CONCISE ENCYCLOPEDIA OF SPECIAL EDUCATION

SECOND EDITION

CONCISE ENCYCLOPEDIA OF SPECIAL EDUCATION

SECOND EDITION

A Reference for the Education of the Handicapped and Other Exceptional Children and Adults

Edited By

Cecil R. Reynolds
Texas A&M University
Bastrop Mental Health Associates

Elaine Fletcher-Janzen
University of Northern Colorado

John Wiley & Sons, Inc.

Published simultaneously in Canada.

No part of this publication may be reproduced, stored in a retrieval system or
transmitted in any form
or by any means, electronic, mechanical, photocopying, recording, scanning or
otherwise, except as permitted under Sections 107 or 108 of the 1976 United
States Copyright Act, without either the prior written permission of the
Publisher, or authorization through payment of the appropriate per-copy fee
to the Copyright Clearance Center, 222 Rosewood Drive, Danvers, MA 01923,
(978) 750-8400, fax (978) 750-4744. Requests to the Publisher for permission
should be addressed to the Permissions Department, John Wiley & Sons, Inc.,
605 Third Avenue, New York, NY 10158-0012, (212) 850-6011,
fax (212) 850-6008, E-Mail: PERMREQ@WILEY.COM.

This publication is designed to provide accurate and authoritative information
in regard to the subject matter covered. It is sold with the understanding that the
publisher is not engaged in rendering professional services. If legal, accounting,
medical, psychological or any other expert assistance is required, the services of
a competent professional person should be sought.

Designations used by companies to distinguish their products are often claimed
as trademarks. In all instances where John Wiley & Sons, Inc. is aware of a
claim, the product names appear in initial capital or all capital letters. Readers,
however, should contact the appropriate companies for more complete
information regarding trademarks and registration.

Library of Congress Cataloging-in-Publication Data
Concise encyclopedia of special education / [edited by] Cecil Reynolds, Elaine
Fletcher-Janzen.—2nd ed.
    p. cm.
    Updated abridgement of Encyclopedia of special education, 2nd ed.
©2000.
    Includes bibliographical references and index.
    ISBN 0-471-39261-8 (cloth : alk. paper)
      1. Handicapped children—Education—United States—Encyclopedias.
2. Special education—United States—Encyclopedias. 3. Handicapped—
Education—United States—Encyclopedias. I. Reynolds, Cecil R., 1952–
II. Fletcher-Janzen, Elaine. III. Encyclopedia of special education.

LC4007 .E53 2002
371.9'03—dc21

                                        2001026647

CONTRIBUTORS

Susanne Blough Abbott
Bedford Central School District
Mt. Kisco, New York

Marty Abramson
University of Wisconsin at Stout
Menomonie, Wisconsin

Patricia Ann Abramson
Hudson Public Schools
Hudson, Wisconsin

Patricia A. Alexander
University of Maryland
College Park, Maryland

Nancy Algert
Texas A & M University
College Station, Texas

Thomas E. Allen
Gallaudet College
Washington, DC

Marie Almond
The University of Texas of the Permian
   Basin
Odessa, Texas

C.H. Ammons
Psychological Reports/Perceptual and
   Motor Skills
Missoula, Montana

Carol Anderson
Texas A & M University
College Station, Texas

Kari Anderson
University of North Carolina
Wilmington, North Carolina

J. Appelboom-Fondu
Université Libre de Bruxelles
Brussels, Belgium

James M. Applefield
University of North Carolina
Wilmington, North Carolina

Kim Ryan Arredondo
Texas A & M University
College Station, Texas

Gustavo Abelardo Arrendondo
Monterrey, Mexico

Bernice Arricale
Hunter College, City University of New
   York
New York, New York

H. Roberta Arrigo
Hunter College, City University of New
   York
New York, New York

Alfredo J. Artiles
University of California
Los Angeles, California

Michael J. Ash
Texas A & M University
College Station, Texas

Adel E. Ashawal
Ain Shams University
Cairo, Egypt

William G. Austin
Cape Fear Psychological Services
Wilmington, North Carolina

Dan G. Bachor
University of Victoria
Canada

Rebecca Bailey
Texas A & M University
College Station, Texas

Timothy A. Ballard
University of North Carolina
Wilmington, North Carolina

Deborah E. Barbour
University of North Carolina
Wilmington, North Carolina

Charles P. Barnard
University of Wisconsin at Stout
Menomonie, Wisconsin

David W. Barnett
University of Cincinnati
Cincinnati, Ohio

Ellis I. Barowsky
Hunter College, City University of New
   York
New York, New York

Lyle E. Barton
Kent State University
Kent, Ohio

Vicki Bartosik
Stanford University
Stanford, California

Anne M. Bauer
University of Cincinnati
Cincinnati, Ohio

Elizabeth R. Bauerschmidt
University of North Carolina
Wilmington, North Carolina

Michael Bauerschmidt
Brunswick Hospital
Wilmington, North Carolina

Monique Bauters
Centre d'Etude et de Reclassement
Brussels, Belgium

John R. Beattie
University of North Carolina
Charlotte, North Carolina

George R. Beauchamp
Cleveland Clinic Foundation
Cleveland, Ohio

Shari A. Beirns
Private Practice
Las Vegas, Nevada

Ana Yeraldina Beneke
University of Oklahoma
Norman, Oklahoma

Randy Elliot Bennett
Educational Testing Service
Princeton, New Jersey

Richard A. Berg
West Virginia University Medical Center,
   Charleston Division
Charleston, West Virginia

John R. Bergan
University of Arizona
Tucson, Arizona

Dianne E. Berkell
C.W. Post Campus, Long Island
  University
Greenvale, New York

Gary Berkowitz
Temple University
Philadelphia, Pennsylvania

Kristen Biernath
The Hughes Spalding International
  Adoption Evaluation Center
Georgia

Erin D. Bigler
Austin Neurological Clinic
University of Texas
Austin, Texas

Roseann Bisighini
The Salk Institute
La Jolla, California

L. Worth Bolton
Cape Fear Substance Abuse Center
Wilmington, North Carolina

Gwyneth M. Boodoo
Texas A & M University
College Station, Texas

Jeannie Bormans
Center for Developmental Problems
Brussels, Belgium

Morton Botel
University of Pennsylvania
Philadelphia, Pennsylvania

Daniel J. Boudah
Texas A & M University
College Station, Texas

Bruce A. Bracken
University of Memphis
Memphis, Tennessee

Mary Brady
Pennsylvania Special Education Assistive
  Device Center
Elizabethtown, Pennsylvania

Janet S. Brand
Hunter College, City University of New
  York
New York, New York

Don Braswell
Research Foundation, City University of
  New York
New York, New York

Warner H. Britton
Auburn University
Auburn, Alabama

Debra Y. Broadbooks
California School of Professional
  Psychology
San Diego, California

Michael G. Brown
Central Wisconsin Center for the
  Developmentally Disabled
Madison, Wisconsin

Robert T. Brown
University of North Carolina
Wilmington, North Carolina

Ronald T. Brown
Emory University School of Medicine
Atlanta, Georgia

Robert G. Brubaker
Eastern Kentucky University
Richmond, Kentucky

Catherine O. Bruce
Hunter College, City University of New
  York
New York, New York

Andrew R. Brulle
Eastern Illinois University
Charleston, Illinois

Laura Kinzie Brutting
University of Wisconsin
Madison, Wisconsin

Donna M. Bryant
University of North Carolina
Chapel Hill, North Carolina

Milton Budoff
Research Institute for Educational
  Problems
Cambridge, Massachusetts

Carolyn Bullard
Lewis & Clark College
Portland, Oregon

Thomas Burke
Hunter College, City University of New
  York
New York, New York

James Button
United States Department of Education
Washington, DC

Anne Campbell
Purdue University
West Lafayette, Indiana

Frances A. Campbell
University of North Carolina
Chapel Hill, North Carolina

Steven A. Carlson
Beaverton Schools
Beaverton, Oregon

Douglas Carnine
University of Oregon
Eugene, Oregon

Janet Carpenter
University of Oklahoma
Norman, Oklahoma

Tracy Calpin Castle
Eastern Kentucky University
Richmond, Kentucky

John F. Cawley
University of New Orleans
New Orleans, Louisiana

Constance Y. Celaya
Private Practice
Irving, Texas

James C. Chalfant
University of Arizona
Tucson, Arizona

Chris Cherrington
Lycoming College
Williamsport, Pennsylvania

Robert Chimedza
University of Zimbabwe
Havare, Zimbabwe

Kathleen Chinn
New Mexico State University
Las Cruces, New Mexico

LeRoy Clinton
Boston University
Boston, Massachusetts

Renato Cocchi
Pesaro, Italy

Christine L. Cole
University of Wisconsin
Madison, Wisconsin

Jane Close Conoley
University of Nebraska
Lincoln, Nebraska

Vivian I. Correa
University of Florida
Gainesville, Florida

Lawrence S. Cote
Pennsylvania State University
University Park, Pennsylvania

Katherine D. Couturier
Pennsylvania State University
King of Prussia, Pennsylvania

Anne B. Crabbe
St. Andrews College
Laurinburg, North Carolina

Sergio R. Crisalle
Medical Horizons Unlimited
San Antonio, Texas

Chara Crivelli
Vito de Negrar
Verona, Italy

Jack A. Cummings
Indiana University
Bloomington, Indiana

Jacqueline Cunningham
University of Texas
Austin, Texas

Susan Curtiss
University of California
Los Angeles, California

Rik Carl D'Amato
University of Northern Colorado
Greely, Colorado

Elizabeth Dane
Hunter College, City University of New
  York
New York, New York

Craig Darch
Auburn University
Auburn, Alabama

Jacqueline E. Davis
Boston University
Boston, Massachusetts

Raymond S. Dean
Ball State University
Indiana University School of Medicine
Muncie, Indiana

Jozi Deleon
New Mexico State University
Las Cruces, New York

Bernadette M. Delgado
Puerto Rico

Randall L. De Pry
University of Colorado
Colorado Springs, Colorado

Lizanne DeStefano
University of Illinois, Urbana-Champaign
Champaign, Illinois

S. De Vriendt
Vrije Universiteit Brussel
Brussels, Belgium

Caroline D'Ippolito
Eastern Pennsylvania Special Education
  Resources Center
King of Prussia, Pennsylvania

Mary D'Ippolito
Montgomery County Intermediate Unit
Norristown, Pennsylvania

Marilyn P. Dornbush
Atlanta, Georgia

Susann Dowling
University of North Carolina
Wilmington, North Carolina

Jengjyh Duh
National Taiwan Normal University
Taiwan

Mary K. Dykes
University of Florida
Gainesville, Florida

Peg Eagney
School for the Deaf
New York, New York

Ronald C. Eaves
Auburn University
Auburn, Alabama

Jana Echevarria
California State University
Long Beach, California

John M. Eells
Souderton Area School District
Souderton, Pennsylvania

Stephen N. Elliott
University of Wisconsin
Madison, Wisconsin

Ingemar Emanuelsson
Goteburg University
Sweden

Carol Sue Englert
Michigan State University
East Lansing, Michigan

Christine A. Espin
University of Minnesota
Minneapolis, Minnesota

Rand B. Evans
Texas A & M University
College Station, Texas

Katherine Falwell
University of North Carolina
Wilmington, North Carolina

Stephen S. Farmer
New Mexico State University
Las Cruces, New Mexico

MaryAnn C. Farthing
University of North Carolina
Chapel Hill, North Carolina

Lisa Fashnacht Hill
California School of Professional
  Psychology
San Diego, California

Mary Grace Feely
School for the Deaf
New York, New York

John F. Feldhusen
Purdue University
West Lafayette, Indiana

Donna Filips
Steger, Illinois

Sally L. Flagler
University of Oklahoma
Norman, Oklahoma

Dennis M. Flanagan
Montgomery County Intermediate Unit
Norristown, Pennsylvania

David Fletcher-Janzen
Colorado Springs, Colorado

Elaine Fletcher-Janzen
University of Northern Colorado
Colorado Springs, Colorado

Wendy Flynn
Staffordshire University
England

Thomas A. Frank
Pennsylvania State University
University Park, Pennsylvania

Mary M. Frasier
University of Georgia
Athens, Georgia

Joseph L. French
Pennsylvania State University
University Park, Pennsylvania

Alice G. Friedman
University of Oklahoma Health Services
Center
Norman, Oklahoma

Douglas L. Friedman
Fordham University
Bronx, New York

Douglas Fuchs
Peabody College, Vanderbilt University
Nashville, Tennessee

Lynn S. Fuchs
Peabody College, Vanderbilt University
Nashville, Tennessee

Gerald B. Fuller
Central Michigan University
Mt. Pleasant, Michigan

Rosemary Gaffney
Hunter College, City University of New
York
New York, New York

Diego Gallegos
Texas A & M University
College Station, Texas
San Antonio Independent School District
San Antonio, Texas

Shernaz B. Garcia
University of Texas
Austin, Texas

Katherine Garnett
Hunter College, City University of New
York
New York, New York

Melissa M. George
Montgomery County Intermediate Unit
Norristown, Pennsylvania

Harvey R. Gilbert
Pennsylvania State University
University Park, Pennsylvania

Joni J. Gleason
University of West Florida
Pensacola, Florida

Sharon L. Glennen
Pennsylvania State University
University Park, Pennsylvania

Rick Gonzales
Texas A & M University
College Station, Texas

Libby Goodman
Pennsylvania State University
King of Prussia, Pennsylvania

Carole Reiter Gothelf
Hunter College, City University of New
York
New York, New York

Steve Graham
University of Maryland
College Park, Maryland

Jeffrey W. Gray
Ball State University
Muncie, Indiana

P. Allen Gray, Jr.
University of North Carolina
Wilmington, North Carolina

Darielle Greenberg
California School of Professional
Psychology
San Diego, California

Laurence C. Grimm
University of Illinois
Chicago, Illinois

John Guidubaldi
Kent State University
Kent, Ohio

Deborah Guillen
The University of Texas of the Permian
Basin
Odessa, Texas

Steven Gumerman
Temple University
Philadelphia, Pennsylvania

Thomas Gumpel
The Hebrew University of Jerusalem
Israel

Patricia A. Haensly
Texas A & M University
College Station, Texas

George James Hagerty
Stonehill College
North Easton, Massachusetts

Winnifred M. Hall
University of West Indies
Jamaica

Richard E. Halmstad
University of Wisconsin at Stout
Menomonie, Wisconsin

Glennelle Halpin
Auburn University
Auburn, Alabama

Donald D. Hammill
Pro-Ed, Inc.
Austin, Texas

Harold Hanson
Southern Illinois University
Carbondale, Illinois

Elise Phelps Hanzel
California School of Professional
Psychology
San Diego, California

Janice Harper
North Carolina Central University
Durham, North Carolina

Gale A. Harr
Maple Heights City Schools
Maple Heights, Ohio

Karen L. Harrell
University of Georgia
Athens, Georgia

Frances T. Harrington
Radford University
Blacksburg, Virginia

Patti L. Harrison
University of Alabama
University, Alabama

Beth Harry
University of Miami
Miami, Florida

Lawrence C. Hartlage
Evans, Georgia

Patricia Hartlage
Medical College of Georgia
Evans, Georgia

Dan Hatt
University of Oklahoma
Norman, Oklahoma

Anette Hausotter
BIS Beratungsstelle für Intergration
Germany

Jeff Heinzen
Indianhead Enterprise
Menomonie, Wisconsin

Rhonda Hennis
University of North Carolina
Wilmington, North Carolina

E. Valerie Hewitt
Texas A & M University
College Station, Texas

Julia A. Hickman
Bastrop Mental Health Association
Bastrop, Texas

Alan Hilton
Seattle University
Seattle, Washington

Delores J. Hittinger
The University of Texas of the Permian
  Basin
Odessa, Texas

Harold E. Hoff, Jr.
Eastern Pennsylvania Special Education
Resources Center
King of Prussia, Pennsylvania

Elizabeth Holcomb
American Journal of Occupational Therapy
Bethesda, Maryland

E. Wayne Holden
University of Oklahoma Health Sciences
  Center
Norman, Oklahoma

Ivan Z. Holowinsky
Rutgers University
New Brunswick, New Jersey

Wayne P. Hresko
Journal of Learning Disabilities
Austin, Texas

Jan N. Hughes
Texas A & M University
College Station, Texas

Kay E. Hughes
The Riverside Publishing Company
Itasca, Illinois

Aimee Hunter
University of North Carolina
Wilmington, North Carolina

Nancy L. Hutchinson
Simon Fraser University
Buraby, British Columbia

Beverly J. Irby
Sam Houston State University
Texas

Paul Irvine
Katonah, New York

Lee Anderson Jackson, Jr.
University of North Carolina
Wilmington, North Carolina

Markku Jahnukainen
University of Helsinki
Finland

Diane Jarvis
State University of New York
Buffalo, New York

Elizabeth Jones
Texas A & M University
College Station, Texas

Gideon Jones
Florida State University
Tallahassee, Florida

Philip R. Jones
Virginia Polytechnic Institute and State
  University
Blacksburg, Virginia

Shirley A. Jones
Virginia Polytechnic Institute and State
  University
Blacksburg, Virginia

James W. Kalat
North Carolina State University
Raleigh, North Carolina

Maya Kalyanpur
Towson University
Towson, Maryland

Randy W. Kamphaus
University of Georgia
Athens, Georgia

Stan A. Karcz
University of Wisconsin at Stout
Menomonie, Wisconsin

Maribeth Montgomery Kasik
Governors State University
University Park, Illinois

Alan S. Kaufman
Yale University School of Medicine
New Haven, Connecticut

James Kaufman
Yale University
New Haven, Connecticut

Nancy J. Kaufman
University of Wisconsin
Stevens Point, Wisconsin

Kenneth A. Kavale
University of Iowa
Iowa City, Iowa

Hortencia Kayser
New Mexico State University
Las Cruces, New Mexico

Forrest E. Keesbury
Lycoming College
Williamsport, Pennsylvania

Kay E. Ketzenberger
The University of Texas of the Permian
  Basin
Odessa, Texas

Peggy Kipling
Pro-Ed, Inc.
Austin, Texas

Gonul Kircaali-Iftar
Anadolu University
Turkey

Margie K. Kitano
New Mexico State University
Las Cruces, New Mexico

F.J. Koopmans-Van Beinum
Amsterdam, The Netherlands

Mark A. Koorland
Florida State University
Tallahassee, Florida

L. Koulischer
Institut de Morphologie Pathologique
Belgium

Martin Kozloff
University of North Carolina
Wilmington, North Carolina

Howard M. Knoff
University of South Florida
Tampa, Florida

Thomas R. Kratochwill
University of Wisconsin
Madison, Wisconsin

James P. Krouse
Clarion University of Pennsylvania
Clarion, Pennsylvania

Louis J. Kruger
Tufts University
Medford, Pennsylvania

Timothy D. Lackaye
Hunter College, City University of New
    York
New York, New York

C. Sue Lamb
University of North Carolina
Wilmington, North Carolina

Nadine M. Lambert
University of California
Berkeley, California

Rafael Lara-Alecio
Texas A & M University
College Station, Texas

Franco Larocca
The University of Verona
Italy

Jeff Laurent
University of Texas
Austin, Texas

Samuel LeBaron
University of Texas Health Science Center
San Antonio, Texas

Yvan Lebrun
School of Medicine
Brussels, Belgium

Linda Leeper
New Mexico State University
Las Cruces, New Mexico

Ronald S. Lenkowsky
Hunter College, City University of New
    York
New York, New York

Mary Louise Lennon
Educational Testing Service
Princeton, New Jersey

Richard Levak
California School of Professional
    Psychology
San Diego, California

Allison Lewis
University of North Carolina
Wilmington, North Carolina

Collette Leyva
Texas A & M University
College Station, Texas

Elizabeth Lichtenberger
The Salk Institute
La Jolla, California

Ping Lin
Elmhurst College
Elmhurst, Illinois

Ken Linfoot
University of Western Sydney
Australia

Janet A. Lindow
University of Wisconsin
Madison, Wisconsin

Daniel D. Lipka
Lincoln Way Special Education Regional
    Resources Center
Louisville, Ohio

Cornelia Lively
University of Illinois, Urbana-Champaign
Champaign, Illinois

Jeri Logemann
Northwestern University
Evanston, Illinois

Charles J. Long
University of Memphis
Memphis, Tennessee

Emilia C. Lopez
Fordham University
New York, New York

Patricia Lowe
Texas A & M University
College Station, Texas

Marsha H. Lupi
Hunter College, City University of New
    York
New York, New York

Ann E. Lupkowski
Texas A & M University
College Station, Texas

Philip E. Lyon
College of St. Rose
Albany, New York

John MacDonald
Eastern Kentucky University
Richmond, Kentucky

Taddy Maddox
Pro Ed, Inc.
Austin, Texas

Susan Mahanna-Boden
Eastern Kentucky University
Richmond, Kentucky

Charles A. Maher
Rutgers University
Piscataway, New Jersey

David C. Mann
St. Francis Hospital
Pittsburgh, Pennsylvania

Douglas L. Mann
V.A. Medical Center, Medical University of
    South Carolina
Charleston, South Carolina

Lester Mann
Hunter College, City University of New
    York
New York, New York

Ellen B. Marriott
University of North Carolina
Wilmington, North Carolina

Tamara Martin
The University of Texas of the Permian
    Basin
Odessa, Texas

Patrick Mason
The Hughes Spalding International
   Adoption Evaluation Center
Georgia

Deborah C. May
State University of New York
Albany, New York

Joan W. Mayfield
Baylor Pediatric Specialty Service
Dallas, Texas

Liliana Mayo
Centro Ann Sullivan
Peru

James K. McAfee
Pennsylvania State University
King of Prussia, Pennsylvania

Eileen F. McCarthy
University of Wisconsin
Madison, Wisconsin

Elizabeth McClellan
Council for Exceptional Children
Reston, Virginia

George McCloskey
The Psychological Corporation
San Antonio, Texas

Linda McCormick
University of Hawaii, Manoa
Honolulu, Hawaii

Phillip J. McLaughlin
University of Georgia
Athens, Georgia

James A. McLoughlin
University of Louisville
Louisville, Kentucky

Frederic J. Medway
University of South Carolina
Columbia, South Carolina

Brenda Melvin
New Hanover Regional Medical Center
Wilmington, North Carolina

Judith Meyers
San Diego, California

Danielle Michaux
Vrije Universiteit Brussel
Brussels, Belgium

Jennifer Might
University of North Carolina
Wilmington, North Carolina

Stephen Miles
Immune Deficiency Foundation
Towson, Maryland

James H. Miller
University of New Orleans
New Orleans, Louisiana

Ted L. Miller
University of Tennessee
Chattanooga, Tennessee

Norris Minick
Center for Psychosocial Studies
The Spencer Foundation
Chicago, Illinois

Anjali Misra
State University of New York
Potsdam, New York

Linda Montgomery
The University of Texas of the Permian
   Basin
Odessa, Texas

Richard J. Morris
University of Arizona
Tucson, Arizona

Lonny W. Morrow
Northeast Missouri State University
Kirksville, Missouri

Sue Ann Morrow
EDGE, Inc.
Bradshaw, Michigan

Tracy Muenz
California School of Professional
   Psychology
San Diego, California

Mary Murray
Journal of Special Education
Ben Salem, Pennsylvania

Jack Naglieri
George Mason University
Fairfax, Virginia

Sigamoney Naicker
Western Cape Educational SI Department
South Africa

Michael Nall
Louisville, Kentucky

Robert T. Nash
University of Wisconsin
Oshkosh, Wisconsin

Joyce Ness
Montgomery County Intermediate Unit
Norristown, Pennsylvania

Robert C. Nichols
State University of New York
Buffalo, New York

Etta Lee Nurick
Montgomery County Intermediate Unit
Norristown, Pennsylvania

Thomas Oakland
University of Florida
Gainesville, Florida

Festus E. Obiakor
Emporia State University
Nigeria

Salvador Hector Ochoa
Texas A & M University
College Station, Texas

Masataka Ohta
Tokyo Gakujei University
Tokyo, Japan

John O'Neill
Hunter College, City University of New
   York
New York, New York

Alba Ortiz
University of Texas
Austin, Texas

Lawrence J. O'Shea
University of Florida
Gainesville, Florida

Kathleen D. Paget
University of South Carolina
Columbia, South Carolina

Douglas J. Palmer
Texas A & M University
College Station, Texas

Hagop S. Pambookian
Elizabeth City, North Carolina

Ernest L. Pancsofar
University of Connecticut
Storrs, Connecticut

Sara Pankaskie
Florida State University
Tallahassee, Florida

Daniel R. Paulson
University of Wisconsin at Stout
Menomonie, Wisconsin

Nils A. Pearson
Pro-Ed, Inc.
Austin, Texas

Mary Leon Peery
Texas A & M University
College Station, Texas

Olivier Périer
Université Libre de Bruxelles
Centre Comprendre et Parler
Brussels, Belgium

Joseph D. Perry
Kent State University
Kent, Ohio

Richard G. Peters
Ball State University
Muncie, Indiana

Jeffry L. Phillips
University of North Carolina
Wilmington, North Carolina

Yongxin Piao
Beijing Normal University
Beijing, China

Sip Jan Pijl
Glon University of Groningen
Groningen, The Netherlands

John J. Pikulski
University of Delaware
Newark, Delaware

Sally E. Pisarchick
Cuyahoga Special Education Service Center
Maple Heights, Ohio

Brenda M. Pope
New Hanover Memorial Hospital
Wilmington, North Carolina

John E. Porcella
Rhinebeck County School
Rhinebeck, New York

James A. Poteet
Ball State University
Muncie, Indiana

David P. Prasse
University of Wisconsin
Milwaukee, Wisconsin

Marianne Price
Montgomery County Intermediate Unit
Norristown, Pennsylvania

Philip M. Prinz
Pennsylvania State University
University Park, Pennsylvania

Antonio E. Puente
University of North Carolina
Wilmington, North Carolina

Krista L. Puente
University of North Carolina
Wilmington, North Carolina

Craig T. Ramey
University of North Carolina
Chapel Hill, North Carolina

Arlene I. Rattan
Ball State University
Muncie, Indiana

Gurmal Rattan
Indiana University of Pennsylvania
Indiana, Pennsylvania

Anne Reber
Texas A & M University
College Station, Texas

Robert R. Reilley
Private Practice
Atlanta, Georgia

Fredricka K. Reisman
Drexel University
Philadelphia, Pennsylvania

Kimberly M. Rennie
Texas A & M University
College Station, Texas

Daniel J. Reschly
Vanderbilt University
Nashville, Tennessee

Cecil R. Reynolds
Texas A & M University
College Station, Texas

Robert Rhodes
New Mexico State University
Las Cruces, New Mexico

William S. Rholes
Texas A & M University
College Station, Texas

James R. Ricciuti
United States Office of Management and Budget
Washington, DC

Teresa K. Rice
Texas A & M University
College Station, Texas

Paul C. Richardson
Elwyn Institutes
Elwyn, Pennsylvania

Pamela Richman
University of North Carolina
Wilmington, North Carolina

Bert O. Richmond
University of Georgia
Athens, Georgia

Catherine Hall Rikhye
Hunter College, City University of New York
New York, New York

Gary J. Robertson
American Guidance Service
Circle Pines, Minnesota

Kathleen Rodden-Nord
University of Oregon
Eugene, Oregon

Jean A. Rondal
Laboratory for Language, Psychology, and Logopedics
University of Liege
Liege, Belgium

Sheldon Rosenberg
University of Illinois
Chicago, Illinois

Bruce P. Rosenthal
State University of New York
New York, New York

Kathy L. Ruhl
Pennsylvania State University
University Park, Pennsylvania

Joseph M. Russo
Hunter College, City University of New York
New York, New York

Robert B. Rutherford, Jr.
Arizona State University
Tempe, Arizona

Anne Sabatino
Hudson, Wisconsin

David A. Sabatino
West Virginia College of Graduate Studies
Institute, West Virginia

Lisa J. Sampson
Eastern Kentucky University
Richmond, Kentucky

Alfred Sander
Universität des Saarlandes
Saarbruecken, Germany

Polly E. Sanderson
Research Triangle Institute
Research Triangle Park, North Carolina

Scott W. Sautter
Peabody College, Vanderbilt University
Nashville, Tennessee

Robert F. Sawicki
Lake Erie Institute of Rehabilitation
Lake Erie, Pennsylvania

Patrick J. Schloss
Pennsylvania State University
University Park, Pennsylvania

Ronald V. Schmelzer
Eastern Kentucky University
Richmond, Kentucky

Carol S. Schmitt
Eastern Kentucky University
Richmond, Kentucky

Sue A. Schmitt
University of Wisconsin at Stout
Menomonie, Wisconsin

Eric Schopler
University of North Carolina
Chapel Hill, North Carolina

Fredrick Schrank
The Riverside Publishing Company
Itasca, Illinois

Louis Schwartz
Florida State University
Tallahassee, Florida

June Scobee
University of Houston, Clear Lake
Houston, Texas

Thomas E. Scruggs
Purdue University
Lafayette, Indiana

Denise M. Sedlak
United Way of Dunn County
Menomonie, Wisconsin

Robert A. Sedlak
University of Wisconsin at Stout
Menomonie, Wisconsin

Sandra B. Sexton
Emory University School of Medicine
Atlanta, Georgia

Susan Shandelmier
Eastern Pennsylvania Special Education
    Regional Resources Center
King of Prussia, Pennsylvania

Deborah A. Shanley
Medgar Evers College, City University of
    New York
New York, New York

William J. Shaw
University of Oklahoma
Norman, Oklahoma

Ludmila Shipitsina
International University for Family and
    Child
Russia

Edward Shirkey
New Mexico State University
Las Cruces, New Mexico

Dakum Shown
University of Jos
Nigeria

Lawrence J. Siegel
University of Texas Medical Branch
Galveston, Texas

Rosanne K. Silberman
Hunter College, City University of New
    York
New York, New York

Paul T. Sindelar
Florida State University
Tallahassee, Florida

Jerry L. Sloan
Wilmington Psychiatric Associates
Wilmington, North Carolina

Craig D. Smith
Georgia College
Milledgeville, Georgia

Maureen A. Smith
Pennsylvania State University
University Park, Pennsylvania

Judy Smith-Davis
Counterpoint Communications Company
Reno, Nevada

Barbara S. Speer
Shaker Heights City School District
Shaker Heights, Ohio

Kenneth O. St. Louis
West Virginia University

Harrison C. Stanton
Private Practice
Las Vegas, Nevada

J. Todd Stephens
University of Wisconsin
Madison, Wisconsin

Cecelia Steppe-Jones
North Carolina Central University
Durham, North Carolina

Linda J. Stevens
University of Minnesota
Minneapolis, Minnesota

Rachael J. Stevenson
Bedford, Ohio

Roberta C. Stokes
Texas A & M University
College Station, Texas

Laura M. Stough
Texas A & M University
College Station, Texas

Edythe A. Strand
University of Wisconsin
Madison, Wisconsin

Sheela Stuart
George Washington University
Washington, DC

Sue Stubbs
Save the Children Fund
London, England

Shelly Suntup
California School of Professional
  Psychology
San Diego, California

Emily G. Sutter
University of Houston, Clear Lake
Houston, Texas

Mark E. Swerdlik
Illinois State University
Normal, Illinois

Henri B. Szliwowski
Hôpital Erasme, Université Libre de
  Bruxelles
Brussels, Belgium

Pearl E. Tait
Florida State University
Tallahassee, Florida

Paula Tallal
University of California
San Diego, California

Mary K. Tallent
Texas Tech University
Lubbock, Texas

C. Mildred Tashman
College of St. Rose
Albany, New York

James W. Tawney
Pennsylvania State University
University Park, Pennsylvania

Ellen A. Teelucksingh
University of Minnesota
Minneapolis, Minnesota

Cathy F. Telzrow
Kent State University
Kent, Ohio

Jo Thomason
CASE

Spencer Thompson
The University of Texas of the Permian
  Basin
Odessa, Texas

Steven R. Timmermans
Mary Free Bed Hospital and Rehabilitation
  Center
Grand Rapids, Michigan

Gerald Tindal
University of Oregon
Eugene, Oregon

Francine Tomkins
University of Cincinnati
Cincinnati, Ohio

Carol Tomlinson-Keasey
University of California
Riverside, California

Bruce Thompson
Texas A & M University
College Station, Texas

Jose Luis Torres
Texas A & M University
College Station, Texas

Stanley O. Trent
University of Virginia
Charlottesville, Virginia

Timothy L. Turco
Louisiana State University
Baton Rouge, Louisiana

Lori E. Unruh
Eastern Kentucky University
Richmond, Kentucky

Greg Valcante
University of Florida
Tallahassee, Florida

Hubert B. Vance
East Tennessee State University
Johnson City, Tennessee

K. Sandra Vanta
Cleveland Public Schools
Cleveland, Ohio

Don Viglione
California School of Professional
  Psychology
San Diego, California

Judith K. Voress
Pro-Ed, Inc.
Austin, Texas

Emily Wahlen
Hunter College, City University of New
  York
New York, New York

Deborah Klein Walker
Harvard University
Cambridge, Massachusetts

Donna Wallace
The University of Texas of the Permian
  Basin
Odessa, Texas

Marjorie E. Ward
The Ohio State University
Columbus, Ohio

Sue Allen Warren
Boston University
Boston, Massachusetts

Lauren Webster
University of North Carolina
Wilmington, North Carolina

Danny Wedding
Marshall University
Huntington, Virginia

Frederick F. Weiner
Pennsylvania State University
University Park, Pennsylvania

Bahr Weiss
University of North Carolina
Chapel Hill, North Carolina

Shirley Parker Wells
University of North Carolina
Wilmington, North Carolina

Louise H. Werth
Florida State University
Tallahassee, Florida

Larry J. Wheeler
Southwest Texas State University
San Marcos, Texas

Susie Whitman
Immune Deficiency Foundation
Towson, Maryland

Thomas M. Whitten
Florida State University
Tallahassee, Florida

Greta N. Wilkening
Children's Hospital
Denver, Colorado

Mary Clare Williams
Ramey, Pennsylvania

Diane J. Willis
University of Oklahoma Health
  Sciences Center
Oklahoma City, Oklahoma

Victor L. Willson
Texas A & M University
College Station, Texas

John D. Wilson
Elwyn Institutes
Elwyn, Pennsylvania

Margo E. Wilson
Lexington, Kentucky

Joseph C. Witt
Louisiana State University
Baton Rouge, Louisiana

Benice Woll
University of Bristol
Bristol, England

Bernice Y.L. Wong
Simon Fraser University
Buraby, British Columbia

Mary M. Wood
University of Georgia
Athens Georgia

Frances F. Worchel
Florida State University
Tallahassee, Florida

Eleanor Boyd Wright
University of North Carolina
Wilmington, North Carolina

Logan Wright
University of Oklahoma
Norman, Oklahoma

Karen F. Wyche
Hunter College, City University of New
  York
New York, New York

Martha Ellen Wynne
Loyola University of Chicago
Chicago, Illinois

James E. Ysseldyke
University of Minnesota
Minneapolis, Minnesota

Roland K. Yoshida
Fordham University
New York, New York

Thomas Zane
Johns Hopkins University
Baltimore, Maryland

Kenneth A. Zych
Walter Reed Army Medical Center
Washington, DC

PREFACE

The *Encyclopedia of Special Education* was originally published in 1987. It was the first major, comprehensive reference work for the field of special education subsequent to the passage of the Education for All Handicapped Children Act of 1974. Because of the success of the original edition, which was named one of the top 25 reference works in all disciplines by the American Library Association, a 2nd edition, updated and expanded, of the *Encyclopedia* was published in 2000. The 2nd edition of the *Encyclopedia of Special Education* followed in the tradition of the 1st edition, giving authors as much space as necessary to cover their desired topic. As happened with the 1st edition, it became apparent that the full set of encyclopedias could not sit on the desk of many professionals in special education and that it was too expensive for the typical parent to acquire and consult. To make the broad array of information in the *Encyclopedia of Special Education* available to a more varied group of professionals and more accessible to parents, the *Concise Encyclopedia of Special Education* was published. Following in this tradition, and once again hoping to enhance the accessibility and availability of information relevant to special education, this 2nd edition of the *Concise Encyclopedia* is offered as a desk reference for special educators, school psychologists, educational and clinical psychologists, educational diagnosticians, resource and related teachers, and the parents of children receiving or in need of special education services.

As with the 1st edition of the *Concise,* individual authors were not asked to condense their articles. The editors culled the text themselves reducing publication and production time, thus allowing timely presentation of the *Concise Encyclopedia of Special Education, 2nd edition.* This also allowed us to enhance the uniformity of content and style across the volume. Articles were updated where appropriate and some key references were added. For the most part, however, it was a task of condensation and abridgement, intended to hold forward the basic ideas and most fundamental information for the reader. Much more detailed information is available as may be required by consulting the complete *Encyclopedia of Special Education.* The majority of the topics were retained, however, we did delete biographies of living individuals and collapsed some highly related topics into a single entry. We accept responsibility for all errors of commission and omission as all development of new material, rewriting, abridgements, and related tasks were solely our responsibility and not that of the original authors. We did, however, work hard to maintain the integrity and intent of the original presentation. In part to add to our ability to condense the work into a more affordable volume, original author names and affiliations have been deleted which resulted in a surprising savings with regard to length of the work. It is in no way intended to denigrate the contributions of the original authors whose names and affiliations can be located in the complete *Encyclopedia of Special Education, 2nd edition.*

The field of special education continues to evolve on many fronts and the advancement of knowledge continues to amaze us as professionals in the field. The breadth and depth of services to children with various disabilities and handicaps have also grown tremendously since the original encyclopedia was presented. We hope that we have encompassed the vast majority of these advances into the *Encyclopedia of Special Education, 2nd edition,* and its follow up volume presented here, the *Concise Encyclopedia of Special Education, 2nd edition.* More and more the general public comes into contact with disabled children and they are being provided full access to society and the many collateral activities associated with positive growth and development in childhood. Anyone who comes into contact with these children on a professional or even paraprofessional basis will have questions and a need for information and guidance. Obviously, there is no simple answer to how to locate the best information for each and every problem encountered. However, we offer these encyclopedias as ready resources which will in some cases answer or resolve the question at hand and in other instances provide background information and material for a further, more detailed search of the literature and improved access to information.

It is our hope that our colleagues will continue to participate with us in the preparation of reference works such as the *Encyclopedia of Special Education* series. Without their hard work and cooperation, reference works such as these could never exist at the level of quality we hope we have been able to offer. Our sincere gratitude to our colleagues is offered for their hard work and cooperation. We must also express our appreciation to our families for their encouragement and support during the time spent on such projects which could alternatively be spent with them: to Julia, Chris, David, Emma, and Leif, thank you immensely again and again.

The efforts of John Wiley and Sons, both in the editorial division and in the production division was absolutely necessary to the initiation and completion of these projects. In particular we offer our appreciation to Jennifer Simon and her staff at Wiley. We also acknowledge our appreciation and offer it on behalf of the underlying sciences that contribute to special education as well, to disabled children throughout the world and to their parents who have allowed their children to participate in the multitude of research tasks that have built the scientific literature upon which the disciplines that contribute to special education have been based. Without their agreement, cooperation, and participation in research on diagnosis, etiology, and amelioration of disabilities, special education would not have progressed beyond its late 1800s conceptualization at the hands of Lightner Witmer and his "experimental classroom for backwards children." We thank all of you and hope that you will find this work useful to you in some regard as you interact with children in need of special education services and their parents and extended families.

CECIL R. REYNOLDS, PhD,
Bastrop Mental Health Associates

ELAINE FLETCHER-JANZEN, EdD,
University of Northern Colorado, Colorado Springs

A

AAAS.

See also American Association for the Advancement of Science.

AAMD CLASSIFICATION SYSTEMS

The American Association on Mental Deficiency (AAMD) was founded in 1876 to support and promote the general welfare of people who are mentally retarded through professional programs, dissemination of research and program advances, and development of standards for services and facilities. The organization is comprised of approximately 10,000 professionals from many different disciplines who are concerned with the prevention and treatment of mental retardation. The association publishes two research journals, *Mental Retardation* and *American Journal of Mental Deficiency.*

The first diagnostic and classification system was published in 1921. It was reviewed and revised in 1933, 1941, 1957, 1959, 1973, 1977, and 1983. Major revisions over the years have centered around the presentation of a dual classification system, medical and behavioral; clarification of the definitions of adaptive and measured intelligence; the addition of an extensive glossary; an illustration of levels of adaptive behavior; and procedures for diagnosing mental retardation in the behavioral system.

The 1983 AAMD classification system continues to reflect current thinking in the field. The 1983 edition was an attempt to provide an acceptable system to be used worldwide. It was developed in coordination with the International Classification of Diseases-9 (ICD-9) of the World Health Organization, the American Psychiatric Association's *Diagnostic and Statistical Manual-III* (DSM-III), and the American Association on Mental Deficiency's Classification in Mental Retardation.

A second purpose was to improve opportunities to gather and disseminate information regarding diagnosis, treatment, and research activities. The third purpose of this classification system was to provide opportunities for the identification of causes of mental retardation with implications for prevention.

The definition of mental retardation accepted by most authorities is the one used by the American Association on Mental Deficiency. The definition was presented first by Heber in 1961 and later revised by Grossman in 1973 to read: "Mental retardation refers to significantly subaverage general intellectual functioning resulting in or associated with concurrent impairments in adaptive behavior and manifested during the developmental period." Based on the definition, to be classified mentally retarded, the person must be below average in both measured intelligence and adaptive behavior. The descriptive terms used by the AAMD are mild, moderate, severe, and profound.

REFERENCE

Grossman, H. (Ed.). (1983). *Classification in mental retardation.* Washington, DC: American Association on Mental Deficiency.

See also AAMD Adaptive Behavior Scales; Mental Retardation

AAMR ADAPTIVE BEHAVIOR SCALES–RESIDENTIAL AND COMMUNITY: SECOND EDITION (ABS–RC:2)

The *AAMR Adaptive Behavior Scales–Residential and Community: Second Edition* (ABS–RC:2) (Nihira, Leland, & Lambert, 1993) is the revision of the 1969 and 1974 *AAMD Adaptive Behavior Scales.* The latest version of the adaptive behavior scales is the product of a comprehensive review of the earlier versions of the rating scales relating to persons with mental retardation in the United States and other countries. The items of the ABS–RC:2 have undergone numerous modifications since the 1969 edition as a result of intensive item analyses over time, with different group results varying with respect to adaptive behavior levels. This scale is appropriate for individuals from ages 18 through 80.

This scale was reviewed in *The Thirteenth Mental Measurements Yearbook* (Impara & Plake, 1998) by Carey (1998) and Harrison (1998). Carey stated that the scale is technically adequate for this type of assessment; Harrison reported that the ABS–RC:2 has many features that enhance the assessment of adults with developmental disabilities.

REFERENCES

Carey, K.T. (1998). Review of the AAMR Adaptive Behavior Scale–Residential and Community, Second Edition. In J.C. Impara & B.S. Plake (Eds.), *The thirteenth mental measurements yearbook* (pp. 3–5). Lincoln: Buros Institute of Mental Measurements, University of Nebraska Press.

Harrison, P.L. (1998). Review of the AAMR Adaptive Behavior Scale–Residential and Community, Second Edition. In J.C. Impara & B.S. Plake (Eds.), *The thirteenth mental measurements yearbook.* Lincoln: Buros Institute of Mental Measurements, University of Nebraska Press.

Impara, J.C., & Plake B.S. (Eds.). (1998). *The thirteenth mental measurements yearbook* (pp. 1–3). Lincoln: Buros Institute of Mental Measurements, University of Nebraska Press.

Nihira, K., Leland, H., & Lambert, N. (1993). *AAMR Adaptive Be-

havior Scales–Residential and Community: Second Edition. Austin, TX: Pro-Ed.

AAMR ADAPTIVE BEHAVIOR SCALES–SCHOOL: SECOND EDITION (ABS–S:2)

The *AAMR Adaptive Behavior Scales–School: Second Edition* (ABS–S:2) (Lambert, Nihira, & Leland, 1993) is used for assessing the current adaptive functioning of children being evaluated for evidence of mental retardation, for evaluating adaptive behavior characteristics of children with autism, and for differentiating children with behavior disorders who require special education assistance. The scale is appropriate for children ages 3 years to 18 years 11 months.

This revision is divided into two parts. Part One focuses on personal independence; it is designed to evaluate coping skills considered important to independence and responsibility in daily living. The skills within Part One are grouped into nine behavior domains: Independent Functioning, Physical Development, Economic Activity, Language Development, Numbers and Time, Prevocational/ Vocational Activity, Self-Direction, Responsibility, and Socialization. Part Two measures socially maladaptive behaviors. The behaviors assessed were identified through a survey of the social expectations placed upon persons with mental retardation in public and special schools, public and private residential institutions, and a wide range of local rehabilitative and recreational services. The descriptions of those expectations were obtained from an analysis of a large number of critical incident reports provided by personnel in residential, community, and school settings. The behaviors in Part Two are assigned to seven domains, which are measures of those adaptive behaviors that relate to the manifestation of personality and behavior disorders: Social Behavior, Conformity, Trustworthiness, Stereotyped and Hyperactive Behavior, Self-Abusive Behavior, Social Engagement, and Disturbing Interpersonal Behavior. The domains in Part One and Part Two are combined into five factors: Personal Self-Sufficiency, Community Self-Sufficiency, Personal-Social Responsibility, Social Adjustment, and Personal Adjustment.

REFERENCE

Lambert, N., Nihira, K., & Leland, H. (1993). *AAMR Adaptive Behavior Scales–School: Second Edition.* Austin, TX: PRO-ED.

See also **AAMD Classification Systems; Adaptive Behavior**

ABAB DESIGN

The ABAB design is one of the oldest and most widely used single-case designs developed in behavioral psychology. It was initially used in laboratory studies with animals (Sid-man, 1960); however, as the applied behavior analysis movement got under way (Baer, Wolf, & Risley, 1968), it became a prototype for applied behavioral investigations conducted in the natural environment. Although the number of single-case designs has increased markedly since the early days of applied behavior analysis (e.g., Kazdin, 1980), the ABAB design still occupies a prominent place in applied behavioral research. Moreover, because of the high degree of experimental control that it provides, it has been widely used with individuals manifesting various types of handicaps (Bergan, 1977). For example, the ABAB design has been particularly useful in studying environmental variables affecting language acquisition in retarded children (Bergan, 1977).

The ABAB design is intended to reveal a functional relationship between an experimental treatment and a behavior targeted for change. For example, it might be used to establish a functional relationship between the use of the plural form of a noun and a treatment such as praise following the occurrence of a plural noun. The demonstration of a functional relationship between praise and plural nouns would require an association between the frequency of plural-noun production and the occurrence of verbal praise. Given that a functional relationship were established, verbal praise could be assumed to function as a positive reinforcer increasing the probability of occurrence of plural nouns by the subject or subjects participating in the experiment.

As the letters in its name suggest, the ABAB design includes four phases. The initial A phase is a baseline period that records behavior across a series of points in time in the absence of intervention. The length of the baseline period varies depending on the variability of the behavior being recorded. If the behavior is highly variable, a longer baseline is required than if the behavior is highly stable. More data are required to get a sense of the fluctuations that may be expected without intervention for a highly variable behavior than for a highly stable behavior. The second phase, denoted by the letter B, is a treatment phase. During this phase the treatment is introduced. The third phase, also denoted by the letter A, constitutes a return to baseline. The return to baseline may be brought about by various means. One is to withdraw the treatment. Another procedure is to introduce another treatment intended to bring the target behavior back to baseline level. For example, reinforcement of a behavior that is incompatible with the target behavior may be introduced during the return-to-baseline phase. The final phase in the ABAB design, denoted by the second occurrence of the letter B, is a second implementation of the treatment. The second implementation is intended to demonstrate treatment control over the target behavior by minimizing the possibility that environmental influences occurring coincidentally with the treatment could be responsible for the observed behavior change. The major advantage of the ABAB design lies in the fact that it minimizes the likelihood of coincidental environmental influences on the target behavior.

REFERENCES

Baer, D.M., Wolf, M.M., & Risley, T.R. (1968). Some current dimensions of applied behavior analysis. *Journal of Applied Behavior Analysis, 8,* 387–398.

Bergan, J.R. (1977). *Behavioral consultation.* Columbus, OH: Merrill.

Kazdin, A.E. (1980). *Research design in clinical psychology.* New York: Harper & Row.

Sidman, M. (1960). *Tactics of scientific research.* New York: Basic.

See also **Research in Special Education**

ABECEDARIAN PROJECT

For the past quarter century, American education has been especially concerned with the academic performance of children from disadvantaged families. This special concern stems from the well-established fact that this group of children typically performs well below average on standardized tests of academic achievement. They also are overrepresented in special education classes. The root causes of this poor performance are not well understood but their consequences are costly, in terms both of economics and psychological dysfunction. Such consequences have frequently been called developmental retardation.

To ameliorate these costly consequences, a wide variety of special education programs have been investigated under the rubric of compensatory education. Most of these programs have concentrated on the so-called preschool and/or early elementary school years. The primary hypothesis has been that educational experiences that augment and/or supplement the educational experiences of the home will better prepare disadvantaged children for academic accomplishment in the public schools. The Abecedarian project has been such an experiment. Abecedarian means one learning the rudiments of something (the alphabet).

The specific aims of the Abecedarian project have been:

To determine whether developmental retardation and school failure can be prevented in children from socially and economically high-risk families by means of educational day care.

To determine whether a follow-through program for early elementary school is necessary to maintain preschool intellectual gains in high-risk children.

To determine whether school-age intervention alone can significantly improve academic and/or intellectual performance in children who did not have preschool intervention.

To identify a sample of families at high risk for having a developmentally retarded child, a high-risk screening index (Ramey & Smith, 1977) was developed. This index included social, environmental, and psychological factors judged on the basis of the developmental literature to be associated with poor intellectual and scholastic progress. Each factor was assigned a weight based on professional consensus as to its likely importance in determining intellectual and scholastic outcomes. Thirteen factors were included; among them were paternal and maternal education; family income; father's absence; retardation among other family members; family disorganization; maladaptive or antisocial behavior within the family; and unstable job history.

It is a special feature of the Abecedarian project that participants were assigned to the preschool experimental educational treatment or control condition at random. Fifty-seven children were randomly assigned to the preschool experimental group, 54 were preschool controls. Ninety-six children remained in the study to be randomly assigned to a school-age treatment group.

The preschool program may be characterized as a comprehensive, whole child program. The aim was to create a rich, stimulating, yet orderly environment in which the children could grow and learn. The curriculum was designed to enhance cognitive and linguistic development and to provide the children with many opportunities for successful mastery experiences. The curriculum materials included those for infants and preschoolers developed by Sparling and Lewis (1979). In addition, there was an enriched language environment that was responsive to the children's needs and interests (Ramey et al., 1982).

In many ways the program was not unlike other high-quality infant daycare and preschool programs. Child/caregiver ratios ranged from 1:3 for infants to 1:6 for four year olds. Teachers typically had early childhood education experience and participated in an extensive in-service education program. The children's experiences became increasingly more structured over the preschool years, eventually coming to include prephonics programs and science and math experiences in addition to an emphasis on language and linguistic development. The presumption was that when the child left the preschool, he or she would be able to enter kindergarten without experiencing an abrupt transition.

Children attended the preschool program beginning between 6 weeks and 3 months of age. Children attended the daycare program 5 days per week, 50 weeks per year. The center was open from 7:30 A.M. to 5:15 P.M. Free transportation to and from the center was provided for families who needed it. Almost all of the children were transported by center staff. This portion of the program has been described in more detail by Ramey, MacPhee, and Yeates (1982).

The school-age intervention program began in kindergarten. It consisted of providing a home/school resource teacher to each child and family in the two Abecedarian school-age experimental groups (EE and CE). These teachers filled many roles: they were curriculum developers who prepared an individualized set of home activities to supplement the school's basic curriculum in reading and math; they taught parents how to use these activities with their children; they tutored children directly; they met regularly with classroom teachers to ensure that home activities matched the skills being taught in the classroom; they served as consultants for the classroom teacher when problems arose; and they advocated for the child and family within the school and community. Thus, they facilitated communication between teacher and parent, providing an important support for disadvantaged parents who frequently lacked the skills and confidence needed to advocate for their children within the school system, an institution seen by many as both monolithic and difficult to comprehend. Each home/school resource teacher had a caseload of approximately 12 families per year. The home/school resource teachers were experienced educators familiar with the local school system.

The supplemental curriculum delivered as home activities concentrated on two basic subjects: reading and math. These subjects were emphasized because it seemed likely that high-risk children might need extra reinforcement of these basic concepts to master and to remember them. The program sought to provide such reinforcement, presuming that scholastic performance would best be enhanced by direct teaching and practice of needed basic skills. The curriculum packets contained teaching activities that parents and children could share and enjoy. In addition, work sheets to give extra drill and practice were often included.

Home/school teachers made approximately 17 school visits per year for each child. During these visits they met with the classroom teacher to identify the skills currently being taught and to learn which areas needed extra work or review. A variety of specialists within the system were contacted, including special education resource personnel, reading teachers, and school counselors. Efforts were made to coordinate the child's program and to make sure the best available resources were being used.

The home component of the program was equally intense. Home visits were made about 15 times each school year. A typical visit lasted approximately 30 to 45 minutes, with the mother being the most likely participant. Teachers reviewed the classroom situation and showed the parent the materials in the activity packet, explaining the purpose and directions for each activity. The child was present and participated in about one-quarter of the home visits; this was often helpful because it allowed the teacher to demonstrate how an activity was to be carried out. Parents reported spending an average of 15 minutes a day working with their children on home activities. Parent response to the activities was very positive; very few reported that they failed to use the activities although direct verification was not possible.

Many forces other than intellectual ability and encouragement to learn can have an impact on a child's scholastic performance: emotional upset within the home, parental unemployment, the death of a family member, or instability of living arrangements, to name a few. Home/ school resource teachers sometimes helped families deal with personal crises. Extra home visits occurred if and when the home/school teacher attempted to help the family solve such real-life problems. Home/school teachers also helped to provide the children with a variety of summer experiences, including summer activity packets, summer camp, trips to the public library, and, for some children, a six-week tutorial in reading.

Overall, outcome data on IQs, academic achievement, and retention in grade suggest that preschool intervention exerts a positive influence on intelligence and school success in the first 2 years of public school. Preschool intervention supplemented by continued help in the early grades via a home/school resource teacher program shows promise for being the most effective intervention. This intensity of effort apparently enabled the high-risk children in this sample to maintain a level of achievement near the national average. In addition, the likelihood of being retained in grade was less by a factor of approximately three for children who had early and continued educational intervention.

REFERENCES

Ramey, C.T., MacPhee, D., & Yeates, K.O. (1982). Preventing developmental retardation: A general systems model. In L.A. Bond & J.M. Joffe (Eds.), *Facilitating infant and early childhood development* (pp. 343–401). Hanover, NH: University Press of New England.

Ramey, C.T., McGinness, G.D., Cross, L., Collier, A.M., & Barrie-Blackley, S. (1982). The Abecedarian approach to social competence: Cognitive and linguistic intervention for disadvantaged preschoolers. In K. Borman (Ed.), *The social life of children in a changing society.* Hillsdale, NJ: Erlbaum.

Ramey, C.T., & Smith, B. (1977). Assessing the intellectual consequences of early intervention with high-risk infants. *American Journal of Mental Deficiency, 81,* 318–324.

Sparling, J., & Lewis, I. (1979, February). Six learning games to play with your baby. *Parents* (pp. 35–38).

See also **Mental Retardation**

ABILITY TRAINING

Many educators believe that most academic and social learning is based on factors such as student aptitudes or abilities, instructional environment, and teaching methodology. While these three variables do not form a complete structure capable of containing all those factors contributing to learning, they certainly account for many of the variables educators would agree are important to success in school.

Learner aptitudes or abilities are those personological variables that frequently are called intelligence(s), traits, gifts, and characteristics. Frequently, educators will talk about a child's potential to learn, using the term ability as if it were a predetermined factor waiting to be drawn on at some point. The logic, then, is that if learning is a result of the presence and development of certain mental abilities, school failure (both academic and social) may be the result of disabilities, with disability implying an academic or social handicap.

If regular (elementary and secondary) educators teach to the abilities of students to learn, then special educators may direct more of their instruction to the disabilities that inhibit learning, hence the term and concept of ability training. How valid is this construct of ability training? A short response to that question is impossible. Any field involving relatively newly defined services to persons, especially children, in particular handicapped children, will generate professional controversy. Any field struggling with the pressures associated with economic, political, social, legislative, litigative, and basic human rights and values will face diversity. Any field that requires its many disciplines to unite in purpose will experience communicative stress. But, few professionals will purposely question their field's major methodology to the degree special and remedial educators have, for the period of time they have done so, and in the face of such a degree of controversy.

Some special educators believe avidly in ability training of all types; some reject it totally; but almost all, no matter what they believe, practice ability training. The truth in that observation is vividly displayed when we recognize that the value of ability training to handicapped persons has been questioned repeatedly for over the last 100 years. What then is in ability training that has caused the field of special education to tenaciously and steadfastly maintain its cause? Ability training is routed in the historic search for the structure and function of the mind. Educators, in particular special educators, have sought to diagnose specific abilities and provide remediation to those abilities, or disabilities as the case may be.

The history of ability training parallels that of the field of special education. The pioneers in ability training were the pioneers of the field. Itard, Howe, Sequin, Montessori, Binet, Wepman, Kirk, Strauss, Fernald, Frostig, and Cruickshank were all advocates of special education as it grew, and responsible for advancing ability training simultaneously. Tests used to describe a disability were followed by commercially prepared curricula to train the ability and remove the disability. The logic is obvious. The problem is in the scientific validation, or lack of it.

The early 1960s brought with it a concern for neurologically impaired children. The mid-1960s added the term learning disabled as a category of handicapping conditions. Both of these conditions required an increased emphasis on psychoneurological and psychoeducational assessment. Those that developed psychoeducational and psychoneurological tests to diagnose these conditions fueled the fire for ability training by describing conditions which, by their description, must exist.

Curricula designed to modify and treat patterns of disability were soon commercially available. Whole classes of children were exposed to Montessori, Frostig, and Fernald techniques, and administered Frostig, Kephart, and Delacato assessment procedures. Tests such as the Illinois Test of Psycholinguistic Abilities became common place, much as the Woodcock-Johnson test batteries of today. The prevailing belief was that specific mental processes must be diagnosed in order for modification of a specific disability to result in quantum jumps in academic remedial achievement

and potential normalization. Thus, the so-called diagnostic-prescriptive process is one form of ability training.

What then is the difficulty with visual and auditory perceptual training, perceptual motor training, language training, and the other forms of sensory, motor, perceptual, and language ability training? The problem is that data arrived at through quasi-scientific means are controversial concerning the results of ability training. There are data to support ability training, if the objective to be achieved is a change in an ability, and that ability alone. There are relatively few data to support that transfer of training occurs between training of a perceptual or cognitive ability and an academic achievement skill, for instance reading.

It is not clear which age groups profit most; there are some data to suggest that perceptual motor training is most effective between 3 and 7 years of age, and language training, 18 months to 14 or 15 years of age. There is no clear pattern as to the intelligence level needed for a student to profit from ability training, since specific abilities constitute statements of global intelligence. Cultural and ethnic factors have been found: urban black children may need auditory perceptual training; Native Americans outperform age norms of Anglos on visual perceptual tests.

The overall interaction among these abilities being training and other abilities remains unknown, except it does seem that auditory perceptual training is related to language growth much more than visual perceptual training. Language training seemingly has the greatest transference to academic remediation. But even the search for generalities would produce only controversy. The fact is, ability training makes sense logically but has not been sufficiently researched devoid of other educational practices with school-age children to permit definitive statements. And yet, the practice does not only continue, it continues to thrive.

See also **Diagnostic-Prescriptive Teaching; Fernald Method; Illinois Test of Psycholinguistic Abilities; Intelligence; Remediation, Deficit-Centered Models**

ABSENCE SEIZURES

Absence seizures (also known as petit mal seizures) are a form of epilepsy characterized by brief losses of consciousness unaccompanied by large convulsive movements. Absence seizures are generalized; involving abnormal activity throughout the brain. They are characterized by lack of any aura (sensation that a seizure is to occur), brevity (absence seizures typically last 5–10 seconds [Menkes, 1985]), and abrupt termination. After an absence seizure has occurred, there is no postictal period, the individual does not complain of fatigue or the need to sleep, and he or she can resume the activity being engaged in prior to the seizure. Children with absence seizures often are unaware of their lapses of consciousness.

Although absence seizures are nonconvulsive during the

seizure, some movement will be seen in about 70% of diagnosed children. When the seizure begins, an observer may notice a vacant look in the child's eyes. Minor motor movements such as lip smacking, eye blinking, or twitching of the eyelids or face sometimes occur. There may be a slight loss of body tone, with the child perhaps dropping something he or she is holding. Absence seizures often can be precipitated by sustained hyperventilation, and less frequently by photic stimulation.

Absence seizures are more common in girls, and onset is generally between 5 and 15 years of age. There frequently is a family history of a seizure disorder. Most often the neurologic exam and CAT scan is normal. The EEG shows a characteristic three-cycle per second spike and wave pattern during seizures. Generally IQs are reported to be within normal limits, though some studies suggest a mild depression when compared with siblings (Dreifuss, 1983). The most frequent school problem is difficulty in paying attention. There is some evidence that this is related to abnormal brain function (Mirsky, 1969). With frequent seizures, schoolwork often is disrupted.

The medications used in absence seizures include ethosuximide (Zarontin), valproate (Depakene), clonazepam (Clonopin), paramethadione (Paradione), and methsuximide (Celontin). There are other types of seizures that include staring, but these are not simple absence seizures.

REFERENCES

Dreifuss, F.E. (1983). *Pediatric epileptology.* Boston: Wright.

Menkes, J.H. (1985). *Textbook of child neurology.* Philadelphia: Lee & Febiger.

Mirsky, A.F. (1969). Studies of paroxysmal EEG phenomena and background EEG in relation to impaired attention. In C.R. Evans & T.P. Mullholland (Eds.), *Attention in neurophysiology* (pp. 310–322). London: Butterworth.

See also **Electroencephalograph; Grand Mal Seizures; Seizure Disorders**

ABSENTEEISM/ATTENDANCE OF HANDICAPPED CHILDREN

Compulsory school attendance laws have been enacted in all states. The scope of those laws was narrowed in most states by the introduction of exemption clauses. These clauses excuse children considered unfit or uneducable because of physical or mental handicaps from school attendance. Legal challenges by handicapped children for extension and protection of the right established under state law of equal access to educational opportunity ensued during the early 1970s. Those cases were followed by federal and state laws that mandate free appropriate public education to handicapped children and ensure their right to attend school regardless of the severity or type of their disability.

Under IDEA and Section 504 of the Rehabilitation Act of 1973, a handicapped child must be educated in the least restrictive environment his or her needs allow. Children with serious, often chronic, health impairments who require special education and related services may receive instruction in hospitals or in the home. Schools use various approaches, including home visitations, school-to-home telephone communication, and interactive television to connect a homebound or hospitalized student with the classroom. Federal law recognizes that there are instances when, because of the nature or severity of a child's handicap, the child must be educated in a setting other than the regular classroom. However, the least restrictive environment provisions prohibit placement of a child on homebound instruction or other exclusion from the regular educational environment solely because the child is handicapped. Homebound instruction may not be appropriate for the instructional needs of that child.

Under the IDEA and Section 504, mandatory procedural safeguards exist that allow parents to challenge school disciplinary actions that would interrupt a handicapped child's education. Expulsions, suspensions, and transfers to settings outside a regular classroom or school are considered placement changes since such measures remove students from their current school program or curtail attendance (Simon, 1984). A series of court decisions on this sensitive area have provided important guidelines for determining when and for what length of time handicapped students may be expelled or suspended under federal law (Reschly & Bersoff, 1999; Simon, 1984).

REFERENCES

Reschly, D., & Bersoff, D. (1999). Law and school psychology. In C.R. Reynolds & T.B. Gutkin (Eds.), *The Handbook of School Psychology* (3rd ed.) (pp. 1077–1112). New York: Wiley.

Simon, S.G. (1984). Discipline in the public schools: A dual standard for handicapped and nonhandicapped students? *Journal of Law & Education, 13,* 209–237.

See also **Homebound Instruction; Individuals with Disabilities Education Act; Summer School for Handicapped**

ABSTRACTION, CAPACITY FOR

Abstract reasoning refers to the ability to identify common features of two or more concepts, and has been considered an essential component of intelligence (e.g., Thorndike, 1927). Abstract reasoning ability can be assessed through at least three types of tasks: those which require a person to identify a general concept common to several exemplars, e.g., sorting objects according to categories; to state common features among different concepts. While general abstraction ability varies across persons, ability to reason abstractly in specific tasks appears to vary with subject area expertise.

REFERENCE

Thorndike, E.L. (1927). *The measurement of intelligence.* New York: Bureau of Publications, Teachers College, Columbia University.

See also Educable Mentally Retarded; Intelligence Testing

ABUSED CHILDREN

Today abused children are typically regarded as suffering from a primary illness (Quirk, 1980). A primary illness refers to the notion that living with a certain circumstance for a prolonged period of time creates a situation in the victim requiring primary treatment. The primary illness of child abuse has identifiable symptoms and etiology along with an official diagnosis and prescribed treatments.

The first step in treatment is proper identification of child abuse as the problem to be treated. Children who have been abused relive their abuse over and over in clear or symbolic ways. They dream abusive dreams, remember abusive situations, and in adulthood go so far as to recreate abusive relationships. They manifest little positive affect in interpersonal relationships, and they lack intimacy and express difficulty in trusting others (Herman, 1981). They are depressed and have difficulty in developing meaningful relationships or experiences in their lives. Insomnia is another frequently reported symptom, even in the absence of distressing nightmares. Abused children are also guilt-ridden, and experience much shame and self-hatred. Concentrating and following a task through to its completion is another problem area for this population.

Acting out the abuse in self-destructive ways such as drug abuse is frequently observed in this population, which is disproportionately represented in chemical dependency treatment facilities. As teenagers, abused children often become runaways and act out their rage in criminal behavior. Abused children are also disproportionately represented in facilities for delinquents. A disproportionately large group in this population may attempt suicide, hallucinate, manifest seizures, and ultimately be placed in psychiatric hospitals. While these obvious problematic behaviors will occur at high rates, another observed phenomena of this population is the frequency with which they become quiet, good children who then marry an abusive partner. Other compulsive behaviors are frequently manifested by these children and subsequently they will be found as adults in Al-anon, Alcoholics Anonymous, Narcotics Anonymous, Overeaters Anonymous, Gamblers Anonymous, and other self-help treatment programs.

Because young and abused children live and grow with a wounded and fragmented personality, they often need intensive treatment efforts. The client who clings or annoys the clinician, reporting that something is missing from treatment, will often be a person who was abused. This person will often complain about the deficiencies of treatment and report that he or she has not been responded to reasonably. This type of reporting should be expected in view of the fact that abused children are wounded people who will have difficulty objectifying their relations: after all, their primary objects, mom or dad, abused them.

Abused children often feel at fault for their experience of child abuse. They live with much guilt, shame, self-blame, and self-loathing. Often their abusers told them it was their fault. Child molesters use guilt as a tool with their victims in order to keep the secret, while parents who physically beat their children do so in the name of discipline. Yet, abused children mentally make their parents correct and good. Generally, therapists should enjoy relationships with people, but it is even more important for therapists of abused children to like their clients: While one might think that all therapists would like their clients, fragile clients often find themselves disliked by their therapists. Since they do not grow as the therapist expects, they experience rejection in the context of the therapeutic relationship.

Most children learn to cope by making decisions separate from the influence of their parents. Abused children have more to cope with, and fewer skills to do so. Reparenting applies here also. Regardless of age, abused children need to learn to live and cope in the real world, and come to recognize that not all people are as threatening as their abusive parents. Therefore, learning coping skills is essential to any successful treatment program.

Because abuse occurs in the context of an interpersonal relationship, the environment of a therapeutic group has proven itself a particularly helpful treatment modality. In view of the characteristics of this population, the following are important considerations for the leader of a group of abused children. The group should be initially supportive, gentle, homogeneous, and closed to new members after the group has begun. These elements are necessary to address the difficulty in trusting manifested by this population. The group needs to project an image of safety and members must be monitored from inappropriately expressing the rage some may possess. Confrontation must be kept well managed to further reduce regression that may be promoted by some of the more fragmented members. The group leader must monitor the development of any situation that may resemble the childhood abuse of any member in the group. A primary goal of the group is to develop understanding of the personal dynamics of abuse and coping skills that may prevent the development of similar abusive situations in the future.

REFERENCES

Herman, J.L. (1981). *Father-daughter incest.* Cambridge, MA: Harvard University Press.

Quirk, J.P. (Ed.). (1980). *Reading in child abuse.* Guilford, CT: Special Learning.

See also Acting Out; Child Abuse; Etiology; Neglect

ACADEMICALLY TALENTED CHILDREN

Academically talented children usually possess superior intellectual ability or a specific subject matter aptitude. This point of view is supported by the continuing general acceptance of Witty's (1940) definition of giftedness as performance by a child that is consistently remarkable in a potentially valuable line of human activity. Included in the scope of Witty's definition are those who are academically talented, and, therefore, have the ability to do well in one or more academic subjects in school. This label distinguishes these children from those who may be talented in other areas designated by the U.S. Office of Education such as creative or productive thinking, leadership, visual and performing arts, and psychomotor activities (Renzulli, 1978).

Identification of academic ability can include the use of IQ tests, achievement test scores, evidence of academic achievement, and products successfully completed in an academic area. In addition, students who are academically talented are sometimes 2 to 8 years ahead of chronological age peers in academic subjects (Clark, 1983).

REFERENCES

Clark, B. (1983). *Growing up gifted.* Columbus, OH: Merrill.

Renzulli, J.S. (1978). What makes giftedness? Reexamining a definition. *Phi Delta Kappan, 60,* 180–184.

Witty, P. (1940). Some considerations in the education of gifted children. *Educational Administration and Supervision, 26,* 512–521.

See also **Acceleration of Gifted Children; Gifted and Talented Children**

ACADEMIC ASSESSMENT

The global function of achievement testing is to assess a student's attainment of academic content areas. Reading, written language, and mathematical functioning are the major domains under the rubric of academic achievement. Anastasi (1982) notes that traditionally academic assessment has been differentiated from aptitude/ability testing by the degree to which a measure is designed to assess uniform versus diverse antecedent experiences. To be categorized as a measure of academic achievement, a measure is designed to test a fairly uniform previous experience (e.g., first grade instruction in reading). In contrast, an aptitude test would be designed to assess the impact of multiple or diverse antecedent experiences. Contemporary measurement specialists recognize that both achievement and aptitude tests assess acquired knowledge, but differ on the degree of specificity and abstraction.

Salvia and Ysseldyke (1981) have described four functions that achievement tests fulfill within the schools. They are used for screening students who may need more in-depth assessment to determine whether special services are appropriate; determining whether a child is eligible for placement in a special education class based on local criteria; assessing a child's strengths and weaknesses to facilitate decisions regarding his or her placement in an instructional sequence; and determining the impact of educational intervention on a class or group of students.

Achievement testing may be conceptualized along several lines: norm-referenced versus criterion referenced; in-

dividual versus group administered; and informal teacher-constructed versus standardized instruction. Each of these dimensions will be discussed to highlight the multifaceted construct of academic achievement assessment.

The most salient characteristic of norm-referenced achievement tests is that an examinee's performance on the test is interpreted by comparing his or her relative standing to a given reference group. The reference group or standardization sample is usually composed of representative peers of the same chronological age, or peers in the same grade placement. Performance on a norm-referenced test is typically expressed in scores based on the normal curve such as stanines, T-scores, and/or standard scores (which usually have a mean of 100 and a standard deviation of 15, or sometimes 16). Performance on a norm-referenced test may also be expressed in percentiles, which tell a student's standing relative to a hypothetical group of 100 children. For instance, a score at the 86th percentile indicates that the examinee scored better than 86 out of 100 of his or her hypothetical same-aged peers.

A primary difference between norm-referenced and criterion-referenced tests lies in the way they are interpreted. As noted, the norm-referenced achievement test is designed to give information on a given student's performance relative to a representative group of same-aged peers. In contrast, the criterion-referenced achievement test is designed to give information on a given student's performance in terms of whether he or she has learned a given concept or skill. Thus, the criterion-referenced measure is designed to tell what the student can and cannot do. For instance, the student can add single digit numerals with sums less than 10, but has not learned to regroup or perform simple subtraction problems. Since discrimination among students is not the purpose of a criterion-referenced test, the difficulty level of items and the power of items to separate students are not as important as they are in norm-referenced measures. The major issue in criterion-referenced measurement is whether items reflect a specified instructional domain. Most of the major group-administered achievement tests have been adapted to yield criterion-referenced information. The problem with adapting norm-referenced tests is that there are a multiplicity of instructional objectives (Cunningham, 1986). Since each objective requires several test items to achieve an adequate level of reliability, the length of the test becomes unmanageable.

Academic achievement testing may also be examined from the viewpoint of the administration format, either individual or group. While group achievement tests are usually given to a whole class by the regular education teacher, individual achievement measures are administered by specially trained personnel (special education teachers, educational diagnosticians, and school psychologists) to a child on a one-to-one basis. Typically, the child has been referred for testing because of academic or behavioral problems manifested in the regular classroom. A general distinction between group and individual measures relates to their use in the decision-making process. Group measures are designed to make decisions about groups, while individual tests are more appropriate for decisions concerning an individual. Therefore, caution must be exercised when attempting to interpret the results of a single child's performance on a group-administered measure. There are many variables that may influence a child's performance on a group-administered measure and result in an inaccurate portrayal of that child's academic skills. Misunderstanding instructions, fatigue, random guessing, class distractions, looking on a neighbor's response sheet, etc., may invalidate a child's scores. When a child is being considered for placement in a special education program, a poor performance on a group-administered measure should be followed up with an individual assessment.

Finally, the academic achievement test may be approached by examining the degree to which the directions to students are standardized. The standardized test is one where the instructions and test questions are presented in the same manner to all examinees. On the other hand, in the teacher constructed test, there is unlimited latitude in the construction and administration of test items. Both standardized and informal teacher-made tests have advantages and disadvantages. However, they should share certain attributes, i.e., clear directions to students, careful development of items based on a table of specifications, and the type or format of test items.

A major difference between standardized and informal, teacher-developed tests is that the former usually represents many more hours of item development, refinement, empirical tryouts, and final selection of test items. In developing standardized achievement tests, considerable weight is placed on both content validity (the representativeness of the items to the domain being tested, and the appropriateness of the format and wording of items relative to the age level of the prospective examinees), and the empirical tryout of the items in terms of reliability. The advantage of the standardized test lies in its documented reliability (presented in an accompanying technical manual), and its ability to compare a student's performance with that of a reference group or specified criterion. Whereas standardized tests measure content that is common to reading and mathematics programs from around the country, the teacher-constructed tests can be specifically targeted to the content of the local curriculum, or to a specific teacher's class.

In addition to defining informal assessment as the administration of a teacher-constructed measure, the term may also be applied to diagnostic processes. These include error analysis (Table 1), behavioral observation, and the learner's relations to various instructional strategies (Sedlak, Sedlak, & Steppe-Jones, 1982).

Another strategy that is being touted for assessment of academic skills is curriculum-based assessment (CBA). CBA attempts to link assessment more directly to classroom instruction and to provide a more direct assessment of a student's instructional needs (Shapiro & Elliott, 2000). Although touted as an alternative to traditional norm-referenced testing, CBA and NRT are seen best as complementary models, and not as competitive ones.

Table 1   Samples of Common Arithmetic Error Patterns That Give Insight into the Student's Incorrect Problem-Solving Strategy

Addition

$$\begin{array}{r} 56 \\ + \ 7 \\ \hline 513 \end{array} \qquad \begin{array}{r} 24 \\ + \ 5 \\ \hline 11 \end{array}$$

(Addition of all numerals without regard for place value)

Subtraction

$$\begin{array}{r} 53 \\ - \ 5 \\ \hline 52 \end{array} \qquad \begin{array}{r} 522 \\ - 101 \\ \hline 401 \end{array}$$

(Failure to group)   (Misunderstanding of zero as a subtrahend)

Multiplication

$$\begin{array}{r} 34 \\ \times \ 3 \\ \hline 122 \end{array} \qquad \begin{array}{r} 93 \\ \times \ 8 \\ \hline 101 \end{array}$$

(Addition of the regrouped number prior to multiplication)   (Use of inappropriate algorithm)

Division

$$\begin{array}{r} 21 \\ 2\overline{)24} \\ 20 \\ \hline 4 \end{array} \qquad \begin{array}{r} 5 \\ 3\overline{)18} \end{array}$$

(A right to left recording pattern is employed)   (Basic fact mistake)

In summary, academic achievement assessment is used to make decisions about students. These decisions may be made from a normative perspective or in terms of students' mastery of a specified skill. Depending on the administration, format decisions can be made for an individual student or for groups of students. Norm-referenced achievement tests provide information about a student's relative standing compared with that of a reference group, while criterion-referenced tests and informal assessments may be used to make informed decisions about a student's future instructional needs. Specific achievement tests are described throughout this work.

REFERENCES

Anastasi, A. (1982). *Psychological testing* (5th ed.). New York: Macmillan.

Cunningham, G.K. (1986). *Educational and psychological measurement.* New York: Macmillan.

Salvia, J., & Ysseldyke, J.E. (1981). *Assessment in special and remedial education* (2nd ed.). Boston: Houghton Mifflin.

Sedlak, R.A., Sedlak, D.M., & Steppe-Jones, C. (1982). Informal assessment. In D.A. Sabatino & L. Mann (Eds.), *A handbook of diagnostic and prescriptive teaching.* Rockville, MD: Aspen Systems.

Shapiro, E., & Elliott, S.N. (2000) Curriculum based assessment and other performance based assessment strategies. In C.R. Reynolds & T.B. Gutkin (Eds.), *The Handbook of School Psychology* (3rd ed.) (pp. 383–408). New York: Wiley.

See also **Achievement Tests; Criterion-Referenced Testing; Norm-Referenced Testing**

ACADEMIC LANGUAGE

Academic language (instructional discourse, cognitive-academic language, or school language) is the way teachers and students organize their communication interactions within educational environments. The purpose is to transmit scientific or logically based knowledge and skills. In contrast, everyday discourse (conversation, social discourse, or basic interpersonal communication) has as its general purpose the regulation of social interaction or interpersonal functions.

Academic communication-learning problems are associated with many developmental and acquired disorders. Academic language use and rules vary from culture to culture. However, the consensus is that to succeed in mainstream educational settings in the course of life students must be able to understand and use the cognitive, linguistic, and contextual conventions associated with academic language.

See also **Discourse**

ACADEMIC SKILLS

While to some individuals the definition of academic skills conjours up the three Rs, to others the delineation of the academic skills most important to the process of special education is a task that poses an awesome definitional problem. To the preschool special educator, for example, certain fine motor skills may be defined as important academic skills. On the other hand, for the special educator working at the secondary level, the ability to accept positive and negative feedback (social skills), driving skills, or home economics may be considered important academic skills that warrant inclusion in the secondary special education curriculum.

One comprehensive sourcebook on research on teaching presents detailed analyses of seven academic skill areas: written composition, reading, mathematics, natural sciences, arts and aesthetics, moral and values education, and social studies (Wittrock, 1986). At least a few of these areas would be considered by most individuals to be core or basic academic skills. The fact that these academic skill areas have entire chapters devoted to them also indicates that there is enough research, theory, or perhaps controversy regarding them as to allow them to be studied and discussed extensively.

Beyond the issue of defining academic skills are the related issues of the rise and fall of skills across generations (which is constantly addressed by the popular media), and equally important, the procedures by which these skills are taught and acquired by students in special education. Cartwright, Cartwright, and Ward (1981) list several approaches used by special education teachers to impart academic skills; these include the diagnostic teaching model, remedial and compensatory education models, direct instruction, task analysis, perceptual-motor training, inquiry, modeling, media-based instruction, education games, and computer-assisted and computer-managed instruction. Two additional instructional approaches that were popularized in the 1970s include mastery learning and cooperative learning (Stallings & Stipek, 1986).

With regard to learner characteristics that affect the acquisition of academic skills, Wittrock (1986) suggests the following broad categories for consideration: students' perceptions and expectations, attention, motivation, learning and memory, comprehension and knowledge acquisition, learning strategies, and metacognitive processes. In summary, special educators must first define the academic skills that their students must acquire and then consider instructional, student, and other variables in planning for the optimal acquisition of academic skills.

REFERENCES

Cartwright, P.G., Cartwright, C.A., & Ward, M.E. (1981). *Educating special learners.* Belmont, CA: Wadsworth.

Stallings, J.A., & Stipek, D. (1986). Research on early childhood and elementary school teaching programs. In M.C. Wittrock (Ed.), *Handbook of research on teaching.* New York: Macmillan.

Wittrock, M.C. (1986). Students' thought processes. In M.C. Wittrock (Ed.), *Handbook of research on teaching.* New York: Macmillan.

See also **Memory Disorders; Metacognition**

ACALCULIA

Acalculia is defined by Hallahan, Kauffman, and Lloyd (1985) as "complete inability to use mathematic symbols and perform mathematical computations" (p. 267). Hallahan et al. distinguish acalculia from dyscalculia by stating that the term dyscalculia is "reserved for less severe problems in these areas" (p. 267).

Strauss and Werner (1938) described acalculia as "deficiency in number operations" (p. 719) and provided evidence of the association between acalculia and finger agnosia (inability to recognize fingers on one's own hands), which was said to be caused by a lesion within an area around the angular gyrus. Strauss and Werner (1938) provided some evidence of a correlation between finger agnosia and acalculia.

According to Strauss and Lehtinen (1948), disturbance in visual perception was a major contributing factor to acalculia. They developed several principles for instruction based on organized perceptual experiences. Terms such as acalculia and dyscalculia have declined in popularity with the increasing attention given to more educationally relevant orientations. Generally, deficits in mathematical functioning have been remediated with the use of task-specific instructional strategies. Mercer (1979, chapter 8) provides an overview of some of these strategies. More recent nomenclature includes these disorders under the more general rubric of specific developmental disorders.

REFERENCES

Hallahan, D.P., Kauffman, J.M., & Lloyd, J.W. (1985). *Introduction to learning disabilities* (2nd ed.). Englewood Cliffs, NJ: Prentice Hall.

Mercer, C. (1979). *Children and adolescents with learning disabilities.* Columbus, OH: Merrill.

Strauss, A.A., & Lehtinen, L.E. (1948). *Psychopathology and education of the brain-injured child.* New York: Grune & Stratton.

Strauss, A.A., & Werner, H. (1938). Deficiency in the finger schema in relation to arithmetic disability (finger agnosia and acalculia). *American Journal of Orthopsychiatry, 8,* 719–724.

See also **Arithmetic Remediation; Dyscalculia**

ACCELERATION OF GIFTED CHILDREN

Acceleration is any process whereby a child makes educational progress faster than usual, whether measured by advancement in school grade or by actual achievement (Ward, 1980). Presently, there are numerous avenues for acceleration in schools for those students who exhibit general intellectual ability and/or outstanding aptitude in one or more subject areas.

For students who exhibit high levels of general intellectual ability, three of the existing options are telescoping, grade skipping, and early admission to formal schooling. Telescoping involves the completion of three years of schooling in two years or four years of schooling in three years (Fox, 1979). Those who skip grades are promoted two grade levels in one year. These children are usually given credit for the skipped year and are able to complete formal schooling in fewer years than usual. Early entrance to formal schooling occurs when children are allowed to enter kindergarten or first grade at an age lower than is usually allowed by the school or school system. These children may merit early entrance because of advanced scores on IQ or abilities tests.

For pupils with outstanding aptitude in one or more subject areas, six options exist: concurrent enrollment, correspondence courses, special schools or classes, independent study, tutorials, and credit by exam. Other options may be created within each individual class, school, or school system.

Concurrent enrollment for secondary school students occurs when high schools and universities cooperate to allow students to be concurrently enrolled both in a high school and in a college. These pupils receive college credit for courses taken on the college campus; in some cases they receive college credit for courses taught by a university faculty member on the high school campus. Correspondence courses provide another option for acceleration when secondary school students enroll through the continuing education division of participating universities. They receive lessons by mail, and, on completion of all requirements, receive a grade after taking a final examination graded by the same university professor who planned the lessons.

Another acceleration practice takes place in special schools or classes where students are allowed to complete more than one year of credit in a subject area class by working in a compacted curriculum and successfully passing examinations. One of the most well known of these special school and class arrangements is Julian Stanley's Study of Mathematically Precocious Youth, conducted at Johns Hopkins University (Stanley, 1977). Students who have qualified for participation in this program by scoring at least 550 on the Scholastic Aptitude Test in mathematics have the opportunity to study higher level mathematics in college classes during the summer and/or complete college correspondence courses during the school year. Since the inception of the program at Johns Hopkins, it has expanded to include students with high verbal aptitude, and subjects other than mathematics are offered. Two other programs have replicated Stanley's work: the Midwest Talent Search at Illinois' Northwestern University and the Talent Identification Program at North Carolina's Duke University.

Talented students may also do independent study or be provided with a special tutor to complete course requirements in an advanced curriculum area. Finally, other credit-by-examination options are available to students who wish to advance beyond their peers through acceleration. These include advanced placement in secondary schools in states that provide their own examinations to receive credit for high school classes, advanced placement in college courses through the Advanced Placement Program, and the College Level Examination Program that allows students to receive credit in 15 fields by taking exams at university testing centers.

Although there are no clear answers concerning the effects of acceleration on social and emotional growth, there are answers to questions about whether acceleration is beneficial academically. In a meta-analysis of 26 controlled studies, evidence showed that examination performance of accelerates surpassed by nearly one grade level the performance of nonaccelerates of equivalent age and intelligence. Furthermore, the examination scores of accelerates were equivalent to those of same-grade, but older, talented nonaccelerates (Kulik & Kulik, 1984).

REFERENCES

Fox, L.H. (1979). Programs for the gifted and talented. In A.H. Passow (Ed.), *The gifted and talented: Their education and development.* Chicago: National Society for the Study of Education.

Kulik, J.A., & Kulik, C.C. (1984). Effects of accelerated instruction on students. *Review of Educational Research, 54,* 409–425.

Stanley, J.C. (1977). Rationale of the study of mathematically precocious youth (SMPY) during its first five years of promoting educational acceleration. In J.C. Stanley, W.C. George, & C.H. Solano

(Eds.), *The gifted and creative: A fifty-year perspective.* Baltimore, MD: Johns Hopkins University Press.

Ward, V.S. (1980). *Differential education for the gifted.* Ventura, CA: Ventura County Superintendent of Schools Office.

See also **Academically Talented Children; Gifted and Talented Children; Sidis, William James**

ACCESSIBILITY OF BUILDINGS

The accessible building is a structure that is readily usable by individuals possessing a wide range of physical disabilities or other limitations (such as sensory handicaps). A building or other site designed to accommodate ambulant or sensorily disabled persons is equally convenient and accessible to the nonhandicapped population. The design criteria used to meet the needs of handicapped populations are essentially no different from those of the general, nondisabled citizenry; they are only more pronounced.

The generally accepted minimum standards for ensuring the accessibility of buildings are incorporated in the American National Standards Institute (ANSI) specifications. Originally adopted in 1961 and subsequently revised and expanded during 1970s, the ANSI standards serve as a foundation for state laws and federal guidelines concerning building accessibility. A federal entity, the National Commission on Architectural Barriers (CAB), was created by an act of Congress to promote and evaluate voluntary and, in the case of federally owned or subsidized buildings, mandatory compliance with the ANSI standards.

Guided by the ANSI standards, architects and facility planners must ensure that the entrances to and the interiors of buildings allow for the uninhibited mobility, orientation, comfort, and performance of all facility users. As reviewed by Cotler and DeGraff (1976), the structural dimensions, interior design, entranceways and the layout of furniture in all buildings should be integrated to accommodate the physical limitations in mobility, reach and posture experienced by most wheelchair users and individuals aided by crutches, walkers and canes. It is of equal importance to the sensorily handicapped population (e.g., individuals who are blind or deaf) that building environments offer a simple, regular, well-lighted and marked design that enhances orientation and ready access to sources of visual, aural and tactile information.

REFERENCE

Cotler, S.R., & DeGraff, A.H. (1976). *Architectural accessibility for the disabled on college campuses.* Albany, NY: State University Construction Fund.

See also **Americans with Disabilities Act; Architectural Barriers; Architecture and the Handicapped**

ACCESSIBILITY OF PROGRAMS

Section 504 of the Rehabilitation Act of 1973, as amended, provides that

no otherwise qualified handicapped individual . . . shall, solely by reason of his handicap, be excluded from participation in, be denied the benefits of, or be subjected to discrimination under any program or activity receiving federal financial assistance or under any program or activity conducted by any executive agency or the United States Postal Service.

The substantive provisions apply to two distinct sets of entities: recipients of federal financial assistance (federally assisted programs) and the operations of government agencies (federally conducted programs).

The concept of program accessibility is a key requirement of the implementing regulations for both federally assisted and federally conducted programs (U.S. Government, 1978; U.S. Government, 1985). In both cases, the requirement is not that every existing building or classroom be physically accessible, but rather that "the program or activity, when viewed in its entirety, is readily accessible to and usable by handicapped persons" (28 CFR 41.57(a)). All new buildings and facilities must be designed and constructed to be readily accessible to and usable by handicapped persons.

Since the late 1970s, federal court decisions and regulatory policy have interpreted and qualified the precise requirements of program accessibility. Of particular importance is the U.S. Supreme Court decision in *Southeastern Community College v. Davis* (1979), which held that the school was not required to modify a nurse training program as sought by a hearing-impaired individual because such modification would constitute "a fundamental alteration in the nature of the program." In discussing program modification, the Court also referenced attaining desirable goals "without imposing undue financial and administrative burdens" (pp. 410, 412).

In a prototype regulation distributed to all agencies as nonbinding guidance, and in its own regulation on federally conducted programs promulgated in 1984 (U.S. Government, 1985), the Department of Justice employs criteria from the *Davis* decision. The program accessibility requirement for existing programs explicitly does not "require the agency to taken any action that it can demonstrate would result in a fundamental alteration in the nature of the program or in undue financial and administrative burdens" (28 CFR 39.150(a)(2)).

Some commentators on the Department of Justice's proposed regulation objected to the inclusion of the *Davis* criteria. They argued that the language must be identical to the Department of Justice's government-wide coordinating regulation on federally assisted programs, which does not include such criteria (U.S. Government, 1985, p. 357). The Department of Justice's position is that "judicial interpretation of Section 504 [including circuit court decisions following *Davis*] compels it to incorporate the new language" and that the regulations for federally assisted programs must now be interpreted consistent with the federally conducted rule and *Davis* (U.S. Government, 1985, p. 357).

A good discussion of these issues is in the editorial note to 28 CFR 39 (U.S. Government, 1985). Other precedents have established the rights of all students to accessibility of educational programs (Sales et al., 1999).

REFERENCES

Sales, B., Krauss, D.A., Sacken, D., & Overcast, T. (1999). The legal rights of students. In C.R. Reynolds & T.B. Gutkin (Ed.), *The Handbook of School Psychology* (3rd ed.) (pp. 1113–1144). New York: Wiley.

Southeastern Community College v. Davis (1979). United States Supreme Court, 442 U.S. 397.

U.S. Government. (1978). Code of Federal Regulations Title 28, Part 41. *Implementation of Executive Order 12250, Non-Discrimination on the Basis of Handicap in Federally Assisted Programs.*

U.S. Government. (1985). Code of Federal Regulations Title 28, Part 39. *Enforcement of Non-Discrimination on the Basis of Handicap in Programs or Activities Conducted by the Department of Justice.*

See also Accessibility of Buildings; Americans with Disabilities Act; Special Education, Legal Regulation of

ACCOMMODATION

Accommodation is one of two complementary processes proposed by Jean Piaget to account for an individual's adaptation to the environment; its counterpart is assimilation. Accommodation involves changing or transforming cognitive or sensorimotor schemes according to the demands of the environment; assimilation involves incorporating external elements into existing conceptual schemes.

The difference between accommodation and assimilation can be illustrated by an example of an infant's response to a rattle (Ginsburg & Opper, 1969). When a rattle suspended from an infant's crib begins to shake after the infant's arm movement causes it to move, the infant looks at and listens to the toy rattling, assimilating the event into his or her schemes of looking and listening. To repeat the movement of the rattle, the infant must make the necessary hand and arm movements, accommodating his or her actions according to the demands of the situation.

Assimilation and accommodation were viewed by Piaget as inseparable aspects of a single process of adaptation, separable only for purposes of discussion (Brainerd, 1978). Assimilation and accommodation occur simultaneously; a balance between the two is necessary for adaptation.

REFERENCES

Brainerd, C.J. (1978). *Piaget's theory of intelligence.* Englewood Cliffs, NJ: Prentice-Hall.

Ginsburg, H., & Opper, S. (1969). *Piaget's theory of intellectual development: An introduction.* Englewood Cliffs, NJ: Prentice-Hall.

See also Assimilation; Cognitive Development; Piaget, Jean

ACETYLCHOLINE

Acetylcholine (ACh) is a neurotransmitter, a chemical that is released from one neuron to pass a message to another neuron. Acetylcholine is naturally synthesized in living cells in cholinergic nerve terminals that are located primarily in the autonomic nervous system. It also is evident at parasympathetic postganglionic synapses, and at neuromuscular junctures (Cooper, Bloom, & Roth, 1982).

REFERENCE

Cooper, J.R., Bloom, F.E., & Roth, R.H. (1982). *The biochemical basis of neuropharmacology.* New York: Oxford University Press.

See also Central Nervous System

ACHIEVEMENT NEED

Achievement need is also known as achievement motivation, the need for achievement and n:Ach. The concept was first defined by Murray (1938) as the need, "to overcome obstacles, to exercise power, to strive to do something difficult as well and as quickly as possible" (pp. 80–81). Murray, however, chose not to attempt to conduct applied research in achievement motivation and the concept did not receive much attention until McClelland (1951) developed a cognitive theory of motivation in which the need for achievement is one element. McClelland's theory states that a person's tendency to approach a task (effort) is a function of the strength of the achievement need, the strength of the need to avoid failure, the person's subjective belief about the probability of success or failure, and the value of the incentives associated with either success or failure. According to McClelland (1951) and Atkinson (1964), achievement need is intrinsic. It is not associated with extrinsic rewards that accrue as a result of achievement. Achievement need is generally measured through the Thematic Apperception Test (TAT).

Many researchers have attempted to determine how achievement need develops. Crandall (1963) discovered that children with high achievement needs had mothers who rewarded achievement and achievement activities at an early age. These mothers also did not attend to their children's pleas for help when the children faced a difficult problem. Crandall further concluded that middle- and upper-class parents were more likely to engage in behaviors that develop achievement motivation than were parents of lower economic status. Weiner (1970) found that high-need achievement persons persist in the face of failure while low-need achievement persons become more inhibited in their responses. Both high- and low-achievement need children attribute failure to themselves, but high-need achievement children attributed failure to lack of effort while low-achievement children attributed it to lack of ability.

REFERENCES

Atkinson, J.W. (1964). *An introduction to motivation.* Princeton, NJ: Van Nostrand.

Crandall, V.J. (1963). Achievement. In H.W. Stevenson (Ed.), *Child psychology* (pp. 416–459). Chicago: University of Chicago Press.

McClelland, D.C. (1951). *Personality.* New York: Dryden.

Murray, H.A. (1938). *Exploration in personality.* New York: Oxford University Press.

Weiner, B. (1970). New conceptions in the study of achievement motivation. In B.A. Maher (Ed.), *Progress in experimental personality research* (Vol. 5). New York: Academic.

See also **Learned Helplessness; Motivation; Self-Concept; Self-Control Curriculum**

ACHIEVEMENT TESTS

Achievement tests are individually- or group-administered standardized instruments intended to measure the effectiveness of former training. Achievement tests are the dominant form of standardized assessment in education. Measures of achievement have been used to evaluate student performance, school instruction efficacy, candidates for scholarship awards, admission to academic programs, and applicants for industrial and government employment. Group administered achievement tests are more likely to be employed for the evaluation of a scholastic program, whereas individually administered achievement tests are typically used to assist in appropriate grade placement in schools and the identification and diagnosis of learning disabilities.

See also **Academic Achievement Tests; Assessment; Criterion-Referenced Tests; Norm-Referenced Tests**

ACHONDROPLASIA

Achondroplasia, also called chondrodystrophy, refers to a defect in the formation of cartilage in the epiphyses of long bones, such that a type of dwarfism results. This most common form of dwarfism is usually inherited as an autosomal dominant trait, or it may result from spontaneous mutation (Avioli, 1979; Magalini, 1971). Clinical features of achondroplasia include absolute diminution of extremities; normal trunk and head size; a prominent, bulging forehead; and a flattened, saddle nose. Hands and feet typically are short, and fingers tend to be nearly equal in length (trident hands). Adult height generally does not exceed 1.4 meters.

The intelligence of affected persons is reported to be normal (Avioli, 1979; Lubs, 1977), although there is evidence of occasional neurologic complications during early adulthood (Magalini, 1971). The fertility of achondroplastic dwarfs is reported to be 30% of normal. Of offspring of two affected persons, two-thirds will exhibit the syndrome (Lubs, 1977). In educational settings, afflicted children may require adaptive equipment to accommodate their short stature. While there is no evidence to suggest that achondroplasia places individuals at increased risk for learning problems, a multifactored evaluation is appropriate for children who experience difficulty in school.

REFERENCES

Avioli, L.V. (1979). Diseases of bone. In P.B. Beeson, W. McDermott, & J.B. Wyngaarden (Eds.), *Cecil textbook of medicine* (pp. 2225–2265). Philadelphia: Saunders.

Lubs, M. (1977). Genetic disorders. In M.J. Krajicek & A.I. Tearney (Eds.), *Detection of developmental problems in children* (pp. 55–77). Baltimore, MD: University Park Press.

Magalini, S. (1971). *Dictionary of medical syndromes.* Philadelphia: Lippincott.

See also **Congenital Disorders; Minor Physical Anomalies**

ACTING OUT

Acting out has been defined by Harriman (1975) as the "direct expression of conflicted tensions in annoying or antisocial behavior in fantasies" (p. 30). A child who exhibits acting-out behavior is one who cannot easily accept structural limits and is difficult to manage in the classroom. Acting-out behaviors are similar to conduct disorders, but not necessarily as severe. One reason for the similarity is that acting-out behavior is one of the characteristics clustered under the broader grouping of conduct disorders. Acting-out behaviors usually are of high frequency and of significant duration, and do not include minor daily misbehavior.

Usually, when a behavior is identified as an acting-out behavior, it is operationally defined, observed, and recorded by the classroom teacher in specific and observable terms. Some of the behaviors that can be identified as acting-out behaviors include fighting, lying, temper tantrums, pouting, stealing, hyperactivity, threatening, and bullying (Quay, 1979).

REFERENCES

Harriman, P.L. (1975). *Handbook of psychological terms.* Totowa, NJ: Littlefield, Adams.

Quay, H.C. (1979). Classification. In H.C. Quay & J.S. Werry (Eds.), *Psychopathological disorders of childhood* (2nd ed.). New York: Wiley.

See also **Applied Behavior Analysis; Conduct Disorder**

ADAPTED PHYSICAL EDUCATION

Adapted physical education is a

diversified program of developmental activities, games, sports, and rhythms suited to the interests, capacities, and limitations of students with disabilities who may not safely and successfully engage in unrestricted participation in vigorous activities of the general physical education program. (Hurley, 1981, p. 43)

The focus of adapted physical education is on the development of motor and physical fitness and fundamental motor patterns and skills in a sportslike environment (Sherrill, 1985).

Adapted physical education implies the modification of physical activities, rules, and regulations to meet existing limiting factors of specific handicapped populations. By definition, adapted physical education includes activities planned for persons with learning problems owed to mental, motor, or emotional impairment, disability, or dysfunction; planned for the purpose of rehabilitation, habilitation, or remediation; modified so the handicapped can participate; and designed for modifying movement capabilities.

Adapted physical education primarily occurs within a school setting, but it may also occur in clinics, hospitals, residential facilities, daycare centers, or other centers where the primary intent is to influence learning or movement potential through motor activity (AAHPER, 1952).

In the school setting, adapted physical education differs from regular physical education in the following manner. It has a federally mandated base through PL 94-142. It serves students who are primarily identified as having a handicapping condition but may serve students such as the obese, who are not identified as handicapped but are in need of physical activity modification within a restricted environment. Adapted physical education classes are usually separate and educationally distinct from regular physical education owing to the need to modify the curriculum to suit the individual interests and capabilities of the student.

REFERENCES

AAHPER. (1952, April). *Guiding principles for a physical education journal of health, physical education, recreation.* Author.

Hurley, D. (1981). *Guidelines for adapted physical education.* New York: *Journal of Health, Physical Education, Recreation, and Dance* (pp. 43–45).

Sherrill, C. (1985). *Adapted physical education and recreation* (3rd ed.). Dubuque, IA: Brown.

See also **Physical Education for Students with Disabilities**

ADAPTIVE BEHAVIOR

Adaptive behavior, or the daily activities required for personal and social sufficiency, is an integral part of the evaluation and planning for handicapped and nonhandicapped individuals. It is not a new concept and has its roots in historical views concerning the treatment of the mentally retarded. The increased emphasis now placed on the use of the adaptive behavior concept in special education and programs for the handicapped is resulting in attempts to better understand the characteristics of adaptive behavior and in the publication of many new instruments for measuring adaptive behavior (Meyers, Nihira, & Zetlin, 1979).

Edgar Doll, the major pioneer in adaptive behavior assessment, disagreed with the use of IQs only, and, in the 1930s, indicated that a person's social competence, or adaptive behavior, should be the first and most important criterion for mental retardation. It was not until 1959 that the American Association on Mental Deficiency published its official manual and formally included deficits in adaptive behavior, in addition to low intelligence, as an integral part of the definition of mental retardation (Heber, 1961). Subsequent editions of the manual have further emphasized the importance of adaptive behavior.

Several issues in the 1960s and 1970s precipitated an upsurge of interest in adaptive behavior and adaptive behavior assessment (Witt & Martens, 1984). A concern arose about "6-hour retarded children" or minority group and low socioeconomic status children who were labeled as retarded in the public schools but exhibited adequate adaptive behavior at home and in the community (Mercer, 1973). This concern eventually led to litigation such as the Guadalupe and Larry P. cases and court decisions that indicated that results of intelligence tests cannot be the primary basis for classifying children as mentally retarded and that adaptive behavior must be assessed. The 1960s and 1970s saw a trend toward the normalization of handicapped individuals and the awareness that effective programs for teaching adaptive skills allow handicapped individuals to participate as fully as possible in normal environments. A third issue was the need for a nonbiased and multifaceted assessment of all handicapped children to facilitate the fairness of decisions based on the results of tests and to investigate functioning in all areas related to a particular handicap.

The passage of the Education of All Handicapped Children Act of 1975 (Public Law 94-142) represented the culmination of the issues of the 1960s and 1970s. Public Law 94-142 and its successor, the current Individuals with Disabilities Education Act, commonly known as IDEA, have stringent guides for the assessment of handicapped children and stipulates that deficits in adaptive behavior must be substantiated before a child is classified as mentally retarded. Further, it recognizes the importance of adaptive behavior assessment for children other than the mentally retarded. Since the passage of the law, most states have developed guidelines for adaptive behavior assessment (Patrick & Reschly, 1982) and many have strict criteria for the types of adaptive behavior instruments and scores to be used.

Sparrow, Balla, and Cicchetti (1984) discuss several characteristics that are inherent in concepts of adaptive behavior. Adaptive behavior is an age-related construct; as normally developing children grow older, adaptive behavior increases and becomes more complex. Adaptive behavior is determined by the standards of other people, those who live, work, play, teach, and interact with an individual. Finally, adaptive behavior is defined as what an individual does day by day, not by an individual's ability or what he or she can do. If a person has the ability to perform a daily task, but does not do it, adaptive behavior is considered to be inadequate.

REFERENCES

Heber, R.F. (1961). A manual on terminology and classification in mental retardation (Monograph Suppl.) *American Journal of Mental Deficiency.*

Mercer, J.R. (1973). *Labeling the mentally retarded.* Berkeley, CA: University of California Press.

Meyers, C.E., Nihira, K., & Zetlin, A. (1979). The measurement of adaptive behavior. In N.R. Ellis (Eds.), *Handbook of mental deficiency: Psychological theory and research* (2nd ed.) (pp. 215–253). Hillside, NJ: Erlbaum.

Patrick, J.L., & Reschly, D.J. (1982). Relationship of state educational criteria and demographic variables to school system prevalence of mental retardation. *American Journal of Mental Deficiency, 86,* 351–360.

Sparrow, S.S., Balla, D.A., & Cicchetti, D.V. (1984). *Vineland Adaptive Behavior Scales.* Circle Pines, MN: American Guidance Service.

Witt, J.C., & Martens, B.K. (1984). Adaptive behavior: Test and assessment issues. *School Psychology Review, 13,* 478–484.

See also Adaptive Behavior Inventory for Children; Mental Retardation

ADAPTIVE BEHAVIOR INVENTORY FOR CHILDREN (ABIC)

The Adaptive Behavior Inventory for Children (ABIC), a component of the System of Multicultural Pluralistic Assessment (SOMPA; Mercer & Lewis, 1977), is a 242-item rating scale for children ages 5 to 11 years. It provides an indication of a child's adaptation to social systems involving the family, peer group, and community. The ABIC items are administered to a child's parents or guardians; the questions are read to a parent and he or she indicates whether the child's role in the activity described by the item is latent, emergent, or mastered. The administration requires about 1 hour. The ABIC contains six scales: Family, Community, Peer Relations, Nonacademic School Roles, Earner Consumer, and Self-Maintenance. A measure of veracity (or a lie scale) is also included.

Scaled scores (with a mean of 50 and a standard deviation of 15) are available for each of the six scales; the ABIC Average Scaled Score, a measure of overall adaptive behavior, is the mean of the six scaled scores. The ABIC was standardized with a sample of 2085 California schoolchildren (696 black, 700 Spanish surname, and 689 white). The SOMPA *Technical Manual* reports average split-half reliability coefficients ranging from 0.82 to 0.89 for the six scales and a reliability coefficient of 0.97 for the ABIC Average Scaled Score. No validity data are reported in the manual, but the ABIC has been used in numerous studies that investigated, for example, the relationship between the ABIC and intelligence and achievement (e.g., Harrison, 1981; Oakland, 1983) and the representativeness of the ABIC norms (Oakland, 1979). Use of the ABIC has declined considerably as its parent system, SOMPA, has lost favor in the profession.

REFERENCES

Harrison, P.L. (1981). Mercer's adaptive behavior inventory, the McCarthy scales, and dental development as predictors of first grade achievement. *Journal of Educational Psychology, 73,* 78–82.

Mercer, J.R., & Lewis, J.E. (1977). *System of Multicultural Pluralistic Assessment.* New York: Psychological Corporation.

Oakland, T. (1979). Research on the adaptive behavior inventory for children and the estimated learning potential. *School Psychology Digest, 8,* 63–78.

Oakland, T. (1983). Joint use of adaptive behavior and IQ to predict achievement. *Journal of Consulting and Clinical Psychology, 51,* 298–301.

See also **Adaptive Behavior; Behavioral Observation; System of Multicultural Pluralistic Assessment; Vineland Social–Emotional Early Childhood Scales**

ADAPTIVE BEHAVIOR SCALE

See also Vineland Adaptive Behavior Scales

ADAPTIVE DEVICES

Adaptive, assistive, augmentative, prosthetic, and orthotic devices are all aids to help those with a variety of disabilities to overcome problems of everyday living. Examples range from leg braces to highly sophisticated microcomputers adapted for the disabled. Included are hearing aids, Braille books, glasses, wheelchairs, specialized eating utensils, braces, positioning devices, page turners, tape recorders, typewriters, and the artificial larynx.

Two sources of information for this wide range of adaptive devices are *The Directory of Living Aids for the Disabled Person,* published by the Veterans Administration (U.S. Government Printing Office, 1982), which provides an extensive list of aids for daily living, and *The Information System for Adaptive, Assistive and Rehabilitative Equipment (ISAARE)* (Melichar, 1977, 1978), an information storage and retrieval system that lists devices by categories such as "travel" and "communication."

The type of adaptive devices currently experiencing the greatest technological advances as well as the greatest emphasis in rehabilitation is augmentative communication systems. Three general modes of nonvocal or augmentative communication have been developed for those for whom intelligible speech is not an option. They are manual communication, communication boards, and electronic systems. Manual communication includes gestures, signs, and finger spelling; it is used extensively with nonhearing-impaired as well as hearing-impaired populations, but it does not include an adaptive device. Communication boards are boards, or booklets, that come in a wide range of sizes, shapes, and materials, and make use of a variety of symbol systems. These symbols include objects, drawings and photographs, rebus symbols, Blissymbols, letters, and words. Sources of information on the design and use of communication boards include the *Language Board Instruction Kit* (Oaklander, 1980), Carlson (1981); Musselwhite & St. Louis (1982), Silverman (1980), and *Non Oral Communication* (Plavan Schools, 1980).

The tremendous growth of computer technology is providing the impetus for the development of communication systems for the physically disabled that can be individually tailored to their abilities. Input devices for those who do not have sufficient motor control for direct selection (pointing or using a keyboard) include paddle switches, joy sticks, moisture switches, optical switches, eyebrow or tongue-controlled switches, sip and puff switches, and voice-controlled switches, among others. These augmentative systems are also tailored to the user's output needs and may include a combination of hard copy printout, synthesized speech output, display screens, and so on. The selection of an appropriate system to include the most effective and efficient symbol system, input technique, and output capabilities is a complex process requiring the services of a team of experts. The American Speech-Language-Hearing Association (ASHA) Ad Hoc Committee on Communication Processes and Non-Speaking Persons (1980) identifies possible team members as well as essential components of the assessment process. Depending on the individual's needs, most of the following people should be involved in the assessment and training process: speech-language pathologist, occupational therapist, physical therapist, parents, teacher, system user, psychologist, rehabilitation engineer, and social worker.

Ongoing research on the design and use of augmentative communication systems makes any list or discussion of specific systems quickly obsolete.

REFERENCES

American Speech-Language-Hearing Association. (1980). Non-speech communication: a position paper. *ASHA, 22,* 267–272.

Carlson, F. (1981). *Alternate methods of communication.* Danville, IL: Interstate.

Directory of living aids for the disabled person. (1982). U.S. Government Printing Office.

Fraser, B.A., & Hensinger, R.N. (1983). *Managing physical handicaps: A practical guide for parents, care providers, and educators.* Baltimore, MD: Brookes.

Haring, N.G. (Ed.). (1982). *Exceptional children and youth.* Columbus, OH: Merrill.

Melichar, J.F. (1977). *ISAARE,* San Mateo, CA: Adaptive Systems.

Melichar, J.F. (1978). *Challenges in mental retardation: Progressive ideology and sources.* New York: Human Services Press.

Musselwhite, C.R., & St. Louis, K.W. (1982). *Communication programming for the severely handicapped: Vocal and nonvocal strategies.* San Diego: College Hill Press.

Non Oral Communication: A Training Guide for the Child Without Speech. (1980). Plavan School, 9675 Warner Ave., Fountain Valley, CA 92708.

Oakander, S. (1980). *Language Board Instruction Kit.* Non-Oral Communication Center, 9675 Warner Ave., Fountain Valley, CA 92708.

Silverman, F.H. (1980). *Communication for the speechless.* Englewood Cliffs, NJ: Prentice Hall.

***See also* Augmentative Communication Systems; Blissymbols; Communication Boards**

ADDERALL

Adderall is a stimulant medication that is a different mixture of amphetamine isomers than the common stimulants such as dexedrine, benzedrine, methamphetamine, methylphenidate, and magnesium pemoline. It is available in 5, 10, 20, and 30 mg tablets. Adderall is used primarily in the treatment of attention-deficit hyperactivity disorder (ADHD) and narcolepsy. Adderall has been shown in clinical trials to increase alertness, improve attention span, decrease distractibility, and increase the ability to follow directions among children ages 3 years and up. Adderall is popular among many children and families because it may need to be taken only once or twice a day, eliminating the need for dosing at school. Since it is a different chemical preparation, Adderall has been found to be effective with patients who do not respond to more popular stimulant treatments, such as Ritalin. However, Adderall may take as long as 3 to 4 weeks to become effective, while other stimulants tend to take effect more immediately. Adderall has a similar side-effect profile to other common stimulants, the most common of those being appetite suppression, growth retardation, insomnia, and headache.

Adderall may be habit-forming and is classified as a central nervous system stimulant. Monitoring of dose response, side effects, and polypharmacy by a physician is crucial to safe use of Adderall and other drugs in its class. Additional information is available in Arky (1998) and Cahill (1997).

REFERENCES

Arky, R. (1998). *Physicians desk reference.* Montvale, NJ: Medical Economies Data Production.

Cahill, M. (Ed.). (1997). *Nursing 97 drug handbook.* Springhouse, PA: Springhouse Corporation.

ADDITIVE-FREE DIETS

During the 1970s and 1980s, a very important and particularly controversial theory of the management of learning and behavioral disorders in children was the theory of the additive-free diet proposed by Feingold (1975). Specifically, Feingold has maintained that children with hyperactivity and other behavioral disorders have a natural toxic reaction to artificial food colors, flavorings, preservatives, and other substances that are added to food to enhance their shelf-life. The additive-free diet regimen proposed by Feingold purports to eliminate artificial flavors and salicylates (compounds naturally occurring in certain fruits and vegetables) from a child's diet as a treatment for hyperactivity and learning disabilities. Feingold has advocated his additive-free diet for a number of other conditions, including mental retardation, early infantile autism, and delinquency (Barkley, 1990).

However, this treatment has been widely assailed in scholarly literature. On the basis of empirically unsubstantiated claims concerning the efficacy of this diet, Feingold has insisted that nearly 50% of hyperactive children in his clinical private practice sample displayed a complete remission of symptoms as a result of the additive-free dietary regimen. Such improved symptoms, according to the Feingold group, include markedly enhanced cognitive and academic functioning. Further, Feingold has insisted that the younger the child, the more expedient and complete the improvement that occurs. Nonetheless, several investigators (Harley & Matthews, 1980) have attributed this dramatic success to a placebo effect, or even the changed aspects of family dynamics that often result from the additive-free diet. Also contributing to widespread acceptance of the Feingold diet is our culture's current obsession with diet consciousness and health food fads.

The publicity and heated debate resulting from Feingold's claims have resulted in a proliferation of empirical studies among investigators in the scientific community that have assessed the efficacy of additive-free diets in hyperactive children (Conners, 1980; Conners, Goyette, Southwick, Lees, & Andrulonis, 1976). In a cogent summary of a series of studies conducted by these researchers, Conners (1980) has concluded that only a small number of children (less than 5%) respond specifically to the additive-free diet. More important, many investigators now recognize that those foods that Feingold has recommended be eliminated from children's diets are often high in important nutrients necessary for normal growth and development. Thus, placing children on the additive-free diet may compromise their nutritional needs.

REFERENCES

Barkley, R.A. (1990). *Hyperactive children: A handbook for diagnosis and treatment* (2nd ed.). New York: Guilford.

Conners, C.K. (1980). *Food additives and hyperactive children.* New York: Plenum.

Conners, C.K., Goyette, C.H., Southwick, D.A., Lees, J.M., & Andrulonis, P. (1976). Food additives and hyperkinesis. *Pediatrics, 58,* 154–166.

Feingold, B.F. (1975). *Why your child is hyperactive.* New York: Random House.

Harley, J.P., & Matthews, C.G. (1980). Food additives and hyperactivity in children. In R.M. Knights & D.J. Bakker (Eds.), *Treatment of hyperactive and learning disordered children.* Baltimore, MD: University Park Press.

See also **Feingold Diet; Hyperactivity**

ADJUSTMENT OF THE HANDICAPPED

By virtue of their "differentness," handicapped individuals and their families must make certain special adjustments to lead fulfilling and satisfying lives. The most obvious and important of these adjustments is the appraisal and acceptance of the handicapping condition itself. Such acceptance is prerequisite to seeking and obtaining appropriate care and services.

Another necessary adjustment requires recognizing and dealing with influences of a handicapping condition on all aspects of the individual's development. For example, a physical handicap affects social development and interactions in ways that have only recently been addressed scientifically and professionally, but have long been sources of confusion and frustration to the handicapped.

The development of the child with a handicap occurs along the same lines as that of the nonhandicapped child. However, an individual handicapped child's development will exhibit qualitative variations from the norm. The specific deviations from typical development depend both on the nature and severity of the handicapping condition and on the level of adjustment achieved by the child and his or her family and teachers. Of particular significance in the adjustment of the handicapped child are personality and social development. Also of concern are possible physical and/or medical adjustments that may be required, and special educational adjustments.

A handicapping condition may limit a child's or adolescent's physical activities. The handicap may impose restrictions owing to physical limitations or medical complications that limit freedom to get about in the environment. Physical and/or medical limitations may reduce opportunities for interaction and exploration in both the physical and social realms and thus curtail experiences that stimulate and promote cognitive growth and personal-social development. Handicapped children must be encouraged not to retreat from any activities that are accessible, although inconvenient, because of physical restrictions. Professionals and others can help them to participate in an adapted way, if necessary, in order not to deprive them of beneficial experiences.

Handicapped children may have to adjust medical interventions or therapies such as drugs, braces, physical therapy, surgical procedures, hearing appliances, etc. The child's adjustment to the medical aspect of his or her program is absolutely essential because the child must cooperate in order to achieve the maximum benefits of the prescribed treatment(s).

A handicapped child is very likely to have to make an adjustment involving his or her educational programs. The adjustment may range from simply modifying his or her study habits or methods to full-time participation in a special self-contained program. Professionals who work with the child should strive to minimize whatever educational disadvantage(s) may be imposed by the handicap. The goals of the child's educational program should emphasize activities to compensate for and/or overcome his or her handicap.

The effectiveness of the child's program will be amplified by the active involvement of parents in consistently following through on behavioral and educational interventions in the home environment. Concrete benefits are derived from the parents' participation. Parents are able to provide additional reinforcement and practice for skills learned during the school day, helping their child consolidate gains more rapidly. In addition, their involvement is a signal to the child of their commitment to his or her development and the high value they place on educational achievement. These attitudes are highly motivating and will help see the child through difficult periods.

Parents who do not accept and adjust to the child's handicap escalate their child's difficulties. Maladaptive behavior patterns that emerge in the relationship between parents and their handicapped child can arise from either of two opposite, but equally harmful, reactions. Parents may either overestimate or underestimate their child's abilities and potential. Overestimates may be due to parents' denial of their child's problems. Such parents are prone to establish unreasonably high standards for their child's behavior or development. Because the child wants to please the parents but is not capable of fulfilling their expectations, he or she continually faces feelings of frustration, inadequacy, and other negative emotions such as guilt, disappointment, and uncertainty as to his or her place in the affections of the parents. On the other hand, some parents seem to overcompensate for their handicapped child. Some typical behaviors of these parents include setting goals that are too easily attained, praising or rewarding the child for work that is below his or her level of functioning, and intervening unnecessarily when the child is working on difficult tasks. Such behaviors convey the message, albeit indirectly, that the parents do not recognize or appreciate the child's actual abilities. These signals undermine the development of high self-esteem and a positive self-concept.

Due to increasing recognition of social and emotional problems that may be secondary to other disabilities, the IDEA requires a behavioral assessment of all children with a disability, regardless of their handicapping condition. It has become commonplace to use objective behavior rating scales and personality assessments during the initial referral and evaluation process (e.g., Reynolds & Kamphaus, 1992). Also, as a direct result of recognition of behavioral and emotional concomitants of various disabilities, IDEA now requires a behavioral assessment prior to disciplining a child with a disability, so that it can be determined whether the behavior of concern is a result of the child's disability. When behavioral problems are disability-related, children must be treated, not punished. Teachers will have the primary role to play in such interventions at school.

REFERENCE

Reynolds, C.R., & Kamphaus, R.W. (1992). *Behavior assessment system for children.* Circle Pines, MN: American Guidance Service.

See also **Behavior Assessment System for Children; Family Response to a Child with Disabilities; Handicapism; Individuals with Disabilities Education Act; Teacher Expectancies**

ADMINISTRATION OF SPECIAL EDUCATION

Public school services for exceptional children began in the latter part of the nineteenth century (Gearheart & Wright, 1979). By the middle of the twentieth century, public school classes became the primary mode of education for exceptional children. With this change, the administration of special education programs fell to educators and school psychologists. Although special education programs were held in public school buildings, they were usually separate, and writers of the time advocated separate administration and supervision systems (Ayer & Barr, 1928).

The rise of special education administration as a discipline occurred simultaneously with the rise of segregated public school programs. Special education administrators during the first quarter of the twentieth century were not trained generally as administrators; it was not until 1938 that any professional identity was established. In that year, the National Association of State Directors of Special Education was founded. In 1951 the Council of Administrators of Special Education (CASE) convened as a special interest group within the Council for Exceptional Children.

Although special education administration has developed a uniqueness and identity, there is considerable variety within the discipline. This variety is expressed across governmental levels and organizational arrangements. There are three governmental levels in special education administration: federal, state, and local. Within each level the tasks of the administrator may vary considerably depending on the specific role of the administrator, the organization of the agency for which the administrator works, and the ways in which the agency delivers services.

Presently, the federal role in special education administration is executed primarily by the Office of Special Education and Rehabilitation of the U.S. Department of Education. The administrative roles of this office include monitoring state compliance with IDEA; generating research; providing public information; formulating regulations; promoting personnel development; and drafting legislation. As a result of PL 94-142 and IDEA, the federal role in administration of special education has grown substantially. Nearly every administrative decision in special education must be made with consideration for the regulations propagated by IDEA. Because of this, the majority of the administrators at the federal level are involved in activities related to providing services to the states in order that they may carry out the provisions of IDEA, or in evaluating/monitoring the state's efforts.

Administration of special education programs at the state level occurs in three places: at the state education agency (SEA); at state-operated schools; and at state-operated regional centers. At the SEA, the roles of administration are to develop legislation; to develop state plans; to obtain and administer financial resources; to develop personnel preparation systems and standards; to develop plans for improving instruction; to enforce and monitor regulations; and to develop public relations (Gearhart & Wright, 1979; Podemski, Price, Smith, & Marsh, 1984). The SEAs also directly administer programs such as state schools for the deaf or blind (e.g., Pennsylvania). These programs are usually for low-incidence populations. In Georgia, the SEA administers both state schools and regional centers that provide direct service to low-incidence populations, especially in rural areas. Regional centers also serve as resource centers for local education agencies (LEAs).

Many rural school systems and suburban systems enter into cooperative agreements in order to provide more cost-effective programs, especially for low-incidence populations (Howe, 1981). Cooperative programs engender the same problems as do IEUs. Additionally, they must often contend with long distances for busing students.

The competencies of LEA and IEU special education administrators are similar. The differences are probably in terms of the amount of time devoted to different tasks rather than the tasks themselves. This may be true also for administrators of state-operated direct service programs (e.g., state schools). The competency areas for such administrators include organization theory and behavior; budget development; curriculum development; supervision; personnel administration; community relations; community resources; change processes; physical plant management; research; professional standards; and policy development.

IDEA requires all LEAs to have available the complete range of service-delivery options. This includes self-contained classes, resource rooms, part-time classes, residential programs, and other options (Deno, 1970). Before PL 94-142 it was possible for LEAs to offer only one service-delivery option (most often self-contained classes). This change and the variability of placement options has brought new problems to the forefront of special education administration. These problems include team-work with regular educators; appropriate placement; coordination with general education administrators; and increased parental involvement (Mingo & Burrello, 1985).

Specialized graduate training for administrators of programs for exceptional children began in 1965. The impetus for such training was provided by a journal article by Milazzo and Blessing (1964). Subsequent to the publishing of that article, the U.S. Office of Education awarded grants to universities for the purpose of developing training programs (Burrello & Sage, 1979). Although most states do have certification requirements for special education leadership positions, requirements can be met with a general administrative certificate or a collection of courses and experience. Because market demands are limited, most training programs have not reached a high degree of articulation, sophistication, or visibility. A number of writers have articulated the desired content of special education administra-

tion training programs. Among the more notable training programs is the Special Education Supervisory Training Project (SEST, 1974), which was based on a human/conceptual/technical model (Burrello & Sage, 1979).

REFERENCES

Ayer, F.C., & Barr, A.S. (1928). *The organization of supervision.* New York: Appleton.

Burrello, L.C., & Sage, D.D. (1979). *Leadership and change in special education.* Englewood Cliffs, NJ: Prentice-Hall.

Deno, E. (1970). Special education for the mildly retarded: Is much of it justifiable? *Exceptional Children, 37*(3), 229–237.

Gearheart, B.R., & Wright, W.S. (1979). *Organization and administration of educational programs for exceptional children* (2nd ed.). Springfield, IL: Thomas.

Howe, C. (1981). *Administration of special education.* Denver: Love.

Milazzo, T.C., & Blessing, K.R. (1964). The training of directors and supervisors of special education programs. *Exceptional Children, 31,* 129–141.

Mingo, J., & Burrello, L.C. (1985) *Determining the relationship between special education administrator, supervisor, and building principal role and responsibilities in the administration of educational programs for the handicapped.* Bloomington, IN: Council of Administrators of Special Education, Inc., Indiana University.

Podemski, R.S., Price, B.J., Smith, T.E.C., & Marsh, G.E. (1984). *Comprehensive administration of special education.* Rockville, MD: Aspen.

SEST Project (1974). *Professional supervisor competencies.* Austin, TX: University of Texas.

See also **Individuals with Disabilities Education Act; Politics and Special Education; Special Education Programs; Supervision in Special Education**

ADULT BASIC EDUCATION (ABE)

Adult basic education (ABE), a part of the adult education movement, is designed and intended for those individuals who may lack the basic education needed to function appropriately in society. For many adults, particularly those with handicapping conditions, adult education serves as a substitute for the education that was missed in earlier years or never completed. For others, adult education implies further or continuing education.

Adult education encompasses all organized learning, including vocational education (Stubblefield, 1981). During the formative years of what became the adult education movement (mid-to-late 1920s), adult education revolved around a belief that individual growth and improvement was paramount; that is, individuals would respond to education that would assist in helping them to understand their life experiences and improve themselves through the acquisition of knowledge, enjoyment, power, etc.

Later, the adult education movement emphasized a variety of other themes, including psychological and physical maturity, service to society, and civic life. Those who have tried to identify a central focus within adult education have most often portrayed the adult learner as an individual who seeks out education and has a desire to accommodate to a changing society and value system. Thus one major issue has centered around whether the goal of adult education should be to satisfy individual needs or societal needs.

There are many adult education service providers, although most can be assigned to one of four categories: (1) agencies that serve the needs of adults; (2) agencies that serve the needs of adolescents, but have some responsibility for serving the needs of adults; (3) agencies that serve the educational and noneducational needs of the community; and (4) agencies that serve the special interest needs of particular groups. In the first category are agencies such as proprietary schools (i.e., business schools, technical schools) and independent education centers. The second category consists of public schools, community colleges, and institutions of higher education. The third category includes libraries and museums, while the fourth category includes unions, churches, business and industry, and so on. In essence, adult education is found in a variety of organizations that provide education for adults.

There are numerous categories of individuals who provide potential populations of adult learners. These include:

Those desiring to overcome educational limitations

College and high school dropouts

Career changers or career updaters

Institutionalized populations

Elderly persons

Those who simply enjoy learning

The handicapped

All possible knowledge could be included in an ABE program. However, few programs have the resources to provide such an extensive range of services for all types of adult learners. Limiting services, however, tends to limit the types of individuals who can participate; thus, handicapped adults may not be recruited for ABE programs that require students who have needs that are linked to a program's goals or capacities. While some ABE programs for adult handicapped persons are available, they have not been a major focus of ABE programs.

REFERENCE

Stubblefield, H.W. (1981). The focus should be on life fulfillment. In B.W. Kreitlow & Associates (Eds.), *Examining controversies in adult education.* San Francisco: Jossey-Bass.

See also **Community-Based Services; Rehabilitation; Vocational Village**

ADULT PROGRAMS FOR THE DISABLED

There are numerous programs of several types that serve adults with disabilities. Many such programs are financed by federal, state, and local governments; many others are funded by private business, private nonprofit organizations, and charities.

The Social Security Act authorizes several major programs providing cash payments and health insurance to adults on the basis of disability. The disability insurance (DI) program replaces in part income lost when a person with a work history can no longer work because of a physical or mental impairment. Many individuals have separate commercial disability insurance policies provided by an employer or purchased on their own. After receiving Social Security DI benefits for 24 months, regardless of age, an individual becomes eligible for government-provided health insurance under the Medicare program, which normally covers persons 65 and over. The Social Security Act also contains the Supplemental Security Income (SSI) program, which provides cash income support payments to needy individuals who are aged, blind, or disabled. Income is provided regardless of work history to those who meet means and asset requirements. In most states, with SSI eligibility comes eligibility for the Medicaid program (federal-state matching required), which provides health insurance for low-income individuals. Included in Medicaid is support for intermediate care facilities for the mentally retarded (ICFs/MR), which provide residential care and service programs. Many disabled individuals benefit from programs for which they may be eligible without regard to their disability, for example, Social Security Old Age and Survivors insurance payments and Medicare (persons 65 and older).

There are four other major federal programs of this type for special groups of disabled individuals. Veterans with service-connected disabilities are eligible for special cash payments under the Veterans Compensation program. Veterans of wartime service with nonservice-connected disabilities are eligible for a special pension program. Coal miners disabled by black lung or other lung disease are eligible for one of two separate special payment programs (one administered by the Social Security Administration, the other by the Labor Department), depending on circumstances.

Special programs of postsecondary education for the deaf and hearing impaired, supported with significant federal funding, are provided at Gallaudet College, the National Technical Institute for the Deaf, and four special regional postsecondary institutions. In addition, educational programs that are recipients of federal financial assistance at public and private colleges and universities must be accessible to and usable by individuals with disabilities of all types. Some schools are making adaptations and providing support services that go beyond legal requirements.

Rehabilitation and job training services are available from a number of sources. Under Title I of the Rehabilitation Act, the federal government and the states provide vocational rehabilitation services such as physical restoration, job training, and placement to persons with mental and physical disabilities, regardless of prior work history. Physical rehabilitation is covered by most accident and health insurance policies; vocational rehabilitation is sometimes covered. Rehabilitation is available and in fact required under some state workers' compensation laws. Rehabilitation services financed by various forms of insurance are provided by private, for-profit companies and facilities, private nonprofit agencies, and state agencies. Provision of rehabilitation services by private, profit-making (proprietary) firms has been a growing phenomenon (Taylor et al., 1985) for many years now.

Private nonprofit entities play a significant role in providing job training, rehabilitation, and other skill development to adults with disabilities. Included in this group are organizations such as the Association for Retarded Citizens, Easter Seals, Goodwill Industries, and United Cerebral Palsy. Some activities of these organizations are financed by the government; others are funded by contracts with businesses for work performed.

Major employers, faced with rising costs of disability, will find it in their interest to pay greater attention to management, rehabilitation, and disability prevention (Schwartz, 1984). Many are increasing efforts in these areas, including rehabilitation, job, and work-site modification efforts to facilitate entry or return to jobs by individuals with disabilities. Contracts with the federal government of more than $2500 must operate with an affirmative action program to employ and advance individuals with disabilities.

Self-help, referral, and training services are available to people with very severe disabilities to improve their capacity for independent living. These services are available through a network of community-based nonprofit centers and from state rehabilitation agencies. In addition, supported employment is an important new program for individuals with disabilities so severe they were previously thought incapable of working. These individuals (especially those with mental impairments) are likely to need continual support, but they are able to work on regular jobs in integrated settings if given a highly structured training program and some support on the job site (Mank 1986).

Special housing and transportation programs are available for individuals with disabilities, financed by both the federal government and states and localities. The same is true for special recreation programs for the disabled, in which local governments, service organizations, charities, and private businesses play a large role. Therapeutic recreation is also part of some rehabilitation programs. In addition, many local recreation facilities and organizations, including those involved with the arts, are adapting programs so that the disabled can participate or attend with the general public.

REFERENCES

General Services Administration. (1985). *Catalog of federal domestic assistance.* Washington, DC: U.S. Government Printing Office.

Mank, D. (1986). Four supported employment alternatives. In W. Kiernan & J. Stark (Eds.), *Pathways to employment for developmentally disabled adults.* Baltimore, MD: Brooks.

National Council on the Handicapped. (1986). *Toward independence: An assessment of federal laws and programs affecting persons with disabilities.* Washington, DC: U.S. Government Printing Office.

Schwartz, G. (1984, May). Disability costs: The impending crisis. *Business and Health* (pp. 25–28).

Taylor, L.J., Golter, M., Golter, G., & Backer, T. (Eds.). (1985). *Handbook of private sector rehabilitation.* New York: Springer.

See also **Accessibility of Programs; Americans with Disabilities Act; Habilitation of the Handicapped; Rehabilitation**

ADVANCED PLACEMENT PROGRAM

The Advanced Placement Program was established in 1955 as a program of college-level courses and examinations for secondary school students. It is administered by the College Board, a nonprofit membership organization composed of public and private secondary schools, colleges, and universities. This program gives high school students the opportunity to receive advanced placement and/or credit on entering college.

Advanced Placement courses offer demanding academic opportunities for abler students. Students who complete these courses are not required to take advanced placement examinations, but those who choose to take them and who receive a passing score, have the opportunity to receive advanced placement and/or credit on entering college.

REFERENCES

College Entrance Examination Board (1985). *School administrator's guide to the advanced placement program* (Edition G). New York: Author.

The College Board Review (quarterly publication)

The College Board
888 Seventh Avenue
New York, NY 10106

Advanced Placement Program
Harlan P. Hanson, Director
45 Columbus Avenue
New York, NY 10023-6917

See also **Acceleration of Gifted Children; Gifted and Talented Children**

ADVANCE ORGANIZERS

Advance organizers are general overviews or conceptual models of new information presented to learners immediately prior to receiving new information. Ausubel (1960) originally proposed the concept of the advance organizer for use with reading material. The principle of advance organizers is that learning is enhanced when information is linked to learners' existing cognitive structures, thereby enabling the learner to organize and interpret new information (Mayer, 1979). Thus advance organizers prepare the learner for the meaningful reception of new learning. They can either present salient prerequisite knowledge not known to the learner (known as expository organizers), or help the learner establish connections between relevant dimensions of existing knowledge and the new information (known as comparative organizers) (Ausubel, Novak, & Hanesian, 1979).

Advance organizers may be either verbal or graphic, and can take a variety of formats, including overviews, outlines, analogies, examples, thought-provoking questions, concrete models, and figures such as cognitive maps (Alexander, Frankiewicz, & Williams, 1979; Zook, 1991). Although originally conceptualized as abstract introductions, advance organizers tend to be more effective if they are concrete and if they are both familiar to the learner and well-learned. In this way, advance organizers provide frameworks or cognitive maps for new content.

REFERENCES

Alexander, L., Frankiewicz, R., & Williams, R. (1979). Facilitation of learning and retention of oral instruction using advance and post organizers. *Journal of Educational Psychology, 71,* 701–707.

Ausubel, D.P. (1960). The use of advance organizers in the learning and retention of meaningful verbal material. *Journal of Educational Psychology, 51,* 267–272.

Ausubel, D.P., Novak, J.D., & Hanesian, H. (1979). *Educational psychology: A cognitive view* (2nd ed.). New York: Holt, Rinehart & Winston.

Mayer, R.E. (1979). Can advance organizers influence meaningful learning? *Review of Educational Research, 49,* 371–383.

Zook, K.B. (1991). Effects of analogical processes on learning and misrepresentation. *Educational Psychology Review, 3,* 41–72.

ADVENTITIOUS DISABILITIES

Disabilities may present themselves at birth or be acquired through disease or accident. Those acquired later in life are known as adventitious disabilities. Among these is brain damage produced by extremely high and consistent temperatures or a lack of needed oxygen to the brain. Adventitious disabilities may also be a consequence of trauma to the brain or injury to other parts of the body. A major cause of adventitious disabilities is child abuse. Child abuse is emotionally or physically damaging and can cause durable learning problems. An area of childhood exceptionality often associated with an adventitious disability is hearing impairment or deafness. Hearing losses may be present at birth or adventitiously acquired later on in life through disease or accident. Adventitious disabilities and congenital disabilities that appear similar (but are obviously of different etiologies) may well have different outcomes.

See also **Brain Damage/Injury; Child Abuse; Postinstitutionalized Children**

ADVOCACY FOR CHILDREN WITH DISABILITIES

Advocacy for handicapped people has become a multifaceted reality in today's world of concern about the legal rights of those with disabilities. The term actually has a variety of meanings, depending on who is providing the advocacy. In its essence, advocacy refers to attempts by an individual handicapped person, by another person, or by a group to guarantee that all rights due a handicapped person are realized. Roos (1983) traces the origins of the advocacy movement to the 1930s, when parents of mentally retarded children began to react against neglectful or inappropriate actions by professionals who claimed to be helping these children and their families. Frustrated with the professionals' response, parents turned to each other for help.

Herr (1983) describes several different kinds of advocacy that have evolved from earlier movements. Though definitions and actual practice may vary, the following types of advocacy approaches for the handicapped can be identified:

1. *Self-advocacy:* "part consciousness-raising, assertiveness-training . . . and springboard to direct consumer involvement. . . ." (Herr, 1983).

2. *Family advocacy:* the oldest and most well understood.

3. *Friend advocacy:* personal, voluntary assistance by altruistic citizens; also referred to as *citizen advocacy.*

4. *Disability rights advocacy:* trained advocacy specialists dealing with individual needs and human service systems.

5. *Human rights advocacy:* usually citizen review committees composed of volunteers and professionals.

6. *Internal advocacy:* individuals within, rather than external to, human service agencies who attempt to guarantee clients' rights (sometimes referred to as ombudsmen).

7. *Legal advocacy:* primarily nonprofit, public-interest law projects, including some private or government lawyers (Herr, 1983).

Although individual special educators, acting alone or through professional organizations, may also view themselves as advocates for the handicapped children they serve, there may be inherent conflicts in attempting to play the two roles simultaneously (Bateman, 1982). Special educators must keep current on ethical practices and legal developments in their field, and on law and education in general.

REFERENCES

Bateman, B. (1982). Legal and ethical dilemmas of special educators. *Exceptional Education Quarterly, 2*(4), 57–67.

Herr, S.S. (1983). *Rights and advocacy for retarded people.* Lexington, MA: Lexington Books.

Roos, P.R. (1983). Advocate groups. In J.L. Matson & J.A. Mulick (Eds.), *Handbook of mental retardation.* New York: Pergamon.

AFFECTIVE DISORDERS

Affect is the externally observable, immediately expressed component of human emotion (e.g., facial expression, tone of voice). Mood is considered to be a sustained emotion that pervades an individual's perception of the world. Affective disorders, as defined by the American Psychiatric Association (1994) are the class of mental disorders where the essential feature is a disturbance of mood.

Emotions and their expression are an integral part of human experience. It is only under certain conditions that the expression of emotion is considered maladaptive; in some instances, in fact, a lack of affect might be viewed as abnormal. It is only when an emotional reaction is disproportionate to the event, when the duration of the reaction is atypical, or when it interferes with a person's psychological, social, or occupational functioning that an emotional response may be labeled symptomatic of an affective disorder.

Affective disorders are comprised of two basic elements, depression and mania, which can be conceptualized as opposite ends of a continuum paralleling the normal happiness/sadness continuum. Both depression and mania have their counterparts in everyday life: The parallels for depression are grief and dejection; the experience corresponding to mania is less clear-cut, but probably could be described as the feverish activity with which people sometimes respond to stress.

Formally, both mania and depression can be characterized by symptoms at the emotional, cognitive, and somatic/motivational levels. The major emotional components of depression are sadness and melancholy, often accompanied by feelings of guilt and worthlessness. These emotions permeate the individual's total experience of life. Cognitively, depressed persons are characterized by a negatively distorted view of themselves, the world, and the future. Their outlook is generally one of unrealistic hopelessness. In terms of their physical functioning, depressed persons frequently suffer appetite and sleep disturbances, fatigue, apathy, and a general loss of energy. Cognitively, manic individuals characteristically show wildly inflated self-esteem, believing themselves to be capable of great accomplishments or possessed of exceptional talent.

Mood disorders have long been the most common of mental illnesses, but they are on the increase in modern society (Keller & Baker, 1992). Depression has been referred to as the common cold of mental illness. Around 10% of the males and perhaps 22% of the females living in the United States will at some point in their lives experience an episode of major depression. This one-to-two ratio has been found in many different cultures, in Europe and Africa as well as North America. (There are, however, a few notable exceptions such as the Amish in Pennsylvania.) It has been hypothesized that more women experience depression than men because it is more socially acceptable for women to respond to negative life experiences with passive, depressive symptoms. Men may be less likely to experience or express depressive symptoms because they may receive more social rejection (or less social reinforcement) than women for acting depressed. Instead, men may respond to stressful events more actively, with substance abuse (e.g., alcoholism) or antisocial behavior.

Most theorists believe that the cognitions that depressed persons experience are a consequence of depression. Beck (1967), however, believes that negative cognitions and thought patterns are the cause of unipolar depression rather than a consequence of depression. He has proposed that individuals prone to depression have negative schema that are activated by stress. Once activated, the individual tends to interpret his or her experience in the worst possible light, using errors of logic (e.g., drawing sweeping conclusions based on one or two events) to do so. This negative interpretation occurs even when more plausible explanations for experiences are available; the person chooses his or her explanation on the basis of its negativity rather than its validity.

From the viewpoint of the individual working with children, what may be most important regarding affective disorders is an awareness of and ability to recognize signs of childhood affective disorders. It should be noted first that it is rare for children, particularly prior to puberty, to experience manic episodes. When a young child exhibits overactive behavior that appears manic, it is probably more appropriately considered a symptom of hyperactivity. (It is also possible for overactive behavior to result from an endocrine dysfunction.) Depressivelike syndromes, on the other hand, have been reported in children 3 years of age and younger. The symptoms of these syndromes vary in part as a function of age; the older a depressed child, the more closely his or her symptoms will parallel those of adults. Consequently, this discussion will focus on the symptoms of younger school-aged children (i.e., approximately ages 6 to 14).

A major distinction between depressed children and adults is that children, in contrast to adults, seldom seek help or complain about feelings of depression. Instead, they may become apathetic regarding school or socially withdrawn, sometimes preferring to remain in their rooms at home rather than playing with friends. They may make vague physical complaints about head or stomach pains, seem overly self-conscious, and cry inexplicably. Older children may see themselves as bad kids—incompetent in school and unworthy of the love of adults or the friendship of other children. Some, but not all, depressed children may simply look sad, particularly in their facial expressions, for extended periods of time with little apparent fluctuation in mood. Overall, a child will usually exhibit only some of the symptoms noted, and the symptom pattern may vary across a period of weeks.

Such symptoms are expressed in what is essentially a passive manner. Though there is far from universal agreement on the issue, certain professionals believe that in some instances children may express depression through aggressive misbehavior. While it is usually difficult to distinguish between genuine misbehavior and misbehavior that is an expression of so-called masked depression, children who are acting out as a symptom of depression often are more responsive to firm (but not overly authoritarian) limit-setting than children who are misbehaving for other reasons.

REFERENCES

American Psychiatric Association (1994). *Diagnostic and statistical manual of mental disorders* (4th ed.). Washington, DC: Author.

Beck, A.T. (1967). *Depression: Clinical, experimental, and theoretical aspects.* New York: Harper & Row.

Keller, M., & Baker, L. (1992). The clinical course of panic disorder and depression. *Journal of Clinical Psychiatry, 53,* 5–8.

See also **Childhood Neurosis; Childhood Psychosis; Depression; Emotional Disorders**

AFFECTIVE EDUCATION

Affective education promotes emotional development by educating students about attitudes, thoughts, values, feelings, beliefs, and interpersonal relationships (Morse, Ardizzone, Macdonald, & Pasick, 1980). Through it, students are provided experiences in which cognitive, motor, social, and emotional elements are interrelated and balanced (Morse et al., 1980), leading to the enhancement of self-concept (what one is) and self-esteem (how one feels about what one is) and the development of social skills essential to meeting basic needs in a satisfying and socially responsible way (Wood, 1982). Affective education helps youngsters to establish value systems, morals, independence, a sense of responsibility, and self-direction (Morse et al., 1980; Wood, 1982). Although the need for affective education is not limited to students in special education programs, it is especially relevant for them because social skills are essential for success in mainstream placements.

Although most educators agree on the importance of affective education and understand its general purpose, there is less agreement among them on the specific objectives or how best to realize them. In part, this ambiguity derives from the persistent difficulty of defining such terms as self-concept, self-esteem, affect, and attitude. The general lack of systematic programming should not, however, be an indication that affective goals are unimportant (Francescani, 1982). Affective education is commonplace in regular education classrooms and is routinely addressed in teacher education programs (e.g., Woolfolk, 1995). Morse et al. (1980) have argued that affective education represents serious obligation and is an essential component of special education. Essentially, all children deserve the right to more "systematic assistance with their affective growth" (Morse et al., 1980, p. 6).

Systematic instruction in the affective domain is especially important for emotionally handicapped students like Ann. Emotionally handicapped students include those who have not learned essential skills for social and emotional growth, or how to control their behavior in times of stress, how to communicate their feelings and needs in a socially acceptable manner, how to bring interpersonal problems to a satisfying solution, or how to encounter others without conflict (Francescani, 1982). It is difficult to imagine how a student with deficits as pervasive as these can survive in an environment for which he or she is so poorly equipped. Yet it is in the highly socialized classroom world in which affective education must occur, and most proponents recognize the need to integrate affective learning into everyday classroom life.

Affective education has grown out of the school mental health movement, but has not yet evolved into a well-formulated program intrinsic to the ongoing school process (Morse, 1980). Instead it tends to be relegated to the periphery of the basic curriculum. If affective education is to realize its potential, deliberate efforts must replace the haphazard, casual, and indirect approaches currently in operation.

REFERENCES

Francescani, C. (1982). M A R C: An affective curriculum for emotionally disturbed adolescents. *Teaching Exceptional Children, 14,* 217–222.

Morse, W.C., Ardizzone, J., Macdonald, C., & Pasick, P. (1980). *Affective education for special children and youth.* Reston, VA: Council for Exceptional Children.

Wood, F.H. (1982). Affective education and social skills training. *Teaching Exceptional Children, 14,* 212–216.

Woolfolk, A.E. (1995). *Educational Psychology* (6th ed.). Boston: Allyn & Bacon.

See also **Developing Understanding of Self and Others; Self-Concept; Social Skills**

AFRICA, SPECIAL EDUCATION IN

Special education is relatively new in most African countries. The need for a major commitment to special education by African countries to provide handicapped learners with a variety of programs and services has been recognized for some time now (Anderson, 1983; Joy, 1979; Shown, 1980; UNESCO, 1979, 1986), though progress toward realization has been slow and halting. The UNESCO definition of special education is one that generally adheres to western European and American expectations. Thus the Nigerian National Policy on Education (1981) has defined special education as "education of children and adults who have learning difficulties as a result of not coping with the normal school organization and methods" (Nigerian Year Book, 1984). In Nigeria's Plateau State (Nigeria), special education is defined as including "the course and content of education, including specially defined classroom, material, and equipment designed to meet the unique needs of a handicapped child" (Shown, 1986).

Despite such broad perspectives, special education in Africa is more likely to be concerned with children who are physically and sensorially handicapped rather than suffering from mild cognitive deficits. Children with more severe cognitive deficits are likely to be cared for in other contexts than those of formal special education. Expressing this fact,

Shown observes: "To acquire education in the modern sense one must possess and make full use of all his senses. This is beside being fully mobile" (Shown, in press). Sambo (1981) has pointed out "when one loses two or more of these senses, then the acquisition of education in the normal sense becomes a problem entirely different from those problems normally encountered in the acquisition of education. For such a person, there is a need for a viable alternative for educating him."

Anderson (1973) observed that the majority of African teachers were not familiar with the special techniques and methods required to assist handicapped students to become educationally competent. Furthermore, as Shown (1986) has pointed out, a lack of clear educational objectives has hampered the delivery of educational services to handicapped learners.

Because most African nations have faced major fiscal difficulties for many years, improvements in special education have been difficult to achieve. Nations like Nigeria have, however, made serious efforts at both federal and local levels to teach the elements of special education in teacher training institutions (Nigeria Federal Ministry, 1977). Nigeria has established training programs at the universities of Jos and Ibadan. These universities provide training and research on scientific education of the handicapped at undergraduate and graduate levels.

In most places in Africa, there are not likely to be clearly defined admission policies for the handicapped or age limits for education of the handicapped as it now exists in Africa. It is not uncommon, therefore, to find a handicapped adult in a special education class with much younger students. Furthermore, the personnel providing special education services are likely to come from the middle or lower ranks of school staffs rather than the higher. The burden of education for handicapped students is thus frequently carried by less well-trained aides and members of the local community, rather than by highly skilled teachers.

Special education teachers working in regular school settings have been reported to be facing emotional and psychological problems (Joy, 1972). They may face neglect and even hostility on the part of other teachers who resent having handicapped students and special education teachers in regular schools. Also, nonspecialist teachers are often resentful of the fact that special education teachers receive extra pay.

Many of the special education services provided in Africa on a noninstitutional basis must be on an itinerant basis because of the scarcity of educational facilities able to serve handicapped students. A dearth of itinerant teachers has limited the extent and effectiveness of such education. Recent efforts have been made in certain African countries to mainstream handicapped students. Thus the Federal Ministry of Information, Lagos, Nigeria (1977) mandates that handicapped school children, where possible, should be mainstreamed along with their nonhandicapped peers. Some African educators have expressed disagreement with this policy (Shown, 1980). There is concern about the dangers that the physical hazards of African terrain may pose for mainstreamed handicapped students who are not carefully supervised, e.g., most parts of Nigeria have dangerous structures and hazards such as rocks, forests, and rivers. Also, the application of mainstreaming policies in Africa places an inordinate burden on most handicapped students unless they are able to use the same materials as their nonhandicapped peers or can be assisted to achieve comparable levels of attainment; this is difficult to achieve in light of the current dearth of trained professionals and the lack of proper facilities and materials. As UNESCO has pointed out (1979), mere physical placement in a mainstreamed school environment is not an answer to providing services to handicapped African children. Provisions at African colleges for handicapped students are essentially nonexistent. There are no ramps, suitable steps elevators, or toilet facilities with special accommodations.

Despite efforts to improve the education of the handicapped, the outlook of Africans respecting the needs of handicapped students and adults is not such as to raise hopes for serious concern regarding their transition into productive roles in society.

REFERENCES

Anderson, E. (1983). *The disabled school child. A study in integration.* Open University Set Book, Jos, Nigeria.

Federal Government of Nigeria. (1984). *Nigerian year book:* Lagos, Nigeria: Author.

Joy, D.C. (1979, August 9). Experiment with blind children. *New Nigerian.*

Nigeria Federal Ministry of Information. (1977). *The republic of Nigeria national policy on education,* Lagos, Nigeria: Author.

Sambo, E.W. (1981, April). *What is special education?* Paper presented at the workshop on the integration of elements of special education into teachers education curriculum in plateau state, University of Jos, Jos, Nigeria.

Shown, D.G. (1980). *A study of effectiveness of mainstreaming of visually handicapped children in Plateau State of Nigeria with a view toward determining quality education for these children.* Jos, Nigeria: University of Jos.

Shown, D.G. (1986, April). *Integrating handicapped children in Plateau State.* Paper presented at the workshop on the integration of elements of special education into teachers education curriculum in plateau state, University of Jos, Jos, Nigeria.

UNESCO. (1979, October 15–20). Expert meetings of special education, UNESCO headquarters, Paris. *Final Report.*

UNESCO. (1981, July 20–31). *Sub-regional seminar on planning for special education.* Nairobi, Kenya.

UNESCO. (1986, April). *Expert meeting on special education.* Plateau State, Nigeria: University of Jos.

See also **Nigeria, Special Education in**

AGE-APPROPRIATE CURRICULUM

An age-appropriate curriculum is a special-education curriculum that consists of activities that are matched to both the students' chronological ages and their developmental or skill levels. This match has been difficult to achieve, especially for older trainable and severely handicapped students who continue to function on preschool levels. The older students with severe handicaps often need continued training in fine motor, cognitive, and language skills, but also need to acquire skills that can be used immediately and will transfer to later community and vocational placements (Drew, Logan, & Hardman, 1984).

IDEA mandates an appropriate education for all handicapped students, but wide differences remain when defining this term. The justification for using an age-appropriate education lies in the principle of normalization, which Nirje (1979) has defined as follows: "Making available to all mentally retarded people patterns of life and conditions of everyday living which are as close as possible to the regular circumstances of society" (p. 73). Although it may appear unrealistic to teach age-appropriate behaviors to students with severe developmental delays, Larsen and Jackson (1981) argue that this is the mission of special education: "No, we will not be completely successful (but) . . . our goals for students will stress skills relevant to the general culture, rather than skills that have a proven value only in special-education classrooms" (p. 1).

Our current knowledge of developmental milestones, task analysis procedures, and behavior modification principles can be used in adopting this approach if we also examine the "age-appropriateness" of the materials, skills, activities, environments, and reinforcers used during instruction. For example, in learning visual discrimination of shapes, elementary-age students may use form boards and shape sorters, while older students use community signs and mosaic art activities. For other skills, calculators may be used instead of number lines; colored clothing can be sorted rather than colored cubes; and the assembly of vocational products may replace peg boards and beads (Bates, Renzaglia, & Wehman, 1981).

Because there are many skills that older severely handicapped youths will never acquire (e.g., reading a newspaper and buying groceries), the curriculum focuses on those abilities that can be learned (e.g., reading survival signs or following directions). To identify these skills for each group of students, Brown et al. (1979) employ an ecological inventory approach listing the environments and subenvironments where the students currently (or will eventually) function. An inventory of the activities in each environment and a listing of skills needed to participate in those activities provide the framework for selecting curriculum goals. In this approach, for example, the basic skill of matching pictures leads to finding grooming items in a drugstore, and identifying different foods leads to ordering in a fast-food restaurant.

Classroom design and decor also should reflect the chronological age of the students. For older youths, pictures of teen activities and movie celebrities are more age-appropriate decorations than cartoon characters. Many special-education classrooms have moved into secondary buildings, opening up opportunities to use age-appropriate training sites such as home economics rooms.

Severely handicapped students may have extremely slow learning rates and much difficulty in generalizing learned skills to new situations. Therefore, their education must include the teaching of critical skill clusters and opportunities to practice functional skills in natural settings such as sheltered workshops, supermarkets, and public transportation. For a more detailed description of curricular approaches to teaching functional skill clusters see Guess and Noonan (1982).

REFERENCES

Bates, P., Renzaglia, A., & Wehman, P. (1981). Characteristics of an appropriate education for severely and profoundly handicapped students. *Education & Training of the Mentally Retarded, 16,* 142–149.

Brown, L., Branston, M.B., Homre-Nietupski, S., Pumpian, I., Certo, N., & Grunewald, L. (1979). A strategy for developing chronological age appropriate and functional curriculum content for severely handicapped adolescents and young adults. *Journal of Special Education, 13,* 81–90.

Drew, C.J., Logan, D.R., & Hardman, M.L. (1984). *Mental Retardation: A Life Cycle Approach* (3rd ed.). St. Louis: Times Mirror/Mosby.

Guess, D., & Noonan, M.J. (1982). Curricula and instructional procedures for severely handicapped students. *Focus on Exceptional Children, 14,* 9–10.

Larsen, L.A., & Jackson, L.B. (1981). Chronological age in the design of educational programs for severely and profoundly impaired students. *PRISE Reporter, 13,* 1–2.

Nirje, B. (1979). Changing patterns in residential services for the mentally retarded. In E.L. Meyen (Ed.), *Basic Readings in the Study of Exceptional Children and Youth.* Denver: Love.

See also **Adaptive Behavior; Functional Instruction; Functional Skills Training; Mental Retardation**

AGE AT ONSET

Age at onset refers to the point in an individual's life when a specific condition began. Age at onset can be compared with a child's chronological age to establish the duration of a condition. It is a significant variable in making diagnostic judgments and prognostic statements. Within a school setting, age at onset is typically a consideration in: (1) understanding behavioral disorders; (2) understanding the prognosis for adequate intellectual and learning performance in children with neurologic and chronic medical conditions; and (3) assessing and programming for children with learning disabilities.

For many disorders, age of onset will influence diagnostic decisions, treatment choices, and prognostications.

See also **Assessment; Medical History; Mental Status Exam**

AGGRESSION

Aggression is usually defined as any form of behavior designed to harm or injure some living being (Baron & Byrne, 1991), although some also include aggressive acts turned toward objects (intentional destruction of property) or toward the self (Ruhl & Hughes, 1985). This intentional definition of aggression includes two categories: hostile aggression and instrumental aggression. If the goal of an aggressor is to injure a victim, the behavior constitutes hostile aggression, whereas instrumental aggression involves acts perpetrated as a means to some end (to get an object or protect one's play space). Hollandsworth (1977) differentiates aggression from assertiveness by emphasizing the former's threatening, punitive, and coercive qualities.

Aggression is sometimes correlated with other disordered behavior patterns. It is frequently associated with hyperactivity and is also related to excessive distractibility and impulsivity. Positive correlations have been found between impulsive cognitive tempo and both aggression and lack of concern for the consequences of aggression (Messer & Brodzinsky, 1979).

While some instances of aggressive behavior are a common and normal part of the behavioral repertoire of children, it is only when the behavior occurs at high frequency or has extreme potential for harm that the aggressive child label is applied.

Explanations of aggressive behavior can be classified into five theoretical perspectives: (1) ethological/biological, (2) psychodynamic, (3) drive theory, (4) social learning theory, and (5) social-cognitive perspective. Lorenz (1966) has proposed the ecological view that aggression stems from an innate fighting instinct. Aggressive energy is thought to build up over time and must eventually be released directly or indirectly. But evidence for causative evolutionary or genetic factors in humans is weak. It is far more likely that environmental histories determine specific aggressive acts and targets (Simmel, Hahn, & Walters, 1983).

According to social learning theory (Bandura, 1973) acquiring aggressive behavior is a function of learning from models, the child's reinforcement history, and current contingencies of reinforcement that maintain aggression. It is well established that children can learn aggressive responses from live or filmed models, and from adults, peers, or cartoon characters. They are also more likely to imitate aggressive models who have high social status and who either receive no punishment or are reinforced for their behavior. Further, when specific or generalized imitation of aggression goes unpunished or is rewarded, a child will be more likely to engage in that behavior. Aversive stimulation in the form of taunts or threats, or the removal of salient reinforcers, may also evoke aggressive behavior.

Once aggression has become a regular aspect of one's behavioral repertoire, it will be perpetuated to the extent that it continues to be reinforced. Paradoxically, some uses of corporal punishment can increase the probability of future aggressive behavior (Axelrod & Apsche, 1983). Aggression can also be maintained through mental processes that serve to justify one's behavior. As Bandura has continued to develop this theory, primary emphasis has shifted from behavioral contributions to the importance of cognitive processes, including a person's thoughts, perceptions, attitudes and self-efficacy.

Interpersonal cognitive problem solving focuses on children's ability to generate multiple strategies for solving social problems. Skills associated with social problem solving include sensitivity to social problems, recognizing alternative solutions, identifying means to reach a social goal, considering the consequences of possible actions, and considering possible causes of other people's behavior. The more strategies children know for solving social problems and hence the greater their social competence, the less likely they are to resort to aggressive or impulsive behaviors.

A related approach emphasizes teaching children healthy ways to manage frustration (Fagen & Hill, 1987). By training children to recognize feelings of frustration, accept those feelings, tolerate frustrating experiences, and build coping skills, teachers can enable aggressive students to respond in more adaptive ways to inevitable frustrations.

REFERENCES

Axelrod, S., & Apasche, J. (Eds.). (1983). *The effect of punishment on human behavior.* New York: Academic.

Bandura, A. (1973). *Aggression: A social learning analysis.* Englewood Cliffs, NJ: Prentice-Hall.

Baron, R.A., & Byrne, D. (1991). *Social psychology: Understanding human interaction* (5th ed.). Newton, MA: Allyn & Bacon.

Fagen, S.A., & Hill, J.M. (1987). Teaching acceptance of frustration. *Teaching Exceptional Children, 19,* 49–51.

Hollandsworth, J.G., Jr. (1977). Differentiating assertion and aggression: Some behavioral guidelines. *Behavior Therapy, 8,* 347–352.

Lorenz, K. (1966). *On aggression.* New York: Harcourt, Brace & World.

Messer, S.B., & Brodzinsky, D.M. (1979). The relation of conceptual tempo to aggression and its control. *Child Development, 50,* 758–766.

Ruhl, K.L., & Hughes, C.A. (1985). The nature and extent of aggression in special education settings serving behaviorally disordered students. *Behavioral Disorders, 10,* 95–104.

Simmel, E.C., Hahn, M.E., & Walters, J.K. (1983). Synthesis and new direction. In E.C. Simmel, M.E. Hahn, & J.K. Walters (Eds.), *Aggressive behavior: Genetic and neural approaches* (pp. 183–190). Hillsdale, NJ: Erlbaum.

See also Cognitive Behavior Therapy; Conduct Disorder; Social Cognitive Theory

AGRAPHIA

The *Cyclopedia of Education* (1915) defines agraphia as a disorder of the associations of speech in which there is a partial or complete inability to express ideas by means of written symbols in an individual who had previously acquired this mode of speech expression. This definition continues to apply. Agraphia is often associated with apraxia and with so-called motor aphasia.

REFERENCE

Cyclopedia of Education (1915). New York: Macmillan.

See also Dysgraphia; Handwriting

AICARDI SYNDROME (CALLOSAL DYSGENESIS)

Aicardi Syndrome (AS) is the most common of syndromes involving agenesis or dysgenesis of the corpus callosum and is sometimes used interchangeably with the designation *callosal dysgenesis*. The corpus callosum is the largest of the cerebral commissures and is the major communication link between the left and the right hemispheres of the brain.

Depending upon the level of dysgenesis, symptoms may vary considerably in their severity but among the most common are: mental retardation, autistic syndromes, severe obsessive compulsive disorders, seizure disorder, and macrocephaly (Gillberg, 1995). When limited to the extreme posterior portions of the corpus callosum, ADHD is a more common result. Girls tend to be overrepresented in callosal dysgenesis syndromes and, in Aicardi Syndrome proper, only girls occur since it is an X-linked, dominant mutation. AS, among the callosal dysgenesis syndromes, is among the most severe and typically results in moderate to severe mental retardation and numerous physical abnormalities, especially of the spine and the orofacial area. Diagnosis is by CAT scan or MRI. Neuropsychological testing is recommended due to the possible range of reaction.

Treatment is entirely symptomatic and virtually all such children will require special education services and may qualify under multiple areas of disability. In less severe cases of callosal dysgenesis, asymptomatic presentations have been reported, emphasizing the need for ongoing neuropsychological follow-up and periodic reassessment of intervention plans. Symptoms not appearing by puberty typically do not occur and the disorder is not progressive. In the most severe forms of callosal agenesis, death in infancy is common.

REFERENCE

Gillberg, C. (1995). *Clinical child neuropsychiatry.* Cambridge, UK: Cambridge University Press.

AIDES TO PSYCHOLINGUISTIC TEACHING

Psycholinguistics focuses on the interactions and psychological functions underlying communication. It attends to the processes by which a speaker or writer emits signals or symbols, and the interpretation of those signals by the receiver.

Language programs and assessment techniques have been derived from these psycholinguistic principles and have been applied to education. A basic tenet of psycholinguistics is that language is made up of discrete components that may be identified and measured; further, it is assumed that if one is deficient in a given component, the deficiency can be remediated. This leads to two more assumptions, that a child's failure to learn stems from his or her own weaknesses, and that strengthening weak areas will result in improved classroom learning (Hammill & Larsen, 1974). If these assumptions are valid, programs aimed at mitigating psycholinguistic weaknesses are both necessary and desirable. If the assumptions are invalid, however, a great deal of time and money is being wasted on the application of these programs in educational settings.

In their review of research, Hammill and Larsen (1974) showed that the efficacy of psycholinguistic training had not been adequately demonstrated. They pointed out that many exceptional children are being provided with training programs aimed at increasing their psycholinguistic competencies. On the basis of their review, the authors claimed that it is essential to determine whether the constructs are trainable by present programs. It is also necessary, they said, to identify the children for whom such training would prove worthwhile.

Arter and Jenkins (1977), in their examination of the benefits and prevalence of modality considerations in special education, concluded that research evidence failed to support the practice of basing instructional plans on modality assessment. Thirteen of the 14 studies they reviewed indicated that students were not differentially assisted by instruction congruent with their modality strengths. Further, they stated that "increased efforts in research and development of test instruments and techniques may be warranted but, as far as the practitioner is concerned, advocacy of the (modality) model cannot be justified." (p. 295)

Recent reviews using a quantitative statistic known as effect size (ES) have been conducted to summarize educational research. This statistic is computed to quantitatively determine how much improvement occurs across different investigations, based on two indices: the direction of improvement (+ or −) and the amount of improvement with an ES of 1.00 revealing a 34% improvement. Kavale and Glass (1982) refer to a meta-analysis performed by Kavale in 1981 that investigated the effectiveness of psycholinguistic training. Kavale's studies yielded 240 effect sizes with an overall ES of 0.39. Kavale and Glass conclude by asserting that there are specific situations where psycholinguistic training is effective and that it should be included within a total remedial program. The findings from this research should be qualified, however, because of the lack of consideration of research methodologies across the different investigations. Furthermore, the outcome measures were based on performance on the process tests (i.e., Illinois Test of Psycholinguistic Abilities—ITPA), not on academic tests. Further analyses of studies using achievement outcomes have found negligible effect sizes. It remains open to question whether such improvement on psycholinguistic process tasks would translate into improved performance on academic tasks in the classroom.

REFERENCES

Arter, J.A., & Jenkins, J.R. (1977). Examining the benefits and prevalence of modality considerations in special education. *Journal of Special Education, 11*(3), 281–298.

Hammill, D.D., & Larsen, S.C. (1974). The effectiveness of psycholinguistic training. *Exceptional Children, 41,* 5–14.

Kavale, K.A., & Glass, G.V. (1982). The efficacy of special education interventions and practices: A compendium of meta-analysis findings. *Focus on Exceptional Children, 15*(4), 1–16.

See also **Fernald Method; Orton-Gillingham Method; Psycholinguistics**

AIDS

See also **Pediatric Acquired Immune Deficiency Syndrome.**

AL-ANON

Al-Anon originally was an adjunct of Alcoholics Anonymous, but in 1954 it incorporated as a separate fellowship. The central headquarters, known as the World Service Office (WSO), serves Al-Anon groups all over the world. The WSO is guided by a voluntary board of trustees, a policy committee, and an executive committee that makes administrative decisions. There is a paid staff with an executive director. Although there is a central headquarters, all local groups operate autonomously. The only requirement for membership is the belief that one's life has been or is being deeply affected by close contact with a problem drinker.

Al-Anon groups help affected by someone else's drinking to:

Learn the facts about alcoholism as a family illness

Benefit from contact with members who have had the same problem

Improve their own attitudes and personalities by the study and practice of the "twelve steps"

Reduce tensions and improve the attitudes of the family through attendance at Al-Anon meetings

Al-Anon is primarily a self-help/support group that focuses on assisting family members in dealing with the problems that an alcoholic brings to the family. It is based on anonymity and sharing.

ALATEEN

Alateen is a self-help, self-support group for young Al-Anon members whose lives have been affected by someone else's drinking. Each Alateen group has an active, adult member of Al-Anon who serves as a sponsor and who is responsible for guiding the group and sharing knowledge of the twelve steps and traditions. The basis purpose of this group is to help Alateens to cope with the turmoil created in their lives by someone else's drinking. Meetings are voluntary and generally are held in community buildings. Alateen members openly discuss their problems, share experiences, learn effective ways to cope with their problems, encourage one another, and help each other to understand the principles of the Al-Anon program.

In a survey conducted by World Service Office it was found that 46% of the Alateens held membership for between 1 and 4 years, 57% were female, most were children of alcoholics, 27% were the brother, sister, or other relative of an alcoholic, and the average age of a member was 14, with 71% between the ages of 13 and 17. Furthermore, 31% of the Alateen members had participated in treatment/counseling before or since coming to Alateen. Fully 94% of the Alateen respondents indicated that personal influences were responsible for their attendance at their first Alateen meeting, with Alcoholics Anonymous members, Al-Anon/Alateen members, or family members being the most frequently identified influence.

See also **AL-ANON**

ALBINISM

Albinism is a genetic disorder that affects the pigmentation, of the skin, hair, or eyes or any combination of the three. Individuals with albinism often have significant visual impairment. Problems with acuity are common, as is pendular nystagmus. Central nervous system involvement may be present. Although one would typically require intense illumination for such problems, persons with albinism are severely photosensitive, i.e., intolerant of light. Special education services will often be necessary, particularly if the visual impairments so often accompanying albinism are severe. Social and behavioral problems related to the odd physical appearance concomitant with albinism are common, as are problems with anxiety and self-esteem. Children with albinism will vary as much as normal individuals in the vast majority of human characteristics. Some will not require special education.

ALBRIGHT'S HEREDITARY OSTEODYSTROPHY (PSEUDOHYPOPARATHYROIDISM)

Albright's hereditary osteodystrophy is believed to be an X-linked inherited disorder that results in a low level of calcium and a high level of phosphorus in the blood. Varying degrees of mental retardation, ranging from slight to severe, are associated with the condition, and hearing and vision problems are found in a number of afflicted children. At times, hyperthyroidism is associated with Albright's, therefore alterations in personality and behavior may be seen (Carter, 1978).

Children with this condition are usually short and stocky with skeletal abnormalities often observed in both upper and lower extremities and prominent foreheads. Calcium deposits may be present in the brain, skin, and organs. Calcification is often found in hands, wrists, and feet. Toes and fingers are short and stubby. There may be impairment in the sense of sour and bitter taste and the sense of smell. Glandular disorders may be seen and sexual glands may be poorly developed (Lemeshaw, 1982).

Neurological, sensory, and motor problems often accompanying this syndrome will require related attention. Developmental and mental status evaluations will be necessary to measure the degree of disability each child has. Because seizures may be present, drug therapy may be necessary and must be known and monitored.

REFERENCES

Carter, C. (Ed.). (1978). *Medical aspects of mental retardation* (2nd ed.). Springfield, IL: Thomas.

Lemeshaw, S. (1982). *The handbook of clinical types in mental retardation.* Boston: Allyn & Bacon.

See also **Hyperthyroidism; Physical Anomalies**

ALEXANDER GRAHAM BELL ASSOCIATION FOR THE DEAF

The Alexander Graham Bell Association for the Deaf is a nonprofit membership organization established in 1890. The Association's mission is to empower persons who are hearing impaired to function independently by promoting universal rights and optimal opportunities to learn, use, maintain, and improve all aspects of their verbal communications, including their abilities to speak, speechread, use residual hearing, and process both spoken and written language. Towards this end, the Association strives to promote (1) better public understanding of hearing loss in children and adults, (2) detection of hearing loss in early infancy, (3) prompt intervention and use of appropriate hearing aids, (4) dissemination of information on hearing loss, including causes and options for treatment, and (5) inservice training for teachers of children who are deaf or hard of hearing. The organization also collaborates on research relating to auditory/verbal communication and with physicians, audiologists, speech/language specialists, and educators to promote educational and social opportunities for individuals of all ages who are hearing impaired.

The Alexander Graham Bell Association for the Deaf may be contacted by writing 3417 Volta Place, N.W., Washington, DC 20007-2778 or by calling (202) 337-5220 (Voice and TTY).

ALEXIA

Alexia is used often in a general sense to refer to reading disabilities of adult onset (Lezak, 1995). As such, the term serves to differentiate between adult reading disorders and developmental reading disabilities commonly denoted by the term dyslexia. Literally, however, the term *alexia* derives from the Greek and can be approximately translated as "no reading." Thus, in a more precise sense, alexia denotes a total inability to read brought about by an abnormality in the central nervous system (Thomas, 1977). The term can be correctly applied to individuals regardless of age.

REFERENCES

Lezak, M.D. (1995). *Neuropsychological assessment* (3rd ed.). New York: Oxford University Press.

Thomas, C.L. (Ed.) (1977). *Tabor's cyclopedic medical dictionary.* Philadelphia: Davis.

See also **Dyslexia**

ALLERGIC DISORDERS

An allergy is a hypersensitivity to a specific substance (an antigen) that in a similar quantity does not affect other people. The abnormal reactions are usually in the form of asthma, hay fever, eczema, hives, or chronic stuffy nose (allergic rhinitis). Technically, the use of the term should be limited to those conditions in which an immunological mechanism can be demonstrated. Allergies are common to 20 to 25% of the children in the United States and are inherited. The tendency to develop allergies is present at birth but may appear at any age.

Allergies can be classified into two types: immediate hypersensitivity (such as allergic rhinitis, asthma, and food allergies) and delayed hypersensitivity (such as reactions to poison ivy). Patients with the former have more of the antibody IgE in their systems. This antibody reacts with whatever patients are allergic to, whether it is something that they breathe, eat, or have skin contact with. This reaction causes certain cells in the body to release chemical mediators such as histamine and serotonin. These chemicals cause the dilation of the small blood vessels, increased secretion from the mucous glands, and smooth muscle contractions that produce the allergy symptoms.

Allergies often play a role in the etiology of asthma, especially in childhood. The chemical mediators released upon the allergic reaction cause contraction of the smooth muscles in the walls of the bronchial airways, swelling of the bronchial tubes, and an increase in the rate of secretion of mucous by submucosal glands. This produces obstruction and causes the characteristic wheezing and shortness of breath. Asthma may be mild (one or two mild attacks per year) or severe with intractable wheezing daily. The severe form may greatly restrict physical activity and make school attendance difficult for school-age children. Physical exertion may precipitate wheezing and become a problem in physical education classes. Skin allergies are common, especially in younger children.

Food allergies are perhaps the most controversial area of allergy study. Some allergists feel that allergic reactions to foods are rare, while others feel they are a common cause of illness. The frequency of food allergy seems to decrease as children grow older. The most common symptoms of food allergy include gastrointestinal symptoms such as abdominal pain, vomiting and diarrhea, and rashes such as hives. Food may play a role in other allergic conditions such as allergic rhinitis, asthma, and eczema, especially during the first 3 or 4 years of life. The most serious allergic reaction to foods and drugs is an anaphylactic one, in which the person experiences a shocklike reaction that can result in death. Any food can cause an allergic reaction, but the foods most apt to cause one in children include milk, eggs, fish, wheat, corn, peanuts, soy, pork, and chocolate.

Stinging insect allergies may cause a severe anaphylactic reaction to the sting of a bee, wasp, hornet, or yellow jacket. The reaction may occur within minutes after the sting and allergic persons need immediate medical attention.

A thorough history and physical examination are important components of a diagnosis. Seasonal patterns of symptoms, exposure to animals, and usual diet are useful information in identifying causes. Laboratory analysis of nasal secretions, sputum, and blood may establish the presence of eosinophil cells that appear in increased numbers with allergic reactions. Pulmonary function tests are also helpful. Scratch and intradermal skin tests for the suspected allergens can confirm a diagnosis. Another tool is the radioallergoabsorbant (RAST) test, which measures the level of IgE in the blood for a particular allergen (Tuft, 1973). The elimination-challenge diet is used for suspected food allergies; after avoiding a particular food for two to three weeks, the patient consumes it and is observed for reactions. Awareness of environmental conditions from change of seasons, foliage in different parts of the country, and environmental factors in homes, schools, and the work place also assists the diagnostician.

While there is no cure for allergies, symptoms may be controlled in a variety of ways. First, symptomatic treatment involves using medication. Antihistamines are the most commonly prescribed drugs for the treatment of allergic reactions. They inhibit some of the actions of histamine but frequently have negative side effects such as sedation, excitation, and insomnia. Antihistamines are often combined with decongestant drugs. Asthmatics are usually treated with bronchodilator drugs that cause relaxation of the smooth muscle surrounding the bronchial tubes. Acute asthmatic attacks and anaphylactic reactions are frequently treated with epinephrine. Both drugs may have negative side effects. For severe allergic problems, corticosteroids may be used, but on a limited basis because of adrenal suppression and limitation of physical growth in children.

The second method of treatment is environmental control, that is, removal of troublesome antigens such as pet hair, dust, and pollen. Good housekeeping practices, use of air conditioning at home and in the car, and other careful planning can prevent many allergic problems. A third and related approach is to teach self-regulation strategies to persons with asthma and other types of allergies. They include

relaxation training, biofeedback procedures to modify physiological reactions, and general education about the medical condition. A fourth treatment is immunotherapy, which involves injecting the patient with small amounts of an antigen that has been processed into a dilute form. These injections stimulate the immune system to produce another type of antibody that inhibits the reaction between the allergic antibody and the antigen. While initially the shots are taken once or twice a week, the regimen is gradually phased out over a 2- to 3-year period (Patterson et al., 1978).

Higher rates of school absenteeism are reported for asthmatic children and those with chronic rhinitis (Shapiro, 1986). Asthmatic children may be absent 10% of the time; such absenteeism is a direct cause of school problems. Additionally, the seasonal occurrence of allergic reactions (especially in the fall) and the typical pattern of frequent, brief absences are disruptive to classroom performance, attending skills, and social development. Milder forms of allergies may not cause significant school absenteeism, particularly with improved medical treatment, self-management programs, and parent education (McLoughlin, Nall, & Petrosko, 1985). Furthermore, some previous estimates of higher absenteeism of allergic children may have been confused with the effects of socioeconomic status.

Hearing difficulties are frequently associated with otitis media resulting from allergies (Northern, 1980). Among allergic students, Szanton and Szanton (1966) found many cases of intermittent hearing loss that had been undetected on screening measures. Articulation and/or vocal quality problems have also been reported among allergic students (Baker & Baker, 1980). Recurrent otitis media among three year olds has been associated with lower speech and language performance (Teele, et al., 1984).

Allergy history seems present among cases of behavioral and emotional disorders (Mayron, 1978). King (1981) estimated that 70% of students with such disorders have personal or family allergy histories; cognitive-emotional symptoms were noted after allergic exposure under double-blind conditions. Psychological and personality changes are frequently reported by asthmatic children and their parents (Creer, Marion, & Creer, 1983). However, comparisons of reports and ratings of behavioral problems, placement in services for behavior disorders, and school suspensions between allergic and nonallergic students have not yielded significantly different profiles (McLoughlin et al., 1985).

Hyperactivity has been particularly connected with food allergies. Feingold (1975b) drew attention to the ingestion of artificial food additives (color and flavors) and naturally occurring salicylates in food and proposed the Feingold Kaiser-Permanente (K-P) diet based on clinical observations and anecdotal accounts (Crook, 1977; Feingold, 1975a). However, reviews of controlled studies (Kavale & Forness, 1983; Mattes, 1983) dismiss these claims, as do the findings of the Consensus Development Conference sponsored by the National Institutes of Health (Office for Medical Applications of Research, 1982).

Allergy medication may have adverse effects on behavior and exacerbate existing behavioral problems (McLoughlin et al., 1983). Theophylline has been significantly correlated with inattentiveness, hyperactivity, irritability, drowsiness, and withdrawal behavior; the negative side effects increase with length of use. Furakawa and his colleagues (1984) found decreased test performances under the influence of theophylline. Terbutaline created socially inappropriate behavior in a comparison group (Creer, 1979), and corticosteroids negatively affected academic performance (Suess & Chai, 1981). Ladd, Leibold, Lindsey, and Ornby (1980) also reported euphoria, insomnia, and visual disturbances with corticosteroids. Antihistamines may cause sedation, dry mouth, and irritability (Weinberger & Hendeles, 1980). Visual hallucinations occur among some children receiving decongestants (Sankey, Nunn, & Sills, 1984).

Allergic disorders have important implications for the professional assessment and intervention of exceptionalities as well as for parental involvement. Certain types of allergies and/or the side effects of medication may be contributing factors in behaviors of concern and may require special consideration when designing special services. The self-monitoring and management skills taught in special education may be mutually beneficial in coping with this medical condition.

REFERENCES

Baker, M., & Baker, C. (1980). Difficulties generated by allergies. *Journal of School Health, 50*, 583–585.

Creer, T.L. (1979). *Asthma therapy.* New York: Springer.

Creer, T.L., Marion, R.J., & Creer, P.P. (1983). The asthma problem behavior checklist. Parental perceptions of the behavior of asthmatic children. *Journal of Asthma, 20*, 97–104.

Crook, W.G. (1977, January). Letter to the editor. *News and Comment.* American Academy of Pediatrics.

Feingold, B.F. (1975a). Hyperkinesis and learning disabilities linked to artificial food flavors and colors. *American Journal of Nursing, 75*, 797–803.

Feingold, B.F. (1975b). *Why your child is hyperactive.* New York: Random House.

Furakawa, C.T., Shapiro, G.G., DuHamel, T., Weimer, L., Pierson, W.E., & Bierman, C.W. (1984, March). Learning and behavior problems associated with theophylline therapy. *Lancet, 621.*

Kavale, K.A., & Forness, S.R. (1983). Hyperactivity and diet treatment: A meta-analysis of the Feingold hypothesis. *Journal of Learning Disabilities, 16*, 324–330.

King, D.S. (1981). Can allergic exposure provoke psychological symptoms? *Biology Psychiatry, 16*, 3–19.

Ladd, F.T., Leibold, S.R., Lindsey, C.N., & Ornby, R. (1980). RX in the classroom. *Instructor, 90*, 58–59.

Mattes, J.A. (1983). The Feingold diet: A current reappraisal. *Journal of Learning Disabilities, 16*, 319–323.

Mayron, L. (1978). Ecological factors in learning disabilities. *Journal of Learning Disabilities, 11*, 40–50.

McLoughlin, J.A., Nall, M., Isaacs, B., Petrosko, J., Karibo, J., & Lindsey, B. (1983). The relationship of allergies and allergy treatment to school performance and student behavior. *Annals of Allergy, 51*, 506–510.

McLoughlin, J.A., Nall, M., & Petrosko, J. (1985). Allergies and learning disabilities. *Learning Disability Quarterly, 8*, 255–260.

Northern, J.L. (1980). Diagnostic tests of ear disease. In C. Bierman & D. Pearlman (Eds.), *Allergic diseases of infancy, childhood and adolescence* (pp. 492–501). Philadelphia: Saunders.

Office for Medical Applications of Research, National Institutes of Health. (1982). Defined diets and childhood hyperactivity. *Journal of the American Medical Association, 245*, 290–292.

Patterson, R., Lieberman, P., Irons, J., Pruzansky, J., Melam, H., Metzger, W.J., & Zeiss, C.R. (1978). Immunotherapy. In E. Middleton, Jr., C. Reed, & E. Ellis (Eds.), *Allergy principles and practice* (Vol. 2, pp. 877–897). St. Louis: Mosby.

Sankey, R.J., Nunn, A.J., & Sills, J.A. (1984): Visual hallucinations in children receiving decongestants. *British Medical Journal, 288*, 1369.

Shapiro, G. (1986). Understanding allergic rhinitis. *Pediatrics in Review, 7*, 212–218.

Suess, W.M., & Chai, H. (1981). Neuropsychological correlates of asthma: Brain damage or drug effects? *Journal of Consulting and Clinical Psychology, 49*, 135–136.

Szanton, V.J., & Szanton, W.C. (1966). Hearing disturbances in allergic children. *Journal of Asthma Research, 4*, 25–28.

Teele, D.W., Klein, J.O., Rosner, B.A., & the Greater Boston Otitis Media Study Group. (1984). *Pediatrics, 74*, 282–287.

Tuft, L. (1973). *Allergy management in clinical practice.* St. Louis: Mosby.

Weinberger, M., & Hendeles, L. (1980). Pharmacologic management. In C. Bierman & D. Pearlman (Eds.), *Allergic diseases of infancy, childhood and adolescence* (pp. 311–332). Philadelphia: Saunders.

ALPHABETIC METHOD

The alphabetic method of teaching children to read is historically connected with the development of an alphabet. Once letters and sounds were fixed in a structure (an alphabet), a method to master this structure emerged. The first recorded use of the alphabetic method was in ancient Greek and Roman civilizations. Reading instruction began by teaching children all the letters in their proper alphabetical order. After a complete mastery of the alphabet, children learned to group the letters to form syllables, words, and finally sentences. Reading instruction was considered primarily an oral process; the child recited the spelling of each syllable or word and then pronounced it. This progression of teaching letters, syllables, words, and sentences was the predominant method of teaching reading from Greek and Roman times until the late 1800s (Huey, 1980).

In using this method, sixteenth- and seventeenth-century teachers drilled children unmercifully on the names of the letters (Matthews, 1966). Instructional materials that presented lists of letters, syllables, and words to be memorized before advancing to the text were developed. The *New England Primer* was one of the most widely used reading texts in seventeenth-century America. Each reading selection focused on a moral or religious lesson, and was preceded by an alphabet, lists of the vowels and consonants, and lists of syllables such as ab, eb, and ib. The lists of words for spelling began with one-syllable words and progressed to two- and three-syllable words (Huey, 1980).

As the English language evolved, letter names no longer directly represented speech sounds; therefore, children became more and more confused as they tried to read modern literature by simply reciting the names of the letters. Realizing that this confusion hindered efforts to teach reading effectively, the alphabetic method was gradually replaced by phonetically based methods of reading instruction. By the beginning of the twentieth century, the classic alphabetic method was seldom used.

REFERENCES

Huey, E.B. (1980). *The psychology and pedagogy of reading.* New York: Macmillan.

Matthews, M.M. (1966). *Teaching to read.* Chicago: University of Chicago Press.

See also **Distar; Reading Remediation; Whole Word Teaching**

ALTERNATIVE COMMUNICATION METHODS IN SPECIAL EDUCATION

Individuals with severe communication disorders are those who may benefit from AAC (augmentative and alternative communication)—those for whom gestural, speech, and/or written communication is temporarily or permanently inadequate to meet all of their communication needs. For those individuals, hearing impairment is not the primary cause for the communication impairment. Although some individuals may be able to produce a limited amount of speech, it is inadequate to meet their varied communication needs. Numerous terms that were initially used in the field but are now rarely mentioned include speechless, nonoral, non-vocal, nonverbal, and aphonic (ASHA, 1991, p. 10).

In the mid 1970s, alternative methods of communication began to be explored with the nonspeaking population. These methods are termed augmentative communication systems. They are currently being used with children and adults who have physical, mental, emotional, and linguistic handicaps. ASHA (1991) defines an AAC system as "an integrated group of components, including the symbols, aids, strategies, and techniques used by individuals to enhance communication" (p. 10). Unaided communication systems use only the physical body for communication. They include sign languages, gestures, and facial expressions. Aided systems require additional equipment for communication. There are many advantages to using unaided systems for communication. Social interaction is enhanced because the rate of communication is typically fast. Speaker-listener eye contact is maintained when using unaided systems. The meaning of many signs and gestures are concrete, making learning and recall of vocabulary easier. In addition, during training, sign and gesture response can be physically prompted and shaped by the instructor.

Aided communication systems require additional devices or equipment for communication. Computers, writing with pen and paper, and communication boards are all examples of aided communication systems. An aided communication system consists of a communication aid, which is the mechanism used for communication, and a symbol system, which is the language used for communication.

The communication aid can consist of three major components: the interface, the communication device, and the output system. Complex electronic systems usually have all three components. Simple communication boards may consist of the communication device alone. The interface is used to control the system. A head stick, joystick, or computer keyboard are examples of interfaces. They are used to select symbols on the communication device. Direct selection allows the user to directly choose symbols for communication. Scanning systems present symbol choices to the user, who then activates a response when the desired symbol is reached. A scanning system resembles an advanced form of the guessing game "Twenty Questions." The communication device can display all of the available vocabulary options, or it can display a few symbols that are combined into codes to access vocabulary. Electronic devices often indicate, by small lights or LCD display screens, which symbol has been selected. Once the entire message to be communicated is completed, an output device such as a speech synthesizer, computer modem, or printer is used to convey the message to others.

There are also many disadvantages to using aided communication systems. The devices themselves are often physically cumbersome and difficult to transport. Communication through a mechanical device also reduces speaker-listener eye contact and affects the location and distance from the speaker or a listener. The primary disadvantage of aided communication systems is an extremely slow rate of communication. Normal verbal communication rates range from 150 to 200 words per minute (Goldman-Eisler, 1986). Direct selection aided systems have rates that range from 6 to 25 words per minutes; scanning systems can be as slow as two words per minute (Foulds, 1987). This slow rate of communication tends to affect the style and amount of communicative interaction that occurs when using aided communication systems. Methods of increasing communication rate will be discussed later.

Before an augmentative communication system can be developed, a complete evaluation of the user's physical, linguistic, cognitive, and academic skills must be completed. This requires a team of professionals including speech-language pathologists, physical therapists, occupational therapists, and school psychologists. The physical evaluation should determine the user's gross motor skills, range of motion, adaptive posturing and seating, fine motor accuracy, and speed of movement. An evaluation of language skills should determine the user's current communication strategies and receptive language skills, and the communicative needs of the user (Beukelman & Mirenda, 1998). Academic and cognitive skills should be evaluated with a language specialist to determine a language symbol system that is within the user's capabilities. In addition, the academic and vocational skills and needs of the user should be identified. The evaluation results are then used to determine the communication aid, or unaided system, and symbolic system that best fits the user's needs.

The ability to communicate with others is a binding element within members of a society. The development of augmentative communication systems has opened many avenues of communication for the nonspeaking population. While most augmentative systems are not yet perfect replacements for oral speech, they do provide a means of communication and interaction with others.

REFERENCES

American Speech-Language-Hearing Association. (1991). Report: Augmentative and Alternative Communication. *Asha, 33* (Suppl. 5), 9–12.

Beukelman, D. & Mirenda, P. (1998). *Augmentative and alternative communication.* Baltimore: Paul H. Brookes Publishing Co.

Foulds, R. (1987). Guest editorial. *Augmentative and Alternative Communication, 3,* 169.

Goldman-Eisler, F. (1986). *Cycle linguistics: Experiments in spontaneous speech.* New York: Academic Press.

AMAROUTIC FAMILIAL IDIOCY

See also Tay-Sachs Syndrome

AMBLYOPIA

Amblyopia, also called suppression blindness (Harley & Lawrence, 1977), is a visual condition that occurs when an anatomically healthy eye cannot see because of some other defect (Eden, 1978). Amblyopia is commonly called "lazy eye"; however, this is a misnomer (Eden, 1978) because it implies that amblyopia results from a muscular problem. Actually, amblyopia can have a number of causes. For example, strabismus (a condition in which the two eyes are not parallel when viewing an object) can lead to amblyopia. The brain ignores the visual signals of one of the two eyes to reduce the annoyance of double vision. Other factors such as astigmatism can also lead to amblyopia.

The degree of visual impairment associated with amblyopia can vary a great deal from losses that are just below normal to those in which only large objects can be identified. Treatment of amblyopia consists of treating the causal factors. It must be accomplished early in life, (before the age of six) because the child is likely to permanently lose the ability to process a 20/20 image from the affected eye.

REFERENCES

Eden, J. (1978). *The eye book.* New York: Viking.

Harley, R.K., & Lawrence, G.A. (1977). *Visual impairment in the schools.* Springfield, IL: Thomas.

See also Blind; Cataracts

AMERICAN ACADEMY FOR CEREBRAL PALSY AND DEVELOPMENTAL MEDICINE (AACPDM)

The American Academy for Cerebral Palsy, founded in 1947, changed its name in 1976 to the American Academy for Cerebral Palsy and Developmental Medicine (AACPDM). This is a professional organization of physicians, diplomates of specialty boards, and persons holding a Ph.D. degree in specialties concerned with diagnosis, care, treatment, and research into cerebral palsy and developmental disorders. The AACPDM's 1,200 members also include associate members from the fields of occupational and physical therapy and speech-language pathology.

The AACPDM's activities and services include the presentation of awards and grants for research, demonstration, and personnel preparation. The organization also supports or conducts continuing education activities. The AACPDM holds an annual convention. The office address is 6300 N. River Road, Suite 727, Rosemont, IL 60018.

AMERICAN ANNALS OF THE DEAF

The American *Annals of the Deaf* is a professional journal dedicated to quality in education and related services for hearing impaired children and adults. First published in 1847, the publication is the oldest and most widely read English language journal dealing with deafness and the education of deaf persons. The *Annals* is the official organ of the Convention of American Instructors of the Deaf and the Conference of Educational Administrators of Schools and Programs for the Deaf. Members of the executive committees of both organizations comprise the Joint *Annals* Administrative Committee charged with the direction and administration of the publication.

For 150 years, the *Annals* has primarily focused on the education of deaf students as well as dissemination of information for professionals associated with the educational development of this population. Concurrently, the *Annals* extends its range of topics beyond education, incorporating the broad interests of educators in the general welfare of deaf children and adults, and representing the diverse professional readership of the publication. Topics covered include communication methods and strategies, language development, mainstreaming and residential schools, parent-child relationships, and teacher training and teaching skills.

Four literary issues are published by the journal each year in March, July, October, and December. An annual reference issue, a comprehensive listing of schools and programs in the United States and Canada for students who are deaf or hard of hearing and their teachers, is also published by the *Annals.* In addition to the listings, the reference issue provides demographic, audiological, and educational data regarding students who are deaf and hard of hearing and the schools they attend. The data are compiled annually by the Center for Assessment and Demographic Studies, a component of the Gallaudet Research Institute.

AMERICAN ASSOCIATION FOR THE ADVANCEMENT OF SCIENCE (AAAS)

The American Association for the Advancement of Science (AAAS) was founded in Philadelphia in 1848, making it one of the oldest professional societies in the United States. AAAS is a nonprofit society dedicated to the advancement of scientific and technological quality across all fields of science, and to increasing the general public's understanding of science and technology. The mission of the organization, according to its Constitution, is to "further the work of scientists, facilitate cooperation among them, foster scientific freedom and responsibility, improve the effectiveness of science in the promotion of human welfare, advance education in science, and increase the public's understanding and appreciation of the promise of scientific methods in human progress" (AAAS, 1995).

Today AAAS's membership is international, and is composed of over 145,000 scientists, science educators, engineers, and interested others; membership is open to anyone interested in scientific and technological progress. The Association publishes many science books and reference works, the most prestigious being the weekly *Science,* a highly respected publication which disseminates state-of-the-art scientific research.

REFERENCE

American Association for the Advancement of Science. (1995). General information. (http://www.aaas.org/aaas/geninfo.html)

AMERICAN ASSOCIATION OF COLLEGES FOR TEACHER EDUCATION (AACTE)

The American Association of Colleges for Teacher Education is a national, voluntary association of colleges and universities with undergraduate and/or graduate programs committed to the preparation of professional educators, including teachers and other educational personnel. The Association is composed of over 700 member institutions representing both private and public colleges and universities of every size and located in every state, the District of Columbia, Puerto Rico, the Virgin Islands, and Guam. As a group, the AACTE institutions produce more than 85% of new educators each year.

AMERICAN ASSOCIATION FOR MARRIAGE AND FAMILY THERAPY

The American Association for Marriage and Family Therapy (AAMFT), founded in 1942, is the national organization representing marriage and family therapists. The association seeks to (1) advance marriage and family therapy through increased understanding, research, and treatment, (2) establish and maintain standards for the education and training of marriage and family therapists, and (3) promote professional development, ethics, and conduct among marriage and family therapists. The AAMFT has over 23,000 members and offers four membership categories. Clinical, Associate, and Student members are mental health therapists or therapists-in-training who have met varying levels of AAMFT credential standards. Affiliate members are individuals in allied mental health professions who are interested in marriage and family therapy.

AMERICAN ASSOCIATION ON MENTAL RETARDATION (AAMR)

The American Association on Mental Retardation was founded in 1876, and claims over 9,500 members both in the United States and throughout the world. Its membership is composed of professionals from a large variety of academic disciplines who are interested in the field of mental retardation, as well as nonprofessionals who are involved in and care about mental retardation. One of its primary goals is to expand the possibilities for people with mental retardation to live fulfilling and productive lives.

The AAMR offers strong support to research in mental retardation in the service of increasing the knowledge and skills of all who are involved in the field of mental retardation, through the publication of two professional journals and the Association's newspaper *News and Notes.* The *American Journal on Mental Retardation* is a scholarly research journal, and *Mental Retardation* includes research, book reviews, and conceptual articles aimed at practitioners.

The AAMR is organized into 10 regions that cover the United States, Canada, and parts of the Pacific, and contains over 85 local, state, or provincial chapters. There are 16 divisions, the topics of which include, among others, administration, communication disorders, legal process and advocacy, medicine, psychology, occupational and physical therapy, and vocational rehabilitation. The Association also offers eight special interest groups, focused on creative arts therapies, direct support professionals, Down Syndrome, families, health promotions, mental health services, multicultural concerns, and sexual/social concerns. Membership in the American Association on Mental Retardation is open to anyone concerned about mental retardation.

AMERICAN BOARD OF PROFESSIONAL NEUROPSYCHOLOGY (ABPN)

The American Board of Professional Neuropsychology (ABPN) is a credentialing board that examines doctoral-level psychologists with specialized training in the field of clinical neuropsychology and awards diplomas if examination performance is satisfactory. Examinations consist of an essay exam concerning clinical casework, a work sample examination (wherein examinees submit for scrutiny two actual cases from their practice), and a 3-hour oral examination. Additionally, documentation of appropriate credentials and training is required. Incorporated in 1982, ABPN was the first (and as of this writing, the only) psychology credentialing board that has applied to be approved and certified by the National Commission of Certifying Agencies, the certification arm of the National Organization for Competency Assurance, an organization charged by the federal government with oversight and accreditation of health care certification bodies. The ABPN central office address is Care of the Executive Director, Dr. Michael Raymond, John Heinz Institute of Rehabilitation Medicine, Neuropsychology Services, 150 Mundy Street, Wilkes-Barre, PA 18702.

AMERICAN BOARD OF PROFESSIONAL PSYCHOLOGY (ABPP)

Originally named the American Board of Examiners in Professional Psychology, this organization was renamed the American Board of Professional Psychology in 1968. Founded in 1947 with the support of the American Psychological Association, it is comprised of a board of 15 trustees with headquarters in Columbia, Missouri. This certification board conducts oral examinations and awards specialty certification in eleven specialties: behavioral psychology, clinical psychology, clinical neuropsychology, counseling psychology, family psychology, forensic psychology, health psychology, industrial/organizational psychology, psychoanalysis in psychology, rehabilitation psychology, and school psychology.

AMERICAN EDUCATIONAL RESEARCH ASSOCIATION (AERA)

The American Educational Research Association (AERA) was founded in 1915 as the National Association of Directors of Educational Research. The AERA is an international organization of educators, professors, research directors, specialists, and graduate students interested in educational research. The objectives of AERA include improving the status and quality of research and promoting application and findings of research to educational problems (American Education Research Association, undated).

REFERENCE

American Educational Research Association (Undated brochure). *American Educational Research Association: A membership for your discipline.* Washington, DC: Author.

AMERICAN FOUNDATION FOR THE BLIND (AFB)

The American Foundation for the Blind (AFB), a nonprofit organization, was founded in 1921 to serve as the national partner of local services for the blind and visually impaired. The organization is a leading national resource for people who are blind or visually impaired, the organizations that serve them, and the general public. The mission of the organization is to enable people who are blind or visually im-

paired to achieve equality of access and opportunity in order to ensure freedom of choice in their lives.

The AFB traces its origins to a meeting of a group of professionals in Vinton, Iowa, in the summer of 1921 (Koestler, 1976). This meeting, comprised primarily of officers of the American Association of Workers for the Blind (AAWB), resulted in the recognition of the pressing need for a national organization that was not affiliated with special interest groups, professional organizations, or any local, regional, or state organization currently serving the needs of the blind (Hagerty, 1987).

Helen Keller was closely identified with AFB from the early 1920s until her death, and the organization is recognized as her cause in the United States. Working with AFB for over 40 years, she represented the organization in their efforts to educate legislators and the public about services needed for people who are blind.

AFB fulfills its mission through four primary areas of activity regarding the nonmedical aspects of blindness and visual impairment. Development, collection, and dissemination of information are accomplished by responding annually to 100,000 inquiries from people who are blind or visually impaired, their family and friends, professionals in the blindness field, and the general public requesting information about AFB's programs, services, and other topics related to blindness and visual impairment.

AFB activities in this area also include the publication of books, pamphlets, videos, and periodicals about blindness for professionals and consumers. The AFB publishes the leading professional journal of its kind, *Journal of Visual Impairment and Blindness.* In addition, the organization is responsible for maintaining and preserving the Helen Keller Archives, an invaluable collection of personal material donated by Helen Keller. AFB also houses the M.C. Migel Memorial Library, one of the world's largest collections of print materials on blindness.

Identification, analysis, and resolution of issues critical to people who are blind or visually impaired is achieved by setting priorities, analyzing policy options, and promoting feasible solutions in conjunction with experts and constituents in the field of blindness. Expertise is offered in program areas such as education, employment, aging, and technology; and policy research that positively affects the quality of life of people who are blind or visually impaired is conducted, evaluated, and published by the AFB. The organization also serves as an advocate for and evaluator of the development of assistive products and technology. Maintenance of the Careers & Technology Information Bank, a network of individuals who are blind from all 50 states and Canada who use assistive technology at home, school, or work and are able and willing to serve as mentors to others, is another function of the AFB.

In the accomplishment of its mission, the AFB also strives to educate policymakers and the public as to the needs and capabilities of people who are blind or visually impaired. Consulting on legislative issues and representing blind and visually impaired persons before Congress and government agencies accomplishes this goal. Corporate and public awareness of the capabilities of people who are blind or visually impaired is also increased through publications, audio/visual presentations, exhibits, and public service announcements.

AFB production and distribution of books and other audio materials includes recording and duplicating Talking Books under contract to the Library of Congress. The organization also records and duplicates annual reports and other publications for various corporations and nonprofit organizations, thus making them accessible to print-handicapped employees, clients, and shareholders.

For more information about AFB, write the American Foundation for the Blind, 11 Penn Plaza, Suite 300, New York, NY 10001 or call 1-800-AFB-LINE (232-5463); in New York State, (212) 502-7657.

REFERENCES

Hagerty, S.J. (1987). American Foundation for the Blind. In C.R. Reynolds & L. Mann (Eds.), *Encyclopedia of Special Education* (1st ed.). New York: Wiley.

Koestler, F.A. (1976). *The Unseen Minority.* New York: McKay.

AMERICAN GUIDANCE SERVICE (AGS)

American Guidance Service, Inc. is an educational publishing company founded in 1957, and is an employee-owned company that encourages partnership and ongoing dialogue with the professionals that use its products. AGS publishes a wide variety of norm-referenced assessment instruments for the identification of special needs students, focusing primarily on cognitive ability, achievement, behavior, and personal and social adjustment, with many publications also available in Spanish. Their better-known tests include the Peabody Picture Vocabulary Test (PPVT-III), Vineland Adaptive Behavior Scales, the Kaufman Test of Educational Achievement (K-TEA), and the Developmental Indicators for the Assessment of Learning (DIAL-III). AGS also publishes The Behavioral Assessment System for Children, known popularly as the BASC, which became their best selling test during 1999, and is now used with over one million children annually.

In addition to testing materials, AGS publishes a great many instructional materials, including over 900 textbooks, as well as programs for parenting and family living. Much of their material is focused on children with learning/emotional problems or in special education, though they also publish material geared to all ages. AGS can be reached at 4201 Woodland Road, Circle Pines, MN 55014-1796, or by phone at (800) 328-2560.

AMERICAN INSTITUTE—THE TRAINING SCHOOL AT VINELAND

The American Institute—The Training School at Vineland, is located in Vineland, New Jersey (Main Road and Landis Avenue, Vineland, NJ 08360). The school and training facility were founded in 1887; they are under the supervision and administrative management of Elwyn Institutes. The facility serves children and adults who are mentally retarded, brain damaged, emotionally disturbed, physically handicapped, and learning disabled.

The school programs are ungraded at the elementary and secondary levels. The school features education and training programs that are designed to train young people to return to the community. The training programs serve mildly handicapped to the severely retarded students. The range of educational programs and vocational training experiences are developed with individualized educational plans and rehabilitation services. The facility is internationally recognized for the pioneering works of Binet and Doll. The Stanford Binet tests were translated and norms were developed at the school. Dr. Edward Doll is recognized as the pioneer in the development of the Vineland Social Maturity Scale.

AMERICAN JOURNAL OF MENTAL RETARDATION (AJMR)

Originally known as the *American Journal of Mental Deficiency,* AJMR is published on a bimonthly basis by the American Association on Mental Retardation (AAMR). The original title reflected the original name of the sponsoring organization, which was changed from the American Organization on Mental Deficiency (AAMD) to its current name in 1987. The primary purpose of the journal is to publish theoretical manuscripts and research in the area of mental retardation, with an emphasis on meterial of an objective, scientific, and experimental nature. Book reviews are included. The journal address is 1719 Kalorama Road, N.W., Washington, D.C. 20009.

AMERICAN JOURNAL OF OCCUPATIONAL THERAPY (AJOT)

The *American Journal of Occupational Therapy (AJOT)* is an official publication of the American Occupational Therapy Association. *AJOT* is published monthly except for July/August and November/December, when it appears in bimonthly issues. Manuscripts are subjected to anonymous peer review. Accepted articles pertain to occupational therapy and may include reports of research, educational activities, or professional trends; descriptions of new occupational therapy approaches, programs, or services; review papers that survey new information; theoretical papers that discuss or treat theoretical issues critically; descriptions of original therapeutic aids, devices, or techniques; case reports that describe occupational therapy for a specific clinical situation; or opinion essays that discuss timely issues or opinions and are supported by cogent arguments. In addition, the journal contains letters to the editor, publication reviews, and product advertising.

AMERICAN JOURNAL OF ORTHOPSYCHIATRY (AJO)

The *American Journal of Orthopsychiatry (AJO)*, is the quarterly journal of the American Orthopsychiatric Association. The association was founded in 1926 and began publication of *AJO* in 1930. The *AJO* is a quarterly, refereed, scholarly journal written from a multidisciplinary perspective. The *AJO* is dedicated to public policy, professional practice, and information that relates to mental health and human development. Clinical, theoretical, research, review, and expository papers are published in *AJO.* These papers are essentially synergistic and directed at concept and theory development, reconceptualization of major issues, explanation, and interpretation.

The *AJO* concentrates on many topics of concern to special educators. During its lifetime, *AJO*'s articles have centered around the topics of social issues and the handicapped, childhood psychosis, psychopharmacology, school phobia, depression, suicide, child abuse, mental retardation, and treatment of all of these disorders. The contributors' list and editorial board have, over the years, featured some of the finest scholars from developmental medicine, developmental psychopathology, child development, school psychology, clinical psychology, special education, neurology, psychiatry, and related mental health fields. The *AJO* is an influential journal that publishes top scholars' writing on special education.

***See also* American Orthopsychiatric Association**

AMERICAN JOURNAL OF PSYCHIATRY

The *American Journal of Psychiatry* began publication in 1844 as the *American Journal of Insanity,* changing to its current title in 1921. It is the official journal of the American Psychiatric Association, and is the most widely read psychiatric journal in the world. Published monthly, the *American Journal of Psychiatry* publishes peer-reviewed research studies and articles that focus on developments in the biological aspects of psychiatry, on treatment issues and innovations, and on forensic, ethical, social, and economic topics. Letters to the editor, book reviews, and official American Psychiatric Association reports are also included. Of special interest to many readers are the overview and special lead articles, which address major psychiatric syndromes and issues in depth.

AMERICAN OCCUPATIONAL THERAPY FOUNDATION

The American Occupational Therapy Foundation was founded in 1965 as the American Occupational Therapy Association's (AOTA) philanthropic sister organization. The foundation has devoted its energies to raising funds and resources in three program areas—publications, research,

and scholarships—associated with the profession of occupational therapy and health-care delivery.

The foundation's publication program aims to increase public knowledge and understanding of the occupational therapy profession. In addition to various reports and documents, it publishes *The Occupational Therapy Journal of Research,* and has produced a major bibliography of completed research in the field. The foundation supports the Occupational Therapy Library, which supplies requested materials through interlibrary loan.

The American Occupational Therapy Foundation is located at 4720 Montgomery Lane, P.O. Box 31220, Bethesda, MD 20824.

AMERICAN ORTHOPSYCHIATRIC ASSOCIATION (ORTHO)

The American Orthopsychiatric Association (Ortho) was formed at the invitation of Herman Adler and Karl Menninger at the Institute for Juvenile Research in Chicago in 1924 under the name of the Association of American Orthopsychiatrists. The group operated informally, debating its name and purpose and finally founding Ortho a year later. In 1926 Ortho amended its constitution, which limited membership to physicians, to redefine membership to include psychiatrists, psychologists, social workers, and other professional persons "whose work and interests lie in the study and treatment of conduct disorders." According to Eisenberg and DeMaso (1985), the first published membership roster, published October 1, 1927, included 45 psychiatrists, 12 psychologists, 5 social workers, and several lawyers and penologists. Ortho had as its purpose the centralization of the techniques, objectives, and aspirations of psychiatrists, psychologists, and related mental health workers whose primary interests were in the area of human behavior, providing a common meeting ground for students of behavior problems and for fostering scientific research and its dissemination. The early membership included names familiar to special educators, including such notables as Edgar Doll, Lightner Witmer, and Carl Murchison.

Lightner Witmer, noted among historians of psychology as the man who coined the term clinical psychology, founded school psychology, and established the first psychological clinic, he also coined the term orthogenics and established the team approach to children's problems when he invited neurologists to collaborate on case studies (Eisenberg & DeMaso, 1985). Ortho subsequently became a major force in the establishment of the child guidance movement in the early 1900s. In 1930 Ortho established the *American Journal of Orthopsychiatry,* a widely read and respected journal that in its early years vigorously debated the roles and functions of various professionals (e.g., psychiatrists, psychologists, social workers, etc.) in the treatment of childhood mental health disorders.

Presently, many special educators belong to Ortho. It is involved in social, scientific, and public policy issues, including diagnosis, evaluation, and treatment, relevant to the improvement of the lives of the handicapped. The *American Journal of Orthopsychiatry* is provided as a benefit of membership; it contains many articles of interest to special educators. The association is located at 330 7th Ave., 18th Floor, New York, NY 10001-5010.

REFERENCE

American Orthopsychiatric Association. (1998). *About Ortho.* http//www.amerortho.org/ortho2.htm.

Eisenberg, L., & DeMaso, D.R. (1985). Fifty years of the *American Journal of Orthopsychiatry:* An overview and introduction. In E. Flaxman & E. Herman (Eds.), *American Journal of Orthopsychiatry: Annotated index: Vols. 1–50. 1930–1980.* Greenwich, CT: JAI.

See also **American Journal of Orthopsychiatry; Witmer, Lightner**

AMERICAN PHYSICAL THERAPY ASSOCIATION

The American Physical Therapy Association (APTA) endeavors to improve physical therapy services and education through accrediting academic programs in physical therapy; assisting states in preparing certification examinations; and offering workshops and continuing education courses for therapists at the national and local level. Information is available about careers in physical therapy, accredited preparation programs, sources of student financial aid, and employment opportunities. A variety of pamphlets are available on prevention of injuries and chronic or degenerative conditions. The association publishes a newsletter and journal. Bibliographies have been prepared on topics including resources for stroke victims, quadriplegics, paraplegics, amputees, parents, and educators. Members benefit from information on questions regarding practice and disabilities. The association also serves as a referral source for individuals who require physical therapy services. Association offices are located at 1111 North Fairfax Street, Alexandria, VA 22314. Telephone: (703) 684-2782; e-mail: www.apta.org.

AMERICAN PRINTING HOUSE FOR THE BLIND (APH)

The American Printing House for the Blind (APH), the oldest private, nonprofit institution for the blind in the United States, was founded in Louisville, Kentucky in 1858. It is the world's largest company devoted solely to creating products and services for people who are visually impaired. The Act to Promote the Education of the Blind, mandated by Congress in 1879, enabled the American Printing House for the Blind to receive grants for education texts and aids for those with visual impairments from the federal government. Funds appropriated under the Act are used by each state to purchase educational materials from APH for their blind students below the college level (American Printing House for the Blind, 1998).

The Company's mission is to promote the independence of blind and visually impaired persons by providing special media, tools, and materials needed for education and life. A wide variety of products and services are available through APH, including braille, large type, recorded, computer disk, and tactile graphic publications as well as a wide assortment of educational and daily living products. Various services designed to assist consumers and professionals in the field of vision are also offered, including *Louis,* a database listing materials available from accessible media across North America and *Patterns,* a reading instruction program developed through APH research.

APH's Talking Books on cassette tape, produced in agency recording studios, are a popular reading medium for blind and visually impaired people of all ages. Fiction and nonfiction topics, ranging from romance to cookbooks, are produced by professional narrators who are also teachers, actors, and media personalities. Most Talking Books can be obtained on a free loan basis from the National Library for the Blind and Physically Handicapped, a division of the Library of Congress. Three magazines are offered by APH directly to eligible blind readers. They include *Readers Digest, Newsweek,* and *Weekly Reader.*

REFERENCE

American Printing House for the Blind. (1998). *What is the American Printing House for the Blind?* Louisville, KY: Author.

AMERICAN PSYCHIATRIC ASSOCIATION (APA)

The American Psychiatric Association was founded in 1844 as the Association of Medical Superintendents of American Institutions for the Insane, and changed to its current name in 1921. The APA is a national medical specialty society that had over 40,000 members in 1998; members are physicians who specialize in the diagnosis and treatment of mental, emotional, and substance abuse disorders. The Association's major focus areas include mental health, psychopharmacology, psychotherapy, and health professions development, and its primary objectives include the advancement and improvement of care for people with mental illnesses through the provision of nationwide education, public information, and awareness programs and materials. The APA can be contacted at their national offices at 1400 K Street, NW, Washington, DC, 20005.

AMERICAN PSYCHOLOGICAL ASSOCIATION

The American Psychological Association (APA) is the nation's largest psychology organization. The APA works to advance psychology as a science and a profession, and to promote human welfare. When the APA was established in 1892, psychology was a new profession and the organization had fewer than three dozen members. Over the years the organization has grown rapidly: In 2000 the APA had more than 155,000 members, 54 divisions in specialized subfields and interest areas, and 58 affiliated state, provincial, and territorial psychological associations. The Association's general headquarters are at 750 First Street, NE, Washington, DC, 20002-4242.

AMERICAN PSYCHOLOGIST

American Psychologist is the official journal of the American Psychological Association. Published monthly, it is the most widely circulated psychological journal in the world, going out to the more than 155,000 members of the Association around the globe. It is a primary source of discussion on cutting-edge issues in psychology, and it publishes empirical, theoretical, and practical articles on broad aspects of psychology. It is indexed in over 20 abstracting/indexing services, including PsycINF0, Index Medicus, Academic Index, Social Sciences Index, and Applied Social Science Index & Abstracts, making its contents easily discoverable and thus highly available to users. As the official journal of the association, it contains archival documents, including the minutes of the annual business meeting, and reports of the officers, directorates, and committees whose work involves policies and practices affecting members of the association. The journal also publishes a commentary section, obituaries of well-known psychologists, and (in each year's December issue) a listing of all APA-approved doctoral training programs in clinical, counseling, and school psychology in the United States and Canada.

AMERICAN SIGN LANGUAGE

During the past 20 years, there has been a rapid and widespread increase in the use of sign language as a viable means of communication by deaf and hearing individuals. American Sign Language (ASL), also known as Ameslan, has been recognized as a natural language with its own unique grammatical structure. Approximately half a million deaf Americans and Canadians currently use ASL.

Sign language is composed of specific movements and shapes of the hands, arms, eyes, face, head, and body that correspond to the words and suprasegmental features of spoken languages. In delineating the major components of ASL, linguists find it useful to differentiate between manual and nonmanual aspects of signing. Sign formation, originally called "cherology" by Stokoe (1960), corresponds to the phonological system of oral languages. Each sign consists of four basic parameters: hand shape (dez); location or place of articulation (tab); movement in a particular direction (sig); and palm orientation occurring with various hand shapes.

Some families of signs are based on the location of the sign in space. Masculine and feminine signs are differentiated on the basis of location. For example, the sign for "man" is made at the forehead by grasping the imaginary brim of a hat with four fingers and the thumb and then

bringing the flat hand, palm down, away from the head at the level of the imaginary hat. The sign of "woman" is produced at the level of the cheek by moving the inside of the thumb of the right "A" hand shape down along the right cheek toward the chin and then bringing the flat hand, palm down, away from the face.

There are similarities in some of the syntactic mechanisms used in ASL and English; others are specialized to accommodate communication in the visual—gestural mode. It has been argued that sign order is relatively flexible and that several built in syntactic devices help to convey information efficiently. One such device is the deletion of grammatical morphemes such as articles and the copular verb "to be." Information is preserved by establishing positions of reference in space and referring to them through pointing and eye gaze. A second device is the incorporation of location, number, manner, size, and shape of signs. A third syntactic device is the use of nonmanual signals, for example, facial expressions and body posture. These are important in terms of syntactic as well as semantic and pragmatic functions in ASL, and they frequently assume a role similar to the suprasegmentals in speech (Liddell, 1980). Eye gaze is used to perform indexic reference or even to establish the reference in a conversation. Raising the eyebrow is used as a topic marker and in forming questions. Eye blinking is relevant to the proper interpretation of conditional sentences and interrogatives. A head shake over part or all of a signed utterance may negate that part or the entire sign communication. Also, certain nonmanual behaviors are associated with particular lexical items. For example, the sign for "bite" is accompanied by a biting motion of the mouth. The sign for "relieved" is accompanied by rapid exhaling and a burst of air through pursed lips. Frequently, a combination of nonmanual signals is used to convey specific linguistic constructions and semantic relations.

REFERENCES

Liddell, S. (1980). *American Sign Language syntax.* The Hague: Mouton.

Stokoe, W.C. (1960). Sign language structure: An outline of the visual communication systems of American deaf. *Studies in Linguistics, Occasional Papers, 8.*

***See also* Alternative Communication Methods in Special Education; Augmentative Communication Systems**

AMERICAN SOCIETY FOR DEAF CHILDREN (ASDC)

The American Society for Deaf Children is a national nonprofit organization of parents and families of deaf or hard of hearing children, founded in 1967. Its stated purpose is to provide support, encouragement, and information to families of deaf children, and to advocate for their total high-quality participation in education and the community. ASDC furnishes information upon request to help families base their decisions on current and accurate information, supports the use of signing, and promotes a positive attitude toward deaf culture.

The ASDC operates a Parents Hotline at (800) 942-ASDC, and their national offices are located at 1820 Tribute Road, Suite A, Sacramento, CA 95815. The ASDC can be contacted at (916) 641-6084 (Business V/TTY).

AMERICAN SPEECH-LANGUAGE-HEARING ASSOCIATION (ASHA)

The American Speech-Language-Hearing Association is the professional and scientific association for more than 96,000 speech-language pathologists, audiologists, and speech, language, and hearing scientists in the United States as well as internationally. Its stated mission is to promote the interests of professionals in audiology and speech-language pathology, and work for the provision of the highest quality services for people with communication disorders.

One of ASHA's most important actions was the development of standards for a Certificate of Clinical Competence in Speech Pathology (CCC-SP) and Audiology (CCC-A). Professionals in communication disorders must meet stringent training and experience standards in order to qualify for these prestigious certifications. ASHA continues to work actively with state governments on licensing procedures for communication disorder professionals, and remains the voice of the professions of speech-language pathology and audiology.

The ASHA offices are located at 10801 Rockville Pike, Rockville, MD 20852, and may be reached by telephone at (800) 498-2071, for hearing impaired individuals at (301) 897-5700 (TTY), or by fax at (301) 571–0457.

AMERICANS WITH DISABILITIES ACT (ADA)

The Americans with Disabilities Act of 1990 (ADA) is a comprehensive civil rights law designed to prohibit discrimination against people with disabilities. ADA is a civil rights law; therefore, it preempts any other local, state, or federal law that grants lesser rights to individuals with disabilities (National Association of State Directors of Special Education [NASDSE], 1992). Federal funding is not provided to carry out the ADA mandates; however, a wide range of public and private institutions, including educational institutions, are required to comply with the ADA provisions. The purpose of ADA is "1) to provide a clear and comprehensive national mandate for the elimination of discrimination against individuals with disabilities; 2) to provide clear, strong, consistent, enforceable standards addressing discrimination against individuals with disabilities; 3) to ensure that the federal government plays a central role in enforcing the standards established in this Act on behalf of

individuals with disabilities; and 4) to invoke the sweep of congressional authority, including the power to enforce the 14th Amendment, to address the major areas of discrimination faced by people with disabilities" (42 U.S.C. §§ 12101 Sec 2 [b] [1–4]). ADA derives its substance from Section 504 of the Rehabilitation Act of 1973, but its procedures from Title VII of the Civil Rights Act of 1964, amended in 1991 (First & Curcio, 1993).

The ADA consists of five titles. The areas addressed in these five titles include employment, public services, public accommodations, telecommunications, and miscellaneous provisions. Title I prohibits discrimination in employment of persons with disabilities. Under this title, employers must reasonably accommodate the disabilities of the "otherwise qualified" applicants or employees unless "undue hardship" would result. An example of an "undue hardship" would be a significant difficulty or excessive expense to the employer associated with making alterations or modifications at the job site to accommodate a qualified applicant who is also an individual with a disability. All school districts, regardless of the number of personnel employed, are subject to Title I standards.

Title II prohibits discrimination in programs, activities, and services provided by state and local governments and their instrumentalities. Title II applies to all public entities, such as public schools, regardless of federal funding status. Under Title II, school facilities, whether existing facilities or under construction, must meet accessibility requirements for individuals with disabilities consistent with Section 504 of the Rehabilitation Act (First & Curcio, 1993). Public transportation, like buses and rail vehicles, must also meet accessibility requirements. Title II requires school districts to provide appropriate aids so that individuals with disabilities have equal opportunities to participate in available programs and services. Likewise, districts are required to give primary consideration to disabled individuals' requests and to ensure that individuals with hearing or visual impairments receive information in an appropriate and understandable format about available programs and services. Examples of public school programs, services, and activities covered by Title II include public entertainment or lectures sponsored by the school district, afterschool activities and social events offered by the schools, parent-teacher conferences, classroom activities, field trips, and any other service provided for students or staff (Office of Civil Rights [OCR], 1996).

Title III prohibits discrimination based on disability in privately owned public accommodations. Nonsectarian private schools and school bus transportation, as well as other privately owned public accommodations must make reasonable alterations in policies, practices, and procedures to avoid discrimination. Nonsectarian private schools must provide auxiliary aids and services to individuals with visual or hearing impairments. In addition, physical barriers must be removed unless readily unachievable. If not readily achievable, alternate methods of providing services must be offered. All new construction and alterations in existing facilities must be handicap-accessible. School bus transportation services, such as bus routes, must be comparable in duration and distance, for disabled and nondisabled individuals.

Title IV requires telephone companies to provide telecommunication relay services for hearing and speech impaired individuals. Closed-captioned public service announcements must also be provided. Under Title IV, schools must ensure that communication with disabled individuals is just as effective as communication with nondisabled individuals.

Title V consists of a variety of provisions. The title identifies the federal agencies responsible for the enforcement and technical assistance related to ADA. The federal agency responsible for the enforcement of Title II, Subtitle A, programs, activities, and services provided by state and local governments and their instrumentalities, which extends to all public school systems, is the Office of Civil Rights (OCR) in the Department of Education. The OCR not only enforces the ADA provisions under Title II, Subtitle A, but it also handles complaints filed with regard to alleged violations of this title. Title V also dictates that state governments are not immune from legal actions related to ADA. In addition, individuals with disabilities have the right to accept or reject accommodations and services offered under ADA. Furthermore, individuals with or without disabilities cannot be coerced or retaliated against for exercising their rights under ADA. The title also addresses the relationship between ADA and other laws and its impact on insurance providers and benefits.

In examining the relationship between ADA and other federal laws affecting persons with disabilities, ADA is viewed as a complementary law (Cunconan-Lahr, 1991). ADA does not diminish any of the rights of disabled individuals under the Civil Rights Act of 1964, as amended in 1991, Individuals with Disabilities Education Act (IDEA), or Section 504 of the Rehabilitation Act of 1973 (NASDSE, 1992).

Section 504 and ADA espouse the same underlying principle, which is that entities under their jurisdiction cannot discriminate against individuals with disabilities in their programs, activities, and services (Cunconan-Lahr, 1991). To eliminate discrimination, both laws stress the importance of equal opportunity, not just equal treatment, for disabled and nondisabled individuals. However, ADA does create a higher standard of nondiscrimination than does Section 504 in several respects. First, Section 504 applies only to recipients of federal funding, whereas ADA applies to employment, public services, public accommodations, and transportation, regardless of whether or not federal funding is received. Second, Section 504 covers qualified individuals with disabilities, whereas ADA extends protection to a person without a disability who is related to or associated with an individual with a disability (OCR, 1996).

With the aforementioned exceptions, Title II of ADA, which extends to public schools, does not impose any new major requirements on school districts (OCR, 1996). Much

of the language in Title II and Section 504 are similar and school districts that receive federal funding have been required to comply with Section 504 for over the past 25 years. In the area of education, nondiscrimination requirements related to disabled individuals are detailed more specifically under Section 504 than under Title II. However, Title II requirements are not to be interpreted as applying a lesser standard or degree of protection for disabled individuals. In fact, if a rule issued under Section 504 imposes a lesser standard than the ADA regulation, the language in the ADA statute replaces the language in Section 504 (NASDSE, 1992).

The ADA statute does not directly specify procedural safeguards related to special education, evaluation and placement procedures, due process procedures, and responsibility and requirements under the provision of a free, appropriate public education (FAPE) as does Section 504 and IDEA. ADA incorporates the specific details of these concepts from Section 504 and IDEA into Title II, Subtitle A. ADA also provides additional protection in combination with the actions brought under Section 504 and IDEA. For example, reasonable accommodations must be made for eligible individuals with disabilities to perform essential functions of a job. Special education programs that are community-based and involve job training or placement are covered under the ADA statute. ADA protections are also applicable to nonsectarian private schools, but not to organizations or entities controlled by religious affiliations (Henderson, 1995).

Section 504 and IDEA provide specific details regarding procedural safeguards, whereas ADA does not. Procedural safeguards involve notification to parents regarding identification, evaluation, and placement of a child in special education programs and related services. ADA, on the other hand, specifies administrative requirements, complaint procedures, and consequences for noncompliance related to services (Henderson, 1995).

ADA does not specify evaluation and placement procedures as does Section 504 and IDEA. However, ADA does specify reasonable accommodations for individuals with disabilities across educational settings and activities. Reasonable accommodations are not limited to, but may include, modifying equipment, hiring one-on-one aids, modifying tests, providing alternate forms of communication, relocating services in more accessible areas, altering existing facilities, and constructing new facilities (Henderson, 1995). ADA does not delineate specific due process procedures; however, IDEA and Section 504 do. According to ADA, individuals with disabilities who are discriminated against in an educational setting have the same recourse that is available under Title VII of the Civil Rights Act of 1964, as amended in 1991. Individuals may file complaints with the OCR or sue in federal court. The OCR encourages informal mediation and voluntary compliance (Henderson, 1995). However, administrative remedies do not have to be exhausted prior to filing a lawsuit (28 C.F.R. § 35.172). Federal funds may be removed from schools for noncompliance with the ADA mandates and individuals with disabilities may be awarded attorney fees if they prevail in any action filed under ADA (28 C.F.R. § 35.175)

Title II, Subtitle A of ADA is the section of the statute pertaining to public schools. The statute prohibits discrimination against any "qualified individual with a disability." ADA's definition of an individual with a disability is essentially the same as Section 504's definition. The ADA definition of a disability consists of three prongs. ADA defines a disability as "a physical or mental impairment that substantially limits one or more major life activities, a record of such an impairment, or being regarded as having such an impairment" (42 U.S.C. § 12102 [2]).

The first prong of the ADA definition, which is a physical or mental impairment, includes physiological disorders, cosmetic disfigurement, or anatomical loss that affects body systems as well as mental or psychological disorders (28 C.F.R. § 35.104 [1] [i]). Examples of physical or mental impairments under the ADA definition of a disability are epilepsy, muscular dystrophy, multiple sclerosis, cancer, heart disease, diabetes, mental retardation, emotional illness, specific learning disabilities, drug addiction, HIV disease (symptomatic or asymptomatic), alcoholism, and orthopedic, visual, speech, and hearing impairments (OCR, 1996). The preceding examples are not an exhaustive list of physical and mental impairments under the ADA definition of a disability.

Another key concept in the ADA definition of a disability is "a substantial limitation in a major life activity." A "major life activity" refers to a basic activity that the "average person performs with little or no difficulty" such as walking, speaking, seeing, breathing, working, and learning (28 C.F.R. § 35.104). A person who has "a substantial limitation" that is determined by the nature, severity, duration, and long-term or permanent impact of the impairment on a major life activity is protected under ADA (OCR, 1996).

In the second prong, a person with a record or history of an impairment that substantially limits a major life activity also meets ADA's definition of an individual with a disability (28 C.F.R. § 35.104 [3]). Examples include a person who has a history of a mental or emotional illness, drug addiction, alcoholism, heart disease, or cancer. An individual who has been misclassified as having an impairment, (such as a person misdiagnosed as being mentally retarded or emotionally disturbed) is also protected under ADA (OCR, 1996).

The third prong of the definition of a disability under ADA protects a person who has an impairment that does or does not substantially limit a major life activity, but is perceived by the public or public entity as being substantially limiting (28 C.F.R. § 35.104 [3]). For example, a girl who walks with a limp but is not substantially limited in her ability to walk is not allowed to participate on the school's soccer team out of fear by school personnel that she will be injured. Under ADA, the third prong of the definition of an individual with a disability applies and thus protects the girl. The third prong of the definition of a disability also protects an individual who does not have an impairment, but the public or public entity perceives the individual as having an impairment (28 C.F.R. § 35.104 [3]).

Title II and Section 504 use the three-prong definition of a disability, whereas IDEA uses the 13 recognized disability categories and the "need" criteria, in other words there must be a need for special education and related services. Based on these differences in the definition of a disability, there may be some students who qualify for regular or special education and related services under Section 504 and Title II but do not have one of the 13 disabilities recognized by IDEA (OCR, 1996).

Protection under Title II, Subtitle A is afforded to *qualified* individuals with disabilities. An individual with a disability is qualified to receive services and/or participate in an elementary and secondary education program if the student meets the eligibility requirements of a qualified individual with a disability established under Section 504. As previously mentioned, Title II incorporates the more specific details and standards in Section 504. A qualified individual with a disability is an individual who has a disability and is of the appropriate age (school-aged), and "who, with or without reasonable modifications to rules, policies, or practices, the removal of architectural, communication, or transportation barriers, or the provision of auxiliary aids and services, meets the essential eligibility requirements for the receipt of services or the participation in programs or activities provided by a public entity" (28 C.F.R. § 35.104).

Parents or other associates of a student who are disabled themselves and who are invited to attend a school event or choose to participate in a school event open to the public are also qualified as individuals with disabilities and are protected under ADA. Under these circumstances, the school district must ensure program accessibility and provide auxiliary aids and services to ensure effective communication for these individuals with disabilities. For example, if a parent is deaf and is invited to attend a parent-teacher conference for his or her child, who may or may not be a student with a disability under ADA, then the school is responsible for providing an interpreter at the parent's request in order for the parent to participate in the meeting (OCR, 1996).

Title II also extends protection to, but does not provide accommodations for, an individual who is not disabled but who assists or lives with someone with a disability (28 C.F.R. § 35.130 [g]). Family members, friends, or any other person or entity who associates with an individual with a disability are protected under this federal regulation. Likewise, Title II extends protection to an individual with or without a disability who takes action to oppose any act or practice prohibited by the statute or assists or encourages others to exercise their rights under the ADA regulations (28 C.F.R. § 35.134). For example, if an educator encourages a family to exercise their rights under ADA regarding a school policy, then the educator and the family, including the individual with the disability, are protected under ADA from any coercion or retaliation from the school district.

To bring a school district into compliance with the ADA

statute, five action steps must be taken by the district. First, the school district must designate a responsible employee to coordinate ADA compliance. Under Title II, if the school district has 50 or more employees, then at least one coordinator must be designated (28 C.F.R. § 35.107 [a]). The ADA coordinator's role includes planning and coordinating compliance efforts, implementing and ensuring completion of the five action steps, and receiving and investigating complaints of possible discrimination against individuals with disabilities. Second, the school district, regardless of size, must provide notice of ADA requirements to all interested parties including participants, beneficiaries, employees, applicants, and the public. Specific information on how Title II requirements apply to particular programs, services, and activities must be included (28 C.F.R. § 35.106). Appropriate methods to disseminate this information include publications, public posters, or media broadcast. The most effective methods for making people aware of their rights and protections under ADA, however, are determined by the head of the school district or delegated to the ADA coordinator. Third, school districts with 50 or more employees must adopt and publish grievance procedures providing for prompt and equitable resolution of complaints alleging violations of ADA (28 C.F.R. § 35.107). These grievance procedures are available to school district employees, students, or the public. Fourth, all school districts, regardless of size, must conduct a self-evaluation of its policies and practices, including communications and employment, and correct any inconsistencies in its policies and practices in relation to the ADA statute (28 C.F.R. § 35.105 [a]). However, if the school district has received federal funding and has conducted a self-evaluation as required under Section 504, then only those programs and new or modified policies or practices since the Section 504 self-evaluation must be reviewed and corrections made to be consistent with the ADA regulations (28 C.F.R. § 35.105 [c]). School districts should have completed Title II self-evaluations by January 26, 1993 (28 C.F.R. § 35.105 [c]) for current programs, policies, and practices in existence at that time. Fifth, a transition plan must be developed to bring existing facilities into structural compliance with the ADA statute. A transition plan is needed to ensure that programs, services, or activities are accessible to individuals with disabilities (28 C.F.R. § 35.150 [d] [1]). Structural changes outlined in the transition plan should have been completed by January 26, 1995 for existing facilities (28 C.F.R. § 35.150 [c]).

Nondiscrimination requirements are used to analyze the policies, programs, and practices of a public school district. Specific nondiscrimination requirements imposed on a school district under Section 504 are applicable under Title II. According to Section 504, a school district is obligated to provide a free, appropriate public education (FAPE) to school-aged children with disabilities. The school district's responsibilities are specifically described under Section 504 and are incorporated into the general provisions of Title II (28 C.F.R. § 35.130; 28 C.F.R. § 35.103 [a]; see 34 C.F.R. §§ 104.31–104.37).

Title II also requires a school district to ensure that qualified individuals with disabilities are not excluded from participation in or denied any benefits from the district's programs, services, or activities based on their disability (28 C.F.R. § 35.130 [a]). This requirement applies to programs, services, and activities operated or provided directly by the district as well as those operated or provided by another entity on behalf of the district under contractual agreement or other arrangements (28 C.F.R. § 35.130 [b]). For example, if a student with a disability is excluded from bus service by a private school bus company that is under contract with the school district to provide this service, then the school district would be liable for the alleged discriminatory act under Title II (OCR, 1996).

The school district must also ensure that qualified individuals with disabilities have an equal opportunity to participate in the district's programs as do nondisabled individuals. Likewise, individuals with disabilities must have an equal opportunity to benefit from any aids, benefits, or services provided by the school district as do nondisabled individuals. For example, if a student with a severe visual impairment is evaluated and it is determined, in order to provide FAPE, visual aids and services must be provided, and the school district refuses to pay for the visual aids, citing expenses, then under these circumstances, the school district is in violation of Title II standards because the district has denied related aids and services to the student. As a result, the student does not have an equal opportunity as does a nondisabled student to participate in or receive benefits from the school program (OCR, 1996). Similarly, a school district's benefits and services must be effective enough to afford equal opportunity to obtain the same results, benefits, or levels of achievement for both individuals with and without disabilities.

Under Title II, a school district may not operate different or separate programs or provide different or separate benefits or services, unless the programs, benefits, or services are needed to provide equal benefits to individuals with disabilities (28 C.F.R. § 35.103 [a]; 28 C.F.R. § 35.130 [b] [1] [iv]). If separate or different programs, services, or benefits are needed, then the school district must provide them in the most integrated setting for individuals with disabilities (28 C.F.R. § 35.103 [a]; 28 C.F.R. § 35.130 [d]). However, in the establishment of separate or different programs, services, or benefits, individuals with disabilities may not be denied participation in the regular programs or access to regular benefits and services.

Another nondiscrimination requirement under Title II includes the prohibition of surcharges. A school district is not allowed to place a surcharge on an individual with a disability to cover the costs of measures that are necessary to provide nondiscriminatory treatment (28 C.F.R.§ 35.130 [f]). For example, if an evaluation is conducted and it is determined that a student with a disability should be placed in a regular education program with related aids and services, including a computer, then the school district cannot charge the student or his/her parents for the use of the computer, as the computer is a necessary aid in order to provide FAPE. Similarly, modifications that would fundamentally alter a specific benefit, program, service, or activity are prohibited. On the other hand, if failure to modify a specific benefit, program, service, or activity results in the denial of FAPE, then the school district must make modifications. However, a school district is not required to provide a personal device, such as wheelchair, or service of a personal nature, such as toileting, unless the device or service is necessary to provide FAPE to the student.

Nondiscriminatory requirements also apply to eligibility criteria. A school district may not use eligibility criteria to screen out individuals with disabilities from participation in its programs or receipt of its benefits or services (28 C.F.R. § 35.103 [a]; 28 C.F.R. § 35.130 [b] [8]). However, a school has the right to impose legitimate safety requirements needed for the safe operation of its services, benefits, or programs, but these safety requirements must be based on actual risks, not stereotypes. For example, if a school offers a course in scuba diving and demonstrates that a certain level of swimming ability is needed for safe participation in the class, then those individuals who cannot pass a swimming test, including some individuals with disabilities, could be screened out without violating the law (OCR, 1996).

Besides nondiscriminatory requirements, a school district must ensure that their programs, services, and activities are accessible to individuals with disabilities. This includes not only students, but parents, guardians, and members of the public with disabilities. According to Title II, two standards are used to determine program accessibility. One standard deals with existing facilities and the other standard deals with new construction and alterations. For existing facilities, when viewed in their entirety, the program or activity must be accessible to and usable by individuals with disabilities, unless a fundamental alteration in the program or undue financial or administrative burden would result (28 C.F.R. § 35.130). The burden of proof, according to Title II, is placed on the school district. For new or altered facilities, the same standard applies, however, the fundamental alteration or undue burden is not applicable.

Based on the program accessibility standard, numerous misconceptions have evolved, such as the view that buildings must be completely accessible and barrier-free. As long as the program, class, or function is accessible, Title II does not require that existing buildings offer a barrier-free environment. In other words, if the program can be held in another classroom or building, and this classroom or building meets accessibility requirements, then the school district's fundamental alteration in the program is in compliance with the standards set forth under Title II (OCR, 1996).

In addition to program accessibility requirements, transition services are also addressed under Title II as well as Title III of ADA. Transition services are defined as "a set of coordinated activities that promote movement from school to postschool activities" (Jacob-Timm & Hartshorne, 1995). Transition services for youth with disabilities are provided in more specific details under IDEA. The enactment of ADA is expected to lead to the expansion of opportunities for youth with disabilities in their transition to postschool activities (American Council on Education, 1993). Postschool activities may include vocational training, continuing education, integrated employment, independent living, community participation, and postsecondary education.

For postsecondary education, the enactment of ADA has translated into renewed attention focused on disability access to facilities and programs as well as employment and promotion issues. In addition, ADA has resulted in a greater number of opportunities for students with disabilities due to increased access to employment, public accommodations, transportation, and telecommunications. Thus, an expanded pool of qualified college-educated disabled workers is expected in the future to address anticipated manpower shortages in the next decade (American Council on Education, 1993).

Numerous implications exist for education officials under Title II. First, local agencies may witness an increase in the number of requests for public hearings to determine student eligibility for special education. A potential increase in the number of students served may occur. Second, parents and other adults' requests to participate in school activities may increase. Since public schools offer programs and opportunities to the community, many adults with disabilities may desire greater participation due to the enactment of the statute. As a result, the public school's responsibilities may increase in meeting program accessibility, service, and benefit requirements. Third, ADA encourages full participation in society of individuals with disabilities. Thus, parents' requests for their children with disabilities to participate in school activities (e.g., athletic events, field trips, recreational offerings, etc.) may increase and transportation issues will also need to be addressed (NASDSE, 1992).

The implementation of ADA has expanded the role of the schools in the preparation of students with disabilities to take full advantage of employment opportunities, to participate more fully in school programs, to achieve greater independence through the use of public transportation, and to learn and to communicate more effectively through the use of telecommunication systems (First & Curcio, 1993). ADA encourages the education system to become more actively involved in the lives of individuals with disabilities and to assist in the empowerment of students with disabilities. Educators and parents are challenged to bring real meaning into the lives of students with disabilities and to the school environment, not only for the students' benefit, but also for the benefit of all people.

REFERENCES

American Council on Education (1993). *Americans with Disabilities* (Report No. H030C3002–94). Washington D.C.: HEATH Resource Center. (ERIC Reproduction Document Service No. ED 381 919)

Americans with Disabilities Act of 1990, 28 C.F.R. § 35; 34 C.F.R. §§ 104.31–104.37 (1993).

Americans with Disabilities Act of 1990, 42 U.S.C. § 12101 *et seq.* (West 1994).

Cunconan-Lahr, R. (1991). *The Americans with Disabilities Act: Educational implications and policy considerations.* (ERIC Document Reproduction Service No. Ed 333 665)

First, P.F. & Curcio, J.L. (1993). *Individuals with disabilities: Implementing the newest laws.* Newbury Park, CA: Corwin.

Henderson, Kelly (1995). *Overview of ADA, IDEA, and Section 504* (Report No. EDO-EC-94–8). Washington, D.C.: Office of Educational Research and Improvement. (ERIC Document Reproduction Service No. ED 389 142)

Jacob-Timm, S., & Hartshorne, T. (1995). *Ethics and law for school psychologists.* Brandon, VT: Clinical Psychology Publishing.

National Association of State Directors of Special Education. (1992). The Americans with Disabilities Act: New challenges and opportunities for school administrators. *Liaison Bulletin, 18*(4), 1–11.

Office of Civil Rights. (1996). *Compliance with the Americans with Disabilities Act: A self-evaluation guide for public elementary and secondary schools.* Washington DC: U.S. Government Printing Office.

See also **Adult Basic Education; Architectural Barriers; Legislation**

Louise Bates Ames

AMES, LOUISE BATES (1908–1996)

Born in Portland, Maine, Louise Ames received her BA in 1930 from the University of Maine. She then went on to receive her MA in 1933 and PhD in 1937 in experimental psychology from Yale University, where she studied with Arnold Gesell. Her relationship with Gesell resulted in the founding of the Gesell Institute in 1950.

Working with Frances Ilg and Arnold Gesell, Dr. Ames developed the important developmental theory that patterned, predictable behaviors are associated with chronological age, with the explicit implication that human development unfolded in discrete, recognizable stages. Such ideas were relatively novel at the time and have had great impact since their development. Dr. Ames' greatest impact was in teaching parents and teachers about the course of child development, primarily through her prolific publications, which included *Infant and Child in the Culture of Today* (1940), *School Readiness* (1956), the syndicated newspaper column "Child Behavior" in collaboration with her colleagues (which later became a weekly half-hour television show in the 1950s), *Child Behavior* (1981), and *Don't Rush Your Preschooler* (1980), co-authored with her daughter Joan Ames Chase. Ames also had a strong interest in projective assessment and provided normative data in *Child Rorschach Responses* (1974). This interest extended to assessment of the elderly (*Rorschach Responses in Old Age*, 1973) and a series of articles developing test batteries for assessing deterioration of functions in old age.

Over her long career, Dr. Ames authored some 300 articles and monographs, co-authored/collaborated on 25 books, and received honorary degrees and many awards for service. One of the most publicized women in psychology, Louise Bates Ames died of cancer in November, 1996, at the age of 88.

REFERENCES

Ames, L.B. (1940). *Infant and child in the culture of today.* New York: Harper & Row.

Ames, L.B. (1974). *Child Rorschach responses.* New York: Brunner/Mazel.

Ames, L.B. (1981). *Child behavior.* New York: Harper Perennial.

Ames, L.B., & Chase, J.A. (1980). *Don't rush your preschooler.* New York: Harper & Row.

Ames, L.B., & Ilg, F. (1956). *School readiness.* New York: Harper & Row.

Ames, L.B., Metraux, R.W., Rodell, J.L., & Walker, R.W. (1973). *Rorschach responses in old age.* New York: Brunner/Mazel.

AMNESIA

Amnesia is a disorder of memory that occurs in the absence of gross disorientation, confusion, or dementia. Amnesia may be retrograde, where the individual has difficulty remembering events and information learned prior to the onset of the amnesia, or it may be anterograde, where the individual is unable to learn new information from the point of onset of the amnesia. Amnesics do not have difficulty with immediate memory. Digit span and immediate repetition are intact. Rather, individuals with amnesia are unable to remember after a delay filled with interference.

Amnesia is fascinating because observation of amnesics may help us understand how new information is learned (e.g., what brain structures are involved and what processes facilitate new learning). Amnesics are also of interest because the sense of continuity and time passing, remembering experiences, and hence, self-identity (Walton, 1977) depend on continuous access to information about the remote and recent past. The difficulties that amnesic patients encounter in awareness of their own experiences emphasizes just how important memory is.

Amnesia as an isolated neurologic symptom can be mistaken for a psychiatric disorder (DeJong, Itabashi, & Olson, 1969). There are hysterical amnesias that are a consequence of psychiatric distress alone. Fugue states are 20 dissociative episodes during which an individual forgets his or her identity and past. Hysterical amnesia is discriminable from neurologic conditions causing amnesia in that the total loss of self-identity rarely occurs in neurologically based amnesias, and because the end of the fugue state is abrupt. In the neurologically based amnesias that remit, the cessation of memory loss is gradual, with the period of time for which the individual is amnesic shrinking only gradually.

Anterograde amnesia that gradually remits is a frequent occurrence after closed head injuries (Levin, Benton, & Grossman, 1982; Reynolds & Fletcher-Janzen, 1997). There often is a more limited retrograde amnesia for the period just prior to the injury. Anterograde amnesia secondary to closed head injury (also called posttraumatic amnesia) is a good index of the severity of the injury and useful in the prediction of long-term recovery. After the amnesia has remitted, there is often a residual memory disorder.

Transient global amnesia is a neurologic condition that is now assumed to be a consequence of transient ischemia (Heathfield, Croft, & Swash, 1973). The presentation of an individual with transient global amnesia is characteristic. There is an abrupt onset of amnesia, both retrograde and anterograde, with perhaps only initial, mild clouding of consciousness, and no change in cognition or speech. Episodes typically last for several hours only, and the retrograde amnesia gradually shrinks, leaving individuals amnesic only for the period during which they had anterograde amnesia (Hecaen & Albert, 1978).

A great deal has been learned about amnesia and memory through the study of groups of patients with unremitting forms of amnesia: amnesia secondary to Korsakoff's syndrome, amnesia secondary to neurosurgery for control of epilepsy, traumatic brain lesions resulting in amnesia, and generalized dementing processes (especially Huntington's disease and Alzheimer's disease) in which memory deficits are disproportionately problematic (at least during specific stages of the disease). Careful investigation of these patients clearly reveals that though the average clinician thinks of memory as a unitary phenomenon, memory loss is a multidimensional symptom with different etiologies resulting in characteristic, discriminable patterns of memory loss and skill (Butters, 1984).

One pattern of amnesia reflects hemispheric differences. Individuals with amnesia secondary to isolated damage to the right hemisphere have deficient skills in nonverbal memory when the information is presented visually. Those amnesic secondary to isolated left hemisphere damage have greater difficulty with verbal memory. Verbal memory deficits are seen regardless of the sensory modality used to present the information; e.g., visual presentation of verbal information (Hecaen & Albert, 1978).

Amnesic patients of differing etiologies demonstrate differential responses to manipulations aimed at facilitating memory. For example, Korsakoff's amnesics are assisted in memorization by increasing rehearsal time, intertrial rest intervals, and a structured orientation procedure. They are not aided, however, by the provision of verbal mediation. Conversely, Huntington's disease patients are not assisted as are Korsakoff's patients; neither increased rehearsal time, increased intertrial intervals, nor general orientation aids their performance. They are assisted, however, by verbal mediation. Patients with Alzheimer's disease are not assisted by verbal mediation.

Another difference between amnesic syndromes is related to the ability to acquire procedural versus declarative memories (Squire, 1982). Declarative memory pertains to specific facts and data. Procedural memory refers to the rules for completing a specific type of task. Studies of amnesic patients indicate that patients with amnesia secondary to Korsakoff's disease acquire procedural information but have great difficulty in learning declarative data. Huntington's disease patients do not remember procedural rules, but do learn (or at least recognize) previously presented data of a declarative type.

The study of patient populations with known etiologies has been useful in increasing our understanding of what brain structures are involved in the elaboration and retrieval of memory. Evidence from neurosurgical intervention to control severe epilepsy has demonstrated that damage to the medial aspects of both temporal lobes, especially the hippocampus, results in profound amnesia (Hecaen & Albert, 1978; Squire, 1982). This amnesia is distinguished by rapid and abnormal forgetting. Other amnesics appear to have diencephalic damage with some disagreement as to exactly which structures are affected. The mammillary bodies and dorsal-medial nucleus of the thalamus are involved, though the relative contributions of either structure are not known. Damage to the dorsal-medial nucleus appears sufficient to cause amnesia (Squire, 1982). Amnesia secondary to diencephalic damage is notable for a normal forgetting curve, but difficulty with encoding. Identification of structures involved in memory is useful not only in terms of understanding specific syndromes, but also in considering pharmacologic manipulations to assist in treatment.

With the exception of posttraumatic amnesia, amnesia in its pure form is not reported to occur in children. Subsequent to head injuries, children do exhibit posttraumatic amnesia and have difficulty learning new information in school and remembering what they learned just prior to their injuries. Consequently, they will be confused in the school setting. Posttraumatic amnesia generally will remit. Such children should be allowed to recover after their injuries (with the most rapid recovery occurring in the first 6 months) without the expectation that by studying harder they will remember significantly better. Once the major recovery period is over (after 6 to 9 months), cognitive rehabilitation programs aimed at providing strategies to assist in memory may be useful. There are limited data available on how generalizable the effect of cognitive rehabilitation is in the adult population, and less data regarding children.

It should be clear that the short-term memory impairments described in the learning of disabled children bear little resemblance to amnesic disorders. Amnesic patients are capable of short-term memory performance. Children with severe brain injury may become amnesic, but it is most often within the context of general dementia with difficulties in a variety of areas.

REFERENCES

Butters, N. (1984). The clinical aspects of memory disorders: Contributions from experimental studies of amnesia and dementia. *Journal of Clinical Neuropsychology, 6,* 17–36.

DeJong, R.N., Itabashi, H.H., & Olson, J.R. (1969). Memory loss due to hippocampal lesion. *Archives of Neurology, 20,* 339–348.

Heathfield, K.W.G., Croft, P.B., & Swash, M. (1973). The syndrome of transient global amnesia. *Brain, 96,* 729–731.

Hecaen, H., & Albert, M.I. (1978). *Human neuropsychology.* New York: Wiley.

Levin, H.S., Benton, A.L., & Grossman, R.G. (1982). *Neurobehavioral consequences of closed head injury.* New York: Oxford University Press.

Reynolds, C.R., & Fletcher-Janzen, E. (Eds.). (1997). Handbook of Clinical Child Neuropsychology. New York: Plenum Press.

Squire, L. (1982). The neuropsychology of human memory. *Annual Review of Neurosciences, 5,* 241–273.

Walton, J.N. (1977). *Brain's diseases of the nervous system.* Oxford: Oxford University Press.

See also Memory Disorders

AMNIOCENTESIS

Amniocentesis is the sampling of amniotic fluid surrounding a fetus. A physician anesthetizes a small area of the pregnant woman's abdomen, inserts a small needle through the abdominal wall, and, with the aid of ultrasonography, enters the amniotic sac and removes 30 ccs (approximately 1 oz) of fluid. It is performed most frequently between 15 and 18 weeks gestation to detect hereditary disease or congenital defects in the fetus. One disadvantage is that analysis of the fluid takes 2 to 4 weeks. Damage to the fetus also may occur, but the risk is small (Pritchard, MacDonald, & Gant, 1985).

Midtrimester amniocentesis plays an important role in genetic and other prenatal counseling by providing potential parents with reproductive options. It should be considered when the pregnant woman is over 35, or a family history of genetic or congenital disorders is apparent (Kaback, 1979). Cytogenetic analysis of fetal fluid leads to prevention of birth of approximately 15,000 chromosomally abnormal infants each year in the United States alone (Pritchard et al., 1985).

Amniocentesis allows identification of about 300 chromosomal, single-gene, and other congenital abnormalities (Pritchard et al., 1985). The list grows with the discovery of new markers. Chromosomally based disorders are identified through karyotyping and resultant abnormal appearance of one or more chromosomes; other disorders are identified through elevated or reduced levels of particular substances. Among the disorders that can be reliably diagnosed are (1) all chromosomally based disorders such as Down's syndrome and cri du chat; (2) about 75 inborn errors of metabolism, including galactosemia, Tay-Sachs disease, and Lesch-Nyhan syndrome (X-linked), but not phenylketonuria; (3) some central nervous system defects including meningocele (a form of spina bifida) and anencephaly; (4) some fetal infections (cytomegalovirus, herpes simplex, and rubella); (5) and some hematologic disorders (e.g., sickle-cell anemia; Pritchard et al., 1985).

A new diagnostic technique, chorion-villus biopsy, usable as early as 8 weeks gestation, may be preferable in some cases because of the emotional and medical problems presented with a midtrimester abortion.

REFERENCES

Kaback, M.M. (1979). Predictors of hereditary diseases or congenital defects in antenatal diagnosis (National Institute of Child Health and Human Development, U.S. Department of HEW, NIH Publication No. 79–1973). *Antenatal Diagnosis,* 39–42.

Pritchard, J.A., MacDonald, C., & Gant, N.F. (Eds.). (1985). *Williams obstetrics* (17th ed.) (pp. 267–293). Englewood Cliffs, NJ: Appleton-Century-Crofts.

See also Chronic Villus Sampling; Genetic Counseling; Inborn Errors of Metabolism

AMPHETAMINE PSYCHOSIS

Amphetamine psychosis results from the neurochemical and behavioral interaction of large doses of amphetamines. The toxic reaction, induced by chronic amphetamine abuse or by an acute overdose, leads to transitory symptoms that are clinically indistinguishable from those of paranoid schizophrenia. Such symptoms, occurring as early as 36 to 48 hours after a large dosage, include vivid auditory, visual, and tactile hallucinations, changes in affect, loosening of associations with reality, and paranoid thought processes (Gilman, Goodman, & Gilman, 1980). Affected individuals may also show behavioral stereotypes such as continuous rocking or polishing motions, repetitive grooming activities (rubbing or picking of the skin), and other locomotor irregularities. Biochemical correlates of amphetamine psychosis, including increased dopaminergic activity, are similar to those of schizophrenia (Kokkinidis & Anisman, 1980).

In addition to reducing amphetamine intake, treatment includes sedatives, psychotherapy, and custodial care. Acidification of the urine will speed excretion of the amphetamines. The psychotic state usually clears in about a week after beginning treatment, with hallucinations being the first symptom to disappear (American Medical Association, 1980).

REFERENCES

American Medical Association. (1980). *AMA drug evaluations* (4th ed.). New York: Wiley.

Gilman, A.G., Goodman, L.S., & Gilman, A. (1980). *Goodman and Gilman's pharmacological basis of therapeutics* (6th ed.). New York: Macmillan.

Kokkinidis, L., & Anisman, H. (1980). Amphetamine models of paranoid schizophrenia: An overview and elaboration of animal experimentation. *Psychological Bulletin, 88,* 551–579.

See also Childhood Schizophrenia; Drug Abuse; LSD; Psychotropic Drugs

AMSLAN

See AMERICAN SIGN LANGUAGE.

ANDERSON, META L. (1878–1942)

Meta L. Anderson, while a teacher in the New York City public schools, enrolled in a course in the education of mentally retarded children at The Training School at Vineland, New Jersey. There, Edward R. Johnstone and Henry H. Goddard, recognizing her unusual ability, recommended her to the Newark, New Jersey, Board of Education, which employed her to begin special classes for mentally retarded children. In 1910 she established two special classes and Newark joined the handful of school systems that provided special programs for handicapped students.

Anderson developed an instructional approach based on careful analysis of the abilities and limitations of each student and devised trade classes and a work experience program to provide vocational preparation. Her book, *Education of Defectives in the Public Schools* (1917), described the program and added impetus to the growing special class movement in the United States. In the closing months of World War I, Anderson was appointed head of reconstruction aid in Europe. After the war she served for a year in Serbia. She returned to the Newark schools in 1920 to become director of the city's comprehensive special education program. She received her PhD from New York University in 1922. She served as president of the American Association on Mental Deficiency in 1941.

REFERENCE

Anderson, M.L. (1917). *Education of defectives in the public schools.* Yonkers, New York: World Book.

ANENCEPHALY

Anencephaly is a congenital disorder marked by the absence of the cerebral cortices. It belongs to a class of disorders that are termed neural tube defects (NTD) and results from the failure of the neural tube to close during embryogenesis. The neural tube, which is the precursor to the brain and spinal cord, usually closes by the 28th day after conception (Kloza, 1985). If this does not occur completely, various defects to the central nervous system (CNS) become manifest. If this occurs "lower" on the neural tube, spina bifida will be present. However, if the "top" of the neural tube remains open, anencephaly results. Anencephaly with spina bifida, rarely occurs (Swaiman & Wright, 1973).

As anencephaly is ostensibly marked by the absence of the cerebral cortices, the centers of higher cognitive functioning are absent. Therefore, while certain subcortical structures may remain intact (producing the reflex patterns and responses often indicative of neonates), higher cerebral activity is precluded by the absence of structures subserving those functions. Many anencephalics are stillborn, as they lack the brain structures necessary to maintain respiration and other functions vital to survival. On the occasion that the newborn is physiologically viable, it should be remembered that associative processes, reasoning, and cognitive and language development are not possible. Therefore, educational services are not a practical consideration and absolute custodial supervision and care are indicated. Ethical considerations pertaining to care must also come into play. Anencephaly remains a medical disorder where special educational services are not practical.

REFERENCES

Kloza, E.M. (1985). Prenatal screening: neural tube defects. *Disorders of Brain Development and Cognition.* Boston: Eunice Kennedy Shriver Center and Harvard Medical School.

Swaiman, K.F., & Wright, F.S. (1973). Neurologic diseases due to developmental and metabolic defects. In A.B. Baker & L.H. Baker (Eds.), *Clinical neurology.* New York: Harper & Row.

See also Baby Jane Doe

ANGELMAN SYNDROME

Angelman Syndrome is an emerging disorder, little studied, with no good population studies completed to allow proper prevalence or incidence estimates. Many, but not all, Angelman Syndrome individuals have deletions on chromosome 15 in maternally related regions (q11–q12) while others are of unknown pathogenic origin. The disorder is characterized by physical, motoric, and behavioral features. Physical features include a wide mouth, prominent lower jaw, and microbrachycephalia. Motor problems are related to diverse, jerky, sometimes rhythmic movements. Some children experience particular difficulties with inadequate control of chewing and swallowing which creates feeding problems. However, these problems abate after infancy in most cases. Acquisition of walking is delayed, and mild to severe ataxia after learning to walk is common.

Most children with Angelman Syndrome have severe to profound levels of mental retardation, although some patients may reach moderate and, rarely, mild levels of mental retardation. Spoken language is absent in 75–80% of children with Angelman Syndrome, but receptive language is typically superior to expressive language. Some do develop skills in sign language but normal levels of communication have not been seen in any published case. Behavioral presentation of Angelman Syndrome often includes hyperactivity, impulsivity, episodic pica, random bursts of laughter (in nearly all cases), jerky nighttime movements, and a generally happy disposition.

Diagnosis is sometimes very difficult, as Angelman has similarities of presentation to Rett Syndrome and to Prader-Willi Syndrome in a number of cases. Detailed cytogenic studies are often necessary for proper diagnosis and even then the diagnosis may still be only inferred rather than confirmed. EEG is helpful as a common pattern with posterior slow wave activity used as a marker variable. CT and MRI are normal in 30–35% of cases, and others show mixed results with diffuse atrophy, deep white matter lesions (periventricular leukomalacia), and cerebellar growth retardation all having been documented in various cases.

At present 100% of children with Angelman Syndrome are believed to require special education services, typically as children with mental retardation, although numerous related services may be required. Intervention is largely related to symptom management and the teaching of fundamental adaptive behavior and communication skills. Sheltered employment is possible in many but not all cases. However, more and better longitudinal studies of Angelman Syndrome individuals are needed to document the long-term effects of interventions and general life outcomes.

See also **Prader-Willi Syndrome; Rett Syndrome**

ANIMALS FOR THE HANDICAPPED

Today, animals are being used to assist the handicapped with daily living. For centuries, the blind have used dogs to assist them in ambulation. Programs using domesticated monkeys to assist moderately to severely disabled persons in the home to perform rote chores has been a successful innovation. Horseback riding has emerged as a leisure-time pursuit for many types of disabled persons.

The benefits of human/animal interaction are now being realized, especially for special education purposes. Lowered blood pressure has been documented in studies where the participants had regular contact with dogs. In another study, Friedman (1980) found that the survival rate of hypertensive persons increased dramatically with pet ownership. Pets have been considered effective agents in the reduction of everyday stress. They provide a sense of relaxation (Kidd, 1981). They also provide a chance to exercise, and for many a sense of security (White & Watson, 1983).

According to Levinson (1969), the introduction of animals into a residential setting for the handicapped indicates that the staff believes that anything of possible treatment value to the handicapped can and should be used. It reveals an awareness of the potential healing properties of pet ownership, even if those benefits have not been scientifically documented in the laboratory.

A handicapped child is not constantly reminded of his or her handicap in the interaction with a pet. A deaf child can care for a dog competently and receive all of the rewards that a hearing child would for the same efforts. The same is true for a variety of handicaps; only the type of pet might have to be changed. A child confined to a wheelchair may interact well with a rabbit or an aquarium and achieve a sense of purpose and responsibility previously unrealized.

The teaching of the emotionally disturbed child provides a setting in which the use of animals may be especially beneficial. Typically, motivating this student to participate in class can be a difficult task for the teacher. Often, these students have never learned to care for or share with others. The animal in the class may provide both the subject matter and the motivation to learn. The child who had previously trusted no one can begin to trust the teacher for the first time when he or she sees the teacher's concern in dealing with the classroom pet. This could be the first step by the child in accepting the structure of the class (Levinson, 1969).

REFERENCES

Friedman, E. (1980, July/August). Animal companions and one year survival of patients after discharge from a coronary care unit. *Public Health Reports, 44*(4), 37–42.

Kidd, A. (1981). Dogs, cats and people. *Mills Quarterly, 23*(8), 23–28.

Levinson, B. (1969). Pet oriented child psychotherapy. Springfield, IL: Thomas.

White, B., & Watson, T. (1983). *Pet love, how pets take care of us.* New York: Pinnacle.

See also **Equine Therapy; Therapeutic Recreation**

ANNALS OF DYSLEXIA

Originating in 1950 as the *Bulletin of the Orton Society* under the editorial leadership of June Lyday Orton, the annual periodical of the Orton Dyslexia Society was renamed the *Annals of Dyslexia* in 1981. It was designed as a means to enhance communication among the members of the Orton Dyslexia Society, an organization founded in 1949 to further research and work with children with specific language disabilities. The *Annals of Dyslexia* ceased publication in 1988.

ANNUAL DIRECTORY OF EDUCATIONAL FACILITIES FOR THE LEARNING DISABLED

See BIENNIAL DIRECTORY OF EDUCATIONAL FACILITIES FOR THE HANDICAPPED.

ANOMALIES, PHYSICAL

See PHYSICAL ANOMALIES.

ANOREXIA NERVOSA (AN)

Anorexia nervosa (starvation due to nerves) is a condition in which an individual eats little or no food for prolonged periods. No physical basis for the abnormal eating can be found. This disorder can be life-threatening, is increasing in incidence, and is a serious problem for medical and psychological professionals.

Although famous and tragic cases such as that of singer Karen Carpenter have made anorexia familiar, little can confidently be said about specific etiology or overall effective treatment. Anorexics share certain personality characteristics and frequently have families with a particular complex of unhealthy attitudes and behaviors. The physical appearance of anorexics is emaciated. Right hemisphere neuropsychological deficits are common but it is not clear if they are a related cause or a result of AN.

Anorexia is largely a disorder of middle- and upper-class adolescent females. It occurs approximately nine times more often in women than in men, and may affect one in one hundred white women between the ages of 12 and 18 years (Newman & Halvorson, 1983). The most common age of onset for anorexia is early adolescence (Newman & Halvorson, 1983).

Diagnostic criteria for anorexia nervosa may be summarized as involving intense fear of becoming obese, which does not diminish as weight loss progresses; disturbed body image (e.g., feeling fat even when emaciated); refusal to maintain normal body weight; and in postmenarcheal females, amenorrhea (i.e., the absence of at least three consecutive menstrual cycles) (American Psychiatric Association, 1994).

Anorexics are subject to numerous additional complications, including malnutrition, edema, loss of hair, hyperactivity, hypoglycemia, vitamin deficiencies, constipation, weakness, and fatigue. In extreme cases, death may result from starvation, electrolyte depletion, or cardiac arrhythmia (Newman & Halvorson, 1983).

The specific etiologies of anorexia nervosa are not known, but are thought to be biopsychosocial diseases. Unknown biological predispositions may interact with both individual psychological states and needs and our culture's emphasis, especially for females, on thinness as a worthy or desirable characteristic (Wooley & Wooley, 1985). Several etiological factors can be described:

1. According to Bruch (1985), in the past 20 years the average female under 30 years of age has become heavier; at the same time, the ideal shape for women has been in the direction of being thinner. To be thin is to increase women's desirability both in their eyes and the eyes of others. The result is demonstrated in the mushrooming of the weight reduction industry and the numerous books and magazine articles that have appeared on losing weight and dieting.

2. Wooley and Wooley (1985) quote from Ambrose Bierce's Devil's Dictionary: "To men a man is but a mind, who cares what face he carries? Or what form he wears? But woman's body is the woman." For many centuries females' cultural conditioning has tied self-esteem to physical attractiveness. Many therapists think that recent cultural emphasis on "thinness is beautiful and good" has contributed to the increased incidence of eating disorders (Wooley & Wooley, 1985). The message to woman in particular is that in order to be popular, attractive, accepted, sexy, healthy, and desired in the world of work, they must be thin. The ideal of feminine beauty increasingly conforms each year to the adolescent male physique, implying emulation of men both behaviorally and physically (Wooley & Wooley, 1985). This change may be due to broader social changes involving competition between women and men for prestige and power. Also involved for many young women is the resolution of intense identification conflicts with their parents. Young women today are the first generation raised by extremely weight-conscious mothers who additionally view themselves as failures by current social standards of beauty.

3. Bruch (1985) says that cultural emphasis for slimness as determining factor does not explain the more severe disturbance of "frantic preoccupation with excessive slenderness of the anorexic." She believes that the changing status of expectations for women is important in understanding the etiology. Females, says Bruch, who have been raised as "clinging vines" and future wives, and who find themselves during their teens with the expectation to demonstrate that they are women of achievement, may find that they are filled with self-doubt and uncertainty. By bowing to the dictum to be thin, they are validating that they deserve respect.

According to Bemis and colleagues, who have studied hypothalamic functions in anorexics, starvation may actually damage the hypothalamus, and emotional stress may interfere with hypothalamic functioning. Further, psychological aberrations associated with anorexia may be relatively independent expressions of a primary hypothalamic deficiency that is of unknown origin (Bemis, 1978).

Certain family factors facilitate the development of anorexia. If a parent has had the disorder or is either extremely thin or obese, the chances of a young woman becoming anorexic increase (Neuman & Halvorson, 1983). In families of anorexics, food is usually a primary issue. The family may use food for other than nutritional purposes. For example, eating may be a way of dealing with personal problems or negative or positive feelings, or it may be a method of presenting the appearance of a happy family. Power struggles over eating are extremely common.

Families of anorexics show certain personality patterns, although no one pattern appears consistently. Mothers are frequently intrusive and dominating and have experienced clinical depressions, whereas fathers appear passive and aloof from the family. Less frequently, these patterns may be reversed (Newman & Halvorson, 1983).

Family interpersonal dynamics are a significant contributing factor. Features that appear to be correlated with the development of the disorder are rigidity, lack of conflict resolution, overprotectiveness, and enmeshment (appearing to be a very close family). Keeping the peace at any cost is a high priority in these families; conflicts are not dealt with openly. In many families of anorexics, the anorexic generally feels powerless and ineffective, and behaves primarily on the basis of what other people want or need. Often the family has not encouraged or allowed the young woman to develop her autonomy or individuality. Only compliance is tolerated. Anorexia may develop as a result of a young woman's attempt to take control of her own life and achieve her own sense of identity. She learns that one thing she can control is her weight. Families must realize that this is an emotionally based disorder with the attempt to control, hide, avoid, and forget emotional pain. Nobody can make these anorexics eat, therefore it is important not to immediately focus on the food (Something Fishy Website).

In some cases the family unconsciously does not want the child to grow up. This message is received by the child, who in turn exhibits anorexic behavior, which then leads to failure to develop secondary sexual characteristics. Some anorexics enjoy being viewed as special by their families. Thus being anorexic can bring a great deal of attention, leading to self-perpetuation of the disorder.

Adolescent peer memberships are viewed as being critical in making the transition from childhood to adulthood. Some investigators have noted that anorexics have few if any close peer friendships (Newman & Halvorson, 1983). Adolescent anorexics' overdependence and involvement with their families may prevent the formation of normal adolescent peer relationships. Thus, these youngsters may be at great disadvantage in making the essential developmental transition to adulthood.

Fifty percent of women diagnosed and treated for anorexia nervosa can be expected to recover completely within 2 to 5 years. Nutritional improvement or recovery can be expected in approximately two thirds of treated cases. Usually, after adequate body weight has been attained, menstruation will resume within a year.

As many as half of all anorexics experience a relapse. Approximately 38% may be re-hospitalized at some point during the next 2 years. Three to 25% of anorexia nervosa cases end in death from medical complications or suicide. This disorder has the highest death rate in psychiatry.

No consensus exits regarding the most effective form of treatment for anorexia nervosa (Vandereycken & Meermann, 1984). The course of treatment typically begins with stabilizing the patient's health, and then it is important that a course of therapy takes place (Something Fishy Website). Current treatment is aimed at first normalizing body weight, correcting the irrational thinking about weight loss, and finally preventing relapse. To obtain these goals, one must be admitted to a hospital or a day treatment program where the disorder can be monitored (Walsh & Devlin, 1998).

Many forms of treatment for anorexia are used. Therapists have used behavioral therapy, diet counseling, cognitive therapy, cognitive-behavioral treatment, drug treatment, and family therapy with varying degrees of success (Garner & Garfinkel, 1985). Whatever the treatment approach, the usual goals are aimed at increasing confidence and self-esteem, challenging irrational or "anorexic" thinking, developing autonomy, and teaching coping skills. Further, Vandereycken and Meermann (1984, p. 219) suggest that the "best guarantees of success in therapy are a constructive patient/therapist working relationship and an explicit but consistent treatment plan/contract." In the case of drug treatment, the therapist is not trying to treat the eating disorder with medication, but the emotional disorder that they are suffering from that causes the eating disorder (Something Fishy Website).

Because eating-disordered individuals are usually perfectionists, teachers can help by advising and encouraging them to take fewer courses and to balance academic loads by combining difficult classes with classes that are less demanding. If hospitalization becomes necessary, and the anorexic student expresses fear that she will be unable to maintain her academic standing, the teacher can point out that usually hospital personnel are more than willing to assist the patient by insuring that the patient will be provided the opportunity to continue uninterrupted with academic requirements. Major treatment centers as well as many hospitals have educational components and academic teachers on their staff.

REFERENCES

American Psychiatric Association. (1994). *Diagnostic and statistical manual of mental disorders* (4th ed.). Washington, DC: Author.

Bemis, K.M. (1978). Current approaches to the etiology and treatment of anorexia nervosa. *Psychological Bulletin, 35,* 395–617.

Bruch, H. (1985). Four decades of eating disorders. In D.M. Garner & P.E. Garfinkel (Eds.), *Handbook of psychotherapy for anorexia and bulimia* (pp. 7 18). New York: Guilford.

Garner, D.M., & Garfinkel, P.E. (Eds.). (1985). *Handbook of psychotherapy for anorexia nervosa and bulimia.* New York: Guilford.

Newman, P.A., & Halvorson, P.S. (1983). *Anorexia nervosa and bulimia: A handbook for counselors and therapist.* New York: Van Nostrand Reinhold.

Vandereycken, W., & Meermann, R. (1984). *Anorexia nervosa: A clinician's guide to treatment.* Berlin: de Gruyter.

Walsh, B.T., & Devlin, M. (1998). Eating disorders: Progress and problems. *Science, 280,* 1387–1391.

Wooley, S.C., & Wooley, O.W. (1985). Intensive outpatient and residential treatment for bulimia. In D.M. Garner & P.E. Garfinkel (Eds.), *Handbook of psychotherapy for anorexia nervosa and bulimia* (pp. 391–430). New York: Guilford.

See also **Bulimia Nervosa; Eating Disorders; Obsessive-Compulsive Disorders**

ANOSMIA

The term *anosmia* derives from the Greek *an* (without) and *osme* (odor); it refers to the absence or impairment of the sense of smell. Synonyms for this condition include anodmia, anosphrasia, and olfactory anesthesia (*Dorland's,* 1981). Organic forms of anosmia are categorized as afferent (related to impaired conductivity of the olfactory nerve), central (due to cerebral disease), obstructive (related to obstruction of the nasal fossae), and peripheral (due to diseases of peripheral olfactory nerves) (*Blakiston's,* 1979).

The most common cause of anosmia is a severe head cold or respiratory infection, which intranasal swelling blocks the nasal passages, preventing odors from reaching the olfactory region. This type of anosmia is temporary. Other organic causes of this condition include neoplasms (tumors), head injuries, or chronic rhinitis associated with granulomatous diseases (Levin, Benton, & Grossman, 1982; *Mosby's,* 1983; Thomson, 1979). Anosmia also is a characteristic of olfactogenital dysplasia, also known as *Kallman's syndrome* or anosmia-eunuchoidism. This condition, more prevalent in males, is associated with lack of development of secondary sexual characteristics and anosmia. The apparently *X*-linked autosomal dominant or recessive inheritable condition is associated with dysfunction of the hypothalamus and the pituitary (Magalini, 1971). Anosmia with these etiologies typically is a permanent condition. Decreased sense of smell, microsmia, is also common with aging and among smokers.

REFERENCES

Blakiston's Gould medical dictionary (4th ed.). (1979). New York: McGraw-Hill.

Levin, H.A., Benton, A.L.M. & Grossman, R.G. (1982). *Neurobehavioral consequences of closed head injury.* New York: Oxford University Press.

Magalini, S. (1971). *Dictionary of medical syndromes.* Philadelphia: Lippincott.

Thomson, W.A.R. (1979). *Black's medical dictionary* (32nd ed.). New York: Barnes & Noble.

ANOXIA

Anoxia literally means an absence of oxygen, a condition that is incompatible with life. Recent terminology more correctly uses the term hypoxia to refer to a condition of lowered oxygen intake. Although hypoxia is compatible with life, long-term sequelae may result depending on the degree and duration of the condition.

See also Asphyxia; Hypoxia

ANTECEDENT TEACHING

Antecedent stimuli are those events that occur before a response that affect the probability of the occurrence of that response. Skinner (1953) described the response sequence as having three parts: the antecedent events, the response, and the consequences. Although much has been written concerning the management of the consequences and their effects on a student's responses, Repp (1983) emphasized that teaching is actually the effective arrangement of both antecedent *and* consequent events in a manner that allows the student to learn to the full extent of his or her capabilities.

Teachers exert tremendous control over the antecedents to which their students are exposed. Some antecedent stimuli commonly seen in classrooms include instruction, curriculum, instructional objectives, commands, modeling, and materials (Repp, 1983; Snell, 1983). As teachers manipulate these antecedents, students learn to respond differentially to the differing stimuli. When their behaviors are consistently affected by the antecedents, their responses are considered to be under stimulus control. Kazdin (1975) noted one particularly effective antecedent strategy, response priming. He stated that "response priming refers to any procedure which initiates early steps in a sequence of responses" (Kazdin, 1975, p. 135). The use of various prompts or directions, while not inclusive of the total concept of response priming, is one area that has received considerable attention.

Kazdin (1975) described another effective subset of response priming, reinforcer sampling. In this procedure, the subject is allowed to experience a small portion of the reinforcer in an effort to have the subject initiate the full sequence of responses necessary to earn the entire reinforcer. Teachers could easily incorporate this procedure into their classrooms, particularly before difficult behavioral sequences are begun (e.g., a verbal description of a movie to be seen after the upcoming math quiz has concluded).

The curriculum and materials that are used in the classroom are other powerful antecedent stimuli that can be easily controlled. In an interesting exposition on classroom materials, Vargas (1984) proposed that many current textual materials actually have a number of errors that result in faulty stimulus control. She stated that if any one of five questions could be answered affirmatively concerning particular textual material, then that material would not be appropriate for use. The questions she listed were:

1. Can students use pictures or diagrams instead of text to complete an exercise?

2. Does highlighting or physical layout give away answers, making it unnecessary to read through an assignment?

3. Are students able to answer questions on a passage without reading it?

4. Do all of the problems on a page require the same process for solution, making it unnecessary to discriminate between strategies?

5. Are the questions Jabberwocky comprehension questions—that is, can they be answered using grammatical cues alone? (p. 130)

Even a casual analysis of many commercially prepared and teacher-made materials will reveal that they provide improper antecedent stimuli for the responses they were designed to elicit.

The area of antecedent teaching is both broad and important. For more information on how this strategy blends with the area of behavioral teaching, the reader is referred to Skinner (1953; 1968), Repp (1983), and Martens et al. (1999).

REFERENCES

Kazdin, A.E. (1975). *Behavior modification in applied settings.* Homewood, IL: Dorsey.

Martens, B., Witt, J., Daly, E., & Vollmer, T. (1999). Behavior analysis: Theory and practice in educational settings. In C.R. Reynolds & T.B. Gutkin (Eds.), *Handbook of School Psychology* (3rd ed.) (pp. 638–663). New York: Wiley.

Repp, A.C. (1983). *Teaching the mentally retarded.* Englewood Cliffs, NJ: Prentice-Hall.

Skinner, B.F. (1953). *Science and human behavior.* New York: Macmillan.

Skinner, B.F. (1968). *The technology of teaching.* New York: Appleton-Century-Crofts.

Snell, M.E. (1983). *Systematic instruction for the moderately and severely handicapped* (2nd ed.). Columbus, OH: Merrill.

Vargas, J.S. (1984). What are your exercises teaching? An analysis of stimulus control in instructional materials. In W.L. Heward, T.E. Heron, D.S. Hill, & J. Trap-Porter (Eds.), *Focus on behavior analysis in education.* Columbus, OH: Merrill.

See also **Applied Behavior Analysis; Behavior Modeling**

ANTHROPOSOPHIC MOVEMENT

The anthroposophic movement was founded by Rudolf Steiner (1861–1925). Steiner defined anthroposophy as knowledge produced by the higher self in man, and a way of knowledge that undertakes to guide man's spirit to communion with the spirit of the cosmos (Wannamaker, 1965). Anthroposophy postulates a spiritual world beyond man's sensory experiences. Steiner proposed that, through proper training, each person could develop an enhanced consciousness that would restore values and morality to materialistic society.

Steiner became involved in the education of both adults and children. Anthroposophic education for adults took place at the Goetheanum, a school for physical science, near Basal, Switzerland. The Waldorf School, founded in Stuttgart, Germany, in 1919, was the first of several schools for children that sought to reach the inner nature of the child and provide guidance to maturity. By 1965, 80 Waldorf Schools had been attended by more than 25,000 children in the United States and Europe (Wannamaker, 1965). Eurythmy (movement of speech and music) was used to develop concentration, attention, imitation, and an awareness of position in space (Ziegler, 1979). The schools included programming for the emotionally disturbed, socially maladjusted, and other exceptional children.

REFERENCES

Steiner, R. (1972). *Outline of occult science.* New York: Anthroposophical Society.

Wannamaker, O.D. (1965). *The anthroposophical society: The nature of its objectives.* New York: Anthroposophical Society.

Ziegler, E.F. (1979). *A history of physical education and sport.* Englewood Cliffs, NJ: Prentice-Hall.

See also **Camphill Community Movement**

ANTICONVULSANTS

Anticonvulsants are medications used to control seizure activity. Phenytoin (Dilantin) is the most widely used anticonvulsant in the world (Bennett & Ho, 1997; Dodrill, 1981; Hartlage & Hartlage, 1997). It has been shown to be effective with a broad range of attacks including generalized tonic-clonic seizures, most types of partial seizures, and some other less frequently observed seizure types. Acute intoxication with phenytoin leads to a confusional state, occasionally referred to as encephalopathy, which is associated with neurological symptoms of toxicity, especially ataxia and nystagmus (Corbett & Trimble, 1983). It also has been demonstrated that prolonged use of this medication, even in low doses (Logan & Freeman, 1969; Vallarta, Bell, & Reichert, 1974), may result in a clinical picture of a progressive degenerative disorder that may occur without the classic signs of such a disorder. Rosen (1968) and Stores (1975) have both reported impaired intellectual performance on long-term treatment with phenytoin. Dodrill (1975) reports that phenytoin has behavioral effects specifically related to motor performance decrements.

Ethosuximide (Zarontin), an anticonvulsant used with children for control of absence (petit mal) seizures, has been shown to impair memory and speech as well as result in affective disturbances (Guey et al., 1967). Soulayrol and Roger (1970) reported intellectual impairment in children treated with this medication; however, other studies have not confirmed this (e.g., Brown et al., 1975).

Carbamazepine (Tegretol) has been reported to have psychotropic effects. About half of 40 studies cited by Dalby (1975), in a major review of the literature, reported a beneficial psychologic effect. Typically, improvements in mood and behavior have been noted, as manifested by greater cooperativeness, reduced irritability, and a possible decrease in aggression. Increases in cognitive skill levels have been reported as well (Bennett & Ho, 1997). There have been no reported studies of the effects of primidone (Mysoline) on behavior in children, although adults occasionally have been reported to develop a florid confusional state on doses within the normal therapeutic range (Booker, 1972). It is well recognized that the drug initially may cause drowsiness and have effects similar to phenobarbital in causing restlessness in some children.

Trimble and Corbett (1980a, 1980b) studied the relationship between anticonvulsant drug levels and the behavior and cognitive performance of 312 children with seizures. The drug most commonly prescribed was phenytoin, followed by carbamazepine, valproic acid, primidone, and phenobarbital. A decrease in IQ was noted in 15% of the

204 children studied; these children had significantly higher mean phenytoin and primidone levels than other subjects. A distinct relationship between an increase in serum drug levels and a decline in nonverbal skills was reported.

Despite these side effects associated with anticonvulsants, they are recognized as essential in the management of epilepsy. According to Dodrill (1981), when anticonvulsant blood serum levels fall within therapeutic ranges and when there are no overt signs of toxicity, the chances of deleterious effects are minimal if detectable at all. Furthermore, the deleterious effects are distinctly offset by decreased seizure frequency, which has known effects on the deterioration of mental functions. It is far preferable to have modest drug side effects than seizures. Other, low incidence drugs used as anticonvulsants are reviewed in detail by Bennett and Ho (1997).

REFERENCES

Bennett, T. & Ho, M. (1997). The neuropsychology of pediatric epilepsy and antiepileptic drugs. In C.R. Reynolds & E. Fletcher-Janzen (Eds.), *Handbook of Clinical Child Neuropsychology* (2nd ed.) (pp. 517–538). New York: Plenum.

Booker, H.E. (1972). Primidone toxicity. In D.M. Woodbury, J.K. Penry, & R.P. Schmidt (Eds.), *Antiepileptic drugs* (pp. 169–204). New York: Raven.

Brown, T.R., Dreifuss, F.E., Dyken, P.R., Goode, D.J., Penry, J.K., Porter, R.J., White, B.J., & White, P.T. (1975). Ethnosuccimide in the treatment of absence (petit mal) seizures. *Neurology, 25,* 515–525.

Corbett, J.A., & Trimble, M.R. (1983). Epilepsy and anticonvulsant medication. In M. Rutter (Eds.), *Developmental neuropsychiatry* (pp. 112–129). New York: Guilford.

Dalby, M.A. (1975). Behavioral effects of carbamazepine. In J.K. Penry & D.D. Daley (Eds.), *Advances in neurology* (Vol. 11, pp. 130–149). New York: Raven.

Dodrill, C.B. (1975). Diphenylhydantoin serum levels, toxicity, and neuropsychological performance in patients with epilepsy. *Epilepsia, 16,* 593–600.

Dodrill, C.B. (1981). Neuropsychology of epilepsy. In S.B. Filskov & T.J. Boll (Eds.), *Handbook of clinical neuropsychology* (pp. 366–395). New York: Wiley.

Guey, J., Charles, C., Coquery, C., Roger, J., & Soulayrol, R. (1967). Study of the psychological effects of ethosuccimide on 25 children suffering from petit mal epilepsy. *Epilepsia, 8,* 129–141.

Hartlage, R.L., & Hartlage, L.C. (1997). The Neuropsychology of epilepsy: Overview and psychosocial aspects. In C.R. Reynolds & E. Fletcher-Janzen (Eds.), *Handbook of Clinical Child Neuropsychology* (2nd ed.) (pp. 506–516). New York: Plenum.

Logan, W.J., & Freeman, J.M. (1969). Pseudodegenerative diseases due to diphenylhydantoin intoxication. *Archives of Neurology, 21,* 631–637.

Rosen, J.A. (1968). Dilantin dementia. *Transactions of the American Neurological Association, 93,* 273–277.

Soulayrol, R., & Roger, J. (1970). Effets psychiatriques defavorables des medications antiepileptiques. *Revue de Neuropsychiatrie Infantile* (English abstract), *18,* 599–603.

Stores, G. (1975). Behavioral effects of anticonvulsant drugs. *Developmental Medicine & Child Neurology, 17,* 547–658.

Trimble, M.R., & Corbett, J.A. (1980a). Behavioral and cognitive disturbances in epileptic children. *Irish Medical Journal, 73,* 21–28.

Trimble, M.R., & Corbett, J.A. (1980b). Anticonvulsant drugs and cognitive function. In J.A. Wada & J.K. Penry (Eds.), *Advances in epileptology: The X International Symposium.* New York: Raven.

Vallarta, J.M., Bell, D.B., & Reichert, A. (1974). Progressive encephalopathy due to chronic hydantoin intoxication. *American Journal of Diseases of Children, 128,* 27–34.

See also **Dilantin; Drug Therapy; Medication; Phenobarbitol; Seizure Disorders; Tegretol**

ANTIHISTAMINES

Antihistamines are a class of pharmaceutical agents that block the effect of histamine. Histamine is a naturally occurring body substance that is released in certain allergic reactions. Typically, antihistamines are more effective in preventing rather than in reversing the action of histamine. Unfortunately, antihistamines have not been found to have any dramatic effects in children with asthma or other severe diseases of an allergic nature (Markowitz, 1983). For pediatric populations, antihistamines may be effective in the treatment of hay fever or mild recurrent hives of unknown etiology. Some antihistamines, particularly Atarax and Vistaril, are used as safe, alternative antianxiety medications without withdrawal (Cepeda, 1997). Some research also has suggested the potential efficacy of antihistamines in the prevention of motion sickness in children (Macnair, 1983).

Typically, antihistamines are found in cold preparations prescribed for children (Pruitt, 1985). Children who are treated with antihistamines are likely to have less severe runny noses, yet the other features of the common cold are not significantly affected by this class of drugs. Antihistamines have atropine like effects that diminish the amount of secretions produced by the irritated lining of the nose or bronchial passages. Although some antihistamines have been marketed as cough suppressants, a number of studies have shown that antihistamines are no better than placebos in relieving children of the symptoms of the common cold (Markowitz, 1983).

Because the use of minor and major tranquilizers carries significant disadvantages in the treatment of behavioral and anxiety disorders in children (Popper, 1985), it has been suggested that antihistamines be used short term for calming acutely anxious children (Cepeda, 1997) and for controlling agitation in severely psychotic children (Popper, 1985). Risks of recreational abuse, management abuse, tolerance, and dependence are also lower than for anti-anxiety agents and major tranquilizers (Cepeda, 1997; Popper, 1985), making this class of drugs more appealing for use by the practicing physician. The enduring cognitive effects of antihistamines are not well documented in the empirical literature, although some recent research has suggested an amelioration of behavioral difficulties and improved academic performance in response to antihistamine therapy (McLoughlin et al., 1983). Further, some investigators (Millichap, 1973; Mattes, 1979) have found antihistamines to be efficacious in the treatment and management of hyperactivity. While the effects of antihistamines on cognitive and learning outcome appear to be somewhat promising, more research must be mounted before any definitive conclusions can be made in this area. Moreover, while the use of antihistamines in the treatment of psychiatric disorders of children may provide a safer alternative than the use of other psychotropic agents, including neuroleptic agents and antianxiety drugs, it still entails some of the same risks and the physician must carefully weigh the potential benefits against any possible risks.

Although the long-term effects of antihistamines have received little systematic study, the use of these agents appear to provide primarily short-term benefits. They are typically safe and consequently are often sold without a prescription. They may have adverse effects, although these usually occur with higher doses. Sedation is the most common side effect in children, but some tolerance may develop. Combinations of antihistamines with other central nervous system depressants (e.g., alcohol) should be avoided. In high doses, or for children who are particularly sensitive to these agents, antihistamines may cause undesirable side effects. These may include excitation, nervousness, palpitations, rapid heartbeat, dryness of the mouth, urinary retention, and constipation. In rare instances, red blood cells can burst (hemolytic anemia) or bone marrow can be depleted of blood-forming cells (arganulocytosis) (Markowitz, 1983). Sustained antihistamine usage with pediatric populations may be associated with persistent daytime drowsiness, "hangover," or mild enduring effects on cognition (Popper, 1985). Although such side effects are better tolerated by younger children than by adolescents, the occurrence of these effects should result in the prompt cessation of antihistamine therapy.

REFERENCES

Cepeda, M. (1997). Nonstimulant psychotropic medication: Desired effects and cognitive/behavioral adverse effects. In C.R. Reynolds & E. Fletcher-Janzen (Eds.), *Handbook of Clinical Child Neuropsychology* (2nd ed.) (pp. 573–586). New York: Plenum Press.

Macnair, A.L. (1983). Cinnarizine in the prophylaxis of car sickness in children. *Current Medical Research Opinion, 8,* 451–455.

Markowitz, M. (1983). Immunity, allergy, and related diseases. In R.E. Behrman & V.C. Vaughn (Eds.), *Nelson textbook of pediatrics* (pp. 497–594). Philadelphia: Saunders.

Mattes, J. (1979). Trial of diphenpyraline in hyperactive children (letter). *Psychopharmacology Bulletin, 15,* 5–6.

McLoughlin, J., Nall, M., Isaacs, P., Petrosko, J., Karibo, J., & Lindsey, B. (1983). The relationship of allergies and allergy treatment to school performance and student behavior. *Annals of Allergy, 51,* 506–510.

Millichap, J.G. (1973). Drugs in management of minimal brain dysfunction. *Annals of the New York Academy of Science, 205,* 321–334.

Popper, C.W. (1985). Child and adolescent psychopharmacology. In R. Michels & J.O. Cavenar (Eds.), *Psychiatry* (Vol. 2, pp. 1–23). New York: Lippincott.

Pruitt, A.W. (1985). Rational use of cold and cough preparations. *Pediatric Annals, 14,* 289–291.

See also Drug Therapy; Tranquilizers

ANTISOCIAL BEHAVIOR

A study by Peterson (1961, reviewed in Quay & Werry, 1972) considered a sampling of many behaviors of children that could be considered as antisocial. More than 400 representative case folders from files of a child-guidance clinic were inspected and the referral problems of each child noted. Peterson's results indicated that the interrelationship among 58 items could be reduced to two independent clusters: conduct problems and personality problems. The two dimensions of problems most frequently reported among the public school students in these two major clusters were aggression and withdrawal. Each child could be placed somewhere in these two dimensions regardless of the number of problem behaviors or other dimensions the child manifested. Children's behaviors differ quantitatively not qualitatively. The degree of quantitative difference between normal and abnormal is usually slight.

Definitions are particularly difficult to generate when context is general and critical, as is the case when the word "social" is used. While there is a need to convey with words what is meant by antisocial behavior, the intensity, timeliness, and impact of a behavior on others in the culture/society/group where the behavior is experienced determines the definition: therefore, a static meaning is not effective. Antisocial behaviors or misbehaving (disliked performances) are accepted daily by society. A behavior is labeled antisocial when the tolerance level of an observer is exceeded with respect to that observer's interpretation of societal rules.

For example, aggressive antisocial behavior is manifested when a student stands and yells a phrase of profanity during a school assembly. The consequences of such behavior could be removal from the audience (peer group), immediate verbal reprimand by adult authorities, a quick trip to the administrator's office, or dismissal from a school. In contrast, if the same pupil were to stand during a professional ball game and yell the same phrase of profanity, not only might the audience approve of the behavior, it might even reward the verbal expressiveness.

Variables in the environment that define the tolerance level of observers when a behavior is judged antisocial are many: time, social status, money, event, location, age, reputation, intensity, duration, frequency, and group expectations. When the cumulative effect of these variables is negative, exceeding the dynamic acceptable definition of the moment, a person's behavioral performance is judged antisocial. For example, when a behavior is poorly timed, appropriate social status is not recognized, intensity is high and loud, the behavior is against school rules, reputation is known, duration is long; frequency is perceived as too often, and other students are conforming to rules of the environment, an antisocial behavior is said to exist. To identify specific factors related to perceptions of antisocial behavior, recent investigation has emphasized those behaviors that teachers and students find most disturbing. Aggressive behavior is most often primary, but withdrawal behaviors such as fear, anxiety, and tension are also defined as antisocial.

This second type of antisocial behavior is reported to be more tolerable to society. The child suffering from withdrawal may be in deeper pain, despair, or depression than an aggressive individual, however, such a child is less aversive to adults and peers, and less likely to excite the environment into action. These children have too little behavior rather than too much. Characteristics accompanying withdrawal are feelings of inferiority and self-consciousness, social withdrawal, shyness, anxiety, weeping, hypersensitivity, infrequent social smiles, nail chewing, depression and chronic sadness, drowsiness, sluggishness, daydreaming, passivity, short attention span, preoccupation, and somber quietness. These children are also picked on by others.

The term antisocial behavior is often applied when behaviors remain inflexible, or frozen, and the person performing the behaviors continues to react to the environment in a manner judged by the group to be displeasing, inappropriate and uncomfortable. The label antisocial behavior is attached to the person displaying the behavior and the definition itself magnifies the individual's differences. Not only does the behavior classify a person, but the antisocial definition itself accentuates differences. Only if classification leads to positive action through school programs on the behalf of the child is this definition constructive.

CHARACTERISTICS

Patterns of antisocial behavior have received a variety of labels: e.g., unsocialized aggressive, conduct disorder, aggressive, unsocialized psychopathic, psychopathic delinquent, antisocially aggressive, and sadistically aggressive. Children exhibiting antisocial behaviors apparent to school officials and teachers may demonstrate one or more of the following characteristics:

1. An inability to learn that cannot be explained by conventional intellectual, sensory, or health factors. A learning-disabled child seldom escapes recognition. He or she is frequently labeled learning disabled, thus lowering self-esteem. The inability to learn is perhaps the single most significant characteristic of antisocial children, with the learning disability manifested as the inability to profit from social experiences and/or academic instruction.

2. An inability to build and maintain satisfactory interpersonal relationships with peers and teachers; to demonstrate sympathy and warmth toward others; to stand alone when necessary; to have close friends; to be aggressively constructive; to enjoy working and playing with others as well as working and playing alone. Children who are unable to build and maintain satisfactory interpersonal relationships are easily defined as different by teachers and peers.

3. "Inappropriate" behaviors or feelings that occur under normal conditions. What is appropriate is judged by the teacher and the student's peers. This judgment is sensed by children because their ability to profit from school experiences and relate to their teachers. Children classified as antisocial often cannot learn what is appropriate because of their inability to relate to and profit from cultural experiences. This amplifies the daily failures of children who fail to conform to social/cultural rules and exacerbates their lack of socialization.

4. Lack of flexibility. When behaviors become frozen into patterns of inappropriateness of such intensity, duration, and frequency that they interfere with social activities of a group, those behaviors are identified as antisocial.

5. Depression and general moods of unhappiness, characteristics of withdrawal. When children seldom smile and express unhappiness in play, art work, group discussions, and language arts, the observer should watch for antisocial expression.

6. A tendency to develop physical symptoms, pains, or fears, especially in reaction to school situations or authority figures. These symptoms may indicate potential antisocial behaviors.

7. Disobedience, disruptiveness, fighting, temper tantrums, irresponsibility, impertinence, jealousy, anger, bossiness, the use of profanity, attention-seeking behavior, boisterousness, defiance of authority, feelings of guilt and inadequacy, irritability, and quarrelsomeness. These descriptors are often associated with antisocial phenomena.

Behaviors described by these characteristics may formulate a pattern of active antisocial behavior that results in conflict with parents, peers, and social institutions. Children and adolescents who represent extreme patterns of antisocial behaviors are likely to have difficulty with law-enforcement agencies. Extreme antisocial behavior will be defined as criminal conduct and result in arrest, incarceration, recidivism, and failure to become a good citizen.

Children with antisocial behaviors are most visible when required to pay strict attention, follow directions, demonstrate control, exhibit socially acceptable behavior, and master academic skills. School, the primary socializing agency for society, emphasizes conformity and educational achievement. These expectations are basic to the order of formal training. When children are unable to meet these expectations, concerns frequently arise among teachers. Questions educators pose may include: How many children are there? How do they behave? How can they be controlled and managed in the classroom? How should they be classified to deduce effects created by labels? What support systems can provide these children with needed programs?

Terms used in educational settings to describe children

with antisocial behaviors are emotionally disturbed, socially maladjusted, minimally neurologically impaired, culturally disadvantaged, behavior disordered, educationally handicapped, and conduct disturbed. Such labels represent different orientations that exist among educators confronted with the task of providing educational programs for children with antisocial behaviors. All these labels could be used collectively for a single child experiencing difficulty in school. For qualification for programs, labels and treatments should be closely related to how the antisocial child (in classroom, community, or at home) is perceived (by educators, social groups, or family). Educational offerings frequently depend on how a child is perceived and the attitude of the referring school toward the child.

When an individual has appropriate behavioral responses in his or her repertoire and exhibits these responses under appropriate circumstances, antisocial behavior is interpreted. Through systematic and explicit application of the principles of learning, behavior management can be applied in educational settings to treat antisocial behaviors.

The individual can be helped to change deficient or maladaptive behavior by receiving assistance to modify his or her responses to specific sound cues. In the case of maladaptive behavior, for example, aggression could be modified to be elicited or emitted under appropriate circumstances only. This type of behavioral learning, unlearning, or relearning is known as behavior management. The teacher or behaviorist operates on the assumption that the behavior can be modified without understanding why the behavior is antisocial. The antecedents to the behavior need not be reconstructed to initiate corrective action. Teaching the child to react more appropriately is the only relevant issue, not finding out how the child came to behave antisocially. The focus during behavior therapy is on teaching new behaviors and eliminating old ones. The first task of the therapist (teacher) is to decide which behavior should be modified. Once a target behavior is defined, the treatment goal can be specified. Treatments are based on principles of learning: respondent learning, operant conditioning, interrelationships of operation and respondent factors, social reinforcement, desensitization, and aversive and contingency control. The treatment goal is assessed when the antisocial behavior has become adapted. If in the process of identifying target behaviors the teacher discovers antecedents as causes, the organization of the classroom environment, stimuli, and consequences can be arranged so that the learning situation supports the child's development. An engineered, structured classroom with clear-cut expectations and rewarding consequences for appropriate behavior and academic accomplishment can result in definite academic and behavioral gains. Primary or tangible rewards, teacher attention, "game" approaches, and high-interest activities can become successful interventions for adapting antisocial behaviors. Precision teaching involves selecting a behavior, charting it on a graph, recording changes and occurrences, analyzing the child's performance, and changing the program according to program effects. Some schools use a resource room concept, in which the child participates part time in a special program and part time in a regular class program.

Completely self-contained classrooms for children with more severe learning and behavioral problems can be successful. The engineered classroom directs attention to the establishment of specific goals or develops a sequence of behavioral objectives, for example, attention, response, order, exploratoration, social activity, mastery, and achievement. This engineering translates behavior modification strategy into realistic use in the classroom. There is constant manipulation of stimuli and intervention in the class to assure a child's continued success.

If a tree crashes in the forest but there is no human ear to hear it, is there a noise? When an individual behaves in an antisocial fashion, does the disturbance exist without a reactor to register the event? Does the disturbance reside in the child or the reactor, or is it a product of both?

REFERENCE

Quay, H.C., & Werry, J.S. (1972). *Psychopathological disorders of childhood.* New York: Wiley.

See also **Conduct Disorder; Emotional Disorders; Seriously Emotionally Disturbed**

ANTISOCIAL PERSONALITY

The antisocial personality is characterized by a recurring pattern of antisocial behaviors and a general disregard for the rights of others. This pattern of behavior has, in the past, been referred to as psychopathy or sociopathy. It emerges during childhood in the form of truancy and other school-related academic and behavior problems such as delinquency, lying, fighting, sexual promiscuity, substance abuse, and running away from home. The DSM-IV (American Psychiatric Association, 1994) requires at least four of the following nine manifestations of the disorder be present before a diagnosis of antisocial personality disorder (APD) is made: inability to sustain consistent work behavior; lack of ability to function as a responsible parent; failure to accept social norms with respect to lawful behavior; inability to maintain enduring attachment to a sexual partner; irritability or aggressiveness; failure to honor financial obligations; failure to plan ahead, or impulsivity; disregard for the truth; and recklessness. The diagnosis of APD is typically reserved for individuals age 18 and over. Younger children and adolescents who manifest signs of APD are diagnosed as conduct disorder. There are four subtypes of conduct disorder depending on the presence or absence of normal social attachments and aggressive behavior. Many, but not all, children who manifest conduct disorder go on to develop an antisocial personality disorder (Loeber, 1982). Research has identified five factors that appear to play a role in the etiology of APD including heredity, brain abnormalities, autonomic nervous system underarousal, and family, and environmental influences.

REFERENCES

American Psychiatric Association. (1994). *Diagnostic and statistical manual of mental disorders* (4th ed.). Washington, DC.

Loeber, R. (1982). The stability of antisocial and delinquent behavior: A review. *Child Development, 53,* 1431–1446.

See also Aggression; Conduct Disorder; Personality Disorders

ANXIETY

There is probably no aspect of the human experience more universal than that of anxiety. In every culture and throughout recorded time, the human organism has been subject to real and imagined threats that may produce the arousal state that is labeled anxiety. By the midpoint of the present century, many authors, philosophers, psychologists, and others were referring to the twentieth century as the age of anxiety. Auden (1947) explained that the age of anxiety was reflected in heightened feelings of loneliness. This increase in anxiety, or perhaps an increased awareness of its existence, was often attributed to loneliness, uncertainty, and bureaucratic interference with the individual's efforts toward self-recognition and self-realization. Anxiety may be both a symptom and a disorder.

Both Kierkegaard (1944) and May (1977) noted the potential for human growth inherent in a satisfactory response to anxiety-producing stimuli. In support of this notion is the considerable research and theory of Torrance (1965) affirming that creative problem solving serves as an antidote for anxiety. Thus anxiety is not always defined as a destructive or debilitating force in human behavior. Many psychologists and educators today describe a curvilinear relationship between learning and anxiety. Both very high and very low levels of anxiety are negatively related to learning, resulting in the well-known inverted or U-shaped curve between anxiety and performance on complex tasks.

One of the more prevalent conceptualizations of anxiety today embodies the state-trait distinction. Here we may refer to Spielberger (1972), who states the differences between state and trait anxiety very clearly. Essentially, state anxiety is a complex system of emotional reactions that arise when an individual perceives a situation as threatening, regardless of whether a real threat exists. Thus, state anxiety is a transitory condition and may vary greatly from individual to individual and from one condition to another. Not all conditions are equally threatening to all individuals.

In contrast, anxiety may be understood to be more of a personality trait. This notion suggests that it is a more permanent construct of the individual's usual manner of functioning. Trait anxiety is a term used to define the personality of one who frequently experiences anxiety, often where the strength of the stimulus for evoking anxiety is relatively weak. It refers to the propensity of the individual to feel anxiety. This trait appears to vary among persons on a continuum from highly infrequent to an almost constant level

of anxiety. Several researchers, including Gottschalk and Gleser (1969), view anxiety as a multi-modal concept. It has been theorized that such emotions as anger, guilt, shame, and shyness are really components of anxiety.

In an effort to understand more clearly the nature and impact of anxiety, several researchers have developed measures of anxiety. Some of these measures record physiological manifestations of anxiety such as changes in temperature or heart rate. Taylor (1951) is credited with an early effort to measure anxiety through a self-report technique. Behavior, task performance, clinical intuition, and stress responses are also used to measure anxiety.

Among the most widely researched measures of anxiety are the *State-Trait Anxiety Inventory for Children* (Spielberger et al., 1973), the *State-Trait Anxiety Inventory* (Spielberger et al., 1970) and the *Revised Children's Manifest Anxiety Scale* (Reynolds & Richmond, 1978, 1985), the latter being the most widely used measure of children's anxiety throughout the world. For behavioral representations of anxiety, the Behavior Assessment System for Children is widely used, especially in the public schools (Reynolds & Kamphaus, 1992). These and other instruments continue to be used by researchers and clinicians in their efforts to specify the nature of anxiety and to record and remediate its debilitating effects on the individual.

REFERENCES

Auden, W.H. (1947). *The age of anxiety.* New York: Random House.

Gottschalk, L.O., & Gleser, G.C. (1969). *The measurement of psychological states through the content analysis of verbal behavior.* Los Angeles: University of California Press.

Kierkegaard, S. (1944). *The concept of dread* (translated by Walter Lowrie). Princeton, NJ: Princeton University Press (originally published in Danish in 1844).

May, R. (1977). *The meaning of anxiety.* New York: Norton.

Reynolds, C.R., & Kamphaus, R.W. (1992). *Behavior assessment system for children.* Circle Pines, MN: American Guidance Service.

Reynolds, C.R., & Richmond, B.O. (1978). What I think and feel: A revised measure of children's manifest anxiety. *Journal of Abnormal Child Psychology, 6,* 271–280.

Reynolds, C.R., & Richmond, B.O. (1985). *Manual, revised children's manifest anxiety scale.* Los Angeles: Western Psychological Services.

Spielberger, C.D. (1972). Anxiety as an emotional state. In C.D. Spielberger (Ed.), *Anxiety: Current trends in theory and research* (p. 30). New York: Academic.

Spielberger, C.D., Edwards, C.D., Lushene, R.E., Montuori, I., & Platzek, D. (1973). *Manual, state trait anxiety inventory for children.* Palo Alto, CA: Consulting Psychologists Press.

Spielberger, C.D., Gorsuch, R.L., & Lushene, R.E. (1970). *Manual, for the state-trait Anxiety inventory.* Palo Alto, CA: Consulting Psychologists Press.

Taylor, J.A. (1951). The relationship of anxiety to the conditioned eyelid response. *Journal of Experimental Psychology, 41,* 81–92.

Torrance, E.P. (1965). *Mental health and constructive behavior.* Belmont, CA: Wadsworth.

See also Phobias and Fears; Revised Children's Manifest Anxiety Scale; Test Anxiety

ANXIETY DISORDERS

Anxiety is an emotional condition experienced by all children and adults to some degree. It results when people's responses to internal or external events produce a negative arousal state. It is a state of general emotional arousal that is experienced as unpleasant to some degree by the individual. Internal or external conditions that create fear are the most common sources of anxiety. When individuals experience anxiety to a significant degree, they often show a wide range of possible responses that are exaggerated in proportion to the objective situation. These diffuse effects may include emotional responses, including physiological changes; cognitive changes in perceptions of objects or thoughts about a situation; motor responses such as irritable behavior or hyperactivity, or the opposite including lethargy or withdrawn behavior. A certain degree of anxiety has motivating properties and can have a positive value such as enhancing performance on educational tasks. Anxiety becomes a clinical problem when it reaches a significant degree on a regular basis and interferes with normal adaptive behavior. The anxiety disorders have their own psychiatric classification (American Psychiatric Association, 1994).

CHILDHOOD STRESS

Stress refers to environmental pressures and changes that produce emotional and physiological coping responses in the child. Circumstances often produce anxiety reactions. Changes that produce stress frequently occur in normal child development. For example, the young infant experiences anxiety in the form of separation anxiety from the mother. Healthy child development depends on the child's learning effective ways to cope with stressful changes so as to keep anxiety at manageable levels.

Much research exists on the effects of change and stressors on adults, and a variety of stress scales have been developed. Less is known about the clinical effects of stress and changes in child development, although Bowlby (1980) has studied the role of separation and loss on the development of childhood depression. Clinicians, teachers, and guidance counselors should be aware of the role of change, loss, and stress in the development of anxiety disorders. The loss of a parent through death or divorce, chronic illness, and school failure all place the child at risk of developing anxiety reactions. The Behavior Assessment System for Children (Reynolds & Kamphaus, 1992) includes standardized measures of stress in children of school age.

SEPARATION ANXIETY DISORDER

The main symptom of this syndrome is excessive anxiety when the child is separated from a major attachment figure such as a parent. Common behaviors include fear that harm will come to the parent; worry that a major trauma such as an automobile accident will occur; refusal to go to school; sleep disturbance; reluctance to be left alone; physical symptoms, such as stomach aches, headaches, or dizziness; and withdrawal from normal social activities. This disorder may develop anytime from infancy through adolescence. It is usually not caused by a single event, but gradually emerges as a behavioral pattern stemming from a disturbed child-parent relationship. Cases often appear to have been set off by a particular upsetting event, but close examination reveals the longstanding pattern.

SCHOOL PHOBIA

Children refusing to go to school or asking to leave school once they arrive is one of the most common and sometimes most difficult to treat of childhood disorders. Children sometimes develop a negative association based on a frustrating school experience and then refuse to go to school. This could be the case where a child has a serious learning disability of an attention deficit disorder in which self-esteem is adversely affected. Generally, however, a school-refusal or school-phobic child is acting out of anxiety relating to separation.

School phobic cases can be classified into two types. The first is generally seen in younger children with more cooperative parents; it responds better to intervention. The second type occurs in late childhood (ages 10 to 12) or adolescence. The parents tend to be less cooperative; there may be conflict in the marital relationship; and response to treatment is slower and may require hospitalization.

AVOIDANT DISORDER OF CHILDHOOD AND ADOLESCENCE

This disorder occurs from age 2 and a half through adolescence. A behavioral pattern of shrinking away from social contacts and withdrawing from others is the central characteristic. Children with this disorder are not merely shy, they actively retreat from social contacts and are very cautious in dealing with peers. Nonverbal body movements may be characterized by the avoidance of eye contact, poor posture, and childlike mannerisms.

OVERANXIOUS DISORDERS

Children with this syndrome show excessive worry about performance, potential injuries, and acceptance by others. The difference between this disorder and the avoidant one is that the primary problem is worry or anxiety rather than avoidant behavior. Children who show this problem syndrome tend to come from families having a high emphasis on performance, achievement, and socially acceptable behavior. The worry tends to be generalized, not specifically associated with a particular situation. It often involves overconcern with being a highly competent individual and sensitivity to criticism. Children with this disorder also may show psychophysiological symptoms such as stomach aches or general nervousness. There are signs of obsessional thoughts about oneself, a tendency toward perfectionism, and approval-seeking behavior. Such children also are prime examples of people who are always imagining the worst; they may have fears of death or impending disaster. Children with this psychological problem share many of the same concerns as those with the avoidant disorder, but they persevere in their efforts to achieve or to please despite their excessive worry instead of withdrawing from social contacts.

CHILDHOOD PHOBIAS

Phobias reflect intense anxiety associated with a fear about a specific object or situation that is out of proportion to the apparent objective danger. In this sense, phobias are irrational fears. In evaluating whether or not a childhood fear is a phobia, the clinician must keep in mind the fears that normally would be apparent at different developmental ages. For example, fear of loud noises and strangers are the norm in infancy; fear of animals and fear of darkness in toddlerhood; and fear of social embarrassment in adolescence. A phobia is distinguished by the severity of the anxiety and a sense of panic that seems to overwhelm the child when faced with the object or situation. There is an obsessional quality to the phobia as the child may spend unusual amounts of time worrying about exposure to the object. Common phobias include fear of animals, heights, and insects.

REFERENCES

American Psychiatric Association. (1994). *Diagnostic and statistical manual of mental disorders* (4th ed.). Washington, DC: Author.

Bowlby, J. (1980). *Attachment and loss: Vol. 3. Loss: Sadness and depression.* New York: Basic Books.

Reynolds, C.R., & Kamphaus, R.W. (1992). *Behavior assessment system for children.* Circle Pines, MN: American Guidance Service.

See also **Behavior Assessment System for Children; Childhood Psychosis; Depression; Emotional Disorders; Psychoneurotic Disorders; School Phobia**

APGAR RATING SCALE

The Apgar Rating Scale was specifically designed to assess medical distress in newborns. Ratings are made by attending nurses or physicians at 1 minute after birth, with possible further ratings at 3, 5, and 10 minutes. Five vital signs, heart rate, respiratory effort, reflex irritability, muscle tone, and color, are rated on a 3-point scale: 2 if present, 1 if not fully present, and 0 if absent. Thus the range of possible scores is 0–10, with scores greater than 7 (about 70% of all newborns) indicating excellent condition, 3–7 (24% of all newborns) indicating a moderately depressed condition, and less than 3 (6% of all newborns) indicating a severely depressed condition (Apgar, 1953; Apgar, Holaday, James, & Weisbrott, 1958).

REFERENCES

Apgar, V. (1953). A proposal for a new method of evaluation of the newborn infant. *Current Researches in Anesthesia and Analgesia, 32,* 260–267.

Apgar, V., Holaday, D., James, L., Weisbrott, I., & Berrien, C. (1958). Evaluation of the newborn infant—second report. *Journal of the American Medical Association, 168,* 1985–1988.

See also **Low Birth Weight Infants; Neonatal Behavioral Assessment Scale; Prematurity**

APHASIA

Everyone with the diagnosis of aphasia has an acquired language disorder, but the type of language disorder (problems understanding talking, problems talking, problems reading, problems writing) and the severity of these difficulties vary, reflecting the different locations and the extent of the damage to the brain. There also are similarities in the type of problems using language among persons whose brain has been damaged in the same location. Aphasiologists are persons who study aphasia and attempt to provide a structure for understanding and diagnosing this language disorder upon the basis of these variations and similarities. As a result of their studies, there are many different definitions of aphasia and many different classification systems offering a means of subdividing aphasia (Chapey, 1994; Davis, 1993).

Literature within the last decade reflects a general agreement on the following: The term aphasia (acquired language disorder due to brain damage) applies to persons who formerly had intact, developed language functioning and, therefore, the term aphasia does not apply to language disorders experienced by children (Davis, 1993). Some aphasiologists (Darley, 1982; Schuell, 1972) set forth arguments against subdividing or classifying aphasia according to differences or similarities of symptoms. In the opinion of these experts, the variations in symptoms reflect degrees of problems in the total, integrated brain function.

However, if classification is considered, one common basis is nonfluent versus fluent. In this case, separation is made on the basis of whether the symptoms of a person's language disorder result in a disruption of fluency (Hegde, 1994). Rosenbek, Wertz, and LaPointe (1989) define being fluent as producing five or more connected words. Obviously, persons who have aphasia and who cannot produce five or more connected words have nonfluent aphasia. Further common subdivision types within nonfluent aphasia include Broca's, global, isolation, and transcortical motor. Subdivisions of fluent aphasia include Wernicke's transcortical sensory and conduction.

Other common perspectives seen in the literature for defining symptoms of aphasia are those in terms of cognitive impairments (Chapey, 1981; Davis, 1993) and linguistic analysis of the disordered language (Jakobsen, 1971; Caplan, 1991). Cognitive definitions of aphasia are based on the idea that cognition underlies language and that if language is impaired, some aspects of cognition also must be impaired. Descriptions of symptoms are reported as impairments in long- and short-term memory for words, phrases, and sentences and as impairments in processing linguistic information (Hegde, 1994). Research done from the linguistic point of view is called "neurolinguistic," and it analyzes the symptoms from a perspective of whether a patient shows difficulties in linguistic units if they are shorter or longer, simple or complex, active or passive, embedded or unembedded, and so forth (Hegde, 1994).

The types of language disorders encountered by persons with aphasia include difficulties in comprehending spoken language (for example, the patient cannot point to a picture or object named, or the person may not know the meaning of ordinary words) and difficulties in talking (the patient may substitute sounds or words and create new words that do not mean anything to the listener, or the person may omit sounds within words or whole words). Persons with aphasia may struggle to get out any words and speak very little, or they may talk a great deal with ease, but the words and grammar do not have meaning for the listener. Persons with aphasia may also experience difficulties in reading or writing and doing number calculations (Hegde, 1994). In addition, there are often many related disorders that occur from the damage to the overall neurological network, such as motor speech problems or paresis of the oral structure and/or arm and leg.

Over one million people in the United States suffer from aphasia and each day almost 300 new cases occur. Rehabilitation requires commitment and support from professionals and family. In an effort to provide a better understanding of this disorder, a national organization, the National Aphasia Association has been formed (LaPointe, 1997). This organization can be reached at P.O. Box 1887, Murray Hill Station, New York, NY 10156-0611.

REFERENCES:

Caplan, D. (1991). Agrammatism is a theoretically coherent aphasic category. *Brain and Language, 40,* 274–281.

Chapey, R. (1981). Assessment of language disorders in adults. In R. Chapey (Ed), *Language intervention strategies in adult aphasia* (pp. 31–84). Baltimore: Williams & Wilkins.

Chapey, R. (1994). *Language intervention strategies in adult aphasia* (3rd ed.) Baltimore: Williams & Wilkins.

Darley, F. (1982). *Aphasia.* Philadelphia: W.B. Saunders.

Davis, G. (1993). *A survey of adult aphasia and related language disorders* (2nd ed.). Englewood Cliffs, NJ: Prentice Hall.

Hegde, M. (1994). *A coursebook on aphasia and other neurogenic language disorders.* San Diego: Singular.

Jakobsen, R. (1971). Two aspects of language and two types of aphasic disturbances. In R. Jakobson & M. Halle (Eds.), *Fundamentals of language* (2nd ed.). The Hague, Netherlands: Mouton.

LaPointe, L. (1997). *Aphasia and related neurogenic language disorders* (2nd ed.). New York: Thieme.

Rosenbek, J., LaPointe, L. & Wertz, R. (1989). *Aphasia: A clinical approach.* Austin, TX: Pro-Ed.

Schuell, H. (1972). *The Minnesota Test of Differential Diagnosis of Aphasia.* Minneapolis: University of Minnesota Press.

See also Developmental Aphasia; Language Disorders

APHASIA, DEVELOPMENTAL

See CHILDHOOD APHASIA; LANGUAGE DISORDERS.

APNEA

Apnea is defined as a lack of respiration for a period of 20 to 30 seconds with or without an accompanied decrease in heart rate to ≤ 80 beats per minute with resultant cyanosis. Twenty-five percent of infants in premature nurseries, but only a small percentage of full-term infants, exhibit apnea. Apnea, therefore, appears in most cases to stem from actual immaturity of the neural mechanism responsible for regulation of respiration. When immature, this mechanism is vulnerable to metabolic disturbances in calcium and blood-sugar levels, changes in body temperature, or disturbances in brain-wave patterns that occur during seizures or normal REM (rapid eye movement) sleep. The association between apnea and sleep is significant because premature sleep up to 80% of the time and REM sleep are the predominant sleep states of these infants (Parry, Baldy, & Gardner, 1985). Apnea is less frequently caused by actual obstruction of the airway itself either from excessive mucus or improper body positioning, as premature infants have very flexible tracheas.

Prognosis is generally good for infants who do not experience prolonged apnea and who are otherwise healthy. It becomes less favorable with increased frequency and duration of apneic episodes (Parry, Baldy, & Gardner, 1984). However, at least one study suggests that infantile apnea may be associated with deficiencies in later gross motor, and perhaps some cognitive, functions and behavior (Deykin, Bauman, Kelly, Hsieh, & Shannon, 1984). Since apnea produces transient anoxia, it can, when extensive, cause many of the problems associated with that disorder.

REFERENCES

Deykin, E., Bauman, M., Kelly, D., Hsieh, C., & Shannon, D. (1984). Apnea of infancy and subsequent neurologic, cognitive and behavioral status. *Pediatrics, 73,* 638–645.

Parry, W., Baldy, M., & Gardner, S. (1985). Respiratory diseases. In G.B. Merenstein, & S.L. Gardner (Eds.), *Handbook of neonatal intensive care.* St. Louis: Mosby.

See also Anoxia; Infant Stimulation

APPLIED BEHAVIOR ANALYSIS

Applied behavior analysis is an approach for changing behavior that involves the systematic application of a set of principles derived from psychological theories of learning. Applied behavior analysis has been demonstrated to be a highly effective, management system in both school (Alberto & Troutman, 1982; Martens et al., 1999) and home situations (Becker, 1971). Its principles have been successfully applied to a wide range of children's problems, including academic problems such as reading, handwriting, and task completion, and social and behavioral problems such as aggression, shyness, and school avoidance.

Applied behavior analysis and behavior modification are closely related terms. Both involve the application of principles of learning to the changing of behavior. Technically, behavior modification is the broader term, including behavior change strategies that are not based on learning principles (e.g., chemotherapy, the use of physical restraints, and brain surgery). Behavior modification in schools has become synonymous with reinforcement programs derived from operant conditioning principles. Operant conditioning procedures change behavior through changing the events that follow behaviors (i.e., consequences of behavior). Applied behavior analysis applies principles derived from operant conditioning, social learning theory, and respondent conditioning. The applied behavior analyst assesses and treats behavior in terms of both consequences and antecedents (i.e., events that precede behavior). These antecedent events may be environmental events or cognitive events (i.e., thoughts, attitudes, or perceptions) that are thought to influence behavior.

The principles of learning that are applied to problem behaviors include positive reinforcement, negative reinforcement, shaping, prompting, fading, extinction, punishment, modeling, discrimination learning, task analysis, and self-instructional talk. Most of these terms are described in more detail in separate entries in this encyclopedia but they are summarized here. Then the steps in behavior analysis are outlined. Finally, applied behavior analysis is illustrated with a case study.

Positive reinforcement involves presenting a reward to a child after the child performs a specific desired behavior. If that behavior occurs more frequently after the reward, positive reinforcement has occurred. A reinforcer, or reward, is defined in terms of its effect on the behavior it follows. If something (a stimulus) follows a specific behavior and the rate of that behavior increases, that stimulus is a reinforcer. There are no universal reinforcers; children can react differently to such potential reinforcers as adult praise and bubble gum. Allowing a child 5 extra minutes of free time when he or she completes an arithmetic assignment with 80% accuracy is an example of positive reinforcement. It is important that the positive reinforcer be contingent on the specific desired behavior. If the behavior occurs, then the reinforcer is given. If the behavior does not occur, or does not occur at the specified frequency, then the reinforcer is not given. Sometimes teachers and parents will inadvertently follow an undesired behavior with a positive reinforcer. For example, when a child gets out of his or her seat, the teacher calls out that child's name. If the out-of-seat behavior occurs more frequently, the teacher calling out the child's name is a reinforcer. When reinforcement is used, the rein-

forcement can follow every appropriate behavior (continuous reinforcement schedule) or only a portion of the appropriate behaviors (intermittent reinforcement). Continuous reinforcement results in a quick increase in the rate of the reinforced behavior, and intermittent reinforcement results in maintenance of the behavior change when the behavior is no longer being reinforced.

When a behavior that has been followed by a reinforcer in the past no longer is reinforced, *extinction* has occurred. Often the immediate result of extinction is a temporary increase in the previously reinforced behavior. If a teacher who has attended to a child's temper tantrums begins to ignore the temper tantrums, the child is likely to increase the frequency and duration of tantrum behavior; however, if the teacher continues to ignore the tantrums (and there are no other reinforcers that follow the tantrums, like peer attention), the tantrums should decrease in frequency.

Negative reinforcement, like *positive reinforcement,* is a procedure for increasing the rate of a desired behavior. In negative reinforcement, some unpleasant event (stimulus) is terminated following the desired behavior. For example, a teacher tells students that children who complete their assignments at 85% accuracy will be relieved of their homework assignment.

Punishment is a process in which the consequences of a behavior reduce the future rate of that behavior. There are three types of punishment procedures. In the application of an unpleasant consequence, a behavior is followed by some unpleasant stimulus, such as extra work, a verbal reprimand, or physical punishment. In response cost, a teacher removes a reinforcer contingent on a specified behavior. Children may lose 3 minutes of recess each time they receive a check next to their names on the board. In *time out,* the child is denied the opportunity to participate in positive reinforcement for a specified period of time, contingent on a specified undesired behavior. Requiring a child to sit on a bench at recess when playing roughly or to sit on a mat during art are examples of time out.

When a child has learned to say "red" only to colors in the red spectrum, the response of saying "red" is under the *stimulus control* of the color red. This control is established by reinforcing the correct response and/or punishing the incorrect response. The reinforcer may be praise or a star. The punisher may be "no" or an X on the paper. When the child learns to respond differently to red and not red, this shows *discrimination learning.* The child who goes to the cookie box when Mother is occupied on the telephone has also mastered a discrimination learning task. Going to the cookie box is reinforced with a cookie when Mother is on the phone. When Mother is not on the phone, she either prevents the child from getting a cookie or reprimands the child.

Shaping involves reinforcing improvement in behavior. For example, a child may work only three math problems during a 30-minute period. The teacher would like the child to work 15 problems. (It is assumed the teacher has determined that the problems are at the appropriate level of difficulty for the child.) If reinforcement were contingent on the child working 15 problems, reinforcement would not occur. The teacher establishes a series of steps between the current level of performance and the goal behavior and applies differential reinforcement at each step. Only if the child performs the behavior at or above the behavioral criterion at the operative step in the hierarchy does the child receive the reinforcer. When the child is consistently successful at one step, the next step is operative, and the child's behavior must meet or exceed the criterion for reinforcement at that step. A related procedure is *task analysis,* which involves specifying the prerequisite behaviors to successful performance of a given behavior. Many instructional tasks are composed of several smaller steps that occur in a specific order. Often the difficulty of the task is the reason a child is having difficulty mastering the task. A *skill hierarchy* breaks a complex skill, such as two-digit multiplication, into sequential steps in which each step is a prerequisite for the next higher step in the hierarchy. Skill hierarchies exist in all areas of human learning, including reading, penmanship, dressing, and eating. Task analysis is a useful tool for selecting what skill to teach. Shaping procedures involve the application of reinforcement and extinction to teaching the selected skill.

Prompting involves the use of additional cues to increase the probability the child will respond appropriately to the discriminative stimulus. These extra cues increase the saliency of the discriminative stimuli and are phased out as soon as the behavior is under control of the discriminative stimulus. Prompts may be visual, verbal, or physical. The first-grade teacher who places pictures with letters of the alphabet is using visual prompts to increase the probability that the child will make the correct letter-sound association. The phasing out of prompts involves gradually decreasing the saliency of the prompt.

Modeling involves having a teacher or peer demonstrate the desired behavior to a child. Models can be live or filmed. When models are present at the time the child imitates the modeled behavior, the model serves as a special type of visual prompt. The effects of modeling extend beyond the direct and immediate imitation of specific behaviors. Children can learn complex sequences of behavior (e.g., participating in a game or ordering a meal in a restaurant) through observation. Furthermore, modeling effects do not depend on the child or the model receiving reinforcement for the imitated behaviors. An impulsive child who is paired with a more reflective child to work on puzzles and games may later adopt a more reflective problem-solving approach.

In recent years behavior analysts have attempted to modify cognitions (i.e., thoughts, attitudes, and perceptions) that are thought to influence overt behavior (Meyers & Craighead, 1985). For example, an impulsive child may be instructed to imitate a model who talks out loud while solving a problem. The model provides the child with an example of helpful *self-instructional talk* (Hughes, 1999; Meichenbaum & Goodman, 1971).

REFERENCES

Alberto, P.A., & Troutman, A.C. (1982). *Applied behavior analysis for teachers.* Columbus, OH: Merrill.

Becker, W.C. (1971). *Parents are teachers.* Champaign, IL: Research Press.

Hughes, J.N. (1999). *Child psychotherapy.* In C.R. Reynolds & T.B. Gutkin (Eds.), *The Handbook of School Psychology* (3rd ed.) (pp. 745–763). New York: Wiley.

Martens, B., Witt, J., Daly, E., & Vollmer, T. (1999). Behavior analysis: Theory and practice in educational settings. In C.R. Reynolds & T.B. Gutkin (Eds.), *The Handbook of School Psychology* (3rd ed.) (pp. 638–663). New York: Wiley.

Meichenbaum, D.N., & Goodman, J. (1971). Training impulsive children to talk to themselves: A means of developing self-control. *Journal of Abnormal Psychology, 77,* 115–126.

Meyers, A.W., & Craighead, W.E. (1985). *Cognitive behavior therapy with children.* New York: Plenum.

See also **Behavioral Assessment; Behavioral Objectives; Behavior Modification; Task Analysis**

APPLIED PSYCHOLINGUISTICS

Applied Psycholinguistics publishes original articles on the psychological processes involved in language. Articles address the development, use, and impairment of language in all its modalities, including spoken, signed, and written. *Applied Psycholinguistics* is of interest to professionals in a variety of fields, including linguistics, psychology, speech and hearing, reading, language teaching, special education, and neurology. Specific topics featured in the journal include language development (the development of speech perception and production, the acquisition and use of sign language, studies of discourse development, second language learning); language disorders in children and adults (including those associated with brain damage, retardation and autism, specific learning disabilities, hearing impairment, and emotional disturbance); literacy development (early literacy skills, dyslexia and other reading disorders, writing development and disorders, spelling development and disorders); and psycholinguistic processing (bilingualism, sentence processing, lexical access).

APRAXIA

See DEVELOPMENTAL APRAXIA.

APTITUDE TESTING

The term *aptitude test* has been traditionally employed to refer to tests designed to assess the level of development attained by an individual on relatively homogenous and clearly defined segments of ability, such as spatial visualization, numerical aptitude, or perceptual speed. Aptitude tests measure the effects of learning under the relatively uncontrolled and unknown conditions of daily living. In this sense, they differ from achievement tests that measure the effects of a relatively standardized set of experiences encountered in an educational program. The two types of test differ in use as well. Achievement tests generally represent a terminal evaluation of an individual's status on the completion of training. Aptitude tests serve to predict subsequent performance. They are employed to estimate the extent to which an individual will profit from a specific course of training, or to predict the quality of achievement in a new situation.

The term "special aptitude" originated at a time when the major emphasis in testing was placed on general intelligence. Traditional intelligence tests were designed primarily to yield a single global measure of an individual's general level of cognitive development such as an IQ. Although they were comprised of a heterogeneous grouping of subtests, both practical and theoretical analysis soon revealed that intelligence tests were limited in their coverage of abilities, and that more precise measures were required. This development led to the construction of separate tests for measuring areas of ability that were not included in the intelligence batteries. Traditional intelligence tests oversampled abstract functions involving the use of verbal or numerical symbols; therefore, a particular need was felt for tests covering the more concrete or practical abilities. The earliest aptitude tests were those measuring mechanical aptitude, but soon tests to measure clerical, musical, and artistic aptitude were developed. These special aptitudes were regarded as supplementary to the IQ in a description of an individual, and were usually administered in conjunction with a standard intelligence battery.

A strong impetus to the construction of special aptitude tests was provided by the problems of matching job requirements with the specific pattern of abilities that characterize each individual, a task commonly faced by psychologists in career counseling or in the classification of industrial and military personnel. Intelligence tests were not designed for this purpose. Aside from the limited representation of certain aptitudes discussed earlier, their subtests or item groups were often too unreliable to justify the sort of intraindividual analysis required for classification purposes. To respond to this need, the testing field turned to the development of multiple aptitude batteries.

Like intelligence tests, multiple aptitude batteries measure a number of abilities, but instead of a total score, they yield a profile of scores, one for each aptitude; thus they provide a suitable instrument for making intra-individual analysis (Anastasi, 1997). In addition, the abilities measured by multiple aptitude batteries are often different than those measured by intelligence batteries. Aptitude batteries tend to measure more concrete skills, such as arithmetic reasoning, numerical aptitude, perceptual speed, and spatial visualization, thereby placing less emphasis on verbal skills than intelligence tests.

Nearly all multiple aptitude batteries have appeared since 1945. Much of the test research and development began in the armed forces during World War II, when the Air Force designed special batteries to select training candidates to be pilots, bombardiers, radio operators, and range finders. The armed services still sponsor a considerable amount of research in this area, but a number of multiple aptitude batteries have been developed for civilian use in educational and vocational counseling and in personnel selection and classification (Murphy, 1994).

Many aptitude tests have been designed explicitly for counseling purposes in which classification decisions are preeminent. In a counseling situation, the profile of test scores is used to aid the counselor in choosing among several possible fields of educational or occupational specialization. The General Aptitude Test Battery (GATB; U.S. Department of Labor, 1980) was developed by the U.S. Employment Services (USES) for use by employment counselors in state employment services offices. The GATB is comprised of 12 tests that combine to yield nine factor scores: Intelligence, Verbal Aptitude, Numerical Aptitude, Spatial Aptitude, Form Perception, Clerical Perception, Motor Coordination, Finger Dexterity, and Manual Dexterity. The profile of these subtest scores can then be compared with profiles corresponding to a huge number of job categories. An alternative form is available for nonreading adults. A host of studies have been conducted on the GATB, which have consistently shown that the test is a valid predictor of performance across a range of jobs (Bemis, 1968).

Unlike the multiple aptitude batteries, special aptitude tests typically measure a single aptitude. Certain areas such as vision, hearing, motor dexterity, and artistic talents are often judged to be too specialized to justify inclusion in standard aptitude batteries, yet often these abilities are vital to a certain task. Special aptitude tests were designed to measure such abilities. They are often administered in conjunction with an aptitude battery, either to assess a skill not included in the battery or to further probe a skill or interest. Special aptitude tests may also be custom-made for a particular job, and be constructed using a simulation of the requisites of the job, such as the Minnesota Clerical Test (The Psychological Corporation, 1959), the Meier Art Judgment Test (Meier, 1942), or the Seashore Measure of Musical Talents (Seashore, 1938). Despite wide use in education, counseling, and industry, the development of aptitude tests has been slow (Murphy, 1994). Many of the aptitude tests currently in use were developed in the 1940s and 1950s and have been revised and reissued in subsequent years.

REFERENCES

Anastasi, A. (1997). *Psychological testing* (7th ed.). Saddle River, NJ: Prentice Hall.

Bemis, S.E. (1968). Occupational validity of the General Aptitude Test Battery. *Journal of Applied Psychology, 52,* 240–244.

Meier, N.C. (1942). *Art in human affairs.* New York: McGraw-Hill.

Murphy, K.R. (1994). Aptitude interest measurement. In D.J. Keyser & R.C. Sweetland (Eds.), *Test critiques: Volume 10* (pp. 31–38). Austin, TX: Pro-Ed.

Seashore, C.E. (1938). *Psychology of music.* New York: McGraw-Hill.

See also Achievement Tests; Assessment; Criterion Reference Testing; Vocational Training of Handicapped

APTITUDE-TREATMENT INTERACTION

Aptitude-treatment interaction refers to an educational phenomenon in which students who are dissimilar with regard to a particular aptitude perform differently under alternate instructional conditions. The alternate instructional conditions are specifically designed to reflect the students' aptitude differences. Thus, if a significant performance difference between the groups results under alternate instructional conditions, an aptitude by treatment interaction has occurred.

Aptitude-treatment interactions have been discussed at length by Bracht (1970), who defines an aptitude-treatment interaction as "a significant disordinal interaction between alternate treatments and personological variables" (p. 627). A personological variable is any measure of an individual characteristic such as learning style, intelligence, achievement anxiety, or locus of control. Disordinal interactions refer to performance differences between groups that denote the significantly better performance of one group under one set of conditions and the significantly better performance of the second group under alternate conditions. Figure 1 graphically displays a disordinal aptitude-treatment interaction.

Figure 1 depicts hypothetical data for two groups of students who differ on a particular aptitude, one group being high and the other being low. Alternate treatments, matched to the students' aptitude, were provided. Students with low aptitude performed better under treatment number 1. Students with high aptitude performed better under treatment number 2. The data confirm the occurrence of an aptitude-treatment interaction and support the use of different instructional approaches for these two groups of students.

Figures 2 and 3, respectively, display hypothetical experimental outcomes that are not indicative of an aptitude-treatment interaction. In Figure 2, both groups of students, despite the aptitude difference, performed better under treatment number 1. In Figure 3, treatment number 1 was again superior for both groups of students. However, the differences for the low-aptitude students under treatment conditions number 1 and number 2 were not significant. The aptitude difference does not suggest the use of different treatments for the two groups; other factors may dictate the use of one or the other treatment for both groups. In this instance, the aptitude dimension did not clarify the choice between treatments.

Interest in aptitude-treatment interactions is fueled by the widely espoused commitment to individualization of instruction and the quest for teaching adaptations that enhance individual student performance. Appreciation for individual differences is a relatively recent development (Snow, 1977). Snow believes that the "recognition that indi-

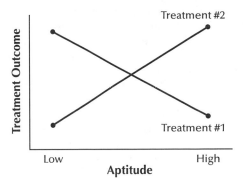

Figure 1. Disordinal aptitude-treatment interaction.

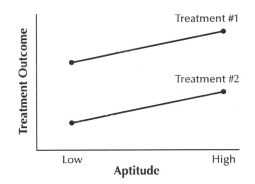

Figure 2. Hypothetical experimental outcome that is not indicative of an aptitude-treatment interaction.

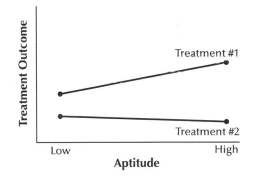

Figure 3. Hypothetical experimental outcome that is not indicative of an aptitude-treatment interaction.

vidual differences in aptitude not only predict learning outcomes but also often interact with instructional treatment variations" (p. 11). This concept makes adaptive instruction a possibility. Teachers have long recognized individual differences and have accommodated such differences in a myriad of ways. Nowhere is the concern for individual differences greater than in special education. The Individual Educational Program requirement of PL 94-142 has mandated individualized educational planning for all exceptional children. Adaptation and accommodation to individual learner needs and characteristics is at the heart of the special education instructional process. Corno and

Snow (1986), in a discussion of adapted teaching, view adaptations as involving either direct aptitude development or circumvention of inaptitude. In special education, the adage "teach to the strengths and remediate the weaknesses" prevails. Teachers generally seek intact or relatively strong abilities as avenues for instruction. Accompanying remediation is most often focused on specific skill or knowledge deficits that impede academic performance or independent functioning. Unfortunately, the commitment among educators, particularly teachers of the exceptional, to individualized instruction in practice is not matched by a strong commitment to educational research. "While it is clear that teachers adapt their behavior to students' individual differences at virtually all levels of education, what is less clear is the underlying logic and intentionality that governs these adaptations" (Corno & Snow, 1986, p. 614).

The meager results from studies specifically designed to demonstrate the interaction between modalities and instruction have not been a deterrent to practitioners. Despite the lack of supportive research, instruction based on the modality concept has been widely implemented. The instructional approach involved children who were tested to determine modality preferences and instruction provided via the preferred modality. It also involved training of perceptual and perceptual-motor skills to enhance the child's readiness for later academic instruction. An extensive body of literature relates to the efficacy of perceptual-motor training. Kavale and Mattson (1983) applied the technique of meta-analysis to 180 efficacy studies. Meta-analysis permits the integration of the results from a large number of independent research studies to reveal the presence of treatment effects that might be obscured in traditional research reviews with a narrative format. The authors found that perceptual-motor interventions were not effective in improving academic, cognitive, or perceptual-motor variables. The results of this review are consistent with the conclusions drawn by others in earlier reviews of perceptual-motor training (Hallahan & Cruickshank, 1973; Myers & Hammill, 1976). The negative or negligible results of efficacy studies should not be surprising in light of the paucity of aptitude-treatment interactions found in studies designed to demonstrate the efficacy of the modality-instructional match. The modality model of instruction is founded on aptitude-treatment interaction theory, but the applicability of aptitude-treatment interaction theory to modality-based instruction has yet to be demonstrated and validated.

Aptitude-treatment interaction research is by no means confined to special education or to investigations of modality-based instruction. Aptitude-treatment interaction research has been conducted in other academic areas such as math (Holton, 1982) and reading (Blanton, 1971). The results generally have been disappointing.

Even though the number of research studies that have successfully demonstrated aptitude-treatment interactions is limited, the research has provided considerable insight into the complexities of the interaction phenomenon and the conditions that favor the occurrence of aptitude-treatment interactions.

In discussing the relationship of aptitude-treatment interaction research to instructional theory, Snow (1977) cautions educators not to expect general theories of instruction to evolve from aptitude-treatment interaction investigations. The research findings to date suggest that each aptitude-treatment interaction, when found, will be valid only in a specific context. Each finding will pertain to a particular group of students under particular instructional conditions. Generalizations, if made at all, will be limited. Educators should not anticipate general educational theories with potential for broad application to emerge from aptitude-treatment interaction research. Those who initiate "blanket treatments" (Snow, 1984) on the premise of aptitude-treatment interactions are likely to be disappointed, as were the proponents of perceptual-motor training. Rather, aptitude-treatment interaction theory implies ongoing evaluation of student and instructional variables and a constant readiness to adjust to meet changing conditions.

REFERENCES

Blanton, B. (1971). Modalities and reading. *Reading Teacher, 25*(2), 210–212.

Bracht, G.H. (1970). Experimental factors related to aptitude-treatment interactions. *Review of Educational Research, 40*(50), 627–645.

Corno, L., & Snow, R.E. (1986). Adapting teaching to individual differences among learners. In M.C. Wittrock (Ed.), *Handbook of research on teaching* (3rd ed.). New York: Macmillan.

Hallahan, D.P., & Cruickshank, W.M. (1973). *Psychoeducational foundations of learning disabilities.* Englewood Cliffs, NJ: Prentice-Hall.

Holton, B. (1982). Attribute-treatment-interaction research in mathematics education. *School Science & Mathematics, 82*(7), 593–601.

Kavale, K., & Mattson, P.D. (1983). "One jumped off the balance beam": Meta-analysis of perceptual-motor training. *Journal of Learning Disabilities, 16*(3), 141–188.

Myers, P.I., & Hammill, D.D. (1976). *Methods for learning disorders* (2nd ed.). New York: Wiley.

Snow, R.E. (1977). Individual differences and instructional theory. *Educational Researcher, 6*(10), 11–15.

Snow, R.E. (1984). Placing children in special education: Some comments. *Educational Researchers, 13*(3), 12–14.

***See also* Diagnostic-Prescriptive Teaching; Direct Instruction; Remediation, Deficit-Centered Models of; Teacher Effectiveness**

ARC, THE

The ARC was founded in 1950 as the National Association of Parents and Friends of Mentally Retarded Children. The organization has undergone several name changes, but its mission has remained constant: to improve the quality of life for children and adults with mental retardation, as well as their families, through education, research, and advocacy.

From 1952 to 1974, the organization was known as the Association for Retarded Children. The name was then changed to the National Association for Retarded Citizens (NARC) in order to reflect a growing service to adults as well as children. In 1980, NARC became the Association for Retarded Citizens of the United States. In 1991, the word "retarded" was removed, and the organization changed its name to The ARC.

Among the association's goals are:

- Increasing the availability of health care for people with mental retardation
- Helping people understand and comply with the public accommodations requirements of the Americans with Disabilities Act
- Ensuring the legal rights of criminal offenders with mental retardation
- Reducing the incidence of fetal alcohol syndrome
- Providing all children, regardless of disability, with a free and appropriate public education
- Protecting the rights of people with mental retardation to enjoy community living, obtain employment, vote, and be protected from abuse and neglect

In 1998, The ARC had 1100 state and local chapters, with over 140,000 members. Information on membership, publications, and topics of interest can be obtained from The ARC National Headquarters, 500 E. Border Street, Suite 300, Arlington, TX, 76010.

ARCHITECTURAL BARRIERS

Recent efforts to fully integrate disabled individuals into the societal mainstream have demanded the elimination of physical barriers that impede access to facilities and the surrounding environment. Common barriers to facility or service accessibility confronted by handicapped citizens include constricted entranceways, ill-equipped public facilities (e.g., restrooms and parking areas), limited passageways, poor room spacing and layout, inadequate lighting, and limitations in the availability of supplementary mediums for providing public information (e.g., braille directions, visual warning or evacuation alarms).

Prior to the 1960s, the vast majority of buildings and thoroughfares were designed for the "ideal user" (i.e., an able-bodied young adult). However, over the past two decades, the National Center for Law and the Handicapped (1978) and the U.S. Department of Housing and Urban Development (1983) have reported that the confluence of federal and state legislation, judicial pronouncements, and publicly accepted standards of accessibility have brought about significant and permanent changes in the architectural design of structures and thoroughfares. These changes have prompted the removal of barriers that inhibit the ac-

cessibility (e.g., mobility and orientation) of physically and sensorily impaired citizens.

The American National Standards Institute (ANSI) specifications, originally adopted in 1961 and updated in the 1970s, establish barrier-free criteria for buildings, entraceways, and thoroughfares. These standards are designed to eliminate all architectural barriers that have historically impeded the access of the following populations:

Nonambulatory Disabled: People with physical impairments that confine them to wheelchairs.

Semiambulatory Disabled. People with physical impairments that cause them to walk with insecurity or difficulty and require the assistance of crutches, walkers, or braces.

Coordination Disabled. Those with impairments of muscle control result in faulty coordination and that create an increased potential for personal injury.

Sight Disabled. Those with impairments that affect vision, either totally or partially, to the extent that an individual functioning in the environment is insecure or liable to injury.

Hearing Disabled. People with impairments that affect hearing, either totally or partially, to the extent that an individual functioning in the environment is insecure or liable to injury.

Modifications that may be required to eliminate architectural barriers in facilities and along public accessways include, but are not limited to, the construction of ramps, wheelchair lifts, and curbing cutouts; the improvement of transfer areas and enlarged spaces for parking facilities; the enhancement of public facilities such as restrooms, telephones, physical education facilities, and dining areas; and the improvement of passageways, entrances (e.g., doors, doorways), room designs (e.g., spacing and layout), facility lighting, and public/user information systems.

REFERENCES

National Center for Law and the Handicapped. (1978, July/August). *Moving toward a barrier free society: Amicus.* South Bend, IN: Amicus.

U.S. Department of Housing and Urban Development. (1983). *Access to the environment.* Washington, DC: U.S. Government Printing Office.

See also **Accessibility of Buildings; Americans with Disabilities Act; Architecture and the Handicapped**

ARCHITECTURE AND THE HANDICAPPED

Approximately 10% of the population has some degree of physical handicap (Moe, 1977). These physical handicaps are of three general types: visual, hearing, and physical/orthopedic. Of these individuals 22 million persons in the United States have some limitation of mobility, with approximately 400,000 confined to wheelchairs. In addition, there are 5½ million individuals who are visually handicapped and 8 million deaf or hearing-impaired persons (Sorensen, 1979).

Apart from the visually handicapped/blind, hearing impaired/deaf, and physically/orthopedically impaired, are those individuals who have health impairments involving cardiopulmonary disorders or neuromuscular diseases. These disorders may permit some mobility but may result in diminished stamina, poor coordination, or limited grasping and manipulative capacity.

Architectural considerations vary and are dependent on whether the handicap is physical, visual, or aural. In fact, such considerations can involve competing requirements that necessitate the establishment of unique environments for the physically handicapped in comparison with the visually handicapped. For example, a physically handicapped person confined to a wheelchair may function best in spaces that are open and large. In contrast, individuals who are blind may do better in smaller spaces where key elements of the sensory environment are within close range. Similarly, an environment that reflects noises may be advantageous for the blind but a disadvantage to the hearing impaired, who have difficulty in attenuating to multiple acoustical cues.

There are a number of general factors to be considered in designing or adapting environments:

1. Many handicapped persons may be smaller or weaker than average; therefore, slopes, reach distances, and forces necessary to open and close objects should be reduced.

2. A number of individuals who use mobility-assist devices (e.g., wheelchairs) may have secondary disabilities that involve difficulty in strength, grasping, etc.

3. Most persons blind at birth, or shortly after birth, know braille, while those adventitiously blind often do not know braille.

4. Tactile signals and signs should be few in number and their location carefully considered to ensure uniformity of placement throughout a building.

5. Audible signals should be in the lower frequencies, because persons lose the capacity to hear higher frequencies with increasing age.

6. Many deaf and blind persons can hear and see in favorable environments such as acoustically "dead" surroundings for the deaf and well-lit and magnified print environments for the blind.

7. Visual and aural signals are best to provide redundancy of cues and to accommodate deaf or blind persons (Sorensen, 1979, p. 2).

Much of the impetus for the modification of buildings and facilities for the physically handicapped is attributable to the Architectural Barriers Act of 1968 (PL 90-480) and its subsequent amendments. The act specifies that buildings financed with federal funds must be designed and constructed to be accessible to the physically handicapped.

Many states, by state statute, require that accessibility for the physically handicapped be provided in newly constructed, privately funded buildings that are open to the public. All states require that publicly funded buildings be accessible to the handicapped. A number of states require that when extensive remodeling is undertaken, such remodeling will include making the building accessible.

Funds for state education agencies have been appropriated for the removal of architectural barriers in schools. This one-time, nonrecurring appropriation was authorized by Section 607 of the Education for All Handicapped Children Act (PL 94-142) as amended by Section 5 of the Education of the Handicapped Act amendments of 1983, PL 98-199. The American with Disabilities Act requires accessibility.

REFERENCES

Moe, C. (1977). *Planning for the removal of architectural barriers for the handicapped.* Monticello, IL: Council of Planning Librarians.

Sorensen, R.J. (1979). *Design for accessibility.* New York: McGraw-Hill.

See also **Accessibility of Buildings; Americans with Disabilities Act; Mobility Training**

ARCHIVES OF CLINICAL NEUROPSYCHOLOGY (ACN)

Archives of Clinical Neuropsychology (*ACN*) is the official journal of the National Academy of Neuropsychology, a 4000+ member organization composed primarily of practicing clinical neuropsychologists. The journal was founded in 1985 under the NAN Presidency of Raymond Dean, who became its first editor. Originally a quarterly, the journal increased to 8 times a year in 1996, and also enlarged its page format to accommodate more articles. It is free as a benefit of membership in the Academy and available by subscription to nonmembers. Cecil R. Reynolds assumed the role of editor-in-chief in 1990. The editorial address is care of Dr. Reynolds at the Department of Educational Psychology, Texas A & M University, College Station, TX, 77843-4225. The journal is owned by the Academy and published by Elsevier Science, the largest scientific publisher in the world today.

The journal publishes original research dealing with psychological aspects of the etiology, diagnosis, and treatment of disorders arising out of dysfunction of the central nervous system. Manuscripts that provide new and insightful reviews of existing literature or raise professional issues are also accepted on occasion. The journal reviews books and tests of interest to the field, and publishes the abstracts of the annual meeting of the Academy. A Grand Rounds section is also included that provides in-depth information about individual or small groups of patients with unique, unusual, or low incidence disorders. According to impact factors calculated by the Social Science Citation Index, the journal is one of the most influential in the field of clinical neuropsychology.

ARGENTINA, SPECIAL EDUCATION SERVICES FOR YOUNG CHILDREN IN

Among the countries of Latin America, Argentina has a well-established record of providing educational services to its citizens. Mandatory school attendance was established in 1884 and Argentina has the highest literacy rate (84%) in Latin America (UNESCO, 1984). The National Directorate of Special Education is responsible for the special instruction of mentally, physically, and socially handicapped students. Services are provided from preschool through adulthood.

Early intervention services for children from birth to age 3 were scarce in Argentina and poorly organized (UNESCO, 1981). There was a need for early educational intervention services for children and their families prior to enrolling a child in a nursery school or special center. As a result, services were developed for early stimulation and education. These services are divided by handicapping condition and are provided in infant consultation units. For children with slight to moderate mental handicaps, services focus on sensory and motor stimulation, socialization skills, and speech development. Parents are involved in these activities so that follow through can be done at home. For children with physical handicaps (blind, partially sighted, deaf or hard of hearing), the education is divided into two stages. The first stage is early neurological and sensory stimulation; it is continued until the child has reached a developmental level of 18 months (UNESCO, 1981). The next stage involves stimulation of sensorimotor activities, language development, and the development of self-care and socialization skills. Guidance and educational services also are given to the families.

The primary goal of these intervention programs is to raise the child's level of developmental functioning so that he or she can enter a prenursery special education program. Along with outreach to parents is the involvement and continuing education of special education teachers. There is a central registry of handicapped children so that they may be referred to the appropriate resources. Primary prevention programs are initiated via the media, with special programs for or articles on handicapped children. Public meetings on issues relating to handicapped students constitute an ongoing effort at general education as to the needs of handicapped children.

REFERENCES

UNESCO. (1981). *Handicapped children: Early detection, intervention and education in selected case studies from Argentina, Canada, Denmark, Jamaica, Jordan, Nigeria, Sri Lanka, Thailand, and the United Kingdom* (Report No. ED/MD/63). Paris: Author.

UNESCO. (1984). Wastage in primary education from 1970 to 1980. *Prospects, 14*, 348–367.

See also **Latin America, Special Education in**

ARITHMETIC REMEDIATION

Remediation in arithmetic has evolved into an instructional system comprised of goals and objectives; tests at various levels and of kinds that assess the objectives; instructional activities that represent curriculum at the concrete, pictorial, and abstract levels; and summative evaluations. Instructional goals are based on the general mathematics goals of a school district or similar educational agency. These goals usually emerge from curriculum groups of teachers, supervisors, administrators, and content specialists from outside the school district. In some cases, goals are determined by available textbooks. Objectives are translations of the goals into observable performance statements.

According to the National Council of Supervisors of Mathematics (NCSM, 1979), the goal of the mathematics curriculum should be to ensure that each student is able to:

1. Solve problems
2. Apply mathematics to everyday situations
3. Determine if results are reasonable
4. Estimate
5. Compute
6. Use geometry
7. Measure
8. Read, interpret, and construct tables, charts, and graphs
9. Use mathematics to predict
10. Understand the role of computers

Diagnostic assessments may include survey tests, concept tests, interviews, attitude scales, and learning style inventories. Survey tests tap broad ranges of mathematics competence and serve to present an overview of students strengths and weaknesses. Survey tests also are referred to as screening tests, where there are relatively few items for each of a great number of objectives.

Concept tests may be used for diagnosing in more depth weaknesses identified in the survey test. Concept tests tap objectives with a greater number of items than survey tests. There may be five items on the concept test as compared with two on the survey test for each objective. Furthermore, a greater number of objectives are assessed on a concept test. Examples of concept tests include the *Diagnostic Test of Arithmetic Strategies, KeyMath Diagnostic Arithmetic Test,* and *Individual Assessment Battery: Standardized Form.*

See also **Acalculia; Mathematics, Learning Disabilities in**

ARMITAGE, THOMAS RHODES (1824–1890)

Thomas Rhodes Armitage, an English physician forced by failing sight to leave the practice of medicine, founded the British and Foreign Blind Association in 1868. This organization, which became the Royal National Institute for the Blind, had as its major purposes the establishment of an effective educational program for the blind and the elimination of the existing confusion over printing systems of the blind.

Armitage established the Royal Normal College and Academy of Music to provide vocational preparation for blind students. Eighty percent of its graduates became self-supporting, a unique accomplishment in that time. After conducting an extensive study of printing systems for the blind, Armitage and his association became the leading English proponents of braille. They were instrumental in the ultimate adoption of that system throughout Britain.

REFERENCES

Armitage, T.R. (1886). *Education and employment for the blind* (2nd ed.). London: Harrison.

Ross, I. (1951). *Journey into light.* New York: Appleton-Century-Crofts.

ARMSTRONG V. KLINE (1979)

Armstrong v. Kline was filed on behalf of handicapped children seeking special education services during the summer term. The plaintiffs argued that handicapped children needed continuous, year-round programming in order to receive an appropriate education. The state countered that summer school was beyond the needs of these children and was not made available to nonhandicapped children free of charge and therefore was not required. In finding that some handicapped children are in need of year-round services, the court used the reasoning that "the normal child, if he or she has had a loss, regains lost skills in a few weeks, but for some handicapped children, the interruption in schooling by the summer recess may result in a substantial loss of skills previously learned."

The court was referring principally to the severely handicapped, concluding that they would most likely require summer sessions. Of particular importance is that the court's finding seems to shift the burden of proof from the parents (to show need) to the school district (to show a lack of necessity for year-round programming). These rulings have been upheld in the appeals process thus far. The court did not issue a blanket requirement for summer sessions for all handicapped children, but rather required a determination to be made on the basis of the needs of the individual child. This ruling ultimately forced the development of better techniques for assessing retention and regression among disabled students.

See also **Summer School for the Handicapped**

ARMY GROUP EXAMINATIONS

The Group Examination Alpha, better known as the Army Alpha, was the first group test of intelligence for adults. The examination was one of a battery of tests developed as a result of the armed forces's need during World War I to have an objective means of classifying vast numbers of recruits for military service.

The original examination, consisting of 13 subtests, was developed between June and September 1917 by the Committee on the Psychological Examining of Recruits. The committee was chaired by R.M. Yerkes and included W.V. Bingham, H.H. Goddard, A.S. Otis, T.H. Haines, L.M. Terman, F.L. Wells, and G.M. Whipple. Although experience among measurement experts with group examination procedures was rare, the committee relied heavily on A.S. Otis's group adaptation to the Binet scales for content and standards for administration (Yoakum & Yerkes, 1920). The committee worked continuously for almost a month developing, selecting, and adapting methods for the test content, and another month thoroughly testing the efficacy methods in military stations across the United States. The resulting version of the test consisted of eight subtests: (1) oral directions, (2) disarranged sentences, (3) arithmetic reasoning, (4) information, (5) Otis synonyms and antonyms, (6) practical judgment, (7) number series complete, and (8) analogies. There were five alternative forms provided and the average administration time was 40 to 50 minutes for groups of up to 500 recruits (Linden & Linden, 1968). Between April 1 and December 1, 1918, Army Alpha was administered to approximately 1,250,000 military recruits.

ARMY BETA

The Army Alpha had more than adequately addressed the need for an instrument with which large numbers of individuals could be evaluated in a short period of time, but another problem quickly emerged. Army psychologists did not know what to do about the approximately 30% of the draftees who either could not read English or read so slowly that they could not perform on the Army Alpha. The Army Group Examination Beta, or Army Beta, was prepared to meet this need. The development of an instrument that could be group-administered without a heavy emphasis on reading or understanding verbal language presented special problems. These problems were mainly eliminated through the use of demonstration charts and pantomime to convey instructions (Yoakum & Yerkes, 1920).

The final version of the examination consisted of seven subtests: (1) maze test, (2) cube analysis, (3) X-O series, (4) digit symbol, (5) number checking, (6) pictorial completion, and (7) geometrical completion. The Beta also took approximately 50 minutes to administer and yielded the same type of numerical scores as the Alpha. Although the ability scores obtained on the Beta were somewhat less accurate than on the Alpha for the higher range of intelligence.

The general administration procedure for the Army examinations soon became routine. Groups of draftees (100 to

500) reported to a special building to take the mental test(s). Based on whether the draftees could speak and/or write English, they were assigned to take either the Army Alpha for literates or Army Beta for illiterates or foreign-born recruits. Depending on the individual's performance on one of these tests, a decision was made regarding classification in the military or on the need for further testing to ascertain mental capacity for military service. Individuals failing the Alpha exam were automatically administered the Beta exam to factor out the possible role of reading and oral language in their poor performance. Anyone failing the Alpha exam and the Beta exam initially was given one of three individual performance examinations. Thus, no individual was designated as mentally incompetent solely based on performance on the group examinations.

The influence of the army group examinations is not all positive. Anastasi (1976) reminds us that often tests modeled after the army examinations failed to acknowledge and account for the limitations of the technical properties of the group examination methods. This failure resulted in much of the negative sentiment toward ability testing in the United States. That sentiment threatened the demise of psychological testing. Thus the army examinations may have done as much to retard as to advance the progress of psychological tests. The ease and efficiency of these group techniques also created a preference for impersonal testing as opposed to the more clinical, individual testing methods promoted by pioneers such as Binet (Matarazzo, 1972).

REFERENCES

Anastasi, A. (1976). *Psychological testing* (4th ed.). New York: MacMillan.

Linden, K.W., & Linden, J.D. (1968). *Modern mental measurement: A historical perspective.* Boston: Houghton-Mifflin.

Matarazzo, J.D. (1972). *Wechsler's measurement and appraisal of adult intelligence* (5th ed.). Baltimore: Williams & Wilkins.

Yoakum, C.S., & Yerkes, R.M. (1920). *Army mental tests.* New York: Holt.

See also Intelligence Tests; Measurement

ARTHRITIS, JUVENILE

Juvenile rheumatoid arthritis (JRA) is a systemic disease that causes inflammation of one and usually more joints. The manifestations of JRA vary considerably among patients. The most common symptoms include joint swelling, warmth, tenderness, and pain, which may lead to stiffness, contractures, and retardation of growth. This disease is usually accompanied by fever bursts, rash, and visceral symptoms.

This form of arthritis is the most common connective tissue disease in children and is the most prevalent of the arthritic diseases. It has been estimated that around 250,000 Americans suffer from JRA with an incidence of 1.1 cases per year 1000 school-age children (Varni & Jay, 1984). The disease affects more girls than boys. It is similar to adult rheumatoid arthritis except that it typically appears before puberty and is more likely to stay in remission.

There are basically three forms of JRA: systemic, polyarticular, and pauciarticular. The systemic form accounts for approximately 20% of the population with JRA. High fevers, rashes, stomach pains, and severe anemia are usually present in this type. Pauciarticular accounts for 30 to 40% of the cases. It begins by affecting only a few joints, usually the large ones (knees, ankles, or elbows). Polyarticular is the most common type, accounting for 40–50% of children with JRA. This type affects several joints (five or more), usually small joints of the fingers and hands (Arthritis Foundation, 1983).

The long-term effects of JRA vary greatly depending on the type as well as the individual. There is no way to know the outcome of the disease in its early stages. However, the overall prognosis for children with JRA is good. Most will be able to go through adulthood without any severe physical limitations. Only about 25% will suffer any significant disability (Jay, Helm, & Wray, 1982). In most cases the disease will go into permanent remission but structural damages and functional limitations will remain. In other cases the disease may continue to be active throughout the individual's life (Rennebohm, 1994).

In addition to physical considerations, certain psychological aspects of JRA are also important. McAnarney, Pless, Satterwhite, and Friedman (1974) found that children who have JRA but no disabilities have more emotional problems than disabled arthritics. They also found that parents of the nondisabled children had a poorer understanding of the disease and were less likely to acknowledge its impact on the child's behavior, schooling, and social relations. Litt, Cuskey, and Rosenburg (1982) found that good self-image and greater autonomy coincided with higher compliance in treatment.

Wilkinson (1981) studied the emotional and social behavior of adolescents with chronic rheumatoid arthritis. She found that one of the major complaints among these adolescents was people's tendency to treat them as younger than their age because of their smaller size. She also reported a high anxiety level because of restricted mobility and fears about an uncertain future. Children with JRA are at increased risk of emotional and behavioral problems but there is considerable variability in the response to the disorder psychologically (Varni, Rapoff, & Waldrov, 1994).

In the classroom as well as at home, children should not be unnecessarily restricted from activities. They should be encouraged to find alternatives when they cannot participate in regular play. Periodically calling on the child to do an activity requiring movement may help relieve stiffness whenever the child is not in pain. Beales, Keen, and Holt (1983) have stressed the importance of being aware of the child's perception of pain. Children may be less likely to interpret internal sensations as pain and therefore may fail to recognize it as a warning sign. Often, even when children know they are in pain they may not complain and may even try to conceal it. Some visible signs that may help determine the presence of pain are walking with a stiff gait, taking short steps, tense muscles, and inability to perform certain tasks. Cognitive behavior therapies may be useful in controlling chronic pain in JRA (see Varni et al., 1994).

Another important consideration is JRA's erratic and unpredictable changes from day to day and even throughout the day. Usually the most severe stiffness occurs in the morning. Finally, it is very important for people supervising individuals with JRA to know the signs of aspirin overdose: rapid or deep breathing, ringing in the ears, decrease in hearing, drowsiness, nausea, vomiting, irritability, and unusual behavior.

REFERENCES

Arthritis Foundation. (1983). *Arthritis in children* and *When your student has childhood arthritis.* Atlanta, GA: Patient Services Department.

Beales, J.G., Keen, J.H., & Holt, P.L. (1983). The child's perception of the disease and the experience of pain in juvenile arthritis. *Journal of Rheumatology, 10*(1), 61–65.

Jay, S., Helm, S., & Wray, B.B. (1982). Juvenile rheumatoid arthritis. *American Family Physician, 26*(2), 139–147.

Litt, I.F., Cuskey, W.R., & Rosenberg, A. (1982). Role of self-esteem and autonomy in determining medication compliance among adolescents with juvenile rheumatoid arthritis. *Pediatrics, 69*(1), 15–17.

McAnarney, E.R., Pless, I.B., Satterwhite, B., & Friedman, S.B. (1974). Psychological problems of children with chronic juvenile arthritis. *Pediatrics, 53,* 523–528.

Rennebohm, R.M. (1994). Juvenile rheumatoid arthritis: Medical issues. In R. Olson, L. Mullins, J. Gillman, & J. Chang (Eds.), *The Sourcebook of Pediatric Psychology* (pp. 70–74). Boston: Allyn & Bacon.

Varni, J., Rapoff, M., & Waldron, S. (1994). Juvenile rheumatoid arthritis: Psychological issues. In R. Olson, L. Mullins, J. Gillman, & J. Chang (Eds.), *The Sourcebook of Pediatric Psychology* (pp. 75–89). Boston: Allyn & Bacon.

Varni, J.W., & Jay, S.M. (1984). Biobehavioral factors in juvenile rheumatoid arthritis: Implications for research and practice. *Clinical Psychology Review, 4,* 543–560.

Wilkinson, V.A. (1981). Juvenile chronic arthritis in adolescence: Facing the reality. *International Rehabilitation Medicine, 3,* 11–176.

See also **Physical Handicaps**

ARTICULATION DISORDERS

Articulation involves the study of (1) the phonemes in a given language, (2) the manner in which they are produced, (3) the order in which they are acquired by the members of a culture, and (4) the disorders which may occur. There are forty phonemes in the English language, consisting of twenty-six consonants and fourteen vowels. (Bernthal & Bankson, 1998). A phoneme is defined as the smallest difference conveying a change of meaning. This is in contrast to an allophone which includes all of the acceptable productions of a given phoneme. Allophonic variations do not impact meaning.

The consonant sounds may be differentiated on the basis of three distinctive features: place, manner and voicing. A vowel varies according to tongue height, placement, and whether the tongue is tense or lax. There are also other characteristics of phonemes, known as suprasegmentals, that cause variations in sounds but do not signal a difference of meaning in English. Suprasegmentals are distinctive in some languages. For example, in tonal languages, the pitch of a phoneme signals a change in meaning.

If a traditional view of articulation development is taken, the age of emergence of specific phonemes may be identified. For example, /p/, / b/, and /m/ are early developmental phonemes and are typically in a child's repertoire by age 3. In contrast, the /s/ phoneme may not emerge until a child is 8 years of age or older. Numerous studies, including one by Sander (1972), have examined the age of emergence of various phonemes. All children have articulation errors when they are young and are moving through the normal developmental process. The errors decrease in number as the child matures. Generally, articulation development is thought to be complete by age 8, although some children continue to develop articulation skills beyond this age.

When a child or adult has an articulation disorder, it is characterized by sound production errors, usually involving less than 10 phonemes. The individual's underlying rule system for combining sounds into words is thought to be intact. That is, the speaker understands how sounds are put together to make words which convey meaning, but the speaker is having trouble making individual sounds. The errors can further be classified as phonetic or phonemic in nature.

The more common sources of articulation errors are (1) inaccurate learning, (2) incorrect speech models, (3) structural deficits of the speech and hearing mechanism, and (4) imprecise and/or poor coordination of motor movements. In the first instance, inaccurate learning, something interferes with the process as the child is acquiring a sound. For example, if a child has fluid in his or her ears or brain injury at a critical point in the acquisition of a phoneme, the child may not hear the sound or its replication accurately. It is thought that children rely heavily on the auditory modality when sounds are being learned, but later shift their focus to the proprioceptive/kinesthetic aspects for monitoring the accuracy of their productions. Thus, initially they focus on how their sound matches up auditorily to that produced by others, but later, once the phoneme is learned, they pay less attention to the auditory aspects and focus on how it feels both proprioceptively and kinesthetically. They then are thought to make the assumption that if the phoneme felt like last time, it must be correct. An erroneously learned production is thus maintained. Second, a child may have a family member or significant other who has an articulation error and is providing incorrect models for the child. Learning of faulty articulation is likely to occur because the child will imitate the errored phoneme and incorporate it into his or her repertoire. Third, structural abnormalities of the speech and hearing mechanism may be a contributing factor to articulation errors. Examples are teeth that do not occlude properly or inadequate velopharyngeal closure. The structure may interfere with the ability to produce acceptable phonemes. Fourth, imprecise motor movements and/or the coordination of these movements may cause articulation errors. Correct articulation requires precise placement, timing, and accurate movement of the articulators. Persons with cerebral palsy, dysarthria, or apraxia, for example, have difficulty in these domains, and their speech production is affected to varying degrees.

The treatment for articulation errors generally consists of teaching the phoneme in isolation, and then assisting the client in generalizing the new sound throughout their sound system. Traditional strategies, such as those suggested by Van Riper (1978) or Bankson and Bernthal (1998), may be used. Minimal pairs and co-articulation strategies may also be utilized. Typically, the prognosis for resolving the errors is good.

REFERENCES

Bernthal, J., & Bankson, N. (1998). *Articulation and phonological disorders* (4th ed.). Boston, MA: Allyn & Bacon.

Sander, E. (1972). When are speech sounds learned? *Journal of Speech and Hearing Disorders, 37,* 55–63.

Van Riper, C. (1978). *Speech correction: Principles and methods* (6th ed.). Englewood Cliffs, NJ: Prentice Hall.

See also **Communication Disorders; Speech and Language Handicaps**

ART THERAPY

Art therapy is a technique developed by Margaret Naumberg (1917), who applied her experience as an art teacher and psychologist to treating children with behavior problems. Naumberg used the art of children as a tool to guide therapy. The techniques of art therapy are based on the knowledge that every person has the capacity to project his or her inner feelings into visual form.

Naumberg's first book was published in 1947; it describes the application of psychoanalytical principles to the use of art therapy (Detre, 1983). Naumberg is also credited with developing active teaching methods to facilitate artistic expression, i.e., the scribble technique and rhythmic exercises to enhance creativity and guide imagination.

There are two approaches to art therapy. The psychoanalytical approach, which was developed by Naumberg, uses art work to symbolize the unconscious. However, in 1958 Edith Kramer began using art therapy as a way of helping individuals to express current life experiences and to solve life problems (Dalley, 1984). Tukianen (1980) divided art therapy into three separate modalities. These are the supportive, active, and psychoanalytical elements. The supportive modality is aimed at social rehabilitation; the active form concentrates on ego development; and the analytical

form uses patients' drawings as a diagnostic tool. All patients who participate in art therapy are required to draw. It is claimed that these techniques are useful in preventing suicide and in diagnosing depression and schizophrenia in adults.

Art therapy has also been used in special education. Art therapy has been helpful in treating children with learning disabilities (Mullin, 1974) as well as children who are mentally retarded. Mullin found that children who are mentally limited or too depressed to make even simple drawings can use pictures from magazines to stimulate their thought processes. Children are encouraged to communicate to one another through art work, which has been found to be helpful in reducing emotional stress. Salant (1974) used art therapy with preschool children to help them with their problems. The art therapist, a teacher, and a parent work together in helping children develop through their art work. Art therapy is based on the idea that man's most fundamental thoughts and feelings can be transferred from the unconscious into images rather than words (Dalley, 1984).

The work pioneered by Naumberg is now being used in schools, hospitals, and institutions. Art therapists must have advanced training (Rubin, 1984) and practical experience with supervision, working directly with patients from early childhood through adulthood. There is little research establishing the effectiveness of art therapy.

REFERENCES

Dalley, T. (1984). Art as therapy. The introduction to the use of art as a therapeutic technique. London: Tavistock.

Detre, K.C. (1983). Roots of art therapy. *American Journal of Art Therapy, 22,* 111–123.

Mullin, J.B. (1974). The expressive therapies in special education, *American Journal of Art Therapy, 13,* 54–58.

Naumberg, M. (1917). *A direct method of education* (Bulletin #4). New York: Bureau of Educational Experiments.

Rubin, J.A. (1984). *The art of art therapy.* New York: Brunner/Mazel.

Salant, E.G. (1975). Preventive art therapy with a preschool child. *American Journal of Art Therapy, 14,* 67–70.

Tukianen, K. (1980). Art therapy. *American Journal of Art Therapy, 32,* 300–314.

See also **Psychoanalysis and Special Education; Psychotherapy with the Handicapped; Therapeutic Recreation**

ASPHYXIA

Asphyxia is a medical emergency requiring immediate intervention to prevent infant mortality and morbidity (Golden & Peters, 1985). Asphyxia occurs with inadequate oxygenation and cellular perfusion. This article deals specifically with asphyxia that occurs during the time of birth or shortly thereafter. Many terms are associated with oxygen deprivation during this period; pertinent information can be found in different sources under the headings of neonatal asphyxia, asphyxia neonatorium, perinatal asphyxia, intrapartum asphyxia, and hypoxic ischemic encephalopathy (HIE). Asphyxia has been hard to define accurately, which has caused difficulty in research on its effects and prognosis for recovery. The classical definition of asphyxia has been a low Apgar score with more emphasis on the 5- or even 10-minute scores than on the 1-minute (Fitzhardinge & Pape, 1981). As low Apgar scores are not necessarily associated with asphyxia, however, this definition is not always accurate and is a poor predictor for neurological outcome. Predicting outcome is very difficult. Even infants with 0 Apgar scores at birth have survived after efficient intervention with no serious handicaps (Rosen, 1985). Incidence of damage is generally overestimated when compared with actual findings (Brann, 1985). HIE, whose description follows, is predictive of later deficits.

Four basic mechanisms underlie asphyxia during the immediate perinatal period: (1) interruption of umbilical blood flow; (2) failure of placental exchange because of premature separation of the placenta from the uterus; (3) inadequate perfusion or oxygenation of the maternal side of the placenta as in severe hypotension; and (4) infant failure to inflate the lungs and complete transition to extrauterine life. In early stages, asphyxia may reverse spontaneously if the cause is removed, but later stages require varying degrees of medical intervention because of circulatory and neurological changes (Fitzhardinge & Pape, 1981).

Cerebral palsy (CP) is the most frequent complication of asphyxia. Even then, risk is high only when the Apgar score is low (<3) for prolonged periods (>10 to 15 minutes) (Freeman, 1985). The incidence of CP may be as high as 38% in infants with Apgar scores of 0 to 3 at 20 minutes, and often occurs in conjunction with mental retardation and seizures. Asphyxia does not seem to be associated with severe mental retardation in the absence of CP (Paneth & Stark, 1983).

HIE may result from severe asphyxia. Children diagnosed with HIE show signs of neurologic dysfunction within 1 week, and often within 12 hours, after birth. The major signs of dysfunction include seizures, altered states of consciousness, and abnormalities in tone, posture, reflexes, and respiration. Infants who exhibit seizures have a 30 to 75% likelihood of long-term sequelae. Mortality is high among infants who had definite neurologic abnormality at discharge. Full-term infants with a history of asphyxia and an abnormal neurologic exam during the first week of life show a 7% incidence of early death and a 28% incidence of neurological handicaps. The most common deficits seen in severely affected children include spastic quadriplegia (a form of CP), severe mental retardation, seizures, hearing deficits, and microcephaly. Treatment for HIE is improving but research is difficult. Identification of infants at risk for neurological handicaps is becoming increasingly important as early intervention techniques improve (Brann, 1985).

Overall, the majority of asphyxiated infants suffer no detectable neurologic or intellectual sequelae. Prognosis is good even in relatively serious cases if neurologic examination is normal by 1 week of age. As would be expected, prognosis is poor when the asphyxia is long and severe or subsequent abnormal clinical features appear (Paneth & Stark, 1983). Much about asphyxia and its sequelae is still not well understood. However, adequate pre-natal care, careful monitoring during labor and delivery with prompt obstetrical intervention, and immediate intervention after delivery by professionals skilled in resuscitation all contribute to lowering the incidence of asphyxia and lessening its long-term effects (Phibbs, 1981).

REFERENCES

Brann, A., Jr. (1985). Factors during neonatal life that influence brain disorders. In J. Freeman (Ed.), *Prenatal and perinatal factors associated with brain disorders* (NIH Pub #85–1149, pp. 263–358). Bethesda, MD: National Institutes of Health.

Fitzhardinge, P.M., & Pape, K.E. (1981). Follow-up studies of the high risk newborn. In G. Avery (Ed.), *Neonatalogy: Pathophysiology and management of the newborn* (2nd ed.) (pp. 350–367). Philadelphia: Lippincott.

Freeman, J. (1985). Summary. In J. Freeman (Ed.), *Prenatal and perinatal factors associated with brain disorders* (NIH Pub #85–1149, pp. 13–32). Bethesda, MD: National Institutes of Health.

Paneth, N., & Stark, R.I. (1983). Cerebral palsy and mental retardation in relation to indicators of perinatal asphyxia. *American Journal of Obstetrics & Gynecology, 146,* 960–966.

Phibbs, R.H. (1981). Delivery room management of the newborn. In G. Avery (Ed.), *Neonatalogy: Pathophysiology and management of the newborn* (2nd ed.) (pp. 350–367). Philadelphia: Lippincott.

Rosen, M.G. (1985). Factors during labor and delivery that influence brain disorders. In J. Freeman (Ed.), *Prenatal and perinatal factors associated with brain disorders* (NIH Pub #85–1149, pp. 13–32). Bethesda, MD: National Institutes of Health.

See also **Apgar Rating Scale; Cerebral Palsy; Low Birth Weight Infants; Prematurity**

ASSESSMENT, CURRICULUM BASED
See CURRICULUM BASED ASSESSMENT.

ASSESSMENT, EDUCATIONAL
The need for assessment of students' abilities was recognized long before Congress passed the Education of All Handicapped Children Act, PL 94-142. Thomas Jefferson saw the virtues of identifying gifted students and allotting financial aid to those who needed it in order to ensure that these students further their education (Cronbach, 1984). While the need for special services for exceptional children has been long recognized, little was done on a uniform basis in the United States until the passing of PL 94-142.

An important question should be asked: Why assess? Taylor (1984) answers this query by considering the stages assessment should take and explaining why. The first stage of assessment is to screen and identify those students with potential problems. This stage may be formal, as with group testing, or informal, as when conducting behavioral observations. The next reason for assessment is to determine and evaluate the appropriate teaching programs and strategies for a particular student. At this point it is possible to implement strategies in the classroom before making a formal referral. This stage also allows for information about previously successful strategies to be incorporated into teaching programs.

The third stage involves determining the current level of functioning and the educational needs of the student. Possible strategies for remediation and the student's strengths and weaknesses should be identified at this point. In the next stage, assessment is used to make decisions about placement within special education and student classification; i.e., what would be the least restrictive environment for the student? The last step is to develop individual educational programs (IEP) for the student using the information obtained in the assessment process.

This is not to imply that all students with educational problems must go through all of these stages of assessment. If a problem can be remediated within the regular classroom, then it is pointless to continue assessment. Evaluations should be done completely and carefully to ascertain exactly what the student needs and how to meet those needs in the best possible way.

A number of important historical events played a part in determining how the special needs of exceptional children are currently evaluated. These events have been outlined in a number of sources (Cronbach, 1984; Graham & Lily, 1984; Nitko, 1983; Nunnally, 1970; Sattler, 1982; Wisland, 1977)

Test publishing has become a flourishing and lucrative industry since World War I. With this growth has come some substantial advantages, the most significant of these being the increased emphasis on test standardization and the provision of norms for purposes of comparison of individuals with the populations within which they exist. This has been pervasive in all areas of assessment used with exceptional children in the education system.

Consideration of more than just a student's intellectual capacity has also become prevalent as other aspects of the individual and his or her capabilities are assessed in conjunction with this area. Other areas that are relevant to evaluation for special education are the student's current level of academic functioning, the level of adaptive behavior, and, in some cases, the evaluation of personality and behavioral factors. All of these areas play an integral part in the assessment of exceptional students.

Intellectual assessment has played a key role since the beginning of interest in special children. There have been many changes within the intellectual assessment field as well. With the growth of the test publishing industry, instruments used to assess intelligence have increased in number. Along with this increase have come changes in the content of the instruments as well as the way the concept of intelligence has been defined. While the Binet-Simon Intelligence Scale purported to measure an overall concept of intelligence, later instruments attempted to further refine this construct. Witness, for example, the sub-scores of the Wechsler scales, which give not only a full-scale score but also verbal and performance scores. The McCarthy Scales of Children's Abilities yield not only a general cognitive index but also information about a student's abilities in verbal, perceptual-performance, quantitative memory, and motor development areas. The Kaufman Assessment Battery for Children has drawn from past research to develop an instrument that yields not only a global mental processing composite score but also scores pertaining to the processing of information presented sequentially and simultaneously. With these changes has come the advancement of not only how the concept of intelligence is evaluated, but also how intelligence test results relate to intervention in special education.

Tests of educational achievement are also an important aspect of the evaluation of the special education needs of children. There are numerous tests that have been developed to assess a child's level of academic functioning compared with other students of the same age or grade. The content of such measures is usually related to actual academic curricula. There are instruments available that assess many academic areas within one test, while others merely concentrate on one specific area. The number of available instruments of these various types is multitudinous and they have been compiled in various tests elsewhere (Compton, 1984). The relevance of such tests when assessing the needs of exceptional children is evident. Information gained from such measures can lead to more effective educational planning for individual students. These instruments allow for the careful scrutinization of students' strengths and weaknesses in academic areas to establish those who are in need of remediation.

Adaptive behavior may also be an integral part of the assessment of exceptional students. It is essential that this area be assessed for the classification of the mentally retarded as the American Association on Mental Deficiency (AAMD) defines mental retardation as not only low intellectual functioning but also subaverage functioning in adaptive behavior (Sattler, 1982). Other educational classifications such as emotionally disturbed and behavior disordered also make it necessary to evaluate this area of functioning. As with intelligence and achievement, there are a number of instruments available to use to assess adaptive behavior levels. Some examples are the AAMD Adaptive Behavior Scales and the Vineland Adaptive Behavior Scales. These allow specific behavior deficits or strengths to be evaluated; such information is imperative for designing proper behavior management or training programs within educational settings.

The evaluation of personality and emotional disorders also has benefited from the growth of the test publishing industry. While such tests play a role in the educational system, it is to a much lesser extent than those previously mentioned. The relevance of using such measures depends on the type of problem a particular student has. This type of instrument is most likely to be used in evaluating those students who may be classified as emotionally disturbed. While the other areas (intelligence, adaptive behavior, and academic achievement) are more likely to be assessed using instruments that are objective in nature, this has not necessarily been true of personality instruments.

Since the early 1990s, objective evaluation of behavior and personality has become the norm, whereas prior efforts in the affective domain relied heavily upon projective techniques and subjective interpretation. The use of behavior rating scales (e.g., Behavior Assessment System for Children; Reynolds & Kamphaus, 1992) and objective self-report (e.g., Reynolds & Richmond, 1985) is now commonplace in school settings, and has led to objective determination of emotional disability and stronger methods of intervention.

All of these types of assessments are an important part of special education evaluation. They can all give useful information about the students and their specific needs within the educational setting.

REFERENCES

Compton, C. (1984). *A guide to 75 tests for special education.* Belmont, CA: Lake.

Cronbach, L.J. (1984). *Essentials of psychological testing* (4th ed.). New York: Harper & Row.

Graham, J.R., & Lily, R.S. (1984). *Psychological testing.* Englewood Cliffs, NJ: Prentice Hall.

Nitko, A.J. (1983). *Educational tests and measurement: An introduction.* New York: Harcourt Brace Jovanovich.

Nunnally, J.C., Jr. (1970). *Introduction to psychological measurement.* New York: McGraw-Hill.

Reynolds, C.R., & Kamphaus, R.W. (1992). *Behavior assessment system for children.* Circle Pines, MN: American Guidance Service.

Reynolds, C.R., & Richmond, B.O. (1985). *Revised children's manifest anxiety scale.* Los Angeles: Western Psychological Services.

Sattler, J.M. (1982). *Assessment of children's intelligence special abilities* (2nd ed.). Boston: Allyn & Bacon.

Taylor, R.L. (1984). *Assessment of exceptional students: educational and psychological procedures.* Englewood Cliffs, NJ: Prentice Hall.

Wisland, M.V. (1977). *Psychological diagnosis of exceptional children* (2nd ed.). Springfield, IL: Thomas.

See also Achievement Tests; Behavior Assessment System for Children; "g" Factor theory; Intelligence Testing; Kaufman Assessment Battery for Children; Vineland Adaptive Behavior Scales; Wechsler Adult Intelligence Scale; Wechsler Intelligence Scale for Children

ASSIMILATION

Assimilation is one of two complementary processes of adaptation to the environment in Jean Piaget's theory of intellectual development; its counterpart is accommodation. Assimilation involves incorporating external elements (objects or events) into existing cognitive or sensorimotor schemes; incoming information is interpreted or adjusted in a manner consistent with current cognitive structures. In contrast, accommodation involves changing the structures that assimilate information (Brainerd, 1978).

The distinction between assimilation and accommodation can be illustrated by a physiological example: digestion of food (Ginsburg & Opper, 1969). Acids (or the body's current schemes or structures) transform the food into a form that can be used; thus elements of the external world are assimilated. Accommodation occurs in this example when, in order to deal with a foreign substance, stomach muscles contract, acids are released by certain organs, etc. Physical structures (the stomach and other organs) accommodate to an external element (food).

Assimilation involves both constraints on the nature and range of a child's interactions with the environment and the seeking out of new stimuli that can be assimilated into existing schemes (Gelman & Baillargeon, 1983). Piaget discusses three forms of assimilation: functional assimilation; which involves a basic tendency to use an existing structure such as a sucking reflex; recognitory assimilation, which involves recognizing particular situations in which the scheme should be applied; and generalizing assimilation, which involves a tendency to generalize a scheme to new objects and situations (Ginsburg & Opper, 1969).

REFERENCES

Brainerd, C.J. (1978). *Piaget's theory of intelligence.* Englewood Cliffs, NJ: Prentice Hall.

Gelman, R., & Baillargeon, R. (1983). A review of some Piagetian concepts. In P.H. Mussen (Ed.), *Handbook of child psychology: Vol. III. Cognitive development* (pp. 167–230). New York: Wiley.

Ginsburg, H., & Opper, S. (1969). *Piaget's theory of intellectual development: An introduction.* Englewood Cliffs, NJ: Prentice Hall.

See also Accommodation; Piaget, Jean

ASSISTIVE DEVICES

The term assistive device has been applied to a wide range of highly specialized mechanical, electronic, and computer-based consumer tools that are now commonly used in rehabilitation and special education settings. The assistive device is typically designed to perform a particular prosthetic or orthotic function, but it is not a prosthesis or an orthosis in the traditional medical sense (Webster, Cook, Tompkins, & Vanderheiden, 1985). For example, an artificial arm that is operated by electric impulses generated by the user's nervous system (a myoelectric prosthesis) is not considered an assistive device in the same sense that a robotic arm is. The arm is completely separate from the user's body and can be operated by a number of alternative control mechanisms. While it may be configured or applied with a specific individual's needs in mind, it is essentially modular and noncustomized in nature. The myoelectric arm must be carefully designed and fitted to the individual using it (Caldwell, Buck, Lovely, & Scott, 1985; Apostolos, 1985).

A communication aid is used with a person having limited or total inability to speak, usually from lack of motor control. This condition may be a result of congenital anomaly, accident, or a temporary condition.

Speechlessness may or may not be accompanied by cognitive language impairment; frequently nonspeaking students are multiply handicapped. Such students have needs in two of three areas: speech, mobility, and self-care. There is no typical candidate for a communication aid. The student may have cerebral palsy, mental retardation, or any of a number of disabilities that severely limit conversation, writing, and interaction with instructional or vocational materials. The communication device serves a prosthetic function, replacing natural speech, writing, and drawing with output in the form of audible speech (synthetic or recorded), written text, or graphics (Randal, 1983).

The terms nonvocal or nonverbal have been used to describe the student requiring an augmentative speech device. Such terms are not satisfactory because the student may have vocalizations, some intelligible speech that is functional, and even intact verbal skills including reading and writing. The term allolingual has been suggested by Baker (1982), but it has not found widespread acceptance. The most acceptable current term to describe students having no functional speech and those using augmentative communication systems is nonspeaking. Augmentative communication systems may incorporate any existing speech as one mode of communication.

The multiply physically handicapped student requires access not only to speaking and writing, but also to devices in the environment: appliances, lights, doors, alarm systems, telephones, and transportation systems. In this area, assistive devices provide control of such necessary implements through the same mechanism or control interface that the individual may use to obtain control of his or her communication aid.

The third area of assistive device application is in providing access to the large body of educational materials and vocational opportunities afforded by the computer. Many assistive devices, from simple mechanical keyguards to sophisticated high-technology devices such as keyboard emulators and infrared data transmitters, have been designed solely for this purpose and are now readily available. Computer technology and its availability has broadened the sophistication of assistive devices substantially, and change is now quite rapid.

REFERENCES

Apostolos, M.K. (1985). An application of aesthetics in the use of a robotic arm. *Proceedings of the Eighth Annual Conference on Rehabilitation Technology.* Memphis, TN: Rehabilitation Engineering Society of North America.

Baker, B. (1982). Is a rose a rose? *Communication Outlook, 4*(2), 3–18.

Caldwell, R.R., Buck, C.S., Lovely, D.F., & Scott, R.N. (1985). A myoelectric b/e prosthesis system for young children. *Proceedings of the Eighth Annual Conference on Rehabilitation Technology.* Memphis, TN: Rehabilitation Engineering Society of North America.

Randal, J. (1983). *Health technology case study 26: Assistive devices for severe speech impairments.* Washington, DC: U.S. Congress, Office of Technology Assessment, OTA-HCS-26.

Webster, J.G., Cook, A.M., Tompkins, W.J., & Vanderheiden, G.C. (1985). *Electronic devices for rehabilitation.* New York: Wiley.

See also **Augmentative Communication Systems; Communication Boards; Electronic Communication Aids**

ASSOCIATION FOR CHILDHOOD EDUCATION INTERNATIONAL (ACEI)

Founded in 1892, The Association for Childhood Education International (ACEI) is a not-for-profit professional education association of educators, parents, and other caregivers interested in promoting quality education practices for children. The organization was originally conceived to provide a formal organization to promote the interest and professionalism of the kindergarten movement throughout the world. With over 11,000 members in the United States and Canada, ACEI is the oldest organization of its kind. Members participate in local and state group activities, including meetings, workshops, and regional conferences. Annual Study Conferences have been held each year since 1896 to share ideas and contribute to the standard of excellence in teaching in all arenas, such as public and private day care centers, kindergartens, elementary schools, middle schools, high schools, and university-level teacher education programs.

The mission of ACEI is to promote the inherent rights, education, and well-being of all children, from infancy through early adolescence, in the home, school, and community. The organization is member-driven and is guided by a dynamic philosophy of education that is flexible and responsive to human needs in a changing society. Members are dedicated to a holistic, child-centered approach to education that considers the child's experiences in the home, school, community, and world.

A library, including volumes on childhood and elementary education, is maintained at association headquarters. Association offices are located at 17904 Georgia Avenue, Suite 215, Olney, MD 20832.

ASSOCIATION FOR CHILDREN AND ADULTS WITH LEARNING DISABILITIES (ACLD)

See LEARNING DISABILITIES ASSOCIATION.

ASSOCIATION FOR THE ADVANCEMENT OF BEHAVIOR THERAPY (AABT)

The Association for Advancement of the Behavioral Therapies was founded in 1966 and renamed the Association for the Advancement of Behavior Therapy (AABT) in 1968.

Headquartered in New York City, the AABT is a not-for-profit organization of over 4,500 mental health professionals and students who utilize and/or are interested in empirically based behavior therapy and cognitive behavior therapy. Membership is interdisciplinary and consists of psychologists, psychiatrists, social workers, physicians, nurses, and other mental health professionals who treat over 90 mental health problems. AABT does not certify its members.

Among its activities, the AABT sponsors training programs and lectures aimed at professionals and semiprofessionals, provides communication accessibility among behavior therapists interested in similar areas of research or specific problems, and maintains a speaker's bureau. Affiliates of the Association conduct training meetings, workshops, seminars, case demonstrations, and discussion groups. In addition, the AABT holds committees on continuing and public education and provides referrals to the general public upon request (a $5 postage and handling fee is required). A Fact Sheet regarding the problem for which help is being sought and the pamphlet, *Guidelines for Choosing a Behavior Therapist,* are included with mailed referrals. Beginning in approximately September 1998, referrals can be obtained by visiting AABT's website at www.aabt.org/aabt.

ASSOCIATION FOR THE GIFTED, THE

Founded in 1958, The Association for the Gifted is one of the 17 divisions of The Council for Exceptional Children. The purposes of this association are to (1) promote the welfare and education of children and youth with gifts, talents, and/or high potential; (2) improve educational opportunities for individuals from all diverse groups with gifts, talents, and/or high potential; (3) sponsor and foster activities to develop the field of gifted education, such as the dissemination of information, the conduct of research, and other scholarly investigations; (4) support and encourage specialized professional preparation for educators of individuals with gifts, talents, and/or high potential, as well as for professional persons in related fields; and (5) work with organizations, agencies, families, or individuals whose purposes are consistent with those of The Association for the Gifted.

Membership inquiries should be made to The Association for the Gifted, The Council for Exceptional Children, 1920 Association Drive, Reston, VA 20191-1589. Only members of The Council for Exceptional Children are eligible to join. Special membership categories for students and parents and professionals are available for those who qualify for these discounted membership rates.

ASSOCIATION OF BLACK PSYCHOLOGISTS

The Association of Black Psychologists (ABPsi) was founded in San Francisco in 1968 when a number of black psychologists from across the country met to discuss the serious problems facing black psychologists and the larger black community. The founding members began building an organization through which they could confront the long-neglected needs of black professionals. They also hoped to have a positive impact on the mental health of the black community through programs, services, training, and advocacy. The Association is organized into four regions as well as a student division. From the original group, the membership of ABPsi has grown into an international organization of over 1,300 psychologists and mental health professionals, committed to addressing the mental health issues of individuals throughout the African diaspora.

The main offices of the Association of Black Psychologists can be reached at P.O. Box 55999, Washington, DC 20040-5999, or by telephone at (202) 722-0808.

ASSOCIATIVE LEARNING

Associative learning, as demonstrated in the classical conditioning experiments of Pavlov (1927), is based on the concept that events or ideas that are experienced at the same time tend to become associated with each other. When a new (conditioned) stimulus is presented with an old (unconditioned) stimulus, the conditioned stimulus assumes the capability of eliciting a (conditioned) response almost identical to the original (unconditioned) response. The conditioned stimulus should be presented about half a second before the unconditioned stimulus for maximum effectiveness.

Associative learning is routinely applied when students recognize words, spell, and recall math facts. A number of remedial techniques are also based on the associative principle. Multisensory approaches to reading, which presume the formation of associative bonds across sensory modalities, have been successful in remediating deficits in mildly and severely reading-disabled children and in retarded students (Sutaria, 1982). Visual imagery training, in which children learn to associate mental pictures with printed text, has been shown to improve learning-disabled students' reading comprehension (Clark, Warner, Alley, Deshler & Shumaker, 1981).

Retarded children, for whom associative skills are often an area of relative strength, have improved their memory performance when taught to pair words according to their conceptual similarity (Lathey & Tobias, 1981). Associative learning is a fundamental principle of teaching, and children's associative learning skills can be corrected and compensated for by using a variety of techniques (Woolfolk, 1995).

REFERENCES

Clark, F., Warner, M., Alley, G., Deshler, D., Shumaker, J., Vetter, A., & Nolan, R. (1981). *Visual imagery and self questioning.* Washington, DC: Bureau of Education for the Handicapped. (ERIC Document Reproduction Service No. ED 217 655)

Lathey, J.W., & Tobias, S. (1981, April). *Associative and conceptual training of retarded and normal children.* Paper presented at the annual meeting of the American Educational Research Association, Los Angeles. (ERIC Document Reproduction Service No. ED 206 139)

Pavlov, I.P. (1927). *Conditioned reflexes.* London: Oxford University Press.

Sutaria, S. (1982). *Multisensory approach to teaching of reading to learning disabled students.* Paper presented at the annual meeting of the World Congress on Reading, Dublin, Ireland. (ERIC Document Reproduction Service No. ED 246 600)

Woolfolk, A.E. (1995). *Educational psychology* (6th ed.). Boston: Allyn & Bacon.

See also **Conditioning; Revisualization**

ASTHMA

Asthma has been recognized and described for more than 200 years and is one of the most common lung diseases of childhood. It is a difficulty in breathing caused by obstruction to the flow of air in the bronchial tubes because of swelling of the lining membranes, contraction of the surrounding musculature, and plugging of the tubes by mucus. This is inevitably accompanied by wheezing. Other symptoms are sometimes present such as a persistent cough and shortness of breath. The distress of asthma attacks is sometimes worsened by simple activities like laughing or lying down (Asthma and Allergy Foundation of America, 1980).

Asthma can be classified on a continuum, with intrinsic or perennial asthma (a type of asthma that presents symptoms all year round) at one end and extrinsic or seasonal asthma (which tends to be aggravated during certain seasons, especially the fall) at the other. Treatment for asthma must be continuously evaluated because of its variability. Medical treatment falls into two categories: the first is immunotherapy, which is the process of desensitizing the child's allergies by injecting the child with progressively increasing amounts of the allergen. Effectiveness of this treatment is limited by compliance to the administration of allergen shots. The second category is pharmacologic therapy. The most common drug prescribed is theophyllene, which is a bronchodilator that reduces the frequency and the severity of attacks. If this or other medication fails to control the attacks, then corticosteroids are used.

Psychological factors are usually not sufficient by themselves to cause asthma. For this and other reasons psychotherapy is not used as a way to control the disease. It has, however, proven effective with psychological problems resulting from the disorder. Broncho constriction in asthmatic patients can result in anxiety in both patients and their parents. Relaxation techniques, biofeedback, and systematic desensitization have also proven effective in managing some cases. Parentectomy (Kapotes, 1977), the removal of patients from the home environment that appears to trigger the attack, is sometimes recommended. Recently, a number of comprehensive self-management programs for asthma have been developed. These are designed to provide patients with the skills to assume responsibility for controlling the affliction. Such programs as the *Living with Asthma* project

(Greer, Backial, & Leung, 1984; Greer, Ullman, & Leung, 1984) evolved from the treatment and rehabilitation program established at CARIH. Patients are provided with information about the mechanics of breathing, the changes that occur during attacks, triggers of attacks, and the medication to control them. When an asthmatic knows his or her condition is due to allergies, then an effective way to control attacks is to avoid the allergens that he or she is sensitive to (Flod, Franz, & Yalant, 1976).

Asthmatic children in educational settings face the problem that teachers may be unfamiliar with the condition and frightened by attacks. It is very important that teachers have meetings with the parents, the child, and the physician to learn about the child's condition and to become familiar with procedures to be followed in case of an attack. Physical education teachers can usually respect a child's knowledge of his or her condition even though exercise can trigger attacks. Preexercise medication can sometimes be useful in preventing attacks. School absenteeism could be reduced by realizing that, through medication, attacks can be controlled. If asthma is under control, a child should be capable of participating in all educational activities. Children with asthma are at increased risk of behavioral and emotional problems but asthma is too complex to allow specification of specific outcomes without considering the individual child (Greer, 1994).

REFERENCES

Asthma and Allergy Foundation of America. (1980). Handbook for the asthmatic. *Asthma and Allergy Foundation of America Publication.*

Evans, H.F. (1981). What happens when a child has asthma. *American Lung Association Publication.*

Flod, N.E., Franz, M.L., & Yalant, S.P. (1976). Recent advances in bronchial asthma. *American Journal of Diseases of Children, 130,* 890–899.

Greer, T. (1994). Asthma: Psychological issues. In R. Olson, L. Mullins, J. Gillman, & J. Chaney (Eds.), *The sourcebook of pediatric psychology* (pp. 61–69). Boston: Allyn & Bacon.

Greer, T.L., Backiel, M., & Leung, P. (1984). *Living with asthma: Manual for teaching self-management skills to children.* Washington, DC: U.S. Department of Health and Human Services.

Greer, T.L., Ullman, S., & Leung, P. (1984). *Living with asthma: Manual for teaching adults the self-management of childhood asthma.* Washington, DC: U.S. Department of Health and Human Services.

Kapotes, C. (1977). Emotional factors in chronic asthma. *Journal of Asthma Research, 15,* 5–14.

See also **Allergic Disorders; Biofeedback**

ASTIGMATISM

Astigmatism is a refractive error that causes reduced visual acuity and a lack of sharply focused, clear vision. In astigmatism, the curve of the cornea is irregular. Because of this irregularity, some light rays may come to focus in front of the retina, some on the retina, and some at the theoretical point behind it. The result is distorted or blurred vision and headache or eye fatigue after intensive close work.

Astigmatism does not seem to be clearly related to difficulties in learning to read. In some cases it has even been associated with better than average reading (Lerner, 1985). The special educator should be aware of the symptoms of astigmatism (Rouse & Ryan, 1984): headaches; discomfort in tasks that demand visual interpretation; problems seeing far as well as near; red eyes; distortion in size, shape, or inclination of objects; frowning and squinting at desk tasks; and nausea in younger or lower-functioning students. Astigmatism is generally correctable with eyeglasses or contact lenses, which should be worn full-time by affected students. These students may be helped in the classroom by being moved closer to the front of the room and by a reduction in the amount of time spent on near tasks.

REFERENCES

Lerner, J. (1985). *Learning disabilities: Theories, diagnoses, and teaching strategies.* Boston: Houghton Mifflin.

Rouse, M.W., & Ryan, J.B. (1984). Teacher's guide to vision problems. *Reading Teacher, 38*(3), 306–317.

See also Visual Acuity; Visual Training

ASYMMETRICAL TONIC NECK REFLEX (ATNR)

Asymmetrical tonic neck reflex (ATNR) is one of a group of postural central nervous system reflexes that in the normal child is inhibited and incorporated into more sophisticated motor skills. The ATNR can be demonstrated easily in normal infants to about 40 weeks by placing the child on the back and turning the head to the left or right. As the face is turned to the left, the left arm extends and the right arm flexes, bringing the right hand flexed to the skull side of the head simultaneous with flexion of the leg on that and the opposite side. In the normal child with no pathology, this reflex is gradually inhibited; thus, children of 24 to 36 months can reach for toys in front of them; look to the side and still bring a cracker or spoon to the mouth when the head is in midposition; and cross the midline. Later on, the child can sustain weight on the arms and knees, and rotation of the head will not result in collapse or support on the skull side arm.

The child who has central nervous system damage above the level of the midbrain (usually considered to be in the basal ganglia, cerebral cortex, or both) will demonstrate a persistent ATNR well beyond the age of 1 year, with accompanying profound damage into adult life. The child with severe ATNR finds self-feeding impossible. Persistence of ATNR can interfere with sitting and standing balance and dressing and writing, and make voluntary motion difficult or impossible.

See also Central Nervous System

ATARAX

Atarax (hydroxyzine hydrochloride) may be used for symptomatic relief of anxiety and tension associated with psychoneurosis and as an adjunct in organic disease states in which anxiety is manifested. It also may be used as a sedative; the most common manifestation of overdosage is extreme sedation. Other uses include treatment of pruritis owed to allergic conditions such as chronic urticaria and dermatoses. Although not a cortical depressant, its action may be due to suppression of activity in certain key regions of the subcortical area of the central nervous system. Adverse reactions may include dryness of mouth and drowsiness, with the possibility of tremor, involuntary motor activity, and convulsions reported in cases where higher than recommended doses have been used.

A brand name of Roeris Pharmaceuticals, it is available in tablets of 10, 25, 50, and 100 milligrams, and as a syrup. The recommended dosage for children under 6 years of age is 50 mg daily in divided doses, and for children over 6 years of age 50 to 100 mg daily in divided doses. When used as a sedative, dosage is recommended to be 0.6 mg/kg (milligram per kilogram of body weight) at all childhood ages, and 50 to 100 mg for adults.

See also Antihistamines; Benadryl; Drug Therapy

ATAXIA

Ataxia is a type of cerebral palsy caused by the loss of cerebellar control. It is characterized by an unbalanced gait. An ataxic gait is often referred to as a drunken gait, as it resembles the walk of someone who is intoxicated.

According to Batshaw and Perret (1981), "The cerebellum coordinates the action of the voluntary muscles and times their contractions so that movements are performed smoothly and accurately" (p. 163). That is, the cerebellum senses where the limb is in space (based on input to the cerebellum), estimates where the target is, integrates the information, and then carries out the infinitesimal corrections necessary to compensate for inaccuracies in motor output, thereby maintaining fluid movement.

A child whose primary diagnosis is ataxia has poor righting and equilibrium reactions, and a staggering, lurching, irregular, and broad-based gait (Brown, 1973). According to Connor, Williamson, and Siepp (1978), the child has difficulty sustaining posture, as well as shifting posture in a coordinated manner. He or she often stumbles and falls. This postural instability may make the child overly cautious. The child may stiffen his or her trunk abnormally in order to increase stability. When walking, the child may visually fix on an object in the environment in an effort to maintain postural control. According to Walsch (1963), when an older child attempts purposeful reaching, he or she often overshoots the mark because of the presence of a distal, wavering tremor. Nystagmus is often present.

REFERENCES

Batshaw, M.L., & Perret, Y.M. (1981). *Children with handicaps: a medical primer.* Baltimore: Brookes.

Brown, J.E. (1973). Disease of the cerebellum. In A.B. Baker & L.H. Baker (Eds.), *Clinical neurology, Vol. II.* New York: Harper & Row.

Connor, F.P., Williamson, G.G., & Siepp, J.M. (1978). *Program guide for infants and toddlers with neuromotor and other developmental disabilities.* New York: Teachers College Press.

Walsch, G. (1963). *Cerebellum, posture, and cerebral palsy* (Clinics in Developmental Medicine, No. 8). London: Heinemann Medical Books.

See also **Cerebral Palsy; Cerebellar Disorders**

ATHETOSIS

Athetosis is a central nervous system disorder characterized by slow, writhing movements, most notable in the extremities. These involuntary muscle movements have been described also as wormlike or snakelike. The actual movements consist of alternating flexion–extension and supination–pronation of the limbs, and are usually associated with increased, though variable, muscle tone (Chow, Durard, Feldman, & Mills 1979).

This is the most common form of cerebral palsy (CP) and accounts for approximately 15 to 30% of children with that diagnosis; however, the overall incidence rate is declining, probably because of improved neonatal intensive care (Batshaw & Perret, 1981). The condition, also known as choreo-athetoid CP, often occurs in conjunction with other forms of CP, especially spasticity. As a form of cerebral palsy, athetosis is one of a group of nonprogressive neuromotor disorders caused by earlier brain damage. Unlike other common forms of CP, the athetoid type presents a problem of controlling movement and posture rather than a difficulty in initiating voluntary movement. The uncontrolled, purposeless, involuntary movements associated with athetosis are not evidenced during sleep. Although the precise nature of the central nervous system insult is often indeterminable, among known causes may be various prenatal factors (e.g., anoxia, blood group incompatibilities, excessive radiation dosage during gestation, physical injuries, various maternal infections); perinatal factors (e.g., prematurity, head trauma, asphyxia, kernicterus); and postnatal factors (e.g., head trauma, hemorrhage, infections of the brain or cranial linings). In the United States, one to two children per thousand may be affected by CP, including athetosis or mixed cerebral palsy with athetosis. It is believed that in the more pure athetoid type of CP, the site of lesion is generally in the basal ganglia or extrapyramidal track (Kandel, Schwartz, & Jessell, 1991; Vaughan, McKay, & Behrman, 1979).

Secondary problems important to the special educator frequently accompany athetosis. Early difficulties may be observed in sucking, feeding, chewing, and swallowing. Special techniques to deal with these problems may come from speech/language pathologists, occupational therapists, physical therapists, or physicians. Speech articulation is often impaired and drooling may be present. In addition, hearing loss, epilepsy, and mental retardation may exist simultaneously. However, careful assessment of cognitive functioning is essential because both speech and motor skills are affected.

REFERENCES

Batshaw, M.L., & Perret, Y.M. (1981). *Children with handicaps: A medical primer.* Baltimore: Brookes.

Chow, M.P., Durand, B.A., Feldman, M.N., & Mills, M.A. (1979). *Handbook of pediatric primary care.* New York: Wiley.

Kandel, E., Schwartz, J., Jessell, T. (1991). *Principles of Neural Science* (3rd ed.). New York: Elsevier.

Vaughan, V.C., McKay, R.J., & Behrman, R.E. (1979). *Nelson textbook of pediatrics.* Philadelphia: Saunders.

See also **Central Nervous System; Cerebral Palsy**

ATTENTION-DEFICIT/ HYPERACTIVITY DISORDER (ADHD)

Attention-Deficit/Hyperactivity Disorder (ADHD) is the most recent diagnostic label for children who exhibit developmentally inappropriate levels of inattention, impulsivity, and hyperactivity (American Psychiatric Association, 1994). Children with ADHD display diminished persistence of effort or have difficulty sustaining attention to tasks with little intrinsic value, exhibit excessive motor and/or vocal activity, and experience difficulty in inhibiting behavior to situational demands (Barkley, 1997). Behavioral disinhibition exhibited by these children is the sine qua non of the disorder (Barkley, 1998). Behavioral disinhibition, overactivity, and inattentiveness are the cardinal characteristics of this disorder, and these characteristics occur across a variety of settings (for example, home and school) with the magnitude of symptom presentation significantly fluctuating in different settings and with different caregivers (Barkley, 1998; Zentall, 1985).

Prevalence rates have been difficult to ascertain, as ADHD has not only been difficult to define but has also been difficult to precisely and objectively measure (Barkley, 1998). Prevalence estimates of ADHD in school-aged children have ranged from a low of 1% to a high of 12% (Frick, Strauss, Lahey, & Christ, 1993). Consensus among many experts in the field, however, suggests that approximately 3–5% of the school-aged population has ADHD (American Psychiatric Association, 1994).

Gender differences have also been reported. The proportion of males to females manifesting the disorder range from 2.5:1 to 5.1:1 with an average of approximately 3.4:1 among non-referred children (Szatmari, Offord, & Boyle, 1989). In clinic-referred samples, however, boys are six to nine times more likely than girls to be diagnosed with the disorder (Barkley, 1998). Research has found that girls with

ADHD are more impaired in their intelligence, less hyperactive, and less likely to exhibit other externalizing symptoms (like aggression, defiance, and conduct problems) and internalizing symptoms (like anxiety, depression, and withdrawn behaviors) than boys (Gaub & Carlson, 1997).

From a historical perspective, the concept of ADHD and the terms used to describe the disorder have undergone a series of revisions. These revisions have been in response to changes in the conceptualization of the disorder among clinical researchers. ADHD was first described in the scientific literature in 1902 (Still, 1902). Still described a group of children whose major difficulties were in the control of their own behavior. These children were of normal intelligence and poor child-rearing techniques had been ruled out. Still believed the major defect displayed by these children was in the moral control of their behavior or volitional inhibition. According to Still, the most distinguishing attribute of these children was their inappropriate social conduct.

Ebaugh (1923) and Strecker and Ebaugh (1924) reported on a group of children who were described as inattentive, impulsive, and socially disruptive. These children had survived the encephalitis outbreak in 1917–1918 in North America, but were left with significant behavioral and cognitive sequelae as a result of brain damage. Many of the characteristics displayed by these children are now incorporated into the concept of ADHD.

Research on the disorder showed resurgence in the 1940s and 1950s with the work of Laufer, Denhoff, and Solomons (1957) and Strauss and Lehtinen (1955). Strauss and Lehtinen described a group of children who were restless, impulsive, overactive, distractible, and inattentive. The researchers attributed the children's problems to brain damage, although direct evidence was weak or nonexistent. The term Minimal Brain Damage (MBD) was coined during this period of time and used to describe these children of the postencephalitic period. These children's greatest problem was their excessive activity levels.

In the 1960s, a number of disagreements arose in the psychiatric community regarding the Minimal Brain Damage label. The crux of the disagreements was due to the fact that there was a lack of clear evidence demonstrating a link between organic impairment and excessive activity levels. Thus, the Minimal Brain Damage label was replaced with a new term, Minimal Brain Dysfunction. The rationale behind the change in terminology was that behavioral symptoms alone could not be used to imply neurological impairment (Copeland & Love, 1991).

The term Minimal Brain Dysfunction was replaced with the term Hyperkinetic Reaction of Childhood in 1968 in the revised nomenclature of the American Psychiatric Association, Diagnostic and Statistical Manual of Mental Disorders, Second Edition (DSM-II; American Psychiatric Association, 1968). The primary diagnostic symptom of ADHD in the DSM-II was hyperactivity.

In the next decade, however, a shift in focus occurred in which attention problems became the most salient symptom of ADHD. Research suggested the inability to sustain and regulate attention was the critical feature of this disorder, rather than hyperactivity (Douglas & Peters, 1979). As a result, the term and description of the disorder was changed to Attention Deficit Disorder (Diagnostic and Statistical Manual of Mental Disorders, Third Edition [DSM-III]; American Psychiatric Association, 1980). The DSM-III also recognized a dichotomy in the disorder in which some children displayed only attention problems, whereas others exhibited both inattention and hyperactivity. The children with attention problems and hyperactivity were given the diagnostic label of Attention Deficit Disorder with Hyperactivity. In contrast, those children with attention problems only were labeled Attentional Deficit Disorder without Hyperactivity. The essential features of Attention Deficit Disorder included inattention, impulsivity, and hyperactivity.

Later in the decade, the DSM criteria for ADHD was revised again (Diagnostic and Statistical Manual of Mental Disorders, Third Edition, Revised [DSM-III-R]; American Psychiatric Association, 1987). In the DSM-III-R, Attention Deficit Disorder with Hyperactivity became known as Attention-Deficit Hyperactivity Disorder and Attention Deficit Disorder without Hyperactivity was removed as a subtype and relegated to a vaguely defined category known as Undifferentiated Attention Deficit Disorder. Attention-Deficit Hyperactivity Disorder was now classified as a disruptive behavioral disorder along with conduct disorder and oppositional defiant disorder. In the revised diagnostic criteria, which were empirically derived, children with affective disorders were now eligible to receive the diagnosis of ADHD, whereas in the past, these children were excluded from the ADHD diagnosis. Moreover, the revisions stressed the importance of assessing the developmental appropriateness of a child's symptoms relative to his or her mental age in determining whether he or she met the diagnostic criteria for the disorder.

The current definition of ADHD is found in the Diagnostic and Statistical Manual of Mental Disorders, Fourth Edition (DSM-IV; American Psychiatric Association, 1994). In the DSM-IV, ADHD symptoms are divided into two main categories, inattention and hyperactivity-impulsivity. Children must exhibit six of the nine symptoms in one or both categories to meet the criteria for one of the three subtypes of ADHD: ADHD-Predominately Inattentive Type, ADHD-Predominately Hyperactive-Impulsive Type, and ADHD-Combined Type. Moreover, the inattentive and/or hyperactive-impulsive symptoms must be present on a frequent basis for at least six months to be considered clinically significant. The symptoms must also be cross-situational (i.e., occur across two or more settings, such as the home and school settings). Some of the symptoms must also have been present before the age of seven.

Of the three subtypes, the ADHD-Combined Type is the most common. Children who meet the criteria for this subtype display both inattentive and hyperactive-impulsive behaviors. In contrast, the Predominately Inattentive Type describes those children who exhibit inattention but do not meet the diagnostic criteria for hyperactivity-impulsivity. These children have difficulty concentrating and completing work. Under the old DSM-III criteria, these children would have met the criteria for Attention Deficit Disorder without Hyperactivity. Currently, little is known about the third subtype, the Predominately Hyperactive-Impulsive Type. These children supposedly exhibit hyperactive-impulsive behavior but do not meet the diagnostic criteria for inattention. McBurnett, Lahey, and Pfiffner (1993) indicate a number of preschoolers fit this subtype.

Children with ADHD are at risk for developing comorbid disorders. Over 50% of the children with ADHD have at least one additional disorder (Barkley, 1998). The most prevalent comorbid psychiatric disorders seen with children with ADHD include conduct disorders, oppositional defiant disorders, anxiety disorders, major depression, bipolar disorders, and somatization disorders. Of these disorders, oppositional defiant disorders and conduct disorders are the most common disorders associated with ADHD. On the other hand, the co-occurrence of mood and anxiety disorders occurs somewhat less frequently in children with ADHD.

In addition to comorbid psychiatric disorders, children with ADHD are more likely to have significant social impairments. Poor peer relationships and misinterpretation of social cues have been reported (Barkley, 1998). These children are more likely to exhibit aggression toward their peers, which in turn, leads to peer rejection. In their relationships with adults, these children are less compliant to parental and teacher requests and receive a greater share of commands, reprimands, and punishment (Barkley, 1998). For parents, parent-training programs are available to address noncompliance. In addition, family therapy and individual counseling for children with ADHD are also available to address difficulties some children and families may encounter in association with the disorder.

A host of etiologies have been proposed throughout the years, including neurological aberrations (Werry et al., 1972), food additives (Feingold, 1975), fluorescent lighting (Frick et al., 1993), and environmental stressors (Barkley, 1981). Recently, neurological and genetic factors have received substantial empirical support as the greatest contributors to this disorder (Barkley, 1998). Possible genetic and neurological etiologies include pregnancy and birth complications (Hartsough & Lambert, 1985), acquired brain damage (Cruickshank, Eliason, & Merrifield, 1988), exposure to environmental toxins (Needleman, Schell, Bellinger, Leviton, & Alfred, 1990), infections (Mick, Biederman, & Faraone, 1996), and genetic effects (Edelbrock, Rende, Plomin, & Thompson, 1995). Genetic and/or neurological factors are thought to disrupt a final common pathway in the nervous system known as the prefrontal cortical-striatal network, and this disruption in the neural pathway may give rise to the disorder (Barkley, 1998). Based on family aggregation studies, adoption studies, twin studies, and molecular genetic research, hereditary factors appear to play the major role in the occurrence of ADHD symptoms in chil-

dren (Barkley, 1998). On the other hand, environmental factors, such as social adversity and family factors, have received some support in the literature as possible etiologies (Carlson, Jacobvitz, & Sroufe, 1995). Family dynamics, parental characteristics, and parenting styles have been highlighted in this line of research (Silverman & Ragusa, 1992). Barkley (1998), however, believes psychosocial factors play a secondary role to the genetic and neurological factors. According to Barkley, environmental factors are contributors to the persistence of the disorder over development, and may simply intensify the symptoms that already exist.

Perhaps the changing diagnostic nosology and the variability in prevalence rates for this very complex disorder have been a function of inadequate assessment techniques in child psychology, psychiatry, and special education. Although new assessment instruments have been developed, the search continues for accurate and reliable measures of ADHD, as no single test has been devised that definitely tells a clinician that a child has ADHD (Gordon & Barkley, 1998). Thus, a multimethod assessment approach has been recommended in which information from a variety of measures, sources, and settings is collected and analyzed (Bradley & DuPaul, 1997).

According to Barkley and Edwards (1998), a comprehensive evaluation of a child with ADHD involves three critical components: the clinical interview, the medical examination, and the completion of behavioral rating scales. When feasible, psychological tests and observations may be included to aid in differential diagnosis or yield additional information about the presence and severity of cognitive impairments associated with some cases of ADHD. Psychological tests incorporated into ADHD-related evaluations tend to fall into four categories: (1) intelligence/achievement measures, (2) neuropsychological batteries, (3) individual neuropsychological tests, and (4) projective/personality measures (Gordon & Barkley, 1998).

Clinical interviews are conducted with parents and teachers to obtain highly descriptive information about the child and the child's psychological adjustment at home and at school. Information about school, family, and treatment histories are also gleaned from these interviews. The child is also interviewed, with the content of the interview being dependent upon the child's age. For a preschooler, the interview is a means of establishing rapport and noting the child's appearance, behavior, developmental characteristics, and general demeanor. For an older child or adolescent, the purpose of the interview is to obtain information about the child or adolescent's perspective of the reason for the referral, evaluation, and difficulties encountered (Barkley & Edwards, 1998).

In addition to the interview, it is imperative that a child has a complete medical examination. In the past, these examinations tended to be extremely brief and produced unreliable or invalid results (Costello et al., 1988). The pediatric medical examination should consist of two parts, the medical interview and the physical examination. The purpose of the medical interview is to focus on differential diagnosis, to evaluate possible coexisting medical conditions, and to determine if any physical conditions exist that preclude the use of medication in the treatment of a child with ADHD. The physical exam, on the other hand, includes numerous screening tests, a neurological examination, and a neurodevelopmental exam (Barkley & Edwards, 1998).

The third component of a comprehensive evaluation is the completion of behavioral rating scales. Child behavior checklists and rating scales provide a wealth of information with little investment of time required. Barkley and Edwards (1998) recommend that parents, teachers, and children, if applicable, complete a broad band rating scale, a narrow band rating scale, and additional scales depending upon the child's problems. Broad band rating scales provide coverage of the major dimensions of child psychopathology. Examples of broad band rating scales include the *Behavior Assessment System for Children*–Parent Rating Scale, Teacher Rating Scale, and Self-Report of Personality (BASC; Reynolds & Kamphaus, 1994) and the *Child Behavior Checklist*–Parent Report Form (Achenbach & Edelbrock, 1983), Teacher Report Form (Achenbach & Edelbrock, 1986a), and Youth Self-Report (Achenbach & Edelbrock, 1986b). In contrast, narrow band scales are used to assess specific symptoms of ADHD. Examples of narrow band scales include the *Disruptive Behavior Rating Scale* (Barkley & Murphy, 1998) and the *Child Attention Profile* (Barkley, 1990). Additional behavioral ratings may be included to address specific areas of concern, for example, peer relations or adaptive functioning.

Besides Barkley and Edwards's (1998) approach to assessing children with ADHD in a clinical setting, DuPaul (1992) presented a model for assessing ADHD within the school setting. DuPaul's model is based on a multimethod assessment approach and includes five stages. Following the initial referral of the child, Stage One of the model involves screening. The child's teacher is asked to complete teacher-rating scales, which assess ADHD symptomatology. Stage Two involves the multimethod assessment of ADHD. Stage Two includes teacher and parent interviews and completion of behavior rating scales, a review of the child's educational records, observations of the child in the school setting, and a review of the child's academic portfolio. During Stage Three, the assessment data are evaluated and interpreted with respect to the DSM-IV diagnostic criteria for ADHD. A treatment plan is developed in Stage Four followed by an assessment of treatment outcome during Stage Five. Based on a multiassessment model, a variety of interventions may be developed and implemented to optimize the child's learning and educational success.

Various treatments for children with ADHD have been widely researched. Interventions have ranged from fluorescent lighting (Sprague, 1979) to dietary regimens (Feingold, 1975). Stimulant medication is the most common form of treatment for ADHD (Milich, Licht, Murphy, & Pelham, 1989). It has been estimated that between 1% and 2% of the school-age population receive stimulant medication for the treatment of ADHD, with methylphenidate (Ritalin) being the most commonly used medication (Safer & Krager, 1988). The primary response to stimulant medication has included an increase in attention and a decrease in impulsive, disruptive, and inappropriate behavior (DuPaul & Rapport, 1993). Collaboration among medical and school personnel and parents is needed to implement clinical drug trials to ensure that the optimal drug dosage level is obtained to optimize a child's learning (DuPaul, Barkley, & Connor, 1998). Research has demonstrated short-term enhancement of behavioral, academic, and social functioning of children with ADHD who are treated with stimulant medication (Pelham, 1993). In contrast, limited long-term effectiveness of stimulant medication has been reported (Evans & Pelham, 1991). The medication's failure to "normalize" children's behavior and academic performance relative to their peers has led to an active search to identify more viable alternatives (Evans & Pelham, 1991).

In 1991, the U.S. Department of Education recognized for the first time that children with ADHD may be entitled to special assistance at school under Section 504 of the Rehabilitation Act of 1973 or special education and related services under the category of "Other Health Impaired" of the Individuals with Disabilities Education Act (IDEA; Davila, William, & McDonald, 1991). Children with ADHD, however, do not automatically qualify for services under these two pieces of legislation. Significant impairment in school performance along with a diagnosis of ADHD is a necessary condition for children with ADHD to qualify for special services. Specifically, if it can be demonstrated that a child's handicap significantly interferes with learning, then the child can be classified under IDEA as Other Health Impaired. On the other hand, if the child is classified as handicapped and the child's handicap results in a substantial limitation in learning, but the child is not eligible for special education services, then the child qualifies for special services under Section 504. It is estimated that 35–57% of the children with ADHD receive special services, with the majority of these children receiving special services in the general education classroom or through "pullout" resource/content mastery programs (Barkley, DuPaul, & McMurray, 1990; Reid, Maag, Vasa, & Wright, 1994).

Children with ADHD are at risk for a number of cognitive and academic problems. In the cognitive domain, children with ADHD are more likely to be behind in comparison to their classmates in intellectual development. Academic difficulties in reading, spelling, mathematics, and handwriting have been reported (Barkley, 1998). It had been estimated that up to 80% of children with ADHD might have an associated learning disability or achievement problems (Semrud-Clikeman et al., 1992). Deficits in both reading and mathematics have been reported in children with ADHD (Reid et al., 1994). Semrud-Clikeman et al. (1992) found 38% of children with ADHD have a reading disability. Students with ADHD may also have a poor sense of time, decreased nonverbal and verbal working memory, impaired planning ability, reduced sensitivity to errors, decreased attention span, difficulty with simultaneous and sequential tasks, and possible impairment in goal-directed behavior (Barkley, 1998; Reardon & Naglierli, 1992). Language and motor difficulties may be present as well (Barkley, 1998). Researchers have found these children are more likely to have academic difficulties, failing grades, grade retention, and dropping out (Barkley, 1990). Moreover, behaviorally, children with ADHD show increased motor and vocal behavior, poor response inhibition, limited persistence, and diminished compliance with rules (Pfiffner & Barkley, 1998). The question then arises whether the symptoms of ADHD interfere with a child's learning, or if a child with learning problems exhibits ADHD symptoms in response to his or her learning difficulties (Frick & Lahey, 1991). This may be the case for some children; however, researchers have noted that many children with ADHD achieve just as well academically as children without ADHD (Reid et al., 1994)

In the classroom, a child with ADHD can be a challenge. Educational success for a child depends not only on the child but on the teacher who is knowledgeable about ADHD and who is willing to develop and foster a positive teacher-student relationship with the child. Pfiffner and Barkley (1998) suggest teachers should be aware of the following:

1. Children with ADHD may experience some difficulty in their academic and social endeavors, even when intervention strategies have been implemented, due to the refractory nature of ADHD symptomatology.

2. Children with ADHD have difficulty sustaining attention, effort, and motivation, and inhibiting behavior in a consistent manner over time. Thus, children with ADHD may encounter difficulty in performing tasks due to limited attention and lack of motivation rather than lack of ability.

3. Children with ADHD need more structure, more frequent positive consequences, more consistent negative consequences, and modifications in assigned work.

4. Interventions implemented in the school setting must be applied with consistency.

Many schools have adopted collaborative consultation models whereby a consultant (i.e., a school psychologist) works with consultees (i.e., regular and special education teachers; see Kratochwill & Bergen, 1990; or parents and regular and special educators, see Conoley & Conoley, 1992; Sheridan, 1993) to address the difficulties encountered by a child, such as a child with ADHD (Dunson, Hughes, & Jackson, 1994). Through collaborative consultation, the consultant and consultees work together to improve the fit between the child's characteristics and the school and/or home settings. The consultant and consultees assess the child's needs and design and implement intervention strategies to increase the child's success in academic and nonacademic endeavors.

A variety of nonpharmacological interventions have been used with children with ADHD in the school and home settings. Modifications in the environment and/or task characteristics associated with a child's difficulties are one group of viable behavioral strategies (Bradley & DuPaul, 1997). These strategies focus on the antecedents of behavior. An example of these strategies may include moving a child's desk closer to the teacher and away from distractors to increase the opportunity for a child to maintain his or her attention.

Another approach used with children with ADHD is teacher administered consequences contingent upon children's performance of particular target behaviors. These strategies are the most commonly used behavioral interventions with students with ADHD. A combination of positive consequences (like teacher praise, tangible rewards, and token economies) and negative consequences (such as response costs, reprimands, and time out) administered immediately after the behavior, with more positive consequences than negative consequences being delivered, seem to be the most effective (Pfiffner & Barkley, 1998).

Peer strategies represent another group of behavioral interventions used with children with ADHD. Peer tutoring and classwide peer tutoring have produced positive effects on both classroom behavior and academic performance for students with ADHD (DuPaul & Henningson, 1993). Peer tutoring strategies appear to be most effective when children with ADHD are paired with well-balanced and conscientious students (Pfiffner & Barkley, 1998).

Home-school contingencies represent a fourth group of strategies used with students with ADHD. Home-school contingency programs are among the most widely used strategies (Pfiffner & Barkley, 1998). Home-school contingencies require collaboration between the home and school systems in order to implement and to produce effective results. A home-school note is an example of a home-school contingency program. The advantages associated with these interventions are that they address the behavior across a variety of settings, which increases the probability of generalization and maintenance of the desired behavior(s). These strategies are less labor-intensive for teachers as well (Kelley, 1990).

Self-management strategies are also used with children with ADHD. These strategies are derived from cognitive or cognitive-behavioral approaches. Self-management interventions emphasize the development of self-control and include self-monitoring, self-instruction, self-reinforcement, and problem-solving strategies. Self-management strategies, such as self-instruction and problem solving approaches, that focus on cognitive control rather than contingency management, such as self-monitoring and self-reinforcement, have shown less positive results with children with ADHD (DuPaul & Stoner, 1994). Overall, self-management strategies have fallen short of initial expectations (Abikoff & Gittelman, 1985; Braswell et al.,

1997). Cognitive or cognitive-behavioral interventions are not as strong, durable, or generalizable as once believed, and these strategies are not superior to the traditional behavioral programs used with children with ADHD (Pfiffner & Barkley, 1998).

Based on the research to date, however, no single treatment has been documented to be overwhelmingly successful with children with ADHD (Bradley & DuPaul, 1997). Instead, research shows the need for multi-modal approaches implemented across a variety of settings (Abikoff, 1991). Multi-modal approaches may involve the integration of medication, such as Ritalin, with specific therapies. Studies have generally indicated that cognitive therapy in combination with stimulant medication is more efficacious than stimulant medication alone (Rapport, Carlson, Kelly, Pataki, 1993). Similarly, behavior therapy in combination with stimulant medication has been shown to be more effective than stimulant medication alone (Carlson, Pelham, Milich, & Dixon, 1992). Thus, multi-modal approaches offer a glimmer of hope in the empirical horizon to address the short- and long-term effects of this disorder.

The clinical myth that ADHD bears a benign prognosis in adolescence and adulthood has not been empirically supported. Over 70% of ADHD children are likely to display the ADHD symptomatology in adolescence (Barkley, Fisher, et al., 1990; Barkley, Anastopoulous, Guevremont, & Fletcher, 1991), but the symptoms dissipate to some extent with age (Hart, Lahey, Loeber, Applegate, & Frick, 1995). Lower levels of hyperactivity and improvement in attention span and impulse control have been reported among adolescents with ADHD (Hart et al., 1995). Cognitive and behavioral difficulties, however, persist with some adolescents. Oppositional and antisocial behavior have been reported in 25–45% of teenagers with ADHD (e.g., Biederman et al., 1996). Moreover, academic outcomes are considerably poorer for adolescents with ADHD in comparison to normal adolescents, as teenagers with ADHD are more likely to fail a grade, be suspended, or be expelled from school (Barkley, 1998). Contradictory findings for alcohol and drug use among adolescents with ADHD have been reported; however, more recent research indicates cigarette and alcohol use is more prevalent among these teenagers (Barkley, Fisher, et al., 1990). Poorer social relationships have also been documented with these adolescents (Barkley, 1998). These results run contrary to the clinical lore that ADHD dissipates during the teenage years. For many, this disorder lasts a lifetime (Weiss & Hechtman, 1993).

REFERENCES

Abikoff, M. (1991). Cognitive training in ADHD children: Less to it than meets the eye. *Journal of Learning Disabilities, 24*(4), 205–209.

Abikoff, M., & Gittelman, R. (1985). Hyperactive children treated with stimulants: Is cognitive training a useful adjunct? *Archives of General Psychiatry, 42,* 953–961.

Achenbach, T.M., & Edelbrock, C.S. (1983). *Child Behavior Checklist–Parent Report Form.* Burlington, VT: University of Vermont.

Achenbach, T.M., & Edelbrock, C.S. (1986a). *Child Behavior Checklist–Teacher Report Form.* Burlington, VT: University of Vermont.

Achenbach, T.M., & Edelbrock, C.S. (1986b). *Child Behavior Checklist–Youth Self-Report.* Burlington, VT: University of Vermont.

American Psychiatric Association. (1968). *Diagnostic and Statistical Manual of Mental Disorders* (2nd ed.). Washington, DC: American Psychiatric Association.

American Psychiatric Association. (1980). *Diagnostic and Statistical Manual of Mental Disorders* (3rd ed.). Washington, DC: American Psychiatric Association.

American Psychiatric Association. (1987). *Diagnostic and Statistical Manual of Mental Disorders* (3rd ed., Revised). Washington, DC: American Psychiatric Association.

American Psychiatric Association. (1994). *Diagnostic and Statistical Manual of Mental Disorders* (4th ed.). Washington, DC: American Psychiatric Association.

Barkley, R.A. (1981). *Hyperactive children.* New York: Guilford.

Barkley, R.A. (1990). *Attention deficit hyperactivity disorder: A handbook for diagnosis and treatment.* New York: Guilford.

Barkley, R.A. (1997). *ADHD and the nature of self-control.* New York: Guilford.

Barkley, R.A. (1998). *Attention-deficit hyperactivity disorder.* New York: Guilford.

Barkley, R.A., Anastopoulos, A.D., Guevremont, D.C., & Fletcher, K.E. (1992). Attention-deficit hyperactivity disorder in adolescents: Mother-adolescent interactions, family beliefs and conflicts, and maternal psychopathology. *Journal of Abnormal Child Psychology, 20,* 263–288.

Barkley, R.A., DuPaul, G.J., & McMurray, M.B. (1990). A comprehensive evaluation of attention deficit disorder with and without hyperactivity as defined by research criteria. *Journal of Consulting and Clinical Psychology, 58,* 775–789.

Barkley, R.A., & Edwards, G. (1998). Diagnostic interview, behavior rating scales, and the medical examination. In R.A. Barkley (Ed.), *Attention-deficit hyperactivity disorder* (pp. 263–293). New York: Guilford.

Barkley, R.A., Fischer, J., Edelbrock, C., & Smallish, M. (1990). The adolescent outcome of hyperactive children diagnosed by research criteria: An eight year follow-up study. *Journal of the American Academy of Child & Adolescent Psychiatry, 29,* 546–557.

Barkley, R.A., Murphy, K.R. (1998). *Attention-deficit hyperactivity disorder: A clinical workbook* (2nd ed.). New York: Guilford.

Biederman, J., Faraone, S.V., Milberger, S., Curtis, S., Chen, L., Marrs, A., Ouellette, C., Moore, P., Spencer, T., Norman, D., Wilens, T., Kraus, I., & Perrin, J. (1996). A prospective 4-year follow-up study of attention-deficit hyperactivity and related disorders. *Archives of General Psychiatry, 53,* 437–446.

Bradley, K.L., & DuPaul, G.J. (1997). Attention-deficit/ hyperactivity disorder. In G.G. Bear, K.M. Minke, and A. Thomas (Eds.), *Children's needs II: Development, problems and alternatives* (pp. 109–117). Bethesda, MD: National Association of School Psychologists.

Braswell, L., August, G.J., Bloomquist, M.L., Realmuto, G.M., Skare, S.S., & Crosby, R.D. (1997). School-based secondary prevention for children with disruptive behavior. *Journal of Abnormal Child Psychology, 25,* 197–208.

Carlson, E.A., Joacobvitz, D., & Stroufe, L.A. (1995). A developmental investigation of inattentiveness and hyperactivity. *Child Development, 66,* 37–54.

Carlson, C.L., Pelham, W., Milich, R., & Dixon, M. (1992). Single and combined effects of methylphenidate and behavior therapy on the classroom behavior, academic performance and self-evaluations of children with attention-deficit hyperactivity disorder. *Journal of Abnormal Child Psychology, 20,* 213–232.

Conoley, J.C., & Conoley, C.W. (1992). *School consultation: Practice and training* (2nd ed.). New York: Allyn and Bacon.

Copeland, E.D., & Love, V.L. (1991). *Attention please! A comprehensive guide for successfully parenting children with attention deficit disorders and hyperactivity.* Atlanta, GA: Southeastern Psychological Institute Press.

Costello, E.J., Edelbrock, C.S., Costello, A.J., Dulcan, M.K., Burns, B.J., & Brent, D. (1988). Psychopathology in pediatric primary care: The new hidden morbidity. *Pediatrics, 82,* 415–424.

Cruickshank, B.M., Eliason, M., & Merrifield, B. (1988). Long-term sequelae of water near-drowning. *Journal of Pediatric Psychology, 13,* 379–388.

Davila, R.R., William, M.L., MacDonald, J.T. (1991). *Memorandum of chief state school officers re: Clarification of policy to address the needs of children with attention deficit disorder within general or special education.* Washington, DC: U.S. Department of Education.

Douglas, V.I., & Peters, K.G. (1979). Toward a clearer definition of the attentional deficit in hyperactive children. In G.A. Hale & M. Lewis (Eds.), *Attention and the development of cognitive skills* (pp. 173–247). New York: Plenum.

Dunson, R.M. III, Hughes, J.N., & Jackson, T.W. (1994). Effect of behavioral consultation on student and teacher behavior. *Journal of School Psychology, 32*(3), 247–266.

DuPaul, G.J. (1992). How to assess attention-deficit hyperactivity disorder within school settings. *School Psychology Quarterly, 7,* 60–74.

DuPaul, G.J., Barkley, R.A., & Connor, D.F. (1998). Stimulants. In R.A. Barkley (Ed.), *Attention-deficit hyperactivity disorder* (pp. 510–552). New York: Guilford

DuPaul, G.J., Barkley, R.A., & McMurray, M.B. (1991). Therapeutic effects of medication on ADHD: Implications for school psychologists. *School Psychology Review, 20,* 203–219.

DuPaul, G.J., Henningson, P.N. (1993). Peer tutoring effects on the classroom performance of children with attention deficit hyperactivity disorder. *School Psychology Review, 22,* 134–143.

DuPaul, G.J., & Rapport, M.D. (1993). Does methylphenidate normalize the classroom performance of children with attention deficit disorder? *Journal of the American Academy of Child and Adolescent Psychiatry, 32,* 190–198.

DuPaul, G.J., & Stoner, G. (1994). *ADHD in the schools: Assessment and intervention strategies.* New York: Guilford Press.

Ebaugh, F.G. (1923). Neuropsychiatric sequelae of acute epidemic encephalitis in children. *American Journal of Diseases of Children, 25,* 89–97.

Edelbrock, C.S., Rende, R., Plomin, R., & Thompson, L. (1995). A twin study of competence and problem behavior in childhood and early adolescence. *Journal of Child Psychology and Psychiatry, 36,* 775–786.

Evans, S.W., & Pelham, W.E. (1991). Psychostimulant effects on academic and behavioral measures for ADHD junior high school students in a lecture format classroom. *Journal of Abnormal Child Psychology, 19,* 537–552.

Feingold, B.F. (1975). *Why your child is hyperactive.* New York: Random House.

Frick, P.J., Lahey, B.B. (1991). The nature and characteristics of attention-deficit hyperactivity disorder. *School Psychology Review, 20,* 163–173.

Frick, P.J., Strauss, C.C., Lahey, B., & Christ, M. (1993). Behavior disorders of children. In P.B. Sutker and H. Adams (Eds.), *Comprehensive Handbook of Psychopathology* (2nd ed.) (pp. 765–789). New York: Plenum.

Gaub, M., & Carlson, C.L. (1997). Gender differences in ADHD: A meta-analysis and critical review. *Journal of the American Academy of Child and Adolescent Psychiatry, 36,* 1036–1045.

Gordon, M., & Barkley, R.A. (1998). Tests and observational measures. In R.A. Barkley (Ed.), *Attention-deficit hyperactivity disorder* (pp. 345–372). New York: Guilford.

Hart, E.L., Lahey, B.B., Loeber, R., Applegate, B., & Frick, P.J. (1995). Developmental change in attention-deficit hyperactivity disorder in boys: A four-year longitudinal study. *Journal of Abnormal Child Psychology, 23,* 729–750.

Hartsough, C.S., & Lambert, N.M. (1985). Medical factors in hyperactive and normal children: Prenatal, developmental, and health history findings. *American Journal of Orthopsychiatry, 55,* 190–210.

Kelley, M.L. (1990). *School-home notes: Promoting children's classroom success.* New York: Guilford.

Kratochwill, T.R., & Bergen, J.R. (1990). *Behavioral consultation in applied settings: An individual guide.* New York: Plenum.

Laufer, M.W., Denhoff, E., & Solomons, G. (1957). Hyperkinetic impulse disorder in children's behavior problems. *Psychosomatic Medicine, 19,* 38–49.

McBurnett, K., Lahey, B.B., & Pfiffner, L.J. (1993). Diagnosis of attention deficit disorders in DSM-IV: Scientific basis and implications for education. *Exceptional Children, 60,* 108–117.

Mick, E., Biederman, J., & Faraone, S.V. (1996). Is season of birth a risk factor for attention-deficit hyperactivity disorder? *Journal of the American Academy of Child and Adolescent Psychiatry, 35,* 1470–1476.

Milich, R., Licht, B.G., Murphy, D.A., & Pelham, W.E. (1989). Attention-deficit hyperactivity disordered boys' evaluations and attributions for task performance on medication versus placebo. *Journal of Abnormal Psychology, 98,* 280–284.

Needleman, H.L., Schell, A., Bellinger, D.C., Leviton, L., & Alfred, E.D. (1990). The long-term effects of exposure to low doses of lead in childhood: An 11-year follow-up report. *New England Journal of Medicine, 322,* 83–88.

Pelham, W.E. (1993). Pharmacotherapy for children with attention-deficit hyperactivity disorder. *School Psychology Review, 22,* 199–227.

Pfiffner, L.J., Barkley, R.A. (1998). Treatment of ADHD in school settings. In R.A. Barkley (Ed.), *Attention-deficit hyperactivity disorder* (pp. 458–490). New York: Guilford.

Rapport, M.D., Carlson, G.A., Kelly, K.L., & Pataki, C. (1993). Methylphenidate and desipramine in hospitalized children: 1. Separate and combined effects on cognitive function. *Journal of the American Academy of Child and Adolescent Psychiatry, 32,* 333–342.

Reardon, S.M., & Naglieri, J.A. (1992). PASS cognitive processing characteristics of normal and ADHD males. *Journal of School Psychology, 30,* 151–163.

Reid, R., Maag, J.W., Vasa, S.F., & Wright, G. (1994). Who are the children with attention deficit-hyperactivity disorder? A school-based survey. *Journal of Special Education, 28,* 117–137.

Reynolds, C.R., & Kamphaus, R.W. (1994). *Behavior Assessment System for Children.* Circle Pines, MN: American Guidance Service.

Safer, D.J., & Krager, J.M. (1988). A survey of medication treatment for hyperactive/inattentive students. *Journal of the American Medical Association, 260,* 2256–2258.

Semrud-Clikeman, M., Bierderman, J., Sprich-Buckminster, S., Lehman, B.K., Faraone, S.V., & Norman, D. (1992). Comorbidity between ADHD and learning disability: A review and report in a clinically referred sample. *Journal of the American Academy of Child and Adolescent Psychiatry, 31,* 439–448.

Sheridan, S.M. (1993). Models for working with parents. In J.E. Zins, T.R. Kratochwill, S.N. Elliott (Eds.), *Handbook of consultation services for children* (pp. 110–133).

Silverman, I.W., & Ragusa, D.M. (1992). A short-term longitudinal study of the early development of self-regulation. *Journal of Abnormal Child Psychology, 20,* 415–435.

Sprague, R.L. (1979). Assessment of intervention. In R.L. Trites (Ed.), *Hyperactivity in children: Etiology, measurement, and treatment implications* (pp. 217–299). Baltimore: University Park Press.

Strauss, A.A., & Lehtinen, L.E. (1947). *Psychopathology and education of the brain-injured child.* New York: Grune & Stone.

Strecker, E., & Ebaugh, F. (1924). Neuropsychiatric sequelae of cerebral trauma in children. *Archives of Neurology and Psychiatry, 12,* 443–453.

Szatmari, P., Offord, D.R., & Boyle, M.H. (1989). Correlates, associated impairments, and patterns of service utilization of children with attention deficit disorders: Findings from the Ontario Child Health Study. *Journal of Child Psychology and Psychiatry, 30,* 205–217.

Weiss, G., & Hechtman, L.R. (1993). *Hyperactive children grown up* (2nd ed.). New York: Guilford.

Werry, J.S., Minde, K., Guzman, A., Weiss, G., Dogan, K., & Hoy, E. (1972). Studies on the hyperactive child–VII: Neurological status compared with neurotic and abnormal children. *American Journal of Orthopsychiatry, 42,* 441–451.

Zentall, S.S. (1985). A context for hyperactivity. In K.D. Gadow & I. Bialer (Eds.), *Advances in learning and behavior disabilities* (Vol. 4, pp. 273–343). Greenwich, CT: JAI Press.

See also Attention Span; Hyperactivity; Ritalin

ATTENTION SPAN

Adequate attention span requires optimal arousal, selection of task-relevant information, maintenance of attention long enough to get a task done, and central processing of the task (Cohen, 1993; Posner & Boies, 1971). Arousal is assessed by heart rate, respiration, or other indicators of autonomic arousal, and there is a level that is optimal for learning. At very low levels of arousal, learning is inefficient and attention to environmental stimuli is diffuse; at very high levels, attention is narrowed but learning becomes inefficient, particularly for complex tasks. Teachers can increase arousal by increasing the novelty of classroom activities, by asking students questions to generate curiosity (Berlyne, 1960), by rotating students in and out of the "action zone" (the T-shaped front-row-and-center region of the classroom) (Piontrowski & Calfee, 1979), or by directing questions to students outside the action zone.

Selective attention is assessed most frequently by use of incidental learning tasks. The child is instructed to recall a specific set of items (e.g., pictures of animals), but other incidental items (e.g., household items) are actually paired with the target (central) items during presentation. After being given tests of recall for central items, the child is tested for recall of the central-incidental pairs. The assumption is that only items that are attended to will be recalled. Recall for central items increases steadily from preschool age through adolescence, while memory for incidental items remains stable. The correlation between central and incidental recall becomes increasingly negative between ages 6 and 13 in normal children, indicating an increasing ability to screen out distractions with age. Adolescents and adults appear to screen out distractors by rehearsing central stimuli (Hagen & Stanovich, 1977). Hallahan et al. (1980) have found selective attention problems to be common in children with learning problems. They also found that these children can be trained to improve their attention to central stimuli by using task-relevant self-talk and by being reinforced for recall of central items (Hallahan & Reeve, 1980).

Maintenance of attention can be assessed by observation, by interviewing, by self-monitoring, or through formal testing (see Reynolds & Bigler, 1997, 1994). In observational methods, eye contact with assigned task materials, with the teacher during instruction, or during task-relevant interaction with peers, is scored as engaged (on-task); other activities are scored as nonengaged (Piontrowski & Calfee, 1979). Observed engaged time is related to achievement; for example, Leach reports that 58% of the variance in primary mathematics achievement is accounted for by academic engaged time (Leach & Dolan, 1985). Observed on-task attention increases from ages 5 to 11 (Higgins & Turnure, 1984), although students may become more adept at appearing to maintain attention with development (Hudgins, 1967). Self-monitoring of "paying attention" improved observed engaged time among second graders, and reinforcement for self-monitoring accuracy improved engaged time more than self-monitoring alone (Rooney, Hallahan, & Lloyd, 1984).

REFERENCES

Berlyne, D. (1960). *Conflict, arousal, and curiosity.* New York: McGraw-Hill.

Cohen, R.A. (1993). *The neuropsychology of attention.* New York: Plenum Press.

Hagen, J.W., & Stanovich, K.E. (1977). Memory: strategies of acquisition. In R.V. Kail & J.W. Hagen (Eds.), *Perspectives on the development of memory and cognition.* Hillsdale, NJ: Erlbaum.

Hallahan, D.P., & Reeve, R.E. (1980). Selective attention and distractibility. In B.K. Keogh (Ed.), *Advances in special education, Vol. 1.* Greenwich, CT: JAI Press.

Higgins, A.T., & Turnure, J.E. (1984). Distractibility and concentration of attention in children's development. *Child Development,* 55, 1799–1810.

Hudgins, B.B. (1967). Attending and thinking in the classroom. *Psychology in the Schools,* 66, 29–32.

Leach, D.J., & Dolan, N.K. (1985). Helping teachers increase student academic engagement rate: The evaluation of a minimal feedback procedure. *Behavior Modification,* 9, 55–71.

Piontrowski, D., & Calfee, R. (1979). Attention in the classroom. In G.A. Hale & M. Lewis (Eds.), *Attention and cognitive development* (pp. 297–329). New York: Plenum.

Posner, M.I., & Boies, S.J. (1971). Components of attention. *Psychological Review,* 78, 391–408.

Reynolds, C.R., & Bigler, E.D. (1994). *Test of memory and learning.* Austin, TX: Pro-Ed.

Reynolds, C.R., & Bigler, E.D. (1997). Clinical neuropsychological assessment of child and adolescent memory with the Test of Memory and Learning. In C.R. Reynolds & E. Fletcher-Janzen (Eds.), *The Handbook of Clinical Child Neuropsychology* (3rd ed.) (pp. 296–319). New York: Plenum.

Rooney, K.J., Hallahan, D.P., & Lloyd, J.W. (1984). Self-recording of attention by learning disabled students in the regular classroom. *Journal of Learning Disabilities,* 17, 360–364.

See also **Attention-Deficit Hyperactivity Disorder; Hyperactivity; Hyperkinesis; Test of Memory and Learning**

ATTITUDES TOWARD THE HANDICAPPED

With the passage of P.L. 94-142 and Section 504, the visibility of disabled children and adults increased in mainstream American society. This has precipitated a need for the examination of attitudes, reactions, and behaviors toward the disabled to foster their integration into a society that has traditionally excluded them (Hazzard, 1983).

Siller (1976) points out that attitudes and reactions to the handicapped are wide ranging and complex. They are based on variables considered related to and important to attitudinal formation (e.g., family background, culture, and personality). Age, sex, and other demographic variables appear to be significant determinants in the manner in which attitudes toward the disabled are expressed rather than in their formation.

Personal contact with the disabled may either substantially improve or worsen attitudes, depending on the quality of the previous interaction. As more handicapped children are both mainstreamed into regular classes (as in the case of the mildly handicapped) or placed within the elementary/secondary school setting (as with the more severely handi-

capped), attention must be placed on assisting regular teachers in accommodating these children in the general school program and on to fostering positive attitudes in nonhandicapped students. Reynolds, Martin-Reynolds, and Mark (1982) report that the most important ingredient in making mainstreaming work is teacher attitude. Some studies have indicated that it is difficult for regular classroom teachers to accept the handicapped in their classrooms (e.g., Alexander & Strain, 1978). This may be due to teachers' feeling inadequately prepared to serve the needs of handicapped children rather than any general negative attitude toward disability. Attitudes of children toward the handicapped have also been affected positively through a variety of programs aimed at increasing contact with the disabled and offering quality of interaction.

Investigations by Gottlieb (1974) and others on the social effects of the integration of mildly handicapped children into classroom settings with nonhandicapped peers are inconclusive (Voeltz, 1980). Furthermore, it may be inaccurate to generalize data involving mildly handicapped children to the social integration of severely handicapped children (Voeltz, 1980). One may assume with confidence that negative attitudes toward the disabled represent a real barrier to their filling appropriate roles in society (Siller, 1976). Positive teacher intervention efforts and structured, long-term contact with handicapped peers (Fenrick & Petersen, 1984) may serve as viable means to breaking down barriers.

REFERENCES

Alexander, C., & Strain, P.S. (1978). A review of educators attitudes towards handicapped children and the concept of mainstreaming. *Psychology in the Schools, 15, 390–396.*

Fenrick, N.J., & Petersen, T.K. (1984). Developing positive changes in attitude towards moderately/severely handicapped students through a peer tutoring program. *Education and Training of the Mentally Retarded, 19*(2), 83–91.

Gottlieb, J., Cohen, L., & Goldstein, L. (1974). Social contact and personal adjustment as variables relating to attitudes toward EMR children. *Training School Bulletin, 71,* 9–16.

Gottlieb, J., & Gottlieb, B. (1977). Stereotype attitude and behavioral intentions toward handicapped children. *American Journal of Mental Deficiency, 82,* 65–71.

Hazzard, A. (1983). Children's experience with, knowledge of, and attitude toward disabled persons. *Journal of Special Education, 17*(2), 131–139.

Reynolds, B.J., Martin-Reynolds, J., Mark, F.D. (1982). Elementary teachers' attitudes toward mainstreaming educable mentally retarded students. *Education and Training of the Mentally Retarded, 17*(3), 171–177.

Siller, J. (1976). Attitudes towards disability. In H. Rusalem & D. Malikin (Eds.), *Contemporary vocational rehabilitation* (pp. 63–79). New York: New York University Press.

Voeltz, L.M. (1980). Children's attitudes toward handicapped peers. *American Journal of Mental Deficiency, 84*(5), 455–464.

See also **Scapegoating; Teacher Expectancies**

ATTRIBUTIONAL RETRAINING

Many handicapped pupils perceive themselves to be incompetent in a variety of school-related activities. While these self-perceptions may accurately reflect limited skills in these areas, they may also affect youngsters' willingness to engage in learning tasks. When presented with school tasks, even tasks in which they have evidenced recent success, many pupils will state that they cannot do the work and as a consequence will not even try. To address the learning needs of their pupils, special education teachers need to focus on their pupils' cognitive and motivational characteristics. An intervention procedure entitled attributional retraining has been used to influence pupils' self-perceptions and their subsequent motivation to learn.

Attribution retraining may be defined as a systematic set of procedures designed to influence individuals' perceptions concerning the causes of their performance on tasks. Many of the procedures are derived from research in the area of cognitive behavior modification. In attributional retraining the focus is on modifying learners' thoughts concerning why they have succeeded or failed on a task. Although attributional retraining procedures have been used in treatment programs for a variety of problems including alcoholism, anxiety, depression, and diet management, the focus on this presentation will be on the use of these procedures with youngsters who evidence severe learning problems.

See also **Learned Helplessness; Motivation**

ATYPICAL CHILD SYNDROME

Atypical child syndrome is a term borrowed from the medical profession and is no longer in common usage. The current term referring to this group is exceptional children. An exceptional child is one who deviates from the norm and could be categorized on the basis of a set of physical and/or behavioral characteristics. There are a variety of specific disorders in the area of special education that use the term syndrome as a part of the classification. Hunter's syndrome, Down's syndrome, Turner's syndrome, Lesch-Neyhan syndrome, Cornelin deLange syndrome, Sturge-Weber syndrome, and Klinefelter's syndrome are but a few that are discussed in the special education literature.

See also **Evaluation; Learning Disabilities; Mental Retardation**

AUDIOGRAM

An audiogram is a graphic representation of the threshold of hearing for each ear, measured at discrete frequencies using pure-tone signals, and transduced through an earphone for determining air conduction (AC) and through a bone vibrator for determining bone conduction (BC) thresholds. The audiogram form and symbols plotted on the audiogram, representing hearing thresholds, have been standard-ized (ANSI S3.6-1996) and are shown in Figure 4. The abscissa of the audiogram shows frequency in hertz (Hz) from 125 to 8000 Hz. The ordinate shows hearing level (HL) in decibels (dB) from −10 to 120 dB. 0-dB HL for each frequency represents the statistical average of normal hearing. If an individual has normal hearing, all pure-tone thresholds would be plotted on the 0-dB HL line. Thresholds <zero-dB HL would mean better hearing than normal and thresholds >zero-dB HL would mean poorer hearing than normal, or the amount of hearing loss. AC hearing thresholds between −10 and 20 are considered within a normal range, while thresholds from 25 to 40 indicate a mild hearing loss; 41 to 55 dB, a moderate one; 56 to 70, moderate to severe; 71 to 90 severe, and greater than 91 dB, profound.

Air-conduction thresholds are obtained through earphones so that sound is conducted to the inner ear by the air in the ear canal and recorded as "O" for the right and "X" for the left ear. Bone-conduction thresholds are obtained through a bone vibrator, usually placed on the mastoid behind the ear so that sound is conducted to the inner ear by the cranial bones and recorded as "<" for the right and ">" for the left ear. When the possibility exists that a pure-tone presented to one ear may be heard in the other ear, a narrow-band masking sound is directed to the non-test ear to eliminate it from responding to the pure-tone presented to the test ear. AC and BC thresholds obtained with masking have different symbols than those obtained unmasked. Once thresholds have been obtained, the AC thresholds for each ear are connected with a solid line and BC thresholds are connected with a dotted line. Sometimes audiologists color code their symbols so that all right ear thresholds are plotted in red and left ear in blue.

REFERENCE

American National Standards Institute. (1996). *Specifications for audiometers.* S3.6–1996. New York.

See also **Audiometry; Auditory Abnormalities**

AUDIOLOGY

Audiology is the study of hearing and hearing disorder, including assessment procedures, hearing conservation, and the habilitation and rehabilitation of individuals having impairment. The field of audiology can be differentiated into specialty areas.

Clinical audiology is concerned with assessing the degree, type, and site of lesion of hearing loss, and determining appropriate rehabilitation procedures. Emphasis is placed on testing, diagnostic procedures, interpretation of results, and counseling. Pediatric audiology is like clinical audiology, except emphasis is placed on special procedures for assessment of hearing in infants and young children. Experimental audiology concerns itself with investigations designed to advance testing, diagram procedures, and increase knowledge of normal and abnormal auditory systems. Educational audiology provides appropriate therapies to pre-

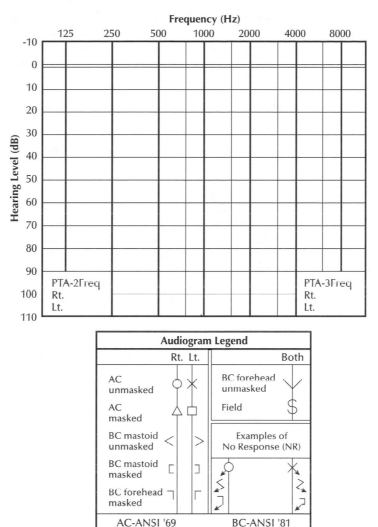

Figure 4. Audiogram form and symbols.

school and school-age children having educationally significant hearing impairments. Industrial audiology deals with the effects of noise on humans, hearing conservation programs, noise control, interpretation of state and federal programs, and noise standards. Rehabilitative audiology has as its primary goal providing therapies for children and adults with hearing impairments. Therapies include speech reading, auditory training, and speech-language therapy.

See also **Audiometry; Auditory Abnormalities**

AUDIOMETRY

Audiometry is the collection of techniques and procedures used for measuring hearing. Traditionally, measurements are done with a calibrated electronic instrument called an audiometer. Generally, two types of audiometry, called pure-tone and speech audiometry, and measurements of the middle ear, collectively called acoustic immittance measurements, are done during an audiological evaluation.

Pure-tone audiometry is the measurement of the threshold of hearing for air- and bone-conducted pure tones. Air-conducted pure tones are transmitted through an earphone so that sound is conducted to the inner ear by the air in the ear canal as part of the pathway. Bone-conducted pure tones are transmitted by a bone vibrator usually placed on the mastoid process behind the outer ear so that sound is conducted to the inner ear by the crania bones.

The American National Standards Institute (ANSI) has specified the methods for manual pure-tone audiometry (ANSI, S3.21–1978, R1992). As a result of pure-tone audiometry, the severity and type of hearing loss can be classified for each ear. Speech audiometry is concerned with determining the threshold of hearing for speech and with measuring speech discrimination ability. The threshold of speech can be measured by determining the lowest hearing level that causes an individual to detect speech. This level is known as a speech awareness threshold (SAT) or speech detection threshold (SDT). Another speech threshold measure, spondee threshold (ST), is found by determining the lowest level at which an individual can just hear and understand bisyllabic words spoken in spondaic stress 50% of the time. If speech stimuli other than bisyllabic words are used (e.g., body parts), this measure is known as a speech reception threshold (SRT). Speech discrimination testing is done to determine the percentage of words (usually monosyllabic) correctly identified when the words are presented loud enough to be heard at normal conversational level. This measure is also known as word or speech recognition or identification; it can be used to judge social adequacy, for hearing-aid fitting, and for diagnostic site-of-lesion testing.

Acoustic immittance measurements are done on a special instrument. It is not truly a measurement of hearing, but rather a test battery to obtain diagnostic information about eardrum mobility (tympanogram) and middle- and inner-ear function (acoustic reflex tests). The result of acoustic immittance measurements can be used alone for diagnostic purposes; however, when used in conjunction with pure-tone and speech audiometry results, the type, degree, site-of-lesion, and in some cases the underlying pathology of the hearing loss can be determined.

REFERENCE

American National Standards Institute. (1992). *Methods for manual pure-tone threshold audiometry* (1978, R 1992). New York: Author.

See also Audiology; Auditory Abnormalities

AUDITORY ABNORMALITIES

Auditory abnormalities are disorders or dysfunctions of the ear that affect the hearing mechanism or sense of hearing. Auditory abnormalities can occur in just one part of the ear or in several parts of the ear simultaneously.

A congenital abnormality of the outer ear is called a microtia. If a patient has a microtia and an intact ear canal, he or she usually does not have a hearing loss. A smaller than normal ear canal, common in Down's Syndrome, is known as a stenotic canal; it usually does not cause hearing impairment. An absent ear canal, or a canal that "dead-ends," is known as an atresia; it causes a moderate to severe conductive hearing loss. An overabundance of wax (cerumen) in the ear canal can cause a mild to moderate conductive loss if it is impacted.

The most common auditory abnormality in children is the presence of fluid in the middle ear space, usually due to Eustachian tube dysfunction; however, there are many causes of middle-ear fluid. Middle-ear fluid is especially prevalent in children having craniofacial disorders (Down's, cleft palate, etc.). Usually, middle-ear fluid can cause a mild to moderate educationally significant conductive hearing loss because movement of the eardrum and middle ear bones bones are restricted. A hole in the ear drum, known

as a perforation or rupture, can cause a mild to severe conductive hearing loss, depending on its location and size. A fixation of the stapes in the oval window of the inner ear is a condition known as otosclerosis, and this usually produces a progressive mild to severe conductive hearing loss. If the joint between the incus and stapes becomes disarticulated, usually by a blow to the head, a moderate to severe conduction hearing loss occurs. There are many congenital middle-ear abnormalities, including absent, fixed, or distorted middle-ear bone malformations. Generally, auditory abnormalities that involved the outer or middle ear and produced conductive hearing losses are amenable to drug therapy or surgical correction to restore hearing.

There are many auditory abnormalities that may be part of an overall syndrome involving other sensory systems, skeletal formation, internal organs, or the nervous system. Generally, inner-ear abnormalities affect the sensory hair cells in the Organ of Corti, causing a sensorineural hearing loss that can range from mild to profound and that can be unilateral (one ear) or bilateral (both ears). In children, about 50% of educationally significant inner-ear hearing losses are inherited and about 50% are acquired. If a child is born with an absent inner ear (cochlea), the condition is known as an inner-ear aplasia. Common genetic causes of inner-ear hearing loss are syndromes (such as Usher's or Waardenburg's Syndromes) and interfamily marriages. Common acquired causes are due to prematurity, meningitis, and birth injury. An inner-ear hearing loss owed to aging is called presbycusis. One from excessive noise exposure is called acoustic or noise-induced trauma.

See also Audiogram; Audiometry

AUDITORY DISCRIMINATION

Auditory discrimination is the process of an individual's ability to recognize, interpret, and distinguish among auditory stimuli, and to respond appropriately. Most often, auditory discrimination is thought to involve the ability to differentiate speech sounds leading to an understanding of the speech message. However, auditory discrimination also involves an individual's ability to differentiate nonspeech sounds of varying intensities, frequencies, and durations. In part, the study of psychoacoustics is devoted to understanding human perception of acoustic stimuli.

Applied to speech, auditory discrimination is the process that enables an individual to recognize, interpret, and distinguish differences among all of the phonemes that make up speech segments. In a broader sense, it is the ability to distinguish and understand speech. Auditory discrimination also involves the process of selecting relevant stimuli from nonrelevant stimuli in the environment. This process is called auditory figure-ground, auditory differentiation, auditory selective listening, competing message integration, and listening in noise.

Auditory discrimination can be tested in several ways,

using a variety of specially designed tests in quiet or noisy backgrounds using an open- or closed-set response. Some auditory discrimination tests employ a rhyming word format so that the individual has to hear a pivotal phoneme to distinguish between two words or to identify the stimulus word from rhyming word alternatives. Some auditory discrimination tests require the listener to hear key words in a sentence or phrase.

Generally, auditory discrimination is tested by presenting a list of monosyllabic words through an earphone or loudspeaker at various sound pressures or hearing levels corresponding to a normal conversational levels, most comfortable levels, or sensational levels above an individual's speech threshold. The monosyllabic word lists can be presented by tape or by monitored live voice. Usually the word lists are phonetically balanced, meaning that the phonetic elements of the words on the list are balanced in relation to their occurrence in normal speech. An auditory discrimination score is the percentage of words correctly identified. A normal discrimination score is usually considered to be 86% to 100% and in some cases 80% to 100%. A discrimination loss is the difference between an individual's score compared with a normal score under the same conditions; it can be classified in severity from mild to profound. Auditory discrimination tests can also be scored by determining the number of phonemes correctly and incorrectly identified.

See also **Auditory Perception; Auditory Processing**

AUDITORY PERCEPTION

Auditory perception relates to the processing of auditory stimuli though the auditory nervous system, including the brainstem and central auditory cortex. Perception follows a sequence of steps from detection of the acoustic signal to discrimination. Children with auditory perceptual and processing disorders often exhibit language and learning disabilities (Garstecki & Erler, 1997; Cherry, 1992).

The sequence of auditory processing includes detection of a single auditory event; temporal resolution of the offset of the first auditory event to the onset of a second; the discrimination of the two events (whether they are the same or different); and temporal order (which signal came first versus second). The process with two signals may be followed by three or more auditory events depending on one's ability to store and recall (i.e., auditory memory).

Auditory perception is the processing of auditory stimuli at the brain stem and cortical levels. There is a hierarchy of steps through which the stimulus is processed between detection of the signal to storing the auditory information in memory. Deficits in the perception processing steps have been linked to specific language and reading disabilities. It has been suggested that it is important to evaluate basic auditory perception separately from speech and language perception to pinpoint deficits. Afterward, it is the responsibility of educators and other related ancillary service providers to ensure that children with auditory processing deficits receive special accommodations or speech language services in order to ensure their classroom success.

REFERENCES

Cherry, R. (1992). Screening and evaluation of central auditory processing disorders in young children. In Jack Katz, Nancy Steckler, & Donald Henderson (Eds.), *Central auditory processing: A transdisciplinary view* (pp. 129–140). St. Louis: Mosby Year Book.

Garstecki, D.C., & Erler, S.F. (1997). Hearing loss management in children and adults. In G.T. Mencher, S.E. Gerber, & A. McCombe (Eds.), *Audiology and auditory dysfunction* (pp. 220–232). Needham Heights, MA: Allyn & Bacon.

See also **Auditory Abnormalities; Auditory Discrimination; Auditory Processing**

AUDITORY PROCESSING

Auditory processing is the means in which auditory information is collected, converted, and sent to the auditory portion of the brain (Bess & McConnell, 1981) where it is perceived as information, whether from speech or nonspeech stimuli. In the educational environment the majority of information is conveyed via an auditory modality. If there is a breakdown in the auditory system, whether due to a specific hearing loss or a central auditory processing disorder, the learning process will be affected (Garstecki & Erler, 1997).

The auditory process can be briefly and clearly described. The acoustic signal is collected at the outer ear, channeled through the outer ear canal to the eardrum, the border of the middle and outer ear, where it is converted to mechanical energy. After transformation to mechanical energy in the form of ossicular vibration, the signal is transferred to the inner ear (the cochlea) at the point of the oval window. The cochlea is filled with fluid, and therefore the signal is then conducted via hydraulic energy. The hydraulic waves cause movement of the hair cells in the cochlea which in turn cause an electrical impulse to travel up the VIII Nerve, thus transferring the signal to the brain stem and then to the auditory cortex. At different points of the brain stem, the signal begins to be processed for temporal elements and localization. As the signal transfers further up to the temporal auditory cortex, decoding and information transfer for speech and language reception takes place.

Hearing loss may occur if there is a breakdown in any part of the system. Sometimes there are lesions in the neurological tract or in the cortex which do not result in a noticeable hearing loss, but which do result in disruptions in processing the signal at a higher level (i.e., the brain stem or auditory cortex). These processing disruptions may be manifested by disabilities in the following listening skill areas:

- Discrimination—the ability to differentiate among sounds not having the same intensity, duration, or frequency

- Auditory discrimination—the ability to differentiate between words and sounds that are similar
- Auditory association—the ability to identify a sound with its source
- Auditory closure—the ability to understand a word or message when part of the signal is missing
- Auditory memory; sequential memory—the ability to store and recall auditory stimuli in exact order
- Auditory localization—the ability to determine the source of a sound
- Auditory figure-ground—the ability to discriminate a speaker's voice from background noise
- Auditory attention—the ability to attend to sound, particularly speech, over a long period of time
- Auditory blending—the ability to synthesize phonemes into words
- Auditory analysis—the ability to identify phonemes or morphemes within words (Keith, 1988; Garstecki & Erler, 1997)

These areas are interrelated; thus, problems in one area may lead to problems in others.

Auditory processing is the sequence by which an acoustic signal is taken in through the outer ear, processed through the middle and inner ear, and transmitted via neurological pathways to the auditory cortex. Lesions or disruptions in the neurological pathways and auditory cortex can lead to problems in auditory discrimination, localization, attention, closure, analysis, figure-ground, and memory. These problems usually manifest in the form of learning disabilities. Thus, educators may need to provide learning style accommodations for children with disabilities related to auditory processing problems.

REFERENCES

Bess, F.H., & McConnell, F.E. (1981). *Audiology, education, and the hearing-impaired child.* St. Louis: Mosby.

Garstecki, D.C., & Erler, S.F. (1997). Hearing loss management in children and adults. In G.T. Mencher, S.E. Gerber, & A. McCombe. (Eds.), *Audiology and auditory dysfunction* (pp. 220–232). Needham Heights, MA: Allyn & Bacon.

Keith, R.W. (1988). Central auditory tests. In L.N. McReynolds & D. Yoder (Eds.), *Handbook of speech language pathology and audiology* (pp. 1215–1236). Toronto, Ontario: BC Decker.

See also **Auditory Discrimination; Central Auditory Dysfunction; Learning Disabilities**

AUGMENTATIVE COMMUNICATION SYSTEMS

Augmentative communication systems are methods of communication that are used as a supplement to vocal speech. These systems are used with persons who are unable to use speech as their primary communication method. They are used to compensate (either temporarily or permanently) for the impairment and disability patterns of individuals with severe expressive communication disorders (i.e., the severely speech-language and writing impaired) (ASHA, 1989, p. 107).

Augmentative communication systems are used with many types of persons to enhance communication and the development of language skills. A child or adult who is unable to communicate at a chronologically age-appropriate level due to physical or other disabilities is at risk for developing poor social interactions and language skills. Even when it seems likely that oral speech may eventually develop, augmentative communication systems are used to prevent delayed communication development. Several studies have shown that the use of augmentative communication systems can sometimes lead to improved oral communication skills (Silverman, McNaughton, & Kates, 1978).

There are two categories of augmentative communication systems: unaided and aided. Unaided communication systems use only the physical body for communication. Sign language, gestures, vocalizations, and facial expressions are unaided communication methods. Aided communication methods require additional tools or equipment to convey a message. Typewriters, communication boards, pen and paper, and computers can all be used as aided communication methods. Although aided communication systems are physically cumbersome, they have the advantage of being easily understood by most listeners. Unaided systems usually require familiarity with the nonspeaking person for the communication system to be understood.

Effective augmentative communication systems should promote social and communicative interactions. To enhance interaction across many social situations, more than one type of augmentative communication system may be needed. The person should be able to use a variety of augmentative communication methods and apply them appropriately. They might rely on a computer for lengthy conversations, school work, and phone calls through a modem. The same person may have a communication board to take shopping or to go outside. In addition, head nods, simple gestures, and vocalizations might be used for rapid communication with friends and family who are familiar with the person. Through using all available augmentative communication methods, social interaction can be enhanced and communication can become effective.

REFERENCES

American Speech-Language-Hearing Association (ASHA). (1989). Competencies for speech-language pathologists providing services in augmentative communication. *Asha, 31,* 107–110.

Silverman, H., McNaughton, S., & Kates, B. (1978). *Handbook of Blissymbolics.* Toronto, Ontario: Blissymbolics Communication Institute.

See also **Alternative Communication Methods in Special Education; Blissymbols**

AUSTRALIA, SPECIAL EDUCATION IN

BACKGROUND AND CONTEXT

Like many western countries, Australia's early provisions for children with special education needs were through institutions and schools established by charitable organizations for people with disabilities in vision or hearing. For example, in Sydney, New South Wales (NSW), a school for deaf children was opened by the Institution for Deaf, Dumb, and Blind in 1860 (Drummond, 1978; Snow, 1990). That organization continues today as the Royal NSW Institute for Deaf and Blind Children, providing a range of on-site and community-based services for dead, blind, deaf-blind and other multiply-handicapped children. Similar developments took place in other states, such as Victoria, where a school for the blind was established in 1866 by the Victorian Royal Blind Society, and in South Australia where a school for deaf children was established in 1874 (Drummond, 1978).

The separate development of Australia's states from beginnings as English colonies meant that each developed its own set of governmental powers and responsibilities, gradually emerging as sovereign states and agreeing to form the federation of states which became known as the Commonwealth of Australia in 1901. While the advent of federation meant that some governmental powers became the province of the new federal government, many, such as the responsibility for universal public education, remained within the jurisdiction of individual states. As a result, the states' public education systems, which were established independently in the late nineteenth century, continued to grow under their own administrations. Services for children with disabilities were slow to be introduced by these state governments, until influences such as the reorganization of schooling into primary and secondary levels and an age-grade placement model identified particular problems for schools in providing for students with intellectual disabilities. Not surprisingly for that time, a segregated special education model was widely adopted for those students (see Snow, 1990, for a fuller discussion of these events in one Australian state between 1880 and 1940).

Special education services in Australia have been broadly influenced by developments in countries such as the United Kingdom, where the Warnock report publicized debate on special education services (Committee of Enquiry into the Education of Handicapped Children and Young People, 1978) and the United States, whose series of public laws prescribing educational provisions for students with disabilities are well-known (Ysseldyke, Algozzine & Thurlow, 1992). In Australia, there has been no equivalent national legislation on special education, nor a Bill of Rights-style document guaranteeing similar individual expectations of their society. In 1992, however, the Australian federal parliament passed the Disability Discrimination Act, making unlawful discrimination against people with disabilities in access to employment, housing, and education. While offering some protection to the access rights of students with disabilities to education in regular schools, the legislation also provides for *exemption* from its provisions to educational institutions which might suffer an unjustifiable hardship in providing the special services needed to sustain a particular student's enrollment (Commonwealth of Australia, 1992). Most Australian states have developed their own legislation in support of the Commonwealth's Disability Discrimination Act (for example, the Disability Services Act, 1993, in NSW) and these have been influenced by the principles and language of normalization (Wolfensberger, 1972). In most Australian states, the principle of the continuum of special education services is supported, involving the placement of each student in a setting best suited to individual needs but as close as possible to a least restrictive or regular class setting. Nevertheless, there is considerable variation between the states in the extent to which this principle is applied. This is most clearly seen in changing trends in special school enrollments as shown below.

Particularly Australian issues in special education services relate to the needs of indigenous Australians with special education needs and the problems of providing special education services in remote and rural areas, where a sparsely distributed population is scattered over an area the size of western Europe. The compounded disadvantage of disability, geographic isolation, and membership of marginalized groups including women and those of different ethnic and cultural backgrounds have been well described by Germanos-Koutsounadis (1990). The national government initiatives include the English as a Second Language Program; the Special Education Program (e.g., recurrent grants including integration support; pre-school special education; children in residential institutions; children with severe disabilities; other training services); the Disadvantaged Schools program (special projects in literacy, numeracy, money management, initiatives to improve retention rates) for schools meeting criteria in relation to socioeconomic disadvantage; and the Country Area program, designed to provide resources to attempt to "minimize the imbalance between rural and urban education" (Australian Education Council, 1989, pp. 156–158).

Considerable differences exist between the various states' special education enrollment data for 1992. These show that special class provisions were rarely used at all (just 2%) by students in government schools in Victoria, with most students placed in special schools (44%), or in regular classes with support (54%). By contrast, in NSW, around 46% were in special classes, 21% in special schools and 33% in regular classes. Most other Australian states fell between these two positions, although South Australia reported 68% of its students with disabilities in regular schools, with special classes and special schools used for 19% and 13% respectively (McRae, 1996, p. 25). Non-government schools across Australia accounted in 1992 for

28% of the school population generally but under 17% of those students identified with disabilities. Of these, most were provided for in regular classes (Catholic schools) though 40% of the small number enrolled in independent schools (2,377 nationally) were in special schools (DeLemos, 1994, cited in McRae, 1996).

These data show, then, that there is quite some disparity between Australian states. The wish of state governments to maintain their responsibilities for public education administration suggests that these differences will continue as each tries to reflect its own community's attitude to issues such as special education services, while the national government role remains restricted to special initiative funding to extend state services to areas considered to have been overlooked by states. The extent to which national governments may continue such a role may well be limited in future years as current constraints on domestic public expenditure continue.

REFERENCES

Australian Education Council. (1989). *National report on schooling in Australia.* Canberra: Author.

Committee of Enquiry into the Education of Handicapped Children and Young People. (1978). *Special education needs.* London: HMSO.

DeLemos, M. (1994). *Schooling for students with disabilities.* Melbourne: Australian Council for Educational Research.

Disability Discrimination Act. (1992). Section 22, Division 2- Discrimination in other areas. Canberra: Commonwealth of Australia. (Internet: http://www/austlii.edu.au/au/legis/cth/ consol_act/dda1992264/s22.html)

Drummond, N.W. (1978). *Special education in Australia.* Sydney: Royal Far West Children's Health Scheme.

Germanos-Koutsounadis, V. (1990). "Fair Go" access and equity issues for Australians with disabilities who are from non-English speaking backgrounds (NESB), aboriginal, Torres Strait Islanders, women and from remote areas. *Australian Disability Review, 390,* 3–10.

McRae, D. (1996). *The integration/inclusion feasibility study.* Sydney: NSW Department of School Education.

Snow, D. (1990). Historicising the integration debate. *Australasian Journal of Special Education, 13*(2), 28–38.

Ysseldyke, J.E., Algozzine, B., & Thurlow, M.L. (1992). *Critical issues in special education* (2nd ed.). Boston: Houghton Mifflin.

See also **New Zealand, Special Education in**

AUTISM

Leo Kanner's 1943 paper, "Autistic disturbances of affective contact," made autism a medical entity. It took twenty more years for autism to become a cultural entity—an intriguing (to outsiders) and devastating (to families) aberration of child development whose incidence, causes, and treatment were mysteries demanding solutions. Prevalence estimates for autism have ranged from the earlier figure of approximately 4 or 5 per 10,000 children to more recent findings of about 1 per 1,000 children (Bryson, 1996), with a ratio of 3 or 4 males to each female. Differences in rates over time may reflect expansion of the list of criteria that define autism, increased reporting (Coleman & Gillberg, 1985), environmental pollution, and iatrogenic (illness-producing) effects of antibiotics (Rimland, 1997). The onset of autism (the beginning of a child's atypical trajectory of psychosocial development) often occurs in the first months of the child's life (Coleman & Gillberg, 1985). Early abnormalities of development crystallize into autism around two and a half years (Folstein & Rutter, 1987).

The lives of many individuals with autism are characterized by marginality with respect to ordinary adolescent and adult activities. Several decades ago, for example, Rutter et al. (1967) stated that a minority of persons with autism reached a good level of social adjustment by adolescence, and even fewer entered paid employment. Recent research is more encouraging. As an autistic child grows through adolescence and adulthood, activity level decreases, ease at managing undesirable behavior increases, and language, sociability, and activities of daily living improve (Mesibov, 1983). Good outcomes (e.g., social relatedness and independent living) appear to be predicted by reactions to sound, less problem behavior at earlier ages, language, schooling, and higher IQ in early childhood (Coleman & Gillberg, 1985).

The most striking and pervasive feature of autism is a child's difficulty participating in the social world. Even with his or her parents, an autistic child may seem alone; in social relationships generally, he or she may be unattached or have a difficult time sustaining attachment. In particular, a child may (1) pay little attention to other persons; (2) avoid physical contact and even the gaze of other persons (Lord, 1993); (3) fail to initiate interaction with others, or initiate interaction in ritualized ways (Hauck, Fein, Waterhouse, & Feinstein, 1995); (4) fail to imitate simple routine actions, e.g., waving bye-bye (Coleman & Gillberg, 1985); (5) fail to follow simple instructions (Coleman & Gillberg, 1985); and (6) have much difficulty taking the role or standpoint of the other person (Mesibov, 1983), as indicated by not sharing attention with others to the same task at hand, not displaying empathy, and seemingly not understanding emotions displayed by other persons (Lord, 1993). In summary, the child with autism, perhaps from infancy, is not geared into the patterns of interaction—the various forms of turn-taking during meals, play and other social activities—which are the vehicle that brings children into the already organized social world.

Second features of autism are overselectivity and overreactivity in attention and attachment. For example, a child with autism may (1) pay attention to stimuli that are irrelevant to a task (e.g., a shiny bolt on a refrigerator door, rather than the handle); (2) stare fixedly and for long periods at spinning objects and flapping hands; (3) have "bizarre attachments to certain objects, such as stones, curls of hair, pins, pieces of plastic toys, or metals," apparently on the basis of color or texture (Coleman & Gillberg, 1985, p. 21);

and (4) pay little attention and underreact to relevant events (e.g., verbal, facial, and postural cues signifying intentions, expectations and feelings of other persons) (Green, Fein, Joy, & Waterhouse, 1995).

Third, individuals with autism show uneven levels of competence across functional domains (Rutter, 1983). Approximately 75 percent of autistic children are mentally retarded (Rutter, 1983).

REFERENCES

Bryson, S.E. (1996). Brief report: Epidemiology of autism. *Journal of Autism and Developmental Disorders, 26,* 165–167.

Coleman, M. (1987). The search for neurological subgroups in autism. In E. Schopler & G. Mesibov (Eds.), *Neurobiological issues in autism* (pp. 163–178). New York: Plenum.

Folstein, S.E. & Rutter, M. (1987). Familial aggregation and genetic implications. In E. Schopler & G. Mesibov (Eds.), *Neurobiological issues in autism* (pp. 83–105). New York: Plenum.

Green, L., Fein, D., Joy, S., & Waterhouse, L. (1995). Cognitive functioning in autism. In E. Schopler & G. Mesibov (Eds.), *Learning and cognition in autism* (pp. 13–31). New York: Plenum.

Hauck, M., Fein, D., Waterhouse, L., & Feinstein, C. (1995). Social initiations by autistic children to adults and other children. *Journal of Autism and Developmental Disorders, 25,* 579–595.

Lord, C. (1993). Early social development in autism. In E. Schopler, M.E. Van Bourgondien, & M.M. Bristol (Eds.), *Pre-school issues in autism* (pp. 61–94). New York: Plenum.

Mesibov, G.B. (1983). Current perspectives and issues in autism and adolescence. In E. Schopler & G.B. Mesibov (Eds.), *Autism in adolescents and adults* (pp. 37–53). New York: Plenum.

Rimland, B. (1997, October). Historical perspectives and techniques that work. Paper presented at the International Symposium on Autism, Illinois Center for Autism, McKendry College, Lebanon, IL.

Rutter, M. (1983). Cognitive deficits in the pathogenesis of autism. *Journal of Child Psychology and Psychiatry, 24,* 513–531.

Rutter, M., Greenfield, D., & Lockyer, L. (1967). A five to fifteen year follow-up study of infantile psychosis. *British Journal of Psychiatry, 113,* 1183–1199.

Schopler, E., & Mesibov, G. (1995). Introduction to learning and cognition in autism. In E. Schopler & G. Mesibov (Eds.), *Learning and cognition in autism* (pp. 3–11). New York: Plenum.

See also **Autistic Behavior; National Society for Children and Adults with Autism**

AUTISM SOCIETY OF AMERICA (ASA)

The Autism Society of America was founded in 1965 to help parents, family members, professionals, and caregivers learn about autism and how to effectively deal with the disability. The Society has over 24,000 members joined through a network of 225 chapters in 46 states across the country. The mission of ASA is to promote lifelong access and opportunities for persons within the autism spectrum and their families to be fully included, participating members of their communities through advocacy, public aware-

ness, education, and research related to autism. ASA believes that each person with autism is a unique individual, and its policies promote the active and informed involvement of family members and those with autism in the planning of individualized, appropriate services and supports.

The ASA provides current information about autism through distribution of free packets of materials on a variety of topics; a comprehensive, bimonthly newsletter, the *Advocate;* and an annual national conference each July. An extensive library of information on issues affecting children and adults with autism, Pervasive Developmental/Disorder-not otherwise specified (PDD-NOS), Asperger's, or other related disorders is maintained by the Society. In addition, ASA furnishes national legislators and government agencies with information about the needs of people with autism and their families and promotes medical research in the field.

Headquarters of the Autism Society of America are located at 7910 Woodmont Avenue, Suite 650, Bethesda, Maryland 20814-3015. ASA may be reached by phoning 1-800-3AUTISM or on the internet at http://www.autism-society.org/.

AUTISM TREATMENT OPTIONS (ATO)

Autism Treatment Options (ATO) is a nonprofit organization that was established in 1994 by parents of autistic children. The main objective of ATO is to provide parents and others interested in the field of autism with information on different types of treatments. ATO publishes the *Autism Options Guide Resource Handbook,* a book that provides readers with a great deal of information on available autism resources.

ATO seeks to increase the awareness of available options for parents and professionals, and also to provide support for family members of autistic persons. Members of ATO are continually updated on current research and new treatments and finding in the field. Membership is open to parents, relatives, and professionals with an interest in autism. For further information about ATO, contact them at Autism Treatment Options Inc., P.O. Box 10772, Goldsboro, NC 2753-0772.

AUTISTIC BEHAVIOR

Autistic behavior is the name for those activities and characteristics frequently associated with the developmental disorder known variously as autism, early infantile autism, or Kanner's (1943) syndrome. Although autism is a specific syndrome having well-defined diagnostic criteria, a wide variety of behaviors are said to be autistic. Further, many of the behaviors are occasionally exhibited by children with other developmental syndromes and disorders such as mental retardation, cerebral palsy, and serious disorders of receptive and/or expressive language. A particular pattern of symptoms, including an early age of onset as well as social and language peculiarities, characterizes the syndrome known as autism and distinguishes it from all other childhood psychotic disorders. Thus, the mere presence of behaviors called autistic in a child's repertoire does not guarantee that autism is the appropriate diagnosis for that child. Further, it is very unusual for any child diagnosed as autistic to show all of the behaviors that have been associated with autism.

One of the first attempts to compile the range of behaviors observed among autistic children was made by Creak (1964) and her colleagues in Great Britain. Similar sets of observations have been reported since that time by others. The observations may be summarized as follows:

1. Unusual and/or self-stimulatory behaviors such as rocking to and fro, flicking fingers in front of the eyes, flapping arms or hands rapidly at particular frequencies, adopting unusual postures, or toe walking.

2. Reluctance to use the distance receptors of vision and hearing. This translates into an avoidance of eye contact and inattention to auditory and visual cues and information. By contrast there is often an excessive and age-inappropriate reliance on near receptors such as taste, touch, and smell for exploration. The threshold for pain may also be unusually high.

3. A preoccupation with certain objects or the operations of objects, often without respect to their intended function. For example, a child may be fascinated by an empty record turntable spinning or may play with a toy truck only by turning it on its side to spin its wheels.

4. The absence of speech or, where speech exists, delays and/or peculiarities such as the use of jargon, the repetition of phrases or whole passages (echolalia), the reversal or misuse of personal pronouns, and idiosyncratic use of words (neologisms).

5. Unusual anxieties, often unrelated to actual environmental circumstances. For instance, a child may become unusually upset if furniture is rearranged in a room, but may remain calm and seemingly unconcerned while involved in an auto accident or while performing dangerous activities such as climbing or balancing at great heights.

6. An unwillingness to have familiar routines changed or delayed and a reluctance to participate in new activities or to process unexpected events. Thus a child may insist on walking exactly the same route to school daily, may wish to constantly possess a particular toy, or consume only certain foods. Any changes or interruptions of these routines produce extreme anxiety.

7. A pattern of uneven intellectual development characterized by general mental retardation with "islands" of near normal, normal, or even supranormal functioning. A child may not be able to answer simple questions (why, when, where, etc.), but the same child may perform complex mathematical calculations or read large and unfamiliar words, though this skill is usually not accompanied by adequate comprehension.

REFERENCES

Creak, M. (1964). Schizophrenic syndrome in childhood: Further progress report of a working party. *Developmental Medicine and Child Neurology, 6,* 530–535.

Kanner, L. (1943). Autistic disturbances of affective contact. *Nervous Child, 2,* 217–250.

See also **Autism; National Society for Children and Adults with Autism**

AUTOMATICITY

Automaticity is an aspect of perceptual and motor processing that occurs outside of conscious awareness. Factors such as stimulus novelty and response practice have been found to be related to automaticity in cognitive functioning (Neiser, 1976). When aroused by a novel or difficult stimulus, extensive cognitive processing occurs, forcing the event into conscious awareness. However, an habitual response elicited by an expected stimulus may be performed at an automatic level requiring little or no attention.

Since humans have a limited attention capacity, automatic functions add to the efficiency of the information processing system (Kutas & Hillyard, 1980). Many simple perceptual processes are innately automatic, while even complex activities such as reading can become automatic with sufficient practice. In fact, Hancock and Byrd (1984) state that reading efficiency is dependent on the extent to which decoding skills become automatized, and Garnett and Fleischner (1980) have related automatization to basic math facts acquisition.

Learning disabilities, and mental retardation, have been discussed in terms of deficient automatization processes. Learning-disabled children have been found to take longer to produce acquired math facts than their non-disabled peers (Garnett & Fleischner, 1980). Their inability to perform this well-drilled task at an automatic level suggests that learning-disabled children's thinking processes are more circuitous and attention demanding. Severely disabled readers have been found to have difficulty processing letters within words, while less impaired readers, who have automatized letter recognition, read whole words in a controlled, attention-demanding manner (Hancock & Byrd, 1984).

Other researchers have suggested that automatic functions may be available to learning-disabled and retarded students, but that other factors impede their effects. Thus, retarded children have been found to perform as well as their nonretarded peers on a measure of perceptual memory automatization (Stein, Laskowski, & Trancone, 1982). The retarded children, however, had more difficulty organizing new skills, thereby preventing the automatization of more complex processes. In another study, learning-disabled children were found to produce the correct definitions of familiar words at a rate equal to that of non-disabled children, but showed a rapid decline in rate and accuracy when unfamiliar words were introduced

(Ceci, 1983). As more purposeful processing was required, the learning-disabled students failed to decode the words, and instead substituted words that could be processed at an automatic level.

REFERENCES

Ceci, S.J. (1983). Automatic and purposeful semantic processing characteristics of normal and language/learning disabled children. *Developmental Psychology, 19*(3), 427–439.

Garnett, K., & Fleischner, J. (1980). *Automatization and basic fact performance of normal and learning disabled children* (Technical Report No. 10). Washington, DC: Office of Special Education. (ERIC Document Reproduction Service No. ED 210 839)

Hancock, A.C., & Byrd, D. (1984, April). *Automatic processing in normal and learning disabled children.* Paper presented at the annual meeting of the Southwestern Psychological Association, New Orleans. (ERIC Document Reproduction Service No. ED 246 414)

Kutas, M., & Hillyard, S.A. (1980). Reading senseless sentences: Brain potentials reflect semantic incongruity. *Science, 207,* 203–204.

Neiser, U. (1976). *Cognition and reality.* San Francisco: Freeman.

Stein, D.K., Laskowski, M.A., & Trancone, J. (1982). *Automatic memory processes in mentally retarded persons.* Paper presented at the annual meeting of the American Psychological Association, Washington, DC. (ERIC Document Reproduction Service No. ED 227 604)

See also **Cognitive Strategies; Conditioning; Transfer of Learning**

AUTOMUTISM

See ELECTIVE MUTISM.

AUTONOMIC REACTIVITY

The autonomic nervous system consists of the sympathetic nervous system and the parasympathetic nervous system. The sympathetic nervous system increases heart rate, adrenal secretions, sweating, and other responses that prepare the body for vigorous activity. The parasympathetic nervous system increases salivation, digestion, and other vegetative responses while antagonizing many effects of the sympathetic nervous system.

The sympathetic system can be activated by sudden sensory stimuli or by emotional experiences. The response to a stimulus depends on one's interpretation of the stimulus and not on just the stimulus itself. Shock believed to be escapable increases heart rate; shock believed to be inescapable decreases it (Malcuit, 1973). A task given to fifth-grade boys as a test increased heart rate; a similar task given to them as a game decreased it (Darley & Katz, 1973).

The sympathetic nervous system is apparently most reactive in early childhood, when gauged by variability of heart rate (Shields, 1983). Sympathetic reactivity is fairly stable over time and may be related to personality traits.

Many people with an antisocial personality have a weak sympathetic response to frightening stimuli. Some authors link high sympathetic responsiveness with impulsiveness and distractibility (Shields, 1983).

REFERENCES

Darley, S.A., & Katz, K. (1973). Heart rate changes in children as a function of test versus game instructions and test anxiety. *Child Development, 44,* 784–789.

Malcuit, G. (1973). Cardiac responses in aversive situation with and without avoidance possibility. *Psychophysiology, 10,* 295–306.

Shields, S.A. (1983). Development of autonomic nervous system responsivity in children: A review of the literature. *International Journal of Behavioral Development, 6,* 291–319.

See also **Central Nervous System; Learned Helplessness**

AVERSIVE CONTROL

The use of aversive stimuli to control behavior is one of the most controversial techniques employed by teachers, researchers, psychologists, therapists, and others. The effectiveness of this procedure is defined by its effect on behavior: it suppresses the behavior that it follows. This definition is similar to that for punishment. Indeed, aversive control is one form of punishment.

The controversy surrounding the use of aversive control is illustrated by Wood and Lakin (1982). They indicate that, although most states approve of the use of moderate corporal punishment, it is specifically forbidden by statutes in others (e.g., Maine and Massachusetts).

The use of aversive consequences for behavior control generally is viewed as a technique to be used only when other techniques have not been successful. Snell (1983) indicates that:

Aversive conditioning using strong primary aversion (such as electric shock and slapping) to eliminate behavior is very defensible in two general instances: when the behavior is so dangerous or self-destructive that positive reinforcement and extinction are not feasible and when all other intervention methods (reinforce competing response, extinction, milder punishment forms) have been applied competently and have been documented as unsuccessful (p. 140).

Despite the reservations that have been expressed regarding the use of aversives, aversives have been used to control behavior, particularly self-injurious behavior (SIB). Lemon juice (Sajwaj, Libet, & Agras, 1974), noxious odors (Baumeister & Baumeister, 1978), and electric shock (McConaghy, Armstrong, & Blaszcynski, 1981) are examples of aversive methods that have been used. At times and under certain conditions, aversive procedures have been found to be the treatment of choice. However, aversive control should be reduced or eliminated when the desired behavior change has occurred or when the target behavior responds to less severe techniques.

The use of aversives to control behavior raises many ethical questions. The basic rationale for the use of aversives is that other methods have failed, the child is at risk, and the aversive to be used is not as harmful as the behavior that is targeted for change.

REFERENCES

Baumeister, A., & Baumeister, A. (1978). Suppression of repetitive self-injurious behavior by contingent inhalation of aromatic ammonia. *Journal of Autism & Childhood Schizophrenia, 8,* 71–77.

McConaghy, N., Armstrong, M., & Blaszczynski, A. (1981). Controlled comparison of aversive therapy and covert sensitization in compulsive homosexuality. *Behavior Research & Therapy, 19,* 425–434.

Sajwaj, T., Libet, J., & Agras, S. (1974). Lemon juice therapy: The control of life threatening rumination in a six-month old infant. *Journal of Applied Behavior Analysis, 1,* 557–566.

Snell, M. (Ed.). (1983). *Systematic instruction of the moderately and severely handicapped* (2nd ed.). Columbus, OH: Merrill.

Wood, F.H., & Lakin, K.C. (Eds.). (1982). *Punishment and aversive stimulation in special education: Legal, theoretical and practical issues in their use with emotionally disturbed children and youth.* Reston, VA: Council for Exceptional Children.

See also **Behavior Modification; Operant Conditioning; Punishment**

AVERSIVE STIMULUS

An aversive stimulus, whether unconditioned (e.g., bright lights) or conditioned (e.g., a frown or gesture) is "an unpleasant object or event" (Sulzer-Azaroff & Mayer, 1986) that can be used to decrease or increase a behavior. When presented as a consequence of, or contingent on, a specific behavior, it may be used to reduce or eliminate the rate of that behavior. However, when an aversive stimulus is removed contingent on the emission of a behavior, it may increase the rate of that behavior. In any case, an aversive stimulus is typically referred to as a punisher.

The application of aversive stimuli to effectively reduce or eliminate severe self-destructive behaviors and/or severe chronic behaviors has been demonstrated by several researchers including Lovaas and Simmons (1969) and Risley (1968). However, the many disadvantages of applying aversive stimuli to reduce behaviors (e.g., withdrawal, aggression, generalization, imitation, negative self-statements; Sulzer-Azaroff & Mayer, 1986) seem to outweigh the advantages. Aversive stimuli to reduce behaviors should be reserved for serious destructive behaviors and employed only when other less aversive procedures have been tried. A more detailed presentation of the use of aversive stimuli may be found in Sulzer-Azaroff & Mayer (1986).

REFERENCES

Lovaas, O.I., & Simmons, J.O. (1969). Manipulation of self destruction in three retarded children. *Journal of Applied Behavior Analysis, 2,* 143–157.

Risley, T. (1968). The effects and side effects of punishing the autistic behaviors of a deviant child. *Journal of Applied Behavior Analysis, 1,* 21–35.

Sulzer-Azaroff, B., & Mayer, G.R. (1986). *Achieving educational excellence using behavior strategies.* New York: Holt, Rinehart, & Winston.

See also **Behavior Modification; Operant Conditioning; Punishment**

AVEYRON, WILD BOY OF
See WILD BOY OF AVEYRON.

AYRES, A. JEAN (1920–1988)

A. Jean Ayres died on December 16, 1988 at the age of 68. Ayres obtained her BS (1945) and MS (1954) in Occupational Therapy, and went on to earn her PhD (1961) in Educational Psychology from the University of Southern California. She worked as an occupational therapist in several California rehabilitation centers, and between 1955 and 1985, she taught and conducted research at the University of Southern California in the Departments of Occupational Therapy and Special Education, achieving the rank of emeritus professor after her retirement in 1985. Ayres was also in private practice in occupational therapy from 1977 to 1984.

Occupational therapy, particularly as related to perceptual and sensory integrative dysfunction and neuromuscular integration, was the focus of her work. From 1964 to 1966, she was a postdoctoral trainee at the University of California, Los Angeles Brain Research Institute, which led to her discovery of sensory integration dysfunction, a neurological disorder of the senses characterized by learning and behavioral problems as well as pain associated with the performance of even simple daily tasks. Ayres had struggled with learning problems similar to those caused by the disease, ultimately identifying an inefficient organization of

A. Jean Ayers

sensory information received by the nervous system as its cause. Perhaps her greatest contribution was the development of sensory-integrative therapy, a neurologically-based treatment for learning disorders widely used among occupational therapists. She is also credited with devising the Southern California Sensory Integration Tests and the Sensory Integration and Praxis Tests, tools used for identifying the disorder.

Distinguishing her work from others, Ayres (1972) used a neurological as opposed to an educational or psychodynamic approach to learning and behavior disorders, emphasizing the normalization of the sensory integration process in the brain stem while not excluding cortical integrative processes. Her research found that students with certain identifiable types of sensory integrative dysfunctions who received occupational therapy specifically for the integrative dysfunction, showed greater gains in academic scores than those who received an equal amount of time in academic work.

During her distinguished career, Ayres published over 50 tests, articles, and films. She was the recipient of the Eleanor Clarke Slagle Lectureship and the Award of Merit, the highest honors conferred by the American Occupational Therapy Association, and she was named to the 1971 edition of *Outstanding Educators of America.* Ayres was a charter member of the honorary Academy of Research of the American Occupational Therapy Association.

REFERENCE

Ayres, A.J. (1972). Improving academic scores through sensory integration. *Journal of Learning Disabilities, 5,* 338–343.

See also **Occupational Therapy; Sensory-Integrative Therapy**

B

BABINSKI REFLEX

The Babinski reflex was first recognized in 1896 by a French neurologist of Polish descent, Joseph Francois Felix Babinski. The Babinski sign, or extensor plantar response, is a phenomenon observed when the sole of the foot is stroked from below the heel toward the toes on the lateral (outside) side. The big toe turns upward or toward the head with the other toes fanned out and extended and the leg is withdrawn.

As the nervous system matures and the pyramidal tract gains more control over spinal motorneurons, the Babinski reflex will not be observed. Indeed, scratching the sole of the foot of a normal person with a dull object will produce a downward flexion of all toes. The presence of Babinski's reflex after the first year of life is an indication of damage to cortical motor neurons and a dysfunction of the pyramidal tract, and further neurological evaluation is required.

See also **Apgar Rating Scale;Developmental Milestones; Plantar Reflex**

BABY DOE

The term *Baby Doe* has come to signify the issue of denying life-sustaining treatment to infants born with permanent handicaps combined with life-threatening but surgically correctable conditions. On October 11, 1983, "Baby Jane Doe" was born in Port Jefferson, New York. She was born with myelomeningocele, hydrocephaly, microcephaly, bilateral upper extremity spasticity, a prolapsed rectum, and a malformed brain stem. Her parents chose a course of conservative treatment as an alternative to surgery. Based on anonymous information, the Department of Health and Human Services filed a complaint with the state Child Protection Agency. The July, 1983 ruling made it clear that the federal government was ready to step in if the decision of a state agency was considered insufficient. This case focused attention on the question of the federal government's right to intrude into the private realm of family decision-making.

In 1983, the President's Commission for the Study of Ethical Problems in Medicine and Biomedical Research issued, as part of its report, a statement on the decision to forgo life-sustaining treatment in critically ill newborns. It contrasted the presumption that parents are the appropriate decision makers for their infants with the *parens patriae* power of the state. That is, while laws concerning the family protect a substantial range of discretion for parents, the state may supervise parental decisions before they become operative to ensure that the choices made are not neglectful or abusive to the child. It concluded that public policy should resist state intervention into family decisions unless serious issues are at stake and the intervention is likely to achieve better outcomes. Additionally, the commission suggested that infants with handicaps be treated no less vigorously than their nonhandicapped peers. However, it also suggested that futile therapies that merely delay death without offering a reasonable probability of saving a baby's life should be avoided. Finally, in ambiguous cases, where the course of action that would benefit the infant is not chosen by the parents, authorized persons acting for the state as *parens patriae* must step in.

On April 15, 1985, the Department of Health and Human Services issued the final rule and model guidelines that encouraged hospitals to establish infant care review committees (ICRCs). This was part of the child abuse and neglect prevention and treatment program included in the Child Abuse Amendments of 1984 (PL 98-457). This legislation attempted to protect the rights of infants with disabilities and limit governmental intervention into the practice of medicine and parental responsibilities. The purpose of the ICRCs was to educate hospital personnel and families of infants with disabilities and life-threatening conditions, to recommend guidelines concerning the withholding from infants of medically indicated treatment (including appropriate hydration, nutrition, and medication), and to offer counsel and review in cases involving infants with disabling and life-threatening conditions.

Recent research (Carter, 1993) has surveyed military and civilian neonatologists and found that, despite frequency of potential cases for review, ICRCs were seldom consulted. In fact, 67% of neonatologists surveyed indicated that the Baby Doe regulations has affected neither their thinking about ethical issues nor their practice.

The practice of decision making continues to be primarily led by the parents and neonatologist or by multidisciplinary conferences that typically do not include the nurses who deliver care (Martin, 1989). The use of multidisciplinary conferences predates the Baby Doe regulations.

The Child Abuse Amendments of 1984 (PL 98-45) state three circumstances under which treatment is not considered medically indicated: the infant is chronically and irreversibly comatose, the treatment would prolong dying but not be effective in ameliorating life-threatening conditions, and the treatment itself would be futile and inhumane. However, when even one of these three circumstances exists (and therefore failure to provide treatment would not be considered withholding medically indicated treatment), the infant must be provided with appropriate hydration, nutrition, and medication. Additionally, the law states that the withholding of treatment must not be based on subjective opinions about the future quality of life of such a person but is to be based on the treating physicians' "reasonable medical judgment." These guidelines are advisory and not mandatory in any way because Congress did not make the rules binding on the states. Rather, it conditioned the receipt of federal funds upon incorporation of the rule into each state's law. Most states have accepted the condition, largely through rulemaking by state child abuse agencies. The rules continue to be vigorously debated (Newman, 1989).

REFERENCES

Carter, B.S. (1993). Neonatologists and bioethics after Baby Doe. *Perinatol, 13*(2), 144–150.

Martin, D.A. (1989). Nurse's involvement in ethical decision-making with severely ill newborns. *Issues in Pediatric Nursing, 12*(6), 463–473.

Newman, S.A. (1989). Baby Doe, Congress and the states: Challenging the federal treatment standard for impaired infants. *American Journal of Law and Medicine, 15*(1), 1–60.

See also **Legislation Regarding the Handicapped; Parents of the Handicapped**

BACKWARD READERS

Backward readers is an archaic term that was commonly used in the first quarter of the twentieth century; its use gradually declined. It is used far less frequently by teachers and psychologists in contemporary special education settings.

In its broadest usage, backward reader referred to anyone with a significant reading problem. The term was derived from the tendency of young children with reading problems to reverse letters and words. Many children will read *was* for *saw* and frequently confuse d, b, p, and q during the early stages of learning to read. If such reversals persist past the age of nine, they are highly significant as indicators of dyslexia. Such reversals have also been termed strephosymbolia. When encountering the term in evaluations, reports, or school records, it is a good idea to query the individual using the term to clarify the specific meaning intended. Backward readers has been found to be a frequently misinterpreted term in both educational and clinical settings.

See also **Dyslexia; Reading Disorders; Strephosymbolia**

BARDON, JACK I. (1925–1993)

Jack I. Bardon earned his BA in psychology at Cleveland College of Western Reserve University in 1949, with a minor in education. He continued his professional education at the University of Pennsylvania, earning the MA in psychology in 1951 and a PhD in clinical psychology in 1956. From 1952 until 1958, Bardon was a school psychologist in the Princeton, New Jersey schools and served as coordinator of special education services from 1958 to 1960. In 1960 he became director of the Rutgers University doctoral program in school psychology with the academic rank of associate professor. He was promoted to professor in 1963 and became head of the department in 1968.

During his tenure at Rutgers, Bardon began to have an impact nationally on the delivery of school psychological services to handicapped children. Bardon was instrumental in developing the primary role definitions of school psychologists (Bardon, 1982; Bardon & Bennett, 1974). Bardon was involved in work to help differentiate school psychology from other disciplines (Bardon, 1983). His work has benefited special education and regular education by improving the ability of school psychologists to provide services to children at all levels. In Bardon's most recent work (1992), he discussed the rationale for successes and failures in educational undertakings and how they relate to the field of school psychology.

Bardon left Rutgers in 1976 to accept a professorship at the University of North Carolina at Greensboro, where he became an Excellence Foundation Professor in 1983. Bardon was editor of the *Journal of School Psychology* from 1968 to 1971, was president of the Division of School Psychology of the American Psychological Association in 1969, and served on the board of directors of the American Orthopsychiatric Association from 1981 to 1984.

Jack Bardon retired from the University of North Carolina at Greensboro in 1991, and died in November, 1993. He worked hard throughout his career to apply psychological theory, principles, and practice to the field of education, and is credited by his colleagues with having made a substantial impact in the definition of school psychology, professional organizational issues, and in the debate over levels of training in school psychology.

REFERENCES

Bardon, J.I. (1992). Solving educational problems: Working across institutional, cultural and political differences. *School of Psychology Quarterly, 7,* 137–147.

Bardon, J.I. (1982). The psychology of school psychology. In C.R. Reynolds & T.B. Gutkin (Eds.), *The handbook of school psychology.* New York: Wiley.

Bardon, J.I. (1983). Psychology applied to education: A specialty in search of an identity. *American Psychologist, 38,* 185–196.

Bardon, J.I., & Bennett, V.C. (1974). *School psychology.* Englewood Cliffs, NJ: Prentice Hall.

BARRIER-FREE EDUCATION

The delivery of special education services to all handicapped children in the least restrictive environment means that school buildings and facilities must be designed or altered to make those services accessible. Barrier-free design standards typically give technical specifications that cover building entrances and exits, parking, curbs, stairs, elevators, lavatories, drinking fountains, hazard warnings, and building elements and fixtures. In both new construction and modifications of existing facilities, buildings may be subject to a variety of definitions and design standards (Redden, 1979). In 1973, the American National Standards Institute (ANSI) criteria were cited in the regulations for Section 504 of the Rehabilitation Act of 1973 as the minimum access standard to assure compliance with nondiscrimination provisions. The design standards set forth in the Uniform Federal Accessibility Standards (UFAS, 1984) generally were consistent with federal standards in effect, major model building codes, and most state and local codes;

they were based on ANSI A117.1–1980. The 1984 UFAS criteria were geared to adult dimensions and anthropometrics. Some states, however, developed design guidelines for special education facilities that considered the total learning environment for children with all types of handicaps (Abend et al., 1979). A barrier-free environment require the removal of all architectural barriers to accessibility (Redden, 1979).

The passage of the Americans with Disabilities Act of 1990 (ADA) substantially supported the intent of accessibility spelt out in Section 504. Title II of the ADA did not impose any major new requirements on school districts because school districts received federal funds and were required to provide accessibility under Section 504 as far back as 1973. However, as the ADA expanded nondiscriminatory protection to school students, it also took precedent over any lesser stringent rules in Section 504. The ADA reiterated that:

"A school district must ensure that students with disabilities are not excluded from participation in, or denied the benefits of, its services, programs, and activities. It must also ensure that they are not subjected to discrimination by the school system." (Office for Civil Rights, p. 45)

The ADA provided new guidelines and self-evaluation surveys based on the Americans with Disabilities Act Accessibility Guidelines for Buildings and Facilities (ADAAG) (U.S. Department of Education, 1996).

The Office for Civil Rights (OCR) enforces Title II of the ADA and Section 504 of the Rehabilitation Act of 1973. The OCR investigates complaints filed by individuals or their representatives, who believe that they have been discriminated against because of a disability. The OCR can be reached at U.S. Department of Education, Office for Civil Rights, 330 C Street, S.W., Room 5000, Washington, DC 20202. Their telephone is (202) 205-5413 and TDD number is (800) 358-8247.

In addition, an internet resource designed to accommodate specific disabilities that can help teachers, parents, and students overcome educational obstacles is called "Barrier Free Education." The creators of the web site initiated the internet resource because they believe that "the academic community has a responsibility to take a leadership role in making accessible environments a reality" (Ira, 1998).

REFERENCES

Abend, A.C., Bedner, M.J., Froehlinger, V.J., & Stenzler, Y. (1979). *Facilities for special educational services: A guide for planning new and renovated schools.* Reston, VA: Council for Exceptional Children.

Ira, V. (1998). Barrier free education. *The Exceptional Parent, 28,* 30.

Redden, M.R. (Ed.). (1979). *Assuring access for the handicapped.* San Francisco: Jossey-Bass.

Uniform Federal Accessibility Standards. (1984, August 7). 49 F.R. 31528–31621.

U.S. Department of Education, Office for Civil Rights. (1996). Compliance with the Americans with Disabilities Act: A self evaluation guide for Public Elementary and Secondary Schools. Washington, DC: U.S. Government Printing Office.

See also Accessibility of Buildings; Accessibility of Programs; Americans with Disabilities Act

BARRIERS, ARCHITECTURAL

See ARCHITECTURAL BARRIERS.

BASC

See BEHAVIOR ASSESSMENT SYSTEM FOR CHILDREN.

BASAL READERS

Basal reader programs are comprehensive, meaningfully sequenced collections of stories, frequently arranged in groups according to a central theme or topic. Smith and Johnson (1980) described these programs as being based on the belief that a controlled vocabulary of high-frequency words, coupled with the presentation of easily decodable pattern words, facilitates learning to read and the improvement of reading skills.

Basal reader programs are intended to be used to instruct children from the stage of nonreading, through the acquisition of developing skills, to the level of mature, flexible reading. Typically, these programs include various correlated and supplementary materials including teachers' manuals, workbooks, skills sheets, activity boxes, criterion-referenced monitoring systems, and even computer software management programs. This self-contained aspect of basal reader programs is intended to provide all that is necessary for a core reading program. Teachers are carefully guided through instructional directed reading activities as outlined in the accompanying manuals. The structure of these lesson plans, explained by both Stauffer (1969) and Harris (1970), follows the sequence of prereading preparation, guided silent reading, oral rereading and comprehension assessment, skill development activities, and enrichment. In addition, teachers are usually provided with suggestions for choosing related books and other materials to use in conjunction with the basal reader. A survey of 500 educators by Bauman and Heubach in 1996 found that teachers believed that these materials have an empowering effect by providing additional instructional ideas to draw from, adapt, or extend (Bauman & Heubach, 1996).

In recent years basal readers have been analyzed in terms of cultural competence. Foley and Boulware (1996) found that gender equity reflected in basal readers has not essentially changed since the 1960s. In addition, analyses of basal readers regarding race and ethnicity indicate that these aspects of culture are omitted from the majority of basal texts. The omission of race and/or ethnicity from basal selections and teacher manuals may not meet the needs of many children (McDermott, 1997). Other criticisms of basal readers suggest that publisher censorship still exists and essential components of literary works are being eliminated by widespread anthologization (Reutzel & Larsen, 1995). However, others (Risner & Nicholson, 1996) applaud the addition of questions to the readers that support higher levels of comprehension than previously found. Therefore, research still suggests that basal readers support the development of additional teacher materials and engaging activities that, in turn, elevate student reading comprehension. Cultural competence appears to be the most important future development for basal readers.

REFERENCES

Bauman, J.F., & Heubach, K.M. (1996). Do basal readers deskill teachers? A national survey of educator's use and opinions of basals. *Elementary School Journal, 96,* 511–526.

Foley, C.L., & Boulware, B.J. (1996). Gender equity in 1990 middle school basal readers. *Reading Improvement, 33,* 220– 223.

Harris, A.J. (1970). *How to increase reading ability* (5th ed.). New York: McKay.

McDermott, P. (1997). The illusion of racial diversity in contemporary basal readers: An analysis of teacher manuals. Evaluative/feasibility report: speech/conference paper. Abstract from: ERIC Item No. ED407473.

Reutzel, D.R., & Larsen, N.S. (1995). Look what they've done to real children's books in the new basal readers. *Language Arts, 72,* 495–507.

Risner, G.P., & Nicholson, J.I. (1996). *The new basal readers: What levels of comprehension do they promote? Evaluative/feasibility report.* (ERIC Item No. ED403546)

Smith, R.J., & Johnson, D.D. (1980). *Teaching children to read* (2nd ed.). Reading, MA: Addison-Wesley.

Stauffer, R.G. (1969). *Directing reading maturity as a cognitive process.* New York: Harper & Row.

See also Reading Disorders; Reading Remediation

BASELINE DATA

A baseline measurement occurs prior to the beginning of an intervention. It involves precise counting of the target behavior (i.e., dependent variable) during whatever current conditions exist. Baselines are meant to be representative measures of the target behavior. As such they should also be reliable and valid. Reliability should be scored by having two persons simultaneously record the data and by comparing those data records using different calculation procedures (e.g., Kappa), dependent on which recording technique was used (e.g., momentary time sampling) and the properties of the data. Validity, in its simplest form, requires that a measure be that which was purported. If after writing the behavioral definition of the target behavior the definition was compared to the behavior to determine whether the behavior written was that which the student exhibited, the primary form of validation would be completed. If the definition is given to another person and he or she is asked whether the written definition was observable in he student's behavior, and if that person found it to be so, the second form of validation would be completed.

Baseline data should be stable prior to the initiation of intervention. Stability is said to have occurred when there is an absence of directionality or trend in the data and when there is restricted variation in the pattern of the data. Trend is said to occur when there are three or more data points patterned in a specific direction. This is also referred to as celeration and is illustrated by data that accelerated or decelerated. Baseline data that are either accelerating or decelerating are generally not useful as preintervention data. The trend in the data suggests that there is already something that is influencing the target behavior. However, when the trend is countertherapeutic (i.e., moving in the undesired direction), the need for protracted baseline data collection is negated. Therefore, if the trend of the baseline data is therapeutic, continuation of the baseline is indicated until such time as the behavior becomes acceptable or until it levels off and becomes stable. If the data are countertherapeutic, this is not necessary and intervention can be begun in 5 to 10 sessions or days.

Variability in the data during baseline in the absence of a significant trend must be measured by examining its degree to determine its effect on the baseline. Baseline data should be stable so that the practitioner can say with reasonable certainty that the target behavior occurred in a specific condition prior to intervention. Stability is measured as the degree of variability about the mean. In research and teaching with humans we would look for +/− 50% variability about the baseline mean (Alberto & Troutman, 1982). Baseline stability or countertherapeutic trend is a basic requirement prior to the initiation of intervention programming.

REFERENCE

Alberto, P.A., & Troutman, A.C. (1982). *Applied behavior analysis for teachers.* Columbus, OH: Merrill.

See also **Applied Behavior Analysis; Behavior Modification**

BASE RATE

A base rate is a baseline measurement of a target behavior's rate of responding. This measurement is useful when the student's behavior of interest is one for which frequency recording is the appropriate recording strategy and for which rate of responding is the appropriate datum. The latter case is true when the response frequency dependent on duration of observation is important.

To determine the base rate, data would be gathered over a period of days or sessions and would be examined to meet the criterion for stability for any baseline data; that is, the data must be stable (have limited variability) or countertherapeutic. Stability is said to occur when the data vary no more than +/− 50% of the baseline mean (Alberto & Troutman, 1982). A countertherapeutic trend is said to occur when the data are not stable but moving in the opposite direction. Base-rate data are usually reported as a mean figure (e.g., "the mean base rate was . . ."), however, these data may be reported as including the range and the usual data display via a graph.

REFERENCE

Alberto, P.A., & Troutman, A.C. (1982). *Applied behavior analysis for teachers.* Columbus, OH: Merrill.

See also **Applied Behavior Analysis; Behavior Modification**

BASIC SKILLS TRAINING

Historically, the term "basic skills" refers to the traditional disciplines of reading, writing, and arithmetic that are stressed in the early years of formal education. The exceptional child or adult may require a completely different type of basic skill training than the traditional disciplines deemed necessary for functioning within society. Depending on the severity of the handicapping condition, basic skills for special education may vary little or greatly from those of regular students and adults. Basic skills training for exceptional children could best be termed those activities and subject areas that provide for each child's individual learning abilities (allowing for his or her weaknesses) in such a way that deviation from the norm is as limited as possible. This training allows children to accomplish what Blake (1981) refers to as "cultural tasks," in which needs are met through means that are acceptable to society.

Specifically, basic skills for the exceptional child might include those skills noted by Berdine and Blackhurst (1981): training in attention skills, increased memory capacity, the ability to transfer and generalize recently learned skills, and language. In addition, study skills, self-management skills and computer competence are needed as basic skills. Therefore, for the special education student, the basic skills required for academic success are more process-orientated than for regular education students.

In recent years, inclusive programming has sought to assist the special education student in the acquisition of basic skills. Instead of pulling special education students out of the content classes, they have remained with specialized assistance (McCollum & Tindal, 1996). Unfortunately, little data exists to support the effectiveness of this programming for basic content skills at this time.

REFERENCES

Berdine, W.H., & Blackhurst, A.E. (1981). *An introduction to special education.* Boston: Little, Brown.

Blake, K.A. (1981). *Educating exceptional pupils: An introduction to contemporary practices.* Reading, MA: Addison-Wesley.

McCollum, S., & Tindal, G. (1996). Supporting students in content areas classes using an outcome-based system of collaboration. *Special Services in the Schools, 12,* 1–17.

See also **Functional Domains; Functional Instruction**

BATTERED CHILD SYNDROME

In 1962, pediatrician C. Henry Kempe published an article entitled "The Battered Child Syndrome." This marked the first official recognition by the medical establishment of the problem of child abuse. Kempe's article focused on abuse as a deliberate, violent attack on a child by a malicious adult and criticized the medical profession for failing to diagnose and report such cases. Child abuse is a broad term currently used to describe incidents of violent attack, neglect, or sexual abuse that may result in psychological and behavioral disturbances as well as physical or even life-threatening injury. Ellerstein (1981) states that between 1 and 3% of children in the United States are abused. Figures vary depending on laws governing reporting and definitions of child abuse. Indeed, the incidence of severe violence against children declined in the mid to late 1980s. Possible reasons cited for the lower rate were an increased reluctance to report, differences in the methods of study, years of prevention and treatment efforts, and effects of changes in American society and family patterns that produce lower rates of violence towards children. However, regardless of decline, about 4,000 children die each year as a result of abuse.

Researchers have investigated several factors associated with child abuse. Various models, each emphasizing the importance of particular factors, have been formulated to explain the phenomenon. The psychopathological model focuses on the personality characteristics of the perpetrator. Attributes such as personal history of abuse, low self-esteem, and inability to cope with frustration are seen as important contributing factors (Gil, 1970). In the sociological model, environmental factors such as poverty, acceptance of corporal punishment, and overcrowding in the home receive emphasis (Gil, 1970). The cognitive-behavioral model takes into account style of responding to stress and the belief systems of abusive parents (Green, 1984). A broader model encompassing the preceding elements and accounting for the significance of interactions between parents and children is referred to as the ecological model (Roscoe et al., 1985).

Investigators have found that some children are more likely than others to become victims of child abuse. Children at increased risk for abuse often come from larger than average families, have low birth weights or were premature as infants, and fail to form attachment bonds with a caregiver. A comparison of incidence rates suggests that age, family income, and ethnicity were risk factors for both sexual and physical abuse. Gender was a risk factor for sexual abuse but not physical abuse (Cappelleri, Echenrode, & Powers, 1993). Males are more likely to be abused, as are handicapped, retarded, and otherwise different or difficult children (Newberger, 1982).

In 1997, child protection professionals were surveyed regarding their opinions about the best papers and chapters on child abuse available. Kempe's 1962 article was cited as one of the best resources on child abuse and a seminal work (Oates & Donnelly, 1997).

REFERENCES

Cappelleri, J.C., Echenrode, J., & Powers, J.L. (1993). The epidemiology of child abuse: Findings from the second national incidence and prevalence study of child abuse and neglect. *American Journal of Public Health, 83,* 1622–1624.

Ellerstein, N.S. (Ed.). (1981). *Child abuse and neglect: A medical reference.* New York: Wiley.

Gil, D. (1970). Unraveling child abuse. *American Journal of Orthopsychiatry, 45,* 345–356.

Green, A. (1984). Child maltreatment: Recent studies and future directions. *Journal of the American Academy of Child Psychiatry, 23,* 675–678.

Kempe, C.H. (1962). The battered child syndrome. *Journal of the American Medical Association, 181,* 17–24.

Newberger, E.H. (Ed.). (1982). *Child abuse.* Boston: Little, Brown.

Oates, R.K., & Donnelly, A.C. (1997). Influential papers in child abuse. *Child Abuse and Neglect, 21,* 319–326.

Roscoe, B., Callahan, J., & Peterson, K. (1985). Who is responsible? Adolescents' acceptance of theoretical child abuse models. *Adolescence, 20,* 188–197.

See also **Child Abuse; Child Care Agencies; Child Caretaker**

BAYLEY SCALES OF INFANT DEVELOPMENT–SECOND EDITION

The Bayley Scales of Infant Development–Second Edition (BSID-II; Bayley, 1993) is an individually administered test of developmental functioning. It is designed to be administered to infants and children between the ages of 1 month through 42 months.

The BSID-II consists of three scales: the Mental Scale, Motor Scale, and Behavior Rating Scale, formerly called the Infant Behavior Record in the first edition of the Bayley Scales. The Mental Scale assesses the child's current level of cognitive, language, and personal social development and includes items that measure memory, problem solving, early number concepts, generalization, classification, vocalizations, language, and social skills. The Motor Scale measures the child's level of gross and fine motor development via items associated with crawling, sitting, standing, walking, and so on, for gross motor movement and items related to the use of writing, grasping, and imitation of hand movements for fine motor movement. The Behavior Rating Scale is completed by the examiner regarding the child's behaviors during the test administration and assesses the child's attention/arousal (for children under 6 months of age), orientation/engagement toward the tasks and the examiner, emotional regulation, and quality of motor movement. Both the Mental and Motor Scales combined take between 25 and 60 minutes to administer, with estimated time for children under age 15 months between 25 and 35 minutes.

The BSID-II was standardized on a sample of 1,700 children, including 100 children (50 boys and 50 girls) in each of the 17 age groups between 1 month and 42 months of age. Data from the 1988 U.S. Census Bureau was used to stratify the sample on the following variables: age, gender, race/ethnicity, geographic region, and parent education variables. The BSID-II Manual (Bayley, 1993) contains specific characteristics of the sample. Data regarding reliability and validity of the BSID-II appear to be good and are described in detail in two chapters of the BSID-II Manual. However, BRS stability coefficients are consistently lower than coefficients for the Mental and Motor scales. This is addressed in the BSID-II Manual.

The BSID-II, like its predecessor, is likely the most widely used scale of infant development. Its primary use remains as a classification tool to describe normal child development and identify children with developmental delays. Several strengths of the BSID-II are important to mention. First, items are based from a wide range of theory and research on infant development. Second, it has the best, most updated norms of the available scales for assessing very young children. Last, it offers flexible administration of items, yet still allowing examiners to follow standardized procedures. Thus, while there is a specified set of items to administer, the order in which one administers the items can be modified, which helps to maintain the child's attention and rapport during the testing. The most notable limitations of the BSID-II include the following: (1) Many of the items require either expressive language or a good understanding of spoken language for success. However, many high risk and developmentally delayed young children have speech and/or language delays or impairments, making it difficult to assess their cognitive abilities using the BSID-II. (2) Mental and Motor Development Indices do not go below 50. Therefore, only mild mental retardation can be accurately assessed. (3) Noted by Dunst (1998) is "the implicit assertion that the scales have value for developing Individualized Family Service Plans (IFSPs). . . ." However, he notes that the Bayley Scales have not demonstrated treatment utility and they "are not appropriate as instruments for identifying behavior goals for intervention." Thus, although the BSID-II has diagnostic utility and is an excellent measure for assessing infant development, it should not be used to plan specific interventions.

REFERENCES

Bayley, N. (1993). *Bayley Scales of Infant Development–Second Edition Manual.* San Antonio, TX: Psychological Corporation.

Dunst, C.J. (1998). Bayley Scales of Infant Development, Second Edition. In J.C. Impara & B.S. Plake (Eds.), *The Thirteenth Mental Measurements Yearbook.* Lincoln, NE: Buros Institute of Mental Measurements.

BECHTEREV (BEKHTIAREV) VLADIMIR M. (1857–1927)

Vladimir M. Bechterev was born in Viatka province, Russia. He was a noted physiologist and neuropathologist and the founder of the School of Reflexology. Bechterev obtained his PhD at the Military Medical Academy in St. Petersburg in 1881. In 1885 Bechterev became professor at the University of Kazan and in 1893, professor at the Military Medical Academy. The same year he began to publish a journal, *Neurological Review.* Bechterev was also interested in the education of exceptional children. His work in this area is referred to as pedagogical reflexology. In 1911 he addressed the International Congress of Pedology in Brussels, Belgium. His pioneering work contributed immensely toward the future development of Soviet defectology.

Bechterev made an important contribution to the knowledge of anatomy and physiology of the nervous system. He conducted research on localization function of the brain and became famous for his work on nerve currents. He also identified the layer of fibers in the cerebral cortex known as Bechterev's fibers.

Bechterev was a prolific writer who produced over 135 publications and papers, including *General Principles of Reflexology* (1918) and *Objective Psychology* (1913).

REFERENCES

Bechterev, V.M. (1913). *Objective psychologie oder psychoreflexologia.* Leipzig/Berlin: Verlag Teubner.

Bechterev, V.M. (1918). *Obshtchie osnovi reflexologii* (General principles of reflexology). St. Petersburg.

BEERS, CLIFFORD W. (1876–1943)

Clifford W. Beers founded the mental hygiene movement following 3 years as a patient in mental hospitals in Connecticut in the early part of the twentieth century. Because of the abuses that he suffered, he left the hospital determined to reform the system, to see harsh custodial care replaced with medical treatment. His book, *A Mind that Found Itself,* published in 1908, gives a vivid account of his experiences, and at the time created a public outcry against inhumane treatment of mental patients.

A gifted speaker and organizer, Beers obtained the support of eminent psychiatrists and other prominent people to form the Connecticut Society for Mental Hygiene in 1908, the National Committee for Mental Hygiene in 1909, and the International Committee for Mental Hygiene in 1930.

REFERENCE

Beers, C.W. (1981). *A mind that found itself* (5th ed.). Pittsburgh: University of Pittsburgh Press.

BEERY-BUKTENICA DEVELOPMENT TEST OF VISUAL-MOTOR INTEGRATION

The Beery-Buktenica Development Test of Visual-Motor Integration (VMI; Beery, 1997) assesses a child's ability to integrate visual and motor skills. The VMI consists of 27 geometric forms that increase in complexity, which the examinee is asked to copy in a space provided underneath each item. Group and individual administrations are equally acceptable. Administration time varies depending upon the age and ability of the examinee, but usually takes 15 minutes. Supplemental tests of Visual Perception and Motor Coordination represent the newest additions to this test, and are recommended by the author for use in individuals that perform poorly on the VMI. These supplemental tests (containing the same geometric figures as the VMI) separate the visual from the motor aspects of the VMI, allowing the examiner to identify which area contributes most to poor performance. The author advises that these tests should be given in the order for which they were normed: VMI, Visual Perception, and Motor Coordination.

Reliability of the VMI and its supplemental tests are reported as high. The manual reports internal consistency at .88 for the VMI, .85 for the Visual Perception Test and .87 for the Motor Coordination Test. Test-retest at a 3 week interval for the VMI, Visual Perception, and Motor Coordination, were reported at .87, .84, and .83, respectively. Concurrent validity is reported through moderate median correlation with the Bender Gestalt (Armstrong & Knopf, 1982; Wesson, 1986) and significant correlations with WISC-R performance IQ (Breen et al., 1985). Predictive validity was established through relation of low VMI scores and grade failure (Fowler et al., 1986) and academic readiness (Weerdenburg & Janzen, 1985; Simner, 1983). Ease of administration, simplistic score structure, and its culture-free nature have facilitated its wide use as a screening and research measure.

REFERENCES

Armstrong, B.B., & Knopf, K.F. (1982). Comparison of the Bender-Gestalt and Revised Developmental Test of Visual-Motor Integration. *Perceptual and Motor Skills, 55,* 164–166.

Beery, K.E. (1997). *The Beery-Buktenica Developmental Test of Visual-Motor Integration Administration Scoring and Teaching Manual.* Modern Curriculum Press, Parsippany, NJ.

Breen, M., & Carlson, M., & Lehman, J. (1985). The Revised Developmental Test of Visual-Motor Integration: Its relation to the VMI, WISC-R, and Bender Gestalt for a group of elementary aged learning disabled students. *Journal of Learning Disabilities, 3,* 136–138.

Fowler, M.G., & Cross, A.W. (1986). Preschool risk factors as predictors of early school performance. *Journal of Developmental and Behavioral Pediatrics, 4,* 237–241.

Simner, M.L. (1983). The warning signs of school failure: An updated profile of at risk kindergarten child. *Topics in Early Childroom Special Education, 3,* 17–27.

Weerdenburg, G., & Janzen, H.L. (1985). Predicting grade 1 success with a selected kindergarten screening battery. *School Psychology International, 1,* 12–23.

Wesson, M.D., & Kispert, K. (1986). The relationship between the Test for Visual Analysis Skills (TVAS) and standardized visual-motor tests in children with visual perception difficulty. *Journal of the American Optometric Association, 11,* 844–849.

BEHAVIORAL ASSESSMENT

Behavioral assessment is distinguished from other types of assessment by the assumptions on which it is based and the purposes for which it is designed (Nelson & Hayes, 1979). It has been used in the assessment of problems as varied as social withdrawal, insomnia, learning disabilities, and seizure disorders (Mash & Terdal, 1981). Behavior domains assessed include cognitive and affective as well as motor behaviors (Cone, 1979).

Assessment is performed to generate treatment plans. This means that the quality of assessment is judged by the effectiveness of the intervention plans that it generates (treatment utility). Internal consistency, stability, interrater agreement, criterion-related validity, content validity, and construct validity are all necessary to establish treatment utility, and thus are as important as traditional assessment.

Controlling events are events that precede the behavior signaling its occurrence (antecedents), and that follow the occurrence of the behavior and have either the effect of strengthening or weakening the behavior (consequences). Different characteristics of a single target behavior may be under different controls. For example, tantrum behavior may be precipitated by the presentation of a frustrating task and the demand to perform it, but duration may be maintained by staff attention. Controlling events can be identified if changes in the occurrence of controlling events are made and the target behavior changes. The goal is to link assessment with intervention by determining what supports and what compromises a child's performance (Westbury, Stevens, & Oetter, 1996).

Skill deficits may preclude a desirable behavior from being performed. Techniques of task analysis (Resnick, Wang, & Kaplan, 1973) decompose behaviors into the simple parts that are necessary for performing the behavior. The client is assessed for performance of these prerequisite behaviors, thus yielding information that can be used to train the more complex skill. Among other methods, information from criterion-referenced tests can be useful for this purpose.

To evaluate intervention effects, data about the target behaviors must be collected prior to the start of an intervention, during a baseline period, as well as after the intervention has begun. Because a behavioral intervention may have inadvertent side effects, it is important for the clinician to hypothesize these and to assess them as well as intended treatment effects. For example, a plan may be to reduce a child's inappropriate talking out in class; the clinician should consider that talking out in class discussions and talking out on the playground may reduce also. Behavior change is evaluated using experimental designs that attempt to remove the threats to validity encountered in single-subject research (Barlow & Hersen, 1984).

Three of the most commonly used behavioral assessment techniques are interviewing, observation, and behavior products. Techniques that are occasionally used include self-monitoring, psychophysiological assessment, checklists and questionnaires, sociometry, and psychoeducational assessment. Interviewing may be the only assessment method available when the behavior is covert, occurs at a low rate, or occurs in a setting in which it is not feasible to observe. Also, the selection and definition of target behaviors must take place in an interview with the client or with someone responsible for the client's welfare. The clinician must decide who will be most informative regarding the client's behavior, and must consider interviewing several persons if any one person's knowledge of the problem is incomplete. Behavioral interviews proceed from an initial phase of problem identification, in which the clinician attempts to elicit all problems of concern to the interviewee, to problem specification, in which the problem behaviors are sufficiently specified so that the clinician and interviewee would agree on occurrences of the behavior if it were observed. Then comes the problem analysis phase, in which the clinician and interviewee attempt to identify controlling events and skill deficits. In consultation and some forms of direct service, the interview also may be used to generate plans for intervention. A fifth phase of interviewing involves evaluating the effectiveness of an intervention. Of these five phases, the most important for successful problem solution appears to be problem specification. The success of this phase depends on the clinician's ability to ask questions eliciting specific descriptions of behavior and controlling events while at the same time maintaining rapport (Haynes, 1978; Tombari & Bergan, 1978).

Observations serve two main purposes in behavioral assessment: to assess characteristics of target behaviors as they change following intervention, and to identify the controlling events of a behavior. In addition, observations can be used to identify goals for behavior change by identifying group norms for behavior. For example, a teacher may want to increase a child's participation in class discussions, but 100% would be too much. Observations reveal that classmates spend 4% of class time participating in discussions; therefore, reaching this level may be a suitable goal. Observation methods vary according to the rate of the behavior, the characteristics being assessed, the training and experience of the observer, and the observer's purpose. Behaviors that are low-rate (e.g., less than one occurrence an hour) will usually need to be recorded by participant observers (e.g., parents, staff) and be tallied on a daily or weekly basis to yield a measure of behavior frequency. Duration and latency of behaviors will need to be timed. Intensity can be rated by an observer, and topography can be described in a verbal narrative. Identifying controlling events requires being able to track immediately preceding and following events. These events, if observers are trained to look for them, can be recorded in an anecdotal record, a narrative report of each occurrence of a behavior. A houseparent, reporting an incident of running away, can note the time and setting of the occurrence, immediately preceding events, the chain of running-away behaviors, the duration of the incident, and likely consequent events. Current observational methods many times rely on computer programs such as the

Direct Observation Data System (DODS). These programs save time, increase reliability and validity, and are user friendly (Munoz & Garcia, 1996).

Sampling is required in observation of high-rate behaviors because it is not convenient or possible to observe target behaviors continuously. In time sampling, a decision must first be made about the length of an observation session (e.g., 20 minutes). This will depend on the rate of the behavior; the session should be long enough to observe many occurrences. A second decision concerns dividing the observation session into smaller units (intervals), deciding on the length of each interval and the interval sampling method to be used. Interval length needs to be short (e.g., 3 seconds) for high-rate behaviors, but can be long (e.g., 1 hour) for low-rate behaviors. The shorter the interval length, the closer the agreement between time sampling and continuous monitoring, but the more tedious observation becomes. In whole-interval sampling, a behavior is recorded only if it has been occurring during the entire interval. In partial-interval sampling, a behavior is recorded if it occurred at any time during the interval. Compared with continuous monitoring, whole-interval sampling consistently underestimates time, while partial-interval sampling overestimates time (Powell, 1984). A method of sampling that provides an unbiased estimate of frequency is momentary time sampling. In this method, an observation is made at the precise onset of an interval. If the behavior is occurring at the moment, it is recorded. Each method generates a summary score indicating the proportion of intervals in which the behavior occurred. If intervals are short (much shorter than average behavior duration), an estimate of behavior duration can be made if one counts consecutive intervals in which the behavior occurred.

Behavior products, such as a math worksheet completed by a student or number of pounds gained by a person with an eating disorder, are less reactive than interviews, observations, self-monitoring, or client-completed checklists (Webb et al., 1966). Such measures are most often used as measures of behavior change in addition to more reactive measures. Although in many instances producing little information about controlling events, some products may produce clues about such events. For example, examination of a child's math worksheet may reveal consistent misapplications of a math rule (Brown & Burton, 1978); or an examination of absentee records may reveal that a child's nonattendance tends to occur following weekends and holidays.

REFERENCES

Barlow, D.H., & Hersen, M. (1984). *Single case experimental designs.* New York: Pergamon.

Brown, J.S., & Burton, R.R. (1978). Diagnostic models for procedural bugs in basic mathematical skills. *Cognitive Science, 2,* 155–192.

Cone, J.D. (1979). Confounded comparisons in triple response mode assessment research. *Behavioral Assessment, 1,* 85–95.

Haynes, S.N. (1978). *Principles of behavioral assessment.* New York: Gardner.

Mash, E.J., & Terdal, L.G. (Eds.). (1981). *Behavioral assessment of childhood disorders* (pp. 441–482). New York: Guilford.

Munoz, A.M., & Garcia, J. (1996). The Direct Observation Data System (DODS). *Journal of Computing in Childhood Education, 8,* 14–18.

Nelson, R.O., & Hayes, S.C. (1979). Some current dimensions of behavioral assessment. *Behavioral Assessment, 1,* 1–16.

Powell, J. (1984). On the misrepresentation of behavioral realities by a widely practiced direct observation procedure: Partial interval (one-zero) sampling. *Behavioral Assessment, 6,* 209–220.

Resnick, L.B., Wang, M.C., & Kaplan, J. (1973). Task analysis in curriculum design: A hierarchically sequenced introductory math curriculum. *Journal of Applied Behavior Analysis, 6,* 679–709.

Tombari, M.L., & Bergan, J.R. (1978). Consultant cues and teacher verbalizations, judgments, and expectancies concerning children's adjustment problems. *Journal of School Psychology, 16,* 212–219.

Webb, E.J., Campbell, D.T., Schwartz, R.D., & Sechrest, L. (1966). *Unobtrusive measures: Nonreactive research in the social sciences.* Chicago: Rand McNally.

Westbury, C.E., Stevens, D.M., & Oetter, P. (1996). A performance/competence model of observational assessment. *Language, Speech, and Hearing in The Schools, 27,* 144–156.

See also **Behavioral Consultation; Behavior Charting; Behavior Modification; Functional Behavioral Assessment**

BEHAVIORAL CONSULTATION

Over the last three decades, consultation has become an increasingly important tool in the provision of psychological services to children and youths in educational settings (Meecham & Peckham, 1978; Ramage, 1979). School-based consultation may be rendered from a variety of theoretical perspectives. These include mental health consultation, which is linked to psychodynamic theories of personality (Caplan, 1970), organization development consultation (Schmuck, 1982), which has its origins in social psychological theory strongly influenced by the Lewinian perspective, and behavioral consultation, which is linked to behavioral theory (Bandura, 1977; Skinner, 1953). The following discussion describes the behavioral approach to consultation services.

Consultation services are generally rendered in a series of stages, each of which is designed to address a particular aspect of the problem-solving endeavor. Four stages are generally recognized in consultation (Bergan, 1977; Dorr, 1979; Goodwin & Coates, 1976; Tombari & Davis, 1979). They are (1) problem identification, (2) problem analysis, (3) plan implementation, and (4) problem evaluation.

Problem identification sets the direction that consultation will take. Within the behavioral perspective, a problem is defined in terms of a discrepancy between observed behavior and desired behavior. The problem is to eliminate the discrepancy. Determining the existence of a discrepancy between observed and desired behavior requires that the concerns communicated by the consultee be expressed in behavioral terms. During problem identification, the consultant assists the consultee to describe current client functioning and desired functioning in terms of current behaviors and desired behaviors. Data are generally collected to document the status of current behavior. A problem exists if the data reveal a difference between current and desired behavior that the consultee regards as a significant discrepancy.

Problem analysis follows problem identification. During this stage of consultation, the factors that may be influencing client behaviors of concern are identified and a plan is formulated to effect desired changes in behaviors. Behavioral principles are heavily relied on in determining influences on behavior. Problem analysis generally begins with the specification of antecedent and consequent environmental conditions that may be affecting behavior. However, client skills and behavioral patterns may also be the subject of analysis (Piersel, 1985). After hypothesized influences on client behavior have been identified, a plan is formulated to change client behavior. The consultant is generally responsible for specifying the strategies that may be used to achieve behavior change. However, the consultee often plays a major role in identifying specific tactics that may be useful in implementing a plan. For example, a consultant may determine that positive reinforcement may be useful in increasing a particular behavior of concern to the consultee. The consultee may then identify the type of reinforcement to be used with the behavior.

After a suitable plan has been formulated, it is implemented. Implementation is generally the responsibility of the consultee. However, the consultee may direct an implementation effort in which others actually carry out the plan. For instance, a teacher may direct a peer tutoring program designed to increase the reading skills of a group of children. The principal role of the consultant during implementation is one of monitoring what is occurring and of assisting the consultee to make minor revisions in the plan in those instances in which the plan is not working as expected.

The final stage in consultation is problem evaluation. During this phase of consultation, the consultant and the consultee determine the extent to which the goals of consultation have been achieved and the extent to which the plan implemented to attain goals has been effective. Evaluation data guide the course of consultation. If the goals of consultation have been achieved, a new problem may be identified or services may terminate. If the goals of consultation have not been achieved, consultation generally returns to problem analysis.

There is a large body of research documenting the effectiveness of behavioral consultation (Feld, Bergan, & Stone, 1984). Research on the effectiveness of behavioral consultation is of two types. The first involves studies of the application of behavioral principles in consultation to achieve changes in behavior. Research of this kind has shown the behavioral approach to be effective in remediating a large variety of behavioral and academic problems (Bergan & Tombari, 1976; Conoley & Conoley, 1982; Medway, 1979; Medway & Forman, 1980).

The second body of research on the effectiveness of the behavioral approach compares the effectiveness of behavioral consultation with that of other forms of service. Many of the comparative studies have methodological flaws (Medway, 1979) and therefore results and generalization are inconclusive.

Recent developments in behavioral consultation focus on collaborative arrangements between parents of special education students and educators. Specific emphasis has been placed on cultural-ethnic lifestyle considerations (Fine & Gardner, 1994).

REFERENCES

Bandura, A. (1977). *Social learning.* Englewood Cliff, NJ: Prentice-Hall.

Bergan, J.R. (1977). *Behavioral consultation.* Columbus, OH: Merrill.

Bergan, J.R., & Tombari, M.L. (1976). Consultant skill and efficiency and the implementation of outcomes of consultation. *Journal of School Psychology, 14,* 3–13.

Caplan, G. (1970). *The theory and practice of mental health consultation.* New York: Basic Books.

Conoley, J.C., & Conoley, C.W. (1982). The effects of two conditions of client-centered consultation on student teacher problem descriptions and remedial plans. *Journal of School Psychology, 20,* 323–328.

Dorr, D. (1979). Psychological consulting in the schools. In J.J. Platt & R J Wicks (Eds.), *The psychological consultant.* New York: Grune & Stratton.

Feld, J.D., Bergan, J.R., & Stone, C.A. (1984). Behavioral approaches to school based consultation: Current status and future directions. In C.A. Maher (Ed.), *Behavioral approaches to providing educational services in schools.* Hillsdale, NJ: Erlbaum.

Fine, M.J., & Gardner, A. (1994). Collaborative consultation with families of children with special needs: Why bother? *Journal of Educational and Psychological Consultation, 5,* 283–308.

Goodwin, D.L., & Coates, T.J. (1976). *Helping students help themselves.* Englewood Cliffs, NJ: Prentice-Hall.

Meecham, M.L., & Peckham, P.D. (1978). School psychologists at three-quarters century: Congruence between training, practice, preferred role and competence. *Journal of School Psychology, 16,* 195–206.

Medway, F.J. (1979). How effective is school consultation: A review of recent research. *Journal of School Psychology, 17,* 275–282.

Medway, F.J., & Forman, S.G. (1980). Psychologists' and teachers' reactions to mental health and behavioral school consultation. *Journal of School Psychology, 18,* 338–348.

Piersel, W.C. (1985). Behavioral consultation: An approach to problem solving in educational settings. In J.R. Bergan (Ed.), *School psychology in contemporary society.* Columbus, OH: Merrill.

Ramage, J.C. (1979). National survey of school psychologists: Update. *School Psychology Digest, 8,* 153–161.

Schmuck, R.A. (1982). Organizational development in the schools. In C.R. Reynolds & T.B. Gutkin (Eds.), *The handbook of school psychology.* New York: Wiley.

Skinner, B.F. (1953). *Science and human behavior.* New York: Macmillan.

Tombari, M.L., & Davis, R.A. (1979). Behavioral consultation. In G.D. Phye & D.J. Reschly (Eds.), *School psychology: Perspectives and issues.* New York: Academic.

See also **Behavior Assessment; Consultation; Consultation, Mental Health**

BEHAVIORAL DEFICIT

The terminology associated with behavioral deficit has become confused as a result of various incomplete usages. The original usage was associated with the 1961 American Association on Mental Retardation inclusion of adaptive behavior in their definition of mental retardation. Adaptive behavior implies that many educational, psychological, sociological, and biological influences interact on the child, affecting function and performance. Principally, it is a term designed to offset the dependence the public schools, mental health agencies, and social welfare institutions had placed on measured intelligence.

In 1974, Gleason and Haring provided the first general behavioral definition of learning disabilities and in so doing used the term behavioral deficit as the principal construct associated with the concept learning disabilities. "We define a learning disability as a behavioral deficit almost always associated with academic performance and that can be remediated by precise, individualized instructional programming" (p. 226).

There are two major issues that surround the construct of behavioral deficits. The first is the possibility or utility of cognitive skills being broken into specific component parts. It should be remembered that all assumed cognitive behaviors are named, usually after a test or subtest designed to measure them. They are not occurrences in nature that are directly observable. The second issue is the reliability of most tests designed to ascertain or describe a basic behavior and therefore illustrate a behavioral deficit. As the reliability decreases, so does the validity.

A behavioral deficit then is a concept suggesting that human abilities are not all the same, and in some cases fall to a deficit level. Operationally defining a deficit has not been well done through the use of tests or subtests in terms of when a deficit statistically or clinically exists. Therefore, while the concept itself has driven several major thrusts (both diagnostic and treatment), including the term developmental disability to some degree, and theoretically is responsible for describing learning disability, it remains an incomplete term, less than fully developed by those who use it on a clinical basis.

REFERENCE

Gleason, C., & Haring, N. (1974). Learning disabilities. In N.G. Haring (Ed.), *Behavior of exceptional children* (pp. 245–295). Columbus, OH: Merrill.

See also **Ability Training; Behavioral Objectives**

BEHAVIORAL DISORDERS

Behavioral Disorders is the official journal of the Council for Children with Behavioral Disorders (CCBD) of the Council for Exceptional Children. Founded in 1975, *Behavioral Disorders* serves as a resource for those professionals interested in the education and treatment of behaviorally disordered children and youth.

The journal, with a quarterly distribution to the 8,400 members of CCBD and hundreds of individual and institutional subscribers, was developed under the editorships of Albert Fink of Indiana University (1975–1978), Denzil Edge of the University of Louisville (1978–1981), and Robert B. Rutherford, Jr., of Arizona State University (1981–1987) into a forum for the publication of manuscripts derived from documented thought and empirical evidence. These data-based articles are presented in several forms: experimental research (either original or replications), research and practice reviews and analyses, program or procedure descriptions, and scholarly reviews of texts, films, and other media.

BEHAVIORAL OBJECTIVES

In the broadest sense, an objective is a statement of an aim or desired outcome. In an educational sense, an instructional objective may be a quantifiable and/or an observable academic or social achievement that specifies the enabling steps necessary to accomplish the objective in a stated period of time. All instructional or behavioral objectives must have observable or measurable outcomes. The difference between an instructional and a behavioral objective is the result to be achieved. The latter may be broader in scope and not confined to an educational effort; it may rather include a wide range of specified behavioral outcomes, for example, speech, language, perceptual development, motor training, and social skill development.

The purpose for developing behavioral objectives is to increase teaching efficiency by having educators and behavioral scientists determine what it is that will be learned, how it will be taught, what materials will be used, and the length of time within which it should be learned against a predetermined criteria or standard. Behavioral objectives become targets to which teachers can direct their instruction. In the process of instruction, their use requires educators to determine whether outcomes or observations of performance are being effectively and efficiently provided and creating an exactness for what is learned and how it is taught. Thus, a teaching methodology may be used for a specified amount of time under conditions that will permit the educator to judge the amount of progress being made.

One of the most common points of confusion is between a course description (or what a course is about) and behavioral objectives (those specific, measurable, or observable performances a student will demonstrate at the completion of a course). Behavioral objectives must contain statements of concrete, measurable, or observable performances. In contrast, nonbehavioral goals are broad, abstract statements; they are not derived from previous observations or performance test data. They do not consider the skills necessary to enter into a next level of work. Nonbehavioral objectives are based on philosophy, ideology, and attitude, not the proficiency of task to be taught.

A behavioral objective is one activity in a series of, or sequence of, activities to be learned. That sequence can become the curriculum. The principal reason for having many small, tightly sequenced steps in the curriculum is that learner performance is examined frequently. More important, the learner is provided with corrective feedback after every trial. That point is critical. What the learner knows does not fall to an assumption that cannot be proven. Behavioral or instructional objectives, once sequenced, become important interlocking steps. Because the ability of children to learn varies widely, particularly when materials change, each objective permits the individual student the necessary time on tasks.

The three major advantages of a behavioral objective are:

1. Students are not compared with others, but with themselves and the speed with which they may learn a given task comfortably.
2. Each tightly sequenced step is validated in the curricular process; all assumptions about learning rate or about what has been learned are rejected.
3. There is a starting point, something the student knows, and a stopping point, a task within the comfort level to be learned.

A curriculum based on a series of behavioral objectives is a scientific approximation of the art of teaching. For that reason, PL 94-142 (1975), and its revisions in 1990 and 1997 called the Individuals with Disabilities Education Act (PL 101-476) required that an individual educational program (IEP) be written for every handicapped child served under this legislation. An IEP is a behavioral objective and/or an instructional objective that requires a specific diagnostic process (with a multidisciplinary team) and a preparation procedure. It ensures the availability of data for accountability.

***See also* Age-Appropriate Curriculum; Teaching Strategies**

BEHAVIORAL OBSERVATION

Behavior observation is at the core of behavioral assessment. Behavior observation is a procedure for categorizing motor and verbal behavior into an organized permanent record. A behavior observation system meets three criteria (Jones, Reid, & Patterson, 1974). These include "recording of behavioral events in their natural settings at the time they occur, not retrospectively; the use of trained impartial observer-coders, and descriptions of behaviors which (sic) require little if any inference by observers to code the events" (p. 46). Excluded from this definition are narrative recordings, anecdotal records, checklists and rating scales, and procedures that require a person to observe and record his or her own behavior.

Behavior observations occur in diverse settings and for numerous purposes. In educational settings, behavior observations are used for purposes of diagnosing individual students, planning an intervention to modify a pupil's behavior, evaluating interventions, consulting with teachers, and conducting research.

Although specific observational procedures and instruments vary in many important ways, they all require selectivity. The observation instrument structures the observer's attention to those selected aspects of behavior and the setting that are presumed to be most relevant to the purposes of the observation. Behavior occurs in a continuous stream, yet the observer must categorize behavior into objectively defined behavioral codes and encode it into an organized, permanent record. Care in defining what is to be observed is critical to measurable results. Narrative recordings and checklists can assist in selecting the most significant behavioral codes as well as the contextual, or environmental, events thought to be associated with the selected behaviors. Data on these antecedent and consequent events are useful in designing a plan for modifying the behaviors of concern.

To minimize observer subjectivity, the selected behaviors are defined as objectively as possible. "Aggressive behavior" is not as objective a definition as "hits, shoves, grabs, and tackles." Although "aggressive behavior" can serve as useful shorthand in coding behavior, the clear specification of the behaviors encompassed by this term gives the observer an objective definition of aggression. When the behavioral codes are objectively defined, any two trained observers should agree on the presence or absence of a behavior. Behavior observations can occur in natural settings (e.g., classroom, peer group, or home) or in simulated or role playing settings.

Observational instruments vary in their degree of formality from homemade teacher-used instruments to published instruments requiring highly trained observers. Three major types of observational procedures are frequency recordings, duration recordings, and interval recordings (Barton & Ascione, 1984). In frequency recordings, the number of times a behavior occurs within the observational period is recorded. Frequency recordings are best suited to behaviors that have a discrete beginning and end, that last approximately the same amount of time each time they occur, and that do not occur so frequently that separating each occurrence becomes difficult. Hand raises, inappropriate noises, bed-wetting, and hitting are examples of frequency target behaviors. Observations should continue over several days to obtain a reliable measure.

A duration recording is a direct measure of the amount of time an individual engages in the target behavior. Duration recordings are most appropriate for behaviors that have a clear beginning and ending and that last for more than a few seconds. If a child gets out of his or her seat and stays out of the seat for periods of time ranging from 1 to 6 minutes, a duration count would indicate the percentage of time the child was out of the seat during the observational period.

In interval recordings, the occurrence or nonoccurrence of selected behaviors during a series of equal time intervals is recorded. Interval recording is recommended when several behaviors need to be observed, when behaviors occur at a high rate, or when behaviors do not have clear-cut beginnings and ends. There are several variations of interval recording procedures. Typically, some sort of signaling device (e.g., an audio timer or beeps on a prerecorded cassette) cues the observer to make a recording. The observer records which target behavior occurred during the preceding interval (usually 10 seconds).

Frequency, duration, and interval recordings can be adapted to a format that allows recording of selected antecedents and consequences of the behavioral codes. At the same time the observed child's behavior is coded, the antecedent and consequent circumstances are coded. Barton and Ascione (1984) provide examples of these different observational instruments.

Observational procedures are measurement procedures, and their reliability and validity need to be established. An important part of establishing reliability is determining the extent to which two observers agree in their use of the instrument while observing the same behavior and context. Recent advances in computer technology have supported reliable data collection by the use of software such as the Direct Observation Data System (DODS). This program saves time, standardizes input, and is preferred by educators over other methods (Johnson, Brady, & Larson, 1996). Validity issues include the relationship of the behavioral code to the referral problem (face validity) and the normality of the observed behavior. One way of determining whether a child's behavior in particular settings (e.g., a classroom) is atypical is to observe other children in the same settings. If the observer alternates between observing the target child and observing other children in a classroom, the observer will have a composite observation of the typical child to compare with the referred child. The observer must also be culturally competent so as to include the sociocultural context to the observation process.

REFERENCES

Barton, C.J., & Ascione, F.R. (1984). Direct observation. In T.H. Ollendick & M. Hersen (Eds.), *Child behavioral assessment* (pp. 166–194). New York: Pergamon.

Johnson, H., Brady, S., & Larson, E. (1996). A microcomputer-based system to facilitate direct observation data collection and assessment in inclusive settings. *Journal of Computing in Childhood Education, 7,* 3–4.

Jones, R.R., Reid, J.B., & Patterson, G.B. (1974). Naturalistic observation in clinical assessment. In P. McReynolds (Ed.), *Advances in psychological assessment.* San Francisco: Jossey-Bass.

See also **Applied Behavior Analysis; Behavior Therapy**

BEHAVIORAL SUPPORT

See SUPPORT, BEHAVIORAL.

BEHAVIOR ANALYSIS, APPLIED

See APPLIED BEHAVIOR ANALYSIS.

BEHAVIOR ASSESSMENT SYSTEM FOR CHILDREN (BASC)

The BASC (Reynolds & Kamphaus, 1992) is a multidimensional, multimethod coordinated system of instruments (that may be used collectively or as individual instruments) designed to evaluate the behaviors, thoughts, and emotions of children and adolescents from ages 2.5 years up to the age of 19 years. The BASC uses both traditional norm-referenced, standardized behavior checklists and omnibus self-report personality scales, interview/questionnaire data, and structured student observations. Designed to provide a comprehensive view of children's and adolescents' behavior and affect when used as a system, each instrument is also designed to stand alone as an individual component when necessary.

The BASC consists of the following components:

1. *Parent Rating Scale (PRS).* Available in three forms, Preschool (ages 2.5 through 5 years), Child (ages 6 through 11 years), and Adolescent (ages 12 to 19 years), the PRS is a traditionally formatted behavior rating scale completed by a parent or other caregiver in 10 to 20 minutes. Broad and narrow bands of behavior and externalizing and internalizing dimensions are all represented. Specific scales are also devoted to school problems and the BASC PRS assesses positive behavioral dimensions through its Adoptive Skills scales.

2. *Teacher Rating Scale (TRS).* The TRS is available in parallel forms to the PRS from ages 2.5 to 19 years and measures primarily the same sets of behaviors as the PRS (adding scales for Learning Problems and Study Skills) but from the perspective of the teacher. 3. *Self-Report of Personality (SRP).* The SRP is an omnibus self-report of thoughts, feelings, and behaviors completed by children (ages 8 through 11 years) and adolescents (ages 12 to 19 years) in about 15–20 minutes. Traditional concepts such as anxiety and depression are assessed alongside newer concepts such as sensation seeking and sense of inadequacy. Other scales with special relevance to the school setting are included as well.

4. *Student Observation Scale (SOS).* The SOS can be used in any structured setting with ages 2.5 years and up as long as the individual is in a learning environment. The SOS is a carefully, conveniently structured observation and coding system that uses an efficient time-sampling approach to observing and counting behaviors. The SOS encourages coding of positive as well as negative behaviors and interac-

tions in classrooms and other structured settings. A child can be assessed with the SOS in about 15 minutes.

5. *Structured Developmental History (SDH).* The SDH is a comprehensive review of developmental, personal, medical, and social histories provided by a knowledgeable caregiver. The SDH is designed so that most caregivers can complete the form independently, but it has also been designed for use as a structured interview. The SDH provides the examiner or clinician with a comprehensive review of the examinee's lifelong developmental path and key family and social history information enhancing diagnostic accuracy and choice of interventions.

The BASC PRS is available in Spanish at all age levels. For those who prefer it, the PRS and SRP are also available on audiotape. The Spanish translations were field tested in all four geographic regions of the United States and in Puerto Rico. They have since been used successfully with a variety of Hispanic and Latino populations including several in South America.

Each of the norm-referenced components of the BASC (each level of the PRS, TRS, and SRP) is available in a hand-scored version, computer-entry scored version, and on scannable forms, all for Windows or Macintosh users. Earlier DOS programs are no longer supported.

The BASC was designed to: (a) facilitate the objective identification of children who are emotionally disturbed according to special education placement criteria; (b) facilitate differential diagnosis among various clinical disorders of behavior, mood, or affect that may affect children; (c) facilitate treatment planning and monitor treatment effectiveness; (d) assess important traditional emotional and behavioral constructs as well as newer constructs that have strong research support; and (e) assess behavioral and emotional strengths as well as the presence of psychopathology.

The psychometric characteristics of the BASC are particularly strong. During 7 years of development, earlier versions of the BASC were administered to nearly 33,000 children.

Normative Data. The BASC scales were standardized on just over 19,000 children and youth from the United States and southern Canada, drawn in a double randomized stratified sampling plan designed to mimic the 1990 U.S. Bureau of the Census population statistics. The sample matched population demographics on the basis of ethnicity, socioeconomic status, parent's educational level, gender, geographic region of residence, and community size. This is overall the largest known standardization sample for an individually administered test.

Scaling. The BASC composite scores and individual scale raw scores are converted to T-scores via a linear transformation. T-scores have a mean of 50 and a standard deviation of 10. Percentiles corresponding to each T-score are provided.

Unlike most tests, the BASC provides the user with multiple sets of T-scores based on 4 normative samples. BASC users have the option of using scores based upon a combined gender sample, gender specific norms (male and female separately), and norms based on a separate sample of children with clinical diagnoses.

Reliability. Scores on the various BASC scales are assessed in the BASC Manual (Reynolds & Kamphaus, 1992) for internal consistency and for temporal stability. Internal consistency reliability estimates for the individual BASC scales are high, averaging about .80 for each gender for the SRP, with composite scores averaging above .90. Test-retest reliability is high as well. The TRS and PRS have comparable reliability associated with their scores as well and follow a common pattern in the research literature, scores on externalizing scales tend to be more reliable than scores on the internalizing scales.

Validity. The BASC Manual provides extensive data regarding the content, construct, and criterion-related validity of score interpretations on the various BASC scales. Follow-up research published since 1992 along with data in the manual are strongly supportive of the use of the BASC in determination of eligibility for special education services. The BASC has proven to be particularly effective, relative to other popular scales, in the differential diagnosis of attention deficit hyperactivity disorder. Although the BASC is more accurate in the diagnosis of all forms of this disorder, it performs especially well in detecting attention deficit hyperactivity disorder, primarily inattentive type.

The BASC has achieved widespread use in the public schools and is used with over 1 million children per year at this time. A growing presence in the private clinical market is also apparent. The BASC is being employed as the major assessment tool in several longitudinal studies including the Minnesota long-term study of ADHD children and the CHAMPUS study of the effectiveness of residential treatment for adolescents. The BASC affords the clinician with reliable and valid scores, comprehensive assessment that is developmentally sensitive to age-related changes in behavior, and with flexible choices of assessment devices.

REFERENCE

Reynolds, C.R., & Kamphaus, R.W. (1992). *Behavior assessment system for children.* Circle Pines, MN: American Guidance Service.

BEHAVIOR CHARTING

Behavior charting is a term commonly used as an equivalent to describe a graphic representation of behavioral data. Graphing behavioral data allows the special educator to see changes easily in target behaviors (behaviors that are to be increased or decreased in frequency or duration). The ordinate, or vertical line, of the graph is labeled with the behavioral measurement scale. This could be the number of occurrences of off-task behavior, the number of fights a child has, or the percentage of time that a child follows instructions. The abscissa, or horizontal line, is labeled with the unit of time. This could be treatment sessions, days, weeks, minutes, or other intervals over which changes in behavior can be measured (Sulzer-Azaroff & Mayer, 1977). A behavioral chart will allow the special educator to evaluate the effectiveness of any treatment that may eventually be implemented (Anguiano, 2001).

REFERENCE

Anguiano, P. (2001). A first year teacher's plan to reduce misbehavior in the classroom. *Teaching Exceptional Children.* 33(3) pp. 52–55.

Sulzer-Azaroff, B., & Mayer, G.R. (1977). *Applying behavior-analysis procedures with children and youth.* New York: Holt, Rinehart and Winston.

See also **Applied Behavior Analysis**

BEHAVIOR, DESTRUCTIVE
See DESTRUCTIVE BEHAVIORS.

BEHAVIOR DISORDERS

The terms behaviorally disordered, emotionally disturbed, emotionally handicapped, and socially maladjusted are used synonymously by practitioners in special education. One of the reasons that different terms are used interchangeably is that various states use a variety of terms in their legal language to describe students who are drawing attention to themselves in matters of personal/social adjustment.

Special education has in the last 50 years developed a repertoire of interchangeable terms. Behavioral disorder implies that a student's social/personal regulative and adjustive mechanisms are poorly defined and generally faulty, given a specific social or environmental condition. The relativity of the term behavioral disorders begins with the displaying situationally and socially of unacceptable behaviors. There are sharp contrasts in what may reflect acceptable behaviors in such settings as urban, rural, large school, small school, etc. In addition, young teacher, old teacher, autocratic or democratic philosophy of the principal, type of community, etc. affect acceptable behaviors. In short, immediate cultural-linguistic circumstances of the child and community are all relative factors.

When do we say a student is failing to make a satisfactory adjustment? The words satisfactory adjustment should signal a recognition that such an expression requires a socially relative value judgment. What goes into that value judgment rests on many factors, including the proximity to the rules being broken and whose rules are being broken.

In 1977, Epstein, Cullinan, and Sabatino attempted to survey the use of the definition behavior disorders among states. The District of Columbia and 45 states replied. The component most prevalent in state definitions was disorder of emotion/behavior; the least common component was prognosis.

These researchers (Epstein, Cullinan, & Sabatino, 1977) identified two definitive types of definitions:

First, numerous authoritative individuals or groups have defined behavior disorders; these statements generally reflect the theoretical positions and professional experiences of their authors and are often intended to structure an exposition of behavior disorders or to provoke thoughtful exploration of a particular position. Another (the second) kind of definition functions primarily to guide the delivery of resources or services to behaviorally disordered children—for example, a state educational agency's definition. (p. 418)

Fifteen definitional components were identified and reported in the data from the study.

Three components, disorders of emotion/behavior, interpersonal problems, and learning/achievement problems, appeared to be separate major areas of child functioning in which problems could occur. Disorders of emotion/behavior was found in all definitions, but the language of the definitions hardly indicated widespread agreement across states. For example, 15 definitions used the word emotion and/or a related reference to interpersonal or mental condition, excluding reference to behavior problems; 18 definitions used behavior and/or alluded to various overt behavior problems, with no mention of difficulties of emotion; 16 definitions referred to both types of problems. Among those definitions that referred to emotional or behavioral disorders, a wide variation in terms and emphases was evident. A majority of state definitions included the components interpersonal problems and learning/achievement problems. A wide range of terms were employed, representing quite different viewpoints that in turn emphasized treatment forms and even expected results.

The components deviation from norm, chronicity, severity, etiology, prognosis, and exclusions functioned as qualifiers in the majority of definitions. The fact that deviation from norm appeared in almost half of the definitions indicated awareness that emotional or behavioral disorders must not only consider the home, school, and social environment, but any discrepancy between a particular child's functioning and that of other pupils of that age in a particular environment. Absent from the definitions were specific statements addressing normal behavioral and emotional patterns. This means the boundaries of diagnosing these behavioral patterns do not have many boundaries wherein the deviation from norm components can be consistently considered. Severity and chronicity components appeared in well over one-third of the definitions. These were apparently intended to distinguish the mild from severe: those in need of in-class support and/or in-school therapy from those who require institutionalization.

The intent of the etiology component may have been to assure that children receiving special education for the behaviorally disordered were truly behaviorally disordered, i.e., that their disturbed functioning arose from some of the classical causes of a behavioral disorder such as organic damage, parental pathology, family breakdown, cultural deprivation, etc. Across the eight definitions that contained this component, however, divergent and even contradictory etiologies were emphasized. Prognosis apparently was included to provide special education primarily to the mildly behaviorally disordered in contrast to the more severely involved. This component is at odds with severity, a principal identification factor in behavioral disorders that affords a reduced likelihood of favorable response to treatment. Over one-third of the definitions contained an exclusions component, which stated that a child should not be identified as behaviorally disordered, regardless of emotional and behavioral problems, if he or she manifests concomitant handicaps. The most common of these handicaps are mental retardation, sensory disabilities, orthopedic disabilities, brain damage, delinquency, social maladjustment, and drug abuse.

Special education needed and certification components require that before formal identification is accomplished, certain individuals or groups designated as official labelers have to verify that a pupil is behaviorally disordered. Specific assessment procedures were not recommended by many states. In fact, diagnostic procedures were rarely addressed.

Behavioral disorders is a practical term, favored currently by many educators instead of more clinical or medically oriented (psychological/psychiatric) terminology. The reason is that all children and youths display a wide range of behaviors, the majority of which are normal. That is, children learn to respond by displaying an acceptable repertoire of behaviors to social cues. Children need the latitude to select a behavior in the learning process and try it; if acceptability or appropriate behaviors are displayed, normal adjustment is assumed to be manifest. A behavioral disorder exists when chronic, or inappropriate persistence is practiced. Certainly, home conditions, intelligence, appropriate modeling, and all important classroom management can inhibit or inadvertently reinforce many unwanted behaviors.

Behavioral disorders are transitory, temporal responses, many of which disappear with age and changes in environmental conditions. Therefore, definitions of behavioral disorders must distinguish between those that are referencing age-specific developmental periods and those that persist over time. There is the stigma and social learning significance of a pejorative label that serves no other purpose but to classify a child diagnostically. Generally, social interaction and self-concept research has shown these labels to set negative self-fulfilling prophecies into motion. Behavioral disorder is not meant to be anything more than a vague categorical descriptor of a handicapping condition for legal and educational purposes. The importance of this definition educationally is that it promotes defining precisely those targeted behaviors that are in need of modification. The term suggests that the educator must observe what is drawing unfavorable attention to the child, or delaying social and academic learning, and prepare specific behavioral objectives to combat the problem.

Behavioral disorders is a useful construct for the current state of knowledge that guides current special educational practices. It contains many improvements over earlier classification systems. It is not, however, a replacement for sophisticated statistical and clinical nomenclatures such as those found in the fourth edition of the *Diagnostic and Statistical Manual of Mental Disorders* (1994; DSM-IV) prepared by the American Psychiatric Association. A number of subclassification systems exist within the broad category of behavioral disorders. Most of these attempt to suggest, if not prescribe, the general course of diagnosis and treatment. The DSM-IV is a psychiatrically derived classification system for use with children and adults with emotional disorders. It is the standard classification system within mental health facilities in the United States, though it has far less official influence in public education.

Behaviorally disordered children may constitute one of the major national issues confronting the schools and society. Observation, diagnosis, and intervention strategies are poorly defined nationally. There is evidence that aggressive children are often detected. Unfortunately, there is also evidence that withdrawn children may not be recognized. The validity of treatment, indeed the value of any one approach may be questioned. Services too frequently are based on eliminating a problem student, not on teaching appropriate behaviors. Behavioral disorders as a loose configuration of symptoms may be the least developed special educational practice at this time. These disorders have the capability of being larger in incidence than any other, and most costly in both resources needed and loss of productivity. In addition, the pressure to place students with behavior disorders in inclusive programming has not borne any research results that suggest inclusion is appropriate for severe behavioral problems (MacMillan, Gresham, & Forness, 1996).

Finally, behavioral disorders are difficult to distinguish from learning disabilities. Frequently, the terms are used together. Certainly, children do react to the frustration of school failure by displaying inappropriate behaviors. There is no question that the symptoms of restlessness, aggressiveness, conflict, and other manifestations of behavioral disorders influence academic learning. Algozzine and Korinck (1985) note a national expansion, if not explosion, in learning disabilities, and fewer behavioral disorders (about 10% of the school-age population). Why? Probably because behavioral disorders remain an unsavory, mixed-bag issue, poorly understood by the schools and community and therefore threatening. Behavioral disorders, unlike learning disabilities, is not yet a concept whose time has come.

REFERENCES

Algozzine, B., & Korinck, L. (1985). Where is special education for students with high prevalence handicaps going? *Exceptional Children, 51,* 388–394.

American Psychiatric Association. (1994). *Diagnostic and statistical manual of mental disorders* (4th ed.). Washington, DC: Author.

Epstein, M.H., Cullinan, D., & Sabatino, D.A. (1977). State definitions of behavior disorders. *Journal of Special Education, 11,* 417–425.

MacMillan, D.L., Gresham, F., & Forness, S. (1996). Full inclusion: An empirical perspective. *Behavior Disorders, 21*(2), 145–159.

See also Diagnostic and Statistical Manual of Mental Disorders (DSM-IV); Emotional Disorders

BEHAVIORISM

The root of behaviorism is the term behavior, which may be defined as the set or universe of things an organism can do, or more simply, what an organism does. Typically, behavior is a term used in the fields of psychology or sociology to describe human or animal activity, but it is important to note that the term can be, and is, applied to a wide range of other things, including plants, simple microorganisms, machines, and even subatomic particles. The critical attribute is that the activities or functions of the organism must be observable and therefore capable of being measured. Just as it is possible to speak of the behavior of single organisms of varying complexity and composition, it is also possible to examine the behavior of organisms in groups. The empirical emphasis of the term behavior is especially prominent in the United States, where the term is associated with a particular school of psychology known as behaviorism.

Early in the twentieth century, the young discipline of psychology was quite concerned with the existing dominance of such concepts as will and mind, notably in the work of introspectionists such as Titchner. However, when Pavlov and his colleagues demonstrated that some learning was a process whose parameters could be empirically specified and whose results could be reliably predicted, psychologists such as John Watson saw that some aspects of human behavior could be studied in a simpler, more elegant way, as other sciences were being studied. Watson's fervent rejection of the idea of introspection, mental states, or any other nonempirical behavior analysis has earned him general recognition as the founder of behaviorism.

It remained for later thinkers, notably Edward L. Thorndike and B.F. Skinner, to refine and clearly articulate behaviorism. Watson had emphasized stimulus conditions (following Pavlov's respondent conditioning principles) in his work; the most famous example was his introduction of the fear of a white rat in a young boy (Watson & Rayner, 1920). Thorndike (1935), through is Law of Effect, and Skinner (1953), through his Principle of Reinforcement, argued that the consequences of response determine much of what we learn. Skinner in particular has written extensively of the many ways in which this operant conditioning can be observed and applied in our daily affairs. Like Watson before him, Skinner adamantly rejects the need for a psychology of the mind or any other attempt to understand behavior in subjective terms. For Skinner, behavior is conditioned by external events, and as such it can be controlled, predicted, and studied by empirical methods. The wide range of studies of both human and animal learning (Kazdin, 1975; Kimble, 1961) as a function of behavioral methods demonstrate how powerful the principles of behaviorism can be when effectively applied.

More recently, behaviorists cautiously have begun to reexamine the role of mental processes in determining behavior. Members of this school of thought, sometimes called cognitive behaviorism, include psychologists such as Albert Bandura (1977) and Donald Meichenbaum (1977). Reconsideration of the role of mental process in behavior has come about for two reasons. First, certain kinds of learning, such as modeling, occur in the absence of typical observable consequences. It is thought that in some cases a form of self-reinforcement (or perhaps self-punishment) through language is responsible for strengthening the behavior (Bandura, 1977). Others (e.g., Meichenbaum, 1977) have noted that traditional behavioral learning paradigms have been too simplistic to account for the wide array of individual differences in behavior, especially among humans. Even unyielding behavioral analyses such as Skinner's make use of variables such as reinforcement history, which imply some sort of cognitive process in mediating across gaps in time.

The influence of behavioristic thought in psychology is undeniable. The emphasis on empirical research conditions that seemed so strident and incongruous in Watson's time is now taught as the basis of good research, and the importance of both Pavlovian and Skinnerian conditioning has been observed even in popular literature. Behavioristic methods of treatment occupy a place in the study of psychopathology, and behavioral principles are being applied in educational and industrial/organizational settings. As the school of thought broadens its consideration of variables involved in behavior, it holds a better promise as a tool for understanding what we do and why we do it.

REFERENCES

Bandura, A. (1977). Self-efficacy: Toward a unifying theory of behavioral change. *Psychological Review, 84,* 191–215.

Kazdin, A. (1975). *Behavior modification in applied settings.* Homewood, IL: Dorsey.

Kimble, G.A. (1961). *Hilgard and Marquis' conditioning and learning* (2nd ed.). New York: Appleton-Century-Crofts.

Meichenbaum, D. (1977). *Cognitive behavior modification: An integrative approach.* New York: Plenum.

Skinner, B.F. (1953). *Science and human behavior.* NY: Free Press.

Thorndike, E.L. (1935). *The psychology of wants, interests and attitudes.* New York: Appleton-Century.

Watson, J., & Rayner, R. (1920). Conditioning emotional responses. *Journal of Experimental Psychology, 3,* 1–14.

See also **Behavior Modification; Psychoanalysis; Social Learning Theory**

BEHAVIOR MODELING

Modeling is a training intervention that was popularized by social learning theory and the works of Albert Bandura (Bandura, 1971). When using this procedure, the practitioner physically demonstrates or shows a visual representation (e.g., photo sequence, videotape, movie) of the production of the behavior. In essence, the practitioner shows the student the appropriate way to respond. The demonstration often includes secondary informational sources such as feedback about the model's success and the environmental and contextual cues that led the model to behave in the particular fashion demonstrated.

Student factors are important to the modeling process. First, the student must be sufficiently motivated to become an active participant in the modeling process. An absence of sufficient motivation will negate the qualities of the model and the modeling event. Second, the attention of the student must be keyed to the relevant properties of the modeled behavior. Third, the student must have sufficient motor abilities to replicate the modeled behavior. Finally, the ability of the student to remember and recall the modeled act will greatly affect the general and functional utility of the modeled behavior. This retention is based on two processes: imagination and verbalization. In the first case, when stimuli are consistently paired, the occurrence of one of the paired stimuli will signal the other. In the second case, labeling of an event (a verbal process whether vocalized or not) lends saliency to the event.

Factors related to the instructional variables can also affect the effectiveness of modeling. Reinforcement for the modeled behavior must be sufficient in quantity and quality to bring about student participation. For example, Lovaas (1967) has shown that children imitate precisely when they are rewarded for precise replication of modeled behaviors. However, when children are reinforced non-differentially (i.e., for approximations of the response), they produce poorly matched responses. Modeled behavior is most effectively acquired and maintained when the modeled behaviors are familiar and functional to the target student. Overt rehearsals of the modeled response can considerably enhance the acquisition and maintenance of the modeled behavior.

Modeling, therefore, is a useful instructional procedure. As a technology for instruction, it requires that its users follow specific procedures to produce maximum results. These procedures are neither esoteric nor difficult to follow. Because modeling is thought to be a "least restrictive" instructional prompting procedure, and because it is usable in most environments, it should be considered to be an instructional procedure of choice under most circumstances.

REFERENCES

Bandura, A. (1971). Analysis of modeling processes. In A. Bandura (Ed.), *Psychological modeling: Conflicting theories.* Chicago: Aldine-Atherton.

Lovaas, O.I. (1967). A behavior therapy approach to the treatment of childhood schizophrenia. In J.P. Hill (Ed.), *Minnesota symposia on child psychology* (Vol. 1). Minneapolis: University of Minnesota Press.

See also **Cognitive Behavior Therapy; Social Learning Theory; Theory of Activity**

BEHAVIOR MODIFICATION

Behavior modification is generally regarded as a term that encompasses the various methods derived from learning theory that are used to alter the response patterns of humans and other animals. The term has been used in this way by Bandura (1969); he and other behaviorists such as Skinner (1965) have enumerated a wide variety of learning principles that have been translated into methods for learning or changing behavior.

Although behavior modification is sometimes considered as a unitary position in discussions of certain issues in psychology, the techniques involved are derived from several different theoretical approaches to learning. Each approach tends to emphasize environmental determinants, as opposed to person-based determinants, of individual differences among organisms in the way in which they learn behavior. On the other hand, each approach also emphasizes the importance of determining the specific environmental variables that influence the behavior of an individual.

One such approach (Wolpe, 1982) is based on classical or respondent conditioning, which was studied extensively early in the twentieth century by Ivan Pavlov, the Russian psychologist, and John Watson, the American sometimes known as the father of behaviorism. In this type of learning, a neutral stimulus is paired in time with another stimulus (called the unconditioned stimulus) already able to elicit a particular response, usually unlearned, from an organism's repertoire. Through repeated pairings, this neutral stimulus also acquires the capability of eliciting the original (or unconditioned) response; this neutral stimulus is called the conditioned stimulus.

A second major approach to behavior modification (Skinner, 1965) is based on operant or instrumental conditioning. The basis of this approach is the so-called law of effect articulated by Thorndike (1935). He proposed that responses followed by pleasurable consequences would be strengthened, whereas responses followed by unpleasant consequences would be weakened. This formulation was refined and greatly expanded by others, notably Skinner, who had demonstrated that consequences (Thorndike would have called them effects) are important in learning a wide variety of behaviors. Most of these behaviors involve some activity or operation (hence the term operant conditioning) in the form of a skill the organism learns.

The modification of behavior using the outlined principles of operant conditioning is sometimes called applied behavior analysis. Usually this involves detailed empirical specification of the behavior to be changed (or to be learned), careful observation of the contributing conditioning elements, and the development of a strategy (changing antecedent stimulus conditions, response consequences, or both) to achieve the desired results. It is important to note that the use of behavior modification techniques does not require the use of terms such as normal or abnormal to describe the behavior being examined. In fact, the learning theorists who have contributed to the development of behavior modification techniques assume that behavior is learned according to principles that operate nearly identically in all situations, even though a given observer may have a higher or lower value to place on a particular learned behavior. As a result, descriptive terms such as abnormal are frequently rejected because their use tempts us to infer that different laws of learning have governed the behavior so described.

REFERENCES

Bandura, A. (1969). *Principles of behavior modification.* New York: Holt, Rinehart, & Winston.

Skinner, B.F. (1965). *Science and human behavior.* New York: Free Press.

Thorndike, E.L. (1935). *The psychology of wants, interests and attitudes.* New York: Appleton, Century.

Wolpe, J. (1982). *The practice of behavior therapy* (3rd ed.). New York: Pergamon.

See also **Applied Behavior Analysis; Operant Conditioning**

BEHAVIOR PROBLEM CHECKLIST, REVISED

The Revised Behavior Problem Checklist (RBPC; Quay & Peterson, 1983) is a widely researched rating scale for the clinical evaluation of deviant behavior. The original Behavior Problem Checklist (BPC) was developed in 1967 and the RBPC is the revised version of this scale. The RBPC consists of four major scales and two minor scales. The major scales include: Conduct Disorder (22 items), Socialized Aggression (17 items), Attention Problems–Immaturity (16 items), and Anxiety–Withdrawal (11 items). The two minor scales are Psychotic Behavior (6 items) and Motor Tension–Excess (5 items). In addition, twelve items are included for research purposes, and do not contribute to the overall score.

Estimates of internal consistency reliability range from .68 to .95. Interrator reliabilities range from .52 to .85. Test-retest reliabilities (two-month interval) range from .49 to .83 (N = 149). Support for validity includes a substantial relationship between the RBPC and the BPC, discrimination between normal children and clinical groups, and support from numerous studies for many facets of validity (Dezolt, 1992; Hinshaw et al, 1987; Lahay & Piacentini, 1985). The authors do not provide representative norms based on Census data, but recommend developing local norms. However, the use of local norms without reference to a normative sample may be complicated by such things as cultural variation within communities and transient populations. The manual provides means and standard deviations for scale scores from clinical and nonclinical samples, and from parent and teacher ratings. However, little demographic information is included; thus, it is unclear whether these samples are representative.

The RBPC is a useful screening instrument for assessing behavior problems along four independent dimensions commonly associated with emotional disturbance (Quay, 1983). However, the absence of a well-defined normative sample is cause for some concern (Shapiro, 1992).

REFERENCES

Dezolt, D.M. (1992). Review of the Revised Behavior Problem Checklist. In J.J. Kramer & J.C. Conoley (Eds.), *The eleventh mental measurements yearbook* (pp. 764–765). Lincoln, NE: Buros Institute of Mental Measurements.

Hinshaw, S.P., Morrison, D.C., Carte, E.T., & Cornsweet, C. (1987). Factorial dimensions of the Revised Behavior Problem Checklist: Replication and validation within a kindergarten sample. *Journal of Abnormal Child Psychology, 15,* 309–327.

Lahey, B.B., & Piacentini, J.C. (1985). An evaluation of the Quay-Peterson Revised Behavior Problem Checklist. *Journal of School Psychology, 23,* 285–289.

Quay, H.C. (1983). A dimensional approach to behavior disorder: The Revised Behavior Problem Checklist. *School Psychology Review, 12,* 244–249.

Quay, H.C., & Peterson, D.R. (1983). *Interim manual for the Revised Behavior Problem Checklist.* Coral Gables, FL: University of Miami.

Shapiro, E.S. (1992). Review of the Revised Behavior Problem Checklist. In J.J. Kramer & J.C. Conoley (Eds.), *The eleventh mental measurements yearbook* (pp. 765–766). Lincoln, NE: Buros Institute of Mental Measurements.

BEHAVIOR THERAPY

Behavior therapy encompasses a broad range of philosophical, theoretical, and procedural approaches to the "alleviation of human suffering and the enhancement of human functioning" (Davison & Stuart, 1975, p. 755). An approach to assessment, therapy, ethics, and professional issues, it has been used successfully with a variety of populations (adults, children, adolescents, mentally retarded, etc.) in diverse settings (schools, hospitals, psychiatric facilities, mental health centers, etc.) and for various problems (anxiety, depression, addictive disorders, social skills deficits, psychotic behaviors, marital dysfunction, academic skills, parent-child problems, etc.).

At least four major models within behavior therapy can be identified: (1) applied behavior analysis, (2) neobehavioristic mediational model, (3) social learning theory, and (4) cognitive-behavior therapy (Agras, Kazdin, & Wilson, 1979; Wilson, 1997). The models differ on the bases of historical tradition, fundamental principles, and therapeutic procedures.

Despite the diversity of models in the behavioral construct system and the inability to provide a single definition of behavior therapy, a number of characteristics and assumptions of behavior therapy can be delineated (Agras et al., 1979; Haynes, 1984; Kazdin & Hersen, 1980). No one of these characteristics is definitive of the field, nor does any one necessarily differentiate behavior therapy from other systems. Nevertheless, taken together, they represent the common core of behavior therapy.

One set of characteristics concern methods of inquiry:

1. There is a commitment to empiricism and scientific methodology as the primary basis for developing and evaluating concepts and therapeutic techniques.
2. There is a commitment to an explicit, testable, and falsifiable conceptual foundation.
3. Therapeutic procedures and hypotheses with sufficient precision to make evaluation, replication, and generalization possible are specified.
4. There are close ties to the experimental findings of the science of psychology.
5. There is a low level of inference about data so as to minimize biases.

These epistemological principles imply that behavior therapy will continue to evolve as new knowledge is gained from empirical findings.

A second set of characteristics concerns the assumptions about behavior and behavioral disorders:

1. There is a deterministic model of behavior in which environmental antecedents and consequences are assumed to have the greatest impact on behavior. Recently, interactional models have been introduced in which behavior, the environment, and the person (most notably cognitive events and physiological conditions) are all presumed to influence one another.
2. There is an emphasis on current determinants of behavior as opposed to historical determinants (i.e., early childhood experiences).
3. The same principles that govern normal behavior also govern abnormal behavior. That is, no qualitative difference separates normal from abnormal behavior.
4. There are multiple determinants of behavior. The determinants of behavioral disorders may vary from individual to individual, and from one disorder to another.
5. Both the disease model of abnormal behavior and the implication that dysfunctional behavior is a sign or symptom of an underlying illness are rejected. Instead, dysfunctional behavior is construed as a "problem in living" or as learned, maladaptive behavior. Thus the dysfunctional behavior itself is targeted for behavior change.
6. Psychological disorders can be expressed in behavioral, cognitive, and affective modes. These modes can covary to differing degrees owing to situational factors and individual differences.
7. There is the relative specificity of behavior to the situation in which it occurs as opposed to the belief that behavior is consistent across situations.

A third set of characteristics concerns the methods of behavior change:

1. Therapeutic procedures are derived from experimental-clinical psychology.

2. Therapy is conceptualized as an opportunity to unlearn maladaptive behaviors and to learn adaptive behaviors.

3. The importance of tailoring therapy to the individual based on an assessment of the idiosyncratic determinants of the individual's dysfunctional behavior is emphasized.

4. The importance of the therapist-client interaction as one source of behavior change is emphasized.

5. There is an ongoing evaluation of intervention results in order to modify procedures as needed.

6. Intervention results are generalized from the intervention setting to the client's natural environment.

In conclusion, behavior therapy is a multifaceted and diverse system linked by a common core of assumptions. It is a viable system that has withstood numerous criticisms to emerge as a major approach within the psychological treatment field.

REFERENCES

Agras, W.S., Kazdin, A.E., & Wilson, G.T. (1979). *Behavior therapy: Toward an applied clinical science.* San Francisco: Freeman.

Davison, G.C., & Stuart, R.B. (1975). Behavior therapy and civil liberties. *American Psychologist, 30,* 755–763.

Haynes, S.N. (1984). Behavioral assessment of adults. In M. Hersen & G. Goldstein (Eds.), *Handbook of psychological assessment.* New York: Pergamon.

Kazdin, A.E., & Hersen, M. (1980). The current status of behavior therapy. *Behavior Modification, 4,* 283–302.

Wilson, G.T. (1997). Behavior therapy at century close. *Behavior Therapy, 28*(3), 449–457.

See also Applied Behavior Analysis; Behavior Modification; Desensitization; Social Learning Theory

BEHAVIOR THERAPY

Behavior Therapy is the journal of the Association for Advancement of Behavior Therapy. The journal is an interdisciplinary publication for original research of an experimental and clinical nature that deals with theories, practices, and evaluation of cognitive-behavior therapy, behavior therapy, or behavior modification. *Behavior Therapy* is published in four issues (Winter, Spring, Summer and Fall) and edited by J. Gayle Beck, Ph.D., Department of Psychology, State University of New York at Buffalo, Buffalo, NY 14260-4110.

BELL, ALEXANDER GRAHAM (1847–1922)

Alexander Graham Bell, inventor of the telephone, educator, and spokesperson for the deaf, was born and educated in Scotland. After emigrating to the United States, he opened a school in Boston for the training of teachers of the deaf in 1872; he became a professor at Boston University and married one of his students, Mabel Hubbard, who was deaf, as was his mother.

Bell used his vast influence to foster his major interest, the teaching of the deaf. An avid proponent of oral methods of teaching the deaf, Bell became the acknowledged leader of the oral movement in the United States. He also campaigned tirelessly for the establishment of day schools for the deaf to provide an alternative to residential school placement. Bell was a founder of the American Association to Promote the Teaching of Speech to the Deaf, later renamed the Alexander Graham Bell Association for the Deaf, and of the *Volta Bureau,* which he established for the dissemination of knowledge about the deaf.

BELL, TERREL H. (1921–1996)

Terrel H. Bell was born in Lava Hot Springs, Idaho, and received a master's degree from the University of Idaho in 1954 and a PhD in Educational Administration from the University of Utah in 1961.

After serving in World War II as a U.S. Marine, Bell was a superintendent of schools in Idaho, Wyoming, and Utah. He was U.S. Commissioner of Education from 1974 to 1976 and secretary of the U.S. Department of Education from 1981 to 1984. He appointed members, wrote the national charter, and provided support and leadership for the work of the National Commission on Excellence in Education. The commission report, "A Nation At Risk," found serious flaws in the education system and concluded that schools were mired in mediocrity. Twelve national forums were sponsored to disseminate the commission report, which is credited with prompting a movement to overhaul education. Over 12 million copies of the report have been printed, reprinted, and widely distributed.

Bell's numerous honors and awards include the Department of Defense Distinguished Public Service Medal awarded by Secretary of Defense Casper Weinberger in 1984. He authored numerous books and publications, and remained active in promoting education and learning after leaving the government. He subsequently taught Educational Administration at the University of Utah, and founded the educational consulting firm of T.H. Bell and Associates. In 1991, he wrote *How to Shape Up Our Nation's Schools: Three Crucial Steps for Renewing American Education.*

REFERENCES

Bell, T.H. (1956). *The prodigal pedagogue.* New York: Exposition.

Bell, T.H. (1960). *A philosophy of education for the space age.* New York: Exposition.

Bell, T.H. (1972). *Your child's intellect: A parent's guide to home based preschool education.* Salt Lake City, UT: Olympus.

Bell, T.H. (1974). *Active parent concern.* Englewood Cliffs, NJ: Prentice-Hall.

Bell, T.H. (1984). *Excellence.* Salt Lake City, UT: Deseret.

BELLEVUE PSYCHIATRIC HOSPITAL

The Public Workhouse and House of Correction, which opened in 1736, ultimately became Bellevue Hospital. It contained a six-bed unit designed to provide care for "the infirm, the aged, the unruly, and the maniac." By 1826, a total of 82 of the 184 patients were listed as insane. In 1879 a pavilion for the insane was erected within hospital grounds. The concept of including the care and treatment of psychiatric patients in a general hospital rather than entirely apart from the treatment of the physically ailing was revolutionary.

The Children's Inpatient Psychiatric Service began at Bellevue in 1920. Separate male and female adolescent wards were maintained providing for 30 patients each. In 1935 the New York City Board of Education established a special school for emotionally disturbed children at Bellevue. Now designated as P.S. 106, the school continues to function at Bellevue.

In establishing itself as a psychiatric prison ward, Bellevue has contributed to forensic medicine via the Psychiatric Clinic of the Court of General Sessions, established in 1931. This psychiatric prison ward encouraged the development of rigid safeguards for the rights of all psychiatric patients, including prisoners.

Among many firsts at Bellevue, in 1936 Karl Murdock Bowman was the first physician in the country to use insulin shock therapy for treatment of mental illness. In 1939 David Wechsler developed the Wechsler-Bellevue Scale of Intelligence, later called the Wechsler Adult Intelligence Scale, a test still widely used today. Wechsler went on to develop a number of intelligence tests often used with handicapped children including the Wechsler Intelligence Scale for Children and the Wechsler Pre-School Scale of Intelligence. Lauretta Bender, a pioneer in work with autistic children and youths, worked at Bellevue during the 1950s and 1960s. In 1984, when its facilities in the New Bellevue Hospital at 27th Street and East River Drive in New York City were completed, Bellevue's psychiatric department was united for the first time with the rest of Bellevue. Psychiatry was truly integrated into a full-service hospital setting.

In recent years, Bellevue has continued to lead the field of psychiatric treatment. In the 1990s Bellevue was innovative in developing treatment modalities for individuals with substance abuse and mental illness with peer-led milieu therapy (Bellevue, 1993). In addition, "social marketing" was promoted by developing educational print materials for immigrant, low-literate, and other hard-to-reach groups (Dooley, 1996). The institution also developed a model for hospital-based alcoholism outpatient treatment services for homeless alcoholics (Miescher & Galanter, 1996). A vivid portrait of the everyday life of the staff and patients at Bellevue is portrayed in the 1995 book by the chief psychologist at Bellevue, Frederick Covan, and is entitled *Crazy All the Time: Life, Lessons, and Insanity on the Psych Ward of Bellevue Hospital.*

REFERENCES

Bellevue Hospital Center. (1993). *Bellevue hospital center.* New York: Author.

Covan, F.L., & Kahn, C. (1995). *Crazy all the time: Life, lessons, and insanity on the psych ward of Bellevue Hospital.* New York: Simon & Schuster.

Dooley, A.R. (1996). A collaborative model for creating patient education resources. *American Journal of Health Behavior, 20,* 15–19.

Miescher, A., & Galanter, M. (1996). Shelter-based treatment of the homeless alcoholic. *Journal of Substance Abuse Treatment, 13,* 135–140.

BENADRYL

Benadryl (diphenhydramine hydrochloride) is used for perennial or seasonal (hay fever) allergic rhinitis, motion sickness, and allergic conjunctivitis owed to inhalant allergens and foods. An antihistamine, it has anticholinergic (drying) and sedative side effects. In isolated cases, it has been used as a sedative for treatment of hyperactivity. Adverse reactions include diminished mental alertness in both adults and children, with occasional excitation in the young child. A 1993 study (Vuurman, van Veggel, Uiterwijk & O'Hanlon, 1993) found that allergic reaction reduces learning ability in children. In addition, this effect is aggravated by diphenhydramine. Therefore, parents and educators should be aware that while Benadryl relieves some of the uncomfortable symptoms of allergies it increases problems in learning. Accommodations for the child with allergies should be specifically targeted to sedation if the child is taking Benadryl. These accommodations could include decreasing workload, increasing time for rehearsal of learning material and communications with parents on a daily basis to assist in the monitoring of side effects and learning retention. Overdose with this or other antihistamines may cause hallucinations, convulsions, and death.

REFERENCES

Physician's desk reference (1997). Oradell, NJ: Medical Economics.

Vuurman, E.F., van Veggel, L.M., Uiterwijk, M.M., Leutner, D., & O'Hanlon, J.F. (1993). Seasonal allergic rhinitis and antihistamine effects on children's learning. *Annals of Allergy, 71*(2), 121–126.

BENDER, LAURETTA (1897–1987)

Born in Butte, Montana, in 1897, Lauretta Bender obtained her BS and MA degrees from the University of Chicago in 1922 and 1923, respectively. She obtained her MD degree at the State University of Iowa in 1926 and returned to Chicago (Billings Hospital) for her internship (1927–1928) and residency in neurology (1928). A residency in psychiatry at Boston's Psychopathic Hospital preceded another psychiatric residency, in 1929–1930, at Johns Hopkins' Phipps Clinic. She also received postgraduate training in neuroanatomy, physiology, and pathology at the University of Amsterdam on a Rockefeller grant in 1926–1927.

With over 100 chapters and articles, Bender is widely published in the fields of child psychiatry, neurology, and psychology. She is best known for her Visual Motor Gestalt Test (1937), several books, including *Psychopathological Disorders of Children with Organic Brain Disease* (1956), and studies of learning disabilities (1970). Her theory of the role of brain pathology in the development of childhood schizophrenia is less known but also important. In addition, she developed the Face-Hand Test, which examines double simultaneous tactile sensation (face and hand). A variation of this test, the Fink-Green-Bender Test, has been used to discriminate between children with neurologic and schizophrenic disorders.

REFERENCES

Bender, L. (1937). *A visual motor gestalt test and its clinical use.* New York: American Orthopsychiatric Association.

Bender, L. (1956). *Psychopathological disorders of children with organic brain disease.* Springfield, IL: C. Thomas.

Bender, L. (1970). Use of the visual motor gestalt test in diagnosing learning disability. *Journal of Special Education, 4,* 29–39.

See also **Bender Gestalt**

BENDER GESTALT

The Bender Gestalt is a brief, nonverbal, perceptual-motor assessment instrument. Originally developed by Lauretta Bender (1938) as a measure of visual-motor maturation in children, the test has become one of the most widely used assessment techniques for individuals of all ages. The Bender has, for example, been used with adults as a projective personality technique, and with children as an indicator of school readiness, emotional problems, and learning difficulties. However, it has been most widely used as a screening measure for brain dysfunction in both adults and children.

The test consists of nine figures, each of which is printed on a separate 4-inch by 6-inch card. Cards are presented one at a time and subjects are instructed to copy each figure as accurately as possible. Variations on this basic procedure include having subjects reproduce the figures from memory, embedding the figures in distracting backgrounds, and placing time limits on performance (Dana, Field, & Bolton, 1983). The test is typically administered individually, however, group administration procedures have also been developed (Koppitz, 1975). Although Bender did not provide a formal scoring method for the test, a number of objective scoring systems have since been devised (Lacks, 1984). The Developmental Bender Test Scoring System (Koppitz, 1963) has become the preferred scoring method for children's protocols. Designed for use with children between ages 5 and 10, the system identifies 30 scoring items (errors in the drawings; for example, rotations, distortions in shape, and failure to integrate the components of the design). Each item is worth one point and enters into a composite developmental score that may then be compared with age-appropriate norms provided by Koppitz (1975). A review of 31 studies revealed high interrater reliability for the developmental system (correlations ranged from .79 to .99; 81% of the correlations were at .89 or above). Despite the availability of objective scoring techniques, many practitioners prefer a global, intuitive interpretation based on clinical judgment (Dana et al., 1983).

Although the Bender Gestalt has been an integral part of standardized test batteries for the past 50 years, there has been considerable criticism on issues of inappropriate admission, scoring, and interpretation (Pitrowski, 1995). However, recent studies indicate reliability of group and individual administration (Brannigan & Brannigan, 1995), reliability of scoring systems (Fuller & Vance, 1995), neuropsychological clinical utility (Bowers, 1994) and intellectual assessment of adults (Bobic, Pavicevic, & Drenovac, 1997). In recent surveys of test use, the Bender Gestalt remains ranked in the top ten assessment instruments (Pitrowski, 1995).

REFERENCES

Bender, L. (1938). *A visual motor Gestalt test and its clinical use.* New York: American Orthopsychiatric Association.

Bobic, J., Pavicevic, L., Drenovac, M. (1997). Intellectual deterioration in alcoholics. *European Journal of Psychiatry, 11*(1), 21–26.

Bowers, W.A. (1994). Neuropsychological impairment among anorexia nervosa and bulimia patients. *Eating Disorders: The Journal of Treatment and Prevention, 2*(1), 42–46.

Brannigan, G.G., & Brannigan, M.J. (1995). Comparison of individual versus group administration of the modified version of the Bender Gestalt Test. *Perceptual & Motor Skills, 80*(3), 1274.

Dana, R.H., Field, K., & Bolton, B. (1983). Variations of the Bender-Gestalt Test: Implications for training and practice. *Journal of Personality Assessment, 47*(1), 76–84.

Fuller, G.B., & Vance, B. (1995). Interscorer reliability of the modified version of the Bender Gestalt. *Psychology in the Schools, 32*(4), 264–266.

Koppitz, E.M. (1963). *The Bender Gestalt Test for young children.* New York: Grune & Stratton.

Koppitz, E.M. (1975). *The Bender Gestalt Test for young children. Vol. 2: Research and application. 1963–1973.* New York: Grune & Stratton.

Lacks, P. (1984). *Bender Gestalt screening for brain dysfunction.* New York: Wiley.

Pitrowski, C. (1995). A review of the clinical and research use of the Bender Gestalt Test. *Perceptual and Motor Skills, 81*(3), 1272–1274.

See also **Visual Motor Problems; Visual Perception and Integration**

BENZEDRINE

Benzedrine is a psychostimulant that acts on the central nervous system. It was the subject of widespread abuse and distribution under the slang term "bennies" until the 1970s. Its previous legitimate uses included, at times, the treatment of hyperactivity and obesity. Recent study indicates some evidence to support the judicious use of psychostimulants in "selected clinical instances of several adult psychiatric syndromes." It is no longer in use in the treatment of childhood or adolescent disorders.

See also **Attention Deficit Disorder; Dexedrine**

BETTELHEIM, BRUNO (1903–1990)

Bruno Bettelheim received his doctoral degree from the University of Vienna in 1938. He was strongly influenced by Freudian thought. Bettelheim was a psychiatrist who gained his fame from work with emotionally disturbed children, particularly those with autism.

During his long association with the University of Chicago, Bettelheim acted as principal of the University of Chicago's Sonia Shankman Orthogeneic School, a residential treatment center for severely emotionally disturbed children. The philosophy and operation of the Shankman School are described in Bettelheim's book *Love Is Not Enough* (1950).

Bettelheim sought in his treatment of severely disturbed children to create a particular social environment, a society with its own definite set of mores, closely paralleling those of society at large. He believed that social norms and standards are important to the treatment of emotionally disturbed children just as they are important in normal populations. He died in 1990 at the age of 87.

REFERENCES

Bettelheim, B. (1950). *Love is not enough: The treatment of emotionally disturbed children.* Glencoe, IL: Free Press.

Bettelheim, B. (1955). *Truants from life: The rehabilitation of emotionally disturbed children.* Glencoe, IL: Free Press.

BIBLIOTHERAPY

Bibliotherapy is an approach to helping pupils understand themselves and their feelings and to providing in-classroom counseling to meet their emotional and social needs (Lerner, 1985). Readings and other media materials in which the characters learn to cope and deal effectively with problems similar to those which are, or will be, encountered by the students are used.

As with psychotherapy, bibliotherapy includes three main components: identification, catharsis, and insight. Identification with characters, situations, or elements of a story enables the reader to view his or her problem from a new and different perspective and thus gain hope and tension release (catharsis). Such tension reduction allows the student to gain insight into his or her motivations and actions and allows for positive change in attitude and behavior. This process is structured and guided by the teacher through the use of classroom discussion, example, and illustration (Lenkowsky & Lenkowsky, 1980).

Bibliotherapy offers many advantages for special education. It is effective in the reduction and management of the stress that often accompanies and impairs learning, development, and adjustment in handicapped children (Humphrey & Humphrey, 1985). It may be used individually or with small groups or classes of children. Bibliotherapy can be modified to the needs of children at any age and little formal training or experience is required for teachers to become proficient bibliotherapists. There is a large body of literature available that presents the problems, feelings, and situations faced by handicapped children and adolescents. In addition, research application demonstrates the potential for bibliotherapy to be a powerful agent for behavior change (Lombana, 1982; Cuijpers, 1997).

REFERENCES

Cuijpers, P. (1997). Bibliotherapy in unipolar depression: A meta-analysis. *Journal of Behavior Therapy & Experimental Psychiatry, 28*(2), 139–147.

Humphrey, J.H., & Humphrey, J.N. (1985). *Controlling stress in children.* Springfield, IL: Thomas.

Lenkowsky, B., & Lenkowsky, R. (1980). Bibliotherapy for the learning disabled adolescent. In C.H. Thomas & J.L. Thomas (Eds.), *Meeting the needs of the handicapped: A resource for teachers and librarians.* Phoenix, AZ: Oryx.

Lerner, J. (1985). *Learning disabilities* (4th ed.). Boston: Houghton Mifflin.

Lombana, J.H. (1982). *Guidance for handicapped students.* Springfield, IL: Thomas.

See also **Counseling the Handicapped; Social Skills**

BIELSCHOLWSKY SYNDROME

See JUVENILE CEREBROMACULAR DEGENERATION.

BIENNIAL DIRECTORY OF EDUCATIONAL FACILITIES FOR THE LEARNING DISABLED

The *Biennial Directory of Educational Facilities for the Learning Disabled* is published by Academic Therapy Publications. It contains a listing of nonpublic educational facilities that specialize in programs for individuals with learning disabilities. A copy of the directory can be obtained from Academic Therapy Publications for a small fee to cover postage and handling (currently $5.00), at 20 Commercial Boulevard, Novato, CA 94949.

BILINGUAL ASSESSMENT AND SPECIAL EDUCATION

The assessment of children who are culturally and linguistically diverse for special education services has been a controversial issue for nearly thirty years. This controversy first received national attention via the case of Diana v. California in 1970 involving the identification of Spanish-speaking children as mentally retarded on the basis of being assessed in English. The safeguards decreed in this case had an impact on both legal requirements and professional ethical standards. Public Law 94-142 mandated that children be assessed in their primary language. Chapter 13 of the American Psychological Association's *Standards for Educational and Psychological Testing* (1985) acknowledges the need for assessing the native language of children.

USE OF INTERPRETERS

The use of interpreters is common practice in bilingual assessment. This is not surprising due to the many different low-incidence language groups school psychologists have to assess (Ochoa, Gonzalez, Galarza, & Guillemard, 1996). Ochoa, Gonzalez, et al. (1996) reported that 53% of school psychologists use interpreters. They found that 77% of school psychologists who use interpreters self-reported that they were clearly not trained by their university training program on how to do so. Moreover, approximately two-thirds of the interpreters used by the school psychologists did not have training to work in this capacity. Ochoa, Gonzalez, et al. (1996) and Nuttall (1987) state the need for interpreter training. When school psychologists must resort to using interpreters, they should review the literature pertaining to the skills they should acquire in this situation (Figueroa, Sandoval, & Merino, 1984) as well as the skills that the interpreter should possess (Chamberlain & Medeiros-Landurand, 1991; Medina, 1982; Miller & Abudarham, 1984; Scribner, 1993; Wilen & Sweeting, 1986).

LANGUAGE PROFICIENCY ASSESSMENT

Language proficiency assessment is an essential component of bilingual assessment because it provides the school psychologist with information about (a) the appropriateness of the child's current educational placement with respect to his/her language development (Ochoa, Galarza, & Gonzalez, 1996) and (b) the child's native and second language development with respect to whether the student has achieved Cognitive Academic Language Proficiency (CALP). Cummins (1984) states that it is important to differentiate between CALP, which takes 5 to 7 years to acquire and is the type of proficiency which one needs to be successful in an academic context, and Basic Interpersonal Communication Skills (BICS), which is the proficiency one needs in social settings and only takes about two years to acquire. If a bilingual student does not have CALP in English, he or she will find the linguistic demands of his instructional arrangement to be difficult, which could result in academic failure. Ochoa, Galarza, and Gonzalez (1996) concluded from their study of the language proficiency assessment practices of school psychologists when conducting bilingual assessment that they ". . . are not implementing the following recommended language proficiency practices: (a) conducting their own testing rather than relying on external data, (b) obtaining information about the LEP child's CALP level, and (c) utilizing informal language assessment methods . . ." (p. 33).

INTELLECTUAL FUNCTIONING, ACADEMIC AND ADAPTIVE BEHAVIOR ASSESSMENT

With respect to intellectual functioning, Ochoa, Powell, and Robles-Pina's (1996) study noted the following assessment trends used with bilingual and LEP students: (a) multiple measures are utilized; (b) nonverbal measures are commonly used; and (c) formally, informally translated tests and alternative/dynamic methods (i.e., Learning Potential Assessment Device and System of Multicultural Pluralistic Assessment) are often not used. In the area of academic assessment of second language learners, approximately 75% of school psychologists reported that they used the Woodcock instruments in both English and Spanish (Ochoa, Powell, et al., 1996). Moreover, the use of curriculum-based measurement (66% of school psychologists) and criterion reference testing (49% of school psychologists) in Spanish are also common practice to assess achievement (Ochoa, Powell, et al., 1996). With respect to adaptive behavior, the most commonly used measure with bilingual students is the Vineland Adaptive Behavior Scales–Survey Edition (Ochoa, Powell et al., 1996).

SECTION FOUR OF THE EXCLUSIONARY CLAUSE

Section Four of the exclusionary clause of Public Law 94-142 states that a student should not be identified as learning disabled if the "discrepancy between ability and achievement is primarily the result of environmental, cultural, or economic disadvantage" (U.S. Office of Education, 1977). Ochoa, Rivera, and Powell's (1997) study examined how school psychologists complied with this legal requirement. They identified 36 factors that school psychologists used which could be summarized by the following six major themes: "(a) family and home factors, (b) language instruction and language-related factors, (c) assessment instrument and procedural safeguards, (d) educational history factors, (e) general educational factors, and (f) other" (p. 163). Ochoa, Rivera, et al., (1997) conclude that "the extent to which many of these factors are used, however, appears to be low. Moreover, many additional important factors are completely overlooked by school psychologists" (p. 163).

CONCLUSION

A review of the aforementioned research concerning the assessment practices used with bilingual and/or LEP students suggests that this area will continue to be controversial. Perhaps the words of Chinn and Hughes' (1987) words best summarize this situation: "The assessment of minority children for educational placement continues to be one of the more volatile issues in special education" (p. 45).

REFERENCES

American Psychological Association. (1985). *Standards for educational and psychological testing.* Washington, DC: American Psychological Association.

Chamberlain, P., & Medeiros-Landurand, P. (1991). Practical considerations in the assessment of LEP students with special needs.

In E.V. Hamayan & J.S. Damico (Eds.), *Limiting bias in the assessment of bilingual students* (pp. 111–156). Austin, TX: Pro-Ed.

Chinn, P.C., & Hughes, S. (1987). Representation of minority students in special classes. *Remedial and Special Education, 8,* 41–46.

Cummins, J. (1984). *Bilingual special education issues in assessment and pedagogy.* San Diego: College-Hill.

Figueroa, R.A., Sandoval, J., & Merino, B. (1984). School psychology and limited-English-proficient (LEP) children: New competencies. *Journal of School Psychology, 22,* 131–143.

Medina, V. (1982). *Issues regarding the use of interpreters and translators in a school setting.* (ERIC Reproduction No. ED 161191)

Miller, N., & Abudarham, S. (1984). Management of communication problems in bilingual children. In N. Miller (Ed.), *Bilingualism and language disability: Assessment and remediation* (pp. 177–198). San Diego: College-Hill.

Nuttall, E.V. (1987). Survey of current practices in the psychological assessment of limited-English-proficiency handicapped children. *Journal of School Psychology, 25,* 53–61.

Ochoa, S.H., Galarza, A., & Gonzalez, D. (1996). An investigation of school psychologists' assessment practices of language proficiency with bilingual and limited-English-proficient students. *Diagnostique, 21*(4), 17–36.

Ochoa, S.H., Gonzalez, D., Galarza, A., & Guillemard, L. (1996). The training and use of interpreters in bilingual psychoeducational assessment: An alternative in need of study. *Diagnostique, 21*(3), 19–40.

Ochoa, S.H., Powell, M.P., & Robles-Pina, R. (1996). School psychologists' assessment practices with bilingual and limited-English-proficient students. *Journal of Psychoeducational Assessment, 14,* 250–275.

Ochoa, S.H., Rivera, B., & Powell, M.P. (1997). Factors used to comply with the exclusionary clause with bilingual and limited-English-proficient pupils: Initial guidelines. *Learning Disabilities Research & Practice, 12,* 161–167.

Scribner, A.P. (1993). The use of interpreters in the assessment of language minority students. *The Bilingual Special Education Perspective, 12*(1), 2–6.

U.S. Office of Education. (1977). Assistance to states for education of handicapped children: Procedures for evaluating specific learning disabilities. *Federal Register, 42,* 65083.

Wilen, D.K., & Sweeting, C.V.M. (1986). Assessment of limited English proficient Hispanic students. *School Psychology Review, 15,* 59–75.

BILINGUAL SPECIAL EDUCATION

By the year 2025, approximately 40% of the total United States population will be African American, Hispanic, or Asian American (Townsend, 1995) and by 2080, non-Hispanic Whites will be a minority. Every region of the country has experienced significant increases in the number of individuals from minority backgrounds, and schools are reporting dramatic increases in the number of language minority students they serve. "Language minority" refers to students who come from homes or communities where a language other than English is spoken. A subset of this population are limited English proficient (LEP) students, whose English skills are so limited they cannot profit from instruction delivered entirely in English and thus require the support of special language programs such as bilingual education or English as a second language instruction. LEP students represent some 200 language groups with Spanish being the most common language spoken (approximately 75%), followed by Vietnamese, Hmong, Cantonese, Cambodian, and Korean.

There is substantial evidence that educational services currently being provided to language minority students are not sufficient to meet their needs. These students experience higher rates of retention and school attrition, score poorly on standardized tests, are underrepresented in colleges and universities, and complete post-secondary studies at low rates. They are also disproportionately represented in special education.

PREVENTION AND PREREFERRAL

With increasing frequency, service delivery models such as the Assessment and Intervention Model for the Bilingual Exceptional Student (Ortiz & Wilkinson, 1991) emphasize proactive steps to ensure that all students are academically successful by creating school climates that reflect awareness and acceptance of diversity, high expectations for all students, a challenging curriculum, quality bilingual education and ESL programs, and involvement of parents and communities. Prereferral interventions are designed to strengthen teachers' abilities to provide appropriate educational opportunities to a diverse student population. If LEP students are ultimately referred for a comprehensive individual assessment, prereferral data help document that external factors such as limited English proficiency or lack of appropriate instruction have already been eliminated as possible causes of problems.

ASSESSMENT

Although inappropriate assessment is one of the primary causes of disproportionate representation of language minority students in special education, research on best practices in assessment of these students is still limited (Ortiz, 1997). Adaptation of standardized procedures is quite common (e.g., translations, use of interpreters, modification of test content). However, such adaptations invalidate the test, making scoring and interpretation of outcomes difficult and error-prone (Damico, 1991). Only those instruments which include appropriate samples of language minority students in the norming sample should be used in making eligibility decisions. If test norms are not appropriate, or if standardized administration procedures are violated, it is recommended that patterns of performance be described and used diagnostically to support eligibility decisions rather than reporting test scores. If performance on the formal and informal measures are positively correlated, multidisciplinary teams can be more confident that the student has a disability.

INSTRUCTION

Individualized education programs (IEPs) for language minority students specify goals and objectives for native language and ESL instruction and include instructional recommendations that reflect understanding of cultural differences, socioeconomic background, preferred modalities, learning styles, and appropriate reinforcements (Yates & Ortiz, 1998). Because of the need to accommodate students' limited English proficiency, a combination of "reciprocal interaction" teaching approaches and basic skills instruction seem to be most beneficial for LEP students with disabilities (Robertson, Wilkinson, & Ortiz, 1991; Willig, Swedo, & Ortiz, 1987; Cummins, 1984). Approaches that focus solely on teaching discrete skills in English are problematic for LEP students because activities that are simplified to focus on specific skills are frequently stripped of context and lose their meaning and purpose, becoming incomprehensible to the second language learner. Lessons that focus on specific skills (e.g., phonology or grammar) and accuracy may actually interfere with the second language acquisition process, because instruction attempts to correct "errors" that are, in reality, developmental. Reciprocal interaction approaches, on the other hand, are characterized by genuine dialogue between students and teacher, in both oral and written communication, opportunities for meaningful language use, collaborative learning groups, the teaching of basic skills in the context of lessons that focus on higher order thinking, and the incorporation of language use and development across the curriculum.

Service delivery models and alternative instructional arrangements are being explored in an effort to ensure that language minority students are served by special educators who have expertise in how language and culture influence learning (Yates & Ortiz, 1998). For effective service delivery, linkages between special education, special language programs, and general education must be established, instructional and related services must be coordinated, and the roles and responsibilities of all personnel who work with these students must be defined. Additionally, teacher education programs must prepare both monolingual and bilingual special educators to serve linguistically and culturally diverse learners.

REFERENCES

Cummins, J. (1984). *Bilingualism and special education: Issues in assessment and pedagogy.* Clevedon, Avon, England: Multilingual Matters Ltd.

Damico, J.S. (1991). Descriptive assessment of communicative ability in limited English proficient students. In E.V. Hamayan & J.S. Damico, *Limiting bias in the assessment of bilingual students* (pp. 157–217). Austin, TX: Pro-Ed.

Ortiz, A.A. (1997). Learning disabilities occurring concomitantly with linguistic differences. *Journal of Learning Disabilities, 30*(3), 321–332.

Ortiz, A.A., & Wilkinson, C.Y. (1991). Assessment and intervention model for the exceptional bilingual student (AIM for the BESt). *Teacher Education and Special Education, 14*(1), 11–18.

Robertson-Courtney, P., Wilkinson, C.Y., & Ortiz, A.A. (1991). Reciprocal interaction-oriented strategies for literacy development: Teacher training outcomes. *The Journal of the New York State Association for Bilingual Education, 7*(1), 95–109.

Townsend, W.A. (1995). *Pocket digest: Digest of education statistics for limited English proficient students.* Washington, D.C.: Office of Bilingual Education and Minority Languages Affairs.

Willig, A.C., Swedo, J.J., & Ortiz, A.A. (1987). *Characteristics of teaching strategies which result in high task engagement for exceptional limited English proficient Hispanic students.* Austin, TX: The University of Texas, Handicapped Minority Research Institute on Language Proficiency.

Yates, J.R., & Ortiz, A.A. (1998). Developing individualized educational programs for the exceptional bilingual student. In L. Baca & H. Cervantes (Eds.), *The Bilingual Special Education Interface* (3rd ed.) (pp. 188–212). Columbus, OH: Merrill Publishing Company.

BILINGUAL SPEECH LANGUAGE PATHOLOGY

Bilingual speech language pathology is an emerging field within the profession of speech language pathology. It is recognized as an area of the field that serves individuals who are bilingual and have a communication disorder. The American Speech-Language Hearing Association approved a position statement that defines who can be a bilingual speech language pathologist and/or audiologist. The definition states (ASHA, 1989): "Speech-language pathologists or audiologists who present themselves as bilingual for the purposes of providing clinical services must be able to speak their primary language and to speak (or sign) at least one other language with native or near-native proficiency in lexicon (vocabulary), semantics (meaning), phonology (pronunciation), morphology/syntax (grammar), and pragmatics (uses) during clinical management." (p. 93). The academic requirements (ASHA, 1985) include the following: (1) language proficiency: native or near native fluency in both the minority language and the English language; (2) normative processes: the ability to describe the process of normal speech and language acquisition for both bilingual and monolingual individuals and how those processes are manifested in oral and written language; (3) assessment: the ability to administer and interpret formal and informal assessment procedures to distinguish between communication difference and communication disorders; (4) intervention: the ability to apply intervention strategies for treatment of communicative disorders in the minority language; and (5) cultural sensitivity: the ability to recognize cultural factors that affect the delivery of speech-language pathology and audiology services to the minority language speaking community.

REFERENCES

American Speech-Language-Hearing Association. (1985). Clinical management of communicatively handicapped minority language populations. *Asha, 27*(6), 29–32.

American Speech-Language-Hearing Association. (1989). Definition: Bilingual speech-language pathologists and audiologists. *Asha, 31*(3), 93.

BILL OF RIGHTS FOR THE DISABLED

The Bill of Rights for the Disabled is a codification by the United Cerebral Palsy Association of rights that have been won for the handicapped in court cases and before legislatures during the 1960s and 1970s. These rights are as follows:

1. The right to prevention, early diagnosis, and proper care.
2. The right to a barrier-free environment and accessible transportation.
3. The right to an appropriate public education.
4. The right to necessary assistance, given in a way that promotes independence.
5. The right to a choice of lifestyles and residential alternatives.
6. The right to an income for a lifestyle comparable to that of the able-bodied.
7. The right to training and employment as qualified.
8. The right to petition social institutions for just and humane treatment.
9. The right to self-esteem.

BINET, ALFRED (1857–1911)

Alfred Binet, the founder of French experimental psychology, became director of the Laboratory of Physiological Psychology at the Sorbonne in Paris in 1895.

In 1904, the minister of public instruction appointed him to a commission created to formulate methods for identifying mentally retarded children in the public schools so that these children could be given a special school program. Out of Binet's work with this commission came the first scale for measuring intelligence, based on the idea of classifying children according to individual differences in performance of tasks requiring thinking and reasoning. On the assumption that intelligence increases with age, he employed the concept of mental age.

The scale was first published by Binet and Theodore Simon in 1905 and was revised in 1908 and 1911. It was translated into English by H.H. Goddard in the United States. In 1916, L.M. Terman at Stanford University published his *Stanford Revision of the Binet Scales*. For half a century dozens of translations and revisions of Binet's scales dominated the field of intelligence testing; they are still extensively used.

REFERENCES

Varon, E.J. (1935). The development of Alfred Binet's psychology. *Psychological Monographs* (No. 207). Princeton, NJ: Psychological Review.

Watson, R.I. (1963). *The great psychologists.* New York: Lippincott.

BIOCHEMICAL IRREGULARITIES

It has been long recognized that a large number of metabolic diseases have characteristic clinical, pathological, and biochemical irregularities that can be attributed to the congenital deficiency of a specific enzyme. This inadequacy is in turn owed to the presence of a particular abnormal gene. The identification and consequent understanding of such biochemical problems began in the early part of the twentieth century with the first demonstration of Mendelian inheritance in humans. A.E. Garrod (Roberts, 1967) derived the basic concept of these disorders through studies on the rare condition known as alcaptonuria (Garrod, 1909). His classical investigation of this abnormality has provided an elegant and simple model for the interpretation of a great variety of different inherited diseases subsequently discovered.

Eventually Garrod described a number of metabolic peculiarities and called them inborn errors of metabolism. He viewed the inborn errors as conditions in which the specific enzyme deficiency effectively blocked at a particular point a sequence of reactions that form part of the normal course of metabolism. As a result, metabolites immediately preceding the block would accumulate and metabolites subsequent to the block would not be formed (Harris, 1975). The various biochemical, clinical, and pathological manifestations of the condition could be regarded as secondary consequences of this primary metabolic defect. These secondary changes might be complex and widespread and would depend in general on the nature and the biochemical effects of the metabolites that tended to accumulate or whose formation was restricted (Harper, Rodwell, & Mayes, 1977).

It is now understood that the end products of gene action are proteins, either structural cell components, elements of extracellular matrices, or enzymes. Since genes are potentially mutable units, a change in a gene will disturb the synthesis of the specific protein for which it is responsible. This results in the formation of a different protein (or no protein at all), which alters the process or processes that depend on it. When the protein is absent or deficient, the normal process is impaired. The expression of such a mutation is a phenotypic effect of more or less consequence to the individual. Such defects in cellular enzyme formation are most often characterized by abnormal protein, carbohydrate, or fat metabolism.

All biochemical processes are under genetic control and each consists of a complex sequence of reactions. A substrate, the substance on which an enzyme acts, is converted into a product through the activity of a specific enzyme. A metabolic pathway consists of many such reactions or steps, each being dependent on the previous reaction and each catalyzed by a specific enzyme (Jenkins, 1983). A block in the normal pathway may produce an accumulation of the substances preceding the block, such as the monosaccharide (simple sugar) galactose in galactosemia or the amino acid phenylalanine in phenylketonuria. In other cases, the block may create a deficiency in the normal product, such as the pigment melanin in albinism or the hormone thyroxine in familial cretinism. Sometimes alternative metabolic pathways are used that result in an increase in the products of these processes such as phenylketones in phenylketonuria.

The effects of defective gene action are often observable in the individual as diseases.

There are many inherited disorders caused by an inborn error of metabolism that involves either the accumulation or degradation of metabolic processes. For the most part, they are rare diseases, and the mode of transmission is almost always autosomal recessive genes. This may be best understood by considering the double-dose effect as it relates to the concept that one gene is responsible for one enzyme. If a specific gene controls the formation of an essential enzyme, and each individual has two such genes (the normal homozygote), then the enzyme is produced in normal amounts. The heterozygote, who has only one gene with a normal effect, is still capable of producing the enzyme in sufficient amounts to carry out the metabolic function under normal circumstances. However, the abnormal homozygote, who inherits a defective gene from each parent, has no functional enzyme and is, thus, clinically affected. It is becoming increasingly possible to detect and, therefore, to screen for a large variety of such inborn errors of metabolism. This should lead to the detection of the presence of the disease in the heterozygote (who is a carrier), the newborn, and the fetus before birth, thus allowing for proper genetic counseling of the parents and successful treatment of affected individuals (Goodenough, 1978).

REFERENCES

Garrod, A.E. (1909). *Inborn errors of metabolism.* New York: Oxford University Press.

Goodenough, U. (1978). *Genetics* (2nd ed.). New York: Holt, Rinehart, & Winston.

Harper, H.A., Rodwell, V.W., & Mayes, P.A. (1977). *Review of physiological chemistry* (16th ed.). Los Altos, CA: Lange Medical.

Harris, H. (1975). *The principles of human biochemical genetics* (2nd ed.). New York: American Elsevier.

Jenkins, J.B. (1983). *Human genetics.* New York: Benjamin/Cummings.

Roberts, J.A.F. (1967). *An introduction to medical genetics* (4th ed.). New York: Oxford University Press.

See also **Congenital Disorders; Cretinism; Inborn Errors of Metabolism; Phenylketonuria**

BIOFEEDBACK

Biofeedback is a highly structured form of therapy that provides immediate feedback about involuntary biological functions such as heart rate, blood pressure, or brain waves. The feedback generally uses visual and auditory devices to show the subject what is happening to normally autonomic bodily functions as the patient attempts to influence them.

In the field of special education, the effectiveness of biofeedback has been exaggerated, but a few procedures do seem to offer promise. The two most frequently used types of biofeedback with learning-disabled and gifted populations are passive and active. During passive electromyographic (EMG) biofeedback, the subject is asked to maintain a signal indicating a low level of tension or other required response. During active electromyographic biofeedback, the subject is asked to produce different levels of tension and or other required responses and to perform differential relaxation. For example, in biofeedback treatment of migraine headaches, patients are taught to warm their hands through temperature feedback. This hand warming is associated with increased blood flow to the hands which in turn leads to a lessening of arterial pressure in the brain (Allen & Shriver, 1997; Blanchard et al., 1978).

Electromyographic biofeedback has been used as an intervention strategy for hyperactivity (Braud, Lupin, & Braud, 1975; Christie, Dewitt, Kaltenbach, & Reed, 1984; Kaduson & Finnerty, 1995; Omizo & Michael, 1982; Rivera & Omizo, 1980). Braud et al. (1975) studied the effects of biofeedback on muscular activity and tension in a hyperactive boy. When the child's forehead muscle group exceeded a certain point, a tone sounded and the child was instructed to "keep the tone off" by sitting and relaxing. Muscular tension and activity decreased both within and across training sessions. It was found that continued practice using laboratory techniques was needed to maintain treatment results. Without parent and school cooperation, the treatment effects deteriorated.

Bhatara, Arnold, Lorance, and Gupta (1979) reviewed the literature on EMG biofeedback and concluded that there is insufficient evidence to support the clinical utility of EMG feedback in hyperactive children. Biofeedback is seen as a promising technique in this area but the problems found in the research to date must be solved (Kaduson & Finnerty, 1995). There must be more tightly controlled designs to rule out the influence of task-motivated suggestions and expectant attitudes. There must be adequate follow-ups carried out on larger populations. Researchers must question the influence of suggestion, motivation, and emotion. Finally, most of the successful results with biofeedback techniques are closely related to relaxation therapies. Thus it would be fruitful to combine biofeedback with older proven therapies.

A relatively recent area of investigation is the use of urodynamic biofeedback with children with myelomeningocele (spina bifida), the most common congenital central nervous system defect. Neurogenic urinary and fecal incontinence is prevalent in the majority of these children. The impact of the physical and psychosocial difficulties associated with chronic incontinence in spina bifida children can cause great distress (Hunt, 1981).

Rectosphincteric biofeedback was used to reduce the number of accidents in eight spina bifida children with chronic fecal incontinence. Six of the eight children reduced the number of accidents and two children became continent (Varni, 1983). Wald (1981) used a similar procedure and found four of eight children had a good clinical response, defined as the disappearance of fecal soiling or a greater than 75% reduction in the frequency of soiling. The results of these studies are encouraging.

In the Killam, Jeffries, and Varni (1985) study using urodynamic biofeedback training, six of eight children demonstrated improved self-regulation of detrusor or sphincter functioning, but only one child demonstrated improvements in urinary incontinence. Unexpectedly, chronic neurogenic fecal incontinence was reduced in four children owing to placement of the surface electrodes in the perianal position.

Recent studies have suggested the clinical utility of biofeedback with children in the reduction of anxiety (Wenck, Leu, & D'Amato, 1996), chronic pain management (James, Sharpley, & Sullivan, 1997), and asthma (Culpert, Kajander, & Reaney, 1996).

REFERENCES

Allen, K.D., & Shriver, M.D. (1997). Enhanced performance feedback to strengthen biofeedback treatment outcome with childhood migraine. *Headache, 37,* 169–173.

Bhatara, V., Arnold, L.E., Lorance, T., & Gupta, D. (1979). Muscle relaxation therapy in hyperkinesis: Is it effective? *Journal of Learning Disabilities, 11,* 182–186.

Blanchard, E.B., Theobald, D.E., Williamson, D.A., Silver, B.V., & Brown, D.A. (1978). Temperature biofeedback in the treatment of migraine headaches. *Archives of General Psychiatry, 35,* 581–588.

Braud, L.W., Lupin, M.N., & Braud, W.G. (1975). The use of electromyographic biofeedback in the control of hyperactivity. *Journal of Learning Disabilities, 8,* 420–425.

Christie, D.J., Dewitt, R.A., Kaltenbach, P., & Reed, D. (1984). Using EMG biofeedback to signal hyperactive children when to relax. *Exceptional Children, 50,* 547–548.

Culpert, T.P., Kajander, R.L., & Reaney, J.B. (1996). Biofeedback with children and adolescents: Clinical observations and patient perspectives. *Journal of Developmental and Behavioral Pediatrics, 17,* 342–350.

Hunt, G.M. (1981). Spina bifida: Implications for 100 children at school. *Developmental Medicine & Child Neurology, 23,* 160–172.

James, R.J., Sharpley, C.F., & Sullivan, M.F. (1997). The effects of self-efficacy and gender upon ability to increase and decrease heart-rate. *Scandinavian Journal of Behaviour Therapy, 26,* 11–16.

Kaduson, H.G., & Finnerty, K. (1995). Self-control game interventions for attention-deficit hyperactivity disorder. *International Journal of Play Therapy, 4,* 15–29.

Killam, P.E., Jeffries, J.S., & Varni, J.W. (1985). Urodynamic biofeedback treatment of urinary incontinence in children with myelomeningocele. *Biofeedback & Self-Regulation, 10,* 161–171.

Omizo, M.M., & Michael, W.B. (1982). Biofeedback-induced relaxation training and impulsivity attention to task, and locus of control among hyperactive boys. *Journal of Learning Disabilities, 15,* 414–416.

Rivera, E., & Omizo, M.M. (1980). An investigation of the effects of relaxation training on attention to task and impulsivity among male hyperactive children. *Exceptional Child, 27,* 41–51.

Varni, J.W. (1983). *Clinical behavioral pediatrics: An interdisciplinary biobehavioral approach.* New York: Pergamon.

Wald, A. (1981). Use of biofeedback of treatment of fecal incontinence in patients with myelomeningocele. *Pediatrics, 68,* 45–49.

Wenck, L.S., Leu, P.W., & D'Amato, R.C. (1996). Evaluating the efficacy of a biofeedback intervention to reduce children's anxiety. *Journal of Clinical Psychology, 52,* 469–473.

See also Hyperactivity; Spina Bifida

BIOGENIC MODELS

Contemporary models of behavior are rarely in absolutely biological or psychological terms, but when a model is primarily biogenic in nature there are important implications for the user's conceptual framework in understanding behavior and implementing behavioral change programs. Biogenic models place the locus of the cause of problem behavior squarely within the individual's biological status and give only minimal roles to other parts of the ecosystem such as family or school. Most contemporary biogenic models are reductionistic and pin their ultimate hopes on an understanding of the relationships among biological, biochemical, and behavioral phenomena. Alterations, which are observed in cognitions or social relations, can be viewed as symptoms of physiological actions. Although our current understanding of biological factors may not allow for biochemical cures for all behavioral problems, the ultimate direction of the biogenic approach lies in biomedical interventions (Engel, 1977).

Critics of the biogenic model have difficulty denying that in a physical sense all behavior can ultimately be traced to biological processes. They do contend, however, that reductionist approaches may not always be the most fruitful guides to practice in education. Biogenic models tend to blame the victim by emphasizing changing the organism and not the environment or situation in which the individual exists (Albee, 1980; Millon & Davis, 1995). It is often the case that concepts of the biogenic model are confused with those of the medical or disease model. Engel (1977), however, proposed a disease model that replaced a biomedical with a biopsychosocial approach to the understanding of disordered behavior.

Biogenic models may be of value to the classroom special education teacher as the basis for planning interventions. Reed (1979) noted the role of neuropsychological diagnoses in developing educational techniques that take into account deficits in brain function. In a rejoinder, Balow (1979) pointed out that such biogenic models were of limited use to the classroom teacher because of their lack of relevance for educational practice and their unclear specification of the link between specific biological dysfunctions and differential educational planning.

REFERENCES

Albee, G. (1980). A competency model to replace the deficit model. In M. Gibbs, J. Lachenmeyer, & J. Sigal (Eds.), *Community psychology: Theoretical and empirical approaches* (pp. 213–238). New York: Gardner.

Balow, B. (1979). Biological defects and special education: An empiricist's view. *Journal of Special Education, 13,* 35–40.

Engel, G. (1977). A need for a new medical model: A challenge for biomedicine. *Science, 96,* 129–136.

Millon, T., & Davis, R.D. (1995). The development of personality disorders. *Developmental Psychopathology,* Vol. 2. New York: Wiley.

Reed, H. (1979). Biological defects in special education: An issue in personnel preparation. *Journal of Special Education, 13,* 9–33.

See also Biological Basis of Emotional Disturbance; Biological Basis of Learning and Memory; Medical Model, Defense of

BIOLOGICAL BASIS OF EMOTIONAL DISORDERS

Biological factors contribute to emotional disorders in various ways. A genetic predisposition has been strongly implicated for schizophrenia, depression, and manic-depressive illness. There is at least moderate evidence of a genetic contribution to childhood autism, obsessive-compulsive disorder, (Franzblau, Kanadanian, & Rettig, 1995) panic disorder, disability (Heubner & Thomas, 1995) and other conditions.

Whether because of genetics, improper nutrition, or other sources, certain areas of the nervous system can misfunction in ways that lead to behavioral abnormalities. For example, individuals who are subject to panic disorder have an overresponsive sympathetic nervous system. Even at rest, they have an elevated heart rate and blood epinephrine level compared with controls (Nesse et al., 1984). They may respond with anxiety, agitation, and palpitations to injections that produce only mild signs of arousal in other people (Charney, Heninger, & Breier, 1984; Liebowitz et al., 1984).

Many types of emotional disorders have been linked to abnormalities affecting one or more synaptic transmitter systems in the brain. One example is depression. Most antidepressant drugs prolong the activity of the monoamine transmitters (dopamine, norepinephrine, and serotonin) in the brain. One interpretation of the effect of antidepressant drugs has been that they counteract an initial deficiency in the activity at monoamine synapses. That interpretation may be incorrect, however; a prolonged increase in the abundance of synaptic transmitter molecules at a synapse leads to a compensatory decline in the later release of that transmitter and to a decline in the number of receptors sensitive to that transmitter. Because of the multitude of effects, it is uncertain whether the antidepressant drugs help to repair an initial overactivity or underactivity of the monoamine synapses. Nevertheless, it is likely that some disorder of those synapses is responsible for many manifestations of depression.

The biological basis of an emotional disorder need not be a permanent chemical disorder of the brain, however, and drugs are not always the best remedy even for a biological disorder. Many cases of depression have been linked to inadequate or poorly timed sleep. Occasionally, individuals suffer from winter depressions as a result of inadequate sunlight. Uncorrected visual problems may lead to headaches. Many adolescents experience moodiness and aggressive outbursts that may be triggered by hormonal changes. A lack of exercise may predispose the body to overreact to stress. Malnutrition can aggravate psychological disorders as well. In certain cases, emotional disorders can be alleviated by altering sleep, diet, exercise, and other habits without resorting to tranquilizers, antidepressant drugs, or other medical interventions. For further information, see Kalat (1984), Pincus and Tucker (1985), or Snyder (1980).

REFERENCES
Charney, D.S., Heninger, G.R., & Breier, A. (1984). Noradrenergic function in panic anxiety. *Archives of General Psychiatry, 41,* 751–763.

Franzblau, S.H., Kanadanian, M., Rettig, E. (1995). Critique of the reductionist models of obsessive compulsive disorder. *Social Science and Medicine, 41,* 99–112.

Heubner, R.A., & Thomas, R. The relationship between attachment, psychopathology, and childhood disability. *Rehabilitation Psychology, 40,* 111–124.

Kalat, J.W. (1984). *Biological psychology* (2nd ed.). Belmont, CA: Wadsworth.

Liebowitz, M.R., Fyer, A.J., Gorman, J.M., Dillon, D., Appleby, I.L., Levy, G., Anderson, S., Levitt, M., Palij, M., Davies, S.O., & Klein, D.F. (1984). Lactate provocation of panic attacks: Vol I. Clinical and behavioral findings. *Archives of General Psychiatry, 41,* 764–770.

Nesse, R.M., Cameron, O.G., Curtis, G.C., McCann, D.S., & Huber-Smith, M.J. (1984). Adrenergic function in patients with panic anxiety. *Archives of General Psychiatry, 41,* 771–776.

Pincus, J.H., & Tucker, G.J. (1985). *Behavioral neurology* (3rd ed.). New York: Oxford University Press.

Snyder, S.H. (1980). *Biological aspects of mental disorder.* New York: Oxford University Press.

See also Diagnostic and Statistical Manual of Mental Disorders (DSM-IV); Emotional Disorders

BIOLOGICAL BASIS OF LEARNING AND MEMORY

To understand the biological basis of learning and memory, two largely independent questions must be dealt with: (1) How does a pattern of experience alter the future properties of cells and synapses in the nervous system? (2) How do populations of altered cells work together to produce adaptive behavior?

Striking progress has been made toward answering the first question. According to studies of invertebrates, short-term increases in behavior can be induced by chemical changes that block the flow of potassium across the presynaptic membrane of certain neurons. Longer lasting changes in behavior require the synthesis of proteins in the neurons to be changed (Kandel & Schwartz, 1982). Protein synthesis also appears to be necessary for learning by vertebrates, especially for long-term retention (Davis & Squire, 1984).

Certain of the brain changes associated with learning or the ability to learn are large enough to be visible under a light microscope. Enhanced learning ability is associated with a proliferation of glial cells and increased branching of dendrites (Uphouse, 1980). Impaired learning associated with the opposite anatomical changes. The extent of branching of dendrites is highly correlated with the number of synapses found in the brain.

Memory, on the other hand, is "attention" that leaves tracks or traces in the brain. Biologically, memory functions at two broad levels, one at the cellular level and one at a systems level. The creation of memories changes individual cell membranes and synaptic physiology (Reynolds & Bigler, 1997).

Investigators have not determined how the changed neurons operate together to produce the overall changes in behavior identified as learning. They have, however, identified areas of the mammalian brain that are necessary for certain aspects of learning. Experiments with animals have indicated that amnesia is most severe if damage to the hippocampus is combined with damage to the amygdala. Damage to those two areas impairs animals' ability to store sensory information and respond to it a few minutes later (Zola-Morgan & Squire, 1985). Various other patterns of learning and memory loss occur after damage to the frontal lobes of the cerebral cortex and to numerous subcortical structures.

Majovski (1997) has suggested that:

Data collected from studies of heredity and environment show that morphogenetic development of the brain's intellectual nature is attributable to both genetic and social environmental influences, the former having slightly greater effect than the latter. What this suggests is that several different cortical and cortical-subcortical systems are operative during the process of learning and information storage. What the infant senses, then, may be in part the result of what is neurally "set" to sense or competent to sense via a selective attention process. (p. 83)

The interactive process of learning and memory with the environmental and physical factors in childhood suggests a highly interactive biological set.

Impaired learning and memory among children and adolescents are not generally caused by discretely localized brain damage. Exposure to alcohol and other toxins in utero can greatly impair brain development, as can phenylketonuria, severe malnutrition, or a chronic lack of social stimulation in early childhood. Head injury leading to a temporary loss of consciousness is a commonly overlooked source of minor, diffuse brain damage. These factors coupled with the process of brain development and acculturation makes the diagnosis of learning and memory problems very difficult.

REFERENCES

Davis, H.P., & Squire, L.R. (1984). Protein synthesis and memory: A review. *Psychological Bulletin, 96,* 518–559.

Kandel, E.R., & Schwartz, J.H. (1982). Molecular biology of learning: Modulation of transmitter release. *Science, 218,* 433–443.

Majovski, L.V. (1997). Development of Higher Brain functions in children: Neural, Cognitive, and Behavioral Perspectives. In C.R. Reynolds & E. Fletcher-Janzen (Eds.), *Handbook of Clinical Child Neuropsychology* (2nd ed.) (pp. 63–101). New York: Plenum.

Reynolds, C.R., & Bigler, E.D. (1997). Clinical neuropsychological assessment of child and adolescent memory with the Test of Learning & Memory. In C.R. Reynolds & E. Fletcher-Janzen (Eds.), *Handbook of Clinical Child Neuropsychology* (2nd ed.) (pp. 296–329). New York: Plenum.

Uphouse, L. (1980). Reevaluation of mechanisms that mediate brain differences between enriched and impoverished animals. *Psychological Bulletin, 88,* 215–232.

Zola-Morgan, S., & Squire, L.R. (1985). Medial temporal lesions in monkeys impair memory on a variety of tasks sensitive to human amnesia. *Behavioral Neuroscience, 99,* 22–34.

BIOLOGICAL FACTORS AND SOCIAL CLASS

See SOCIAL CLASS AND BIOLOGICAL FACTORS

BIRCH, HERBERT G. (1918–1973)

Herbert G. Birch was born in New York City on April 21, 1918. He graduated from New York University (NYU) in 1939, and received the PhD degree in psychology in 1944. In 1960 Birch received the MD degree from the New York College of Medicine. He served as a research associate at the Yerkes Laboratories for Primate Biology from 1944 to 1946, as an instructor in psychology at NYU the next year, and as an assistant and associate professor at the City College of New York from 1947 to 1955. For the following 2 years, Birch was research associate at Bellevue Medical Center in New York City. From the time he received the MD degree in 1960 until his death, he was a member of the faculty of the Albert Einstein College of Medicine in New York City, first as an associate research professor and then as a full professor of pediatrics and director of the Center for Normal and Aberrant Behavioral Development. Concurrently, he was professor of psychology and education at the Ferkauf Graduate School of Humanities and Social Sciences, Yeshiva University.

An internationally known researcher in child development and brain injury, Birch was the author of 200 articles and coauthor of six books, the latter including *Brain Damage in Children* (1964), *Disadvantaged Children: Health, Nutrition, and School Failure* (1970), and *Children with Cerebral Dysfunction* (1971). He served in an editorial capacity for a number of journals, including the *Journal of Special Education,* the *American Journal of Mental Deficiency,* the *American Journal of Child Psychology and Human Development,* and the *International Journal of Mental Health.* In 1971 he received the Kennedy International Award for Scientific Research for outstanding scientific research contributing to the understanding and alleviation of mental retardation. Birch died at his home in Suffern, New York, on February 4, 1973.

REFERENCES

Birch, H.G. (Ed.). (1964). *Brain damage in children.* Baltimore: Williams & Wilkins.

Birch, H.G., & Diller, K. (1971). *Children with cerebral dysfunction.* New York: Grune & Stratton.

Birch, H.G., & Gussow, J.D. (1970). *Disadvantaged children: Health, nutrition and school failure.* New York: Grune & Stratton.

Wang, M.C., & Birch, J.W. (1985). *Reports on the implementation and effects of the adaptive learning environments model in general and special education settings.* Pittsburgh, PA: University of Pittsburgh.

BIRCH, JACK W. (1915–1998)

A native of Glassport, Pennsylvania, Jack W. Birch began his career as an elementary education teacher after receiving a BS (1937) with majors in English and science and a minor in special education from California University of Pennsylvania. He later went on to earn his MEd from Pennsylvania State University (1941) and a PhD in Psychology from the University of Pittsburgh (1951).

Birch taught classes for educable mentally retarded children, and was a psychologist and supervisor of special education. From 1948 to 1958 he was director of special education for the Pittsburgh Public Schools, and spent the remainder of his career at the University of Pittsburgh as a professor of psychology and education, chairman of the Department of Special Education, and an associate dean in the School of Education. He was among the initial faculty organizers of the University Senate and served as its vice president. Birch became an emeritus professor in 1985 at the age of 70. He was active in the field of education and community service until his death on April 1, 1998.

Birch published over 120 articles and books on topics including gifted and talented persons and individuals with mental retardation, speech handicaps, blindness, deafness, and physical handicaps. *Teaching Exceptional Children in All America's Schools* and *Reports on the Implementation and Effects of the Adaptive Learning Environments Model in General and Special Education Settings* are two of his major books. His writings also included books related to aspects of academia, including writing better dissertations and how to make the best use of retired professors.

Believing that students with handicaps should have an opportunity to display skills society assumed they were incapable of developing, Birch was among early advocates of mainstreaming students with handicaps.

During his lifetime, Birch traveled to numerous countries, frequently as a consultant in special education to various foreign governments and schools, and from 1985 to 1986, he was the Belle van Zuijlen professor of clinical child psychology and pedagogy at the University Utrecht, Netherlands. For his contributions to special education and rehabilitation, Birch received an award from the Pennsylvania Federation of the Council for Exceptional Children, and he was also honored for his service with an award from The National Accreditation Council of Services to the Blind and Visually Handicapped.

REFERENCES

Birch, J.W. (1978). Mainstreaming that works in elementary and secondary schools. *Journal of Teacher Education, 29,* 18–21.

Reynolds, M.C., & Birch, J.W. (1982). *Teaching exceptional children in all America's schools.* Reston, VA: Council for Exceptional Children.

BIRTH INJURIES

Birth injuries are the traumatic injuries to the brain, skull, spinal cord, peripheral nerves, and muscle of the newborn that occasionally occur during the birth process. These injuries include cephalohematoma, skull fracture, central nervous system hemorrhage, spinal cord injury, peripheral nerve injury, bony injury, abdominal injury, cerebral palsy, and seizure disorders. The frequency of these birth injuries has greatly decreased with the declining use of high and midforceps, better monitoring during labor, and decreased vaginal breech deliveries (Brann, 1985). However the frequency of birth injuries may vary depending on the introduction of new techniques to assist delivery such as vacuum extraction (Hes, de Jong, Paz, & Avezaat, 1997).

Cephalohematoma usually refers to a benign traumatic lesion to the skull in which blood pools under the periosteum and is confined by suture boundaries. But 10 to 25% of all cephalohematomas are associated with an underlying skull fracture. These fractures rarely pose major problems but if depressed can result in compression of the skull (Menkes, 1984).

Central nervous system hemorrhage may be caused by mechanical trauma to the infant's brain during the birth process. The hemorrhage may occur in the subarachnoid space, the subdural space, or the dural space, or it may be intracerebral. The most common type of traumatic central nervous system hemorrhage is the subarachnoid hemorrhage resulting from tears in the meninges. Usually this is a benign condition unless it is associated with perinatal hypoxia or meningitis (Oxorn, 1986).

Subdural hemorrhage, now uncommon, may result in hydrocephalus and seizures. Intracerebral hemorrhage, one of the rarest types of traumatic central nervous system hemorrhage in the newborn, may result in increased intracranial pressure, hemiparesis, and convulsions. Hemorrhage into the dural space is also rare, but it usually results in massive hemorrhage and early neonatal death (Brann, 1985).

Traumatic spinal cord injuries are unusual. The most common sites of damage are the lower cervical and upper thoracic regions. These injuries can lead to stillbirth, respiratory failure, paralysis, or spasticity (Oxorn, 1986).

Peripheral nerve injuries can involve trauma to the brachial plexus, the phrenic nerve, the facial nerve, or the radial nerves. The nerve injuries are usually caused by traction or direct compression of the nerve itself. Trauma to the brachial plexus may cause muscle atrophy, contractures, and impaired limb growth (Menkes, 1984).

Trauma to the phrenic nerve may cause diaphragm paralysis and mimic congenital pulmonary or heart disease, resulting in long-term ventilatory support. Damage to the facial nerve results in weakness of the muscles to the affected side of the face, causing failure on the affected side of the mouth to move and the eyelid to close. Radial nerve injury may result in wrist drop and the inability to extend the fingers and the thumb (Menkes, 1984).

Traumatic bony injuries include fractures of the clavicle, humerus, and femur. Fracture of the clavicle is the most common bony injury; it usually occurs in association with shoulder dystocia. Fractures of the humerus and femur are rare and result from traumatic delivery (Oxorn, 1986).

Traumatic abdominal injuries are uncommon but they can have serious consequences. The traumatic abdominal injuries include hepatic or splenic rupture; they result from traumatic delivery. These injuries are usually life-threatening conditions (Oxorn, 1986).

Cerebral palsy is a chronic nonprogressive disorder of the pyramidal motor system resulting in lack of voluntary muscle control and coordination. The cause is uncertain but cerebral anoxia during the perinatal period has been associated with the resulting cerebral damage (Rosen, 1985).

Seizure disorders may result from many causes, including perinatal asphyxia, intracranial hemorrhage, infection, congenital defects, metabolic disorders, drug withdrawal, inherited defects, and kernicterus. Perinatal asphyxia is the most frequent cause of seizures in the pre- and full-term infant. Perinatal asphyxia as the cause of neonatal seizures has the poorest prognosis. Approximately 60% of those infants with seizures caused by perinatal asphyxia have permanent neurologic sequelae and lifelong seizure disorders (Brann, 1985).

REFERENCES

Brann, A.W. (1985). Factors during neonatal life that influence brain disorders. In J.M. Freeman (Ed.), *Prenatal and perinatal factors associated with brain disorders* (NIH Publication No. 85–1149, pp. 263–358). Bethesda, MD: U.S. Department of Health and Human Services.

Hes, R., de Jong, T.H., Paz, D.H., & Avezaat, C.J. (1997). Rapid evolution of a growing skull fracture after vacuum extraction. *Pediatric Neurosurgery, 26,* 269–274.

Menkes, J.H. (1984). Neurologic evaluation of the newborn infant. In M.E. Avery & H.W. Taeusch (Eds.), *Schaffer's diseases of the newborn* (5th ed.) (pp. 652–661). Philadelphia: Saunders.

Oxorn, H. (1986). *Human labor and birth* (5th ed.). Norwalk, CT: Appleton-Century-Crofts.

Rosen, M.G. (1985). Factors during labor and delivery that influence brain disorders. In J.M. Freeman (Ed.), *Prenatal and perinatal factors associated with brain disorders* (NIH Publication No. 85–1149, pp. 359–440). Bethesda, MD: U.S. Department of Health and Human Services.

See also Absence Seizures; Brain Damage; Cerebral Palsy; Grand Mal Seizures

BIRTH ORDER

Birth order, or sibling status, refers to a child's ordinal position in the family. There has been much speculation about the effects of birth order on important variables such as personality characteristics, mental illness, intelligence, achievement, and occupational status; but consistent relationships have been difficult to establish unequivocally.

Various personality profiles, though sometimes overlapping and inconsistent, have been suggested for prominent ordinal positions. The proposed profiles follow:

Firstborn. Firstborns are said to exhibit higher standards of moral honesty, have higher need for achievement, earlier social maturation, better work habits, and higher need for recognition and approval (Forer, 1976; Harris, 1973). Firstborns are also considered to rate higher in leadership, independence, and sensitivity to stress (Sutton-Smith & Rosenberg, 1970), and tend to be dominant, more aggressive, ambitious and conservative (Koch, 1955).

Secondborn. Secondborns are believed to have good social skills, seek out group activities, and maintain better relationships in life than do firstborns. They also show more dependency behavior and seek more adult help and approval (Forer, 1976; McGurk & Lewis, 1972).

Middleborn. Middleborns, like secondborns, show better interpersonal skills and tend to express greater sensitivity to the feelings and needs of others (Falbo, 1981; Miller & Maruyama, 1976). Middle children generally have the fewest behavior problems, enjoy a healthier adjustment to life and as adults experience less anxiety in new or threatening situations (Touliatos & Lindholm, 1980; Yannakis, 1976). They also show more concern for peer norms and consequently accept peer advice more readily (Harris, 1973).

Lastborn. The youngest child is more likely to exhibit dependency and be peer oriented (Schacter, 1959). This birth order also has been associated with higher propensity to use alcohol and cigarettes (Ernst & Angst, 1983).

Onlyborn. Only children have a tendency to be leaders rather than joiners and show considerable affinity for independent behavior (Falbo, 1981). Schacter (1959) reports that only children experience more fear and anxiety during adolescence and adulthood than laterborn children. Conventional wisdom that singletons are selfish, lonely, and uncooperative is unsupported (Falbo, 1981).

Many factors affect a child's perception of ordinal position and associated family dynamics. Sex of siblings and spacing are important, as is the status of adopted children and stepchildren. For example, Adler (1958) has suggested that the male child with all female siblings may place more emphasis on his masculinity. A secondborn might assume the responsibilities of a firstborn who is developmentally delayed. With adopted children or stepchildren, previous family interactional patterns may have consequences for adjustment to new ordinal positions.

Several large-scale studies have found relationships between birth order and intelligence and achievement. (Belmont & Marolla, 1973; Zajonc & Markus, 1975; Berbaum & Moreland, 1980). On the average, oldest children have higher IQ's and have higher achievement in school and in careers. Only children also tend to be high achievers (Zajonc & Markus, 1975). However, a more recent study using a large data set from 1973 found that birth-order effects, when measured by educational attainment (i.e., total years of education), are negligible for small sib sizes, such as one to four children. For large families, it was found that lastborns and next-to-lastborns did considerably better than firstborns (Blake, 1989). Birth order and SAT data showed virtually no correlation. When these data were collected, presumably more resources were available for the lastborn child and more educational opportunities were afforded them.

It must be remembered that even the reported differences in IQ correlated with birth order are quite small and have been obtained only when large numbers of families are compared. It is therefore unwise to make predictions for individuals on the basis of birth order. Family size, family structure and income have far greater effects on IQ than birth order. Wide spacing of siblings also tends to eliminate any evidence of birth order effects (Shaffer, 1993). To the degree that birth order may have consequences for achievement, it should not be assumed that such effects occur cross-culturally (LeVine, 1990).

As for personality, some research has found that firstborn infants, preschoolers, and adults are more socially outgoing and more interested in peer contacts than laterborns (Schachter, 1959; Snow, Jacklin, & Maccoby, 1981; Vandell, Wilson, & Whalen, 1981). There is some evidence that laterborn children tend to be somewhat more popular on average than firstborn children (Miller & Maruyama, 1976). And birth order may be a factor that contributes to children's acceptance by peers. One rationale offered is that laterborn children must learn to negotiate with older, more powerful siblings, and hence learn how to cooperate. Acquiring and using more conciliatory interpersonal skills may enable laterborns to be more popular than firstborns, who may use their greater power to dominate their younger siblings and use coercive ways with peers (Berndt & Bulleit, 1985).

Frank Sulloway (1996), in his book *Born to Rebel,* marshals persuasive evidence for the contributions of birth order to personality development. His meta-analysis leads him to conclude that for the personality dimension of openness to experience, laterborns are more nonconforming, adventurous, and unconventional. And firstborns tend to be more responsible, achievement-oriented, and organized; in a word, conscientious. They also tend to be more emotionally unstable, anxious, and fearful. In short, "firstborns tend to be dominant, aggressive, ambitious, jealous, and conservative" (p. 79). He also claims that birth order effects are 5 to 10 times greater for the key personality dimensions of openness to experience, conscientiousness, agreeableness, and neuroticism than they are for academic achievement and IQ.

However, as with correlations reported between birth order and measures of intelligence, ordinal position effects reported for sociability are quite small. Thus, one must conclude that birth order plays at best only a minor role in determining how sociable a child is likely to become. The same is true for effects on peer popularity. More research is needed before we can understand how children's experiences in their families are translated into patterns of behavior and social standing outside the family.

It does appear that birth order, at certain times and in some cultures, has been a significant developmental variable. In societies where primogeniture has been important, the life experiences of firstborn males were vastly different from those of other siblings and were no doubt instrumental in promoting their success. There is also some evidence to support the influence of birth order, as mediated through the complex dynamics of family experience, on certain dimensions of human personality. Although birth order can affect developmental outcomes, its importance cannot be systematically predicted, and thus should be considered with reasonable caution as a potential contributor to personality development.

REFERENCES

Adler, A. (1958). *What life should mean to you.* New York: Capricorn.

Belmont, L., & Marolla, F.A. (1973). Birth order, family size, and intelligence. *Science, 182,* 1096–1101.

Berbaum, M.L., & Moreland, R.I. (1980). Intellectual development within the family: A new application of the confluence model. *Developmental Psychology, 16,* 506–518.

Berndt, T.J. & Bulleit, T.N. (1985). Effects of sibling relationships on preschoolers' behavior at home and at school. *Developmental Psychology, 21,* 761–767.

Blake, J. (1989). *Family size and achievement.* Berkeley: University of California.

Ernst, C., & Angst, J. (1983). *Birth order: Its influence on personality.* Berlin: Springer-Verlag.

Falbo, T. (1981). Relationship between birth category, achievement, and interpersonal orientation. *Journal of Personality & Social Psychology, 41,* 121–131.

Forer, L.K. (1976). *The birth order factor.* New York: McKay.

Harris, I.D. (1973). Differences in cognitive style and birth order. In J.C. Westman (Ed.), *Individual differences in children* (pp. 199–210). New York: Wiley.

Koch, H.L. (1955). Some personality correlates of sex, sibling position, and sex of sibling among five- and six-year old children. *Genetic Psychology Monographs, 52,* 3–50.

LeVine, R.A. (1990). Enculturation: A biosocial perspective on the development of self. In D. Cicchetti & M. Beeghly (Eds.), *The self in transition: Infancy to childhood* (pp. 99–117). Chicago: University of Chicago.

McGurk, H., & Grandon, G.M. (1979). Birth order: A phenomenon in search of an explanation. *Developmental Psychology, 7,* 33, 366.

Miller, N., & Maruyama, G. (1976). Ordinal position and peer popularity. *Journal of Personality & Social Psychology, 33,* 123–131.

Schacter, S. (1959). *The psychology of affiliation.* Stanford, CA: Stanford University.

Shaffer, D.R. (1993). *Developmental psychology: Childhood and adolescence* (3rd ed.). Pacific Grove, CA: Brooks/Cole.

Snow, M.E., Jacklin, C.N., & Maccoby, E.E. (1981). Birth-order differences in peer sociability at thirty-three months. *Child Development, 52,* 589–595.

Sulloway, F.J. (1996). *Born to rebel: Birth order, family dynamics, and creative lives.* New York: Pantheon.

Sutton-Smith, B., & Rosenberg, B.G. (1970). *The sibling.* New York: Holt, Rinehart, & Winston.

Touliatos, J., & Lindholm, B.W. (1980). Birth order, family size, and children's mental health. *Psychological Reports, 46,* 1097–1098.

Vandell, D.L., Wilson, K.S., & Whalen, W.T. (1981). Birth-order and social experience differences in infant-peer interaction. *Developmental Psychology, 17,* 438–445.

Yannakis, A. (1976). Birth order and preference for dangerous sports among males. *Quarterly Research, 47,* 42–67.

Zajonc, R.B., & Markus, G.B. (1975). Birth order and intellectual development. *Psychological Review, 82,* 74–88.

See also **Personality Assessment; Socioeconomic Status; Temperament**

BIRTH TRAUMA

According to Freudian psychodynamic theory, early traumatic and painful events produce memories that, when repressed into the unconscious, may affect later life. Otto Rank (1929) elaborated on the proposition that birth is itself traumatic: It suddenly and painfully thrusts the infant from the warm, secure womb into a cold, hostile, and frustrating world. When frustrated later in life, people may in some ways behave as though they wished to return to the womb.

Leboyer (1975) argued that birth should be as gentle as possible for both mother and infant. In his birthing technique, the shock of birth is reduced by, among other things, keeping light and noise levels in the delivery room low. At birth, the newborn is placed on the mother's breast, massaged to decrease initial crying, and placed in a warm bath. The father attends and assists in handling the newborn.

Leboyer infants evidence normal physiological functioning (Kliot & Silverstein, 1984) and no differences in either maternal or infant morbidity or infant behavior (Nelson et al., 1980). At present, with the exception of shorter active labors among mothers expecting a Leboyer delivery (Nelson et al., 1980), advantages of the method appear more psychological than physiological (Grover, 1984). Indeed, evidence of long-term consequences of both conventional and Leboyer births are notably lacking, and the concept of birth trauma, particularly the Rankian version, is largely in disrepute.

REFERENCES

Grover, J.W. (1984). Leboyer and obstetric practice. *New York State Journal of Medicine, 84,* 158–159.

Kliot, D., & Silverstein, L. (1984). Changing maternal and newborn care. *New York State Journal of Medicine, 84,* 169–174.

Leboyer, F. (1975). *Birth without violence.* New York: Knopf.

Nelson, N.M., Enkin, M.W., Saigal, S., Bennett, K.J., Milner, R., & Sackett, D.L. (1980). A randomized clinical trial of the Leboyer approach to childbirth. *New England Journal of Medicine, 302,* 655–60.

Rank, O. (1929). *The trauma of birth.* New York: Harcourt, Brace.

BLATT, BURTON (1927–1985)

Burton Blatt, widely known as a leader in the movement for deinstitutionalization of people with mental retardation, began his professional career as a special class teacher in the public schools of New York City. After earning the doctorate in special education at Pennsylvania State University in 1956, he served on the faculties of Southern Connecticut State College and Boston University before joining the faculty of Syracuse University in 1969, where he served as dean of the School of Education from 1976 until his death in 1985.

In 1971 he formed the Center on Human Policy at Syracuse University, devoted to the study and promotion of open settings for people with mental retardation and other disabilities. His work was characterized by an inspirational humanism that contributed greatly to his effectiveness as a leader.

REFERENCES

Blatt, B. (1984). Biography in autobiography. In B. Blatt & R.J. Morris (Eds.), *Perspectives in special education: Personal orientations* (pp. 263–307). Glenview, IL: Scott, Foresman.

Blatt, B., & Kaplan, F. (1966). *Christmas in purgatory: A photographic essay on mental retardation* (2nd ed.). Boston: Allyn & Bacon.

Semmel, M.I. (1985). In memoriam: Burton Blatt, 1927–1985. *Exceptional Children, 52,* 102.

BLIND

Blind is a term used to refer to those students who have either no vision or, at most, light perception (the ability to tell light from dark) but no light projection (the ability to identify the direction from which light comes) (Faye, 1970; Colenbrander, 1977; NICHCY, 1998). Educationally, one who is blind learns primarily through tactual, auditory, and kinesthetic experiences, without the use of vision. The legal term for blindness is corrected visual acuity of 20/200 or less in the better eye and/or field of vision of 20 degrees or less (Goble, 1984; NICHCY, 1998). Severe visual impairments (legally or totally blind) occur at a rate of .06 per 1,000 (NICHCY, 1998). Individuals classified as blind under this legal definition receive certain benefits such as special educational materials and an extra income tax deduction.

Historically, academically oriented blind and low-vision students have been mainstreamed successfully into regular classes. They obtain their specialized skills in a variety of placement options. These include

1. *Itinerant Program.* The blind or low-vision student is enrolled in the regular class in the neighborhood school and an itinerant teacher who travels from school to

school provides direct instruction and serves as a consultant to the regular teachers several times a week.

2. *Resource Room Program.* The blind or low-vision student is enrolled in the regular class in a school within the district or town and a resource room teacher is housed in the school and is readily available to work with the student on a daily basis at regularly scheduled times and when needed.

3. *Special Class.* The blind or low-vision student is enrolled in a self-contained class in a public or private school setting for most of the day. Usually, those students with multiple impairments in addition to a visual handicap are placed in this type of setting.

4. *Residential School.* The blind or low-vision student enrolled in this placement usually has additional disabilities and/or cannot be cared for adequately at home. Sometimes blind students attend residential schools for short periods of time to develop intensive skills in such areas as orientation and mobility, vocational training, and technology (Cartwright, Cartwright, & Ward, 1981).

The unique curriculum for blind students includes reading and writing braille; typing; listening skills using human and synthetic speech; map and chart reading; domestic skills; orientation and mobility; career education; and instruction in the use of special aids and equipment such as the Cranmer abacus, talking calculators, cassette tape recorders, electronic reading machines, and other hardware and software adaptations that access computers (Heward & Orlansky, 1984).

Major resources relevant to blind students cited by the National Information Center for Children and Youth with Disabilities (1998) are:

American Council of the Blind Parents
c/o American Council of the Blind
1155 15th Street N.W., Suite 720
Washington, DC 20005
(202) 467-5081; 1-800-424-8666
Web Address: *http://www.acb.org*

American Foundation for the Blind
11 Penn Plaza, Suite 300
New York, NY 10001
1-800-AFBLIND (Toll Free Hotline)
To order publications, call: 1-800-232-3044
E-mail: *afbinfo@afb.org*
Web Address: *http://www.afb.org/afb*

Blind Children's Center
4120 Marathon Street
Los Angeles, CA 90029-0159
(213) 664-2153; 1-800-222-3566
E-mail: *info@blindcntr.org*
Web Address: *http://www.blindcntr.org/bcc*

Division for the Visually Handicapped
c/o Council for Exceptional Children
1920 Association Drive
Reston, VA 22091-1589
(703) 620-3660

National Association for Visually Handicapped
22 West 21st Street, 6th Floor
New York, NY 10010
(212) 889-3141
E-mail: *staffnavh@org*
Web Address: *http://www.navh.org*

National Braille Press
88 St. Stephen Street
Boston, MA 02115
(617) 266-6160; 1-800-548-7323

National Federation of the Blind, Parents Division
c/o National Federation of the Blind
1800 Johnson Street
Baltimore, MD 21230
(410) 659-9314
E-mail: *epc@roudley.com*
Web Address: *http://www.nfb.org*

National Library Services for the Blind and
Physically Handicapped
Library of Congress
1291 Taylor Street, N.W.
Washington, DC 20542
(202) 707-5100; 1-800-424-8567
E-mail: *nls@loc.gov*
Web Address: *http://www.loc.gov/nls*

Prevent Blindness America
500 E. Remington Road
Schaumburg, IL 60173
(708) 843-2020; 1-800-221-3004 (Toll Free)
E-mail: *info@preventblindness.org*
Web Address: *http://www.prevent-blindness.org*

REFERENCES

Cartwright, G.P., Cartwright, C.A., & Ward, M. (1981). *Educating special learners.* Belmont, CA: Wadsworth.

Colenbrander, A. (1977). Dimensions of visual performance. *Archives of American Academy of Ophthalmology, 83,* 332–337.

Faye, E.E. (1970). *The low vision patient.* New York: Grune & Stratton.

Goble, J.L. (1984). *Visual disorders in the handicapped child.* New York: Marcel Dekker.

Heward, W.L., & Orlansky, M.D. (1984). *Exceptional children.* Columbus, OH: Merrill.

National Information Center for Children and Youth with Disabilities (NICHCY). (1998). General information about visual impairments Fact Sheet Number 13. Washington, DC: Author.

See also American Printing House for the Blind; Blindisms; Braille; Electronic Travel Aids

BLIND INFANTS

An increase in the birth of blind infants can be related to four major factors: (1) prematurity; (2) family history of a visual defect; (3) infection during pregnancy; and (4) difficult or assisted labor (Ellingham et al., 1976). With increasing medical advances in saving premature infants, the incidence of retinopathy of prematurity (previously termed retrolental fibroplasia) is rising (Morse & Trief, 1985). In fact, it is estimated that in the 1990s there will be somewhere between 12,000 and 19,000 visually impaired preschoolers (up to 5 years of age) (Hill et al., 1984).

The increase of visually impaired infants demands focused attention toward early intervention efforts. Unfortunately, many of the infants born prematurely are also born with deafness, mental retardation, and blindness (Morse & Trief, 1985). Programs for both normally developing blind infants and multiply handicapped infants require intervention in areas including motor, sensory, communication, and conceptual development. Parent involvement is a critical component in the early intervention of blind infants (Moore, 1984; CEC, 1987). As an example, Ferrell (1985) developed a training handbook for parents of visually impaired and multiply handicapped children, describing several intervention strategies. Research is clearly needed in this area because much of what we know about the development of blind infants is currently based on research efforts from the 1960s (Fraiberg, 1977). Other and more current research has focused on orientation and motility training for infants (CEC, 1987).

REFERENCES

Council for Exceptional Children. (1987). *Orientation and mobility for blind infants.* Reston, VA: Author.

Council for Exceptional Children. (1992). *Visual Impairments.* (ERIC Digest No. E511)

Ellingham, T., Silva, P., Buckfield, P., & Clarkson, J. (1976). Neonatal at risk factors, visual defects and the preschool child: A report from the Queen Mary Hospital multidisciplinary child development study. *New Zealand Medical Journal, 83,* 74–77.

Ferrell, K. (1985). *Reach out and teach: Meeting the training needs of parents of visually and multiply handicapped young children.* New York: American Foundation for the Blind.

Fraiberg, S. (1977). *Insights from the blind.* New York: Basic Books.

Hill, E., Rosen, S., Correa, V., & Langley, M.B. (1984). Preschool orientation and mobility: An expanded definition. *Education of the Visually Handicapped, 16,* 58–72.

Moore, S. (1984). The need for programs and services for visually handicapped infants. *Education of the Visually Handicapped, 16,* 48–57.

Morse, A., & Trief, E. (1985). Diagnosis and evaluation of visual dysfunction in premature infants with low birth weight. *Journal of Visual Impairment and Blindness, 79,* 248–251.

See also Blind; Visual Impairment

BLINDISMS

Blindisms is a term used to describe a group of simple or complex repetitive behaviors that involve both small movements of various parts of the body, such as eye rubbing, head turning, and hand flapping, and large body movements such as rocking or swaying (Warren, 1984). This term is actually a misnomer because these behaviors occur in other types of children as well, including those who are autistic, retarded, and without any handicapping conditions. More appropriate terms that do not single out blind children are stereotypic behaviors or mannerisms.

One of the most common mannerisms in blind children is pressing on one or both eyes. Pressure on the eyeball results in a pleasurable sensation to the child, i.e., the child may find it entertaining and relaxing. The most active eye pressers are children with retinal disorders (Scott, Jan, & Freeman, 1985). Children who are continual eye pressers tend to have deeply depressed eyes and black circles around their eyes; this detracts from their overall appearance. Another common mannerism, not considered by parents to be unusual when it first develops, is rocking. Whereas sighted children find other pleasurable activities to replace rocking, blind children tend to persevere in this activity.

Mannerisms frequently occurring in children with low vision, particularly those with rubella, are light gazing at the sun or fluorescent lights and waving of fingers in front of their eyes against the lights. Many become so involved in these behaviors that it is extremely difficult to direct their attention to more appropriate activities within the environment (Scott et al., 1985).

There are several theories regarding the causes of stereotypic behaviors in blind children. One of them is that these behaviors are efforts to increase the level of sensory stimulation (Burlingham, 1967; Curson, 1979; Scott et al., 1985). It has also been suggested that stereotypic repetitive behaviors are pleasurable because of the motor discharge (Burlingham, 1965). Another theory related to cause of stereotypic behaviors is that the behaviors are a result of social rather than sensory deprivation (Warren, 1984). However, according to Webster (1983), one cannot separate the sensory stimulation factor from the social stimulation factor in the case of blind infants. Williams (1978) has indicated that mobility plays a role in inhibiting stereotypic behavior patterns, and that lack of early mobility causes these behaviors to perpetuate.

Stereotypic behaviors tend to increase in both sighted and blind children when they are under stress. However, these repetitive patterns are fewer, and more intensely practiced, in blind children (Warren, 1984). They continue because they become self-reinforcing and therefore self-sustaining (Eichel, 1979). Research studies have shown that behavior modification approaches can reduce or eliminate some stereotypic behaviors in visually handicapped children (Caetano & Kaufman, 1975; Miller & Miller, 1976; Williams, 1978).

Parents and teachers are advised to work together to help blind and low-vision children develop positive exploratory and mobile behaviors. These efforts will enable this population to become more socially accepted by their peers, to attend more to the outside environment, and to prevent possible physiologic damage caused by excessive eye poking or rubbing, or head banging (Warren, 1984).

REFERENCES

Burlingham, D. (1965). Some problems of ego development in blind children. *Psychoanalytic Study of the Child, 20,* 194–208.

Burlingham, D. (1967). Developmental considerations in the occupations of the blind. *Psychoanalytic Study of the Child, 22,* 187–198.

Caetano, A.P., & Kaufman, J.M. (1975). Reduction of rocking mannerisms in two blind children. *Education of the Visually Handicapped, 7,* 101–105.

Curson, A. (1979). The blind nursery school child. *Psychoanalytic Study of the Child, 34,* 51–83.

Eichel, V.J. (1979). A taxonomy for mannerisms of blind children. *Journal of Visual Impairment and Blindness, 72,* 125–130.

Miller, B.S., & Miller, W.H. (1976). Extinguishing "blindisms": A paradigm for intervention. *Education of the Visually Handicapped, 8,* 6–15.

Scott, E.P., Jan, J.E., & Freeman, R.D. (1985). *Can't your child see?* Austin, TX: Pro-Ed.

Warren, D.H. (1984). *Blindness and early childhood development.* New York: American Foundation for the Blind.

Webster, R. (1983). What—no blindisms in African blind children? *Imfama, 7,* 16–18.

Williams, C.E. (1978). Strategies of intervention with the profoundly retarded visually-handicapped child: A brief report of a study of stereotypy. *Occasional Papers of the British Psychological Society, 2,* 68–72.

See also **Blind; Self-Stimulation; Visual Impairment; Visual Training**

BLIND LEARNING APTITUDE TEST (BLAT)

The Blind Learning Aptitude Test (BLAT) was developed in 1969 by T. Ernest Newland as a nonverbal, individually administered multiple aptitude battery for use with blind and partially sighted children and adolescents. The age range of BLAT is from 6 to 20 years, but it is most often recommended for use between the ages of 6 and 12. The test was designed to objectively measure learning process rather than learning product in blind children by minimizing the influence of experiences to which the sighted child is subjected. In fact, the majority of the items were taken from tests designed to minimize cultural bias. The BLAT items are presented in an embossed format involving dots and lines similar to those used in braille; however, no knowledge of braille is required to complete the test. The test consists of 61 tactile stimulus items, and 49 of those are scored while 12 are used for training purposes. The items measure abilities such as discrimination, generalization, and sequencing (Buros, 1978).

Standardized on a sample of 961 blind students in a number of residential and day schools for the blind across the United States, the author reports reliability coefficients ranging from 0.86 to 0.93. However, much of the reliability data is indeterminate, as many tables lack information such as Ns, means, and standard deviations. Data on the validity of the BLAT is also incomplete. Factor analysis indicated some tendency for the items to fall into groups that relate to the six different items used in the test. However, information is not provided on the nature or size of the sample, nor how the factors were extracted or rotated.

Although it was welcomed as an alternative to traditional tests for the blind on its development in 1969, the BLAT is not widely used in education or research today.

REFERENCES

Buros, O.K. (1978). *The eighth mental measurements yearbook.* Highland Park, NJ: Buros Foundation.

Newland, T.E. (1971). *Manual for the Blind Learning Aptitude Test: Experimental edition.* Urbana, IL: Author.

See also **Blind; Visual Impairment; Visual Perception and Discrimination**

BLISSYMBOLS

Blissymbols, or Blissymbolics, is a graphic symbol system that was originally created by Charles K. Bliss in 1942 (Bliss, 1965). Blissymbols consist of 100 meaningful picture symbols that are combined in a logical manner for communication. Not simply a set of symbols, Blissymbolics is a language that has its own linguistic rule system. Blissymbolics was originally developed to be a language that could be easily learned and understood for international communication. In 1971, Blissymbols were first used as an augmentative communication symbol system for nonspeaking handicapped persons at the Ontario Crippled Children's Center in Toronto, Canada (Silverman, McNaughton, & Kates, 1978). Currently, Blissymbolics is one of many picture graphic symbol systems that have been developed for use with augmentative communication systems.

Many studies have documented the effectiveness of using Blissymbols with individuals who are nonspeaking and who have physical handicaps (Silverman et al., 1978). In addition, they have been used with individuals who are mentally retarded, autistic (Kozleski, 1991), hearing impaired, and adults with aphasia. Blissymbols are best suited for persons who are unable to use traditional written language as an alternative communication method but are capable of learning large vocabularies.

REFERENCES

Bliss, C.K. (1965). *Semantography-Blissymbolics.* Sydney, Australia: Semantography.

Kozleski, E.B. (1991). Visual symbol acquisition by students with autism. *Exceptionality, 24*(4), 173–194.

Silverman, F., McNaughton, S., & Kates, B. (1978). *Handbook of*

Blissymbolics. Toronto, Canada: Blissymbolics Communications Institute.

See also Alternative Communication Methods in Special Education; Augmentative Communication Systems

BOBATH METHOD

Karel Bobath, a neuropsychiatrist, and Berta Bobath, a physiotherapist, developed an assessment and treatment program in England based on central nervous system (CNS) functioning. Their approach focuses on the whole child and is referred to as neurodevelopmental treatment (NDT) (Bobath, 1980).

In the Bobath method, the central nervous system functioning is regarded as the basis of all motor functioning. It provides the individual with the ability to perform all posture and movement tasks, from the most simple to the most highly integrated complex ones. The individual is able to maintain the head and trunk in a mid-line or balanced position while pursuing a motor task because of the working of the CNS.

A major emphasis of NDT when employed with children is that parents and teachers be taught appropriate handling techniques by the therapist with the physician's approval. For carryover and integration of new skills to occur, the same handling procedures used by the therapist should be used at home and in the classroom. The Bobath method has been criticized as being "insufficient in meeting the special cognitive, social, and emotional problems and integrating these variables into patient examination and physical rehabilitation" (Rasmussen, 1994).

REFERENCES

Bobath, K. (1980). *A neurophysiological basis for the treatment of cerebral palsy.* Philadelphia: Lippincott.

Rasmussen, G. (1994). A new approach to physical rehabilitation. In A.L. Christensen & B. Uzzell (Eds.), *Brain injury and physical rehabilitation.* Hillsdale, NJ: Erlbaum.

See also Cerebral Palsy; Occupational Therapy; Physical Therapy

BODER TEST OF READING-SPELLING PATTERNS

The Boder Test of Reading-Spelling Patterns (the Boder Test) is subtitled "A diagnostic test for subtypes of reading disability," a designation that reflects the medical orientation of the test's senior author and the need for a typology of dyslexia. Boder and Jarrico (1982), in devising the Boder Test, relied on several assumptions about children and about reading.

The first assumption is that each dyslexic reader has a distinctive pattern of cognitive strengths and weaknesses across the two primary factors of the reading process: the visual gestalt and the auditory analytic functions. In Boder's scheme, the former underlies the development of a sight vocabulary and the latter the development of phonic word analysis or word attack. The Boder Test thus gives the following as its operational definition of developmental dyslexia:

A reading disability in which the reading and spelling performance gives evidence of cognitive deficits in either the visual gestalt function or auditory analytic function, or both. A corollary of this definition is that when the reading-spelling pattern of poor readers gives no evidence of such cognitive deficits, the reading disability is regarded as nonspecific rather than dyslexic. (Boder & Jarrico, 1982, p. 5)

Accordingly, the Boder Test is intended to allow for differential diagnosis of developmental dyslexia by analyzing together a child's reading and spelling performances as interdependent functions. The manual describes what is offered as "a systematic sequence of simple reading and spelling tasks . . ." giving "an essentially qualitative analysis of the ability to learn to read and spell, for which quantitative criteria are provided" (Boder & Jarrico, 1982, p. 5).

Although the Boder Test is the product of much clinical experience with children and reflects great insight into abnormal reading processes, the technical development of the Boder Test was inadequate to support its use in other than research settings. The use of antiquated quotients for scaling, the failure to collect normative data, and significant problems with the development of reliability and validity data (Flynn, 1992) all argue strongly against use of the scale. Boder's model of reading disabilities may still be useful in the conceptualization and treatment of children's reading difficulties, particularly in learning disabilities placements where differentiated instruction is possible, although the visual learner–auditory learner aspects of the approach are antiquated and have not been supported over the years (Reynolds, 1981). The use of the Boder Test in the diagnosis or evaluation of dyslexia or other reading difficulties is insupportable at this time and other means of implementing Boder's model of dyslexia should be pursued.

REFERENCES

Boder, E., & Jarrico, S. (1982). *Boder Test of reading-spelling patterns.* New York: Grune & Stratton.

Flynn, J.M. (1992). Electrophysiological correlates of dyslexic subtypes. *Journal of Learning Disabilities, 25*(2), 133–141.

Reynolds, C.R. (1981). Neuropsychological basis of intelligence. In G. Hynd & J. Obrzunt (Eds.), *Neuropsychological assessment and the school aged child: Issues and procedures.* New York: Grune & Stratton.

See also Grade Equivalents; Ratio IQ, Reading Disorders

BODY IMAGE

Body image as defined by Galloway and Bean is "the individual's awareness and knowledge of the physical and spatial characteristics" of his or her own body (1974, p. 126). Included in this definition is the idea of knowing body parts and the relationships among body parts. Thus, laterality and directionality stem from body image (Marshall, 1975). In addition, body image is often considered a component of self-concept.

The body awareness and knowledge of an exceptional child may be distorted because of sensory, perceptual, or cognitive dysfunctions inherent in the handicapping condition. Visual or hearing impairments, for example, may deprive a developing child of sensory information necessary for a complete and functional body image. Children with learning disabilities may have problems with body image that influence their learning and development (Cruickshank, 1977). Mentally retarded children, when compared with normal children, have been found to express body images of larger size and less detail and symmetry (Wysocki & Wysocki, 1973). Children and adolescents who are cancer survivors may experience body image issues as far as seven years post incident (Pendley, Dahlquist, & Dreyer, 1997). Body image distortions may also be culturally bound as researchers are finding that Anglo and Mexican-American female students are more likely to develop body image distortion that leads to eating disorders than Black American female students (Guinn, Semper, Jorgenson, & Skaggs, 1997; Greenberg & LaPorte, 1996).

Typically, body image is assessed by a student's drawing of a person; problems in body image are suspected when a student evidences laterality and directionality confusion. When such basic problems are encountered, the educational plan may include developmental approaches typically associated with preschool education and physical motor development.

Beyond a definition of body image emphasizing body awareness and knowledge, a more popular definition includes the feelings that accompany a person's body knowledge. Conceptualized in this light, body image is a precursor to self-concept (Morse, 1975). Thus, accurate body image is not only necessary for foundations basic to learning, but also essential for self-concept development and, ultimately, self-acceptance.

REFERENCES

Cruickshank, W.M. (1977). *Learning disabilities in home, school, and community.* Syracuse: Syracuse University Press.

Galloway, H.F., & Bean, M.F. (1974). The effects of action songs on the development of body-image and body-part identification in hearing-impaired preschool children. *Journal of Music Therapy, 11,* 125–134.

Greenberg, D.R., & LaPorte, D.J. (1996). Racial differences in body type preferences of men for women. *International Journal of Eating Disorders, 19*(3), 275–278.

Guinn, B., Semper, T., Jorgenson, L., & Skaggs, S. (1997). Body image perception in female Mexican-American adolescents. *Journal of School Health, 67,* 112–115.

Marshall, E.D. (1975). Teaching materials for children with learning disabilities. In W.M. Cruickshank & D.P. Hallahan (Eds.), *Percep-*

tual and learning disabilities in children (Vol. 1, pp. 279–307). Syracuse: Syracuse University Press.

Morse, W.C. (1975). The learning disabled child and considerations of life space. In W.M. Cruickshank & D.P. Hallahan (Eds.), *Perceptual and learning disabilities in children* (Vol. 1, pp. 337–353). Syracuse: Syracuse University Press.

Pendley, J.S., Dahlquist, L.M., & Dreyer, Z. (1997). Body image and psychosocial adjustment in adolescent cancer survivors. *Journal of Pediatric Psychology, 22,* 29–43.

Wysocki, B.A., & Wysocki, A.C. (1973). The body-image of normal and retarded children. *Journal of Clinical Psychology, 29*(1), 7–10.

See also **Draw-a-Person; Mental Status Exams**

BODY TYPES

The most recent and notable attempt to classify people according to bodily characteristics and their associated personality types was conducted by the American psychologist and physician William Sheldon. A system was developed to measure and classify the human body along three dimensions (Sheldon, 1940); this provided an individual's somatotype. A person receives a score ranging from one to seven on each of three bodily characteristics: endomorphy, mesomorphy, and ectomorphy. Endomorphy refers to a soft and rounded appearance. The extreme endomorph would be rated as 7–1–1 on the three components; the associated personality type would be considered viscerotonic, meaning a love of comfort and relaxation, sociability, and extroversion. The typical stereotype would be the jolly, gregarious fat person.

The second bodily characteristic, mesomorphy, refers to a strong muscular anatomy. At the extreme it would be rated as 1–7–1. Somatotonia is the related personality. This denotes a physically active individual who is assertive and adventuresome. The stereotype is a loud, aggressive athlete.

Ectomorphy is the third bodily characteristic. It gets rated as 1–1–7 at the extreme and refers to the thin, delicate person. Cerebrotonia is the associated personality type. This includes individuals who are restrained, private, and intellectually intense. The stereotype would be that of a shy, introverted scholar. The three bodily characteristics can vary along a seven-point scale, creating the possibility of many different combinations of these types with a hypothetically average person rated at 4-4-4.

Originally, Sheldon's theory hypothesized a relatively direct relationship between body type and behavior. Once the body build is created through genetic, biochemical, and physiological processes, certain behavior tends to follow. Even though there is some support for a correlation between body type and behavior (Shasby & Kingsley, 1978; Sheldon, Lewis, & Tenney, 1969; Walker, 1963), current authors (Cortes & Gatti, 1972; Glueck & Glueck, 1956; McCandless, 1961) have modified the genetic and physiological explanation by emphasizing a reciprocal relationship between people with different body types and the socialcultural milieu. Certain body types may arouse negative or positive social reactions in others; this fosters differential personality development (Collins, & Plahn, 1988; Butler & Ryckman, 1993; McCandless, 1961). In support of this social learning explanation, several studies (Brodsky, 1954; Lerner & Korn, 1972; Staffieri, 1967) have verified the existence of a body build-behavior stereotype. People with certain physiques create stereotype expectations in others of how they will behave.

REFERENCES

Brodsky, C. (1954). *A study of norms for body form-behavior relationships.* Washington, DC: Catholic University of America.

Butler, J.C., & Ryckman, M. (1993). Perceived and ideal physiques in male and female university students. *Journal of Social Psychology, 133,* 751–752.

Collins, J.K., & Plahn, M.R. (1988). Recognition accuracy, stereotypic preference aversion, and subjective judgment of body appearance in adolescents and young adults. *Journal of Youth and Adolescence, 17,* 317–334.

Cortes, J., & Gatti, F. (1972). *Delinquency and crime: A biopsychosocial approach.* New York: Seminar.

Glueck, S., & Glueck, E. (1956). *Physique and delinquency.* New York: Harper.

Lerner, R.M., & Korn, S.J. (1972). The development of body-build stereotypes in males. *Child Development, 43,* 908–920.

McCandless, B. (1961). *Children and adolescents.* New York: Holt, Rinehart, & Winston.

Shasby, G., & Kingsley, R.F. (1978). A study of behavior and body type in troubled youth. *Journal of School Health, 48,* 103–107.

Sheldon, W.H. (1940). *The varieties of human physique: An introduction to constitutional psychology.* New York: Harper & Brothers.

Sheldon, W.H., Lewis, N.D.C., & Tenney, A.M. (1969). Psychotic patterns and physical constitution: A thirty-year follow-up of thirty-eight-hundred psychiatric patients in New York State. In D.V. Siva Sanker (Ed.), *Schizophrenia: Current concepts and research.* New York: PJD.

Staffieri, J. (1967). A study of social stereotype of body image in children. *Journal of Personality & Social Psychology, 7,* 101–104.

Walker, R. (1963). Body build and behavior in young children. *Child Development, 34,* 1–23.

See also Heredity; Physical Anomalies

BONET, JUAN P. (1579–1629)

Juan Pablo Bonet, a Spanish philologist, instructed deaf students in language and articulation, and taught them a manual alphabet and system of signs that he had developed. He wrote the first book on the education of the deaf, *Simplification of the Letters of the Alphabet and Method of Teaching Deaf-Mutes to Speak.* This work, which appeared in 1620, provided a basis for the developments relating to the education of the deaf in Europe and Great Britain during the eighteenth century (Lane, 1984).

REFERENCE

Lane, H. (1984). *When the mind hears.* New York: Random House.

BORDERLINE PERSONALITY DISORDER

Borderline personality disorder is a diagnostic classification included in the *Diagnostic and Statistical Manual of Mental Disorders* (DSM-IV; American Psychiatric Association, 1994). The diagnosis of borderline personality disorder requires the presence of at least five of the following: impulsive or unpredictable behavior, unstable interpersonal relationships, difficulty in controlling anger or inappropriate anger, identity disturbance, unstable mood (including depression, anxiety, and irritability), physically self-damaging acts, chronic feelings of boredom, and intolerance of being alone. As is the case with other personality disorders, the borderline disorder represents a chronic, pervasive pattern of behavior that emerges during late childhood/adolescence and interferes with social and occupational functioning for much of the individual's adult life.

Despite the presence of symptoms during adolescence, the DSM-IV recommends that this diagnosis be reserved for individuals 18 years of age and older. For those under 18, the diagnosis of identity disorder, characterized by a similar clinical picture (e.g., mild depression, anxiety, self-doubt, negative/oppositional behavior), is preferred. Identity disorder reflects an inability to establish an acceptable sense of self and includes uncertainty about such issues as career goals, sexual orientation or behavior, moral values, friends, and long-term goals. Contrary to DSM-IV recommendations, however, the borderline diagnosis is often used with children and adolescents (Bradley, 1981), a practice that has received some empirical support (Archer et al., 1985).

The advent of managed care companies has severely restricted the ability of the helping professions to give significant and long-term care to individuals with this condition (Gabbard, 1997). Consequently many individuals with borderline personality disorder are left to fend for themselves after short-term treatment. Hopefully this poor state of affairs will change in the future.

REFERENCES

American Psychiatric Association. (1994). *Diagnostic and statistical manual of mental disorders* (4th ed.). Washington, DC: Author.

Archer, R.P. Ball, J.D., & Hunter, J.A. (1985). MMPI characteristics of borderline psychopathology in adolescent inpatients. *Journal of Personality Assessment, 49,* 47–55.

Bradley, S.J. (1981). The borderline diagnosis in children and adolescents. *Child Psychiatry & Human Development, 12*(2), 121–127.

Gabbard, G.O. (1997). Borderline personality disorder and rational managed care policy. *Psychoanalytic Inquiry, 10,* 17–28.

See also Childhood Psychosis; Childhood Schizophrenia; Diagnostic and Statistical Manual of Mental Disorders (DSM-IV)

BOWER, ELI M. (1917–1991)

Eli M. Bower obtained a BS degree from New York University in 1937 and an MA from Columbia University in 1947.

He continued his education at Stanford University, receiving his EdD in counseling psychology in 1954. Bower was a pioneer in the field of early childhood education of handicapped children. His major areas of study included orthopsychiatry, enhancing growth and learning for the disabled, and engaging children in the school setting with games. By bringing together mental health professionals and parents of disabled children, orthopsychiatry was founded in 1924. Orthopsychiatry is defined as the science of the study and treatment of behavior disorders, particularly those involving young people.

Bower's interest in this area was focused on behavioral and social problems and their daily resolution (Bower, 1971). He also believed that games should be encouraged as teaching devices, allowing children the freedom to be involved while learning to relate to the real world. Bower looked at the question of whether children with learning disabilities could be helped in an economical, effective, and institutionally acceptable manner early enough to change their course of school development.

Bower wrote several books and more than 100 articles. Some of his major works include *Games in Education and Development, Early Identification of Emotionally Handicapped Children in School,* and *Orthopsychiatry and Education.* Eli Bower died at his home in Alameda, California, on December 20, 1991 at the age of 74.

REFERENCES

Bower, E.M. (1971). *Orthopsychiatry and education.* Detroit: Wayne State University Press.

Bower, E.M. (1974). *Early identification of emotionally handicapped children in school.* Springfield, IL: Thomas.

Bower, E.M., & Shears, L.M. (1974). *Games in education and development.* Springfield, IL: Thomas.

BRACKEN BASIC CONCEPT SCALE-REVISED

The Bracken Basic Concept Scale (BBCS; Bracken, 1984) was designed to assess children's (ages two and a half to 8 years) understanding of 258 foundational language terms in eleven distinct conceptual domains. After 14 years of clinical use and research by early childhood educators, speech-language pathologists, and psychologists, the BBCS was revised (BBCS-R; Bracken, 1998). The revised instrument retained many of the characteristics of the previous test, but added several significant improvements (e.g., larger, full-color stimulus manual, 50 additional concepts, minor reorganization of content and subscales, Spanish form) and was renormed. The BBCS-R, like its predecessor, assesses children's conceptual knowledge in eleven categorical areas (i.e., colors, letters, numbers/counting, sizes, comparisons, shapes, direction/position, self/social awareness, texture/material, quantity, and time/sequence).

The BBCS-R was normed on a nationally representative sample of children from across the United States. The sample included 200 children from each year level, for a total of 1,100 children. Also included in the normative sample were proportionate samples of exceptional children (e.g., developmentally delayed, learning disabled, autistic). A separate sample of Spanish-speaking children (i.e., Caribbean, Mexican, Puerto Rican, Central American, South American) was tested to establish the technical qualities of the instrument for use with Hispanic youth.

The BBCS-R demonstrates strong psychometric qualities. Subtest internal consistencies across the age levels range from .78 to .98. Total test internal consistencies range from .96 to .99 across the age span for the English speaking sample and .95 to .99 for the Spanish speaking sample. BBCS-R stability coefficients similarly range from .78 to .88 for the subtests, and .94 for the total test.

The BBCS-R is intended to be used as a language measure, school readiness screener, and intellectual screener, in addition to its primary use as a measure of basic concept acquisition. When used with the Bracken Concept Development Program (Bracken, 1986), the BBCS-R also can be employed as a curriculum-based measurement tool.

REFERENCES

Bracken, B.A. (1984). *Bracken Basic Concept Scale.* San Antonio, TX: The Psychological Corporation.

Bracken, B.A. (1986). *Bracken Concept Development Program.* San Antonio, TX: The Psychological Corporation.

Bracken, B.A. (1998). *Bracken Basic Concept Scale-Revised.* San Antonio, TX: The Psychological Corporation.

BRAIDWOOD, THOMAS (1715–1806)

Thomas Braidwood, a Scottish teacher, established Great Britain's first school for the deaf in Edinburgh in 1760. Unaware of the methods of teaching the deaf that had been developed on Europe by Heinicke, Epée, and others, Braidwood developed his own techniques, through which his students learned to speak and lip read, and to read and write. Once he had established the effectiveness of his methods, Braidwood published a proposal for the provision of public funds for the education of those deaf students whose families could not afford to pay for schooling, and for the training of teachers in his methods. When public funding was not granted, Braidwood declared that the system would remain his property, and swore to secrecy the family members and others at the school who had learned his techniques (Bender, 1970).

Braidwood moved his school to Hackney, near London, in 1783. Because of his obsession with secrecy, it was not until after Braidwood's death that the details of his methods became known. The writings of his nephew, Joseph Watson, who assisted him at Hackney and later established England's first school for the indigent deaf, showed that Braidwood had developed an elaborate oral method of instruction that generally paralleled the development of the oral approach elsewhere.

REFERENCE

Bender, R. (1970). *The conquest of deafness.* Cleveland: Case Western Reserve University.

BRAILLE

Braille is a tactile system that individuals who are blind use to read and write. The basis of braille is a rectangular "cell" consisting of six raised dots, two vertical rows of three dots each. The official code, Standard English Braille (Grade 2), consists of alphabet letters, numbers, punctuation, composition signs, and 189 contractions and short-form words, both of which are abbreviations of whole words to increase the speed of reading and writing braille. The Nemeth Braille code is used to transcribe mathematics and science; other codes are used to transcribe foreign languages and musical notation.

The majority of experienced braille readers use two hands. A skilled two-handed reader usually begins reading a line of braille by placing both hands at the beginning of the line; when the middle of the line is reached, the right hand continues across the line, while the left hand moves in the opposite direction and locates the beginning of the next line. After the entire first line has been read by the right hand, the left hand reads the first several words on the next line, while the right hand moves quickly back to meet the left hand (Mangold, 1982). Important mechanical skills needed by braille readers include light finger touch, finger curvature, smooth independent hand movements, and page turning.

A major disadvantage of braille reading is that its average speed is two to three times slower than that of print reading. An average speed of 90 words per minute has been reported as typical for readers in the upper elementary grades (Harley, Henderson, & Truan, 1979). Braille books are also large and cumbersome, and they require large amounts of storage space. However, Mellor (1979) reports that braille as a medium for reading and recording information is superior to other mediums for providing random access to a page; skimming a page; labeling; filing; writing memorandums; reading tables and diagrams; reading technical or difficult material; allowing the reader to be an active participant in reading; and providing deaf-blind individuals with their only means of reading. In addition, braille-reading students have been found to be significantly ahead of their sighted peers in spelling; braille students make less than half the spelling mistakes of their sighted peers. (Grenier & Giroux, 1997)

There have been several innovations in braille reading, writing, and production. One of them is an electronic braille device that can send and retrieve information to and from a computer. This device can store information on audio cassette tapes and present it in a braille display of 20 or more characters in a single line of movable pins representing braille dots. The blind individual presses on a keyboard similar to the Brailler and the information is converted to a digital code that is recorded on the tape in a cassette. The encoded information moves the six pins up and down so that the reader can read the configurations on the one-line display. When the reader gets to the end of the line, he or she touches a switch, which then presents the next line of braille stored on the cassette. Blind students can write and edit their papers with ease using one of these machines. (Olson, 1981; Ruconich, 1984). The electronic braille device reduces considerably the storage space needed for braille materials since an ordinary 60-minute audio cassette tape can store the equivalent of 400 pages of bulky paper braille. It is marketed by several commercial companies.

Another recent invention is an electronic braille printer that enables a person to produce hard-copy braille in either six- or eight-dot computer code. It also provides an onboard Grade 1 translator. Using translation software, the user can produce Grade 2, Nemeth, or music braille codes in six-dot computer braille code mode.

Another innovation is a paperless braille device that provides access to the screen of a computer by directly reading the computer's memory. It enables the blind person to access information on a full screen in increments of up to 20 characters while maintaining orientation to screen format through the use of auditory and tactile cues.

While the cost of such electronic braille devices is currently extremely high, their benefits are overwhelmingly positive in enabling blind individuals to access the available technology. As a result, more and more of this equipment will become available for use by blind students in special education programs yearly.

REFERENCES

Grenier, D., & Giroux, N. (1997). A comparative study of spelling performance of sighted and blind students in senior high school. *Journal of Visual Impairment and Blindness, 91,* 393–400.

Harley, R.K., Henderson, F.M., & Truan, M.B. (1979). *The teaching of braille reading.* Springfield, IL: Thomas.

Mangold, S. (1982). Teaching reading via braille. In S. Mangold (Ed.), *A teachers' guide to the special educational needs of blind and visually handicapped children.* New York: American Foundation for the Blind.

Mellor, C.M. (1979). Technical innovations for braille reading, writing, and production. *Journal of Visual Impairment and Blindness, 73,* 339–341.

Olson, M.R. (1981). *Guidelines and games for teaching efficient braille reading.* New York: American Foundation for the Blind.

Ruconich, S. (1984). Evaluating microcomputer access technology for use by visually impaired students. *Education of the Visually Handicapped, 15,* 119–125.

See also **Blind; Versabraille**

BRAILLE, LOUIS (1809–1852)

Louis Braille, blinded in an accident at the age of three, developed his system of reading and writing for the blind while serving as a teacher at the Institution National des Jeunes Aveugles, the school for the blind in Paris. Dissatisfied with earlier approaches that were cumbersome and difficult to read, Braille developed a code employing one or more raised dots in a cell three dots high and two wide. An accomplished musician, he also worked out an application of his system to musical notation. Ironically, his school did not accept his system and actually forbade its use. Braille feared that his invention would die with him, but it survived, although it did not immediately flourish. It was not until 1916 that braille was officially adopted by the schools for the blind in the United States. A universal braille code for the English-speaking world was adopted in 1932.

BRAIN DAMAGE/INJURY

The expression brain injury denotes a condition where extragenetic influences arrest or impair the normal structure, growth, development and functioning of brain tissue (Cruickshank, 1980). Damage to the brain can be either congenital or acquired after birth, with acquired damage resulting most frequently from trauma (Rourke, Bakker, Fisk, & Strang, 1983). The severity of dysfunction and prognosis for recovery following trauma depend on many variables, including the nature, location, and extent of the injury, the developmental level, and demographic factors such as age and sex (Rourke et al., 1983).

The brain of a child shows a capacity for development and recovery of function following brain injury. It has been argued (the Kennard principle) that early brain damage produces less dramatic behavioral effects and better prospects for recovery than damage in later life. This claim is only partially correct. The prognosis of early brain damage depends on many variables, including the type, location, and extent of the injury (Rourke et al., 1983). Most brain-injured children show some capacity for development of functions or recovery of functions, although it is difficult to predict the extent, rate, and degree of improvement because it depends on a number of neurological and psychological factors (Kolb & Fantie, 1997; Rourke et al., 1983).

Early brain damage may produce permanent dysfunction, delayed onset of dysfunction, or no dysfunction, depending on the maturational status of the system (Teuber & Rudel, 1962). For example, the effect of brain damage initially may be mild until functions subserved by damaged tissue become crucial for behavioral performance during development.

The term growing into a deficit has been used to emphasize the importance of the maturational status of the brain area at the time of damage (Rourke et al., 1983). Rourke (1983) argues that attentional deficits are a special problem for the young brain-damaged child, while older brain-damaged children show cognitive deficits. Rourke contends the young brain-injured child also has cognitive deficits, but they may not be apparent because of the generalized effects of attentional deficits. As attentional deficits resolve, the previously masked cognitive deficits become evident. Part of the process of recovery may involve the brain-injured child's learning to solve old problems in new ways by reorganizing functional elements of the behavioral repertoire (Luria, 1973).

There are few common behavior patterns characterizing brain damage. However, most changes suggest a loss of the normal inhibitory influence of the cortex on behavior (Rutter, 1983). There is also frequently a deficit in attention that can lead to perseveration, hyperactivity, and impaired sensory processing (Cruickshank, Bentzen, Ratzeburg & Tannhauser 1961; Gordon, White, & Diller, 1972; Haskell, Barrett, & Taylor, 1977).

Attention deficit disorders or hyperactivity represent early and common consequences of brain injury. Such behaviors may reflect a deficit in planning and regulation of behavior, a deficit in memory, or loss of inhibitory control on the brain stem reticular system. In cases where a major behavioral component of the dysfunction is attention deficits, other deficits may not be observable or may not be easily measured.

Deficits affecting primarily the diencephalon often produce impaired memory consolidation. Individuals with such deficits may be able to attend to a task but they do not benefit from their experiences. As with attentional deficits, memory deficits can be pervasive and lead to more generalized deficits unless effectively remediated.

Higher level functions involve more complex cortical processing of information. The left hemisphere processes verbal material and deals with material in a discrete manner. The right hemisphere deals with nonverbal and new material in a more global manner. Functions can be divided further in each hemisphere; thus cortical damage can have dramatically different effects on behavior and learning depending on the brain area damaged. Cognitive functions relate primarily to cortical processing and include a broad range of behaviors. Early deficits in acquired brain damage may be generalized, but most pronounced recovery is noted in sensory and motor function and speech comprehension. Often recovery of language is given precedence and other functions may suffer. Left hemisphere damage is likely to impair syntactical functions, although with increasing severity, more general language processing may be involved. Furthermore, right-sided sensory and motor deficits may be observed as well as processing of verbally labeled material. Right hemisphere impairment results in deficits in visuospatial functions and spatial memory. Recovery of these functions is likely to lag behind language. Developmental changes appear to shift from right hemisphere global functions to left hemisphere linguistic functions. Rourke (1983) postulates that the left hemisphere functions in an automated manner, thus freeing the right hemisphere to deal with novelty, complexity, and intermodal integration.

Brain damage not only attenuates intellectual functions but also increases the chance of problems in emotional adjustment (Rutter, 1981). While brain damage can cause emotional lability, emotional problems are usually secondary or reactive to intellectual impairment, physical handicaps, or altered peer relations. The emotional consequences of brain injury are substantially influenced by the child's level of preinjury functioning as well as post-injury social support systems. Social learning is a complex cognitive

Table 1 Essential Areas of Neuropsychological Assessment

Basic sensory and motor function
Perceptual and perceptual-motor functions
Attention
Language abilities
Intelligence
Problem-solving and abstract reasoning
Memory
Emotional adjustment

function that involves learning social cues and gestures and modifying social behavior. Head-injured children are most likely to retain characterological deficits that limit full remediation (Lezak, 1976).

An adequate evaluation of children with brain injuries involves assessing intelligence (verbal and nonverbal), memory, academic achievement, and emotional adjustment. In some cases more specific neuropsychological functions also must be tested (Table 1). In addition, consideration must be given to social/environmental factors and their contribution to overall performance. The assessment must produce a valid and reliable picture of the individual's strengths and weaknesses, and allow inferences about underlying brain functions to be made. It is important to differentiate between behavioral problems that reflect structural lesions and behaviors having no direct relationship to the brain's continuity.

Assessment of intellectual and academic strengths and weaknesses for remedial or rehabilitative purposes, such as constructing an individual educational program (IEP), is maximally useful only when certain requirements are met (Hartlage, 1981). First, a majority of the child's educationally related cognitive abilities and methods of higher order information processing skills must be assessed in a quantifiable, replicable, and valid manner. Second, the assessment should be translated into a relevant and valid educational plan. Third, the assessment procedures should be reasonably efficient in terms of time and effort needed to administer and interpret them. In essence, the neuropsychological assessment process should be designed to test the specific referral problem and to provide the information needed to devise an appropriate program for the child in question (Hartlage, 1981).

Comprehensive neuropsychological batteries developed for use with children such as the Reitan-Indiana Neuropsychological Battery and the Luria-Nebraska Neuropsychological Battery-Children's Revision add significantly to the evaluation and remedial planning process (Berg et al., 1984; Lezak, 1976). The major drawback to the use of these and similar batteries is the great deal of time and training required for administration and interpretation (Hartlage, 1981; Reynolds, 1981).

Hartlage (1981) suggests an alternative approach in the application of neuropsychological principles to the interpretation of developmental, behavioral, and test data that can provide a systematic framework for understanding patterns of learning strengths and weaknesses and for making direct translations of the findings into intervention strategies that are uniquely relevant to the child's cerebral organization. By knowing the neuropsychological implications of common psychoeducational tests, such as the Wechsler Intelligence Scale for Children—III (WISC-III), Bender-Gestalt, Wide Range Achievement Test, and Peabody Picture Vocabulary Test, the neuropsychologist can determine which additional tests, if any, are needed to complete an adequate neuropsychological diagnostic profile (Hartlage, 1981). Detection with an accurate description of dysfunction leads to a remediation program to enhance the child's acquisition of skills using the child's intact areas and capitalizing on the child's neuropsychological strengths.

Intervention and remediation in brain-impaired children involve standard procedures with adjustment in manner or mode of presentation. These children need sustained study on material where they receive effective feedback, and where material is interesting and presented on their level. Computer systems are an ideal tool for special education with such children, as they can provide individualized courses of study. Such systems should be viewed as an adjunct rather than a replacement for the educator.

REFERENCES

Berg, R.A., Bolter, J.F., Chien, L.T., Williams, S.J., Lancster, W., & Cummins, J. (1984). Comparative diagnostic accuracy of the Halstead-Reitan and Luria-Nebraska neuropsychology adult and children's batteries. *International Journal of Clinical Neuropsychology, 6,* 200–204.

Cruickshank, W.M. (Ed.). (1980). *Psychology of exceptional children and youth.* Englewood Cliffs, NJ: Prentice-Hall.

Cruickshank, W.E., Bentzen, F.A., Ratzeburg, E.H., & Tannhauser, M.T. (1961). *A teaching method for brain-injured and hyperactive children: A demonstration-pilot study.* Syracuse, NY: Syracuse University Press.

Gordon, R., White, D., & Diller, L. (1972). Performance of neurologically impaired preschool children with educational material. *Exceptional Child, 38,* 428–437.

Hartlage, L.C. (1981). Neuropsychological assessment techniques. In C.R. Reynolds & T. Gutkin (Eds.), *Handbook & School Psychology* (pp. 296–320). New York: Wiley.

Haskell, S.H., Barrett, E.K., & Taylor, H. (1977). *The education of motor and neurologically handicapped children.* New York: Wiley.

Kolb, B., & Fantie, B. (1997). Development of the child's brain and behavior. In C.R. Reynolds & E. Fletcher-Janzen (Eds.), *Handbook of Clinical Child Neuropsychology.* New York: Plenum.

Lezak, M.D. (1976). *Neuropsychological assessment.* New York: Oxford University Press.

Luria, A.R. (1973). *The working brain: An introduction to neuropsychology.* New York: Basic Books.

Reynolds, C.R. (1981). Neuropsychological assessment and the habilitation of learning: Considerations in the search for the aptitude × treatment interaction. *School Psychology Review, 10,* 343–349.

Rourke, B.P. (1983). Reading and spelling disabilities: A developmental neuropsychological perspective. In U. Kirk (Ed.), *Neu-*

ropsychology of language, reading and spelling (pp. 209–234). New York: Academic.

Rourke, B.P., Bakker, D.J., Fisk, J.L., & Strang, J.D. (1983). Child neuropsychology: An introduction to theory, research, and clinical practice. New York: Guilford.

Rutter, M. (1981). Psychological sequelae of brain damage in children. American Journal of Psychiatry, 138, 1533–1544.

Rutter, M. (1983). Developmental Neuropsychiatry. New York: Guilford.

Stevens, M.M. (1982). Post concussion syndrome. Journal of Neurosurgical Nursing, 14, 239–244.

Teuber, H.L., & Rudel, R. (1962). Behavior after cerebral lesions in children and adults. Developmental Medicine & Child Neurology, 4, 3–20.

See also Neuropsychology

BRAIN DISORDERS (DEGENERATIVE MOTOR DYSFUNCTION)

Degenerative disorders of the central nervous system are a group of diseases of unspecified etiology leading to progressive deterioration and, eventually, death. Many of these disorders demonstrate a familial pattern and for some there is evidence of heritability (Slager, 1970; Gelbard, Boustany, & Shor, 1997). Recent studies that began with attempts to understand cell loss during normal development have now began to contribute to the understanding of the process of pathological cell loss (Gelbard, Boustany, & Shor, 1997). Specific degenerative disorders are characterized by their unique clinical and pathological features associated with age of onset and type and progression of symptoms (Alpers & Mancoll, 1971; Slager, 1970).

Several genetically determined disorders are associated with progressive cerebral degeneration in children. Major types are the lipid storage disease, the leukodystrophies, and progressive degeneration of the gray matter (Sandifer, 1967). Tay-Sachs disease, a major example of cerebral lipidosis that is confined to children of Jewish descent, is an infantile variety of cerebromacular degeneration (Walton, 1971). Symptoms, which emerge during early infancy and result in death during the second or third year of life, include spastic paralysis, epilepsy, dementia, and optic atrophy leading to blindness (Sandifer, 1967). Alper's disease is an example of a disorder characterized by gray matter degeneration. Onset of symptoms occurs during infancy or early childhood. Symptoms include mental deficiency, cerebral palsy, ataxia, blindness, and epilepsy (Slager, 1970). Death typically occurs within a few months to several years (Sandifer, 1967). Hallervorden-Spatz disease encompasses a group of degenerative disorders that affect boys more than girls (Halliday, 1995; Sandifer, 1967). Symptoms occur between the ages of 8 and 10 and include spastic paralysis, choreo-athetosis, and slowly developing dementia (Sandifer, 1967). The development of magnetic resonance imaging has increased the number of reports of this disease and the case-to-case variability is considerable. Demyelinating leukodystrophies are disorders associated with progressive paralysis and increased mental impairment (Conway, 1977). One example in metachromatic leukodystrophy, inherited as an autosomal recessive trait. Apparently normal development up until about 2 years is followed by onset of symptoms that include ataxia, impairment in swallowing and speaking, tonic seizures, and mental regression (Conway, 1977). Other examples of the demyelinating leukodystrophies include Krabbe's disease, Grienfield's disease, and Alexander's disease (Conway, 1977).

Spinocerebellar ataxias are a group of degenerative disorders involving the cerebellum and associated pathways. Friedreich's ataxia is an autosomal recessive disorder with symptoms developing between ages 7 and 15 (Conway, 1977). Early symptoms include ataxia, gait disturbances, and poor coordination, including frequent falling (Rosenberg, 1979). Other cerebellar signs, including nystagmus, dysarthria, and sensory impairments distally may be evident. Other forms of progressive ataxia affecting children include Ramsay Hunt syndrome, hereditary cerebellar ataxia, and Louis-Bar syndrome (Conway, 1977).

Demyelinating encephalopathies are a group of progressive degenerative disorders resulting in death. One example is Leigh's disease (subacute necrotizing encephalopathy), an autosomal recessive condition with onset occurring during infancy. Characteristics of this disorder include hypotonia, ataxia, and spasticity. Respiratory or feeding problems may be associated with this condition, resulting in failure to thrive (Conway, 1977; Slager, 1970). Schilder's disease is another example of the demeylinating encephalopathies. The progressive deterioration associated with this condition may result in significant behavioral disturbance in children during the middle years of childhood (Conway, 1977). More advanced symptoms of Schilder's disease include ataxia, cortical blindness, seizures, and deafness.

Such disorders may be expressed with wide degrees of severity, hence individual monitoring is essential. In summary, degenerative disorders of the nervous system are progressive, frequently hereditary conditions that produce significant mental, motor, and behavioral impairments that frequently result in death. Because of the genetic component associated with the transmission of many of these conditions, genetic counseling may be advisable for parents who have one affected child. Special education and related services may be required for children with degenerative disorders who survive to school age. The assistance of a variety of social service agencies may be of value to the families of afflicted children for counseling and group and individual support.

REFERENCES

Alpers, B.J., & Mancoll, E.L. (1971). Clinical neurology (6th ed.). Philadelphia: Davis.

Conway, B.L. (1977). Pediatric neurologic nursing. St. Louis: Mosby.

Gelbard, H.A., Boustany, R.M., & Shor, N.F. (1997). Apoptosis in childhood neurologic disease. Pediatric Neurology, 16, 93–97.

Halliday, W. (1995). The nosology of Hallervorden-Spatz disease. *Journal of the Neurological Sciences, 134,* 84–91.

Rosenberg, R.N. (1979). Inherited degenerative diseases of the nervous system. In P.B. Beeson, W. McDermott, & J.B. Wyngaarden (Eds.), *Cecil textbook of medicine* (15th ed.) (pp. 764– 772). Philadelphia: Saunders.

Sandifer, P.H. (1967). *Neurology in orthopaedics.* London: Butterworths.

Slager, U.T. (1970). *Basic neuropathology.* Baltimore, MD: Williams & Wilkins.

Walton, J.N. (1971). *Essentials of neurology* (3rd ed.). Philadelphia: Lippincott.

See also **Congenital Disorders; Gait Disturbances; Heredity; Neuropsychology; Physical Anomalies**

BRAIN GROWTH PERIODIZATION

Brain growth periodization refers to the rapid unequal development of the central nervous system (CNS) in general and the brain in particular. Following the moment of conception, neuronal cells begin an accelerated developmental course of division and reorganization (Gardner, 1969). This process involves the sequence of neuronal cell proliferation, migration, differentiation, axonal growth, formation of synapses, process of elimination, and, finally, myelination. Complexity of this emerging system is immense, and it grows within the context of plasticity and modifiability that exists throughout prenatal, perinatal, and early postnatal development (Moore, 1985).

The formation of the neural plate, which is marked by rapid neuronal cell proliferation, is evident within 16 days following conception. This plate then folds over into a tube shape. After a month, it closes toward the front and rear. The majority of cells attach themselves to the front of the tube and eventually form the brain.

Cell differentiation occurs at variable rates, as dictated by the location of cells within the CNS, where the cortical areas change rapidly and other areas mature more slowly. Next, the axonal growth and dendritic formations of the cells expand to make synaptic connections to one another. This highly ordered circuitry, which links up the brain electrochemically, is controlled by genetic programming and is largely influenced by the environment. One function of the synapses is related to specificity of action, which changes relative to location in the CNS (Sidman & Rakic, 1982). The primary sensory and motor structures are examples of highly specific functioning areas.

Genetic programming initiates the processes of brain growth, but environmental influences modify its form and function. Myelination can be thought of as insulating the neuronal cells to increase the conductivity of sending or receiving electrochemical messages. Early influences of nutrition and mother's health and lifestyle impinge on prenatal development; social, cultural, and economic factors further refine brain growth through postnatal life (Avery, 1985; Freeman, 1985).

The observation of a growing and changing system that is adapting to environmental influences before and after birth complicates the prediction of any pathological outcome (i.e., early insult resulting in later specific learning disorders). Special educators should be aware of the periodic growth of the brain in the framework of a dynamic interaction between genetics and environment. Recognition of this complex process promotes understanding of students' individual differences and necessitates the development of unique perspectives for intervention.

REFERENCES

Avery, G. (1985). Effects of social, cultural and economic factors on brain development. In J.M. Freeman (Ed.), *Prenatal and perinatal factors associated with brain damage* (Publication No. 85–1149) (pp. 163–176). Washington, DC: National Institutes of Health.

Freeman, J.M. (1985). *Prenatal and perinatal factors associated with brain damage* (Publication No. 85-1149). Washington, DC: National Institutes of Health.

Gardner, E. (1968). *Fundamentals of neurology.* Philadelphia: Saunders.

Moore, R.Y. (1985). Normal development of the nervous system. In J.M. Freeman (Ed.), *Prenatal and perinatal factors associated with brain damage* (Publication No. 85-1149, pp. 33–51). Washington, DC: National Institutes of Health.

Sidman, R.L., & Rakic, P. (1982). Development of the human central nervous system. In W. Haymaker & R.D. Adams (Eds.), *Histology and histopathology of the nervous system* (pp. 3–145). Springfield, MA: Thomas.

See also **Brain Damage; Brain Disorders (Degenerative Motor Dysfunction); Neurological Organization**

BRAIN INJURY ASSOCIATION (BIA)

The Brain Injury Association (BIA), formerly the National Head Injury Foundation, was founded in 1980 by concerned parents and professionals as the first national organization to advocate for persons with head injuries and their families. Today its mission is "to promote awareness, understanding, and prevention of brain injury through education, advocacy, research grants, and community support services that lead toward reduced incidence and improved outcomes for children and adults with brain injury." The BIA is the only national nonprofit organization working on behalf of those with brain injury, maintaining 42 state affiliates and several hundred local support groups nationwide (BIA, 1998).

Increasing awareness, education, and prevention of brain injury is accomplished through the organization's work in conjunction with a diverse group of individuals, including persons with brain injury and their families, rehabilitation providers, physicians, attorneys, educators, therapists, case managers, counselors, government organizations, corporate partners, and citizens. Prevention and education is attained through public awareness initiatives, training seminars, and publications, while advocacy results from work with government entities at all levels. BIA efforts in these areas have resulted in such important measures as safety belt and car seat legislation and heightened awareness of the dangers of drinking and driving. Also in the area of education, the Violence and Brain Injury Institute, founded by the BIA in conjunction with other institutions, is currently developing the Headsmart® Schools Program, a brain injury and violence prevention program for elementary and preschools focusing on brain development and both intentional and unintentional injuries (BIA, 1998).

Information on brain injuries is provided by the organization's interactive multimedia software program, the Brain Injury Resource Center, available in certain emergency and trauma centers as well as state association offices throughout the nation. The BIA also publishes *Brain Injury Source,* a magazine devoted to professionals in the field, and a catalog of current educational resources. The organization annually confers several prestigious awards to those who have made outstanding contributions to the field of brain injury. The Brain Injury Association headquarters are located at 105 North Alfred Street, Alexandria, VA 22314 (BIA, 1998).

REFERENCE

The Brain Injury Association. (1998, October 1). *Welcome to the Brain Injury Association, Inc.* web site. Retrieved December 29, 1998 from http://www.biausa.org/.

BRAIN ORGANIZATION

See NEUROLOGICAL ORGANIZATION.

BRAIN STEM AUDIOMETRY

Brain stem audiometry is an electrophysiologic measurement of hearing function currently known as auditory brain stem response (ABR) audiometry. As a diagnostic procedure, brain stem audiometry is used for the assessment of a peripheral hearing function (especially for high-risk infants, (Durieux-Smith, Picton, Edwards, & MacMurray, 1987) individuals with mental retardation, and those individuals who are unable to respond appropriately to traditional tests) and to determine the neurological integrity of the auditory nerve and brain stem (especially for adults suspected of having an auditory nerve or brain stem tumor or other neural pathology). Brain stem audiometry can be done when the patient is lightly sedated, asleep, or awake.

A brain stem audiometer contains an averaging computer that triggers stimulus-generating instrumentation that transduces an acoustic stimulus through an earphone, loudspeaker, or bone vibrator. The patient is fitted with an active surface electrode along the midline of the head (usually at the vertex) and reference surface electrodes (usually on each mastoid or earlobe). The output of the electrodes are amplified, filtered, and directed to the averaging computer, which is programmed to present many repetitions of the same stimulus and average the response of the neural ac-

tivity for each stimulus for a period of about 10 milliseconds following the onset of the stimulus. The resultant pattern, known as the ABR waveform, is characterized by six to seven identifiable peaks having different latencies and amplitudes. Each peak is thought to originate from a neural generator starting with the auditory nerve through the brain stem. Peak I and especially Peak V are the most robust in reference to stimulus level and procedural variables.

If brain stem audiometry is done to determine the existence of a peripheral hearing impairment, an ABR waveform is obtained to high level auditory stimuli and to the same stimuli at lower levels until an ABR waveform cannot be determined for each ear. Then the latency of Peaks I and V at each stimulus level (intensity) are usually plotted on an intensity-latency graph referenced to age-appropriate norms. This procedure allows for determining the degree and type of peripheral hearing loss. When used to determine neurological integrity, an ABR waveform is usually obtained for one or two high-level auditory stimuli for each ear. The amplitude and latency of the ABR peaks are analyzed individually and compared across ear and to norms to determine whether a pathologic condition exists.

REFERENCE

Durieux-Smith, A., Picton, T., Edwards, C.G., & MacMurray, B. (1987). Brainstem electric-response audiometry in infants of a neonatal intensive care unit. *Audiology, 26,* 284–297.

See also Audiology; Audiometry

BRAIN TUMORS

Brain tumors are the most frequent type of childhood cancer, after leukemia. Over half of the brain tumors in childhood occur in the area of the cerebellum and brain stem; the rest occur higher in the brain, primarily in the cerebrum. Presenting symptoms for children with cerebellar tumors include early morning headaches, nausea and vomiting, vision problems, and loss of balance. Children with tumors located higher in the brain may experience more focal symptoms such as weakness on one side of the body or vision problems. For any child with a brain tumor, these symptoms are often accompanied by changes in mood and academic performance.

Many brain tumors are treated successfully with various combinations of surgery, radiation, and chemotherapy. Depending on the type and location of the tumor, and the treatment, most children are able to resume schooling (at least on a limited basis) within a few months following treatment. Teachers need to be aware of the treatment regimen and possible side effects for a child recovering from a brain tumor. For a period of 2 to 4 months following surgery, mood and behavior changes are frequently observed, presumably a result of cranial irradiation and the psychological impact of having been diagnosed with a severe illness (Katz, 1980; Mulhern, Crisco, & Kun, 1983). Some of these children will receive chemotherapy for 1 to 3 years following surgery. Most children experience at least one of the following side effects: hair loss (usually reversible), nausea, behavioral changes, and painful mouth sores. Cortisone, taken to reduce the traumatic effects of surgery, also may cause changes in mood and physical appearance.

As these children resume school, they need regular, detailed assessment of their abilities and deficits. A complete neuropsychological assessment should be obtained every few years. There have not been enough studies to predict what specific deficits will occur; however, available data suggest that most children recovering from brain tumors suffer from at least one of the following: (1) poor coordination, (2) poor memory, (3) difficulty in acquiring and integrating new concepts, (4) a decline in overall IQ (ranging from only a few to 20 or more points), (5) emotional problems, especially somatic worries and low self-esteem (Mulhern, Crisco & Kun, 1983). Most of these children will require either special education placement and a learning program that emphasizes gradual acquisition and practice of basic skills or placement in a regular classroom with the ready availability of additional resources. Parents can play a significant role in helping the child to perform at a maximal level.

REFERENCES

Katz, E.R. (1980). Illness impact and social reintegration. In J. Kellerman (Ed.), *Psychological aspects of childhood cancer* (pp. 14–46). Springfield, IL: Thomas.

Mulhern, R.K., Crisco, J.J., & Kun, L.E. (1983). Neuropsychological sequelae of childhood brain tumors: A review. *Journal of Clinical Child Psychology, 12*(1), 66–73.

See also **Brain Disorders (Degenerative Motor Dysfunctions); Chemotherapy**

BRIDGMAN, LAURA DEWEY (1829–1899)

Laura Dewey Bridgman, deaf and blind from the age of 2, entered the Perkins Institution and Massachusetts School for the Blind at the age of 7. The director of the institution, Samuel Gridley Howe, developed an educational program for Bridgman and she quickly learned to read from raised letters and to communicate with manual signs. She related well to people and developed into a cheerful, intelligent woman who used her talents to teach other deaf-blind students at Perkins.

Bridgman was the first deaf-blind person to become well educated, and her achievement received wide attention. Charles Dickens visited her and published an account of their meeting. That publication led Helen Keller's mother to appeal to Howe to find a teacher for Helen; the teacher he recommended was Anne Sullivan Macy, who, as a student at Perkins had lived in the same house as Bridgman. What Bridgman accomplished was later repeated by Helen Keller and other similarly handicapped persons. But Bridgman was the first to demonstrate that proper education could enable a deaf-blind person to lead a happy and productive life.

REFERENCE

Ross, I. (1951). *Journey into light.* New York: Appleton-Century-Crofts.

BRIGANCE DIAGNOSTIC INVENTORIES

The Brigance Inventories are a comprehensive set of individually administered criterion-referenced tests. There are several inventories, each covering a specific age range, that are used for assessment, diagnosis, record keeping, and instructional planning.

Reviewers of the Brigance Diagnostic Inventories consistently have noted that the lack of reliability or validity data for these measures is troubling (Berk, 1995; Carpenter, 1995; Watson, 1995). Also questioned by one reviewer was the appropriateness of the instruments for students who do not speak English as a first language (Berk, 1995). The instruments are generally viewed as viable tool because of their flexibility and planning utility (Carpenter, 1995). One reviewer viewed the Brigance Inventories as positive methods for identifying a child's strengths and weaknesses (Penfield, 1995). Because of the lack of validity data, these inventories are perhaps best used as informal screening measures to provide assistance to teachers in planning curriculum objectives. Also because of the lack of data, placement decisions based on the inventories are inappropriate (Watson, 1995).

REFERENCES

Berk, R. (1995). Review of the Revised Brigance K & 1 Screen for Kindergarten and First Grade Children-Revised. In J.C. Conoley & J.C. Impara (Eds.), *The twelfth mental measurements yearbook* (pp. 133–134). Lincoln, NE: Buros Institute of Mental Measurements.

Carpenter, C.D. (1995). Review of the Revised Brigance Diagnostic Inventory of Early Development. In J.C. Conoley & J.C. Impara (Eds.), *The twelfth mental measurements yearbook* (pp. 852–853). Lincoln, NE: Buros Institute of Mental Measurements.

Penfield, D.A. (1995). Review of the Revised Brigance Diagnostic Inventory of Early Development. In J.C. Conoley & J.C. Impara (Eds.), *The twelfth mental measurements yearbook* (pp. 853–854). Lincoln, NE: Buros Institute of Mental Measurements.

Watson, T.S. (1995). Review of the Revised Brigance K & 1 Screen for Kindergarten and First Grade Children-Revised. In J.C. Conoley & J.C. Impara (Eds.), *The twelfth mental measurements yearbook* (pp. 134–135). Lincoln, NE: Buros Institute of Mental Measurements.

See also **Criterion-Referenced Testing; Grade Equivalents**

BRITTLE BONE DISEASE (OSTEOGENESIS IMPERFECTA)

Osteogenesis imperfecta appears in several forms, one that is nearly always fatal to the neonate (osteogenesis imperfecta congenita), and a later appearing variation (osteogenesis imperfecta tarda) in which the affected individual may live a normal life (Behrman & Vaughan, 1983). The congenital variety results from an autosomal recessive gene; the later appearing from an autosomal dominant gene.

The later appearing type (OI Type I) is present in 1 out of 30,000 births. Bone fractures are present at birth about 10% of the time and scoliosis is seen in about 20% of affected adults. There is a distinct blue coloring and bulging appearance of the white portion of the eyes (sclera). One-third of this group will show hearing impairment after age 10; earlier onset is uncommon. "Occurrence of neonatal fractures does not predict more deformity or more handicap" (Behrman & Vaughan, 1983).

In the second type (OI Type II), the condition is generally fatal. Half of the infants survive the birth process but expire soon afterward, usually to respiratory difficulties associated with the skeletal anomalies. The limbs are usually severely deformed. There is no effective treatment for Type II.

Management of the disorder centers around proper support and support of skeletal growth. Parents must learn first aid for fractures. The youngster must learn to engage in activities that minimize the risk of fracture without becoming inactive. Nutrition and genetic counseling are essential, as is a careful monitoring of the hearing loss (Bennett, 1981).

Recent studies have suggested that early diagnosis is very important to prevent families from being suspected of child abuse (Brodin, 1990). A 30-year-old Nigerian woman in England had her 3-week-old infant removed from her care when the infant was presented at a hospital with multiple fractures of the femurs and ribs. It was only several months later that osteogenesis imperfecta was diagnosed. The disruption in the mother-child bonding was not measurable (Minnis, Ramsay, Ewije, & Kumar, 1995).

REFERENCES

Behrman, R., & Vaughan, V. (1983). *Nelson textbook of pediatrics* (12th ed.). Philadelphia: Saunders.

Bennett, P. (1981). *Diseases, The nurse's reference library series.* Philadelphia, Pennsylvania: Informed Communications Book Division.

Brodin, J. (1990). Children with osteogenesis imperfecta and their daily living. *Handicap Research Group Report, 4,* 2.

Minnis, H., Ramsay, R., Ewije, P., & Kumar, C. (1995). Osteogenesis imperfecta and non-accidental injury. *British Journal of Psychiatry, 166,* 824–825.

See also Osteoporosis

BROCA, PIERRE PAUL (1824–1880)

Pierre Paul Broca, a French surgeon and physical anthropologist noted for his studies of the brain and skull, was a member of the Academy of Medicine in Paris and professor of surgical pathology and clinical surgery. Through postmortem examinations he learned that damage to the third convolution of the left frontal lobe of the brain (Broca's convolution) was associated with loss of the ability to speak; this was the first demonstration of a connection between a specific bodily activity and a specific area of the brain. His announcement of this finding in 1861 led to a vast amount of research on cerebral localization.

Broca was a key figure in the development of physical anthropology in France. He founded a laboratory, a school, a journal, and a society for the study of anthropology. He originated techniques and invented instruments for studying the skull, and helped to establish that the Neanderthal man discovered in his time was a primitive ancestor of modern man.

REFERENCE

Talbott, J.H. (1970). *A biographical history of medicine: Excerpts and essays on the men and their work.* New York: Grune & Stratton.

BROCA'S APHASIA

Broca's aphasia is one of several subdivisions of nonfluent aphasia. Originally the symptoms associated with this acquired language disorder were believed to occur as a result of damage to Broca's Area, the posterior-inferior (third) frontal gyrus of the left hemisphere, also known as Broadman's area 44 (Hegde, 1994).

The major language characteristics most often associated with this diagnosis are: nonfluent and effortful speech, many inappropriate pauses, short mean length of utterance, telegraphic speech limited to nouns and verbs, omission of grammatical function words (articles, pronouns, auxiliary verbs, and some prepositions), impaired repetition of words and sentences, and impaired confrontation naming. Although these persons may have some problems in the area of auditory comprehension, silent reading comprehension, and writing, these persons most often have better skills in these areas and than in their expressive communication (Kearns, 1997, Hegde, 1994). Other types of nonfluent aphasia include the following.

TRANSCORTICAL MOTOR APHASIA

Originally the symptoms associated with this acquired language disorder were believed to occur as a result of damage to the watershed regions between the middle cerebral and anterior arteries and in the premotor area in front of the motor cortex. However, as Kearns reports (1997), as modern neuroradiographic techniques obtain sophisticated data related to symptoms characteristic of damage to this area, it is often evident that many different parts of the brain may be damaged while still resulting in the type of symptoms classified as transcortical motor aphasia.

The major language characteristics most often associated with this diagnosis are nonfluency, paraphasia, agrammaticisms, telegraphic (similar to those described in Broca's aphasia) and intact repetition (differing from Broca's aphasia), and echolalia. Comprehension may be impaired for complex speech but is generally good for simple conversation (Chapey, 1994; Hegde, 1994).

GLOBAL APHASIA

Originally, the symptoms associated with this acquired language disorder were believed to occur as a result of damage to the entire perisylvian region.

Persons with this diagnosis have profoundly impaired language skills in all ways, and fluency is greatly reduced (naming, repetition, auditory comprehension, reading, and writing are impaired). Language is limited to a few words, exclamations or automatic speech. (Chapey, 1994; Hegde, 1994).

ISOLATION APHASIA

This is a rare type of nonfluent aphasia with severe impairment to all language functions except preservation of the skill to repeat words. It is this characteristic that discriminates between global aphasia and isolation aphasia. This subdivision is not acknowledged by all aphasiologists (Hegde, 1994).

REFERENCES

Chapey, R. (1994). *Language intervention strategies in adult aphasia* (3rd ed.). Baltimore: Williams & Wilkins.

Hegde, M. (1994). *A coursebook on aphasia and other neurogenic language disorders.* San Diego: Singular Publishing Group, Inc.

Kearns, K.P. (1997). Broca's aphasia. In L.L. LaPointe (Ed.), *Aphasia and related neurogenic language disorders* (pp. 1–41). New York: Thieme.

BROWN V. BOARD OF EDUCATION

In 1954, *Brown v. Board of Education* was brought to the Supreme Court by a Kansas City black family, the Browns. It was joined by other cases from South Carolina, Virginia, and Delaware (Alexander, Corns, & McCann, 1969; Zirkel, 1978). The plaintiffs, African American students from various states, were seeking admission to public schools that had been restricted to white students. African American students had been denied admission to attend these schools under the "separate but equal" doctrine that had been adopted in a previous court case (Bolmeier, 1973). Under this doctrine, schools claimed that black students were being treated equally through the provision of equal facilities, even though these facilities were separate. The plaintiffs claimed that, by being denied equal facilities, they were also being deprived of their right to an equal education.

The *Brown v. Board of Education* 347 U.S. 483 decision (1954) was unanimously in favor of the plaintiffs. The Court declared that separate educational facilities were unequal because they violated the black students' right to an equal education under the Fourteenth Amendment of the Constitution, which guarantees equal protection of the law to all American citizens.

The complexities of case law and practice in the nearly fifty years after the decision suggest that the Brown case represented a significant shift in the national attitude towards students from ethnic minorities. However, studies of the effect of desegregation on intergroup attitudes are generally inconclusive and inconsistent. The fortieth anniversary of the Brown decision brought forth discussion groups that analyzed the promise of *Brown* and strategies for achieving the promise in a more current context (Johnson, 1995). The Department of Education stated that the "Brown decision was a crowbar for change, and we are all the better for it" (Riley, 1994). However others (Ruiz, 1994) suggested that although 500 school districts were ordered to desegregate, very few of those schools were found by the courts to have completed the process. Ruiz (1994) suggests that the central tenet of *Brown* is in danger of being lost amidst "voluminous paperwork and clever legal arguments." Race discrimination issues are still prominent, however the issues have evolved into conflicts about ability grouping, bilingual education, harassment, educational services for undocumented immigrants and different kinds of educational remedies in school desegregation cases (*Milliken II*) (Heubert, 1994).

REFERENCES

Alexander, K., Corns, R., & McCann, W. (1969). *Public school law: Cases and materials.* St. Paul, MN: West.

Bolmeier, E.C. (1973). *Landmark decisions on public school issues.* Charlottesville, VA: Michie.

Heubert, J.P. (1994). *"Brown" at 40: The tasks that remain for educators and lawyers.* (ERIC Clearinghouse No. EA026514)

Johnson, D. (1995). *The promise of Brown: Has it been fulfilled?* New York, NY: Metropolitan Center for Urban Education.

Riley, R.W. (1994). *Fulfilling the promise of Brown.* Washington DC: Department of Education.

Ruiz, C.M. (1994). *Equity, excellence and school reform: A new paradigm for desegregation.* (ERIC Clearinghouse No. EA026648)

Zirkel, P.A. (1978). *Supreme Court Decisions affecting education.* Bloomington, IN: Phi Delta Kappa.

***See also* Culture Fair Tests; Disproportionality; Socioeconomic Status**

BRUININKS-OSERETSKY TEST OF MOTOR PROFICIENCY

The Bruininks-Oseretsky Test of Motor Proficiency (Bruininks, 1978) is an individually administered test of gross and fine motor functioning of children from 4 and a half to 14 and a half years of age. It is the latest revision of the Oseretsky tests of motor proficiency published in Russia in 1903 (later translated into English by Edgar Doll in 1946). The complete battery comprises 46 items subdivided into 8 subtests: Running Speed and Agility (1 item), Balance (8 items), Bilateral Coordination (8 items), Strength (3 items), Upper-Limb Coordination (9 items), Response Speed (1 item), Visual-Motor Control (8 items), and Upper Limb Speed and Dexterity (8 items). In addition to subtest scores, composite scores are available for the gross motor subtest scores, the fine motor subtests, and the total battery. The complete form takes from 45 to 60 minutes to administer. There is also a 14-item short form, requiring 15 to 20 minutes, which provides a single index of general motor proficiency.

The battery was standardized on a sample of 765 children, and was distributed across ten age groups from 4–6 to 14–15 years. The sample was stratified by age, sex, race, community size, and geographic region according to the 1970 U.S. Census and is therefore out of date. Test-retest reliability coefficients for the separate subtests range from .58 to .89 for Grade 2, and from .29 to .89 for Grade 6. The lower reliability scores for Grade 6 are probably a result of the maximum point scores achieved by many older children (Anastasi, 1997). Validity was investigated using factor analysis of items, age differentiation, and comparative studies with retarded and learning-disabled children.

The Bruininks-Oseretsky Test is a useful tool for measuring gross and fine motor skills, developing and evaluating motor training programs, and screening for special purposes (Sabatino, 1985). It should be noted, however, that the test is a product measure of motor development as opposed to a process measure. Product measures focus on the outcome of movement, while process measures emphasize the movement of the body when performing particular motor tasks or skills (Harrington, 1985). Thus the Bruininks-Oseretsky is best combined with other measures of sensory and motor development in order to provide an appropriate indication of motor development.

REFERENCES

Anastasi, A. (1997). *Psychological testing* (7th ed.). Saddle River, NJ: Prentice Hall.

Bruininks, R.H. (1978). *Bruininks-Oseretsky Test of Motor Proficiency.* Circle Pines, MN: American Guidance Services.

Harrington, R.G. (1985). Bruininks-Oseretsky Test of Motor Proficiency. In D.L. Keyser & R.C. Sweetland (Eds.), *Test critiques* (Vol. 3, pp. 99–110). Kansas City, MO: Test Corporation of America.

Sabatino, D. (1985). Review of the Bruininks-Oseretsky Test of Motor Proficiency. In J.V. Mitchel (Ed.), *The ninth mental measurements yearbook.* (Vol. 1, pp. 235–236). Lincoln, NE: Buros Institute of Mental Measurements.

BRUXISM

Bruxism can be defined as "the nonfunctional gnashing and grinding of teeth occurring during the day or night" (Richmond et al., 1984). The adverse effects of bruxism include severe dental wear, damage to the alveolar bone, temporomandibular joint disorders, and hypertrophy of masticatory muscles, as well as occasional infection. It can also result in significant pain, permanent damage to the structures of the mouth and jaw, and lost teeth (Richmond et al., 1984; Rugh & Robbins, 1982). Dental wear is the most commonly used measure to determine the extent of bruxism.

Estimates of the frequency of bruxism in the nonretarded population have ranged between 5% (Reding et al., 1966) to a high of 21% (Wigdorowicz-Makowerowa et al., 1977), with no significant differences between sexes (Bober,

1982) or age groups (Lindqvist, 1971). Investigators have reported more dental wear as a consequence of bruxism in severely mentally retarded children than in nonretarded children (Lindqvist & Heijbel, 1974). An informal survey by Blount et al. (1982) indicated that 21.5% of a profoundly retarded group engaged in bruxism.

Behavioral methods to reduce bruxism have been favored in recent years (Rugh & Robbins, 1982). Thus positive reinforcement has been used to reduce its incidence in retarded individuals (i.e., to reinforce nonbruxist behaviors) and to encourage incompatible behaviors such as keeping the mouth open. Problems with positive reinforcers include the fact that social and tactile reinforcers usually do not have strong effects with severely retarded individuals. Edibles result in further chewing, thus reinforcing behaviors that are not compatible with efforts to reduce bruxism. Unfortunately, the treatment ideology and modalities has been haphazard for bruxism; therefore, most treatment effects are short-lived (Glaros & Melamed, 1992).

REFERENCES

Blount, R.L., Drabman, R.S., Wilson, N., & Stewart, D. (1982). Reducing severe diurnal bruxism in two profoundly retarded females. *Journal of Applied Behavior Analysis, 15,* 565–571.

Bober, H. (1982). Cause and treatment of bruxism and bruxomania. *Dental Abstracts, 3,* 658–659.

Glaros, A.G., & Melamed, B.G. (1992). Bruxism in children, Etiology and treatment. *Applied and Preventive Psychology, 1,* 191–199.

Lindqvist, B. (1971). Bruxism in children. *Odontologisk Revy, 22,* 413–424.

Lindqvist, B., & Heijbel, J. (1974). Bruxism in children with brain damage. *Acta Odontologica Scandinavica, 32,* 313–319.

Reding, G.R., Rubright, W.C., & Zimmerman, S.O. (1966). Incidence of bruxism. *Journal of Dental Research, 45,* 1198–1204.

Richmond, G., Rugh, J.D., Dolfi, R., & Wasilewsky, J.W. (1984). Survey of bruxism in an institutionalized retarded population. *American Journal of Mental Deficiency, 88,* 418–421.

Rugh, J.D., & Robbins, W.J. (1982). Oral habit disorders. In B. Ingersoll (Ed.), *Behavioral aspects in dentistry* (pp. 179–202). New York: Appleton-Century-Crofts.

Wigdorowicsz-Makowerowa, N., Grodzki, C., & Maslanka, T. (1977). Frequency and etiopathogenes of bruxism (on the basis of prophylactic examinations of 1000 middle-aged men). *Czaopismo-Stomatologiczne, 25,* 1109–1112.

See also **Dentistry and the Handicapped Child; Self-Injurious Behavior**

BUCKLEY AMENDMENT

See FAMILY EDUCATIONAL RIGHTS & PRIVACY ACT (FERPA).

BULIMIA NERVOSA

Bulimia nervosa, a term of Greek origin meaning "ox hunger," is an eating disorder that is also referred to as the binge-purge syndrome. It is a condition in which an individual alternately binges (grossly overeats) and purges (rids the body of food or fluids). Although difficult to comprehend, bulimics apparently may ingest as many as 20,000 calories in one binge episode. Bulimics commonly chew and spit out food (Mitchell, Halsukami, Eckert, & Pyle, 1985). Bingeing is mainly on foods rich in carbohydrates; purging may be through vomiting, abuse of laxatives or diet tablets, or excessive exercise, regardless of fatigue (Garner & Garfinkel, 1985). No physical basis for the abnormal eating can be found. This disorder can be life-threatening, is increasing in occurrence and is a serious problem for medical and psychological professionals who are attempting to treat it. Unlike anorexia, which has been known for centuries, bulimia is of relatively recent origin. Indeed, professional journals have commonly reported on bulimia only since the 1970s. This recency is partly responsible for the relatively little firm knowledge about bulimia and the absence of generally effective treatments. Incidence rates that vary with age, race, job status, and ethnic background further hamper general understanding of the disorder.

Bulimia characteristically is largely a disorder of women, with 9–17 times more women than men hospitalized for an eating disorder (Goetestan, Erikson, Heggestad, & Neilson, 1998). It is largely restricted to white women from middle- and upper-class social classes, although it is becoming more common among women from lower social economic status. Further, incidence is increasing among African American women as they become acculturated into the dominant Anglo society. Onset of bulimia is generally between 18 and 20 years of age, with a peak onset at about the age of 18 years of age (Neuman & Halvorson, 1993). Bulimia is more common than anorexia nervosa and may affect 5% of college women and 1% of young employed women (Hart & Ollendick, 1985). Twenty to 30% of college women may occasionally engage in bulimic behavior.

However, some general etiological factors and occasionally effective treatments have been described. Bulimics share personality characteristics and have families with a particular complex of unhealthy attitudes and behaviors. Bulimics can suffer from gastrointestinal problems and serious potassium depletion and damage to their teeth due to the acid nature of the regurgitated food. In extreme cases, death may result. As is the case with anorexia, bulimia is viewed as a biopsychosocial disorder.

DSM-IV (American Psychiatric Association, 1994) criteria for bulimia include: (a) recurrent episodes of secretive binge eating (rapid consumption of a large amount of food in a short period of time); (b) termination of bingeing because of abdominal pain, sleep, or social interruptions; and (c) recurrent episodes of purging as an attempt to lose weight or avoid gaining weight through self-induced vomiting, severe diets, abuse of laxatives, cathartics, or diuretics, or excessive exercise. The bulimic suffers frequent weight fluctuations owing to alternating binges and fasts, awareness that the eating pattern is abnormal, and fear of not being able to stop eating voluntarily. Depression and self-deprecating thoughts may follow eating binges (American Psychiatric Association, 1994). DSM-IV distinguishes between purging and non-purging types of bulimia. A purging type periodically engages in the act of self-induced vomiting or the use of laxatives, whereas a non-purging type uses diets, exercise, and fasting instead of regular self-induced vomiting.

Considering biological aspects, bulimia leads to a variety of physiological complications, including cardiac irregularities, kidney dysfunction, neurological abnormalities, gastrointestinal pain, salivary gland enlargement (appearance of a chipmunk), edema and bloating, electrolyte imbalance, amenorrhea, dermatological disorders, and finger clubbing or swelling. Finger abnormalities result from the pressure against the mouth during self-induced vomiting. Abuse of laxatives can lead to permanent nerve damage in the colon, chronic stomach overloading, and potential of stomach rupture. Several of these complications can result in death.

No consensus exists regarding the most effective form of treatment for eating disorders (Vandereycken & Meermann, 1984). Therapists have used behavioral therapy, diet counseling, cognitive therapy, cognitive-behavioral treatment, drug treatment, and family therapy with varying degrees of success (Garner & Garfinkel, 1985). Whatever the treatment approach, the usual goals are aimed at increasing confidence and self-esteem, challenging irrational or anorectic thinking, developing autonomy, and teaching coping skills. Unfortunately, group therapy sessions may provide an environment in which bulimics can feed on each other's effective purging techniques and become essentially schools for training better bulimics. Further, Vandereycken and Meermann (1984, p. 21) suggest that the "best guarantees of success in therapy are a constructive patient/therapist working relationship and an explicit but consistent treatment plan/contract."

REFERENCES

American Psychiatric Association. (1994). *Diagnostic and statistical manual of mental disorders* (4th ed.). Washington, DC: Author.

Garner, D.M., & Garfinkel, P.E. (Eds.). (1985). *Handbook of psychotherapy for anorexia nervosa and bulimia.* New York: Guilford.

Goetestan, K.G., Erikson, L., Heggestad, T., & Neilson, S. (1998). Prevalence of eating disorders in Norwegian general hospitals 1990–1994: Admissions per year and seasonality. *International Journal of Eating Disorders, 23,* 57–64.

Hart, K.J., & Ollendick, T.H. (1985). Prevalence of bulimia in working and university women. *American Journal of Psychiatry, 142,* 851–854.

Mitchell, J.E., Halsukami, D., Eckert, E.D., & Pyle, R.L. (1985). Characteristics of 275 patients with bulimia. *American Journal of Psychiatry, 142,* 251–255.

Neuman, P.A., & Halvorson, P.S. (1983). *Anorexia nervosa and bulimia: A handbook for counselors and therapists.* New York: Van Nostrand Reinhold.

Vandereycken, W., & Meermann, R. (1984). *Anorexia nervosa: A clinician's guide to treatment.* Berlin: de Gruyter.

BUREAU OF EDUCATION FOR THE HANDICAPPED (BEH)

The Bureau of Education for the Handicapped (BEH) was created in 1966 to administer all U.S. Office of Education programs designed for the handicapped. During the late 1960s and early 1970s, BEH administered newly created federal programs for the handicapped, including regional resource centers that provided testing to determine the special education needs of handicapped children. It also administered service centers for the deaf-blind; offered technical assistance on programs for the gifted and talented; provided funds for recruiting and training special education personnel; created experimental preschool and early education programs that could serve as models for school districts; and mounted research projects concerning the handicapped. Eventually, BEH's responsibility was extended to include the provision of technical assistance, compliance monitoring, and evaluation of state education agency and local school district implementation of PL 93-380, the Education Amendments of 1974, and PL 94-142, the Education of All Handicapped Children Act of 1975. The BEH was succeeded in name but not in authority and responsibility by the Office of Special Education when the U.S. Department of Education was created in 1980. For a more detailed description of federal legislation and the role of BEH, see Weintraub, Abeson, Ballard, and LaVor (1976).

REFERENCE

Weintraub, F.J., Abeson, A., Ballard, J., & LaVor, M.L. (1976). *Public policy and the education of exceptional children.* Reston, VA: Council for Exceptional Children.

BUREAU OF INDIAN AFFAIRS: OFFICE OF INDIAN EDUCATION PROGRAMS

The mission of the Office of Indian Education Programs (OIEP) is to:

provide quality education opportunities from early childhood throughout life in accordance with the Tribe's needs for cultural and economic well-being in keeping with the wide diversity of Indian Tribes and Alaska Native villages as distinct cultural and governmental entities. OIEP manifests consideration of the whole person, taking into account the spiritual, mental, physical, and cultural aspects of the person within a family and Tribal or Alaska Native village contexts. (OIEP, 1998)

The OIEP has developed an extensive list of goals and benchmarks for the year 2000. These goals do not address exceptional children per se, but do include goals that pertain to areas that overlap with special education programs such as behavioral management, alcohol and drug abuse, culturally appropriate assessment instrument for reading and language arts, attendance issues, and staff development (OIEP, 1998).

The OIEP supervises the Branch of Exceptional Education (BEE). The mission of this branch is to assure that:

Indian children with disabilities, who are between the ages of 5 and 22 are enrolled in Bureau funded schools and have available to them a free appropriate education in the least restrictive environment in accordance with an Individual Education Program. This mission includes: Monitoring to assure the rights of children with disabilities and their parents or guardians are protected; providing technical assistance to provide for the education of all children with disabilities; and assessing the effectiveness of efforts to educate children with disabilities. (OIEP, 1998)

In 1994, 7,933 students with disabilities were served. Those children with severe disabilities requiring residential care were also provided services through contracts with state or private institutions. In 1993, 371 students received residential services. The Branch of Exceptional Education (BEE) also provides programs for gifted and talented students. In 1994, 4,703 students were served in Gifted and Talented Programs (Branch of Exceptional Education, 1998).

The Bureau of Indian Affairs Office of Indian Education Programs maintains an informative webpage at http://shaman@unm.edu. An extensive newsletter *American Indian Education News* is available from this website. The information in this entry was taken from the OIEP webpage with gracious permission from the BIA.

See also Cultural Bias in Testing; Special Education, Legal Regulations of

BURKS' BEHAVIOR RATING SCALES (BBRS)

The Burks' Behavior Rating Scales (BBRS), Preschool and Kindergarten Form and Grades One–Nine Form, are rating inventories used to identify the type and severity of problem behaviors exhibited by referred children ages 2 to 15. The scales may be completed by parents, teachers, or any responsible person who knows the rated child well.

Individual items are clustered together to form 19 (18 for the Preschool and Kindergarten Form) factor-analytically derived behavior categories bearing diagnostic labels such as excessive withdrawal, excessive dependency, poor coordination, poor academics, poor impulse control, poor reality contact, or excessive aggressiveness. Items are summed for each behavior category (usually by someone other than the rater) and transferred to a profile sheet. The profile sheet orders each category score along a continuum indicating the degree of significance of the presence of each negative behavior. Significance ratings can be used in differential diagnosis and in prioritizing intervention needs. The BBRS manual includes a lengthy discussion of the possible meanings of category scores and intervention suggestions for each problem behavior area. The BBRS has received favorable reviews as a clinical tool to aid in behavior assessment (Lerner, 1985).

REFERENCES

Burks, H.F. (1977). *Burks' Behavior Rating Scales.* Los Angeles: Western Psychological Services.

Lerner, J.V. (1985). Review of the Burks' Behavior Rating Scales. In D.J. Keyser & R.C. Sweetland (Eds.), *Test critiques. Vol. II* (pp. 108–112). Kansas City, MO: Test Corporation of America.

See also **Behavior Problem Checklist, Revised; Child Behavior Checklist**

BUROS, OSCAR K. (1905–1978)

Oscar K. Buros is remembered internationally as the foremost proponent of critical analyses of educational and psychological tests. Buros attended the State Normal School in Superior, Wisconsin, from 1922 to 1924 and completed his undergraduate education at the University of Minnesota in 1925. Buros received his graduate degree from the Teachers College, Columbia University. He accepted a faculty appointment at Rutgers University in 1932 and was a member of that faculty until his retirement in 1965. During World War II, he was in charge of testing for the U.S. Army's specialized training program, and later an adviser on the assessment of leadership at West Point.

He married Luella Gubrud who, an accomplished artist in her own right, later shared with him the responsibilities for the famous *Buros Mental Measurements Yearbook* (MMY) series. It was she who saw the last edition through to its completion following his death on March 19, 1978. Buros published the first *MMY* in 1938. Seven other *Yearbooks* followed, as well as the *Mental Measurements Yearbook* monographs series and the *Tests in Print* series.

In 1979, the Buros Institute of Mental Measurements was moved to the University of Nebraska-Lincoln. The institute has continued the Buros tradition by publishing *Tests in Print III* (Mitchell, 1983) and up to twelve *Mental Measurements Yearbooks* (Conoley, Impara & Murphy, 1995).

REFERENCES

Buros, O.K. (1938). *The 1938 mental measurements yearbook.* Highland Park, NJ: Gryphon.

Conoley, J.C., Impara, J.C., & Murphy L.L. (Eds.). (1995). *The twelfth mental measurements Yearbook.* Lincoln, NE: Buros Institute of Mental Measurements.

Mitchell, J.V. Jr. (1983). *Tests in print III.* Lincoln, NE: Buros Institute of Mental Measurements.

See also **Tests in Print**

BUROS MENTAL MEASUREMENTS YEARBOOK

There are twelve *Mental Measurements Yearbooks* (MMYs) The yearbooks, which originated in 1938 (Buros, 1938), provide test users with factual information on all known tests published separately in the English-speaking countries of the world. In addition, the books contain test reviews written by professionals representing a variety of viewpoints. The volumes are also sources of comprehensive bibliographies for specific tests, and references relevant to the tests.

The books are published by the Buros Institute of Mental Measurements, located since 1979 at the University of Nebraska, Lincoln, Department of Educational Psychology. The institute, established originally by Oscar K. Buros, has published over 20 volumes (edited by Buros) relating to test description and review.

REFERENCE

Buros, O.K. (1938). *The 1938 mental measurements yearbook.* Highland Park, NJ: Gryphon.

BURT, SIR CYRIL (1883–1971)

Sir Cyril Burt became the first psychologist in the world to be employed by a school system when he was appointed to the position of psychologist with the London County Council in 1913. Burt's career centered around the application of psychology to the study and education of children. He made pioneering investigations in the areas of mental retardation, delinquency, and the genetics of intelligence, and conducted studies that served as models of the application of the scientific method to the study of human characteristics. Burt developed numerous tests for use by school psychologists and published his influential *Factors of the Mind* in 1941. He was co-editor of the *British Journal of Statistical Psychology.*

From 1931 until his retirement in 1950, Burt was professor of psychology at University College, London, where he devoted most of his attention to the training of psychologists and the continuation of his research and writing. He was knighted in 1946.

Sadly, Burt's work and reputation are marred by recent findings that he deliberately fabricated data in some of his best known studies. These acts of fraud cast doubt on his research findings, but do not erase his great contributions to psychology as a clinician, theoretician, and teacher (Hearnshaw, 1979).

REFERENCES

Burt, C. (1941). *The factors of the mind: An introduction to factor analysis in psychology.* New York: Macmillan.

Hearnshaw, L.S. (1979). *Cyril Burt, psychologist.* Ithaca, NY: Cornell University Press.

C

CAFÉ AU LAIT SPOTS

Café au lait spots are areas of patchy pigmentation of skin, usually light brown in color. They are so-named because of their resemblance in color to coffee with cream. They are of diagnostic significance because they may indicate the presence of serious disease such as neurofibromatosis, polyostotic fibrous dysplasia, or tuberous sclerosis (*Blakiston's*, 1979; Johnson, 1979). Café au lait spots may also be found in normal individuals.

When six or more café au lait spots are present and they are larger than 1.5 cm in diameter, neurofibromatosis is suspected (Johnson, 1979). Neurofibromatosis, also known as Von Recklinghausen's disease, is a genetic disorder inherited as an autosomal dominant trait (Batshaw & Perret, 1981). In addition to the presence of café au lait spots, which exist at birth and hence aid in the diagnosis of this condition, other symptoms include multiple skin-colored tumors or nodules and freckles of the axillae (armpits), which represent the Crowe's sign of neurofibromatosis.

Neurofibromatosis may have numerous neurological, psychological, and educational implications. Tumors or neurofibromas typically develop prior to puberty. These tumors may be associated with the spinal or cranial nerves and hence may result in sensory deficits such as visual or hearing impairment. Enlargement and deformation of the bones and scoliosis (curvature of the spine) may occur. Hypertension may be present in young victims of this condition. There is reported to be an increased incidence of mental retardation (Johnson, 1979) and school problems associated with neurofibromatosis (Batshaw & Perret, 1981). In severe cases, the presence of multiple contiguous tumors produces elephantiasis neuromatosa, a cosmetically disfiguring condition. While skin tumors may be removed, there is some evidence these may recur and multiply (*Fact Sheet*, 1983).

In addition to neurofibromatosis, café au lait spots also have been observed in other neurocutaneous syndromes such as tuberous sclerosis (Bourneville's disease) (Rosenberg, 1979). Also inherited as an autosomal dominant trait, tuberous sclerosis is characterized by nevi or moles on the face, epilepsy, and mental retardation (Rosenberg, 1979). The course of tuberous sclerosis begins with the onset of epilepsy and declining mental ability during the first decade, with development of facial lesions around the cheeks and nose several years later (Rosenberg, 1979). Educational management of children who have been diagnosed as having neurofibromatosis or tuberous sclerosis should be conducted on an individual basis because the severity and expression of symptoms vary widely.

REFERENCES

Batshaw, M.L., & Perret, Y.M. (1981). *Children with handicaps: A medical primer.* Baltimore, MD: Brookes.

Blakiston's Gould medical dictionary (4th ed.). (1979). New York: McGraw-Hill.

Fact Sheet: Neurofibromatosis. (1983). Bethesda, MD: National Institute of Neurological and Communicative Disorders and Stroke.

Johnson, M. (1979). Certain cutaneous diseases with significant systemic manifestations. In P.B. Beeson, W. McDermott, & J.B. Wyngaarden (Eds.), *Cecil textbook of medicine* (15th ed.) (pp. 2266–2312). Philadelphia: Saunders.

Rosenberg, R.N. (1979). Inherited degenerative diseases of the nervous system. In P.B. Beeson, W. McDermott, & J.B. Wyngaarden (Eds.), *Cecil textbook of medicine* (15th ed.) (pp. 764–772). Philadelphia: Saunders.

***See also* Minor Physical Anomalies; Neurofibromatosis**

CAMPBELL, SIR FRANCIS JOSEPH (1832–1914)

Francis J. Campbell was born on a farm in Tennessee on October 9, 1832. Blinded in an accident at the age of 3, he was educated at the newly opened Tennessee State Institution for the Blind, where he later served as a teacher of music while studying at the University of Tennessee. Following a period as a student at Harvard University and then as a teacher of the blind in Wisconsin, he became an instructor at Perkins Institution and Massachusetts Asylum for the Blind, where he served for 11 years as head of the music department.

A talented pianist, Campbell left Perkins to continue his music education in Europe and to study methods of teaching the blind. While in London he met Thomas Rhodes Armitage, a blind physician who had just completed joining together Britain's numerous organizations for the blind into a federation that ultimately became known as the Royal National Institute for the Blind.

Campbell's account of the large number of students at Perkins whom he had helped prepare for successful careers as professional musicians led Armitage to establish a music school to train blind children, with Campbell as headmaster. Starting in 1872 with two students, the school ultimately became the Royal Normal College and Academy of Music, with an enrollment, by 1885, of 170 students. Campbell's original faculty included a number of teachers from Perkins, and through the years he maintained a continuing exchange of teachers with Perkins and other schools in the United States. As a result, the Royal Normal College and Academy of Music probably had more influence on American teaching methods than any other foreign school. The institution, under Campbell, combined gen-eral education and physical training with careful vocational preparation, job placement, and follow-up after graduation. Between 80 and 90% of the graduates became self-supporting, mostly as musicians, teachers, and technicians trained in piano tuning and repair. This unprecedented achievement stimulated an emphasis on vocational preparation in schools for the blind throughout the world.

In recognition of his work on behalf of the blind, Campbell was knighted by King Edward VII in 1909. Campbell retired as headmaster in 1912. He died on June 30, 1914.

REFERENCES

Koestler, F.A. (1976). *The unseen minority: A social history of blindness in America.* New York: McKay.

Ross, I. (1951). *Journey into light.* New York: Appleton-Century-Crofts.

CAMPHILL COMMUNITY MOVEMENT

The Camphill Community (movement) was founded by Karl Koenig (1902–1966) after he fled the Nazi powers of central Europe in 1939. The name Camphill refers to the group's first house in Aberdeen, Scotland (Baron & Haldane, 1991).

The Camphill Community is based on the writings of Rudolph Steiner (1861–1925). It works for a full understanding of people's spiritual being, eternal purpose, and earthly tasks. The goals of Steiner's work (known as anthroposophy) include allowing all human beings, handicapped or not, to develop to their potential and to find a productive place in society. The fostering and development of individual human dignity is of paramount importance.

The Camphill Special School, Glenmoore, Pennsylvania, currently serves 72 children from elementary through high school age. Its program complements the philosophies of the larger Camphill Community and provides the "structure, rhythm, regularity, and consistency" needed for curative education. Each child works from an individual education program based on an adaptation of the Waldorf School movement. The education of the whole child is stressed; specific therapies (painting, speech, medicine, music) are provided depending on need. Older students are prepared vocationally for life after graduation through training in groundskeeping, woodwork, and household activities.

A 4-year training seminar is currently offered in the Beaver Run, Pennsylvania school. It is designed to train the individual in curative education using the Waldorf curriculum, as well as in all aspects of community living in the Camphill tradition.

Persons interested in joining or learning more about the Camphill communities are encouraged to contact them directly.

Camphill Special Schools	Camphill Village USA
Beaver Run	Copake, NY 12516
Glenmore, PA 19343	
Camphill Village USA	Camphill Village Minnesota
Kimberton Hills	Route 3
PO Box 155	PO Box 249
Kimberton, PA 19442	Sauk Centre, MN 56378

REFERENCE

Baron, S., & Haldane, D. (1991). Approaching Camphill: From the boundary. *British Journal of Special Education, 18, 2,* 75–78.

CAMPING FOR THE HANDICAPPED

Camping for the handicapped is divided into two types—individual and organized camping. The camping areas used for individualized camping are either in developed or wilderness states. Developed campsites are usually near conveniences that facilitate their use by handicapped campers, e.g., they offer amenities such as tent pads, electrical and water outlets, and restroom facilities. Their nature paths are wide and smooth to facilitate travel for children and youths who are wheelchair-bound or impaired in motor functioning (Gerstein, 1992; Sessoms, 1984).

Organized camping has been defined as the merging of outdoor recreation and education in a campsite setting (Sessoms, 1984). Organized camping is carried out on day and residential bases. Activities at organized camps for the handicapped range from general activities (such as sports and games, hobbies, arts and crafts, and drama) to special-purpose activities such as computer training and weight control. Such camps are also likely to emphasize education and rehabilitation (Wiseman, 1982). Major emphases in organized camps are to foster socialization skills, the acceptance of responsibilities, and the learning of leisure skills, and to facilitate living in communal atmospheres.

Organized camping programs for the handicapped are sponsored by the following types of agencies: (1) private or commercial campers agencies, whose fees come from their clients; (2) quasipublic agencies, some of whose funds come from donations and endowments, while the balance is paid by the participants, e.g., Easter Seals and American Red Cross camps; and (3) public-camping programs supported and sponsored by either local or municipal parks and recreation systems, or by organizations serving the handicapped and parent groups.

Four different types of organized camping programs for the handicapped may be distinguished. One type is camps that are located within communities where campers participate on a daily basis; these have accessible toilets, play, and eating areas. Another type is resident camps for the handicapped. These have cabins, dining halls, staff quarters, and indoor and outdoor recreation facilities. Their sessions last from 1 to 8 weeks. A third type is combination resident and daycamping opportunities that permit some campers to attend daily while others remain overnight. Finally, there are special purpose camps that promote a single concept or activity such as a specific sport or religion (Wiseman, 1982).

In integrative camping, handicapped campers participate in all activities together with able-bodied campers. Handicapped campers in the halfway group may have the potential for regular group participation but still lack some ability to fully engage in activities. Usually, they engage in the same activities as the regular group and share the same facilities, but they do so separately (Sessoms, 1984).

Handicapped campers in the special group require a segregated and supervised program because of the severity and complexity of their condition. All camping activities are modified to the capabilities and interests of this group.

REFERENCES

Gerstein, J. (1992). *Direction of experiential therapy and adventure-based counseling programs.* (ERIC Clearinghouse No. ED39 80 21)

Sessoms, H. (1984). *Leisure services* (3rd ed.). Englewood Cliffs, NJ: Prentice-Hall.

Wiseman, D. (1982). *A practical approach to adapted physical education.* Reading, MA: Addison-Wesley.

See also **Equine Therapy; Recreational Therapy**

CANADA, SPECIAL EDUCATION IN

Canada is one of the few countries in the world that does not have a national education system; education is the exclusive jurisdiction of the 10 provinces and 2 territories[1] that make up the country. The only common vehicle that exists to discuss educational policy at the national level is the Council of Ministers of Education, Canada;[2] however, this body serves only as a mechanism to discuss issues of concern to the provinces and territories as it has no regulatory power over special education. The lack of a Canadian office of education results in considerable diversity in the organization and governance of special education across the country.

A combination of geographical and language factors continue to influence special education in Canada (Hutchinson & Wong, 1987). The majority of Canada's population is concentrated in the southern portion of the country, which results in a reasonable efficient pool of services for the majority of the population, which tends to be clustered in urban areas. Using geography as a framework, however, providing special education services for the minority of the population is both costly and inefficient. For example, there are several areas of the country where school authorities serve a sparse population spread over several hundred miles. Within such a service area there may be only a few people who require special education support service; however, they may be located in opposite ends of the catchment area. This geographic spread might be further complicated by the language(s) spoken and by an increasing cultural diversity. In addition to the two national official languages (English and French), a growing number of individuals have another native language and speak English or French only secondly or thirdly. There also are areas of the country where the majority cultural group is, for example, Indo-Canadian or Inuit. The change in cultural diversity is not limited to the sparsely populated regions of the country; because of immigration, English has now been reduced to a minority language status in Vancouver and Richmond, British Columbia ("English," 1998). The end result of this amalgamation is that service providers must be aware of diverse cultural values and be sensitive to the possibility that different languages are spoken at home, at school, and in the community, while providing the required services at a reasonable cost in an era of diminished fiscal resources.

One of the most significant influences on Canadian special education was introduced in 1982. The full impact of the Canadian Charter of Rights and Freedoms (1982), however, was not felt by special educators until Section 15 was implemented in 1985 (MacKay, 1987). Section 15 of the Charter contained this key clause: "Every individual is equal before and under the law and has the right to the equal protection and equal benefit of the law with discrimination and, in particular, without discrimination based on race, national or ethnic origin, colour, religion, sex, age, or mental or physical disability." MacKay noted that Section 15 could provide the legal grounds on which to request the provision of well-funded special education programs and to challenge the segregation of children. Provinces/territories, however, can sidestep the implications of the Charter by invoking the "notwithstanding" clause, declaring that the education statute operates notwithstanding the Charter. There were also shifts in the preparation of materials to prepare special educators that had a Canadian flavor. For the first time, Canadian special educators introduced professional texts that initially were adaptations of work published in the United States (for example, Hammill, Bartel, & Bunch, 1984) but subsequently were written specifically for Canadian audiences (for example, Bachor & Crealock, 1986). This trend has continued with both adapted (Friend, Bursuck, & Hutchinson, 1998) and unique texts (for example, Andrews & Lupart, 1993; Crealock & Bachor, 1995) continuing to be published.

During this period, policies and practices established in the United States and (to a lesser extent) Europe, continued to influence service delivery models adopted in Canada as well. One notable example was the regular education initiative which led to the introduction of the full-service school (school-based service provision). Further, partly as a result of a British influence, Canadian schools have changed to school-based management, which has resulted in increased parental advocacy for all children and, in some provinces, the establishment of parent advisory councils. Deinstitutionalization gained momentum with the closure of provincial schools for the deaf and/or blind, with services being shifted to local school jurisdictions and of provincial institutions for the mentally disabled, and with accommodation and services being provided in the local community through group homes.

During the 1990s, the dominant theme in special education at the school level was the evolution of services known as inclusion, in which most students remain in the regular classroom. Current policies across the country were designed to support inclusion. For example, the policy of the Northwest Territories includes the following statement: "Inclusive schooling is both a philosophy and a practice. However, including all students in regular classrooms with their age peers, and responding to individual needs and strengths, requires a number of conditions and practices. . . ." A listing of territorial, regional, and school-based requirements for inclusion is given in the policy. (Northwest Territories, Department of Education, Culture, and Employment, 1998). As a consequence, the regular classroom became the home base of most children and adolescents with special needs, and curriculum adaptations made if required. Given this trend, it is not possible to estimate realistically the percentage of individuals with special educational needs being served in total; however, about 1 to 3 percent of students are still being provided services within non-graded special education classrooms.

The scope and substance of special education in Canada has changed substantially, and likely will continue to reform in at least two ways. First, special education no longer applies to school-aged children exclusively. It has been expanded to include services for younger children and to respond to meeting the needs of adults. Second, the substance of special education is being expanded to address a wider mandate of social and economic issues that affect the quality of life of both children and adults with special needs. As noted above, however, this expanded mandate comes in a period of fiscal conservatism and the impact on social services generally and on service provision for people with various challenges is unknown.

NOTES

[1]The provinces in Canada from east to west are Newfoundland and Labrador, Prince Edward Island, Nova Scotia, New Brunswick, Quebec, Ontario, Manitoba, Saskatchewan, Alberta, and British Columbia. Currently there are two Canadian territories, from west to east the Yukon and the Northwest Territories. It should be noted, however, that in 1993, there was an agreement passed to separate the Northwest Territories (NWT) into two independent jurisdictions. This agreement will come into effect on April 1, 1999. The new territories are Nunavut and an as yet unnamed western section of NWT, now the Mackenize Delta area.

[2]This Canadian federal agency has its own webpage and can be found at http://www.cmec.ca/ in both English and French.

REFERENCES

Andrews, J. & Lupart, J. (Eds.). (1993). *The Inclusive Classroom: Educating Exceptional Children* (pp. 293–329). Toronto: Nelson Canada.

Bachor, D. & Crealock, C. (1986). *Instructional strategies for students with special needs.* Scarborough, Ontario: Prentice Hall, Canada.

Canadian Charter of Rights and Freedoms. (1982). Schedule B of *Canada Act, 1982* (U.K.) c. 11 (1982).

Crealock, C. & Bachor, D. (1995). *Instructional strategies for students with special needs* (2nd ed.). Scarborough, Ontario: Allyn and Bacon.

English now minority tongue. (1998, March 3). *The Globe and Mail,* p. A3.

Friend, M., Bursuck, W., & Hutchinson, N. (1998). Including exceptional students: A practical guide for classroom teachers (Canadian ed.). Scarborough, Ontario: Prentice Hall, Canada.

Hammill, D.D., Bartel, N.R., & Bunch, G.O. (Eds.). (1984). *Teaching children with learning and behavior problems* (Canadian ed.). Toronto: Allyn & Bacon.

Hutchinson, N.L., & Wong, B. (1987). Special education in Canada. In C.R. Reynolds & L. Mann (Eds.), *Encyclopedia of special education: A reference for the education of the handicapped and other exceptional children and adults.* New York: Wiley.

MacKay, A.W. (1987). The charter of rights and special education: Blessing or curse? *Canadian Journal for Exceptional Children, 3,* 118–127.

Northwest Territories, Department of Education, Culture, and Employment. Inclusive schooling. http://siksik.learnnet.nt.ca/DOCS/juniorHandbook/InclusiveSchooling.html, retrieved March 11, 1998.

See also **Politics and Special Education**

CANCER, CHILDHOOD

Cancer is a leading cause of mortality in children between the ages of 1 and 15 years, exceeded only by accidents as a cause of death in this age group. The incidence is 130 cases for each 1 million children who are under the age of 15. Approximately 40% of these cases will be leukemia.

The medical treatment of cancer involves radiation, chemotherapy, and—rarely in children—surgery. The treatment often causes weight loss, fatigue, nausea, and emotional distress, among other significant problems (Link, 1982). The physical discomfort suffered by the child and the resulting irritability require extremely sensitive attitudes on the part of teachers. Additionally, the disease, both in its manifestations and the time required to treat it, may result in lost time from school or instruction (Armstrong & Horn, 1995; Bigge & Sirvis, 1986).

Children who have cancer are likely to be referred for instruction and related services of a special education nature when they are unable to deal with the demands of regular school work. Under the guidelines established by IDEA they would receive these under the category of health impairments and would partake of inclusionary services as much as they are able (Peckham, 1993).

REFERENCES

Armstrong, D.F., & Horn, M. (1995). Educational issues in childhood cancer. *School Psychology Quarterly, 10,* 4, 292–304.

Bigge, J., & Sirvis, B. (1986). Physical and health impairments. In N.G. Haring & L. McCormick (Eds.), *Exceptional children and youth* (4th ed.). Columbus, OH: Merrill.

Link, M.P. (1982). Cancer in childhood. In E.E. Bleck & D.A. Nagel (Eds.), *Physically handicapped children: A medical atlas for teachers* (2nd ed.) (pp. 121–144). New York: Grune & Stratton.

Peckham, V.C. (1993). Children with cancer in the classroom. *Teaching Exceptional Children, 26,* 1, 26–32.

See also **Brain Tumors; Chemotherapy; Chronic Illness**

CARDIAC DISORDERS

Congenital cardiac disorders, with their subsequent physical impairments, constitute some of the most common and serious childhood illnesses. Congenital cardiac disorders are those in which defects in the structure of the heart and/or great vessels alter the normal flow of blood through the cardiorespiratory system. Whaley and Wong (1983) report the incidence of congenital heart disease to occur in approximately 8/1000 to 10/1000 live births. They also report that congenital anomalies are the major cause of death outside of prematurity. However, with the evolution of palliative and varied surgical techniques, the percentage of those infants who survive cardiac malformations/lesions in the neonatal period has dramatically increased; therefore, serious complex defects currently account for a large number of individuals passing through infancy and childhood into full maturity (Nelson, Behrman, & Vaughn, 1983). Surgically corrected congenital defects constitute the largest group of those surviving until adulthood.

The cause of congenital cardiac anomalies is still relatively unknown at this time; however multifactorial patterns have been associated with an increased incidence of the disease. The following prenatal factors have been identified as having causal relationships of varying degrees: maternal rubella infection and other viruses such as cytomegalovirus, coxsackle virus B, and nerpesvirus nomines B (Nelson, Behrman, & Vaughn, 1983; Nora, 1971); poor maternal nutrition (Reeder, Mastroianni, & Martin, 1983); alcohol, dextroamphelamine, lithium chloride, progesterine/estrogen, and warafin, which are suspected teratogenic agents, as well as maternal overexposure to radiation (Taybi, 1971).

Genetic factors have also been associated with an increased incidence of cardiac disorders. Those parents who already have a child with a cardiac defect have a higher incidence of a second child with a cardiac malformation than parents with an unaffected child (King, 1975). Although this incidence is higher than the general population, it is still quite low (2 to 5%) (King, 1975, p. 87; Nelson et al., 1983, p. 1121). Other factors predisposing children to congenital heart disease are parents who have congenital cardiac disease themselves or chromosomal aberrations such as Down's syndrome and/or other noncardiac anomalies. Rowe and Uchida (1961) found that between 30 and 40% of all children with Down's syndrome have heart defects of some kind.

The general signs and symptoms associated with congenital cardiac defects in children have been outlined by Miller (1985): (1) dyspnea, especially on exertion; (2) feeding difficulties or a general failure to thrive; (3) stridor or choking spells; (4) increased heart and respiratory rate (tachypnea) with retractions when the ribs show with each breath; (5) numerous respiratory tract infections; (6) in older children, delayed or poor physical and/or mental development with a decreased exercise tolerance; (7) cyanosis, posturing (particularly a squatting position and clubbing of fingers and toes); (8) heart murmurs; and (9) dyaphoresis.

The type of medical intervention or surgical treatment required for congenital heart disease depends on the type or severity of the cardiac lesion. The majority of children with mild congenital heart disease require no treatment. Children with severe heart defects may develop congestive heart failure, which is frequently treated with a cardiac glycoside (digoxin) and furesmide (lasix). Selective palliative surgical procedures may be done to improve oxygenation temporarily until the child grows. Total correction of the heart defect is usually postponed until the benefits of surgery outweigh the risks, or until the child is between the ages of 3 and 5 years (Rowe, 1978).

Parents of children with congenital heart defects are encouraged to treat their children normally. In all but the most severe cases (Morris 1993), a normal life can be expected. Restriction of the child's activities is rarely suggested, but it is often implemented as a control measure by parents. Discipline problems are common, and sibling rivalry is seen frequently because of the attention given the child with the cardiac disorder by parents, health care workers, and educators. The best means of avoiding overprotection of the child is to have a functional knowledge of the child's unique disorder. Overprotection frequently results in increased anxiety in the child and interferes with a normal lifestyle. Parents are recommended to manage their child's heart condition by providing a well-balanced diet, prevention of anemia, and the usual childhood immunizations.

Additional, but imperative, guidelines for all children with cardiac lesions include treating bacterial infections vigorously but not prophylactically to prevent infective endocarditis. Specifically, cyanotic children should be alert for dehydration and iron deficiencies, which may interfere with activity tolerance. As maturity is achieved, women should be counseled regarding the risks of childbearing and the use of contraceptives.

REFERENCES

King, O.M. (Ed.). (1975). *Care of the cardiac surgical patient.* St. Louis: Mosby.

Miller, A. (Ed.). (1985). *Mosby's comprehensive review of nursing* (11th ed.) (pp. 400–405). St. Louis: Mosby.

Morris, R.D. (1993). Neuropsychological, academic, and adoptive functioning in children who survive in-hospital cardiac arrest and resuscitation. *Journal of hearing Disabilities, 26,* 1, 46–51.

Nora, J.J. (1971). Etiologic factors in congenital heart diseases. In S. Kaplin (Ed.), *Pediatric clinics of North America* (Vol. 18, pp. 1059–1074). Philadelphia: Saunders.

Reeder, S.J., Mastroianni, L., & Martin, L. (Eds.). (1983). *Maternity nursing* (15th ed.). Philadelphia: Lippincott.

Rowe, R.D. (1978). Patent ductus arteriosus. In J. Keith, R. Rowe, &

R. Vlad (Eds.), *Heart disease in infancy and children* (3rd ed.). New York: Macmillan.

Rowe, R.D., & Uchida, I.A. (1961). Cardiac malformation in mongolism: A prospective study of 184 mongoloid children. *American Journal of Medicine, 31,* 726–735.

Taybi, H. (1971). Roentgen evaluation of cardiomegaly in the newborn period and early infancy. In S. Kaplin (Ed.), *Pediatric clinics of North America, 18*(4), 1031–1058. Philadelphia: Saunders.

Whaley, L.F., & Wong, D.L. (1983). The child with heart disease. In L.F. Whaley & D.L. Wong (Eds.), *Nursing care of infants and children* (2nd ed.) (pp. 1279–1337). St. Louis: Mosby.

See also **Physical Education of the Handicapped; Physical Handicaps**

CAREER EDUCATION FOR THE HANDICAPPED

Career education is a comprehensive educational program aimed beyond work. It includes the whole person, who functions in a society in a variety of roles such as citizen, family member, student, and advocate (Kokaska, 1980). Career education is often thought of as an introduction to vocational education. In context, it is much broader than vocational education. This comprehensive and functional orientation in career education has received wide acceptance as a major curricular emphasis in special education (Clark, 1980).

Career education is divided into three phases: elementary career awareness, junior high or middle school career exploration, and high school and postsecondary career preparation (Phelps & Lutz, 1977).

There are three major elements within each phase of career education: the school, the family, and community experiences. Career education creates and uses educational experiences in the community, business and industry, the family, and the school for each phase and level in career education sequence. The list of potential sources of assistance and experiences is extensive (Brolin & Kokaska, 1979). This functional, community-based educational emphasis forms the foundation for programs for severely handicapped individuals (Wilcox & Bellamy, 1982).

The infusion of career education into the curriculum creates a systematic curriculum organized through the postsecondary levels that emphasizes process rather than content Miller and Schloss (1982) believe that the integrated curriculum enhances the likelihood that instructional goals will be achieved and maintained.

Brolin and Kokaska (1979) identified 22 career education competencies in three major clusters: daily living skills, personal/social skills, and occupational guidance and preparation. It is reported that these competencies represent the major goals and outcomes that should be completed by students if they are to be successful in community life. Although many local school jurisdictions create their own career counseling programs, successful programs such as "Pathways" (Hutchinson and Freeman, cited in

Hutchinson, 1995) are recommended because outcomes for special education students have already been established (Hutchinson, 1995).

Career education is a concept that provides an alternative curricular orientation for educating handicapped students. While encompassing all of the basic skills, social skills, and content areas, it provides a functional, practical, and still holistic orientation to developing curriculum and instruction for handicapped students. It is much more than the mere preparation for vocational training. Career education is general curriculum development orientation that holds great promise for not only secondary aged and postsecondary handicapped students, but all handicapped individuals.

REFERENCES

Brolin, D.E., & Kokaska, C.J. (1979). *Career education for handicapped children and youth.* Columbus, OH: Merrill.

Clark, G.M. (1980). Career education: A concept. In G.M. Clark & W.J. White (Eds.), *Career education for the handicapped: Current perspectives for teachers.* Boothwyn, PA: Educational Resources Center.

Hutchinson, N.L. (1995). *Career counseling of youth with learning disabilities.* (ERIC Digest No. ED 400470)

Kokaska, C.J. (1980). A curriculum model for career education. In G.M. Clark & W.J. White (Eds.), *Career education for the handicapped: Current perspectives for teachers.* Boothwyn, PA: Educational Resources Center.

Miller, S.R., & Schloss, P. (1982). *Career-vocational education for handicapped youth.* Rockville, MD: Aspen.

Phelps, L.A., & Lutz, R.J. (1977). *Career exploration and preparation for the special needs learner.* Boston: Allyn & Bacon.

Wilcox, B., & Bellamy, G. (Eds.). (1982). *Design of high school programs for severely handicapped students.* Baltimore, MD: Brookes.

See also **Rehabilitation; Vocational Evaluation**

CARIBBEAN, SPECIAL EDUCATION IN THE

Recognition of special education is a relatively recent phenomenon in the Caribbean. Although services for persons with special needs were evident in the first half of the twentieth century, increased government involvement began in the second half of the century. Nongovernmental organizations and individuals with humanitarian concerns were the architects of special education services in the region, and these groups are still involved. Consequently, national associations for the deaf and local chapters of the Salvation Army, for example, continue to play indispensable roles in educating persons with hearing and visual impairments. Activities relating to physical disabilities, mental retardation, learning disabilities, and multiple disabilities have gained prominence over the years.

There is no island with a legislated policy exclusively for special education. However, interest groups use existing legislation relating to general education, as well as statements made by governments relating to "education for all," as fuel in their quest for appropriate support. Governments are committed, therefore, to the concept of equal educational opportunities for children with special needs in the school system. This commitment is displayed in special education units (departments responsible for national special education affairs) in the Education Ministries of the Republic of Trinidad and Tobago and Jamaica, and at least one special education officer in some of the other islands. Education officers work in close collaboration with special and mainstream schools and other relevant institutions. Most of the special education schools and institutions are incorporated into the public system; therefore, governments are responsible for recurrent expenditure including the payment of salaries. There are, however, some institutions operating independently by private sector and nongovernmental organizations.

In the Caribbean, most of the children with special needs are in mainstream schools without adequate support. For example, in the Republic of Trinidad and Tobago, the Ministry of Education (1993) reports that approximately "13.1% of special needs children are not in school; 5.8% are in preschool; 5.1% are attending special schools; 6.7% are in other facilities, while 67.2% are in mainstream schools in which there are no provisions for them." The implication is that only 2.1% of children with special needs are in the mainstream with adequate support.

Overall, the support provided in the region is at varying levels of quality and organization, both within schools and institutions. In Jamaica, for example, there is a national braille and large print service, and to date over 400 texts have been printed and distributed to schools. Furthermore, at the Mona Campus of the University of the West Indies (UWI), there is a very active committee for students with special needs comprised of students and staff. Over the years, the committee has been acquiring resource materials to enhance the learning environment of the students. In January 1998, a member of the committee, who is blind and also a graduate student, created history when he was appointed Senator by the Jamaican Prime Minister.

The training of special education teachers began in 1971 with the introduction of a one-year certificate program at UWI Mona Campus for teachers of the deaf. In 1976, Mico Teachers College began offering a 3-year program in mental retardation, learning disabilities, hearing impairment, and physical disabilities. These initial training program are still available, and recently visual impairment was included. In 1986, Mico, in collaboration with UWI, began a Bachelor in Education program in special education. Each of the program mentioned has had large financial support from the Government of the Netherlands and regional governments, and is accessed by students throughout the region. In 1994, a B.Ed. in "Managing Learning Difficulties" began at Mona, UWI. The program focuses on learners in mainstream classes. Graduate level courses in special education are offered at Mona, and Cave Campus in Barbados introduced a Master in Education in special education during the 1997–98 academic year. In Trinidad and Tobago the local teachers' association, working in collaboration with a university in the United Kingdom, offers graduate level training to its teachers.

There are other training programs throughout the region. For example, the Caribbean Association for the Mental Retarded or Developmental Disabilities (CAMRODD), a regional association, has a 3-year Parent Empowerment Program for 1997–99. In a recent session, pairs of parents and professionals from several islands including Antigua, Saba, St. Lucia, Barbados, St. Vincent, and Trinidad and Tobago were involved (CAMRODD, 1997). The general plan is for participants involved in training to implement parent training workshops in their communities.

Future directions in the field must encompass aspects of early identification of special needs, more community involvement, inclusion, giftedness, and public education. In Barbados, for example, there are plans to assess annually children in the 3 to 7 year age group for visual, hearing, and speech impairments (Ministry of Education, Youth Affairs, & Culture, 1995). The Republic of Trinidad and Tobago has plans to establish regional diagnostic prescriptive centers. The Mico College Centre for Child Assessment and Research, a diagnostic and therapeutic center, is committed to intensify its efforts in the area of research and its dissemination. The UWI, working with both governmental and nongovernmental agencies, is continuing to set standards and respond to needs with the delivery of relevant research and pedagogy. Finally, if work in progress in the area of special needs continues unabated, and plans articulated are implemented, interest groups within the region can greet the end of the millennium with optimism.

REFERENCES

Caribbean Association for the Mentally Retarded or Developmental Disabilities. (1997). *CAMRODD's parent empowerment programme.* Jamaica: 3D's Documentation Unit.

Ministry of Education. (1993). *Education Policy Paper: 1993–2003.* Trinidad and Tobago: Author.

Ministry of Education, Youth Affairs, & Culture. (1995). *White Paper on education reform: preparing for the 21st century.* Barbados: Government of Barbados.

CARROW ELICITED LANGUAGE INVENTORY (CELI)

The Carrow Elicited Language Inventory (CELI; Carrow, 1974) is a diagnostic test of expressive language, containing 51 sentences and one phrase that the child is required to repeat.

The CELI was normed in 1973 on 475 Anglo middle-class Texans between 3 years and 7 years 11 months. Children who were identified with speech or language disorders were excluded from the normative sample. Validity of the CELI has been established by its ability to discriminate between children with and without language disorders and to identify children at high risk for learning disorders (Blau,

1984; Swift, 1984). Test-retest reliability at 2 week intervals is reported at .98, but this should be interpreted with caution because of the small sample size employed.

A major assumption underlying the CELI is that a child's imitations of model sentences will closely resemble his or her proficiency in spontaneous speech. However, numerous studies question the validity of the sentence imitation tasks as a valid measure of spontaneous language (Kuczaj, 1975; Haniff, 1975; Connell, 1982; Prutting, 1975; McDade, 1983). A weakness of this test is that the normative data is limited (small sample size, restricted geographic region, and limited SES) and out of date.

REFERENCES

Blau, A.F., & Lahey, M., Oleksiuk-Velez, A. (1984). Planning goals for intervention: Language testing or language sampling? *Exceptional Children, 1,* 78–79.

Carrow, E. (1974). *Carrow Elicited Language Inventory.* Boston: Teaching Resources Corporation.

Connell, P.J., & Myles-Zitzer, C. (1982). An analysis of elicited imitation as a language evaluation procedure. *Journal of Speech and Hearing Disability, 47,* 390–396.

Haniff, M.H., & Seigel, G.M. (1981). The effect of context on verbal elicited imitation. *Journal of Speech and Hearing Disability, 46,* 27–30.

Kuczaj, S., & Maratsos, M. (1975). What children can say before they will. *Merrill-Palmer Quarterly, 21,* 89–112.

McDade, H.L., & Simpson, M..A. (1983). Reply to Carrow-Woolfolk. *Journal of Speech and Hearing Disorders, 3,* 334–335.

Prutting, C.A., Gallagher, T.M., & Mulac, A. (1975). The expressive portion of the NSST compared to a spontaneous language sample. *Journal of Speech and Hearing Disabilities, 40,* 40–48.

Swift, C. (1984). Sentence imitation in kindergarten children at risk for learning diability: A comparative study. *Language, Speech, & Hearing Services in Schools, 1,* 10–15.

CASCADE MODEL OF SPECIAL EDUCATION SERVICES

The Cascade Model of Special Education Services is a conceptualization of the range of placement and service options that used to be available for handicapped children. The placement options were presented in hierarchical form and ranged from the least restrictive placement in the regular education classroom to the most restrictive placement in hospital or institutional settings. The Cascade Model was first proposed by Reynolds in 1962 and an amended version was proposed by Deno in 1970. Both proposals predated the passage of the Education of All Handicapped Children Act of 1975 (PL 94-142), a time when placement and service options for the handicapped were scarce. Reynolds and Birch (1977) characterized the pre-PL 94-142 administrative arrangements as a two-box system in which parallel but separate educational programs for regular and special education were in operation within school buildings. Interaction and movement of children between the two systems was difficult at best, and more often, nonexistent. The Cascade

Model helped create understanding of and support for a better system that "facilitates tailoring of treatment to individual needs rather than a system for sorting out children so they will fit conditions designed according to group standards not necessarily suitable for the particular case" (Deno, 1970, p. 235).

The Cascade Model visually appeared as a triangular form that contained two essential elements: the degree of placement specialization and the relative number of children in the various placement options. The base of the triangle coincided with regular classroom placement, the preferred placement for the largest number of handicapped students. Progressively more specialized placements were included as the triangle extended toward the apex. The decreasing width of the triangle reflected the decreasing numbers of children to be placed in progressively more restrictive environments. Deno's Cascade Model was widely cited and reproduced; it has become a fundamental concept for the field of special education.

The basic concepts of specialization embodied in the Cascade Model were subsequently incorporated into federal and state laws as the least restrictive environment principle (Peterson, Zabel, Smith, & White, 1983). Variations of the Cascade Model have been presented by other authors (Cartwright, Cartwright, & Ward, 1985). However, the basic elements of degree of restrictiveness and relative numbers of children in the different placement options were retained.

Despite its popularity and utility, the Cascade Model was criticized. Reynolds and Birch (1977) viewed the original Cascade Model as "too place oriented" because of its "clearest focus on administrative structures and places." They offered an alternative conceptualization of the Cascade Model in which instructional diversity was emphasized.

The Instructional Cascade envisioned the regular education classroom as the primary and optimal setting for the delivery of specialized services to handicapped children. Children were seen as moving among the levels of the cascade for educational purposes. Ideally, a child would be moved to a more restrictive setting only for compelling educational reasons and was moved back as quickly as possible. The introduction of inclusive programming in the past few years has created a debate as to whether special education should abolish the Cascade Model. On one hand are conservative educators who believe in the original model that provided integration on a case by case method. On the other hand are abolitionists who believe in full inclusion for all special education students. At this time, federal law still supports individualization and many follow its lead (Fuchs, 1994). Outcome evaluation studies in the next few years will probably determine the debate and also determine how the cascade of services will change.

REFERENCES

Cartwright, G.P., Cartwright, C.A., & Ward, M.E. (1985). *Educating special learners* (2nd ed.). Belmont, CA: Wadsworth.

Deno, E. (1970). Special education as developmental capital. *Exceptional Children, 37*(3), 229–237.

Fuchs, D. (1994). *Best practices in school psychology: Peabody reintegration project.* (ERIC document No. ED378774)

Peterson, R.L., Zabel, R.H., Smith, C.R., & White, M.A. (1983). Cascade of services model and emotionally disabled students. *Exceptional Children, 49*(5), 404–408.

Reynolds, M.C. (1962). A framework for considering some issues in special education. *Exceptional Children, 28*(7), 367–370.

Reynolds, M.C., & Birch, J.W. (1977). *Teaching exceptional children in all America's schools.* Reston, VA: Council for Exceptional Children.

See also **Inclusion; Least Restrictive Environment; Philosophy of Education for the Handicapped; Special Class**

CASE HISTORY

Case histories serve several purposes: to provide information about rare disorders, individual differences in treatment responsiveness, or the natural course for a disorder (Kratochwill, 1985); to provide information necessary to plan and monitor appropriate treatment; to provide data needed by external agencies; to illuminate pitfalls to be avoided; and to provide information for scientific, administrative, and instructional purposes.

Identification information in a complete case history should include client's name, date of birth, sex, ethnicity, dominant language, marital status, guardians' names if a minor, residence, phone number, persons to notify in an emergency, medical status, and current program status (e.g., grade or placement if an educational setting); this information should be in an easily located part of the record. Historical data, as determined relevant for client welfare by a multidisciplinary committee, should include developmental, health, and educational history; work history if an adult; and significant family events.

Specific statements of the concerns of the referral agent should be included. The client's status at the time of referral should include information about current health, including current medications; sensory or perceptual abilities; motor abilities; language skills; current adaptive behavior; intellectual abilities and academic skills; other cognitive data, such as current belief systems or attributions as may be pertinent to the referral problem; emotional behavior; social skills and behavior; family status; and vocational aptitudes, skills, and interests. A description of the client's current status with respect to the referring problem should always be included. The preintervention frequency of the problem behavior should be recorded to establish treatment effectiveness at a later time.

To establish intervention effectiveness, a record must be maintained of changes in the client's behavior or level of skill. Data from observations, self-monitoring, or other methods can be collected and recorded and effectiveness assessed by means of single-subject designs (Barlow & Hersen, 1984). These techniques have the advantage of demonstrating that specific treatments have been tried and have been effective or noneffective; of being sensitive to subtle changes in behavior; and of allowing the comparison of several alternative treatments.

REFERENCES

Barlow, D.H., & Hersen, M. (1984). *Single-case experimental designs: Strategies for studying behavior change* (2nd ed.). New York: Pergamon.

Kratochwill, T.R. (1985). Case study research in school psychology. *School Psychology Review, 14,* 204–215.

See also **Medical History; Mental Status Exam**

CATALOG OF FEDERAL DOMESTIC ASSISTANCE

The *Catalog of Federal Domestic Assistance* is a compendium of over 1,300 programs, projects, and activities of the federal government that provide benefits or assistance to the public (U.S. Government Printing Office, 1985). The catalog provides basic descriptive information on each program or activity, such as the purposes of the program, eligible applicants, total funds available, examples and dollar range of prior awards, and person to contact. The catalog covers programs providing both financial and nonfinancial forms of assistance (e.g., information, technical assistance, transfer of real property). It is updated and published twice a year by the General Services Administration, an agency of the federal government.

The catalog is distributed free of charge on a limited basis to state and local officials. It can be purchased on machine readable tape, diskettes and/or CD ROM from the General Services Administration, Ground Floor, Reporters Building, 300 7th Street, SW, Washington, DC 20407. Their telephone number is 202-708-5126.

REFERENCE

General Services Administration. (1998). *Catalog of federal domestic assistance.* Washington, DC: Author

CATARACTS

A cataract is an imperfection in the clarity or a clouding of the lens of the eye. It will be experienced by a majority of people who live to an old age (Eden, 1978). Surgically removing the affected lens is the only treatment.

Eden (1978) defines three types of cataracts. Senile cataracts are those that occur as part of the normal aging process. Cell layers form around the lens as people grow older; this is similar to rings forming in the trunks of trees. The lens becomes opaque and loses its resiliency. Secondary cataracts are those that result from some other trauma or disease. For example, persons with diabetes often develop cataracts. Secondary cataracts can also result from excessive radiation, electrical shock, and the side effects of some drugs. Excessive use of cortisone, for example, has been related to the development of lens opacity. Congenital cataracts are those that are present from birth. This type of cataract is very rare. Illnesses during pregnancy such as German measles (rubella) can cause congenital cataracts (Harley & Lawrence, 1977).

Post operative treatment of cataract removal involves the use of regular glasses or contact lenses, or the insertion of artificial plastic lenses in the eye itself. Such treatments are effective in restoring vision to the affected eye.

REFERENCES
Eden, J. (1978). *The eye book.* New York: Viking.

Harley, R.K., & Lawrence, G.A. (1977). *Visual impairment in the schools.* Springfield, IL: Thomas.

See also Amblyopia; Blind

CATEGORICAL EDUCATION

Categorical education was the practice of separating handicapped children into subgroups representing different types of disability. Each subgroup had a specific categorical designation and its members were reviewed as a cohesive group for instructional purposes. The traditional categorical group structure presumed that there were significant homogeneity of student characteristics within each subgroup and that there was significant heterogeneity among the groups. That is, the members of one group shared common qualities that distinguished them from the members of all other groups. The assumptions of homogeneity within categories and heterogeneity among categories were not well founded (Iano, 1972; Hallahan & Kauffman, 1977; Kirk & Elkins, 1975; Leland, 1977), particularly for the mildly handicapped.

The Education for All Handicapped Children Act of 1975 (PL 94-142) stipulated 11 handicapping conditions: mentally retarded, hard of hearing, deaf, speech impaired, deaf-blind, learning disabled, visually handicapped, seriously emotionally disturbed, orthopedically handicapped, other health impaired, and multihandicapped. These categories became the prototype for the nation and were reflected in state and local plans for the education of handicapped children. They also continue to grow and change.

A long-term disaffection with traditional categorical education has led to the development of alternative practices. Critics of traditional categorical labels such as mentally retarded, learning disabled, or socially emotionally disturbed emphasize that such labels are of little use to the teacher who must plan appropriate instructional programs. Therefore the shift to inclusive practices of placement has placed emphasis on outcome rather than diagnosis or label. Alternate assessments (such as curriculum-based assessment) has also de-emphasized labels and classification, and have attempted to individualize instructions to learner needs as opposed to label.

REFERENCES
Hallahan, D.P., & Kauffman, J.M. (1977). Labels, categories, behaviors: ED, LD, and EMR reconsidered. *Journal of Special Education, 11*(2), 139–149.

Iano, R.P. (1972). Shall we disband special classes? *Journal of Special Education, 6*(2), 167–177.

Kirk, S.A., & Elkins, J. (1975). Characteristics of children enrolled in the child service demonstration centers. *Journal of Learning Disabilities, 8*(10), 630–637.

Leland, H. (1977). Mental retardation and adaptive behavior. *Journal of Special Education, 6*(1), 71–80.

See also Cascade Model of Special Education Services

CATECHOLAMINES

Epinephrine (adrenaline) and norepinephrine (noradrenaline) are hormones of the sympathetic division of the autonomic nervous system. Epinephrine was the first hormone to be isolated, and by 1897 Abel had separated it from the adrenal gland and found it to be represented by the formula C17 H15 No4. By 1905, the Japanese chemist Takamine treated Abel's abstract and named the product adrenaline, with the formula C9 H13 No3 (Krantz & Carr, 1961). Norepinephrine was not identified until 1942; it derives its name from the German expression Nitrogen ohne radikal, referring to the fact that the molecule is identical to that of epinephrine except for missing the methyl group on the nitrogen atom.

Epinephrine produces a variety of metabolic effects useful in an emergency: increased epinephrine levels result in what is often called the "fight, flight, or fright" reaction (West & Todd, 1963). Epinephrine stimulates the effector cells of the pilomotor nerves to cause hair erection, and also causes pupillary dilation, giving rise to the picture of a fright reaction. By also causing a rapid rise in blood pressure and an increase in the rate and amplitude of respiration, it prepares for more effective fright or flight from danger. The metabolic behavioral effects of epinephrine and norepinephrine are in some ways opposite, in that while epinephrine is associated with tachycardia (rapid heartbeat), norepinephrine is associated with brachycardia (slow heart action) (Eranko, 1955). In children, normal levels in plasma are 3–6 m/l for norepinephrine, and >1 m/l for epinephrine (Cone, 1968).

REFERENCES
Cone, T.E. (1968). The adrenal medulla. In R. Cooke & S. Levin (Eds.), *The biologic basis of pediatric practice* (pp. 1171–1177). New York: McGraw-Hill.

Eranko, O. (1955). Distribution of adrenaline and noradrenaline in the adrenal medulla. *Nature, 88,* 175.

Krantz, R.C., & Carr, C.J. (1961). The *pharmacologic principles of medical practice* (5th ed.). Baltimore, MD: Williams & Wilkins.

West, E.S., & Todd, W.R. (1963). *Textbook of biochemistry* (3rd ed.). New York: Macmillan.

See also Epinephrine

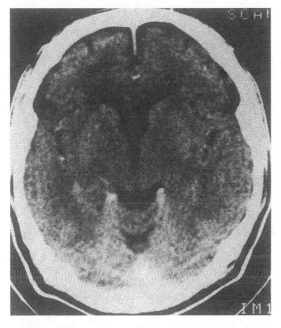

Figure 1. CAT scan image of the brain in horizontal plane. The two upside down L-shaped dark areas represent the anterior horns of the lateral ventricles. The light area just adjacent and lateral to these structures is the caudate nucleus. The centrally located dark area just below the anterior horns in this figure represents the third ventricle. On either side of the third ventricle is the thalamus. The angular slightly darker area that runs from the outside top of the caudate nucleus down and adjacent to the outside of the thalamus is the internal capsule. Lateral to the internal capsule is the putamen-globus pallidus complex.

CAT SCAN

Computerized axial tomography (CAT) scanning is an imaging technique (Binder, Haughton, & Ho, 1979) that permits visualization of many of the important landmarks and structures of the brain (see Figure 1). This is a technique that did not become commercially available until 1973 (Hounsfield, 1973).

CAT scanning is accomplished by passing a narrow X-ray beam directed toward a detector on the other side through the patient's head (or body). The detector is sensitive to the number of X-ray beam particles that pass through the tissue; this in turn is related to the density of the tissue (e.g., the greater the density the fewer the X-ray particles that pass through). The X-ray beam is passed through the head (or body) in numerous planes so as to examine the same point from multiple directions, thus allowing a specification of density for any given point on the surface of a plane. Next, each density point is color-coded depending on the degree of density; these various density points are used to computer generate an "image" of the tissue being examined (see Figure 2).

CAT scanning has numerous useful applications. The CAT image approximates an actual anatomic specimen taken in a similar plane; thus significant structural abnor-

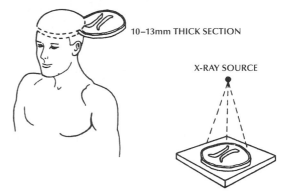

Figure 2. Diagrammatic representation of the position of the view of the CAT image.

malities can be detected. This is particularly true in cases of cerebral trauma, vascular infarctions, congenital and neoplastic disorders, and degenerative brain diseases. For children with developmental disorders, CAT scanning may reveal any major structural anomalies of the brain, but it has not been found to be routinely diagnostic in children in which the only problem is a learning disability (Denkla, LeMay, & Chapman, 1985). These observations suggest that, in general, there is no gross anatomic derangement associated with learning disorders.

REFERENCES

Binder, G.A., Haughton, V.M., & Ho, K-C. (1979). *Computed tomography of the brain in axial, coronal and sagittal planes* Boston: Little, Brown.

Denkla, M.B., LeMay, M., & Chapman, C.A. (1985). Few Ct scan abnormalities found ever in neurologically impaired learning disabled children. *Journal of Learning Disabilities, 18,* 132–135.

Hounsfield, G.N. (1973). Computerized transverse axial scanning (tomography). I. Description of system. *British Journal of Radiology, 46,* 1016–1022.

See also **Nuclear Magnetic Resonance (NMR); X-Ray Scanning Techniques**

CATTELL, JAMES MCKEEN (1860–1944)

James McKeen Cattell was educated at Lafayette College in Pennsylvania and the University of Leipzig in Germany. He worked under Wilhelm Wundt at Leipzig and at Sir Francis Galton's psychological laboratory in London. He held the world's first professorship in psychology, at the University of Pennsylvania, and later was professor of psychology and head of the department of psychology at Columbia University (Woodworth, 1944).

A devoted researcher, Cattell conducted significant investigations in areas such as reaction time, perception, association, and individual differences. He developed numerous tests and coined the term mental tests. He studied the backgrounds and characteristics of eminent scientists, and published the widely used directory *Biographical Dictionary of American Men of Science.* To promote the practical application of psychology, he founded the Psychological Corporation and served as its president for many years. Cattell, through his students, research, and writing and editing, was a major figure in the development of psychology as a profession in the United States (Watson, 1968).

REFERENCES

Watson, R.I. (1968). *The great psychologists.* New York: Lippincott.

Woodworth, R.S. (1944). James McKeen Cattell, 1860–1944. *Psychological Review, 51,* 201–209.

CAWLEY'S PROJECT MATH

Project MATH (Mathematics Activities for Teaching the Handicapped) is a comprehensive developmental mathematics program for children with special needs. The program was developed by Dr. John Cawley and his associates at the University of Connecticut under a federal grant operated from 1970 to 1975. The project was entitled "A Program Project Research and Demonstration Effort in Arithmetic Among the Mentally Handicapped"; it is available commercially.

The teaching model used in the curriculum is called the *Interactive Unit* (IU). This teaching model allows for the presentation of information to the learner in four different ways and also allows the learner to respond to questions or information in four different ways. There are 16 possible interactions that can take place between the teacher and the learner for any concept being taught. No interaction is considered to be cognitively superior to another. The interactive unit teaching model offers several advantages for the instructor. Chief among these advantages is that the model allows an instructor to teach around a disability. Learners who have difficulty in reading or writing may be taught by any of the remaining nine interaction possibilities. The instructor components of the IU are state, construct, present, and graphically symbolize. The learner components are state, construct, identify, and graphically symbolize.

The goal of the curriculum is to give a balanced emphasis to the development of skills, concepts, and social growth. The content of the math strands addressed are patterns, numbers, operations, measurements, fractions, and geometry. There are multiple lessons and support materials for concepts taught in each strand. A math concept inventory accompanies each level of the curriculum. This inventory is essentially a criterion-referenced test used to make initial placement decisions in the curriculum and to measure growth.

Two years of field testing, from 1972 to 1974, was undertaken. It involved 1917 children instructed by 116 teachers in seven states. In addition to the curricular development thrust of the project, a large number of research studies were undertaken and published, primarily in the area of verbal problem solving. Cawley has continued to build on the Pro-

ject MATH materials and to expand the basic model so that it can be used by a wide variety of special educators (Thornton, 1995). Cawley continues to develop ways to reduce the inconvenience between special and general education mathematics instruction (Palmer & Cawley, 1995).

REFERENCES

Palmer, R.S., & Cawley, J.F. (1995). Mathematics curricula frameworks: Goals for general and special education. *Focus on Learning Problems in Mathematics, 17,* 2, 50–66.

Thornton, C.A. (1995). Promising Research, programs, and projects. *Teaching Children Mathematics, 2,* 2, 134–135.

See also **Mathematics, Learning Disabilities in**

CENTER FOR APPLIED SPECIAL TECHNOLOGY (CAST)

The Center for Applied Special Technology (CAST) is a nonprofit organization founded in 1984, with the mission of expanding opportunities for people with disabilities through the development of and innovative uses of technology. Center activities include research, product development, and work with educational settings in the service of furthering universal design for learning.

CAST works from the premise that the most effective way to expand educational opportunities is " . . . through universal design for learning. The phrase 'universal design' refers to the creation of computer software and learning models that are usable by everyone, including individuals of all ages, whether they are gifted, are typical learners, or have special needs." (CAST, 1998).

The CAST offices are located at 39 Cross Street, Suite 201, Peabody, MA 01960, and may be reached at (978) 531-8555, or (978) 538-3110 (TTY).

REFERENCE

Center for Applied Special Technology. (1998). About CAST—Mission and history.

CENTILE SCORES

See PERCENTILE SCORES.

CENTRAL AUDITORY DYSFUNCTION

Central auditory dysfunction is a term used to describe a broad spectrum of difficulties that may arise when an individual attempts to process an auditory signal. This disorder occurs even in people without measurable hearing loss. The term implies that when an individual has normal hearing status, but exhibits certain difficulties in correctly interpreting an auditory signal, there is some type of damage in the brain.

In the past 25 years, there have been attempts to determine whether children with language disorders also have a central auditory dysfunction. If they did, the question pertains to the relationship between the two and what remedial strategies could be used successfully. Language acquisition, language disorders of various types, and learning disabilities have all been considered to be directly related to various types of central auditory dysfunction (Cherry, 1992; Garstecki & Erler, 1997).

Two basic types of tests are given to evaluate the central auditory functioning of an individual. The first type is designed to evaluate the auditory neuromaturational level of the individual. Keith (1981) suggests that these tests should (1) not be loaded with language comprehension items; (2) not require linguistic manipulation of the signal; (3) not require, or least minimize, cross-modal input or response; (4) use nonlinguistic signal; and (5) be primarily a speech imitative task using nonmeaningful material or speech material so familiar that comprehension plays no role in the process. To that end, Keith (1986) developed a Central Auditory Processing Disorder (CAPD) assessment instrument called the SCAN: A Screening Test for Auditory Processing Disorders. The SCAN includes three subtests: a filtered word test, an auditory figure-ground test, and a competing word test. The SCAN was originally normed on children ages 3 to 11 (Cherry, 1992). Another CAPD test, the Selective Auditory Attention Test (SAAT) was developed by Cherry (1980). The SAAT is used to assess auditory distractibility and Attention Deficit Hyperactivity Disorder. The SAAT includes two subtests, a monosyllabic word test given in quiet and a similar monosyllabic word list with a semantic distractor.

The second type of test can be categorized as auditory-language tests. These tests are heavily loaded both cognitively and linguistically. Examples are tests in which the child must point to a series of pictures in the order in which the words are heard. It should be noted that this task is not simply a single-factor auditory-perceptual test, but requires memory and comprehension.

While noting that a number of children with language problems do poorly on tests of central auditory functioning, Rees (1981) observes that it is not at all clear whether the deficits actually produce the language disorders or whether they are simply behavioral correlates of these and other disabilities. She further criticizes these tests, stating that "no one has developed an intelligible account of how these central auditory processing skills, or the lack of them, relate to language acquisition or academic learning" (p. 118). She considers the tests that are heavily loaded with linguistic and cognitive material to be tests designed more to evaluate an individual child's metalinguistic ability (the ability to analyze and talk about language) than to measure directly the child's ability to learn language. While these tasks may be good indicators of the individual child's ability to function successfully in school, she questions whether they have a fundamental relationship with central auditory processing. Rees notes that in some ways all the phenomena that have been clustered under the rubric of central auditory functioning have only one thing in common. They all involve data taken in through the ear.

In summary, central auditory dysfunction refers to problems individuals may exhibit in processing an auditory signal even when they have no specific hearing loss. When adults with known brain lesions were asked to perform specific tasks, related to auditory functioning, it was found that they exhibited specific problems. Some children with learning problems performed similarly on tests of auditory processing. It was presumed they also might have some kind of brain damage. Two types of tests are given to test auditory functioning. The first evaluates auditory maturational level. The second tests language-related auditory functions. It is not clear whether there is a cause-and-effect relationship between auditory functioning and learning disorders.

REFERENCES

Cherry, R. (1980). *Selective Auditory Attention Test (SAAT)*. St. Louis: Auditec of St. Louis.

Cherry, R. (1992). Screening and evaluation of central auditory processing disorders in young children. In J. Katz, N. Steckler, & D. Henderson (Eds.), *Central auditory processing: A transdisciplinary view* (pp. 129–140). St. Louis: Mosby.

Garstecki, D.C., & Erler, S.F. (1997). Hearing loss management in children and adults. In G.T. Mencher, S.E. Gerber, & A. McCombe (Eds.), *Audiology and auditory dysfunction* (pp. 220–232). Needham Heights, MA: Allyn & Bacon.

Keith, R.W. (1981). *Central auditory and language disorders in children*. San Diego, CA: College Hill.

Keith, R.W. (1986). *SCAN: A screening test for auditory processing disorders*. San Diego: The Psychology Corp.

Rees, N.S. (1981). Saying more than we know: Is auditory processing a meaningful concept? In R.W. Keith (Ed.), *Central auditory and language disorders in children* (pp. 94–120). San Diego: College Hill.

See also **Auditory Abnormalities; Auditory Discrimination; Auditory Perception**

CENTRAL NERVOUS SYSTEM

The central nervous system (CNS) refers to the brain, including the cerebral cortex, cranial nerves, cerebellum, spinal cord, and other subcortical structures contained within the cranial vault. It consists of more than 12 billion neurons and approximately 10 times that number of glial cells. The cerebral cortex represents the CNS structure underlying most adaptive behavior, including sensation, perception, judgment, intellective functioning, and purposeful movement. Divided into two cerebral hemispheres, the respective cerebral cortices tend to be differentiated in terms of functions. As with other CNS structures that develop embryologically from the prosencephalon, the cerebral hemispheres have contralateral representation, i.e., the left side of the cortex controls the right side of the body, and vice versa. Each cerebral hemisphere is divided into anterior and posterior regions by the central sulcus or fissure of

Rolando. Those cortical areas just anterior to the Rolandic fissure are specialized for motor functions, with motor enervation proceeding from superior areas of the motor strip, which control lower extremity movement, downward to more inferior areas, which control movement of the face. Just posterior to the Rolandic fissure is the sensory area, which controls such phenomena as sensitivity to stimulation for body areas corresponding to those enervated by the motor strip.

In addition to lateralized representation of motor and sensory functions, the cerebral cortex areas are also specialized for processing given types of information, and for processing information in given ways. In essentially all right-handed and in most left-handed individuals, the left cerebral hemisphere is more efficient in processing verbal or linguistic types of information, with the right hemisphere more specialized for the processing of spatial types of information. This specialization of function can be demonstrated in normal individuals by injecting fast-acting barbiturate types of drugs such as sodium amytal into a selected cerebral hemisphere. Following such an injection to the left cerebral hemisphere, for example, individuals will normally experience a brief period of aphasia, during which they are both unable to comprehend spoken language and to formulate verbalizations. Within a few minutes, all verbal functions return to preinjection levels. Similar temporary impairment of spatial function is demonstrated on right hemisphere injection (Hartlage & Flanigin, 1982).

There is good evidence that in most individuals the cerebral hemispheres are not symmetrical (Geschwind & Levitsky, 1968; Von Bonin, 1962). This asymmetry has been related to differences in facility with processing certain types of information and other psychological characteristics (Lansdell & Smith, 1975; Levy, 1974; Reynolds, 1981; Reynolds, Kamphaus, Rosenthal, & Hiemenz, 1997). This hemispheric asymmetry has been postulated as being etiologic in certain mental disorders such as schizophrenia (Gruzelier, 1984; Newlin, Carpenter, & Golden, 1981), autism (Colby & Parkinson, 1977; Dawson, Warrenburg, & Fuller, 1982), and a number of other maladaptive behaviors (Sandel & Alcorn, 1980).

Although much adaptive behavior is attributed to the cerebral hemispheres, other portions of the central nervous system mediate behaviors of crucial importance to the individual. The 12 cranial nerves (olfactory, optic, oculomotor, trochlear, trigeminal, abducens, facial, acoustic, glossopharyngeal, vagus, accessory, and hypoglossal) control such functions as smell, visual acuity, eye movement, facial sensation and movement, and hearing.

The cerebellum, located posteriorly and partially under the occipital lobe, with connections to many portions of the cerebral cortex, is involved with balance and with coordination of some motor activities (because some areas of the cerebellum are uniquely sensitive to the effects of alcohol, law enforcement officers often check some aspects of cerebellar function when screening drivers suspected of intoxication). A number of brain areas often referred to as subcortical (e.g., amygdala, hippocampus, thalamus) because of their location under the cortex, have been identified as playing important roles in such behaviors as emotion, memory, movement, and the integration of information from diverse cortical areas (Riklan & Levita, 1965). The medulla, that portion of the central nervous system that bridges with the spinal cord, is more involved with lower sensory and motor functions than with higher cognitive abilities.

Although some areas of the CNS have been shown to be crucial for the performance of given tasks, the CNS functions in an interrelated way for the execution of most complex tasks. Damage to the CNS will almost always result in a complex disorder requiring special educational services.

REFERENCES

Colby, K.M., & Parkinson, C. (1977). Handedness in autistic children. *Journal of Autism and Childhood Schizophrenia, 7,* 3–9.

Dawson, G., Warrenburg, S., & Fuller, D. (1982). Cerebral lateralization in individuals diagnosed as autistic in early childhood. *Brain and Language, 15,* 353–368.

Geschwind, N., & Levitsky, W. (1968). Human brain: Left-right asymmetries in temporal speech region. *Science, 161,* 186–187.

Gruzelier, J.H. (1984). Hemispheric imbalances in schizophrenia. *International Journal of Psychophysiology, 1,* 227–240.

Hartlage, L.C., & Flanigin, H. (1982, October). *An abbreviated intracarotical amytal testing procedure.* Paper presented at the annual meeting of the National Academy of Neuropsychologists, Atlanta, GA.

Lansdell, H., & Smith, F.J. (1975). Asymmetrical cerebral function for two WAIS factors and their recovery after brain injury. *Journal of Consulting and Clinical Psychology, 43,* 931.

Levy, H. (1974). Psychological implications of bilateral asymmetry. In S.J. Dimond & J.G. Beaumont (Eds.), *Hemispheric function in the Human Brain.* London: Elek Science.

Newlin, D.B., Carpenter, B., & Golden, C. (1981). Hemispheric asymmetries in schizophrenia. *Biological Psychiatry, 16,* 561–581.

Reynolds, C.R. (1981). The neuropsychological basis of intelligence. In G. Hynd & J. Obrzut (Eds.), *Neuropsychological assessment of the school aged child: Issues and procedures.* New York: Grune & Stratton.

Reynolds, C.R., Kamphaus, R.W., Rosenthal, B.L., & Hiemenz, J.R. (1997). Applications of the Kaufman Assessment Battery for Children (K-ABC) in Neuropsychological Assessment. In C.R. Reynolds & E. Fletcher-Janzen (Eds.), *Handbook of Clinical Child Neuropsychology* (2nd ed.). New York: Plenum.

Riklan, M., & Levita, E. (1965). Laterality of subcortical involvement and psychological functions. *Psychological Bulletin, 64,* 217–224.

Sandel, A., & Alcorn, J. (1980). Individual hemispherity and maladaptive behaviors. *Journal of Abnormal Psychology, 9,* 514–517.

Von Bonin, G. (1962). Anatomical asymmetries of the cerebral hemispheres. In V.B. Mountcastle (Ed.), *Interhemispheric relations and cerebral dominance* (pp. 1–6). Baltimore, MD: Johns Hopkins Press.

See also **Aphasia; Brain Organization; Cerebral Dominance; Cerebral Function**

CENTRAL PROCESSING DYSFUNCTIONS IN CHILDREN

The world is a colorful, noisy, and interesting place. To learn and respond to the world around them, infants, children, adolescents, and adults receive information about their world through the senses of vision, hearing, smell, touch, and bodily movement.

When the brain does not function properly in receiving, analyzing, and storing sensory information or sending messages to the bodily parts, a dysfunction is said to exist. Because the brain is part of the central nervous system, which processes sensory information, a breakdown in this system is often referred to as a central processing dysfunction.

Central processing dysfunctions can be caused by damage to the brain, but brain damage is not always the cause. There are many cases in which individuals behave as if they had a central processing dysfunction, but show no evidence of brain damage. All of the causes of central processing dysfunctions are not yet known.

With visual processing dysfunctions, a student may have normal visual acuity but have difficulty processing and obtaining meaning from visual information. Some of the major characteristics of visual processing dysfunctions are difficulty in (1) attending to or focusing on what is seen; (2) seeing the difference between printed numbers, letters, and words; (3) learning spatial relationships such as left-right, up-down, far-near; (4) distinguishing a figure or object from the background within which it is embedded; (5) reorganizing a whole when one or more of its parts are missing, as in constructing a puzzle; (6) remembering what has been seen; and (7) responding quickly to visual stimuli. Visual processing dysfunctions may result in academic learning disabilities in reading, writing, and arithmetic (Kirk & Chalfant, 1984).

In auditory processing dysfunctions, a student may have normal hearing, but have difficulty in processing what is heard. Auditory processing dysfunctions are characterized by difficulty in (1) listening or attending to sound; (2) locating the origin or source of sound; (3) hearing the differences or similarities between pitch, loudness, rhythm, melody, rate, or duration of sounds; (4) listening to a teacher's instructions (figure) through the interferences of classroom noises (background); (5) reorganizing a spoken word when only part of the word is heard, e.g., telepho—; (6) remembering what has been heard; and (7) associating sounds to experiences such as "ding-dong" to a bell. Dysfunctions in auditory processing may result in learning disabilities in understanding spoken language, expressing oneself through oral language, forming concepts, and developing abstract thinking skills (Kirk & Chalfant, 1984).

In the haptic processing system, the term haptic processing refers to the information received from both touch and movement. Dysfunctions in the haptic system will result in difficulty in performing fine motor tasks such as writing, manipulating tools and equipment, or learning motor performance skills.

In summary, central processing dysfunctions can have a wide range of impact on a child or student. Young children often will be delayed in developing an understanding of and the use of oral language, visual-motor coordination, and/or cognitive abilities such as attention, discrimination, memory, conceptualization, and problem-solving skills. Students of school age may present academic disabilities in reading, writing, spelling, or arithmetic.

REFERENCE

Kirk, S.A., & Chalfant, J.C. (1984). *Academic and developmental learning disabilities.* Denver: Love.

See also **Brain Damage; Learning Disabilities; Learning Styles**

CENTRAL TENDENCY

Measures of central tendency are used to describe the typical or average score in a sample or population of scores. Many measures of central tendency exist, but the three most popularly used in the behavioral sciences are the mean, the median, and the mode.

The mean is the most widely used measure of central tendency. It is the arithmetic average of a given set of scores.

The median of a set of scores is the score that divides the set into two groups with each group containing the same number of scores. To compute the median, first rank the set of scores from smallest to largest. When the number of scores is odd and there are no ties, the median is the middle score. For example, the median of the above scores is 110. When the number of scores is even, with no ties, the median is the average of the two middle scores. Thus, the median score of 87, 96, 98, 110, 113, 114, 119, 120 is 110 + 113/2 = 111.50.

The mode is the score that occurs most frequently in a set of scores. For the scores 87, 96, 98, 98, 98, 110, 113, 114, 119, the mode is 98. When there are two modes, the distribution of scores is said to be bimodal. All three measures may be used when the data are quantitative. The median and mode are used with ranked data, whereas only the mode is applicable to nominal data.

The mean is the preferred measure of central tendency when the variable measured is quantitative and the distribution is relatively symmetric. It is relatively stable and reflects the value of every score in the distribution and, unlike the median and the mode, it is amenable to arithmetic and algebraic manipulations. These qualities make the mean useful not only for describing the average of a set of scores, but also for making inferences about population means.

For skewed distributions, the median is used. This is because the median is not affected by the scores falling above and below it. When the distribution is symmetric and unimodal, the median, mean, and mode are the same. When the distribution is skewed, however, the median and mean are unequal with median > mean in negatively skewed distributions and mean > median in positively skewed distributions.

See also **Standard Deviation**

CEREBELLAR DISORDERS

The cerebellum is an oval-shaped portion of the brain under the occipital lobe of the cerebrum and behind the brain stem. It has a right and left hemisphere and a central section. The cerebellum integrates information vital to the control of posture and voluntary movement. The cerebellum is responsible for maintaining equilibrium and trunk balance; regulating muscle tension, spinal nerve reflexes, posture, and balance of the limbs; and regulating fine movements initiated by the frontal lobes.

Persons with cerebellar dysfunction may show any or all of the following deficits: wide-based clumsy gait; tremor on attempted motion; clumsy, rapid alternating movements; inability to control the range of voluntary movements with overshooting the goal most common; low muscle tone; and scanning speech with inappropriate accenting of syllables. Rapid alternating eye movements (nystagmus) may be observed as a component of closely associated vestibular involvement.

Tumors of the cerebellum, heavy metal poisoning, repeated high fever or head trauma, and hypothyroidism can affect the cerebellum directly. Since the cerebellum receives postural and movement information from many parts of the brain, integrates them and sends information out to motor coordinating areas, the function of the cerebellum may be impaired by a wide range of neurological conditions. Multiple sclerosis, blood clots, and congenital anomalies of other parts of the brain can influence the cerebellum via input/output tracts as well. The spinocerebellar diseases are a family of degenerative hereditary diseases that affect (to varying degrees) the cerebellum, spinal cord, brain stem, and other parts of the nervous system. Most of these diseases have their onset in childhood, are slowly progressive, and have no known specific inheritance patterns, cause, or treatment, although in some individual family studies clinical findings and inheritance patterns are consistent. It is believed that inherited biochemical abnormalities are causal, and some have been identified. Some diseases in this category with early onset, rapid progression, and strong familial tendencies are Marie's ataxia, Roussy-Levy syndrome, and Friedreich's ataxia. Although progression results in clumsiness, poor balance, later use of a wheelchair for safety, slurred speech, and loss of skilled hand function, there is usually no related impairment to intelligence.

Dr. John C. Eccles (1973), a recognized authority on the cerebellum, believes that the relative simplicity of neuronal design, together with its well-defined action in control of movement, will result in the cerebellum becoming one of the first parts of the brain where linkage between structure and function can be documented. The rapid growth of specific knowledge about cerebellar diseases suggests that differential diagnosis by a skilled neurologist together with genetic studies when indicated are imperative in children with cerebellar disorders, as there are treatable conditions that may present symptoms similar to the degenerative disorders.

REFERENCE

Eccles, J.C. (1973). *The understanding of the brain.* New York: McGraw-Hill.

See also **Ataxia; Brain Organization; Friedreich's Ataxia**

CEREBRAL DOMINANCE

Cerebral dominance refers to the asymmetrical lateralization of language and perceptual functions in the human brain. Cerebral dominance, or hemispheric specialization, was initially applied to language functions that are served by the left hemisphere in most individuals. However, the term was later expanded to include cognitive functions of nonverbal reasoning and visual-spatial information processing that are associated with the right hemisphere. In short, functions associated with the left hemisphere involve processing linguistic, analytical, and sequential information while the right hemisphere is responsible for processing nonlinguistic or spatial information in a holistic fashion (see Witelson, 1976).

Research using direct electric stimulation of the brain was pioneered by Penfield (Penfield & Roberts, 1959). This technique was developed to map the centers of the brain that controlled specific functions prior to surgical procedures. Since the brain does not contain pain receptors, the patient was conscious when a small electrical current was applied to the surface of the brain to determine areas of the brain associated with such functions as vision, hearing, olfaction, or haptic sensations. Applications of electrical stimulation to areas believed to control speech would be verified by the patient's inability to talk. These "aphasic arrests" would occur only when areas of the brain associated with speech were electrically stimulated. In this way, hypotheses about other functions of the brain could also be verified if responses associated with those functions were absent during stimulation.

Another invasive technique to study brain functioning has been to anesthetize one hemisphere by injecting sodium amytal in the carotid artery located on either the right or left side of the patient's neck. This procedure, known as the Wada test, quickly anesthetized that side of the brain. For example, if the left side or the side dominant for language was infused, the individual would become speechless while the drug was in effect, while the functions of the right hemisphere would remain intact. Wada and Rasmussen (1960) hypothesized that the left hemisphere is dominant for processing verbal information and the right hemisphere for nonverbal information. To demonstrate this, Wada and his associate injected sodium amytal into the left hemisphere and asked the patient to sing "Happy Birthday"; the patient was able to hum the tune without producing the words. When the right hemisphere was anesthetized and the patient was required to perform the same task, the patient was only able to recite the words of "Happy Birthday" in a monotone without producing a tune. Using this procedure, Milner (1974) found that 95% of right-handed and 70% of left-handed individuals are left hemisphere dominant for language.

Split-brain surgery or commissurotomy is another invasive technique used to study cerebral dominance. A commissurotomy is a surgical procedure used to stop the spread of seizure activity from a focal point in one hemisphere to the other hemisphere via the corpus callosum. This procedure involves the severing of the corpus callosum, a large band of nerve fibers that connects the left and right hemispheres, thereby preventing any communication between the hemispheres.

Much research was conducted by Speery in the 1950s. Researchers were able to localize functions of language, motoric control of the same or opposite sides of the body, and visual discrimination (Hacaen, 1981). In one study that examined visual perception, Levy and her associates (Levy, Trevarthen, & Speery, 1972) used stimulus figures in which the left half of one face was joined with the right half of another. The patient was required to gaze at a dot on the center of the screen before a figure was flashed on the screen. The presentation was such that each half of the face would be projected to only one hemisphere. When the patient was asked to respond by pointing to the correct picture from available alternatives, the left sides of faces, which are processed by the right hemisphere, were correctly chosen more often than the right sides regardless of the hand used for pointing. However, when the patient was required to verbally identify the picture, the face on the right side (left hemisphere) was chosen, although the number of errors made by this response mode was much higher. These results were subsequently replicated using other stimuli, suggesting that the right hemisphere is superior in processing nonverbal visual stimuli.

A noninvasive technique in the study of brain-behavior relationships has been dichotic listening. This procedure involves the simultaneous presentation of verbal or nonverbal information to each ear. Similar but different information is presented to each ear and the subject's task is to identify or recall what was heard. This technique was initially developed by Broadbent (1954) to study auditory attention and later adapted by Kimura (1961) to study cerebral lateralization. Studying normal individuals, Kimura found that subjects were more able to identify correctly verbal information when it was presented to the right ear (left hemisphere). If the information was nonverbal, however, a left-ear advantage (right hemisphere) was found. Kimura also showed that if patients having neurological disorders were found to be left hemisphere dominant for language (via the Wada test), a right-ear advantage was noted for verbal information. Similarly, if the patient was right hemisphere dominant for language, a left-ear advantage (right hemisphere) was found for verbal information. These findings suggested that superiority for each ear varies with the specialization in function for the opposite hemisphere.

Studies that have examined language lateralization for dyslexic children using a dichotic listening paradigm have found mixed results. Dyslexic or reading-disabled children are usually characterized by a two-year lag in reading achievement despite average intelligence and an absence of any sensory-motor, neurological or emotional difficulties (Hynd & Cohen, 1983). Some studies (e.g., Witelson & Rabinovitch, 1972) have reported that dyslexic children show a left-ear advantage for verbal information. Other researchers (e.g., Leong, 1976) have demonstrated a right-ear advantage for verbal information for both dyslexic and normal readers. Differential findings may be partially due to differences in methodology and criteria of subject selection.

Another noninvasive technique in studying cerebral dominance has been split-visual field research. This involves a tachistoscopic presentation of verbal or spatial information to either the right-half or left-half visual fields. The visual pathways are such that information perceived in the left-visual field is processed by the right hemisphere while right-visual field information is processed by the left hemisphere. Studies have demonstrated that while word recognition levels were lower for the dyslexic children when compared with normal readers, both readers showed a right-visual field superiority for words (Marcel & Rajan, 1975). However, when pictures were presented to either visual field, Witelson (1976) reported that while normal readers had a significant left visual-field advantage, this difference was not significant for a dyslexic group. These results suggest that while dyslexic readers, like normal readers, have a left-hemisphere representation for language, the dyslexic group appears to lack right-hemisphere specialization for visual-spatial information.

In sum invasive and noninvasive techniques have made significant contributions in mapping functions of the brain. However, our knowledge of hemispheric specializations is far from complete. Given the inter-individual differences in cognitive processing, the brain's ability to compensate for damage, and developmental factors, the assessment of hemispheric specializations remains a complex and sometimes chaotic (Reynolds, Kamphaus, Rosenthal, & Hiemenz, 1997) endeavor.

REFERENCES

Broadbent, D.E. (1954). The role of auditory localization in attention and memory. *Journal of Experimental Psychology, 47,* 191–196.

Hacaen, H. (1981). Apraxias. In S.B. Filskov & T.J. Boll (Eds.), *Handbook of clinical neuropsychology.* New York: Wiley.

Hynd, G., & Cohen, M. (1983). *Dyslexia: Neuropsychological theory, research, and clinical differentiation.* New York: Grune & Stratton.

Jackson, J.H. (1874). On the duality of the brain. *Medical Press Circulator, 1,* 19, 41, 63.

Kimura, D. (1961). Cerebral dominance and the perception of verbal stimuli. *Canadian Journal of Psychology, 15,* 166–171.

Leong, C.K. (1976). Lateralization in severely disabled readers in relation to functional cerebral development and synthesis of information. In R.M. Knights & D.J. Bakker (Eds.), *Neuropsychology of learning disorders: Theoretical approaches.* Baltimore, MD: University Park Press.

Levy, J., Trevarthen, C., & Speery, R.W. (1972). Perception of bilateral chimeric figures following hemispheric disconnection. *Brain, 95,* 61–78.

Marcel, T., & Rajan, P. (1975). Lateral specialization of recognition of words and faces in good and poor readers. *Neuropsychologia, 13,* 489–497.

Milner, B. (1974). Hemispheric specialization scope and limits. In F.O. Schmitt & F.G. Warden (Eds.), *The neurosciences: Third study programme.* Cambridge, MA: MIT Press.

Penfield, W., & Roberts, L. (1959). *Speech and brain mechanisms.* Princeton, NJ: Princeton University Press.

Reynolds, C.R., Kamphaus, K.W., Rosenthal, B.L., & Hiemenz, J.R. (1997). Applications of the Kaufman Assessment Battery for Children in neuropsychological assessment. In C.R. Reynolds & E. Fletcher-Janzen (Eds.), *Handbook of Clinical Child Neuropsychology* (2nd ed.). New York: Plenum.

Wada, J.A., & Rasmussen, T. (1960). Intracarotid injection of sodium amytal for lateralization of cerebral speech dominance: Experimental and clinical observations. *Journal of Neurosurgery, 17,* 266–282.

Witelson, S.F. (1976). Abnormal right hemisphere specialization in developmental dyslexia. In R.M. Knights & D.F. Bakker (Eds.), *Neuropsychology of learning disorders: Theoretical approaches.* Baltimore, MD: University Park Press.

Witelson, S.F. & Rabinovitch, M.S. (1972). Hemispheric speech lateralization in children with auditory-linguistic deficits. *Cortex 8,* 412–426.

See also **Central Nervous System**

CEREBRAL FUNCTION, LATERALIZATION OF

The human brain is divided longitudinally into two distinct hemispheres. Research over the past century has confirmed early speculations that each of these cerebral hemispheres serve specialized functions (Dean, 1984). Although anatomical differences have been identified between hemispheres at birth, more complex patterns of functional specialization may well continue to develop throughout childhood (Dean, 1985).

Hemispheric lateralization has been argued to be an interactive process in which the mode is dependent on the degree of cognitive reformulation, constraints of attention, and actual hemispheric differences in function (Dean, 1984; Gordon, 1974; Kinsbourne, 1997; Paivio; 1971). It has been suggested that normal individuals can employ different strategies that make differential use of one hemisphere or the other regardless of the form of the original stimulus (Dean, 1984). Clearly, information presented in a visual fashion may be encoded almost entirely in semantic terms (Conrad, 1964). So, too, it has been shown that verbal stimuli may be encoded and recalled as visual memory traces (Bower, 1970; Dean, 1983). As Dean (1984) points out,

"even young learners can generate visual or verbal encoding strategies which correspond to hemispheric specific abilities regardless of the form of the original stimulus array" (p. 249). This point of view acknowledges independent cognitive processes served by each hemisphere while it stresses the importance of interhemispheric communication. It seems, therefore, that the verbal-nonverbal or left-right hemispheric differences may well be an exaggeration of reality. That is, cerebral lateralization may be more heuristically attributed to modes of processing information than to lateralization for specific stimuli. Therefore, the total task demands for the process of a given bit of information are necessary prior to assuming hemispheric lateralization.

The lateralization of functions is dependent in part on the degree to which cognitive processing is necessary for interpretation and encoding (e.g., Gordon, 1974). Indeed, few differences have been found between hemispheres for lower level information processing. For example, in the discrimination of sensory elements such as brightness, color, pressure, sharpness, pitch, and contour, little lateralization exists in processing (e.g., Dean, 1984; Rabinowicz, 1976). However, when learners are required to form generalizations, categorize, reorder, or integrate, or when they are called on to abstract common elements, clear hemispheric differences emerge. As would be expected, cerebral lateralization is dependent on the amount of interpretation or prior knowledge that the subject must draw on in dealing with the incoming information. Such cognitive processing enhances the degree to which functionally lateralized abilities are relied on (e.g., Moscovitch, 1979).

Although less than complete agreement exists among neuroscientists, it would seem that functional lateralization of cerebral hemispheres of the brain corresponds to the developmental pattern of consolidation that occurs from birth and progresses through adolescence (Dean, 1985). Dean (1984) argues that the rate of lateralization in the child varies with the specific function being examined. In keeping with this hypothesis, Krashen (1973) has offered data favoring a progressive decrease in the role played by the right cerebral hemisphere in verbal-analytic tasks with the child's increasing neurological development. The progressive lateralization of cerebral functions seems concomitant with the rate and variable progression in the maturation of the commissure-association cortex (Sperry, 1969).

Gender differences have been reported for the lateralization of cerebral functions. The force of the data in this area suggests less secure hemispheric specialization for females than for males (e.g., Witelson, 1976). Although anatomical gender differences exist (e.g., MacLusky & Naftolin, 1981), the functional differences found for males and females seem more heuristically attributed to organizational factors than differences in structure (e.g., Kolata, 1979). A convincing argument may be made for a genetic-hormonal cultural locus for observed gender differences (Dean, 1984).

In sum, the functioning of the left hemisphere seems predisposed to process information in a sequential, temporal, or analytic fashion; as such, language is an excellent tool for such forms of cognition. The right hemisphere, in contrast, is best prepared to function in a more simultaneous, holistic, or nonverbal fashion, with spatial reasoning and imagery being the most consistently reported mode of thought. This pattern corresponds with a large body of research in both cognitive psychology and the neurosciences. A good deal of interhemispheric communication should be recognized and functional lateralization is exhibited only as the individual must employ higher order cognitive skills in an attempt to comprehend or learn the incoming information.

REFERENCES

Bower, G.H. (1970). Analysis of a mnemonic device. *American Scientist, 58,* 496–510.

Conrad, R. (1964). Accoustic confusions in immediate memory. *British Journal of Psychology, 55,* 75–83.

Dean, R.S. (1983, Feb.). *Dual processing of prose and cerebral laterality.* Paper presented at the annual meeting of the International Neuropsychological Society, Mexico City, Mexico.

Dean, R.S. (1984). Functional lateralization of the brain. *Journal of Special Education, 18*(3), 239–256.

Dean, R.S. (1985). Foundation and rationale for neuropsychological bases of individual differences. In L.C. Hartlage & C.F. Telzrow (Eds.), *The neuropsychology of individual differences: A developmental perspective.* New York: Plenum.

Gordon, H.W. (1974). Auditory specialization of the right and left hemispheres. In M. Kinsbourne & W.L. Smith (Eds.), *Hemispheric disconnection and cerebral function.* Springfield, IL: Thomas.

Kinsbourne, M. (1975). Cerebral dominance, learning, and cognition. In H.R. Myklebust (Ed.), *Progress in learning disabilities.* New York: Grune & Stratton.

Kolata, G.B. (1979). Sex hormones and brain development. *Science, 205,* 985–987.

Krashen, S.D. (1973). Lateralization, language learning, and the critical period: Some new evidence. *Language Learning, 23,* 63–74.

MacLusky, N.J., & Naftolin, F. (1981). Sexual differentiation of the central nervous system. *Science, 211,* 1294–1302.

Moscovitch, M. (1979). Information processing and the cerebral hemispheres. In M.S. Gazzaniga (Ed.), *Handbook of behavioral neurobiology, Vol. 2: Neuropsychology.* New York: Plenum.

Paivio, A. (1971). *Imagery and verbal processes.* New York: Holt, Rinehart, & Winston.

Rabinowicz, B.H. (1976). *A non-lateralized auditory process in speech perception.* Unpublished master's thesis, University of Toronto.

Sperry, R.W. (1969). A modified concept of consciousness. *Psychological Review, 76,* 532–536.

Witelson, S.F. (1976). Early hemisphere specialization and interhemisphere plasticity: An empirical and theoretical review. In S. Segalowitz & F. Gruber (Eds.), *Language and development and neurologic theory.* New York: Academic.

See also **Hemispheric Asymmetry; Hemispheric Functions; Laterality; Neuropsychology**

CEREBRAL INFARCTION

Cerebral infarction refers to the death of brain tissues resulting from a sudden onset of a circulation disorder that often leads to a neurological deficit. Infarction is caused by conditions of anoxia, hypoglycemia, or ischemia (Toole, 1984; Toole & Patel, 1974). Anoxic infarction results from a lack of oxygen to the brain, whereas hypoglycemic infarction occurs when an insufficient level of blood glucose exists for a prolonged period of time despite normal circulation. The most prevalent of the infarctions, however, is ischemic infarction, which results from a sudden interruption of blood supply owed to an obstruction in an artery. Cerebral infarction can occur in any of the cerebral blood vessels of the carotid (anterior portion of the brain) or vertebral basilar (posterior portion of the brain) systems. It may be confused with symptomology resulting from cerebral hemorrhage, tumor, or other space-occupying lesions.

Medical therapy usually involves a regimen of drugs that have the properties of inhibiting the formation or aggregation of red blood cells and the narrowing of arteries. Such drugs consist of aspirin, Anturane, Persantine, and Conmadin (Lubic & Palkovitz, 1979).

REFERENCES

Lubic, L.G., & Palkovitz, H.P. (1979). *Discussions in patient management: Stroke.* New York: Medical Examination.

Toole, J.F. (1984). *Cerebrovascular disorders* (3rd ed.). New York: Raven.

Toole, J.F., & Patel, A.N. (1974). *Cerebrovascular disorders* (2nd ed.). New York: McGraw-Hill.

See also **Anoxia**

CEREBRAL LESION, CHRONIC

A chronic cerebral lesion is one that has been in existence beyond what might be considered to be the amount of time required for recovery of lost function.

Chronic cerebral lesions, much like acute cerebral lesions, are likely to influence behavior in ways related to their location and extent or size. Unlike acute cerebral lesions, however, chronic cerebral lesions may have greater effects on behavior than effects related to their location and extent. Increased effects on behavior can result from two conditions. The primary behavioral loss can be due to the interruption of developmental schemata, whereby a child who sustains a chronic cerebral lesion at an early age may be precluded from development of the normal repertoire of behaviors dependent on the integrity of the area of lesion. Since the normal sequence of ontogenetic recapitulation of phylogenetic phenomena is interrupted, not only is there limitation of the behavior dependent on the specific area of cerebral tissue that sustains a lesion, but also of the subsequent behaviors dependent on the development of that initial behavior. The secondary loss from a chronic cerebral lesion results from a disuse atrophy phenomenon, whereby deterioration of muscle tissue or degeneration of neuro-transmitter receptor sites, resulting secondary to the lesion, inhibits the development, performance, or acquisition of given behavioral skills.

Although chronic cerebral lesions can have onset at any age, many such lesions of congenital or prenatal onset result in death or profound developmental handicap. Onset age appears to be related to the severity of the handicap imposed by the lesion. Although it has been traditional to believe that the effects of chronic brain lesions are less severe in children because of presumed greater plasticity in the organization of their central nervous systems (Lyons & Matheny, 1984), there is accumulating evidence that a chronic cerebral lesion acquired early in childhood may have more severely debilitating effects (Cermak, 1985; Levin, Benton, & Grossman, 1982). There is also evidence that such lesions limit the development of memory and intellectual ability to a greater extent with early age onset than with later age onset (Levin, Eisenberg, Wigg, & Kobayashi, 1982). Further, there is evidence to suggest a greater likelihood of emotional problems resulting from chronic cerebral lesions at an early age (Rutter, 1981). These problems may interact with cognitive problems, depending on the age at which the lesion was acquired (Lyons & Matheny, 1984). The selective results of unilateral cerebral lesions on such specific aspects of behavior as language development, previously thought to be less specific when acquired at an early age, have been found to be similar in early childhood onset to those of later age onset (Aram et al., 1985). Even for those children who appear to show good recovery from early onset chronic cerebral lesions, there is a strong likelihood that special educational placement may be necessary (Lehr, 1984). The etiology of the chronic cerebral lesion, whether from head injury, brain tumor, or radiation therapy, appears to be unrelated to the neuropsychological outcome (Bruce, 1982).

REFERENCES

Aram, D.M., Ekelman, B.L., Rose, D.F., & Whitaker, H.A. (1985). Verbal and cognitive sequelae following unilateral lesions acquired in early childhood. *Journal of Clinical and Experimental Neuropsychology, 7,* 55–78.

Bruce, D.A. (1982). Comment. *Neurosurgery, 11,* 672–673.

Cermak, L.A. (1985, Feb.). The effects of age at onset and causal agent of brain injury on later adaptive functioning in children. Paper presented at the International Neuropsychological Society, San Diego. Abstract in *Proceedings* (p. 10).

Lehr, E. (1984, August). Good recovery from severe head injury in children and adolescents. Paper presented at American Psychological Association meeting, Toronto, Ontario.

Levin, H.S., Benton, A.L., & Grossman, R.G. (1982). *Neurobehavioral consequences of closed head injury.* New York: Oxford University Press.

Levin, H.S., Eisenberg, H.M., Wigg, N.R., & Kobayashi, K. (1982). Memory and intellectual ability after head injury in children and adolescents. *Neurosurgery, 11,* 668–672.

Lyons, M.J., & Matheny, A.P. (1984). Cognitive and personality differences between identical twins following skull fracture. *Journal of Pediatric Psychology, 9,* 485–494.

Rutter, M. (1981). Psychological sequelae of brain damage in children. *American Journal of Psychiatry, 138,* 1533–1544.

See also **Birth Injuries; Brain Damage; Cerebral Infarction; Head Injury**

CEREBRAL PALSY (CP)

Cerebral palsy (CP), sometimes called congenital spastic paralysis, is characterized by varying degrees of disturbance of voluntary movements caused by damage to the brain. Cerebral refers to the brain and palsy refers to weakness or lack of control. Cerebral palsy was originally called Little's disease after the English surgeon William John Little, who first described it. Later, Winthrop Phelps, an orthopedic surgeon, coined the term cerebral palsy and brought it into common usage as a result of his extensive work with this population in the United States.

There is agreement among experts in the field that cerebral palsy is a complex of characteristics attributed to brain injury. It has been defined by the United Cerebral Palsy Research and Educational Foundation as having the following elements: (1) being caused by injury to the brain; (2) causing motor disturbance, including paralysis, weakness, and uncoordination; (3) consisting of a cluster of symptoms; (4) usually originating in childhood; and (5) perhaps including learning difficulties, psychological problems, sensory defects, convulsions, and behavioral disorders of organic origin. In addition to these elements, cerebral palsy is nonprogressive, static, and unamenable to treatment.

There are two major types of CP: spastic, characterized by sudden, violent, involuntary muscular contractions, and athetosic, characterized by ceaseless, involuntary, slow, sinuous, writhing movements. The physical symptoms of CP can be so mild that they are detected only with difficulty, or they can be so profound that the affected individual is almost complete physically incapacitated. It is not unusual for a cerebral palsied individual to function normally intellectually. However, this intelligence is often masked (at least to the lay person) by uncontrolled physical characteristics, involuntary movements of the body and extremities, speech disorders, and drooling. Cerebral palsy is not a disease, and it is not curable.

The incidence of cerebral palsy varies; a conservative estimate of its occurrence is 1.5 to 2.0 cases per 1000 live births. It has been estimated that the incidence may be higher in areas where there is inadequate prenatal care and accompanying prematurity. It is estimated that there are 500,000 children and adolescents with cerebral palsy in the United States (UCP, 1998). While CP occurs at every socioeconomic level, it is more prevalent among lower socioeconomic groups. Children born in poverty situations have a greater chance of incurring brain damage from factors such as malnutrition, poor prenatal and postnatal care, and environmental hazards during infancy. Cerebral palsy occurs slightly more frequently in males than in females, and more white than black children are affected. Cerebral palsy makes up the largest category of physical disabilities, representing 30 to 40% of all children in programs for the physically disabled.

In most cases, cerebral palsy is congenital (approximately 85% of all cases), meaning damage to the brain occurs during pregnancy or at birth. However, infectious diseases or severe head injuries can cause cerebral palsy at any time in life. Postnatal causes are said to be acquired, whereas those present at birth are congenital. It is generally agreed that CP cannot be inherited.

It is estimated that as many as three-quarters of all persons with CP have additional disabilities such as retardation, seizures, auditory and visual handicaps, or communication disorders (UCP, 1998). Approximately 50 to 60% of CP children are retarded. Mental retardation has been difficult to diagnose in the population since intelligence tests were standardized on children with adequate speech, language, and motor abilities. Seizures are associated with approximately 25 to 35% of individuals with cerebral palsy and are much more prevalent with spastic CP persons. Strabismus (squinting) occurs in approximately 30 to 35% of cerebral-palsied individuals. Some athetotic CPs experience farsightedness while spastic CPs are nearsighted. Visual field reduction also can occur in some types of CP (Capute, 1975).

Speech disorders are found in 70% of cerebral-palsied children. It has been reported that speech defects are found in 88% of persons with athetosis, 85% of those with ataxia, and 52% of those who are spastic. Most of the speech problems are caused by problems controlling the muscles used to make speech sounds.

Minear (1965) developed a classification scheme for cerebral-palsied individuals based on motor characteristics as well as the area of the body where the problem is located. The six types within the motor component were adopted by the American Academy for Cerebral Palsy and have been described by others (Bleck, 1975; Denhoff, 1976; Healy, 1983). The six types include spasticity, athetosis, ataxia, rigidity, tremor, and mixed.

Spasticity is the most common type of CP, occurring in approximately 40 to 60% of the total. Stiffness of the muscles in spastic children occurs when the injury is on the brain surface or when it involves those nerves leading from the surface through the substance of the brain and onto the spinal cord. The spastic type is characterized by a loss of voluntary motor control. When the child initiates voluntary movement, it is likely to be jerky, with lack of control in the body extremities. This disability may affect any or all limbs. Involvement in the upper extremities may include varying degrees of flexing of the arms and fingers, depending on the severity of the disability. When lower extremities are involved, there may be a scissoring movement of the legs, caused by muscle contractions.

Athetosis is the second largest group in the CP population, occurring in approximately 15 to 20% of the total. This type is caused by injury to the brain's motor switchboard. Athetoid children are characterized by involuntary jerky, writhing movements, especially in the fingers and wrists. The head is often drawn back with the neck extended and mouth open. There are generally two types of athetosis: tension and nontension. The tension athetoid's muscles are always tense; this reduces contorted movement of limbs. The nontension athetoid has contorted movements without muscle tightness. Unlike the spastic child, all movements cease during sleep. The movements occur only in a conscious state; when emotionality increases, athetosis movements become intensified. Athetoids are usually higher in intelligence than spastic CP victims.

Ataxia is less prevalent than spasticity and athetosis. Together with tremor and rigidity, it makes up approximately 8% of the total CP population. The injury is in the cerebellum. Ataxic children are characterized by a lack of coordination and sense of balance. The eyes are often uncoordinated and the child may stumble and fall frequently.

Rigidity and tremor types of CP are extremely rare. Rigidity is unlike the other types in that the lower level of muscles stiffen and a rigid posture is maintained. The rigid type is usually severely retarded with a high incidence of convulsions. In tremor, there is involuntary movement in one extremity, usually one hand or arm. The motion may vary in its consistency and pattern. In intention tremor, the involuntary movement happens only when the child attempts an activity while in constant tremor. The involuntary movement is continuous.

Mixed is another variation of CP. It is a combination of the other five types with one type predominating. Approximately 30% of individuals with CP have more than one type.

The movement or motor component of the clinical classification system is composed of two types, pyramidal and extrapyramidal. The pyramidal type refers to the spastic cerebral-palsied group because the usual nerve cell involved in this disorder is shaped like a pyramid. Extrapyramidal refers to all other types of CP, athetosis, rigidity, tremor, ataxia, and mixed, in which the area of the brain affected is composed of conglomerates of nerve cells (Capute, 1975).

When planning and implementing educational programs for cerebral-palsied individuals, a cadre of persons working in a multidisciplinary approach must be used. Many educators and physicians (Capute, 1975; Gearheart, 1980; Healy, 1983) have delineated the specific roles of the individuals who must work together in the education of cerebral-palsied children. The degree of CP and physical characteristics will determine the extent of participation by the physician. The physician may prescribe drugs for the patient to relax and to control the convulsions as well as treat overall health problems. Braces and other mechanical devices that provide support and allow children to walk are usually prescribed by medical doctors. The physical therapist works to facilitate motor development, to prevent or slow orthopedic problems, and to improve posture and positioning so that the child may benefit from other intervention activities. The occupational therapist uses creative, educational, and recreational activities to enhance self-help skills and teach parents to handle the child's daily living activities. The speech pathologist will monitor the child's progress in speech and language and provide therapy if the child is able to benefit from it. The speech therapist also may work with parents and other educational personnel on how to stimulate language development. An audiologist, learning disabilities specialist, and teacher of the mentally retarded may be needed to provide some direct and indirect services to the primary teacher when required. Biofeedback clinicians may be useful in teaching the individual what muscle groups are voluntarily effected (UNC, 1998).

A variety of specialized equipment is available to teachers, including adapted typewriters, pencil holders, book holders, page turners, and special desks to make cerebral-palsied individuals more self-sufficient.

The success achieved by the cerebral-palsied child depends largely on the extent of his or her physical and mental disability. While some cerebral-palsied people will need constant care in a protected environment, many can lead relatively normal lives and become productive citizens if given the opportunity.

REFERENCES

Bleck, E.E. (1975). Cerebral palsy. In E.E. Bleck & D.A. Nagel (Eds.), *Physically handicapped children: A Medical atlas for teachers.* New York: Grune & Stratton.

Capute, A.J. (1975). Cerebral palsy and associated dysfunctions. In R.H. Haslam & P.G. Valletutti (Eds.), *Medical problems in the classroom.* Baltimore, MD: University Park Press.

Denhoff, E. (1978). Medical aspects. In W.M. Cruickshank (Ed.), *Cerebral palsy: A developmental disability* (3rd ed.). Syracuse, NY: Syracuse University Press.

Gearheart, B.R. (1980). *Special education for the 80s.* St. Louis: Mosby.

Healy, A. (1983). Cerebral palsy. In J.A. Blackman (Ed.), *Medical aspects of developmental disabilities in children—birth to three.* Iowa City, IA: University of Iowa Press.

Minear, W.L. (1956). A classification of cerebral palsy. *Pediatrics, 18,* 841–852.

United Cerebral Palsy. (1998). *Comments on biofeedback.* www.ucpa.org.

See also **Habilitation of the Handicapped; High Incidence Handicaps Conditions; Multiple Handicapping Conditions; Physical Handicaps; United Cerebral Palsy**

CERTIFICATION/LICENSURE ISSUES

With only a few exceptions, the issues and standards involving special education programs do not differ from those that apply to teacher education programs nationwide. These issues include teacher testing, the use of teaching personnel having college degrees but lacking teacher preparation courses, standards used to approve teacher education programs, and state certification requirements.

A number of states have moved toward, or implemented, the use of tests as part of the certification process.

Some states require a test of basic skills prior to entering a teacher education program (e.g., California, Missouri), while other states require teachers to achieve a passing score on a content area test. It has been suggested that such tests will have a significant impact on the qualifications of individuals desiring to become teachers, particularly minority populations (Feistritzer, 1983). Feistritzer (1983) has suggested that the number of minority candidates entering teacher preparation programs has declined considerably in recent years. The Center for Minority Research in Special Education (COMRISE, 1998) is attempting to increase the number and research capacity of minority scholars in institutions of higher education with high minority enrollments and is trying to improve the quality and effectiveness of these programs.

An issue that has importance to special education is that of appropriate certification in the actual field of teaching. While most teachers are certified to teach in some field, not all teachers have been trained and certified to teach in the field to which they are assigned. For example, large numbers of special education teachers are not certified in special education or are not teaching the types of handicapped children and youths for which they hold a special education certificate. Thus teachers who are qualified to teach non-handicapped children in elementary schools may be teaching learning-disabled, emotionally disturbed, or some other type of handicapped children. While emergency, temporary, or provisional certificates permit regular education teachers to teach handicapped learners, there is some question as to whether this constitutes the most appropriate and effective instruction for these students. An analysis of the changes made in the past twenty years to special education coursework for regular educators seeking recertification shows dramatic advances (Patton & Braithwaite, 1990).

The development of inclusionary education has changed the requirements of teacher preparation from a focus of individual mastery to a consultation/collaboration format. The inclusion of special education students in the regular classroom has mandated teacher preparation to prepare students for collaborative teaching arrangements (Campbell & Fyfe, 1995). Programs that involve students in practicum supervision involving regular-education cooperating teachers, special-education cooperating teachers, and university supervisors are growing in number (Ludlow, Wienke, Henderson, & Klein, 1998). The reflection of educational service delivery trends such as inclusion in teacher preparation, however, is not uniform and assessing competency is difficult at best.

REFERENCES

Campbell, D.M., & Fyfe, B. (1995). *Reforming teacher education: The challenge of inclusive education.* Paper presented at the Annual Meeting of the Association of Independent Liberal Arts Colleges for Teacher Education (Washington, DC, February 12, 1995).

COMRISE. (1998). *Center of Minority Research in Special Education.* Charlottesville, VA: University of Virginia, Curry School of Education.

Feistritzer, C.E. (1983). *The condition of teaching.* Lawrenceville, NJ: Princeton University Press.

Ludlow, B.L., Wienke, W.D., Henderson, J., & Klein, H. (1998). A collaborative program to prepare mainstream teachers: Using peer supervision by general and special educators. In American Council on Rural Special Education Conference Proceedings *Coming together: Preparing for Rural Special Education in the 21st Century.* March 25–28.

Patton, J.M., & Braithwaite, R. (1990). Special education certification/recertification for regular educators. *Journal of Special Education, 24,* 117–124.

See also **Professional Standards for Special Educators; Personnel Training in Special Education**

CHEMICALLY DEPENDENT YOUTHS

Chemically dependent youths are children and adolescents who want and need continued use of a psychoactive substance to sustain or maintain a chronic state of euphoria or intoxication. Alcohol and drug use by young people must be viewed not in isolation but in concert with that period of life known as adolescence. Substance use and addiction have profound effects on development and have serious implications for the future functioning of the abuser (Cohen, 1983).

Two types of chemical dependency occur, physical and psychological. Some substances induce tolerance and create a physical craving and addiction cycle, whereas others create a psychological dependency in which the user experiences changes in mood. Further, some compounds create both a physical and psychological dependency. In the latter case, chemically dependent youths may undergo detoxification to treat the physical craving and resultant withdrawal symptoms, but may continue to experience a craving or felt need to use again. This process sets up a cycle of dependency, detoxification, and return to use that accounts for the recidivism rate among addicted youths.

Psychological dependence is characterized by a drive to continue taking a drug when the user feels the effects of the drug are needed to maintain his or her sense of well being at an optimal level. The complex interaction of drug effects, personality, and stage of development constitute the degree of psychic craving or compulsion the user may experience. Drug-seeking behavior or compulsive drug use develops when the user comes to believe that the drug can produce pleasure and deter discomfort such that continuous or periodic administration of the drug is required. This mental state is the most powerful of all the factors involved in chronic intoxication with psychoactive drugs (Adesso, 1985).

Physiological dependence is characterized by reliance of body tissue on the continued presence of a drug within the user's system. Its presence is unknown to the user as long as the drug continues to be taken and is of no immediate consequence until the drug is withdrawn or no longer available. The magnitude of the dependence and the severity of the withdrawal symptoms vary directly with the type, amount, frequency, and duration of the drug use. Physiological dependence manifests itself as severe and immediate physical pain and discomfort, commonly referred to as withdrawal symptoms or abstinence syndrome. Symptoms may include fever, chills, gastrointestinal cramps, watery eyes, runny nose, and muscle cramping or spasms. They are frequently accompanied by psychological dependence. For drugs like alcohol, barbiturates, narcotic analgesics (morphine, Percodan, heroin) and cocaine, withdrawal symptoms and accompanying psychological dependence are so uncomfortable and threatening that they motivate young drug users to continue to seek and administer the drug. For drugs like stimulants (speed), and to a lesser degree marijuana and hallucinogenics (LSD, mescaline, psilocybin, peyote), the primary disturbance is psychological rather than physiological. But it should be noted that although the symptoms are not as severe as with physiological withdrawal, the user does experience discomfort of a mental or emotional nature (Bardo & Risner, 1985).

A single episode of intoxication does not produce either physical or psychological dependency. Several stages occur in the move from no use to dependency. The initial reason to try any drug depends more on the value the youth places on its use than on its pharmacological properties. Curiosity and availability, key factors at this stage, are influenced by the social factors of peer pressure and acceptance, adult role models, and family norms or values. Adolescents with learning disabilities are at particularly high risk for chemical dependency (Karacostas & Fisher, 1993). The majority of youthful experimenters do not proceed through all stages to dependence because of the drug effects themselves not being valued and the fact that most peer-group norms do not support continued use (Kandel et al., 1978).

Experimental use may proceed to casual or occasional use, frequently referred to as socio-recreational use. This pattern usually involves imitation of adult role models who drink during social gatherings or use other drugs as mood enhancers. The youthful user may use drugs while at a party once or twice a month, or while attending a movie or listening to music with friends. Such use tends to be spontaneous and in a social context where drugs are readily available. Reasons for use are primarily social in that friends use and approve of use. Also, the drugs enhance self-confidence and social interaction during the identity phase of adolescence. The youthful user does not avidly seek drugs at this stage but will participate with a group if drugs are available.

The third stage, regular use, is distinguished from sociorecreational use by several features. The user at this stage actively seeks drugs, and is rarely seen in a social context without being intoxicated. Psychological dependence occurs. The user perceives that he or she functions better in social gatherings while intoxicated. Regular use also may involve physiological dependence if the user develops tolerance to a drug and experiences physical discomfort with cessation. The pharmacological properties of the drug become critical at this point. Whether the user proceeds into the final stage, dependency, is partly a function of what the drug does for the user's personality and the user's stage in adolescence.

The final stage is physical and/or psychological reliance on the drug to produce the user's desired effect. Heavy or compulsive use implies daily intoxication, although the user may indulge in binge-type use. Although only a minority of users become chemically dependent youths, the central factor is the degree to which use dominates the life of the adolescent. Intoxication may avoid other critical issues of adolescence (e.g., responsibilities of school and family, stress, lack of self-confidence) or mask the pain and discomfort of other pathological personality or mental disorders. Psychological and physical dependence are critical at this stage because regardless of reasons for continued use, the youthful user will have to continue to take the drug in order to avoid the newly acquired set of symptoms and difficulties associated with chemical dependency (Kandel, 1984). Although chemical dependency is not an official handicapping condition under federal legislation, it has been considered (Williams, 1990), and specialized programs for individuals with disabilities have been developed (Campbell, 1994).

REFERENCES

Adesso, V.J. (1985). Cognitive factors in alcohol and drug use. In M. Galizio & S.A. Maisto (Eds.), *Determinants of substance abuse* (pp. 179–208). New York: Plenum.

Bardo, M.T., Risner, M.E. (1985). Biochemical substrates of drug abuse. In M. Galizio & S.A. Maisto (Eds.), *Determinants of substance abuse* (pp. 65–99). New York: Plenum.

Campbell, J. (1994). Issues in Chemical dependency treatment and aftercare for people with learning differences. (1994). *Health and Social Work, 19,* 1, 63–70.

Cohen, S. (1983). *The alcoholism problems.* New York: Haworth.

Kandel, D.B., Kessler, R.C., & Margulies, R. (1978). Adolescent initiation into stages of drug use: A developmental analysis. In D.B. Kandel (Ed.), *Longitudinal research in drug use: Empirical findings and methodological issues* (pp. 73–99). Washington, DC: Hemisphere.

Karacostas, D.D., & Fisher, G.L. (1993). Chemical dependency in students with and without hearing disabilities. *Journal of hearing Disabilities, 26,* 491–495.

See also **Alcohol and Drug Abuse Patterns; Drug Abuse; Substance Abuse**

CHEMOTHERAPY

The treatment of cancer in children usually includes chemotherapy, which consists of drugs that are administered to the child intravenously, intramuscularly, or orally on a repeated schedule (e.g., every 10 days or every month). The purpose of chemotherapy is to poison the cancer cells. Unfortunately, it also is toxic to healthy cells of the body. As a result, many children receiving chemotherapy experience unpleasant side effects.

Two common side effects of chemotherapy are nausea and vomiting. Children differ in the extent to which they have these symptoms. Furthermore, the degree of nausea and vomiting for a given child may vary widely from one course of chemotherapy to the next, even when there are no changes in chemotherapy. Many children feel intensely ill during the days they receive chemotherapy and for a few days afterward. Other children are able to carry on with play and other normal activities to varying degrees (Zeltzer, LeBaron, & Zeltzer, 1984).

Another possible side effect is a temporary susceptibility to bacterial infection or excessive bleeding. During such a period, physicians usually will advise the child not to participate in any contact sports or activities (e.g., gymnastics) that might increase the risk of bleeding. Because children on chemotherapy also are sometimes at risk for severe illness with certain viral infections, doctors often advise these children to stay home from school for a period of time if there is an outbreak of chicken pox. However, for the majority of time the child is receiving chemotherapy, the doctor usually will permit the child to engage in all normal school activities, including sports.

What are the effects of chemotherapy on the child's behavior and academic performance? Many of these children are absent from school at regular intervals because of medical appointments and chemotherapy side effects. Some children also stay home because of embarrassment over hair loss and fear of being rejected by peers. A further reason for school absence is a fear of failure because of the large amount of school material missed (Deasy-Spinetta, 1981; Deasy-Spinetta & Spinetta, 1980; Katz, Kellerman, Rigler, Williams, & Siegle, 1977).

For some children, radiation to the head produces cognitive deficits, especially when combined with injections of chemotherapy into the spinal canal. Many children with cancer show little or no evidence of cognitive deficits, but these are problems that can occur gradually and may be long-lasting. During the acute phase of radiation therapy, there often is transient swelling of the brain, which could produce additional temporary cognitive deficits.

Educators need to be aware that hospitalization or confinement to bed at home because of nausea and vomiting does not necessarily preclude school work. On the contrary, involvement in school work, at least at a minimal level, can have therapeutic value. By attending school a few hours a day, having a homebound teacher, or doing some school work in the hospital, children can be distracted from unpleasant physical symptoms or worries. Some adolescents who receive chemotherapy in the morning prefer to come to school in the afternoon rather than to spend the rest of the day at home feeling sick. If the student experiences some nausea, he or she may need to leave the class abruptly. If these considerations are discussed in advance, then involvement in school can be therapeutic for the many children and may reduce the severity of nausea and vomiting.

Teachers can be most helpful to children receiving chemotherapy by maintaining a flexible attitude and realistic expectations. Most children receiving chemotherapy can maintain a normal educational load. However, specific expectations regarding homework and exams need to be flexible because of the intermittent nature of treatment-related problems. Frequent consultation with the student and parent will help to define reasonable and appropriate education goals.

REFERENCES

Deasy-Spinetta, P. (1981). The school and the child with cancer. In J.J. Spinetta & P. Deasy-Spinetta (Eds.), *Living with childhood cancer* (pp. 153–168). St. Louis: Mosby.

Deasy-Spinetta, P.M., & Spinetta, J.J. (1980). The child with cancer in school: Teachers' appraisal. *American Journal of Pediatric Hematology/Oncology, 2,* 89–94.

Katz, E.R., Kellerman, J., Rigler, D., Williams, K., & Siegle, S.E. (1977). School intervention with pediatric cancer patients. *Journal of Pediatric Psychology, 2,* 72–76.

Zeltzer, L.K., LeBaron, S., & Zeltzer, P.M. (1984). The adolescent with cancer. In R. Blum (Ed.), *Chronic illness and disabilities in childhood and adolescence* (pp. 375–395). Orlando, FL: Grune & Stratton.

See also **Cancer, Childhood; Homebound Instruction**

CHILD ABUSE

The age-old phenomenon of child maltreatment has only recently attracted the attention of mental health professionals. Psychiatric and psychological exploration of child battering has lagged two decades behind the pioneering efforts of pediatricians and radiologists in establishing medical diagnostic criteria for physical abuse in children. Between 1963 and 1965, the passage of laws by all 50 states requiring medical reporting of child abuse ultimately subjected the abusing parents to legal process; these laws were also the catalyst for the formation of child protective services throughout the nation. The first psychological studies of abusing parents were carried out during this period.

Child abuse is currently regarded as the leading cause of death in children and a major public health problem. The proliferation of child abuse and neglect might bear some relationship to the alarming general increase of violence in our society demonstrated by the rising incidence of violent crimes, delinquency, suicide, and lethal accidents. In the last 20 years, child abuse has become a major focus of research and clinical study. A concerted effort is being made by federal, state, and local governments to develop programs for the study, prevention, and treatment of child abuse.

Child protective services are specialized agencies existing under public welfare auspices; they are responsible for receiving and investigating all reports of child abuse or maltreatment for the purpose of preventing further abuse, providing services necessary to safeguard the child's well-being, and strengthening the family unit. These agencies are responsible for maintaining service until the conditions of maltreatment are remedied. They also have the mandate to invoke the authority of the juvenile or family court to secure the protection and treatment of children whose parents are unable or unwilling to use their services.

The wide variety of behavior and personality traits observed in abusing parents suggests that a specific abusive personality does not exist. Rather, individuals with a certain psychological makeup operating in combination with the burden of a painfully perceived childhood and immediate environmental stress might be likely to abuse the offspring who most readily elicits the unhappy childhood imagery of the past.

The stress argument has at least in part been predicated on the high percentage of low socioeconomic status (SES), multiple problem families in child abuse registers throughout the country. It is probable that reporting procedures themselves have led to the greater emphasis on socioeconomic determinants. Any controlled study that matches for SES is compelled to look beyond such variables as family income for the origins of child abuse. The conclusion that Spinetta and Rigler (1972) reach in their review of the literature is far more likely—that environmental stress is neither necessary nor sufficient for child abuse but that it does, in some instances, interact with other factors such as parent personality variables and child behaviors to potentiate child battering.

Justice and Duncan (1975) described the contribution of work-related pressures to environmental stress in situations of child abuse. They cited four types of work-related situations: unemployed fathers caring for children at home; working mothers with domestic obligations; overworked husbands who neglect their wives; and traumatic job experiences resulting in undischarged tension. Justice and Justice (1979) were able to document the importance of stress in terms of excessive life changes in child-abusing families by means of the *Social Readjustment Rating Scale* developed by Holmes and Rahe (1967).

The greatest area of agreement in the field of child abuse has pertained to the history and background of the abusive parents themselves. These individuals have usually experienced abuse, deprivation, rejection, and inadequate mothering during childhood. As children they were subjected to unrealistic expectations and premature demands by their parents. Parents with these characteristics are said to have "abuse-prone" personality traits.

The psychodynamics in a given case of child abuse are largely determined by the abuse-prone personality traits of the parent. The relationship between the abusing parent and his or her child is distorted by the cumulative impact of the parent's own traumatic experiences as a child reared in a punitive, unloving environment. Individuals who abuse their children cannot envision any parent-child relationship as a mutually gratifying experience. The task of parenting mobilizes identifications with the parent-aggressor, child-victim dyad of the past. The key psychodynamic elements in child abuse are role reversal, excessive use of denial and projection as defenses, rapidly shifting identifications, and displacement of aggression from frustrating objects onto the child.

Role reversal occurs when the unfulfilled abusing parent seeks dependency gratification, which is unavailable from his or her spouse or family, from the "parentified" child. It is based on an identification with the child-victim. The child's inability to gratify the father or mother causes the youngster to be unconsciously perceived as the rejecting mother. This intensifies the parent's feelings of rejection and worthlessness, which further threaten his or her narcissistic equilibrium. These painful feelings are denied and projected onto the child, who then becomes the recipient of the parent's self-directed aggression.

A wide range of psychotherapeutic and educational techniques have proven successful in reducing the symptoms and problems of abused children. In general, these children present with ego deficits and cognitive impairment to such a degree that an emphasis on ego integration, reality testing, containment of drives and impulses, and strengthening of higher level defenses (similar to those techniques applied to borderline and psychotic children) proves necessary.

The ideal objective in studying and treating child abuse on a nationwide scale is, as with any major public health problem, the development of a strategy for prevention. Thus far, early case findings and protective intervention in abusing families have been the primary areas of interest for workers in this field. As more basic knowledge is accumulated about the child-abuse syndrome, through clinical experience and research, one can envision a logical shift in focus from treatment and rehabilitation (secondary prevention) to primary intervention.

REFERENCES

Holmes, T., & Rahe, R. (1967). The social readjustment rating scale. *Journal of Psychosomatic Medicine, 11*, 213–218.

Justice, B., & Duncan, D. (1975). *Child abuse as a work-related problem.* Paper presented at American Public Health Association, Chicago.

Justice, B., & Justice, R. (1979). *The broken taboo: Sex in the family.* New York: Human Science Press.

Spinetta, J., & Rigler, D. (1972). The child abusing parent: A psychological review. *Psychological Bulletin, 77*, 296–304.

See also **Abused Children; Battered Child Syndrome; Child Care Agencies**

CHILD ANXIETY SCALE (CAS)

The Child Anxiety Scale (CAS) is a 20-item self-report inventory of anxiety for young children. The CAS was published in 1980 by the Institute for Personality and Ability Testing.

The norms for the CAS were derived from a standardization study involving 2105 cases (1097 boys and 1008 girls). The test manual does not do an adequate job of describing the standardization sample. The manual also admits that the geographic representation of the sample did not mimic the national population. The authors tested for significant score differences by region by randomly selecting 30 cases from each region and testing for differences with an ANOVA (Analysis of Variance procedure). The results were insignificant but this may be due to a lack of statistical power because of small sample sizes rather than a lack of real differences. The match of the CAS sample to U.S. Census statistics by socioeconomic status or ethnic group is not shown. In light of other evidence, one cannot help but assume that the sample was selected on a convenience basis as much as on the basis of important stratification variables.

Results of a test-retest study were favorable with coefficients ranging from .82 at grade 1 to .92 at grade 3. Estimates of internal consistency were somewhat lower.

A variety of types of validity evidence are reported in the manual. First, the correlations between each of the 20 items and the ESPQ are reported. These range from .17 to .49. In addition, a study was conducted correlating CAS scores with parent mobility but a significant relationship was not found. In addition, the CAS scores of children in single versus dual parent families were compared and no significant differences between the groups were reported. Taken together, the results of these validity studies appear mixed at best and unimpressive at worst.

In summary, as a brief measure of children's anxiety the CAS shows some potential but suffers from problems with a poor standardization sample and poor evidence of validity.

REFERENCE

Gillis, J.S. (1980). *Child Anxiety Scale.* Champaign, IL: Institute for Personality and Ability Testing.

See also **Revised Children's Manifest Anxiety Scale**

CHILD BEHAVIOR CHECKLIST/4–18

The Child Behavior Checklist/4–18 (CBCL; Achenbach, 1991) is a standardized measure designed to elicit information from parents regarding their child's competences and problems. The checklist contains 20 competence items which target domains such as activities, school performance, and ability to establish and maintain friendships. These items yield a standardized T-score (mean of 50 and standard deviation of 10) on three scales: Activities, Social, and School. The remaining 118 problem items are rated on a 3-point Likert scale (not true, sometimes true, very true). These items yield standardized T-scores on 8 syndrome scales (Withdrawn, Somatic Complaints, Anxious/Depressed, Social Problems, Thought Problems, Attention Problems, Delinquent Behavior, and Aggressive Behavior). Combinations of these subsets comprise two other broader indices, Internalizing and Externalizing, as well as an overall Total Problem score.

The CBCL was normed on 2,368 individuals from 4 to 18 years of age, representing 48 states. These individuals were stratified according to socioeconomic status, ethnicity, region, and CBCL respondent. Individuals receiving professional services for behavioral or emotional problems within the year prior to data collection, were excluded.

Detailed reliability and validity data are provided. Test-retest reliability at 7-day and one-year intervals for the competence and problem scales are reported at .87, .89, and .62, .75, respectively. Inter-rater reliability (agreement between mother's and father's ratings) is .75 for the Competence scale and .70 for the Problem scale. Criterion-related validity was established through its ability to discriminate between referred and nonreferred children. Although well-established as an effective clinical and research tool, the author emphasizes that the CBCL's utility is enhanced when used in combination with other measures and clinical observations (Achenbach, 1991; Lowe, 1998).

REFERENCES

Achenbach, T.M. (1991). *Manual for the Child Behavior Checklist/ 4–18 and 1991 Profile.* Burlington, VT: University of Vermont Department of Psychiatry.

Achenbach, T.M. (1991). *Integrative guide for the 1991 CBCL/4–18, YSR, and TRF profiles.* Burlington, VT: University of Vermont Department of Psychiatry.

Lowe, L.A. (1998). Using Behavior Checklists in assessing conduct disorder: Issues of reliability and validity. *Research on Social Work Practice, 8,* 286–301.

CHILD DEVELOPMENT

Since its inception in 1930, *Child Development* has been published six times a year by the University of Chicago Press. It is a professional journal sponsored by the Society for Research in Child Development. As an interdisciplinary group, the Society for Research in Child Development uses the *Child Development* journal to publish manuscripts from all academic and professional disciplines that study developmental processes. The articles range from empirical and theoretical to reviews of previous research. The scholarly papers that appear in *Child Development* focus on the growth and development of children from conception through adolescence, including the development of language, thinking and reasoning, moral judgment, social skills, and family relationships.

The editor of *Child Development* is Marc H. Bornstein and subscription information can be obtained from The University of Chicago Press Journals Division, P.O. Box 37005 Chicago, IL 60637.

CHILD FIND

Child Find is a term used since 1974 to describe a federal requirement for states to institute systematic procedures in order to locate all children with disabilities or at risk for disabilities from birth to age 21. In 1986, Congress expanded support for early intervention by creating the Infants and Toddlers with Disabilities Program, authorized under Part H of the Individuals with Disabilities Education Act (IDEA). The Part H program promotes a comprehensive and culturally appropriate approach to meeting the needs of infants and toddlers with disabilities through statewide systems of coordinated, comprehensive, multidisciplinary and interagency programs. In any given state, there are about half a dozen state agencies that participate in the financing and delivery of early intervention services under the Part H umbrella. Unfortunately, each state has created its own definition of developmental delay; therefore, variation in eligibility exists across the United States. Today, about 155,000 infants and toddlers birth through age 2 and their families are receiving early intervention services under Part H.

A comprehensive child find system includes many different aspects and methods of locating at-risk infants and toddlers. Interagency Coordinating Councils (authorized by Part H of IDEA) reveal that a wide variety of public awareness and child-find strategies have been utilized to improve program participation of culturally/linguistically diverse groups (Bernstein & Stettner-Eaton, 1994). Low-cost strategies such as mailings, home visit, and on-site questionnaires have had success in identifying children (Squires, 1996). Programs such as the Infant Follow Along Program (Lytwyn, 1992) combines agencies for referral and follow-up of identified children.

Feasibility studies about Part H of IDEA are being conducted by state departments of health and education departments (Hawaii Department of Health, 1993; Michigan Department of Education, 1991). The effectiveness of child find and Part H of IDEA is addressed regularly in annual reports to Congress (Eighteenth Annual Report, 1996).

REFERENCES

Bernstein, H.K., & Stettner-Eaton, B. (1994). Cultural inclusion in Part H: Systems development. *Infant-Toddler Intervention: The Transdisciplinary Journal, 4,* 1, 1–10.

Eighteenth Annual Report to Congress on the Implementation of the IDEA. (1996). Washington, DC: U.S. Department of Education.

Hawaii Department of Health. (1993). *A feasibility study for an evaluation of family needs in early intervention.* Hawaii: Author.

Lytwyn, P. (1992). *Infant follow along program: A computer assisted child find system using parent completed questionnaires.* Project description. (ERIC Document No. ED350734)

Michigan Department of Education. (1991). *Barriers and resources underlying Part H implementation: A utilization-focused evaluation study.* Michigan: Author.

Squires, J. (1996). Parent-completed developmental questionnaires: A low-cost strategy for child-find and screening. *Infants and Young Children, 9,* 1, 16–28.

See also **Early Identification of Handicapped Children; Education for All Handicapped Children Act of 1975**

CHILD GUIDANCE CLINIC

Child guidance clinics are the result of the blending of several historical forces. By 1921 there were a number of clinics for children that were attached to mental hospitals, social agencies, schools, and colleges. Child guidance clinics were formally organized under that name in 1922 by the National Committee for Mental Hygiene and the Commonwealth Fund. These early clinics emphasized a team approach to the diagnosis and treatment of children's problems. A social worker and psychologist (under the supervision of a psychiatrist) constituted the treatment team. Thus, the interdisciplinary team concept was initiated, and it was revolutionary for its time. While interdisciplinary teams today have considerable overlap in role and function, the early teams were regimented so that the psychologist did the necessary testing, the social worker dealt with the parents (typically just the mother), and the psychiatrist worked with the child.

The Philadelphia Child Guidance Clinic was one of these early clinics; it has survived the years and seems reflective of the changes that have evolved. This is the clinic that is identified strongly with one of the major orientations to working with families: primarily structural family therapy as developed by Salvador Minuchin (1974). As Minuchin was an employee of the Philadelphia-based clinic, so were other influential persons in the development of family therapy such as Jay Haley, Harry Aponte, and Braulio Montalvo. This clinic also demonstrates the great overlap of functioning by various disciplines; social workers, psychologists, and psychiatrists all share equally in the delivery of services. In fact, a project supervised by Haley and Minuchin in the early 1970s focused on the training of lay people as significant helpers with troubled families. The Philadelphia Child Guidance Clinic, with its emphasis on one-way mirrors, live supervision, and video taping has also distinguished itself as a significant training institution. While not on the same scale as the Philadelphia clinic, many other clinics have followed the lead and developed themselves as centers of treatment and training (Chandra, Srinath & Kinshore, 1993). Certainly, the early child guidance clinics initiated the development of a far more elaborate treatment delivery system, but their influence still seems easily distinguishable as one considers the many community mental health centers that feature the multidisciplinary treatment teams that are now considered standard practice.

REFERENCES

Chandra, P.S., Srinath, S., & Kinshore, A. (1993). Disturbed children grown up: Follow up of a child guidance clinic population into adulthood. *NIMHANS Journal, 11*, 1, 43–47.

Minuchin, S. (1974). *Families and family therapy.* Cambridge, MA: Harvard University Press.

See also **Child Psychiatry; Child Psychology**

CHILDHOOD APHASIA

Childhood aphasia, a label used in the pediatric and neurologic literature to describe disorders of speech and language in children, covers various disorders of communication. It is applied to children who have impairment of previously normal language and to children who failed in the normal acquisition of language.

In the adult there are mainly two groups of aphasia. The first, in which the patient is more affected in the comprehension of oral language, is called receptive, sensory, or Wernicke's aphasia. The patient is able to speak fluently but speech may have no connection with the questions asked. The pathology involves the posterior-superior portion of the first temporal gyrus (Wernicke's area). In the second group, the aphasic patient has great difficulties with speech but is able to write or to show the answers indicating that comprehension is correct. This is expressive, motor, or Broca's aphasia. The underlying pathology affects mainly the prerolandic region of the brain (frontal operculum or Broca's area).

Acquired aphasia in children is defined as impairment of previously normal language. Even in similar pathologic processes, as in adults, the clinical symptoms of aphasia in children depend on the degree of language development prior to cerebral insult. Childhood aphasia is characterized by an absence of spontaneous expressive language (oral, written, and gestural), producing a clinical syndrome of nonfluent speech or mutism (Wright, 1982). In all cases, the lexicon is reduced and the syntax is simplified; there is no logorrhea and even the lesion is temporal. Recovery is more frequent and rapid than in the adult, but when children regain language they rarely return to the premorbid level. Guttmann (1942) showed that disorders of language are mainly a reduction of the verbal expression of speech (thus, mainly a motor disorder). The prognosis is good unless there are simultaneous expressive and comprehension disorders.

Developmental language disorders or dysphasias are seen in children who have never acquired normal language function. They have been described under various terms: congenital or developmental aphasias, specific language disorders, and dysphasias. From the literature it appears that the capability for human language is partially an innate cognitive skill (Mayeux & Kandel, 1985). The process of acquisition of normal language function (Rapin, 1982; Wright, 1982) starts at birth. Infants with normal hearing are sensitive to sounds and react to them; they progressively become able to discriminate the acoustically subtle phonetic cues crucial for the comprehension of human language. This sensitivity is lost as language is acquired. Children learn to associate meaningful visual precepts (visual memory) with discriminable auditory ones (auditory memory), and to demonstrate this by pointing to objects on verbal command. Therefore, language acquisition is not a passive operation based on imitation. The child will only start to repeat syllables and words when he or she is able to segment speech sounds and elemental units of meaningful language extracted from the casual conversation all around. Auditory comprehension precedes speaking. An infant understands the meaning of a word before vocalizing it and initially learns to comprehend the spoken symbol of a word (decoding). When the child comprehends the word, he or she is able to express the language symbol (encoding) (Wright, 1982). Children progressively acquire the rules of grammar and form sentences by age 4. It will take a child much longer to perfect articulatory skills and to learn to produce highly complex sentences. The addition of new words throughout the vocabulary continues throughout life. The process of acquisition follows a progression related to the overall maturation and development of the infant, but it also requires normal functioning and control of the structures involved in sound production.

Developmental language disorders traditionally have been divided into two groups. The first is disorders of receptive language, in which impaired comprehension is the essential feature; however, one may find some degree of verbal language and articulation dysfunction. The second group is expressive language disorders, characterized by delayed talking; poverty of words (especially in naming); and agrammatical spontaneous speech but normal comprehension, provided the child has no deafness, no mental retardation, no cerebral palsy and is not psychiatrically disturbed and did not suffer from environmental deprivation. As this type of classification has not satisfied clinicians or linguists, other subgroups have been proposed (Aram & Nation, 1975; Rapin, 1982, 1985).

In verbal auditory agnosia (word deafness), one is incapable of decoding the sounds around him or her (phonologic level, first necessary step to comprehension of language). The child does not understand phonemes or verbal words; therefore, he or she cannot reproduce them, is mute, or utters single words with phonologic distortion. The syntax is poor. These children learn gestural language and can express themselves through drawings. Their comprehension of symbols and cognitive functions is good and is expressed through games. They will benefit from teaching techniques for deaf children.

In semantic-pragmatic syndrome, the child has an impaired comprehension of the meaning and intent of communication but has good phonology and syntax. The child has a fluent language and often reproduces what is said, but is echolalic for even well-constructed sentences. As the deficit affects comprehension and use of language, the syndrome will be mainly observed with sophisticated questions. If these are put in a simply way, the child can answer yes or no, showing the deficit is not a cognitive one. These children have good auditory memory and are able to repeat long sentences, but their spontaneous speech often lacks precision. As pragmatics is affected in this syndrome, the subject cannot read facial expression or recognize tone of voice, so speech can be unadapted to the situation, creating difficulties in social contacts and behavioral problems. These children also can learn to read, but they do not totally understand what they read.

In semantic-syntactic-organizing syndrome, the deficit lies at two levels: syntax, necessary to organize words into meaningful sentences, and semantics, which is concerned with the meaning of sentences. Therefore, children are dysfluent using incorrect words in an inadequate order. The repetition of words is better than spontaneous speech.

Mixed receptive-expressive (phonologic-syntactic) syndrome is the most frequently seen syndrome of the developmental dysphasias. Comprehension is always better than expression, and can even be normal. The children are dysfluent, have a reduced vocabulary, and an elementary syntax. The phonology is also impaired, producing some distortions of poorly articulated words. Speech may be telegraphic.

In severe expressive syndrome (verbal apraxial), children with normal comprehension have a deficiency in coding language symbols into words. Their speech is extremely poor; often the children are mute. They learn to read and sign.

Phonological programming deficit syndrome is a subgroup of severe expressive syndrome. Children have a good comprehension, are fluent, and are able to speak in sentences. Phonologic disorder produces distorted pronunciation with substitutions or omissions in words; speech is uncomprehensible to other than family members.

The classifications used in developmental language disorders are still descriptive and the anatomic clinical correlations are less well understood than in adult or childhood acquired language disorders. The mechanisms involved are not only dependent on the left hemisphere, they have still to be elucidated.

REFERENCES

Aram, D.M., & Nation, J.E. (1975). Patterns of language behavior in children with developmental language disorders. *Journal of Speech & Hearing Research, 18,* 229–241.

Guttmann, E., (1942). Aphasia in children. *Brain, 65,* 205.

Mayeux, R., & Kandel, E.R. (1985). Natural language, disorders of language, and other localizable disorders of cognitive functioning. In E.R. Kandel & J.H. Schwartz (Eds.), *Principles of Neural Science.* New York: Elsevier.

Rapin, I. (1982). *Children with brain dysfunction: Neurology, cognition, language and behavior.* New York: Raven.

Rapin, I. (1985). Communication disorders in children. In H. Szliwowski & J. Bormans (Eds.), *Progrès en neurologie pédiatrique.* Brussels: Prodim.

Wright, F.S. (1982). Disorders of speech and language. In K.F. Swaiman & F.S. Wright (Eds.), *The Practice of pediatric neurology.* St. Louis: Mosby.

See also **Aphasia; Language Disorders; Mutism**

CHILDHOOD NEUROSIS

See PSYCHONEUROTIC DISORDERS.

CHILDHOOD PSYCHOSIS

Researchers in child psychology and psychiatry agree that there exist identifiable clinical syndromes where children are out of touch with reality, withdraw from the social world around them, and show unusual and bizarre behaviors. These psychotic children present great challenges to their caretakers: parents who try to provide for the psychotic child's needs and integration into the family system; teachers who try to educate the child and provide basic social skills training; and mental health professionals who try to treat the child clinically.

Consider the following case that the author supervised at a community mental health center. A 9-year-old boy was referred by foster parents following a sudden onset of bizarre destructive behavior and hallucinations. He thought monsters lurked behind doors, heard voices, and displayed bizarre speech during psychotic episodes. This child had been placed in several different foster homes since being abused and neglected as an infant. Two of his siblings were being legally adopted by one set of foster parents, but this child's behavior had led them to decide not to adopt him. He showed poor social skills, was intrusive with others (i.e., did not keep his hands to himself), and had a short attention span. He tolerated stress poorly and would sometimes lash out at others in a violent manner when frustrated. Several psychiatric hospitalizations had only temporarily stabilized self-control and reality orientation. This child was psychotic.

Incidence of childhood psychosis is estimated at a maximum of 6 in 10,000 children (Werry, 1972), with a more probable estimate of 1 in 1,000 children (Quay & Werry, 1979). Unfortunately, methodological difficulties impede accurate estimates of incidence. However, research consistently shows that more boys than girls are diagnosed for each of the psychotic disorders. Estimated differences vary considerably, but it appears that at least twice as many boys are diagnosed as psychotic (Wing, 1968).

The evolution of theoretical syndromes points to three general types of childhood psychosis: (1) childhood schizophrenia, (2) early infantile autism, and (3) atypical or symbiotic psychosis.

Interest in childhood schizophrenia followed Potter's (1933) paper. The schizophrenic child was seen as someone who was disinterested in the environment, manifested disturbed thought processes and frequently poor verbal skills, had difficulty in forming emotional attachments to others, and showed bizarre behaviors with a tendency to perseverate in various activities. This view of childhood schizophrenia was modeled after adult schizophrenia.

Research on childhood autism was pioneered by Kanner (1943), who described autistic children as generally having a limited ability to relate to other people beginning in infancy, a language disturbance making it difficult to communicate with others, and conspicuous and obsessive behavior for repetition and maintaining sameness.

Symbiotic psychosis is a rare subtype described by Mahler (1952) as a disturbance owed to intense resistance by the child to becoming psychologically independent of the mother. The number of cases reported is small. The syndrome may be due to repeated early traumatic events and also may stem from a constitutional predisposition to fail to

see the mother as a separate object (Mahler, 1965). The onset of this syndrome occurs between 2 1/2 and 5 years of age, preceded by fairly normal development during the first 2 years of life. The onset of symptoms can be set off by such events as illness of a mother, birth of a sibling, or the beginning of school.

The *Diagnostic and Statistical Manual of Mental Disorders* (DSM-IV; American Psychiatric Association, 1994) attempted to integrate the various approaches to childhood psychosis. This was not an easy task because of the complexity of the subject matter and the distinct points of view on such disorders as childhood schizophrenia. The resulting classification system is organized under the concept of pervasive developmental disorders, with separate subcategories for infantile autism and childhood onset pervasive developmental disorder. This latter category is very general and appears to reflect early research on childhood schizophrenia represented by the work of Lauretta Bender; it excludes work on symbiotic psychosis by Mahler. A separate less specifically defined category, atypical pervasive developmental disorder, allows the clinician to use diagnostic flexibility in describing the individual case, including a symbiotic psychotic child. The clinician can draw on the diagnostic criteria for adult schizophrenia in determining the appropriateness of this category for a child. The DSM-IV represents the most current thinking of the mental health profession on these disorders, and contains specific criteria for each psychotic disorder.

TREATMENT APPROACHES

Psychotherapy. Individual psychotherapy has been widely used in the treatment of childhood psychosis. Treatment approaches differ depending on the clinician's theory of the causes of the disorder, but they have in common an attempt to resolve psychic turmoil. Psychoanalytic-based approaches focus on the individual child and the presumed intrapsychic conflicts created by a fractured mother-child relationship (Mahler, 1965). Other approaches focus more on interpersonal skills and involve other family members in the treatment (Reiser, 1963).

Research on the effectiveness of psychotherapy with psychotic children has produced differing estimates of improvement. Most writers agree that it often helps to improve symptoms, but there is disagreement on how much it contributes beyond an untreated recovery rate. Some reported recovery rates have been astoundingly high, but the research is difficult to evaluate because of differing criteria used to measure success and lack of untreated control groups.

Milieu and Educational Therapy. This approach manipulates the total environment in a residential setting. It addresses impairments to all areas of functioning and employs multiple treatments (individual, educational, and group therapy). Children referred for these programs are usually the most disturbed; this may partly explain why clinical improvement occurs in a high percentage of cases. Milieu therapy often focuses on improving adaptive self-care skills and improving reality orientation to facilitate better relatedness to others (Zimmerman, 1994). Research on the effectiveness of such programs is difficult to evaluate owing to lack of experimental controls, diverse groups of psychotic children, and small sample sizes. However, more structured programs appear to be more effective (Schopler, 1974).

Behavior Therapy. Principles of learning theory have been successfully applied to treating the symptoms of psychotic children, especially autism (Ferster, 1961). The application of behavioral contingencies has helped child care workers and parents to shape the behavior of disturbed children in positive ways, but research suggests that the effects are not easily generalizable across settings.

Organic Treatments. A wide variety of physical treatments have been attempted. Electroconvulsive shock therapy, sensory deprivation, vitamin therapy, hallucinogenic drugs (LSD), and antipsychotic drugs all have been used. Campbell (1973) concluded that little success can be attributed to any of these treatments though antipsychotic drugs are effective in alleviating the worst of some symptoms such as aggressiveness and hallucinations.

In summary, biological, genetic, (Crow, Done & Sacker, 1995) and family factors combine to produce psychotic disturbance in children. A small percentage of children appear to be at risk of developing psychotic symptoms owed to these etiological factors when exposed to extreme environmental stress. Although a variety of treatments may produce some positive changes, long-term prognosis is generally poor for psychotic children. A high percentage continue to show psychotic symptoms or minimal social adjustment over time. With onset before age 10, the prognosis appears to be particularly poor. When a therapist and/or parent demonstrates a high degree of emotional involvement over time, the prognosis improves.

REFERENCES

American Psychiatric Association. (1994). *Diagnostic and statistical manual of mental disorders* (4th ed.). Washington, DC: Author.

Campbell, M. (1973). Biological interventions in psychoses of childhood. *Journal of Autism & Childhood Schizophrenia, 3,* 347–373.

Crow, T.J., Done, D.J., & Sacker, A. (1995). Childhood precursors of psychosis as clues to its evolutionary origins. *European Archives of Psychiatry & Clinical Neuroscience, 245,* 2, 61–69.

Ferster, C. (1961). Positive reinforcement and behavioral deficits of autistic children. *Child Development, 32,* 437–456.

Kanner, L. (1943). Autistic disturbances of affective contact. *Nervous Child, 2,* 217–250.

Mahler, M. (1952). On child psychosis in schizophrenia: Autistic and symbiotic infantile psychosis. *Psychoanalytic Study of the Child, 7,* 286–305.

Mahler, M. (1965). On early infantile psychosis: The symbiotic and autistic syndromes. *Journal of the American Academy of Psychiatry, 4,* 554–568.

Potter, H.W. (1933). Schizophrenia in children. *American Journal of Psychiatry, 12,* 1253–1270.

Quay, H.C., & Werry, J.S. (1979). *Psychopathological disorders of childhood* (2nd ed.). New York: Wiley.

Reiser, D. (1963). Psychosis of infancy and early childhood. *New England Journal of Medicine, 269,* 790–798, 844–850.

Schopler, E. (1974). Changes of direction with psychotic children. In A. Davids (Ed.), *Child personality and psychopathology: Current topics* (Vol. 1). New York: Wiley.

Werry, J.S. (1972). Childhood psychosis. In H.D. Quay & J.S. Werry (Eds.), *Psychopathological disorders of childhood.* New York: Wiley.

Wing, J. (1968). Review of B. Bettelheim. *The empty fortress. British Journal of Psychiatry, 114,* 788–791.

Zimmerman, P.D. (1994). Bruno Bettelheim: The mysterious other: Historical reflect on the treatment of childhood psychosis. *Psychoanalytic Review, 81,* 3, 411–413.

See also **Autism; Borderline Personality Disorder; Depression; Emotional Disorders; Mental Status Exams; Psychoneurotic Disorders**

CHILDHOOD SCHIZOPHRENIA

The term childhood schizophrenia is one that is, at present, the subject of considerable dispute among authorities in the fields of child psychiatry and psychology. The dispute has mainly to do with the boundaries of this term and the validity of the concept of a childhood onset schizophrenic disorder. As a result of the uncertainty and differences of opinion, firm conclusions have not been reached, and the variation in interpretation of the term childhood schizophrenia has made compilation of a data base problematic.

In the fourth edition of the *Diagnostic and Statistical Manual of Mental Disorders* (DSM-IV), childhood schizophrenia is not set apart as a separate category, but is diagnosed using the adult criteria for schizophrenia. These include:

A. Characteristic symptoms: Two (or more) of the following, each present for a significant portion of time during a 1-month period (or less if successfully treated):

   (1) delusions

   (2) hallucinations

   (3) disorganized speech (e.g., frequent derailment or incoherence)

   (4) grossly disorganized or catatonic behavior

   (5) negative symptoms, i.e., affective flattening, alogia, or avolition

B. *Social/occupational dysfunction:* For a significant portion of the time since the onset of the disturbance, one or more major areas of functioning such as work, interpersonal relations, or self-care are markedly below the level achieved prior to the onset (or when the onset is in childhood or adolescence, failure to achieve expected level of interpersonal, academic, or occupational achievement).

C. *Duration:* Continuous signs of the disturbance persist for at least 6 months. This 6-month period must include at least 1 month of symptoms (or less if successfully treated) that meet Criterion A (i.e., active phase symptoms) and may include periods of prodromal or residual symptoms. During these prodomal or residual periods, the signs of the disturbance may be manifested by only negative symptoms or two or more symptoms listed in Criterion A present in an attenuated form (e.g., odd beliefs, unusual perceptual experiences).

D. *Schizoaffective and Mood Disorder exclusion:* Schizoaffective Disorder and Mood Disorder with Psychotic Features have been ruled out because either (1) no Major Depressive, Manic, or Mixed Episodes have occurred concurrently with the active-phase symptoms; or (2) if mood episodes have occurred during active-phase symptoms, their total duration has been brief relative to the duration of the active and residual periods.

E. *Substance/general medical condition exclusion:* The disturbance is not due to the direct physiological effects of a substance (e.g., a drug of abuse, a medication, or a general medical condition.

F. Relationship to a Pervasive Developmental Disorder: If there is a history of autistic disorder or another pervasive developmental disorder, the additional diagnosis of Schizophrenia is made only if prominent delusions or hallucinations are also present for at least a month (or less if successfully treated). (DSM-IV, 1994, p. 285–286)

DSM-IV suggests that this approach to diagnosis is controversial. Part of the problem involves the inherent difficulty in identifying delusions, hallucinations, and thought disorders in children whose language abilities are very limited. Another shortcoming involves the inability to diagnose organic disorders in children, especially at an early age. Finally, a number of authors (e.g., Fish & Ritvo, 1979) have noted the crossover of children from one category to another. This crossover does not occur often in samples of more retarded children, who tend to show more autistic symptoms, but it occurs often enough among samples with average intelligence to prompt concern about the diagnostic criteria.

Demographic data using the DSM-IV criteria for schizophrenia in children are virtually nonexistent except insofar as they may be inferred from data obtained for adults. The overall incidence of schizophrenia is thought to range between 15 and about 1% of the population, with an equal sex distribution and a higher incidence rate in lower socioeconomic classes. It also appears to have a higher incidence in some families, but the concordance rate, even in monozygotic twins, is not perfect, implying intervening environmental and/or biological factors. The lower limit for the age of onset using the DSM-IV criteria appears to be 8 or 9 years, but there are isolated reports of much earlier onset. As Rutter (1974) notes, the differences in age of onset between autism and schizophrenia and the low incidence of any severe disorder between ages three and early adolescence suggest that both autism and schizophrenia are etiologically distinct and valid syndromes. Unfortunately, little of substance can be said regarding the prognosis or etiology of schizophrenia in children or adults. Whereas autism has been linked to a number of organic and/or genetic conditions, the changing definition of childhood schizophrenia has prevented the compilation of a large enough data base to permit inferences about etiology. The same general state of affairs exists concerning prognosis, although in adults, schizophrenia is thought to have a very poor outcome and a high relapse rate, as noted in DSM-IV.

As noted previously, early in this century it was common to lump all severe childhood disorders together diagnostically; it was assumed that these were earlier forms of adult schizophrenia. In the last 20 years, however, it has become clear that distinctions should be made among these disorders. The most important differential diagnoses are between schizophrenia and disorders such as autism, mental retardation, and pervasive developmental disorders or disintegrative diseases of organic origin such as Heller's syndrome. Some of these disorders are documented in DSM-IV and some are not, but delineation of the differences among them may illuminate the nature of schizophrenia in children.

Because of the heterogeneity of the cases that have been labeled as schizophrenia, a wide variety of treatments have been employed, as has been the case with autism. Insofar as schizophrenic children may have more intact intellectual/language skills than children with other severe disorders, the traditional play, insight-oriented, and "talking" therapies might be expected to be more effective. Unfortunately, no good studies documenting the utility of this approach are available, again owing in part to differences in diagnostic terminology over the years. Similarly, since drugs such as the phenothiazines have demonstrated value with adult schizophrenic populations, one might expect them to be effective with younger patients diagnosed with schizophrenic symptoms. Campbell (1975), Fish et al. (1968), and others have noted the favorable effects of such drugs with children, but it is again not clear how their samples fit into the DSM-IV scheme. It is noteworthy that most antipsychotic drugs are apparently not especially effective in reducing the symptoms of autism, except in isolated cases (Rutter & Schopler, 1985). The most common form of treatment today involves parental support, counseling, and special psychoeducational strategies, much as with autistic children. In fact, many classes for severely disturbed or psychotic children contain a mix of autistic, schizophrenic, and other types of children. Whether the use of DSM-IV nosology will lead to enhanced and differentiated treatment for these diagnostic groups remains to be seen.

REFERENCES

American Psychiatric Association. (1994). *Diagnostic and Statistical Manual of Mental Disorders* (4th ed.). Washington, DC: author.

Campbell, M. (1975). Pharmacotherapy in early infantile autism. *Biological Psychiatry, 10,* 399–423.

Fish, B., & Ritvo, E. (1979). Psychoses of childhood. In J. Noshpitz (Ed.), *Basic handbook of child psychiatry.* New York: Basic Books.

Fish, B., Shapiro, T., & Campbell, M. (1968). A classification of schizophrenic children under five years. *American Journal of Psychiatry, 124,* 1415–1423.

Rutter, M. (1974). The development of infantile autism. *Psychological Medicine, 4,* 147–163.

Rutter, M., & Schopler, E. (1985). Autism and pervasive developmental disorders: Concepts and diagnostic issues. Paper prepared for National Institute of Mental Health Research Workshop, Washington, DC.

See also Autism; Childhood Psychosis; Psychoneurotic Disorders

CHILD PSYCHIATRY

Child psychiatry is a subdiscipline of psychiatry, a branch of medicine focusing on human emotional development and pathology. As a subspecialty, child psychiatry is approximately 75 years old, with Freud's treatment of a young boy in 1909 marking its genesis (Jones, 1959). The practitioner of child psychiatry must have comprehensive training both in general psychiatry and child development. This includes a firm understanding of trends in cognitive, language, and motor development. Training in neurology is also essential in understanding which diagnoses may be attributed to organic as opposed to psychogenic etiology (Knapp & Harris, 1998).

REFERENCES

Jones, E. (Ed.). (1959). *Sigmund Freud: collected papers* (5 vols). New York: Basic Books.

Knapp, P.K., & Harris, E.S. (1998). Consultation—liaison in child psychiatry: A review of the past 10 years. *Journal of the American Academy of Child and Adolescent Psychiatry, 37,* 2, 139–146.

See also Cascade Model of Special Education Services; Mental Status Exams; Multidisciplinary Teams

CHILD PSYCHOLOGY

Child psychology is concerned with answering two basic questions: How do children change as they develop, and what are the determinants of these developmental changes? (Hetherington & Parke, 1979). Modern child psychology is particularly concerned with understanding the processes that produce and account for age-related changes in children. Child psychology is concerned with development from conception to adolescence.

Child psychologists recognize the influence of heredity on setting the foundation for the course of development. These genetic factors interact with the child's learning experiences to determine actual developmental outcomes. Learning processes (e.g., conditioning mechanisms, imitation), are therefore an important area of study by child psychologists.

During the past two decades, five areas of development have received considerable attention by child psychologists. These areas are emotional development, language development, cognitive development, moral development, and the development of sex role behaviors (Mussen, 1970).

In the area of emotional development, research has focused on the manner in which positive and negative emotions originate and how the expression of emotions changes with age (Yarrow, 1979). Another area that has attracted considerable interest is the development of attachment, in which infants show a specific desire to be near particular caretakers in their environment. Related to this issue is the study of the development of fears in the young child, particularly the fear of strangers. Child psychologists also have been interested in the ways that children learn to label and recognize their own and other people's emotions.

Language development represents one of the most significant achievements of childhood because of its importance in communication, thinking, and learning.

Research in children's cognitive development has dominated the field of child psychology. The area of cognition pertains to the mental activity and behavior through which knowledge is acquired and processed, including learning, perception, memory, and thinking. The psychological processes that underlie cognitive development are of particular interest to the child psychologist, including the operations involved in receiving, attending to, discriminating, transforming, storing, and recalling information.

Child psychologists have noted individual differences in the cognitive styles that children use to process information. One of the most frequently studied dimensions of cognitive style is reflectivity-impulsivity. Reflectivity-impulsivity is associated with a number of intellectual, social, and personality factors.

Cognitive problem-solving abilities, as reflected in the concept of intelligence, have attracted the attention of psychologists for nearly a century. Child psychologists have addressed such issues as whether intelligence is a unitary, generalized ability, or a group of relatively separate abilities. In addition, the modifiability of intelligence has attracted much research attention in recent years (Lewis, 1976). There have been debates between those groups who argue that intelligence is genetically determined and, therefore, not alterable, and those who suggest that intelligence is more dependent on learning experiences. Similarly, the development and use of intelligence tests has generated considerable controversy within the field, with some investigators arguing that such tests are culturally biased toward anglo middle-class experiences. Intelligence tests, based on the concept of global intelligence, yield a single IQ score and continue to be widely used by practicing psychologists in clinical and academic settings. Tests of intellectual ability generally have been shown to be good predictors of achievement in academic settings.

The development of sex roles also has been an area of study in child psychology. Sex-role typing is the process by which children acquire the values and behaviors that are regarded as appropriate to either males or females in a specific culture. Characteristics of masculinity and femininity appear to be developed very early in life and are stable over time. Research indicates that the development of sex roles and sex differences in behavior is a complex phenomenon that involves the interaction of biological, social, and cognitive factors (Maccoby & Jacklin, 1974).

One component of the socialization process of children that has been of particular interest to child psychologists is the development of moral values and moral behaviors. Psychological research has focused on three basic aspects of morality: (1) cognitive factors including knowledge of ethical rules and judgments about whether various acts are right or wrong; (2) behavioral factors involving negative acts such as cheating, lying, resisting temptation, and controlling aggression, and behaviors involved in prosocial acts such as sharing, cooperation, altruism, and helping; and (3) emotional factors of morality such as feelings of guilt following a transgression (Hoffman, 1979).

There is a long history of interest by child psychologists in the family's role in the socialization process. Of particular interest has been the relationship between child-rearing attitudes and practices and children's cognitive, personality, and social development. Contemporary issues pertaining to the family that have been investigated by child psychologists include the effects of child abuse, divorce, single-parent families, and maternal employment on the child's development.

Relationships with age mates are another important influence on the development of children. Age-related changes in peer interactions and the role of play behaviors have been the focus of much research. The influence of peers as models for negative and prosocial behaviors, and factors affecting peer group acceptance, also have been investigated.

The major research interests in child psychology have changed over the course of time, often in response to social and historical pressures. Much of the knowledge that has accumulated in this field has been used to meet the needs of children in today's society and improve their well being through the implementation of various programs and services. In recent years, child psychologists have become increasingly interested and influential in the formulation of social policies affecting children (Seitz, 1979). A review of development in child psychology from the 1960s to 1990s can be found in Reese (1993).

REFERENCES

Hetherington, E.M., & Parke, R.D. (1979). *Child psychology: A contemporary viewpoint* (2nd ed.). New York: McGraw-Hill.

Hoffman, M.L. (1979). Development of moral thought, feeling, and behavior. *American Psychologist, 34,* 958–966.

Lewis, M. (Ed.). (1976). *Origins of intelligence.* New York: Plenum.

Maccoby, E.E., & Jacklin, C.N. (1974). *The psychology of sex differences.* Stanford: Stanford University Press.

Mussen, P.H. (Ed.). (1970). *Carmichael's handbook of child psychology.* New York: Wiley.

Reese, H.W. (1993). Developments in child psychology from the 1960s to the 1990s. *Developmental Review, 13,* 4, 503–524.

Seitz, V. (1979). Psychology and social policy for children. *American Psychologist, 34,* 1007–1008.

Yarrow, L.J. (1979). Emotional development. *American Psychologist, 34,* 951–957.

See also **Child Psychiatry; Clinical Psychology; Pediatric Psychologist**

CHILDREN OF A LESSER GOD

Children of a Lesser God is a play by Mark Medoff that was a hit on the Broadway stage in 1980. It is about the meeting, courtship, and marriage of James Leeds, a speech teacher at a state school for the deaf, and Sarah Norman, a maid at the school who has been deaf from birth and who refuses to lip read or speak.

Mark Medoff, the author of *Children of a Lesser God,* found sign language an interesting theatrical device, and used deafness as a symbol for the problems inherent in all human communication. He wrote the play for Phyllis Frelich, a founding member of the National Theater of the Deaf, in response to her difficulty in finding roles.

REFERENCE

Medoff, M. (1980). *Children of a Lesser God.* New York: Dramatists Play Service.

See also **Deaf; Deaf Education; Sign Language**

CHILDREN OF THE HANDICAPPED

Parents have the responsibility of providing care, love, and social training for their children. It is commonly assumed that many of a child's developmental abilities (e.g., expressive language, reasoning, social and emotional) will be enhanced through formal and informal activities initiated by parents. This may not be assumed for children of handicapped individuals who may grow up in environments where stimulation in communication areas and training in the socialization processes are less accessible. However, this does not mean that a child of a handicapped person will be deficient in cognitive and affective development. It may mean that the child will have to adapt to different methods of learning and rely more on relatives, teachers, and others who can provide the necessary stimulation. Individual differences in intelligence, physical abilities, and temperament will play an important role in how well children adapt to the environment and how growth and development proceed when confronted with obstacles. The type of disability of the parent, the parent's intellectual ability, and the parent's motivation to rear children properly are also crucial factors.

To minimize the probability that children of handicapped parents will experience developmental deficits, emphasis must be placed on adequate parenting and improving the quality of the child-rearing environment. This can be done through parent training that emphasizes effective parenting skills. This training will not only eliminate developmental disabilities in some children, but also make individuals with disabilities more responsible and effective parents.

See also **Family Response to a Child with Disabilities**

CHILDREN'S DEFENSE FUND (CDF)

The Children's Defense Fund (CDF) is an advocacy organization for poor, minority, and handicapped children. The mission of the CDF is to "Leave No Child Behind" (CDF, 1999). Efforts are undertaken on behalf of large numbers of children as opposed to individual children. Relevant to special education, the organization has addressed exclusion of children from school as well as the labeling and treatment of children with special needs (Staff, 1974). The CDF maintains a lobbying organization, pursuing an annual legislative agenda in the U.S. Congress; works with state and local child advocates, providing information, technical assistance, and support; monitors the development and implementation of federal and state policies; and litigates selected cases (Children's Defense Fund, undated).

The CDF also develops information on key issues affecting children. It has published books and handbooks of interest to special education, including *94–142 and 504: Numbers that Add Up to Educational Rights for Handicapped Children, How to Help Handicapped Children Get an Education.* A monthly newsletter, *CDF Reports,* is also published.

The CDF was founded in 1973. Until 1978 CDF was known as the Children's Defense Fund of the Washington Research Project. It is a private organization, with its main office in Washington DC at 25 E. Street NW, Washington DC 20001. The CDF has a very informative website at www.childrensdefense.org.

REFERENCES

Children's Defense Fund. (1999). *About the Children's Defense Fund.* Washington, DC: Author.

Staff. (1974). An interview with Marian Edelman Wright. *Harvard Educational Review, 44,* 53–73.

CHILDREN'S EARLY EDUCATION DEVELOPMENTAL INVENTORY

See BATTELLE DEVELOPMENTAL INVENTORY.

CHILDREN'S MANIFEST ANXIETY SCALE (CMAS)

Originally published in 1956 by Castaneda, McCandless, and Palermo as a downward extension of Taylor's Manifest Anxiety Scale for adults (Taylor, 1951), the Children's Manifest Anxiety Scale (CMAS) was substantively revised in 1978 (Reynolds & Richmond). The *Revised Children's Anx-*

iety Scale (RCMAS) was published in 1985 (Reynolds & Richmond). Since its first publication, more than 150 articles using the CMAS or the RCMAS have been published in various scholarly journals. These scales have been used in studies of the effects of anxiety on children's learning, behavior in the classroom, and response to a variety of treatment programs, and in descriptive studies of anxiety and its relationship to behavior, gender, ethnicity, age, socioeconomic status, and other variables.

Designed to measure anxiety of long-standing duration (i.e., trait as opposed to state or situational anxiety), the RCMAS has four empirically derived subscales titled: Concentration/Social, Worry and Oversensitivity, Physiological Anxiety, and Lie or Social Desirability. Standard scores are provided for a total anxiety score and for each subscale. Reliability data are good with most studies reporting internal consistency estimates in the .80s across age (5 to 19 years), gender, and race (black, white, and Hispanic). Extensive validity data are provided in the test manual (Reynolds & Richmond, 1985).

REFERENCES

Castaneda, A., McCandless, B., & Palermo, D. (1956). The children's form of the Manifest Anxiety Scale. *Child Development, 27,* 327–332.

Reynolds, C.R., & Richmond, B.O. (1978). What I think and feel: A revised measure of children's manifest anxiety. *Journal of Abnormal Psychology, 43,* 281–283.

Reynolds, C.R., & Richmond, B.O. (1985). *Revised Children's Manifest Anxiety Scale.* Los Angeles. Western Psychological Services.

Taylor, J.A. (1951). The relationship of anxiety to the conditioned eyelid response. *Journal of Experimental Psychology, 41,* 18–92.

See also **Anxiety**

CHILD SERVICE DEMONSTRATION CENTERS (CSDC)

Child Service Demonstration Centers (CSDCs) (1971–1980) were federally funded operations that, in their totality, represented the largest single national commitment specifically made to the education of the learning disabled (Mann et al., 1984).

Their beginnings are to be found in several pieces of legislation. PL 88-164, passed in 1963, which predated the introduction of the modern term learning disabilities (LD), provided assistance to learning-disabled children in a bill directed at the educational needs of handicapped children under the rubric of "crippled and other health impaired." Then, under PL 91-230, passed in 1969, the U.S. commissioner of education was enjoined by Congress "to seek to make equitable geographic distribution of training programs, and train personnel throughout the nation, and . . . to encourage the establishment of a model training center in each of the states." This was to be done by making grants or contracts available to public schools, state educational agencies, nonprofit organizations, and colleges and universities. Such model centers for the learning disabled were then authorized, and ultimately created, under PL 91-230, Title VI-G.

This law made possible Child Service Demonstration Centers to serve learning-disabled students. Under the law, the to-be-created centers were to (1) provide testing and educational evaluation to identify learning-disabled students; (2) develop and conduct model programs designed to meet their special educational needs; (3) assist appropriate educational agencies, organizations, and institutions "in making such model programs available to other children with learning disabilities"; and (4) disseminate new methods or techniques for overcoming learning disabilities and evaluate their effectiveness.

From 1971 to 1980, 97 CSDCs were created in all, with each of the 50 states being served by at least one during that time. The majority operated under the auspices of state educational agencies (SEAs). A good number also operated out of universities, and sometimes out of local educational agencies (LEAs), often on the basis of their serving as agencies of the states. The private sector was only minimally represented.

The federal government had high hopes for the CSDCs. They were expected to assume major responsibility for trailblazing in the creation of service models, programs, and technologies; the identification, diagnosis, and remediation of learning disabilities; and the training of regular as well as special education teachers, specialists, and administrators. They were also expected to play a major role in research on the learning disabled. Furthermore, they were cast as both transformation instigators and partners for state educational agencies. In these roles they were expected to help the state agencies to plan and implement statewide learning disabilities programs and services; indeed, the initial CSDCs were granted to state educational agencies to further this expectation.

The intervention models stressed by the CSDCs were strongly academic, as might be expected since students receiving services from the CSDCs usually had been referred because of academic problems. Remedial reading was the treatment of choice, on similar grounds. Perceptual motor training, including ITPA-based interventions, held the second highest priority, particularly in the early projects, when perceptual motor training was still the vogue. Surprisingly, the behavioral movement that so dominated special education during much of the CSDCs' sway does not appear to have greatly influenced most of the CSDCs, though some had strong behavioral emphases. While only several projects have averred ecological orientations, there was an ecological shift over the course of CSDC operations. Earlier projects were committed to overcoming learning disabilities through direct intervention, while later ones were more likely to emphasize helping learning-disabled students to adjust to academic and school environments and assisting schools in their accommodations to the special needs of learning-disabled students.

While there were some exemplary research efforts, the CSDCs remained essentially service agencies and, generally speaking, did not assume the research leadership originally expected of them. This was not surprising since neither their funding, personnel capabilities, nor the nature of local conditions were such as to encourage earnest research. The Learning Disability Institutes, funded in 1977, were created in response the federal government's recognition of these facts and a desire to seek wider research efforts from other sources.

The federal government clearly expected the CSDCs to have a major national impact on LD practices. That they did not fulfill such expectations can be attributed to a variety of causes. One was the fact that their allocation of funds was far below original authorizations. Another was that individual centers came on line too slowly and irregularly, thus any collaborative thrust on their part was weakened. Still another reason was that they did not affect state educational policies as had been hoped, the states usually pursuing their own LD agendas rather than those of the federal government or of the CSDCs. Furthermore, the demands made on the CSDCs regularly changed as a consequence of changes in federal direction and because of disagreements among recognized LD specialists as to the nature of learning disabilities and the goals of intervention. Finally, most of the projects were funded for only 3 years, and several were funded for 2 or less, hardly time to create forceful and enduring efforts. Nevertheless, they did sensitize many areas of the nation and its schools to the needs of learning-disabled children and provided them with guidance, training, programs, materials, and direct services during a period when the field of learning disabilities was still emerging as an area of educational concern in the United States. Undoubtedly, they also shaped current concepts and services.

The CSDCs were subject to a number of external evaluations. A study of the CSDCs' intervention efforts was carried out by Kirk and Elkin in 1975. In 1976 a major yearlong effort was made by the American Institute of Research to examine the operations of the CSDCs. In 1979 Ysseldyke et al. began their studies of the CSDCs' assessment approaches (Thurlow & Ysseldyke, 1979). At the final closing of the CSDCs, Mann et al. published several summative articles reviewing the status and contributions of the CSDCs (Boyer et al., 1982; Mann et al., 1983; Mann et al., 1984).

REFERENCES

Boyer, C.W., Mann, L., Davis, C.H., Metz, C.M., & Wolford, B. (1982). The Child Service Demonstration Centers: Retrospect of an age. *Academic Therapy, 18,* 171–177.

Kirk, S.A., & Elkin, V. (1975). Characteristics of children enrolled in the Child Service Demonstration Centers. *Journal of Learning Disabilities, 16,* 63–68.

Mann, L., Davis, C.H., Boyer, C.W., Metz, C.M., & Wolford, B. (1983). LD or not LD, that was the question: A retrospective analysis of the Child Service Demonstration Centers' compliance with the federal definition of learning disabilities. *Journal of Learning Disabilities, 16,* 14–17.

Mann, L., Cartwright, G.P., Kenowitz, L.A., Boyer, C.W., Metz, C.M., & Wolford, B. (1984). The Child Service Demonstration Centers: A summary report. *Exceptional Children, 50,* 532–540.

Thurlow, M.L., & Ysseldyke, J.E. (1979). Current assessment and decision making practices in model LD programs. *Learning Disability Quarterly, 4,* 15–24.

See also Diagnosis in Special Education; Learning Disabilities

CHILD VARIANCE PROJECT

The Conceptual Project in Child Variance was undertaken from 1970 to 1972 at the University of Michigan under the direction of William C. Rhodes. It was funded as a special project by the (then) Bureau of Education for the Handicapped to "order and organize the vast but scattered literature on emotional disturbance and other types of variance in children" and to "serve as a prototype for combining the functions of graduate training and professional research" (Rhodes & Tracy, 1974, p. 1). The product of this prodigious undertaking is a series of five volumes in which the literature on explanations of variance, intervention with variant children, and service provision are integrated and synthesized.

The first volume, *Conceptual Models,* has had a significant impact on subsequent treatments of childhood emotional disturbance and the education of disturbed children. The volume is comprised of papers in which explanatory models from five perspectives are presented. These models include biological, behavioral, psychodynamic, sociological, and ecological accounts of deviance.

The organization of the second volume, *Interventions,* derives from the first. In it, intervention with variant children is considered from biophysical, behavioral, psychodynamic, environmental, and countertheoretical perspectives. Of course, the rapid and multifaceted advance in the treatment of disturbed children in the decades since the publication of this volume has limited its usefulness.

In the third volume, *Service Delivery Systems,* the development of contemporary services for children provided by educational, correctional, mental health, and social welfare systems and religious institutions is analyzed from a historical perspective. The fourth volume, *The Future,* is a treatise by Rhodes on the somewhat profound cultural and philosophical changes that must be realized for our soci-ety to fulfill its caretaking role. The fifth volume, *Exercise Book,* presents a series of exercises through which the sometimes complex and abstract content of the previous volumes may be brought to life for students.

Although the project did not realize the ultimate and far-reaching goals set forth by Rhodes in *The Future,* its impact on our thinking about emotional disturbance, the education of emotionally disturbed children, and the training of teachers of the emotionally disturbed has been significant and enduring. The organization of explanatory theory and its application to the understanding of intervention approaches are legacies of the Child Variance Project. Fur-thermore, its emphasis on the understanding of problems in their broadest context provided impetus to the subsequent development of ecological theory and intervention approaches.

REFERENCES

Rhodes, W.C. (1975). *A study of child variance. Exercise book.* Ann Arbor: University of Michigan Press.

Rhodes, W.C., & Tracy, M.L. (1974). Preface. In W.C. Rhodes & M.L. Tracy (Eds.), *A study of child variance. Vol. 2. Interventions* (pp. 1–15). Ann Arbor: University of Michigan Press.

Rhodes, W.C., & Tracy, M.W. (Eds.). (1974). *A study of child variance. Vol. 1. Conceptual models.* Ann Arbor: University of Michigan Press.

Rhodes, W.C., & Tracy, M.L. (1974). *A study of child variance. Vol. 2. Interventions.* Ann Arbor: University of Michigan Press.

Rhodes, W.C., & Tracy, M.W. (Eds.). (1974). *A study of child variance. Vol. 3. Service delivery systems.* Ann Arbor: University of Michigan Press

Rhodes, W.C., & Tracy, M.L. (1974). *A study of child variance. Vol. 4. The future.* Ann Arbor: University of Michigan Press.

See also Affective Education; Emotional Disorders

CHINA, SPECIAL EDUCATION IN

HISTORY OF SPECIAL EDUCATION SERVICES

China has a history of civilization exceeding five thousand years. The description of disabled people (deaf and blind) was first documented in the fourth century BC in Zuo. The progressive thought that all people with disabilities should be well taken care of was explicitly stated in the Book of Rites, in the second century BC. In 1859, Hong Rengan proposed that institutions for disabled people be established. However, the first school for the blind was founded by a British missionary named William Murray in Beijing, in 1874. Thirteen years later (1887), an American, C. R. Mills, became the founder of the first school for the deaf in Shandong. It was not until 1916 when the first Chinese, Zhang Jian, opened Nantong School for the Deaf in Jiangsu, which is still in operation. By 1948, there were a total of 42 special schools for the deaf and blind, with an enrollment of 2,380 students and 360 faculty/staff members. Among these schools, eight were funded by the public. At that time, special education was categorized as social education.

After the People's Republic of China was founded in 1949, the government integrated special education into the general educational system and new special education programs were created in the Department of Education. The number of schools for the deaf and blind increased significantly from 64 to 253 between 1953 and 1963. According to statistics in 1984, the enrollment of deaf and blind students was 33,055, served by 8,000 faculty and staff. Meanwhile, four schools for students with other disabilities came into existence. In 1997, there were a total of 1,440 special education schools—27 higher education institutions, 845 schools for the deaf, 143 schools for the deaf and blind, and 425 schools for children with disabilities. The number of disabled students enrolled also increased to 340,621, along with 43,296 faculty and staff members.

In 1987, the survey results showed that there were 52 million disabled people in China, 4.9% of the national population. It was estimated that 60 million people were handicapped out of 1.2 billion Chinese; among them 12.3 million were under 18, which was 2.58% of the total population. The enrollment rate of school-age children with visual, hearing, speech, and mental disabilities increased from 20% (1991) to nearly 60% (1995).

PRESENT STRUCTURE

Special education can be defined in the following two ways: (a) in a broad sense, it may indicate the education of all children who have special needs including the gifted and talented and juvenile criminals, or (b) in a narrow sense, it may imply the education of all kinds of mentally and physically disabled people. Currently, the emphasis in special education is placed on the training of people, especially children, with various disabilities, though the study of all who need special care in education is being conducted simultaneously.

China is developing a special education system with its own characteristics, responding to the situation of a large number of disabled children, a developing economy, and a developing educational foundation. This system is neither complete segregation nor mainstreaming and inclusiveness; it is a combination of general education and special education—each is independent but also integrated. Special education is in one of three forms: special education schools, special education programs, and learning in regular class. However, the majority of the students are enrolled in either special programs or regular classes in general education schools.

The focus of special education is within the nine-year compulsory education. Early childhood education is considered critical and the early intervention and training of deaf and mentally disabled children have received a great deal of attention. Meanwhile, disabled adult vocational education also grows rapidly. In 1997, 610 adult vocational education institutions were registered and 1.5 million disabled people were trained. In addition to advancing their education in regular higher educational institutions, disabled people also enjoy the privilege of attending two universities founded exclusively for them. Although the national educational department established standard curriculum and instruction materials in special education, local educational institutions are encouraged to make any changes to accommodate their specific needs.

TRENDS AND GOALS FOR THE PRESENT AND NEAR FUTURE

A Chinese-style special education system is being established on the basis of adapting models from other countries to serve the needs of China. The national government has set the following five priorities in developing special education for the near future:

1. The expansion of special education in rural areas will be emphasized before the year 2000. For those places where special education has been available, the focus will be placed on educational improvement and reform. The goal is to increase the enrollment rate of disabled children to that of regular children. By the year 2000, approximately 80% of all blind, deaf, and mentally handicapped children are expected to attend schools.

2. Early childhood special education will be improved considerably, and families and communities are encouraged to participate in early intervention.

3. Vocational training for the disabled will be strengthened, with short-term training as the primary means.

4. Promotions systems will be established for special education teachers to improve their benefits.

5. Further research will be conducted on the education of children with learning disability, autism, and other disabilities.

Due to historical reasons, special education in Taiwan, Hong Kong, and Macao shares similar cultural tradition and background with that in P.R. China. However, each has formed its own characteristics in classification, standards, and educational methods in their process of development. In December of 1997, a symposium was held at Taibei Normal University to discuss special education in mainland China and Taiwan. The theme of the conference was to create a brand new world of special education with love and wisdom. The interaction among Chinese and international special education professionals has increased significantly in recent years. These educators' interactions enhance mutual understanding and advance the knowledge of special education by all nations.

See also Japan, Special Education in

CHLAMYDIA TRACHOMATIS INFECTIONS

Chlamydia trachomatis is the most prevalent sexually transmitted infection in the United States today. The annual incidence is estimated to be as high as 3 million (Washington, Gove, Schachter, & Sweet, 1985). Of sexually active adolescents who were examined, about 22% had a chlamydia infection (Fraser, Rettig, & Kaplan, 1983).

The bacteria can cause painful urination and pelvic, urinary, eye, and respiratory infections in both sexes. Additional symptoms in women may include vaginal discharge, lower abdominal pain or sensitivity, abnormal Pap smear (often described as heavy or moderate inflammation), vaginal bleeding between periods even when taking birth-control pills regularly, and uterine infection. Symptoms in men may include penile discomfort and/or discharge.

If silent or not correctly diagnosed and treated, the disease can lead to such serious complications as pelvic inflammatory disease, ectopic (tubal) pregnancy, infertility, and, possibly, cervical cancer in women and urethritis and sterility in men. Though common, the disease may not be recognized among the mentally handicapped, often thought of as asexual by many medical or social work personnel. Mentally retarded adolescents, and young adults in particular, should receive education in the recognition of chlamydia and other venereal diseases.

Chlamydia infections are curable with a full 21-day treatment with tetracycline. A 7-day treatment may be effective for men, but not for women. Sulfisoxazole and erythromycin are also effective, but penicillin is not.

REFERENCES

Fraser, J., Rettig, P., & Kaplan, D. (1983). Prevalence of cervical chlamydia trachomatis and Neisseria gonorrheae in female adolescents. *Pediatrics, 71,* 333–336.

Washington, E., Gove, S., Schachter, J., & Sweet, R. (1985). Oral contraceptives, chlamydia trachomatis infection, and pelvic inflammatory disease. *Journal of the American Medical Association, 253,* 2246–2250.

See also **Herpes**

CHLORPROMAZINE

Chlorpromazine (CPZ) is the generic name for Thorazine, a phenothiazine used in the treatment of psychoses and other psychiatric disorders (Conley, Tamminga, Bartro, Richardson, Peszke, Lingle, Hegerty, Love, Gounaris, & Zaremba, 1998).

Though the actions of CPZ on the central nervous system (CNS) are not completely understood, it tends to produce the following behavioral changes: decreases apparent agitation, decreases perceptions of anxiety, decreases reports of hallucinatory experiences, produces mild to moderate sedating effects that appear to be both dosage and clinical condition dependent, and decreases spontaneous motor activity.

Because CPZ and all phenothiazines appear to block dopamine receptors in the CNS, a number of motor-related adverse effects are noted, especially during initial usage, chronic usage, or at high dosages. Three general reactions may be observed: dystonic reactions (most often with children, especially during acute infections or while dehydrated; these include spasms of neck muscles, rigidity with extension of back muscles, jaw tics, difficulty in swallowing or talking, and facial spasms with tongue protrusion, and may be accompanied by sweating or pallor); feelings of motor restlessness (e.g., agitation, inability to sit still, tapping of feet, insomnia, strong desire to move about without reported anxiety; often occurs within 2 to 3 days of initiating treatment); parkinsonlike symptoms (most frequent with elderly persons; include masked facial appearance, increased salivation/drooling, motor slowing, including slowed speech, swallowing difficulties, and cogwheel rigidity) (McEvoy, 1985). In addition, blurred vision and dry mouth are reported during early stages of treatment. A persistent motor syndrome called tardive dyskinesia, characterized by rhythmic involuntary movements of facial and oral musculature and occasionally the limbs, may develop in conjunction with CPZ administration. The elderly, especially females, on high dosages are reported as most at risk for this condition.

REFERENCES

Conley, R.R., Tamminga, C.A., Bartro, J.J., Richardson, C., Peske, M. Lingle, J., Hegerty, J., Love, R., Gounaris, C., & Zaremba, S. (1998). Olanzapine compared with chlorpromazine in treatment-resistant schizophrenia. *American Journal of Psychiatry, 155,* 7, 914–920.

McEvoy, G.K. (1985). *American hospital formulary service: Drug information 85.* Bethesda, MD: American Society of Hospital Pharmacists.

See also **Phenothiazines; Stelazine**

CHOLINESTERASE

Neurons are the basic information processing and transmitting elements of the central nervous system. The transmission of impulses across these nerve cells is a biochemical process. As such, a neurochemical process is the foundation of all human behavior.

Impulses travel from one neuron to another across a biochemical junction (synapse). Specifically, when an impulse reaches the terminal button of a neuron, it releases a transmitter substance called acetylcholine (ACh), which causes a temporary change in the membrane of the receiving neuron. If there is sufficient chemical stimulation, the second neuron will subsequently fire. Following the alteration of the membrane potential, the enzyme *cholinesterase* (ChE) neutralizes (destroys) the transmitter substance and thus restores the synapse to a resting state. In this way a single impulse is transmitted through the nervous system.

Neuroscientists have long hypothesized that this biochemical process underlies learning and memory functioning in the brain (Hillgard & Bower, 1975). While a clear relationship has not been established between cholinesterase activity and memory functioning, a number of investigators have consistently found a cholinergic deficit in dementia patients (e.g., Giacobini, Gracon, Smith, & Hoover, 1997; Perry et al., 1978). Based on postmortem examination, these investigators found reduced cholinesterase levels in those areas of the brain typically associated with memory (e.g., the hippocampus). Thus, it appears that a reduction in cholinesterase activity may be related to memory dysfunctions. Research efforts are presently under way that examine the relationship between increased cholinergic activity and memory and learning functions, and the role of cholinesterase in obsessive-compulsive disorder (Erzegovesi, Bellodi & Smeraldi, 1995).

REFERENCES

Erzegovesi, S., Bellodi, L., & Smeraldi, E. (1995). Serum cholinesterase in obsessive-compulsive disorder. *Psychiatry Research, 58,* 3, 265–268.

Giacobini, E., Gracon, S., Smith, F., & Hoover, T. (1997). Cholinesterase inhibitors in Alzheimer disease treatment. In R.E. Becker & E. Giacobini (Eds.), *Alzheimer Disease: From molecular biology to therapy.* Boston, MA: Birkhauser.

Hillgard, E.R., & Bower, G.H. (1975). *Theories of learning.* Englewood Cliffs, NJ: Prentice-Hall.

Perry, E.K, Tomlinson, B.E., Blessed, G., Bergmann, K., Gibson, P.H., & Perry, R.H. (1978). Correlation of cholinergic abnormalities with senile plaques and mental test scores in senile dementia. *British Medical Journal, 2,* 1457–1459.

See also **Neurological Organization; Synapses**

CHOREA

Choreiform movement is a term used to describe a disorder characterized by quick, sudden, random, purposeless, jerky, irregular, spasmodic movement. Choreiform movement can occur in any body part and often is observed in shoulders, arms, and hands, or in the tongue and face as grimaces. Clark (1975) reports a hemichorea may occur on one side of the body with vascular lesions of the basal ganglia of the brain. There are a number of diseases in which choreiform movement is a part of the descriptive syndrome, including hysterical chorea, which is a kind of conversion hysteria with the movement disorder a primary symptom (Hensyl, 1982).

Two major kinds of chorea are of primary interest to school personnel because of their possible school-age onsets and their markedly different outlook for recovery or prognosis. Sydenham's chorea (also known as chorea minor, rheumatic chorea, or St. Vitus's dance) is a disease of the central nervous system that usually occurs following streptococcal inflammation. Its slow start, often several months after the initial infection, begins with choreiform movements after the initial infection, begins with choreiform movements involving all muscles except those of the eyes, and may involve obsessive-compulsive symptoms (Swedo & Leonard, 1994). There are seldom any specific laboratory findings. There is no specific treatment except for sedation and protection from injury, together with prophylactic follow-up for identified residual infection. Recovery is slow and spontaneous, usually within 3 to 6 months, with no permanent damage to the central nervous system. Medical follow-up is recommended, and return to regular school is encouraged as soon as the transitory motor symptoms permit. The disease is reported to be more common in girls, with onset most frequent in summer and early fall (Berkow, 1982).

The second major type of chorea is Huntington's chorea (also known as chorea degenerative, progressive, or hereditary). The age of insidious onset of Huntington's chorea is reported by most sources to be between 30 and 50 years

(Barr, 1979; Chusid, 1976; Clark, 1975). However, a subtype of this disease has been described with onset in childhood, with initial symptoms of stiffness (rigidity), slowed movement (bradykinesia), and later choreiform movement (Berkow, 1982). The disease is characterized by progressive choreiform movement, progressive mental deterioration, and marked personality changes. Swallowing becomes difficult, walking impossible, and dementia profound with progression. Death usually follows within 10 to 15 years. Treatment is symptomatic for motor symptoms. There is no known treatment for the dementia.

Clinical experience suggests that the subtypes with early childhood onset appears to progress more rapidly to early death. The presence of several children with the disorder in one family is a devastating experience. The serious implications of Huntington's chorea should serve to reinforce the importance of differential diagnosis of choreiform movement disorders by a skilled neurologist with appropriate medical follow-up. Supportive special education services should be provided.

REFERENCES

Barr, M.L. (1979). *The human nervous system* (3rd ed.). Hagerstown, MD: Harper & Row.

Berkow, R. (Ed.). (1982). *The Merck manual of diagnosis and therapy* (14th ed.). Rahway, NJ: Merck, Sharp & Dohme.

Chusid, J.G. (1976). *Correlative neuroanatomy and functional neurology* (16th ed.). Los Angeles: Lang Medical.

Clark, R.G. (1975). *Manter and Gatz's essentials of clinical neuroanatomy and neurophysiology* (5th ed.). Philadelphia: Davis.

Hensyl, W.R. (1982). *Stedman's medical dictionary* (24th ed.). Baltimore, MD: Williams & Wilkin.

Swedo, S.E., & Leonard, H. (1994). Childhood movement disorders and obsessive compulsive disorder. *Journal of Clinical Psychiatry, 55,* 3, 32–37.

See also **Genetic Counseling; Heredity; Huntington's Chorea**

CHORIONIC VILLUS SAMPLING (CVS)

Chorionic villus sampling (CVS), sometimes called chorion-villus biopsy, is a relatively new technique that allows diagnosis of chromosomal abnormalities, many inborn errors of metabolism, and other disorders, in the first trimester of pregnancy.

CVS has clear advantages over amniocentesis as a technique for antenatal (prenatal) diagnosis. It can be performed optimally at 9 weeks of pregnancy as opposed to 16 to 18 weeks, and results, including chromosomal analyses, are available in about a week after testing, as opposed to the 2 to 4 weeks for amniocentesis (*Lancet,* 1986). Thus genetic counseling can be provided early in pregnancy in cases where disorders are identified, avoiding some of the ethical and emotional concomitants of later abortion.

Risk of CVS is not established, although the likelihood

of it infecting the embryo appears low. Of particular concern is the suggestion of greater risk of test-induced abortion following CVS than following amniocentesis (Clarke, 1985), although at least one study has found no difference between the two techniques (Jahoda, Vosters, Sacks, & Galjaard, 1985). A number of questions, particularly regarding safety, remain unanswered (*Lancet,* 1986). Widespread availability of CVS will depend on the outcome of large-sample controlled studies of risk and accuracy. Research reports are appearing frequently, and coordinated evaluation studies in Europe, Canada, and the United States began in 1985 (Clarke, 1985).

REFERENCES

Clarke, M. (1985). Fetal diagnosis trial. *Nature, 315,* 269.

Jahoda, M.G., Vosters, R.P.L., Sacks, E.S., & Galjaard, H. (1985). Safety of chorionic villus sampling. *Lancet, 2,* 941–942.

***See also* Amniocentesis; Chromosomal Abnormalities; Maternal Serum Alpha-Fetroprotein (AFP) Screening**

CHROMOSOMES, HUMAN, ANOMALIES AND CYTOGENETIC ABNORMALITIES

Chromosomal (cytogenetic) abnormalities are the most frequent cause of congenital (present at birth) malformations, affecting some 1 in 200 newborns (Moore, 1982). Their importance is reflected in the fact that they account for at least 10 to 15% of individuals with mental retardation severe enough to require institutionalization (Moore, 1982; Pueschel, 1983) and for about 8 to 10% of newborn and early infant deaths (Sperling, 1984). Further, some 30% of spontaneously aborted embryos/fetuses had a chromosomal abnormality, an incidence 50 times higher than that in live births, meaning that incidence in all pregnancies must be about 5% (Sperling, 1984).

Because chromosomal abnormalities involve disruption in the action of many genes, most are associated with severe and varied effects (Brown, 1986). These frequently, but not always, involve general and specific intellective deficits, particular facial anomalies and cardiovascular, digestive, and pulmonary defects. Further, people with a chromosomal abnormalities usually have such characteristic phenotypes (physical appearance and physiological and behavioral functioning) that they frequently look more like unrelated persons with the same chromosomal abnormality than like their own siblings (Moore, 1982). The common characteristics that differentiate individuals with one abnormality from normal people or those with a different abnormality are called syndromes. Some two dozen chromosomally based syndromes have been identified. Although some, particularly the familiar Down's, Klinefelter's, and Turner's syndromes are relatively common, others are so rare that only 50 or so cases have been reported (Smith, 1982).

Vogel and Motulsky (1979, p. 18) elegantly describe hu-

man cytogenetics as "a successful late arrival." Although the chromosome theory of inheritance had been proposed in 1902, cytogenetics really began in 1956 with the discovery that the diploid number of human chromosomes was 46 instead of the commonly accepted 48. When in 1959 researchers discovered chromosomal bases for three common and well-established human syndromes (Down's, Klinefelter's, and Turner's), human cytogenetics really came into its own. Since then, a variety of chromosomally based syndromes have been discovered on the basis of now routine cytogenic analysis of spontaneously aborted fetuses, early death newborns and infants, and individuals with physical and behavioral abnormalities. A number of children traditionally labeled by diagnosticians as "syndromish in appearance" (something looks wrong but no etiology is known) now are identified as having a chromosomal abnormality. In most cases, the description of the physical and behavioral characteristics of the syndrome has followed, rather than preceded, chromosomal analysis. Further, subsequent studies have identified multiple chromosomal bases for syndromes such as Down's, Klinefelter's, and Turner's that help to account for high variability among and even within affected individuals. A variety of technical advances account for much of our knowledge about these abnormalities (Sperling, 1984; Vogel & Motulsky, 1979).

NORMAL AND ABNORMAL KARYOTYPES

Normal humans have 23 pairs of chromosomes in all body cells, 22 pairs of autosomes, and one pair of sex chromosomes. Females normally have two long X sex chromosomes and males one long X and one shorter Y sex chromosomes. Chromosomes (colored bodies) are visible only early in mitosis, when cell samples are subjected to certain stains. A karyotype is a picture of chromosomes arranged by pair. The 22 autosomal pairs are arranged from the longest (1) to the shortest (22), followed by the sex chromosomes. Chromosomes are grouped into three types: metacentric (e.g., numbers 1 and 3), where the arms are nearly equal in length; submetacentric (e.g., numbers 4 and 5), where the "p" arm is distinctly shorter than the "q"; and acrocentric (e.g., numbers 14 and 21), which have a secondary constriction and abbreviated and apparently genetically inactive satellite "p" arms.

Normal Cell Division. During mitosis, the process of duplication of body cells, each of the 46 chromosomes divides and one member of each migrates to a pole of the cells. When the cell divides, each offspring cell contains the same 23 pairs of chromosomes. Thus mitosis is a process of chromosome duplication. In meiosis, the process of production of germ cells (sperm and eggs), each of the 23 chromosome pairs divides and one member of each pair migrates to a pole of the cell. When the cell divides, each offspring has 23 chromosomes. Thus each germ cell has 23 chromosomes. Meiosis is a process of chromosome reduction. Women's eggs will all have 22 autosomes and an X chromosome; men's sperm all have 22 autosomes and can have either an X or Y. In sexual recombination, when a sperm penetrates an egg, the resulting zygote normally has the appropriate 46 chromosomes. Thus gender of offspring is determined by the father's sperm.

Abnormal Karyotypes. Abnormalities can be: (1) an abnormal total number of chromosomes in an individual's body cells; (2) structural aberrations resulting from breakage in one or more chromosomes; or (3) populations of cells of different chromosome numbers in the same individual (mosaicism).

Aneuploidies refers to deviations, greater or fewer, in number of chromosomes from the normal 46. The most common aneuploidy is trisomy 21, which accounts for the greatest number of chromosomal abnormalities in spontaneous abortions as well as in live births. Trisomies on most pairs are prenatally lethal. Similarly, monosomy, absence of one of a pair, resulting in fewer that 46 chromosomes, is virtually always prenatally lethal, except for Turner's syndrome, in which one X chromosome is missing (45,X). Even then, only one in 150 to 200 45,X embryos survives to fullterm birth. The most common cause of aneuploidy is nondisjunction, the failure of a chromosome pair to split during formation of germ cells in meiosis. Thus one offspring germ cell will have a "double dose" of one chromosome and the other will have none. Anaphase lag can also produce monosomy.

Mosaicism results from nondisjunction occurring mitotically in a cell in an embryo in an early stage of development. As a result, if the embryo survives and continues to develop, it will have both normal and abnormal, generally trisomic, cell populations. Because of the presence of normal cells, individuals with mosaicism will generally show less severe symptoms than those with the pure syndrome.

The basis for nondisjunction is not known, but is presumed to be manifested biochemically. In nondisjunction Down's syndrome, approximately 80% of the cases result from maternal and 20% from paternal nondisjunction (Sperling, 1984). Since all autosomal trisomies (not just Down's syndrome) increase dramatically with maternal age, research focuses on factors that correlate with aging, including potential problems with aging oocytes themselves. Hypothesized links with irradiation, chemical agents, methods of birth control, and endocrine factors have not been fully confirmed, but some evidence suggests they play a role (Hassold & Jacobs, 1984).

Chromosomes may break, with material being either lost or attached to another chromosome. The most common structural aberrations are translocations, which result when two chromosomes break and parts of one are transferred to another. A reciprocal translocation occurs when two nonhomologous chromosomes exchange pieces. Individuals with such translocation chromosomes themselves have an appropriate balance of chromosomes and are phenotypically normal. Since they are carriers of a translocation chromosome, their offspring may suffer from duplication-deficiency syndromes, notably partial trisomies.

Important because of clinical implications are centric fusions, or Robertsonian translocations. Centric fusion occurs when two acrocentric chromosomes each break near the centromere and rejoin. Generally, the short arms of both and the centromere of one are lost. Again, individuals may be unaffected, although they have one fewer than normal chromosome, but they are carriers. Their offspring may have a trisomy syndrome. Monosomies are also possible, but appear to be prenatally lethal. The best known translocation is Down's syndrome, resulting from centric fusion of chromosome 21 with chromosome 14 or, less frequently, 15.

Several other structural aberrations also may occur. Simple loss of part of a chromosome may result in a deletion syndrome. Isochromosomes occur when instead of a chromosome pair dividing longitudinally through the centromere, it divides horizontally, producing two chromosomes with identical arms. Fertilization will produce a cell with three "p" or "q" arms and only one of the other. When the segment between two breaks in a chromosome becomes inverted, reversing the gene order, an inversion results. Ring chromosomes occur when both ends of a chromosome break off and the tips of the centric segment rejoin. The resulting circular chromosome is unstable and has material from both ends deleted.

Standard Nomenclature. Normal and abnormal human karyotypes are described using a standard system, general aspects and examples of which are given here. More detailed descriptions are in Cohen and Nadler (1983), Smith (1982), Vogel and Motulsky (1979), and most human genetics textbooks.

As shown in Table 1, the order of information is (1) total number of chromosomes; (2) sex chromosomes; and (3) any abnormalities. Extra or missing chromosomes are indicated by "+" and "−", respectively, before the affected chromosome's number; extra or missing parts are indicated by "+" and "−", respectively, after the affected part. Structural aberrations are indicated by a standard abbreviation followed, parenthetically, by the number of the affected chro-

Table 1 Examples of Karyotype Nomenclature

Karyotype	Description
46,XX; 46,XY	Normal female and male
47,XX,+21	Female with trisomy 21 (Down's syndrome)
46,XY/47,XY+21	Male with mosaic trisomy 21 (Down's syndrome)
46XY,+t(14q21q)	Male with Down's syndrome owed to centric-fusion type translocation between chromosomes 14 and 21
46,XX,del(5p) or 46,XX,5p—	Female with cri du chat owed to deletion of part of short arm of chromosome 5
46,XY,fra X(q27)	Male with fragile X syndrome, involving constriction at distal end of long arm of chromosome

mosome(s). Then, also parenthetically, the affected arm(s) and, if known, the chromosomal band numbers, are stated. Mosaics are indicated by a (/) mark separating descriptions of the two cell populations.

ABNORMALITIES AND THEIR CHARACTERISTICS

Although chromosomal syndromes vary widely in their effects, the various types share some characteristics. Because much genetic material has been either added or is missing, many are lethal and most of the rest involve multiple and severe complications. However, as normal individuals vary in their physical and behavioral characteristics, so do those affected by chromosomal abnormalities. Not all will show even all of the major effects.

The description and characteristics of major cytogenic abnormalities occurring in live births are in Tables 2 and 3. It is important that different sources vary in their estimates of incidence and specification of major characteristics. In a number of cases, subsequent cases have led to changes in what were initially thought to be defining characteristics. For example, Cat-eye syndrome (trisomy 22p) was named for the striking coloboma of the iris seen originally. However, it has occurred only in a minority of the 40 cases that had been reported at the time of Smith's summary (1982).

Chromosomal Aneuploidies. The most common abnormalities are aneuploidies, involving an added or missing chromosome (Table 2). Multiple forms of some may occur. By far the most common is Down's syndrome (trisomy 21), but several others have been reported. Early death is common in all, and in some types virtually all die in early infancy. Although each has individual characteristics, all involve brain damage generally resulting in moderate to severe mental retardation, congenital heart disease, and malformed ears. Specific facial, limb, and digit abnormalities are also common. All increase dramatically in incidence with maternal age (Vogel & Motulsky, 1979).

Turner's and Klinefelter's syndromes have clear phenotypic characteristics and were described before the development of modern cytogenic techniques. Both are associated with absence of puberty and sterility. Unfortunately, as pointed out by Brown (1986), textbook authors have frequently described sex-chromosome aneuploidies in chapters on mental retardation. However, standard forms are associated with low average intelligence (IQ ≈ 90), not mental retardation, although incidence of mental retardation is higher than among the normal population. Many affected individuals will complete high school and college. Mosaic Turner females and Klinefelter males will be less affected. Klinefelter males and Poly-X females with extra X chromosomes above trisomy for sex chromosomes are much more adversely affected and likely to be retarded.

Klinefelter and Poly-X syndromes increase with maternal age (Hassold & Jacobs, 1984). However, incidence of neither Turner's nor XYY syndrome correlates with maternal age, consistent with largely paternal origin (Hassold & Jacobs, 1984; Simpson, 1982).

Abnormal Parts of Chromosomes. Several partial trisomy syndromes, involving extra chromosomal material, and deletion syndromes are known, as shown in Table 3. Mental retardation of some degree is common to all. Low birth weight and specific facial and digital anomalies are also frequent.

Of particular current interest is Fragile X syndrome, resulting from a constriction in the X chromosome, which cytogenic studies reveal to be relatively common. Associated with mental retardation in affected males, it appears to be second only to Down's syndrome as a cytogenic cause of mental retardation.

IMPLICATIONS FOR SPECIAL EDUCATORS

As cytogenic analyses become more standard, increasing numbers of children will be identified as having some chromosomal disorder. Many minor ones will have few implications for teachers. Others will be associated with general and specific intellectual deficits, coordination problems, and emotional disorders. Special educators and others in education generally may need to become familiar with the syndrome and standard nomenclature. Further, research will doubtless render some current knowledge incorrect and we must be ready to accept new information. It should be kept in mind that syndromes can induce stereotypes, and that affected children should be treated on the basis of their individual characteristics, not the general ones of a syndrome.

REFERENCES

Brown, R.T. (1986). Etiology and development of exceptionality. In R.T. Brown & C.R. Reynolds (Eds.), *Psychological perspectives on childhood exceptionality: A handbook* (pp. 181–229). New York: Wiley.

Cohen, M.M., & Nadler, H.L. (1983). Chromosomes and their abnormalities. In R.E. Behrman & V.C. Vaughn, III (Eds.), *Nelson textbook of pediatrics* (12th ed.) (pp. 288–310). Philadelphia: Saunders.

Hassold, T.J., & Jacobs, P.A. (1984). Trisomy in man. *Annual Review of Genetics, 18,* 69–97.

Moore, K.L. (1982). *The developing human* (3rd ed.). Philadelphia: Saunders.

Pueschel, S.M. (1983). The child with Down syndrome. In M.D. Levine, W.B. Carey, A.C. Crocker, & R.T. Gross (Eds.), *Developmental-behavioral pediatrics* (pp. 353–362). Philadelphia: Saunders

Simpson, J.L. (1982). Abnormal sexual differentiation in humans. *Annual Review of Genetics, 16,* 193–224.

Smith, D.W. (1982). *Recognizable patterns of human malformation* (2nd ed.). Philadelphia: Saunders.

Sperling, K. (1984). Frequency and origin of chromosome abnormalities in man. In G. Obe (Ed.), *Mutations in man* (pp. 128–146). Berlin and New York: Springer-Verlag.

Vogel, F., & Motulsky, A.G. (1979). *Human genetics.* Berlin and New York: Springer-Verlag.

See also **Chromosomal Abnormalities; Cri Du Chat; Down's Syndrome; Etiology; Fragile X**

Table 2 Chromosomal Aneuploidies and Characteristics

Syndrome	Incidence (live births)	Source	Characteristics
Autosomal Trisomies			
Trisomy 8	Very rare	Mosaicism (mainly)	Variable height; MR (M → S); CHD; poor coordination; prominent forehead; deep-set eyes; digital abnormalities
Trisomy 9	Very rare	Mosaicism (mainly)	LBW; MR (S); CHD; low-set malformed ears; joint contractures; majority die in infancy
Trisomy 13 (Patau syndrome)	1:7000 to 20,000	Nondisjunction	LBW; MR (S); CHD; apnea; seizures; bilateral cleft lip and/or palette; failure to thrive; majority die in infancy
Trisomy 18 (Edwards syndrome)	1:8000	Nondisjunction	Three times more frequent in females; LBW; MR (S); failure to thrive; CHD; prominent occiput, majority die in infancy
Trisomy 21 (Down's syndrome)	1:650–800	Nondisjunction—94% Mosaicism—2.4% Translocation—3.3%	MR (M → Mod); CHD; hypotonia; flat occiput; epicanthic fold; large tongue; above average infant death rate
Trisomy 22	Very rare	Nondisjunction (?)	MR; growth retardation; microcephaly; CHD; cleft palate; digit abnormalities; majority die in infancy
Sex Chromosome Aneuploidies			
Turner's syndrome	1:10,000	Various	Short stature; sterility; short webbed neck; broad, flat chest; IQ ≈ 90
(45,X)	57% of cases	Missing paternal X	
(45,X/46XX, others)	12% of cases	Mosaicism	
(45,X/46,XY)	4% of cases	Mosaicism	
(other)	27% of cases	Inversion and deletion	
Klinefelter's syndrome	1:1000	Various	Sterility; hypogonadism; decreased facial and pubic hair; IQ ≈ 90; behavior problems
(47,XXY)	82% of cases	Nondisjunction	
(48,XXXY)`	3% of cases	Nondisjunction	More problems with added X chromosomes
(49,XXXXY)	<1% of cases	Nondisjunction	
(47,XXY/46,XY)	8% of cases	Mosaicism	
(Others)	6% of cases		
Poly X Syndrome	1:1000	Nondisjunction	No characteristic features; some delayed speech and motor development; more problems with added X chromosomes
(47,XXX)	98+% of cases		
(48,XXXX)	Rare		
47,XYY syndrome	1:1000	Nondisjunction	Variable features; tall; impulsive behavior; IQ ≈ 90

MR = mental retardation (S = severe; Mod = moderate, M = mild); CHD = congenital heart disease; LBW = low birth weight. Information from Cohen and Nadler (1983), Gerald and Meryash (1983), and Smith (1982).

Table 3 Syndromes Involving Abnormal Part of Chromosomes

Syndrome	Incidence	Source	Characteristics
Autosomal Partial Trisomies			
Trisomy 9p	Rare	Translocation (?)	MR (S); delayed growth and puberty; delayed language; digital abnormalities
Partial trisomy 10q	Rare	Translocation (?)	LBW; MR (S); flat occiput; digital abnormalities; CHD; 50% die in infancy
Trisomy 20p	Rare	Translocation (?)	MR (M → Mod); hypotonia; facial abnormalities; digital deformities
Cat-eye syndrome (trisomy 22p)	Rare	Translocation (?)	MR (M); emotional retardation; normal growth; CHD; coloboma of iris; other eye defects
Autosomal Partial Deletion			
4p-	Rare (?)	Partial deletion	LBW; MR (S); beaked nose; microcephaly; cleft palate; hypotonia; seizures; early death
Cri du chat (5p-)	Rare	Partial deletion	LBW; MR (S); catike cry; hypotonia; epicanthal folds; microcephaly
9p-	Rare	Partial deletion	Normal growth; MR (S); micronathia; trignocephaly; wide-spaced nipples
11p- (Andiria-Wilms Tumor Association)	Rare	Partial deletion	MR (Mod → S); growth deficiency; microcephaly; eye defects: micronathia; andiria; Wilms tumor
13p-	Rare	Partial deletion	LBW; MR (S); failure to thrive; microcephaly; CHD; facial and digital abnormalities
18p-	Rare	Partial deletion	Variability in effect; LBW; MR (variable); epicanthal folds; large, floppy ears
18q-	Rare	Partial deletion	LBW; MR (S); seizures; CHD; microcephaly; limb, digital, and genital abnormalities
21q-	Rare	Partial deletion	MR; hypertonia; growth retardation; microcephaly; micrognathia; large ears
22q-	Rare	Partial deletion	MR; hypotonia; microcephaly; epicanthal folds; digital abnormalities
Constriction Syndrome			
Fragile X	1:1000 males	Constriction at distal end of long arm of X chromosome	Long face; prominent chin; MR (M → S); developmental delay; language problems; specific learning problems

MR = mental retardation (S = severe; Mod = moderate, M = mild); CHD = congenital heart disease; LBW = low birth weight. Information from Cohen and Nadler (1983), Gerald and Meryash (1983), and Smith (1982).

Syndrome; Klinefelter's Syndrome; Turner's Syndrome; XYY Syndrome

CHRONIC ILLNESS IN CHILDREN

There are many chronic illnesses that children may suffer from. They include some but not all of the conditions regarded as being within the traditional scope of special education. Among important chronic illnesses are asthma, cystic fibrosis, diabetes, epilepsy, leukemia, juvenile rheumatoid arthritis, muscular dystrophy, sickle cell anemia, and thalassemia.

Each group within the broad constituencies of chronic illness by itself may not constitute a large number of children, but together they represent a large group. Thus, Gortmaker (1985) and Pless and Roghmann (1971) have estimated that some 10 to 15% of children have chronic health impairments of some sort. While many of these impairments are mild, others are severe and debilitating. Hobbs, Perrin, and Ireys (1985) estimate that at least 1 million children have severe diseases and that many of these diseases are chronic. This number expands if Hobbes et al. include children who might otherwise be considered physically handicapped, e.g., children with spina bifida, and others who have suffered severe and catastrophic trauma from injuries.

Many of the children who suffer from chronic illness, e.g, asthma or diabetes, have their health needs reasonably well met within the mainstream of society (by medical practitioners and public health agencies). The more severe of these illnesses, however, require more persistent, pervasive, and demanding care. The severity of a child's medical condition does not directly relate to the type and severity of the problem encountered. Some children with severe medical conditions may have little difficulty in participating within the mainstream of everyday living, including at school. Others with relatively mild physical or physiological disturbances may have their lives severely affected by their problems. There is no direct correlation between chronic illness and poor psychosocial functioning (Midence, 1994).

Despite the fact that some chronically ill children are being effectively served under current special education laws and regulations, there are those who believe that the parents and policy makers who were the prime movers in the creation of state and federal programs for the education of the handicapped largely overlooked the needs of chronically ill children (Walker & Jacobs, 1985). Hobbes, Perrin, and Ireys claim that chronically ill children and youths have "shared in relatively little of the sustained attention given to children with other handicapping conditions, such as mentally retardation" (1985, pp. 4–5).

REFERENCES

Gortmaker, S.L. (1985). Demography of chronic childhood diseases. In N. Hobbes & J.M. Perrin (Eds.), *Issues in the care of children with chronic illness: A sourcebook on problems, services and policies.* San Francisco: Jossey-Bass.

Hobbs, N., Perrin, J.M., & Ireys, H.T. (1985). *Chronically ill children and their families.* San Francisco: Jossey-Bass.

Midence, K. The effects of chronic illness on children and their families: An overview. *Genetic, Social, & General Monographs, 120,* 3, 309–326.

Pless, I.B., & Roghmann, K.J. (1971). Chronic illness and its consequences: Some observations based on three epidemiological surveys. *Journal of Pediatrics, 79,* 351–359.

Walker, D.K., & Jacobs, F. (1985). Public school programs for chronically ill children. In N. Hobbes & J.M. Perrin (Eds.), *Issues in the care of children with chronic illness: A sourcebook on problems, services and policies.* San Francisco: Jossey-Bass.

See also **Asthma; Diabetes; Other Health Impaired**

CHURCH WORK WITH THE HANDICAPPED

During the early development of Christianity, the influence of Christ's healing works and the Apostle Paul's writings shaped the Christian attitude toward handicapped persons.

However, as Christianity spread across Europe, especially during the Middle Ages, Christian attitudes varied. Religious teaching led to persecution (witnessed in the Inquisition), isolation (lest a clean person be tainted), and protection (many monasteries tended to the handicapped) (Hewett & Forness, 1977; Scheerenberger, 1982). It was during this time (1377 AD) that the first asylum (Hospital of St. Mary of Bethlehem, known as Bedlam) was founded. In the early part of the seventeenth century, St. Vincent dePaul initiated a program for "idiots." In the eighteenth century William Tuke, a Quaker, established a program for the humane treatment of the mentally retarded and the mentally ill (Scheerenberger, 1982). Also in the eighteenth century, the charitable work that had been the purview of the church began to receive attention from governments (Hewett & Forness, 1977). Religious organizations such as the St. Vincent dePaul Society, and much later the YMCA and YWCA, provided services, but their roles were diminished.

In addition to the hundreds of religious schools that provide special education and residential services for handicapped children, and the hundreds of hospitals and medical care facilities that are church supported, there are a large number of organizations dedicated to service/advocacy for the handicapped. The following is a list of some of these organizations:

1. Board of Missions, Ministry of the Deaf, Lutheran Church–Missouri Synod
2. Department of Urban Ministries, Board of Missions, United Methodist Church
3. Ephphatha Missions for the Deaf and Blind
4. Episcopal Conference of the Deaf
5. International Catholic Deaf Association
6. National Congress of Jewish Deaf
7. Xavier Society for the Blind
8. National Apostolate with Mentally Retarded Persons
9. Advisory Committee on Ministry with Handicapped Persons, United States Catholic Conference
10. Task Force on Church and Disability, World Council of Churches

REFERENCES

Hewett, F.M., & Forness, S.R. (1977). *Education of exceptional learners.* Boston: Allyn & Bacon.

Scheerenberger, R.C. (1982). Treatment from ancient times to the present. In P.T. Cegelka & H.J. Prehm (Eds.), *Mental retardation: From categories to people* (pp. 44–75). Columbus, OH: Merrill.

CITIZEN ADVOCACY GROUP

See ADVOCACY GROUP, CITIZEN.

CIVIL RIGHTS OF THE HANDICAPPED

A person with disabilities has certain rights guaranteed by law that relate to education, employment, health care, senior citizen activities, welfare, and any other or private services, programs, or activities that receive federal assistance.

Individuals with disabilities have the right to travel assisted or unassisted on airplanes, trains, buses, and taxi cabs. Persons with disabilities have a right to gain entrance to public facilities without being inconvenienced, and buildings should be free of architectural barriers. Handicapped individuals have a right to receive equal treatment by doctors and hospitals. This will require that medical personnel acquire understanding and knowledge of disabilities. Handicapped persons have a right to apply for any license (e.g., marriage, fishing) made available to nonhandicapped individuals without additional requirements or embarrassment. It is unlawful to discriminate against the handicapped regarding employment practices. It is also unlawful for the owner of commercial property to refuse to sell, rent, lease, or in any way discriminate because of a disability. As important as the services needed is the right to feel assured that the members of society will look on the handicapped as responsible people capable of making a contribution to society.

It is the responsibility of the Office for Civil Rights in the Department of Education and the Office for Civil Rights in the Department of Health and Human Services to enforce federal laws prohibiting discrimination against persons on the basis of race, color, national origin, sex, age, or handicap in federally assisted programs or activities, and to investigate discrimination complaints brought by individuals under these statutes (Office of Civil Rights, 1998).

REFERENCE

Office of Civil Rights. (1998). Mission Statement. Washington, DC: U.S. Department of Education.

See also **Accessibility of Buildings; Accessibility of Programs; Americans with Disabilities Act; Attitudes Towards the Handicapped; Social Behavior of the Handicapped**

CLASS-ACTION SUITS

Class actions are lawsuits in which a class of persons is represented by one or more of its members. In federal and in most state courts, groups of persons who have similar interests in the law and fact of the lawsuit can sue or be sued through a representative who acts on their behalf. A class action offers the following: the benefits of a clear resolution of a specific issue; the convenience of a useful method to assert legal rights in cases that have common interest where small individual claims might otherwise preclude judicial relief; and the saving of time, money, and effort by eliminating repetitious lawsuits (Redden & Vernon, 1980).

Court rulings in class-action suits have stimulated both litigation and legislation on behalf of handicapped individuals. During the 1950s courts were confronted with class actions concerning the civil rights of handicapped children and adults. The majority of the actions were focused on the public's responsibility to provide education and treatment

for handicapped citizens. The legal doctrines which courts have relied in substantiating the right to an education for the handicapped stem, in part, from the Supreme Court ruling in *Brown v. Board of Education.* The Supreme Court ruled in this landmark decision that all children are constitutionally entitled to an equal educational opportunity (Abeson & Bolick, 1974; Kirp, 1976). Subsequent class-action suits addressed the enforcement of the ruling in *Brown v. Board of Education* (Martin, 1980). Handicapped children were no longer denied a public education, however, many issues remained unresolved, and new issues surfaced in the courts, as well. For example, several state laws still regarded the severely handicapped as uneducable and thereby excluded this group from public schools. Questions regarding racial overrepresentation in special programs were also subjects of extensive litigation (Kirp, 1976).

The major legislation that governs our present delivery of services to exceptional children, Individuals with Disabilities Education Act (IDEA), precipitated litigation that was more diverse and more individualized, thereby decreasing the numbers of representative classes. With the advent of the earlier version of IDEA, PL 94-142, class-action suits declined and individual legal claims were filed in matters of due process, Individual Education Plan (IEP) challenges, placement, and related services.

REFERENCES

Abeson, A., & Bolick, N. (1974). *A continuing summary of pending and completed litigation regarding the education of handicapped children,* Reston, VA: Council for Exceptional Children.

Kirp, D. (1976). *Trends in education: The special child goes to court.* Columbus, OH: University Council for Educational Administration.

Martin, R. (1980). *Educating handicapped children the legal mandate.* Champaign, IL: Research Press.

Redden, K. & Vernon, E. (1980). *Modern legal glossary.* Charlottesville, VA: Michie.

See also **Brown v. Board of Education; Education for All Handicapped Children Act of 1975; Larry P.**

CLASSROOM MANAGEMENT

Broadly conceived, classroom management refers to the orderly organization of materials and activities and the development of acceptable student behavior within the school learning environment. Although a deceptively simple concept, any consideration of the purposes and techniques of classroom management suggests numerous other educational concerns. Classroom management techniques must be in harmony with the school's perception of the nature and purpose of instruction and must satisfy a significant number of ethical and legal concerns. Similarly, the school's organizational structure must be constructed in a manner that will allow meeting the psychoeducational assumptions implicit in any selected alternative. For these reasons, classroom management techniques must be selected with regard to many considerations. Few authors advocate a single approach as optimal for all settings.

Although classroom management can be broadly conceived, the usual topic of interest is the behavior of students and, specifically, discipline in the classroom. Clearly, the control of student behavior receives far more emphasis than other potential events that could be associated with classroom management. Public opinion consistently notes school discipline, often described as student control, to be a major problem in schools. In addition, a 1981 survey of teachers conducted by the National Education Association found 90% of the respondents indicating negative instructional outcomes as a result of student misbehavior. Cruickshank (1981) found similar results in that the control of students was seen to be one of the five most important issues identified by teachers throughout the course of a 15-year longitudinal study. Clearly then, classroom management is now virtually synonymous with discipline. Why discipline is a problem in contemporary U.S. schools is not fully understood.

All models of classroom management have had significant influence on the development of techniques for classroom management. The sociological and ecological models, though theoretically suggesting great promise, have generally not spawned specific procedures widely placed into practice. The biophysical model has largely remained the purview of physicians. Both the psychodynamic and the behavioral models have, however, demonstrated immense appeal to educators and have generated many variations in approach. Of the two, the behavioral model is now the more dominant in the special education literature, but is now taking into account social constructivist classrooms (Brophy, 1998). Early conceptualizations that relied on the teacher's control of contingencies have been augmented in recent years through the widespread use of modeling techniques (e.g., Bandura, 1969), cognitive behavior modification (e.g., Meichenbaum, 1977), group contingency programs (e.g., Litow & Pumroy, 1975), and other advances. Significant problems in transfer of training and generalization of learned behaviors remain obstacles to the use of the approach. An excellent overview of representative classroom management techniques can be found in Charles (1985) and Walker and Shea (1984).

REFERENCES

Bandura, A. (1969). *Principles of behavior modification*. New York: Holt.

Brophy, J. (1998). Classroom management as socializing students into clearly articulated roles. *Journal of Classroom Interaction, 33*, 1, 1–4.

Charles, C.M. (1985). *Building classroom discipline: From models to practice* (2nd ed.). New York: Longman.

Cruickshank, D. (1981). What we know about teachers' problems. *Educational Leadership, 38*, 402–405.

Litow, L., & Pumroy, D.K. (1975). A brief review of classroom group-oriented contingencies. *Journal of Applied Behavior Analysis, 8*, 341–347.

Meichenbaum, D. (1977). *Cognitive-behavior modification: An integrative approach*. New York: Plenum.

Walker, J.E., & Shea, T.M. (1984). Behavior management: *A practical approach for educators* (3rd ed.). St. Louis: Times Mirror/Mosby.

See also **Applied Behavior Analysis; Behavior Assessment; Discipline**

CLEFT LIP/PALATE

The phenomenon of cleft lip and palate is rather frequent all over the world: 0.1% of all neonates are born with a more or less severe cleft, ranging from a cleft uvula or a partly cleft upper lip to a two-sided complete cleft of upper lip, jaw, and hard and soft palate. Normally, three main groups are discerned: cleft lip only (CL), cleft palate only (CP), and cleft lip and palate combined (CLP). Cleft lip and palate malformations are congenital and originate in the fourth to seventh week (CL) and in the seventh to twelfth week (CP) of embryonic development. Although in some cases viral, medical, and X-ray influences may play a role in causing these malformations, they are generally believed to have a hereditary basis. The chance of cleft lip and palate increases accordingly as the occurrence of clefts in a family are more frequent and more severe, and with the closeness of the relationship (mother or father). The occurrence of clefts is more frequent in boys than in girls, and, moreover, types of clefts are not equally divided between the sexes.

Problems arising from being born with a cleft lip and palate are highly dependent on the part of the world in which the baby is born. In Third World countries, where no surgery is done on cleft lip and palate children, the main problem is survival and nourishment. In highly developed countries, the problems for cleft lip and palate children mainly concern communication and socialization. But even in these countries, a large differentiation can be found in the treatment of children with cleft lip and palate depending on the scientific ideas and theories of the treating medical team.

In most countries where surgery is applied, the child passes through a whole program of treatment and rehabilitation during the first years of life, often starting with healing of the lip followed by closure of the soft palate some months later, and sometimes the hard palate as well. The schedule and type of treatment depends to a large extent on the philosophy of the medical team. For example, the plastic surgeon will stress the aesthetic and visible aspects, the orthodontist the dental aspects, the speech pathologist the importance of the development of language and speech, and so on. Nevertheless, it will be clear that the best results are achieved by an interdisciplinary team of experts in close cooperation, all aiming to establish normal appearance, normal dental function, and good language and communication skills. The whole rehabilitation program is normally spread over more than 15 years.

As for the speech and language development and related verbal expression abilities of children with cleft lip and palate, a clear delay is found compared with the average population. One of the causes might be hearing problems, since children with cleft lip and palate have increased chances of inflammation of the middle ear combined with hearing impairment. Nevertheless, these possible hearing losses are not considered to be the main cause of the speech and language delays. Nor are the pronunciation problems that result from the abnormalities of the speech production mechanism, although a thorough speech training program will nearly always be necessary. No one-to-one relationship can be found between the severity of the malformation or the proportions of the cleft and the degree of delay in language and speech development. More and more, the psychosocial development of the child is believed to be a ground for speech and language problems.

Because interaction between parent and child is the cradle of the development of communication, it is clear that acceptance of the infant and his or her difficulties is a must. The birth of a child with a cleft lip and palate will undoubtedly cause the parents a degree of concern. The questions of the parents, their anxieties and concerns, require immediate professional counseling to create safe and adjusted surroundings for the child. Well-balanced interaction between parents and infant provides the possibility for the cleft palate child to develop normal linguistic, communicative, and social skills.

See also **Language Deficiencies and Deficits; Language Disorders, Expressive; Physical Anomalies**

CLERC, LAURENT (1785–1869)

Laurent Clerc, deaf from the age of one, was educated at the Institution Nationale des Sourdes Muets in Paris; following graduation served as a teacher there. He traveled to the United States with Thomas Hopkins Gallaudet to open the nation's first school for the deaf, now the American School for the Deaf, at Hartford, Connecticut, in 1817. Schooled in the teaching methods of Epée and Sicard, Clerc was the school's first teacher and was responsible for the training of new teachers.

Clerc was the first educated deaf person to be seen in the United States. He exemplified the potential of education for the deaf, and was influential in the movement to establish public responsibility for the education of the deaf.

REFERENCES
Lane, H. (1984). *When the mind hears.* New York: Random House.

Turner, W.W. (1871). Laurent Clerc. *American Annals of the Deaf, 15,* 14–25.

CLINICAL EVALUATION OF LANGUAGE FUNDAMENTALS

The Clinical Evaluation of Language Fundamentals, Third Edition (CELF-3) is an individually administered diagnostic battery designed for the identification, diagnosis, and follow-up evaluation of language skill deficits in the areas of listening (receptive) and speaking (expressive). The CELF-3 can be administered to persons aged 6 through 21 and takes approximately 30 to 45 minutes to administer. The full battery contains 11 subtests, but only 6 are needed to obtain the global standard scores for Receptive Language, Expressive Language, and Total Language Scores. The CELF-3 is comprised of sentence structure, word structure, concepts and directions, formulated sentences, word classes, recalling sentences, sentence assembly, semantic relationships (core subtests) and word associations, listening to paragraphs, and rapid, automatic naming (supplementary subtests).

The CELF-3 was standardized on 2450 students ranging in age from 6 to 21 years. The entire standardization sample consisted of normally achieving children. Thus, an issue of generalizability results from the use of the test to identify those who are impaired. Tests of internal consistency ranged from .83 to .95 for the global standard scores and from .54 to .95 for the individual subtests. Test-retest reliability (based on repeated administration with 152 of the examinees form the standardization set) ranged from .52 to .90 for the individual subtests and from .80 to .91 for the global standard scores. Validity was examined through the comparison of the CELF-3 with the Wechsler Intelligence Scale for Children (WISC-III). A strong correlation of $r = .75$ resulted. Gillam noted that the CELF-3's relationship to the WISC-III supports of the idea that the CELF-3 is a good measure of verbal ability but leaves much to be desired, as a measure of criterion-related validity (relating the CELF-3 to an achievement test) would have been more convincing (1998).

REFERENCE
Gillam, R.B. (1998). Review of the Clinical Evaluation of Language Fundamentals, Third Edition. In J.C. Impara & B.S. Plake (Eds.), *The thirteenth mental measurements yearbook* (pp. 261–263). Lincoln, NE: Buros Institute of Mental Measurements.

CLINICAL INTERVIEW

Assessment interviews are conducted to identify and define current problems, to collect information concerning why current problems exist, or to make a diagnostic decision. The focus can be on information the client provides directly (content interviews), or on information that the client's behavior provides (process interviews, also known as mental status exams), or both. Manuals for conducting process interviews with children include Beiser's (1962), Goodman & Sours' (1967), and Greenspan's (1981). Content interviews have been emphasized in the literature on behavioral assessment of adult disorders (e.g., Haynes, 1978); prior to 1975, however, there were few references to content interviews with children. Since then, a number of studies have demonstrated that children can directly provide reliable information (e.g., Abu-Saad & Holzemer, 1981; Herjanic &

Campbell, 1977), particularly when describing publicly observable events.

As with any assessment instrument, the quality of an interview depends on getting accurate information with the least amount of error. Three major sources of error are present in the interview: the interviewer, the interviewee, and the interview setting. One obvious interviewer error is the failure to ask for necessary information. It is unlikely that information that is not specifically asked for will be obtained; thus the information needed from an interview should be well planned. Some interviews are highly structured (e.g., the Vineland Adaptive Behavior Scales); oth-ers use rough organizing frameworks such as BASIC ID (Lazarus, 1973) or S-O-R-K-C (Kanfer & Saslow, 1969); the interview also may be organized ad hoc by the clinician. Several structured interviews for the assessment of child psychopathology exist (e.g., Edelbrock & Costello, 1984; Orvaschel, Sholomskas, & Weissman, 1980). The specific plan an interviewer uses will depend on the interviewer's purpose and theoretical model (Ventura, Lieberman, Green, Shaner & Mintz, 1998). A second information-gathering error is the failure to recognize and clarify ambiguous responses. This source of error can be reduced by asking questions that clarify contradictory information.

A great deal of information can be given during interviews; thus, the storage and retrieval system used by the clinician is a third potential source of error.

In addition, an interviewer may use tactics that initially result in accurate information, but the information quality will deteriorate throughout the interview if the interviewer does not maintain a relationship in which the client continues to want to give accurate information. Maintaining warmth, empathy, genuineness and person reinforcement may help maintain rapport. The interviewer must remain alert to changes in affect and change tactics to maintain an appropriate and culturally competent (Lesser, 1997) relationship.

Sources of interviewee error fall into categories of effects of developmental deficits, client perceptions of the nature and consequences of the interview, and fatigue. These sources of error can be partly controlled by ensuring that vocabulary used by the interviewer is familiar to the client, by keeping cognitive demands low (e.g., by asking for single bits of information at once rather than multiple bits), and by clearly explaining what information the interviewer knows and what information is needed. There is evidence that closed-ended or multiple-response format questions (e.g., "When the other kids call you that name, do you feel angry, sad, or something else?") obtain more reliable responses from developmentally younger persons than open-ended questions (e.g., "How do you feel when they call you that name?"), and some evidence that open-ended questions produce more refusals and less complete information than closed-ended ones (Ammons, 1950; Miller & Bigi, 1979). However, there is a tendency for developmentally delayed adults and children to give acquiescent responses to yes-no questions, and to give the last choice in multiple-response formats (Sigelman et al., 1981).

The interviewee's expectations about the interview and about what will be done with the information obtained is also likely to affect validity. Clinicians should ensure that clients understand what will happen during the interview, why the interview is being conducted, and how the information will be used, and should elicit any concerns the client has about the interview. In interpreting data, the clinician should consider the likelihood that the client may have been giving biased responses because of the demands of the setting. Bias owed to ecological demand characteristics can be reduced if the interview is designed so that the client believes the interview will be ecologically helpful. If the clinician begins the interview by asking whether there are problems in the setting that the client would like to have ameliorated, the client is more likely to be cooperative in sharing information.

The interview setting influences the interview, and can therefore be a source of error. Interviewer and interviewee should generally be alone unless the presence of other persons is expected to enhance the quality of the interview (e.g., a young child may be very fearful unless mother is present). The clinician needs to consider how the presence of other persons may affect the demand characteristics of the interview when interpreting the results. The client's prior experience with the clinician may also bias results; this problem is minimal in situations in which interviewer and interviewee have never met. The location of the interview may also affect the information that is elicited; interviewing a child in a classroom, for example, may generate a client expectation that the interviewer is a teacher; on the other hand, the setting can be used to prompt information that may not be normally accessible. It's possible, for example, that a child will give more reliable information about what has occurred in a classroom when the child is interviewed alone in the classroom. The setting for the interview should be carefully planned by the clinician.

REFERENCES

Abu-Saad, H., & Holzemer, W.L. (1981). Measuring children's self-assessment of pain. *Issues in Comprehensive Pediatric Nursing, 5,* 337–349.

Ammons, R.B. (1950). Reactions in a projective doll-play interview of white males two to six years of age to differences in skin color and facial features. *Journal of Genetic Psychology, 76,* 323–341.

Beiser, H.R. (1962). Psychiatric diagnostic interviews with children. *Journal of the American Academy of Child Psychiatry, 1,* 656–670.

Edelbrock, C., & Costello, A.J. (1984). *A review of structured psychiatric interviews for children.* Unpublished manuscript.

Goodman, J., & Sours, J. (1967). *The child mental status examination.* New York: Basic Books.

Greenspan, S.I. (1981). *The clinical interview of the child.* New York: McGraw-Hill.

Haynes, S.N. (1978). The behavioral interview. In S.N. Haynes (Ed.), *Principles of behavioral assessment.* New York: Gardner Press.

Herjanic, B., & Campbell, W. (1977). Differentiating psychiatrically disturbed children on the basis of a structured interview. *Journal of Abnormal Child Psychology, 5,* 127–134.

Kanfer, F.H., & Saslow, G. (1969). Behavioral diagnosis. In C.M. Franks (Ed.), *Behavior theory: appraisal and status.* New York: McGraw-Hill.

Lazarus, A. (1973). Multimodal behavior therapy: Treating the BASIC ID. *Journal of Nervous and Mental Disease, 156,* 404–411.

Lesser, I.M. (1997). Cultural considerations using The Structured Clinical Interview for DSM-III for mood and anxiety disorder assessment. *Journal of Psychopathology & Behavioral Assessment, 19,* 2, 149–160.

Miller, P.H., & Bigi, L. (1979). The development of children's understanding of attention. *Merrill-Palmer Quarterly, 25,* 235–250.

Orvaschel, H., Sholomskas, D., & Weissman, M.M. (1980). *The assessment of psychopathology and behavioral problems in children: A review of epidemiological and clinical research (1967–1979).* Rockville, MD: National Institute of Mental Health, Division of Biometry and Epidemiology (DHHS Publication No. (ADM)80–1037).

Sigelman, C.K., Schoenrock, C.J., Winer, J.L., Spanhel, C.L., Hromas, S.G., Martin, P.W., Budd, E.C., & Bensberg, G.J. (1981). In R.H. Bruininks, C.E. Meyers, B.B. Sigford, & K.C. Lakin (Eds.), *Deinstitutionalization and community adjustment of mentally retarded people.* Washington, DC: American Association on Mental Deficiency.

Ventura, J., Liberman, R.P., Green, M.F., Shaner, A., & Mintz, J. (1998). Training and quality assurance with Structured Clinical Interview for DSM-IV (SC ID-I/P). *Psychiatry Research, 19,* 2, 16–17.

See also Assessment; Mental Status Exams

CLINICAL PSYCHOLOGY

Clinical psychology is the branch of psychology devoted to the scientific study, assessment, diagnosis, and treatment of mental disorders. Clinical psychology has its origins in 1896 with the construction of the first psychological clinic by Lightner Witmer at the University of Pennsylvania (Benjamin, 1997). In 1907, Witmer founded and served as editor of *The Psychological Clinic,* a journal describing the types of problems and work performed at the clinic. Witmer wrote the initial article in the new journal and described his work with a child referred for treatment of bad spelling in school (Witmer, 1907). The article was titled "Clinical Psychology," wherein Witmer applied this name to his work, and became known as the founder of clinical psychology (Benjamin, 1997).

Initially, clinical psychology was most interested in the development and assessment of human abilities, and provided the government the means to test intelligence, achievement, vocational interests, and personality characteristics of recruits during both world wars. After World War II, the Veterans Administration hired large numbers of clinical psychologists to work with disabled veterans, and the psychologists' roles expanded beyond assessment to psychotherapy (Phares, 1979). During this time, clinical psychology gained professional status by obtaining licensure in most states, and establishing independent practice activities.

Training for clinical psychology is normally four years of graduate coursework followed by a full-time year of internship. Courses taken for the degree include basic psychological areas such as social, learning, methodology, and biological with advanced coursework in assessment and psychopathology (Matthews & Walker, 1997). The PhD (Doctor of Philosophy) degree is the traditional degree for clinical psychology and usually involves a scientist-practitioner model of training. The PsyD (Doctor of Psychology) is a newer degree focusing more on practitioner training with less emphasis on research productivity. Current requirements for licensure usually involves both a written and oral examination followed by a year of postdoctoral supervision. Additionally, the American Psychological Association provides accreditation for clinical psychology programs, allowing for common goals and training among diverse graduate programs.

REFERENCES

Benjamin, L.T., Jr. (1997). *A history of psychology: Original sources and contemporary research* (2nd ed.). New York: McGraw-Hill.

Matthews, J.R., & Walker, C.E. (1997). *Basic skills and professional issues in clinical psychology.* Boston: Allyn and Bacon.

Phares, E.J. (1979). *Clinical psychology: Concepts, methods, and profession* (Vols. 1–2). Homewood, IL: Dorsey Press.

Witmer, L. (1907). Clinical psychology. *The Psychological Clinic, 1,* 1–9.

See also Clinical Interview; Diagnostic and Statistical Manual of Mental Disorders (DSM-IV); Mental Status Exams

CLINICAL TEACHING

Clinical teaching is teaching prescriptive (diagnosis → prescription → remediation), with the intent of matching the student's strengths and weaknesses to a specific type of instruction. Clinical teaching is therefore often called diagnostic-prescriptive teaching. It is a continuous test-teach-test process. This process was influenced by Johnson and Myklebust (1967), Smith (1968, 1974), Learner (1985), and many others. Teaching strategies in clinical teaching include task analysis and applied behavior analysis.

Learner (1985) views the clinical teaching process as a five-stage repetitive cycle of decision making that consists of assessment, planning, implementation, evaluation, and modification of the assessment. She further adds that the clinical teacher considers the student's ecological, home, social, and cultural environments.

Smith (1983) offers eight steps in the clinical teaching process: (1) the clinical teacher should objectively observe and analyze the student's classroom abilities; (2) the teacher should objectively observe and analyze the nature of the student's successes and difficulties on different types of tasks; (3) the teacher should scrutinize the characteristics of alternative tasks and settings; (4) compare and contrast how information gained from step (3) might interact with the observations in steps (2) and (1) so as to result in more favorable achievement; (5) the teacher should consult with the student whenever possible, present the choices for modification, and together decide which ones to try; (6) the teacher should set short-term goals, make the modifications; and (7) teach; (8) evaluate progress after a reasonable time interval; if successful, continue teaching similar but higher level objectives; if unsuccessful retrace steps 1–7 (p. 361).

REFERENCES

Johnson, D., & Mykelbust, H. (1967). Learning disabilities: Educational principles and practices. New York: Grune & Stratton.

Learner, J. (1985). Learning disabilities: Theories, diagnosis, and teaching strategies (4th ed.). Boston: Houghton Mifflin.

Smith, C.R. (1983). Learning disabilities: The intervention of learner, task and setting. Boston: Little, Brown.

Smith, R.M. (1968, 1974). Clinical teaching: Methods of instruction for the retarded. New York: McGraw-Hill.

See also **Diagnostic Prescriptive Teaching**

CLOZE TECHNIQUE

The cloze technique is a procedure that is used for both the assessment and instruction of reading comprehension skills. Based on the psychological construct of closure, the technique was first developed by Taylor (1953), who believed that a person reading a narrative or expository selection psychologically endeavors to complete a pattern of thought and language that is left incomplete. With the cloze technique, such a language pattern is typically a reading passage from which words have been deleted. Typically, in a reading selection of approximately 250 words, e.g., every tenth lexical word would be deleted and it would be the reader's task to fill in the missing words.

Cloze exercises may be developed from basal reader texts, trade books, content area materials, and any other reading selections that are appropriate for a given population of readers. Often, the cloze procedure has been used as a device for the assessment of reading comprehension. As described by Smith and Johnson (1980), it may involve the use of a variety of cloze passages taken from the same reading material. For example, three different passages of approximately 100 words in length may be taken from the beginning, middle, and end of a selection. Then, certain words are deleted, e.g., every fifth or tenth lexical word. The reader's task is to read the passage and write in the missing word on a blank. Ekwall (1985) elaborated on this procedure by stating that the first and last sentences of the selection should be left intact, with every fifth word omitted to be replaced with a blank of 10 spaces in length. Again, the reader is required to read the selection and fill in blank spaces with a word that would seem to fit.

Cloze exercises can be used with either individual students or groups of students. As an assessment tool, there is usually no time limit for the completion of a cloze exercise.

The evaluation or scoring of a cloze passage is usually based on a percentage of blank spaces that have been completed correctly. If a student is able to complete approximately 45 to 50% of the omitted spaces correctly, the reading material is judged to be at the reader's instructional level. If 60% or more of the blanks have been filled in correctly, the selection is probably at the reader's independent reading level. If fewer than 45% of the blanks are completed correctly, the material is at the reader's frustration reading level.

The cloze technique, therefore, based on the construct of perception and closure as defined by the gestalt psychologists, assumes the ability of a fluent reader to predict or anticipate what is coming next in a reading passage. This requires the use of various reading skills, including context clues, knowledge of linguistic patterns, and the ability to comprehend in general what is being read. As Rye (1982) describes, the activity involves a sampling of information from a contextual setting and the formation of hypotheses, a prediction of what will appear subsequently in the selection both linguistically and conceptually. The value of the cloze technique as both a diagnostic and instructional device lies in its demand on the reader's comprehension abilities and a variety of language skills.

REFERENCES

Ekwall, E.E. (1985). *Locating and correcting reading difficulties* (4th ed.). Columbus, OH: Merrill.

Rye, J. (1982). *Cloze procedure and the teaching of reading.* Exeter, NH: Heinemann.

Smith, R.J., & Johnson, D.D. (1980). *Teaching children to read* (2nd ed.). Reading, MA: Addison-Wesley.

Taylor, W.L. (1953). Cloze procedure: A new tool for measuring readability. *Journalism Quarterly, 30,* 415–433.

See also **Reading Disorders; Reading Remediation**

CLUTTERING

Cluttering is a speech disorder—or, more specifically, a fluency disorder—related to stuttering. Importantly, the two disorders are not the same. Cluttering is characterized by excessive breaks in the normal flow of speech that result from disorganized speech planning, talking too fast or in a jerky fashion, or simply being unsure of what one wants to say. By contrast, the person who stutters typically knows exactly what he or she wants to say but is temporarily unable to say it, thus repeating or prolonging sounds or syllables, blocking, and/or using accessory (secondary) devices (e.g., eye-blinks, synonyms for difficult words, or abnormal facial postures) (Daly, 1996; St. Louis & Myers, 1997). Because cluttering is not well-known, there is much ambiguity about the disorder. For example, the speech of many people who clutter is often described by themselves or others as stuttering. Moreover, cluttering frequently coexists with stuttering. And some authorities question whether or not a reliable definition of cluttering has been established (e.g., Curlee, 1996).

The definition of cluttering recently adopted by the fluency disorders division of the American Speech-Language-Hearing Association is "a fluency disorder characterized by a rapid and/or irregular speaking rate, excessive disfluencies, and often other symptoms such as language or phonological errors and attention deficits" (St. Louis, Hanley, & Hood, 1998). Clutterers' speech does not sound fluent; in other words, they do not appear to be clear about either what they want to say or how to say it. They manifest excessive levels of normal disfluencies, such as interjections (e.g., "um," or "you know") and revisions (e.g., "We went over . . . we started to go to grandma's.") (St. Louis, Hinzman, & Hull, 1985); they manifest little or no physical struggle in speaking; and they have few, if any, accessory behaviors. A rapid and/or irregular speaking rate would be present in a speaker who shows symptoms of speaking too fast, whether based on actual syllable-per-minute counts or simply an overall impression; sounding jerky; or using pauses during speech that are too short, too long, or improperly placed.

These fluency and rate deviations are often considered to be the essential symptoms of cluttering (St. Louis, 1992). Other characteristics may also be present but are not mandatory. These include confusing, disorganized language or conversational skills, often with word-finding difficulties; limited awareness of fluency or rate problems; temporary improvement when asked to slow down or to pay attention to speech (or when being tape recorded); specific sound misarticulations, slurred speech, or deleting nonstressed syllables in longer words (e.g., "ferchly" for "fortunately"); speech that is difficult to understand; a family history of stuttering and/or cluttering; social or vocational problems; learning disabilities; attention deficit/hyperactivity disorder; sloppy handwriting; difficulty with organizational skills for daily activities; and/or auditory perceptual difficulties (Daly, 1992; St. Louis & Myers, 1995, 1997; Weiss, 1964).

Therapy for clutterers generally addresses the contributing problems before focusing directly on fluency. Ordinarily, one of the first goals of therapy is to reduce the speaking rate, although this may not be easy for the clutterer to achieve. Some clutterers respond well to "timing" their speech to a delayed auditory feedback (DAF) device; some do not. Another technique that has been found helpful with younger clutterers is to use the analogy of a speedometer wherein rapid speech is above the speed limit, and "speeding tickets" are given for exceeding the limit (St. Louis & Myers, 1995, 1997).

It is currently impossible to predict with accuracy whether or not a clutterer will benefit from speech therapy. Most who benefit have become convinced from friends, family, or employers (or on their own) that they do have a significant speech problem. Also, motivation is a key element; successful clients typically have good reason for working hard to change, such as the likelihood of a job promotion. On the other hand, clutterers who are not sure that they have a problem, or are relatively unconcerned about it, tend not to improve as much or as easily from therapy (Daly, 1992; St. Louis & Myers, 1997).

REFERENCES

Curlee, R.F. (1996). Cluttering: Data in search of understanding. In K.O. St. Louis (Ed.), *Research and opinion on cluttering: State of the art and science,* Special issue of the *Journal of Fluency Disorders, 21,* 315–327.

Daly, D.A. (1992). Helping the clutterer: Therapy considerations. In F.L. Myers & K.O. St. Louis. *Cluttering: A clinical perspective* (pp. 107–124). Kibworth, Great Britain: Far Communications. (Reissued in 1996 by Singular Press, San Diego, California)

St. Louis, K.O. (1992). On defining cluttering. In F.L. Myers & K.O. St. Louis, *Cluttering: A clinical perspective* (pp. 37–53). Kibworth, Great Britain: Far Communications. (Reissued in 1996 by Singular Press, San Diego, California)

St. Louis, K.O., Hanley, J.M., & Hood, S.B. (1998). *Terminology pertaining to fluency and fluency disorders.* Final report of the Terminology Task Force of the Special Interest Division on Fluency and Fluency Disorders of the American Speech Language Hearing Association.

St. Louis, K.O., Hinzman, A.R., & Hull, F.M. (1985). Studies of cluttering: Disfluency and language measures in young possible clutterers and stutterers. *Journal of Fluency Disorders, 10,* 151–172.

St. Louis, K.O, & Myers, F.L. (1995). Clinical management of cluttering. *Language, Speech, and Hearing Services in Schools, 25,* 187–195.

St. Louis, K.O., & Myers, F.L. (1997). Management of cluttering and related fluency disorders. In R. Curlee & G. Siegel (Eds.), *Nature and treatment of stuttering: New directions* (pp. 313– 332). New York: Allyn & Bacon.

Weiss, D. (1964). *Cluttering.* Englewood Cliff, NJ: Prentice Hall.

COCKAYNE SYNDROME (CS)

Cockayne Syndrome (CS) is rare genetic disorder, autosomally recessive, of unknown prevalence. Males and females are equally affected. In CS, growth and development are normal for at least the first year followed by neurodevelopmental retardation that may not become especially prominent in many cases until 4 or 5 years of age.

In the early stages of CS, these children are often misdiagnosed with ADHD or with various coordination disorders. Typically, mental retardation develops in the childhood years and may be mild to severe. Photosensitivity is common and peripheral neuropathy develops. Small stature with large ears occurs routinely. Leukodystrophy occurs in all cases along with premature death. There is no cure, and the only treatment is symptom management. Diagnosis is by physical examination and CT or MRI (Gillberg, 1995). Symptoms are usually well-expressed by age 10 years.

Special education will typically be required for intellectual impairment and externalizing behavior problems. Dwarfism and emotional symptoms may occur as well, and may require special assistance. Thorough psychoeducational evaluations on a yearly basis are required due to the severity of the disorder and the rapid changes that may occur in behavior, intellect, and motor skills.

REFERENCE

Gillberg. C. (1995). *Clinical child neuropsychiatry.* Cambridge, UK: Cambridge University Press.

COGENTIN

Cogentin is the proprietary name of benztropine mesylate, a skeletal muscle relaxant used in the treatment of Parkinson's disease (Modell, 1985). Cogentin acts on the basal ganglia of the brain. By restoring more normal chemical balance in the basal ganglia, specific movement disorders associated with parkinsonism are relieved. Cogentin reduces tremors, gait disturbances, and rigidity in afflicted individuals (Ellis & Speed, 1998; Long, 1982). Common side effects, especially during initial drug use, include blurred vision, nervousness, constipation, and dryness of the mouth. On rare occasions more serious side effects may occur, including confusion, hallucinations, nausea, and vomiting (Long, 1982). Common cold and cough remedies may interact unfavorably with Cogentin. The drug is not recommended for use in children under 3 years of age, and should be used with caution in older children (Long, 1983; *Physician's Desk Reference,* 1983).

REFERENCES

Ellis, K.L., & Speed, J. (1998). Pharmacologic management of movement disorder after midbrain haemorrhage *Brain Injury, 12,* 7, 623–628.

Long, J.W. (1982). *The essential guide to prescription drugs.* New York: Harper & Row.

Modell, W. (Ed.). (1985). *Drugs in current use and new drugs* (31st ed.). New York: Springer.

Physician's desk reference (37th ed.). (1983). Oradell, NJ: Medical Economics.

See also **Drug Therapy; Medication**

COGNITIVE ASSESSMENT SYSTEM (CAS)

The Cognitive Assessment System (CAS; Naglieri & Das, 1997a) is an individually administered test of ability for children ages 5 though 17 years that is given by psychologists and similarly trained professionals when conducting clinical, psychoeducational, or neuropsychological evaluations. The 1997 edition of the CAS is the first published version of the test, which was designed to measure Planning, Attention, Simultaneous, and Successive (PASS) cognitive processes. The PASS theory was used to identify subtests for the CAS, organize these tests into scales, and guide interpretation and intervention efforts. This test differs from traditional measures of ability because it (a) is built on a theory of ability reconceptualized as PASS cognitive processes; (b) is designed to measure specific cognitive processes rather than general ability; (c) was built to reflect contemporary understanding of cognitive processes that have been obtained from recent research in psychology and education; (d) does not include subtests that involve academic content, such as vocabulary and arithmetic; (e) was designed to be sensitive to the specific strengths and weaknesses of children that are related to academic success and failure; and (f) was built to have relevance to instruction and identification of specific interventions.

The PASS theory is based on the concept that these processes are very important to competent functioning and both influence and rely on the person's base of knowledge. The processes are defined as follows: Planning–mental process by which the person determines, selects, and uses efficient solutions to problems; Attention–a mental process by which the person selectively attends to some stimuli and ignores others; Simultaneous processing–a mental activity by which the person integrates stimuli into groups; and Successive processing–a mental activity by which the person integrates stimuli in a specific serial order.

The CAS is comprised of a Planning, Attention, Simultaneous, and Successive scale, each of which represents the theory upon which the test was built. These four scales are further comprised of three subtests, each of which has undergone extensive development and validation (see Das, Naglieri, & Kirby, 1994; Naglieri & Das, 1997b). Each subtest yields a standardized score with a mean of 10 and standard deviation of 3. Subtests are combined into specific PASS Scales and a Full Scale, each of which are expressed as standard scores with a mean of 100 and standard deviation of 15. There are two versions of the test, a Standard Battery (12 subtests) and a Basic Battery (8 subtests), which are administered in 60 and 45 minutes, respectively. Each subtest is described by PASS Scale below.

The CAS was standardized on 2,200 persons aged 5 years 0 months to 17 years 11 months who closely match the United States population on the basis of gender, race, region, community setting, classroom placement, educational classification, and parental education. The CAS Full Scale internal reliability is .96 and the separate PASS Scale reliabilities are as follows: Planning = .88; Simultaneous = .93; Attention = .88; and Successive = .93. The test meets or exceeds recognized standards for reliability.

There are a number of important validity studies of the CAS reported by Naglieri and Das (1997b). In summary, these authors have shown that the PASS scales are powerful predictors of achievement. Naglieri (1997) showed that the CAS Full Scale correlated .73 with the Woodcock-Johnson Tests of Achievement–Revised, in contrast to correlations between the WISC-III and WIAT correlation of .59 as well as the Woodcock-Johnson Cognitive Battery correlation of .62 with the Woodcock-Johnson Tests of Achievement. These data showed that the CAS accounted for more than 50% of the variance in achievement while the WISC-III and WJ-R Cognitive only accounted for about 35% of the variance. Importantly, Naglieri and Das (1997b) also showed that the CAS yields distinctive PASS profiles for children with Attention-Deficit Hyperactivity Disorders and reading disabilities. Finally, Naglieri and Gottling (1995, 1997) have clearly demonstrated that the CAS has important instructional implications. Thus, the CAS appears to offer a new way to conceptualize ability as well as a new way to measure it. Future research is needed to further explore these initial findings.

REFERENCES

Das, J.P., Naglieri, J.A., & Kirby, J.R. (1994). *The assessment of cognitive processes: The PASS theory of intelligence.* Boston: Allyn & Bacon.

Naglieri, J.A. (1997). *Relationships between achievement and the Cognitive Assessment System.* American Psychological Association, Chicago, IL.

Naglieri, J.A., & Das, J.P. (1997a). *Cognitive Assessment System.* Chicago: Riverside.

Naglieri, J.A., & Das, J.P. (1997b). *Cognitive Assessment System: Interpretive handbook.* Chicago: Riverside.

Naglieri, J.A., & Gottling, S.H. (1997). Mathematics instruction and PASS cognitive processes: An intervention study. *Journal of Learning Disabilities, 30,* 513–520.

Naglieri, J.A., & Gottling, S.H. (1995). A cognitive education approach to math instruction for the learning disabled: An individual study. *Psychological Reports, 76,* 1343–1354.

COGNITIVE BEHAVIOR THERAPY

The term cognitive behavior therapy refers to a diverse assemblage of theoretical and applied orientations that share three underlying assumptions. First, a person's behavior is mediated by cognitive events (i.e., thoughts, images, expectancies, and beliefs). Second is a corollary to the first; it states that a change in mediating events results in a change in behavior. Third, a person is an active participant in his or her own learning. The third assumption recognizes the reciprocal relationships among a person's thoughts, behavior, and environment and runs counter to the behaviorist's unidirectional view of the individual as a passive recipient of environmental influences.

A variety of therapies derived from research in cognitive psychology and taking advantage of the broadened behavioral perspective were developed and subjected to empirical test. These therapies attempt to modify thinking processes as a mechanism for effecting cognitive and behavioral changes. Particular therapeutic approaches that are closely identified with cognitive behavior therapy include modeling, self-instructional training, problem-solving training, rational emotive therapy, cognitive therapy, self-control training, and cognitive skills training. Because self-instructional training and problem-solving training illustrate the dual focus on cognitions and behavior, have been researched in schools, and are particularly well suited to classroom application, they will be briefly described in this entry.

In self-instructional training, the child is taught to regulate his or her behavior through self-talk. The child is taught to ask and to answer covertly questions that guide his or her own performance. The questions are of four types:

1. Questions about the nature of the problem (OK. Now what is it I have to do? I have to find the two cars that are twins.)

2. Plans, or self-instructions for solving the task (How can I do it? I could look at each car carefully, looking at the hood first, and then the front wheels, until I get to the end.)

3. Self-monitoring (Am I using my plan?)

4. Self-evaluation. (How did I do? I did fine because I looked at each car carefully and I found the twins.)

The particular self-statements vary according to the type of task.

The steps in teaching children to use self-speech to guide problem-solving behavior are derived from research in the developmental sequence by which language regulates one's behavior. First, an adult talks out loud while solving a task, and the child observes (modeling). Next, the child performs the same task while the adult verbally instructs the child. Next, the child performs the task while instructing himself or herself out loud. Then the child performs the task while whispering. Finally, the child performs the task while talking silently to himself or herself, with no lip movements.

Research in self-instructional talk has demonstrated that it helps impulsive children to think before acting (Meichenbaum & Goodman, 1971). While treated children have improved on novel problem-solving tasks and academic performance (Camp, Blom, Hebert, & Van Doorninck, 1977; Douglas, Parry, Marton, & Garson, 1976; Meichenbaum & Goodman, 1971), results of treatment on classroom behavior have been inconclusive (Camp, 1980; Camp et al., 1977).

Problem-solving training is similar to self-instructional training in that the child is taught to think through problems following a systematic problem-solving process. In a series of studies, Spivack and Shure (Spivack, Platt, & Shure, 1976; Spivack & Shure, 1974) taught preschool children the following interpersonal cognitive problem-solving skills: problem identification, means-end thinking, alternative thinking, and consequential thinking. Means-end thinking includes the ability to plan, step-by-step, ways to reach an interpersonal goal. Alternative thinking includes the ability to generate different plans for solving a given interpersonal problem. Consequential thinking is the ability to anticipate and evaluate consequences of a given interpersonal solution. These skills are taught in game-type interactions involving pictures, puppets, and stories depicting interpersonal problem situations. Research on problem-solving training has demonstrated improvement on teacher ratings, academic performance, and behavior observations (Shure, 1981).

In terms of psychotherapeutic intervention, cognitive behavior therapy has been shown to be very helpful with pain control (Tan & Leucht, 1997), depression (Murphy, Carney, Kreserich, & Wetzel, 1995), body dysmorphic disorder (Neziroglu, McKay, Todaro, & Yaryura-Tobias, 1996), and eating disorders (Eldredge, Agras, Arnow, Telch, Bell, Castonguay, & Marnell, 1997). However, there are two caveats for using cognitive behavior therapy with school-aged populations. The first is including both the assessment of logical/analytical thought structures *and* social perspective-taking abilities of the child when planning a course of cognitive behavior therapy (Kinney, 1991). The second, (which pertains to any age of client/subject) is that multicultural influences and diversity must be taken into account and formally addressed if the course of treatment is to be successful (Hays, 1995).

REFERENCES

Camp, B.W. (1980). Two psychoeducational treatment programs for young aggressive boys. In C.K. Walen & B. Henker (Eds.), *Hyperactive children—The social psychology of identification and treatment.* New York: Academic.

Camp, B.W., Blom, G.E., Hebert, F., & Van Doorninck, W.J. (1977). "Think Aloud": A program for developing self-control in young aggressive boys. *Journal of Abnormal Child Psychology, 5,* 157–169.

Douglas, V.I., Parry, P., Marton, P., & Garson. C. (1976). *Journal of Abnormal Child Psychology, 4,* 389–410.

Eldredge, K.L., Agras, W.S., Arnow, B., Telch, C.F., Bell, S., Castonguay, L., & Marnell, M. (1997). The effects of extending cognitive-behavior therapy for binge eating disorder among initial treatment nonresponders. *International Journal of Eating Disorders, 21,* 4, 347–352.

Hays, P.A. (1997). Multicultural applications of cognitive behavior therapy. *Professional Psychology: Research & Practice, 26,* 3, 309–315.

Kinney, A. (1991). Cognitive-behavior therapy with children: Developmental considerations. *Journal of Rational-Emotive & Cognitive Behavior Therapy, 9,* 1, 51–61.

Meichenbaum, D.H., & Goodman, J. (1971). Training impulsive children to talk to themselves: A means of developing self-control. *Journal of Abnormal Psychology, 77,* 115–126.

Neziroglu, F., McKay, D., Todaro, J., & Yaryura-Tobias, J.A. (1996). Effect of cognitive behavior therapy on persons with body dysmorphic disorder and comorbid Axis II diagnosis. *Behavior Therapy, 27,* 1, 67–77.

Shure, M.B. (1981). Social competence as a problem-solving skill. In J.D. Wine & M.D. Smyne (Eds.), *Social competence* (pp. 158–185). New York: Guilford Press.

Spivack, G., Platt, J.J., & Shure, M.B. (1976). *The problem-solving approach to adjustment.* San Francisco: Jossey-Bass.

Spivack, G., & Shure, M.B. (1974). *Social adjustment of young children: A cognitive approach to solving real-life problems.* San Francisco: Jossey-Bass.

Tan, Siang-Yang, & Leucht, C.A., (1997). Cognitive-behavioral therapy for clinical pain control: A 15-year update and its relationship to hypnosis. *International Journal of Clinical & Experimental Hypnosis, 45,* 4, 396–416.

See also **Cognitive Retraining; Cognitive Strategies; Self-Control Curriculum**

COGNITIVE DEVELOPMENT

Cognitive development consists of numerous overlapping conceptual and theoretical processes involving changes that occur in mental capacity and facility between birth and death. Cognition, the product of cognitive development, refers to mental processes by which individuals acquire knowledge. Moreover, cognition is the process of acquiring a conscious awareness that helps us to "know" and "understand" in a wide spectrum of activities such as remembering, learning, thinking, and attending. As a human phenomenon, cognition is comprised of unobservable events, their subsequent comprehension, and resultant response (Flavell, 1982). These covert behaviors characterize the activities of human thought processes.

In an effort to present general parameters of childhood cognitive development as it pertains to special education, several cognitive perspectives must be addressed. The human is an active problem solver who attempts to discriminate, extract, and analyze information; subsequently, directed planful action undergoes developmental change. Three contemporary theoretical orientations are consistent with the theme of the child as an active problem solver: Piaget's theory of cognitive development; information-processing approaches, and social learning theory.

One of the most influential descriptors of how development occurs is Piaget's theory of cognitive development (Piaget, 1970). In his work, cognitive structures are represented in the symbolic medium of formal logic, where each structure is regarded as a broad system of logical operations that mediates and unites a whole range of more specific intellectual behaviors and characteristics. Even though research with large samples of infants have confirmed Piaget's theories, certain aspects of his developmental accounts have come under scrutiny (Flavell, 1980; Gelman, 1978) and warrant revision or reinterpretation. Nevertheless, the Piagetian approach remains an important scientific paradigm on human intellectual development. The formative phases of the domain of study known as cognitive development are rooted in Piaget's theoretical formulations.

INFORMATION-PROCESSING APPROACH TO COGNITIVE DEVELOPMENT

As a model of human cognitive development, information processing explains decision making, knowing, and remembering as processes. In this approach to the study of cognitive development, the mind is conceived of as a complex cognitive system, analogous in some ways to a computer. In essence, human cognition becomes what the computer must know in order to produce behavior y. Information from the environment is abstracted from sensory systems and "flows" through a variety of proposed information-processing components. Information is transformed and analyzed at each step; feedback and feedforward loops among the components influence these transformations and analyses. Planning and purposeful thinking are derived by executive functions. The executive system contains sets of elementary information-processing rules that construct, execute, and monitor the flow of information to achieve objectives.

Most of the information-processing research builds directly on Piaget's contributions to the understanding of cognitive development. Contrary to Piaget's structural explanation underlying the thought structure of logic in thought processes and operational reversibility, information processing accounts for and identifies specific mental processes by which cognition is processed. Some researchers, such as Pascual-Leone (1980) and Case (1978), have modified Piagetian theory to take into account information-processing considerations (also called neo-Piagetian theories). One such approach is Siegler's (1981) rule-assessment approach. In essence, Siegler's work examines a child's problem-solving skills within a domain at different ages. A child's pattern of responses across problems helps to determine which of information-processing rules the child is using.

Several other information-processing perspectives have examined cognitive development. For example, researchers have found that young children have limited attention and persistence at tasks (Wellman, Ritter, & Flavell, 1975) and that their curiosity interferes with systematic problem solving. Thus, contrary to Piagetian theory, very young children may fail to solve many problems because they are unable to sustain their attention long enough to gather the necessary information. By about age 5 children become more persistent in their attempts to solve problems. Hence younger children may know to look first at relevant stimuli and label them; whereas, older children are better at selectively attending without special training.

SOCIAL LEARNING THEORY

Social learning theorists suggest that cognitive development is much more than a result of some combination of individual characteristics and environmental influences. They view all three as existing within a mutually interdependent network; they exist as a set of reciprocal determinants. Thus cognitions, beliefs, and expectations influence behavior and vice versa. Behavior partially determines the nature of the environment, whereas cognitions determine the psychological definitions of the environment.

Learning takes place either directly (through association of behaviors and consequences) or through modeling. The direct consequences of behavior, or reinforcements, are not conceptualized in the more traditional fashion that ignores awareness of the contingencies on the part of the child. Hence consequences of behavior explicitly carry information and function to provoke the individual into formulating and testing hypotheses. Thus reinforcement influences whether or not a response will elicit cognitions or thoughts about stimulus associations.

Learning is thought to be acquired through modeling. All new behaviors are observed along with their consequences. Inherent symbolic abilities facilitate abstraction and representation of information and provide an efficient means for retaining that information. From a social learning perspective, the anticipation of reinforcement may serve as a stimulus to direct attention to a model's behavior; hence, reinforcement may facilitate learning.

In summary, social learning theory places a great deal of emphasis on symbolic and self-regulatory processes. Cognitive development is important to the extent that changes in cognitive functioning influence changes in those processes. In children, development becomes more refined with experience and actual manipulation; consequently, children are better able to represent efficiently and retain observational experiences. Additionally, symbolic processes, attentional processes, and motivational processes change with observational learning.

IMPLICATIONS FOR SPECIAL EDUCATION

Traditional stages of cognitive development apply to individuals with and without disabilities alike. Handicapping conditions, however, may result in irregularities or delays in cognitive development, particularly in profoundly mentally retarded or multiply impaired persons. Some profoundly mentally retarded handicapped never progress into the higher stages of cognitive development such as preoperational or operational thought. Other handicapped children acquire skills by rote or through carefully structured instruction, but have difficulty in applying them to new situations (Brown, Campione, & Murphy, 1977).

Most mildly and moderately retarded children do progress through Piaget's lower stages of cognitive development; however, their rate of skill acquisition is much slower. As the child gets older, the gap between the age at which specific skills are expected to be learned and the age at which they are actually learned increases. The retarded child also performs cognitive tasks with less efficiency than the nonretarded child (Campione & Brown, 1978).

Individuals with learning disabilities (LD) represent the largest percentage of the handicapped population (U.S. Office of Special Education, 1996); they evidence a broad array of cognitive dysfunctions. These deficits emerge when academic learning lags with age. Children who are learning disabled may not exhibit specific cognitive problems early in development; however, skills acquired during Piaget's preoperational stage (intuitive thinking) are learned at a slower pace. Thus, problems in areas such as mathematics, reading, and memory are more prevalent.

During the primary years, children with LD have problems with seriation and classification tasks that are essential for mathematics. They cannot sort objects by size, match objects, or grasp the concept of counting and addition. In reading, LD children evidence word recognition errors (omissions, insertions, substitutions, reversals, and transpositions) and comprehension errors (inability to recall facts, sequences, or main ideas).

Word recognition difficulties suggest that LD children are unable to make a word or a letter stand for or represent something else. These are preconceptual skills (ages 2 to 7) of cognitive development in which symbolic thought develops. Problems with centration may inhibit reading comprehension.

Students with learning disabilities generally have problems with recalling auditory and visual stimuli. They also have problems with tasks requiring production or generation of specific learning or memorization strategies that influence the efficient organization of input for retrieval and recall. Bauer (1979) found that poor readers perform poorly on memory tasks that require complex organizational and retrieval strategies. Kauffman and Hallahan (1979) suggest that LD students fail to engage in strategies that enhance attention and recall. These deficits are evident when applied to academic tasks.

Cognitive development may be viewed from numerous perspectives and subsequently applied to academic problems encountered in the field of special education. The information-processing approach to cognitive development is still in the early stage. It is best described as a complement to, rather than a replacement for, Piaget's earlier framework. However, recent research suggests that infants and young children are more competent and adults less competent that once thought (Flavell, 1992). Growth and extension of the cognitive development literature continues and quite often fills in some of the gaps in Piaget's model (Siegler & Crowley, 1991); hence, advances in empirical findings will eventually aid in the development of successful school-based interventions.

REFERENCES

Bauer, R.H. (1979). Memory, acquisition, and category clustering in learning disabled children. *Journal of Experimental Child Psychology, 217,* 365–383.

Brown, A., Campione, J., & Murphy, M. (1977). Maintenance and generalization of training meta-mnemonic awareness of educable retarded children. *Journal of Experimental Child Psychology, 24,* 191–211.

Campione, J.C., & Brown, A. (1978). Toward a theory of intelligence: Contributions from research with retarded children. *Intelligence, 2,* 279–304.

Case, R.S. (1978). Intellectual development from birth to adulthood: A neo-Piagetian interpretation. In R.W. Siegler (Ed.), *Children's thinking: What develops?* Hillsdale, NJ: Erlbaum.

Flavell, J. (1980, Fall). A tribute to Piaget. *Society for Research in Child Development Newsletter.*

Flavell, J. (1982). On cognitive development. *Child Development, 53,* 1–10.

Flavell, J. (1992). Cognitive development. *Developmental Psychology, 28,* 998–1005.

Kauffman, J.M., & Hallahan, D.P. (1979). Learning disabled and hyperactivity. In B.B. Lahey & A.E. Kazdin (Eds.), *Advances in clinical child psychology* (Vol. 2). New York: Plenum.

Pascual-Leone, J. (1980). Constructive problems for constructive theories: The current relevance of Piaget's work and a critique of information-processing simulation psychology. In R.H. Kluwe & H. Spada (Eds.), *Developmental models of thinking.* New York: Academic.

Piaget, J. (1970). Piaget's theory. In P.H. Mussen (Ed.), *Carmichael's manual of child psychology* (Vol. 1). New York: Wiley.

Siegler, R.S. (1981). Developmental sequences within and between concepts. *Monographs for the Society for Research in Child Development, 46* (Serial No. 189).

Siegler, R.S., & Crowley, K. (1991). The microgenetic method. *American Psychologist, 46,* 6, 606–620.

U.S. Office of Special Education. (1996). *Eighteenth annual report to Congress on the implementation of Public Law 94-142: The Education for All Handicapped Children Act.* Washington, DC: U.S. Department of Education.

Wellman, H.M., Ritter, K., & Flavell, J. (1975). Deliberate memory in the delayed reactions of very young children. *Developmental Psychology, 11,* 780–787.

See also **Cognitive Strategies; Cognitive Styles; Information Processing; Intelligence; Piaget, Jean; Social Learning Theory**

COGNITIVE IMPAIRMENT AND METAL POLLUTANTS

It is well known that children who are exposed to high doses of lead and other metal pollutants may suffer permanent neurological sequelae and cognitive impairments (Hartman 1995; Moon, Marlow, Stellern, & Errera, 1985). The causes of metal pollution are often associated with substandard living conditions: e.g., living in dilapidated substandard housing with peeling lead-based paints or plaster, living with household dust carrying metal pollutants, and living in proximity to heavy traffic or factories with noxious emissions. Inadequate nutrition also contributes to the effects of metal pollution.

Some of the physical difficulties associated with metal pollution are loss of appetite, chronic abdominal pain, headache, and anemia. Reported behavior difficulties associated with high levels of such poisoning are decreased learning performance, deficient attention, irritability, and clumsiness. Investigators have implicated metal toxicity in nonadaptive behavior as manifested in classroom situations (Marlowe, Moon, Errera, Cossairt, McNeil, & Peak, in press), associated with learning-disabled children (Marlowe, Errera, Cossairt, & Welch, in press) and with emotional disturbances in children (Marlowe, Errera, & Jacoby, 1983).

The assessment of metal concentrations in humans is easily carried out through various bodily analyses, e.g., of blood, teeth, and hair. The study of hair is both easy and noninvasive: samples are subjected to the study of atomic absorption spectroscopy (Laker, 1982). Trace elements such as metals accumulate in hair at concentrations that are usually higher than in the blood serum. Hair thus can provide a record of a child's nutrient and mineral status. A method appropriate to classroom use to help teachers identify children who are potentially suffering from metal pollution is the Metal Exposure Questionnaire (Marlowe et al., 1983). This provides quantitative information about the possibility that a schoolchild is suffering significantly from metal pollutants.

Many of studies of metal pollutant effects suffer from methodological errors. One of the more significant of these is that while investigators study the effects of one toxic metal, they often fail to take into account the effects of other toxic metals on a child's behavior (Hartman, 1995; Moon et al., 1985).

While there is clear evidence indicating that high doses of metal pollution are physically and cognitively deleterious, there is less certainty as to whether low doses of such metals have significant effects. A number of studies have suggested that they do. Low levels of arsenic, cadmium, mercury, aluminum, and lead have been implicated in cognitive, perceptual, and behavioral childhood developmental deficits (Marlowe, Errera, J., Stellern, & Beck, 1983; Winneke et al., 1983). Some investigators also have hypothesized that metal combinations have interactive effects, thereby increasing the total toxicity in a child (Moon et al., 1985).

The potential widespread nature of metal pollutants' toxic effects has been demonstrated by Moon, Marlowe, Stellern, & Errera (1985). These investigators, studying a randomly selected sample of elementary school children, found significant relationships between low metal concentrations and diminished performance on a variety of cognitive and academic tasks. They also discovered interactive effects. Thus, both increases in arsenic and its interaction with lead were significantly related to decreased reading and spelling achievement. Increases in aluminum and the interaction of aluminum with lead were associated with decreased visual motor performance. An excellent review of the neuropsychological segnelae of toxic substance exposure can be found by Hartman (1995).

REFERENCES

Hartman, D.E. (1995). *Neuropsychological Toxicology* (2nd ed.). New York: Plenum.

Laker, M. (1982). On determining trace element levels in man: The uses of blood and hair. *Lancet, 12,* 260–263.

Marlowe, M., Errera, J., Cossairt, A., & Welch, K. (in press). Hair mineral content as a predictor of learning disabilities. *Journal of Learning Disabilities.*

Marlowe, M., Errera, J., & Jacoby, J. (1983). Increased lead and cadmium levels in emotionally disturbed children. *Journal of Orthomollecular Psychiatry, 12,* 260–267.

Marlowe, M., Moon, C., Errera, J., Cossairt, A., McNeil, A., & Peak, R. (in press). Main and interaction effects of metallic toxins on classroom behavior. *Journal of Abnormal Child Psychology.*

Moon, C., Marlowe, M., Stellern, J., & Errera, J. (1985). Main and interaction effects of metallic pollutants on cognitive functioning. *Journal of Learning Disabilities, 18,* 217–220.

Winneke, G., Kramer, U., Brockhaus, U., Evers, U., Kujanek, G., Lechner, H., & Janke, W. (1983). Neuropsyhological studies in children with elevated tooth-lead concentrations. *International Archives of Occupational environmental Health, 51,* 231–252.

See also **Lead Poisoning; Poverty, Relationship to Special Education**

COGNITIVE RETRAINING

Cognitive retraining involves remediation of acquired cognitive dysfunction arising from brain injury, cerebrovascular accidents, or other less common neurological disorders. Referred to by different terms, cognitive retraining is synonymous with cognitive redevelopment, cognitive remediation, neurological retraining, and cognitive rehabilitation. In each case, the goal is to produce functional changes in verbal (e.g., verbal problem solving) and/or nonverbal (e.g., visual-spatial reasoning) skills or abilities. The approach attempts to strengthen premorbid patterns of mental functioning or the design of compensatory strategies to circumvent permanently impaired functions (i.e., return is unlikely). Cognitive retraining may involve remediation of deficits, capitalization on individual strengths, or the training of compensatory approaches. With dysfunction differing from one individual to the next, the therapist may design a program integrating more than one of these approaches. Indeed, rarely will a brain-damaged patient be presented with a specific area of impairment that is not reflected in other areas of cognitive functioning (e.g., abstract reasoning and memory).

Cognitive retraining is a recent endeavor and therefore many of its methods continue to be developed. Most approaches involve controlling materials, such as computer programs, and strategies in therapy such that optimal conditions exist to facilitate task performance (Diller & Gordon, 1981; Nieman, Ruff, & Baser, 1990). The cognitive therapist seeks to move the patient in small enough steps to the final goal so that the opportunity for failure is rare. Although retraining packages have been developed, the majority of cognitive retraining involves a task analysis approach to the specific disorder (Dean, 1982). Task analysis involves (1) assessing the patient's modality specific cognitive functioning; (2) defining content elements necessary (terms, rules, and the like) to achieve the objective of therapy; (3) identifying the level of cognitive functioning and modality (visual memorization, etc.) necessary to master content; (4) specifying relationships between content and cognitive functions for the patient; (5) using small steps and correction feedback in retraining procedures; and (6) chaining small components together to encompass the final goal (Dean, 1982). Specific approaches may vary from teaching specific verbal strategies as compensation for spatial deficits to relearning phonetic skills necessary in reading.

From the above description, it should be clear that the present state of the art of cognitive retraining remains at a clinical level. Thus, most retraining procedures are applied without benefit of a consistent research base. In fact, the research that does address the effectiveness of cognitive training procedures is limited by a lack of control for spontaneous recovery. That is to say, following brain damage, a degree of functional recovery occurs without intervention. Clearly this recovery must be accounted for in evaluating the effectiveness of any retraining procedure (Dean, 1986).

REFERENCES

Dean, R.S. (1982). Neuropsychology and the rehabilitation process. *Bulletin of the National Academy of Neuropsychologists,* 161–162.

Dean, R.S. (1986). Neuropsychological assessment. In J.D. Cavenar & S.B. Guze (Eds.), *Psychiatry.* Philadelphia: Lippincott.

Diller, L., & Gordon, W.A. (1981). Rehabilitation and clinical neuropsychology. In S.B. Filskov & T.J. Boll (Eds.), *Handbook of clinical neuropsychology* (pp. 702–703). New York: Wiley.

Nieman, H., Ruff, R.M., & Baser, C.A. (1990). Computer-assisted attention retraining in head-injured individuals: A controlled efficacy study of an outpatient program. *Journal of Consulting & Clinical Psychology, 58,* 6, 811–817.

See also **Brain Injury; Cognitive Strategies; Neuropsychology**

COGNITIVE STRATEGIES

Cognitive strategies are cognitive processes that we use to monitor, control, and manage our cognitive functioning. They mediate both learning and performance. While cognitive strategies have been studied under various names for a long time, credit should probably go to Bruner, Goodnow, and Austin (1956) for first using the construct in the modern-day sense of the term. During recent years, there has been considerable interest in the training and remediation of such strategies.

While a variety of cognitive theories have influenced work on cognitive strategies, information processing theories have been the most influential of all. Defining cognitive strategies from an information processing point of view, Young has pointed out that most tasks and problems can be carried out and solved in a variety of different ways and that individuals "have at their command a number of different strategies from which to choose for these purposes . . . there is an analogy between strategies and the subroutines used by computer programmers to organize [their programs]" (1978, pp. 357–358).

Cognitive strategies are theoretically distinguished from cognitive capacities (abilities) and knowledge information). They are regarded as cognitive techniques that guide the ways our capacities are exercised and our knowledge is used. Strategies are learned both informally and formally. Most important from the standpoint of special education is that they are susceptible to training and improvement.

A number of classification systems have been suggested for cognitive strategies. Baron (1978) has suggested that we categorize them in three ways: (1) central strategies that are basic to the development of others strategies; (2) general strategies applicable to a variety of situations; and (3) specific strategies pertaining to particular types of applications.

Newell (1979) has addressed the classification of strategies using an analogy of an inverted cone of strategic skills. At the bottom of the cone are a large number of strategies that apply only to certain problems or situations, e.g., a carrying strategy for two-column addition. Such narrow strategies may be powerful and, if properly used, should effectively solve the problems to which they are applied. They are, however, limited to specific types of problems or work only under particular conditions.

As we move up Newell's inverted cone to its tip we find more generalizable but less effective strategies; there is a tradeoff between generalizability and effectiveness. At the very tip of the cone we find a few highly general strategies that are applicable to almost any problem or situation but that are weak and by themselves unable to solve any specific problem. Checking one's school work to see that it is accurate is an example of a general beneficial cognitive strategy, but it has weak effects and by itself can solve no specific problem. In between lie a variety of intermediate-level strategies that vary in specificity and power. It has been suggested that the most useful approach to cognitive strategy training from a general remedial standpoint might be to address such intermediate level strategies (Brown & Palincsar, 1982). Thus scanning written pages in a systematic left to right fashion is a strategy that has some specificity, i.e., it applies to reading; it also has some generality in that it applies to a wide range of reading.

In determining what type of strategies to use with special education students, the cognitive trainer is confronted with decisions as to optimal training programs. Teachers engaged in the cognitive training of learning-disabled children might well stick to specific and intermediate-level strategies that are directly applicable to particular types of school work. Psychologists might be interested in more general types of cognitive strategic training such as is involved in problem solving, test taking, etc.

A distinction has been made between blind and informed cognitive strategy training. Blind training programs are ones in which the subjects do not know the purpose of the training they are receiving. Informed cognitive strategy training not only trains the pupils strategically but helps them to understand the purpose of the training and the benefits to be derived from it. There is evidence that both types of training programs can be effective. However, students trained under informed conditions are likely to use their strategies more effectively and to continue to use them after their formal training is over (Kendall, Borkowski, & Cavanaugh, 1980).

A number of researchers have offered recommendations to guide cognitive strategy training with handicapped students (Belmont & Butterfield, 1979; Brown & Palincsar, 1982; Borkowski & Cavanaugh, 1980; Kreiner, 1992). Some investigators have advised that teachers of handicapped students may wish to use cognitive strategy curricula (Borkowski & Cavanaugh, 1979; Winschel & Lawrence, 1975).

The most active interest in cognitive strategies currently is in metacognition, which represents a supraordinate realm of executive cognitive strategies that monitor and regulate lower level strategies, and in cognitive behavioral interventions, which involve strategic training.

REFERENCES

Baron, J. (1978). Intelligence and general strategies. In G. Underwood (Ed.), *Strategies of information processing* (pp. 403–450). London: Academic.

Belmont, J.M., & Butterfield, E.C. (1979). Learning strategies as determinants of memory deficiencies. *Cognitive Psychology, 2,* 411 420.

Borkowski, J.G., & Cavanaugh, J.C. (1979). Maintenance and generalization of skills and strategies by the retarded. In W.R. Ellis (Ed.), *Handbook of mental deficiency* (2nd ed.). Hillsdale, NJ: Erlbaum.

Brown, A.C. & Palincsar, A.S. (1982). Inducing strategic learning from texts by means of informed, self control training. *Topics in Learning & Learning Disabilities, 2,* 1–17.

Bruner, J.S., Goodnow, J.J., & Austin, G.A. (1956). A study of thinking. New York: Wiley.

Kendall, C.R., Borkowski, J.G., & Cavanaugh, J.C. (1980). Metamemory and the transfer of an interrogative strategy by EMR children. *Intelligence, 4,* 255–270.

Kreiner, D.S. (1992). Reaction times measures of spelling. *Journal of Experimental Psychology: Learning, Memory, & Cognition, 18,* 4, 765–776.

Newell, A. (1979). One final word. In D.T. Tuma & F. Reid (Eds.), *Problem solving and education: Issues in teaching and research.* Hillsdale, NJ: Erlbaum.

Winschel, J.F., & Lawrence, E.A. (1975). Short-term memory: Curricular implications for the mentally retarded. *Journal of Special Education, 9,* 395–408.

Young, R.M. (1978). Strategies and the structure of a cognitive skill. In G. Underwood (Ed.), *Strategies of information processing* (pp. 357–401). London: Academic.

See also **Cognitive Style; Information Processing; Metacognition**

COGNITIVE STYLES

Cognitive styles are constructs that help to explain the ways that personality variables affect cognition. Kogan has defined them as reflecting "individual variations in *modes* of attending, perceiving, remembering and thinking" (1980, p. 64). Two individuals who score identically on intelligence and other cognitive aptitude or achievement tests and are the same in information processing capabilities may nevertheless differ significantly in school work, success on the job, and other behaviors because they differ in their cognitive styles (Mann & Sabatino, 1985).

The study of cognitive styles began in earnest following World War II, urged on by concern about the psychiatric casualties of that war and postwar interest in personal self-development and psychotherapy. Personality assessment had become exceedingly popular. Thus interest developed respecting the ways that personality variables affect cognitive variables. Studies of what came to be known as cognitive styles emerged.

Interest in cognitive styles first appeared most promi-

nently in the work of George Klein et al. at the Menninger clinic. While the original work was conceptualized in terms of perceptual attitudes (perceptual types of tests being used as the most prominent way of assessing cognitive styles), later research emphasized the cognitive aspects of the research and the term cognitive controls became the dominant descriptor applied to work seeking to determine how personality factors interact with and influence cognitive skills.

Many definitions of cognitive styles have been offered. They generally agree that cognitive styles should be thought of as personality characteristics or traits that are related to other personality characteristics. Furthermore, while cognitive styles cannot always be distinguished or separated from cognitive skills, they are distinct from cognitive contents.

Though there has been disagreement on the issue, Kogan has suggested that cognitive styles can be classified on the basis of whether the results obtained are judgmental, i.e., have positive or negative implications attached to particular styles and their scores. Thus certain cognitive styles clearly suggest good or poor cognitive performance, e.g., Witkin's field dependence-independence continuum. Other cognitive styles, however, only indirectly imply cognitive strength or weakness, while still others appear to be truly stylistic, i.e., inputing neither cognitive strength nor weakness but rather suggesting different ways of thinking. Still other cognitive styles can be interpreted either in terms of cognitive strengths and weaknesses or in purely stylistic terms, depending on the circumstances of usage and interpretation.

While the study of cognitive styles began with adult populations, it gradually moved over to juvenile populations as well, including those of children with learning problems and handicaps. This has been more for research rather than diagnostic purposes. The two most popular of cognitive-style study approaches to schoolchildren and special education students are those of field independence dependence and conceptual tempo. Blackman and Goldstein (1982) have suggested that a major reason for their popularity is the easy availability of instruments to assess them. Another reason seems to be that they appear to be cognitive styles that may have particular relevance to school work.

There have been many studies suggesting that field-independent students are better and more self-dependent learners than field-dependent ones; that they are better decoders in reading than field-dependent students; and that they are better at math and science as well. Field-independent students have been found to do better in "discovery" types of learning situations; while field-dependent students are benefited by structured learning situations. Gifted children are more likely to be field independent than mentally retarded ones (Mann & Sabatino, 1985). Learning-disabled pupils are more likely to be field dependent than normal readers.

In respect to conceptual tempo, this cognitive-style dimension characterizes children on the basis of their placement on a reflection-impulsivity dimension, according to their performance on problem-solving tests, etc. As might be expected, reflective children are usually better students, while impulsive ones are more likely to read inaccurately and to manifest behavior problems.

While the research into cognitive styles has been very active, and results are regularly found indicating that cognitive styles are significantly related to school and academic variables that are important to both normal and handicapped children, the sum and substance of this research does not appear to support a position that knowledge of a handicapped child's particular cognitive style, in and of itself, is particularly helpful in respect to predicting school achievement (Swanson, 1980) or in guiding day-to-day instruction or management. Socioeconomic and general cognitive factors play roles of far greater importance in the school lives of special education students. Indeed, many of the significant differences found in the school performances of special education students who differ in cognitive style appear to be the result of consequences of investigators confounding their variables.

The most popular variant or offshoot of cognitive styles currently are identified as learning styles based on objective imaging and EEG examinations. (Riding, Glass, Butler, Pleydell-Pearce, 1997). Since learning styles tend to be educationally oriented, they have received a great deal of attention in educational circles. Learning style constructs, which emphasize learning preferences rather than personality characteristics, have taken much of the attention away from other types of cognitive styles among researchers concerned with school and academic achievement.

REFERENCES

Blackman, S., & Goldstein, K.M. (1982). Cognitive styles and learning disabilities. *Journal of Learning Disabilities, 15,* 106–113.

Kogan, N. (1980). Cognitive styles and reading performance. *Bulletin of the Orton Society, 39,* 63–77.

Mann, L., & Sabatino, D.A. (1985). *Foundations of cognitive processes in remedial and special education.* Rockville, MD: Aspen.

Riding, R.J., Glass, A., Butler, S.R., & Pleydell-Pearce, C.W. (1997). Cognitive style and individual differences in EEG alpha during information processing. *Educational Psychology, 17,* 219–234.

Swanson, L. (1980). Cognitive style, locus of control, and school achievement in learning disabled females. *Journal of Clinical Psychology, 36,* 964–967.

See also **Learning Styles; Personality Tests; Sperry, R.; Split-Brain Research; Temperament**

COLITIS

Ulcerative colitis is a chronic inflammatory disease of the colon (large intestine). It is a progressive disease, spreading to include part or all of the colon and rectum. It is charac-

terized by alternating remissions and relapses. The disease is usually more severe in children than adults, carrying an increased risk of malignancy because of the greater severity and duration of the disease (Dixon & Walker, 1984). A disease closely related to ulcerative colitis is Crohn's disease, which involves the small intestine as well as the large. Symptomatology and progression in Crohn's closely resembles that in ulcerative colitis.

The cause of ulcerative colitis is unknown. Symptoms of the disease include diarrhea with blood and mucous, abdominal pain preceding defecation, anemia, and rectal urgency. Weight loss is apparent in some children owing to reduced caloric intake or to limitation of food eaten to avoid discomforts of the disease (Dixon & Walker, 1984).

Treatment of colitis varies with severity and extent of the disease. The goal of treatment for children is to bring about remission to allow normal growth and development. Medical therapy includes use of corticosteroids to control inflammation and sulfasalazine to control flare-ups. Undesirable side effects of the two precipitate cautious use with children. Corticosteroids interfere with growth, increase susceptibility to infection, and cause temporary alterations in physical appearance. Sulfasalazine can cause headaches, nausea, vomiting, anorexia, and rash.

If the disease does not respond to medical therapy, or if it involves complications, surgery is required. Part or all of the colon is removed and then resected together or attached to the abdominal wall. If attached to the abdominal wall, a stoma is formed to allow excretion of waste products into an external collecting apparatus. With surgery, the effects of the disease disappear.

Children and their families need a great deal of emotional support and understanding in dealing with the manifestations of the disease and the effects of treatment (Burke, Neigut, Kocoshis, & Chandra, 1994). Children need special understanding and encouragement when dealing with side effects of steroid treatment or adjusting to the use of an external collecting apparatus. Advances in development of collection apparatus now make it possible for most children to participate in many activities and sports. Most individuals with colitis live a normal life under prolonged medical care.

REFERENCES

Burke, P.M., Neigut, D., Kocoshis, P.R., & Chandra, R. (1994). Correlates of depress in new onset pediatric bowel disease. *Child Psychiatry and Human Development, 24,* 4, 275–283.

Dixon, M.L., & Walker, W.A. (1984). Ulcerative colitis and Crohn's disease. In S.S. Gellis & B.M. Kagan (Eds.), *Current pediatric therapy* (pp. 195–198). Philadelphia: Saunders.

See also **Family Response to a Child with Disabilities; Physical Handicaps**

COLLABORATION

See INCLUSION.

COLLABORATIVE PERINATAL PROJECT

The main purpose of the Collaborative Perinatal Project is to evaluate factors in pregnancy that may relate to cerebral palsy and other abnormalities of the central nervous system. The project is sponsored by the National Institute of Neurological and Communicative Disorders and Strokes. Over 50,000 pregnant women were recruited (from January 1959 to December 1965) for the largest prospective study of its kind.

Data collected at the 14 university-affiliated hospitals include information on the mother's social and medical background; coexisting diseases; complications of pregnancy; current drug/medication use; and previous use of drugs (extending beyond the mother's last menstrual period). Each participant was interviewed at least monthly throughout pregnancy, at scheduled intervals during the infant's first 2 years, and annually until the child reached 8 years. Records on each child until the age of 8 years include birth and developmental history, diseases, noted congenital defects, and information on siblings and father. Infants received daily examinations for the first 7 days of life (and weekly for prolonged postnatal hospitalizations), with an extensive, standard pediatric exam at age one. Of the mortality rate (4.4% or 2227 stillborn or died before age 4), 81% came to autopsy.

The study (1) provided quantitative information, much not previously available, on relationships among birth defects; (2) confirmed and elaborated on, in quantitative terms, factors such as single umbilical artery and birth defects; (3) raised, in quantitative terms, hypotheses concerning risk factors, some previously suspected but without quantitative information and some not previously suspected; and (4) concluded that birth defects are rarely attributable to a single cause and that many malformation outcomes appear to have multiple risk factors that are interrelated.

Heinonen et al. (1977) were commissioned by the National Institutes of Health to document all findings. Their text contains detailed information on methods, malformations, drugs used, etc. The data from the project continue to be analyzed (Friedman, Granick, Bransfield & Kreisher, 1995), and debated (James, 1996).

REFERENCE

Friedman, H.S., Granick, S., Bransfield, S., & Kreisher, C. (1995). Gender difference in early life risk factors for substance use/abuse: A Study of an African-American Sample. *American Journal of Drug & Alcohol Abuse, 21,* 4, 511–531.

Heinonen, O.P., Slone, D., & Shapiro, J. (1977). *Birth defects and drugs in pregnancy.* Littleton, MA: Publishing Sciences Group.

James, W..H. (1996). Debate and argument: The sex ratio of the sibs of neurodevelopmentally disordered children. *Journal of Child Psychology & Psychiatry & Allied Disciplines, 37,* 5, 619.

See also **Congenital Disorders; Low Birth Weight; Prematurity**

COLLEGE PROGRAMS FOR DISABLED COLLEGE STUDENTS

Following the end of World War II, the majority of colleges and universities in the United States became more sensitive to the needs of students who would have been financially disabled without the original G.I. bill. This same sensitivity, however, on the part of colleges and universities for those who were physically, socially, and/or academically handicapped did not manifest itself to any major degree until the 1970s.

In April 1978 the Association on Handicapped Student Service Programs, in Post-Secondary Education (AHSSPPE) came into existence. This organization, along with others, provided professional support for full implementation of the Architectural Barriers Act of 1968 as upgraded and expanded on by Section 504 of the Vocational Rehabilitation Act of 1973, which became operational in April of 1977. The net effect of this act was to ensure the access and use of public schools (elementary through college) by the physically disabled through assurance that the schools would be constructed to accommodate the handicapped person.

Similarly, by the late 1970s a few colleges and universities began formal programs to serve college-bound students who had academic deficits resulting from either some innate and formal learning (language) disability and/or environmentally induced one. Those higher education institutions having programs for this population were identified in part by research projects sponsored by the National Association of College Admission Counselors (NACAC) (Mangrum, 1984). Two agencies that contributed to the development of the NACAC directory of college programs were the Post Secondary School Committee of the Association for Children with Learning Disabilities (ACLD) and the Loyola Academy of Wilmette, Illinois. Other references that identify colleges and universities having academic support services are Liscio's *A Guide to Colleges for Learning Disabled Students;* Mangrum and Strichart's *College and the Learning Disabled Student;* the *FCLD's Guide for Parents of Children with Learning Disabilities;* and *Peterson's Guide to Colleges with Programs for Learning Disabled Students.*

The college-aged learning-disabled student who is looking for a school to attend will find that the majority of two- and four-year higher education institutions (both public and private) that offer support services will be of the type just depicted; for example, those that provide assistance and support that is not necessarily intended to be remedial. The student who wishes to become language independent, academically as well as socially, might want to consider the other major type of service.

Those institutions that intend to remediate the student's language handicap and his or her accompanying social and psychological deficits, will be characterized by instruction that is designed to remediate the student's reading, spelling, written expression, and arithmetic deficits. The kind of instruction that would be most commonly used would directly reteach the basic or requisite information that must be known to read, spell, write, and carry out mathematical operations. Other probable aspects of this second service posture would be the use of tutors who have been trained to carry out direct remediation of the students academic deficits and formal support programs that deal directly with the student's social habilitation and psychological needs. Both types of schools offer their learning-disabled students the opportunity to take exams in a private setting without time constraints; use tape recorders to record lectures; take a reduced load as necessary; and partake in the institution's traditional student support services. Beyond the traditional academic assistance and/or remediation, most institutions of higher learning also offer counseling and testing support services.

REFERENCES

The FCLD guide for parents of children with learning disabilities. (1984). New York: Foundation for Children with Learning Disabilities.

Liscio, M.A. (1984). *A guide to colleges for learning disabled students.* Orlando, FL: Academic.

Mangrum, C.T., & Strichart, S.S. (1984). *College and the learning disabled student.* Orlando, FL: Grune & Stratton.

Peterson's guide to colleges with programs for learning disabled students. (1985). Princeton, NJ: Peterson's Guide.

See also **Continuing Education for the Handicapped**

COLOR BLINDNESS

The inability to perceive or discriminate colors is known as color blindness. There are four main types of color blindness, each containing a number of subtypes. The most rare type is known as *achromotopsia*. In this condition, the subject sees no color; everything is perceived as black, white, or shades of gray. This condition can result from a degenerative process. In the absence of such pathology, the condition is due to an autosomal recessive gene and is extremely rare.

The more common types of color vision disturbances are closely related to retinal physiology, specifically, to the structure and function of the cones. Since the cones are not evenly distributed in the retina, color vision in the visual field is somewhat variable. Color perception is not possible in the periphery of the visual field and diminishes as the object moves away from the point of fixation (Wald, 1968). The perception of color is dependent on not only the presence of different types of cone cells, but of complex chemical pigments thought to respond selectively to the different wavelengths of light.

Protanopia refers to the condition in which the individual has difficulty in distinguishing red. *Deuteranopia* is the condition in which the individual has difficulty in distinguishing green. *Tritanopia* is the condition in which the individual cannot distinguish blue; it is a severe and rare form of colorblindness, affecting less than .1% of the population. Tritanopia is considered to be an autosomal dominant trait.

Red-green color disturbances occur in both protanopia and deuteranopia. The former is more severe and less common than the latter. Both are sex-linked (X) recessive, traits, explaining their nearly exclusive presence in males. The prevalence of protanopia is about 1:100; deuteranopia about 1:20 (Linksz, 1964).

Determination of the condition is easily made using pseudoisochromatic plates (Isihara test) that present colored patterns or numbers to the individual. The normal person sees one pattern or number; those with color disturbances see the stimulus differently (Thuline, 1972).

Color blindness is not generally considered to be a significant handicap. Some authors (Cooley, 1977) feel that the tests are far too sensitive and that some persons have been needlessly denied employment. The classroom teacher, especially in the early grades, should expect to find at least one color-blind male in the classroom. Tasks involving color discrimination must be eliminated. The literature is replete with retinal changes owed to phenothiazine (Mellaril, Thorazine) administration (Apt, 1960; Weekly et al., 1960). Color vision anomalies may occur if a youngster is under phenothiazine therapy.

REFERENCES

Apt, R. (1960). Complications of phenothiazine tranquilizers ocular side effects. *Survey Ophthalmology, 5,* 550.

Cooley, D. (Ed.). (1977). *Family medical guide.* New York: Better Homes and Gardens.

Linksz, A. (1964). *An essay on color vision and clinical color vision tests.* New York: Grune & Stratton.

Thuline, H. (1972). Color blindness in children: The importance and feasibility of early recognition, *Clinical Pediatrics, 11*(5), 295–299.

Wald, G. (1968). The receptors of human color vision. *Science Magazine, 145,* 1007.

Weekly, R., Potts, A., Rebotem, J., & May, R. (1960). Pigmentary retinopathy in patients receiving high doses of a new phenothiazene. *Archives of Ophthalmology, 64,* 65.

See also **Mellaril; Thorazine; Visual Perception and Discrimination; Visually Impaired**

COMMUNICATION AIDS, ELECTRONIC

See ELECTRONIC COMMUNICATION AIDS.

COMMUNICATION BOARDS

Communication boards are simple, nonelectronic, augmentative communication systems used by nonspeaking persons. They are usually made individually according to the skills and needs of the nonspeaking user. The advantages of communication boards are their flexibility and low cost. Any symbol system ranging from objects and pictures to written alphabet letters can be used as message symbols. The communication board can be accessed by direct selection, through scanning, or by an encoding process. As the nonspeaking person's skills change over time, the communication board can be easily adapted to reflect those changes.

See also **Augmentative Communication Devices; Computer Use with the Handicapped**

COMMUNICATION DISORDERS

Communication disorders are defined as an observed disturbance in the normal speech, language, or hearing processes as determined by (1) objective signs (i.e., measurable characteristics that can be observed by other persons), (2) social signs (i.e., failing to understand a speaker's meaning and responding inappropriately resulting in mutual embarrassment), and (3) personal signs (i.e., a person's reactions to a self perceived disorder) (Plante & Beeson, 1999). Communication disorders may involve the processes of listening, speaking, reading, writing, and thinking. The American Speech-Language-Hearing Association (ASHA) estimates that about 10% of the population in the United States (approximately 25 million individuals of all ages) has some form of communication disorder involving speech, language, and/or hearing (Shames, Wiig, & Secord, 1994). Severity of communication disorders ranges from mild to severe/profound across different levels of communication (prelinguistic, sounds and letters, words, phrases and sentences, oral and literate discourse [conversation, narration, exposition] and discourse plus [non-literal language, math-language (including time and money), computer language, foreign language, and career or employment language]). Communication disorders are categorized as impairment (abnormality of structure or function at the organ level), disability (functional consequences of an impairment), or handicap (social consequences of impairment or disability) (Gelfer, 1996).

SPEECH DISORDERS

Speech disorders are variations from commonly used acoustic characteristics of the utterances one makes, rather than of the meaning of the utterances (Hegde, 1995; Silverman, 1995). Speech disorders include articulation (the process of producing vowels and consonants that result in meaningful language morphemes, words, phrases, sentences, and discourse), stuttering (the interruption of the flow of speech, characterized by sound or word repetitions, prolongations, and blocking of sound), and voice (production of the frequency and intensity of speech sounds that is atypical of sex, physical maturity, and age resulting in disorders of phonation and resonance). Associated features of speech disorders may be rate of speaking (too fast or too slow for communicative purposes) and dysphagia (disordered swallowing because of inflammation, compression, paralysis, weakness, or hypertonicity of the esophagus).

LANGUAGE DISORDERS

Language disorders involve the impaired ability to receive, process, and use auditory, visual, and haptic (touch and movement) symbols in order to negotiate meaning for social interaction and/or academic/professional communication learning. Language disorders may involve nonverbal symbols or verbal language (phonologic, semantic, syntactic, morphologic, and pragmatic linguistic rule systems). Language disorders are often classified as receptive (watching, listening, reading), expressive (moving/gesturing, speaking, writing), or a combination of receptive and expressive (Palmer & Yantis, 1990).

Auditory language disorders include problems making sense of speech sounds, single words, phrases, sentences, thoughts, concepts, and ideas. Visual language disorders include problems making sense of the nonverbal dimensions of communication that are critical in the pragmatic dimensions of communication (i.e., who can communicate what, with whom, how, when, where, and why), as well as decoding and encoding the graphemic and geometric visual symbols used for Augmentative/Alternative Communication (AAC) systems, reading, writing, mathematics, and the physical and technological sciences. Haptic language disorders include problems receiving, interpreting, and using nonverbal symbols involved in pragmatics, the linguistic symbols and motor acts associated with cursive and manuscript writing, and with specialized systems such as braille and manually-coded communication.

Language disorders and learning disabilities are integrally related. Preschool-aged children with a diagnosed language disorder (learning to communicate) will likely encounter problems with academic language (communicating to learn) when they enter a formal education system. Although the underlying problem is the encoding and decoding of symbols (language disorder), the disorder may be termed a learning disability because of the problems encountered learning academic material. The preferred term is language-learning disorder (Gelfer, 1996; Nelson, 1998; Plante & Beeson, 1999). Because individuals do not outgrow language-learning disorders, they continue to encounter social or academic problems as adults. The communication-learning deficits that are evident at the adult level are referred to as adaptive communication-learning disorders (Weller, Crelly, Watteyne, & Herbert, 1992).

HEARING DISORDERS

Hearing disorders stem from problems within the auditory system. Although this is usually associated with the ear, it may also be located in the areas of the peripheral and central nervous system where the perception of word meanings and associations occur. Individuals with ear infections or allergy/cold related symptoms may have temporary or chronic problems with hearing. Hearing impairments may slowly develop with advancing age. Irreversible impairment can occur following unusual levels of noise exposure, or from ototoxic drugs. Hearing impairments can easily lead to serious difficulties in the ability to perceive and understand the speech and language of others, resulting in speech and/or language disorders (Gelfer, 1996; Minifie, 1994; Plante & Beeson, 1999).

Early identification and intervention are important to maximize the successful management of both individuals with communication disorders and their families. Communication disorders should be assessed and treated by speech-language pathologists and audiologists who hold state licensure or who hold the certificate of clinical competence in speech-language pathology (CCC-SLP) or audiology (CCC-A) from the American Speech-Language-Hearing Association (ASHA). Speech-language pathologists and audiologists work in schools, hospitals, rehabilitation centers, long-term care facilities, through contract health care companies, and in private practice (Boone & Plante, 1993; Gelfer, 1996; Hegde, 1995; Minifie, 1994; Palmer & Yantis, 1990; Shames et al., 1994; Silverman, 1995).

REFERENCES

Boone, D.R., & Plante, E. (1993). *Human communication and its disorders* (2nd ed.). Englewood Cliffs, NJ: Prentice Hall.

Gelfer, M.P. (1996). *Survey of communication disorders: A social and behavioral perspective.* New York: McGraw-Hill.

Hegde, M.N. (1995). *Introduction to communicative disorders* (2nd ed.). Austin, TX: Pro-Ed.

Minifie, F.D. (Ed.). (1994). *Introduction to communication sciences and disorders.* San Diego: Singular Publishing Group.

Nelson, N.W. (1998). *Childhood language disorders in context: Infancy through adolescence* (2nd ed.). Boston: Allyn and Bacon.

Palmer, J.M., & Yantis, P.A. (1990). *Survey of communication disorders.* Baltimore: Williams & Wilkins.

Plante, E., & Beeson, P.M. (1999). *Communication and communication disorders: A clinical introduction.* Boston: Allyn & Bacon.

Shames, G.H., Wiig, E.H., & Secord, W.A. (1994). *Human communication disorders: An introduction* (4th ed.). New York: Merrill/Macmillan.

Silverman, F.H. (1995). *Speech, language, & hearing disorders.* Boston: Allyn & Bacon.

Weller, C., Crelly, C., Watteyne, L., & Herbert, M. (1992). *Adaptive language disorders of young adults with learning disabilities.* San Diego: Singular.

See also **Aphasia; Audiology; Auditory Abnormalities; Language Deficiencies and Deficits; Language Disorders; Speech and Language Disorders**

COMMUNICATION METHODS IN SPECIAL EDUCATION, ALTERNATIVE

See ALTERNATIVE COMMUNICATION METHODS IN SPECIAL EDUCATION.

COMMUNICATION SPECIALIST

A communication specialist is any one of a number of professionals who deal with aspects of both normal and disordered human communication. Such an individual may have expertise in communication theory, small group communication, organizational communication, or rhetoric. This individual may call himself or herself a linguist, a psycholinguist, a sociolinguist, a cultural linguist, or a rhetorician. The specialist is concerned with the influence of such diverse disciplines as linguistics, psychology, and sociology on human communication in general and language and speech in particular. In addition, these professionals study the development of normal communication theories and processes.

The study of disordered communication can also be considered in the realm of the communication specialist. The individual typically has expertise in communication disorders, education of the hearing impaired, or neurolinguistics. Speech and language disorders in children and adults can be studied from an organic (anatomic and physiologic) or functional (psychological, learning) perspective. The specialist in disordered communication may be concerned with such problems as language delay in children from multiple articulation errors or delay in (or loss of) the acquisition of morphologic, syntactic, or semantic rules of language. The communication specialist will also be concerned with language disorders owed to neurologic factors (e.g., brain damage).

See also **Communication Disorders; Speech and Language Handicaps; Speech Language Pathologist**

COMMUNITY-BASED INSTRUCTION

Community-based instruction refers to the opportunity for students to have direct interaction with resources in the community while participating in educational programs. With the current emphasis on education in the least restrictive environment for all students with handicaps, community-based instruction has been implemented in many special education programs, especially in those that serve students with moderate to severe handicaps. For students with moderate and severe handicaps to perform adequately in normalized postschool environments, skills must be taught in locations where they will naturally occur (Brown et al., 1983). Indeed, community-based instruction is a more powerful predictor of education/adaptive gains than intelligence quotient, level of ambulation, or presence of behavior problems (McDonnell, 1993).

Community-based instruction may be implemented using a number of models (Brown et al., 1983). These include consecutive instruction, whereby skills are taught in a simulated setting within the school facility until a certain skill level is reached; instruction in nonschool settings then follows. Concurrent instruction can occur where instruction takes place in both school and nonschool settings at daily or weekly intervals. Nonschool instruction can be implemented with direct training in nonschool (community) settings only students must have current access or have contact with the setting in the future.

A number of advantages in using community-based instruction with students who have moderate to severe handicaps have been cited by professionals in the field of special education. If training takes place in heterogeneous, nonschool environments, student adaptive functioning will be more likely in current and subsequent community settings. Transfer and generalization of community skills will be more likely to occur when taught in natural rather than simulated settings (Brown et al., 1979; Brown et al., 1976; Council for Exceptional Children, 1990). In addition, handicapped students participating in community-based instruction will have frequent access to nonhandicapped peers who may serve as role models. In turn, the awareness by nonhandicapped people of their peers with handicaps will be enhanced. This will enable the nonhandicapped peers to be cognizant of the abilities of individuals with handicaps, thus promoting a smoother transition to postschool environments on the part of handicapped individuals. Parent and teacher expectations of student abilities may be increased when community-based instruction occurs. Finally, the opportunity for students to sample the reinforcing aspects of activities in the community can be an advantage in achieving acquisition of functional skills (Wehman & Hill, 1982; Wehman et al., 1985).

REFERENCES

Brown, L., Branston, M.B., Hamre-Nietupski, S., Pumpian, I., Certo, N., & Gruenwald, L. (1979). A strategy for developing chronological age-appropriate and functional curricular content for severely handicapped adolescents and young adults. *Journal of Special Education, 13,* 81–90.

Brown, L., Nietupski, M., & Hamre-Nietupski, S. (1976). Criterion of ultimate functioning. In M.A. Thomas (Ed.), *Hey, don't forget me!* Reston, VA: Council for Exceptional Children.

Brown, L., Nisbet, J., Ford, A., Sweet, M., Shiraga, B., York, J., & Loomis, R. (1983). The critical need for nonschool instruction in educational programs for severely handicapped students. *Journal of the Association for Persons with Severe Handicaps, 8*(3), 71–77.

Council for Exceptional Children (1990). Designing Community-based instruction. Research brief for teachers. Reston, VA: Author.

McDonnell, J. (1993). Impact of Community-based instruction on the development of adaptive behavior of Secondary-Level students with mental retardation. *American Journal on Mental Retardation, 97,* 5, 575–584.

Wehman, P., & Hill, J. (1982). Preparing severely handicapped youth for less restrictive environments. *Journal of the Association for Persons with Severe Handicaps, 7*(1), 33–39.

Wehman, P., Renzaglia, A., & Bates, P. (1985). *Functional living skills for moderately and severely handicapped individuals.* Austin, TX: Pro-Ed.

See also Competency Education; Non-Sheltered Employment; Sheltered Workshops; Vocational Training of Handicapped

COMMUNITY-BASED JOB TRAINING FOR STUDENTS WITH AUTISM AND DEVELOPMENTAL DISABILITIES

In the past few years, the need to better prepare persons with disabilities for life after high school has become recognized by federal and local agencies and has been well documented in the professional literature. Now the development of programs to facilitate the transition from school to adult living has received substantial funding and attention. A major component of this transition movement involves vocational preparation of handicapped students.

Traditionally, vocational training efforts have centered on nonhandicapped and mildly handicapped students, with little or no related instruction being provided to persons having more severe handicaps. In fact, sheltered workshops and day treatment centers have served as the primary vehicles for the delivery of adult services for persons who are developmentally disabled, with few other placement alternatives (Schutz & Rusch, 1982). However, as generations of students served by the Individuals with Disabilities Education Act (IDEA) have begun to graduate from school, it has become clear that additional educational and vocational programs are required so that these individuals may also become employed.

The purpose of community-based job training is to prepare students for employment through the provision of instruction in actual job tasks at work sites within the local community. Research has shown that, because students with developmental disabilities often have difficulty transferring skills learned in one situation to another (Koegel, Rincover, & Egel, 1982), it is advantageous to assess and to teach job skills in the settings in which they will ultimately have to be performed (Black & Langone, 1995). Through the provision of vocational training in job sites within the community, teachers can facilitate student mastery of specific job skills, as well as the development of interpersonal job-related skills required to maintain various employment positions.

There are five major phases involved in community-based job training: (1) student evaluation, (2) job development, (3) instruction at the work site, (4) supervision reduction, and (5) client follow-up. Each of these phases must be addressed by the vocational trainer regardless of the student's ability level.

In contrast to job training programs for mildly handicapped persons, students with autism and developmental disabilities may require systematically planned job retention and follow-up services for many years following graduation from school. Methods of determining follow-up intervention strategies include periodic employee evaluations and progress reports, parent/guardian questionnaires, on-site visits, and telephone contacts with employers and family members or group home staff (Moon, Goodall, Barcus, & Brooke, 1985).

Preparation of students with developmental disabilities for productive employment has become a major educational concern. Issues regarding the selection of instructional locations and the types of assessment and training methods used in vocational preparation programs have received increased attention in the past decade. Research has shown that, because students with autism and developmental disabilities often have difficulty in transferring skills learned from one situation to another, it is advantageous to teach job skills in community-based settings rather than in the classroom even though inclusive educational settings may support generalization (Bang & Lamb, 1997). By providing vocational training in the job sites within the community, teachers can help students to master the necessary competencies for specific jobs and to learn job-related skills necessary to maintain various employment positions.

REFERENCES

Bang, Myong-Ye, & Lamb, P. (1997). *Impacts of an inclusive school-to-work program.* Paper presented at the Annual Convention of the Council for Exceptional Children, Salt Lake City, UT, April 9–13.

Black, R.S., & Langone, J. (1995). *Generalization of work-related social behavior for persons with mental retardation.* Paper presented at the Annual International Conference of the Division on Career Development and Transition. Raleigh, NC, October 19–21.

Koegel, R.L., Rincover, A., & Egel, A.I. (1982). *Educating and understanding autistic children.* San Diego, CA: College Hill.

Moon, S., Goodall, P., Barcus, M., & Brooke, V. (Eds.). (1985). *The supported work model of competitive employment for citizens with severe handicaps: A guide for job trainers.* Richmond, VA: Rehabilitation and Training Center, Virginia Commonwealth University.

Schutz, R.P., & Rusch, F.R. (1982). Competitive employment: Toward employment integration for mentally retarded persons. In K.P. Lynch, W.E. Kiernan, & J.A. Stark (Eds.), *Prevocational and vocational education for special needs youth: A blueprint for the 1980's* (pp. 133–160). Baltimore, MD: Brookes.

See also **Sheltered Workshops; Unemployment of the Handicapped; Vocational Rehabilitation**

COMMUNITY-BASED SERVICES

The concept of normalization has led to the current trend of serving individuals who might have been institutionalized in the community. These individuals must be provided with support services to help them successfully adjust to community life. To achieve the goal of normalization, the handicapped should be involved in developmental activities that are closely associated with those of nonhandicapped individuals

Pollard, Hall, & Kiernan (1979) state that there are many services available to the handicapped from various separate systems such as health, education, rehabilitation, recreation, employment, and housing. However, when these systems are working separately, there is little chance for them to solve the varied problems of the handicapped. There is a great need for these human services to work together to provide comprehensive community services (Pires, 1992). According to Schalock (1985), comprehensive community-based services for the handicapped include community living alternatives, habilitation programs, and support programs. Community living alternatives range from the highest level of independence, independent living, to congregate living, home care, supervised living, staffed apartments, and group homes, to the lowest level of independence, community institutional facilities. The habilitation programs in education range from the highest level of community integration, mainstreamed classes in public schools, to resource rooms, day training programs, and residential programs, to the lowest level of community integration, homebound instruction. The habilitation programs in employment range from the highest level of productivity, competitive employment, to transitional employment, sheltered workshop, and work activity, to the lowest level of activity, day training programs. The last category of comprehensive community services, support services, includes health and mental health care, legal services, home assistance (respite care), early identification/intervention, and transportation. In addition, the importance of the following points in designing and providing community living and habilitation alternatives are crucial:

Natural environments are the preferred service settings

Generic services should be used as much as possible

Assistance to the client should be provided only at the level actually needed to promote independence and self-sufficiency

Training should focus on increasing the client's independence, productivity, and community integration

Everyone has potential for growth regardless of his or her current functioning level (Schalock, 1985 p. 38)

REFERENCES

Pires, S. (1992). *Issues related to community-based service delivery for children and adolescents with mental illness and their families.* Washington, DC: Georgetown University Child Development Center.

Pollard, A., Hall, H., & Kiernan, C. (1979). Community services planning. In P.R. Magrab & J.O. Elder (Eds.), *Planning services to handicapped persons: Community, education, health.* Baltimore, MD: Brookes.

Schalock, R.L. (1985). Comprehensive community services: A plea for interagency collaboration. In R.H. Bruininks & K.C. Lakin (Eds.), *Living and learning in the least restrictive environment.* Baltimore, MD: Brookes.

See also **Deinstitutionalization; Normalization; Rehabilitation**

COMMUNITY PLACEMENT

The term community placement is generally used to denote those living, working, and recreational/leisure arrangements found in community environments as opposed to institutions. It refers to those environments in which persons with disabilities work, live, and recreate within a community. Community placement has received increased attention as the most appropriate and desirable treatment setting for persons with disabilities (Lakin et al., 1982; Prouty & Lakin, 1997; Larson & Lakin, 1991). As early as 1969 Wolfensberger stressed the importance of community services and facilities as a viable alternative to institutionalization. Others quickly recommended that such a movement be guided by the principle of normalization (Wolfensberger, 1972). The deinstitutionalization movement has created a need for a variety of community placement options. Community placement not only permits easier access to those experiences that lead to a more normal lifestyle, but also may sensitize nonhandicapped persons to those with handicapping conditions.

The array of services provided in the community typically includes vocational opportunities, residential options, and recreational/leisure activities. Community vocational opportunities should include competitive employment (Hill & Wehman, 1983), long-term supported employment (Wehman & Kregel, 1985), small enterprise-contract shops (Wald & Rhodes, 1984), and mobile work crews (Wald & Rhodes, 1984).

Educational opportunities available in the community should consist of classes in age-appropriate regular education buildings (Brown, Ford, et al., 1983). Curricular priorities should stress functional life skills with training conducted in the natural environments in which behaviors will ultimately be performed (Brown, Nisbet, et al., 1983; Lynch, Kellow, & Willson, 1997). Residential options in the community range from natural homes or foster care (one to six persons) to group homes and domiciliary care facilities. The appropriateness of each option is determined by the individual needs of the residents.

REFERENCES

Brown, L., Ford, A., Nisbet, J., Sweet, M., Donnellan, A., & Gruenewald, L. (1983). Opportunities available when severely handicapped students attend chronological age appropriate regular schools. *Journal of the Association for Persons with Severe Handicaps, 8*(1), 16–24.

Brown, L., Nisbet, J., Ford, A., Sweet, M., Shiraga, B., York, J., & Loomis, R. (1983). The critical need for nonschool instruction in educational programs for severely handicapped students. *Journal of the Association for Persons with Severe Handicaps, 8*(3), 71–78.

Hill, M., & Wehman, P. (1983). Cost benefit analysis of placing moderately and severely handicapped individuals into competitive employment. *Journal of the Association for the Severely Handicapped, 8*(1), 30–38.

Lakin, K.C., Krantz, G.C., Bruininks, R.H., Clumpner, J.L., & Hill, B.K. (1982). One hundred years of data on populations of public residential facilities for mentally retarded people. *American Journal of Mental Deficiency, 87,* 1–8.

Larson, S.A., & Lakin, K.C. (1991). Parent attitudes about residential placement before & after deinstitutionalization. *Journal of the Association for Persons with Severe Handicaps, 16,* 1, 25–38.

Lynch, P., Kellow, J.T., Willson, V.L. (1997). The impact of deinstitutionalization on the adaptive behavior of adults with mental retardation: A meta-analysis. *Education and Training in Mental Retardation and Developmental Disabilities, 32,* 3, 255–262.

Prouty, R., & Lakin, K.C. (1997). *Residential Services for Persons with Developments Disabilities: Status and Trends Through 1996, Report #49.* Minneapolis, MN: University of Minnesota.

Wald, B.A., & Rhodes, L.E. (1984). *Developing model vocational programs in rural settings for adults with severe retardation: The mobile crew model.* Paper presented at the meeting of the Association for Persons with Severe Handicaps, Chicago, IL.

Wehman, P., & Kregel, J. (1985). A supported work approach to competitive employment of individuals with moderate and severe handicaps. *Journal of the Association for Persons with Severe Handicaps, 10*(1), 3–12.

Wolfensberger, W. (1969). Twenty predictions about the future of residential services in mental retardation. *Mental Retardation. 6*(7), 51–54.

Wolfensberger, W. (1972). *The principle of normalization in human services.* Toronto, Ontario: National Institute on Mental Retardation.

See also **Community-Based Services; Community Residential Programs; Deinstitutionalization**

COMMUNITY RESIDENTIAL PROGRAMS

There is an array of community residential options available. Foster homes, also known as personal care homes or family care homes (McCoin, 1983), are private homes rented or owned by a family with one or more persons with disabilities living as family members (Hill & Lakin, 1984). The number of residents rarely exceeds six (Miller & Intagliata, 1984). These residences are licensed by a state agency or a local facility (e.g., a hospital). Foster homes are available for both children and adults. They tend to be homelike, with the person with the disability being "one of the family."

Group homes are residences with staff to provide care and supervision of one or more persons with disabilities (Hill & Lakin, 1984). Financial support comes from a variety of sources, including churches, states, private nonprofit organizations, and private for-profit organizations (Miller & Intagliata, 1984). It is not uncommon to find group homes staffed with house parents (a man and a woman who live in the residence, with one having an additional outside job) and one or two additional staff members for the hours when the majority of residents are home. The number of residents living in groups varies from home to home. Most of the research conducted has involved group homes serving under 20 residents (Miller & Intagliata, 1984).

Domicilary care facilities are community-based facilities whose primary function is to provide shelter and protection to the residents. There are no training or rehabilitation activities conducted (Miller & Intagliata, 1984). Since there is a lack of emphasis on training or rehabilitation, these types of facilities are deemed most appropriate for persons with high levels of independent living skills who need little or no additional training, or for those persons who, because of severe medical or physical needs or age, would not benefit from additional skill training (Miller & Intagliata, 1984). The number of residents in these facilities ranges from 5 to 200. Most of these facilities are operated by individual proprietors (Hill et al., 1984).

Although there are a variety of names given to domiciliary care facilities, there are generally two broad categories. Board and care facilities are also known as boarding homes and adult homes. As a general rule, these facilities provide a room and meals to the residents. Some also provide limited supervision. The major source of support for most residents is Social Security. (Miller & Intagliata, 1984). Health care facilities are also known as convalescent care homes, nursing homes, skilled nursing facilities, intermediate care facilities, and health-related facilities (Miller & Intagliata, 1984). In addition to providing a room and meals, these facilities also provide some level of nursing care to the residents. Generally, these facilities are funded through Medicare and Medicaid.

Halfway houses are short-term residential options available to persons leaving institutional settings (Katz, 1968). The setting is supervised with emphasis on facilitating the person's reentry into the community. The number of residents ranges from 12 to 25. An extensive report on residential services can be found by Prouty and Lakin (1997).

REFERENCES

Hill, B.K., & Lakin, K.C. (1984). *Classification of residential facilities for mentally retarded people* (Brief No. 24). Minneapolis, MN: Center for Residential and Community Services, University of Minnesota, Department of Educational Psychology.

Katz, E. (1968). *The retarded adult in the community.* Springfield, IL: Thomas.

McCoin, J.M. (1983). Adult foster homes: *Their managers and residents.* New York: Human Sciences.

Miller, B., & Intagliata, T. (1984). *Promises and realities for mentally retarded citizens: Life in the community.* Baltimore, MD: University Park Press.

Prouty, R., & Lakin, K. (1997). *Residential Services for Persons with Development Disabilities: Status and Trends through 1996, Report #49.* Minneapolis, MN: University of Minnesota.

See also Independent Living; Residential Facilities

COMPAZINE

Compazine (prochlorperazine) is used for the short-term treatment of generalized nonpsychotic anxiety, the control of severe nausea and vomiting, and the management of the manifestations of psychotic disorders (Servis & Miller, 1997). Compazine may impair mental or physical abilities, especially during the first few days of therapy. Adverse reactions can include drowsiness, dizziness, blurred vision, restlessness, agitation, jitteriness, insomnia, and motor dysfunctions such as muscle spasms, pseudo-parkinsonism, and tardive dyskinesia. Overdose can produce coma.

A brand name of Smith Kline and French, Compazine is available in tablets of 5, 10, and 25 mg, in sustained release capsules of 10, 15, and 30 mg in injectible ampuls, and in suppositories of 2 and a half, 5, and 25 mg. Dosage may vary, ranging from 2 and a half mg, according to the symptom being treated. It is given one or two times per day for severe nausea and vomiting in young children to a maximum of 25 mg per day in children 6 to 12 years of age being treated for psychosis.

REFERENCE

Physicians' desk reference. (1984). (pp. 1874–1877). Oradell, NJ: Medical Economics.

Servis, M., & Miller, B. (1997). Treatment of psychosis with prochlorperazine in the ICU setting. *Psychosomatics, 38,* 6, 589–590.

See also Atarax; Benadryl; Navane

COMPENSATORY EDUCATION

Compensatory education usually refers to supplemental educational services provided through federal, state, or local programs to educationally disadvantaged children in schools with concentrations of children from low-income families.

The largest such program is that authorized by Chapter 1 of the Education Consolidation and Improvement Act, formerly known as Title I of the Elementary and Secondary Education Act. Federal grants are made through state education agencies to local school districts based on the number of children from families in poverty. About 90% of all districts, receive Chapter 1 funds.

Local educational agencies then allocate funds to schools based on poverty and educational criteria. Schools provide services to children based not on family income, but on extent of educational deprivation. This determination is made at the local level within broad federal guidelines. In general, schools with the greatest concentrations of children from poor families and children most in need of services receive priority in program delivery.

The law allows for a wide range of services to be provided: instructional services, purchase of materials and equipment, teacher training, construction, and social and health services. However, about 80% of funds are spent on instructional services (White, 1984), with particular emphasis on reading and math. About three-fourths of participants receive compensatory reading and almost one-half receive compensatory math, with language arts the next most common service (Carpenter & Hopper, 1985). Almost two-thirds of districts pull students out of regular classrooms to provide services in classes that are likely to be smaller and more personnel-intensive than regular classes.

Title I average class size was about 10 children, with a 4.5 to 1 student to instructor ratio (White, 1984).

Chapter 1 programs resemble special education programs for learning-disabled children in several ways. They attempt to address a similar symptom: low or lower than expected achievement. There is a special concentration on attacking difficulties with reading and mathematics skills. Children are often removed from regular classrooms for part of the school day for more personnel-intensive services in smaller classes. That is not to suggest that children served, educational needs, or instructional content of programs for learning-disabled children and compensatory education are identical, or that learning-disabled children are interchangeable with children receiving compensatory education. They are not. But in terms of difficulty addressed, administrative design, or general approach to service delivery, there are important similarities.

Given the Chapter 1 eligibility criterion of educational disadvantagement, nothing prohibits a handicapped child who receives special education and related services from also being served as an educationally deprived child through compensatory education. Anecdotal evidence suggests this may not be common.

Evaluation of the federal compensatory education program has improved over the years. Findings from a large new federal study required by law are due in early 1987. This will be of particular interest to those in special education because the study includes the first school-based comparison of compensatory education, special education, bilingual education, and regular education programs.

It is also important to remember the many compensatory education programs run by state and local educational agencies complement and extend Chapter 1. Information on children served, services provided, and evaluation results of these programs is available from state and local education agencies (Federal Register, 1998).

REFERENCES

Carpenter, M., & Hopper, P. (1985). *Synthesis of state Chapter 1 data: Draft summary report.* Washington, DC: Advanced Technology.

Federal Register (1998). Title I helping disadvantaged children meet high standards; Final Rule. Federal Register, Part IV: 34 CFR. Washington, DC: Department of Education.

Riddle, W. (1985). *Elementary and Secondary Education Act: A condensed history of the original law and major amendments.* Washington, DC: Congressional Research Service.

White, B.F. (1984). *Compensatory education.* Washington, DC: Office of Management and Budget.

See also **Bilingual Special Education; Migrant Handicapped; Socioeconomic Status**

COMPETENCY EDUCATION

Implementation of educational curricula in secondary special education programs requires a shift from traditional content-based curricula to more process-based approaches. Moore and Gysbers (1972) cautioned against viewing students as needing to be brought up to a grade level by the end of the school year, thereby creating passive-dependent students who may evidence apathy, irresponsibility, or rebellious behavior. A process-oriented approach, which relates curriculum directly to the outside world and focuses on each student's unique learning and motivational methods, is recommended for exceptional learners.

Competency education emphasizes developing skills; acquiring knowledge and information (or content) becomes secondary. In curriculum development and planning, the programming concerns revolve around what skills, or competencies, are essential to the student in order to make him or her a more effective person and community member. In competency-based education, the content of a curriculum is selected for its utility in bringing about and exercising those skills. The competencies become the goals, and the curriculum becomes the vehicle by which the goal of skill development may be realized (Cole, 1972).

The responsibility is fixed on the educational system to ensure that the student gains those skills, or competencies, essential for adequate community adjustment (Brolin, 1976). It is frequently proposed that a secondary-level educational curriculum that best meets the life career development needs of special education students should revolve around career education concepts that emphasize three primary curriculum areas and one support area. The three curriculum areas are daily living skills; occupational guidance and preparation; and personal-social skills. A fourth curriculum area that lends itself to competency-based educational programming and is supportive to the other three is academic skills. As many as 22 major competencies have been identified as important to acquire at the secondary level under one of these major areas (Brolin, 1974).

REFERENCES

Brolin, D. (1976). *Vocation preparation of the retarded citizen.* Columbus, OH: Merrill.

Brolin, D., & Kokaska, C. (1974). Critical issues in the job placement of the educable mentally retarded. *Rehabilitation Literature, 10*(2), 16–18.

Cole, H.P. (1972). *Process education: The new direction for elementary-secondary schools.* Englewood Cliffs, NJ: Educational Technology.

Moore, E.J., & Gysbers, N.C. (1972). Career development: A new focus. *Educational Leadership, 30,* 108.

See also **Curriculum-Based Assessment; Vocational Evaluation; Vocational Training of Handicapped**

COMPETENCY TEST

Testing for competence is a method of evaluating individuals to assess the attainment of minimal skills in a given area. Usually, this type of testing occurs in grade school (first through twelfth grade) for the purpose of advancement from one grade to another, as a condition of promotion from one level of schooling to another (e.g. elementary school to junior high school), or the conferring of a high school diploma. This diploma is the most common occasion for minimum competency testing, as it is often seen as the final hurdle in the schooling process. Widespread use of competency testing arose out of a concern regarding the low competence level of high school graduates in reading, writing, and arithmetic skills (Lazarus, 1988). Although competence is tested in many states, regulations are far from uniform.

McClung (1977) has suggested that minimum competency tests should at least reflect the topics studied in the school curriculum (curriculum validity) and should ensure that the topics tested are actually taught (instructional validity). The legitimacy of minimum competency testing will be compromised until these issues are addressed.

In terms of content validity, the advent of computers has complicated the issue of minimum competency. Obviously, computers and computer skills are essential for the modern student, and most school systems recognize the importance of computers in our society by including computer classes in the curriculum. Despite this fact, there are very few, if any, minimum competency tests in the school systems designed to measure one's proficiency in computer usage.

The predictive validity of minimum competency tests is also at issue. The use of competency tests rests on the assumption that performance on such tests predicts later life success. Lazarus suggested that predicting life success would be a difficult, if not impossible, endeavor (1981).

Performance standards are another problematic issue of competency tests. Glass reviewed methods for establishing pass-fail cutoffs and found these methods to be arbitrary (1978). Milder critics concede that the process of establishing performance standards is subjective and vulnerable to social and political influences.

Minimum competency testing is supposed to be a means of improving the educational system. Currently there is too much variability among minimum competency tests in order to establish their worthiness as an improvement in education. In order to be truly worthy of their intention, minimum competency tests will need to resolve their deficits in validity.

REFERENCES

Glass, G.V. (1978). Minimum competency and incompetence in Florida. *Phi Delta Kappan, 63*(2), 134–135.

Lazarus, M. (1981). *Goodbye to excellence: A critical look at minimum competency testing.* Boulder, CO: Westview.

McClung, M. (1977). Competency testing: Potential for discrimination. *Clearinghouse Review, 2,* 439–448.

See also Achievement Tests; Minimum Competency Testing

COMPETENCY TESTING FOR TEACHERS

Competency testing for teachers is an educational and political practice that has been implemented in some states but not others. While all states in the United States have certification requirements for teachers, many states have delegated decision-making and testing to teacher training institutions within the states. In other states, the decision has returned to state agencies in the form of competency tests administered at the completion of teacher training (Lines, 1985). Those states given the responsibility of determining competency have differing methods of evaluation. For example, Arkansas, along with other states, proposed a system of certifying teachers and then recertifying them at intervals to continue or withhold one's credentials. In Texas, prospective teacher trainees are tested prior to entry into teacher education programs for minimum competency in basic arithmetic, writing, and reading skills. In South Carolina, competency testing is also used to determine salary levels.

Generally, competency testing for prospective or active teachers is oriented toward basic skills content and knowledge of pedagogy. The most widely used test in this regard is the National Teacher Examination (NTE). Educational Testing Services (ETS) developed the NTE and stated that the test should be used only to test entering teachers on academic knowledge. ETS does not set cutoff scores for passing, as each state is given the responsibility of determining its own competency level.

The validity of the NTE is a major issue in competency testing for teachers. The NTE, along with other such tests, has been challenged in court cases regarding its validity. Content validity has never been seriously challenged, mostly because the content being tested is fairly low in difficulty in arithmetic, spelling, grammar usage, and reading comprehension. Supreme Court decisions, notably *United States vs. South Carolina* (1976), have affirmed that a test such as the NTE may be used even though it does not have predictive validity of later job performance. The only validity reported for the NTE has been for performance in teacher training. The same decision affirmed that the test may be used as a basis for salary determination.

Minimum competency tests for teachers have not been able to produce respectable predictive validity estimates for effective teaching in the classroom. While some lawsuits have been based on this lack of validation, the South Carolina decision indicates that states may implement such a test without requiring predicative validity. The court uses the standard that it is reasonable that teachers possess knowledge such as that measured in such tests at the time of certification. Whether a minimum competency test is appropriate for continued certification of already-practicing teachers continues to be an issue.

REFERENCE

Lines, P.M. (1985). Testing the teacher: Are there legal pitfalls? *Phi Delta Kappan, 66,* 618–622.

See also Criterion-Referenced Testing; Teacher Effectiveness

COMPREHENSIVE RECEPTIVE AND EXPRESSIVE VOCABULARY TEST (CREVT)

The Comprehensive Receptive and Expressive Vocabulary Test (CREVT; Wallace & Hammill, 1994) measures both receptive and expressive oral vocabulary. The CREVT is used to identify students who are significantly below their peers in oral vocabulary proficiency, to note receptive vocabulary and expressive oral vocabulary strengths and weaknesses, and to document progress in oral vocabulary development as a consequence of intervention programs.

A review of the CREVT by Kaufman (1998) found the test to be reliable and stable with good norms and attractive pictorial stimuli. He did find problems with specific items in Receptive Vocabulary, and cautions that additional research is needed to establish the instrument's validity. The CREVT is easy to use and nicely packaged, reports McLellan (1998). The test has reasonable statistical properties and conforms to standards of testing. An adult version of the instrument is available. The CREVT-A (Wallace & Hammill, 1997) was standardized on adults aged 18 through 89.

REFERENCES

Kaufman, A.S. (1998). Review of the Comprehensive Receptive and Expressive Vocabulary Test. In J.C. Impara & B.S. Plake (Eds.), *The thirteenth mental measurements yearbook* (pp. 301–304). Lincoln: Buros Institute of Mental Measurements, University of Nebraska Press.

McLellan, M.J. (1998). Review of the Comprehensive Receptive and Expressive Vocabulary Test. In J.C. Impara & B.S. Plake (Eds.), *The thirteenth mental measurements yearbook* (pp. 304–305). Lincoln: Buros Institute of Mental Measurements, University of Nebraska Press.

Wallace, G., & Hammill, D.D. (1994). *Comprehensive Receptive and Expressive Vocabulary Test.* Austin, TX: Pro-Ed.

Wallace, G., & Hammill, D.D. (1997). *Comprehensive Receptive and Expressive Vocabulary Test–Adult.* Austin, TX: Pro-Ed.

COMPREHENSIVE TEST OF NONVERBAL INTELLIGENCE (CTONI)

The *Comprehensive Test of Nonverbal Intelligence* (CTONI; Hammill, Pearson, & Wiederholt, 1996) is a test that measures nonverbal reasoning abilities of individuals aged 6 through 90 for whom most other mental ability tests are either inappropriate or biased. The CTONI measures analogical reasoning, categorical classifications, sequential reasoning in two different contexts: pictures of familiar objects (e.g., people, toys, and animals) and geometric designs (e.g., unfamiliar sketches and drawings).

Results of the CTONI are used to estimate the intelligence of individuals who experience undue difficulty in language or fine motor skills, including individuals who are bilingual, who speak a language other than English, or who are socioeconomically disadvantaged, deaf, language-disordered, motor-disabled, or neurologically impaired. No oral responses, reading, writing, or object manipulation are required to take the test.

The CTONI is easy to administer and score. It can be administered orally to students who speak English or in pantomime to those who speak a language other than English or those who are deaf, aphasic, or neurologically impaired.

The reliability of the CTONI has been studied extensively, and evidence relating to content sampling, time sampling, and interscorer reliability is provided. The reliability coefficients are all .80 or greater, indicating a high level of test reliability. Evidence of content, criterion-related, and construct validity also is reported.

The CTONI was reviewed in *The Thirteenth Mental Measurements Yearbook* by Aylward (1998) and von Lingen (1998). These reviewers state that the test seems particularly useful in testing bilingual students because there are fewer intervening variables than found on other tests or batteries.

REFERENCES

Aylward, G.P. (1998). Review of the Comprehensive Test of Nonverbal Intelligence. In J.C. Impara & B.S. Plake (Eds.), *The thirteenth mental measurements yearbook* (pp. 310–312). Lincoln: Buros Institute of Mental Measurements, University of Nebraska Press.

Hammill, D.D., Pearson, N.A., & Wiederholt, J.L. (1996). *Comprehensive Test for Nonverbal Intelligence.* Austin, TX: Pro-Ed.

van Lingen, G. (1998). Review of the Comprehensive Test of Nonverbal Intelligence. In J.C. Impara & B.S. Plake (Eds.), *The thirteenth mental measurements yearbook* (pp. 312–314). Lincoln: Buros Institute of Mental Measurements, University of Nebraska Press.

COMPULSORY ATTENDANCE (AND STUDENTS WITH DISABILITIES)

Compulsory school attendance laws have been in effect in nearly every state and in most other parts of the western world for the bulk of the twentieth century. These laws require the parents or legal guardians of all children to send them to school or to provide an equivalent education. The ages of children for whom school attendance is compulsory varies as well, but includes children between the ages of 7 and 16 years in the vast majority of states. The courts have exempted some religious groups from the enforcement of compulsory attendance laws, notably the Amish nationwide and in some states the Mennonites. The states differ greatly in what constitutes a legal school under their compulsory attendance laws. Some states recognize only state certified and supervised schools (public or private), while some allow children to attend noncertified church-supported schools. Others are even more liberal and allow home schooling accomplished by lay parents. Compulsory attendance laws have been the subject of much litigation since their initial enactment.

Many consider compulsory attendance laws to be an infringement on various rights granted to the general populace in the first 10 amendments to the U.S. Constitution (the Bill of Rights). However, the courts have held, with minor religious exceptions, that the state has a compelling interest in the welfare of all children within its jurisdiction and that the provision for education under compulsory circumstances is an acceptable part of this compelling interest and is a legal extension of the police powers of the state. The full extent of the state's compelling interest in education has yet to be defined in adequate detail by the courts, but it is related to the provision of an education that allows individuals to become contributing members of society, preventing them from becoming burdens on the state.

In most states, children with disabilities are included in the compulsory attendance laws and the failure (or refusal) of the parents or legal guardians to present these children for school attendance is likely actionable on civil and/or criminal bases in most states. However, school officials or child welfare workers will, in the typical case, have to take the lead in seeking the enforcement of compulsory attendance laws for children with disabilities. It is clear, however, that unless specifically exempted by the wording of the state statute, handicapped children are required to attend school. What constitutes a school or an equivalent educational program may be different for the handicapped than the non-handicapped given the broad authority granted to multidisciplinary teams to diagnose and prescribe educational plans.

See also **Individuals with Disabilities Education Act (IDEA)**

COMPUTER-ASSISTED INSTRUCTION

Computer-assisted instruction (CAI) refers to educational software that can be run by students with little or no teacher assistance. In CAI, the computer presents information, asks questions, and verifies responses in much the same way a teacher does. Unlike traditional means of instruction, however, CAI allows students to work at their own levels and paces. This mode of instruction can be beneficial to handicapped students who have difficulty in working at the same pace as their nonhandicapped peers. Because CAI can be geared toward students' needs, interests, and expertise, it is generally considered to increase students' motivation to learn.

There are six types of computer-assisted instruction: informational, drill and practice, tutorial, instructional gaming, simulation, and problem solving. The various types of CAI represent a continuum of instructional formats, ranging from the highly structured to the unstructured (Levy & Lahm, 1984).

In the past few years, as researchers have begun to explore the potential applications of artificial intelligence, they have pointed out some of the *shortcomings of CAI*. For example, with traditional CAI, students cannot ask questions. Further, CAI programs usually cannot handle unanticipated answers. Often, CAI programs do not have any information base of a particular subject; they simply offer questions and answers that have been preprogrammed. Researchers are now looking at ways of improving CAI by giving it the capability of responding to the idiosyncrasies of each student's learning style. In the future, educators can look forward to programs that combine the best features of traditional CAI with new developments in artificial intelligence. These programs are expected to include a problem-solving model appropriate for the target domain of knowledge; a tutoring or teaching model; and a model of the student, including individual student characteristics such as knowledge about the content to be learned (Roberts, 1984). Intelligent computer-assisted instruction programs will allow users to communicate with the computer in natural English sentences Borchardt & Johnson, 1993. Programs will be able to accommodate random student questions on a given topic. Intelligent computer-assisted instruction will be more teacherlike in that programs will keep track of what the student knows and needs to know. The program will also have the capability of understanding when and how to provide a student with information and when to ask a question (McGrath, 1984).

REFERENCES

Borchardt, F.L., & Johnson, E.M. (1993). *Assessment proceedings of the computer-assisted learning and instruction consortium (CALICO) Annual conference, March 8–13, 1993.* Durham, NC: Duke University.

Levy, S.A., & Lahm, E.A. (1984). Microcomputers in special education curriculum. In E. McClellan (Ed.), *Microcomputer applications in special education* (pp. 21–43). Reston, VA: Council for Exceptional Children.

McGrath, D. (1984). Artificial intelligence: A tutorial for educators. *Electronic Learning, 4,* 39–43.

Roberts, F.C. (1984, June). *An overview of intelligent CAI systems.* Paper presented at the Special Education Technology Research and Development Symposium, Washington, DC.

See also **Computer Literacy; Computer-Managed Instruction; Computer Use with Students with Disabilities**

COMPUTERIZED AXIAL TOMOGRAPHY

See CAT SCAN.

COMPUTER LITERACY

The state of the art of computer technology and the internet are constantly changing, therefore so too is the definition of computer literacy. The major thrust in computer literacy today has shifted away from programming and toward the applications of computer technology in various settings, particularly the home, school, and office. The primary reason for this shift has been the increased availability of good software, inexpensive hardware, and access to the internet.

The problem of defining computer literacy is compounded by the fact that individuals with different educational levels have differing computer needs. Meeting these needs requires varying levels of expertise. For example, for the high-school student, computer literacy encompasses the following areas: basic knowledge of how to operate a computer; an understanding of how computers are used in work and for leisure; an appreciation of the ethical, social, and economic ramifications of computer usage; and an ability to use computers and the internet for instruction, information collection and retrieval, word processing, decision making, and problem solving.

For teachers, computer literacy means being knowledgeable about the capabilities of hardware and software and understanding how computers and the internet can enhance students' educational experiences. For those who work with handicapped students, computer literacy also implies an understanding of the ways in which technology can be used to improve services to special needs learners. Specifically, to be computer literate, special educators should acquire the following competencies:

1. Understand the fundamental operation and care of computers and software.

2. Become fluent in the basic terminology of computer technology.

3. Be able to apply computer technology to improve instruction.

4. Be able to use computers for management of instruction.

5. Understand how microprocessor-based technology can compensate for motoric, sensory, and cognitive disabilities.

6. Become proficient in evaluating software and hardware.

7. Be able to use an authoring system or language to develop instructional programs.

8. Understand the principles of telecommunication, especially as they apply to the improvement of instruction and learning.

9. Be able to access and utilize information retrieved from the internet.

See also **Computer-Assisted Instruction; Computer Use with Students with Disabilities**

COMPUTER-MANAGED INSTRUCTION

Computer-managed instruction (CMI) refers to a category of computer programs that are used by educators to organize and manage data related to instruction. In the early days of microcomputers in the schools, CMI was limited to pack-

ages that helped teachers monitor students' grades or those that allowed administrators to keep track of students' schedules and records. In the past few years, however, sophisticated CMI packages have been created that not only facilitate recordkeeping but also aid in the diagnosis of students' strengths and weaknesses. In special education in particular, CMI is used to analyze test data, determine goals and objectives based on the data, generate individualized educational plans (IEPs) monitor student progress, and generate reports (Gibbons, 1993; McClellan, 1984).

The key to the successful implementation of computer-managed instruction is not with single-purpose computer programs but with integrated packages. Software developers have created sophisticated, and often expensive, packages that can be customized to meet the specific needs of the teacher, administrator, or school system. These programs usually call for the creation of large data bases that integrate classroom and administrative information. Information stored in these master files might include student tracking data, assessment and diagnostic information, IEP goals and objectives, and classroom performance data. Integrated packages can also include instructional sequences and performance data (Lahm & Levy, 1984). The computer's capacity to analyze data rapidly and to present them in ways that are easily used suggests a tremendous potential for reducing the amount of time and paper work required to generate reports. More important, however, teachers and administrators can use the data compiled and analyzed by computer-managed instruction packages as a basis for making decisions that affect teaching and learning (Gibbons, 1993).

REFERENCES

Gibbons, A.S. (1993). The future of computer managed instruction (CMI). *Educational Technology, 33,* 5, 7–11.

Lahm, E.A., & Levy, S.A. (1984). Microcomputers in special education management. In E. McClellan (Ed.), *Microcomputer applications in special education* (pp. 44–59). Reston, VA: Council for Exceptional Children.

McClellan, E. (1984). Introduction to microcomputers. In E. McClellan (Ed.), *Microcomputer applications in special education* (pp. 1–21). Reston, VA: Council for Exceptional Children.

See also **Computer Literacy; Computer Use with Students with Disabilities**

COMPUTERS AND EDUCATION, AN INTERNATIONAL JOURNAL

Computers and Education is a scholarly journal published by the Pergamon division of Elsevier Publishing. Since 1977, the journal has provided a forum for communication in the use of all forms of computing. *Computers and Education* publishes papers in the language of the academic computer user on educational and training system development using techniques from and applications in many knowledge domains including: graphics, simulation, computer-aided design, computer integrated manufacture, and artificial intelligence and its applications. The journal is published 8 times a year and subscriptions can be ordered on-line from www.elsevier.nl/inca/publications/ store/.

COMPUTERS IN HUMAN BEHAVIOR

Computers in Human Behavior is a scholarly journal devoted to research that attempts to articulate the relationship between psychology, the science of human behavior, and technological advances in computer science. Articles are concerned with advances in research design and the technology of research, but also with the effects of computers on the topics chosen for study by psychologists, such as the use of health promotion programs to promote behavioral change, and use of virtual reality programs. Changes in clinical practice, ethics, and standards related to computers are also examined. Articles appearing in the journal have also included studies of the equivalence of testing conditions (computerized vs. standard administration), computerized interpretation of tests. The latter two areas are of interest to special educators as several articles have addressed placement decisions and educational diagnosis using computer programs to interpret tests. *Computers in Human Behavior* is a Pergamon Press journal; it began publication in 1985.

COMPUTER USE WITH STUDENTS WITH DISABILITIES

For handicapped persons, computers have three main functions: compensation for disabilities, management, and instructional delivery.

In terms of compensation for disabilities, one of the most exciting aspects of computer technology is the use of augmentative devices for communication and control. Computers, particularly microcomputers, help users overcome communication problems associated with limited mobility and sensory impairment. To increase the speed and accuracy of using computers, engineers and educators have developed special input and output devices. Innovative input devices include voice recognition; speech synthesizers (Schery & Spaw, 1993), the mouse, joysticks and game paddles, mechanical keyboard aids such as guards, mouths, and headsticks, and splints. Examples of computer output devices are synthetic speech, Blissymbols, tactile display (Opticon), braille, and portable computer printers (Brady, 1982).

For individuals with cerebral palsy, amyotrophic lateral sclerosis, or severe paralysis, one of the biggest problems of computer usage is the multiple simultaneous key strokes required to run many pieces of standard software. To take advantage of the computer's capacity to control the environment, a person with limited mobility must have an adaptive firmware card. The card is a device that enables a person with limited mobility to run software by activating a single switch (Schwedja & Vanderheiden, 1982). Single switches

and expanded keyboards require only slight movement, such as the blinking of an eye.

Access to standard software allows handicapped individuals to use the computer for information management. The four primary areas of information management are word processing, data base management, financial management, and telecommunication. Word processing packages allow users to draft, edit, and print text with relative ease. Changing margins and moving sentences or paragraphs are a matter of a few key strokes. Learning-disabled students can use word processing packages to overcome some of the problems associated with writing and spelling (Arms, 1984). Financial management programs such as speadsheets allow users to create, monitor, and change budgets. Other programs help with checkbook balancing and income tax preparation.

In addition to the functions that allow the computer to aid in communication and information management, the computer has certain characteristics that enhance the delivery of instruction. Interaction means that the computer can perform many of the functions that are typically performed by the teacher such as providing immediate feedback. Software can be designed so that rates of response and level of difficulty can be varied according to the student. One of the characteristics that tends to motivate students is branching capability (i.e., the capability of moving from one part of a program to another). Branching allows learners to decide whether they need to repeat material or move on to new material. Moreover, the computer is tireless; it does not become irritated when asked to repeat information or activities.

REFERENCES

Arms, V.M. (1984). A dyslexic can compose a computer. *Educational Technology, 24,* 39–41.

Brady, M. (1982). The Trace Center International Hardware/Software Registry: Programs for handicapped students. *Journal of Special Education Technology, 5,* 16–21.

Schery, T., & Spaw, L. (1993). Computer talk: Helping young handicapped children communicate. Paper presented at the Council for Exceptional Children Conference (San Diego, CA. December 14).

Schwejda, P., & Vanderheiden, G. (1982). Adaptive-firmware card for the Apple II. *Byte, 7,* 276–314.

***See also* Computer Literacy; Computer-Managed Instruction**

CONCEPT FORMATION

A concept would appear to be a mental construct that serves to group together similar entities. Having knowledge of a concept means having at least knowledge of the common elements that define inclusion or exclusion of an entity from a category. The presence of a concept is tested by observing which objects are placed in the same category or are acted on similarly. The individual carrying out such an activity may or may not have any idea what the concept is that he or she is using for categorization, nor what the common elements may be.

The relationship between a concept and language is a culturally contextual and problematical one, however. Gagne (1970), for example, has argued that there are two types of concepts, concrete ones such as "dog," which are based on direct empirical experience, and those such as "uncle" or "democracy" which cannot exist without language. It is further argued by some that the way language organizes and categorizes information actually effects the way one perceives incoming data.

Two general approaches for concept formation have been described (Martorella, 1972). The first is inductive, the second deductive. Concepts learned inductively start with a group of facts, data, or concepts that are already understood. Through the use of certain intellectual skills, new, more abstract concepts are developed. For example, to assist a child in learning the rule that "e" in a VCVe word usually makes the vowel long, the child could compare two lists of similar words, one containing the final "e," the other not. The deductive approach, on the other hand, begins by presenting the more abstract principle. The learner develops an understanding of the principle through repeated mental operations on examples pertinent to the concept. In this case, a child would be presented with the rule about the final "e" first, and then would be shown a number of examples. Research has not yet determined that teaching using either type of model is clearly superior. There is, in fact, some indication in cognitive style research that the success of one method over the other is at least to some degree dependent on a person's individual learning style (Witkin, Moore, Goodenough, & Cox, 1977).

Vygotsky (1962) made a similar distinction between two types of conceptual learning. He described two methods for learning concepts depending on whether the concept is spontaneous or scientific. Spontaneous concepts are learned from day-to-day concrete exposure to specific examples of the concept. An example of this type of concept would be that of "dog." The individual learns what a dog is by living with a dog and by seeing pictures of many different kinds of dogs. However, a term like exploitation is probably learned through a mediated situation in a formal learning environment. The individual is presented with only the beginning schematics of the term's meaning. A fuller understanding is gained over time with examples not directly experienced by the learner, but learned through discussion and reading.

Behaviorists have attempted to explain the development of concepts in strict stimulus-response terms. Vygotsky and others have objected to this explanation on the grounds that while the mental processes described by behaviorists are necessary, they are not sufficient for explaining how external phenomena become categorized into conceptual frameworks. These thinkers find the stimulus-response paradigm an inadequate explanation for how the brain arrives at the essence of concepts such as dogginess or exploitation.

Festinger (1957), in describing the process of concept formation, borrowed from the Piagetian notion of equilibrium. Festinger stated that if an organism has two cognitions that are perceived as being dissonant with one another, there is a tendency to attempt a modification of the cognitive structures to reduce the dissonance. This process, he states, creates new concepts. For example, if a child calls all animals doggie but notices others call some of those cats, the child will in time modify his or her notion of what characteristics identify members of the class of dogs.

DeCecco (1968) has proposed the following general model for teaching concepts:

1. Describe what performance is expected after the concept is taught.

2. For complex concepts, reduce the number of attributes to be taught; emphasize dominant attributes.

3. Provide clear verbal associations.

4. Give positive and negative examples of the concept.

5. Present the examples either in close succession or simultaneously.

6. Present a new positive example, asking the student to identify it.

7. Verify the student's understanding of the concept.

8. Ask the student to define the concept.

9. Provide opportunities for the student to practice the concept with appropriate reinforcement (p. 58).

There was considerable interest in the process of concept formation during the late 1960s and early 1970s, when new mathematics and social studies curricula were being developed. The back-to-basics movement led to a declining interest in this field of inquiry. Recently, with the introduction of problem solving into the curriculum, a renewed interest in concept formation has developed. The hope is that, particularly for students with special needs, understanding how concept formation occurs in a culturally competent context (Gonzales & Schallert, 1993) will guide teachers in helping their students become more effective learners.

REFERENCES

DeCecco, J.P. (1968). *The psychology of learning and instruction.* Englewood Cliffs, NJ: Prentice-Hall.

Festinger, L. (1964). The motivating factor of cognitive dissonance. In R.C. Harper, et al. (Eds.), *The cognitive processes.* Englewood Cliffs, NJ: Prentice-Hall.

Gagne, R.M. (1970). *The conditions of learning* (2nd ed.). New York: Holt, Rinehart, & Winston.

Gonzales, V., & Schallert, D. (1993). *Influence of Linguistic, and Cultural Variables on Conceptual Learning in Second Language Situations.* Paper presented at the Annual Meeting of the American Educational Research Association (Atlanta, GA, April 12–16, 1993).

Martorella, P.H. (1972). *Concept learning: Designs for instruction.* Scranton, PA: Intext Educational.

Vygotsky, L.S. (1962). *Thought and language.* Cambridge, MA: MIT Press.

Witkin, H.A., Moore, C.A., Goodenough, D.R., & Cox, P.W. (1977). Field-dependent and field-independent cognitive styles and their educational implications. *Review of Educational Research, 47*, 1–64.

See also **Thought Disorders; Vygotsky, L.S.**

CONCEPT OF ACTIVITY

See THEORY OF ACTIVITY; VYGOTSKY, L.S.

CONCRETE OPERATIONS

Concrete operations is the third of four invariant stages of Piaget's theory of cognitive development. According to Piaget, the distinctive features of children's thought occurring during the period of concrete operations are logic and objectivity that includes the ability to perform mental manipulations directly related to objects and events. These manipulations, which emerge between the ages of approximately 7 to 11 years, are termed operations by Piaget. To qualify as an operation, an action must be internalizable, reversible, and part of an overall system of actions. By internalizable Piaget meant that a child can think about the action "without losing their original character of actions" (1953, p. 8). An example of internalization during the concrete operations stage is the performance of mental arithmetic. Essential to understanding number and size relationships are transitivity and associativity. Transitivity, the basis for seriation, is the ability to arrange a series of events or objects in a continuum such as "less than," "greater than," "fewer than," or "more than." Associativity is demonstrated by understanding that parts of a whole may be combined in different ways without effecting a change on the whole.

The classic measure of whether a particular child is capable of concrete operational thinking is provided by the task of conservation. There are more than 1000 published studies on conservation (Yussen & Santrock, 1982). In a classic study, a child is seated before two same size beakers equally filled with water and a taller empty beaker. The experimenter pours one of the beakers into the tall empty one and asks the child if the amounts in the tall beaker and the unpoured beaker are the same or different. The conserver, i.e., the concrete operational thinker, knows that the amount of liquid has not changed and that if it were poured back into the original container (internalization of a reversible action) it would be the same.

In recent years, several aspects of Piaget's theory of cognitive development have been challenged (Flavell, 1992). As early as 1964, Jerome Bruner showed that children who should not be able to conserve, according to Piaget, could do so if the transformation of the object (pouring the beaker of water) were hidden from view. Since then, there has been considerable debate as to the accuracy of Piaget's four-stage model. It now seems clear that many specifics of Piaget's theory such as the age of onset of concrete operations, are in doubt. Nonetheless, the elegance and insight that Piaget brought to the study of children's thinking was immense.

REFERENCES

Bruner, J.S. (1964). The course of cognitive growth. *American Psychologists, 19*, 1–15.

Flavell, J.H. (1992). Cognitive development: Past, present, and future. *Developmental Psychology, 28*, 6, 998–1005.

Piaget, J. (1953). *Logic and psychology.* Manchester, England: Manchester University.

Yussen, S.R., & Santrock, J.W. (1982). *Child development: An introduction.* Dubuque, IA: Brown.

See also **Cognitive Development**

CONDITIONING

Conditioning is a general term that describes a strengthening (through a predictive relationship) of an association between a stimulus and a response or between two stimuli. With conditioning, responses become increasingly likely to occur under appropriate circumstances. In operant conditioning, the probability of a response that has been followed by reinforcement increases. In Pavlovian (or respondent or classical) conditioning, the probability of a response to an initially neutral stimulus increases when that neutral stimulus is followed by one that reliably elicits a response in reflex fashion. Pavlovian conditioning is named after the great Russian physiologist Ivan Pavlov (1927), whose research established the basic phenomena associated with this type of conditioning. However, the phenomenon itself had been discovered and described some years earlier by an American psychologist, E. B. Twitmeyer.

BASIC ASPECTS FOR PAVLOVIAN CONDITIONING

The paradigm for Pavlovian conditioning is:

$$CS \rightarrow UCS \rightarrow UCR \qquad \text{(before conditioning)}$$

$$CS \rightarrow CR \qquad \text{(after conditioning)}$$

Pairing of an initially neutral conditional stimulus (CS) with an unconditional stimulus (UCS) that reliably elicits a response (UCR) leads to a conditional response (CR) occurring to the CS. Frequently, but not always, the CR is similar to the UCR in form. For example, Pavlov would sound a bell (CS) and then give a dog food (UCS) that elicited salivation (UCR). After several pairings of the bell with food, the bell itself elicited salivation. Using the paradigm

CS	→	UCS	→	UCR	(before conditioning)
(bell)		(food)		(salivation)	
CS	→	CR			(after conditioning)
(bell)		(salivation)			

we can see that through pairing, a response can occur to a stimulus that never occurred to it before.

Watson (1916) made Pavlovian conditioning the basic form of learning in his formulation of behaviorism. In 1920 Watson and Rayner published a classic article on conditioning of an emotional response in a human infant. While one experimenter held a white rat (CS) toward 11-month-old Albert, the other experimenter hit a bar with a hammer, making a very loud noise (UCR) that elicited crying (UCS) from Albert. After only five pairings, the rat itself elicited crying (CR).

The basic aspects of conditioning can be briefly described:

Acquisition. With repeated trials, strength of the CR increases to some maximum level.

Extinction. Presentation of the CS without the UCS leads to a decrease in intensity of the CR until no response is observed.

Spontaneous Recovery. Presenting the CS after some delay following extinction may revoke a CR, although it will be of relatively low intensity.

Reacquisition. Repairing of the CS and UCS generally leads to more rapid reconditioning than original conditioning.

Generalization. After conditioning, a CR will tend to occur, but at lower intensity, to similar stimuli.

Discrimination. Presentation of one CS (CS1) followed by a UCS and of another (CS2) not followed by a UCS will generally result in the subject developing a discrimination such that it produces a CR to CS1 but not CS2.

APPLICATIONS TO CHILDREN'S DEVELOPMENT

Development of emotions. Since the time of Watson, Pavlovian conditioning has played an important role in accounting for the association of positive and negative emotional reactions with particular stimuli. Watson and Rayner demonstrated how conditioning could lead to negative emotions such as fear. Indeed, conditioning is viewed as a major process underlying the development of severe fears or phobias.

As conditioning may induce phobias, so it may be used to reduce them. As early as 1924, Jones "counterconditioned" a severe fear of rabbits in a child, Peter, by pairing a rabbit with pleasurable stimuli such as peer play and ice cream cones. By the end of the process, Peter no longer feared rabbits and, indeed, was petting them. This procedure, now called desensitization, is one of the most effective means of treating phobias in children and adults. Conditioning may also produce positive emotional responses, as shown, for example, in children's excitement at the sight of a favored food, person, or toy.

Development of meaning. Conditioning is one process thought to underlie the attachment of meaning to words (Mowrer, 1954). Pairing a word (CS) with the object (UCS) signified by the word will result in responses elicited by the object becoming attached to the word as a CR. Thus, pairing the word *doll* with an actual doll leads to responses elicited by the doll becoming associated with *doll*. Although a conditioning model cannot deal with all meaning, particularly that involving abstract concepts, it does provide a framework for understanding how reactions to stimuli can become attached to symbols for them. If an object comes to elicit an emotional response, then the word for the object may also elicit that response. If a child who has been painfully knocked to the ground by a large dog now fears all large dogs, he or she may show fear at the phrase *large dog.* On the other hand, a child who likes ice cream cones might well show positive anticipation to the phrase *ice cream cone.*

Also important is the related concept of mediated or semantic generalization. Once a CR occurs to a word, it will occur to words similar in meaning if the individual has developed a concept involving that word. Thus, if conditioned to respond to the word *shoe,* an individual will respond more to *boot,* or other words similar in meaning, than to *shoot,* a word similar in physical characteristics. Already apparent by at least age eight semantic generalization becomes stronger with age (Osgood, 1953).

IMPLICATIONS FOR EDUCATORS

Those dealing with children need to be sensitive to the fact that they and the situation they are in are paired with what they say and do to the children. So is the situation paired with peers' reactions to children. Thus, teachers who use aversive means of classroom management may condition children to be anxious about them and their classrooms. Similarly, children who are ridiculed in class or on the playground or who experience much failure and little success may become conditioned to fear school itself and teachers generally. In extreme, a school phobia may result.

We should also be aware that children will arrive at school with conditioned likes and dislikes and emotional responses. Some may have been specifically food poisoned or have had gastric distress after eating and may have strong aversions to certain foods. Others may have strong fears. However controversial it may be, those in special education should consider the roles of conditioning when predicting the effects of inclusion on children with disabilities. Those children who succeed socially and academically will have a positive conditioning experience, whereas those who are not accepted and/or fail academically may suffer from negative conditioning and develop conditioned responses associated with anxiety and fear of failure.

REFERENCES

Mowrer, O.H. (1954). The psychologist looks at language. *American Psychologist, 9,* 660–694.

Osgood, C.E. (1953). *Method and theory in experimental psychology.* New York: Oxford University Press.

Pavlov, I.P. (1927). *Conditioned reflexes* (translated by G.V. Anrep). New York: Oxford University Press.

Watson, J.B. (1916). The place of the conditioned reflex in psychology. *Psychological Review, 23,* 89–116.

Watson, J.B., & Rayner, R. (1920). Conditioned emotional reactions. *Journal of Experimental Psychology, 3,* 1–14.

See also Behavior Modification; Operant Conditioning

CONDUCT DISORDER

Conduct disorder is a behavioral disorder in youth characterized by a "repetitive and persistent pattern of behavior in which the basic rights of others or major age-appropriate societal norms or rules are violated." (American Psychiatric Association, 1994, p. 85). The behaviors fall into four basic groups: (1) aggressive behaviors that cause or threaten physical harm to people or animals; (2) nonaggressive behaviors that cause harm to property; (3) deceitfulness or theft; and (4) serious violations of rules. Three or more of the characteristics must have been present for 12 months or more, and at least one of the characteristics for 6 months for a diagnosis to be made. Overall, the disturbance in conduct must significantly impair the youth's social, academic, or occupational functioning. The prevalence of conduct disorder has increased over the past few decades: For males under the age of 18, rates changed from 6% to 16%, and females from 2% to 9% (American Psychiatric Association, 1994).

Individuals with conduct disorder may not be the best informants about their own behavior; therefore, it is important that diagnosticians conduct assessments that are multi-setting, multi-modal, and multi-method to accurately assess functioning (Sommers-Flanagan & Sommers-Flanagan, 1998). Many individuals with conduct disorder have little empathy for the feelings of others, and may negatively distort the positive intentions of others. The disorder is also highly correlated with early and risky sexual behavior, substance abuse, recklessness, and illegal acts. The onset of conduct disorder may occur as early as age 5, but it usually begins in late childhood or early adolescence. Many youth diagnosed with this disorder continue to show similar behaviors in adulthood (Storm-Mathisen, & Valglum, 1994) and meet the criteria for Antisocial Personality Disorder (American Psychiatric Association, 1994). There is a significant overlap of other psychiatric disorders (such as depression) with conduct disorders (Offord, Boyle, & Racine, 1991), especially in incarcerated juvenile populations (Eppright, Kashani, Robison, & Reid, 1993). Substance abuse is a significant precursor for disorders of conduct (Storm-Mathisen, & Valglum 1994), especially in Hispanic populations (Stewart, Brown, & Myers, 1997).

There is a great deal of research activity devoted to the treatment of youth with conduct disorders, and there are constant calls citing the need for new models of treatment delivery (Kazdin, 1997). Treatments include problem-solving skills training, parent management training, functional family therapy, and multisystemic therapy (Kazdin, 1997). The treatments are usually delivered in residential facilities and are subject to the common criticism of not being amenable to demonstrating clinically significant change that generalizes to every patient's situation. In addition, research about the treatments are not longitudinal in nature (Kazdin, 1993; 1997), which compromises the certainty of results. There have been some promising psychopharmacological treatments that are being researched (Shah, Seese, Abikoff, & Klein, 1994), but no conclusive results are available because of the multiple etiologies of conduct disorder (Stoewe, Kruesi, & Lelio, 1995). An exciting line of research stems from the field of neuropsychiatry where organic etiologists, such as early traumatic brain injury, are being studied with reasonable treatment success (Wood & Singh, 1994). Some researchers of conduct disorders, after reviewing treatment effectiveness, suggest that prevention is a far more an effective and economical use of resources (Dodge, 1993; Offord, 1994).

Special education services may be available to students with conduct disorders usually because of the comorbidity with handicapping conditions such as serious emotional disturbance, attention-deficit hyperactivity disorder, and learning disabilities. However, far too many of these students are underidentified and they subsequently enter the juvenile justice system where specific treatments that are linked to the etiology of the disorder are seldom available. School psychologists and support personnel can best serve these students by using multiple sources of information and assessment, not only for diagnosis, but also for treatment. Success in the demands of everyday living for these students requires that the school, community, and home work in unison.

REFERENCES

American Psychiatric Association. (1994). *Diagnostic and Statistical Manual of Mental Disorders* (4th ed.). Washington DC: Author.

Dodge, K.A. (1993). The future of research on the treatment of conduct disorder. *Development and Psychopathology, 5,* 1–2, 311–319.

Eppright, T.D., Kashani, J.H., Robison, B.D., & Reid, J.C. (1993). Comorbidity of conduct disorder and personality disorders in an incarcerated juvenile population. *American Journal of Psychiatry, 150,* 8, 1233–1236.

Kazdin, A.E. (1993). Treatment of conduct disorder: Progress and directions in psychotherapy research. *Development & Psychopathology, 5,* 1–2, 277–310.

Kazdin, A.E. (1997). Practitioner review: Psychosocial treatments for conduct disorder in children. *Journal of Child Psychology & Psychiatry & Allied Disciplines, 38,* 2, 161–178.

Offord, D.R., Boyle, M.H., & Racine, Y.A. (1991). *The epidemiology of antisocial behavior in childhood and adolescence.* Hillsdale, NJ: Erlbaum.

Offord, D.R., & Bennett, K.J. (1994). Conduct disorder: Long-term outcomes and intervention effectiveness. *Journal of the American Academy of Child & Adolescent Psychiatry, 33,* 8, 1069–1078.

Shah, M.R., Seese, L.M., Abikoff, H., & Klein, R.G. (1994). Pemoline for children and adolescents with conduct disorder: A pilot investigation. *Journal of Child & Adolescent Psychopharmacology, 4,* 4, 255–261.

Sommers-Flanagan, J., & Sommers-Flanagan, R. (1998). Assessment and diagnosis of conduct disorder. *Journal of Counseling & Development, 76,* 2, 189–197.

Stewart, D.G., Brown, S.A., & Myers, M.G. (1997). Antisocial behavior and psychoactive substance involvement among Hispanic and non-Hispanic Caucasian adolescents in substance abuse treatment. *Journal of Child and Adolescent Substance Abuse, 6,* 4, 1–22.

Storm-Mathisen, A., & Vaglum, P. (1994). Conduct disorder patients 20 years later: A personal follow-up study. *Acta Psychiatrica Scandinavica, 89,* 6, 416–420.

Stoewe, J.K., Kruesi, M.J.P., & Lelio, D.F. (1995). Psychopharmacology of aggressive states and features of conduct disorder. *Child & Adolescent Psychiatric Clinics of North America, 4,* 2, 359–379.

Wood, I.K., & Singh, N.N. (1994). The impact of neuropsychiatry upon forensic issues related to children and adolescents. In L.F. Koziol & C.E. Stout (Eds.), *The neuropsychology of mental disorders: A practical guide.* Springfield, IL: Charles C. Thomas.

See also **Antisocial Personality; Emotional Disorders; Substance Abuse**

CONDUCTIVE HEARING LOSS

Auditory functioning can be altered at several levels: the ear, the auditory nerve, or the brain. In the ear, there are two types of anatomical structures—those concerned with the mechanical transmission of sound (a physical process) and those concerned with the transformation of the sound waves into nervous impulses (a biological process). Conductive hearing loss (CHL) applies to the condition resulting from an alteration of the former in opposition to sensory-neural hearing loss, which results from pathology of the latter. The combination of CHL with sensory-neural hearing loss is called mixed hearing loss. For more details about terms and causes of the different types, see Davis and Silverman (1960).

The mechanical transmission of the sound vibrations obeys the laws of acoustics. It is effected by the external and middle ear, the fluids of the inner ear, and the combined displacements of the cochlea's basilar and tectorial membranes. These bring the vibrations to bear on the sensory cells of the organ of Corti, the hair cells. There the conduction process ends; the hair cells are the transducers that transform the acoustic phenomenon into a biochemical and bioelectrical event. The CHL alone is never greater than 60 dB hearing loss, for higher intensity sounds reach the inner ear directly through the skull (von Békésy, 1948). In small children, it is often superimposed on sensoryneural hearing loss, thereby producing an additional deficiency.

Interference with the conduction process most commonly occurs at the level of external or middle ear structures.

One of the most frequent causes of temporary CHL is the external obstruction of the external ear canal (the auditory meatus) by cerumen, a waxlike secretion, especially in individuals with mental retardation (Crandell & Roesner, 1993). Obstruction by foreign bodies is also relatively frequent, especially in children. Various malformations of the external ear can affect hearing, the most serious being nondevelopment of the external auditory meatus.

Numerous pathological processes can produce conductive hearing loss. The eardrum can be swollen by inflammation, stiffened by sclerosis, or perforated. The ossicles may be partly or totally absent or malformed. The mobility of the chain may be reduced by fixation of the stapes in the oval window owing to abnormal bone proliferation at that level. This occurs in otosclerosis (otospongiosis), a frequent condition in adults and a rare one in children.

The accumulation of fluid in the ear occurs in several different forms of otitis media. One of them, serous otitis media, is a frequent chronic or semichronic disease of small children up to 5 or 6 years of age. It is often associated with obstruction of the eustachian tube. These conditions can usually be alleviated or cured relatively easily by medical and/or surgical treatment. However, since the CHL caused by them is mild or moderate, it is often ignored or neglected: This could have serious consequences in later life.

While most causes of CHL can be efficiently corrected by medical and/or surgical treatment, the latter may have to be delayed, especially in children where plastic reconstruction surgery can only be done at a certain age level. For these patients, as well as for those where medico-surgical therapy has failed, is contraindicated, is impossible for practical reasons, or is refused by the patient, a well-adapted hearing aid is an excellent solution.

While CHL alone does not prevent spoken language development, it may severely slow down its progression and affect speech skills if undiagnosed or inadequately treated. In the latter case, speech and hearing therapy, following the appropriate medical and/or surgical treatment and/or hearing aid fitting, may be required. Special education may also be necessary as a temporary measure for those children whose speech and language deficiencies prevent them from holding their own in a school for those who hear normally. The great majority of children with CHL, however, can follow their whole curriculum in a mainstream situation, for instance, in ordinary schools with hearing children.

REFERENCES

Crandell, C.C., & Roesner, R.J. (1993). Incidence of Excessive/ Impacted Cerumen in Individuals with mental retardation: A longitudinal study. *American Journal on Mental Retardation, 97,* 5, 568–574.

Davis, H., & Silverman, S.R. (1960). *Hearing and deafness.* New York: Holt, Rinehart and Winston.

von G. Békésy, (1948). Vibration of the head in a sound field and its role in hearing by bone conduction. *Journal of the Acoustical Society of America, 20,* 749–760.

See also **Deaf; Deaf Education; Deprivation, Bioneural Results of**

CONFIDENTIALITY OF INFORMATION

One major right guaranteed all citizens under the U.S. Constitution is the right to privacy. Included within this privilege is the right to have certain information held confidential. Two basic forms of confidential information are covered in the legislation: information held by educational or residential institutions; and certain information discussed by individuals with certain school officials.

The Buckley Amendment (FERPA, 1976) was enacted in direct response to this practice by educational institutions or agencies that appeared to be in violation of their clients' constitutional rights. It now stands as the major legal document that provides parents and eligible students with the right to: review and inspect educational records; amend inaccurate records; and control disclosure of personally identifiable information in educational records. More specific to children with disabilities, parts of this document are reiterated in the Individuals with Disabilities Education Act (IDEA). This act specifically extends parents of handicapped children the right to control or participate in major educational decisions directly affecting their child. Under this law, as in the Buckley amendment, consent must be given before certain filed information can be revealed to individuals outside the educational institution. In addition, under IDEA, parents must be able to inspect and amend all information in their child's file.

In addition to these legal documents that ensure the right to have recorded information held confidential, there are also certain guidelines intended to protect the confidentiality of information disclosed by students to certain educational personnel (e.g., counselors, school psychologists). The issue of what and how much information is confidential is not entirely clear. In general, professionals (e.g., psychologists) are bound by their particular ethical standards to protect the confidentiality of information revealed to them in private sessions. This information can usually be revealed without the individual's consent unless there is evidence that the information would result in harm or danger to the patient or others (Reynolds et al., 1984, p. 259). When this information is revealed to school personnel, there seems to be even more ambiguity regarding what is to be held confidential. Overcast and Sales (1982) state:

It is simply not clear how much confidentiality a student may expect in dealing with school personnel. It depends on the nature of the communication, to whom the communication is directed, and the particular status of the state law (p. 1089).

REFERENCE

Reynolds, C.R., Gutkin, T.B., Elliot, S.N., & Witt, J.C. (1984). *School psychology: Essentials of theory and practice.* New York: Wiley.

See also **Buckley Amendment; Individuals with Disabilities Education Act (IDEA)**

CONGENITAL DISORDERS

Two concepts are joined together in the expression congenital disorders, making it pertinent to begin this entry with a short comment on each. Congenital stands for present at birth. This definition does not imply any causal relationship. Nevertheless, for a long time, the terms congenital and hereditary have been confused. Indeed, some congenital disorders may be hereditary, but in many others heredity is not involved. Thus the clear recognition of the absence of any familial factor allows many couples to be reassured concerning the possible recurrence of congenital disorders.

According to Warkany (1971), "Congenital malformations are structural defects present at birth. They may be gross or microscopic, on the surface of the body or within it, familial or sporadic, hereditary or nonhereditary, single or multiple." Only the molecular level must be added to this definition to include all congenital disorders.

There are many causes of congenital disorders. It is possible to distinguish three broad categories: (1) disorders genetically transmitted following classical Mendelian modes (McKusick, 1983), (2) disorders owed to anomalies of the genetic material but usually not transmitted (e.g., chromosome anomalies), and (3) disorders owed to environmental factors. Many can be recognized at birth by at least one characteristic symptom and some others are detected only later in life.

Dominant heredity is most frequently observed in the case of minor anomalies that do not impair normal life (e.g., supernumerary or fused fingers or toes). A dominant congenital defect is theoretically transmitted to half the offspring, and may be followed through many generations. Sometimes, one generation seems skipped over, or, on the contrary, more severely affected: this is due to variations in penetration or expressivity of the gene. However, severe congenital disorders can be transmitted through a dominant mode. This is the case in Huntington's chorea, a disease of the nervous system. Strictly speaking, Huntington's chorea is a congenital disorder, the gene responsible for it being present at birth. However, carriers of the mutation enjoy a normal life until 30 or 40 years of age and in reproduction transmit the gene to half their offspring.

Recessive heredity is characterized by the birth of affected children to normal parents. Indeed, the father and the mother are heterozygous for a common mutant gene, and 25% of their offspring are homozygous and affected. Hundreds of examples are found in McKusick's catalog of Mendelian diseases in man (1983). When the disorder is severe, people with the disease usually do not reproduce and the genes are eliminated: the reservoir of the disease is thus found in the heterozygous carriers. Many recessive disorders are rare: consanguineous marriages are a well-known favoring factor, as is a common ethnic background (e.g., Tay-Sachs disease is more frequent in Ashkenazi Jews, sickle-cell anemia in blacks, thalassemia in Mediterranean populations). However, this is not a general rule, and unrelated parents from different ethnic backgrounds may be heterozygous for a common recessive gene (a well-known example is mucoviscidosis).

Congenital disorders may be sex-linked, either dominant or recessive. In the first case, females and males are affected, in the second only males. Some common congenital malformations such as cleft lip and palate, clubfoot, spina bifida cystica, anencephaly, and pyloric stenosis are not transmitted through simple Mendelian inheritance, but nevertheless show a clear familial aggregation (Carter, 1976).

A number of congenital disorders are due to environmental factors. The term environmental must, however, be understood in a broad sense: everything that alters the normal parameters of the body, the body being considered a conglomerate of cells. Clearly, this means that environmental factors can originate from the surrounding area in which the patient lives (e.g., radiation, viruses, drugs), or inside his or her own body (e.g., diabetes, hypothyroidism). This creates abnormal environmental conditions for the cells and, if the patient is a pregnant woman, for the fetus.

In experiments with animals, many agents are known to cause congenital disorders when they are administered to pregnant females (Warkany, 1971). The systematic study of these effects is called teratology. A catalog of teratogenic agents is regularly published and kept up to date (Shepard, 1983). Many drugs are known to be associated with fetal malformations. Pregnant women are usually warned to seek medical advice before taking any medication. Nevertheless, some compounds, although carefully tested before marketing, escape detection and are responsible for the birth of malformed babies. The case of thalidomide is well known. This sedative drug, used also by pregnant women for nausea and vomiting, was found to induce severe anomalies in the human fetus when ingested between the 35th and the 50th day after the last menstrual period (the 23rd to 38th day after conception). Rat and mouse embryos did not seem to suffer from thalidomide administered to pregnant females. However, when the relationship between human malformations and thalidomide was established, the effect of the drug was studied again on macaques. They showed the same sensibility as man. Rabbits also suffered, but to a lesser degree. This demonstrates the importance of selecting a good experimental model. All teratogenic agents cannot be reviewed here; only a few will be discussed.

Ionizing radiations have a well-known teratogenic effect. However fear of congenital malformations in the fetus must not stop pregnant women from having examinations needed for their health (and thus for their baby's health). The teratogenic effect is dose-dependent; it also depends on the site of irradiation and the advancement of the pregnancy. As all this has been extensively demonstrated, it is best to advise the radiologist about a pregnancy or to perform a pregnancy test in case of doubt. Some viruses, but not all, also present with teratogenic activity. The example of rubella is well known; however, the risk is not the same throughout pregnancy. The maximum fetal sensitivity is during the first trimester. Alcohol ingestion may be harmful and cause fetal alcohol syndrome. Heavy smoking is also responsible for fetal damage and low birth weight. Diseases of the mother may affect the fetus if not corrected. Diabetes causes the birth of large infants, higher mortality at birth, and a tendency to hypoglycemia and respiratory distress after delivery (Delaney & Ptacek, 1970). Moreover, some authors are convinced that congenital malformations are more frequent in children of diabetic mothers or at least that some diabetic mothers are more at risk than others. However, if the ingestion of some drugs is known to be teratogenic, the absence of other elements, like vitamins, is harmful. Nutritional deficiencies as a cause of congenital malformations in experimental animals are well documented (Warkany, 1971). These situations are seldom encountered under normal human living conditions, but they explain why a vitamin supplement is advised for pregnant women.

The prevention of congenital malformations has many aspects. An important and simple means of prevention is regular medical surveillance during pregnancy. Another mode of prevention is to avoid any known teratogenic agent and to have balanced nutritional intake. If the birth of a child with severe congenital disorder is followed by death, necropsy is of paramount importance to determine the recurrence risk for the parents. However, sophisticated means of surveillance have been developed for the at-risk mother to be. Prenatal diagnosis is offered, including chromosome analysis of the fetus, research on abnormal genes at the molecular level with recombinant DNA techniques, blood sampling or biopsy of the fetus, follow-up of the anatomical growth of the fetus with ultrasound, various biochemical dosages in the amniotic fluid, and direct viral research on fetal tissues. For some defects, no known treatment is possible, and interruption of pregnancy may appear as the most appropriate solution. For others, treatment is possible either directly with the fetus or just after birth. Thus if a curable congenital heart malformation is diagnosed before birth, the mother can be delivered in a hospital specializing in the correction of such an anomaly.

Neonatal screening is important in some metabolic or endocrine disorders. For instance, hypothyroidism at birth is responsible for future mental retardation of the child, known as cretinism. Nevertheless, after delivery, hypothyroidic children are potentially normal, the maternal thyroid having supplemented the fetus. Immediate substitution treatment allows normal intellectual development. Hypothyroidism can be diagnosed just after birth by the increase of the hormone stimulating the thyroid activity (the thyreostimulating hormone [TSH]) in the blood. Testing is possible on a few drops of blood taken in the perinatal period, and the affected babies, duly treated, enjoy normal development (Delange et al., 1979). Many other disorders can be detected by neonatal screening (Bickel et al., 1980), and progress in this area is promising. This compensates for the high incidence of congenital disorders at birth.

REFERENCES

Bickel, H., Guthrie, R., & Hammersen, G. (1980). *Neonatal screening for inborn errors of metabolism* (Vol. 1). Berlin: Springer-Verlag.

Carter, C.O. (1976). Genetics of common single malformations. *British Medical Bulletin, 32,* 21–26.

Delange, F., Beckers, C., Höfer, R., König, M.P., Monaco, F., & Varrone, S. (1979). Neonatal screening for congenital hypothyroidism in Europe. *Acta Endocrinologica, 90* (Suppl. 223), 1–27.

Delaney, J.J., & Ptacek, J. (1970). Three decades of experience with diabetic pregnancies. *American Journal of Obstetrics & Gynecology, 106,* 550.

McKusick, V. (1983). *Mendelian inheritance in man* (6th ed.). Baltimore, MD: Johns Hopkins University Press.

Shepard, T.H. (1983). *Catalog of teratogenic agents* (4th ed.). Baltimore, MD: Johns Hopkins University Press.

Warkany, J. (1971). *Congenital malformations* (Vol. 1). Chicago: Year Book Medical.

See also **Genetic Counseling; Genetic Variations; Heredity**

CONGENITAL WORD BLINDNESS, HISTORY OF

This term refers to "a condition in which, with normal vision and therefore seeing the letters and words distinctly, an individual is no longer able to interpret written or printed language" (Hinshelwood, 1917, p. 2). The term was the title of a book written by Hinshelwood (1917) in which he described case studies and intervention techniques with individuals who evidenced word blindness. Hinshelwood's clients showed such disability subsequent to strokes or brain damage induced by chronic alcoholism. He extended the use of this term to children who showed the same reading disability. However, "congenital word blindness" was originally used by Morgan (1896), whose paper was one of the first to document a clear case of severe reading disability in a 14-year-old boy of apparent brightness.

Hinshelwood believed that intensive practice and the development of the brain's visual memory would enable individuals with congenital word blindness to reach reading proficiency (Mercer, 1983). Specifically, he suggested a three-stage approach to the remediation of deficits: teaching the individual letters for storage in the supposed visual-memory center of the brain; teaching word recognition by spelling the printed words aloud so as to use the individual's good auditory memory for letter sounds; and enabling storage of the reading words using oral and written practice. It has been suggested that Hinshelwood's emphasis on visual memory and generally visual interpretations of reading disability had a significant impact on subsequent visual-perceptual theories of learning disabilities (Smith, 1983).

REFERENCES

Hinshelwood, J. (1917). *Congenital word blindness.* London: Lewis.

Mercer, C.D. (1983). *Students with learning disabilities* (2nd ed.). Columbus, OH: Charles E. Merrill.

Morgan, W.P. (1896). A case of congenital word blindness. *British Medical Journal, 2,* 1378.

Smith, C.R. (1983). *Learning disabilities: The interaction of learner, task and setting.* Boston: Little, Brown.

See also **Dyslexia; Reading Disorders**

CONNERS' PARENT-RATING SCALES-REVISED, CONNERS' TEACHER-RATING SCALES-REVISED, CONNERS'-WELLS' ADOLESCENT SELF-REPORT SCALE

The revised Conners' rating scales follow the original aims of the earlier versions in assessing attention-deficit/hyperactivity disorder (ADHD) (Conners, 1997). Both the Conners' Parent-Rating Scale Revised (CPRS-R) and the Conners' Teacher-Rating Scales Revised (CTRS-R) are designed to assist in the assessment of ADHD and related behavioral problems for children ages 3 to 17. This measure should be used as an ancillary source of information rather than the sole means of diagnosing ADHD.

Both parent and teacher scales include Oppositional, Cognitive Problems, Hyperactivity, Anxious-Shy, Perfectionism, Social Problems, the Conners' Global Index, Restless-Impulsive, Emotional Liability, DSM-IV symptom subscale, DSM-IV Inattentive and DSM-IV Hyperactive-Impulsive. For the parent scale, there is an additional Psychosomatic scale.

The validity of this measure was determined by its ability to discriminate between clinically referred and non-referred children. (Miller et al., 1997). Correlations (concurrent validity) between parent and teacher ratings for individual subscales ranged from .12 to .47 for males, and .21 to .55 for females, indicating that teacher and parent raters often perceived the same children quite differently.

The Conners'-Wells' Adolescent Self-Report Scale (CASS) is a new addition to the parent and teacher rating scales. It contains 10 subscales including Family Problems, Emotional Problems, Conduct Problems, Cognitive Problems, Anger Control Problems, Hyperactivity, ADHD Index, DSM-IV Symptom Subscale, DSM-IV Inattentive, DSM-IV Hyperactive-Impulsive and takes approximately 20 minutes to complete.

The CASS long form contains 87 items that are rated using an adapted Likert 4 point scale (from never to very often) by adolescents between 12 and 17 years of age. The CASS long form was normed on 3,394 adolescents between the ages of 12 and 17 (1558 males and 1836 females). Sixty-two percent of this sample were Caucasian. Internal reliability (Cronbach's alpha coefficient) are reported for each scale, by gender and range from .75 to .92. Test-retest intervals between 6 and 8 weeks were studied for each subscale using 50 children (mean age 14.8) and ranged from .73–.89.

Until recently, only one form was available for the parent and teacher ratings. The revised version, however, now includes both long and short versions of these scales. The CPRS and CTRS short forms cover a smaller scope of problems (only the Oppositional, Cognitive Problems, Hyperactivity and ADHD Index are measured) then does the long form. The short forms can be completed in significantly less time than the long forms. The CASS is also available in a short form and includes only 4 subscales, Conduct Problems, Cognitive Problems, Hyperactivity-Impulsive, and the ADHD Index.

REFERENCES

Conners, C.K. (1997). *Conners' Rating Scales-Revised Technical Manual.* North Tonawanda, NY: Multi-Health Systems.

Miller, L.S., Koplewicz, H.S., & Klein, R.G. (1997). Teacher ratings of hyperactivity, inattention, and conduct problems in preschoolers. *Journal of Abnormal Child Psychology, 2,* 113– 119.

See also **Attention Deficit Disorder; Hyperkinesis**

CONSCIENCE, LACK OF IN HANDICAPPED

Society is particularly concerned that children develop the skills to regulate their own behavior or, stated differently, internalize moral principles. Situations often arise that pose a conflict between the individual desires of the person and the requirements of society. These circumstances call for the exercise of self-control as the person suppresses self interested behavior in favor of actions that serve the needs of others. Two areas of research bear directly on this problem—altruism and resistance to temptation.

ALTRUISM

Altruism refers to behavior that is carried out to benefit another in the absence of threat or expected reward. Altruism entails self-control since the helper must weigh the costs of helping (e.g., material loss or physical danger) against the benefits (e.g., self-satisfaction) of helping (Kanfer, 1979).

One research finding that is unequivocal is that the altruistic behavior of children can be modified. Numerous studies have shown that children will imitate an altruistic model (Harris, 1971). In fact, the influence of a model was shown in one study to extend up to 4 months, even though posttesting was conducted under very different circumstances (Rushton, 1975). These results have obvious implications for child-rearing practices.

RESISTANCE TO TEMPTATION

Resistance to temptation is another example of self-control. Here the child is required to exercise self-restraint in the absence of immediate surveillance. Several studies have examined variables that promote this form of self-control. From a developmental perspective, the emergence of language is important in that it allows the child to regulate his or her behavior by stating rules of conduct (Kanfer & Phillips, 1970). The ability to verbalize rules may be necessary but usually is not sufficient for resisting temptation.

The importance of verbal controlling strategies in resistance to temptation is underscored by a study comparing Down's syndrome children to nonretarded children matched for level of cognitive development. On the average, the retarded children were less able to resist temptation than were the nonretarded children, a finding consistent with the Franzini et al. (1980) study. Interestingly, those Down's syndrome children that were most successful were observed to spontaneously engage in verbal and non-verbal behaviors

that served to distract them from the desired object (Kopp, Krakow, & Johnson, 1983).

In considering the research in both the areas of altruism and resistance to temptation, a clear directive for teachers and parents is evident. In order to enhance self-control one should not think in terms of building the child's character. Instead, the child should be taught specific verbal and nonverbal behavioral skills that can be used for self-regulation in tempting situations.

REFERENCES

Franzini, L.R., Litrownik, A.J., & Magy, M.A. (1980). Training trainable mentally retarded adolescents in delay behavior. *Mental Retardation, 18,* 45–47.

Harris, M. (1971). Models, norms and sharing. *Psychological Reports, 29,* 147–153.

Kanfer, F.H. (1979). Personal control, social control, and altruism: Can society survive the age of individualism? *American Psychologist, 34,* 231–239.

Kanfer, F.H., & Phillips, J.S. (1970). *Learning foundations of behavior therapy.* New York: Wiley.

Kopp, C.B., Krakow, J.B., & Johnson, K.L. (1983). Strategy production by young Down syndrome children. *American Journal of Mental Deficiency, 88,* 164–169.

Rushton, J.P. (1976). Socialization and the altruistic behavior of children. *Psychological Bulletin, 83,* 898–913.

See also **Impulse Control; Moral Reasoning; Self-Control Curriculum**

CONSENT, INFORMED

Increased parental involvement through informed consent began with the Education for All Handicapped Children Act of 1975 and consistently has been supported and enforced by subsequent legislation in the firm of the Individuals with Disabilities Education Act (IDEA) and amendments. The intent of the informed consent requirement is to change the relationship between schools and parents from one of the schools as the primary authority in determining the appropriate education for handicapped students to one of shared decision making. Prior to the passage of PL 94-142, some schools consulted with parents and told them about their children's special education placement and some did not, carrying the doctrine of *in loco parentis* to an intolerable extreme. However, court decisions and decrees have stated that the consequences of possible labeling, segregation, and exclusion of handicapped children from other children, and changes in their curriculum, may infringe on their constitutional rights of life, liberty, or property, and that individuals who may be subject to such deprivation must consent to any process with these possible results.

To protect students from arbitrary changes in placement, parental consent must be received before conducting a preplacement evaluation, before placing a child in a program providing special education and related services and before re-valuation of services. If the parents refuse to give their consent to evaluation or placement, the school system may request a due process hearing to obtain the authority to proceed with the assessment and placement process without parental consent.

Bersoff (1978, 1982), Overcast and Sales (1982), and Kotin (1978) suggest various procedures for securing informed consent and corresponding criteria and assessment techniques to determine the extent to which the informed consent principle has been implemented. Current practice in special education varies greatly from school district to school district. Ethics consultation (Heron, 1996) and specialized policies for students with handicapping conditions and aversive procedures are necessary (Braaten, 1991). Careful attention to obtaining informed consent is not just good professional practice, it is a requirement of federal law.

REFERENCES

Bersoff, D.N. (1978). Procedural safeguards. In L.G. Morra (Ed.), *Developing criteria for the evaluation of due process procedural safeguards provisions of Public Law 94-142* (pp. 63–142). Washington, DC: U.S. Office of Education.

Bersoff, D.N. (1982). The legal regulation of school psychology. In C.R. Reynolds & T.B. Gutkin (Eds.), *The handbook of school psychology.* New York: Wiley.

Braaten, S. (1991). A policy model for use of aversive and deprivation procedures to decrease problem behaviors of students in special education. *Preventing School Failure, 35,* 3, 27–31.

Heron, T.E. (1996). Ethical and legal issues in consultation. *Remedial and Special Education, 17,* 6, 377–385.

Kotin, L. (1978). Recommended criteria and assessment techniques for the evaluation by LEAs of their compliance with the notice and consent requirements of PL 94-142. In L.G. Morra (Ed.), *Developing criteria for the evaluation of due process procedural safeguards provisions of Public Law 94-142* (pp. 143–178). Washington, DC: U.S. Office of Education.

Overcast, T.D., & Sales, B.D. (1982). The legal rights of students in the schools. In C.R. Reynolds & T.B. Gutkin (Eds.), *The handbook of school psychology.* New York: Wiley.

See also **Individuals with Disabilities Education Act (IDEA)**

CONSENT AGREEMENT

See CONSENT DECREE.

CONSENT DECREE

A consent decree is a legal mandate or court order issued by a judiciary authority that has jurisdiction over the particular civil matter resolved in the decree. It is a legally enforceable order of that court. Consent decrees derive from the agreement of the adversarial parties to a civil lawsuit to end their disagreement provided that certain acts are performed by one or both parties and agreed to in order to avoid continuing litigation. The agreement is drawn up by the two

parties, signed by the appropriate legal representatives, and submitted to the court for review. If the court decides the agreement is fair and entered into with appropriate understanding and representation by both parties, the court will then mandate and enforce the decree by court order.

Many special education cases are decided by consent agreements that become enforceable court decrees. Among the best known and most influential are *Diana and Guadalupe.* Consent decrees are binding only on the parties to the decree, however, and do not make case law or set legal precedent.

See also **Diana *v.* State Board of Education**

CONSTITUTIONAL LAW (IN SPECIAL EDUCATION)

Judicial interpretations of the Constitution and its amendments have played a major role in the comparatively recent efforts to obtain and maintain appropriate special education programs and services for handicapped children and youth and their families. The groundwork for this role was laid in the 1954 Supreme Court decision in *Brown v. Board of Education;* the decision made clear that separate education facilities for children of different races are inherently not equal (Lippman & Goldberg, 1973). This decision affirmed that, because of the importance of education today, education "is a right which must be available to all on equal terms" (*Brown v. Board,* 347 U.S. 483). Citing this decision almost 20 years later, attorneys in two class-action suits built their arguments for landmark special education cases that were resolved in federal district courts: *PARC v. Board* (*PARC v. Commonwealth,* 334 F. Supp. 1257, E.D. Pa., 1971), which made clear that mentally retarded children in Pennsylvania are entitled to free education programs appropriate for their needs; and *Mills v. Board* (*Mills v. Board of Education, District of Columbia,* 348 F. Supp. 866, 1972), which extended free and appropriate education to all handicapped children in the District of Columbia.

Both the *PARC and Mills* cases have been cited in subsequent litigation involving similar and related principles that eventually were incorporated into federal legislation. Of particular importance to special education are the Rehabilitation Act of 1973, which requires access to programs and facilities, and more recently the Individuals with Disabilities Education Act (IDEA) and subsequent amendments, the latest being in 1997 (Martin, 1996). They embody the principles of zero project, nondiscriminatory testing, individualized and appropriate education planning and programming, least restrictive alternative as preferred educational placement, and procedural due process.

For a detailed discussion of litigation in special education and its reliance on constitutional guarantees and interpretations of the Supreme Court, see Turnbull and Fiedler (1984). Recent litigation has focused on the constitutionality of State financing systems (Verstegen, 1998).

REFERENCES

Lippman, L., & Goldberg, I. (1973). *Right to education: Anatomy of the Pennsylvania case and its implications for exceptional children.* New York: Teachers College Press.

Martin, E.W. (1996). The legislative and litigation history of special education. *Future of Children, 6,* 1, 25–39.

Turnbull, J.R., III, & Fiedler, C.R. (1984). *Judicial interpretation of the Education for All Handicapped Children Act.* Reston, VA: Council for Exceptional Children.

Verstegen, D.A. (1998). Landmark court decisions challenge state special education funding. *Center for Special Education Brief.* Palo Alto, CA: American Institutes for Research.

See also **Brown *v.* Board of Education; Larry P.; Mills *v.* Board of Education; Pase *v.* Hannon; The Pennsylvania Association for Retarded Citizens *v.* Pennsylvania**

CONSULTATION

Consultation refers to a professional relationship in which a specialist attempts to improve the functioning of another professional. Although there are many models of school consultation, each with different sets of assumptions, techniques, and goals, Bergan and Tombari's definition (1976) is general enough to encompass the idiosyncrasies of these various models. "Consultation refers to services rendered by a consultant (e.g., school psychologist) to a consultee (e.g., teacher) who functions as a change agent with respect to the learning or adjustment of a client (e.g., a child) or a group of clients" (p. 4).

Consultation in school settings is an indirect model of providing broadly defined mental health services to children. The consultant attempts to effect a change in children's behavior and learning by attempting to change the teacher's (or administrator's) attitudes, perceptions, and behaviors. One of the rationales for consultation is the economy of resources it offers. By improving teacher and administrator functioning, the psychologist can affect many more children than possible in the traditional counseling and testing models of service delivery.

Consultation involves two jobs: working on the content, or specific problem brought to consultation, and working on the process of helping the consultee improve his or her job-related performance. It is important for the consultant to have specialized knowledge that is relevant to the consultation content (e.g., the particular behavior, learning, or programmatic concern). Indeed, the reason the consultee asked for the consultant's help is that the consultee believes the consultant has such relevant knowledge. Knowledge bases the psychologist-consultant might draw from in teacher consultation include child development, theories of learning, childhood psychopathology, tests and measurements, diagnosis of learning and behavior, group processes, individual instructional programming, and treatment of childhood learning and behavioral disorders.

In addition to content skills, the consultant must have skills necessary for establishing and maintaining rapport with the consultee and for facilitating the consultee's professional growth. Thus the consultant (1) seeks clarification, encouraging consultees to see problems from new or broader perspectives; (2) supports the consultee while he or she is grappling with the problem, boosting consultee motivation and self-confidence; (3) asks questions that require consultees to validate information; (4) probes for feelings to help consultees accept their emotional reactions to children; (5) provides choices to increase consultee freedom to choose and commitment to choices made; and (6) confronts consultees either directly or indirectly to increase consultee objectivity. An example of an indirect confrontation is telling a female teacher who is inappropriately "mothering" a young girl that the girl is expecting the teacher to do too much for her and the girl needs to learn that the teacher cannot be her mother. An example of a direct confrontation is telling a male teacher that he seems to be apologizing to his students when he assumes an authoritative role, and that perhaps students are misbehaving because they are picking up on his discomfort in the authoritarian role.

Five models of school consultation are described with respect to their primary purpose and the roles and skills required of the consultant. Psychoeducational consultation is the type of consultation most frequently practiced in schools. After the psychologist has evaluated a child, the psychologist interprets the evaluation results to the teacher, presents recommendations to the teacher, and engages the teacher in a discussion of these recommendations so that the teacher will be able to choose and implement one or more recommendations. The primary purpose is remedial. The consultant's primary role is to diagnose the problem and recommend treatment.

Behavioral consultation is based on social learning theory. The behavioral consultant applies the technology of applied behavior analysis to the task of changing student and teacher behavior. The consultant observes the child as well as the teacher in the classroom to identify and count target behaviors, determine antecedents and consequences of those target behaviors, and recommend changes expected to result in a change in target behaviors. Because the teacher is ultimately responsible for making any changes that are recommended by the consultant, the consultant needs to establish a collaborative working relationship with the teacher. The primary goal in behavioral consultation is remedial; however, the consultant expects consultees will improve their skills in applied behavior analysis and will apply their new skills to similar problems in the future.

In educational consultation, the consultant presents new information or teaches new skills to consultees by conducting in-service workshops. The effective consultant-trainer carefully assesses educational needs of the workshop audience as well as the expectations of the administrators, and provides training that matches those needs and expectations. It is important, in cases of individual student consultation, that the question of needing informed consent from the parents is considered (Heron, 1996).

The mental health consultant's primary purpose is to improve the consultee's ability to effectively cope with similar problems in the future without the consultant's continued help. The particular problem discussed in consultation acts as leverage for changing the consultee's behavior. A secondary goal is to change the child's behavior. Because the focus is on the consultee, the consultant's process skills are especially important. The mental health consultant uses clinical interviewing skills to determine the reason a teacher is experiencing difficulty and employs different consultation approaches depending on the presumed reason for the consultee's difficulty. When the consultee's problem is presumed to be a lack of objectivity, the consultant uses specialized skills that require specialized training in consultation techniques. The consultant attempts to minimize the teacher's displacement of personal problems onto the work setting.

In program consultation, the consultant is requested by the administration to design or to evaluate a specific program such as a gifted education program, a race relations program, or a truancy program. The consultant must have experience and skills relevant to the particular program. The consultant issues a written report that contains recommendations for the school to implement.

Process consultation, like program consultation, is initiated by an administrator. It attempts to effect a change in the system rather than in the individual teacher or child. Process consultation is based on social psychological and general systems theory. The process consultant attempts to improve interpersonal and group processes used by administrators, teachers, parents, and students to reach educational objectives. Thus the consultant will involve the administrators and teachers in a mutual problem-solving effort aimed at diagnosing and changing such human processes as communication, leadership, decision making, and trust. The process consultant does not deal directly with the subject matter of the interactions of an organization. Rather, the consultant provides help with the methods of communication, problem solving, planning, and decision making (Schmuck, 1976).

Consultation is a term that encompasses a diverse set of models for delivering psychological services to a school (or other organization). The common thread is that the psychologist attempts to affect change in clients of the organization (e.g., students) by influencing the behaviors of persons who have a responsibility for client care.

REFERENCES

Bergan, J.R., & Tombari, M.L. (1976). Consultant skill and efficiency and the implementation and outcomes of consultation. *Journal of School Psychology, 14*(1), 3–14.

Heron, T.E. (1996). Ethical and legal issues in consultation. *Remedial and Special Education, 17,* 6, 377–385.

Schmuck, R.A. (1976). *Process consultation and organization development.* Reading, MA: Addison-Wesley.

See also Multidisciplinary Teams; Prereferral Interventions; Preschool Screening; Professional School Psychology

CONSULTATION, INCLUSION AND
See INCLUSION.

CONSULTATION, MENTAL HEALTH

Mental health consultation is an indirect mode of providing mental health services to clients served by some agency. The mental health consultant attempts to improve the psychological adjustment of persons in the community (i.e., students, parishioners, probationers, or patients) by consulting with professional caregivers in the community (i.e., teachers, clergymen, probation officers, or doctors).

The mental health consultant may be a psychiatrist, psychologist, or social worker, and the consultee may be any person whose ministrations to lay persons in the community have mental health implications. Mental health consultation is more prevalent in schools than in other settings. Reasons for its prevalence in schools include the opportunity provided in schools to affect the mental health of large numbers of children through consultation with a small number of teachers, the recognition of the importance of schooling on children's mental health, the presence of psychologists in schools, and the demonstrated relevance of psychological theories and knowledge to educational goals and practices. Consistent with the focus of this work, the following discussion of consultation will be specific to mental health consultation in schools.

There are several key elements in the previous definition of consultation that distinguish consultation from other professional activities. First, the consultee (teacher, principal, other administrator) invokes the consultant's help. Because consultation is a professional-to-professional interaction, the consultee is responsible for determining whether the assistance of the consultant would be helpful.

Caplan (1970) categorized mental health consultation as to the kind of problem dealt with (a case or an administrative problem) and as to the focus (the client or program on the one hand or the consultee on the other). This resulted in four categories of consultation.

In *client-centered case* consultation, the focus is on a child's problems. The goal of change in the teacher is secondary to the goal of formulating the problem. A written report to the teacher summarizes the diagnostic findings and recommendations for the teacher's handling of the problem.

In *consultee-centered case* consultation, the focus is on the student; however, the consultant's primary goal is change in the teacher's knowledge, skills, self-confidence, or objectivity. The problem case is a leverage point for effecting a change in the teacher that will enable the teacher to work more effectively, not only with the particular child who is the focus of consultation, but also with similar children in the future. This expected ripple effect in consultation extends the impact of consultation to an indefinite number of children. Because a change in the teacher is the primary goal, the consultant spends considerable time with the teacher, helping the teacher gain new perspectives, insights, knowledge, and skills that will generalize to similar problems in the future.

In *program-centered administrative* consultation, the focus is on a particular program for which the administrator-consultee has responsibility. The primary goal is the assessment of obstacles to achieving goals of a particular program. After a site visit and interviews with persons in the school, a written report summarizing the consultant's findings and recommendations is prepared. As in client-centered case consultation, the goal of educating administrators to handle similar problems in the future is secondary.

In *consultee-centered administrative* consultation, the focus is on the administrator's skills in areas such as group processes, leadership, and interpersonal relationships. This model of consultation is frequently referred to as organizational development consultation. It assumes that change in social structures and human processes within a school will result in the greatest positive impact on the mental health of students and teachers.

Although consultation is different from teaching, the consultant has an educational role. As teacher, the consultant instructs, shares information, translates psychological theories into educationally relevant practices, models approaches, offers ideas, and interprets data. As facilitator, the consultant provides a model of professional objectivity, guides teachers in problem solving, encourages, helps consultees deal with affect that may decrease their ability to deal effectively with a problem, and helps consultees avoid displacement of personal problems in the work setting. The consultant also facilitates communication among different organizational units within the school (i.e., regular and special education teachers, grade level teachers, and administrators).

REFERENCE

Caplan, G. (1970). *The theory and practice of mental health consultation.* New York: Basic Books.

See also **Consultation; Psychology in the Schools; School Psychology**

CONTINGENCY CONTRACTING

A contingency contract is a written agreement between parties that details specific behaviors that are expected and the various reinforcers or punishers that are associated with compliance or noncompliance with the terms of the contract. Contingency contracts have been used successfully with a wide variety of subjects to help manage diverse behaviors such as Attention-deficit/Hyperactivity Disorder (Gardill, 1996) homework compliance (Miller & Kelley, 1994) and reduction of suspension (Novell, 1994); they have become exceptionally popular management alternatives in special education.

Stuart (1971) has delineated five components that should be incorporated into an ideal contract. First, an exact explanation of the behaviors, rewards, punishers, and privileges must be provided. For example, if a teacher wanted a student to remain in his or her seat in exchange for extra time at the microcomputer, the time of in-seat behavior that must be exhibited before a specified amount of time at the computer can be earned must be detailed. Closely related to the first point is the second requirement: that all behaviors must be observable and measurable and that all terms must be specified. For example, once computer time has been earned, one should be able to refer to the contract to learn when the time may be claimed. Also, in-seat behavior can be operationally defined and measured accurately. However, a behavior such as "attending" is more nebulous and would be difficult to measure reliably enough for use in a contract. Third, contingencies for failure to meet with the terms of the contract should be specified for both parties. Just as a child must suffer the consequences if he or she does not perform as required, the manager must also be willing to suffer consequences (e.g., double reinforcement for the subject) if his or her part of the agreement is not fulfilled. Fourth, a bonus clause for consistent performance may be included if the subject or the manager feels it may be beneficial. This addition would help to stress the positive aspects of the contract. Finally, either the contract or the manager should provide a means of monitoring the effectiveness of the contract. By providing for this feedback, the contract can help to induce more positive comments on the part of the involved parties when each is in compliance with contract terms. Kazdin (1975) notes that well-developed contingency contracts offer a number of advantages over traditional management strategies: subject input into the contract can enhance performance and motivation; subject negotiation of contingencies will result in the contingencies being truly reinforcing; contracts can be flexible; contracts specify both behaviors and contingencies; and the logistics of contract implementation can help to structure interactions between parties and thus lead to more successful and lasting changes.

REFERENCES

Gardill, M.C. (1996). Classroom strategies for managing students with ADHD. *Intervention in School and Clinic, 32,* 89–94.

Miller, D. & Kelley, M.L. (1994). Use of goal setting and contingency contracting for improving children's homework performance. *Journal of Applied Behavior Analysis, 27,* 1, 73–84.

Novell, I. (1994). *Decreasing school suspension among middle school children by implementing a rehabilitative in-room suspension.* (ERIC Clearinghouse No. PSO 22397)

Stuart, R.B. (1971). Behavioral contracting within the families of delinquents. *Journal of Behavior Therapy and Experimental Psychiatry, 2,* 1–11.

See also **Applied Behavior Analysis; Behavior Modification**

CONTINUING EDUCATION FOR THE HANDICAPPED

The types of continuing education available to handicapped learners is dependent on the community in which an individual resides and the resources available. In general, however, programs of continuing education can include academic education, creative arts, economic education, basic and literacy education, home and family life education, human relations training, recreation education, and occupational education.

For those individuals exhibiting more severe handicapping conditions or requiring a unique form of assistance, continuing education consists of specific training/education in independent living, communication skills, or vocational employment. This type of continuing education is offered through public and private vocational rehabilitation facilities as well as social service organizations. For the most part, these programs of continuing education are supported by public funds intended to promote greater self-sufficiency and independence.

See also **Adult Basic Education; Adult Programs for the Disabled; Vocational Rehabilitation**

CONTINUUM OF SPECIAL EDUCATION SERVICES

See INCLUSION.

CONTRACT PROCUREMENT

Contract procurement is a term used in vocational rehabilitation facilities, sheltered workshops, and work activities centers. The term is simply defined; however, the concept and process are more complex. The word contract refers to jobs that are used in the cited facilities to teach work habit skills or trade skills, or provide activities that result in reimbursement to persons with disabilities. The term procurement refers to the act of attaining contracts. The term contract procurement, as it relates to programs for the disabled, refers to the process of attaining work from businesses to be done by persons with disabilities. Subcontracts and prime manufacturing are two categories of contracts.

Understanding that sales is a key concept in contract procurement is important. Often work programs fail to understand that attaining work is a process of identifying, attaining, working, and delivering. Some programs still use nonsales people to attain work and deliver a product, thus causing contract procurement for persons with disabilities to be thought of as cheap, subsidized labor.

The process of attaining work is subdivided into time and motion studies, and submitting a bid for subcontract or setting a price for prime manufacturing. Time and motion refers to setting up the work in the most efficient manner and then timing the steps in completing the work. The federal Department of Labor publications explain the rules for time and motion studies. A bid should include the following information: labor rate, overhead, materials, handling and waste, freight, and profit.

The bid also should include any conditions that may need to be included in the subcontract that concern the workshop regulations.

See also **Habilitation; Rehabilitation**

CONTROL GROUPS

Control groups are aggregates of subjects who do not receive the treatment of interest in an experimental or quasi-experimental intervention. They are used in research and program evaluation to provide baselines against which to measure the impact of an experimental manipulation and as a means to rule out alternative explanations of "treatment" effects. Control groups are useful particularly in field settings, where there may be a number of plausible rival accounts for the meaning of the researcher's observations. Whether the study is an elaborate investigation or the simple introduction of classroom innovation, control groups are often crucial to the interpretation of results.

Particularly in the case of quasiexperimental designs, where random assignment of subjects is not possible, a number of control groups are often used to rule out different competing interpretations. For example, members of a placebo control group receive an irrelevant treatment that gives an amount of time and attention similar to that of the experimental group (Cook & Campbell, 1979).

It is commonplace to introduce innovative programs in special education. By following proper control group design, one can judge the effectiveness of "reforms as experiments" and make policy decisions on a more rational basis (Campbell, 1969).

REFERENCES

Campbell, D.T. (1969). Reforms as experiments. *American Psychologist, 24,* 409–429.

Cook, T.D., & Campbell, D.T. (1979). *Quasiexperimentation: Design and analysis issues for field settings.* Chicago: Rand McNally.

See also **Measurement; Research in Special Education**

CONVERGENT AND DIVERGENT THINKING

Emerging from Guilford's structure of intellect model of human intelligence, the concepts of convergent and divergent thinking are often applied to the education of gifted children. Both are viewed as high-level cognitive operations that individuals use when making decisions (Guilford, 1966, 1984).

Convergent thinking requires a narrowing process by which an individual develops classification rules that explain the relationships among objects and concepts. Essential to this process is the invocation of recall and recognition strategies. As such, the products of convergent thinking tend to be in the form of single "correct" answers. Critics have argued that typical school instruction demands an inappropriate proportion of convergent thinking at the expense of more creative (divergent) processes (Steffin, 1983).

Divergent thinking involves a broad scanning operation, enabling an individual to generate multiple possible solutions. It has received a major share of research attention in creativity, problem solving, and critical thinking (Steffin, 1983).

Several studies have shown that young children's divergent productions can be increased by the use of open-ended questions in class discussions (Pucket-Cliatt, Shaw, & Sherwood, 1980; Thomas & Holcomb, 1981). These studies have also suggested that teachers can become increasingly comfortable using open-ended questions and that they can decrease their reliance on rote memory activities.

While learning-disabled (Jaben, 1983) and language-deficient (Burrows & Wolf, 1983) children have shown gains in creativity following training in divergent thinking, the observation and development of creative thinking in gifted students continues to dominate the research literature at the present time (Hildebrand, 1991).

REFERENCES

Burrows, D., & Wolf, B. (1983). Creativity and the dyslexic child: A classroom view. *Annals of Dyslexia, 33,* 269–274.

Guilford, J.P. (1966). Basic problems in teaching for creativity. In C.W. Taylor & F.E. Williams (Eds.), *Instructional media and creativity.* New York: Wiley.

Guilford, J.P. (1984). Varieties of divergent production. *Journal of Creative Behavior, 18,* 1–10.

Hildebrand, V. (1991). Young children's care and education: Creative teaching and management. *Early Child Development and Care, 71,* 63–72.

Jaben, T.H. (1983). The effects of creativity training on learning disabled students' creative written expression. *Journal of Learning Disabilities, 16,* 264–265.

Pucket-Cliatt, M.J., Shaw, J.M., & Sherwood, J.M. (1980). Effects of training on the divergent thinking abilities of kindergarten children. *Child Development, 51,* 1061–1064.

Steffin, S.A. (1983). Fighting against convergent thinking. *Childhood Education, 59,* 255–258.

Thomas, E., & Holcomb, C. (1981). Nurturing productive thinking in able students. *Journal of General Psychology, 104,* 67–79.

See also **Creative Problem Solving; Teacher Expectancies; Teaching Strategies**

CONVULSIONS, FEBRILE
See FEBRILE CONVULSIONS.

CONVULSIVE DISORDERS
See SEIZURE DISORDERS.

COOPERATIVE TEACHING
See INCLUSION.

COPROLALIA

Coprolalia is a condition characterized by an irresistible urge to utter obscene words and phrases and uncontrollable performance of obscene gestures (Singer, 1997), which are frequently observed together. Obscenities are interspersed randomly within a dialogue, interrupting the normal flow of conversation. The cursing is usually uttered during a break between sentences and in a loud, sharp tone in contrast to normal voice. The frequency of obscene utterances has a tendency to vary from low to high frequencies for extended periods of time. Coprolalic episodes are positively associated with periods of anxiety and anticipation.

Coprolalia is most often associated with Gilles de la Tourette's syndrome (TS) and is evident in some patients following a stroke. As with other tics associated with TS, coprolalia can be controlled by TS patients for brief intervals. Lees, Robertson, Trimble, and Murray (1984) report that TS patients exhibiting coprolalia attempt to substitute euphemisms or somewhat disguised neologisms for obscenities. Early estimates of the prevalence of coprolalia in Tourette syndrome patients were approximately 60%, but more recently have been revised to approximately 33% (Lees et al., 1984). Coprolalia tends to peak in adolescence and to wane in adulthood (Singer, 1997).

Both medical and behavioral treatments have been used successfully to control coprolalic expressions. Erenberg, Cruse, and Rothner (1985) report that the preferred medical treatment is the use of dopamine-blocking agents such as haloperidol, a drug used in treating hyperkinetic and manic disorders. Comings and Comings (1985) recommend starting with low doses of haloperidol (.05 mg daily for 1 week) and increasing the dosage by .05 mg at weekly intervals until a 70 to 90% reduction of symptoms occurs. Because of the sedative side effects of haloperidol, stimulant drugs may be given simultaneously.

Behavioral treatments have included the use of self-management and negative practice techniques. Friedman (1980), for instance, had a patient substitute socially acceptable utterances for obscenities whenever she had the urge to curse. Evans and Evans (1983) decreased the rate of utterances of an expletive using a self-counting procedure. The patient simply recorded each frequency of his use of the target expletive. Storms (1985) had patients practice their tics until they were tired, had them rest, and then repeated the practice.

REFERENCES

Comings, D.E., & Comings, B.G. (1985). Tourette syndrome: Clinical and psychological aspects. *Human Genetics, 37,* 435–450.

Erenberg, G., Cruse, R.P., & Rothner, A.D. (1985). Gilles de la Tourette's syndrome: Effects of stimulant drugs. *Neurology, 35,* 1346–1348.

Evans, W.H., & Evans, S.S. (1983). Self-counting in the treatment of

Gilles de la Tourette syndrome. *Journal of Precision Teaching, 4,* 14–17.

Friedman, S. (1980). Self-control in the treatment of Gilles de la Tourette's syndrome: Case study with 18-month follow-up. *Journal of Consulting & Clinical Psychology, 48,* 400–402.

Lees, A.J., Robertson, M., Trimble, M.R., & Murray, N.M.F. (1984). A clinical study of Gilles de la Tourette syndrome in the United Kingdom. *Journal of Neurology, Neurosurgery, & Psychiatry, 47,* 1–8.

Singer, C. (1997). Coprolalia and other coprophenomena. *Neurologic Clinics, 15,* 2, 299–308.

Storms, L. (1985). Massed negative practice as a behavioral treatment for Gilles de la Tourette's syndrome. *American Journal of Psychotherapy, 39,* 277–281.

See also **Stimulant Drugs; Tics; Tourette's Syndrome**

COPROPRAXIA

See COPROLALIA.

CORE SCHOOL

The core educational concept has two basic components: time and philosophy (Oliver, 1965). Time is usually administered through a "block time class," for example, two or more class periods are joined together in order to study a wide range of related subjects. The philosophy of core involves the breaking down of strict boundaries between disciplines. Thus, students may study a topic from literary, historical, mathematical, and artistic viewpoints concurrently rather than as separate topics in isolated classes (Manning, 1971; Oliver, 1965).

Beyond these two basic components, cores are identified as having the following characteristics (Hass, 1970; Manning, 1971; Oliver, 1965):

1. They are problem centered.
2. Learning is done through firsthand experiences by the learner.
3. Students are involved in the planning, teaching, and evaluation processes.
4. Students are provided with opportunities for total growth by way of lifelike environments.
5. The instruction is more personal, allowing for individual guidance.
6. There are opportunities for integrated knowledge across subject lines.

REFERENCES

Hass, G., Wiles, K., & Bondi, J. (1970). *Reading in curriculum* (2nd ed.). Boston: Allyn & Bacon.

Manning, D. (1971). *Toward a humanistic curriculum.* New York: Harper & Row.

Oliver, A.I. (1965). *Curriculum improvement: A guide to problems, principles, and procedures.* New York: Dodd, Mead.

See also **Ecological Education for the Handicapped; Holistic Approach and Learning Disabilities; Test-Teach-Test Paradigm**

CORNELIA DE LANGE SYNDROME

Cornelia De Lange syndrome is a developmental disability first reported by Brachman in 1916 and further investigated by De Lange in 1933 (Goodman & Gorlin, 1977). It may also be referred to as *Amsterdam dwarfism* (Clarke & Clarke, 1975). Currently, no definitive test or genetic analysis to confirm the diagnosis exists. However, it is suspected of being an autosomal dominant disorder associated with mutations on chromosome 3 (Gillberg, 1995).

Cornelia De Lange infants show a lower than normal birth weight and length, and can be described as failing to thrive. The majority are found to be functioning in the lower reaches of the moderately retarded range. A few reported cases have shown functioning levels approaching the low average range. Motor problems are pronounced.

These children appear remarkably similar in appearance, substantiating the probability of a genetic etiology as well as a syndrome. Nearly all of the children show thick curly eyebrows, long eyelashes, and increased facial hair. They have thin lips forming a downward slanting mouth, with smaller than normal-sized limbs, hands, feet, and head. Many exhibit a characteristic low-pitched gravelly voice early in infancy (Smith & Jones, 1982).

Behaviorally, these children may demonstrate autistic-like behaviors as well as the potential for self-abusive behaviors. They may be stubborn and difficult to manage and may bruise easily, an observation that may be of particular interest to the special educator. The syndrome tends to be relatively uncommon, with reported incidence rates varying from 1:30,000 to 1:50,000 live births (Goodman, 1977). There is no syndrome-specific treatment and outcome is poor in many respects.

REFERENCES

Clarke, A., & Clarke, D.B. (1975). *Mental deficiency, the changing perspectives* (3rd ed.). New York: Free Press.

Gillberg, C. (1995). *Clinical child neuropsychiatry.* Cambridge, UK: Cambridge University Press.

Goodman, R., & Gorlin, R. (1977). *Atlas of the face of genetic disorders.* St. Louis: Mosby.

Smith, D., & Jones, R. (1982). *Recognizable patterns of human malformation* (3rd ed.). Philadelphia: Saunders.

See also **Autism**

CORRECTIONAL EDUCATION

The Correctional Education Association (1983) defined correctional education as a coordinated system of individualized learning services and activities conducted within the walls of a correctional facility. Services are provided by certified educational staff and are designed to meet the identified needs of the inmate population in the areas of basic education leading to a high-school credential; vocational training geared toward obtaining entry-level skills and maintaining competitive employment; and development of attitudes, skills, and abilities in the context of sociopersonal development.

Estimates indicate that 85 to 95% of the incarcerated adults do not have high-school diplomas. Many of them can neither read nor write after completing their sentences (Loeffler & Martin, 1982). From a survey conducted by Bell (1979), it was found that 50% of the adults in federal and state institutions were illiterate. Researchers such as Roberts (1973) state that the average inmate is unable to complete a job application, read and understand newspapers, or apply for an automobile operator's license (Day & McCane, 1982). In addition, 70% of the inmates have had no vocational training prior to sentencing. The National Advisory Council on Vocational Education found that the typical inmate is male, poor, and with less than 10 years of schooling. Gehring (1980) described correctional students as frequently afflicted by special learning and/or drug-related problems, accustomed to violence, and lacking in academic skills.

According to the U.S. Department of Justice (1983), the incarceration rate for individuals not completing elementary school is 259 per 1000 for males between the ages of 20 to 29 years; for elementary school graduates, it is 83 per 1000; for those completing 9 to 11 years in school, it is 70 per 1000; for high school graduates, it decreased to 11 per 1000; and for persons with 16 years of schooling, the rate drops to 1 per 1000.

Numerous research studies on correctional education programs have documented the effectiveness of both juvenile and adult correctional programs (Correctional Education Association, 1983). Correctional education programs have resulted in increased employment and improved quality of life for released inmates.

REFERENCES

Bell, R. (1979, June). *Correctional education program for inmates* (National Evaluation Programs, Phase I). Washington, DC: U.S. Department of Justice.

Correctional Education Association. (1983). Lobbying for correctional education: A guide to action. (Available from Correctional Education Association, 1400 20th Street, NW, Washington, DC 20009.)

Day, S.R., & McCane, M.R. (1982). *Vocational education in corrections* (Information Series 237, 11–12). Columbus, OH: State University, National Center for Research in Vocational Education.

Gehring, T. (1980, September). Correctional education and the U.S. Department of Education. *Journal of Correctional Education, 35*(4), 137–141.

Loeffler, C.A., & Martin, T.C. (1982, April). *The functional illiterate: Is correctional education doing its job?* Huntsville, TX: Marloe Research.

Roberts, A.R. (1973). *Readings in prison education.* Springfield, IL: Thomas.

U.S. Department of Justice. (1983, October). *Report to the nation on crime and justice. The data* (NCJ-87060, p. 37). Rockville, MD: Bureau of Justice Statistics.

See also **Juvenile Delinquency; Right to Education**

CORRECTIONAL SPECIAL EDUCATION

A large portion of the incarcerated population is handicapped for educational purposes. Morgan's (1979) survey indicated that 42% of incarcerated juveniles met PL94-142 definitional criteria as handicapped. Surveys of adult correctional facilities in Oregon (Hurtz & Heintz, 1979) and Louisiana (Klinger, Marshall, Price, & Ward, 1983) suggest similar proportions of handicapped persons in adult prisons, for example, between 30 and 50%.

Correctional education, which consists of formal educational programs ranging from basic literacy training to postsecondary vocational and university education, is offered in the vast majority of correctional facilities in the United States. Such programs typically are voluntary in adult facilities, but mandatory for juveniles. The federal administrative regulations for special education specifically include correctional education programs in the mandate for a free and appropriate public education for handicapped persons 21 years of age and under; however, less than 10% of the state departments of juvenile and adult corrections are in compliance (Coffey, 1983). States not in compliance are experiencing heightened pressure through litigation (Wood, 1984) and administrative sanction to provide special education programs. Increased interest in correctional special education is reflected in federally funded demonstration and training projects, receipt of federal to state flow-through monies by correctional education programs, and the development of training programs for correctional special educators.

In 1984 the Correctional/Special Education Training (C/SET) Project staff (Rutherford, Nelson, & Wolford, 1985) surveyed the 85 state departments of juvenile and/or adult corrections and the 50 state departments of education to determine the number of handicapped offenders in juvenile and adult correctional facilities.

There were 33,190 individuals incarcerated in state juvenile correctional facilities. Of this number, 30,681 or 92%, were in correctional education programs. The estimated number of handicapped juvenile offenders is 9443, or 28% of the total incarcerated population. The number of juveniles receiving special education services was 7750, or 23% of the number of juveniles in corrections. Thus, according to state administrators' estimates, approximately 80% of handicapped juvenile offenders were being served.

Currently a need exists for correctional special education services in juvenile and adult correctional institutions, raising the question of what constitutes an effective correctional special education program. Some researchers (e.g., Gerry, 1985; Smith & Hockenberry, 1980; Smith, Ramirez, & Rutherford, 1983) have delineated essential compliance issues with regard to implementation of special education laws in correctional education programs. There are six factors that are important to the implementation of meaningful correctional special education programs. These are (1) procedures for conducting functional assessments of the skills and learning needs of handicapped offenders; (2) the existence of a curriculum that teaches functional academic and daily living skills; (3) the inclusion of vocational special education in the curriculum; (4) the existence of transitional programs and procedures between correctional programs and the public schools or the world of work; (5) the presence of a comprehensive system for providing institutional and community services to handicapped offenders; and (6) the provision of in-service and preservice training for correctional educators in special education.

REFERENCES

Coffey, O.D. (1983). Meeting the needs of youth from a corrections viewpoint. In S. Braaten, R.B. Rutherford, & C.A. Kardash (Eds.), *Programming for adolescents with behavioral disorders* (pp. 79–84). Reston, VA: Council for Children with Behavioral Disorders.

Gerry, M.H. (1985). *Monitoring the special education programs of correctional institutions.* Washington, DC: U.S. Department of Education.

Hurzt, R., & Heintz, E.I. (1979). Incidence of specific learning disabilities at Oregon State Correctional Institution. Paper presented at the National Institute of Corrections Conference, Portland, OR.

Klinger, J.H., Marshall, G.M., Price, A.W., & Ward, K.D. (1983). A pupil appraisal for adults in the Louisiana Department of Corrections. *Journal of Correctional Education, 34*(2), 46–48.

Morgan, D.J. (1979). Prevalence and types of handicapping conditions found in juvenile correctional institutions: A national survey. *Journal of Special Education, 13,* 283–295.

Rutherford, R.B., Nelson, C.M., & Wolford, B.I. (1985). Special education in the most restrictive environment: Correctional/special education. *Journal of Special Education, 19,* 60–71.

Smith, B.J., & Hockenberry, C.M. (1980). Implementing the Education for All Handicapped Children Act, P.L. 94-142, in youth corrections facilities: Selected issues. In F.J. Weintraub, A. Abeson, J. Ballard, & M.L. LaVor (Eds.), *Public policy and the education of exceptional children* (pp. 1–36). Reston, VA: Council for Exceptional Children.

Smith, B.J., Ramirez, B., & Rutherford, R.B. (1983). Special education in youth correctional facilities. *Journal of Correctional Education, 34,* 108–112.

Wood, F.J. (1984). *The law and correctional education.* Tempe, AZ: Correctional Special Education Training Project.

See also **Correctional Education; Juvenile Delinquency**

COSTA RICA, SPECIAL EDUCATION IN

Costa Rica has the strongest public education system in Central America. The 1869 constitution mandated a free, obligatory, and state-supported educational system—making Costa Rica one of the first countries in the world to pass such legislation (Biesanz, Biesanz, & Biesanz, 1982; Creedman, 1991). Approximately 25% of the national budget is dedicated to education (United Nations Educational and Scientific Organization [UNESCO], 1997) and elementary schools can be found even in the most isolated regions of the country. As a result, Costa Rica's literacy rate of 93% is one of highest in all of Latin America (Economic Commission for Latin America and the Caribbean [ECLAC], 1996; UNESCO, 1997).

Costa Rica is equally progressive in the area of special education. Special education services were formally established in 1939 when the Fernando Centeno Güell School for children with mental retardation was created near the capital city of San José (Asesoría General de Educación Especial, 1992). Public special education services were first ensured through the Fundamental Law of Education of 1957, which declared that students had the right to a special education, if so needed, and the right to special didactic techniques and materials; and that parents had the right to information on how to care for their child. Costa Rica has continued to pass progressive legislation for individuals with disabilities. The recently enacted Equal Opportunity Law for Persons with Disabilities (1996) includes antidiscriminatory clauses and guarantees equal rights for individuals with disabilities across all sectors of public life. Special education has been redefined in this law as "the combination of assistance and services at the disposal of students with special educational needs, whether they be temporary or permanent" (Sección VI, Artículo 27). The Equal Opportunity Law also strongly suggests that students with disabilities should be integrated into regular education classrooms that are "preferentially in the educational center closest to their home" (Capítulo I, Artículo 18).

Approximately 20,000 students with disabilities receive services through the public education system in Costa Rica (Asesoría General de Educación Especial, 1993). The Department of Special Education uses the diagnostic categories of learning disabilities, mental retardation, emotional disturbance, speech impaired, auditory impaired, visually impaired, physically disabled, psychosocially disordered, and multiply handicapped. Eligibility for services is determined through a psychological and educational assessment conducted by a diagnostic team consisting of a psychologist, social worker, educator, and psychiatrist (Mainieri Hidalgo & Méndez Barrantes, 1992). Children with disabilities are eligible to receive educational services beginning at birth and these services continue through age 18, when most Costa Ricans finish high school.

While the Ministry of Education promotes programs which are "integrated into the community, always using the least restrictive methods" (Asesoría General de Educación

Especial, 1993), the reality is that the delivery of special education services usually segregates students with disabilities from their same-age peers.

Special education in Costa Rica suffers from the same obstacles that have been described in other developing countries: limited material resources, geographic isolation of large segments of the population, and insufficient training programs (see González-Vega & Céspedes, 1993; Marfo, Walker, & Charles, 1986). The greatest national need is for trained professionals. Few special education teacher training programs exist outside of the capital city and teachers in rural areas usually have had no formal training with students with disabilities (Stough, 1990; Villarreal, 1989).

Recent educational initiatives have exponentially increased the number of students receiving special education in Costa Rica and the Ministry of Education is making a focused effort to coordinate these services. Undeniably progressive legislation now supports the rights of individuals with disabilities to work, receive public health services, and to be educated. While special education continues to expand in Costa Rica, untrained personnel limit the effectiveness of this instruction. The current challenge for Costa Rica is to ensure the quality of these special services, as well as the accessibility to them.

REFERENCES

Asesoría General de Educación Especial. (1992). *Estructura, principios, normas y procedimientos de la educación especial en Costa Rica* [Structure, principles, norms and procedures of special education in Costa Rica]. San José, Costa Rica: Ministerio de Educación Pública.

Asesoría General de Educación Especial. (1993, March). *La educación especial en Costa Rica* [Special education in Costa Rica]. Paper presented at the meeting of the Conferencia Hemisférica sobre Discapacidad, Washington, DC.

Biesanz, R., Biesanz, K.Z., & Biesanz, M.H. (1982). *The Costa Ricans.* Englewood Cliffs, NJ: Prentice Hall.

Creedman, T.S. (1991). *Historical dictionary of Costa Rica* (2nd ed.). Metuchen, NJ: The Scarecrow Press.

Economic Commission for Latin America and the Caribbean [ECLAC]. (1996). *Statistical yearbook for Latin America and the Caribbean.* Chile: United Nations Publication.

González-Vega, C., & Céspedes, V.H. (1993). Costa Rica. In S. Rottenberg (Ed.), *A World Bank comparative study. The political economy of poverty, equity, and growth. Costa Rica and Uruguay.* New York: Oxford University Press.

Mainieri Hidalgo, A., & Méndez Barrantes, Z. (1992). *Detección de problemas de aprendizaje: Antología* [Detection of learning disabilities: Anthology]. San José, Costa Rica: Editorial Universidad Estatal a Distancia.

Marfo, K., Walker, S., & Charles, B. (1986). *Childhood disability in developing countries: Issues in habilitation and special education.* New York: Praeger.

Stough, L.M. (1990, January). *Special education and teacher training in the third world: Costa Rican and Honduran rural education programs.* Paper presented at the annual meeting of the Southwest Educational Research Association, Austin, TX.

United Nations Educational and Scientific Organization [UNESCO]. *UNESCO Statistical Yearbook.* (1997). Lanham, MD: Bernan.

Villarreal, B. (1989). *An analysis of the special education services for children and youth in Costa Rica.* Unpublished doctoral dissertation, University of San Diego, CA.

COUNCIL FOR CHILDREN WITH BEHAVIORAL DISORDERS

Founded in 1961, the Council for Children with Behavioral Disorders (CCBD), a division of the Council for Exceptional Children (CEC), is the professional organization of teachers, teacher educators, administrators, parents, and mental health personnel concerned with the education and general welfare of children and youth with behavioral and emotional disorders. The goals of CCBD include: promoting quality educational services and program alternatives for persons with behavioral disorders; advocating for the needs of children and youth with behavioral disorders and their families; encouraging research and professional growth as vehicles for better understanding behavioral disorders; disseminating relevant and timely information through professional meetings, training programs, and publications; providing professional support for persons who are involved with and serve children and youth with behavioral disorders; and supporting the activities, policies, and procedures of CEC and other CEC divisions.

Membership inquiries should be made to the Council for Children with Behavioral Disorders, The Council for Exceptional Children, 1920 Association Drive, Reston, VA 20191-1589. Only members of The Council for Exceptional Children are eligible to join the Council for Children with Behavioral Disorders. Special membership categories for students, parents, and professionals are available for those who qualify for these discounted membership rates.

COUNCIL FOR EXCEPTIONAL CHILDREN

The Council for Exceptional Children (CEC) is the world's largest professional organization dedicated to the welfare of exceptional children. The CEC was founded in 1922 at Teachers' College, Columbia University. Today, its United States and Canadian membership includes approximately 50,000 persons, including over 9,000 members of the organization's 288 student chapters. There are also 269 state, local, and provincial chapters in the U.S. and Canada. The organization is further divided into special interest groups, including divisions on the physically handicapped, behavior disorders, mental retardation, communication disorders, learning disabilities, visually handicapped, talented and gifted, early childhood education, special education administration, career development, technology and media, educational diagnostic services, teacher education, international special education, cultural and linguistic diversity, research, and pioneers of the CEC.

CEC members include educators, parents, students, and others concerned with the education of children with disabilities and gifted and talented children and youth. The CEC's membership is dedicated to increasing educational opportunities for all exceptional children and youth and to improving conditions for the professionals who work with them. The CEC advocates for appropriate governmental policies, sets professional standards, provides continual professional development, advocates for newly and historically underserved individuals with exceptionalities, and helps professionals obtain conditions and resources necessary for effective professional practice.

CEC has been highly visible as an advocate for federal legislation and funding for the gifted and the handicapped. The organization issues two respected periodicals, *Exceptional Children and Teaching Exceptional Children.* The former is more research and policy oriented, while the latter is geared more toward practitioners' needs. In addition, several hundred books, multimedia packages, bibliographies, and fact sheets are available from CEC. Access to nearly one half a million references on handicapped and gifted children can be obtained from ERIC (Educational Resources Information Center) and CEC Information Services. Each year, a national convention sponsored by CEC attracts thousands of professionals, paraprofessionals, and parents.

The Council for Exceptional Children's headquarters are now located at 1920 Association Drive, Reston, VA 20191, and may be reached by phone at (703) 620-3660.

COUNCIL FOR LEARNING DISABILITIES

In 1968 educators formed the Division for Children with Learning Disabilities (DCLD) within the Council for Exceptional Children (CEC) (Hallahan, Kauffman, & Lloyd, 1985). Both groups believed that without a name to identify a group of children who did not fit into any other handicapping condition, there would be difficulty in obtaining needed funds for special services.

During the early 1980s emerged the realization that not only did children have learning disabilities but so did adults. Consequently, the Division for Children with Learning Disabilities became the Council for Learning Disabilities (CLD). Besides this change of name, CLD changed its affiliation: as it seceded from the Council for Exceptional Children (Lerner, 1985). The majority of CLD's membership voted to become a separate and independent organization.

Conferences and newsletters sponsored by CLD provide a valuable means of sharing information and serve as a stimulus for research, program development, and advocacy. In addition, CLD formed a strong national lobbying group to promote legislative recognition of learning disabilities.

REFERENCES

Hallahan, D.P., Kauffman, J.M., & Lloyd, J.W. (1985). *Introduction to learning disabilities.* Englewood Cliffs, NJ: Prentice-Hall.

Learner, J.W. (1985). *Learning disabilities.* Dallas: Houghton Mifflin.

COUNCIL OF ADMINISTRATORS OF SPECIAL EDUCATION (CASE)

The Council of Administrators of Special Education (CASE) was founded in 1952 as a division of the Council for Exceptional Children (CEC). The CASE membership of 5,200 includes administrators, directors, supervisors, and coordinators of local private and public special education programs, schools, or classes serving children and youth with special needs. The purpose of CASE is to promote professional leadership, provide opportunity for the study of problems common to its members and to provide information for developing improved services to exceptional children. CASE has 41 Subdivisions in the U.S. and Canada.

CASE provides six newsletters and two issues of its refereed journal *CASE in POINT* to its members annually. CASE maintains a web site at <http://www.members. aol.com/casecec/index. htm> where members may obtain current information on a variety of topics and activities of the Council.

The office staff is directed by the Executive Director, Dr. Jo Thomason. The office may be contacted at 615 16th St. NW, Albuquerque, New Mexico, 87104 or via e-mail through its web site.

COUNSELING THE HANDICAPPED

With so much emphasis placed on handicapped individuals' educational, adaptive behavior, and social skill needs, their emotional needs are often forgotten. Indeed, handicapped individuals often have issues that affect their lives that could be addressed and resolved through the counseling process. For example, some individuals with mental retardation experience feelings of frustration because of their handicap and its limitations and could benefit from counseling support. Learning-disabled students, given the peer rejection sometimes associated with their academic difficulties, also might benefit from therapeutic attention. Clearly, counseling should be a central intervention for behaviorally and emotionally disturbed persons.

From a purely counseling perspective, a number of therapeutic approaches are available. Prout and Brown (1983) identified six major theoretical approaches to counseling and psychotherapy that can be adopted when handicapped individuals are the primary clients: behavior therapy, reality therapy, person-centered therapy, rational-emotive therapy, Adlerian therapy, and psychoanalytic/psychodynamic therapy. Behavior therapy has been especially useful with behaviorally disturbed individuals. Using operant or classical conditioning, cognitive, or social learning behavioral approaches, positive behaviors are taught and/or reinforced while disruptive or disturbing behaviors are altered or extinguished. The other psychotherapeutic approaches have been used, in addition to the behavioral, for emotionally disturbed individuals who manifest an assortment of affectively based difficulties and issues. Additionally, all of these approaches can be applied to the emotional issues that often coexist or result from other handicapping conditions.

Besides the psychotherapeutic approaches, a number of more specialized approaches are available when counseling handicapped individuals. Briefly reviewed in Reynolds and Gutkin (1982), these include family therapy approaches, sociodrama, developmental therapy, art therapy, music therapy, and holistic or milieu therapy. Again, these approaches often become part of a comprehensive program that addresses handicapped children's educational, social-emotional, affective, family, and adaptive needs. In many cases, the use of counseling occurs only as an afterthought to what is otherwise a comprehensive program. Clearly, the possibility that handicapped children have related or separate counseling needs must be emphasized in research programs and in applied settings.

REFERENCES

Prout, H.T., & Brown, D.T. (1983). *Counseling and psychotherapy with children and adolescents.* Tampa, FL: Mariner

Reynolds, C.R., & Gutkin, T.B. (1982). *The handbook of school psychology.* New York: Wiley.

See also **Behavior Modification; Family Therapy; Psychotherapy**

CREATIVE PROBLEM SOLVING (CPS)

Creative problem solving (CPS) is a structured model for using knowledge and imagination to arrive at a creative, innovative, or effective solution to a problem. Developed by Alex F. Osborn (1953), the original process consisted of three steps: fact finding, including problem definition and preparation; idea finding, including idea production and idea development; and solution finding, including evaluation and adoption. Parnes (1967) developed and refined this sequential problem-solving process into a five-step comprehensive model that incorporates findings from applied and theoretical research on creative thinking and behavior. The five steps are fact finding, problem finding, idea finding, solution finding, and acceptance finding.

Also known as the Osborn-Parnes Model, CPS is the most widely used method to encourage the application of creative thinking skills in the solving of problems. Fundamental to the CPS process is the principle of deferred judgment. This principle is based on Osborn's original notion that when judgment is withheld during ideation, at least 70% more good ideas are produced (Osborn, 1953). Throughout the process both divergent thinking and convergent thinking constantly occur as the problem solver moves from one step to the next.

The literature on CPS is extensive. Reviews of the CPS process have been completed by Parnes (1981) and Noller (1977), among others. Edwards (1986) has provided an extensive review of information on approaches to enhance creative thinking and ideation during the CPS process.

REFERENCES

Edwards, M.O. (1986). *Idea power: Time tested methods to stimulate your imagination.* Buffalo, NY: Bearly.

Noller, R.B. (1977). *Scratching the surface of creative problem solving.* Buffalo, NY: D.O.K.

Osborn, A.F. (1953). *Applied imagination.* New York: Scribner.

Parnes, S.J. (1967). *Creative behavior guidebook.* New York: Scribner.

Parnes, S.J. (1981). *The magic of your mind.* Buffalo, NY: Bearly.

See also **Creative Problem Solving Institute; Creativity; Sociodrama**

CREATIVE PROBLEM SOLVING INSTITUTE (CPSI)

The Creative Problem Solving Institute (CPSI) is a multidisciplinary, multilevel program designed to familiarize participants with the principles and techniques of creative problem solving (CPS). Founded in 1955 by Alex Osborn, the institute is sponsored by the Creative Education Foundation in cooperation with the State University College, Buffalo.

Sidney J. Parnes, who succeeded Osborn as the director of the institute, retained the basic principles of the original model while extending the process to encompass a more eclectic approach. Kitano and Kirby (1986) summarized Parnes's approach as follows: "The Model consists of six steps and incorporates a variety of research-supported techniques for stimulating creativity, including brainstorming, synectics, incubation, imaging, deferred judgment, forced relationships and practice" (p. 205). The six steps as outlined by Parnes (1977) are objective finding, fact finding, problem finding, idea finding, solution finding, and acceptance finding.

The annual summer institute has four major areas: (1) the Springboard Program, (2) the CPSI Youth Program, (3) the Extending Program, and (4) the Leadership Development Program Facilitating Creative Problem Solving. The Springboard Program and the CPSI Youth Program (ages 7 to 16) are designed for participants who have little or no previous experience in the study of creative problem solving. The Extending Program is designed to help participants expand their options through a variety of approaches to creativity. This program consists of different interest groups in which participants practice skills in the creative problem-solving process. The Leadership Development Program emphasizes self-growth and the development of skills for teaching creative problem solving to others.

REFERENCES

Kitano, M.K., & Kirby, D.F. (1986). *Gifted education: A comprehensive review.* Boston: Little, Brown.

Parnes, S.J. (1977). Guiding creative action. *Gifted Child Quarterly,* *21*(4), 460–476.

See also **Concept Formation; Creative Problem Solving; Osborn, Alexander F.**

CREATIVE STUDIES PROGRAM

The Creative Studies Program was inaugurated in September 1969 by Stanley J. Parnes at Buffalo (N.Y.) State University College to enhance various aspects of college students' present and future behaviors both in college and the general community (Parnes & Noller, 1972a). Parnes et al. developed the Creative Studies Program curriculum based on an earlier project, Creative Problem Solving.

The Creative Studies Program appears to be a successful method to increase the creative performance of college students (Maher, 1982; Parnes & Noller, 1972b). These students do better in school, perform better on three out of five mental operations (cognition, divergent production, and convergent production) in Guilford's Structure of Intellect Model (Guilford, 1967), and are more productive in nonacademic settings calling for creative performance. Torrance (1972) notes that the Creative Problem Solving curriculum or its modifications (e.g., the Creative Studies Program) is successful in teaching children to think creatively 91 to 92% of the time.

REFERENCES

Guilford, J.P. (1967). *The nature of human intelligence.* New York: McGraw-Hill.

Maher, C.J. (1982). *Teaching models in the education of the gifted.* Rockville, MD: Aspen.

Parnes, S.J., & Noller, R.B. (1972a). Applied creativity: The Creative Studies Project: Part I—The development. *Journal of Creative Behavior, 6,* 11–22.

Parnes, S.J., & Noller, R.B. (1972b). Applied creativity: The Creative Studies Project: Part II—Results of the two-year program. *Journal of Creative Behavior, 6,* 164–186.

Torrance, E.P. (1972). Can we teach children to think creatively? *Journal of Creative Behavior, 6,* 114–143.

See also **Creativity Tests**

CREATIVITY

Creativity is a complex and multifaceted phenomenon of human behavior. Theories explaining creativity have ranged from those that define it as the innovative combination of knowledge and imagination applied to the solution of problems to those that view creativity as an "unconscious process through which libidinal or aggressive energies are converted into culturally sanctioned behaviors" (Freud, 1924).

What happens in the creative process? Wallas (1926) described the process as consisting of four stages: preparation, incubation, illumination, and verification. Torrance defined the process as "one of becoming sensitive to or aware of problems . . . bringing together available information . . . searching for solutions . . . and communicating the results" (Torrance & Myers, 1970, p. 22).

While Taylor (1960) supported the notion of stages, he added that creativity exists at five levels with each level involving different psychological processes that may change the steps in the process. The five levels are (1) expressive creativity, a form of spontaneous expression without reference to originality and quality of the product; (2) technical or productive creativity, where the emphasis is on skill rather than spontaneity and novelty; (3) inventive creativity, with an emphasis on the new use of old things; (4) innovative creativity, where new ideas or principles are developed; and (5) emergentive creativity, which describes creative formulation using the most abstract ideational principles or assumptions underlying a body of art or science.

Research into hemispheric functioning has provided the most recent perspectives on creativity and the creative process. The notion that creative individuals are right-hemisphere dominant while logical, rational thinkers are left-hemisphere dominant has led to current theories that define the creative act as the result of interactions between hemispheres. For detailed reviews of current studies on hemisphericity, the reader is referred to Clark (1983) or Kitano and Kirby (1986).

Consistent among the many descriptions of creative persons are traits and behaviors such as unusual sensitivity to their environment, independence in thinking, nonconforming in their behaviors, and persistence at tasks. Creative people tend to be open to new ideas and experiences and less accepting of traditional points of view. Exploring ideas for their own sake, a marked sense of humor, a high tolerance for ambiguity, and strong self-confidence in their own work are other common traits of highly creative people.

An environment or situation that is open and accepting is critical for the release and development of creative potential. Kneller (1966) suggested that the main obstacles to creativity appear to be cultural and biological. Arieti (1976) presented the concept of the creativogenic society to describe his holistic view of cultural traits that support the development of creativity. Such a society is distinguished by its lack of emphasis on immediate gratification, its tolerance for and interest in divergent points of view, and its use of incentives and rewards for creativity. Torrance (1962) has suggested that other important variables are those that encourage unusual questions and ideas and those that allow performance to occur without constant threat of evaluation.

Much of the discussion regarding the relationship between creativity and intelligence relates to assessment. There have been several measures developed to assess creativity, but questions still arise regarding whether creativity should be measured by recognized achievement or by tests of divergent or creative thinking. The most frequently used measure of creativity is the Torrance Tests of Creative Thinking (1974), which provides a single score index of creative potential on both the figural and verbal versions.

Other measures of creativity are batteries developed by Guilford (1959) and by Wallach and Kogan (1965).

REFERENCES

Arieti, S. (1976). *Creativity: The magic synthesis.* New York: Basic Books.

Clark, B. (1983). *Growing up gifted* (2nd ed.). Columbus, OH: Merrill.

Freud, S. (1924). The relations of the poet to day-dreaming. In *Collected papers* (Vol. 2). London: Hogarth. (Original work published 1908)

Guilford, J.P. (1959). Three faces of intellect. *American Psychology, 14,* 469–479.

Kitano, M.K., & Kirby, D.F. (1986). *Gifted education: A comprehensive view.* Boston: Little, Brown.

Kneller, G.F. (1966). *The art and science of creativity.* New York: Holt, Rinehart, & Winston.

Taylor, I.A. (1960). The nature of the creative process. In P. Smith (Ed.), *Creativity: An examination of the creative process.* New York: Hastings House.

Torrance, E.P. (1962). *Guiding creative talent.* Englewood Cliffs, NJ: Prentice-Hall.

Torrance, E.P. (1974). *Torrance Tests of Creative Thinking: Norms-technical manual.* Bensenville, IL: Scholastic Testing Service.

Torrance, E.P. (1979). An instructional model for enhancing incubation. *Journal of Creative Behavior, 13*(1), 23–35.

Torrance, E.P., & Myers, R.E. (1970). *Creative learning and teaching.* New York: Dodd, Mead.

Wallach, M.A., & Kogan, N. (1965). *Modes of thinking in young children.* New York: Holt, Rinehart, & Winston.

See also Creative Studies Program; Investment Theory of Creativity

CREATIVITY TESTS

Most of the tests of creativity currently available were developed in the course of large-scale research projects on the nature of creativity. The two major batteries to be developed were the University of Southern California tests, devised by Guilford et al. as part of the Aptitude Research Project, and the Torrance Tests of Creative Thinking, devised by E. Paul Torrance in his efforts to design curriculum and teaching methods for the improvement of creative functioning in children. Torrance's research program has been designated the Georgia Studies of Creative Behavior since the late 1960s.

These tests and many others are commercially available and often used in the assessment of creativity; however, many psychometricians consider all such tests to be experimental (Anastasi, 1982). The items in creativity tests, with very few exceptions (such as the Welsh Figure Preference Test), are open-ended and thus on the subjective side of the scoring continuum. It is particularly important for this reason to assess the interscorer reliability of creativity tests before placing them into practice. Normative data for creativity tests generally fall significantly short of what has become the accepted psychometric standard for good tests of intelligence and achievement. Reliability and validity data are extensive for some tests such as the Torrance Tests of Creative Thinking, but for others they are extremely limited.

The major creativity scales attempt to measure multiple dimensions of creativity, including such variables as fluency, originality, unusual responses, flexibility, resistance to premature closure, etc. It remains unclear whether these dimensions are sufficiently independent to warrant differentiation in the measurement process. The measurement of creativity also has been found to be relatively task specific; i.e., performance on creativity measures does not generalize well to tasks outside of the test and the test setting.

Despite these problems, the use of creativity tests continue to be a popular activity in programs for the gifted and talented. Creativity has proven a difficult concept to master and the state of the psychometric data regarding creativity tests generally reflects the nature of the concept. Creativity tests are probably better than most psychometricians believe (Bennett, 1972; Wallach, 1968). The relatively weak results of research on this genre of tests, compared with the outcome of research on tests of intelligence and academic achievement, are more reflective of the difficult nature of the concept than of any inherent weakness in the major scales in use today such as the Torrance Tests of Creative Thinking. Little progress has occurred in the development or refinement of creativity testing since the work of Torrance.

REFERENCES

Anastasi, A. (1982). *Psychological testing* (5th ed.). New York: Macmillan.

Bennett, G.K. (1972). Review of the Remote Associates Test. In O.K. Buros (Ed.), *Seventh mental measurements yearbook.* Highland Park, NJ: Gryphon.

Wallach, M.A. (1968). Review of the Torrance Test of Creative Thinking. *American Educational Research Journal, 5,* 272–281.

See also Creative Problem Solving; Torrance Tests of Creative Thinking; Welsh Figure Preference Test

CRETINISM

Cretinism is a metabolic endocrine abnormality that is caused by a thyroid gland disorder. It exists in many forms. Athyrotic hypothyroidism is the congenital absence or partial absence of the thyroid gland. Endemic cretinism is a dietary deficiency of iodine. Familial hypothyroidism is an inborn error of thyroid metabolism and iodine transport. Intrauterine hypothyroidism occurs in infants whose mothers were on antithyroid therapy during pregnancy. Prior to the advent of diets containing iodine and the addition of iodine to table salt within the last hundred years, the endemic form was most common in areas where iodine-rich seafoods were difficult to obtain, for example, the mountainous regions of western Europe and the mid-western United States.

Individuals with untreated congenital hypothyroidism have characteristic features: wide-set eyes, broad nose bridge, and protruding tongue. The head appears to be oversized. The abdomen is large and protrudes with frequent umbilical hernia. Extremities look as though they are shortened and there is general low muscle tone. Mental retardation is a frequent result of the untreated condition.

Treatment consists of replacement of the thyroid hormone, thyroxin, with synthetic preparations. The results of treatment depend not only on the length of time before treatment is begun but on the severity and type of hypothyroidism. Occurring in one in every 6000 children, hypothyroidism is one of the most common inborn errors of metabolism. The direct result of early identification is the opportunity for early treatment. This, in turn, allows children born with hypothyroidism to develop normally, obviating the need for special education.

See also Hypothyroidism; Inborn Errors of Metaolism

CRI DU CHAT SYNDROME (CAT CRY SYNDROME)

Discovered by Jerome Lejeune, director of the department of genetics at the University of Paris, and his coworkers, Gautier and Turpin, in 1963, cri du chat syndrome is associated with a partial deletion of one of the chromosomes in the B group; specifically, there is a deletion of the short arm of chromosome 5 (5p-). Cri du chat syndrome is the most frequently reported of the autosomal deletion syndromes. The name was derived from the characteristic high-pitched, mewing cry, closely resembling the cry of a kitten, that is heard in the immediate newborn period, lasts several weeks, and then disappears with the exception of some cases, in which the catlike cry persists into adulthood. Incidence is estimated at 1:50,000 births (Hynd & Willis, 1987).

Affected infants show low birth weight, failure to thrive, hypotonia, microcephaly, a round or moon-faced appearance with hypertelorism (wide-set eyes), antimongoloid or downward sloping palpebral fissures with or without epicanthal folds, strabismus, and a broad-based nose. Ears are low-set and abnormally shaped with malformations, including narrow external canals and preauricular tags. Micrognathia, a short neck, and varying degrees of syndactyly are present. Various types of congenital heart defects and abnormal dermatoglyphics are frequently noted. Major diagnostic features include severe mental retardation and markedly delayed motor development.

A significant number of cri du chat infants survive to adulthood and continue to demonstrate microcephaly. They also have short stature, facial asymmetry, dental malocclusions, skeletal problems such as scoliosis, eye defects, and a waddling gait. These individuals are at or below the trainable level. As school-aged children, they are found in classes for the moderately and severely retarded. According to Gearheart and Litton (1975), the incidence of cri du chat is not known. Berg et al. (1970) found that 7 of the 744 patients with IQs below 35 had this defect. Goodman and

Gorlin (1970) reported that a preponderance of patients were female. No treatment is presently available for this syndrome.

REFERENCES

Berg, J.M., McCreary, B.D., Ridler, M.A., & Smith, G.F., (1970). *The deLange syndrome.* Oxford, England: Pergamon.

Gearheart, B.R., & Litton, F.W. (1975). *The trainable retarded: A foundations approach.* St. Louis, MO: Mosby.

Goodman, R.M., & Gorlin, R.J. (1970). *The face in genetic disorders.* St. Louis, MO: Mosby.

Hynd, G., & Willis, G. (1987). *Pediatric neuropsychology.* Boston: Allyn & Bacon.

See also Chromosomal Abnormalities; Mental Retardation

CRIME AND THE HANDICAPPED

Public Law 94–142 first mandated that educational services be provided to all handicapped youths no matter where they reside, a mandate continued by its successor, IDEA. Johnson (1979) indicates that about one third of incarcerated youths are thought to have serious learning disabilities, in contrast to only 16% of the unincarcerated population.

Much speculation exists as to the relationship between criminal behavior and handicapping conditions. Siegal and Senna (1981) assign theories that attempt to determine the cause of delinquency into four categories: individualized, social structure, social process, and social reaction. Unfortunately, the variables and factors that impact on these theories are the same that are used to describe the educable mentally retarded and the emotionally handicapped.

Keilitz and Miller (1980) present three rationales as the most prominent explanations of the disproportionate prevalence of handicapping conditions among youths in the justice system. The three are school failure, suspectibility, and differential treatment.

Despite these attempts to account for unexpectedly high prevalence, there is no definitive explanation for the disproportionate number of handicapped youths in the justice system. There is clear evidence that services (Johnson, 1979) mandated under IDEA must be provided and that these services have not been fully implemented. The problem of handicapping conditions as they relate to crime is serious and needs much more attention, especially in the areas of research, programs, and prevention (Brown & Robbins, 1979).

REFERENCES

Brown, S., & Robbins, M. (1979). Serving the special education needs of students in correctional facilities. *Exceptional Children, 45,* 574–579.

Johnson, J. (1979). An essay on incarcerated youth: An oppressed group. *Exceptional Children, 45*(7), 566–571.

Keilitz, I., & Miller, S.L. (1980). Handicapped adolescents and young adults in the justice system. *Exceptional Education Quarterly, 1*(2), 117–126.

Siegal, L.J., & Senna, J.J. (1981). *Juvenile delinquency: Theory, practice, and law.* St. Paul, MN: West.

See also **Educationally Disadvantaged; Juvenile Deliquency**

CRISIS INTERVENTION

Crisis intervention is a service spontaneously available to individuals and students who are in need of immediate assistance (Kelly & Vergason, 1978). Caplan defines a crisis as a sudden onset of behavioral imbalance in a child where previous function was stable (Caplan, 1963). The intent of intervention in a crisis is to provide knowledge of coping behaviors of enduring value. According to Swanson and Reinert (1976), a child in conflict is one "whose manifested behavior has a deleterious effect on his/her personal or educational development and/or the personal or educational development of his peers" (p. 5).

Intervention at the point of disruption or crisis is not new. Traditionally, the crisis was handled by an administrator or teacher. The crisis concept has changed in four ways. The first is in consultation, which has gone from supervisory to strategic planning. In other words, clinicians and teachers work together toward resolution. The second is in the use of the helping teacher, who becomes responsible for the disturbed child. The third change is in the style of interviewing proposed by Redl called life space interviewing (LSI). The fourth change occurs in a system to manage the confrontation situations that are found in secondary education.

The holding of crisis meetings is one way to develop a positive, success-oriented classroom. When disruptions such as fights, serious arguments, misunderstandings, and expressions of angry feelings (verbal or physical) occur, impromptu crisis meetings help students understand and resolve serious conflicts (Redl, 1959). These meetings, which involve only those students who were actually involved in the problem situation, can take place in the classroom, lunchroom, or playground. To conduct a crisis meeting, the following steps are usually taken:

1. *Cooling Off.* Students should be given a few minutes to cool off if they are very upset and not ready to engage in thoughtful discussion. If necessary, students can be sent to their desks, a quiet area, or the principal's office.

2. *Setting Rules.* The meeting is initiated by speaking in a calm manner. Ground rules for the discussion are set. These may include avoiding arguing and listening to what each person has to say.

3. *Listening Actively.* The student is asked to describe the incident, what led up to the incident, and how he or she feels. After listening carefully, the listener rephrases what the student has said to show understanding. Other students may be asked to summarize or repeat what the first student said. Then the second student is asked to give his or her recollection of the incident. During the active listening phase, the main goal is to obtain a clarification of what happened and how the participants are feeling. Helping students clarify their feelings may also serve to drain off some anger or frustration.

4. *Exploring Problem.* At this step, the problem is considered at length. Questions such as how the problem could have been avoided, what can be done the next time the problem begins, and what consequences should be expected (Glass et al., 1982) can be addressed.

Another form of crisis intervention is the life space interviewing (LSI) method which was developed to help teachers become effective in talking to children and to help teachers use these skills as a specific management tool (L'Abate & Curtis, 1975). There are two main goals: clinical exploitation of life events and immediate emotional first aid. There are both long-range and immediate goals. This kind of therapy may help the student to express hostility, frustration, or aggression; provide support while helping the student to avoid panic or guilt; help the student to maintain relationships; allow teachers to supervise behavior and ensure conformity to rules; and help teachers in settling complex situations (L'Abate & Curtis, 1975).

The resource classroom is yet another way to help exceptional children. Here the child is provided with instruction and emotional support by the resource teacher for part of the day. The child may move between the classrooms and receive instruction from both teachers. It is even possible that the child can be placed on a limited day schedule in cases where he or she cannot handle either the resource or regular classroom. In summary, crisis intervention can be the most appropriate kind of action if all psychological, sociological, and educational knowledge is applied at the correct moment in time.

REFERENCES

Caplan, G. (1963). Opportunities for school psychologists in the primary prevention. *Mental Hygiene, 47*(4), 525–539.

Glass, R., Christiansen, J., & Christiansen, J.L. (1982). *Teaching exceptional students in the regular classroom.* Boston: Little, Brown.

Kelly, L.J., & Vergason, G.A. (1978). *Dictionary for special education and rehabilitation.* Denver: Love.

L'Abate, L., & Curtis, L.T. (1975). *Teaching the exceptional child.* Philadelphia: Saunders.

Redl, F. (1959). Concept of the life space interview. *American Journal of Orthopsychiatry, 29*(1), 1–18.

Swanson, L.H., & Reinert, H.R. (1979). *Teaching strategies for children in conflict curriculum methods, and materials.* St. Louis: Mosby.

See also **Life Space Interviewing; Redl, F.**

CRISIS TEACHER

The concept of the crisis teacher/helping teacher was initiated, according to Long, Morse, and Newman (1976), as the result of the efforts of a staff of elementary teachers in a high problematic school. The crisis teacher is first an educator trained in psychoeducational theory and practice who provides direct assistance to regular classroom teachers and students that might exhibit disruptive (crisis) behaviors. Ultimately, this educator will enhance the learning environment by providing a liaison between the crisis teacher and the regular classroom teacher. This brings to the classroom teacher immediate peer help as opposed to the consultants, such as the school psychologist, school counselor, or principal, ordinarily sought out.

Long, Morse, and Newman (1976) has suggested the crisis/helping teacher model include the following features: (1) emphasizes direct assistance to pupils; (2) has an eclectic approach to intervention strategies; (3) is concerned with the prevention of problems as well as their remediation; (4) tends to be broadly concerned with the total life space of the child rather than targeted on specific discrepancies or deficits. It appears that the concept of the crisis teacher has had a positive effect in that it tends to promote healthy self-concepts and lends itself to future self-management and authentic human relationships.

An important footnote includes the crisis teacher's ability to know when an incident is not a crisis and does not warrant his or her attention. Of importance then is to avoid conceiving of all events of a disruptive nature as being catastrophic and in need of special attention.

REFERENCE

Long, N.J., Morse, W.C., & Newman, R.G. (1976). *Conflict in the classroom: The education of emotionally, disturbed children* (3rd ed.). Belmont, CA: Wadsworth.

See also **Crisis Intervention; Resource Room; Special Class**

CRITERION-REFERENCED TESTING

Criterion-referenced testing is a method for examining a person's performance with respect to a standard or criterion. It is commonly contrasted with norm-referenced testing, in which a person's performance is compared with that of other persons who make up a norm group. While this concept has been used in pedagogy for millennia, it has been most recently formalized by Glaser and Klaus (1962). In their conception, a criterion is a level of performance achieved only when the person being examined is able to perform certain tasks. These tasks have been determined to be necessary for learning. During the course of study there may be many criteria, which may be viewed as stages or intermediate steps. The assessment of the performance on the tasks necessary to achieve criteria is commonly called criterion referenced testing (CRT). A criterion referenced test is thus a test constructed to assess the performance level of examinees in relation to a well-defined domain of content (Hambleton, 1999).

The major issues in CRT are definition of the content, development of the tests, evaluation of test characteristics, and standard setting. A useful text on these issues has been compiled by Berk (1984a); more current thinking by researchers in the CRT field is reviewed by Hambleton (1999).

Definition of the content for criterion-referenced tests is closely tied to instruction. If one uses the Glaser and Husek concept of CRT, a careful analysis of the tasks being required of the students forms the basis for the test. Those tasks are separated either hierarchically or organizationally into stages or steps. Tests are constructed that sample the behaviors the student must exhibit to demonstrate knowledge or mastery for each step. In hierarchical content, the student must know certain content or be able to perform certain tasks before the next content or task can be attempted. Many courses in mathematics exhibit such structure. Other content may have an organizational sequence that is not inherent to it such as English literature. It may be studied historically, thematically, or by type such as poetry, novel, and essay. Criterion-referenced testing may be used to indicate level of achievement for each part. Nitko (1984) refers to ordering and definition for domains. A domain may be ordered or unordered and well-defined or ill-defined. He asserts that CRT should be used only with well-defined content domains.

There has been relatively little research on developing items or questions for CRTs, and most test developers have used item-writing technology developed for norm-referenced achievement tests. Analysis of item and test characteristics has received considerable attention from psychometricians. Both classical reliability theory and item characteristic curve theory have been applied to the analysis of items and of the entire test. Reliability of CRT tests has been derived for test scores (Berk, 1984b) and for the classification decision (Hambleton, 1999; Subkoviak, 1984).

REFERENCES

Berk, R.A. (Ed.). (1984a). *A guide to criterion-referenced test construction.* Baltimore, MD: Johns Hopkins University Press.

Berk, R.A. (1984b). Conducting the item analysis. In R.A. Berk (Ed.), *A guide to criterion-referenced test construction* (pp. 97–143). Baltimore, MD: Johns Hopkins University Press.

Glaser, R. (1963). Instructional technology and the measurement of learning outcomes. Some questions. *American Psychologist, 18,* 519–521.

Glaser, R., & Klaus, D.J. (1962). Proficiency measurement: Assessing human performance. In R.M. Gagne (Ed.), *Psychological Principles in Systems Development* (pp. 419–474) New York: Holt, Reinhart & Winston.

Hambleton, R. (1999). Criterion-referenced testing: Principles, technical advances, and evaluation guidelines. In C.R. Reynolds & T.B. Gutkin (Eds.), *The Handbook of School Psychology* (3rd ed.) (pp. 409–433). New York: Wiley.

Nitko, A.J. (1984). Defining "Criterion-Referenced Test." In R.A. Berk (Ed.), *A guide to criterion-referenced test construction* (pp. 8–28). Baltimore, MD: Johns Hopkins University Press.

Subkoviak, M.J. (1984). Estimating the reliability of mastery nonmastery classifications. In R.A. Berk (Ed.), *A guide to criterion referenced test construction* (pp. 267–291). Baltimore, MD: Johns Hopkins University Press.

See also **Minimum Competency Testing; Norm-Referenced Testing**

CROSS CATEGORICAL PROGRAMMING

Public Law 94-142 and its update, IDEA, identifies 11 categories of special-needs students. The categories include deaf, deaf-blind, hard of hearing, mentally retarded, multihandicapped, orthopedically impaired, other health impaired, emotionally disturbed, specific learning disability, speech impaired, visually impaired, and traumatic brain injury (Federal Register, 1977).

It is becoming increasingly common for school districts and special education cooperatives to group students with diverse handicaps in a single classroom or program. One classroom, for example, may serve both moderately mentally retarded and severely emotionally disturbed youths. A resource program may serve both mildly mentally retarded and learning-disabled individuals. The practice of grouping children and youth with diverse handicaps is referred to as cross categorical programming. For many years inclusive programming has made the cross categorical approach redundant. Many school districts continue to explore hybrid models that suggest cross categorical and inclusive practices. Outcome studies, however, are lacking in these areas.

REFERENCE

Federal Register. (1977, August). Washington, DC: U.S. Government Printing Office.

See also **Generic Special Education; Inclusion; Individualization of Instruction; Least Restrictive Environment**

CROSS-CULTURAL ADAPTABILITY INVENTORY

The Cross-Cultural Adaptability Inventory (Kelly & Meyers, 1992) is a 50-item self-scored inventory that measures the ability of an individual to live and work in a cross-cultural environment. The CCAI is a self-assessment inventory. The instrument was first developed in 1987 by Dr. Colleen Kelly, a human resource specialist, and Dr. Judith Meyers, a clinical psychologist with a specialty in diagnostics. The instrument met the needs of cross-cultural specialists who needed a training tool to promote cross-cultural understanding and insight. The CCAI focuses on four skill areas which research has shown to be critical in adapting to other cultures. The CCAI is based on a cultural general approach, which purports that there are certain commonalities to all areas across cultural transitions, regardless of the culture of origin. It provides a frame of reference for evaluating individuals adapting from one culture to another or working in a multicultural setting.

The CCAI is a popular instrument among trainers and cross-cultural specialists because it is research-based, easy to understand and administer, self-scoring, inexpensive, and easily available. It was normed on a population of 653 cross-cultural specialists, foreign students, educators, missionaries, and business people. The test underwent two revisions where factor analysis, principle components analysis, and item analysis were performed. The final version was published by NCS in 1992. The instrument has excellent alpha reliability, face validity, and construct validity. Predictive validity has not been established, and it is not recommended that the CCAI be used for selection purposes.

The CCAI is used to develop insight into the adaption process, increase awareness of cross-cultural issues, and provide training for individuals living and working in other cultures. It also has application for multicultural work groups. The CCAI has been used to train foreign students and to prepare business people and their families for relocation abroad. The CCAI has trained volunteer groups working abroad (such as missionaries) and has assisted social service groups working with immigrant populations. The CCAI is also an excellent tool for training counselors, teachers, and principals in the issues of cross-cultural competency. Psychotherapists have found the CCAI useful in working with foreign-born patients as a feedback tool.

The CCAI has a manual that provides thorough information on the development of the instrument, the theories underlying the instrument, and the statistical data supporting it. Training tools are available that provide a full-day training design, as well as follow-up materials in the form of action planning. A feedback form is also available.

REFERENCE

Kelly, C., & Meyers, J. (1992). *The Cross-Cultural Adaptability Inventory* (CCAI). Minneapolis, MN: National Computer Systems.

CROSS-CULTURAL SPECIAL EDUCATION

Public Law 94–142 was implemented to provide equal educational opportunities for all handicapped children. Legislation including IDEA and the ADA, and litigation continues to focus on educational opportunities for exceptional children, however, equal educational opportunity is not a reality for all. Many exceptional students continue to be discriminated against or receive inadequate services based solely on their race, social class, or creed (Heward & Orlansky, 1984).

It seems unlikely that any teacher would possess the skills or background to deal adequately with the unique aspects of the many and varied cultures that may be encountered. As such, it may be useful to use as many community resources as possible in any attempt to meet these culturally diverse needs. King-Stoops (1980) devised a strategy for working with children of migrant farmers. She suggests that high school or college students with similar migrant backgrounds be used as aides or volunteers in the classroom setting. While King-Stoops speaks only to migrant children, it seems clear that such an approach could be easily and successfully used with a wide variety of cultures. While this may serve well in certain circumstances, this strategy may be impossible to implement in all settings. Heward and Orlansky (1984) suggest that the implementation of effective instructional techniques would likely benefit all students regardless of cultural background. It is important to note that effective instruction is based on and stems from effective assessment. Diversity in the provision of services in school also has began to receive special attention (e.g., Henning-Stout and Brown-Cheatham, 1999).

REFERENCES

Henning-Stout, M., & Brown-Cheatham, M. (1999). School psychology in a diverse world: Considerations for practice, research, and training. In C.R. Reynolds & T.B. Gutkin (Eds.), *The Handbook of School Psychology* (3rd ed.) (pp. 1041–1055). New York: Wiley.

Heward, W.L., & Orlansky, M.D. (1984). *Exceptional children.* Columbus, OH: Merrill.

King-Stoops, J. (1980). *Migrant education: Teaching the wandering ones.* Bloomington, IN: Phi Delta Kappa.

See also **Cultural Bias in Testing; System of Multicultural Pluralistic Assessment**

CROSS MODALITY TRAINING

Cross modality training refers to teaching the neurological process of converting information received through one input modality to another system within the brain. The process is also referred to as intersensory integration, intermodal transfer, and transducing. Cross modality integration problems have been linked historically to learning disabilities. It has been hypothesized that certain learners may process visual and auditory information accurately when each type of information is presented distinctly, but that those students may be deficient in tasks requiring them to shift or cross information between sensory systems (Chalfant & Scheffelin, 1969).

Cross modality training programs have been devised to address intersensory integration problems. For example, Frostig (1965, 1968) advocated cross modality exercises, including activities such as describing a picture (visual to auditory), following spoken directions (auditory to motor), and feeling objects through a curtain and drawing their shapes on paper (tactile to visual-motor). Scant research is available to support the use of cross modality training as a strategy to improve students' academic skills. Additionally, few, if any, tests are designed to assess cross-modal perception.

REFERENCES

Chalfant, J., & Scheffelin, M. (1969). *Central processing dysfunction in children* (NINDS Monograph NO. 9). Bethesda, MD: U.S. Department of Health, Education, and Welfare.

Frostig, M. (1965). Corrective reading in the classroom. *Reading Teacher, 18,* 573–580.

Frostig, M. (1968). Education for children with learning disabilities. In H. Myklebust (Ed.), *Progress in learning disabilities.* New York: Grune & Stratton.

See also **Developmental Test of Visual Perception-2; Frostig Remedial Program; Multisensory Instruction**

CROUZON'S SYNDROME (CRANIOFACIAL DYSOSTOSIS) (CS)

Crouzon's syndrome (CS) is believed to be a congenital disability that follows a pattern of autosomal dominance. The major physical characteristics are a result of premature closing of the skull, which causes cranial deformity, widely spaced eyes (which may protrude), and a misshapened face. The nasal bridge may be flat and the nose beaked with underdeveloped nasal sinuses. Malformation of the ear canals and eyes as a result of hypertension and orbital deformity is said to occur in 70 to 80% of the cases (along with optic atrophy); this may cause visual and hearing problems. The upper jaw and bones of the midface may be underdeveloped and the lower jaw may be prominent. Crowding, misalignment of upper teeth, and an enlarged tongue may cause some problems with eating and speech development. Higher incidence of infections also may occur, and in some cases congenital heart disease has been reported. Mental retardation may be noted in some children, but most have average mental abilities. In rare instances, spina bifida may be present (Carter, 1978).

REFERENCE

Carter, C. (Ed.). (1978). *Medical aspects of mental retardation* (2nd ed.). Springfield, IL: Thomas.

CRUICKSHANK, WILLIAM M. (1915–1992)

William M. Cruickshank received his BA in 1937 from Eastern Michigan University, his MA in 1938 from the University of Chicago, and his PHD in 1945 from the University of Michigan.

Since 1937 Cruickshank's main interests have been in the area of brain-injured children, neurologically handicapped children, and the neurophysiological characteristics of accurately defined learning-disabled children. Author of over 200 books, articles, and edited books (some of which are translated in several languages), Cruickshank's major publications include *Teaching Methods for Brain-Injured and Hyperactive Children* (1961), *Learning Disabilities in Home, School, and Community* (1977), and *Psychoeducational Foundations of Learning Disabilities* (1973).

Holder of six honorary degrees, he taught in many countries and remained active as a visiting professor and lecturer for a number of years following his retirement from the University of Michigan. As the founder, first president (1975–1985), and executive director of the International Academy for Research in Learning Disabilities, he was an international authority on the problems of learning-disabled children and youths. Dr. William Cruickshank passed away in 1992, after a long and productive career.

REFERENCES

Cruickshank, W.M. (1977). *Learning disabilities in home, school, and community* (Rev. ed.). Syracuse, NY: Syracuse University.

Cruickshank, W.M., et al. (1961). *Teaching methods for brain-injured and hyperactive children.* Syracuse, NY: Syracuse University.

CRYPTOPHASIA

Cryptophasia is a language disorder characteristic of twins. Twins often have delayed language development accompanied by what appears to be a jargon that only the twins understand. This jargon is a form of imitation of adult language with its own syntax, a type of "pidgin." The language may become elaborate and complex but remains, for the most part, understandable only to the twins. The language develops as they attempt to imitate the speech sounds of adults. Twins spend an inordinate amount of time together therefore they begin to understand approximations of mature language and reinforce each other for use of this lesser form of communication. Cryptophasia retards normal language development.

See also Language Delays; Language Disorders; Twins

CRYSTALLIZED V. FLUID INTELLIGENCE

The theory of fluid and crystallized intelligence was proposed over 40 years ago by Raymond Cattell. It is based on the work of Charles Spearman (1932), who concluded that intelligence has a unitary, comprehensive ability common to all tests. He called his universal factor "g" for general ability factor.

This factor was the basis for the two-factor theory proposed by Cattell. This theory states that every mental test measures two factors: a general factor g, which is common to all tests, and a specific factor s, which is peculiar to each test (Cattell, 1963). Cattell defined intelligence by dividing the general ability factor into two categories. These are now designated crystallized intelligence (*Gc*) and fluid intelligence (*Gf*).

Cattell and Horn (1978) suggested that *Gf* is the major measurable outcome of the influence of biological factors and that *Gc* is the primary manifestation of educational and cultural influence. They indicated that fluid intelligence pertains to the individual ability to perceive and extract rules and relationships, while crystallized intelligence arises from the individual application of fluid intelligence in learning symbols, language, and mathematics. Cattell and Horn suggested that *Gf* may be determined by heredity, and may be defined by tasks in which analytical ability is emphasized, while *Gc* is determined by education, and is similar to achievement in that it is the accumulated knowledge of an individual.

Current research on *Gf* and *Gc* is focused on ability factors and cognitive processes (Lansman, 1982), primacy/recency components of short-term memory (Crawford & Stankov, 1983), and speed of information processing in sixth graders. This last study (Jenkinson, 1983) measured memory scanning and picture identification. It eliminated the effects of *Gf* and *Gc* and failed to support any causal relationship between fluid and crystallized abilities.

REFERENCES

Cattell, R.B. (1963). Theory of fluid and crystallized intelligence: A critical experiment. *Journal of Educational Psychology, 54,* 1–22.

Cattell, R.B., & Horn, J.L. (1978). A check on the theory of fluid and crystallized intelligence. *Journal of Educational Measurement, 15,* 139.

Crawford, J., & Stankov, L. (1983). Fluid and crystallized intelligence and primacy/recency components of short-term memory. *Intelligence, 7,* 227–252.

Jenkinson, J.L. (1983). Is speed of information processing related to fluid or to crystallized intelligence? *Intelligence, 7,* 91–106.

Lansman, M., Donaldson, G., Hunt, E., & Yantis, S. (1982). Ability factors and cognitive processes. *Intelligence, 6,* 347–386.

Spearman, C. (1932). *The abilities of man.* London. Macmillan.

See also Intelligence; Intelligence Quotient

CUED SPEECH

Cued speech was developed in 1967 by R. Orin Cornett at Gallaudet College in Washington, DC. It was designed to clarify ambiguity experienced by severely and profoundly hearing-impaired individuals relying on lipreading as a means of comprehending speech (Evans, 1982). During speechreading, hearing-impaired individuals may confuse many sounds such as /p/, /m/, and /b/, because they are visually similar. Users of cued speech attempt to overcome this confusion by providing a visual supplement to information presented through speechreading.

There are advantages and disadvantages associated with the use of cued speech. Its advantages include an adherence to the philosophy of oralism. Cued speech supplements information presented through speechreading; however, it cannot be used and understood in the absence of speech. In addition, use of cued speech has been associated with increases in speechreading accuracy (Clarke & Ling, 1976; Ling & Clarke, 1975), vocabulary, and intelligibility (Rupert, 1969). Disadvantages include the questionable phonetic competence of users, lack of transfer potential to reading (Wilbur, 1979), and an overdependence on cues (Clarke & Ling, 1976).

REFERENCES

Clarke, B.R., & Ling, D. (1976). The effects of using cued speech: A follow-up study. *Volta Review, 78,* 23–34.

Cornett, R.O. (1967). Cued speech. *American Annals of the Deaf,* *112,* 3–13.

Evans, L. (1982). *Total communication: Structure and strategy.* Washington, DC: Gallaudet College Press.

Ling, D., & Clarke, B.R. (1975). Cued speech: An evaluative study. *American Annals of the Deaf, 120,* 480–488.

Rupert, J. (1969). Kindergarten program using cued speech at the Idaho School for the Deaf. *Proceedings of the 44th Meeting of American Instructors of the Deaf.* Berkeley, CA.

Wilbur, R.B. (1979). *American Sign Language and sign systems.* Baltimore, MD: University Park Press.

See also Sign Language; Total Communication

CUISENAIRE RODS

Cuisenaire rods, named for the Belgian mathematician who designed them, consist of a set of small colored wooden rods of varying lengths. Gattegno, a British psychologist, popularized their use for both mathematics and language instruction through combinations of size and color. Karambelas (1971) described how the rods are used in language instruction.

There have been many studies of the use of Cuisenaire rods in mathematics instruction. Hawkins (1984) introduced the relationship in the Pythagorean theorem to low-ability seventh graders using Cuisenaire rods. Sweetland (1984) used the rods in teaching multiplication of fractions. LeBlanc (1976) designed a teacher preparation program in elementary school mathematics using Cuisenaire rods as the vehicle for actively engaging prospective teachers in mathematics with the goal of applying that mathematics in the elementary school. McDonald (1981) incorporated the rods in teaching binomial expressions and Ginther (1970) designed applications of the rods in advanced mathematics. Urion (1979) developed a Cuisenaire rod activity for generating approximations of pi. Knowles (1979) described the use of the rods and the calculator in examining decimals that result from division of whole numbers. Ewbank (1978) and Hater (1970) drew attention to the use of color in mathematics instruction including Cuisenaire rods, number lines, magic squares, and combinatorial problems. Davidson (1977) suggested uses for the rods in teaching mathematics from basic arithmetic through algebra.

REFERENCES

Davidson, P.S. (1977). Rods can help children learn at all grade levels. *Learning, 6*(3), 86–88.

Ewbank, W.A. (1978). The use of color for teaching mathematics. *Arithmetic Teacher, 26*(1), 53–57.

Ginther, J.L. (1970). An application of Cuisenaire rods in advanced mathematics. *School Science & Mathematics, 70*(3), 250–253.

Hater, M.A. (1970). Investigation of color in the Cuisenaire rods. *Perceptual & Motor Skills, 31*(2), 441–442.

Hawkins, V.J. (1984). The Pythagorean theorem revisited: Weighing the results. *Arithmetic Teacher, 32*(4), 36–37.

Karambelas, J. (1971). Teaching foreign languages "the silent way."
Association of Departments of Foreign Languages Bulletin, 3(1), 41.

Knowles, F. (1979). Coloured rods, a calculator, and decimals. *Mathematics Teaching, 86,* 28–29.

LeBlanc, J.F. (1976). *Addition and subtraction Mathematics-methods program unit.* Bloomington, IN: Mathematics Education Development Center, Indiana University.

McDonald, J.R. (1981). Sharing teaching ideas: Factor cards: A device for GFC; A model of 3-space; Discovery in advanced algebra with concrete models. *Mathematics Teacher, 74*(5), 349–358.

Sweetland, R.D. (1984). Understanding multiplication of fractions. *Arithmetic Teacher, 32*(1), 48–52.

Urion, D.K. (1979). Using the Cuisenaire rods to discover approximations of pi. *Arithmetic Teacher, 27*(4), 17.

CULTURAL ATTITUDES TOWARDS SPECIAL EDUCATION

The children and youth of the United States represent an increasingly diverse variety of cultural and linguistic groups. The 1990 Census (U.S. Bureau of the Census, 1990) determined that the school-age population within the United States included 6,914,000 African American children, 5,390,000 children of Hispanic descent (including children of Mexican, Cuban, and Puerto Rican origin), 1,550,000 children of Asian/Pacific Island descent (including children of Japanese, Chinese, Korean, and Filipino origin), and 522,000 Native American children (including American Indians, Eskimos, and Aleuts). This large number of school-age children (and the kaleidoscope of cultures and languages which they represent) offer unique challenges and opportunities for educational professionals.

Underscoring the need to appropriately address these challenges and opportunities is the rate at which the culturally and linguistically diverse school-age population is growing. Between 1995 and 2050 the overall U.S. population is forecast to grow by almost 50%, with the Anglo (White, Not of Hispanic Origin) population experiencing the smallest proportional increase (approximately 7%; U.S. Bureau of the Census, 1994). This is in sharp contrast to the proportional increase forecast for the African American population (70%), Native American population (83%), Hispanic population (258%), and the Asian/Pacific Islander population (269%) during the same time period.

In order to provide appropriate educational services for such a heterogeneous population, an understanding of cultural affiliation and corresponding cultural attitudes as related to special education is necessary. A cultural group, for the purpose of this entry, is defined as a group set apart from others because of its national origin or distinctive cultural patterns (Schaefer, 1990). It is furthermore recognized that although members of a cultural group may have common values, beliefs, and behaviors, no individual member exemplifies all of the groups modal practices (Wehrly, 1995). The following sections include a discussion of the literature related to cultural attitudes toward special education, a summary of common attitudes reported for various cultural groups, and an analysis of the benefits and limitations of our current knowledge base.

The present body of literature related to cultural attitudes towards special education is largely focused on suggestions for practice in the special education arena and can be generally categorized as either (a) theory-based (e.g., "best practice" papers in which general knowledge of specific cultural groups is applied to the school setting), or (b) research-based (i.e., the presentation of data to demonstrate specific relationships between cultural attitudes and educational strategies). Thus, cultural attitudes towards special education are presented within the framework of these two categories.

PARENTAL ATTITUDES

Research-based studies regarding culturally and linguistically diverse parental attitudes towards special education have addressed various topics.

Meanings attached to labels. Studies on the meanings attached to special education labels by culturally and linguistically diverse parents reveal that (a) their concept and boundaries of "normal" may be different from that of the educational system (Bennett, 1988; Danseco, 1997; Harry, 1992; Rodriguez, 1995; Zetlin, Padron & Wilson, 1996); (b) they are often confused by the specific terminology or labels common to special education (e.g., handicapped, disabled, impaired, retarded) and may associate these labels with more severe, as opposed to mild, manifestations of impairments (Danseco, 1997; Harry, 1992); (c) they may perceive the label as somehow reflective of family inadequacies (Harry, 1992); and (d) may attach biomedical and sociocultural (e.g., spiritual) causes to the labels (Danseco, 1997; Rodriguez, 1995).

Perceived role of language and culture. Several studies (e.g., Harry, 1992; Rodriguez, 1995; Zetlin, Padron, & Wilson, 1996) revealed parental perceptions that their child was placed in special education as a result of a language and cultural difference and not because of a true handicapping condition. This sentiment was reported by parents from various cultural and linguistic backgrounds (e.g., Hispanic and Southeast Asian).

Instructional format concerns. While parents tend to report positive feelings regarding the smaller group size for instruction found in special education, they also expressed concern that the slower pace, and lack of actual individualization of instruction might hinder, rather than help, their children (Harry, 1992; Zetlin, Padron, & Wilson, 1996). Confusion seems to exist among some parents as to how native language and culture should be utilized in their child's instruction (Zetlin, Padron, & Wilson, 1996), while others felt that instruction should focus on English and reading (Harry, 1992; Rodriguez, 1995).

Factors affecting parental participation. Parental opportunities for participation in the special education process was often reported by parents as (a) impersonal and one-sided (e.g., during meetings), with school personnel underestimating parental capabilities and limiting parental voice and power in decision-making; (b) overwhelming with regard to the number of letters and forms involved; (c) constrained by the parents' limited knowledge of the special education process (e.g., legal rights and necessity of attendance at meetings) (Bennett, 1988; Danseco, 1997; Harry, 1992; Rodriguez, 1995); and (d) permeated with distrust (Bennett, 1988; Harry, 1992).

SCHOOL PERSONNEL ATTITUDES

Research-based studies within this area are generally focused on the attitudes of culturally and linguistically diverse school personnel, primarily teachers, towards special education. Two recent studies provide an example of this type of research. Rodriguez (1995) and Paez, Flores, & Trujillo (2000) surveyed culturally and linguistically diverse teachers employed in bilingual education programs. Both studies revealed that the teachers' knowledge of special education services and processes were limited and that the older the age group (Rodriguez, 1995) or the longer the time since college graduation the less informed they generally were.

According to Rodriguez (1995), there was significant variation among 100 teachers of Southeast Asian origin with regard to the belief that spiritual forces or destiny cause a child's disability with approximately one third agreeing, over one third disagreeing, and the rest being ambivalent on this point. Many of these teachers felt that children were often misplaced in special education and were discriminated against because of lower English proficiency. Moreover, they reported that lower levels of English proficiency among some students of Southeast Asian origin resulted in lower expectations for these students on the part of other school personnel.

CONCLUSION

It is clear that cultural attitudes play an important role in a family's adjustment to a child with a disability and the impact the situation has on the family's responsiveness and receptivity to sources of help (Fine & Gardner, 1994). The work of Harry (1992) serves as an example of the use of theory-based knowledge to construct data-based research. It is this type of application which will allow accurate and pertinent knowledge regarding cultural attitudes to be applied to the special education setting. Regardless of the informational source, whether it be theory- or research-based literature, the attitudes of culturally and linguistically diverse parents towards special education must be viewed within the context of the current life situation of the individual caregiver (Fracasso & Busch-Rossnagel, 1992). Dennis & Giangreco (1996) expand on this sentiment by noting that contextual considerations which should be considered include the emotional climate of racial or ethnic discrimination experienced by the individual, the implications of poverty, the neighborhood and living environment, and the degree and duration of acculturation into the dominant cultural group. Added to this list is the universal and very individual experience of caring for a child with special needs (Lynch & Hansen, 1992).

REFERENCES

Bennett, A.T. (1988). Gateways to powerlessness: Incorporating Hispanic deaf children and families into formal schooling. *Disability, Handicap, and Society, 3*(2), 119–151.

Danseco, E.R. (1997). Parental beliefs on childhood disability: Insights on culture, children development, and intervention. *International Journal of Disability, Development and Education, 44,* 41–52.

Dennis, R.E., & Giangreco, M.F. (1996). Creating conversation: Reflections on cultural sensitivity in family interviewing. *Exceptional Children, 63*(1), 103–113.

Fine, M.J., & Gardner, A. (1994). Collaborative consultation with families of children with special needs-why bother? *Journal of Educational and Psychological Consultation, 5,* 283–308.

Fracasso, M., & Busch-Rossnagel, N. (1992). Parents and children of Hispanic origin. In M. Procidano & C. Fisher (Eds.), *Contemporary families: A handbook for school professionals* (pp. 83–98). New York: Teachers College Press.

Harry, B. (1992). *Cultural diversity, families and the education system: Communication and empowerment.* New York: Teachers College.

Lynch, E.W., & Hansen, M.J. (1992). *Developing cross-cultural competence: A guide for working with young children and their families.* Baltimore: Paul H. Brookes.

Paez, D., Flores, J., & Trujillo, T. (2000). Rural school personnel's conceptions of issues of diversity. *Rural Special Education Quarterly, 17.*

Rodriguez, J. (1995). *Southeast Asian's conception of disabilities and special education intervention in American schools.* Lowell, MA: University of Massachusetts, College of Education. (ERIC Document Reproduction Service No. 388 740)

Schaefer, R.T. (1990). *Racial and ethnic groups* (4th ed.). Glenview, Scott Foresman.

U.S. Bureau of the Census. (1990). *1990 United States census.* Washington, DC: U.S. Department of Commerce, Economics and Statistics Administration.

U.S. Bureau of the Census. (1994). *Population projections of the United States by age, sex, race, and Hispanic origin: 1995–2050.* Washington, DC: U.S. Department of Commerce, Economics and Statistics Administration.

Wehrly, B. (1995). *Pathways to multicultural counseling competence: A developmental journey.* Pacific Grove, CA: Brookes/Cole.

Zetlin, A., Padron, M., & Wilson, S. (1996). The experience of five Latin American families with the special education system. *Education and Training in Mental Retardation and Developmental Disabilities, 31,* 22–28.

CULTURAL BIAS IN TESTING

The cultural test bias hypothesis is the contention that racial and ethnic group differences in mental test scores are the result of inherent flaws in the tests themselves. These flaws bias, or cause systematic error, in a manner that causes ethnic minorities to earn low scores. Mean differences in scores among groups are then interpreted as artifacts of the test and not as reflecting any real differences in mental abilities or skills.

Mean differences in mental test scores across race are some of the most well-established phenomena in psycho-logical research on individual differences. One of the primary explanations of these differences is that they are produced by people who are reared in very different environments, with lower scoring groups having been relatively deprived of the quantity and quality of stimulation received in the formative years by higher scoring groups. Another explanation is that lower scoring groups reflect a difference in the genetic potential for intellectual performance. Most contemporary views take an environment X genetic interaction approach.

Additionally, it has been argued (see Reynolds, Lowe, & Saenz, 1999, for a discussion) that minority and majority groups have qualitatively distinct forms of intelligence and personality and thus cannot be assessed with the same methods, negating any attempt to compare groups or test performance.

Research on race bias in testing was, and continues to be, of major importance to psychology as well as to society. The cultural test bias hypothesis is probably one of the most crucial scientific questions facing psychology (Reynolds, 1981). If this hypothesis ultimately is accepted as correct, then the past 100 years or so of research into the psychology of individual differences (or differential psychology, the basic psychological science underlying all fields of applied psychology) must be dismissed as artifactual, or at least as confounded, since such research is based on standard psychometric methodology. Race bias in testing is being tested in the judicial courts as well as in the scholarly court of open inquiry. Two major court decisions, known as *Larry P.* (1979) and *PASE* (1980), have given conflicting opinions regarding the issues. Of two federal district courts, one decided that intelligence tests are racially biased and the other decided they are not biased.

Contrary to the position of the late 1960s, considerable research is now available regarding race bias in testing. For the most part, this research has failed to support the test bias hypothesis, revealing that (1) well-constructed, well-standardized educational and psychological tests predict future performance in an essentially equivalent manner across race for U.S.-born ethnic minorities; (2) the internal psychometric structure of the tests is essentially invariant with regard to race; and (3) the content of these tests is about equally appropriate across these groups (Reynolds, 1982a; Reynolds et al., 1999).

Race bias in testing is one of the most controversial and violently emotional issues in psychology. It will not be resolved entirely on the basis of research and data, as tests have unquestionably been abused in their past use with minority groups. Much of the controversy centers around the placement of minority children in special education programs. Thus, special consideration must be given to ensure that the misuses and abuses of the past are thwarted by "intelligent testing" (Kaufman, 1979).

REFERENCES

Kaufman, A.S. (1979). Intelligence testing with the WISC-R. *Interscience.* New York: Wiley.

Reynolds, C.R. (1981). In support of bias in mental testing and scientific inquiry. *Behavioral & Brain Sciences, 3,* 352.

Reynolds, C.R. (1982). The problem of bias in psychological assessment. In C.R. Reynolds & T.B. Gutkin (Eds.), *The handbook of school psychology.* New York: Wiley.

Reynolds, C.R., Lowe, P., & Saenz, A. (1999). The problem of bias in psychological assessment. In C.R. Reynolds & T.B. Gutkin (Eds.), *The Handbook of School Psychology* (3rd ed.) (pp. 549–595). New York: Wiley.

See also **Larry P.; Marshall *v.* Georgia; Pase *v.* Hannon**

CULTURAL DEPRIVATION

See EARLY EXPERIENCE AND CRITICAL PERIODS; SOCIO-ECONOMIC STATUS.

CULTURE FAIR TEST

The Culture Fair Intelligence Test (Cattell, 1973) is a measure virtually devoid of examinee verbal content (the test uses a paper and pencil format). It consists of novel problem-solving items that do not occur in any particular culture. The test format is multiple choice and includes four subtests: Series Completion, Classification, Matrices, and Conditions. Different levels are administered depending on the subject's age: 4 to 8 years, 8 to 14 years, or 14 to adult. Similar to other standardized tests, the results of the Culture Fair Intelligence Test are expressed as deviation IQs with a mean of 100 and a standard deviation of 16.

Lewis (1998) notes that there are some serious weaknesses of the Culture Fair Intelligence Test. One is that it uses fairly extensive verbal instructions during administration of the test. This causes difficulty for linguistically different clients. Therefore, although the test does not have culturally loaded information items or verbal components, the verbal nature of the directions themselves are problematic. Also, the subtests emphasize speed. This emphasis on speed can differ cross-culturally, and thereby reduces the cultural fairness of the instrument. These potential problems should be taken into account when assessing clients of different cultural backgrounds. Anastasi (1988) has noted that the interpretation of test scores are "by far the most important considerations in the assessment of culturally diverse groups" (p. 66). Misinterpretation of scores with these groups is a serious concern.

REFERENCES

Anastasi, A.A. (1988). *Psychological testing* (6th ed.). New York: Macmillan.

Cattell, R.B. (1973). *Technical supplement for the Culture Fair Intelligence tests Scales 2 and 3.* Champaign, IL: Institute for Personality and Ability Testing.

Lewis, J.E. (1998). Nontraditional uses of traditional aptitude tests. In R.J. Samuda, R. Feurerstein, A.S. Kaufman, J.E. Lewis, & R.J. Sternberg (Eds.), *Advances in Cross Cultural Assessment.* Thousand Oaks, CA: Sage.

See also **Cultural Bias in Testing**

CULTURAL-FAMILIAL RETARDATION

The term cultural-familial retardation has long been used to indicate mild retardation of unknown etiology that is associated with a family history of mild retardation, and a home environment that provides adverse experiences that are believed to inhibit mental development. The word cultural suggests an environmental basis; familial implies a genetic origin. Synonyms include sociocultural or psychosocial, intrinsic, subcultural, endogenous, and familial retardation. Individuals in this population usually have IQs in the range of mild retardation (about 55 to 70), have no demonstrable biological pathology to account for the retardation, usually have a parent or sibling who is retarded, and come from low socioeconomic status homes (Gillberg, 1995; Westling, 1986).

The specific cause of cultural-familial retardation is uncertain, but it probably involves interactive factors; each factor alone is not sufficient to explain the intellectual and behavioral deficits. The present consensus is that the interactions among psychosocial, environmental, and genetic factors are so great and begin so early in life that one cannot place responsibility on any single cause in individual cases (Grossman, 1983). A few decades ago it was believed that this type of retardation was inherited, and environmental factors were discounted. Polygenic inheritance is suggested because this type of retardation is not randomly distributed among the poverty stricken, but most often found in families where the mother is retarded.

Some psychologists and educators have proposed that much of the responsibility for retardation in culturally disadvantaged families is with the environment outside the home, particularly the educational system. Mildly retarded students have been called "six-hour retarded children," implying that they are retarded only during school hours; however, there is little evidence for assuming that those children cope as well as others outside of school. Criticism of schools is partially based on the fact that prevalence studies have shown a higher percentage of identified cases during school years than before or after those years (Richardson, 1968). School demands may tax the abilities of mildly retarded individuals more than some activities of later life; for example, good reading comprehension and high mathematics are important, but they are not essential for some occupations. If we classify as retarded any adults who are competitive and consistently employed full-time, many former EMR students would not be considered retarded as adults, whatever an earlier classification, and whatever their IQs as adults. Levine (1985) reported a high correlation between stress and anxiety, especially for unemployed mildly retarded adults; therefore, personality factors as well as job skills and IQ may be relevant in the classification of adults.

Some sociologists and educators have argued that children in this group are not really retarded, but that intelligence tests are biased against poor children, especially minority ones. This argument seems to ignore the fact that some children from the same families and communities are successful with the same test items that others fail. Careful empirical evaluations of tests and test items offer little support for claims of test bias in well-constructed, properly standardized tests (Reynolds, 1983; Reynolds, Lowe, & Saenz, 1999). Modifying (raising) scores because of economic disadvantages would merely make it more difficult for low-scoring and disadvantaged students to meet eligibility criteria for services they need.

Since mid-century, extensive efforts have been made to interrupt the vicious cycle of poverty, social incompetence, and prejudice associated with cultural-familial retardation. The establishment of the federal Office of Economic Opportunity (OEO) in the 1960s illustrates a massive effort to provide health, educational, and social intervention. The OEO's most visible and enduring program is Project Head Start: a preschool program for young children. Federal and state programs have had impact, but have not even approached the goal of reducing mental retardation by half, as was predicted in 1962 by the President's Panel on Mental Retardation. Project Head Start is now one of the largest health service providers for young children in America. It has been very successful in health areas, but its effects on intellectual functioning and academic achievement are less certain. However, there have been positive results in federally funded research in rigorously controlled experimental preschool programs. In addition, a collaborative study of the pooled data from 11 major studies on the long-term effects of early educational intervention projects designed to prevent the progressive decline in cognitive skills of children from low-income families (primarily minorities) suggests that carefully planned early intervention may have a positive effect on school competence. The competence was measured by assignment to special education programs or repeated grades, the development of abilities as measured by standardized tests, and the effect of attitudes and values of children and on families, both measured by questionnaires (Lazar & Darlington, 1982).

Studies of socially competent children who are at high risk for retardation may provide especially useful information. Werner and Smith (1982) described the "resilient" children in a 20-year study of 698 multiracial children in Hawaii. The resilient children grew to successful, competent adulthood despite poverty, parents with little formal education, and a good deal of stress. Factors associated with resilience were fewer serious childhood illnesses, development of more internal locus of control, well-spaced families of less than five children, and high-achievement motivation.

Das (1973), who has lived in several cultures, has suggested that the technology and cultural demands of society may be important factors in determining whether individuals are classified as mildly retarded. He noted that "biases" in the West emphasize verbal abilities and reasoning, and that the educational systems selectively refer children showing deficiencies in these areas for special education. School experiences are an integral part of a child's growth and development; they transmit the values of the majority culture. Cultural-familial children generally are less adept in language and reasoning than those from higher socioeconomic status families; thus, they start school at a disadvantage. In a technological society in which high-level verbal and reasoning skills are needed and valued, these children begin at a disadvantage that might not be such a problem in a simpler society. It is unlikely that we will soon prevent cultural-familial retardation in America, but progress is being made in reducing associated medical problems and perhaps ameliorating some of the severe learning and educational problems of children from families in which the risk of cultural-familial retardation is high.

REFERENCES

Das, J.P. (1973). Cultural deprivation and cognitive competence. In N.R. Ellis (Ed.), *International review of research in mental retardation* (Vol. 6). New York: Academic.

Gillberg, C. (1995). *Clinical child neuropsychiatry.* Cambridge, UK: Cambridge University Press.

Grossman, H.J. (Ed.). (1983). *Classification in mental retardation.* Washington, DC: American Association on Mental Deficiency.

Lazar, I., & Darlington, R. (1982). Lasting effects of early education: A report from the consortium for longitudinal studies. *Monographs of the Society for Research in Child Development, 47*(serial nos. 2–3).

Levine, H.G. (1985). Situational anxiety and everyday life experiences of mildly mentally retarded adults. *American Journal of Mental Deficiency, 90,* 27–83.

Reynolds, C.R. (1983). Test bias: In God we trust; all others must have data. *Journal of Special Education, 17,* 241–260.

Reynolds, C.R., Lowe, P., & Saenz, A. (1999). The problem of bias in psychological assessment. In C.R. Reynolds & T.B. Gutkin (Eds.), *The handbook of School Psychology* (3rd ed.) (pp. 549–595) New York: Wiley.

Richardson, S.A. (1968). The influence of social-environmental and nutritional factors on mental ability. In N.S. Scrimshaw & J.E. Gordon (Eds.), (1968). *Malnutrition, Learning, and behavior.* Cambridge, MA: MIT Press.

Werner, E.E., & Smith, R.S. (1982). *Vulnerable but invincible: A longitudinal study of resilient children and youth.* New York: McGraw Hill.

Westling, D.L. (1986). *Introduction to Mental Retardation.* Englewood Cliffs, NJ: Prentice-Hall.

See also Abcedarian Project; Goddard, H.H.; Mental Retardation

CULTURALLY/LINGUISTICALLY DIVERSE ISSUES IN EARLY CHILDHOOD

See EARLY CHILDHOOD, CULTURALLY/LINGUISTICALLY DIVERSE ISSUES IN.

CULTURALLY/LINGUISTICALLY DIVERSE STUDENTS AND LEARNING DISABILITIES

Students who are culturally and linguistically diverse (CLD) who experience academic difficulties are often misidentified, misplaced, and misinstructed. Historically, these students been overrepresented in special education (Mercer & Rueda, 1991), although for many, their academic problems were more a result of limited English proficiency than a learning disability.

One critical issue for providing appropriate services for CLD students with learning disabilities is first determining if a student's academic difficulties are the result of a specific learning disability or other causal factors. Has the student had sufficient educational opportunity? Is the student literate in his or her native language? Does the student have the requisite English proficiency to successfully complete academic tasks in English? Is the student familiar with the content presented in academic subject areas? Is the student's behavior significantly different from peers from the same language and/or cultural group?

If the answer to any of these questions is no, then prereferral interventions are in order. Prereferral interventions are systematic, documented modifications suggested by a site based team, often called a Student Study Team, to ensure student success. Such interventions may include adapting assignments in ways that capitalize on the student's strengths, involving parents in the teaching and learning process, and using teaching approaches known to be effective with CLD learners.

If difficulties persist after appropriate interventions have been exhausted, a referral for special education services may be in order. Assessment of CLD students includes testing in the student's native language as well as English, to ensure the problem is evident in both languages. Also, informal measures should be used to support or refute the findings of standardized measures.

Once a learning disability has been diagnosed, a linguistically appropriate Individualized Education Plan, (IEP) is developed to reflect the student's cultural and language needs. The IEP addresses areas (such as language support options) that meet students' cultural and linguistic needs, including primary language support, ESL, and/ or sheltered instruction. The IEP should also specify the language of instruction for each instructional goal, the specifics of the systematic development of English language skills, and how progress in these language-related areas will be measured.

Special educators and paraprofessionals working with students with learning disabilities often are overlooked or excluded from general education professional development sessions that deal with culturally and linguistically diverse students. Special educators and paraprofessionals must be trained in current instructional practices in working with CLD students. Moreover, little interface occurs between special educators and those professionals who have expertise in working with CLD students (Gersten & Woodward, 1994). The focus needs to be on meeting the individual student's needs, not on purview. Increased communication and collaboration between programs and service providers, as well as support from administrators, would alleviate some of the issues relative to educating CLD students with learning disabilities.

REFERENCES

Gersten, R., & Woodward, J. (1974). The language minority student and special education: Issues, trends and paradoxes. *Exceptional Children, 60*(4), 310–322.

Mercer, J., & Rueda, R. (1991, November). *The impact of changing paradigms of disabilities on assessment of special education.* Paper presented at the Council for Exceptional Children Topical Conference on At-Risk Children & Youth, New Orleans.

See also Disproportionality; Learning Disabilities

CULTURALLY/LINGUISTICALLY DIVERSE GIFTED STUDENTS

Students with special gifts and talents come from all populations, and as society becomes increasingly diverse, educators are faced with a challenge in meeting the needs of students who have special gifts from all populations represented in society. However, government and media reports indicate that systems are not effectively identifying and serving minority students, particularly those who are either considered limited English proficient, or those who are from low socioeconomic status (SES) backgrounds and/or from other cultures out of the mainstream middle-class Anglo American culture. In fact, these groups are not fairly represented in programs for the gifted and talented (Irby, 1993; Ortiz & González, 1989; USDE, 1993).

Because of the misunderstandings among educational systems regarding this population (García, 1994), and furthermore, because Borland and Wright (1994) suggested that the potential for giftedness is present in roughly equal proportions in all groups of our society, there is a need to develop valid and reliable methods of screening and identifying culturally and linguistically diverse potentially gifted students (Irby, Hernandez, Torres, & González, 1997). Additionally, with increasing reliance on nominations from teachers who are guided by a checklist of behaviors commonly attributed to exceptional children (Strom, Johnson, Strom, & Strom, 1992), it becomes important for teachers to have valid, defining characteristics with which to screen culturally and linguistically diverse populations.

Several formal instruments or techniques for identifying

potentially gifted individuals who are culturally and linguistically diverse have surfaced over the past two decades and include the child's cultural context. Among those are the Baldwin Matrix (Baldwin, 1977), the System of Multicultural Pluralistic Assessment (SOMPA; Mercer & Lewis, 1978), Kranz Talent Identification Instrument (KTII; Kranz, 1981), the Structure of the Intellect Test (Meeker, 1985), Torrance Tests of Creative Thinking (Torrance, 1970; Torrance, 1997), Group Inventory for Finding Talent (Rimm, 1976), and Fraiser's Talent Assessment Profile (1990). For screening purposes, the Hispanic Bilingual Gifted Screening Instrument (Irby & Lara-Alecio, 1996) is under development and has been specifically designed for Hispanic linguistically and culturally diverse students (Irby, Hernandez, González, & Torres, 1997). Eleven characteristic aspects of gifted students have been determined to be significant for identifying potential within the population of diverse students: Motivation for Learning, Social and Academic Language, Cultural Sensitivity, Familial, Collaboration, Imagery, Achievement, Creative Performance, Support, Problem Solving, and Locus of Control (Lara-Alecio, Irby, & Walker, 1997).

There are several principles that may be followed to improve the numbers of culturally and linguistically diverse students served in gifted education programs:

1. The definition used in the school district should be inclusive. Renzulli (1986) noted that the definition of giftedness must be based on research about characteristics of gifted individuals; in this case, those individuals would be representative the diverse group to be served. Furthermore, researchers should identify ecological characteristics of the diverse group.

2. Definitions should be connected to the identifica-tion procedures and those identification procedures should be diverse (Fraiser, 1990). Look for the diversity.

3. Identification procedures should be multifaceted or multidimensional, including objective and subjective data. Data should also be gathered from those who know the child on a personal/cultural level (Frasier, 1990). Additionally, the instruments used should be based on sociocultural and linguistic characteristics of the referent population; seek out valid and reliable instruments in the child's native language or use nonverbal measures.

4. Implement an identification program early that includes a screening phase, an evaluation phase, and a recommendation phase (Frasier, 1990).

5. Make sure that all relevant information on a student has been reviewed prior to making a decision (Frasier, 1990).

6. Train teachers in general and specific diverse population characteristics of giftedness (Lara-Alecio & Irby, 1993; Rogers, 1986). Use a send-in model with the teacher of the gifted—send them into the classrooms and have them observe functional levels of children within the classroom on various types of activities. When observing, have them focus on products and performance. Additionally, have the teacher solicit products and performances demonstrated away from school.

7. Program options must match district definitions and identification procedures (Frasier, 1990; Lara-Alecio & Irby, 1993). The best learning environment should be provided for the student (Frasier, 1990).

8. Bilingual/bicultural instruction should be provided in early programming, in particular, which suggests a two-way bilingual campus program. Trained bilingual, biliterate, and bicultural teachers are needed for the gifted program (Lara-Alecio, & Irby, 1993). Curriculum for the general education program should have a multicultural perspective, which would urge educators to modify their opinions regarding cultural diversity (Kitano, 1991).

9. Include staff development for mainstream and gifted education teachers with a suggested model that includes workshops on research in this field, exploration of negative myths about the culturally and linguistically diverse, how to develop supportive environments, how to help alter attitudes about specific diverse populations, and how to utilize bilingualism in the classroom.

10. Come to a point of viewing cultural and linguistic diversity as an asset, not as a liability or as a need for remediation. Educators need to celebrate differences and develop a secure communicative environment in which the diverse gifted can thrive.

REFERENCES

Baldwin, A.Y. (1977). *Baldwin identification matrix inservice kit for the identification of gifted & talented students.* East Aurora, NY: Trillium.

Borland, J.H., & Wright, L. (1994). Identifying young, potentially gifted, economically disadvantaged students. *Gifted Child Quarterly, 38,* 164–171.

Frasier, M. (1990). *Frasier's Talent Assessment Profile.* Athens, GA: University of Georgia.

García, E. (1994). Understating & meeting the challenge of student cultural diversity. Boston: Houghton Mifflin.

Irby, B. "Hispanic LEP Gifted Students." Education Week. May 1993.

Irby, B., Hernández, L., Torres, D., & González, C. The correlation between teacher perceptions of giftedness & the Hispanic bilingual screening instrument. Unpublished manuscript, Sam Houston State University.

Irby, B. & Lara-Alecio, R. (1997). Attributes of Hispanic gifted bilingual students as perceived by bilingual educators in Texas. *NYSABE Journal, 11,* 120–142.

Kitano, M.K. (1991). A multicultural education perspective on serving the culturally diverse gifted. *Journal for the Education of the Gifted, 15*(1), 4–19.

Kranz, B. (1981). *Kranz talent identification instrument.* Moorhead, MN: Moorhead State College.

Lara-Alecio, R., & Irby, B. (1993). Reforming identification procedures for the bilingual gifted child. Paper presented at BEAM,

The Ninth Annual Bilingual/ESL Spring Conference, Denton, TX.

Lara-Alecio, R. & Irby. B. (1996). Bilingual education & multicultural education: An inclusively oriented educational delivery System. *The Journal of Educational Issues of Language Minority Students, 17,* 11–24.

Mercer, J.R., & Lewis, J.F. (1978). Using the system of multicultural pluralistic assessment. (SOMPA) to identify the gifted minority child. In A.Y. Baldwin, G.H. Gear, & L.J. Lucito (Eds.), *Educational planning for the gifted* (pp. 7–14). Reston, VA: Council for Exceptional Children.

Meeker, M.N., Meeker, R., & Roid, G. (1985). Structure-of-intellect learning abilities test (SOI-LA). Los Angeles: Western Psychological Services.

Ortíz, V., & González, A. (1989). Validation of a short form of the WISC-R with accelerated & gifted Hispanic students. *Gifted Child Quarterly, 33,* 152–155.

Renzulli, J.S. (1986). The three-ring conception of giftedness: A developmental model for creative productivity. In R.J. Sternberg & J.E. Davidson (Eds.), *Conception of Giftedness.* Cambridge, UK: Cambridge University Press.

Rimm, S.B. (1976). *GIFT: Group Inventory for Finding Creative Talent.* Watertown, WI: Educational Assessment Service.

Rogers, K. (1986). *Review of research on the education of intellectually & academically gifted students.* Minnesota State Department of Education, St. Paul.

Strom, R., Johnson, A., Strom, S., & Strom, P. (1992). *Educating gifted children: Genetic studies of genius* (Vol. 1). Stanford CA: Stanford University Press.

Torrance, E.P. (1970). *Encouraging creativity in the classroom.* Dubuque, IA: William C. Brown.

Torrance, E.P. (1997). *Discovery & nurturance of giftedness in the culturally different.* Reston: VA: Council for Exceptional Children.

U.S. Department of Education, Office of Educational Research & Improvement. (1993). *National excellence: A case for developing America's talented.* Washington, DC: U.S. Government Printing Office.

See also **Creativity; Disproportionality; Gifted and Talented Children; Gifted Handicapped**

CULTURALLY AND LINGUISTICALLY DIVERSE STUDENTS IN SPECIAL EDUCATION, FAMILIES OF

Since the mid-1980s, because of PL 99-457, the ideal of parent participation has evolved into a vision of family-centered practice with issues of diverse family beliefs and practices becoming a crucial focus in the effort to address the problems listed above. Family-centered practice revolves around the concept of family empowerment, or the process of helping families increase control over their lives and take action to get what they want. Empowerment occurs when professionals (a) give families information about services and their rights; (b) facilitate their participation; for instance, by arranging transportation and/or childcare and scheduling meetings at times convenient to parents; and (c) develop collaborative relationships with families by af-

firming and building on family strengths, honoring cultural diversity, creative and cooperative problem-solving, and establishing trust and respect (Dunst & Trivette, 1987; Lynch & Hanson, 1992; Salend & Taylor, 1993; Turnbull & Turnbull, 1996). Evidence for the continuing centrality of this ideal is the 1997 re-authorization of IDEA. This current focus has generated the need for reconceptualizing culture—whether it is perceived as a static or discrete phenomenon—in order to prevent families from being presented in stereotypic ways. The original notion of culture as a process of stages (for instance, from traditional to bicultural to assimilation) through which individuals from minority groups might move, has gradually been superceded by a less discrete view of culture where boundaries are variable according to different dimensions of individual identity, thus acknowledging that an individual may assume multiple group memberships simultaneously (Banks & Banks, 1992).

This definition has also provided a need for context, which brings the focus of study to the precise realm of the individual family, rather than assuming that a generalized concept of the family's cultural tradition will be adequate. By applying Bronfenbrenner's theory of nested systems and Vygotsky's concept of the zone of proximal development, all development is seen as being based in participation in specific social and cultural settings or an individual's "ecocultural niche" (Tharp & Gallimore, 1988), combining the family's ecology and culture. This perspective takes into account more than just the ethnic status of the family by including contextual variables, such as education, acculturation, socioeconomic status, or geographic location, and the effects of these on the daily routines of families to describe a family in all its individuality, as opposed to generalizations about what a family from "this" or "that" cultural group would be expected to look like. The importance of examining contextual influences to avoid cultural stereotypes is well-illustrated, for instance, by Mardiros' (1989) study of Mexican-American parents which demonstrated that parents from a relatively homogenous cultural group, who held similar beliefs regarding the causation of a disability, still displayed a range of responses, some very proactive and creative, others passive and resigned. Similarly, Harry, Allen, & McLaughlin (1995) offer evidence of effective single parenting when they note that the six "living alone" mothers were the most proactive advocates in a sample of 24 African American families of preschoolers with mild disabilities.

Several writers have identified strategies that specifically accommodate this new concept of contextualized culture toward increasing the participation of culturally and linguistically diverse parents in the special education process:

1. Developing self-awareness as a first step towards understanding one's personal and professional values (Caple, Salsido, & di Cecco, 1995). This can involve examining genealogical records and asking oneself questions like "When I was growing up, what did my family say about

people from different cultures?" (Hyun & Fowler, 1995), or "Why do I want 21-year-old Husain to move into a group home?" to recognize the cultural value that underlies one's professional recommendation (Kalyanpur & Harry, 1997).

2. Engaging in conversations with families to learn about their culture and values. This involves using naturalistic means for collecting information about families' situations, including open-ended interviewing (Harry, 1992), and identifying and involving key and/or extended members of the family (Linan-Thompson & Jean, 1997). Professionals should identify and accommodate the family's preferred method of communication, whether written or verbal, English or native language (Barnwell & Day, 1996); make time to listen to parents' stories (Caple, Salsido, & di Cecco, 1995; Kalyanpur & Rao, 1991; Thorp, 1997); and respect their input in the decision-making process (Correa, 1987; Harry, 1992).

3. Making available services and professional recommendations that are compatible with families' values. This involves working with the family to identify their resources and supports and modifying service options or developing creative, individualized alternatives (Correa, 1989; Harry, 1992; Rueda & Martinez, 1994). Comer and Haynes (1991) describe the successful efforts of the Yale Child Study Center Team to "change the ecology of a school" and empower low-income parents by improving parental status and meaningful collaboration between parents and professionals in special education. The program contained three mechanisms for change: a governance mechanism, the school planning and management team, that represented all the adult stakeholders in the school to develop a plan for restructuring the school; a mental health team to address the developmental and behavioral needs of students; and a parent program which focused on supporting the social program of the school restructuring plan and on the academic program as needed. The parent program created social occasions for families and professionals to meet, developing a sense of community, and encouraged parent volunteers to participate in a broad range of school activities from helping in classrooms to participation on the school planning and management team. The authors attribute the success of the entire program to allowing parents to participate in the way they were comfortable and effective and to play meaningful roles, with staff support, with a clear direction and purpose. Unfortunately, efforts to replicate this model have not been as successful in involving special education teachers and parents (Ware, 1994).

In conclusion, school involvement by families from culturally and linguistically diverse backgrounds continues to be problematic. However, parental participation can be enhanced when professionals use naturalistic collection of information about families' situations in order to find out where a family stands on a given issue, are aware of their own cultural influence in the decision-making process, and are committed to flexibility and responsiveness to the need for change.

REFERENCES

Banks, J., & Banks, C.A. (1992). *Multicultural education: Issues and perspectives* (2nd ed.). Boston: Allyn & Bacon.

Barnwell, D.A., & Day, M. (1996). Providing support to diverse families. In P.J. Beckman (Ed.), *Strategies for working with families of young children with disabilities* (pp. 47–68). Baltimore: Brookes.

Caple, F.S., Salsido, R.M. & di Cecco, J. (1995). Engaging effectively with culturally diverse families and children. *Social Work in Education, 17*(3), 159–170.

Comer, J.P. & Haynes, N.M. (1991). Parent involvement in schools: An ecological approach. *The Elementary School Journal, 91*(3), 271–277.

Correa, V.I. (1989). Involving culturally diverse families in the educational process. In S.H. Fradd & M.J. Weismantel (Eds.), *Meeting the needs of culturally and linguistically different students: A handbook for educators* (pp. 130–144). Boston: College-Hill.

Dunst, C.J., & Trivette, C.M. (1987). Enabling and empowering families: Conceptual and intervention issues. *School Psychology Review, 16*, 443–456.

Harry, B. (1992). *Cultural diversity, families, and the special education system: Communication and empowerment.* New York: Teachers College.

Harry, B., Allen, N., & McLaughlin, M. (1995). Communication versus compliance: African American parents' involvement in special education. *Exceptional Children, 61*(4), 364–377.

Hyun, J.K., & Fowler, S.A. (1995). Respect, cultural sensitivity, and communication: Promoting participation by Asian families in the Individualized Family Service Plan. *Teaching Exceptional Children, 28*(1), 25–28.

Kalyanpur, M. & Harry, B. (1997). A posture of reciprocity: A practical approach to collaboration between professionals and parents of culturally diverse backgrounds. *Journal of Child and Family Studies, 6*(4), 485–509.

Kalyanpur, M. & Rao, S.S. (1991). Empowering low-income, black families of handicapped children. *American Journal of Orthopsychiatry, 61*, 523–532.

Linan-Thompson, S. & Jean, R.E. (1997). Completing the parent participation puzzle: Accepting diversity. *Teaching Exceptional Children, 52*(6), 46–50.

Lynch, E.W. & Hanson, M.J. (1992). Developing cross-cultural competence: A guide for working with young children and their families. Baltimore: Brookes.

Mardiros, M. (1989). Conception of childhood disability among Mexican-American parents. *Medical Anthropology, 12*, 55–68.

Rueda, R. & Martinez, I (1994). Fiesta educativa: One community's approach to parent training in developmental disabilities for Latino families. *JASH, 17*(2), 95–103.

Salend, S.J. & Taylor, L. (1993). Working with families: A cross-cultural perspective. *Remedial and Special Education, 14*(5), 25–32.

Tharp, R.G. & Gallimore, R. (1988). *Rousing minds to life: Teaching, learning and schooling in social context.* Cambridge, UK: Cambridge University Press.

Thorp, E.K. (1997). Increasing opportunities for partnership with culturally and linguistically diverse families. *Intervention in School and Clinic, 32*(5), 261–269.

Turnbull, A.P. & Turnbull, H.R. (1997). *Families, professionals, and exceptionality: A special partnership* (3rd ed.). Upper Saddle River, NJ: Merrill.

Ware, L.P. (1994). Contextual barriers to collaboration. *Journal of Educational and Psychological Consultation, 5*(4), 339–357.

See also **Family Counseling**

CULTURALLY/LINGUISTICALLY DIVERSE STUDENTS, REPRESENTATION OF

Special educators have debated for decades about the disproportionate representation of ethnic and linguistic minority students in special and gifted education programs. This phenomenon refers to unequal proportions of culturally diverse students in these special programs. Two patterns are associated with disproportionality, namely over- and underrepresentation of minority students. The former tends to occur in special education; specifically, in the mild disability categories—i.e., mild mental retardation (MMR), specific learning disabilities (SLD), and serious emotional disturbances (SED). Underrepresentation is generally observed in programs for students with gifts and talents (G&T). Historically, certain ethnic minority groups (particularly African American) and poor and male students have been most affected by disproportionality.

Litigation (particularly placement bias cases) has been at the center of disproportionality discussions. For instance, some of the most important rulings in *Diana v. California Board of Education* (1970) and *Larry P. v. Riles* (1979) (which involved Latino and African American students respectively) included (a) intelligence tests were culturally and linguistically biased, (b) biased assessment resulted in the overrepresentation of Latino and African American students in MMR programs, (c) alternative procedures were needed to assess students' abilities (e.g., nonverbal tests, assessment in native language), and (d) many students needed to be retested and reclassified. These cases were very influential in the passage of federal legislation designed to protect the rights of individuals with disabilities, specifically in the inclusion of a requirement that identification and assessment procedures must be nondiscriminatory.

DISPROPORTIONALITY: PATTERNS AND CAVEATS

Formulas to estimate disproportionality typically aim to answer two questions: (a) "What proportion of students in a special education program is [say, Black]?" and (b) "What percent of the [Black] population is placed in a special education program?" (Reschly, 1997). The former is called the percent of program by group, and is calculated by contrasting the proportion of a particular ethnic group in the general education student population with the percentage of the same group of students enrolled in a special education program. The latter question is concerned with the percent of group in program. This figure is obtained by calculating the percent of, say, the Latino population that is enrolled in a special education program.

The percent of program by group is usually larger than the percent of group in program. To illustrate, Table 4 presents national enrollment data using both formulas on three ethnic groups at four points in time. These data suggest that Black students are overrepresented in MR and SED programs whereas Latinos are not overrepresented in any of the mild disability categories. A closer look at the total percent

Table 4 Percent of Mild Disability Program by Ethnic Group (A) and Percent of Ethnic Group in Mild Disability Program (B), 1986–1994

	1986[a]						1990[b]						1992[c]					
	Black (16)*		Latino (10)		White (70)		Black (16)		Latino (12)		White (68)		Black (16)		Latino (12)		White (67)	
	A	B	A	B	A	B	A	B	A	B	A	B	A	B	A	B	A	B
MMR**	35	2.30	5	0.56	58	0.87	35	2.10	8	0.65	56	0.81	32	1.62	5	0.39	61	0.75
SLD	17	4.43	10	4.31	71	4.29	17	4.95	11	4.68	70	4.97	18	5.79	12	5.29	68	5.32
SED	27	1.04	7	0.46	65	0.57	22	0.89	6	0.33	71	0.69	24	1.02	7	0.41	67	0.70
Total	—	7.77	—	5.33	—	5.73	—	7.94	—	5.66	—	6.47	—	8.43	—	6.09	—	6.77

[a,b] The data in the A columns are from Harry (1994) as presented in Reschly (1997, p. 54). The data in the B columns were obtained from Reschly (1997, p. 55).
[c] These data were obtained from USDOE (1997) (Table I-5, p. I-43).
[d] These date were obtained from OCR (1997, p. 1) (Revised data, July 22, 1997).
* Numbers in parenthesis are percents of the total student population.
A = percent of mild disability program by ethnic group; B = Percent of ethnic group in mild disability program.
**MMR = Mild mental retardation; SLD = Specific learning disabilities; SED = Serious emotional disturbances.
†The consulted 1994 OCR table (revised on July 22, 1997) only reported data for the whole mental retardation category.

of ethnic group in mild disability program data presented in the B columns suggests that the difference between Black and White students with mild disabilities declined from 1986 to 1990 but it has been increasing in the 1990s. Such differences were 2.04 (1986), 1.47 (1990), 1.66 (1992), and 1.77 (1994).

Interestingly, somewhat distinct patterns emerge when we disaggregate the data by disability category to examine Black/White differences in the 1986–1994 period. On the one hand, with the exception of 1994, Black/White differences decreased across time in the MR category (i.e., 1.43, 1.29, 0.87, and 1.40 respectively). However, similar to the national data, Black/White differences in the SED category decreased from 1986 to 1990 but it has increased in the 1990s—i.e., it was 0.47 in 1986, 0.20 in 1990, 0.32 in 1992, and 0.36 in 1994. It seems, therefore, that African Americans continue to be overrepresented in mild disability programs and that Black/White differences are increasing in the present decade.

CAUSES OF DISPROPORTIONATE REPRESENTATION

The most widely used explanation of this problem is based on the deficit thinking that has characterized theories about minority students' educational performance (Trent, Artiles, & Englert, in press): It has been concluded that many of these students lack the abilities and skills needed to succeed in the general educational system; hence, they need to receive specialized services. The most favored argument to explain minority students' deficits is the nefarious effects of poverty which is rampant among these groups. Because of their higher levels of poverty, the argument follows, we should expect a higher incidence of negative developmental outcomes (e.g., disabilities) among these groups. In this vein, research has linked poverty to placement in special education; however, we need more inquiries to understand (a) the complex nature of this association, (b) minorities' resilience to the negative effects of poverty, and (c) the role of structural factors in the production of higher rates of poverty among minority groups.

An alternative position posits that deficit explanations oversimplify this complex problem by blaming the student and disregarding the significant impact of contextual, technical, structural, and ideological factors. For example, a critical technical factor is related to the procedures used in the special education field. A case in point is the variability in the operationalization and implementation of eligibility and placement criteria: Analyses of the 1996 and 1997 US-DOE reports to Congress indicate that students served in SED programs in Mississippi and Connecticut differ by a factor of 41 and 33 respectively. Similar, though less dramatic, variability patterns are observed in the MMR and SED categories (MacMillan & Reschly, 2000, USDOE, 1997). Also, such patterns seem to vary according to school location. For example, it has been found that the psychometric profiles of students with LD in urban and suburban schools differ to the point that many identified students in urban schools did not fit the established eligibility criteria for LD (e.g., in terms of ability levels) (Gottlieb, Alter, Gottlieb, & Wishner, 1994).

Another factor that complicates disproportionality analyses is our limited understanding of the role of culture in human development. For instance, an analysis of 22 years of research in four major special education journals showed a paucity of studies on ethnic minority students, a narrow scope of research topics, and a disregard for potential interactions between sociocultural variables (e.g., ethnicity and language, gender, or social class) (Artiles, Trent, & Kuan, 1997). How, then, can educators discern the influence of language, cognitions, social class, and ethnicity on students' competence and performance? How can educators make decisions about students' competence based on culturally-insensitive criteria? Indeed, this paucity of knowledge has enormous implications for the identification of students' needs and the provision of adequate educational services.

Other factors could impinge upon this predicament, though they have received scant attention by the research community. For instance, we need to investigate how disproportionality can be exacerbated, masked, or reduced in distinct contexts by (a) the quality of the instructional context, (b) the role of racism and discrimination, (c) the dismissal of alternative ways of knowing in the design and implementation of school rules, curricula, assessment practices, and expectations, (d) the inattention to the influence of sociocultural variables in researchers' labor (e.g., investigators' beliefs or values about cultural diversity), (e) the disregard for within-cultural-group variability, (f) the failure to include minority students' perspectives in investigations, and (g) the availability of alternative services (e.g., prereferral, bilingual education, and Chapter 1 programs).

REFERENCES

Artiles, A.J., Trent, S.C., & Kuan, L.A. (1997). Learning disabilities research on ethnic minority students: An analysis of 22 years of studies published in selected refereed journals. *Learning Disabilities Research & Practice, 12*, 82–91.

Gottlieb, J., Alter, M., Gottlieb, B.W., & Wishner, J. (1994). Special education in urban America: It's not justifiable for many. *The Journal of Special Education, 27*, 453–465.

MacMillan, D., & Reschly, D.J. (2000). Overrepresentation of minority students: The case for greater specificity or reconsideration of the variables examined. *The Journal of Special Education.*

Reschly, D.J. (1997). *Disproportionate minority representation in general and special education: Patterns, issues, and alternatives.* Des Moines, IA: Iowa Department of Education.

Trent, S.C., Artiles, A.J., & Englert, C.S. (in press). From deficit thinking to social constructivism: A review of special education theory, research and practice. *Review of Research in Education.*

CULTURAL PERSPECTIVES ON BEHAVIORAL DISORDERS

Children with behavioral disorders constitute one of the major national issues confronting the schools and society.

There is increasing concern about the academic failure and school dropout rate of U.S. children and adolescents identified with behavioral disorders (BD). Observation, diagnosis, and intervention strategies for these students are poorly defined nationally (Sabatino, 1987). The current definition of BD may encourage the underidentification of students with behavioral disorders from the entire school-age population, while promoting an overrepresentation of students identified as BD from culturally diverse groups (Algozzine, Ruhl, & Ramsey, 1991). The rates of identification, placement, and achievement of children and adolescents with BD are strongly correlated with gender, race, and other cultural dimensions. However, these issues are often neglected in our educational system (Singh, Oswald, Wechsler, & Curtis, 1997).

The public school system needs to continue to move away from a cultural deficit model to a cultural difference model. A cultural difference model accepts that the cognitive, learning, and motivational styles of students are different from those often expected by the teacher, who is usually from the dominant culture (Singh et al., 1997) while a cultural deficit model uses the culture as the explanation for school failures. The idea that all students should assimilate and fit into the majority culture has been successfully challenged by the concept of cultural pluralism.

The United States is becoming a country where minority groups are becoming the majority (Robinson & Bradley, 1997). These demographic changes require adaptations in assessment and teaching in our public schools. Current trends lead to an overrepresentation of culturally diverse students being misidentified as emotionally or behaviorally disordered. In most cases, culturally divergent behaviors can be respected (McIntyre, 1996). Acknowledging culture as a predominant factor in shaping behaviors and values and respecting culturally defined traits will yield a more productive learning and teaching environment for culturally diverse students, students with BD, and teachers. This change also should result in more accurate identification of all students and more appropriate support for students who have BD, and it potentially will decrease the misdiagnosis of culturally diverse students (Singh et al., 1997).

REFERENCES

Algozzine, B., Ruhl, K., & Ramsey, R. (1991). *Behaviorally disordered? Assessment for identification and instruction.* Reston, VA: The Council for Exceptional Children.

McIntyre, T. (1996). Guidelines for providing appropriate services to culturally diverse students with emotional and/or behavioral disorders. *Behavioral Disorders, 21*(2), 137–144.

Robinson, B., & Bradley, L.J. (1997). Multicultural training for undergraduates: Developing knowledge and awareness. *Journal of Multicultural Counseling and Development, 25*(4), 281–289.

Sabatino, D.A. (1987). Behavior disorders. In C.R. Reynolds & Lester Mann (Eds.), *The Encyclopedia of Special Education* (Vol. 1). New York: Wiley.

Singh, N.N., Ellis, C.R., Oswald, D.P., Wechsler, H.A., & Curtis, W.J. (1997). Value and address diversity. *Journal of Emotional and Behavioral Disorders, 5*(1), 24–35.

CURRICULUM

Educational curriculum is what students learn, or the content of instruction. Historically, the curriculum of U.S. public education was specified in broad, global terms, addressing abstract notions such as Americanization and instilling of democratic values in youths (Mulhern, 1959). In the twentieth century, however, developments in learning theory such as Thorndike's demonstration of the specificity of transfer promoted a reconceptualization of learning from concurrent strengthening of global faculties to sequential mastery of numerous, definite, and particularized skills and knowledge (Fuchs & Deno, 1982). This reconceptualization has led to alternative ways of specifying school curricula for distinct behavioral outcomes (Bloom, Hastings, & Madaus, 1971). Current curriculum statements typically represent carefully sequenced, calibrated, and organized sets of tasks, regularly called objectives (Johnson, 1967).

In special education, as in regular education, curriculum is derived from an analysis of the needs of society. This analysis, however, renders considerably different instructional focuses for mildly and severely handicapped students. For the mildly handicapped, analysis of the needs of society results in a curriculum similar, if not identical, to that of normally developing pupils; it includes curricular tasks such as reading, writing, and mathematics. For the more severely handicapped, this analysis results in a curriculum that addresses basic survival skill requirements. These alternative educational focuses often are referred to as developmental curriculum (which identifies tasks for normally performing children) (Snell, 1983) and functional curriculum (which addresses skills necessary for ultimate attainment of self-sufficiency) (Holvoet, Guess, Mulligan, & Brown, 1980).

REFERENCES

Bloom, B.S., Hastings, J.T., & Madaus, G.F. (1981). *Handbook on formative and summative evaluation of student learning.* New York: McGraw-Hill.

Fuchs, L.S., & Deno, S.L. (1982). *Developing goals and objectives for educational programs.* Washington, DC: American Association of Colleges for Teacher Education.

Holvoet, J., Guess, D., Mulligan, M., & Brown, F. (1980). The Individualized Curriculum Sequencing model (II): A teaching strategy for severely handicapped students. *Journal of the Association for the Severely Handicapped, 5,* 337–351.

Johnson, M. (1967). Definitions and models in curriculum theory. *Educational Theory, 7,* 127–140.

Mulhern, J. (1959). *A history of education* (2nd ed.). New York: Ronald.

Snell, M.E. (1983). *Systematic instruction of the moderately and severely handicapped* (2nd ed.). Columbus, OH: Merrill.

***See also* Curriculum for the Mildly Handicapped; Curriculum for the Severely Handicapped**

CURRICULUM, AGE APPROPRIATE

See AGE APPROPRIATE CURRICULUM.

CURRICULUM-BASED ASSESSMENT (CBA)

Curriculum-based assessment (CBA) uses instructional materials and course content as the basis for testing. According to Shinn and Good, the prominence of CBA has grown in the last 10 years and within the last five years entire volumes of journals have been devoted to CBA (1993).

As an alternative to commercial norm-referenced tests, CBA addresses at least the last two problems (Fuchs, 1986). With CBA, student's programmatic objectives are matched with measurement procedures. Alternative test forms are drawn directly from curricula specified in objectives and are administered repeatedly. Student progress data are evaluated with reference to the performance criteria specified in objectives and with respect to classroom peer's progress within the same curriculum. To ensure effective instructional programs and attainment of objectives, individualized programs are tested carefully and modified over time as required.

The following set of assumptions provide the basis for CBA: (1) the instructional and curricular validity of CBA is stronger than with traditional assessment methods, (2) each student's needs are defined best in terms of the context of local educational programs, (3) the essential measure of educational success is the student's progress in the school's curriculum, and (4) the appropriate reference group with which to judge the adequacy of students' rates of curricular progress is their local school district peers' progress through the same material (Deno, 1985).

Research indicates that at least some forms of ongoing CBA can be used effectively to address several different assessment functions. It can be used reliably to identify students in need of special education (Marston, Tindal, & Deno, 1984; Tindal & Marston, 1986), to clearly demarcate the criteria for entering special education (Shapiro, 1993), to specify target skills for students and write useful individual education program goals and objectives (Fuchs, Deno, & Mirkin, 1984), to monitor pupil progress toward goals and formatively develop effective instructional programs, and to evaluate the effectiveness of special education programs on an individual and district-wide basis (Tindal & Marston, 1986).

REFERENCES

Deno, S.L. (1985). Curriculum-based measurement: The emerging alternative. *Exceptional Children, 52,* 219–232.

Fuchs, L.S. (1986). Monitoring progress among mildly handicapped pupils: Review of current practice and research. *Remedial & Special Education, 7,* 5–12.

Fuchs, L.S., Deno, S.L., & Mirkin, P.K. (1984). The effects of frequent curriculum-based measurement and evaluation on pedagogy, student achievement and student awareness of learning. *American Educational Research Journal, 21,* 449–460.

Martson, D., Tindal, G., & Deno, S.L. (1984). Eligibility for learning disability services: A direct and repeated measurement approach. *Exceptional Children, 50,* 554–555.

Shapiro, E.S. (1993). Curriculum-Based Assessment: Implications for psychoeducational practice. In J.J. Kramer (Ed.), *Curriculum based measurement* (pp. 123–138). Lincoln, NE: Buros Institute of Mental Measurements.

Tindal, G., & Martson, D. (1986). Approaches to assessment. In J. Torgeson & B. Wong (Eds.), *Psychological and educational perspectives on learning disabilities.* Orlando, FL: Academic.

See also **Age-Appropriate Curriculum; Assessment; Norm-Referenced Testing**

CURRICULUM FOR STUDENTS WITH MILD DISABILITIES IN SPECIAL EDUCATION

Special education curriculum for the mildly handicapped learner consists of learning tasks, activities, or assignments that are directed toward increasing a student's knowledge or skills in a specific content or subject area. It is the special educator's task to identify the differences between the regular and special education curriculum and to make educational decisions based on available assessment data.

The decision to provide variation in content may be less significant in educating mildly handicapped learners than the decision to provide variation in the conditions under which learning can be best facilitated. A critical issue involves the determination of the need for compensatory versus remedial curricula (Case, 1975). Many of the strategies and techniques used with mildly handicapped learners in special education overlap with Chapter I, other remedial programs, and regular education.

Mainstreaming has encouraged efforts to help the over 70% of special education students who spend at least part of the day in regular classrooms to master the regular curriculum or "face curricular isolationism" (O'Connell-Mason & Raison, 1982).

Howell, Kaplan, and O'Connell (1979) indicate that to date, the research has not demonstrated the superiority of one type of curriculum modification over another. However, there are a number of general types of modifications that have been found useful: (1) eliminate or reduce the subjects in the student's curriculum; (2) develop or identify an alternative curriculum; (3) alter expectations for the quantity or quality of work; (4) teach subject matter more slowly; (5) teach only the most essential subject matter; (6) develop a parallel curriculum; (7) provide a supplemented curriculum; or (8) adjust materials and/or response modes.

Growth in the field of special education curriculum for the mildly handicapped learner has become an integral part of regular education. It is clear that the similarities are greater than the differences. The same principles and procedures, with some modifications, can be used to instruct all children. All children can reach their potential given the opportunity, effective teaching, and proper resources (Berdine & Blackhurst, 1985).

REFERENCES

Berdine, W.H., & Blackhurst, A.E. (1985). *An introduction to special education.* Boston: Little, Brown.

Case, R. (1975). Gearing the demands of instruction to the developmental capacities of the learner. *Review of Educational Research, 45,* 3–9.

Howell, K.W., Kaplan, J.S., & O'Connell, C.Y. (1979). *Evaluating exceptional children: A task analysis approach.* Columbus, OH: Merrill.

O'Connell-Mason, C., & Raison, S.B. (1982). *Curriculum assessment and modification.* Washington, DC: American Association of Colleges for Teacher Education.

See also **Age-Appropriate Curriculum; Mainstreaming; Task Analysis**

CURRICULUM FOR STUDENTS WITH SEVERE DISABILITIES

In special education, as in regular education, curriculum is derived from an analysis of the needs of society. For the severely handicapped individual, this analysis results in curriculum that addresses basic survival skill requirements. This educational focus, which represents an alternative to the normal or developmental educational curriculum (Snell, 1983), is referred to as a functional curriculum. The basic assumptions of a functional curriculum for the severely handicapped are that the school's responsibility is to teach skills that optimize a person's independent and responsible functioning in society (Hawkins & Hawkins, 1981) and that, for the severely handicapped, these skills must be chosen from a group of tasks and activities that have a high probability of being required and that increase self-sufficiency (Brown et al., 1979).

This functional curriculum is determined individually and addresses objectives that (1) represent practical or functional skills most likely to be needed currently or in the near future; (2) are suitable for the student's chronological age; (3) address the pupil's current performance levels and are reasonably thought to be attainable; and (4) span four instructional domains (Snell, 1983).

The four domains of instructional content are domestic, leisure/recreational, community, and vocational. The domestic domain includes skills performed in and around the home, including self-care, clothing care, housekeeping, cooking, and yard work. In the leisure-recreational domain are skills needed to engage in spectator or participant activities performed for self-pleasure. Skills required in the community domain include street crossing, using public transportation, shopping, eating in restaurants, and using other public facilities such as parks. The vocational domain addresses skills necessary for employment such as appropriate work dress and demeanor, assembly line behavior, in-

terviewing for jobs, completing work applications, and punctuality.

The process of determining appropriate functional curricula on an individual basis has been conceptualized as comprising five steps (Brown et al., 1979): (1) selecting curriculum domains; (2) identifying and surveying current and future natural environments; (3) dividing the relevant environments into subenvironments; (4) inventorying these subenvironments for the relevant activities performed there; and (5) examining the activities to isolate the skills required for their performance.

To address the functional curriculum for the severely handicapped, instructional strategies typically have been based on behavioral methodology. The instructional process begins with a descriptive analysis of the environmental events subsequent to, antecedent to, or during recurring behavioral events, with the purpose of identifying possible discriminative and reinforcing stimuli. Then, a task analysis of terminal objectives is conducted; in it subskills necessary for successful mastery of the final objectives are identified. Next, subskill instructional objectives are established and initial teaching strategies are specified. Then ongoing assessments of pupils' progress toward goals are collected as the instructional hypothesis is implemented. Finally, ongoing assessment data are evaluated and employed formatively to redesign instructional procedures in order to increase the probability of goal attainment.

REFERENCES

Brown, L., Branston, M.B., Hamre-Nietupski, S., Pumpian, I., Certo, N., & Gruenewald, L. (1979). A strategy for developing chronological age appropriate and functional curricular content for severely handicapped adolescents and young adults. *Journal of Special Education, 13,* 81–90.

Hawkins, R.P., & Hawkins, K.K. (1981). Parental observation on the education of severely retarded children: Can it be done in the classroom? *Analysis & Intervention in Developmental Disabilities, 1,* 13–22.

Johnson, M. (1967). Definitions and models in curriculum theory. *Educational Theory, 7,* 127–140.

Snell, M.E. (1983). *Systematic instruction of the moderately and severely handicapped* (2nd ed.). Columbus, OH: Merrill.

See also **Curriculum; Curriculum for the Mildly Handicapped; Functional Instruction; Functional Skills**

CURRICULUM IN EARLY CHILDHOOD INTERVENTION

The curricula used in early intervention vary depending on the needs of the children served. Generally, however, they address developmental areas critical to the child's psychological/behavioral maturation and later school success (Bailey & Wolery, 1984). Early intervention curricula are likely to emphasize motor, cognitive, language, social, and self-help skill development. Early intervention instructors will likely address the development of gross and fine motor skills, eating and self-help skills, toileting, dressing, and undressing. A distinction has been made between developmental and functional approaches in early childhood curricula. The first emphasizes developmental progress; the second is more concerned with training for independent functioning (Bailey & Wolery, 1984).

The purposes of early intervention curricula are to develop, habilitate, or accelerate young children's development. In the case of handicapped children, the intent is to minimize the effects of children's disabilities on later development and learning and academic performance. With mildly to moderately handicapped children, early curriculum is more likely to emphasize developmental training. With more severely handicapped children, the emphasis is likely to be on functional training, for example, facilitating independent functioning.

REFERENCES

Bailey, D.B., Jr., & Wolery, M. (1984). *Teaching infants and preschoolers with handicaps.* Columbus, OH: Merrill.

See also Early Identification of Handicapped Children; Preschool Assessment; Preschool Special Education

CUSTODIAL CARE OF THE HANDICAPPED

Organized care for the handicapped goes back no more than 150 years. If we consider the handicapped to include the insane, mentally infirm, orphans, the poor, and those found to be criminal in nature, then we can easily locate the second American Revolution as during the Jackson presidency (Rothman, 1971). Prior to this period, care of handicapped individuals was managed primarily by families, neighbors, and friends of the handicapped. In the case of criminals, the offenders were put to death.

It was not until the late 1800s that the mentally retarded were beginning to be seen as a group separate, at least in name, from other of society's deviant groups. There is reason to suspect that the mentally retarded had often been punished severely and in some instances hanged for criminal activities beyond their comprehension. The first institutions constructed solely for the mentally retarded seem to have been built for educational purposes. These temporary boarding school-type facilities were established primarily for the "improvables." The schools rejected admittance to those who could not be cured and returned to their families. Even the famed Fernald State School sought to create an institution that would not serve uncurables. When the effort to educate the mentally retarded and return them to society failed, retarded individuals' care deteriorated. The retarded were viewed as subhuman and unable to be taught productive skills. The failure was probably due to the unrealistically high expectations of complete recovery.

The perception of failure and disappointment prevailed after these early attempts at cure failed. Along with this perception came a dramatic change in the care of retarded individuals. People that had the potential to be developmentally changed were treated accordingly, while those thought of as having subhuman qualities were treated as animals.

In the early 1900s perceptions of the mentally retarded again changed and custodial care was said to have deteriorated. The moron and imbecile were soon made the source of all social ills. Leaders in the field such as M.W. Barr, a past president of the American Association for Mental Deficiency (AAMD), issued indictments of imbeciles as a threat to home and community. Calling for action, Johnson (1901) spoke bluntly when he stated that in order to prevent the propagation of idiocy and imbecility it might be "necessary to kill them or to resort to the knife" (Kugel & Shearer, 1976, p. 57). With attitudes such as these, it is little wonder that retarded individuals received deplorable care for the next 50 years.

The severely retarded were gradually dehumanized and moved to the back wards. These wards as well as other asylum cells were filthy and overcrowded. Such facilities were often referred to as the land of the living dead. In the fall of 1965 Senator Robert Kennedy visited several of his state's institutions; he was appalled at the conditions he encountered. Additional investigations by Blatt (1970) further delineated the horrors: "in toilets, I frequently saw urinals ripped out, sinks broken and toilet bowls backed up . . . I found incredible overcrowding" (p. 13). The national average cost of caring for the mentally retarded in 1962 was less than $5 per day per patient. Some states managed to lower that to less than $2.50 per day.

Blatt (1970) further described conditions in several institutions. He saw 7 foot by 7 foot isolation cells that seldom included beds, washstands, or toilets. Restraints were common. There were alarming shortages of staff and one supervisor for each 100 severely retarded individuals was not uncommon. It is small wonder that patients were locked up, restrained, or sedated. The odors of the wards and dayrooms were overpowering even though rooms were hosed down daily to move the human excretions to sewers located in the center of the rooms.

Blatt's (1966) photographic essay, "Christmas in Purgatory" did much to alert professionals and the general public to the deplorable conditions existing for the institutionalized retarded. Those pictures of the stark gray, high walls, barred windows, beds pushed head to head, patients lying unclothed in feces, and rooms full of young children, left their mark. The ensuing years have seen a movement away from those custodial conditions. Even in the 1960s, many institutions such as the Seaside, also chronicled by Blatt, were providing residential treatment that encouraged more and better trained staff, family participation, fewer closed wards, sunlit areas, medical and dental attention, and daily hygienic care. Within the last 20 years, the mentally retarded have been part of a deinstitutionalization movement unlike that of any era in U.S. history. Residential homes for the handicapped are commonplace and the U.S. educational system now provides especially designed curricula to teach basic independent living skills. In addition, government-supported projects have proliferated throughout the United States and now include not only programs for assessment and training but opportunities in employment that were nonexistent only a few years ago.

REFERENCES

Blatt, B., & Kaplan, F. (1966). *Christmas in purgatory.* Boston: Allyn & Bacon.

Blatt, B. (1970). *Exodus from pandemonium.* Boston: Allyn & Bacon.

Kugel, R.B., & Shearer, A. (Eds.). (1976). *Changing patterns in residential services for the mentally retarded.* Washington, DC: President's Committee on Mental Retardation.

Rothman, D.J. (1971). *The discovery of the asylum.* Boston: Little, Brown.

See also **Deinstitutionalization; Institutionalization**

CYLERT

Cylert (Pemoline) is a mild central nervous system stimulant medication that is used in the management of hyperactive children. While the onset of effectiveness of Cylert has been found to be slower than that of some other central nervous system stimulants, it also has been found to have a longer half-life, 12 hours compared with 4 hours for other stimulants (Ross & Ross, 1982). Because of this longer half-life, Cylert need be administered only on a once daily basis. For hyperactive children, this eliminates the social stigma associated with taking medication at school. In addition, parents are better able to supervise drug administration, thereby reducing the possibility of drug abuse and increasing the probability of compliance. Another advantage of Cylert therapy over other psychostimulants in pediatric populations is its long duration of therapeutic action without sympathomimetic cardiovascular effects. In fact, therapeutic effects of Cylert have been found to be similar to those of amphetamines and methylphenidate (Ross & Ross, 1982). Clinical trials have yielded data to indicate that Cylert enhances short-term memory, attentiveness to cognitive and academic tasks, and social functioning (Ross & Ross, 1982).

As with other psychostimulants, one concern with Cylert administration has been the occurrence of side effects. While mild side effects, including insomnia, headaches, anorexia, abdominal pains, dizziness, and nausea have been reported, of greater concern is the elevation of liver enzymes, which must be regularly checked, and sometimes necessitates the withdrawal of medication. Indeed, there have been deaths associated with poor monitoring of liver functioning. Severe dysphoric effects following the cessation of Cylert also have been reported in some isolated cases (Brown, Borden, Spunt, & Medenis, 1985).

REFERENCES

Brown, R.T., Borden, K.A., Spunt, A.L., & Medenis, R. (1985). Depression following Pemoline withdrawal in a hyperactive child. *Clinical Pediatrics, 24,* 174.

Ross, D.M., & Ross, S.A. (1982). *Hyperactivity: Current issues, research and theory* (2nd ed.). New York: Wiley-Interscience.

See also **Hyperactivity; Medical Management**

CYSTIC FIBROSIS

Cystic fibrosis is a fatal genetic disorder that involves almost all organ systems. Pulmonary infection and obstruction generally cause most of the complications and are ultimately the cause of death (Doershuk & Stern, 1982). Repeated hospitalizations and crises, financial burdens, as well as the fatal nature of the disease itself, have an extreme emotional impact on the child and his or her family. Parents must deal with the anxiety, depression, and self-blame associated with having a terminally ill child with an illness that is genetically determined.

Frequent hospitalizations along with physical difficulties such as chronic cough, clubbed fingertips, shortness of breath, and short stature clearly set the cystic fibrosis child apart from his or her peers. Although the disease apparently has little effect on intellectual functioning, the child may fall behind his or her peers academically if home instruction is not instituted during absences from school. Adolescence may be a particularly difficult period for both child and parents. The increasingly debilitating nature of the disease may thwart the child's natural striving for independence and make planning for the future difficult (Wright, Schaefer, & Solomons, 1979).

REFERENCES

Doershuk, C.F., & Stern, R.C. (1982). Cystic fibrosis. In S.S. Gellis & B.M. Kagan (Eds.), *Current pediatric therapy* (Vol. 10, pp. 207–218). Philadelphia: Saunders.

Wright, L., Schaefer, A.B., & Solomons, G. (1979). *Encyclopedia of pediatric psychology.* Baltimore, MD: University Park Press.

See also **Adapted Physical Education; Cystic Fibrosis Foundation; Health Maintenance Procedures**

CYSTIC FIBROSIS FOUNDATION

The Cystic Fibrosis Foundation is a voluntary, nonprofit health organization that actively supports research and treatment for cystic fibrosis. Founded in 1955 by a small group of parents of children with cystic fibrosis, it was originally conceived to raise money for research to find a cure and improve the quality of life for individuals with the disease. With the help of more than 250,000 volunteers operating in 65 chapters and branch offices across the United States, the organization depends on public support to implement its programs.

The Foundation actively supports the advancement of medical science by funding research centers at leading universities and medical centers throughout the United States and providing a variety of grants to scientists for research on the disease. It also offers comprehensive diagnosis and treatment for people with cystic fibrosis through a nationwide network of 113 cystic fibrosis care centers. In addition to the research, diagnostic, and treatment services provided, the centers also offer professional medical education and training and conduct clinical trials testing new drug therapies. The Therapeutic Development Program, which provides matching funds to biotechnology companies to stimulate development of new therapies, furnishes the infrastructure needed to conduct these clinical trials in the early phases.

Information on a variety of subjects related to cystic fibrosis, including updates on research, clinical trials, public policy issues, and ways to become involved with the Cystic Fibrosis Foundation may be obtained through its web site at www.cff.org. The Foundation may be contacted at its national offices at 6931 Arlington Road, Bethesda, MD 20814, by telephone at (800) FIGHTCF, (301) 951-4422, or fax at (301) 951-6378.

CYTOMEGALOVIRUS

The cytomegalovirus is a filterable DNA virus in the family of herpes viruses. It is responsible for the infectious disease known as cytomegalic inclusion disease. The virus is not easily eliminated and persists in host tissues for months, years, or even a lifetime. It produces a chronic infection with a variable incubation period, outcome, and course. The infection may be a significant form of congenital disease in newborns whose immune system is incompletely developed or in adults who are immunosuppressed.

There are two patterns of infection: localized and gener-

alized. In the localized form, inclusion bodies are found only in the salivary glands; this clinical entity sometimes is referred to as generalized salivary gland disease. The second, generalized, form is represented in two principal types: that accompanied by necrotizing and calcifying encephalitis and that associated with enlargement of the spleen and the liver, lymphadenopathy, and blood dyscrasias. There is increasing recognition of the association of this infection with acquired immune deficiency syndrome (AIDS). Where there is significant cerebral damage, there is often ocular involvement.

It is generally agreed that the virus is widespread; the localized form of the disease is both frequent in occurrence and asymptomatic. Ten to thirty-two percent of autopsied infants show evidence of localized disease. Although the generalized form of the disease may occur in adults, it is characteristically seen in infants and children, occurring in up to 1% of children. Cytomegalovirus has been detected in up to 90% of immunosuppressed kidney transplant patients; active infection may predispose these patients to bacterial superinfection and transplant rejection. The virus also alters the immune system, although apparently only during the acute phase of infection; the mechanism for immunosuppression is not fully understood.

The diagnosis is best established by recovery of the virus from the urine, saliva, or aqueous humor of the eye. Congenital toxoplasmosis is difficult to differentiate, but radiologic evidence of periventricular calcification suggests cytomegalic inclusion disease. Other diseases to be differentiated include generalized bacterial infection, herpes simplex encephalitis, congenital liver deformities, and diseases of the reticuloendothelial system. No treatment has been effective in controlling this disease. Several antiviral medications used to control the herpes virus have been tried with minimal success.

See also **Herpes**

D

DAILY LIVING SKILLS

The term daily living skills refers to those skills that individuals use in their personal self-care and occasionally in their interactions with others. A wide range of specific behaviors may be included under each of these headings. The skills might appear to be very straightforward (e.g., grasping a

brush handle) or extremely complex (e.g., developing healthy eating habits). The range of skills and behaviors that are often included under the rubric of daily living skills is best conceptualized as points along a continuum. At one end of the continuum essential daily living skills might include toileting, feeding, and dressing. Moving along the continuum toward increasing independence, a second level of skills could include hand washing, toothbrushing, etc. Daily living skills that might be taught at a higher level of independence include menstrual hygiene, shaving, and other more complex tasks.

Nonexceptional children typically learn these skills (as a matter of course) through the instruction and modeling of parents, siblings, and peers, and through their own natural exploration of their environment. The exceptional child, however, often has handicaps that impair his or her ability to observe, explore, internalize, and use the skills that might otherwise be acquired. Physical handicaps may prevent the exceptional child from making use of information that he or she is able to absorb. The emotionally disordered child may exhibit problem behaviors that actively interfere with the learning of daily living skills. In addition, some exceptional children, notably those in institutions and segregated classrooms, may lack role models and/or access to the type of environments that allow the sort of exploration and experimentation necessary for the acquisition of daily living skills. Indeed, some environments actually discourage the development of such skills by prohibiting, in the interest of efficiency, neatness, etc., the exceptional individual from becoming involved in any aspect of his or her own care. Thus, the exceptional child often requires systematic instruction and/or various forms of environmental adaptation to enable him or her to reach the full development of potential in the area of daily living skills. As Bigge and O'Donnell (1976) have pointed out, not only is it necessary to teach exceptional children daily living skills in order to enable them to cope effectively with their present day-to-day experiences, but it is also necessary to provide them with the chance to survive in society and contribute to it. Failure to assist exceptional children in learning these skills can only result in their becoming unnecessarily dependent adults.

Owing to the complexity, the uniqueness of mental and physical conditions and limitations, and the variety of skills to be taught, a wide range of goals exists in the area of daily living skills. Some children may become self-reliant; others may be able to accomplish only the most basic of daily living tasks (Bigge & O'Donnell, 1976). In addition, the techniques used in teaching these skills will vary widely in accordance with the child's abilities, attention motor imitation, and verbal comprehension (Snell, 1978).

Prior to beginning training in daily living skills, there must be an initial period of assessment. At times it will be more efficient to first strengthen verbal skills, attending, and imitation. Likewise, behaviors such as those that are disruptive, aggressive, or nonresponsive may not only interfere with the teaching process but may lead to inaccurate test results and confused training methods. Thus, these behaviors are best decreased or eliminated before assessment begins. The assessment itself should produce not only a detailed analysis of existing daily living skills and needs, but also an estimate of additional factors that might affect training—current level of development and functioning in relevant areas, physical limitations, problem behaviors, and practical considerations such as accessibility of needed facilities and specialized equipment.

Once the assessment is complete, the child's individual needs can be clearly defined and appropriate goals set. A task analysis of the skill(s) to be taught can then be completed and any necessary adaptive equipment (e.g., a special spoon handle or clothing with velcro fastenings) can be obtained. Following this, the child is guided through the successive steps, with assistance being gradually cut back until the child is able to perform the task independently and across settings. The issues of generalization and maintenance are of utmost importance in the teaching of daily living skills. Teachers of exceptional students should consider, at all times, the learning characteristics of the students in conjunction with the potential for new behavior.

REFERENCES

Bigge, J.L., & O'Donnell, J.G. (1976). *Teaching individuals with physical and multiple disabilities.* Columbus, OH: Merrill.

Snell, M.E. (1978). *Systemic instruction of the moderately and severely handicapped.* Columbus, OH: Merrill.

See also Ecological Assessment; Functional Domains; Functional Skills Training

DANCE THERAPY

Dance therapy is a method by which movement is incorporated into a therapeutic or educational program. As a therapy approach, dance has been used to enhance traditional methods of medical and verbal group therapies with numerous populations, including the aged, the mentally ill, and the mentally retarded. Dance especially useful with individuals who are retarded because it does not require verbal abilities (Rogers, 1977). Benefits noted through informal observations of dance therapy programs have included improvements in general motility, speech patterns, locomotion, and social ability (Barteneiff & Lewis, 1980). Dance therapy has also resulted in reduction of muscle tension and trait anxiety (Kline et al., 1978).

Dance therapy is useful with special populations both as an adjunct to normal group verbal therapies and as a method to enhance physical, social, and educational development (Gladding, 1992).

REFERENCES

Barteneiff, I., & Lewis, D. (1980). *Body movement: Coping with the environment.* New York: Gordon & Breach.

Gladding, S.T. (1992). *Counseling as an art: The creative arts in counseling.* Alexandria, VA: American Counseling Association.

Kline, F., Burgoyne, R.W., Staples, F., Moredock, P., Snyder, V., & Ioerger, M. (1978). A report on the use of movement therapy for chronic, severely disabled outpatients. *Art Psychotherapy, 5,* 181–183.

Rogers, S.B. (1977). Contributions of dance therapy in a treatment program for retarded adolescents and adults. *Art Psychotherapy, 4,* 195–197.

See also Recreation for the Handicapped; Recreational Therapy

DANDY-WALKER SYNDROME (DWS)

DWS is a congenital anomaly that involves the formation of a large cyst in the posterior region of the brain (known as a Dandy-Walker Formation) that results in hydrocephalus and agenesis of the central region or vermis of the cerebellum (Greenspan, 1998). It is similar to Joubert Syndrome in the latter respect and has some overlapping symptoms. Etiology is unknown, but DWS is thought to be, not genetic, but related to some invasive organism, possibly cytomegalovirus. It is sometimes diagnosable via ultrasound in utero but is more likely to be detected in infancy and early childhood.

There are significant impairments associated with most cases of DWS including mental retardation of varying degrees (in about 50% of cases), nonverbal learning disabilities in higher functioning DWS patients, and many social and behavioral problems.

Specific psychoeducational recommendations cannot be made for all DWS patients due to the degree of variability in outcome. Most will require special education services, often as Other Health Impaired, but consistent assessment and modification of programming are typically necessary. The successfulness of the shunt for the hydrocephalus is crucial to a positive outcome, and the earlier the shunting takes place, the better the prognosis.

REFERENCE

Greenspan, S. (1998). Dandy-Walker syndrome. In L. Phelps (Ed.), *Health-related disorders in children and adolescents.* (pp. 219–223). Washington, DC: American Psychological Association.

DATA-BASED INSTRUCTION

Data-based instruction is a way of describing, measuring, and assessing behavior for instructional purposes. The system is based on the behavioral theories of B.F. Skinner (1938). Data-based instruction emerged from the concept of precision teaching. Precision teaching involves operationally defining behavior and measuring, recording, and assessing behavior to determine the success of an instructional program (Idol-Maestas 1983).

Lilly (1979) listed the eight basic steps of data-based instruction. The first step is to define the instructional problem in behavioral terms. The use of behavioral terms allows the teacher to pinpoint specific descriptions of behaviors that need addressing. The behavior should be defined in such a manner that anyone observing the child would be able to determine what the behavior is and when it occurs.

The second step involves assessing the problem so the teacher will have some idea of the student's present level of performance before intervention. There must be a pattern of behavior established during baseline. Therefore, one to five instances of baseline data of each behavior is required. Baseline data collected before intervention will serve as a measure of the student's progress after intervention has been implemented.

Once the behavior has been defined and baseline data collected, the next step is to state the objectives of the instructional program. What are the teacher's expectations as a result of the educational intervention? These objectives should be clear and specific. In breaking down instructional objectives into teachable components, instructional objectives may become simple and clear or complex and detailed. Therefore, some objectives may need to be broken down into small teachable steps. This process is called task analysis. In the determination of teaching-learning procedures, the teacher should determine the instructional strategies that will be used. In data-based instruction there are no specific instructional strategies that must be used. Any strategy that produces good results is acceptable. The emphasis is placed on determining the instructional objectives first; then instructional strategies and materials are selected based on the objectives.

Once the instructional program is implemented, it is very important to collect data on a continuous basis. This information is used to assess the effectiveness of the instructional program. The more often the data are collected, the more reliable and consistent the information. These data should be collected in the same manner as the baseline data to ensure appropriateness and the accuracy of the conclusions. Lilly (1977) states that it is important for the teacher to record the data so that it can be used for instructional decisions. Recording the data is done by charting the information on a graph. There are many formats used to chart data, however, the most important consideration is that the data display a visual presentation of the student's behavior for a specific amount of time.

At all times, precision teaching and data-based instruction involves "being aware of the relationship between teaching and learning, measuring student performance regularly and frequently, and analyzing the measurements to develop instructional and motivational strategies" (West, 1990).

REFERENCES

Idol-Maestas, L. (1983). *Special educator's consultation handbook.* Rockville, MD: Aspen.

Lilly, M.S. (1977). Evaluating individual education programs. In S. Torres (Ed.), *A primer on individualized education programs for handicapped children* (pp. 26–30). Reston VA: Council for Exceptional Children.

Lilly, M.S. (1979). Learning and behavior problems, current trends. In M.S. Lilly (Ed.), *Children with exceptional needs: A survey of special education.* New York: Holt, Rinehart & Winston.

Skinner, B.F. (1938). *The behavior of organisms.* New York: Appleton Century.

West, R. (1990). Precision teaching: An introduction. *Teaching Exceptional Children, 22,* 4–9.

See also **Diagnostic Prescriptive Teaching; Precision Teaching**

DAY-CARE CENTERS

Day-care programs exclusively for disabled children excluded from school began in the 1950s. Sponsored and conducted by parent groups, most were for moderately retarded children. In the 1960s the Massachusetts Department of Mental Health added a day-care program to its preschool program because many severely retarded children were excluded from schools. After implementation of PL 94-142 in 1977, school systems supported educational programs that replaced (and were often similar to) the private day-care facilities for school-age children. Then day-care services were developed for preschool- and postschool-age handicapped groups. This is noted in the American Association on Mental Deficiency's definition of day care: "extended care services provided on an ongoing basis for individuals residing in the community and not eligible for school programs or workshops; involves social, physical, recreational, and personal-care training and activity" (Grossman, 1983, p. 167).

Efforts at integrating handicapped and nonhandicapped preschool day-care programs have increased in recent years (Branca, 1988; Guralnick, 1978; 1994; 1995; Templeman, 1989). A national survey of day-care facilities for young children and infants showed that some handicapped children were eligible for integrated services. About 21% of the centers reported accepting physically and emotionally handicapped children; about 14% would accept retarded children (Coelen, Galantz, & Calore, 1979). The tendency for separation of handicapped from nonhandicapped children is still reflected in professional literature, with almost no mention of handicaps in day-care journals and books. A few booklets (e.g., Granato, 1972) offer common-sense suggestions for day-care providers working with integrated handicapped children.

Empirical studies evaluating the effects of day-care programs for handicapped children and adults are rare, but comments on scientific and social policy issues in a book by Zigler and Gordon (1982) suggest that the research trend is toward identifying factors associated with different outcomes rather than simply attempting to determine whether day care is good for children. Guralnick (1994, 1995) studied the parent's perception of early integration of exceptional preschoolers. Notwithstanding the parental concerns of peer rejection, most parents perceived positive gains for their children.

In addition, Zigler (1991, 1995) cites the 1990 Child Care and Development Act as a step towards the solutions of day/child care problems. Indeed, Zigler predicted the inclusion of integrated child care provided by the public schools and supported by parents and family. Community placements also give services for young children with severe disabilities that are successful (Branca, 1988). Best practices for the inclusion of preschoolers with moderate to profound disabilities can be found in Templeman (1989).

REFERENCES

Branca, R.A. (1988). Implementing a program of supportive services to severely handicapped preschool age children in community programs. (Eric Clearinghouse No. EC212115)

Coelen, C., Galantz, F., & Calore, D. (1979). *Day care centers in the United States: A national profile.* Cambridge, MA: Abt Associates.

Granato, S. (1972). *Day care: Serving children with special needs.* Washington, DC: U.S. Government Printing Office.

Grossman, H.J. (1983). *Classification in mental retardation.* Washington, DC: American Association on Mental Deficiency.

Guralnick, M.J. (1978). *Early intervention and the integration of handicapped and nonhandicapped children.* Baltimore, MD: University Park Press.

Guralnick, M.J. (1994). Mother's perceptions of the benefits and drawbacks of early childhood mainstreaming. *Journal of Early Intervention, 18,* 2, 168–38.

Guralnick M.J. (1995). Parent perspectives of peer relationships and friendships in integrated and specialized programs. *American Journal on Mental Retardation, 99,* 5, 457–476.

Templeman, T.P. (1989). Integration of children with moderate and severe handicaps into a daycare center. *Journal of Early Intervention, 13,* 4, 315–328.

Zigler, E.F., & Finn-Stevenson, M. (1995). The child care crisis: Implications for the growth and development of the nation's children. *Journal of Social Issues, 51,* 3, 215–231.

Zigler, E.F., & Gilman, E. (1991). Beyond academic instruction: The twenty first century school model for preschoolers. *New Directions for Child Development, 53,* 75–82.

Zigler, E.F., & Gordon, E.W. (Eds.). (1982). *Day care: Scientific and social issues.* Boston: Auburn House.

See also **Head Start; Least Restrictive Environment; Mainstreaming; Respite Care**

DAYDREAMING

The literature on daydreaming from the special educator's perspective tends to fall into three categories. In the first, daydreaming is seen as a symptom of disability. In the second, it is associated with creativity and giftedness. In the third, it is reported to be an effective therapeutic device. As a symptom of disability, daydreaming is associated with both physical and cognitive disorders. It has been suggested that a central nervous system dysfunction may cause a lag in brain structure development leading to behavior such as daydreaming that inhibits learning. Petite mal epileptic seizures are also often mistaken for daydreaming. As a result, medical screening might be appropriate for chronic daydreamers. Cognitively, Blanton (1983) and others classify daydreaming as an immature behavior—along with hyperactivity, distractibility, impulsivity, procrastination, messiness, and sloppiness—that becomes a problem in educational situations. Besides possible physiological causes, inordinate daydreaming may be due to shyness (Sheridan, Kratochwill, & Elliot, 1990), deep emotional problems, or to a student's inability to focus attention on a task for any length of time.

Suggested treatments for problem daydreaming vary as widely as suggested causes. Mock et al. (1982) found that among hyperactive students with distractible cognitive styles (characterized by daydreaming, slow response time, and high error rates), the use of Ritalin improved performance on some school-related tasks, decreasing both decision time and error rates. Practical suggestions for teachers include calling the student's attention to the task at hand in some inconspicuous way such as placing a hand on the student's paper or using physical proximity to convey expectations. Allowing students to choose activities that are inherently interesting to them also fosters prolonged attention.

Daydreaming itself has been used in a variety of ways as a clinical device. Programmed imaging, as McQueen (1983) describes it, is often used to develop skills in the psychomotor domain. Subjects practice basketball free throws in their mind's eye, for example, before going onto the court. Controlled experiments have shown this to be highly effective. Guided daydreaming, which until recently was a more common technique in Europe than in the United States, is controlled by someone who stays outside the activities of the participants. The leader, usually a teacher or therapist, talks the subjects through an experience. This is often useful for relaxation and as an aid to memory, self-awareness, and clarifying goals or realizing internal conflicts. Once a subject becomes adept at disciplined daydreaming, it can be used as a powerful tool. Therapists have reported decreased incidence of depression, phobias, and psychosomatic disorders in patients trained to use their imaginations. Neurotic or otherwise undesirable behaviors have also been modified with clinical use of imagery. One technique is to have the subjects practice substitute behaviors mentally before incorporating them into their daily activities. A more extreme method is the use of aversive imagery techniques, in which highly negative mental pictures are evoked to discourage maladaptive behaviors such as compulsive stealing (Singer, 1974).

REFERENCES

Blanton, G.H. (1983, February). *Social and emotional development of learning disabled children.* Paper presented at the annual convention of the Association for Children and Adults with Learning Disabilities, Washington, DC. (ERIC Document Reproduction Service No. ED 232 336)

McQueen, D. (1983, March). *Imaging as a heuristic.* Paper presented at the annual meeting of the Conference on College Composition and Communication, Detroit, MI. (ERIC Document Reproduction Service No. ED 234 429)

Mock, K.R., Swanson, J.M., & Kinsbourne, M. (1978, March). *Stimulant effect on matching familiar figures: Changes in impulsive and distractible cognitive styles.* Paper presented at the annual meeting of the American Educational Research Association, Toronto, Canada. (ERIC Document Reproduction Service No. ED 160 189)

Sheridan, S.T., Kratochwill, T., & Elliott, S. Behavioral Consultation with parents and teachers. *School Psychology Review, 19,* 33–52.

Singer, J.L. (1974). Imagery and daydream methods in psychotherapy and behavior modification. New York: Academic.

See also Hypnosis; Imagery

DEAF

The word deaf is applied to persons who cannot hear or have a major hearing impairment. In classical writings as well as in common talk, until only a few years ago, the word deaf frequently had a strongly pejorative connotation, either in its figurative sense of deaf to the word of God or in locutions such as deaf and dumb. The latter clearly indicated a belief that those who are deaf from birth also have an intellectual defect. The term deaf-mute (used either as an adjective or as a noun), carried the notion of a double infirmity, until it was realized that the absence of speech, in those born deaf, was not related to a deficiency of the vocal organs and was only the consequence of the lack of hearing. Deaf now is used alone mostly since a majority of deaf persons have no other infirmity aside from possibly an oral language deficiency.

There is as yet no universally accepted definition of the different categories of hearing impairment. All the existing classifications are based on the mean speech range frequency thresholds obtained for the best ear by pure tone. The classification of the Bureau International d'Audiophonologie (BIAP; International Office for Audiophonology) is based on the mean hearing loss for 500, 1000, and 2000 Hz (ISO standards). It uses the terms recommended by the World Health Organization for the grading of all types of impairments: mild (20–40 dB), moderate (40–70 dB), severe (70–90 dB), and profound (more than 90 dB). The last category is itself divided in three subgroups, because there are large differences in the possibilities of residual hearing use among those whose average loss is only slightly superior to 90 dB and those who have a more than 100 dB hearing loss. Other classifications use different gradings and terms for the less than 70 dB categories, but there is fair agreement concerning the definition of the severe and profound groups.

Pure-tone audiometry, however, provides only a partial picture of the residual hearing capacity. It does not reflect the variable potential gain that can be brought by adequate hearing aid fitting. Several authors such as Pollack (1964), advocate the aided audiogram as a more meaningful measure of functional hearing capacity. Even this, however, does not reflect the qualitative aspects of residual hearing, which may vary extensively among individuals with the same pure-tone audiometric thresholds. Some insight about the quality of hearing may be gained by investigation of psychoacoustic tuning curves (Harrison, 1984), but these measures cannot presently be applied to small children because they require the subjects' active and informed cooperation.

These difficulties in establishing a well-founded functional classification have led several authors to adopt simpler general definitions for educational purposes. According to the Conference of Executives of American Schools for the Deaf (Frisina, 1974), a deaf person is one whose hearing is disabled to an extent (usually 70 dB International Standards Organization or greater) that precludes the understanding of speech through the ear alone, without or with the use of a hearing aid; a hard-of-hearing person is one whose hearing is disabled to an extent (usually 35 to 69 dB International Standards Organization) that makes difficult, but does not preclude, the understanding of speech through the ear alone, without or with a hearing aid.

It is necessary to stress the importance in both of these definitions of the word usually because there is a large overlap in the degree of pure-tone hearing loss of people who functionally correspond to one or the other category. Recently, Quigley and Kretschmer (1982) stated that for educational purposes, "a deaf child or adult is one who sustained a profound (91 dB or greater) primarily sensorineural hearing impairment prelingually" (p. 2). This trend toward considering as deaf only those with a larger than 90 dB hearing impairment is probably related to development of early intervention programs and improvement of hearing aids, resulting in earlier and better spoken language acquisition for an increasing number of the less profoundly hearing impaired.

Among deaf and hard-of-hearing children and adults, it is important to distinguish between those who were affected from birth or shortly thereafter (before language was established) and those who became hearing impaired later on. These groups are commonly called prelingually and postlingually deaf, respectively. The prelingually deaf child cannot acquire language by the same natural process as the normally hearing. Their auditory pathways in the brain, as well as those parts of the cerebral cortex concerned with the processing of spoken language, are not adequately stimulated in the early years most favorable for language development. This lack of adequate stimulation during the sensitive period not only results in great difficulties in the acquisition of spoken language skills, but may also produce permanent structural changes in the central nervous system. These changes could diminish the capacity of the brain to efficiently process speech-linked information later on, even if normal hearing could be restored, or artificial hearing produced (Périer et al., 1984).

Because of the interference of deafness with language acquisition prelingually deaf children and adults markedly differ from the postlingually deafened. The latter have a sensory impairment that interferes with their ability to perceive speech and other sounds, but they have a normally and completely developed language function. Although the quality of their speech may become distorted after some time because of the lack of auditory feedback, they usually remain intelligible. Their reading and writing capacities remain intact. By contrast, prelingually deaf children have such difficulties in acquiring spoken language that most of them, when they leave school as adolescents or young adults, have a linguistic insufficiency in addition to their sensory impairment (Conrad, 1979). Not only are they deficient in oral language skills, but also in reading and writing capacities. This linguistic insufficiency constitutes a serious handicap for their integration within the society of the normally hearing. It can, however, be attenuated and largely prevented by early and adequate education. When this includes sign language, a normal linguistic function may be developed in that modality, allowing full participation in the sociocultural life of the deaf community.

Deafness is related to a physical impairment, like other disabilities requiring rehabilitative and educational measures. It differs, however, from all these by a unique feature: the fact that this disability has given birth to a specific language, sign language (Bellugi, 1972). Just as a wide variety of spoken languages have evolved among the normally hearing world population, different sign languages have originated among the scattered communities of deaf people (Stokoe, 1972). However, many western world sign languages have a partly common trunk because of the important influence of the Abbé de l'Epée, the first educator of the deaf to recognize, in the late eighteenth century in France, the sign language of the deaf. There are, therefore, more common or similar signs among western sign languages than there are common or similar words in spoken languages. This facilitates communication among deaf people of different nationalities.

In the past, many deaf individuals did not themselves realize the value of their manual language (Meadow, 1980). They were influenced by the hearing society's contempt for what was regarded as a primitive and crude mode of communication, incapable of expressing abstraction and therefore unsuitable for high-level intellectual processes. The new status of sign language has done much not only to promote its diffusion and enrichment, but also to upgrade its users' self-confidence and self-esteem. This has given new impetus to deaf organizations and prompted the birth of such movements as Deaf Pride. This movement promulgates the notion that the deaf are equal but different and want this difference to be recognized and taken into account in the organization of society as a whole. Sign language supports deaf culture, mainly characterized by social and artistic events. It is, however, more appropriate to speak of cultural values rather than of a complete culture because the deaf share many ingredients of the hearing majorities' cultures such as their literature and their religions.

While some of the deaf reject spoken language and refuse to make any efforts at participation in sociocultural activities with the hearing, most of them aspire to bilingualism (i.e., the use of both sign and spoken languages) and biculturalism. Individuals who are deaf are considered bilingual if they are able to communicate effectively in both American Sign Language (ASL) and English or the spoken language of their country. They are considered bicultural if they are capable of functioning in both the deaf community and the majority culture (Baker & Baker, 1997). Bilingual-bicultural programs in the schools differ from other programs most notably by the approach to first language acquisition. These programs advocate for ASL to be the first language of children who are deaf because cognitive research indicates that "effective language has to be fast and clear. ASL is an efficient language for visual learning and is easier for deaf children to acquire as a first language than any form of English" (Finnegan, 1992, in Baker & Baker, 1997).

Bilingual-bicultural programs are generally found outside mainstream education and are relatively new. The gain in popularity may well be hampered or supported by achievement outcome studies. Baker and Baker (1997) suggest that students in rural areas may not have access to this approach, and classes for caregivers (especially in rural areas) are necessary for success.

Better information for society at large and sensitization to the rightful demands of the deaf has contributed in recent years to strengthening biculturalism. An important event in bringing the deaf to the attention of the hearing world was the success of Mark Medoff's play *Children of a Lesser God,* in which a deaf actress held the principal part. The play was awarded the Tony Award for best play of the year in 1980. In addition, the "Deaf Prez Now" or Gallaudet University protest in 1988 galvanized individuals who are deaf in ways that have not impacted the hearing community. In 1988 students at Gallaudet University protested the hiring of a hearing University President. They were successful in removing the President from office. The students removed hearing members of the board of trustees as well.

The concept of "identity formation" is starting to be realized in the deaf and hearing communities. Professionals are being invited to take a more "ethical and positive view of sign language and the deaf community" (Carver, 1999). It is clearly felt that Deaf culture adds to, and does not detract from, a child's education and identity formation (Carver, 1999).

REFERENCES

Baker, S., & Baker, K. (1997). *Educating children who are deaf or hard-of-hearing: Bilingual-bicultural education.* Reston VA: ERIC Clearinghouse on Disabilities and Gifted Education. (ERIC Digest No. E 553)

Bellugi, U. (1972). Studies in sign language. In T.J. O'Rourke (Ed.), *Psycholinguistics and total communication: The state of the art. American Annals of the Deaf* (pp. 68–74).

Carver, R. (1999). Identity and deafness: Who am I? *Deaf World Web:* dww.org.

Conrad, R. (1979). *The deaf school child.* London: Harper & Row.

Finnegan, M. (1992). Bilingual-bicultural education. *The Endeavor, 3,* 1–8.

Frisina, R. (1974). *Report of the committee to redefine deaf and hard of hearing for educational purposes.* (Mimeo).

Harrison, R.V. (1984). Objective measures of cochlear frequency selectivity in animals and in man. A review. *Acta Neurological Belgica, 84,* 213–232.

Meadow, K.P. (1980). *Deafness and child development.* London: Arnold.

Périer, O., Alegria, J., Buyse, M., D'Alimonte, G., Gilson, D., & Serniclaes, W. (1984). Consequences of auditory deprivation in animals and humans. *Acta Oto-Laryngologica* (Suppl. 411), 60–70.

Pollack, D. (1964). Acoupedics: A uni-sensory approach to auditory training. *Volta Review, 66,* 400–409.

Quigley, S.P., & Kretschmer, R.E. (1982). *The education of deaf children: Issues, theory and practice.* London: Arnold.

Stokoe, W.C. (1972). *Semiotics and human sign language.* Paris: Mouton.

See also Conductive Hearing Loss; Deaf Education

DEAF, INTERPRETERS FOR
See INTERPRETERS FOR THE DEAF.

DEAF-BLIND
There exists a broad range of visual and auditory impairments among deaf-blind persons, indicating an enormous diversity in the severity of disabilities within this population. The term deaf-blind (also called dual sensory impairment) covers persons with severe visual and hearing disabilities who are unable to profit from special programs designed solely for deaf or blind children and youths (*Federal Register,* 1975).

It is estimated that there are over 5,000 children and youth who are deaf-blind in the United States (Arizona Deaf-Blind Project, 1998). Maternal rubella, CHARGE Association, Usher's Syndrome, and meningitis are among the top four causes of deaf-blindness in the United States. Additionally, deaf-blind persons often are afflicted with congenital heart disease, mental retardation (Vernon, Grieve, & Shaver, 1980), physical handicaps, social/emotional issues, and communication delays (Arizona Deaf-Blind Project, 1998).

Deaf-blindness has often been associated with Helen Keller and her teacher Anne Sullivan (Lash, 1980). Although some deaf-blind people function within or above normal intelligence, many require extraordinary educational training. The separate handicaps are not additive but multiplicative in nature (Warren, 1984), and often cause severe learning problems. Deaf-blind children have often been referred to as the most difficult group of children to educate (Sims-Tucker & Jensema, 1984). They frequently engage in stereotypic behaviors that interfere with learning and communication. In an attempt to meet the special needs of this population, Regional Centers for Services for Deaf-Blind Children was established in 1967 (Sims-Tucker & Jensema, 1984).

The Arizona Deaf-Blind Program has recently been established as a federally-funded free resource for professionals and families working with deaf-blind individuals. It is housed at the Arizona School for the Deaf and Blind. The program provides consultation services for families of deaf-blind children, provides a lending library, and maintains an on-line interactive webpage. The project can be contacted at P.O. Box 87010, Tucson, AZ, 85754 or at www.azdb.org. Their telephone is 520–770–3680. Other resources are:

American Association of the Deaf-Blind, Inc.
Silver Spring, Maryland 20901
Telephone: 301-588-6545
TTY: 301-523-1265

Helen Keller National Center for Deaf-Blind
111 Middle Neck Road
Sands Point, New York 11050
Telephone: 516-944-8900
TTY: 516-944-8637

REFERENCES

Arizona Deaf-Blind Program. (1998). Deaf-blindness Fact Sheet. www.azdb.org.

Lash, J.P. (1980). *Helen and teacher: The story of Helen Keller and Anne Sullivan Macy.* New York: Delacorte.

Sims-Tucker, B., & Jensema, C. (1984). Severely and profoundly auditorially/visually impaired students: The deaf-blind population. In P. Valletutti & B. Sims-Tucker (Eds.), *Severely and profoundly handicapped students: Their nature and needs* (pp. 269–317). Baltimore, MD: Brookes.

Vernon, M., Grieve, B., & Shaver, K. (1980). Handicapping conditions associated with the congenital rubella syndrome. *American Annals of the Deaf, 125*(8), 993–997.

Warren, D. (1984). *Blindness and early childhood development.* New York: American Foundation for the Blind.

See also **Deaf; Keller, Helen; Movement Therapy; Visually Handicapped**

DEAF EDUCATION

It is generally accepted today that many hearing-impaired children, with early education, proper hearing aid fitting, and continued support, can successfully be educated with the normally hearing (Nix, 1976; Webster & Ellwood, 1985). While the degree of hearing loss is an important factor in determining which hearing-impaired children can be mainstreamed, it is generally recognized that this factor is by no means decisive in itself. Some profoundly deaf children can succeed in ordinary schools, while others with more residual hearing may not be able to do so (Périer et al., 1980). There is, therefore, no consensus concerning the proportion of deaf and hard-of-hearing children that should be integrated. The present situation varies greatly among nations. In some such as Italy, the official policy is that all handicapped children should be mainstreamed. Other countries, like West Germany, maintain separate special school systems for the profoundly deaf and the hard of hearing, so that even the majority of the latter are not educated with the normally hearing. Several developing countries where special education has yet to be organized view mainstreaming as a tempting alternative to the building and maintaining of special schools. Caution against the excesses of such a trend is voiced by numerous educators of the deaf, who argue that most of the profoundly deaf will continue to need special education. The pros and cons of mainstreaming have been aptly described by Meadow (1980), who argues that the options should carefully be weighed for each child.

Sign language interpretation services for the deaf have been developed primarily in the United States to assist the deaf in all circumstances in which they may benefit from them. Legal provisions ensuring that a deaf child has the right to the best possible education has made it possible in some cases to provide support services in schools or universities, allowing more deaf children and students to be mainstreamed than was formerly possible. In addition to sign language interpretation, other forms of interpretation are beginning to be developed in some countries: oral interpretation and oral interpretation with cued speech.

While the trend toward mainstream education has steadily increased over the years, the hope that early speech and hearing training would solve the language and education difficulties of most hearing-impaired children has proved overly optimistic. Several studies, among them Conrad's (1979), demonstrated that whatever method was used, whether oral or manual, the majority of deaf school graduates reached a mean reading age equivalent only to that of 9- to 10-year-old hearing children. Thus, the existing methods had not prevented relative failure to develop good command of the societal language (English in this case), even in its written form. Other studies reviewed by Quigley and Kretschmer (1982) showed that deaf children of deaf parents who had had signs as their first language were not disadvantaged in the oral skills and had slightly but significantly better gradings in overall language evaluation when compared with deaf children of hearing parents.

These results, together with the rehabilitation of sign language, were largely instrumental in the birth and development of the total communication (TC) philosophy. This, as defined by Denton (1970), is the right of a deaf child to learn to use all forms of communication available to develop language competence. This includes the full spectrum: child-devised gestures, speech, formal sign language, finger spelling, speech reading, reading, writing, as well as any other methods that may be developed in the future. Every deaf child should also be provided with the opportunity to learn to use any remnant of residual hearing he or she may have by employing the best possible electronic equipment for amplifying sound. Many schools in the United States, and a growing number throughout the world, have adhered to the principle of TC, although there are various interpretations of its meaning. More and more infant programs throughout the world are using it from the earliest age; many are urging parents to learn to communicate with their children through signs in addition to speech. Such combination of signs and speech has been termed bimodal communication by Schlesinger (1978).

Table 1 is an attempt at classification of the methods currently used. It must be borne in mind, however, that various combinations are possible; some techniques developed within the framework of a given method are applicable in other contexts.

1. Auditory unisensory or acoupedic methods rely on auditory training to develop spoken language. Speech reading is either not encouraged or suppressed during training periods (Pollack, 1964). In the verbo-tonal method (Guberina et al., 1972), perception of acoustic features through the tactile sense is used in addition to hearing. The auditory global approach of Calvert and Silverman (1975) stands at the margin between the acoupedic and the oral-aural, since "the primary, although not always the exclusive, channel for speech development is auditory."

2. Oral also called oral-aural (Simmons-Martin, 1972). Auditory perception and speech reading are used as well as other modalities, but signs are excluded. Ling (1976) describes systematic speech development procedure primarily based on audition though not neglecting tactile and visual support, as in Calvert and Silverman's multisensory approach, used when the auditory global is not sufficient. Van Uden's maternal reflective method (1970) insists on the necessity of active oral-aural dialogue and natural prosody.

3.1 Oral-aural plus lip-reading complements. In cued speech (Cornett, 1967) and related systems, the oral-aural approach is combined with a system of hand shapes executed near the mouth, synchronously with speech. The hand brings only that part of the information that is not supplied by lip reading. The combination of this information allows the deaf child to unequivocally identify by sight the speech sounds and syllables that the hearing identify through the ear (Nicholls & Ling, 1982; Périer et al., 1986).

3.2 Oral-aural plus manual representation of phonemes. In the French Borel-Maisonny method (1979), and in the German Phonembestimmte Manual System (PMS) of Schulte (1974), the oral-aural methodology is aided by contrived gestures that correspond to some of the characteristics of speech sounds and thus help in their identification and production. The gestures bring independent information that is not linked to lip reading.

3.3 Oral-aural plus finger spelling. These are the U.S. Rochester (Scouten, 1942) and U.S.S.R. neo-oralism (Morkovin, 1960) methods. Finger spelling is executed by the teacher simultaneously with speech; the child is asked to accompany his or her own speech by finger spelling. Since the latter is a representation of written language, reading and writing are strongly emphasized.

4.1 Unilingual bimodal communication or simultaneous method. One language, that of the hearing society and of most deaf children's parents, is simultaneously expressed in speech and signs. There are numerous vari-

Table 1 Classifications of Methods Used in Deaf Education

1. Auditory		Auditory unisensory or acoupedic
2. Oral		Oral-aural, multisensory
3. Oral + Manual Aids	3.1	Oral-aural + lip-reading complements
	3.2	Oral-aural + manual representation of phonemes
	3.3	Oral-aural + finger spelling
4. Combined	4.1	Unilingual bimodal communication or simultaneous method
	4.2	Bilingual bimodal communication
5. Manual		Visual unisensory communication by sign language alone

eties of signed representations of spoken language. Some are close to the regional sign language of the deaf, differing mostly in word order; others use additional signs to convey syntactical and morphological information; still others are wholly contrived (Crystal & Craig, 1978).

4.2 Bilingual bimodal communication. Spoken language in an oral-aural approach is used in certain situations by hearing persons, while sign language is used in other situations by deaf and hearing persons. In early education, it is often considered acceptable for hearing parents who have not yet mastered sign language to use those signs they have learned in combination with their spoken language (Bouvet, 1981; Erting, 1978).

5. Visual unisensory communication by sign language alone. While no educators advocate that deaf children should not learn the major societal language, a few favor the exclusive use of sign language for early education. Only when sign language is firmly established as a first language is the majority's societal language taught as a second language (Ahlgren, 1980). In some programs, teaching is first done in the written form, spoken language being delayed (Mali & Rickli, 1983).

The status of deaf education is characterized by a great vitality and a large diversity, although the antagonism between methods has somewhat abated. The oral-manual controversy is not as bitter as before, with most people on each side now recognizing the merits of the other (Tervoort, 1982a, 1982b). The question today is not so much of a choice between exclusively oral and combined oral-manual methods as of deciding for whom, when, how, and how much each modality should be used. General agreement exists on the paramount importance of early detection, assessment, and intervention, including proper hearing aid fitting and maintenance. The role of parents as the first educators of their deaf children, already stressed by Whetnall and Fry and the John Tracy Clinic, is now widely recognized (UNESCO, 1985). Their full participation is essential for the success of any method.

REFERENCES

Ahlgren, E. (1980). The sign language group in Stockholm. In E. Ahlgren & Bengman (Eds.), Papers from the first international symposium on the sign language research (pp. 3–7). Leksand.

Borel-Maisonny, S. (1979). *Absence d'expression verbale.* Paris: A.R.P.L.O.E.

Bouvet, D. (1981). *La Parole de l'enfant sourd.* Paris: Presses Universitaires de France, Collection Le Fil Rouge.

Calvert, D.R., & Silverman, S.R. (1975). *Speech and deafness: A text for learning and teaching.* Washington, DC: A.G. Bell Association.

Conrad, R. (1979). *The deaf school child.* London: Harper & Row.

Cornett, R.O. (1967). Cued speech. *American Annals of the Deaf, 112,* 3–13.

Crystal, D., & Craig, E. (1978). Contrived sign language. In I.M. Schlesinger & L. Namir (Eds.), *Sign language of the deaf* (pp. 141–168). New York: Academic.

Denton, D. (1970). Remarks in support of a system of total communication for deaf children. Communication Symposium. Frederick, MD: Maryland School for the Deaf.

Erting, C. (1978). Language policy and deaf ethnicity in the United States. *Sign Language Studies, 19,* 139–152.

Guberina, P., Skaric, I., & Zaga, B. (1972). *Case studies in the use of restricted bands of frequencies in auditory rehabilitation of the deaf.* Zagreb, Yugoslavia: Institute of Phonetics Faculty of Arts.

Ling, D. (1976). *Speech and the hearing-impaired child: Theory and practice.* Washington, DC: A.G. Bell Association.

Mali, A., & Rickli, F. (1983). *Introduction au bilinguisme: Langue des signes française—français oral, à l'école de Montbrillant.* Geneva, Switzerland: Départment de l'Instruction Publique.

Morkovin, B. (1960). Experiment in teaching deaf preschool children in the Soviet Union. *Volta Review, 62,* 260–268.

Nicholls, G.H., & Ling, D. (1982). Cued speech and the reception of spoken language. *Journal of Speech and Hearing Research, 25,* 262–269.

Nix, G. (1976). *Mainstream education for hearing impaired children and youth.* New York: Grune & Stratton.

Périer, O., Capouillez, J.M., & Paulissen, D. (1980). The relationship between the degree of auditory deficiency and the possibility of successful mainstreaming in schools for hearing children. In H. Hartmann (Ed.), *1st International Congress of the Hard of Hearing* (pp. 348–353). Hamburg: Deutscher Schwerhorigenbund.

Périer, O., Charlier, B., Hage, C., & Alegria, J. (1986). Evaluation of the effects of prolonged cued speech practice upon the reception and internal processing of spoken language. *Proceedings of the 1985 International Congress of Educators of the Deaf.* Manchester, England.

Pollack, D. (1964). Acoupedics: An unisensory approach to auditory training. *Volta Review, 66,* 400–409.

Quigley, S.P., & Kretschmer, R.F. (1982). *The education of deaf children: Issues, theory and practice.* London: Arnold.

Schlesinger, H.S. (1978). The acquisition of bimodal language. In I.M. Schlesinger & L. Namir (Eds.), *Sign language of the deaf.* New York: Academic.

Schulte, K. (1974). *The phonemetransmitting manual system* (PMS). Heidelberg: Julius Verlag.

Scouten, E. (1942). *A reevaluation of the Rochester method.* Rochester, NY: Rochester School for the Deaf.

Simmons-Martin, A. (1972). The oral/aural procedure: Theoretical basis and rationale. *Volta Review, 74,* 541–551.

Tervoort, B.T. (1982a). Communication and the deaf. *Proceedings of the International Congress on Education of the Deaf* (pp. 219–229). Hamburg. Heidelberg: Julius Verlag.

Tervoort, B.T. (1982b). The future: Oralism versus manualism? *Proceedings of the International Congress on Education of the Deaf* (pp. 544–547). Hamburg. Heidelberg: Julius Verlag.

UNESCO (1985). Consultation on alternative approaches for the education of the deaf. Paris: UNESCO.

Van Uden, A. (1970). New realizations in the light of the pure oral method. *Volta Review, 72,* 524–536.

Webster, A., & Ellwood, J. (1985). *The hearing-impaired child in the ordinary school.* London: Croom Helm.

See also American Sign Language; Deaf; Fingerspelling; Total Communication

DEBORAH P. V. TURLINGTON

Deborah P. (1979) is the federal district court case that struck down the competency testing program requirements for high-school graduation in the state of Florida. Deborah P. represented the class of all students in the state who were in danger of failing the test, including students of all ethnic backgrounds. The federal district court found that the competency testing program was unconstitutional for two reasons. The program had failed to provide students with adequate notice of the changes in requirements for a diploma, and the program was held to be racially discriminatory under the Fourteenth Amendment. According to the court, the competency testing program tended to perpetuate preexisting patterns of racial discrimination within the Florida school system. Children in special education programs were not specifically addressed in *Deborah P.*, however, similar issues may be raised if special education students are required to pass competency tests or denied diplomas on the basis of testing programs that discriminate on the basis of race or handicapping condition.

REFERENCE

Deborah P. v. Turlington. (1979). #78–892-CIV-T-C, U.S. District Court, Middle District, Tampa Division, July 12 (slip opinion).

DECROLY, OVIDE (1871–1932)

Ovide Decroly, a Belgian physician whose hospital work brought him into contact with many handicapped children, reasoned that the best treatment for such children would be a sound educational program. He established a special school for "the retarded and abnormal" in 1901. A few years later, he founded a school for normal children, where he demonstrated that the methods he was using successfully with handicapped children were equally effective with the nonhandicapped.

Decroly's educational methods were unique. The cornerstone of his method was what he called the "center of interest." Centers of interest were developed around four basic needs: food, protection from the elements, defense against common dangers, and work. Emphasis was placed on learning through activities that grow out of the interests and needs of the students. As much as a year's study could grow out of one topic or theme.

REFERENCES

Hamaide, A. (1924). *The Decroly class.* New York: Dutton.

Kajava, K. (1951). *The traditional European school and some recent experiments in the new education.* Doctoral dissertation. New York: Columbia University.

DEFINITION OF HANDICAPPING CONDITIONS

See SPECIFIC HANDICAP.

DEINSTITUTIONALIZATION

The trend toward deinstitutionalization of retarded persons began approximately 35 years ago when President Kennedy remarked that the practice of institutionalized segregation from the rest of society was immoral. In 1974 President Nixon announced the goal of returning half of all institutionalized retarded individuals to community settings (Braddock, 1977). The basic construct for the deinstitutionalization movement included: (1) the creation and maintenance of environments that did not impose excessive restrictions on disabled persons; (2) the creation of arrangements that brought persons as close as possible to the social and cultural mainstream; and (3) guaranteed that the human and legal rights of disabled citizens were protected (Neufeld, 1979, p. 115).

Numerous studies have been conducted over the past 35 years to assess outcomes for individuals who were a part of deinstitutionalization. The results of these studies are mixed. Many studies cite improvement in quality of life, adaptive behavior skills, and self-care skills (Fine, 1990; Larsen & Lakin, 1989; Lord & Pedlar, 1991).

Other studies present a more negative outcome, with deinstitutionalized mentally retarded individuals being overrepresented in the homeless (Roleff, 1996). Indeed, Craig and Paterson (1988) cited lack of long-term support for mentally ill individuals, and estimated that there are 300,000 mentally ill homeless persons in the United States. Perhaps the most disturbing of studies regarding deinstitutionalization is by Strauss and Kastner. In 1996 they compared risk-adjusted odds of mortality of people with mental retardation living in institutions or the community from 1980 to 1992 in California. It was estimated that the mortality was 72% higher in the community. It was suggested that the reason for the difference was the availability and adherence to health care (Strauss & Kastner, 1996).

For children, deinstitutionalization has had mixed results. Many children return to their families and research suggests that one-third will return to state schools. However, daily living skills training and vocational training are widely available, and many children who were originally placed in contained classrooms are included in the mainstream in less than a year (Laconia State School, 1987).

For deinstitutionalization to produce effective results, several issues should be considered. Adequate alternatives that are properly designed, properly maintained, and properly supervised should be developed. In addition, comprehensive evaluations of the individual's ability to succeed in a community-based facility should be made.

REFERENCES

Braddock, D. (1977). *Opening closed doors: The deinstitutionalization of disabled individuals.* Reston, VA: Council of Exceptional Children.

Craig, R.T., & Paterson, A. (1988). The homeless mentally ill; No longer out of sight and out of mind. *State Legislative Report, 13,* 30; National Conference of State Legislatures, Denver, Co.

Fine, M. (1990). Changes in adaptive behavior of older adults with mental retardation following deinstitutionalization. *American Journal on Mental Retardation, 94,* 6, 661–668.

Laconia State School. (1987). Deinstitutionalization of minors with Mental retardation. *Abstract X: Research & Resources on Special Education.* Reston, VA: ERIC Clearinghouse on Handicapped and Gifted Children.

Larsen, S.A., & Lakin, C. (1989). Deinstitutionalization of persons with mental retardation; The impact on daily living skills. *Policy Research Brief, 1,* 1.

Lord, J., & Pedlar, A. (1991). Life in the community: Four years after closure of an institution. *Mental Retardation, 29,* 4 213–221.

Neufeld, G.R. (1979). Deinstitutionalization procedures. In R. Wiegerink & J.W. Pelosi (Eds.), *Developmental disabilities: The DD movement* (pp. 115–126). Baltimore, MD: Brookes.

Roleff, T.L. (1996). *The homeless: Opposing viewpoints.* San Diego, CA: Greenhaven Press.

Strauss, D., & Kastner, T.A. (1996). Comparative mortality of people with mental retardation in institutions and the community. *American Journal on Mental Retardation, 101,* 1, 26–40.

See also Community-Based Services; Normalization; Rehabilitation

DELAYED LANGUAGE

See LANGUAGE DELAYS.

DE LEON, PEDRO

See PONCE DE LEON, PEDRO DE.

DE L'EPÉE, ABBÉ CHARLES MICHEL (1712–1789)

Abbé Charles Michel de l'Epée founded in Paris in 1755 the first public school for the deaf, the *Institution Nationale des Sourds Muets.* The Abeé developed a systematic language of signs based on the earlier work of Jacob Rodrigues Pereire. His system of signs was the basis of the instructional system in the United States' first school for the deaf, the American School for the Deaf. It is still in use today in modified form.

REFERENCE

Lane, H. (1984). *When the mind hears.* New York: Random House.

DELINQUENCY, HANDICAPPING CONDITIONS AND

It has been estimated that between 30% and 60% of juvenile offenders have handicapping conditions that require special education services (OJJDP, 1998). This number may be low because many youths are identified with a handicapping condition before their incarceration (Perryman, Di-Gangi, & Rutherford, 1989). In addition, it is estimated that 22% of incarcerated youth have significant mental health problems (OJJDP, 1998). Estimates of prevalence of handicapping conditions among juvenile delinquents vary dramatically (Crawford, 1982; Murphy, 1986; Nelson & Rutherford, 1989; OJJDP, 1998). These disparities largely can be attributed to methodological inconsistencies in identification of the major handicapping conditions. Further methodological inconsistencies exist in the defining of juvenile delinquency. The criteria for identifying juvenile delinquents are not uniform across state departments of correction (Murphy, 1986). Indeed, differential diagnosis of handicapping conditions as well as juvenile delinquency appear, in part, to be a state phenomenon.

Leone (1991) suggests that the social disadvantages and characteristics associated with juvenile delinquents may lead to increased likelihood of contact with the criminal justice system. Although there is a correlation between poor social and conflict resolution skills and delinquent behavior, no causality can be inferred. Several studies are available that address the effectiveness of special education programs in corrections. Bachara and Zaba (1978) found that the juvenile offenders who were offered remediation in the form of special education, tutoring, or perceptual-motor training exhibited a significantly lower recidivism rate than those who were not offered these programs (Karcz, 1987). Other researchers of the juvenile delinquent population have found that there exists an overall impoverishment of adaptive skill behaviors for this population (Baerman & Siegal, 1976). More recent studies (Forbes, 1991; Grande & Koorland, 1988) suggest that the uniqueness of the correctional setting realizes special problems with staff training, special educator training for correctional settings, curriculum design, and interagency cooperation.

The Office of Juvenile and Delinquency Prevention (1998) has suggested the following recommendations to parents or guardians of incarcerated youth who have handicapping conditions:

Discuss the need for appropriate services at the facility with:
- Teachers and tutors at the facility.
- A facility administrator.
- A special education attorney in the area or a law school clinical program.
- A professor of education.
- Parents.

Obtain the Correctional Education Association standards on correctional education programs.

Review the facility's educational standards.

Establish a committee of educators, advocates, and administrators to:
- Ensure that IEPs are conducted in a timely fashion by qualified personnel.
- Revise the educational standards of the facility.
- Simplify the eligibility determination for special education services.
- Ensure that the facility has qualified teachers.

Involve local advocacy groups that support children and persons with disabilities.

Contact an attorney who can assist you in bringing litigation against the facility if education services not improve.

REFERENCES

Bachara, G.H., & Zaba, J.N. (1978). Learning disabilities and juvenile delinquency. *Journal of Learning Disabilities, 11,* 58–62.

Crawford, D. (1982). *Prevalence of handicapped juveniles in the justice system: A study of the literature.* Phoenix, AZ: Research & Development Training Institutes.

Forbes, M.A. (1991). Special education in juvenile correctional facilities: A literature review. *Journal of Correctional Education, 42,* 1, 31–35.

Grande, C.G., & Koorland, M.A. (1988). A complex issue: Special education in corrections. *Children and Youth Services Review, 10,* 4, 345–350.

Karcz, S.A. (1987). Delinquency and special education. In C.R. Reynolds & Lester Mann (Eds.), *Encyclopedia of Special Education* (1st ed.). New York: Wiley.

Leone, P.E. (1991). Juvenile corrections and the exceptional student. (ERIC Digest No. E509)

Murphy, D.A. (1986). The prevalence of handicapping conditions among juvenile delinquents. *Remedial and Special Education, 7,* 7–17.

Nelson, C.M. & Rutherford, R.B. (1989). Impact of the correctional special education training (C/SET) project on correctional special education. Paper presented at the CEC/CCBD National Topical Conference on Behavior Disorders, Charlotte, NC.

Office of Juvenile Justice and Delinquency Prevention (OJJDP). (1998). *Educational advocacy for youth with disabilities. Beyond the walls: Improving conditions of confinement for youth in custody.* Rockville, MD: Juvenile Justice Clearing House.

Perryman, P., DiGangi, S.A., & Rutherford, R.B. (1989). Recidivism of handicapped and nonhandicapped juvenile offenders: An exploratory analysis. Paper presented at the Learning Handicapped Offender Conference, Pittsburgh, PA.

See also **Juvenile Delinquency; Learning Disabilities**

DEMENTIA

Dementia is a generic term applied to a pattern of observable abnormalities in mental abilities, with impairment in at least three of the following five functions: memory, visuospatial skills, emotion or personality, language, and cognition. Combinations of symptoms are caused by many different etiologies (Hegde, 1994). Recent literature agrees that irreversible dementia can be subdivided into three major areas: primary degenerative dementia, multi-infarct dementia, and all other dementia diagnoses of terminal diseases collectively (Shekim, 1997). Dementia of the Alzheimer's type is the most common, and it is caused by structural and chemical changes in the brain. The second most common, multi-infarct dementia, is caused by repeated focal lesions from strokes. Dementia is associated with acquired immunodeficiency syndrome (AIDS), Pick's disease, Parkinson's disease, supranuclear palsy, Binswanger's disease, Creutzfeldt-Jakob disease, Huntington's disease, and Korsakoff's disease (Payne, 1997). In addition, reversible dementias arise from adverse drug interactions or toxicity, metabolic and endocrine disorders, infections, intracranial masses, normal-pressure hydrocephalus, alcohol abuse, vitamin deficiencies, neurosyphilis, arteriosclerotic complications, and epilepsy (Tonkovich, 1988).

Assessment and diagnosis of dementia is a team effort involving physicians, speech-language pathologists, psychologists, and other specialists. The final determination is made on the basis of case history, clinical examination, neurological tests, brain imaging, laboratory tests, communication assessment, and assessment of intellectual functions. Analysis of higher intellectual and language functions include verbal description of common objects, immediate and delayed story retelling, and verbal fluency ("Tell me all the words you can think of beginning with T.") (Hegde, 1994).

Language problems frequently observed in early stages of dementia are mild naming problems, verbal paraphasia (saying words that are similar to the target word), subtle problems in comprehending abstract meanings, impaired picture description, difficulty in topic maintenance, and repetitious speech. As the disease progresses, symptoms include severe memory problems in all forms of memory; generalized intellectual deterioration; profound disorientation to place, person, and time; speech at a rapid rate with echolalia (repeating what was said to them); pallilalia (repeating one's own utterances); jargon; and inattention to social conventions (Hegde, 1994).

REFERENCES

Hegde, M.N. (1994). *A coursebook on aphasia and other neurogenic language disorders.* San Diego: Singular.

Payne, J.C. (1997). *Adult neurogenic language disorders: Assessment and treatment.* San Diego: Singular.

Shekim, L. (1997). Dementia. In L.L. LaPointe (Ed.), *Aphasia and related neurogenic language disorders* (2nd ed.) (pp. 238–249). New York: Thieme.

Tonkovich, J.L. (1988). Communication disorders in the elderly. In B.B. Shadden (Ed.), *Communication behavior and aging: A sourcebook for clinicians* (pp. 197–218). Baltimore: Williams & Wilkins.

DEMOGRAPHY OF SPECIAL EDUCATION

Demographic characteristics relating to handicapped children and youths include (1) the number and types of handicapped children and youths served; (2) the services received by these children and youths; (3) the personnel who provide services; and (4) the settings in which special education and related services are provided.

A total of 5,439,626 children and youth ages 3–21 were served under IDEA Part B during the 1994–95 school year. This figure was a 3.2 percent increase over the previous year, and a 12.7 percent increase since the 1990–91 school year. These figures do not include more than 100,000 infants and toddlers who were served under Part H of IDEA.

During the 1994–95 school year, approximately 12 percent of elementary and secondary students received special education services, and 95 percent of these students were served in regular school buildings. For several years in a row, the percentage of special education students served in the regular classroom increased and the percent served in resource rooms decreased.

Placement patterns vary by disability. The majority of students with speech and language impairments are served in regular classes. Students with learning disabilities, orthopedic impairments, serious emotional disturbance, and traumatic brain injury are generally placed in regular school buildings, but are then spread across regular classes, resource rooms, and separate classes. Separate classroom placements are most prevalent for students with mental retardation, autism, and multiple disabilities. However, resource room placements are also commonly used to serve students with mental retardation and multiple disabilities.

The category of disability that increased the most from 1990–91 to 1994–95 was Other Health Impaired. Much of the increase may be related to an increased number of students diagnosed with attention-deficit/hyperactivity disorder.

There are unique issues in the information available about inner city students' special education services. The Eighteenth Annual Report to Congress (1996) makes the following points:

- Inner-city and non-inner-city areas appear to have similar percentages of students in special education—10.4 percent and 10.8 percent, respectively. Little variation exists between the two types of areas by disability.

- Thirty percent of all inner-city students live in poverty, compared to 18 percent of students living outside inner cities. Data from the NLTS on secondary education students indicate that families of students with disabilities in urban areas are more likely to live in poverty than families of students with disabilities in suburban or rural areas.

- Inner-city districts enroll a greater percentage of limited English proficient students than non-inner-city districts, and data suggests that 5 percent of special education students in inner-city districts have limited English proficiency, compared to 1 percent in non-inner-city districts.

- Public schools in inner cities enroll almost twice as many African American and Hispanic students as do non-inner-city schools. The percentage of African American students enrolled in special education is generally high relative to their representation in the general student population. In some individual states and in some disability categories, Hispanics are over- and underrepresented relative to their proportion of the total population. In general, Asian American students are represented in special education at a lower rate proportional to the general population.

• Although a large number of African American and Hispanic students attend inner-city schools and are reportedly overrepresented in special education, two types of areas apparently enroll virtually the same percentage of students in special education. According to an analysis of NLTS data, the disproportionate representation of African Americans in special education is a function of relatively low income and the disabilities associated with poverty. When income is accounted for, disproportionate representation remains in the categories of speech or language impairments, visual impairments, and mental retardation.

• IDEA and its implementing regulations require that the special education assessment process be conducted in a nondiscriminatory manner. However, in inner-city schools and school districts, identification and assessment of students for special education is complicated by the effects of poverty, race/ethnicity, and limited English proficiency. A central concern over the disproportionate representation of minority students in special education is the role of intelligence tests in identifying students with disabilities.

• Current research suggests that for limited English proficient students, it is very difficult to distinguish between the effect of a disability on the student's achievement and the student's failure to understand the majority language and culture. This difficulty is a serious impediment to accurately assessing the student's disability.

• Data from the Office of Civil Rights suggest that students with disabilities living in inner cities are more likely to be placed in restrictive environments. NLTS data confirm that urban secondary students with disabilities spend less time in regular education classrooms than students living in nonurban areas.

• Special education teachers are in particularly short supply in inner-city areas. Also, schools have failed to attract a sufficiently diverse work force, and over the past 20 years the proportion of African American college graduates entering teaching has declined to a lower level than that of whites.

• Two national datasets on parental reports of disability among their children provide inconsistent results. In the Current Population Survey data, which includes families of children ages 5–17, white families reported that their children had a disability at a higher rate (5.6 percent) than African American families (4.6 percent) or Hispanic families (2.7 percent). In the National Household Education Survey data, which includes families of children age 3 through grade 2, white and African American parents reported prevalence rates of 12.4 and 12.1 percent respectively, while Hispanics reported a prevalence rate of 14.4 percent. In both sets of data, reports of disability diminish as income increases, and rates by race/ethnicity become more similar in the higher income ranges.

• According to NLTS data, youth in urban areas were less likely than their peers in suburban and rural areas to graduate from high school and were more likely to drop out of school. Suburban youth with disabilities who were out of secondary school two years or more reported taking any postsecondary courses in the past year at a slightly higher rate (17 percent) than urban youth with disabilities (14 percent) or rural youth with disabilities (12 percent).

It is clear that the disproportionality of ethnic minorities and inner-city youth in special education continues to be a source of investigation. Issues such as socioeconomic status and assessment bias are ongoing even after being subject to close scrutiny by researchers in the field and the U.S. Department of Education.

The demography of special education allows us to examine our advances in the understanding of handicapping conditions (such as the addition of Traumatic Brain Injury as a handicapping condition); it allows us to examine how we define disability from year to year; it allows us to track the impact of shifts in paradigms (such as inclusion); and it allows us to hold the field accountable for culturally competent services.

The Annual Report to Congress, written by Office of Special Education of the U.S. Department of Education, is published every year and is available on-line for inspection at www.ed.gov/pubs. The facts in this entry were taken verbatim from the *Eighteenth Annual Report to Congress* (1996).

REFERENCE

U.S. Department of Education. (1996). *Eighteenth annual report to Congress: To assure the free appropriate public education of all children with disabilities: Implementation of the Individuals with Disabilities Education Act (IDEA).* Washington, DC: Author.

See also **Politics and Special Education; Special Education, Federal Impact on**

DENDRITES

The nucleus of a brain cell, called the soma or perikaryon, has various protruding elements. The main protruding element is the axon. Typically surrounding the soma, except where the axon exits, are a variety of smaller protruding elements that form the dendritic network of the neuron. The dendrites have an appearance somewhat akin to branches of a leafless tree and *dendron* is the Greek stem meaning tree (see Figure 1). The dendrites serve as the neurotransmitter receptacle sites, as does the soma itself, from neurotransmitter release from the axon of a different neuron. The synaptic termination actually occurs on little spines that arise from the dendrite. These spines are numerous. For example, a single motor neuron may have as many as 4000 spines on its dendrites. Although it was originally assumed that the dendrite served a rather passive role in neuronal transmission, it is now speculated that the dendritic processes play a much more dynamic and active role in neurotransmission (Cooper, Bloom, & Roth, 1978; Cotman & McGaugh, 1980) and neurobehavioral (i.e., learning) functions.

REFERENCES

Cooper, J.R., Bloom, F.E., & Roth, R.H. (1978). *The biochemical basis of neuropharmacology* (3rd ed.). New York: Oxford University Press.

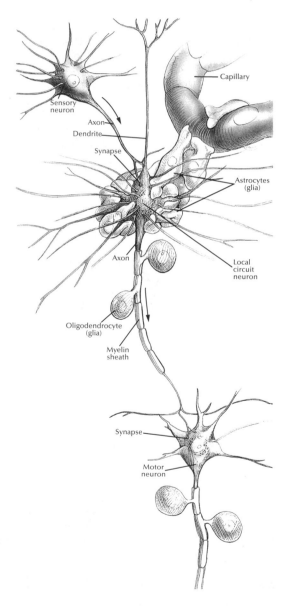

Figure 1. A neural circuit.

Cotman, C.W., & McGaugh, J.L. (1980). *Behavioral neuroscience.* New York: Academic.

See also **Central Nervous System; Glial Cells**

DENTISTRY AND THE HANDICAPPED CHILD

Dental disease represents a serious health problem for many handicapped children. A comprehensive survey by the National Center for Health Statistics (1979) estimated that oral disease is 40% higher among mentally retarded individuals, across all ages, than in the population at large. In a more recent report (Callahan, 1983a), the incidence of dental disease was almost 20% higher in the mentally retarded population than in comparably aged nonhandicapped individuals.

The 1970s were a particularly active period with respect to comprehensive investments of time and effort in improving dental care for handicapped individuals. One of the most important efforts in this respect was the funding by the Robert Wood Johnson Foundation during 1974–1978 of 11 dental schools across the country. This funding was to support the development of comprehensive dental school training programs relative to the provision of services to handicapped individuals; i.e., to develop specialized skills and technology, to create positive attitude change in dental professionals, to develop referral and service delivery capabilities at dental schools, and to institutionalize aspects of these programs at dental schools following funding.

Apropos of the Robert Wood Johnson Foundation's work, Stiefel and Truelove (1985) reported on the 5-year postgraduate program at the University of Washington that resulted in significant cognitive changes and gains in confidence respecting the treatment of handicapped individuals by dentists, dental hygienists, and assistants who participated in a postgraduate program. Curricula guidelines are also available (Jolly, 1990).

While there has been a steady if meager stream of publications concerning the dental management of handicapped children, a resurgence of interest is to be observed in the work of such investigators as Price (1978) and Pugliese (1978). Much of this interest, as might be expected, has been in the direction of preventive dentistry, and in the participation of home, school, and community in the dental management of handicapped individuals. The Association for Retarded Citizens' position is that dental treatment should "be of the same quality as received by other people, preserve or enhance the individual's health and be administered only with the *informed consent* of the person or his or her surrogate decision maker" (p. 1 ARC, 1992). Callahan (1983a, 1983b), among others, has emphasized that effective dental care for handicapped individuals must go beyond the improvement of dental services per se and improved technology to improving the willingness of dental practitioners to engage school and other service providers in the dental care of handicapped students. Callahan emphasizes the value of preventive services that will improve the dental status of the handicapped and reduce the costs of their dental care. For those handicapped individuals who will remain school and community based (this means most handicapped children and adults), programs of comprehensive preventive dental care should be emphasized over those of costly treatment.

What can be accomplished through preventive programs has been demonstrated through model outreach programs implemented by the National Foundation of Dentistry for the Handicapped (Callahan, 1983b). These programs have incorporated daily oral hygiene programs into the practices at a variety of special education schools, sheltered workshops, and group homes at relatively modest costs. They rely on periodic screening to detect dental disorders while they are still easily manageable. They use referral networks to coordinate the delivery of dental treatment to those handicapped individuals who require it. Most important, they use teachers, counselors, vocational rehabilitation personnel, houseparents, and other service personnel, in addition to those from the dental professions, on their service delivery teams. Similar concerted efforts might be valuable in bringing special education and special educators fully into the teaching and training of oral hygiene methods and precepts.

Recent interest in applying dental and oral hygiene principles in work with more severely handicapped populations is evidenced by the work of Feldman and Elliot (1981). Finally, because the vast majority of special education students these days reside at home, it is encouraging to observe recent efforts directed toward parents as oral hygiene trainers and monitors. Thus an article by Stark et al. (1985) provides guidelines to parents respecting their children's dental needs with regard to nutrition, medication, visits to the dentist, and the inculcation of proper dental care habits.

REFERENCES

Association for Retarded Citizens. (1992). *Position paper on Medical and dental treatment.* Arlington, Texas; ARC.

Callahan, W.P. (1983a). Dental disease: A continuing education problem for the disabled individual. *Journal of Special Education, 17,* 355–359.

Callahan, W.P. (1983b). The effectiveness of instructional programming on the reduction of dental diseases in mentally retarded individuals. *Mental Retardation, 21,* 260–262.

Campbell, J.Y., Esser, B.F., & Flaugher, R.L. (1982). *Evaluation of a program for training dentists in the care of handicapped patients* (Report No. QAT24225). Princeton, NJ: Educational Testing Service.

Feldman, D., & Elliot, T.A. (1981). A multidimensional oral hygiene curriculum for the severely and profoundly handicapped. *Journal of Special Education Technology, 4,* 33–45.

Jolly, D.E. (1990). Curriculum guidelines for training general practice residents to treat the person with a handicap. *Journal of Dental Education, 54,* 5, 293–297.

Price, J.H. (1978). Dental health education for the mentally and physically handicapped. *Journal of School Health, 48,* 171–173.

Pugliese, R. (1978). Oral health status in a group of mentally retarded patients. *Rhode Island Dental Journal, 11,* 6–9.

Stark, J., Markel, G., Black, C.M., & Greenbaum, J. (1985). Day to day dental care: A parents' guide. *Exceptional Parent, 15,* 15–17.

Stiefel, D.J. (1980). Dental care for the handicapped at the University of Washington. *Journal of Dental Medicine, 44,* 141–145.

Stiefel, D.J., & Truelove, E.L. (1985). A postgraduate dental training program for treatment of persons with disabilities. *Journal of Dental Education, 49,* 85–90.

See also Bruxism; Individual Education Plan (IEP); Self-Help Training

DEPAKENE

Depakene is an antiepileptic agent known generically as valproic acid. Depakene is the most recently introduced anticonvulsant medication. It differs both chemically and in clinical action from most other anticonvulsants (Goldensohn, Glaser, & Goldberg, 1984). Generally this medication is used either as the sole or adjunctive treatment for simple (petit mal) and complex absence seizures as well as generalized seizure disorders. The precise mechanism by which Depakene works is unknown; however, some research has suggested that its activity is related to increased brain levels of gamma-aminobutyric acid.

Nausea and gastrointestinal irritation are common side effects of Depakene, but these can be controlled through dosage or by giving the drug with food. If Depakene is given with other medications, particularly phenobarbital, there can be extreme, temporary sedation as well as awkward motor movements. Some of the more extreme side effects include a disruption of platelet functioning, liver damage, and pancreas failure, all of which have the potential to be fatal. For these reasons, Depakene typically is held in reserve as a medication of final resort for those individuals with seizures that cannot be controlled by other medication. For those who are using the ketogenic diet there may also be possible interactions (Ballaban-Gil, O'Dell, Pappo, Moshe, & Shinnar, 1998).

REFERENCES

Ballaban-Gil, K., Callahan, C., O'Dell, C., Pappo, M., Moshe, S., & Shinnar, S. (1998). Complications of the ketogenic diet. *Epilepsia, 39,* 7, 744–748.

Goldensohn, E.S., Glaser, G.H., & Goldberg, M.A. (1984). Epilepsy. In L.P. Rowland (Ed.), *Merritt's textbook of neurology* (7th ed.) (pp. 629–650). Philadelphia: Lea & Febiger.

See also Anticonvulsants; Epilepsy

DEPRESSION

Depression has been considered to be the major psychiatric disease of the 20th century. Recent studies have indicated that greater than 20 percent of adolescents have emotional problems and one-third of adolescents attending psychiatric clinics suffer from depression (Blackman, 1995).

Depression is the leading cause of suicide (National Institute of Mental Health, 1998). The suicide rate for adolescents has increased more than 200 percent over the last decade (Blackman, 1995). Each year 250,000 teens attempt suicide, and 2,000 complete the act. Females are more likely to attempt suicide, but males kill themselves four times more often, usually with guns (NetHealth, 1998).

Symptoms of depression vary from individual to individual in terms of frequency, number, and intensity. Common symptoms are:

- Persistent sad, anxious, or "empty" mood
- Feelings of hopelessness, pessimism
- Feelings of guilt, worthlessness, helplessness
- Loss of interest or pleasure in hobbies and activities that were once enjoyed, including sex
- Insomnia, early-morning awakening, or oversleeping
- Appetite and/or weight loss or overeating and weight gain
- Decreased energy, fatigue, being "slowed down"
- Thoughts of death or suicide; suicide attempts
- Restlessness, irritability
- Difficulty concentrating, remembering, making decisions
- Persistent physical symptoms that do not respond to treatment, such as headaches, digestive disorders, and chronic pain

The causes of depression are numerous. There is some indication that there is a genetic component; some 30 to 40 percent of depressed children will have a biologic parent who is also depressed at the time the child presents for initial evaluation (Weinberg, Harper, Emslie, & Brumback, 1995). Twin studies suggest that heredity partly determines how often normal children become mildly depressed and how their moods fluctuate. For both level of depression and fluctuations of symptoms, the correlation among identical twins in one study (Wierzbicki, 1987) was about .68 which suggested that up to two-thirds of the variance was genetic.

Psychological makeup also plays a role in the possibility of developing depression. Children and adolescents who have low self-esteem and are easily overwhelmed by stress are prone to depression (NetHealth, 1998). Serious losses, chronic illness, or unwelcome changes in life patterns can also trigger depressive episodes.

Many adolescents and their families do not realize that depression is a treatable condition (NIMH, 1998). There are a variety of antidepressant medications which, when used in conjunction with psychotherapy, are very effective. The medication gives relatively quick symptom relief and the psychotherapy helps the individual and their family learn more effective ways to deal with life's problems (NIMH, 1998). Researchers have also been optimistic about light therapy for seasonal affective depression (Swedo, 1997).

In terms of the educational system, many times teachers are the first to notice that children and adolescents are hav-

ing problems. Academic performance is very susceptible to disruption from depression. Teachers should receive training as to the unique symptomatology of depression in youth, and training to support the student who needs assistance (Willis, 1996).

Special education students may be particularly susceptible to depression. As mentioned previously, chronic illnesses such as diabetes, eating disorders, or cerebral palsy present long-term difficulties and problems that the child must overcome. The concurrent incidence of chronic illness and depression has been well established in the scientific literature. Learning disabilities are commonly diagnosed concurrently in youth with depression. Weinberg et al. (1995) report that 60 to 80 percent of learning-disabled children failing in school will fulfill criteria for depression at the time of initial clinical evaluation. School is a very frustrating place for many of these students, as repeated failure lowers motivation and self-esteem. This condition spirals downward as the child develops negative thinking about those academic tasks on which he or she cannot perform adequately

Strength models of remediation in special education have primarily focused on the neurological and neuropsychological rationale for teaching to a child's strengths (Reynolds, 1992). The latter also focuses on the inherent positive feedback that a learner receives when the educational intervention matches the psychoeducational diagnosis. The child understands the material, performs to expectations, and receives positive feedback. This, in turn, enhances self-esteem and motivation, and recreates a positive and flexible mindset when the child approaches an academic task. Over a period of time, negative thoughts are not the norm for the child and depression can only exist when rigid and chronic negative thoughts are present. Therefore, for the special education learner, it is critical that any treatment for depression (psychopharmacology, family therapy, and/or individual therapy) also takes into account the individual education plan that is based on a strength model. The interplay between success in school and success in treatment is crucial for the special education student who is depressed.

REFERENCES

Blackman, M. (1995). Adolescent depression. *The Canadian Journal of CME.* Internet Mental Health: www.mentalhealth.com.

National Institute of Mental Health. (1998). *Plain talk about depression.* Washington DC.: Author.

NetHealth. (1995). *Depression.com.* www.depression.com.

Reynolds, C.R. (1992). Two key concepts in the diagnosis of learning disabilities and the habilitation of learning. *Learning Disability Quarterly, 15,* 1, 2–12.

Swedo, S.E. (1997). Light therapy may help kids with seasonal depression. *Journal of the American Academy of Child and Adolescent Psychiatry, 5,* 2, 112–115.

Weinberg, W.A., Harper, C.R., Emslie, G.J., & Brumback, R.A. (1995). Depression and other affective illnesses as a cause of school failure and maladaptation in learning disabled children, adolescents and young adults. *Secondary Education and Beyond.* Pittsburgh, PA: Learning Disabilities Association.

Wierzbicki, M. (1987). Similarity of monozygotic and dizygotic child twins in level and liability of subclinically depressed mood. *American Journal of Orthopsychiatry, 57,* 33–40.

Willis, S.M. (1996). Childhood depression in school age children. (ERIC Clearinghouse No. PS026156)

See also **Drug Abuse; Serious Emotional Disturbance**

DEPRIVATION

See NEGLECT; POST INSTITUTIONALIZED CHILD.

DEPRIVATION, BIONEURAL RESULTS OF

The term deprivation is usually used to mean the absence or reduction of normal sensory input to the nervous system. Its meaning is sometimes extended to include restriction or suppression of opportunities for normal motoric activities associated with exploration, play, and social intercourse. The bioneural results of deprivation have mostly been investigated through animal experiments.

The visual system has been studied extensively. Various changes reviewed by Vrensen and De Groot (1974) have been observed in the visual cortex of animals reared in the dark. Monocular deprivation has been shown to produce more salient changes than binocular; competition between the two sides seems to be a more important factor than deprivation per se. The changes are particularly marked, and largely irreversible, when deprivation occurs during a critical period of early life.

In the auditory system, complete suppression of input is impossible without destruction of both inner ears, since otherwise there is always some perception of the sounds produced in the animal's own body. Temporary restriction of auditory stimuli can be achieved by rearing in a sound-attenuated environment or by interfering with the external or middle ear structures that transmit sound to the inner ear. Both methods produce perturbations of the auditory function and neuronal alterations of brain stem auditory nuclei (Webster & Webster, 1979). Significant changes in the microscopic structure of the auditory cortex have been observed in mutant mice with hereditary deafness owed to inner ear degeneration (Périer et al., 1984). As in the visual system, there are critical or sensitive periods of development during which plasticity is greatest and the results of deprivation most evident (Eggermont, 1986).

In man, the counterpart of animal experiments on the visual system is functional amblyopia, a condition observed in some children who have suffered from unattended squinting or other conditions interfering with the vision of one eye. Even after correction of the pathological condition, the deprived eye may remain largely nonfunctional. Partial auditory deprivation is a frequent occurrence in small children as a result of serous otitis media. It seems to cause long-lasting learning difficulties, even after normal hearing has been restored. All degrees of hearing loss, from mild to profound, might affect the human auditory pathways and cortex, as shown in animals. These possible effects in man have been discussed by Ruben & Rapin (1980). Studies in language development indicate that infants possess a capacity for making phonetic distinctions which must, to persist, be confirmed by the corresponding sounds of language spoken in their environment. Some studies indicate that children with congenital or early acquired hearing loss might lose this early competence (Serniclaes et al., 1984).

Examples of extreme multisensory and social deprivation in man are afforded by "wolf" children and exceptional cases such as that of Genie, a girl maintained in isolation for years by psychotic parents (Curtiss, 1977). The complexity of such cases as well as the lack of sufficient information about their early life make their interpretation difficult. Less severe but more frequent deprivation situations occur in hospitalism (Spitz, 1945) and in poorly stimulating familial background. It is probable, though yet unproven, that these have bioneural consequences in addition to the well-known psychological ones.

REFERENCES

Curtiss, S. (1977). *Genie, a psycholinguistic study of a modern day "wild child."* New York: Academic.

Eggermont, J. (1986). Critical periods in auditory development. Proceedings of the Nijmegen Workshop. *Acta Otolaryngologica* (Stockholm) (Suppl., in press).

Périer, O., Alegria, J., Buyse, M., D'Alimonte, G., Gilson, D., & Serniclaes, W. (1984). Consequences of auditory deprivation in animals and humans. *Acta Otolaryngologica* (Stockholm), *411,* 60–70.

Ruben, R.J., & Rapin, I. (1980). Plasticity of the developing auditory system. *Annals of Otology Rhinology and Laryngology, 89,* 303–311.

Serniclaes, W., D'Alimonte, G., & Alegria, J. (1984). Production and perception of French stops by moderately deaf subjects. *Speech Communication, 3,* 185–198.

Spitz, R.A. (1945). Hospitalism—An inquiry into the genesis of psychiatric conditions in early childhood. *Psychoanalytic Study of the Child, 1,* 53–74.

Vrensen, G., & De Groot, D. (1974). The effect of dark rearing and its recovery on synaptic terminals in the visual cortex of rabbits. A quantitative electron microscopic study. *Brain Research, 78,* 263–278.

Webster, D.B., & Webster, M. (1979). Effects of neonatal conductive hearing loss on brain stem auditory nuclei. *Annals of Otology Rhinology, & Laryngoly, 88,* 684–688.

See also **Genie; Language, Absence of; Language Delays**

DESENSITIZATION

Desensitization is a procedure that combines guided participation, modeling, and the graduated approach to a desired response (e.g., shaping). The technique has been used primarily with fear responses in children and adults, and its primary targets have been phobic reactions to various stimuli. While undergoing this therapy, the individual is first introduced to the process by beginning under the least demanding conditions. The therapist models the desired behavior and the individual is guided through his or her responses. These responses are gradually modified to approximate the real circumstances under which the feared stimuli might be encountered. The gradual modification takes place with the therapist modeling each successive response and guiding the student through the appropriate response. The therapist also makes encouraging statements and uses other reinforcing methods (Kratochwill, 1975). These supportive techniques are gradually withdrawn. The two procedures used are generally referred to as shaping a correct response and fading the prompts that have been used to support the acquisition of the behavior (Alberto & Troutman, 1982).

Desensitization, as a behavioral procedure, has a substantive body of research to support its feasibility in fear reduction treatment. Desensitization is currently used for many situations, such as test anxiety (Austin, 1995), math anxiety (Schneider, 1993), general school anxieties (Ross, 1990), and in attempts to control negative effects of mass media (Wilson, 1993). Therefore, desensitization is a procedure that combines several common behavioral techniques to assist in the development of appropriate responses to currently feared or anxiety-provoking situations (e.g., riding in a bus, entering a swimming pool, going to a movie).

REFERENCES

Alberto, P.A., & Troutman, A.C. (1982). *Applied behavior analysis for teachers*. Columbus, OH: Merrill.

Austin, J.S. (1995). Prevent school failure: Treat test anxiety. *Preventing School Failure, 40,* 1, 10–13.

Kratochwill, T.R. (1975). Contact desensitization. In A.S. Bellack & M. Hersen (Eds.), *Dictionary of behavior therapy techniques*. New York: Pergamon.

Ross, D.B. (1990). *Controlling School Anxiety: A practical guide for counselors and teachers*. Grayslake, IL: College of Lake County.

Schneider, W.J. (1993). Overcoming math anxiety: A comparison of stress inoclution training and systemic desensitization. *Journal of College Student Development, 34,* 4, 283–288.

Wilson, B.J. (1989). Densensitizing children's emotional reactions to the mass media. *Communicating Research, 16,* 6, 723–745.

See also **Behavior Modification; Phobias and Fears**

DES LAURIERS–CARLSON HYPOTHESIS

The work of Des Lauriers and Carlson (1969) came after Kanner (1943) identified the behavioral characteristics of children who were qualitatively different from other childhood clinical populations. These symptoms included the inability to develop relationships, a delay in speech acquisi-

tion, echolalia, and repetitive play activities. These have become identifying characteristics of early infantile autism.

Although much of the early research focused on family and environmental causes, more recent research identifies possible involvement with neurochemistry, developmental biology, neurophysiology, and neuroanatomy (Hanson & Gottesman, 1976). In 1983 Gillberg and Gillberg reported an increase in pre and perinatal hazards that are suggestive of brain dysfunction in infantile autism. Recent advances in cytogenetics have resulted in the identification of a specific biological marker or fragile site on the X chromosome. These are indicators that there is a coexistence of autism with the fragile X chromosome, suggesting an etiological link (August & Lockhart, 1984). Sherman, Nass, and Shapiro (1984) researched cerebral blood flow in autistic children. Their research suggested depressed gray matter cerebral blood flow in autistic subjects; this may reflect their mental retardation. These findings lend support to the hypothesis of Damasio and Maurer (1978), who suggested that autism is the result of abnormalities of the mesolimbic dopaminergic system.

Currently, it is generally accepted that early infantile autism is a behavioral syndrome reflecting abnormal brain functioning (Sherman, Nass, & Shapiro, 1984) and multiple causes (Schopler, 1990).

REFERENCES

August, J.A., & Lockhart, H.L. (1984). Familial autism and the fragile X chromosome. *Journal of Autism & Developmental Disorders, 14,* 197–203.

Damasio, A.R., & Maurer, R.G. (1978). A neurological model for children with autism. *Archives of Neurology, 35,* 771–776.

Des Lauriers, A.M., & Carlson, C.F. (1969). *Your child is asleep: Early infantile autism*. Homewood, IL: Dorsey.

Gillberg, C., & Gillberg, C.I. (1983). Infantile autism: A total population study of reduce optimality in the pre-peri and neonatal period. *Journal of Autism & Developmental Disorders, 13,* 153–166.

Hanson, D.R., & Gottesman, I.I. (1976). The genetics, if any, of infantile autism and childhood schizophrenia. *Journal of Autism & Developmental Disorders, 6,* 209, 231.

Kanner, L. (1943). Autistic disturbances of affective contact. *Nervous Child, 2,* 217–250.

Schopler, E. (1990). *Neurobiological correlates of autism*. Reston, VA: ERIC Publications. (ERIC Clearinghouse No. EC300540)

Sherman, M., & Nass, R., & Shapiro, T. (1984). Brief report: Regional cerebral blood flow in autism. *Journal of Autistic & Developmental Disorders, 14,* 439–446.

See also **Autism; Reticular System**

DESPERT, JULIETTE L. (1892–1982)

Juliette L. Despert, MD, child psychiatrist and researcher, received her education in her native France and in the United States. During her many years as a practicing psychiatrist, she contributed numerous articles to professional journals and published over half a dozen books, including

The Emotionally Disturbed Child: An Inquiry into Family Patterns, Schizophrenia in Childhood, and *Children of Divorce,* and developed the Despert Fables.

REFERENCES

Despert, J.L. (1953). *Children of divorce.* New York: Doubleday.

Despert, J.L. (1968). *Schizophrenia in childhood.* New York: Brunner.

Despert, J.L. (1970). *The emotionally disturbed child: An inquiry into family patterns.* New York: Doubleday.

DESTRUCTIVE BEHAVIORS

To specify all acts in which persons engage that could be considered destructive is impossible; the topography of various destructive behaviors is at least as diverse as the people who exhibit them. A number of factors mitigate against a universally acceptable definition of destructive behaviors and are generally accounted for in operational definitions of such acts. There are at least three elements that should be implicitly or explicitly incorporated into operational definitions of destructive behaviors. One element is that of intentionality. For example, a child who accidentally breaks a dish is not generally considered destructive, but one who deliberately breaks a dish is considered destructive. Second, characteristics of the behavior itself (e.g., intensity, frequency) play a definitional role. For instance, children who occasionally bite their fingernails are not considered to be self-destructive, while those who often bite their hands until they bleed generally are considered self-destructive. Third, situational factors influence definitions. Persons who intentionally break a glass in a restaurant are considered destructive; in contrast, in some wedding ceremonies the intentional breaking of a glass is a socially sanctioned event. Much has been asserted in recent years that society has redefined destructive behavior in a more innocuous fashion: a statement about society's increasing tolerance for deviant behaviors (Moynihan, 1994).

There have been many examples of positively-based programs to reduce destructive behaviors. An interesting large-scale program to reduce acts of vandalism was reported by Mayer, Butterworth, Nefpaktitis, and Sulzer-Azaroff (1983). Selected teachers in 18 schools participated in workshops and consultation sessions. Over the three-year study, the teachers significantly increased their rates of praise. Acts of vandalism were significantly reduced and decreases in other disruptive and destructive student behaviors were also observed. Russo, Cataldo, and Cushing (1981) reported that positively reinforcing compliance resulted in decreased acts of self-destruction among three children, although no contingencies were in effect for the self-destructive behaviors. Using a DRO procedure (reinforcement delivered for nonoccurrence of behavior), Frankel, Moss, Schofield, and Simmons (1976) eliminated aggressive and self-destructive acts.

Extinction combined with positive reinforcement was used by Martin and Treffry (1970) to eliminate poor posture and self-destructive behaviors in a 16-year-old partially paralyzed mentally retarded girl with cerebral palsy. She was positioned in such a manner that if she slouched she was not visible to the persons administering the reinforcers. If she was engaging in self-destructive behaviors, she was also not reinforced.

A variety of destructive behaviors exhibited by five mentally retarded boys were reduced by a nonexclusionary timeout procedure (Foxx & Shapiro, 1978). A number of advantages are associated with this technique compared with other forms of timeout procedures.

An overcorrection procedure (a punishment technique involving the correction of the undesirable behavior followed by practicing the desirable behavior) was used by Foxx and Azrin (1972) to eliminate the destructive behavior of a profoundly retarded adult female.

Irrespective of the particular type of destructive behavior, these responses merit our best professional interventions. A variety of treatments (in addition to the ones mentioned here) have proven successful, but careful attention to aspects of individual cases is essential.

REFERENCES

Foxx, R.M., & Azrin, N.H. (1972). Restitution: A method of eliminating aggressive-disruptive behavior of retarded and brain damaged patients. *Behavior Research and Therapy, 10,* 15–27.

Foxx, R.M., & Shapiro, S.T. (1978). The timeout ribbon: A nonexclusionary timeout procedure. *Journal of Applied Behavior Analysis, 11,* 125–136.

Frankel, F., Moss, D., Schofield, S., & Simmons, J.Q. (1976). Use of differential reinforcement to suppress self-injurious and aggressive behavior. *Psychological Reports, 39,* 843–849.

Martin, G.L., & Treffry, D. (1970). Treating self-destruction and developing self-care skills with a severely retarded girl: A case study. *Psychological Aspects of Disability, 17,* 125–131.

Mayer, G.R., Butterworth, T., Nafpaktitis, M., & Sulzer-Azaroff, B. (1983). Preventing school vandalism and improving discipline: A three-year study. *Journal of Applied Behavior Analysis, 16,* 355–369.

Moynihan, P. (1994). Defining deviancy down: How we've become accustomed to alarming levels of crime and destructive behavior. *American Educator, 17,* 10–18.

Russo, D.C., Cataldo, M.F., & Cushing, P.J. (1981). Compliance training and behavioral covariation in the treatment of multiple behavior problems. *Journal of Applied Behavior Analysis, 14,* 209–222.

See also **Acting Out; Applied Behavior Analysis; Emotional Disorders; Reality Therapy**

DETROIT TESTS OF LEARNING APTITUDE–FOURTH EDITION (DTLA–4)

The DTLA-4, like its predecessors, was designed to assess an individual's cognitive strengths and weaknesses and can be used to help identify children and adolescents with learning problems or special needs.

The DTLA-4 consists of ten discrete subtests that measure specific cognitive abilities. The subtests assess such areas as vocabulary, auditory and visual memory, visual closure, and visual problem solving. The DTLA-4 yields subtest scores, a global ability score, and six domain composite scores involving linguistic, attentional, and motoric aspects. Also, by regrouping the subtests in a variety of ways, theory-based composites can be generated that represent some of the major theories in intelligence, including Cattell and Horn's model of fluid and crystallized intelligence, Jensen's model of associative and cognitive levels, Das' model of simultaneous and successive processing, and Wechsler's verbal and performance scales. Each of the ten subtests yields a raw score that is converted to a standard score ($M = 10$, $SD = 3$). The global ability score is generated by combining all ten of the subtest standard scores, which are converted to a standard score or quotient ($M = 100$, $SD = 15$). The domain and theoretical composites are obtained by combining specific subtest standard scores, also converted to quotients ($M = 100$, $SD = 15$). Percentile ranks, age equivalents, and descriptive ratings (ranging from very superior to very poor) are provided for subtests and composites along with the above-mentioned standard scores.

According to the author, the DTLA-4 improved the test in many significant ways (e.g., norms were stratified and keyed to the 1996 census data relative to gender, race, ethnicity, and family income). However, no critiques of the DTLA-4 have been published as of yet. The author contends that "because the DTLA-4 retained all the items on DTLA-3, the reviews of DTLA-3 have relevance to DTLA-4." The primary criticisms raised in recent reviews of the DTLA-3 include statements concerning the norms, the factor structure of the test, and administration time.

DEVELOPING UNDERSTANDING OF SELF AND OTHERS–REVISED (DUSO-R)

The DUSO-R is a colorful, easily administered program that assesses three main subject areas (Krismann, 1983): affective education, guidance and counseling, and health. It is based on an inquiry, experiential, and discussion approach to learning. The program can be used to teach appropriate social skills and problem-solving techniques, as well as to give insight into self-concept, interpersonal relationships and conflict resolution. As it is more of a teaching instrument than a testing instrument, objective interpretations are based on individual responses rather than norms. The DUSO-R can be a useful, valuable tool that can be added to a teacher's daily, weekly, or periodic schedule.

REFERENCE

Krisman, C. (1983). Developing Understanding of Self and Others-Revised. *Social Science Education Consortium* (Suppl.), 39–40.

See also **Counseling the Handicapped; Social Skills**

DEVELOPMENTAL APHASIA

See CHILDHOOD APHASIA; LANGUAGE DISORDERS.

DEVELOPMENTAL APRAXIA

Developmental apraxia is a childhood disorder of sensory integration interfering with ability to plan and execute skilled or non-habitual motor tasks in the absence of muscle weakness or paralysis (Davis, Jakielski, & Marquardt, 1998; Hall, Jordan, & Robin, 1993). Voluntary or purposeful motor acts are inconsistently produced while involuntary movements remain intact. The condition is characterized by difficulty in articulation of speech (oral, speech, or verbal apraxia); formation of letters in writing; difficulty with visual-spatial tasks such as drawing, block arrangements, assembling stick designs or shapes in drawing; or problems in sequential movements of gesture, pantomime, dressing, grooming, or eating (Hall et al., 1993; Shriberg, Aram, & Kwiatkowski, 1997). In less severe forms, apraxia may be referred to as dyspraxia (Dewey, 1995; Missiuna & Polatajko, 1995).

This condition is also referred to as clumsy child syndrome, mild motor problems, incoordination, developmental apraxia or dyspraxia, perceptual motor dysfunction, visual-motor problems and sensory-integrative dysfunction. The *Diagnostic and Statistical Manual of Mental Disorders* (DSM-IV) (American Psychiatric Association, 1994) description of DCD implicitly excludes the coordination disturbances affecting speech motor skill development, even though phonological awareness deficits are frequently found in children diagnosed with DCD. A consensus does not exist for etiology of the condition (Davis et al., 1998; Dewey, 1995; Hall et al., 1993; Shriberg et al., 1997). Developmental apraxia of speech and developmental coordination disorders can impact on the social and academic dimensions of the communication-learning process across the life course, but particularly do so in childhood.

REFERENCES

American Psychiatric Association. (1994). *Diagnostic and statistical manual of mental disorders* (4th ed.) (DSM-IV). Washington, CD: Author.

Davis, B.L., Jakielski, K.J., & Marquardt, T.P. (1998). Developmental apraxia of speech: Determiners of differential diagnosis. *Clinical Linguistics and Phonetics, 12,* 25–45.

Dewey, D. (1995). What is developmental dyspraxia? *Brain and Cognition, 29,* 254–274.

Hall, P.K., Jordan, L.S., & Robin, D.A. (1993). *Developmental apraxia of speech: Theory and clinical practice.* Austin, TX: Pro-Ed.

Missiuna, C., & Polatajko, H. (1995). Developmental dyspraxia by any other name: Are they all just clumsy children? *The American Journal of Occupational Therapy, 49,* 619–627.

Shriberg, L., Aram, D., & Kwiatkowski, J. (1997). Developmental apraxia of speech: I. Descriptive and theoretical perspectives. *Journal of Speech, Language and Hearing Research, 40,* 273–285.

DEVELOPMENTAL DELAY

The concept of developmental delay refers to a maturational lag, an abnormal, slower rate of development in which a child demonstrates a functioning level below that observed in normal children of the same age (Thompson & O'Quinn, 1979). Suggesting no cerebral dysfunction or structural damage, proponents of the concept maintain that discrepant abilities manifested by the delayed child occur because of neurological immaturity associated with slower development (Golden & Wilkening, 1986; Lerner, 1985; Thompson & O'Quinn, 1979).

In terms of handicapping conditions and eligibility for services, the term developmental delay was adapted in an amendment to the Individuals with Disabilities Education Act (IDEA) in 1986. The new PART H, which became PART C in 1998, addressed the needs of infants and toddlers with disabilities and their families through a "Statewide system of coordinated, comprehensive, multidisciplinary, interagency programs providing appropriate early intervention services to all infants and toddlers with disabilities and their families" (20 U.S.C. § 1476(a)).

The amendment was based on Congress' findings that services to families and children below the age of 2 were not organized, economic, or meeting the needs of initiatives designed to prevent the need for special education services. The criteria for eligibility in the Act laid the groundwork for clearer definitions of developmental delay to emerge. The Act states:

Infants and toddlers from birth through age 2 are eligible for PART H services if they:

(1) Are experiencing developmental delays, as measured by appropriate diagnostic instruments and procedures in one or more of the following areas:
  (i)   Cognitive development,
  (ii) Physical development, including vision and hearing,
  (iii) Communication development,
  (iv) Social or emotional development,
  (v)   Adaptive development, or
(2) Have a diagnosed physical or mental condition that has a high probability of resulting in developmental delay. (34 CFR 303.16)

States have the discretion to serve infants and toddlers and their families who are at risk of having substantial developmental delays if early intervention services are not provided (34 CFR 303.16). At this time, there are 13 states serving at-risk infants and toddlers (Nineteenth Annual Report, 1997).

Children eligible to receive these services under Part H must have an individualized family service plan (IFSP) in place. The IFSP is based on a family systems theoretical basis because infants and toddlers can only be assessed and assisted within the context of their environment. It is a requirement of the Act that professionals collaborate with the family (Nineteenth Annual Report, 1997).

Today, 50 states and 7 jurisdictions participate in the Part H program. In general, the participants identify three categories of risk for adverse developmental outcomes: established risk, biological/medical risk, and environmental risk. Many state definitions of developmental delay address multiple risk factors (Shackelford, 1998).

The Council for Exceptional Children in 1996 made recommendations concerning the use of the developmental delay eligibility category:

(1) that a **developmental delay** category of eligibility should be available for children in this age group; (2) that informed clinical opinion, culturally and linguistically appropriate test performance, and observation should be utilized in determining eligibility; (3) that a team process should be used as children move from IDEA Part H to Part B services; and (4) that personnel preparation programs should train professionals to use a multi-setting, multi-measure, and multi-informant model for identification and evaluation of **developmental delay.** (Abstract)

There have been many calls for clarification of eligibility criteria in the past few years (Larson, 1993; Harbin & Maxwell, 1991). In general, a 25% delay in one or more areas of development has been the most frequently used type of test-based criteria (Harbin & Maxwell, 1991). However, surveys of state consultants have shown a need for assessment instruments that assist with parental involvement and that are culturally competent (Harrington & Tongier, 1993).

In summary, the term developmental delay has a long history based in the understanding of normal developmental theory. In the mid 1980s the importance of serving infants and toddlers became patent, and service was mandated to these and at-risk children in a way that would maximize familial involvement. The current status of services to these children includes the evolution of a nationwide understanding of eligibility criteria, the establishment of appropriate assessment instruments, and a culturally competent awareness of the familial context of developmental delays.

REFERENCES

Council for Exceptional Children. (1996). *Developmental delay as an Eligibility Criteria.* Reston, VA: Council for Exceptional Children. (ERiC No. EC305927)

Golden, C.J., & Wilkening, G.N. (1986). Neuropsychological bases of exceptionality. In R.T. Brown & C.R. Reynolds (Eds.), *Psychological perspectives on childhood exceptionalities: A handbook* (pp. 61–90). New York: Wiley.

Harbin, G.L., & Maxwell, K. (1991). *Progress towards developing a definition for developmentally delayed: Report #2.* Carolina Institute for Child and Family Policy. Chapel Hill, NC: North Carolina University.

Harrington, R.G., & Tongier, J. (1993). The compatibility between State eligibility criteria for developmental delays and available early childhood assessment instrumentation. *Diagnostique, 18,* 3, 199–217.

Larson, L. (1993). *Part H of the Individuals with Disabilities Education Act: House research information brief.* St. Paul, MN: Minnesota House of Representatives Research Dept.

Lerner, J. (1985). *Learning disabilities: Theory, diagnosis & teaching strategies* (4th ed.). Boston: Houghton Mifflin.

Nineteenth Annual Report to Congress on the Implementation of the Individuals with Disabilities Education Act. (1997). Washington DC: U.S. Dept. of Education.

Shackelford, J. (1998). State and jurisdictional eligibility definitions for infants and toddlers with disabilities under IDEA. *NEC*TAS Notes*, 5.

Thompson, R.J., & O'Quinn, A.N. (1979). *Developmental disabilities.* New York: Oxford University Press.

See also **Deprivation; Individuals with Disabilities Education Act (IDEA); Early Experiences**

DEVELOPMENTAL DISABILITIES

Developmental disabilities is a generic term that refers to "all of the lifelong disabling conditions that require similar treatment or helping services and that occurred prior to age 22" (Ehlers, Prothero, & Langone, 1982). According to Boggs (1972), the concept of developmental disabilities has no etiological basis and includes all children and adults with a substantial continuing disability originating in childhood. The term is not to include disabilities that effectively could be overcome with rehabilitation or that are not both apparent and disabling prior to age 18. This concept of developmental disabilities has evolved since its inception in 1969 from a coalition of representatives of the National Association for Retarded Children, American Association on Mental Deficiency (AAMD), National Association of Coordinators of State Programs for the Mentally Retarded, National Association of State Mental Health Program Directors, Council for Exceptional Children, and United Cerebral Palsy Association.

In 1969 the concept of developmental disabilities as previously described by Boggs was introduced by this coalition; its members developed an amendment to the Mental Retardation Facilities Act (PL 88-164). The reasons for amending PL 88-164, according to Boggs, were as follow: (1) to give states greater incentive to continue planning and greater authority to use federal funds in accordance with state plans, (2) to expand the list of eligible services and not have the services tied to a specialized facility, (3) to have available monies allocated in response to the same plan, and (4) to use a functional approach associating the handicapped by common service needs to define eligibility for service rather than categorization by diagnosis.

In the proposed legislation the term mental retardation was replaced by the term developmental disabilities. Developmental disability was seen as a functional definition of a person needing specific services. According to a report issued by the President's Committee on Mental Retardation (1976), the rationale for use of the term developmental disability was to avoid categorical fractioning of service organizations and funding among similar and overlapping disabilities and to clearly distinguish developmental disabilities from the field of mental health. This concept as incorporated into the Developmental Disabilities Services and Facilities Construction Amendments of 1970 (PL 91-517) was broader than the one (mental retardation) used in previous legislation, but it did not reflect a truly functional definition of developmental disabilities

The concept of developmental disabilities as reflected in this legislation was criticized because while expanding the population eligible for services, it was still essentially categorical. Neisworth and Smith (1974) point out that the definition as used in PL 91-517 lacked precision and included requirements based on assumptions that "invite inconsistent and tenuous interpretations and applications" (p. 345). They further point out the lack of functionality in the definition and suggest a redefinition of developmental disabilities that would, in their opinion, lead to more specificity and reliability of interpretation and implementation:

Developmental disability refers to significantly deficient locomotor, communicative, adjustive, or academic functioning that is manifested during the developmental period, and that has continued or can be expected to continue indefinitely. (p. 346)

Since the introduction of the term developmental disability in federal legislation, it has been altered so that the definition used more clearly reflects the concept held by the coalition. The first alteration occurred when autism, any other condition closely related to mental retardation or requiring similar services and treatment, and dyslexia resulting from other disabilities included in the definition were added to the earlier definition and used in the Developmentally Disabled Assistance and Bill of Rights Act (PL 94-103). However, this altered definition still did not reflect the thinking of the coalition or address issues described by Neisworth and Smith.

A major alteration occurred when the National Task Force on the Definition of Developmental Disabilities was established in response to one of the requirements of PL 94-103. According to Thompson and O'Quinn (1979), members of this task force opposed the use of the term developmental disabilities as a "catch-all for an arbitrary collection of existing labels or conditions" (p. 14) and advocated a generic or functional definition be formulated to cut across specific categories or conditions. Members of this task force defined the developmentally disabled as "a group of people experiencing a chronic disability which substantially limits their functioning in a variety of broad areas of major life activity central to independent living" (p. 14). Subsequently, the thinking of the task force was reflected in the Rehabilitation Comprehensive Services and Developmental Disabilities Amendments of 1978 (PL 95-602) and retained in the Developmental Disabilities Act of 1984 (PL 98-527), and later Acts culminating in 1994. The definition reads as follows:

The term developmental disability means a severe, chronic disability of a person which:

—is attributable to a mental or physical impairment or combination of mental and physical impairments;

—is manifested before the person attains age twenty-two;

—is likely to continue indefinitely;

—results in substantial functional limitations in three or more of the following areas of major life activities; (i) self-care, (ii) receptive and expressive language, (iii) learning, (iv) mobility, (v) self-direction, (vi) capacity for independent living, and (vii) economic sufficiency; and

—reflects the person's need for a combination and sequence of special, interdisciplinary, or generic care, treatment, or other services which are of lifelong or extended duration and are individually planned and coordinated.

Seltzer (1983) describes this definition as functionally oriented with emphasis on chronicity, age-specific onset, multiple areas of functional limitations, and need for an extended array of long-term services from a multiplicity of service providers. Seltzer points to this functional orientation as an advantage of this latest definition but cites its lack of operational clarity as a disadvantage. However, Seltzer goes on to point out that with use and the development of operational guidelines, the disadvantages are hoped to diminish.

The overlap in various definitions of developmental disabilities and other handicapping conditions has caused considerable confusion. Grossman (1983) points out that basic characteristics of mental retardation overlap with the legislative definition of developmental disabilities. Grossman goes on to say that the areas of limitations described in the legislative definition of developmental disabilities apply to more severe forms of mental retardation and to some mildly retarded individuals during certain periods of their lives. Grossman describes the parallel aspects of mental retardation and developmental disabilities as that of being developmental in origin and stressing impairment in adaptive behavior. He also indicates that the subgroup of persons with more severe forms of mental retardation will have a permanent and substantial handicap, as do many children with autism and cerebral palsy. Thus persons in this subgroup may be considered developmentally disabled. However, those with milder mental retardation and less severe conditions of cerebral palsy, epilepsy, and autism would fall outside the definition of developmental disability.

In summary, the concept of developmental disability is a generic one that evolved from the area of mental retardation and focuses on the needs of persons with serious and ongoing disabilities that originated before age 22. Thompson and O'Quinn (1979) point out that as the concept of developmental disabilities continues to evolve, efforts at defining developmental disabilities in cultural contexts are likely to continue as well.

REFERENCES

Boggs, E.M. (1972). Federal legislation 1966–1971. In J. Wortis (Ed.), *Mental retardation: An annual review* (Vol. 4). New York: Grune & Stratton.

Ehlers, W.H., Prothero, J.C., & Langone, J. (1982). *Mental retardation and other developmental disabilities* (3rd ed.). Columbus, OH: Merrill.

Grossman, H.J. (Ed.). (1983). *Classification in mental retardation.* Washington, DC: American Association on Mental Deficiency.

Neisworth, J.T., & Smith, R.M. (1974). An analysis and redefinition of "developmental disabilities." *Exceptional Children, 40,* 345–347.

Seltzer, G.B. (1983). Systems of classification. In J.L. Matson & J.A. Mulick (Eds.), *Handbook of mental retardation.* New York: Pergamon.

Thompson, R.J., & O'Quinn, A.N. (1979). *Developmental disabilities.* New York: Oxford University Press.

See also AAMD; Cerebral Palsy; Mental Retardation; Physical Handicap

DEVELOPMENTAL DISABILITIES ASSISTANCE ACT AND BILL OF RIGHTS

The Developmental Disabilities Assistance and Bill of Rights Act Amendments of 1994 was originally enacted as Title 1 of the Mental Retardation Facilities and Construction Act of 1963, Public Law, 88-164 and was amended in 1981, 1987, 1990, and 1994. The purpose of the Act is to:

assure that individuals with developmental disabilities and their families participate in the design of and have access to culturally competent services, supports, and other assistance and opportunities that promote independence, productivity, and integration and inclusion into the community. (Part A. p. 1)

This is carried out through the participation of State Developmental Disabilities Councils, the development of state protection and advocacy systems, the support of university-affiliated programs, and the support of national initiatives to collect data and provide technical assistance to state Councils.

The Act also states the rights of individuals with developmental disabilities as:

(1) Individuals with developmental disabilities have a right to appropriate treatment, services, and habilitation for such disabilities.

(2) The treatment services, and habilitation for an individual with developmental disabilities should be designed to maximize the developmental potential of the individual and should be provided the setting that is least restrictive of the individual's personal liberty.

(3) The Federal Government and the States both have an obligation to assure that public funds are not provided to any institutional or other residential program for individuals with developmental disabilities that—

(A) does not provide treatment, services, and habilitation which is appropriate to the needs of such individuals, or

(B) does not meet the following minimum standards:

(i) Provision of a nourishing, well-balanced daily diet to the individuals with developmental disabilities being served by the program.

(ii) Provision to such individuals of appropriate and sufficient medical and dental services.

(iii) Prohibition of the use of physical restraint on such individuals unless absolutely necessary and prohibition of the use of such restraint as a punishment or as a substitute for a habilitation program.

(iv) Prohibition on the excessive use of chemical restraints on such individuals and the use of such restraints as punishments or as a substitute for a habilitation program or in quantities that interfere with services, treatment, or habilitation for such individuals.

(v) Permission for close relatives of such individuals to visit them at reasonable hours without prior notice.

(vi) Compliance with adequate fire and safety standards as may be promulgated by the Secretary.

(4) All programs for individuals with developmental disabilities should meet standards which are designed to assure the most favorable possible outcome for those served, and—

(A) in the case of residential programs serving individuals in need of comprehensive health-related, habilitative, or rehabilitative services, which are at least equivalent to those standards applicable to intermediate care facilities for the mentally retarded promulgated in regulations of the Secretary on June 3, 1988, as appropriate when taking into account the size of the institutions and the service delivery arrangements of the facilities of the programs;

(B) in the case of other residential programs for individuals with developmental disabilities, which assure that care is appropriate to the needs of the individuals being served by such programs, assure that the individuals admitted to facilities of such programs are individuals whose needs can be met through services provided by such facilities, and assure that the facilities under such programs provide for the humane care of the residents of the facilities, are sanitary, and protect their rights; and

(C) in the case of nonresidential programs, which assure the care provided by such programs is appropriate to the individuals served by the programs. The rights of individuals with developmental disabilities described in findings made in this section are in addition to any constitutional or other rights otherwise afforded to all individuals. (Part A, Section 110)

Under Part B of the Act, the Developmental Disabilities Council program provides financial assistance to each state to support the activities of a Developmental Disabilities Council. The councils are made up of individuals who have developmental disabilities, family members, and representatives of State agencies that provide services to individuals with developmental disabilities. The Council develops and implements a state-wide plan to address employment (which is a federally mandated priority) and case management, child development and community living. Fiscal year 1998 appropriation provided $64,803,000 to support these plans.

See also Individuals with Disabilities Education Act (IDEA); Office of Civil Rights

DEVELOPMENTAL DISABILITIES LEGAL RESOURCE CENTER

See PROTECTION AND ADVOCACY SYSTEM—DEVELOPMENTALLY DISABLED (P&A).

DEVELOPMENTAL DYSLEXIA

Developmental dyslexia is typically perceived as a complex heterogeneous reading disorder. It appears to stem from a selective disturbance of the maturation of neurological functions thought to be responsible for the acquisition of reading and writing skills. It is genetically determined and thus distinct from acquired alexia from traumatic brain injury (Gaddes, 1976). Critical components of the disorder that are relative to the individual's unique patterns of intrinsic abilities and extrinsic assets dictate that the dyslexic must have at least average intelligence; sufficient cultural and linguistic opportunity; emotional stability; access to appropriate instruction; and approximately normal sensory acuity (Rourke & Gates, 1981). Prognosis of relative success in compensating for the disorder's consequences is based on early identification, delineation of the individual's unique pattern of strengths and weaknesses, capitalization on unique educational strategies, and concomitant appropriate socio-cultural/familial support systems.

Educational and clinical psychologists' interest in dyslexia gained momentum during the first two decades of the twentieth century. Research focused on the basic underlying factors that presumably caused failure in learning to read, and two schools of thought emerged. The first emphasized the relation of perceptual and cognitive disabilities and the second concentrated on environmental factors (Benton, 1980). A new perspective on dyslexia was formulated by Orton toward the end of the second decade.

Orton related reading disability to a defective interhemispheric organization of cerebral function. It was assumed to be the result of a faulty maturational process of establishing specialization of function in a single hemisphere. The consequences of incomplete hemispheric dominance were said to lead to confusion and failure to read effectively (Johnson & Myklebust, 1967).

From the 1960s to the present, research proceeded by varied means. Renewed interest in Orton's work followed advances in asymmetrical hemispheric specialization research (e.g., dichotic listening, dichaptic discrimination, and tachistoscopic methods). Medical technology has furthered investigations in the neurological basis of dyslexia by means of electroencephalography, computerized tomography scanning, cerebral blood flow studies, positron emission tomography, and autopsies on dyslexic and normal brains. Current research in the educational/neuropsychological literature (Hynd & Obrzut, 1981; Knights & Bakker, 1976) has supported the involvement of higher cortical impairment in developmental dyslexia. There are a select few that contend that dyslexia stems from sub-cortical impairment involving the cerebellar-vestibular system (Frank &

Levinson, 1973); however, independent validation of this research has not yet been published.

Sex differences are apparent in that males are disproportionately represented in reading-disabled populations. Data exist that indicate even normal girls are more adept at the learning-to-read process than normal boys. Anatomical data further substantiate those claims, since myelination occurred more rapidly in the left hemisphere for girls and the right hemisphere for boys (Dalby, 1979). Other sex differences have been hypothesized to be maturational lags in hemispheric specialization shifts in the learning-to-read process (Rourke, 1982), where girls pass through the stages faster than boys (Gaddes, 1976). These hypotheses suggest that the right hemisphere-mediated functions may have a critical role in the initial stages of the acquisition of the reading process, whereas the left hemisphere-mediated functions may be more efficient in using a routinized mode that stems from that acquisition. This right-to-left shift in hemispheric specialization may be a function of increased competence with the learning-to-read process.

The current perspective on developmental dyslexia has focused on more stringent methods of research in the identification of distinct subtypes (Rourke & Gates, 1981). Converging data from this body of research suggested a need for a multidimensional definition; it was clear that appropriate identification of dyslexics could not be made solely on the basis of poor reading achievement with approximately average intelligence (Yule & Rutter, 1976). The presence of differences in the types of dyslexia necessitates different strategies of educational interventions. Recognition of these differences became more pronounced following multivariate analyses of clinical neuropsychological methods (Petrauskas & Rourke, 1979) and important developmental changes, described in longitudinal research (Satz, Taylor, Friel, & Fletcher, 1978).

The neuropsychological evidence has suggested the presence of several subtypes of dyslexic readers, two of which are fairly distinct in older children and adults: auditory-linguistic deficient (dysphonetic) readers and visual-spatial deficient (dyseidetic) readers, as described by Pirozzolo (1981). Others have described a mixed dyslexic group (both dysphonetic and dyseidetic); an unspecified group (of which subcortical impairment cannot be completely ruled out), and a normal group; or linguistic, perceptual, and mixed groups (Masutto, 1994); and phonological and surface types (Murphy & Pollatsek, 1994).

Hartlage and Telzrow (1983) have elucidated various means of using neuropsychological data for successful educational intervention. They hypothesized that a child's neuropsychological strengths should be emphasized in matching complementary curricula to that pattern, without total rejection of tasks using weaker neuropsychological abilities. As an example, auditory-linguistic deficient dyslexics typically have stronger right hemisphere-mediated functions; thus, a "whole word" or "look and say" method of reading would be recommended. This would occur without rejecting the teaching of sounds of letters and blends when decoding new words. Other techniques (Aaron & Poostay, 1982) advocate a careful review of the individual child's functional behaviors. Task analysis of these behaviors indicates where the functional breakdown has occurred in the learning process and represents the focus of intervention. The most widely used teaching method is the Orton-Gillingham method, which uses a simultaneous association of visual, auditory, and kinesthetic language stimuli (Griesbach, 1993).

REFERENCES

Aaron, I.E., & Poostay, E.J. (1982). Strategies for reading disorders. In C.R. Reynolds & T.B. Gutkin (Eds.), *The handbook of school psychology* (pp. 410–435). New York: Wiley.

Benton, A.L. (1980). Dyslexia: Evolution of a concept. *Bulletin of the Orton Society, 30,* 10–26.

Dalby, J.T. (1979). Deficit or delay: Neuropsychological models of development dyslexia. *Journal of Special Education, 3,* 239–264.

Frank, J., & Levinson, H. (1973). Dysmetric dyslexia and dyspraxia: Hypothesis and study. *Journal of the American Academy of Child Psychiatry, 12,* 690–701.

Gaddes, W.H. (1976). Prevalence estimates and the need for definition of learning disabilities. In R. Knights & D. Bakker (Eds.), *The neuropsychology of learning disorders: Theoretical approaches* (pp. 3–24). Baltimore, MD: University Park Press.

Griesbach, G. (1993). *Dyslexia: It's history, etiology, and treatment.* (ERIC Clearinghouse No. CS011300)

Hartlage, L.C., & Telzrow, C.F. (1983). The neuropsychological basis of educational intervention. *Journal of Learning Disabilities, 16,* 521–523.

Hynd, G.W., & Obrzut, J.E. (1981). *Neuropsychological assessment and the school-age child: Issues and procedures.* New York: Grune & Stratton.

Johnson, D.J., & Myklebust, H.R. (1967). *Learning disabilities: Educational principles and practices.* New York: Grune & Stratton.

Knights, R., & Bakker, D. (1976). *The neuropsychology of learning disorders: Theoretical approaches.* Baltimore, MD: University Park Press.

Orton-Gillingham Practitioners and Educators (1998). Dyslexia. www.ols.net./users/orton/index.htm

Masutto, C. (1994). Neurolinguistic differentiation of children with subtypes of dyslexia. *Journal of Learning Disabilities, 27,* 8, 520–526.

Murphy, L., & Pollatsek, A. (1994). Developmental dyslexia: Heterogeneity without discrete subgroups. *Annals of Dyslexia, 44,* 120–146.

Petrauskas, R.J., & Rourke, B.P. (1979). Identification of subtypes of retarded readers: A neuropsychological multivariate approach. *Journal of Clinical Neuropsychology, 1,* 17–37.

Pirozzolo, F.J. (1981). Language and brain: Neuropsychological aspects of developmental reading disability. *School Psychology Review, 3,* 350–355.

Rourke, B.P. (1982). Central processing deficiencies in children: Toward a developmental neuropsychological model. *Journal of Clinical Neuropsychology, 4,* 1–18.

Rourke, B.P., & Gates, R.D. (1981). Neuropsychological research and school psychology. In G.W. Hynd & J.E. Obrzut (Eds.), *Neu-*

ropsychological assessment and the school-age child: Issue and procedures (pp. 3–25). New York: Grune & Stratton.

Satz, P., Taylor, H.G., Friel, J., & Fletcher, J.M. (1978). Some developmental and predictive precursors of reading disabilities: A six year follow-up. In A.L. Benton & D. Pearl (Eds.), *Dyslexia: An appraisal of current knowledge* (pp. 313–347). New York: Oxford University Press.

Yule, W., & Rutter, M. (1976). Epidemiological and social implications of specific reading retardation. In R. Knights & D. Bakker (Eds.), *The neuropsychology of learning disorders: Theoretical approaches* (pp. 25–39). Baltimore, MD: University Park Press.

DEVELOPMENTAL MILESTONES

Adults who have kept infant diaries have watched with pride as their children reached particular developmental milestones. The first responsive smile, the initial unsure steps, and the dawning of language are three of the most obvious milestones. Psychologists take an interest in these early milestones, but their perspective extends beyond the infant years to the whole life span. Their research includes a host of physical, biological, mental, emotional, and social milestones which, taken together, form a normative picture of the child's development.

Milestones that involve a physical or biological change are the most salient because the newly acquired behavior is so clear. One day infants are holding onto the coffee table investigating magazines or curios, and the next day they are launching themselves into a void where no support exists. This adventure constitutes the first step. The first step, typically achieved at 11.7 months is, however, a culmination of the series of physical milestones outlined in the Table below (Bayley, 1969). This table gives the average age when infants master the physical skills that precede walking as well as an age range when different children master the skills. Notice that these normal ranges are often several months apart. For example, occasionally children will pull themselves to a standing position at the age of 5 months. At the other end of the scale, some perfectly normal children do not accomplish this same feat until they are a year old. This range of normality attests to the individual differences that exist in attaining all developmental milestones.

At birth, the brain weighs about 12 ounces (350 grams). Most of this brain tissue is generated in the last 3 months of pregnancy. In fact, forming the 10 billion cells that comprise the human brain means that during the last months of pregnancy and the first months of life, about 250,000 neurons must be generated each minute (Cowan, 1979). In the first 2 years of life, the weight of the brain will triple, reflecting a surge in the number of dendrites (Conel, 1967). As the infant matures, the dendrites intertwine into more extensive networks, until each neuron is connected by its dendrites with thousands of other cells. When one cell is activated, the effect can be spread through the entire dendritic network.

This brief sketch of how the brain develops fits into The-len's (1981) discussion of rhythmical behavior. She argues that the development of the brain presages the physical developments we regard as milestones. In newborns, the brain's neurons are relatively isolated, hence the child's behaviors are reflexive and uncoordinated. As the dendritic networks begin to form, the child's behavior takes on more rhythmical patterns. At this point, the child will practice activating a particular part of the body in a rhythmical way. When neuronal networks for a particular area mature, physical skills will be controlled by the infant and will be integrated with the actions of other parts of the body (Hofer, 1981). Many of the milestones in physical development reflect, then, the developmental milestones of the brain.

The sensory motor period of development refers to the first 2 years of life. During this period, the child changes dramatically, from a wordless newborn, whose behaviors are primarily reflexive, to a talking 2 year old who has developed an amazing mastery of the immediate environment. In these 2 growth-filled years, the biggest mental milestones are the development of the object concept and the beginnings of language.

The object concept, described by Piaget (1954), reflects the infant's growing mental awareness. In the first few months of life, the infant is unconcerned about the comings and goings of people and objects. "Out of sight, out of mind" is an appropriate description for the infant's understanding of objects. Shortly after the first 6 months, infants' behaviors begin to change. Now, when their mothers disappear, infants stare at the doorway. They may cry, hoping that the combination of looking and crying will make their mother reappear. This change in behavior signals the realization, on the infant's part, that their mother is a separate entity.

Piaget (1954) followed the development of the object concept in his own three children. Using an infant version of hide-and-seek, he hid his children's favorite toy under a cloth or pillow. The hiding involved no deception; the infant could follow the toy visually as Piaget slowly slid it under the cover. Prior to 8 months, Piaget's children often reached for the cloth, but abandoned the search in a moment or two. By 10 months, however, they quickly pulled the cloth away and grabbed the toy. Piaget interpreted this change as indicating that his children could hold an image of the toy in their memories long enough to search for the object. They had developed a concept of an object that endured even when the object disappeared.

The object concept is a landmark in the development of memory. Once infants can represent objects in their minds, they are no longer limited to a reacting role; they can plan a course of action. Combine this initiative with the fact that 8 to 10 month olds have some mobility and you have the foundation for the avid exploration and curiosity of the 2 year old. The exploration and action of the 2 year old may seem like play to adults, and it is; but it is play with a serious purpose. It serves as the foundation for the abstract logic that is still many years in the future (Langer, 1980).

It is not coincidental that the second milestones of infancy, the child's first word, appears shortly after the object concept. In order to name an object, you must have a clear concept of that object. In most children, the appearance of the first word occurs between 10 and 15 months (de Villiers & de Villiers, 1979). But these early words are tied to a specific context and really do not function as symbols. For example, Nicky at 13 months would wave and say "bye-bye" when his father left for work in the morning. But Nicky couldn't say "bye-bye" without waving. "Bye-bye" was associated with the morning, the waving, and the father leaving (Anisfeld, 1984). It took several more months for Nicky to use "bye-bye" in a symbolic way, to mean goodbye.

With the acquisition of language, the child moves into a period called the intuitive or preoperational stage of mental development. This stage of development, which lasts from approximately 2 to 5 years, stands in stark contrast to the sensory motor period because language begins to direct the child's behavior. The preoperational period begins with a child whose language skills are just emerging and ends with a child who relies on language instead of action to understand the world (Anisfeld, 1984). Two and 3 year olds buttress their beginning language skills by combining words and actions. These toddlers comprehend an airplane by saying "airplane," sticking out their arms, running around the room, and making sounds like a roaring engine. The action of imitating the airplane helps them form an image of an airplane and helps them attach the label "airplane" to the scene. Similarly, 3 and 4 year olds playing with blocks or dolls keep a running monologue going to describe the action they are orchestrating. By tying language to the action-based concepts that were developed during the sensory motor period, the child can gain confidence in the use of language. When language emerges as the primary means of understanding the world, the child's behavior changes dramatically. Four year olds who ask their parents endless questions about the car, the refrigerator, the dog, and the weather, are demonstrating that they can now learn about the world using language. When language skills are mature, the child is ready to transcend the constraints of time and space, to think about situations that cannot be experienced, and to let logic become the guide to mental operations.

Between 5 and 7 years of age, a third mental milestone is reached—concrete operational thought. Having mastered language and action, children begin to operate symbolically. They classify and order their environments and, in the process, enhance their awareness of the world. Understanding the days of the week and the months of the year allows adults to bring order to the daily chaos of life. Knowing that it is Monday supplies a great deal of information. It is the beginning of the week, tomorrow is Tuesday, and the weekend is 5 days away. The knowledge that today is Monday allows us to draw many other conclusions, because Monday is part of a larger organization of knowledge encompassing months, seasons, and years. Preoperational children lack these higher level organizations. But with the onset of concrete operational thought, children begin to sort out the world, order it for their use, and develop multilayered concepts (Kuhn, 1972).

The real hallmark of concrete operational thought is the ability to transform information. One woman can simultaneously be mother, Mrs. Lindsay, and Aunt Carol, and each of these classifications is appropriate. Each label is understood as part of a larger organization. The concrete operational child not only uses language to guide actions, but coordinates different bits of information.

Mastering concrete operations moves the child toward more logical thought processes, but the advances of concrete operational thought are really a stepping stone to the culmination of mental development—formal operational thought. Formal thought processes are the final mental milestone; they begin between 12 and 16 years of age (Inhelder & Piaget, 1958). During this period of development, mental operations are completely integrated and thought attains a flexibility unrealized at the earlier stages. Students can abstract from the reality of a problem and consider alternatives to a problem. Furthermore, they can systematically test their ideas and discover which of several hypotheses is correct.

Developmental milestones take many forms. The rapid physical changes that occur during infancy and the biological milestones that herald a new period of life are readily identified because they represent an abrupt break with the past. Mental development is characterized by just as many milestones, but they tend to emerge gradually. The object concept, the first word, and concrete operational thought processes are each noticeable points on the continuous tableau of development. As with most milestones, cognitive advances represent both the culmination of earlier processes and the foundation for further development. Social and emotional milestones include attachment behaviors and friendships. It is essential that these milestones are investigated and assessed in a culturally competent fashion. Family and social relationships are contextually and culturally-loaded concepts (Nissani, 1993; Rocco, 1993; Winborne & Randolf, 1991). The first cries for attention and the devoted camaraderie of adolescence are both milestones that attest to the child's interactions with others. Examined together, the succession of physical, mental, and social milestones chart an individual's progress on the road of life.

REFERENCES

Anisfeld, M. (1984). *Language development from birth to three.* Hillsdale, NJ: Erlbaum.

Bayley, N. (1969). *Manual for the Bayley scales of infant development.* New York: Psychological Corporation.

Conel, J.L. (1967). *The postnatal development of the human cortex* (Vol. 8). Cambridge, MA: Harvard University Press.

Cowan, W.M. (1979). The development of the brain. *Scientific American, 241,* 112–133.

de Villiers, P.A., & de Villiers, J.G. (1979). *Early language.* Cambridge, MA: Harvard University Press.

Hofer, M.A. (1981). *The roots of human behavior.* San Francisco: Freeman.

Inhelder, B., & Piaget, J. (1958). *The growth of logical thinking from childhood to adolescence.* New York: Basic Books.

Kuhn, D. (1972). Mechanisms of change in the development of cognitive structures. *Child Development, 43,* 833–844.

Langer, J. (1980). *The origins of logic: Six to twelve months.* New York: Academic.

Nissani, H. (1993). Early childhood programs for language minority students. *ERIC clearinghouse on languages and linguistics.* (ERIC Digest No. ED355836)

Piaget, J. (1954). *The construction of reality in the child.* New York: Ballantine.

Rocco, S. (1993). *New visions for the developmental assessment of infants and young children.* (ERIC Clearinghouse No. EC302834)

Thelen, E. (1981). Rhythmical behavior in infancy: An ethological perspective. *Developmental Psychology, 17,* 237–257.

Winborne, D.G., & Randolf, S.M. (1991). Developmental expectations and outcomes for African-American infants. (ERIC Clearinghouse No. PS019880)

DEVELOPMENTAL NORMS

Developmental norms describe the position of an individual along a continuum of development. Two fundamental types of developmental norms are age equivalents and grade equivalents. They are obtained by administering a test to several successive age or grade groups; the average, or typical, performance of each age or grade group is subsequently determined and becomes the norm for a particular age or grade group (Anastasi, 1982).

A number of human traits demonstrate growth with increasing age, including abstract intelligence, vocabulary or language acquisition, and motor skill development. Age equivalents have frequently been used to interpret performance for age-related traits. The average test score obtained by successive age or grade groups is determined based on the performance of a carefully selected sample of individuals. The age (in years and months) for which a particular test score was the average becomes the age equivalent for that particular test score; e.g., a child who answered 35 questions correctly on a receptive language test received an age equivalent of 4–6, meaning that 35 was the average, or typical, score for children aged 4 years, 6 months tested in the norming program. The term mental age refers to an age equivalent obtained from an intelligence test. A child with a mental age of 6 years, 3 months, for example, performed as well as the average child aged 6 years, 3 months.

Skills that develop as a direct result of school instruction such as reading or mathematics have frequently been assessed with tests that yield grade equivalents. The typical, or average, performance of successive grade groups is determined for a carefully selected sample of pupils. The grade for which a certain test score was the average becomes the grade equivalent for that particular test score (Thorndike & Hagen, 1977); e.g., a pupil who answered 40 questions correctly on a mathematics concepts test received a grade equivalent of 6.2, meaning that 40 was the average score for pupils in the second month of grade 6.

Age and grade equivalents have come into disfavor for a number of reasons:

1. They represent scales having unequal units because human traits typically develop faster in the earlier years and slow down in adolescence and adulthood.

2. They are not as rich in meaning as within-group norms (standard scores and percentile ranks) because they "match" the individual's performance to the age or grade group for which that performance was just average.

3. They can imply a level of functioning or skill development that is misleading. A fifth-grade pupil who receives a reading comprehension grade equivalent of 10.8 is not necessarily reading at the same level as a student in the eighth month of the tenth grade. The grade equivalent of 10.8 is to some extent a contrivance of the grade equivalent score scale and simply means the pupil is reading very well for a fifth grader (Cronbach, 1984).

In summary, age and grade equivalents are developmental norms that, when interpreted cautiously, can sometimes provide useful information; however, within group norms such as standard scores and percentile ranks are the preferred method of test interpretation.

REFERENCES

Anastasi, A. (1982). *Psychological testing* (5th ed.). New York: Macmillan.

Cronbach, L.J. (1984). *Essentials of psychological testing* (4th ed.). New York: Harper & Row.

Thorndike, R.L., & Hagen, E.P. (1977). *Measurement and evaluation in psychology and education.* New York: Wiley.

See also **Grade Equivalents; Norm-Referenced Testing**

DEVELOPMENTAL OPTOMETRY

The relationship between vision, sight, and learning took on a new meaning in 1922 when A.M. Skeffington, an optometrist who help found the Postgraduate Optometric Extension Program, lectured on the concept that Snellen visual acuity (sight) and visual effectiveness (vision) were not one in the same. In the 1930s George Crow and Margaret Eberl expanded this concept by instituting the use of preventive lenses and visual training to enhance visual abilities, promote visual efficiency, and reduce or eliminate visual anomalies such as amblyopia, strabismus, and binocular dysfunction.

Clinical studies in the visual development of the school-age child took a dramatic step forward in the 1940s at the Clinic of Child Development at Yale University. Gesell et al. (1949) established that the eye and the other sensory modalities take turns in the development of the mind. Gesell et al. stated that vision is so fundamental in the growth of the mind that the child takes hold of the physical world with his eyes long before he takes hold with his hands. The eyes lead in the patterning of behavior.

The optometrist specializing in the field of developmental vision, today, includes in the basic vision examination a careful case history that covers any significant information on the prenatal, perinatal, and postnatal disorders and any delays in the developmental milestones. The visual examination includes the standard testing procedures such as visual acuity, ocular health status of the eyes, binocular status, refractive status, and accommodative facility. Additional tests may probe the child's concept of laterality, directionality, dominance, eye-hand coordination, and visual perception.

Training of the child with developmental vision problems encompasses the standard visual training procedures. These include enhancement of ocular motility, stereopsis, eye-hand coordination, and accommodation. Additional techniques may emphasize bilateral and binocular integration. It is also important for the optometrist to collaborate with special services personnel to assist in the psychological conditions that sometimes exist with vision difficulties (Biaggo & Bittner, 1990).

The optometrist, as Solan (1979) states, blends professional and intellectual skills to develop in the learning-disabled child a suitable level of visual functional readiness for learning, the sensory-motor skills necessary for a child to respond to classroom instruction, and cognitive skills and conceptual tempo required for assimilation and generalization in learning reasoning and problem solving.

REFERENCES

Biaggio, M.K., & Bittner, E. (1990). Psychology and optometry: Interaction and collaboration. *American Psychologist, 45,* 12, 1313–1315.

Gesell, A., Ilg, F.L., & Bullis, G.E. (1949). *Vision: Its development in infant and child.* New York: Harper & Brothers.

Solan, H. (1979). *Learning disabilities: The role of the developmental optometrist, 50*(11), 1265. St. Louis: American Optometric Association.

DEVELOPMENTAL TEST OF VISUAL PERCEPTION: SECOND EDITION (DTVP-2)

The *Developmental Test of Visual Perception: Second Edition* (DTVP-2) (Hammill, Pearson, & Voress, 1993) is the most recent revision of *The Marianne Frostig Developmental Test of Visual Perception* originally authored by Frostig, Maslow, Lefever, & Whittlesey (1963). The new edition includes numerous improvements, is suitable for children ages 4 to 10, measures both visual perception and visual-motor integration skills, has eight subtests, is based on updated theories of visual perception development, and can be administered to individuals in 35 minutes. The DTVP-2 subtests are Eye-Hand Coordination, Copying, Spatial Relations, Position in Space, Figure-Ground, Visual Closure, Visual-Motor Speed, and Form Constancy.

This test was reviewed in *The Twelfth Mental Measurements Yearbook* by Bologna (1995) and Tindal (1995). Bologna stated that the revised test was an impressive revision of a previously weak instrument; Tindal described the test as useful in determining General Visual Perception, Motor Reduced Visual Perception, and Visual-Motor Integration.

REFERENCES

Bologna, N.B. (1985). Review of the Developmental Test of Visual Perception: Second Edition. In J.C. Conoley & J.C. Impara (Eds.), *The twelfth mental measurements yearbook* (pp. 289–292). Lincoln, NE: Buros Institute of Mental Measurements, University of Nebraska Press.

Frostig, M., Maslow, P., Lefever, D.W., & Whittlesey, J.R.B. (1963). *The Marianne Frostig Developmental Test of Visual Perception.* Palo Alto, CA: Consulting Psychologists Press.

Hammill, D.D., Pearson, N.A., & Voress, J.K. (1993). *Developmental Test of Visual Perception Second Edition.* Austin, TX: Pro Ed.

Tindal, G. (1985). Review of the Developmental Test of Visual Perception: Second Edition. In J.C. Conoley & J.C. Impara (Eds.), *The twelfth mental measurements yearbook* (pp. 289–292). Lincoln, NE: Buros Institute of Mental Measurements, University of Nebraska Press.

DEVELOPMENTAL PSYCHOLOGY

Developmental Psychology is a publication of the American Psychological Association. Founded in 1968, its first editor was Boyd R. McCandless of Emory University.

The journal's primary purpose is to publish reports of empirical research on topics pertaining to developmental psychology. Developmental psychology is defined as including variables pertaining to growth and development broadly cast. Not only chronological age and physical growth variables are included, but also other factors, such as sex and socioeconomic status.

Developmental Psychology is published bimonthly. Manuscripts may be sent to *Developmental Psychology,* American Psychological Association, 1200 Seventeenth Street, NW, Washington, DC 20036.

DEVELOPMENTAL THERAPY

Developmental therapy is a method of educating severely socially, emotionally, and behaviorally handicapped children. It has normal social-emotional development as its goal. Developmental sequences in behavior, social communication, socialization, and cognition provide the framework for the curriculum. Devised by Mary M. Wood and associates (1979, 1986), developmental therapy links theory and research about normal social-emotional development to classroom practices.

Developmental therapy has been used successfully with severely emotionally disturbed and autistic children from age 2 to 16 years in preschool, elementary, middle school, and high-school classes. It also has been used effectively in day-treatment settings and residential facilities. Educators have adapted aspects of developmental therapy to resource rooms, self-contained classrooms, and regular education classes. It has extensive applications in the therapeutic arts, including art, music, and recreation therapies. It has also been adapted for use in camp settings and leisure programs, and for parents in home programs with autistic children. It was approved by the U.S. Office of Education, National Institute of Education Joint Dissemination Review Panel in 1975 as an exemplary educational program with documented effectiveness. It received validation again in 1981 from the same panel as an exemplary training model for teachers.

Students are grouped for developmental therapy according to their stage of social-emotional development. Groups range in size from 4 to 12 students, with the smaller groups used for students at lower developmental stages and those with severe psychopathology. Each group is conducted by a lead teacher-therapist and a support teacher aide. The goals and specific program (treatment) objectives and procedures for each stage are based on individual assessment of each student's social-emotional development. Characteristic roles for adults and the activities, materials, schedules, and behavior management strategies are specified by the stage.

The instrument used to assess each student's social-emotional development is the Developmental Therapy Objectives Rating Form (DTORF). This instrument provides specific individual education plan (IEP) short-term objectives and long-range program goals. Since the first field testing, the DTORF has been used with several thousand students ages 2 to 16 with a range of handicapping conditions, including children who are autistic, mentally retarded, severely multihandicapped, deaf, schizophrenic, nonhandicapped, and gifted. Several studies provide adequate support for the effectiveness of developmental therapy (Kaufman, Paget, & Wood, 1981; Wood & Swan, 1978; Wood, 1997).

Developmental therapy has received contextual endorsement because of the directives for Part H of the Individuals with Disabilities Education Act and its amendments. Professionals working with young children with behavioral disorders and their families have adopted developmental therapy because it is based on the child's current level of performance rather than chronological age. This concept is conducive to the practicalities of working within the family system as mandated by IDEA (Hanft & Striffler, 1995; Zabel, 1991).

REFERENCES

Hanft, B., & Striffler, N. (1995). Incorporating developmental therapy in early childhood programs: Challenges and promising practices. *Infants and Young Children, 8,* 2, 37–47.

Kaufman, A., Paget, C., & Wood, M.M. (1981). Effectiveness of developmental therapy for severely emotionally disturbed children. In F.H. Wood (Ed.), *Perspectives for a new decade: Education's responsibility for seriously emotionally disturbed and behaviorally disordered children and youth.* Reston, VA: Council for Exceptional Children.

Wood, M.M. (1979). *The developmental therapy objectives: A self-instructional workbook.* Austin, TX: Pro-Ed.

Wood, M.M. (1986). *Developmental therapy in the classroom.* Austin, TX: Pro Ed.

Wood, M.M. (1997). *Social competence for young children: An outreach project for inservice training.* (ERIC Clearinghouse No. EC305787)

Wood, M.M., & Swan, W.W. (1978). A developmental approach to educating the disturbed young child. *Behavioral Disorders 3,* 197–209.

Zabel, M.K. (1991). Teaching young children with behavior disorders: Working with behavior disorders. *ERIC Clearinghouse on Handicapped and Gifted Children.* Reston, VA: Council for Exceptional Children. (ERIC Document No. EC300413)

See also **Emotional Disorders; Social Development; Social Learning Theory**

DEVEREUX FOUNDATION, THE

The Devereux Foundation was founded in 1912 by Helena T. Devereux (1885–1975), a public school teacher who resigned her position to begin a school for emotionally disturbed and mentally retarded children. Devereux was considered a pioneer in the field of education, operating on the premise that every student can learn and grow in an environment tailored to his or her needs. In 1938, the school was chartered as a Pennsylvania nonprofit foundation and currently maintains its headquarters in Devon, Pennsylvania. With locations in 12 states and the District of Columbia, today's Foundation is the largest independent nonprofit provider of treatment services for individuals with emotional, behavioral, and developmental disabilities in the United States.

In addition to the provision of educational and treatment services, Devereux was involved in various research and publishing efforts, such as publication of the *Devereux Behavior Rating Scale* and the *Individual Motor Achievement Guided Education* (IMAGE) program (Sargent, 1984). The Foundation may be contacted via email at info@devereux.org.

REFERENCE

Sargent, J.K. (1984). *The directory for exceptional children* (10th ed.). Boston: Porter Sargent.

DEVIATION IQ

A standard score, known as a deviation IQ, was introduced to overcome the technical problems inherent in the ratio IQ. A standard score is obtained by converting raw test scores from a standardization sample to a normalized score distribution with a fixed mean and standard deviation. Deviation IQs typically have a mean of 100 and a standard deviation of the authors' choosing such as 15 for Wechsler tests and 16 for the Stanford-Binet. Standard scores are used to convert ordinal to interval data. Standard (normalized) scores provide equal variability at each age level and standard scores from one test can be directly compared with standard scores from another. In individual assessment, David Wechsler introduced the deviation IQ with his Wechsler-Bellevue scale in 1939. (The deviation IQ had been used with some group tests earlier.) Wechsler chose to use a standard score with a standard deviation of 15 (instead of 16, the median standard deviation of the contemporary Binet) because most people are more familiar with units of 5 (i.e., 5, 10, 15) than of 4 (i.e., 4, 8, 12, 16). Today most test authors use a deviation IQ with a standard deviation of either 15 or 16, but some use 20 and even 24.

Because of the popularity among professionals of the concept of the standard score with a mean of 100 and a standard deviation of 15 or 16, and because of the lack of popularity of the letters I and Q, some contemporary test authors have changed the name of the score from IQ to Learning Quotient (LQ), General Cognitive Index (GCI), Mental Processing Composite, etc. Whatever standard scores may be called, when they are derived from a test of mental ability, they are interpreted in the same way as deviation IQs, i.e., as indicating where the individual stands in relation to others of his or her age on the content of the test.

Since an IQ is a score from a test and since the content of tests of mental ability differ not only from each other but also within a test from childhood to adolescence, the term IQ should be preceded by the name of the test from which it was derived and accompanied by the age at which it was obtained. As a score, an IQ indicates both an individual's ability level at a given point in time and the relationship of the individual's score to those obtained by others of his or her age. As such, an IQ should be considered as a descriptive rather than an explanatory term. An IQ can be used to help understand a person's current level of cognitive functioning associated with learning in the mainstream culture. Scores from mental ability scales are to some extent reflections of previous learning within the culture in which the test was standardized, and they are predictors of subsequent educational performance in that culture over the next few years.

IQs are often thought of as indicators of scholastic or educational aptitude. However, they do not reflect important variables such as mechanical, motor, musical, and artistic aptitudes. IQs do not reflect skills in building or maintaining inter- or intrapersonal relationships. Only to a limited extent do IQs reflect such catalytic variables as persistence, enthusiasm for a particular kind of effort, or divergent thinking. Decisions about an individual need to be based on more than scores from one test of cognitive ability.

See also Intelligence Quotient; Ratio IQ

DEXEDRINE

(Dextroamphetamine sulfate), an amphetamine, is used in the treatment of attention deficit disorder with hyperactivity (Rxlist, 1997), narcolepsy, and as short-term therapy for exogenous obesity. Although amphetamines are known to work as central nervous stimulants, the mechanism whereby they produce mental and behavioral effects in children is not known. Adverse reactions can include palpitations and rapid heartbeat; euphoria, restlessness, and insomnia; and exacerbation of motor and vocal tics and Tourette's syndrome. Overdose may result in assaultiveness, confusion, hallucinations, and panic states usually followed by fatigue and depression.

REFERENCE

Physicians' desk reference. (1984). (pp. 1878–1880). Oradell, NJ: Medical Economics.

RXLIST. (1997). Internet Drug Index. www.rxlist.com/.

See also **Attention Deficit Disorder; Hyperactivity; Ritalin**

DIABETES

Diabetes is a chronic metabolic disease affecting approximately 12 million Americans. Common symptoms of diabetes include extreme hunger and thirst, frequent urination, irritability, weakness, fatigue, nausea, and high blood and urine sugar levels. Two major types of diabetes have been identified. Type I, or insulin dependent diabetes, was formerly called juvenile-onset because it usually occurred in children and adolescents. Type II, or non-insulin dependent, was formerly called maturity-onset. In Type I diabetes, the pancreas does not function properly, resulting in little to no insulin production and a build-up of sugar in the bloodstream. Treatment involves insulin injections, diet, and regular exercise. Approximately 1 million Americans are Type I diabetics. It is thought that there is a genetic predisposition for diabetes. At present there is no known cure. Obesity and stress can contribute to the onset of diabetes.

Hypoglycemia (low blood sugar) and hyperglycemia (high blood sugar) are the two most common emergencies encountered by diabetics. Hypoglycemia occurs when the blood sugar drops too low because of too much insulin, not enough food, or too much exercise. Symptoms include anger or bad temper, sudden staggering and poor coordination, pale color, disorientation, confusion, and sweating, eventually leading to stupor or unconsciousness, also called insulin shock. This condition is treated by administering some form of sugar such as fruit juice or candy. If unconsciousness occurs, a child should receive emergency medical care.

Hyperglycemia occurs when there is too little insulin, when infection or illness is present, or when too much food or drink is consumed. Symptoms of hyperglycemia include drowsiness, extreme thirst and frequent urination, fruity or wine-smelling breath, heavy breathing, flushed skin, vomiting, and eventually stupor or unconsciousness, called a diabetic coma. Treatment of this condition is usually the administration of insulin with the supervision of a healthcare professional.

Some diabetics develop complications such as retinopathy, that sometimes result in blindness, diabetic neuropathy or nerve disease, diabetic nephropathy or kidney disease, cardiovascular disease, or respiratory failure. Diabetes and its complications is the number three cause of nonaccidental death among children in the United States (Wright, Schafer, & Solomons, 1979).

It has been suggested by researchers that by the time a child reaches the developmental age of 12, he or she should be able to take the lead by doing his or her own urine or blood sugar tests and administration of insulin. Keep in mind that children in special education classes may reach these developmental ages at slower rates and thus may be more reliant on teachers and parents for assistance in complying with their diabetic regimen. In such cases teachers must be aware of the regimen. Parents should inform teachers about their child's needs, which may include a special diet, especially at lunch and snack time, time to run tests and take insulin injections, exercise, and signs of emergency, especially hyperglycemia and hypoglycemia. However, teachers should make every effort not to separate the child from the peer group. The diabetic child has the same needs for support, encouragement, and understanding as other children and should be encouraged to participate in all activities. When treats are offered, the teacher might offer a "diabetic" treat such as raisins, peanuts, or sugarless candy or gum.

Indeed, school districts have been found in violation of the Americans with Disabilities Act (1990) with respect to their treatment of students with diabetes (Vennum, 1995). In addition, most parents surveyed by the American Diabetes Association (1996) indicate dissatisfaction with their child's diabetes management in school. Certainly, higher expectations for school involvement are the current trend.

REFERENCES

American Diabetes Association. (1996) This can't be happening in our schools! *Diabetes Forecast, 49,* 2, 61–66.

Vennum, M.K. (1995). Students with diabetes: Is there legal protection? *Journal of Law and Education, 24,* 1, 33–69.

Wright, L., Schafer, A., & Solomons, G. (1979). *Encyclopedia of pediatric psychology.* Baltimore, MD: University Park Press.

See also Family Response to a Child with Disabilities; Health Problems of the Handicapped

DIAGNOSIS IN SPECIAL EDUCATION

The diagnostic procedure traditionally employed in special education has been one based on a medical model (Reynolds, 1984; Ysseldyke & Algozzine, 1982). This model is one borrowed from psychological diagnostic systems. It consists of preparing catalogs of systems of various special and remedial conditions and determining the extent to which an individual has characteristics similar to those of the known condition (Ysseldyke & Algozzine, 1982). According to Reynolds (1984), the focus has been on "intrapsychic causes of psychological dysfunction to the exclusion of extraper-

sonal factors, and on the deficiencies and weaknesses of individuals rather than on their strengths (p. 453)."

There have been many problems associated with the use of this type of a diagnostic model in special education. One problem centers around the fact that a wide variety of diagnostic systems have been developed. This has resulted in a situation in which the assessment of one student can produce very different diagnoses depending on the diagnostic system being referred to. There also tends to be considerable variations among the diagnoses of individuals classified under the same diagnostic system (Edgar & Hayden, 1985; Reynolds, 1984). These inconsistencies have made the process of special education diagnosis complicated and controversial.

The evaluations and diagnoses of children with disabilities that determine eligibility for special education services must adhere to guidelines according to IDEA that include the following points.

1. Individual testing. The student must be tested individually, not as part of a larger group. [Section 614(a)(1)(A)]

2. Evaluation in the native language. The evaluation must be conducted in the child's native language (for example, Spanish) or other mode of communication (for example, sign language for a student who is deaf), unless it is clearly not feasible to do so. [Section 614(b)(3)(A)(ii)]

3. Nondiscriminatory evaluations. Tests and other evaluation materials must be selected and administered so as not to be discriminatory on a racial or cultural basis. [Section 614(b)(3)(A)(i)]

4. Using tests correctly. Any standardized tests given to the child must be validated for the specific purpose for which they are being used. [Section 614(b)(3)(B)(i)]

5. Appropriate evaluation. Any standardized tests given to the child must be administered by trained and knowledgeable personnel, in keeping with the instructions provided by the producer of the test. [Section 614(b)(3)(B)(ii) and (iii)] (NICHCY, 1998).

The emphasis on cultural competency in diagnosis is not new, but it is much more emphasized in the scientific literature and in the law. Cultural competence also refers to the individual who is conducting the evaluation. The individual must have professional training in multicultural issues and demonstrate competence in assessment and diagnosis of children and adolescents of different socioeconomic status, gender, ethnicity, handicapping condition, and acculturation.

School psychologists traditionally have been the gatekeeper in the diagnosis/eligibility process. School psychology emphasized classification. Rosenfield and Nelson (1995) state:

But as the current ethical, political, legal and educational context has evolved, there has been a re-examination of the purposes and applications of data gathered during assessment process (Taylor et al., 1993). In a position paper on the Role of the School Psychologist in Assessment (1994), the National Association of School Psychologists endorsed the proposition that assessment practices must be linked to prevention and intervention to provide positive outcomes for students. Thus, there is an increasing emphasis on information that is "useful in designing, implementing, monitoring, and evaluating interventions" (Reschly, Kicklighter, & McKee, 1988, p. 9–50).

Diagnosis in special education therefore, has taken on a broader definition and is linked much more to intervention than ever before. Rosenfield and Nelson (1995) suggest that there are three purposes of school psychological assessment: informing/entitlement/classification decisions, planning interventions, and evaluating outcomes. Diagnosis and outcome are on the same continuum as opposed to being discrete entities. This shift in paradigm has also changed assessment instrument usage. The use of more natural and dynamic forms of assessment that directly impact instructional delivery and behavior management are common (Rosenfield & Nelson, 1995).

REFERENCES

National Information Center for Children and Youth with Disabilities (1998). Evaluation and Testing Guidelines. Washington, DC: Author.

Reynolds, C.R. (1984). Critical measurement issues in learning disabilities. *Journal of Special Education, 18,* 451–475.

Rosenfield, S., & Nelson, D. (1995). *The school psychologist's role in school assessment.* (ERIC Digest No. ED391985)

Ysseldyke, J.E., & Algozzine, B. (1982). *Critical issues in special and remedial education.* Boston: Houghton Mifflin.

See also AAMD; Diagnostic and Statistical Manual of Mental Disorders (DSM-IV); Mental Status; Severe Discrepancy Analysis

DIAGNOSTIC ACHIEVEMENT BATTERY–SECOND EDITION (DAB-2)

The *Diagnostic Achievement Battery–Second Edition* (DAB-2; Newcomer, 1990) uses 12 subtests divided into five areas: listening (Story Comprehension, Characteristics), speaking (Synonyms, Grammatic Completion), reading (Alphabet/Word Knowledge, Reading Comprehension), writing (Capitalization, Punctuation, Spelling, Writing Composition), and mathematics (Mathematics Calculation, Mathematics Reasoning) for children between the ages of 6 and 14. By combining subtests, composite scores (M = 100, SD = 15) are generated that reliably assess global strengths and weaknesses. The composites are Listening, Speaking, Reading, Writing, Mathematics, Spoken Language, Written Language, and Total Achievement.

The test was normed on 2,623 students residing in 40 states. The sample is representative of the nation as a whole with regard to gender, race, ethnicity, geographic region, and urban/rural residence. Reliability coefficients are high.

Evidence of content, concurrent, and construct validity also is provided.

Compton (1996) reports that the DAB-2 measures a wide variety of skills that are directly related to classroom performance. Bernier and Hebert (1995) find that the DAB-2 is a well-designed individual diagnostic test. Brown (1995) reports that the subtests seem to measure common constructs.

REFERENCES

Bernier, J., & Hebert, M. (1995). Review of the Diagnostic Achievement Battery, Second Edition. In J.C. Conoley & J.C. Impara (Eds.), *The twelfth mental measurements yearbook* (pp. 294–295). Lincoln: Buros Institute of Mental Measurements, University of Nebraska Press.

Brown, R. (1995). Review of the Diagnostic Achievement Battery, Second Edition. In J.C. Conoley & J.C. Impara (Eds.), *The twelfth mental measurements yearbook* (pp. 295–296). Lincoln: Buros Institute of Mental Measurements, University of Nebraska Press.

Compton, C. (1996). *A guide to 100 tests for special education.* Upper Saddle River, NJ: Globe Fearon.

Newcomer, P.L. (1990). *Diagnostic Achievement Battery: Second Edition.* Austin, TX: Pro-Ed.

DIAGNOSTIC AND STATISTICAL MANUAL OF MENTAL DISORDERS (DSM-IV)

The most widely used system for psychiatric diagnosis and classification in the United States is the fourth edition of the Diagnostic and Statistical Manual of Mental Disorders (DSM-IV; American Psychiatric Association, 1994). The first edition of the DSM was published in 1952, with the first revision appearing in 1968. All revisions of the DSM were developed for use with children, adolescents, and adults. The revision process included literature reviews, data reanalyses, and field trials. The APA also publishes the DSM-IV Sourcebook, which provides a comprehensive and convenient reference record of the clinical and research support for the various revision decisions.

The purpose of the DSM "is to provide clear descriptions of diagnostic categories in order to enable clinicians and investigators to diagnose, communicate about, study, and treat people with various mental disorders" (APA, 1994). The DSM uses a multiaxial classification system. Each axis refers to a different domain of information that may help the professional plan treatment plans and advice, and predict outcomes for the patient or student.

Axis I:	Clinical Disorders
	Other Conditions that May Be a Focus of Clinical Attention
Axis II:	Personality Disorders
	Mental Retardation
Axis III:	General Medical Conditions
Axis IV:	Psychosocial and Environmental Problems
Axis V:	Global Assessment of Functioning

The multiaxial system assists the clinician in making a diagnosis that is biopsychosocial in nature. In other words, the information given is holistic and takes the mental, physical, and social aspects of the individual's life into consideration. This is particularly appropriate for the 1990s, where the field of psychology has recognized the need for cultural competence in diagnosis.

The DSM-IV includes a section on "Disorders Usually First Diagnosed in Infancy, Childhood, or Adolescence." The diagnoses included in this section are: Mental Retardation, Learning Disorders, Motor Skills Disorder, Communication Disorders, Pervasive Developmental Disorders, Attention-Deficit and Disruptive Behavior Disorders, Feeding and Eating Disorders of Infancy or Early Childhood, Tic Disorders, Elimination Disorders, and a category of Other Disorders of Infancy Childhood or Adolescence. The latter diagnoses include Separation Anxiety Disorder, Selective Mutism, Reactive Attachment Disorder of Infancy or Early Childhood, Stereotypic Movement Disorder and Disorder of Infancy, Childhood, or Adolescence NOS.

A criticism of this definition of mental disorder that is particularly relevant to children is that it includes areas not typically regarded as mental disorders such as developmental disorders and learning disabilities. Concerns have been expressed that children diagnosed with specific developmental or learning problems will be diagnosed and stigmatized as having a mental disorder. The issue of labeling children for special education placement decisions has been controversial over the years, and it continues to be a source of frustration for many students, professionals, and parents. Therefore, the DSM-IV is probably best used in clinical settings where specific psychiatric treatment plans follow the specific psychiatric diagnoses.

REFERENCES

American Psychiatric Association. (1994). *Diagnostic and statistical manual of mental disorders* (4th ed.). Washington, DC: Author.

See also **Clinical Psychology; Mental Illness; Mental Status Exams**

DIAGNOSTIC ASSESSMENTS OF READING WITH TRIAL TEACHING STRATEGIES (DARTTS)

The Diagnostic Assessments of Reading with Trial Teaching Strategies (DARTTS; Roswell & Chall, 1992) program is designed to assess students' relative strengths and weaknesses in reading and to discover methods and materials that will be effective in helping students grow as readers.

DARTTS is intended for use in regular classrooms, Title I programs, special education, reading clinics, placement situations, adult education, and other settings where a detailed diagnostic picture of reading achievement is needed.

The two components of DARTTS are the Diagnostic Assessments of Reading (DAR) and the Trial Teaching Strategies (TTS). The DAR is comprise of six formal individually-administered tests in reading and language: Word Recognition, Word Analysis, Oral Reading, Silent Reading Comprehension, Spelling, and Word Meaning. Administration of the DAR is untimed and takes about 20 minutes. The questions are primarily open-ended, with the test administrator noting students' correct responses and recording incorrect responses verbatim. Scoring is based on mastery criteria. The subtests are multilevel, and each student is administered only the portion of each subtest that is needed to determine mastery. Because of the nature of the questions and administration procedures, standard Kuder-Richardson Formula 20 (K-R 20) reliability data were not published in the Technical Manual (Roswell & Chall, 1994). Unpublished K-R 20 data for Silent Reading Comprehension, the only DAR subtest that uses multiple-choice questions, are provided below. Validity information in the Technical Manual includes a description of the test development process. Validity data are provided in the form of correlations with a nationally standardized norm-referenced reading test and intercorrelations between the DAR and the TTS and among the DAR subtests.

The TTS is a group of informal lessons designed to explore effective reading comprehension strategies with the student. The timing of the TTS is completely flexible depending on the needs of the student, but basic information can be obtained in about 30 minutes. The DAR and TTS may be used together or separately, depending on circumstances.

Two reviews of the DAR, including brief mention of the TTS, can be found in the Buros Institute's *Twelfth Mental Measurements Yearbook* (Conoley & Impara, 1995). A paper describing the validation research was presented at the 1992 meeting of the American Educational Research Association in San Francisco (Hennings & Hughes, 1992).

REFERENCES

Conoley, J.C. and Impara, J.C. (Eds.). (1995). *Twelfth mental measurements yearbook*. Lincoln, NE: Buros Institute of Mental Measurements.

Hennings, S.S., and Hughes, K.E. (1992). Building a performance-based assessment system to diagnose strengths and weaknesses in reading achievement. Paper presented at meeting of the American Educational Research Association. (ERIC Document Reproduction Service No. TM 018521)

Roswell, Florence G., and Chall, Jeanne S. (1992) *Diagnostic Assessments of Reading with Trial Teaching Strategies.* Itasca, IL: The Riverside Publishing Company.

Roswell, Florence G., and Chall, Jeanne S. (1994). *Technical manual: DARTTS.* Itasca, IL: The Riverside Publishing Company.

DIAGNOSTIC PRESCRIPTIVE TEACHING

Diagnostic prescriptive teaching "refers to the practice of formulating instructional prescriptions on the basis of differential diagnostic results" (Arter & Jenkins, 1979, p. 518). Although any educational plan for an individual learner should spring from assessment, diagnostic prescriptive teaching has had a more specific meaning. The key idea underlying diagnostic prescriptive teaching is that a given diagnostic pattern is linked differentially to a specific instructional strategy (methods, materials, techniques, etc.). That a given set of assessment findings implies an accompanying set of instructional strategies is assumed.

Since the early 1970s, diagnostic prescriptive teaching has taken on a meaning broader than the two theoretical models. Smead and Schwartz (1982) have developed a model that is integrative in nature. Moving beyond the ability training model with its focus nearly completely on perceptual or psycholinguistic processes. They have identified three learner-focused areas from which diagnostic information has relevance for instruction: motivational-emotional, cognitive-perceptual, and neurological-physical. In a similar manner, they have focused on a greater variety of dimensions than did those previously concerned solely with the application of task analysis to special education. In addition, they have suggested that a third set of factors must be considered: the environmental characteristics of the learning situation, which include sociological, emotional, pedagological, contingency, standing patterns of behavior, and physical factors. Finally, they have suggested that the interactions among these three sets of factors—learner focused, task focused, and environmental focused—must also be diagnosed and related to the instructional prescription.

Thus, diagnostic prescriptive teaching has become better understood with the realization that a series of diagnostic patterns with related prescribed activities is simplistic given the complexity and variety of learners, tasks, and environments—and how they interact. Prescribed instructional goals must flow from assessment, addressing the learner and his/her style of learning, the skills or abilities that must be learned, and the situation and contingencies under which learning will be best facilitated. Recent studies (Covey, 1991; Fox & Thompson, 1994) suggest that diagnostic-prescriptive teaching techniques such as multisensory approaches, mapping strategies, peer learning, and process writing have achieved good outcomes with learning disabled students.

REFERENCES

Arter, J.A., & Jenkins, J.R. (1979). Differential diagnosis-prescriptive teaching: A critical appraisal. *Review of Educational Research, 49*, 517–555.

Covey, D.G. (1991). *The influence of teaching the main idea, drawing conclusions, and making inferences on the improvement of writing skills.* (ERIC Clearinghouse No. CS213114)

Fox, L.H., & Thompson, D.L. (1994). *Bringing the lab school method to an inner-city school.* (ERIC Clearinghouse No. EC304266)

Smead, V.S., & Schwartz, N.H. (1982, August). *An integrative model for instructional planning.* Paper presented at the 19th Annual Meeting, of the American Psychological Association, Washington, DC.

See also **Diagnostic Remedial Approach;
Diagnostic Teaching; Direct Instruction**

DIAGNOSTIC TEACHING

Diagnostic teaching is the name given an instructional process used to discover the instructional and environmental conditions under which student learning is most productive. Diagnostic teaching is also referred to as clinical teaching and data-based instructional decision making.

Diagnostic teaching is a cyclical process that is continued throughout the duration of student instruction. It involves planning, executing and evaluating teaching hypotheses (Wixson, 1991). It is used to find the most effective match of learner characteristics and instructionally relevant variables. However, there is a recognition that because the difficulty of material and the demands of schooling change over time, the most appropriate combinations of instructional variables will change over time as well.

Since diagnostic teaching is an ongoing process, the diagnostician is most properly a skilled teacher rather than a diagnostic specialist who does not have continual contact with the student. The child's teacher is also in the best position to judge whether student performance or a particular instructional interchange is typical and of significance or merely an exception to the norm. The teacher's ability to note student habits and learning strategies, likes and dislikes, reactions to grouping arrangements, etc., provides the basis on which trial modifications in instruction can be made.

Diagnostic teaching requires the diagnostician to be familiar with a variety of different curricular approaches. For any given approach, the diagnostician must be able to determine where the student might encounter difficulty. This allows the teacher to provide instruction at an appropriate level of difficulty using curricula that require different student behaviors, capacities, and experiences. Howell and Kaplan (1980) demonstrate how basic skills can be analyzed for use in diagnostic teaching.

Diagnostic teaching also requires the diagnostician to be culturally competent (Baca & Valenzuela, 1994) and familiar with instructional variables that can be used differently in conjunction with various curricular approaches. Among these are engaged time, the immediacy and nature of performance feedback, grouping practices, and presentation and questioning techniques. For example, one exploratory combination within the diagnostic teaching process might be an increase in the engaged time a student spends being directly taught (instructional variables) phonics (curricular approach). If student learning did not meet expectations, one or more of the critical variables would be systematically altered.

Procedures for the collection of student performance data are integral to most models of diagnostic teaching. These range from the use of special recording paper and elaborate techniques for performance analysis (White & Haring, 1980) to the use of checklists and behavioral tallies (Zigmond, Vallecorsa, & Silverman, 1983). Decision rules are usually presented within the context of a particular model but generally indicate what to do if student performance is deficient and how long instruction should continue before some systematic modification in instruction is made.

REFERENCES

Baca, L., & de Valenzuela, J.S. (1994). Reconstructing the bilingual special education interface. Washington, DC: National Clearinghouse for Bilingual Education.

Howell, K.W., & Kaplan, J.S. (1980). *Diagnosing basic skills.* Columbus, OH: Merrill.

White, O.R., & Haring, N.G. (1980). *Exceptional teaching.* Columbus, OH: Merrill.

Wixson, K.K. (1991). Dignostic teaching. *Reading Teacher, 44,* 6, 420–422.

Zigmond, N., Vallecorsa, A., & Silverman, R. (1983). *Assessment for instructional planning in special education.* Englewood Cliffs, NJ: Prentice-Hall.

See also **Diagnostic Prescriptive Teaching; Direct Instruction; Teacher Effectiveness**

DIALYSIS AND SPECIAL EDUCATION

Dialysis, the process of flushing kidney wastes by artificial means in cases of acute or chronic renal failure, has been increasingly used with children during the last 25 years. Dialysis methodology is viewed as a drastic mode of treatment for children, necessitated in advanced cases of kidney disease prior to, or as the result of, failed transplantation (Czaczkes & De-Nour, 1979).

While individual differences make generalization difficult, Whitt (1984) indicates that the complex and time-consuming dialysis schedule places most children at educational and emotional risk, as the time spent in hemodialysis treatment interrupts the normal pace and progress of the child's schooling. Hobbs and Perrin (1985) found the result of this loss of school time and educational opportunity to be academic underachievement and missed and splintered basic skills. In addition, the disruption of normal school progress and success weakens children's emotional stability and their feelings of competence and control (Stapleton, 1983).

During periods of school attendance, the primary role of special education is to maintain the independence of the child in dialysis. This is best accomplished by providing resource assistance to allow that child to function effectively within the regular classroom whenever possible while remediating educational weaknesses and gaps (Kleinberg, 1982). As the school experience for the dialysis child represents one of the few opportunities for that child to be in control of the environment, to gain competence and skill, and to prepare for the future in a normalized setting, special education must be used to modify programs, instruction, and the learning environment to ensure optimal educational progress (Sirvis, 1989; Van Osdol, 1982).

REFERENCES

Czaczkes, J.W., & De-Nour, A.K. (1979). *Chronic hemodialysis as a way of life.* New York: Brunner/Mazel.

Hobbs, N., & Perrin, J.M. (Eds.). (1985). *Issues in the care of children with chronic illness.* San Francisco: Jossey-Bass.

Kleinberg, S. (1982). *Educating the chronically ill child.* Baltimore, MD: Aspen Systems.

Sirvis, B. (1989). Students with specialized health care needs. *ERIC Clearinghouse on Handicapped and Gifted Children:* Reston, VA: Council for Exceptional Children. (ERIC Digest No. 458)

Stapleton, S. (1983). Recognizing powerlessness: Causes and indicators in patients with chronic renal failure. In J.F. Miller (Ed.), *Coping with chronic illness: Overcoming powerlessness.* Philadelphia: Davis.

Van Osdol, W.R. (1982). *Introduction to exceptional children* (3rd ed.). Dubuque, LA: Brown.

Whitt, J.K. (1984). End stage renal disease. In M.G. Eisenberg, L.C. Sutkin, & M.A. Jansen (Eds.), *Chronic illness and disability through the life span: Effects on self and family.* New York: Springer.

See also **Adaptive Physical Education; Physical Disabilities**

DIANA V. STATE BOARD OF EDUCATION

Diana (1970) and *Guadalupe v. Tempe Elementary School District* (1972) were highly similar cases that were never actually brought to trial but that have nevertheless had a significant impact on special education assessment and placement procedures. In each case, civil rights organizations filed suit in federal courts on behalf of all bilingual students attending classes for the mildly mentally retarded (or the respective state's cognate designation). Both cases noted disproportionate representation of bilingual, Spanish-surnamed children in programs for the mentally retarded. Additionally, the plaintiffs in each case argued that intelligence tests administered in English to Spanish-speaking children were the principal reason for the overrepresentation. As Reschly (1979) has noted, in both cases the school districts involved were engaged in unsound, unprofessional assessment procedures and had developed much of their special education processes around what most in the field would consider poor professional practice.

Guadalupe, in the consent decree, mandated the same changes in testing practices as *Diana. Guadalupe* went on to add four additional statements:

1. IQ tests were not to be the exclusive or the primary basis for the diagnosis of mild mental retardation.

2. Adaptive behavior in other than school settings would be assessed.

3. Due process procedures were to be developed and instituted before individual assessment or any movement toward diagnosis and placement could occur.

4. Special education would be provided to each child in the most normal setting or environment possible.

Since *Diana* and *Guadalupe* were settled by consent decrees, no judicial opinion is available and there are no findings to be reviewed and discussed. Neither case set legal precedent. Both were strongly influential, however, in subsequent legislation passed at the state and federal levels. Wording from the two decrees is now commonplace in many state and federal regulations governing the education of the handicapped.

REFERENCE

Reschly, D.J. (1979). Nonbiased assessment. In G. Phye & D. Reschly (Eds.), *School psychology. Perspectives and issues.* New York: Academic.

See also Consent Decree; Education for All Handicapped Children Act of 1975; Equal Protection; Larry P.; Marshall *v.* Georgia

DIAZEPAM

Diazepam (Valium) is a minor tranquilizer with relatively few side effects compared with other psychotropic medications. It is prescribed primarily with adult populations for symptoms of anxiety. Although the use of diazepam continues to be widespread (Yaffe & Danish, 1977), few studies regarding its therapeutic efficacy can be found in pediatric literature. Clinically, diazepam seems to be prescribed infrequently as a psychotropic, particularly as an antianxiety drug in children.

While diazepam is used only infrequently as a psychotropic agent in pediatric populations, it is often used as an adjunct in the treatment of seizure disorders. When administered intravenously in repeated dosages as deemed necessary, diazepam has been found to be effective in the initial management of uncontrolled, continuous seizures, or status epilepticus (Behrman, Vaughn, Victor, & Nelson, 1983). In general, diazepam is not used in the long-term management of seizure disorders because of the likelihood of the development of tolerance to the drug. Tolerance often develops very rapidly, sometimes as quickly as 3 to 14 days after initiation of therapy (Behrman et al., 1983). Increasing the dosage when the tolerance develops may help control the seizures, but, frequently, side effects such as drowsiness, ataxia, and slurred speech make the increased dosage intolerable. Occasionally, diazepam may be indicated therapeutically in the treatment of petit mal seizures, refractory to Zarontin and other agents, and in combination with phenobarbital and phenytoin in the treatment of seizures associated with central nervous system disease (Behrman et al., 1983).

The side effects attributed to diazepam are often further elaborations of the desired therapeutic effects. Those of primary concern include disinhibition, incoordination, drowsiness, and depression (Jaffe & Magnuson, 1985; Rapoport, Mikkelsen, &. Werry, 1978). Both physiological and psychological dependence may also develop as a function of prolonged usage (Rapoport et al., 1978). Following prolonged usage, diazepam should be discontinued slowly with decreasing dosages because seizures may occur in response to abrupt withdrawal.

REFERENCES

Behrman, R.E., Vaughn, V.C., Victor, B., & Nelson, W.E. (1983). Convulsive disorders. In R. Behrman & V. Vaughn (Eds.), *Nelson textbook of pediatrics* (pp. 1531–1545). Philadelphia: Saunders.

Jaffe, S., & Magnuson, J.V. (1985). Anxiety disorders. In J. Wiener (Ed.), *Diagnosis and psychopharmacology of childhood and adolescent disorders* (pp. 199–214). New York: Wiley.

Rapoport, J.L., Mikkelsen, E.J., & Werry, J.S. (1978). Anti-manic, antianxiety, hallucinogenic, and miscellaneous drugs. In J. Werry (Ed.), *Pediatric psychopharmacology* (pp. 316–355). New York: Brunner/Mazel.

Yaffe, S.J., & Danish, M. (1977). The classification and pharmacology of psychoactive drugs in childhood and adolescence. In J. Wiener (Ed.), *Psychopharmacology in childhood and adolescence* (pp. 41–57). New York: Basic Books.

See also Anticonvulsants; Phenobarbital; Tranquilizers; Zarontin

DICHOTIC LISTENING

Dichotic listening involves the simultaneous presentation of similar stimuli to both ears. An advantage of one ear over another is assumed by faster or more correct recall for a given ear. This technique has been used to draw conclusions concerning an individual subject's auditory asymmetry and cerebral lateralization for a given stimuli. Originally devised by Broadbent (1954) to examine auditory attention and memory deficits, the dichotic listening paradigm was later adapted by Kimura (1961) to examine hemispheric lateralization of language.

Research using a dichotic listening task has typically focused on "ear advantages" or the number of correct responses for each ear. Most normal (nonbrain injured) individuals demonstrate a right ear advantage (REA) (left-hemisphere) for verbal material and a left ear advantage (LEA) for nonverbal material (Kimura, 1961). This effect is thought to reflect the functional specialization of the cerebral hemisphere opposite the favored ear. Neurologically, this favored access is due to greater numbers of contralateral ear to hemisphere connections and a blocking of ipsilateral signals.

The dichotic listening paradigm has been demonstrated to have both clinical and research application. Clinical use of dichotic listening tasks attempt to differentiate disorders that involve the central auditory system (at the cerebral level) from those that are primarily peripheral (sensory organs). It is expected that achieved scores will be lower for input presented to the ear that is contralateral to a temporal lobe lesion than scores for input presented to the ear ipsilateral to the lesion. This difference in scores is referred to as the lesion or contralateral effect (Speaks, Niccum, & Van Tasell, 1985).

REFERENCES

Broadbent, D.E. (1954). The role of auditory localization in attention and memory span. *Journal of Experimental Psychology, 47,* 191–196.

Kimura, D. (1961). Cerebral dominance and the perception of verbal stimuli. *Canadian Journal of Psychology, 15,* 166–171.

Speaks, C., Niccum, N., & Van Tasell, D. (1985). Effects of stimulus material on the dichotic listening performance of patients with sensorineural hearing loss. *Journal of Speech & Hearing Research, 28,* 16–25.

See also **Cerebral Function, Lateralization of; Developmental Dyslexia**

DICTIONARY OF OCCUPATIONAL TITLES

The *Dictionary of Occupational Titles* (DOT) is prepared and published by the U.S. Department of Labor, Employment and Training Administration. It provides comprehensive occupational information to serve the labor market in job placement, employment counseling, and guidance. Concise standardized definitions (12,741) are alphabetized by title with coding arrangements for occupational classifications. Blocks of jobs are assigned to one of 550 occupational groups using 5- or 6-digit code. Skilled, semiskilled, or unskilled categories are specified. The format for each definition is occupational code number; occupational title; industry designation; alternate title (if any); body of the definitional lead statement; task element statement; undefined related title (if any).

Consumers may reproduce any part of this public document without special permission from the federal government. Source credit is requested but not required. The *Dictionary of Occupational Titles* has 1,404 pages. A new computerized version of the DOT is available and provides the benefit of a searchable database.

REFERENCE

U.S. Department of Labor, Employment, and Training Administration. (1996). *Dictionary of occupational titles* (4th ed.). Washington, DC: Author.

DIFFERENTIAL ABILITIES SCALES (DAS)

The Differential Abilities Scales (DAS; Elliott, 1990a) is an individually administered battery of cognitive and achievement tests designed to be administered to children and adolescents between the ages of 2 years, 6 months through 17 years, 11 months. The British Ability Scales (BAS; Elliott, 1979) was published in Great Britain and was the forerunner to the DAS.

The DAS cognitive battery consists of 17 subtests that divide into three levels: Preschool Level (ages 2:6 to 3:5), Upper Preschool Level (3:6 to 5:11), and School-Aged Level (ages 6:0 to 17:11). Depending on the child's age, the core battery consists of four to six subtests. The cognitive battery yields a composite score or General Conceptual Ability score (GCA), in addition to lower-level composite scores, called Cluster scores. For preschool-aged children, two Cluster scores, Verbal Ability and Nonverbal Ability, are yielded from 4 to 6 subtests. For school-aged children, three cluster scores, Verbal Ability, Nonverbal Reasoning Ability and Spatial Ability, are yielded from 6 subtests. The composite scores are comprised of "core" subtests, only those subtests with relatively high *g* loadings. There are also 2 to 5 "diagnostic" subtests for each level, which measure specific abilities that are less related to *g,* such as speed of information processing and short-term memory; however, the diagnostic subtests do not contribute to the composites. The cognitive battery takes approximately 25 to 65 minutes to administer. The brief school achievement battery consists of 3 subtests that measure basic skills of spelling, arithmetic, and word reading. It is administered only to school-aged children and takes approximately 15 to 25 minutes to administer.

There are some key differences between the DAS and other widely used cognitive batteries such as the Wechsler tests, Kaufman tests, and Stanford-Binet. First, in the DAS, an estimate of the child's ability is based on performance on a set of targeted items, or item set. The DAS does not assume that the child would pass all items below the item set or fail all items above the item set. Thus, children may take different sets of items ranging in difficulty. Second, administration differs in that there is not the use of traditional basal and ceiling rules (e.g., five consecutive failures for ceiling). Rather, if a child passes more than two items and fails more than two items in the item set, the item set would be considered an accurate set of items for the child and the test would be discontinued. A third difference in the DAS concerns scoring. Raw scores are converted to ability scores, which take into account both the difficulty of the items and the number of items answered correctly. However, ability scores are not norm-referenced. Therefore, ability scores for cognitive subtests must then be converted to T-scores (M = 50, SD = 10) in order to make comparisons with other children or between subtests. T-scores are then summed and converted to a standard score (M = 100, SD = 15) for both cluster scores and the GCA.

The DAS was standardized on a sample of 3,475 children and adolescents. *The Differential Ability Scales Introductory and Technical Handbook* (Elliott, 1990b) contains specific characteristics of the sample.

Reliability and validity data appear to be good and are described in detail in two full chapters of the DAS handbook. Additional studies not included in the handbook have shown high correlations between the DAS and WISC-III, with the highest correlations between DAS GCA and WISC-III FSIQ, DAS Verbal Composite and WISC-III VIQ, DAS Spatial Composite and WISC-III PIQ (correlations ranging from .82 to .92; Wechsler, 1991).

The DAS was designed as a classification and diagnostic tool. For classification purposes, it is intended to provide a single overall score of conceptual and reasoning abilities, in combination with other data, to determine if a child falls into a category such as learning disabled, mentally retarded, or gifted. For diagnostic purposes, the child's profile of cognitive strengths and weaknesses should be examined. The DAS has several strengths that are noteworthy: its division of fluid ability into two factors, nonverbal reasoning and spatial ability; its measurement of nonverbal reasoning without using time limits or requiring visual-motor coordination; and its use of subtests that load high on *g* for the overall GCA score. The most notable limitations of the DAS relate to the difficult scoring and conversion system. Five subtests have open-ended responses requiring some judgment by the examiner. Additionally, converting cognitive subtest scores from a raw score to an ability score to a T-score to a standard score is tedious for examiners. The utility of the ability score, which uses an arbitrary numbering system and does not allow for norm-referenced comparisons, does not appear to warrant the "extra" step involved in converting the raw score to its final norm-referenced score.

REFERENCES

Elliott, C.D., Murray, D.J., & Pearson, L.S. (1979). *British Ability Scales.* Windsor, England: National Foundation for Educational Research.

Elliott, C.D. (1990a). *DAS: Administration and scoring manual.* San Antonio, TX: Psychological Corporation.

Elliott, C.D. (1990b). *Differential Ability Scales: Introductory and technical handbook.* San Antonio, TX: Psychological Corporation.

Wechsler, D. (1991). *Manual for the Wechsler Intelligence Scale for Children–Third Edition (WISC-III).* San Antonio, TX: Psychological Corporation.

DIGEORGE SYNDROME

See VELOCRANIAL FACIAL SYNDROME.

DILANTIN

Dilantin is an antiepileptic drug that can be useful in the treatment of seizure disorders. Generically, it is known as phenytoin. It has proven remarkably effective in treating both partial seizures and generalized tonic-clonic seizure activity. Dilantin appears to work primarily in the motor cortex of the brain; it acts to inhibit the spread of seizure activity by preventing the extension of seizure activity from abnormally discharging neurons to surrounding cells. (Mosby, 1997) It is thought that Dilantin tends to stabilize the threshold of neurons against the hyperexcitability caused by excessive stimulation or environmental changes that can lead to seizures. Additionally, Dilantin appears to reduce brain stem center activity responsible for the tonic phase of tonic clonic (grand mal) seizures.

Some minor toxic symptoms such as gastric discomfort and nausea are frequent at the onset of Dilantin therapy. These tend to disappear rapidly. In children, a common effect of chronic use is gingival hyperplasia, which may cause bleeding gums. This condition generally can be prevented by good oral hygiene. Hirsutism occurs frequently, and may be aesthetically distressing, especially in girls. Toxic reactions to Dilantin include blurring of vision or ataxia. The onset of pruritus (severe itching), rash, or fever is an indication for immediate drug withdrawal, as liver damage or bone marrow suppression may occur, as may a syndrome resembling systemic lupus. However, drug withdrawal should always be done on physician's orders. Abrupt withdrawal of Dilantin may precipitate status epilepticus (Mosby, 1997).

REFERENCE

Mosby's GenRx. (1997). Phenytoin Sodium. Rx List Monographs. Linn, MO: Mosby.

See also **Anticonvulsants; Epilepsy**

DIPLEGIA

Diplegia is a topographic term used to describe a movement disorder predominantly affecting the lower extremities, with only mild involvement of the upper extremities. The term diplegia frequently is used as a description of a kind of cerebral palsy in which the arms are less involved than in a quadriplegia and more involved than in a paraplegia.

The etiology of diplegia may be developmental delay, anoxia, trauma, jaundice, neonatal seizures, reflex suppression, or other factors that suggest the possibility of certain progressive biochemical disorders or spinocerebellar degenerative diseases. Differential diagnosis by a skilled pediatric neurologist, with ongoing follow-up by appropriate therapists, is essential to provide appropriate medical and educational intervention for children with diplegia.

See also **Chorea; Dyskinesia; Neuropsychology**

DIPLOPIA

Diplopia, double vision, may be physiologic or pathologic (Von Noorden, 1985). Physiologic diplopia is normal and results from stimulation and appreciation of objects simultaneously with the area of disparities that may be fused within the cortex and those outside. Object points in visual space stimulating corresponding retinal elements may be constructed to form a plane known as horopter. Both in front of and behind this plane is Panum's fusional space, an area in space that can be integrated cortically without perceiving objects as double. Physiologic diplopia occurs outside this space, and may be appreciated by observing an object in the distance and holding a pencil near. While attending to the distant object, the pencil will be seen as double. Most of the time, physiologic diplopia is cortically suppressed and not appreciated. Its clinical significance is twofold. Occasionally, schoolchildren become aware of and concerned about physiologic diplopia; reassurance is warranted. Second, diplopia may be useful from a diagnostic and therapeutic perspective in the presence of strabismus.

Pathological diplopia may be characterized as either

monocular or binocular. Monocular diplopia results from defects in the refractive media or retinal pathology. Examples are high astigmatic refractive error, cataract, ectopic lens position, or macular edema. If diplopia is binocular, image positions may be separated horizontally, vertically, or obliquely; may vary with different directions of gaze and head position; and may be constant or variable.

Extraocular muscle paresis in adults almost always yields diplopia. However, patients with strabismus from early life rarely perceive diplopia. A series of adaptive mechanisms in infancy and childhood avoid this symptom: abnormal head position, binocular rivalry, suppression, and abnormal retinal correspondence. In the presence of a weak extraocular muscle, moving the head to a position that avoids the field of action of the paretic muscle often will prevent diplopia; therefore, an abnormal head position may be an indicator of extraocular muscle paresis. Binocular rivalry is a function that can be present normally or abnormally. When viewing with one eye through a monocular telescope or microscope, it often is unnecessary to close the other eye to avoid confusion of images. This cortical phenomenon, known as retinal rivalry, is a normal adaptation to avoid diplopia. In the presence of strabismus, particularly in a strabismic circumstance where there is alternation of fixation from one eye to the other, retinal rivalry is apparently the operant mechanism. In a constant strabismic circumstance, one eye assumes fixation to the exclusion of the other, and the image from the deviating eye is suppressed. Suppression is a mechanism, largely limited to infancy and youth, one consequence of which is decreased vision (amblyopia). Thus, amblyopia develops and is treatable in infancy and early childhood; however, once maturation of the system is complete (about age 9 years), amblyopia is neither a threat nor effectively treated.

Where strabismus is of early onset and longstanding duration, the cortical adaptation of abnormal retinal correspondence may ensue. In this instance, noncorresponding retinal points are cortically integrated, presumably to avoid diplopia. Thus diplopia may be monocular or binocular, physiologic or pathologic. The presence of diplopia may be detrimental to school performance. It is generally avoidable by closing one eye, and this behavior may be observed. Generally, however, adaptations are readily achieved to conditions producing diplopia in children, and the symptom does not represent a significant barrier to learning.

REFERENCE

Von Noorden, G.K. (1985). *Binocular vision and ocular motility.* St. Louis: Mosby.

DIRECT INSTRUCTION

The term direct instruction arose from two complementary lines of research and development. Rosenshine (1976) introduced the term into the mainstream of educational research. His synthesis of many classroom observation studies indicated that students consistently demonstrate higher reading achievement scores when their teachers do the following:

1. Devote substantial time to active instruction
2. Break complex skills and concepts into small, easy-to-understand steps and systematically teach in a step-by-step fashion
3. Ensure that all students operate at a high rate of success
4. Provide immediate feedback to students about the accuracy of their work
5. Conduct much of the instruction in small groups to allow for frequent student-teacher interactions

The other source of direct instruction derives from the work of curriculum developers rather than researchers. In the early 1960s in Israel, Smilarsky taught preschoolers from peasant immigrant families from surrounding Arab nations. The method, called direct promotion, taught in a direct manner toward specific goals. In the mid-1960s Bereiter and Engelmann (1966) formed an academically oriented preschool based on direct-instruction principles. In the late 1960s, Engelmann articulated the concept of direct instruction in the form of specific curricular materials and in a comprehensive model for teaching low-performing students. Direct instruction was incorporated as part of the acronym for DISTAR (Direct Instruction System for Teaching and Remediation) and as part of the title of the direct instruction model that took part in the U.S. Office of Education Follow Through Project. The key to direct instruction, as envisioned by Engelmann and his colleagues, is a comprehensive intervention, addressing teacher expectations for student learning, the curriculum, teaching skills, time spent engaged in academic activities, administrative support, and parental involvement.

Direct instruction materials also teach students strategies that allow them to handle a wide range of tasks. In intermediate spelling, students learn a few rules and 655 word roots; they then can spell over 10,000 words. The instructional design principles are articulated in several books: *Theory of Instruction* (Engelmann & Carnine, 1982), *Direct Instruction Reading* (Carnine & Silbert, 1979), *Direct Instruction Mathematics* (Silbert, Carnine, & Stein, 1981), and *Applied Psychology for Teachers: A Behavioral Cognitive Approach* (Becker, in press).

Direct instruction teaching techniques are designed to maximize the quality and amount of academic engaged time. The amount of time is increased by showing teachers how to schedule instructional time more effectively and how to keep students attending by using reinforcement, rapid pacing, challenges, etc. The quality of learning is particularly influenced by how teachers react to student errors. For memorization errors, teachers give the answers and periodically review the missed questions. For errors reflecting inappropriate strategy selection or application, the teacher asks questions based on prior instruction to guide the student in using the strategy to arrive at an appropriate answer.

Although some sources point to the success (broad-ranged) of direct instruction (Adams & Siegfried, 1996), others have suggested that there are no significant differences between direct instruction and regular classroom reading outcomes (Mosley, 1997). Findings suggest that students have to be taught by direct instruction for 2 years before effects are noted (Mosley, 1997).

REFERENCES

Adams, G.L., & Siegfried, L. (1996). *Research on direct instruction: 25 years beyond DISTAR.* Seattle, Washington: Educational Achievement Systems.

Bereiter, C., & Engelmann, S. (1966). *Teaching disadvantaged children in the preschool.* Engelwood Cliffs, NJ: Prentice-Hall.

Carnine, D.W., & Silbert, J. (1979). *Direct instruction reading.* Columbus, QH: Merrill.

Engelmann, S., & Carnine, D.W. (1982). *Theory of instruction.* New York: Irvington.

Mosley, A.M. (1997). *The effectiveness of direct instruction on reading achievement.* (ERIC Clearinghouse No. CS012664)

Rosenshine, B. (1976). Classroom instruction. In N.L. Gage (Ed.), Psychology of teaching. The 77th yearbook of the National Society for the Study of Education. Chicago, IL: National Society for the Study of Education.

Silbert, J., Carnine, D.W., & Stein, M. (1981). *Direct instruction mathematics.* Columbus, OH: Mcrrill.

See also Distar; Reading Remediation

DISABILITY

The term disability is derived from the Latin prefix *dis-*, meaning negation, separation, lack of, or opposite of; and the Latin *habilitas,* meaning fitness, and *habere,* indicating to have or to be easily handled. Disability today indicates the lack of power or ability to do something. It is usually regarded as a negative attribute.

The World Health Organization (WHO) has made efforts to clarify terms and extend the medical model of disease per se to account for the consequences of disease (1980). In 1980, the International Classification of Impairments, Disabilities, and Handicaps (ICIDH) was formed. The ICIDH bridged the former medical model with a social model and facilitated the recognition of the contributions of medical services, rehabilitation agencies, and social welfare personnel to the care of people with conditions that interfere with everyday life, especially those people who have chronic, progressive, and irreversible conditions. The medical model of disease may be illustrated as:

$$etiology \rightarrow pathology \rightarrow manifestation$$
$$(WHO, 1980, p. 10).$$

The extended model, a biopsychosocial model, may be presented as:

$$disease \rightarrow impairment \rightarrow disability \rightarrow handicap$$
$$(WHO, 1980, p. 11).$$

Disability in the WHO classification system denotes the "consequences of impairment in terms of functional performance and activity by the individual" (p. 14). An impairment is defined as "any loss or abnormality of psychological, physiological, or anatomical structure or function" (p. 47). Handicap is defined as "a disadvantage for a given individual, resulting from an impairment or a disability, that limits or prevents the fulfillment of a role that is normal (depending on age, sex, and social and cultural factors) for that individual" (p. 183). Thus impairment represents "exteriorization of a pathological state" (p. 47) and occurs at the tissue level; disability refers to "excesses or deficiencies of customarily expected activity, performance, and behavior" (p. 142) and is located at the level of the person; and handicap "reflects the consequences for the individual—cultural, social, economic, and environmental—that stem from the presence of impairment and disability" (p. 183).

The ICIDH is again, in the process of revision. Suggested revisions include:

the need to keep in mind users who are not health professionals, the presentation of handicap as a set of circumstances that individuals encounter as part of an interaction between their impairments and disabilities and their physical and social environment, the reflection of the major revision in the mental health sections of the ICD in the ICIDH as this is especially important for legislation and the protection of human rights, newer understanding of the biology of illness mechanisms and ensure that the classification is appropriate across cultures and no inappropriate gender references are made. (p. 1, WHO, 1998)

The emphasis on cultural competence is noted. The draft of the revision has been renamed the "International Classification of Impairments, Activities and Participation A Manual for Dimensions of Disablement and Functioning" (WHO, 1998). The term disability has been replaced by "limitation in activity" and the term handicap has been replaced by "restriction in participation" (WHO, 1998). The revision is currently undergoing extensive field testing and the final draft will be presented in 1999.

In the present context of special education and rehabilitation, the term disability is frequently changed to the adjectival form and used to describe individuals. Thus we hear talk about disabled persons. Note, however, the affect of this change; instead of considering a disability or the lack of power to act, attention is directed to people who are characterized as not having power to act, with no distinction as to what actions might be limited. Wright (1960), in her discussion of physical disabilities, has pointed out the distinction between calling someone a physically disabled person as opposed to a person with a physical disability: "it is precisely the perception of a person with a physical disability as a *physically disabled person* that has reduced all his life to the disability aspects of his physique."

Attempts to define the term disability and differentiate it from related terms is more than an exercise in semantics. Precise definitions are needed for determining who is eligible for services; what the incidence and prevalence of conditions are; what projected health care, educational, rehabilitation, and welfare assistance may be required from a local, state, national, or international perspective; and what efforts might facilitate the development of appropriate housing and employment opportunities. It seems likely that as long as the term disability carries a strong pejorative connotation, attempts will be made to limit its denotation and increase the objectivity of its meaning.

REFERENCES

World Health Organization. (1980). *International classification of impairments, disabilities, and handicaps: A manual of classification relating to the consequences of disease.* Geneva, Switzerland: Author.

World Health Organization. (1998). *ICIDH-2 Beta 1 Field Trials.* www.who.org.

Wright, B. (1960). *Physical disability—A psychological approach.* New York: Harper & Row.

See also **Handicapped, Definition; Individuals with Disabilities Education Act (IDEA); Labeling**

DISADVANTAGED CHILD

Most writings about disadvantaged children first gained attention during the 1940s and 1950s; lower-class youths and racial minorities were identified as the populace of this educationally disenfranchised group of learners. Historically we can identify the roots of this population in terms of their educational needs, but it was not until the mid 1960s that writers such as Riessman and Havighurst had their turns at defining the characteristics that constitute this deprived population. As indicated by Riessman (1962), the terms culturally deprived, educationally deprived, deprived, underprivileged, disadvantaged, lower class, and lower socioeconomic group, could all be used interchangeably.

Although Riessman has made great efforts to identify some characteristics that might be construed as potentially positive qualities, he also is cognizant of the negative criteria used by Havighurst and others. An examination of *The Culturally Deprived Child* (1962), results in the reader's awareness that Reissman understood the enormity of the problems encountered by the deprived children of our nation.

Without many of the precise criteria needed to identify the disadvantaged population, the educational community moved ahead with special programs with a financial base from congressional legislation. In 1965 Congress passed the Elementary and Secondary Education Act (ESEA) and for the first time in U.S. history, federal financial support was provided to both public and nonpublic schools. From this legislation came Title I—Education of Children of Low-Income Families. Title I was designed to support and provide financial incentives for special programs to meet the special needs of socially and educationally deprived children of low-income families. Congress amended and expanded the ESEA many times over the next 30 years. The

major criticism of the Act was that funds were spread thinly instead of being focused in areas of most need (Department of Education, 1993). In addition, a crisis developed in urban schools, where an exodus of white middle-class families from the city to private and/or suburban schools created a buildup of educationally disadvantaged minority students (Ornstein, 1989). Issues of cultural competence have also been included recently to the evaluation of services to disadvantaged children. There have been requests (Lake, 1990) to distinguish between the terms "culturally disadvantaged" and "culturally different."

Specific learning characteristics of the deprived or disadvantaged student might include many of the following: (1) oriented to the physical and visual rather than to the oral; (2) content-centered rather than form-centered; (3) externally oriented rather than introspective; (4) problem-centered rather than abstract-centered; (5) inductive rather than deductive; (6) spatial rather than temporal; (7) slow, careful, patient, and persevering (in areas of importance) rather than quick, clever, facile, and flexible; (8) inclined to communicate through actions rather than words; (9) deficient in auditory attention and interpretation skills; (10) oriented toward concrete application of what is learned; (11) short attention span; (12) characteristic gaps in knowledge and learning; (13) lacking experiences of receiving approval for success in tasks (Conte & Grimes, 1969).

Meeting the needs of the disadvantaged child is a relatively new educational approach when viewed within the context of America's education history. Efforts to define this population have not been without conflict, and massive expenditures of monies by the federal government has also stirred controversy. However, studies indicate that enrichment programs (Kaniel & Richtenberg, 1992), mentoring (Shaughnessy, 1992), and appropriate curricula design (Gemma, 1989) have very positive outcomes with children who are disadvantaged.

REFERENCES

Conte, J.M., & Grimes, G.H. (1969). *Media and the culturally different.* Washington, DC: National Education Association.

Department of Education. (1993). *Improving America's Schools Act of 1993: The Reauthorization of the Elementary and Secondary Education Act.* Washington, DC: U.S. Department of Education.

Gemma, A. (1989). *A comparison of the child-centered curriculum model, the direct instruction curriculum model, and the open-framework curriculum model: Three curriculum models for disadvantaged preschool children.* (ERIC Clearinghouse No. PS018905)

Kaniel, S., & Richtenberg, R. (1992). Instrumental enrichment: Effects of generalization and durability with talented adolescents. *Gifted Education International, 8,* 3, 128–35.

Lake, R. (1990). An Indian father's plea: *Teacher Magazine, 2,* 1, 48–53.

Ornstein, A.C. (1989). Enrollment trends in big city schools. *Peabody Journal of Education, 66,* 4, 64–71.

Riessman, F. (1962). *The culturally deprived child.* New York: Harper & Row.

Shaughnessy, M.F. (1992). *Mentoring disadvantaged gifted children and youth.* (ERIC Clearinghouse No. UD028765)

DISCIPLINE

The noun discipline comes from the Latin word *disciplina,* meaning teaching, learning. However, a more common use of the word connotes either training that corrects or molds or punishment for transgressions against societal or parental rules.

Discipline, like control, is often incorrectly used to mean various aspects of classroom management. Good discipline may be considered maintaining an orderly classroom. A classroom and/or school environment that supports good student behavior must also expect the student to make good choices. Students that only respond to external structures such as rewards or punishments learn very little self-discipline and the gains are usually only short-term (Short, 1994).

A more acceptable use of the term in the educational setting would describe discipline as an imposition of self-control in order to promote efficient habits of learning, proper conduct, consideration for others, and a positive learning environment. From the educator's point of view, preventing misbehavior is much more important than imposing control after the fact (Baron, 1992). Teachers working in teams to create positive classroom climates have much better support and success than individual efforts (Bell-Ruppert, 1994). In addition, democratic rather than authoritarian values have emerged in recent classroom discipline models. However, democratic values require flexible problem-solving skills that both the teacher and the students must value (Lewis, 1997).

To maintain discipline in the classroom, the student must be given as much independence as the teacher and child can tolerate. Classroom management should yield neither highly structured teacher-dominated environments nor completely permissive ones. To facilitate the development of self-control and discipline, a teacher's managerial style should attempt to promote active participation and a positive learning environment.

REFERENCES

Baron, E.B. (1992). *Discipline strategies for teachers.* (ERIC Clearinghouse No. SP034413)

Bell-Ruppert, N. (1994). *Discipline plans in middle schools.* Paper presented at the Annual Conference and Exhibit of the National Middle School Association, November, 1994.

Lewis, R. (1997). *The discipline dilemma: Control Management, Influence* (2nd ed.). Melbourne, Australia: Australian Council for Educational Research.

Short, P. (1994). *Rethinking student discipline: Alternatives that work.* (ERIC Clearinghouse No. EA026417)

***See also* Classroom Management; Self-Control Curriculum; Self-Monitoring**

DISCOURSE

Two major types of discourse exist: Basic Interpersonal Communication Skills (BICS) or "everyday language," and Cognitive Academic Language Proficiency (CALP) or "instructional language" (Cummins, 1983; Chamot & O'Malley, 1994). Both BICS and CALP contribute to education success. Characteristics of discourse associated with BICS and CALP are divided into three categories that occur across a developmental continuum: Conversation, Narration, and Exposition (Larson & McKinley, 1995; Merritt & Culatta, 1998; Naremore et al., 1995; Nelson, 1998; Wallach & Butler, 1994).

Conversation is used to request and report concrete items and actions (informal or personal oral or written interactions) (Halliday, 1975; Hoskins, 1996; Naremore, Densmore, & Harman, 1995; Nelson, 1998; Tough, 1979). Conversation is a type of BICS that can be oral (e.g., social group, family conferences, telephone calls, "rap" sessions, gossip) or literate (e.g., personal notes, a diary, e-mail). Conversational discourse is context-embedded and has a structure of topics, initiations, responses, turns, exchanges, topic maintenance, reaction time latency, breakdowns, repairs, pacing/leading, and closure. Conversation competence is measured by quantity, quality, relationship, and manner, as well as nonverbal dimensions of communication. Individuals who do not develop conversational skills may experience difficulty with the second level of discourse, narration.

Narration is used to report what happened, to talk or write about, or to read about the there and then (recounts, eventcasts, accounts, fictional stories) (Esterreicher, 1995; Hedberg & Westby, 1993; Hughes, McGillivray, & Schmidek, 1997; Naremore et al., 1995; Nelson, 1998). Narrative competence includes the understanding and use of *story grammars* (characters, place, time, initiating event, problem, internal response, resolution, and ending). Story grammars develop through the process of centering and chaining involved in learning *story types* (heaps, sequences, primitive narratives, unfocused chains, focused chains, and eventually true narratives represented by complex, multiple, embedded, or interactive episodes). Narration, a combination of BICS and CALP discourse, is a bridge between conversation and exposition because narration develops the cognitive, linguistic, and contextual structures introduced in conversation and required by exposition. For some individuals, reading problems may be related to poorly developed productive narrative abilities.

Exposition, an oral and literate CALP communication form, is a context-reduced and abstract form of language used to generalize about and infer what happens in the there and then (Chamot & O'Malley, 1994; Cummins, 1983; Larson & McKinley, 1995; Merritt & Culatta, 1998; Naremore et al., 1995; Nelson, 1998; Ripich & Creaghead, 1994; Wallach & Butler, 1994). Expository language includes understanding and producing speeches, lectures, discussions, classroom discourse, textbooks, reaction papers, essays, and technical, (research, or term papers). Expository forms are structured through genres such as description, collection, sequence/procedure, compare-contrast, cause-effect, problem-solution, and argue-persuade. Exposition competence requires the understanding and use of precise vocabulary (often associated with academic content or career areas), pronunciation, grammar, organization, sequencing, transitions, cohesion, coherence, spelling, proofreading, and editing. Individuals who have not developed the oral and literate communication skills associated with narration may experience difficulties with expository language.

Discourse problems may be caused by developmental or acquired conditions. Oral and literate discourse rules and use vary from culture to culture (Hedberg & Westby, 1993). However, the consensus is that for social and academic success throughout life, individuals must be able to understand and use the communication-learning conventions associated with conversation, narration, and exposition (Nelson, 1998; Wallach & Butler, 1994).

REFERENCES

Chamot, A.U., & O'Malley, J.M. (1994). *The CALLA handbook: Implementing the cognitive academic language learning approach.* Reading, MA: Addison-Wesley.

Cummins, J. (1983). Language proficiency and academic achievement. In Oller, J.W., Jr. (Ed.), *Issues in language testing research.* Boston, MA: Newbury House.

Esterreicher, C.A. (1995). *Scamper Strategies: FUNdamental activities for narrative development.* Eau Claire, WI: Thinking Publications.

Halliday, M.A.K. (1975). *Learning how to mean: Explorations in the development of language.* London: Edward Arnold.

Hedberg, N.L., & Westby, C.E. (1993). *Analyzing Storytelling skills: Theory to practice.* Tucson, AZ: Communication Skill Builders.

Hoskins, B. (1996). *Conversations: A framework for language intervention.* Eau Claire, WI: Thinking Publications.

Hughes, D., McGillivray, L., & Schmidek, M. (1997). *Guide to narrative language.* Eau Claire, WI: Thinking Publications.

Larson, V.L., & McKinley, N. (1995). *Language disorders in older students: Preadolescents and adolescents.* Eau Claire, WI: Thinking Publications.

Merritt, D.D., & Culatta, B. (1998). *Language intervention in the classroom.* San Diego: Singular.

Naremore, R.C., Densmore, A.E., & Harman, D.R. (1995). *Language intervention with school-aged children: Conversation, narrative, and text.* San Diego: Singular.

Nelson, N.W. (1998). *Childhood language disorders in context: Infancy through adolescence* (2nd ed.). Boston: Allyn and Bacon.

Ripich, D.N., & Creaghead, N.A. (Eds.). (1994). *School discourse problems* (2nd ed.). San Diego: Singular.

Tough, J. (1979). *Talk for teaching and learning.* Portsmouth, NJ: Heinemann.

Wallach, G.P., & Butler, K.G. (1994). *Language learning disabilities in school-age children and adolescents: Some principles and applications.* New York: Merrill/Macmillan College.

DISCREPANCY ANALYSIS

See LEARNING DISABILITIES, SEVERE DISCREPANCY ANALYSIS IN.

DISCREPANCY FROM GRADE

Discrepancy model analysis is used in the assessment of learning disabilities to determine if a difference exists between the level of achievement and ability. Levels of achievement and intelligence are measured reliably by using standardized tests. Results, however, may not always be accurate owing to error in measurement (Connell, 1991). Attempts to measure discrepancy may also be complicated by age or grade level. A discrepancy of one year at the third grade for a 9 year old is more severe than a similar discrepancy for a 16 year old. In addition, cognitive language relationships change over time, which may make eligibility decision-making inappropriate using these models (Cole, 1992).

Several techniques using expectancy analysis are used in quantifying learning disabilities (Mercer, 1983). They are the mental grade method, the learning quotient method, and the Harris method. Harris (1961) provided a method to determine an individual's reading expectancy grade (RE). The examiner subtracts five years from the individual's mental age:

$$RE = MA - 5$$

To determine if a discrepancy exists, a comparison is made between the individual's reading expectancy and the present reading level. The learning quotient method was developed by Myklebust (1968); it includes mental age, chronological age, and grade age (GA). The learning quotient is the ratio between the present achievement age and expectancy age with a score of 89 or below resulting in classification as learning disabled.

A third technique once commonly used to determine discrepancy in learning disabilities was proposed by Harris (1970). This method includes both mental age and chronological age but gives priority to mental age:

$$EA = \frac{2MA + CA}{3}$$

These methods for determining discrepancy have been criticized in that difference scores between two tests were less reliable than each score separately (Salvia & Clark, 1973). It has also been noted that a large number of children might exhibit discrepancy by pure chance. These techniques were also criticized because of their failure with nonreaders.

REFERENCES

Cole, K. (1992). Stability of the intelligence quotient-language quotient relation. *American Journal of Mental Retardation, 97,* 2, 131–143.

Connell, P.H. (1991). *An analysis of aptitude-achievement discrepancy formulas in learning disability assessment.* (ERIC Clearinghouse No. TM017793)

Harris, I. (1961). *Emotional blocks to learning.* New York: Free Press.

Harris, A.J. (1970). *How to increase reading ability* (5th ed.). New York: McKay.

Mercer, C.D. (1983). *Students with learning disabilities* (2nd ed.). Columbus, OH: Merrill.

Myklebust, H. (1968). Learning disabilities: Definition and overview. In H. Myklebust (Ed.), *Progress in learning disabilities.* New York: Grune & Stratton.

Salvia, J., & Clark, J. (1973). Use of deficits to identify the learning disabled. *Exceptional Children, 39,* 305–308.

See also **Classification, Systems of; Grade Equivalents; Learning Disabilities; Learning Disabilities, Problems in Definition of; Learning Disabilities, Severe Discrepancy Analysis in Diagnosis of**

DISCRIMINANT ANALYSIS

Discriminant analysis is a statistical technique used to predict group membership from two or more interval dependent variables. It is similar to multiple regression in conception. For example, a researcher might be interested in determining if dyslexic students are distinguishable from other learning-disabled students using the subtests of the WISC-R. Discriminant analysis can be used to determine the optimal set of weights for the WISC-R subtests that maximally separate the two groups on a new variable composed of the weighted sum of the WISC-R subtests.

Discriminant analysis may also be viewed as a data reduction technique. Instead of needing a large number of variables to categorize subjects, the researcher applies discriminant analysis so that a new variable or set of variables is created that uses the information of the original variables. The new variables are linear combinations, or weighted sums, of the original variables. It is anticipated that fewer new variables are needed than in the original set, hence the idea of data reduction. Mathematically, more than one unique solution to the problem is possible. The number of solutions will be equal to the smaller of two numbers: the number of predictors or the degrees of freedom for groups (number of groups minus one). Each solution corresponds to a new variable independent statistically of all the other new solution variables. For two groups there is only one solution since the smaller of the two numbers is equal to one (two groups minus one). This solution is also equal to the multiple regression of the group variable (mathematically defined as, for example, one or two on the predictor variables. The regression weights and the discriminant analysis weights in this case are identical.

For three or more groups, there will be two or more solutions to the problem of maximally distinguishing between the groups. Each solution corresponds to constructing a straight line on which the groups differ most in the sense of squared distance from the mean of the groups on the line. Each solution line is perpendicular in a Euclidean geometric sense from each other solution line. Computer programs are used to solve these problems, and the programs are designed to find the best solution first. The best solution is one in which the variance between the groups is greatest in rela-

tion to average variance within the groups for all possible lines. Once this solution is found, the next one is found from the residuals of fit to the first solution. A statistical test, Wilks lambda, is a multivariate analog to the ratio of the sum of squares within groups to the sum of the squares' total. An F-test may be used to test significance. For each new solution, test the additional error reduced in a manner similar to that employed in multiple regression to test a new predictor's additional contribution to prediction. Also, stepwise procedures can be employed in discriminant analysis to select the subset of predictors that maximally separate the groups. Predictors that do not contribute to separation in a given solution are dropped.

Discriminant analysis is widely used in both social and physical sciences. Its mathematical solutions are straightforward for a computer; discriminant analysis programs for microcomputers are widely used (Huberty & Lowman, 1997).

REFERENCE

Huberty, C., & Lowman, L.L. (1997). Discriminant analysis via statistical packages. *Educational and Psychological Management, 57,* 759–784.

See also **Factor Analysis; Multiple Regression; WISC-WISC-R**

DISCRIMINATION LEARNING

Discrimination learning refers to the process of learning to respond differentially to relevant dimensions of a stimulus event. As a fundamental construct of behaviorally oriented learning explanations, this type of learning emphasizes events that occur before a behavior(s), the relationship of these events to the strength and contextual appropriateness of the behavior(s); and the resulting consequences that serve to maintain, strengthen, or punish the behavior(s).

During the teaching of discriminations, a stimulus event is presented to the student. Following this presentation, the student independently or, if necessary, with prompts, exhibits a behavioral response. If the behavior that the individual engages in is appropriate relative to the stimulus event, the learner is rewarded with a potentially reinforcing outcome. If the behavior is not appropriate with regard to the stimulus event, the consequent alternatives might include not attending to the response (ignoring), or systematic presentation of consequences aimed at reducing the future probability of the behavior occurring (punishment).

Planned teaching of discriminations has involved simple to complex presentations of the attributes of the stimulus events (e.g., size, shape, volume, color, or combinations of these) and varied reinforcement schedules (e.g., movement from fixed to variable schedules of reinforcement) aimed at strengthening the discriminative potential of the stimulus event. Following accurate individualized assessment, discriminations are taught beginning at a level that increases the opportunity for success. Based on continuing assessment, teaching complexity is systematically moved in the direction of more normative skill development.

Teaching of discriminated responses has been used in vocationally oriented, curricula, social skills programs, and many other curriculum areas targeted for the exceptional needs learner. By teaching individuals to exhibit specified behaviors under certain stimulus conditions, many of the inconsistent and inappropriate behaviors exhibited by this diverse group have been strengthened or replaced with more environmentally appropriate responses. For a comprehensive explanation of discrimination learning, the reader is referred to texts by Alberto and Troutman (1977) and Sulzer-Azaroff and Mayer (1977). Both texts provide clear examples of the application of this learning principle to educational programming. McDonald and Martin (1993) recommend the use of the Assessment of Basic Learning Abilities Test to assess discrimination acquisition with individuals who have profound disabilities.

REFERENCES

Alberto, P.A., & Troutman, A.C. (1977). *Applied behavior analysis for teachers: Influencing student performance.* Columbus, OH: Merrill.

McDonald, L., & Martin, G.L. (1993). Facilitating discrimination learning for persons with developmental disabilities. *International Journal of Rehabilitation Research, 16,* 2, 160–164.

Sulzer-Azaroff, B., & Mayer, G.R. (1977). *Applying behavior-analysis procedures with children and youth.* New York: Holt, Rinehart & Winston.

See also **Applied Behavior Analysis; Behavior Modification; Data-Based Instruction; Precision Teaching**

DISPROPORTIONALITY

Disproportionality in special education denotes unequal percentages of students with various demographic characteristics in special education classifications and programs. Disproportionality most often occurs in the mildly handicapping classifications of mild mental retardation (MMR), emotionally disturbed (ED), and specific learning disability (SLD), or in programs for the talented and gifted (TAG). The demographic variables in which disproportionality is most often observed, and sometimes seen as a problem, are ethnic/racial status, sex, and socioeconomic status. Disproportionality related to these student characteristics is well known, but highly controversial (Reschly, 1986; 1991; 1997).

Disproportionality, particularly overrepresentation of minority students in programs for the mildly mentally retarded, has provoked extensive and enormously expensive litigation beginning in about 1968 and continuing through present day (Bersoff, 1982; Prasse & Reschly, 1986; Reschly, 1986; 1991). The common features of the placement bias cases are (1) overrepresentation of minority students, usually blacks, in self-contained MMR special classes; (2) class-action suits filed in federal district courts; and (3) allegations of bias in various aspects of the referral, pre-placement evaluation, and classification/placement decision making. The outcomes of these cases have been extremely diverse, ranging from judicial decrees banning overrepresentation and forbidding the use of individually administered intelligence tests in certain circumstances to judicial decrees indicating that overrepresentation as such is not discriminatory and upholding the use of IQ tests along with other measures as an important protection for all children in the referral and classification/placement process. Federal circuit courts have upheld trial decisions in two cases, *Larry P. v. Riles* (1984) and *Marshall v. Georgia* (1985). However, the *Larry P.* and *Marshall* opinions reached opposite conclusions on a similar set of issues. Further litigation is likely.

Research methods designed to develop valid ways to screen, refer, and classify/place students that also eliminate disproportionality have been unsuccessful to date. However, inclusive programming (Kovach, 1997; Markowitz, 1997) has reduced many instances of placement from service provision to special education outcomes. Processes and procedures that maintain the integrity of programs in meeting the needs of students, apply reliable and valid screening, referral, and classification/placement procedures, and are being consistently implemented and assessed. Centers such as COMRISE (Center of Minority Research in Special Education) are attempting to increase the number and research capacity of minority scholars in institutions of higher education with high minority enrollments. They are building a community of minority scholars within the larger special education research community and are trying to improve the quality and effectiveness of culturally competent special education services for minority students (COMRISE, 1998). The U.S. Department of Education reports disproportionality statistics on an annual basis, and is currently focusing much attention to the less than adequate special education services delivered to inner-city students (U.S. Dept. of Education, 1996). The Office of Civil Rights conducts compliance reviews on such issues as ensuring nondiscriminatory practices are followed in the placement of minority students in special education and low-track courses, ensuring that access to English language instruction as well as content courses and other educational benefits are afforded to limited-English proficient students, ensuring student assessment practices are nondiscriminatory and providing nondiscriminatory access to gifted and talented and other high ability programs (OCR, 1998). There also has been a national shift towards prereferral intervention, better interventions in regular education, orienting assessment procedures towards intervention rather than classification, the use of court orders, and the use of alternative criteria and assessment procedures (Reschly, 1991; 1997).

REFERENCES

Bersoff, D.N. (1982). The legal regulation of school psychology. In C.R. Reynolds & T.B. Gutkin (Eds.), *The handbook of school psychology* (pp. 1043–1074). New York: Wiley.

COMRISE. (1998). *Center of Minority Research in Special Education.* Charlottesville, VA: University of Virginia, Curry School of Education.

Kovach, J.A., & Gordon, D.E. (1997). Inclusive education: A modern-day civil-rights struggle. *Educational Forum, 6,* 3, 247– 257.

Markowitz, J. (1997). *Addressing the disproportionale representation of students from racial and ethnic minority groups in special education: A resource document.* Alexandria, VA: National Association of State Directors of Special Education.

Office of Civil Rights. (1998). Annual report to Congress, Fiscal Year 1996. Washington, DC: Department of Education.

Prasse, D.P., & Reschly, D.J. (1986). *Larry P:* A case of segregation, testing, or program efficacy? *Exceptional Children, 52,* 333–346.

Reschly, D.J. (1986). Economic and cultural factors in childhood exceptionality. In R.T. Brown & C.R. Reynolds (Eds.), *Psychological perspectives on childhood exceptionality: A handbook* (pp. 423– 466). New York: Wiley-Interscience.

Reschly, D.J. (1991). Bias in cognitive assessment: Implications for future litigation and professional practices. *Diagnostique, 17,* 1, 86–90.

Reschly, D.J. (1997). *Disproportionate minority representation in general and special education: Patterns, issues, and alternatives.* Des Moines, IA: Iowa State Department of Education.

U.S. Department of Education. (1996). *Eighteenth annual report to Congress: To assure the free appropriate public education of all children with disabilities: Implementation of the Individuals with Disabilities Education Act (IDEA).* Washington, DC: Author.

See also **Cultural Bias in Tests; Culturally/ Linguistically Diverse Students, Representation of; Larry P.; Marshall *v.* Georgia; Nondiscriminatory Assessment**

DISTAR

DISTAR (Direct Instructional System for Teaching and Remediation) is a product name for an instructional system published by Science Research Associates Inc. (SRA).

The DISTAR system was originally designed to teach basic skills and concepts in reading, arithmetic, and language to disadvantaged preschoolers (Guinet, 1971). However, the scope has broadened to include average, above average, learning-disabled, and educable and trainable mentally retarded children (Kim et al., 1972). Current reviews of research (Cotton & Savard, 1982; Gersten, 1981) have revealed that the direct instruction method has proven successful with socioeconomically disadvantaged primary age children and special education students through age 13.

The system is grounded in the ideas that children learn what they are taught, that the necessary basic skills and concepts are the same for all children, that IQ is a function of teaching, and that it is possible to teach all of the necessary skills and concepts by means of a suitable instructional program. The required small group instruction ensures maximum student participation. Immediate reinforcement or correction ensures the prevention of error patterns (*Direct Instruction Management Handbook,* 1981; Guinet, 1971; Kim et al., 1972; Moodie & Hoen, 1972). The 30-minute les-

sons consisting of verbal interaction between teacher and students provide immediate teacher feedback. Lessons are carefully sequenced in a step-by-step fashion requiring mastery of basic skills before presentation of more complex ones. The well-defined small learning stages ensure daily successes that reinforce student self-concept. Limited visuals control distractions and are provided only at the end of lessons as rewards. The rewards are similar to the worksheets completed in class and taken home in recognition of doing well (Williamson, 1970). The presentation of tasks and the use of praise is highly structured. The teacher's manual instructs the teacher how to present the tasks, what to say, what signals and cues to use, what to expect from the children, and how to correct errors. Research results comparing the DISTAR program with other direct instruction curricula indicate that DISTAR is comparable in outcomes (Kuder, 1990; Traweek & Berniger, 1997).

REFERENCES

Cotton, K., & Savard, W.G. (1982). *Direct instruction: Research on school effectiveness project.* Portland, OR: Northwest Regional Educational Lab. (ERIC Document Reproduction Service No. ED 214 909)

Direct instruction management handbook. (1981). Chicago: Science Research Associates.

Gersten, R.M. (1981, April). *Direct instruction programs in special education settings: A review of evaluation research findings.* Paper presented at the annual international convention of the Council for Exceptional Children, New York. (ERIC Document Reproduction Service No. ED 204 957)

Guinet, L. (1971). *Evaluation of DISTAR materials in three junior learning assistance classes* (Report No. 71–16). Vancouver, BC: Board of School Trustees, Department of Planning and Evaluation. (ERIC Document Reproduction Service No. ED 057 105)

Kim, Y., Berger, B.J., & Kratochvil, D.W. (1972). *DISTAR instructional system* (Report No. OEC-0-70-4892). Washington, DC: Office of Education, Office of Program Planning and Evaluation. (ERIC Document Reproduction Service No. ED 061 632)

Kuder, S.J. (1990). Effectiveness of the DISTAR reading program for children with learning disabilities. *Journal of Learning Disabilities, 23,* 1, 69–71.

Moodie, A., & Hoen, R. (1972). *Evaluation of DISTAR programs in learning assistance classes of Vancouver 1971–72* (Report No. 72-18). Vancouver, BC: Board of School Trustees, Department of Planning and Evaluation. (ERIC Document Reproduction Service No. ED 088 911)

Traweek, D., & Berniger, V. (1997). Comparisons of beginning literacy programs. *Learning Disability Quarterly, 20,* 2, 160–168.

Williamson, F. (1970). *DISTAR Reading—Research and Experiment.* Urbana: University of Illinois. (ERIC Document Reproduction Service No. ED 045 318)

See also **Direct Instruction; Follow Through**

DISTRACTIBILITY

Attention is considered the most basic prerequisite for learning (Hewett, Taylor, & Artuso, 1969). As a disorder of attention, distractibility has been extensively studied by special educators and psychologists.

Definitions of distractibility include difficulty in tuning out or forced responsiveness to unessential or extraneous stimulation such as environmental noises or stimuli such as hunger pangs, that may produce a motor activity within the individual (Cruickshank, Bentzen, Ratzeburg, & Tannhauser, 1961). In a classroom setting, distractibility typically refers to behavior that reflects the child's interest in things other than those on which the child should be concentrating (Bryan, 1974).

The presumed causes of distractibility are many and varied. There exists some evidence for a developmental trend in distractibility, with children becoming less distractible as they grow older (Well, Lorch, & Anderson, 1980). Distractibility in boys has also been associated with congenital characteristics such as minor, physical anomalies as well as gross motor incoordination (O'Donnell, O'Neill, & Staley, 1979). Other suspected etiologies include metabolic disturbances interacting with diet (Wunderlich, 1981), gross brain damage or an underlying neurological condition such as minimal brain dysfunction, and environmental variables such as child-rearing practices. Ross (1976) postulates that distractibility is due to a delayed development in selective attention.

Selective attention refers to a child's age-appropriate ability to focus on relevant information in the environment while excluding irrelevant or distracting information. As a child is listening to a teacher-directed lesson in the classroom, numerous stimuli impinge on the child's senses such as the noise from the overhead lights, the child's classmate across the row shifting in his or her chair, or a feeling of hunger. In order for the child to learn and attend to the teacher, the child must screen out all the irrelevant stimuli and focus on the relevant stimuli. The ability to screen out the irrelevant while focusing on the relevant stimuli requires selective attention.

Although there exists wide agreement that attention/distractibility and learning are strongly related, the precise nature of this relationship remains unclear. Distractibility has been demonstrated to negatively affect memory (Torgesen, 1981), and achievement in arithmetic and reading (Stedman, Lawlis, & Cortner, 1978). The exhibiting of distractible behaviors also affects adult behavior, with distractible children eliciting greater amounts of attention and instruction from adults in a one-to-one setting but less attention and interaction in a group setting (Ianna, Hallahan, & Bell, 1982). Distractibility typically occurs following head trauma in children and in adults.

The most common types of interventions for distractibility are pharmacotherapy, consisting of the administration of stimulant medication such as Ritalin and Mellaril (Gadow, 1981), and behavior-management techniques. Behavior-management techniques include making rewards contingent on attentive behaviors and cognitive behavioral interventions such as self-instruction, self-correction, and self-monitoring (Kneedler & Hallahan, 1981). Other types of interventions have included reducing distracting input by environmental modifications such as changing the seating arrangement (Sandoval, 1982), having youngsters work in plain, nonstimulating cubicles, changing the student's diet (Wunderlich, 1981), introducing sensory integrative therapy, which involves gross, fine and visual-motor activities (Ainsa, 1983) and introducing attentional skills as learning objectives (Wolfson, 1995). Although all of these interventions have enjoyed some success, the most successful are pharmacotherapy and behavior management. Further, although these two types of interventions have often reduced distractibility in particular children, they frequently do not produce increases in learning unless they are combined with increased direct academic instruction, and interventions that require various degrees of monitoring and supervision (Faison & Barniskis, 1993).

REFERENCES

Ainsa, T. (1983). Sensory integration: A home intervention program. *Academic Therapy, 18,* 495–498.

Bryan, T.S. (1974). An observational analysis of classroom behaviors of children with learning disabilities. *Journal of Learning Disabilities, 7,* 35–43.

Cruickshank, W.M., Bentzen, F.A., Ratzeburg, F.H., & Tannhauser, R. (1961). *A teaching method for brain-injured and hyperactive children.* Syracuse, NY: Syracuse University Press.

Faison, M.W., & Bernikis, E.A. (1993). *A systematic approach to the treatment of ADHD: An intervention model.* (ERIC Clearinghouse No. EC30311)

Gadow, K. (1981). Effects of stimulant drugs on attention and cognitive deficits. *Exceptional Child Quarterly, 2*(3), 83–93.

Ianna, S.O., Hallahan, D.P., & Bell, R.Q. (1982). The effects of distractible child behavior on adults in a problem-solving setting. *Learning Disabilities Quarterly, 5,* 126–132.

Kneedler, R.D., & Hallahan, D.P. (1981). Self-monitoring of on-task behavior with learning-disabled children: Current studies and directions. *Exceptional Child Quarterly, 2*(3), 73–82.

O'Donnell, J.P., O'Neill, S.O., & Staley, A. (1979). Congenital correlates of distractibility. *Journal of Abnormal Child Psychology, 7,* 465–470.

Ross, A.O. (1976). *Psychological aspects of learning disabilities and reading disorders.* New York: McGraw-Hill.

Sandoval, J. (1982). Hyperactive children. 12 Ways to help them in the classroom. *Academic Therapy, 18,* 107–113.

Stedman, J.M., Lawlis, G.F., & Cortner, R.H. (1978). Relationships between WISC-R factors, Wide Range Achievement Test scores, and visual-motor maturation in children referred for psychological evaluation. *Journal of Consulting & Clinical Psychology, 46,* 869–872.

Torgesen, J.K. (1981). Relationship between memory and attention in learning disabilities. *Exceptional Child Quarterly, 2*(3), 51–59.

Well, A.D., Lorch, E.P., & Anderson, D.R. (1980). Developmental trends in distractibility: Is absolute or proportional decrement the appropriate measure of interference? *Journal of Experimental Child Psychology, 30,* 109–124.

Wolfson, L. (1995). Attentional skills and 5–14. *Scottish Educational Review, 27,* 2, 138–145.

Wunderlich, R.C. (1981). Nutrition and learning. *Academic Therapy, 16,* 303–307.

See also Attention-Deficit Hyperactivity Disorder; Attention Span; Connors Rating Scale; Hyperkinesis; Impulse Control; Wechsler Intelligence Scale for Children—Third Edition

DIVISION OF INTERNATIONAL SPECIAL EDUCATION AND SERVICES (DISES)

In June, 1978, the Council for Exceptional Children held the first World Congress on Future Special Education in Stirling, Scotland (Fink, 1978). Following that meeting in order to preserve the momentum created by this Congress, some university faculty members organized a special interest group within the CEC's Teacher Education Division. This group was concerned primarily with the international aspects of delivery of special education services to children with disabilities. Since the scope of interest went beyond teacher education, a separate division of the CEC, known as the Division of International Special Education and Services (DISES), was formed in 1990 with the mission of assisting in the improvement of the quality of special education and services to individuals with disabilities throughout the world.

DISES has also been active in disseminating information about special education programs worldwide through its newsletter and special publications. Four monographs have been published, and a professional journal, *The Journal of International Special Needs Education (JISNE)* began publication in 1998. The editors of the DISES newsletter are Bob Henderson of the University of Illinois (bob-h@uiuc.edu), Lisa Dieker of the University of Wisconsin-Milwaukee (dieker@csd.uwm.edu), and Yash Bhagwanj (bhagwanj@students.uiuc.edu); and the editor of *JISNE* is Robert Michael (michaelr@npvm.newpaltz. edu).

REFERENCE

Fink, A.H. (1978.) *International Perspectives on Future Special Education.* Reston, VA: Council for Exceptional Children.

DIVORCE AND SPECIAL EDUCATION

Since the mid 1970s, the impact of parental divorce on children has been an area of concern for professionals in psychology and education. This interdisciplinary consensus has been generated in part by alarming census descriptions of rapidly changing adult lifestyles. For example, census reports indicate that the divorce rate more than quadrupled from 1970 to 1994. Since these figures do not account for those who were divorced and remarried at the time of the survey, they actually underestimate the total incidence of divorce in our society. Similarly, the incidence of single-parent child rearing has also increased markedly, from 11.9% in 1970 to 29% in 1994. These figures do not include those who have previously experienced a single-parent situation but are now living in reconstituted two-parent families.

A central issue is whether adjustment to divorce represents a transitory stressor or is associated with long-term disorders. Longitudinal studies provide a consensus that divorce should be conceptualized as a multistage process. These studies, conducted over periods of 6 and 10 years, respectively, reveal complex interactions and altered family relationships that result in long-term maladjustment for children. They also illustrate substantial age and sex differences in adjustment.

Wallerstein and Kelly (Wallerstein & Kelly, 1976) conducted a 10-year longitudinal study of 131 children residing in Marin County, California, whose parents were divorced. This was a nonclinical sample of children, ages 2 1/2 to 18 years, from white, middle-class families. Clinical interviews were conducted just after separation, and at 1-, 5-, and 10-year intervals following divorce. Initial results revealed that children responded differently by age. At the 1-year follow-up, adjustment problems persisted, although most adolescents had made adequate adjustments (attributed to distancing from parents and successful mastery experiences during the past year). At the 5-year follow-up, variables that mediate children's adjustment to divorce were identified—resolution of parental conflict, child's relationship with noncustodial parent, quality of parenting by custodial parent, personality and coping skills of the child, child's support system, diminished anger and depression in the child, and age and sex of the child. A positive relationship with the father was more important for boys than girls. Results of the 10-year follow-up (of 113 original subjects) confirmed the long-term impact of divorce. Difficulties at 10 years were characterized by poor parenting (diminished capacity to parent) and an overburdened child (taking on of adult responsibility).

Critical reviews of past research have consistently indicated severe methodological limitations (Atkeson, Forehand, & Rickard, 1982; Clingempeel & Reppucci, 1982). Major limitations include (1) small and biased samples that limit generalizability of the findings; (2) inadequate or nonexistent control groups, which precludes the study of divorce-specific effects; (3) failure to control for socioeconomic status in comparisons between divorced and intact families; and (4) failure to include multimethod, multifactored criteria to control for measurement bias.

The NASP-KSU (National Association of School Psychologists—Kent State University) Impact of Divorce Project was directed at minimizing the limitations of the cited research in order to provide more definitive conclusions about the long-term impact of divorce on children (Guidubaldi, 1983, 1985). Results on 699 children from 38 states at the initial data-gathering period (Time-1) demonstrated more conclusively than previous studies that, during middle childhood (ages 6 to 11), youths are adversely affected by divorce. Because the average length of time in a single-parent home at Time-1 was 3.98 years (sd = 2.54), these effects were interpreted as long term. Specific criteria on which children from divorced homes performed more poorly than those from intact homes are as follows: (1) social-behavioral measures from parent and teacher ratings of peer popularity status, anxiety, dependency, aggression, withdrawal, inattention, and locus of control; (2) Wechsler IQ scores; (3) Wide Range Achievement Test scores in reading, spelling, and math; (4) school performance indexes, including grades in reading and math and repeating of a school grade; (5) adaptive behaviors (measured by the Vineland Teacher Rating Scale) in the areas of daily living, social skills, and communication; and (6) physical health ratings of the children in the study as well as of parents and siblings. Intact-family children showed superior performance on 21 of 27 social competence criteria and 8 of 9 academic competence criteria. Additionally, analyses revealed that divorced-family children were far more likely to have been previously referred to a school psychologist, to have been retained in grade, and to be in special class placements, including programs for reading difficulties.

Definition of the sequelae of divorce is a complex process, and assessment must therefore include not only multidimensional aspects of child and parent adjustment but also a longitudinal-ecological approach. The NASP-KSU Impact of Divorce study included follow-up samples of 229 children at 2- and 3-year intervals, and examined environmental factors as mediators of children's postdivorce adjustment. Major findings from this nationwide study are as follows:

1. The negative, differential effects of divorce on children and young adolescents are long term where the average length of time since divorce was 6.41 years (sd = 2.35) at Time-2 of this study.

2. Children's reactions to divorce are especially influenced by sex and age, with boys during late childhood and early adolescence being more adversely affected on multiple criteria than 6- and 7-year-old boys. Late childhood and young adolescent girls were much better adjusted than those at the 6- and 7-year age levels.

3. Single-parent, divorced-family households have significantly less income than intact families. This difference accounts for significant academic achievement variance between divorced- and intact-family children.

4. The socioeconomic measures of parents' educational and occupational levels moderate some of children's divorce adjustment. This is especially apparent in regard to the educational level of the same sex parent.

5. A positive relationship with both the custodial and noncustodial parent predicted positive adjustment for both girls and boys of divorce concurrently and across time. The noncustodial parent-child relationship was noticeably more important for boys.

6. More frequent and reliable visitation with the noncustodial parent (typically, the father) was associated with better adjustment for both girls and boys.

7. Diminished degree of conflict between parents predicted improved children's adjustment, especially for boys across time to early adolescence.

8. Authoritarian (i.e., punitive) child-rearing styles in comparison with authoritative (i.e., more democratic) and permissive styles predicted more adverse child adjustment, especially for boys.

9. The home routines of less television viewing, regular bedtimes, maternal employment, and helpfulness of maternal grandfather predict positive adjustment for both boys and girls.

10. Family support factors that promote positive postdivorce adjustment are availability of helpful relatives, including in-laws, availability of friends, paid child care assistance such as nursery schools and babysitters, and participation in occupational and educational endeavors by the custodial parent.

11. When the total sample of male and female divorced-family children are considered, school environment variables of smaller school population, safe and orderly atmosphere, fewer miles bused to school, and traditional rather than open classroom structure are associated with better adjustment. However, several school and classroom climate factors relate to better adjustment for girls only. These include safe and orderly environment, frequent monitoring of student progress, high expectations for academic achievement, and time on task.

The impact of divorce on children has appropriately become a central concern of mainstreamed education. Special educators perhaps need to focus even more on this rapidly increasing disruption of children's lives. As evidenced in the NASP-KSU nationwide study and in Beattie & Maniscalo (1985), children in special education programs disproportionately come from divorced, single-parent homes. Income levels, home routines, and parental supports are adversely affected by this condition and children from these homes, particularly boys, show overwhelming evidence of maladjustment in both academic and social-emotional areas of performance. Understanding conditions that can ameliorate the negative impact of divorce on children may be one of the most critical bases for development of preventive mental health interventions as well as remedial techniques for children already identified as special.

REFERENCES

Atkeson, B.M., Forehand, R.L., & Rickard, K.M. (1982). The effects of divorce on children. In B.B. Lahey & A.E. Kazdin (Eds.), *Advances in clinical child psychology* (Vol. 5). New York: Plenum.

Beattie, J.R., & Maniscalo, G.O. (1985). Special education and divorce. Is there a line? *Techniques, 1,* 5, 342–345.

Clingempeel, W.G., & Reppucci, N.D. (1982). Joint custody after divorce: Major issues and goals for research. *Psychological Bulletin, 91,* 102–127.

Guidubaldi, J. (1983, July). Divorce research clarifies issues: A report on NASP's nationwide study. *Communique, 10,* 1–3.

Guidubaldi, J. (1985). Differences in children's divorce adjustment across grade level and gender: A report from the NASP-Kent State University Nationwide Project. In S. Wolchik & P. Karoly

(Eds.), *Children of divorce: Perspectives on adjustment.* Lexington, MA: Lexington.

Wallerstein, J.S., & Kelly, J.B. (1976). The effects of parental divorce experiences of the child in later latency. *American Journal of Orthopsychiatry, 46,* 256–267.

DIX, DOROTHEA L. (1802–1887)

Dorothea Dix, a humanitarian and social reformer, was responsible for major reforms in the care of the mentally ill in the United States and abroad. Shocked by the common practice of incarcerating mentally ill people in jails with criminals, she spent a year and a half investigating conditions in her home state of Massachusetts and, in 1843, reported her findings to the state legislature. Her description of the abhorrent conditions that existed (including the use of chains for restraint) and her argument that mentally ill persons could be properly treated and cared for only in hospitals, resulted in substantial enlargement of the state hospital at Worcester, which was one of only eight mental hospitals in the United States at that time. Capitalizing on her success in Massachusetts, Dix turned her attention to other states and countries. She was responsible for the construction of 32 hospitals in the United States and others in Canada, Europe, and Japan.

During the Civil War, Dix served as superintendent of women nurses, the highest office held by a woman during the war. After the war she returned, at age 65, to her work with hospitals. In 1881 she retired to the New Jersey State Hospital at Trenton, the first hospital established through her efforts, where she remained until her death.

REFERENCE

Marshall, H.E. (1937). *Dorothea Dix, forgotten samaritan.* Chapel Hill, NC: University of North Carolina Press.

DOCTORAL TRAINING IN SPECIAL EDUCATION

Over 80 special education programs in colleges and universities in the United States award the doctoral degree (Sindelar & Schloss, 1986). The common purpose of these programs is to prepare leaders for the field, but the programs themselves are as diverse as the roles their graduates assume. Many local, state, and federal administrators, college and university teacher trainers, scholars, and researchers hold the doctorate in special education. Both the doctor of philosophy (PhD) and the doctor of education (DEd or EdD) are awarded. Although the PhD is considered an academic degree and the DEd a professional degree, this distinction does not hold up in practice because many prominent scholars hold the DEd and many practitioners the PhD.

A program of study is planned under the direction of an advisor (or major professor) and a supervisory committee.

The program typically derives from the aspirations of the student and the strengths of the program offerings. In addition to special education course work, doctoral programs may include concentrations in a related field of study or cognate area and work in research methodology and statistics. The successful completion of coursework, however, represents only a fraction of the formal requirements that a doctoral candidate must meet. Many programs require a qualifying examination before formal admission to candidacy and, later in the program, a comprehensive examination to determine mastery of the program of studies. Doctoral programs culminate with the completion of an independent research project and the preparation and defense of the dissertation. The supervisory committee evaluates the student's performance at each of these checkpoints.

These formal requirements represent only part of what students learn during their doctoral studies. Many have the opportunity (often as graduate assistants) to develop skills in teaching, supervision, administration, and research. Initially, their participation in these activities is guided by the faculty. With experience, candidates may take on more responsibility and operate with greater independence. Many programs provide financial support for graduate assistants with funds from leadership preparation grants awarded by the U.S. Department of Education's Office of Special Education and Rehabilitative Services.

It must be emphasized that leadership preparation programs have undertaken a critical self-evaluation in response to the common and difficult problems they face: the quantity and quality of students, the poor focus of their offerings, faculty dissatisfaction, and low faculty productivity (Prehm, 1984). With regard to this final concern, research (Schloss & Sindelar, 1985) has shown that productive researchers are the exception and not the rule, even for faculties of doctoral-granting programs. The recent efforts of the Higher Education Consortium for Special Education, an organization representing institutions with comprehensive programs in special education, in developing indicators of quality in leadership training represent a positive first step in addressing these issues. There has been a call for a national data collection system to address a critical shortage of doctoral-level specialists (Smith, 1990).

REFERENCES

Prehm, H.J. (1984). Preparation for leadership in personnel preparation. *Teacher Education & Special Education, 7,* 59–65.

Schloss, P.J., & Sindelar, P.T. (1985). Publication frequencies of departments conferring the PhD in special education. *Teacher Education and Special Education.*

Sindelar, P.T., & Schloss, P.J. (1986). The reputations of doctoral training program in special education. *Journal of Special Education, 20,* 49–59.

Smith, D.D. (1990) *History and future needs of doctoral training in special education.* (ERIC Clearinghouse No. EC301042)

See also **SpecialNet; Supervision in Special Education; Teacher Centers**

DOG GUIDES FOR THE BLIND

The use of dogs to guide blind persons has a long history. However, it was not until after World War I that the dog was systematically trained to guide blinded German veterans. The veterans were taught to follow the trained dog's movements through the use of a specially designed harness.

An American, Dorothy Harrison Eustis, living in Switzerland, described the use of German shepherds as dog guides for the blind in a 1927 article published in the *Saturday Evening Post.* One of the Americans who got in touch with Eustis after the publication of the article was Morris Frank, a young man from Tennessee who had been recently blinded. He persuaded Eustis to have a dog trained for him and traveled to Switzerland to be trained with the dog.

After Frank's success with the first American dog guide, the legendary Buddy, Eustis returned to the United States in 1929 and established The Seeing Eye Inc., the first school to train dog guides for the blind in America. The twenty-second edition of the American Foundation for the Blind *Directory of Agencies Serving the Blind in the United States* lists eight programs in the United States that prepare dog guides. There are similar training programs throughout the world.

The dog guide, because of a variety of limitations, provides mobility assistance to only about 1% of the blind population (Whitstock, 1980). However, the introduction of guide dogs has led to a greater acceptance of blind travelers and has helped a shift in perception of the blind (Blasch & Stuckey, 1995). Personal preferences, remaining vision, vocation, and life circumstances often dictate the advisability of the use of a dog guide. Very few school-aged visually impaired persons use dog guides, although the practice is not prohibited.

REFERENCES

American Foundation for the Blind. (1984). *Directory of agencies serving the visually handicapped in the U.S.* (22nd ed.). New York: Author.

Blasch, B.B., & Stuckey, R.A. (1995). Accessibility and mobility of persons who are visually impaired: A historical analysis. *Journal of Visual Impairment, 89,* 5, 417–422.

Whitstock, R.H. (1980). Dog guides. In R.L. Welsh & B.B. Blasch (Eds.), *Foundations of orientation and mobility.* New York: American Foundation for the Blind.

See also **American Foundation for the Blind; Mobility Training**

DOLCH WORD LIST

The Dolch Word List of 220 common words constitutes over 65% of the words found in elementary reading materials and 50% of all reading materials (Dolch, 1960). These high-frequency words form the framework for all reading materials. The list, developed by Edward W. Dolch, includes prepositions, conjunctions, pronouns, adjectives, adverbs, and the most common verbs. There are no nouns included in this list since each noun, according to Dolch, is tied to subject matter (Johns, 1971). The list is comprised of structure words, words that hold language together, as opposed to content words.

The average third-grade reader should be able to identify these 220 service words at sight. Many of the words have irregular spellings and cannot be learned by picture cues. Dolch (1939) reports that if the reader is able to recognize more than half the words at the sight reading rate of 120 words per minute, he or she will have confidence and will be able focus on the meaning of the material.

The Dolch Word List is frequently used as a diagnostic tool to identify poor readers (Elmquist, 1987). Many readers with mental retardation are deficient in recognizing and understanding the proper use of these words. The list also serves as the basis of remedial instruction. Garrard Publishers produces several materials, Popper Words, Basic Sight Vocabulary Cards, and Basic Sight Word Test, based on the list.

REFERENCES

Dolch, E.W. (1939). *A manual of remedial reading.* Champaign, IL: Garrard.

Dolch, E.W. (1960). *Teaching primary reading.* Champaign, IL: Garrard.

Elmquist, E. (1987). Improving reading skills and attitudes through the reading and writing connection. (ERIC Clearinghouse No. CS010210)

Johns, J.L. (1971). The Dolch Basic Word List—Then and now. *Journal of Reading Behavior, 3,* 35–40.

See also **Reading Disorders; Reading Remediation**

DOLL, EDGAR A. (1889–1968)

Edgar A. Doll joined the staff of the Training School at Vineland, New Jersey, as research and clinical psychologist in 1913. There he worked with E.R. Johnstone and H.H. Goddard in the Vineland Laboratory: the first laboratory devoted solely to the study of mental retardation.

Following service in World War I, three years with New Jersey's State Department of Classification and Education, completion of the doctorate in psychology at Princeton University, and two years of teaching at Ohio State University, Doll returned to Vineland as director of research. His studies of social competence led to the publication, in 1935, of the *Vineland Social Maturity Scale,* a revolutionary instrument that provided an objective basis for measuring social functioning which was more useful than mental age for classifying people for purposes of training and care.

Doll left Vineland in 1949 to serve as coordinator of research for the Devereux Schools. He was later consulting psychologist for the Bellingham, Washington, public schools. He served as president of the American Association of Applied Psychology, the American Association on Mental Deficiency, and the American Orthopsychiatric Association.

REFERENCES

Doll, E.A. (1953). *The measurement of social competence: A manual for the Vineland Social Maturity Scale.* Minneapolis: Educational Test Bureau.

Doll, E.E. (1969). Edgar Arnold Doll, 1889–1968. *American Journal of Mental Deficiency, 73,* 680–682.

DOPAMINE

Dopamine (DA) is a catecholamine class neurotransmitter. Dopamine has been one of the most studied neurotransmitters because of observed roles for DA in schizophrenia, obessive-compulsive behavior (Lewis, 1996), conduct disorder (Galvin, 1995) tardive dyskinesia, and Parkinson's disease. Dopaminergic pathways are located throughout the limbic system (area of the brain often associated with emotional reactivity and memory), the basal ganglia (area of the brain associated with motor timing and complex integration), and frontal brain areas. Animal studies of DA depletion and studies of neurological disorders with motor manifestations (i.e., Parkinson's disease) produce results supportive of DA's contributory role in brain systems involved in normal locomotion (Seiden & Dykstra, 1977). Similarly, researchers working with drugs that stimulate DA in animal brains have noted increases in spontaneous aggression during chemical stimulation of DA receptor sites (Senault, 1970). Introduction of haloperidol (Haldol), a DA-blocking agent, reduces the frequency of such fighting (Leavitt, 1982). In addition, DA appears to play a role in the regulation of food intake. Investigators (Seiden & Dykstra, 1977) also have noted a role for DA in the maintenance of avoidance behavior and in the facilitation of behavior on positive reinforcement schedules.

REFERENCES

Galvin, M. (1995). Serum dopamine beta Hydroxylase and maltreatment in psychiatrically hospitalized boys. *Child Abuse & Neglect: The International Journal, 19,* 7, 821–832.

Leavitt, F. (1982). *Drugs and behavior.* New York: Wiley.

Lewis, M.H. (1996). Plasma HVA in adults with mental retardation and stereotyped behaviors: Biochemical evidence for a dopamine deficiency model. *American Journal on Mental Retardation, 100,* 4, 413–418.

Seiden, L.S., & Dykstra, L.A. (1977). *Psychopharmocology: A biochemical and behavioral approach.* New York: Van Nostrand Reinhold.

Senault, B. (1970). Comportement d'aggressivité intraspécifique induit par l'apomorphine chez le rat. *Psychopharmocologia, 18,* 271–287.

See also **Haldol; Tranquilizers**

DOUBLE-BLIND DESIGN

One frequently encountered problem in research involving the administration of medication, particularly psychotropic drugs, is that some children or adults may be improved solely as a function of their knowledge that a drug has been administered. The degree to which this effect, frequently referred to as a placebo effect, is present and affecting the outcome of research is unknown and uncontrolled in any specific situation. Experimenters may also be influenced by administration of medication, particularly if the researcher developed the pharmaceutical agent or has other subjective reasons to be biased toward a particular outcome. In such cases, investigators may observe differential rates of behavioral or physiological change in those subjects receiving medication in comparison with those individuals receiving no drug therapy (Babbie, 1979). In either of these cases, the subject's or experimenter's expectation of a certain outcome represents a threat to the validity of the research design. Validity is compromised when the effect of the drug administered is confounded with the expectation of what, if any, the effects of the drug might be.

To control for the effect of patients merely taking medication, as would be the case if those taking medication were compared with a nonmedicated control group, subjects who are not receiving an active drug substance are administered a placebo that appears identical to the active medication in every regard, with the exception that its active ingredients are inert. Thus, the drug under study is not present in the placebo dose and the patients are unaware of whether their medication is in fact active or a placebo. In research terminology, then, the patients are blind to their own drug condition. In order to control for the effect of experimenter bias, it is also necessary for the investigators who administer medication and those who evaluate the outcome (the presence or absence of the drug effect) to be blind to the drug condition of the patients. When these precautions are followed, the research design is said to employ a double-blind procedure, since neither the patients nor the researchers are cognizant of the drug condition to which patients may be assigned (Sprague, 1979).

Obviously, there must be records of which patients have received active medication and which have received placebos in order for the results of the study to be interpretable. However, it is critical that this information not be available to researchers who may have contact with the patients or to the patients themselves until after the study has been completed. Thus, by following a strict double-blind research design, drug effects may be distinguished from actual patient and experimenter expectations regarding the drug under investigation (Sprague, 1979). Unless these two types of effects can be separated, the validity of such a study would be compromised seriously (Sprague, 1979; Sprague & Werry, 1971).

REFERENCES

Babbie, E.R. (1979). *The practice of social research.* Belmont, CA: Wadsworth.

Sprague, R.L. (1979). Assessment of intervention. In R.L. Trites (Ed.), *Hyperactivity in children: Etiology, measurement and treatment implications* (pp. 217–229). Baltimore, MD: University Park Press.

Sprague, R.L., & Werry, J.S. (1971). Methodology of psychopharmacological studies with the retarded. In N.R. Ellis (Ed.), *International review of research in mental retardation* (Vol. 5). New York: Academic.

See also ABAB Design; Hawthorne Effect; Research

DOWN, J. (JOHN) LANGDON, (1828–1896)

J. (John) Langdon Down, an English physician, in 1866 described the condition that he called mongolism and that is now known as Down syndrome or Down's syndrome. Although there had been earlier descriptions in the medical literature of individuals who appeared to belong to the same category, Down is credited with the discovery and description of this clinical entity.

Down was concerned with the prevention of mental retardation. He recommended attention to good parental health and sound prenatal care and child-rearing practices. He advocated education for mentally retarded individuals and recognized the efficacy of early training.

REFERENCES

Down, J.L. (1866). Observations on an ethnic classification of idiots. *London Hospital Clinical Lecture Reports, 3,* 259–262.

Down, J.L. (1887). *Mental affectations of childhood and youth.* London: Churchill.

Penrose, L.S., & Smith, G.F. (1966). *Down's anomaly.* Boston: Little, Brown.

DOWN'S SYNDROME

Down's syndrome, a chromosomal anomaly, accounts for one-third of all cases of genetic-origin mental retardation (Hayden & Beck, 1981). Zarfas and Wolf (1979) reported a frequency of 2/1000 live births. The Centers for Disease Control in Atlanta currently report statistics of 1/1000. In 1866 J. Langdon Down, the first person to describe the characteristics of the syndrome. Down's recognition of the pattern of characteristics clearly delineated the condition as a distinct and separate entity (Pueschel, Canning, Murphy, & Zausmer, 1978).

Of the more than 50 known characteristics (Koch & Koch, 1974), the most common are a small skull with a flat back of head; slanting, almond-shaped eyes; white speckled irises; flat-bridged nose and ears slightly smaller than average; small mouth with protruding, fissured tongue; drooping corners of the mouth; shortness of stature; stubby hands; little finger curved inward; a single crease along the palm of the hand rather than the average double palm crease; fingerprints and footprints differing from the norm; hypotonia (too little muscle tone); and an unsteady, jerky gait. Not all characteristics are present in each Down's syndrome individual and some of the symptoms may be less pronounced. Some level of mental retardation is inevitable but the degree of mental retardation may vary greatly. Studies have shown that cognitive development advances steadily until it levels off at mental ages of about 3 and a half to 5 years (Cornwell & Birch, 1969; Zeaman & House, 1962). Connally (1978) suggests that despite the generally found IQ deficit, the abilities of Down's syndrome children are not as limited as once suggested. Some IQs may be as high as borderline normal. Skill development may continue well into the third and fourth decade but abstract abilities may remain severely limited (Cornwell, 1974).

Lejeune, Gautur, and Turpin (1963) discovered that individuals with Down's syndrome had 47 rather than 46 chromosomes in each cell. All of the types of chromosomal abnormalities that cause Down's syndrome result in an extra 21 chromosome, or trisomy 21. Hereditary types account for less than 4%. In such cases, genetic counseling can be given. Amniocentesis may be helpful, as Down's syndrome is detectable in utero.

Nondisjunction, the most common form of Down's syndrome, found in 95% of afflicted persons, is not inherited. Trisomy 21 occurs when in place of the chromosome 21 pair, there is a trisomy (three individual 21 chromosomes). Nondisjunction can occur during formation of the egg or the sperm, or during the first few cell divisions after conception. The older the female, the more likely Down's syndrome will occur. During aging, the ova are exposed to stressors that may damage the chromosomes. Recent studies that examined chromosomes from both parents indicate that there may be a link between the age of the male and Down's syndrome as well (Pueschel, 1982).

Translocation, the inherited form of Down's syndrome, occurs during normal cell reproduction when two chromosomes overlap and break at the point of contact. Instead of reuniting properly, the broken ends unite with the wrong chromosome. The translocation usually occurs between the 14th and 21st chromosomes. A 14th may break and unite with a 21st or may become attached to a 21st without breaking, resulting in an abnormal chromosome (a 14-21 combination). The abnormal chromosome will reproduce itself. Therefore, an individual who inherits it will be a carrier of translocation Down's syndrome. Either a male or female can be a carrier, but it is more common in the female (Koch & Koch, 1974).

Mosaicism is the least common type of Down's syndrome. The mosaic has some normal 46 chromosome cells and some abnormal 47 chromosome cells, as detailed by Koch and Koch (1974). At some point during prenatal cell division (mitosis), and after a number of normal cells are produced, a mutation occurs. Generally, the result is a milder form of Down's syndrome. In some cases, a mosaic may have normal intelligence and exhibit few or no Down's syndrome characteristics. This type of Down's syndrome is not initially hereditary and there is little chance that it will occur in a second birth to the same parents. However, mosaics can pass on Down's syndrome to their offspring.

Although the exact cause of Down's syndrome is unknown, possible causes include radiation, gene mutation, viruses, drugs and other chemicals, autoimmune mechanisms, existing aberrations, aged gametes, and factors such as economic, thermal, temporal, and geographic conditions (American Association of Mental Deficiency, 1983). Advances in technology have made it possible to photomicrograph and more accurately study chromosomes.

Parent support is a vital need (Turnbull & Turnbull, 1978) to ensure that infant stimulation programs emphasizing self-help skills, motor training (Sanz & Menendez, 1992) language acquisition, feeding, toilet training, and positive socialization, are provided. Down's syndrome individuals are educable and should have exposure to their nonhandicapped peers from their early years. Generally, there is no reason that most Down's syndrome individuals cannot attend regular preschools and later local neighborhood schools. Custodial care is seldom warranted unless severe medical, psychological, or social problems occur. Carefully supervised, comprehensive special education, K–12, should include inclusion (Cheney & Demchak, 1996) and prevocational and vocational skill development. Adult living may include working in a sheltered workshop or in a well-organized and supervised private work place in business or industry. The greatest general development is found in Down's syndrome individuals who are reared at home and well stimulated (Connally, 1978). Optimum progress occurs when facilities are positive, view Down's syndrome as a part of a rich inheritance, (Stratford, 1994) and training begins early and is comprehensive.

REFERENCES

American Association of Mental Deficiency. (1983). Classification in mental retardation (Rev. ed.). *American Journal of Mental Deficiency, 89,* 242–256.

Cheney, C., & Demchak, M. (1996) *Providing appropriate education in inclusive settings: A rural case study.* (ERIC Clearinghouse No. RC020560)

Connally, J. (1978). Intelligence levels of Down's syndrome children. *American Journal of Mental Deficiency, 83,* 193–196.

Cornwell, A.C. (1974). Development of language abstraction and numerical concept formation in Down's syndrome children. *American Journal of Mental Deficiency, 79,* 179–190.

Cornwell, A.C., & Birch, H.G. (1969). Psychological and social development in home reared children with Down syndrome (mongolism). *American Journal of Mental Deficiency, 74,* 314–350.

Hayden, A.H., & Beck, G.R. (1981). Finding and educating high risk infants. In R. Meyer, C. Ramsey, & P. Throames (Eds.), *Finding and educating high risk infants* (pp. 19–51). Baltimore, MD: University Park.

Koch, R., & Koch, K. (1974). *Understanding the mentally retarded child. A new approach.* New York: Random House.

Lejeune, J., Gautur, M., & Turpin, R. (1963). Study of the somatic chromosomes of nine mongoloid idiot children. In S.H. Bayer (Ed.), *Papers on human genetics* (pp. 238–240). Englewood Cliffs, NJ: Prentice-Hall.

Pueschel, S., Canning, C., Murphy, A., & Zausmer, E. (1978). *Down syndrome growing and learning.* Fairway: Andrews, McMeel, & Parker.

Sanz, M.T., & Menendez, F.J. (1992). *Early motor training in Down's Syndrome babies: Results of an intervention program.* (ERIC Clearinghouse No. EC301660)

Stratford, B. (1994). Down syndrome is for life. International *Journal on disability, development & Education, 41,* 1, 3–14.

Turnbull, A., & Turnbull, H. (1978). *Parents speak out: Growing with a handicapped child.* Columbus, OH: Merrill.

Zarfas, D.E., & Wolf, L.C. (1979). Maternal age patterns and the incidence of Down's syndrome. *American Journal of Mental Deficiency, 83,* 353–359.

Zeaman, D., & House, B. (1962). Mongoloid mental age is proportional to log cognitive age. *Child Development, 33,* 481–488.

See also **Genetic Counseling; Mental Retardation; Mosaicism; Trisomy 21**

DRAW-A-PERSON TEST

The draw-a-person (DAP) is an assessment technique used with both children and adults for a variety of purposes. Harris (1963) provided a set of instructions, a scoring system, and norms for using the technique as a measure of children's intelligence. The test has also been widely used as a projective personality assessment technique following a suggestion by Machover (1949). Although specific instructions vary, the examinee is typically asked to draw a picture of a person. The examiner provides as little structure as possible; however, if necessary, the subject is encouraged to draw an entire person and not to use stick figures. The subject is then asked to draw a person of the opposite sex. These basic instructions are often embellished to include a drawing of oneself and an inquiry phase during which the subject may be asked to make up a story about the person in the drawing or to explain various details included in the picture. Several scoring systems are available (Naglieri, 1988; Shaffer, Duszynski, & Thomas, 1984), and they have moderate to high test-retest reliability based on global quantitative ratings (Naglieri, 1988; Swenson, 1968).

The DAP is still popular and may provide a reasonable estimate of the cognitive abilities of people across a wide age range. Unfortunately, its effectiveness in diagnosing emotional disorders is limited at best (Groth-Marnat, 1997). Commonly used with standardized tests such as the MMPI, the DAP can be used alone as a means of initiating rapport with a child or adult in a counseling situation (Groth-Marnat, 1997).

REFERENCES

Groth-Marnat, G. (1997). *Handbook of psychological assessment* (3rd ed.). New York: Wiley.

Harris, D.B. (1963). *Children's drawings as measures of intellectual maturity.* New York: Harcourt, Brace, & World.

Machover, K. (1949). *Personality projection in the drawing of the human figure.* Springfield, IL: Thomas.

Naglieri, J.A. (1988). *Draw a person: A quantitative scoring system.* San Antonio, TX: The Psychological Corporation.

Shaffer, J., Duszynski, K., & Thomas, C. (1984). A comparison of three methods for scoring figure drawings. *Journal of Personality Assessment, 48,* 245–254.

Swenson, C.H. (1968). Empirical evaluation of human figure drawings. 1957–1966. *Psychological Bulletin, 70,* 20–44.

***See also* Bender Gestalt; House-Tree-Person; Kinetic Family Drawing**

DROPOUT

A dropout is generally considered to be an individual who leaves school before graduation. In recent years the dropout rate has been declining. For example, the event dropout rate for ages 15 through 24 in grades 10 through 12 has fallen from 6.1% in 1972 to 4.5% in 1993. However, these figures still constitute a large number of individuals. In 1993, approximately 381,000 students in grades 10 through 12 dropped out of school (National Center for Education Statistics, 1993).

For special education students and children with disabilities, the dropout rate is twice that of their non-disabled peers (OSERS, 1997). In addition, dropouts with disabilities do not return to school, and females became unwed mothers at a much higher rate than non-disabled peers (OSERS, 1997).

Dorn (1996) argues that "instead of seeing different educational outcomes as evidence of remaining inequities in schooling, Americans have focused instead on the social costs of dropping out." Schools are expected to ameliorate problems that are essentially socioeconomic in nature and many times beyond their scope and jurisdiction.

REFERENCES

Dorn, S. (1996). *Creating the dropout: An institutional and social history of school failure.* Westport, CT: Praeger.

Office of Special Education. (1997). *An overview of the bill to provide a broad understanding of some of the changes in IDEA '97.* http://www.ed.gov/offices/OSERS/IDEA/overview.html.

U.S. Department of Education National Center for Education Statistics. (1993). *High School Dropout Rates.* Washington D.C.: National Institute on the Education of at-risk students.

DRUG ABUSE

Drug abuse, or more currently substance abuse, is defined by the Diagnostic and Statistical Manual of Mental Disorders Fourth Edition (DSM-IV; American Psychiatric Association, 1994) as "a maladaptive pattern of substance use manifested by recurrent and significant adverse consequences related to the repeated use of substances" (p. 182). The criteria for a substance abuse diagnosis are the following:

A. A maladaptive pattern of substance use leading to clinically significant impairment or distress, as manifested by one (or more) of the following, occurring within a 12-month period:

(1) recurrent substance use resulting in a failure to fulfill major role obligations at work, school, or home (e.g., repeated absences or poor work performance related to substance use; substance-related absences, suspensions, or expulsions from school; neglect of children or household)

(2) recurrent substance use in situations in which it is physically hazardous (e.g., driving an automobile or operating a machine when impaired by substance use)

(3) recurrent substance-related legal problems (e.g., arrests for substance-related disorderly conduct)

(4) continued substance use despite having persistent or recurrent social or interpersonal problems caused or exacerbated by the effects of the substance (e.g., arguments with spouse about consequences of intoxication, physical fights)

B. The symptoms have never met the criteria for Substance Dependence for this class of substance (pp. 182–183)

Drug abuse is one of the six categories of behaviors that contribute to the leading causes of morbidity and mortality in the United States (National Clearinghouse for Alcohol and Drug Information [NCADI], 1998). It has only been in the 1980s and 1990s that the neuropsychological effects of drug abuse have started to be understood. This new understanding has been due to technological advances in the study of the brain, and the rise and development of pediatric neurology and neuropsychology. It is during adolescence that the more abstract and sophisticated cognitive skills develop in the human brain. Planning, evaluation, flexibility, internalized behavioral controls, higher-level abstracting skills, and higher levels of moral awareness are some of these sophisticated skills. The use of drugs during this period many have long-lasting effects on frontal and prefrontal regions of the brain (Elliott, 1998). For each insult to the brain there is a concomitant negative consequence for cognitive functions and behavior; therefore, the prevention of drug abuse in youth is extremely important if individual and social consequences are to be avoided.

The Centers for Disease Control (CDC) has developed a Youth Risk Behavior Surveillance System (YRBSS) to monitor the health-risk behaviors among youth and young adults (CDC, 1996). The system includes national, state, and local school-based surveys of high school students and gives a shocking picture of how students in the United States are involved in drug abuse.

According to the 1995 YRBSS, over 80% of high school students have used alcohol; over 40% have used marijuana; 16% have used cocaine, crack, or freebase; and over 20% have sniffed or inhaled intoxicating substances. Of the students who had experienced drug abuse, 40% initiated drug-related behaviors before the age of 13. Over 30% of the students reported using alcohol or drugs at the last episode of sexual intercourse. In addition, over 40% of the students had ridden with a driver who had been drinking alcohol.

For the past twenty years, significant efforts have been made with private and public monies to prevent drug abuse. Schools have been a primary vehicle for prevention monies because education has been shown to assist in prevention, and education is a compatible goal with school missions (Bosworth, 1997). Education programs begin as early as the elementary years, and try to eliminate myths that support student use (such as "everybody is doing it") with normative information that gives students statistics. There is no conclusive evidence on what types of programs or strategies are effective or ineffective; however, there is some evidence that scare tactics, providing only information on drugs and their effects, self-esteem building, values clarification, large assemblies, and didactic presentation of material have not been shown to be particularly effective (Tobler & Stratton, 1997, cited in Bosworth, 1997). Skill building and experiential teaching techniques (role-playing, simulations, and so on) have been successful in helping students utilize positive approaches to avoiding drug use (Bosworth, 1997).

For educators exploring possible drug prevention approaches and curricula, several excellent guides to curriculum selection are available from the National Clearinghouse for Alcohol and Drug Information (NCADI), P.O. Box 2345, Rockville, MD 20852, (800) 729–6686. [NCADI is the public information arm of the U.S. Department of Health and Human Services.

REFERENCES

American Psychiatric Association. (1994). *Diagnostic and statistical manual of mental disorders* (4th ed.). Washington D.C.: Author.

Bosworth, K. (1997). Drug abuse prevention: School-based strategies that work. *ERIC Clearinghouse on Teaching and Teacher Education,* Washington D.C. (ERIC Digest No. ED409316)

Centers for Disease Control. (1996). *Youth Risk Behavior Surveillance United States, 1995.* 45, SS-4.

Elliot, R. (1998). Neuropsychological sequelae of substance abuse by youths. In C.R. Reynolds & E. Fletcher-Janzen (Eds.), *Handbook of Clinical Child Neuropsychology* (pp. 311–331). New York Plenum.

National Clearinghouse for Alcohol and Drug Information. (1998). *Youth risk Behavior Surveillance United States, 1995.* http://www.health.org/pubs/yrbbs/index.htm

See also AL-ANON; Alcohol and Drug Abuse Patterns; Chemically Dependent Youth; Substance Abuse

DRUGS

See SPECIFIC DRUGS.

DRUG THERAPY

Drug therapy is the most common medical intervention for altering the behavior of children. Despite its relatively short history (usually traced to the mid-1930s), drug treatment is widely practiced today. Exact prevalence data do not exist, yet most estimates indicate that in any given year about 2% of all schoolchildren receive medication for hyperactivity alone. The major categories of drugs most often used with handicapped children are anticonvulsants, stimulants, antipsychotics, and antidepressants. Of these classes of drugs, stimulants are the most frequently prescribed.

Anticonvulsants are used in the treatment of disorders such as epilepsy. Beyond their use as antiepileptics, there is little evidence indicating desirable effects of these drugs. In fact, research indicates that adverse short-term side effects such as anxiety, nausea, and increased disorganization may result from these medications.

Ritalin (methylphenidate), Dexedrine (dextroamphetamine), and Cylert (magnesium pemoline) are the stimulants most often prescribed for hyperactivity. Used for this purpose, these drugs have sparked the most controversy and also have been the most thoroughly researched of all psychoactive medications. Many earlier researchers referred to the calming effects of stimulants with hyperactive children as paradoxical, and suggested this response had diagnostic merit. However, because increased sustained attention is seen in both hyperactive and non-hyperactive children who are given stimulants, the paradoxical effect and its diagnostic implications have been seriously questioned.

Other frequently reported effects of stimulants include improvement in impulse control, increased compliance, and decreased disruptive behavior. The learning of new skills or improvements in memory or intelligence test performance are generally not influenced beyond that which can be ascribed to improvements in attention. Adverse side effects associated with stimulants include increases in heart rate and blood pressure, insomnia, decreases in appetite, heightened emotionality, nervous habits, and assorted somatic complaints (e.g., headaches, stomach aches). One potential side effect, although rare, is the risk of producing an irreversible form of Tourette's syndrome.

Antipsychotics are most often used to treat extreme excitability, stereotypic behavior, delusions, hallucinations, and other schizophrenic characteristics. Among a number of possible negative side effects of antipsychotics are impairments in learning, enuresis, drowsiness, retarded speech and movement, rashes, sensitivity to sunlight, drooling, and tardive dyskinesia.

Antidepressants are generally prescribed to children to treat hyperactivity (when the use of stimulants is not appropriate), enuresis, and anxiety. In reports of the efficacy of antidepressants, it is generally concluded that both enuresis and anxiety (e.g., school phobia) respond to drug therapy but only while the drug is administered. Reported side effects include dry mouth, decreased appetite, nausea, seizures, and even death in rare instances.

In sum, the following conclusions appear justified. Alternative treatments must be attempted before drug therapy is initiated; drug therapy alone is insufficient; careful monitoring by both physicians and persons in the child's daily environment of both intended and unintended effects is essential; the prolonged use of psychoactive medications should be minimized; medications should not be used as punishment, as an alternative for active programming, or in dosages larger than necessary.

See also Anticonvulsants

DUE PROCESS

Due process is the shorthand term applied to the procedural safeguard and due process procedures stated in the Individuals with Disabilities Education Act (IDEA) reauthorizations and regulations. These procedures offer parents the right to share with schools in decision making that could result in their children's being found eligible for and placed in special education classes. Because these placements may segregate children from the typical school environment, courts and laws have mandated that schools follow particular procedures to ensure that parents have the opportunity to review and give their consent to changes in their child's educational program.

The due process requirements can be classified under six headings: prior notice, opportunity to examine records, independent educational evaluation, informed consent, impartial due process hearing and appeal, and surrogate parents. First, the educational agency must provide written notice a reasonable time before any action is initiated to propose or reject (e.g., when parents request special education for their child) a change in the identification, evaluation, or educational placement of a child. The notice must be written in the parents' native language or other mode of communication such as braille and in a way that results in parents understanding the notice. The notice must contain a description of the action proposed or refused by the agency, an explanation of why such action was considered, a description of any options to be considered in making a decision, and a full explanation of all procedural safeguards available to the parents. These procedural safeguards allow the parents, at no cost, the opportunity to inspect and review all education records of their child and to obtain an independent educational evaluation conducted by a qualified examiner who is not employed by the agency. The intent of these provisions is to fully inform parents.

With this information, the parents are presumed able to give voluntary informed consent to the actions proposed. Consent must be obtained before the agency conducts a preplacement evaluation and before initial special education placement.

When parents and schools disagree about any issue concerning the evaluation, placement, or educational program for a special education student, either party may request an impartial due process hearing. A hearing officer is presented evidence under conditions that are similar to those in a court. Either party can call witnesses and cross-examine. A verbatim record is taken of the proceedings. The hearing officer writes a decision that may be appealed to the state education agency and, if desired, to a civil court. Given the emotional and financial costs of this procedure, several states have initiated a mediation process as an alternative for settling disputes before a due process hearing is conducted; however, mediation is not a substitute for a due process hearing. Recent U.S. Department of Education Reports to Congress (up to 1996) have reported on the extent to which mediations are used and have described issues concerning implementation.

Finally, public agencies are required to identify surrogate parents to represent a handicapped child when no parent or guardian can be located. Several issues have been raised about this requirement, such as qualifications to be a surrogate parent, training for this role, and liability protection, among others (U.S. Department of Education, 1977).

REFERENCES

U.S. Department of Education. (1984). *Fifth annual report to Congress on the implementation of Public Law 94-142: The Education for All Handicapped Children Act.* Washington DC: Author.

U.S. Department of Education. (1985). *Sixth annual report to Congress on the implementation of Public Law 94-142: The Education for All Handicapped Children Act.* Washington, DC: Author.

U.S. Department of Education. (1986). *Seventh annual report to Congress on the implementation of Public Law 94-142: The Education for All Handicapped Children Act.* Washington, DC: Author.

U.S. Department of Health, Education, and Welfare. (1977). Education of handicapped children: Implementation of Part B of the Education of the Handicapped Act. *Federal Register, 42*(163), 42474–42518.

See also **Individuals with Disabilities Education Act (IDEA); Informed Consent; Legal Regulations of Special Education; Surrogate Parents**

DUSO

See DEVELOPING UNDERSTANDING OF SELF AND OTHERS.

DWARFISM

Dwarfism is a condition of extreme smallness of stature in an individual. There are several kinds of dwarfism, and systems of categorization vary. In general, however, two distant types exist: dwarfism, usually seen in specific groups such as pygmies, in which individuals have normal psychic development, physiological functioning, and regular physical proportions; and dwarfism owed to a disorder of the pituitary gland, also called hypopituitarism (Guyton, 1977).

Guyton (1977) describes several kinds of pituitary disorders in which the rate of secretion of one or more of the eight hormones produced by this gland is affected. Disorders in the production of human growth hormone during childhood can lead to childhood dwarfism. Hypopituitarism can be caused by genetic factors in which normal parents may produce an individual with dwarfism. In this type of dwarfism, the individual usually is of normal intelligence with disproportionate growth of body parts, usually the legs. Some of these cases are marked by sexual immaturity as well.

A variety of metabolic disturbances owed to organic disease may also result in hypopituitarism, and may result in mental deficiency as well as suppressed growth. In recent years, experimentation with human growth hormone obtained from cadavers has resulted in near normal growth in children with hypopituitarism. Various organizations have been formed recently to promote acceptance and understanding of "little people" (as they prefer to be called) and to dissipate stereotypical ideas that have arisen from the centuries of sideshow ostracism that little people have received (Ablon, 1984).

REFERENCES

Ablon, J. (1984). *Little people in America: The social dimension of dwarfism.* New York: Praeger.

Guyton, A.C. (1977). *Basic human physiology.* Philadelphia: Saunders.

See also **Physical Anomalies**

DYSCALCULIA

Dyscalculia is a term that applies to disturbances of quantitative thinking stemming from dysfunction of the central nervous system. The term precludes limited intellectual capacity, primary language disorders, anxiety, or poor teaching as causes of arithmetic failure. Kosc (1974) describes developmental dyscalculia as a disorder owed to heredity or congenital impairment of the brain centers that are the organic substrates of mathematical abilities. In cases of developmental dyscalculia, these abilities fail to develop within the normal limits of time and sequence. The term acalculia generally is used to describe an acquired disorder of calculating ability resulting from traumatic brain damage (Gaddes, 1980).

Studies of traumatically brain-damaged adults indicate that specific areas of damage are associated with specific arithmetical disabilities. Lesions of the parieto-occipital areas of the left hemisphere are likely to be related to disabilities in counting, ordering, or reading numbers. Posterior right hemisphere lesions may result in spatial difficulties associated with poor computation skills (Lezak, 1983). While these studies give insight into the organic origins of developmental dyscalculia, precise localization is difficult to ascertain. However, limited postmortem study suggests that developmental dyscalculia is related to abnormality or underdevelopment of parietal, temporal, and occipital cortices of both hemispheres and the intracerebral mechanisms associated with hearing and language (Gaddes, 1980).

Rourke and Strang (1983) and Rourke and Conway (1997) suggest the existence of subtypes of arithmetical disabilities on the basis of neuropsychological characteristics. Research has demonstrated that children who have similarly low levels of performance in arithmetic may differ widely in neuropsychological abilities and deficiencies (Rourke & Finlayson, 1978; Rourke & Strang, 1978). Children who performed poorly on most measures of verbal and auditory-perceptual abilities made arithmetical errors involving memory for number facts, sequencing steps necessary to do complex written computation, and word problems. Their deficient language skills were reflected in these errors. Conversely, those children who performed poorly on visual-spatial, visual-perceptual, complex psychomotor, and bilateral tactile-perceptual tasks showed an impoverished understanding of mathematical concepts; difficulty with column alignment, number formation, and directionality; and general visual-spatial disorganization. It is possible that different and additional subtypes may emerge as a result of further research in this area.

The existence of different sets of central processing skills in dyscalculic children points to the importance of differential diagnosis and the selection of appropriate methods of intervention and instruction. Johnson and Myklebust stress the use of auditory verbalization as a mediating process to help children with visual-spatial problems learn numerical relationships they are unable to generalize through observation and manipulation. This theory is consistent with recent data suggesting that teaching approaches emphasizing neuropsychological strengths in the instruction of specific academic subjects may result in the greatest gains for individual students (Hartlage & Telzrow, 1983, Reynolds, 1992).

REFERENCES

Gaddes, W.H. (1980). *Learning disabilities and brain function: A neuropsychological approach* (2nd ed.). New York: Springer-Verlag.

Hartlage, L.C., & Telzrow, C.F. (1983). The neuropsychological bases of educational intervention. *Journal of Learning Disabilities, 16*(9), 521–528.

Kosc, L. (1974). Developmental dyscalculia. *Journal of Learning Disabilities, 7*(3), 164–177.

Lezak, M.D. (1983). *Neuropsychological assessment* (2nd ed.). New York: Oxford University Press.

Reynolds, C.R. (1992). Two key concepts in the diagnosis of learning disabilities and the habilitation of learning. *Learning Disability Quarterly, 15,* 1, 2–12.

Rourke, B., & Conway, J.A. (1997). Disabilities of arithmetic and mathematical reasoning; Perspectives from neurology and neuropsychology. *Journal of Learning Disabilities, 30,* 1, 34–46.

Rourke, B.P., & Finlayson, M.A.J. (1978). Neuropsychological significance of variations in patterns of academic performance: Verbal and visual-spatial abilities. *Journal of Abnormal Child Psychology, 6,* 121–133.

Rourke, B.P., & Strang, J.D. (1978). Neuropsychological significance of variations in patterns of academic performance: Motor, psychomotor, and tactile-perceptual abilities. *Journal of Pediatric Psychology, 3,* 62–66.

Rourke, B.P., & Strang, J.D. (1983). Subtypes of reading and arithmetical disabilities: A neuropsychological analysis. In M. Rutter (Ed.), *Developmental neuropsychiatry analysis* (pp. 473–488). New York: Guilford Press.

See also **Arithmetic Remediation; Mathematics, Learning Disabilities and**

DYSCOPIA

See APRAXIA.

DYSFLUENCY

See STUTTERING.

DYSGRAPHIA

Dysgraphia is the impaired ability to express ideas in writing (Gaddes, 1980). The ability to communicate thoughts to others through the written word is a highly complex process involving the integration of auditory, visual, and motor skills (Myklebust, 1965). The nature of the underlying deficits in dysgraphia is related to one or more of these factors. Writing disturbances are commonly observed when children are required to copy written or printed material, write words and sentences to dictation, or write spontaneously (Luria, 1966).

To learn to write, children must have developed many prerequisite skills in language, perception, sequencing, memory, and motor coordination. Slowed or delayed development interferes with the acquisition of readiness skills needed for writing (Myklebust, 1965). Writing requires a variety of verbal functions, including verbal comprehension and expression, auditory phonetic discrimination, oral sequencing, and verbal memory. A deficit in any one of these functions may result in impaired ability to convey ideas in spontaneous writing while the ability to copy accurately remains unimpaired (Johnson & Myklebust, 1967).

Children with auditory discrimination deficits have difficulty distinguishing the sounds in words and confuse similarly sounding letters. Spontaneous writing and writing to dictation frequently reveal misspellings characterized by the omission and insertion of letters and syllables (Luria, 1973). Children who cannot hear the sequence of sounds in words are unable to write letters in the correct order. Auditory memory problems often are associated with this difficulty (Gaddes, 1980).

Writing also requires many nonverbal functions, including visual discrimination, visual-spatial orientation, visual memory, motor control, and visual-motor integration. Impairments in these skills not only are evidenced in writing to dictation and writing spontaneously, but are manifested in difficulty reproducing and copying written or printed materials (Johnson & Myklebust, 1967). Writing requires children to visually recognize and distinguish the differences between letters and words. Children with visual-spatial disturbances frequently confuse letters of the same shape but different orientation, make directional errors, and have difficulty maintaining horizontal and vertical positions.

Impaired visual memory is reflected in an inability to recall and reproduce the visual image or sequence of letters and words. Children with memory problems often can copy but lack the ability to write spontaneously or from dictation because they cannot visually remember letter and word forms (Johnson & Myklebust, 1967). Visual skills must be integrated and coordinated with motor skills. Children with disorders of motor control may be able to read and may possess the auditory and visual skills needed for writing but are unable to make the appropriate motor movements needed to produce letters and words (Luria, 1973; Myklebust, 1965; Smits-Engelsman & Van Galen, 1997). Computers have helped dysgraphic students with word processing capabilities and are now used in the classroom and at home (NEC Foundation, 1994).

REFERENCES

Gaddes, W.H. (1980). *Learning disabilities and brain function: A neuropsychological approach.* New York: Springer-Verlag.

Johnson, D.J., & Myklebust, H.R. (1967). *Learning disabilities: Educational principles and practices.* New York: Grune & Stratton.

Luria, A.R. (1966). *Higher cortical functions in man.* New York: Basic Books.

Luria, A.R. (1973). *The working brain.* New York: Basic Books.

Myklebust, H.R. (1965). *Development and disorders of written language* (Vol. I). New York: Grune & Stratton.

NEC Foundation (1994). *Adaptive technology that provides access to computers.* Seattle, WA: Author.

Smits-Engelsman, B.C.M., & Van Galen, G.P. (1997). Dysgraphia in children: Lasting psychomotor deficiency of transient developmental delay? *Journal of Experimental Child Psychology, 67,* 2, 164–168.

See also **Visual-Motor and Visual-Perceptual Problems; Writing Disorders; Writing Remediation**

DYSKINESIA

Dyskinesia refers to a difficulty in performing voluntary movements. Dyskinetic syndromes refer to a large group of different problems that interfere with the performance of voluntary motion. When used in descriptions of cerebral palsy, the dyskinetic syndrome may include the slow writing movements of athetosis, which affects extremities; the proximal and trunk movements (dystonia); or the abrupt, sudden, unpatterned choreiform movements. In this context, the dyskinesia is most apparent with emotional tension and disappears during sleep. Such movements are felt to be due to pathological states of the basal ganglion and associated neurological systems (Berkow, 1982).

Tardive dyskinesia sometimes is used to describe a kind of involuntary movement of the jaw or other tremors, including rigidity that contributes to difficulty in performance of voluntary movements. Tardive dyskinesia may result from adverse side effects of certain antipsychotic drugs (Berkow, 1982). Dyskinesis intermittens sometimes is used to describe a movement difficulty owed to poor circulation (Hensyl, 1982). All of the aforementioned terms are medical and imply special cause/effect relationships, therefore the use of these terms is most appropriate within a medical context. Observations of such movement disorders by teachers or therapists should be communicated to appropriate medical personnel in a clear, descriptive manner.

REFERENCES

Berkow, R. (Ed.). (1982). *The Merck manual of diagnosis and therapy* (14th ed.). Rahway, NJ: Merck, Sharp & Dohme.

Hensyl, W.R. (Ed.). (1982). *Stedman's medical dictionary* (24th ed.). Baltimore, MD: Williams & Wilkins

See also **Cerebral Palsy; Chorea**

DYSLEXIA

See DEVELOPMENTAL DYSLEXIA.

DYSLOGIC SYNDROME

Dyslogia refers to an impairment in the ability to express ideas in speech (*Blakiston's*, 1979; Hinsie & Campbell, 1960). Most authors, however, use the term to denote an impairment in the ability to use language that is of a central nervous system etiology and cannot be explained by specific sensory deficits (e.g., deafness) or mental deficiency (Nicolosi, Harryman, & Kresheck, 1978). Hence dyslogia is a seldom used synonym for aphasia. Eisenson (1972) used the term dyslogia to describe youngsters with congenital or developmental aphasia. He argued that by definition aphasia denotes a loss of language function, and thus use of this term to describe children who had never developed language would not be accurate. Hence, in the strictest use, dyslogic syndrome refers to children with congenital or developmental aphasia (Eisenson, 1972).

REFERENCES

Blakiston's Gould medical dictionary (4th ed.). (1979). New York: McGraw-Hill.

Eisenson, J. (1972). *Aphasia in children.* New York: Harper & Row.

Hinsie, L.E., & Campbell, R.J. (1960). *Psychiatric dictionary* (3rd ed.). New York: Oxford University Press.

Nicolosi, L., Harryman, E., & Kresheck, J. (1978). *Terminology of communication disorders.* Baltimore, MD: Williams & Wilkens.

See also **Aphasia; Developmental Aphasia; Dysphasia; Language Disorders**

DYSMETRIA

Dysmetria is a term derived from the Greek *dys-* (difficult) and *metron* (measure). It refers to a condition in which an individual has difficulty in gauging distance for bodily movements. Dysmetria is a form of dysergia, in which an individual is unable to stop muscular movement at a desired point. Signs of dysmetria are elicited by asking the afflicted individual to raise both arms rapidly, stopping at the shoulders so the arms are extended horizontally. Difficulty in controlling the range of movement in such a task may be indicative of dysmetria. In some expressions of dysmetria, the individual may overshoot the intended goal (hypermetria). Undershooting the intended goal is referred to as hypometria. Individuals with dysmetria may perform rapid, brusque movements with more force than is typically seen in voluntary movement. Dysmetria may be associated with cerebellar dysfunction.

See also **Ataxia; Gait Disturbances**

DYSMORPHIC FEATURES

Dysmorphic features are those physical anomalies that identify the presence of congenital syndromes or acquired disabilities.

While dysmorphic features may occur in the absence of any known syndrome and without apparent mental or physical impairment, in most cases such anomalies are suggestive of moderate to severe impairment. Dysmorphic features may represent malformations that occur during the first trimester (Batshaw & Perret, 1981). Malformations may result from genetic abnormalities (e.g., Down's syndrome, phenylketonuria); cell migration defects (e.g., cleft palate, spina bifida); maternal infection (e.g., rubella, cytomegalovirus); drugs (e.g., fetal alcohol syndrome, fetal dilantin syndrome); and other teratogens (Batshaw & Perret, 1981; Casey & Collie, 1984). The presence of dysmorphic features often is used to infer level and type of associated impairment. A study of the relationship between physical appearance and mental retardation syndromes reported that atypical appearance increases with the severity of mental retardation; greater atypical appearance is associated with more severe organic impairment in populations of severely and profoundly retarded persons; and mildly retarded persons with positive neurologic findings demonstrated greater degrees of atypical appearance (Richardson, Koller, & Katz, 1985).

Dysmorphic features of a less severe nature also have been identified in populations of mildly handicapped children. Waldrop and Halverson (1971) described findings from five separate studies in which congenital anomalies such as epicanthus, curved fifth digits, and a wide gap between the first and second toes were associated with hyperactive behavior in children. The authors suggest that "the same factors operating in the first weeks of pregnancy influenced the occurrence of *both* the morphological aberrations and the predisposition for impulsive, fast-moving behavior" (Waldrop & Halverson, 1971, p. 343). Subsequent studies demonstrated such minor physical anomalies could be identified in infants, were stable overtime, and were associated with infant irritability (Quinn, Renfield, Burg, & Rapaport, 1977). While these and other authors (e.g., Rosenberg & Weller, 1973) suggest minor congenital anomalies may be useful in predicting at-risk status for mild learning problems, other findings suggest the quality of the child's environment may represent an important intervening variable (LaVeck, Hammond, Telzrow, LaVeck, 1983).

REFERENCES

Batshaw, M.L., & Perret, Y.M. (1981). *Children with handicaps: A medical primer.* Baltimore, MD: Brooks.

Casey, P.H., & Collie, W.R. (1984). Severe mental retardation and multiple congenital anomalies of uncertain cause after extreme parental exposure to 2, 4-D. *The Journal of Pediatrics, 104,* 313–315.

LaVeck, F., Hammond, M.A., Telzrow, R., & LaVeck, G.D. (1983). Further observations on minor anomalies and behavior in different home environments. *Journal of Pediatric Psychology, 8,* 171–179.

Quinn, P.O., Renfield, M., Burg, C., & Rapaport, J.L. (1977). Minor physical anomalies: A newborn screening and 1-year follow-up. *Journal of Child Psychiatry, 16,* 662–669.

Richardson, S.A., Koller, H., & Katz, M. (1985). Appearance and mental retardation: Some first steps in the development and application of a measure. *American Journal of Mental Deficiency, 89,* 475–484.

Rosenberg, J.B., & Weller, G.M. (1973). Minor physical anomalies and academic performance in young school-children. *Developmental Medicine & Child Neurology, 15,* 131–135.

Waldrop, M.F., & Halverson, C.F. (1971). Minor physical anomalies and hyperactive behavior in young children. In J. Hellmuth (Ed.), *The exceptional infant* (Vol. 2, pp. 343–380). New York: Brunner/Mazel.

See also **Congenital Disorders; Minor Physical Anomalies; Physical Anomalies**

DYSNOMIA

Dysnomia and anomia are used interchangeably to denote problems in finding and using an intended word. Eisenson (1973) defines dysnomia as "difficulty in invoking an appropriate term regardless of its part of speech" (p. 19). It is frequently evidenced in dysphasic patients as a residual of central nervous system dysfunction. The dysphasic individual may substitute a word related by class or function to the intended word (e.g., knife for fork; Eisenson, 1973). Fewer problems were noted on common words than those used less frequently in the language (Jenkins, Jiménez-Pabón, Shaw, & Sefer, 1975).

A dysphasic individual tends to talk around the elusive word and sometimes may remark that he or she knows it but cannot say it. He or she may attempt a gesture to illustrate the word's meaning or may give several functional cues, sometimes achieving successful recall through associations. Some dysphasics recognize the word when it is said to them. Word-finding difficulties also have been found among learning-disabled children with language disorders (Wiig & Semel, 1984) and among children diagnosed as being developmentally dysphasic (Myklebust, 1971). In such cases, the child cannot name an object or picture, but is aware of the error and can recognize the intended word when it is supplied because auditory monitoring processes are intact (Myklebust, 1971).

Word-finding problems in spontaneous speech may be signaled by inappropriate pauses, use of filler ("um" and "er") and nonmeaningful phrases ("whatchama call it"), substitution of a functional description (circumlocution), or overuse of nonspecific words ("stuff," "place," "some-thing," "thing") (Wiig & Semel, 1984). Classroom tasks involving rhyming words, silent picture naming, matching initial-, medical-, and final-consonant sounds, and look-say methods of reading may prove troublesome for dysnomic children (Wiig, Semel, & Nystrom, 1982). German (1982) suggests that a thorough evaluation of a child's pattern of word substitutions may prove helpful in intervention techniques.

REFERENCES

Eisenson, J. (1973). *Adult aphasia: Assessment and treatment.* New York: Appleton-Century-Crofts.

German, D. (1982). Word-finding substitutions in children with learning disabilities. *Language, Speech & Hearing Services in Schools, 13,* 223–230.

Jenkins, J.J., Jiménez-Pabón, E., Shaw, R.E., & Sefer, J.W. (1975). *Schuell's aphasia in adults: Diagnosis, prognosis, and treatment.* Hagerstown, MD: Harper & Row.

Myklebust, H. (1971). Childhood aphasia: An evolving concept. In L.E. Travis (Ed.), *The handbook of speech pathology and audiology* (pp. 1181–1201). New York: Appleton-Century-Crofts.

Wiig, E., & Semel, E. (1984). *Language assessment and intervention for the learning disabled* (2nd ed.). Columbus, OH: Merrill.

Wiig, E., Semel, E., & Nystrom, L.A. (1982). Comparison of rapid naming abilities in language learning disabled and academically achieving eight-year olds. *Language, Speech & Hearing Services in Schools, 13,* 11–25.

See also **Aphasia; Speech and Language Handicaps**

DYSPHAGIA

Dysphagia is difficulty in swallowing (Arvedson & Brodsky, 1993; Logemann, 1998). It is specifically defined as difficulty moving food from the mouth through the pharynx and esophagus and into the stomach. Recently, some clinicians and investigators have suggested that the act of eating and swallowing actually begins with the development of appetite, the increase in oral secretions prior to eating, as well as the action of placing food in the mouth (Logemann, 1998).

Dysphagia can occur in a variety of different populations as a result of structural or neurologic damage (Perlman & Schulze-Delrieu, 1997). Infants can be born with various disturbances in swallowing, including difficulty controlling the oral musculature, difficulty in triggering the pharyngeal stage of swallowing, problems in the motor movements characteristic of the pharyngeal stage of swallowing, as well as either anatomic or physiologic abnormalities in the esophagus.

Children and adults of all ages may acquire swallowing difficulty as a result of stroke; head injury; head and neck cancer and its treatment; degenerative neurologic diseases such as motor or neuron disease, multiple sclerosis, or Parkinson's disease; dementias such as Alzheimer's disease; and a wide range of other medical problems. Almost all neurologic diseases can result in changes in the swallow in any of its various stages.

As the health care system has changed and encouraged sick children to be treated in schools, many children must receive their swallowing assessment and treatment in public school systems. This has expanded the scope of practice of school speech-language pathologists.

Treatment for dysphagia typically involves a variety of compensatory and direct exercise programs. Compensatory strategies are designed to eliminate the symptoms of the problem (such as food entering the airway) without necessarily changing or eliminating the underlying disorder. Included in compensatory strategies are postural techniques, sensory enhancement techniques, swallowing maneuvers, and dietary changes. Direct therapy strategies include exercise programs to improve the range, rate, and coordination of movements of structures in the oral cavity and pharynx, as well as swallowing maneuvers. Swallowing maneuvers arc voluntary controls over selected aspects of the oropharyngeal swallow.

REFFERENCES

Arvedson, J.C., & Brodsky, L. (Eds.). (1993). *Pediatric swallowing and feeding: Assessment and management.* San Diego: Singular.

Logemann, J.A. (1998). *Evaluation and treatment of swallowing disorders* (2nd ed.). Austin, TX: Pro-Ed.

Perlman, A.L., & Schulze-Delrieu, K.S. (Eds.). (1997). *Deglutition and its disorders.* San Diego: Singular.

DYSPEDAGOGIA

Dyspedagogia refers to poor teaching. It has been cited as a major cause of reading retardation and other learning disorders. Though the term is used as one of the etiological agents for a wide array of problems, dyspedagogia is most commonly associated with the field of learning disabilities (Epstein et al., 1980).

Cohen (1971) believes that dyspedagogia is the norm for most children, both in regular and special education. Many children, however, learn well enough despite poor or inappropriate teaching. The problem lies in the fact that those children who come to the educational setting with negatively predisposing social, psychological, neurological, or linguistic differences need effective, intensive teaching, and will suffer inordinately from dyspedagogia (Wertsch, 1985). The presenting background problems are not ignored, but the burden falls on educators to minimize their deleterious effects on learning by providing sound, skill oriented instruction.

REFERENCES

Cohen, S.A. (1971). Dyspedagogia as a cause of reading retardation: Definition and treatment. In B. Bateman (Ed.), *Learning disorders* (Vol. 4). Seattle, WA: Special Child Publications.

Epstein, M.H., Cullinan, D., Hessen, E.L., & Lloyd, J. (1980). Understanding children with learning disabilities. *Child Welfare, 59*(1), 3–14.

Wertsch, J. (1985). *Vygotsky and the social formation of mind.* London, England: Harvard University Press.

DYSPHASIA

See LANGUAGE DISORDERS.

DYSPHONIA

See VOICE DISORDERS.

DYSPRAXIA

See APRAXIA.

DYSTONIA MUSCULORUM DEFORMANS (DMD)

Dystonia musculorum deformans (DMD) is a progressive neurological disease primarily reflected in movement disorders. In addition to impaired motor function, twisting of the limbs is often seen. In its early stages, DMD may be mistaken for hysteria or psychosomatic movement disturbances. Well learned, previously smooth, coordinated movements become difficult and awkward in appearance. Individuals in the early stages of DMD may lose the previously acquired ability to write legibly; one hand may be affected prior to the other, even more confusing in the early stages of the disorder. Other apparently confusing symptoms appear; some children may be able to walk backward and even run without visible difficulty, but ordinary forward walking may be severely impaired (Hartlage & Hartlage, 1986). Children with DMD are often misdiagnosed as having emotional disorders. Proper diagnosis requires not only a psychological assessment but a thorough evaluation by a pediatric neurologist. Children with DMD have a serious orthopedic neuromuscular disorder that requires adaptive physical education and other accommodations at school in order for the child to function successfully in formal educational environments.

Families and professionals may find support and information from the Dystonia Society at Weddel House, 13–14 West Smithfield, London ECIA 9HY, United Kingdom. Their telephone number is 0 (171) 329 0797, and they can be faxed at 0 (171) 329-0689.

REFERENCE

Hartlage, P.L., & Hartlage, L.C. (1986). Epilepsy and other neurological and neuromuscular handicaps. In R.T. Brown & C.R. Reynolds (Eds.), *Psychological perspectives on childhood exceptionality.* New York: Wiley-Interscience.

See also **Adaptive Physical Education**

E

EAR AND HEARING

The ear is the sensory organ of hearing, and hearing is the sense by which sound waves are recognized and interpreted. The ear can be divided into four parts: the outer, middle, and inner ear, and central pathways. Sound waves enter the outer ear via the auricle (or pinna) on the side of the head and then go through the ear canal (external auditory meatus) to the middle ear. The middle ear consists of the eardrum (tympanic membrane) and three articulated bones (malleus, incus, and stapes), collectively called the ossicles. The middle ear transforms the acoustic energy of sound waves to mechanical energy.

The inner ear is divided into a vestibular (balance) and cochlear (hearing) section. The cochlea consists of three fluid-filled ducts. The middle duct contains the Organ of Corti, which houses the sensory nerve endings for hearing. The cochlea transforms the mechanical sound wave energy from the middle ear to electrical energy to initiate a neural response. The neural response of the cochlea is carried by the central auditory pathways to the brain. The central pathways consist of the auditory nerve (eighth cranial nerve), which starts in the inner ear, interacts with neural complexes in the brain stem, and terminates in Heschel's gyri, which is the primary auditory reception center in the temporal cortex on each side of the brain.

See also **Deaf; Deaf Education**

EARLY CHILDHOOD, CULTURALLY AND LINGUISTICALLY DIVERSE ISSUES IN

Two important factors have increased professional awareness of the responsibility to better meet the needs of young children from culturally and linguistically diverse backgrounds. The first factor includes the group of dramatic demographic changes occurring in the United States (Lynch, 1992). The second is the passage of the 1986 amendments to the Education of the Handicapped Act Amendments (EHA; Gettinger, Elliot, & Kratochwill, 1992).

Due to linguistic, cultural, and economic barriers, children from cultural and linguistically diverse backgrounds are at greater risk to experience difficulties and to be identified for intervention (Cook, Tessier, & Klein, 1992; NICHCY, 1987). As the number of culturally and linguistically diverse children increases, early interventionists are faced with issues surrounding the delivery of comprehensive early intervention services to children and their families (Gettinger et al., 1992). Evaluation and assessment of infants, toddlers, and preschoolers who are culturally and linguistically diverse presents complex responsibilities to early childhood professionals. Determining eligibility for special education and related services for diverse children poses particular challenges to early interventionists. On the one hand, children who are culturally and linguistically diverse are overrepresented in special education (Yansen & Shulman, 1996). On the other hand, a genuine delay or disability may be overlooked if the child's cultural and/or linguistic context is poorly understood. The provision of early intervention services to young children who are culturally and linguistically diverse requires sensitivity to cultural and linguistic factors that may explain behaviors that might appear to indicate disability or delay.

Service delivery to families of children who are disabled or at risk for disabilities has moved toward a much more family-centered approach. Part H of PL 99-457 strongly emphasizes the involvement of families in the service delivery process. The Individualized Family Service Plan (IFSP), a key feature of Part H, must be designed to meet the developmental needs of the child and also the family's needs (Lynch, 1992). Approaches to early childhood intervention with culturally and linguistically diverse children and families, therefore, require an understanding of the child within the family and cultural context. An understanding of the cultural beliefs and practices of families from diverse backgrounds is needed to develop and implement high quality services that are culturally appropriate and effective. For children and families from culturally and linguistically diverse backgrounds, critical issues including language learning and the impact of culture on early development and behaviors must be addressed (Bergeson, Gutting, Gill, & Shureen, 1997).

General considerations for evaluation and intervention with young children who are culturally or linguistically diverse include an effort to avoid mistaking differences in culture and language with genuine disabilities and delays in development (Bergeson et al., 1997). Comprehensive assessment of young culturally and linguistically diverse children must include a determination of language proficiency and dominance in order to assist early childhood specialists in deciding which language to use for evaluation and instruction (Yansen & Schulman, 1996). Alternative procedures, such as observations, interviews, profiles, and professional judgment, should be utilized due to the limited number of norm-referenced tests standardized to include specific cultural and linguistic factors. The results of the assessment must provide for appropriate interventions that honor the child's primary language and culture (Bergeson et al., 1997).

REFERENCES

Bergeson, T., Gutting, J.M., Gill, D.H., & Shureen, A. (1997). *Evaluation and assessment in early childhood special education: Children who are culturally and linguistically diverse.* Olympia, WA: State Superintendent of Public Instruction.

Children's Defense Fund. (1994). *State of the children report.* Washington, DC: Author.

Cook, R.E., Tessier, A., & Klein, M.D. (1992). *Adapting early childhood curricula for children with special needs* (3rd ed.). New York: Merrill.

Gettinger, M., Elliot, S.N., & Kratochwill, T.R. (1992). *Preschool and early childhood treatment directions.* New Jersey: Erlbaum.

Lynch, E.W. (1992). Developing cross-cultural competence. In E.W. Lynch & M.J. Hanson (Eds.), *Developing cross-cultural competence: A guide for working with young children and their families* (pp. 35–62). Baltimore: Brookes.

Yansen, E., & Shulman, E. (1996). Language assessment: Multicultural considerations. In L. Suzuki, P. Meller, & J. Ponterotto (Eds.), *The handbook of multicultural assessment* (pp. 353– 393). San Francisco: Jossey-Bass.

EARLY IDENTIFICATION OF HANDICAPPED CHILDREN

Early identification became a topic of increasing interest with the community mental health movement of the 1960s and again with the passage of PL 94-142 in 1975. This law contained components requiring that schools take aggressive action to identify handicapped children needing services; it recommended that such children be provided services from ages 4 through 19, and severely handicapped children from birth through age 21. In addition, several early childhood intervention programs that targeted at-risk children began yielding impressive evidence by the late 1970s of the cost-effectiveness of early intervention (Edmiaston & Mowder, 1985).

Effective early intervention programs require identification methods with high predictive validity. Given possible undesirable outcomes (such as labeling effects) and the extensive costs of intervention programs, the number of false positives (students predicted to become handicapped but who do not) should be kept low (Mercer, Algozzine, & Trifiletii, 1979b). The identification procedure must also be cost-efficient; screening procedures should use readily available information or tests that are quick and inexpensive to administer.

There have been a large number of attempts to construct easily administered tests and test batteries that accurately identify children needing special services. Mercer et al. (1979a) reviewed 70 studies. They suggest that screening should take place in mid-kindergarten, as this allows intervention to begin at the earliest time that teacher ratings become reliable as predictors. Share, Jorm, Maclean, and Matthews (1984) provide data indicating that more than half the variance in first grade reading scores can be predicted by direct assessment of phonemic naming and letter copying in kindergarten; Mercer et al. suggest that useful ratings of these skills can be made by classroom teachers, freeing professional examiners' time.

REFERENCES

Edmiaston, R.K., & Mowder, B.A. (1985). Early identification for handicapped children: Efficacy issues and data for school psychologists. *Psychology in the Schools, 22,* 171–178.

Mercer, C.D., Algozzine, B., & Trifiletti, J.J. (1979a). Early identification—An analysis of the research. *Learning Disabilities Quarterly, 2*(2), 12–24.

Mercer, C.D., Algozzine, B., & Trifiletti, J.J. (1979b). Early identification: Issues and considerations. *Exceptional Children, 46,* 52–54.

Share, D.L., Jorm, A.F., Maclean, R., & Matthews, R. (1984). Sources of individual differences in reading acquisition. *Journal of Educational Psychology, 76,* 1309–1324.

***See also* Abecedarian Project; Early Screening Profiles; Prereferral Interventions; Preschool Assessment; Preschool Screening**

EARLY INFANTILE AUTISM
See AUTISM.

EARLY SCREENING PROFILES (ESP)

The Early Screening Profiles (ESP; Harrison et al., 1990) is a developmental screening test of young children ages 2 years 0 months through 6 years 11 months of age. It is designed to identify children who require further testing or early intervention services. The ESP is comprised of seven components: the Cognitive/Language Profile, Motor Profile, Self-Help/Social Profile, Articulation Survey, Home Survey, Health History Survey, and Behavior Survey. The parts may be used independently or in combination with other parts. Only three components (Cognitive/Language Profile, Motor Profile, and Articulation Survey) are administered directly to the child. Test administration time for these three components ranges from 15 to 30 minutes. The Cognitive/Language Profile consists of 2 cognitive subtests that measure nonverbal reasoning (Visual Discrimination and Logical Relations) and two language subtests that measure receptive and expressive language (Verbal Concepts and Basic School Skills). The Motor Profile consists of two subtests, assessing gross motor and fine motor skills. The Articulation Survey measures the child's speech production. The Behavior Survey is completed by the examiner regarding the child's behaviors during the test administration. The Home Survey (assessing aspects of home environment and parent-child interactions) and Health History Survey (a list of past and present health problems) are both brief questionnaires completed by the parent. The Self-Help/ Social Profile is also a questionnaire completed by the parent and/or the child's teacher. It measures the child's performance of everyday activities required to take care of oneself and interact with others. The parent and teacher questionnaires take 10 to 15 minutes to complete.

The ESP was standardized on a sample of 1,149 children from 2 years 0 months through 6 years 11 months of age. The number of subjects in each of the five one-year intervals ranged from 163 to 303. There were approximately equal distributions of males and females per group. Data from the 1985 and 1990 U.S. Census Bureau was used to stratify the sample on variables including age, sex, parent education, geographic region, and race/ethnicity. The sample matches the U.S. population well on all variables, although there are slight differences in parental education. The manual contains specific characteristics of the sample. A high degree of reliability was found of the profiles and Total Screening, with the exception of the Motor Profile and Behavior Survey, which were less reliable, and the Home Survey, which was quite low, which the author notes may be due to the diverse items on the scale.

Critiques of the ESP have been mixed. Telzrow (1995) reveals a favorable impression. She notes that the manual is comprehensive and detailed in its discussion of its development, technical adequacy, and scoring, including limitations to using age equivalents, which makes the ESP a "comprehensive addition to a total program in early childhood identification and service delivery." However, Barnett (1995) criticizes that the ESP lacks ecological validity and does not improve on the limitations of most screening instruments.

REFERENCES

Barnett, D.W. (1995). AGS Early Screening Profiles. In J.C. Conoley & J.C. Impara (Eds.), *The twelfth mental measurements yearbook.* Lincoln, NE: Buros Institute of Mental Measurements.

Harrison, P.L., Kaufman, A.S., Kaufman, N.L., Bruininks, R.H., Rynders, J., Ilmer, S., Sparrow, S.S., & Cicchetti, D.V. (1990). *Early Screening Profiles manual.* Circle Pines, Minnesota: American Guidance Service.

Telzrow, C. (1995). AGS Early Screening Profiles. In J.C. Conoley & J.C. Impara (Eds.), *The twelfth mental measurements yearbook.* Lincoln, NE: Buros Institute of Mental Measurements.

EATING DISORDERS

Quite different forms of eating disorders occur in young children and in adolescents/adults. *DSM-IV* (1994) lists them under two headings: Feeding Disorders of Infancy or Early Childhood, comprising pica, rumination disorder, and feeding disorder of infancy or early childhood; and Eating Disorders, comprising anorexia nervosa and bulimia nervosa. In all of these conditions, no physical basis for the abnormal eating is apparent. Each disorder is described in a separate entry; brief descriptions follow.

FEEDING DISORDERS OF INFANCY OR EARLY CHILDHOOD

In *pica,* children persistently eat nonnutritive substances. Substances consumed tend to vary with age. Pica often ac-

companies mental retardation. *Rumination disorder,* usually seen in infants and children with mental retardation, is characterized by repeated voluntary regurgitation of food. Both pica and rumination disorder can have a variety of serious medical consequences. *Feeding disorder of infancy or early childhood* refers to a persistent failure to consume an amount of food adequate to maintain appropriate weight or weight gain.

EATING DISORDERS

In *anorexia nervosa* (starvation due to nerves) an individual eats little or no food for prolonged periods, whereas in *bulimia nervosa* (ox hunger), an individual alternately binges (grossly overeats) and purges (rids the body of food or fluids through behaviors such as induced vomiting). Both can be life threatening, are more prevalent in females than males, are increasing in incidence, and are serious problems for medical and psychological professionals.

REFERENCE

American Psychiatric Association. (1994). *Diagnostic and statistical manual of mental disorders* (4th ed.). Washington, DC: Author.

***See also* Anorexia Nervosa, Bulimia Nervosa; Family Counseling; Malnutrition; Pica**

ECHOLALIA

Echolalia is a strong, almost mandatory, tendency to repeat spontaneously what has been said by another person (Benson & Ardila, 1996). Echolalia has been noted in those with degenerative brain disease, psychosis (both children and adults), Gilles de la Tourette syndrome, childhood dysphasia, severe mental retardation, and some forms of aphasia, as well as in some congenitally blind children (Cummings & Benson, 1989; Fay, 1980). It is a prominent characteristic of all of these children's speech, with the vast majority who eventually acquire speech having a history of echoing. Many children who acquire normal speech and language practice some echolalia during the developmental speech and language period of infancy and early childhood, although these echolatic behaviors generally disappear by 2 and a half to 3 years of age (Fay, 1980; Loveland, McEvoy, & Tunali, 1990). A message may be repeated in its entirety or partially, with repetition usually following immediately after the initial presentation. An echoed utterance preceded or followed by an appropriate self-formulated comment evidences comprehension. The repetition seems to facilitate understanding in much the same manner as in normal adults and children when confronted with difficult messages.

REFERENCES

Benson, D.F., & Ardila, A. (1996). *Aphasia: A clinical perspective.* New York: Oxford University Press.

Cummings, J.L., & Benson, D.F. (1989). Speech and language alterations in dementia syndromes. In A. Ardila & F. Ostrosky (Eds.),

Brain organization of language and cognitive processes (pp. 107–120). New York: Plenum.

Fay, W.H. (1980). Aspects of speech. In R.L. Schiefelbush (Ed.), *Language intervention series* (Vol. 5, pp. 21–50). Baltimore, MD: University Park Press.

Loveland, K.A., McEvoy, R.E., & Tunali, B. (1990). Narrative story telling in autism and Down's syndrome. *British Journal of Developmental Psychology, 8,* 9–23.

See also **Autism, Autistic Behavior; Speech and Language Handicaps**

ECHOPRAXIA

Echopraxia can be defined as the involuntary and spasmodic imitation of movements made by another person (Goodwin, 1989). The echolalia of a child with autism, in which the child echo-speaks phrases and words, might be viewed as a specific kind of echopraxia. Another echo of movement that is specific to some hearing-impaired persons has been observed clinically. In this form, the individual imitates the facial and mouth movements of the speaker. These movements may be a means of reinforcing meaning and subsequent content for the hearing-impaired individual.

REFERENCE

Goodwin, D.M. (1989). *A dictionary of neuropsychology.* New York: Springer-Verlag.

See also **Childhood Schizophrenia; Echolalia**

ECOLOGICAL ASSESSMENT

The purpose of ecological assessment is to understand the complex interactions that occur between an individual who is the focus of assessment and his or her environment. Representing what is essentially an expansion of traditional behavior assessment techniques, ecological behavior assessment is similar to behavioral assessment with two important distinctions. First, in ecological behavior assessment, emphasis is placed on the quantification of behavior and its controlling environmental factors from a systems level perspective. That is, rather than focusing exclusively on molecular units of targeted behaviors and consequences directly responsible for their maintenance, the goal of ecological behavior assessment is to generate an understanding of the total behavior-environment system. This "system mapping" is typically accomplished through the measurement of behaviors and persons other than those to which an intervention is to be applied. For example, research conducted by Wahler and his associates (Wahler, 1975) in which observational data were taken on a variety of child behaviors has suggested that behavioral interventions targeted at a single response are likely to result in complex patterns of collateral and inverse changes in behavior within a child's repertoire. Second, in ecological behavior assessment, emphasis is placed on the measurement of existing patterns of teacher and student behavior with the goal of using this information in the development of intervention alternatives.

Ecological assessment can be time-consuming and complex, but it is often a rewarding process for truly understanding the behavior of children. The present summary draws heavily on the work of Kounin (1970), Gump (1975), Martens et al. (1999), and Reynolds, Gutkin, Elliott, and Witt (1984). The interested reader is referred to these sources for additional detail on the application of the ecological perspective to assessment.

REFERENCES

Gump, P.V. (1975). Ecological psychology and children. In M. Hetherington (Ed.), *Review of child development research* (Vol. 5). Chicago: University of Chicago Press.

Kounin, J.S. (1970). *Discipline and group management in classrooms.* New York: Holt, Rinehart & Winston.

Martens, B., Witt, J., Daly, E., & Vollmer, T. (1999). Behavior analysis: Theory and practice in educational settings. In C.R. Reynolds & T.B. Gutkin (Eds.), *The handbook of school psychology* (3rd ed.) (pp. 638–663). New York: Wiley.

Reynolds, C.R., Gutkin, T.B., Elliott, S.N., & Witt, J.C. (1984). *School psychology: Essentials of theory and practice.* New York: Wiley.

Wahler, R.G. (1975). Some structural aspects of deviant child behavior. *Journal of Applied Behavior Analysis, 8,* 27–42.

See also **Applied Behavior Analysis; Clinical Interview**

ECOLOGICAL EDUCATION FOR THE HANDICAPPED

Ecology refers, generally, to the study of the relationship between an organism and its environment. Although the roots of ecology as a field of study are found in early anthropology, the application of ecological theories, models, and principles in special education is relatively new. The first attempt to examine the interaction of environmental effects and certain handicapped persons, and to specify related treatment approaches, is found in the works of Heinz Werner, Alfred A. Strauss, Lora Lehtinen, and William M. Cruickshank. These researchers of the 1940s, 1950s, and 1960s studied brain-injured children and adults and the effects that various environmental stimuli had on their learning and overall behavior. An important concept derived from their research was the idea of the "stimulus-reduced" environment, first prescribed for classically brain-injured adults and children, then extended to certain "exogenous" mentally retarded children, and finally to children with "minimal brain damage" or learning disabilities. Although this work began in the 1940s, these researchers, and those who built on their pioneering efforts, did not refer formally to their efforts as ecological in nature. The term ecology itself, derived primarily from the biological sciences, surfaced as an educational variable with studies of emotionally disturbed children in the late 1960s and early 1970s.

The most notable contributions to the field include the

work of Hobbs (1966) with Project Re-Ed and the University of Michigan studies in child variance (Feagans, 1972). Project Re-Ed recognized that many of the socialization problems experienced by so-called emotionally disturbed children did not have a locus within the child. Rather, problems existed in the interaction between the labeled child and the important social institutions in which he or she acted. Since there was a bad fit between child and environment (i.e., home, family, school, community), it was necessary to remove the child temporarily from this failure situation, not just to work with the child, but also to change contributing factors in the environment. While specially trained teachers aided the student, social services personnel and mental health consultants worked with the significant others in the child's world before re-merging the two again. Segregation was to be as brief as possible; normalization was always the goal.

The Michigan work, accomplished within the university's Institute for Mental Retardation and Related Disorders, reviewed, integrated, and synthesized the research, theories, and conceptual models bearing on childhood emotional disturbance. The group then developed and implemented various dissemination and training activities based on their synthesis of differing approaches to emotional disturbance. Though ecological theory was only one of six major approaches studied, the Michigan efforts helped in large part to enhance the role of ecological theory in special education.

Broadly, the ecological approach to the study and treatment of emotionally disturbed and other handicapped children attempts to break down traditional views of handicaps as something found exclusively in the involved child. The disturbance is not intrinsic per se, but a description of the interaction of a particular child with a particular environment. The search is for the source of the mismatch in the ecosystem. The study of the child occurs not in the sterility of the psychological laboratory, but in the naturalistic, real-world, holistic settings in which the child's problems occur. This is not to deny that emotional disturbance, or mental retardation, or learning disabilities are not real, or that problems in learning or adjustment that certain children experience may not have contributing neurological or biochemical substrata. The ecological focus in special education tries to show that looking only at internal factors cannot give the whole picture, and that treatment approaches based on simplified, historical, etiological views can limit the success parents and professionals might have with handicapped learners.

REFERENCES

Feagans, L. (1972). Ecological theory as a model for constructing a theory of emotional disturbance. In W.C. Rhodes & M.L. Tracy (Eds.), *A study in child variance* (Vol. 1). Ann Arbor: University of Michigan.

Hobbs, N.L. (1966). Helping disturbed children: Psychological and ecological strategies. *American Psychologist, 21,* 1105–1115.

See also **Ecological Assessment**

EDUCABILITY

In its broadest sense, educability refers to the likelihood of a handicapped child benefiting from and progressing in a course of education. As such, it is appropriate to refer to the educability of a blind child or a hearing child. However, the concept is most closely related to mental retardation and has become part of the classificatory nomenclature in that area. In fact, the concept of educability can be viewed as the driving force behind the development and growth of psychometrics. The term itself is now largely archaic.

EDUCABLE MENTALLY RETARDED (EMR)

Educable mentally retarded (EMR) was a popular term in the 1960s and 1970s, referring to those people whose IQ scores ranged between 50 and 80 (based on the IQ tests of those days) (Smith, 1998), and who were assessed in school as being unlikely to profit from a regular academic curriculum. With the passage of the Education for All Handicapped Children Act of 1975, classification of mental retardation subtypes changed to mild, moderate, severe, and profound mental retardation, and a diagnosis of mild MR required that, in addition to an IQ score ranging from 50 to 70, a person must also exhibit significant deficits in adaptive behavior that affect everyday activities of living (American Psychiatric Association, 1994). "Educable" mental retardation is most similar to the more current category of "mild mental retardation." The term is seldom used in current discussions of mental retardation.

REFERENCES

American Psychiatric Association. (1994). *Diagnostic and statistical manual of mental disorders* (4th ed.). Washington, DC: Author.

Smith, D.D. (1998). *Introduction to special education: Teaching an age of challenge.* Boston: Allyn and Bacon.

See also **Mental Retardation; Trainable Mentally Retarded**

EDUCATEUR

The educateur, sometimes referred to as the psychoeducateur, is a trained generalist whose primary concern goes beyond that of the traditional teacher's interest in student learning to include a focus on the personality and emotional development of the child (Morse & Smith, 1980). The role of the educateur dates to the years immediately following World War II, when the presence of large numbers of displaced emotionally disturbed children (victims of the psychological traumas of war) were identified in France and Scotland (Daly, 1985). Inadequate numbers of qualified mental health workers to meet the many needs of these children led to the development of a new profession, that of the educateur, a professional trained in the skills of teaching, social work, psychology, and recreation.

In the mid 1950s in Canada, Guindon (1973) adapted

the European educateur model for use with delinquent and emotionally handicapped children and youths. Guindon's psychoeducateur intervention had an ecological orientation, emphasizing the significance of change in the child's environment and using interventions associated with other perspectives.

Linton (1971) described the educateur working in these specialized facilities as being trained to effect positive changes by focusing specifically on the interaction between child and environment and on the natural support systems such as family and community. Thus the educateur functions as a child advocate and environmental change agent to reduce discord and restore harmony in a manner that ultimately permits complete withdrawal of external intervention. The educateur's goal is to help the child acquire problem-solving skills and behavioral repertoires for successfully meeting both known and unfamiliar situations (Goocher, 1975).

Project Re-ED (Hobbs, 1982) is considered by some individuals to represent an Americanized version of the educateur model with the term teacher-counselor replacing educateur. For those individuals interested in acquiring educateur skills, Daly (1985) reports that at least four American colleges or universities (Ohio State University, Southern Connecticut State College, Western Michigan University, and the University of Virginia) provide training programs using the term educateur. The training in these programs includes recreation, special education, and behavioral sciences as well as an internship in a child service agency.

REFERENCES

Daly, P.M. (1985). The educateur: An atypical childcare worker. *Behavioral Disorders, 11*, 35–41.

Goocher, B.E. (1975). Behavioral applications of an educateur model in child care. *Child Care Quarterly, 4*, 84–92.

Guindon, J. (1973). The reeducation process. *International Journal of Mental Health, 2*(1), 15–26, 27–32.

Hobbs, N. (1982). *The troubled and troubling child.* San Francisco: Jossey-Bass.

Linton, T.E. (1971). The education model: A theoretical model: A theoretical monograph. *Journal of Special Education, 5,* 155–190.

Morse, W., & Smith, J. (1980). *Understanding child variance.* Reston, VA: Council for Exceptional Children.

See also Project Re-ED

EDUCATIONAL AND PSYCHOLOGICAL MEASUREMENT

Educational and Psychological Measurement is a bi-monthly journal devoted to the development and application of measures of individual differences. Articles published in the journal are divided into sections.

The first section consists of articles reporting the results of research investigations into problems in the measurement of individual differences in education and psychology.

The second section is devoted to validity studies on new or existing tests for measuring individual differences. This section is published at least twice a year, in the summer and winter issues. A third section is devoted to computer studies, with reports on the use(s) of already existing or new computer programs available on a mainframe, mini-, or microcomputer. These programs may be used for carrying out computations in statistical analyses when assessing the measurement of individual differences.

The journal also publishes occasional book reviews. Correspondence should be submitted to: Bruce Thompson, *EPM* Editor, Department of Educational Psychology, Texas A & M University, College Station, TX 77843-4225. Copies of the various journal guidelines and editorials are available on the Internet at http://acs.tamu.edu/~bbt6147/.

EDUCATIONAL DIAGNOSTICIAN

An educational diagnostician is an individual who often functions as a member of the multidisciplinary team that determines whether a child is eligible for special education programs. The educational diagnostician differs from the school psychologist both in preparation and function. Generally, the educational diagnostician is a certified or licensed regular or special education teacher with three or more years of experience in the classroom. Graduate training, typically a two-semester master of education program, is focused on content and techniques concerned with diagnosis and remediation of learning problems. The school psychologist is generally not a certified or licensed teacher but has graduate or advanced graduate training of two or more years, the focus of which is on the content and techniques related to assessment of intellectual and behavioral functioning of children and training in psychological interventions including both direct and indirect service delivery. While most states offer certification for school psychologists, fewer states actually offer formal certification, licensure, or endorsement for educational diagnosticians.

In most school districts using educational diagnosticians, their primary role relates to the evaluation of students referred for special education programs or services, though in most states they are prohibited from working with emotionally disturbed children, a task more suited to the school psychologist. The educational diagnostician can perform a valuable function in working with other students who may be experiencing learning problems but who would not be considered in need of special education.

See also **Multidisciplinary Teams; School Psychology**

EDUCATIONALLY DISADVANTAGED

According to the Office of Elementary and Secondary Education, educationally deprived children are children whose educational attainment is below the level that is appropriate for children their age. These children are often referred to as educationally disadvantaged. A cause for this scholastic retardation in depressed areas is attributed to the attitudes and behavior of school personnel (Passow, 1967). These children often come from culturally deprived homes that fail to equip the children to fit into and adapt well into the school environment (Passow, 1967). Daniels (1967) adds that the disadvantaged have become handicapped because of social or environmental conditions in their ability to learn and to acquire skills and abilities for coping with the problems of earning a living and enjoying a satisfying life. He accepts the estimate that the disadvantaged constitute 25% of the school population and in larger cities 30 to 40%.

Title I of the Elementary and Secondary Education Act was designed to overcome the debilitating burdens placed on educationally disadvantaged students by certain school personnel and culturally deprived families. Title I was one in a series of legislative efforts aimed at addressing the needs of the culturally disadvantaged. Some of the others were the Civil Rights Act of 1964, the Economic Opportunity Act of 1964, the Vocational Act of 1963, and the National Defense Act (revised in 1965). Additional related legislation aimed at reducing discrimination policies toward the educationally disadvantaged and other specific targeted populations were Title IX of the Education Amendments of 1972 (PL 92-318), the Education for All Handicapped Children Act (PL 94-142), the Rehabilitation Act of 1973 (PL 93-112), and IDEA.

Chapter 1 of PL 97-35 addresses the issue of financial assistance to meet the educational needs of disadvantaged children. This legislation replaced Title I of the Elementary and Secondary Act of 1965. Chapter 1 continues to be the main legislation addressing the educational needs of deprived children. The act will fund local education agency school programs to meet the needs of educationally deprived children. According to PL 97-35:

Such programs and projects may include the acquisition of equipment and instructional materials, employment of special instructional and counseling and guidance personnel, employment and training of teacher aides, payments to teachers in amounts in excess of regular salary schedules (as a bonus for service in schools serving project areas), the training of teachers, the construction, where necessary, of school facilities, other expenditures authorized under Title I. . . .

Passow's (1967) assessment of the underlying causes for educational deprivation and cultural deprivation still appear to be valid, even though much federal legislation has been written to address this American educational need. Passow has stated that "their problems stem from poverty and unemployment; segregation, discrimination, and lack of equal opportunity in housing and employment, as well as education; discontinuities with the 'dominant' culture, rising out of difference in life style, child rearing practices and skills for urban living; and inadequate educational attainment of those skills essential in a technical society." Promising practices, he states, fall into nine categories.

The current literature suggests that schools can increase their effectiveness by changing their focus from considering the culturally disadvantaged as disadvantaged to considering them as culturally different. This shift in focus permits one to accept the fact that the culturally different may continue having disadvantages but they also have benefits for society. Programs that include emphasis on the benefits to society by the culturally different are basically encompassed in the concept of multicultural education.

Rodriguez (1983) defines multicultural education as education that values cultural pluralism. Multicultural education recognizes that cultural diversity is a valuable resource and should be extended into American society. Schools should not melt away cultural differences or merely tolerate cultural pluralism. Each cultural unit lives as part of an interrelated whole. According to Bennett (1986), the goal of multicultural education is to change the total educational environment so that it will develop competencies in multiple cultures and provide members of all cultural groups with equal educational opportunity. Equity is at the heart of multicultural education.

It appears, therefore, that effective programming for the educationally disadvantaged can be enhanced if the needs of the disadvantaged are perceived in an educational milieu that also recognizes the benefits to society of the students' culture.

REFERENCES

Bennett, C.I. (1986). *Comprehensive multicultural education: Theory and practice* (p. 53). Boston: Allyn & Bacon.

Daniels, W.G. (1967). Some essential ingredients in educational programs for the socially disadvantaged. In J. Hellmuth (Ed.), *Disadvantaged child. Vol. 1: Special child* (pp. 202–221). Seattle, WA: Seattle Seguin School.

Passow, H.A. (1967). Education of the culturally deprived child. In J. Hellmuth (Ed.), *Disadvantaged child, Special child.* Seattle, WA: Seguin School.

Rodriguez, F. (1983). *Education in a multicultural society.* Lanham, MD: University Press of America.

See also **Cultural Bias in Testing; Pluralism, Cultural**

EDUCATIONAL PRODUCTS INFORMATION EXCHANGE (EPIE)

Established in 1967 and chartered by the New York Board of Regents, the Educational Products Information Exchange (EPIE) is devoted to helping educators effectively select and use instructional materials. Its members are primarily educational practitioners in local school districts.

The EPIE is a source of information, advocacy, and training concerning instructional materials. The organization has emphasized the need for consumers and producers to examine products with respect to the congruence of instructional design, intrinsic quality dimensions, practicality, and user effects. The EPIE Institute publishes a newsletter, "Epiegram," which reviews research findings derived from product development and evaluation studies and from practitioners' uses of products. The EPIE Institute may be contacted at 475 Riverside Drive, New York, New York 10027.

EDUCATIONAL RESOURCES INFORMATION CENTER (ERIC)

The Educational Resources Information Center (ERIC) is a national information system that provides access to the literature of education. Operating since 1965 and funded by the National Institute of Education, the ERIC system consists of a coordinating staff in Washington, DC, and 16 clearinghouses located at universities or professional organizations, each specializing in a major area of the field of education. The clearinghouse responsible for selecting, acquiring, cataloguing, abstracting, and indexing documents related to handicapped and gifted children is located at the Council for Exceptional Children (CEC) in Reston, Virginia.

The 16 clearinghouses prepare abstracts of relevant documents for two monthly ERIC publications. *Current Index to Journals in Education* (CIJE), a guide to current periodical literature in education, covers approximately 780 major educational and education-related journals; *Resources in Education* (RIE), a guide to other current literature in education, covers research findings, project and technical reports, speeches, unpublished manuscripts, and books. The clearinghouses also prepare interpretive summaries and annotated bibliographies on high-interest topics. The ERIC Clearinghouse on Handicapped and Gifted Children prepares a quarterly publication, *Exceptional Child Education Resources* (ECER), that includes indexes and abstracts of material included in both RIE and CIJE. The RIE and CIJE can be searched manually using author, subject, and institution indexes; they are also available for on-line computer searching through major commercial database brokerage systems. The ERIC system also produces a thesaurus of descriptors used to index documents. Documents indexed and abstracted in RIE are available from the ERIC Document Reproduction Service, except when noted, in both microfiche and paper copy, or in microfiche only. The ERIC microfiche collections are maintained at numerous university libraries across the country. ERIC is available for online search through the internet.

See also Council for Exceptional Children

EDUCATIONAL TESTING SERVICE (ETS)

Educational Testing Service (ETS) is a nonprofit corporation established in 1947; it originally intended to carry out the College Entrance Examination Board (CEEB) testing program. The ETS also was involved in assisting the testing functions of the Carnegie Corporation and the American

Council on Education. In addition to providing contract services to these, and now many other agencies (ETS develops and is responsible for carrying out the Law School Admissions Test, Graduate Record Examination, and numerous other programs), ETS has a world-renowned research and development staff. In recent years, ETS has undergone a streamlining that has reduced its basic research programs and led to a cutback in all research and development activities not aimed at marketable products, a change that represents a great loss to testing and to measurement theory.

The largest percentage of ETS's activity is devoted to developing, administering, scoring, and reporting services for the Scholastic Aptitude Test (SAT). The SAT is administered regularly at more than 5000 testing centers to more than 1 million college applicants each year. The use of ETS-administered admissions testing programs periodically stirs great controversy, mostly centering around charges of unfairness to certain classes of individuals.

In all of its testing programs, ETS regularly makes accommodations for handicapped individuals. Not only are readers or recorded tests provided for the blind and for the dyslexic, but prostheses and special administrative procedures for orthopedically handicapped individuals are provided as well; such special arrangements must be requested far in advance of the intended testing date.

ETS has become heavily involved in competency testing and examinations for licensure and certification of professions. The ETS prepares exams for teachers and has proposed competency exams for school psychologists as well.

EDUCATION AND TRAINING IN MENTAL RETARDATION AND DEVELOPMENTAL DISABILITIES

Education and Training in Mental Retardation and Developmental Disabilities is the quarterly journal published by the Division on Mental Retardation and Developmental Disabilities, a division of The Council for Exceptional Children. The journal began its twentieth volume in 1985. Content focuses on the education and welfare of retarded persons through data-based and expository articles as well as critical reviews of the literature. The editorial policy statement places major emphasis on identification and assessment, educational programming, characteristics, training of instructional personnel, habilitation, prevention, community understanding, and legislation. Editorial offices are located at 1920 Association Drive, Reston, VA 22091.

EDUCATION AND TREATMENT OF CHILDREN (ETC)

Education and Treatment of Children (ETC) is a refereed, scholarly journal published quarterly by Clinical Psychology Publishing Company for the Pressley Ridge School in Pittsburgh, Pennsylvania. The journal's goal is to disseminate reliable information related to educational and treatment services for children and youths. Manuscripts accepted for publication are judged on their relevance to a variety of child care professionals for improving the effectiveness of teaching and training techniques.

The responsibilities of the editorship of *ETC* are shared by R.F. Dickie and Daniel Hursh in cooperation with several specific area editors. The scholarly review process is further facilitated by 10 editors and numerous individuals serving on the editorial review board. These individuals include academicians, educators, practitioners, and others representing most geographic areas of the United States and portions of Canada.

Since its initial publication in 1976, *ETC* has published manuscripts describing a wide variety of experimental studies as well as nonexperimental procedures and/or services and programs for exceptional and normal children and youths. A considerable portion of each issue is devoted to reviews of books and other published materials in the areas of education and treatment of children and youths. The content of the journal is informative and practical for practitioner and researcher alike and should prove useful in improving treatment practices.

EDUCATION FOR ALL HANDICAPPED CHILDREN ACT OF 1975 (PL 94-142)

See INDIVIDUALS WITH DISABILITIES EDUCATION ACT (IDEA).

EDUCATION FOR "OTHER HEALTH IMPAIRED" CHILDREN

"Other Health Impaired" children include those pupils whose health problems severely affect their learning. Federal law designates this group as children with severe orthopedic impairments, illnesses of a chronic or acute nature that require a prolonged convalescence or which limit that child's vitality and strength, congenital anomalies (e.g., spina bifida and clubfoot), other physical causes (e.g., amputation and cerebral palsy), and other health problems including, but not limited to, hemophilia, asthma, severe anemia, and diabetes. This category constitutes about 5% of children classified as handicapped. Unfortunately, the terminology used for children suffering other health impairments does not indicate any commonality in student need, as the categorization is based on recognizable differences in condition and not on necessary educational interventions (Reynolds & Birch, 1982).

Other health impairments may be the result of congenital defects or adventitious (acquired) disabilities. The tremendous heterogeneity associated with the term requires attention to the one obvious common factor of such children, a physical condition that interferes with normal functioning. This limits the child's opportunity to participate fully in learning activities by affecting the body's supply of

strength and energy or the removal of wastes, reducing mobility, and creating severe problems in growth and development (Kneedler, 1984).

Although the continuum of degree may range from mild to severe, educational principles for other health impaired children include:

1. Placement and education within the mainstream of the public school to the maximum capability of the child. In addition, for those children requiring a special class, school, or home/hospital instruction, directing efforts to return them as soon as possible to regular education (Heron & Harris, 1982).
2. Architectural modifications including the removal of all architectural barriers for full school integration and the modification of classroom structure and environment to allow optimal mobility and exploration.
3. Parent and family education is assumed by the school to provide for coordination of effort, resources, and services.
4. Trained teachers and paraprofessionals who will assist other health impaired children within the school setting.
5. Coordination and utilization of all necessary support and resource personnel by school districts serving such children include transportation modifications, physical and occupational therapy, adaptive physical education, and vocational education and counseling (Gearheart & Weishahn, 1980).

REFERENCES

Gearheart, B.R., & Weishahn, M.W. (1980). *The handicapped child in the regular classroom* (2nd ed.). St. Louis: Mosby.

Heron, T.E., & Harris, K.C. (1982). *The educational consultant: Helping professionals, parents, and mainstreamed students.* Boston, Mass: Allyn & Bacon.

Kneedler, R.D., Hallahan, D.P., & Kauffman, J.M. (1984). *Special education for today.* Englewood Cliffs, NJ: Prentice-Hall.

Reynolds, M.C., & Birch, J.W. (1982). *Teaching exceptional children in all America's schools.* Reston, VA: Council for Exceptional Children.

See also **Categorical Education; Cerebral Palsy; Education for the Terminally Ill; Other Health Impaired; Spina Bifida**

EDUCATION FOR THE HANDICAPPED LAW REPORT (EHLR)

Education for the Handicapped Law Report (EHLR) is a compilation of current documents concerning special education law. The *EHLR* loose-leaf volumes contain federal statutes and regulations relevant to the education of handicapped children and youths; policy letters, state monitoring reports, rulings, and other documents issued by the Office for Civil Rights and Special Education Programs in the U.S. Department of Education; major court decisions; and current decisions of administrative hearings and appeals from selected state educational agencies.

Other features of the *EHLR* are lists of relevant cases pending before or acted on by the U.S. Supreme Court during each term, a newsletter that reports events and items of special interest, and directories of groups and agencies involved or interested in education of the handicapped. The binder contents are continually updated by 24 supplements annually. The extensive *EHLR* indexes serve as a convenient search system for users.

EDUCATION FOR THE TERMINALLY ILL

The teacher confronted by the crisis of a terminally ill child is faced with a complex and difficult situation. The role of the educator requires interaction with the life-threatened child and that child's family, peers, and classmates. Medical and technological advances have increased the life expectancy of terminally ill children and allowed many to return to school during periods of remission or control of their illness (Desy-Spinetta & Spinetta, 1983). To be helped and comforted by a return to the familiar atmosphere of school, the dying child requires the active support and assistance of school personnel (Eklof, 1984).

There are several stages of instruction to be observed in the education of terminally ill children. The initial phase should begin with the instruction and counseling of those who will teach them. It is necessary for educators to face, express, and deal with their own feelings toward death and dying before they can effectively identify and meet the emotional needs and presenting problems of such children. Denial, avoidance, fear, and helplessness are attitudes commonly encountered in unprepared teachers that directly affect the quality of the terminally ill child's experiences in school (Cairns, 1980). Instructional modules devoted to teacher self-awareness and the reality of facing and coping with death and dying are recommended for inclusion in teacher preparation programs (Sirvis, 1981).

As terminally ill children often choose a caring adult other than a parent with whom to communicate and express their feelings, the second stage in teacher preparation must be familiarization and understanding of the psychological stages encountered by the terminally ill and the "language of feelings" employed by such children. Professionals must be aware of the different ways children may select to communicate those feelings in order to be helpful and supportive (Kubler-Ross, 1983).

The second phase in a comprehensive education program for the terminally ill must address the needs and fears of the peers and classmates of the dying child. Wass and Corr (1982) stress the need for curriculum units on death and terminal illness to prepare teachers to instruct on such topics, while Jeffrey and Lansdown (1982) also recommend the inclusion of curriculum units on death and dying for both regular and special education class pupils.

The final phase in educating the terminally ill child offers directed strategies for the teacher. These include: (1) the maintenance of regular classroom routines for such children and the continued application of rules, limits, and reasonable goal-setting (Noore, 1981); (2) the use by teachers of such methods as life space interviews, adjunctive therapy, expressive writing, bibliotherapy (literature), role playing, magic circle discussions, art therapy, and play therapy to cope with the child's presenting problems (Ainsa, 1981); (3) the preparation by teachers to deal effectively with behaviors that may range from withdrawal to defiance while helping friends and classmates grieve and recover on the death of the child; (4) the maintenance by teachers of a primary role and the fulfillment of teaching responsibilities while emphasizing views in the classroom that stress maintaining meaning in the life of the terminally ill child. Most terminally ill children continue to receive educational services until they are too ill to benefit from them and may receive in-home teaching services as Other Health Impaired through special education.

REFERENCES

Ainsa, T. (1981). Teaching the terminally ill child. *Education, 101,* 397–401.

Cairns, N. (1980). The dying child in the classroom. *Essence: Issues in the study of aging, dying, and death, 4,* 25–32.

Desy-Spinetta, P., & Spinetta, J.J. (1983). The child with cancer returns to school: Preparing the teacher. In J.E. Schowalter, P.R. Patterson, M. Tallmer, A.H. Kutscher, S.V. Gullo, & D. Peretz (Eds.), *The child and death.* New York: Columbia University Press.

Eklof, M. (1984). The terminally ill child: How peers, parents and teachers can help. *PTA Today, 10,* 8–9.

Jeffrey, P., & Lansdown, R. (1982). The role of the special school in the care of the dying child. *Developmental Medicine & Child Neurology, 24,* 693–696.

Kubler-Ross, E. (1983). *On children and death.* New York: Macmillan.

Noore, N. (1981). The damaged child. *Journal for Special Educators, 17,* 376–380.

Sirvis, B. (1981). Death and dying: An instructional module for special educators. *Dissertation Abstracts International,* Order no. 76–21039, *39,* 164 pp.

Wass, H., & Corr, C.A. (1982). *Helping children cope with death: guidelines and resources.* New York: Hemisphere.

***See also* Family Counseling; Family Response to a Child with Disabilities; Physical Handicaps**

EDUCATION OF THE BLIND/ VISUALLY HANDICAPPED

Educationally significant, noncorrectable vision impairments are prevalent in approximately 1 student in 1000. The U.S. Department of Education (1985) reports that approximately 32,000 students between the ages of 3 and 21 are identified as visually handicapped. Educators use one of two basic classifications in identifying students who are visually handicapped: blind and visually impaired/low vision.

Those who are blind may have no light perception or may have some light perception without projection. The low-vision learner is considered severely impaired (even with corrective assistance such as glasses), but is able to read print (often in modified form).

According to Kirk and Gallagher (1986), research on the impact of visual handicaps indicates that, for the vast majority of students, (1) intellectual abilities are not markedly affected; (2) the perception of other senses is not substantially different from that of seeing persons; (3) language development is affected only in those areas where the meanings of words are dependent on visual concepts; and (4) self-esteem and self-confidence are not distorted except when a peer group has negatively influenced the individual's attitude.

The influence of social and educational movements to serve disabled citizens in less restrictive settings has realized a particular impact on the education of visually handicapped students. Prior to 1960, approximately 80% of visually handicapped learners were prepared in residential schools; currently over 70% of visually handicapped learners are served in local educational programs. The integration of visually handicapped students into regular school environments such as the innovative local programming promoted by Barraga (1983) focuses on adaptations in the presentation of learning experiences, modifications in instructional materials, and refinements in the learning environment.

Depending on the nature and severity of the visual handicap, Reynolds and Birch (1982) have identified the continuum of services that should be available to appropriately serve the blind or low-vision student placed in local school programs. The range of services and other resources includes specialized instruction directed to the unique learning needs and style of the visually impaired. This instruction may be offered by consultants, itinerant teachers, resource teachers, or specially assisted regular classroom teachers or teacher aides. Particularly important in the development of effective programming for this population is the substitution of auditory or tactual learning programs to compensate for the loss of visual capabilities.

The range of services also includes instruction in orientation and mobility and the availability of readily accessible programs and facilities. To ensure the maximum possible classroom integration, modifications in facility structure, classroom arrangement, and lighting may be necessary. In addition, specialized materials and technologies such as braille, advanced reading machines (e.g., Kurzweil Reader, Optacon), recorded information, and large print documents and magnifiers are offered, along with comprehensive early intervention programming for infants and young children and a strong, ongoing program of career preparation and placement.

REFERENCES

Barraga, N. (1983). *Visual handicaps and learning* (Rev. ed.). Austin, TX: Exceptional Resources.

Kirk, S.A., & Gallagher, J.J. (1986). *Educating exceptional children* (5th ed.). Boston: Houghton Mifflin.

Reynolds, M.C., & Birch, J.W. (1982). *Teaching exceptional children in all America's schools* (Rev. ed.). Reston, VA: Council for Exceptional Children.

U.S. Department of Education. (1985). *Seventh annual report to Congress on the implementation of the Education of the Handicapped Act.* Washington, DC: U.S. Government Printing Office.

See also **Visual Impairment**

EDUCATION WEEK

Education Week is a weekly newspaper published 42 times during the typical academic year. It is published by Editorial Projects in Education Inc., a Washington, DC based corporation, and edited by Ronald Wolk. *Education Week* carries news, comment, and editorials of interest and concern to professional educators and researchers in the field. The paper monitors budgetary concerns and federal policy. Special education news is regularly included, as are position papers on topics of special interest such as learning disabilities diagnosis and mainstreaming. Letters to the editor and commentary on current events in education and previously published news items, features, or commentaries are accepted. Classified ads and listings of job openings are also included.

EEG ABNORMALITIES

The EEG is a graphic representation of the electrical activity of the brain that is generated in the cortex by the flow of synaptic currents through the extracellular space. Electrical changes in the brain that manifest in EEG abnormalities represent the heart of the epileptic attack (Bennett & Ho, 1997; Kandel, Schwartz, & Jessell, 1991). When an epileptic seizure occurs, large populations of neurons are activitated synchronously in regions of the cortex. During the evaluation of a patient, it is not uncommon to find an abnormal EEG when there is no overt evidence of a seizure disorder. The criteria for determining the presence of a seizure disorder in an individual with an abnormal EEG are rarely stated explicitly. Hill (1957) has reported that a high percentage of schizophrenic patients show paroxysmal abnormalities in their EEGs (e.g., synchronous spikes, spike and wave complexes, and slow wave bursts). The relationship between an abnormal EEG and behavioral disturbances in nonepileptic individuals is more difficult to define. It also has been demonstrated that commonly used drugs can often cause EEG changes that can mimic seizure activity (Fink, 1963; Ulett, Heusler, & Word, 1965). Some of these changes are described in Table 1.

Defining the limits of normality in an EEG presents a major problem with which clinicians and investigators have struggled for years. There is no doubt that spikes, spike-wave discharges, focal slowing with phase reversal, and

Table 1 Effect of Commonly Used Drugs on the EEG[a]

Drug Type	Effect on Basic Frequencies	EEG Changes Synchronization	New Waves	Persistence After Drug Discontinued
Phenothiazine	Beta slowing (occasional)	Increased	High voltage sharp	6–10 weeks
Tricyclics	Increased beta	Increased	Sharp	Unknown
Barbiturates	Increased beta; slowing	Increased in low doses; decreased in high doses	Spindles	3–6 weeks
Meprobamate	Increased beta	Increased	Spindles	3–6 weeks
Benzodiazepines	Increased beta	Increased	Fast, sharp	3–6 weeks

[a]All of these drugs except barbiturates tend to increase preexisting dysrhythmias. Withdrawal from high levels of barbiturates and meprobamate can induce increased slowing, synchronization, and paroxysmal activity, and may result in seizures.

paroxysmal activity during wakefulness are always abnormal; however, there are many instances and EEG patterns that do not contain any of the above but still may be considered abnormal. In patients who drink alcohol heavily or who have received tranquilizers or other medications, EEG abnormalities may be seen and represent the effect of these drugs or withdrawal from them. EEG abnormalities seen in some psychopathic individuals with a history of aggressive behavior may be due to brain damage. Positive electroencephalographic abnormalities and brain damage thus may be a result and not the cause of emotional disturbance. Even with these possibilities there remains impressive literature correlating EEG abnormalities with certain psychiatric symptomatology (e.g., Dodrill, 1981; Hartlage & Hartlage, 1997).

REFERENCES

Dodrill, C.B. (1981). Neuropsychology of epilepsy. In S.B. Filskov & T.J. Boll (Eds.), *Handbook of clinical neuropsychology* (pp. 366–395). New York: Wiley.

Fink, M. (1963). Quantitative EEG in human psychopharmacology: Drug patterns. In G.H. Glaser (Ed.), *EEG and behavior* (pp. 143–169). New York: Basic Books.

Hartlage, P.L., & Hartlage, L.C. (1997). The neuropsychology of epilepsy: Overview and psychosocial aspects. In C.R. Reynolds & E. Fletcher-Janzen (Eds.), *Handbook of clinical child neuropsychology* (2nd ed.) (pp. 506–516). New York: Plenum.

Hill, D. (1957). Electroencephalogram in schizophrenia. In R. Richter (Ed.), *Schizophrenia: Somatic aspects* (pp. 30–72). London: Pergamon.

Kandel, E., Schwartz, J., & Jessell, T. (1991). *Principles of neural science* (3rd ed.). New York: Elsevier.

Ulett, G.A., Heusler, A.F., & Word, T.J. (1965). The effect of psychotropic drugs on the EEG of the chronic psychotic patient. In W.P. Wilson (Ed.), *Applications of electroencephalography in psychiatry: A symposium* (pp. 23–36). Durham, NC. Duke University Press.

See also **Epilepsy; Neuropsychology**

EEOC

See EQUAL EMPLOYMENT OPPORTUNITY COMMISSION.

EFFECTIVENESS OF SPECIAL EDUCATION

The question of the effectiveness of special education brings to mind Dickens' opening lines in *A Tale of Two Cities:* "It was the best of times, it was the worst of times." Much the same can be said about the effectiveness of special education: it is effective, it is not effective. The reasons for this equivocation are varied. One primary source is the vaguely defined parameters of the group labeled mildly handicapped. For some 90% of pupils labeled mildly handicapped who fall under the rubric of educable mentally retarded (EMR), learning disabled (LD), or behaviorally disordered (BD), there is considerable controversy surrounding specific identification criteria; the result is a lack of homogeneous classification. The heterogeneity present in these populations makes it difficult to assess treatment effectiveness even though these groups are presumed to possess similar problems. Those children with sensory deficits, physical disabilities, or severe and profound handicaps do not suffer from as many classification problems. Their conditions are better defined and more specific than the arbitrary and nonspecific symptoms that surround the mildly handicapped. This does not mean that it is impossible to treat conditions difficult to diagnose. It does mean, however, that the differences across mildly handicapped populations may mask specific treatment effectiveness, and, consequently, not provide an accurate picture of intervention efficacy in general. Therefore, it is possible for special education to be both effective and ineffective. The problem is not the lack of research investigating the effectiveness of special education practices but rather the lack of definitive conclusions that may be drawn from such research.

In an effort to delineate more fully the magnitude of the effectiveness (or the ineffectiveness) of special education, methods of quantitative research synthesis have been developed; they add clarity, explicitness, and definition to the review process. Because such methods, which have come to be known as meta-analysis (Glass, McGaw, & Smith, 1981), increase the objectivity, verifiability, and replicability of the review process, the conclusions drawn are more systematic and unequivocal. Meta-analysis is based on a metric "effect size" (*ES*), which transforms individual study data into standard deviation units (z-scores). The individual *ES* calculations may then be combined and recombined into different aggregations that reveal important information about the problem under study. For example, suppose a hypothetical evaluation of a special education intervention (temporal centripetal therapy) revealed an average ES () of +1.00. This would indicate a one standard deviation superiority of the treatment group. This relationship suggests that the average treated child was better off than 84% of the control (comparison) group, while only 16% of the control group was better off than the average treated child.

By summarizing the findings of several meta-analyses investigating the effectiveness of special education, it is possible to delineate the magnitude of treatment efficacy for common practices in special education, and place the question of the effectiveness of special education into a different context (Kavale, 1999).

Special education is not characterized by precise relationships wherein the efficacy of any intervention is easily calculated (e.g., do A in circumstance X and Y, and do B in circumstance Z). Although this may appear to be a serious shortcoming, practical applications in special education do not require prescriptive pronouncement; i.e., a single course of action under a wide range of circumstances. Because special education is unpredictable, it must be approached with a degree of uncertainty. The uncertainty introduces risk into the system (i.e., not knowing whether the intervention will work or not), and means that it is necessary for the practice of special education to be based on rational action. Such rational action demands that the special education practitioner possess a variety of options in order to remain flexible and versatile in the face of uncertainty. When it is realized that the success or failure of special education is contingent on relatively uncontrolled (and unknown) factors, the task of the practitioner becomes one of minimizing the risk by providing the most satisfactory solution for the child's problem under the present circumstances. The best means of achieving a satisfactory solution is to replace dogmatic beliefs with an array of rational choices that interpose between the intricate concatenation of events involved in the special education teaching-learning process and the practitioner's wisdom and experience. Given the nature of special education, it is likely that intervention practices will remain variable and unpredictable. Consequently, when considering the question of the effectiveness of special education, it is also likely that the answer will remain, it is effective, it is not effective. The equivocation necessary when evaluating special education practice means that for the practitioner, it is the best of times, it is the worst of times. Kavale (1999) presents a lengthy delineation of suggestions for creating more of the former.

REFERENCES

Glass, G.V., McGaw, B., & Smith, M.L. (1981). *Meta-analysis in social research.* Beverly Hills, CA: Sage.

Kavale, K.A. (1981). Functions of the Illinois Test of Psycholinguistic Abilities (ITPA): Are they trainable? *Exceptional Children, 47,* 496–510.

Kavale, K.A. (1999). Effectiveness of special education. In C.R. Reynolds & T.B. Gutkin (Eds.), *The Handbook of school psychology* (3rd ed.) (pp. 984–1024). New York: Wiley.

See also **Feingold Diet; Perceptual Training; Psycholinguistics; Research in Special Education; Standard Deviation**

ELABORATED *V.* RESTRICTED VERBAL CODES

The expressions "elaborated" and "restricted" code were introduced by the British sociologist Basil Bernstein in 1974 and were defined:

on a linguistic level, in terms of the probability predicting for any one speaker which syntactic elements will be used to organize meaning. In the case of an elaborated code, the speaker will select from a relatively extensive range of alternatives and therefore the probability of predicting the pattern of organizing elements is considerably reduced. In the case of a restricted code, the number of these alternatives is often severely limited and the probability of predicting the pattern is greatly increased. (pp. 76–77)

Bernstein hypothesized that these different codes were functions of different social structures. Comparisons of groups of middle-class and working-class children showed significant differences for grammatical and lexical features. Middle-class children used a significantly higher proportion of subordinations, complex verbal stems, the passive voice, uncommon adjectives, adverbs and conjunctions, and the pronoun I.

In later publications, Bernstein refined and extended his theory. A code was then said to be "a regulative principle controlling speech realizations in diverse social contexts" (Bernstein, 1974, p. 12). "Elaborated codes give access to universalistic orders of meaning, which are less context bound, whereas restricted codes give access to particularistic orders of meaning, which are far more context bound, that is, tied to a particular context" (p. 197).

Bernstein was criticized, on the one hand, for the vagueness of his definitions and the crudeness of the linguistic distinctions he operated with, and on the other hand, for having given scientific support to the theory of linguistic deprivation (Labov, 1970) and eventually to compensatory education programs (Bereiter & Engelmann, 1966). The latter criticism does not seem to be justified, as it ignores the evolution in Bernstein's ideas after 1962.

REFERENCES

Bereiter, G., & Engelmann, S. (1966). *Teaching disadvantaged children in the pre-school.* Englewood Cliffs, NJ: Prentice-Hall.

Bernstein, B. (1974). *Class, codes and control* (Vol. 1). London: Routledge & Kegan Paul.

Labov, W. (1970). The logic of non-standard English. In J. Alatis (Ed.), *Report of the 20th Annual Round Table Meeting on Linguistics and Language Studies*. Washington, DC: Georgetown University Press.

See also **Expressive Language Disorders; Language Deficiencies and Deficits; Language Delays**

ELAVIL

Elavil is the trade name for the generic tricyclic antidepressant amitriptyline. Elavil and other tricyclic antidepressants (TCA) usually are prescribed for endogenous depressions. These are affective disorders that present with vegetative disturbance (i.e., psychomotor slowing, poor appetite/weight loss, loss of sexual interest) and usually cannot be ascribed to a situational cause. Persons with endogenous depression often have positive familial histories for an affective disorder.

Therapeutically, TCAs are intended to reduce symptom intensity, increase mood elevation and physical activity, reestablish appetite and sleep patterns, and, in general, facilitate activity levels that will promote social adjustment (Blum, 1984). Such effects are assumed to be a result of TCA's blocking brain amine re-uptake, thus making more of the various catecholamines available at their specific receptor sites (Seiden & Dykstra, 1977).

Elavil differs from other TCAs in that it tends to produce greater sedation and a greater degree of anticholinergic side effects: visual blurring, urinary retention, constipation, concentration difficulties (Katzung, 1982). The TCAs are not often used in the treatment of children, because children appear to be more at risk for cardiovascular side effects and seizure-facilitating side effects of high doses (Blum, 1984). However, in titrated doses, TCAs have been used to treat enuresis and severe obsessive-compulsive disorders in children (Detre & Jarecki, 1971). In the 1990s, widespread use of TCAs was curtailed in favor of the SSRIs, selective serotonin reuptake inhibitors, such as Prozac.

REFERENCES

Blum, K. (1984). *Handbook of abusable drugs*. New York: Gardner Press.

Detre, T.P., & Jarecki, G.H. (1971). *Modern psychiatric treatment*. Philadelphia: Lippincott.

Katzung, B.G. (1982). *Basic and clinical pharmacology*. Los Altos, CA: Lange Medical.

Seiden, L.S., & Dykstra, L.A. (1977). *Psychopharmocology: A biochemical and behavioral approach*. New York: Van Nostrand Reinhold.

See also **Dopamine; Haldol; Tranquilizers**

ELECTIVE MUTISM

Elective mutism is a psychological disorder most often encountered in early childhood. It is marked by the refusal of the individual to speak. The child has both the physical capacity to produce speech and comprehends the spoken language. To maintain a diagnosis of elective mutism, according to the *Diagnostic and Statistical Manual of Mental Disorders* of the American Psychiatric Association (*DSM-III*, 1980), more pervasive developmental disorders, including language disorders and mental retardation, must first be eliminated as primary diagnoses.

While elective mutism is generally regarded as a disorder primarily found in the preschool and younger elementary school child, an adolescent variation of mutism has been identified by Kaplan and Escoll (1973). However, as its discussion precedes the more contemporary psychiatric definition, it is not elaborated on.

Symptomatology indicative of elective mutism was first identified in German literature in the late nineteenth century by Kussmaul, who referred to it as *aphasia voluntaria,* although the present term of elective mutism was not used until 1934 by Tramer (Silver, 1985). Careful review of the literature indicates the presence of elective mutism in many countries such as Israel (Hesse, 1981; Meijer, 1979), Great Britain (Wilkins, 1985), Switzerland (Hesselman, 1983), Canada (Zondlo & Scanlan, 1983), France (Myquel et al., 1982), and Japan (Ohi et al., 1982). The variety of languages represented in this childhood disorder suggests that culture does not have an overwhelming influence on its development. Rather, elective mutism is psychogenic, with its etiology linked to socioemotional and other developmental factors.

The treatment of elective mutism depends on the provision of a nonthreatening milieu at home and in the situations under which the behaviors become manifest. Attempts to be intrusive into the child's silence only serve to strengthen the resistance and will generally result in greater withdrawal and the absence of speech.

REFERENCES

American Psychiatric Association (1980). *Diagnostic and statistical manual of mental disorders* (3rd ed.). Washington, DC: Author.

Hesse, P.P. (1981). Colour, form and silence: A formal analysis of drawings of a child who did not speak. *Arts in Psychotherapy, 8,* 175–184.

Hesselman, S. (1983). Elective mutism in children 1877–1981. A literary summary. *Acta Paedopsychiatra, 49,* 297–310.

Kaplan, S.I., & Escoll, P. (1973). Treatment of two silent adolescent girls. *Journal of the American Academy of Child Psychiatry, 12,* 59–71.

Meijer, A. (1979). Elective mutism in children. *Israeli Annals of Psychiatry, 17,* 93–100.

Myquel, M., & Granon, M. (1982). Le mutisme electif extrafamilial chez l'enfant. *Neuropsychiatre Enfant Adolesce, 30,* 329–339.

Ohi, M., Fujita, T., Tanaka, T., & Kobayashi, I. (1982). A clinical and psychopathological consideration on elective mutism in adolescence: Five cases who have poor volition to seek socialization. *Seishin Shinkeigaku Zasshi, 84,* 114–133.

Silver, L.B. (1985). Speech disorders. In H.J. Kaplan & B. Sadock (Eds.), *Comprehensive textbook of psychiatry/IV* (pp. 1716–1721). Baltimore, MD: Williams & Wilkins.

Wilkins, R. (1985). A comparison of elective mutism and emotional disorders in children. *British Journal of Psychiatry, 146,* 198–203.

Zondlo, F.C., & Scanlan, J.M. (1983). Elective mutism in a 26 year old deaf female. *Canadian Journal of Psychiatry, 28,* 49–51.

See also Language Disorders; Mutism

ELECTROCONVULSIVE THERAPY (ECT)

Though developed as a treatment for schizophrenia, electroconvulsive therapy (ECT) has not been consistently demonstrated to be a successful intervention for that disorder. Major affective disorders, however, have been amenable to a course of ECT; thus, it is considered an adjunctive somatic therapy in the treatment of depression. As described by the American Psychiatric Association Task Force on Electroconvulsive Therapy (1978), a course of ECT consists of a series of treatments, usually 6 to 10, occurring two to three times per week. During each treatment, a major motor seizure is induced. Electrode placement has evolved from bitemporal placement (Cerletti & Bini, 1938) to unilateral placement over the nondominant hemisphere (Goldman, 1949; Lancaster, Steinert, & Frost, 1958). The latter placement was an attempt to avoid the gross confusional symptoms created by bilateral placement or unilateral placement over the dominant hemisphere.

Though beneficial effects have been reported subsequent to a course of ECT, the cost-benefit question involved in the treatment has not been resolved. The majority of reviews suggest that no permanent structural changes may be attributed directly to the electrical stimulation. Memory disturbance (both retrograde and anterograde) appears severe immediately after treatment; however, memory processes appear to reintegrate between 1 and 3 months following cessation of treatment (Halliday et al., 1968; Squire, 1977). Electrode placement is related to both the degree and the modality of memory interference. Bitemporal placement produces the greatest interference, which disrupts both verbal and nonverbal recall. Unilateral electrode placement appears to produce effects consistent with assumed brain-behavior interactions (i.e., dominant placement produces greater interference in verbal recall, while nondominant placement produces greater interference in nonverbal recall).

REFERENCES

American Psychiatric Association Task Force on Electroconvulsive Therapy. (1978, September). *Electroconvulsive therapy.* Task Force Report 14. Washington, DC: Author.

Cerletti, U., & Bini, L. (1938). L'electroshock. *Archivo Generale di Neurologia Psychiatria e Psychoanalisi, 19,* 266–268.

Goldman, D. (1949). Brief stimulus electroshock therapy. *Journal of Nervous & Mental Disease, 110,* 36–45.

Halliday, A.M., Davison, K., Browne, M.W., & Keeger, L.C. (1968). A comparison of the effects on depression and memory of bilateral ECT and unilateral ECT to the dominant and non-dominant hemispheres. *British Journal of Psychiatry, 114,* 997–1012.

Lancaster, N.P., Steinert, R.R., & Frost, I. (1958). Unilateral electronconvulsive therapy. *Journal of Mental Science, 104,* 221–227.

Squire, L.R. (1977). ECT and memory loss. *American Journal of Psychiatry, 134,* 997–1001.

See also Brain Organization; Depression; EEG Abnormalities

ELECTROENCEPHALOGRAPH

An electroencephalograph is a machine that is used to measure the electrical activity of the brain. Fluctuations in brain electrical activity are recorded by electrodes attached to the scalp. The placement of the electrodes has been standardized for clinical use and is accepted internationally (Jasper, 1958). The potentials of the brain are shown on paper in a record called an electroencephalogram (EEG). The amplitude of the brain's electrical activity is small; it is measured in microvolts (millionths of a volt) and must be amplified by the electroencephalograph. The fluctuations in voltage that appear on the EEG have a fairly rhythmic character. The wavelike patterns that are produced will vary with the brain region being recorded as well as with the age and state of alertness of the patient.

The primary information in the EEG is its frequency, which varies from 0.5 to 60 Hz (cycles per second). Attempts have been made to provide rough categories for the classification of frequency. The characteristic pattern for adults in the waking state is dominated by the so-called alpha frequencies, a roughly sinusoidal shape pattern ranging from 8 to 12.5 Hz. Current usage usually identifies five frequency bands that are used in both clinical practice and research, particularly sleep research: delta, 0.5–4 Hz; theta, 4–8 Hz; alpha, 8–13 Hz; beta 1, 13–20 Hz; and beta 2, 20–40 Hz (Greenfield & Sternbach, 1972).

As a general rule, it is possible to predict what sort of brain wave pattern an individual will produce in the absence of brain damage. Variations from expected patterns can constitute a basis for postulating impaired brain functioning. Lewinsohn (1973) notes that the major pathologic changes include waves that are too fast, too slow, or too flat, with all of these conditions being either focal or diffuse.

A major limitation of the EEG is that normal-appearing records may be obtained in the presence of clear-cut evidence of severe organic brain disease (Chusid, 1976). Additionally, about 15 to 20% of the normal population produce abnormal EEG recordings (Mayo Clinic, 1976). Diagnostically, EEGs have been found to be about 60% accurate (Filskov & Goldstein, 1974). EEGs have proven most useful in the diagnosis of seizure disorders.

REFERENCES

Chusid, J.G. (1976). *Correlative neuroanatomy and functional neurology.* Los Altos, CA: Lange Medical Publications.

Filskov, S.B., & Goldstein, S.G. (1974). Diagnostic validity of the Halstead-Reitan Neuropsychological Battery. *Journal of Consulting & Clinical Psychology, 42,* 382–388.

Greenfield, N.S., & Sternbach, R.A. (1972). *Handbook of psychophysiology.* New York: Holt, Rinehart & Winston.

Jasper, H.H. (1958). The ten twenty electrode system of the International Federation. *Electroencephalography & Clinical Neurophysiology, 10,* 371–375.

Lewinsohn, P.M. (1973). *Psychological assessment of patients with brain injury.* Washington, DC: Division of Research, Department of Health, Education and Welfare.

Mayo Clinic. (1976). *Clinical examinations in neurology.* Philadelphia: Saunders.

See also **Absence Seizures; Epilepsy; Grand Mal Seizures**

ELECTROMECHANICAL SWITCHES

Simple technologies like electromechanical switches and battery interrupters are an easy and relatively inexpensive means of providing physically disabled students with access to battery-operated toys, small appliances, assistive communication devices, and computers. Electromechanical switches, which are often referred to simply as controls, can be purchased or made in a variety of styles, sizes, and shapes. The majority of physically disabled students use some type of push switch. The selection of a particular switch is based on the student's movement capabilities and the device the switch will operate.

Battery-operated toys with electromechanical switches are interesting and fun for physically disabled and sensory-impaired students. They are effective in teaching cause-effect relationships and independent environmental control and motor skills such as reaching and grasping. Switches attached to toys can also provide one way for a student to practice using an adaptation for computer access.

See also **Computer Use with the Handicapped; Electronic Communication Aids**

ELECTRONIC COMMUNICATION AIDS

Electronic communication aids consist of several related electronic components used by nonspeaking persons to communicate. These components are the communication aid, an interface, and an output device. An interface is a device used by a nonspeaking person to control the communication aid. The interface could consist of a simple on/off electronic switch, a headstick pointer, or a computer keyboard. An electronic signal is sent to a communication aid, which processes and may display the selected message signal. The symbol can be indicated by a small light emitting diode (LED) light, an electronic pointer, or liquid crystal display (LCD) display. The message can then be sent to one or more output devices such as a computer printer or speech synthesizer.

Electronic communication aids can be categorized by implementation level and by symbol selection technique (Harris & Vanderheiden, 1980). There are two implementation levels: simple and independent. Simple electronic aids consist of an interface and the communication aid. No output devices are used. An example of a simple electronic device is a joystick interface, which controls a light indicator on a vocabulary display. The disadvantage of a simple electronic system is that the listener must be present to observe the communication aid, and must sequence the selected symbols together to understand the message. Independent electronic aids are similar to simple electronic aids except that a spoken or written output device is added. This allows the nonspeaking person to communicate without listener assistance. These devices may or may not be portable.

Symbol selection methods for electronic communication aids can be categorized as direct selection or scanning selection systems. Direct selection allows the nonspeaking user to directly choose symbols for communication. Finger-pointing, pointing with a headstick, or typing on a keyboard are direct selection methods. Scanning selection systems are designed for persons with very limited motor control. The interface for a scanning system is typically a simple electronic switch. When the switch is activated, the communication aid will scan the available symbols one at a time. The nonspeaking person then uses the switch to stop the scanning once the symbol to be communicated is reached.

REFERENCE

Harris, D., & Vanderheiden, G. (1980). Augmentative communication techniques. In R.L. Schiefelbush (Ed.), *Nonspeech language and communication: Analysis and intervention.* Baltimore, MD: University Park Press.

See also **Augmentative Communication Systems; Communication Boards**

ELECTRONIC TRAVEL AIDS

Blind persons who travel independently rely on essentially three kinds of travel aids: long canes, dog guides, and electronic travel aids. Electronic travel aids serve as guidance devices that extend the range of perception of the environment beyond the fingertip, tip of the long cane, or handle of the dog guide's harness. These sensory aids enable the blind person to determine the approximate elevation, dimensions, azimuth, and possibly surface texture of objects detected within the range that the ultrasonic or electromagnetic waves penetrate. Information put out as auditory sounds or tactile vibrations permits the user to decide whether to avoid direct contact with the source of the signal, make contact with it, or simply use it as a reference point for orientation and navigation purposes.

See also **Mobility Training; Vision Training**

ELEMENTARY AND SECONDARY EDUCATION ACT (ESEA)

The Elementary and Secondary Education Act (ESEA; PL 89-10) of 1965 included the first major program of federal assistance to local school districts (Eidenberg & Morey, 1969). Title I of ESEA, amended and renamed Chapter 1 of the Education Consolidation and Improvement Act (ECIA) in 1981, provides federal grants through states to school districts based on the number of children from families in poverty. The grants are to provide compensatory education services to educationally deprived children. Children are determined to be eligible for services based not on family income but on local determination, within federal guidelines, that they are educationally disadvantaged.

Also included in this statute is the authorization for the Chapter 1 state agency program for handicapped children in state-operated or state-supported schools. Grants are made to the states to provide supplementary educational services based on the number of handicapped children in such programs. This authority predates the Education for All Handicapped Children Act (PL 94-142) and was aimed primarily at children in institutional settings. Children served in Chapter 1 state agency programs are subject to all the requirements of IDEA. For purposes of federal reimbursement, however, a handicapped child may be counted in either the Chapter 1 state agency grant (250,000 children in December 1984) or in the IDEA state grant (4.1 million children in December 1984), but not both.

REFERENCE

Eidenberg, E., & Morey, R. (1969). *An act of congress.* New York: Norton.

See also **Individuals with Disabilities Education Act (IDEA); Legal Regulations of Special Education**

THE ELEPHANT MAN

Renowned in both late Victorian England during his lifetime and contemporarily more by his "professional name," the "Elephant Man," than his real one, Joseph Carey Merrick has been fascinating to both professionals and the public for over 100 years. First brought to recent attention by Ashley Montagu (1972) in his biography, *The Elephant Man: A Study in Human Dignity,* Merrick has been the subject of at least one other biography (Howell & Ford, 1980), a successful play and subsequent movie, and numerous professional and popular articles. Howell & Ford's book not only contains a detailed biography, but many photographs and drawings, contemporary accounts, and Merrick's autobiography, which serve as the sources for this entry.

Merrick may well as an adult have been the "ugliest man in the world," as he was frequently called. Born normal to lower-class parents in Leicester, England in 1860, Merrick began to develop deformities in the head, limbs, and back such that regular employment became impossible, although he held several jobs for a short time in early adulthood. His mother died when he was young, and his father virtually abandoned him when he remarried. Unable otherwise to make a living, Merrick allowed himself for many years to be exhibited as a sideshow freak as the "Elephant Man." When a London physician, Frederick Treves, saw him in Whitechapel, he left Merrick one of his cards. When the show was closed in England as an affront to human decency, Merrick and a manager went to Belgium, where the manager abandoned him when the show was again pursued by police. Merrick, with money gained by pawning some possessions, made his way back to London. This time, he was pursued and jeered by curious crowds. Finally, he ended up at London Hospital where Treves worked. After some difficulty, Treves arranged for a room to be furnished in the hospital, where Merrick spent most of the rest of his life.

Treves at first thought Merrick was retarded, but found that he was intelligent, and perhaps surprising given his years of mistreatment, sensitive, friendly, and sociable. Indeed, he became a society celebrity, and was visited by many notables, including the Prince and Princess of Wales and the Duke of Cambridge in 1887. Visitors frequently brought small gifts, which Merrick treasured. His head was so large that he could only sleep with his head between his knees. Unfortunately, his condition became progressively more serious and debilitating. He was found dead in his room, lying flat on his bed, on April 11, 1890.

What caused his deformities? He thought that he knew. In his words:

The deformity which I am now exhibiting was caused by my mother being frightened by an Elephant; my mother was going along the street when a procession of animals were passing by, there was a terrible crush of people to see them, and unfortunately she was pushed under which frightened her very much; this occurring during a time of pregnancy was the cause of my deformity. (Howell & Ford, 1980, p. 168)

But, however popular such explanations were at the time, he was, of course, wrong. Treves had viewed the disorder as being congenital, but neither he nor anyone else at the time could suggest a specific disorder. However, as early as 1909, a diagnosis of neurofibromatosis was suggested. Now known to be a single-gene dominant disorder, it is a likely candidate since many of the symptoms fit with Merrick's condition and it frequently arises through spontaneous mutation. The most characteristic manifestation is neurofibromas, masses of tumors comprised of densely packed nerve and fibrous tissue. Common also are patches of darkened skin, termed *café au lait* spots. Recently, however, alternatives have been suggested, most notably Proteus syndrome. Proteus is characterized by "macrocephaly, hyperostosis of the skull; hypertrophy of long bones; and thickened skin and subcutaneous tissues, particularly of the hands and feet, including plantar hyperplasia, lipomas, and other unspecified subcutaneous masses" (Tibbles & Cohen, 1986, p. 683). Over a hundred years after his death, Joseph Merrick indeed remains a subject of fascination.

REFERENCES

Howell, M., & Ford, P. (1980). *The true history of the elephant man.* London: Allison & Busby.

Montagu, A. (1972). *The elephant man: A study in human dignity.* New York: Outerbridge & Dienstfrey.

Tibbles, J.A., & Cohen, M.M., Jr. (1986). The Proteus syndrome: The Elephant Man diagnosed. *British Medical Journal (Clinical Research Edition), 293,* 683–685.

ELWYN INSTITUTES

Elwyn Institutes was founded in 1852. It is located on a 400-acre campus near Media, Pennsylvania. It is a comprehensive service facility, and it provides day and residential programs for children and adults who are learning handicapped, developmentally delayed, retarded, deaf/ blind, neurologically disabled, brain damaged, visually impaired, physically handicapped, deaf, hard of hearing, or multi-handicapped and deaf.

Elwyn Institutes' continuum of services features rehabilitation programs that coordinate residential and community living arrangements with special education, vocational training, and sequential programs that lead to independence in the community. Students in residence live in modern living accommodations on campus and in apartments within the local communities.

Elwyn Institutes maintains programs in Philadelphia; Wilmington, Delaware; Fountain Valley, California; and Israel. Management and administrative supervision is provided at the American Institute for Mental Studies, also known as the Vineland Training School, in Vineland, New Jersey.

Elwyn Institutes' educational programs are offered to students with day and residential accommodations from preschool years through to 21 years. These programs provide a wide range of educational services, including comprehensive evaluations, preschool programs, daycare facilities, and elementary and secondary levels of education and training. Ancillary services include audiological evaluations, speech and language therapy, mobility training, occupational therapy, psychiatric and psychological services, and medical and dental care.

Elwyn Institutes is located at 111 Elwyn Road, Elwyn, PA 19063.

EMBEDDED FIGURES TEST (EFT)

The Embedded Figures Test (EFT) was designed to measure individual differences in cognitive style, specifically, field dependence-independence. Developed by Herman Witkin in 1950, the EFT requires subjects to locate a simple geometric figure embedded within a larger, more complex figure. Field-independent subjects are able to perform this task more quickly than field-dependent subjects. A recent review by LaVoie (1985) suggested that the EFT may be related to learning and instructional preferences and serve as

an indicator of analytic ability. Witkin, Moore, Goodenough, and Cox (1977) also discussed the educational implications of cognitive style.

Test materials include 24 complex figure cards (two sets of 12, Form A and Form B), a set of eight simple figure cards, and a stylus used by the subject to trace the embedded figure. An average time of disembedding is calculated (total search time divided by 12) and converted into a standard score. Reliability studies indicate good internal consistency and test-retest stability. The test correlates significantly with more cumbersome measures of field dependence. The EFT can be used with individuals ages 12 and up, however, adaptations of the test are available for younger children (the Children's Embedded Figures Test for ages 5 through 11 and the Preschool Embedded Figures Test for ages 3 through 5). There is also a group test. All four versions are available from Consulting Psychologists Press, Inc.

REFERENCES

LaVoie, A.L. (1985). Embedded Figures Test. In D.J. Keyser & R.C. Sweetland (Eds.), *Test critiques* (Vol. II). Kansas City, MO: Test Corporation of America.

Witkin, H.A. (1950). Individual differences in ease of perception of embedded figures. *Journal of Personality, 19,* 1–15.

Witkin, H.A., Moore, C.A., Goodenough, D.R., & Cox, P.W. (1977). Field-dependent and field-independent cognitive styles and their educational implications. *Review of Educational Research, 47,* 1–64.

See also Assessment; Visual Perception and Discrimination

EMOTIONAL DISORDERS

The greatest amount of progress on behalf of the emotionally disturbed (ED) has occurred in the twentieth century. Assessment instruments, residential schools for the emotionally disturbed, special classes in public schools, child guidance clinics, juvenile courts and legal statutes specifically written for delinquent and abused children, and hundreds of texts dealing with the etiology, diagnosis, and treatment of children are all products of the twentieth century.

By the 1960s and 1970s, dramatic progress had been made on behalf of children and youth. Behavior modification techniques became a popular treatment method and ecological approaches to treatment of the disturbed child were developed. Public Law 94-142 mandated an appropriate education for all children. Efforts were made to deinstitutionalize children and to mainstream them in the public schools. By the late 1970s and early 1980s, a family systems approach to treatment of the disturbed child came into vogue. Today efforts are being made to educate the emotionally disturbed child in the classroom and to supplement education with a therapeutic treatment program.

The problems in defining normal functioning in children make it difficult to classify abnormalities. This is particularly the case in emotional disturbance, where behavioral rather than academic criteria are primarily employed. Stemming from the realities of providing educational remediation, however, Bower (1969) spearheaded efforts to conceptualize emotional disturbances in children. He provided a practical definition consisting of the following five characteristics: (1) learning problems are not explained by intellectual, sensory, or health factors; (2) there are difficulties in initiating and maintaining interpersonal relationships; (3) behavioral or emotional reactions are not appropriate to circumstances; (4) there is pervasive unhappiness or depression; and (5) there is the development of physical symptoms or fears related to school or personal problems. Any one or more of these five characteristics occurring to a marked extent over a long period of time are sufficient for diagnosis. Bower's criteria were adopted verbatim in PL 94-142. Public Law 94-142 additionally labeled schizophrenic and autistic children as seriously emotionally disturbed and differentiated socially maladjusted from emotionally disturbed children. Autistic children were dropped from the emotionally disturbed category and placed in the health-impaired category in 1981, and later received their own category.

Despite its official sanction as a category of childhood exceptionality, the label emotional disturbance has evoked considerable debate in the literature. It has been reported that the differentiation of emotional and behavioral disorders in children is difficult to make (Boyle & Jones, 1985), and that the distinction between primary and secondary emotional disturbance in learning disabilities is similarly confused (Chandler & Jones, 1983). Inadequacies in definition may have resulted in the underdetection and underserving of emotionally disturbed children (Long & McQueen, 1984). Although Bower (1981) has openly discussed the nebulous nature of basing a classification category on disturbances in emotion, he has continued to advocate the application of the revised term emotionally handicapped and his original diagnostic criteria.

Incidence rates of emotional disturbances, or the number of newly diagnosed cases at any point in time, are practically nonexistent because of the difficulties in accurately defining the onset and duration of childhood psychiatric disorders. Estimates of prevalence, or the number of existing cases at any point in time, however, are available and are based on data collected from educational and psychiatric perspectives.

A number of individual difference variables have been identified as significant correlates of childhood emotional disturbance. Sex is a particularly important factor. Males are more likely than females to be identified throughout the school years, with more males receiving the psychiatric diagnosis of conduct disorder and more females receiving the psychiatric diagnoses of specific emotional disorders, especially during adolescence (Offord, 1983). Racial and family characteristics have also been implicated. Blacks are more likely than whites to be identified, and identification varies inversely with parent education level as well as family so-

cioeconomic status (Zill, 1985). The importance of family variables is supported by the strong association between childhood psychiatric diagnoses in general and broken homes, marital discord, and parental deviance (Offord, 1983).

The etiology of mild to moderate emotional disturbances may not always be precise, but two major causative factors seem to predominate. These include socioenvironmental factors and biological factors. Genetic factors are important, but from the information to date, only the more severe forms of psychopathology seem to result from a genetic predisposition.

REFERENCES

Bower, E.M. (1969). *Early identification of emotionally handicapped children in school* (2nd ed.). Springfield, IL: Thomas.

Bower, E.M. (1981). *Early identification of emotionally handicapped children in school* (3rd ed.). Springfield, IL: Thomas.

Boyle, M.H., & Jones, S.C. (1985). Selecting measures of emotional and behavioral disorders of childhood for use in general populations. *Journal of Child Psychology & Psychiatry, 26,* 137–159.

Chandler, H.N., & Jones, K. (1983). Learning disabled or emotionally disturbed: Does it make any difference? *Journal of Learning Disabilities, 16,* 432–434.

Offord, D.R. (1983). Classification and epidemiology in child psychiatry: Status and unresolved problems. In P.D. Steinhauer & Q. Rae-Grant (Eds.), *Psychological problems of the child in the family* (2nd ed.). New York: Basic Books.

Zill, N. (1985). *The school-age handicapped.* Prepared by Child Trends, incorporated under Department of Education contract number 300-83-0198. Washington, DC: U.S. Department of Education.

See also **Childhood Psychosis; Childhood Schizophrenia; Conduct Disorder; Psychoneurotic Disorders; Seriously Emotionally Disturbed**

EMOTIONAL LABILITY

Emotional lability refers to rapidly shifting or unstable emotions (American Psychiatric Association, 1994). It is a psychiatric term that developed from attempts to classify the qualitative aspects of inappropriate emotional functioning in clinical cases. Lability has been most frequently applied in descriptions of serious emotional disturbance where rapid changes in emotional status are readily apparent. Unstable emotions are also characteristic of less severe psychopathologies and can be used to describe normal children's functioning during periods of stress or crisis. Sustained emotional lability, however, is considered to be pathological and results from a number of different causative factors. The primary etiological agents in children are fragile central nervous system functioning and frustration in meeting environmental demands (Swanson & Willis, 1979).

REFERENCES

American Psychiatric Association. (1994). *Diagnostic and statistical manual of mental disorders* (4th ed.). Washington, DC: Author.

Swanson, B.M., & Willis, D.J. (1979). *Understanding exceptional children and youth.* Chicago: Rand McNally.

See also **Acting Out; Emotional Disorders; Seriously Emotionally Disturbed**

ENCEPHALITIS

Encephalitis is an inflammation or infection of the brain, as contrasted with meningitis, which is an infection of the meninges or tissue covering the brain and spinal cord. Numerous types of encephalitides have been identified, and these tend to be classified by the etiologic agent. The two most common types are viral encephalitis, which is the result of a virus infection, and postinfectious encephalitis, which occurs as a complication of another infectious disease (e.g., chicken pox, measles). Encephalitis lethargica (also known as Von Economo's disease or sleeping sickness) is a rarely occurring type of encephalitis that appears in epidemics, generally in the spring of the year (Brown, 1971; Thomson, 1979). The last known outbreak of encephalitis lethargica occurred in Great Britain in the 1920s; it is presumed to be associated with a viral infection that attacks cortical and subcortical brain structures (Thomson, 1979).

The course of encephalitis is highly variable, and is associated with the etiologic agent and age of onset, among other factors. Mortality rates for victims of herpes simplex encephalitis are reported to be as high as 30 to 70% (Baringer, 1979). Survivors tend to demonstrate significant neurologic impairment of memory, cognition, and behavior, although total recovery in selected individuals has been reported (Baringer, 1979). Mortality rates for St. Louis and western encephalitides are much lower, approximately 10% of those afflicted (Johnson, 1979), although higher rates may occur in infants below 1 year. More than half the children surviving western equine encephalitis are reported to have significant neurologic sequelae, including mental retardation, spastic paralyses, and behavioral problems (Johnson, 1979). Many survivors of encephalitis may require special education or related services. Because of the variable sequelae associated with this condition, a multifactored evaluation is essential to planning an appropriate educational program.

REFERENCES

Baringer, J.R. (1979). Herpes simplex encephalitis. In P.B. Beeson, W. McDermott, & J.B. Wyngaarden (Eds.), *Cecil textbook of medicine* (pp. 821–824). Philadelphia: Saunders.

Brown, J.A.C. (1971). *The Stein and Day international medical encyclopedia.* New York: Stein & Day.

Johnson, R.T. (1979). Viral meningitis and encephalitis. In P.B. Beeson, W. McDermott, & J.B. Wyngaarden (Eds.), *Cecil textbook of medicine* (pp. 817–821). Philadelphia: Saunders.

Thomson, W.A.R. (1979). *Black's medical dictionary* (32nd ed.). New York: Barnes & Noble.

See also **Herpes; Meningitis**

ENCOPRESIS

Encopresis refers to the repeated (voluntary or involuntary) passage of feces into places not socially appropriate among persons for whom there is no organic pathology. Reported prevalence estimates range from 1 to 5%, depending on the particular sample studied (i.e., children in the general population or in institutional settings). Encopresis is more prevalent among males than females.

See also **Applied Behavior Analysis; Enuresis**

ENDOCRINE DISTURBANCES

Diabetes mellitus (a disease of the pancreas) and delayed growth are two common endocrine disturbances. In healthy individuals, the pancreas secretes insulin in response to the amount of glucose in the blood. Insulin is essential in helping the glucose enter the cell for use in cell growth. In children with diabetes, this insulin/glucose regulatory mechanism is lost and insulin is produced/released in insufficient amounts. Thus, the child must rely on an external source of insulin that is injected daily into an arm or thigh. The child must eat the right amount of certain foods in order to regulate his or her blood glucose and thus insulin requirements.

Such regimentation of daily insulin injections and diet can pose problems for children and their families. Arguments can occur between the child and parents over diet, regular testing of blood or urine glucose, and insulin injections. Child/parent conflict may be accompanied by poor academic performance or other behavioral problems. Poor diabetic control also may negatively affect the child's energy level, concentration, and neuropsychological functioning (Rosenbloom, 1984).

Management of the child's diabetes may be a significant source of stress and friction in some families, especially those in which adolescent diabetics use their disease management as an outlet for demonstrating independence and individuation from parents. Some children are embarrassed by their illness and are teased by peers. If the diabetes is not well controlled, the child may miss school frequently; in that case, he or she should have the opportunity for homebound education. Even though most children with diabetes lead a relatively normal life, some continue to feel different, and all such children, in reality, have some diabetes-required regimentation that their peers do not share (Stein & Jessop, 1984). For example, they need to eat three meals per day, to avoid a sugar overload, and to awaken early for an insulin injection. The child and his or her parents should be consulted to determine the diabetic student's individual academic and personal requirements at school.

Delayed growth or short stature is another common endocrine disturbance. Most children with this disturbance eventually will have normal stature, but the onset of their pubertal development is delayed. A smaller group of children have specific hormonal deficits such as Turner's syndrome (a chromosomal abnormality in girls) and hypopituitarism (insufficient quantities of growth hormone).

Girls with Turner's syndrome have some difficulties with spatial relationships; these difficulties can affect school performance in areas such as geometry or geography (Holmes, Karlsson, & Thompson, 1985). It should be emphasized that a girl with Turner's syndrome who is bright and functioning well in other areas may compensate for this difficulty, although these areas still may be much harder for her than for her peers.

Relatively few data exist regarding types of behavioral problems or cognitive deficits in children with hypopituitarism. A variety of areas of the brain may be involved for children with this problem. Ideally, a child with hypopituitarism should receive a comprehensive neuropsychological assessment of academic achievement, cognitive ability, memory, motor and sensory functioning, and social abilities. Because of the markedly small size of these children, they may be teased by their peers and their parents may expect less of them. These children may compensate by becoming the "class clown" or "school mascot." The educator should make note of his or her own reactions to the student with short stature to ensure that the student is treated according to age rather than size.

Interpersonal difficulties may occur in children with short stature as they enter adolescence. Inability to participate in age-appropriate activities and low self-esteem may result in behavior problems, withdrawal from social contacts, or poor school performance (Holmes, Karlsson, & Thompson, 1985). Some of these children are able to cope well with their dwarfism by finding areas in which they excel.

REFERENCES

Holmes, C.S., Karlsson, J.A., & Thompson, R.G. (1985). Social and school competencies in children with short stature: Longitudinal patterns. *Journal of Developmental and Behavioral Pediatrics, 6*(5), 263–267.

Rosenbloom, A.L. (1984). Primary and subspeciality care of diabetes mellitus in children and youth. *Pediatric Clinics of North America, 31,* 107–117.

Stein, R.E., & Jessop, D.J. (1984). General issues in the care of children with chronic physical conditions. *Pediatric Clinics of North America, 31,* 189–198.

See also **Diabetes; Dwarfism; Family Response to a Child with Disabilities**

ENGINEERED CLASSROOM

The engineered classroom designed by Frank M. Hewett is a developmental strategy for educating children with maladaptive behavior. Hewett (1968) identifies other strategies, sensory-neurological, psychodynamic-interpersonal, and behavior modification, as having contributed successfully to the amelioration of some emotionally handicapped students' problem behaviors, but found that all had limitations relating to their goals or methodologies. The engineered

classroom is designed to provide a more complete strategy in terms of establishing goals and procedures for the treatment of handicapped students in educational settings. Although the original concept was applied to work with emotionally handicapped students, Hewett (1968) expresses a belief that many of the components of the engineered classroom could also be applied to students classified as mentally handicapped and learning disabled.

The engineered classroom is designed as a "learning triangle" consisting of curriculum, conditions, and consequences (Hewett & Forness, 1984). Three fundamental precepts underlie the engineered classroom curriculum:

1. Teachers need to think and provide instruction in small steps.
2. The steps are basic to instruction.
3. The steps and procedures are to be sequential.

The curriculum areas are designed as a sequence of instruction for developing students' learning competence. The five levels in the sequence include goals and activities designed to develop students' skills in attending to tasks, responding to tasks, following ordered steps in tasks, exploring the environment, interacting socially with others, and attaining mastery of basic academic skills. The conditions under which the curriculum is to be implemented entail a set of variables to be controlled by the teacher or "engineer." These include *when* students are to complete tasks, *where* they are to complete tasks, *how* students are to complete tasks, *how long* they are to work on tasks, *how much* teachers expect students to do, and *how well* students are to complete a task. The third component of the learning triangle, consequences for behavior, is provided in the form of positive reinforcement or punishment based on the completion or incompletion of tasks. Within each of the curricular levels of learning competence, Hewett and Taylor (1980) describe specific goals and methods.

At the response level, motor coordination, verbal and nonverbal language, and task response skills are developed. Development of response skills helps students to interact more appropriately by improving basic response systems used in educational settings. This is accomplished by teachers providing extensive cues to guide responding (errorless learning) and by controlling requirements for success (successive approximations). In addition, response barriers are reduced by building motor and language response skills.

The order level consists of following directions and school adjustment tasks. Students are required to demonstrate skills in locating, copying from a model, and following multistep directions. The process of skill development entails students determining starting points for specific tasks and following tasks through to completion. Teachers must present task procedures clearly to students to minimize confusion or conflict. Perceptual motor training tasks are used frequently to develop order-level competence.

The next level within the curriculum, the exploratory level, is designed to develop active participation in classroom and community activities and students' knowledge of their environment. Objectives at this level focus on students demonstrating curiosity about objects, events, and experiences available to them. Teachers expose students to a wide range of multisensory experiences and encourage them to use their sensory channels to explore and learn about their environment. As with other levels, the teacher structures the choices available to students to reduce confusion and conflict. Activities with predictable outcomes are used to develop an understanding of cause/effect relationships. Discovering predictable cause and effect relationships helps students' awareness of reality and reduces fantasy experiences. This focus on reality helps students to overcome irrational fears and misperceptions about their world. Science and art activities are used as vehicles to guide students to explore the world around them (Hewett, 1968; Hewett & Taylor, 1980).

At the social level of learning competence, students develop skills in establishing and maintaining relationships with peers, teachers, and significant others (Hewett & Taylor, 1980). Students' positive self-concepts are also developed in terms of self-confidence, reactions to frustration, and emotional mood. Teachers structure activities to encourage communication among students and with others in the environment. Students use novel communication devices (e.g., walkie-talkies, invisible ink, telephones) to participate in activities requiring cooperation and communication between two or more individuals. Cooperative activities also are used to develop turn-taking skills and tolerance for delays in receiving rewards. Development and maintenance of appropriate social behaviors are facilitated through modeling, coaching, and role-playing techniques. Also, between-student competition is replaced by within-student competition.

The mastery level entails development of the basic academic skills needed to function successfully in school. Skill areas include reading, written language, mathematics, and vocational skills. There is an emphasis on structuring learning through the use of extensive response cues and consequences. Extensive use of errorless learning strategies is typical at this level. The specific structure of individual tasks is determined by the operations associated with the task and deals primarily with the *how* and *how well* conditions. Mastery level assignments are broken down into tiny steps to encourage and simplify learning.

One of the most salient characteristics of the engineered classroom is the physical arrangement of its learning centers (part of the conditions side of the learning triangle). The room is structured to encourage the development of skills within different levels of the curriculum.

Consequences for behavior are an additional component of the engineered classroom. Behavior in the engineered classroom is followed by either positive consequences or punishment. Students are rewarded for appropriate behaviors through task-embedded reinforcement (e.g., acquisition of knowledge, knowledge of results, multisensory stimulation, task completion) or external rein-

forcers provided by the teacher (e.g., tangible reinforcers, points, social approval). The primary punishment techniques include response cost, time-out, and overcorrection. Teachers monitor behavior through the use of a check-mark system that features a work record card. Teachers give or withhold check marks contingently for a 15-minute fixed interval. Each instructional hour, therefore, is divided into three 15-minute work periods, each followed by a 5-minute monitoring period (Hewett & Taylor, 1980).

REFERENCES

Hewett, F.M. (1968). *The emotionally disturbed child in the classroom.* Boston: Allyn & Bacon.

Hewett, F.M., & Forness, S.R. (1984). *Education of exceptional learners* (3rd ed.). Boston: Allyn & Bacon.

Hewett, F.M., & Taylor, F.D. (1980). *The emotionally disturbed child in the classroom: The orchestration of success* (2nd ed.). Boston: Allyn & Bacon.

See also **Behavior Modification; Classroom Management; Multisensory Instruction; VAKT**

ENGRAMS

Psychologists have long questioned how information is stored and subsequently retrieved from the brain. As early as 1900, Müller and Pilzecker argued that memory involves an unobservable physical change in the central nervous system that becomes relatively permanent as a result of repeated presentation of information. In keeping with this notion, most neurobiological theories of memory have hypothesized the existence of a memory trace or engram. Generally, this term is used to denote the relatively permanent structural or biochemical change in the brain consistent with the long-term storage of information (Hillgard & Bower, 1975). Information in short-term memory, on the other hand, appears to be less stable and is inaccessible unless converted into the enduring long-term store.

Retrieval of the memory trace is seen to be based on a reactivation of the same physical structure or biochemical conditions that were responsible for the initial storage or encoding process (Bloch & Laroche, 1984). This reactivation process seems to be triggered by stimuli that are the same or similar to the original stimulus event. From this point of view, both storage and retrieval are based on similar "neuronal circuits."

REFERENCES

Bloch, V., & Laroche, S. (1984). Facts and hypotheses related to the search for the engram. In G. Lynch, J.L. McGaugh, & N.M. Weinberger (Eds.), *Neurobiology of learning and memory* (pp. 249–260). New York: Guilford Press.

Hillgard, E.R., & Bower, G.H. (1975). *Theories of learning.* Englewood Cliffs, NJ: Prentice-Hall.

Müller, G.E., & Pilzecker, A. (1900). Experimentelle beitrage zur lehre von gedachtniss. *Zeitschrift fur Psychologie, 1,* 1–300.

See also **Memory Disorders**

ENRICHMENT

Enrichment is a term that is frequently used to denote one form or approach to differentiating instruction for gifted youth. It is also often used to denote supplementary curriculum for youth at any level of ability. When the term refers to a form of instruction for gifted youth, it may be defined, by contrast, with terms such as acceleration, individualization, or grouping. These terms may, however, relate chiefly to administrative arrangements just as enrichment may relate to an approach that administratively refers to provision for the gifted by the regular teacher in a typical heterogeneous classroom. Administrative acceleration may simply refer to a gifted child's early admission to school, grade skipping in the elementary school, or early admission to college. Individualization may refer to the administrative arrangement of continuous progress in an ungraded school. Finally, grouping may refer to the gathering of all mathematically talented youth into a single "honors" mathematics class in seventh grade. While these administrative approaches may stem in part from concern with the nature or needs of gifted youth, they tend to acquire a functional autonomy that makes them independent alternatives or options, regardless of gifted youths' specific needs.

Massé and Gagné (1983) assert that proper definitions of the term enrichment and the associated terms, acceleration, individualization, and grouping, must grow out of consideration of the special and unique characteristics of the gifted and their correlated special needs. They noted, however, that lists of characteristics of gifted (and talented) youths can be extensive and even contradictory. From their own review of research on characteristics of the gifted they concluded that there are four basic and pervasive characteristics: (1) rapid learning; (2) ease in learning complex material; (3) diversity of interests; and (4) depth of specific interests. Renzulli's (1979) three-ring conception of giftedness would probably be similar in stressing the components of ability (rapid learning, complex learning and task commitment) and depth of interest, but Renzulli's third component, creative ability, is probably not reflected in Massé and Gagné's concept. However, in his enrichment triad instructional model, Renzulli (1977) proposed a Type 1 enrichment that provides gifted youths with an opportunity for exploratory learning in areas of varied interests. Such activity might meet the need generated by the characteristic of "varied interests" noted by Massé and Gagné. Type II enrichment in the triad model refers to group instructional activities to teach thinking and feeling processes, while Type III refers to enrichment through opportunities to investigate real problems. Type III probably relates well to Massé and Gagné's characteristic of the gifted, depth of specific interest.

Stanley (1979) proposed four types of enrichment. The first is busywork, or simply more of the same type of work done by all students. A second type is irrelevant academic enrichment, which is supplementary instruction that pays no attention to the special talents or characteristics of gifted youth. The third type is cultural enrichment, which ignores the student's talents or abilities but offers curriculum in the arts and foreign languages. The fourth type, relevant enrichment, provides special instruction directly related to gifted youths' special talents or characteristics (e.g., an enriched mathematics course for mathematically talented youths). In contrast to these four types of enrichment, Stanley proposes that acceleration is always vertical, moving a gifted youth to higher levels. In contrast to his use of the term of vertical to refer to acceleration, the term horizontal is often used to refer to enrichment. Stanley characterizes it as a process of teaching more content but at the same level of difficulty or complexity.

Tannenbaum (1983) argued that enrichment for the gifted always requires a curriculum that is differentiated from the regular curriculum in that it is designed to meet the special needs of gifted youths. Tannenbaum (1983) went on to propose an enrichment matrix that can be used to design a curriculum for the gifted. The matrix calls for five type of content adjustment: (1) expansion of basic skills; (2) teaching core content in less time; (3) broadening the knowledge base; (4) teaching content related to the teacher's special expertise; (5) out-of-school mentoring experiences. The matrix also attends to higher level thinking skills and social-affective modification. These modifications can be applied to all curricular areas.

The term enrichment is best used to refer to curriculum experiences that are supplements to or replacements for the regular curriculum. Enrichment for the gifted should be designed to meet their specific needs and their capacity to learn more and more complex material. The term acceleration refers to learning or delivery processes: instruction or learning earlier than normal and at a faster pace. Administrative acceleration should be used to meet the needs of gifted youths for instruction at a level that matches their readiness or achievement levels and their need to learn rapidly or at a faster pace. However, it should also be recognized that gifted youths do not wait for the school to initiate acceleration. Alone or with the help of parents or siblings, they learn new skills or information ahead of the normal schedule. At home and at school, they usually comprehend and learn new skills and information much more rapidly than other youths.

The ideal educational program for gifted youths offers a combination of enriched curriculum and accelerated instruction. That is, these students are allowed to move into higher and appropriate levels of the regular school curriculum, to be taught at a pace that matches their capacity to learn, and to experience an enriched or augmented curriculum that meets their need for extended and more complex learning.

REFERENCES

Massé, P., & Gagné, F. (1983). Observations on enrichment and acceleration. In B.M. Shore, F. Gagné, S. Larivee, R.H. Tali, & R.E. Tremblay (Eds.), *Face to face with giftedness* (pp. 395–413). New York: Trillium.

Renzulli, J.S. (1977). *The enrichment triad model: A guide for devel-*

oping defensible programs for the gifted and talented. Mansfield Center, CT: Creative Learning Press.

Renzulli, J.S. (1979). *What makes giftedness.* Los Angeles, CA: National State Leadership Training Institute for the Gifted/Talented.

Stanley, J.C. (1979). Identifying and nurturing the intellectually gifted. In W.C. George, S.J. Cohn, & J.C. Stanley (Eds.), *Educating the gifted, acceleration and enrichment* (pp. 172–180). Baltimore, MD: Johns Hopkins University Press.

Tannenbaum, A.J. (1983). *Gifted children, psychological and educational perspectives.* New York: Macmillan.

See also Accelerated Placement of Gifted Children; Gifted and Talented Children

ENRICHMENT TRIAD MODEL

The Enrichment Triad Model is a teaching-learning model developed by J.S. Renzulli (1977) specifically for teaching gifted children. Renzulli's model is designed to be used with students who have three interacting clusters of traits—creativity, high ability, and task commitment. Identified students with these traits take part in a program based on three interrelated categories of enrichment that are depicted in Figure 1. These categories include (1) Type I, general exploratory activities; (2) Type II, group training activities; and (3) Type III, individual and small group investigations of real problems. The first two categories (Types I and II) are considered appropriate for all learners, whereas the third category (Type III) consists of advanced-level experiences that gifted students pursue on a self-selected basis.

To obtain additional information related to the model, Renzulli requests that interested persons write to him at the University of Connecticut, Storrs, CT 06268.

REFERENCE

Renzulli, J.S. (1977). *The Enrichment Triad Model.* Wethersfield, CT: Creative Learning Press.

See also Gifted and Talented Children

ENURESIS

Enuresis may be broadly defined as the repeated involuntary voiding of urine that occurs beyond the age at which bladder control is expected and for which there is no organic or urologic explanation. According to the American Psychiatric Association (1994), diagnostic criteria include at least two events per month for children between the ages of 5 and 6, or at least one monthly episode for older children.

Childhood enuresis is classified as either nocturnal (occurring during sleep) or diurnal (occurring during waking hours). Distinctions have also been made between primary enuresis (child has always been enuretic) and secondary enuresis (child loses previously acquired control). According to Sorotzkin (1984), the view that secondary enuresis is related to higher levels of psychological stress or organic eti-

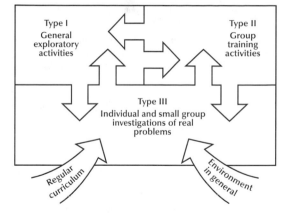

Figure 1. The Enrichment Triad Model.
Note: From *The Enrichment Triad Model,* by J.S. Renzulli. Copyright 1977 by Creative Learning Press. Reprinted with permission.

ology is not based on empirical evidence. Furthermore, the lack of prognostic value of distinguishing primary and secondary enuresis also attests to not making such a distinction.

REFERENCES

American Psychiatric Association. (1994). *Diagnostic and statistical manual of mental disorders* (4th ed.). Washington, DC: Author.

Sorotzkin, B. (1984). Nocturnal enuresis: Current perspectives. *Clinical Psychology Review, 4,* 293–315.

See also Applied Behavior Analysis; Encopresis

EPICANTHIC FOLD

The epicanthic fold, also known as epicanthus, refers to the vertical fold of skin from the upper eyelid covering the lacrimal caruncle at the inner canthus of the eye (the point where the upper and lower eyelids meet). The expression of epicanthus may be extreme, covering the entire canthus, or mild. It is a normal feature in some ethnic groups, such as those of Asian descent. Epicanthus also is commonly seen in infants under approximately 3 years (Waldrop & Halverson, 1971).

In persons for whom there is no evidence of ethnic etiology, the presence of epicanthus may represent a congenital anomaly. Epicanthus is a physical anomaly that typically is observed in persons with Down's syndrome, for example (*Blakiston's,* 1979). Epicanthus also is one of several minor physical anomalies that has been associated with learning and behavior problems in children (Rosenberg & Weller, 1973; Waldrop & Halverson, 1971).

REFERENCES

Blakiston's Gould medical dictionary (4th ed.). (1979). New York: McGraw-Hill.

Rosenberg, J.B., & Weller, G.M. (1973). Minor physical anomalies and academic performance in young school children. *Developmental Medicine & Child Neurology, 15,* 131–135.

Waldrop, M.F., & Halverson, C.F. (1971). Minor physical anomalies and hyperactive behavior in young children. In J. Hellmuth (Ed.), *The exceptional infant* (Vol. 2, pp. 343–380). New York: Brunner/ Mazel.

See also **Dysmorphic Features; Minor Physical Anomalies**

EPIDEMIOLOGY

Epidemiology is the study of specific disorders within communities to measure risk of attack and to uncover etiological clues and modes of spread. Reid (1960) defines epidemiological inquiry as "the study of the distribution of diseases in time and space, and of the factors that influence this distribution."

REFERENCE

Reid, D.D. (1960). *Epidemiological methods in the study of mental disorders.* Geneva, Switzerland: World Health Organization.

See also **Diagnosis in Special education; Etiology; Research in Special Education**

EPILEPSY

See SEIZURE DISORDERS.

EPILEPSY FOUNDATION OF AMERICA (EFA)

The Epilepsy Foundation of America (EFA) is a nonprofit, voluntary health organization devoted to epilepsy care, treatment, research, and education. The national foundation, together with its numerous local chapters, provides information on a wide variety of issues related to epilepsy, including low-cost anticonvulsant medication, legal rights, and employment. The foundation provides a discount drug pharmacy service for its members.

Numerous excellent publications relevant to the school-age child with epilepsy are available from the foundation. These include pamphlets such as "What Everybody Should Know About Epilepsy," "Epilepsy: The Teacher's Role," and "Epilepsy School Alert." School Alert is one of two major annual educational programs sponsored by the foundation. In operation since 1972, the School Alert program was developed in conjunction with the Department of School Nurses and the National Education Association; it is designed for EFA chapter use with schools in the local chapter vicinity. Some state departments of education have officially endorsed the School Alert program.

The address for the Epilepsy Foundation of America is 1828 L Street, N.W., Washington, DC 20036.

EPINEPHRINE

Epinephrine is one of the naturally occurring catecholamines (together with norepinephrine and dopamine). Its action sites are mainly in the sympathetic nervous system (Katzung, 1982). Leavitt (1982) suggests wider involvement of epinephrine in automatic processes owing to its presence in the hypothalamus. The gross actions of epinephrine are to relax bronchial muscles, constrict bronchial vasculature, and increase cardiac output, thus increasing overall oxygenation. Secondary central nervous system effects may occur through the overall increase in blood pressure and oxygen availability (McEvoy, 1984). Thus, the overall action of epinephrine is that of a mild stimulant. Because of its action as a bronchodilator, one of the chief uses of epinephrine is in providing symptomatic relief for sufferers of asthma and chronic obstructive pulmonary diseases.

REFERENCES

Katzung, B.G. (1982). *Basic and clinical pharmacology.* Los Altos, CA: Lange Medical.

Leavitt, F. (1982). *Drugs and behavior.* New York: Wiley.

McEvoy, G.K. (1984). *American hospital formulary service: Drug information 84.* Bethesda, MD: American Society of Hospital Pharmacists.

See also **Catecholamines; Dopamine**

EQUAL EDUCATIONAL OPPORTUNITY

In its earliest form, equal educational opportunity referred to a belief that education would "close no entrance to the poorest, the weakest, the humblest. Say to ambition everywhere, the field is clear, the contest fair; come, and win your share if you can!" (Woodard & Watson, 1963). A number of judicial decisions have affirmed this basic premise that underlies equal educational opportunity (e.g., *Brown v. Board of Education,* 1954, 1955; *Lau v. Nichols,* 1974; *Regents of California v. Bakke,* 1978).

While there is general agreement on what constitutes equal educational opportunity, there is some uncertainty as to whether this implies equal access to education, the process of education, or the outcomes of education (Hyman & Schaaf, 1981). In the case of handicapped learners, the concept of equal opportunity has focused on equal access and equity in the process of education.

The first equal opportunity decision involving handicapped students (*PARC v. Commonwealth,* 1971) resulted in an order providing that the state of Pennsylvania could not postpone or deny handicapped children access to a publicly supported education. In addition, those school districts that provided education to preschool children were required to provide such education for handicapped children. A similar case in the District of Columbia (*Mills v. Board of Education,* 1972) resulted in a similar judicial order, with the court indicating that if sufficient funds are not available to finance all of the services and programs that are needed and desirable in the system, then the available funds must be expended equitably in such a manner that no child is entirely excluded from a publicly supported education consistent with his needs and ability to benefit therefrom.

Apart from protections afforded by the judiciary, attorney generals in a number of states interpreted state laws, regulations, and administrative guidelines to include the public education of handicapped children and youths (e.g., Arkansas, 1973; Wisconsin, 1973).

With the passage of PL 94-142, the Education of All Handicapped Children Act, the federal government extended the concept of equal educational opportunity to include the process by which education is delivered. These rights are reaffirmed in the Individuals with Disabilities Education Act and in the Americans with Disabilities Act. Not only was access to education required, but it was to be provided, to the extent possible, with nonhandicapped students in regular education classrooms. Moreover, handicapped students were to receive specially designed instruction to meet their unique needs, as well as the related services (e.g., audiology, psychological services) required for handicapped students to benefit from special education.

REFERENCES

Hyman, J.B., & Schaaf, J.M. (1981). *Educational equity: Conceptual problems and prospects for theory.* Washington, DC: National Institute of Education.

Woodard, C.V., & Watson, T. (1963). *Agrarian rebel.* New York. Oxford University Press.

See also **Americans with Disabilities Act; Brown v. Board of Education; Individuals with Disabilities Education Act (IDEA); Mainstreaming; Mills v. Board of Education; Pennsylvania Association for Retarded Citizens v. Pennsylvania**

EQUAL EMPLOYMENT OPPORTUNITY COMMISSION (EEOC)

The purposes of the Equal Employment Opportunity Commission (EEOC) are to eliminate discrimination based on race, color, religion, national origin, and age in hiring, promoting, firing, wages, testing, training, apprenticeship, and all other conditions of employment. The commission also promotes voluntary action programs by employers, unions, and community organizations to make equal employment opportunity an actuality. The EEOC also is responsible for all compliance and enforcement activities relating to equal employment among federal employees and applicants, including handicap discrimination (*Federal Register,* 1985, p. 398).

The EEOC was created under Title VII of the Civil Rights Act of 1964. Title VII was amended by the Equal Employment Opportunity Act of 1972 and the Pregnancy Discrimination Act of 1978. The commission consists of five commissioners appointed by the president with advice and consent of the Senate to five-year terms. The president designates a commissioner as chairperson and appoints a counsel general. The work of the commission has been credited with widespread banning of various forms of discrimination against a variety of groups. Reorganization Plan One of 1978 transferred to the EEOC Section 501 of the Rehabilitation Act of 1973, which pertains to employment discrimination against handicapped persons in the federal government.

The EEOC has field offices that receive written complaints against public or private employers, labor organizations, joint labor-management, and apprenticeship programs for charges of job discrimination or age discrimination. Charges of Title VII violations in private industry or state or local government must be filed with the commission within 180 days of the alleged violation. The commission has the authority to bring suit in federal district court if a negotiated settlement cannot be found. The commission encourages settlements prior to determination by the agency through fact-finding conferences and informal methods of conciliation, conference, and persuasion.

The EEOC has issued several guidelines on employment policies and practices, the most comprehensive of which are the Guidelines on Discrimination Because of Sex (April 5, 1972) and the Guidelines on Employee Selection Procedures (August 1, 1970). The commission is also a major publisher of employment data on minorities and women. For further information, contact the Director, Office of Public Affairs, Equal Employment Opportunity Commission, Room 412, 2401 E. Street NW, Washington, DC 20507.

REFERENCES

Equal Employment Opportunity Commission. (1983). 17th annual report. *American statistics index* (10th Suppl.).

Federal Register. *The United States government manual 1985–86.* Washington, DC: U.S. Government Printing Office.

See also **Civil Rights of the Handicapped; Equal Education Opportunity**

EQUAL PROTECTION

Equal protection is a term often applied to the need for due process in the differential treatment of any persons in society. In special education, equal protection applies to placement proceedings or any other action that might result in differential treatment of a child. The term is derived from the Fourteenth Amendment to the U.S. Constitution.

The Fourteenth Amendment equal protection clause provides, in a simple, straightforward statement, the far-reaching assertion that "no state shall . . . deny to any person within its jurisdiction the equal protection of the laws." The court system has interpreted this statement in numerous cases and generally holds that it does not require that all persons be treated equally under all laws at all times. According to Overcast and Sales (1982), the essence of the constitutional guarantee provided by the equal protection clause of the Fourteenth Amendment is that any classifications made in a rule or a law must be reasonable and not of an arbitrary nature. In determining the reasonableness of a classification, the courts normally look to see whether (1) the classification itself is a reasonable one, (2) the classification furthers an appropriate or legitimate government purpose, and, (3) the classification's subgroups, or classes, are treated equally (Overcast & Sales, 1982; Sales et al., 1999).

Whenever the classification affects a fundamental right or is related to suspect criteria (e.g., is statistically related to membership in a protected class such as race or handicap), the judiciary also will examine two additional criteria. The court wishes to determine in these circumstances, which circumstances are always extant in special education, whether the classification is necessary to promote some compelling state interest, and whether the classification represents the least burdensome alternative available or that can be designed. Suspect criteria that have been identified by the courts include race, religion, national origin, alien status, legitimacy, poverty, and sex. Discrimination related to these categories takes place almost daily in the schools, however, it must be based on a valid distinction among the groups.

The courts have held that they have the right to intervene in the actions of schools and others when any basic constitutional safeguard is violated, including the equal protection clause (e.g., *Epperson v. Arkansas,* 1968; *Ingraham v. Wright,* 1977). The equal protection clause has been used to protect students' right to an education on a number of occasions; this clause may be (and certainly has been) interpreted as granting the right to equal educational opportunity. School systems cannot discriminate among groups of people when providing an education unless there is a substantial and legitimate purpose for the discrimination (Bersoff, 1982). Prior to the passage of PL 94-142, the Education for All Handicapped Children Act of 1975, advocates fighting for the right of the handicapped to attend public schools, from which they were frequently excluded, relied heavily on the equal protection clause of the Fourteenth Amendment in winning their cases. The equal protection clause also has been invoked in favor of children classified as handicapped who have argued they are not handicapped and claimed that by placing them in special education programs, they have been denied equal protection through exclusion from access to regular education with normal children (Bersoff, 1982; Reschly & Bersoff, 1999).

REFERENCES

Bersoff, D.N. (1982). The legal regulation of school psychology. In C.R. Reynolds & T.B. Gutkin (Eds.), *The handbook of school psychology.* New York: Wiley.

Overcast, T.D., & Sales, B.D. (1982). The legal rights of students in the elementary and secondary public schools. In C.R. Reynolds &

T.B. Gutkin (Eds.), *The handbook of school psychology.* New York: Wiley.

Reschly, D., & Bersoff, D. (1999). Law and school psychology. In C.R. Reynolds & T.B. Gutkin (Eds.), *The handbook of school psychology* (3rd ed.). New York: Wiley.

Sales, B.D., Krauss, D., Sacken, D., & Overcast, T. (1999). The legal rights of students. In C.R. Reynolds & T.B. Gutkin (Eds.), *The handbook of school psychology* (3rd ed.). New York: Wiley.

See also Larry P.; Marshall *v.* Georgia; Matty T. *v.* Holladay

EQUINE THERAPY

Equine therapy refers to prescribed medical treatment that uses horsemanship to alleviate an extensive array of physical, psychological, cognitive, and social disabilities. Brought to the United States from Europe, it has grown steadily in this country in popularity and credibility since 1970. Its effectiveness depends on the integration of services provided by a physician who prescribes treatment, a physical therapist who designs the therapeutic regimen, and an instructor who implements the program.

Additional information may be obtained from the Cheff Center for the Handicapped, Augusta, MI; the North American Riding for the Handicapped Association (NARHA), Ashburn, VA; and Winslow Therapeutic Riding Unlimited, Inc., Warwick, NY.

See also **Occupational Therapy; Physical Therapy**

ERRORLESS LEARNING

Errorless learning is the practice of structuring a task so that the learner is taught a skill or concept without having the opportunity to make errors. A detailed analysis of all subskills is made and then ordered into a task analysis. The presentation of the task by the teacher to the learner follows a paradigm that maximizes the probability of success. The plan calls for interrupting a response on the part of the learner if it appears that the wrong response will be given. The system uses a cuing system to maximize success. It also structures response options to maximize success. The first response would require no discrimination on the part of the learner but would consist merely of the model (correct response) presented to the learner. In a second stage, the correct response and a foil would be presented with a cue to the correct response. As the teaching progresses, the discriminations that must be made become more complex. The model has been used with the severely retarded and the young learner. The rationale for the model is that by structuring a task so that errors are not committed, the learning is more efficient. Learners do not commit errors and therefore do not waste time practicing errors.

See also **Direct Instruction; Learned Helplessness; Task Analysis**

ERTL INDEX

The problem of cultural bias in traditional measures of intelligence has led to the development of alternative assessment strategies. One rather exotic strategy is the use of the Neural Efficiency Analyzer (NEA). Introduced by Ertl (1968), this instrument is purported to measure the reaction time of brain waves to 100 randomly presented flashes of light. Ertl argued that in contrast to traditional methods of intellectual assessment, the score obtained from the Neural Efficiency Analyzer (Ertl Index) was free of cultural influences and thus was appropriate for use with any ethnic group regardless of age.

The Ertl Index consists of the average time from the onset of the stimulus light to the appropriate brain wave change. Based on this average evoked potential, an estimate of the subject's performance on a more traditional measure of cognitive functioning (e.g., Wechsler Intelligence Scale for Children) is also calculated.

While the Neural Efficiency Analyzer appeared to be an innovative attempt to minimize the cultural bias in intelligence testing, empirical evidence does not support the use of this measure on a clinical basis. Indeed, Evans, Martin, and Hatchette (1976) showed that the Ertl Index did not discriminate between children with learning problems and normal controls. Similarly, it was found that the Ertl Index did not significantly predict college grade point averages (Sturgis, Lemke, & Johnson, 1977). A review of more than a dozen major texts in assessment, psychophysiology, and learning disabilities published in 1990s failed to produce a reference to this method, and it appears to have faded from any serious consideration at this point.

REFERENCES

Ertl, J. (1968). *Evoked potential and human intelligence.* Final Report, USOE, Project No. 6–1454.

Evans, J.R., Martin, D., & Hatchette, R. (1976). Neural Efficiency Analyzer scores of reading disabled, normally reading and academically superior children. *Perceptual & Motor Skills, 43,* 1248–1250.

Sturgis, R., Lemke, E.A., & Johnson, J.J. (1977). A validity study of the Neural Efficiency Analyzer in relation to selected measures of intelligence. *Perceptual & Motor Skills, 45,* 475–478.

See also Intelligence; Intelligence Testing; Neural Efficiency Analyzer

ESQUIROL, JEAN E. (1722–1840)

Jean E. Esquirol, a French psychiatrist, studied under Philippe Pinel in Paris, and succeeded him as resident physician at the Salpetriere. His exposure of inhumane practices in French institutions for the mentally ill contributed greatly to the development of properly run hospitals in France. Esquirol identified and described the main forms of mental illness, and in 1838 published *Des Maladies Mentales,* the first scientific treatment of the subject.

REFERENCE

Esquirol, J.E. (1838). *Des maladies mentales.* Paris: Bailliere.

ETHICS

In its broadest sense, ethics is that branch of philosophy concerned with the study of how people ought to act towards each other. To state this point in the traditional manner, we would say that ethics is interested in "what ought to be" rather than simply "what is, has been, and will be" (Sidgwick, 1902, p. 22). Within the educational, medical, and mental health professions that most often work with special education populations, ethics is more often discussed in terms of ethical principles and the formal ethical codes of the various professions, which provide standards and guidelines by which professionals can guide their practice. Though it is true that ethics is concerned with telling the difference between "right and wrong," the more important, and much more difficult, ethical distinctions which the special education professions must make involve decision-making when all the alternatives are either good or bad (Steininger, Newell, & Garcia, 1984). Such situations are true ethical dilemmas, in that a reasonable case can be made for choosing each alternative, yet the ethical principles underlying each choice are in conflict. And usually, one choice precludes the other.

Special education professionals include special education teachers, counselors, social workers, psychologists, and researchers, and they work in a variety of settings that range from working with special needs children in mainstream classrooms, self-contained classrooms, residential settings, rehabilitation hospitals, homes of chronically ill children, and juvenile justice educational settings, among others. While the demands and organizational structures of the settings within which special education services are offered vary tremendously, the ethical principles and standards by which professionals guide their practices are very similar. Originating in and published by the various professional organizations, all the ethical codes embody the fundamental ethical principles of autonomy, justice, fidelity, nonmaleficence (the duty to do no harm), and beneficence (the duty to do good) identified by Kitchener (1984), who built upon the work of earlier ethicists Beauchamp & Childress (1983) and Drane (1982).

The various ethical codes, including those of the American School Counselors Association (1992), the American Counseling Association (1995), the National Education Association (1985), the American Psychological Association (1992), the National Association of Social Workers (1993), and others, are periodically revised to reflect changes in social values and priorities, as well as evolving legal rulings and statutory requirements. All professionals have a responsibility to be knowledgeable about the ethical codes of their particular profession, as those codes represent the profession's expectations of its members. In certain cases, these codes mandate or prohibit specific behaviors, and in less clear-cut situations they provide direction for further thought and consideration.

REFERENCES

American Counseling Association (ACA). (1995). *Code of ethics and standards of practice.* Alexandria, VA: Author.

American Psychological Association (APA). (1992). *Ethical principles of psychologists and code of conduct.* Washington, DC: Author.

American School Counselors Association (ASCA). (1992). *Ethical standards for school counselors.* Alexandria, VA: American Counseling Association.

Beauchamp, T.L., & Childress, J.F. (1983). *Principles of biomedical ethics* (2nd ed.). Oxford, England: Oxford University Press.

Drane, J.F. (1982). Ethics and psychotherapy: A philosophical perspective. In M. Rosenbaum (Ed.), *Ethics and values in psychotherapy.* NY: Free Press.

Kitchener, K. (1984). Intuition, critical evaluation and ethical principles: The foundation for ethical decisions in counseling psychology. *The Counseling Psychologist, 12,* 43–55.

National Association of Social Workers (NASW). (1993). *Code of ethics.* Silver Spring, MD: Author.

National Education Association. (1985). *NEA Handbook: 1985–86.* Washington, DC: Author.

Sidgwick, H. (1902). *Philosophy: Its scope and relations.* New York: Macmillan.

Steininger, M., Newell, J.D., & Garcia, L.T. (1984). *Ethical issues in psychology.* Boston: Wadsworth.

ETIOLOGY

Etiology is the study of causes of diseases and impairments. When considering those with handicaps, however, one must consider not only the specific cause, if known, but the affected individual's developmental history and exposure to intervention. Increasingly, technology is not only leading to increasing knowledge about the origins of various disorders, but also to increasing ability to ameliorate some of the conditions. Only in the most severe cases is the relationship between cause and outcome one-to-one. Research is also leading to reconsideration of some presumed origins of disorders and the extent to which various factors may underlie these origins. In particular, findings from behavior genetics research is leading to changed views of both normal and abnormal development.

EUGENICS

The term eugenics refers to attempts to improve the hereditary characteristics of man. The idea of improving the human stock arose from the observation of the great diversity of human characteristics and abilities and the tendency for characteristics to run in families. Thus the human population might be improved by breeding from the best stock, as is commonly done with considerable success in plants and animals. This idea was expressed by the Greek poet Theognis as early as the sixth century BC, and various eugenics plans for the ideal state were included in the writings of Plato.

Although eugenics is an ancient idea, it gained intellectual credibility with the general acceptance of the Darwinian theory of evolution and the idea that man is a product of an evolutionary process that continues in the present and will extend into the future. The term eugenics was coined in 1883 by Francis Galton, who was greatly influenced by the work of his cousin, Charles Darwin. Galton's eugenics proposals centered around providing scholarships and other inducements for superior young people to marry and raise large families, as well as assistance to those of low ability in limiting family size.

It seems clear that a properly administered eugenics program could achieve considerable success over a period of time, but it is instructive to note that no such program has been properly administered for a long enough time to demonstrate success on even a small scale. To have any effect on the course of human evolution, a eugenics program would have to alter the relative fertility of substantial segments of the world population over a long period of time. The human population is now so large and so disorganized politically that it is difficult to imagine how any of the past eugenics proposals could have a significant impact. Human reproductive patterns appear to be governed by forces that are still beyond human control.

Homo sapiens evolved from a common ancestor with modern apes over a period of about a million years. Although little is known about the details of this process, the early humanoids probably lived dangerously as hunters and gatherers in small isolated groups dispersed over a wide area. There must have been extremely strong selection for intelligence, language usage, and cooperativeness, since evolution of these traits was rapid. It seems likely that favorable cultural adaptations were selected along with favorable genetic traits, so that human culture evolved along with human biology.

For the past 10,000 years, humans have lived as farmers in fixed abodes. Osborn (1968) has reviewed studies of the fertility of agrarian primitive peoples performed before they were subjected to modern influences. These studies show that the more successful farmers tended to have larger families than the less successful, and that their offspring tended to have a better chance for survival. Statistics from the past century also tend to show that the more successful in terms of education and income tended to have more surviving children than did the less successful. Thus, during most of its history, humankind appears to have had a eugenic reproductive pattern. This is undoubtedly the basic cause of the current level of human achievement.

The future of human heredity is exceptionally difficult to forecast at this time because of the rapid advances that are being made in genetics and biology that will likely result in new technologies of reproduction. Already we have in vitro fertilization, which could be used to separate genetic selection from childbearing and child rearing. Perhaps the future will bring the ability to clone humans and to alter the human genetic code. With these possibilities on the horizon, and others that cannot be foreseen, the present may not be the opportune time to undertake the politically awesome task of reversing the current dysgenic reproductive trends.

REFERENCE

Osborn, F. (1968). *The future of human heredity.* New York: Weybright & Talley.

See also **Genetic Counseling; Genetic Factors in Behavior; Heredity**

EUSTIS, DOROTHY HARRISON (1886–1946)

Dorothy Harrison Eustis introduced the use of guide dogs for the blind in the United States. Born in Philadelphia, Eustis established an experimental breeding kennel for dogs at her estate in Switzerland. With her husband, George Morris Eustis, and Elliott S. (Jack) Humphrey, an American horse breeder and trainer, she began a program of experimental breeding of dogs for police and army duty. She was also aware that trained guide dogs had been used successfully by the blind in Germany.

Convinced that guide dogs could make the difference between independent and dependent living for the blind, she wrote an article, "The Seeing Eye," for *The Saturday Evening Post,* urging the use of dogs as guides for the blind. The resulting deluge of mail from blind Americans led to the establishment, in 1929, of the United States' first guide-dog training school, in Nashville, Tennessee. Seventeen men and women and their dogs were trained the first year, after which the school was moved to Morristown, New Jersey, where it continues to the present day.

REFERENCES

Eustis, D.H. (1927, November 5). The seeing eye. *The Saturday Evening Post,* 43–46.

Putnam, P.B. (1979). *Love in the lead.* New York: Dutton.

EVALUATION

In the broadest sense, evaluation is concerned with the determination of worth or merit. It includes obtaining information for use in judging the value of a program, product, procedure, or objective. To the extent that such judgments are based on accurate information, and that that information was collected in a systematic manner, evaluation can be said to have taken place, since the real worth of alternatives can be determined.

Evaluation is thus a form of disciplined inquiry, but it should not be confused with research aimed at obtaining generalizable knowledge by testing claims about functional relationships among variables describing a phenomenon. Evaluation and research possess differences in their focus, generalizability, and value emphasis. The focus of evaluation is on decisions; research seeks conclusions. The gener-

alizability of evaluation decisions is low, while research conclusions aim at high generalizability. The value of evaluation is on determining worth, while research seeks truth in the form of lawful relationships.

Although there is consensus about the nature of evaluation in general, a variety of models exist with respect to the specific nature of evaluation. For example, one model views evaluation as roughly synonymous with education measurement (e.g., Ebel, 1965), while another model bases evaluation on professional judgment (e.g., Eisner, 1975) and represents an alternative to precise measurement. This model often is used by accreditation agencies, where judgments are based on opinions of experts, whether or not the data and criteria used in making those judgments are clear. During the 1930s, Tyler (1942) introduced evaluation models based on an assessment of whether or not goals have been attained. Evaluation is viewed as a process of comparing performance data with clearly specified objectives and it may take any number of forms (e.g., Hammond, 1973; Metfessel & Michael, 1967; Popham, 1975).

The use of extrinsic criteria in evaluation was emphasized in other models (Cronbach, 1973). One model was elucidated by Scriven (1967, 1973), who described the formative-summative distinction (i.e., evaluators who formatively try to improve a still-under-development curriculum and evaluators who summatively assess the worth of a completed curriculum). He also described goal-free evaluation (i.e., focus on program outcomes both intended and unanticipated).

Stake (1967) developed the Countenance Model of evaluation, which emphasized two primary operations, descriptions and judgments that incorporate antecedent, transaction, and outcome phases of an educational program. Each of the primary operations is placed in a data matrix with intents and observations on the description side and standards and judgments on the judgment side. Based on the data matrices, it is possible to perform either relative comparisons (i.e., one program versus another), absolute comparisons (i.e., one program versus perceived standards of excellence), or both.

Another class of evaluation models is concerned not with the determination of worth per se but rather with the collection and presentation of data necessary to facilitate decisions (Alkin, 1969). An example is Stufflebeam et al.'s (1971) CIPP model, which represents four types of evaluation: context evaluation (a rationale for determining objectives); input evaluation (information on how to employ resources to achieve program objectives); process evaluation (identification of defects in the procedural design of the program); and product evaluation (measurement and interpretation of the attainments yielded by the program). These evaluations are performed in a context of delineating (i.e., focusing), obtaining (i.e., collecting, organizing, and analyzing), and providing (i.e., synthesizing) information. Another example is the Discrepancy Model (Provus, 1971), which is particularly concerned with the comparison between posited standards and actual performance. The comparison of performance with standards and resulting (if any) discrepancy leads to four alternatives: proceed unaltered, alter performance, alter standards, or terminate program.

For special education, evaluation is an important and necessary process. The variety of service delivery systems as well as the specialized curriculum, methods, and materials used need to be evaluated to determine their worth. The efficacy of such procedures cannot be assumed. Evaluation in special education is also necessary on an individual level, as evidenced by the provision in PL 94-142 that the individual education plan (IEP) contain criteria and procedures for determining, at least on an annual basis, whether goals and objectives are being achieved. The evaluation schemes for an IEP are varied (Jenkins, Deno, & Mirkin, 1979; Maher & Barbrack, 1980), but all are conceptually related to the evaluation models previously described. The evaluation should be designed to determine the effective portions of the IEP so they may be continued or expanded, and the ineffective portions, which must be revised, deleted, or completely restructured when a change in procedure is indicated.

REFERENCES

Alkin, M.C. (1969). Evaluation theory development. *Evaluation Comment, 2*(1), 2–7.

Cronbach, L.J. (1973). Course improvement through evaluation. In B.R. Worthen & J.R. Sanders (Eds.), *Educational evaluation: Theory and practice.* Belmont, CA: Wadsworth.

Ebel, R.L. (1965). *Measuring educational achievement.* Englewood Cliffs, NJ: Prentice-Hall.

Eisner, E.W. (1975). *The perceptive eye: Toward the reformation of educational evaluation.* Palo Alto, CA: Stanford Evaluation Consortium.

Hammond, R.L. (1973). Evaluation at the local level. In B.R. Worthen, & J.R. Sanders (Eds.), *Educational evaluation: Theory and practice.* Belmont, CA: Wadsworth.

Jenkins, J.R., Deno, S.L., & Mirkin, P.K. (1979). Measuring pupil progress toward the least restrictive alternative. *Learning Disability Quarterly, 2,* 81–91.

Maher, C.A., & Barbrack, C.R. (1980). A framework for comprehensive evaluation of the individualized education program (IEP). *Learning Disability Quarterly, 3,* 49–55.

Metfessel, N.S., & Michael, W.B. (1967). A paradigm involving multiple criterion measures for the evaluation of the effectiveness of school programs. *Educational & Psychological Measurement, 27,* 931–943.

Popham, W.J. (1975). *Educational evaluation.* Englewood Cliffs, NJ: Prentice-Hall.

Provus, M.M. (1971). *Discrepancy evaluation.* Berkeley, CA. McCutchan.

Scriven, M. (1967). The methodology of evaluation. In R.E. Stake (Ed.), *Curriculum evaluation.* American Education Research Association Monograph Series on Evaluation No. 1. Chicago: Rand McNally.

Scriven, M. (1973). Goal-free evaluation. In E.R. House (Ed.), *School evaluation: The politics and process.* Berkeley, CA: McCutchan.

Stake, R.E. (1967). The countenance of educational evaluation. *Teachers College Record, 68,* 523–540.

Stufflebeam, D.L., Foley, W.J., Gephart, W.J., Guba, E.G., Hammond, R.L., Merriman, H.O., & Provus, M.M. (1971). *Educational evaluation and decision making.* Itasca, IL: Peacock.

Tyler, R.W. (1942). General statement on evaluation. *Journal of Educational Research, 35,* 492–501.

***See also* Program Evaluation; Research in Special Education**

EXCEPTIONAL CHILDREN (EC)

Exceptional Children is the official scholarly journal of the Council for Exceptional Children (CEC), and has been published continuously since 1934. The quarterly journal will solicit and publish the following types of articles: scholarly data-based research papers in the field of special education, papers that will have a broad base of interest among practitioners in special education, major research projects that are of specific interest, papers that integrate previously published research into a set of conclusions, and illustration of the applications of research to educational practice. The current editors are Martha Thorlow and Bob Algozzine.

EXPECTANCY AGE

Expectancy age refers to a method used to compare performance on an intelligence or scholastic aptitude measure with performance on an achievement measure. The practice most likely had its origins in the accomplishment ratio proposed by Raymond Franzen in 1920. Franzen advocated dividing a pupil's subject age, obtained from an achievement test, by his or her mental age, obtained from an intelligence test (Formula 1):

$$100 = \left(\frac{\text{Subject age}}{\text{Mental age}} \right) = \text{Subject ratio.}$$

Formula 1 was applied to each subject matter domain measured by a particular achievement test. Separate ratios were computed for reading, mathematics, and other subjects for which achievement test results were available. Subject ratios above 100 denoted performance greater than expected for the pupil's mental age, while subject ratios below 100 signified performance lower than expected for the pupil's mental age. The average of a pupil's subject ratios was termed the accomplishment quotient, an overall index of achievement in relation to mental age. A number of serious technical flaws resulted in the abandonment of the use of ratios in relating achievement to intellectual ability or capacity.

Present-day test developers and users, like their 1920 counterparts, continue to search for meaningful ways to relate intelligence and achievement test results. Government intervention in establishing procedures for identifying children with severe learning disabilities in connection with PL 94-142 has undoubtedly served to intensify pressures placed on test users. The proliferation of several discrepancy formulas that use age equivalents or grade equivalents has resulted in further confusion and inappropriate practices (Reynolds, 1981). For example, the use of a mental age, obtained either directly from an intelligence test or indirectly when only an IQ is available, to establish an expectancy age has sometimes occurred from solving for *MA* in Formula 2:

$$MA = \frac{(CA)(IQ)}{100}$$

Age equivalents in various achievement domains (e.g., reading, mathematics, spelling) are then compared one by one with the expectancy age to identify discrepancies between intelligence and achievement. Such practices are technically indefensible for the following reasons.

Age equivalents constitute a scale of unequal units. The difference in performance between an age equivalent of 6-0 and 7-0 is, for example, much greater than the difference in performance between an age equivalent of 14-0 and 15-0 for both the intelligence and the various achievement domains. In fact, an age equivalent must be extrapolated after about age 16 for most traits because there is little real growth beyond this age. Both the unequal units of the age equivalent scale and their artificial extension, or extrapolation, render them unsuitable for any sort of statistical manipulation. Thus the simple arithmetic operation of subtraction needed to search for discrepancies between ability and achievement is untenable.

Further difficulties with age equivalents result from their unequal variability, both at successive age levels within one subject matter domain as well as among different subject matter domains. The variability of age equivalents in arithmetic computation, for example, will be considerably smaller at a particular age level than that for reading comprehension. For this reason, there is no technically sound method to interpret discrepancies at different age levels within a single subject matter domain or across subject matter domains.

An added difficulty occurs when an attempt is made to compare age equivalents from tests having dissimilar norm groups. If the norming sample for an intelligence test differs from that for an achievement test, then observed discrepancies between age equivalents on the two measures may merely represent systematic differences between the two norm groups.

One other difficulty that must be mentioned in connection with such comparisons is the correlation between intelligence and achievement in various subject matter domains. Because the relationship between intelligence and reading comprehension, for example, differs from that for intelligence and arithmetic computation, the magnitude of observed discrepancies cannot be accepted at face value without taking into account the phenomenon known as regression to the mean. Interpretation of differences is thus difficult because the correlation between each intelligence-achievement pairing differs both within a single age level as well as across age levels. For these reasons, the practice of using an expectancy age as a benchmark for undertaking achievement test comparisons to identify pupils with suspected learning disabilities or atypical ability-achievement relationships cannot be recommended on technical or logical grounds.

REFERENCES

Franzen, R. (1920, November). The accomplishment quotient. *Teachers College Record,* 114–120.

Reynolds, C. (1981). The fallacy of "two years below grade level for age" as a diagnostic criterion for reading disorders. *Journal of School Psychology, 19*(4), 350–358.

See also **Grade Equivalents; Severe Discrepancy Analysis**

EXPRESSIVE DYSPHASIA

Expressive dysphasia is used in this discussion to refer to the problem of language production encountered by those who have experienced language dysfunctions as a result of central nervous system damage. Verbal expression difficulties may be placed on a continuum ranging from mild to severe.

Brookshire (1978) considers dysphasia to be a verbal information processing disorder affecting comprehension and production of words, whether they be in isolation, phrases, or sentences.

Reductions in available vocabulary, impairment of auditory retention span, and impairments in perception and production of messages are common characteristics of dysphasic individuals (Jenkins et al., 1975).

Word-finding problems are common, and recall problems involving grammatical structures may be present, reducing the number of such structures available to express a message (Brookshire, 1978). A loss of grammatical forms is felt to be a more severe disruption of the language process than dysnomia (Jenkins et al., 1975).

Problems in using correct verb tenses may be noted, with the individual producing sentences such as "He run." Other grammatical problems such as pronoun confusion or difficulties using articles, prepositions, conjunctions, and demonstratives also have been noted (Brookshire, 1978). More complex sentence structures such as those containing dependent or relative clauses may be troublesome for the dysphasic individual to understand and use. Certain types of grammatical transformations such as questions, negations, and passive constructions also are likely to cause problems.

Speech may be fluent, except for pauses owed to word-finding difficulties. Grammar, articulation, and rhythm may be intact, but semantic problems result in speech that is devoid of meaning. This group of symptoms has been labeled Wernicke's aphasia (Brookshire, 1978). Speakers are unaware of their errors as a result of poor auditory comprehension and monitoring. The term Broca's aphasia has been used to characterize verbal expression that is labored, halting, misarticulated, and often telegraphic. In the absence of paralysis of the speech mechanism, these difficulties seem to be related to deficiencies in planning and executing voluntary motor movements required for speech production. Darley, Aronson, and Brown, cited in Brookshire (1978), argue that Broca's aphasia can be more accurately classified as apraxia of speech rather than a true aphasia.

Paraphasia also may be present. In this condition, a substitution for a target word is produced, which maintains some relationship to the word intended. The condition may take the form of reversing syllables within the same word (e.g., tevelison for television), telescoping elements of adjacent words together; omitting sounds; or substituting a word for another word with a similar sound structure. At times, a new word may be produced, called a neologism. Such errors generally are confined to specific naming attempts and may not be a part of habitual language usage (Eisenson, 1973).

REFERENCES

Brookshire, R.H. (1978). *An introduction to aphasia* (2nd ed.). Minneapolis, MN: BRK.

Eisenson, J. (1973). *Adult aphasia: Assessment and treatment.* New York: Appleton.

Jenkins, J.J., Jiménez-Pabón, E., Shaw, R.E., & Sefer, J.W. (1975). *Schuell's aphasia in adults: Diagnosis, prognosis and treatment.* Hagerstown, MD: Harper & Row.

See also **Communication Disorders; Dysnomia**

EXPRESSIVE LANGUAGE DISORDERS

See LANGUAGE DISORDERS.

EXTENDED SCHOOL YEAR FOR THE HANDICAPPED

Following the passage of the Education for all Handicapped Children Act of 1975, and between 1977 and 1981, 46 cases were filed in state and federal courts to contest the unwillingness of local educational agencies to provide special education for a period beyond the traditional school year (Marvell, Galfo, & Rockwell, 1981). The issue in those cases was whether a state or local policy of refusing to consider or provide education beyond the regular school year (usually 180 days) for handicapped children violated mandates under Part B of the Education of the Handicapped Act (EHA).

In the leading case, *Battle v. Pennsylvania* (1980), a third circuit court of appeals held that Pennsylvania's inflexible application of a 180-day maximum school year prevented the proper formulation of appropriate educational goals and was, therefore, incompatible with the EHA's emphasis on the individual. Most of the courts that have considered limitations on the length of the school year, as applied to handicapped children, have invalidated them for essentially the reasons stated in the *Battle* decision.

The court decisions have provided some general guidelines, but controversial areas remain relative to the provision of extended-year services to the handicapped. One major issue relates to determining which handicapped children are eligible for extended-year services. Generally, the individual plaintiffs or class of plaintiffs involved in those lawsuits consisted of severely handicapped children, a term that generally is not confined to a separate and specific category but indicates a degree of disability that necessitates intensified services. Courts have made it clear that determination of whether a child will receive a program in excess of the traditional school year must be made on an individual basis. To prevail, an individual must demonstrate that such a program is required for a particular child to benefit from the education provided during the preceding school year, in accordance with the interpretation of "free appropriate public education" set forth by the U.S. Supreme Court in *Board of Education v. Rowley* (1982).

Courts generally have accepted the argument advanced in the *Battle* case that severely handicapped children, as compared with nonhandicapped children, have greater difficulty in acquiring and transferring skills, are more likely to lose a greater number of skills over time (or regress), and take a longer time to recoup those skills. There is disagreement, however, as to whether a continuous program of education, without extended breaks, would lessen the likelihood of regression in certain severely handicapped children. In accordance with the *Rowley* decision, courts have stressed the importance of the individualized education program (IEP) process in educational decision making regarding extended-year services (e.g., *Crawford v. Pittman*, 1983).

Another major area of controversy concerns the cost of extended-year services. Courts have rejected arguments by school officials that limited fiscal resources justify limitations on the services that may be provided for handicapped children. Since *Mills v. Board of Education* (1972), courts have almost uniformly held that lack of funds may not limit the availability of appropriate educational services for handicapped children more severely than for nonhandicapped children (Sales et al., 1999).

REFERENCES

Marvell, T., Galfo, A., & Rockwell, J. (1981). *Student litigation: A compilation and analysis of civil cases involving students, 1977– 1981.* Williamsburg, VA: National Center for State Courts.

Sales, B., Krauss, D., Sacken, D., & Overcast, T. (1999). The legal rights of students. In C.R. Reynolds & T.B. Gutkin (Eds.), *The Handbook of School Psychology* (3rd ed.). New York: Wiley.

See also **Mills *v.* Board of Education District of Columbia; Legal Regulations of Special Education**

EXPRESSIVE VOCABULARY TEST

The Expressive Vocabulary Test (EVT) is an individually administered measure of expressive vocabulary and word retrieval for ages 2.5 through 90. It contains 190 items. Administration time varies depending on the age and ability of the examinee, but usually takes between 10–25 minutes to complete. Younger children are asked to label stimulus pictures or body parts presented, while older individuals are required to provide a synonym for the word provided that is also accompanied by a target picture. The quality of test materials reflects forethought in practical test principles. The presentation easel includes colorful stimuli that maintain interest and facilitate administration. The record form supplies the examiner with both the correct and most frequently given incorrect answers, which aids in easy, on-line scoring. The form also provides specific cues on prompting for further responses, when appropriate.

The EVT was co-normed with the Peabody Picture Vocabulary Test-III (PPVT-III), a receptive vocabulary measure, on a sample of 2,725 individuals between 2.5 and 90 years of age. The sample was representative of the 1994 U.S. census with respect to gender, race, geographic region, and socioeconomic status. Because the EVT and PPVT-III were normed on the same population, scores on these two measures are directly comparable. Both yield standard scores (with a mean of 100 and standard deviation of 15) for 25 age bands. When used together, the PPVT-III should be administered first.

REFERENCE

Williams, K. (1997). *Expressive Vocabulary Test Manual.* American Guidance Service, Inc.

EXTINCTION

Extinction, also termed planned ignoring, is a behavior reductive procedure that occurs when a behavior that has been previously reinforced is no longer reinforced in order to reduce or eliminate the occurrence of that behavior (Sulzer-Azaroff & Mayer, 1986). Extinction has been used to effectively reduce a wide variety of inappropriate behaviors, usually those that are maintained by social attention (Spiegler, 1983).

REFERENCES

Spiegler, M.D. (1983). *Contemporary behavioral therapy.* Palo Alto, CA: Mayfield.

Sulzer-Azaroff, B., & Mayer, G.R. (1986). *Achieving educational excellence using behavioral strategies.* New York: Holt, Rinehart, & Winston.

See also **Aversive Control; Aversive Stimulus; Behavior Modification; Punishment**

EYE-HAND COORDINATION

Eye-hand coordination refers to the ability of an individual to direct fine motor activities of the hand in response to directive input and feedback provided by the visual system. Eye-hand coordination is a subskill of the larger concept of visual-motor coordination. The latter concept refers to the role of vision in directing and controlling voluntary movements of the body.

A deficiency in eye-hand coordination can arise from many sources, including deficiency in visual perception, acuity, figure-ground distortion, and discrimination. Similarly, underdeveloped muscles of the hand or damage in the lower sensory-neural pathways can affect the outcome of eye-hand coordination efforts. However, excluding obvious visual defects and/or disturbance in the lower neural or musculature systems, eye-hand coordination difficulty is most likely traceable to disruption within the cerebellum.

The cerebellum is a small mass attached to the brain stem near the (dorsal, inferior) base of the cerebrum. According to Gaddes (1985), the cerebellum collects sensory inputs not only from haptic sensitivity (touch) but also from the perception of visual stimuli. The structure is apparently capable of rapid activity following relatively limited input. The cerebellum apparently "acts as a filter to smooth and coordinate muscular activity" (Gaddes, 1985, p. 53). Moreover, dysfunction in the mid-cerebellum may produce generalized motor clumsiness. If the clumsiness is manifested in a visual motor disability, the result is a decrement in manual dexterity (apraxia). Perceptual activities, writing, and other fine motor activities are generally affected. Although such conditions do disrupt the development of school progress, Gaddes (1985) maintains that little empirical evidence specifically relates dysfunction of the cerebellum to the special education classification of learning disabilities. Exceptions to this view, however, have been offered (Ayres, 1972; Valk, 1974).

As noted, eye-hand coordination has generally been studied under the more comprehensive topic of visual- (or visuomotor) motor deficiency. Several academic and behavioral deficits have been associated with this problem, including speech and language problems as well as problems in reading, arithmetic, spelling, and handwriting. Additionally, elements of emotional disorders have been associated with visual-motor difficulties. These disorders appear to stem largely from the negative attitudes developed toward academics.

The importance of eye-hand coordination is apparent. However, central issues pertaining to assessment and training remain a source of empirical controversy. Informal assessment often proceeds from the observation of daily skills thought to be dependent on eye-hand coordination ability. Activities that might be used for informal diagnosis (and perhaps training) include tracing, scissor use, lacing, design copying, and other similar tasks (Lerner, 1981). More formal assessment might be approached through laboratory-derived procedures (e.g., use of the rotary pursuit) or published tests (e.g., the *Developmental Test of Visual-Motor Integration* [Beery, 1982]). It should be noted that a review of the formal tests associated with eye-hand coordination generally reveals a lack of evidence of appropriate development, reliability, and validity (Salvia & Ysseldyke, 1985).

A number of authors have argued strongly the importance of visual-motor activities as a basis for academic deficiency and as a trainable (remediable) skill. Among the more forceful proponents of this theory was Getman (1965), who emphasized the importance of visual training, a developmental model that employed the training of a visuomotor learning schema. In Getman's view failures in visuomotor activities, of which eye-hand coordination is an element, can result in behavioral, cognitive, and academic failure.

Despite Getman's (1965) and other theorists' models, the efficiency of visuo-training approaches is a controversial topic. This is particularly true where the purpose of the training program is to improve readiness skills, intelligence test scores, or academic achievement. Additionally, there may be doubt that the programs actually train the abilities in question. Somewhat countering the research base that suggests the ineffectiveness of past efforts, Hallahan and Cruickshank (1973) have suggested that the data are limited and often too flawed to provide an adequate assessment of the potential value of training programs.

REFERENCES

Ayres, A.J. (1972). *Sensory integration and learning disorders.* Los Angeles: Western Psychological Services.

Beery, K.E. (1982). *Revised administration, scoring and teaching manual for the developmental test of visual-motor integration.* Cleveland: Modern Curriculum Press.

Gaddes, W.H. (1985). *Learning disabilities and brain function: A neuropsychological approach* (2nd ed.). New York: Springer-Verlag.

Getman, G.N. (1965). The visuomotor complex in the acquisition of learning skills. In J. Hellmuth (Ed.), *Learning disorders* (Vol. 1). Seattle, WA: Special Child Publications.

Hallahan, D.P., & Cruickshank, W. (1973). *Psychoeducational foundations of learning disabilities.* Englewood Cliffs, NJ: Prentice-Hall.

Lerner, J. (1981). *Learning disabilities: Theories, diagnosis and teaching strategies* (3rd ed.). Boston: Houghton Mifflin.

Salvia, J., & Ysseldyke, J.E. (1985). *Assessment in special and remedial education* (3rd ed.). Boston: Houghton Mifflin.

Valk, J. (1974). Neuroradiology and learning disabilities. *Tydschrift Voor Orthopedagogiek, 11,* 303–323.

See also Visual-Motor and Visual-Perceptual Problems; Visual Perception and Discrimination

EYSENCK, HANS J. (1916–1997)

Eysenck was born and educated in Berlin, Germany, openly opposing Hitler and his requirement of Nazi party membership for university admission, and moving to England in the late 1930s in protest. He received his BA in 1938 and PhD in Psychology in 1949 from the University of London. In 1946 Eysenck became senior research psychologist at Maudsley Hospital, a year later becoming head of the psychology department, founded by him within the Institute of Psychiatry at that hospital. For over 30 years he was professor of psychology at the University of London and director of the psychology unit at Maudsley Hospital. Hans J. Eysenck died on September 4, 1997 at the age of 81.

Eysenck has been described as one of the most influential, provocative, and controversial psychologists of his generation. He was a persistent critic of psychoanalysis, psychotherapy, and projective assessment, and a moving force in the establishment of clinical psychology and behavior therapy. As a behaviorist, he advocated scientific methods of personality assessment and denied the theory of the subconscious, denouncing Freud as a charlatan in the process. Eysenck applied research methods traditionally used in the study of intelligence to the study of personality, utilizing factor analysis and discriminant function analysis to identify major factors. He attempted to develop hypotheses linking those factors to widely accepted psychological and physiological concepts. This approach to the treatment of scientific data was a general theme throughout his research.

Eysenck was a pioneer in defining the structure of personality, attracting students and collaborators from around the world with his analysis of the layers of personality. *Dimensions of Personality* (1947) and *The Structure of Human Personality* (1970) provide explanations of his theory of personality, identifying the measurable areas as intelligence, neurosis, psychosis, extroversion, and introversion, all later components of psychological tests. In the behaviorist tradition, Eysenck was unconcerned about aspects of personality that could not be measured, claiming that what was not measurable did not exist. His belief in interventions based on unlearning the maladaptive behaviors that had been learned, drew criticism that he was merely treating symptoms of mental disorders, not the disease itself. He argued, however, that the symptoms are the disorder.

During his career, Eysenck published some 80 books and 1,600 journal articles dealing with a vast array of subjects. In *Decline and Fall of the Freudian Empire* (1985), he proposed that Freud was "a genius, not of science, but of propaganda," and despite his rationalism, in his later work he concluded that powerful evidence exists to support extrasensory perception and found a significant correlation between personality and the position of the planets. His self-help books such as *Check Your Own IQ* (1966) sold in the millions, and he founded two journals, *Behavior Research and Therapy* and *Personality and Individual Differences.* In 1990 he published his autobiography, *Rebel With a Cause.*

REFERENCES

Eysenck, H.J. (1947). *Dimensions of personality.* London: Routledge & Kegan Paul.

Eysenck, H.J. (1966). *Check your own IQ.* Harmondsworth, England: Penguin.

Eysenck, H.J. (1970). *The structure of human personality* (Rev. ed.). London: Methuen.

Eysenck, H.J. (1985). *Decline and fall of the Freudian empire.* Harmondsworth, England: Penguin.

Eysenck, H.J. (1990). *Rebel with a cause: The autobiography of H.J. Eysenck.* London: Allen.

F

FACILITATED COMMUNICATION

Facilitated communication (FC) is among the most controversial techniques in special education in particular, and in education and psychology in general. In FC, a trained person, called a "facilitator," supports the hand, wrist, or arm of a communication-impaired individual, most commonly one with autism or another developmental disability. The individual is thus allegedly enabled to use a finger to point to or press the keys of a typewriter, computer keyboard, or alphabet facsimile. Supporters (e.g., Biklen & Cardinal, 1997) allege that this method allows the impaired individual to communicate by typing letters, words, sentences, and numbers.

FC first emerged in the 1970s in Australia. Rosemary Crossley initiated use of the technique while working with physically disabled persons (Prior & Cummins, 1992). Douglas Biklen, who observed Crossley's methods during a trip to Australia, introduced FC to the United States in 1989. Biklen extended use of the therapy to include those afflicted with cerebral palsy, autism, and Down's Syndrome (Kerrin et al., 1998).

Biklen's results using FC were purportedly successful. As Jacobson et al. (1995, p. 753) state, ". . . previously non-verbal students were typing, with facilitation, words, sentences, and paragraphs of remarkable clarity and intellect." Reports of FC's successes and Biklen (e.g., 1993) and his Syracuse University group's workshops, publications, and conferences led to widespread adoption of, and support for, the new technique. The media, combined with hopeful parents and teachers, aroused further excitement about FC's possibilities (Rimland, 1991).

With all of the support for FC, attention began to turn to exactly what the students were typing. Biklen (1993) stated that autistic individuals reported through their facilitators that they are of normal intelligence and social competence. Some children and adolescents using FC apparently claimed that they had been physically and sexually abused for many years, although unable to report it (Zirkel, 1995). Outrage began to spread as criminal charges were filed against parents who were forcibly separated from their children. In one case, "Michael" supposedly alleged through FC that his father was sexually abusing him (Zirkel, 1995). Michael's father was criminally charged and Michael sent to live in a foster home. In an attempt to confirm Michael's alleged claim of abuse, two different facilitators working with Michael reported that he claimed to have been abused. However, prior to working with Michael, both facilitators had been informed of his previous claims. Importantly, the details of the reported abuse varied drastically between the facilitators (Zirkel, 1995). Michael's father was later cleared of all criminal charges, and he pressed charges against the facilitation agency.

Skepticism of FC developed as quickly as had initial support. The results of numerous experiments suggested that FC was, in terms if actually enabling those with disabilities to communicate, a hoax. Well-controlled, double blind studies of FC demonstrated consistently that messages were coming not from the students, but from their facilitators. On trials where both the student and the facilitator had correct information, the facilitated message was correct, but on those trials on which only the student had correct information, the message was incorrect (Thompson, 1994). In other studies, researchers used screens to separate the student's and the facilitator's visual fields, showed them both a series of pictures, and asked the student to type what s/he saw. When student and facilitator saw the same picture, the facilitated answer was correct, but when the pictures were different, the answer corresponded to what the facilitator, not the student, had seen. Further, observations of students and facilitators consistently indicated that although the facilitators consistently looked at the keyboard, the students generally did not and had no home base, as do skilled typists. Without either looking at the board or having such a base, accurate typing is virtually impossible. Individuals with impairments using various methods of adapted communication always look at the instrument through which they are communicating. Much of this evidence may be seen in the videotape, *Prisoners of Silence* (Palfreman, 1993).

Virtually all well-controlled research indicated that the facilitators were themselves, although wholly without awareness, producing the messages (Jacobson, Mulick, & Schwartz, 1995). As several authors have suggested, this unconscious motor movement is similar to what occurs in dowsing, automatic writing, and Ouija.

With all of the evidence against FC, however, Biklen and the Syracuse University group still support the technique, as reflected in a recent book (Biklen & Cardinal, 1997) and current website (http://web.syr.edu/~thefci/cfacts.htm;). In addition, Vermont, Washington, and Indiana have facilitated communication coalitions where FC is still taught and implemented (http://www.bloomington.in.us; http://moose.uvm.edu). Perhaps Biklen and others are correct in claiming that FC is effective in some cases, but they need to provide stronger and more consistent evidence than they have to date. Unfortunately, the best conclusion at this time appears to be that, in spite of its hopes and bandwagon support, FC, as have so many other methods, appears to be wholly ineffective in enabling those with severe disabilities to communicate at all, let alone normally.

REFERENCES

Biklen, D.P. (1993). *Communication unbound: How FC is challenging traditional views of autism and ability/disability.* New York: Teachers College Press.

Biklen, D., & Cardinal, D.N. (Eds.). (1997). *Contested words, contested science: Unraveling the facilitated communication controversy.* New York: Teachers College Press.

Jacobson, J.W., Mulick, J.A., & Schwartz, A.A. (1995). A history of facilitated communication: Science, pseudoscience, and antiscience. *American Psychologist, 50,* 750–765.

Kerrin, R.G., Murdock, J.Y., Sharpton, W.R., & Jones, N. (1998). Who's doing the pointing? Investigating facilitated communication in a classroom setting with students with autism. *Focus on Autism and Other Developmental Disabilities, 13,* 73–75.

Palfreman, J. (1993, October 19). *Prisoners of silence.* Frontline, Public Broadcasting Service.

Prior, M., & Cummins, R. (1992). Questions about facilitated communication and autism. *Journal of Autism and Developmental Disorders, 22,* 331–336.

Rimland, B. (1991). Facilitated communication: Problems, puzzles and paradoxes: Six challenges for researchers. *Autism Research Review International, 5*(2), 3.

Thompson, T. (1994). Reign of error: Facilitated communication. *American Journal on Mental Retardation, 98,* 670–673.

Zirkel, P.A. (1995). Facilitated communication of child abuse. *Phi Delta Kappan, 76,* 815–818.

FACTOR ANALYSIS

Factor analysis is a statistical technique intended to reduce mathematically the interrelationships within a set of variables to a simpler structure. This structure is assumed to represent one or more variables not directly measurable; hence, they may be termed latent factors. Each observed variable in the original set is related mathematically to each of the latent factors. The relationship may be zero. Factor analysis may be applied to summarize relationships among variables in a data set (Everitt, 1998).

Factor analysis was developed from practical problems in psychology and the physical sciences. When scientists measured many different variables they were unable to discern patterns of relationships because of the sheer number of correlations. Because the information in some variables might be redundant, scientists sought a method to reduce the number of variables needed to describe things they observed. This method is termed dimensional reduction. Its initial solution, mathematically straightforward, is now called principal components analysis.

REFERENCE

Everitt, B.S. (1998). Latent variables, factor analysis, and causal modeling. In N. Schooler (Ed.), *Research and Methods,* volume 5 of A. Bellack & M. Hersen (Eds.), *Comprehensive Clinical Psychology* (pp. 287–312). New York: Elsevier.

***See also* Discriminant Analysis; Multiple Regression**

FAILURE TO THRIVE

Failure to thrive (FTT) is defined as "a progressive decline in responsiveness, accompanied by loss of weight and retardation in physical and emotional development among infants who have been neglected, ignored, or institutionalized" (Goldenson, 1984, p. 283). A common diagnostic criterion is that affected children are below the fifth percentile for height and weight (Committee on Nutrition, American Academy of Pediatrics, 1985). The incidence is greatest in infancy and early childhood. It can occur in children who were normal at birth although incidence is higher in premature infants (Kotelchuck, 1980). The low growth rate has no obvious organic basis and may occur even when affected children are provided with adequate food. Regardless of the definition, FTT "has become a catchall term for all growth failures of unknown origin in young children . . . [Its] cause has remained perplexing" (Kotelchuck, 1980, pp. 29–30), and it has been linked to numerous physical problems with the direction of causality still in question (e.g., Domek, 1994).

In the 1950s, FTT and similar conditions came to be viewed psychodynamically as an outcome of maternal deprivation: the infant or young child reacted emotionally to the lack of maternal affection and contact (Bowlby, 1951). The nutritional and growth problems were said to result from the disturbed mother-infant interactions. However, the effects of maternal deprivation itself are not as great or persistent as originally reported (Rutter, 1972). Further, some studies report that mothers of FTT children, contrary to the maternal deprivation or neglect model, are not identifiably different from mothers of normal children (Kotelchuck, 1980). Affected children frequently have histories of infant feeding problems, including vomiting and poor appetite, suggesting that infants' own characteristics may be partly responsible for the condition (Pollitt & Eichler, 1976). Unfortunately, relatively few well-controlled studies of FTT and its correlates are available, resulting in uncertainty and contradictory conclusions (Kotelchuck, 1980).

Frequently associated with failure to thrive is deprivation dwarfism (Patton & Gardner, 1969). Indeed, the two may be different terms for the same basic condition (Pollitt & Eichler, 1976), since deprivation dwarfism is presumed also to result from psychosocial deprivation. In deprivation dwarfism, however, the child is stunted to the point of literally appearing dwarflike. Notable is the fact that when removed from the disturbed home setting and placed in a hospital or foster home, such children frequently show "catch-up growth" (Patton & Gardner, 1969), which tends to return them to their expected growth level.

Failure to thrive is best viewed as a heterogeneous disorder with multiple causes. Psychosocial neglect is clearly indicated as a potential issue, particularly when hospitalization is followed by catch-up growth, but it may account for only one-third of the cases. Organismically based factors associated with, among other things, feeding problems, general lack of responsiveness, hormonal disturbance, or prematurity, are more common likely causes (Kotelchuck, 1980). In cases resulting from neglect, "there is a fine line between failure to thrive and child abuse" (Committee on Nutrition, American Academy of Pediatrics, 1985, p. 199).

Regardless of uncertainty regarding FTT, educators and counselors should be sensitive to the possibility that extremely short and thin children may be suffering from psychosocial deprivation or neglect rather than from either primary malnutrition, an organically based growth disorder, or genetically determined smallness. Social and cognitive deficits occur in chronic cases (Drotar & Sturm, 1994) and may lead to special education concerns.

REFERENCES

Bowlby, J. (1951). Maternal care and mental health. *Bulletin of the World Health Organization, 3,* 355–534.

Committee on Nutrition, American Academy of Pediatrics. (1985). *Pediatric nutrition handbook* (2nd ed.). Elk Grove Village, IL: American Academy of Pediatrics.

Domek, D. (1994). Failure to thrive: Medical issues. In R. Olson, L. Mullins, J. Gillman, & J. Chaney (Eds.), *The Sourcebook of Pediatric Psychology* (pp. 26–28). Boston: Longwood.

Drotar, P., & Sturm, L. (1994). Failure to thrive: Psychological issues. In R. Olson, L. Mullins, J. Gillman, & J. Chaney (Eds.), *The sourcebook of pediatric psychology* (pp. 29–41). Boston: Longwood.

Goldenson, R.M. (Ed.). (1984). *Longman dictionary of psychology and psychiatry.* New York: Longman.

Kotelchuck, M. (1980). Nonorganic failure to thrive: The status of interactional and environmental etiologic theories. In B.W. Camp (Ed.), *Advances in behavioral pediatrics* (Vol. 1, pp. 29–51). Greenwich, CT: JAI Press.

Patton, R.G., & Gardner, L.I. (1969). Short stature associated with maternal deprivation syndrome: Disordered family environment as cause of so-called idiopathic hypopituitarism. In L.I. Gardner (Ed.), *Endocrine and genetic diseases of childhood* (pp. 77–89). Philadelphia: Saunders.

Pollitt, E., & Eichler, A. (1976). Behavioral disturbances among failure-to-thrive children. *American Journal of Diseases of Children, 130,* 24–29.

Rutter, M. (1972). *Maternal deprivation reassessed.* New York: Penguin.

See also **Deprivation, Bioneural Results of; Developmental Delay; Malnutrition; Neglect**

FALSE POSITIVE AND FALSE NEGATIVE

The term false positive, developed in the vocabulary of medicine, is often confusing when used in other circles. In medicine, a condition is reported as positive when the condition is present. When the condition is reported as negative it is in the normal or average range. Therefore, a false positive refers to a judgment about the presence of an exceptional attribute that is actually in the average range or a score or judgment that incorrectly indicates a diagnosis (or a classi-

fication) of an individual who has been diagnosed as brain injured when in fact he or she is only exhibiting reasonably normal developmental delays. A false negative, the opposite of a false positive, results when an individual is determined to be average when in fact the individual is exceptional. For example, occasionally a child with cerebral palsy (who by medical diagnosis and by definition is brain injured) will reproduce, almost perfectly, drawings of geometric figures from a test for brain injury. By the results of the drawing test, the individual is a false negative. Whereas a negative interpretation of a clinical test indicates that nothing unusual has been found, a positive interpretation indicates exceptionality or pathology.

Further confusion may result when terms used in personnel selection are mixed with clinical terminology. In personnel selection, false rejections corresponds to false positives in clinical terminology. In the language of personnel specialists, a false rejection is an individual who has a score on a selection instrument that is below the cutoff (e.g., too exceptional to be successful on the job) but who is eventually successful on the job. False acceptances are those individuals who have scores on the selection tests above the cutoff but who are failures on the job. Even though nonnumerical conditions may influence the cutoff score, or various conditions may determine success on the job, such individuals are known as false negatives.

Figure 1 gives an illustration of the concept of false negative and false positive as it has been used in the diagnosis of learning disabilities (Reynolds, 1984). Four cells are illustrated: students who are learning disabled and are so diagnosed are true positives; students who are learning disabled but are diagnosed as normal are false negatives; students who are not in fact learning disabled are false positives; students who are not learning disabled and are not diagnosed as learning disabled are true negatives. Frequently, in deciding on a diagnosis, assessment results are interpreted in a way to minimize either false negatives or false positives. In special education, learning disability diagnosis is best structured to minimize false negatives (Reynolds, 1984) while the diagnosis of mental retardation is best designed to minimize false positives.

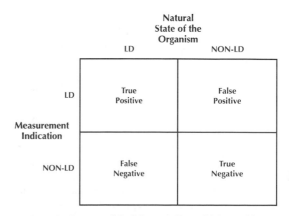

Figure 1. Concept of the false negative and false positive.

REFERENCE

Reynolds, C.R. (1984). Critical measurements issues in learning disabilities. *Journal of Special Education, 18,* 451–476.

See also **Learning Disabilities, Severe Discrepancy Analysis**

FAMILIAL DYSAUTONOMIA

Familial dysautonomia was first identified as a syndrome by Riley and his associates in 1949; it was termed Riley-Day syndrome (Riley, Day, Greeley, & Langford, 1949). The symptomatology, which is extensive, results from involvement of the central (CNS) and peripheral nervous systems (PNS) and impacts on other developing systems of the body. Primarily found in Jews of eastern European extraction, dysautonomia is transmitted genetically, with the mode of inheritance believed to be autosomal recessive. The disorder is prominently marked by the individual's insensitivity to pain, absence of lacrimation, and absence of taste buds, in addition to many functional incapacities from birth. Dysautonomia is rarely diagnosed during the neonatal period (Perlman, Benady, & Sassi, 1979), although early identification is important to its management and to provision of appropriate treatment and educational services. The disorder is progressive, with those involved rarely living beyond the fourth decade of life. Exceptions have been noted, however, and since improvement can occur, an optimistic attitude may enhance the emotional relationship between family members (Meijer & Hovne, 1981).

Neonatal functioning, when identified, may be marked by unusual posture and limb movements as well as difficulties in swallowing (Perlman et al., 1979). The latter may be associated with other oropharyngeal deficits, may interfere with subsequent normative speech development, and may require the assistance of speech therapy. With regard to problems of swallowing, early identification and the provision of a feeding program would greatly assist the young child, as feeding problems have also been found in a large percentage of this population (Ganz, Levine, Axelrod, & Kahanovitz, 1983). As an adult, the dysautonomic may be dysarthric, resulting from involvement of the CNS. The presence of altered posture and limb movements may further interfere with the integration of more complex motor patterns, and delayed developmental milestones may also be noted (Ganz et al., 1983).

Orthopedic problems, including scoliosis and kyphosis, may also develop, thus requiring the use of adaptive aids for positioning and, in severe cases, to aid in locomotion. Physical therapy input would probably be indicated by this time, as might occupational therapy to assist the individual in maintaining range of motion. If the disorder progresses to the point where hospitalization becomes necessary, as much contact as possible should be maintained with the child or adolescent's educational placement and home setting by the hospital. Decreased vitality, resulting from compromised vital functions that may occur with severe scoliosis and kyphosis, as well as with cardiovascular and pulmonary problems associated with dysautonomia, may dictate adjustment of the individual's activity levels and routines. Additionally, the presence of ataxia (difficulties with balance and maintaining position in space) presents problems of both coordination and safety to the dysautonomic individual.

Since dysautonomia is generally not marked by a decrease in IQ, individuals can benefit from educational programming geared to the mainstream student. They may also take an active role in the treatment and educational process and thus feel more in control of the disorder that has altered their lives. The maintenance of maximal functional ability can best be attained by the active involvement of dysautonomics on their own behalf, rather than through their passive compliance, often ascribed to the old medical model of treatment. Thus, individuals with familial dysautonomia require specialized educational, medical, and psychological treatment through their lifespans: the absence of any of these components represents a marked deficit in the management process.

REFERENCES

Ganz, S.B., Levine, D.D., Axelrod, F.B., & Kahanovitz, N. (1983). Physical therapy management of familial dysautonomia. *Physical Therapy, 63*(7), 1121–1124.

Meijer, A., & Hovne, R. (1981). Child psychiatric problems in "autonomous dysfunction." *Child Psychiatry & Human Development, 12*(2), 96–105.

Perlman, M., Benady, S., & Sassi, E. (1979). Neonatal diagnosis of familial dysautonomia. *Pediatrics, 63*(2), 238–241.

Riley, C.M., Day, R.L., Greeley, D.M., & Langford, W.S. (1949). Central autonomic dysfunction with defective lacrimation. I. Report of five cases. *Pediatrics, 3,* 468–478.

See also **Central Nervous System; Orthopedic Impairments**

FAMILIAL RETARDATION

The term familial is used in the field of retardation as a synonym for cultural-familial retardation and also to refer to retardation associated with known heredity disorders. Discussions about whether retardation is inherited or owed to inappropriate environmental stimulation are a part of the debate on the basis of intelligence—the nature-nurture or heredity-environment controversy—that dates back to the 1930s. That debate is unresolved, but it is now abundantly clear that some medical disorders associated with mental retardation are transmitted genetically, whereas the etiology of others is uncertain (Westling, 1986).

Numerous studies have found evidence suggesting hereditability in the cultural-familial group with mild, or educable, retardation. Reed and Reed (1965) provided extensive data on the issue. Of their 289 probands (initial cases), there were 55 who had the diagnosis of "cultural-familial, probably genetic" and had no other medical diagnosis associated with retardation. All of the 55 probands had at least one retarded primary family member, and retardation was found across two or three generations. The Reeds estimated that when both parents have cultural-familial retardation, the probability of retardation in a child born to them is about 40%, in contrast to a probability of about 1% if neither parent is retarded. The Reeds estimated that retardation incidence could be reduced by one-third to one-half if retarded couples chose not to have children. Analysis of the results of over 40 studies (excluding the challenged British studies) of identical and fraternal twins and other family relationships strongly suggests that hereditary factors are associated with intelligence, so the existence of a polygenic factor in cultural-familial retardation is credible. Consensus now seems to be that a polygenic pattern in combination with adverse environmental factors best explains retardation in the cultural-familial group.

Diagnosis of genetically based medical syndromes is more probable in cases where the degree of mental impairment is severe. Among the genetically determined disorders with which mental retardation is associated are metabolic disorders such as phenylketonuria (PKU) and chromosomal anomalies such as cri du chat (5p monosomy). Genetic defect may be inherited from the parents, or it may be due to a mutation caused by viruses, certain chemicals, or radiation. Mutant genes may be dominant or recessive, and inheritance thereafter follows normal Mendelian laws. Familial retardation continues to be considered of unknown causes (Gillberg, 1995).

Heredity is clearly a factor in some disorders with retardation as a concomitant condition. However, those are the minority of retardation cases, usually associated with severe retardation, and found primarily in cases of chromosomal defects and endocrine dysfunction. In other disorders, genes are indicated, but the mechanism is unclear. It is probable that there is a hereditary component in cultural-familial retardation, but the mechanism and amount of genetic contribution is uncertain.

REFERENCES

Gillberg, C. (1995). *Clinical child neuropsychiatry.* Cambridge, UK: Cambridge University Press.

Reed, E.W., & Reed, S.C. (1965). *Mental retardation: A family study.* Philadelphia: Saunders.

Westling, D.L. (1986). *Introduction to mental retardation.* Englewood Cliffs, NJ: Prentice-Hall.

See also **Congenital Disorders; Cretinism; Cri Du Chat Syndrome; Down's Syndrome; Heredity; Phenylketonuria; Tay-Sachs Disease**

FAMILIES OF CULTURALLY/ LINGUISTICALLY DIVERSE STUDENTS IN SPECIAL EDUCATION

See CULTURALLY/LINGUISTICALLY DIVERSE STUDENTS, FAMILIES OF.

FAMILY COUNSELING

Family counseling is an interactive process that aims to assist families in regaining a balance comfortable to all members (Perez, 1979). Family counseling is a therapeutic technique for exploring and alleviating the current interlocking emotional problems within a family system by helping family members to change dysfunctional transaction patterns together (Goldenberg & Goldenberg, 1985).

Family counseling is usually indicated when the family's ability to perform becomes inadequate. Unlike individual counseling, which focuses on the person's intrapsychic difficulties, family counseling emphasizes the relationships that transpire during therapeutic settings (Goldenberg & Goldenberg, 1983). Family counseling evolved from an extension of psychoanalytic treatment to coverage of a full range of emotional problems. The field includes work with families, the introduction of general systems theory, the evolution of child guidance and marital counseling, and an increased interest in new clinical techniques such as group therapy. It grew out of a need to expand traditional therapy from a linear approach to a multifactor systematic view of individuals and their families (Frank, 1984).

Families of children in special education require family counseling frequently simply because of the multiplicity of crises with which they are faced. Black (1982) indicates that the treatment of handicapped children and their families is as complex and diverse as are the disorders from which they suffer. The communication problems indigenous to handicapping conditions (sensory, affective, or cognitive) cause enormous problems of communication within the family. These problems can be mitigated through the use of family therapy. A frame of reference must be retained, however, in that the presence of a handicapped child does not presume family problems.

Through the use of family counseling, parents and other family members may alter their behavior patterns to produce positive changes in the behaviors of their children (Kozloff, 1979).

REFERENCES

Black, D. (1982). Handicap and family therapy. In A. Bentovin, G. Barnes, & A. Cooklin (Eds.), *Family therapy* (Vol. 2). New York: Grune & Stratton.

Frank, C. (1984). Contextual family therapy. *American Journal of Family Therapy, 12*(1), 3–12.

Goldenberg, I., & Goldenberg, H. (1983). Historical roots of contemporary family therapy. In B.B. Solman & G. Stricker (Eds.), *Handbook of family and marital therapy.* New York: Plenum.

Goldenberg, I., & Goldenberg, H. (1985). *Family therapy: An overview.* Monterey, CA: Brooks/Cole.

Kozloff, M.A. (1979). *A program for families of children with learning and behavior problems.* New York: Wiley.

Perez, J. (1979). *Family counseling: Theory and practice.* New York: Van Nostrand.

See also **Counseling the Handicapped; Family Response to a Child with Disabilities; Family Therapy**

FAMILY EDUCATIONAL RIGHTS AND PRIVACY ACT (FERPA)

The Family Educational Rights and Privacy Act (FERPA), also known as the Buckley Amendment, is a 1974 amendment to the Elementary and Secondary Education Act of 1965 (ESEA; Jacob-Timm & Hartshorne, 1995). The purpose of FERPA is to ensure that parents and eligible students have access to the education records of the student, to give parents and eligible students the right to challenge the accuracy of the content of the education records of the student at a hearing, and to limit disclosures of the student's education records to others for unauthorized purposes (Rosenfield, 1989). FERPA applies to public schools and state and local educational agencies (SEAs and LEAs) that receive federal funding (National Center for Educational Statistics [NCES], 1997). Federal funds are not made available to public schools, SEAs, or LEAs that are not in compliance with the record-keeping procedures outlined in FERPA (Jacob-Timm & Hartshorne, 1995).

Prior to the enactment of FERPA, numerous anomalies existed in the schools' record-keeping policies and procedures. First, many schools had exercised the authority of denying parents access to their child's educational records, while allowing many third parties, such as government agents and prospective employers, unlimited access to the education records. Second, certain types of information tended to accrete in the student's education records, and the information was not always based on fact or used for educational purposes. Third, the right of access to a student's education records varied from state to state and was often based on common case law and/or local policy. Fourth, parents were often denied the opportunity to challenge the accuracy of the content of their child's education records, and the parents' requests and the schools' denials went unrecorded (Rosenfield, 1989).

To address the preceding irregularities or anomalies in schools' record-keeping policies and procedures, the U.S. Congress passed FERPA, sponsored by U.S. Senator James Buckley, in 1974. The final version of the FERPA regulations were published in 1988.

The 1988 final version of the FERPA regulations were more simplified and clearer than the initial regulations issued in 1976. The 1988 final version of FERPA also reduced some of the regulatory burden placed on colleges and universities (American Association of Collegiate Registrars and Admissions Officers [AACRAO], 1995).

Since 1988, various acts and other amendments have modified FERPA. The Crime Awareness and Campus Security Act amended FERPA in 1990. This act led to modifications in the FERPA disclosure rules. In 1992, the Higher Education amendments also led to modifications in the FERPA provisions. The amendments excluded certain law enforcement records of institutes of higher education from being categorized as student education records. In 1995, modifications were made in the exclusion of certain law enforcement records as well (AACRAO, 1995). The Improving America's Schools Act in 1994 also had a major impact on the FERPA regulations. The Improving America's Schools Act essentially tightened privacy assurances for students and their families.

With the passage of the Improving America's Schools Act of 1994, a critical piece of legislation for the schools, several key components in FERPA were amended. First, parents or eligible students are now given the right to review the education records of the student maintained by the SEAs. Second, a stiff penalty is imposed on third parties who release through inappropriate means personally identifiable information from the student's education records. Third parties who release information in the student's education records through inappropriate means are not allowed to have access to education records for the next five years. Third, information on the disciplinary actions against students may now be shared with other education institutions without prior consent from a parent or eligible student. Fourth, schools may release education records of the student in order to be in compliance with certain law enforcement judicial orders or subpoenas without notifying parents or eligible students. The Improving America's Schools Act of 1994 plus the other acts and amendments enacted since 1988 are not only attempts to tighten privacy assurances for students and their families but also to extend protection to the public (NCES, 1997).

Under FERPA, parents and eligible students have four basic rights. These four basic rights include: (1) the right to examine the education records of the student; (2) the right to consent to disclosure of personally identifiable information in the education records of the student; (3) the right to challenge the content of the education records of the student at a hearing; and (4) the right to know their rights under FERPA (Rosenfield, 1989).

Parents and eligible students must be informed of their rights under FERPA, how they can act on these rights, and where they can view a copy of the school district's policies and procedures with regard to their rights. Schools must provide parents and eligible students with an annual notice informing them of their rights to examine, review, and request changes in the student's school records (34 C.F.R. § 99.7). In addition, schools must provide parents and eligible students with a written copy of the district's policies and procedures for inspection and amendment of the education records of the student, a list of the type of school records held, and location of these records upon request (34 C.F.R. § 99.6).

Another right granted under FERPA is the right of access to school records by parents and eligible students. Parental separation, divorce, or custody does not affect parents' rights to inspect and review their child's school records. Both parents have equal access to their child's records unless a court order, state statute, or legally binding document states otherwise (34 C.F.R. § 99.4). In the absence of notification, school personnel may assume that the noncustodial parent has the right to examine his or her child's school records (see *Fay v. South Colonie Central School District,* 1986). An eligible student, on the other hand, is defined as "a student who is 18 years or older or a student who is enrolled in a postsecondary education institution." When a student turns 18 years old, the rights of the parents are transferred to the student (34 C.F.R. § 99.5). However, parents retain their rights of access to the student's records as long as the student is claimed as a dependent for federal tax purposes (34 C.F.R. § 99.32). Specifically, the law requires that an educational agency or institution comply with a parent or eligible student's request for access to education records within 45 days of the formal request. The educational agency or institution must provide explanations and interpretations of the records upon request to ensure that parents or eligible students understand the content of the records.

The right to inspect and review education records is limited in a number of different areas at the postsecondary level (see AACRAO, 1995; Rosenfield, 1989) as well as the elementary and secondary levels (Rosenfield, 1989). There are also certain limitations to access that are inherent in the law's definition of what constitutes an education record (Hickman, 1987). Education records are defined as "any records maintained by an educational agency or institution or by a person acting for such an agency or institution that contains information directly related to a student" (34 C.F.R. § 99.3). Education records may come in a variety of record forms including handwritten, print, computer media, video- or audiotape, film, microfilm, and microfiche. Education records may include the results of a student's psychological evaluation or individualized education program (IEP), a videotape of a student's classroom behavior, or an audiotape of a student's oral reading performance in the classroom (Hartshorne & Boomer, 1993). Records collected or used, but not originating in the school district, are also considered to be education records, such as juvenile court or social service agency reports that the schools maintain in their files. Therefore, it is the use of the record rather than its source of origin that defines an education record under FERPA (Hartshorne & Boomer, 1993).

However, there are a number of different records which are maintained by the schools that are excluded from the definition of education records under FERPA. Law enforcement records of school-based law enforcement units that are kept apart from the education records of the student and maintained solely for law enforcement purposes are excluded (AACRAO, 1995). School employee records are also excluded. However, records of students who are employed as a result of their status as students are not exempted. Certain medical and psychological records of students who are 18 or older and/or are attending postsecondary institutions are exempted if the records made or maintained by a physician, psychiatrist, psychologist, or related professional are made, maintained, or used in connection with the provision of treatment for the student (Rosenfield, 1989). However, if the medical or psychological records are made, maintained, or used in the student's treatment, and that treatment consists of remedial education or instructional programming, then the records are not ex-

cluded (Jacob-Timm & Hartshorne, 1995). Directory information records are another category of records which are not considered to be education records as well under the FERPA definition. Directory information records are records that include personal information about students such as their name, address, telephone number, major field of study, degrees and awards received, and activities and sports participation. Schools are allowed to release this information about students without the consent of parents or eligible students as long as public notice of the categories of information to be disclosed has been given and a reasonable amount of time has been allowed for parents or eligible students to object to the disclosure (34 C.F.R. § 99.37). Prior to disclosure, however, a school official should check to see if the parents or eligible student have requested that the information be withheld. Disclosure of what appears to be common, ordinary information may in actuality be harmful to the student and may be an invasion of privacy. For example, if a student attended a special school for youth with severe emotional problems, then the disclosure of the name of the student's previous school in the directory of information would be considered an invasion of privacy (Hartshorne & Boomer, 1993). The last category of education records not subject to FERPA regulations is sole possession records. Sole possession records are "records of instructional, supervisory, and administrative personnel and educational personnel ancillary, which are in the sole possession of the maker and which are not accessible or revealed to any other person except a substitute" (34 C.F.R. § 99.3). Teachers, counselors, and other school personnel's private notes about students (e.g., observations in the classroom) that are not revealed to another individual except a substitute are considered to be sole possession records. Once teachers, counselors, or other school personnel reveal their private notes to another individual, then their notes are no longer sole possession records. Under these circumstances, the notes become part of the student's education record (Hummel, Talbutt, & Alexander, 1985).

Another area of concern in record keeping is the parents' or eligible student's access to test protocols. Psychological and educational test protocols are not private notes but are considered to be part of a student's education records (*John K. v. Board of Education from School District 65, Cook County*, 1987). For school psychologists, the parent access requirements of FERPA appear to conflict with the profession's obligation to maintain test security and observe the copyright laws of tests and test protocols (Jacob-Timm & Hartshorne, 1995). Numerous sources are available that discuss the impact of the FERPA regulations on the functioning of certain school personnel, such as school psychologists (see Bersoff & Hofer, 1990; Jacob-Timm & Hartshorne, 1995).

Even though private notes are sole possession records, not education records as defined by FERPA, private notes may be subpoenaed in a court of law. Definitive case law is limited with regard to private notes, thus, confusion surrounds the permissible nature or scope of private notes of school personnel under FERPA (Jacob-Timm & Hartshorne, 1995). Therefore, school personnel must exercise extreme caution and good judgment in the creation and maintenance of these notes.

If upon review of education records as defined by FERPA, the parents or eligible student find the information in the records to be inaccurate, misleading, or to violate the privacy or other rights of the student, then the parents or eligible student have the right to challenge the content of the records and request changes or corrections be made in the records. These requests should be made in writing according to the agency's annual notice of procedures for exercising rights to amend records. Schools must respond within a reasonable amount of time, which is not clearly defined in the law, to the parents' or eligible student's request. The school, based on its own assessment of the accuracy of the records, may agree with the parents or eligible student and amend the record, or may disagree, advise the parents or eligible student of the denial of their request, and inform the parents or eligible student of their right to a hearing. If a hearing is conducted, any party, including an official of the educational agency or institution, who does not have a direct interest in the outcome of the hearing, may conduct the hearing. The parents or eligible student are afforded the opportunity in a hearing to present evidence relevant to the issues raised and may be assisted or represented by individuals of their own choosing at their own expense, including an attorney. Once the evidence has been presented, the educational agency or institution makes a decision on amending the record. The educational agency or institution must present its findings related to its decision in writing. If the educational agency or institution agrees with the parents or eligible student that the education record is inaccurate, misleading, or in some way violates the student's rights, then the education record is amended and written notification is given to the individuals initiating the request. On the other hand, if the educational agency or institution disagrees with the parents or eligible student, the agency or institution informs the parents or eligible student of their decision in writing and allows the parents or eligible student to add a written statement to the education record explaining their objection to the content in the record (34 C.F.R. § 99.20–99.22). This written statement must be maintained as long as the record is maintained and is subject to the same guidelines if disclosed to a third party (Hickman, 1987).

A fourth right granted to parents and eligible students under FERPA is the right to confidentiality of records, or the right to consent to disclosure of personally identifiable information in the education records of the student to a third party. Personally identifiable information includes the student's name, family members' names, student personal identification numbers, personal characteristics of the student that would easily lead to the identification of the student, and other information that would make the student's identity known (34 C.F.R. § 99.3). Disclosures of personally identifiable information are prohibited without informed consent of the parents or eligible student unless specifically authorized by the Act. When the educational agency or institution releases information from the student's record at the request of the parents or eligible student, the educational agency or institution must obtain a signed written consent from the parents or eligible student. The written consent form must specify the records to be disclosed, state the purpose of the disclosure, and identify the third party to whom the disclosure is to be made (34 C.F.R. § 99.30). A copy of the information disclosed to a third party must be provided to the parents or eligible student upon their request.

Schools may also disclose information from a student's education records without informed consent from the parents or eligible student in response to a subpoena or court order. School officials must make a reasonable effort, however, to contact the parents prior to complying with the subpoena or court order, unless the subpoena is issued to enforce a law and specifies not to notify the parents. In emergency situations or crisis situations, information in a student's education records may be released without consent to protect the health or safety of the student or others (34 C.F.R. § 99.36). Organizations conducting appropriate research studies for or on behalf of the school may have access to information in a student's records, as long as the personally identifiable information on the student and student's family is destroyed when it is no longer needed (Rosenfield, 1989). However, if research is not conducted on behalf of the school, informed consent is needed for the release of personally identifiable information from the education records of the student. For example, if a school or school district decides it is in the public's interest to participate in policy evaluations or research studies and student records are to be released for these purposes, then the school or school district must obtain prior consent from the parents and eligible students before records are released (NCES, 1997). Testing organizations may also receive information if anonymous. The education records of the student may be released to certain accrediting organizations as well. Parents of a dependent student who attends a postsecondary institution may also have access to the student's education records without the consent of the student.

In general, an educational agency or institution must maintain a record that is kept with the student's education record indicating each request for record access and each disclosure of information from the student's education record. However, the requests and disclosures of parents, eligible students, and school officials who have a legitimate educational interest are exempted from this provision. The record of access must include the name of the individual who is seeking information about the student, the date access was given, and the purpose of access (Hartshorne & Boomer, 1993). The record of access must be maintained until the school or agency destroys the student's education record. Third parties who receive education records of the student must also receive a written explanation of the restrictions on the re-release of personally identifiable information from the student's records (NCES, 1997).

The Family Policy Compliance Office in the U.S. Department of Education handles complaints filed about alleged violations of FERPA. Complaints filed by parents or eligible students must be submitted to the Family Policy Compliance Office in writing. Once received, this office notifies each complainant and the educational agency or institution against which the violation has been alleged in writing about the complaint. The educational agency or institution is then given an opportunity to submit a written response (34 C.F.R. § 99.63).

The Family Policy Compliance Office conducts investigations based on alleged violations of FERPA and provides each complainant and educational agency or institution with written statements regarding the findings of their investigation. If an educational agency or institution is found to be out of compliance, then the Family Policy Compliance Office provides specific steps for an agency or institution to follow to remedy the situation. If an educational agency or institution does not voluntarily comply within a specified period of time, the matter is referred to a review board for a hearing (34 C.F.R. § 99.63).

Hearing panels designated by the chairman of the review board conduct the hearings (34 C.F.R. § 99.65). In a hearing, the hearing panel affords each party the opportunity to present their case. The hearing panel then prepares an initial written decision. Copies of the initial decision are submitted to each party as well as to the Secretary of the Department of Education. The Secretary of the Department of Education has the right to modify or reverse the hearing panel's decision. If no action is taken by the Secretary, then the initial decision of the hearing panel stands and becomes the final decision of the Secretary (34 C.F.R. § 99.67). If the Secretary finds the educational agency or institution out of compliance and it is evident that voluntary compliance cannot be secured, then federal funding is terminated until the educational agency or institution comes into compliance (34 C.F.R. § 99.64).

Portions of the FERPA regulations were incorporated into the Education for All Handicapped Children Act of 1975 (PL 94-142; Hickman, 1987), now known as the Individuals with Disabilities Education Act or IDEA. IDEA is the major special education law in the United States. Under the Act, parents are guaranteed certain procedural safeguards. One of the procedural safeguards guaranteed to parents is the opportunity for parents to examine all relevant records of their child with respect to the identification, evaluation, placement, and provision of a free appropriate public education (FAPE). With the passage of the 1997 Amendments to IDEA, a change or modification has been made in this procedural safeguard. Parents are now given the opportunity to examine all, not just relevant, records of their child with respect to the identification, evaluation, placement, and provision of FAPE (National Association of State Directors of Special Education [NASDSE], 1997).

The Family Educational Rights and Privacy Act is one of the nation's strongest privacy protection laws. Since its passage in 1974, Congress has strengthened the privacy safeguards of the education records of students as well as refined and clarified family rights and agency responsibilities to protect those rights. Educational agencies and institutions must have a written policy consistent with the FERPA regulations. School personnel should be familiar with and comply with the FERPA provisions. Under FERPA, parents and eligible students have the right to review, confirm the accuracy, and limit the disclosure of the education records of students. FERPA has made major strides in eliminating the anomalies existing in the U.S. schools' record keeping policies and procedures.

REFERENCES

American Association of Collegiate Registrars and Admissions Officers. (1995). *Implementation of the Family Educational Rights and Privacy Act of 1974 as amended—revised edition* (Report No. ISBN-0-929851-26-9). Annapolis Junction, MD: AACRAO Distribution Center. (ERIC Document Reproduction Service No. ED 384 333)

Bersoff, D N., & Hofer, P.T. (1990). The legal regulation of school psychology. In T.B. Gutkin & C.R. Reynolds (Eds.), *The handbook of school psychology* (2nd ed., pp. 939–961). New York: Wiley.

Family Educational Rights and Privacy Act of 1974, 34 C.F.R. § Part 99 (1993).

Hartshorne, T., & Boomer, L. (1993). Privacy of school records: What every special education teacher should know. *Teaching Exceptional Children, 25*(4), 32–35.

Hickman, J.A. (1987). Buckley Amendment. In C.R. Reynolds & L. Mann (Eds.), *Encyclopedia of special education* (pp. 256–258). New York: Wiley.

Hummel, D.L., Talbutt, L.C., & Alexander, M.D. (1985). *Law and ethics in counseling.* New York: Van Nostrand-Reinhold.

Jacob-Timm, S., & Hartshorne, T. (1995). *Ethics and law for school psychologists.* Brandon, VT: Clinical Psychology Publishing.

John K. v. Board of Education for School District 65, Cook County, 504 N.E. 2d. 797 (Ill. App. 1 Dist. 1987).

National Association of State Directors of Special Education. (1997). *Comparison of key issues: Current law & 1997 IDEA Amendments.* Washington, DC: National Association of State Directors of Special Education.

National Center for Education Statistics. (1997). Protecting the privacy of student education records—revised. (Report No. NCES-97–859). Washington, DC: Council of Chief School Officers. (ERIC Document Reproduction Service No. ED 405 643)

Rosenfield, S. (1989). *EHA and FERPA Confidentiality.* Washington, DC: EDLAW.

See also **Buckley Amendment; Individuals with Disabilities Education Act (IDEA)**

FAMILY POLICY COMPLIANCE OFFICE (FPCO)

The Family Policy Compliance Office (FPCO) is an office of the U.S. Department of Education whose mission is to meet the needs of learners of all ages by effectively implementing legislation that seeks to ensure student and parental rights in education: the Family Educational Rights and Privacy

Act (FERPA) and the Protection of Pupil Rights Amendment (PPRA).

Parents and eligible students who need assistance and/or wish to file a complaint under FERPA or PPRA should do so in writing to the FPCO at:

Family Policy Compliance Office
U.S. Department of Education
600 Independence Avenue. S.W.
Washington, D.C. 20202-4605

FAMILY RESPONSE TO A CHILD WITH DISABILITIES

Youngsters with disabilities have the potential to substantially alter the dynamics of family life (Knoblock, 1983). Changes in the family structure typically start with the parents' reactions to the handicapped child. Initially there is the impact of a handicapped child on parental adjustment; then there is the combined influence of the handicapped child and the resulting parental reactions on other siblings in the family.

Parents are often slow to recognize that their child is not developing normally. Typically, someone outside of the family unit (e.g., pediatrician, teacher, psychologist, etc.) will make the initial diagnosis (Cartwright, Cartwright, & Ward, 1985). Once the parents acknowledge that a problem exists, they may be initially comforted in knowing that a more severe disorder is not present. For example, a husband and wife may be relieved that their child is learning disabled but not mentally retarded. They may also be initially consoled in the belief that the problem can be cured relatively quickly. Unfortunately, many handicapping conditions cannot be corrected. Others may require years of education or therapy before the child is no longer affected by the disorder. The parents' recognition that the problem will not go away easily may trigger a crisis reaction. This reaction has been described by Luterman (1979) with reference to deaf youngsters and Kubler-Ross (1969) with reference to the terminally ill.

A state of shock is typically the first reaction of parents to learning that their child is handicapped. This period often lasts from a couple of hours to a few days and is characterized by a calm detachment from the actual problem. Parents eventually become aware that a real problem exists. Their emotional reaction at this time is heightened. Typical emotional reactions include inadequacy when faced with the demands of raising a child with special needs, confusion in light of the vast amount of new and highly technical information offered by professionals about the disorder, anger that the child does not conform to the parents' expectations, and guilt that the parents could have avoided or prevented the disability.

Parents eventually become committed to providing the experiences and opportunities necessary to maximizing the child's potential. The acknowledgment and constructive action phases are likely to recur throughout the child's development. Each time a new stage is reached (e.g., adolescence, adult independence, etc.), the parents will again have to acknowledge the problem and initiate an appropriate course of action.

Parental reaction to the handicapped child may have an equally strong influence on siblings in the family (Wolfensberger, 1967). As parents progress through the preceding stages, their relationship with other children in the family is likely to change. In general, the more time parents spend in constructive action, the more favorable the influence of siblings. Parents who actively support the development of their handicapped child are likely to provide the siblings with numerous opportunities to observe and model positive attitudes and behaviors. Siblings able to benefit from these experiences are likely to develop a positive relationship with their handicapped brother or sister. Further, these experiences may result in the siblings' developing problem-solving skills that enhance their own adjustment.

Conversely, parents who fail to reach the stage of constructive action are likely to have an adverse influence on their other children. A parent's denial, for example, may involve the handicapped youngster in the sibling's social activities. This, of course, may cause the sibling to resent his or her handicapped brother or sister. Recognition of the problem without constructive action may cause a parent to have unrealistic expectations for the handicapped child's siblings. The nonhandicapped child's exceptional performance may be expected to offset the guilt and disappointment resulting from the handicapped child's limited performance.

The care and attention required by many handicapped children may substantially diminish the time available for nonhandicapped family members. When a parent spends an excessive amount of time with a handicapped youngster, it may deprive the other children of opportunities and experiences important for their own growth and development.

In conclusion, parents of handicapped children are likely to experience a crisis reaction. This reaction begins with the initial shock and ends in acknowledgment of the handicap and constructive action. The parents' ability to move quickly through the stages of the crisis reaction to the point of constructive action will, to a large extent, determine the overall adjustment of the family.

REFERENCES

Cartwright, G.P., Cartwright, C.A., & Ward, M.E. (1985). *Educating special learners* (2nd ed.). Belmont, CA: Wadsworth.

Knoblock, P. (1983). *Teaching emotionally disturbed children.* Boston: Houghton Mifflin.

Kubler-Ross, E. (1969). *On death and dying.* New York: Macmillan.

Luterman, D. (1979). *Counseling parents of hearing impaired children.* Boston: Little, Brown.

Wolfensberger, W. (1967). Counseling the parents of the retarded. In A.A. Baumeister (Ed.), *Mental retardation: Appraisal, education and rehabilitation.* Chicago: Aldine.

See also **Parent Counseling; Parent Effectiveness Training**

FAMILY SERVICE AMERICA (FSA)

Founded in 1911 as the Family Welfare Association of America, and then the Family Service Association of America, the current name is Family Service America. The association is a federation of 280 local agencies located in over 1,000 communities. The local agencies provide a variety of services designed to resolve problems of family living, including family counseling, family life education, and family advocacy services dealing with parent-child, marital, and mental health problems.

The association compiles statistics, conducts research, sponsors competitions, and bestows awards. Publications include books, the journal *Families in Society: The Journal of Contemporary Human Services,* and a directory of member agencies. Public information activities include the production and dissemination of manuals, pamphlets, brochures, and public service releases. Biennial meetings are held in odd-numbered years. The association maintains a library with primary holdings in social work, family life, psychology and nonprofit agency management. A placement service is also available. Association offices are located at 11700 W. Lake Park Drive, Milwaukee, WI 53224, and the organization may be contacted by telephone at (414) 359-1040.

FAMILY THERAPY

Family therapy offers a distinctive theoretical approach for working with human problems, with the focus on the individual and their relationships with others, especially within the family structure. This interpersonal and systemic perspective challenged and revolutionized the etiology and treatment of psychological difficulties, and created advances in the way we view human functioning.

Prior to family therapy, methods of helping individuals focused on the individual, and sought to help the person resolve personal or intrapsychic conflicts. Thus, most therapists would treat the individual, and refuse to see the client's spouse or family members. Family therapy, however, believes that problems and solutions lie in the patterns and connections among people, that people exist in a context of mutual influence and interaction, and thus the individual must be considered part of a larger system, such as the family.

The theoretical foundations for family therapy began in the 1920s and came from diverse areas. First, research exploring the dynamics of small groups found similarities with family functioning, in that the individual exists as part of a social structure, and group membership defines various roles and interactions. Second, the child guidance movement discovered that families often played a part in the successful treatment of childhood difficulties. Third, social work, with their tradition of community service, provided additional support that the family is an important focus of intervention. Finally, research investigating family functioning and schizophrenia observed dramatic differences in the patient's behavior when family members were present, and concluded that families were a major influencing factor

in mental disorders. All of these different sources suggested families play an important part in life and development, and an interpersonal approach to solving problems is the most appropriate model from which to provide treatment.

Family therapy and the systemic principles on which it is founded continue to be utilized today in mental health centers, community agencies, and educational settings. Family therapy represents a challenging and beneficial method of intervention for many personal difficulties.

See also **Parental Counseling**

FARRELL, ELIZABETH E. (1870–1932)

Elizabeth E. Farrell, who began her teaching career in an ungraded rural school in upstate New York, accepted a position as an elementary teacher in New York City in 1900. Observing that some children were unable to make satisfactory progress in the elementary classes, Farrell, using her experience in the rural school in which she had taught all grades, formed an ungraded class for these children, the first special class in the public schools of New York City. In 1906 a Department of Ungraded Classes was formed with Farrell as director, a position she held until her death.

Farrell designed the nation's first training program for special class teachers in 1911 at the Maxwell Training School in New York City, and she taught the first university courses for special class teachers at the University of Pennsylvania in 1912. Largely through her efforts, a program to prepare special class teachers was established at the Oswego (New York) Normal School in 1916.

Farrell originated and edited *Ungraded,* the journal of the Ungraded Class Teachers' Association. She was a founder of the Association of Consulting Psychologists. In 1922 she was one of 12 special educators who founded the International Council for Exceptional Children, and she served as its first president.

REFERENCE

Warner, M.L. (1944). Founders of the International Council for Exceptional Children. *Journal of Exceptional Children, 10,* 217–223.

FEARS

See PHOBIAS AND FEARS.

FEBRILE CONVULSIONS

Febrile convulsions are seizures associated with fevers or high body temperature in childhood. Single or multiple generalized seizures in infancy or early childhood may be associated only with fever in about 4% of the population. Typically, febrile convulsions occur soon after the onset of a fever-producing illness not directly affecting the central nervous system. Usually the seizure occurs 3 to 6 hours after the onset of the fever (Livingston, 1972), although such seizures can be seen during the second or third day of an illness (Lennox-Buchtal, 1973). When the seizure begins, body temperature is usually at its peak at 39 to 40 degrees C. Acute upper respiratory infection, tonsillitis, otitis media, and bronchial pneumonia are some common causes of febrile convulsions. The seizure is usually generalized and of short duration. The movements seen with these convulsions are bilateral but may show unilateral elements. Males have been found to be more susceptible to febrile seizures than females.

Typically, this form of seizure activity is benign. Initially, it is difficult to separate these benign febrile convulsions from seizures caused by brain damage owed to unrecognized meningitis or congenital brain defects. The signs of a benign prognosis include (1) onset of the convulsions between the ages of 6 months and 4 years; (2) a normal EEG within a week after the seizure; (3) the absence of clinical signs of brain damage; and (4) the lack of atypical features or excessive duration of the attack. The chances of additional febrile seizures are about one in two if the first episode occurs before the age of 14 months, and much lower if the first attack occurs after 33 months of age. Few children have attacks later in life; however, it is not always possible to predict whether subsequent febrile or nonfebrile seizures will follow (Goldensohn, Glaser, & Goldberg, 1984).

Children who have a single febrile seizure have an excellent prognosis, as there appears to be little, if any, lasting neurological or mental deficit (National Institutes of Health, 1980). For those children who have a febrile convulsion in conjunction with a febrile seizure, preexisting central nervous system abnormalities, or a fever-inducing illness involving the central nervous system resulting in a convulsive episode, the prognosis is much less positive. Multiple febrile seizures may have a more deleterious effect.

REFERENCES

Goldensohn, E.S., Glaser, G.H., & Goldberg, M.A. (1984). Epilepsy. In L.P. Rowland (Ed.), *Merritt's textbook of neurology* (7th ed.) (pp. 629–650). Philadelphia: Lea & Febiger.

Lennox-Buchtal, M. (1973). Febrile convulsions: A reappraisal. *Electroencephalography & Clinical Neurophysiology, 32* (Suppl. 1).

Livingston, S. (1972). Epilepsy in infancy, childhood, and adolescence. In B. Wolman (Ed.), *Manual of child psychopathology* (pp. 45–69). New York: McGraw-Hill.

National Institutes of Health. (1980). Febrile seizures. A consensus of their significance, evaluation, and treatment. *Pediatrics, 66,* 1009–1030.

See also **Absence Seizures; Epilepsy; Grand Mal Seizures**

FEDERAL INTERAGENCY COORDINATING COUNCIL

In 1987, the U.S. Department of Education and the U.S. Department of Health and Human Services signed a Memorandum of Understanding endorsing the establishment of a Federal Interagency Coordinating Council (FICC). The FICC was established to mirror the role that Congress stipulated for State Interagency Coordinating Councils (SICC) who were advising and assisting state lead agencies in achieving coordinated service delivery systems to infants and toddlers served under Part H of the Education of the Handicapped Amendments passed in 1986. Reauthorization of the Act, which became the Individuals with Disabilities Education Act Amendments of 1991, statutorily established the FICC and expanded its membership.

The FICC serves by facilitating the coordination of resources at the Federal level. The FICC maintains a website on the internet at http://www.nectas.unc.edu.

FEDERAL REGISTER (FR)

The *Federal Register* (*FR*) is a uniform system for publishing all executive orders and proclamations, proposed rules, regulations, and notices of agencies authorized by Congress or the president, documents required to be published by an act of Congress, and other documents deemed by the director of the *FR* to be of sufficient interest. It does not contain rules of Congress or of the courts. As such, it serves as formal notice to the public of legally significant actions and is typically the first place of public appearance of these documents (Cohen & Berring, 1984).

Since the *FR* publishes notices promulgated by federal agencies such as the U.S. Department of Education, it is an important source for laws pertaining to special education. The Education for All Handicapped Children Act (PL 94-142), for example, was first published here. Also, the *FR* is the primary source for the announcement of grant and contract competitions administered by special education programs. Guidelines and priorities for the spending of federal special education monies are contained therein as well.

The *FR* was established by the Federal Register Act of 1935 and is considered prima facie evidence of the filing and text of the original documents. It is issued each federal working day.

REFERENCE

Cohen, M.L., & Berring, R.C. (1984). *Finding the law.* St. Paul, MN: West.

FEEBLE-MINDED

Feeble-minded is the historical term applied to individuals of borderline or mild mental retardation. The term was used as early as the sixteenth century. The Swiss physician Aurealus Theophastus Bombastus von Hahenheim, better known as Paracelsus (1493–1541), used the term feeble-minded to describe individuals who act as "healthy animals." It is no longer in common use.

See also **Idiot; Mental Retardation**

FEINGOLD DIET

One of the most widely acclaimed (particularly in the popular press) yet least empirically supported treatment modes for hyperactive children is the Feingold diet (Feingold, 1975, 1976). Specifically, Feingold (1975, 1976) has insisted that children with learning and behavioral disturbances have a natural toxic reaction to artificial food colors, flavorings, preservatives, and other substances that are added to foods to enhance their shelf life. The Feingold diet purports to be an additive-free dietary regimen that attempts to eliminate artificial flavorings, colorings, and even several nutritional fruits and vegetables containing salicylates. While the use of the Feingold diet has been frequently advocated in the therapeutic treatment of hyperactivity, learning disabilities, and other behavioral disorders, Feingold (1975) has claimed his additive-free diet to be effective in treating other handicapping conditions, including mental retardation, autism, and conduct disorders.

Feingold's unempirically substantiated claims have suggested that nearly 50% of hyperactive children in his clinical population have displayed marked improvements, and that in the majority of cases, the children have had a complete remission of symptoms as a result of the additive-free dietary regimen (Feingold, 1975, 1976). According to the Feingold group, these improvements have been demonstrated in both the social and cognitive domains. Feingold has even claimed striking academic improvements as a function of the additive-free diet, despite the fact that academic achievement has been an area little influenced by therapeutic efforts with this population (Barkley & Cunningham, 1978). Further, Feingold has insisted that the younger the child, the more expedient and pervasive the improvement that may be observed. For example, according to Feingold (1975), the efficacy of the additive-free diet in infants and toddlers may be documented in as little as 24 hours to one week. Feingold has noted that in adolescents, where improvement is predicted to be least successful, notable effects often take as long as several months to be seen.

The intense debate resulting from Feingold's claims has spawned a number of empirical studies supported by the federal government. A consensus of these studies (Conners, 1980) did not support Feingold's claims, and criticized Feingold's earlier work on the basis of its marginal research methodology, including poor placebo controls. Although Conners (1980) has accused Feingold of making "gross overstatements" (p. 109) regarding his diet, Conners does concede that a small number of hyperactive children (less than 5%) do respond favorably to the diet. Nonetheless, it is still unclear whether it is the Feingold diet that is responsible for the observed improvements in this small percentage of children or the regimen associated with the laborious preparations surrounding this special diet. For example, one research group (Harley & Matthews, 1980) has attributed any success of the Feingold diet to a placebo effect. They claim altered aspects of family dynamics often result from special procedures and efforts in implementing the Feingold diet. Others have attributed its effects to the familiar Hawthorne effect. A careful review and meta-analysis of purported support for the Feingold diet by Kavale and Furness (1999) conclude there is little support for the Feingold hypothesis. Further, it must be cautioned that many practitioners have recognized that several of the foods Feingold has recommended for elimination from children's diets contain important nutrients necessary for their growth and development. Consequently, there has been concern in the pediatric community that the Feingold diet may not fulfill the nutritional needs of children treated with this approach.

Despite the frequent failures to corroborate Feingold's (1975, 1976) original claims (Conners, 1980; Kavale & Furness, 1999) the Feingold diet continues to have loyal followers. Many parents have even formed a national association, frequently contacting food manufacturers to provide additive-free food products. Perhaps contributing to its widespread acceptance is the fact that the Feingold diet is commensurate with society's penchant for dieting, health food fads, and natural foods. Further, the Feingold diet offers an alternative to psychotropic medication, which many parents perceive as risky and having side effects, although this has not been verified in the research literature (Ross & Ross, 1982). Citing the etiology and treatment of hyperactivity as an allergic reaction to food may be more palatable to parents than neurological or psychogenic hypotheses, but it is almost certainly less valid.

REFERENCES

Barkley, R.A., & Cunningham, C.E. (1978). Do stimulant drugs improve the academic performance of hyperactive children? A review of outcome studies. *Clinical Pediatrics, 17,* 85–92.

Conners, C.K. (1980). *Food additives and hyperactive children.* New York: Plenum.

Feingold, B.F. (1975). *Why your child is hyperactive.* New York: Random House.

Feingold, B.F. (1976). Hyperkinesis and learning disabilities linked to the ingestion of artificial food colors and flavors. *Journal of Learning Disabilities, 9,* 551–559.

Harley, J.P., & Matthews, C.G. (1980). Food additives and hyperactivity in children. In R.M. Knights & D.J. Bakker (Eds.), *Treatment of hyperactive and learning disordered children.* Baltimore, MD: University Park Press.

Kavale, K., & Furness, S.A. (1999). Effectiveness of special education. In C.R. Reynolds & T.B. Gutkin (Eds.), *Handbook of School Psychology* (3rd ed.). New York: Wiley.

Ross, D.M., & Ross, S.A. (1982). *Hyperactivity: Current issues, research and theory* (2nd ed.). New York: Wiley-Interscience.

See also Hyperactivity; Hyperkinesis; Impulse Control

FENICHEL, CARL (1905–1975)

Carl Fenichel was founder and director of the League School for Seriously Disturbed Children in Brooklyn, New

York. At the school, Fenichel provided one of the early demonstrations that it is feasible to educate severely emotionally disturbed children in a day program when the parents are given intensive training in appropriate home management and care.

Educated at the City College of New York, the New School for Social Research, and Yeshiva University, where he earned the doctorate in education, Fenichel began his professional career as a teacher and psychologist. During his years at the League School, he served as professor of education at Teachers College, Columbia University, and as a lecturer at the Downstate Medical College in Brooklyn. Fenichel's pioneering League School, which he founded in 1953, served as a model for many of the first day programs for severely emotionally handicapped children in the United States.

FERAL CHILDREN

From Peter in 1724 to Victor in 1799, Kasper Hauser in 1828, and Amala and Kamala—the "Wolf Children"—in 1920, feral children have fascinated philosophers, physicians, anthropologists, educators, and psychologists. Many have looked to them for answers to questions about the nature of man, the permanence of early experience, the efficacy of education in overcoming early deprivation, and, perhaps most basically, what each of us owes to heredity and what we owe to environment. Feral children have spent various, usually unknown, amounts of their childhood living in wild or at least uncivilized conditions.

For convenience, feral children may be divided into two basic groups: (1) those who have grown up in open "wild" settings such as jungles or forests, and (2) those who have grown up under extreme environmental and social deprivation. Victor and Kasper Hauser are examples of the two groups respectively. In addition, a subgroup of "wild" children has supposedly been raised by animals. Amala and Kamala, the wolf girls of Midnapore are but two recent examples. Such so-called wolf children continue to fascinate the public at large.

The antiquity of interest in using conditions of early rearing to learn of man's nature is indicated by King Psammitichus's experiment, as reported by Herodotus. To determine what language was the most ancient, the king ordered that two infants be nursed by goats and separated from all contact with humans. Supposedly the first word they said was Phrygian for bread, and the Egyptians yielded to the primacy of the Phrygians. Ireland (1898) indicated that similar experiments were conducted by Emperor Frederick II and James IV of Scotland. Interest in feral children peaked in the eighteenth century with scientific uncertainty about who are and are not humans (the word orangutan comes from Malaysian for wild man). There were attempts to discriminate between Descartes' endowment of humans with innate ideas and Locke's empiricist concept of the human mind as a blank slate. Feral children were studied as models of Rousseau's noble savage (Lane, 1986; Shattuck, 1980).

Unfortunately, we probably will never have clear answers to any of the questions asked of feral children. Their stories have the shortcomings of all retrospective case histories—lack of complete information, potentially biased observers, the lack of repeatability and control, the impossibility of knowing how the children would have behaved if raised under normal conditions, and the virtual impossibility of empirical verification of events in the children's lives before their discovery. As one example, Dennis (1951) has pointed out that many of the children apparently did not disappear from their families until they were several years of age. How, then, can the supposed permanence of their primitive characteristics be attributed to their normal early experience? As another example, we do not know whether Genie, a contemporary deprived child, would have developed normal language under normal conditions. Given the limits of the data, the problem of direction of causality seems unsolvable. Attributing all behavioral deficits to these children's unnatural rearing environment is a clear case of illogical *post hoc ergo propter hoc* (after this, because of this) reasoning. Thus cases of feral children are almost inevitably open to alternative interpretations.

We do know from reports of numerous modern cases that considerable intellective, motor, social-emotional, and even language development can occur in formerly severely deprived, abused or neglected, and institutionalized children. Early deprivation, if not extremely prolonged, can be overcome, particularly with special and intensive intervention. Early adverse learning experiences are not irreversible, a message of considerable optimism to those in special education. Candland (1993) has sensitively portrayed the lives of many feral children and their relationships not only to the questions listed at the beginning of this entry but also to other interesting cases of humans and nonhumans.

REFERENCES

Candland, D.K. (1993). *Federal children and clever animals.* New York: Oxford University Press.

Dennis, W. (1951). A further analysis of reports of wild children. *Child Development, 22,* 153–159.

Ireland, W.W. (1898). *Mental affections of children, idiocy, imbecility, and insanity.* London: J. & A. Churchill.

Lane, H. (1976). *The wild boy of Aveyron.* Cambridge, MA: Harvard University Press.

Shattuck, R. (1980). *The forbidden experiment.* New York: Farrar Straus Giroux.

See also **Early Experience and Critical Periods; Genie; Itard, Jean M.G.; Kaspar Hauser Children; Wild Boy of Aveyron**

FERNALD, GRACE MAXWELL (1879–1950)

Grace Maxwell Fernald received her PhD in psychology from the University of Chicago in 1907. In 1911 she became head of the psychology department and laboratory at the

Grace Maxwell Fernald

Walter E. Fernald

State Normal School at Los Angeles. The remainder of her career was spent at the Normal School and the University of California at Los Angeles.

Fernald's lasting contribution to the field of education is her method for teaching disabled readers, a method that uses not only visual and auditory approaches, but kinesthetic and tactile cues as well. In 1921, UCLA's Clinic School, later renamed the Fernald School, was founded by Grace Fernald.

REFERENCES

Fernald, G. (1943). *Remedial techniques in basic school subjects.* New York: McGraw-Hill.

Sullivan, E.B., Dorcus, R.V., Allen, R.M., Bennet, M., & Koontz, L.K. (1950). Grace Maxwell Fernald. *Psychological Review, 57,* 319–321.

FERNALD, WALTER E. (1859–1924)

Walter E. Fernald received his medical degree from the Medical School of Maine, served as assistant physician at the State Hospital in Minnesota, and then became the first resident superintendent of the Massachusetts School for the Feeble-Minded (later renamed the Walter E. Fernald State School). A leader in the movement for humane treatment of mentally retarded persons, he developed an educational plan that provided a 24-hour-a-day program for each child. He devised a system for diagnosing and classifying mentally retarded people on the basis of total development rather than test results alone. Under his leadership, the Massachusetts school became an international center for the training of workers in the field of mental retardation. Fernald was also influential in the development of federal and state legislation relating to mental retardation (Wallace, 1924).

REFERENCE

Wallace, G.L. (1924). In memoriam Walter E. Fernald. *American Journal of Mental Deficiency, 30,* 16–23.

FERNALD METHOD

Multisensory remedial reading methods, commonly used in remedial and special education, are based on the premise that some children learn best when material is presented in several modalities. Typically, kinesthetic and tactile stimulation are used along with visual and auditory modalities. The multisensory programs that feature tracing, hearing, writing, and seeing are often referred to as VAKT (visual-auditory-kinesthetic-tactile) (Hallahan, Kauffman, & Lloyd, 1985).

One of the most widely known and used multisensory approaches to teaching handicapped children to read is the Fernald method (Gearheart, 1985). The rationale for the Fernald Word Learning Approach, which is usually known as the VAKT approach, was described by Fernald in 1943; it is based on the belief that if a child learns to use all senses, the child will make use of these experiences in learning to read. If one modality is weak, the others will help to convey the information. In practice, the VAKT approach is not confined to reading, but includes spelling and writing instruction. In essence, it is a language experience and whole-word approach (Kirk & Chalfant, 1984).

REFERENCES

Fernald, G. (1943). *Remedial techniques in basic school subjects.* New York: McGraw-Hill.

Gearheart, B.R. (1985). *Learning disabilities.* St. Louis: Times Mirror/Mosby.

Hallahan, D.P., Kauffman, J.M., & Lloyd, J.W. (1985). *Introduction to learning disabilities.* Englewood Cliffs, NJ: Prentice-Hall.

Kirk, S., & Chalfant, J.C. (1984). *Academic and developmental learning disabilities.* Denver: Love.

See also **Hegge-Kirk & Kirk Approach; Orton-Gillingham Method**

FETAL ALCOHOL SYNDROME (FAS)

Fetal alcohol syndrome (FAS) is a complex of physical anomalies and neurobehavioral deficits that may severely affect the children of heavy-drinking mothers. FAS is the leading type of mental retardation in the Western world (Abel & Sokol, 1987). FAS is certainly the most prevalent environmental and preventable type of mental retardation. In 1987, Abel and Sokol estimated that as much as 11% of the annual cost of mental retardation in the United States might be devoted to FAS cases, and that the annual cost of treatment of all FAS-related effects was $321 million. Prenatal exposure to alcohol has a range of effects, with less serious sequelae termed fetal alcohol effects (FAE) or alcohol-related neurodevelopmental disorder (ARND; Batshaw & Conlon, 1997). FAS is associated with three major effects, known as "the triad of the FAS" (Rosett & Weiner, 1984, p. 43): (1) growth retardation of prenatal origin, (2) characteristic facial anomalies, and (3) central nervous system dysfunction. First described in 1973 (Jones, Smith, Ulleland, & Streissguth, 1973), FAS has since been the subject of over 2,000 scientific reports (Streissguth et al., 1991). Follow-up studies, described below, confirm that alcohol is a teratogen that produces lifelong impairments.

DIAGNOSTIC CRITERIA AND COMMON CHARACTERISTICS

The Fetal Alcohol Study Group of the Research Society on Alcoholism (Rosett, 1980) established minimal criteria for diagnosis of FAS (see Figure 2), based largely on Clarren and Smith's (1978) summary of 245 cases. FAS should be diagnosed only when all three criteria are met:

1. Prenatal and/or postnatal growth retardation (below 10th percentile for body weight, length, and/or head circumference, when corrected for gestational age). However, although growth retardation has been viewed as the most common characteristic of FAS, some suggest that it may not be a primary feature and perhaps not a defining characteristic (Carmichael Olson & Burgess, 1997).

2. Central nervous system dysfunction (neurological abnormality, developmental delay, or mental impairment < 10th percentile).

3. Characteristic facies (at least two of the following three facial dysmorphologies: a. Microcephaly [head circumference < 3rd percentile]; b. Microphthalmia and/or short palpebral fissures; c. Poorly developed philtrum, thin upper lip, and flattening of the maxillary area).

In addition to these three diagnostic criteria, a history of drinking during pregnancy should be present for confident diagnosis, since no individual feature is specific to prenatal exposure to alcohol (Sokol et al., 1986).

Although estimates vary widely across study and country, worldwide incidence of FAS is estimated as approximately 1.02 per 1,000 live births. However, most cases are in the United States, where incidence is estimated to be 1.9 per 1000 births (Abel & Hannigan, 1995). The varying estimates may reflect sampling error and use of different diagnostic criteria as well as actual national/regional differences. As would be expected, incidence varies most with degree of prenatal maternal drinking. Full-blown FAS appears to be associated only with heavy maternal drinking; no cases have been reported among moderate drinkers (Abel & Sokol, 1987). FAS may occur in 30–50 percent, and

FAE in 50–70 percent, of offspring of truly alcoholic women who consume eight or more drinks daily (Little et al., 1990). Some studies report incidence as high as 80% in low SES samples (Bingol et al., 1987).

FAS has effects, although in somewhat modified form, that last into adulthood. According to longitudinal studies (e.g., Streissguth, 1986; Streissguth et al., 1991; Streissguth, Clarren, & Jones, 1985), FAS/FAE adolescents and adults were about two standard deviations below the mean in height and head circumference, although variability was high; little overall catch-up growth had occurred. The characteristic low weight of FAS/FAE children had largely disappeared, although weight/height ratios were even more variable than other measures.

The facial dysmorphologies characteristic of FAS children became less distinctive with age. Although some features, such as short palpebral fissure length, remained, growth in a number of facial areas reduced the extent of the overall abnormal appearance.

The average IQ of the 61 FAS/FAE adolescents and adults reported by Streissguth et al. (1991) was 68, just into the mild retardation level. The FAS mean was 66 and the FAE was 73. Variability was again high, with IQ ranging from 20 to 105; no FAS individual's IQ was above the low 90s. Those with the most severe growth retardation and facial dysmorphologies in childhood continued to have the lowest later IQ scores. Only 6% of the 61 were in regular classes and not receiving special help; 28% were in self-contained special education classes, 15% were neither in school nor working, and 9% were in sheltered workshops. Although academic deficits were broad, arithmetic deficits were particularly large. Academic performance had not improved since childhood.

Children and adolescents with FAS/FAE show a number of additional behavioral deficits and excesses that present serious educational and other challenges (Carmichael Olson, & Burgess, 1997; Mattson & Riley, 1998). Among the more common features are hyperactivity, inattention, impaired learning (but not impaired memory of verbal material), a wide variety of receptive and expressive language problems, and fine motor coordination. Of particular concern are reports of temper tantrums in younger affected children and serious conduct disorders in older ones. Not surprisingly, FAS children have difficulty conforming to social norms.

In Streissguth et al. (1991), even FAS/FAE adolescents and adults who were not mentally retarded showed poor socialization scores and an unusually high level of maladaptive behaviors, including poor concentration and attention, sullenness, impulsivity, lying, and cheating. However, their family environments were highly unstable, making difficult the determination as to whether these effects owed to prenatal alcohol exposure, postnatal environment, or an interaction between difficult infants and inadequate parenting. Only 9% were still living with both parents; the mothers of 66% had died, many from alcohol-related causes.

Of particular concern for those in special education are

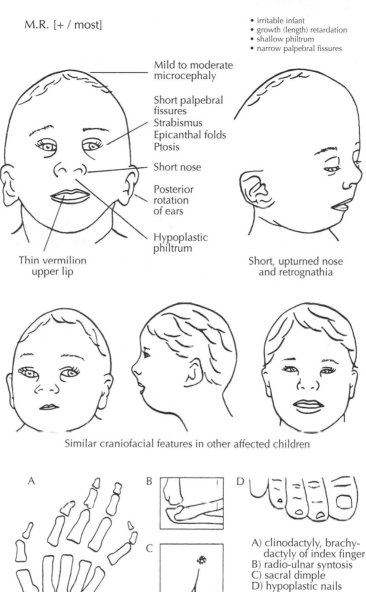

M.R. [+ / most]

- irritable infant
- growth (length) retardation
- shallow philtrum
- narrow palpebral fissures

Mild to moderate microcephaly

Short palpebral fissures
Strabismus
Epicanthal folds
Ptosis

Short nose

Posterior rotation of ears

Hypoplastic philtrum

Thin vermilion upper lip

Short, upturned nose and retrognathia

Similar craniofacial features in other affected children

A) clinodactyly, brachy-dactyly of index finger
B) radio-ulnar syntosis
C) sacral dimple
D) hypoplastic nails and 5th toe

Figure 2. Fetal alcohol syndrome.

the wide variety of behavioral sequelae, their varying degree, and the extent to which some may not be related to physical characteristics of FAS individuals. The suggestion that early stimulation may reduce the extent of some effects indicates the need for early and continued intervention (Phelps, 1995).

PREVENTION

Although 100 percent preventable theoretically, FAS may prove resistant to reduction efforts in practice. Alcohol abuse is notably resistant to treatment, and relapse rates 12 months after treatment are as high as 75% (Tucker, Vuchinich, & Harris, 1985). Thus, education programs on the

adverse effects of prenatal alcohol may lower alcohol consumption of moderately drinking women during pregnancy, but are unlikely to affect alcohol-abusing or alcoholic women, whose infants are most at risk. Although a variety of general approaches are available (Cox, 1987; Milkman & Sederer, 1990), treatment/prevention programs targeted specifically at women (Kilbey & Asghar, 1992; National Institute on Alcohol Abuse and Alcoholism, 1987) may be necessary if we wish to decrease the incidence of this tragic condition.

For more information, contact the National Organization on Fetal Alcohol Syndrome at http://www.nofas.org/what.htm.

REFERENCES

Abel, E.L., & Hannigan, J.H. (1995). Maternal risk factors in fetal alcohol syndrome: provocative and permissive influences. *Neurotoxicology and Teratology, 17,* 445–462.

Abel, E.L., & Sokol, R.J. (1987). Incidence of fetal alcohol syndrome and economic impact of FAS-related anomalies. *Drug and Alcohol Dependence, 19,* 51–70.

Batshaw, M.L., & Conlon, C.J. (1997). Substance abuse: A preventable threat to development. In M.L. Batshaw (Ed.), *Children with disabilities* (4th ed.) (pp. 143–162). Baltimore: Brookes.

Bingol, N., Schuster, C., Fuchs, M., Iosub, S., Turner, G., Stone, R.K., & Gromisch, D.S. (1987). The influence of socioeconomic factors on the occurrence of fetal alcohol syndrome. *Advances in Alcohol and Substance Abuse, 6*(4), 105–118.

Carmichael Olson, H., & Burgess, D.M. (1997). Early intervention for children prenatally exposed to alcohol and other drugs. In M.J. Guralnick (Ed.), *The effectiveness of early intervention* (pp. 109–145). Baltimore: Brookes.

Clarren, S.K. & Smith, D.W. (1978). The fetal alcohol syndrome. *New England Journal of Medicine, 298,* 1063–1067.

Cox, W.M. (Ed.). (1987). *Treatment and prevention of alcohol problems.* New York: Academic.

Jones, K.L., Smith, D.W., Ulleland, C.N., & Streissguth, A.P. (1973). Pattern of malformation in offspring of chronic alcoholic mothers. *Lancet, 1,* 1267–1271.

Kilbey, M.M., & Asghar, K. (Eds.) (1992). *Methodological issues in epidemiological, prevention, and treatment research on drug-exposed women and their children.* Research monograph 117. Rockville, MD: National Institute on Drug Abuse.

Little, B.B., Snell, L.M., Rosenfeld, C.R., Gilstrap, L.C. III, & Gant, N.F. (1990). Failure to recognize fetal alcohol syndrome in newborn infants. *American Journal of Diseases in Children, 144,* 1142–1146.

Mattson, S.N., & Riley, E.P. (1998). A review of the neurobehavioral deficits in children with fetal alcohol syndrome or prenatal exposure to alcohol. *Alcoholism: Clinical and Experimental Research, 22,* 279–294.

Milkman, H.B., & Sederer, H.B. (Eds.). (1990). *Treatment choices for alcoholism and substance abuse.* New York: Lexington.

National Institute on Alcohol Abuse and Alcoholism. (1987). *Program strategies for preventing fetal alcohol syndrome and alcohol-related birth defects.* Rockville, MD: National Institute on Alcohol Abuse and Alcoholism.

Phelps, L. (1995). Psychoeducational outcomes of fetal alcohol syndrome. *School Psychology Review, 24,* 200–212.

Rosett, H.L., & Weiner, L. (1984). *Alcohol and the fetus.* New York: Oxford University Press.

Sokol, R.J., Ager, J., Martier, S., Debanne, S., Ernhart, C., Kuzma, J., & Miller, S.I. (1986). Significant determinants of susceptibility to alcohol teratogenicity. In H.M. Wisniewski & D.A. Snider (Eds.), *Mental retardation: Research, education, and technology transfer* (pp. 87–100). *Annals of the New York Academy of Sciences, 477.*

Streissguth, A.P. (1986). The behavioral teratology of alcohol: Performance, behavioral, and intellectual deficits in prenatally exposed children. In J.R. West (Ed.), *Alcohol and brain development* (pp. 3–44). New York: Oxford University Press.

Streissguth, A.P., Aase, J.M., Clarren, S.K., Randels, S.P., LaDue, R.A., & Smith, D.F. (1991). Fetal alcohol syndrome in adolescents and adults. *Journal of the American Medical Association, 265,* 1961–1967.

Streissguth, A.P., Clarren, S.K., & Jones, K.L. (1985). Natural history of fetal alcohol syndrome: A 10-year follow-up of eleven children. *Lancet, 2,* 85–91.

Tucker, J.A., Vuchinich, R.E., & Harris, C.V. (1985). Determinants of substance abuse relapse. In M. Galizio & S.A. Maisto (Eds.), *Determinants of substance abuse* (pp. 383–421). New York: Plenum.

See also **Attention Deficit Disorder; Fetal Hydantoin Syndrome; Teratogen**

FETAL HYDANTOIN SYNDROME

The anticonvulsant agent phenytoin (Dilantin) has teratogenic effects. Uncertainty whether negative effects in infants and children was caused by medication or seizures themselves has been eliminated, owing in part to successful animal models (e.g., Adams, Vorhees, & Middaugh, 1990). Children of epileptic mothers who took phenytoin during pregnancy may show a complex of anomalies, known as fetal hydantoin syndrome (FHS) or fetal Dilantin syndrome, that include (1) mild to moderate growth deficiency, microcephaly (with associated mental deficiency); (2) cleft lip and palate, wide anterior fontanel, depressed nasal bridge, and other facies; (3) limb abnormalities, including hypoplasia of nails and terminal digits, a digitalized thumb, and dislocation of the hip; and (4) a variety of other abnormalities (Jones, 1997). Risk of damage to infants exposed prenatally to hydantoin is relatively low; exposed infants are estimated to have about a 10% chance of developing the syndrome and approximately a 33% chance of showing some effects (Jones, 1997). The fetal genotype is an important influence on susceptibility to prenatal hydantoin (Jones, 1997), and rodent models additionally indicate a dose-response relationship (Adams et al., 1990).

The biggest concern for infants diagnosed with the syndrome is the degree of mental deficiency. Although effects are generally mild relative to some other teratogens, IQs of children with the full syndrome is 71 (Jones, 1997). The infants also show a failure to thrive in the early months of life for unknown reasons.

For more information, contact the National Organization for Rare Disorders, Inc. (http://ericps.ed.uiuc.edu/npin/reswork/workorgs/nord.html).

REFERENCES

Adams, J., Vorhees, C.V., & Middaugh, L.D. (1990). Developmental neurotoxicity of anticonvulsants: Human and animal evidence on phenytoin. *Neurotoxicology and Teratology, 12,* 203–214.

Jones, K.L. (1997). *Smith's recognizable patterns of human malformation,* 5th ed. Philadelphia: W.B. Saunders.

See also **Dilantin; Fetal Alcohol Syndrome**

FIELD DEPENDENCE–INDEPENDENCE

The concepts field dependence (FD) and independence (FI) were introduced into psychology and education by H.A. Witkin (1954). He identified FD and FI as two distinct cognitive polarities that developed out of the theory of psychological differentiation. They were the terms used to accommodate broad patterns of psychological functioning associated with individual differences.

Witkin's research began with investigations of individual differences in the perception of the "upright" in the rod and frame, body adjustment, rotating room, and embedded figures tests. In each of these tests, subjects differed in the extent to which they used the external visual field or the body itself for locating the upright in space. The rod and frame test was used in early FD–FI research. Seated in darkness, the subject looks at a rod suspended in a frame. The rod and frame are independent of one another. The subject has the examiner adjust the rod to a perceived vertical position. How the subject rotates the rod in relation to the frame indicates field dependence or independence. At one extreme, when perception of the upright is dominated by the previous field (frame), this is designated field dependence. When the person sees the items as distinct from the surrounding field, this is designated field independence. The Embedded Figures Test (Witkin et al., 1977) is used more frequently and especially with younger children because of its simplicity. In this test, subjects are asked to locate a simple figure in a complex background. Witkin used this test to determine FD–FI in children between 3 and 9 years of age.

Many of the concepts derived from FD–FI styles are useful to special education. These are applicable to such issues as how children think, perceive, solve problems, and learn to relate to others. Field dependence-independence has been applied to the education of various groups, including the mentally retarded, gifted, physically disabled, and emotionally disturbed.

Tests used to determine FD–FI have aided in program planning both in school and at home. Moskowitz et al. (1981) used the embedded figures test with preschool children to determine FD–FI. He explored the early precursors of field dependence, which suggest that field-dependent children seek more emotional reassurances from their mothers than field-independent children.

Keough (1982) discussed the importance of individual differences in educational and instructional planning and practical decisions for classroom management for exceptional children. This research stressed an increased need for the sensitivity to behavioral styles of children that is essential for teachers in diagnostic and remedial planning, as well as understanding children's interpersonal demands.

The embedded figures test and Piers-Harris Self-Concept Scale were used by Guyot et al. (1984) to access FD–FI in boys and girls in grades four to six. Results suggested that field independent girls had significantly higher self concept scores than field-dependent girls. Field dependent-independent boys showed no significant difference in self-concept scores.

Gargiulo (1982) used the Children's Embedded Figures Test to measure FD–FI in retarded and nonretarded children of equal mental age. The educable mentally retarded were found to be significantly more field dependent, as were subjects characterized as impulsive.

The FD–FI may be helpful in planning and predicting concepts outcomes of cognitive restructuring programs for people with neurological impairment. Field independents will show greater lateral specialization of the hemispheres compared with field dependents (Witkin, 1979). Results showed that the left hemisphere would be for verbal and motor control processing and the right hemisphere for configuration-gestalt processing. People who are more field independent may have more developed cognitive restructuring skills, while people with more field dependence may lean toward interpersonal competencies, making this work very important for program planning.

Fitzgibbons (1965) found that field-dependent individuals are particularly attuned to social aspects of their surroundings. These persons are also better at learning materials with social content than field-independent people. This is a valuable finding for classroom learning. Fitzgibbons found that field-independent children often exhibit a function of lack of attention rather than ability. By bringing social material to attention, the performance of children who are field independent could be improved.

A final variable that has implications for education is how teachers and their related FD–FI styles affect students. Mahlios (1981) found that there were differences obtained regarding instructional behaviors among FD–FI teachers. The FD teachers seem to prefer greater interaction with pupils, while FI teachers preferred a more impersonal teaching situation. Consideration will be given to the combined effects of matched and mismatched teacher-student cognitive orientation in classroom interaction. Field dependent-independent students and teachers who were matched responded more positively to one another in both cognitive and personal characteristics (Distefano, 1970). This may create an environment more conducive to learning.

REFERENCES

Distefano, J.J. (1970). Interpersonal perceptions of field independence and field dependence among teachers and students. *Dissertation Abstracts International, 31,* 463a–464a.

Fitzgibbons, D. (1965). Field dependence and memory for incidental material. *Perceptual & Motor Skills, 21,* 743–749.

Gargiulo, M. (1982). Reflection-impulsivity and field dependence-field independence in retarded and non-retarded of equal mental age. *Bulletin of the Psychonomic Society, 19,* 74–77.

Guyot, G.W., Fairchild, L. & Johnson, B. (1984). Embedded figures test performance and self concept of elementary school children. *Perceptual and Motor Skills, 58,* 61–62.

Keough, B.K. (1982). Temperament: An individual difference of importance in intervention programs. *Topics in Early Childhood Special Education, 2,* 25–31.

Mahlios, M.C. (1981). Instructional design and cognitive styles of teachers in elementary schools. *Perceptual & Motor Skills, 52,* 335–338.

Moskowitz, D.S., Dreyer, A.S., & Kronsberg, S. (1981). Preschool children's field independence prediction from antecedent and concurrent maternal and child behavior. *Perceptual & Motor Skills, 52,* 607–616.

Witkin, H.A. (1954). *Personality through perception.* Westport, CT: Greenwood.

Witkin, H.A. (1979). Psychological differentiation: Current status. *Journal of Personality & Social Psychology, 37,* 1127–1145.

Witkin, H.A., Moore, C.A., Goodenough, D.R., & Cox, P.W. (1977). Field dependent and independent cognitive styles. *Review of Educational Research, 47,* 1–64.

See also Perception; Visual-Motor and Visual-Perceptual Problems; Visual Perception and Discrimination

FILIAL THERAPY, SPECIAL EDUCATION AND

Filial therapy was developed in the 1960s by Bernard Gurney and Michael Andronico (Andronico & Gurney, 1967). It is a "psychotherapeutic technique utilizing parents as therapeutic agents for their own children" (Hornsby & Applebaum, 1978). Primarily intended for emotionally disturbed children and their parents in outpatient school settings, filial therapy has been adapted to residential settings with borderline mentally retarded and autistic children (Hornsby & Applebaum, 1978; White, Hornsby, & Gordon, 1972). This approach is considered integrative; it empowers the parents as therapists and enlists them as agents of change. Instead of the child being taken away from the family to be helped, the message is clear that the parents are a necessary and integral part of the process. Filial therapy is a method of treatment that can be used as a preventive or remedial approach to help parents become more effective in their parenting skills.

Although filial therapy has been used in the schools (Andronico & Gurney, 1967) to lighten the work loads of school psychologists, current usage is mainly in residential facilities where psychological therapy is the central treatment focus. A typical filial therapy session has a multiimpact format. After the family has undergone initial evaluation, designed to determine the internal dynamics of the family members, the filial sessions begin. The parent who is considered to be the most distant from the child is used as the "primary therapist." It is this parent who will work with the child in the therapy playroom. The psychologist supplies this patient with a "bug" (a hearing device placed in the ear) and retires with the other parent to an observation room. The psychologist gives suggestions and directions to the parent engaging in play with the child, and uses the other parent as a co-observer and resource. After the play session is over,

the family and therapist process feelings, observations, and thoughts regarding the relationship and communication patterns between the primary therapist and the child. In addition, there is an emphasis on overall reactions to the filial therapy process. As sessions progress, the bug is removed and therapy focuses on generalizing what has been learned by the parent and child to the home setting. Ultimately, the goals of filial therapy are to enhance and improve family relations, communications, and behavior management and to increase motivation of the parents to succeed and be responsible for changes in the family system.

Special education personnel may use the principles of filial therapy in one of three ways: (1) as a continuation of filial therapy with emotionally disturbed children reentering the public schools from residential or outpatient treatment; (2) where academic and behavioral deficits require support from the home environment; and (3) as a preventive measure in classes with behaviorally disturbed children. Modifications will certainly have to be made in the school setting. For example, the bug could be replaced by the teacher modeling appropriate academic or behavioral instruction in front of the parent or the parent and child engaging in academic or behavioral instruction with the educator observing and making suggestions. The benefits of filial therapy to the special educator include enhanced rapport with the child and parents, emphasizing a cooperative and holistic effort; reinforcement of appropriate learning from home, thereby assisting the child in generalization and transfer of training; and improved communication and interaction among family members.

In the last 20 years filial therapy has come full circle. The catalyst for its possible reentry into the public schools parallels deinstitutionalization. Residential care facilities have recognized the need to reintegrate the child back into the public sector. By parents acting as coagents of change, therapeutic gains are maintained in the family and the public schools.

REFERENCES

Andronico, M.P., & Gurney, B. (1967). The potential application of filial therapy to the school situation. *Journal of School Psychology, 6,* 7–12.

Hornsby, L.G., & Applebaum, A.S. (1978). Parents as primary therapists: Filial therapy. In N.L.E. Arnold (Ed.), *Helping parents help their children.* New York: Brunner/Mazel.

White, J.H., Hornsby, L.G., & Gordon, R. (1972). Treating infantile autism with parent therapists. *International Journal of Child Psychotherapy, 1,* 83–95.

FINGERSPELLING

The American manual alphabet consists of 26 distinct hand configurations that represent the letters of the alphabet. Fingerspelling is the rapid execution of a series of these configurations to communicate words visually. As such, it is more a representation of written language than of spoken language because it excludes the phonological alterations and prosodic aspects of speech. Fingerspelling skills include the hand configurations, the characteristic positioning of the hand in a fixed central location, and the set of possible transition movements from one configuration to the next (Padden & LeMaster, 1985).

There are numerous manual alphabets in use in different countries around the world. The American manual alphabet, however, with only two exceptions (t and d), was adopted by the Fourth Congress of the World Federation of the Deaf in 1963 as the international hand alphabet. This was in part because English and French (which uses a very similar system) are the official languages of the federation, and in part because the American alphabet was already in use in many countries (Carmel, 1975; Schein, 1984).

Fingerspelling is generally used as an adjunct to sign language, especially to render proper nouns, technological terms for which no signs exist, and slang. To the uninitiated, fingerspelling seems an indistinguishable part of sign language. There are, however, several differences between signing and fingerspelling. Signs usually use one or two distinct hand configurations, while in fingerspelling there are as many configurations as there are letters in the word. Fingerspelling is done in a much smaller space than signing, with the hand remaining in a nearly fixed position as only the configuration changes. Palm orientation in fingerspelling is restricted almost exclusively to a palm out position, in contrast to signing, in which there is no such restriction. Another important difference is that while signing evolved as a means of communication in the deaf community, fingerspelling originated as an instructional tool (Padden & LeMaster, 1985).

Although fingerspelling is used primarily as a supplement to sign language, a method of manual communication exists that relies exclusively on the use of fingerspelling. This is known as the Rochester Method, after the Rochester School for the Deaf where the superintendent of the school, Zenas Westervelt, initiated its use in 1878. The method gradually fell into disuse after Westervelt's death in 1912, and though proponents of it still exist, it is seldom used today, not even in the school for which it was named (Schein, 1984).

REFERENCES

Carmel, S.J. (1975). *International hand alphabet charts.* Rockville, MD: Studio Printing.

Padden, C.A., & LeMaster, B. (1985). An alphabet on hand: The acquisition of fingerspelling in deaf children. *Sign Language Studies, 47,* 161–172.

Schein, J.D. (1984). *Speaking the language of sign.* New York: Doubleday.

See also **American Sign Language; Deaf Education**

FINLAND, SPECIAL EDUCATION IN

The first act for public education in Finland dates from the middle of the nineteenth century. The first schools for children with disabilities started at that time, beginning with special provision for deaf and blind. Compulsory education was enacted in 1921. After that, every community had to organize primary education and every municipality with more than 10,000 inhabitants had to arrange education for persons with mental retardation. There has been a strong emphasis in welfare of students in compulsory education. The schooling itself, medical care, school transportation, and hot meals are free for all pupils.

However, the equality of educational opportunities for all children was not ensured until the Comprehensive School Act of 1970 (CSA). Since then, the nine-year comprehensive school has been compulsory for all children except the severely mentally retarded, who have eleven-year compulsory schooling beginning at age six.

Special education in Finland's current comprehensive system is complementary to the mainstream education by nature, meeting the diverse needs of an entire age group and helping to fulfill the demand for organizing education to match the student's age and developmental stage (CSA, 3).

Part-time special education is concentrated in the early years of primary level comprehensive schooling, and is therefore remedial (speech disorders and specific reading and writing difficulties) and preventative by nature. At the secondary level (stages 7–9), the clinic-type part-time education mostly deals with academic learning difficulties (for example, difficulties in foreign languages and mathematics) and with behavioral problems (see figure). In most cases, the pupils have this clinic-type special education only one or two hours per week and not necessarily throughout the whole school year.

Full-time special education exists in special classes in comprehensive schools or in separate special schools. The proportion of independent and segregated special schools is decreasing in recent years. Currently, they are often located as a functional part of a bigger comprehensive school complex. According to the latest statistics (year 1994–1995), 12.2% (11,000 pupils) were enrolled at special schools, and 6.6% of students were enrolled in integrated special classes in comprehensive schools. The most important forms of full-time special education are special provisions for slow learners (so-called adjusted education), for children with emotional and behavioral disorders, and for children with disabilities.

The dropout rate in comprehensive schooling is quite low. A little more than 100 pupils of whole age groups (less than 0.3%) leave school every year without completing their compulsory studies. The dropout problem is more serious in later education and with the former students of special education, especially vocational education. According to different investigations, the admission or acceptance to further studies is not a problem. However, former students of special classes, especially former pupils of classes for emotionally and behaviorally disordered students, are at the highest risk to interrupt their studies at the vocational level. Although since 1988 the state has guaranteed that every young person with special education needs will have a place in further studies, more efforts have been put towards building transition programs for students with special needs.

The New Comprehensive Education Act was enacted August 1, 1998. The most important change is the demand of individualized education plans for pupils with special needs. The new law gives more power to municipalities for arranging the best possible education for all children. Thus, the role of special educator is reformed to more consultative and collaborative work with other school personnel as well as with other professionals.

The preparation for this kind of work is one of the key topics in the Quality of Special Education Project funded by the National Board of Education. Also, regular school teachers at primary or secondary schools, as well as teachers at schools for further education, will need more education for teaching students with special needs and, in particular, for working as a team member in IEP and ITP processes. This could be the next step in building inclusive schooling in Finland.

FITZGERALD KEY

The Fitzgerald key is used to teach deaf children to generate correct language structures. Developed by Elizabeth Fitzgerald, a deaf teacher, the key was originally described in 1926 in Fitzgerald's book, *Straight Language for the Deaf.* For the next 40 years it was widely used throughout the United States and Canada in schools and programs for the deaf (Moores, 1978; Myers & Hammill, 1976).

The key provides the deaf child with a visual guide for structuring sentences, thus helping to compensate for the lack of hearing. Fitzgerald (1976) recommended that it be used for all subjects and at all age levels. To facilitate its use she suggested that the key be painted in washable yellow paint across the top of the most prominent blackboard in the classroom.

The key consists of ordered (left-to-right) headings (key words) and six symbols that constitute a sentence pattern. Key words are used to classify new vocabulary. Nouns, for example, are classified under the keywords what and who; adjectives under the key words how many, what kind, what color. Symbols are used to classify parts of speech for which there are no associated key words. For example, the symbol for verb is =; for pronoun –. Fitzgerald was careful to point out that each of the six written symbols should always be verbally paired with the name of the part of speech it represents. The teacher may also pair the symbol with its written name. Fitzgerald believed that the use of symbols helps children at beginning levels of instruction to sense the difference between parts of speech more easily than terms such as verb, participle, etc.; however, she recommended that their use be dropped as soon as possible.

In 1947 Pugh (1955) published *Steps in Language Development for the Deaf,* a book of carefully sequenced language lessons using the key and based on the principles of instruction set forth by Fitzgerald. Although Pugh slightly modified Fitzgerald's approach, her book complemented Fitzgerald's so well that both books are traditionally used together.

The Fitzgerald key also has been recommended as an instructional program for learning-disabled students with either severe auditory or visual modality problems (Myers & Hammill, 1976). The extent of its use with this population and the degree of success achieved in remediating learning disabilities has not been documented.

REFERENCES

Fitzgerald, E. (1976). *Straight language for the deaf.* Washington, DC: Alexander Graham Bell Association for the Deaf.

Moores, D.F. (1978). *Educating the deaf: Psychology, principles, and practices.* Boston: Houghton Mifflin.

Myers, P.I., & Hammill, D.D. (1976). *Methods for learning disorders* (2nd ed.). New York: Wiley.

Pugh, B.L. (1955). *Steps in language development for the deaf.* Washington, DC: Volta Bureau.

See also **Deaf Education; Language Deficiencies and Deficits; Written Language of Handicapped**

FOCUS ON AUTISM AND OTHER DEVELOPMENTAL DISABILITIES

In 1988, Pro-Ed, Inc. bought the quarterly newsletter, *Focus on Autistic Behavior,* from Aspen Press. In 1996, the publication was upgraded to a 64 page-per-issue quarterly journal to respond to multidisciplinary matters related to autism as well as to other types of developmental disabilities. The journal was retitled *Focus on Autism and Other Developmental Disabilities.* This journal covers practical elements of management, treatment, planning, and education of interest to practitioners, researchers, higher education personnel, parents, and other persons concerned with understanding and improving practices and conditions affecting persons with autism and other developmental disorders. Included are articles on a variety of topics, including assessment, vocational training, curricula, educational strategies, treatments, integration methods, and parent/family involvement.

FÖLLING DISEASE

See PHENYLKETONURIA.

FOLLOW THROUGH

Follow Through was initiated through an amendment to the Economic Opportunity Act. Project Head Start had begun as an early intervention program for children from low-income families under this legislation (Rhine, 1981). Early reports on small groups of Head Start children had shown an average increase in IQ of about 10 points after a year of preschool, but the first major evaluation of Head Start showed initial gains dissipating soon after the children entered elementary school. Follow Through was intended to provide continued support when children were in the elementary grades to help preserve and enhance any gains made in preschool (Haywood, 1982). Follow Through was plagued by insufficient funds and by conflicting interpretations of data gathered in evaluation studies of planned variations of different educational models.

Probably the safest statement to make about the Follow Through planned variation experiment is that with structured approaches such as applied behavior analysis or direct instruction models, scholastic achievement is facilitated, but clearly there is still much to be learned about compensatory programs and their effects.

REFERENCES
Haywood, H.C. (1982). Compensatory education. *Peabody Journal of Education, 59,* 272–300.

Rhine, W.R. (1981). Follow Through: Perspectives and possibilities. In W.R. Rhine (Ed.), *Making schools more effective.* New York: Academic.

See also Abecedarian Project; Head Start; Head Start for the Handicapped

FOOD ADDITIVES
In the 1970s and 1980s, one particularly fashionable explanation in the etiology of a number of learning disorders was proposed by Feingold et al. (Feingold, German, Brahm, & Slimmers, 1973). They contended that naturally occurring salicylates in fruits, vegetables, and other foods, artificial food colorings, and preservatives could produce a toxic reaction of cerebral irritability that could result in hyperactivity and other learning disorders in genetically predisposed children. This hypothesis has been subsequently revised by Feingold (1975a, 1976) to mitigate the importance of naturally occurring salicylates and to emphasize the role of two antioxidant preservatives, BHA (butylated hydroxyanisole) and BHT (butylated hydroxytoluene) (Feingold and Feingold, 1979). It is important to note that there has been a significant distinction made between food additives' allergic effect, which does occur for a small percentage of hyperactive children (Conners, 1980), and the toxic effect of these additives, which Feingold and Feingold (1979) have more recently hypothesized to explain the origins of learning disorders.

There has been some evidence posited (Brenner, 1979) to suggest that those children who appear to be affected by food additives differ biochemically from children who are not affected. Evidence that low concentrations of food dye (frequently referred to as Red Dye No. 3) used in a number of confections prevent brain cells from ingesting dopamine, a substance having significant effects on motor activity, provide this biochemical hypothesis with further impetus. In fact, in one seminal piece of research, Lafferman and Silbergeld (1979) concluded that the food dyes' blocking of dopamine is consistent with the notion that the dye could induce hyperactivity in some children.

Although some research has tentatively supported the mechanism of the toxic effect of certain food dyes for particular children, Feingold (1975a) has made a plethora of unsupported statements attesting to the efficacy of his additive-free therapeutic diet. In fact, Feingold (1975a) has even suggested that nearly half of his clinical practice evidenced complete remission of symptoms as a function of a diet that was additive-free. Despite the fact that these claims were not based on empirical data and were refuted later by other investigators (National Advisory Committee on Hyperkinesis and Food Additives, 1980), the claims from Feingold (1975b) still continued at high pitch; he contended that eliminating food additives would decrease motor incoordination and increase academic achievement for hyperactive children (Feingold, 1975b).

Feingold's claims resulted in a proliferation of reports by the popular press attesting to the potential link of food additives to hyperactivity (Ross & Ross, 1982). Further, there were also reports of behavioral improvements ascribed to additive-free diets (Ross & Ross, 1982). Understandably, the food industry perceived these claims as a direct threat and thus organized with the Food and Drug Administration committees to review the evidence pertaining to Feingold's claims. The committees concluded that there was no empirical evidence linking food additives to behavioral or learning dysfunctions in children. The committees further recommended (Ross & Ross, 1982) that carefully controlled empirical studies be conducted to test any validity of food additives in causing hyperactivity or other learning disorders in children.

Subsequently, a series of methodologically sophisticated studies were funded by the federal government. In them Feingold's hypotheses regarding food additives were put to careful tests. The results of these recent studies, which were reviewed by the National Advisory Committee on Hyperkinesis and Food Additives (1980), have generally "refuted the claim that artificial food colorings, artificial flavorings, and salicylates produce hyperactivity and/or learning disability." Based on their findings, the National Advisory Committee also recommended that further funding efforts in this area cease.

REFERENCES
Conners, C.K. (1980). *Food additives and hyperactive children.* New York: Plenum.

Feingold, B.F. (1975a). *Why your child is hyperactive.* New York: Random House.

Feingold, B.F. (1975b). Hyperkinesis and learning disabilities linked to artificial food flavors and colors. *American Journal of Nursing, 75,* 797–803.

Feingold, B.F. (1976). Hyperkinesis and learning disabilities linked to the ingestion of artificial food colors and flavors. *Journal of Learning Disabilities, 9,* 551–559.

Feingold, H., & Feingold, B.F. (1979). *The Feingold cookbook for hyperactive children and others with problems associated with food additives and salicylates.* New York: Random House.

Feingold, B.F., German, D.F., Brahm, R.M., & Slimmers, E. (1973).

Adverse reaction to food additives. Paper presented to the annual meeting of the American Medical Association, New York.

Lafferman, J.A., & Silbergeld, E.K. (1979). Erythrosin B inhibits dopamine transport in rat caudate synaptosomes. *Science, 205,* 410–412.

National Advisory Committee on Hyperkinesis and Food Additives. (1980). New York: Nutrition Foundation.

Ross, D.M., & Ross, S.A. (1982). *Hyperactivity: Current issues, research and theory* (2nd ed.). New York: Wiley-Interscience.

See also **Dopamine; Feingold Diet; Hyperactivity**

FORREST V. AMBACH

Muriel Forrest, a school psychologist with the Edgemont Union Free School District in Winchester, New York, was dismissed with only a five-day notice in May 1979. The district dismissed Forrest ostensibly because her work was unsatisfactory and she had refused to follow orders directing her to change. The dismissal was appealed to the Commissioner of Education for the State of New York (*In re Forrest,* 1980). Forrest based that appeal on three points. First was her contention that she had acquired tenure status. As a four-fifths-time employee, the district argued no, while Forrest argued yes on the basis of being included in the collective bargaining agreement (tenure status would mandate a formal hearing prior to dismissal). The second point (the crux of system procedure/professional standard interaction) involved the district's order that Forrest shorten reports, delete technical language, and refrain from making recommendations to parents prior to referrals being made to the Committee on the Handicapped. Forrest's position was that these requirements forced her to perform in a manner that violated her professional organization's ethical standards and state and federal law. The third issue was the district's refusal to permit her to present a paper at a professional conference, infringing, therefore, on a constitutionally protected right. In April 1980, Commissioner Ambach dismissed the appeal on the basis that Forrest had failed to demonstrate that the speech in question is constitutionally protected and that her exercise of her rights was a substantial or motivating factor in the respondent board's decision to terminate her services.

Forrest sought judgment in the court to invalidate Ambach's decision (*Forrest v. Ambach,* 1981). Appearing as *amici curiae* were the National Association of School Psychologists, American Psychological Association, New York State Psychological Association, and the Westchester County Psychological Association. Justice Kahn rendered his decision late in 1980. In finding in part for Forrest, the court ordered that Commissioner Ambach review and reconsider the dismissal of Forrest from her position as a school psychologist. The court addressed two issues in the written opinion. First, whether Forrest was a tenured employee and therefore not subject to dismissal without a due process hearing, and second,

whether the Commissioner was correct in declining to consider petitioner's specific allegations concerning the reason for her dismissal by holding that she lacked standing to challenge respondents' alleged neglect of their statutory duties regarding handicapped children (p. 920).

With regard to the first question, the court upheld the commissioner's ruling that Forrest had not gained tenured status. However, the court went on to quickly add that the commissioner should have provided a forum for a review of the allegation made by Forrest. Forrest claimed that she was injured (loss of job) by the board's (district's) alleged misconduct. Justice Kahn identifies this as the "hub of her claim" and the commissioner's decision not to review whether the district was neglecting its statutory duties "resulted in a failure to have her grievance aired." Therefore, the opinion identifies the commissioner's determination as "a 'Catch 22' and is arbitrary and capricious in that there is not a rational basis therefore" (p. 920).

While a school board is in the position of an employer, those professionals employed by a school board do have a level of professional competence and standards which must be recognized and respected, not only for the profession itself, but for the purpose of rendering the best service to the school board and ultimately to the students they service. *The ethical standards of any professional employed by a school board cannot be cavalierly dismissed as irrelevant to the employer-employee relationship, and may indeed become quite relevant in certain circumstances* (emphasis added). If, in fact, petitioner was dismissed solely due to her own professional standards as a psychologist, then her dismissal by said school board would be arbitrary, capricious and unconstitutional (p. 920).

Justice Kahn affirms the special education legislation and regulation and the explicit requirement of equal educational opportunity with a relevant reminder that "a school board should not be permitted to, in any way, impede the noble goals of such a law" (p. 920). Subsequent to the court's decision and directives, Ambach reheard Forrest's appeal and once again ruled in favor of the school district. Forrest appealed the decision to the state supreme court, and then the appellate division, losing each time. New York's highest court, the Court of Appeals, declined to review the case. The decision of Forrest accentuates the importance of professional standards and serves to underline the real and potential conflict that exists between such standards and system policy and procedure. In that sense, the decision provides an important foundation for establishing legal precedent in similar situations.

REFERENCES

Forrest v. Ambach, 436 N.Y.S. 2d 119, 107 Misc. 2d 920 (Sup. Ct. 1981).

In re Forrest. New York Education Department No.10237 (April 2, 1980).

See also **Ethical Issues; National Association of School Psychologists**

FOSTER HOMES FOR THE HANDICAPPED

Foster homes for handicapped children and adults have been used for many years (Sanderson & Crawley, 1982). With the advent of deinstitutionalization in the 1970s, alternatives to housing had to be considered. Although group homes were predicted to be the primary providers for this population, Roos (1978) affirmed that adoption or foster care would be the preferred residential placement. Willer and Intagliata (1982) compared group home and foster home placements on clients' achievement of self-care skills, adaptive behavior, community living skills, social skills, and community access. Interestingly, few differences were found across the two residential settings. Nevertheless, the authors concluded that family-care homes provided more opportunities to develop age-appropriate personal and interpersonal behaviors, while group homes provided more opportunities to develop community and independent living skills. Two major implications were made from these results. First, placement of handicapped persons into community residential facilities must be based on the individual needs of the client. Second, "group-home staff members could benefit from training in behavior-management techniques, whereas family-care providers could benefit from training in how to encourage residents to develop and utilize more independent community living skills" (Willer & Intagliata, 1982, p. 594). Although cost-effectiveness data were not examined, the authors concluded that the cost for foster care was significantly lower than for group-home placement.

Despite the issues of best placement, handicapped children and adults continue to be placed in foster homes. Many questions arise when considering these placements. What kinds of handicapped children are being placed in foster homes? What kinds of families take handicapped foster children? What are the needs of families with handicapped foster children?

Foster homes for children with retardation and motor delays have been a constructive alternative to residential placement. For example, in a report by Taylor (1980), two case studies were presented from a foster parent's perspective. The achievements made by each of Taylor's foster children were remarkable. To meet the needs of foster parents such as these, Arizona developed a curriculum for foster parents of children with retardation (Drydyk, Mendeville, & Bender, 1980). The curriculum, Foster Parenting a Retarded Child, is available for purchase from the Child Welfare League of America, 67 Irving Place, New York, NY 10003.

Medically fragile children also have been placed in foster homes. Often it is a nurse who will take a foster child with medical needs such as tracheotomy care, tube feeding, sterile dressing, and physical therapy. In many cases, these children would remain hospitalized indefinitely because of the biological parents' inability to provide care. Additionally, it was estimated that in 1983 the cost of foster care for these children was $1000 per month, while the average cost of a month's hospitalization was $10,500 (Whitworth, Foster, & Davis, 1983).

Foster homes provide an invaluable service to children with handicaps. Professionals serving handicapped children need to recognize the needs of foster parents in order to enhance the services provided to them and their foster children.

REFERENCES

Drydyk, J., Mendeville, B., & Bender, L. (1980). Foster parenting a retarded child. *Children Today, 9,* 10, 24–26.

Roos, S. (1978). The future residential services for the mentally retarded in the United States: A Delphi study. *Mental Retardation, 16,* 355–356.

Sanderson, H.W., & Crawley, M. (1982). Characteristics of successful family-care parents. *American Journal of Mental Deficiency, 86,* 519–525.

Taylor, S.W. (1980). Foster care: A foster mother's perspective. *Exceptional Parent, 10,* L4–L8.

Whitworth, J.M., Foster, P.H., & Davis, A.B. (1983). *Medical foster care for abused and neglected children of dysfunctional families.* Washington, DC: U.S. Department of Health and Human Services. Federal Grant #90-CA-0932.

Willer, B., & Intagliata, J. (1982). Comparison of family-care and group homes as alternative to institutions. *American Journal of Mental Deficiency, 86,* 588–595.

See also **Family Counseling**

FOUNDATION FOR CHILDREN WITH LEARNING DISABILITIES (FCLD)

The Foundation for Children with Learning Disabilities (FCLD) is a charitable foundation incorporated in the state of New York and holding tax exempt status with the Internal Revenue Service. The FCLD is located at 99 Park Avenue, New York, NY 10016. It was founded in 1977 by Carrie Rozelle, who remains the president of the organization. The FCLD publishes *Their World,* an annual devoted to developing public awareness of learning disabilities. An annual benefit and other activities are carried out each year to raise funds to support the goals of FCLD.

In 1985 FCLD launched two major efforts aimed at service as well as public relations for the learning disabled. The FCLD has a grant program for public libraries to develop live programs for parents, teachers, learning disabled children, and the public about learning differences. A second grant program has been designed and implemented to educate both the public and the judiciary about the potential link between learning disabilities and delinquency. The organization is devoted to developing public awareness of the problems associated with learning disabilities and to providing general educational services to the public on the topic. The FCLD does not provide direct services to learning-disabled children.

See also **Their World**

FOUNTAIN VALLEY TEACHER SUPPORT SYSTEM IN MATHEMATICS

The 1967–1968 mathematics program teacher's guide for the Fountain Valley School District, California, includes the following mathematics content: numbers and numerals, geometry, measurement, applications, statistics and probability, sets, functions and graphs, logic, and problem solving. The teacher's guide also lists manipulative aids, audio-visual materials, and demonstration materials for use with elementary school-age students.

The outstanding feature of the Fountain Valley program is the mainstreaming of 60 educable mentally handicapped (EMH) and 30 educationally handicapped (EH) students into regular classes. The goal of the project was to determine whether they could be effectively educated in those settings. Effective education was defined as improvement in mathematics, reading, peer and teacher acceptance, and self-concept. The students were provided with individually prescribed programs of instruction that were based on daily assessment and prescription by a resource teacher. The resource teacher worked with regular classroom teachers to coordinate pupils' programs of instruction with regular classroom activities. Regular classroom teachers attempted to help handicapped students feel that they were valuable class members. Information available includes descriptions of scope, personnel, organization, services, instructional equipment and materials, budget, parent-community involvement, and evaluation.

Pre- and posttest assessments were administered to evaluate project objectives that were concerned with pupils' growth in academic achievement, acceptance by regular classroom teachers and students, and self-concept. Data indicate that EMR and EH students progressed an average of 12 months in mathematics and 9 to 11 months in reading. No difference was apparent in teachers' overall perception of handicapped versus nonhandicapped students as measured by Osgood's Semantic Differential. Also reported was the fact that the majority of students reached criterion levels of self-concept measures.

See also **Arithmetic Remediation**

FOURTEENTH AMENDMENT RIGHTS

See EQUAL PROTECTION.

FRAGILE X SYNDROME

Little known until the 1980s, fragile X [fra(X)] is a chromosomal abnormality that is now seen to be the most common heritable cause, and second only to Down's Syndrome as a genetically-based cause, of mental retardation. (Down's Syndrome, generally arising through nondisjunction of chromosome pair 21 during meiosis, is genetic but not inherited.) Based in a weak or fragile site on the X chromosome, fra(X) is sex-linked and thus expressed more frequently in males. It is the only one of the more than 50 X-linked disorders associated with mental retardation that occurs frequently (e.g., Brown et al., 1986) and it is largely responsible for the higher prevalence of mental retardation in males than females. Although estimates vary across studies, incidence is about 1 in 1,500 in males and 1 in 2,000 in females (Fryns, 1990). Fragile X may account for over 5% of retarded males and about 0.3% of retarded females (Jones, 1997). Of males with mental retardation serious enough to require extensive support, 6–14% have fra(X), as do 3–6% of individuals with autism (Batshaw, 1997). Individuals with mental retardation of unknown cause are now routinely screened for fra(X).

GENETICS OF FRA(X)

Fra(X) is unusual genetically in several ways. In typical X-linked disorders, a carrier female who has no characteristics of the disorder passes the defective gene on average to half of her children. Of those children who inherit the defective gene, males will express any effects, whereas females will be unaffected but carriers. In fra(X), however, the situation is more complicated. Heterozygotic (carrier) females, who have one normal X chromosome and one with the fragile site, may manifest some fra(X) characteristics, including impaired intelligence and specific learning disabilities. About 20 percent of males who inherit the fragile site show no apparent physical or psychological effects and no evidence of fragility. They do, however, pass the X chromosome on to their daughters who may have affected sons (Brown, 1990). As a further complication, repeated cytogenetic testing fails to reveal the fragile site in more than 50 percent of unaffected carrier females.

Research in the 1990s has clarified the basis and inheritance patterns of fra(X) and its precursors. The description that follows is closely modeled after Batshaw's (1997) exposition. Initially, the specific defective gene, the FMR1 (fragile X mental retardation gene) was found in all males who expressed the fra(X) syndrome. The defective gene was later found to interfere with a particular protein apparently important in brain development. Fragile sites themselves were found to be abnormal expansions of perseverations or repetitions commonly seen in three nucleotide base pairs of the genetic code. The expansion of the triplet repeat is likely to increase over generations. The fragile X site (FRAXA) normally contains some 6–50 repeats of the cytosine-guanine-guanine (CGG) triplet base pair sequence. Asymptomatic transmitting males and carrier females have 50–90 and 50–200 CGG repeats, respectively; do not show a fragile X site; and are said to have a premutation. Such premutations are relatively common, occurring in about 1 in 500 males and 1 in 250 females. Males and females who have the full mutation of 200–3000 CGG fragile X repeats have observable fragile X sites and show various symptoms. All males and 50% of females will show mental retardation.

The increased expansion of CGG repeats over successive generations leads to increased fra(X) symptomatology over the same generations. Premutations of more than 100 CGG repeats almost always expand into full mutation range in the next generation. Transmitting males usually have less than 100 CGG repeats, so their daughters will tend also to have premutations and be asymptomatic. Since these daughters will likely have CGG repeats expanded into the 90–200 range, their male and female children who inherit the fra(X) site are likely to have CGG repeats of over 1000. That, of course, is in the full mutation range, and those children will display fra(X) symptoms. As Batshaw (1997, p. 379) observed, "Thus, transmitting males tend to have grandchildren manifesting fragile X syndrome, a very unusual pattern for an X-linked disorder!"

CHARACTERISTICS OF AFFECTED MALES

About two thirds of affected adult males show a "clinical triad": 1) moderate to severe mental retardation; 2) characteristic craniofacial features, including large forehead, protruding chin, and elongated ears; and 3) large testes (macroorchidism) (Curfs, Wiegers, & Fryns, 1990; Fryns, 1990; Sutherland & Hecht, 1985). However, affected individuals show such a variety of characteristics that diagnosis can firmly be based only on cytogenetic analysis. Females and prepubertal males are even more variable. Although most males show an "overgrowth syndrome" from birth, with head size, fontanel, and body measurements exceeding the 97th percentile, macroorchidism and craniofacial features are much less distinct in prepubertal boys (Curfs et al., 1990). The following summary of characteristics of affected individuals is based on information in Batshaw (1997); Bregman, Dykens, Watson, Ort, & Leckman (1987); Brown et al. (1986), Curfs et al. (1990); Dykens & Leckman (1990); Fryns (1990); and Hagerman (1990).

Physical features. In addition to the characteristic craniofacial features, macroorchidism, and overgrowth described above, males with fra(X) may show a variety of other features, such as hyperextensible joints, high arched palate, mitral valve prolapse (a form of heart murmur), flat feet, and low muscle tone. Female carriers, particularly those with subnormal intelligence, may also show facial features, including high broad forehead and long face, and hyperextensibility.

Cognitive features. Approximately 95% of affected males have mental retardation, but the degree of retardation varies from mild to profound, with a small percent of cases in the low normal range of intelligence. Males frequently show a decline in intelligence quotient, but not absolute intelligence, with age. Affected males have particular difficulty with sequential processing and short-term memory for information presented serially, performing poorly on tasks requiring recall of series of items or imitation of a series of motor movements. This deficit in sequential processing differentiates fra(X) individuals from those with other forms of mental retardation (Zigler & Hodapp, 1991). Affected males perform relatively well on tasks requiring simultaneous processing and integration, such as block design. Auditory memory and reception is poor.

Language. About 95% of affected males show some form of communication disorder. Language development in general is delayed beyond their mental retardation. Additionally, specific problems such as perseverations, repetitions, echolalia, cluttered speech, and dysfluencies are often shown, some of which may stem from general deficits in sequential processing. Word-finding problems and irrelevant associations are exacerbated by anxiety.

Behavioral characteristics. About 75% of affected individuals show serious behavior problems, including hyperactivity and attention deficits, stereotyped self-stimulatory behaviors, and aggression. About 60% show autistic features and 20% have seizures. The combination of features leads many to be diagnosed with pervasive developmental disorder (Batshaw, 1997). Many affected individuals are also socially withdrawn, show gaze aversion, and engage in self-injurious behavior, particularly self-biting.

CHARACTERISTICS OF AFFECTED FEMALES

About 70% of carrier females show no clear physical, cognitive, or behavioral problems. The remaining 30% show a variety of symptoms, which manifest less severely than in males. About 10% show mild mental retardation, 20% have learning disabilities, 30% have communication problems, and 30% have emotional disturbances. Frequent learning disabilities include problems in visual-spatial skills, executive function, and simultaneous processing. Language problems, similar to males, include cluttered and perseverative speech. Some evidence suggests that, unlike males, intelligence quotient of affected carrier females increases with age.

SOME IMPLICATIONS

Psychological approaches are of importance in dealing with fra(X) for at least two reasons (Curfs et al., 1990): (1) The diffuse and variable physical effects of fra(X) in children place additional significance on the role of psychological assessment in identifying potentially fra(X) children for cytogenetic analysis; and (2) cognitive characteristics of those with fra(X) have important implications for treatment and educational programs. Owing to the variety and variation in problems exhibited by those with fra(X), a team approach is recommended for treatment (Hagerman, 1990). Further, the clear distinction between characteristics of those with fra(X) and those with Down's Syndrome indicates heterogeneity among groups with organic retardation, which may have theoretical implications (Burack, Hodapp, & Zigler, 1988; Dykens & Leckman, 1990; Zigler & Hodapp, 1991). Fra(X) can be identified antenatally with a special test (Brown et al., 1986), but the incomplete penetrance in males, phenotypic effects in a significant number of carrier females, and difficulty of diagnosis in unaffected females all complicate genetic counseling.

Numerous websites are available for additional information on fragile X. One useful site is http://www3.ncbi.nlm.nih.gov:80/htbin-post/Omim/dispmim?309550.

REFERENCES

Batshaw, M.L. (1997). Fragile X syndrome. In M.L. Batshaw (Ed.), *Children with disabilities* (4th ed.) (pp. 377–388). Baltimore: Brookes.

Bregman, J.D., Dykens, E., Watson, M., Ort, S.I., & Leckman, J.F. (1987). Fragile-X syndrome: Variability of phenotypic expression. *Journal of the American Academy of Child and Adolescent Psychiatry, 26,* 463–471.

Brown, W.T. (1990). Invited editorial: The fragile X: Progress toward solving the puzzle. *American Journal of Human Genetics, 47,* 175–180.

Brown, W.T., Jenkins, E.C., Krawczun, M.S., Wisniewski, K., Rudelli, R., Cohen, I.R., Fisch, G., Wolf-Schein, E., Miezejeski, C., & Dobkin, C. (1986). The fragile X syndrome. In H.M. Wisniewski & D.A. Snider (Eds.), *Mental retardation: Research, education, and technology transfer* (pp. 129–149). *Annals of the New York Academy of Sciences, 477.*

Burack, J.A., Hodapp, R.M., & Zigler, E. (1988). Issues in the classification of mental retardation: Differentiating among organic etiologies. *Journal of Child Psychology and Psychiatry, 29,* 765–779.

Curfs, L.M.G., Wiegers, A.M., & Fryns, J.P. (1990). Fragile-X syndrome: A review. *Brain Dysfunction, 3,* 1–8.

Davies, K.E. (Ed.). (1990). The fragile X syndrome. Oxford, UK: Oxford University Press.

Dykens, E., & Leckman, J. (1990). Developmental issues in fragile X syndrome. In R.M. Hodapp, J.A. Burack, & E. Zigler (Eds.), *Issues in the developmental approach to mental retardation* (pp. 226–245). Cambridge, UK: Cambridge University Press.

Fryns, J.P. (1990). X-linked mental retardation and the fragile X syndrome: A clinical approach. In K.E. Davies (Ed.), *The fragile X syndrome* (pp. 1–39). Oxford, UK: Oxford University Press.

Hagerman, R. (1990). Behaviour and treatment of the fragile X syndrome. In K.E. Davies (Ed.), *The fragile X syndrome* (pp. 66–75). Oxford, UK: Oxford University Press.

Jones, K.L. (1997). *Smith's recognizable patterns of human malformation* (5th ed.). Philadelphia: W.B. Saunders.

Sutherland, G.R., & Hecht, F. (1985). *Fragile sites on human chromosomes.* New York: Oxford University Press.

Zigler, E., & Hodapp, R.M. (1991). Behavioral functioning in individuals with mental retardation. *Annual Review of Psychology, 42,* 29–50.

See also **Autism; Chromosomal Abnormalities; Congenital Disorders; Down's Syndrome; Mental Retardation**

FRAIBERG, SELMA HOROWITZ (1918–1981)

Selma Horowitz Fraiberg received her BA (1940) and MSW (1945) from Wayne State University. She was a professor of child psychoanalysis at the University of Michigan, Ann Arbor.

As a social worker, Fraiberg advocated using appropriately trained social workers to work with children. Realizing that most caseworkers are trained to help adults, Fraiberg

Selma Horowitz Fraiberg

noted that resources are usually not available for a child with problems to be seen by any professional other than a caseworker. Fraiberg saw the difficulty in determining where casework ends and other professions begin when addressing children's problems. She contended that a child with problems affects the lifestyle of an entire family, and that, she believed, is a casework problem that is difficult to resolve without the involvement of a caseworker. She stressed that the effective caseworker must have appropriate training.

Fraiberg's 1977 book, *Every Child's Birthright: In Defense of Mothering,* was written to publicize the practical aspects of research on the rearing of children. Much of the research studied the development of children from the Depression and the two world wars who grew up without their parents and frequently without other family as well. Her belief is that the survival of humankind depends at least as much on the nurturing care and love given to a child in infancy and childhood as it does on preventing war and surviving natural disasters. Another of Fraiberg's interests, how blind children develop and form bonding attachments when they cannot see their parents, was the basis of *Insights from the Blind: Comparative Studies of Blind and Sighted Infants* (1977). *The Magic Years* (1969) was another important work by Fraiberg. Among her honors, Fraiberg was elected to *Who's Who of American Women* (1975), and *Who's Who in World Jewry: A Biographical Dictionary of Outstanding Jews* (1972). A native of Detroit, Michigan, Selma Horowitz Fraiberg died on December 19, 1981 in San Francisco, California.

REFERENCES

Fraiberg, S.H. (1969). *The magic years: Understanding and handling the problems of early childhood.* New York: Scribner's Sons.

Fraiberg, S.H. (1977). *Every child's birthright: In defense of mothering.* New York: Basic Books.

Fraiberg. S.H., & Fraiberg, L. (1977). *Insights from the blind: Comparative Studies of blind and sighted infants.* New York: Basic Books.

Karpman, I.J. Carmín. (Ed.). (1972). *Who's who in world Jewry: A biographical dictionary of outstanding Jews.* New York: Pitman.

Who's Who of American Women, Ninth Edition. (1975). Wilmette, IL: Marquis Who's Who.

FRANCE, SPECIAL EDUCATION IN

Special education in France can be defined as "education combining pedagogical, psychological, social, medical, and paramedical actions. It is provided either by conventional establishments or by specialized establishments or departments" (Article 4, Law of Orientation, 1975). Recipients are "young subjects who, at a certain period of their life, in view of their active participation and integration in the community, are temporarily or lastingly in need of particular medical, social, pedagogical, or education procedures other than those provided for the general population" (Article 4, Law of Orientation, 1975). These definitions evolved over the past hundred years and are important in understanding how special education is provided in France at the present time.

Until the nineteenth century, assistance to handicapped children was dispensed by charitable institutions, mainly religious communities or philanthropic organizations, and was principally custodial. Saint Vincent de Paul (1581–1660) was one of the first to take interest in the plight of abandoned children. The Abbe de l'Epee (1712–1789) founded the deaf and dumb institution of Paris, teaching language through dactylic signs. Valentin Hauy (1745–1752), founder of the Institute for Blind Youths, invented printing in relief for their instruction.

The mentally deficient, children then termed idiots or degenerates, were confined with adults to asylums, the precursors of modern psychiatric hospitals. There they received neither care nor education. However, the works of Esquirol, Itard, Seguin, and Bourneville foreshadowed a change in how handicapped children were to be treated. Bourneville considered the possibility of creating special classes providing the "necessary assistance and treatment to satisfy all the needs of the insane" (CRESAS, 1984).

The law of March 28, 1882, decreed compulsory education for all children. It highlighted the incapacity of some to follow the school curriculum and the fact that many children simply did not attend school. As a result of this law, some believed that a mentally defective child was a product of public, compulsory education. During this period, when mental specialists were turning their attention toward schooling, a number of educators were in favor of weeding out these "disturbing" elements. In 1905 Alfred Binet developed a system of identifying children maladjusted to conventional school: the metric intelligence scale. This instrument enabled qualifying all children less than 9 years old who were 3 years behind in their studies as feebleminded. The notion of an IQ is a logical outcome of this scale. The work of a committee led by Alfred Binet resulted in the promulgation of the law of April 15, 1909, relating to the creation of "refresher courses" for "backward" children of both sexes to be handled by teachers having undergone appropriate complementary training.

An educational system of segregated classes for the handicapped subsequently developed. From 25 special education classes in 1914, the number grew to 240 in 1939, 1145 in 1951, over 4000 in 1963, and over 16,000 in 1973. Recent statistics indicate a sharp decline in this number.

Whereas in 1975–1976 a total of 141,007 pupils were in special public and private education courses, the figure dropped to 86,011 in 1983–1984. This is due to a general reduction of staff as well as to the creation of new institutions (notably psychopedagogical assistance groups and adaptation classes) and the development of a school integration policy.

During the 1970s, a vast movement in favor of integration, or the right to be different, developed in France, as elsewhere. It was ratified by the law of July 31, 1975. This law, decreeing compulsory education for all handicapped children and adolescents, accredits the principle of integration. It gives priority to upkeep in a normal working and living milieu, and, while assisting children and adolescents in finding the right solutions for their problems, maintains them in normal classes pending their admission to special establishments (using the cascade system). The primary aim of the integration principle is maintaining the largest possible number of handicapped children—taken in the most general sense of the term, from intellectual deficiency to physical disability—in ordinary schools. The main means to this end is through a transformation of the conventional school system.

For the most part, special education is the responsibility of the education ministry (on which public education is directly dependent), the health, social affairs, and solidarity ministries (under trusteeship), and the law ministry. The institutions and structures under the trusteeship of the health, social affairs, and solidarity ministries include the private medical and educational establishments in which education and medical care go hand in hand, the cost being reimbursed by health insurance and social assistance. These are the medico-pedagogical, medico-professional, and medico-educational institutions. Medical organizations include children's homes dispensing medical care (chronic afflictions), functional readaptation homes, treatment and postcure centers, etc. Organizations having a social and educational calling include children's villages, social assistance centers for children, etc. Reeducation of individual cases is handled in the medico-psycho-pedagogical centers (CMPM) and in daytime hospitals.

Altogether, these organizations handle approximately 40% of the children and adolescents in special education, primarily those who are physically handicapped, totally deficient, moronic, feebleminded, or afflicted with serious psychiatric or behavioral disorders; they also handle social classes. Few slightly deficient children are under their auspices. National education facilities coming under the heading of special education include the following:

1. For beginning or elementary schooling, there are special "refresher courses," mainly in nursery schools or various specialized schools. Slightly more than 90% of handicapped children provided with schooling by the ministry of education attend these classes.

2. At the secondary level, specialized education sections (SES) in the secondary schools provide slightly intellec-

tually deficient children with general education, prepro-fessional training, and workshop courses (Moallen & Moallen, 1998); there are also 81 state refresher schools for backward and slightly backward children who are also social cases. In addition, psychopedagogical assistance groups were set up as of 1970 to anticipate un-adapted cases. Adaptation classes are attended on a temporary basis to enable especially difficult cases to follow the regular school courses.

This organizational structure forms a dense, complex network. It underwent considerable development up to the 1970s; at present, it is experiencing profound modifications. Special education will likely continue to undergo major structural changes in the coming years.

The notion of a team is the very hub of all special education procedures. In addition to specialized educators, the teams include school psychologists, social workers, school medical service doctors, and various medical and therapeutic personnel, depending on objectives and need.

Several questions arise regarding special education in France. They may well provide a summary. What are special education methods in France? Personalized teaching takes into account the difficulties of each subject and the rate of acquisition and apprenticeship; progressive apprenticeship is based on analytical programming of subject matter; there is recourse to things concrete, to experimentation, to action on matter; there is an accent on motivation of the pupil, on teacher/pupil relations, on the lifestyle of the institution and its emotional climate; permanent attention to continuous observation and elaboration of an educational program based on teamwork are considered important. There is also prompt initiation of the necessary compensatory measures and therapy, flexible institutional or therapeutic solutions, and the taking into account of the evolutive and relative character of all maladjustments.

REFERENCES

CRESAS Researchers. (1984). *Integration or marginalization? Aspects of special education* (Collection No. 2). Paris: l'Harmattan & INRP.

Moallen, A., & Moallen, M. (1998). Systemic change in vocational training institutions in France. *International Journal of Disability Development & Education, 45*(1), 17–33.

See also **Binet, Alfred; Cascade Model of Special Education Services**

FREE APPROPRIATE PUBLIC EDUCATION

One of the major provisions incorporated in the Education for All Handicapped Children Act (PL 94-142) and re-inforced in its reauthorization, the Individual in with Disabilities Education Act, is the requirement that all handicapped children and youths, ages 3 through 21, be af-forded a free and appropriate public education (FAPE). Ini-tial federal statutory requirements were that services be pro-vided to all children ages 3 through 5 and youths ages 18 through 21 apply to all states and U.S. territories except where state law or court order expressly prohibits the provi-sion of FAPE to children or youths within these age ranges. The U.S. Congress then passed legislation (P.L. 99-457) to extend federally-supported services to handicapped infants and toddlers, aged birth through two years of age.

The definition of a free and appropriate public educa-tion is comprised of three discrete, yet interrelated, provi-sions:

1. *Free.* Essentially this component of the FAPE mandate requires that special education and related services be provided at no cost to the parent or guardian.

2. *Appropriate.* This component of the FAPE principle re-quires that all special education and related services (1) be specifically tailored to the student's unique needs and capabilities (as established during the evaluation process); (2) conform to the content of the student's individualized education program (IEP); and (3) be provided in the least restrictive environment (LRE).

3. *Public Education.* The public education requirement mandates that all local, intermediate, or state agencies that directly or indirectly provide special education or related services must provide for FAPE. In meeting the FAPE requirements, public agencies (e.g., local school districts) may contract with private day or residential fa-cilities to appropriately address the unique educational needs of a handicapped child or youth. Although the provision of FAPE does not fully apply to those handi-capped children who, by parental discretion, are en-rolled in private or parochial schools, these students must (by federal statute and regulation) be afforded gen-uine opportunities to participate in special education activities supported under Education for All Handi-capped Children Act and IDEA funding.

Turnbull, Leonard, and Turnbull (1982) indicate that the provisions contained in the federal free and appropriate public education requirements have their foundations in several prominent civil rights court cases. These judicial de-cisions include *PARC v. Commonwealth* of *Pennsylvania, Mills v. D.C. Board of Education, Wyatt v. Stickney, New York State Association for Retarded Citizens v. Rockefeller, Diana v. State Board of Education,* and *Larry P. v. Riles.*

In establishing the concept of free and appropriate pub-lic education, the U.S. Congress (1983) statutorily defined FAPE as:

Special education and related services which (A) have been pro-vided at public expense, under public supervision and direction, and without charge, (B) meet the standards of the State educa-tional agency, (C) include an appropriate preschool, elementary, or secondary school education in the state involved, and (D) are provided in conformity with the individualized education pro-gram required under section 614(a)(5).

In expanding on the legislative and judicial foundations supporting the provision of FAPE, Turnbull, Leonard, and Turnbull (1982) specify six major principles for the administration of special education: implementation of the zero reject concept, development of nondiscriminatory evaluation models, preparation of IEPs, maintenance of the full continuum of least restrictive placement options, administration of compliant due process systems, and the assurance of full parent participation in all programming decisions.

REFERENCES

Turnbull, A., Leonard, J.L., & Turnbull, H.R, (1982). *Educating handicapped children: Judicial and legislative influences.* Washington, DC: American Association of Colleges for Teacher Education.

U.S. Congress (1983). The Education of the Handicapped Amendments of 1983 (Public Law 98-199). Washington DC: Government Printing Office.

See also **Individual Education Plan; Individuals with Disabilities Education Act (IDEA); Least Restrictive Environment; Zero Reject**

FREEDOM FROM DISTRACTIBILITY

Numerous factor-analytic studies of the Wechsler Intelligence Scales have revealed freedom from distractibility as an additional, smaller factor that underlies test performance, separate from the two larger factors that reflect the Verbal and Performance constructs that underlie all of Wechsler's scales. The first two factors that correspond to Verbal IQ and Performance IQ are typically labeled verbal comprehension and perceptual organization; each is robust in its makeup and generally invariant in its subtest composition. The third, or distractibility factor, usually consists of the arithmetic, digit span, and coding/digit symbol subtests, although some distractibility factors are composed only of the first two of these subtests. Indeed, the Wechsler Intelligence Scale for Children–Third Edition (WISC–III) includes four factor indexes in addition to the IQs, one of which is composed of the arithmetic and digit span subtests and is labeled *freedom from distractibility.* Coding is not aligned with this factor, but instead joins a new speeded subtest (symbol search) to form the fourth factor index, processing speed. Similarly, arithmetic and digit span (plus a new subtest, letter-number sequencing) form a distractibility-like factor index on the Wechsler Adult Intelligence Scale–Third Edition (WAIS–III). However, in a departure from tradition, the WAIS–III uses the name working memory for that factor index.

Although the exact meaning of the so-called freedom from distractibility factor (or memory or stimulus trace factor) remains to be discovered, it has sometimes been identified as the capacity to resist distraction (Wechsler, 1958) and is sometimes referred to as the anxiety triad (Lutey, 1977), although Lutey stressed that the factor may be primarily a measure of number ability. Bannatyne (1974) interpreted

the factor as measure of sequential ability. Kaufman (1979, 1990, 1994) suggests that the factor may reflect a variety of cognitive faculties in addition to number facility, such as sequential processing and short-term memory, rather than just the behavioral attributes of distractibility or anxiety. Horn (1989) considers the factor to be primarily a memory dimension, which he labels short-term apprehension and retrieval, one of about eight aspects of intelligence that define his fluid-crystallized (Gf–Gc) theory. Wielkiewicz (1990) emphasizes that the distractibility factor may be thought of as a measure of executive processing.

REFERENCES

Bannatyne, A. (1974). Diagnosis: A note on recategorization of the WISC scaled scores. *Journal of Learning Disabilities, 7,* 212–274.

Horn, J.L. (1989). Cognitive diversity: A framework of learning. In P.L. Ackerman, R.J. Sternberg, & R. Glaser (Eds.), *Learning and individual differences* (pp. 61–116). New York: Freeman.

Kaufman, A.S. (1979). *Intelligent testing with the WISC–R.* New York: Wiley.

Kaufman, A.S. (1990). *Assessing adolescent and adult intelligence.* Boston: Allyn & Bacon.

Kaufman, A.S. (1994). *Intelligent testing with the WISC–III.* New York: Wiley.

Lutey, C. (1977). *Individual intelligence testing: A manual and source-book* (2nd ed.). Greeley, CO: Lutey.

Wechsler, D. (1958). *The measurement and appraisal of adult intelligence* (4th ed.). Baltimore, MD: Williams and Wilkins.

Wielkiewicz, R.M. (1990). Interpreting low scores on the WISC–R third factor: It's more than distractibility. *Psychological Assessment, 2,* 91–97.

See also **Factor Analysis; Profile Analysis; Profile Variability; Wechsler Adult Intelligence Scale–Revised; Wechsler Adult Intelligence Scale–Third Edition; Wechsler Intelligence Scale for Children–Revised; Wechsler Intelligence Scale for Children–Third Edition**

FREEMAN SHELDON SYNDROME

Freeman Sheldon Syndrome, also known as Whistling Face Syndrome, is a rare inherited condition that includes a very small mouth, mask-like face, joint contractures, and hypoplasia of the nasal cartilage. Crossed eyes, drooping eyelids, and development of scoliosis may also be encountered. Intelligence is usually normal, although some patients have been mentally retarded. Usually inherited in an autosomal dominant pattern, there are also sporadic cases and others with an autosomal recessive pattern of inheritance. There is no laboratory test to confirm the disorder.

The small mouth causes difficulties with speech, oral hygiene, and dental care. Contractures of the fingers complicate fine motor function. Orthopedic and plastic surgery can improve appearance and function but a potentially fatal reaction (malignant hyperthermia) to certain inhaled anesthetic agents necessitates careful preoperative planning with a knowledgeable anesthesiologist. There are several voluntary health agencies focusing on children with craniofacial abnormalities which offer additional information for families and professionals. Two such resources are Children's Craniofacial Association (P.O. Box 280297, Dallas, Texas 75228, (800)535-3643) and AboutFace International (99 Crowns Lane, 4th Floor, Toronto, Ontario, Canada M5R 3P4, (800)665-3223).

FRENCH, EDWARD LIVINGSTON (1916–1969)

Edward Livingston French began his professional career as a teacher at Chestnut Hill Academy in Philadelphia. Following three years of military service in World War II, he served as chief psychologist at the Training School at Vineland, New Jersey, where he was associated with Edgar A. Doll. In 1949 both French and Doll joined the Devereux Schools in Pennsylvania, French as director of psychology education. French became a member of the board of trustees of the Devereux Foundation in 1954. Three years later he was made director of the foundation; in 1960 he became president and director.

French received his PhD in clinical psychology from the University of Pennsylvania in 1950. He co-authored *How You Can Help Your Retarded Child.* His chapter on the Devereux Schools in *Special Education Programs within the United States* describes the principles of residential therapy on which the Devereux program is based. He served as president of both the Clinical Biochemistry and Behavioral Institute and the Division of School Psychologists of the American Psychological Association, and he was a trustee of the National Association of Private Psychiatric Hospitals.

Edward Livingston French

REFERENCES
French, E.L. (1968). The Devereux Schools. In M.V. Jones (Ed.), *Special education programs within the United States.* Springfield, IL: Thomas.

French, E.L., & Scott, J.C. (1967). *How you can help your retarded child: A manual for parents.* New York: Lippincott.

FREUD, ANNA (1895–1982)

Anna Freud was the youngest of Sigmund Freud's six children. She was educated at the Cottage Lyceum, and although an excellent student, left without a degree in 1912. Her father was her mentor in psychoanalytic theory and practice. Following the Nazi takeover of Austria, the family moved to London in 1938. Anna and her father remained professionally active and influential after their emigration. She was her father's devoted companion and associate until his death in 1939.

Anna Freud's many professional contributions resulted from her interest in applying psychoanalytic theory to the study of child development and in formulating and conducting psychotherapy appropriate to the special needs of young patients. Her work stimulated others, including Erik Erikson, whose study of psychoanalysis she encouraged. Her theoretical contributions included elaborating and extending her father's concept of ego defense mechanisms, particularly displacement and identification. She wrote prolifically, producing more than 100 articles and many important books, including *Introduction to the Technique of Child Analysis* (1927), *Psychoanalysis for Teachers and Parents* (1931), *The Ego and the Mechanisms of Defense* (1936), and *Psychoanalytic Treatment of Children* (1946). She also edited the 24-volume edition of her father's works (1953–1956).

Her interest in promoting child psychoanalysis led her to found in 1947 a clinic and a serial publication, both of which are still active. The Hampstead Child-Therapy Course and Clinic in London treats children and trains psychoanalytic child therapists; *The Psychoanalytic Study of the Child* is a scholarly forum for theoreticians and practitioners.

Anna Freud received the highest professional recognition of her contemporaries in 1970 when she was named the most outstanding living child psychoanalyst. Other distinctions include awards, medals, and honorary degrees from Clark, Yale, Columbia, and Harvard universities, and an honorary MD in 1972 from the University of Vienna.

Because of Anna Freud's modest and private nature, frustratingly little is known about her personal and professional development (Jackson, 1982). However, a memorial section of Volume 39 of *The Psychoanalytic Study of the Child* (1984) includes five papers discussing her contributions to the fields of law, developmental psychology, politics, and training in child analysis.

REFERENCE
Jackson, D.J. (1982). Psychology of the scientist: XLVI. Anna Freud. *Psychological Reports, 50,* 1191–1198.

FREUD, SIGMUND (1856–1939)

Sigmund Freud, the founder of psychoanalysis, entered medical practice as a neurologist in Vienna in 1886. Psychoanalysis, developed out of Freud's clinical practice, revolutionized not only psychiatric treatment but man's view of himself. Freud introduced the concept of the unconscious mind and its influence on behavior. Free association and dream interpretation were developed as techniques for reaching the unconscious. Freud demonstrated the role of mental conflict in human development and identified the motivating forces of sexuality and aggression. He also identified the existence and importance of infantile sexuality, and the influence of childhood development on adult behavior. After the annexation of Austria by Nazi Germany in 1938, Freud moved to London, where he resided until his death the following year.

REFERENCES

Freud, S. (1933). *New introductory lectures on psychoanalysis.* New York: Norton.

Freud, S. (1970). *An outline of psychoanalysis.* New York: Norton.

Jones, E. (1953–1957). *The life and work of Sigmund Freud* (3 vols.). New York: Basic Books.

FRIEDREICH'S ATAXIA (FA)

Friedreich's ataxia (FA) applies to a varied group of problems whose major symptoms usually appear in the late childhood or early adolescent years. The condition is generally transmitted along family lines through Mendelian inheritance as an autosomal recessive trait, though some cases of dominant mode transmission have been recognized. At the core of the disorder is progressive dysfunction of the spinal cord and cerebellum. Cardiac muscle fiber degeneration may also be present.

The early signs of FA are an increasing disturbance of normal gait followed by progressive loss of muscular coordination in the upper extremities and trunk. Skeletal anomalies such as club foot, hammer toes, and highly arched feet, along with scoliosis, may be present. Cardiac failure, enlargement of the heart (or arrhythmias), nystagmus of the eyes, optical nerve atrophy, tremors, dysarthria, and feeding disorders may be noted. Loss of sensation, especially in the feet, is common in this disorder, and the risk of development of seizure disorders is high. The diagnosis of FA is completely reliant on these clinical manifestations. Lab findings are generally of little assistance in diagnosis, except for cases where electrocardiogram changes indicating myocarditis are observed. Most individuals with FA become wheelchair-bound and eventually bedridden. There is no known cure for this disorder, with death from myocardial failure in childhood, adolescence, or early adulthood the usual result.

Friedreich's ataxia has been separated diagnostically from other similar disorders such as ataxia-telangiectasia, Roussy-Levy syndrome, and Bassen-Kornzweig syndrome.

See also **Gait Disturbances; Genetic Counseling**

Marianne Frostig (right)

FROSTIG, MARIANNE (1906–1985)

Born in Vienna, Austria, Marianne Frostig received a degree as a children's social worker from the College of Social Welfare, Vienna, Austria, in 1926. Several years later, she and her neuropsychiatrist husband worked in a psychiatric hospital in Poland before he accepted a position in the United States. When the Nazis invaded Poland, they killed everyone in the hospital. In the United States, Frostig earned the first BA ever issued by the New School for Social Research (1948). She received her MA (1940) from Claremont Graduate School and her PhD (1955) from the University of Southern California. She became ill and died while on a lecture tour in Germany.

Believing that every person is a unique individual who needs to be assessed and treated as such, Frostig was interested in finding the most appropriate education/treatment for each child. She thought that education should be adjusted to meet the needs of all children, especially those who, for various reasons, find learning difficult. To Frostig, a problem child is a child whose needs are not being met. *Education for Dignity* was intended to be a practical guide for the regular classroom teacher to meet those needs.

The Marianne Frostig Developmental Test of Visual Perception was the first test to segregate different visual abilities. Prior to this, all visual problems were grouped together. Frostig retired as director of the Marianne Frostig Center for Educational Therapy in 1972.

Frostig received the *Los Angeles Times* Woman of the Year Award and the Golden Key Award of the International Association for Children with Learning Disabilities. She has been included in *Who's Who of American Women, American Men and Women of Science,* and the *Dictionary of International Biography.*

REFERENCES

Frostig, M. (1976). *Education for dignity.* New York: Grune & Stratton.

Frostig, M., Lefever, D.W., & Whittlesey, J.R.B. (1964). *The Marianne Frostig Developmental Test of Visual Perception* (3rd ed.). Palo Alto, CA: Consulting Psychologists.

FROSTIG REMEDIAL PROGRAM

The Frostig Program of Visual Perception, developed in 1964, is designed to train children who have visual problems in perceptual and motor skills. Using a series of workbooks and worksheets, the program focuses on five areas. First, eye motor coordination, which involves drawing lines in carefully prescribed boundaries. Second, figure-ground, in which the child finds hidden figures in distracting and overlapping backgrounds. Third, perceptual constancy; here the child learns to recognize that an object remains the same even if its shape or color changes. Fourth, position in space; in this part of the program the child discovers that figures and objects remain the same although they may occupy different positions. Often, the child is provided with a model, then given several other models and is asked to select the shape or design that is exactly like the original. The fifth area is spatial relationships; at this point the child develops skills in perceiving positional relationships between objects or points of reference such as the arrangement of material or figures on a printed page (Bannatyne, 1971; Hallahan & Kaufman, 1976).

The assumption underlying the Frostig program is that brain damage in children results in neurological disabilities giving rise to visual perceptual problems. This assumption, based on the seminal works of Goldstein, Strauss, Werner, and Cruickshank, concludes that manifestations of brain dysfunctions, usually perceptual problems, can occur even if no specific damage to the brain can be found (Hallahan & Kaufman, 1976). The Frostig program is one of several commercially developed training programs to aid learning-disabled children who exhibit perceptual deficiencies (Frostig & Maslow, 1973).

REFERENCES

Bannatyne, A. (1971). *Language, reading and learning disabilities.* Springfield, IL: Thomas.

Frostig, M., & Maslow, P. (1973). *Learning problems in the classroom.* New York: Grune & Stratton.

Hallahan, D., & Kaufman, J. (1976). *Introduction to learning disabilities.* Englewood Cliffs, NJ: Prentice-Hall.

See also **Developmental Test of Visual Perception-2; Movigenics; Visual-Motor and Visual-Perceptual Problems; Visual Perception and Discrimination**

FUNCTIONAL ANALYSIS

Functional analysis is a procedure that involves the experimental manipulation of contextual variables which have been hypothesized to predict and/or maintain persistent problem behavior. Typically, these hypotheses are derived from indirect and/or direct functional assessments. Using functional analysis, educators can systematically identify associations or functional relationships between environmental events (i.e., antecedent and/or consequent events) and persistent problem behavior (Fowler & Schnacker, 1994;

O'Neill et al., 1997). Upon demonstration of a functional relationship, interventions are developed and incorporated into a behavior support plan for the targeted individual (Wacker, Berg, Asmus, Harding, & Cooper, 1998).

Miltenberger (1998) outlines three features that need to be in place when conducting a functional analysis: (a) objective measurement of the problem behavior under experimental conditions, (b) demonstration of a change in the problem behavior following the systematic manipulation of antecedent and/or consequent events, and (c) systematic replication of the above process. Two different experimental designs are used to establish a functional relationship between hypothesized environmental events and the problem behavior. The two design approaches used in functional analysis include the ABAB reversal design and the multielement (alternating treatments) design (Alberto & Troutman, 1999).

REFERENCES

Alberto, P.A., & Troutman, A.C. (1999). *Applied behavior analysis for teachers* (5th ed.). Upper Saddle River, NJ: Merrill.

Fowler, R.C., & Schnacker, L.E. (1994). The changing character of behavioral assessment and treatment: An historical introduction and review of functional analysis research. *Diagnostique, 19,* 79–102.

Miltenberger, R.G. (1998). Methods for assessing antecedent influences on challenging behaviors. In J.K. Luiselli & M.J. Cameron (Eds.), *Antecedent control: Innovative approaches to behavioral support* (pp. 47–65). Baltimore: Brookes.

O'Neill, R.E., Horner, R.H., Albin, R.W., Sprague, J.R., Storey, K., & Newton, J.S. (1997). *Functional assessment and program development for problem behavior: A practical handbook* (2nd ed.). Pacific Grove, CA: Brooks/Cole.

Wacker, D.P., Berg, W.K., Asmus, J.M., Harding, J.K., & Cooper, L.J. (1998). Experimental analysis of antecedent influences on challenging behaviors. In J.K. Luiselli & M.J. Cameron (Eds.), *Antecedent control: Innovative approaches to behavioral support* (pp. 67–86). Baltimore: Brookes.

FUNCTIONAL ASSESSMENT

Functional assessment is a systematic process for gathering information about the contextual factors that predict and/or maintain persistent problem behavior. Data from functional assessments are used to develop comprehensive behavior support plans that outline the hypothesized function or purpose that a targeted problem behavior serves for an individual. This includes data of any distal and immediate predictors that occasion the behavior and/or consequent events that are hypothesized to maintain the problem behavior. The behavior support plan also outlines proposed environmental modifications, curricular adaptations, and instructional strategies for teaching replacement responses that serve the same function or purpose of the problem behavior, but are more socially acceptable given the individual's home, school, and work environments.

O'Neill et al. (1997) write that all functional assessments should include the following features: (a) an operational definition of the problem behavior; (b) an identification of any events, persons, times, or situations that predict when the problem behavior occurs and when the problem behavior does not occur; (c) identification of the consequences that maintain the problem behavior; (d) summary or hypothesis statements that include any setting events, predictors, and maintaining consequences; and (e) direct observation data that support the summary statements. A comprehensive functional assessment includes both indirect and direct methods for gathering information about the contextual features of the problem behavior. Indirect methods target persons that are familiar with the student (e.g., teacher, parent, caregiver, paraprofessional) and incorporate interviews, behavioral rating scales, and questionnaires. Direct observation methods incorporate the use of systematic direct observation procedures that are conducted in the environment where the problem behavior occurs and other environments when feasible. Data from indirect and direct functional assessment procedures are used to develop behavior support plans.

The inclusion of functional assessment requirements in the 1997 reauthorization of the Individuals with Disabilities Education Act (IDEA) provides a unique opportunity for special educators to improve current policies, programs, and practices for children and youth with persistent problem behavior. Tilly et al. (1998) indicate that this new requirement will provide the individualized education program (IEP) team with useful information regarding (a) why a student engages in persistent problem behavior, (b) when the student is least and most likely to engage in the behavior, and (c) hypothesis or summary statements that guide the IEP team as they collaboratively develop instructional strategies that can be used to teach the student more appropriate responses within the context of individualized behavioral support planning (Sugai & Horner, 1994).

REFERENCES

O'Neill, R.E., Horner, R.H., Albin, R.W., Sprague, J.R., Storey, K., & Newton, J.S. (1997). *Functional assessment and program development for problem behavior: A practical handbook* (2nd ed.). Pacific Grove, CA: Brooks/Cole.

Sugai, G., & Horner, R. (1994). Including students with severe behavior problems in general education settings: Assumptions, challenges, and solutions. In J. Marr, G. Sugai, & G. Tindal (Eds.), *The Oregon Conference monograph* (pp. 102–120). Eugene, OR: University of Oregon.

Tilly III, W.D., Kovaleski, J., Dunlap, G., Knoster, T.P., Bambara, L., & Kincaid, D. (1998). *Functional behavioral assessment: Policy development in light of emerging research and practice*. Alexandria, VA: National Association of State Directors of Special Education.

See also Functional Analysis

FUNCTIONAL CENTERS HYPOTHESIS

The functional centers hypothesis, the Soviet view of learning disorders expounded by and associated primarily with Vygotsky and Luria, was further investigated and supported by other researchers in the Soviet Union (Holowinsky, 1976). It is based on Pavlovian psychology and on the dialectical-materialistic interpretation of human behavior: behavior, that is, on the elementary and higher levels, the product of phylogenetic, ontogenetic, and sociohistorical influences.

Central to the understanding of the hypothesis is the notion that an individual's mental functions (i.e., attention, memory, perception, thinking) are not only adaptive and acquired, but also are localized in and mediated by areas of cerebral cortex centers. Speech problems, language disorders, learning dysfunctions, and other handicaps are related to such centers but have psychoneurological etiologies. However, the functions "as complex functional systems with dynamic levels of localization in the brain" (Luria, 1980) are differentially related to various areas of the brain that are themselves highly differentiated in their structure. Mental functions are not, therefore, totally localized in particular/isolated areas of the brain (e.g., neuron, cortex), but operate as systems of functional combination centers. Localization in the Lurian brain for higher cortical function is dynamic, not static (Reynolds, 1981).

Mental functions appear in the developmental process first in elementary form as a result of natural development (determined by environmental stimulation). They then are changed primarily because of cultural development and self-regulated stimulation by the individual into a higher form (Vygotsky, 1978). Vygotsky considered voluntary control, conscious realization, social origins and nature, and mediation by psychological tools as characteristics of higher mental functioning (Wertsch, 1985). The development of speech is crucial because it provides new tools and signs that on mastery will clarify the operations of mental functioning to the individual.

Society plays a preeminent role in human development and functioning. In fact, higher mental functions (e.g., abstract thought, voluntary action) are formed during everyday activities. In a social context, they enable individuals to use a high level of organization, find new ways of regulating behavior, and establish new functional systems (Luria, 1978). Thus human beings can develop extracerebral connections and have the capacity to form numerous new functional systems and new functional centers in the cerebral cortex.

As a function is "a complex and plastic system performing a particular adaptive task and composed of a highly differentiated group of interchangeable elements" (Luria, 1980, p. 24), damage to any part of the cortical area can lead to a disintegration of the functional system. However, such a disturbance is likely to differ depending on the factors and on the role each part of the brain plays in the organization of the system during different stages of functional development (early or late).

In treating the learning disabled and mentally handicapped, the practitioner operates on the premise that a mental function may be performed by one of several intercenter connections in the functional centers. If one such connection is damaged—the damage or loss is not permanent—another system or cortical function can be trained to compensate for the deficit and take over the lost function. Thus restoring the disturbed or disorganized function is merely reorganizing that function and forming a new functional system.

REFERENCES

Holowinsky, I.Z. (1976). Functional centers hypothesis: The Soviet view of learning dysfunctions. In L. Mann & D.A. Sabatino (Eds.), *The third review of special education* (pp. 53–69). New York: Grune & Stratton.

Luria, A.R. (1978). L.S. Vygotsky and the problem of functional localization. In M. Cole (Ed.), *The selected writings of A.R. Luria* (pp. 273–281). White Plains, NY: Sharpe.

Luria, A.R. (1980). *Higher cortical functions in man* (2nd ed.) (B. Haigh, Trans.). New York: Basic Books. (Original work published 1962)

Reynolds, C.R. (1981). The neuropsychological basis of intelligence. In G.W. Hynd & J.E. Obrzut (Eds.), *Neuropsychological assessment and the school-aged child: Issues and procedures.* New York: Grune & Stratton.

Vygotsky, L.S. (1978). *Mind in society: The development of higher mental processes.* Cambridge, MA: Harvard University Press.

Wertsch, J.V. (1985). *Vygotsky and the social formation of mind.* Cambridge, MA: Harvard University Press.

See also Activity, Theory of; Luria, A.R.; Zone of Proximal Development

FUNCTIONAL DOMAINS

Educators, psychologists, and other health professionals will often assess and describe a child's performance in a number of areas, called functional domains, in addition to describing the child's overall performance and development in a global fashion. Theoretically, an assessment of the child's strengths and weaknesses in the various domains gives a snapshot of the child's functional status or the child's performance and ability to do things most other children do. Functional status is closely related to the concept of health status in the health field (Starfield, 1974; Stein & Jessop, 1984) and to the concept of social competence in the early childhood field (Zigler & Trickett, 1978).

Although typologies for the number and name of the functional domains vary, they generally are divided into four major areas: physical, cognitive, social, and emotional. Sometimes, the social and emotional areas are considered together and called psychological or mental health. The key to assessments in all functional domains is that behavior should be seen in a developmental context or framework so that the dynamic qualities of a child's development are considered (Walker, Richmond, & Buka, 1984).

REFERENCES

Starfield, B. (1974). Measurement of outcome: A proposed scheme. *Millbank Memorial Fund Quarterly, 52,* 39–50.

Stein, R.E.K., & Jessop, D.J. (1984). Assessing the functional status of children. In D.K. Walker & J.B. Richmond (Eds.), *Monitoring child health in the United States.* Cambridge, MA: Harvard University Press.

Walker, D.K., Richmond, J.B., & Buka, S.L. (1984). Summary and recommendations for next steps. In D.K. Walker & J.B. Richmond (Eds.), *Monitoring child health in the United States.* Cambridge, MA: Harvard University Press.

Zigler, E.F., & Trickett, D.K. (1978). IQ, social competence and evaluation of early childhood intervention programs. *American Psychologist, 33,* 789–798.

See also Adaptive Behavior; Assessment; Intelligence; Mental Status Exams

FUNCTIONAL INSTRUCTION

Functional instruction refers to the use of activities that involve skills of immediate usefulness to students as well as the employment of teaching materials that use real rather than simulated materials (Wehman, Renzaglia, & Bates, 1985). For example, a student could be taught to increase fine motor skills by assembling vocational products from local industry rather than by placing pegs in a board or stringing beads. Or a student could be required to place one cup at each place setting as opposed to placing one chip on each colored circle in an effort to teach one-to-one correspondence.

The use of functional materials and instruction involves the examination of individual needs in current and future environments. An ecological inventory (Brown et al., 1979) or ecological analysis (Wehman, Renzaglia, & Bates, 1985) can be conducted to determine individual student needs. By looking at aspects of the student's current environments (e.g., home, school, vocational site) and his or her future environments (e.g., group home, community recreation facility, vocational site), one can determine which skills will enable that student to function independently. By further breaking down current and future environments into subenvironments (e.g., group home: bathroom, living room, bedroom) and determining what activities are necessary in those subenvironments, one can determine the types of functional materials to be used during instruction. Careful consultation with parents or guardians as well as staff at future residential sites is also needed to ensure the functionality of skills targeted for instruction during the school years.

REFERENCES

Brown, L., Branston-McClean, M.B., Baumgart, D., Vincent, L., Falvey, M., & Schroeder, J. (1979). Using the characteristics of current and subsequent least restrictive environments in the development of curricular content for severely handicapped students. *AAESPH Review, 4,* 407–424.

Wehman, P., Renzaglia, A., & Bates, P. (1985). *Functional living skills for moderately and severely handicapped individuals.* Austin, TX: Pro-Ed.

See also Ecological Education of the Handicapped; Educable Mentally Retarded; Trainable Mentally Retarded; Transfer of Learning; Transfer of Training

FUNCTIONAL SKILLS TRAINING

Functional skills are generally considered to be those skills and competencies that are necessary for everyday living. These competencies are also referred to by many as "survival skills." The skills could be relatively simple for many people, such as counting change from a basic purchase, reading the sign for a restroom in an unfamiliar location, or realizing when to walk across an unfamiliar intersection. They could also be more complicated and involve the balancing of a checkbook, the completion of an application for employment, or comparative shopping. Many students are able to acquire these types of skills either within their normal environment, through incidental learning, or through general instruction within a formal classroom setting. The exceptional child, however, may not be able to acquire these competencies through incidental learning in his or her environment, and may not be able to generalize and transfer classroom learning to everyday situations out of the formal learning situation. Thus, the exceptional child may lose the opportunity to learn the very skills necessary for existence within our society.

Techniques for instruction of functional skills within the special education classroom will vary with the degree of impairment of the students involved. The techniques would include teaching of the "3 R's," generally referred to as the basics of academic instruction. Additionally, the social skills that are usually acquired by nonhandicapped students through environmental influences may require specific instruction by the special education teacher. Essentially, the teacher must decide whether to remediate deficits in academic subject areas or to concentrate on instruction in areas that could enable the student to function in as independent a manner as possible considering the limits of his or her abilities.

In functional reading, the sight-word approach is generally used to give a reading vocabulary. Teachers should consider the purpose of the instruction before selecting a method of instruction. In many cases, the level of literacy should be the level necessary for personal protection and information. Reading for protection requires minimal competence in reading itself, and must be practical for the survival of the individual (Palloway, Payne, Patton, & Payne, 1985). The sight vocabulary must include words such as restroom, men, women, danger, exit, walk, do not enter, and poison. For most special education students, vocational application of sight word skills would be a reasonable expectation. These skills would include those required to obtain and hold employment, to pass a driver's test, to complete a job application, and to order from a menu.

Functional skills training in mathematics should include those skills needed to provide a foundation for competence in vocational areas and daily living. Instruction should provide an understanding of measurement (both in carpentry and cooking), ordering, checking, paying bills, time, budgeting, purchasing, and making change. Mathematics is used much more in daily life than is realized by individuals who are able to assimilate knowledge without formal instruction. Consider the complexities involved in calculating a grocery bill, including taxes, without the ability to perform multiplication procedures, much less percent calculations. It is highly recommended that the use of a hand-held calculator be included in all programs of mathematics for special education students. A project for developing survival skills for "regular" students is discussed by Frey-Mason (1985). This technique could easily be adapted for the special education population.

Training in functional skills in written language should emphasize legibility. A student should be instructed in signing his or her name, completing an employment application, taking an order, writing a personal check, and executing basic personal correspondence. The signature should be accomplished in cursive style; however, all other writing can be in either cursive or manuscript, whichever is more legible. A student will be able to write only what he or she is able to read in most cases; therefore, the amount of written language will depend to a great extent on reading skills. The use of microcomputers is encouraged for the handicapped in writing tasks. Lerner (1985) provides an overview of methods and theories of written language for the special child.

Frequently, the handicapped individual will require specific training in social skills. These should include specific instruction in developing appropriate peer relationships, classroom behaviors, and relationships with adults. While many children are able to learn these skills from their environment, specific techniques should be considered for the special education child to enable him or her to function in a socially acceptable manner.

REFERENCES

Frey-Mason, P. (1985). Teaching basic mathematics and survival skills. *Mathematics Teacher, 78,* 669–671.

Lerner, J. (1985). *Learning disabilities: Theories, diagnosis, and teaching strategies* (4th ed.). Boston: Houghton Mifflin.

Palloway, E.A., Payne, J.S., Patton, J.R., & Payne, R.A. (1985). *Strategies for teaching retarded and special needs learners* (3rd ed.). Columbus, OH: Merrill.

See also Functional Domains; Functional Vocabulary

FUNCTIONAL VISION

The term functional vision is associated with the name of Natalie Barraga, a pioneer figure in emphasizing the importance of helping children with severe visual limitations to use their residual visual abilities as effectively as possible

(Barraga, 1980). The term functional vision, as defined by Barraga (1976, p. 15) denotes "how a person uses whatever vision he may have."

The federal regulations for IDEA have defined visual handicaps for school purposes so that the consideration of functional vision is primary. As defined in that law, "Visually handicapped means a visual impairment which, even with correction, adversely affects a child's educational performance." Thus the concept of functional vision is one that emphasizes what the visually handicapped child can do, rather than a particular type of physical visual limitation.

A functional vision assessment of children with visual problems attempts to determine how well a visually handicapped student is able to use the visual abilities and skills he or she possesses (Livingston, 1986). It usually involves the use of informal checklists that professionals working with the visually handicapped (e.g., teachers of visually impaired students, low-vision specialists, optometrists, orientation and mobility specialists) are asked to complete as per their particular observations.

The California Ad Hoc Committee on Assessment (Roessing, 1982) has developed a comprehensive criterion-referenced checklist for functional vision assessment. This covers the skills required for activities of daily living within a school setting, mobility, and academics. Barraga (1983) has developed the Program to Develop Efficiency in Visual Functioning, which provides an observational checklist and a diagnostic assessment procedure (DAP) for the developmental assessment of a wide range of visual skills. She also provides lesson plans to develop visual efficiencies.

Since children with multiple handicaps require specialized assessment, a number of functional vision assessment devices have been created to meet their needs. Among them is Langley's (1980) Functional Vision Inventory for the Multiply and Severely Handicapped.

REFERENCES

Barraga, N.C. (1976). *Visual handicaps and learning: A developmental approach.* Belmont, CA: Wadsworth.

Barraga, N.C. (1980). *Source book on low vision.* Louisville, KY: American Printing House for the Blind.

Barraga, N.C. (1983). *Visual handicaps and learning.* Austin, TX: Exceptional Resources.

Langley, M.B. (1980). *Functional vision inventory for the multiply and severely handicapped.* Chicago: Stoelting.

Livingston, R. (1986). Visual impairments. In N.G. Haring & L. McCormick (Eds.), *Exceptional children and youth* (4th ed.) (pp. 398–429). Columbus, OH: Merrill.

Roessing, L.J. (1982). Functional vision: Criterion-referenced checklists. In S.S. Mangold (Ed.), *A teacher's guide to the special educational needs of blind and visually handicapped children.* New York: American Foundation for the Blind.

See also **Individuals with Disabilities Education Act (IDEA); Visual Impairment**

FUNCTIONAL VOCABULARY

The development of functional reading vocabularies acquired significance as a result of the realization that the acquisition of functional academic skills was the upper limit of academic achievement for moderately/severely retarded persons. Prior to the time of that realization (late 1950s and 1960s) many curricula for the trainable retarded, although watered down, were not designed for functionality.

The content of an appropriate functional vocabulary (whether reading or speaking) is determined by analyzing the current and expected environmental demands for the student. Factors that influence the content include the age of the student, the degree of mobility independence the student has, the expected adult environment (e.g., sheltered workshop, competitive employment, custodial care), and the student's likes and dislikes. According to Musselwhite and St. Louis (1982), functional vocabulary content for severely handicapped persons should be based on client preferences and should be in the here and now rather than the future or past directed. They should also be words that occur with frequency. Many writers (Baroff, 1974; Holland, 1975; Lichtman, 1974; Schilt & Caldwell, 1980; Snell, 1983) have attempted to develop core functional lexicons or lists of sources for such lexicons. However, most researchers (including the mentioned writers) would agree that for a vocabulary to be truly functional, it must be based on an individual's experience and not on assumed common experience.

REFERENCES

Baroff, G.A. (1974). *Mental retardation: Nature, cause and management.* New York: Holsted.

Holland, A. (1975). Language therapy for children: Some thoughts on context and content. *Journal of Hearing Disorders, 40,* 514–523.

Lichtman, M. (1974). The development and validation of R/EAL: An instrument to assess functional literacy. *Journal of Reading Behavior, 6,* 167–182.

Musselwhite, C.R., & St. Louis, K.W. (1982). *Communication programming for the severely handicapped: Vocal and non-vocal strategies.* San Diego, CA: College-Hill.

Schilt, J., & Caldwell, M.L. (1980). A word list of essential career/vocational words for mentally retarded students. *Education & Training of the Mentally Retarded, 15*(2), 113–117.

Snell, M.E. (1983). Functional reading. In M.E. Snell (Ed.), *Systematic instruction of the moderately and severely handicapped* (pp. 445–487). Columbus, OH: Merrill.

See also **Functional Domains; Functional Instruction; Functional Skills; Functional Vision**

FUTURE PROBLEM SOLVING PROGRAM (FPSP)

The Future Problem Solving Program (FPSP) is a year-long program for gifted children. Begun by E. Paul Torrance in 1974 as a high-school classroom project, the program has spread to all grade levels in all areas of the United States and more than 14 other countries. In 1985, it was estimated that approximately 120,000 students were participating in the program.

Based on the creative problem-solving process developed by Osborn (1967), the program challenges youngsters to follow a six-step process to solve futuristic problems. The regular program is divided into three age divisions: Juniors (grades 4–6), Intermediates (grades 7–9), and Seniors (grades 10–12). Each team receives three practice problems that are to be completed and sent to evaluators by designated due dates. After evaluation, the work is returned with scores and suggestions for improvement.

The most proficient teams are invited to participate in state FPSP Bowls held each spring. The three winning teams, one from each level, receive invitations to attend the International FPSP Conference, usually held in June, now at the University of Michigan.

The selection of topics to be studied each year is determined by a vote of students, coaches, and state FPSP directors. Topics have included such concerns as genetic engineering, artificial intelligence, feeding the world, and organ transplants.

The program also offers a purely instructional and non-competitive component for younger children, the Primary Division. Designed for children in grades K–3, the Primary Division also serves older children who are not yet ready for the complexity of the regular program. Like the regular program, the Primary Division provides three practice problems, which, when completed, are sent to evaluators who score them and return them with constructive comments. The topics for this division are of current concern and geared to the children's interests.

Crabbe (1985) provides a more detailed description of the program. Information regarding participation may be obtained from FPSP, 2500 Packard, Suite 110, Ann Arbor, MI 481004–6827 or on the web at www.fpsp.org.

REFERENCES

Crabbe, A. (1985). *The coach's guide to the Future Problem Solving Program.* Laurinburg, NC: Future Problem Solving Program.

Osborn, A. F. (1967). *Applied imagination* (3rd ed.). New York: Scribner's.

See also **Creative Problem Solving; Creativity**

G

GAIT DISTURBANCES

Walking depends on the integration of sensory-motor-vestibular brain systems, as well as the functional strength and range of motion of the component body parts (Stolov & Clowers, 1981). Normal walking is developmentally linked to the orderly sequential integration of postural reflexes into automated smooth, adaptive responses that permit movement forward, backward, and up and down stairs by approximately 3 years of age.

Any skeletal or joint injury defect or disease that limits the normal range of joint motion produces a lack of fluidity in walking, or limping gait, because of necessary compensatory movements to maintain balance. Examples may be seen in children with arthritis, arthrogryposis, achondroplastic drawfism, and fractures. The shortening of one leg produces a characteristic pelvic tilt that can contribute to scoliosis or spinal curvature in a growing child. Pain or foot deformities can also produce a limping gait.

Cerebellar gait or ataxia is a wide-based gait with irregular steps and unsteadiness, with staggering on turning; it is characteristic of children who lack balance.

In hemiplegic gait, the child with spastic hemiplegia leans to the afflicted side and swings the affected leg out to the side and in a semicircle (circumduction).

In scissors gait, the legs are adducted and internally rotated so that with each step the child tends to trip over the opposite foot. Toe walking increases the balance difficulty. Steps are short, jerky, and slow, with many extraneous movements of the upper extremities to facilitate balance. This is the typical pattern for the child with spastic paraplegia or mild quadriplegic cerebral palsy.

Staggering or drunken gait is seen in persons with alcohol intoxication. It may also be observed in children with brain tumor, drug poisoning, or other central nervous system impairment.

Steppage gait is characterized by lifting the knees high to flop the foot down; foot drop is evident. Some children with initial stage muscular atrophy walk in this manner. Children with Duchenne muscular dystrophy show a gait somewhat similar to the steppage gait in initial stages. As their heel cords tighten these children walk more on their toes and often fall. To maintain their tenuous balance they lean back in lordosis. As weakness progresses, these children find it increasingly difficult to come to an erect position after a fall. They use their hands to "walk up their legs" to push themselves into an erect position and achieve balance. This process is the Gower's sign. These children are vulnerable in a regular school setting because a slight touch may disturb their precarious balance and weakness prevents their using their arms to catch themselves when falling; hence, serious head injuries and fractures can result.

The gait patterns of children with involuntary movement disorders are highly variable. Some individuals with athetoid and choreiform movements, which are severe and extensive, walk with a fair degree of speed and safety while their windmill involuntary movements occur. Others with less involuntary movement may have severe concomitant balance problems that require supportive safety devices.

Specific description, diagnosis, and medical intervention relative to gait disturbances usually occurs as a result of consultation among the pediatrician, orthopedist, and neurologist. Assistive devices such as braces, corsets, splints, canes, crutches, and wheelchairs require individualized fitting and training to provide the most effective locomotion compatible with health and safety. Readjustments in the nature and use of these devices must be adapted to changes owed to growth and disease status.

REFERENCE

Stolov, W.C., & Clowers, M.R. (Eds.). (1981). *Handbook of severe disability* (stock #017-090-00054-2). Washington, DC: U.S. Government Printing Office.

See also **Adaptive Physical Education; Ataxia; Muscular Dystrophy; Physical Anomalies**

GALACTOSEMIA

Galactosemia, first described in 1908, is an inborn error of galactose metabolism resulting in an accumulation of galactose in the blood, tissue, and urine. Three types of galactosemia are known, each due to a specific enzyme deficit. Classic galactosemia (the primary emphasis of this review) is the most prevalent and most severe form. It occurs in approximately 1/70,000 births and is attributed to a marked deficiency of galactose-1-phosphate uridyl transferase. Galactosemia is caused by an autosomal recessive gene, and heterozygotes for the trait exhibit reduced enzyme activity (VHGI, 1999). Galactokinase deficiency, less severe, occurs in 1/155,000 births and leads to the development of cataracts. The overall incidence of variant forms of galactosemia is approximately 1/16,000 (Desposito & Cho, 1996).

Symptoms of classic galactosemia begin within two weeks after birth and may include jaundice, vomiting, hypoglycemia, lethargy, hepatosplenomegaly, cataracts, and failure to thrive (Desposito & Cho, 1996; VHGI, 1999). Without treatment, the disorder is usually lethal, and many affected infants die during the first few weeks of life. Failure to thrive, liver failure, and sepsis are associated with additional abnormalities, such as Fanconi syndrome and cere-

bral edema, and may be fatal if untreated (Holton & Leonard, 1994; Desposito & Cho, 1996). The potential prenatal origin may account for the lack of relationship between either the age at which treatment begins or the severity of the neonatal disorder and the long-term outcome (Holton & Leonard, 1994). Other clinical manifestations include cataracts, liver damage, ataxia, seizures, cerebral palsy, proteinuria, and aminoaciduria (Desposito & Cho, 1996). Continued ingestion of galactose may lead to mental retardation, malnourishment, progressive failure, and death. Even among treated children, mental retardation and learning disabilities are common (VHGI, 1999).

Diagnosis is determined by severity of the symptoms, previous diagnosis of galactosemia in siblings or parents, amniocentesis, and neonatal screening. The prevalent screening technique is a blood analysis for elevated galactose followed by a test for deficient enzyme activity.

Treatment consists of elimination of galactose and lactose from the diet as early as possible. Since galactose is mainly formed by digestion of disaccharide lactose found in milk (milk sugar), a formula made from cow's milk is replaced with a meat-based or soybean formula. On dietary intervention, most physical symptoms subside. The infant gains weight; vomiting, diarrhea, and liver anomalies disappear; and cataracts regress, although any brain damage is permanent. Since the monosaccharide galactose does not occur in free forms in food, certain carbohydrates, lipids, and proteins that eventually metabolize to galactose must also be eliminated. A balanced galactose-free diet should be maintained throughout life (Desposito & Cho, 1996). The diet does not in any way cure the disorder, but reduces its effects on the developing person. Galactosemic women should adhere to the diet when they become pregnant to reduce levels of circulating toxins and resulting damage to the unborn fetus. Although affected women bear children, the frequency of ovarian failure is high (Desposito & Cho, 1996). Mothers of galactosemic children should also adhere to the diet during subsequent pregnancies to lessen symptoms present at birth (American Liver Foundation, 1995).

Even early dietary intervention may only partially reduce the degree and severity of cognitive damage. IQs cluster in the below normal to low-normal range, although variability is high (Staff, 1982; Desposito & Cho, 1996). Normal IQ has been reported in some cases where treatment was started before ten days of age (Desposito & Cho, 1996). Other specific difficulties may interfere with the education of treated galactosemic children. About 50% of treated children are developmentally delayed, and learning difficulties increase with age. These effects are apparently due to progressive neurological disease or brain damage sustained at an earlier age that becomes more apparent with age (Holton & Leonard, 1994). Additionally, galactosemic children may show growth retardation; visual-perceptual, speech, motor function, balance, and language difficulties; short attention spans; and difficulty with spatial and mathematical relationships. They generally present no significant behavior problems except for occasional apathy and withdrawal that in some severe cases is shown as a personality disorder characterized by timidity and lack of drive (Holton & Leonard, 1994). According to Roth and Lampe (1995), "[G]alactosemia has humbled us. It has evaded all attempts to categorize and systematize it, consistently becoming more, rather than less, complicated." In other words, "[W]e still have much to learn" (Holton & Leonard, 1994). Those in special education should be aware of the many and varied problems that treated galactosemic children may have.

REFERENCES

American Liver Foundation. (1995). Galactosemia. http://www. gastro.com/liverpg/galactos.htm, accessed 1/20/99.

Desposito, F., & Cho, S. (1996). Newborn screening fact sheets. *Pediatrics, 28*, 473–501.

Holton, J.B., & Leonard, J.V. (1994). Clouds still gathering over galactosemia. *Lancet, 344*, 1242–1243.

Roth, K.S., & Lampe J.B. (1995). Literature reviews: The gene—a multipurpose tool. *Clinical Pediatrics, 34*, 567.

Staff. (1982). Clouds over galactosemia. *Lancet, 2*, 1379–1380.

VHGI. (1999). Vermont newborn screening program: Galactosemia online.http://www.vtmednet.org/~m145037/vhgi_mem/nbsman/galacto.htm, accessed 1/20/99. 344, Issue 8932, p1242.

See also Biochemical Irregularities; Congenital Disorders; Inborn Errors of Metabolism

GALLAUDET, EDWARD M. (1837–1917)

Edward Miner Gallaudet, the originator of higher education for the deaf, was the youngest son of Thomas Hopkins Gallaudet, founder of the first school for the deaf in the United States. While teaching in his father's school, Gallaudet was chosen to organize a new school for the deaf in Washington, DC, the Columbia Institution, which came into existence in 1857 with Gallaudet as superintendent. Believing that deaf students should have the same opportunity as hearing students to receive a higher education, Gallaudet obtained legislation, approved by President Lincoln, giving the Columbia Institution the power to grant college degrees. A higher education department was created, and in 1894 it was named Gallaudet College, in honor of Edward Gallaudet's father.

An early eclectic in the education of the deaf, Gallaudet advocated a system of instruction that combined the language of signs with speech and speech reading. He was primarily responsible for the adoption of oral teaching methods by the state residential schools for the deaf in the United States.

REFERENCE

Boatner, M.T. (1959). *Voice of the deaf: A biography of Edward Miner Gallaudet.* Washington, DC: Public Affairs Press.

GALLAUDET, THOMAS HOPKINS (1787–1851)

Thomas Hopkins Gallaudet established the first school for the deaf in the United States in Hartford, Connecticut, in 1817, using methods that he had learned when visiting the *Institution Nationale des Sourds Muets* in Paris, and assisted by a teacher from that school, Laurent Clerc. Gallaudet served as principal of the Hartford school, later named the American School for the Deaf, until 1830, and continued on its board of directors for the rest of his life.

Gallaudet married one of his first students at the school. His oldest son, Thomas, became a minister to the deaf. His youngest son, Edward, established a school for the deaf in Washington, DC, the advanced department of which became Gallaudet College, named in honor of Thomas Hopkins Gallaudet.

REFERENCES

DeGerring, E.B. (1964). *Gallaudet, friend of the deaf.* New York: McKay.

Lane, H. (1984). *When the mind hears.* New York: Random House.

GALLAUDET COLLEGE

Gallaudet College, in Washington, DC, is the only liberal arts college for the deaf in the world. The college was formed in 1864 as a department of the Columbia Institution for the Deaf, now the Kendall School for the Deaf, by Amos Kendall, who had been postmaster general under President Andrew Jackson, and Edward Miner Gallaudet, superintendent of the Columbia Institution. The two men obtained the necessary federal legislation, which was signed by President Lincoln, to establish this national college for the deaf. In 1894 the college department became Gallaudet College, named in honor of Edward Miner Gallaudet's father, Thomas Hopkins Gallaudet, who established the first school for the deaf in the United States.

In addition to a distinguished record of success in the education of its students, Gallaudet College has provided much of the leadership in the education of the deaf in the United States. Its teacher-training program has provided both deaf and hearing teachers of the deaf. Many of the leaders in the field during the past century have been products of the Gallaudet College program.

REFERENCES

Boatner, M.T. (1959). *Voice of the deaf: A biography of Edward Miner Gallaudet.* Washington, DC: Public Affairs.

Gallaudet, E.M. (1983). *History of the College for the Deaf, 1857–1907.* Washington, DC: Gallaudet College Press.

See also Deaf; Deaf Culture

GALTON, FRANCIS (1822–1911)

Sir Francis Galton, born in England in 1822, came from an intellectual family; his mother, Violetta Darwin, was the aunt of Charles Darwin, and his grandfather, Samuel Galton, was a fellow of the Royal Society. The youngest of a family of nine, he was brought up in a large house near Birmingham, where his father ran a bank. Galton was a precocious child. From material in Pearson's biography, Terman (1917) estimated Galton's childhood IQ at 200. He was the author of over 300 publications, including 17 books covering a broad range of topics.

Galton pioneered the development of psychological testing and the formulation of the major genetic principle of segregation of inherited characteristics. He is perhaps best known for his work on the genetic basis of individual differences in intelligence as discussed in his book, *Hereditary Genius* (1869). He was an early proponent of eugenics, a term coined by him. He is also largely credited with having invented the stopwatch for his research on reaction time.

In his research on the relationship of the characteristics of parents and offspring, Galton discovered the phenomenon of regression toward the mean and developed the concept of correlation, a term first used by him. Galton's measure of correlation was later given mathematical refinement by Karl Pearson, who later wrote a biography of Galton (Pearson, 1914). A more recent biography was prepared by Forrest (1974).

REFERENCES

Forest, D.W. (1974). *Francis Galton: The life and work of a Victorian genius.* New York: Toplinger.

Galton, F. (1869). *Hereditary genius: An inquiry into its laws and consequences.* London: Macmillan.

Galton, F. (1908). *Memories of my life.* London: Methuen.

Pearson, K. (1914). *The life, letters and labours of Francis Galton.* Cambridge, England: Cambridge University Press.

Terman, L.M. (1917). The intelligence quotient of Francis Galton in childhood. *American Journal of Psychology, 28,* 209.

GAMMA-AMINOBUTYRIC ACID (GABA)

Gamma-aminobutyric acid (GABA) is a major inhibitory neurotransmitter in the central nervous system. Specific functions of the brain depend on adequate levels of neurotransmitters in the areas that control such functions. This knowledge has stimulated a search for drugs that can augment or reduce the supply of particular neurotransmitters. A deficiency of GABA has been associated with several diseases, including schizophrenia and epilepsy (Hammond & Wilder, 1985).

REFERENCE

Hammond, E.J., & Wilder, B.J. (1985). Gamma-vinyl GABA: A new antiepileptic drug. *Clinical Neuropharmacology, 8*(1), 1–12.

GARGOYLISM

See HURLER'S SYNDROME.

GARRETT, EMMA (1846–1893)

Emma Garrett, seeking a way to demonstrate the effectiveness of the oral method of teaching the deaf, obtained a grant that enabled her, with her sister Mary, to establish the Pennsylvania Home for the Training in Speech of Deaf Children Before They Are of School Age, also known as the Bala Home. Located in Philadelphia, the home began operation in 1891. Emma Garrett was superintendent, and both sisters served as teachers. The Bala Home was widely influential as an example of the effectiveness of the oral method of teaching the deaf and of the efficacy of early intervention. Following Emma Garrett's death in 1893, her sister became superintendent of the Bala Home and carried on the work that the two of them had begun.

REFERENCE

Fay, E.A. (1893). *Histories of American schools for the deaf, 1817–1893* (Vol. 3). Washington, DC: Volta Bureau.

GARRETT, MARY SMITH (1839–1925)

Mary Smith Garrett, with her sister Emma, in 1891 founded in Philadelphia the Pennsylvania Home for the Training in Speech of Deaf Children Before They Are of School Age, also known as the Bala Home. Mary Garrett succeeded her sister as superintendent after Emma died in 1893. She continued in this position for the remainder of her life.

Mary Garrett was a leading advocate of the oral method of teaching the deaf and helped to develop a curriculum based on this approach. Her system of teaching oral communication was based on early intervention, with speech training beginning as early as 2 years of age. Through the efforts of Mary and her sister, Pennsylvania became the first state to appropriate funds for preschool speech and language training for deaf children.

Mary Garrett was instrumental in the enactment of legislation establishing a juvenile court and probation system for Pennsylvania. She was also a leader in the National Congress of Mothers, the forerunner of the National Congress of Parents and Teachers, where she promoted such social reforms as child labor laws and juvenile court legislation.

REFERENCE

Fay, E.A. (1893). *Histories of American schools for the deaf, 1817–1893* (Vol. 3). Washington, DC: Volta Bureau.

GARRISON, S. OLIN (1853–1900)

S. Olin Garrison, minister and educator, founded in New Jersey in 1887 the school for retarded children that later became the Training School at Vineland. The school featured a cottage system of small, homelike facilities, a strong educational program, and a research department that published some of the nation's most influential works on mental retardation. Garrison served as superintendent of the Training School until his death in 1900. He was also responsible for the establishment by New Jersey of the State Home for Girls and of a school for epileptic children.

REFERENCE

McCaffrey, K.R. (1965). *Founders of the Training School at Vineland, New Jersey: S. Olin Garrison, Alexander Johnson, Edward R. Johnstone.* Unpublished doctoral dissertation. Teachers College, Columbia University, New York.

GATES-MACGINITIE READING TESTS (GMRT)

The Gates-MacGinitie Reading Tests (GMRT; MacGinitie & MacGinitie, 1988; 1989) are designed to evaluate reading achievement in grades K through 12. They are appropriate for use in regular classrooms, Title I programs, special education programs, and other educational settings where an evaluation of reading is needed.

The subtests at Levels PRE and R assess students' knowledge of print, print conventions, and the alphabetic principle. The Vocabulary tests at Levels 1 and 2 assess word decoding skills; the Comprehension tests gauge the ability to read and comprehend sentences and brief paragraphs. At Levels 3 and up, the Vocabulary tests measure knowledge of the meaning of words. The reading passages for the Comprehension tests at Levels 3 and up are all taken from published text that reflects the kinds of materials students read in and outside of school, including fiction and content materials in social studies, science, and the humanities.

Three test levels are provided for grade 1—Level PRE, which is appropriate for students who have little or no background knowledge or have had minimal formal instruction in reading; Level R, which is appropriate for students who have had some training in letters and sounds; and Level 1, which is appropriate for students who are beginning readers. One test form of each of these levels is provided. For Levels 2 and up, two statistically equivalent test forms are provided for evaluating growth at different times of the school year.

A description and review of the third edition are included in the Buros Institute's *Eleventh Mental Measurements Yearbook* (Kramer & Conoley, 1992). The entry includes 78 test references up through 1991. The third edition is also reviewed in *The Teacher's Guide to Reading Tests* (Cooter, 1990).

REFERENCES

Cooter, R.B. (1990). *The teacher's guide to reading tests.* Scotsdale, AZ: Gorsuch Scarisbrick.

Kramer, J.J., & Conoley, J.C. (Eds.). (1992). *Eleventh mental measurements yearbook.* Lincoln, NE: Buros Institute of Mental Measurements.

MacGinitie, W.H., & MacGinitie, R.K. (1988). *Gates-MacGinitie Reading Tests* (3rd ed.). Itasca, IL: Riverside.

MacGinitie, W.H., & MacGinitie, R.K. (1989). *Technical report: Gates-MacGinitie Reading Tests.* Itasca, IL: Riverside.

GAZE AVERSION

Eye contact, the study of facial characteristics during human intercourse, has been a topic that has always captivated inquiry. Why do we maintain eye contact during social interaction? What is there in facial cues that provide others social clues and what do these clues address? Are there normal patterns of gaze aversion?

The answer to the last question is a definite yes. It is neither socially correct nor communicatively enriching to look continuously at another person's face. Researchers (Beattie, 1979) have advanced a hypothesis that gaze aversion is a technique that reduces distractibility and permits thinking and speech planning. Ehrlichman (1981) advanced this hypothesis, which his data supported, as a statement of cognitive interference. Simply, the hypothesis postulates that people look away more often during periods of speech hesitancy than during periods of fluency. Gaze aversion is used while thinking and planning the next speech pattern.

Coss (1979) believed that the dimensions of gaze in psychotic children were different in several respects. He ran three studies. The first examined 10 normal and 10 psychotic children during presentations of five models comprising a blank model and models with one through four concentric discoid elements separated by the same interpupillary distance as human eyes. The second experiment examined 15 psychotic children using models presenting two concentric discoid elements in vertical, diagonal, and horizontal orientations. The third experiment examined 10 normal and 10 psychotic children using five models comprising two schematic facing eyes as represented by concentric discoid elements. The psychotics looked longer at the models than did the normals. However, these groups did not differ for the model with two concentric discoid elements. Both groups, particularly the psychotics, looked less at the model presenting two concentric discoid elements than at the models presenting other arrangements of concentric discoid elements in the first experiment. Similarly, in the third experiment, both groups looked less at the model with two concentric discoid elements than at models with staring and averted irises. In sum, normals and psychotics did not differ appreciably in their gaze under varying conditions.

Currently, there is no data to support the long-standing belief that gaze aversion occurs with greater duration or more frequency among emotionally disturbed than among normal children. Scheman and Lockhard (1979) generated data from 573 children suggesting that gaze or stare is developmentally determined. Children under 18 months of age rarely establish eye contact. Children 18 months to 5 years do not avert their gaze. From 5 to 9 years, behavioral patterns specific to the youth are well established. This study took place in a suburban shopping center where the children were unprotected by parents' wishes when confronted by gazes from strange adults. This work lends strong support to the communication theory of gaze aversion. That, in turn, suggests that gaze aversion is not solely a function of development, conditions, or emotional problems, but is a device that provides and protects concentration and is instrumental in speech production. Therefore, children with fluency difficulties, e.g., stutters, may have increased gaze aversion, a contention that is also supported in the research literature.

REFERENCES

Beattie, G.W. (1979). Planning units in spontaneous speech: Some evidence from hesitation in speech and speaker gaze direction in conversation. *Linguistics, 17,* 61–78.

Coss, R.G. (1979). Perceptual determinants of gaze aversion by normal and psychotic children: The role of two facing eyes. *Behavior, 3–4,* 228–253.

Ehrlichman, H. (1981). From gaze aversion to eye movement suppression: An investigation of the cognitive interference explanation of gaze patterns during conversation. *British Journal of Social Psychology, 20,* 233–241.

Scheman, J.D., & Lockhard, J.S. (1979). Development of gaze aversion in children. *Child Development, 50,* 594–596.

GENERAL APTITUDE TEST BATTERY

The General Aptitude Test Battery (GATB) was developed by the U.S. Employment Services as a means of assisting clients (and those at state employment offices) in identifying possible successful occupation areas. The battery is composed of 12 separately timed and scored tests that measure nine aptitudes for individuals age 13 through adulthood. Scores are then used to point out areas of client strengths and weaknesses. There are two forms. The following nine vocational aptitudes are measured:

1. intelligence—the general learning ability of the client;

2. verbal aptitude—the ability to understand words and their relationships;

3. numerical aptitude—the ability to perform arithmetic quickly and accurately;

4. spatial aptitude—the ability to think visually of geometric forms and to recognize relationships resulting from the movement of objects in space;

5. form perception—the ability to perceive pertinent details and make visual discriminations;

6. clerical perception—the ability to discriminate similarities and differences in verbal material;

7. motor coordination—the ability to coordinate eyes and hands rapidly and accurately;

8. finger dexterity—the ability to move and manipulate small objects with the fingers rapidly and accurately;

9. manual dexterity—the ability to move the hands skillfully in placing and turning motions.

In the manual for the GATB (1967), scores on the various subtests are correlated with occupations, and tentative cutoff scores are provided for each occupational area. The test was validated to predict performance in over 400 professional, semi-, and unskilled occupations (Buros, 1978). A Spanish version of the GATB is available, as is a non-reading measure of the same aptitudes. There is also a special edition for deaf persons. The GATB takes approximately two hours to complete. To administer the GATB, one must obtain certification by attending a workshop that teaches administration and interpretation of the GATB. State employment offices present these workshops.

REFERENCES

Buros, O.K. (1978). USES General Aptitude Test Battery. In O.K. Buros (Ed.), *The eighth mental measurements yearbook* (Vol. II, pp. 675–680). Highland Park, NJ: Gryphon.

United States Employment Services. (1967). *Manual for the USES General Aptitude Test Battery.* Minneapolis: Intran.

GENERAL CASE PROGRAMMING

The essence of general case programming is generalization. A teacher or trainer engaging in general case programming is systematically increasing the probability of skills learned in one setting being successfully performed in different settings with different target stimuli (Horner, Sprague, & Wilcox, 1982).

There are several trends in special education that coalesce to underscore the importance of general case programming. There has been a growing interest in training relevant age-appropriate skills that can be immediately used by a student in his or her real-life environment (Brown et al., 1979; Brown et al., 1983). For many students, particularly at the secondary level and above, this call for relevancy translates into community-based skills. Even though the community is the desired environment for performance, it presents a demanding set of circumstances for instruction. There are just too many different forms of transportation, restaurants, stores, people, jobs, etc., to train in all situations. Therefore, any training strategy must be efficient and promote generalization. The training examples a teacher selects must increase the likelihood of students performing correctly on similar but untrained examples and must be the fewest number of examples necessary to create this generalization. It is these two criteria that general case instruction is designed to meet.

Stimulus control is an important concept for general case programming. This control is achieved when environmental events, or discriminative stimuli, are able to cue correct performance. All stimuli have certain characteristics that are either relevant or irrelevant for correct performance. General case instruction teaches students to respond to the relevant stimulus characteristics and ignore the irrelevant by systematically varying the dimensions and levels of stimuli presented during instruction. By varying the dimensions and levels of stimuli, students come to identify a group or class of stimuli that share certain relevant characteristics and set the occasion for correct responding. The stimulus class comes to control the selection of correct responses because response characteristics have been automatically varied along with the variation in stimulus characteristics, creating a class of relevant or effective responses from the pool of all possible responses.

There are several guidelines that have been identified by Horner et al. (1982) for creating a general case curriculum:

1. Define the instructional universe by identifying all the situations in which a student is expected to produce a particular behavioral outcome.
2. Identify the range of relevant stimulus and response variation in the instructional universe by systematically analyzing the situations within which a student is expected to perform.
3. Select the minimum number of logistically feasible examples for training and testing that will sample the full range of stimulus and response variation.
4. Sequence teaching examples to produce the most efficient training possible.
5. Teach the examples using the most current instructional technology.
6. Test on nontrained probe examples to identify and eliminate error patterns.

Research has shown that general case programming is more effective in obtaining generalized responding than single instance training or training on several similar instances of a particular skill. Generalized responding has been obtained via general case instruction for vending machine use (Sprague & Horner, 1984), preparing electronic capacitors for insulation (Horner & McDonald, 1982), and grocery shopping (McDonnell, Horner, & Williams, 1984), among others.

REFERENCES

Brown, L., Branston, M.B., Hamre-Nietupski, H., Pumpian, I., Certo, N., & Gruenwald, L.A. (1979). A strategy for developing chronological age-appropriate and functional curricular content for severely handicapped adolescents and young adults. *Journal of Special Education, 13,* 81–90.

Brown, L., Nisbet, J., Ford, A., Sweet, M., Shiraga, B., York, J., & Loomis, R. (1983). The critical need for non school instruction in educational programs for severely handicapped students. *Journal of the Association for the Severely Handicapped, 8,* 71–77.

Horner, R.H., & McDonald, R.S. (1982). Comparison of single instance and general case instruction in teaching a generalized vocational skill. *Journal of the Association for the Severely Handicapped, 8,* 7–20.

Horner, R.H., Sprague, J., & Wilcox, B. (1982). General case programming for community activities. In B. Wilcox & G.T. Bellamy (Eds.), *Design of high school programs for severely handicapped students.* Baltimore, MD: Paul H. Brookes.

McDonnell, J.J., Horner, R.H., & Williams, J.A. (1984). Comparison of three strategies for teaching generalized grocery purchasing to high school students with severe handicaps. *Journal of the Association for the Severely Handicapped, 9,* 123–133.

Sprague, J.R., & Horner, R.H. (1984). The effects of single instance, multiple instance, and general case training on generalized vending machine use by moderately and severely handicapped students. *Journal of Applied Behavior Analysis, 17,* 273–278.

See also **Generalization; Programmed Instruction**

GENERALIZABILITY THEORY

Generalizability theory was developed by Cronbach and his associates (Cronbach, Gleser, Nanda, & Rajaratnam, 1972) to evaluate the generalizability of results obtained when measurement is carried out for assessing, for example, differences among students. The theory is primarily concerned with identifying and estimating the variances associated with the effects present in the design used to collect the evaluation data. Variances are estimated within an analysis of variance (ANOVA) framework. These estimated variances are then used to describe the relative contribution of each effect to the observed variance and to compute measurement error variance and, if desired, generalizability coefficients for each factor of interest.

Two types of studies are conducted using generalizability theory: G(generalizability)-studies and D(decision)-studies. A G-study is carried out when developing a measurement procedure for use in a D-study later on. Thus, a G-study is designed to encompass the "universe of admissible observations" (Cronbach et al., 1972, p. 20); for instance, a universe including all the variables (factors) under which observations could be collected in subsequent D-studies. A D-study draws observations from the "universe of generalization," i.e., the universe to which we wish to generalize the results in a specific situation. The universe of generalization is then a subset of, or the same as, the universe of admissible operations. The results of a G-study are used to design D-studies. In many instances, however, a G- and D-study may be conducted using the same data set; for instance, the data are used both for making decisions and for improving the design of future D-studies so that the universe of admissible observations is the same as the universe of generalization.

From a generalizability analysis we estimate variance associated with each factor in the design, measurement error, and a generalizability coefficient associated with the factor of interest. The practitioner or researcher wishing to conduct generalizability analysis should read Brennan (1983), Fyans (1983), and Shavelson and Webb (1981).

REFERENCES

Brennan, R.L. (1983). *Elements of generalizability theory.* Iowa City, Iowa: American College Testing Program.

Cronbach, L.J., Gleser, G.C., Nanda, H., & Rajaratnam, N. (1972). *The dependability of behavioral measurements: Theory of generalizability for scores and profiles.* New York: Wiley.

Fyans, L.J. (Ed.). (1983). *Generalizability theory: Inferences and practical applications.* San Francisco: Jossey-Bass.

Shavelson, R.J., & Webb, N.M. (1981). Generalizability theory: 1973–1980. *British Journal of Mathematical & Statistical Psychology, 34,* 133–166.

See also **Research in Special Education**

GENERALIZATION

Generalization is the demonstration of a behavior in circumstances other than those in which it was trained. The term is also used to refer to the occurrence of a behavior similar to, but different than, the learned behavior under the same circumstances as during training (Rutherford & Nelson, 1988; Scruggs & Mastropieri, 1984). These two types of generalization are referred to as stimulus generalization and response generalization. Stimulus generalization, the type most commonly studied by special education researchers, may be said to have occurred when a learner demonstrates a skill or behavior in different surroundings, at different times, or with different people. For example, a student who is trained to insert the correct amount of change into a soda machine at school and subsequently performs the same skill at a recreation center is said to have generalized the response. Response generalization refers to the spread of effects to other related behaviors and is exemplified by a student opening a large can after having successfully learned to open a small can.

Generalization is necessary to the development of a wide repertoire of behavior. It was once assumed that generalization occurred automatically with the learning of a behavior, but this principle has not proven true, especially for handicapped learners (Stokes & Baer, 1977). If generalization is to occur, it must be a component of the actual training process (Baer, Wolf, & Risley, 1968).

Success in training for generalization has varied and researchers differ in their opinions regarding its efficacy (Scruggs & Mastropieri, 1984). Some propose that failure to train for generalization is due to a lack of educational technology; others contend that inherent deficiencies in the intellectual functioning of handicapped persons make generalization difficult. The former analysis implies that new and better training techniques are needed and that the problem is a teaching one. The latter implies a learning problem and that attempts to train for generalization should be replaced by more effort spent training desired behaviors in the environments in which they are required (Scruggs & Mastropieri, 1984). The failure of generalization has been a major drawback in the application of strictly behavioral methods to learning (Martens & Witt, 1988).

REFERENCES

Baer, D.M., Wolf, M.M., & Risley, T.R. (1968). Some current dimensions of applied behavior analysis. *Journal of Applied Behavior Analysis, 1,* 91–97.

Martens, B., & Witt, J. (1988). On the ecological validity of behavior modification. In J. Witt, S. Elliott, & F. Graham (Eds.), *Handbook of behavior therapy in education* (pp. 325–339). New York: Plenum.

Rutherford, R., & Nelson, C. (1988). Generalization and maintenance of treatment effects. In J. Witt, S. Elliott, & F. Graham (Eds.), *Handbook of behavior therapy in education* (pp. 277–324). New York: Plenum.

Scruggs, T.E., & Mastropieri, M.A. (1984). Issues in generalization: Implications for special education. *Psychology in the Schools, 21,* 397–403.

See also **General Case Programming; Transfer of Learning; Transfer of Training**

GENERIC SPECIAL EDUCATION

Generic special education is a cross-categorical orientation to training teachers and delivering special education services to mild/moderately handicapped youngsters. This approach came about as a result of a variety of educational movements in special education. In the 1960s, there was growing dissatisfaction among educators with the use of traditional medical-model categories to identify handicapped pupils. This concern was due, in part, to increased recognition of the heterogeneity of learner characteristics within a specific handicap classification and to reports that many pupils have similar educational needs despite differences in their handicapping conditions (Hewett & Forness, 1984).

Legal requirements to educate handicapped children in the least restrictive educational environment according to an individualized educational plan (IEP) further eroded the historical categorical boundaries to instruction. According to IDEA, selection of instructional services for the handicapped is based on pupils' educational needs as determined by a committee of educators and parents who develop the IEP. After analyzing pupils' levels of performance, the appropriate educational placement is prescribed. A variety of instructional options have been developed to meet pupils' individual needs, including placement in regular classes, the use of consulting and itinerant special education teachers, resource and self-contained special education classes, special day schools, residential centers, hospital schools, and homebound instruction (Deno, 1973; Reynolds & Birch, 1982). The specific nature of instructional services, including decisions concerning curricula and teaching strategies, should be determined by the individual needs and instructional characteristics of the pupil; they should not be arbitrarily prescribed on the basis of the child's handicapping condition.

Concern for individualization is evident throughout the entire continuum of services provided by schools and agencies. From infant stimulation to vocational preparation programs that emphasize the transition from school to work, pupils who require special education services receive them based on their individual needs rather than on their categorical label. Within this context of individualization of instruction, generic special education focuses on identifying and meeting the learning needs and characteristics of specific pupils regardless of disability category. For example, owing to similarities in performance characteristics, many learning-disabled, mildly retarded, and emotionally disturbed youngsters may be effectively served in the same classroom with the same curricula.

As special education instructional services evolved from a rigid categorical approach to a functional orientation, so did teacher training programs change. With the support of federal funds in the early 1970s, several institutions of higher education initiated cross-categorical special education teacher training programs (Brady, Conroy, & Langford, 1984). These programs exhibited a variety of characteristics differentiating them from the traditional categorical orientation to teacher education. For example, each program's name described the role or function of the teacher rather than a particular handicapping condition (e.g., diagnostic-prescriptive teacher, consulting teacher). The programs were primarily developed at the master's degree level for already certified teachers, and although students were trained noncategorically, their certification remained categorical. Later, teacher training programs emphasized greater interaction with regular education, offered programs at both bachelor's and master's levels, and were located in states that began initiating noncategorical certification, primarily by collapsing certain categories into a general one. These training programs tended to collapse categorical course offerings to meet the challenge of noncategorical certification.

Associated with these movements in service delivery and teacher training has been a trend for state education agencies to develop noncategorical teacher certification in special education, growing from only 12 states in 1979 to 34 states and the District of Columbia in 1983 (Idol-Maestas, Lloyd, & Lilly, 1981). Nearly all states now provide some form of generic certification. Names of these new certificates range from descriptions of pupils (e.g., learning handicapped, mildly handicapped) to descriptions of programs (e.g., resource room specialist, diagnostic prescriptive teacher) to nonspecific terms such as generic special educator.

REFERENCES

Brady, M.P., Conroy, M., & Langford, C.A. (1984). Current issues and practices affecting the development of noncategorical programs for students and teachers. *Teacher Education & Special Education, 7*(1), 20–26.

Deno, E.N. (Ed.). (1973). *Instructional alternatives for exceptional children.* Arlington, VA: Council for Exceptional Children.

Hewett, F.M., & Forness, S.R. (1984). *Education of exceptional learners* (3rd ed.). Boston: Allyn & Bacon.

Idol-Maestas, L., Lloyd, S., & Lilly, M. (1981). A noncategorical approach to direct service and teacher education. *Exceptional Children, 48*(3), 213–220.

Reynolds, M., & Birch, J.W. (1982). *Teaching exceptional children in all America's schools* (2nd ed.). Reston, VA: Council for Exceptional Children.

See also **Holistic Approach and Learning Disabilities**

GENETIC COUNSELING

There have been many advances in the management of hereditary disorders in the past 25 years (e.g., plastic surgery, dietary manipulation, prenatal diagnosis, and most recently, gene therapy). Genetic counseling provides the vehicle for the transmission of relevant information needed by the client to make an informed decision about the treatment and prevention of hereditary disorders.

The first American genetic counseling center on record

was the Eugenic Records Office in Cold Spring Harbor, New York, founded by Dr. Charles B. Davenport in 1915. Genetic counseling fell out of favor in the 1930s as the role of environment in human behavior became better understood. During the next 20 years, the study of genetics was predominantly an academic pursuit. Informal counseling was done by academicians who were primarily involved in basic genetic research rather than clinical medicine.

By the 1960s, great strides had been made in understanding human genetics. The new information gave counselors a broader and more scientific basis for telling families about the recurrence, risks, and inheritance patterns of an increasing number of diseases. The development of genetic tests based on blood and cell samples introduced the field of prospective counseling and helped shift counseling from primarily nonmedical settings to medical screening programs in hospitals and universities. Today, there are approximately 800 centers and satellite facilities specializing in genetics in the United States. Both the National Foundation—March of Dimes, 1275 Mamaroneck Avenue, White Plains, New York 10605, and the National Genetics Foundation, 250 West 57th Street, New York, NY, can direct those in need of counseling to an appropriate source.

Until recently, a professional providing genetic counseling was typically a physician with an interest in genetics, or a PhD geneticist with an interest in medicine. In the past 20 years, postdoctoral fellowship positions have prepared physicians and PhD geneticists in the full range of clinical genetics. In addition, genetic counselors with MS degrees emerged in response to a substantial increase in the number of individuals seeking genetic counseling and screening. The varied training and backgrounds of genetic counselors, and recognition by the American Society of Human Genetics for the need to certify counselors, led to the creation of a board certification process. Since 1981, hundreds of professionals have been certified by the American Board of Medical Genetics.

See also **Genetic Factors in Behavior; Heredity; Tay-Sachs Syndrome**

GENETIC FACTORS IN BEHAVIOR

Little is known about the genetics of human behavior, either normal or abnormal, and it is unlikely that there are specific genes for behavior or any other phenotypic trait. Behavior genetics is more complex than the study of genetic influences on physical traits because it is hard to define behavioral traits reliably, to assess them validly, and to control situational influences. Nonhuman species offer advantages of convenience and control for genetic research, but the lack of precise analogs between human and animal behavior, especially pathological behavior, limits the value of animal research for human behavior genetics.

However, a number of human pathological genes have more or less specific effects on behavior. The child with Phenylketonuria (PKU) is likely to be hyperactive and irritable, have outbursts of temper, abnormal postural attitudes, and agitated behavior; about 10% of those affected show psychotic behavior. Characteristic behavioral changes often precede the choreic movements in Huntington's chorea. Congenital cretinism, which may be recessively inherited, produces effects on personality. Perhaps the most striking example of a gene-induced behavioral defect is the bizarre tendency for self-mutilation in Lesch-Nyhan syndrome.

Chromosomal aberrations also have effects on behavior. Children with Down's syndrome are thought to be happier and more responsive to their environment than other children of comparable IQ; they often display musical ability. Girls with Turner's syndrome rate high on verbal IQ tests but below average on performance measures; they seem to have a deficit in perceptual organization. The XYY karyotype is alleged to show a predisposition to criminality and aggressive behavior; however, a causal link between an excess or deficiency of chromosomal material and a behavior phenotype is obscure.

There is more information about the genetics of abnormal behavior than about how normal behavior is encoded in the gene loci. Schizophrenia, with incidence in the 1% range, has been studied in families, and 2 to 5% of the parents and 6 to 10% of the siblings are affected. If a propositus and parent are both affected, the risk for the siblings is higher. Concordance is much greater for monozygotic than for dizygotic twin pairs. Children of schizophrenic parents raised by their natural parents and those raised by adoptive parents show the same incidence of schizophrenia. This finding seems to establish a role for heredity in schizophrenia. However, questions of genetic heterogeneity, the role of environmental stress, and the nature of the biochemical abnormalities associated with schizophrenia remain to be answered. At present, it does not seem reasonable to suspect a single gene-determined basic defect.

The affective disorders are somewhat similar to schizophrenia in terms of population incidence and frequency within families. It has been suggested that bipolar disease is an x-linked dominant disease, but so simple a hypothesis seems implausible on the basis of current evidence. Biochemical evidence of a single-gene basis for either the bipolar or the unipolar type is still lacking.

Developmental aphasia appears to be caused by the inability of the aphasic child to process auditory stimuli presented at a normal rate. This ability does develop eventually, but at a later age than average, and it is suspected to be an autosomal dominant trait (Thompson & Thompson, 1980). The evidence favoring the familial nature of dyslexia is compelling, but the factors that account for the aggregation of cases remain unclear. Some types of dyslexia seem to be influenced by the genes and it is speculated that dyslexia is an autosomal dominant condition with some degree of sex limitation (males are affected far more frequently).

A number of disorders that are considered behavioral, such as the pervasive developmental disorders and conduct disorders, have genetic links that are almost certainly poly-

genetic and cannot be linked to a single gene (Gillberg, 1995). This has made studying the genetic basis of complex human behavior at the single gene level quite complex. It is difficult to predict precise behavioral outcomes or patterns for children, even with extensive data on parents.

By the application of biometrical genetics and twin studies, evidence for heritability has been found for infant behavior and temperament, introversion-extroversion, and neuroticism. Empirical evidence on sibling resemblance in intelligence published since 1915 in the United States and Europe, including more than 27,000 sibling pairs, showed that genetic factors are the major source of individual differences in intelligence. The most likely estimate of the sibling correlation for IQ in the population is +0.49 (Paul, 1980).

REFERENCES

Gillberg, C. (1995). *Clinical child neuropsychiatry.* Cambridge: Cambridge University Press.

Paul, S.M. (1980). Sibling resemblance in mental ability: A review. *Behavior Genetics, 10*(3), 277–290.

Thompson, J.S., & Thompson, M.W. (1980). *Genetics in medicine* (3rd ed.). Philadelphia: Saunders.

See also **Autism; Conduct Disorders; Cretinism; Emotional Disorders; Fragile X; Genetic Counseling; Huntington's Chorea; Lesch-Nyhan Syndrome**

GENETIC TRANSMISSIONS

Genetics, the scientific study of heredity, is the phenomenon wherein biological traits appear to be transmitted from one familial generation to the next. Gregor Mendel, the nineteenth-century Austrian monk, did the seminal studies leading to the founding of the field of genetics. The history of human genetics since that time has included the development of cytogenetics, biochemical genetics, molecular genetics, immunogenetics, population genetics, applied genetics, and clinical genetics. The science of genetics has shown that inherited traits result from the transmission of the parents' genes to their offspring. Genes interact with one another and with their environment to produce distinctive characteristics or phenotypes. Therefore, offspring tend to exhibit phenotypes similar to those of their parents.

There are two types of cell division that occur within the human body. Mitosis is the process of cell division that occurs in all cells, except for the sex cells or gametes. Gametes are divided during the process of meiosis.

Critical to genetic transmission are chromosomes, which are the small, rod-shaped bodies located in the nuclei of each cell. Each normal human body cell has 23 pairs or 46 chromosomes. During mitosis, cells divide by duplicating themselves, and each daughter cell contains 46 chromosomes that are identical to the 46 chromosomes contained in the original cell. During meiosis, the gametes divide by splitting into two separate distinct cells that each contain 23 chromosomes of the original cell. During reproduction, the male and female gametes join and produce a zygote that contains 46 chromosomes. One pair of the 23 chromosomes is different in size and shape and this atypical pair is related to sex determination. In all mammals, the female has two similarly sized chromosomes, called X, while the male has one X and a smaller Y chromosome. If an ovum is fertilized by a Y-bearing sperm, the zygote will be a male, but if the ovum is fertilized by an X-bearing sperm, the zygote will be female.

The actual units of hereditary transmission are the deoxyribonucleic acid (DNA) molecules or genes residing at specific loci on the chromosome. A recent estimate has indicated there are over 30,000 structural genes per haploid set of 23 chromosomes. The different variants of genes that control a particular trait and occupy corresponding loci on the paired chromosomes are called alleles. For example, one allele, or variant, of the gene for eye color produces blue eyes, while a different allele produces brown eyes. The paternal and maternal alleles for eye color are aligned beside each other in two adjoining chromosomes of the offspring.

According to Mendel's laws, one allele dominates the other in the phenotypic expression of a heterozygous genotype (genetic constitution). Dominant alleles are represented by capital letters and recessive alleles with small letters. Whenever one or both parents are heterozygous for a trait, as often occurs, their children are not all likely to inherit the same genotype as distinguished from its physical appearance (phenotype). For example, a male inherits blue-eyed (b) alleles from both his mother and father. He is therefore homozygous for eye color (bb); both alleles are the same, the zygote is homogeneous for eye color. The boy will have blue eyes and can pass only an allele for blue eyes to his offspring. If the boy mates with a girl who has alleles only for brown eyes, she can pass only a brown-eyed (B) allele to their child. Since this child receives the blue allele (b) from one parent and the brown allele (B) from the other, the child is heterozygous for eye color (Bb). The child will have brown eyes because brown eye color is a dominant trait. Because so many different gene combinations can arise from two parents, two siblings seldom have the same genes, unless they come from the same zygote; these offspring are identical or monozygotic twins.

See also **Chromosomal Abnormalities; Genetic Counseling; Karyotype**

GENETIC VARIATIONS

The independent assortment of chromosomes during meiosis is a major reason for the variation of the genetic constitution in different individuals. Each gamete has 8 million possible combinations of chromosomes from the 23 pairs, and each set of parents has 7 ´ 1013 possible chromosome combinations to offer their children. Thus, with the incomplete exception of monovular twins, every person is and will be potentially genetically unique.

While genetics is the study of biological variations, medical genetics is the study of those variations that result in, or predispose one to, disease. Genetic diseases make a considerable contribution to the burden of mortality and morbidity in childhood. Mendelian and chromosomal diseases account for about 12% to 15% of childhood mortality, with congenital malformations contributing an additional 25% to 30%. Of all individuals with IQs below 50, at least 40% have a chromosomal disorder (of which Down's syndrome accounts for about three-quarters); 15% have a single-gene disease (e.g., Huntington's disease, x-linked mental retardation, Tay-Sachs disease); and 45% have severe developmental malformation (Porter, 1982).

Generally, three major varieties of genetic disease afflict humans: Mendelian disorders caused by a single gene, cytogenetic disorders caused by chromosomal abnormalities, and multifactorial genetic diseases. In Mendelizing or single-gene diseases, the genetic factor is relatively simple. Three distinct patterns are recognized: dominant, recessive, and x-linked, of which there are 800, 550, and 100 known conditions, respectively. The most important of the genetic disorders of early development affect metabolism (e.g., phenylketonuria [PKU], a disorder of amino acid metabolism). Untreated, PKU results in severe mental retardation, decreased attention, and lack of responsiveness to the environment. Well-known autosomal dominant diseases are Huntington's disease, deafness (dominant forms), and neurofibromatosis (Von Recklinghausen disease). Cystic fibrosis is the most prevalent autosomal recessive disorder in white children. Tay-Sachs disease, also an autosomal recessive disorder, has a high prevalence rate among Ashkenazi Jews. Hemophilia is an x-linked recessive disease in which the blood fails to clot normally. Another genetic blood disease characterized by a tendency of the red cells to become grossly abnormal in shape is sickle cell disease, which affects about 0.25% of American blacks.

The second category of diseases results from failure of chromosomes to develop properly (chromosomal dysgenesis) during the formation of the oocyte or spermatocyte, or during conception and germination, resulting in an irreversibly abnormal chromosome makeup in the embryo. Extra and mismatched chromosomes, as well as structural anomalies, are major forms of dysgenesis. Examples of dysgenesis are trisomy 21, 18, and 13, as well as partial trisomies, mosaicisms, monosomies, deletions, and inversions. Sex chromosomal anomalies include Turner's syndrome and Klinefelter's syndrome (XXY). For the most part, the disorders in this category are not inherited, but they involve the genetic material, the chromosomes. Mental retardation and physical abnormalities are the most common consequences of chromosomal disorders.

The more common abnormal genetic conditions are multifactorial in their causation and are characterized by a complex interaction of genetic and environmental factors. The genetic effects are complex and determined by the interaction of many genes, each contributing a small effect. Cleft lip and palate, congenital dislocation of the hip, pyloric stenosis, talipes, and equinovarus are well-known examples; perhaps the best known examples are anencephaly and meningomyelocele, known collectively as neural tube defects. Carcinogens have been found to induce some kind of chromosomal rearrangements that are associated with a variety of human cancers (Radman, Jeggo, & Wagner, 1982).

REFERENCES

Porter, I.H. (1982). Control of hereditary disorders. *Annual Review of Public Health, 3,* 277–319.

Radman, M., Jeggo, P., & Wagner, R. (1982). Chromosomal rearrangement and carcinogenesis. *Mutation Research, 98,* 249–264.

See also **Genetic Counseling; Genetic Factors in Behavior**

GENIE

The case of Genie involves an adolescent who experienced a degree of social isolation and experiential deprivation so far unparalleled in medical literature. The case came to light in 1970, when Genie was 13 and a half years of age.

From the age of 20 months to 13 years, 7 months, Genie was confined to a small bedroom at the rear of the family home. There, she was physically harnessed to an infant potty seat. At night, when she was not forgotten, she was removed from the harness and put into a sleeping bag which had been modified to hold Genie's arms stationary. She was then put into a crib with wire mesh sides and a wire mesh cover.

Genie received a minimum of care and stimulation. She was fed only infant food and wore no clothing. There was no TV or radio in the home, and as there were two doors separating her bedroom from the front of the house, where the remainder of the family lived, she could hear little of any family conversations. As her bedroom was set in the back of the house, away from the street, she heard few environmental noises. Her room contained only the potty and crib—no carpet, no pictures on the walls. The room's two windows were covered up except for a few inches at top. Genie's mother, having become blind shortly after Genie's birth, was unable to care for Genie, and so it was Genie's father and brother who were her primary caretakers. Together, they committed many acts of cruelty and abuse, among which was their consistent unwillingness to talk to her and beatings inflicted on Genie for making noise.

When Genie was found, she was extremely malnourished. She weighed only 59 pounds and was only 54 inches tall. Never having been fed solid food, she was unable to chew or bite. She could not stand erect, and could barely walk. She was incontinent for feces and urine. Having been beaten for making noise, she was silent. She knew only a few words. She was essentially unsocialized and untrained.

Genie's case caught the attention of the scientific community because of the unique opportunity it offered for studying the human potential to "catch up" as it were—to develop social, cognitive, and linguistic knowledge after the typical points in development. Particular interest in Genie's potential for linguistic development was fostered by Lenneberg's (1967) critical age hypothesis for language acquisition. Lenneberg proposed that, as is the case with many maturationally timed species-specific behaviors, there is a critical period for first language acquisition—between the ages of two and puberty, beyond which a first language could not be learned. Genie faced the task of first language acquisition at 13 and a half. Thus, her ability to learn language directly tested Lenneberg's hypothesis.

In the 9 years she was studied, Genie showed very uneven language learning ability. Most important in this regard is the striking contrast between her acquisition of morphology and syntax on the one hand and her acquisition of semantic knowledge on the other. Genie's acquisition of vocabulary and of how to express meaningful relations through words steadily progressed and increased, whereas her utterances remained largely ungrammatical and hierarchically flat (Curtiss, 1977, 1981, 1982). Genie's case, then, supports a weak form of Lenneberg's hypothesis in that while she developed some language, she did not acquire language fully or normally. Her case also suggests that different components of language are differentially vulnerable to the age at which language acquisition is carried out. In particular, her case points to the separability of a conceptual or referential linguistic component (which involves lexical knowledge and knowledge of semantic roles, and which is resilient in its developmental potential) from a grammatical component, which involves the constraints and rules of grammar, for which the acquisition potential appears to be far more maturationally constrained.

Although most of the scientific investigation carried out with Genie concentrated on her language development, a considerable number of standardized intelligence tests and tests of Piagetian operations were also administered. Remarkably, Genie evidenced 1 year's mental growth every year past her discovery and demonstrated full operational intelligence in spatial knowledge, with less developed ability in some other areas, specifically, those relying on verbal mediation.

The cognitive profile that Genie displayed lends support to a modular view of the mind in which grammar represents a distinct faculty of mind, separate from other components of language and separate from other mental abilities. For details regarding Genie's case history and language acquisition, see Curtiss, 1977. For details regarding her nonlinguistic cognitive abilities, see Curtiss, 1979. For a discussion of Genie's case and the critical age hypothesis, see Fromkin et al., 1974. For a discussion of Genie's case in connection with theories of language learning and cognitive development, see Curtiss, 1981 and 1982. Unfortunately, relations between Genie's mother and the research team studying her soured, and some disputes among those working with her arose. Lawsuits and other disruptions followed, and as a result, not only research on Genie but contact between her and the research team was legally restricted. For an interesting story of this aspect of Genie, see Rymer (1993).

REFERENCES

Curtiss, S. (1977). *Genie: A psycholinguistic study of a modern-day "wild child."* New York: Academic.

Curtiss, S. (1979). Genie: Language and Cognition. *UCLA Working Papers in Cognitive Linguistics, 1,* 16–62.

Curtiss, S. (1981). Dissociation between language and cognition. *Journal of Autism & Developmental Disorders, 11,* 15–30.

Curtiss, S. (1982). Developmental dissociations of language and cognition. In L. Obler & L. Menn (Eds.), *Exceptional Language and Linguistics.* New York: Academic.

Fromkin et al. (1974). The development of language in Genie: A case of language acquisition beyond the critical period. *Brain & Language, 1,* 81–107.

Lenneberg, E.H. (1967). *Biological foundations of language.* New York: Wiley.

Rymer, R. (1993). *Genie: An abused child's flight from silence.* New York: HarperCollins.

See also **Expressive Language Disorders; Language Deficiencies and Deficits; Linguistic Deviance**

GENIUS

The term genius is used chiefly to denote exceptionally high talent, ability, or achievement. However, it has been largely supplanted by the terms gifted or giftedness. As originally used in his research on heritability, Galton (1892) intended that genius should denote an "ability that was exceptionally high, and at the same time inborn" (p. VIII). However, he also suggested that it should not be considered a technical term. Galton attempted to demonstrate that genius or exceptional ability is inherited.

In approaching his monumental longitudinal study of gifted children, Terman (1925) used the term gifted, but he nevertheless titled the entire series of books that resulted *Genetic Studies of Genius.* It should be noted, however, that Terman had extended the concept of the origins of genius, "The origins of genius, the natural laws of its development, and the environmental influences by which it may be affected for good or ill, are scientific problems of almost unequalled importance for human welfare" (1925, p. v). Terman went on to suggest that there were three problems related to genius: its nature, its origins, and its cultivation. Clearly then, the stage was set for nature-nurture research.

Research on the origins and nurturance of genius has often taken the form of studies of eminent people or very high achievers. In Volume II of *Genetic Studies of Genius* (1926), Catherine Cox and others (including Lewis Terman) studied the early mental traits of 300 geniuses. Galton had also pioneered in this approach to the study of genius (1869). More recently the biographical research of the Goertzels (1962) continues this tradition, as reported in *Cradles of Eminence.*

Research by Bloom (1985), however, focused on living subjects who have achieved world recognition. The research by Bloom and his predecessors agrees in the finding that genius, giftedness, special talent, and high ability often appear as precocious behavior; for instance, accomplishments in youth that far exceed normal achievements. There is also increased recognition of the influence of family, schooling, and other variables in determining giftedness. The term genius is now used less frequently than it was, although it is sometimes evoked to denote truly exceptional giftedness.

REFERENCES

Bloom, B.S. (Ed.). (1985). *Developing talent in young people.* New York: Ballantine.

Cox, C.M. (1926). *Genetic studies of genius: Vol. 2. The early mental traits of three hundred geniuses.* Stanford, CA: Stanford University Press.

Galton, F. (1869). *Hereditary genius.* London: Macmillan.

Galton, F. (1892). *Hereditary genius* (2nd ed.). London: Macmillan.

Goertzel, V., & Goertzel, M.G. (1962). *Cradles of eminence.* Boston: Little, Brown.

Terman, L.M. (1925). *Genetic studies of genius: Vol. 1. Mental and physical traits of a thousand gifted children.* Stanford, CA: Stanford University Press.

See also **Gifted and Talented Children**

GEORGE, WILLIAM REUBEN (1866–1936)

William Reuben "Daddy" George was born on June 4, 1866, in the hamlet of West Dryden in central New York. As a young man, he moved to New York City, where he established a small manufacturing business. Through his church, George began working with children in one of the city's most oppressive slums. He had notable success with city

William Reuben George

gangs, forming his own "law and order" gangs, which transformed young people from lawbreakers to law enforcers. Because children from the slums were often not accepted into the summer fresh air programs for city children, George started a program that provided a camping experience in a rural setting for these needy young people. George's summer program began in 1890 on a farm at Freeville, near West Dryden, and continued until he conceived the idea of a permanent community for young people based on the structure of the U.S. government: "our glorious republic in miniature—a junior republic."

In 1895 George gave up his business to remain at Freeville at the end of the summer with a number of students to begin a year-round program. The community that they developed was based on the principles of self-support—the students worked for their food and lodging—and self-government—the students made and enforced the laws governing the community.

George's ideas attracted the attention of educators and social reformers, and of prominent men and women who provided much of the financial support for the "junior republic." There was great interest in other parts of the country as well, and George supervised the establishment of nine similar communities in other states. None of these institutions consistently followed George's principles, however, and he considered the expansion effort a failure.

At the Freeville junior republic, George developed an elaborate educational and social system based on the principles of self-government and self-support. "Nothing without labor" became the junior republic's motto. The students, or citizens, as they came to be called, attended school, worked in the various jobs that made the junior republic almost entirely self-sufficient, and ran their own government.

George's junior republic, an early demonstration of the progressive education principle of learning by doing, was a major force in the development of programs for deprived, delinquent, and troubled youths in schools and institutions in the first part of the century. George headed the junior republic until his death on April 25, 1936. It is a tribute to the power of his ideas that George's junior republic, which today enrolls 170 adolescents referred by public schools, courts, and parents, still carefully adheres to its founder's precepts of self-support and self-government.

REFERENCES

Holl, J.M. (1971). *Juvenile reform in the progressive era: William R. George and the junior republic movement.* Ithaca, NY: Cornell University Press.

Van Dyck, H.D., & Van Dyck, R. (1983). George junior republic: Fresh start for troubled teens. *Journal of the New York State School Boards Association,* pp. 15–20.

GEORGIA STUDIES OF CREATIVE BEHAVIOR

The Georgia Studies of Creative Behavior is a research program devoted to the study of creativity. Established at the University of Georgia in 1966 by Torrance (1974), it continued and expanded a similar program of research and development at the University of Minnesota—the Minnesota Studies of Creative Behavior (1958–1966). The Minnesota and Georgia research program has been concerned with the identification of creative potential, developmental patterns in creative thinking abilities, predictions of adult creative achievement, future imaging, instructional models and strategies to enhance creative thinking, the presence of creativity in various population groups, teacher training, creative problem solving, and cross-cultural studies of creative behavior.

The contributions to theory and practice regarding creative behavior from the Minnesota and Georgia studies have been numerous. Significant achievements and events have included the development and refinement of a battery of creative thinking tests, the Torrance Tests of Creative Thinking (TTCT) (1966), for use from kindergarten through adulthood; a 22-year longitudinal study to assess the creative achievement of adults whose IQs and creativity had been tested in elementary school; the Incubation Model, an instructional model to enhance creative thinking and incubation; the wide-scale application of this model into the Ginn Reading 360 and 720 series; the Ideal-Pupil Checklist and the Torrance Checklist of Creative Positives; and the founding of the Future Problem Solving Program and the International Network of Gifted Children and their Teachers.

The program of the Georgia studies has been supported and directed by Torrance with the assistance of J. Pansy Torrance, numerous graduate research assistants from different countries, postdoctoral students, and visiting scholars. Torrance (1984) observed that graduate students throughout the world have participated in the studies through their questions, suggestions and research findings.

Headquarters for the Georgia Studies of Creative Behavior are now located at the University of Georgia. Current activities are concerned with investigating the nature of mentoring relationships; sociodrama as an instructional strategy; developing and revising the streamlined scoring procedures for the TTCT; and verbal and figural and work with the Torrance Center for Creative Studies at the University of Georgia in developing the Torrance Creative Scholars Program and the Torrance Creative Scholar-Mentor Network.

The work of the Minnesota and Georgia studies has resulted in the publication of over 1600 articles, over 40 books, monographs, instructional materials, films, filmstrips, and other creative learning materials. The collection of these materials and other references on creativity, giftedness, and future studies are contained in the library and archives of Torrance, which are housed at the University of Georgia Library and coordinated through the Torrance Center for Creative Studies. E. Paul Torrance, founder of these programs, is now Emeritus Alumni Foundation Distinguished Professor at the University of Georgia and continues to be active in the study of creativity.

REFERENCES

Torrance, E.P. (1974). *Georgia studies of creative behavior: A brief summary of activities and results (1966–1974).* Unpublished paper, Department of Educational Psychology, University of Georgia, Athens.

Torrance, J.P. (1984). A retrospective view of the Minnesota and Georgia Studies of Creative Behavior. In *New directions in creativity research* (pp. 65–73). Ventura, CA: National/State Leadership Training Institute on the Gifted and Talented.

See also Creativity; Torrance Center for Study of Creative Behavior

GERMANY, SPECIAL EDUCATION IN

Germany provides a well-equipped system of institutions for special education of disabled children and youth. Traditional special education services were developed under the concept of segregation. Not until the 1970s did a movement for integration emerge. It slowly moves forward, against quite a resistance.

Special education in Germany for many children starts in their first years of life. Early intervention for infants who run the risk of becoming handicapped or who are handicapped takes place in the child's home. Young children should not be institutionalized, if possible. In periodical turns—for instance, once a week for one hour—the early educator leaves the responsible resource center to meet the family, provided they agree, in order to give pedagogical and therapeutic help in a playing manner. In practice, this spread method of early intervention can be stonewalled if the family's living circumstances are not suitable or if the adults refuse regular house visits. In these cases, parents can visit the resource center with their handicapped child regularly. Special early intervention can also take place in an institution. In some regions of Germany, this centralized form is still preferred to the early home intervention. The reasons for this preference are more organizational than pedagogical.

Special early intervention also reaches clinical instiutions, especially sociopediatrical clinics, where handicapped children and children at risk can get medical treatment, psychological consultation, and pedagogical support.

Early educational attention often continues during kindergarten time (three to six years old). The early educator can visit the child at home; however, often this educator visits the child in the ordinary kindergarten and gives support in the children's group. The other children may participate in the pedagogical and therapeutic games and exercises. This prevents the handicapped child from being seen by other students as "special" and improves the child's social integration.

In addition, however, there are also many special kindergartens, each of which specializes in one specific kind of handicap. There are working governesses, most of whom have completed an additional course in special education, with groups of, for example, only mentally handicapped infants or only hearing-impaired infants. In some parts of Germany, special kindergartens have begun to open themselves to children without handicaps in order to promote integration. In Germany, for school-aged children and youth with special educational needs, there exist two main options: separate education in special schools, or integrative education with special educational support in ordinary schools. Special educational classes in regular schools exist as well, but are rare. Segregated schooling is built on a 200-year long tradition and still is quite prevalent. In the 1995/96 school year, 391,100 pupils attended special schools; that equals 3.94% of all 9,931,500 pupils of general schools in Germany (Bundesministerium, 1996.) The number of integratively-educated children represents only one-tenth of all students; nevertheless, the number is slowly increasing. Exact official statistics showing the number of integrated pupils with special educational needs in Germany does not yet exist.

Since the German reunion in 1990, the Federal Republic of Germany (F.R.G.) consists of 16 Laender. In their territories, the Laender maintain the sovereignty for culture and education. Some Laender with conservative school politics keep special needs students in compulsory special schools; other Laender are promoting integration in regular schools. The Conference of the Ministers for Culture and Education in the F.R.G. (KMK) intends to avoid development in different directions. According to a recommendation given in 1972 by the KMK, 10 types of special schools exist in Germany.

1. Schools for learning disabilities:

   With about 221,000 pupils (95/96), schools for learning disabilities are the most common type of special schools, but at the same time they are especially criticized, because learning disabilities are only defined in relation to school, and because before education age they cannot actually be diagnosed. Learning deficiencies fundamentally depend on the efficiency of regular schools, which can either support slow learners adequately or not. Through administrative trials, low performance in school is reduced to an intellectual handicap, which is indicated by an IQ between 55 to 85.

2. Schools for the mentally handicapped:

   Schools for the mentally handicapped were not founded until the 1960s. These schools take pupils who are not able to follow classes in schools for learning disabilities (IQ usually under 60). Nearly 60,000 children attend these schools.

3. Schools for speech problems:

   About 32,000 pupils in Germany attend these special schools. For many of them, it is a school to pass through on their way to another (regular) school or another type of special school.

4. Schools for behavioral disorders:

   In Germany, about 21,000 students with behavioral disorders attend this type of special school, which is in several Laender called *school for (special) educational support*. This type of special school is meant to be a temporary school, like the schools for speech problems; it should educate the pupils on the learning level of regular schools and send them back to a regular school after a few years' time. However, this happens very rarely.

5. Schools for physically handicapped students:

Schools have about 20,000 pupils who are all very different from each other in the degree of their physical handicap as well as in their learning abilities. Many children in the schools for physically handicapped students suffer from additional disorders such as speech development, sensory organ impairment, and mental retardation.

6. & 7. Schools for the hard of hearing and deaf:

Both types of schools together teach about 10,000 pupils, most of them hard of hearing children. In the official statistics, hearing impaired and deaf students are not separated from each other. The Institution for the Deaf and Dumb, founded in 1778 in Leipzig, is considered the oldest special school in Germany. Special schools for hard of hearing children in Germany did not originate until 1900.

8. & 9. Schools for the visually impaired and blind:

These two types of special schools are attended only by about 4,000 pupils; only about 1,000 of them attend schools for the blind. Quite often, schools for the blind and schools for the visually impaired are situated next to one another, so single students can easily change from one school to the other according to their educational needs.

10. Clinic Schools:

For most ill young people, this is a transitory school, because they are educated there only during the time of their medical treatment in the hospital. Instruction takes place in the clinic part for children, or if necessary, at the bed or their home.

Besides these 10 special schools, there exist further specialized institutions; for instance, schools for multiple-disordered students, such as deaf-blind students.

GERSTMANN SYNDROME

The Gerstmann syndrome consists of a constellation of problems including finger agnosia, right-left orientation problems, inability to calculate or do math (acalculia), and inability to write (agraphia). When first described by Gerstmann (1940), Gerstmann syndrome was believed to be a discrete, localized neurological problem denoting damage specific to the left parietal lobe of the brain. Considerable disagreement currently exists regarding the specific nature and causes of Gerstmann syndrome. Benton (1961) argued that the syndrome was prematurely described and was based on a serendipitous combination of learning and behavior problems with a variety of causes. Others have argued over its precise nature, some holding that the underlying deficit is aphasic in nature and others arguing that Gerstmann syndrome is related to left-hemisphere neglect. The constellation of behaviors occurring in concert is rare and whether or not they represent a true syndrome is difficult to discern.

REFERENCES

Benton, A.L. (1961). The fiction of the Gerstmann syndrome. *Journal of Neurology, Neurosurgery, & Psychiatry, 28,* 339–346.

Gerstmann, J. (1940). Syndrome of finger agnosia: Disorientation for right and left, agraphia, and acaculia. *Archives of Neurology & Psychiatry, 44,* 398–408.

See also Acalculia; Agraphia

GESELL, ARNOLD LUCIUS (1880–1961)

Arnold Lucius Gesell was a high-school teacher and principal before entering graduate school at Clark University, where he received his doctorate in psychology in 1906. In 1911 he became assistant professor of education at Yale University, where he founded the Yale Clinic of Child Development and began the studies of child development that were to occupy him for the rest of his life. To improve his qualifications for this work, Gesell studied medicine at Yale, receiving his MD degree in 1915. Gesell made a detailed, step-by-step analysis of infant behavior, establishing that infant behavior develops in an orderly manner through stages that are alike from child to child.

Gesell became a household name in the United States, primarily because of three books that he coauthored: *Infant and Child in the Culture of Today* (1943), *The Child from Five to Ten* (1946), and *Youth: The Years from Ten to Sixteen* (1956).

In addition to his studies of normal development, Gesell made numerous investigations of deviations in development, including mental retardation, Down's syndrome, cretinism, and cerebral palsy. Following his retirement from Yale in 1948, Gesell continued his work at the Gesell Institute of Child Development, which was founded in his honor in 1950.

REFERENCES

Ames, L.B. (1961). Arnold L. Gesell: Behavior has shapes. *Science, 134,* 266–267.

Langfield, H.S., Boring, E.G., Werner, H., & Yerkes, R.M. (1952). *A history of psychology in autobiography* (Vol. 4). Worcester, MA: Clark University Press.

See also Gesell Developmental Schedules

GESELL DEVELOPMENTAL SCHEDULES

The Gesell Developmental Schedules were first published by Gesell and his colleagues in 1940, although updated administration and norms are reported by Gesell, Ilg, and Ames (1974) and Ames, Gillespie, Haines, and Ilg (1979). The schedules provide an empirical method of measuring the development of infants and young children from 4 weeks through 5 years of age. Items on the schedules are ordinally arranged, with behaviors typical of successive ages (e.g., 42 months, 48 months, 54 months) listed. The administration of the schedules requires direct observations of children's responses to stimulus objects such as toys and parent interviews.

Four areas of development are included in the schedules: motor, adaptive, language, and personal/social. Items include walking up and down stairs, saying words and sentences, and imitating drawing circles and crosses. Behavioral norms for ages 2½ through 5 years of age are reported in Ames et al. (1979). Interrater reliability coefficients over .95 have been found (Knobloch & Pasamanick, 1974). The scales are quite dated and no longer useful in this form.

REFERENCES

Ames, L.B., Gillespie, B.S., Haines, J., & Ilg, F.L. (1979). *The Gesell Institute's child from one to six: Evaluating the behavior of the preschool child.* New York: Harper & Row.

Gesell, A., Ilg, F., & Ames, L.B. (1974). *Infant and child in the culture of today* (Rev. ed.). New York: Harper & Row.

Knobloch, H., & Pasamanick, B. (Eds.). (1974). *Gesell and Amatruda's developmental diagnosis* (3rd ed.). Hagerstown, MD: Harper & Row.

See also **Bayley Scales of Infant Development**

GESELL SCHOOL READINESS TEST

The Gesell School Readiness Test (Ilg, Ames, Haines, & Gillespie, 1978), a behavior test for children ages 5 through 10 years, determines children's readiness for school and promotions to succeeding grade levels according to developmental level. The administration of the test requires about half an hour. The test consists of an interview with the child (questions about the child's age, birthday, number of siblings, and father's occupation); paper and pencil tests (writing name, address, date, and numbers); copying of forms (e.g., circle, triangle, square); finishing of a drawing of an incomplete man; right and left orientation; the Monroe Visual Tests; and questions about what the child likes to do best at home and at school.

Behavioral norms (i.e., the typical scores for children at each year from 5 through 10 years of age) are provided for each section of the instrument. Ilg et al. (1978) provide detailed descriptions of average children at each year from 5 through 10 years of age. Ilg et al. (1978) also report several psychometric characteristics of the tests. These include a description of the standardization sample and sex and group differences.

REFERENCE

Ilg, F.L., Ames, L.B., Haines, T., & Gillespie, C. (1978). *School readiness: Behavior tests used at the Gesell Institute* (Rev. ed.). New York: Harper & Row.

See also **Gesell Developmental Schedules**

GETMAN, GERALD N. (1913–1990)

A native of Larchwood, Iowa, Gerald M. Getman earned his doctor of optometry degree from Northern Illinois College of Optometry (NICO) in 1937. He was subsequently awarded an honorary doctor of ocular sciences degree (1957) from NICO as well as the honorary doctor of sciences degree (1986) from the State University of New York College of Optometry. Getman conducted most of his work in Minnesota, Pennsylvania, and California, spending three years as director of research and child development (1967–1970) at the Pathway School in Norristown, Pennsylvania, and ten years in education and research in California, first as a member of the faculty at Southern California College of Optometry and subsequently (1978–1985) as part of a group practice in developmental optometry in Newport Beach specializing in children's learning disabilities. He served as a consultant on visually related learning problems to numerous public and private schools and taught special courses and seminars on children's learning problems as a visiting member of the faculties at Ohio State University, Yale University, Temple University, the University of Chicago, and institutions of higher learning in Australia and The Netherlands. Prior to his death in April 1990, Getman had moved to the Washington area where he continued to lecture and consult.

Getman's principal contributions to special education have been equally divided between developmental/behavioral optometry and education. He is widely considered as the father of developmental optometry, with his concept of vision development strongly influenced by his pioneering work with Arnold Gesell on the visual development of infants and children. Their joint research, conducted from 1944 to 1950 at the Yale Clinic of Child Development, contributed to the vision care of children that now enjoys widespread availability from optometrists (Getman, Gesell, Ilg, Bullis, & Ilg, 1949). Getman also had a significant influence on educational procedures used to guide children with learning problems. In order to best prepare children for an increasingly technological and abstract culture, he advocated a parental role in planning their learning programs. In establishing these programs, he viewed clinical labels as ambiguous and useless, creating confusion instead of understanding (Getman, 1976).

Getman authored more than 300 professional papers as well as the book *How to Develop Your Child's Intelligence,* which has become important internationally to both teachers and parents (Getman, 1962). His numerous publications include *Smart in Everything . . . Except School* and *Developmental Optometry* (both 1992). He is the recipient of the Pioneer Award of the National Association for Children with Learning Disabilities, the Special Award of Distinction of the International Federation of Learning Disabilities, and the Apollo Award, the highest commendation given by the American Optometric Association. Getman has also been recognized in *Who's Who in the Midwest.*

REFERENCES

Getman, G.N. (1962). *How to develop your child's intelligence.* Luverne, MN: Getman.

Getman, G.N. (1976). *Teaching children with learning disabilities: Personal perspectives.* Columbus, OH: Merrill.

Getman, G.N. (1992). *Developmental optometry: The optometric appraisal of vision development and visual performance.* Santa Ana, CA: Optometric Extension Program.

Getman, G.N. (1992). *Smart in everything . . . Except school.* Santa Ana, CA: VisionExtension.

Getman, G.N., Gesell, A., Ilg, F., Bullis, G., & Ilg, V. (1949). *Vision, its development in infant and child.* New York: Hoeber.

g FACTOR THEORY

Charles Spearman (1863–1945) proposed a general intellectual ability, *g*, to account for the fact that all mental abilities are to some degree positively intercorrelated (Spearman, 1904, 1927). Spearman considered *g* to be a hereditary general mental energy that is manifest most strongly in tasks involving "the education of relations and correlates" (i.e., inductive and deductive reasoning) and "abstractness."

Spearman developed the statistical method of factor analysis by which it is possible to determine the *g* loading of a test, or the proportion of variation in the test score that is shared with all other tests in the analysis. This led to Spearman's two-factor theory of mental ability, in which the variation of each measured ability is divided into two parts: a part owed to *g* and a part specific to the particular test. The two-factor theory was later expanded to admit the possibility of group factors, representing groups of tests that share variation in addition to their general and specific variation.

More recent studies confirmed Spearman's observation that nearly all mental abilities are positively correlated. It has proved to be virtually impossible to devise a test that appears to involve mental ability that is not positively correlated with all other such tests when administered to a representative sample of people. Factor analysis of such positively correlating tests can always be made to yield a large general factor representing the variation that the tests share in common as indicated by their positive correlations. In such analyses, the tests with the highest *g* loadings tend to involve comprehension and abstract reasoning across a broad range of content. The greater the degree of mental manipulation of the input elements of the test items, the higher the general factor loading tends to be.

The observations that led Spearman to develop the theory of *g* are now well established; however, rival conceptualizations of the same observations have gained wide acceptance among psychologists. Thurstone (1938) extended Spearman's method of factor analysis to accommodate correlated factors and adopted the criterion of simple structure to determine the best set of multiple factors to represent the abilities contained in the tests being analyzed. The name primary mental abilities, which Thurstone attached to these factors, focused attention on the multiple differential abilities. The general factor, although still present, was hidden in the correlations among the primary factors. Following Thurstone, the number of known ability factors steadily increased. They have been organized into a model of the structure of intellect by Guilford (1967).

There is now general agreement that there are a number of distinct factors of mental ability that are substantially correlated with each other and that the correlation among the distinct factors represents a large general factor. The disagreement centers on which is most important, the multiple distinct factors or the single underlying general factor, *g*.

Jensen (1979, 1985) interpreted *g* as the basic biological factor of intelligence and attempted to relate it to general speed of mental processing. He pointed out that *g*, more than any other factor of ability, corresponds to the commonsense notion of intelligence, that it is most predictive of success in academic and occupational situations demanding mental ability. He also presented evidence concerning inbreeding depression that suggests that *g* is the ability that has been most subject to natural selection during the course of human evolution.

REFERENCES

Guilford, J.P. (1967). *The nature of human intelligence.* New York: McGraw-Hill.

Jensen, A.R. (1979). *g:* Outmoded theory of unconquered frontier? *Creative Science & Technology, 2,* 16–29.

Jensen, A.R. (1985). The nature of the black-white difference on various psychometric tests: Spearman's hypothesis. *Behavioral & Brain Sciences, 8,* 193–219.

Spearman, C. (1904). General intelligence, objectively determined and measured. *American Journal of Psychology, 27,* 229–239.

Spearman, C. (1927). *The abilities of man.* New York: Macmillan.

Thurstone, L.L. (1938). Primary mental abilities. *Psychometric Monographs, 1.*

See also **Culture Fair Tests; Intelligence Testing**

GIFTED AND TALENTED, UNDERACHIEVEMENT IN THE

Student underachievement is failure to perform at expected levels in a given area, when these expectations are based on the student's past performance or area related aptitude measures. This failure to perform is not the result of sensory acuity limitations, health status, or a specific cognitive disability.

"Underachievement," or failure to perform (FTP), is a

sociologically based concept in which a status is assigned to an individual based on the perception of him or her by others. "Failure to perform" is a label that is based on a performance predictor. It is possible that the predictor may be neither accurately measured nor relevant to performance in given task areas under specific conditions of instruction.

In a population free of cognitive disabilities, FTP may reflect a number of factors. These factors include motivational, personality, interpersonal, and curricular instructional considerations. Failure to achieve appears to be a relatively complex phenomenon with multiple dimensions.

Motivation has two basic aspects: "direction or location" and "degree of need for success." Motivation may be of an extrinsic or external nature, or it can be characterized as intrinsic or internal (Newland, 1966). External motivation refers to a student responding to forces and demands outside of himself or herself. Extrinsic motivation is typified by students studying simply to pass an examination. In contrast, an example of intrinsic motivation would be a student's efforts to master an area to satisfy his or her personal achievement needs.

Achievement has interpersonal, motivational, and personality influences, as well as curriculum influences. It is arguable that the needs of the gifted and talented might be best met through an individual educational plan approach (Swassing, 1985). This plan is based on a curriculum with the characteristics of content acceleration, content enrichment, content novelty, and content sophistication (Gallagher, 1984). Flexibility in programming, such as community-based programs or other alternative educational approaches, permit wider curriculum/program options to more fully motivate larger numbers of gifted and talented pupils (Swassing, 1985). Social and affective curriculum goals are also desirable to facilitate the more effective adult functioning of the gifted and talented, as well as their more integrated and more effective function in school (Lacy, 1979).

REFERENCES

Gallagher, J.J. (1984). *Teaching the gifted child.* Boston. Allyn & Bacon.

Lacy, G. (1979). *The social and emotional development of the gifted and talented.* Albany, NY: University of the State of New York, State Education Department.

Newland, T.E. (1966). *The gifted in socioeconomic and educational perspective.* Englewood Cliffs, NJ: Prentice Hall.

Swassing, R.H. (1985). *Teaching gifted children and adolescents.* Columbus, OH: Merrill.

GIFTED AND TALENTED CHILDREN

Gifted and talented children are now recognized in thousands of American schools as having learning and personal characteristics that are different from those of children of average and low ability. As a result of these differential characteristics, they have special educational needs and therefore a need for differentiated educational programs. Among the special characteristics of the gifted and talented are the following:

1. They learn new material rapidly and easily.
2. They are precocious. Talents appear early and advanced skills and achievement levels are much higher than grade placement.
3. They have large vocabularies, read early, are verbally fluent, and write well.
4. They reason well, understand easily, have intellectual depth, and are logical.
5. They have extended awareness of the world, respond to more elements of a situation, and are socially aware.

These characteristics lead to a set of special educational needs. Van-Tassel (1979) proposed the following list of special educational needs of gifted and talented children:

1. To be challenged to operate cognitively and affectively at complex levels of thought and feeling
2. To be challenged through opportunities for divergent production
3. To be challenged through work that demonstrates process/product outcomes
4. To be challenged by discussions among intellectual peers
5. To be challenged by experiences that promote understanding of human value systems
6. To be challenged by the opportunity to see interrelationships in all bodies of knowledge
7. To be challenged by special courses that accelerate pace and depth
8. To be challenged by exposure to new areas of learning
9. To be challenged by applying abilities to real problems
10. To be taught critical thinking, creative thinking, research, problem solving, coping with exceptionality, decision making, and leadership

Gifted children are those who have superior general intellectual ability. Talented children are those who show signs of special aptitude or ability in a specific area of the arts, sciences, business, etc. (Gagne, 1985). Renzulli (1979) suggests that giftedness also includes high levels of task commitment (motivation) and creativity. Feldhusen (1986) extended the conception of giftedness to include a self-concept that recognizes and accepts special talents or abilities. Gagne (1985), however, proposed that personal factors such as motivation, task commitment, and self-concept are not elements or factors of giftedness but rather are catalysts that facilitate the emergence and growth of general ability toward specialized talent or aptitude in a special area of human endeavor.

Schools sometimes identify the gifted and talented as early as kindergarten or first grade and provide special educational programs of service to them. Richert, Alvino, and

McDonnel (1982) conducted a survey of the methods used to identify gifted and talented youths in the United States. They found a wide diversity of tests and rating scales being used (and misused) to identify gifted and talented children. They particularly noted that tests are often used in ways for which they were not intended and that the most significant deficiency in identification occurs in the area of leadership talent. However, they acknowledge that this is the most difficult area of giftedness to define.

Gallagher, Weiss, Oglesby, and Thomas (1983) conducted a survey of schools in the United States to determine which practices characterized special programs for the gifted. They found that the resource room/pullout model was most popular, followed by special advanced classes for the gifted at the elementary level. At the secondary level the most widely used provision was advanced or honors classes, while opportunities for independent study and research came in second.

Some states now mandate that all schools must provide special program services for gifted and talented youths. Many provide formula funding to the schools for the special education of these youths. There is increasing recognition that these youths need to be identified early and given differentiated educational opportunities if they are to realize their full potential. Research by Bloom (1985) indicates that gifted and talented youths should be identified early and given specialized instruction in their areas of special talent or ability. Through such special programming at school, and with support at home, gifted and talented children can reach high achievement as adults.

REFERENCES

Bloom, B.S. (Ed.). (1985). *Developing talent in young people.* New York: Ballantine.

Feldhusen, J.F. (1986). A conception of giftedness. In R.S. Sternberg & J.S. Davidson (Eds.), *Conceptions of giftedness.* New York: Cambridge University Press.

Gagne, G. (1985). Giftedness and talent: Reexamining a reexamination of the definitions. *Gifted Child Quarterly, 29,* 103–112.

Gallagher, J.J., Weiss, P., Oglesby, K., & Thomas, T. (1983). *The status of gifted/talented education.* Los Angeles: National/State Leadership Training Institute for the Gifted/Talented.

Renzulli, J.S. (1979). *What makes giftedness.* Los Angeles: National/ State Leadership Training Institute for the Gifted/Talented.

Richert, E.S., Alvino, J.J., & McDonnel, R.C. (1982). *National report on identification.* Sewell, NJ: Educational Improvement Center-South.

Van-Tassel, J.L. (1979). A needs assessment model for gifted education. *Journal for the Education of the Gifted, 29,* 103–112.

See also **Genius; Intelligence**

GIFTED CHILD QUARTERLY

Gifted Child Quarterly is a major publication in the field of the education of gifted children. It is published by the National Association for Gifted Children, 1707 L St. NW, Ste. 550, Washington, DC 20036-4201. The quarterly was first published in 1958 with an emphasis toward education-alresearchers, administrators, teachers, and parents of gifted children. The journal publishes manuscripts that offer new or creative insights about giftedness and talent development in the context of the school, the home, and the wider society. The journal also publishes quantitative or qualitative research studies as well as manuscripts which explore policy and policy implications. It is a refereed publication with a panel of 30 reviewers and an editor elected by the association board. All members of the association receive the quarterly as part of their membership privileges.

GIFTED EDUCATION RESOURCE INSTITUTE

The Gifted Education Resource Institute was founded at Purdue University, West Lafayette, Indiana, in 1978 to (1) conduct research on gifted children; (2) provide graduate programs in gifted education at the MS and PhD levels; (3) offer services to schools in developing programs for the gifted; (4) conduct special programs for gifted youths on Saturdays and in summers; (5) make psychological services available for gifted youths in the areas of testing and counseling; and (6) disseminate information to schools and parents concerning the identification and education of gifted children. The institute is directed by Dr. John F. Feldhusen. Eight other professors in related disciplines serve as associated faculty at the institute. Approximately 15 graduate students are in residence each year working on grants and projects conducted by the institute. The institute also works closely with the Indiana Department of Education and Indiana schools in training teachers for work with the gifted and in developing educational programs for gifted and talented youth.

GIFTED HANDICAPPED

The gifted handicapped have been defined as "those who exhibit unusual gifts/talents in spite of physical, mental, emotional, or experiential handicaps" (Blacher-Dixon, 1977). This definition, however, is far too simplistic for one to understand the complexity of this seemingly contradictory category. To understand the category of gifted handicapped, one must understand each of the categories separately.

The experts in the field of gifted education disagree among themselves as to the appropriate definition of a gifted child. Burroughs (1979) writes of over 113 definitions of gifted children. Terman identified gifted as the 2% who score the highest on tests of intelligence (Clark, 1983). The federal government, through the Educational Consolidation and Improvement Act of 1983 (PL 97-35) defines the gifted as "children who give evidence of high performance capability in areas such as intellectual, creative, artistic, leadership capacity, or specific academic fields, and who require services or activities not normally provided by the school in order to fully develop such capabilities" (Section 582). Some define a gifted child as one possessing a cluster of characteristics (Renzulli, 1978), while others point to the latest research in biological differences in defining giftedness (Clark, 1983). All seem to agree, however, that giftedness implies superior ability and/or functioning in at least one specific area. Children are considered handicapped when their normal learning and development are impaired by one or more specific conditions so that special educational programming and related services are required to develop their abilities (Whitmore & Maker, 1985). "Gifted learners appear in every population of handicapped students with the obvious exceptions of the mentally retarded and severely developmentally disabled" (Clark, 1983). Different handicapping conditions affect the gifted child in varying ways. For example, the blind and visually impaired may possess the same levels of cognitive ability as the sighted, but they attain their maximum levels later. Among the deaf, there is a slower rate of development and difficulty in dealing with abstractions. Among the learning disabled and emotionally disturbed, problems are found in attention, perception, and ability to evaluate. For the physically handicapped, the rate and type of cognitive processes is comparable to that of the normal population (Maker, 1977).

Concern for the gifted handicapped surfaced in 1974 when Ed Martin, of the Bureau of Education for the Handicapped, spoke on historic patterns of discrimination affecting such youngsters. In 1975 a TAG (The Association of Gifted) committee on the gifted handicapped was formed. A TAG-sponsored topical conference was held in New Orleans in 1976. By 1977 the term gifted handicapped appeared in ERIC and Exceptional Children Educational Research indices (Porter, 1982).

Children classified as gifted and handicapped require special educational programming both to accommodate one or more disabling conditions and to develop fully their potential for exceptional achievement in one or more areas (Whitmore & Maker, 1985). The deficit needs of these children are often so immediate that remediation becomes the primary concern. In this climate, evidence of giftedness is often overlooked (Clark, 1983) and those needs are not addressed.

Identification of the gifted handicapped learner will follow many of the same procedures of screening and multiple data collection that are typically used in identifying the gifted population. There are, however, some special factors that need to be considered in order to unmask the ability obscured by the disability. Pendarvis & Grossi (1980) present detailed identification procedures specific to each disability area. The federal government has supported some programs for identifying, diagnosing, and programming for gifted handicapped children. Three of the best known are the Chapel Hill, North Carolina, Training and Outreach Program; the RAPYHT (Retrieval and Acceleration of Promising Young Handicapped and Talented) Project; and the Rural School Gifted and Talented Project for Handicapped Children. All three programs were developed to identify and serve gifted, handicapped pre-school-age children (Porter, 1982).

More and more attention is being given to this particular field; however, it is evident from the studies of people such as Whitmore and Maker (1985) that those disabled gifted who have become high achievers have done so despite discouragement, resistance, and rejection by many of those around them. Much work is yet to be done in the fields of identification, acceptance, and programming for the gifted handicapped if they are to fulfill the promise of their potential.

REFERENCES

Blacher-Dixon, J. (1977). *Preschool for the gifted handicapped: Is it untimely or about time?* Paper presented at the 55th Annual International Convention of the Council for Exceptional Children. (ERIC Document Reproduction Service No. ED 139 170)

Burroughs, M. (1979). *Restraints on excellence.* Hingham, MA: Teaching Resource.

Clark, B. (1983). *Growing up gifted.* Columbus, OH: Merrill.

Maker, J. (1977). *Providing programs for the gifted handicapped.* Reston, VA: Council for Exceptional Children.

Pendarvis, E., & Grossi, J. (1980). Designing and operating programs for the gifted and talented handicapped. In J. Jordan & J. Grossi (Eds.), *An administrative handbook on designing programs for the gifted and talented* (pp. 66–88). Reston, VA: Council for Exceptional Children.

Porter, R. (1982). The gifted handicapped: A status report. *Roper Review, 4*(3), 24 25.

Renzulli, J. (1978). What makes giftedness? Reexamining a definition. *Phi Delta Kappan, 60,* 180 184.

Whitmore, J., & Maker, J. (1985). *Intellectual giftedness in disabled persons.* Rockville, MD: Aspen.

See also **Americans with Disabilities Act**

GIFTED INTERNATIONAL

Gifted International is a journal published by the World Council for Gifted and Talented Children. The founding and current editor is Dr. Dorothy Sisk of the University of South Florida. The journal publishes theory, research on, and discussions of problems and practices in gifted education from around the world. In the first issue Sisk stated the following specific aims of the journal:

1. Provide a forum for the exchange of research, identification procedures, curriculum, and good educational practices for the gifted and talented.

2. Generate cooperative sharing of gifted and talented practices and resources.

3. Stimulate cross-cultural research and provide opportunities for dissemination of findings.

The secretary of the World Council is Sisk; subscription orders for *Gifted International* should be addressed to her at the College of Education, University of South Florida, Tampa, Florida.

GILLINGHAM-STILLMAN: ALPHABETIC APPROACH

Anna Gillingham and Bessie Stillman derived their remedial training for children with specific disabilities in reading, spelling, and penmanship from the work of Dr. Samuel T. Orton. Orton was a neurologist who spent his career studying and treating children and adults with specific difficulties in reading, writing, and spelling (Orton, 1937). Both Gillingham and Stillman were teachers at the Ethical Culture Schools in New York City. Gillingham left the schools to become a research fellow under Orton at the Neurological Institute at Columbia-Presbyterian Medical Center, New York. She worked closely with Orton and then Stillman to devise and refine their teaching approach for children with specific language disabilities.

The Gillingham-Stillman approach is remedial, designed for children from third through sixth grades who have normal intelligence, normal sensory acuity, a tendency for letter or word reversals, and an inability to acquire reading and spelling skills by ordinary methods, for instance, "sight word methods even when these are reinforced by functional, incidental, intrinsic, or analytic phonics, or by tracing procedures" (Gillingham & Stillman, 1960, p. 17).

The technique is based on the close association of visual, auditory, and kinesthetic elements forming what has been called the language triangle. The following is the description of phonogram presentation from the manual by Gillingham and Stillman (1960):

Each new phonogram is taught by the following processes, which are referred to as associations and involve the associations between visual (V), auditory (A), and kinesthetic (K) records on the brain. Association I. This association consists of two parts—association of the visual symbol with the name of the letter, and association of the visual symbol with the sound of the letter: also the association of the feel of the child's speech organs in producing the name or sound of the letter as he hears himself say it. Association I is V-A and A-K. Part b. is the basis for oral reading.

Part a. The card is exposed and the name of the letter is spoken by the teacher and repeated by the pupil.

Part b. As soon as the name has been really mastered, the sound is made by the teacher and repeated by the pupil.

Association II. The teacher makes the sound represented by the letter (or phonogram), the face of the card not being seen by the pupil, and says "Tell me the name of the letter that has this sound." Sound to name is A-A, and is essentially oral spelling. Association III. The letter is carefully made by the teacher and its form, orientation, etc., explained. It is then traced by the pupil, then copied, written from memory, and finally written again with eyes averted while the teacher watches closely. This association is V-K and K-V. . . . Now, the teacher makes the sound, saying "Write the letter that has this sound." This association is A-K, and is the basis of written spelling (p. 40).

REFERENCES

Gillingham, A., & Stillman, B. (1960, 1970). *Remedial training for children with specific disability in reading, spelling and penmanship* (7th ed.). Cambridge, MA: Educators Publishing Service.

Orton, S.T. (1937). *Reading, writing and speech problems in children.* New York: Norton.

See also Reading Disorders; Reading Remediation

GLAUCOMA

See VISUALLY IMPAIRED.

GLIAL CELLS

In addition to the neuron, there are a variety of brain cells that function in a supportive role. These are the glial or neuroglial cells (Brodal, 1981). The glial cells are 5 to 10 times more numerous than neurons. The name is derived from the Greek derivative *glia,* which means glue. Originally, the glial cells were thought to function only as supportive tissue for the intricate neuronal matrix of the brain. While glial cells do play an important supportive role, it is now known that glial cells may play an even more dynamic, interactive, and regulatory role in brain function. For example, it is now known that many glial cells surround synaptic areas in an apparent network to restrict the escape of and specify the direction of neurotransmitter release between neurons. Glial cells may also play a nutritive role, providing a pathway from the vascular system to individual nerve cells (Rosenzweig & Leiman, 1982). Similarly, glial cells may assist in directing or redirecting blood flow, especially to active cerebral regions (Bloom, Lazerson, & Hofstadter, 1985). Glial cells also participate in regulating neuronal growth and direction of neuronal interaction (Cotman & McGaugh, 1980).

Anatomic findings in the brain of dyslexic individuals have demonstrated significant abnormalities in not only neuronal microstructure, but also glial cell development (Duffy & Geschwind, 1985; Galaburda & Kemper, 1979). These and similar findings suggest that glial cell abnormalities may play an important role in the expression of certain neurobehavioral disorders.

REFERENCES

Bloom, F.E., Lazerson, A., & Hofstadter, L. (1985). *Brain, mind, and behavior.* New York: Freeman.

Brodal, A. (1981). *Neurological anatomy* (3rd ed.). New York: Oxford University Press.

Cotman, C.W., & McGaugh, J.L. (1980). *Behavioral neuroscience.* New York: Academic.

Duffy, F.H., & Geschwind, N. (1985). *Dyslexia: A neuroscientific approach to clinical evaluation.* Boston: Little, Brown.

Galaburda, A.M., & Kemper, T.L. (1979). Cytoarchitectonic abnormalities in developmental dyslexia: A case study. *Annals of Neurology, 6,* 94–100.

Rosenzweig, M.R., & Leiman, A.L. (1982). *Physiological psychology.* Lexington, MA: Heath.

See also **Central Nervous System; Dendrites; Multiple Sclerosis**

GOALS, ANNUAL

See ANNUAL GOALS.

GOALS, USE OF

Educational goals serve three important functions: (1) to structure teaching and curriculum development, (2) to guide learners by helping them recognize errors and discriminate among responses, and (3) to structure the evaluation process (Bloom, Hastings, & Madaus, 1971).

The use of goals in special education was mandated in 1975 by the Education for All Handicapped Children Act (PL 94-142). Incorporation of educational goals into PL 94-142 was prompted by congressional concern for accountability, not by a desire to facilitate the educational purposes cited previously (Fuchs & Deno, 1982). In its fact finding for PL 94-142, Congress found that the special education needs of handicapped children were not being met fully and that the goal specification component of the law would ensure that schools would be accountable for the quality of the programs they provide to handicapped pupils (Turnbull & Turnbull, 1978).

Given this legal mandate, within the past 10 years, the writing of goals has become standard special education practice; i.e., teachers routinely write goals on students' individual educational programs (IEPs). Additionally, as mandated by PL 94-142 and subsequently IDEA, teachers are required to monitor their students' progress toward those goals. This typically translates into informal evaluations of student goal mastery approximately two to three times each year (Fuchs & Fuchs, 1984).

REFERENCES

Bloom, B.S., Hastings, J.T., & Madaus, G.F. (1971). *Handbook on formative and summative evaluation of student learning.* New York: McGraw-Hill.

Fuchs, L.S., & Deno, S.L. (1982). *Developing goals and objectives for educational programs.* Washington, DC: American Association of Colleges for Teacher Education.

Fuchs, L.S., & Fuchs, D. (1984). Criterion-referenced assessment without measurement: How accurate for special education? *Remedial & Special Education, 5*(4), 29–32.

Turnbull, H.R., & Turnbull, A.P. (1978). *Free appropriate public education: Law and implementation.* Denver: Love.

See also **Individual Education Plan; Teacher Effectiveness**

GODDARD, HENRY H. (1866–1957)

Henry Herbert Goddard received his PhD in psychology at Clark University. He taught at the Pennsylvania State Teachers College at West Chester before becoming director of research at The Training School at Vineland, New Jersey, in 1906. Specializing in the study of atypical children, his work at the Training School was a major influence on the education of mentally retarded children and adults in the United States. He established the first psychological laboratory devoted to the study of the mentally retarded, and developed and tested educational methods for their instruction. He translated and adapted the Binet-Simon Intelligence Scale and inaugurated its use in the United States. He also participated in the development of the group tests used to classify the men in the U.S. armed forces in World War I. Goddard conducted a classic study of mental retardation as an inherited trait, reported in 1912 in *The Kallikak Family: A Study in the Heredity of Feeblemindedness.*

In 1918 Goddard was appointed director of the State Bureau of Juvenile Research in Ohio. From 1922 until his retirement in 1938, he was professor of abnormal and clinical psychology at Ohio State University.

REFERENCE

Goddard, H.H. (1912). *The Kallikak family: A study in the heredity of feeblemindedness.* New York: Macmillan.

GOLD, MARC (1931–1982)

Vocational training, job placement, and respect for the moderately, severely, and profoundly mentally handicapped was a vision Marc Gold forged into a reality. His interests during his teaching of the mentally retarded in Los Angeles led him to pursue a doctoral degree in experimental child psychology and special education. In 1969 he joined the University of Illinois faculty as a research professor and began working at the Institute for Child Behavior and Development.

Gold's strong philosophy of respect for persons with mental retardation acted as the foundation for all of his efforts. Gold (1980) believed that (1) the mentally handicapped are served best by training them in marketable skills; (2) individuals identified as mentally handicapped respond to learning best in a situation based on respect of their worth and capabilities; (3) given the appropriate training, the mentally retarded have the capability to demonstrate competence; (4) when a lack of learning occurs, it should first be interpreted as a result of inappropriate or insufficient teaching strategies rather than the individual's inability to learn; (5) intellectual testing is limiting to the mentally retarded; (6)) the labeling of people as mentally retarded is unfair and counterproductive; and (7) trainers should never assume that they are approaching the maximum potential of their learner.

Extolling this philosophy, Gold developed Try Another Way, a systematic training program for individuals who find it difficult to learn (1980). The strategies employed were physical prompts, modeling, manipulation of the learner's hands, and short specific phrases like, "Try another way."

Task completion was met with silence as Gold believed no news is good news. The Try Another Way system is based on task analysis. Components of task analysis include method (the way the task is performed), content (the amount of steps the method is divided into), and process (the way the task is taught). Process is subdivided into format (the presentation of the material), feedback (cues so the learner knows what is wanted), procedure (description of the proposed training plan), criterion (the predetermined point when learning takes place), and data collection (the charting of steps accomplished and still to be mastered).

Gold's research (1972, 1973, 1974, 1976, 1980) consistently supports task analysis as a learning strategy with the autistic, deaf/blind, and multihandicapped for tasks such as self-help, mobility, and vocational and social skills.

In addition to the development of the Try Another Way system, Gold created an organization that disseminated information regarding the program, was the president of the Workshop Division of the Illinois Rehabilitation Association, was a member of the Executive Board of the American Association for the Education of the Severely/Profoundly Handicapped, was vice president of the Vocational Rehabilitation Division of the American Association on Mental Deficiency, and was consulting editor or member of the editorial board of *The American Journal of Mental Deficiency, Mental Retardation,* and *Education and Treatment of Children.*

REFERENCES

Gold, M.W. (1972). Stimulus factors in skill training of retarded adolescents on a complex assembly task: Acquisition, transfer, and retention. *American Journal of Mental Deficiency, 76,* 517–526.

Gold, M.W. (1973). Factors affecting production by the retarded: Base rate. *Mental Retardation, 11*(6), 41–45.

Gold, M.W. (1974). Redundant cue removal in skill training for the mildly and moderately retarded. *Education & Training of the Mentally Retarded, 9,* 5–8.

Gold, M.W. (1976). Task analysis of a complex assembly task by the retarded blind. *Exceptional Children, 4,* 78–84.

Gold, M.W. (1980). *Did I say that?* Champaign, IL: Research.

GOLDENHAR SYNDROME (GS)

Goldenhar Syndrome (GS) is a relatively recently enumerated syndrome that is somewhat more common among children with diagnoses of autism than in the general population. The diagnosis of GS is made in the presence of a pattern of 3 physical anomalies: ocular abnormalities that include the epibulbar dermoid; auricular abnormalities including microtia, periauricular tags and similar abnormalities of the ear; and vertebral abnormalities.

Cases are sporadic and the cause of GS is unknown but anticipated at this time to be due to a teratogen (Gillberg, 1995). Hearing loss of varying degrees is common, and callosal agenesis has also been reported. An increased prevalence of mental retardation, especially in the mild range,

occurs, and there is increased incidence of autism and autistic-like behavior, although the latter tends to improve with age, especially after puberty. GS occurs in boys and girls with about equal frequency. There is no cure and treatment is entirely symptomatic. Special education is typically required but may be associated with one or more of the symptoms noted above. GS has highly variable expressivity and testing is necessary to establish which of the behavioral and mental symptoms are present and to what degree. Outcome is related directly to the degree of hearing loss, the level of intellectual impairment, and the number and severity of any autistic symptoms.

REFERENCE

Gillberg, C. (1995). *Clinical child neuropsychiatry.* Cambridge: Cambridge University Press.

GOLDMAN-FRISTOE TEST OF ARTICULATION (GFTA)

The Goldman-Fristoe Test of Articulation (GFTA) (1986 edition) was designed to provide a systematic method for identifying and recording an individual's articulatory proficiency as a basis for establishing remedial strategies (Goldman & Fristoe, 1986). Normative data for GFTA are provided for individuals ranging in age from 2 to 16 years and above. Administration and scoring can be completed in approximately 45 minutes. The GFTA is comprised of three subtests that elicit spontaneous productions of 23 consonants and 12 consonant blends in various positions of words and sentences. Although this tool was not specifically designed to assess vowel and diphthong productions most can be observed and evaluated.

The sounds-in-words subtest consists of 35 large colored line drawings depicting objects and activities that are familiar to young children. Subjects are required to name the pictures as the examiner records misarticulations of target sounds. Evaluation of an individual's articulation skills in connected speech is obtained using the sounds-in-sentences subtest. Two narrative stories complemented by visual illustrations are read aloud by the examiner. As the client retells each story, the examiner evaluates accuracy of productions and records errors. The stimulability subtest yields information about the relative ease with which the client is able to produce a previously misarticulated sound at the syllable, word, and sentence level when provided with auditory and visual stimulation.

According to the authors, interpretation of test results is made by comparisons of responses across subtests. This assists the examiner in determining overall patterns of misarticulations and consistency of individual articulatory errors. Normative data and statistical analysis are provided in the examiner's manual.

REFERENCE

Goldman, R., & Fristoe, M. (1986). *Goldman-Fristoe Test of Articulation examiner's manual.* Circle Pines, MN: American Guidance Service.

See also Articulation Disorders; Goldman-Fristoe-Woodcock Auditory Skills Test Battery

GOLDMAN-FRISTOE-WOODCOCK AUDITORY SKILLS TEST BATTERY (G-F-W BATTERY)

The Goldman-Fristoe-Woodcock Auditory Skills Test Battery (G-F-W Battery), now dated, was designed to measure a broad spectrum of auditory abilities while providing detailed diagnostic information useful for instructional programming (Goldman, Fristoe, & Woodcock, 1974a). Normative data are provided for ages 3 through 80. The G-F-W Battery was compromised of 12 tests that are self-contained in five easel kits. Administration time is approximately 15 minutes per test.

The G-F-W Auditory Selective Attention Test measures an individual's ability to attend to and understand a message in the presence of systematically varied competing noise. The G-F-W Auditory Discrimination Test consists of three parts: part one provides a simple assessment of an individual's ability to discriminate among frequently confused speech sounds; parts two and three, used only with subjects exhibiting difficulty on part one, analyze the pattern of specific speech-sound discrimination errors. The G-F-W Auditory Memory Tests, designed to identify children and adults with short-term memory deficits, assess recognition memory, memory for content, and memory for sequence.

The seven tests comprising the G-F-W Sound-Symbol assessment were designed to measure prerequisite abilities for advanced language processes, including reading and spelling. These tests are described by the authors (1974b) as follows:

Test 1—Sound Mimicry measures the ability to imitate nonsense syllables immediately after auditory presentation

Test 2—Sound Recognition measures the ability to recognize isolated sounds comprising a word

Test 3—Sound analysis measures the ability to identify component sounds of nonsense syllables

Test 4—Sound blending measures the ability to synthesize isolated sounds into meaningful words

Test 5—Sound-Symbol Association measures the ability to learn associations between unfamiliar auditory and visual symbols

Test 6—Reading of Symbols measures the ability to make grapheme to phoneme translations

Test 7—Spelling of Sounds measures the ability to make phoneme to grapheme translations

The G-F-W Battery was a test designed to evaluate various auditory abilities. It was useful to speech-language pathologists, audiologists, educational diagnosticians, reading specialists, learning-disability teachers, school psychologists, and counselors.

REFERENCES

Goldman, R., Fristoe, M., & Woodcock, R.W. (1974a). *Technical manual for Goldman-Fristoe-Woodcock Auditory Skills Test Battery.* Circle Pines, MN: American Guidance Service.

Goldman, R., Fristoe, M., & Woodcock, R.W. (1974b). *Goldman-Fristoe-Woodcock Auditory Skills Test Battery: Sound-symbol tests.* Circle Pines, MN: American Guidance Service.

See also Goldman-Fristoe Test of Articulation

GOLDSTEIN, MAX A. (1870–1941)

Max A. Goldstein, an otolaryngologist, originated the acoustic method of teaching the deaf. The major significance of this method was that it used the student's residual hearing, an avenue largely neglected by educators of the deaf at the time. Goldstein employed amplification to train the student to use any remaining sound perception to understand spoken language and to guide his or her own voice in the production of speech. In 1914 Goldstein founded the Central Institute for the Deaf in St. Louis, where he demonstrated his methods and where he established the first two-year training program for teachers of the deaf and began the first nursery school for deaf children.

Goldstein was founder and editor of *The Laryngoscope,* a journal devoted to disorders of the ear, nose, and throat. To promote closer cooperation between teachers of the deaf and physicians, and to standardize teaching methods used in schools for the deaf, Goldstein established the professional society that later became the National Forum on Deafness and Speech Pathology. Goldstein served as president of the American Otological Society, the American Laryngological, Rhinological, and Otological Society, and the organization that was the forerunner of the American Speech and Hearing Association.

REFERENCES

Goldstein, M.A. (1939). *The acoustic method.* St. Louis: Laryngoscope Press.

In memoriam: Dr. Max A. Goldstein, 1870–1941. (1941). *Laryngoscope, 51,* 726–731.

GOODENOUGH, FLORENCE LAURA (1886–1959)

Florence Laura Goodenough obtained the PhD degree in psychology under Lewis M. Terman at Stanford University after a number of years of experience as a teacher in the public schools and at the Training School at Vineland, New Jersey. Goodenough is well known for her Draw-A-Man Test, published in 1926, and the Minnesota Pre-school Scale. As a researcher and an authority on research methodology, she was an innovator, applying a variety of research techniques to diverse research questions. Her *Experimental Child Study,* written with John E. Anderson, evaluated the pros and cons of numerous research methodologies. Goodenough served as president of the school psychology division of the American Psychological Association.

REFERENCES

Goodenough, F.L. (1926). *Measurement of intelligence by drawings.* Yonkers, NY: World Book.

Goodenough, F.L., & Anderson, J.E. (1982). *Experimental child study.* Darby, PA: Arden Library.

GOWAN, JOHN C. (1912–1986)

John C. Gowan earned his BA at Harvard University and his EdM and EdD at the University of California at Los Angeles. During his distinguished career in education, Gowan's interest focused on the areas of psychic science, guidance, and creativity, particularly as related to gifted learners (Gowan, 1980). Prior to his death in 1986, he was a professor at California State University, Northridge, for over 25 years.

Gowan is known for his work in the area of guidance for gifted children (Gowan, Demos, & Kokaska, 1980). He emphasized special problems such as a the disparity between social and intellectual development sometimes associated with these children and examined the influence of right-hemisphere imagery on creativity (Gowan, Khatena, & Torrance, 1981). Gowan also noted the importance of using developmental stage theory to enhance creativity in gifted children, and his theories on the subject were explored in his book *Trance, Art, and Creativity,* a psychological analysis of the relationship between the individual ego and the numinous element (Gowan, 1987).

Among his contributions, Gowan served as president of the Association for the Gifted (1971–1972), president of the National Association for Gifted Children (1974–1975), and editor of *Gifted Child Quarterly* (1974–1979). Additionally, he was a Fulbright lecturer at the University of Singapore (1962–1963) and a visiting lecturer at the University of Hawaii (1965, 1967), Southern Connecticut State College (1969), and the University of Canterbury (1970) and Massey University (1975), both in New Zealand. A compilation of his work related to gifted children was published in the 1971 book, *Educating the Ablest.*

REFERENCES

Gowan, J.C. (1971). *Educating the ablest: A book of readings on the education of gifted children.* Itasca, IL: Peacock.

Gowan, J.C. (1980). The use of developmental stage theory in helping gifted children become creative. *Gifted Child Quarterly, 24,* 22–28.

Gowan, J.C. (1987). *Trance, art, and creativity: A psychological analysis of the relationship between the individual ego and the numinous element in three modes—prototaxic, parataxic, and syntaxic.* Buffalo, NY: Creative Education.

Gowan, J.C., Demos, G.D., & Kokaska, C.J. (1980). *The guidance of exceptional children: A book of readings* (2nd ed.). New York: Longman.

Gowan, J.C., Khatena, J., & Torrance, E.P. (Eds.). (1981). *Creativity: Its educational implications* (Rev. ed.). Dubuque, IA: Kendall-Hunt.

GRADE EQUIVALENTS (GES)

Grade equivalents (GEs) represent a popular, though much abused and often misinterpreted, score system for achievement tests. A GE is a representation of an average level of performance of all children at a specific grade level. For example, if, on a test of reading, the average number of questions correct (the mean raw score) for children in the third month of fourth grade (typically written as 4.3) is 40, then a raw score of 40 is assigned a GE of 4.3. If the average number correct for children in the second month of fifth grade is 43, then all scores of 43 are henceforth assigned a GE of 5.2, and so forth.

Grade Equivalents have numerous problems of interpretation and use. Many users assume that GEs have the characteristics of standardized or scaled scores when, in fact, they do not. Often GEs are treated as being on an interval scale of measurement when they are only on an ordinal scale; i.e., GEs allow the ranking of individuals according to their performance but do not tell us anything about the distance between each pair of individuals. This problem can be illustrated as follows. If the mean score for beginning fourth graders (grade 4.0) on a reading test is 37, then any person earning a score of 37 on the test is assigned a GE score of 4.0. If the mean raw score of a fifth grader (grade 5.0) is 38, then a score of 38 would receive a GE of 5.0. A raw score of 37 could represent a GE of 4.0, 38 could be 5.0, 39 could be 5.1, 40 be 5.3, and 41, 6.0. Thus, differences of one raw score point can cause dramatic differences in the GE received. The differences will be highly inconsistent across grades with regard to magnitude of the difference in grade equivalents produced by constant changes in raw scores.

Table 1 illustrates the problems of using GEs to evaluate a child's academic standing relative to his or her peers. Frequently, in both research and clinical practice, children of normal intellectual capacity are diagnosed as learning disabled through the use of grade equivalents such as "two years below grade level for age" on a test of academic attainment. The use of this criterion for diagnosing learning disabilities or other academic disorders is clearly inappropriate (Reynolds, 1981, 1984). As seen in the table, a child with a GE score in reading 2 years below the appropriate grade placement for age may or may not have a reading problem. At some ages this is within the average range, whereas at others a severe reading problem may be indicated.

Grade equivalents tend to become standards of performance as well, which they are not. GE scores on a test do not indicate what level of reading text a child should be using. Grade equivalent scores on tests do not have a one-to-one correspondence with reading series placement or the various formulas for determining readability levels.

Table 1   Standard Scores and Percentile Ranks Corresponding to Performance "Two Years Below Grade Level for Age" on Three Major Reading Tests

Grade Placement	Two Years Below Placement	Wide Range Achievement Test		Woodcock Reading Mastery Test[a]		Stanford Diagnostic Reading Test[a]	
		SS[b]	%R[c]	SS	%R	S	%R
2.5	K.5	72	1	—		—	
3.5	1.5	69	2	64	1	64	1
4.5	2.5	73	4	77	6	64	1
5.5	3.5	84	14	85	16	77	6
6.5	4.5	88	21	91	27	91	27
7.5	5.5	86	18	94	34	92	30
8.5	6.5	87	19	94	34	93	32
9.5	7.5	90	25	96	39	95	37
10.5	8.5	85	16	95	37	95	37
11.5	9.5	85	16	95	37	92	30

Note: Reprinted from *Journal of School Psychology*, Vol. 19, Cecil Reynolds, "The Fallacy of 'Two Years below Grade Level for Age' as a Diagnostic Criterion for Reading Disorders," pp. 250–258, Copyright 1981, with permission from Elsevier Science.
[a] Total test.
[b] All standard scores in this table have been converted for ease of comparison to a common scale having a mean of 100 and an SD of 15.
[c] Percentile rank.

Grade equivalents are also inappropriate for use in any sort of discrepancy analysis of an individual's test performance and for use in many statistical procedures for the following reasons (Reynolds, 1981):

1. The growth curve between age and achievement in basic academic subjects flattens out at upper grade levels. This can be seen in the table, where there is very little change in standard score values corresponding to 2 years below grade level for age after about grade 7 or 8. In fact, GEs have almost no meaning at this level since reading instruction typically stops by high school. This difficulty in interpreting GEs beyond about grade 10 or 11 is apparent in an analogy with age equivalents (Thorndike & Hagen, 1977). Height can be expressed in age equivalents just as reading can be expressed as GEs. It might be helpful to describe a tall first grader as having the height of an 8 and a half-year-old, but what happens to the 5 ft, 10 in. 14-year-old female? At no age does the mean height of females equal 5 ft, 10 in. Since the average reading level in the population changes very little after junior high school, GEs at these ages become virtually nonsensical, with large fluctuations resulting from a raw score difference of two or three points on a 100-item test.

2. Grade equivalents assume the rate of learning is constant throughout the school year and that there is no gain or loss during summer vacation.

3. Grade equivalents involve an excess of extrapolation, especially at the upper and lower ends of the scale. However, since tests are not administered during every month of the school year, scores between the testing intervals (often a full year) must be interpolated on the assumption of constant growth rates. Interpolation between sometimes extrapolated values on an assumption of constant growth rates is a somewhat ludicrous activity.

4. Different academic subjects are acquired at different rates and the variation in performance varies across content areas so that "two years below grade level for age" may be a much more serious deficiency in math than in reading comprehension.

5. Grade equivalents exaggerate small differences in performance among individuals and for a single individual across tests. Some test authors even provide a caution on record forms that standard scores only, and not grade equivalents, should be used for comparisons.

Standard scores are a superior alternative to the use of GEs. The principal advantage of standardized or scaled scores with children lies in the comparability of score interpretation across age. By standard scores is meant scores scaled to a constant mean and standard deviation (SD), such as the Wechsler Deviation IQ, and not to ratio IQ types of scales employed by the early Binet and the Slosson Intelligence Test, which give the false appearance of being scaled scores. Ratio IQs or other types of quotients have many of the same problems as grade equivalents and should be avoided for many of the same reasons. Standard scores of the deviation IQ type have the same percentile rank across age since they are based not only on the mean but the variability in scores about the mean at each age level. For example, a score that falls two-thirds of a standard deviation below the mean has a percentile rank of 25 at every age. A score falling two-thirds of a grade level below the average grade level has a different percentile rank at every age.

Standard scores are more accurate and precise. When constructing tables for the conversion of raw scores into standard scores, interpolation of scores to arrive at an exact score point is usually not necessary. The opposite is true of GEs. Typically, extrapolation is not necessary for scores within three SDs of the mean, which accounts for more than 99% of all scores encountered. Scaled scores can be set to any desired mean and standard deviation, with the fancy of the test author frequently the sole determining factor. Fortunately, a few scales can account for the vast majority of standardized tests in psychology and education.

Nevertheless, GEs remain popular as a score reporting system in special education. This popularity seems owed to the many misconceptions surrounding their use rather than any true understanding of children's academic attainment or how better to instruct them.

REFERENCES

Reynolds, C.R. (1981). The fallacy of "two years below grade level for age" as a diagnostic criterion for reading disorders. *Journal of School Psychology, 19,* 350–358.

Reynolds, C.R. (1984). Critical measurement issues in learning disabilities. *Journal of Special Education, 18,* 451–476.

Thorndike, R.L., & Hagen, E.P. (1977). *Measurement and evaluation in psychology and education.* New York: Wiley.

See also Diagnosis in Special Education; Severe Discrepancy Analysis

GRADE RETENTION

Grade retention involves the repetition of a particular grade level in school by a student. The practice is also known as grade repetition and nonpromotion, and by the commonly used terms of flunking, failing, or holding back a student. Typically, the term grade retention is used when the student is of elementary school age and is required to spend another academic year going over the same material. Such students may receive some individualized attention or curriculum the second year in the grade, but this is the exception rather than the rule. In a few school districts, retained students are promoted at midyear or on skill mastery to the next grade. The term subject repetition is used when a secondary school student fails one or more subjects, but not the grade, and has to repeat them.

Historically, the practice of grade retention can be traced back to the late sixteenth century, when schools in England first began grouping students according to age or lessons mastered. Students were placed in different rooms rather than taught all together, as had been the earlier European practice. With the assignment of students to graded classes in England during this period and in America during the nineteenth century, grade retention became a convenient and popular way of attempting to correct academic failure. From 1840 to 1930, approximately one out of two children was retained at least once during the first eight years of school, and little attention was paid to learning difficulties associated with immigrant status, native language differences, cultural factors, or intellectual handicaps. Over the next 30 years, the retention rate began to drop as its effect on children's social and emotional welfare was questioned. Many students, regardless of classroom performance, were "socially promoted" if they were overaged, oversized, or overly sensitive to failure. However, as the numbers of socially promoted students increased, standardized achievement test scores decreased and social promotion was singled out as one reason why some students who were awarded high-school diplomas were unable to adequately read, write, and compute.

In the late 1970s, federal, state, and local government agencies called for upgraded teaching standards, educational accountability, and a renewed emphasis on basic academic skills. Many states now require students to pass minimum competency tests to graduate from high school or be promoted from one grade to the next.

Grade retention has been and continues to be a controversial educational practice. The arguments in favor of grade retention involve the following: (1) it allows the immature or developmentally delayed child time to catch up; (2) it prevents the child who is having difficulty from experiencing undue failure and frustration; (3) it makes classes homogeneous and easier to teach; (4) it preserves the meaning of school diplomas; and (5) children who repeat learn more than those who are promoted. The arguments against retention are (1) it can stigmatize and lower the self-image of the student; (2) it is an ineffective remediation strategy; (3) it discriminates against males, minorities, and the disadvantaged; (4) it is associated with students dropping out of school and committing crime; and (5) it delays a needed thorough psychological assessment of the child (Carstens, 1985).

The existing research literature, despite methodological problems (Jackson, 1975), generally supports the antiretention position. Promoted students obtain scores on achievement tests that are, on the average, 34% greater than those of retained students (Holmes & Matthews, 1984). Research indicates academic benefits of retention for students in kindergarten, first, and second grades, but few benefits after sixth grade. Students who have been retained obtain lower scores on measures of personal adjustment than those who have been promoted (Holmes & Matthews, 1984), although the young child does not appear to suffer emotionally. Students placed in special educational programs, rather than just retained or promoted, usually fare the best, both academically and emotionally.

Research is just beginning to address the issue of what types of children are helped the most by grade retention. The best candidates for retention are children who are young, who have made some progress the first year in school, whose intelligence is at least low-average, who are not behavior problems, and who have parents who agree with the decision and help the child at home (Medway & Rose, 1986). There is no support for the position of retaining children who are small in stature, siblings of other retainees, or labeled "immature." No child should be retained before his or her teacher has tried alternative teaching approaches.

Handicapped students may be given minimum competency tests and may be subject to the same promotion and graduation standards as nonhandicapped students (McCarthy, 1983). However, students should be given at least a year's notice prior to the enforcement of the promotion standard and grade requirements should be taught as part of the individualized educational program.

Numerous alternatives to grade retention and social promotion have been proposed; they attempt to directly remediate learning and adjustment problems. These include preventive programs such as preschool, readiness, and early childhood enrichment classes, and early identification of children in need of special education; remedial programs, transition classes, and tutoring; and intensive summer programs (Medway & Rose, 1986). For additional information on this topic see Germain and Merlo (1985) and Thompson (1980).

REFERENCES

Carstens, A.A. (1985). Retention and social promotion for the exceptional child. *School Psychology Review, 14,* 48–63.

Germain, R., & Merlo, M. (1985). Best practices in assisting in retention and promotion decisions. In A. Thomas & J. Grimes (Eds.), *Best practices in school psychology.* Stratford, CT: NASP Publications.

Holmes, C.T., & Matthews, K.M. (1984). The effects of nonpromotion on elementary and junior high school pupils: A meta-analysis. *Review of Educational Research, 54,* 225–236.

Jackson, G.B. (1975). The research evidence on the effects of grade retention. *Review of Educational Research, 45,* 613–635.

McCarthy, M.M. (1983). The application of competency testing mandates to handicapped children. *Harvard Educational Review, 53,* 146–164.

Medway, F.J., & Rose, J.S. (1986). Grade retention. In T.R. Kratochwill (Ed.), *Advances in school psychology* (Vol. 5). Hillsdale, NJ: Erlbaum.

Thompson, S. (1980). Grade retention and social promotion. *ACSA School Management Digest, Series 1, 20,* 1–36.

See also Retention in Grade

GRAND MAL SEIZURES

See SEIZURE DISORDERS.

GRANULOMATOUS DISEASE, CHRONIC

An inherited disease of white blood cell bacteria-killing function, chronic granulomatous disease (CGD) results in chronic infections and granuloma formation in skin, lymphatic tissues, respiratory and gastrointestinal tracts, and bones. White blood cells ingest bacteria normally but cannot kill them because of the cell's inability to generate hydrogen peroxide. Some bacteria, like pneumococci and streptococci, produce their own hydrogen peroxide and are normally disposed of by CGC white cells, while many other bacteria, including staphylococci, which do not produce hydrogen peroxide, cannot be killed.

Early in life, eczema-like rashes, enlarged lymph nodes, and perirectal abscesses may be initial signs. Respiratory infections are the most common symptom, and there is gradual enlargement of the liver and spleen. Infections in the central nervous system and the anemia of chronic disease may have cognitive sequelae.

Prophylactic antibiotic treatment, usually with sulfa methoxazole/trimethaprim, has greatly improved life expectancy and steroids are used to shrink granulomas obstructing the airways or gastrointestinal tract. Bone marrow transplant and interferon gamma treatments have been used with success in some patients.

Information for families and professionals is available from the Chronic Granulomatous Disease Association, Inc., 2616 Monterey Rd., San Marino, CA 91108, or at www.pacific.net.net/amhurley.

GRAPHESTHESIA

Graphesthesia is a medical term used to define an individual's ability to identify numbers or figures written on the skin (Hensyl, 1982). For many years, tests of graphesthesia have been a part of the clinical neurological examination to determine the intactness and integration of sensory neural systems related to sensations from within the body, at a distance from the body, and outside the body.

See also **Halstead-Reitan Neuropsychological Battery; Luria-Nebraska Neuropsychological Battery; Neuropsychology**

GRAY ORAL READING TESTS– THIRD EDITION (GORT-3)

The Gray Oral Reading Tests—Third Edition (GORT-3; Wiederholt & Bryant, 1992) is the latest revision of the reading test created by William S. Gray. The third edition provides an objective measure of growth in oral reading and is an aid in the diagnosis of oral reading difficulties. The GORT-3 is comprised of two alternate, equivalent forms, each of which contains 13 developmentally sequenced passages with five comprehension questions. The GORT-3 yields clinically useful information about oral reading rate and accuracy, oral reading comprehension, total oral reading ability, and oral reading miscues.

A reader's ability to read passages orally with speed and accuracy is measured by the GORT-3 with three scores: Rate, Accuracy, and a Passage Score (a score that Gray originally reported, which reflects a combination of rate and accuracy). The scores are generated by determining first how long it takes a student to read each passage and then how many deviations from print are made. A 5-point system is used to convert time (i.e., the time in seconds it takes to read the story) to rate, and to convert deviations from print (i.e., the number of oral reading errors) to accuracy. The two scores are summed to produce a Passage Score.

The GORT–3 assesses oral reading comprehension by having the student respond to five multiple-choice questions following each story. The examiner reads aloud the stem and response choices for each question as the student follows along in the Student Book. The student selects the response choice that best completes the idea expressed by the stem. The questions tap a variety of comprehension forms (i.e., literal, inferential, critical, and affective). The number of questions answered correctly is summed, and the resulting raw score is called a Comprehension Score.

The GORT–3 also provides a total measure of oral reading performance by combining the Passage Score and Comprehension Score. This total score, called the Oral Reading Quotient (ORQ), provides an overall index of the student's ability to read orally. In addition, the GORT–3 provides a means to conduct an analysis of oral reading miscues. Five types of miscues can be recorded: meaning similarity, function similarity, graphic/phonemic similarity, multiple sources, and self-correction.

Reviewers were generally complimentary of this revision of the instrument. King (1995) states that the GORT–3 appears to be a generally successful revision. He reports that the test is easier to use than previous editions and provides more detailed information concerning the standardization sample and the psychometric properties of the test. Kundert (1995) summarized that the GORT–3 may be an appropriate measure to use when examining oral reading and comprehension.

REFERENCES

King, J.D. (1995). Review of the Gray Oral Reading Test, Third Edition. In J.C. Conoley & J.C. Impara (Eds.), *The twelfth mental measurements yearbook* (pp. 422–423). Lincoln: Buros Institute of Mental Measurements, University of Nebraska Press.

Kundert, D.K. (1995). Review of the Gray Oral Reading Test, Third Edition. In J.C. Conoley & J.C. Impara (Eds.), *The twelfth mental measurements yearbook* (pp. 423–425). Lincoln: Buros Institute of Mental Measurements, University of Nebraska Press.

Wiederholt, J.L., & Bryant, B.R. (1992). *Gray Oral Reading Test–Third Edition.* Austin, TX: Pro-ed.

GRIEVING PROCESS

It has been recognized for some time that parents of handicapped children often experience intense traumatic reactions to the diagnosis of their children. Further, these initial feelings are not the only ones that parents experience. It appears that parents go through a continual process of emotional fluctuation in the process of coming to terms with having a handicapped child (Searl, 1978). The intensity or degree of handicap does not seem to affect directly the appearance of these feelings. These reactions seem to occur regardless of when the parents become aware of the handicapping condition or how intense the condition is. For example, parents who have been informed that their expected child will be handicapped early enough into a pregnancy to make numerous physical and financial preparations still have intense emotional reactions to the child's condition at the time of the child's birth. These reactions continue during the child's maturation (Roos, 1977). These feelings have often been likened to the mourning process experienced at the death of a loved one. Hence the reactions and the subsequent process of coming to terms with a handicapped person within the family has been labeled the grieving process. Several authors have taken Kubler-Ross's developmental stage model of reaction to dying and have applied it to the loss associated with parenting a handicapped child.

Professionals need to be aware that the grieving process may adversely affect their relationship and interactions with parents of handicapped children. At least three considerations must be understood. First, parents may be experiencing a variety of emotional states at a given time. Single interactions may not be representative of the parents' levels of cooperation or enthusiasm, but rather a stage in grieving (e.g., anger or guilt). Second, interaction with specific agency representatives may cause emotional responses that are not expected by the professionals involved. This may not mean that a parent's total life is focused in that direction, but that current interactions are bringing out certain feelings. Third, parents may spend a prolonged amount of time in one stage or another. A parent may appear to be angry or sad during dealings with a professional. This does not mean that the parent will always remain in this emotional stage; the parent eventually may move on to other feelings in the process. Those who deal with parents must realize that not only do emotions affect interactions, but varied behaviors are normal and to be expected (Searl, 1978).

The implications of the grieving process to those who deal with the parents of the handicapped may be summarized as follows. First, parents often experience deep and intense feelings that may require counseling. Second, these feelings may continue for long periods of time. Third, feelings change at differing rates and/or varied sequences, necessitating flexibility in interpersonal dealings. Fourth, the grieving process is experienced by parents in an individual manner, necessitating interactions with parents to reflect an individual approach.

REFERENCES

Roos, P. (1977). Parents of mentally retarded people. *International Journal of Mental Health, 6,* 96–119.

Searl, S. (1978). Stages of parent reaction. *Exceptional Parent, 8,* 27–29.

See also **Family Counseling; Family Response to a Child with Disabilities**

Mildred A. Groht

GROHT, MILDRED A. (1890–1971)

Mildred A. Groht, a prominent educator of the deaf and developer of one of the major methods of teaching language to deaf children, was a graduate of Swarthmore College, with an honorary doctorate from Gallaudet College. She began her career as a teacher at the New York School for the Deaf and later taught at the Maryland School for the Deaf. In 1926 she joined the faculty of the Lexington School for the Deaf in New York City, where she served as principal until her retirement in 1958.

A talented teacher, she proposed and developed the influential natural language method of teaching language to the deaf. Based on the premise that deaf children can best acquire language through activities that are a natural part of a child's life, Groht's method uses a variety of activities. The teacher consistently creates situations that provide the students with language experiences and continually talks to the children and encourages them to respond with speech. Such practice in real-life situations was seen as more effective than the traditional grammatical or analytical approach, with its emphasis on language analysis and drill. The use of natural methods has increased markedly, and most programs today use a mixture of natural and analytical approaches.

Groht described the natural method in her book *Natural Language for Deaf Children.* In its foreword, Clarence D. O'Connor, then superintendent of the Lexington School for the Deaf, called Groht, "one of America's most distinguished teachers of the deaf, particularly in the field of communication arts." He went on to say:

She has increasingly expounded the philosophy that deaf children can acquire fluent use of English comparable to that of the hearing through what has come to be known as the 'natural' method, and through her own skillful teaching of deaf children

and guiding of teachers she has demonstrated that this can be done without question. Through her writings, her demonstrations, and her lecture courses, and now through the chapters of this excellent book, she has very generously passed on to her coworkers the benefits of her rich experience in this specialized field.

Active in the Alexander Graham Bell Association for the Deaf, Groht served on the association's auxiliary board for a number of years and was named to its honorary board in 1965. She died in Ossining, New York, on December 11, 1971.

REFERENCE

Groht, M.A. (1958). *Natural language for deaf children.* Washington, DC: Alexander Graham Bell Association for the Deaf.

GROUP HOMES

The group home design is one model of alternate living environments designed to promote independent living for handicapped individuals in our society. As an alternative to large institutions, group homes provide a residential environment within a community that allows handicapped individuals to function as independently as possible while protecting their civil rights (Youngblood & Bensberg, 1983).

Historically, the developmentally disadvantaged in our society were placed in large institutions housing vast numbers of handicapped individuals. In 1969 Kugel and Wolfensberger reported that in the United States, 200,000 persons lived in over 150 public institutions for the retarded. An additional 20,000 resided in private institutions, with tens of thousands awaiting admittance to institutions for the mentally ill. For the most part, these institutions have been shown to be understaffed, overcrowded, and poorly managed. Violation of the rights of handicapped individuals came into serious question (e.g., *Wyatt v. Stickney,* 1972). As a direct result of this, and in keeping with the civil rights movement that was raging in the late 1960s, a large deinstitutionalization movement began.

The current philosophy is one of normalization, which maintains that developmentally disabled persons have the same legal and civil rights as any other citizen as guaranteed under the Fourteenth Amendment of the U.S. Constitution. Because most alternative living arrangements involve some departure from culturally normative practices, special attention to implementation of normalization and use of the "least restrictive environment" concept must underlie all such arrangements (Accreditation Council for Services for Mentally Retarded and Other Developmentally Disabled Persons, 1984).

To qualify for federal assistance, group homes must be established according to specific guidelines set forth by the Federal Agency of the Administration of Developmental Disabilities (WAC 275.36.010). According to these guidelines, a group home is defined as a residential facility in the form of a single dwelling, series of apartments, or other sound structures that allow for a pleasant and healthful environment for human life and welfare. This structure may be owned, leased, or be part of a larger facility serving other disabled individuals.

A group home is designed to serve a maximum of 20 mentally or physically disabled individuals who participate in various jobs, sheltered workshops, daycare centers, activity centers, educational facilities, or other community-based programs that are designed for their training, rehabilitation, and/or general well-being. These facilities must be located within reasonable proximity to those community resources that are necessary adjuncts to a training, education, or rehabilitation program. The living quarters should provide a homelike atmosphere and the residents should participate in the care of the facility and of themselves.

There are two major types of group home facilities. Both are designed to house 8 to 10 individuals. The first is a transitional group home. As the name implies, this home is designed to house adults (18 or older) with the goal that the handicapped person will move on to more independent living quarters (e.g., an apartment) once he or she has mastered important independent living skills. For individuals who exhibit less potential for being capable of independent living, long-term group homes are provided. These more permanent residences offer less restrictive environments than institutions, but not as independent an environment as transitional group homes. There are provisions even with long-term group homes that individuals be allowed to develop to their maximum potential. Thus, there are instances when individuals in long-term group homes have developed independent living skills to the extent that they can enter a transitional group home or can move directly into an independent living setting. Certain other groups of disabled individuals (e.g., deaf-blind) are also afforded chances for group home living. These facilities differ only in that they generally provide additional services to the transitional or long-term group home.

Group home facilities provide a wide range of services from legal assistance to sex education/family planning. The facilities, depending on states' funding patterns, are staffed by individuals ranging from house parents to supervisory professional staff members. Pros and cons of various staffing patterns are discussed by Youngblood and Bensberg (1983).

Establishing alternative living facilities (i.e., group homes) has not been always met with wholesale support, particularly by residents of communities where these residences are to be located. In keeping with the normalization principles and in accordance with state and federal guidelines for their establishment, group homes are to allow disabled individuals to experience community living to the maximum extent possible. Often residents of the community are concerned that their property values will fall because of group homes (Conroy & Bradley, 1985), or that a disabled resident might be dangerous. Researchers in the Pennhurst study found that resident attitudes following actual establishment of a group home were more positive than

were attitudes toward the proposal of the same facility. The more negative attitudes were also directed toward group homes for the more severely disabled or mentally ill.

Research regarding the effects of group home living versus institutional living has been overwhelmingly positive. For example, the Pennhurst study (Conroy & Bradley, 1985) investigated whether disabled individuals ordered released from an institution following a court ruling and placed in alternative living environments, including group homes, were better off than a matched group of their peers who remained in the institution. Factors such as adaptive behavior, satisfaction with living arrangements, costs, and family and neighbor attitudes were examined. The study concluded: "the people deinstitutionalized under the Pennhurst court order *are* better off in *every* way measured . . . the results are not mixed" (pp. 322–323).

Just as residential services for the developmentally disabled today have met Kugel and Wolfensberger's 1969 predictions, Willer (1981) has proposed that the concept of normalization and alternative living arrangements will again change in the future, out of necessity. He predicts "quality of life" concepts with emphasis on the individual will replace the group homes of today. Group homes as we know them, according to Willer, will be reserved for only the more severely disabled.

REFERENCES

Conroy, J.W., & Bradley, V.J. (1985). *The Pennhurst longitudinal study: A report of five years of research and analysis.* Philadelphia: Temple University, Developmental Disabilities Center. Boston: Human Services Research Institute.

Kugel, R.B., & Wolfensberger, W. (1969). *Changing patterns in residential services for the mentally retarded.* Washington, DC: President's Committee on Mental Retardation.

Standards for services for developmentally disabled individuals. (1984). Washington, DC: Accreditation Council for Services for Mentally Retarded and Other Developmentally Disabled Persons.

Willer, B. (1981). The future of residential services for mentally retarded persons. *Forum, 1*(4), 8–10.

Wyatt v. Stickney. 325F. Supp 781 (1972).

Youngblood, G.S., & Bensberg, G.J. (1983). *Planning and operating group homes for the handicapped.* Lubbock, TX: Research and Training Center in Mental Retardation.

See also **Adaptive Behavior; Deinstitutionalization; Least Restrictive Environment**

GROUP THERAPY

Group therapy is a general term that refers to any of the various types of therapeutic groups that share the broad purpose of increasing people's knowledge of themselves and others and giving people the skills necessary to enhance their personal competence. According to this general definition, group counseling, encounter groups, human relation groups, and skill-oriented groups are all types of group therapy. There are as many theoretical orientations to group therapy as there are to individual therapy. These include existentialism-humanism, gestalt, psychoanalytic, behavioral, rational-emotive therapy, reality therapy, transactional analysis, and others (Corey & Corey, 1977). The several types of group therapies plus the various theoretical orientations that may characterize group therapy make it difficult to make meaningful statements that generalize to the various types and models.

There are three major types of group therapy used in school settings: skill-oriented groups, personal growth groups, and specific focus therapy groups. The use of all three in schools is justified by the recognition that emotional and behavioral adjustment is important to a child's educational performance. Social-emotional problems like depression, loneliness, or anxiety affect school learning and adjustment.

Skill-oriented group therapy is the most widely accepted type of group therapy in school settings as it focuses on teaching specific adaptive skills such as communication, problem-solving, or social skills. An example of a skill-oriented therapy program is the structured learning therapy model developed and popularized by Goldstein (1981). In this model children with deficient social skills are taught skills through a procedure that employs instruction, modeling, behavior rehearsal, and feedback. Children in the group discuss each skill (e.g., expressing anger, offering help, disagreeing with another), citing their own examples of each skill. The skills are broken into component steps, and members practice the skills in role playing. They receive feedback from the group on their performance. Another example of a skill-oriented group is a communication skill group for adolescents. Members practice such skills as listening and perception-checking in the group setting and discuss how these skills apply outside the group.

In the personal growth group, the group setting provides the emotional support and encouragement necessary for the type of self-exploration that leads to a change in attitudes and behaviors. In schools, members of the group might share a common problem or situation such as having parents who are recently divorced. The group provides members with a place where they can express their feelings regarding their situations and discover that other people experience similar problems and feelings. These groups attempt to help members integrate their thinking and feelings and to experience greater self-acceptance. They are often directed to the normal person who is experiencing unusual stress or who wishes to become more self-actualized.

The specific focus therapy group attempts to correct an emotional or behavioral problem. An example is a group for highly anxious children. Children might share anxiety-producing situations and their reactions to those situations. They learn that different children are afraid of different situations, test the reality of their fears, and learn from other children how to cope with their anxieties. The group thera-

pist might teach children how to use specific anxiety-management techniques such as relaxation, self-talk, or problem solving.

REFERENCES

Corey, G., & Corey, M.S. (1977). *Groups: Process and practice.* Belmont, CA: Wadsworth.

Goldstein, A.P. (1981). *Psychological skill training: The structured learning technique.* New York: Pergamon.

See also Family Counseling; Psychotherapy

GUADALUPE *V.* TEMPE ELEMENTARY SCHOOL DISTRICT

See DIANA *V.* STATE BOARD OF EDUCATION.

GUGGENBÜHL, JOHANN J. (1816–1863)

Johann Guggenbühl, a Swiss physician, was the originator of institutional care for the mentally retarded. Following an extensive study of cretinism, Guggenbühl established a hospital and school for mentally retarded children, the Abendberg, in the mountains of Switzerland. There he instituted for his students a program that combined healthful living, good diet, and medicine with an educational program that emphasized cognitive, sensory, and physical training. Guggenbühl found that his students, especially those who entered his school at an early age, showed improvement in both physical and mental development. Guggenbühl publicized his results widely, and institutions similar to his were established in many of the countries of Europe and in the United States.

Guggenbühl was much in demand and was often away from the Abendberg for extended periods, during which time the institution was poorly administered. This situation caused problems that, in conjunction with the high expectations that Guggenbühl had fostered, led to the closing of the Abendberg and the departure in disgrace of its founder. Nevertheless, Guggenbühl's contribution was monumental. He originated institutional care for the mentally retarded, demonstrated that young mentally retarded people could be helped to develop both physically and mentally, and developed a system of care and education that served as a model throughout the western world.

REFERENCE

Kanner, L. (1964). *A history of the care and study of the mentally retarded.* Springfield, IL: Thomas.

GUILFORD, J.P. (1897–1987)

A native Nebraskan, J.P. Guilford obtained his degree in psychology at the University of Nebraska and later did graduate work at Cornell University. While attending Nebraska, his association with Winifred Hyde led to an interest in psychological testing, with Karl Dallenbach and Kurt Koffka, both of whom he met at Cornell, strongly influencing his later work. Guilford died in 1987.

Guilford spent most of his academic career at the University of Southern California. In addition to writing what some consider classic texts in psychological measurement (e.g., Guilford, 1942, 1948), he is best known for his extensive work in factor analysis, the method used to develop his structure of intellect (SOI) model (Guilford, 1967, 1988). Guilford's model of intelligence postulates some 120 distinct human abilities that contribute to overall intellectual ability and was later revised to contain five content properties, including visual, auditory, symbolic, semantic, and behavioral. In the field of special education, his SOI model, particularly the concepts of convergent and divergent thought, was used to develop programs to foster creativity and improve learning of gifted and creative children.

In 1983, Guilford received the Gold Medal Award of the American Psychological Association. His numerous publications include *The Nature of Human Intelligence* (1967), *Intelligence Education is Intelligent Education* (1980), and *Fundamental Statistics in Psychology and Education* (1942). A compilation of his work in scholarly journals was recently published in German (Primmer, 1995).

REFERENCES

Guilford, J.P. (1942). *Fundamental statistics in psychology and education.* New York: McGraw-Hill.

Guilford, J.P. (1967). *The nature of human intelligence.* New York: McGraw-Hill.

Guilford, J.P. (1980). *Intelligence education is intelligent education.* Tokyo: International Society for Intelligence Education.

Guilford, J.P. (1988). Some changes in the structure-of-intellect model. *Educational & Psychological Measurement, 48,* 1–4.

Guilford, J.P., Anastasi, A., English, H., & Freeman, G. (1948). *Fields of psychology.* New York: Van Nostrand.

Primmer, H. (1995). *Kreativitatsforschung und Joy Paul Guilford.* Munchen: Akademischer Verlag.

See also **Convergent and Divergent Thinking; Structure of Intellect**

GUILLAIN-BARRÉ SYNDROME

Guillain-Barré syndrome is described as a peripheral polyneuritis resulting in symmetrical pain and weakness of the extremities (*Mosby's,* 1983). The condition was originally described by Guillain, Barré, and Strohl in 1916. It sometimes bears the names of all three physicians; other synonyms include acute febrile polyneuritis and Landry's paralysis (Durham, 1969; Magalini, 1971). Onset of Guillain-Barré syndrome may occur one to three weeks following a mild fever associated with immunization or viral infection (*Mosby's,* 1983). The presence of an upper respiratory infection prior to onset of symptoms has been reported in approximately half the cases (Dyck, 1979). Early signs are mild, and include weakness of the lower extremities, characterized by difficulty in walking, climbing stairs, or rising from a seated position. Weakness and paralysis develop in an ascending fashion either rapidly (within hours) or more gradually, over a period of 7 to 10 days (Magalini, 1971). Bladder incontinence may occur, tendon reflexes are absent, and ocular nerves may be involved (Durham, 1969).

The course of Guillain-Barré syndrome varies widely; some individuals have extreme impairment (e.g., near total paralysis) and require nursing care, while others exhibit less severe symptoms. In nearly all cases, total remission occurs within a few weeks or months. The small number of patients for whom Guillain-Barré syndrome is fatal succumb to respiratory paralysis (Durham, 1969; Lechtenberg, 1982). The cause of Guillain-Barré syndrome is unknown, although exposure to a virus or bacterial infection is suspected (Dyck, 1979). Males and females, children and adults are affected equally. Treatment typically is limited to maintaining respiration and maximizing comfort. The administration of corticosteroid hormones has been associated with enhanced rate of recovery (Dyck, 1979). Physical therapy is advisable during the recovery period. During the acute and recuperative stages of Guillain-Barré syndrome, affected children may require special education, including homebound instruction for limited periods and related services (e.g., physical therapy). Educational programming should follow a multifactored evaluation and consultation with appropriate medical personnel.

REFERENCES

Durham, R.H. (1969). *Encyclopedia of medical syndromes.* New York: Harper & Row.

Dyck, P.J. (1979). Diseases of the peripheral nervous system. In P.B. Beeson, W. McDermott, & J.B. Wyngaarden (Eds.), *Cecil textbook of medicine* (pp. 899–913). Philadelphia: Saunders.

Lechtenberg, R. (1982). *The psychiatrist's guide to diseases of the nervous system.* New York: Wiley.

Magalini, S. (1971). *Dictionary of medical syndromes.* Philadelphia: Lippincott.

Mosby's medical and nursing dictionary. (1983). St. Louis: Mosby.

See also **Central Nervous System; Physical Disability**

H

HABILITATION OF THE HANDICAPPED

Habilitation is the process of using various professional services to help disabled persons maximize their vocational, mental, physical, and social abilities (Rosen, Clark, & Kivitz, 1977). Whereas the term rehabilitation connotes restoration of abilities, habilitation refers to the development of abilities that never existed. The term usually refers to programming for those with developmental disabilities such as cerebral palsy, mental retardation, epilepsy, autism, or sensory impairment.

Present-day habilitation programs have evolved from a decade of legislation and litigation addressing the rights and needs of the developmentally disabled. Three major pieces of legislation promoted early habilitation efforts: the Rehabilitation Act Amendments of 1973 (PL 93-112), the Education for all Handicapped Children Act of 1975 (PL 94-142), and the Education Amendments of 1976 (PL 94-482), efforts which continue to be supported by the Individuals with Disabilities Education Act (IDEA) and the Americans with Disabilities Act (ADA).

Habilitation programs for handicapped students vary, but are similar in format to those described by Miller and Schloss (1982). Current programs focus not only on vocation, but also on academic, social, leisure, and interpersonal skills. Teaching procedures include identification of the handicap, assessment of skills, program design based on needs, interests, and skills of the individual, instruction, and behavior management and evaluation. Career education includes career awareness and exploration, development of vocational prerequisites, and preparation training.

REFERENCES

Miller, S.R., & Schloss, P.J. (1982). *Career vocational education for handicapped youth.* Rockville, MD: Aspen.

Rosen, M., Clark, G.R., & Kivitz, M.S. (1977). *Habilitation of the handicapped: New dimensions in programs for the developmentally disabled.* Baltimore, MD: University Park.

See also **Rehabilitation; Vocational Training**

HABITUATION

Habituation is a decline in response to a stimulus that is presented repeatedly but that signals the onset of no other stimulus. For example, a loud noise may evoke a startle response at first but little response after its twentieth repetition. A new cuckoo clock may awaken people on the hour for the first few nights but not on later nights.

Because habituation is generally perceived as a relatively simple example of learning, it has been a popular focus for study by investigators interested in the physiology of learning. For example, the gill-withdrawal response of the sea slug *Aplysia* habituates after a tactile stimulus is repeated many times. The habituation can be traced to a single, identifiable synapse at which the pre-synaptic end bulb shrinks and releases less than normal amounts of its synaptic transmitter (Castellucci & Kandel, 1974).

Some investigators have used rate of habituation as a diagnostic technique to identify infants or young children who may have been exposed to factors that impair brain maturation. One study examined the rate of habituation by newborns as a function of alcohol use by their mothers during pregnancy (Streissguth, Barr, & Martin, 1983). Habituation was slightly but significantly slower among infants whose mothers drank alcohol during pregnancy, even if they drank a mean of less than one ounce of alcohol per day.

REFERENCES

Castellucci, V.F., & Kandel, E.R. (1974). A quantal analysis of the synaptic depression underlying habituation of the gill-withdrawal reflex in *Aplysia. Proceedings of the National Academy of Sciences, U.S.A., 71,* 5004–5008.

Streissguth, A.P., Barr, H.M., & Martin, D.C. (1983). Maternal alcohol use and neonatal habituation assessed with the Brazelton scale. *Child Development, 54,* 1109–1118.

See also **Attention-Deficit Hyperactivity Disorder; Behavior Modification; Distractibility**

HALDERMAN *V.* PENNHURST STATE SCHOOL AND HOSPITAL (1977)

The *Halderman* case was filed as a class-action suit by a resident, T.L. Halderman, of the Pennhurst State School and Hospital (operated by the Commonwealth of Pennsylvania), the Pennsylvania Association of Retarded Citizens, and the United States of America against the Pennhurst State School and Hospital. The residents made a variety of claims that centered around the lack of rehabilitative and educational efforts at Pennhurst. The plaintiffs argued that custodial care was insufficient for involuntary placement in the Pennhurst institution since the plaintiffs were retarded and not considered dangerous.

In deciding the case, the federal judge for the eastern district of Pennsylvania, R.J. Broderick, made three rulings that have been of major importance in modifying special education services to the institutionalized retarded. Broderick ruled that retarded residents of state institutions have constitutional rights to minimally adequate habilitation services, to freedom from harm, and to the receipt of habilitation services in a nondiscriminatory manner. Broderick went on to rule in the *Halderman* case specifically that the resident's rights at Pennhurst had been violated because of failure to provide even minimally adequate habilitative services. In making his rulings, Broderick rejected the argument that improvements at Pennhurst were being made gradually and should be allowed to proceed at an incremental pace, that state law restricted the programs that could be offered, and that funding levels prevented minimally adequate habilitation programs. Broderick wrote a lengthy decision that reviews assessment practices, programming, and management in institutional settings. All were directed at the provision of habilitative services and special education.

Broderick placed many restrictions on the use of punishment, drugs, and physical restraints. He particularly ruled that lack of sufficient staff did not allow the use of otherwise inappropriate methods of control. Physical constraints, for example, could not be used just because insufficient staff were available to supervise self-injurious residents.

Broderick made strong statements indicating favorable sentiments toward the principles of normalization as applied to the severely and profoundly retarded as well. Since the court found that the environment at Pennhurst was not conducive to normalization, Broderick ruled that the residents were to be moved to community-based living facilities as part of the injunctive relief. He noted that each community facility would be required to provide minimally adequate habilitative services. Broderick's extensive rulings regarding the provisions of habilitative services, including detailed multidisciplinary assessment and movement toward normalization, have had significant impact on the deinstitutionalization of all but the most severely and profoundly mentally retarded.

See also Normalization

HALDOL

Haldol (haloperidol) is considered a major tranquilizer. Unlike thorazine, which is a phenothiazine, haldol is of the drug class butyrophenone, which tends to have a greater neuroleptic effect than phenothiazine (Bassuk & Schoonover, 1977). Haldol is similar in effect to the piperazine subgroup (e.g., Stelazine) of phenothiazines. Like similar antipsychotic drugs, haldol appears to block dopamine receptors in the brain. In contrast to chlorpromazine, haldol tends to produce less sedation, less decrease in blood pressure, and less change in temperature perception (McEvoy, 1984). Haldol is used primarily for symptomatic management of psychotic conditions. Haldol also appears to have more specific effects on agitated behavior. Thus, it tends to be used with psychotic individuals who also show assaultive behavior, with combative adolescents, and with hyperactive brain-impaired children (Bassuk & Schoonover, 1977). Haldol also has been used as an adjunct with manic-depressive patients in the manic phase during the initiation of lithium treatment (Jefferson, Greist, & Ackerman, 1983). Although haldol was once the most popular of the neuroleptic drugs for the treatment of psychotic processes (such as schizophrenia) due to its low side-effect profile, newer drugs with even fewer side effects, such as Risperidone, have gained popularity.

REFERENCES

Bassuk, E.L., & Schoonover, S.C. (1977). *The practitioner's guide to psychoactive drugs.* New York: Plenum.

Jefferson, J.W., Greist, J.H., & Ackerman, D.L. (1983). *Lithium encyclopedia for clinical practice.* Washington, DC: American Psychiatric Press.

McEvoy, G.K. (1984). *American hospital formulary service: Drug information 84.* Bethesda, MD: American Society of Hospital Pharmacists.

See also Dopamine; Stelazine

HALL, FRANK H. (1843–1911)

Frank Haven Hall, inventor of the braille typewriter, was a school superintendent prior to becoming superintendent of the Illinois Institution for the Education of the Blind in 1890. In 1892 Hall introduced the braillewriter, a braille typewriter that quickly replaced the laborious writing device then in use—a slate and hand-held stylus—and greatly speeded up the writing of braille. Hall then adapted his machine to print multiple copies. With its speed and efficiency, Hall's machine revolutionized book-making for the blind and made feasible the mass production of braille materials.

Hall's experience at the Illinois institution convinced him that blind students should have the opportunity of participating fully in the activities of sighted individuals. He persuaded the school authorities of Chicago, who were considering the establishment of a boarding school for blind students, to establish day classes instead. As a result, the first public school day class for blind students was initiated in Chicago in 1900, with one of Hall's teachers as supervisor. The last decade of Hall's life was spent as superintendent of the Farmers' Institute of Illinois, where he effectively promoted the cause of agricultural education.

REFERENCE

Hendrickson, W.B. (1956). The three lives of Frank H. Hall. *Journal of the Illinois State Historical Society, 44,* 271–293.

HALL, G. STANLEY (1844–1924)

G. Stanley Hall established one of the first psychology laboratories in the United States, at Johns Hopkins University. Later, as the first president of Clark University, he instituted the first child psychology laboratory in the nation. A former student of Wilhelm Wundt in Leipzig, Hall was influential in introducing European theories and methods of psychology into the United States. He carried out pioneering studies of childhood, adolescence, senescence, human genetics, and the psychology of religion. Among Hall's students were many of the next generation of leaders in psychology and education, including John Dewey, James McKeen Cattell, Henry H. Goddard, and Lewis Terman. Hall published nearly 500 articles and books and founded four psychological journals. He was a leading figure in the formation of the American Psychological Association and was its first president.

REFERENCES

Hall, G.S. (1923). *Life and confessions of a psychologist.* New York: Appleton.

Watson, R.I. (1968). *The great psychologists.* New York: Lippincott.

HALLERMANN-STREIFF SYNDROME (OCULO-MANDIBULO-FACIAL SYNDROME) (HSS)

Hallermann-Streiff syndrome (HSS) is a syndrome whose etiology is presently unknown. Children with HSS have multiple craniofacial malformations that often include a short head, thin skin, small face, eyes, and mouth, a reduction of hair, and a thin "beaked" nose that produces a bird-like appearance (Carter, 1978). Teeth may be present at birth; the small mouth, high palate, and absence of some teeth often result in dental problems. Congenital cataracts are frequently present, causing severe visual problems. In addition, hearing problems often occur.

Children with HSS are generally short in stature (usually less than the third percentile for height) with proportional dwarfism of extremities and hyperextensibility of joints. Small sexual organs are noted and spina bifida has been reported in some cases. Mental range extends from normal to moderate and, in some cases, severe retardation.

Special services will be required for hearing, vision, and speech problems. Because varying degrees of mental retardation may be present in HSS children, good diagnostic evaluations are important. In addition, there is a relatively substantial difference in the physical appearance of HSS children, therefore, psychological and guidance counseling may be necessary as the children mature because joint, motor, and spinal problems may develop. Mainstreamed settings with proper support services are usually the preferred educational settings.

REFERENCES

Carter, C. (Ed.). (1978). *Medical aspects of mental retardation* (2nd ed.). Springfield: IL: Thomas.

See also **Physical Anomalies; Spina Bifida**

HALLUCINOGENS

Blum (1984) describes three classes of hallucinogenic drugs: adrenergic compounds (e.g., mescaline, adrenaline); indole types (e.g., lysergic acid diethylamide [LSD]); and anticholinergic hallucinogens (e.g., scopolamine, atropine). An additional hallucinogen, which has been sold as everything from cocaine to LSD, is phencyclidine (PCP), which was originally marketed as an animal anesthetic. For a complete review of hallucinogenic agents, see Blum (1984).

In reviewing the personality characteristics of the users of hallucinogenic drugs, several trends have been noted. LSD users tend to be more introverted and artistic (McGothlin, Cohen, & McGothlin, 1966). Comparisons of personality test findings suggest that persons using hallucinogens are more socially distant, interpersonally suspicious, dominant, anxious, creative, and accident-prone (Kleckner, 1968). These trends have been replicated in additional studies (Pittel et al., 1970, cited in Leavitt, 1982), suggesting a contributory role for childhood chaos and above average stress in substance abuse.

REFERENCES

Blum, K. (1984). *The handbook of abusable drugs.* New York: Gardner.

Kleckner, J. (1968). Personality differences between psychedelic drug users and non-users. *Psychology, 5,* 66–71.

Leavitt, F. (1982). *Drugs and behavior.* New York: Wiley.

McGothlin, W., Cohen, S., & McGothlin, M. (1966). Personality and attitude changes in volunteer subjects following repeated administration of LSD. *Excerpta Medica International Continuing Reports, 129,* 425–434.

See also **Drug Abuse**

HALSTEAD APHASIA TEST

The Halstead Aphasia Test, Form M, was developed by Ward C. Halstead in cooperation with J.M. Wepman, R.M. Reitan, and R.F. Heimburger. It was published by the Industrial Relations Center, University of Chicago, in 1955. It is the pocket-size version of the Halstead-Wepman Screening Test for Aphasia (1949), which itself was a version of a 1935 test.

This test uses basically the same 51 test items and order of presentation as its predecessor. Test materials consist of plastic stimuli cards, which the patient views through a 2-inch by 1 and a half-inch window, a manual, and scoring sheets. Criteria for evaluating subjects' responses and a diagnostic code and profile by which patients are classified into four aphasic categories (global, expressive-receptive, expressive, and receptive) are included in the manual. Administration time is 30 to 60 minutes.

REFERENCES

Halstead, W.C., Wepman, J.J., Reitan, R.M., & Heimburger, R.F. (1955). *The Halstead Aphasia Test.* Chicago: University of Chicago Press.

HALSTEAD-REITAN NEUROPSYCHOLOGICAL TEST BATTERY

Collectively, three separate test batteries are commonly referred to as the Halstead-Reitan Neuropsychological Test Battery. The adult battery (ages 15 and older) is entitled the

Halstead Neuropsychological Test Battery for Adults; the older children's battery (ages 9 through 14) is called the Halstead Neuropsychological Test Battery for Children. A third battery for younger children (ages 5 through 8) is the Reitan-Indiana Neuropsychological Test Battery for Children. This differential terminology, which has resulted in confusion and inconsistent use of the proper battery name, is the result of an agreement between W.C. Halstead and his protégé, R.M. Reitan (Reitan, 1979), the two individuals credited with various aspects of the development and refinement of these batteries.

Despite terminology differences, the three batteries reflect conceptual similarities in their approaches to the assessment of brain-behavior relationships. The nuclear tests of the three batteries were originally developed by Halstead (1947) and later standardized and modified by Reitan. The adult battery is composed of the following tests: Category Test, Tactual Performance Test, Seashore Rhythm Test, Speech-Sounds Perception Test, Finger Oscillation Test, Trail-Making Test, Aphasia Screening Test, Sensory-Perceptual Disturbances Test, Lateral Dominance Test, and Strength of Grip Test. Reitan simplified several of these tests to create the battery for older children. The younger children's battery involved many more modifications of the original tests and the development of some entirely new tests (Reitan, 1979). It is common to use any of the three batteries in conjunction with the appropriate Wechsler Intelligence Scale, an achievement measure for children, or the Minnesota Multiphasic Personality Inventory (MMPI) for adults (Boll, 1981).

All three batteries have proven to be effective in differentiating brain-damaged from normal functioning individuals, provided they are administered and interpreted properly by trained professionals. Reitan and Davison (1974) provide a detailed examination of the limitations and validity of these batteries.

REFERENCES

Boll, T.J. (1981). The Halstead-Reitan Neuropsychology Battery. In S.B. Filskov & T.J. Boll (Eds.), *Handbook of clinical neuropsychology* (pp. 577–607). New York: Wiley.

Halstead, W.C. (1947). *Brain and intelligence.* Chicago: University of Chicago Press.

Reitan, R.M. (1979). *Manual for administration of neuropsychological test batteries for adults and children.* Tucson, AZ: Reitan Neuropsychology Laboratories.

Reitan, R.M., & Davison, L.A. (1974). *Clinical neuropsychology.* New York: Hemisphere.

See also **Luria-Nebraska Neuropsychological Battery; Neuropsychology**

HANDEDNESS AND EXCEPTIONALITY

Handedness, though seemingly a phenomenon in its own right, is actually one component of a more general pattern of lateralization. Lateralization refers to the fact that most people tend to favor one side of their body over the other. A minority of individuals demonstrate inconsistent or weak lateralization, meaning they have a mixed pattern of hand dominance, foot dominance, eye dominance, or cerebral hemisphere dominance.

Research has documented that the left side of the brain controls the right side of the body, and vice versa, for basic sensory and motor activity, and that the left side of the brain is generally more efficient than the right side at processing language. These two facts, considered along with estimates that right-handers constitute approximately 90% of all humans, indicate that the most common pattern of lateralization includes both right-handedness and left hemisphere cerebral dominance for language. Left-handers, who are more apt to use both hemispheres of the brain for language than right-handers, might then be thought of as having weak or "deviant" lateralization. It is this deviant lateralization, of which handedness is but one component, rather than handedness per se, that has been linked to exceptionalities throughout the literature.

Deviant or weak lateralization may be inherited (Annett, 1964) or it may be caused by injury to the brain (Corballis & Beale, 1983). Whatever the etiology, deviation from the usual pattern of right-handedness and left hemisphere language representation can be manifested in a number of ways. On the positive side, weakly lateralized left-handers tend to be overrepresented among highly gifted and creative individuals. Leonardo da Vinci, Harpo Marx, and Charlie Chaplin are examples. On the negative side, left-handers may be particularly susceptible to a myriad of pathological conditions. Throughout the ages, left-handers have been overrepresented among schizophrenics, epileptics, and various types of criminals (Corballis & Beale, 1983).

Investigations have revealed a higher incidence of left-handedness in special education populations. Fein, Waterhouse, Lucci, Snyder, and Humes (1984) found 18% of a sample of school-age autistic children were left-handed. This figure is consistent with previous studies of autistic children, and is comparable to Satz's (1973) estimate of 83% right-handedness in retarded and epileptic populations. Those findings represent an approximate doubling of the left-handedness consistently found in normal populations. Other studies have found markedly greater frequencies of immune disease, migraine, and learning disabilities among left-handers (Geschwind & Behan, 1982).

Two other pathological conditions that have been linked to the deviant lateralization associated with left-handedness are dyslexia, a form of reading disability, and stuttering. The concept of dyslexia, first formulated about 100 years ago, has been surrounded by a great deal of controversy. Disagreement as to whether the disorder actually exits, its nature, and how it should be diagnosed and treated abound. A distinction can be drawn between developmental dyslexia, which implies a developmental or maturational anomaly, and acquired dyslexia, which implies brain damage.

Despite the fact that it is still widely believed that stuttering is related to left-handedness, and in particular that it is caused by forcing a natural left-hander to write with the right hand, there is no evidence to show that changed handedness has any influence on cerebral representation of speech control. Moreover, it is difficult to separate left- or changed-handedness from the more general condition of weak or deviant lateralization (Dean & Reynolds, 1997).

Both dyslexia and stuttering occur more frequently among males than females. Since both of these conditions have been linked to weak or deviant lateralization, it seems contradictory that evidence suggests that generally females have weaker lateralization than males, both with respect to left hemispheric representation of language and right hemispheric representation of spatial functions (Corballis & Beale, 1983). This contradiction may be attributed to several different factors. First, males tend to be more susceptible to pathological influences at birth resulting in injury-induced deviant lateralization (Annett, 1964). Second, weaker female lateralization is specific to adults, as boys tend to lag behind girls in the development of lateralization (Bakker, Teunissen, & Bosch, 1976). The development of lateralization may be complete earlier in girls than in boys since girls generally reach puberty before boys. Dyslexia and stuttering typically develop well before puberty, when lateralization may be more highly developed in girls than in boys. Third, a factor more closely associated with males than females may actually trigger these two conditions. Geschwind and Behan (1982) believe that the male hormone, testosterone, slows development of the brain's left side, allowing the right hemisphere to assume some typically left-brain functions. The end result can be left-handedness or simply weaker or deviant cerebral lateralization.

Overall, there is convincing evidence that weak or deviant lateralization, of which handedness is one important component, is linked to various exceptionalities. While deviant lateralization should not be taken as a sufficient cause of learning disabilities, dyslexia, stuttering, or any of the other pathological conditions herein mentioned, it cannot be overlooked that those who manifest weak cerebral dominance are more apt to develop one of these afflictions than those who manifest strong lateralization. Deviant lateralization is most likely a comorbid symptom, however, and not the fundamental cause of these problems (Dean & Reynolds, 1997).

REFERENCES

Annett, M. (1964). A model of the inheritance of handedness and cerebral dominance. *Nature, 204,* 59–60.

Bakker, D.J., Teunissen, J., & Bosch, J. (1976). Development of laterality-reading patterns. In R.M. Knights & D.J. Bakker (Eds.), *The neuropsychology of learning disorders* (pp. 207– 220). Baltimore, MD: University Park Press.

Corballis, M.C., & Beale, I.L. (1983). *The ambivalent mind.* Chicago: Nelson-Hall.

Dean, R.S. & Reynolds, C.R. (1997). Cognitive processing and self-report of lateral preference. *Neuropsychology Review, 7,* 127–142.

Fein, D., Waterhouse, D., Lucci, D., Snyder, D., & Humes, M. (1984, February). *Cognitive functions in left and right-handed autistic*

children. Presentation at the annual meeting of the International Neuropsychological Society, Houston, TX.

Geschwind, N., & Behan, P. (1982). Left-handedness: Association with immune disease, migraine, and developmental learning disorder. *Proceedings of the National Academy of Science, U.S.A., 79,* 5097–5100.

Satz, P. (1973). Left-handedness and early brain insult: An explanation. *Neuropsychologia, 11,* 115–117.

See also **Dyslexia; Stuttering**

HANDICAPISM

Handicapism is a term created by Biklen and Bogdan (1976) to identify both an evolving social movement and a set of behaviors toward those with disabilities. It has been defined by its authors as "a theory and set of practices that promote unequal and unjust treatment of people because of apparent or assumed physical or mental disability" (p. 9). Handicapism is evident in our personal lives, social policy, cultural norms, and institutional practices (Biklen & Bogdan, 1976). Like racism and sexism, handicapism is evident in the language often used to describe disabled individuals. Such language tends to be discriminatory and serves to devalue the capabilities of the person (Heward & Orlansky, 1984; Mullins, 1979).

Common words and phrases that devalue rather than enhance a disabled person's characteristics include, "had a fit," "a basket case," and "ree tard." Handicapist phrases such as "he's a moron," handicapist humor such as "what did the twit say," and handicapist behavior, for instance, avoiding contact with a disabled person, are examples of handicapism in our personal lives. People with physical disabilities are often confronted with inaccessible entrances to buildings, bathrooms that do not accommodate wheelchairs, and public transportation systems that are difficult to use. Handicapism is also evident in the limited employment opportunities that prevail for the disabled, in media reporting that often transforms the severely disabled into objects rather than people, and in the attitudes of helping professions that often overlook the disabled person's need for privacy and human dignity.

REFERENCES

Biklen, D., & Bogdan, R. (1976, October). Handicapism in America, *WIN,* 9–13.

Heward, W., & Orlansky, M.D. (1984). *Exceptional children* (2nd ed.) (p. 7). Columbus, OH: Merrill.

Mullins, J.B. (1979). Making language work to eliminate handicapism. *Education Unlimited,* June 1979, 20–24.

See also **Civil Rights of the Handicapped; Individuals with Disabilities Education Act (IDEA)**

HANDICAPPED, DEFINITION OF

The Education for All Handicapped Children Act of 1975 originally defined the handicapping conditions that are eligible for services that are reimbursable by the federal government. IDEA maintained essentially the same wording in its 1993 federal regulations. This law defines a handicapped individual:

as being mentally retarded, hard of hearing, deaf, speech impaired, visually handicapped, seriously emotionally disturbed, orthopedically impaired, other health impaired, deaf-blind, multi-handicapped, or as having specific learning disabilities, who because of those impairments need special education and related services.

(b) The terms used in this definition are defined as follows:

(1) "Deaf " means a hearing impairment which is so severe that the child is impaired in processing linguistic information through hearing, with or without amplification, which adversely affects educational performance.

(2) "Deaf-blind" means concomitant hearing and visual impairments, the combination of which causes such severe communication and other developmental and educational problems that they cannot be accommodated in special education programs solely for deaf or blind children.

(3) "Hard of hearing" means a hearing impairment, whether permanent or fluctuating, which adversely affects a child's educational performance but which is not included under the definition of "deaf " in this section.

(4) "Mentally retarded" means significantly subaverage general intellectual functioning existing concurrently with deficits in adaptive behavior and manifested during the developmental period, which adversely affects a child's educational performance.

(5) "Multihandicapped" means concomitant impairments (such as mentally retarded–blind, mentally retarded–orthopedically impaired, etc.), the combination of which causes such severe educational problems that they cannot be accommodated in special education programs solely for one of the impairments. The term does not include deaf-blind children.

(6) "Orthopedically impaired" means a severe orthopedic impairment which adversely affects a child's educational performance. The term includes impairments caused by congenital anomaly (e.g., clubfoot, absence of some member, etc.), impairments caused by disease (e.g., poliomyelitis, bone tuberculosis, etc.), and impairments from other causes (e.g., cerebral palsy, amputations; and fractures or burns which cause contractures).

(7) "Other health impaired" means (i) having an autistic condition which is manifested by severe communication and other developmental and educational problems; or (ii) having limited strength, vitality or alertness, due to chronic or acute health problems such as a heart condition, tuberculosis, rhematic fever, nephritis, asthma, sickle cell anemia, hemophilia, epilepsy, lead poisoning, leukemia, or diabetes, which adversely affect a child's educational performance.

(8) "Seriously emotionally disturbed" is defined as follows:

(i) The term means a condition exhibiting one or more of the following characteristics over a long period of time and to a marked degree, which adversely affects educational performance:

(A) An inability to learn which cannot be explained by intellectual, sensory, or health factors;

(B) An inability to build or maintain satisfactory interpersonal relationships with peers and teachers;

(C) Inappropriate types of behavior or feelings under normal circumstances;

(D) A general pervasive mood of unhappiness or depression; or

(E) A tendency to develop physical symptoms or fears associated with personal or school problems.

(ii) The term includes schizophrenia. The term does not include children who are socially maladjusted, unless it is determined that they are seriously emotionally disturbed.

(9) "Specific learning disability" means a disorder in one or more of the basic psychological processes involved understanding or in using language, spoken or written, which may manifest itself in an imperfect ability to listen, think, speak, read, write, spell, or to do mathematical calculations. The term includes such conditions as perceptual handicaps, brain injury, minimal brain dysfunction, dyslexia, and developmental aphasia. The term does not include children who have learning problems which are primarily the result of visual, hearing, or motor handicaps, of mental retardation, of emotional disturbance or of environmental, cultural, or economic disadvantage.

(10) "Speech impaired" means a communication disorder such as stuttering, impaired articulation, a language impairment, or a voice impairment, which adversely affects a child's educational performance.

(11) "Visually handicapped" means a visual impairment which, even with correction, adversely affects a child's educational performance. The term includes both partial sight and blind children. (20 U.S.C. 1401(1), (15))

See also **Education for All Handicapped Children act of 1975; Individuals with Disabilities Education Act (IDEA)**

HANDICAPPED CHILDREN, SOCIAL MAINSTREAMING OF

Mainstreaming is a special education procedure designed to ensure that special students are serviced in the least restrictive environment in accordance with IDEA. Traditionally, a student who demonstrates academic proficiency in the special education class may qualify for regular classroom placement. Throughout this transition, academic performance is closely monitored but the affective domain may be ignored. Commonly, disregard for the affective development of the special education student socially segregates the student entering the regular classroom (Cartwright, Cartwright, & Ward, 1995).

A plethora of social skills training strategies have emerged to train social skills in the handicapped. Traditionally, social skills training has involved instrumental and classical learning techniques as well as modeling. More recently, the concern over social mainstreaming has contributed to interest in cooperative learning strategies (Cartwright, Cartwright, & Ward, 1995).

REFERENCE

Cartwright, P., Cartwright, C., & Ward, M. (1995). *Educating special learners.* NY: Wadsworth.

See also **Individuals with Disabilities Education Act (IDEA); Inclusion; Mainstreaming; Social Skills Training**

HANDICAPPED CHILDREN'S EARLY EDUCATION ASSISTANCE ACT (PUBLIC LAW 90-538)

The Handicapped Children's Early Education Program (HCEEP) began in 1968 with the passage of the Handicapped Children's Early Education Assistance Act (PL 90-538). The major goals of the program were to design experimental approaches to meet the special needs of young children with handicaps; to develop programs to facilitate the intellectual, mental, social, physical, and language development of the children; to acquaint the community with the problems and potential of young handicapped children; to coordinate with the local school system in the community being served; and to encourage parental participation in the development of programs. The program originally was comprised of one of its five current components—demonstration projects.

DEMONSTRATION PROJECTS

To accomplish HCEEP's goals, the Act authorized grants and contracts to public and private agencies and organizations for the establishment of experimental preschool and early education demonstration projects. The chosen projects showed promise of developing comprehensive and innovative approaches for meeting the special needs of handicapped children from birth to eight years of age. These projects were expected to serve as models providing highly visible examples of successful practices, and encouraging others to initiate and/or improve services to young handicapped children. In this respect, HCEEP was viewed not as a direct service mechanism, but as an indirect mechanism for expanding and improving the quality of services.

OUTREACH PROJECTS

The Outreach Component, developed in 1972, had two goals: to stimulate and increase high quality services to preschool handicapped children, birth through eight years, and to stimulate replication of innovative models developed in the demonstration projects. Successful demonstration projects were expected to apply for outreach funds at the end of three years. To be even eligible for consideration, a demonstration project had to obtain funds from other sources to continue providing direct services to children and their families. Projects not funded previously as early childhood demonstration projects have been allowed to compete for outreach funds.

STATE PLAN GRANTS

The third component of HCEEP had its roots prior to 1976. Aware of the need for state planning to consider the needs of young handicapped children, HCEEP had made technical assistance available to states which desired to improve or expand services to the early childhood age range. The expectation was that federal funds would be available in the immediate future to help implement these states' plans. When such funds did become available in 1976 through the State Implementation Grant (SIG) initiative, states applying were awarded grants on a competitive basis. The goal of SIG was to assist state education agencies in building a capacity to plan for the initiation and expansion of early intervention services. To some degree, this planning process was expected to be enhanced simply by creating financial resources for an early childhood planning position within each state.

Public law 98–199 carried this initiative further with the creation of the current State Plan Grant Component. The state plan grant is intended to enable each state and territory to plan, develop, or implement a comprehensive service delivery system for special education and related services to handicapped children from birth to five years of age. States may apply for a grant to support planning, to support development, or to support implementation activities depending on their assessment of appropriateness and readiness. At least 30 percent of the HCEEP appropriation must be used for this component in recognition of the need for state commitments to serving these children.

RESEARCH INSTITUTES

In 1977, the fourth component of HCEEP was initiated. In cooperation with the Research Projects Branch of the Office of Special Education Programs, HCEEP funded four research institutes to carry out longitudinal research. Topics of research included social, emotional, physical, cognitive, and behavioral aspects of the child; theories and methods of intervention; parent-child interaction; and assessment techniques.

The institutes were seen as investments in the future, paying off not only in terms of the immediate research results, but in terms of the training of future special education researchers and service providers. A second generation of institutes was funded in 1982 to investigate problems concerning services for autisticlike children, cost and efficacy data for early childhood interventions, and programming for parental involvement. In addition, another institute was funded in 1985 to focus on evaluating the impact of various methods of early intervention for handicapped children as a whole and in various subgroups.

TECHNICAL ASSISTANCE

In 1971, the Technical Assistance Development System (TADS) was funded to assist demonstration projects. From 1977 to 1982, two technical assistance systems, TADS and WESTAR, were operating in order to provide geographical coverage for the large number of demonstration projects and SIGs. When the number of demonstrations decreased in 1982, the need for technical assistance also was reduced and TADS again became the sole designated external provider of technical assistance to demonstration projects. A new technical assistance effort, the State Technical Assistance Resource Team (START), was funded in 1985 to provide assistance to the state plan grant projects.

HANDICAPPED CHILDREN'S EARLY EDUCATION PROGRAM (HCEEP)

The federal initiatives for research and service to young children with handicaps began in 1968 with the establishment of the Handicapped Children's Early Assistance Act. This act created the Handicapped Children's Early Education Programs (HCEEP) that were to develop, implement, and evaluate model preschool services. These services took direction from previous research and documentation of the positive results possible when children with handicaps received intervention early (Tjossem, 1976).

The stated purposes for HCEEP were to focus on all of the developmental aspects of the child, to provide parents with support and strategies to meet the needs of their child, to provide the parents with opportunities to participate in providing their child with an education, and to provide the community with information regarding the difficulties and potentials of young children with handicaps (Jordan, Hayden, Karnes & Wood, 1977). Individuals who have applied for funds to implement one of the programs provided statements of how they planned to meet the HCEEP purposes. These purposes were implemented with young children experiencing a variety of educational and developmental needs.

Information collected on these programs has expanded the knowledge and data base on successful intervention strategies with young handicapped children. These programs developed assessment tools, curricula, programming, and data collection strategies that serve as a foundation for today's early intervention services. This occurred as a result of the model services developed by the first group of funded projects. These projects demonstrated how to develop and operate model programs and provided technical assistance for the replication of their model. Some examples of projects are the Chapel Hill-Carrboro Outreach Project of North Carolina, the Rutland Center For Severely Emotionally Disturbed Children, the Curative Workshop, the Ski-Hi Project, the Portage Project, and the University of Washington (DeWeerd, 1981).

REFERENCES

DeWeerd, J. (1981). Early education services for children with handicaps: Where have we been, where are we now, and where are we going? *Journal of the Division for Early Childhood, 2,* 15–24.

Jordan, J.B., Hayden, A.H., Karnes, M.B., & Wood, M.M. (Eds.). (1977). *Early education for exceptional children: A handbook of exemplary ideas and practices.* Reston, VA: Council for Exceptional Children.

Tjossem, T.D. (1976). *Intervention strategies for high risk infants and young children.* Baltimore: University Park Press.

See also **Early Childhood, Special Education Topics in**

HANDICAPPING CONDITIONS, HIGH INCIDENCE

See HIGH INCIDENCE HANDICAPS.

HANDICAPS, LOW INCIDENCE

See LOW INCIDENCE HANDICAPS.

HAND TEST

The Hand Test (Wagner, 1962) is unique among projective techniques that require storytelling. The stimuli provided to the individual are not whole scenes or figures but nine cards with line drawings of single hands. Each card shows a hand in a different position. A tenth blank card is included. Reaction time and responses are recorded during the administration, which averages about 10 minutes per case. Responses are scored into four categories for normative comparisons: impersonal, environmental, maladjusted, and withdrawal.

Another score that has received some support is the Acting-Out Score (AOS). The AOS seems to do well in differentiating between aggressive and nonaggressive children and between assaultive and nonassaultive delinquents. The AOS is also positively related to recidivism among juvenile offenders. The Hand Test is quick and easy to administer and is useful in the evaluation of children and adolescents with emotional and behavioral problems.

REFERENCE

Wagner, E.E. (1962). *The Hand Test: Manual for administration, scoring, and interpretation.* Akron, OH: Mark Jones.

HANDWRITING

Handwriting is an essential tool for recording, expressing, and communicating human thought. It is a traditional element of the elementary school curriculum, and considerable time and energy are devoted to its mastery. Handwriting is not a discrete and separate skill, however, but an integral part of the writing process. A general goal of writing instruction is to make the act of handwriting so automatic that it can be produced with maximum efficiency and minimum effort, enabling students to deploy more of their attention to higher order writing processes such as purpose, content, or organization (Graham, 1982).

Although it is generally assumed that a large percentage of handicapped children and youths have handwriting difficulties, it is difficult to substantiate or refute this assumption. Very little empirical evidence on the handwriting characteristics of handicapped students is available, and an examination of the information that has been gathered suggests that students with different disabilities may have different characteristics and ultimately different instructional needs.

With the exception of specific technological adaptations for the physically disabled and the use of braille with the blind, handwriting instruction for the handicapped has, in large part, been based on traditional procedures and techniques used to teach normally achieving students. Instruction has been aimed at assisting students to develop a handwriting style that is, first and foremost, legible and that can be produced quickly and fluently. Furthermore, most handicapped students are taught two styles of writing: manuscript in the lower primary grades and cursive in middle and upper elementary grades. There is considerable controversy, however, surrounding this practice. Some experts have indicated that it is more difficult to master two styles than it is to perfect one. Nevertheless, it is not clear which style should be taught. According to Graham and Miller (1980), the evidence is not conclusive and the relative effectiveness of the two styles has not been adequately established.

REFERENCES

Graham, S. (1982). Composition research and practice: A unified approach. *Focus on Exceptional Children, 14,* 1–16.

Graham, S., & Miller, L. (1980). Handwriting research and practice: A unified approach. *Focus on Exceptional Children, 13,* 1–16.

See also Dysgraphia; Reversals in Reading and Writing

HAPPY PUPPET SYNDROME

See ANGELMAN SYNDROME.

HARD OF HEARING

See DEAF.

HARVARD EDUCATIONAL REVIEW

The *Harvard Educational Review* was first published in 1931 under the name of *Harvard Teachers Record* by the offices of the Harvard Graduate Schools of Education. The present name was taken in 1937. This journal consists of opinions and research related to the field of education. Articles are read blind, then selected, edited, and published by an editorial board of graduate students from various Harvard schools. The selection process of the editorial board involves the distribution of letters to the faculty requesting nominations from the student body and the posting of information on bulletin boards at Harvard schools asking the students to apply for consideration. Students are then selected according to their ability and by their diversity of interests. The board of 20 students is balanced among men and women and minorities, each of whom receives a small stipend. There is one chairperson who receives a slightly larger stipend. This position changes yearly.

Sixty-seven volumes have now been published and there are an estimated 10,000 in circulation annually. Each journal, published quarterly, contains on the average three manuscripts equaling 500 to 550 pages a year.

HAÜY, VALENTIN (1745–1822)

Valentin Haüy, a French pioneer in the education of the blind, developed a system of raised letters with which he taught blind students to read and write, providing one of the earliest demonstrations that it is possible for a blind person to be educated. It was one of Haüy's students, Louis Braille, who later developed the system in use today, replacing Haüy's raised letters with a system of dots.

HAVIGHURST, ROBERT J. (1900–1991)

Robert J. Havighurst was born in De Pere, Wisconsin; graduated from Ohio Wesleyan University; and received his doctorate from The Ohio State University in 1924. Although trained as a chemist and physicist, he ultimately became interested in the broader aspects of general education. He was a professor of education and psychology at the University of Chicago for over forty years: he retired in 1983 but continued to teach and conduct research until 1990. Before joining the University of Chicago faculty in 1941, he had taught at Miami University, the University of Wisconsin, and The Ohio State University. Robert Havighurst died in 1991 at the age of 90.

In 1943, Havighurst introduced his theory of developmental tasks, which he continued to develop throughout his career (Havighurst, 1979). Described as skills, knowledge, functions, or attitudes normally acquired by an individual during a specific period of life, he believed in the existence of "teachable moments," meaning those periods when a person is most able and receptive to learning new skills. According to the theory, if a task is not learned at the appropriate time, it is much more difficult to learn later.

Havighurst was an early advocate of integrated public schools, believing they were crucial in creating opportunities for poor children. He proposed that children's performance in school depends not upon the socioeconomic status of the child or the child's family, but rather upon the socioeconomic status and character of the school itself. He also focused on the sociological aspects of old age and retirement, identifying and discussing the need for retirees to develop new roles as they aged and new ways of obtaining satisfaction once those previously achieved through work were no longer available.

Havighurst was a student of social and economic conditions in Germany and was Director of the Rockefeller Foundation's European Rehabilitation Program. In the late 50s, he was codirector of the Brazilian government's effort to prepare a national system of elementary and secondary schools.

REFERENCES

Havighurst, R.J. (1970). Minority subcultures and the law of effect. *American Psychologist, 25,* 313–322.

Havighurst, R.J. (1979). Developmental tasks and education (4th ed.). New York: Longman.

HAWTHORNE EFFECT

The experimental findings that led to the use of the term Hawthorne effect resulted from research done primarily between 1927 and 1932 at the Hawthorne plant of Western Electric. Investigators isolated a group of workers and then systematically varied such working conditions as rest periods and length of the work day. Over time, productivity steadily increased even in instances where more favorable working conditions were replaced with those originally in effect. The researchers in the Hawthorne study explained these results in terms of the workers' response to the special attention that they received in a novel situation (Roethlisberger & Dickson, 1939).

The Hawthorne effect is demonstrated when people are highly compliant in settings that they perceive to be innovative or experimental. As originally studied in industry, it resulted in greater worker productivity regardless of specific experimental manipulations. Writers now use the term Hawthorne effect in nonindustrial research contexts to indicate increased subject compliance with the perceived wishes of the experimenter (Sears, Freedman, & Peplau, 1985). In some cases, these subject responses might represent a rival account for results attributed to manipulations of the independent variable(s).

Although it has been difficult in specific instances to demonstrate the Hawthorne effect, the concept has important implications for the evaluation of educational and treatment innovations. To be certain that experimental interventions are responsible for observed changes, researchers must employ control groups where subjects receive attention, but not intervention, in a novel situation. A Hawthorne effect in special education classroom innovations would initially accelerate the benefits of a given program, but as the program became routine, the positive effects of its novelty would be expected to dissipate.

REFERENCES

Roethlisberger, F., & Dickson, W. (1939). *Management and the worker.* Cambridge, MA: Harvard.

Sears, D., Freedman, J., & Peplau, L. (1985). *Social psychology* (5th ed.). Englewood Cliffs, NJ: Prentice-Hall.

See also Motivation; Program Evaluation; Research in Special Education

HAYDEN, ALICE HAZEL (1909–1994)

Alice Hazel Hayden received her MS degree in chemistry from Oregon State University at the age of 19, and later received her PhD from Purdue University. She began teaching at the University of Washington in 1946, and was eventually awarded Professor Emeritus in education from that institution. She stayed at the University of Washington for 33 years, retiring in 1979. Alice Hayden died in 1994, at the age of 85.

Hayden was well known for her research on mental retardation in children, particularly the education of children with Down's Syndrome. In contrast to the prevailing views of the day, she emphasized the importance of recognizing the disability as early as possible, and strongly advocated that intervention begin in infancy for those identified with Down's Syndrome. In 1960, she codirected the experimental Pilot School for children with disabilities, which was the forerunner to the Experimental Education Unit at the Child Development and Mental Retardation Center at the University of Washington, where she served as associate director following her retirement.

One of her principal publications was *The Improvement of Instruction,* coedited with Norris G. Haring, a book of readings from a workshop designed to provide the classroom teacher with information about various ways of choosing instructional programs to accomplish teaching objectives and to assist teachers in arranging better classroom conditions to improve instruction. Her book *Systematic Thinking about Education,* coedited with Gerald M. Torkelson, discusses the technology of education and technology in teaching. It suggests that teachers and the school as an institution must be responsive to the world community and the advancing instruments and processes that people continue to create for a better life, in order to convey the most current techniques and advancements in education to students.

REFERENCES

Hayden, A.H., & Haring, N.G. (1972). *The improvement of instruction.* Special Child.

Hayden, A.H., & Torkelson, G.M. (Eds.). (1973). *Systematic thinking about education.* Phi Delta Kappa Educational Foundation.

HEAD INJURY

See TRAUMATIC BRAIN INJURY.

HEAD START

Head Start began in 1965 as a federally funded 8-week summer program for over 550,000 children from low-income families. Its initiation reflected the era's optimism for the role of preschool education in fighting the effects of poverty. It also reflected the environmentalist view of intellectual development, a belief in a critical period for human learning, the recommendations in the 1962 report of the President's Panel on Mental Retardation, and the need for a highly visible symbol of President Lyndon Johnson's war on poverty. By 1972 most programs ran the full year.

Head Start was intended to counteract negative environmental effects because of the well-known relationships between low school achievement and such factors as poverty, racial/ethnic membership, and socioeconomic status. Those factors were believed to be related to developmental and ecological variables that should be subject to modification. Early intervention was expected to eliminate the progressive decline in intellectual functioning and academic achievement that was typical of many children from poor families. Head Start emphasized local community involvement and autonomy; therefore, programs varied greatly across sites. The government encouraged parent volunteers and parent training, and published numerous training materials.

Research support for the expectation that preschool education would counteract effects of environmental disadvantages came from early reports of experimental preschool programs for poor, black children begun in 1958 by Susan Gray in Tennessee, Martin Deutsch in New York City, and David Weikart in Michigan (Lazar & Darlington, 1982). Their experimental work was theoretically anchored, carefully monitored, designed, and implemented by skilled professional educators and psychologists. However, for early Head Start programs there was not enough time for advance planning of curriculum and evaluation and limited direct supervision and monitoring of actual experiences of children. There were also too few teachers trained in early childhood education and a limited amount of in-service training for teachers and volunteers. Ironically, a program for disadvantaged children began at a disadvantage.

Head Start placed strong emphasis on medical, dental, and social services; initially, these were the most readily documented benefits. Millions of children were vaccinated, had vision and hearing tests, and received medical and dental examinations. A substantial percentage also received medical and dental treatment.

Early evaluation of sustained effects on cognitive and academic skills raised serious doubts about the program's effect on academic skills (Cicirelli, 1969). Media coverage was extremely negative. The program was modified. A Planned Variations project was devised to seek factors related to successful intervention. Training programs for Head Start personnel were greatly expanded.

Data from dozens of Head Start studies comparing group averages of Head Start graduates with averages of children without preschool programs lead to these conclusions: Head Start has positive effects on intellectual development (although in most studies average test scores are somewhat below the national average); Head Start children have fewer retentions in grade and fewer special education placements (although they still contribute disproportionately to special education and retention); some Head Start programs produce advantages in reading or arithmetic as measured by standardized tests; different curricula do not appear to produce differential effects (although such differences are found in experimental pre-school programs for high-risk children); most parents of Head Start children are highly supportive; and full-year Head Start program are superior to short summer ones. Positive effects reported in some studies include improvement in social behavior, parent-child interactions, skills of parents, and nutrition (Haywood, 1982; Hubbell, 1983).

As evidence of program efficacy increased, criticisms from professionals decreased and public approval increased. A highly laudatory article in the national newspaper USA Today (Kanengiser, 1985) described Martin Deutsch's report that his group of Head Start graduates were more likely to finish high school, go to college, and hold full-time jobs than similar children who had no preschool experience. Such findings suggest that Head Start may affect motivation for education.

Edward Zigler, who was Head Start's first federal administrator, viewed Head Start's goal as the development of social competence. He commented that when one realistically examines its true effectiveness, it cannot be dismissed as a failure, but neither should so fragile an effort over one year of a child's life be viewed as the ultimate solution to poverty, illiteracy, and failures in life (Zigler, 1979). Dozens of additional studies have shown overwhelmingly that Head Start has myriad of positive effects (Cartwright, Cartwright, & Ward, 1995).

REFERENCES

Cartwright, P. Cartwright, C., & Ward, M. (1995). Educating special learners. New York: Wadsworth.

Cicirelli, V.G. (1969). Project Head Start, a national evaluation: Summary of the study. In D.G. Hayes (Ed.), Britannica review of American education (Vol. 1). Chicago: Encyclopedia Britannica.

Haywood, H.C. (1982). Compensatory education. Peabody Journal of Education, 59, 272–300.

Hubbell, R. (1983). A review of Head Start research since 1970. Washington, DC: Administration for Children, Youth, and Families (Superintendent of Documents, U.S. Government Printing Office.

Kanengiser, A. (1985, October 3). Head Start really gives a head start. USA Today, 4D.

Lazar, I., & Darlington, R. (1982). Lasting effects of early education: A report from the consortium for longitudinal studies. Monographs of the Society for Research in Child Development. 47 (serial nos. 2–3).

Zigler, E. (1979). Project Head Start: Success or failure? In E. Zigler & J. Valentine (Eds.), Project Head Start: A legacy of the war on poverty. New York: Free Press.

See also **Early Identification of Handicapped Children; Preschool Assessment**

HEALTH IMPAIRMENTS

Public Law 94–142 and IDEA divide the classification of physical handicaps into two categories for purposes of special education: orthopedic impairments and health impairments (Bigge & Sirvis, 1986). The second category of health impairments consists of physical conditions that affect a child or youth's educational performance such as "limited strength, vitality or alertness due to chronic or acute health problems such as a heart condition, tuberculosis, rheumatic, fever, nephritis, asthma, sickle cell anemia, hemophilia, epilepsy, lead poisoning, leukemia, or diabetes" (*Federal Register,* 1977, p. 42478). Such children are often diagnosed and managed medically and socially as chronically ill children. Phelps (1998) provides a review of the educational consequences of more than 95 health impairments of children.

REFERENCES

Bigge, J., & Sirvis, B. (1986). Physical and health impairments. In N.G. Haring & L. McCormick (Eds.), *Exceptional children and youth* (4th ed.) (pp. 313–354). Columbus, OH: Merrill.

Phelps, L. (1998). *Health-related disorders in children and adolescents: A guidebook for understanding and educating.* Washington, DC: American Psychological Association.

See also Chronic Illness in Children; Orthopedic Impairments

HEALTH MAINTENANCE, INVASIVE PROCEDURES FOR

In accordance with PL 94-142 and IDEA, some invasive procedures for health maintenance are required to be performed by the teacher or other school personnel during the school day if required for the child to attend school and if no health care professional is available. Procedures that do not require a sterile field and that may be routinely performed by parents may be required to be performed by school-based personnel. Procedures such as ostomy maintenance, injection, catheterization, suctioning, or tube feeding may need to be conducted by the teacher, an aide, or a trained volunteer for the child to be in school all day.

Specific health maintenance activities have been deemed a part of the teacher's responsibility if no health care specialist is available. Whenever possible, the child should perform the maintenance activities independently. When this is not possible because of the child's age, physical, sensory, or cognitive functioning, the teacher should (1) provide only the level of supervision, support, or intervention required by the student; (2) develop a program or procedure wherein the child learns to take care of as much of the maintenance activity as possible; (3) carry out the procedure when required under the direction of the parents, school system health officer, and child's physician and therapist; (4) obtain training in basic first aid and cardiopulmonary resuscitation as a general protection prior to conducting any health maintenance activity; and (5) have a school board and school-based policy in writing defining procedures to be followed. Depending on school or district policy, aides, volunteers, or secretaries may be trained to carry out a specific procedure so that the teacher may continue to teach and supervise academic activities during the time of the procedure.

Depending on local, state, and federal policy, the teacher may be required to (1) have a witness when carrying out any invasive procedure, and (2) record all procedures, including time, observations of health, and general impressions of the adequacy of the intervention. Record keeping systems must be employed each time a procedure is conducted (Dykes & Venn, 1983).

REFERENCE

Dykes, M.K., & Venn, J. (1983). Using health, physical and medical data in the classroom. In J. Unbreit (Ed.), *Physical disabilities and health impairments: An introduction.* Columbus, OH: Merrill.

See also Health Maintenance Procedures; Medically Fragile Student

HEALTH MAINTENANCE PROCEDURES

Under PL 94-142 and IDEA, educators may be held responsible for monitoring specific health maintenance activities required in order for the child to attend school. Teachers may oversee students taking medication, conducting bowel and bladder maintenance procedures, and adjusting braces. In addition, monitoring of such health maintenance equipment as ventilators, cardiac monitors, reciprocal braces, and shunts may be a part of required teacher activity. Before monitoring or helping with any health maintenance activity, the teacher should have a written school district and school policy to follow, have completed first aid and cardiopulmonary resuscitation courses, have been trained by parents and a school health official, and have written, dated, and signed specific directions requesting that a procedure be carried out while the child is at school.

Whenever possible, the student should be responsible for carrying out all health maintenance activities. Medications should be taken by the student in the presence of an adult who checks the prescription bottle for name, directions for administration, and the log for last time taken. If students are incapable of carrying out the required procedure (e.g., catheterization), they should be taught the procedure as soon as possible if there is enough potential motor and intellectual skill to carry out the task.

See also Medically Fragile Students

HEARING IMPAIRED

See DEAF.

HEBER, RICK F. (1932– 1992)

Rick Heber was born January 12, 1932. He received his BA degree from the University of Arkansas in 1953. After a year as principal of the Manitoba School for Mental Deficiency, Heber attended Michigan State University, obtaining his MA degree there in 1955. He then went on to achieve his PhD in 1957 from George Peabody College. Heber joined the faculty of the University of Wisconsin, Madison in 1959 as coordinator of the special education program.

Heber is best known for his work as principal investigator of the Milwaukee Project and the subsequent controversies surrounding the project. A major finding of the project was that the variable of maternal intelligence proved to be by far the best single predictor of the level and character of intellectual development in the offspring. Heber believed that the prevalence of mental retardation associated with the slums of American cities is not randomly distributed but is actually strikingly concentrated within individual families who can be identified on the basis of maternal intelligence (1988). Heber was a member of the faculty of the University of Wisconsin at Madison when he was indicted on charges stemming from the misuse of federal funds allocated to the project. He was subsequently convicted and served time in the federal prison in Bastrop, Texas. Previously a respected scholar in the field of mental retardation, his academic work on the Milwaukee Project has been called into serious question. It is now questionable whether the project ever actually existed as it had been described by Heber.

REFERENCES

Heber, R.F. (1970). *Epidemiology of mental retardation.* Springfield, IL: Thomas.

Heber, R.F., & Garber, H. (1975). The Milwaukee Project: A study of the use of family intervention to prevent cultural-familial mental retardation. In B.Z. Friedlander, G. Kirk, & G. Sterritt (Eds.), *The exceptional infant* (Vol 3). New York: Brunner/Mazel.

Heber, R.F. (1988). Mental retardation in the slums. In G.W. Albee & J.M. Joffe (Eds.), *Prevention, powerlessness, and politics: Readings on social change.* Newbury Park, CA: Sage.

See also **Milwaukee Project, The**

HEELCORD OPERATION

The heelcord operation is an orthopedic surgical treatment for children with spastic cerebral palsy. It is performed to compensate for equinus, a condition in which the foot is involuntarily extended owing to contracted tendons in the heel. Palsied children with equinus often have severe gait problems. The operation itself involves cutting and lengthening the Achilles tendon and rotating the heel to a normal position. The operation is typically followed by 6 weeks in a cast and roughly 6 months of physical therapy.

Without surgery, treatment of this condition is often painful and unsuccessful. It involves the use of braces, splints worn at night, and regular heelcord stretching exercises. The success rate of the operation is very high. Research has shown an overall recurrence rate for patients receiving surgery of only 9%, although recurrence is related to age; 2 year olds, for example, have a recurrence rate of 75%. Improvements in mobility improve multiple outcomes in cerebral palsy.

See also **Cerebral Palsy**

HEGGE, KIRK, KIRK APPROACH

Hegge, Kirk, and Kirk (1936) formulated the phonographo-vocal method of remedial reading while teaching educable mentally retarded children. Emphasizing programmed learning techniques, this method incorporates sound blending and kinesthetic experiences (Kirk & Gallagher, 1983). Basic to this method is a set of remedial read-

ing drills presented in four parts. Part I provides drills in sounding out consonants, short vowels, and vowel combinations such as *ee, ay, ow, ing, all, ight, ur,* and the final *e* marker. Drills in Part I are printed on one line from left to right, reinforcing directional patterns in reading. Early drills are simple, showing that only the initial consonant changes in words such as sat-mat-rat. More complex drills are successively introduced by changing the first and last consonant of words. After repeated drills on the consonants, the short vowels, a, e, i, o, and u, are emphasized.

In Part II words are presented using the sounds already learned in Part I. Children are taught to read hand as-h-an-d instead of h-a-n-d. Through frequent review and drills (the hallmark of this method) children move from vocalizing and recognizing simple sounds to incorporating these sounds into words.

Parts III and IV are for those children who, after having been repeatedly drilled on the sound blends in Parts I and II, are beginning to read by rapidly sounding out words. Part III requires children to read new words in syllables or wholes.

In Part IV of this approach children are drilled on sounds that could not be systematically presented in earlier drills. Reinforcement drills are used with children who exhibit problems in specific areas such as confusing b, d, and p or m and n (Kirk, 1940).

Kirk (1940) warns that the Hegge, Kirk, Kirk method, developed in 1936, should not be used as a general teaching method or for children in higher grade levels.

REFERENCES

Hegge, T., Kirk, S., & Kirk, W. (1936). *Remedial reading drills.* Ann Arbor, MI: Wahr.

Kirk, S. (1940). *Teaching reading to slow-learning children.* Cambridge, MA: Riverside.

Kirk, S., & Gallagher, J. (1983). *Educating exceptional children* (4th ed.). Boston: Houghton Mifflin.

See also **Orton-Gillingham Method; Reading Disorders; Reading Remediation**

HEINICKE, SAMUEL (1727–1790)

Samuel Heinicke, a German educator, founded the first oral school for the deaf about 1755. He established Germany's first public school for the deaf in 1778 at Leipzig. Using published accounts of the teaching of deaf children by Jacob Pereire and others, Heinicke devised a highly successful method for teaching reading, writing, speech, and speech reading to deaf students, a method that formed the basis for the later development of the oral method in Germany by Moritz Hill.

Some of Heinicke's ideas anticipated later educational practice. He taught the reading of whole words before teaching the letters. He advocated classes at the University of Leipzig for preparing teachers of the deaf, and attempted, apparently unsuccessfully, to establish with the university provision for his deaf students to participate in university activities. Heinicke's work was continued after his death by his widow, who took charge of his school, and his son-in-law, who established a school for the deaf near Berlin.

REFERENCE

Bender, R.E. (1970). *The conquest of deafness.* Cleveland, OH: Case Western Reserve University Press.

HELEN KELLER INTERNATIONAL

Founded in 1915, Helen Keller International assists governments and agencies in developing countries in providing services to prevent or cure eye diseases and blindness and to educate or rehabilitate the blind and visually impaired. Subsumed under Helen Keller International are the Association for Chinese; Permanent Blind Relief War Fund; American Braille Press for War and Civilian Blind; and the American Foundation for Overseas Blind (Gruber & Cloyd, 1985).

The organization offers courses for teachers of blind children and adults as well as for field workers dealing with the rural blind. A training focus is prevention and treatment of blindness caused by malnutrition, trachoma, cataracts, and other eye diseases. Additionally, there are programs to prepare volunteers to counsel families of blind babies.

An important function of this international agency is the collection and compilation of statistics on blindness throughout the world. Publications include an annual report, a newsletter, fact sheets, technical reports, educational materials, and training information. There is one annual conference and an annual board meeting. Headquarters are at 15 West 16th Street, New York, NY 10011.

REFERENCE

Gruber, K., & Cloyd, I. (1985). *Encyclopedia of associations* (Vol. 1, 20th ed.). Detroit, MI: Gale Research.

See also Deaf-Blind

HEMIBALLISMUS

Hemiballismus is a rare condition that is characterized by violent, flinging, involuntary movements in the extremities on one side of the body. The movements are typically more pronounced in the arm than in the leg and may be severe enough to cause bruising of the soft tissues or exhaustion. Involvement also has been reported in the muscles of the neck. Hemiballistic movements disappear during sleep.

Chlorpromazine and haloperidol have been reported to substantially reduce or eliminate hemiballistic movements over a period of 3 months to more than 1 year. In some individuals, medications have been reduced gradually and ultimately eliminated with no recurrence of the condition. The prognosis has become more optimistic in recent years owing to increased use of these medications. There is also

some optimism that newer classes of neuroleptics may also be beneficial (e.g., Risperdal).

See also Chorea; Multiple Sclerosis

HEMIPARESIS

Hemiparesis is a topographic term used to describe a person who has a slight paralysis affecting one side of the body (with muscular weakness on that side). Hemiparesis may be facial in nature and vision and hearing deficits may be contributory deficits. The cause (etiology) of the hemiparesis may be a disease, injury, or congenital defect that occurred before, at, or after birth. The nature of the etiology is important to educational and vocational plans, and is best determined during evaluation by a skilled neurologist. Two questions are relevant: Is the causal agent progressive? In addition to the evident weakness, what sensory/motor/vestibular damage, if any, is also present?

Weakness on one side of the body may be accompanied by a loss of pain sensitivity (hemianalgesia). Hemianesthesia, one-sided anesthesia, or loss of tactile sensibility on one side of the body, also may be a component feature. The pattern of sensory loss may not be on the same side as the motor loss. The importance of knowing about pain, heat, and cold sensibility loss relates to protection of the individual from burns, freezing, and injuries that could be more serious impairments than the obvious weakness. Both sensory deprivation and balance deficits (cerebellar/vestibular) have profound implications for safety in transportation to and from school, school activities, self-care, and realistic vocational plans for the individual child.

See also Adapted Physical Education; Hemipelgia; Physical Anomalies

HEMIPLEGIA

Hemiplegia is a topographic term used to describe a person who has a movement disorder or paralysis of both limbs on the same side of the body owing to congenital defect, disease, or injury to the brain or central nervous system (CNS). The extent and nature of the disturbance of functional performance experienced by the individual is determined by the age at which the impairment occurs, the severity and location of the damage of the CNS, and the etiology of the injury.

The increased muscle tone in the antigravity muscles on the affected side is the most obvious symptom of the child with spastic hemiplegia; however, the associated damage and sensory deficits may have more profound impact on plans for educational and vocational intervention. Vision, hearing, and touch, hot/cold and position sense and balance may be impaired and seriously affect a child's ability to learn complex motor skills. Specific aphasias, language processing problems, and seizures are common concomitants of this condition. It would be expected that close medical, school, and parent cooperation would need to be established, with appropriate evaluation and intervention of related service therapists to prevent deformity and maximize opportunity for a schoolchild with hemiplegia and associated deficits.

See also **Adapted Physical Education; Hemiparesis**

HEMISPHERECTOMY

Hemispherectomy (surgical removal of one cerebral hemisphere) is an uncommon procedure, usually reserved for children with widespread damage affecting one cerebral hemisphere, such as intracerebral tumor(s) (Gott, 1973), intractable seizures, or congenital/infantile hemiplegia (Ameli, 1980). Adult hemispherectomy patients generally demonstrate severe, non-recoverable deficits (e.g., hemiparalysis and cognitive impairment) after surgery. In contrast, some hemispherectomized children show good recovery of sensorimotor function with fairly normal development of many cognitive abilities. For example, Smith (1974) described a case of juvenile hemispherectomy in which the patient developed above average verbal and normal nonverbal capabilities and went on to graduate from college.

While there is considerable variability in the findings, the extent of recovery after hemispherectomy appears to be, at least in part, age related. Young children clearly show better recovery than adults.

REFERENCES

Ameli, N.O. (1980). Hemispherectomy for the treatment of epilepsy and behavior disturbance. *Canadian Journal of Neurological Sciences, 7,* 35–38.

Gott, P.S. (1973). Cognitive abilities following right and left hemispherectomy. *Cortex, 9,* 266–274.

Smith, A. (1974). Dominant and nondominant hemispherectomy. In M. Kinsbourne & W.L. Smith (Eds.), *Hemispheric disconnection and cerebral function* (pp. 5–33). Springfield, IL: Thomas.

See also **Cerebral Dominance**

HEMISPHERIC ASYMMETRY, SEX DIFFERENCES IN

Hemispheric asymmetry refers to the fact that the left and right hemispheres of the brain specialize in different forms of information processing. For most individuals, the left hemisphere is more efficient at processing information logically and sequentially (e.g., spoken and written language), while the right hemisphere is better suited to processing spatially and holistically (e.g., visual spatial tasks). However, because most tasks include both linguistic and spatial aspects, cognitive processing generally involves both hemispheric functions, though they may vary in emphasis from moment to moment (Gaddes, 1985).

Considerable research exists to support a sex difference in hemispheric asymmetry at all age levels. The evidence indicates that males characteristically are more proficient

with their right hemispheres and females with their left, suggesting a male spatial superiority and a female verbal superiority. Thus, when a task can be performed either by left or right hemisphere mechanisms, males are more likely to use a nonverbal, spatial strategy for problem solving, while females are more apt to use a verbal strategy (McGlone & Davison, 1973).

REFERENCES

Gaddes, W.H. (1985). *Learning disabilities and brain function: A neuropsychological approach* (2nd ed.). New York: Springer-Verlag.

McGlone, J., & Davison, W. (1973). The relation between cerebral speech laterality and spatial ability with special reference to sex and hand preference. *Neuropsychologia, 11,* 105–113.

See also **Cerebral Dominance**

HEMISPHERIC FUNCTIONS

Hemispheric functions refers to the specialization of each cerebral hemisphere of the brain for various processes. The right hemisphere usually has been associated with processing information in a simultaneous, spatial, and holistic fashion (Speery, 1974). In contrast, the left hemisphere of the brain has been shown to best process information in a sequential, temporal, and analytic mode (Speery, Gazzaniga, & Bogen, 1969).

The notion of lateralization of functions within cerebral hemispheres can be dated back to the late 1800s, when Broca and Wernicke demonstrated that aphasia (or the inability to express or comprehend language) resulted from lesions to the left hemisphere. Moreover, the left hemisphere was portrayed as the dominant hemisphere by virtue of its leading role in such activities as speech and calculation, whereas the right hemisphere was seen as the minor hemisphere, serving activities associated with perception and sensation (Geschwind, 1974).

Research from invasive techniques has found that the right hemisphere plays a dominant role in processing certain information. Specifically, the right hemisphere is dominant for processing nonlinguistic information involving nonverbal reasoning, visual-spatial integration, visual-constructive abilities, haptic perception, pattern recognition, and other related tasks (Dean, 1984). Conversely, the left hemisphere has been shown to be responsible for tasks that require speech, general language, calculation, abstract verbal reasoning, etc. (Dean, 1984).

Differences in hemispheric specializations may be due, in part, to anatomical differences of the cortical hemispheres. In examining anatomical differences, it was found that the left temporal planum structure that serves language functions is larger than the right temporal planum (Geschwind & Levitsky, 1968). Similarly, the Sylvian fissure, a large lateral depression in the brain that contains the major speech area, is found to be larger for the left side of the Sylvian fissure than the right. (Geschwind, 1974). In addition, the left hemisphere is noted to be approximately 5 gr heavier than the right hemisphere. Another anatomical difference is the projection of nerve fibers from the left hemisphere that cross over earlier at the base of the brain than do nerve fibers from the right hemisphere. Such structural differences between the hemispheres may partially account for cerebral lateralization of specific functions.

When gender differences are examined, subtle anatomical dissimilarities between males and females are found to exist shortly after birth. Perhaps more striking than anatomical are functional changes that exist between adult male and female brains (Kolata, 1979). As a group, males have been shown to perform better on tasks of spatial ability than females, who present superior verbal facility (Witelson, 1976). The spatial ability of males may be partially due to an earlier right hemisphere lateralization of spatial functions. Males also have been shown to have an earlier hemispheric specialization for language, while females are noted to be less consistent in lateralization for language activities (Levy, 1973). This less established hemispheric specialization for females, however, can be contrasted to their firmer lateralization for peripheral activities such as handedness (Annett, 1976) and visually guided motor activities (Dean & Reynolds, 1997). That is, while females are more bilateral for cognitive activities such as language, they have more established preference than do males for consistently using the same hand, ear, eye, etc., for related activities.

This paradoxical finding for females seems to be a function of the tenuous relationship between lateral preference patterns for peripheral activities and hemispheric specialization for language. Inferring hemispheric lateralization from lateral preference patterns from simple measures of handedness should be cautioned against. Dean (1982) has shown that lateral preference is a factorially complex variable and a function of the system (e.g., eyes, ears, hands, etc.) under study. Lateral preference patterns, then, may be more heuristically represented on a continuum from entirely left to entirely right instead of categorically as either left or right (Dean & Reynolds, 1997).

REFERENCES

Annett, M. (1976). Hand preference and the laterality of cerebral speech. *Cortex, 11,* 305–329.

Dean, R.S. (1984). Functional lateralization of the brain. *Journal of Special Education, 18,* 239–256.

Dean, R.S., & Reynolds, C.R. (1997). Cognitive processing and self-report of lateral preference. *Neuropsychology Review, 7,* 127–142.

Geschwind, N. (1974). The anatomical basis of hemispheric differentiation. In S.J. Dimond & J.G. Beaumont (Eds.), *Hemisphere function in the human brain.* New York: Wiley.

Geschwind, N., & Levitsky, W. (1968). Human brain: Left-right asymmetries in temporal speech region. *Science, 161,* 186–187.

Kolata, G.B. (1979). Sex hormones and brain development. *Science, 205,* 985–987.

Levy, J. (1973). Lateral specialization of the human brain: Behavioral manifestations and possible evolutionary basis. In J.A. Kriger (Ed.), *The biology of behavior.* Corvallis, OR: Oregon State University Press.

Speery, R.W. (1974). Lateral specialization in the surgically separated hemispheres. In F.O. Schmitt & F.G. Worden (Eds.), *The neurosciences: Third study program.* New York: Wiley.

Speery, R.W., Gazzaniga, M.S., & Bogen, J.H. (1969). Interhemispheric relationships: The neocortical commissures: Syndromes of hemisphere disconnection. In P. Vinken & G.W. Bruyn (Eds.), *Handbook of clinical neurology* (Vol. 4). New York: Wiley.

Witelson, S.F. (1976). Abnormal right hemisphere specialization in developmental dyslexia. In R.M. Knights & D.F. Bakker (Eds.). *Neuropsychology of learning disorders: Theoretical approaches.* Baltimore, MD: University Park Press.

See also **Cerebral Dominance**

HEMOPHILIA AND SPECIAL EDUCATION

Hemophilia ("bleeder's disease") is an hereditary disorder of the blood clotting process caused by an inadequacy of certain coagulation factors within the blood. The deficiency may be in one or more of the 10 blood plasma proteins required for normal clotting. Hemophilia may be classified as severe, moderate, or mild based on the degree of factor deficiency, but actual bleeding episodes will vary in affected persons. The disorder is genetically transmitted in a sex-linked recessive pattern from mothers to male offspring, accounting for 85 to 90% of all cases. In rare instances, girls may have other forms of the condition. (Cartwright, Cartwright, & Ward, 1995; Lindemann, 1981).

Evidence indicates that children with hemophilia require mainstreamed educational opportunity. School achievement is at risk only as the result of possible school absences and the debilitating effects of pain associated with the swelling of tissues and joints. Major school modifications may be required in transportation, mobility, and physical education activities. Maintenance of normalized school involvement to the greatest extent possible is essential for educational and psychosocial development (Walker & Jacobs, 1984); however, referrals to support groups are often helpful, especially during adolescence and for children who undergo routine injections (Randolph & Talamo, 1998).

The emotional adjustment of the child with hemophilia is of central concern to special education. Low self-esteem, delays in masculine identification, denial, prolonged immaturity, and depression characterize the emotional development of many hemophiliacs. The psychological implications of the disorder are particularly important for the preschool, early childhood, and adolescent patient, and for the family. In the early childhood period (ages 4 to 8), the hemophiliac experiences the limitations imposed by the condition; these include the inability to engage in many physical and exploratory activities important for both learning and social adjustment (Cerreto, 1986). Possible special educational opportunities for limited physical participation or the presentation of equivalent educational activities may be desirable.

The adolescent with hemophilia must face the usual emotional stress of that period with the complications of a chronic disorder, including its implication of lifelong restrictions, its limitations on physical activity, and the potential danger of using alcohol or drugs that may interact with medication. Concentrated emotional guidance and support is fundamental to the adolescent hemophiliac (Eisenberg, Sutkin, & Jansen, 1984; Lindemann, 1981).

The role of the special educator is seen primarily as maintaining the child in the regular program with support and resource assistance if necessary, as helping the classroom teacher bridge periods of absence, and as promoting home-school contact to offer support and relief to the parents of children with hemophilia.

REFERENCES

Cartwright, G.P., Cartwright, C.A., & Ward, M.J. (1995). *Educating special learners* (4th ed.). Belmont, CA: Wadsworth.

Cerreto, M.C. (1986). Developmental issues in chronic illness: Implications and applications. *Topics in Early Childhood Special Education, 5,* 4.

Eisenberg, M.G., Sutkin, L.C., & Jansen, M.A. (Eds.). (1984). *Chronic illness and disability through the life span: Effects on self and family.* New York: Springer.

Lindemann, J.E. (1981). *Psychological and behavioral aspects of physical disability.* New York: Plenum.

Randolph, M., & Talamo, Y. (1998). Hemophilia. In L. Phelps (Eds.), *Health-related disorders in children and adolescents.* Washington, DC: American Psychological Association.

Walker, D.K., & Jacobs, F.H. (1984). Chronically ill children in school. *Peabody Journal of Education, 61,* 28–74.

See also **Attitudes Toward the Handicapped; Family Response to a Child with Disabilities**

HEREDITY

Heredity refers to the phenomenon of progeny being biologically similar to their parents. Genetics is the science or study of heredity; it includes the study of the variation of inherited characteristics. Genetics has shown that units called genes, which store information and control heredity, are transmitted from parent to progeny during the reproductive process. These genes interact with each other and with the environment to produce distinctive characteristics.

Genetics is a relatively recent science with most discoveries occurring in the twentieth century. Advances in genetics since 1950 have dramatically increased our understanding of phenomena such as the origin of life, the structure of living material, and evolution. The application of genetic theory has yielded a better understanding of certain human diseases, a clearer picture of the nature versus nurture controversy, and improvements in plant and animal breeding.

See also **Congenital Disorders; Phenylketonuria**

HERPES SIMPLEX I AND II

Although clinically and pathologically described as early as 100 BCE, herpesvirus hominus (HVH) was not identified until the 1920s; the existence of two antigenic types was not known until the 1960s; and genital herpes was not recognized as a venereal disease until the late 1960s. In the past, infections above and below the waist have generally been attributed to oral herpes (HVH-1) and genital herpes (HVH-2), respectively. However, the site of the infection does not always point to the particular type of herpes. HVH-1 and 2 now appear in both genital and oral areas, perhaps owing to increased frequency of oral-genital sexual contact (Bahr, 1978). Oral herpes most commonly causes cold sores in infants and children; however, it may cause eye infections and lesions on the fingers as well. Genital herpes has serious effects on both affected individuals and the offspring of affected women; both types of effects are described in this entry. Genital herpes is a highly contagious and prevalent venereal disease characterized by the appearance of pus-containing sores in the genital region.

Adolescents with genital herpes are frequently concerned about transmitting the disease to close friends or family members. This may be a genuine concern. However, careful and precise hygienic methods usually prevent the spread of the infection. The herpes victim should thoroughly clean bathroom facilities after using them. During periods when the disease is active or their genital sores are at the weeping stage, victims should not bathe with others in hot tubs or sit on edges of hot tubs and swimming pools.

As of yet, no cure for the herpes simplex virus is available. Two types of drug intervention are currently being used for treatment. Acute therapy involves taking a drug to diminish the symptoms of an outbreak, as well as to reduce the duration of the occurrence. This type of therapy requires taking medication for a short length of time, beginning immediately with the first signs of a potential outbreak. The other alternative is suppressive therapy, which requires a daily dose of medication to help prevent reactivation of the virus.

In previous years, the medication acyclovir (Zovirax) was the only option available for treatment. Acyclovir is available by prescription only, and is offered in both oral and topical forms. It works by impeding the spread of the virus in cells without damaging normal cells (Griffith, 1996).

The U.S. Food and Drug Administration has recently approved two new drugs for treatment of the virus. Famciclovir (Famvir) and Valacyclovir (Valtrex) are now being prescribed more frequently than acyclovir. They have been proven to be more effective in absorption by the body, and require fewer daily doses for effectiveness.

PSYCHOLOGICAL CONSEQUENCES

Herpes can have serious psychological consequences, especially for adolescents. Luby (1981) has noted a sequence of responses to genital herpes: (1) shock and emotional numbing; (2) search for an immediate cure; (3) development of feelings of isolation and loneliness and fear that companionship, sexual relations, and children are not in one's future; (4) anger, which can reach homicidal proportions, directed toward the person who is believed to be the transmitter of the disease (at this point fear generalizes and anxiety may result); (5) a "leper" effect, accompanied by depression, which may deepen with time and recurrences. Common feelings at this point include hopelessness, guilt, unworthiness, and self-hatred. Finally, developing herpes can make manifest any latent psychopathology.

Not all victims are emotionally affected, but for many adolescents, it can become a psychologically crippling experience. Individual counseling or membership in a herpes self-help group may be helpful. Herpes self-help groups generally work to achieve several goals, including relief from isolation and loneliness, establishment of a new social network, provision of mentors, and ventilation of rage. If depression with sleep disorder, loss of appetite, psychotic symptoms, or suicidal ideation occur, a psychiatric referral may be required (Luby, 1981). Stress of a variety of kinds appears to increase reactivation of the infection (Keller, Shiflett, Schleifer, & Bartlett, 1994).

SUGGESTIONS FOR WORKING WITH AFFECTED STUDENTS

Teachers, coaches and others who work with students who have herpes can help by being sympathetic listeners and having an understanding of the disease that enables them to dispel myths and untruths regarding herpes. Also, they can help students develop a realistic view of their situation by stressing that the disease can be medically managed and is not fatal.

Adolescents' self-esteem can be deeply affected. If this occurs, referral to the school's guidance counselor or family physician should be arranged. Suicide cannot be ruled out. The teacher or coach should not hesitate in making a referral to the guidance counselor or to a mental health professional if emotional disturbances are noted. Remind the victims that they need to isolate active lesions, not themselves.

REFERENCES

Bahr, J. (1978). Herpesvirus hominis type 2 in women and newborns. *American Journal of Maternal Child Nursing,* pp. 16–18.

Griffith, H.W. (1996). *Complete guide to prescription and nonprescription drugs.* Triangle Park: Putnam Berkeley.

Keller, S.E., Shiflett, S.C., Schleifer, S.J., & Bartlett, J.A. (1994). Stress, immunity, and health. In R. Glaser & J. Kiecolt-Glaser (Eds.), *Handbook of human stress and immunity* (pp. 217–244). San Diego, CA: Academic.

Luby, E. (1981). *Presentation at the National Genital Herpes Symposium,* Philadelphia. *The Helper, 3*(4), 2–3.

See also **Depression; Storch Complex**

HESS, ROBERT (1920–1993)

Robert Hess received his BA at the University of California at Berkeley in 1947 and his PhD in developmental psychol-ogy at the University of Chicago in 1950. He was the Lee L. Jacks Professor Emeritus of Child Education at Stanford University and codirector of the graduate training program in Interactive Educational Technology. Robert Hess died in 1993 at the age of 73.

Hess' major interests focused on the relationships of teachers who interact with young children's home lives, external realities, and inner lives within the atmosphere of the classroom. He believed that the future of a society rests in its ability to train or socialize the young. He held that the growth of programs in early education and the large-scale involvement of schools and the federal government represented a fundamental shift in the relative roles and potential influence of the two major socializing institutions of society, the family and the school (Hess & Bear, 1968). Thus, he saw the need for social experimentation in order to deal effectively with this shift.

Hess was best known for his work in the late 50s and early 60s at the University of Chicago. There he conducted a number of studies on the environmental deprivation of children in poverty, consequently helping to establish the theoretical background for Head Start and other similar government programs. Later research included a 1965 study of communication and instruction methods used by mothers with their children and a longitudinal cross-cultural study, conducted in the 1970s in Japan and the United States, on the interactions of mothers and their children. The latter was one of the first major collaborations between child development researchers in the two countries.

In more recent years, Hess' interests broadened to include research involving the use of computers in the classroom. Results of this work indicated a distinct gender gap in computer interest and usage among young people.

Some of his major writings include *Early Education: Current Theory, Research, and Action* (1968), *Family Worlds: A Psychosocial Approach to Family Life* (1995), and *Teachers of Young Children* (1972).

REFERENCES

Hess, R.D., & Bear, R.M. (1968). *Early education: Current theory, research, and action.* Chicago: Adline.

Hess, R.D., & Croft, D.J. (1972). *Teachers of young children.* Boston: Houghton Mifflin.

Hess, R.D., & Handel, G. (1995). *Family worlds: A psychosocial approach to family life.* Lanham, MD: University Press.

HETEROPHORIA

See STRABISMUS, EFFECT ON LEARNING.

HIGHER EDUCATION, MINORITY STUDENTS WITH DISABILITIES AND

College campuses are quickly becoming multiracial, multicultural, and multilingual societies (Sue, Arredondo, & Mc-

Davis, 1992). The number of students with disabilities and the number of minority students entering colleges and universities are increasing. It is natural to assume that the two groups will overlap; however, research devoted to ethnic/racial minorities with disabilities in higher education is limited. While special education in public schools continues to battle the overrepresentation of minority students in special education programs, institutions of higher education often fail to acknowledge the presence of minorities with disabilities and their needs for specialized attention. This is exhibited when disability service providers fail to recognize the need for service provision appropriate to the individual student's culture.

Disability service providers in higher education must recognize the need for multicultural awareness and prepare themselves for the pivotal role they may play in the success of minority students with disabilities. Sue and Sue (1990) indicate that preparation for this type of role involves confronting, becoming aware of, and taking actions in dealing with personal biases, stereotypes, values, and assumptions about human behavior, as well as being aware of the culturally different student's worldview, values, and assumptions about human behavior. Harry (1992) adds that it is perhaps more important for service professionals to recognize the cultural base of their own belief systems than to know the particular characteristics of any one cultural group.

A disability in any culture is considered different than the norm; however, disability service providers must continually be aware that there is no universal measure of normality. This notion must be accepted for all cultures. It will continue to be essential that professionals working with multicultural students with disabilities be sensitive to concepts of disability and to traditional communication patterns among different cultural groups. We must understand and respect the traditional values of these cultures while succeeding in achieving collaboration between disability service provider and student.

REFERENCES

Harry, B. (1992). *Cultural diversity, families, and the special education system: Communication and empowerment.* New York: Teachers College Press.

Sue, D.W., Arredondo, P., & McDavis, R.J. (1992). Multicultural counseling competencies and standards: A call to the profession. *Journal of Counseling & Development, 70,* 477–486.

Sue, D.W., & Sue, D. (1990). *Counseling the culturally different* (2nd ed.). New York: Wiley.

HIGH-INCIDENCE HANDICAPS

The expression high-incidence handicapped refers to an exceptionally large proportion of a particular type of exceptionality during some particular period of time relative to the incidence of other conditions. The expression high incidence is arbitrarily defined, however, as no specific numerical proportion is required. Unfortunately, the special education literature provides mention of both high-incidence and high-prevalence handicaps; therefore, the reader must keep this distinction in mind.

High-incidence handicapped can only be meaningful when thought of in connection with other handicapping conditions. These conditions are often referred to as categories of exceptionality. Currently, the U.S. Department of Education accepts 10 categories of handicapping conditions, although individual states often alter these basic categories. Garrett and Brazil (1979), for example, identified 13 categories used across the 50 states. Most states did not recognize all 13 categories, and two states recognized no multiple categories of exceptionality, preferring instead to offer special education to children in need of special assistance.

Despite difficulties in establishing precise incidence rates, several categories possess generally accepted levels that represent a significant proportion of the school-aged handicapped population. Approximately 11% (Algozzine & Korinek, 1985) of the total school-aged population now receives special education services in the public schools. Some handicapping conditions (e.g., visual and hearing impairments) represent a long-standing pattern of low incidence rates. Others, notably language disorders, learning disabilities, mental retardation, and behavioral (emotional) *disorders* occur in sufficient numbers to be considered high incidence.

Strictly, the concepts of low incidence or high incidence might have little more than a descriptive capacity for denoting the likelihood (probability) of occurrence. There are, however, at least two fundamental considerations that will help the value of the term. The first is the rapid expansion of the number of high-incidence handicaps. Ysseldyke and Algozzine (1984) suggest that a high-incidence group might include the learning disabled, the mentally retarded, the behaviorally (emotionally) handicapped, and the language disordered. A high-incidence group constituted in this way would represent in excess of 90% of the handicapped students served in the public schools. Algozzine and Korinek (1985) reached a similar conclusion. However, the authors also noted that of the categories included in high-incidence exceptionalities, learning disabilities was by far the most rapidly expanding and largest category, and emotional disturbance the smallest. Within the high-incidence handicapped group, both learning disabilities and emotional disorders are rapidly expanding, learning disabilities phenomenally. Two are decreasing (mental retardation and speech-language disordered). Yet overall incidence of high-incidence handicaps is increasing at a rate in sharp contrast to the near stable levels of the low-incidence handicapped. Current statistics and projections of future trends demonstrate the group's influence on the special education service delivery system.

Beyond the sheer size of the high-incidence group, a second important matter, that of programming through combining several traditional high-incidence categories, has emerged. Sometimes this is viewed as noncategorical special education, though that seems to be a misnomer (Hallahan & Kauffman, 1982) as most special educators do not mean to imply the deletion of all categories of exceptionality. Lilly (1979), for example, presented a limited noncategorical or high-incidence approach that included the educable mentally retarded, the behaviorally (emotionally) disordered, and the learning disabled. In Lilly's view, the prevalence of the groups, the identification techniques that are used, the behavioral characteristics, and the instructional strategies are sufficiently similar to make further nosological classification unnecessary. In stressing the use of a data-based instructional model, Lilly observed little to encourage the continuation of traditional categorical classification and programming for these groups. It should be noted that speech- and language-impaired individuals were not included in Lilly's (1979) proposal, presumably because the similarity of this category to the high-incidence group lies only in the matter of incidence/prevalence.

Miller and Davis (1982) generally found points of agreement with Lilly's (1979) position. Among the more convincing evidence was the observation of Connor (1976) that cross-categorical teacher education had gained momentum and the results of a survey by Belch (1979) that identified an increasing number of states offering cross-categorical (comprehensive) certification. Both trends may be interpreted as heightened interest in the viability of the high-incidence handicapped concept, although the majority of states continue to organize services in line with the traditional handicapping conditions.

REFERENCES

Algozzine, B., & Korinek, L. (1985). Where is special education for students with high prevalence handicaps going? *Exceptional Children, 51,* 388–394.

Belch, P.J. (1979). Toward noncategorical teacher certification in special education—Myth or reality? *Exceptional Children, 46,* 129–131.

Connor, F.P. (1976). The past is prologue: Teacher preparation in special education. *Exceptional Children, 42,* 366–378.

Garret, J.E., & Brazil, N. (1979). Categories used for identification and education of exceptional children. *Exceptional Children, 45,* 291–292.

Hallahan, D.P., & Kauffman, J.M. (1982). *Exceptional children: Introduction to special education* (2nd ed.). Englewood Cliffs, NJ: Prentice-Hall.

Lilly, M.S. (1979). *Children with exceptional needs.* New York: Holt.

Miller, T.L., & Davis, E.E. (1982). The mildly handicapped: A rationale. In T.L. Miller & E.E. Davis (Eds.), *The mildly handicapped student* (pp. 3–16). New York: Grune & Stratton.

Ysseldyke, J.E., & Algozzine, B. (1984). *Introduction to special education.* Boston: Houghton Mifflin.

See also Categorical Education; Low-Incidence Handicaps

HIGH INTEREST–LOW VOCABULARY

High interest–low vocabulary refers to reading materials that have been designed to interest older students who have low vocabularies and low reading levels. Often, adolescents who have reading levels in the lower elementary grade levels become even more frustrated if given the reading books that have been designed for their reading levels. Such reading books can insult the adolescents since they are geared for the interest level of a third grader, not a ninth grader.

Many publishers have designed materials to deal with this problem. For example, the *Corrective Reading* series (Engelmann et al., 1978) is designed for students from fourth to twelfth grade who have not developed adequate reading, decoding, and comprehension skills. The vocabulary introduced in these stories is very controlled. Only word patterns that have been taught and practiced are included in the lessons (low vocabulary). More important, however, the interest level of the stories is geared to the older reader; the topics covered do not insult the older reader by assuming his or her interests are similar to those of a third grader.

REFERENCE

Engelmann, S., Johnson, G., Hanner, S., Carnine, L., Meyers, L., Osborn, S., Haddox, P., Becker, W., Osborn, W., & Becker, J. (1978). *Corrective reading program.* Chicago, IL: Science Research.

See also Reading Disorders; Reading in the Content Areas; Reading Remediation

HIGH-RISK REGISTRY

A high-risk registry is based on the premise that early identification of infants and young children with handicaps is critical to the success of an early intervention treatment program. The registry contains factors associated with an increased risk for the development of a handicapping condition (Feinmesser & Tell, 1974). These factors typically include birth weight of less than 1500 gr; billirubin level of less than 20 mg/100 ml of serums; exposure to or the presence of bacterial infections such as meningitis; exposure to or the presence of nonbacterial infections such as rubella or herpes; multiple apneic spells; and 5-minute Apgar scores less than 5.

The Apgar score (Apgar, 1953) is a simple measure of neonatal risk routinely obtained during the medical assessment of a newborn infant 1 and 5 minutes after delivery. The infant's heart rate, respiration, reflex irritability, muscle tone, and skin color are rated on the basis of 0, 1, or 2. For example, a heart rate between 100 and 140 beats per minute is rated a 2, while a heart rate less than 100 beats per minute is rated 1; no heartbeat is rated 0. A composite score reflects the infant's ability to adapt to the postnatal environment (Gorski, 1984).

The staff at a hospital participating in a high-risk registry typically completes a card after each live birth. Information regarding birth weight, billirubin levels, the presence of bacterial or nonbacterial infections, apneic spells, and Apgar scores is provided by the obstetric staff or the attending physician. Maternal interviews provide addi-

HISPANIC STUDENTS WITH DISABILITIES

tional information regarding exposure to bacterial or non-bacterial infections and any parental concern for the health of the baby. The presence of any one of these factors tentatively identifies an infant as at risk and warrants referral for additional evaluation at 6, 9, and 12 months of age. If during subsequent evaluation, the baby no longer displays any abnormal characteristics, and if parents express no concern, the baby's name is removed from the files. If subsequent evaluation does indicate the presence of a handicap, the parents are encouraged to pursue additional assessment, a medical evaluation, and a treatment program.

REFERENCES

Apgar, V. (1953). A proposal for a new method of resolution of the newborn infant. *Current Researchers in Anesthesia & Analgesia, 32*, 260–267.

Feinmesser, M., & Tell, L. (1974). Evaluation of methods for detecting hearing impairment in infancy and early childhood. In G.T. Mencher (Ed.), *Early identification of hearing loss* (pp. 102–113). Pratteln, Switzerland: Thur AG Offsetdruck.

Gorski, P.A. (1984). Infants at risk. In M.J. Hanson (Ed.), *Atypical infant development* (pp. 59–75). Baltimore, MD: University Park Press.

See also **Early Identification of Handicapped Children; Infant Stimulation; Prematurity**

HISKEY-NEBRASKA TEST OF LEARNING APTITUDE

The Hiskey-Nebraska Test of Learning Aptitude (HNTLA) is individually administered to assess the learning aptitude of persons age 3 through 17. The test is appropriate for use with deaf and hard of hearing persons as well as those without sensory defects. The HNTLA is composed of 12 subtests; 3 of the 12 are administered to subjects of all ages; 5 are administered only to children under age 12; and 4 are administered only to students over age 11. Items are uniformly administered either in pantomime fashion or by verbal directions. Examinees respond to items motorically, by pointing to one of several response alternatives, drawing picture parts, or manipulating objects such as beads, colored sticks, picture cards, or wooden blocks. The type of tasks on the HNTLA range from memory for color sequences to puzzle completion, picture analogy, and spatial reasoning. The tasks administered to children ages 3 to 11 primarily involve short-term visual memory, perceptual organization, visual discrimination abilities, and freedom from distractibility. The tasks administered to older examinees primarily involve perceptual organization, visual discrimination abilities, and analogical reasoning.

An examinee's raw score is based on the median subtest performance and converted to a learning age (LA) if pantomimed directions were used or a mental age (MA) if verbal directions were used. Learning ages are based on norms for deaf children; MAs are based on norms for hearing children. By using norms tables, LAs and MAs can be con-

verted to learning quotients and IQs respectively. The current edition of the HNTLA was normed in 1966 for hearing and deaf children. Reviewers have consistently noted the lack of more current reliability or validity for the test, but frequently acknowledge it as the best, and only appropriate, device available for the assessment of deaf children. It is a useful instrument for evaluating the intellectual functioning of children with language disorders. It is now in revision and published by PRO-ED publishing company.

See also **Assessment; Intelligence Testing**

HISPANIC STUDENTS WITH DISABILITIES

Hispanic students make up a large and growing segment of the school population. While they do not share a singular cultural tradition nor an identical linguistic code, these students who have ties to Mexico, South and Central America, and the Caribbean share a variety of common characteristics. Unfortunately, many of these characteristics place them at risk in America's schools. Many are poor, have limited proficiency in English, and are acculturated into a system of values and cognitive styles that may conflict with the dominant culture in schools. Owing, in part, to these characteristics, controversy has surrounded the delivery of special education services to these children. Specifically, the adequacy of assessment and intervention practices for handicapped Hispanic children are two issues that have received a great deal of attention.

Due to their unique ethnic, linguistic, and socioeconomic status, Hispanic handicapped children may also have instructional needs that differ from those of their peers. However, the capability of school districts to meet those needs is limited by such factors as lack of trained personnel in special and bilingual education, appropriate materials, and policies within state education agencies. Proponents of bilingual education claim that children who are not proficient in English need to receive instruction in their primary mode of communication to be able to maximize their learning. While this position is a basis for the bilingual instruction of many children, handicapped Hispanic youngsters have not been systematically included in specially designed programs for bilingual handicapped youngsters (Bergin, 1980).

A review by Chinn (1982) identified unique instructional programs used with culturally different handicapped children. One instructional approach for Hispanic handicapped pupils with limited English proficiency involves interfacing bilingual and special education programs to apply the intervention techniques inherent in those programs. The goal is to provide the needed cultural and linguistic emphasis as well as special instructional methods. Examples of exemplary bilingual-special education efforts include the Responsive Environment Program for Spanish American Children (REPSAC) in Clovis, New Mexico; the Psycholinguistic Learning Disabilities in Mexican American Students program in Coachella, California; Early On (for severely and multiply handicapped) in San Diego, California; and the Coordinated Services for Handicapped LESA Students in Houston, Texas.

Excellent guides to resources for intervention efforts, research, and training concerning Hispanic handicapped pupils include publications from the National Clearing House for Bilingual Education and The Council for Exceptional Children, Reston, Virginia.

Meeting the educational needs of handicapped Hispanic youngsters will require extensive study of the impact of cultural and linguistic factors on the cognitive functioning and socialization of these pupils in America's schools. Unfortunately, there is limited research information in these areas. As such, one of the critical problems is the lack of educational leadership personnel to engage in research and development efforts.

REFERENCES

Bergin, V. (1980). *Special education needs in bilingual programs.* National Clearinghouse for Billingual Education. Lanham, MD: Eagle One Graphics.

Chinn, P.C. (1982). Curriculum development for culturally different exceptional children. In C.H. Thomas & J.L. Thomas (Eds.), *Billingual special education resource guide.* Phoenix, AZ: Oryx.

See also Bilingual Assessment in Special Education; Bilingual Education; Cultural Bias in Tests; Culturally/Linguistically Diverse Students

HIRSCHSPRUNG'S DISEASE

Hirschsprung's disease is a congenital genetic disorder characterized by a lack of nerve cells in a segment of the bowel resulting in constipation, diarrhea, and abdominal distention. This condition was originally named for Harold Hirschsprung, a Danish physician in Copenhagen who first described the disease in 1886 (Passarge, 1993). It is also referred to as aganglionic megacolon.

Hirschsprung's disease is caused by the absence of nerve cells, called ganglia, in the wall of the intestines. From the fifth to the twelfth week of pregnancy, nerve cells form in a downward manner through the alimentary tract from the mouth to the anus. These nerve cells control the squeezing and relaxation of the intestinal wall, which moves the stool through the bowel. In the baby with Hirschsprung's disease, the downward migration of nerve cells is not completed, and a portion of the intestine remains aganglionic, or lacking nerve cells. The portion of intestine that is aganglionic is unable to relax and the stool is unable to pass through. This condition causes a build-up of bowel contents behind the obstruction. Most often the disease begins in the last foot or two of the bowel, called the sigmoid colon and the rectum, and always ends at the anus. The length of the aganglionic portion of the bowel varies, but rarely involves the entire bowel.

Treatment may include a temporary colostomy (surgically opening the large intestine) or ileostomy (opening the lower part of the small intestine), which will later be surgically closed. Surgical removal of the diseased section of the intestine may also be necessary. For most children with Hirschsprung's disease, there are no long-term complications after successful surgery. A small but significant minority of children, however, do experience persistent constipation, encopresis, or persistent enterocolitis.

REFERENCE

Passarge, E. (1993). Wither polygenic inheritance: Mapping Hirschsprung disease. *Nature Genet, 4,* 325–326. PubMed ID: 8401573.

HISTORY OF SPECIAL EDUCATION

Prehistoric societies, whose survival could depend on the fitness of each member, did not protect children who were born with defects, generally allowing them to die at birth or in infancy. Some ancient peoples, believing that physical deformities and mental disorders were the result of possession by demons, rejected, punished, or killed those who were afflicted. However, there is some evidence of persons with disabilities being treated with kindness, or even revered as being possessed of supernatural powers.

The ancient Greek and Roman societies gave us the first recorded attempts at the scientific understanding and treatment of disability in children. Some physicians and scholars in these cultures began to look on such conditions as treatable, and although infanticide was common, some efforts were made to preserve the lives of children with disabilities.

In the Middle Ages, persons with disabilities were often objects of amusement, and sometimes were used for entertainment. More often, however, they were derided, imprisoned, or executed. During this period, the church began to foster humane care for people with disabilities and to provide asylums for them. The Renaissance brought a greater belief in the value of human life, and laid the groundwork for the popular revolutions that later overthrew the domination of royalty in much of Europe and in America. Interest in educating children with disabilities, then, grew out of the new humanism of the Renaissance, the belief in the worth of every individual, and the associated struggles for freedom for the common man.

EDUCATION OF INDIVIDUALS WITH HEARING IMPAIRMENTS

Special education, as the scientific study and education of exceptional children, started about 1555 when a Spanish monk, Pedro Ponce de Leon (1520–1584), taught a small number of children who were deaf to read, write, speak, and to master academic subjects. Another Spaniard, Juan Pablo Bonet (1579–1629?), wrote the first book on the education of individuals who were deaf in 1620. He described his methods, probably derived from those of Ponce de Leon, and set forth a one-handed manual alphabet that provided the basis for the one used today.

In 1644 in England, John Bulwer (1614–1684) published the first book in English on the education of the deaf. This was followed in 1680 by the most significant of the early books in English, *Didasopholus; or, The Deaf and Dumb Man's Tutor,* by George Dalgarno (1628?–1687). The author made the startling assertion that people who are deaf have as much capacity for learning as those who can hear, and outlined instructional methods that came to be widely used by subsequent educators.

The first permanent school for the deaf in Great Britain was established in 1767 in Edinburgh by Thomas Braidwood (1715–1806). Braidwood's school was successful from the beginning, and in 1783 he moved it to Hackney, near London, to draw students from the larger population of the London area. Braidwood's nephew and assistant, Joseph Watson (1765–1829), later established the first school in Great Britain for children who were poor and deaf, in the London area. Braidwood's method combined manual and oral elements, teaching his students a manual alphabet and signs as well as articulation.

In Germany, at about the same time, Samuel Heinicke (1729–1784) developed a purely oral method of instruction, emphasizing the development of lip reading and speaking skills. Heinicke's method, as further developed by Friedrich Moritz Hill (1805–1874), was the basis for the oral method that became accepted practice throughout the world.

In France, Abbé Charles Michel de l'Epée (1712–1789) and Abbé Roch Ambroise Sicard (1742–1822) were developing the modern language of signs. Based on earlier work by Jacob Pereire (1715–1790), the instructional system was characterized by use of signs and a manual alphabet for communication. The French system also emphasized training of the senses of sight and touch, a forerunner of the sensory training that became an integral part of special education in the next century.

Organized education for children who were deaf in the United States began with the training of Thomas Hopkins Gallaudet (1787–1851) by Sicard in the French method of teaching persons who were deaf. Gallaudet, who had been chosen to start America's first school for the deaf, returned to Hartford, Connecticut, well trained in Sicard's methods and accompanied by a recruit from France, Laurent Clerc (1785–1869), a teacher of the deaf who was deaf himself. In 1817, they established the first school for children who were deaf in the United States, now the American School for the Deaf. This was the first educational program for exceptional children established in the United States. The New York Institution for the Deaf opened the next year, and by 1863, 22 schools for the deaf existed in the nation. In 1867, the first oral schools for the deaf were established in the United States, the Clarke School for the Deaf in Massachusetts and the Lexington School for the Deaf in New York. Gallaudet College, the only liberal arts college for students who are deaf in the world, was established in 1864. The first day school classes for any exceptionality in the United States

were established for children who were deaf in Boston in 1869. Adult education for persons who were deaf began in New York City in 1874.

The subsequent development of services for persons who were deaf in the United States was aided immeasurably by a number of prominent advocates, most notably Alexander Graham Bell (1847–1922), inventor of the telephone and tireless worker for education for the deaf, and Helen Keller (1880–1957), who, deaf and blind from early childhood, was a living example of the effectiveness of special educational methods in overcoming even the most severe handicaps.

The development of services for persons who were deaf were hindered in the United States and elsewhere by bitter disagreements between advocates of oral and manual methods of instruction, with a resulting lack of cohesive effort toward common goals. These disagreements continue to this day, with some educators advocating oral speech-language and others promoting gestural language or a combination of methods. Most educators agree that the goal is to provide an adequate means of communication for the individual, and the predominant teaching method today is total communication which incorporates various modes of communication.

EDUCATION OF CHILDREN WITH VISUAL IMPAIRMENTS

Education for children who were blind began in France with the work of Valentin Haüy (1745–1822), a French philanthropist who, in 1784, founded the National Institution for the Young Blind in Paris. The school admitted students who were both blind and sighted so as not to isolate students who were blind from their peers with sight. Its success led to the formation of seven similar schools in Europe during the next 15 years. The first school for children who were blind in the United States, now the Perkins School for the Blind in Watertown, Massachusetts, was begun in 1829 with Samuel Gridley Howe (1801–1876) as its first director. There followed a rapid development of residential schools, which soon began also to enroll students who were partially sighted. These residential schools provided the nation's only education services to children with visual impairments until the development of special classes in the public schools, a movement that began with the formation of a special class for children who were blind in Chicago in 1900. The first special class for children with partial sight was opened 13 years later in Boston.

Crucial to the education of students who are blind was the development of a system of reading and writing. Haüy developed a system of embossed letters to be read with the fingers and, using this system, he printed the first books for the blind. Raised letters proved to be extremely difficult to read, however, and Louis Braille (1809–1852), blind from childhood and one of Haüy's students, developed the system of reading that has become universal. Known as braille, the system uses raised dots to represent the letters of the alphabet. For many years all braille materials had to be prepared individually by hand. Two inventions by Frank H. Hall (1843–1911) greatly expanded the amount of materials in braille: a braille typewriter (1892) and a braille printing system (1893). English language braille, which developed in many variations, was standardized in 1932 with an international agreement on the code that is now called Standard English Grade Two.

EDUCATION FOR CHILDREN WITH MENTAL RETARDATION

Education for children with mental retardation began with the attempt by a French physician, Jean Marc Gaspard Itard (1775–1838), to educate an 11-year-old boy who had been found living as a savage in the woods. Itard's efforts to educate and civilize the boy were only partially successful, apparently because the boy was mentally retarded. Itard documented his methods in a book, *The Wild Boy of Aveyron* (1801). His instructional materials and procedures formed the basis for more than a century of development in the education of those with mental retardation, most notably by Edouard Seguin (1812–1880) in France and the United States and by Maria Montessori (1870–1952) in Italy. Seguin, in his influential book, *Idiocy and Its Treatment by the Physiological Method,* published in 1866, enunciated many ideas that have persisted to the present time: education of the whole child, individualization of instruction, beginning instruction at the child's current level of functioning, and the importance of rapport between teacher and pupil. These concepts and Seguin's emphasis on sensory training were incorporated in the twentieth century into the famous Montessori method, used worldwide in the education of children both with and without disabilities. Ovide Decroly (1871–1932) in Belgium developed an effective curriculum for children with mental retardation early in the twentieth century and established schools that served as models throughout Europe. Alfred Binet (1857–1911), working in the public schools of Paris, made an immense contribution with the invention of intelligence testing, providing in 1905 the first objective instrument for selecting children for placement in special education programs.

The first instance of schooling for children with mental retardation in the United States took place in 1839 with the admission of a student who was blind and mentally retarded to the Perkins Institute for the Blind in Massachusetts. The first school designed specifically for children with mental retardation, a residential facility, was opened in 1848 in Barre, Massachusetts, by Hervey Backus Wilbur (1820–1883). Public residential facilities for children and adults with mental retardation were opened in all parts of the country during the next half century, and by 1917 all but four states were providing institutional care for individuals with mental retardation.

The first public school special class for children with mental retardation was formed in Germany in 1859, and a small number of such classes were formed in other European nations during the next several decades. In the United States the first public school special class for children with mental retardation was opened in 1896 in Providence, Rhode Island. Several cities followed suit between 1896 and 1900. During this same period "streamer classes" were set up for non-English speaking children. These special education facilities soon were a "hodgepodge bin" for nearly every sort of variant child that could not be handled with regular classrooms.

In the 1930s special education was incorporated into the secondary schools primarily in the large cities. Up until that time special education programs serving adolescents were primarily residential or housed in elementary schools. Martens (1947) cited the inclusion of exceptional students in secondary schools as a significant and gratifying indication that secondary schools were being modified to meet the needs of handicapped adolescents. Special divisions in city high schools were set up for the "mentally subnormal" coming from elementary schools, and some city junior high schools offered modified programs of instruction.

In the years that followed, children with milder forms of mental retardation were educated primarily in separate classes in public schools or in residential facilities. Children with more severe mental retardation were kept at home, provided for in private programs, or were institutionalized. The normalization and deinstitutionalization movements, which began in the 1940s and continue to the present, led to an increasing number of children classified as mentally retarded being educated in the public schools. The passage of PL 94-142 in 1975 began a major shift in special educational services received by children classified as mentally retarded. More and more children classified as "educable" by the school systems were "mainstreamed" into general education and fewer were placed in separate classes and schools. Children classified as "trainable" and "severe" were educated in the public schools and no longer expected to be educated in segregated facilities.

EDUCATION OF CHILDREN WITH ORTHOPEDIC HANDICAPS AND OTHER HEALTH PROBLEMS

Few special educational provisions for children with orthopedic handicaps and health impairments existed prior to the twentieth century. In the United States, the first special class for orthopedically-handicapped children was established in the Chicago public schools in 1899 or 1900. A class for students with lowered vitality was initiated in Providence, Rhode Island in 1908, and one for children with epilepsy was formed in Baltimore, Maryland in 1909. Special educational and related services, such as occupational and physical therapy for children with a wide variety of orthopedic and health-related problems, expanded with the passage of PL 94-142 and IDEA.

EDUCATION OF EMOTIONALLY HANDICAPPED/BEHAVIORALLY DISORDERED CHILDREN

References to emotionally disturbed children do not appear in the scientific literature until the nineteenth century; there is a puzzling absence of references to the subject in any literature prior to that time. The first description of childhood psychosis was published in 1838 by Jean Etienne Esquirol (1772–1840) in *Des Maladies Mentales,* a work that constituted the first scientific treatment of mental illness.

The development of school services for children with emotional handicaps is not easy to trace because of imprecision in the classification of handicaps, difficulty in diagnosis, and a tendency to place children with these types of problems in classes designed for children with other handicaps. Late in the nineteenth century, a few schools in the United States began to make formal provision for students with emotional handicaps. The New Haven, Connecticut public schools established a class in 1871 to provide for children exhibiting unmanageable behavior and the New York City public schools formed classes for unruly boys in 1874. It is noteworthy that these were the first public school special classes for exceptional students to be established in the United States.

Children with severe emotional problems began to be studied in a systematic way only in the 1930s, and even then public schools were slow to accept responsibility for educating them. But with psychiatry developing as a discipline, with individual differences a central topic in psychology, and with psychological testing increasingly useful as a diagnostic tool, schools began to assume responsibility for educating these students and for developing programs based on psychiatric diagnosis and treatment recommendations.

In 1975, ten categories of handicapped children were recognized as eligible for special education, and in 1990 PL 101-476 defined the categories of disabilities which qualify children for special education. These disabilities are mental retardation, hearing impairments (including deafness), speech or language impairments, visual impairments (including blindness), serious emotional disturbance, orthopedic impairments, autism, traumatic brain injury, other health impairments, or specific learning disabilities.

PARENT INVOLVEMENT

The years since World War II have been characterized by the rapid development of services for children with disabilities in the United States, with greatly increased involvement of parents and governmental entities. Parents of children with disabilities, who had long been in the background of special education, began in the 1940s and 1950s to organize themselves to represent the needs of their children and, where necessary, to provide educational services for those children not being served by the public schools. Organizations such as the National Association of Retarded Citizens (now known as The Arc), the United Cerebral Palsy Association, and the Association for Children with Learning Disabilities (now known as the Learning Disabilities Association) have been major forces in the development of public school services for all handicapped children. They have had great influence in establishing the educational rights of all children and their families, obtaining legislation relating to the rights of persons with disabil-

ities, changing attitudes toward those with disabilities, and establishing the right of parents to participate in public school decisions about their child.

LEGISLATIVE AND GOVERNMENTAL ACTION

The federal government conducted a variety of programs designed to improve educational services for children with disabilities in the years following World War II. These governmental activities included grants to the states to assist in the development of new programs for children with disabilities, funding of research and demonstration projects, funding of training of special education personnel, establishment of regional resource centers for teachers, and establishment of a network of centers for children who are deaf-blind. In 1967, the Bureau of Education for the Handicapped was established in the U.S. Office of Education to administer the training, research, and educational programs supported by the federal government throughout the nation.

The landmark legislation for children with disabilities in the United States is PL 94-142, the Education for All Handicapped Children Act, enacted by Congress in 1975. Its stated purpose is ensuring that all handicapped children have available a free appropriate public education that provides special education and related services as needed to meet the student's unique needs. Public Law 94-142 required that state and local education agencies ensure that all children who are handicapped be identified and evaluated; that a comprehensive, nondiscriminatory, multidisciplinary educational assessment be made; that a reassessment be made at least every 3 years; that a written individualized educational plan (IEP) be developed and maintained for each child who has been determined to be handicapped; and that each child be educated in the least restrictive environment that is consistent with his or her handicap. The law also granted certain rights to parents to review their child's school record, to obtain an independent evaluation of the child, to receive written notice prior to placement in special education services, and to have an impartial hearing if they wish to challenge the proposed classification or placement of their child. Compliance with the requirements of PL 94-142 has brought modest amounts of federal financial aid to the states, to be used with state and local funds to support the cost of educating handicapped children. A far-reaching effect of PL 94-142 has been the virtual elimination of the exclusion of handicapped children from school. As the title of the act states, the legislation provides for the education of all handicapped children.

PL 94-142 was amended a number of times to increase the age of children covered under the provisions of the law and to emphasize transition services and assistive technology. A major reauthorization of PL 92-142 in 1990 changed the name of the law from Education of All Handicapped Children Act to Individuals with Disabilities Education Act, or IDEA (PL 101-476). This act increased the number of categories of disabilities to include autism and traumatic brain injury and attempted to address what were perceived to be injustices in the previous act. Amendments to IDEA in 1997 significantly changed the requirements for the IEP (Individualized Education Plan) and combined the "categorical" approach with the "functional" approach. A "child with a disability" between the ages of 3 through 9 may include a child experiencing developmental delays in one or more of the following areas: physical development, cognitive development, communication development, social or emotional development, or adaptive development. This provision allows states to serve "at-risk" children.

A number of court decisions laid the groundwork for the enactment of PL 94-142. The decision in *Pennsylvania Association for Retarded Children v. Commonwealth of Pennsylvania* in 1972 established that the public schools have the responsibility to provide appropriate programs for handicapped children and that a child may not be excluded from school without due process. *Mills v. Board of Education* in the same year established that a handicapped child may not be denied an appropriate, publicly supported education, and that the school system may not use lack of funds as a reason for failing to provide the services to which a handicapped child is entitled.

Section 504 of the Vocational Rehabilitation Act of 1973 (PL 93-112) serves as a statement of civil rights for the handicapped, providing that no otherwise qualified handicapped individual will, because of his or her handicap, be denied participation in any activity or program that receives federal financial assistance. This provision established public education as a right for all handicapped children, regardless of how serious the handicap might be, and is also the basis for a nationwide effort to make school buildings accessible to the handicapped.

The Americans with Disabilities Act (ADA) of 1990 extended the nondiscriminatory provisions of Section 504 of the Rehabilitation Act amendment in 1975 to the private sector and with its emphasis on accessibility impacts on the provision of special education. IDEA and the Rehabilitation Act deal with education and training for employment and Section 504 and ADA make sure that students with disabilities can put their education and training to use.

GROWTH IN SERVICES

Special education services expanded rapidly after World War II, both in number and types of children served. New special classes and special schools dramatically increased, as did college and university preparation programs for special education personnel. Additional types of children included in the population served were children classified as trainable mentally retarded, previously served primarily in institutions or in special schools operated by parent groups, and, beginning in the 1960s, children with learning disabilities, a group that had mostly been achieving poorly in regular classes or misplaced in special classes for students with other kinds of disabilities. In addition, interest increased in providing special programs for a group of students who are not disabled but who are generally included in the definition of exceptional children: gifted and talented children.

Programs for these students appeared only slowly, as they lacked strong support from most educators. Consequently, programs for the gifted and talented have not shown the rapid growth that took place in programs for students with disabilities.

Early or preschool education for children with disabilities, long provided for children who had hearing impairments or cerebral palsy and other physical handicaps, became generally available for other categories of children with disabilities in the 1970s. This development was based on research findings corroborating commonly-held beliefs that the development of young children can be changed through early educational intervention. Often initiated with federal funding, these programs provided several new emphases in special education, including organized "child-find" procedures to locate young children in need of special programming, improved multidisciplinary approaches, and parent education.

Under the provisions of PL 94-142 and Section 504 of the Vocational Rehabilitation Act, public schools are required to make appropriate educational services available to students with severe, profound, and multiple handicaps, a category that includes various degrees and combinations of mental retardation, behavior disorders, physical disabilities, and sensory disabilities. Programs for such children with severe disabilities, many of whom were previously unserved by the public schools, have become a major element of special education, and have brought with them services (such as physical therapy and occupational therapy) that had not previously been considered within the province of the schools. These programs also have necessitated the downward extension of the curriculum to include instruction in infant-level self-help skills.

Increased enrollment of students with disabilities in vocational education programs was fostered by the Vocational Education Amendments of 1976 (PL 94-482), which require each state to allocate 10% of its vocational funds for the education of students with disabilities. Increasingly since the enactment of these amendments, high-school students with disabilities have had a variety of occupational preparation options available to them, in both regular and special vocational education programs.

The explosion of technology that characterizes our time has directly benefited students with disabilities in some significant ways. The use of computers by children with disabilities is becoming commonplace, as it is for all students. Adaptive technology, including improved prostheses, motorized wheelchairs, and other transportation devices, has greatly increased the mobility of children with physical disabilities. Persons who are hearing impaired have benefited from vastly improved hearing aid technology, advances in surgical techniques, and increased captioning of films and television programs. Of special significance are telecommunication devices for persons who are deaf or hearing impaired, the best known being the teletypewriter and teleprinter (TTY), a device that enables the deaf to communicate by telephone, typing into the system messages that are then printed at the receiving end. Reading for persons with visual impairments is being made more effective by a number of devices. The recorded "talking book" can now be enhanced by a technique known as compressed speech, which can double the speed at which the recording is played without producing distortion in pitch or quality. The Optacon converts print into a vibrating image that can be read with the fingers. The Kurzweil Reading Machine converts print into spoken English. In the important area of mobility, the Sonicguide aids those with visual impairments by producing a sound that indicates the presence and distance of an object that lies in their path. Other technologies include translation of printed language into spoken language and braille, synthetic speech, speech-producing hand-held calculators, closed-circuit television with enlargers, optical-to-tactile and print-to-braille converters, and various portable devices. Although the cost of such devices remains high in some instances, they are enhancing the quality of services to children with disabilities in a variety of educational and community settings.

The 1970s saw the emergence of mainstreaming and least restrictive environment as dominant concepts in special education. The requirement in PL 94-142 that handicapped students be educated in the least restrictive environment was a reaction to doubts about the educational and social efficacy of the existing special class model and about the willingness of the schools to give handicapped students access to the regular school program. The least restrictive environment requirement has led to a significant shift in special education placements in the last decade. The shift is towards a reduction in placements in residential schools and special day schools, and increased enrollment of handicapped students in special classes in regular school buildings and in regular classes, usually with assistance in the form of some type of supplementary special instruction. Placement in less restrictive environments and the provision of appropriate educational services in this context, while not without its difficulties, is serving to eliminate needless segregation of handicapped students.

The debate still continues regarding the best environments in which to educate children with disabilities. IDEA creates a presumption in favor of educating students with disabilities with those who do not have disabilities to the maximum extent possible and of the school providing supplementary aids and support services. The presumption in favor of inclusion can only be set aside if the student cannot benefit from regular education. In this case the student may be placed in a less typical, more specialized, less inclusive program. IDEA also set forth the provision that schools must offer a continuum of services from more to less typical and inclusive. On the other hand, organizations such as the Learning Disabilities Association (LDA) believe that the regular classroom is not the appropriate place for many students with learning disabilities. They advocate for alternative instructional environments or teaching strategies that cannot be provided with the regular classroom. Other organizations and professionals support the LDA position,

but do not advocate a return to the previous total segregation models of special education.

The history of special education reveals evolution from initial education of specific groups in segregated settings to a movement toward total inclusion within public schools. The restructuring of general education taking place in the 1990s (Goals 2000, etc.) and the accompanying reforms have impacted special education. These reforms are cooperative learning, cooperative/collaborative teaching, site-based management, outcomes-based education and assessment, academic standards, effective assessment tools, accountability, and state and federal legislation. The future should hold much research to evaluate current reforms.

REFERENCES

Bender, R. (1970). *The conquest of deafness.* Cleveland, OH: Case Western Reserve.

Blatt, B., & Morris, R.J. (1984). *Perspectives in special education: Personal orientations.* Glenview, IL: Scott, Foresman.

Despert, J.L. (1965). *The emotionally disturbed child: Then and now.* New York: Brunner.

Fancher, R.E. (1979). *Pioneers of psychology.* New York: Norton.

Fancher, R.E. (1985). *The intelligence men: Makers of the I. Q. controversy.* New York: Norton.

Gannon, J.R. (1981). *Deaf heritage: A narrative history of deaf America.* Silver Spring, MD: National Association of the Deaf.

Hatlen, P.H., Hall, A.P., & Tuttle, D. (1980). Education of the visually handicapped: An overview and update. In L. Mann & D.A. Sabatino (Eds.), *The fourth review of special education* (pp. 1–33). New York: Grune & Stratton.

Irwin, R.B. (1955) *As I saw it.* New York: American Foundation for the Blind.

Jan, J.E., Freeman, R.D., & Scott, E.P. (1977). *Visual impairment in children and adults.* New York: Grune & Stratton.

Kanner, L. (1964). *A history of the care and study of the mentally retarded.* Springfield, IL: Thomas.

Kanner, L. (1970). Emotionally disturbed children: A historical review. In L.A. Faas (Ed.), *The emotionally disturbed child: A book of readings.* Springfield, IL: Thomas.

Kirk, S.A., & Gallagher, J.J. (1983). *Educating exceptional children* (4th ed.). Boston: Houghton Mifflin.

Kirk, S.A., Gallagher, J.J. & Anastasiow, N.J. (1997). *Educating exceptional children* (8th ed.). Boston: Houghton Mifflin.

Koestler, F.A. (1976). *The unseen minority: A social history of blindness in the United States.* New York: McKay.

Lane, H. (1984). *When the mind hears.* New York: Random House.

Lerner, J. (1985). *Learning disabilities: Theories, diagnosis, and teaching strategies* (4th ed.). Boston: Houghton Mifflin.

Lowenfeld, B. (1976). *The changing status of the blind: From separation to integration.* Springfield, IL: Thomas.

Meyen, E.L., & Skrtic, T.M. (Eds.). (1995). *Special education and student disability: Traditional, emerging, and alternative perspectives.* Denver: Love.

Moores, D.F. (1982). *Educating the deaf—Psychology, principles, and practices* (2nd ed.). Boston: Houghton Mifflin.

Reynolds, M.C., & Birch, J.W. (1977). *Teaching exceptional children in all America's schools.* Reston, VA: Council for Exceptional Children.

Rhodes, W.C., & Head, S. (1974). *A study of child variance.* Ann Arbor: University of Michigan.

Rosen, M., Clark, G.R., & Kivitz, M.S. (Eds.). (1976). *The history of mental retardation: Collected papers.* Baltimore, MD: University Park Press.

Ross, I. (1951). *Journey into light: The story of the education of the blind.* New York: Appleton-Century-Crofts.

Scheerenberger, R.C. (1983). *A history of mental retardation.* Baltimore, MD: Brookes.

Smith, S. (1983). *Ideas of the great psychologists.* New York: Harper & Row.

Swanson, B.M., & Willis, D.J. (1979). *Understanding exceptional children and youth.* Chicago: Rand McNally.

Turnbull, A., Turnbull, R., Shank, M., & Leal, D. (1999). *Exceptional lives: Special education in today's schools* (2nd ed.). Upper Saddle River, NJ: Merrill.

Turnbull, R. & Cilley, M. (1999). *Explanations and implications of the 1997 Amendment to IDEA.* Upper Saddle River, NJ: Merrill.

Wallin, J.E.W. (1955). *Education of mentally handicapped children.* New York: Harper & Row.

Watson, R.I. (1968). *The great psychologists: From Aristotle to Freud* (2nd ed.). Philadelphia: Lippincott.

Wiederholt, J.L. (1974). Historical perspectives on the education of the learning disabled. In L. Mann & D.A. Sabatino (Eds.), *The second review of special education* (pp. 103–152). Philadelphia: JSE.

Wright, E.B. (1980). *Noncategorical special education programs for the mildly handicapped in secondary schools: A review of the literature.* Unpublished manuscript.

See also **Americans with Disabilities Act; Inclusion; Individuals with Disabilities Education Act (IDEA); Politics and Special Education**

HOBBS, NICHOLAS (1915–1983)

Nicholas Hobbs began his professional career as a high school teacher, earned his PhD degree in clinical psychology from Ohio State University in 1946, and served on the faculties of Teachers College, Columbia University, Louisiana State University, and George Peabody College of Vanderbilt University. From the time of his arrival at George Peabody College in 1951 until his retirement in 1980, he held a number of positions, including chairman of the division of human development, director of the Center for the Study of Families and Children, which he created, and provost of Vanderbilt University.

Hobbs was widely known for his pioneering Project Re-ED, dedicated to "the reeducation of emotionally disturbed children." An educational approach to the treatment of emotionally disturbed children, Project Re-ED, which grew into a nationwide program, is described in Hobbs's *The Troubled and Troubling Child.*

Hobbs was appointed to a number of presidential panels and commissions and participated in the creation of the Peace Corps. He served as president of the American Psychological Association.

REFERENCES

Hobbs, N. (1982). *The troubled and troubling child.* San Francisco: Jossey-Bass.

The legacy of Nicholas Hobbs: Research on education and human development in the public interest, Part I. (1983). *Peabody Journal of Education, 60*(3).

The legacy of Nicholas Hobbs: Research on education and human development in the public interest, Part II. (1984). *Peabody Journal of Education, 61*(3).

HOBSON V. HANSEN

Hobson v. Hansen (1967) was the first case in which the federal courts chose to become involved in the racial issues of testing for placement in educational programs. *Hobson* centered around the controversial practice in the District of Columbia of using educational tracking. *Hobson* subsequently challenged the legality of within school district disparities in the allocation of financial and educational resources. These disparities resulted in greater resources being given to white children placed in higher level programs than black children, who were disproportionately placed in lower level educational tracks. All placements had been made on the basis of group-administered standardized tests of intelligence and achievement. In considering this case, the court expressed much concern that the placement had occurred primarily, or in some cases exclusively, on the basis of standardized tests.

As Bersoff (1982) has reported, despite the genuine intent of the Washington, DC school district in remediating severe academic deficiencies of black children, the court, in *Hobson,* eventually ruled against the district because of the resultant disproportionality in the different educational tracks. The court wrote that "in those schools with a significant number of white and Negro students a higher proportion of Negroes will go into the Special Academic (EMR) Tract than will white students" (p. 456). The court determined that the placement system as actually practiced violated the equal protection clause of the Fourteenth Amendment to the Constitution. The court ruled that ability grouping was justified when it resulted in racial disproportionality only when the assessment measures and judgments of ability were based on children's innate ability or genetic endowment and not current skill or ability levels. Though many special educators and psychologists would continue to take issue with this position, the court ventured into even more controversial ground when it asserted that only when ability grouping is based on innate ability would special education be "reasonably related to the purposes of education" (p. 512).

Bersoff (1982) has asserted that when viewed in its entirety, *Hobson* was not nearly so much a rejection of testing practices as it seems, but was more "the condemnation of rigid, poorly conceived classification practices that negatively affect the educational opportunities of minority children. The court's major concern was not the tests but the inflexibility of ability grouping as practiced by the school system, the stigmatizing effect on blacks, and its failure to provide sufficient resources to those in the lower tracks, resulting in generally poor teaching" (pp. 1047–1048). The court held that the end result was to relegate EMR students to a permanent class of inequality.

The court in *Hobson* was more impressed with the results of individual assessment, however, and did favor the use of individually administered tests by psychologists for placement in special educational programs. When reevaluated by psychologists under the conditions of individual assessment, the court found that nearly two-thirds of the children placed into EMR programs on the basis of group test results had been misclassified.

REFERENCE

Bersoff, D.N. (1982). The legal regulation of school psychology. In C.R. Reynolds & T.B. Gutkin (Eds.), *The handbook of school psychology.* New York: Wiley.

See also **Intelligence Testing; Larry P.; Marshall v. Georgia; Mental Retardation; Six-Hour Retarded Child**

HOLISTIC APPROACH AND LEARNING DISABILITIES

Holism is defined as "a theory that the universe and especially living nature is correctly seen in terms of interacting wholes . . . that are more than the mere sum of elementary particles" (*Webster's New Collegiate Dictionary,* 1979). Holism, as applied to teaching and learning, suggests an approach whereby variables are not broken down into their component parts, but are examined within the context in which they occur. This type of learning is ongoing and is not fragmented into discrete segments or skills (McNutt, 1984). In contrast, behaviorists contend that each learning task can be analyzed, segmented, and sequenced in a hierarchical order; the individual parts must be learned before the whole (the sum of the parts) can be understood. Holists believe this to be a piecemeal approach that results in learning that is irrelevant and boring.

Until recently the major approaches used with children who are learning disabled have been reductionist in their orientation. According to Poplin (1984a), the psychological process approach, the behaviorist approach, and the cognitive-strategies approach, all of which have been used in treating learning disabilities, share several assumptions: the learning process is divided into segments; the focus is on deficits of the individual instead of strengths; and there are right and wrong ways to process information. Holists do not agree with these assumptions and, in fact, would argue that operating in this manner hinders learning in the learning-disabled student.

Applied to learning disabilities, holistic inquiry lends credence to the argument that processes such as memory can neither be viewed experimentally nor taught separately, and that a child's memory for academic tasks may depend more on what the child already knows and feels and her/his interests than on the function or dysfunction of any hypothetical construct (Poplin, 1984a, p. 290).

Those advocating a holistic approach for teaching children with learning disabilities (Heshusius, 1984; Leigh, 1980; Poplin, 1984a, 1984b; Rhodes & Dudley-Marling [in press]) argue that these students need a curriculum that is rich in language and that provides frequent opportunities to engage in reading and writing. Learning-disabled students, however, often read in a slow, laborious, and dysfluent manner. Rhodes and Dudley-Marling (in press) posit that disfluent readers are afraid to take risks in the process of reading and writing. These readers believe that reading and writing are done in order to practice the form of language, word recognition, spelling, and mechanics. They do not understand that the goal is to derive and communicate meaning from their reading. According to Pflaum and Bryan (1982), fluent readers use the three language systems, graphophonics, syntax, and semantics, in an interrelated way to determine meaning, while disabled readers rely mainly on graphophonics. Holists feel that learning-disabled students need to learn to treat reading and writing as language rather than as discrete sets of skills that have little meaning or relevance to the reader.

A holistic classroom provides opportunities for students to engage in reading and writing. There are reading centers that contain a variety of reading materials, e.g., books, newspapers, magazines, comics, and cookbooks. Writing centers are complete with pencils, papers, and reasons for writing. Students write journals, stories, notes, poems, plays, or recipes. Students read and write together in groups to help one another be creative or to overcome obstacles. Holistic teachers plan activities that show reading and writing is useful. For example, a cooking project includes finding recipes in books, writing grocery lists, writing and reading recipes, and talking about the experience.

The holistic classroom is a place where teaching and learning is an interactive process with the emphasis on the meaning, not the form, of language. Learning-disabled students benefit in this meaningful environment. Segmenting learning into discrete parts can discourage reluctant learners with its repetition and boredom. Holistic learning, on the other hand, motivates students because it is meaningful, purposeful, and relevant.

REFERENCES

Heshusius, L. (1984). Why would they and I want to do it? A phenomenological-theoretical view of special education. *Learning Disability Quarterly, 7*(4), 363–368.

Leigh, J.E. (1980). Whole-language approaches: Premises and possibilities. *Learning Disability Quarterly, 3*(4), 62–69.

McNutt, G. (1984). A holistic approach to language arts instruction in the resource room. *Learning Disability Quarterly, 7*(4), 315–320.

Pflaum, S.W., & Bryan, T.H. (1982). Oral reading research and learning disabled children. *Topics in Learning and Learning Disabilities, 1,* 33–42.

Poplin, M.S. (1984a). Summary rationalizations, apologics and farewell: What we don't know about the learning disabled. *Learning Disability Quarterly, 7*(2), 130–135.

Poplin, M.S. (1984b). Toward a holistic view of persons with learning disabilities. *Learning Disability Quarterly, 7*(4), 290–294.

Rhodes, L.K., & Dudley-Marling, C.C. (in press). *Teaching literacy to learning disabled and remedial students.* Portsmouth, NH: Heinemann Educational Books.

Webster's New Collegiate Dictionary (1979). Springfield, MA: Merriam.

See also **Ecological Assessment; Ecological Education for the Handicapped**

HOLLAND, SPECIAL EDUCATION IN

See NETHERLANDS, SPECIAL EDUCATION IN.

HOLLINGWORTH, LETA A.S. (1886–1939)

Leta A.S. Hollingworth, psychologist, received her PhD from Teachers College, Columbia University, in 1916, after serving as a high-school teacher in Nebraska and as a clinical psychologist in New York City. She was a member of the faculty of Teachers College from 1916 until her death in 1939.

Hollingworth made pioneering studies of the psychology of women, correcting prior misconceptions regarding differences in abilities between the sexes and providing the basis for her strong advocacy of professional equality between men and women. She was a leader in the establishment of standards for clinical psychologists and carried out significant investigations of both mentally retarded and gifted children.

REFERENCES

Gates, A.I. (Ed.). (1940). Education and the individual. *Teachers College Record, 42,* 183–264.

Hollingworth, H.L. (1943). *Leta Stetter Hollingworth.* Lincoln: University of Nebraska Press.

Hollingworth, L. (1926). *Gifted children: Their nature and nurture.* New York: Macmillan.

HOLT, WINIFRED (1870–1945)

Winifred Holt founded the New York Association for the Blind in 1905. She was responsible for the creation of the committee that eventually became the National Society for the Prevention of Blindness. With a special interest in training and employment for the blind, she developed the New York Lighthouse, a workshop devoted to education, em-

Winifred Holt

ployment, and recreation for the blind. Dedicated by President William Howard Taft in 1913, the Lighthouse was so successful that Lighthouses were established in many cities in the United States, and eventually in 34 other countries.

A leader in the campaign to get blind children into the public schools, Holt helped the New York City Board of Education to establish its program for the education of blind students in classes with sighted children. She wrote two influential books, a biography of Henry Fawcett, the blind English postmaster-general, and *The Light Which Cannot Fail,* which contained stories about blind men and women and a useful "handbook for the blind and their friends." In 1922 Holt married Rufus Graves Mather, a research and lecturer on art who joined her in her work for the blind.

REFERENCES

Bloodgood, E.H. (1952). *First lady of the Lighthouse.* New York: The Lighthouse, New York Association for the Blind.

Holt, W. (1914). *A beacon for the blind: Being a life of Henry Faucett, the blind postmaster-general.* Boston: Houghton Mifflin.

Holt, W. (1922). *The light which cannot fail.* New York: Dutton.

HOMEBOUND INSTRUCTION

Homebound instruction is defined as education for the child confined to home owing to illness, physical injury, or emotional condition provided by an itinerant or visiting teacher. A child is eligible for a home instruction program if school attendance is made impossible by such physical or emotional conditions. Public Law 94-142 and IDEA have categorized home instruction as one of the most restrictive in the available cascade of services; as a result, such placement is to be considered temporary whenever possible (Berdine & Blackhurst, 1985).

The homebound teacher is used as the provider of this instruction in those areas or school districts where such services are available. The homebound instructional component must consist of direct service to the child and regular consultation with in-school personnel, as the nature of the service will vary from helping students at home for short periods of time to maintain the pace and assignments of their classes, to providing a complete instructional program for those confined for longer periods. Authorities agree that regular liaison with school and peers to maintain contacts and social skills is vital to the student on homebound instruction, who must be brought back to school as quickly as the handicapping condition allows (Polloway, Payne, Patton, & Payne, 1985).

New directions in special education are extending traditional homebound instruction to include home-based services for severely handicapped children, deaf and blind infants and preschool children, the mentally retarded, and other high-risk infants (Cartwright, Cartwright, & Ward, 1995). These services include the use of teacher-trainers to teach parents and children, with emphasis on self-help skills, communications, and language arts using the natural surroundings of the home environment to promote development (Kiernan, Jordan, & Saunders, 1984).

Technological advances in telecommunications and computer-linked instruction increasingly assist the homebound child and teacher until a return to a less restrictive environment is accomplished (Kirk & Gallagher, 1986).

REFERENCES

Berdine, W.H., & Blackhurst, A.E. (1985). *An introduction to special education* (2nd ed.). Boston: Little, Brown.

Cartwright, G.P., Cartwright, C.A., & Ward, M.J. (1995). *Educating special learners* (4th ed.). Belmont, CA: Wadsworth.

Kiernan, C., Jordan, R., & Saunders, C. (1984). *Stimulating the exceptional child: Strategies for teaching communication and behavior change to the mentally disabled.* Englewood Cliffs, NJ: Prentice-Hall.

Kirk, S.A., & Gallagher, J.J. (1986). *Educating exceptional children* (5th ed.). Boston: Houghton Mifflin.

Polloway, E.A., Payne, J.S., Patton, J.R., & Payne, R.A. (1985). *Strategies for teaching retarded and special needs learners.* Columbus, OH: Merrill.

See also **Cascade Model of Special Education; Least Restrictive Environment**

HOMEWORK

Time spent on homework is generally related to academic achievement. This conclusion has been supported in studies conducted since the early 1900s. Keith (1982) found that homework has a higher correlation with better grades in school than any other factor except intellectual ability. Walberg (1984) found, after a review of 15 studies on graded homework, that such assignments have three times more influence on student achievement than the education, income level, or occupational status of the parents. The relative effectiveness of assigning homework versus not assigning homework results in an achievement gain of approximately .30 of a standard deviation. By grading homework, a teacher can almost triple the effectiveness of this strategy over merely assigning it for practice.

It is not simply a question of requiring more homework to achieve higher performance. The benefits depend on how well designed, supervised, and monitored such assignments are. Keith (1982) has concluded that at some point, increased homework will probably bring smaller and smaller returns. It is probably safe to assume, however, that most students are a long way from the point of diminishing returns regarding homework. Some general rules for homework assignments are (1) require it on a regular schedule; (2) evaluate it by grades or feedback as soon as possible after the assignment; (3) make it an integral part of the in-class activities; and (4) base it on content that will be evaluated on tests.

REFERENCES

Keith, T.Z. (1982). Time spent on homework and high school grades: A large sample path analysis. *Journal of Educational Psychology, 74*(2), 246–253.

Walberg, H.J. (1984). Improving the productivity of America's schools. *Educational Leadership, 41*(8), 19–27.

See also **Achievement Need; Teacher Effectiveness**

HORSEBACK RIDING FOR THE HANDICAPPED

See EQUINE THERAPY.

HORTICULTURAL THERAPY

Horticultural therapy is also known as hortitherapy, agritherapy, therapeutic horticulture, plant therapy, and hort-therapy. Horticultural therapy for handicapped persons has its roots in the nineteenth century, during the rise of the large state institutions. Many of these institutions were located in rural areas and included areas for propagation of crops. Residents were trained to plant, care for plants, and harvest. The purpose of this farming was primarily economic rather than therapeutic. However, as a secondary benefit many residents were able to obtain work in agriculture and, in fact, before World War II, agriculture was one of the strongest occupational areas for the handicapped.

Contemporary hortitherapy has several underpinnings. It may be a branch of occupational therapy (Burton & Watkins, 1978) used to enhance motor development. It has also been employed as a form of psychotherapy (Watson & Burlingame, 1960) to develop motivation and provide clients with a sense of responsibility for living things (Saever, 1985). Horticultural therapy has also been used as a vocational activity (Downey, 1985; Good-Hamilton, 1985; Schrader, 1979). Such training may be in a sheltered work setting or in a vocational school program for competitive employment.

There are a number of unique hortitherapy programs. Burton and Watkins (1978) described a public school program for physically handicapped students in which academic concepts were taught while students were involved in plant care. The program was designed from a Piagetian point of view and was transdisciplinary, incorporating physical, occupational, and speech therapy, and classroom instruction. Saever (1985) employed agritherapy with learning-disabled students (8 to 12 years old) as a means of promoting responsibility, order, and structure, following through on plans, respect for nature, cooperative effort, and positive relationships with adults. Good-Hamilton (1985) described another public school program in which trainable mentally retarded students and learning-disabled students worked in greenhouse production to develop vocational skills (primarily work habits). More than 50% of the students were able to obtain employment at the conclusion of training. There is a professional hortitherapy organization, the National Council for Therapy and Rehabilitation Through Horticulture (NCTRH), which was started in 1973.

REFERENCES

Burton, S.B., & Watkins, M. (1978). *The green scene: Horticultural experiences for the physically impaired student.* Paper presented at the 56th annual International Conference, Council for Exceptional Children, Kansas City, MO.

Downey, R.S. (1985). Teaching the disadvantaged and handicapped. *Agricultural Education Magazine, 57*(8), 5–7.

Good-Hamilton, R. (1985). Plants breed success. *Agricultural Education Magazine, 57*(8), 8–10.

Saever, M.D. (1985). Agritherapy, plants as learning partners. *Academic Therapy, 20*(4), 389–397.

Schrader, B. (1979). *Working hands and 3,000 chrysanthemums. Special report: Fresh views on employment of mentally handicapped people.* Washington, DC: President's Committee on Employment of the Handicapped.

Watson, D.P., & Burlingame, A.W. (1960). *Therapy through horticulture.* New York: Macmillan.

See also Occupational Therapy; Vocational Therapy

HOSPITALIZATION AND SPECIAL EDUCATION

Hospital instruction involves teaching the special education pupil who is recovering from illness or accident in the hospital setting. Typically, such instruction is viewed as part of a temporary delivery system (Cartwright, Cartwright, & Ward, 1995). As long-term hospital placements are by far the most restrictive environments available to the handicapped child, the provisions of PL 94-142 and IDEA require increasingly more sophisticated in-district school special education programs and shorter durations for hospital or homebound physically or emotionally handicapped children (Kirk & Gallagher, 1986).

REFERENCES

Cartwright, G.P., Cartwright, C.A., & Ward, M.J. (1995). *Educating special learners* (4th ed.). Belmont, CA: Wadsworth.

Kirk, S.A., & Gallagher, J.J. (1986). *Educating exceptional children* (5th ed.). Boston: Houghton Mifflin.

See also Homebound Instruction; Individuals with Disabilities Education Act (IDEA)

HOUSE-TREE-PERSON (HTP)

The House-Tree-Person (HTP), devised by J.N. Buck (1948, 1966), is a projective drawing technique widely used, albeit controversially, as a measure of personality adjustment in children and adults. Although a variety of administration procedures exist, the individual is typically asked to draw (in pencil) a picture of a house, a tree, and a person, either on a single $81/2 \times 11$ in. sheet of paper or, as originally proposed by Buck, on three separate sheets. An inquiry phase may follow during which the individual is asked to describe and interpret the drawings. A quantitative scoring system was devised by Buck and a set of qualitative interpretations has been provided by Jolle (1971). Bieliauskas (1980) has compiled a bibliography and review of research on the HTP that remains current.

REFERENCES

Bieliauskas, V.J. (1980). *The House-Tree-Person research review.* Los Angeles: Western Psychological Services.

Buck, J.N. (1948). The H-T-P technique: A qualitative and quantitive scoring manual. *Journal of Clinical Psychology, 4,* 317–396.

Buck, N.N. (1966). *The House-Tree-Person technique: Revised manual.* Los Angeles: Western Psychological Services.

Jolle, I. (1971). *A catalogue for the qualitative interpretation of the House-Tree-Person (H-T-P).* Los Angeles: Western Psychological Services.

See also Personality Assessment

HOWE, SAMUEL GRIDLEY (1801–1876)

Samuel Gridley Howe, pioneer educator of the blind and the mentally retarded, was a Massachusetts physician who became superintendent of that state's first school for the blind, which opened in Howe's home in 1832. Later named the Perkins Institution and Massachusetts School for the Blind, Howe's school led in the development of programs to enable blind students to become academically competent, self-reliant, and competitively employable. Howe's most famous student was a deaf-blind child, Laura Bridgeman, and the school's success in educating her led Helen Keller's father (50 years later) to appeal to the Perkins Institution for help, with the result that Anne Sullivan became young Helen's teacher.

Howe published books for the blind, and through appeals to Congress was instrumental in the establishment of the American Printing House for the Blind in 1879. Howe accepted a blind, mentally retarded student in 1839, demonstrated that such a child could be successfully educated, and, in 1848, established an experimental program at Perkins for blind, mentally retarded students. With encouraging results in this program, Howe convinced the legislature that education of the mentally retarded should be a public responsibility, and a state school for the mentally retarded was authorized. That school, established in 1855, became the Walter E. Fernald State School.

REFERENCES

Kanner L. (1964). *A history of the care and study of the mentally retarded.* Springfield, IL: Thomas.

Scheerenberger, R.C. (1983). *A history of mental retardation.* Baltimore, MD: Brookes.

Schwartz, H. (1956). *Samuel Gridley Howe, social reformer.* Cambridge, MA: Harvard University Press.

HUMAN RESOURCE DEVELOPMENT (HRD)

Human resource development (HRD) in special education involves the implementation of approaches and interventions designed to improve the functioning of professionals and paraprofessionals in their delivery of special education services. The need for HRD in special education has been exacerbated by four historical trends and events: (1) the changing nature of special education, (2) burnout of special services providers, (3) new professional and legal requirements, and (4) the increasing demand for special education services. The changing nature of special education is evident in many ways, including the introduction of new technologies such as microcomputers. For special services providers to keep abreast of advances, it is important that they participate in skill and knowledge development activities. Burnout and stress have been recognized as important problems for many types of employees, and a recent review of the literature suggests that special services providers are not exempt from burnout and high levels of job-related stress (Cherniss, 1985).

The HRD approaches and interventions may have the potential for reducing burnout and stress in special education by enriching the work experience of special services providers. The significance of HRD for special education is further underscored by changing professional and legal requirements. The advent of PL 94-142, for example, placed new demands on many special services providers such as multidisciplinary team decision making. It has been argued (Yoshida, 1980) that special services providers and others may have been ill prepared to participate in team decision making. The need for HRD in special education is evident from the increasing demand for special education services. As Sarason (1982) has noted, it is unlikely that traditional approaches to training will be able to generate the number of individuals needed to provide the requested services. Therefore, it is also important to engage various nonprofes-

sional groups (e.g., classroom instructional aides, parents, and even students) in special education HRD.

REFERENCES

Cherniss, C. (1985). Stress, burnout, and the special services providers. *Special Services in the Schools, 2,* 45–61.

Sarason, S.B. (1982). *The culture of the school and the problem of change* (2nd ed.). Boston: Allyn & Bacon.

Yoshida, R.K. (1980). Multidisciplinary decision making in special education: Review of the issues. *School Psychology Review, 9,* 221–227.

See also **Multidisciplinary Teams; Personnel Training in Special Education**

HUMPHREY, ELLIOTT S. (1888–1981)

Elliott S. (Jack) Humphrey, after early experiences as a jockey and a cowboy, made a career of the breeding and training of animals. He trained lions and tigers for circuses, and bred some of the dogs used by Admiral Richard E. Byrd in his Antarctic expedition. Dorothy Eustis, who later founded The Seeing Eye, the first American organization to train dogs as guides for the blind, hired Humphrey to breed and train guide dogs for the blind. His teaching methods are credited with the immediate success of The Seeing Eye when it was established in 1928. His methods are used today by more than half a dozen other programs that train guide dogs. Faced with difficulty in finding competent instructors for The Seeing Eye, Humphrey designed and operated a school for instructors that provided not only teachers needed at The Seeing Eye but staff for other guide-dog programs as well. Humphrey published a book on the breeding of working dogs, and lectured on his specialty at Columbia University. During World War II he served as a commander in the Coast Guard, with responsibility for organizing and directing a school for dog trainers for the armed forces.

REFERENCES

Humphrey, E.S., & Warner, L.H. (1934). *Working dogs.* Baltimore, MD: Johns Hopkins University Press.

Putnam, P.B. (1979). *Love in the lead.* New York: Dutton.

HUNGERFORD, RICHARD H. (1903–1974)

Richard H. Hungerford, a leader in the field of mental retardation, served from 1942 to 1953 as director of the Bureau for Children with Retarded Mental Development in the New York City public schools. Subsequently he was superintendent of the Laconia, New Hampshire, State School; executive director of the Gulf Bend Center for Children and Youth in Victoria, Texas; executive director of Mental Health and Mental Retardation Services for the diocese of Galveston-Houston; and professor of special education at Boston University.

During the 1940s, Hungerford developed for New York City's schools a comprehensive curriculum for mentally retarded students that emphasized specific occupational preparation, training in home living skills, and activities aimed at the development of social competence. In 1943 he co-founded, with Chris J. DeProspo, *Occupational Education,* a journal for teachers of mentally retarded pupils. Hungerford's thoughtful writings, especially his beautifully written essays, such as "On Locusts," inspired both laymen and colleagues in the field of mental retardation. Hungerford served as president of the American Association on Mental Deficiency and was editor of its *American Journal of Mental Deficiency* from 1948 to 1959.

REFERENCES

Blatt, B. (1975). Toward an understanding of people with special needs: Three teachers. In J.M. Kauffman & J.S. Payne (Eds.), *Mental retardation: Introduction and personal perspectives.* Columbus, OH: Merrill.

Hungerford, R.H. (1950). On locusts. *American Journal of Mental Deficiency, 54,* 415–418.

HUNT, JOSEPH MCVICKER (1906–1991)

Joseph McVicker Hunt was born in Scottsbluff, Nebraska, on March 19, 1906. He attended the University of Nebraska, receiving his BA degree there in 1929 and his MA in 1930. He then received his PhD degree in 1933 from Cornell University. On graduating, he became a National Research Council fellow in psychology, spending the year 1933–1934 at New York Psychiatric Institute and Columbia University and 1934–1935 at Worcester State Hospital and Clark University. After a year as visiting assistant professor of psychology at the University of Nebraska in 1935, Hunt went to Brown University as an instructor in psychology in 1936, advancing to assistant professor in 1938 and associate professor in 1944. While at Brown, Hunt became associated with Butler Hospital in Providence, Rhode Island, acting as research associate (1944–1946) and as director (1946–1951). In 1951, Hunt joined the department of psychology at the University of Illinois as professor of psychology, a position he held until gaining Professor Emeritus status in 1974. Hunt died in 1991.

Hunt is well-known for his many studies in child psychology. Aside from being professor of psychology, he was also professor of early education at the University of Illinois (1967–1974). He was chair of the White House Task Force on Early Childhood Education and was instrumental in the preparation of the report "A Bill of Rights for Children." That report recommended extending Head Start programs to very young children and promoted a follow-through program that would extend the age limits of Head Start children.

Hunt's long list of publications have dealt with problems of clinical psychology, child psychology, social casework, personality and behavior disorders, and intelligence.

REFERENCES

Hunt, J.McV. (1950). *Measuring results in social casework: A comparison of diagnostic and functional casework concepts.* New York: Family Service Association of America.

Hunt, J.McV. (1965). *Intrinsic motivation and its role in psychological development.* Proceedings of the Nebraska Symposium on Motivation. Lincoln: University of Nebraska Press.

Hunt, J.McV. (1986). Effect of variations in quality and type of early child care on development. *New Directions for Child Development, No. 32,* 31–48.

Hunt, J.McV. (1987). Effects of differing kinds of experience in early rearing conditions. In I.C. Uzgiris & J.McV. Hunt (Eds.), *Infant performance and experience: New findings with the ordinal scales.* Urbana, IL: University of Illinois Press.

Hunt, J.McV. (1988). Relevance to educability: Heritability or range of reaction. In S.G. Cole & R.G. Demaree (Eds.), *Applications of interactionist psychology: Essays in honor of Saul B. Sells.* Hillsdale, NJ: Erlbaum.

HUNTER'S SYNDROME (MUCOPOLY SACCHARIDOSIS II)

Hunter's syndrome (mucopoly saccharidosis II), which belongs to a general family of mucopolysaccharide disorders (including Hurler, Scherie, Hurler-Scheire, Marquio, and Sanfillipo Syndromes; Brown & Trivette, 1998), is transmitted as an X-linked recessive trait that occurs primarily in males. Growth during the first 2 years is normal, with malformations occurring during years 2 to 4. There are two types of Hunter's syndrome, A (severe) and B (mild). In type A, there is no clouding of corneas and death usually occurs before year 15. Concomitant mental retardation and learning levels are higher than for children with Hurler's syndrome (Carter, 1978). However, behavior disorders and hyperactive and destructive behavior are often seen as a result, and the children tend to become difficult to manage as they mature. With type B, survival rates may extend to age 50, with fair intelligence possible. (Wortis, 1981).

Children having Hunter's syndrome will appear short in stature with stiff joints and a large abdomen (associated with enlarged organs like the spleen and liver). Children have a large head, prominent forehead, long skull, and coarse eyebrows. Thick lips, broad flat nose, and misaligned teeth are seen as the child develops. Hairiness, especially in brows and lashes, is characteristic and usually apparent by 2 to 4 years of age. Hands are clawlike, with short and stubby fingers; stiff hands and feet may present mobility and coordination problems (Lemeshaw, 1982).

Mental retardation occurs in varying degrees but because development is normal to age 2 or beyond, cognitive and verbal capabilities may be higher than in other syndromes having similar physical characteristics. Motor retardation may be more likely as the child matures. Seizures also have been noted in older children. Progressive nerve deafness and occasional vision problems are present in some Hunter's syndrome children (Illingworth, 1983). Many learning-disabled like symptoms (low attention span, hyperkinesis, negative behavior) may also be displayed.

Health and behavior problems, coupled with the motoric and mental disabilities that occur later in development, may require placement in a more restricted setting than the regular classroom. Visual, speech, and hearing impairments that may occur will need to be assessed and remediated by a special education specialist. Physical and occupational therapy may also be necessary. Hunter's Syndrome is quite rare, occurring in about 1 per 140,000 male births (Brown & Trivette, 1998).

REFERENCES

Brown, M.B., & Trivette, P.S. (1998). Mucopolysaccharide disorders. In L. Phelps (Eds.), *Health-related disorders in children and adolescents.* Washington, DC: American Psychological Association.

Carter, C. (Ed.). (1978). *Medical aspects of mental retardation* (2nd ed.). Springfield, IL: Thomas.

Lemeshaw, S. (1982). *The handbook of clinical types in mental retardation.* Boston: Houghton Mifflin.

Wortis, J. (Ed.). (1981). *Mental retardation and developmental disabilities: An annual review.* New York: Brunner/Mazel.

See also **Hurler's Syndrome; Mental Retardation; Physical Anomalies**

HUNTINGTON'S CHOREA (HC)

Huntington's chorea, or Huntington's disease, is a degenerative condition, the progression of which is insidious. Its onset generally occurs between 25 and 50 years of age and is characterized by involuntary, irregular, jerking movements (i.e., chorea). Although the condition is often not correctly diagnosed until the onset of the chorea, Bellamy (1961) found that 29% of his patients manifested emotional disturbance prior to the abnormal motor movements. As the disease progresses, mental deterioration occurs and, after 10 to 20 years, ends with the death of the afflicted individual.

Huntington's chorea is rare; most prevalence studies agree that it occurs in from 4 to 7 individuals per 100,000 in the population. Although it was long thought not to occur among certain ethnic groups (e.g., Jewish families), such is not the case. However, it is apparently true that, among Japanese, the disease occurs at a much lower rate (about .4 per 100,000).

The major symptoms of the disease had been reported in earlier literature by several individuals: Charles O. Waters in 1841, Charles L. Gorman in 1848, George B. Wood in 1855, and Irving W. Lyon in 1863. Nevertheless, George S. Huntington is widely considered to deserve the use of his name in the medical nomenclature because his 1872 description of the symptoms of the disease was so accurate (DeJong, 1973).

Huntington's chorea is transmitted by a dominant autosome. That is, half of the children of a parent who carries the gene will become afflicted (Coleman, 1964). The prevalence could be reduced to zero in one generation if affected individuals would forego bearing children. Nevertheless, this solution is difficult to implement because the carrier is often unaware of the problem until after the prime reproductive years. In addition, since the disease originates as a defective gene mutation, abstinence on the part of the gene carrier from parenthood remains only a partial solution. Unfortunately, there is no cure for Huntington's chorea.

The juvenile form of HC is rare and represents about 5% of cases of HC. Slurred speech and dysasthria are the most easily recognized symptoms in children but diagnosis is very difficult before age 20. Depression and anxiety are especially prominent in juvenile HC and seizures develop in 25 times more cases of juvenile HC (50%) as compared to adult HC (2%). Special education is typically required, but symptom management is the only form of treatment (Nation, Turk, & Reynolds, 1998).

REFERENCES

Bellamy, W.E., Jr. (1961). Huntington's chorea. *North Carolina Medical Journal, 22,* 409–412.

Coleman, J.C. (1964). *Abnormal psychology and modern life* (3rd ed.). Chicago: Scott, Foresman.

DeJong, R.N. (1973). The history of Huntington's chorea in the United States of America. In A. Barbeau, T. Chase, & G.W. Paulson (Eds.), *Advances in neurology—Huntington's chorea* (Vol. 1). New York: Raven.

Nation, P. Turk, K. & Reynolds, C.R. (1998). Huntington's disease. In L. Phelps (Ed.), *Health-selected disorders in children and adolescents* (pp. 337–42). Washington, DC: American Psychological Association.

See also **Chorea; Genetic Counseling**

HURLER'S SYNDROME

Hurler's syndrome (gargoylism; lipochondrodstrophy), a mucopolysaccharide disorder of the same family as Hunter's syndrome, is an inherited metabolic disorder that can affect an individual's physical or mental development. There are two distinct forms of this disease (Stanbury, Wyngaarden, & Fredrickson, 1966). The milder form of this disorder results from an inherited sex-linked recessive gene commonly carried by the X chromosome of the twenty-third pair of chromosomes. It is more likely to be expressed in the male population. The more severe form is inherited by way of an autosomal recessive gene that may affect any one of the 22 genes inherited from either parent (Robinson & Robinson, 1965).

In its milder form, clinical indicators of Hurler's may not be evident at birth, although symptoms generally begin to appear by 6 months of age. By 2 years of age, affected children may reflect retarded physical or mental growth. In its more severe form, individuals may manifest a variety of physical characteristics. Owing to a build up of mucopolysaccharides throughout the body, abnormal growths will result. Tissues in the liver, heart, lungs, and spleen are most often the areas affected. Abnormal lipid deposits may result in lesions in the gray matter of the brain. Even in its severe form, this genetic defect accounts for less than 1% of the severe mental retardation in children.

Physical characteristics of this disorder typically include an underdeveloped body with significant disproportion between the head and body. Limbs are short and mobility may be limited as fingers and toes are often fixed in a partial flexed position. Bone abnormalities may affect the vertebrae and result in a shortened neck and protruding belly, with possible umbilical hernia.

Individuals severely affected by Hurler's disease often have an enlarged head and protruding forehead. Facial characteristics may include bushy eyebrows, a saddle-shaped nose, double chin, and enlarged tongue. The more common form of this disorder is characterized by dwarfism and corneal clouding. In this more severe form of the disorder, individuals may live only into their teens, with death resulting from heart failure or respiratory disease. In milder cases, there is an absence of corneal clouding and dwarfism, but there is a high frequency of deafness from nerve damage.

Recent diagnostic advances in detecting fetal abnormalities have accurately confirmed the presence of Hurler's as early as 14 to 16 weeks into gestation. This diagnosis is made on the basis of finding elevated levels of the compound mucopolysaccharide in amniotic fluid (Henderson & Whiteman, 1976). A positive in vitro diagnosis of Hurler's syndrome is questionable owing to the variety of related diseases. As advances are made in microtechnology, the efficacy of in vitro diagnosis will increase.

REFERENCES

Henderson, H., & Whiteman, P. (1976). Antenatal diagnoses of Hurler's disease. *Lancet, 2,* 1024–1025.

Robinson, H.B., & Robinson, N.M. (1965). *The mentally retarded child.* New York: McGraw-Hill.

Stanbury, J.B., Wyngaarden, J.B., & Fredrickson, D.S. (Eds.). (1966). *The metabolic bases of inherited diseases* (2nd ed.). New York: McGraw-Hill.

See also Amniocentesis; Chromosomal Abnormalities; Hunter's Syndrome

HYDROCEPHALUS

Hydrocephalus is a condition in which there is an abnormal accumulation of cerebrospinal fluid within the skull. As the fluid accumulates, the upper portion of the skull gradually increases in size out of proportion to the rest of the body. Left untreated, the condition usually produces several sequelae that end in the death of the patient. The three primary causes of the accumulation of fluid are overproduction of cerebrospinal fluid, defective absorption of the fluid, and interference with the circulation of the fluid. Underlying causes of the accumulation are often associated with meningitis, spina bifida, or tumors.

Although the pathology was not fully understood, the basic approach to the treatment of hydrocephalus has been known for at least 150 years. For example, Meindl, cited by Jordan (1972), recounted two successful surgical treatments of hydrocephalus by tapping the ventricles of the brain as early as 1829. However, the procedure, which was introduced by a Dr. Conquest, was criticized and eventually abandoned. Unfortunately, the technology that would make successful treatment commonplace was not to become available until the 1950s.

Many ingenious procedures have been devised to diagnose and treat hydrocephalus. MRI now provides definitive evidence for diagnosis.

An early treatment approach reported by Ingraham and Matson (1954) is the ventriculo-ureterostomy procedure, in which, following the removal of one kidney, the ventricular cavity of the skull is connected to the ureter via a plastic tube. Thus, the excess cerebrospinal fluid is drained into the bladder and evacuated along with the urine produced by the remaining kidney. This procedure and the others to follow are referred to as shunt procedures because the excess fluid is diverted from the cranium to a part of the body that can absorb or excrete it. The two procedures most common today both employ a unidirectional valve (usually the Hakim or the Prudenz, sometimes in combination with the anti-siphon valve). In ventriculo-atrial shunting, the cerebrospinal fluid is diverted to the right atrium of the heart. When the ventriculo-peritoneal shunt is used, the fluid is passed into the peritoneal cavity (stomach).

Although successful shunts often result in the arrest of the normal course of the condition, three problems may complicate the treatment: 1) extreme care is necessary to avoid infection; 2) revision or replacement of a valve is necessary when it becomes blocked or malfunctions in some way, and the tube used to drain the fluid may become dislodged and require adjustments; and, 3) epilepsy is a frequent sequela to operative treatment and shunt-related infection (Blaauw, 1978).

REFERENCES

Blaauw, G. (1978). Hydrocephalus and epilepsy. In R. Wullenweber, H. Wenker, M. Brock, & M. Klinger (Eds.), *Treatment of hydrocephalus—Computer tomography* (pp. 37–41). Berlin: Springer-Verlag.

Ingraham, F.D., & Matson, D.M. (1954). *Neurosurgery of infancy and childhood.* Springfield, IL: Thomas.

Jordan, T.E. (1972). *The mentally retarded* (3rd ed.). Columbus, OH: Merrill.

See also Meningitis; Spina Bifida

HYPERACTIVITY

See ATTENTION-DEFICIT HYPERACTIVITY DISORDER.

HYPERCALCEMIA

See INFANTILE HYPERCALCEMIA.

HYPERKINESIS

Hyperkinesis, previously believed to be a behavioral pattern associated with neurological dysfunction, is an archaic diagnostic classification for children with a high degree of activity combined with disordered or unmanageable behavior. It is now subsumed under the classification of Attention-Deficit Hyperactivity Disorder.

HYPERLEXIA

Hyperlexia is a condition characterized by precocious word calling skills that exceed levels of performance expected on the basis of intellectual ability. Although reading, or word calling, skills are high, there is usually poor reading comprehension. The condition has been reported since the 1940s (Bergman & Escalona, 1948), with more reports in the next decade (Eisenberg & Kanner, 1956). The term hyperlexia was first used by Silberberg and Silberberg (1967), who suggested that the condition might be related to a neurological abnormality characterized by advanced development of specific brain functions. As recently as 1969, Cain reviewed the literature to date and concluded that there was no explanation for the phenomenon. Since that time there have been a number of studies of hyperlexic children (Hartlage & Hartlage, 1973; Richman & Kitchell, 1981), but there is still no consensus concerning the exact nature or etiology of the condition.

REFERENCES

Bergman, P. & Escalona, S. (1948). Unusual sensitivities in very young children. *Psychoanalytic Study of the Child.* New York: International Universities Press.

Eisenberg, L., & Kanner, L. (1956). Early infantile autism, 1943–1955. *American Journal of Orthopsychiatry, 26,* 556–566.

Hartlage, L.C., & Hartlage, P.L. (1973, May). *Hyperlexia in severely, moderately, and mildly retarded children.* Paper presented at American Association on Mental Deficiency, Minneapolis.

Richman, L.C., & Kitchell, M.M. (1981). Hyperlexia as a variant of developmental language disorder. *Brain & Language, 12,* 203–212.

Silberberg, N.E., & Silberberg, M.C. (1967). Hyperlexia: Specific word recognition skills in young children. *Exceptional Children, 34,* 41–42.

See also Reading Disorders; Reading Remediation

HYPEROPIA

Hyperopia is a visual disorder that results from an error of refraction. Refraction is a process by which light rays are gathered and focused onto certain portions of the retina. The hyperopic eye is too short and too weak to allow this process to take place normally (Heward & Orlansky, 1984). As a result, hyperopia develops. This impedes near vision and is commonly referred to as farsightedness.

The average, normal infant is born farsighted. As the child matures, the hyperopia decreases. This is especially true during puberty, when children who began life without the hyperopic trait will become nearsighted (Michelson, 1980). Children who are left with some farsightedness will become aware of it at different times depending on severity or occupational demands.

Hyperopia is easily treated through the prescription of glasses or contact lenses. However, if untreated, hyperopia can have significant impact on classroom performance. Since a hyperopic student will have difficulty in focusing on near objects, it may become difficult to perform certain academic functions.

REFERENCES

Heward, W.L., & Orlansky, M.D. (1984). *Exceptional children.* Columbus, OH: Merrill.

Michelson, P.E. (1980). *Insight into eyesight.* Chicago: Nelson-Hall.

See also Visual Acuity; Visual Efficiency

HYPERTELORISM

Hypertelorism is a descriptive term designating wide orbital separation characterized by separation of the eyes. This represents a retention of the wide, primitive inter-orbital angle. While early studies suggested a single cause, subsequent evaluations show great variety in the clinical and radiologic appearances of the skull. The condition is distinguished from telecanthus (lateral displacement of the medical canthal tissue), where the interocular (between the eyes) distance is normal (Duke-Elder, 1963).

Divergent strabismus is the most common associated ocular disorder, although other abnormalities such as microphthalmos, microcornea, and optic atrophy may occur. Mentation is generally good and most patients are described as even-tempered and gentle.

The significance of this anomaly is minimal to the educator except as a clue to other developmental defects. In general, the eye, face and brain develop concurrently; defects in one area suggest the possibility of defects in another. Only if associated with ocular or central nervous system defects would this anomaly be of particular significance.

REFERENCE

Duke-Elder, S. (1963). *System of ophthalmology: Vol. III, Part 2, Congenital deformities.* St. Louis: Mosby.

HYPERTHYROIDISM

Hyperthyroidism is an endocrinological disorder that is characterized by excessive functional activity in the production of thyroid hormones. The resulting condition is generally marked by increased metabolic rate, protrusion of the eyes, enlargement of the thyroid gland, high blood pressure, and rapid heart rate. Other symptoms may include an exaggerated startle response and quick, jerky movements of the extremities, face, and neck. Increased agitation and behavioral problems may appear (Hutchens & White, 1998). This disease is genetically determined, runs in families, affects females more than males, and requires a physician's diagnosis and subsequent treatment. Parents, teachers, and the school psychologist should work closely with the child's physician in providing intervention (Gardner, 1969).

Children with congenital hyperthyroidism have been observed to be restless, to overeat without weight gain, and to experience high temperatures. Hyperthyroidism is extremely rare before age 5; approximately 10% of patients are under 10. Although females have a disproportionate representation of 6:1 over males, the prevalency is equal between the sexes for children ages 10 to 15 years. The disorder progresses rapidly from early symptoms to the expression of behavioral problems and subsequent decline in school performance. Accelerated body growth without modification of final height has been reported (Mornex & Orgiazzi, 1980).

Confusion of hyperthyroidism with emotional disorders is common and necessitates a careful diagnosis by a physician. Research has shown that abnormally high levels of thyroid hormones in the body are associated with and may precipitate psychopathology in hyperthyroidism (Zeitlhofer, Saletu, Stary, & Ahmandi, 1984). Psychopathology sometimes masks the underlying disorder of hyperthyroidism, and the aberrant behavior diminishes following antihyperthyroid treatment. It is assumed that the chemical imbalance inhibits efficient processing of the central nervous system and that pathological behaviors result.

Treatment of hyperthyroidism is either ablative (surgery, radioactive iodine) or conservative (drug therapy), or a combination of both. When a tumor is thought to be the cause of hyperthyroidism, surgery is necessary. However, the removal of the thyroid gland then may reverse its symptomatology, resulting in hypothyroidism. Antihyperthyroid medication is generally the treatment of choice, in combination with supportive counseling.

Prognosis is poor owing to the lack of a completely satisfactory treatment. The disorder is probably lifelong and requires lengthy treatment. Special educators should work closely with the physician and school psychologist in adapting the educational environment to the unique needs of the child with hyperthyroidism.

REFERENCES

Gardner, L. (1969). *Endocrine and genetic disease in childhood.* Philadelphia: Saunders.

Hutchens, T., & White, J. (1998). Metabolic disorders. In L. Phelps (Ed.), *Health-related disorders of children and adolescents.* Washington, DC: American Psychological Association.

Mornex, R., & Orgiazzi, J.J. (1980). Hyperthyroidism. In M. De Visscher (Ed.), *The thyroid gland* (pp. 275–369). New York: Raven.

Zeitlhofer, J., Saletu, B., Stary, J., & Ahmandi, R. (1984). Cerebral function in hyperthyroid patients: Psychopathology, psychometric variables, central arousal and time perception before and after thyreostatic therapy. *Neuropsychobiology, 2,* 89–93.

See also **Emotional Disorders; Hypothyroidism**

HYPERTONIA

Hypertonia, or hypertonicity, is a nonspecific state of increased skeletal muscle tone or partial contraction. The term often is used interchangeably with spasticity, but spasticity generally is viewed as a more pronounced degree of pathologic hypertonicity. Hypertonia occurs because of excessive motor unit activity within the muscle fibers; it is an indicator of neurologic dysfunction. Hypertonia is best represented by a continuum, from slightly above normal muscle tone to severely rigid. Muscle tone is often variable throughout different locations of the body. A person's level of arousal, body position in relation to gravity, and activity often will influence the degree of hypertonia that is present.

See also **Hypotonia; Physical Disabilities**

HYPNOSIS

While no generally accepted definition exists, hypnosis is usually considered to be an altered state of consciousness characterized by a heightened susceptibility to suggestion. As an altered state of consciousness, hypnosis is seen as a condition distinct from sleep or wakefulness, perhaps similar to deep meditation, yoga, or some other trancelike state. The heightened susceptibility characteristic relates to the observation that the hypnotized person accepts ideas more uncritically and wholeheartedly than ordinarily (American Society of Clinical Hypnosis, 1973).

Little agreement about the nature of hypnosis exists among the authorities in the field. Numerous competing theories have been proposed, but none seem to explain adequately the phenomenon and no theory has gained wide acceptance. Many theories fit into one of two categories, physiological and psychological. Physiological theories of hypnosis emphasize physical changes that are reported to occur during or as a result of hypnosis: alteration in metabolism, changes in the nervous system, and unusual electrical activity in the brain. Psychological theories stress the importance of psychological factors: learning, suggestion, role-playing, and modeling.

Ernest R. Hilgard, a leader in the scientific study of hypnosis, has proposed a neodissociation theory, which holds that hypnotic procedures rearrange control systems in the brain (Hilgard, 1977). Research by Hilgard and others supports this model. However, at the present time, the scientific understanding of hypnosis is at an early stage of development.

Regardless of the true nature of hypnosis, it can be used to produce some conditions in a subject that are helpful and therapeutic: relaxation, concentration, the ability to put oneself in imaginary situations, and the capacity to accept suggestions more fully. These conditions provide a basis for the application of hypnosis to the treatment of a number of medical and psychological problems.

Hypnosis has been used successfully alone or in combination with other treatment methods in dealing with the following: emotional problems, including anxiety; control of pain; surgery; psychosomatic problems; obesity and dietary problems; smoking; pediatric problems; neurological problems; rehabilitation; conditions related to obstetrics and gynecology; skin problems; sexual dysfunction; and dental procedures. Practical application of hypnosis is extensive.

REFERENCES

American Society of Clinical Hypnosis–Education and Research Foundation. (1973). *A syllabus on hypnosis and a handbook of therapeutic suggestions.* Des Plains, IL: Author.

Hilgard, E.R. (1977). *Divided consciousness.* New York: Wiley.

See also **Psychosocial Adjustment; Psychotherapy**

HYPOACTIVITY

Hypoactivity is a condition characterized by insufficient or inadequate motor activity and the inability to focus and sustain attention on external stimuli. Myers and Hammill (1969) describe the hypoactive child as one who is lethargic and quiet, and who causes little disturbance in the classroom. These children are more difficult to recognize and identify than are their hyperactive counterparts, and their problems may escape detection.

Although hyperactive and hypoactive children are at opposite ends of an activity level continuum, both show attentional deficits that may interfere with learning. Dykman, Ackerman, Clements, and Peters (1971) discuss the child who is unable to focus attention on the written or spoken word, and who, therefore, cannot easily learn to read or spell. Most frequently, such attention deficits take the form of impulsivity and overreaction to stimuli. However, in the case of hypoactive children, inhibition, passivity, and underreaction to stimuli are symptomatic of the deficit.

The Russian psychologist A.R. Luria (1959, 1961) has written extensively on attention deficits, and has addressed the problem of hypoactivity specifically. He refers to the syndrome of cerebral asthenia, characterized by an inability to concentrate, distractibility, and short attention span. Luria points out that this syndrome often can be expressed in two externally different but essentially similar forms. He states that nervous processes are reducible to the two basic components of excitation and inhibition, present in all individuals. The strength, concentration, equilibrium, and mobility of excitation and inhibition may be affected by brain pathology. If the pathological state of the cortical cells primarily affects the inhibitory processes, the child displays excessive impulsivity and the loss of control associated with hyperactivity. However, if the pathology is expressed in a decline of the excitatory processes, the child experiences a sharp fall of the tone of the nervous processes and enters into a state of passivity. Luria refers to such children as inhibitory types and describes them as sluggish, torpid, and slow to form new positive reactions to stimuli, much like the hypoactive, learning-disabled child.

Although the literature reflects considerable research focused on hyperactivity, there have been relatively few studies dealing with the hypoactive child. Luria (1961) investigated the role of speech as an influence on the disequilibrium between the basic nervous processes. In experiments that required sustained, focused attention, he found inhibited children failed to make correct motoric responses to stimuli. However, when these children were asked to respond verbally as well as motorically, the accuracy and frequency of their responses increased significantly. Luria concluded that the combination of verbal and motoric responses tones up the activity level of the child, and that the compensatory influence of speech serves to heighten the level of the excitatory processes.

REFERENCES

Dykman, R.A., Ackerman, P.T., Clements, S.D., & Peters, J.E. (1971). Specific learning disabilities: An attentional deficit syndrome. In H.R. Myklebust (Ed.), *Progress in learning disabilities* (Vol. 2, pp. 56–94). New York: Grune & Stratton.

Luria, A.R. (1959). Experimental study of the higher nervous activity of the abnormal child. *Journal of Mental Deficiency Research, 3,* 1–22.

Luria, A.R. (1961). *The role of speech in the regulation of normal and abnormal behavior.* New York: Liveright.

Myers, P.I., & Hammill, D.D. (1969). *Methods for learning disorders.* New York: Wiley.

See also **Attention-Deficit Hyperactivity Disorder; Attention Span**

HYPOGLYCEMIA

Hypoglycemia is a physiological disorder in which a sudden rise and then rapid decrease in blood glucose level occurs within 1 to 3 hours. This abrupt drop in blood glucose sends the body into a condition of near shock that may be exacerbated by stress (Sorochan, 1981). Concomitant symptomatology may include lethargic behavior (unmotivated, fatigued, withdrawn, depressed); erratic behavior (mental confusion, unprovoked anxiety, hyperactivity, aggression); and a craving for sweets (Knapczyk, 1979). This condition of low blood glucose level marks the disorder of hypoglycemia. It is differentiated from hyperglycemia, in which the body has abnormally high blood glucose levels.

The diagnosis of hypoglycemia is made by a physician, who measures the blood glucose level at different times (e.g., before eating, immediately after eating, and a few hours after eating). Before eating, the level is low; it rises after eating and then falls after a few hours. If the rate of the drop in blood glucose level exceeds the normal range for the individual's age group, then the diagnosis of hypoglycemia is positive.

Some researchers have investigated the relationship between hypoglycemia and behavioral disorders (Knapczyk, 1979) and aggression and psychiatric symptoms (Virkkunen, 1982). Many researchers have concentrated on the area of diet, particularly the reduction of carbohydrates. One of the most effective treatments of hypoglycemia may be a well-controlled elimination diet that advocates six or more meals a day instead of three. The intention is to reduce sugar consumption as well as decrease the amount of time in which the individual is in the low blood glucose state.

Even though hypoglycemia should be diagnosed by a physician, school administrators, psychologists, and teachers also should be aware of the disorder. Consistent observation of a child's erratic behavior following eating may indicate hypoglycemia, and referral to a physician may be in order.

REFERENCES

Knapczyk, D.R. (1979). Diet control in the management of behavior disorders. *Behavioral Disorders, 1,* 2–9.

Sorochan, W.D. (1981). *Promoting your health.* New York: Wiley.

Virkkunen, M. (1982). Reactive hypoglycemic tendency among habitually violent offenders: A further study by means of the glucose tolerance test. *Neuropsychobiology, 1,* 35–40.

See also Acting Out; Behavioral Disorders; Diabetes

HYPOTHYROIDISM

Congenital hypothyroidism is an endocrinological disorder resulting from a deficient production of thyroid hormones. If left untreated for a period of 1 to 3 months postnatally, severe mental retardation occurs. Acquired hypothyroidism in childhood does not have as devastating an effect on intelligence as the congenital form. However, this condition is associated with fatigue, poor growth, cold intolerance, aggressive behavior, and depression. Research has shown that acquired hypothyroidism impairs psychological, neurological, and behavioral patterns (Gardner, 1969).

There appear to be sufficient data to support the hypothesis of critical periods of brain development that require adequate supplies of thyroid hormones (Hulse, 1983). The fetus is largely dependent on its own thyroid gland because little of the mother's thyroxine crosses the placenta. Thyroid hormones have been determined to be critical in the development of the central nervous system. It has been postulated that even before birth, hypothyroidism may cause cerebral and cerebellar impairment. Current research is examining the extent to which changes in brain-behavioral relationships are reversible through early treatment. Evidence suggests that early diagnosis through neonatal screening and subsequent treatment is of major importance for the prevention of lifelong complications of congenital hypothyroidism.

The effects of hypothyroidism on the developing brain are accumulated through complex interactions. The diversity and speed at which brain growth is delayed by the absence or lack of thyroid hormones adversely affects dendritic growth and synaptic connections (Birrell, Frost, & Parkin, 1983). The overall consequence is severe mental retardation.

Hulse (1983) reported that early researchers investigating hypothyroidism recognized that both age and severity of the retardation were important variables at the time of treatment, but were not always predictive in the assumed direction. Later, more detailed studies demonstrated the need for treatment prior to 1 to 3 months postnatally for good prognosis of congenital hypothyroidism (Rovet, Westbrook, & Ehrlich, 1984). The diagnosis and treatment are conducted by a physician. School personnel should work closely with the physician in designing and implementing intervention programs.

A good prognosis will stem from continued early diagnosis and treatment from routine neonatal screening. The successfully treated cases have had normal intelligence, some behavioral disorders, and minor motor incoordination. If remedial programs are required, careful delineation of the child's strengths and weaknesses may indicate specific interventions. Participation in the daily activities of school and its general milieu will promote mental and physical growth of the child with treated hypothyroidism.

REFERENCES

Birrell, J., Frost, G.J., & Parkin, J.M. (1983). The development of children with congenital hypothyroidism. *Developmental Medicine & Child Neurology, 4,* 512–519.

Gardner, L. (1969). *Endocrine and genetic disease in childhood.* Philadelphia: Saunders.

Hulse, A. (1983). Congenital hypothyroidism and neurological development. *Journal of Child Psychology & Psychiatry, 4,* 629–635.

Rovet, J.F., Westbrook, D.C., & Ehrlich, R.M. (1984). Neonatal thyroid deficiency: Early temperamental and cognitive characteristics. *Journal of the American Academy of Child Psychiatry, 1,* 10–22.

See also Hypoactivity; Hypoglycemia

HYPOTONIA

Hypotonia, or hypotonicity, is a nonspecific state of decreased skeletal muscle tone or partial contraction. The term may occasionally be used interchangeably with flaccidity, but flaccidity is generally viewed as an absence of muscle tone. Hypotonia occurs because of reduced motor unit activity within the muscle fibers. It is an indicator of neurologic dysfunction or muscle disease. Hypotonia is best represented by a continuum, from slightly below normal muscle tone to complete flaccidity; it is often variable throughout different locations of the body. Although hypotonia occurs in the absence of voluntary control, a person's level of arousal, body position in relation to gravity, and activity may influence the degree of hypotonia that is present.

Some people may have a lower state of normal muscle tone (resulting in poor posture), but this is generally not considered to be pathologic hypotonicity. Normal muscle tone is a state of tension or partial contraction that provides postural stability and allows a person to maintain himself or herself in an upright position against the force of gravity. When damage occurs to parts of the central nervous system (CNS), especially the cerebellum of the brain, hypotonia may be seen in the trunk or extremities. Peripheral nerve injuries typically result in flaccidity in the involved extremity. Some congenital impairments or syndromes such as muscular dystrophy or Down's syndrome have varying degrees of muscular hypotonia. The decreased muscle tone associated with hypotonia reduces the amount of stability and increases the mobility in the joints of the affected extremity. This decreased stability and increased mobility reduce the postural capacity of the individual and often makes movement of body parts more strenuous.

Treatment for hypotonia includes a variety of surgical or therapeutic approaches. Splinting and bracing may be used to prevent spinal curvature and permanent deformity, but these approaches only address the symptoms and not the condition itself. Physical management or manipulation techniques such as neurodevelopmental treatment (NDT) and proprioceptive neuromuscular facilitation (PNF) also have been tried, but the effectiveness has been less than with hypertonia. When permanent orthopedic deformities occur secondary to hypotonia, orthopedic surgery may be necessary to insert a pin or surgically fuse the spine or other joints to prevent further deformity or dislocation. Educational performance may be influenced by hypotonia in regard to activities involving sensory motor functioning. Hypotonia may be mild enough to have no discernible effect on educational performance or may be so severe as to prevent a person from sitting or holding his or her head upright. Mental retardation or other disturbances in intellectual functioning may exist concurrently with hypotonia, requiring multidisciplinary educational intervention.

See also **Muscular Dystrophy**

HYPOXIA

Hypoxia means lowered levels of oxygen intake. Lowered oxygen levels cause changes in pH balance, energy use, and tissue perfusion (Freeman, 1985a). The degree of change varies with the duration and severity of the episode. In extreme, it can lead to death. Hypoxia may occur in infants (1) requiring mechanical ventilation because their lungs are unable to absorb inspired oxygen; (2) with recurring apnea; (3) with heart disorders that prevent oxygenated blood from reaching vital tissues; and, more rarely (4) with severe anemia. In the last case, the underlying factor is the blood's inability to transport oxygen even though the heart and lungs are functioning normally (Parry & Adams, 1985).

Neonatal hypoxia may cause irreversible damage, especially to the brain. Developing brain tissue is particularly susceptible to lowered oxygen levels as well as other insults. The effects of hypoxia are highly variable; some infants who experience hypoxia do poorly, but most recover well. Recent research suggests a threshold effect: A range of degrees of hypoxia can be tolerated without obvious effect, but severity beyond the threshold produces damaging effects. Normal term infants of normal weight are presumed to have the highest threshold, and thus can best withstand minor degrees of hypoxia. Conditions that lower the threshold are those that "weaken" the infant and his or her ability to handle stress. Two such conditions are prematurity and low birth weight (Freeman, 1985b).

Maternal hypoxia, caused, for example, by severe pneumonia, may adversely affect the developing fetus, causing severe malformations in the brain itself (Goodlin, Heidrick, Papenfuss, & Kubitz, 1984).

Cerebral palsy is the most common defect associated with hypoxia; it is seen in 10 to 26% of survivors. Other possible sequelae are hydrocephalus, seizures, brain hemorrhage, and mental retardation. Hypoxia may also be one cause of learning disorders and deficits in fine and gross motor coordination (Parry, Baldy, & Gardner, 1985). Hypoxia is one component in a series of events that often progress to a condition termed asphyxia.

REFERENCES

Freeman, J. (1985a). Introduction. In J.F. Freeman (Ed.), *Prenatal and perinatal factors associated with brain damage* (NIH Publication No. 85–1149, pp. 1–11). Bethesda, MD: National Institutes of Health.

Freeman, J. (1985b). Summary. In J. Freeman (Ed.), *Prenatal and perinatal factors associated with brain damage* (NIH Publication No. 85–1149, pp. 13–32). Bethesda, MD: National Institutes of Health.

Goodlin, R.C., Heidrick, W.P., Papenfuss, H.L., & Kubitz, R.L. (1984). Fetal malformation associated with maternal hypoxia. *American Journal of Obstetrics and Gynecology, 149*(2), 228–229.

Parry, W., & Adams, N. (1985). Acid-base homeostasis and oxygenation. In G. Merenstein & S. Gardner (Eds.), *Handbook of neonatal intensive care* (pp. 239–252). St. Louis: Mosby.

Parry, W., Baldy, M., & Gardner, S. (1985). Respiratory diseases. In G. Merenstein & S. Gardner (Eds.), *Handbook of neonatal intensive care* (pp. 301–344). St. Louis: Mosby.

See also **Apnea; Asphyxia; Prematurity**

HYSTERICAL PERSONALITY

See HISTRIONIC PERSONALITY DISORDER.

I

IDIOT

Idiot is an archaic term used from the turn of the century through the 1950s to denote a retarded individual whose measured IQ fell below 25 or 30. It represented the most severe level of mental retardation and was used comparatively with lesser degrees of retardation (i.e., imbecile and moron). The term acquired a pernicious quality among lay people over the years of its use and, during the 1950s, led to several revised systems of nomenclature.

See also **AAMD Classification Systems; History of Special Education**

IDIOT SAVANT

This apparent contradiction in terms refers to an individual who, though performing as a psychotic or retarded individual in most respects, displays one or more skills at a much more advanced level. The savant behavior may take the form of outstanding memory, quantitative ability, musical or other artistic talent, or mechanical facility. The term, idiot savant behavior, is not commonly found in the literature today. In order to avoid the stigma and other emotionality associated with the term, it has been replaced by the rubric, splinter skill.

The skill displayed by such individuals is isolated. In most respects, the so-called idiot savant manifests behavior that is consistent with the labels of mental retardation or psychosis. Although severely mentally handicapped people may demonstrate savant behavior, generally, their levels of retardation are mild. There is no known cause for the phenomenon; it has received relatively little attention from scientists, probably because it is generally harmful to no one and beneficial to many.

See also **Autism; Mental Retardation**

IEP

See INDIVIDUALIZED EDUCATIONAL PLAN.

ILLINOIS TEST OF PSYCHOLINGUISTIC ABILITIES (ITPA)

The Illinois Test of Psycholinguistic Abilities (ITPA; Kirk, McCarthy, & Kirk, 1968) was designed to measure a child's verbal and nonverbal language comprehension and production abilities.

The ITPA has been the subject of extensive research and debate since its publication. Critics have questioned its theoretical foundation, technical adequacy, and educational relevance. As to theory, the model of psycholinguistic functioning on which the ITPA was based is widely regarded as outmoded (see Reid & Hresko, 1981, for a detailed review of Osgood's model and an examination of the ITPA). Technical adequacy has been called into question with respect to the test's validity, reliability, and standardization (Sattler, 1982). Finally, studies of remediation programs based on the ITPA have not supported the value of this assessment approach for improving either psycholinguistic or academic skills (Newcomer & Hammill, 1976). While the ITPA represented an early and significant attempt to assess underlying cognitive processes and to forge a link between assessment and instruction, it has retained little support as a diagnostic instrument or intervention model.

REFERENCES

Kirk, S., McCarthy, J., & Kirk, W. (1968). *The Illinois Test of Psycholinguistic Abilities.* Urbana, IL: University of Illinois Press.

Newcomer, P.L., & Hammill, D.D. (1976). *Psycholinguistics in the schools.* Columbus, OH: Merrill.

Reid, D.K., & Hresko, W.P. (1981). *A cognitive approach to learning disabilities.* New York: McGraw-Hill.

Sattler, J.M. (1982). Assessment of children's intelligence and special abilities (2nd ed.). Boston: Allyn & Bacon.

See also **Kirk, Samuel; Measurement; Psycholinguistics**

IMAGERY

Imagery is the mental representation of objects, events, or concepts in some nonverbal form, a process thought to be basic to human functioning. While this representation is often assumed to be visual such as a picture according to Klinger (1981), mental imagery includes any of the almost unceasing sensationlike experiences that are a part of our stream of consciousness and that are representative of any of our sense modalities.

Mental imagery appears to play a critical role in the creative processes in diverse fields, from architecture and sports (Hall, Mack, Paivio, & Housenblas, 1998), to molecular science (Shepard, 1978). The ability to process information through imagery has been used to predict and enhance creative imagination in children and adults (Khatena, 1979). In addition, directed focusing of imagery has been found to be a powerful enhancer, eliciting from the individual a holistic and directly felt bodily sense of a situation or issue (Gendlin, 1980). Perfection of various athletic or performance skills, as well as a wide variety of classroom applications, have evolved, and scripts have been developed for using such guided imagery (Roberts, 1983). Rose (1980) describes his technique for using guided fantasies in the elementary classroom to acquire new concepts, build confidence for oral reports, or handle conflicts. In special education, imagery can be used to help individuals identify negative or positive attitudes regarding a physical disability (Morgan, 1980).

Imagery has been a particularly useful tool for the psychotherapist: the patient expresses in drawings or paintings, to be interpreted clinically, information unlikely to have been offered verbally. The advantage of this type of communication is that it is given in less threatening situations, avoiding times when the patient may be withdrawn, overly aroused, or frightened. In addition, imagery can be used to establish empathetic understanding, manage anxiety and stress, and even reduce pain, giving symptomatic relief to patients. Through imagery, then, humans can alter in positive ways both mental and physical functioning, their own as well as that of others.

REFERENCES

Gendlin, E.T. (1980). Imagery is more powerful with focusing: Theory and practice. In J.E. Schorr, G.E. Sobel, P. Robin, & J.A. Connella (Eds.), *Imagery. Its many dimensions and applications.* New York: Plenum.

Hall, C.R., Mack, D.E., Paivio, A., & Housenblas, H.A. (1998). Imagery use by athletes: Development of the Sport Imagery Questionnaire. *International Journal of Sport Psychology, 29*(1), 73–89.

Khatena, J. (1979). *Teaching gifted children to use creative imagination imagery.* Starkville, MI: Allan.

Klinger, E. (Ed.). (1981). *Imagery. Concepts, results and applications.* New York: Plenum.

Morgan, C. (1980). Imagery experiences of disabled persons. In J.E. Schorr, G.E. Sobel, P. Robin, & J.A. Connella (Eds.), *Imagery. Its many dimensions and applications.* New York: Plenum.

Roberts, N.M. (1983). Imagery: A second look: Expanding its use in the classroom. *Reading Improvement, 20*(1), 22–27.

Rose, R. (1980). Guided fantasies in elementary classrooms. In J.E. Schorr, G.E. Sobel, P. Robin, & J.A. Connella (Eds.), *Imagery. Its many dimensions and applications.* New York: Plenum.

Shepard, R.N. (1978). Externalization of mental images and the act of creation. In B.S. Randhawa & W.E. Coffman (Eds.), *Visual learning, thinking, and communication.* New York: Academic.

See also **Creativity; Hypnosis**

IMPERSISTENCE

See PERSEVERATION.

IMPULSE CONTROL

An impulse is a psychological term given to a feeling that results in an action. Research about impulse control can be found as it relates to many psychiatric disorders such as attention-deficit/hyperactivity disorder (Pulkkinen, 1996), manic depression (McElroy, Pope, Keck, & Hudson, 1996) and so on. As used here, it refers to a trait normally measured by a test such as the Matching Familiar Figures Test. The resulting outcome of the test is an indication of whether the learner is reflective or impulsive. A reflective learner examines a stimulus slowly and takes more time to make a decision than an impulsive learner. Generally, there is some relationship between impulsive responders and high error rates. Thus, there is a need to control the response rate of the learner to cut down on errors (Kagan, Pearson, & Welch, 1966; Kendall & Wilcox, 1979).

The predominant method for the control of impulsive behavior is cognitive training (Kendall & Finch, 1978; Kendall & Wilcox, 1979, 1980). Investigators have combined cognitive and behavioral methods. Two of the most successful strategies for the control of impulsive behavior are modeling and self-instructional training. Modeling is based on social learning theory. A learner observes a high-status adult or peer engaging in acts that are reflective and purposeful. If the tasks performed by the model are similar to the types of tasks to be performed by the learner, there is a likelihood that the reflective behavior will be modeled by the learner. As the tasks become dissimilar, the degree of transfer decreases.

Self-instructional training is based on a theory that states that voluntary control over motor behavior requires the internalization of verbal commands (Meichenbaum & Goodman, 1971). To improve impulsive behavior by self-instruction, the learner verbalizes either aloud, in a whisper or subvocally. The practice becomes a thinking-out-loud intervention that reminds a learner to slow down, to be careful, and to follow the steps in a process.

Another approach to cognitive training involves the following six-step problem-solving sequence (Meichenbaum & Goodman, 1971): (1) problem definition; (2) problem approach; (3) focusing attention; (4) problem solution; (5) self-reinforcement; and (6) coping with errors. In studies following this sequence, there is a greater generalization of reflective behavior if the training deals with self-statements that are global rather than problem specific. If training focuses only on a specific problem situation, the generalization of reflective behavior is restricted. If the problem situations are broad and the strategies applicable to a wide range of behavior, generalization will be enhanced.

REFERENCES

Kagan, J., Pearson, L., & Welch, L. (1966). Modifiability of an impulsive tempo. *Journal of Educational Psychology, 57,* 359–365.

Kendall, P.C., & Finch, A.J. (1978). A cognitive-behavioral treatment for impulsivity: A group comparison study. *Journal of Consulting & Clinical Psychology, 46,* 110–118.

Kendall, P.C., & Wilcox, L.E. (1979). Self-control in children: Development of a rating scale. *Journal of Consulting & Clinical Psychology, 47,* 1020–1029.

Kendall, P.C., & Wilcox, L.E. (1980). Cognitive-behavioral treatment for impulsivity: Concrete versus conceptual training in non-self-controlled problem children. *Journal of Consulting & Clinical Psychology, 48,* 80–91.

McElroy, S.L., Pope, H.G., Keck, P.E., & Hudson, J.I. (1996) Are impulse-control disorders relaxed to bipolar disorder? *Comprehensive Psychiatry, 37*(4), 229–240.

Meichenbaum, D.H., & Goodman, J. (1971). Training impulsive children to talk to themselves: A means of developing self-control. *Journal of Abnormal Psychology, 77,* 115–126.

Pulkkinen, L. (1996). Impulse control in children. *Journal of Forensic Psychiatry, 7*(2), 228–233.

See also Behavior Modeling; Behavior Modification; Self-Monitoring

IMPULSIVITY-REFLECTIVITY

Impulsivity-reflectivity is a cognitive dimension defined by Kagan (1965) that describes the way children resolve uncertainty. Impulsivity-reflectivity describes the tendency to reflect on the validity of problem solving when several choices are presented. The instrument most often used to measure reflectivity and impulsivity in children is the Matching Familiar Figures Test (MFFT) which also comes in a computerized version (Hummel-Schulgar & Baer, 1996). Based on test performance, reflective children will make fewer errors and have longer response latencies than impulsive children (Kagan, 1965).

Reflectivity and impulsivity seem to develop with age as children typically become more reflective as they grow older (Messer, 1976). Messer reported that response times increased with age, while the amount of errors decreased. Siegelman (1969) examined the ways in which reflective and impulsive children of different ages actually deploy alternatives and scan the objects presented to them. The hypothesis was that impulsive children devote a greater amount of time to a chosen stimulus and ignore the alternatives, in contrast to the reflectives, who spent more time weighing alternatives. Results suggested that impulsive and reflective children may be using different search strategies. This indicates that the impulsive dimension may be modifiable. Kagan (1983) and Messer (1976) found that impulsivity may be modified by teaching impulsives to improve their scanning strategies. The researchers accomplished this by having children who were impulsive verbalize what they were doing.

Impulsivity and reflectivity have also been examined from a teaching perspective that has implications for classroom learning. Teachers need to be aware of individual differences among children to cope with each individual learner. Readance and Bean (1978) reported that the impulsive child has a tendency to act on his or her initial response with little reflection when solving problems. A reflective child usually delays, weighing all choices available. Reflective children are not necessarily brighter or better learners; however, the research did suggest that teachers may perceive impulsive children less favorably. Reflective students were seen as highly attentive. Impulsive boys were seen as less able to concentrate in class. This supported the notion that this particular individual difference of impulsivity and reflectivity is important for classroom learning. Evidence supports the contention that the cognitive and metacognitive (Palladino, Poli, Masi, & Marcheschi, 1997) dimensions of impulsivity and reflectivity are important individual differences. These dimensions will play a role in helping assess a child's ability, ultimately improving the learning process within the field of special education.

REFERENCES

Hummel-Schulgar, A.O., & Baer, J.S. (1996). A computer-controlled administration of the Matching Familiar Figures Test. *Behavior Research Methods, 28*(1), 93–95.

Kagan, J. (1965). *Conceptual development in children.* New York: International University Press.

Kagan, J. (1983). Reflection-impulsivity and reading ability in primary grade children. *Child Development, 54,* 609–628.

Messer, S.B. (1976). Reflection-impulsivity: A review. *Psychological Bulletin, 83,* 1026–1052.

Palladino, P., Poli, P., Masi, G., & Marcheschi, M. (1997). Impulsive-reflective cognitive style, metacognition and emotion in adolescence. *Perceptual and Motor Skills, 84*(1), 47–57.

Readance, J.E., & Bean, T.W. (1978). Impulsivity-reflectivity and learning: An individual difference that matters. *College Student Journal, 11,* 367–371.

Siegelman, E. (1969). Reflective and impulsive observing behavior. *Child Development, 40,* 1213–1222.

See also Creative Problem Solving; Impulse Control

INBORN ERRORS OF METABOLISM

Inborn errors of metabolism are classified as a group of genetic diseases and involve single-gene defects that interfere with the process of metabolism. Metabolism refers to the process in which the body breaks down food into fats, proteins, and carbohydrates. The conversion of the food into energy to maintain the life cycle of body cells is carried out by enzymes. The enzymes assist in the maintenance of homeostasis and the control of functions of blood pressure, blood sugar levels, and rate of growth. A single-gene defect may lead to a missing or malfunctioning enzyme, which if left untreated, may result in severe mental retardation or impaired bodily functions such as poor digestion. Such disorders occur in approximately 1 in 5000 births (Batshaw & Perret, 1981).

Robinson and Robinson (1965) divided metabolic disorders into three areas: (1) ongoing faulty digestive processes identified by biochemical substances in the urine or the bloodstream; (2) storage diseases in which materials are stored because of decreased rate of metabolism or overproduction; and (3) disorders in endocrine secretions that result in anomalies in the structure of the brain and cranium or other difficulties.

Koch and Koch (1974) reported that 40 to 50 such serious diseases often are passed on by consanguineous parents. The body is constantly producing, maintaining, and recycling cells. In the metabolic process of mitosis, the cell dies and is recycled and changed into chemicals and proteins. These components are then absorbed and reused by the body. Any genetic disease that interferes with the process is called an inborn error of metabolism. For many metabolic disorders, there is no effective therapy. For some, therapy is successful only if begun immediately. When untreated, profound mental retardation, seizures, aberrant behavior, and stunted growth may accompany the metabolic abnormality. Some inborn errors of metabolism (e.g., Gaucher's) are asymptomatic and may pose little threat to a reasonably normal existence. However, many of these disorders have serious consequences and may be fatal if untreated. Age of onset affects severity. In several of the lipid storage diseases such as Gaucher's and Niemann-Pick disease, if the disorder is manifested during the infantile period when the brain is being myelinated, the result is a much more serious disability. Conversely, many of the hereditary metabolic disorders such as gout, hemochromatosis, or familial periodic paralysis do not become fully manifest until adulthood.

Inborn errors of metabolism are the subject of continued intensive research. Reports of newly discovered syndromes frequently are announced. Screening still offers the best hope. The most direct method detects qualitative changes in the structure of the protein (Bearn, 1979). Mass screening for all possible single gene defects is still prohibitive financially. Therefore, with the exception of PKU, the focus is on families and at-risk populations. Bearn (1979) suggests that amniocentesis and the use of cultured fibroblasts will increase in the years ahead as a means of making screening programs more comprehensive. Currently, scientists apply a sophisticated battery of laboratory procedures to identify and elucidate suspected metabolic disorders.

REFERENCES

Batshaw, M.L., & Perret, Y.M. (1981). *Children with handicaps: A medical primer.* Baltimore, MD: Brooks.

Bearn, A.G. (1979). Inborn errors of metabolism and molecular disease. In P. Beeson, W. McDermott, & J. Wyngaarden (Eds.), *Cecil textbook of medicine* (15th ed.) (pp. 40–48). Philadelphia: Saunders.

Koch, R., & Koch, K. (1974). *Understanding the mentally retarded child: A new approach.* New York: Random House.

Robinson, H.B., & Robinson, N.M. (1965). *The mentally retarded child: A psychological approach.* New York: McGraw-Hill.

See also **Galactosemia; Genetic Counseling; Genetic Transmissions; Hurler's Syndrome; Metabolic Disorders; Phenylketonuria**

INCIDENCE

The term incidence refers to the estimated number of people in a given population who possess or exhibit a given characteristic at some point during their lives (Blackhurst & Berdine, 1981). Schifani, Anderson, and Odle (1980) define incidence as the number of new cases of handicapped children identified in a given period of time—usually a year. Incidence most often relates to the occurrence of some characteristic.

Incidence is often confused with prevalence but the two terms have different meanings. Prevalence refers to currently existing handicapped children as opposed to those who might be considered exceptional at some point in their lives. Incidence results in a higher figure since it estimates future occurrence, where prevalence deals with a point in time figure.

Because incidence is an estimate, it is more difficult to validate or substantiate. Meyen (1978) states that state education agencies and school districts generally establish prevalence rates when conducting needs assessment surveys. He suggests that surveys and studies would be better able to establish incidence rates given the data becoming available from referral requests for service under IDEA. For general education planning purposes prevalence estimates continue to be used.

REFERENCES

Blackhurst, A.E., & Berdine, W.H. (1981). (Eds.). *An introduction to special education.* Boston: Little, Brown.

Meyen, E.L. (1978). *Exceptional children and youth: An introduction.* Denver: Love.

Schifani, J.W., Anderson, R.M., & Odle, S.J. (Eds.). (1980). *Implementing learning in the least restrictive environment.* Baltimore, MD: University Press.

See also **Demography of Special Education**

INCLUSION

Generally speaking, inclusion refers to the placement and education of students with disabilities in general education classrooms with students of the same age who do not have disabilities. The underlying premise of inclusion is that all children can learn and belong in the mainstream of school and community life. The goal of inclusion, then, is to ensure that all students, regardless of any individual differences they may have, are fully included in the mainstream of life (Stainback & Stainback, 1992; Villa, 1993; Sailor, 1991). Inclusion, however, has been greatly debated in special education. Many educators, professionals, and professional organizations have developed different definitions and positions in favor of it and against it.

ARGUMENTS IN FAVOR OF INCLUSION

According to Stainback & Stainback (1990), if a society supports integration of all individuals, then segregated schools and classrooms have no place in that society. They asserted that, therefore, there is no defensible rationale, excuse, nor scientific research that can be conducted that will in the final analysis justify segregation (Stainback & Stainback, 1990). Accordingly, there are a number of potential benefits for students and schools that can occur as a result of inclusion. A few of these include delabeling, social acceptance, independence, and service integration (Blesz, Boudah, & Harrell, 1993).

Delabeling students eliminates the need for disability determination, which only serves to stigmatize (Villa, 1993). Social acceptance in the workplace and the community at large is born out of opportunities for people with disabilities to function, perform normalized tasks, and interact with their peers in school. Equally important is for their peers to learn how to interact with them (Wood, 1998). Independence is fostered when classroom educators focus on lifelong learning, work habits, and teaching children how to spend their leisure time (Villa, 1993). Inclusion can also facilitate service integration in school systems when general and special education personnel, as well as curriculum and instructional procedures, are combined to design educational experiences to meet the needs of students in integrated settings (Stainback & Stainback, 1992).

ARGUMENTS AGAINST INCLUSION

Inclusion opponents tend to argue against inclusion practices based on pragmatic, sociopolitical, and empirical reasons. First, a number of researchers have questioned the willingness and capability of general education teachers to make the necessary adaptations to accommodate greater student diversity, including the integration of all, or most, children with disabilities (Baker & Zigmond, 1990; Fuchs & Fuchs, 1991; Schumaker & Deshler, 1988; Schumm & Vaughn, 1991). Some writers, such as MacMillan, Semmel, and Gerber (1994), claimed that most classroom teachers lack the time, training, or right attitude to work effectively with extremely low-achieving students. In addition, there are few resources or incentives for regular educators to change.

Some opponents (e.g., MacMillan, Semmel, & Gerber, 1994) have contended that inclusive education has not been thoroughly evaluated in a methodologically sound manner. Indeed, much of the research in inclusive education is survey research on attitudes toward inclusion. Moreover, Kauffman (1989) has charged inclusion proponents as possessing "a cavalier attitude toward experimentation and research."

THE IMPORTANCE OF SPECIAL EDUCATION LAW FOR INCLUSION

The enactment of IDEA has resulted in several key regulatory principles: (a) free and appropriate education in a public school, (b) appropriate and nondiscriminatory evaluation, (c) individualized education programs, (d) least restrictive alternative/environment, (e) procedural due process, and (f) parent and student participation. The principle that seems to continue to require the most clarification is Least Restrictive Alternative/Environment (LRA/ LRE) which is fundamental to inclusive education.

In short, LRE does not specifically imply a particular setting, but rather a way for schools to ensure the integration of students with disabilities (Yell, 1998). IDEA states that

to the maximum extent appropriate, children with disabilities, including children in public or private institutions or other care facilities, are educated with children who are not disabled, and that special classes, separate schooling, or other removal of children with disabilities from the regular educational environment occurs only when the nature or severity of the disability is such that education in regular classes with the use of supplementary aids and services cannot be achieved satisfactorily. (IDEA, 20 U.S.C. 1412)

The environment in which a child is educated (i.e., placement) is a decision to be made by the IEP team in accordance with the child's Individualized Education Plan. Therefore, each placement decision should be based first on individual service needs, rather than determining what educational environment a child will be educated in and then deciding which services are available. To ensure that each child's placement is based on an individual basis, IDEA also provides a continuum of alternative placements. Regulations state that

(a) each school district shall ensure that a continuum of alternative placements is available to meet the needs of children with disabilities for special education and related services

(b) the continuum required must include the alternative placements (i.e., instruction in regular classes, special classes, special schools, home instruction, and instruction in hospitals and institutions); and make provision for supplementary services (e.g., resource room or itinerant instruction) to be provided in conjunction with regular class placement. (IDEA Regulations, 34 C.F.R. 300.551)

The Office of Special Education Programs (Department of Education, 1997) has defined a general education placement as one in which a student receives special education and related services outside of the general education classroom for zero (0) to 20% of the school day. Resource room placements are defined as those in which students receive special education and related services for 21% to 60% of the school day outside the general education setting. Students who receive special education and related services outside the general education classroom for more than 60% of the school day are considered to be placed in a separate class.

Therefore, school districts are not mandated by IDEA to provide inclusion to every student with disabilities (Gore, 1996), but are required to educate students with disabilities in regular education classrooms to the maximum extent possible. The implementation regulations of the law, however, also specify a range, or continuum, of services for individuals with disabilities. Supplementary aid and services may include prereferral interventions, consultation, behavior management plans, paraprofessionals, itinerant teachers, and resource rooms (Yell, 1998). Therein lies one of the key issues: What is the maximum extent of education possible with supplementary aids and services to achieve a satisfactory or beneficial education?

Court decisions have provided some direction in addressing this question, but not for every child with a disability. One court remedy is to compare the educational benefits of the general education classroom (with supplementary aids and services) to the benefits received in the special education classroom. If the special education classroom provides more benefits and the student is more successful, then the regular education classroom would not be appropriate (Yell, 1998).

CURRENT STATUS OF STUDENTS IN INCLUSIVE SETTINGS

Since the passage of EHA/IDEA, the Department of Education has annually compiled and reported national statistics about the implementation of the law, including the percentage of students participating in various school environments such as general education classes. Each year, reports have shown an increase in the number of students receiving services and, since the late 1980s, a noticeable rise in the number of students included in general education classes for at least part of the school day. Based on cumulative placement rates (number of students with disabilities per thousand in a given setting; McLeskey, Henry, & Hodges, 1998) from the Department of Education statistics (1997), greater numbers of students with disabilities have received special education services in general education placements. In fact, the cumulative placement rate (CPR) for all students with disabilities in general education classrooms rose from 30 to 48 between the 1988–89 and 1994–95 school years, representing a 60% increase. Concurrently, the CPR for students placed in resource rooms dropped significantly (37 to 31, a 16% decrease).

This trend toward more inclusive education was also consistent across disability categories between the 1988–89 and 1994–95 school years, with the largest movements occurring among students with learning disabilities, speech and language disabilities, other health impairments, orthopedic impairments, and visual impairments (McLeskey, Henry, & Hodges, 1999). Students with mental retardation, multiple disabilities, and deaf-blindness continued to have the smallest percentages of students moving to and placed in inclusive general education classrooms (McLeskey, Henry, & Hodges, 1999).

Advocates and opponents of inclusion share a vision for educational reforms that focus on effective teaching practices for all children. The most important question is not whether a student with disabilities can best be served in the general education classroom or some type of special education classroom, but whether that child's education is appropriate and beneficial. Inclusion is not an either/or choice, but a viable option within the cascade of available services ensured by the Individuals with Disabilities Educational Act. Furthermore, inclusion may be appropriate during one phase of a student's school program but not at other times.

REFERENCES

Baker, J.M., & Zigmond, N. (1990). Are regular education classes equipped to accommodate students with learning disabilities? *Exceptional Children, 56*(6), 515–526.

Blesz, D., Boudah, D., & Harrell, L.G. (1993). *Inclusive education: Issues, trends, and concerns.* Unpublished manuscript. University of Kansas.

Dunn, L.M. (1968). Special education for the mildly retarded- Is much of it justifiable? *Exceptional Children, 35,* 5–22.

Fuchs, D., & Fuchs, L. (1991). Framing the REI debate: Abolitionists versus conservationists. In J.W. Lloyd, N.N. Singh, & A.C. Repp (Eds.), *The regular education initiative: Alternative perspectives on concepts, issues, and models* (pp. 241–255). Sycamore, IL: Sycamore.

Gore, S. (1996). *What do I do when: The answer book on special education law.* Horsham, PA: LRP.

Kauffman, J.M. (1989). The regular education initiative as Reagan-Bush education policy: A trickle down theory of the hard-to-teach. *The Journal of Special Education, 23*(3), 256–278.

MacMillan, D.L., Semmel, M.I., & Gerber, M.M. (1994). The social context of Dunn: Then and now. *The Journal of Special Education, 27,* 466–480.

McLeskey, J., Henry, D., & Hodges, D. (1999). Inclusion: What progress is being made across disability categories? *Teaching Exceptional Children, 31*(3), 60–64.

McLeskey, J., Henry, D., & Hodges, D. (1998). Inclusion: Where is it happening? *Teaching Exceptional Children, 31*(1), 4–10.

Sailor, W. (1991). Special education in the restructured school. *Remedial and Special Education, 12*(6), 8–22.

Schumaker, J.B., & Deshler, D.D. (1988). Implementing the regular education initiative in secondary schools: A different ball game. *Journal of Learning Disabilities, 21,* 36–42.

Schumm, J.S., & Vaughn, S. (1991). Making adaptations for mainstreamed students: General classroom teachers' perspectives. *Remedial and Special Education, 12*(4), 18–27.

Stainback, W., & Stainback, S. (1990). *Support networks for inclusive schooling: Interdependent integrated education.* Baltimore: Brookes.

U.S. Department of Education. (1997). *To assure the free appropriate public education of all children with disabilities: Nineteenth annual report to Congress on the implementation of The Individuals with Disabilities Education Act.* Washington, DC: Office of Special Education Programs.

Villa, R. (1993, April). Inclusive education: Issues, trends and concerns. A public forum sponsored by the Kansas State Board of Education and the University of Kansas Department of Special Education. Lawrence, KS.

Wood, J.W. (1998). *Adopting instruction to accommodate students in inclusive settings* (3rd ed.). Upper Saddle River, NJ: Prentice Hall.

Yell, M.L. (1998). *The law and special education.* Upper Saddle River, NJ: Prentice Hall.

INCLUSION & CO-TEACHING

See TEACHING: INCLUSION AND CO-TEACHING.

INCORRIGIBILITY

See CONDUCT DISORDER.

INDEPENDENT LIVING

According to Cartwright, Cartwright, and Ward (1984), the majority of individuals with disabilities desire to live independently. However, to achieve independence, adaptations must be made in the home living environment. For example, adaptations for a severely handicapped person would include an intercom system, kitchen with adapted appliances and controls, accessible sinks and showers, and wheel-in showers. Outside the home environment, other areas of consideration are transportation and employment. In terms of transportation, personal mobility may be achieved with computer-controlled wheelchairs, Sonicguide electronic glasses, and other technological devices such as the Voice Data Entry Terminal System. This system allows the handicapped individual a way to control the immediate environment.

Sections 503 and 504 of the Vocational Rehabilitation Act of 1973 guarantee that individuals with disabilities cannot be denied access to housing, jobs, or transportation because of their disability. Employment is also an essential component of independent living. There is a wide range of possible jobs appropriate for the handicapped. However, this depends on the skill and knowledge level of the individual. The major goal of rehabilitation agencies is to assist the handicapped individual with obtaining and keeping a job. Some handicapped individuals will be able to compete in the regular job market. There are others with more serious disabilities who are unable to compete and are limited to sheltered workshops and work activity centers. The sheltered workshop employs disabled adults to perform various jobs that have been subcontracted from companies and firms. All employees of the workshop receive wages based on attendance, satisfactory job performance, and adequate social behavior. The work activity center, which is often operated by the workshop, is designed for those who are not able to perform satisfactorily in a sheltered workshop or who may be in need of additional training before entering a workshop.

REFERENCE

Cartwright, G.P., Cartwright, C.A., & Ward, M.E. (1984). *Educating special learners* (2nd ed.). Belmont, CA: Wadsworth.

See also **Americans with Disabilities Act; Community Placement; Deinstitutionalization; Normalization**

INDIA, SPECIAL EDUCATION IN

HISTORICAL OVERVIEW

In India, during ancient times, the family was the main agency for educating children. This was followed by a period of private tutors, *gurkulas,* and *ashrams* (homes where children were sent to study under a *guru*). Organized educational institutions came into existence with the impact of Buddhist monasteries. In 1910, a Department of Education was created in the central government. In 1935, provincial

autonomy of education was introduced, and the Central Advisory Board of Education was established (Shukla, 1986). The central government was empowered in 1975 to legislate education while maintaining the responsibility of state governments.

Christian missionaries in the 1880s started schools for the disabled as a charitable cause (Mehta, 1982). In 1887, the first school for the blind was established, followed by two more schools at the end of the 19th century and two at the beginning of the 20th century. An Institute for the Deaf and Mute was established in 1888 and another began in 1893. Seven more schools were started between 1904 and 1918, and by 1954 there were 41 schools for deaf children. Services for the physically disabled were initiated in the middle of the 20th century by volunteers and doctors with the establishment of the Society for Rehabilitation of Crippled Children. Because of this organization, many hospitals started physiotherapy and artificial limb manufacturing departments. Individuals with mental retardation were the last to receive attention. Mental retardation was synonymous with mental illness, and these individuals are still considered legally incompetent (*Law handicaps,* 1995). The first school for mental retardation was established in 1934, followed by a home for mentally deficient children in 1944 and the first non-residential school in 1953. After Independence, in 1947, the Ministry of Education set up a small unit to address the problems faced by blind individuals and later included people who were deaf, physically impaired, and mentally retarded (Rohindekar & Usha, 1988). Currently there are an estimated 2,271 institutions for the disabled in the country (Ministry of Welfare, 1995a). Integrated education initiatives were introduced by the government in 1974. An estimated 1,456 schools (less than 1% of all schools) in rural areas and 359 schools in urban areas provide integrated education, primarily at the elementary level. Until 1993, 23 of 25 states were participating in integrated education programs and an estimated 40,000 children had been reached.

PREVALENCE

Precise prevalence figures for disabilities in India are unavailable. The National Sample Survey Organization (NSSO) determined that in 1991 there were 16.15 million people with physical and sensory disabilities. Of these, 4 million were blind. However, the figure generally accepted is 12 million (Ministry of Welfare, 1995). Similarly, NSSO estimated 8.9 million people with locomotor disabilities, but other professional organizations suggest the number may exceed 20 million. The number of hearing impaired individuals, according to NSSO, was 3.2 million. Figures on mental retardation are calculated to be 7.5 million for children under 14 years, based on 2.5% of the total child population (Ministry of Welfare, 1995).

EDUCATIONAL STRUCTURE AND SERVICES

The Ministry of Welfare is responsible for rehabilitation efforts, including administration of special schools, with supporting assistance from the Departments of Health, Labour, and Employment. The precise number of special schools is unknown. There are an estimated 432 institutions (a term which includes schools) for individuals with loco-motor disabilities, 430 for the visually impaired, 728 for the hearing impaired, and 681 for mentally retarded individuals. Existing schools serve about 2% to 4% of all individuals with disabilities (Ministry of Welfare, 1995a). Approximately one-fifth of these schools offer a secondary-level education, and there are two colleges for individuals who are deaf. The National Open Schools for independent study and the National Open University for higher education provide alternative routes to obtain an education. The vast majority of schools are located in urban areas and are unevenly distributed across the country. In fact, 10 states account for more than 90% of these schools (NCERT, 1990).

Nongovernment organizations surpass government-run special schools in both quantity and quality of services. They receive 90% of all government sanctioned monies for the disabled. Most special schools are residential (Rohindekar & Usha, 1988) so they may serve populations from remote rural areas and from states with limited services. Another feature of special schools is that they are categorical. For example, schools for the mentally retarded typically do not admit students who are nonambulatory. Some schools offer vocational training focusing on trades such as chair-caning, candle-making, printing, and loom-weaving. A small number of NGOs offer exceptional programs: these are expensive and usually have long waiting lists.

Integrated education is governed by the Department of Education. A small percentage of all children with physical and sensory disabilities have been integrated into regular schools. Primarily, government-run schools are implementing integration programs. However, children who are integrated face many barriers to true academic and social integration. These barriers include large class sizes (40–60 students), a vast curriculum, bi- and trilingual requirements, competitive learning environment, National essay-format examinations, lecture teaching styles, emphasis on rote memorization, and ignorance regarding disabilities. Integration of children with disabilities in private schools is almost nonexistent. Through rigorous admission and promotion procedures, private schools promote the academically gifted.

ATTITUDES AND FAMILY ISSUES

The society of India in general is not aware of needs of individuals with disabilities. The belief in *karma* (impact of present actions upon one's future) has led to a system of care and protection. People with disabilities are provided shelter in religious places and given charity. Parents may fear that their child's disability is a form of punishment, while others may believe they have been specially chosen by God.

In India the family is primarily responsible for its members irrespective of disability and large institutions for the care of disabled have never existed. The National Institute for the Mentally Handicapped (NIMH) funded a project to obtain information about families (Peshawaria et al., 1995). A majority of parents told stories about incorrect and delayed diagnosis and visits to several specialists. Parents who had girls became socially isolated in their attempts to hide the disability to ensure future marital prospects. The most critical concern of parents was the future of their child. Parents did not want to burden siblings yet were wary when asked about the feasibility of starting group homes, fearing abuse and mistreatment in such settings.

Parents do not have the opportunity to be advocates for their children because of limited options and lack of functional legislative backing. Parent groups are a very recent development in India. The first parent group was started in 1982. NIMH organized the first national meeting of the 23 registered parent associations in 1990. A National Trust for Welfare of Persons with Mental Retardation and Cerebral Palsy has been proposed. Its mission would be to start group homes, assist in establishing guardianships and foster care, provide support to families and parent associations, and manage properties bequeathed for children.

CHALLENGES AND FUTURE TRENDS

To understand the magnitude of the challenge faced by India, it is essential to be familiar with certain facts. India is one of the largest developing countries and is second largest in population (953 million). It is significant to note that 40% of India's population is comprised of children below 14 years of age. Literacy rates in India are low (average of 50% in 1991), with wide regional and gender variations.

Although the constitution mandates compulsory education up to 14 years of age, approximately 30% of all children drop out during their first year, and less than 50% complete 5 years of schooling (NCERT, 1990). It is not surprising that only 2% to 4% of all disabled children attend school: this figure decreases to less than 1% in rural areas. A Department of Education (1992) report estimates that 12.59 million 5- to 14-year-old children with disabilities need to be educated in schools. Another half million need vocational training, and 2 million children need early intervention. To meet this challenge, the new National Policy on Education must be proactive and inclusive of all children. Advocates suggest that the Department of Education must become solely responsible for educational services, because under the poorly funded Ministry of Welfare, children are given an education not as a *right* but as *assistance*. Furthermore, centralization will assist with coordination of services. Similarly, the four national institutes for the disabled must cease to function independently and begin to coordinate their efforts.

India has demonstrated gains in early detection and disability prevention programs, and these efforts must continue. Most disabilities are a result of preventable factors such as malnutrition and iodine deficiency, communicable diseases (polio, leprosy), poverty (37% of people live below poverty level), low quality prenatal care (deliveries done by *dais* or midwives in villages), and accidents (road and agricultural). Access to doctors will be critical in prevention.

Currently 40–50% of disabled people do not seek treatment for disabilities.

To provide educational services, the government faces the challenge of rapidly increasing the number and quality of special schools, especially in rural areas. Many special schools do not have trained staff and necessary equipment and materials. The curriculum is watered down, especially in schools for the mentally retarded. Special services such as speech therapy, physical therapy, and counseling are rare. Schools must be monitored so children with disabilities receive an education geared towards functional, lifelong skills training. Parents must be given a greater role in their child's education.

In conclusion, India has made remarkable efforts to serve individuals with disabilities given its economic and social constraints. The nation must continue to make an investment to improve the lives of its citizens with disabilities.

REFERENCES

Department of Education. (1992). *Revised Programme of Action, 1992.* New Delhi: Ministry of Human Resource Development.

Jangira, N.K. (1996). *Research in special education: A trend report.* New Delhi: National Council for Educational Research and Training.

Law handicaps mentally disabled. (1995, March). *Times of India,* p. 16.

Mehta, V. (1982). *Vedi.* New York, NY: Oxford University Press.

Ministry of Welfare. (1995). *Handbook on disability rehabilitation.* New Delhi: National Information Centre on Disability and Rehabilitation, Government of India.

Ministry of Welfare. (1995a). *Directory of institutions working for the disabled in India.* New Delhi: National Information Centre on Disability and Rehabilitation, Government of India.

Ministry of Welfare. (1995b). *Report published by the Rehabilitation Council of India.* New Delhi: Author.

NCERT. (1990). *Fifth all-India education survey.* New Delhi: National Council of Educational Research and Training.

Peshawaria, R., Menon, D.K., Ganguly, R., Roy, S., Pillay, R., & Gupta, A. (1995). *Understanding Indian families.* Secunderabad, A.P.: National Institute for the Mentally Handicapped.

Rohindekar, S.R., & Usha, M.N. (1988). *Educational and vocational needs of physically handicapped children.* Bangalore, India: Institute for Social and Economic Change.

Shukla, P.D. (1986). *Administration of education in India.* Ghaziabad, U.P.: Vikas.

INDIVIDUALIZATION OF INSTRUCTION

Individualization of instruction is a method of teaching in which instruction is tailored to the unique needs of students, enabling them to advance at their own rates and to achieve their potential. Individualized instruction requires that students be placed individually within a curriculum or sequence of objectives, and that teaching methods be prescribed so as to maximize individual growth and accomplishment.

Public Law 94–142 and subsequent amendments assigned to state and local agencies the responsibility to provide free, appropriate education to meet the unique needs of exceptional children. The act delineated guidelines for individualized placement and prescription by requiring an individual educational program (IEP) for every student. The IEP includes statements of present levels of educational performance, annual goals, short-term objectives, and specific educational services to be provided. Ideally, then, an IEP must embody the elements of individualized instruction and in so doing "represents a formalization of the diagnostic/prescriptive approach to education" (Safer, Morrissey, Kaufman, & Lewis, 1978, p. 1).

Individualization of instruction is not synonymous and should not be confused with one-to-one instruction. The latter may or may not be individualized; the former may be accomplished with groups. Similarly, individualized instruction does not necessarily require that students work independently on seat work tasks. Effective individualized instruction can occur in teacher-led groups (Stevens & Rosenshine, 1980).

REFERENCES

Safer, D., Morrissey, A., Kaufman, J., & Lewis, L. (1978). Implementation of IEPs: New teacher roles and requisite support systems. *Focus on Exceptional Children, 10,* 1–20.

Stevens, R., & Rosenshine, B. (1980). Advances in research on teaching. *Exceptional Education Quarterly, 2,* 1–9.

See also **Data-Based Instruction; Individualized Education Plan; Precision Teaching**

INDIVIDUALIZED EDUCATION PLAN (IEP)

IEP is the acronym for the individualized educational program that must now be written for each identified handicapped child prior to his or her placement in a special education program. Public Law 94–142, the Education of All Handicapped Children Act (1975), and subsequent amendments and laws such as IDEA required that states receiving federal funds for special education services develop and implement a written statement, as to what unique educational services each handicapped child is to receive. At a minimum it is mandatory that each written program include the following:

1. A statement of the child's present levels of performance.
2. A statement of annual goals, including long- and short-term institutional objectives.
3. A statement of special education and related services to be provided to the child, and the extent to which the child will be able to participate in regular education programs.
4. The projected dates for initiation of services and anticipated duration of the services.

5. Appropriate objective criteria and evaluation procedures and schedule for determining, on an annual basis at least, whether the short-term instructional objectives are being achieved. (*Federal Register,* p. 42491)

Under these guidelines, a meeting must be held at least once a year to review and, if necessary, revise the educational program as originally outlined. It is obvious that the goals—long- or short-range—specified in the initial IEP would periodically be in need of revision for a number of reasons: the original goals may be inappropriate for the individual child, or the child may meet or make progress on many of the goals, thus requiring revision and development of new goals.

Although the intent of the law is commendable, the actual implementation is often less than satisfactory. One example involves the extent to which the IEP is in fact individualized for the child. It is not uncommon for educational programs to be designed specific to the child's classification (e.g., learning disabled) rather than the unique abilities of the child involved. Often individualized educational programs will simply be a reflection of the specific district or school the child attends. For example, states will frequently mandate that all children meet certain objectives within a given subject (e.g., reading). Therefore, it is not uncommon to find the short-range objectives specified for the learning-disabled child in reading to be simply a list of the reading objectives common to the district. This practice would seem in direct contradiction to the intent of the law and certainly not always in the best interests of the child with disabilities involved. Indeed, special educators have questioned the general value of these types of IEPs (Ryan & Rucher, 1991).

Various studies have been conducted investigating parental participation in IEP development and planning (e.g., Lusthaus, Lusthaus, & Gibbs, 1981; Polifka, 1981; Roit & Pfohl, 1984; Scanlon, Arick, & Phelps, 1981; Yoshida, Fenton, Kaufman, & Maxwell, 1978; Van Reusen & Bos, 1994). Yoshida et al. (1978) found that educational personnel involved in the planning meeting expected parents to simply provide information as opposed to actively participating in the decisions as to what would constitute the plan. Interestingly, results of a parental survey conducted by Lusthaus et al. (1981) found that parents agreed that their role should be that of information giver and receiver instead of equal decision maker. This has slowly changed (Van Reusen & Bos, 1994). Roit and Pfohl (1984) indicated that printed information provided to parents regarding PL 94-142 and their rights (including their right to participate in the IEP process) was often not comprehensible to a large number of parents. This is one variable that should be addressed in helping agencies meet not only the letter but also the intent of the law (Roit & Pfohl, 1984).

REFERENCES

Federal Register. (1977). Regulations implementing Education for All Handicapped Children Act of 1975. Washington, DC: Department of Health, Education, and Welfare.

Lusthaus, C.S., Lusthaus, E.W., & Gibbs, H. (1981). Parents' role in the decision process. *Exceptional Children, 48*(3), 256–257.

Polifka, J.C. (1981). Compliance with Public Law 94-142 and consumer satisfaction. *Exceptional Children, 48*(3), 250–253.

Roit, M.L., & Pfohl, W. (1984). The readability of PL 94-142 parent materials: Are parents truly informed? *Exceptional Children, 50*(6), 496–506.

Ryan, L.G., & Rucher, C.N. (1991). The development and validation of a measure of special education teachers' attitudes toward the IEP. *Educational and Psychological Measurement, 51*(4), 877–882.

Scanlon, C.A., Arick, J.R., & Phelps, N. (1981). Participation in development of the IEP: Parents' perspective. *Exceptional Children, 47*(5), 373–376.

Van Reusen, A.K., & Bos, C.S. (1994). Facilitating student participation in individualized education programs through motivational strategy instruction. *Exceptional Children, 60*(5), 466–475.

Yoshida, R., Fenton, K., Kaufman, M.J., & Maxwell, J.P. (1978). Parental involvement in the special education pupil planning process: The school's perspective. *Exceptional Children, 44,* 531–533.

See also **Individuals with Disabilities Education Act (IDEA); Parents of the Handicapped**

INDIVIDUAL VARIABILITY

See TEST SCATTER.

INDIVIDUALS WITH DISABILITIES EDUCATION ACT (IDEA), PL 105-17

The Individuals with Disabilities Education Act (IDEA), formerly known as the Education for All Handicapped Children Act of 1975 (EHA; PL 94-142), represents a more than 20 year national commitment, beginning with EHA, to children with disabilities ("Focus on IDEA," 1997). IDEA, a federal statute, is the main special education law in the United States, and when initially enacted in 1975, it represented the most sweeping statement this nation has ever made regarding the rights of children with disabilities (Haring, McCormick, & Haring, 1994). The purpose of the law is:

"1)(a) to ensure that all children with disabilities have available to them a free appropriate public education that emphasizes special education and related services designed to meet their unique needs and prepare them for employment and independent living; (b) to ensure that the rights of children with disabilities and parents of such children are protected; (c) to assist states, localities, educational service agencies and federal agencies to provide for the education of all children with disabilities; 2) to assist states in the implementation of a statewide, comprehensive, coordinated, multidisciplinary, interagency system of early intervention services for infants and toddlers with disabilities and their families; 3) to ensure that educators and parents have the necessary tools to improve educational results for children with disabilities by supporting systemic-change activities; coordinated technical assistance, dissemination, and support; and technology development and media services; and, 4) to assess, and ensure the effectiveness of, efforts to educate children with disabilities" (20 U.S.C. 1400 § Sec 601 [d]).

Under IDEA, the state is responsible for providing for children with disabilities, whether they are attending a public or private school, the opportunity to participate in special education and related services (20 U.S.C. 1400 § Sec 612). Denial of this opportunity by the state results in the forfeiture of federal funds (20 U.S.C. 1400 § Sec 616).

Early legislation and case law, spanning over a 20-year period, foreshadowed the enactment of the initial version of the law, EHA, in 1975 (Jacob-Timm & Hartshorne, 1995). Three landmark court cases, *Brown v. Board of Education of Topeka* (1954); *Pennsylvania Association for Retarded Children v. Commonwealth of Pennsylvania* (PARC; 1971, 1972); and *Mills v. Board of Education* (1972); marked a turning point in the education of children with disabilities and provided the impetus for the development and enactment of federal legislation assuring a free appropriate public education for children with disabilities. Prior to the Brown case, many school districts throughout the nation were operating under the "separate but equal" policy (i.e., segregated classrooms based on race) that were in actuality not equal. Many minorities (Blacks, in the case of Brown) were excluded from an equal educational opportunity in public schools. This practice, according to the Brown ruling, was in violation of the "equal protection clause" of the 14th Amendment to the U.S. Constitution. Education, which is considered to be a property right, is protected under the "equal protection clause" of the 14th Amendment, and in the Brown ruling, the property right of Blacks to an education at the public expense was violated (Jacob-Timm & Hartshorne, 1995).

Following the Brown ruling and other successful court challenges to racial discrimination in the public schools, parents of children with disabilities began to file lawsuits on behalf of their children alleging that the children's right to an education at the public expense was being violated in accordance to the equal protection clause of the 14th Amendment. Prior to the 1970s, many schools denied children with disabilities access to a public education based on school district policies, which required a child to meet certain admission standards (e.g., possession of a certain level of adaptive living and cognitive skills). In PARC, parents of children with mental retardation brought suit against the Commonwealth of Pennsylvania because their children were denied access to a public education. In a consent decree, the parents of the children with mental retardation won access to the public schools for their children. Similarly, in Mills, the parents of children with behavioral, emotional, and learning problems brought suit on behalf of their children against the District of Columbia for denial of access to a public education. In a consent decree followed by a court order, the court ruled that the schools were required to provide each child with a disability a free and public-supported education, regardless of the degree of severity or nature of the child's disability (Jacob-Timm & Hartshorne, 1995).

In response to the successful resolution of the PARC and Mills cases, an additional 36 "right-to-education" cases were filed in 27 different jurisdictions by parents on behalf of their children with disabilities (Martin, 1979). These cases served as a signal to the U.S. Congress that federal legislation was needed to ensure a full educational opportunity to children with disabilities (Jacob-Timm & Hartshorne, 1995).

In addition to case law, early attempts were made by the U.S. Congress to address the needs of children with disabilities. Funds were made available through various education laws and amendments to education laws to develop or improve special education resources, programs, services, and personnel. Beginning as early as the 1960s with the passage of PL 87-276, Congress authorized support for the training of teachers to work with the deaf and for speech pathologists and audiologists to work with individuals with speech and hearing impairments (Abramson, 1987; Reynolds & Fletcher-Janzen, 1990). In 1965, the Elementary and Secondary Education Act (ESEA; PL 89-10), one of the first major federal programs to aid education, was enacted. One year later, Congress amended the ESEA (PL 89-750), and, with these amendments, grants were provided to states to assist in the development and improvement of programs to educate children with disabilities (Jacob-Timm & Hartshorne, 1995). Students with disabilities were also assisted when the 1968 Amendments to the Vocational Education Act (PL 90-576) were passed. With these amendments, funds were made available for students with disabilities in vocational education programs (Abramson, 1987; Reynolds & Fletcher-Janzen, 1990). The needs of young children with disabilities were addressed with the establishment of model programs under the Handicapped Children's Early Education Assistance Act (PL 90-538) in 1968 (Abramson, 1987; Reynolds & Fletcher-Janzen, 1990). In 1970, Congress repealed and replaced the 1966 amendments to the ESEA (PL 89-750; Jacob-Timm & Hartshorne, 1995). Public Law 99-230, which replaced PL 89-750, established a grant program similar to PL 89-750 to encourage states to develop special education resources and personnel (Turnbull, 1990). Federal government assistance to states for special education increased with the passage of the Education Amendments of 1974 (PL 93-380). This act also put schools on notice that federal funding for special education purposes would be contingent on the development of a state plan with the goal of providing children with disabilities a full educational opportunity (Jacob-Timm & Hartshorne, 1995).

Congress also attempted to address the needs of children with disabilities through antidiscrimination legislation (Martin, 1979). An amendment to Title VI of the Civil Rights Act of 1964 was one of the first pieces of legislation that attempted to ensure equal educational opportunities for children with disabilities. Nine years later, this amendment became part of Section 504 of the Rehabilitation Act of 1973. Section 504 is a civil rights act that prohibits discrimination against children with disabilities in schools receiving federal funds. Federal funds are not available to schools not in compliance with the act (Jacob-Timm & Hartshorne, 1995).

Through enactment of antidiscrimination legislation and education laws, passage of amendments to existing education laws, and litigation, the stage was set for the introduction of a comprehensive federal statute that would reaffirm and strengthen the educational rights of children with disabilities and increase the federal government's financial commitment to children with disabilities (Abramson, 1987; Reynolds & Fletcher-Janzen, 1990). The Education for All Handicapped Children Act was originally introduced as a Senate bill in 1972. After three years of extensive hearings, the U.S. Congress passed the bill in 1975 and President Gerald Ford signed the bill into law on November 29, 1975. EHA was amended in 1978 (PL 98-773), 1983 (PL 98-199), twice in 1986 (PL 99-457 and PL 99-372), in 1988 (PL 100-630) and 1990 (PL 101-476; Jacob-Timm & Hartshorne, 1995).

In 1990, President George Bush signed PL 101-476 into law. In signing the 1990 Amendments into law, the law was renamed the Individuals with Disabilities Education Act. IDEA has also been amended with the most recent amendments passed in 1997 (PL 105-17; National Association of State Directors of Special Education [NASDSE], 1997). Public Law 105–17 was signed into law on June 4, 1997 by President Bill Clinton and is the current law. The majority of the IDEA provisions went into effect with the President's signature; however, some provisions addressing the development of an individual program for each disabled student, referred to as an individualized education program (IEP), did not go into effect until July 1998 ("Focus on IDEA," 1997).

The new legislation restructures IDEA into four parts: Part A, General Provisions; Part B, Assistance for Education of All Children with Disabilities; Part C, Infants and Toddlers with Disabilities; and Part D, National Activities to Improve Education of Children with Disabilities (20 U.S.C. 1400 § Sec 101). Part A, General Provisions, contains the definitions used within the law and the law's purpose. With the passage of the 1997 Amendments, a few important changes have been made in Part A. First, a child who is experiencing developmental delays and ranges in age from 3 to 9 years now meets the eligibility criteria for a child with a disability. The age range has been expanded with the new legislation from 3–5 to 3–9 years of age with state and local educational agencies' (SEAs and LEAs) approval. Second, a change of emphasis in the term serious emotional disturbance is referenced in the definitions section under the heading of a child with a disability but thereafter is referred to as an emotional disturbance. Another major change involves policy letters drafted by the U.S. Department of Education (DOE). The DOE must now provide an official notice for public response when it drafts a policy letter used to monitor compliance with the law. This requirement in the new law restricts the power of the DOE in attempts to increase public input (20 U.S.C. 1400 § Sec 601–607).

Part B, Assistance for Education of All Children with Disabilities, includes information on the authorization of federal funds to the states and state requirements to receive federal funds. The federal government provides funds to the states to financially assist the states in the education of children with disabilities. Federal funds are distributed to the states based on a "child-count" formula. The current child-count formula for a state is equal to the number of children with disabilities, aged 3–21, receiving special education and related services in the state multiplied by 40 percent of the average per pupil expenditure (APPE) in public elementary and secondary schools in the United States (NASDSE, 1997). With the new legislation, the current child-count formula is retained; however, when the federal appropriation exceeds $4.9 billion (i.e., $4,924,672,000), additional funds are to be allocated based on a census formula, corrected for poverty ("Focus on IDEA," 1997). When federal funds are received by the state, the state may retain up to 25% of the federal funds for state administrative and state-level activities but must send at least 75% of the funds to the LEAs if the federal appropriation does not exceed the $4.9 billion mark. However, the percentage of allocated funds to SEAs and LEAs will change if the federal appropriation exceeds $4.9 billion (20 U.S.C. 1400 § Sec 611).

In order to receive federal funds, states are required to have a state plan in effect. The state plan must include the following key components:

1. *Free appropriate public education (FAPE).* The state ensures that a free appropriate public education is available to all children with disabilities.

2. *Full educational opportunity goal.* The state establishes policies and procedures to ensure a full educational opportunity is available to all children with disabilities.

3. *Child find.* The state identifies, locates, and evaluates all children with disabilities, regardless of the severity of their disabilities. Under PL 105-17, children in private schools are included in the child find requirement. In addition, nothing in the new amendments requires classification of a child by disability as long as the child is eligible under the federal definition.

4. *Individualized education program (IEP).* An individualized education program or individualized family service plan (IFSP) is developed, reviewed, and revised for each child with a disability.

5. *Least restrictive environment (LRE).* The state establishes procedural safeguards to ensure that children with and without disabilities are educated together to the maximum extent appropriate.

6. *Procedural safeguards.* Children with disabilities and their parents are assured the procedural safeguards required by the law, including the right to nondiscriminatory testing and evaluation. Additional safeguards are listed below.

7. *Confidentiality.* The state protects the confidentiality of any personally identifiable information, data, and records collected or maintained by the federal government, SEAs, and LEAs on students with disabilities.

8. *Transition from infant and toddler program to preschool program.* The state ensures that children who will partic-

ipate in the preschool programs and are currently at-tending infant and toddler programs will experience a smooth and effective transition to the preschool pro-grams. Under the new legislation, the LEAs are required to participate in the transition planning conferences.

9. *Children in private schools.* Children with disabilities who attend private schools are entitled to special edu-cation and related services. The services may be pro-vided on the premises of the private schools, including parochial schools to the extent consistent with the law. According to the 1997 Amendments, however, LEAs are not required to pay for the placement of a child with a disability if the placement was based on a unilateral parent-initiated decision.

10. *State educational agency responsibility.* The state en-sures that all educational programs are under the gen-eral supervision of the SEA.

11. *Ensuring services.* The SEA establishes interagency agreements with public agencies responsible for provid-ing and paying for special education or related services used by children with disabilities. These agreements must be in effect. Under the new legislation, the state Medicaid agency and other public insurers' financial responsibility precedes the LEA and SEA's responsibil-ity, but the SEA remains the payer of last resort.

12. *Comprehensive system for personnel development (CSPD).* The new legislation requires the state to have a CSPD in effect. The CSPD is designed to ensure an adequate supply of qualified personnel to work with children with disabilities.

13. *Personnel standards.* The state ensures that personnel who work with children with disabilities have the high-est qualified standards. Under the new legislation, trained and supervised paraprofessionals may assist in providing services to children with disabilities. In addi-tion, when school personnel shortages exist the SEA may permit a LEA to hire an individual who does not currently have the highest qualified standards but who will reach these standards in three years.

14. *Performance goals and indicators.* Under the new legis-lation, the State is required to establish goals for the performance of children with disabilities and develop indicators to judge children's progress.

15. *Participation in assessments.* According to the new leg-islation, beginning in 1998, the state must ensure that children with disabilities are included in state- and dis-trict-wide assessment programs and that appropriate accommodations are made if necessary.

16. Additional components. Other components that must be included in the state plan are: 1) the establishment of a state advisory panel; 2) examination of suspension and expulsion rates of disabled and nondisabled chil-dren; 3) public comment prior to the adoption of new policies and procedures; 4) regulations regarding sup-plementation of state, local, and other federal funds; 5)

maintenance of state financial support; and 6) notifica-tion and hearing rights of LEAs (20 U.S.C. 1400 § 612).

Section 613 of the Act outlines the conditions LEAs must meet to be eligible for funding. To be eligible for fund-ing, each LEA's plan must be consistent with the state plan. Once funding is received, LEAs are not allowed to reduce fi-nancial support to schools unless the federal appropriation reaches $4.1 billion or special circumstances arise, such as the voluntary departure of school personnel or a decrease in school enrollment. LEAs must provide funding and serve children with disabilities who attend public charter schools in the same manner as children with disabilities who attend public schools. LEA funding, if approved by the state, may also be used to develop school-based improvement plans with significant parent or professional approval (20 U.S.C. 1400 § Sec 613).

The state may require LEAs to meet other conditions as well. The state may require LEAs to include disciplinary in-formation in the records of children with disabilities and to transmit the record with the disciplinary information in-cluded in the same manner that disciplinary information is included in, and transmitted with, the student records of nondisabled children. The information transmitted may in-clude a description of the behavior and disciplinary action taken, and any other additional information that is relevant to the safety of the child or others. When the child with a disability transfers to another school (e.g., to another ele-mentary school), the child's most current IEP and all disci-plinary action would be included in and transferred with the child's records (20 U.S.C. 1400 § Sec 613).

Section 614 of IDEA addresses the evaluation process used to determine a child's eligibility for special education and related services, the IEP developed for the child once el-igibility has been determined, and the educational place-ment or appropriate setting for the child to receive an education. The new legislation has resulted in significant changes in evaluations, reevaluations, eligibility determina-tions, IEPs, and placement decisions. The law requires a full and individual initial evaluation of the child to be con-ducted once informed consent from the parent is obtained before the initial provision for special education and related services is provided. The initial evaluation must be con-ducted with technically sound instruments and the child must be initially assessed in all areas of suspected disability. The child is afforded greater protections in the evaluation process under the new legislation, including non-biased protections as well as the need to address the child's educa-tional experiences and primary language. Parental partici-pation in the assessment process, including information provided by the parents, has also been incorporated into the law (20 U.S.C. 1400 § Sec 614).

Upon completion of the evaluation process, a determi-nation is made as to whether a child qualifies as a child with a disability or not. A team of qualified professionals and a parent of a child make the eligibility determination. The parent is given a copy of the evaluation report and documentation of the determination of eligibility (20 U.S.C. 1400 § Sec 614).

After eligibility for special education and related services has been determined, an IEP must be developed. An IEP is a written statement developed, reviewed, and revised by the IEP team for a child with a disability, and it includes information regarding the child's present level of educational performance, measurable annual goals, special education and related services and supplementary aids and services to be provided to the child, program modifications or supports for school personnel that will be provided to the child, explanations of the extent of the child's nonparticipation with nondisabled children in the regular classroom, modifications in administration of state- or district-wide assessments or an explanation as to why these assessments are inappropriate for the child, transition plans, and progress of the child and means of informing the parents of the child's progress. Several new provisions have been mandated with the passage of PL 105-17 with regard to the IEP team and the IEP. The IEP team must now include, as appropriate, one of the child's regular education teachers in addition to the former requirement that established the composition of the IEP team. New additions or modifications in the IEP are also required. The IEP goals must focus on involvement and measured progress of the child in the general curriculum. Transition plans addressing the child's courses of study will now appear on the IEP beginning at age 14 instead of 16 or younger as required by the former regulations. The IEP, as always, must consider the child's strengths, parent concerns, and initial and most recent evaluation results (20 U.S.C. 1400 § Sec 614).

A reevaluation is conducted for a child with a disability if conditions warrant a reevaluation, a child's parent or teacher requests a reevaluation, or a three-year period has elapsed since the last evaluation. Under the new legislation, additional testing is not required in the reevaluation process to reconfirm a child's disability. The content or components that make up a three-year evaluation will be determined by the IEP team along with other qualified professionals with the parents' approval and may include only existing data, such as classroom assessments and observations. More comprehensive and more frequent reevaluations may still be conducted at the parents' request. Under the new legislation, parents have the right to consent to a reevaluation. A reevaluation must now also be conducted when a child exits eligibility from IDEA (20 U.S.C. 1400 § Sec 614).

Section 614 also addresses the behavioral needs of school children. A new special consideration section including goals for behavioral needs has been added. Strategies, including positive behavioral interventions and supports to address any behavior that interferes with learning, must be considered when and where appropriate (20 U.S.C. 1400 § Sec 614).

Section 615 of IDEA requires procedural safeguards to be put into place to assure the rights of children with disabilities and their parents. The procedural safeguards include:

1. The opportunity for parents to examine all of their child's records and to participate in meetings with respect to the identification, evaluation, placement, and provisions of FAPE to the child. This procedural safeguard has been modified under PL 105-17.

2. Protections of the child's rights when parents or guardians cannot be located. In other words, a surrogate parent is appointed whenever the parent or guardian is unknown.

3. Written prior notice to parents when a change or refusal to make a change in the identification, evaluation, or placement of the child is anticipated by the LEA.

4. Written prior notice to parents is provided in their native language, unless unfeasible, regarding all safeguards.

5. An opportunity for mediation is available to parents. This procedural safeguard is new under the Act. Failure to participate in mediation cannot be used to delay or deny the parents' rights to a due process hearing.

6. An opportunity for parents to present complaints with respect to the identification, evaluation, or placement of the child or provision of FAPE to the child.

7. The SEA requirement to develop a model form to assist parents in filing complaints. This procedural safeguard is another addition to the current law.

8. Parental notice or notice from the parents' attorney when the child or parent encounters a problem. The notice includes a description of the problem and proposed resolution of the problem. This procedural safeguard is new under PL 105-17 (20 U.S.C. 1400 § Sec 615).

The remainder of this section describes procedures parents may use to resolve disputes with LEAs and SEAs as well as placement in alternative educational settings (AES). Procedures for resolving disputes range from voluntary mediation to due process hearings to civil actions. If disputes cannot be resolved through mediation or due process hearings, parents may pursue civil action (20 U.S.C. 1400 § Sec 615). Under the 1990 Amendments to IDEA, states may be sued by private citizens for violations of the law; however, parents are required, except for a few unusual circumstances, to exhaust administrative remedies (e.g., mediation or due process hearings) before pursuing civil action. Parents may recover attorneys' fees if they prevail in court action (Jacob-Timm & Hartshorne, 1995). Court decisions (e.g., Moore v. District of Columbia, 1990) suggest parents may be able to recover attorney fees for both administration proceedings as well as litigation (Jacob-Timm & Hartshorne, 1995).

School personnel may order a change in placement for not more than 10 school days to an interim AES, another setting, or suspension for a child of not more than 45 calendar days to an interim AES for a child who carries a weapon to school or to a school function or possesses, uses, or sells illegal drugs at school or a school function. Within 10 business days after taking the disciplinary action, the LEA must conduct a functional behavioral assessment and implement a behavioral intervention plan or review and revise, as necessary, the existing plan. The IEP team is responsible for developing or reviewing and revising the assessment plan to address the inappropriate behavior. Under these circumstances, FAPE continues to be available to the child (20 U.S.C. 1400 § Sec 615). However, the Secretary of the DOE offers an interpretation of this new provision to the law and proposes that schools be relieved of the obligation to provide FAPE and to consider behavioral interventions or modifications in existing strategies for children who are suspended for 10 or less school days during a given calendar year, whereas schools need to continue FAPE for children who are chronically ill or who have serious behavior problems and are repeatedly excluded from school (*Proposed federal regulations,* 1997).

A hearing officer may also order a change in placement for a child with a disability. The change in placement to an interim AES may not be for more than 45 calendar days. The hearing officer's decision to change a child's placement must be based on the preponderance of evidence suggesting that a child is likely to injure him/herself or others if maintained in the current placement (20 U.S.C. 1400 § Sec 615).

In all disciplinary action against a child with a disability involving a change in placement, a manifestation of determination, a new provision under the 1997 Amendments to IDEA, must be made by an IEP team and other qualified personnel. The manifestation of determination involves a review of diagnostic results, observations of the child, placement, and IEP to determine if appropriate and to consider if the child's inappropriate behavior was the result of the disability. If the behavior is not the result of either the disability or inadequate services, the child may be disciplined under the general code of conduct in the same manner and severity as a nondisabled peer, but the child must continue to receive FAPE. Parents have the right to appeal any step of this process (20 U.S.C. 1400 § Sec 615). The Secretary of the DOE offers an interpretation of this provision of the law and proposes that if the child is removed for 10 or less school days in a given school year or the child has not engaged in repeated or significant misconduct, then the school is not required to conduct a manifestation of determination (*Proposed federal regulations,* 1997).

Section 616 of the Act contains provisions related to withholding payments to the states by the Secretary of the DOE. The Secretary may withhold federal funding in part or whole to the state if the SEA or LEAs are found not to be in compliance with either the provisions of the act or the state plan. If any state does not agree with the Secretary's decision with respect to the state plan, then a state may file a petition with the U.S. Court of Appeals for judicial review of the Secretary's action. The judgment of the court shall be subject to review by the U.S. Supreme Court (20 U.S.C. 1400 § Sec 616).

Section 617 addresses the administrative components of the act. The law outlines the responsibilities of the Secretary, rules and regulations, protection of the confidentiality of personally identifiable information, and the hiring of personnel to collect data. The responsibilities of the Secretary include promotion and dissemination of information about special education. The Secretary is required to issue regulations to the extent that such regulations are necessary to ensure compliance with the act. Personnel are hired to collect data for both evaluation and program information purposes (20 U.S.C. 1400 § Sec 617).

Each state, according to Section 618, is required to provide information on their program (i.e., data) on an annual basis. The purpose of the data collection process is to evaluate the impact of the program, the effectiveness of state efforts, and the progress made since the implementation of the Act. Head counts are taken on the number of children with disabilities, by race, ethnicity, and disability category who are receiving FAPE, participating in regular education, receiving early intervention services, and/or attending separate classes, schools, or facilities or public or private residential facilities. Additional information is obtained on the number of children with disabilities, by race, ethnicity, and disability category who are 14–21 years of age and have stopped receiving special education and related services or who are between birth and two years of age and have stopped receiving early intervention services because of program completion or other reasons. The number of children with disabilities, by race, ethnicity, and disability category, who have been removed to an interim AES or subject to long-term suspensions or expulsions, is computed as well. The number of infants and toddlers who are at risk for substantial developmental delays and are receiving early intervention services are calculated by race and ethnicity. Significant discrepancies in the data collected concerning identification and placement of children with disabilities by race as well as significant discrepancies in the suspension and expulsion rates between disabled and nondisabled children are examined, and based on these examinations, policies, practices, and procedures are reviewed and revisions are made to ensure compliance with the Act. The information obtained through the data collection process is submitted on an annual basis to the U.S. Congress (20 U.S.C. 1400 § Sec 618).

Preschool grants are addressed in Section 619. Preschool grants are available to states to assist the states in providing special education and related services to children with disabilities aged 3 to 5. States at their own discretion may also include two year old children with disabilities who will turn three during the school year. Under the new legislation, the funding formula has changed to conform to the formula change in Part B. In addition, the state/local split of federal funding has also changed to conform to the changes in Part B with the exception of subgrants to LEAs, where the amount to be received is based on a different formula (20 U.S.C. 1400 § Sec 619).

Part C of the Act, Infants and Toddlers with Disabilities, contains information about this program, including eligibility criteria, state requirements, IFSP, state application and assurances, funding issues and responsibilities, procedural safeguards, and coordination efforts among state or federal agencies. Grants are made available to states to develop statewide interagency systems for the provision of early intervention services for infants and toddlers with disabilities and their families. With the passage of the 1997 Amendments to IDEA, several changes have been made. First, Part H is now Part C. Second, at-risk infants and toddlers are now included in the eligibility definition. Third, federal funding has increased for the Infant and Toddler program. Another change is that services provided to infants and toddlers and their families must be maximally provided in natural settings. Highest qualified standards for personnel are also incorporated into Part C (20 U.S.C. 1400 § Sec 631–645).

Part D, National Activities to Improve Education of Children with Disabilities, includes all other discretionary programs (i.e., state improvement grants, personnel preparation, research, technical assistance, parent training, and dissemination). State improvement grants are made available to assist SEAs and their partners in reforming and improving systems for providing educational, early intervention, and transitional services to improve results for students. Grants are also made available for research and innovation and personnel preparation to improve services and results for children with disabilities (20 U.S.C. 1400 § Sec 651–687).

The key provisions of IDEA include FAPE, nondiscriminatory assessment, the IEP, procedural safeguards, confidentiality of records, LRE, and related services. A free appropriate public education is available to all children with disabilities, regardless of the nature or severity of their disability. FAPE is special education and related services, and these services are provided to children with disabilities at no cost to the children's parents or the children. SEAs are responsible for ensuring that LEAs provide FAPE to all children with disabilities (20 U.S.C. 1400 § Sec 602).

Another key provision is nondiscriminatory assessment. Testing and evaluation materials must be selected and administered so as not to be culturally and racially discriminatory. In addition, tests must be administered in the child's native language or other mode of communication, unless unfeasible to do. Besides these requirements, LEAs must ensure that standardized tests given to a child are validated for the purpose for which they are used and are administered by trained personnel in accordance with the test producer's instructions. The child must be assessed in all areas of suspected disability. The child must also be assessed with a variety of assessment tools and strategies, the instruments must be technically sound, and no single procedure must be used as the sole criterion for determining eligibility (20 U.S.C. 1400 § Sec 614).

Procedural safeguards are discussed at length under Section 615. These safeguards are a means of ensuring that children with disabilities and their parents have certain rights and these rights are protected under the law. Parents are given the opportunity to present their complaints regarding possible violations of their rights through mediation, due process hearings, and/or civil action with respect to any matter relating to the identification, evaluation, or placement of a child (20 U.S.C. 1400 § Sec 615).

Parents' rights also extend to the educational records of their child. Educational and psychological records pertaining to the child must remain confidential except to those individuals who are directly involved in a child's education and who have a specific reason for reviewing the records (20 U.S.C. 1400 § Sec 617). Additional limitations regarding the confidentiality of students' records can be found in the entry for the Family Educational Rights and Privacy Act (FERPA). The 1997 Amendments provide parents with the opportunity to examine all records, not just relevant records, with respect to the identification, evaluation, and placement of their child, and the provision of FAPE (20 U.S.C. 1400 § Sec 615).

Special education and related services must be provided in the LRE for children with disabilities in public or private institutions. The act requires, to the maximum extent appropriate, that children with disabilities and nondisabled children be educated together in as normal an environment as possible, and that removal from the regular education environment occurs only when education in the regular education setting with supplementary aids and services cannot be achieved satisfactorily. Therefore, the LRE for a child with a disability does not necessarily require the child to be educated entirely or in part in regular classes. Decisions about what constitutes the LRE are made on an individual basis for each child with a disability. Decisions are based on the child's needs and requirements for an educational program (20 U.S.C. 1400 § Sec 612).

Related services are support services required to assist children with disabilities to benefit from special education. Examples of related services include psychological services, physical and occupational therapy, speech pathology, and audiology. Under the new legislation, orientation and mobility services are added to the definition of related services. Related services cannot stand alone under IDEA-Part B. Those services must be attached to a special education program. In other words, a child must be eligible for special education under IDEA-Part B in order to receive related services (20 U.S.C. 1400 § Sec 602).

An IEP is required for each child with a disability who is receiving special education. Each LEA must have an IEP in place for each child at the beginning of each school year. The child's IEP is reviewed and revised on at least an annual basis by the IEP team, and a reevaluation is conducted at least once every three years. The IEP team consists of the parent of the child, at least one special education teacher and one regular education teacher if the child is or may be participating in the regular education program, a representative of the LEA who is qualified to provide or supervise the provision of specially-designed instruction and who is knowledgeable about the general curriculum and resources available, an individual who can interpret the instructional implications of evaluation results, other individuals at the discretion of the parent or LEA, and the child when appropriate (20 U.S.C. 1400 § Sec 614). The IEP serves as the mechanism by which goals and objectives are established, programs are planned, and progress of the child is monitored (Abramson, 1987; Reynolds & Fletcher-Janzen, 1990).

With the passage of the 1997 Amendments to IDEA, more opportunities for the development of partnerships among parents, educators, related services, and early intervention service providers now exist. The role of parents and students will hopefully be strengthened through these increased opportunities for involvement (*Proposed federal regulations,* 1997). Parents have the opportunity to participate in meetings that are held to address the identification, evaluation, placement, and provision of FAPE to their child. Parents have the right to be part of the teams that determine what additional information is needed as part of their child's evaluation, determine their child's eligibility, and determine their child's educational placement. Parents' concerns and the information provided must be considered in developing and reviewing the child's IEP. Notification must be given to parents about IEP meetings. The purpose, time, location, and attendees must be included in the notice. Documentation of attempts to notify parents to ensure their participation in the meetings is required. Parents have the right to request and receive a copy of their child's IEP. Parents have the right to seek resolution of disagreements with the LEA or SEA through mediation, due process hearings, or civil action. The parents have a right to obtain an independent evaluation. Parents must also be informed on a regular basis of their child's progress in meeting his/her annual goals. Furthermore, parents have the right to participate in an annual review of their child's educational progress. These meetings are to be conducted on an annual basis. Finally, a foster parent may be treated as a parent for IDEA purposes. The addition of a foster parent in the definition of a parent may promote more involvement of foster parents in the education of children with disabilities (*Proposed federal regulations,* 1997).

The IDEA Amendments of 1997 and 1990 have created opportunities to strengthen the involvement of children with disabilities in decisions regarding their own future. Students must be invited to IEP meetings when the purpose of the meetings will be to discuss the need for transition services. Thus, students who are 14 or 15 years old may be invited to participate in these meetings. If the student is unable to attend, steps must be taken to ensure that a student's preferences and interests are considered. Under Part B, states may now transfer most parents' rights to their child when the child reaches the age of majority under state law if the student is mentally competent. Furthermore, at least one year before the child reaches the age of majority, the student must be informed that these rights will be transferred. A statement regarding the transfer of rights must be included in the child's IEP (*Proposed federal regulations,* 1997).

There are some additional changes or modifications that have resulted with the passage of the new amendments. First, parents' right to a due process hearing cannot be de-

layed or denied because the parents failed to give notice to the LEA or SEA as required by the statute. Second, the new law terminates a student's right to FAPE when the student graduates with a regular high school diploma, but not when the student receives some other certificate. The purpose of this regulation is to make clear that the educational expectations for disabled and nondisabled students are the same. Third, SEA reports on state- or district-wide assessment results must include disabled and nondisabled students. Aggregated results are reported to ensure better accountability. Fourth, LEAs may reduce expenditures only when qualified, lower-salaried personnel replace departing personnel. Fifth, written informed consent from parents must be received before an IFSP can be used instead of an IEP. Sixth, parents must receive prior written notice about how to file complaints, and a three-year limitation is placed on the age of complaints. Parents are also made aware of low-cost and less adversarial mechanisms to resolve disputes (*Proposed federal regulations,* 1997).

The 1997 Amendments to IDEA mark an over 20 year national commitment to ensure a full educational opportunity to children with disabilities ("Focus on IDEA," 1997). The impact of these new amendments is unknown at the present time. Additional changes to the law will continue to be made in the future, and these changes will more than likely have a significant influence on children with disabilities as well as their families.

REFERENCES

Abramson, M. (1987). Education For All Handicapped Children Act of 1975 (PL 94-142). In C.R. Reynolds & L. Mann (Eds.), *Encyclopedia of special education* (pp. 583–585). New York: Wiley.

Focus on IDEA. (1997, July). *Span update.* Bethesda, MD: National Association of School Psychologists.

Haring, N.G., McCormick, L., & Haring, T. (1994). *Exceptional children & youth: An introduction to special education* (6th ed.). New York: Prentice Hall.

Individuals with Disabilities Act of 1997, 20 U.S.C. §§ 1400 *et seq.* (West, 1997).

Jacob-Timm, S., & Hartshorne, T. (1995). *Ethics and law for school psychologists.* Brandon, VT: Clinical Psychology Publishing.

Martin, R. (1979). *Educating handicapped children: The legal mandate.* Champaign, IL: Research Press.

Moore v. District of Columbia, 907 F.2d 165 (D.C. Cir. 1990).

National Association of State Directors of Special Education. (1997). *Comparison of key issues: Current law & 1997 IDEA Amendments.* Washington, DC: National Association of State Directors of Special Education.

Proposed federal regulations for the Individuals with Disabilities Education Act. (November, 1997). Washington, DC: Department of Education.

Reynolds, C.R., & Fletcher-Janzen, E. (1990). Education For All Handicapped Children Act of 1975 (PL 94-142). In C.R. Reynolds & L. Mann (Eds.), *Concise encyclopedia of special education* (pp. 386–388). New York: Wiley.

Turnbull, H.R. (1990). *Free appropriate public education* (3rd ed.). Denver, CO: Love.

INFANT ASSESSMENT

The term infant assessment has come to represent a variety of formal and informal screening and diagnostic procedures used for the systematic collection of data. The initial purpose of assessment is to determine whether development of the infant is progressing normally.

Recent advances in genetics and biochemistry have made it possible to begin this assessment process prior to the birth of the infant. Information about the health of the mother and her fetus, including the identification of genetic and chromosomal disorders, can be obtained through prenatal diagnostic techniques.

The common areas of focus for the assessment of infants from birth through 2 years of age include physical and sensory attributes, cognitive and general communication abilities, and social/emotional responses and interactions.

Infant assessment begins with procedures that can be carried out quickly and inexpensively. These screening measures constitute the initial stage of the assessment process and allow for the identification of at-risk infants (i.e., individuals with known or suspected disorders or developmental delays).

For those infants considered to be at risk, the focus of assessment is expanded to include more in-depth or diagnostic procedures. The purpose for using diagnostic measures is to collect information that will help to identify and understand the nature of an impairment as it affects the development of the infant.

Screening and diagnostic information can be gathered through the combined use of direct testing (using standardized norm, criterion, or curriculum reference measures), naturalistic observations, and parent interviews. The resulting information is analyzed and used to make strategic diagnostic, placement, and intervention decisions.

It is clear that the most pervasive issue with respect to the validity of assessing infant behavior is that it may not be possible to accurately predict long-range performance based on early test results. As Sheehan and Gallagher (1984) suggest, it may be more productive for infant assessment to be used to address immediate needs of diagnoses, placement, and intervention rather than long-range predictions of a child's developmental outcome.

As a result of continuing dialogue and research on infant assessment, many guiding principles have been offered in an attempt to achieve greater assessment reliability and validity. Although it is not possible to detail all of the information presented in the literature, the following summary represents an overview of suggestions as discussed by Bailey and Wolery (1984) and Sheehan and Gallagher (1984).

The assessment process should begin with the identification of the specific behaviors to be measured. Following this identification, selection of appropriate screening and diagnostic measures can be made. In-depth, diagnostic procedures must include the use of reliable and valid standardized tests (with appropriate use of adaptive equipment); multiple, systematic observations of the infant in various settings and situations; and parent interviews.

The collection and subsequent analysis of assessment data should be conducted by a multidisciplinary team, which might include a pediatrician, a psychologist, a communications specialist, and a physical therapist as well as the parents of the infant. The resulting information is used for the purpose of establishing appropriate objectives for intervention. This process of assessment also must include an evaluation of the intervention program.

REFERENCES

Bailey, D.B., & Wolery, M. (1984). *Teaching infants and preschoolers with handicaps.* Columbus, OH: Merrill.

Sheehan, R., & Gallagher, R.J. (1984). Assessment of infants. In M.J. Hanson (Ed.), *A typical infant development.* Baltimore, MD: University Park Press.

See also Apgar Rating Scale; Assessment; Developmental Milestones; Infant Stimulation; Measurement

INFANTILE AUTISM

See AUTISM.

INFANTILE HYPERCALCEMIA

Infantile hypercalcemia (also called hypercalcemia, or William's syndrome) is a rare syndrome whose etiology is uncertain. It is characterized by abnormal calcium chemistry and is associated with circulatory and cardiac (particularly supravalvular aortic stenosis) defects. Many children with this syndrome have low birth weights. They may have heart murmurs, kidney problems, and gastrointestinal problems early in life. There may be reduced muscle tone and general motor difficulties (listlessness, lethargy), also noted in infants. Most children will have mild to moderate mental retardation, although some children may have normal intelligence. Some mild neurologic dysfunction has been noted (Bergsma, 1979).

Children are short in stature (and skeletal defects are often seen), with pointed chins and ears, and are often described as having elfinlike features (full cheeks, small, broad foreheads). Wide-spaced and squinted eyes with epicanthal folds are typical. Teeth tend to be underdeveloped but the mouth is wide with a "cupid-bow" upper lip. No significant characteristics in upper or lower extremities are usually noted (Lemeshaw, 1982).

Affected individuals show a severe deficit of spatial cognition but have a modicum of language and face recognition (Atkinson, King, Braddick, Nores, Anker, & Braddick, 1997). Because of the varying degree of mental retardation and concomitant health and skeletal problems that may exist, a comprehensive assessment is necessary for proper placement of these children. Support medical services are usually required, and in some instances children will respond to medical treatment and surgery. Motoric problems may cause extensive immobility and may result in more restricted education placement than in a regular classroom. This decision can be made only by a complete evaluation of all the factors of this syndrome. Related services are often necessary as well.

REFERENCES

Atkinson, J., King, J., Braddick, O., Nores, L., Anker, S., & Braddick, F. (1997). A specific deficit of dorsal stream junction in William's Syndrome. *Neuroreport, 8*(8), 1919–1922.

Bergsma, D. (1979). *Birth defects compendium* (2nd ed.). New York: National Foundation, March of Dimes.

Lemeshaw, S. (1982). The handbook of clinical types in mental retardation. Boston: Allyn & Bacon.

See also **Hunter's Syndrome; Hurler's Syndrome; Low Birth Weight Infants; Mental Retardation; Physical Anomalies**

INFANT STIMULATION

The term infant stimulation is used to represent a variety of early intervention activities (i.e. perceptual, sensorimotor, cognitive, language, and/or social/emotional) that are designed to facilitate development. The value of early intervention is based on a body of research that has demonstrated that infants, including those with disabilities, are capable of learning as a result of sustained, meaningful interactions with people and events within their environment (Osofsky, 1979).

It is believed that early experiences of the infant serve as the foundation for future growth of the individual. According to developmental theory, an infant's early sensorimotor experiences such as visually tracking and reaching for objects are precursors for later cognitive attainments such as object permanence, means-ends, and spatial relationships (Gallagher & Reid, 1981).

Since many at-risk infants (i.e., infants with known or suspected handicapping conditions) manifest deficits in perceptual or sensorimotor areas, early intervention is particularly important. Deficits that limit an infant's interaction with his or her physical and social environment often will result in delayed or deficient development (Bobath & Bobath, 1972).

Currently, there is no clear agreement about how much or what type of stimulation is most effective for facilitating development. This issue is unresolved because it is not known how to validly evaluate the effects of stimulation activities. There is general agreement, however, that the stimulation of infants does have a positive effect on immediate and future development (Alberto, Briggs, & Goldstein, 1983; Hanson & Hanline, 1984; Sheehan & Gallagher, 1983).

Over the years many programs have been developed for the purpose of stimulating the development of handicapped and at-risk infants. Detailed reviews of these programs (Bailey, Jens, & Johnson, 1983; Sheehan & Gallagher, 1983) reveal that they vary greatly in their content and effectiveness.

Infant stimulation programs can be center-based (i.e., carried out by professionals in hospitals, clinics, or schools) or home-based (i.e., conducted by parents and professionals within the infant's home). There are also programs that combine center-based instruction with a home-based component.

Infant stimulation programs have been shown to be successful with low-vision infants (Leguire, Fellows, Rae, Rogers, & Bremer, 1992), with premature infants (Dieter & Emory, 1997), infants with gastric problems (de Roiste & Bushnell, 1995), and many other conditions.

REFERENCES

Alberto, P.A., Briggs, T., & Goldstein, D. (1983). Managing learning in handicapped infants. In S.G. Garwood & R.R. Fewell (Eds.), *Educating handicapped infants* (pp. 417–454). Rockville, MD: Aspen.

Bailey, D.B., Jr., Jens, K.G., & Johnson, N. (1983). Curricula for handicapped infants. In S.G. Garwood & R.R. Fewell (Eds.), *Educating handicapped infants* (pp. 387–416). Rockville, MD: Aspen.

Bobath, K., & Bobath, B. (1972). Cerebral palsy. In P.H. Pearson & C. Williams (Eds.), *Physical therapy services in the developmental disabilities.* Springfield, IL: Thomas.

Dieter, J.N.I., & Emory, K. (1997). Supplemental of stimulation of premature infants: A treatment model. *Journal of Pediatric Psychology, 22*(3), 281–295.

de Roiste, A., & Bushnell, I.W.R. (1995). The immediate gastric effects of a tactile stimulation programme on premature infants. *Journal of Reproductive & Infant Psychology, 13*(1), 57– 62.

Gallagher, J., & Reid, D.K. (1981). *The learning theory of Piaget and Inhelder.* Monterey, CA: Brooks/Cole.

Hanson, M.J., & Hanline, M.F. (1984). Behavioral competencies and outcomes: The effects of disorder. In M.J. Hanson (Ed.), *A typical infant development* (pp. 109–178). Baltimore, MD: University Park Press.

Leguire, L.E., Fellows, R.R., Rogers, G.L., & Bremer, D.L. (1992). The CCH vision stimulation program for infants with low vision: Preliminary results. *Journal of Visual Impairment & Blindness, 86*(1), 33–37.

Osofsky, J.D. (Ed.). (1979). *Handbook of infant development.* New York: Wiley.

Sheehan, R., & Gallagher, R.J. (1983). Conducting evaluations of infant intervention programs. In S. Garwood & R.R. Fewell (Eds.), *Educating handicapped infants.* Rockville, MD: Aspen.

See also **Deprivation; Enrichment; Infant Assessment; Low Birth Weight Infants**

INFORMAL READING INVENTORY (IRI)

Informal reading inventory (IRI) is a generic term that refers to some type of nonstandardized technique used to assess aspects of reading performance. According to Smith and Johnson (1980), the most informal application of the diagnostic method involves having the child read selections of material silently and orally, asking comprehension questions about what has been read, and making note of the quality of reading, particularly word identification errors.

Johnson and Kress (1965) identified four purposes for administering an informal reading inventory. The IRI can be used to determine the level at which a reader can function independently, the level at which he or she can profit from instruction, the level at which the reader is frustrated by the material (Pehrsson, 1994), and the level of listening comprehension. Results of an IRI aid in determining specific strengths and weaknesses in reading, thus leading to a program of instruction or remediation. Also, the results of an IRI enable the reader to become aware of his or her own abilities and can be used as a measure of reading progress.

REFERENCES

Johnson, M.S., & Kress, R.A. (1965). *Informal reading inventories.* Newark, DE: International Reading Association.

Pehrsson, R.S. (1994). Challenging frustration level. *Reading and Writing Quarterly, 10*(3), 201–208.

Smith, R.J., & Johnson, D.D. (1980). *Teaching children to read* (2nd ed.). Reading, MA: Addison-Wesley.

See also **Basal Reader; Cloze Technique; Johnston Informal Reading Inventory; Reading**

INFORMATION PROCESSING

Information processing in the context of psychological study, is the manipulation of incoming stimuli, and existing or stored information, and the creation of new information by the human brain. This would include such common activities as perception, encoding, decoding, retrieval from memory, rehearsal, general reasoning ability, and a growing multitude of "new" cognitive processes. As new theories of cognitive processes occur, new names and new constructs are devised and added to the list. Implicit in theories of information processing is the assumption that each individual's behavior is determined by the information processing that occurs internally. In combination, the form, depth, and breadth of information processing is what controls behavior, overt and covert, though in all likelihood in a reciprocal relationship with the outside world.

Since at least the early 1900s, special educators have been interested in training children in various information-processing methods as a technique for the remediation of learning disorders. Past efforts to improve academic skills through the training of processing have been notable in their failures (Glass, 1983; Mann, 1979; Myers & Hammill, 1969; Reynolds, 1981). With the revival of cognitivism has come a new wave of cognitive processes and higher order information-processing strategies to train. The effectiveness of training cognitive processes for the purpose of improving academic skills has yet to be demonstrated, and the potential of such efforts has been hotly debated (Gresham, 1986; Haywood & Switzky, 1986a, 1986b; Reynolds, 1986).

The information-processing skills of exceptional children will always be of interest to special educators. Most mentally handicapped children have some form of information processing disorder, whether it is a mild deviation from the average skill level of other same-age children or a massive disruption of higher order skills. Treating these children requires extensive knowledge of their information-processing skills.

There are basically only three kinds of models of information processing. The first treats information processing as a linear activity, a form of processing that is serial, wherein stages of processing are linked in a straight line and the output of one stage is the input for the next stage; processing proceeds very much in a sequential step-by-step manner. Each stage must await the outcome of the preceding stage. The second primary model of processing does not need to wait for each link in the chain to be completed, but rather carries on parallel processing, doing many tasks simultaneously without awaiting output from a prior step. In parallel processing, several stages can access output from any other stage at the same time. An information processing theory with both components interlinked (serial stages and parallel stages) is a hybrid model (Kantowitz, 1984). These models tend to be more complex but may not always be more useful. They continue to be challenged by organizations such as Neural Information Processing Systems (NIPS) that study broad-based and inclusive approaches (Tesauro, Touretzky & Leen, 1995).

Information processing has progressed to the point of now being a major force in experimental psychology. It is likely to continue to occupy a significant amount of space in the leading scientific journals of psychology for some years to come. Discussions, reviews, and research related to information processing and its related theories will grow in importance in journals related to the education of exceptional children.

REFERENCES

Glass, G.V. (1983). Effectiveness of special education. *Policy Studies Review, 2,* 65–78.

Gresham, F. (1986). On the malleability of intelligence: Unnecessary assumptions, reifications, and occlusion. *School Psychology Review, 15,* 261–263.

Haywood, H.C., & Switzky, H.N. (1986a). The malleability of intelligence: Cognitive processes as a function of polygenic-experiential interaction. *School Psychology Review, 15,* 245–255.

Haywood, H.C., & Switzky, H.N. (1986b). Transactionalism and cognitive processes: Reply to Reynolds and Gresham. *School Psychology Review, 15,* 264–267.

Kantowitz, B.H. (1984). Information processing. In R. Corsini (Ed.), *Encyclopedia of psychology* (Vol. 2). New York: Wiley-Interscience.

Mann, L. (1979). *On the trail of process.* New York: Grune & Stratton.

Myers, P., & Hamill, D. (1969). *Methods for learning disorders.* New York: Wiley.

Reynolds, C.R. (1981). Neuropsychological assessment and the habilitation of learning: Considerations in the search for the aptitude × treatment interaction. *School Psychology Review, 10,* 343–349.

Reynolds, C.R. (1986). Transactional models of intellectual development, yes. Deficit models of process remediation, no. *School Psychology Review, 15,* 256–260.

Tesauro, G., Touretzky, D., & Leen, T. (Eds.). (1995). *Advances in neural information processing systems.* Cambridge, MA: MIT Press.

See also **Perceptual Development; Perceptual Training; Reciprocal Determinism; Remediation, Deficit-Centered Models of; Sequential and Simultaneous Cognitive Processing**

INFORMED CONSENT

See CONSENT, INFORMED.

INITIAL TEACHING ALPHABET (I/T/A)

The Initial Teaching Alphabet, popularly known as i/t/a, was devised by Sir James Pitman of England. His work was the amalgamation of earlier work done by British advocates of the simplification of English spelling. Pitman promoted the concept of a simplified spelling of the English language requiring the addition of new symbols that augmented the alphabet from 26 characters to 44 characters. These early efforts at changing the orthography of English were known as the Augumented Roman Alphabet (Aukerman, 1971).

Downing (1979) reviewed the use of i/t/a with exceptional children. He reported that even though i/t/a had been successful in teaching reading disabled, mentally retarded, culturally disadvantaged, bilingual, and emotionally disturbed and socially maladjusted children to read, further research is needed. Longitudinal studies in Britain showed that the gifted benefited most from the i/t/a method (Downing, 1979).

REFERENCES

Aukerman, R.C. (1971). *Approaches to beginning reading.* New York: Wiley.

Downing, J. (1979). "i.t.a." in special education. *Special Education in Canada, 53,* 25–27.

See also **Reading Disorders; Reading Remediation**

INSATIABLE CHILD SYNDROME

Insatiable child syndrome has been described by Levine, Brooks, and Shonkoff (1980) as chronic insatiability that may accompany attention deficit disorder. As described by these authors, insatiable children have a persistent quest for satisfaction, never obtained, that may focus on food, specific activities, or material goods. They are often whiny and irritable and are described by parents as unpleasant, demanding, and difficult to live with. Insatiability may be biological (i.e., a constitutional trait) or it may be acquired.

"Chronic insatiability is a difficult management problem" (Levine et al., 1980, p. 239). Teachers and parents of such children are often weary and frustrated from contact with the child. Specific intervention strategies and general goals have been provided by Levine et al. (1980), but their implementation depends on a correct diagnosis. The etiology will dictate in many cases the specific approach to treatment. In general, one must focus on building the child's capacity to delay gratification, build tolerance for not having adult attention, and encourage the sharing of possessions with others. At school, the use of attention and special one-on-one times may be used as reinforcement for more appropriate behavior. If the child's sense of competency, self-sufficiency, and self-esteem can be enhanced through school activities, insatiability may diminish. In all cases, consultation with special education support staff, particularly the school psychologist, will be needed, along with coordination with efforts at home. Well-rounded, comprehensive intervention programs are required for success in treating the insatiable child. An interesting treatise on this subject has been presented by Battegay (1991).

REFERENCES

Battegay, R. (1991). *The hunger diseases.* Lewiston, NY: Hogrefe & Huber.

Levine, M.D., Brooks, R., & Shonkoff, J.P. (1980). *A pediatric approach to learning disorders.* New York: Wiley.

See also **Attention-Deficit Hyperactivity Disorder**

IN-SERVICE TRAINING FOR SPECIAL EDUCATION TEACHERS

In-service training for special education teachers is not clearly defined. Definitions abound (Hite, 1977; Johnson, 1980; Langone, 1983). Significant differences exist on the subjects of purpose, need, responsibility, and format. In general, however, any training of special education teachers after they have begun functioning as full professionals may be labeled in-service training. Over the past decades, the focus of in-service training for special education teachers has ranged from remedying the deficiencies in pre-service training programs (i.e., undergraduate and in some cases graduate degree programs) to implementing new instructional technology.

Three forces within the education community have also increased the need for in-service training of special education teachers: an awareness of the limits of preservice training programs, a shift in service delivery that demands collaborative engagement in regular education classes, and an infusion of instructional technology. For decades teacher educators focused their attention on raising the standards of preservice special education teacher training programs. During this time period, in-service training was primarily viewed as a means to remedy the deficiencies in the preservice programs. In the late 1970s teacher educators began to realize that preservice training programs only prepare beginning teachers, not accomplished teachers (Howey, 1978). In addition, teacher educators also began to realize that some teaching competencies are better learned on the job, with the benefit of experience, and that other competencies cannot be learned anywhere else. For example, it is difficult to see how special education teachers can internalize complex organizational strategies or transfer principles of growth and development to instructional decisions without more substantive teaching experience than is generally provided in preservice training programs. In addition, preservice programs sustained significant problems in attending to training requirements for inclusion teaching practices. Different teaching arrangements such as co-teaching & collaboration require supplemental content and practica.

A final reason why the need for in-service training has been intensified in the 1990s is the infusion of instructional technology into special education programs. Bennett and Maher (1984) have identified training special education teachers for effective use of instructional technology as a critical in-service need. For example, special education teachers must learn to capitalize on the potential of instructional technology. Technology such as computer-assisted instruction can bring about more productive use of the teacher's and the student's time. Of particular importance is its capacity to provide instruction that is truly individualized for each handicapped student.

Frequently used formats for in-service training of special education teachers include on-site after school workshops, release-time activities, teacher centers, and on-site college or university courses (Swenson, 1981). Among these formats, the teacher center reflects the new role played by teachers. Teacher centers are places where teachers determine their own needs, seek assistance, and develop materials or strategies to solve problems. Teacher center instructors are themselves classroom teachers, sharing their own practical, classroom-developed materials; or they are advisors—formerly classroom teachers—who view their job as stimulating, supporting, and extending a teacher's own direction of growth. Attendance at teacher center classes is voluntary, not prescribed by the school district; if indirectly required (e.g., as a way to spend release time), programs offered are based on teachers' expressions of their own training needs (Devaney & Thorn, 1975).

In addition, in-service training to assist in the education of culturally/linguistically diverse students is not as prevalent as it should be (Zimpher & Ashburn, 1992). Future staff development must take into account educational reform (Little, 1993).

REFERENCES

Bennett, R., & Maher, C. (Eds.). (1984). *Microcomputers and exceptional children.* New York: Haworth.

Devaney, K., & Thorn, L. (1975). *Exploring teachers' centers.* San Francisco: Far West Laboratory for Educational Research and Development.

Hite, H. (1977). Inservice education: Perceptions, purposes, and practices. In H. Hite & K. Howey (Eds.), *Planning inservice teacher education: Promising alternatives* (pp. 1–20). Washington, DC: American Association of Colleges for Teacher Education.

Howey, K. (1978, March). *Inservice teacher education: A study of the perceptions of teachers, professors and parents about current and projected practice.* Paper presented at the meeting of the American Educational Research Association, Toronto. (ERIC Document Reproduction Service NO. ED 152 701)

Johnson, M. (1980). *Inservice education: Priority for the '80s.* Syracuse, NY: National Council of States on Inservice Education, Syracuse University.

Langone, J. (1983). Developing effective inservice for special educators. *Journal for Special Educators, 19*(3), 33–47.

Little, J.W. (1993). Teachers' professional development in a climate of educational reform. *Educational Evaluation and Policy Analysis, 15*(2), 129–151.

Swenson, R. (1981). The state of the art in inservice education and staff development in K-12 schools. *Journal of Research & Development in Education, 15*(1), 2–7.

Zimpher, N.L., & Ashburn, E.A. (1992). Countering parochialism in teacher candidates. In M. Dilworth (Ed.), *Diversity in teacher education* (pp. 40–62). San Francisco, CA: Jossey-Bass.

See also **Teacher Centers; Teacher Effectiveness**

INSIGHT (IN THE GIFTED)

Insight has also been described in human beings by researchers such as Wertheimer (1945) and Sternberg and Davidson (1983). Wertheimer studied children's insightful solutions to geometric problems. Some children used a rote fashion to solve problems; others, however, could see the essential structure of a problem situation, and consequently used insight as their approach to learning. Sternberg and Davidson, on the other hand, developed a sub-theory of intellectual giftedness based on the centrality of insight skills.

In a later work, Davidson and Sternberg (1984) proposed that insight involves not one, but three separate but related psychological processes. They refered to the products of the three operations as insights, understood in terms of three types of insight skills: (1) selective encoding, by which relevant information in a given context is sifted from irrelevant information; (2) selective combination, by which relevant information is combined in a novel and productive way; and (3) selective comparison, by which new information is related in a novel way to old information.

The authors' three-process view of insight constitutes what they believe to be a subtheory of intellectual giftedness. Whereas selective encoding involves knowing which pieces of information are relevant, selective combination involves knowing how to blend together the pieces of relevant information. Selective comparison involves relating the newly acquired information to information acquired in the past (as when one solves a problem by using an analogy). In addition, the authors reason that the three processes are not executed in simple serial order, but rather, continually interact with each other in the formation of new ideas. Thus, it is the products of these operations that they refer to as insights.

Davidson and Sternberg (1984) suggest several benefits of their approach to understanding and assessing intellectual giftedness over alternative psychometric and information-processing approaches. First, they propose that their theoretically based approach deals with what it is that makes the gifted special. Second, because their measurement of insight skills has no demands on prior knowledge, their approach is appropriate for individuals with nonstandard backgrounds. Current researchers are using EEG technology to investigate insight in problem-solving (Jansovec, 1997).

REFERENCES

Davidson, J.E., & Sternberg, R.J. (1984). The role of insight in intellectual giftedness. *Gifted Child Quarterly, 28*(2), 58–64.

Jansovec, N. (1997). Differences in EEG activity between gifted and non-identified individuals: Insights into problem solving. *Gifted Child Quarterly, 41*(1), 26–32.

Sternberg, R.J., & Davidson, J.E. (1983). Insight in the gifted. *Educational Psychologist, 18*(1), 51–57.

Wertheimer, M. (1945). *Productive thinking.* New York: Harper & Row.

See also **Culturally/Linguistically Diverse Gifted Students**

INSTITUTES FOR RESEARCH ON LEARNING DISABILITIES

The Institutes for Research on Learning Disabilities were created to encourage basic and applied research in order to develop and validate successful practices with learning-disabled (LD) pupils. Originally sponsored by the Bureau of Education for the Handicapped and later funded through Special Education Programs within the Department of Education, the five 6-year institutes were awarded on a contractual basis to the University of Illinois—Chicago Circle, Teachers College at Columbia University, the University of Kansas, the University of Minnesota, and the University of Virginia.

The work of the five Institutes for Research on Learning Disabilities began amidst considerable controversy about the nature of learning disabilities (McKinney, 1983). Nevertheless, it is generally accepted that the institutes, through the collective resources of many investigators pursuing a complex set of problems in programmatic fashion, contributed significantly to what we now know about the nature and treatment of learning disabilities (Keogh, 1983; McKinney, 1983).

REFERENCES

Keogh, B.K. (1983). A lesson from Gestalt psychology. *Exceptional Education Quarterly, 4*(1), 115–128.

McKinney, J.D. (1983). Contributions of the Institutes for Research on Learning Disabilities. *Exceptional Education Quarterly, 4*(1), 129–144.

INSTITUTIONALIZATION

In the past, persons with disabilities (notably persons with mental retardation or mental illness) were left to fend for themselves, were shut away in rooms or houses, or worse, were placed in prisons (Wolfensberger, 1972). This often resulted in illness or death, a situation that led to the establishment of institutional residences in the nineteenth century. These facilities, called hospitals, asylums, or colonies, were constructed in rural areas with residents having little contact with community members. The original intent of such facilities was to provide a higher level of care for handicapped persons needing such care.

Placement in a residential facility was often for life. Through the 1950s, the number of handicapped persons residing in institutions increased. Then, with the advent of the deinstitutionalization movement, promoted by those who thought the physical and social environment of institutions to be detrimental, the resident institutional population declined. From 1955 to 1973, the resident population declined from 500,000 to 250,000 in spite of a 40% increase in the U.S. population (Telford & Sawrey, 1977). Currently, the emptying of residential institutions has slowed, with most states controlling new admissions instead of removing residents.

While many formerly institutionalized persons with disabilities can be accommodated in the community, care and treatment facilities have not kept pace with the deinstitutionalization movement. Consequently, a number of those who returned to the community have been unable to obtain needed services and have become part of the homeless contingent found in many cities. Institutions will always be required for at least some small segment of the handicapped population. However, with early intervention, education, and community-based alternatives, few individuals will require intensive and lifelong care.

REFERENCES

Telford, C.W., & Sawrey, J.M. (1977). *The exceptional individual* (2nd ed.). Englewood Cliffs, NJ: Prentice-Hall.

Wolfensberger, W. (1972). *The principle of normalization in human services.* Downsview, CT: National Institute of Mental Retardation.

See also **Community Residential Programs; Deinstitutionalization**

INSTITUTION NATIONALE DES SOURDS-MUETS

The Institution Nationale des Sourds-Muets, the first public nonpaying school for the deaf in the world, was founded in Paris in 1755 by the Abbot Charles Michel de l'Epée (1712–1789). Its name was changed in 1960 to Institut National de Jeunes Sourds (INJS) (National Institute for Young Deaf). Despite its location in the heart of Paris, it has retained spacious grounds (19,300 square meters) comprising playgrounds, gardens, orchards, and vegetable gardens.

The INJS deserves the title of cradle of sign language for deaf education. In its front courtyard, visitors are greeted by the statue of the Abbot de l'Epée, to whose robe clings a grateful deaf child. Many deaf people throughout the world consider de l'Epée as their spiritual father, and the INJS as the living historical landmark of his action.

See also **Deaf Education; Total Communication**

INSTRUCTIONAL MEDIA/ MATERIALS CENTER

Virtually every school district, intermediate unit, and cooperative supports an instructional media/materials center as part of its overall educational effort. The implementation of IDEA has expanded the functions of many instructional media/materials centers that today house teacher centers, professional libraries, and collections of textbooks, print materials, and adaptive devices (in addition to audiovisuals). The range of services may include circulation of new products through on-site borrowing, by mail or mobile units; information searches; in-service training; development of print and nonprint products for local use; dissemination of information on promising practices and products; assistance with the selection and adoption of new practices; and participation in school improvement programs. Some instructional media/materials centers also provide microcomputer workshops, software development, software reviews and guides, and microcomputer libraries.

See also **In-Service Training of Special Education; Instructional Technology for Students with Disabilities**

INSTRUCTIONAL PACING

A considerable portion of educational research has focused on validating the effectiveness of specific educational approaches. Instructional pacing, or the rate of stimulus presentation, has been proposed as a teaching behavior that may have a direct impact on student learning (Schnachenberg, 1996).

There are several temporal variables that determine the pacing of a teacher's lesson. Teacher wait-time is generally defined as the amount of time a teacher waits for a student's response after presenting a question or stimulus. Researchers (Fagan, Hassler, & Szabo, 1981; Rowe, 1974) have suggested that extended teacher wait-time leads to more frequent and more accurate responses. These findings also have been substantiated in the field of special education with children with multiple disabilities.

A second temporal variable, the intertrial interval, is the time that elapses between the end of one learning trial and the beginning of the next. In studies with autistic children, short intertrial intervals of 1 to 4 seconds have been shown to result in more rapid learning (Koegel, Dunlap, & Dyer,

1980) and lower levels of self-stimulatory behaviors (Dunlap, Dyer, & Koegel, 1983) than long intervals of 5 to 26 seconds.

Englert (1984) has examined presentation rates in the context of special education. She found that teacher interns who were judged to be more effective, based on their students' achievement, presented a significantly higher number of trials per minute than interns judged to be less effective. The effective interns were said to have maintained a brisker lesson pace.

Although extended teacher wait-times and shortened intertrial intervals may seem to be theoretically opposed, the proponents of the direct instruction model and commercial curricula based on it advocate a similar approach. They suggest allowing students ample time to respond to a task and shortening the time between tasks. Future research may help in establishing firm instructional pacing guidelines for special education professionals.

REFERENCES

Dunlap, G., Dyer, K., & Koegel, R.L. (1983). Autistic self-stimulation and intertrial interval duration. *American Journal of Mental Deficiency, 88,* 194–202.

Englert, C.S. (1984). Effective direct instruction practices in special education settings. *Remedial & Special Education, 5*(2), 38–47.

Fagan, E.R., Hassler, D.M., & Szabo, M. (1981). Evaluation of questioning strategies in language arts instruction. *Research in the Teaching of English, 15,* 267–273.

Koegel, R.L., Dunlap, G., & Dyer, K. (1980). Intertrial interval duration and learning in autistic children. *Journal of Applied Behavior Analysis, 13,* 91–99.

Rowe, M.B. (1974). Wait-time and rewards as instructional variables, their influence on language, logic, and fate control: Part one—wait-time. *Journal of Research in Science Teaching, 11*(2), 81–94.

Schnachenberg, H. (1996). *Matching learner preference to preferred amounts of instruction.* Paper presented at the Annual Conference of the American Educational Research Association, New York, NY, April 8–12.

See also **Autism; Direct Instruction; Teacher Effectiveness**

INSTRUCTIONAL TECHNOLOGY FOR THE HANDICAPPED

Instructional technology, also known as educational technology, is a term that has been used to describe a wide range of tools or techniques developed to simplify or enhance educational efforts by either the learner or the teacher. Although commonly thought of as mechanical or electronic devices (e.g., computers and calculators) and instructional media (e.g., filmstrips and videotapes), certain assessment strategies (e.g., precision teaching and applied behavioral analysis procedures), and curriculum designs (e.g., specific competencies/technology design or objective-based instruction) also may be considered instructional technology.

The key element in classifying something as instructional technology seems to be that the device or technique is the result of the application of a scientific principle to an educational concern.

The *Journal of Special Education Technology,* a quarterly publication of Utah State University, the Association for Special Education Technology, and the Technology and Media Division of the Council for Exceptional Children deal specifically with research and presentations of innovative practices in the application of instructional technology with the handicapped.

See also **Augmentative Communication Systems; Computers and Education; Computers in Human Behavior; Computer Use with Students with Disabilities; Electronic Communication Aids**

INTEGRATED THERAPY

The provision of specialized therapy services in the classroom and in other natural environments has been termed integrated therapy (Nietupski, Schutz, & Ockwood, 1980; Sternat et al., 1977). Integrated therapy has a number of advantages over the isolated therapy model, in which students are removed from their classroom for therapy in a segregated environment, usually a clinic or therapy room. One advantage is the potential for continuous as opposed to episodic training sessions. Therapists and classroom teaching staff are able to coordinate both training goals and procedures. Moreover, in an integrated therapy model, there are more opportunities for sharing of professional skills and information concerning students' programs.

Another important advantage of integrated therapy conditions is the potential to enhance generalization. This is particularly critical for very young students with severe disabilities who often fail to perform new skills in other than the training environment.

REFERENCES

Nietupski, J., Scheutz, G., & Ockwood, L. (1980). The delivery of communication therapy services to severely handicapped students: A plan for change. *Journal of the Association for the Severely Handicapped, 5*(1), 13–23.

Sternat, J., Messina, R., Nietupski, J., Lyon, S., & Brown, L. (1977). Occupational and physical therapy services for severely handicapped students: Toward a naturalized public school service delivery model. In E. Sontag, J.J. Smith, & N. Certo (Eds.), *Educational programming for the severely & profoundly handicapped.* Reston, VA: Council for Exceptional Children.

See also **Inclusion; Least Restrictive Environment; Mainstreaming**

INTELLECTUAL DEFICIENCY

See MENTAL RETARDATION; See INTELLIGENCE.

INTELLIGENCE

Intelligence has proven to be a difficult construct to define. From as early as 1921 (Intelligence and its measurement: A symposium, 1921) to the present (e.g., Detterman, 1994; Sternberg & Detterman, 1986; Neisser et al., 1996), psychologists have consistently failed to agree on a common conceptual definition, general theoretical approach, or assessment device.

Some commonality of agreement at a fairly global level holds both among psychologists and the public at large. Consider the well-known study of implicit theories of intelligence by Sternberg, Conway, Ketron, & Bernstein (1981), who asked lay people at a supermarket, train station, and university library to describe behaviors that they would consider intelligent, academically intelligent, or everyday intelligent. Sternberg et al. (1981) then sent the entire list of behaviors to academic psychologists whose research interest was psychology and asked them to indicate how important each behavior was in characterizing intelligent, academically intelligent, or everyday intelligent people. The authors also asked a group of lay people to do essentially the same task in a laboratory setting. Factor analysis of the psychologists' ratings of intelligence revealed three factors: Verbal Intelligence ("is verbally fluent"), Problem Solving Ability ("is able to apply knowledge to problems at hand"), and Practical Intelligence ("sizes up situations well"). Factor analysis of the lay people's ratings also revealed three factors: Practical Problem-Solving Ability ("reasons logically and well"), Verbal Ability ("speaks clearly and articulately"), and Social Competence ("accepts others for what they are"). Clearly, these factors are similar for the two groups and indicate that professionals and lay people have well-developed and similar implicit theories of intelligence. Sternberg et al. (1981) suggest that problem solving, which they equated to fluid intelligence, and verbal ability, which they equated to crystallized intelligence (see discussion below) are "integral aspects of intellectual functioning" (p. 54). Further, two elements are common to many experts' definitions of intelligence: 1) the ability to learn from experience, and 2) the capacity to adapt to one's environment.

PSYCHOMETRIC APPROACHES

Psychometric theories of intelligence derive from statistical analyses, particularly factor analysis, of scores on intelligence tests. Such theories could be seen as following the Boring prototype of the intelligent person, someone who does well on intelligence tests. Several strong arguments can be made in support of a single general intelligence factor, called *g.* As early as 1904, Spearman reported that scores on a variety of then-available tests all intercorrelated; that is, high scores on one test tended to be associated with high scores on others, and vice versa. The intercorrelations suggested that one intellectual factor predicted performance on the tests. He later (e.g., Spearman, 1927) conducted factor analyses, a technique he invented, on large numbers of intelligence test scores and found that scores intercorrelated, reflecting a general factor of intelligence (*g*), but that each group of tests also tapped a more specific factor (*s*).

Support for a single general intelligence has been offered in studies of reaction time. Reaction time is measured by the time it takes an individual to complete an uncomplicated task. Eysenck (1994) has provided evidence for a biological basis of the *g* factor, and Jensen (1993) claims that the essence of *g* relies on the speed of neural transmission. The faster an individual's neural processes, the faster their reaction time. Reaction time has been related to intelligence through its positive correlation with IQ. Others have argued against this position by claiming it does not make sense that reaction time speed and intelligence should correlate. They counter that intelligence is an engaging process that involves problem solving. Reaction time is different; it is an automatic response over which one has little control. The importance and basis of *g* remain contentious as seen in the pro and con arguments in Modgil and Modgil (1987).

Cattell (1971) proposed a hierarchical model of intelligence in which *g* was divided into two components, fluid intelligence and crystallized intelligence. Fluid intelligence, now referred to as Gf, is the ability to apply cognitions to novel problems, to acquire new information, and to induce new relationships among known information. This type of intelligence is considered abstract and culture-free. Crystallized intelligence, now referred to as Gc, includes skills and knowledge acquired across the lifespan that enable individuals to apply proven problem-solving skills to familiar challenges. This form of intelligence is acquired, and relies heavily on culture and experience. Under each of these two major subfactors are other more specific ones. Horn (1985) has presented new evidence for Gf and Gc, and has suggested that they are highly correlated in young children but tend to become less and less correlated as children grow and have various experiences.

Carroll (e.g., 1993) has developed a hierarchical theory of intelligence based on factor analysis of a large sample of data sets. His model proposes over 40 primary factors in various domains (language competence, reasoning and thinking, memory and learning, visual perception, auditory reception, idea production, and cognitive speed). Analysis of the primary factors revealed seven secondary factors, many of them similar to aspects of the theories of Horn, Cattell, Eysenck, and Jensen: Gf, fluid intelligence; Gc, crystallized intelligence; Gv, visualization capacity; Gs, general cognitive speed; Gm, general memory; Gr, general retrieval capacity; and Ga, general auditory perception capacity. Analyses of these factors revealed, not surprisingly, Spearman's *g*. Carroll (1994, p. 62) suggests that *g* mainly loads on tasks involving "the *level of complexity* at which individuals are able to handle basic processes of induction, deduction, and comprehension."

BEYOND PSYCHOMETRICS: INTELLIGENCE BROADLY CONCEPTUALIZED

Concerned among other things about limitations of *g*, Gardner (1983, 1993) proposed seven "multiple intelli-

gences" (M.I.) as individual components that perform separately at differing levels. He (Gardner, 1983, p. 9) claims support for M.I. through "studies of prodigies, gifted individuals, idiots savants, normal children, normal adults, experts in different lines of work, and individuals from diverse cultures." His M.I. are: 1) linguistic intelligence, reflected in tasks such as reading or language comprehension; 2) logical-mathematical intelligence, involving calculations and logic; 3) spatial intelligence, involving transformations of objects and perception of forms; 4) musical intelligence, which supposedly develops earliest, involving such capabilities as composing or playing an instrument; 5) bodily-kinesthetic intelligence, reflected in control over the motions of one's body as well as ability to manipulate objects; 6) interpersonal intelligence, the ability to understand other individuals; and 7) intrapersonal intelligence, which relates to the ability to view oneself objectively in terms of strengths and weaknesses. Although the seven intelligences are viewed as functioning separately, they often interact to produce particular kinds of intelligent behavior.

Although generating much interest in both psychology and education, Gardner's proposal is questionable from a scientific standpoint. In the first place, he has offered no tests of his intelligences, leaving their presumed independence as well as their very existence in question. The evidence he offers is interesting, but hardly systematic or compelling, particularly because comparable evidence could be found for other presumed "intelligences." As others (e.g., Neisser et al., 1996) have pointed out, separate categories of intelligence are not all that independent; individuals who have talent in one area tend to be talented in other areas as well, relating again to the *g* factor premise.

Also concerned about limitations of *g* Sternberg (1985) has proposed a triarchic componential theory of intelligence. Intelligence is viewed as involving three types of abilities that operate on three different levels and that draw on three components of information processing. The triarchy of abilities are the analytic, creative, and practical abilities. Analytic abilities are used to evaluate and judge information to deal with problems that have only one right answer. Creative abilities are used to deal with novel problems that require thinking in a different way and that may have no one solution. Practical abilities deal with real-world problems that may have various solutions. The three levels on which the abilities operate are the internal world, the external world, and individual experience. The three information-processing components are: 1) metacomponents are executive processes which plan, monitor, and evaluate; 2) performance components implement metacomponents; and 3) knowledge-acquisition components are used for initial learning of problem solving strategies. These three components operate interdependently. Sternberg's argument against the emphasis on *g* is that general reasoning, such as previously noted in crystallized intelligence, may be a highly-regarded aspect in some cultures, but other cultures have no use for it at all.

Proponents of *g* contend that Sternberg's theory lacks

any biological basis and that his concepts are not empirically supported. Some (e.g., Eysenck, 1994) have provided evidence that originality and creativity are not aspects of cognitive ability, but traits of personality. On the other hand, a variety of evidence (Neisser et al., 1996) supports Sternberg's contention that practical intelligence is both largely independent of scores on standard intelligence tests and an important correlate of real-world problem solving.

PREDICTION OF SCHOLASTIC ACHIEVEMENT

Since the time of Binet, the major purpose of intelligence tests has been to predict academic performance. As would be expected, scores on such tests do correlate with scholastic achievement as measured both by grades and standardized achievement tests. Correlations between IQs and measures of school achievement for children average about .50. At a higher educational level, SAT and scores also predict college grades, although the correlations vary considerably from one study to another. These correlations only account for about 25% of the total variance, indicating that a host of other factors, including personality, social, and cultural factors are also important in school performance.

Intelligence test scores correlate with years of education, occupational status, and job performance. They also correlate with socioeconomic status, but interpretation is difficult owing to the number of other correlates. The speed with which people perform a number of cognitive tasks also correlates positively with measured intelligence, and the magnitude of the correlations appears to increase with task complexity.

GENETIC AND ENVIRONMENTAL BASES

Although a topic of much research and controversy, the degree to which genetic and environmental factors contribute to intelligence remains uncertain. Many reasons are responsible for this uncertainty, including the statistical techniques and subject samples used. Further, by necessity, the more environmental factors are similar for subjects in the samples, the larger must be the contribution of genetic ones. That is, if environment differences are negligible, then any variability must owe to genetic differences. Estimates of the proportion of differences in intelligence that may be attributed to differences in genetic background range from .40 to .80, with a mean of about .50. These estimates are, however, based on studies in which subjects from very low socioeconomic levels were underrepresented. Since environmental differences are correlated with socioeconomic status, artifactually small environmental differences would necessarily exaggerate the effect of genetic differences. The proportion tends to increase with age, perhaps because as individuals develop, they increasingly select their own environments, partly to be compatible with other genetically-based traits. Of course, particular genetic conditions, such as Down's syndrome, may be responsible for individual cases of mental retardation.

Although even the highest estimates of the role of differences in genetics indicate a considerable role of environ-

mental differences in determining differences in intelligence, determining the nature of the responsible environmental factors has been difficult. Researchers have identified numerous environmental factors as being potentially important in influencing normal variations in intelligence, including cultural, familial, social, and academic ones, but firm identification remains elusive. Doubtless, environmental factors, such as lead exposure, prenatal alcohol, prolonged malnutrition, perinatal factors (prematurity, very low birth weight) are responsible for individual cases of lowered intelligence and mental retardation, but their role in normal individual differences is small.

GROUP DIFFERENCES

Consistent differences exist among cultural/ethnic subgroups in measured intelligence, although the degree of difference is not as consistent. Mean IQ of Anglos is the same as the standardized mean, 100, whereas that of Asian Americans is somewhat higher, about 105, and that of African Americans considerably lower, about 85. Means for Latinos and Native Americans fall in between. Many explanations, both environmental and genetic, have been offered for these differences, but all are subject to criticism. One consistent finding, however, is that group differences cannot be attributed to bias in the tests, for which no scientific evidence exists. Absence of test bias should not, however, be taken as support of a genetic interpretation. Flynn (1999), for example, has recently offered a cogent criticism of genetic interpretations of group differences. Virtually no direct evidence supports a genetic explanation, but reliable evidence of environmental factors also remains elusive. What can be said at this time is that firm claims to either position likely rest more on belief than on scientifically-supported evidence.

THE RISING IQ

"Perhaps the most striking of all environmental effects is the steady worldwide rise in intelligence test performance" (Neisser et al., 1996, p. 89). The "Flynn Effect," named after the person who first systematically reported it (e.g., Flynn, 1984, 1999), refers to the consistent and sizable increases in measured intelligence that have occurred in the United States and other western countries since at least the 1930s. The gain is approximately 0.3 IQ points each year (Flynn, 1999). Of particular interest, gains on the Ravens Progressive Matrices test, a culture-reduced and thus more g loaded test, are even higher and occur in 20 different countries (Flynn, 1999). The increases must of course be environmental, since positing genetic change over that period of time is simply untenable. Furthermore, the increases occur in the absence of any increases in achievement test scores. The reasons for the increase are unclear. Neisser et al. (1996) argue that increased test sophistication is an unlikely basis and suggest that increased cultural complexity and/or improved nutrition may play a role. But possible also is Flynn's (1987) position that the improved scores cannot reflect a comparable increase in real intelligence, or several countries would be experiencing a true cultural renaissance owing to a dramatic increase in the number of their geniuses. Flynn suggests that what has increased actually may be only a relatively narrow, for practical purposes, type of abstract problem solving. Doubtless, his 1999 paper will evoke further discussion.

SOME IMPLICATIONS

The validity of intelligence tests as predictors of school performance supports their continued use to identify children in need of special education services. The relatively low correlations between IQ and academic performance indicate that many other factors are involved. Although a hierarchical theory of intelligence with g as the highest factor is supported by much research, additional aspects of intelligence, particularly practical intelligence, appear to be important determinants of a wide range of behavior. The Flynn Effect is a clear reflection of environmental influences on measured intelligence for which theories will need to account. Formal adequate schooling, including preschools and appropriate intervention, is an important influence on intellectual development. Finally, a separation of the scientific aspects of the study of intelligence from its political implications is needed.

REFERENCES

Carroll, J.B. (1994). Cognitive abilities: Constructing a theory from data. In D.K. Detterman (Ed.), *Current topics in human intelligence, volume 4: Theories of intelligence* (pp. 43–63). Norwood, NJ: Ablex.

Cattell, R.B. (1971). *Abilities: Their structure, growth, and action.* Boston: Houghton Mifflin.

Eysenck, H.J. (1994). A biological theory of intelligence. In D.K. Detterman (Ed.), *Current topics in human intelligence, volume 4: Theories of intelligence* (pp. 117–149). Norwood, NJ: Ablex.

Flynn, J.R. (1984). The mean IQ of Americans: Massive gains 1932 to 1978. *Psychological Bulletin, 95,* 29–51.

Flynn, J.R. (1999). Searching for justice: The discovery of IQ gains over time. *American Psychologist, 54*(1), 5–20.

Gardner, H. (1983). *Frames of mind: The theory of multiple intelligences.* New York: Basic Books.

Gardner, H. (Ed.). (1993). *Multiple intelligences: The theory in practice.* New York: Basic Books.

Horn, J.L. (1985). Remodeling old models of intelligence: Gf-Gc theory. In B.B. Wolman (Ed.), *Handbook of intelligence* (pp. 267–300). New York: Wiley.

Intelligence and its measurement: A symposium. (1921). *Journal of Educational Psychology, 12,* 123–147; 195–216; 271–275.

Modgil, S., & Modgil, C. (Eds.). (1987). *Arthur Jensen: Consensus and controversy.* Falmer, England: Falmer Press.

Neisser, U., Boodoo, G., Bouchard, T.J., Jr., Boykin, A.W., Brody, N., Ceci, S.J., Halpern, D.F., Loehlin, J.C., Perloff, R., Sternberg, R.J., & Urbina, S. (1996). Intelligence: Knowns and unknowns. *American Psychologist, 51,* 77–101.

Spearman, C. (1904). "General intelligence" objectively determined and measured. *American Journal of Psychology, 15,* 201–293.

Spearman, C. (1927). *The abilities of man: Their nature and measurement.* New York: Macmillan.

Sternberg, R.J. (1985). *Beyond IQ: A triarchic theory of human intelligence.* New York: Cambridge University Press.

Sternberg, R.J., Conway, B.E., Ketron, J.L., & Bernstein, M. (1981). People's conception of intelligence. *Journal of Personality and Social Psychology, 41,* 37–55.

Sternberg, R.J., & Detterman, D.K. (Eds.). (1986). *What is intelligence?* Norwood, NJ: Ablex.

INTELLIGENCE: A MULTIDISCIPLINARY JOURNAL

When *Intelligence* was established in 1977, there were no other journals devoted exclusively to basic research in human intelligence, even though many prestigious journals were available in the field of learning. By establishing a new journal, the founder sought to "formalize the importance of the study of human intelligence and the major role it has played in the development of the behavioral sciences" (Detterman, 1977, p. 2).

Intelligence is a scientifically oriented journal, publishing papers that make a substantial contribution to the understanding of the nature and function of intelligence. The journal is devoted to the publication of original research, but also accepts theoretical and review articles. Studies concerned with application are considered only if the work also contributes to basic knowledge. The journal is multidisciplinary in nature. Of interest to special educators are the many empirical studies published in the field of mental retardation. Other types of studies include early childhood development, measurement of individual differences, and issues in cultural test bias.

REFERENCE

Detterman, D.K. (1977). Is *Intelligence* necessary? *Intelligence. A Multidisciplinary Journal, 1*(1), 1–3.

INTELLIGENCE, EMOTIONAL

The idea that emotion is a significant part of our intellectual being has roots in the works of Darwin (1872/1965) and Freud (1923/1962), and, more recently, in the work of Howard Gardner (1983). In Gardner's (1983) theory of multiple intelligences, two of his proposed seven intelligences involve emotions: Interpersonal intelligence (understanding other people) and Intrapersonal intelligence (understanding one's self). Robert Sternberg's theory of successful intelligence (also known as practical intelligence) is another major theory of intellect that takes into consideration the importance of emotional well-being (Sternberg, 1985, 1996; Sternberg & Kaufman, 1998). The common historical view, however, is that emotions are secondary—indeed, inferior to—intellect (Salovey, Bedell, Detweiler, & Mayer, in press).

In 1990, Salovey and Mayer proposed a model of emotional intelligence that had three factors: appraisal and expression of emotion, regulation of emotion, and utilization of emotion. Appraisal and expression of emotion is comprised of emotion in the self (which can be both verbal and nonverbal), and emotion in others. Emotion in others consists of nonverbal perception of emotion and empathy. The second factor, regulation of emotion, is the ability to regulate emotion in the self, and the ability to regulate and alter emotions in other people. The final factor, utilizing emotional intelligence, has four aspects: flexible planning, creative thinking, redirected attention, and motivation. Flexible planning refers to the ability to produce a large number of different plans for the future, enabling the planner to better respond to opportunities. This production of many plans can result from using emotion and mood changes to one's advantage and from looking at a wide variety of possibilities. Creative thinking, the second aspect, may be more likely to occur if a person is happy and in a good mood. Redirected attention involves the idea that when strong emotions are experienced, a person's resources and attentions may be turned to new problems. People who can use this phenomenon to their own benefit will be able to use a potentially stressful situation to focus on the most important or pressing issues involved. Motivating emotions, the final principle of emotional intelligence, refers to the art of making one's self continue to perform difficult tasks by focusing one's anxiety or tension toward the performance of that task.

Mayer and Salovey (1997) have refined their theory in a chapter in *Emotional Development and Emotional Intelligence* (Salovey & Sluyter, 1997). They compressed their theory into four abilities: (1) perceiving, appraising, and expressing emotions; (2) accessing and producing feelings in aid of cognition; (3) comprehending information on affect and using emotional knowledge; and (4) regulating emotions for growth and contentment (Mayer & Salovey, 1997).

There are some tests of emotional intelligence: The Trait Meta-Mood Scale (TMMS; see Salovey, Mayer, Goldman, Turvey, & Palfai, 1995), The Multifactor Emotional Intelligence Scale (MEIS; Mayer, Caruso, & Salovey, 1998); and the Bar-On Emotional Quotient Inventory (EQ-I; Bar-On, 1997). However, all of these measures are self-report and have psychometric properties that are largely unknown. At this time, no test has been published or significantly researched that uses a more hands-on approach with actual problems or tasks to solve (Salovey, in press).

Future directions in emotional intelligence research, according to Salovey (1999), will likely be concentrated in the following areas: distinguishing emotional intelligence from more traditional types of intelligence; assessing cultural differences and similarities in emotional intelligence (both abilities and definitions); developing more empirical measures of the construct; and seeing how these measures can predict academic, personal, and professional success.

REFERENCES

Bar-On, R. (1997). *EQ-I: Bar-On Emotional Quotient Inventory.* Toronto: Multi-health Systems.

Darwin, C. (1872/1965). *The expression of the emotions in man and animals.* Chicago: University of Chicago Press.

Freud, S. (1923/1962). *The ego and the id.* (J. Strachey, Ed.; J. Riviere, Trans.) New York: Norton.

Gardner, H. (1983). *Frames of mind: The theory of multiple intelligences.* New York: Basic Books.

Mayer, J.D., Caruso, D., & Salovey, P. (1998). *The Multifactor Emotional Intelligence Scale: MEIS.* Unpublished test.

Mayer, J.D., & Salovey, P. (1997). What is emotional intelligence? In P. Salovey & D.J. Sluyter (Eds.), *Emotional development and emotional intelligence* (pp. 3–31). New York: Basic Books.

Salovey, P. (1999). Emotional intelligence. In D. Levinson, J. Ponzetti, & P. Jorgensen (Eds.), *Encyclopedia of human emotions.* New York: Macmillan.

Salovey, P., Bedell, B.T., Detweiler, J.B., & Mayer, J.D. (in press). In M. Lewis & J.M. Haviland-Jones (Eds.), *Handbook of emotions* (2nd ed.). New York: Guilford.

Salovey, P., & Mayer, J.D. (1989–1990). Emotional intelligence. *Imagination, Cognition, and Personality, 9*(3), 185–211.

Salovey, P., Mayer, J.D., Goldman, S.L., Turvey, C., & Palfai, T.P. (1995). Emotional attention, clarity, and repair: Exploring emotional intelligence using the Trait Meta-Mood Scale. In J.W. Pennebaker (Ed.), *Emotion, disclosure, and health* (pp. 125–154). Washington, DC: American Psychology Association.

Salovey, P. & Sluyter, D. (Eds.). (1997). *Emotional development and emotional intelligence.* New York: Basic Books.

Sternberg, R.J. (1985). *Beyond IQ: A triarchic theory of human intelligence.* New York: Cambridge.

Sternberg, R.J. (1996). *Successful intelligence.* New York: Simon and Schuster.

Sternberg, R.J., & Kaufman, J.C. (1998). Human abilities. *Annual Review of Psychology, 49,* 479–502.

INTELLIGENCE, PRACTICAL

See PRACTICAL INTELLIGENCE.

INTELLIGENCE QUOTIENT

The intelligence quotient represents a measurement concept that was used extensively in the early days of intelligence testing but is less commonly used today. After Alfred Binet's death in 1911, Stern (1914) introduced the notion of a mental quotient, suggesting that the index of intellectual functioning derived from the Binet-Simon Scale could be expressed as the ratio of a test taker's mental age to his or her chronological age multiplied by 100 to eliminate decimals ($MQ = 100 \times MA/CA$). This *MQ* represented something about a person's rate of mental growth up to the time of the test. If examinees earned a mental age (MA) equivalent to chronological age (CA), their mental quotient (MQ) would be 100. An MQ of 100 represented average performance.

Working at Stanford University in California, Lewis M. Terman developed what was to become the most widely used American version of the Binet test, the Stanford-Binet. Terman (1916) incorporated Stern's notion of a mental quotient but renamed it, calling it a ratio intelligence quotient, or IQ.

The concept of the ratio intelligence quotient became increasingly popular, but it was used in a number of inappropriate ways. Its decline over the last quarter century can be attributed to a number of inherent characteristics that have been highly criticized by measurement specialists and practitioners.

Owing to these criticisms of the ratio intelligence quotient, most major intelligence tests today yield IQs but not ratio intelligence quotients. For example, since the 1960 revision of the Stanford-Binet, the ratio intelligence quotient has been replaced by the deviation IQ. Major intelligence tests such as the Wechsler and McCarthy scales and the Kaufman Assessment Battery for Children (K-ABC) do not yield ratio intelligence quotients. However, several other intelligence tests in use today retain the concept of the ratio intelligence quotient, including the Leiter International Performance Scale, the Slosson Intelligence Test, and the Quick Test. Because of the inherent limitations of the ratio intelligence quotient, IQs yielded from these tests should be interpreted cautiously.

REFERENCES

Stern, W. (1914). *The psychological methods of testing intelligence*. Baltimore, MD: Warwick & York.

Terman, L.M. (1916). *The measurement of intelligence*. Boston: Houghton Mifflin.

See also Deviation IQ; IQ; Ratio IQ

INTELLIGENCE TESTING

Intelligence tests, both group and individual, are used in many different ways today. The largest users of intelligence tests are schools. Group intelligence tests are used at the preschool and kindergarten levels to distinguish children who are ready to participate in educational activities from those who need remedial preparation. At the elementary, middle, and high-school levels, group tests are used to identify exceptional and handicapped students, and to aid in forming homogeneous ability groups within classrooms. Group intelligence tests are commonly used as one criterion for admission into colleges and universities. Individual intelligence tests have been administered for over half a century by well-trained clinicians for psychological, psychoeducational, and neuropsychological diagnosis. The passage of the Education of All Handicapped Children Act of 1975 (PL 94-142) resulted in the common use of individual intelligence tests as part of larger assessment batteries for the placement of children in special education programs for the mentally retarded, learning disabled, emotionally disturbed, and so forth, and for the development of individual educational programs for these children. For adults, group and individual intelligence tests are used in a variety of settings, including business and industry, prisons, mental health centers, hospitals, and private clinical practice.

Group intelligence tests find their principal application in education, business, government, and military, in circumstances where it is feasible to obtain valid test data from many individuals at once; they are useful as well with individuals who are able to take a test by themselves without need of an examiner. In contrast, individual intelligence tests are used in clinics and special education centers, where an intensive study of individual clients is needed and a trained examiner is necessary to secure valid test results. The reasons for using group and individual tests are many and provide a basis for understanding the type of information provided by the two testing formats. A summary of these reasons, as reported by Anastasi (1982), follows.

Group tests can be administered to a large number of individuals at the same time by using booklets of printed items and forms for the examinee to indicate his or her answer. The training and experience required by the examiner is minimal, as most group tests only require the examiner to read simple instructions and accurately keep time. The minimal role of the examiner in group testing provides more uniform testing conditions than in individual testing.

Objective scoring is a key aspect of group tests. Test items are usually multiple choice, true-false, or some other type that produces responses that can be scored as correct or incorrect with no deliberation. Items on group tests can usually be scored by a clerk or a computer. In addition, group tests typically include answer sheets, separate from the test booklets that contain the items, allowing economical reuse of test booklets.

Because group tests can be administered to large groups of individuals at the same time, larger numbers of individuals can be used in the standardization programs for group tests than for individual tests. Group test norms are generally better established because they are based on standardization samples of 100,000 to 200,000 instead of the 1000 to 4000 used for individual tests.

On the other hand, individual intelligence tests have several characteristics that make them suitable for a variety of clinical purposes. In individual testing, the examiner has the opportunity to obtain cooperation, establish rapport, and enhance motivation of the examinee. The trained examiner in individual testing detects, reports, and uses in the interpretation of test scores the many characteristics of the examinee that may affect test performance such as anxiety, fatigue, and problem-solving style. In addition, some individuals such as emotionally disturbed and mentally retarded children and adults may perform better on individual tests than on group tests. Since most group tests require the examinee to read instructions and test items, individually administered tests, which demand little or no reading, are especially useful for learning-disabled and retarded individuals, and others who may have reading problems.

Individual intelligence tests, because they typically include short questions that require oral and open-ended responses, allow examinees to give creative and original responses to items. In individual testing, examinees are not limited to selecting one of four multiple choice answers or indicating if an item is true or false. The contents of an examinee's response on an individual intelligence test can therefore be analyzed in order to generate hypotheses about, for example, the examinee's creativity, style of thinking, cognitive development, or defense mechanisms.

Another aspect of individual intelligence testing concerns the flexibility of administration. On a group test, an examinee is required to respond to all items, or as many items as he or she can in a certain time limit. On an individual test, testing time is more effectively used because the examinee is administered only those items in the range appropriate to his or her ability level. This characteristic of individual tests helps avoid the boredom an examinee may have when working on items that are too easy or the frustration of working on items that are too difficult.

There are many group intelligence tests, but most have the characteristics noted previously: multiple choice items with four or five choices for each question and test booklets with separate answer sheets for recording responses. Also, most group tests provide deviation IQs or similar standard scores. Since there is no flexibility to present more or less difficult items based on the examinee's performance, most group intelligence tests consist of a series of multilevel tests, each designated for a particular age, grade, or level of difficulty.

Intelligence testing has been a controversial topic since the 1960s (Kaufman, 1979). The most pressing issues that are debated within both professional and public forums concern test bias, the influence of heredity versus environment on IQ, race differences in test scores, and disproportionate placement of minority children into special education classes such as those for the retarded or gifted. These issues have been the subject of research, debate, federal guidelines, laws, and lawsuits. Just as major law cases differ on whether intelligence tests are unfair to minority children (*Larry P. v. Riles;* PASE decision in Chicago), so do professionals in the field of intelligence testing continue to disagree on these issues. It is likely that the future will be filled with arguments on the appropriate use of intelligence tests and claims that they should be banned; at the same time, it is equally certain that there will continue to be a proliferation of new and revised instruments of both the individual and group variety.

REFERENCES

Anastasi, A. (1982). *Psychological testing* (5th ed.). New York: Macmillan.

Kaufman, A.S. (1979). *Intelligent testing with the WISC-R.* New York: Wiley.

See also **Intelligence; Intelligence Quotient; Intelligent Testing**

INTELLIGENT TESTING

Intelligent testing is a philosophy or model of assessment widely espoused and best represented in the writings of Kaufman et al. (Kaufman, 1979, 1994; Kaufman & Kaufman, 1977; Kaufman & Lichtenberger, 1999; Reynolds, 1999; Reynolds & Clark, 1982; Reynolds & Kaufman, 1986). The intent of the intelligent testing model is to bring together empirical data, psychometrics, clinical acumen, psychological theory, and careful reasoning to build an assessment of an individual leading to the derivation of an intervention to improve the life circumstances of the subject. The promulgation of this philosophy was prompted by many factors, but particularly extremist approaches to the use of tests.

With low-IQ children, the primary role of the intelligent tester is to use the test results to develop a means of intervention that will "beat" the prediction made by global IQs. A plethora of research during the twentieth century has amply demonstrated that very low-IQ children show concomitantly low levels of academic attainment. The clinical purpose of administering an intelligence test to a low-IQ child, then, is at least twofold: (1) to determine that the child is indeed at high risk for academic failure, and (2) to articulate a set of learning circumstances that defeat the prediction. For individuals with average or high IQs, the specific tasks of the intelligence tester may change, but the philosophy remains the same. When evaluating a learning-disabled (LD) child, for example, the task is primarily one of fulfilling the prediction made by the global IQs. Most LD children exhibit average or better general intelligence, but have a history of academic performance significantly below what would be predicted from their intelligence test performance. The intelligent tester takes on the responsibility of preventing the child from becoming an "outlier" in the prediction; i.e., he or she must design a set of environmental conditions that will cause the child to achieve and learn at the level predicted by the intelligence test.

When psychologists engage in intelligent testing, the child or adult becomes the primary focus of the evaluation and the tests fade into the background as only vehicles to understanding. The test setting becomes completely examinee oriented. Interpretation and communication of test results in the context of the individual's particular background, referral behaviors, and approach to performance on diverse tasks constitute the crux of competent evaluation. Global test scores are deemphasized; flexibility, a broad base of knowledge in psychology, and insight on the part of the psychologist are demanded. The intelligence test becomes a dynamic helping agent, not an instrument for labeling, placement in dead-end programs, or disillusionment on the part of eager, caring teachers and parents.

Intelligent testing urges the use of contemporary measures of intelligence as necessary to achieve a true understanding of the individual's intellectual functioning. The approach to test interpretation under this philosophy has been likened to the approach of a psychological detective (Kaufman, 1979, 1994). It requires melding of clinical skill, mastery of psychometrics and measurement, and extensive knowledge of cognitive development and intelligence. A far more extensive treatment of this approach to test interpretation appears in the book *Intelligent Testing with the WISC-R* (Kaufman, 1979), a volume updated in 1994 by Kaufman to apply directly to the WISC-III. The philosophy is not, however, test-specific. Discussion of applications of this philosophy to preschool children may be found in Kaufman and Kaufman (1977) and Reynolds and Clark (1982).

Knowledge and skill in psychometrics and measurement are requisite to intelligent testing (Reynolds, 1999). The clinical evaluation of test performance must be directed by careful analyses of the statistical properties of the test scores, the internal psychometric characteristics of the test, and the data regarding their relationship to external factors. As one example, difference scores have long been of inherent interest for psychologists, especially between subparts of an intelligence scale. Difference scores are unreliable, and small discrepancies between levels of performance may be best attributed to measurement error. If large enough, however, difference scores can provide valuable information regarding the choice of an appropriate remedial or therapeutic program. The psychometric characteristics of the tests in question dictate the size of the differences needed for statistical confidence in their reflecting real rather than chance fluctuations. Interpretation of subscale differences often requires integrating clinical observations of the child's behavior with data on the relationship of the test scores to other factors, and with theories of intelligence, but only after first establishing that the differences are real and not based on error.

Through the elements of clinical skill, psychometric sophistication, and a broad base of knowledge of theories of individual differences emerges intelligent testing. None is sufficient, yet, when properly implemented, these elements engage in a synergistic interaction to produce the greatest possible understanding. The intelligent testing model places a series of requirements on the test but also on the tester; not every test can be used intelligently nor can everyone be an intelligent tester. The examiner's breadth of knowledge of psychometrics, differential psychology, child development, and other areas is crucial. Equally, the test must have multiple scales that are reliable, with good validity evidence, and be standardized on a sufficiently large, nationally stratified random sample. The test must offer the opportunity for good clinical observations. Without all of these characteristics, intelligent testing is unlikely to take place; when it does, however, the child is certain to benefit.

REFERENCES

Kaufman, A.S. (1979). *Intelligent testing with the WISC-R.* New York: Wiley-Interscience.

Kaufman, A.S. (1994). *Intelligent testing with the WISC-III.* New York: Wiley.

Kaufman, A.S., & Kaufman, N.L. (1977). *Clinical evaluation of young children with the McCarthy scales.* New York: Grune & Stratton.

Kaufman, A.S., & Lichtenberger, L. (1999). Intellectual assessment. In C.R. Reynolds (Ed.), *Assessment,* Vol. 4 of M. Hersen & A. Bellack (Eds.), *Comprehensive clinical psychology.* Oxford: Elsevier Science.

Reynolds, C.R. (1999). Fundamentals of measurement and assessment in psychology. In C.R. Reynolds (Ed.), *Assessment,* Vol. 4 of M. Hersen & A. Bellack (Eds.), *Comprehensive clinical psychology,* Oxford: Elsevier Science.

Reynolds, C.R., & Clark, J.H. (1982). Cognitive assessment of the preschool child. In K. Paget & B. Bracken (Eds.), *Psychoeducational assessment of preschool and primary aged children.* New York: Grune & Stratton.

Reynolds, C.R., & Kaufman, A.S. (1986). Assessment of children's intelligence with the Wechsler scales. In B. Wolman (Ed.), *Handbook of intelligence.* New York: Wiley-Interscience.

See also Assessment; Cultural Bias in Testing; Intelligence Testing; Remediation, Deficit-Centered Models of; Sequential and Simultaneous Cognitive Processing

INTERACTIVE LANGUAGE DEVELOPMENT

The notion of interactive language development has its roots in the philosophy of pragmatism and in child language pragmatics research. Pragmatics refers to the study of the social uses of language and research in the area of pragmatic language development in children. It is concerned primarily with three major focuses: (1) understanding how children learn to adapt their language to various linguistic and nonlinguistic contexts; (2) tracking development relative to the increasing repertoire of language functions; and (3) determining the role of social context in facilitating various aspects of language development (Bates, 1976; Prutting, 1982).

Interactive language development approaches rely heavily on social psychological research involving the study of adult-child interaction. Rees (1982) found a recurring theme in this literature: that pragmatic considerations have a prominent role in language acquisition "not only as a set of skills to be acquired but as motivating and explanatory factors for the acquisition of the language itself" (p. 8). Rees argues that pragmatic interactional factors assume an important role in the child's mastery of native language. Interactional factors may be seen as the source or origin of language in the child. Bruner (1975) cites the interaction between mother and infant during the first year of life, particularly in shared attention objects, people, and events of interest, as the basis of the child's capacity for reference and more broadly for meaning that eventually characterizes the human use of symbols.

Second, pragmatic interactional factors may be seen as the motivation for language learning as exemplified in the research of Halliday (1975) and Bates (1976). These researchers demonstrate how communicative functions emerge prior to the acquisition of linguistic skills. In addition to forming the basis for the development of particular linguistic structures, pragmatic interactional factors explain the development of linguistic style and code switching ability. As Rees (1982) notes, "language users typically control a range of style and code variants that are appropriate to particular listeners and particular settings, and they use these variants in establishing and maintaining social role relationships. . . ." (p. 10). Children as young as 3 or 4 years have been found to use different styles or "registers" for speaking to their parents, siblings, friends, strangers, younger and older children (Gleason, 1973; Snow & Ferguson, 1977).

Procedures for pragmatic interactional language treatment are discussed in Wilcox (1982).

REFERENCES

Bates, E. (1976). Pragmatics and sociolinguistics in child language. In D. Morehead & A. Morehead (Eds.), *Normal and deficient child language*. Baltimore, MD: University Park Press.

Bruner, J. (1975). The ontogenesis of speech acts. *Journal of Child Language, 2,* 1–20.

Gleason, J. (1973). Code-switching in children's language. In T. Moore (Ed.), *Cognitive development and the acquisition of language*. New York: Academic.

Halliday, M. (1975). *Learning how to mean*. London: Arnold.

Prutting, C. (1982). Pragmatics as social competence. *Journal of Speech & Hearing Disorders, 47,* 123–134.

Rees, N. (1982). An overview of pragmatics or what is in the box? In J.V. Irwin (Ed.), *Pragmatics: The role in language development*. La Verne, CA: Fox Point and University of La Verne Press.

Snow, C., & Ferguson, C. (1977). *Talking to children: Language input and acquisition*. Cambridge, England: Cambridge University Press.

Wilcox, M. (1982). The integration of pragmatics into language therapy. In J.V. Irwin (Ed.), *Pragmatics: The role in language development*. La Verne, CA: Fox Point and University of La Verne Press.

See also Communication Disorders; Language Therapy; Pragmatics; Social Learning Theory; Theory of Activity

INTERDISCIPLINARY TEAMS

Before any child receives special education services, he or she must receive an individual assessment to identify areas of educational need, determine the child's aptitude for achievement, and identify other factors that might be interfering with school performance. This individual assessment is the basis for all instructional planning. With the advent of PL 94-142 came the requirement that an interdisciplinary team (IDT), also known as a multidisciplinary team (MDT), be used to determine pupil eligibility for special education services. Public agencies assessing children suspected of having a handicapping condition must include the following in their interdisciplinary team (Federal Register, 1977, 121a.540):

(A)(1) The child's regular teacher; or

(2) If the child does not have a regular teacher, a regular classroom teacher qualified to teach a child of his or her age; or

(3) For a child of less than school age, an individual qualified by the State Educational Agency to teach a child of his or her age; and

(B) At least one person qualified to conduct individual diagnostic examinations of children such as a school psychologist, speech language pathologist, or remedial reading teacher.

Since PL 94142 and subsequent amendments and legislation (IDEA), IDTs have become incorporated into the organizational routine of most school systems in the United States. Nevertheless, school professionals, parents, and the general public have expressed differing views regarding their value (Masters & Mori, 1986).

While IDT functioning has been widely researched, the results have been mixed; some inquiries into whether IDTs make better decisions than individuals have revealed few differences between decisions made by IDTs and those made by individual decision makers (Pfeiffer, 1982). Some researchers (Pfeiffer & Naglieri, 1983) have demonstrated that teams make more consistent and less variable decisions than do individuals. Interpretive and methodological differences between positive and negative studies make it difficult to arrive at definitive answers.

REFERENCES

Masters, L.F., & Mori, A.A. (1986). *Teaching secondary students with mild learning and behavior problems*. Rockville, MD: Aspen.

Pfeiffer, S.I. (1982). Special education placement decisions made by teams and individuals. *Psychology in the Schools, 19,* 335– 340.

Pfeiffer, S.I., & Naglieri, J.A. (1983). An investigation of multidisciplinary team decision-making. *Journal of Learning Disabilities, 15*(10), 586–590.

See also Assessment; Individuals with Disabilities Education Act (IDEA); Multidisciplinary Teams

INTERNATIONAL CHILD NEUROLOGY ASSOCIATION (ICNA)

The International Child Neurology Association was founded in 1973. ICNA is a nonprofit organization composed of child neurologists and related professionals dedicated to the promotion of research in the field of child neurology and encouraging recognition of the ability and scope of those who practice within the profession. In the interest of advancing and benefiting child and infant neurological science, the association provides a forum for the exchange of scientific and professional opinions by organizing international meetings, international cooperative studies, publications, and translations as well as supporting international exchange of teachers and students in the field. The 8th International Child Neurology Congress (1998) of ICNA was held in Ljubljana, Slovenia (ICNA, 1998).

REFERENCE

International Child Neurology Association (ICNA)(1998, September 9). *8th International Child Neurology Congress*. Retrieved December 5, 1998 from: http://dstumpf.net/icna/index.html.

INTERNATIONAL CLASSIFICATION OF DISEASES (ICD)

The International Classification of Diseases (ICD) is used to classify morbidity and mortality data for statistical purposes and to index hospital records on diseases and operations for information storage and retrieval. Classifying operations for this purpose has traditionally involved structuring according to type of operative procedure, anatomic site, or a combination of these two methods. Surgical specialty serves as the primary axis for classification in the present ICD as well as in most hospitals. The way in which a classification system of diseases is applied depends on the particular data to be classified and on the final product desired. As of yet, there exists no internationally agreed on method for classifying multiple causes of death.

The tenth revision of the ICD is an extension of the system of causes of morbidity and mortality. Furthermore, it provides a means for developing an efficient basis for indexing diagnostic information on hospital charts so that this data may later be reviewed and studied. The ICD is divided into 17 main sections, among them: diseases caused by well-defined infective agents; endocrine, neoplasmic, metabolic, and nutritional diseases; mental diseases; complications of pregnancy and childbirth; diseases of the perinatal period; ill-defined conditions; and a classification of injuries (puncture, burn, or open wound). The last category involves a dual classification system: external cause and nature of injury. This section is designed to bear the numbers 800–999; external cause is distinguished by the prefix "E," while nature of injury is distinguished by the prefix "N." Although the broad section headings aid organization, much significance should not be placed on their inherent value, since they have never represented a consistent collection of disease conditions to serve as statistically stable and usable areas. The detailed list is comprised of 671 categories, in addition to 187 categories characterizing injuries according to the nature of the wound, and 182 categories classifying external causes of injuries. A decimal numbering system is used; thus the categories are designated by three-digit numbers. The initial two digits pinpoint important or summary groups, while the third digit sections each group into categories representing classifications of diseases according to a specific axis of specific disease entities. The three-digit categories are not numbered consecutively. Four-digit subcategories provide additional specificity regarding etiology or manifestations of the condition. While the list of categories in the ICD provides a structure for classification, it is essential to be familiar with the diagnostic terms included within each category before the ICD can be of practical use.

INTERNATIONAL DYSLEXIA ASSOCIATION

The International Dyslexia Association (IDA), formally the Orton Dyslexia Society, is an international, nonprofit organization dedicated to the study and treatment of dyslexia. The IDA was established to continue the pioneering work of Dr. Samuel T. Orton, a neurologist who was one of the first to identify dyslexia and develop effective teaching approaches. Since then, the association has been a strong force in educational and scientific communities. For nearly fifty years, the IDA has been helping individuals with dyslexia, their families, teachers, physicians, and researchers to better understand dyslexia. The association believes that all individuals have the right to achieve their potential; that individual learning abilities can be strengthened; and that social, educational, and cultural barriers to language acquisition and use must be removed.

The mission statement of the association is: "The International Dyslexia Association actively promotes effective teaching approaches and related clinical educational intervention strategies for dyslexics. We support and encourage interdisciplinary study and research. We facilitate the exploration of the causes and early identification of dyslexia and are committed to the responsible and wide dissemination of research-based knowledge."

Information for this entry was provided directly from the International Dyslexia Association's webpage. This internet website is an excellent source of information for individuals interested in dyslexia and the association. The website address is http://www.interdys.org.

INTERNATIONAL JOURNAL OF CLINICAL NEUROPSYCHOLOGY (IJCN)
See ARCHIVES OF CLINICAL NEUROPSYCHOLOGY.

INTERNATIONAL READING ASSOCIATION (IRA)

The International Reading Association (IRA) is a nonprofit professional organization devoted to the improvement of reading instruction (IRA, 1985). Membership in IRA is open to individuals who are interested in the field of reading, including teachers, administrators, reading specialists, special educators, college-level instructors and researchers, psychologists, librarians, and parents. In addition, membership is also available to institutions and agencies that are involved with the teaching of reading or the preparation of reading teachers. The IRA endorses the study of reading as a process, promotes research into improvement of reading programs, and advocates better teacher education. The organization is also closely involved with the worldwide literacy movement and the role of reading in the general welfare of society and individuals, as promulgated in the IRA Code of Ethics (1985).

The IRA is comprised of over 1150 councils and national affiliates in various countries around the world. The four major professional journals and numerous individual volumes on reading-related topics published annually by the IRA provide other means through which members are kept informed of current practices in reading education.

REFERENCES

Committee on Professional Standards and Ethics. (1985). IRA Code of Ethics. *Reading Teacher, 39*(1), 56–57.

International Reading Association. (1985). Newark, DE: Author.

See also Reading; Reading Remediation

INTERNATIONAL TEST USE IN SPECIAL EDUCATION

An international survey of test use in 44 countries, not including the United States, identified 455 tests used frequently with children and youth (Hu & Oakland, 1991; Oakland & Hu, 1991, 1992, 1994). Among these tests, 46% were imported for use as they were developed outside of the countries in which they were being used. Tests commonly imported for use originally were developed in the United States (22%), the United Kingdom (7%), West Germany (7%), France (5%), and Sweden (5%). Foreign developed tests are used more frequently than locally developed tests in 68% of the countries surveyed. Locally developed tests are used more frequently than foreign developed tests in only 27% of the reporting countries. Seven countries report no nationally developed tests.

Test use is not uniform throughout the world. Highest test use was reported by three pre-1990 socialist nations: Yugoslavia (principally Slovenia), East Germany, and Czechoslovakia. Lowest test use was reported by the least developed nations. Reliance on foreign developed tests is most common in the Middle Eastern and least developed nations.

TYPES OF TESTS USED

Measures of intelligence (39%), personality (24%), and achievement (10%) appear most frequently. Tests assessing perceptual-motor abilities, vocational interests and aptitudes, school readiness, and social development are not found commonly. The 10 most frequently used tests, in rank order of frequency of use, are the Wechsler Intelligence Scales for Children, the Raven's Progressive Matrices, Bender Gestalt, Rorschach, Stanford-Binet, Wechsler Adult Intelligence Scales, Thematic Apperception Test, Differential Aptitude Test, Minnesota Multiphasic Personality Inventory, and Frostig Developmental Test of Visual Perception.

Two-thirds of the countries surveyed report a critical need for additional group and individual tests of achievement, intelligence, vocational interest and aptitudes, social development, and personality. The need for tests that assess qualities important to persons who are mentally retarded, blind, deaf, slow learners, emotionally and socially disturbed, physically impaired, and gifted were identified by almost 85% of the countries. Tests to assess students with learning disabilities are needed most, given an estimated 150 million worldwide.

PSYCHOMETRIC STUDIES

Standardized tests are expected to be suitably normed and to have reliability and validity estimates (American Educational Research Association, 1985). As noted below, these important qualities often do not exist. Local norms are available on 80% of achievement tests, 65% of intelligence tests, and 58% of personality tests. Among measures of achievement, studies of concurrent validity are available on 71%, predictive validity on 43%, and construct validity on 48%. Among measures of intelligence, studies of concurrent validity are available on 63%, predictive validity on 56%, and construct validity on 54%. Among measures of personality, concurrent validity studies are available on 53% and predictive and construct validity studies on approximately 39%.

Reliability studies have been conducted on 50% to 60% of measures of intelligence, personality, achievement, vocational interests and aptitudes, and school readiness. Studies examining the reliability of other types of measures appear less frequently. Thus, information often is unavailable to determine the adequacy of measures commonly used with children and youth (Oakland & Hu, 1994).

PROFESSIONALS WHO USE TESTS

At least 16 professional groups commonly use tests with children and youth. School or educational psychologists often assume leadership for testing. Other frequently cited specialists include regular and special education teachers, clinical psychologists, and counselors (Oakland & Hu, 1991).

The educational levels of these professionals differ considerably, ranging from 2.5 years of post-secondary education for nurses to 6.5 years for physicians. The correlation between the number of years of post-secondary education and the perceived competence of the professional groups is substantial ($r = -.50$, $p > .001$). Thus, professions with more education are thought to be more competent in the use of tests. In addition, professionals who use individually administered tests often are educated more highly than those who use only group tests.

IMPLICATION CONCERNING TEST USE IN SPECIAL EDUCATION

The availability and quality of tests used with children and youth internationally varies greatly by region and country. Resources are strongest in Western Europe and some Eastern European countries, in English-speaking countries affiliated with the United Kingdom, and Israel. Fewest resources are found in the Middle East, and Central and South America. The number of studies examining test reliability and validity clearly is deficient. Professionals commonly are required to make decisions about children and youth using measures whose psychometric qualities are unknown and whose norms were developed on children from technologically advanced countries. As a result, professional standards and professional respect are jeopardized along with the quality of services delivered to children, youth, and their families.

Efforts to promote proper test development and use internationally should address three major needs: for additional studies that examine test reliability and validity, for additional measures that have nationally representative norms, and for greater reliance on nationally developed tests.

REFERENCES

American Educational Research Association. (1985). *Standards for educational and psychological testing.* Washington, DC: Author.

Hu, S., & Oakland, T. (1991). Global and regional perspectives on testing children and youth: An empirical study. *International Journal of Psychology, 26,* 329–244.

Oakland, T., & Hu, S. (1991). Professionals who administer tests with children and youth: An international survey. *Journal of Psychoeducational Assessment, 9*(2), 108–120.

Oakland, T., & Hu, S. (1992). The top 10 tests used with children and youth worldwide. *Bulletin of the International Test Commission, 19,* 99–120.

Oakland, T., & Hu, S. (1994). International perspectives on tests used with children and youth. *Journal of School Psychology, 31,* 501–517.

INTERNATIONAL YEAR OF DISABLED PERSONS, 1981

The General Assembly of the United Nations proclaimed 1981 the International Year of Disabled Persons (Resolution 31/123, December 16, 1976). Previous initiatives had set the stage. These included the Declaration on the Rights of Mentally Retarded Persons (Resolution 2856 [xxvi], adopted on December 20, 1971) and the Declaration on the Rights of Disabled Persons (Resolution 3447 [xxx], adopted December 9, 1975).

The resolution on the International Year of Disabled Persons stressed the theme of full participation by persons with disabilities in the social, political, and economic life and development of the societies in which they live. It also promoted national and international efforts to provide disabled persons with proper assistance, training, care, and guidance, and encouraged study and research projects designed to facilitate the practical participation of disabled persons in daily life by improving such things as transport and access. One hundred and thirty-one countries took an active part in the International Year of Disabled Persons. They formed national commissions and carried out national programs, many of them focusing formally on the problem of disability for the first time.

On December 3, 1982, at the conclusion of its 37th session and the end of the International Year of Disabled Persons, the United Nations' General Assembly proclaimed the United Nations Decade of Disabled Persons, 1983–1992. It also formally adopted the World Program of Action, with its stress on the prevention of disability and its effort to identify major problems facing people with disabilities throughout the world, and made recommendations of actions to be taken to respond to these problems. The majority of recommendations address strategies for prevention, rehabilitation, and equalization of opportunity. The last category includes such issues as legislation, the physical environment, income maintenance, social security, education and training, employment, recreation, culture, religion, and sports.

INTERPRETERS FOR THE DEAF

Interpreters for the deaf are hearing individuals who listen to a spoken message and communicate it in some way to hearing-impaired people. In interpreting it is permissible to depart from the exact words of the speaker to paraphrase, define, and explain what the speaker is saying. Interpreting is differentiated from translating, which is a verbatim presentation of another person's remarks (Quigley & Paul, 1984).

The first case involving PL 94-142, the Education for all Handicapped Children Act, decided by the U.S. Supreme Court, was a demand for a sign language interpreter by the parents of a mainstream deaf child, Amy Rowley. The Court decided that this particular deaf child did not need an interpreter. However, in other cases, sign language interpreters have been ordered, even for elementary school students when teachers state that interpreters are needed for pupils to benefit from their classes and actively participate in them (DuBow & Geer, 1983). In 1982 the U.S. Court of Appeals mandated state vocational rehabilitation agencies to provide interpreters for deaf clients attending college.

The Vocational Rehabilitation Act of 1965 provided that interpreter services must be included as part of vocational rehabilitation services. Since then, most states have mandated that deaf individuals must be offered sign language interpreters whenever their civil rights are involved. Interpreter training programs are available throughout the United States. Many colleges offer an AA or BA degree in interpreting.

REFERENCES

DuBow, S., & Geer S. (1983, July). Education decisions after Rowley. *National Center for Law and the Deaf Newsletter* (pp. 1–3).

Quigley, S., & Paul, P. (1984). *Language and deafness.* San Diego, CA: College Hill Press.

See also **Deaf Education; Lipreading/ Speechreading**

INTERVENTION

Intervention consists of all planned attempts to promote the general welfare of exceptional individuals. There are three broad types of interventions: preventive, remedial, and compensatory.

Efforts to thwart the appearance of disabilities are considered preventive. For example, phenylketonuria is an inherited condition that ultimately results in brain damage and arrested mental development. Early diagnosis and intervention via a special diet effectively prevent the otherwise predictable neurological damage and mental retardation. Though it is not invariably so, preventive interventions are most often introduced by the medical profession.

Remedial intervention is the process of overcoming a deficit by correcting or otherwise improving it directly. When a handicapped reader is taught to read at a level that is comparable to that of his or her peer group, it is called remedial intervention. Remedial interventions are generally introduced by the education profession where service delivery, in the form of individualized education programs, is developed for each child independently.

In compensatory intervention, the usual approach is to provide a child with the means to circumvent, substitute, or otherwise offset an irremediable deficit. The best known and most widely used compensatory interventions consist of teaching a child to use technological advances that at least partially obviate the need for remediation. For example, the development of close-captioned television programs effectively compensates for the inability of people who are deaf to hear the program.

Several theoretical models exist by which interventions may be classified. They include biophysical, psychological, behavioral, ecological, and sociological models.

Biophysical theorists believe that abnormalities result from physical anomalies within the organism. The causes of affective, cognitive, and motoric difficulties may be either endogenous (i.e., originating within the body) or exogenous (originating outside of the body), and generally are considered to be genetic, nutritional, neurological, or biochemical in nature.

Genetic counseling is an intervention intended to prevent hereditary disorders from occurring. Prime candidates for genetic counseling are adults who have known hereditary disorders or who find themselves in circumstances that increase the probability of bearing a child with a genetic disorder. Sickle cell anemia, hemophilia, and osteogenesis imperfecta (tarda) are just three conditions that are genetically caused and, therefore, can be prevented through genetic counseling. On the other hand, genetic counselors provide a service to older couples by informing them of the probabilities of bearing a child with a genetic abnormality such as Down's syndrome.

Nutritional deficiencies can result in severe, irreversible intellectual and physical disorders. Although nutritional problems are not particularly extensive in the United States, they do exist; in many third world nations (e.g., Ethiopia) the extent of such disorders is nothing short of catastrophic. The introduction of a balanced, nutritional diet is the obvious biophysical intervention of choice.

Neurological damage incurred following accidents, low levels of oxygen in the blood, etc., also result in behavioral abnormalities. When instruction in sign language is used with victims of electrical shock or stroke in order to circumvent the resulting neurological impairment, a compensatory intervention is implemented.

Remedial interventions are also employed to overcome assumed neurological dysfunctions. For instance, cognitive interventions are those that deal with teaching the individual how to think. Such interventions primarily intend to improve perception, memory, and problem solving. Included here are approaches often referred to as process or ability training (Mann & Sabatino, 1985; Ysseldyke & Algozzine, 1984). Often, the tasks involved are neuropsychologically specific. That is, they are characterized by modality specificity (e.g., auditory, visual, or haptic) or hemisphere specificity (i.e., they are analytical, sequential, and highly language-based or global, simultaneous, and nonlanguage-based). Cognitive intervention strategies cover a wide range of topics (Hallahan, 1980). They remain among the most controversial approaches to intervention.

The core belief in the psychological intervention model is that abnormality is the result of internalized conflicts that prevent the individual from fully participating in the social and academic environment. An outgrowth of Freudian psychology, the psychodynamic model seeks to reduce the individual's conflicts by helping him or her to better understand both behavior and the reasons for exhibiting it. Fritz Redl was one of the primary contributors to this approach, introducing such classroom techniques as the life space interview (LSI). The LSI is actually a set of interventions designed to take place immediately following crisis situations. The interventions have a temporal advantage over traditional therapy in that life events are not allowed to grow distant before the child and the teacher or therapist deal with them.

Although the behavioral intervention tradition in special education is often tied most closely to B.F. Skinner's work in instrumental (or operant) conditioning, its roots are much broader. It is true that most of the interventions known today as behavior modification do stem from Skinner's ground-breaking research in reinforcement, punishment, and extinction. However, many of the more powerful interventions being introduced to the field lately (e.g., in the writings of Kathryn Blake, Siegfried Engelman, and Douglas Carnine) come from the traditional psychological research on concept learning, verbal learning, discrimination learning, and problem solving.

In contrast to proponents of the biophysical and psychological models, ecological theorists consider disturbance to be the result of the dynamic interaction between the child and the environment (Rhodes & Tracy, 1974). According to the ecological intervention approach, such events as physical abuse by the parents, slothful behavior by the child, or the death of a sibling are not isolated phenomena, but are interactive in nature. That is, the individual's behavior and other environmental conditions both affect and are affected by the people and conditions within the ecosphere. Consequently, advocates of this model discuss disturbed environments, not disturbed people.

Three distinct views characterize the sociological intervention model: (1) labeling theory, (2) societal rule breaking and rule following, and (3) anomie. Specific interventions that are the result of these views are difficult to identify. Rather, in labeling theory and societal rule breaking and rule following, the opposite seems true; i.e., it may be the interventions themselves that lead to deviance (as it is termed by sociologists).

Labeling theorists suggest that deviance itself is sometimes the result of the painfully focused attention that the individual's behavior may receive. They contend that labels such as troublemaker and dunce are pejorative and can actually be powerful stimuli for deviant behavior.

Unlike other perspectives, sociological theorists generally view abnormality as behavior that is significantly contrary to the rules established by society. Since normal people break rules some of the time and abnormal individuals follow established rules much or even most of the time, it is important to note the agents who enforce societal rules (e.g., police, teachers) are in the unhappy position of deciding which rule breakers to label as abnormal. Clearly, only a few rule breakers are labeled by society. Since deviance is only a vaguely defined concept, it seems certain that many injustices in the form of false positives and false negatives are committed. In particular, many believe that individuals from poor or culturally different backgrounds are especially susceptible to the application of false labels. Such logic would seem to support the notion of labeling theory.

Interventions based on sociological models are difficult to implement. Nevertheless, society has implemented a number of them in an attempt to prevent or remediate deviance. Local, state, and federal police forces are intended to both prevent and enforce societal rules that have been codified into laws. Our judicial system is intended to mete out justice to those accused of offenses. Public school programs clearly play a similar role, particularly with regard to values and mores that have not been codified as laws. Prison systems and youth detention centers assume both a punitive and a remedial intervention role where lawbreakers are concerned. Some recent attempts by society to intervene more effectively include an increase in mental health centers, better organized community services, crisis intervention centers, suicide help lines, normalization projects, and not least, public school inclusion programming with children who have disabilities.

REFERENCES

Hallahan, D. (Ed.). (1980). *Teaching exceptional children to use cognitive strategies.* Rockville, MD: Aspen.

Mann, L., & Sabatino, D.A. (1985). *Foundations of cognitive processes in special and remedial education.* Rockville, MD: Aspen.

Rhodes, W.C., & Tracy, M.I. (Eds.). (1974). *A study of child variance: Conceptual models* (Vol. 1). Ann Arbor: University of Michigan.

Ysseldyke, J.E., & Algozzine, B. (1984). *Introduction to special education.* Boston: Houghton Mifflin.

See also **Behavior Modification; Child Psychology; Ecological Assessment**

INTERVENTION IN SCHOOL AND CLINIC

In 1988, Pro-Ed, Inc. purchased the journal *Academic Therapy* from Academic Therapy Publications. In 1990, Pro-Ed changed the title of the journal to *Intervention in School and Clinic;* however, the emphasis remained the same as when John Arena began *Academic Therapy* in 1965. *Intervention* is a practitioner-oriented journal designed to provide practical, research-based ideas to those who work with students with severe learning disabilities or emotional and behavioral problems for whom typical classroom instruction is not effective. The articles are easy to read, and the interventions and strategies provided can be implemented in school or special clinical settings. *Intervention* is published five times during a volume year: September, November, January, March, and May.

INTERVENTIONS FOR AUTISM

Persons with autism can make considerable gains in intellectual, motor, and social development when the appropriate intervention is implemented in schools and families (Adams & Toomey, 1995; Kozloff, 1998, Lovaas, 1987; Powers, 1992; Rogers, 1996). Rogers (1996) identified two specific characteristics of interventions that are effective in lessening the debilitating effects of autism and fostering affected children's psychosocial development: (1) *Early* intervention. Children with autism appear to make the greatest gains when treatment is implemented as early as feasible, between the ages of two and four years. (2) *Intense* intervention. Programs that have at least 15 contact hours weekly and low teacher-child ratios have more successful outcomes.

BEHAVIORALLY-ORIENTED PROGRAMS

Dawson and Osterling (1997) identified several elements of early interventions for autism that are present in effective treatments. (1) The content of the curriculum should emphasize five basic skills: a) to attend and follow teaching commands, b) to imitate others, c) to comprehend and use language, d) to play appropriately, and e) to engage in social interactions. (2) The learning environment should be a highly structured one that emphasizes the generalization of mastered skills to other tasks, materials, persons, and locations in a child's environment. (3) Learning environments are tailored to the child's need for routine and predictability. Both (2) and (3) are important owing to the fact that children with autism are generally highly dependent on structure. They appear to benefit greatly from stability or predictability in their environments that enables them properly to induce generalizations and to learn strategies for action. (4) A functional approach is used to modify problem behaviors. Functional analysis consists of a) identifying environmental conditions—such as antecedent events, prompts, and reinforcement contingencies—that are maintaining undesirable behaviors and/or that might be used to strengthen desirable behavior; b) planning ways to alter features of the environment in order to replace problem behaviors and accelerate desirable behaviors; c) instituting the plan and collecting formative evaluation data on effectiveness; and d) revising program plans as indicated by the data.

(5) The treatment program aids in the transition from preschool to kindergarten or first grade. This transition should be a gradual process in which the child is prepared for the change and the teacher is adequately trained to accommodate the child. Many programs offer workshops for teachers and others who will be working with the child. (6) Family involvement may be an essential component of successful programs (Kozloff, 1998). Parental involvement assists in the generalization and maintenance of skills that one-on-one and group therapy sessions cannot always facilitate. Many programs provide family training workshops, which offer assistance in treating behaviors that occur in the home environment.

The Young Autism Project (Lovaas, 1987; Lovaas, 1993; McEachin, Lovaas, & Smith, 1993) is perhaps the best described and evaluated of the autism intervention programs. Beginning in 1970, the project worked with children who had been independently diagnosed as autistic, who were less 40 months chronological age (less than 46 months if echolalic), and whose mental age was at least 11 months at chronological age 30 months. Children were assigned to either an experimental (n = 19) or control (n = 19) group. Although assignment was nonrandom, children in the two groups were highly similar at the outset of the program. Children in the experimental group received at least 40 hours a week of one-on-one therapy, using applied behavioral analysis procedures, in their homes, schools, and communities, whereas those in the control group received only 10 hours a week of treatment.

A double-blind follow-up report when the experimental children averaged 13 years of age and the control group children averaged 10 years of age (McEachin et al., 1993) largely confirmed the dramatic differences between groups when the children averaged about 7 years of age (Lovaas, 1987). Of functional importance, 9 of the 19 experimental children (47%) were in regular classrooms, whereas none of the control children were.

Another effective model of intervention incorporates developmental perspectives into teaching children with autism. The developmental approach stresses the importance of recognizing the uneven developmental patterns of persons with autism. Division TEACCH (Treatment and Education of Autistic and related Communication Handicapped children), founded by Schopler and Reichler, is a particularly well-developed example of a developmentally-focused program (Bashford, Mesibov, Schopler, & Shigley, 1984). The TEACCH method emphasizes the importance of individualizing each child's program to facilitate his or her developmental level. This method also uses some behavioral therapy and special education in the treatment of persons with autism. Parents are trained and considered "cotherapists" in the treatment programs of their children. TEACCH services provide a highly structured learning environment that facilitates the autistic individual's need for predictability and routine. This model also emphasizes the importance of assisting independence at all levels of development. The Health Sciences Center program (University of Colorado) also incorporates developmental principles into the learning environment, using play as a teaching medium to facilitate progress through stages of development. Positive feedback is presented to the child to encourage appropriate social interaction and to aid in the understanding of human relationships. This program also offers parent training and family support groups.

PSYCHOPHARMACOLOGICAL INTERVENTIONS

Numerous drugs have been administered to autistic children in an attempt to decrease the behavioral disturbances of autism. As reported by McDougle (1997), some drug therapies have been successful. Drugs which affect serotonin functioning, such as buspirone, fluoxetine, and lithium, as well as some drugs which affect the dopamine system, have decreased symptoms in some children. Beta-blockers, which interfere with norepinephrine functioning, have led to a reduction in aggression and self-injurious behaviors and an increase in speech and social skills in some autistic persons. Since the neurobiological component of autism is, in large part, a mystery, no drug therapies have been successful in "curing" autism.

It is important to recognize no interventions are effective in treating all children with autism. Interventions that apply behavioral or developmental principles to the treatment of autism in combination with drug therapies have led to encouraging outcomes in those with autism.

REFERENCES

Adams, L., & Toomey, J. (1995). Naturalistic observations of children with autism: Evidence for intersubjectivity. *New Directions for Child Development, 69,* 75–89.

Bashford, A., Mesibov, R., Schopler, E., & Shigley, H. (1984). Helping autistic children through their parents: The TEACCH model. In A. Mesibov & B. Schopler (Eds.), *The effects of autism on the family* (pp. 65–81). New York: Plenum.

Dawson, G., & Osterling, J. (1997). Early intervention in autism. In M.J. Guralnick (Ed.), *The effectiveness of early intervention* (pp. 307–324). Baltimore: Brookes.

Kozloff, M.A. (1998). *Reaching the autistic child* (Rev. ed.). Cambridge, MA: Brookline.

Lovaas, I.O. (1987). Behavioral treatment and normal educational and intellectual functioning in young autistic children. *Journal of Consulting and Clinical Psychology, 55,* 3–9.

Lovaas, I.O. (1993). The development of a treatment-research project for developmentally disabled and autistic children. *Journal of Applied Behavior Analysis, 26,* 617–630.

McDougle, C.J. (1997). Psychopharmacology. In D.J. Cohen & F.R. Volkmar (Eds.), *Handbook of autism and pervasive developmental disorder* (2nd ed.) (pp. 707–729). New York: Wiley.

McEachin, J., Lovaas, I.O., & Smith, T. (1993). Long term outcomes for children with autism who received early intensive behavioral treatment. *American Journal on Mental Retardation, 97,* 359–372.

Powers, M. (1992). Early interventions for children with autism. In A. Berkell (Ed.), *Autism: Identification, education, and treatment* (pp. 282–309). New York: Guilford.

Rogers, S.J. (1996). Brief report: Early intervention in autism. *Journal of Autism and Developmental Disorders, 26,* 243–246.

INTERVENTION PROGRAMS, EARLY

Federal legislation mandates intervention services for children with disabilities. 1986 Amendments to PL 94-142, the Education of All Handicapped Children Act of 1974, extended services to children 3 to 5 years of age, and 1997 Amendments to what had become the Individuals with Disabilities Education Act (IDEA 97, PL 105-17) further mandate services to infants and toddlers who either manifest a developmental delay or have a diagnosed condition likely to lead to a developmental delay. Although some (e.g., Ramey & Ramey, 1998) use the term "intervention program" to describe services for children at risk for developmental delay and "treatment program" to describe services for children who have a specific diagnosed condition, many (e.g., Bryant & Graham, 1993a; Guralnick, 1997b) use "intervention program" inclusively, as will be the case with this entry.

Intervention programs now exist for children with many potentially handicapping and handicapping conditions: (1) disadvantaged at-risk children; (2) premature and low birth weight infants; (3) infants exposed to prenatal alcohol or other substances; (4) infants with various neuromotor disorders, including cerebral palsy; (5) infants whose parents are mentally retarded; (6) infants with HIV infection; (6) infants with Down's Syndrome; (7) infants with autism; (8) young children with communication (speech and language) disorders; (9) young children with conduct problems; (10) children with vision or hearing impairments; and (11) maltreating parents and their children, among others. Summaries and evaluations of these programs are described in individual chapters in Guralnick (1997b). Development of programs has progressed to the point that Bryant and Graham (1993) have collected recommendations for implementing such programs.

Several sets of guiding principles have been proposed to guide intervention programs. The following list was compiled largely from those (a) developed by the Division for Early Childhood Task Force on Recommended Practices as presented in Bryant and Graham (1993b) and (b) presented in Guralnick (1997a).

1. Whatever the service delivery model, it should be the least restrictive and most natural environment for the child and family.

2. Programs should center on the needs of individual families and children, and be responsive to families' priorities.

3. Programs should not only be interdisciplinary, but should fully integrate components from each discipline.

4. Empirical results and professional and family values should guide service delivery practices.

5. Each child's and each family's services should be individualized and developmentally appropriate.

6. Intervention programs should be based in local communities.

7. Intervention programs should integrate services from a variety of agencies using a systems model.

8. Intervention programs should begin as early and be as intense as realistically possible and appropriate for the child and family. However, for some conditions, timing and intensity of treatment must be based carefully on each child's level of development since manipulations that occur too early or are too intense may have iatrogenic effects, being actually harmful.

REFERENCES

Bryant, D.M., & Graham, M.A. (1993a). *Implementing early intervention: From research to effective practice.* New York: Guilford.

Bryant, D.M., & Graham, M.A. (1993b). Models of service delivery. In D.M. Bryant & M.A. Graham (Eds.), *Implementing early intervention: From research to effective practice* (pp. 183–215). New York: Guilford.

Guralnick, M.J. (1997a). Second-generation research in the field of intervention. In M.J. Guralnick (Ed.), *The effectiveness of early intervention* (pp. 3–20). Baltimore: Brookes.

Guralnick, M.J. (1997b). *The effectiveness of early intervention.* Baltimore: Brookes.

INTERVENTION PROGRAMS FOR AT-RISK CHILDREN

Disadvantaged children (those born into poverty conditions) are at risk for developmental delays, school failure, behavioral problems, and a variety of other conditions. These children generally score below average on standardized intelligence and achievement tests, are overrepresented in special education classes, and are likely to drop out of school. In Birch and Gussow's (1970) representation of the poverty cycle, school failure contributed directly to unemployment and underemployment, which in turn were the major perpetuators of the cycle. Such failure and resulting poverty are clearly costly to the affected individuals, their children, and society at large.

Beginning in the 1930s and 40s and expanding greatly in the 1950s and 60s, experimental research demonstrated dramatic effects of early experience and environment on animals' learning and problem solving. Hebb (1949) used that research as the basis for his theory that varied early experience is necessary for adequate "primary learning" that in turn was a necessary precursor to adequate later learning. Hebb proposed that primary learning was perceptual and led to the development of particular structures in the brain. In an influential book, Hunt (1961) integrated Hebb's theory with Piaget's theory of child development and suggested that human intelligence could be modified through varied early experience. The finding that varied early environmental experiences increase brain development in animals (e.g., Bennett, Diamond, Krech, & Rosenzweig, 1964) supported the views of Hebb and Hunt. In addition, a variety of research suggested that environmental factors related to socioeconomic status (SES) might have positive or negative influences on children's cognitive development. For example, Hess and Shipman (1965) reported that relatively high-SES mothers used more complex and child-oriented

Table 1 Summary of Results of the Carolina Abecedarian Project

Measure	Treatment Condition			
	EE	EC	CE	CC
Intelligence at age 15 years	95.0	94.5	87.3	92.0
Woodcock-Johnson reading scores	95.0	92.0	88.8	87.5
Woodcock-Johnson mathematics scores	92.3	92.3	87.0	86.0
Percentage ever retained in grade to age 15	31	30	52	56
Percentage assigned to special education, K–9	36	12	48	48

Note: Data derived from figures in Campbell and Ramey (1995).

language styles with their children than did mothers from poverty-level backgrounds and that these differences correlated with differences in the children's performance on problem-solving tasks. Thus, research of a variety of kinds converged on the possibility that early intervention might raise IQs and school performance of at-risk children. Out of this convergence came Head Start in 1964, now including Early Head Start, and other intervention programs.

The Carolina Abecedarian Project may well be the best-designed, longest duration, and most intense of the intervention programs. Some participants received intervention services from early infancy to eight years of age.

A follow-up evaluation of the participants at age 15 showed significant effects of preschool program on several measures. Major results are shown in Table 1. Participants in the EE and EC groups had higher scores on reading and mathematics achievement tests, fewer assignments to special education programs, and only about half as many grade retentions than did children in the CC and CE groups. Differences in measured intelligence, although small, favored the EE and EC participants. The preschool program had notably large and durable positive effects on participant's academic achievement.

Owing to its long-term effects and demonstrable cost-effectiveness, the Perry Preschool program may be the best known to policy makers (Bryant & Maxwell, 1997). The program, which ran from 1962 thorough 1965, served disadvantaged preschool children whose initial IQs were less than 90. Children were randomly assigned to a preschool that used a specially-designed High/Scope Curriculum or an untreated control group. The High/Scope Curriculum, based on Piaget's constructivist developmental theory, treated participants as active learners and focused on child-initiated learning. Participants planned and carried out their own activities, supervised and encouraged by teachers. Experiences related to broad aspects of development, including initiative, creativity, language, logic and mathematical relations, and social relations. This type of curriculum provided participants with a sense of control, which is especially important for disadvantaged children. Participants attended preschool for 2.5 hours a day, five days a week, for two years before entering school.

Follow-up evaluation indicated that the High/Scope Curriculum was successful on not only academic but also socioemotional levels. During their school years, children who attended the High/Scope preschool spent fewer than half as many years as control children (1.1 vs. 2.8) in special education programs for those with educable mental retardation and scored higher on educational achievement tests on every evaluation. Although by the age of 27, no differences in cognitive scores between the two groups remained, preschool participants had higher rate of completion of grade 12 or more, lower rates of arrest, higher income, higher rate of home ownership, and lower participation in welfare (Schweinhart & Weikart, 1993). These differences are shown in Table 2. Of particular importance are cost-effectiveness analyses that indicate that return on investment for the public was $7.16 for each dollar spent on the program. The program developers (Schweinhart & Weikart, 1993) suggest that the success of the program owes to it having empowered children, parents, and teachers.

PRINCIPLES FOR INTERVENTION PROGRAMS FOR AT-RISK CHILDREN

Based on extensive review of intervention programs for both at-risk children and children with diagnosed disabilities, Ramey and Ramey (1998) developed a set of six general principles that apply to the development, implementation, and effects of intervention programs. The additional seventh is implied by the others, but is of sufficient importance to justify separate status.

1. *Principle of developmental timing.* Generally speaking, the earlier in development intervention begins and the longer it lasts, the more effective it is. In many cases, however, intervention most effectively should begin in early infancy as is the case with premature, low birth weight, or at-risk children.

2. *Principle of program intensity.* Programs increase in effectiveness with increases in number of intervention hours per day and days per week, number of intervention settings, and number of intervention activities.

3. *Principle of direct provision of learning experiences.* Whether conducted in centers or at children's homes, programs whose staff members directly provide learning experiences to participants are more effective than those which train parents to provide the experiences.

4. *Principle of program breadth and flexibility.* As would be expected, programs increase in effectiveness with in-

Table 2 Summary of Results of the Perry Project

Measure	Treatment Condition	
	Preschool	Control
Completed grade 12	71%	54%
Had 5 or more arrests	7%	35%
Earned at least $2,000 month	29%	7%
Owned home	36%	13%
Received welfare as an adult	59%	80%

Note: Data from Schweinhart and Weikart (1993).

creases in the range of services provided and the routes through which intervention is implemented.

5. *Principle of individual differences in program benefits.* Children respond differently to the same programs, related at least in part to their initial degree risk.

6. *Principle of ecological dominion and environmental maintenance of development.* Effects of early intervention will likely decrease or even disappear in the absence of follow-up programming and a supportive environment.

7. *Principle of individuation.* This principle is both so obvious and so considered in programs for handicapped children in general, each of whom after all has an IEP, that it perhaps could go without statement.

SUMMARY AND CONCLUSIONS

Intervention, if early, intense, and of long duration, can benefit at-risk children and thereby society in a number of ways. Several programs have had considerable impact scholastically, improving children's school performance, reducing retention in grade, and reducing referrals for special services or assignment to special education classes. This effect may, although the participants are as yet too young to evaluate, increase their employability and therefore help interrupt the poverty cycle (Birch & Gussow, 1970). Many programs have also significantly reduced conduct and other behavior problems.

As to why the programs haven't had a greater impact on participants' intelligence, some possible answers may be offered: (1) Few of the programs began in infancy, and recent research (e.g., Hart & Risley, 1995) suggests that the first three years of life may be particularly important in children's intellectual development; (2) Relative to the amount of time participant children spend in their home environment, none of the programs has been truly intense or of long duration. Even those programs that run for 40 hours a week for several years cannot compete with the time (128 hours a week) children spend outside of the program subject to deleterious influences of their home and social setting. Given the fact that many of these children come from single-parent homes where the mothers are themselves poorly educated and of limited coping skills, we might be surprised that the programs have effects as extensive as some have.

REFERENCES

Bennett, E.L., Diamond, M.C., Krech, D., & Rosenzweig, M.R. (1964). Chemical and anatomical plasticity of the brain. *Science, 146,* 610–619.

Birch, H.G., & Gussow, J.D. (1970). *Disadvantaged children: Health, nutrition, and school failure.* New York: Gruen & Stratton.

Bryant, D.M., & Maxwell, K. (1997). The effectiveness of early intervention for disadvantaged children. In M.J. Guralnick (Ed.), *The effectiveness of early intervention* (pp. 23–46). Baltimore: Brookes.

Hart, B., & Risley, T.R. (1995). *Meaningful differences in the everyday experience of young American children.* Baltimore: Brookes.

Hebb, D.O. (1949). *Organization of behavior.* New York: Wiley.

Hess, R.D., & Shipman, V.C. (1965). Early experience and the socialization of cognitive modes. *Child Development, 36,* 869–886.

Hunt, J. McV. (1961). *Intelligence and experience.* New York: Ronald.

Schweinhart, L.J., & Weikart, D.P. (1993). Success by empowerment: The High/Scope Perry Preschool study through age 27. *Young Children, 49*(1), 54–58.

INVESTMENT THEORY OF CREATIVITY

Creativity operates just like investment banking, argue Robert J. Sternberg and Todd I. Lubart, with the difference being that the currency of creativity is ideas. A creative person will "buy low" and "sell high," just like a Wall Street trader. The key is knowing when to "invest" in ideas, and when to move on and pursue other projects (Sternberg & Lubart, 1995, 1996). According to the Sternberg-Lubart theory, there are six personal resources that are required for the production of creative work: Intelligence, Knowledge, Thinking Styles, Personality, Motivation, and Environmental Context. Intelligence, Personality, Motivation and Environmental Context are commonly viewed as necessary (but not sufficient) variables in other theories of creativity (e.g., Amabile, 1996; Csikszentmihalyi, 1996; Simonton, 1994). Intelligence, Sternberg and Lubart argue, plays a part in creativity according to the triarchic theory of intelligence (Sternberg, 1984). Synthetic intelligence is involved in casting a problem in a new perspective. Analytical intelligence helps an individual decide which ideas are worth pursuing. Finally, practical intelligence is necessary for conveying an idea to a larger audience. Personality, a commonly studied variable among creative individuals (e.g., Csikszentmihalyi, 1996), is also a factor is the Sternberg-Lubart model. Creative individuals must be risk-taking and persistent, they believe, especially as the most brilliant ideas are also the ones that encounter the most resistance.

One variable that Sternberg and Lubart (1995) discuss is school climate and its relationship to creativity. They report that personal experience has led them to believe that students "often become less able to produce creative work as they progress through school" (p. 267). One reason for this phenomenon may be that teaching usually has an end goal, which is measured through standardized testing. These tests traditionally are more knowledge-based and do not usually give credit for creativity.

REFERENCES

Amabile, T.M. (1996). *Creativity in context.* Boulder, CO: Westview.

Csikszentmihalyi, M. (1996). *Creativity.* New York: HarperCollins.

Simonton, D.K. (1994). *Greatness.* New York: Guilford.

Sternberg, R.J. (1984). Toward a triarchic theory of human intelligence. *Behavioral and Brain Sciences, 7,* 269–287.

Sternberg, R.J., & Lubart, T.I. (1995). *Defying the crowd.* New York: Free Press.

Sternberg, R.J., & Lubart, T.I. (1996). Investing in creativity. *American Psychologist, 51,* 677–688.

IQ

In psychoeducational assessment, a difference exists between an IQ and an intelligence quotient or ratio IQ. Since the ratio IQ or intelligence quotient has decreased in use, the IQ has taken on more of a generic meaning as an index of a test taker's current level of intellectual functioning or general cognitive ability. The IQ has been found useful in understanding and predicting a number of important behaviors such as academic achievement (Sattler, 1982). In addition, diagnoses of a variety of learning disorders such as mental retardation and learning disabilities are dependent in part on determining the IQ of the student.

David Wechsler, author of the Wechsler Intelligence Scales, proposed what he called a deviation IQ. The deviation IQ is a measure that describes how much a test taker's intellectual ability deviates from the average performance of others of the same chronological age within the standardization sample. Initially, developing a test to measure adult intelligence, Wechsler (1939) culled the standardization sample's data and constructed tables so that the person who scored at the average level for his or her age group would receive an IQ of 100. The standard deviation for all age groups was set at 15 by Wechsler. For the Wechsler Intelligence Scale for children, IQs were obtained by comparing a child's performance with the average performance of those in his or her age group. This deviation IQ is a standard score that represents how many standard deviations above or below the average the test taker's intellectual ability falls. To further aid in communicating the meaning of the IQ to nonprofessionals, IQ standard scores are often translated into a descriptive classification such as mentally deficient, a percentile rank, or an age equivalent.

The deviation IQ now represents the most common composite standard score yielded by intelligence tests, including the Wechsler scales and the Stanford-Binet. This popularity can be attributed primarily to the deviation IQ's overcoming many of the criticisms leveled at the ratio intelligence quotient. The means and standard deviations are equal across all age levels for the deviation IQ, allowing comparability for similar IQs across different ages. However, it is important for the test user to remember that deviation IQs yielded by different intelligence tests can only be compared if they have the same or similar standard deviations.

REFERENCES

Sattler, J.M. (1982). *Assessment of children's intelligence and special abilities.* Boston: Allyn & Bacon.

Wechsler, D. (1939). *The measurement of adult intelligence.* Baltimore, MD: Williams & Wilkins.

See also Deviation IQ; Intelligence; Intelligence Testing

IRWIN, ROBERT BENJAMIN (1883–1951)

Robert Benjamin Irwin, blind from the age of five, in 1909 became superintendent of classes for the blind in the Cleveland, Ohio, public schools, one of the first school systems in the United States to educate blind children. He organized braille reading classes and, most significantly, established the first "sight-saving" classes for partially seeing students rather than group them with blind children.

Irwin became director of research and education for the newly formed American Foundation for the Blind in 1923, and served as its executive director from 1929 until his retirement in 1950. He promoted federal legislation relating to the blind, including laws authorizing the Library of Congress to manufacture and distribute "talking books" and books in braille, providing Social Security for the blind, providing income tax exemptions for the blind, and giving priority to the blind in the operation of vending stands in federal buildings. Believing that the blind should not be segregated, he opposed a movement to establish a national college for the blind.

REFERENCES

Allen, A. (1952). Robert B. Irwin–A lifetime of service. *New Outlook for the Blind, 46,* 1–3.

Irwin, R.B. (1955). *As I saw it.* New York: American Foundation for the Blind.

ISRAEL, SPECIAL EDUCATION IN

A key element for understanding the current state of affairs in Israeli special education is the Special Education Law of 1988 (SEL). The SEL was intended to mark a turning point in the provision of special education services to children and adolescents with special needs in Israel. The law was passed with wide multi-party support in 1988 with hopes that it would create procedural certainty and codify guidelines where none had previously existed. The law consists of five subsections: Definitions of Terms, Free Special Education, Diagnosis and Placement, Education in a Special Education Institution, and Miscellaneous. From the law's opening lines which define the scope of the SEL, the discerning reader will notice several problems. The opening section provides operational definitions and begins with the definition of "the handicapped child" and "special education." These two definitions provide an interesting tautology: the "handicapped child" is defined as "A person aged three to twenty-one, whose capacity for adaptive behaviors is limited, due to faulty physical, mental, psychological or behavioral development, and is in need of special education" (Special Education Law of 4358, 1988, p. 2930). On the other hand, "special education" is defined as "methodological teaching, learning and treatment granted by law to the handicapped child . . ." (p. 2930). These circular definitions exemplify the confusion regarding exclusionary versus inclusionary special services: for a child to be defined as "handicapped" he or she must be taught in a "special education" framework, which is subsequently defined as a framework provided only to children with handicaps. It remains unclear whether a child can be described as having special needs if he or she is being educated in regular education classrooms. Moreover, through the examination of Section 3, Chapter B, "The handicapped child is entitled to a free special education in a special education institution in his or her area of residence" (p. 2930), we have further evidence regarding the legislature's opinion regarding exclusive vs. inclusive practices, as the law clearly states that special educational services must be provided in a special education institution. These statements can be contrasted to the legal mandate regarding placement: "On determining the placement of the handicapped child, the placement board will grant priority to his or her placement in an educational institution which is not a special education institution" (p. 2931). These two positions are seemingly at odds with one another: on one hand, the law seems to clearly state that special education services are to be provided only in special education institutions; while on the other hand, the law gives a clear directive for placement in a general education framework. Currently, the Ministry of Education, Culture, and Sport has accepted the more restrictive opinion. What was the actual legislative intent regarding inclusive education? It remains unclear and will be left to the courts to decide.

This issue is further complicated by the strictly categorical nature of Israeli special education. In order to be eligible for services, each child must be classified into one of the 13 special education categories (e.g., "borderline intelligence," "mild mental retardation," "moderate mental retardation," "learning disabilities"). To allow for maximum flexibility, special education services are provided to the child and not the school, and all services are provided according to these categories. Categories entitled to fiscal support specifically for integration are presented in Table 3. As we have seen earlier, this policy is based on category membership and complicates the issue of inclusive education for a wide range of children who may benefit from more mainstreamed settings.

As is common in special education service provision, services are divided between consensual special education groups (e.g., multiple, severe, or sensory handicaps) and

Table 3 Categorical Funding Breakdown by Disability

Type of Disability	Eligible for Integration?
Borderline Intelligence	Yes
Mild Mental Retardation	No
Moderate Mental Retardation	No
Severe & Profound Mental Retardation	No
Emotional/Behavioral Disorders	Yes
Autism/PDD	No
Psychotic/Mentally Ill	No
Learning Disabilities	Yes
Cerebral Palsy	Yes
Deaf & Hard of Hearing	Yes
Blind/Visually Impaired	Yes
Developmental Disabilities	No
Language Disorders	Yes
Chronically Ill	(home bound)

Source: Israeli Special Education Master Plan (Ministry of Education, Culture, and Sport; 1994).

non-consensual special education groups (e.g., learning disabilities, mild mental retardation). The structure of special education placement is changing as the Ministry of Education, Culture, and Sport strives to limit the number of children being placed in segregated settings through two maneuvers: (a) not formally identifying them as children with special needs (and hence not bringing them before the Placement Committee, thereby circumventing the restrictive budgetary aspects of the law), and (b) establishing a series of decentralized resource centers in each community in the country. These Local Support and Resource Centers (LSRC) serve only the non-consensual handicap categories and function in a semi-autonomous manner, and are thus able to allocate resources according to specific local needs. The LSRCs are changing the very nature of service provision in Israel: special education teachers are no longer associated with specific schools, but rather with their LSRC. In this way, teachers and paramedical services are provided from within an itinerant consultative and collaborative framework. Currently, LSRCs are operating in selected communities throughout the country, and expanding rapidly. Little empirically controlled data, however, is being collected regarding the efficacy of the LSRCs.

The LSRC system is designed to primarily benefit children from the non-consensual special education groups. A concurrent improvement in the provision of services to children with consensual disabilities is less noticeable. A firm and clear mandate to strive for each child's education in his or her own least restrictive environment would help to substantially rectify this problem. These children are now almost exclusively educated in segregated special education systems with individual schools having a wide range of autonomy in deciding curricular and transition issues. Legislative intent regarding exclusive versus inclusive education must be clarified and made less categorical.

CONCLUSION

It is an exciting, yet confusing, time to be involved in special education in Israel. Perhaps never before during the last fifty years has the provision of special services to children with handicaps undergone such rapid changes as during the decade since passage of the SEL. Currently, the new national director of the Division of Special Education in the Ministry of Education, Culture, and Sport is dynamically revamping the Ministry's focus and is creating a professionally rich and engaging work atmosphere. Special education in Israel remains highly categorical and segregative, however, and hence has a long way to go.

ITALY, SPECIAL EDUCATION IN

Special education in Italy is an index of political attention to social equity. It concerns every person who evidences handicaps to a complete development of their personality. Special education refers to a science known as the Special Pedagogy. Its historical roots lay part in the general pedagogy (and therefore in philosophy) and part in the medical sciences. The current distinction between disability (physical, sensory, or psychic) and handicap helps to better define the domain of special education.

After World War II, through three decades, special classes and schools arose everywhere in Italy. These served not only the blind and the deaf, but also mentally retarded pupils. Psychiatry and psychology provided the models for special education. In the 60s, after the Unified Junior High School Law (Scuola Media Unica-Law # 1859 of 1962) and other measures concerning special education began, the political and social revolutionary changes of 1968 took place. This led to all special schools gradually closing and disabled pupils being mainstreamed (today only 4% of them attend special schools). The aim was to deinstitutionalize special education by enforcing the right of special needs pupils to attend school with their nondisabled peers. People considered special schools as ghettos where children could not learn because of low social stimulation.

The social attitude gradually changed from a medical model (static and pessimistic) to a more optimistic one. However, the educational system was not well prepared for inclusion. Law # 517 in 1977 stated, on a national basis, what some regions had set up in advance. It gave the constitutional right of being educated without any discrimination to every Italian citizen.

Classes having disabled pupils became smaller (up to 20 individuals). A support teacher to every four disabled pupils joined the regular class teacher, but often this ratio is one to every two or three pupils. As a result, disabled children became more accepted, and a more positive attitude was felt towards them. When teachers learned how to work with the single individual to program school activities and to score the learning rates, pupils had very significant results. However, because most teachers were unprepared for it, success occurred rarely and many disabled pupils spent their time in a resource room with only their support teacher. Special

Table 4 Disabled Individuals at School

School type	No. of Disabled Pupils	%	No. of Support Teachers	Ratio Pupils/ Teachers
Kindergarten (age 3–6)	9,080	1.02	5,498	1.65
Primary School (age 6–11)	48,335	1.86	23,400	2.07
Junior High School (age 11–14)	42,949	2.36	21,665	1.98
Senior High School (age 14–19)	10,300	0.42	5,799	1.78
Totals	110,664		56,353	

Source: Report to Parliament on State of Realization of Law #104, updated 1996.

needs students also experienced a lack of individualized work, few activities for learning skills, an inability to really become integrated in the classroom, and no vocational evaluation.

Today, Italian schools have gone back to selection and competition. Therefore, some people consider inclusion a noble utopia. The last decade, however, found the inclusion policy strengthened by three law acts. In 1987, Law # 215 gave disabled pupils the right to attend senior high schools. Law # 104 (1992) even foresees university access (see Table 4). The 1994 ministry decree, "Atto di indirizzo e di coordinamento," obliges community health units and schools to cooperate. The aim of this decree was the creation of the Functional Diagnosis, the Functional Dynamic Profile, and the Individualized Educational Plan for each disabled pupil.

Drug therapies for cognitive and learning mechanisms, like attention, memory, concentration, and so on, have a pioneering interest. For more than a decade, specific experiences have been documented at AIAS Centre in Castelfranco Veneto, at CIFRRE Centre in Verona, and in the current consultation practice of Cocchi (1990, 1991, 1992, 1993). CIFRRE in Verona uses a multidisciplinary approach involving families in the educational plan. This includes rehabilitative activities, educational activities, medical approaches, and technology-assisted self-care (Crivelli, 1992; Donati, 1992, 1995). Involving the families of disabled children is an important step, leading them to become proponents of the child's life project.

Special education concerns more and more cultural disadvantages (dyslexia, dysgraphia, attention deficit disorders, behavior problems, emotional problems, and so on) even when they have a medical foundation. The challenge of inclusion lies in the innovation of the school system, and, above all, on cultural preparation of teachers and graduates in the science of education.

REFERENCES

Cocchi, R. (1990). The pharmacological approach to treating childhood psychoses: Theoretical basis. *Ital. J. Intellect. Impair.*, 3, 185–193.

Cocchi, R. (1991). Childhood psychoses: Results of drug treatment on school achievement of Down and non-Down subjects. *Ital. J. Intellect. Impair., 4,* 23–30.

Cocchi, R. (1992). School learning in 8 year old Down children treated or not with drugs. *Ital. J. Intellect. Impair., 5,* 143–148.

Cocchi, R. (1993). Drug therapy in Down's syndrome: A theoretical context. *Ital. J. Intellect. Impair., 6,* 143–154.

Crivelli, C. (1992). Obbiettivi di apprendimento per il bambino con grave tetraparesi. In R. Cocchi (Ed.), Il disturbo cognitivo in eta' scolare: Disturbi motori e psicomotori e difficolta' di apprendimento. *Riv. It. Disturbo Intellet., 5,* 85–87.

Donati, A. (1992). L'equilibrio della trasmissione chimica cerebrale e' coinvolto nell'apprendimento: Il Modulatore della Neurotrasmissione come strumento per favorirlo. In R. Cocchi (Ed.), Il disturbo cognitivo in eta' scolare: Disturbi motori e psicomotori e difficolta' di apprendimento. *Riv. It. Disturbo Intellet., 5,* 89–96.

Donati, A. (1995). Il bambino epilettico a scuola: Problemi psicologici e relazionali. In R. Cocchi (Ed.), Il disturbo cognitivo in eta' scolare: Il bambino epilettico a scuola. *Riv. It. Disturbo Intellet., 8,* 65–70.

ITARD, JEAN M.G. (1775–1838)

Jean Itard, a French physician who served on the medical staff of the famous National Institution for Deaf Mutes in Paris, is best known for his work with the wild boy of Aveyron. This child of 11 or 12 was found naked in the woods, where he had been living as a savage. He was brought to Itard for training, and Itard set out to civilize the boy, to teach him to speak and to learn. Five years of work with the boy, whom Itard named Victor, led to the conclusion that his pupil was mentally retarded. Victor learned to read and write many words and could even exchange simple written communications with others, but he never learned to speak. He became socialized to some degree; he could, for example, dine in a restaurant with his tutor. The experiment ended unhappily when, with the onset of puberty, Victor changed from a gentle boy into a rebellious youth. Itard abandoned his work with the boy, and Victor lived in custodial care until his death at the age of about 40.

Itard's work was not in vain, however. He demonstrated that mentally retarded individuals could be trained in both cognitive and social skills, and he provided essential groundwork for the development of the first educational programs for mentally retarded children by Edouard Seguin and others.

REFERENCES

Itard, J.M.G. (1932). *The wild boy of Aveyron.* New York: Appleton-Century-Crofts.

Kanner, L. (1960). Itard, Seguin, Howe—Three pioneers in the education of retarded children. *American Journal of Mental Deficiency, 65,* 2–10.

Lane, H. (1976). *The wild boy of Aveyron.* Cambridge, MA: Harvard Press.

ITINERANT SERVICES

Itinerant services are resource programs on wheels. This program model is most practical in areas that have limited funds for full-time services in each school or that do not have enough eligible children to warrant a full-time teacher. In addition to serving schools, itinerant services can provide instruction in the hospital or home to recuperating and chronically ill children by establishing a curriculum and offering teaching services.

A comparative study, designed by Pepe (1973), concerned the effectiveness of itinerant services and resource room programs serving children with learning disabilities. Each group consisted of 20 students identified as learning disabled, of average ability, and 9 to 12 years of age. There was no significant difference in the treatment effect gains of students, indicating that the itinerant and resource room programs were equally effective in providing services for mildly learning-disabled children. Since there was no significant difference in gains made by students of comparable ability who were afforded less time by the special education teachers, the itinerant programs appeared to be more efficient. Similar results were obtained by Sabatino (1971).

Difficulties in operating itinerant services are described by Wiederholt, Hammill, and Brown (1978). First, teachers must carry their materials from school to school. Second, they frequently must work in the furnace room, in the lunchroom, or in the principal's or counselor's office, and may even share a room with other staff. Third, they are rarely able to provide instruction on a daily basis. Fourth, the fact that they may serve several schools makes it difficult for them to develop social and professional bonds.

An advantage of itinerant services is flexible scheduling, allowing the student's instructional program to be altered to meet changing needs. Because large numbers of young children with developing problems can be accommodated less expensively, later severe disorders may be prevented, making room for the handicapped students for whom self-contained classes were originally developed. Through itinerant services, most students can receive help in their neighborhood schools; thus, the necessity of busing handicapped children is reduced. Finally, in contrast to the self-contained special class program, children start the day in an integrated program with their age mates and become special for specific services. The itinerant service setting helps avoid the stigma of the special class.

REFERENCES

Pepe, H.J. (1973). A comparison of the effectiveness of itinerant and resource room model programs designed to serve children with learning disabilities (Doctoral dissertation, University of Kansas, 1973). *Dissertation Abstracts, 34,* 7612A.

Sabatino, D.A. (1971). An evaluation of resource rooms for children with learning disabilities. *Journal of Learning Disabilities, 4,* 341.

Wiederholt, J.L., Hammill, D.D., & Brown, V. (1978). *The resource teacher.* Boston: Allyn & Bacon.

See also **Homebound Instruction; Itinerant Teacher; Resource Room**

ITINERANT TEACHER

An itinerant teacher has received specialized training in a particular category and provides services to homebound students, or students in hospital programs. The itinerant teacher may also travel between schools within a district, or between districts. The service rendered supplements the instruction provided by the student's classroom teacher. Although teaching is the major responsibility of itinerant teachers, they are involved in related activities such as procuring special materials, conferring with parents, assessing students, or participating in case conferences (Dejnozka & Kapel, 1982). According to Wiederholt, Hammill, and Brown (1978), itinerant teachers must also be able to manage daily details, such as scheduling and grading. In addition, they must possess considerable knowledge of many specific school-related abilities, including reading, spelling, writing, arithmetic, spoken language, and classroom behavior.

The use of itinerant teachers has developed particularly in the field of speech and hearing handicaps, where only small group or individual instruction will work. In the past few years, itinerant teachers have been employed to serve learning-disabled, emotionally disturbed, and gifted students.

REFERENCES

Dejnozka, E.L., & Kapel, D.E. (1982). *American educators' encyclopedia.* Westport, CT: Greenwood.

Wiederholt, J.L., & Hammill, D.D., & Brown, V. (1978). *The resource teacher.* Boston: Allyn & Bacon.

See also **Homebound Instruction; Itinerant Teacher; Resource Room**

J

JACTATIO CAPITIS (JC)

Prior to puberty, it is common for children, especially during the preschool years, to engage in rhythmic body movements and rhythmic vocalizations. Some is inconsequential beyond being annoying to adults (e.g., body rocking or incessant humming). Some will engage in more serious forms of rhythmic behavior that may include head-banging. All of such behaviors are subsumed under the term Jactatio Capitis (JC), with the additional modifier of "nocturna" in those cases where the behavior occurs only at night (Gillberg, 1995).

About 10% of otherwise normal children will display behavior that is consistent with JC; however, a disproportionate percentage of these children go on to develop diagnoses of disorders of attention and motor control (Gillberg, 1995). The male-to-female ratio of JC is estimated to be 3:1. It is suspected to be an inheritable disorder, but its true etiology and pathogenesis are not known. In most cases no intervention beyond reassurance of the parents and the child will be required, as the disorder is most commonly benign. There is no special treatment beyond behavioral interventions when the symptoms may be injurious to the child. Outcome is excellent in those cases that do not progress to motoric and attentional deficiencies, with most cases being entirely asymptomatic by adulthood with no intervention.

REFERENCE

Gillberg, C. (1995). *Clinical child neuropsychiatry.* Cambridge: Cambridge University Press.

JAPAN, SPECIAL EDUCATION IN

SPECIAL EDUCATION WITHIN THE FORMAL EDUCATION SYSTEM

In Japan, the compulsory education system consists of six years of primary school education followed by three years of junior high school education. Children start their compulsory education at the age of 6 and finish it at 15.

School education that is provided for mentally and physically challenged children, in accordance with the type and extent of their disability and their aptitude, is called *tokushu kyoiku,* or special education. This aims to help develop children's potentials and to broaden their abilities.

Unlike the United States and some countries in Europe, Japan does not include vocational training, professional education, or the education of gifted children under the label of special education. Subsequently, in recent years, *tokushu kyoiku* has been more often referred to as *shogaiji kyoiku* or the education of children with physical and/or intellectual disabilities. For the purpose of this paper, the author uses the English term "special education" to describe Japan's formal school education for children with physical and/or intellectual disabilities.

SYSTEM OF SPECIAL EDUCATION

The special education provided for disabled children of school age is given according to the type and extent of their disability. The definition of disability includes visual and hearing impairment, intellectual development disability, physical disability, infirmity/invalidism, and emotional disturbance. Within the school education system, there are special schools, special classes offered by ordinary primary schools and junior high schools, and *tsukyu,* or resource rooms.

The special schools include schools for the visually impaired, schools for the hearing impaired, and schools for mentally and physically disabled children (including children with mental deficiency and children with a weak constitution). These schools cater to relatively seriously disabled children. Some special schools have a kindergarten and a senior high school. For those children who have difficulty commuting to school because of the severity of their impediments, teachers visit the children at their home, hospital or other institution.

The special classes cater to children with relatively mild disabilities. The children are given special education suitable to their individual needs, considering the type and extent of their disability—mental deficiency, physical disability, weak constitution, weak sight, difficulty in hearing, speech impediment, or emotional disturbance. The law provides for ordinary senior high schools to open special classes, but in reality, none offer them.

Tsu-kyu literally means attending class. In the current special education system, it is a form of guidance offered in special classrooms (resource rooms) to school children with weak eyes, difficulty in hearing, a speech impediment or emotional disturbances. These children attend classes in ordinary schools; however, in addition, they may receive a specialist's guidance appropriate to their individual needs.

Incidentally, the use of the Japanese term *seishin hakujaku* (mental deficiency) was banned on April 1, 1999. It is to be replaced by *chiteki shogai* (intellectual disability). Therefore, the school or class for children with mental deficiency will be called the school or class for children with intellectual disability.

HISTORY OF SPECIAL EDUCATION

The first provisions regarding special education were made in 1872, when the modern system of formal education in Japan was inaugurated. In 1878, a school for the visually impaired and the hearing impaired came into being in Kyoto. In 1923, a legal obligation was laid on each prefecture to establish schools for the visually impaired and schools for the hearing impaired.

For children with intellectual developmental disabilities, a private school known as Takinogawa Gakuen was opened in Tokyo in 1891. During the 1920s, special classes for those with intellectual development disabilities were introduced in Tokyo and in many other parts of Japan. Classes for children who stuttered, were weak-sighted, or were hard-of-hearing were also opened one after another. In 1941, immediately before the outbreak of the Pacific War, the National Elementary School decree was instituted. Education for disabled children, in addition to the establishment of schools for the visually impaired and hearing impaired, was incorporated into the nation's school education system. However, because of the war, no progress was made in the area of special education.

AFTER WWII

In the aftermath of World War II, drastic educational reform was introduced. In 1947, the School Education Law was enacted based on the spirit of the new Constitution and the Fundamental Law of Education. Chapter VI, "Special Education" (Articles 77–76), presented the outline of special education. At this time, various forms of education for physically and/or mentally disabled children of school age were put together and termed special education. Thus, special education took its place legally as part of the compulsory education system for the first time in the educational history of Japan.

The law provided for the establishment of special schools which were classified into three divisions—schools for the visually impaired (*mo gakko*), schools for the hearing impaired (*ro gakko*) and schools for physically and/or mentally disabled children (*yogo gakko*). The extent of children's handicaps were also defined by law, providing a standard teachers could use regarding special education.

Compulsory education at schools for the visually impaired and schools for the hearing impaired was introduced in 1948. However, plans for building schools for physically and/or mentally disabled children across the nation made little progress. It was not until 1979 that compulsory education was instituted at these schools. All special schools introduced compulsory education into their syllabus. The home visit system, which had already been put into practice, formally took its place as one method of instruction offered by the schools for physically and/or mentally disabled children.

Children who were expected to attend special classes were divided according to the type of disability—intellectual disability, physical disability, physical weakness, amblyopia (weak sight), impaired hearing, speech impediment, and emotional disturbance. In 1993, the system of *tsu kyu* was inaugurated, under which disabled children enrolled in ordinary schools could receive lessons in special classrooms (resource rooms).

CURRICULUM

The law stipulates that special schools must offer, in principle, the same education as ordinary schools. The objective of each lesson and the curriculum at schools for mentally disabled children are not bound by the government guidelines for teaching. The curriculum can be organized in a flexible manner in accordance with the needs of the children.

The course of study for disabled children who receive lessons in resource rooms under the *tsu-kyu* system includes therapeutic training classes, in addition to ordinary subjects, aimed at encouraging them to improve and to overcome their disabilities. Classes at special schools for disabled children and special classes at ordinary schools are small.

Special school children sometimes have the opportunity to get together with their peers at ordinary primary and junior high schools. Children in special classes also sometimes mix with children in ordinary classes to do schoolwork or engage in other activities together. Disabled children also have opportunities to participate in events organized by neighborhood associations.

These opportunities are helpful not only in enriching the experience and social life of the disabled and building their characters, but also by increasing society's understanding of disabled children as well as special education.

COUNSELING ON EDUCATION AND SCHOOLING

Counseling to parents on education prior to enrollment at school is given by the Board of Education. This counseling before school age is helpful to the parents who have physically and mentally disabled children. Counselors are able to give pertinent advice on the care of disabled children in their infancy, alleviating anxiety experienced by the parents about their children's upbringings, in addition to advice on the right course of education. Whether or not special education should be taken is decided by local Boards of Education, with the parents' opinions always held in high regard.

ADVICE ABOUT WHAT TO DO AFTER GRADUATION

Most of the special school and special class children who completed their compulsory education in March 1996 went on to tertiary education—96.9% of the graduates from the schools for the visually impaired, 98.5% of those from the schools for the hearing impaired, 84.9% of those for mentally and physically handicapped and 73.8% of those at special classes in junior high schools. Although recently the number of graduates from special schools for the intellectually disabled has been decreasing, the percentage of those who go on to the next stage of education has been increasing. The ratio was 56% in 1984, and it rose to 83% in 1996. After graduation from special schools, 43.7% of graduates from the schools for the visually impaired and 43.4% of those from the schools for the hearing impaired went on to special training courses attached to the school or university. Meanwhile, the rate of employment was 21.9% for graduates from the schools for the visually impaired and 35.9% for those from the schools for the hearing impaired.

Most graduates from the senior classes of special schools for the physically and mentally disabled entered social welfare facilities: 63% for the schools for the intellectually disabled, 78.9% for the schools for the physically disabled, and 55.5% for the schools for the physically weak children. The employment rates were 34.4%, 12.1%, and 16.8%, respectively. It has become increasingly difficult for the intellectually disabled to find employment since 1990 because of the long-term business depression in Japan.

See also China, Special Education in

JARGONAPHASIA

Jargonaphasia refers to an expressive language deficit in which a dysphasic individual produces a profusion of unintelligible utterances. Language structure may be retained, but meaning is unclear. Intonation, rhythm, and stress patterns are normal. Speech is fluent with few if any of the hesitations or pauses characteristic of some other dysphasic speech patterns. Bizarre responses, often consisting of clichés, stock phrases, neologisms, and unusual word combination patterns are produced. Speakers seem unaware that their utterances are not meaningful, and receptive language is impaired. Although meaningless to the listener, Eisenson (1973) feels that jargon may not be so to the speaker. Eisenson considers jargonaphasia to be a transitory condition rather than a true aphasic condition.

REFERENCE

Eisenson, J. (1973). *Adult aphasia: Assessment and treatment.* New York: Appleton-Century-Crofts.

See also Aphasia; Communication Disorders; Developmental Aphasia; Dysphasia; Expressive Dysphasia

J.E.V.S.

The J.E.V.S. evaluation was developed by the Jewish Employment Vocational Service in Philadelphia, Pennsylvania, during the 1960s. It takes approximately 2 weeks to evaluate the capabilities of a client in a wide range of employment skills. The initial stages of the procedures are with simple work samples that are gradually advanced to more complex skills.

The J.E.V.S. programs measure many employment variables, including information concerning a person's vocational potential. The work samples provided enable an evaluator to assess the client's potential for competitive employment and to assess functional abilities in spatial and perceptual skills and manual dexterity. The objective areas of the J.E.V.S. program provide information concerning the client's interests, behaviors, and aptitudes in work-related situations. The program is divided into two major review areas: VIEWS (Vocational Information and Evaluation Work Samples) and VITAS (Vocational Interests, Temperaments and Aptitude Systems).

The J.E.V.S. programs evaluate two factors that are inherent in work-related situations: the specific and the global. Specific factors include discrimination skills, counting ability, eye-hand-foot coordination, finger dexterity, following diagrammatic instructions, following a model, motor coordination, manual dexterity, measuring ability, numerical ability, forms perception, clerical perception, spatial discrimination, size discrimination, and the use of hand tools. The four global factors are accuracy, following oral instructions, neatness, and organizational ability.

REFERENCE
Vocational Research Institute. (1973). *Work sample evaluator's handbook*. Philadelphia: Jewish Employment and Vocational Services.

See also **Vocational Evaluation**

JOHNSTON INFORMAL READING INVENTORY

The Johnston Informal Reading Inventory (JIRI; Johnston, 1982) is an informal reading scale that assesses understanding of antonyms and synonyms, and silent reading comprehension skills. The test is designed for use for students in the seventh grade through adulthood. The test can be group-administered or individually administered. Results of the JIRI may be used for diagnostic as well as placement purposes, according to the author.

Three types of tasks are used in the JIRI: word opposites, word synonyms, and graded narrative passages. The Word Opposites test results determine the level of the passages at which the examinee is to begin. The passages contain nine levels that progress from simple stories to more complex narratives. The examinees are asked a series of short-answer questions about the passages that require written responses, assessing the main idea, detail, vocabulary, cause-effect, and inference. The role of the third test, Word Synonyms, is not clearly articulated by the author (Rogers, 1995).

REFERENCES
Johnston, M.C. (1982). *Johnston Informal Reading Inventory.* Tucson, AZ: Educational Publications.

Rogers, M.R. (1995). Review of the Johnston Informal Reading Inventory. In J.C. Conoley & J.C. Impara (Eds.), *The twelfth mental measurements yearbook* (pp. 523–524). Lincoln, NE: Buros Institute of Mental Measurements.

JOHNSTONE, EDWARD RANSOM (1870–1946)

Edward Ransom Johnstone began his career as a teacher and principal in the public schools of Cincinnati. He then served as a teacher in the Indiana School for Feeble Minded Youth, subsequently becoming principal there. In 1898 he moved to the Training School at Vineland, New Jersey, where he was employed as vice principal under the Reverend Stephen Olin Garrison, who had founded the school 10 years before. After Garrison's death in 1900, Johnstone was made superintendent. He became executive director in 1922, and director emeritus in 1944.

During Johnstone's years there, the Training School exerted tremendous influence on the education and training of mentally retarded children and adults, on the preparation of teachers of handicapped children, and on educational testing. Johnstone founded a research laboratory with Henry H. Goddard as director. There numerous studies were conducted using data from the school's mentally retarded population. A summer school was conducted for teachers.

Johnstone inaugurated *The Training School Bulletin,* an influential journal in special education from its inception in 1904. Johnstone served on numerous boards and commissions and was elected to two terms as president of the American Association on Mental Deficiency.

REFERENCES
McCaffrey, K.R. (1965). *Founders of the Training School at Vineland, New Jersey: S. Olin Garrison, Alexander Johnson, Edward R. Johnstone.* Unpublished doctoral dissertation. Teachers College, Columbia University, New York.

The Training School Bulletin. (1947, May). *44.*

JOINT TECHNICAL STANDARDS FOR EDUCATIONAL AND PSYCHOLOGICAL TESTS

See STANDARDS FOR EDUCATIONAL AND PSYCHOLOGICAL TESTING.

JORDAN LEFT-RIGHT REVERSAL TEST

The Jordan Left-Right Reversal Test (the Jordan) is a norm-referenced measure of visual reversal of letters, numbers, and words intended for use with individuals from age 5 years through adulthood. The current version, the second revision, was published by Academic Therapy Publications in 1980. The first edition was published in 1974 (Jordan, 1980). The test is untimed but typically requires about 20 minutes for administration and scoring. Two levels or forms are available, the first for ages 5 to 8 years and the second for ages 9 years and up.

The Jordan was standardized on children ages 5 through 12 years only; it should not be used outside this age range despite the author's claim for utility through adulthood. Very little data are given on the sample, far too little to allow for an adequate appraisal of its quality and representativeness, though the sample was large. Only test-retest reliability data are reported, but even this was miscalculated. Internal consistency evidence, as required by the Standards for Educational and Psychological Testing (Committee to Revise the Standards, 1984), is not reported, although ample data for such calculations were available to the author. Validity evidence is limited and the scaling of the norms is cumbersome. The Jordan is an interesting and innovative test that could have filled a gap in the assessment of children with a variety of learning disabilities. However, the psychometric ineptness apparent in the development, standardization, and investigation of the scale's validity and reliability render it useful only for an informal appraisal.

REFERENCES
Committee to Revise the Standards. (1984). *Standards for educational and psychological testing.* Washington, DC: American Psychological Association.

Jordan, B.T. (1980). *Jordan left-right reversal test.* Novato, CA: Academic Therapy.

JOUBERT SYNDROME (JS)

Joubert Syndrome (JS) is a rare genetic disorder that is autosomal recessive, characterized by partial or complete agenesis of the cerebellar vermis (Gillberg, 1995), but without the formation of cysts and hydrocephalus common in Dandy-Walker Syndrome (Greenspan, 1998). JS results in mental retardation that is typically severe or profound coupled with pronounced autistic-like behaviors, ataxia, hypotonia, tongue protrusion, and abnormal patterns of eye movements. Exceptional cases exist with IQs reported as high as 85, but diagnoses of autism are common in the higher IQ JS patient. Diagnosis may occur prenatally via ultrasound in some cases, but traditionally the diagnosis has been made on the basis of the clinical exam and MRI findings. Academic and psychosocial outcomes are typically quite limited due to the level of retardation and the social deficits noted. Special education services and continuous psychoeducational work-ups are required in all cases.

REFERENCES

Gillberg, C. (1995). *Clinical child neuropsychiatry.* Cambridge: Cambridge University Press.

Greenspan, S. (1998). Dandy-Walker syndrome. In L. Phelps (Ed.), *Health-related disorders of children and adolescents* (pp. 219–223). Washington, DC: American Psychological Association.

JOURNAL FOR EDUCATION OF THE GIFTED (JEG)

The *Journal for Education of the Gifted* (*JEG*) is the official journal of the Association for the Gifted (TAG), a division of the Council for Exceptional Children. Members of TAG receive *JEG* as a benefit of membership. First published in 1978, the journal currently issues quarterly publications.

JEG provides a forum for the analysis and communication of knowledge about the gifted and talented, as well as the exchange of ideas and diverse points of view regarding this special population. Theoretical and position papers, descriptive research, evaluation, and experimental research exemplify the types of writings published in the journal. *JEG* specifically solicits (1) original research relevant to the education of the gifted and talented; (2) theoretical and position papers; (3) descriptions of innovative programming and instructional practices based on existing or novel models of gifted education; (4) reviews of literature related to gifted education; (5) historical reviews; and (6) action research. Submitted writings are refereed following a blind reviewing process, and manuscript preparation follows the American Psychological Association's style manual. Laurence J. Coleman of the University of Tennessee at Knoxville is the current editor.

JOURNAL OF ABNORMAL CHILD PSYCHOLOGY

The *Journal of Abnormal Child Psychology* was established in 1973 by Herbert Quay, PhD. In 1995 the *Journal* became the official publication of the International Society for Research in Child and Adolescent Psychopathology. The *Journal* focuses on child and adolescent psychopathology with an emphasis on empirical studies of the major childhood disorders (the disruptive behavior disorders, depression, anxiety, and pervasive developmental disorders). Research addresses the epidemiology, assessment, diagnosis, etiology, developmental course and outcome, and treatment of childhood disorders. Studies on risk and protective factors, and on the correlates of children's psychiatric disturbances, especially family and peer processes, are of interest. Treatment outcome research is also published, with an emphasis on studies that include randomized clinical trials with appropriate controls. Occasional special issues highlight a particular topic of importance in the field and conceptual articles are included from time to time. The journal is published bimonthly by Plenum Press.

JOURNAL OF APPLIED BEHAVIOR ANALYSIS (JABA)

Founded in 1968, the *Journal of Applied Behavior Analysis* (*JABA*) was established to publish "reports of experimental research involving applications of the experimental analysis of behavior to problems of social importance" (*JABA,* 1998). The journal is published quarterly by the Society for the Experimental Analysis of Behavior (SEAB).

JABA's first issue was published in 1968 with Montrose M. Wolf of the University of Kansas as its first editor. The journal primarily seeks to publish empirical research articles relevant to applied behavior analysis, including behavior therapy and behavior control. Innovative pilot research, replications, controlled case studies, and analogue studies are also accepted as research articles. Other categories of articles accepted for publication include technical articles contributing primarily to research methodology, data analysis, or instrumentation; discussion and review articles; book reviews; and comments from readers (*JABA,* 1998). The current editor is David P. Wacker of the University of Iowa.

REFERENCE

Journal of Applied Behavior Analysis. (1998, July 10). *A bit of history: Who published JEAB and JABA?* http://envmed. rochester.edu/wwwvgl/seab/history/circulation.htm.

JOURNAL OF AUTISM AND DEVELOPMENTAL DISORDERS

The *Journal of Autism and Developmental Disorders* was first published under the title of the *Journal of Autism and Childhood Schizophrenia.* It was born from the collaboration of

Leo Kanner, regarded as the founding father of child psychiatry in the English-speaking world, and publisher V. H. Winston, the father of an autistic child. The journal was dedicated to stimulating and disseminating from diverse sources "ways to understand and alleviate the miseries of sick children." As founding editor and the discoverer of autism, Kanner convened a task force of outstanding researchers and clinicians to contribute from multidisciplinary sources. Fields such as ethology, genetics, psychotherapy, chemotherapy, behavior modification, special education, speech pathology, and neurobiology contributed. Research was conducted by investigators from the professions of medicine, psychology, neuroscience, biochemistry, physiology, and education. The unifying basis for the publication of such diverse material was the direct relevance to the understanding and remediation of autism, childhood psychoses, and related developmental disorders.

In 1974 Eric Schopler took over as editor of the journal, with Michael Rutter collaborating as European editor. Editorial policies remained the same, but there was increasing emphasis on studies demonstrating the connection between basic research and clinical application. Toward that end a "Parents Speak" column was added. It was intended to raise issues of practical concern not always accessible to current research methodologies and research issues not always clear as to their practical implications. The purpose of the column was to provide a forum for parents and researchers. Eric Schopler remains the editor as of 1999.

By 1979 the title of the journal was changed from the *Journal of Autism and Childhood Schizophrenia* to its current title. This change reflected primarily the growth of empirical knowledge. Initially, autism was regarded as the earliest form of childhood schizophrenia. However, increasing data suggested that autism and childhood schizophrenia were different both in onset and symptoms. Autism was usually related to early onset, before age 3, while childhood schizophrenia came with later onset and somewhat different symptoms. Moreover, the effects of development were recognized for a wide range of disorders, as was the coexistence of autism with other developmental disorders such as mental retardation. An unusual convergence of scientific knowledge and political action occurred when autism was included in the Developmental Disabilities Act of 1975. The journal's change of title and scope was intended to proclaim this infrequent marriage of science and policy.

JOURNAL OF CLINICAL CHILD PSYCHOLOGY

The Journal of Clinical Child Psychology (*JCCP*) is the official journal of the Section on Clinical Child Psychology (Section 1), Division of Clinical Psychology (Division 12) of the American Psychological Association. It publishes original research, reviews, and articles on child advocacy and training and professional practice in clinical child psychology. Authors need not be members of the Section. Colleagues in other disciplines, students, and consumers are also encouraged to contribute. *JCCP* is published quarterly in one volume by Lawrence Erlbaum Associates, Inc., 10 Industrial Avenue, Mahwah, NJ 07430-2262. It is edited by Thomas H. Ollendick, Child Study Center, Virginia Polytechnic Institute and State University, 3110 Prices Fork Road, Blacksburg, VA 24061-0355.

JOURNAL OF COMMUNICATION DISORDERS

The *Journal of Communication Disorders,* first published in 1968, serves a readership of health care professionals interested in the prevention and treatment of human communication disorders. The journal contains original articles related to speech, language, and hearing disorders, and special topics issues, entitled *Clinics in Communications Disorders,* provide information pertaining to the assessment, diagnosis, and treatment of these disorders to speech-language pathologists, audiologists, psychotherapists, otolaryngologists, and other professionals in the field. Published bimonthly, the journal is interested in publishing reports of experimental or descriptive investigations, theoretical or tutorial papers, case reports, and letters to the editor.

Originally founded by its first editor, R. W. Riever of John Jay College and Columbia University, the aim of the journal has remained the same since its inception: to publish articles on "problems related to the various disorders of communication, broadly defined." Its interests include the biological foundations of communications as well as psychopathological, psychodynamic, diagnostic, and therapeutic aspects of communication disorders.

The current editor is Theodore J. Glattke of the University of Arizona-Tucson, and the journal is now published by Elsevier Science, Inc. (*Journal of Communication Disorders,* 1998).

REFERENCE
Journal of Communication Disorders. (1998, December 20). *Aims and scope.* http://elsevier.co.jp/.

JOURNAL OF CONSULTING AND CLINICAL PSYCHOLOGY

The *Journal of Consulting and Clinical Psychology* was first published in 1937 by the American Psychological Association (APA) under the name *Journal of Consulting Psychology.* Its original managing editor was J.P. Symonds. The total circulation in 1998 was over 7,000.

The journal publishes original contributions on such topics as the development and use of diagnostic techniques in the treatment of disordered behaviors; studies of populations of clinical interest; studies of personality and of its assessment and development related to consulting and clinical psychology; and cross-cultural and demographic studies of interest for behavioral disorders.

The journal considers manuscripts dealing with diagnosis or treatment of abnormal behavior. Manuscripts are submitted and blind-reviewed by a board of consulting editors. The journal receives approximately 400 manuscripts a year; about 25% of these are published.

JOURNAL OF EMOTIONAL AND BEHAVIORAL DISORDERS

The *Journal of Emotional and Behavioral Disorders (JEBD)* is a refereed, quarterly journal publishing articles on research, practice, and commentary related to children and adolescents with emotional and behavioral disorders. Established in 1993 by Pro-Ed, the journal contains articles with implications for a range of disciplines, including counseling, education, early childhood care, juvenile corrections, mental health, psychiatry, psychology, public health, rehabilitation, social work, and special education. *JEBD* provides an impartial forum and draws on a wide variety of fields to further services for youngsters with emotional and behavioral problems.

JOURNAL OF FLUENCY DISORDERS

The *Journal of Fluency Disorders* was begun in 1974, and is the official journal of the International Fluency Association. The journal is recognized as the leading publication devoted specifically to fluency issues. It provides comprehensive coverage of clinical, experimental, and theoretical aspects of stuttering, including the latest remediation techniques. The journal also features full-length research and clinical reports; methodological, theoretical, and philosophical articles; reviews; sort communications; and more (Journal of Fluency Disorders, 1999). The target audience includes clinicians and researchers working in universities, hospitals, and community clinics.

REFERENCE

Journal of Fluency Disorders. (1999). *Aims and Scope.* Elsevier Science. http://www.elsevier.nl/inca/public/s/store/5/0/7/7/1/505771.pub.htt

JOURNAL OF FORENSIC NEUROPSYCHOLOGY (JFN)

The *Journal of Forensic Neuropsychology* (*JFN*) was founded in 1998 by Jim Hom of the Neuropsychology Center of Dallas. Hom continues as its editor. The journal publishes articles involving legal aspects of the practice of clinical neuropsychology. It is published quarterly by the Haworth Press.

Its interest to special educators lies in its focus on head injury and litigation of head injury cases, many of which involve children and the schooling and education of brain-injured children. The journal includes original research, reviews of research, opinions, and topical presentations on matters of timely interest.

JOURNAL OF INTELLECTUAL DISABILITY RESEARCH

The *Journal of Intellectual Disability Research* is the official journal of the International Association for the Scientific Study of Intellectual Disability and the European Association for Mental Health and Mental Retardation. It began publication as the *Journal of Mental Deficiency Research* in 1956 and was renamed in 1992. This international journal is devoted exclusively to the scientific study of intellectual disability. The journal publishes papers reporting original observations, including clinical case reports; pathological reports; biochemical investigations; genetics; and psychological, educational, and sociological studies. The results of animal experiments or studies in any discipline that may increase knowledge of the causes, prevention, or treatment of intellectual disability are also discussed. Reviews are submitted from experts from time to time on themes in which recent research has produced notable advances. All papers are reviewed by expert referees. The journal also reports the activities of special interest groups and the meetings and conferences of the International Association for the Scientific Study of Intellectual Disability.

The journal is published six times per year. The current editor-in-chief is W. I. Fraser, University of Wales College of Medicine (United Kingdom), and the North American Corresponding Editor is S. Landesman Ramey of the University of Alabama at Birmingham.

JOURNAL OF LEARNING DISABILITIES

The *Journal of Learning Disabilities* (*JLD*), the oldest and most prestigious journal in the area of learning disabilities, contains reports of empirical research, opinion papers, and discussions of issues that are of concern to all disciplines in the field. The journal has been published consecutively since 1968. In 1986, Pro-Ed purchased *JLD* from The Professional Press, a subsidiary of Capital Cities Media, Inc. *JLD* is published six times a year. All published articles are peer reviewed; consulting editors are from North America, Europe, Asia, Africa, and Australia.

JOURNAL OF MENTAL DEFICIENCY RESEARCH

See JOURNAL OF INTELLECTUAL DISABILITY RESEARCH.

JOURNAL OF POSITIVE BEHAVIOR INTERVENTIONS

A new journal published by Pro-Ed, the *Journal of Positive Behavior Interventions (JPBI)* deals exclusively with principles of positive behavioral support in school, home, and community settings for people with challenges in behavioral adaptation. Established in 1999, *JPBI* publishes empirical research reports, commentaries, program descriptions, discussion of family supports, and coverage of timely issues. Contributors and editorial board members are leading authorities representing different disciplines involved with intervention for individuals with challenging behaviors. The journal is published quarterly.

JOURNAL OF PSYCHOEDUCATIONAL ASSESSMENT (JPA)

The *Journal of Psychoeducational Assessment (JPA)* was founded in 1983, and for the past 13 years has continuously published quarterly issues as well as special topic monographs on topics of interest to all assessment specialists, including psychologists, educational diagnosticians, special educators, and academic trainers. The internationally-known journal originated as an outlet for the publication of research on assessment practices and procedures common to the fields of psychology and education. It provides school psychologists with current information regarding psychological and educational assessment practices, legal mandates, and instrumentation; and includes topics such as cross-cultural assessment practices, differential diagnoses, and dynamic assessment neuropsychology.

JPA publishes brief reports, position papers, and book and test reviews routinely addressing issues related to achievement, adaptive behavior, classroom behaviors, creativity, motor skills, intelligence, language skills, memory, and other constructs. An editorial board of some 50 members representing a wide range of expertise in assessment-related issue employs a double-blind peer review process for manuscripts submitted for publication. *JPA* is published by The Psychoeducational Corporation, and Dr. Bruce A. Bracken of the University of Memphis is the current editor (*JPA*, 1998).

REFERENCE

Journal of Psychological Assessment. (1998, June 9). *History and mission.* http://www.psychoeducational.com/Default.htm.

JOURNAL OF SCHOOL PSYCHOLOGY (JSP)

The *Journal of School Psychology* (JSP) is school psychology's oldest and most prestigious journal; it first appeared in 1963. Its 58 original founders and shareholders provided the capital necessary to launch *JSP*. In its first editorial, Smith (1963) states:

The main purpose of the *Journal of School Psychology* is to provide an outlet for research studies and articles in professional school psychology. It is a scientifically oriented journal devoted to the publication of original research reports, reviews, and articles, with the aim of fostering the expansion of school psychology as an applied science. (p. 2)

This statement of purpose has remained largely unchanged during the last 20 years, with *JSP*'s primary goal being the

publication of "original articles on research and practice related to the development of school psychology as both a scientific and an applied specialty" (*JSP*, 1998). *JSP* also reviews tests and books, publishes brief reports and commentaries, and occasionally invites writers to submit manuscripts on timely topics of interest. Particular attention is given to assisting school psychologists who have not published on a regular basis. *JSP* is now published by Elsevier Science on behalf of the Society for the Scientific Study of School Psychology.

REFERENCES

Journal of School Psychology. (1998, December 22). *Aims and scope.* http://elsevier.nl/inca/publications/store/6/9/9/699.pub.htt.

Smith, D. (1963). Editor's comments: Genesis of a new *Journal of School Psychology. Journal of School Psychology, 1,* 1–4.

See also School Psychology

JOURNAL OF SPECIAL EDUCATION

First published in 1966, *The Journal of Special Education* (*JSE*), is internationally known as the prime research journal in the field. In 1987, Pro-Ed, Inc. purchased *JSE* from Buttonwood Farms, Inc. This quarterly, multidisciplinary publication presents primary research and scholarly reviews by experts in all subspecialties of special education for individuals with disabilities ranging from mild to severe. *JSE* includes critical commentaries; intervention studies; integrative reviews of timely problems; traditional, ethnographic, and single-subject research; and articles on families, transition, technology, general/special education interface, and legislation and litigation. All published articles have undergone a rigorous peer review process.

JOURNAL OF SPEECH AND HEARING DISORDERS

The *Journal of Speech and Hearing Disorders* was discontinued in 1990, but was incorporated into the *Journal of Speech, Language, and Hearing Research* in 1991. It is now published by the American Speech, Language and Hearing Association.

Each issue is divided into three major categories: "Language," "Speech," and "Hearing." Articles pertain to studies of the processes and disorders of speech, language, and hearing, and to the diagnosis and treatment of such disorders. Included are reports of original research; theoretical, tutorial, or review articles; research notes; and letters to the editor. Topics covered are screening, assessment, treatment techniques, prevention, professional issues, supervision, and administration. This journal will primarily interest researchers and professional educators.

The current editor is Richard G. Schwartz. The journal is a refereed journal with a circulation of 73,000.

JOURNAL OF THE AMERICAN ASSOCIATION FOR THE SEVERELY HANDICAPPED

See TASH.

JOURNAL OF VISUAL IMPAIRMENT AND BLINDNESS (JVIB)

The *Journal of Visual Impairment and Blindness* (*JVIB*) is a monthly publication of research articles and discussion articles on topics of interest related to the field of visual impairment. *JVIB* provides its interdisciplinary, international subscribers with a forum for the exchange of ideas and information as well as a means of discussing controversies and issues relevant to practitioners and researchers concerned with visually impaired and blind individuals (*JVIB*, 1998).

A publication of the American Foundation for the Blind, *JVIB* contains features pertinent to all ages which cover various aspects of visual impairment, including international news, short reports, research, innovative practice techniques, worldwide events, employment updates, and evaluation of new products and publications. A sampling of past articles finds that topics include parental concerns and involvement, educational issues of the visually impaired and blind, assessment, language development, residential schools, rehabilitation, employment, orientation, mobility, and physical fitness.

Information pertaining to the impact of technology on individuals with visual impairment is continually updated in the segment "Random Access." Another feature, entitled "Research Note," contains brief reports on cutting-edge research and relevant work from other fields. Additionally, *JVIB* presents important statistical information about blindness, and reviews fiction and nonfiction books as well as videos related to blindness (*JVIB*, 1998).

REFERENCE

Journal of Visual Impairment and Blindness (1998, January 17). *About the Journal of Visual Impairment and Blindness.* www.afb.org./a_jbiv.html.

JOURNALS IN EDUCATION OF INDIVIDUALS WITH DISABILITIES AND SPECIAL EDUCATION

See SPECIFIC JOURNAL.

JUKES AND THE KALLIKAKS

In the late nineteenth and early twentieth centuries, Americans became increasingly concerned with overpopulation and unrestricted immigration. It was believed that the high birth rate of the mentally defective would have an adverse impact on the economy and social order. The eugenics movement promoted compulsory sterilization of people with undesirable traits as well as restricted immigration of unwanted races (Bajema, 1976). Research on human pedi-

grees provided scientific support for these efforts by showing that mental retardation and other undesirable traits tend to run in families over a number of generations. Many studies of family degeneracy were published, but the two most influential were based on the pedigrees of the Juke and the Kallikak families.

One of the most influential studies of family degeneration, *The Jukes,* written by Richard L. Dugdale as a report for the Prison Association of New York (Dugdale, 1895), was the first comprehensive study of the history of an entire family over a number of generations. By examining prison records, Dugdale discovered a family with a long history of arrest and dependence on charity. Dugdale traced 709 members of the Juke family, spanning seven generations, who were related by blood, marriage, and cohabitation.

Dugdale found that the Juke family had a high incidence of feeblemindedness, pauperism, prostitution, illegitimacy, and crime among its members. The family tended to marry its own members and produce large numbers of offspring. Dugdale calculated the cost of the Juke family in confinement and charity to be over $1 million (over $12 million in 1985).

The study concluded that crime and poverty are mainly the result of heredity, but that the environment does have some influence. Dugdale argued that crime and poverty are avoidable if the proper environmental conditions are met. He advocated a program of industrial education and personal hygiene, with imprisonment only as a last resort for the habitual criminal. Heredity was viewed as an innate force that impinged on individuals throughout their lives. In spite of Dugdale's emphasis on environmental interventions, his report of the Juke family was widely used in support of the argument that only heredity determines human behavior and consequently poverty and crime.

Although Dugdale claimed that his data-gathering methods were sound, the study has been severely criticized on methodological grounds (Gould, 1981). One problem is that feebleminded individuals were identified mainly on the basis of hearsay, rather than by testing or other standardized methods. In addition, it has been charged that the self-fulfilling prophecy may have biased the results, in that the researcher's strong expectations may have influenced his judgment of the cases.

A follow-up of the Juke family (Estrabrook, 1915) reported that the incidence of feeblemindedness, prostitution, pauperism, illegitimacy, and crime had continued at about the same rate as reported by Dugdale. This report argued against imprisoning people with criminally weak intellects, proposing instead that they receive permanent custodial care and sterilization. Sterilization was particularly advocated because the mentally impaired produced large numbers of offspring and put high demands on charity. It was claimed that the Juke family history demonstrated that criminal fathers would produce criminal offspring, making sterilization the only remedy.

The second most influential study of family degeneracy was Henry Goddard's 1912 book *The Kallikak Family:*

A Study of the Heredity of Feeble-Mindedness (Goddard, 1912). Goddard's work was based on the family background of a young girl with the pseudonym of Deborah Kallikak; she was a resident at the Vineland Training School for Feeble-Minded Girls and Boys in New Jersey. Deborah's family was traced back through six generations to Martin Kallikak. Martin first married a woman of good repute and founded a line of offspring that were upstanding citizens of normal intelligence. Martin Kallikak also had an illegitimate child with a barmaid, and this branch of the family produced large numbers of criminals, feebleminded, and charity cases. Goddard summarized the findings as follows:

The Kallikak family presents a natural experiment in heredity. A young man of good family becomes through two different women the ancestor of two lines of descendants,—the one characterized by thoroughly good, respectable, normal citizenship, with almost no exceptions; the other being equally characterized by mental defect in every generation. . . . In later generations, more defect was brought in from other families through marriage. . . .

We find on the good side of the family prominent people in all walks of life and nearly all of the 496 descendants owners of land or proprietors. On the bad side we find paupers, criminals, prostitutes, drunkards, and examples of all forms of social pest with which modern society is burdened. (Goddard, 1912, p. 116)

It is interesting to note that Goddard interpreted the striking difference between the two lines of the Kallikak family as evidence for the strong influence of heredity, an interpretation uncritically accepted at the time. Later writers have pointed out, however, that this difference is actually stronger evidence for the importance of the environment, since the two lines of the family have a common ancestor, yet differed greatly in social standing (Smith, 1985).

Goddard's methodology has been subject to the same criticism as was Dugdale's study of the Jukes. He relied on untrained field workers to make diagnostic decisions about the mental abilities and personalities of family members, both living and dead. For example, the following report of a home visit was submitted by a research associate.

The girl of twelve should have been at school, according to the law, but when one saw her face, one realized it made no difference. She was pretty, with olive complexion and dark languid eyes, but there was no mind there. . . . Benumbed by this display of human degeneracy, the field worker went out into the icy street. (Goddard, 1912, p. 73)

There is also uncertainty over whether Goddard's original diagnosis of Deborah's feeblemindedness was correct (Smith, 1985). Smith reviewed Goddard's diagnostic evidence and concluded that using modern standards, Deborah would not be classified as mentally retarded.

Although the studies of the Jukes and the Kallikaks are seriously flawed by present-day standards, they provided all the evidence that was needed to convince the eugenicists of the time that something must be done to stem the prolifera-

tion of mental defects. Armed with these inflammatory studies, they successfully lobbied for compulsory sterilization laws in 30 states, and helped pass the Immigration Restriction Act of 1924.

REFERENCES

Bajema, C.J. (1976). *Eugenics then and now.* Stroudsburg, PA: Hutchinson & Ross.

Dugdale, R.L. (1895). *The Jukes: A study in crime, pauperism, disease, and heredity.* (5th ed.). New York: AMS.

Estrabrook, A.H. (1915). *The Jukes in 1915.* New York: Macmillan.

Goddard, H.H. (1912). *The Kallikak family: A study in the heredity of feeble-mindedness.* New York: Macmillan.

Gould, S.J. (1981). *The mismeasure of man.* New York: Norton.

Smith, J.D. (1985). *Minds made feeble: The myth and legacy of the Kallikaks.* Rockville, MD: Aspen.

See also **Eugenics; Heredity; Socioeconomic Status**

JUVENILE ARTHRITIS

See ARTHRITIS, JUVENILE.

JUVENILE CEREBROMACULAR DEGENERATION

Juvenile cerebromacular degeneration (also known as juvenile neuronal ceroid lipofuscinosis) is a progressive disorder transmitted on an autosomal recessive basis. If the onset occurs between the ages of 1 and 3 years, it may be known as infantile cerebromacular degeneration or Bielschowsky syndrome. The juvenile variety occurs at 5 to 7 years of age and may also be known as Spielmeyer-Vogt disease. Both types involve a degenerative process of the gray matter of the brain and are generally classified with the lipid storage diseases, the most common of which is Tay-Sachs or amaurotic familial idiocy (Behrman & Vaughan, 1983). Onset usually begins with visual disturbances (eventually leading to blindness; Gillberg, 1995) because of degenerative changes in the retina. The visual disturbances are followed by a progressive degeneration of cortical gray matter. The child may develop seizures, become hyperactive, and show a severe pattern of cognitive and motor degeneration. Speech is lost as are most other motor functions. The later the onset of the disease, the slower it progresses. Some have survived into adolescence but there remains no cure for the disorder. Treatment consists only of symptom alleviation and supportive care.

REFERENCES

Behrman, R., & Vaughan, V. (1983). *Nelson textbook of pediatrics* (12th ed.). Philadelphia: Saunders.

Gillberg, C. (1995). *Clinical child neuropsychiatry.* Cambridge: Cambridge University Press.

See also **Tay-Sachs Syndrome**

JUVENILE DELINQUENCY

Prior to the enactment of the federal Juvenile Delinquency Act in 1938, juvenile offenders violating the laws of the United States were subject to prosecution in the same manner as adults. Since the act, juvenile delinquents have been treated procedurally as juveniles even though juvenile delinquency is defined as the violation of the law of the United States committed by a person prior to his eighteenth birthday that would have been a crime if committed by an adult (Karcz, 1984). Official delinquency refers to those encounters with the law where the juvenile custody (called an arrest for adults) is entered into the recordbooks. Any act that could place the juvenile who committed it in jeopardy of adjudication if it were to be detected is delinquent behavior (Hopkins, 1983).

Broadly speaking, there are two categories of youngsters committing a delinquent offense: status offenders and juvenile offenders. Status offenses are those subject to legal action only if committed by a juvenile. Examples of status offenses are truancy, incorrigibility, smoking, drinking, and being beyond the control of the parent or guardian (Hopkins, 1983). An adult committing the same offense would not be charged with violation of the law. The category status offender includes the following: minors in need of supervision (MINS), dependent minors, and neglected and abused minors. The Juvenile Justice and Delinquency Act of 1974 requires that status offenders be removed from juvenile detention experiences and from correctional institutions.

A major difference between juvenile offenders and adult offenders is the importance that the juvenile places on gang membership and the tendency of the juvenile to engage in group criminal activity. Violent juvenile offenders, however, have similar characteristics to those of adult felons. Juvenile offenders and adult felons are predominately male, disproportionately black and Hispanic as compared with their proportion in the population, typically disadvantaged, likely to exhibit interpersonal difficulties and behavioral problems both in school and on the job, and likely to come from one-parent families with a high degree of conflict, instability, and inadequate supervision (U.S. Department of Justice, 1983).

In 1981 juveniles under 18 years of age committed 18.5% (or 73,506) of all the violent offenses committed in the United States. Violent offenses include murder, negligent manslaughter, forcible rape, robbery, and aggravated assault. Juveniles under 18 committed 37% (or 567,923) of all property crimes. Property crimes include burglary, larceny-theft, motor vehicle theft, and arson (U.S. Department of Justice, 1983).

The U.S. Juvenile Justice and Delinquency Prevention Office (1977) found that juvenile delinquents are typically males who limited or lowered their educational goals to high school—or whose mothers did—and who showed much higher delinquency rates than those whose aspirations/expectations were college oriented; or blacks from a large family with poor father-son interaction and from a low-quality neighborhood. Ng (1980) supports the position that poor family relationships, undesirable peer associations, poor choice of free time activities, and inadequate moral development are the preconditions of juvenile delinquency. Undesirable peer associations are also an immediate factor contributing to juvenile delinquency. Glueck and Glueck (1968) found that juvenile delinquents come from families characterized by greater family disorganization, greater alcoholism, more criminality, more separations, more divorces, less supervision of children, and fewer home rules such as those relating to meals and bedtime. The Gluecks also found that more delinquents are struck down by motor vehicles than nondelinquents, 14% compared with 5%. Perhaps most strikingly, however, they found that 98% of the juvenile delinquents reported having friends who are delinquents compared with only 7% of the nondelinquents.

REFERENCES

Glueck, S., & Glueck, E. (1968). *Delinquents and nondelinquents in perspective.* Cambridge, MA: Harvard University Press.

Hopkins, J.R. (1983). *Adolescence: The transitional years* (pp. 327, 329, 339). NY: Academic.

Karcz, S.A. (1984, August). *The impact of a special education related service on selected behaviors of detained handicapped youth* (pp. 31, 32). Unpublished doctoral dissertation, University of Syracuse, New York.

Ng, A.M. (1980). *Family relationships and delinquent behavior.* Unpublished doctoral dissertation, Columbia University, New York.

U.S. Department of Justice. (1983, October). *Report to the nation on crime and justice: The data* (p. 33). National Criminal Justice Reference Service, Box 6000, Rockville, MD 20850.

U.S. Juvenile Justice and Delinquency Prevention Office. (1977). *City life and delinquency: Victimization, fear of crime and gang membership* (p. 61). Washington, DC: U.S. Government Printing Office.

See also **Conduct Disorder; Disadvantaged Child; Discipline**

K

KAISER-PERMANENTE DIET

The Kaiser-Permanente (K-P) diet, frequently referred to as the Feingold diet, was proposed by Feingold (1975) for the management of learning and behavioral disorders in children. Feingold's diet essentially eliminates the chemical additives that are frequently added to foods to enhance their longevity. Rooted in the basic premise of the Kaiser-Permanente diet is the assumption that children with hyperactivity, or other learning and behavioral disorders, have a natural toxic reaction to these artificial additives. Specifically, the diet forbids artificial colors and flavorings and foods containing natural salicylates, including a number of nutritious fruits and vegetables.

Despite the vogue of the K-P diet in many households across the country, Feingold's (1976) claim that the diet would ameliorate behavioral and learning disturbances has received scant support in the research literature (Kavale & Forness, 1983). Although Conners (1980) has indicated that a small percentage of hyperactive children do respond to some type of dietary intervention, it still remains unclear whether the improvement is actually a function of the diet itself or the regimen associated with the diet. Nonetheless, despite the dubious validity of Feingold's (1975, 1976) claims, many parents are loyal followers of Feingold's diet and have formed a national association to laud its efficacy and warn the public about the harmful effects of food additives for children. Recent reviews (e.g., Kavale & Forness, 1999) continue to fail to find support for the K-P diet as an effective intervention.

REFERENCES

Conners, C.K. (1980). *Food additives and hyperactive children.* New York: Plenum.

Feingold, B.F. (1975). *Why your child is hyperactive.* New York: Random House.

Feingold, B.F. (1976). Hyperkinesis and learning disabilities linked to the ingestion of artificial food colors and flavors. *Journal of Learning Disabilities, 9*(9), 551–559.

Kavale, K.A., & Forness, S.R. (1983). Hyperactivity and diet treatment: A meta-analysis of the Feingold hypothesis. *Journal of Learning Disabilities, 16*(6), 324–330.

Kavale, K., & Forness, S. (1999). Effectiveness of special education. In C.R. Reynolds & T.B. Gutkin (Eds.), *The handbook of school psychology* (3rd ed.) (pp. 984–1024). New York: Wiley.

See also Additive-Free Diets; Feingold Diet; Hyperactivity; Impulse Control

KANNER, LEO (1894–1981)

Leo Kanner, "the father of child psychiatry," was the founder of the Johns Hopkins Children's Psychiatric Clinic and the author of the widely used textbook *Child Psychiatry.* Born in Austria, he came to the United States in 1924 and was naturalized in 1930.

Associated with Johns Hopkins University from 1928 until his death, Kanner was the first to describe infantile autism, which he characterized as the innate inability of certain children to relate to other people. A prolific author who once hoped to be a poet, Kanner published more than 250 articles and books on psychiatry, psychology, pediatrics, and the history of medicine.

REFERENCES

Kanner, L. (1964). *A history of the care and study of the mentally retarded.* Springfield, IL: Thomas.

Kanner, L. (1979). *Child psychiatry* (4th ed.). Springfield, IL: Thomas.

KARYOTYPE

Karyotype is the chromosome set or constitution of an individual. Each species has a characteristic karyotype, not only with respect to chromosome number and morphology, but also with respect to the genes on each chromosome. Chromosomes are typically visualized in peripheral lymphocytes that have been placed in tissue culture, stimulated to divide, arrested in metaphase, and osmotically swelled. When prepared for analysis, the chromosomes of a human metaphase cell appear under the microscope as a chromosome spread. To analyze such a spread, the chromosomes are cut out from a photomicrograph and arranged in pairs in a standard classification. This process is called karyotyping.

See also Chromosomal Abnormalities; Down's Syndrome; Genetic Counseling

KASPER HAUSER CHILDREN

Children raised under highly deprived conditions are sometimes described, particularly in older literature, as Kasper Hauser children. In 1828, when he was about 17 years of age, Kasper Hauser appeared in rags in Nuremberg. He could write his name primitively, but was poorly coordinated and appeared retarded. Under the care of a local teacher, he learned some speech and social graces. He was able to recall that he lived alone for years in a dark room and was cared for by someone who never spoke or was seen. His story, originally written by Anselm von Feuerbach, is summarized by Shattuck (1980).

Unfortunately, as with most such cases, interpretation of Kasper Hauser's progress is difficult because of lack of knowledge about his early environment, how he had lived prior to isolation, and whether, for example, he had previously acquired language.

REFERENCE

Shattuck, R. (1980). *The forbidden experiment: The story of the Wild Boy of Aveyron*. New York: Farrar Straus Giroux.

See also **Deprivation; Feral Children; Genie; Post-Institutionalized Children**

KAUFMAN ADOLESCENT AND ADULT INTELLIGENCE SCALE

The Kaufman Adolescent and Adult Intelligence Test (KAIT; Kaufman & Kaufman, 1993) is an individually administered test of intelligence for individuals ages 11 to 85 years and older. The KAIT measures general intelligence, crystallized intelligence, and fluid intelligence. Crystallized intelligence is intended to measure those abilities that are dependent on schooling and acculturation for success, whereas fluid intelligence is believed to be those abilities needed to solve new and novel problems.

The KAIT includes a six-subtest core battery that takes about sixty minutes to administer. A ten-subtest expanded battery is also available for the KAIT and takes an additional thirty minutes to administer. The KAIT yields standard IQs (mean = 100; SD = 15) for the Crystallized, Fluid, and Composite scales, which are derived from the six core subtests. The IQs are derived from age-based norms, so that individuals' scores are compared to those from their own age group. Each of the subtests produce standard scores (scaled scores) with a mean of 10 and a standard deviation of 3. In addition to the subtests in the core and expanded batteries, the KAIT provides a supplementary standardized Mental Status test that is intended to produce descriptive categories for examinees who are too low-functioning to be assessed with the full KAIT.

The KAIT was standardized between 1988 and 1991 on a sample of 2,000 adults and adolescents. The standardization sample was stratified by gender, geographic region, socioeconomic status, and race or ethnic group, according to 1988 U.S. Census data. The KAIT manual provides extensive information on the validity and reliability of the test.

Overall, the KAIT is a well-standardized test that provides interesting tasks to keep the attention of adolescents and adults during the process of administration. It is based upon a theoretical groundwork which is helpful in conceptualizing and interpreting the KAIT profile. Keith (1995) comments that although extensive validity information is provided, further information on the validity of the KAIT is needed to fully evaluate its effectiveness in measuring Horn and Cattell's fluid and crystallized constructs. Some of the KAIT's subtests are timed, which may interject components of speed (Gs), rather than being "pure" measures of fluid and crystallized ability. The KAIT provides a suitable alternative and/or supplement to the WAIS-III and the WISC-III, as well as other measures of adolescent and adult intelligence.

REFERENCES

Kaufman, A.S., & Kaufman, N.L. (1993). *Kaufman Adolescent and Adult Intelligence Test*. Circle Pines, MN: American Guidance Service.

Keith, T.Z. (1995). Review of the Kaufman Adolescent and Adult Intelligence Test. In J.C. Conoley & J.C. Impara (Eds.), *The twelfth mental measurements yearbook*. Lincoln, NE: Buros Institute of Mental Measurements.

KAUFMAN ASSESSMENT BATTERY FOR CHILDREN

The Kaufman Assessment Battery for Children (K-ABC; Kaufman & Kaufman, 1983) is a measure of intelligence and achievement for children ages 21/2 to 121/2. The K-ABC was built from psychological theory, which sets it apart from many traditional IQ tests. It was designed to measure ability (intelligence) on the basis of the processing style required to solve tasks.

The theories underlying the K-ABC hold the assumption that intelligence is composed of two types of processes: 1) sequential, analytic, and temporal and 2) simultaneous, holistic, gestalt, and spatial. Hence, the cognitive portion of the K-ABC is divided into two scales: Sequential Processing and Simultaneous Processing. These modes of processing have been identified by Luria and his followers, and also by cognitive psychologists such as Neisser.

The Sequential Processing Scale of the K-ABC is comprised of tasks with problems that must be solved by arranging the input in sequential or serial order, and in which each idea is linearly or temporally related to the preceding one. The unifying process in this scale is the sequential handling of the stimuli, regardless of content.

The Simultaneous Processing Scale includes problems that are spatial, analogic, and organizational in nature, and that require the input to be integrated and synthesized simultaneously to produce the appropriate solution. This scale is illustrated by the Face Recognition subtest which involves selecting from a group photograph the one or two faces that were shown briefly on the preceding page. Another Simultaneous subtest, Gestalt Closure, requires the child to name an object or scene pictured in a partially complete inkblot drawing (Kaufman & Kaufman, 1983). A composite score is formed from the combination of the two processing scales.

A measure of acquired facts and school-related knowledge is provided on a separate K-ABC scale: the Achievement Scale. This scale includes tasks similar to many conventional IQ tests (tests of vocabulary, language concepts), traditional achievement tasks (reading), or both (general information, arithmetic). For example, the Faces and Places subtest involves naming the well-known person, fictional character, or place pictured in a photograph or drawing. The Riddles subtest requires the child to infer the name of a concrete or abstract concept when given a list of its characteristics (Kaufman & Kaufman, 1983).

The K-ABC was standardized on a sample of 2,000 children, stratified according to 1980 U.S. Census data. Reliability and validity data provide considerable support for the psychometric properties of the K-ABC. Split-half reliability coefficients of the K-ABC global scales range from 0.86 to 0.93 (mean = 0.90) for preschool children and from 0.89 to 0.97 (mean = 0.93) for children ages 5 to 121/2. Test-retest reliability of the test is also strong. Considerable research into the validity of the K-ABC has been conducted that shows clear empirical support of two factors at each age level that correspond the Sequential and Simultaneous scales (Kaufman, Lichtenberger, & Naglieri, 1999).

The K-ABC has been shown to be an instrument that is sensitive to minority groups (Kaufman & Lichtenberger, 1998). Data have shown that the large group differences between Caucasians and African Americans on other intelligence tests are not present on the K-ABC and group means of Hispanics on the K-ABC are also quite similar to the total standardization sample, providing evidence that the test is not biased against these ethnic groups (Kaufman & Lichtenberger, 1998). Sternberg (1984, p. 271) stated that in comparison to other existing instruments, the "K-ABC comes closer than most, if not all, existing instruments" to being culture-fair or representative of all groups in its norms. A revision of the K-ABC was begun early in 2001 but a firm publication date for the revised scale was not available when the present work went to press.

REFERENCES

Kaufman, A.S., & Kaufman, N.L. (1983). *Kaufman Assessment Battery for Children*. Circle Pines, MN: American Guidance Service.

Kaufman, A.S., & Lichtenberger, E.O. (1998). Kaufman Assessment Battery for Children (K-ABC): Recent research. In R.J. Samuda (Ed.), *Advances in cross-cultural assessment* (pp. 56–99). Thousand Oaks, CA: Sage.

Kaufman, A.S., Lichtenberger, E.O., & Naglieri, J.A. (1999). Intelligence testing in the schools. In C.R. Reynolds & T.B. Gutkin (Eds.), *The handbook of school psychology* (pp. 307–349). New York: Wiley.

Sternberg, R.J. (1984). The Kaufman Assessment Battery for Children: An information-processing analysis and critique. *The Journal of Special Education, 18,* 269–279.

See also Assessment; Intelligence; Intelligence Quotient; Intelligence Testing; Measurement

KAUFMAN BRIEF INTELLIGENCE (K-BIT)

The Kaufman Brief Intelligence Test (K-BIT, Kaufman & Kaufman, 1990) is a brief, individually-administered test of cognitive ability. The test is designed to be administered to persons ages 4 through 90.

The K-BIT takes approximately 15 to 30 minutes to administer, with older examinees requiring more time. There are no time limits. The K-BIT consists of 2 subtests, Vo-

cabulary and Matrices. Vocabulary, which is composed of two parts, requires examinees to provide the name of a pictured object (Expressive Vocabulary) and to provide the word that best fits two written clues (Definitions). Matrices is a nonverbal measure consisting of items that involve visual stimuli and requires examinees to point to the correct picture (or say its letter). The K-BIT has predetermined starting items according to the examinee's age. In addition, a discontinue rule is used for all K-BIT tasks such that if the examinee fails every item in one unit (consisting of about 4 or 5 items), the task is discontinued. The test yields raw scores which are converted to standard scores (M = 100, SD = 15) and percentile ranks for Vocabulary, Matrices, and an IQ Composite.

The K-BIT was standardized on a sample of 2,022 subjects ages 4 to 90 years and was codeveloped and conormed with the Kaufman Adolescent and Adult Intelligence Test (KAIT). The sample used approximates the 1985 U.S. Census data and 1990 estimates when they were available. Numerous studies have been conducted demonstrating that the reliability and validity of the K-BIT are good.

REFERENCE

Kaufman, A.S., & Kaufman, N.L. (1990). *Kaufman Brief Intelligence Test*. Circle Pines, MN: American Guidance Service.

KAUFMAN FUNCTIONAL ACADEMIC SKILLS TEST (K-FAST)

The Kaufman Functional Academic Skills Test (K-FAST, Kaufman & Kaufman, 1994) is a brief, individually-administered test of functional reading and math abilities of individuals ages 15 to over 85 years. More specifically, it assesses one's acquired knowledge of basic reading and math skills and the ability to apply those skills to everyday problems.

The K-FAST takes approximately 15 to 25 minutes to administer. It is composed of two subtests, Arithmetic and Reading. The Arithmetic subtest measures numerical reasoning, computation skills, and mathematical concepts using pictorial stimuli to lessen the influence of reading ability. The Reading subtest assesses the examinee's ability to recognize and understand certain rebuses, abbreviations, and phrases. The development of both subtests includes many items that reflect social-adaptive behaviors that are assessed on adaptive behavior scales. All examinees begin with item 1 and the subtests are discontinued after 4 consecutive failures. The K-FAST yields raw scores which are converted to standard scores (M = 100, SD = 15) and percentile ranks for Arithmetic, Reading and a Functional Academic Skills Composite.

The K-FAST was standardized on a sample of 1,424 subjects ages 15 to over 85 years, which was stratified within each age group by gender, geographic region, socioeconomic status, and race or ethnic group. The sample closely approximates the 1988 U.S. Census data. The K-FAST has good reliability and validity.

REFERENCE

Kaufman, A.S., & Kaufman, N.L. (1994). *Kaufman Functional Academic Skills Test.* Circle Pines, MN: American Guidance Service.

KAUFMAN SURVEY OF EARLY ACADEMIC AND LANGUAGE SKILLS (K-SEALS)

The Kaufman Survey of Early Academic and Language Skills (K-SEALS, Kaufman & Kaufman, 1993) is a brief, individually-administered test which assesses young children's language, pre-academic, and articulation skills. The test was developed from and is considered an expanded form of the Cognitive/Language Profile of the Early Screening Profiles (ESP, Kaufman & Kaufman, 1990). The K-SEALS was designed for children aged 3 years 0 months to 6 years 11 months.

The K-SEALS takes about 15 to 25 minutes to administer. It consists of three subtests. The Vocabulary subtest assesses the child's receptive and expressive vocabulary. The child points to or names pictures of objects or actions and names objects from verbal descriptions of their characteristics. The Numbers, Letters, & Words subtest assesses the child's knowledge of numbers and number concepts, letters, and words. It requires the child to point to or name numbers, solve number problems, and count. The Articulation Survey subtest assesses the child's ability to clearly articulate words by pronouncing common words. The K-SEALS yields raw scores which are converted to standard scores (M = 100, SD = 15), percentile ranks, age equivalents, and descriptive categories. Interpretive scales include Language Scales (Expressive Skills Scale and Receptive Skills Scale), Early Academic Scales (Number Skills Scale and Letter & Words Skills Scale, for use with children age 5–0 to 6–11 only), and the Early Academic & Language Skills Composite.

Standardization of the K-SEALS was conducted as part of the AGS Early Screening Profiles, resulting in a K-SEALS sample of 1,000 children ages 3–0 to 6–11. The sample was selected to match variables such as age, gender, geographic region, socioeconomic level, and race or ethnic group. Data for the sample was compared to U.S. Census data from 1990; the sample was shown to closely approximate this census data. The K-SEALS has excellent reliability and validity, and, in fact, has been commended for being "remarkably reliable and valid" (Ackerman, 1995).

REFERENCES

Ackerman, P.L. (1995). In J.C. Conoley & J.C. Impara (Eds.), *The twelfth mental measurements yearbook.* Lincoln, NE: Buros Institute of Mental Measurements.

Kaufman, A.S., & Kaufman, N.L. (1990). *Cognitive/Language Profile in the AGS Early Screening Profiles.* Circle Pines, MN: American Guidance Service.

Kaufman, A.S., & Kaufman, N.L. (1993). *Kaufman Survey of Early Academic and Language Skills.* Circle Pines, MN: American Guidance Service.

KAUFMAN SHORT NEUROPSYCHOLOGICAL ASSESSMENT PROCEDURE (K-SNAP)

The Kaufman Short Neuropsychological Assessment Procedure (K-SNAP, Kaufman & Kaufman, 1994) is a brief, individually-administered test designed to assess mental functioning of individuals ages 11 to over 85 years. It assesses functioning at 3 differing levels of cognitive complexity.

The K-SNAP takes approximately 20 to 30 minutes to administer. The test is composed of four subtests, organized by level of complexity. The Mental Status subtest (low complexity) assesses attention and orientation; the Number Recall and Gestalt Closure subtests (medium complexity) measure simple memory and perception skills, respectively; and Four-Letter Words (high complexity) assesses reasoning and planning ability. The K-SNAP yields raw scores which are converted to standard scores (M = 100, SD = 15) for the K-SNAP Composite and to scaled scores (M = 10, SD = 3) for the individual subtests. In addition, percentile ranks and descriptive categories are also available. An Impairment Index can also be calculated with the intent of providing a more objective method to determine a level of cognitive impairment and whether more comprehensive assessment is needed.

Standardization of the K-SNAP included a sample of 2,000 subjects ages 11 to 94 years, which was stratified within each age group by gender, geographic region, socioeconomic status, and race or ethnic group. U.S. Census data from 1988 was used and the sample closely approximated this data. The K-SNAP was conormed and codeveloped along with the KAIT, K-BIT, and K-FAST. It has been demonstrated that the K-SNAP has good reliability and validity.

REFERENCES

Kaufman, A.S., & Kaufman, N.L. (1994). *Kaufman Short Neuropsychological Assessment Procedure.* Circle Pines, MN: American Guidance Service.

Kaufman, A.S., & Kaufman, N.L. (1994). *Manual for the Kaufman Short Neuropsychological Assessment Procedure.* Circle Pines, MN: American Guidance Service.

KAUFMAN TEST OF EDUCATIONAL ACHIEVEMENT/NORMATIVE UPDATE (K-TEA/NU)

The Kaufman Test of Educational Achievement is an individually-administered measure of achievement that is available in two separate and non-overlapping versions; a Brief Form that delivers global scores for Reading, Spelling, and Mathematics; and a Comprehensive Form that provides scores in the more specific domains of Reading Decoding, Reading Comprehension, Mathematics Applications, Mathematics Computation, and Spelling (Kaufman & Kaufman, 1985; 1997). Testing time for the Brief Form is approximately 30 minutes, whereas the Comprehensive

Form takes over an hour for older children, and about 30 minutes for younger children.

The K-TEA offers both age-based norms (6 years 0 months to 18 years 11 months) as well as grade-based norms. Standard scores, with a mean of 100 and a standard deviation of 15, are obtained for each subtest and for the Composite Score. Age-equivalent and grade-equivalent scores are also provided for each raw score.

Separate spring and fall national standardization programs were conducted for the Comprehensive Form of the K-TEA/NU. The spring standardization program included more than 1,400 students at 25 test sites in 15 states. The fall standardization program included more than 1,000 students at 27 sites in 16 states. The national testing program for the Brief Form equating sample consisted of the administration of the three Brief Form subtests to more than 580 students at 27 test sites in 16 states. Kaufman and Kaufman (1997) note that the Brief Form testing was part of the larger Comprehensive Form fall standardization program, and the sample was selected to match the demographic characteristics of the nationally representative Comprehensive Form norm group. Both the Brief and Comprehensive Forms were stratified by grade level, sex, geographic region, socioeconomic status, and race or ethnic group to match 1994 U.S. Census data.

REFERENCES

Kaufman, A.S., & Kaufman, N.L. (1985). *Kaufman Test of Educational Achievement.* Circle Pines, MN: American Guidance Service.

Kaufman, A.S., & Kaufman, N.L. (1997). *Kaufman Test of Educational Achievement/NU.* Circle Pines, MN: American Guidance Service.

KAYSER-FLEISCHER RING

This phenomenon is a visible symptom of Wilson's disease that is present in most cases (and typically in all cases) of Wilson's Disease that have behavioral or psychiatric conditions. It should prompt a referral to an opthalmologist when seen. It is due to a defect in liver cells that causes a disruption in the metabolism and elimination of copper from the body.

See also **Wilson's Disease**

KEARNS SAYRE SYNDROME

Kearns Sayre Syndrome is a relentlessly progressive multi-system disorder with childhood onset. The cardinal features are paralysis of eye muscles, pigmentary degeneration of the retina, and heart block. Other features include ataxia, hearing loss, short stature, endocrine abnormalities, and progressive decline in intellectual function. Annual reassessments of these students are needed because of their changing needs.

Deletions of sizable portions of mitochondrial DNA affect the structure and function of mitochondria, the intracellular energy factories. The cells requiring the most energy, like the brain, heart, and muscle, are most vulnerable. Collections of abnormal mitochondria are seen as ragged red fibers in muscle biopsies. Even at rest, persistent lactic acidosis is present. There is no cure for this life-limiting disorder, but cardiac pacemakers are usually indicated, and some patients have benefited from dietary supplements of coenzyme Q and carnitine.

Nearly all cases occur sporadically and it is important to recognize that there is a great deal of variability in expression in mitochondrial diseases. An apparently identical mitochondrial DNA deletion is seen in progressive external ophthalmoplegia, an adult-onset, very slowly progressive weakness of eye and limb muscles.

Kearns Sayre syndrome is a rare disease, but it has been estimated that up to 1 in 4,000 people are affected by various mitochondrial disorders. *Exceptional Parent* magazine ran a three-part series on these diseases and their management in their June, July, and August 1997 issues which was comprehensive but readable. Their address is P.O. Box 2078, Marion, Ohio, 43306–2178. Extensive information for families and professionals about these disorders is available from The United Mitochondrial Disease Foundation, P.O. Box 1151, Monroeville, Pennsylvania, 15146–1151, and at their website: http://www.biochemgen. ucsd.edu/umdf/.

KELLER, HELEN A. (1880–1957)

Helen Adams Keller, blind, deaf, and mute from the age of 18 months, became one of the world's best known examples of victory over a severe handicap. Under the direction of a dedicated and talented teacher and companion, Anne Sullivan Macy, Keller was not only educated; she also became a successful writer, lecturer, and advocate for the handicapped. She graduated cum laude from Radcliffe College in 1904 and began a long career on behalf of the handicapped. She wrote, lectured on the Chatauqua circuit and in vaudeville, served on Massachusetts' State Commission for the Blind, and worked tirelessly for the American Foundation for the Blind from the time it was formed in 1923. Her lobbying for federal legislation for the blind was instrumental in the creation of federal reading services, including talking-book recordings, and the inclusion of federal grant assistance for the blind in the Social Security Act. She involved herself in numerous social causes, including women's suffrage, pacifist movements prior to both world wars, and the antinuclear movement after World War II. Most important, Keller made herself a living symbol of triumph over handicap, and an inspiration to handicapped people everywhere.

REFERENCES

Brooks, V.W. (1956). *Helen Keller: Sketch for a portrait.* New York: Dutton.

Keller, H. (1904). *The story of my life.* New York: Doubleday.

Lash, J. (1980). *Helen and teacher: The story of Helen Keller and Anne Sullivan Macy.* New York: American Foundation for the Blind.

Sister Elizabeth Kenny

KENNY, SISTER ELIZABETH (1886–1952)

Sister Elizabeth Kenny revolutionized the treatment of poliomyelitis and became an international heroine during the polio epidemics of the 1940s. She began working with polio patients as a nurse in her native Australia—hence the title of "Sister," which is given to nurses in British Commonwealth countries. She developed a method of treatment that, in contrast to the prevailing procedure of immobilizing the muscles with braces or casts, involved stimulating affected muscles to enable them to regain their function. Her success attracted worldwide attention and in 1939 she was invited to the United States by a group of physicians. Her demonstration of her treatment methods to physicians in Minneapolis-St. Paul resulted in a hospital ward dedicated to the Kenny treatment. From this beginning, the world-renowned Kenny Institute was formed, and Sister Kenny's approach became the accepted method of treatment for polio.

REFERENCE

Kenny, E. (1943). *And they shall walk: The life story of Sister Elizabeth Kenny.* New York: Dodd, Mead.

KEPHART, NEWELL C. (1911–1973)

Newell C. Kephart received his PhD from the University of Iowa in 1936. He worked as a mental hygienist at the Wayne County (Michigan) Training School and as a research analyst for the U.S. Employment Service prior to naval service in World War II. In 1946 he joined the faculty of Purdue University, where he served as professor of psychology and education and conducted the Achievement Center for Children, a research and treatment center for handicapped children.

Kephart, who excelled in presenting classroom procedures in a manner readily understood and accepted by teachers, was a leading contributor to the perceptual-motor training movement of the 1960s. Following retirement from Purdue University in 1968, Kephart served until his death as director of the Glen Haven Achievement Center in Fort Collins, Colorado, a school devoted to the education of handicapped children and their parents.

REFERENCES

A special tribute. (1973). *Academic Therapy, 8,* 373–374.

Ball, T.S. (1971). *Itard, Seguin, and Kephart: Sensory education—A learning interpretation.* Columbus, OH. Merrill.

Kephart, N.C. (1971). *The slow learner in the classroom* (2nd ed.). Columbus, OH: Merrill.

KERLIN, ISAAC NEWTON (1834–1893)

Isaac Newton Kerlin, a physician, served as superintendent of the Pennsylvania Training School for Feeble-Minded Children (now Elwyn Institute) from 1863 until his death in 1893. An excellent administrator, Kerlin made Elwyn a model that influenced the planning of institutions for the mentally retarded throughout the country. Through his efforts the Association of Medical Officers of American Institutions for Idiotic and Feeble-Minded Persons (now the American Association on Mental Deficiency) was formed at Elwyn in 1876. Kerlin, as secretary of the young organization, was responsible for the extension of the membership until it included almost all American physicians interested in mental deficiency.

REFERENCES

Historical notes on institutions for the mentally defective: Elwyn Training School. (1941). *American Journal of Mental Deficiency, 45,* 341–342.

Scheerenberger, R.D. (1983). *A history of mental retardation.* Baltimore, MD: Brookes.

KERNICTERUS

Kernicterus is a form of neonatal brain damage that results from destruction of fetal red blood cells in utero and deposits of bilirubin in the basal ganglia (Medway & Thomas, 1998). Excess bilirubin in the blood penetrates the meningeal barrier (blood-brain barrier) and cerebral damage results. This syndrome is usually secondary to RH incompatibility and may be a result of brain lesions. However, it may also occur as a result of drugs, enzyme abnormalities of red blood cells, or liver or other blood infections (Zimmerman & Yannet, 1935). Kernicterus may also manifest athetoid and spastic paralysis in children. It is rarely seen now because it is almost always preventable (Medway & Thomas, 1998).

A broad range of mental retardation can occur, but in many instances it is not seen. Early feeding seems to reduce the depth of jaundice and lower complications (Illingworth, 1983). Several blood problems may occur. However, many of these children possess normal intelligence. A multidisciplinary team of evaluators is necessary to accurately assess the child.

Seizures, hearing impairment, visual, and communication problems will require related services, as will motor impairments. Support services may be required to locomote and feed the child. Program placement will necessitate a cohesive effort from a variety of professionals. Settings will vary based on the degree of impairment.

REFERENCES

Illingworth, R. (1983). *Development of the infant and young child: Abnormal and normal* (7th ed.). New York: Churchill, Livingstone.

Medway, F., & Thomas, S. (1998). Jaundice (neonatal). In L. Phelps (Ed.), *Health-related disorders of children and adolescents.* Washington, DC: American Psychological Association.

Zimmerman, H., & Yannet, H. (1935). Cerebral sequelae ofícterus gravis neonatorum and their relation to kernikterus. *American Journal of Diseases in Children, 49,* 418–423.

See also **Birth Injuries; Neonatal Behavioral Assessment Scales**

KEYMATH-REVISED: A DIAGNOSTIC INVENTORY OF ESSENTIAL MATHEMATICS

The KeyMath-Revised (Connolly, 1988) is an untimed, individually-administered diagnostic test that measures mathematical functioning. The KeyMath consists of 13 subtests examining areas such as knowledge of numbers and fractions, ability to perform operations such as addition and subtraction, and "real life" skills involving money and time. The subtests are classified into three major divisions: content, operations, and applications. The content area focuses on knowledge of basic mathematical concepts that are necessary to perform mathematical operations, such as numeration, rational numbers, and geometry. The mathematical operations area involves the computational processes of addition, subtraction, multiplication, and division, as well as mental computation. The applications area contains problems involving the use of mathematical processes in everyday life, such as estimation, measurement, data interpretation, time, and money.

The KeyMath-Revised is intended for students in grades K–9, and takes approximately 30 to 50 minutes to administer, depending upon the age of the child. There are two versions of this test available, forms A and B, each containing 258 items. Interpretations can be made on four diagnostic levels, which the examiner can use to identify strengths and weaknesses. These four levels include Total Test, Area, Subtest, and Domain. The information generated by the interpretations can be used for assessment for general instruction or as part of a more global assessment, pre- and post-testing, curriculum assessment, or assessment for remedial instruction.

There are two supplementary components to the KeyMath-Revised. One is a Report to Parents for the examiner to communicate the child's results to the parents. The other supplement is the KeyMath-Revised-Assist (automated system for scoring and interpreting standardized tests), which provides automatic conversion, profiling, and record management.

The KeyMath was standardized in fall 1985 and spring 1986. The fall sample included 873 students in grades K–8, and the spring sample involved 925 students in grades K–9. In 1997, new norms were obtained for the KeyMath-Revised, and the newly normed version of the test is referred to as the KeyMath-Revised/Normative Update (NU; Connolly, 1997). Alternate-forms reliabilities for the KeyMath-Revised range from .53 to .80 for the subtests, from .82 to .85 for the area tests, and from .88 to .92 for the total test. For the 1997 normative update, median alternate form reliabilies were .69 for subtests, .82 for the area tests, and .92 for the total test. Split-half reliabilities for the KeyMath-Revised are shown by subtest and by grade, and although these coefficients are generally higher than the alternate forms coefficients, the split-half reliabilities for some subtests in grades K and 1 are low (Larson & Williams, 1994). For the 1997 normative update, the median split-half reliability values were .81 for the subtests, .92 for the area tests, and .97 for the total test. There are some limitations to the validity information available about the KeyMath-Revised, and Larson and Williams (1994) report that the construct validity of the test seemingly would have been enhanced by factor analyses studies.

REFERENCES

Connolly, A.J. (1988). *KeyMath-Revised: A Diagnostic Inventory of Essential Mathematics.* Circle Pines, MN: American Guidance Service.

Connolly, A.J. (1997). *KeyMath-Revised/Normative Update: A Diagnostic Inventory of Essential Mathematics.* Circle Pines, MN: American Guidance Service.

Larson, J.A., & Williams, J.D. (1994). KeyMath-Revised: A Diagnostic Inventory of Essential Mathematics. In D.J. Keyser & R.C. Sweetland (Eds.), *Test critiques, Volume X* (pp. 350–354). Austin, TX: Pro-Ed.

See also **Achievement Tests; Mathematics, Learning Disabilities and**

KEYWORD METHOD

The keyword method is one of several mnemonic (memory-enhancing) techniques used for facilitating the learning and later recall of associative information. First employed by Atkinson (1975) in teaching Russian vocabulary words to college students, the keyword method was first applied to school-age children by Pressley (1977) in the learning of Spanish vocabulary words. Since that time it has been applied in many different content domains with students of several age and ability levels (Pressley, Levin, & Delaney, 1982).

The keyword method employs what Levin (1983) has described as the 3 R's of mnemonic techniques: recoding, relating, and retrieving. For example, in learning the Italian vocabulary word *roccia* (pronounced roach-ia), which means cliff, learners are first provided with (or are asked to generate) a recoded keyword. A keyword is a word that is acoustically similar to the stimulus term, and easily pictured. In this case, *roach* would be a good keyword for *roccia*. In a second step, the keyword is related to the response term via an interactive picture or image. In the *roccia* example, a *roach* could be shown jumping off a cliff. For the final, retrieving step, the learner is asked, when given the stimulus *roccia,* to think back to the keyword *roach,* to think of the picture of the roach, recall what else was in the picture, and respond with the appropriate referent, cliff.

The keyword method has recently been used with learning-disabled (Mastropieri, Scruggs, & Levin, 1985), mentally retarded (Scruggs, Mastropieri, & Levin, 1985), and gifted (Scruggs, Mastropieri, Monson, & Jorgenson, 1985) students. Results to date have suggested that the keyword may be an effective instructional strategy in special education.

REFERENCES

Atkinson, R.C. (1975). Mnemotechnics in second language learning. *American Psychologist, 30,* 821–828.

Levin, J.R. (1983). Pictorial strategies for school learning: Practical illustrations. In M. Pressley & J.R. Levin (Eds.), *Cognitive strategy research: Educational applications.* New York: Springer-Verlag.

Mastropieri, M.A., Scruggs, T.E., & Levin, J.R. (1985). Maximizing what exceptional students can learn: A review of research in mnemonic techniques. *Remedial and Special Education, 6,* 39–45.

Pressley, M. (1977). Children's use of the keyword method to learn simple Spanish vocabulary words. *Journal of Educational Psychology, 72,* 575–582.

Pressley, M., Levin, J.R., & Delaney, H.D. (1982). The mnemonic keyword. *Review of Educational Research, 52,* 61–91.

Scruggs, T.E., Mastropieri, M.A., & Levin, J.R. (1985). Vocabulary acquisition of retarded students under direct and mnemonic instruction. *American Journal of Mental Deficiency, 89,* 546–551.

Scruggs, T.E., Mastropieri, M.A., Monson, J.A., & Jorgenson, C. (1985). Maximizing what gifted students can learn: Recent findings of learning strategy research. *Gifted Child Quarterly, 29,* 181–185.

See also **Memory Disorders; Mnemonics**

KINETIC-FAMILY-DRAWING (KFD)

Family drawings have been used as projective techniques in the diagnosis of children's emotional disorders for many years. Of the various approaches available, the Kinetic-Family-Drawing (KFD), as described by Burns and Kaufman (1970, 1972) is the most popular, particularly among school psychologists. Children are given a blank sheet of paper, a pencil with an eraser, and instructed to "Draw a picture of everyone in your family doing something, including you; try to draw whole people, not cartoon or stick figures, and be sure to have everyone doing something."

The KFDs are analyzed for action, symbols, and style. Action refers to movement of energy among people and/or objects and reflects love, power, and anger. Symbols on the KFD are interpreted according to traditional psychoanalytic theory. For example, the drawing of a bed is associated with sexual and depressive themes. Style on the KFD is reflected in the overall approach to the drawing and may include such characteristics as compartmentalization of figures, underlining, edging figures, lining the bottom of the drawing, and drawing all figures in a small portion of the paper. A quick reference guide to the interpretation of children's KFDs, intended for the already experienced user, has been provided by Reynolds (1978).

REFERENCES

Burns, R.C., & Kaufman, S.H. (1970). *Kinetic Family Drawing (K-F-D): An introduction to understanding children through kinetic drawings.* New York: Brunner/Mazel.

Burns, R.C., & Kaufman, S.H. (1972). *Actions, styles and symbols in Kinetic Family Drawings (K-F-D): An interpretive manual.* New York: Brunner/Mazel.

Reynolds, C.R. (1978). A quick scoring guide to the interpretation of children's Kinetic Family Drawings (KFD). *Psychology in the Schools, 15,* 489–492.

KIRK, SAMUEL A. (1904–1996)

Samuel A. Kirk, often referred to as "the Father of Learning Disabilities," received his BA (1929) and MA (1931) in psychology from the University of Chicago, and his PhD (1935) in physiological and clinical psychology from the University of Michigan. His doctoral studies led him to discount biophysical identifications of disability and to recommend more behavioral descriptions that could lead to remedial planning. In 1935, he began working as the director of a teacher education program at Milwaukee State Teachers College. He joined the faculty of the University of Illinois in 1947 to develop a program in special education for undergraduates and graduates. Much of his pioneering work was done as the founding director of the Institute for Research on Exceptional Children at the University of Illinois, a position he held before and after serving as director of the Federal Office of Education's Division of Handicapped Children in 1963 and 1964. During his tenure in Washington, he contributed to early federal legislation that led to the Early Education Assistance Act of 1968 and the establishment of the Bureau for the Education of Handicapped Children. The work of this bureau eventually culminated in PL 94-142, the Education for All Handicapped Children Act of 1975. After more than 20 years at the University of Illinois, he moved to the University of Arizona at Tucson, where he continued to play an active role even after his retirement. Samuel Kirk died in 1996 at the age of 92, in Tucson, Arizona.

Samuel Kirk published more than 200 books, monographs, and journal articles, and was the recipient of numerous awards, including the First International Award in Mental Retardation from the Joseph P. Kennedy Foundation.

REFERENCES

Kirk, S.A. (1958). *Early education of the mentally retarded—An experimental study.* Urbana: University of Illinois Press.

Kirk, S.A., McCarthy, J.J., & Kirk, W.D. (1968). *The Illinois Test of Psycholinguistic Abilities.* Urbana: University of Illinois Press.

Learning Disabilities Association. (1996). *LDA bids farewell to father of learning disabilities.* http//www.ldantl.org/newsbriefs/oct96/kirk.html.

KLINEFELTER'S SYNDROME

Klinefelter's syndrome (KS) is a chromosomal abnormality occurring in a male who has at least one extra female sex chromosome (i.e., xxy or xxxy) in contrast to the normal male genotype of xy (Reed, 1975). About two thirds of KS patients have an xxy pattern and the remainder have an xxxy pattern (Ginther & Fullwood, 1998). The extra sex chromosome(s) has been attributed to nondisjunction during meiosis, a process that also results in Down's syndrome, although the precise etiology is unknown (Hoaken, Clarke, & Breslin, 1964). This syndrome is characterized by a generally normal-appearing phenotypical male with small and non-functioning testes, gynecomastia (i.e., enlarged breasts), low sex drive, a high-pitched voice, eunuchoid build, obesity, scant facial hair, tallness, and deficiencies of male hormone production. The incidence is reported to vary from 0.15 to 0.3% of the general population or 15 to 30 in every 10,000 males (Lubs & Ruddle, 1970; Reed, 1975); however, incidence is related to maternal age directly (Ginther & Fullwood, 1998). Although it is increasingly being identified during early infancy through genetic screening, Klinefelter's syndrome is typically not diagnosed until after puberty, when the testicles are noted to be abnormally small. It is medically treated with testosterone during adolescence.

Research has consistently indicated that the extra x chromosome(s) material results in proportionately higher risks for a wide variety of developmental and psychological disabilities (Haka-Ikse, Steward, & Cripps, 1979; Money, 1980; Pomeroy, 1980).

Wright et al. (1979) recommended that behavioral practitioners provide comprehensive evaluation of intellectual, academic, and personal-social functioning of xxy persons. They especially recommended that evaluation take place before and after hormone treatment for those first identified during adolescence. Students with KS often require special education placement and counseling, and are at high risk both academically and socially (Ginther & Fullwood, 1998). Anticipatory guidance for the child and parents is especially recommended over time regarding such issues as sterility.

REFERENCES

Ginther, D., & Fullwood, H. (1998). Klinefelter syndrome. In L. Phelps (Ed.), *Health-related disorders in children and adolescents.* Washington, DC: American Psychological Association.

Haka-Ikse, K., Steward, D.A., & Cripps, M.H. (1979). Early development of children with sex chromosome aberrations. *Pediatrics, 62,* 761–766.

Hoaken, P.C.S., Clarke, M., & Breslin, M. (1964). Psychopathology in Klinefelter's syndrome. *Psychosomatic Medicine, 26,* 207–223.

Lubs, H.A., & Ruddle, F.H. (1970). Chromosomal abnormality in the human population: Estimates of rates based on New Haven newborn study. *Science, 169,* 495–499.

Money, J. (1980). Human behavior cytogenetics: Review of psychopathology in three syndromes—47, XXY; 47, XYY; and 45, X. In S.I. Harrison & J.F. McDermott (Eds.), *New directions in childhood psychopathology* (pp. 70–84). New York: International Universities Press.

Pomeroy, J.C. (1980). Klinefelter's syndrome and schizophrenia. *British Journal of Psychiatry, 136,* 597–599.

Reed, E.W. (1975). Genetic anomalies in development. In F.D. Horowitz (Ed.), *Review of child development research* (Vol. 4, pp. 283–318). Chicago: University of Chicago Press.

Wright, L., Schaefer, A.B., & Solomons, G. (1979). *Encyclopedia of pediatric psychology.* Baltimore, MD: University Park Press.

See also **Genetic Counseling; Genetic Factors in Behavior; Genetic Variations; Physical Anomalies**

KNIGHT, HENRY M. (1827–1880)

Henry M. Knight, physician and educator, entered the field of mental retardation as a member of the Connecticut state legislature, when he served on a committee established to ascertain the number of mentally retarded children in that state. Following completion of a census, legislation was proposed for the construction of a school for the retarded. When the legislation failed, Knight gave up his medical practice and, in 1858, established a residential program for retarded children in his home. Through Knight's continuing campaign for public support, the legislature, in 1861, appropriated the necessary funds and Knight's school became the fifth publicly supported institution for the mentally retarded in the United States. Knight served as superintendent until shortly before his death in 1880. The institution was closed in 1917 with the opening of more modern facilities. Knight was one of the founders of the Association of Medical Officers of American Institutions for Idiotic and Feeble-Minded Persons, now the American Association on Mental Deficiency.

REFERENCE

Brown, G. (1964). Memoir of Dr. H.M. Knight. *Association of medical officers of American institutions for idiotic and feeble-minded persons, proceedings, 1876–1886.* New York: Johnson Reprint Corporation.

KOPPITZ, ELIZABETH M. (1919–1983)

Elizabeth M. Koppitz came to the United States from Germany in 1939. She received her PhD from Ohio State University in 1955, and worked as a psychologist in Ohio and in the public schools of New York state until her retirement in 1982. She made major contributions to the field of psychoeducational assessment of children and is best known for the scoring system presented in the *Bender Gestalt Test for Young Children* and her studies of children's human figure drawings.

REFERENCES

In memoriam: Elizabeth M. Koppitz. (1983). *Communique, 12,* 1–3.

Koppitz, E.M. (1964). *The Bender Gestalt Test for young children.* New York: Grune & Stratton.

Koppitz, E.M. (1968). *Psychological evaluation of children's human figure drawings.* New York: Grune & Stratton.

KRAEPELIN, EMIL (1856–1926)

Emil Kraepelin, German psychiatrist, held teaching posts at universities in Dorpat, Heidelberg, and Munich during his long career. Best known for his classification of mental disorders, his descriptions and classifications of the symptoms of mental illness provided a common ground for psychiatric thought; they constitute the basis for the categories in use today. Kraepelin applied the methods of the psychological laboratory to the study of personality, learning, and abnormal behavior. He developed tests to evaluate sensory-motor performance and the psychological deficits of psychiatric patients. He studied the effects of alcohol and tobacco, and was the first to use scientific methods to test the effects of drugs on human behavior. He wrote extensively on the problem of crime, providing much of the basis for the modern study of the relationship between criminality and mental illness.

REFERENCES

Kahn, E. (1959). The Emil Kraepelin memorial lecture. In B. Pasamanick (Ed.), Epidemiology of mental disorders: A symposium organized by the American Psychiatric Association to commemorate the centennial of the birth of Emil Kraepelin. Washington, DC: American Association for the Advancement of Science.

Kraepelin, E. (1962). One hundred years of psychiatry. New York: Citadel Press.

KUHLMANN, FREDERICK (1876–1941)

Frederick Kuhlmann, psychologist and test developer, obtained his PhD from Clark University in Massachusetts. After holding teaching positions there and at the universities of Wisconsin, Illinois, and Minnesota, he became director of research at the Minnesota School for the Feeble-Minded in Faribault, where he specialized in the assessment and education of mentally retarded children and adults. In 1912 and 1922 Kuhlmann published revisions of the 1908 Binet-Simon Scale, which extended the range of the test down to 3 months and represented one of the earliest efforts to develop a standardized test for infants. In 1927 he and Rose Anderson published a widely used group test of intelligence, the Kuhlmann-Anderson Intelligence Tests. Kuhlmann's individually administered Tests of Mental Development appeared in 1939.

In 1921 Kuhlmann's research department at Faribault became a state office, the Bureau of Mental Examinations, which he headed until his death. Kuhlmann's articles and research reports had widespread influence on other state institutions and on the development of services for mentally retarded students in the public schools of Minnesota. In addition, Kuhlmann was responsible for much of the teaching in the training program for teachers of the mentally retarded at Faribault. Kuhlmann was an active member of the American Association on Mental Deficiency and served as its president in 1940–1941.

REFERENCES

Dayton, N. (1940). President Frederick Kuhlmann. *American Journal of Mental Deficiency, 45,* 3–7.

Maxfield, F.N. (1941). Fred Kuhlmann. *American Journal of Mental Deficiency, 46,* 17–18.

KURZWEIL READING MACHINE

Developed by Raymond Kurzweil in the mid-1960s at the Massachusetts Institute of Technology, the Kurzweil Reading Machine (KRM) is a computer for blind and print-handicapped individuals; it converts printed materials directly into synthesized speech. The KRM converts printed materials from a variety of sources, type sizes, and styles into synthetic, full-word, multilingual speech that is readily understandable after a short period of familiarization. The KRM also functions as a talking calculator and can serve as a full word, voice output computer terminal.

The KRM consists of two principal units: the automatic scanning system and the control panel. The scanning system automatically scans documents up to 11 inches × 14 inches and will read print or type from 6- to 24-point. The push-button control panel activates and directs the system (Kurzweil Computer Products). The development of the KRM offers several important advances over Braille or direct-translation reading machines. Because the output of the device is speech, it is more easily understood and requires less special training. Relatively high reading speeds (approximately 250 words per minute) are able to be attained (Goodrich et al., 1979).

Users indicate the major advantages of the KRM include providing equal access to entire print collections, immediate availability of materials, and the ability to read at their own pace, on their own schedule, with privacy and independence (Kurzweil Computer Products, 1985). Limitations pertaining to the KRM involve its cost, size, and ability to produce clear speech from poor or elaborate print. Computer scanning of text and conversion to speech has become common and is now relatively inexpensive as a result of the revolution in personal computer pricing and availability seen in the 1990s.

REFERENCES

Goodrich, G.L., Bennett, R.R., De L'aune, W.R., Lauer, H., & Mowinski, L. (1979). Kurzweil reading machine: A partial evaluation of its optical character recognition error rate. *Journal of Visual Impairment & Blindness, 3,* 389–399.

Kurzweil Computer Products. (1985). Reading Machine Department, Cambridge, MA.

See also **Blind; Electronic Travel Aids; Versabraille**

L

LABELING

Labeling is an imprecise term referring to a series of effects, mostly negative, believed to result from formal classification of students as handicapped. Hobbs (1975), in his classic work that seems as current today as when it was first published, defined classification as "the act of assigning a child or condition to a general category or to a particular position in a classification system" (p. 43). The close relationship of classification and labeling is revealed by Hobbs's (1975) definition of labeling as, "the assignment of a child to a category," which also includes, "the notion of public communication of the way a child is categorized; thus, the connotation of stigma is present" (p. 43).

The somewhat confusing definitions cited are typical of the efforts to separate the effects of classification and labeling. Labeling is the term used to refer to negative effects that are assumed to be associated with the classification of students. These negative effects are most often associated with various mild handicapping classifications, particularly the classification of mild mental retardation (MMR). Labeling effects also are assumed to exist for other classifications such as specific learning disabilities (SLD) and emotionally disturbed (ED), but the negative effects associated with these classifications have not been seen as severe.

Labeling effects depend heavily on social deviance theory (Becker, 1963). Social deviance theory was initiated to explain the effects of the formal justice system on the behavior of persons, often teenagers, who may or may not have been classified as juvenile delinquents. Social deviance theory emphasizes the effects of labels on the behavior of individuals. Formal labels are believed to exert direct influence on behavior through complex processes that, simplified, result in labels creating deviant behavior. The question of whether labels create deviant behavior or whether labels result from significant behavioral deviation is the basic issue in the voluminous professional literature on labeling effects.

One of the strongest statements claiming to show the effects of labels in creating behavior was published by Rosenthal and Jacobson (1968). This widely cited and highly influential study claimed to show the effects of communicating positive information to teachers on the intellectual development of elementary school-aged children. Rosenthal and Jacobson claimed that changes in teachers' beliefs produced by brief statements about children inserted in their educational records led to significant intellectual growth by children, presumably because of subtle changes in how those children were treated by their teachers.

Although the Rosenthal and Jacobson work was severely criticized in the professional literature, and numerous efforts to replicate the findings were unsuccessful, the notion of self-fulfilling prophecy exerted enormous influence on special education in the late 1960s and 1970s, and, to a considerable extent, into the present era. The self-fulfilling prophecy as applied to special education suggests that children and youths acquire deviant behaviors or fail to develop positive behaviors because of the special education classification.

The theme that special education classifications, particularly MMR, have significant negative effects on students was particularly prominent in a widely cited article by Dunn (1968). Dunn argued that MMR special class programs involved stigmatizing labels as well as ineffective interventions. The labeling theme, particularly regarding MMR, was developed further by a 1970 report of the President's Committee on Mental Retardation. This report coined the term six-hour retarded child. Discussions of the labeling effects in the classification/placement process also further developed the theme by Mercer (1973, 1979). Although the conclusions of Dunn, Mercer, and the concept of 6-hour retarded child are widely cited, there is little or no evidence showing direct negative effects of special education labels. A continuing problem in the special education literature is the insufficient attention to empirical studies of labeling effects.

Extensive research attempting to identify effects of special education classifications or placements has been conducted. This research is very complex. Perhaps the most serious complication is the fact that labels are not randomly assigned to students (and indeed could not be due to ethical concerns). In the real world, some students are classified and placed; others are not. There are well-known, significant differences separating those who are classified and placed in special education, and therefore potentially vulnerable to labeling effects, and those who are not classified and placed. Thus, an accurate account of the effects of labels in the real world must somehow take into account the differences among students that led to the original referral and then the classification and placement decisions.

Referrals are almost always initiated because of significant learning or behavioral problems in classroom settings. Only a few students are referred, typically under 10%. Students who are referred receive preplacement evaluations in which a multifactored assessment is conducted. The multifactored assessment information is considered by a multidisciplinary team that may or may not recommend classification as handicapped and placement in special education. Thus the students for whom some labeling effect might occur are a highly selected subsample of the general population. Possible effects of labeling, which presumably occur after formal classification and placement, are contaminated with the behavioral characteristics of students that led to their initial referral and eligibility for special education. It is impossible to separate these effects in the real world.

Research attempting to observe developmental changes in self-concept and peer acceptance before and after labeling has been conducted with mixed results. The balance of evidence would appear to suggest that labeling either improves or has no significant effect on self-concept and peer acceptance (Gottlieb, 1980; Guskin, 1978).

The enormously complex labeling literature does yield at least two fairly well established generalizations. First, children and youth classified as mildly handicapped do not like being labeled. Second, many persons, including professionals such as public school teachers, often misunderstand the common special education labels. These two findings provide ample reason to be cautious about the assignment of labels, to exert strong effort to avoid misclassification, to consider alternatives to the current classification system, and to deliver effective programs if labeling is deemed necessary.

Labeling is an enormously complex phenomena about which much distortion, confusion, and misinformation have been communicated. Much work on the development of better systems of categorizing children and on noncategorical approaches to special education has been completed since passage of PL 94-142 in 1975. Despite more than 25 years of research, little has changed and no better systems have been devised. Pros and cons of the existing systems are reviewed in detail in Cartwright, Cartwright, and Ward (1995).

REFERENCES

Becker, H.S. (1963). *Outsiders: Studies in the sociology of deviance.* Glencoe, IL: Free Press.

Cartwright, G., Cartwright, C., & Ward, M. (1995). *Educating special learners* (4th ed.). Boston: Wadsworth.

Dunn, L. (1968). Special education for the mildly retarded: Is much of it justifiable? *Exceptional Children, 35,* 5–22.

Gottlieb, J. (Ed.). (1980). *Educating mentally retarded persons in the mainstream.* Baltimore, MD: University Park Press.

Guskin, S.L. (1978). Theoretical and empirical strategies for the study of the labeling of mentally retarded persons. In N.R. Ellis (Ed.), *International review of research in mental retardation* (Vol. 9, pp. 127–158). New York: Academic.

Hobbs, N.L. (1975). *The futures of children.* San Francisco: Jossey-Bass.

Mercer, J. (1973). *Labeling the mentally retarded.* Berkeley, CA: University of California Press.

Mercer, J. (1979). *System of multicultural pluralistic assessment technical manual.* New York: Psychological Corporation.

Rosenthal, R., & Jacobson, L. (1968). *Pygmalion in the classroom: Teacher expectation and pupils' intellectual development.* New York: Holt, Rinehart, & Winston.

See also **AAMD Classification System; Mental Retardation; Six-Hour Retarded Child; Systems of Classification**

LAMINAR HETEROTOPIA

Laminar heterotopia are nodules in the brain formed of neurons that were supposed to migrate during gestation or infancy, but did not. They are structurally out of place in the maturing brain and form nodules or laminae. Laminar heterotopia are particularly prominent on the walls of the lateral ventricles of the brain. They are a symptom and do not form a specific syndrome in and of themselves. Outcomes depend on the underlying disorder and the size and number of the nodules.

LANGUAGE, ABSENCE OF

The nondevelopment of a language system in several categories of individuals does not preclude the possibility of producing separate sounds or words. For example, it is generally acknowledged that individuals with profound intellectual disabilities (with IQs below 20 and marked deficiencies in adaptive behavior) do not develop language. Past work with nonspeech language systems (Lloyd, 1976; Rondal, 1985) highlighted the possibility of equipping such individuals with gestural prosthetic communicative systems that in turn proved helpful in establishing limited functional vocal repertoires.

REFERENCES

Lloyd, L. (Ed.). (1976). *Communication assessment and intervention strategies.* Baltimore, MD: University Park Press.

Rondal, J.A. (1985). *Language et communication chez les handicapés mentaux. Théorie, évaluation, intervention.* Brussels: Mardaga.

See also **Communication Disorders; Deaf Education; Language Deficiencies and Deficits; Language Delays; Language Disorders**

LANGUAGE ASSESSMENT

The assessment of language is a multifaceted process (Cole, Dale, & Thal, 1996; Haynes, Pindzola, & Emerick, 1992; Shipley & McAfee, 1998; Tomblin, Morris, & Spriestersbach, 1994). The process begins with *awareness* that an individual's communication is not effective or efficient to negotiate oral, literate, or manually coded meaning within diverse contexts as compared with what is typical for community cultures (ethnicity, age, sex, disability, socioeconomic status). Next, a referral is made to a qualified speech-language pathologist, who will determine which aspects of the communication process (speech, language, hearing) are affecting communication competence. Determination of assessment focus (speech, language, and/or hearing) is made from historical information (observation, interviews, reports) about the client, the client's family or caregivers, and the nature of the communication disorder and associated conditions.

Although all three aspects of the communication process are typically addressed in an assessment of communication, if the historical information suggests that the communication problem is primarily the result of the client's lack of ability to receive, process, and use auditory, visual, and haptic symbols, then a detailed assessment of the *language* components of communication would be in order (Haynes & Shulman, 1998; Nelson, 1998; Paul, 1995). Depending on the presenting condition and age of the client, the following aspects of language would be considered:

1. nonverbal and verbal symbol *systems* (Haynes & Shulman, 1998; Hegde, 1998; Nelson, 1998)

2. symbol use *levels* (prelinguistic; sounds; words; phrases; sentences; literate discourse; and discourse plus, which includes nonliteral language, math language, computer language, foreign language, and career and employment language (Cherney, Shadden, & Coelho, 1998; Larson & McKinley, 1995; Naremore, Densmore, & Harman, 1995; Wallach & Butler, 1994; Wallach & Miller, 1988)

3. receptive/expressive *modalities* (watching/moving, listening/speaking, reading/writing; Hegde, 1998; Nelson, 1998)

4. cognitive/metacognitive (attention, perception, discrimination, memory, executive functions; Gillam, 1998; Hegde, 1998), linguistic (phonology/phonics, semantics, syntax, morphology; Loban, 1976), and social (pragmatics) *dimensions* (Baron & Boschee, 1995; Lund & Duchan, 1993)

5. biological (genetics, heredity), affective (emotion, motivation, attitude, commitment, self-concept/ esteem, honesty, trust, resilience), and contextual (socioeconomic status, ethnicity, gender, family, demographics, environment) *mediators* (Pressley & McCormick, 1995)

6. social, educational, and occupational language *demands* of the client's life (Lane & Molyneaux, 1992; Larson & McKinley, 1995; Wallach & Butler, 1994; Wallach & Miller, 1988; Weller, Crelly, Watteyne, & Herbert, 1992).

ASSESSMENT MODELS

The models of language assessment reflect the concept of "best practices" in communication disorders. Best practices are flexible, consumer-directed, state-of-the-art, and sensitive to cultural diversity (Secord, 1992). Three models of language assessment can be used: Modular Assessment, Synergistic Assessment, and Wholistic Assessment. The model of choice is determined by the purpose of the assessment and the types of data needed to report the outcome.

Modular, or quantitative, assessment is characterized by the use of standardized and norm-referenced instruments that focus on discrete points of language comprehension and production (phonemes, graphemes, semantics, syntax, morphology; Carrow-Woolfolk, 1988; Harris & Shelton, 1996; Loban, 1976; Mattes, 1996). Modular methodology comprises clinical case histories, statistical measures, and a client (inside out; emic) focus. Modular assessment is not functionally related to intervention because it is done outside a client's communicative contexts.

Synergistic, or qualitative, assessment is communication-referenced and uses functional descriptive, authentic, and dynamic methodology (Baron & Boschee, 1995; Bellanca, Chapman, & Swartz, 1994). Synthesis of ethnographic interview domain patterns, teaching-learning style inventories, observation (Lund & Duchan, 1993; Silliman & Wilkinson, 1991), and oral and literate discourse analysis (conversation, narration, exposition; Hedberg & Westby, 1993; Merritt & Culatta, 1998; Ripich & Creaghead, 1994) data are used to describe the inside out (emic; client) and outside in (etic or contextual; Nelson, 1998) facilitative and nonfacilitative language variables operating in the client's communication-learning network. Rubrics (a term that comes from the word "rules") offer very exacting definitions of the outcomes being assessed (Taggart, Phifer, Nixon, & Wood, 1998). Synergistic assessment is functionally related to authentic intervention because it includes a client's communicative contexts. Synergistic and wholistic assessment require knowledge and understanding of typical developmental patterns related to age, gender, disabilities, and ethnicity (Haynes & Shulman, 1998; Lane & Molyneaux, 1992; Owens, 1996).

Wholistic assessment is the combination of select modular and synergistic procedures, processes, and materials. Wholistic assessment is both emic and etic and data lead directly to functional interventions (Baron & Boschee, 1995; Lund & Duchan, 1993; Owens, 1991; Secord, 1992).

The American Speech-Language-Hearing Association provides information about language assessment through print and broadcast media. ASHA can be contacted at 10801 Rockville Pike, Rockville, MD 20852; 301.897.5700 for voice or TTY; FAX 301.571.0481; or via http://www. asha.org/.

REFERENCES

Baron, M.A., & Boschee, F. (1995). *Authentic assessment: The key to unlocking student success.* Lancaster, PA: Technomic.

Bellanca, J., Chapman, C., & Swartz, E. (1994). *Multiple assessments for multiple intelligences.* Palatine, IL: IRI/Skylight.

Carrow-Woolfolk, E. (1988). *Theory, assessment and intervention in language disorders: An integrative approach.* Philadelphia: Grune & Stratton.

Cherney, L.R., Shadden, B.B., & Coelho, C.A. (1998). *Analyzing discourse in communicatively impaired adults.* Gaithersburg, MD: Aspen.

Cole, K.N., Dale, P.S., & Thal, D.J. (Eds.). (1996). *Assessment of communication and language.* Baltimore: Brookes.

Gillam, R.B. (Ed.). (1998). *Memory and language impairment in children and adults: New perspectives.* Gaithersburg, MD: Aspen.

Harris, L.G., & Shelton, I.S. (1996). *Desk reference of assessment instruments in speech and language* (revised). San Antonio, TX: Communication Skill Builders/The Psychological Corporation.

Haynes, W.O., & Shulman, B.B. (1998). *Communication development: Foundations, processes, and clinical applications.* Baltimore: Williams & Wilkins.

Hedberg, N.L., & Westby, C.E. (1993). *Analyzing storytelling skills: Theory to practice.* Tucson: Communication Skill Builders.

Hegde, M.N. (1998). *A coursebook on aphasia and other neurogenic language disorders* (2nd ed.). San Diego: Singular.

Lane, V.W., & Molyneaux, D. (1992). *The dynamics of communicative development.* Englewood Cliffs, NJ: Prentice Hall.

Larson, V.L., & McKinley, N. (1995). *Language disorders in older students: Preadolescents and adolescents.* Eau Claire, WI: Thinking Publications.

Loban, W. (1976). *Language development: Kindergarten through grade twelve.* Urbana, IL: National Council of Teachers of English.

Lund, N.J., & Duchan, J.F. (1993). *Assessing children's language in naturalistic contexts* (3rd ed.). Englewood Cliffs, NJ: Prentice Hall.

Mattes, L.J. (1996). *Sourcebook for speech and language assessment.* Oceanside, CA: Academic Communication Associates.

Merritt, D.D., & Culatta, B. (1998). *Language intervention in the classroom.* San Diego: Singular.

Naremore, R.C., Densmore, A.E., & Harman, D.R. (1995). *Language intervention with school-aged children: Conversation, narrative, and text.* San Diego: Singular.

Nelson, N.W. (1998). *Childhood language disorders in context: Infancy through adolescence* (2nd ed.). Boston: Allyn & Bacon.

Owens, R.E. (1991). *Language disorders: A functional approach to assessment and intervention.* New York: Merrill/Macmillan.

Owens, R.E. (1996). *Language development: An introduction* (4th ed.). Boston: Allyn & Bacon.

Paul, R. (1995). *Language disorders from infancy through adolescence: Assessment and intervention.* St. Louis: Mosby.

Pressley, M., & McCormick, C.B. (1995). *Advanced educational psychology: For educators, researchers, and policymakers.* New York: HarperCollins.

Ripich, D.N., & Creaghead, N.A. (Eds.). (1994). *School discourse problems* (2nd ed.). San Diego: Singular.

Secord, W.A. (1992). *Best practices in school speech-language pathology: Descriptive/nonstandardized language assessment.* The Psychological Corporation.

Shipley, K.G., & McAfee, J.G. (1998). *Assessment in speech-language pathology: A resource manual* (2nd ed.). San Diego: Singular.

Silliman, E.R., & Wilkinson, L.C. (1991). *Communicating for learning: Classroom observation and collaboration.* Gaithersburg, MD: Aspen.

Taggart, G.L., Phifer, S.J., Nixon, J.A., & Wood, M. (Eds.). (1998). *Rubrics: A handbook for construction and use.* Lancaster, PA: Technomic.

Tomblin, J.B., Morris, H.L., & Spriestersbach, D.C. (1994). *Diagnosis in speech-language pathology.* San Diego: Singular.

Wallach, G.P., & Butler, K.G. (1994). *Language learning disabilities in school-age children and adolescents: Some principles and applications* (2nd ed.). New York: Merrill/Macmillan College Publishing.

Wallach, G.P., & Miller, L. (1988). *Language intervention and academic success.* Boston: College-Hill/Little, Brown and Co.

Weller, C., Crelly, C., Watteyne, L., & Herbert, M. (1992). *Adaptive language disorders of young adults with learning disabilities.* San Diego: Singular.

See also Communication Disorders

LANGUAGE DELAYS

Language delays, language disorders, and language differences are not synonyms. *Language delays* exist when receptive and expressive language skills are slow to emerge but the skills are acquired in the same sequence that is associated with typical (normal) development (Reed, 1994). The delay is essentially the same for all features of language (e.g., semantics and syntax). Language delay may be present in one or both languages of children who are bilingual. Children with language delays learn quickly when placed in language-rich environments. There are no known neuropsychological etiological factors. The term *Specific Language Impairment* (SLI; Nelson, 1998; Paul, 1995) may be used to define children whose language skills are at the lower end of a continuum of normal variation.

Language delays can interfere with social and academic dimensions of the communication-learning process during early childhood. Early identification and intervention are recommended to prevent or decrease the negative effects of language delays (Nelson, 1998; Paul, 1995).

REFERENCES

Nelson, N.W. (1998). *Childhood language disorders in context: Infancy through adolescence* (2nd ed.). Boston: Allyn & Bacon.

Paul, R. (1995). *Language disorders from infancy through adolescence: Assessment and intervention.* St. Louis: Mosby.

Reed, V.A. (1994). *An introduction to children with language disorders* (2nd ed.). New York: Merrill/Macmillan College Publishing.

See also Communication Disorders; Expressive Language Disorders; Language Deficiencies and Deficits; Language Disorders; Speech, Absence of

LANGUAGE DISORDERS

"Language disorders" is a term that represents a heterogeneous group of either *developmental* or *acquired* significant deficits in comprehension, production, and/or use of a spoken, written, and/or other symbol system for social, educational, and employment or career purposes (Bernstein & Tiegerman-Farber, 1997; Hegde, 1998; Nelson, 1998; Owens, 1991). Language disorders are chronic and may persist across an individual's lifetime. The symptoms, manifestations, effects, and severity of the problems change over time; changes occur as a consequence of context, content, and the communication-learning demands of tasks.

TERMINOLOGY

A variety of names have been used throughout the history of developmental language disorders, including *language-learning disorder, language impairment, language disability, language disorder, language delay, language deviance, language difference, and childhood* or *congenital aphasia* or *dysphasia* (Bernstein & Tiegerman-Farber, 1997). Language disorders and learning disabilities are integrally related (Nelson, 1998). Preschool children with a diagnosed language disorder (learning to communicate) will likely encounter problems with academic language (communicating to learn) when they enter a formal education system. Although the underlying problem is the encoding and decoding of symbols (language disorder), the disorder may be termed a learning disability because of the problems encountered learning academic material (reading, writing, spelling, math). Currently, the preferred term is *language-learning disorder.* Because individuals do not outgrow language-learning disorders, they continue to encounter social or academic problems as adults. The communication-learning deficits that are evident at the adult level are referred to as *adaptive communication-learning disorders* (Weller, Crelly, Watteyne, & Herbert, 1992). The terms aphasia, dysphasia, dementia, and right hemisphere syndrome refer to *acquired* language disorders (Hegde, 1998).

Language disorder implies a deviation from the usual rate and sequence with which specific language skills emerge (Carrow-Woolfolk, 1988; Owens, 1991; Nelson, 1998). Deviations can include differences within one aspect of language (e.g., semantics or morphology), inordinate difficulties with certain features within one aspect of language, differences in rate of acquisition among various aspects of language (e.g., relationship of semantics/syntax/pragmatics in the development of meaning), and/or age-appropriate skills in one or more aspects but with delays in development of other dimensions of language. Because of the asynchrony in the rate of acquisition within and across various language parameters, the typical developmental sequence is disrupted. Children with language disorders need special intervention.

Language differences are associated with social, academic, and employment contextual (pragmatic) bias; value bias; phonological bias; grammatical bias; and vocabulary bias that differ from Standard American English or mainstream culture communication but are appropriate to another ethnic group (e.g., African American, Asian American, Latino American).

ETIOLOGY

Language disorders, whether developmental or acquired, can interfere with social and academic dimensions of the communication-learning process during early childhood; elementary, secondary, and post-secondary levels of education; and the young adult and adult levels when life roles change. Early identification and intervention are recommended to prevent or decrease the effects of language disorders.

The American Speech-Language-Hearing Association promotes aggressive prevention practices: *primary* prevention targets the management of conditions to prevent problems before they start, *secondary* prevention targets early identification and intervention to foster conditions that will minimize long-term handicaps, and *tertiary* prevention targets remediating current problems and decreasing the possibility of further problems occurring because of the original disorder (Nelson, 1998). The ASHA provides information about language disorders, assessment, and treatment through print and broadcast media. ASHA can be contacted at 10801 Rockville Pike, Rockville, MD 20852; 301.897.5700 voice or TTY; FAX 301.571.0481; or via http://www.asha.org/.

REFERENCES

Bernstein, D.K., & Tiegerman-Farber, E. (1997). *Language and communication disorders in children* (4th ed.). Boston: Allyn & Bacon.

Carrow-Woolfolk, F. (1988). *Theory, assessment and intervention in language disorders: An integrative approach.* Philadelphia: Grune & Stratton.

Hegde, M.N. (1998). *A coursebook on aphasia and other neurogenic language disorders* (2nd ed.). San Diego: Singular.

Nelson, N.W. (1998). *Childhood language disorders in context: Infancy through adolescence* (2nd ed.). Boston: Allyn and Bacon.

Owens, R.E. (1991). *Language disorders: A functional approach to assessment and intervention.* New York: Merrill/Macmillan.

Weller, C., Crelly, C., Watteyne, L., & Herbert, M. (1992). *Adaptive language disorders in young adults with learning disabilities.* San Diego: Singular.

See also Childhood Aphasia; Cleft Lip/Palate; Communication Disorders; Deaf; Expressive

Language Disorders; Language Deficiencies and Deficits; Mutism; Speech, Absence of; Stuttering; Voice Disorders

LANGUAGE DISORDERS, EXPRESSIVE

See LANGUAGE DISORDERS.

LANGUAGE THERAPY

Language therapy (also referred to as language treatment) can take many forms. The primary six perspectives it may take are: (1) Verbal and nonverbal symbol system perspective, (2) Communication Channels perspective, (3) Language Acquisition Theory perspective, (4) Oral-Literate Discourse perspective, (5) Emic-Etic perspective, (6) Non-oral perspective.

Verbal and nonverbal symbol system: Language, defined as a verbal (words) and nonverbal (e.g., paralinguistics, kinesics, proxemics) symbol system, may be treated through the use of verbal symbols or nonverbal symbols. Verbal systems may be used for addressing problems in listening, speaking, reading, writing, and thinking; nonverbal systems may be used for metalanguage and pragmatic language disorders (Hulit & Howard, 1997).

Communication Channels: Language therapy may be approached through a six-channel comprehension (receptive)/production (expressive) paradigm: watching/moving, listening/speaking, reading/writing (Nelson, 1998).

Language Acquisition Theories: Three major categories of language acquisition theories are recognized: Behavioral, Innatist (Nativist, Linguistic), and Cognitive-Social Interactionist (Pragmatic) (Haynes & Shulman, 1998).

The basic focus of the behavioral theory is that language is a learned behavior resulting from antecedents and consequences of language behavior, i.e., learners are taught language through training and shaping by the environment. The differences between the language of a child and that of adult models constitute a disorder. Therapy uses B.F. Skinner's basic S-R-R paradigm of behavior modification to train behaviors (phonological, semantic, syntactic, and morphological) that a child does not perform.

The basic focus of the Innatist (also referred to as the Nativist or Linguistic) theory is that language is a system of abstract rules from which an individual can generate an infinite number of utterances. Noam Chomsky's suggestion that children are born with an innate language acquisition device (LAD) and his later government-binding theory of s-structures (surface) and d-structures (deep) form a foundation for this approach to therapy. Language rules are induced by a child whose own system controls the selection of rules and their internal construction; the process has universal characteristics.

The basic focus of the Cognitive-Social Interactionist (also referred to as the Pragmatic) theory is that the primary function of language is communication (i.e., the negotiation of meaning), and that its basic unit is the speech act that occurs in a context that helps to determine form. Jean Piaget, Brian McWhinney, and Jean Berko-Gleason, as well as others, have contributed to the research that has explored this theory. Language is developed through cognitive (developmental cognition, meta-abilities, and information processing; Wiig, 1989), linguistic (the rules of phonology, semantics, syntax/morphology), and social (pragmatic rules) interaction with the environment.

Oral-Literate Discourse: Language therapy may include both oral and literate (reading and writing) forms of conversation, narration, and exposition discourse (Nelson, 1998). Treatment of discourse disorders focuses on establishing the pragmatic rules (who can communicate what, to whom, how, when, where, and why) associated with oral and written interpersonal communication-learning, understanding and producing diverse story forms, and academic communication-learning, including math language, computer language, foreign language, and employment language. The metaskills of study strategies, time management, teaching-learning styles and strategies, and contextual scripts and schemas are included in this treatment focus.

Emic (Inside-Out)–Etic (Outside-In): An Emic–Etic approach to language therapy, also referred to as Outside-In (client)–Inside-Out (context), includes cognitive, linguistic, and contextual dimensions of the communication-learning process (Nelson, 1998). Two tenets make up this approach: (1) a language breakdown may exist within the child and/or the context (e.g., teacher-talk, curriculum); and (2) the theory of change—first order change (of individual) and second order change (of the system). A child may experience a language-learning breakdown because of innate deficits; however, the disorder may be exacerbated because of contextual conditions (e.g., implicit, vague, or ambiguous teacher directions; complex cognitive and linguistic structures in textbooks and tests; and peer use of nonliteral language forms such as figurative language, humor, sarcasm, and teasing). It is possible to change language behavior of an individual (Inside-Out therapy) but if that person returns to a context that causes or contributes to the disorder, the individual change will not be maintained. Outside-In language therapy involves modifying the contexts in which a client functions. Emic-Etic therapy may target basic interpersonal communication skills (BICS) and/or cognitive academic language proficiency (CALP).

Non-Oral: Non-oral language therapy includes using symbols within a variety of augmentative/alternative communication (AAC) low-tech or high-tech systems, manual communication or sign language systems, and braille symbols (Nelson, 1998).

Language therapy is important in maximizing a person's success in social, academic, and employment situations across the life span. Treatment approaches may vary with culture, etiology, and severity of the communication disorder.

REFERENCES

Haynes, W.O., & Shulman, B.B. (1998). *Communication develop-ment: Foundations, processes, and clinical applications.* Baltimore: Williams & Wilkins.

Hulit, L.M., & Howard, M.R. (1997). *Born to talk: An introduction to speech and language development.* Boston: Allyn & Bacon.

Nelson, N.W. (1998). *Childhood language disorders in context: In-fancy through adolescence* (2nd ed.). Boston: Allyn & Bacon.

Wiig, E.H. (1989). *Steps to language competence: Developing met-alinguistic strategies.* San Antonio: The Psychological Corpora-tion.

See also Communication Disorders; Language Delays; Language Disorders; Learning Disabilities

LARGE-PRINT BOOKS

Many low-vision students learn to read using regular-sized print, with or without the use of optical aids. The print se-lected for low-vision students depends on factors such as the student's motivation and interest, visual acuity and fields of view, reading experience and ability, lighting, and accessibility of print (Jose, 1983).

According to Jose (1983), the advantages of large print are that it is more comfortable and easier to read; it is usu-ally produced on nonglare paper; and it offers a less re-stricted field of view compared to using regular print with a magnifying lens. However, producing large-type textbooks is expensive. As a result, the number and variety of available books is limited, particularly at the high school and college level. Other disadvantages are that the pictures in these textbooks are usually missing or not as clear as the color pictures in regular print textbooks, and large-print books are large and bulky and look so different from regular print books that some students are embarrassed to use them (Barraga, 1983).

REFERENCES

Barraga, N. (1983). *Visual handicaps and learning.* Austin, TX: Ex-ceptional Resources.

Jose, R. (1983). *Understanding low vision.* New York: American Foundation for the Blind.

See also American Printing House for the Blind; Libraries for the Blind and Physically Handicapped; Library Services for the Handicapped; Low Vision

LARRY P.

Larry P. was one of six black children who were plaintiffs in a suit brought in 1971 against Wilson Riles, California state superintendent of public instruction. The suit charged that the IQ tests that were used in determining eligibility for placement in classes for the educable mentally retarded (EMR) were culturally biased. The lawyers for the plaintiffs based their charges of cultural bias on the fact that the av-erage scores for blacks were lower than for whites, and that using the scores resulted in a higher percentage of black children in EMR classes than in regular classes.

As a consequence of the *Larry P. v. Wilson Riles* suit, the federal district court granted an injunction in 1972 that banned the use of individually administered intelligence tests for black children being considered for placement in EMR classes. This resulted in psychologists having to use alternative methods such as classroom observations, adap-tive behavior assessment, and academic achievement mea-sures to determine whether children referred for special education were intellectually retarded and, in turn, eligible for special education services.

In 1976 the case was brought to trial. The plaintiffs were represented by Public Advocates, Inc. and by *pro bono* at-torneys from the San Francisco firm of Morrison and Foer-ster. The state was represented by a deputy attorney general from the state attorney general's office. The plaintiffs' argu-ments centered on the disproportion of black children in EMR classes as well as the lower average IQs earned by blacks on most standardized tests of intelligence. They con-tended that the tests were culturally biased because the items were drawn from white middle-class culture to which black pupils were not exposed. This contention was sup-ported, they argued, by the fact that when the six plaintiffs were retested using the WISC-R (the same test that was used to determine their eligibility for the EMR programs), their IQs were higher because black examiners perceived racial, ethnic, or socioeconomic bias and made modifications in the administration of the test such as rewording items, ac-cepting nonstandard responses, or extending time limits. In addition to arguments that the tests were biased against black children, the plaintiffs maintained that the EMR classes did not cover the same subjects as did regular classes, and that the longer the children attended the EMR classes, the greater the performance gap between EMR children and their regular class peers.

The plaintiffs' legal arguments revolved around showing that blacks were overrepresented in EMR classes and that the IQ test was the sole basis for decisions regarding eligi-bility and placement. If the IQ was the instrument used for placement, and blacks were overrepresented in EMR classes, then, they argued, the tests had to be biased, mak-ing the special education classes suspect. Both IQ tests and special education, therefore, discriminated against black children. From a legal standpoint, the burden shifted to the state of California to show that the tests were not biased, and that even though there were more black children in spe-cial education classes, the children benefited from the spe-cial education programs.

The state's defense rested on data showing that the IQ tests were valid predictors of present and future perfor-mance, and that the tests predicted equally well for blacks and whites. Witnesses for the defense testified that the IQ test was administered only after children had a long experi-ence of failing in regular class programs and were referred for evaluation of their eligibility for EMR classes. The state's witnesses also testified that there was a linear relationship between IQs and severity of mental retardation from the mildly (EMR) to the profoundly retarded. The state's witnesses, moreover, rebutted plaintiff testimony that there should be evidence for a biological or metabolic origin of mental retardation; mildly retarded children fall at one end of the normal distribution of intelligence just as gifted children are at the other, higher, end of the continuum. Having to explain why more black than white children were mildly retarded, the state countered with research that showed a relationship between IQs and poverty, poor nutrition, lack of cognitive stimulation, and other environmental factors.

Ultimately, the state had to contend with two factors: one related to the use of IQ tests for special education placement and the second to the benefits of special education. Plaintiffs built their charges against IQ tests on their cultural bias and the contention that they were the sole criterion for placement of certain children in EMR classes. The state showed that the tests were used to determine eligibility for special education and for a diagnosis of the extent of intellectual retardation. The numerous studies of the validity of IQ tests for distinguishing among individuals varying with respect to academic performance, and, therefore, indicative of the construct and criterion validity of IQ tests for both black and white children, were summarized by several witnesses. But the IQ test was not designed to show whether a child would benefit from or improve as a result of special education placement. A showing of a positive or remedial effect on the academic performance or on the level of intelligence of the child resulting from special education placement was necessary to satisfy the court. As the research on EMR programs had not shown this necessary positive effect, the plaintiffs argued that the IQ tests were not valid for EMR placement even though the state showed convincingly that they were valid for making inferences about current level of intellectual functioning, the only psychological inference required for a determination of mild mental retardation and eligibility for special education.

The state's effort to show that a major source of the overrepresentation was attributable more to the process by which the child was referred for psychological evaluation was not successful. Evidence regarding bias in the referral process (i.e., more black boys than black girls and more blacks than whites were referred resulting in overrepresentation of boys over girls and black boys over white boys in EMR classes) did not convince the court that the IQ was not the primary basis for identifying a child for placement in an EMR class. Testimony that only one-fifth (approximately) of referred children were found eligible after IQ testing did not alter the court's opinion that the IQ test was the culprit.

The plaintiffs' evidence that the IQs of blacks were lower than those of whites was the evidence on which the court ultimately relied to judge that the tests were biased. Since IQs were the most frequent piece of information in the case study records of EMR children, the court concluded that the IQ test was the basis for placement in the special education program even though the state had shown that only a portion of all children with IQ scores in the EMR range were ever placed in special education classes. The overrepresentation of black children could have been tolerated if the state had been successful in demonstrating remediation of EMR children's academic deficiencies. The court, therefore, concluded that the tests were biased and the primary basis for placement in dead-end, stigmatizing special education classes.

The court handed down its opinion in 1979 and prohibited schools "from utilizing, permitting the use of, or approving the use of any standardized intelligence tests...for the identification of black EMR children or their placement into EMR classes, without securing prior approval of the court." Furthermore the court ruled that any tests used for special education purposes should be shown to be valid for the purposes for which they were to be used. The consequences of the *Larry P.* decision in California have been a search for alternative methods, often less reliable and valid, for determining eligibility for special education classes as well as an attempt to select from among those who are eligible, those children who can benefit from special education.

Children who were classified as EMR in 1971, when the suit was filed, were reevaluated by order of the legislature before the trial began in 1976. The reevaluation resulted in a marked reduction in the number of children in special education, but no change in the overrepresentation of minority children in EMR classes. During the trial, the state of California adopted the California Master Plan for Special Education (almost at the same time that Congress passed PL 94-142), eliminating the category of EMR programs and substituting the category of "learning handicapped" to include mildly retarded pupils and those with learning disabilities. There was also a large amount of additional research evidence published during and after the trial on the differential validity of tests of scholastic aptitude, including individual tests of intelligence, using a variety of criterion measures including school grades and adaptive behavior assessments. These data generally have shown that aptitude tests are valid for both blacks and whites.

Have the outcomes of the *Larry P.* case improved the assessment or special education treatment of black children? We have now the burden of showing not only criterion validity, but the validity of IQ tests to identify those who will benefit from special education treatment. Aptitude and IQ tests may be excellent sources of evidence for prediction or diagnosing eligibility, but not necessarily for selecting the children who will profit most from special education. The *Larry P.* decision has not resulted in elimination of minority overrepresentation, only in fewer children being classified as mildly retarded. Some hail this outcome as a beneficial one, while others wonder what will become of children who are categorically denied special education services. Regardless of the psychological tests or procedures used, school psychologists and special education professionals are obligated to show that they are valid and reliable for diagnosing the cause of educational failure, as well as for selecting and placing those who will benefit from special education services.

Larry P. subsequently went to school out of state and was later identified for special education on the basis of his school achievement and classroom performance. By age 19, he still could not pass the test for a driver's license and was not gainfully employed. The one plaintiff who was adapting well in high school had been placed back in special education after leaving San Francisco schools at the request of his mother.

See also Cultural Bias in Tests; Intelligence; Intelligence Tests

LATERALITY

See CEREBRAL DOMINANCE.

LAURENCE-MOON SYNDROME

Laurence-Moon Syndrome (LMS) is an autosomal (non-sex-related chromosome), recessive genetic disorder of unknown etiology characterized by neurological, ophthalmologic, and endocrine abnormalities resulting in a deteriorating handicapping condition. John Zachariah Laurence and Robert Moon first described this condition in 1866.

Laurence and Moon observed four members of the same family who were found to exhibit mental retardation, short stature, obesity, hypogenitalism (unusually small genitalia), and retinitis pigmentosa (narrowing of the visual fields leading to a progressive loss of vision; Nathanson, 1998). LMS is also characterized by progressive neurological involvement, including ataxia (inability to coordinate voluntary muscle movements) and spastic paraplegia (Nathanson, 1998). In the early 1920s, a French physician named George Louis Bardet and Arthur Biedl, a professor of experimental pathology at the University of Prague, independently published descriptions of patients with a similar syndrome that also included polydactyly (having more than five fingers or toes per hand or foot). In the past, these two similar syndromes have been recognized as a single disorder and called the Laurence-Moon-Bardet-Biedl Syndrome; however, they are now considered separate disorders. Although both syndromes include mental retardation, retinal abnormalities, and hypogenitalism, neurological problems are characteristic of Laurence-Moon syndrome but rarely occur in Bardet-Biedl syndrome. Polydactyly is a defining feature of Bardet-Biedl syndrome, but is not characteristic of Laurence-Moon syndrome (Morris & Morris, 1998).

Although there is no medical treatment for LMS, affected individuals of school age will require a multidisciplinary approach to effectively assess, develop, and implement appropriate educational programs and support services. Because mental retardation is characteristic of LMS, affected individuals will frequently benefit from an educational program that emphasizes functional living skills in a self-contained classroom (Nathanson, 1998), with opportu-nities to integrate and interact with nondisabled peers as much as possible. Students with ataxia and spastic paraplegia may require adapted physical education. Physical and occupational therapies may be necessary to develop motor skills and increase muscle tone. Severe visual impairment is also a hallmark of LMS, and affected students will require educational services for the visually impaired. Low vision aids such as magnifiers, large print books, large print computer software, tape players, CDs, and manual and electronic Braille writers must be investigated. Transition planning will also assist the placement of LMS students in supported employment settings to help them become productive members of society. For further information regarding LMS, contact the Laurence-Moon-Bardet-Biedl Syndrome Network, 1006 Duncan Avenue, Perry, GA 31069; or call 912-987-4034.

REFERENCES

Morris, R.J., & Morris, Y.P. (1998). Bardet Biedl syndrome. In L. Phelps (Ed.), *Health-related disorders in children and adolescents.* Washington, D.C.: American Psychological Association.

Nathanson, D.S. (1998). Laurence-Moon syndrome. In L. Phelps (Ed.), *Health-related disorders in children and adolescents.* Washington, D.C.: American Psychological Association.

LEAD POISONING

The health hazards associated with the use of lead have been known for over 2000 years. Gillifan (1965) has speculated that lead poisoning may have contributed to the decline of the Roman civilization after the introduction of lead pipes for the supply of drinking water. Mental retardation, sterility, and infant mortality were frequent among influential Romans, and the unearthed bones of wealthy ancient Romans have high lead content. But the modern history of lead poisoning in children dates only from the late 1800s. Histories of the early reports and resistance of the medical community and others to recognize lead as a toxic agent in children are in Needleman (1998) and Pueschel, Linakis, and Anderson (1996). That lead is toxic at some levels is now not disputed, but the extent to which low blood-lead levels (BLL) produce lasting damage is controversial, as will be described below.

Although not a common element, lead is found in soil, water, and the atmosphere. It occurs more frequently than other heavy metals in the natural environment. Lead is one of the few metals that has toxic effects but seems to have no essential function in an organism. Lead can enter the body through diet, eating of lead-based paint (pica), or exposure to an environment containing a high lead content. Needleman (1980) has reported low-level lead intoxication from automobile exhaust fumes. Various other studies also implicate industrial emission as a possible source of low-level lead intoxication (Berney, 1996).

In the United States, lead poisoning occurs most often in one- to five-year-old children who inhabit slum areas of large cities. However, the adverse effects of lead are a concern for children of all ages and socioeconomic backgrounds. In recent years, severe forms of encephalopathy have declined due to better social and medical care and legislation protecting homebuyers and renters against unknowingly living in a heavily leaded environment.

In children, BLL above 10µg/dl indicate overexposure and may call for nutritional intervention. However, symptoms of lead poisoning are generally not present at BLL below 20, and even at this level most cases are asymptomatic. At BLL above 45 children must have medical intervention, which often includes chelation therapy. Symptoms of lead encephalopathy are generally associated with BLL above 60 µg/dl. BLL below those that produce diagnosable effects have been implicated as a possible cause of subtle behavior and learning difficulties.

The clinical manifestations of lead poisoning in children develop over a period of three to six weeks. The child becomes less playful, more irritable, and often anorexic. These symptoms may be (and often are) misinterpreted as a behavior disorder or mental retardation. Intermittent vomiting, vague abdominal pain, clumsiness, and ataxia may also be exhibited in the early stages of lead poisoning. In the final stages, vomiting becomes more persistent, apathy progresses to drowsiness and stupor, periods of hyperirritability develop, and finally, seizures and coma occur. Severe cases may result in death. In children under the age of two, the syndrome progresses rapidly, whereas in older children, recurrent and less severe episodes are more likely.

Controversial is the extent to which low BLL may have long-term adverse effects. The initial major evidence for such effects was in much-cited research by Needleman (e.g., 1980). However, in 1992 (e.g., Begley, 1992; Sibbison, 1992), two highly regarded researchers, Scarr and Ernhart, claimed that Needleman had made serious methodological errors in his study, and that the results could not be considered reliable. Arguments over the magnitude of effects of low exposure levels, methodological soundness of the research, and interpretation of results continue (e.g., Bellinger, 1995; Ernhart, 1995; Ernhart & Hebben, 1997). Tong and Baghurst (1996) have longitudinally studied the development of children early exposed to lead in Port Pirie, Australia. The study appears to be very well designed and conducted. When aged 11 to 13 years, as at earlier ages, the children showed deficits in IQ correlated with their lifelong BLLs. The deficit for children with BLLs of 10–20µg/dl was about three points, with effects somewhat larger in girls than boys. The obtained graded effect with BLL does not support a threshold effect or a "safe" level of lead. Further supporting conclusions of adverse effects of low-lead exposure in humans are parallel findings in experimental research with animals (e.g., Needleman, 1995). Of importance, several lines of research (e.g., Dietrich, 1996) now indicate that exposure of pregnant women to low levels of lead may have adverse effects on their offspring.

Recent reviews of most topics dealing with lead poisoning in childhood can be found in Pueschel, Linakis, and Anderson (1996). Information is also available from the National Lead Information Center (National Safety Council), 1019 19th St, Suite 401, Washington, DC, 20036–5105; 800-LEAD-FYI.

REFERENCES

Begley, S. (1992). Lead, lies and data tape. *Newsweek, 119*(11), 62.

Bellinger, D.C. (1995). Interpreting the literature on lead and child development: The neglected role of the "experimental system." *Neurotoxicology and Teratology, 17,* 201–212.

Berney, B.L. (1996). Epidemiology of childhood lead. In S. Pueschel, J. Linakis, & A. Anderson (Eds.), *Lead poisoning in childhood* (pp. 15–35). Baltimore: Brookes.

Dietrich, K.N. (1996). Low-level exposure during pregnancy and its consequences for fetal and child development. In S. Pueschel, J. Linakis, & A. Anderson (Eds.), *Lead poisoning in childhood* (pp. 117–139). Baltimore: Brookes.

Ernhart, C.B. (1995). Inconsistencies in the lead-effects literature exist and cannot be explained by "effect modification." *Neurotoxicology and Teratology, 17,* 227–234.

Ernhart, C.B., & Hebben, N. (1997). Intelligence and lead: The "known" is not known. *American Psychologist, 52,* 74.

Gillifan, S.C. (1965). Lead poisoning and the fall of Rome. *Journal of Occupational Medicine, 7,* 53–60.

Needleman, H. (Ed.). (1980). *Low-level lead exposure: The clinical implications of current research.* New York: Raven.

Needleman, H.L. (1995). Making models of real world events: The use and abuse of inference. *Neurotoxicology and Teratology, 17,* 241–242.

Needleman, H.L. (1998). Childhood lead poisoning: The promise and abandonment of primary prevention. *American Journal of Public, 88,* 1871–1878.

Pueschel, S.M., Linakis, J.G., & Anderson, A.C. (1996). Lead poisoning: A historical perspective. In S. Pueschel, J. Linakis, & A. Anderson (Eds.), *Lead poisoning in childhood* (pp. 1–13). Baltimore: Brookes.

Sibbison, J.B. (1992). USA: Legality of misconduct inquiry challenged. *Lancet, 339,* 1102.

Tong, S., & Baghurst, P. (1996). Lifetime exposure to environmental lead and children's intelligence at 11–13 years: The Port Pirie cohort study. *BMJ: British Medical Journal, 312,* 1569–1575.

See also **Brain Damage; Mental Retardation; Pica**

LEAGUE SCHOOL

The League School, now expanded and known as the League Center, was founded in 1953 by Dr. Carl Fenichel. It is a not-for-profit continuum of care serving multiply mentally handicapped children and adults at four facilities in Brooklyn, New York.

The League Center's continuum of services includes a school-based home training program serving parents of severely disturbed children 18 months to 4 years of age. Both the League School Nursery and the Joan Fenichel Therapeutic Nursery provide day treatment for groups of 2 to 4 year olds. The League School is attended by more than 100 students. Since communication disorders are prevalent and contribute significantly to the students' bizarre behavior, language skills are stressed in the school program. Students with little or no language are in classes staffed by both a language and a special educator; those with some developed communication skills receive language therapy and participate in small-group conversation clinics. There are special programs in physical education, travel training, print shop, crafts, and prevocational training. A six-week summer program extends social and life skills training into a wide range of recreational activities.

The Adult Day Treatment Center serves older adolescents and adults with the goal of developing sufficient self-control and socially acceptable behavior for living independently in the community. Fenichel House is a residence for adults who require continuing supervision in order to live and work in the community. This program is small and operates in a homelike setting.

In addition to providing diagnostic, educational, and treatment programs for hundreds of New Yorkers each year, the League Center serves as a model for special day schools and treatment centers throughout the world. It also serves as a training resource for students and professionals, as a research center, and as a valuable resource for public information, leadership, and advocacy on behalf of mentally handicapped and emotionally disturbed people of all ages.

LEARNED HELPLESSNESS

The term learned helplessness refers to a theory that has been broadly applied to the study of motivational and emotional problems in recent years. In essence, the theory maintains that the perception that one is helpless, or unable to control or affect significant events in one's life, leads to low self-esteem, undermines goal-oriented motivation, and produces a depressed emotional state. While the theory is now most often applied to human psychology, its historical roots lie in the animal conditioning laboratory. The work that eventually gave rise to learned helplessness theory was concerned with the impact of uncontrollable aversive stimulation on the conditioning process. The major finding to emerge from this research was that a wide variety of animal species can learn that reinforcements, such as the cessation of aversive stimulation, are uncontrollable or unaffected by any efforts that they might exert. In the typical experiment with dogs, it was shown that dogs given a chance to escape an electrical shock by jumping over a barrier would learn to jump the barrier rather quickly. On the other hand, dogs that were given unavoidable continuous shock in an earlier procedure acted quite differently. These conditioned dogs would jump around briefly, and then give up by lying down and quietly whimpering while shocking continued. They would not even search for an escape. Such learning experiences were found to have important consequences in regard to motivation, cognition, and emotion. Motivationally, experience with uncontrollable reinforcement was found to lead to a passive, non-goal-oriented state. Cognitively, uncontrollability was found to interfere with the subsequent capacity to learn to control reinforcements that were in fact contingent on the animal's behavior. Emotionally, uncon-

trollability led to a state that in some ways resembled human depression.

As the theory moved out of the animal laboratory, higher mental processes were accorded a greater role in the events that produce the helpless state. In particular, understanding why one could not control events, called the causal attribution process, became a focus of theoretical activity. More recent revisions of learned helplessness theory emphasized that it was not merely the lack of control of aversive effects, but one's biased understanding of why one lacks control, that determined passive, helpless-like behaviors (Abramson, Seligman, & Teasdale, 1978). Reactions to unsolvable problems can demonstrate "universal helplessness" or "personal helplessness." Universal helplessness reflects the belief that failure is objectively uncontrollable, due to external causes, and that anyone would fail at the task. Personal helplessness reflects the belief that a person lacks the internal ability and skill to solve the problem, but others have this skill and can find solutions. Thus, the attributed causes for failure may be stable over time, generalized over many areas of life, internal and personal, or external and environmental. While many patterns have been associated with this theory, recent research has focused on changing a person's perception of personal helplessness. For example, a student is taught that success and failure are due to malleable factors such as effort and persistence rather than internal, highly general, and stable factors such as intelligence, ability, and personality.

The theory of learned helpless has received considerable attention from researchers concerned with the nature of children's motivational problems in educational contexts and from persons interested in helplessness as it might relate to clinical depression in both adults and children. The research on motivation has shown that deficits in motivation can be a result of the onset of learned helplessness and that some children are more vulnerable to helplessness than others. The work of Carol Dweck (1986) and her colleagues has been extensive in applying learned helplessness theory to educational settings.

Teachers can affect what kinds of educational goals children seek out and how hard they try to master them. Dweck and others have shown that children can have an "incremental view of ability" or an "entity view of ability." With an incremental view of ability children believe that ability can be improved through effort and practice. An entity view of ability fosters the belief that ability is a highly stable trait that is not influenced much by effort or practice. In one compilation of studies (Mueller & Dweck, 1998) researchers praised fifth grade students for task performance according to entity attributions (intelligence, "You are smart") or incremental attributions (effort, "You worked hard"). Students adopted attributions and achievement strategies consistent with learned helplessness. The intelligence-praised children tended to do tasks for the performance goal of looking good. When they failed, they tended to quit trying and attributed their failure to a lack of intelligence. The effort-praised children sought to do problems as a learning challenge and continued to seek more problems even after they failed. They attributed their failures to a lack of effort rather than to a lack of ability. Indeed, other studies have consistently shown that praise for effort and praise for ability have differential effects on children even though the children have the same actual ability levels. One implication of this is that teachers should emphasize individual mastery and improving one's competency and not just high goals and grades. Learned-helplessness children who think their failures are due to internal, highly general, and stable factors will avoid achievement situations, will become emotionally distressed, and will show less persistence.

The implications of learned helplessness theory are well demonstrated in education but are also relevant to other settings. Parents are advised to adopt authoritative parenting styles that praise a child's successes but more importantly focus on the effort the child makes even if the child fails. Learned helplessness has also been applied to clinical studies of depression and other psychopathologies. Future research will expand the areas in which learned helplessness theory applies. Current studies are optimistic about altering motivational behavior by changing attributions about success and failure.

REFERENCES

Abramson, L.Y., Seligman, M.E.P., & Teasdale, J.D. (1978). Learned helplessness in humans: Critique and reformulation. *Journal of Abnormal Psychology, 87,* 49–74.

Dweck, C.S. (1986). Motivational processes affecting learning. *American Psychologist, 41,* 1040–1048.

Mueller, C.M., & Dweck, C.S. (1998). Praise for intelligence can undermine children's motivation and performance. *Journal of Personality and Social Psychology, 75,* 33–52.

See also **Anxiety Disorders; Attitudes Toward the Handicapped; Attributional Training; Depression; Stress**

LEARNER TAXONOMIES

A taxonomy is any organizational structure that classifies information for some specified purpose. The phrase learner taxonomy refers to the classification of individuals by individual characteristics presumed to represent dimensions of importance to the process of learning. Many learner taxonomies exist in special education; indeed, current learner classification structures (e.g., learning disabilities) represent initial attempts in this vein, though possibly not effective ones.

Several assumptions are implicit in the effort to develop useful learner taxonomies. Among them are the following. Individuals must be viewed as varying on a continuum of individual dimensions that are assumed to be essential to learning. If individuals did not present important individual differences, the need for learner taxonomies would not exist. A second assumption demands that salient individual differences, which are in fact hypothetical constructs, be measurable. Difficulty has traditionally arisen in the validity and reliability associated with such measures. Such difficulty must, in practice, be eliminated. A third prerequisite lies in the presumed capacity of the educator to operate on the elements of the taxonomy. That is, pragmatically, the learner taxonomy must alter the course of instruction in some measurably effective way. If the taxonomy is unable to direct the course of instruction effectively, its purpose, hence activity directed to it, is suspect. Other assumptions are implied; however, the preceding set the initial and important limits for the approach as it is used in education.

Currently, many taxonomies can be described as mostly associated with the cognitive domain; finite, in the sense that some very specific aspect is considered; and heuristic, in the sense that most are based on theoretical models that are as yet unverified. There are exceptions to some of these descriptors however. A widely used taxonomy developed by Krathwohl, Bloom, and Masia (1964) is associated with the affective domain. The taxonomy developed by Bloom et al. (1956) is concerned with a broad realm of cognitive behaviors and learning outcomes. Attempts to qualify children's performance through subscale analysis of tests such as the Wechsler Scales can, in one sense, be seen as an inductive process rather than the more typical deductive process of taxonomy development. That is, the latter represents an attempt to build a model from behaviors rather than predict behaviors from a model.

Despite considerable differences, virtually all learner taxonomies attempt to explain learning behavior and promote an individualized course for instruction. This may be seen in contrast to a behavioral model that emphasizes the relative similarities of the learning process. A task for the educator who accepts the concept of learner taxonomies and related concepts such as cognitive or learning styles is to select the most appropriate model. Comprehensive models generally do not exist and the models now available may offer conflicting recommendations. Because of this and other factors, the actual use of learner taxonomies remains more scarce than the intriguing possibilities the approaches seem to offer.

REFERENCES

Bloom, B.S., Endlehort, M.B., Furst, E.J., Hill, W.H., & Krathwohl, D.R. (1956). *Taxonomy of educational objectives. The classification of educational goals. Handbook I: Cognitive domain.* New York: Longman Green.

Krathwohl, D.R., Bloom, B.S., & Masia, B.B. (1964). *Taxonomy of educational objectives, Handbook II: Affective domain.* New York: McKay.

See also **Piaget, Jean; Systems of Classification**

LEARNING DISABILITIES

According to the definition most often used by state departments of education to guide appropriate services, specific learning disabilities afflict those children who have a disorder in one or more of the basic psychological processes involved in understanding or in using language, spoken or written, which disorder may manifest itself in imperfect ability to listen, think, speak, read, write, spell, or do mathematical calculations. Such disorders include conditions as perceptual handicaps, brain injury, minimal brain dysfunction, dyslexia, and developmental aphasia. Such term does not include children who have learning problems which are primarily the result of visual, hearing, or motor handicaps, of mental retardation, of emotional disturbance, or environmental, cultural or economic disadvantage (Federal Register, 1977).

A conceptualization by the National Joint Committee on Learning Disabilities stresses the heterogeneity, intrinsicness, and presumed neurological basis of this condition (McLoughlin & Netick, 1983). The Association for Children and Adults with Learning Disabilities adds that learning disabilities can continue into adulthood and can involve socialization skills (Association for Children and Adults with Learning Disabilities, 1985). Estimates of incidence range from conservative ones of 3 to 5% of the school-age population to as high as 10%.

Educational assessment is the systematic process of gathering educationally relevant information to make legal and instructional decisions about the provision of special services (McLoughlin & Lewis, 1986). The data are used to answer such questions as "What are the school learning problems?" "Are they related to having a specific learning disability?" "What are the student's needs?" The data are also used to establish a basis for developing an individualized education plan. The selection and use of appropriate assessment procedures are governed by the principles of IDEA and good practice. Specifically, the assessment is to be a team effort (with the student's parents) that is comprehensive in nature, nondiscriminatory to exceptional and other special groups, and subject to due process procedures. Individual standardized tests and informal procedures concerning intelligence and adaptive behavior, specific learning disabilities, classroom behavior, social-emotional development, reading, mathematics, oral and written language, and career-vocational needs may be used. The informal techniques include observations, work sample analyses, task analyses, informal teacher inventories, criterion-referenced tests, diagnostic teaching, checklists, rating scales, interviews, and questionnaires.

Of particular controversy in the assessment of this condition is the poor quality of procedures to establish the existence of a significant level of discrepancy between a learning-disabled person's ability and actual achievement. Early approaches to quantify this gap have been criticized, including the years-below-grade-level procedure and various expectancy formulas based on age, grade level, mental age, etc. (McLoughlin & Lewis, 1986). The use of standard scores and regression analyses have received considerable attention (Cone & Wilson, 1981; Reynolds, 1984). The procedure recommended by Reynolds (1984) is the most sound of these models despite being misunderstood by many in the

field (e.g., Cartwright, Cartwright, & Ward, 1995). Figure 1 shows the various types of scores that have been involved in the statistical analysis of severe discrepancies in learning. Additionally, the tests for visual, auditory, and other information processes are generally considered of questionable validity and reliability, making assessment in these critical areas difficult and reliant on informal techniques (Salvia & Ysseldyke, 1985). Thus, considerable emphasis is being placed on the measurement of cognitive and learning strategies. Other diagnosticians often participate in the assessment, including speech-language-hearing clinicians and counselors; however, full neurological examinations are rare.

School-age students with learning disabilities are served in a variety of ways. According to IDEA, they should receive their instruction as much as possible with their age-appropriate peers and not be isolated from them unnecessarily. The appropriateness of a placement is based on the needs of the student as judged by a team of professionals and parents. Most students spend some time in the regular classroom, and their teachers may be supported by a consulting teacher. Such placements are possible with well-designed cooperative learning activities (Smith, Johnson, & Johnson, 1982), peer tutoring, learning centers, behavior management programs (Demers, 1981), and other suitable modifications.

Generally, the students are directly instructed by an itinerant teacher on a regular basis or by a resident resource room teacher for part of each school day. More severely involved students (and perhaps those beginning their remedial programs) are placed in full-time special classes with some mainstreaming activities or in a special day or residential facility. The relative efficacy of one approach over another is unclear because of differences in teacher training, curriculum, instructional procedures, student assignment composition, and research design employed. The practice of assigning children with other diagnosed conditions (e.g., mild mental retardation or behavior disorders) to the same class is becoming more common and is based on the assumption that instructional objectives and methodologies are similar. Parent groups and others are not in full agreement about such modifications of strictly categorical services. Additionally, concern is being expressed over the loss of gains made once these supportive services are discontinued (Ito, 1980).

Families of persons with learning disabilities have a strong influence on them. The families in turn may experience stress as well as other feelings as they move closer to full acceptance of the learning-disabled person (McLoughlin, 1985). Parents are expected to participate fully in various aspects of the remedial program. The Association for Children and Adults with Learning Disabilities is a major parent-support organization. For professionals there are a variety of groups, including the National Council for Learning Disabilities and a division in the Council for Exceptional Children. Teachers are certified to instruct the learning-disabled student after appropriate training at a

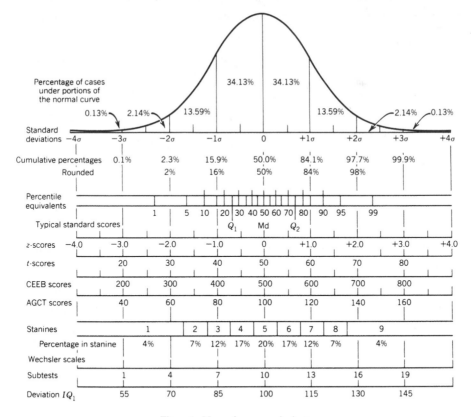

Figure 1. Normal curve equivalents.

recognized university; some states have additional teacher competency tests and internship requirements.

REFERENCES

Association for Children and Adults with Learning Disabilities. (1985). ACLD Vocational Committee Survey of LD Adults. *ACLD Newsbriefs, 145,* 20–23.

Cartwright, P., Cartwright, C., & Ward, M. (1995). *Educating special learners* (4th ed.). Boston: Wadsworth.

Cone, T.E., & Wilson, L.R. (1981). Quantifying a severe discrepancy: A critical review. *Learning Disability Quarterly, 4,* 359–371.

Demers, L.A. (1981). Effective mainstreaming for the learning disabled students with behavior problems. *Journal of Learning Disabilities, 14,* 179–189.

Federal Register. (1977, January 19) Washington, DC: U.S. Government Printing Office.

Ito, R.H. (1980). Long-term effects of resource room programs on learning disabled children's reading. *Journal of Learning Disabilities, 13,* 36–40.

McLoughlin, J.A. (1985). The families of children with disabilities. In W.H. Berdine & A.E. Blackhurst (Eds.), *An introduction to special education* (2nd ed.) (pp. 617–660). Boston: Little, Brown.

McLoughlin, J.A., & Lewis R.B. (1986). *Assessing special students* (2nd ed.). Columbus, OH: Merrill.

McLoughlin, J.A., & Netick, A. (1983). Defining learning disabilities: A new and cooperative direction. *Journal of Learning Disabilities, 16,* 21–23.

Reynolds, C.R. (1984). Critical measurement issues in learning disabilities. *Journal of Special Education, 18,* 451–426.

Salvia, J., & Ysseldyke, J.E. (1985). *Assessment in special and remedial education* (3rd ed.). Boston: Houghton Mifflin.

Smith, K., Johnson, D.W., & Johnson, R. (1982). Effects of cooperative and individualistic instruction on the achievement of handicapped, regular, and gifted students. *Journal of Social Psychology, 116,* 277–283.

See also **Allergies; Brain Damage; Direct Instruction; Feingold Diet; Individuals with Disabilities Education Act (IDEA); Learning Disabilities; Preschool Assessment; Severe Discrepancy Analysis**

LEARNING DISABILITIES AND CULTURALLY/ LINGUISTICALLY DIVERSE STUDENTS

See CULTURALLY/LINGUISTICALLY DIVERSE STUDENTS AND LEARNING DISABILITIES.

LEARNING DISABILITIES ASSOCIATION (LDA)

The Learning Disabilities Association (LDA), formerly the Association for Children and Adults with Learning Disabilities, was organized as a nonprofit association in 1964 by parents of children with learning disabilities. LDA is a national volunteer organization that includes individuals with learning disabilities, their families, and professionals. Its purpose is to advance the education and general welfare of children and adults of normal or potentially normal intelligence who have learning disabilities of a perceptual, conceptual, or coordinative nature. As its mission, the association seeks to enhance the quality of life for persons with learning disabilities and their families, to allay the limiting effects, and to support efforts to determine the causes through advocacy, research, service, and cooperative efforts.

Among its goals, LDA strives to educate individuals about the nature of learning disabilities and inform them of their rights. Additionally, regular and special education are improved through organizational advocacy with the U.S. Department of Education and state departments of education; LDA also promotes education and training in learning disabilities for teachers in regular and special education. Working directly with schools, LDA assists in the planning and implementation of programs to provide early identification and improved services for individuals with learning disabilities, and maintains extensive resources at its national headquarters to aid educators in dealing with all aspects of learning disabilities.

With membership of more than 50,000 in 600 local chapters in 50 states, Washington, D.C., and Puerto Rico, the Learning Disabilities Association is the largest nonprofit volunteer organization for persons with learning disabilities, advocating for over two million students of school age with learning disabilities as well as affected adults. LDA headquarters are located at 4156 Library Road, Pittsburgh, PA, 15204-1349 (LDA, 1996).

REFERENCE

Learning Disabilities Association. (1996, August 29). *About LDA.* http://www.ldanatl.org/lda/.

LEARNING DISABILITIES, PROBLEMS IN DEFINITION OF

There are five reasons why educators have difficulty with identifying children with specific learning disabilities. First, many people have equated learning disabilities with any kind of learning problem. This has tended to obscure the target population. Second, there is no single observable characteristic or syndrome of behaviors that is typical of a learning-disabled child because these children present a variety of diverse behavioral symptoms. Third, each child has his or her own unique learning pattern. The behavioral symptoms depend on the kind of disability, its severity, the child's intact abilities, and how the child tries to cope with the problem. Fourth, some of the behavioral symptoms of specific learning disabilities might also arise from visual or hearing impairments, mental retardation, emotional disturbances, social maladjustment, health problems, cultural

differences, family problems, or poor instruction. Fifth, when a child is multiply handicapped and has other problems in addition to a specific learning disability, the presence of the learning disability may be overlooked because attention is drawn to the more obvious problems in health, vision, hearing, etc. The more subtle learning disability sometimes remains undetected.

The recognition of specific learning disabilities as a type of handicap is relatively recent. The term became popular in 1963 when representatives of several parent organizations dealing with brain-injured and severely handicapped children met in Chicago to discuss their mutual problems and to establish a national organization. The concept and label were introduced to include a large group of children who did not fit other categories of handicapping conditions, but who did need help in acquiring school skills.

In the years since 1963, many people have tried to define learning disabilities, but no one has yet developed a definition that is acceptable to everyone. Professionals working with learning-disabled students tended to define learning disabilities from their own professional points of view. Different definitions, therefore, emphasized different aspects of learning disabilities such as neurological damage in the central nervous system, academic failure, visual perceptual disorders, language disorders, psychological process dysfunctions, behavioral symptoms, and impaired learning efficiency.

The creation of a federal definition of learning disabilities has helped reduce the number of terms and definitions in use, but this definition has serious limitations. The federal definition of learning disabilities included in IDEA reads:

The term "children with specific learning disabilities" means those children who have a disorder in one or more of the basic psychological processes involved in understanding or in using language, spoken or written, which disorder may manifest itself in imperfect ability to listen, think, speak, read, write, spell, or do mathematical calculations. Such disorders include such conditions as perceptual handicaps, brain injury, minimal brain dysfunction, dyslexia, and developmental aphasia. Such term does not include children who have learning problems which are primarily the result of visual, hearing, or motor handicaps, of mental retardation, of emotional disturbance, or of environmental, cultural, or economic disadvantage.

Forty-eight states and the District of Columbia define learning disabilities. Two states do not define the learning-disabled population to serve them through noncategorical programs. Most states and the District of Columbia use the federal definition verbatim. An analysis of the federal definition, the modified definitions, and the "original" definitions written by states revealed five major components that might be included in a definition of learning disability. These components are (1) failure to achieve; (2) psychological process; (3) exclusionary; (4) significant discrepancy; and (5) etiological (Chalfant & Pysh, 1984).

The exclusionary component refers to the handicapping conditions, other than learning disabilities, that cause problems in learning. These include mental retardation; visual impairment; hearing impairment; social-emotional problems; poor instruction; cultural or environmental factors; and physical problems.

The student's learning problem must be evaluated to determine whether the difficulty is due to a specific learning disability or to some other handicapping condition. To be eligible for special education services because of a learning disability, the student's primary problem must be a specific learning disability. It is necessary, therefore, to rule out or exclude all other factors that might cause a similar problem.

It is important to understand, however, that learning disabilities sometimes occur in combination with other problems. A visually impaired child, for example, might have difficulty in processing auditory or haptic information; and a hearing-impaired child might have difficulty in processing visual information. Children with multiple handicaps should receive multiple services because the extent and kinds of services needed may be quite different for each handicapping condition.

The specific criteria for the exclusionary impairments varies from state to state. Although guidelines are rather precise about the criteria for visual and hearing impairments, mental retardation, and motor and health impairments, criteria are not clearly delineated for slow learners, social and emotional maladjustment, and cultural, environmental, and economic factors. Variation from one state to another and imprecise criteria result in inappropriate inclusion or exclusion from services for the learning disabled and further confuse the defining of the population in question.

Although the etiology of learning disabilities is included in the definition of learning disabilities by 44 states, its role as a criterion for supporting the identification of a learning disability is minimal. Most state guidelines mention the need to review a student's developmental history and medical information as they relate to the student's daily functioning. Among the etiological factors frequently mentioned as being found among learning disabled students are:

A history of brain injury or neurological problems

Motor coordination problems

Slow speech and language development

Immature social and emotional development

Hyperactivity or hypoactivity

Frequent periods of illness or absenteeism from school

Surgery at an early age

Early symptoms such as infant or early childhood problems in feeding or sleeping, temper tantrums, frequent crying, prenatal or natal difficulties, low birth weight, or premature birth

Information or data concerning the physiological and medical status of a student is in the realm of the physician. However, educators can obtain important information through interviews with parents, reviews of developmental history, and identification of any information that might be a contributing factor to learning disabilities. Cooperation with the medical profession may link the student's classroom behavior to etiological factors that might contribute to a learning disability. This information may not help the teacher address the problems of the learning disabled, but it may help the multidisciplinary team in distinguishing which students are learning disabled (Chalfant & Pysh, 1984).

One characteristic of the student with a specific learning disability is a severe discrepancy between current achievement and intellectual potential. The finding of a discrepancy between achievement and potential alone, however, does not identify a learning-disabled student, since such a discrepancy also occurs among students whose underachievement is due to frequent absences from school; frequent family relocations; negative attitudes toward school; little motivation; family problems in the home; or instructional discontinuity of any kind. Students with such problems also need help. The basic needs of these students differ from the needs of learning-disabled students. These needs can often be met within the regular classroom or through regular education alternative programs within regular education.

Regression models are used to determine discrepancy between achievement and potential. They take into account the phenomenon of regression toward the mean. It is assumed that regression formulas reduce overidentification of children with IQs over 100, and underidentification of children with IQs below 100 (the opposite of the case for expectancy formulas). In addition, standard score procedures, emphasizing regression analysis, seem to be more statistically appropriate for quantifying severe discrepancies between aptitude and achievement.

Some of the major concerns about analysis follow:

1. "Regression is a precise sophisticated technique being used on tests that are gross measures of behavior" (Lerner, 1984).

2. Regression has an inherent weakness as a way to quantify discrepancy because the intelligence tests that are used have low reliability and fail to meet acceptable psychometric standards (Shepard, 1980; Salvia & Ysseldyke, 1981).

3. There are disagreements among knowledgeable statisticians and psychometrists about certain statistical derivations, concepts, and assumptions with respect to regression. It is not surprising, therefore, that many administrators, special education personnel, teachers, and parents do not understand, use, or interpret regression analysis procedures and results.

4. There is failure to account for the number of years a student has been in school.

5. Although the regression procedure makes no assumptions about the appropriateness of a given severity level, selection of an arbitrary severity level is an arbitrary decision.

6. There is lack of teacher preparation for the use of a formula.

7. There is difficulty in determining when special services should be discontinued.

Advocates for the use of regression would take issue with several of these concerns (e.g., see Reynolds, 1984). Regression is not seen as a precise, sophisticated technique, but as a quantitative reflection of what actually occurs in test data. Also, failure to account for the number of years a student has been in school should not be addressed in a formula; retention is a legitimate regular education intervention and students should not be held accountable for material to which they may not have been exposed.

The presence of a severe discrepancy between achievement and potential is not a sufficient condition for identifying a learning disability. Reynolds (1984) points out that a discrepancy yields only statistical information and must be based on more than one simple calculation by formula involving an IQ. The educational significance of any score must be considered independently of the discrepancy model.

The results of individually administered intelligence tests are analyzed to determine whether a student is learning disabled. An individually administered intelligence test samples many different aspects of verbal and non-verbal mental functioning and provides a measure of general ability. An analysis and grouping of subtest scores can give a clearer interpretation of intraindividual cognitive strengths and weaknesses and provide a measure of general ability.

Specialized abilities tests designed to assess psychological processes are often listed. These tests are in special areas such as language functioning; auditory discrimination; auditory processing; kinesthetic processing; visual processing; and visual-motor integration. Part of the problem with many tests of specialized abilities is that they are not related to a particular academic or school-related task (with the exception of listening tests, comprehension tests, and language tests), and therefore many educators do not know how to relate the results of many specialized tests to day-to-day tasks and behavior in the classroom. For young children, greater reliance should be placed on the developmental scales supported by observation of child behavior at home and at school. Anecdotal records and rating scales also are helpful.

REFERENCES

Chalfant, J.C., & Pysh, M.V. (1984). *Teacher assistance teams* (Workshop materials). Tucson, AZ: University of Arizona.

Lerner, J.W. (1984). *Learning disabilities: Theories, diagnosis, and teaching strategies* (4th ed.). Boston: Houghton Mifflin.

Reynolds, C.R. (1984). Critical measurement issues in learning disabilities. *Journal of Special Education, 18,* 451–476.

Salvia, J., & Ysseldyke, J.E. (1981). *Assessment in special and remedial education* (2nd ed.). Boston: Houghton Mifflin.

Shepard, L. (1980). An evaluation of the regression discrepancy method for identifying children with learning disabilities. *Journal of Special Education, 14,* 79–91.

See also Kirk, Samuel; Learning Disabilities; Regression (Statistical); Severe Discrepancy Analysis

LEARNING DISABILITIES, SEVERE DISCREPANCY ANALYSIS IN

For many years, the diagnosis and evaluation of learning disabilities have been the subjects of almost constant debate in the professional, scholarly, and lay literature, especially since the passage of PL 94-142. The lack of consensus regarding the definition of learning disabilities is reflected in the day-to-day implementation of PL 94-142 and its successor, IDEA; in the absence of a readily acceptable definition, many school districts experience difficulty in deciding who is eligible for services. Both under- and overidentification of learning-disabled (LD) children create significant problems. Undercounting deprives LD children of special services to which they are entitled; overcounting results in the inappropriate placement of students who are not handicapped, the loss of valuable staff time, and the increased expense of operating programs (Chalfant, 1984). Overcounting thus drains resources from other programs and students; if rampant enough, it could result in the demise of LD programs altogether. Errors in LD diagnosis will never be completely eliminated, but the amount of error must be reduced as much as possible while still ensuring that as many LD children as possible receive the special services to which they are entitled.

Two broad factors seem to determine who is LD: (1) the prevailing definition of LD and (2) how that definition is applied on a day-to-day basis. The rules and regulations of implementing PL 94-142 provided a definition of learning disability for use by all states receiving federal funds for special education programs, a definition retained in IDEA. According to this definition, the diagnosis

is made based on (1) whether a child does not achieve commensurate with his or her age and ability when provided with appropriate educational experience, and (2) whether the child has a severe discrepancy between achievement and intellectual ability in one or more of seven areas relating to communication skills and mathematical abilities.

These concepts are to be interpreted on a case by case basis by the qualified evaluation team members. The team must decide that the discrepancy is not primarily the result of (1) visual, hearing, or motor handicaps; (2) mental retardation; (3) emotional disturbance; or (4) environmental, cultural, or economic disadvantage (*Federal Register,* 1977, p. 655082).

While this definition gives states some guidance, generally the field has regarded it as vague, subjective, and resulting in diagnosis by exclusion in many cases. Operationalization of the federal definition has varied tremendously across states, resulting in great confusion and disagreement over who should be served. In fact, the probability of LD diagnosis varies by a factor of nearly five purely as a function of the child's state of residence.

Chalfant's (1984) review of state education agency (SEA) definitions across the United States identifies five major components that appear to be reasonably consistent across states. The first is failure to achieve, or, perhaps more aptly, school failure. This represents a lack of adequate levels of academic attainment in one of the principal areas of school learning. It is sometimes seen as relative to grade placement and sometimes as relative to intellectual potential for achievement. The second component, psychological process disorders, refers to disorders in one or more of the basic psychological processes that are believed to underlie school learning. Though never listed or defined in their entirety, such processes include attention and concentration, understanding and use of written and spoken language, conceptualization, and, in general, information processing of all types.

Exclusionary criteria require that the observed symptoms not be due to other factors such as sensory incapacity, mental retardation, emotional disturbance, or educational, economic, or related disadvantages. Etiology, probably the most ill-defined of all factors, typically reflects the need to evaluate a student's medical and developmental histories in order to locate factors believed to be causative of learning disability. These include history of brain injury or substantive neurological problems, motor coordination problems, hyperactivity, general immaturity, delayed speech and language development, and pre- or perinatal difficulties.

The last component, severe discrepancy, is specified in the federal regulations as a child's failure to achieve commensurate with age and ability to the extent that it results in a severe discrepancy between achievement and intellectual ability in one or more of the seven areas listed in the federal regulations. It is important to note that many states seem to ignore the "and ability" component of this definition, focusing only on the mean achievement level of all children of the same age, regardless of ability. Each of these criteria should have an important role in the diagnosis of learning disabilities and each requires work in terms of definitional and operational clarity.

Although all five components are important, the psychological process component and the severe discrepancy component are the most salient. The severe discrepancy criterion seems a particularly fruitful place to begin in the endeavor to improve methods of diagnosing learning disabilities. The severe discrepancy criterion is the most widely applied across the states. Further, in spite of the fact that severe discrepancy is easily measured relative to other components of the definition of LD, methods of applying the criterion vary widely across states (Reynolds, 1984).

The Federal Work Group on Critical Measurement Issues in Learning Disabilities has recommended a procedure to determine what constitutes a severe discrepancy (Reynolds, 1984); this model seems to be the one preferred by measurement experts (e.g., Willson & Reynolds, 1984).

OBJECTIVE DETERMINATION OF A SEVERE DISCREPANCY

Clinical judgment has a revered and appropriate place in all diagnostic decision making, even though it has been amply demonstrated that statistical or actuarial approaches are always as good as—and often better than—clinical judgment (Meehl, 1954; Wiggins, 1981). Nevertheless, people should hold the central role of decision making about people. Clinical judgment, however, must be guided by statistical criteria whenever possible. Most states require the demonstration of a severe discrepancy for diagnosis of LD. It is important to note, however, that determining a severe discrepancy does not constitute the diagnosis of a learning disability; it only establishes that the primary symptom of LD exists. A severe discrepancy is a necessary but insufficient condition for a diagnosis of LD.

Two conditions must be met in order to establish that a severe discrepancy exists between two test scores for a particular child. First, the simple difference between the two scores must be reliable enough to yield great confidence that the difference is real and not owed to errors of measurement. Second, the difference must be large enough to be considered unusual among non-LD children.

Formulas (such as those considered by the Bureau of Education for the Handicapped in early proposals for the federal regulations pertaining to learning disabilities diagnosis and placement) that in any way involve the use of grade or age equivalent scores can be quickly rejected as inadequate and misleading. The reasons for this are many; in short, age and grade equivalents do not possess adequate mathematical properties for use in discrepancy analysis (Angoff, 1971; Reynolds, 1981, 1984; Thorndike & Hagen, 1977). In essence, one cannot add, subtract, multiply, or divide age or grade equivalents. In addition, grade equivalents have other problems, including ease of misinterpretation, lack of relevance to curriculum markers (though they appear directly related), and general imprecision. Only standard scores have any real potential for answering the question of severe discrepancy. The following presentations deal only in terms of standardized or scaled scores, mostly of the age-corrected deviation score genre such as those employed by the current Wechsler scales, the Kaufman Assessment Battery for Children, and the Stanford-Binet Intelligence Scale—Fourth Edition.

RELIABILITY OF A DISCREPANCY

As noted, the difference between the scores on the aptitude and achievement measures should be large enough to indicate, with a high degree of confidence (i.e., $p < .05$) that the difference is not due to chance or to errors of measurement. This requires an inferential statistical test of the hypothesis that the aptitude and achievement scores for the child in question are the same. Payne and Jones (1957) first introduced such a test to interpret individual tests of intelligence. More complex methods of calculation involving the reliabilities of the respective scales and the correlation between the two measures have been proffered (Salvia & Ysseldyke,

1981), but the simple computational formula shown is the algebraic equivalent of the more complex formulas (Reynolds & Willson, 1984; Willson & Reynolds, 1984; Zimmerman & Williams, 1982). The test for the significance of the difference of two obtained scores $(X_i - Y_i)$ when the scores are expressed as z-scores is shown in equation 1:

$$z = \frac{X_i - Y_i}{\sqrt{2 - r_{xx} - r_{yy}}}. \tag{1}$$

There is no need to be intimidated by such equations; they are easy to calculate and require no more than beginning high-school algebra. In equation 1, X_i and Y_i represent the child's score on an aptitude measure X and achievement measure Y; r_{xx} and r_{yy} represent the respective internal consistency reliability estimates for the two scales. These reliability estimates should be based on the responses of the standardization sample of each test and should be age appropriate for the child being evaluated; these are most often reported in test manuals. The test statistic is a z-score that is referred to the normal curve. For a one-tailed test with $p = .05$, the critical value of $z = 1.65$. If $z > 1.65$, one can be sufficiently confident that the difference is not due to errors inherent in the two tests. Although a one-tailed test at the .05 level is probably justifiable for evaluating children referred for the possibility of a learning disability, a two-tailed test or a higher level of confidence (e.g., $p = .01$) would provide a more conservative measure of observed differences. For a two-tailed test, the critical value of z at $p = .05$ is 1.96. All other critical values can be determined from any table of values of the normal curve.

After reliability has been established, the frequency of occurrence of a difference score must be evaluated. In the following discussion it will become clear that any discrepancy meeting the recommended criteria for frequency will of necessity also have met the criteria of reliability.

FREQUENCY OF A DISCREPANCY

In evaluating the frequency of a discrepancy score, one must first decide what type of discrepancy score to assess (e.g., a residualized difference between predicted and obtained achievement scores, differences between estimated true scores and residualized true scores, true difference scores). In part, this decision depends on how one interprets the PL 94-142 definition of LD.

To establish that a discrepancy is severe, one must decide which of the following two questions to address:

1. Is there a severe discrepancy between this child's score on the achievement measure and the average achievement score of all other children with the same IQ as this child?

2. Is there a severe discrepancy between this child's measured achievement level and this child's measured level of intellectual functioning?

Both of these questions involve intraindividual variations in test performance (as opposed to purely interindividual norm-referenced comparisons). While this is obvious in the case of the second question, it may not be so evident for the first, which involves an intraindividual comparison because the determination of the average achievement level of all other children with the same IQ is based on the IQ obtained by the individual child in question. Though both are clearly intraindividual difference models, the mathematical models for answering these two questions differ considerably.

The former appears to be the most pressing question for evaluating children with learning problems and is the most consistent with the intent of IDEA because the aptitude or ability we want to define is the aptitude or ability in academic areas (Reynolds, 1984). Evaluating the second question is easier in terms of calculation; one can follow Kaufman's (1979) or Reynolds and Gutkin's (1981) recommended methodology for assessing verbal-performance IQ differences on the Wechsler scales. However, this is only the case when no directionality is implied, as in evaluating within test scatter. This is certainly not the case in the diagnosis of learning disabilities, where we are clearly interested in the case in which aptitude exceeds achievement. Thus such models as Linn's Regression Estimates of True Discrepancy Scores, most recently promulgated by the Kansas Institute for Research in Learning Disabilities, that do not account for the regression between aptitude and achievement will be faulty (see Reynolds, 1984, for a review of this model and its problems). An adequate evaluation of the second question, when directionality is known or assumed, is not yet known.

To assess the first question requires a regression model (i.e., a mathematical model that accounts for the imperfect relationship between IQ and achievement). Once regression effects have been assessed, the frequency of occurrence of the difference between the academic performance of the child in question and all other children having the same IQ can be determined. The correct model specifies that a severe discrepancy between aptitude (X) and achievement (Y) exists when, assuming the two tests are scaled to a common metric,

$$\hat{Y} - Y_i \geq SD_y \sqrt{1 - r_{xy}^2}, \tag{2}$$

where Y_i is the child's achievement score

X_i is the child's aptitude score

$\hat{Y}$ is the mean achievement score for all children with IQ = X_i

SD_y is the standard deviation of Y

z_a is the point on the normal curve corresponding to the relative frequency needed to denote "severity"

$r2_{xy}$ is the square of the correlation between the aptitude achievement measures

It is necessary to use $\hat{Y} - Y_i$ as the discrepancy score because IQ and achievement are not perfectly correlated. For example, if the IQ and achievement tests have the same mean and standard deviation $\bar{X} = 100$; $SD = 15$), and if they correlate at .60, then the average achievement score of all children with IQs of 80 is 88 and of all children with IQs of 120 is 112. Therein lies the need to compare the achievement of the child in question with the achievement of all other children with the same IQ. The term $SD_y 1 - r2_{xy}$ is the standard deviation of the distribution $\hat{Y} - Y_i$. Since this distribution is normal, we can estimate the frequency of occurrence of any given difference ($\hat{Y} - Y_i$) that corresponds to the point of "severity" on the normal curve. Next, one must establish a value for z_a, a controversial matter in itself (also see Reynolds, 1986a).

ESTABLISHING A VALUE FOR z_a IN DISCREPANCY MODELS

There are no strictly empirical criteria or research methods for establishing a value for z_a because we have no consensus on a definition of LD. Specifically, we do not have a definition that would allow the generation of a true and globally accepted estimate of the prevalence of the group of disorders subsumed under the term LD. To complicate this issue further, there is no consensus in the LD community regarding whether it is better to risk overidentification (in the hope that nearly all truly LD children will receive services) or to risk underidentification (in order to avoid identifying non-LD children as LD). Taking the second argument to its extreme, the proper procedure would be to identify no children as LD since the proportion of the population exhibiting this disorder is so small (see Schmidt, 1974). Consensus regarding the relative desirability of different diagnostic errors, coupled with valid estimates of prevalence, would provide considerable guidance in establishing a recommended value of z_a. In the absence of such guidance, one can rely only on rational, statistical, and traditional criteria.

It has been argued that a discrepancy should occur relatively infrequently in the normal population of individuals under consideration before being considered severe. Of course, "relatively infrequently" is as open to interpretation as "severe discrepancy." Strong tradition and rational argument in psychology, particularly in the field of mental retardation, argue for a definition of severity as two standard deviations from the mean of the distribution under consideration. With regard to a diagnosis of mental retardation, a score two standard deviations below the mean of an intelligence scale is defined as a severe intellectual problem, which is one of several criteria used for diagnosis. Qualitative descriptions such as mentally or cognitively deficient or lower extreme are common designations below this point in the distribution. At the opposite end of the curve, most definitions of intellectual giftedness refer to IQs falling two or more standard deviations above the mean, with descriptions such as very superior and upper extreme being common. Such practice is widely accepted.

In inferential statistics, confidence levels of .05 in an inference or judgment that a hypothesis can be rejected are the accepted standard. The .05 number corresponds roughly to two standard errors (for a two-tailed test) of the difference being evaluated, or to two standard deviations from the mean of the distribution of the test statistic employed (e.g., z, t, F). There is, thus, considerable precedent in the social as well as physical sciences for using a discrepancy of two standard deviations as a criterion for severity. For a .05 level of confidence, $z = 1.96$; this is close enough to the 2.00 value to support the use of 2.00. The actual 1.96 value is used principally to avoid more fractional alpha levels that may imply an unwarranted level of precision. Thus a value of $z_a = 2.00$ is recommended for determining whether a difference score is severe, though this value needs further qualification.

Since a difference score, whether defined as $\hat{Y} - Y_i$ or as some other value, will be less than perfectly reliable, one must somehow consider this unreliability in defining a severe discrepancy. If one considers underidentification a greater risk than overidentification, then there is a reasonable solution. Otherwise, as mentioned, one would minimize total errors by not identifying any children as LD. While several methods of accounting for potential unreliability in a discrepancy score are possible, the concept of the confidence interval is both popular and applicable. Adopting the traditional .05 confidence level for a one-tailed test, the value of z_a corrected for unreliability can be defined as $z_a - 1.65 SE$ (i.e., z_a minus the z corresponding to the one-tailed .05 confidence interval times the standard error of the relevant difference score). A one-tailed value is clearly appropriate here, since we must decide in advance which side to protect; both sides cannot be protected. Under these assumptions, a discrepancy is defined as severe when, substituting 2 for z_a

$$\hat{Y} - Y_i \geq \left(2 SD_y \sqrt{1 - r_{xy}^2} \right) - 1.65 SE_{\hat{Y} - Y_i}. \qquad (3)$$

The calculation of the standard error of $Y - Y_i$ is given in Reynolds (1984). Its use is clearly optional, although it does seem advisable to account for error in the process. It is important to note here that this is not the type of measurement error assessed by equation 1. This calculation allows us to identify more children than are likely to be true LD children; on the other hand, it accounts for many possible inaccuracies in the process that might inhibit identification of a truly LD child. The other four components of the most prevalent LD definitions, as previously presented, may then be evaluated to make the final judgment regarding whether or not a child is entitled to and needs services for the learning disabled.

The procedure outlined can objectify determination of a severe discrepancy in LD diagnosis. We may think that with regard to LD diagnosis we "know one when we see one," but if there is no "severe discrepancy," chances are we are wrong, and statistical guidance is necessary to aid human judgment.

The procedure outlined provides guidance for the objective determination of severe discrepancy. A computer program by Reynolds and Stowe (1985) will perform these analyses with all tests in use. It is crucial to bear in mind, however, that mathematical manipulations cannot transform the quality of the initial data.

QUALITY OF THE INPUT DATA

The quality of the input or test data used is crucial in assessing a discrepancy. Tests with poor psychometric characteristics can be misleading or can fail to detect a severe discrepancy. The following standards provide guidelines for choosing tests for use in the assessment of a potentially severe discrepancy. Though one will not always be able to choose tests meeting all of these standards, the more that can be met, the better. Of course, the characteristics of the examiner(s), that is, the person(s) gathering the data, are of equal or possibly even greater import.

Tests should meet all requirements stated for assessment devices in the rules and regulations for implementing IDEA. This is not only a requirement of law, but is consistent with good professional practice. For example, administering a test in accordance with the instructions provided by the test maker is prerequisite to interpretation of test scores. If a standardized test is not given explicitly according to the instructions provided, inestimable amounts of error are introduced and norm-referenced scores are no longer interpretable. Thus all personnel evaluating children with educational problems must be conversant with the requirements of IDEA and adhere closely to these standards.

Normative data should meet contemporary standards of practice and be provided for a sufficiently large, nationally stratified random sample of children. In practice, this standard is nearly impossible to meet in all respects. Yet it is important to approximate it as closely as possible because standardization samples are crucial to establishing levels of performance for comparison purposes. To know that an individual answers 60 out of 100 questions correctly on an achievement test and 75 out of 100 questions correctly on an intelligence test conveys very little information. On which test did this individual earn the better score? Without knowledge of how a specified referent group would perform on these tests, one cannot answer this question.

Raw scores on a test, such as the number of correct responses or percentage correct, take on meaning only when evaluated against the performance of a normative or reference group. Once the appropriate reference population has been defined, a random sample of this group is tested under as nearly identical procedures as possible with the same administration, scoring, timing rules, etc., for all. This group is known as the standardization sample. Ebel (1972) and Angoff (1971) have discussed a number of the conditions necessary for the appropriate development and use of normative reference group data.

Standardization samples for tests whose scores are being compared must be the same or highly comparable. Under the best of all conditions, the aptitude, achievement, or other tests on which children are being compared to themselves or to others should be conormed; i.e., their standardization samples should consist of precisely the same children. When this is not possible, the norms for each test should be based on comparable samplings of the same population that meet all of the requirements for normative data. Standardization of the scales should have been undertaken in the same general time period, or else equating studies should be done. Scales normed on different samples and at different times are likely not to have the same mean and standard deviation across samples even though they may be scaled to a common metric within their respective samples. This gives the two tests the appearance of actually having the same mean and the same standard deviation across samples even though they may be scaled to a common metric within their respective samples. This gives the two tests the appearance of actually having the same mean and the same standard deviation, even though this may not at all be true. Ample evidence demonstrates that general levels of performance on aptitude and achievement measures vary in the population across time. As just one example, the population mean level of performance on the 1949 WISC is now very close to 116 and the 1974 revision (the WISC-R) now has a mean of nearly 110, though both are scaled within their respective normative samples to a mean of 100. Use of an achievement test normed in 1984 and an intelligence test normed in 1970 would add approximately three or four points to the size of the intelligence-achievement score difference for children with achievement levels below their IQ, purely as an artifact of when the two tests were standardized. In the face of the paucity of conormed scales, using highly similar samples tested at a similar time (or with equating studies completed) is acceptable, but conorming will always be superior provided the sample meets the conditions of normative data mentioned previously.

For diagnostic purposes, individually administered tests should be used. For purely screening purposes (e.g., referral for comprehensive evaluation), group-administered tests may be appropriate, though for young children, individual screening is preferable (Reynolds & Clark, 1983). For all children, but especially for handicapped children, too many uncontrolled and unnoticed factors can affect test performance in an adverse manner. The test administrator is more likely to detect these factors under the conditions of individual assessment, where close observation of the child is possible. Further, individual assessment is more conducive to the use of special adaptations and testing procedures that may be required. Finally, individual assessment allows for careful clinical observation of the child during performance of a variety of academic and intellectual tasks; this is central to the proper assessment of learning problems for children of all ages (Kaufman, 1979; Reynolds & Clark, 1983). Generally, individual assessment affords better opportunity to maximize the child's performance and provides higher quality data from which to devise interventions.

In the measurement of aptitude, an individually administered test of general intellectual ability should be used. Such a test should sample a variety of intellectual skills; it should be a good measure of what psychologists refer to as "g," the general intellectual ability that permeates performance on all cognitive tasks. If ability tests are too specific, a single strength or weakness in the child's ability spectrum may inordinately influence the overall estimation of aptitude. It is also important to assess multiple abilities in deriving a remedial or instructional plan for a handicapped student and in preventing ethnic bias (Reynolds, 1982). Specific ability measures (e.g., Bender-Gestalt, Columbia Mental Maturity Scale, Peabody Picture Vocabulary Test-III) and memory tests (e.g., Test of Memory and Learning) constitute a necessary complement to a good assessment, but they are inadequate for estimating the general ability level of handicapped children.

Age-based standard scores should be used for all measures and all should be scaled to a common metric. The formulas for deriving severe discrepancies require the use of at least interval data. Scoring systems such as age or grade equivalents, which are essentially ordinal scales, should be avoided whenever score comparisons are to be made. Such scores may be helpful for purely descriptive purposes, but they are unacceptable for comparing scores of individuals or groups except under special, infrequent circumstances. Scores that are ratios of age and/or grade equivalents such as an intelligence quotient derived from the traditional formula of $(MA/CA) \times 100$, are also inappropriate. Grade-based standard scores are inappropriate as well. The criteria for LD given in IDEA specifically denote a discrepancy in achievement for age and ability. Age is properly considered in age-based standard scores. The scores should be age corrected at appropriate intervals. Two to six months are reasonable ranges of time in age groupings for the derivation of standard scores, but in no case should groups extend more than 6 months for children below age 6 years or more than 12 months for children above age 6 years.

Age and grade equivalents remain immensely popular despite their serious psychometric deficiencies and misleading nature. In most instances relevant to diagnosis, grade equivalents are abused because they are assumed to have scaled score properties when in fact they represent only an ordinal scale of measurement. Grade equivalents ignore the dispersion of scores about the mean when the dispersion is constantly changing from grade to grade. Under no circumstances do grade equivalents qualify as standard scores. The calculation of a grade equivalent is quite simple. When a test is administered to a group of children, the mean raw score is calculated at each grade level and this mean raw score then is called the grade equivalent score for a raw score of that magnitude. If the mean raw score for beginning fourth graders (grade 4.0) on a reading test is 37, then any person earning a score of 37 on the test is assigned a grade equivalent score of 4.0. If the mean raw score of fifth graders (grade 5.0) is 38, then a score of 38 would receive a grade equivalent score of 5.0. A raw score of 37 could represent a grade equivalent of 3.8, 38 could be 4.0, and 39 could be 5.0. Thus, differences will be inconsistent across grades with regard to magnitude of the difference in grade equivalents produced by constant changes in raw scores.

The measures employed should demonstrate a high level of reliability, which should be documented in the technical manual accompanying the test. The specific scores employed in the various discrepancy formulas should have associated internal consistency reliability estimates (where possible) of no less than .80 and preferably of .90 or higher. Coefficient alpha is the recommended procedure for estimating reliability, and should be routinely reported for each age level in the standardization sample of the test at not more than 1-year intervals. It is recognized that alpha will not be appropriate for all measures. Test authors and publishers should routinely use alpha where appropriate and provide other reliability estimates as may be appropriate to the nature of the test. When alpha is not reported, an explanation should be given. Internal consistency reliability (e.g., alpha) will almost always be the most appropriate reliability estimate for intelligence and achievement tests. Internal consistency estimates are the most appropriate of all reliability estimates for these tests because they best determine the accuracy of test scores (Nunnally, 1981).

The validity coefficient, r_{xy}, which represents the relationship between the measures of aptitude and achievement, should be based on an appropriate sample. This sample should consist of a large, stratified, random sample of normally functioning children. A large sample is necessary to reduce the sampling error in r_{xy} to an absolute minimum, since variations in r_{xy} will affect the calculation of a severe discrepancy and affect the difference score distribution the most at the extremes of the distribution, the area of greatest concern. Normally functioning children are preferred for the samples because the definition of severe discrepancy is based in part on the frequency of occurrence of the discrepancy in the normal population. When conorming of aptitude and achievement measures is conducted, this problem is simplified greatly since r_{xy} can be based on the standardization sample of the two measures (which should meet the standards of normative data) without any handicapped children included. Some states use validity coefficients based on estimates derived from research using handicapped children. This practice is not recommended because the IQ and achievement score distributions of handicapped children are not normal; thus they restrict the range of scores and alter the correlation between IQ and achievement, making it appear artificially smaller than it is in reality.

The validity of test score interpretations should be clearly established. Though clearly stated in the rules and regulations for IDEA, this requirement should receive special emphasis, particularly with regard to Cronbach's (1971) discussion of test validation. Validation with normal samples is insufficient for application to diagnosis of handicapping conditions; validity should be demonstrated for exceptional populations (for use of equations (2) and (3), however, r_{xy} should again be based on a normal sample). This requirement is an urgent one, especially in certain areas of achievement where a paucity of adequate scales exists. To determine deviations from normalcy, validation with normal samples should typically be regarded as sufficient. This requirement does not require separate normative data for each handicapping condition. The generalizability of norms and of validity data is in part a function of the question one seeks to answer with the test data and is ultimately an empirical question (Reynolds, 1986b; Reynolds, Gutkin, Elliot, & Witt, 1984).

Special technical considerations should be addressed when one uses performance-based measures of achievement (e.g., writing skill). Some measures, such as written expression, involve special problems of reliability and validity. For example, interrater reliability of scoring on any measure calling for judgments by the examiner should be reported and should be .85 to .90 or higher. This would also hold for such tasks as the Wechsler vocabulary and comprehension measures, in which examiners are frequently called on to make fine distinctions between the levels of quality of a response. Highly speeded and primarily memory-based tasks also will pose special technical problems that must be addressed.

Bias studies on the instruments in use should be reported. Criterion-related validity should receive emphasis in this regard, but not to the exclusion of other studies of bias. Bias should be addressed with respect to appropriate demographic variables that may moderate the test's validity. At a minimum, these should include race, sex, and socioeconomic status, though not necessarily simultaneously. In the assessment and diagnosis of LD in particular, sex bias needs to be investigated since boys outnumber girls in classes for the learning disabled by about 3.5 to 1. The procedures for evaluating bias in all aspects of a test are presented in a comprehensive form in Jensen (1980). While measures that exhibit little or no statistical bias are the measures of choice, other measures can be used with the appropriate corrections.

All of the noted points should be considered in the evaluation of test data used for determining a severe discrepancy. It bears repeating that the discrepancy formulas presented here yield results that are only as reliable as the test data used in them. Integrally related to the quality of test data are the characteristics of the examiner.

REFERENCES

Angoff, W.H. (1971). Scales, norms, and equivalent scores. In R.L. Thorndike (Ed.), *Educational measurement* (2nd ed.). Washington, DC: American Council on Education.

Chalfant, J.C. (1984). *Identifying learning disabled students: Guidelines for decision making.* Burlington, VT: Northeast Regional Resource Center.

Cronbach, L.J. (1971). Test validation. In R.L. Thorndike (Ed.), *Educational measurement* (2nd ed.). Washington, DC: American Council on Education.

Ebel, R. (1972). *Essentials of educational measurement.* Englewood Cliffs, NJ: Prentice-Hall.

Federal Register. (1977). Rules and regulations for implementing Public Law 94–142, 42. Washington, DC: U.S. Government Printing Office.

Jensen, A.R. (1980). *Bias in mental testing.* New York: Free Press.

Kaufman, A.S. (1979). *Intelligent testing with the WISC-R.* New York: Wiley-Interscience.

Meehl, P.E. (1954). *Clinical versus statistical prediction.* Minneapolis, MN: University of Minnesota Press.

Nunnally, J. (1981). *Psychometric theory* (2nd ed.). New York: McGraw-Hill.

Payne, R.W., & Jones, H.G. (1957). Statistics for the investigation of individual cases. *Journal of Clinical Psychology, 13,* 155–191.

Reynolds, C.R. (1981). The fallacy of "two years below grade level for age" as a diagnostic criterion for reading disorders. *Journal of School Psychology, 19,* 350–358.

Reynolds, C.R. (1982). The problem of bias in psychological assessment. In C.R. Reynolds & T.B. Gutkin (Eds.), *The handbook of school psychology.* New York: Wiley.

Reynolds, C.R. (1984). Critical measurement issues in learning disabilities. *Journal of Special Education, 18,* 451–476.

Reynolds, C.R. (1986a). Toward objective diagnosis of learning disabilities. *Special Services in the School, 5,* 161–176.

Reynolds, C.R. (1986b). Assessment of exceptional children. In R.T. Brown & C.R. Reynolds (Eds.), *Psychological perspectives on childhood exceptionality.* New York: Wiley-Interscience.

Reynolds, C.R., & Clark, J.H. (1983). Assessment of cognitive abilities. In K.D. Paget & B. Bracken (Eds.), *Psychological assessment of preschool children.* New York: Grune & Stratton.

Reynolds, C.R., & Gutkin, T.B. (1981). Test scatter on the WPPSI: Normative analyses on the standardization sample. *Journal of Learning Disabilities, 14,* 460–464.

Reynolds, C.R., Gutkin, T.B., Elliot, S.N., & Witt, J.C. (1984). *School psychology: Essentials of theory and practice.* New York: Wiley.

Reynolds, C.R., & Stowe, M. (1985). *Severe discrepancy analysis.* Philadelphia: TRAIN.

Reynolds, C.R., & Willson, V.L. (1984, April). *Another look at aptitude-achievement discrepancies in the evaluation of learning disabilities.* Paper presented at the annual meeting of the National Council on Measurement in Education, New Orleans.

Salvia, J., & Ysseldyke, J. (1981). *Assessment in special and remedial education* (2nd ed.). Boston: Houghton Mifflin.

Schmidt, F.L. (1974). Probability and utility assumptions underlying use of the Strong Vocational Interest Blank. *Journal of Applied Psychology, 4,* 456–464.

Thorndike, R.L., & Hagen, E. (1977). *Measurement and evaluation in education and psychology.* New York: Wiley.

Wiggins, J.S. (1981). Clinical and statistical prediction: Where are we and where do we go from here? *Clinical Psychology Review, 1,* 3–18.

Willson, V.L., & Reynolds, C.R. (1984). Another look at evaluating aptitude-achievement discrepancies in the diagnosis of learning disabilities. *Journal of Special Education, 18,* 477–487.

Zimmerman, D.W., & Williams, R.H. (1982). The relative error magnitude in three measures of change. *Psychometrika, 47,* 141–147.

***See also* Deviation IQ; Grade Equivalents; Intelligence Testing; Learning Disabilities;**

Learning Disabilities, Problems in Definition of;
Ratio IQ; Severe Discrepancy Analysis

LEARNING DISABILITIES AND JUVENILE DELINQUENCY

During the late 1960s and early 1970s, increasing attention and concern had been paid to the possibility of a causal link between learning disabilities and juvenile delinquency (Keiltz & Dunivant, 1986). In response to this concern, the National Institute for Juvenile Justice and Delinquency Prevention (NIJJDP), Office of Juvenile Justice and Delinquency Prevention (OJJDP), commissioned Charles Murray of the American Institute for Research to review empirical evidence of a causal relationship between learning disabilities and juvenile delinquency. After evaluating the empirical evidence, Murray (1976) concluded that while prior research clearly indicated that juvenile delinquents have learning problems, a causal relationship between learning disabilities and juvenile delinquency had not been established. His report recommended that carefully designed research be conducted to assess the effects of learning disabilities on juvenile delinquents and that the efficacy of diagnosing and treating delinquents with learning disabilities be studied.

The Foundation for Children with Learning Disabilities provides educational materials to courts and related agencies regarding the relationship between learning disabilities and juvenile delinquency, a relationship that remains controversial.

REFERENCES

Keiltz, I., & Dunivant, N. (1986). The relationship between learning disability and juvenile delinquency: Current state of knowledge. *Remedial & Special Education, 7,* 18–26.

Murray, C.A. (1976). *The link between learning disabilities and juvenile delinquency.* Washington, DC: U.S. Department of Justice.

See also Association for Children and Adults with Learning Disabilities; Foundation for Children with Learning Disabilities

LEARNING DISABILITIES MARKER VARIABLES PROJECT

Marker variables reflect the constructs that define and characterize a particular field and provide operational and conceptual organization to that field by allowing readers to assess comparability of research samples (Bell & Hertz, 1979). The purpose of the Marker Variable Project, conducted by Barbara Keogh at the University of California, Los Angeles (UCLA), was to develop and test a set of marker variables in the field of learning disabilities (Keogh, Major, Omori, Gandara, & Reid, 1980).

This UCLA Marker Variable Project sought to identify possible markers from empirical and conceptual perspectives by reviewing the learning disabilities literature to determine the descriptive variables actually used by researchers for defining and selecting subjects, and reviewing various definitions and theoretical orientations to determine which processes and/or abilities were viewed as primary components of learning disabilities. Based on this procedure, a set of marker variables was proposed and then modified by consultants at a series of conferences.

The resulting set of tentative marker variables was organized along three dimensions: (1) descriptive markers, not specific to learning disabilities research but representative of information reasonably expected in any study involving human subjects, including number of subjects, chronological age, grade level, month/year of study, geographic location, community type, race/ethnicity, source of subjects, socioeconomic status, language background, educational history, current educational status, health status, and exclusionary criteria; (2) substantive markers, particularly relevant to the study of learning-disabled children, including general ability, reading and math achievement, and behavioral and emotional adjustment; and (3) topical markers, relating to specific research areas within the learning disabilities field, including activity level, attention, auditory perception, fine motor coordination, gross motor coordination, memory, oral language, and visual perception (Keogh et al., 1980).

REFERENCES

Bell, R.Q., & Hertz, T.W. (1979). Toward more comparability and generalizability of development research. *Child Development, 47,* 6–13.

Keogh, B.K., Major, S.M., Omori, H., Gandara, P., & Reid, H.P. (1980). Proposed markers in learning disabilities research. *Journal of Abnormal Child Psychology, 8,* 21–31.

See also Learning Disabilities; Research in Special Education

LEARNING DISABILITY QUARTERLY

Learning Disability Quarterly is the official journal of the Council for Learning Disabilities. A publication generally similar to the *Journal of Learning Disabilities,* this journal is more accessible to the frontline educator and equally valuable to the academic. Special issues relating to specific topics are not uncommon. Among recent articles are "Social Skills Deficits in Learning Disabilities: The Psychiatric Comorbidity Hypothesis," and "The Impact of Positive Mood on Learning." The journal's goal is to enhance the education and development of people with learning disabilities.

The quarterly also seeks papers in categories such as (1) techniques in identification, assessment, remediation, and programming; (2) reviews of literature relating directly to people with learning disabilities; (3) theory and discussion of pertinent issues; (4) original research with an applied focus; and (5) practices in personnel preparation. *Learning Disability Quarterly* is a refereed journal with a circulation of 4,000.

LEARNING DISABILITY SUBTYPES

According to a survey of professionals in the field of learning disabilities (Adelman & Taylor, 1985), the search for subtypes of specific learning disabilities emerged in the 1980s as one of the most overriding concerns in the area of practice and related applied research.

Historically, the field has been dominated by single syndrome theories. These theories maintain that there is such a thing as the learning-disabled child (Fisk & Rourke, 1983) and construct appropriate univocal views of major characteristics, etiology, and interventions. Principal among these theories are neurological deficit theories, perceptual deficit theories, and language deficit theories. However, as early as the late 1960s multiple syndrome theories of learning disabilities began to appear in the literature; they have continued to grow in scope and importance. These theories have attempted to deal with the persistently troublesome problem of the heterogeneity of the learning-disabled population by searching for more homogeneous subgroups.

Investigators have used multivariate classification techniques to group subjects empirically (McKinney, 1984). Empirical subtyping studies have been done using a vast array of factors and across a variety of domains. Within the broader domain of learning disabilities, subtypes of reading, arithmetic, and spelling disability have been developed, as well as behavioral subtypes (Rourke, 1985).

Research on learning disability subtypes has shown the feasibility of identifying homogeneous subgroups of learning-disabled students. Developing an adequate taxonomy of learning disability subtypes parallels similar efforts in other areas of exceptionality.

REFERENCES

Adelman, H.S., & Taylor, L. (1985). The future of the LD field: A survey of fundamental concerns. *Journal of Learning Disabilities, 18*, 423–427.

Fisk, J.L., & Rourke, B.P. (1983). Neuropsychological subtyping of learning-disabled children: History, methods, implications. *Journal of Learning Disabilities, 16*, 529–531.

McKinney, J.D. (1984). The search for subtypes of specific learning disability. *Journal of Learning Disabilities, 17*, 43–50.

Rourke, B.P. (Ed.). (1985). Neuropsychology of learning disabilities: Essentials of subtype analysis. New York: Guilford.

See also **Learning Disabilities; Severe Discrepancy Analysis**

LEARNING-DISABLED COLLEGE STUDENTS

Since the 1970s learning-disabled students have become increasingly visible on American college campuses. More learning-disabled individuals are choosing the college option (Astin, Hemond, & Richardson, 1982) and increasing numbers are identifying themselves as learning disabled, both prior to and after admission to college. Concomitantly, a few colleges have developed comprehensive support services for their learning-disabled students (Cordoni, 1982). It was not until the 1980s that most colleges began to consider what might be appropriate accommodations and supports beyond those available for all students.

Most descriptions of learning-disabled college students have come from observation and clinical work with students attending support programs within colleges and universities (Barbaro, 1982; Cordoni, 1979; Vogel, 1982). While these descriptions focus on deficits rather than strengths, clearly it is the presence of substantial talent and fortitude that allows learning-disabled adults to succeed in higher education.

Characteristics of learning-disabled college students vary considerably. These students display a variety of different patterns of difficulty that may include one or more of the following: immaturities and disorganization of spoken or written language, perceptual-motor problems, study and time/space organizational difficulties, social discoordination, and weakness in basic reading, spelling, writing, or mathematical skills.

Underlying causes of these difficulties are presumed, though often not proven, to be of neurological or biochemical origin. They represent differences, tendencies, or deficits that may be either inherited or acquired. IQ levels vary as a function of each college program's view of the level needed to succeed, but none are reported to be less than 85 and many are well above average (Mangrum & Strichart, 1984).

The recent influx of greater numbers of identified learning-disabled students has just begun to affect the shape of college programs and policies. Some programs still do not address student needs. For example, the NCAA did not recognize exceptions for student-athletes with learning disabilities until the 1990s, and accommodating these individuals remains remarkably controversial among coaches and NCAA officials.

REFERENCES

Astin, A.W., Hemond, M.K., & Richardson, G.T. (1982). *The American freshman: National norms for fall 1982.* Los Angeles: University of California at Los Angeles, Higher Education Research Institute.

Barbaro, F. (1982). The learning disabled college student: Some considerations in setting objectives. *Journal of Learning Disabilities, 15*, 599–603.

Cordoni, B. (1979). Assisting dyslexic college students: An experimental program design at a university. *Bulletin of the Orton Society, 29*, 263–268.

Mangrum, C.T., & Strichart, S. (1984). *College and the learning disabled student: A guide to program selection, development, and implementation.* New York: Grune & Stratton.

Vogel, S. (1982). On developing LD college programs. *Journal of Learning Disabilities, 15*, 518–528.

See also **Adult Programs for the Disabled**

LEARNING POTENTIAL

Strategies for the assessment of learning potential have developed as alternatives to standardized norm-referenced assessment. With this method, the student is assessed, coached on assessment tasks, then reassessed. The posttest score is a measure of the student's potential for learning. The objectives of the method are to identify how performance is affected by prior learning experiences, what the processes are by which the student learns, how modifiable the processes are, and how to develop strategies to modify them. The ultimate goal is the prescription of intervention procedures to modify these processes to enhance the efficiency of learning (Haywood, Filler, Shifman, & Chatelanat, 1975).

Although the four most prominent approaches (Budoff, 1968; Feuerstein, 1970; Haywood et al., 1975; Vygotsky, 1978) differ in varying degrees in their theoretical bases and specific techniques, they all operate on the premise that a student's true cognitive ability may be different from what it appears to be from standardized measurement. Investigators view the approach as a way of linking assessment with intervention because the psychologist knows not only what and how much a student needs, but also what instructional strategies work to improve functioning. Although the approach may hold potential as an assessment alternative, research has failed to support its predictive validity, generalizability of training, and use with a variety of populations (e.g., see review by Glutting & McDermott, 1990).

REFERENCES

Budoff, M. (1968). Learning potential as a supplementary strategy to psychological diagnosis. In J. Hellmuth (Ed.), *Learning disorders* (Vol. 3). Seattle, WA: Special Child Publications.

Feuerstein, R. (1970). A dynamic approach to the causation, prevention, and alleviation of retarded performance. In H.C. Haywood (Ed.), *Social-cultural aspects of mental retardation.* New York: Appleton-Century-Crofts.

Glutting, J., & McDermott, P.A. (1990). Principles and problems in learning potential. In C.R. Reynolds & R.W. Kamphaus (Eds.), *Handbook of psychological and educational assessment of children, vol. I.* New York: Guilford.

Haywood, H.C., Filler, J.W., Shifman, M.A., & Chatelanat, G. (1975). Behavioral assessment in mental retardation. In P. McReynolds (Ed.), *Advances in psychological assessment* (Vol. 3). San Francisco: Jossey-Bass.

Vygotsky, L.S. (1978). *Mind in society: The development of higher psychological processes.* Cambridge, MA: Harvard University Press.

See also **Learning Potential Assessment Device; Vygotsky, L.S.; Zone of Proximal Development**

LEARNING POTENTIAL ASSESSMENT DEVICE

The Learning Potential Assessment Device (LPAD) is a direct teaching approach for the assessment of learning potential. The primary premise underlying the LPAD is that human beings are modifiable (Feuerstein, Feuerstein, & Gross, 1997). The LPAD is a dynamic or process approach

to assessment that rests on the idea that cognitive deficiencies result from faulty adult-child mediated learning experiences and that cognitive functioning is modifiable (Lidz, 1997). This approach is different than the goal of traditional assessment, which is to detect the "hard-wired" traits of the individuals (Feuerstein et al., 1997). Designed originally for use with low-functioning adolescents, its major purposes are to determine which of a student's cognitive operations are deficient, estimate the likelihood that the student can master those operations, and design and carry out a modifiable plan.

The LPAD is not standardized in the manner of conventional tests such as the WISC-III; rather, it involves an interactive process wherein the examiner develops and tests hypotheses about the student's cognitive structures. The LPAD tasks were constructed from a model that allows a test-mediate-test technique which requires the examiner not only to observe the individual's behavior, but also to intervene and assess the behavior again to know the outcome of the intervention (Feuerstein et al., 1997). It is not designed for classification or placement purposes since only informal age comparisons can be made. Thus, it is a supplement to, rather than a substitute for, other assessment measures. Because the LPAD is a complex assessment process, extensive training before administration is necessary, even for professionals who already have training and experience in individual psychoeducational assessment.

REFERENCES

Feuerstein, R., Feuerstein, R., & Gross, S. (1997). The Learning Potential Assessment Device. In D.P. Flanagan, J.L. Genshaft, & P.L. Harrison (Eds.), *Contemporary intellectual assessment: Theories, tests, and issues.* New York: Guilford.

Lidz, C.S. (1997). Dynamic assessment approaches. In D.P. Flanagan, J.L. Genshaft, & P.L. Harrison (Eds.), *Contemporary intellectual assessment: Theories, tests, and issues.* New York: Guilford.

See also **Remediation, Deficit-Centered Models of; Theory of Activity; Zone of Proximal Development**

LEARNING STRATEGIES

Learning strategies are strategies used by people to learn or remember things. Gagne (1970) categorizes eight different kinds of learning: signal; stimulus-response; chaining; verbal association; discrimination; concept; rule; and problem solving. For nonhandicapped students, the first four types are less important for school instruction than the last four. In special education, however, all levels of learning need to be considered by the teacher. Problems associated with learning of all types form the basis of special education programs for most handicapped learners.

REFERENCE

Gagne, N.E. (1970). *The conditions of learning* (2nd ed.). New York: Holt, Rinehart, & Winston.

See also Behavior Modeling; Imagery; Learning Styles; Mnemonics; Teaching Strategies

LEARNING STYLES

Learning styles can be defined, in their simplest forms, as ways that students' personal characteristics, including their needs and preferences, stylistically affect their learning. However, a variety of different definitional approaches have been taken.

A learning style has been defined by Bennett (1979) as being a "preferred way of learning. It represents a cluster of personality and mental characteristics that influence how a pupil perceives, remembers, thinks, and solves problems" (Holland, 1982, p. 8). According to Hunt (1974), learning styles represent accessibility characteristics, i.e., specific cognitive and motivational characteristics of the learner.

Learning styles actually represent subsets of cognitive styles. Indeed, inquiry into learning styles often encompasses study of traditional cognitive styles. Nevertheless, learning style constructs tend to be much more classroom and instruction oriented than traditional cognitive style constructs and usually are studied in and applied to instructional contexts. Another characteristic of learning styles that sets them apart from the broader category of cognitive styles is that they tend to be more oriented to environmental events. It may be said at the cost of simplification that cognitive style researchers emphasize the particular ways that individuals respond to and structure their environments, while learning style investigators are more interested in how the environment affects those individuals.

While cognitive styles are currently studied through a variety of paper and pencil methods, they originated in psychological laboratories and have a more rigorous research tradition and deeper data base support than learning styles. The latter are usually dependent on information obtained from behavior checklists, inventories, and questionnaires.

While learning style assessments reveal distinctions between students and their learning preferences, learning style variables may not account for enough learner variances to make them major springboards for educational intervention. Indeed, it is questionable as to how much learning environments can be adjusted to meet particular student needs. In special education, the individualized education plan, which does individualize instruction, conceivably could allow for more adjustment to learning styles than in regular education.

On the positive side, it is both easy and inexpensive to determine students' learning styles through a variety of paper and pencil and observational means. Insight into students' learning styles may provide useful instructional hints for teachers.

REFERENCES

Bennett, C.I. (1979). Individual differences and how teachers perceive them. *Social Studies, 70,* 56–61.

Holland, R.P. (1982). Learner characteristics and learner performance: Implications for instructional placement decision. *Journal of Special Education, 15,* 221–238.

See also Cognitive Styles; Dyspedagogia; Teacher Effectiveness

LEAST RESTRICTIVE ENVIRONMENT (LRE)

The term least restrictive environment (LRE) often has been used synonymously with the term mainstreaming. Although these two terms do refer to the placement of handicapped children, they are not necessarily synonymous. While PL 94-142 and IDEA specifically guarantee the right to an appropriate education in the least restrictive environment, there is no mention of the term mainstreaming.

There is tacit understanding among professional educators that LRE refers to the placement of a handicapped child in a learning situation that most clearly approximates that of a normal child. The ideal conceptualization would be in a regular class. LRE does not necessarily mean that a handicapped child can be placed with normal students for all educational programs.

Public Law 105–17 (the IDEA Amendments of 1997) instructs each local education agency (LEA) to ensure that to the maximum extent appropriate, children with disabilities, including children in public or private institutions, are educated with children who are not disabled. Special classes, separate schooling, or other removal of children with disabilities from the regular educational environment occurs only when the nature of severity of the disability of a child is such that education in regular classes with the use of supplementary aids and services cannot be achieved satisfactorily.

The assumption of the law is that consideration for placement for each student with disabilities will begin in the general education classroom.

See also Cascade Model of Special Education Services

LEFT-HANDEDNESS

Left-handedness, a characteristic of fewer than 10% of humans, is a condition that has generated a tremendous amount of superstition. Negative properties and values have come to be associated with the left, while positive traits are associated with the right. The majority of individuals prefer using their right hands and also are more skilled with their right hands (Corballis & Beale, 1983). Our language also expresses this distinction; for example, a left-handed compliment is an insult, but a right-hand man is a trusted friend. Throughout history the left has represented darkness, evil, demons, death, the Devil, movement, the unlimited, the many, the even, the curved, and the oblong. The left also has been associated traditionally with femaleness and weakness.

Today, there is no dispute that left-handedness is inherited, at least to a degree. An individual is more likely to be left-handed if one parent is left-handed, and more likely still if both parents are left-handed. However, transmission from one generation to the next is not perfect. Even if both parents are left-handed, there is only a 50% chance that an offspring also will be left-handed. Annett (1964) has devised a theory of handedness that explains this circumstance better than others. She suggests that most people inherit a right shift, or tendency to be right-handed, from two right-handed parents. Most will be right-handed, but a small portion may become left-handed owing to environmental influences or left-side brain damage. Right-handedness also is more marked for females than males since the latter are more susceptible to pathological influences at birth. Annett's alternative to the right shift is not a left shift, but rather a lack of the right shift. A minority of people inherit no genetic predisposition to be either left- or right-handed. Owing to various environmental or pathological influences, half will be left-handed and half will be right-handed, although a good many may be better classified as mixed-handed or ambidextrous.

Investigations have revealed a higher incidence of left-handedness in handicapped populations. Fein, Waterhouse, Lucci, Snyder, and Humes (1984) found 18% of a sample of school-age autistic children were left-handed. This figure is consistent with previous studies of autistic children, and is comparable to Satz's (1973) estimate of 83% right-handedness in retarded and epileptic populations. These findings represent an approximate doubling of the left-handedness consistently found in normal populations. Other studies have found markedly greater frequencies of immune disease, migraine, and learning disabilities among left-handers (Geschwind & Behan, 1982). While we can distinguish superstition from fact better than ever before, left-handedness continues to be an elusive phenomenon and a source of fascination and frustration. Results of research studies also may vary dramatically depending upon whether one defines handedness as either/or on a continuum (Dean & Reynolds, 1997).

REFERENCES

Annett, M. (1964). A model of the inheritance of handedness and cerebral dominance. *Nature, 204,* 59–60.

Corballis, M.C., & Beale, I.L. (1983). *The ambivalent mind.* Chicago: Nelson-Hall.

Dean, R.S., & Reynolds, C.R. (1997). Cognitive processing and self-report of lateral preference. *Neuropsychology Review, 7,* 127–142.

Fein, D., Waterhouse, L., Lucci, D., Snyder, D., & Humes, M. (1984, February). *Cognitive functions in left and right handed autistic children.* Presentation at the Annual Meeting of the International Neuropsychological Society, Houston, Texas.

Geschwind, N., & Behan, P. (1982). Left-handedness: Association with immune disease, migraine and developmental learning disorder. *Proceedings of the National Academy of Science, USA, 79,* 5097–5100.

Satz, P. (1973). Left-handedness and early brain insult: An explanation. *Neuropsychologia, 11,* 115–117.

See also **Cerebral Dominance; Handedness and Exceptionality**

LEGAL REGULATIONS OF SPECIAL EDUCATION

See SPECIAL EDUCATION, LEGAL REGULATION OF.

LEGG-CALVÉ-PERTHES DISEASE

Legg-Calvé-Perthes disease, or avascular necrosis of the femoral head, involves loss of blood supply to the proximal epiphysis of the femur. This serious condition has a peak incidence between 3 and 10 years of age, affects males four to five times more than females, and affects white children 10 times more frequently than black children (Wong, 1995). The etiology is unknown (Mayo Physician Group, 1997). A defining characteristic is the disturbance of circulation to the femoral epiphysis, thereby producing an ischemic necrosis of the femoral head (Ball & Bindler, 1999). When the blood supply is diverted, the femoral head in the hip joint dies and intense inflammation and irritation develops (Wong, 1995).

Legg-Calvé-Perthes disease is usually diagnosed when the child is brought to the pediatrician and/or orthopedic surgeon because of pain and limping. This pain may be caused by pathological fractures or by muscle spasms that accompany the hip irritation. Pain may also spread to other parts of the leg such as the groin, thigh, or inner knee (Herring, 1994). When the hip is moved, the pain grows more intense. Rest often relieves the discomfort.

The treatment regime has changed over the past decade and now encompasses several therapies to enhance the healing process (Wong, 1995; Nochimson, 1998; Ball & Bindler, 1999). The initial therapy is rest and non-weight bearing to restore motion and reduce inflammation. Traction is often used to relieve spasms, stretch out contractures, and restore hip motion. Weight bearing should be avoided on the affected limb, so the child is also contained in a non-weight bearing device such as an abduction brace, leg casts, or harness sling. Conservative therapies are usually continued for 2–4 years. Surgical correction may speed the recovery process and allow the child to return to normal activities in 3–4 months (Wong, 1995).

Children who develop Legg-Calvé-Perthes disease before the age of 6 tend to have a better prognosis and a faster recovery (Mayo Physician Group, 1997). The later the diagnosis, the more femoral damage has occurred before treatment is implemented and the poorer the overall prognosis (Wong, 1995). Special education services for the orthopedic handicaps are typically required.

REFERENCES

Ball, J., & Bindler, R. (1999). *Pediatric nursing: Caring for children* (2nd ed.). Stamford, CT: Appleton & Lange.

Herring, J. (1994). The treatment of Legg-Calvé-Perthes disease. *The Journal of Bone and Joint Surgery, 76*(A), 448–458.

Mayo Physician Group. (1997, February 3). Legg-Calvé-Perthes (LCP) condition. http://www.mayohealth.org/mayo/askphys/qa970201.htm

Nochimson, G. (1998, October 29). Legg-Calvé-Perthes disease. http://www.emedicine.com/emerg/topic294.htm

Wong, D. (1995). *Whaley & Wong's nursing care of infants and children* (5th ed.). St. Louis: Mosby-Year Book.

See also **Physical Disorders**

LEISURE-TIME ACTIVITIES

Leisure-time activities, or avocations, represent constructive use of leisure time in the pursuit of recreational activities. In addition to providing enjoyment, enhancing the development of skills, and the opportunity for meeting and interacting with individuals who share similar interests, leisure-time activities can help meet certain self-actualization and therapeutic needs.

In special education, leisure-time activities can provide an especially helpful means for ameliorating personal-social and academic handicaps imposed by the educationally limiting condition or conditions. The child receiving special education services, whether physically segregated from peers by special class placement or identified as being different owing to special educational problems, is at risk for developing a sense of isolation or inferiority. Counseling such a child to engage in leisure-time activities in which the educationally limiting conditions or handicaps will not be limiting may represent one approach toward ameliorating these kinds of problems. Leisure-time activities that provide the child with successful experiences can be especially helpful and can aid in the development of feelings of confidence and self-assurance that may not be facilitated in the academic sphere.

Caution may need to be used in encouraging the child with special educational problems to engage in leisure-time activities lest such activities exacerbate feelings of inability to perform. The caution necessary in such cases involves a consideration of how the child's academically limiting condition may relate to given leisure-time activities. The child with attention-deficit disorder, for example, may become frustrated by leisure-time activities such as chess or table games that require extended periods of concentration over time. Similarly, the child with visual perception difficulty may experience difficulty with some craft projects or jigsaw puzzles, but find satisfaction in word games or crossword puzzles. By focusing on the child's strengths, leisure-time activities can be a source of satisfaction and sense of accomplishment rather than a source of further frustration or sense of inadequacy (Hartlage & Telzrow, 1986).

Leisure-time activities can provide supplementary skills training in academically relevant pursuits. Especially for gifted individuals, leisure-time activities can provide the opportunity for enhancing and expanding areas of academic or career interest. Building electronic systems or doing mechanical repairs may be a source of expansion for a child gifted in and interested in physics or mechanics. It can provide an out-of-school opportunity for skill enhancement and development. Even for the exceptional child with academically limiting problems, the opportunity for developing skills in the nonthreatening context of leisure-time activities can have a positive transfer to school settings. For example, the counting in such table games as Monopoly, or the word building skills involved in Scrabble, can be encouraged as an enjoyable approach toward helping the exceptional child with counting or language difficulties.

Consideration of the child's interests, aptitudes, strengths, and weaknesses, matched with leisure-time activities either by formal matching procedures (Hartlage, 1968; Hartlage & Ells, 1983) or intuitively guided counseling, can help transform leisure-time activities into ones that can simultaneously be enjoyable, provide enhancement of existing strengths, and be a source of remediation for academic weakness and a measure of developing personal and social competence and confidence.

REFERENCES

Hartlage, L.C. (1968). *Computer Research Avocational Guidance Test.* Phoenix, AZ: Computer Research.

Hartlage, L.C., & Ells, A. (1983). *Leisure compatability guide.* Scottsdale, AZ: Afterwork.

Hartlage, L.C., & Telzrow, C.F. (1986). *Neuropsychological assessment and intervention with children.* Sarasota, FL: Professional Resource Exchange.

See also **Enrichment; Motivation**

LEITER INTERNATIONAL PERFORMANCE SCALE–REVISED (LEITER-R)

The Leiter-R is an individually-administered test designed to assess nonverbal intelligence in individuals from 2 years 0 months to 20 years 11 months. It includes measures of fluid reasoning (intelligence), visualization, memory (short and long term), and attention. This instrument was designed to assess the cognitive functions of individuals who cannot be reliably assessed with traditional intelligence measures, such as those with communication disorders, hearing loss, and learning disabilities. Though it is technically a revision of the original Leiter International Performance Scale (Leiter, 1979), this new revision was designed using the hierarchical *g*-factor of intelligence (Carroll, 1993; Horn & Cattell, 1966). The Leiter-R also was carefully standardized on groups of 1,719 individuals (Visualization and Reasoning battery) and 763 individuals (Attention and Memory battery) between ages 2–21. Numerous tests of reliability and validity also were performed to produce a potentially vital tool in nonverbal assessment.

The test includes a total of 20 subtests divided into two groupings: the Visualization and Reasoning battery, which measure the fluid reasoning, visualization, and spatial abilities; and the Attention and Memory battery, which measure attention and memory functioning. Composite scores can be obtained within each of the batteries, including a Brief IQ Screen, Full Scale IQ, Spatial Visualization, and Fluid Reasoning from the Visualization and Reasoning battery, and Memory Screen, Associative Memory, Memory Span, Attention, and Memory Processing scores from the Attention and Memory battery. Exploratory factor analyses yielded three separate age groups (2–5 years, 6–10 years and 11–20 years), with different groupings of subtests most accurately measuring the above abilities for each group. There are also four optional rating scales: an Examiner's Rating Scale, a Parent Rating Scale, a Self Rating Scale, and a Teacher Rating Scale. Normalized standard scores with a mean of 100 and a standard deviation of 15 were developed for each factor score and standard scores with a mean of 10 and a standard deviation of 3 were developed for each subtest. Growth scores based on item response theory (Rasch model) can also be calculated.

There are various options for assessment with the Leiter-R. The Visualization and Reasoning battery provides a Brief IQ Screener for an initial estimate of general intellectual functioning and can be done with a total of 4 subtests in approximately 25 to 35 minutes. The more reliable Full Scale IQ score can be done in 40 to 50 minutes using 6 subtests. The Attention and Memory Battery provides a Memory Process Screener (25 to 35 minutes) as well as a more in-depth assessment of the attention and memory functions. These tests are intended to contribute to the evaluation of learning disabilities, ADHD, and other neuropsychological disorders (Roid & Miller, 1997). A comprehensive assessment can be performed using all appropriate subtests for a given age group in approximately 2 to 2 and a half hours.

REFERENCES

Carroll, J.B. (1993). *Human cognitive abilities: A survey of factor-analytic studies.* New York: Cambridge University Press.

Horn, J.L., & Cattell, R.B. (1966). Refinement and test of the theory of fluid and crystallized intelligences. *Journal of Educational Psychology, 57* (5), 253–270.

Leiter, R.G. (1979). *Instruction manual for the Leiter International Performance Scale.* Wood Dale, IL: Stoelting.

Roid, G.H., & Miller, L.J. (1995, 1997). *Leiter International Performance Scale–Revised.* Wood Dale, IL: Stoelting.

See also **Assessment; Intelligence Testing**

LENZ MICROPHTHALMIA SYNDROME

See RARE DISEASES.

LENNOX-GAUSTAUT SYNDROME

See SEIZURE DISORDERS.

LEOPARD SYNDROME

See RARE DISEASES.

LESCH-NYHAN SYNDROME

Lesch-Nyhan Syndrome, a rare X-linked recessive disorder that occurs in an estimated 1 in 100,000 births (Holmes, 1992), is an inborn error of purine metabolism caused by absence of, or deficiency in, hypoxanthine-guanine phosphoribosyl transferase (HPRT). HPRT metabolizes hypoxanthine and guanine to uric acid (Anderson, Ernst, & Davis, 1992).

The disorder is characterized by behavior abnormalities, the most horrific and prevalent being aggressive, severe, and chronic self-injurious behaviors. Self-injurious behaviors (SIBs) are so persistent and potentially damaging that restraint is necessary. The onset of SIBs may occur as early as infancy or as late as teenage years. The most frequent SIBs are hand biting and lip chewing, which may lead to considerable tissue destruction and loss (e.g., Holmes, 1992). Since pain perception is normal, affected children scream during SIBs (Nyhan, 1973) and may actually beg to be physically restrained. Lip chewing can be so self-mutilating that tooth extraction is necessary. In a particularly severe case, continual self-inflicted oral ulcerations led to removal of all of a 17-month-old infant's teeth (Rashid & Yusuf, 1997). The earlier the onset of SIBs, the worse they become over time (Anderson & Ernst, 1994). Other features include choreoathetosis and spasticity (e.g., Holmes, 1992; Stout & Caskey, 1989). New research showing that cognitive impairment is minimal questions the belief that mental retardation is a regular feature of Lesch-Nyhan Syndrome. Patients have shown normal memory skills, range of emotions, concentration abilities, self-awareness, and social skills (Anderson et al., 1992).

The disease can be inherited or occur through genetic mutation. The expression of the gene is fully recessive, which makes this disease virtually exclusive to males by transmission from their mother. Females can be carriers but rarely ever exhibit the disease. A few recently reported cases in females are believed to have occurred through genetic mutation (Barabas, 1993).

Lesch-Nyhan patients appear normal at birth. The early signs of the disorder are seen when high levels of uric acid cause sand-like deposits in the infant's diaper. Affected infants show normal motor development usually until about six months of age when they begin to lose any previously acquired motor skills. Arching of the back and poor head control are often indicators, and patients are unable to sit or stand without assistance. Speech is greatly limited as well. Involuntary movements are typical as muscle tone increases with maturity. Frequently the disorder is differentiated from cerebral palsy only with onset of self-mutilation.

Treatment of this disorder has had only limited success. Allopurinol effectively reduces HPRT-based hyperuricemia and its various renal effects and gout, but has no effects on the neurologic abnormalities (Schroeder et al., 1990). Serotonin reuptake inhibitors have been used in attempts to correct dopamine and serotonin levels. This treatment has shown short-term improvements, but over time effectiveness significantly diminishes. Benzodiazepines are currently the most prescribed medication for behavior control, although no change in self-injury over time has been noted (Anderson & Ernst, 1994).

Behavior modification has also had limited effectiveness. The best preventative strategy has been stress reduction and protective restraint. Punishment for SIB has only resulted in an increase in the unwanted behavior. However, time-out tactics and reinforcement of non self-injurious behavior have decreased SIBs in certain settings (Luiselli, Matson, & Singh, 1992). Undesired behaviors particularly occur when a patient is not receiving direct attention, indicating that social and environmental factors must be considered in future behavior modification treatments.

REFERENCES

Anderson, L.T., & Ernst, M. (1994). Self-injury in Lesch-Nyhan disease. *Journal of Autism and Developmental Disorders, 24,* 67–81.

Anderson, L.T., Ernst, M., & Davis, S.V. (1992). Cognitive abilities of patients with Lesch-Nyhan disease. *Journal of Autism and Developmental Disorders, 22,* 189–203.

Barabas, G. (Ed.). (1993). Lesch-Nyhan syndrome. *Matheny Bulletin, 3*(2), 1–11.

Holmes, E.W. (1992). Other disorders of purine metabolism. In J.B. Wyngaarden, L.H. Smith, Jr., & J.C. Bennett (Eds.). *Cecil textbook of medicine* (19th ed.) (pp. 1115–1116). Philadelphia, PA: Saunders.

Luiselli, J.K., Matson, J.L., & Singh, N.N. (Eds.). (1992). *Self-injurious behavior.* New York: Springer-Verlag.

Nyhan, W.L. (1973). The Lesch-Nyhan syndrome. *Annual Review of Medicine, 24,* 41–60.

Rashid, N., & Yusuf, H. (1997). Oral self-mutilation by a 17-month-old child with Lesch-Nyhan syndrome. *International Journal of Pediatric Dentistry, 7*(2), 115–117.

See also **Genetic Counseling; Heredity**

LESIONS

The term lesion refers to "an alteration, structural or functional due to a disease" (*Blakiston's,* 1979). Lesions may be acute, subacute, and chronic; these terms are not disease specific. They relate to no specific disease, syndrome, or illness but are only adjectives that describe time of onset and appearance of symptoms.

See also **Brain Damage; Brain Disorders; Central Nervous System; Learning Disabilities**

LEUKEMIC CHILD

Leukemia is a cancer of the white blood cells. In leukemia, normal blood elements are replaced by undifferentiated, or immature, cells. These cells are termed blasts (Pendergrass, Chard, & Hartmann, 1985).

In chronic leukemia, there is a malignant proliferation of differentiated or mature cells. In both acute and chronic leukemia, these abnormal cells increase in number and accumulate in the victim's body. The spread can be very rapid if untreated. It will involve bone marrow, lymph nodes, kidney, liver, spleen, lungs, skin, and gonads.

Acute leukemic conditions predominate in children. Ninety-nine percent of leukemic children suffer from acute conditions, 1% from chronic ones. The most common acute leukemia is acute lymphoblastic leukemia (ALL) (Baehner, 1978), which accounts for almost 80% of all childhood leukemic conditions. Acute leukemias of other types are identifiable as acute nonlymphoblastic leukemias (ANLL; Pendergrass, Chard, & Hartmann, 1985).

The treatment of childhood leukemia traditionally has been one of drug therapy. Prednisone, a steroid, has been found to be the best single drug. It is often used with other drugs to optimize treatment. Sometimes bone marrow transplants also are used; they have been found effective even in late stage anemia. Hopeful expectations have been expressed regarding the use of bone marrow transplants with less advanced leukemic conditions.

The treatment of leukemic conditions has made major strides in recent years, with much longer survival times for leukemic children being reported (Hanson, McKay, & Miller, 1980). As a consequence, leukemia mortality rates are no longer clearly reflective of incidence and new means for establishing the latter have been developed. Data provided by the Third National Cancer Survey (Young & Miller, 1975) and by the Surveillance, Epidemiology, and End Results (SEER) Program of the National Cancer Institute (Silverberg, 1981) show a rise in the incidence for acute lymphoblastic leukemia beginning at approximately 2 years of age with a peaking during the 3- to 4-year age period. The distribution of acute nonlymphoblastic leukemias is fairly flat.

The long-term prognosis for childhood leukemia is still poor. Few individuals who have childhood leukemia survive into adulthood. There are indications that they have a higher risk of manifesting cancer as adults, though there is no clear evidence to indicate that they are susceptible to other diseases.

Of considerable significance to special educators is the fact that central nervous system leukemia has been found to develop in a large percentage of children who have childhood leukemia, even in those who are in states of complete hematologic remission. Research has indicated that this is partly due to the fact that the brain has a protective mechanism that decreases the amount of drugs allowed into brain tissue. The effects of the medications used to treat childhood leukemia thus may be vitiated in respect to their effect on the central nervous system. In attempts to circumvent this problem, medication may be injected directly into the spinal fluid. This procedure has been found to reduce significantly the incidence of central nervous system leukemia and to sustain significantly longer remissions from the disease (Glidewell & Holland, 1973; Pendergrass, Chard, & Hartmann, 1985).

The psychological impact on both the child and the family of those having childhood leukemia is of major proportions. The medical management of the condition is arduous and stressful for child, family, and therapists, and often physically painful for the child. The sequelae of treatment as well as the constant knowledge of the consequences of the diseases—learned early by most children—can be overwhelming. The chronicity of the condition and of its medical management and treatment places great stress on family psyches and finances. The leukemic child's social and academic performances can be expected to suffer. The fact that the child, even when surviving into adulthood, can be expected to have lifelong problems also takes its toll. Fortunately, the great strides forward that have been made in the disease's management encourage a positive outlook.

Children who have leukemia are entitled to special education under the provisions of IDEA. They are specifically identified as health impaired and entitled to special education under this law.

REFERENCES

Baehner, R.L. (1978). Hematologic malignancies: Leukemia and lymphoma. In C.H. Smith (Ed.), *Blood diseases of infancy and childhood* (4th ed.). St. Louis: Mosby.

Glidewell, O.J., & Holland, J.G. (1973). Clinical trials of the acute leukemia group B in acute lymphocytic leukemia in childhood. *Bibliotheca Haemetologica, 39*, 1053–1067.

Hanson, M.R., McKay, F.W., & Miller, R.W. (1980). Three-dimensional perspective of United States cancer mortality. *Lancet, 2*, 246–247.

Pendergrass, T.W., Chard, R.L., & Hartmann, J.R. (1985). Leukemia. In N. Hobbs & J.M. Perrin (Eds.), *Issues in the care of children with chronic illness.* San Francisco: Jossey-Bass.

Silverberg, E. (1981). Cancer statistics, 1981. *CA: A Cancer Journal for Clinicians, 31*, 13–28.

Young, J.L., & Miller, R.W. (1975). Incidence of malignant tumors in United States children. *Journal of Pediatrics, 86*, 254–258.

See also **Cancer, Childhood; Health Impairments**

LEXINGTON SCHOOL FOR THE DEAF

The Lexington School for the Deaf was established in New York City in 1867 to provide oral education for deaf children. There were already more than a dozen schools for deaf students in the United States at that time but all used some form of sign language. The Lexington School was a pioneer in oral education and has remained a strong proponent of speech, speech reading, and aural rehabilitation.

Lexington is a world-renowned leader in the education of deaf infants, children, and adolescents in all levels of educational programs. It offers special programs for multiply handicapped deaf students, including psychiatric and psychological services. Its staff has included such outstanding educators as Mildren Groht, author of *Natural Language for Deaf Children*, Edith Buell, author of *Outline of Language for Deaf Children*, speech teachers Mary New,

Eleanor Vorce, and Janet Head, and superintendents Clarence D. O'Connor and Leo Connor. The Lexington School for the Deaf is now located in Queens, New York.

LIABILITY OF TEACHERS IN SPECIAL EDUCATION

The concern for teacher effectiveness has focused considerable attention on what happens in the special education classroom. As such, teacher performance is monitored and teachers are held accountable for their actions in the classroom. A byproduct of this is a growing wave of legal action against teachers involving teacher liability.

Teacher liability is usually defined in court as involving negligence or lack of appropriate services for the exceptional student. The result is often a malpractice suit against the teacher (Brady & Dennis, 1984). Alexander (1980) and Brady and Dennis (1984) note that malpractice liability in education usually involves negligence, intentional interference or harm, or constitutional infringement. However, if a liability suit is brought against a teacher, it will likely focus on negligence.

Teacher negligence is affirmed if the court is shown that a teacher (1) owed a duty of care to the student, (2) did not carry out that duty, and (3) the lack of completion of that duty resulted in injury to the student (Brady & Dennis, 1984). To conduct appropriately their duties, it is commonly felt that teachers must provide proper instruction, supervision, and maintenance of equipment. If the lack of these duties results in substantial injury to a student, the teacher may be found liable (Alexander, 1980; Brady & Dennis, 1984; Connors, 1981).

Lack of proper instruction has been defined in many ways. As it pertains to teacher liability, violation of duty seems to be primarily a result of exposing students to physical risk during an instructional period. For example, student injuries in sports or laboratory settings may result in a liability suit. Thus far, the failure of a student to learn has not resulted in teacher liability (Brady & Dennis, 1984).

Connors (1981) notes that proper supervision is usually defined as general supervision; for example, a teacher is responsible for being present and overseeing the activities that take place. In so doing, a teacher must be aware of the situation and the inherent risks involved and take every possible step to see that the potential risks are eliminated. If teacher presence were enough to avoid injury, lack of teacher presence often would result in a finding of liability due to negligence.

Finally, teachers must ensure that equipment used in daily activities is not defective and is in proper working order. Cases have been tried in which defective playground equipment has been the cause of an accident (*District of Columbia v. Washington,* 1975). In one case a defective safety guard on a chain saw caused a student to be injured (*South Ripley v. Peters,* 1979).

To avoid liability cases, teachers should engage in sound educational practices, consider each child's individual needs, and document the activities that have been conducted.

REFERENCES

Alexander, K. (1980). *School law.* St. Paul, MN: West.

Brady, M.P., & Dennis, H.F. (1984). Integrating severely handicapped learners: Potential teacher liability in community based programs. *Remedial & Special Education, 5*(5), 29–36.

Connors, E.T. (1981). *Educational tort liability and malpractice.* Bloomington, IN: Phi Delta Kappa.

See also **Dyspedagogia**

LIBRARIES FOR THE BLIND AND PHYSICALLY HANDICAPPED

The National Library Service for the Blind and Physically Handicapped (of the Library of Congress) publishes books and magazines in Braille and in recorded form on disks and cassettes for readers who cannot hold, handle, or see well enough to read conventional print because of a visual or physical handicap. Persons diagnosed as having a reading disability of sufficient severity to prevent their reading printed matter in a normal manner are also eligible for loan services.

Through a nationwide network of over 160 cooperating libraries, the routine services of the National Library Service include book circulation, outreach, publicity, tape duplication, equipment assignment, publications distribution, reader's advisory, reference assistance, and production of local-interest material. Subscribers to the service receive free playback equipment and the bi-monthly *Talking Book Topics* or *Braille Book Review,* which list the latest books and magazines produced by the National Library Service.

In addition to the productions of the National Library Service, the American Foundation for the Blind, the American Printing House for the Blind, and Recording for the Blind also produce a wide variety of taped and recorded materials for disabled readers. While the National Library Service does not produce or distribute textbooks or curriculum materials, the American Printing House for the Blind and Recording for the Blind do.

The following equipment is loaned free of charge to eligible readers as long as Library of Congress materials are being borrowed: talking book machines (for hard and flexible discs), cassette-book machines, headphones, pillow speakers (for handicapped readers who are bedridden), amplifiers (for readers with a significant hearing disability), tone-arm clips (a device attached to talking-book machines for readers who have difficulty grasping the tone arm), and extension levers (for readers who have difficulty operating controls of the cassette-book machine).

LIBRIUM

Librium is the trade name for the generic minor tranquilizer chlordiazepoxide. It was the first benzodiazepine to be synthesized; it was marketed in 1960 (Bassuk & Schoonover, 1977). Librium is a less potent muscle relaxant than Valium, but it shares similar antianxiety properties with other benzodiazepines. Librium is recommended for short-term use to deal with psychic discomfort that accompanies unusual situational stress or crisis (Bassuk & Schoonover, 1977). As is the case with all psychotropic medications, such treatment is symptomatic and does not affect the cause of the discomfort. Additional interventions are necessary to assist the individual in crisis to reestablish equilibrium. There is no evidence to support the development of addiction to Librium; however, as with all tranquilizers, psychological dependence can develop (Blum, 1984).

As with all benzodiazepines, sensitivity or overdosage is characterized by drowsiness, fatigue, confusion, and dizziness. Geriatric patients and children are most likely to experience these adverse effects (McEvoy, 1984). A reversible dementia also has been reported among elderly patients after extended administration.

REFERENCES

Bassuk, E.L., & Schoonover, S.C. (1977). *The practitioner's guide to psychoactive drugs.* New York: Plenum Medical.

Blum, K. (1984). *Handbook of abusable drugs.* New York. Gardner.

McEvoy, G.K. (1984). *American hospital formulary service: Drug information, 84.* Bethesda, MD: American Society of Hospital Pharmacists.

See also **Tranquilizers**

LICENSING AND CERTIFICATION OF SCHOOLS, CENTERS, AND FACILITIES

The licensing or certification of schools is under the purview of state governments. The federal government maintains jurisdiction only over the disbursement of federal funds and over the separation of church and state. Many of these functions have been clarified through litigation. The Supreme Court in 1971 ruled that the relationship between the public schools and private parochial schools must not entangle the state in religious affairs. To determine whether a school is religious or sectarian, the court specified a three-fold test: whether the school has a secular purpose; whether the school advances or inhibits religion; and whether the school fosters excessive government entanglement with religion (*Lemon v. Kurtman*). The Supreme Court has also ruled that it is clearly within the rights of the states to regulate private schools. In *Purce v. Society of Sisters* (1925), the court ruled that

No question is raised concerning the power of the state reasonably to regulate all schools, to inspect, to supervise, and examine them, their teachers, and their pupils, to require that all children of proper age attend some school, that teachers shall be of good moral character and patriotic disposition, that certain studies plainly essential to good citizenship be taught, and that nothing inimical to the public welfare be manifestly taught.

In *State v. Williams* (1960), the court ruled that the "exercise of such power must not be arbitrary and must be limited to the preservation of public safety, public health, and morals."

As a result, each state has established rules, regulations, and supervisory procedures for private and parochial schools. These are established through statutes and state education directives and through the regulation of private nonprofit and for-profit business. Each state has its own rules for the physical facilities, health, and welfare of students, the curriculum, and instructional staff of non-public schools.

See also **Certification/Licensure Issues; Private Schools and Special Education**

LIFE EXPECTANCY AND THE HANDICAPPED

The life expectancy of handicapped individuals is increasing each decade. Research on treatment and etiology of infant disease, better nutrition, improved housing, advanced medical and surgical knowledge, and improved prenatal and neonatal child care practices have contributed to better prognoses for premature infants and to a decrease in the number of infant deaths.

Zill (1985) suggests that it is critical to seek new and better ways to enable handicapped individuals to become economically productive. He indicates it could cost up to $31,000 per year to maintain a handicapped individual in a state-run institution. Opinions regarding institutionalization have changed in recent years. Needed today is a range of services from hospital setting to full-time public school regular education classroom. Such services require a multidisciplinary team approach, including parents as well as medical, agency, and school personnel. A greater number of all types of trained personnel will be called for. Along with more special education teachers, a full range of ancillary personnel such as psychologists, physical, occupational, and speech therapists and a host of other medical and educational specialists will be needed.

Children who were regularly excluded from public education present problems that may require more and varied related services: assessment, transportation, appropriate technological and educational equipment, media and materials, special classroom aids such as adaptive equipment, communication and feeding devices, and wheelchairs. Vocational education for handicapped individuals must shift from traditional career training to a more intensive, creative K-12 approach to preparing for and matching manpower needs to individual abilities. There is also an increased demand for postsecondary school adjustment and greater assistance with the transition from school to work. There is a healthy new demand to attend to quality-of-life issues that will require that attention be given to quality programming and such things as leisure skill development.

REFERENCE

Zill, N. (1985, June). *How is the number of children with severe handicaps likely to change over time?* Testimony presented for the Subcommittee on Select Education of the Committee on Education and Labor, U.S. House of Representatives.

See also **Adult Handicapped; Chronic Illness in Children; Community Placement; Deinstitutionalization; Handicapping Conditions**

LIFE SPACE INTERVIEWING

The life space interview, a form of crisis intervention for emotionally disturbed youngsters, was formulated during the 1950s by Fritz Redl. The term life space refers to events occurring within the child's immediate environment at a specific point in time. Developed in a residential milieu, it is a technique intended for use by classroom teachers and support staff for addressing children's aggressive behavior.

Redl (1966) described the life space interview as a means by which an adult helps a child to mediate an emotionally charged experience. Following a behavioral crisis, the adult and the student engage in an in-depth discussion that focuses on the student's role in the event. The life space interview is viewed as strategically important to the child's therapeutic goals, and themes discussed during the interview may resurface in formal therapy sessions. As behaviorally oriented interventions have gained popularity in schools over the past decade, the life space interview, based in psychoanalytic theory, has gone into decline.

Addressing its infrequent use, Heuchert (1983) has recently written that the life space interview is a technique worth reviving. While acknowledging its psychodynamic heritage, Heuchert views the interview as a simple behavioral intervention that can be implemented in the classroom. The teacher knows the child, has observed the behavior, and is in a temporally close position to the event. As such, the teacher can isolate the child and prompt a retelling of the incident. The goal is to improve the child's understanding of the behavior and to develop a workable solution that will reduce future maladaptive behavior.

REFERENCES

Heuchert, C.M. (1983). Can teachers change behavior? Try interviews. *Academic Therapy, 18*(3), 321–328.

Redl, F. (1966). *When we deal with children.* New York: Free Press.

See also **Psychoanalysis; Redl, Fritz**

LIGHTNER WITMER AWARD

Division 16 (School Psychology) of the American Psychological Association presents an annual award in recognition of the production of significant scholarly works within the broad professional domain of school psychology. The award is named for the late Dr. Lightner Witmer, whose early work with school children is considered by many to have originated the field of school psychology. The award is given to young professional and academic school psychologists who have demonstrated scholarship that merits special recognition. Continuing scholarship, rather than completion of a dissertation alone, is the primary consideration in making the award. However, an individual does not need a doctoral degree to be eligible for the award. Nominees must be no older than 35 as of September 1 in the year in which the award is given. The Division of School Psychology gave the first award in 1973.

LIMITED ENGLISH PROFICIENCY AND SPECIAL EDUCATION

Children in need of programs supporting their acquisition of English are referred to by many acronyms: *NEP* (non-English proficient), *LEP* (Limited English proficient), and *PEP* (potentially English proficient). Their language needs are established by determining the language used in the home as well as directly assessing the language dominance and language proficiency of the student. A rating is generated upon the initial language evaluation which describes the nature of the student's language. These are called Lau ratings and are the direct result of the remedies established by the courts in the Lau vs. Nichols case to ensure that linguistically appropriate instruction is provided to all language minority children. *Lau A* refers to a student who is monolingual in a language other than English, *Lau B* indicates that the student is dominant in a language other than English but has some English language skills, *Lau C* refers to a student who is bilingual in English and the home language, *Lau D* describes a student who is dominant in English, and *Lau E* refers to a student who is monolingual in English. Students labeled Lau A and B are those in need of English as a Second Language (ESL) or other language support programs.

In providing services to children with disabilities who are not dominant in English, educators must first understand the differences in program options. Both bilingual and ESL programs promote the acquisition of English language skills. The difference lies in the language of instruction. Bilingual programs provide instruction in the native language (NL). They often have a strong ESL and transitional component which allows children to move smoothly from NL to English. ESL programs provide instruction exclusively in English (Ovando & Collier, 1985; Baca, 1998). The nature of ESL programs varies. Some are pull-out programs in which the student receives instruction from an hour a day to half a day. Some school systems have devised programs which provide instruction all day or half-a-day intensified instruction in programs called High-Intensity Language Training (HILT; Ovando & Collier, 1985). These programs are much more effective than pull-out programs in ensuring that the students acquire the English language skills they need. Content-area ESL programs are additional

programs that can be very effective for special education students in the upper grades since instruction focuses less on language and more on hands-on, motivating tasks in the content areas resulting in content-area-specific English language skills.

There are different approaches and methods of teaching ESL, and special educators should be aware of the type of program used in their school. Some programs are more amenable than others in instructing special education students. The *Direct Method* is an approach in which students are immersed in English-only instruction. This approach does not rely on drill exercises but rather focuses the learning of English around special topics and materials requiring open-ended spontaneous responses. Students learn about culture and language simultaneously through experiential props focused on real-life situations. The *Audiolingual Method* incorporates an approach in which drill and repetition are used to establish language patterns. Dialogue substitutions and the memorization of grammatical patterns are intended to teach the rules of the language. This approach has been highly criticized for its inability to establish a strong communicative competence. The *Cognitive Approach* facilitates the learning of English through small-group and individualized instruction. Language is viewed as developmental and errors are acceptable. In some cases NL may be used to establish meaning and understanding. The affective aspects of motivation and self-esteem are viewed as key in acquiring a second language. *Total Physical Response* (Asher, 1977) is perhaps most useful for individuals in the early stages of second language acquisition. It is the method that has most frequently been suggested for some special education populations. The students focus on listening comprehension and then learn English by following a command or demonstrating a certain action. The depth and level of English that can be learned using this method is limited. The *Natural Approach* (Terrell & Krashen, 1983) incorporates the use of language within a context that the student can understand and is relevant to his or her experience. Understanding is key in this approach, and the teacher facilitates meaning in whatever way necessary. "Comprehensible input" and the sensitivity to affective factors in the acquisition of a second language are central to this approach. Language is accepted and treated as a developmental process, and the acquisition of English is seen as being developmentally like the acquisition of the first language. This approach has been viewed by bilingual special educators as the most viable for creating communicative competence leading to the development of literacy skills of language minority students (Yates & Ortiz, 1998).

Teachers working with ESL students with disabilities can incorporate ESL techniques in their special education classrooms or work closely with their school ESL program. If students are pulled out or receive instruction in the school's ESL program, the special education teacher needs to work closely with the ESL teacher and become informed about the approach and philosophy of the program. Some programs are more conducive to meeting the needs of special education students, and some approaches are more "special education student friendly." Of special importance is the overlap of the English language skills the student is learning in ESL and the language needed by the student to function in the special education classroom. A careful evaluation of language taught, the transitioning of those skills from one setting to the next, and the generalization of those skills to other areas is critical. Collaboration by both the special education and ESL teacher is needed to ensure that language is not fragmented and that it focuses on functional use.

If teachers are incorporating ESL techniques, they need to determine the types of approaches and methods they will use based on student needs. Training in different techniques may be necessary. In addition, educators need to be aware of aspects of second language research impacting their decisions and teaching methods. Chamot (1981) in her application of second language acquisition research to the classroom, offers these suggestions:

The acquisition of a second language is similar to the first language; therefore, teachers should:

- Expect errors and consider them part of the natural developmental processes.
- Respond to what the child is intending to communicate rather than the specific language used.
- Ensure that children gain meaning by providing context and action-oriented activities.
- Teach in a way that children can gain practice listening and speaking when they are ready. Do not pressure children to speak before they are ready.
- Avoid any drills and repetitive patterns. Use songs, poetry, rhymes, stories, and activities of interest to the children in teaching language.

Social and affective factors influence the acquisition of a second language; therefore, teachers should:

- Foster a positive environment in the classroom, especially ensuring caring attitudes between children limited in their English speaking ability and native speakers of English.
- Have the children work in small groups or conduct paired activities to lessen the anxiety and develop an atmosphere of cooperation and communication.
- Group the children and provide opportunities for language-mixed groups (ESL and native speakers of English) to interact.
- Use a variety of methods and teaching styles so that all the learning styles of the children are reflected in your instruction.
- Foster an atmosphere of understanding and acceptance of the diverse cultures (especially those represented in the class).

The right type of input is essential in ensuring that students acquire the second language; therefore, teachers should:

- Use and model language that is meaningful, useful, and relevant to the students.
- Use language that is slightly above the students' level of functioning, but is understandable or can be made understandable.
- Expose children to different language varieties, formal and informal, standard and nonstandard, and different styles of communicating by bringing different people into the classroom.

Children must reach a level of language that is higher than basic communication skills; therefore, teachers should:

- Ensure that concepts and certain subject matter knowledge has been developed in their stronger language first, if at all possible. These skills will more easily transfer into the second language.
- Use the second language when students have the concepts clearly in place and are therefore ready to attach new labels/terms to those concepts in the second language.
- Ensure that the second language is used first in less linguistically demanding subjects such as music, PE, math, and science. More linguistically demanding subject matter can be added as students become more proficient.
- When children are literate in their first language, it becomes easier to move to the learning of literacy skills in the second language. If at all possible, teach children to learn to read and decode in their stronger language.
- Be aware that children demonstrating communicative competence or the ability to communicate socially may nonetheless not have the ability to meet the linguistic challenge of an academic environment.

In a review of second language learning research and through her own studies of over 200 children acquiring English as a second language, Wong-Fillmore (1991) indicates that learner and setting characteristics play a large role in the acquisition of second language skills. Learner characteristics such as sociability and communicative need, as well as contact with speakers of English and a setting which enables interaction, are key elements in the acquisition of English. These should be especially important in determining program placement and writing IEP goals and objectives for special education students in need of ESL support.

REFERENCES

Asher, J.J. (1977). *Learning another language through actions: The complete teacher's guide.* Los Gatos, CA: Sky Oaks.

Baca, L. (1998). Bilingualism and bilingual education. In L.M. Baca & H.T. Cervantes (Eds.), *The bilingual special education interface* (pp. 26–45). Columbus, OH: Merrill.

Chamot, A.U. (1981, September). Applications of second language acquisition research to the bilingual classroom. (Issue #8). *Focus national clearinghouse for bilingual education.* Washington, DC.

Ovando, C.J., & Collier, V.P. (1985). *Bilingual and ESL classrooms: Teaching in multicultural contexts.* San Francisco, CA: MacGraw-Hill.

Terrell, T.D., & Krashen, S.D. (1983). *The natural approach: Language acquisition in the classroom.* Oxford: Pergamon.

Wong-Fillmore, L.W. (1991). Second-language learning in children: A model of language learning in social context. In E. Bialystok (Ed.), *Language processing in bilingual children* (pp. 49–69). Cambridge: Cambridge University Press.

Yates, J.R., & Ortiz, A.A. (1998). Developing individualized education programs for exceptional language minority students. In L.M. Baca & H.T. Cervantes (Eds.), *The bilingual special education interface* (pp. 188–212). Columbus, OH: Merrill.

LINCOLN OSERETESKY TEST

See BRUININKS—OSERETESKY TEST OF MOTOR PROFICIENCY.

LINDAMOOD PHONEME SEQUENCING PROGRAM FOR READING, SPELLING AND SPEECH (LIPS)

The Lindamood Phoneme Sequencing Program for Reading, Spelling and Speech (LiPS; 1998) by Patricia C. and Phyllis D. Lindamood, is a multicomponent program designed to teach phonemic awareness skills and to facilitate the application of these skills to improve reading, spelling, and speech. The LiPS program is a revision of the Auditory Discrimination in Depth program (Lindamood, 1975), developed by Charles H. and Patricia C. Lindamood, published originally in 1969 and revised in 1975 by Teaching Systems and Resource Corporation, Teaching Resources Division. Pro-Ed, Inc. acquired the ADD program in 1994.

REFERENCES

Lindamood, C.H., & Lindamood, P.C. (1975). *The ADD Program: Auditory Discrimination in Depth.* Austin, TX: Pro-Ed.

Lindamood, P.C., & Lindamood, P.D. (1998). *The Lindamood Phoneme Sequencing Program for Reading, Spelling and Speech (LiPS).* Austin, TX: Pro-Ed.

LING METHOD

The Ling method is a systematic procedure for developing and remediating the speech of hearing-impaired children. The first book describing what has become known as the Ling method was written by Daniel Ling (1976). The method relies heavily, but not exclusively, on the optimal use of the hearing-impaired child's residual hearing. Teachers versed in the Ling method emphasize the sequential acquisition of speech skills, the use of acoustic cues, and the automatic coarticulation of sounds in syllables. The model consists of seven developmental stages on both the phonetic and phonologic levels of speech. The phonetic level is the child's capacity to produce the required sound patterns, while the phonologic level is the systematic and meaningful use of those sound patterns.

The initial steps of the Ling method are concerned with the prosodic elements of speech, which are often neglected (Cole & Paterson, 1984). Neglect of these elements results in monotonic, unnatural sounding speech. Prosodic elements in the Ling method include duration, intensity, and pitch.

Abraham and Stokes (1984) found that consistent and systematic practice with meaningful words, as advocated by the Ling method, can improve phoneme production by deaf students, and that speech drill at the syllable level, also advocated by Ling, appears to be a better way to achieve adequate levels of intelligibility for deaf pupils at the phonologic level of speech development. The Ling method is designed to be taught in several brief periods throughout the day rather than in one extended formal speech period.

REFERENCES

Abraham, S., & Stokes, R. (1984). An evaluation of methods used to teach speech to the hearing impaired using a simulation technique. *Volta Review, 86,* 325–335.

Cole, E., & Paterson, M. (1984). Assessment and treatment of phonologic disorders in the hearing impaired. In J.M. Costello (Ed.), *Speech disorders in children: Recent advances.* San Diego, CA: College Hill.

Ling, D. (1976). *Speech and the hearing-impaired child: Theory and practice.* Washington, DC: Alexander Graham Bell Association for the Deaf.

See also **Deaf; Deaf Education; Speech-Language Services**

LINGUISTIC DEVIANCE

The term linguistic deviance has acquired various meanings in the literature on communicative disorders. The most salient definitions include (1) a general sense in which deviance subsumes all types of linguistic disability (including delay); (2) a more restricted usage where the range of linguistic structures used is comparable to an earlier stage of normal language development, but the frequency of use of specific grammatical forms exceeds normal expectations; and (3) a significantly reduced sense, in which only specific types of structural abnormality are labeled deviant. The last definition of deviance is closest to the general sense of the term in linguistics and in the literature on communicative disorders. Deviance then would include only those utterances that would be both structurally inadmissible in the adult grammar and outside of the expected language development of normal children (Crystal, 1981). For example, if an adult monolingual speaker of English uttered "chicken a," it would be considered deviant on the basis that adult grammar would reject this construction and that this construction is not a regular feature of normal language development in children.

REFERENCE

Crystal, D. (1981). *Clinical linguistics.* Vienna: Springer-Verlag.

See also **Communication Disorders**

LINGUISTIC READERS

Linguistic readers, based on the philosophy that the goal of beginning reading instruction should be the automatic recognition of major spelling patterns of the English language, are intended to be used for beginning reading instruction. They have also been used with disadvantaged children who speak nonstandard English (Center for Field Research and School Services, 1970), bilingual children (Digneo & Shaya, 1968), and children with learning disabilities (Myers & Hammill, 1976).

Following the publication of *Why Johnny Can't Read* (Flesch, 1955), in which the linguistic approach to reading was offered as a solution to the national reading problem, Bloomfield and Barnhart (1961) and Fries (1963) developed the first linguistic readers. In these readers several means were used to achieve the goals set forth for linguistic reading programs. First, the vocabulary in beginning material is controlled through phonetic regularity, i.e., only one phonetic value is associated with each letter. For example, beginning materials containing words with *c*, as in *cot, cat*, and *cut*, would not contain words in which *c* has a different phonetic value, e.g., *cent*. Likewise, material containing words with *i*, as in *kit, zip*, and *dig*, would not include a word like *ride*.

Second, the introduction of spelling patterns is carefully sequenced. For example, in *Let's Read* by Bloomfield and Barnhart (1961), the first 36 lessons concentrate on spelling patterns containing a consonant letter plus a vowel letter plus a consonant letter. Patterns using the vowel *a* as in *cat, fat, hat*, and *cap, lap, map* are presented first. Next, patterns using the vowel *i* as in *bit, hit, sit*, and *fib, rib, bib* are introduced. These are followed by patterns for *u, e*, and *o*.

Third, spelling patterns are introduced within the context of whole words, e.g., the words *can, fan, man*, and *tan* exemplify a particular pattern. Students are guided by the teacher through a process that helps them to discover the pattern. Accompanying reading materials provide practice in applying the knowledge of spelling patterns to the pronunciation of new words and in reading words within the context of phrases and short sentences. Unlike phonics approaches, students are never directed to sound out words or to blend the sounds of individual letters into words.

Fourth, the material is designed to make minimal demands on the child in terms of reading comprehension. The vocabulary is simple. Students are not expected to learn new word meanings. Complex phrases and sentences are avoided. Fifth, oral reading is emphasized as a means of enabling the child to recognize spelling patterns. Finally, the use of pictures and context clues as aids to word recognition are discouraged.

REFERENCES

Bloomfield, L., & Barnhart, C.L. (1961). *Let's read: A linguistic approach.* Detroit: Wayne State University Press.

Center for Field Research and School Services. (1970). *An evaluation of improving the teaching of English as a second language in poverty area schools.* New York: School of Education, New York University. (ERIC Document Reproduction Service No. ED 058 363)

Digneo, E.H., & Shaya, T. (Eds.). (1968). *The Miami Linguistic Reading Program, 1965–1968.* Santa Fe, NM: New Mexico Western States Small Schools Project. (ERIC Document Reproduction Service No. ED 029 724)

Flesch, R. (1955). *Why Johnny can't read and what you can do about it.* New York: Harper & Brothers.

Fries, C.C. (1963). *Linguistics and reading.* New York: Holt, Rinehart, & Winston.

Myers, P.I., & Hammill, D.D. (1976). *Methods for learning disorders* (2nd ed.). New York: Wiley.

See also **Linguistic Deviance; Phonology**

LIPREADING/SPEECHREADING

Lipreading is commonly defined as the art of understanding a speaker's thought by watching his or her mouth. Lipreading, or speechreading, as it is more frequently called, is the use of the visual information available in speech to facilitate its comprehension. Speechreading is a difficult skill that not all hearing-impaired persons master. Even the best speechreader cannot see everything that is said, since only about 25% of all speech is visible on the lips. However, a good speechreader can often identify about 75% of a message because speechreading improves when words, phrases, and sentences are used in context (Bishop, 1979).

Training hearing-impaired students to use their residual hearing in conjunction with speechreading significantly improves their speechreading ability. Profoundly deaf individuals, however, are able to make little use of acoustic cues, and their speechreading performance remains essentially the same whether auditory cues are added or not (Sanders, 1982).

Speechreading is also included in total communication, which involves the simultaneous presentation of information through speech, speechreading, fingerspelling, signing, and other manual forms of communication. Currently, total communication is widely used in schools for deaf students throughout the United States. Recent research into speechreading has emphasized viseme grouping (a viseme is the smallest unit of visible speech); the effectiveness of the use of varying degrees of optical distortion in speechreading training; and the visual intelligibility of deaf speakers themselves (Kanter, 1985).

REFERENCES

Bishop, M. (1979). *Mainstreaming.* Washington, DC: Alexander Graham Bell Association for the Deaf.

Kanter, A. (1985, Summer). Aiming for the best. *N.T.I.D. Focus,* 12–13.

Sanders, D. (1982). *Aural rehabilitation.* Englewood Cliffs, NJ: Prentice-Hall.

See also **Total Communication**

LITERACY

Literacy is the condition or quality of being able to read and write. The term has been used in a narrow fashion (e.g., ability to sign one's name) and in some cases it has taken on much broader meaning (e.g., computer literacy or economic literacy).

LITHANE

Lithane (lithium carbonate) is used in the treatment of manic episodes of manic-depressive illness. Its use is not recommended for children under age 12. Adverse reactions may include fine hand tremor, especially during initial days of treatment. Overdose may result in drowsiness and lack of coordination at lower serum levels, with giddiness, ataxia, blurred vision, and ringing in the ears at higher levels. A brand name of Miles Pharmaceuticals, it is available as scored tablets containing 300 mg. Dosage is recommended in the range of 600 mg three times daily for treatment of acute mania, with approximately half this dosage recommended for long-term control of mania.

REFERENCE

Physicians' desk reference. (1984). (pp. 1368–1369). Oradell, NJ: Medical Economics.

See also **Drug Therapy**

LITHIUM

See LITHANE.

LITHONATE

See LITHANE.

LOCUS OF CONTROL

Locus of control generally refers to the mechanism through which individuals determine or do not determine their actions and behavioral controls. Historically, when behavior was felt to be determined by either person-related or environment-related variables and characteristics, two respective control mechanisms were identified: internal and external locus of control. Internal locus of control refers to an individual's ability to self-determine actions or behaviors through self-mediation (e.g., self-observation, self-cueing, self-encouragement, self-reinforcement, self-punishment) or specific personal characteristics (e.g., intelligence, persistence, wisdom). External locus of control occurs when an individual's actions or behaviors are actually or perceived to be under the control of external reinforcers or reinforcement schedules in the environment. With this individual, behavioral control is attributed to the environment (i.e., it is outside of the person's control) and to specific contingencies within the environment. Naturally, no individual is fully influenced by either internal or external control mechanisms; some feel, however, that one of these controls has dominance in each person.

See also **Cognitive Behavior Therapy; Depression; Learned Helplessness**

LOUIS-BAR SYNDROME

Louis-Bar syndrome, also known as ataxia telangiectasia (AT), is a rare, progressive, autosomal (non-sex-related chromosome) recessive genetic disorder. The hallmarks of AT are ataxia (lack of muscle control) and telangiectasia (tiny, red "spider" veins), which appear in the corners of the eyes or on the surface of the nose, ears, eyelids and inside of the elbows and knees soon after the onset of ataxia.

The earliest signs of Louis-Bar/AT include disturbances in balance, usually before the age of one year. The child's head and upper part of the body bend backwards or to one side while sitting or standing. Eventually the symptoms become so severe that by adolescence the child is confined to a wheelchair. The children also gradually develop tremors of the hands, fingers, and head. Speech becomes increasingly dysarthric (slowed) and slurred. Affected individuals also exhibit repetitive jerky eye movements and have difficulty moving their eyes from side to side without turning their head at the same time.

The great majority of affected individuals, 80% to 90%, also have immunodeficiency, which results in a susceptibility to chronic infections and recurring bacterial and viral infections of the sinuses and lungs (Haugsgjerd, 1999). Persons with Louis-Bar/AT have a strong tendency to develop lymphatic malignancies such as Hodgkin and non-Hodgkin lymphomas and acute lymphoblastic leukemia (Webster, 1999). Other features of the disease may include mild diabetes mellitus, premature graying of the hair, difficulty swallowing—which causes choking and/or drooling—and slowed growth. Children with AT initially exhibit normal intelligence and regress to the mildly mentally retarded range (Gandy, 1999). Physical development includes hypogonadism (underdevelopment of the genitalia) in males and hypoplasia of the ovaries.

Children are usually integrated in normal kindergartens or schools, but will show an increasingly complex pattern of many different disabilities and associated problems as they progress in school. Continuous adjustments to their educational program are needed as the disease progresses. Occupational and physical therapies may be helpful to maintain muscle strength and delay constriction of the limbs. Adapted physical education may also be appropriate to maintain physical activity at the child's level. As the magnitude of the motor problems intensifies and accompanying speech problems emerge, speech therapy may be helpful, as well as possible alternative communication methods such as sign language or communication boards. Children with poor vision may need corrective lenses, books with large print, magnifiers and/or computers.

Many affected children and their families will need prolonged psychological support. The prognosis of Louis-Bar/AT creates a situation of permanent crisis, as one crisis after another develops as the disease progresses. Dermatological abnormalities such as wrinkled skin, gray hair, or dilated blood vessels on the face, ears, and neck may evoke negative reactions from other children and adults. In 1985, the parents of children with AT established their own group in the Cerebral Palsy Association. For more information on the internet see: http://www. med.jhu.edu/ataxia/, or contact: The Johns Hopkins Hospital, Room CMSC 1102, Baltimore, Maryland, 21287; toll-free 800–610–5691; phone 410–614–1922.

REFERENCES

Gandy, A. (1999). *Pediatric database* (PEDBASE). http://www. icondata.com/health/pedbase/files/LAURENCE.HTM.

Haugsgjerd, H. (1999). *Rikshospitalet, The National Hospital University of Oslo.* http://www.rh.uio.no/rhdoks/rhindex.html.

Webster, R.E. (1999). Louis-Bar syndrome (ataxia telangiectasia). In L. Phelps (Ed.), *Health-related disorders in children and adolescents.* Washington, DC: American Psychological Association.

LOW BIRTH WEIGHT INFANTS

Low birth weight (LBW) is a term generally used to describe infants weighing less than 2500 grams at birth. Such infants may be born at term or preterm. Advances in neonatal medicine have improved survival of smaller and smaller infants to the point that further differentiation is needed to discuss populations of low birth weight infants.

LOW BIRTH WEIGHT INFANTS

Low birth weight (LBW) infants weigh between 1501–2500 grams. Infants may be low birth weight for many reasons, including preterm birth, genetic predisposition, or growth retardation. An infant may be growth retarded at any gestation, but in general this term is used for infants greater than 37 weeks gestational age at birth. This group of neonates is often said to be intrauterine growth retarded (IUGR), implying that they have failed to achieve their full growth potential. Causes of this growth failure can be categorized as fetal, maternal, placental, and environmental (Stevenson & Sunshine, 1997). Fetal factors include chromosomal and genetic abnormalities, congenital malformations, nonchromosomal syndromes, and intrauterine infections. Maternal factors are the most common cause of IUGR, with maternal nutrition as a major factor adversely impacting fetal growth. Maternal illness, low socioeconomic status, and labor-intensive occupations also contribute to low birth weight. Abnormalities of placental function such as decreased placental size, poor implantation, and decreased placental blood flow can cause poor fetal growth. Incidence of IUGR increases with multiple gestation and may be as high as 15% to 25% in twins. Incidence increases significantly with triplets and quadruplets. Environmental factors are often hard to separate from maternal factors. Medications and drugs may cause fetal malformation; alcohol and substance abuse are frequently seen in conjunction with poor nutritional status and infections. Cigarette smoking is believed to negatively impact fetal growth (Stevenson & Sunshine, 1997).

VERY LOW BIRTH WEIGHT

Very low birth weight (VLBW) infants are preterm infants weighing between 801–1500 grams (see Prematurity entry for causes and contributing factors for preterm birth). Approximately 42,000 VLBW infants are born each year in the United States. Survival rates are as high as 85%. Of survivors, 5% to 15% will have a form of spastic cerebral palsy and an additional 25% to 50% will display less handicapping but significant cognitive and school-related disorders (Graziani, 1996). Intracranial hemorrhage and periventricular leukomalicia continue to be of major concern in the development of neurological and developmental deficits. Although specific abnormalities are highly correlated to neurologic sequelae, the severity of the eventual handicap is difficult to predict.

EXTREMELY LOW BIRTH WEIGHT

In the last decade, the survival of extremely low birth weight (ELBW) infants, those weighing less than 800 grams at birth, has markedly increased. Survival rates are now reaching 40% for infants at 22 to 25 weeks gestation. These infants, referred to in the literature as "micropremies," are at extremely high risk for serious physical, neurological, and developmental complications. As would be expected, the shorter the gestation period at birth, the greater the number and severity of complications. In one study, 2% of infants born at 23 weeks gestation survived without severe complications, whereas 21% born at 24 weeks and 69% born at 25 weeks survived without severe neurological complications. Although only 10% to 20% of 23 to 25 week survivors have neurodevelopmental problems, almost 60% have some disability, including disorders of sensory integration and learning disabilities that significantly affect their school and psychosocial functioning. Close monitoring and assessment may lead to early identification and interventions that contribute to a more positive outcome for the child and the family (Goldson, 1996).

REFERENCES

Goldson, E. (1996). The micropremie: Infants with birthweights less than 800 grams. *Infants and Young Children, 8*(3), 1–10.

Graziani, L.J. (1996). Intracranial hemorrhage and leukomalacia in preterm infants. In A.R. Spitzer (Ed.), *Intensive care of the fetus and neonate* (pp. 696–703). St. Louis: Mosby.

Stevenson, D.K., & Sunshine, P. (Eds.). (1997). *Fetal and neonatal brain injury: Mechanisms, management, and the risks of practice* (2nd ed.). Oxford, UK: Oxford University Press.

See also **Congenital Disorders; Prematurity**

LOWE SYNDROME

Lowe Syndrome (LS) is an X-linked recessive disorder of unknown etiology which primarily affects males. It is also called the Oculo-Cerebro-Renal syndrome of Lowe (OCRL), reflecting the three major organ systems involved in the disorder (eyes, brain, and kidney). A rare genetic condition that causes physical and mental handicaps and medical problems, Lowe Syndrome was first described in 1952 by Dr. Charles Lowe, Dr. Terrey, and Dr. MacLachlan. Prevalence estimates vary between 200–2,000 cases in the United States. Lowe Syndrome has been reported in 15 females, with only 5 meeting strict diagnostic criteria (Charnas & Gahl, 1991).

The most prominent ocular symptom is congenital cataracts, and this system is mandatory for diagnosis (Lopata, 1999). Associated features include glaucoma, nystagmus (involuntary, rapid, and rhythmic eye movements), corneal keloid (an elevated, irregularly-shaped, progressively enlarging scar), and strabismus (eyes that do not track or focus together). Neurological manifestations involve both the central and peripheral nervous systems (Charnas & Gahl, 1991). These symptoms include hypotonia (less-than-normal muscle tone) and areflexia (reduced or absent deep tendon reflexes) which contribute to a tendency to develop bone fractures, scoliosis, and joint problems. Affected individuals also exhibit borderline to severe mental retardation. Seizures occur in approximately half of the cases of LS/OCRL (Charnas & Nussbaum, 1995). Renal (kidney) manifestations, also characteristic of LS, are usually seen within the first year of life. Renal Fanconi Syndrome, a group of diseases caused by the dysfunction of the renal tubules, can result in episodes of vomiting, dehydration, weakness, and unexplained fever. Affected individuals with LS/OCRL often succumb to complications resulting from slow, progressive renal failure. With aggressive medical care, most of these difficulties can be avoided and life expectancy typically extends into the 20s and 30s, while some have lived into their 40s. In 1992, the gene that causes LS was found on the Xq24–26 region of the X chromosome.

Behavioral problems are also frequently evident with LS-affected individuals, including inattentiveness, unusual obsessions or preoccupations, self-abuse, self-injury, episodic outbursts, aggression, irritability, and repetitive, non-purposeful movements. Some parents of LS/OCRL children report that behavior difficulties often appear by age 5, worsen by age 8, and in two-thirds of the cases improve by age 14 (Lowe Syndrome Association, 1997).

There is no cure for Lowe Syndrome/OCRL, but many of the symptoms can be treated through medication; surgery; speech, physical, and occupational therapies; and special education, often begun prior to entering school. Affected children are often provided special education services in school through the classifications of mental retardation, other health impaired, or multiply disabled. Maintenance of metabolic balance is vital and can be assisted by monitoring the physical health and activity of the child. General nutrition is also required to sustain optimal levels of critical substances. Affected children should have constant access to water in order to prevent dehydration (Charnas & Nussbaum, 1995). Behavior modification may be helpful to address behavior problems. Families of LS-affected children may need psychological support to assist with the emotional demands of caring for a child with a debilitating disease. For further information contact the Lowe Syndrome Association, 222 Lincoln Street, West Lafayette, IN, 47906 or call (765) 743–3634. The organization's email address is lsa@medhelp.org.

REFERENCES

Charnas, L.R., & Gahl, W.A. (1991). The oculocerebrorenal syndrome of Lowe. *Advances in pediatrics, 38,* 75–107.

Charnas, L.R., & Nussbaum, R.L. (1995). The oculocerebrorenal syndrome of Lowe (Lowe syndrome). In C.R. Scriver, A.L. Beaudet, W.S. Sly, & D. Valle (Eds.), *The metabolic and molecular bases of inherited disease* (7th ed.) (pp. 3705–3716). New York: McGraw-Hill.

Lopata, C. (1999). Lowe syndrome. In L. Phelps (Ed.), *Health-related disorders in children and adolescents.* Washington, DC: American Psychological Association.

Lowe Syndrome Association. (1997). *Living with Lowe syndrome: A guide for families, friends, and professionals.* http://www.medhelp.org/ lowesyndrome/.

LOWENFELD, BERTHOLD (1901–1994)

A native of Austria, Berthold Lowenfeld began his career as a teacher of blind children in 1922. He earned his PhD in child psychology from the University of Vienna in 1927. He studied child psychology and the education of the blind in the United States in 1930–1931 as a Rockefeller research fellow. After the Nazi invasion of his homeland in 1938, he emigrated to the United States to become director of educational research for the American Foundation for the Blind in New York City. He also lectured at Columbia University and made an extensive survey for the Canadian National Institute for the Blind of all Canadian schools for the blind.

In 1949, he accepted the position of superintendent of the California School for the Blind, where he remained until 1964. From that time until his death at 93, he engaged in research and writing under the sponsorship of the U.S. Office of Education, the California State Department of Education, and the Social and Rehabilitation Service of the Department of Health and Human Services.

Among the honors Lowenfeld received were the 1965 Ambrose Shotwell Distinguished Service Medal for leadership and service to the blind and the Miguel Medal, the nation's highest award for service to the blind. In his lifetime, Lowenfeld wrote over 100 books and journal articles. A life-long advocate for the visually impaired, Lowenfeld died in 1994.

REFERENCES

Lowenfeld, B. (1981). *Berthold Lowenfeld on blindness and blind people.* New York: American Foundation for the Blind.

Lowenfeld, B. (1994, May 25). *The San Francisco Chronicle.* p. C3. [Newspaper, selected stories online]. Retrieved April 30, 1998 by Nexis-Lexis on the World Wide Web: http://web.lexis-nexis.com/universe.

See also **Visually Impaired; Visual Training**

LOXITANE

A dibenzoxazepine compound, Loxitane represents a subclass of tricyclic antipsychotic agent used as a tranquilizer. Its use is indicated for the management of the manifestations of psychotic disorders. Side effects include rigidity (27%), tremor (22%), and drowsiness (11%), with less frequent incidence of confusion, dizziness, and slurred speech. Overdosage results may induce depression and unconsciousness. A brand name of Lederle Laboratories, Loxitane is supplied in capsules of 5, 10, 25, and 50 mg as an oral concentrate and in injectible units of 1 and 10 ml. Dosage levels are recommended in divided doses, two to four times a day, in initial dosage of 10 mg.

REFERENCE

Physicians' desk reference. (1984). (pp. 1078–1080). Oradell, NJ: Medical Economics.

See also **Drug Therapy**

LSD

Lysergic acid diethylamide (LSD) was initially discovered by accident by the Swiss chemist Albert Hoffman. LSD is a psychotominetic drug that elicits vivid hallucinations and intense emotions. Synesthesia, a phenomenon in which perceptions cross modalities, may occur (e.g., words are seen and colors heard). The drug is extraordinarily potent and a dosage as low as 50 mg can produce marked psychological effects. Some users report kaleidoscopic imagery that appears before their closed eyes; perceptions are reported to be richer and more intense. There is frequently a distorted perception of body parts. Spatial and temporal distortions are common. Depersonalization may result, and there is almost always a heightened suggestibility. In addition, it is common for users to report an increased awareness of the "true nature of things" and to find special significance in trivial events.

Like other psychotominetic drugs, it is clear that response to LSD is contingent on set and setting. The "bad trip" is perhaps the single most common adverse experience encountered by LSD users. The best treatment during this condition is simply companionship and support from someone who is knowledgeable about the drug and its effects. Even the worst effects typically wear off in 8 to 12 hours.

LSD is a drug that produces rapid tolerance and increasingly larger doses are required to produce an effect over the short run. However, once drug use is discontinued, tolerance rapidly abates. There is no physical dependence on the drug, and there is little evidence of long-term organic brain changes of the sort that are found with the abuse of certain other drugs. However, about 25% of users will experience flashbacks during which they may relive the experience of acute LSD intoxication. Flashbacks rarely occur more than a year after the last use of the drug. Some authors have argued the use of LSD may constitute a risk factor in the development of schizophrenia (Kaplan & Sadock, 1981).

REFERENCE

Kaplan, H.I., & Sadock, D.J. (1981). *Modern synopsis of comprehensive textbook of psychiatry.* Baltimore, MD: Williams & Wilkins.

See also **Childhood Schizophrenia; Drug Abuse**

LURIA, ALEXANDER R. (1902–1977)

Alexander Luria was a Russian neuropsychologist. He is best known for his theoretical and practical work on the behavioral consequences associated with focal brain injury. His early work integrated and expanded on the work of other Russian scientists, notably Pavlov and Vygotsky (Hatfield, 1981). Luria incorporated Vygotsky's ideas about the development of the social aspects of speech and Pavlov's neurophysiologic approach to understanding higher cortical processes (Hatfield, 1981).

Luria thought that all higher cortical functions required the concerted and coordinated working of multiple brain areas. His theory is neither a localizationist nor an equipotentialist one. Luria believed that higher cortical functions (e.g., reading) require the operation of functional systems incorporating multiple brain areas. Though specific aspects of the functional system (e.g., movement) are localizable within the brain, the more complex, complete behavior is not localizable. Hence, focal brain damage affects a variety of specific skills because one link in the system is nonfunctional while others are intact (e.g., the brain is not equipotential or homogeneous) (Luria, 1980, 1982). Luria's other contributions include methods for the assessment and treatment of aphasia using his functional systems approach to understanding cortical processes. He also is well known for his seminal work on frontal lobe functions (Pribram, 1978).

REFERENCES

Hatfield, F.N. (1981). Analysis and remediation of aphasia in the USSR: The contribution of A.R. Luria. *Journal of Speech & Hearing Disorders, 46,* 338–347.

Luria, A.R. (1980). *Higher cortical functions in man* (2nd ed.). New York: Basic Books.

Luria, A.R. (1982). *Language and cognition,* New York: Wiley.

Pribram, K.H. (1978). In memory of Alexander Romanovitsch Luria. *Neuropsychologia, 16,* 137–139.

See also **Luria-Nebraska Neuropsychological Battery; Vygotsky, L.S.**

LURIA-NEBRASKA NEUROPSYCHOLOGICAL BATTERY

The Luria-Nebraska Neuropsychological Battery (Golden, Hammeke, & Purisch, 1980) is a set of tasks specifically designed for the assessment of brain-damaged individuals. Like other neuropsychological batteries (e.g., Halstead-Reitan Neuropsychological Test Battery), it was developed to provide information regarding the absence or presence of brain damage. The battery also may be used by trained neuropsychologists to assist in rehabilitation planning, to discriminate between functional and organic disorders, to suggest the localization of brain damage, and to make prognostic statements (Moses, Golden, Ariel, & Gustavson, 1983). Based on the theoretical work of A.R. Luria, the battery, though broken into "scales," is really a set of interrelated items that may be evaluated both qualitatively and quantitatively.

REFERENCES

Golden, C.J., Hammeke, T.A., & Purisch, A. (1980). *The Luria-Nebraska Neuropsychological Battery.* Los Angeles: Western Psychological Services.

Moses, J.A., Golden, C.J., Ariel, R., & Gustavson, J.L. (1983). *Interpretation of the Luria-Nebraska Neuropsychological Battery* (Vol. 1). New York: Grune & Stratton.

See also **Halstead-Reitan Neuropsychology Battery; Luria, A.R.; Neuropsychology**

LURIA-NEBRASKA NEUROPSYCHOLOGICAL BATTERY: CHILDREN'S REVISION

The Luria-Nebraska Neuropsychological Battery: Children's Revision (LNNB-C; Golden, 1987) is an individually-administered battery designed to measure the neurological functions of children ages 8 to 12 years. It may be used for screening and diagnosing general and specific cognitive deficits such as lateralization and localization of focal brain impairments, and brain damage in children with psychiatric impairments. However, this is not a useful test for children who have poor verbal abilities.

The LNNB-C takes approximately 2 hours to administer. It covers a broad range of neurological functions that are assessed by the following subtests: Motor Functions, Rhythm, Tactile Functions, Visual Functions, Receptive Speech, Expressive Speech, Writing, Reading, Arithmetic, Memory, Intellectual Processes, Spelling-Academic Achievement, Integrative Functions, Spatial-Based Movement, Motor Speed and Accuracy, Drawing Quality, Drawing Speed, Rhythm Perception and Production, Tactile Sensations, Receptive Language, Expressive Language, and Word and Phrase Repetition. The results obtained from the LNNB-C are presented in the form of T-scores. There are 11 clinical scales, 11 factor scales, and 3 summary scales for which scores are obtained. The LNNB-C can be hand- or computer-scored. A qualitative scoring system is also presented in the LNNB-C manual, but no data are provided with respect to its use (Hooper, 1992).

Although the LNNB-C is purported to be constructed on the basis of developmental neuropsychology principles, it appears to be simply a scaled-down version of the adult battery (Hooper, 1992). The battery excludes measures of frontal lobe functioning, although evidence is available that shows some frontal lobe functions begin to develop by age 6 or 7. The final version of the LNNB-C was normed on 125 children (25 at each age level). There were only Caucasian children sampled. Reliability values for the clinical and summary scales range from .13 to .92 and range from .70 to .94 for the factor scales. Hooper (1992) agrees that these normative data are inadequate.

Hooper (1992) notes that the LNNB-C manual presents its information in a disorganized manner and also has inconsistencies. However, he further notes that all the necessary information to properly evaluate the instrument is provided. There is validity evidence supporting the LNNB-C as an instrument that discriminates brain dysfunction as well as the Halstead-Reitan Neuropsychological Battery. The factorial validity of the LNNB-C is well done, and Hooper (1992) notes that this provides additional interpretive information. In general, however, it has been suggested by one reviewer that caution be used while using this battery because of its psychometric and conceptual deficiencies (Hooper, 1992).

REFERENCES

Golden, C.J. (1987). *Luria-Nebraska Neuropsychological Battery: Children's Revision.* Los Angeles, CA: Western Psychological Services.

Hooper, S.R. (1992). Review of the Luria-Nebraska Neuropsychological Battery: Children's Revision. In J.J. Kramer & J.C. Conoley (Eds.), *The eleventh mental measurements yearbook* (pp. 479–481). Lincoln, NE: Buros Institute of Mental Measurements.

M

MA

See MENTAL AGE.

MACROGLOSSIA

See RARE DISEASES.

MACY, ANNE SULLIVAN (1866–1936)

Anne Sullivan Macy, Helen Keller's teacher, taught the deaf, blind, and mute child from the age of 6, serving as both teacher and companion until her death in 1936. Trained at the Perkins Institution for the Blind in Boston, where she resided in the same house as Laura Bridgeman, the first deaf-blind person to be educated, the young teacher developed methods that she successfully used to teach Helen Keller to read, write, and speak, and that enabled Keller to become a well-educated and effective person. In Keller's adult years, Macy, whom Keller always addressed as "teacher," served not only as teacher and interpreter for her, but also managed her extremely busy schedule of writing, lecturing, and personal appearances for many educational and social causes.

REFERENCES

Keller, H. (1955). *Teacher: Anne Sullivan Macy.* New York: Doubleday.

Lash, J. (1980). *Helen and Teacher: The story of Helen Keller and Anne Sullivan Macy.* New York: American Printing House for the Blind.

MAGICAL MODEL

The magical model of exceptionality explains deviance in terms of demonic possession and other supernatural causes. Common beliefs include possession by human and animal spirits and victimization by witches and spell casters (Rosenhan & Seligman, 1984). For centuries the model competed only with the biogenic (organic) model as an explanation of exceptional behavior (Brown, 1986).

Although biological, psychological, and ecological models have displaced magical models in the literature of educational professionals, some residual use of supernatural explanations occurs in the general culture. The public's attitudes toward the disabled and the disabled's attitudes toward themselves may be partially shaped by these notions of magic.

REFERENCES

Brown, R.T. (1986). Etiology and development of exceptionality. In R.T. Brown & C.R. Reynolds (Eds.), *Psychological perspectives on childhood exceptionality: A handbook* (pp. 181–229). New York: Wiley.

Rosenhan, D., & Seligman, M. (1984). *Abnormal psychology.* New York: Norton.

***See also* History of Special Education**

MAGNESIUM

Magnesium is a light metal that represents an essential body mineral (Ensminger, Ensminger, Konlande, & Robson, 1983; Thomson, 1979). The body contains approximately 20 to 30 g of magnesium, most of which is present in the skeleton (Yudkin, 1985). Magnesium also is found in cell tissue and it represents an essential component of the body's enzyme systems (Yudkin, 1985). The recommended daily allowances of magnesium range from 50 to 70 mg for infants to approximately 300 mg for adults (Ensminger et al., 1983). Dietary sources include a wide variety of foods, including flours, nuts, and spices. The typical western diet supplies ample magnesium (Yudkin, 1985).

While magnesium deficiency is rare under normal circumstances, it may occur in alcoholics and in persons with acute diarrhea or severe kidney disease (Ensminger et al., 1983; Yudkin, 1985). Symptoms of magnesium deficiency include depression; tremors and muscular weakness; confusion and disorientation; dizziness and convulsions; and loss of appetite, nausea, and vomiting (Ensminger et al., 1983; Yudkin, 1985). The salts of magnesium (magnesium sulfate, magnesium carbonate) are used medicinally for their antacid and laxative properties (Malseed, 1983; Parish, 1977). Use in patients with impaired kidney function is contraindicated (Parish, 1977).

REFERENCES

Ensminger, A.H., Ensminger, M.E., Konlande, J.E., & Robson, J.R.K. (1983). *Foods and nutrition encyclopedia* (Vol. 2). Clovis, CA: Pegus.

Malseed, R. (1983). *Quick reference to drug therapy and nursing considerations.* Philadelphia: Lippincott.

Parish, P. (1977). *The doctors' and patients' handbook of medicines and drugs.* New York: Knopf.

Thomson, W.A.R. (1979). *Black's medical dictionary* (32nd ed.). New York: Barnes & Noble.

Yudkin, J. (1985). *The Penguin encyclopedia of nutrition.* Middlesex, England: Penguin.

MAGNET SCHOOLS

Magnet schools, also referred to as alternative schools, are established within a school district to allow teachers, students, and parents the right to select specific curricula and/or methods of instruction.

Over the years, magnet schools have been developed around many programs. Some of these are science and math, individual guided instruction, environmental education, global education, bilingual or multicultural education, gifted and talented education, health care, marketing, college preparation, performing and visual arts, vocational and work study programs, business and management, human services, law and public administration, transportation, multiple careers for special education, back to basics, and microsociety programs where students design and operate their own democratic society (Clinchy, 1984; Doherty, 1982; Power, 1981). Magnet schools have also used business and industrial resources through special materials, instruction, and/or experiences. This involvement with industry has been called the adopt a school concept (Barr, 1982).

In the 1980s, magnet schools received much criticism in areas related to changes in the organizational and political processes within the school system (Metz, 1984). Current issues include freedom of choice, educational reform, desegregation and forced busing, and involvement of community leaders (Carrison, 1981). Many of these issues revolve around the area of quality of programming. Are these programs really superior to and different from regular programs? Are the poor really being included? Does integration really occur? Why should there be special programs that are superior to regular programs? What does that mean for the educational programs of the students who are not involved in the magnet programs (Carrison, 1981)? All of these questions will continue to be debated as the success or failure of magnet schools continues to be evaluated and public schools compete for pupils.

REFERENCES

Barr, R.D. (1982). Magnet schools: An attractive alternative. *Principal, 61*(3), 37–40.

Carrison, M.P. (1981). Do magnet schools really work? *Principal, 60*(3), 32–35.

Clinchy, E. (1984). Yes, but what about Irving Engelman? *Phi Delta Kappan, 65*(8), 542–545.

Doherty, D. (1982). Flint, Michigan: A case study in magnet schools and desegregation. *Principal, 61*(3), 41.

Metz, M.H. (1984). The life course of magnet schools organization and political influences. *Teachers College Record, 85*(3), 411–430.

Power, J. (1979). Magnet schools, are they the answer? *Today's Education, 68*(3), 68–70.

See also **Private Schools and Special Education**

MAHLER, MARGARET SCHOENBERGER (1897–1985)

A native of Sopron, Hungary, Margaret S. Mahler studied medicine and psychiatry in Germany and Austria. As a child psychiatrist, she headed a well-baby clinic in Vienna in the late 1920s and established the first psychoanalytic child guidance clinic there in the 1930s. In 1938, she emigrated to the United States. From 1941 to 1955, she taught at Columbia University's College of Physicians and Surgeons. From 1955 until her retirement in 1974, she was a clinical professor of psychiatry at the Albert Einstein College of Medicine in New York. Margaret Mahler died in 1985 at the age of 88.

Mahler was one of the earliest pioneers in the recognition and diagnosis of childhood schizophrenia. She was an early advocate of treatment programs that would include the mother, the child, and the therapist. Her research focused on what she called the "psychological birth" of the child, between infancy and age 3, during which a child moves from the experience of full psychological union with the mother to the eventual realization of separate personhood around age 3. This view of infant psychological development required the formulation of concepts about the process of separation/individuation and how it contributes to identity formation.

Mahler's honors include having received the Scroll of the New York Psychoanalytic Institute and the Frieda Fromm Reichman Award of the American Academy of Psychoanalysis.

REFERENCES

Bird, D. (1985, October 3). Margaret Mahler. *The New York Times,* p.23. Retrieved April 30, 1998, by Lexis-Nexis: http://web.lexis-nexis.com/universe.

Mahler, M.S. (1979a). *The selected papers of Margaret Mahler, M.D.: Infantile psychosis and early contributions* (Vol. 1). New York: Aronson.

Mahler, M.S. (1979b). *The selected papers of Margaret Mahler, M.D.: Separation-individuation* (Vol. 2). New York: Aronson.

MAKE-A-PICTURE STORY (MAPS) TEST

The Make-a-Picture Story (MAPS) Test is a variation of other projective storytelling methods used by earlier tests such as the Thematic Apperception Test (TAT) and the Children's Apperception Test (CAT). In the MAPS Test (Shneidman, 1949, 1960), the child selects figures from an array of 67 cutouts in order to make a scene against some 22 background pictures. The child then tells a story for each scene. The MAPS Test was intended to provide greater elicitation of the child's innermost feelings, needs, and desires, enhancing the projective nature of the responding (tests such as the TAT and CAT use ready-made pictures). Since every child responds to different pictures (of their creation), good studies of the reliability and validity of the technique have been nearly impossible to conduct.

The structure of the MAPS Test makes it appealing to elementary and secondary children, however, and it is used periodically in the schools in evaluating seriously emotionally disturbed children (Koppitz, 1982). The MAPS Test stories are scored the same as the TAT stories, except that the number of figures selected by the child for inclusion in the story seems to be of particular significance. There are little data to support the use of the test as other than an adjunct to other clinical methods and in developing a general understanding of a child's general mood and internal drive state. Extensive training is needed to use the MAPS Test appropriately.

REFERENCES

Koppitz, E.M. (1982). Personality testing in the schools. In C.R. Reynolds & T.B. Gutkin (Eds.), *The handbook of school psychology.* New York: Wiley.

Shneidman, E.S. (1949). *The Make-a-Picture Story Test.* New York: Psychological Corporation.

Shneidman, E.S. (1960). The MAPS with children. In A.I. Rubin & M.R. Haworth (Eds.), *Projective techniques with children.* New York: Grune & Stratton.

MAINSTREAMING

Mainstreaming is the popular term used for the legal doctrine of least restrictive environment (LRE). This term and its underlying concept are the products of the civil rights movement of the 1950s and 1960s, during which time courts judged as illegal segregation on the basis of race. Segregation was said to deny some children the opportunity of an education on equal terms with others. This principle was extended to include the handicapped in the cases of *PARC v. Commonwealth of Pennsylvania* (1971) and *Mills v. Board of Education of the District of Columbia* (1972). Educational agencies were encouraged to place students in the most normalized settings possible and discouraged from placing them in stigmatizing or segregated ones. Under the 1975 Education for All Handicapped Children Act, the 1990 Individuals with Disabilities Education Act (IDEA), and the 1997 IDEA Amendments, educational agencies are required to provide the "least restrictive environment" possible for a student's education.

Although the terms mainstreaming and least restrictive environment share historical antecedents, they are not equivalent, and careless use of them often leads to confusion about the LRE provisions of the law. The LRE doctrine mandates that, to the maximum extent possible, children with disabilities be educated with nondisabled children. Mainstreaming, in contrast, is only one of many instructional arrangements which can meet the LRE requirement; the mainstreamed student receives his or her instruction in the regular education classroom, with special education support when necessary.

The interpretation of what constitutes the least restrictive environment has raged throughout the 1990s, and continues to be hotly debated. Some believe that every child, regardless of disability status, should be educated in the regular education classroom, with special supports when necessary; this approach has been termed *full inclusion.* The inclusion model, as a philosophy, seeks to merge special and general education into a unified system for meeting the educational needs of all students regardless of their abilities or disabilities. Many others involved in special education and work with children with disabilities believe that the continuum of alternative placements discussed above best serves the interests of the special education student.

See also **Inclusion; Least Restrictive Environment**

MAINTENANCE

The concept of maintenance as it relates to academic school work is that a student can maintain performance with accuracy, even after task-training procedures are no longer employed. Maintenance (as suggested by Mims, 1991) is related to three other concepts: the concepts of acquisition and proficiency, which are antecedent to maintenance; and the concept of generalization, which is subsequent to maintenance.

Acquisition means that the student can do something that he or she could not do before. For example, a student is pretested on the ability to identify the 17 different ways to spell the schwa /ə/ vowel. The pretest result identifies a knowledge of only four ways to spell the schwa sound. After initial training (i.e., 30 minutes per day for 4 weeks using multisensory practice), the student knows 15 of the 17 ways. At this point the student has demonstrated by way of acquisition the initial mastery of a new skill. As the student is called on to use this newly acquired skill, and does so across time without recourse to the original task-training procedures, the student is evidencing a maintenance skill. The attainment of maintenance will probably involve the student in further appropriate practice work that can be identified as overlearning trials and distributed practice.

Overlearning trials are representative of repeated practice or overlearning work that is about half of what it was at the acquisition stage. For example, the initial learning of the 17 ways to spell the sound of schwa /ə/ required 30 minutes of appropriate practice per day for 4 weeks. We can for maintenance purposes, by way of overlearning trials, reduce the time to 15 minutes per day for 2 weeks. Distributed practice is work that is systematically distributed across a designated period of time, such as several weeks. Therefore, the concept of distributed practice as it relates to maintenance is concomitant with the practice suggested for the aspect of overlearning trials, which involve expanded practice relative to some task that the student is assigned to do.

The practical difference is that instead of designating 15 minutes of appropriate practice per day for 2 weeks, the same practice time can be scheduled two times per week for 5 weeks. A major advantage of distributed practice is that it complements long-term memory, and long-term memory likewise complements the execution of generalization. Generalizing means that a student who was previously handicapped can now perform academic tasks with efficiency and do so independent of assistance. It also means that the student can randomly (or as needed) execute self-directed remedial practices. Thus the concept of generalization and its application represents independence for the learning-disabled (LD) student. When generalization occurs in reference to learning the 17 ways to spell the schwa sound /ə/, the student will spell words with the schwa sound with 96% accuracy across various and random settings that call for the spelling of words with that schwa sound.

What is to be stressed in reviewing the relationship of the continuum of acquisition, maintenance, and generalization is that learning evidenced through correct or corrected work will, under systematic analysis, reveal the interfacing presence of each of the previously mentioned three components.

Many students who have been and are associated with special education do not initially acquire and thus cannot employ generalization of study habits and skills commonly associated with the successful nonhandicapped student (Kavale & Forress, 1985). Thus, maintenance becomes essential. Special education students taught to employ respective concepts associated with maintenance can become independent scholars.

REFERENCES

Kavale, K., & Forness, S. (1985). *The science of learning disabilities.* San Diego, CA: College Hill.

Mims, A. (1991). Effective instruction in homework for students with disabilities. *Teaching Exceptional Children, 24*(1), 42 44.

See also Generalization; Mastery Learning and Special Education

MALADAPTIVE BEHAVIOR

Maladaptive behavior consists of negative behaviors that interfere with normal adaptive functioning. Examples range from swearing and shyness to temper tantrums and theft. Most children exhibit maladaptive behavior at one time or another. Rubin and Balow (1978) indicated that in a study investigating 1586 children, about 60 to 65% were considered to exhibit maladaptive behavior by at least one teacher during a six-year period.

There are three general methods for assessing maladaptive behavior. Behavior checklists are available for teachers and parents to allow them to rate children's maladaptive behavior on a variety of dimensions. Examples are the Child Behavior Checklist (Achenbach & Edelbrock, 1979), which measures aspects of maladaptive behavior such as delinquency, aggression, cruelty, and hyperactivity, and the Behavior Problem Checklist (Quay & Peterson, 1970), which contains four subscales measuring conduct problems, personality problems, inadequacy, and immaturity; and the Behavior Assessment System for Children, (Reynolds & Kamphaus, 1992). Maladaptive behavior may also be assessed through informal interviews with teachers, parents, peers, and the children being assessed. A final method for the assessment of maladaptive behavior is direct observation of children's behavior in different settings such as the classroom, playground, or home.

Intervention techniques for maladaptive behavior vary, usually according to the severity or frequency of the behav-

ior. For example, behavior modification and structuring of the child's environment are often used by classroom teachers to decrease maladaptive behavior. In special education classrooms for emotionally and behaviorally disturbed children, teachers may implement extensive behavior management programs or cognitive behavior modification (Meichenbaum & Burland, 1979). For severe maladaptive behavior, intensive therapy and drugs may be used.

REFERENCES

Achenbach, T.M., & Edelbrock, C.S. (1979). The Child Behavior Profile II: Boys aged 12–16 and girls 6–11 and 12–16. *Journal of Consulting & Clinical Psychology, 47,* 223–233.

Meichenbaum, D., & Burland, S. (1979). Cognitive behavior modification with children. *School Psychology Digest, 8,* 426–433.

Quay, H.C. (1979). Classification. In H.C. Quay & T.S. Werry (Eds.), *Psychopathological disorders of childhood* (2nd ed.). New York: Wiley.

Reynolds, C., & Kamphaus, B. (1992). *Behavior Assessment System for Children.* Circle-Pines, MN: American Guidance Service.

Rubin, R.A., & Balow, B. (1978). Prevalence of teacher identified behavior problems: A longitudinal study. *Exceptional Children, 45,* 102–113.

See also Behavior Assessment System for Children (BASC); Child Behavior Checklist; Conduct Disorder; Discipline

MALE TURNER'S SYNDROME

See NOONAN'S SYNDROME.

MALNUTRITION

Malnutrition is defined as a state of altered nutrition which may occur from either too much or too little nourishment (Williams, 1997). Individuals may become malnourished as a result of the inability to absorb nutrients, refusal to eat foods provided, difficulty in purchasing and preparing food, financial constraints, or even poor cooking facilities (Davis & Sherer, 1994). Each day an estimated 35,000 persons (14 million per year) die of hunger, malnutrition, and its related disease effects (Williams, 1997).

Malnutrition is a disease which affects many children. One out of five American children lives in poverty and suffers from the ill effects of malnutrition (Williams, 1997). Stunted growth, deficiency diseases such as anemia, lowered resistance to infections, impaired learning, and reduced activity levels may all result as by-products of malnutrition. Recent malnutrition research has shown a decline in affective performance and impaired cognition in elderly persons (Salvioli, Ventura, & Pradelli, 1998). Sigman and Whaley's (1998) research on malnutrition also noted a link between nutrition and intelligence. For years, researchers have documented improved academic performance among children who eat a nutritious breakfast (Whitney, Cataldo, & Rolfes,

1998). The federally-funded School Lunch Program resulted from statistics that demonstrated an improvement in scores on achievement tests in children who had eaten a well-balanced breakfast (Whitney, Cataldo, & Rolfes, 1998).

REFERENCES

Davis, J., & Sherer, K. (1994). *Applied nutrition and diet therapy for nurses* (2nd ed.). Philadelphia: Saunders.

Salvioli, G., Ventura, P., & Pradelli, J. (1998). Impact of nutrition on cognition and affectivity in the elderly: A review. *Archives of Gerontology and Geriatrics*, (Suppl. 6), 431–434.

Sigman, M., & Whaley, S. (1998). The role of nutrition in the development of intelligence. In U. Neisser (Ed.), *The rising curve: Long-term gains in IQ and related measures* (pp. 155–182). Washington, DC: American Psychological Association.

Whitney, E., Cataldo, C., & Rolfes, S. (1998). *Understanding normal and clinical nutrition* (5th ed.). Belmont, CA: Wadsworth.

Williams, S. (1997). *Nutrition and diet therapy* (8th ed.). St. Louis: Mosby-Year Book.

MANNOSIDOSIS

See RARE DISEASES.

MANUAL COMMUNICATION

Human language is conceived as being primarily produced and perceived in an oral-aural mode (speaking and hearing). Yet all kinds of information are provided by nonvocal means such as facial expressions, gazes (direction, quality), hand movements, gestures, and body movements. Nonvocal communication and manual communication can have an auxiliary function, completing the information provided through the vocal channel, or be the main and often sole channel of communication.

In the phonology of sign languages (first called cherology, the science of cheremes) each sign has the following features: tabula (location, the place where the sign is made); designator (the shape of the hand); signation (the movement made by the hand); and orientation (of the hand relative to the body). It has been shown that these features can in many ways be compared to the phonemes of spoken languages.

In the morphology, the categories (gender, number, tense) and the formal processes are not necessarily the same as in spoken languages (e.g., sign languages have compounds, but they have no derivation through affixation). Sign languages express a variety of distinctions such as deixis, reciprocity, number, distributional aspect, and temporal aspect (Klima & Bellugi, 1979).

In the syntax of sign languages, the order in which signs are produced is not arbitrary, i.e., sign languages have their own syntax. Sign languages also have their own lexicon. Lexical differences between sign languages or between a sign language and a spoken language are not fundamentally different from lexical differences between spoken languages (Stokoe et al., 1965).

Although hand movements are of primary importance in sign languages, it must be stressed that signers make intensive use of other nonvocal models of expression (gaze, facial expression, movements of head, shoulders, torso, etc.). There are also systems of manual communication, generally called signed languages (e.g., signed French as opposed to the French sign language), that consist of extensions and modifications of a sign language. Most characteristic are the addition of signs for morphological categories that do not exist in the original sign language and a syntax more akin to that of the national spoken language. Signers sometimes use finger spelling, in which one handconfiguration represents one letter in the written version of the spoken language. This is done for most proper names and concepts for which there is no sign or to express a meaning more accurately than a sign allows (e.g., if a sign for poodle does not exist, the sign for dog plus the letters P, O, O, D, L, E would be used).

REFERENCES

Klima, E., & Bellugi, U. (1979). *The signs of language.* Cambridge, MA: Harvard University Press.

Stokoe, W.C., Casterline, D.C., & Croneberg, C.G. (1965). *A dictionary of American sign language on linguistic principles.* Silver Spring, MD: Linstok.

***See also* American Sign Language; Total Communication**

MARASMUS

Marasmus is a form of severe malnutrition. It results from overall food deprivation from birth or early infancy. It is most common in poverty-level infants who are not breast fed. However, marasmus can occur in children of any age whose diet is grossly inadequate, especially with respect to energy intake (Kreutler, 1980).

Marasmus results in wasting of tissues and severe growth retardation. Loss of muscle mass and subcutaneous fat gives children suffering from this condition a shrunken, old appearance in the face. The rest of the body has the skin and bones appearance typical of starvation. Poor nutritional status lowers resistance to disease, making these children particularly vulnerable to infections such as gastroenteritis, diarrhea, and tuberculosis (Pelletier, 1993).

As growth rate declines, both physical stunting and mental and emotional impairment occur if nutrient deprivation continues. Marked retardation in mental development may persist in marasmic children even after physical and biochemical rehabilitation (Cravioto, 1981).

REFERENCES

Cravioto, J. (1981). Nutrition, stimulation, mental development and learning. *Nutrition Today, 16*(5), 4–14.

Kreutler, P.A. (1980). *Nutrition in perspective.* Englewood Cliffs, NJ: Prentice Hall.

Pelletier, J.G. (1993). Severe malnutrition: A global approach. *Children in the Tropics, 12*(1), 208–209.

See also Anorexia Nervosa; Eating Disorders; Malnutrition; Nutritional Disorders; Pica

MARCH OF DIMES

The March of Dimes Foundation was founded by President Franklin D. Roosevelt in 1938 as the National Foundation for Infantile Paralysis to combat the nation's polio epidemic. Basil O'Conner, the President's former law partner, was asked to lead the organization. Roosevelt, a victim of polio, recovered partial use of his legs by swimming in the warm spring waters in Georgia and exercising his leg muscles, thereby becoming a national model for polio patients. Later, he purchased the facility at Warm Springs and established the Warm Springs Foundations. Roosevelt had great compassion for polio patients, many of whom were victims of the nation's economic problems and who could not receive the treatments from which he had so greatly benefited. Moreover, he felt that every city should have hospitals with iron lungs, hot-pack equipment, swimming pools, walking ramps, and lightweight braces. If everyone, Roosevelt reasoned, would give just a little bit, even a dime, a lot of money would be raised for the noble cause.

In 1953 Dr. Jonas Salk, a foundation grantee, developed a killed virus vaccine; it was declared in 1955 to be safe, potent, and effective. Before the discovery and licensing of the Sabine oral vaccine in 1962, the National Foundation, assured of its victory over polio, redirected its efforts from treatment to rehabilitation, the prevention of birth defects, and the overall improvement of the outcome of pregnancy. It changed its name to the National Foundation–March of Dimes. The present name, March of Dimes–Birth Defects Foundation, was adopted in 1979. The March of Dimes–Birth Defects Foundation is one of the 10 largest voluntary associations in America in membership and annual budget with seventy-five percent of all funds raised going to research and programs (MOD, 1998). It provides research, professional education, volunteer services, and public health education. The March of Dimes maintains an Internet website at http://modimes.org.

REFERENCE

March of Dimes Birth Defects Foundation. (1998). *All about the March of Dimes.* New York: Author.

MARFAN SYNDROME

Marfan Syndrome is an autosomal dominant disorder in most cases, although it can occur as a spontaneous mutation (Gillberg, 1995). Involvement of chromosome 15 is theorized but not yet proven. The disorder is characterized by a variety of symptoms, some of which occur inconsistently with the disorder, that include primarily physical markers.

Intelligence and affect are not believed to be directly affected by Marfan Syndrome (Gillberg, 1995). The disorder is well known in part because Abraham Lincoln suffered from Marfan Syndrome (Randall, 1990).

The primary physical hallmarks of the disorder are the elongations of the bones in particular regions of the body, primarily the arms and legs, but also including abnormally long and spindly fingers and toes. The latter is a physical characteristic known as spiderdactyly (a characteristic seen in certain other genetic disorders as well, including Klinefelter's Syndrome). However, there may be more severe physical problems including scoliosis, cardiac deformities, aneurysms, and even abnormal location of the lungs. Vision may be affected in some cases, and often there are dermatological problems. Children with Marfan Syndrome will see an unusual number of physicians and may experience excessive absences from school. As noted, behavior and affect are not directly affected, but due to their unusual appearance, children with Marfan are subject to more emotional difficulties than the average child, especially during adolescence. Special education is not required in most cases of Marfan but may be necessary depending upon the degree of cardiac, lung, or vision impairment. Services are provided in most cases, if necessary, under the rubric of other health impaired. There is no specific treatment for Marfan Syndrome beyond symptom management and possibly surgical corrections of cardiac and spinal defects.

REFERENCES

Gillberg, C. (1995). *Clinical child neuropsychiatry.* Cambridge: Cambridge University Press.

Randall, T. (1990). Marfan gene search intensifies following identification of basic defect. *Journal of the American Medical Association, 264,* 1642–1643.

MARLAND REPORT

The Marland Report was a response to a mandate from Congress that Commissioner of Education S.P. Marland, Jr., conduct a study to:

1. Determine the extent to which special educational assistance programs are necessary or useful to meet the needs of gifted and talented children.

2. Show which federal education assistance programs are being used to meet the needs of gifted and talented children.

3. Evaluate how existing federal educational assistance programs can more effectively be used to meet these needs.

4. Recommend new programs, if any, needed to meet these needs (Marland, 1972, VIII).

The report identified the lack of services for gifted and talented youths as well as widespread misunderstandings about this population. These findings, as well as others, prompted action by the U.S. Office of Education to eliminate the widespread neglect of gifted and talented children.

This report served to focus attention on gifted and talented children. The report's recommendations were important factors in developing state and national programs for the gifted and talented. Moreover, the report was of major significance in involving the federal government in the education of gifted and talented students.

REFERENCE

Marland, S.P., Jr. (1972). Education of the gifted and talented. Report of the Congress of the United States by the U.S. Commissioner of Education. Washington, DC: U.S. Government Printing Office.

MARSHALL v. GEORGIA

Marshall v. Georgia, also known as *Georgia State Conference of Branches of NAACP v. Georgia,* was a class-action suit filed on behalf of African American school-age children in the state of Georgia alleging discrimination in two forms: (1) overrepresentation of African American students in the lower, and underrepresentation in the higher, achievement/ability groups within regular education resulting in separation of African American and Anglo students; and (2) discrimination in the evaluation and placement of African American students resulting in overrepresentation in special education programs for the educable mentally retarded. Both claims were rejected by the trial court in a decision upheld by the Eleventh Circuit Court of Appeals.

The allegations of discrimination for both aspects of the case were based on alleged violations in Thirteenth and Fourteenth Amendment rights, Title VI of the Civil Rights Act of 1964, and the Equal Education Opportunity Act. In addition to these provisions, the special education aspect of the case also was filed on the basis of Section 504 of the Rehabilitation Act of 1973.

The allegations of discrimination against black students who were significantly overrepresented in lower ability/achievement groups, and underrepresented in higher ability/achievement groups, were based on various statistical evidence and expert witness testimony claiming harm to black students as a result of regular education tracking practices. The plaintiffs' expert witness, Martin Shapiro of Emory University, presented data, undisputed by the plaintiffs, that the disproportionality was beyond statistical chance. Another expert witness for the plaintiffs, Robert Calfee, an educational psychologist from Stanford University, argued that the discrepancies in achievement between African American and Anglo students were caused, at least in part, by ability/achievement grouping practices. The plaintiffs' attorneys further argued that the ability/achievement grouping disproportionality is related to past discrimination as well as to impermissible practices leading to separation of black and white students.

The plaintiffs alleged five areas of improper or inappropriate practices carried out by state and local defendants.

The first had to do with the IQ guidelines stated in Georgia regulations and the interpretation and application by local defendants. The Georgia IQ guidelines suggested that significantly subaverage general intellectual functioning had to be two or more standard deviations below the mean. However, some degree of flexibility was common with local defendants and approved by state department officials. The plaintiffs argued for a rigid cutoff score of 70, suggesting that any student with an IQ score of 70 or above was misclassified. They presented several cases in which the full-scale IQ scores of black students in EMR programs was 70 or slightly above. The second issue had to do with the assessment of adaptive behavior, particularly whether a standardized scale must be used in assessing adaptive behavior. The plaintiffs argued for the mandatory use of a standardized scale with a specific, stringent cutoff score.

The third issue also dealt with adaptive behavior, specifically the setting in which adaptive behavior had to be assessed in order to meet state and professional association guidelines. The plaintiffs argued that adaptive behavior assessment should be focused, if not exclusively, at least primarily, on out-of-school adaptive behavior. Further, the plaintiffs' expert witness suggested that for a student to have an adaptive behavior deficit, he or she needed to be performing poorly in all environments. Finally, the plaintiffs argued that various local districts were failing to document properly compliance with all aspects of due process regulations and that there were instances in which triennial reevaluations were not conducted in a timely fashion. As noted earlier, the plaintiffs failed to show that any of the five areas of improper or inappropriate practices occurred more frequently with African American EMR students. Thus discrimination was impossible to infer in the view of the court.

The defendants' case was based on explaining overrepresentation owing to the effects of poverty and the use of various professional standards and guidelines. In particular, the American Association on Mental Deficiency (AAMD; Grossman, 1983) manual, *Classification in Mental Retardation,* as well as the National Academy of Sciences report on special educational overrepresentation (Heller, Holtzman, & Messick, 1982) were relied on heavily by the defendants' expert witnesses, Daniel J. Reschly of Iowa State University and Richard Kicklighter of the Georgia State Department of Education. The defendants' expert witnesses argued that standards for professional practices always have supported viewing results of measures of general intelligence as a range rather than a specific point, and that rigid, inflexible application of numerical guidelines were inappropriate in view of imperfect measurement processes. Specific paragraphs from the AAMD manual were cited as further justification for a flexible IQ guideline.

The court rejected all of the plaintiffs' claims concerning discrimination. In addition, all of the plaintiffs' remedies were rejected, including those related to assessment of adaptive behavior, classification criteria for general intellectual functioning and adaptive behavior, mandatory prereferral strategies, and mandatory reevaluation of all black children. The court's basis for rejecting these claims cited various professional association guidelines, particularly the AAMD. The court explicitly endorsed the AAMD: "the court believes the practices as defined and endorsed by the AAMD evidence best professional practices in this regard" (p. 146).

The Marshall trial and appeals court decisions established certain clear-cut guidelines concerning allegations of discrimination as well as the development and implementation of programs for the educable mentally retarded. Overrepresentation as such clearly was insufficient to prove discrimination. Overrepresentation had to be accompanied by evidence of discrimination, which both courts suggested needed to be based on comparisons of black and white students with retardation. Furthermore, professional association guidelines such as those of the AAMD (Grossman, 1983), and authoritative sources such as the National Academy of Sciences report (Heller, Holtzman, & Messick, 1982), were accorded considerable deference by the courts.

Marshall may well be a landmark decision similar to *Larry P.* in potential impact on classification and placement of students with retardation. Both decisions have been based on lengthy trials and upheld by appeals courts. However, the *Marshall* and *Larry P.* courts reached very different conclusions on similar issues. Future developments are therefore impossible to anticipate.

REFERENCES

Grossman, H.J. (Ed.). (1983). *Classification in mental retardation.* Washington, DC: American Association on Mental Deficiency.

Heller, K., Holtzman, W., & Messick, S. (Eds.). (1982). *Placing children in special education: A strategy for equity.* Washington, DC: National Academy.

Reschly, D.J. (1986). Economic and cultural factors in childhood exceptionality. In R.T. Brown & C.R. Reynolds (Eds.), *Psychological perspectives on childhood exceptionality: A handbook* (pp. 423–466). New York: Wiley-Interscience.

See also **Diana v. State Board of Education; Larry P.; Nondiscriminatory Assessment; Racial Discrimination in Special Education**

MASTERY LEARNING AND SPECIAL EDUCATION

"Mastery learning is an optimistic theory about teaching and learning that asserts that any teacher can help virtually all students to learn excellently, swiftly and self confidently" (Bloom cited in Block, 1984, p. 68). Bloom, Hastings and Medaus (1971) believe that both exceptional and nonexceptional learners can benefit from instruction if it is systematic, if the task is broken down into small steps, if goals are clearly stated, students are given sufficient time to achieve mastery, and there is some criterion of what constitutes mastery.

From a mastery learning perspective, management of learning requires three basic stages (Block, 1984). The first is the orientation stage, where the teacher clearly states what outcomes are expected from the learner. Grading policy and the standards for mastery are explained, and the learner is oriented to the strategies he or she will be using to master the material.

The second teaching stage is where the instructor uses various approaches for teaching the content. Initially, the whole class is taught the material in a sequence and formatively tested. Subsequently, the students are grouped according to their levels of learning. Corrective procedures are used for those who have not attained a predetermined level and enrichment is provided for those who have. In the third stage, grading stage, which occurs after correctives and enrichment, each student is individually evaluated for mastery. A's are given to students who have reached a predetermined level and I's are awarded to students who score below this standard. Steps are taken to help students replace their I's with A's.

Some materials used in special education classes are based on the principles of mastery learning. DISTAR (Englemann & Bruner, 1969), a reading program for elementary-aged students, breaks reading down into its smallest units, sequences those units in hierarchical order, and teaches each unit to mastery. There are programs that teach thinking skills (Black & Black, 1984) as well as programs that teach social skills (Goldstein, Sprafkin, Gershaw and Klein, 1980) that have been developed with mastery learning in mind. The advantages of mastery learning are consistent with the goals of special education programming. More students accomplish designated objectives and earn higher grades. This, in turn, leads to a positive effect on student self-concept and a heightened interest in subjects where success is achieved (Block & Anderson, 1975).

REFERENCES

Black, S., & Black, H. (1984). *Building thinking skills.* Pacific Grove, CA: Midwest.

Block, J.H. (1984). Making school learning activities more play like: Slow and mastery learning. *Elementary School Journal, 85*(1), 65–75.

Block, J.H., & Anderson, L. (1975). *Mastery learning in classroom instruction.* New York: Macmillan.

Bloom, B.S., Hastings, J., & Medaus, G. (1971). *Handbook on formative and summative evaluation of student learning.* New York: McGraw-Hill.

Englemann, S., & Bruner, E.C. (1969). *DISTAR reading I and II.* Chicago: Science Research.

Goldstein, A.P., Sprafkin, R.P., Gershaw, N.J., & Klein, P. (1980). *Skill streaming the adolescent: A structured learning approach to teaching prosocial skills.* Champaign, IL: Research Press.

See also **Competency Education; Data-Based Instruction; Teaching Strategies**

MASTURBATION, COMPULSIVE

Masturbation, or genital stimulation and gratification by oneself, is a common form of sexual behavior that occurs in almost all males and in the majority of females (Taylor, 1970). Young children may handle their genitals, but purposeful masturbation often begins when sexual drives become intense during and after puberty.

Normal adolescence is characterized by a series of developmental phases, which include accommodating the sex drive. These phases are often "long, delayed, and distorted toward passivity" among mentally retarded children (Bernstein, 1985). Such children may engage in masturbation to relieve sexual tension, or simply because it feels good. Gordon (1973) suggested that masturbation is a normal sexual expression no matter how frequently or at what age it occurs, and that all sexual behavior involving the genitals should occur only in private. Motivation for frequent public masturbation, which might be called compulsive masturbation, may be boredom or the lack of anything else interesting to do. In other cases, it may be an attention-getting device.

A recommended approach to the situation is to communicate to the masturbating person that the behavior is not socially acceptable in public (Withers & Gaskell, 1998). Such an approach gives the person exhibiting the behavior the option to continue in private, and attention-getting behavior is not reinforced. Parents of physically handicapped children and adolescents should have education and training on this subject, so they will be able to guide their children appropriately (Hardoff & Milbul, 1997).

REFERENCES

Bernstein, N.R. (1985). Sexuality in mentally retarded adolescents. *Medical Aspects of Human Sexuality, 19,* 50–61.

Gordon, S. (1973). A response to Warren Johnson (on sex education of the retarded). In F. DeLaCruz & G.D. LaBeck (Eds.), *Human sexuality and the mentally retarded.* New York: Brunner/Mazel.

Hardoff, D., & Milbul, J. (1997). Education program on sexuality and disability for parents of physically handicapped adolescents. *International Journal of Adolescent Medicine & Health, 9*(3), 173–180.

Taylor, D.L. (1970). *Human sexual development: Perspectives in sex education.* Philadelphia: Davis.

Withers, P.S., & Gaskell, S.L. (1998). A cognitive-behavioral intervention to address inappropriate masturbation in a boy with mild learning disabilities. *British Journal of Learning Disabilities, 26*(2), 58–61.

See also **Self-Stimulation; Social Skills**

MATERNAL SERUM ALPHA-FETOPROTEIN (AFP) SCREENING

Maternal Serum Alpha-Fetoprotein Screening is a diagnostic blood test performed on pregnant women between the fourteenth and eighteenth weeks of gestation. It determines the presence of alpha-fetoprotein (AFP), a normal protein produced by the fetus that enters the maternal circulatory system early in pregnancy (Jensen & Bobak, 1985).

Elevated levels of maternal AFP have been associated with fetal neural tube defects, the most frequently encountered central nervous system malformations. These defects include anencephaly, encephalocele, and spina bifida (Harrison, Golbus, & Filly, 1984). Anencephaly is the failure of the cerebrum and cerebellum to develop. Encephalocele is the protrusion of the brain through a congenital gap in the skull. Spina bifida is the failure of the lower portion of the spinal column to close, allowing spinal membrane to protrude (Thomas, 1985). Elevated levels indicate the need for the further tests of sonography and amniocentesis to confirm the defect.

REFERENCES

Harrison, M.R., Golbus, M.S., & Filly, R.A. (1984). *The unborn patient, prenatal diagnosis and treatment.* Orlando, FL: Grune & Stratton.

Jensen, M.D., & Bobak, I.M. (1985). *Maternity and gynecologic care, the nurse and the family* (3rd ed.). St. Louis: Mosby.

Thomas, C.L. (Ed.). (1985). *Taber's cyclopedic medical dictionary* (15th ed.). Philadelphia: Davis.

See also **Amniocentesis; Genetic Counseling; Spina Bifida**

MATHEMATICS, LEARNING DISABILITIES IN

Learning disabilities in mathematics manifest themselves in at least three different groupings. One of these groups is characterized by an overall deficiency in mathematics such that progress is slow and labored, but steady. A second group displays deficiencies in specific mathematics topics such as fractions, or within a subtopic such as division. A third group is characterized by comprehensive disorders of thinking, reasoning, and problem solving such that performance in both concepts and skills in mathematics is distorted and illogical.

Mathematics is a comprehensive subject in which emphasis must be given to the development of concepts and principles, accuracy and ease in computation, and the use of concepts and principles and computational proficiency to solve problems and make decisions. The great majority of research and programming in mathematics learning disabilities has focused on arithmetical computation. Within this area, the emphasis has been on whole numbers, where efforts have been further subordinated to addition and subtraction. In spite of the fact that teachers have indicated that division is the primary topic with which learning-disabled students have difficulty (McLeod & Armstrong, 1982), there is a paucity of research and instructional development on this topic. By contrast, the literature is replete with work in addition and subtraction (Thornton & Toohey, 1985). The stress on addition and subtraction is understandable when one considers that these are the two computational skills with which children have their initial difficulties. It has yet to be determined whether the early emergence of learning disabilities in addition and subtraction is due to learner deficiencies in concepts and principles, a more cognitive view, or learner deficiencies in attentional factors or memory capabilities, a more behavioral view. Nor has it been fully determined that children who are successful in their introduction to addition and subtraction are the same learning-disabled children who are successful with multiplication and division.

Appraisal in mathematics needs to be comprehensive. There needs to be some reasonable representation of the full range of content at various developmental levels. At the very least, this should include appraisal of concepts and skills, computation, and problem solving across the topics of numbers, fractions, geometry, and measurement. The use of a single topic measure suggests that a "g" factor is operating and that performance in one topic of mathematics is sufficient to predict performance in another topic, or that the appraisal is conducted from an interest only perspective where one topic is of primary interest to the examiner. The single topic procedure limits the search for patterns of strengths and weaknesses, but enables one to delve more fully into one area of concern. If the Key-Math Diagnostic Arithmetic Test–Revised (Connolly, Nachtman, & Prichett, 1988) is contrasted with other tests, one would note that Key Math covers more topics but does not cover any single topic to the degree that others cover computation. Given these variations, appraisal specialists need to make informed decisions as to the components of their approach.

Instruction and curriculum are interwoven in programs designed to meet the needs of persons having learning disabilities in mathematics. Curriculum choices determine content, the level of the content, and the sequence or sequences in which the content will be presented. With few exceptions (Cawley et al., 1974, 1976) special education has not directed any significant attention to the development of curriculum for mathematics. Two factors tend to influence curriculum choices. One of these is the use of the regular class curriculum, which is largely determined by the textbook in use. The second factor stresses the remedial orientation of computation in whole numbers. This second factor leaves little variation in curriculum.

Instructional choices determine the method by which the content will be presented. It is possible to separate the approaches to instruction into two categories, although it is important to note that more than two categories could be designated and that there is overlap among them. One category of approaches stresses concepts, principles, information processing, and analysis across the topics of mathematics. Another category stresses high rates of correct responses and the habituation of response behavior across a fewer number of mathematics topics, frequently whole number computation and word problem solving.

An area of concern that has recently been raised by the National Council of Teachers of Mathematics is the content validity of standardized tests of mathematics (Parmar, Frazita, & Cawley, 1996) for special education students. Performance in mathematics requires considerable knowledge, competence in prerequisite skills such as language and reading, and the use of a variety of cognitive acts. Proper programming and assessment for the learning disabled requires an approach as comprehensive as the subject itself.

REFERENCES

Cawley, J.F., Fitzmaurice, A.M., Goodstein, H.A., Lepore, A., Sedlak, R., & Althaus, V. (1974, 1976). *Project MATH*. Tulsa, OK: Educational Progress Corporation.

Connolly, A., Nachtman, W., & Prichett, E.M. (1976). *Key Math Diagnostic Arithmetic Test.* Circle Pines, MN: American Guidance Service.

McLeod, T.M., & Armstrong, S.W. (1982). Learning disabilities in mathematics—Skill deficits and remedial approaches at the intermediate and secondary level. *Learning Disability Quarterly, 5,* 305–311.

Parmar, R.S., Frazita, R., & Cawley, J.F. (1996). Mathematics assessment for students with mild disabilities: An exploration of content validity. *Learning Disability Quarterly, 19*(2), 127–136.

Thornton, C.A., & Toohey, M.A. (1985). Basic math facts: Guidelines for teaching and learning. *Learning Disabilities Focus. 1.* 44–57.

See also **Acalculia; Arithmetic Remediation**

MATHEMATICS, REMEDIAL

The traditional model of instruction for remedial mathematics has been a diagnostic one, for example, identifying areas of strengths and weaknesses and, traditionally, focusing instructional attention on weak areas, including mathematical skill deficiencies. However, the diagnostic remedial mathematics specialist also might be interested in remediating such dysfunctional learner characteristics as distractibility, inefficient strategies, and poor short- or long-term memory processes (Reisman, 1982). Much of the remedial effort might then go into teaching the mathematically handicapped student strategies appropriate to coping with and overcoming these and other deficiencies related to poor mathematics performance.

In contrast, there are those who recommend a developmental approach, taking the position that good developmental instruction in mathematics represents the best remediation for handicapped learners. Cawley (1984) objects that one of the problems in helping children with learning problems to learn mathematics is that there has been too much emphasis on "how to" to the neglect of the curriculum. He advocates greater emphasis on "what shall we teach, when shall we teach it, and in what sequence is it best taught" (1984, p. ix) in imparting mathematics to learning-disabled children. Nevertheless, he, too recommends that the mathematical instruction of learning-handicapped children be tailored to their particular strengths and weaknesses. Beyond that, he suggests that mathematics instruction for learning-handicapped students should proceed on the premise that the needs of children with learning problems are interrelated and that the activities from skill areas and topics other than mathematics should be used to reinforce positive mathematics behaviors on their part and to encourage application and generalization.

REFERENCES

Cawley, J.F. (1984). Preface. In J.F. Cawley (Ed.), *Developmental teaching of mathematics for the learning disabled.* Rockville, MD: Aspens.

Reisman, F. (1982). *A guide to the diagnostic teaching of arithmetic.* Columbus, OH: Merrill.

See also **Mathematics, Learning Disabilities in; Reading, Remedial**

MATHIAS AMENDMENT

During the 97th Congress (1981–1982) in the U.S. Senate, Honorable Charles McC. Mathias, Jr., from Maryland introduced Senate Bill S.604:

To amend the Communication Act of 1934 to provide that telephone receivers may not be sold in interstate commerce unless they are manufactured in a manner which permits their use by persons with hearing impairments.

Ironically for Americans with hearing aids, one of five existing telephones did not produce electromagnetic signals compatible with magnetic telephone pick-ups built into most hearing aids. Thus hearing impaired people were denied an essential part of independent living. The passage of the Mathias Amendment corrected this problem.

REFERENCE

Telephone Service for Hearing Impaired. (1982). Hearing Before the Subcommittee on Communications of the Committee on Commerce, Science and Transportation, United States Senate, 97th Congress, Second Session on S.604 and S.2355. Serial No. 97–119. Washington, DC: U.S. Government Printing Office.

MATTIE T. v. HOLLADAY

In April 1975, *Mattie T. v. Holladay* was filled on behalf of all Mississippi school-age children who were handicapped or regarded by their school as handicapped, for alleged violations or failure to enforce the children's rights under PL 94-142, the Education for All Handicapped Children Act. The plaintiffs were named as either handicapped children excluded from school in segregated special programs or ignored in regular classes, or nonhandicapped minority students who had been misclassified as mentally retarded and hence inappropriately placed.

In 1977 the district court ruled that the defendants were indeed in violation of the plaintiffs' federal rights and ordered a comprehensive compliance plan. On February 22, 1979, the judge approved a comprehensive consent decree, which required that (1) these students be placed in the least restrictive environment (e.g., mainstreamed, put in day programs for institutionalized children, given surrogate parents if parentless); (2) the state redesign its child evaluation procedures so as to be nondiscriminatory; (3) compensatory education be required for those students who had been misclassified and inappropriately placed; (4) school suspensions of longer than 3 days be discontinued; (5) a statewide complaint procedure service be instituted; (6) the state monitoring system be strengthened to ensure local school district compliance with federal law; and (7) procedural safeguards be put in as required by the federal statute, to include such features as a parents' rights handbook and community outreach to locate children with special needs.

REFERENCES

Comprehensive consent decree issued to enforce PL 94-142 in Mississippi. (1979, March/April). *Mental Disability Law Reporter,* 3(2), 98–99.

Mattie T. v. Holladay 522 F. Supp. 72 (N.D. Mississippi 1981).

See also **Individuals with Disabilities Education Act (IDEA); Larry P.; Marshall v. Georgia**

MATURATIONAL LAG

See DEVELOPMENTAL DELAY.

MBD SYNDROME

The MBD syndrome or minimal brain dysfunction syndrome, which is obsolete, has for many years been offered as an explanation for and diagnosis of the cluster of behaviors, including hyperactivity, distractibility, and impulsiveness, commonly found in children with academic and behavior problems (Clements, 1966; Cruickshank, 1966; Strauss & Lehtinen, 1947).

In recent years there has been comparatively little interest in the use of MBD as either a diagnostic term in medicine or a classificatory term in special education. Recognizing that differential consequences may result from damage to different brain areas, acute versus chronic brain dysfunction can exert different influences on the nature of brain-behavior relationships. The brain contains millions of neurons, with disabilities reflecting both location and numbers of damaged neurons (Hartlage & Hartlage, 1977). It is not surprising, then, that the concept of MBD may be too broad to relate to any meaningful description of a given child or resultant prescription for intervention. Thus the MBD syndrome may represent a term of historic and heuristic value rather than one with specific implications for special education practice.

REFERENCES

Clements, S.D. (1966, January). *Minimal brain dysfunction in children* (Public Health Service Publication No. 1415). Washington, DC: U.S. Department of Health, Education, and Welfare.

Cruickshank, W.M. (1966). *The teacher of brain injured children.* Syracuse, NY: Syracuse University Press.

Hartlage, L.C., & Hartlage, P.L. (1977). Application of neuropsychological principles in the diagnosis of learning disabilities. In L.

Tarnopol & M. Tarnopol (Eds.), *Brain function and reading disabilities* (pp. 111–146). Baltimore, MD: University Park Press.

Strauss, A.A., & Lehtinen, L.U. (1947). *Psychopathology and education of the brain-injured child.* New York: Grune & Stratton.

See also **Brain Damage; Learning Disabilities**

MCCARTHY, DOROTHEA (1906–1974)

Dorothea McCarthy made her greatest contributions to psychology in the areas of language development and clinical assessment of young children. She earned her PhD in 1928 at the University of Minnesota under the tutelage of Florence Goodenough, who had a strong effect on McCarthy's professional career, convincing her that "cognitive differences among children could be measured at early ages and along several dimensions" (McCarthy, 1972, p. iii).

McCarthy culminated her professional career with the publication in 1972 of the McCarthy Scales of Children's Abilities, a test of the mental and motor abilities of children ages 2½ to 8½ years. This test was developed over a 15-year period and was published one year after her retirement from Fordham University, where she served as associate professor and professor for 40 years (1932–1971).

At Fordham University her colleagues considered her most distinctive characteristics to be the soundness and dependability of her research and the high standards she upheld for herself and for the students whose research she directed. Her clinical sense regarding the needs and interests of preschool children is evidenced by the child-oriented tasks she developed for the McCarthy Scales and the clever way these tasks are sequenced within the test to help establish and maintain rapport.

REFERENCE

McCarthy, D. (1972). *Manual for the McCarthy Scales of Children's Abilities.* New York: Psychological Corporation.

MCCARTHY SCALES OF CHILDREN'S ABILITIES (MSCA)

The McCarthy Scales of Children's Abilities (MSCA; McCarthy, 1972) was designed to measure general intellectual ability of children ages 2.5 to 8.5 years. The MSCA consists of 18 subtests that are grouped into five separate scales: Verbal (V), Perceptual-performance (P), Quantitative (Q), Memory, Motor, and General Cognitive (a composite scale). The General Cognitive Index is derived from 15 of the 18 subtests and provides a normative indicator of a child's cognitive level (M = 100, SD = 16). The five MSCA scale indexes each has a mean of 50 and a standard deviation of 15.

Strengths of the McCarthy are its clearly written format and its well constructed materials that are appealing to children. Weaknesses include excessive clerical work in scoring,

a lack of sufficient ceiling or floor, and the limited age-range for which the test can be used. Kaufman and Kaufman (1977) provide information on methods of interpreting the McCarthy. However, because of the outdated nature of the McCarthy norms and the availability of more up-to-date measures for assessing young children's cognitive abilities, it is suggested that the McCarthy be administered mainly to gain clinical information and that its scores be interpreted with caution.

REFERENCES

Kaufman, A.S., & Kaufman, N.L. (1977). *Clinical evaluation of young children with the McCarthy Scales.* New York: Grune & Stratton.

McCarthy, D. (1972). *Manual for the McCarthy Scales of Children's Abilities.* New York: The Psychological Corporation.

See also **Intelligence Testing; Kaufman Assessment Battery for Children; Stanford Binet Intelligence Scale; Wechsler Intelligence Scale for Children (WISC-III)**

MCCUNE-ALBRIGHT SYNDROME

See RARE DISEASES.

MCGINNIS METHOD

The McGinnis method, also known as the association method, was the recommended teaching approach during the 1950s, 1960s, and early 1970s for children classified as aphasic or diagnosed as suffering from receptive and/or expressive aphasia. Aphasia is defined as an impairment or lesion in the brain causing sensory deprivation.

The association method employs techniques using sight, sound, and kinesthesis as a multisensory teaching approach. The method stresses the importance of attention, recall, and retention. The speech training or oral articulation program emphasizes the kinesthetic sense of movement in the muscular coordination of lip and tongue movements. The student is carefully guided through the training program. The early training establishes the ability to pronounce phonemes in isolation. The memory sequence is established through reading and written form.

The association method further develops language skills through its vertical and horizontal training programs. The vertical program teaches basic language and speech patterns that are to be mastered over a specified period of time. The horizontal training program is the daily teaching paradigm. This program provides for the continuum of grade-level work.

The association method follows seven steps that stress attention, development of specific sounds, the smoothing or combining of sounds into meaningful nouns, the association of appropriate concepts with the noun, the writing of the noun or word using the written word, the development of speech reading, acoustical association, and the association of the meaning of language in both written and oral expression.

REFERENCE

McGinnis, M.A. (1963). *Aphasic children.* Washington, DC: Alexander G. Bell Association for the Deaf.

MEASUREMENT

Measurement is the assignment of numbers to observed behaviors or actions.

Two major characteristics of importance to measurement in special education are reliability and validity. Reliability has a technical meaning that is somewhat different from the dictionary meaning. Reliability commonly means trustworthiness. To the extent that we can believe the measurement of a behavior is consistent, we can consider it trustworthy. Consistency is defined in terms of psychometrics (the mathematical modeling of measurement) as maintenance of relative position of a score with respect to other scores. For example, if five people are observed and their scores are 1, 3, 4, 4, 6, high reliability in the observation process would occur if the people were ordered exactly the same on another measurement, say 2, 4, 5, 5, 7, even though the scores are all different. Reliability is consistency of measurement of a score with respect to all other scores. That the two sets of scores all differ by one point is an issue of validity.

Reliability can be examined in three ways. One is to make the same measurement twice. In mental testing this means the same test is given with some interval between; this is termed test-retest reliability. If a test consists of parts that are independently measured, the consistency of the parts with respect to the whole can be examined; this is termed internal consistency. Finally, a complete second test may be constructed that is intended to measure the same thing as the first. Reliability for the two scores is termed parallel forms reliability.

Validity is a concept with several different applications. For the example given previously, one might ask which set of scores better indicates the behavior. In measuring children's school learning, we may be most interested in the content validity of the test: To what extent do the questions represent the topics the children were taught and should have learned? In measuring mental processing we are interested in the construct validity of the intelligence test used: To what extent does the test measure the mental processes it is intended to measure? In measuring a prospective college freshman's achievement as an indicator of future success in college, we are interested in predictive validity. Finally, in measuring how well a screening test indicates learning disabilities in comparison with the diagnoses of trained clinicians, we are interested in concurrent validity. Validity of a test must be associated with purpose for the test.

Inference in observation of behavior is a complex mental process. Reliability of measurement of a human observer typically decreases as the degree of inference necessary to the task increases. It is possible to achieve high reliability for high inference observation at a cost of extensive training and frequent retraining or maintenance practice.

See also Assessment; Psychoeducational Methods; Reliability

MEDIATION

Mediation is an intellectual activity that can be used to direct, control, or regulate one's behavior or responses by thinking before acting (Meichenbaum & Aronson, 1979). Mediation is particularly useful during the initial phases of learning, when one is trying to acquire new facts, establish associations, remember information, or learn sequences of action. Mediation can be used to direct motor behavior, to control emotional and social behavior, to remember information, and to learn academically. Mediation may be verbal or visual in nature and its effects increase with meaningfulness (Peterson, Colavita, Sheanan, & Blattner, 1964).

Verbal mediation has application in many situations. Children can analyze their situations or experiences and plan their responses by literally talking to themselves. Verbal mediation can be used to help children learn physical movements. If a teacher simply counts "One, two, three, four," this mediation helps students to perform each movement in sequence at the correct time. Soon the children count aloud for themselves. Later the children can count silently to themselves until the movement patterns become automatic.

Mediation also can be used to control emotional and social responses. For example, a child who is pushed or knocked down in a lunch line may become very angry. If the child uses verbal mediation, he or she can: (1) focus on the problem—He knocked me down; (2) analyze the emotions—That really makes me mad; (3) analyze the situation—He was playing tag and wasn't looking where he was going; it was accidental. As a result of mediation, the child might conclude that the student should be more careful, but that the situation is not worth getting upset over. The child has controlled his or her own emotions and regulated the social responses. Instead of hitting back, the child might respond by saying, "Hey, be a little more careful." Both Luria (1966) and Vygotsky (1962) suggest that children learn socialization by using language to mediate and regulate their social actions and behaviors.

Mediation has a number of applications in academic learning, as in reading, writing, spelling, and arithmetic. For example, a child might use mediation to remember the steps in computing an addition problem. In reading, for example, a child who has previously learned to read *cat* and *hat* can use this previous learning to help mediate new but similar words such as *bat* or *fat*. Knowing that the last two letters look alike and sound alike can be used to mediate the rapid learning of the new words.

During the initial stages of learning, mediation is usually conscious and overt. The child may verbally say things out loud. In time, mediation becomes covert and the child silently speaks to himself or herself. When learning has occurred and the response is nearly automatic, mediation is no longer necessary.

REFERENCES

Luria, A.R. (1966). *Higher cortical functions in man*. New York: Plenum.

Meichenbaum, D., & Aronson, J. (1979). Cognitive behavior modification and metacognition development: Implications for the classroom. In P. Kendall & S. Hollon (Eds.), *Cognitive behavior interventions: Theory, research, and procedures*. New York: Academic.

Peterson, M.J., Colavita, F.J., Sheanan, III, D.B., & Blattner, K.C. (1964). Verbal mediating chains and response availability as a function of the acquisition paradigm. *Journal of Verbal Learning & Verbal Behavior, 3*, 11–18.

Vygotsky, L.S. (1962). *Thought and language* (E. Hanfmann & G. Vakar, Eds. and Trans.). Cambridge, MA: MIT Press.

See also **Attention Deficit Disorder; Behavior Modification; Luria, A.R.; Theory of Activity; Vygotsky, L.S.**

MEDIATIONAL DEFICIENCY

Mediational deficiency refers to an inability to use verbal mediators to facilitate learning. Luria (1961) and Vygotsky (1962) proposed that language and thinking are closely related. Progress in one area affects progress in the other. For example, young children use private speech by talking to themselves to direct their activities and formulate their thoughts. This private speech gradually becomes internalized and serves as an effective mediator enabling children to think before they act.

Older children, according to this mediational model, are better learners than young children because they are more likely to use verbal mediators as a learning aid. Consider a concept formation task in which a child is presented with stimuli that combine one of two shapes (triangle, circle) with one of two colors (red, green). The child must choose all instances of the concept, which may be green shapes. Each time the child chooses correctly he or she is reinforced. It has been hypothesized that the older child, using verbal mediators, will label the important features of the situation (in the preceding example, every correct choice is colored green). It has been observed that older children acquire such a concept quicker than younger children. Young children, not using these private labels or mediators, are likely to keep selecting whatever stimulus has been reinforced most often recently.

Mediational research with the mentally retarded began in the early 1960s. Like young children, the retarded were found to have mediational deficiencies. They failed to produce verbal labels that were within their repertoires such as labeling all the responses as instances of a color. A number of studies were carried out to determine whether mentally retarded children and adults could use verbal mediators to facilitate learning if they were instructed to do so. The data indicated that like young children, retarded individuals could use mediational cues to facilitate learning under mediation-prompting conditions. Their problem, then, might be best described as a production deficiency.

The individual who learns a complex skill and uses it effectively under direct instruction may fail to apply the strategy or skill in other situations. This is especially likely when those situations appropriate for strategy application are not identical to the original situation in which the strategy was learned (Campione & Brown, 1978). Mentally retarded learners experience considerable difficulty when required to transfer their learning to a new situation. After they have been instructed to use mediation and their mediation deficiency has largely disappeared, their performance continues to be characterized by production deficiencies.

REFERENCES

Campione, J.C., & Brown, A.L. (1978). Toward a theory of intelligence. Contributions from research with retarded children. *Intelligence, 2*, 279–304.

Luria, A.R. (1961). *The role of speech in the regulation of normal and abnormal behavior*. New York: Liveright.

Vygotsky, L.S. (1962). *Thought and language* (E. Hanfmann & G. Vakaar, Eds. and Trans.) Cambridge, MA: MIT Press.

See also **Language Therapy; Mediators; Metacognition; Theory of Activity; Verbal Ability of the Handicapped**

MEDIATION ESSAY

The mediation essay is a series of printed statements that describe specific desirable and undesirable behaviors and the consequences of each. It is used as a behavior change technique that uses cognitive intervention (Blackwood, 1970).

The format of a mediation essay is that of a Socratic dialogue, with a question posed and a response detailed. The content is centered around four specific questions and their answers, using the student's own vocabulary. Generally the four questions are as follows: (1) What did I do wrong? (2) Why shouldn't I do _____ (inappropriate behavior)? (3) What should I do? (4) What will happen if I do _____ (appropriate behavior)? (Blackwood, 1970; Morrow & Morrow, 1985). Responses to the first two questions focus on a description of the student's inappropriate behavior and the negative consequences to the child of that behavior. Responses to the last two questions present the desirable, alternative behavior and its positive, to the child, consequences.

Research on the efficacy of the mediation essay with both nonhandicapped (Blackwood, 1970; MacPherson et al., 1974) and handicapped (Morrow & Morrow, 1985) students has been promising. The superiority of the mediation essay, with its focus on positive alternative behaviors, over the more traditional punishment essay has been clearly demonstrated in earlier studies.

REFERENCES

Blackwood, R.O. (1970). The operant conditioning of verbally mediated self-control in the classroom. *Journal of School Psychology, 8,* 251–258.

MacPherson, E.M., Candee, B.L., & Hohman, R.J. (1974). A comparison of three methods for eliminating disruptive lunchroom behavior. *Journal of Applied Behavior Analysis, 7,* 287– 297.

Morrow, L.W., & Morrow, S.A. (1985). Use of verbal mediation procedure to reduce talking-out behaviors. *Teaching: Behaviorally Disordered Youth, 1,* 23–28.

See also **Cognitive Behavior Modification; Contingency Contracting; Life Space Interviewing; Self-Control Curriculum; Self-Monitoring**

MEDICAL CONCERNS OF HANDICAPPED CHILDREN

Five percent, roughly 200,000, of school age children are physically disabled. Special education provides for about 150,000 of these children. An increase in certain physical disabilities has been reported in the last two decades (Harkey, 1983; Wilson, 1973). This may be due to improvements in identification, but more likely, medical advances have improved the survival rates of such children. This creates a great need by the schools and their professionals to understand fully the chronically ill, physically handicapped, and sensory-impaired populations, and the problems of these children imposed on the schools. Harkey (1983) feels that at least 1 to 2% of the child population, about 1 million children, have severe enough illnesses to require some kind of additional professional services to function adequately in school. Since 80% of the mildly handicapped are mainstreamed for at least a portion of the day, each teacher's chances of interacting with a handicapped student are very high. Many handicapped children also have concomitant health problems. Thus it is imperative that school professionals become as knowledgeable as possible about handicapping conditions.

Many teachers have concerns about how best to meet these varied needs in order to provide adequate educational programs for handicapped children. Recent state, federal, and Supreme Court decisions have substantiated the right of these multihandicapped and chronically ill children to be mainstreamed where possible and to have support services provided by the schools (computer-assisted instruction, mechanical interpreters, extended school year, etc.). Given all these mandates, the teacher needs to develop a good interdisciplinary cooperative program with the many specialists involved with handicapped children with medical problems. The teacher must know what other disciplines are involved with the child, and he or she needs to be able to communicate professionally with persons in the medical field about the physical, emotional, cognitive, and social development of the handicapped child. Because of the support services needed, the occupational and physical therapists may be able to give valuable suggestions about working with the child in a regular or resource classroom. Continuing therapeutic management in the classroom will be needed so that the child can have a program that encourages independence and skill development.

Good communication must be maintained with the handicapped child's family. Family cooperation and encouragement are necessary for success in school. The most crucial tool for dealing with illness and disabilities is information; thus parents and teachers need to communicate regularly so that information can be shared. Since these children may have erratic attendance, maladaptive social behavior, severe side effects, and isolation owing to equipment needs and geographic location of care facilities, it is important that parents and school personnel work together to make the various transitions as smooth as possible for the child. Hobbs et al. (1984) have pointed out that chronically ill children are often short-changed educationally because teachers and school professionals develop plans for these children based on existing school services instead of what the child needs. Home and hospital programs, though often necessary, can be sketchy, disjointed, and take place in a diversity of settings.

REFERENCES

Harkey, J. (1983). The epidemiology of selected chronic childhood health conditions. *Children's Health Care, 112,* 62–71.

Hobbs, N., Perrin, J., Freys, H., Moynihan, L., & Shayne, M. (1984). Chronically ill children in America. *Rehabilitation Literature, 45,* 206–211.

Wilson, M. (1973). Children with crippling and health disabilities. In L.M. Dunn (Ed.), *Exceptional children in the schools* (2nd ed.). New York: Holt, Rinehart, & Winston.

See also **Abnormalities, Neuropsychological; Adaptive Physical Education; Medical History, Somatic Complaints; Medical Management; Physical Anomalies; Physical Disabilities**

MEDICAL HISTORY, SOMATIC COMPLAINTS

When a student has academic or behavioral problems, or does not look physically well, educators often wonder if they should refer the student to a physician or psychologist for further evaluation. There are several areas of inquiry that could help the educator determine the need for one kind of referral or another (Zeltzer & LeBaron, 1984).

An assessment interview with the student should include an inquiry into the student's interests and favorite activities such as hobbies, favorite books, television programs, friends, and pets. The educator should observe whether the student appears unusually shy, defensive, anxious, or depressed. Next, the educator needs to ask about any current academic or interpersonal problems or physical symptoms in general. Questions regarding physical symptoms should include inquiries about pain, fatigue, recent changes in appetite or sleep patterns (including nightmares), activity changes, bodily concerns, or unusual physical sensations. Questions regarding academic and social concerns should include worries about friends, family, teachers, or school performance, or activity in general. Inquiry also should include recent or anticipated problems or changes such as illness in family members, divorce, unemployment, or change of residence.

A large percentage of visits to general pediatricians are made for nonmedical reasons. In a school setting, one may expect an even greater likelihood that a very large proportion of problems, even when they have a somatic component, are not primarily medical. Somatic complaints are often the manifestation of three types of common problems seen in an educational setting:

1. *Problems Emanating from a Poorly Functioning Family.* Such problems may consist of a poor parent/child relationship, inconsistent parenting, parental discord, physical or sexual abuse, or parental neglect. In problem families, major psychiatric disorders or alcoholism are frequent findings that require serious attention. Suspicion of abuse or neglect should be reported to the Department of Child Welfare.

2. *Anxiety Regarding Change.* Children are often anxious regarding physical or social change. As children and adolescents grow and develop, they are frequently worried about their ability to match perceived standards set by peers, parents, teachers, or themselves. These anxieties may reflect a distorted view of the child's own abilities, but in other cases may represent a realistic self-assessment of the child's own disabilities.

3. *Medical Problems with an Identifiable Organic Basis.* If the student is not feeling well physically, he or she may not be able to concentrate on school work, and a decline in the student's academic performance may result.

In general, any somatic complaints or significant changes in appetite or sleep should be cause for referral to a physician for further evaluation. One exception would be when there is an isolated symptom (e.g., abdominal pain) that is clearly related to a specific source of stress and that disappears when the child no longer has that stress. If the physician is unable to find a cause for the complaints and the problems persist, then the child should be seen by a clinical psychologist or other mental health professional associated with the school. Whether or not a mental health referral is made, maintenance of good physician/educator collaboration can prevent further unnecessary medical work-ups for the child and can facilitate a direct line of medical information when needed (LeBaron & Zeltzer, 1985; Marshall, Wuori, & Carlson, 1984; Parette & Bartlett, 1996).

REFERENCES

LeBaron, S., & Zeltzer, L. (1985). Pediatrics and psychology: A collaboration that works. *Journal of Developmental & Behavioral Pediatrics, 6*(3), 157–161.

Marshall, R.M., Wuori, D.F., & Carlson, J.R. (1984). Improving physician/teacher collaboration. *Journal of Developmental & Behavioral Pediatrics, 5*(5), 241–245.

Parette, H.P., & Bartlett, C.S. (1996). Collaboration and ecological assessment: Bridging the gap between the medical and educational environments for students who are medically fragile. *Physical Disabilities, 15*(1), 33–47.

Zeltzer, L.K., & LeBaron, S. (1984). Psychosomatic problems in adolescents. *Postgraduate Medicine, 75*(1), 153–164.

See also **Medical Management; Mental Status; Prereferral Intervention; Teacher Expectancies**

MEDICALLY FRAGILE STUDENT

The medically fragile student requires monitoring by the teacher during the school day in order to ensure that all of the body's physical systems are stable. The student's specific problem may or may not require that the teacher know special intervention techniques in case of emergency.

Medically fragile students are different from each other. They have different needs, energy levels, and potentials. Some children may exhibit a pervasive fragility (a generalized pattern of slow growth and development) but require no specific intervention. More likely, the child will have a chronic illness or experience an acute episode of a condition that requires that specific procedures be available when needed or that the daily routine be modified in order for the child to participate in school activities.

For each medically fragile child the teacher and school administration should be trained to handle specific procedures that the child may need. For instance, if the student has life-threatening seizures, school personnel need to know exactly what procedures the child's parents and physicians want followed. All directions must be written in detail, signed, dated and discussed with the principal and teacher before the child attends school.

Other health problems that may label a child medically fragile include chronic diseases, terminal conditions, post-surgery recovery, apnea, severe depression, cardiovascular problems, and kidney dysfunction. For some medically fragile children there are periods when they will be hospitalized for a long time, thus requiring hospital-based educational services.

See also **Health Maintenance Procedures**

MEDICAL MANAGEMENT

Because of advances made during the past 10 to 15 years in medical diagnosis and treatment, many childhood diseases formerly considered fatal have now become chronic illnesses such as cystic fibrosis and cancer (Zeltzer, 1978). Because of improved medical management, many children who would have been bedridden are now able to attend school. Examples include those with cyanotic heart disease, chronic renal disease, and rheumatologic diseases such as systemic lupus erythematosis and rheumatoid arthritis. Asthma and diabetes mellitus are the most common chronic illness of childhood. These and others are discussed in a text by Blum (1984) and a volume edited by Haggerty (1984).

When a chronic illness flares up, children often feel anxious or depressed about having to miss out on planned activities. Some children worry about the possibility of dying. Although chronic illness per se does not invariably lead to increased anxiety or poor self-esteem, such feelings, when they do occur, can lead to chronic school absenteeism and poor relationships with peers. The medications that are required to manage most illnesses often have side effects with psychological consequences. For example, some of the medications taken by children with asthma can lead to hyperactivity or periods of irritability and short attention span.

The role of the educator in managing such children in an academic setting is to become as well informed as possible about the particular illness and its treatment. The educator needs to discuss the illness and the treatment with the student and his or her parents and, if possible, with the physician. The educator needs to develop an educational plan that is flexible and highly individualized. This plan needs to be reviewed frequently as the student's needs may change because of variations in the course of the disease. Chronically ill children usually respond well to educators who are personally supportive and interested in them as individuals. It is important for educators to recognize that most children and adolescents are remarkably resilient and that they cope well with illness and its treatment. The most important contribution the educator can make is to become well acquainted with the ill student and to encourage a normal life as much as possible while responding to the child's individual needs.

REFERENCES

Blum, R. (Ed.). (1984). *Chronic illness and disabilities in childhood and adolescence.* Orlando, FL: Grune & Stratton.

Haggerty, R. (Ed.). (1984). Chronic disease in children. *Pediatric Clinics of North America, 31*(1), 1–275.

Zeltzer, L. (1978). Chronic illness in the adolescent. In I.R. Shenker (Ed.), *Topics in adolescent medicine* (pp. 226–253). New York: Stratton Intercontinental Medical.

See also **Chemotherapy; Diabetes; Medical History, Somatic Complaints**

MEDICAL MODEL, DEFENSE OF

The medical model describes a theoretical orientation that focuses on the underlying, frequently physical cause of an observed problem, impairment, or disorder (Davis, 1980). Synonyms for the medical model include the disease model and the pathological model.

Within the field of special education, the medical model is most clearly applicable in cases of physical impairment such as visual, hearing, or orthopedic handicaps. Assessment techniques are designed to identify signs of such phys-

ical disability. Mass screenings in schools for vision or hearing problems, scoliosis, or tuberculosis are conducted within the framework of the medical model. Consistent with the ethical standards of this orientation, conservative decision rules are employed. Children identified as at risk for the disorder as a result of the screening procedure are referred for additional assessment and, if necessary, appropriate treatment (Helton et al., 1982). Application of the medical model in other areas of special education, particularly with the mildly handicapped, has been criticized. Mercer (1973), for example, stated that "the medical model for conceptualizing mental retardation in the community was inadequate" (pp. 20–21). Mercer does note, however, that the use of the medical model is more defensible in cases of mental retardation syndromes where there is "clear evidence of biological dysfunction" (p. 8).

In a detailed discussion of the application of the medical model in the interpretation of specific learning disabilities, Gaddes (1985) and Barbour (1995) indicate that many of the most frequent criticisms of the medical model (e.g., that it does not promote change or growth and minimizes the role of psychoeducational intervention) are not inherent in the model itself, but are a result of abuses in its application. Gaddes indicates that use of a neuropsychological model, which is a special orientation within the generic medical model, has a number of important advantages. Neuropsychology, he argues, is a respected, established scientific field. Because all behavior is a byproduct of brain and central nervous system functioning, understanding brain-behavior relationships is critical to knowledge of children's learning and behavior. A neuropsychological or biopsychosocial diagnostic model helps identify the cause of observed disorders, which in turn leads to the development of more effective interventions.

REFERENCES

Barbour, A.B. (1995). *Caring for patients: A critique of the medical model.* Stanford, CA: Stanford University Press.

Gaddes, W.H. (1985). *Learning disabilities and brain function: A neuropsychological approach* (2nd ed.). New York: Springer-Verlag.

Helton, G.B., Workman, E.A., & Matuszek, P.A. (1982). *Psychoeducational assessment.* New York: Grune & Stratton.

Mercer, J.R. (1973). *Labeling the mentally retarded.* Berkeley: University of California Press.

See also **Biogenic Models; Neuropsychology; Psychogenic Models**

MEDICATION

See SPECIFIC MEDICATION.

MEDIUM CHAIN ACYL-COENZYME A DEHYDROGENASE DEFICIENCY (MCAD)

See RARE DISEASES.

MEGAVITAMIN THERAPY

Megadose vitamin therapy (or orthomolecular treatment) is generally defined as the consumption of a vitamin dose greater than ten times the Recommended Dietary Allowance (RDA; Lutz & Przytulski, 1997). Although megavitamin therapy regimes are often prescribed and closely monitored by physicians, controversy remains related to self-administration. Megadoses of vitamins are often consumed by pregnant women who are trying to eat well and mistakenly assume that with vitamin supplementation, more is better (Whitney, Cataldo, & Rolfes, 1998). Such therapy is hazardous during pregnancy and may cause irreversible damage to the unborn fetus. Therapeutic treatments with megadoses of vitamins should be administered only by physicians conversant with both the treatments' risks and side effects.

Documentation regarding the use of megadose vitamins in the treatment of acute schizophrenia (Hoffer, 1994), cancer, and hardening of the arteries (Hoffer, 1995) remains controversial. In terms of megavitamins and children's intelligence, improved performance occurs primarily in children whose diets were low in vitamins and minerals (Benton, 1995).

Evaluation of the controversial megadose-vitamin treatment of individuals with Down's Syndrome failed to show intellectual improvement (Selikowitz, 1990). Selikowitz cautioned that high-dose vitamins can accumulate in the body causing toxic effects, slowing the child's development, and even causing ill health. Despite inadequate evaluation and negative research findings, elevated doses of vitamins also continue to be frequently prescribed for and taken by individuals affected with pathological conditions such as neurological discomforts, psychosis, alopecia, or inherited metabolic defects (Combs, 1992).

The Council on Scientific Affairs of the American Medical Association (AMA) has stated that support for megadose-vitamin therapy to date is based on anecdotal or nonscientific evidence (Davis & Sherer, 1994). The Council went on to state that use of megadose-vitamin therapies can contribute to false hopes and needless financial expense, as well as produce direct toxic effects or even adverse interactions among vital nutrients (Davis & Sherer, 1994). Research continues on the effects and effectiveness of megadose vitamins. As more is known about the pharmacologic effects of some vitamins, special use of them in larger therapeutic doses is likely to occur.

REFERENCES

Benton, D. (1995). Vitamin/mineral supplementation and the intelligence of children: A review. *Journal of Orthomolecular Medicine, 7*, 21–29.

Combs, G.E. (1992). *The vitamins: Fundamental aspects in nutrition and health.* New York: Academic Press.

Davis, J., & Sherer, K. (1994). *Applied nutrition and diet therapy for nurses* (2nd ed.). Philadelphia: Saunders.

Hoffer, A. (1994). Follow-up reports on chronic schizophrenic patients. *Journal of Orthomolecular Medicine, 9,* 121–123.

Hoffer, A. (1995). The megavitamin revolution. *Journal of Orthomolecular Medicine, 7,* 3–5.

Lutz, C., & Przytulski, K. (1997). *Nutrition and diet therapy* (2nd ed.). Philadelphia: Davis.

Selikowitz, M. (1990). *Down Syndrome: The facts.* New York: Oxford University Press.

Whitney, E., Cataldo, C., & Rolfes, S. (1998). *Understanding normal and clinical nutrition* (5th ed.). Belmont, CA: Wadsworth.

See also **Malnutrition; Nutritional Disorders**

MELLARIL

Mellaril is the trade name for the generic phenothiazine, thioridazine. In addition to its general applications for symptomatic relief in psychotic disorders, Mellaril also appears to show some efficacy in psychotic disorders with depressive components. It also has been used in short-term, symptomatic treatment of agitation, depression, sleep disturbance, and fears in elderly patients, and for the short-term symptomatic treatment of hyperactivity, combativeness, attention problems, mood lability, and poor frustration tolerance in children (McEvoy, 1984).

Like all phenothiazines, Mellaril produces some sedation, especially during early administration. In addition, anticholinergic effects (dry mouth, urinary retention, motor incoordination), extrapyramidal symptoms, dystonic reactions, motor restlessness, and parkinsonlike symptoms are among the adverse effects that may be experienced early in treatment or from overdosage.

REFERENCE

McEvoy, G.K. (1984). *American hospital formulary service: Drug information 84.* Bethesda, MD: American Society of Hospital Pharmacists.

See also **Stellazine; Thorazine; Tranquilizers**

MEMORY DISORDERS

Neuropsychological research suggests that memory disorders may occur with brain injury or neurological disease. Generally speaking, a memory disorder refers to a deficiency in the storage and/or retrieval of information. Impaired memory functioning is one of the most common symptoms of generalized cerebral damage (Straub & Black, 1977).

An understanding of memory disorders is facilitated by an appreciation of the basic memory components. Although a number of memory models have been proposed, three distinct yet interactive memory stores are generally implicated (Shallice, 1979). Incoming sensory information is thought to be held briefly and selected for future processing in a sensory register. Research in this area suggests that information in the sensory register is either transferred to short-term memory or is rapidly replaced by incoming information.

Short-term store, or immediate memory, is portrayed as a temporary working memory of limited capacity. Information in the short-term store has been shown to be accessible for 20 to 30 seconds (Norman, 1973) and limited to approximately five to nine items (Miller, 1956). Information in the short-term memory is rehearsed and subsequently stored in long-term memory or is displaced by incoming information. Thus rehearsal serves to prolong the memory trace as well as to facilitate permanent storage. In sum, information in short-term memory appears to be unstable and lost or inaccessible unless transferred into the more enduring long-term store.

Long-term memory refers to the relatively permanent storage of information. Seen as the result of repeated presentations of information or very salient stimuli, long-term storage involves a relatively permanent structural or biochemical change in the brain (Hillgard & Bower, 1975). The long-term storage of information involves both transfer and consolidation of sensory inputs. Simply stated, transfer refers to the transmission of information from short-term memory to long-term memory or directly to long-term memory from the sensory register. A much more complex process, consolidation involves the progressive strengthening of memory traces over time. Disruption of the consolidation process may impair the ability to learn.

The brain has been clearly linked to memory processing. Indeed, convincing data have been offered that closely tie the temporal area of the brain to memory functioning. Primarily involved in audition, the temporal lobe appears to be instrumental in triggering complex memories. In addition, a substantial amount of research has shown that damage to the hippocampus (structure within the limbic system lying just under the temporal flap) serves in the consolidation and transfer of information to long-term store. It has also been shown that bilateral damage to the hippocampus results in the inability to learn other than simple rudimentary motor skills (Barbizet, 1963). On the basis of such data, it has been concluded that the temporal lobe and specifically the limbic system may be the underlying anatomical substrates of the memory system.

Damage to the temporal lobe or its related structures (e.g., hippocampus, fornix, mammillary bodies, thalamus) often results in memory dysfunction. The most prevalent disorder, retrograde amnesia, refers to an impairment in the ability to retrieve information from the period prior to brain pathology. While most often affecting memories stored up to 30 minutes preceding the damage (Lezak, 1983), retrograde amnesia relates to the disturbance of memories from several months to many years prior to onset. However, older, well-ingrained memories are rarely permanently disrupted.

Anterograde amnesia, a much more serious memory disturbance, is characterized by a profound deficit in the ability to retain new information. While immediate (short-term) memory functioning may be intact, the ability to recall day-to-day events over hours is severely impaired. Thus learning new material is difficult, if not impossible. Interestingly, however, a number of investigators have shown that patients suffering from chronic anterograde amnesia generally are able to retrieve information learned prior to the neuropathology (Squire & Slater, 1978). These data suggest that anterograde amnesia stems from a problem in encoding new information rather than from difficulty in retrieving previously stored information.

In addition to affecting memory processes in circumscribed ways, cerebral pathology may also differentially affect the storage and retrieval of specific types of material. For example, depending on the location of the brain dysfunction, a memory deficit may be limited to either verbal or nonverbal material. So, too, a specific memory deficit may be isolated to previously learned motor behaviors (Corkin, 1968).

Traumatic brain injuries often produce memory impairments (traumatic amnesia). Typically, postconcussion memory loss includes both retrograde and anterograde amnesia. Following a traumatic loss of consciousness, individuals often experience a temporary inability to store and retrieve incoming information. During the posttraumatic period, the individual may appear to behave normally, but may later have little recollection of specific behaviors. A number of investigators have concluded that posttraumatic amnesia is significantly related to the length of coma as well as the severity of the cerebral insult (Evans, 1975).

Older memories usually remain intact after the trauma, however, memories involving the minutes or several hours prior to the cerebral trauma may be inaccessible. Moreover, if the coma lasts for several days or weeks, the retrograde amnesia may be much more pervasive. Over time, however, many of the well-ingrained memories are again accessible. While a number of memory disturbances seem to be concomitant with traumatic head injuries, the specific effects of such trauma are dependent on the severity, age, and site of the damage (Lezak, 1983). There are three basic types of intervention strategies for this population: externally driven interventions aimed at changing the environment, interventions aimed at improving cognitive ability, and interventions that teach compensatory strategies (Mateer, Kerns, & Eso, 1996).

Congenital anomalies may also lead to problems of memory and learning. Clearly, such congenital abnormalities as cerebral palsy, meningitis, and hydrocephalus have been associated with severe learning and memory difficulties. The memory disorders associated with these congenital conditions tend to be pervasive and may make learning difficult at best. Consistent with this pervasive impairment in learning (Maurer, 1992), severe disruption of the storage and retrieval processes have been shown to be characteristic. Because of this diffuse impairment, patients often require special education services or custodial care. Indeed, there are some that posit many learning disabilities and language disorders as memory disorders (Gathercole & Baddeley, 1990).

REFERENCES

Barbizet, J. (1963). Defect of memorizing of hippocampal-mammillary origin: A review. *Journal of Neurology, Neurosurgery, & Psychiatry, 26,* 127–135.

Corkin, S. (1968). Acquisition of motor skills after bilateral medial temporal lobe excision. *Neuropsychologia, 6,* 255–266.

Evans, M. (1975). Discussion of the clinical problem. *In Ciba Foundation Symposium, No. 34 (new series). Symposium on the outcome of severe damage to the CNS.* Amsterdam: Elsevier-Excerpta Medica.

Gathercole, S.E., & Baddeley, A.D. (1990). Phonological memory deficits in language disordered children: Is there a causal connection? *Journal of Memory & Language, 29*(3), 336–360.

Hillgard, E.R., & Bower, G.H. (1975). *Theories of learning.* Englewood Cliffs, NJ: Prentice-Hall.

Lezak, M.D. (1983). *Neuropsychological assessment.* New York: Oxford University Press.

Mateer, C.A., Kerns, K.A., & Eso, K.L. (1996). Management of attention and memory disorders following traumatic brain injury. *Journal of Learning Disabilities, 29*(6), 618–632.

Miller, G.A. (1956). The magical number seven, plus or minus two: Some limits on our capacity for processing information. *Psychological Review, 63,* 81–97.

Norman, D.A. (1973). What have the animal experiments told us about human memory? In J.A. Deutsch (Ed.), *The physiological basis of memory* (pp. 248–260). New York: Academic.

Shallice, T. (1979). Neuropsychological research and the fractionation of memory systems. In L.G. Nilsson (Ed.), *Perspectives on memory research* (pp. 218–236). Hillsdale, NJ: Erlbaum.

Squire, L.R., & Slater, P.L. (1978). Anterograde and retrograde memory impairment in chronic amnesia. *Neuropsychologia, 16,* 313–322.

Straub, R.L., & Black, F.W. (1977). *The mental status examination in neurology.* Philadelphia: Davis.

See also **Amnesia; Cholinesterase; Dysnomia; Learning Disabilities; Test of Memory & Learning**

MENINGITIS

Meningitis is an infection or inflammation of the membranes covering the brain and spinal cord. It may affect the arachnoid, the pia mater, and the cerebrospinal fluid in the subarachnoid space. The infection resulting in meningitis may occur via spinal fluid pathways, directly from a local infection or the bloodstream, or via retrograde thrombophlebitis (*Melloni's,* 1985). Meningitis is classified by the causative agent, and may include bacterial meningitis, meningococcal meningitis, and viral meningitis. A lumbar puncture is conducted to obtain a sample of cerebrospinal fluid in which the causative agent can be identified (Thomson, 1979).

Seventy percent of the cases of bacterial meningitis are caused by Streptococcus pneumoniae, Neisseria meningitidis, and Homophilus influenza type b, collectively (Swartz, 1979). There is a strong age component associated with the etiologic agent in cases of bacterial meningitis. In neonates, gram-negative bacilli are the major bacterial cause of meningitis, with H. influenza type b the most common agent in children under the age of 5 (Swartz, 1979). Neisseria meningitidis is the offending bacterium in meningococcal meningitis, a common form of the disease. Transmission may occur from person to person via hand to hand, hand to mouth, or mouth to mouth contact (Feldman, 1979).

Bacterial meningitis is characterized by an acute onset of fever, headache, vomiting, and stiff neck. Prior history of upper respiratory infection, acute otitis, or pneumonia may be identified (Swartz, 1979). Drowsiness and lethargy may be evident. Seizures may be present in 20 to 30% of affected individuals. Partial or complete sensorineural hearing loss may occur in patients over 3 years of age, and may persist (Swartz, 1979). While rapid recovery from bacterial meningitis typically follows prompt treatment with antibiotics, residual neurologic impairment may be identified in 10 to 20% of recovered individuals (Swartz, 1979).

Viral meningitis, in contrast to the bacterial form, is described as "a benign, self-limited illness" (Johnson, 1979, p. 817). The coxsackie and echoviruses are associated with approximately 50% of the cases of viral meningitis (Johnson, 1979). Symptoms develop rapidly, and include headache, fever, stiff neck, sore throat, nausea, and vomiting; symptoms may persist from 3 to 14 days. Full recovery is typically within 1 to 2 weeks (Johnson, 1979).

Some children with a history of bacterial meningitis may require special education and related services (Gade, Bohr, Bjerrum & Udesen, 1992). Hearing loss may be a residual impairment in some individuals, and generalized intellectual deficiency resulting from high fever or seizures may be identified. A multi-factored evaluation is essential in planning an educational program for affected children.

REFERENCES

Feldman, H.A. (1979). Meningococcal disease. In P.B. Beeson, W. McDermott, & J.B. Wyngaarden (Eds.), *Cecil textbook of medicine* (pp. 417–423). Philadelphia: Saunders.

Gade, A., Bohr, V., Bjerrum, J., & Udesen, H. (1992). Neuropsychological sequelae in 91 cases of pneumococcal meningitis. *Developmental Neuropsychology, 8*(4), 447–457.

Johnson, R.T. (1979). Viral meningitis and encephalitis. In P.B. Beeson, W. McDermott, & J.B. Wyngaarden (Eds.), *Cecil textbook of medicine* (pp. 817–821). Philadelphia: Saunders.

Melloni's illustrated medical dictionary (2nd ed.). (1985). Baltimore, MD: Williams & Wilkins.

Swartz, M.N. (1979). Bacterial meningitis. In P.B. Beeson, W. McDermott, & J.B. Wyngaarden (Eds.), *Cecil textbook of medicine* (pp. 411–416). Philadelphia: Saunders.

Thomson, W.A.R. (1979). *Black's medical dictionary* (32nd ed.). New York: Barnes & Noble.

MENINGOMYELOCELE

Meningomyelocele is an abnormal outpouching of the spinal cord through an opening in the back of the spine. The term is synonymous with myelomeningocele and is a more common form of spina bifida than a meningocele (an outpouching that includes only the protective membranes but not the spinal cord). The outpouching of the spinal cord and its nerve roots into the meningomyelocele causes a flaccid paralysis and loss of sensation in the lower extremities or trunk. This loss of function depends on the level of the spinal cord defect and the number of nerve roots involved.

The cause of a meningomyelocele is essentially unknown. It occurs when the neural tube (the cells that form the spine and spinal cord) fails to develop and close completely in the first few weeks of pregnancy. A meningomyelocele may be detected using several intrauterine tests, most commonly amniocentesis or ultrasound. Early treatment includes closure of the open sack to prevent infection, a procedure that often requires the removal of some neural elements. Additional surgery also may be required subsequently to repair other conditions that are frequently associated with meningomyelocele. These secondary conditions may include hydrocephalus and orthopedic abnormalities in the legs or spine such as club foot or scoliosis.

Loss of bowel and bladder control is common for persons with a meningomyelocele. Management of bowel and bladder function may include a combination of suppositories, diet, medication, and clean intermittent catheterization. Physical and occupational therapy, bracing, wheelchairs, and other assistive devices often promote increased functional independence and permit a productive and rewarding life.

See also **Physical Handicaps; Spina Bifida**

MENTAL AGE

Mental age is an age-equivalent score derived from a general test of intellectual skill or aptitude. The mathematical derivation is the same as for other types of age-equivalent scores. A mental age represents the mean level of performance or a group of children at a particular chronological age on the test in question.

Mental ages have been popular for some time and are necessary in the calculation of ratio IQs, a type of IQ scale abandoned many years ago by all major tests of intelligence. Mental ages are regarded by most psychologists and psychometricians as a poor method of score reporting; standard scores are considered superior in all instances (Reynolds, Gutkin, Elliott, & Witt, 1984).

REFERENCE

Reynolds, C.R., Gutkin, T.B., Elliott, S.N., & Witt, J.C. (1984). *School psychology: Essentials of theory and practice.* New York: Wiley.

See also **Central Tendency; Deviation IQ; Grade Equivalents; Ratio IQ; Standard Deviation**

MENTAL DEFICIENCY

See MENTAL RETARDATION.

MENTAL ILLNESS

Mental illness is a disease or condition that is manifested in disruptions of an individual's behavior, thinking, perception, or emotions. Other terms used synonymously are mental, psychiatric, and psychological disorder or disease.

No other term in psychiatry has prompted more heated debate than mental illness. It has been used as a vehicle for politically based, interprofessional fighting, as well as a means of focusing on differences in theoretical approaches to abnormal behavior. Although the current controversies about the usefulness of the concept of mental illness are recent, the term has a long history.

Several arguments have been offered to the effect that the sickness model, embodied in the term mental illness, has outlived its usefulness. One implication of this model is that physician-psychiatrists should hold primary, if not sole, responsibility for the treatment of people labeled as mentally ill. The terms illness, cure, psychiatric hospital, treatment, remission, and relapse are all borrowed from medicine and applied to the psychotherapeutic endeavor. And who best to administer the treatment but someone trained within the medical profession? Thus, some authors have argued that psychiatry is endorsing a view of abnormal behavior that strengthens their professional territorial boundary (Mowrer, 1960).

Other attacks aimed at the sickness model are rooted in alternate theoretical approaches to mental illness such as replacing the term with the phrase "problems in living" (Kanfer & Phillips, 1970; Szasz, 1961). This learning-based framework holds that abnormal behavior is not a manifestation of an underlying psychic disorder, but is a result of a reciprocal interaction between behavior and environment (Bandura, 1969; Davison & Neale, 1982). Within this framework, terms such as mental illness, disease, symptoms, and cure have little meaning. Symptoms are not the outgrowth of an underlying psychic disease process but are the client's problems. They are learned, maladaptive strategies that may have several purposes such as anxiety reduction, avoiding negative social consequences, or evoking positive consequences from others. The implications for diagnosis and treatment are accordingly different from the traditional sickness model (Kanfer & Grimm, 1977). Recently the debate has become less political, and paradigmatic demarcations are beginning to blur as clinicians strive for a theoretical rapprochement (Wachtel, 1977) and reimbursement for services that are supervised by managed care companies that demand medical model coding.

The *Diagnostic and Statistical Manual* (*DSM-IV*) lists over 30 disorders under the heading "Disorders Usually First Evident in Infancy, Childhood, or Adolescence." The disorders range in severity from infantile autism to developmental arithmetic disorder. It has been charged that knowledge of the *DSM-IV* criteria for neuropsychiatric disorders does not always help diagnosis because children manifest behavior differently than adults (Taylor, 1998).

It is not uncommon for parents to voice concern when

their children exhibit what appears to be deviant behavior. Fortunately, most children's problems are time limited. It is typical for 2 year olds to fear strangers, 4 year olds to fear the dark, and 5 year olds to fear dreams and robbers (Gray, 1971). Symptoms occurring before the age of six have little predictive significance for later problems. There are, of course, notable exceptions. A child with many symptoms at one age is likely to have several symptoms at a later age (Robins, 1972). Mental retardation and Infantile Autism are usually evident at an early age and persist through subsequent developmental periods.

An example of a childhood disorder is attention-deficit/hyperactivity disorder. The main features are short attention span, impulsivity, and excessive motor activity. These children give the impression of not listening and have difficulty in carrying tasks through to completion. Their school work is often sloppy, unorganized, and replete with careless errors of omissions and insertions. Their attention deficit is exaggerated in the classroom and when performing in loosely structured settings. They appear to be perpetually in motion as they run and climb excessively. The disorder is usually evident by age three but may go undiagnosed until the child enters school. It is typical that the child's behavior fluctuates across situations and time. Thus, the disorder is not invariant and periods of well-organized behavior are to be expected. The child may show personality characteristics of stubbornness, bullying, low frustration tolerance, and outbursts of anger. The disorder may persist into adulthood, disappear at puberty, or show a diminution of excessive motor activity while still revealing attentional deficits. Approximately 3% of children have this problem and 90% of them are boys.

Another common childhood disorder is separation anxiety disorder. The essential aspect of this disorder is excessive anxiety surrounding separation from major attachment figures, home, or familiar surroundings. The child may become anxious to the point of panic and refuse to sleep at friends' homes, go to school, or play a few blocks from home. Anticipated separation may evoke physical complaints such as headaches or stomach aches. These children are often preoccupied by thoughts of death and horrible fears of harm befalling the family. The ill-defined fears of the younger child may become more focused in later years and center on potential dangers such as kidnapping, burglars, or car accidents. Adolescent boys may deny feeling anxious when away from their mothers, but their propensity to stay at home, and discomfort when forced to leave the house for a day or two, reflect their separation anxiety. Children with this disorder often fear the dark and prefer to sleep with their parents, even if it requires sleeping on the floor outside their mother and father's bedroom door. These children may be described as clinging, demanding, and in need of constant reassurance. The disorder typically begins after some trauma such as a move, death of a pet, illness, or loss of a friend or relative. The disorder may persist for several years with exacerbations and remissions. Further, sep-

aration anxiety may continue into adulthood and manifest itself in a person's reluctance to move out of the house or excessive dependency on a spouse.

REFERENCES

Bandura, A. (1969). *Principles of behavior modification.* New York: Holt, Rinehart, and Winston.

Davison, G.C., & Neale, J.M. (1982). *Abnormal psychology.* New York: Wiley.

Gray, J. (1971). *The psychology of fear and stress.* New York: McGraw-Hill.

Kanfer, F.H., & Grimm, L.G. (1977). Behavior analysis: Selecting target behaviors in the interview. *Behavior Modification, 1,* 7–28.

Kanfer, F.H., & Phillips, J.S. (1970). *Learning foundations of behavior therapy.* New York: Wiley.

Mowrer, O.H. (1960). "Sin," the lesser of two evils. *American Psychologist, 15,* 301–304.

Robins, L.N. (1972). Follow-up studies of behavior disorders in children. In H.C. Quay & J.S. Werry (Eds.), *Psychopathological disorders in childhood.* New York: Wiley

Szasz, T.S. (1961). *The myth of mental illness: Foundations of a theory of personal conduct.* New York: Hoeber-Harper.

Taylor, E.H. (1998). Advances in the diagnosis and treatment of children with serious mental illness. *Child Welfare, 77*(3), 311–332.

Wachtel, P. (1977). *Psychoanalysis and behavior therapy: Toward an integration.* New York: Basic Books.

See also **Diagnostic & Statistical Manual of Mental Disorders (DSM-IV); Projective Techniques; Sociopathy**

MENTALLY RETARDED, EDUCABLE
See MENTAL RETARDATION.

MENTAL RETARDATION

Mental retardation has been known for centuries, and different terms have been used by professionals to refer to individuals having the condition. Among terms used centuries ago are naturals, idiots, and natural fools. From the early- to mid-20th century, moron, imbecile, and idiot referred to three levels of retardation (from highest to lowest), and until about 1940, the inclusive term was feebleminded. More recent terms include mental deficiency, mental subnormality, mental challenge, and developmental disability, the latter implying a long-term severe disability.

Definitions of mental retardation are designed to reflect current thinking about the condition and to represent the status of knowledge of the field (Grossman, 1983). In adopting this definition and the accompanying classification system, AAMR replaced the mild, moderate, severe and profound classifications in previous definitions with levels of support needed by an individual: intermittent, limited, extensive, and pervasive. These terms may be summarized as follows:

Intermittent: Supports of high or low intensity are provided intermittently as needed. Characterized as episodic or short-term during life-span transitions.

Limited: Supports are provided consistently over time, but may not be extensive at any one time. Supports may require fewer staff members and expense than more intense levels of support.

Extensive: Supports are provided regularly, perhaps daily, in at least some environments such as work or home. Support may not be intensive but will be needed long term.

Pervasive: High intensity supports are provided constantly, across environments, and may be of life-sustaining and intrusive nature. Pervasive supports typically involve a variety of staff members.

Since the 1992 AAMR definition was published, others have been developed in part because of dissatisfaction with it. This dissatisfaction centered around the IQ cutoff level, the adaptive skill areas, and the levels of needed support. The most notable definition is the one proposed by the American Psychological Association (Jackson & Mulick, 1996):

Mental retardation (MR) refers to: (a) significant limitations in general intellectual functioning; (b) significant limitations in adaptive functioning, which exist concurrently; and (c) onset of intellectual and adaptive limitations before the age of 22 years.

This definition essentially restates the 1983 AAMD definition except that it raises the developmental period to age 22, consistent with the federal definition of developmental disabilities.

The American Psychiatric Association in its fourth edition of the *Diagnostic and Statistical Manual of Mental Disorders* (*DSM-IV;* 1994) also retains the essence of the 1983 AAMD definition of mental retardation as well as the levels of severity of mental retardation. Mental retardation is characterized by significantly subaverage intellectual functioning (an IQ of approximately 70 or below) with onset before age 18 and concurrent deficits or impairments in adaptive functioning. Four degrees of severity are specified reflecting the level of intellectual impairment: mild, moderate, severe, and profound. Furthermore, *DSM-IV* and the *International Statistical Classification of Diseases and Related Health Problems, Tenth Revision* (*ICD-10*) have coordinated sections on mental and behavioral disorders so that they both have the same definition and classification system for mental retardation. Definitions of mental retardation have changed over time reflecting both social and political forces, and they likely will continue to change in the future. For example, AAMR is reexamining its definition of mental retardation once again.

Individuals classified as mentally retarded represent a heterogeneous group with respect to both etiology and functioning within their environments. A number of predisposing conditions are associated with mental retardation. Hereditary factors include single-gene recessive inborn er-

rors of metabolism, such as Tay-Sachs Disease and tuberous sclerosis, and chromosomal aberrations, of which nondisjunction Down's syndrome and Fragile X are the best known. Early alterations of embryonic development include chromosomal changes, such as mosaic Down's syndrome, or prenatal damage due to toxins, including maternal alcohol consumption and infections. Fetal malnutrition, prematurity, hypoxia, viral and other infections, and trauma are factors associated with pregnancy and perinatal problems. General medical factors acquired in infancy and childhood include infections, traumas, and poisoning from substances such as lead. Deprivation of nurturance and of social, linguistic, and other stimulation are leading environmental influences associated with mental retardation. Factors associated with other mental disorders, such as autism, are also recognized in medical classification systems.

The two-group approach to mental retardation (e.g., Zigler, 1967; Zigler & Hodapp, 1986) is a useful conceptual framework for describing types of mental retardation and their relation to etiology. The two-group approach suggests that those with mental retardation can be divided into two groups, familial and organic. The familial patients, who comprise the great majority, are generally of relatively mild retardation and have parents and siblings who also have below average levels of intelligence. That is, their intelligence is a familial trait, transmitted from one generation to another as a result of the interaction of many genes with a succession of pre-, peri-, and postnatal environments, as other familial traits such as height. Their intelligence develops through the same general complex of factors as are those of higher intelligence, and they fall on the lower end of the normal distribution of intelligence. The organic patients, on the other hand, have more severe degrees of retardation and form a separate distribution of intelligence at the very low end of the normal distribution. Their retardation is due to some specific organic problem that may be genetic or environmental in origin, and their parents and siblings are likely to have average intelligence. Genetically-based organic conditions include Down's and Fragile X Syndromes and inborn errors of metabolism; environmentally-based ones include fetal alcohol syndrome, effects of prenatal infections such as rubella, and lead poisoning.

Such classification systems are very useful for medical treatments, prevention programs, and research on prevention and treatment, but available psychoeducational research suggests that they offer little aid in the development of educational plans.

Since 1977 when PL 94-142 went into effect, the number of students classified as mentally retarded has significantly decreased, with the group classified as mildly retarded affected the most. This "new" group of students, representing approximately 85% of the population classified as mentally retarded, appears to be lower functioning that those called mildly retarded a decade or more ago. For this reason, much of the previous literature on the earlier group may not be true for the current one. Also, not every individual classified as mildly mentally retarded will present all the characteristics described below. This group is heterogeneous, and generally individuals require few or no support systems in most adaptive skill areas. In the past, individuals who were categorized in the mildly retarded range were referred to as educable or trainable, particularly in the school system. In regard to demographic characteristics, more males than females and a disproportionate number of children from minority groups are identified as mildly retarded.

Motivational characteristics include limited self-regulatory behaviors, outerdirectedness (a tendency to look to others for solutions to problems rather than to oneself), expectancy of failure, and an external locus of control. In the area of learning, various cognitive processes may be limited. These include attention, mediation strategies, memory, transfer of training, and generalization. Certain speech, language, and health conditions may occur with greater frequency with this group. These include delayed language and motor development, cerebral palsy, seizure disorders, and sensory deficits.

In terms of education, the predominance of IEP goals in the elementary grades are academic, and many students can succeed in inclusive educational settings. With systematic instruction, skills training, and transition services, these individuals can succeed in integrated, competitive work settings upon completion of formal schooling.

Individuals previously classified as having severe, profound, or, in some cases, moderate mental retardation would be classified as needing more extensive supports. Neither those in the severely retarded (IQ range about 20 to 35) nor profoundly retarded (IQ below 20 or 25) ranges of intelligence were generally considered public-school responsibility until after the passage of PL 94-142 in 1975. Educators usually referred to all children classified as mentally retarded below the moderate level (IQ range about 35–55) as custodial, and most or all of such children would be educated in residential facilities. With the deinstitutionalization movement, this is no longer true. These children are now the responsibility of the public school system, and as such, must be provided an appropriate education in the least restrictive environment.

Current definitions of mental retardation support the use of terms such as severe/profound, persons with extensive support needs, and individuals with severe disabilities. The needs of this group are in many cases directly related to physical or health-related concerns. The extent of support required is influenced by the environment. Environments that encourage independence, productivity, and social interaction can enhance the development of individuals with severe mental retardation. The supports needed differ from those needed by individuals with less severe forms of mental retardation in their frequency, duration, and intensity; and many supplemental supports related to activities of daily living may be required.

In the area of education, IEP goals should be individualized, functional, and age appropriate. Instruction should be community-referenced and delivered in the settings where the skills will be used. The emphasis in transition planning should be on fostering independence, community integration, and supported employment to the maximum extent possible.

In the past, the potential of persons with mental retardation was grossly underestimated and they were subjected to prejudice, fear, and mistreatment. As children with mental retardation are included in public school classrooms, teachers and other school personnel tend to be wary of using the term "retarded." Some believe that the label is stigmatizing. Alternative terms include mentally challenged, cognitive disability, and mental disability. Available research suggests that the label itself is unlikely to stigmatize when teachers and others have opportunities to interact with children. However, in our society, persons classified as mentally retarded seem to be devalued, so any term that identifies the condition tends to become pejorative. As we learn to value others for what they are, rather than for what they are not, the label can become less onerous.

In summary, mental retardation is a condition associated with cognitive disabilities and impairments in adaptive behavior. Students classified as mentally retarded can be provided an appropriate education that will facilitate their leading as productive, independent lives as possible. Although they may have difficulty in learning, all can learn to some extent and profit from well-designed educational programs and systems of support.

REFERENCES

American Association on Mental Retardation. (1992). *Mental retardation: Definition, classification, and systems of supports* (9th ed.). Washington, DC: American Association on Mental Retardation.

American Psychiatric Association. (1994). *Diagnostic and statistical manual of mental disorders* (4th ed.) Washington, DC: American Psychiatric Association.

Grossman, H.G. (Ed.). (1983). *Classification in mental retardation.* Washington, DC: American Association on Mental Deficiency.

Jackson, J.W., & Mulick, J.A. (1996). *Manual on diagnosis and professional practice in mental retardation.* Washington, DC: American Psychological Association.

MacMillan, D.L. (1982). *Mental retardation in school and society* (2nd ed.). Boston: Little, Brown.

Zigler, E. (1967). Familial mental retardation: A continuing dilemma. *Science, 155,* 292–298.

Zigler, E., & Hodapp, R.M. (1986). *Understanding mental retardation.* Cambridge, UK: Cambridge University Press.

***See also* AAMR Adaptive Behavior Scales; Adaptive Behavior; Inclusion; Intelligence Quotient; Labeling; Vineland Adaptive Behavior Scales**

MENTAL RETARDATION: A JOURNAL OF POLICY, PRACTICES, AND PERSPECTIVES

The journal *Mental Retardation* was first published in 1963 by the Boyd Publishing Company. It is now published bimonthly by the American Association on Mental Retardation. Since its inception, the journal has been devoted to meeting the needs of people with mental retardation and providing their families and educators with information about effective ways to help them. As a journal with an applied focus, *Mental Retardation* publishes articles on new teaching approaches, administrative tools, program evaluation studies, new program developments, service utilization studies, community surveys, public policy issues, case studies, and research studies that emphasize the application of new methods. Articles submitted for publication are subject to peer review, with the editor making final publication decisions. The current editor is Steven J. Taylor of Syracuse University, and subscription information is available from the American Association on Mental Retardation, 444 N. Capitol St., NW, Suite 846, Washington, DC, 20001–1512.

MENTAL RETARDATION, SEVERE

The label of severe mental retardation continues to be used to describe persons who receive intelligence testing scores of more than four and up to five standard deviations below the norm (IQ = 20 to 35 on the Stanford-Binet and 25 to 39 on the Wechsler scales). Also, deficits in adaptive behavior (i.e., a lack of behaviors necessary to meet the standards of personal and social responsibility expected for a given chronological age) are considered in the labeling process according to the classification system of the American Association of Mental Deficiency (AAMD; Grossman, 1977). Adaptive behavior is typically assessed through the administration of the Adaptive Behavior Scale of the AAMD, or a similar instrument that provides a profile of skill levels that can be used to compare an individual's adaptive behavior profile with that of the group of persons who are mentally retarded.

Historically, the care and treatment of persons with severe retardation has largely emphasized deficits in ability. The consequences of such negative attitudes have been neglect, ridicule, segregation in institutional settings, and pessimism regarding habilitative efforts. Kauffman (1981) provides an accounting of the history of mental retardation in the United States since the beginning of the nineteenth century. In the early nineteenth century there was a period of optimism regarding the education of the handicapped. At this time it was assumed that all handicapped persons could be provided with residential care that would make them contributing members of society, or at least greatly improve their skill levels and the conditions under which they lived. This was the period when Dorthea Dix led the movement to institutionalize the handicapped to protect them from abuse, and when successes in teaching the severely retarded were being reported by Samuel Howe and Edouard Seguins. The size of institutions rapidly increased in the late nineteenth century without a corresponding increase in resources. The effect of the cutback in resources relative to the number of persons who were institutionalized resulted in a decline in the quality of care. The focus of institutions changed from that of providing training to that of providing custodial care and permanent segregation from society as

pessimism grew in the face of lack of success in curing the condition of mental retardation.

In the 1960s and 1970s there was a shift to a more optimistic outlook regarding the provision of services to individuals labeled severely mentally retarded. These persons began to receive skill training services in institutional settings in the 1960s and, to a limited extent, educational services in the public schools in the 1970s. The beginning of deinstitutionalization and the provision of community-based services also appeared. This stands in stark contrast to the preceding decades, in which severely retarded persons were provided food, shelter, and medical care in large institutions.

In the 1960s and 1970s several events were responsible for a change to the provision of habilitative programming. These events included (1) continued advocacy by parents' groups; (2) the enactment of legislation such as PL 94-142, the Education Act for All Handicapped Children of 1975, PL 94-103, the Developmentally Disabled Assistance and Bill of Rights Act of 1975, and PL 93-112, Section 504 of the Rehabilitation Act of 1973, which mandated services and guaranteed the rights of persons with handicaps; (3) litigation such as *Brown v. the Board of Education* in 1954, in which the Supreme Court struck down segregated education systems, *Wyatt v. Stickney* in 1974, in which the Supreme Court decided for a constitutional right to treatment, and the *Pennsylvania Association for Retarded Citizens v. Commonwealth of Pennsylvania,* which guaranteed due process in educational placements to prevent exclusion from a free public education; (4) advances in instructional technology by behavioral researchers (Whitman, Sciback, & Reid, 1983); and (5) advocacy for the normalization principle (Wolfensberger, 1969).

During the 1960s and 1970s a number of changes occurred in habilitative programming. The focus of instructional technology changed from basic self-care skills and reduction of inappropriate behaviors in institutional settings to a focus on community living skills for persons working and living in a variety of residential options in the community. These changes were strongly reflective of the instructional approach to the definition of mental retardation (Gold, 1980).

The reforms in treatment models and improvements in instructional technology continued. Models have been developed for the training of vocational and independent living skills. These models actively involve persons with severe retardation in all aspects of community life (Cuvo & Davis, 1983; Rusch, 1986) and represent an optimistic viewpoint that persons with severe retardation can participate more fully in their home communities with appropriate training and support services. To achieve this goal of participation in community life to the fullest extent possible, increased service options in vocational, residential, and community programs need to be developed and expanded to accommodate the needs of persons labeled severely mentally retarded. The Association for Persons with Severe Handicaps has emerged as a dynamic coalition of parents and professionals with the purpose of ensuring full integration of people labeled as severely mentally retarded in school, residential, vocational, and other community environments.

REFERENCES

Cuvo, A.J., & Davis, P.K. (1983). Behavior therapy of community skills. In M. Hersen, R.M. Eisler, & P.M. Miller (Eds.), *Progress in behavior modification* (Vol. 14). New York: Academic.

Gold, M.W. (1980). *Try another way training manual.* Champaign, IL: Research.

Grossman, H.J. (1977). *Manual of terminology and classification in mental retardation.* Washington, DC: American Association on Mental Deficiency.

Kauffman, J.M. (1981). Historical trends and contemporary issues in special education in the United States. In J.M. Kauffman & D.P. Hallahan (Eds.), *Handbook of special education.* Englewood Cliffs, NJ: Prentice-Hall.

Rusch, F.R. (Ed.). (1986). *Competitive employment: Issues and strategies.* Baltimore, MD: Brookes.

Whitman, T.L., Scibuck, J.W., & Reid, D.H. (1983). *Behavior modification with the severely and profoundly retarded: Research and application.* New York: Academic.

Wolfensberger, W. (1969). *Changing patterns in residential services for the mentally retarded.* Washington, DC: President's Commission on Mental Retardation.

See also **Mental Retardation; Profoundly Retarded**

MENTAL STATUS EXAMS

The mental status examination is an attempt to integrate qualitative observation with standardized assessment in a brief form. An examiner attempts to sample a broad enough representation of mental processes and behavioral performance to decide whether a disorder is present. Additionally, a brief examination also allows hypothesis building in the sense that the pattern of findings may be related to a specific syndrome. Historically, the majority of brief examinations were developed with an eye toward psychopathology; currently, more attention is being placed on the efficient identification of neuropsychological disorders, specifically dementia among the elderly.

In a review of mental state tests, Weintraub and Mesulam (1985) include the following general areas for consideration within an examination:

Wakefulness, arousal, and attention

Mood and emotional responsiveness

Learning and recall

Aspects of language and communication, including pragmatics

Arithmetic manipulation/calculation

Complex perceptual tasks

Constructional tasks

Spatial distribution of attention

Conceptual reasoning

Synthetic reasoning (i.e., translating a problem into plans and action)

When selecting procedures and organizing an assessment, the clinician must be prepared to allow assessment items to vary along several dimensions. Assessment techniques must permit observation of both complex performance and very simple performance. Procedures need to vary input and output modalities while attempting to maintain a focus on targeted mental processes. Lateralized performance also must be observed. In creating such an examination, a clinician must not sacrifice depth of observation for brevity. (For applications of mental status examinations, see Weintraub & Mesulam, 1985; Strubb & Black, 1983.) Though these goals sound sensible in terms of a brief diagnostic procedure, the usual mental status exam is a finite set of tasks whose performance generates a score that may be compared with a norm-referenced criterion.

It is interesting to note that if one reviews the development of successive mental status examinations, the usual stimulus for development of a new procedure is that the preceding technique was not extensive enough. In such an evolutionary process, the distinction between a standardized battery and a brief mental status examination is notably blurred.

REFERENCES

Strubb, R.L., & Black, F.W. (1983). *The mental status examination in neurology.* Philadelphia: Davis.

Weintraub, S., & Mesulam, M. (1985). Mental state assessment of young and elderly adults in behavioral neurology. In M. Mesulam (Ed.), *Principles of behavioral neurology* (pp. 71–124). Philadelphia: Davis.

See also **Assessment; Clinical Interview**

MERCER, JANE R.

See SYSTEM OF MULTICULTURAL PLURALISTIC ASSESSMENT.

MERRILL, MAUD AMANDA (1888– 1985)

Maud Amanda Merrill earned her PhD in psychology at Stanford University in 1923 and served on the faculty there until 1947. She was coauthor, with Lewis M. Terman, of the 1937 revision of the Stanford-Binet Tests of Intelligence.

REFERENCE

Terman, L.M., & Merrill, M.A. (1977). *Measuring intelligence.* Cambridge, MA: Riverside.

MERRILL-PALMER SCALE

The Merrill-Palmer Scale is an individually administered intelligence test for children ages 18 months to 6 years.

The test is particularly useful for assessing children lacking verbal skills (e.g., very young, developmentally delayed, or handicapped). Two excellent reviews of the scale (Honzik, 1975; Loeb, 1985) have identified several problem areas, including an excessive number of timed tests that penalize the slow-moving, thoughtful child and inadequate standardization. In addition, the test is difficult to interpret because the standard deviations of the mental age do not increase in proportion to advancing chronological age beyond 54 months. The test is published by Stoelting Company, Chicago.

REFERENCES

Honzik, M.P. (1975). The Merrill-Palmer Scale of Mental Tests. In O.K. Buros (Ed.), *Intelligence tests and reviews.* Highland Park, NJ: Gryphon Press.

Loeb, H.W. (1985). Merrill-Palmer Scale. In D.J. Keyser & R.C. Sweetland (Eds.), *Test critiques* (Vol. 2). Kansas City, MO; Test Corporation of America.

See also **Intelligence; Intelligence Testing**

METABOLIC DISORDERS

The study of metabolic disorders is expanding rapidly and more than 2000 different types of inborn errors of metabolism and morphology have been identified (Ampola, 1982). Most of these diseases are single recessive gene defects that result in impaired metabolism of fat, protein, amino acids, or carbohydrates because of a deficiency in essential enzymes. Some of the more commonly known of these diseases are cystic fibrosis, diabetes, galactosemia, phenylketonuria (PKU), and Tay-Sachs disease.

Metabolic disorders are of relevance to special education practitioners because of the developmental and behavioral sequelae of these diseases. For example, they have been found to be associated with intellectual deficits (Kanner, 1979), social-behavioral problems (Allen et al., 1984), and childhood psychiatric disorders (Nyhan, 1974). Moreover, the siblings of a child with metabolic disorders may experience psychosocial sequelae (Langdell, 1979). The impact of metabolic diseases on development and behavior varies with such factors as the specific type of medical disorder, age of onset, type and efficacy of medical treatment, social support systems, and premorbid level of functioning (Lehr, 1984).

The more common metabolic disorders with known developmental and behavioral sequelae are Cushing's disease, cystic fibrosis, diabetes, galactosemia, and PKU. While cognitive functioning does not appear to be impaired in such diseases as cystic fibrosis, social-emotional adjustment is typically affected owing to associated stressors. There is much still unknown regarding the long-term sequelae of metabolic disorders. For example, while recent advances in the medical treatment of PKU has resulted in decreased mental retardation, hyperactivity, epilepsy, and microcephaly, there is evidence of continued but less severe learning and behavioral problems.

There is presently a lack of effective treatment for most metabolic diseases; the most relevant current emphasis should be directed at prevention through genetic screening and planned parenthood. Practitioners might refer parents to the following two national organizations for reliable information concerning metabolic disorders: Science Information Division, National Foundation–March of Dimes, Box 2000, White Plains, NY, 10602; and National Genetics Foundation, 9 West 57th Street, New York, NY 10019.

REFERENCES

Allen, D.A., Affleck, G., Tennen, H., McGrade, B.J., & Ratzan, S. (1984). Concerns of children with a chronic illness: A cognitive-developmental study of juvenile diabetes. *Child Care, Health, & Development, 10,* 211–218.

Ampola, M.G. (1982). *Metabolic diseases in pediatric practice.* Boston: Little, Brown.

Kanner, L. (1979). *Child psychiatry.* Springfield, IL: Thomas.

Langdell, J.I. (1979). Working with parents to discover and treat inherited metabolic diseases. In J.D. Nosphitz (Ed.), *Basic handbook of child psychiatry* (Vol. IV, pp. 86–90). New York: Basic Books.

Lehr, E. (1984). Cognitive effects of acute and chronic pediatric medical conditions. In P.R. Magrab (Ed.), *Psychological and behavioral assessment: Impact on pediatric care* (pp. 235–278). New York: Plenum.

Nyhan, W.L. (1974). *Heritable disorders of amino acid metabolism: Patterns of clinical expression and genetic variation.* New York: Wiley.

See also **Galactosemia; Genetic Counseling; Inborn Errors of Metabolism; Phenylketonuria; Tay-Sachs Syndrome**

METACOGNITION

Metacognition refers to individuals' knowledge "about knowing and about how to know" (Brown, 1975). With this knowledge, learners allocate and orchestrate their cognitive resources effectively to meet task demands. Metacognition may be viewed as one of many potential domains of knowledge and skill that children may acquire; however, in this case, the domain is not reading or arithmetic, it is thinking. Investigations by cognitive psychologists, developmental psychologists, and special educators indicate that youngsters' metacognitive knowledge and skill may play a critical role in school achievement (Brown, Bransford, Ferrara, & Campione, 1983). Many handicapped pupils with learning problems evidence metacognitive deficiencies.

Educators' and psychologists' interest in metacognition reflects the view that human behavior is the outcome of a variety of mental events and processes. That is, students do not merely react to environmental demands. Rather, they interpret their world. It is these thoughts and perceptions that subsequently guide their behavior. A central tenet of this viewpoint is that individuals actively attempt to understand their environment. While motivational factors may interfere with this problem-solving activity and some learners may not understand task demands or how to perform a task, most students attempt to understand what the task requires and then initiate problem-solving activities.

These metacognitive characteristics of poor readers have been identified in handicapped pupils in the performance of a variety of academic, problem-solving, and memory tasks (Brown et al., 1983; Fisher, 1998). Identification of these characteristics has resulted not only in a better understanding of human learning but in the development of instructional interventions for these pupils. Since the latter part of the 1970s, a variety of metacognitive training programs have been developed. In the area of reading, one training approach that has received considerable attention is the reciprocal teaching program developed by Brown and Palinscar (1982). In this program, pupils and a teacher take turns leading a dialogue on a segment of text that they are jointly attempting to understand. The purpose of this dialogue is to get the child to be aware of and use metacognitive skills that are related to effective reading comprehension. These skills include self-review, self-questioning, clarifying important text information, and predicting events in the text. As pupils' competence to perform these metacognitive tasks increases the teacher decreases his or her level of guidance. This intervention results not only in pupils' increased ability to paraphrase, ask meaningful questions, and predict text materials, but pupils also improve on a variety of comprehension tests immediately after the training and on follow-up assessments several months later.

While many pupils with learning problems may evidence specific deficits in rudimentary skills such as letter and number identification, it has become clear that teaching these individuals to be literate will require instruction in how to think and solve problems. Research in metacognition has helped educators to identify knowledge and skill deficits that may limit handicapped pupils' ability to learn and to design instructional programs that will meet their learning needs.

REFERENCES

Brown, A.L. (1975). The development of memory: Knowing about knowing, and knowing how to know. In H.W. Reese (Ed.), *Advances in child development and behavior* (Vol. 10, pp. 103–152). New York: Academic.

Brown, A.L., Bransford, J.D., Ferrara, R.A., & Campione, J.C. (1983). Learning, remembering, and understanding. In J.H. Flavell & E.M. Markman (Eds.), *Handbook of child psychology: Vol. 1. Cognitive development* (pp. 77–166). New York: Wiley.

Brown, A.L., & Palinscar, A.S. (1982). Inducing strategic learning from texts by means of informed, self-control training. *Topics in Learning & Learning Disabilities, 2*, 1–17.

Fisher, R. (1998). Thinking about thinking: Developing metacognition in children. *Early Child Development & Care, 141*, 1–13.

See also **Reading Disorders; Reciprocal Determinism**

MEXICAN AMERICAN CULTURE AND DISABILITY

An individual's perception of and adaptation to disability is directly related to his or her culture or, more precisely, the individual's level of acculturation. Culture also influences family reaction to disability, help-seeking behaviors, medical compliance, and the degree of rapport between special education professionals and the student. Further, the culture of the individual influences symptom manifestation and the way in which the individual communicates the experience of disability, beliefs about causation and etiology, and the individual's expectation of treatment and educational outcomes.

In discussing the Mexican American culture, it must be clearly stated that there is great intracultural variability related to factors such as generational level of residence in the United States, socioeconomic level, educational attainment, racial identification of the individual, and language ability/preference. Indeed, it has been clearly shown that, when conducting research, differing definitions of "Mexican American" have yielded different results. Therefore, any discussion of the Mexican American culture and disability must be of a general nature. A further caution: Much of our knowledge of the Mexican American culture is based upon research that is of questionable value because of unethical or invalid research methods, such as failure to separate the effects of culture from the effects of socioeconomic factors; undue focus on rural, lower-class Mexican Americans; failure to keep abreast of rapid demographic changes; and an overreliance on survey and impressionistic methods of research.

Nonetheless, special educators need to achieve a balance between respect for the individual and his or her family and some broad knowledge of various cultural/ethnic groups and the ways in which they perceive disability. Six factors may be identified as related to the perception and adaptation to disability in the Mexican American culture. These factors are (a) a familial, cohesive, protective society; (b) a stoic attitude toward life in general; (c) well-defined gender roles; (d) religious views; (e) reliance on physical labor; and (f) lack of a strong distinction between the body and the mind (Smart, 1993).

Special educators will be called upon to serve greater numbers of Mexican Americans due to three factors: (a) their greater absolute numbers in the United States, (b) they tend to be a young population due to high birth rates and immigration and thus a great proportion of Mexican Americans are of school age, and (c) Mexican Americans experience higher disability rates than do White Anglo Americans.

Mexican Americans differ from other American ethnic groups in that they have maintained, over centuries, a strong language loyalty. This may be, in part, due to the geographic proximity of Mexico. Nonetheless, this strong language loyalty will require the use of trained, supervised Spanish-English translators. Since an individual's first language is the language of emotions, bilingual individuals may be able to express their feelings about their disability more completely and fully in the Spanish language.

Special educators should also interpret and use standardized test results of Mexican Americans with caution and recognize that many Mexican Americans have been incorrectly labeled as having learning disabilities, mental retardation, or psychopathology. Language bias, inappropriate standardization samples, and inappropriate test content often render standardized achievement, intelligence, and psychological testing invalid for some Mexican Americans.

REFERENCE

Smart, J.F. (1993). Level of acculturation of Mexican Americans with disabilities and acceptance of disability. *Rehabilitation Counseling Bulletin, 36*, 199–211.

MEXICO, SPECIAL EDUCATION IN

Since 1992, Mexico has recognized a variety of handicapping conditions that require special education intervention and services, which include mental deficiency, visual deficiency, motor impairments, auditory and language delays, learning difficulties, conduct or behavior problems, and autism. Although separate areas of disabilities are recognized, there are no specific criteria for diagnosis or for qualifying for special education services. Under Article 41 of the Mexican General Law of Education, students are identified as needing special education services when they exhibit difficulties relative to their peers when learning grade-level content, and require modifications to the regular curriculum to succeed (Dirección General de Educación Especial, 1994). The point of view of Mexican educators is to assume that the child's difficulties are not within the child, but that they are more likely due to developmental delays based on a Piagetian theoretical framework or inadequate teaching approaches (Fletcher et al., 1995). As a result of this position, intervention efforts are focused more on providing appropriate services than labeling the child.

In 1996, Mexico reported a total of 2,121,365 disabled school-aged children. The state of Mexico, particularly the federal district, reported the highest number of disabled children. The state of Southern Baja California reported the lowest. The disability most often diagnosed was "discapacidad" or general disability including learning disabilities. The records indicate that there were 46,000 children in Mexico identified with autism, and 126,326 children identified as mentally deficient (DIF, 1996).

The identification of the disabled child in Mexico follows the procedures set forth by the General Direction of Special Education. The process begins with a referral made by the general classroom teacher regarding the students who exhibit difficulties in reading, writing, and/or math calculation. The Test of School Knowledge is then administered to assess reading, comprehension, writing, and math calculation. This test will serve as a screen to detect the children who require further assessment. Such further assessment includes administration of the Monterrey Test, which is a more comprehensive test to assess the same areas (Dirección General de Educación Especial, 1984). Mexico has also adapted some of the assessment instruments that are used in the United States, such as the Wechsler Intelligence Scale for Children-Revised Mexican version (WISC-RM), the WISC-R in Spanish, the Kaufman Assessment Battery for Children (KABC) in Spanish, and the System of Multicultural Pluralistic Assessment (SOMPA). To assess psychological functioning, Mexican practitioners sometimes use the Bender-Gestalt Visual Motor Test and the Draw a Person Test.

The lack of trained special education teachers continues to be a critical issue in Mexico. The government sponsors teacher-training institutions called specialized normal schools that train teachers to work with special-needs children. As of 1995, there were 21 states throughout Mexico that have such schools to prepare teachers in the areas of learning disabilities, hearing and language impairment, and mental retardation. Only a few of the state schools prepare teachers in the areas of behavior disorders, visually impaired or blind, or neuromuscular disorders.

Although the special educational system in Mexico has undergone numerous reforms in recent years, there still remain areas of concern. Although Spanish is the native language in Mexico, there are fifty-six ethnic groups dispersed throughout the country. Cultural and economic conditions can vary, in some cases significantly, from one state to the other. Even with all of the aforementioned legislation, the educational programs are directly affected by this diversity, which can even prevent the provision of special education services.

The legislative educational reform in Mexico is clearly in place. However, there is still a large discrepancy between the letter of the law and what is actually put into practice. According to a survey of special education administrators from twenty Latin American countries, including Mexico, some of the major difficulties in implementing legislation into practice include a lack of financial resources, resistance to change, lack of coordination between general and special education, and lack of trained personnel who can formulate and implement curricular adaptations (Ministerio de Educación, 1996). Strong resistance to change also exists among some educators. Some general education personnel are opposed to the integration of disabled students in their classrooms, and some special education teachers become overprotective of the disabled students and also do not support integration. Even though the current emphasis for special education is to integrate disabled students with nondisabled peers, some parents still prefer to send their children to special education schools.

In order for any of the special education services to be provided, the school must have physical space available and have enough students who require the services to form a group to be served, or else services will not be provided. Special education services to integrate disabled children are usually not available in rural areas. The quality of the program, services, and facilities vary widely from state to state, and even from school to school within the same city. Very few schools have ramps and other wheelchair-accessible facilities.

Another area of concern is that while it is estimated that 10% of the school-aged children in Mexico are in need of special education services, only about 1% are actually served (Fletcher et al., 1995). There are still many parents who are unaware that services are available. Some parents are unable to transport their child to the school to receive services, as transportation is not a service provided by the schools.

In the instances where the provisions mandated by law are not followed, the issues have not yet been challenged in the legal system. However, parents of disabled children are beginning to have a voice through advocacy organizations such as the *Asociación de Padres* (Parent Association), which has now gained national status.

In keeping pace with worldwide trends, special education in Mexico is no longer a separate, segregated program, but rather a complementary support service to the general education program. Together, the primary objective is to help disabled students become independent, productive members of society.

REFERENCES

Dirección General de Educación Especial. (1994). *Los grupos integrados.* Mexico City, Mexico: SEP.

Fletcher, T., & Kaufman de Lopez, C. (1995). A Mexican perspective on learning disabilities. *Journal of Learning Disabilities, 28*(9), 530–34.

Ministerio de Educación. (1996). *Informe sobre la situación de la región de américa latina y el caribe en relación con la educación especial y la integración de alumnos con necesidades educativas especiales en la escuela regular.* República de Chile: Ministerio de Educación.

Sistema Nacional para el Desarrollo Integral de la Familia. (DIF). *Menores con discapacidad por entidad federativa de residencia habitual segun tipo de discapacidad.* Published data from the Sistema Nacional para el Desarrollo Integral de la Familia (DIF). Mexico: DIF.

MICROCEPHALY

Microcephaly, a congenital anomaly, is characterized by an abnormally small head in relationship to the rest of the body and by an underdeveloped brain resulting in some degree of mental retardation. The condition is described by Udang and Swallow (1983) as one in which the cranium of the affected individual is less than two standard deviations below the average circumference size for age, sex, race, and period of gestation. The primary or inherited form of microcephaly is transmitted by a single recessive gene, while the secondary form is the result of environmental factors (Gerald, 1982; Robinson & Robinson, 1965; Telford & Sawrey, 1977; Udang & Swallow, 1983). Factors associated with microcephaly include maternal infections; trauma, especially during the third trimester of pregnancy or in early infancy;

anoxia at birth; massive irradiation or indiscriminate use of X-ray; and chemical agents.

Individuals who have the primary form of the disorder are generally more seriously affected (Robinson & Robinson, 1965). In addition to the small, conical-shaped skull, the scalp may be loose and wrinkled. The forehead generally is narrow and receding; the back of the skull is flattened; the facial features can be normal, although frequently the lower jaw recedes. The stature of the affected individual is very small with a curved spine and stooping posture, flexed knees, and disproportionately long arms and legs. Such individuals almost always are severely retarded and may not develop speech or primary self-help skills.

Individuals with the secondary form of microcephaly are not as severely affected. Although the skull is small, other symptoms are less visible or may not be present at all. The degree of mental retardation is less severe. Occasionally such individuals may be found in day classes for the moderately retarded (Dunn, 1973). There is no treatment for microcephaly. Medical care is primarily supportive and educational. A full range of custodial and educational services is needed (Udang & Swallow, 1983).

REFERENCES

Dunn, L.M. (1973). Children with moderate, severe and general learning disabilities. In L.M. Dunn (Ed.), *Exceptional children in the schools: Special education transition* (pp. 65–123). New York: Holt, Rinehart, & Winston.

Gerald, P. (1982). Chromosomes and their disorders. In J. Wyngaarden & L. Smith (Eds.), *Cecil 16th edition textbook of medicine* (pp. 17–22). Philadelphia: Saunders.

Robinson, H., & Robinson, N. (1965). *The mentally retarded child: A psychological approach.* New York: McGraw-Hill.

Telford, C., & Sawrey, J. (1977). *The exceptional individual.* Englewood Cliffs, NJ: Prentice-Hall.

Udang, L., & Swallow, H. (Eds.). (1983). *Mosby's medical and nursing dictionary.* St. Louis: Mosby.

See also **Chromosomal Abnormalities; Congenital Disorders; Physical Anomalies**

MICROTRAINING

Microtraining is a practice teaching method used in a majority of teacher education programs. Teacher trainees involved in microtraining typically prepare a brief lesson, present the lesson to a small group of students, observe a videotape of the lesson, modify the lesson based on their own critique or the critique of a supervisor, and reteach the lesson. As is apparent from these procedures, microtraining emphasizes the use of objective feedback in improving the teacher's future performance. The term microtraining is used because the teacher trainee is involved in a simulated teaching experience that minimizes the complexities of actual teaching. Specifically, only a few students are involved in a brief and highly structured lesson (Gregory, 1972).

Microtraining was introduced in the Secondary Teacher

Education Program at Stanford University in the early 1960s. Keith Acheson, then a graduate student at Stanford, is frequently credited with its development as a preservice teacher training method. Hundreds of research articles evaluating its effectiveness have been reported and over half of the teacher education programs in the United States have incorporated it as a required preservice clinical experience (Turney, Clift, Durkin, & Traill, 1973).

There are a number of variations of the basic microtraining methodology. Jensen (1974) has suggested 24 basic alterations. These result from various combinations of feedback options (e.g., videotapes, audiotapes, peers, critiquer), critique options (e.g., others, self), and reteach options (e.g., teach only, systematic reteach, trials-to-criterion). In addition to these options, microtraining may be conducted with peers versus actual pupils, and with various combinations of feedback modes (e.g., peers using videotape, critiquer using audiotapes, etc.). It is currently being used in culture-specific counseling (Grant, 1991).

REFERENCES

Grant, C.A. (1991). *Toward education that is multicultural.* Wisconsin: National Association for Multicultural Education.

Gregory, T.B. (1972). *Encounters with teaching: A microteaching manual.* Englewood Cliffs, NJ: Prentice-Hall.

Jensen, R.N. (1974). *Microteaching: Planning and implementing a competency-based training program.* Springfield, IL: Charles Thomas.

Turney, C., Clift, J.C., Durkin, M.J., & Traill, R.D. (1973). *Microteaching: Research theory and practice.* Sydney, Australia: Sydney University Press.

See also Teacher Effectiveness; Teaching Startegies

MIDDLE EAST, SPECIAL EDUCATION IN THE

Perhaps no other Third World region has made as much progress over the last decades as the Middle East in the area of special education. With the rapid development of the oil and travel industries, money became readily available to many countries and their individual universities could develop and expand their program offerings in the areas of teacher training rehabilitation services and institutional care for the handicapped. The two countries that led in this movement were Egypt and Israel. Arab countries such as Kuwait, Jordan, and Saudi Arabia have also made significant gains in the programming for and treatment of handicapped youngsters. However, the cutback in oil prices, declining tourism, and the increase in terrorist activities may well affect the continued development of special education programs in the Middle East.

Egypt. The purpose of educational services and programs in the area of special education in Egypt is assessment of abilities and aptitudes to aid the handicapped in developing an independent lifestyle. Basically, there are three major handicapping conditions that the schools in Egypt focus on. Visual education is for those individuals who are classified as blind or visually impaired. These individuals are entitled to 6 years of elementary schooling, 3 years of intermediate and secondary level schooling, and college based on their abilities (visually and intellectually).

The deaf and hearing impaired are entitled to auditory education. This education consists of 8 years of elementary school and 3 years of intermediate vocational school (El-Ashawal, 1986).

Education for the mentally retarded consists of two separate programs. Children and youths who score between 50 and 70 on Egyptian IQ tests can be enrolled in an elementary education program for 8 years. The first 2 years of schooling concentrate on academic skills, the following years on vocational/career opportunities. Education is handled through the Ministry of Education. For children and youths who score below 50 on an IQ test, education consists of vocational training with few academic skills emphasized. These programs are handled through the Social Affairs Ministry. There are hospitals for the more severely and profoundly retarded.

Perhaps the leading university focusing on the education of teachers for the handicapped is Ain Shams University in Roxy-Cairo. This university's training program is under the auspices of a special branch of the Ministry of Education that is responsible for special education. A teacher who plans to teach in the area of special education must be a graduate of a university that has a faculty of education and have at least one additional year of course work within one of the specialized areas. The teacher training programs are weak in practicum experience but strong on the theoretical and philosophical aspects of education.

Saudia Arabia, Bahrain, Kuwait, and Jordan. Perhaps in no area has the influence of the Egyptian scholars in special education been more evident than in Saudia Arabia, Bahrain, Kuwait, and Jordan. These Middle Eastern countries often use Egypt's university personnel to develop their individual special education teacher training programs and service delivery models. Basically, we see the same structure in these countries for teacher education and services for exceptional children as we do in Egypt. When faculty members from Egyptian universities are called on to develop special education programs in their neighboring countries, they use the Egyptian model, administrative structure, and governing procedures and adapt them to the individual country.

In countries such as Saudia Arabia, where the *Koran* is interpreted strictly and the Moslem faith is strongly adhered to, there is a separation of boys and girls, not only at the elementary level but also the university level in terms of education programs, treatment facilities, and, to a lesser degree, opportunities. Special education in most of the Middle East is developing at a rapid pace but it still has a long way to go. However, each government has made a commitment at the program level to develop effective special education program to meet the needs of their handicapped children and youths.

An attempt needs to be made to integrate theories and effective practice in special education throughout the Middle East. In addition, ways in which practices can be adapted to areas with severe economic and social problems must be developed. Mba (1983) indicates that only a small percentage of handicapped children with disabilities receive schooling and that opportunities for training special educators are limited in the African countries. However, most Middle Eastern countries demonstrate a high interest in the areas of gifted education and retardation.

REFERENCES

El-Ashawal, A., & Vance, H. (1986, April). *Special education in Egypt and the Middle East.* Paper presented at the meeting of the Council for Exceptional Children, New Orleans, LA.

Mba, P.O. (1983). Trends in education of handicapped children in developing countries with particular reference to Africa. *Journal of Special Education, 7,* 273–278.

MIGRANT HANDICAPPED

Migratory farmworkers are those individuals who must move their home bases and travel to other locations, usually hundreds of miles away, in search of seasonal farmwork. This mass movement of migratory farmworkers takes place every year during periods that coincide with the planting and/or harvesting of agricultural products; it is commonly referred to as the migrant stream.

There are three major identifiable migrant streams within three broad geographical areas. One stream is found within California, Oregon, and Washington. The other stream begins in the Lower Rio Grande Valley of Texas and farms out into the Midwest, Rocky Mountains, and Red River Valley. The third major stream originates in southern Florida and moves northward along the Atlantic coast as far as New York State (Stoops-King, 1980).

Migrant farmworker families are usually comprised of low socioeconomic ethnic minorities that include Mexicans, Mexican-Americans, Blacks, Native Americans, Indians, and Central and South Americans. The heaviest concentrations of migratory farmworker children reside in the states of Texas, California, Washington, Arizona, Colorado, Florida, and New Mexico (Goldfarb, 1981).

The nature of seasonal migratory labor causes most of the migrant farmworkers to experience considerable deprivation in the basic human needs of nutrition, health, housing, and education. The typical migrant family lives below the poverty level, experiences high infant mortalities, is exposed to the hazards of chemical insecticides and pesticides, and has a low educational level. Children of migrant workers are at high risk for abuse (Larson, Doris, & Alvarez, 1990), mental health disorders such as anxiety (Kupersmidt & Martin, 1997), poor health and nutrition (Leon, 1996), and are rising in numbers of those with disabilities (Interstate Migrant Education Council, 1992). The average life span of a migrant farmworker is thought to be 47 years

(Thedinger, 1982). The critical needs of migrant children prompted Congress to amend Title I of the Elementary and Secondary Education Act of 1965 (currently identified as Chapter I of the Consolidated and Improvement Act of 1981) to address the educational and health needs of these children (U.S. Government Accounting Office, 1983).

The federally funded Migrant Education Program was initiated on the premise that migrant children suffer educational interruptions when forced to move into different school districts. This program provides federal aid for supplementary instructional services, medical and health services, and parent training services provided that the children meet the following specified criteria:

migratory means a child whose parent or guardian is a migratory agricultural worker or a migratory fisher; and who has moved within the past 12 months from one school district to another to enable the child, the child's guardian or a member of the immediate family to obtain temporary or seasonal employment in an agricultural or fishing activity.

Over 711,000 migratory children have been counted as eligible in approximately 3100 projects (U.S. Government Accounting Office, 1983; Interstate Migrant Education Council, 1992). In addition, early childhood education and nutrition intervention efforts are available through selected programs in several states.

Characteristically, migrant children are mobile within the educational systems and, as such, pose unique information management concerns. One of the features of the federal migrant education program is an automated telecommunication system, the Migrant Student Record Transfer System (MSRTS), which transmits data regarding the children. This system, headquartered in Little Rock, Arkansas, enables participating school districts to obtain and forward via computer pertinent educational, medical, and demographic information. This system makes it possible to notify a receiving school that a certain migrant student was enrolled in a special education program in the sending school.

While states generally do not have accurate data on numbers of migrant handicapped pupils, migrant children tend to be underrepresented in special education (U.S. Government Accounting Office, 1981; Interstate Migrant Education Council, 1992). With the national average of 10 to 12% of school-aged children identified as handicapped, surveys indicate that less than 6% of the migrant pupils are identified as handicapped. These children are underrepresented despite the presence of a variety of conditions that place this population at risk.

Addressing this issue of underrepresentation of handicapped migrant youngsters in special education will require better informed parents, teachers, and assessment personnel, and closer coordination and monitoring of services by local school districts and state and federal agencies. Reflecting on the history of special education, complex problems such as those associated with migrant handicapped children may be resolved only through the political and advocacy activities of migrant farmworker organizations.

REFERENCES

Goldfarb, R.L. (1981). *A caste of despair.* Ames IA: Iowa State University Press.

Interstate Migrant Education Council. (1992). *Special education: Migrant education policy brief.* Washington, DC: Author.

Kupersmidt, J.B., & Martin, S.L. (1997). Mental health problems of children of migrant and seasonal farm workers: A pilot study. *Journal of the American Academy of Child & Adolescent Psychiatry, 36*(2), 224–232.

Larson, O.W., Doris, J., & Alvarez, W.F. (1990). Migrants and maltreatment: Comparative evidence from central register data. *Child Abuse and Neglect, 14*(3), 375–385.

Leon, E. (1996). *Challenges and solutions for educating migrant students.* (ERIC Clearinghouse No: RC020477)

Stoops-King, J. (1980). *Migrant education: Teaching the wandering ones.* Bloomington, IN: Educational Foundation.

Thedinger, B. (1982, September 14). Testimony in citing U.S. Public Health Service. Subcommittee on Labor Standards of the Committee on Education and Labor, House of Representatives, 97th Congress, HR 7102.

U.S. Government Accounting Office. (1981, September 30). *Disparities still exist in who gets special education.* Report to Subcommittee on Select Education, Committee on Education and Labor, House of Representatives.

U.S. Government Accounting Office. (1983, May). *Analysis of migration characteristics of children served under the migrant education program.* Report to the Congress of the United States.

See also **Bilingual Education; Cultural Bias in Testing**

MILDLY HANDICAPPED, TEST-TAKING SKILLS AND THE

Test-taking skills, or test-wiseness, has been defined by Millman, Bishop, and Ebel (1965) as "a subject's capacity to utilize the characteristics and formats of the test and/or the test-taking situation to receive a high score" (p. 707). Additionally, they state test-wiseness to be "logically independent of the knowledge of the subject matter for which the items are supposedly measured" (p. 707). Test-taking skills can therefore be seen as a set of abilities that can be applied to a variety of tests regardless of their content.

Currently, most students with mild disabilities spend the largest portion of the school day in general education classrooms (Friend & McNutt, 1984; Heller, 1981). Therefore, they are expected to cope with the same academic demands as students without disabilities. A frequent and important demand in the mainstream class is taking teacher-made, objective (e.g., true-false, multiple-choice, matching) tests. Indeed, academic success is largely measured by how well students perform on these tests (Cuthbertson, 1979; Schumaker & Deshler, 1983). For example, Cuthbertson found that 60% of a student's grade depends solely on test scores. Apart from prior knowledge and amount of studying, a source of variance affecting test scores is the test-taking skills or test-wiseness of the individual taking the test.

Unfortunately, evidence exists that, when compared as a group with nonhandicapped peers, mildly handicapped students lack test-wiseness (Forness & Duorak, 1982; Keogh, 1971; Scruggs, Bennion, & Lifson, 1985). Some general behaviors considered characteristic of the mildly handicapped that may account for poor test-taking ability include distractibility, impulsivity, and anxiety. Specific behaviors noted by researchers include attending to the wrong part of test directions, making an answer choice before reading all available choices, not reading questions carefully, and not using cues when guessing.

REFERENCES

Cuthbertson, E.B. (1979). *An analysis of secondary testing and grading procedures.* Unpublished master's thesis, University of Kansas, Lawrence.

Forness, S.R., & Duorak, R. (1982). Effects of test time limits on achievement scores of behaviorally disordered adolescents. *Behavioral Disorders, 7*(4), 207–212.

Friend, M., & McNutt, G. (1984). Resource room programs: Where are we now? *Exceptional Children, 51*(2), 150–155.

Heller, H.W. (1981). Secondary education for handicapped students: In search of a solution. *Exceptional Children, 47,* 582–583.

Keogh, B. (1971). Hyperactivity and learning disorders: Review and research paradigm. *Developmental Psychology, 10,* 590–600.

Millman, J., Bishop, C.H., & Ebel, R. (1965). An analysis of test-wiseness. *Educational & Psychological Measurement, 25,* 707–726.

Schumaker, J.B., & Deshler, D.D. (1983). *Setting demand variables: A major factor in program planning for the LD adolescent.* Lawrence: University of Kansas, Institute for Research in Learning Disabilities.

Scruggs, T.E., Bennion, K., & Lifson, S. (1985). Learning disabled students' spontaneous use of test-taking skills on reading achievement tests. *Learning Disabilities Quarterly, 8*(3), 205–210.

See also **Measurement; Test Anxiety**

MILLON CLINICAL MULTIAXIAL INVENTORY–III

The Millon Clinical Multiaxial Inventory was originally developed by Theodore Millon in 1977 as a clinical inventory useful for clinical diagnoses and aligned with the classification system of mental disorders (*Diagnostic and Statistical Manual of Mental Disorders,* American Psychiatric Association, 1980). Millon is well known for his work on psychopathology and his theoretical formulation in this area.

The MCMI is most appropriately used with a psychiatric population to assess moderate to severe character pathology or clinical syndromes. It is not a general personality instrument for normal populations. According to the manual, the primary intent of the MCMI is to provide information to clinicians—psychologists, psychiatrists, counselors, social workers, physicians and nurses—who must make assessments and treatment decisions about persons with emotional and interpersonal difficulties. The profile report of scaled scores can serve as a screening device to identify those who may require more intensive evaluation or personal attention. The clinical narrative interpretative report provides a detailed analysis of personality and symptom dynamics, as well as suggestions for therapeutic management (Millon, 1983, p. 2).

The MCMI is based on Millon's theories of psychopathology. His theory sees personality functioning as eight basic styles that can be derived from a 4 × 2 matrix. The first dimension of the matrix refers to the primary source of positive reinforcements: *detached, dependent, independent,* and *ambivalent.* The second dimension deals with the basic pattern of coping behavior, either *active or passive.* The MCMI–III uses 24 scales that are consistent, though not identical, to the classification system in the DSM–IV. Millon describes these scales as defining basic styles of personality. The Clinical Personality Patterns are the basic personality disorders: schizoid, avoidant, depressive, dependent, histrionic, narcissistic, antisocial, sadistic, compulsive, negativistic, and self-defeating. The next three scales, Severe Personality Pathology, deal with more severe and enduring personality disturbances. They are schizotypal, borderline, and paranoid. Clinical Syndrome Scales are extensions of basic personality style, but they are transient and reactive to stress, such as anxiety, dysthymia, alcohol dependence, and post-traumatic stress disorder. The Severe Clinical Syndromes are thought disorder, major depression, and delusional disorder.

The MCMI–III was designed for adults 18 years and older. There is an adolescent version, the Millon Adolescent Clinical Inventory (MACI), for an adolescent population of 13 to 19 years old. The MCMI–III has a reading level of eighth grade and takes 25 minutes to administer. The MACI is at a sixth grade level and takes 30 minutes to administer.

The MCMI was a ground-breaking instrument in that it offered a brief and efficient alternative to more lengthy personality testing. The test has found wide acceptance amongst clinicians who find it valuable for diagnosing personality disorders and evaluating their treatment plans. However, there has been some criticism that the test has a great deal of item overlap, which may detract from the discriminating power of the scales. This was especially true when an individual was anxious or depressed. However, there have been two revisions that have attempted to address these problems. In both revisions, items were changed, scales were added and changes were made in the item weighting. More data is needed, however, about the diagnostic efficacy of the clinical syndrome scales. Another criticism has been directed toward the readily available computer scoring system. While the interpretative report is attractive for the clinician, the user must assume professional responsibility for interpretation of the scales. There has been some criticism of the validity of the interpretative test reports. Thus, it is highly recommended that the MCMI–III not be used as a stand-alone instrument, and that other clinical data be integrated with the test reports before any definitive diagnostic decisions are made.

REFERENCES

American Psychiatric Association. (1980). *Diagnostic and statistical manual of mental disorders* (3rd ed.). Washington, DC: Author.

Millon, T. (1983). *Millon Clinical Multiaxial Inventory manual* (3rd ed.). Minneapolis, MN: National Computer Systems.

MILLS v. BOARD OF EDUCATION OF THE DISTRICT OF COLUMBIA (1972)

In 1972 a class-action suit was brought against the District of Columbia Board of Education by the parents of seven school-aged handicapped children for failure to provide all handicapped children with a publicly supported education. In December 1971 the court issued a stipulated agreement, an order that required that the plaintiffs be provided a publicly supported education; that the District of Columbia Board of Education provide a list of every school-aged child not receiving a publicly supported education; and that the Board of Education attempt to identify other handicapped children not previously identified.

In January 1972 the U.S. District Court issued an order establishing the right of all handicapped children to a publicly supported education. It indicated that the exclusion of children from public school without the provision of a prior hearing and review of placement procedures denied handicapped children the rights of due process and equal protection of the law.

Only three years following the Mills case, the Education for All Handicapped Children Act of 1975 (Public Law 94–142) became federal law.

Mills v. Board of Education has had a strong and lasting impact on how children with disabilities are educated today. Today, every state must ensure the provision of a free appropriate public education to all children with disabilities, and significant progress has been made in addressing many of the educational problems faced by children with disabilities that existed in 1972.

MILWAUKEE PROJECT

The term Milwaukee Project is the popular title of a widely publicized program begun in the mid-1960s as one of many Great Society efforts to improve the intellectual development of low-achieving groups. It was headed by Rick Heber of the University of Wisconsin (UW), Madison, who was also director of the generously funded Waisman Institute in Madison. The Milwaukee Project was a small study with some 20 experimental subjects and 20 control subjects. It was not reported on by the investigators in any refereed scientific journals, yet its cost was some $14 million, mostly in federal funds, and its fame was international, since it claimed to have moved the IQs of its subject children from the dull-normal range of intelligence to the superior range of intelligence.

Enthusiasm, controversy, and scandal subsequently surrounded the history of the project. Its claimed success was hailed by famous psychologists and by the popular media. Later in the project, Heber, the principal investigator, was discharged from UW, Madison and convicted and imprisoned for large-scale abuse of federal funding for private gain. Two of his colleagues were also convicted of violations of federal laws in connection with misuse of project funds. Almost two decades after the beginning of the project, the scientific world had not yet seen the long-promised final report. However, the project received uncritical acceptance in many college textbooks in psychology and education (Page, 1986).

REFERENCE

Page, E.B. (1986). The disturbing case of the Milwaukee Project. In H.H. Spitz (Ed.), *The raising of intelligence.* Hillsdale, NJ: Erlbaum.

See also Heber, R.F.; Intelligence; Mental Retardation

MINIMAL BRAIN DYSFUNCTION

See MBD SYNDROME.

MINIMUM COMPETENCY TESTING

Minimum competency testing is assessment to determine whether students possess skills that have been designated as prerequisites for either grade promotion or graduation with a high-school diploma. Minimum competency testing enjoys widespread public and political support as it is seen as a means of raising academic standards and increasing educational achievement (Haney & Madaus, 1978). A majority of the states have instituted minimum competency testing requirements (Pipho, 1978); however, there is no unanimity as to the purpose and content of the tests, which are determined at the state or local school district level.

The inclusion of handicapped students in minimum competency testing programs is problematic. Some educators are totally opposed to minimum competency testing of the handicapped (Chandler, 1982). However, the tide of opinion favors inclusion provided appropriate accommodations are made to ensure fairness and nondiscrimination in the testing process.

Minimum competency testing of the handicapped has been challenged on the basis of the Education for All Handicapped Children Act (PL 94-142), Section 504 of the Rehabilitation Act of 1973, and Constitutional grounds. The Constitutionally-based objection involves issues of due process and equal protection as set forth in the Fourteenth Amendment. Thus far, the courts have upheld the right of states to establish minimal competency standards. The courts have intervened on behalf of handicapped students only when academic standards have been clearly arbitrary and unfair, when criteria have been applied in a discriminatory manner, or when students have not been provided with sufficient notice of requirements prior to the imposition of sanctions (McCarthy, 1983).

REFERENCES

Chandler, H.N. (1982) A modest proposal. *Journal of Learning Disabilities, 15,* 306–308.

Haney, W., & Madaus, G.F. (1978). Making sense of the competency testing movement. *Harvard Educational Review, 53,* 462–484.

McCarthy, M.M. (1983). The application of competency testing mandates to handicapped children. *Harvard Educational Review, 53,* 146–164.

Pipho, C. (1978). Minimum competency testing in 1978: A look at state standards. *Phi Delta Kappan, 59,* 585–588.

See also Achievement Tests; Competency Testing

MINNESOTA MULTIPHASIC PERSONALITY INVENTORY–2 (MMPI–2)

The Minnesota Multiphasic Personality Inventory–2 (MMPI–2; Butcher, Dahlstrom, Graham, Tellegen, & Kaemmer, 1989) is the revised form of the Minnesota Multiphasic Personality Inventory (MMPI; Hathaway & McKinley, 1940), a personality test originally developed in the 1930s and 1940s to help physicians distinguish psychiatric patients from medical patients (Dahlstrom, Welsh, & Dahlstrom, 1972). The MMPI and its revision, the MMPI–2, is the most widely used and researched objective personality test in the world, with well over 10,000 books and articles on the subject (Butcher & Owens, 1978).

The MMPI–2 consists of 567 dichotomously scored questions, one more than the MMPI. Subjects 18 years and older with at least an eighth-grade education can take the test, and the instructions are to answer all questions if possible. Subjects are to be given a quiet place to self-administer the questionnaire and questions about confidentiality and result usage should be addressed. Test-taking time is usually 60–90 minutes. Answers are then either hand or computer scored, using materials obtained from NCS (P.O. Box 1416, Minneapolis, MN, 55440, (800) 627-7271). Raw scores are converted to T scores with a mean of 50 and a standard deviation of 10, and an individual's scores are compared to a group of modern normals chosen to reflect the current U.S. social and ethnic mix. One of the criticisms is that the new normative group is overeducated compared to the general U.S. population. Scores yield 10 clinical scales measuring personality and psychopathology and 6 validity scales assessing consistency and accuracy of reporting. The 10 clinical scales are:

1. *Hypochondriasis (Hy).* This scale measures an individual's nonreality-based preoccupation with health and body damage.
2. *Depression (D).* This scale measures an individual's level of pessimism, depression, and low self-esteem.

3. *Hysteria (Hy).* This scale measures an individual's tendency to deny, repress, and somatize under stress.

4. *Psychopathic Deviancy (Pd).* This scale measures an individual's tendency to externalize and to act out without adequate empathy and concern for others. In the extreme, it measures the propensity for antisocial behavior.

5. *Masculine/Feminine (Mf).* This scale measures an individual's gender identification, though not necessarily their sexual preference.

6. *Paranoia (Pa).* This scale measures an individual's level of paranoid sensitivity, self-righteousness, and paranoid argumentativeness.

7. *Psychasthenia (Pt).* This scale measures an individual's tendency to worry, feel guilty or inadequate, and to use obsessive-compulsive defenses.

8. *Schizophrenia (Sc).* This scale measures an individual's level of self esteem and tendency to cognitively disorganize under stress.

9. *Hypomania (Ma).* This scale measures an individual's energy level, optimism, grandiosity, and self-centeredness.

10. *Social (Si).* This scale measures an individual's level of shyness and need for social introversion contact.

The six validity scales, three of which are new to the MMPI–2, are:

• *Lie (L).* Measures a person's tendency to give socially desirable responses claiming unlikely virtues.

• *Frequency (F) & Frequency-Back (Fb).* Measures the tendency to over- or underendorse psychopathological items and exaggerate symptomatology.

• *Variable Response Inconsistency (VRIN).* Measures the consistency of item endorsement and if this scale is elevated to unacceptable levels, the test is uninterpretable.

• *True Response Inconsistency (TRIN).* Measures the tendency of an individual to answer "true" or "false" inconsistently throughout the test. If this scale is elevated to unacceptable levels, the test is uninterpretable.

• *Correction (K).* Developed to correct for test misses due to sophisticated defensiveness. A percentage of this correction scale is added to some of the clinical scales, as this increases the power of the test. It also correlates with socioeconomic status and measures a person's tendency to "wear their feelings on their sleeves" or to approach life with a "stiff upper lip."

Two experimental validity scales have recently been added: the Frequency Psychiatric (Fp) and the Superlative (S; Butcher & Han, 1993) scales. The Fp scale has been found useful in detecting exaggeration of symptomatology and the S scale has been found useful in identifying individuals who are presenting themselves with superlative or unrealistically positive adjustment.

The MMPI–2 revision, using a rational, empirical approach, also developed 15 new highly homogeneous, face-valid content scales (Butcher, Graham, Williams, & Ben-Porath, 1990) that measured different attributes than the original 10 clinical scales. These content scales, which are used to enrich interpretation, are:

1. *Anxiety (ANX).* This scale measures an individual's reporting of generalized anxiety, with difficulties in making decisions and concentrating.

2. *Fears (FRS).* This scale measures an individual's level of specific fears, such as fears of mice, spiders, handling money, blood, and so on.

3. *Obsessiveness (OBS).* This scale measures an individual's difficulty in making decisions with a tendency to obsess and worry.

4. *Depression (DEP).* This scale measures an individual's level of depression. The quality of depression is different than the depression measured on scale 2, in that it is more of an angry, negativistic kind of depression.

5. *Health Concerns (HEA).* This scale measures an individual's preoccupation with body symptoms.

6. *Bizarre Mentation (BIZ).* This scale is useful in detecting psychotic and paranoid thought processes.

7. *Anger (ANG).* This scale measures an individual's tendency to be irritable, grouchy, and hotheaded.

8. *Cynicism (CYN).* This scale measures an individual's expectancy that others cheat, lie, steal, and cannot be trusted.

9. *Anti-Social Practices (ASP).* This scale measures an individual's reporting of past problem behaviors and antisocial practices.

10. *Type A (TPA).* This scale measures an individual's tendency to be hard-driving, impatient, and irritable.

11. *Low Self-Esteem (LSE).* This scale measures an individual's low self-esteem and lack of self-confidence.

12. *Social Discomfort (SOD).* This scale measures an individual's level of social discomfort and a tendency to be shy and uneasy around others.

13. *Family Problems (FAM).* This scale measures an individual's level of family discord and feelings of being unsupported by family members.

14. *Work Interference (WRK).* This scale measures an individual's difficulties being efficient, making decisions, and thinking clearly at work.

15. *Negative Treatment Indicators (TRT).* This scale measures an individual's tendency to see doctors generally and mental health professionals specifically as not helpful.

Factor analysis of the MMPI revealed two factors, an anxiety factor (A) and a repression factor (R; Welsh, 1956). Though the MMPI was originally developed to identify psychopathology, it use has expanded to research, diagnosis and treatment planning for individuals in psychotherapy, and hiring nuclear power plant personnel, pilots, and police officers. It is widely used in forensic settings and is also being used in marital and family psychotherapy (Lewak, Marks, & Nelson, 1990). It is an effective tool for short-term treatment planning and recent research (Finn & Tonsager, 1992) has shown that one feedback session with the MMPI–2 can have positive therapeutic effects.

Thousands of empirical studies have shown the MMPI–2 to have high predictive validity and high test-retest reliability. Over a two week period, test-retest reliability averages above .8 for all of the clinical scales.

The original MMPI was developed for use with adults but was applied to adolescent populations early in its development. Much research was done using the MMPI with adolescents (Marks, Seeman, & Haller, 1974), but the need for a revised instrument specifically designed for adolescents became clear as the test items became increasingly outdated and appeared irrelevant to modern adolescents. The MMPI-Adolescent version (MMPI-A) revision committee developed an adolescent version of the MMPI-2 by adding a number of new items to measure more specific adolescent concerns, such as alcohol and drug abuse, family relationship difficulties, school, achievement problems, and eating disorders, and by eliminating items that were not deemed relevant to adolescent issues. This resulted in a 478-item test that requires about 60–90 minutes to self-administer. Adolescents are compared to their peers from a new representative national sample. The clinical scales of the MMPI–A have more or less the same meaning as the clinical scales of the MMPI–2. The MMPI–A validity scales, however, have been empirically renormed for adolescents. New scales developed specifically for the MMPI-A include the immaturity (IMM) scales, the alcohol/drug problem acknowledgment scale (ACK), and the alcohol/ drug problem proneness (PRO) scale. Most of the fifteen content scales developed for the MMPI–A overlap with similar measures developed for the MMPI–2; however, the MMPI–A also has some distinctive features. Adolescent-specific content scales are: Alienation (A-aln), measuring feelings of being isolated and alienated from others; Adolescent Conduct Problems (A-con), measuring impulsivity, risk-taking behavior and antisocial behaviors; Adolescent Low Aspirations (A-las), measuring level of self-esteem and ambition; and Adolescent School Problems (A-sch), measuring the level of negative attitude towards school and scholastic achievement. The MMPI–A is restricted to 14- to 18-year-old adolescents, although a 12- or 13-year-old adolescent can take it if he or she meets all the administration criteria such as adequate reading ability at the 7th grade level. Eighteen-year-old adolescents could be administered the MMPI–2 if they are already emancipated. Scoring the MMPI–A is similar to the MMPI–2 and templates and computer scoring information can be also obtained from NCS (P. O. Box 1416, Minneapolis, MN, 55440, (800) 627-7271). The MMPI–A appears to be an excellent revision of the MMPI for use with adolescents, and the new content

scales appear to be particularly useful in diagnosing modern-day adolescent difficulties.

Although the MMPI–2 and the MMPI–A are proving to be excellent instruments for diagnosis, treatment planning, feedback, and personnel selection, one difficulty that remains is that not all code types are exactly congruent between the original MMPI, the MMPI–2, and the MMPI–A. In only 60% of the cases would an individual taking the MMPI–2 and the MMPI–A get the same code-type as they would have if they had taken the original MMPI. Congruence approaches 100% in elevated and clinically distinct profiles. Consequently, this may not make a great deal of difference in the actual interpretation of the test. However, it is important because much of the original research done on the code types was based on the original MMPI. Until new research develops code type information based on the MMPI–2 and MMPI–A, it is recommended that clinicians replot the MMPI–2 and MMPI–A back to the MMPI using the appropriate tables provided in the manuals.

REFERENCES

Butcher, J.N., Dahlstrom, W.G., Graham, J.R., Tellegen, A.M., & Kaemmer, B. (1989). *MMPI–2: Manual for administration and scoring.* Minneapolis: University of Minnesota Press.

Butcher, J.N., Graham, J.R., Williams, C.L., & Ben-Porath, Y.S. (1990). *Development and use of the MMPI–2 content scales.* Minneapolis: University of Minnesota Press.

Butcher, J.N., & Han, K. (1993). Development of an MMPI-2 scale to assess the presentation of self in a superlative manner: The S scale. *Advances in Personality Assessment, 10,* 25–50.

Dahlstrom, W.G., Welsh, G.S., & Dahlstrom, L.E. (1972). *An MMPI handbook: Vol. I. Clinical interpretation* (rev. ed.). Minneapolis: University of Minnesota Press.

Finn, S.E., & Tonsager, M.E. (1992). Therapeutic effects of providing MMPI–2 test feedback to college students awaiting therapy. *Psychological Assessment, 4,* 278–287.

Hathaway, S.R., & McKinley, J.C. (1940). A multiphasic personality schedule (Minnesota): I. Construction of the schedule. *Journal of Psychology, 10,* 249–254.

Lewak, R.W., Marks, P.A., & Nelson, G.E. (1990). *Therapist guide to the MMPI & MMPI–2.* Muncie: Accelerated Development.

Marks, P.A., Seeman, W., & Haller, D.L. (1974). *The actuarial use of the MMPI with adolescents and adults.* Baltimore: Williams & Wilkins.

Welsh, G.S. (1956). Factor dimensions A and R. In G.S. Welsh & W.G. Dahlstrom (Eds.), *Basic readings on the MMPI in psychology and medicine* (pp. 264–281). Minneapolis: University of Minnesota Press.

MINOR PHYSICAL ANOMALIES

A higher than normal number of minor physical anomalies (MPAs) has been linked with various behavioral disorders including schizophrenia, Down's Syndrome, mental retardation, autism, learning disabilities, and attention-deficit/ hyperactivity disorder (Krouse & Kauffman, 1982). MPAs are now being used to determine individuals at an increased risk for adolescent psychopathology. Thus far, MPAs have led to successful predictions of childhood conduct disorder (Pine, Shaffer, Schonfeld, & Davies, 1997).

Examples of MPAs are soft and pliable ears, a tongue with rough and smooth spots, fine electric hair, high-steepled palate, head circumference larger or smaller that normal, curved fifth finger, single crease across the palm of the hand, epicanthus, and a gap between first and second toe (Waldrop & Halverson, 1971).

Recent research has shown a 60% increase in occurrence of MPAs in people with schizoprenia over the normal population, which typically exhibits only a 5% chance of having MPAs. However, siblings of individuals with schizophrenia also have shown a 38% increased occurrence of MPAs. MPAs exhibited in individuals with schizophrenia frequently pertain to eye, mouth, hand, and foot regions (Ismail, Cantor-Graae, & McNeil, 1998). MPAs can often be detected from various events that occur during pregnancy and may lead researchers to a better understanding of the causes of schizophrenia (Waddington et al., 1998).

REFERENCES

Ismail, B., Cantor-Graae, E., & McNeil, T.F. (1998). Minor physical anomalies in schizophrenic patients and their siblings. *American Journal of Psychiatry, 155,* 1695–1702.

Krouse, J.P., & Kauffman, J.M. (1982). Minor physical anomalies in exceptional children: A review and critique of research. *Journal of Abnormal Child Psychology, 10,* 247–264.

Pine, D.S., Shaffer, D., Schonfeld, I.S., & Davies, M. (1997). Minor physical anomalies: Modifiers of environmental risks for psychiatric impairment? *Journal of the American Academy of Child and Adolescent Psychiatry, 36,* 395–403.

Waddington, J.L., Buckley, P.F., Scully, P.J., Lane, A., O'Callaghan, E., & Larkin, C. (1998). Course of psychopathology, cognition, and neurobiological abnormality in schizophrenia: Developmental origins and amelioration by antipsychotics? *Journal of Psychiatric Research, 32,* 179–189.

Waldrop, M.F., & Halverson, C.F. (1971). Minor physical anomalies and hyperactive behavior in young children. In J. Hellmuth (Ed.), *Exceptional infant: Studies in abnormalities* (Vol. 2, pp. 343–380). New York: Brunner/Mazel.

See also **Down's Syndrome; Dysmorphic Features; Physical Anomalies; Physical Handicaps**

MISCUE ANALYSIS

Miscue analysis is a research technique developed by Kenneth Goodman in 1970 to describe the language and thought processes involved in the act of reading. Based on psycholinguistic theory, Goodman described reading as an interaction between the language of the reader and the language of the author (Goodman & Burke, 1972). To discover how both language and thought processes are involved in reading, children's oral miscues were analyzed as they read unrehearsed passages of text. Miscues were defined as unexpected responses that deviated from the expected responses in the text. Specifically, miscue analysis is used as a means of identifying and evaluating the strategies employed by skilled and unskilled readers as they attempt to construct meaning from written text.

The procedures used in miscue analysis have been simplified for classroom use in a diagnostic instrument called the Reading Miscue Inventory (Goodman & Burke, 1972). Burke (1974) cites procedures that include recording children's oral reading errors and classifying the errors based on the following questions:

1. *Graphic Similarity.* How much does the miscue *look* like the expected response?

2. *Sound Similarity.* How much does the miscue *sound* like the expected response?

3. *Grammatical Function.* Is the grammatical function of the reader's word the same as the grammatical function of the text word?

4. *Syntactic Acceptability.* Is the sentence involving the miscue grammatically acceptable?

5. *Semantic Acceptability.* Is the sentence involving the miscue semantically acceptable?

6. *Meaning Change.* Is there a change in meaning involved in the sentence?

7. *Correction and Semantic Acceptability.* Do corrections by the reader make the sentence semantically acceptable? (p. 23)

These questions are applied to each miscue to determine how readers process three kinds of information from the printed page: grapho-phonic, syntactic, and semantic (Goodman, 1969).

Research on miscue analysis is inconclusive because of inconsistencies in classifying and interpreting specific reading miscues. Wixson (1979) points out that miscue procedures are not designed to account for variables such as instructional methods, type of text, passage length and difficulty, and reader's purpose. It has been suggested (Leu, 1982; Wixson, 1979) that miscue patterns may be a function of these variables rather than a reflection of a particular reader's processing strategies.

One of the most significant findings of miscue analysis research is that the reading strategies of proficient readers are different from those of less skilled readers. Because proficient readers have greater language competency, they tend to make errors that are more syntactically and semantically acceptable than less proficient readers (Goodman, 1969; Goodman & Burke, 1972; Goodman, 1995).

Teachers can use the results of miscue analysis to improve their instructional strategies. After classifying and interpreting students' miscues, teachers should provide the appropriate language experiences necessary to develop the conceptual understandings needed to comprehend the author's message (Martens, 1995). Once teachers know the type of miscues children make, they can provide experiences that build bridges from the language and thought of the child to the language and thought of the author.

REFERENCES

Burke, C. (1974). Preparing elementary teachers to teach reading. In K.S. Goodman (Ed.), *Miscue analysis: Applications to reading instruction.* Urbana, IL: National Council of Teachers of English.

Goodman, K.S. (1969). Analysis of reading miscues: Applied psycholinguistics. *Reading Research Quarterly, 5*(1), 9–30.

Goodman, Y.M. (1995). Miscue analysis for classroom teachers: Some history and some procedures. *Primary Voices, 3*(4), 2–9.

Goodman, Y.M., & Burke, C.L. (1972). *Reading miscue inventory: Procedures for diagnosis and evaluation.* New York: Macmillan.

Leu, D.J., Jr. (1982). Oral reading error analysis: A critical review of research and application. *Reading Research Quarterly, 17*(3), 420–437.

Martens, P. (1995). Empowering teachers and empowering students. *Primary Voices, 3*(4), 39–42.

Wixson, K.L. (1979). Miscue analysis: A critical review. *Journal of Reading Behavior, 11*(2), 163–175.

See also **Linguistic Readers; Reading Disorders; Reading Remediation**

MIXED CONNECTIVE TISSUE DISEASE

See RARE DISEASES.

MNEMONICS

Mnemonics are among the oldest strategies used to enhance recall of information such as facts, names, sequences, and concepts. In recent years they have been helpful to students labeled learning disabled and mildly handicapped (Mastropieri, Scruggs, & Levin, 1985; Rose, Cundick, & Higbee, 1983). Examples of tasks taught by such strategies include reading comprehension and concept formation.

One frequently used mnemonic with learning-disabled students is the rhyming or pegword technique. It consists of remembering a simple rhyme pairing a number and an object such as "one-bun, two-shoe, three-tree." The learner then pairs the new information with each object in the rhyme. Another strategy requires the learner to visually imagine a set of loci in which he or she can place the new information. The keyword method combines a special word for the information (e.g., box for "bauxite") with a pegword. Students find mnemonic strategies entertaining and prefer them over traditional instruction (Scruggs & Mastropieri, 1992).

REFERENCES

Mastropieri, M.A., Scruggs, T.E., & Levin, J.R. (1985). Mnemonic strategy instruction with learning disabled adolescents. *Journal of Learning Disabilities, 18,* 94–100.

Rose, M.C., Cundick, B.P., & Higbee, K.L. (1983). Verbal rehearsal and visual imagery: Mnemonic aids for learning disabled children. *Journal of Learning Disabilities, 16,* 352–354.

Scruggs, T.E., & Mastropieri, M.A. (1992). Classroom applications

of mnemonic instruction, acquisition, maintenance, and generalization. *Exceptional Children, 58*(3), 219–229.

See also **Amnesia; Memory Disorders**

MOBAN

Moban is the proprietary name of molindine, a white crystalline powder used as a tranquilizer (Modell, 1985). The drug acts on the ascending reticular activating system to reduce depression, aggressiveness, and spontaneous locomotion. Tranquilizing effects reportedly are achieved without such negative concomitants as incoordination or muscle relaxation. Moban typically is used in the management of schizophrenia.

Common side effects associated with Moban include initial drowsiness, depression, and hyperactivity. Moban has been associated with seizure activity on occasion. Increased activity may occur in some individuals, and hence protective environments may be necessary. Tardive dyskinesia is a possible side effect. Moban has not been shown to be effective in the management of behavior problems associated with mental retardation. Use of Moban in children under 12 years of age is not recommended.

REFERENCES

Modell, W. (Ed.). (1985). *Drugs in current use and new drugs* (31st ed.). New York: Springer-Verlag.

Physician's desk reference (37th ed.). (1983). Oradell, NJ: Medical Economics.

See also **Thorazine; Tranquilizers; Stelazine**

MOBILE EDUCATION UNITS

As the name implies, mobile education units are vans, buses, recreational vehicles, or trailers that have been converted to house specialized materials, media, and testing equipment to serve handicapped children and youths. They are in use in rural areas primarily, where geographic distances and learner sparsity make the units an efficient means of making special materials and services available to teachers and learners. These units are usually owned by the administrative unit that is responsible for supportive special education services (e.g., BOCES, CESA, Intermediate Unit).

The term mobile special education unit is a generic category of vehicle. The size and purpose of the unit is dependent on the needs of the region being served. Some units are used exclusively for testing. Space is at a premium in many schools and even if space is available, it may not be appropriate for services such as psychological testing or auditory assessments because of noise or distractions. Mobile units that are designed for these purposes have special lighting and noise reduction materials to improve the environment for testing. The unit travels around a geographic region on a schedule and is parked adjacent to a school for an extended period. The psychologist or audiologist may double as the driver of such a unit.

See also **Homebound Instruction; Itinerant Services**

MOBILITY INSTRUCTION

Mobility instruction is a term used to represent specific daily functional living skills that are incorporated into educational programs for moderate and severely handicapped populations. The purpose of this instruction is to allow individuals to safely engage in planned movement from one location to another (Merbler & Wood, 1984).

Included in this group of functional skills are activities that promote independent travel within the immediate home environment as well as the local community. Instruction in toileting and meal preparation, and travel training for shopping, employment, or community recreation are examples of the activities included in mobility instruction.

Within the last 20 years there has been growing support for systematically incorporating functional skills into the existing curriculum for the mentally retarded. A variety of programs have been developed that focus on the direct teaching of these skills. Mobility training programs such as those reviewed by Martin, Rusch, and Heal (1982), include activities that engage individuals in real-life experiences as well simulated travel activities conducted within a classroom setting.

While there is a need for additional research that will evaluate the effectiveness of mobility instruction, there are preliminary indicators that reveal that real-life experiences are more effective than simulation activities for training mobility skills.

Regardless of how simulation and real-life experiences are combined, it is important that the mobility instruction be systematic. Equally important is that parents and group-home workers allow handicapped individuals opportunities to practice these skills independently (Certo, Schwartz, & Brown, 1977).

REFERENCES

Certo, N., Schwartz, R., & Brown, L. (1977). Community transportation: Teaching severely handicapped students to ride a public bus system. In N.G. Haring & L.J. Brown (Eds.), *Teaching the severely handicapped* (Vol. 2, pp. 147–232). New York: Grune & Stratton.

Martin, J., Rusch, F., & Heal, L. (1982). Teaching community survival skills to mentally retarded adults: A review and analysis. *Journal of Special Education, 16*(3), 243–267.

Merbler, J.B., & Wood, T.A. (1984). Predicting orientation and mobility proficiency in mentally retarded visually impaired children. *Education & Training of the Mentally Retarded, 19*(3), 228–230.

See also **Electronic Travel Aids; Travel Aids for the Handicapped**

MOBILITY TRAINERS

Formal training of the blind to help them move independently had its beginnings in the United States with the founding of the first dog guide school, Seeing Eye, Inc. of Morristown, New Jersey (Bledsoe, 1980). Although many blind individuals had traveled independently for centuries, it was not until the founding of this dog guide school that efforts were made to formalize a sequential approach to independent travel.

However, the formal curriculum for mobility training owes its roots to the cane rather than the dog. Over the years, mobility training for the blind has had many names. Sir Francis Campbell, an American who was naturalized and knighted in Britain, wrote extensively in the 1860s about the need for formal mobility training under the broad term "foot travel." Father Thomas Carroll, founder of the Catholic Guide for All the Blind, coined the term peripatology, which could be loosely defined as the study of travel. The most common term today is orientation and mobility. Orientation in this context is the acquisition of knowledge about one's environment; mobility means one's ability to move freely and safely from one place to another. The individual who teaches orientation and mobility is commonly referred to as a mobility specialist, although the terms peripatologist or orientator are also used.

The training, either at the bachelor's or master's level, consists of course work in the nature and needs of the blind, training in the specific skills and techniques of teaching independence, and a block of hours working under a blindfold. The formal course work is followed by a term of practicum supervised by a qualified mobility specialist. The Mobility Interest Group of the Association for the Education and Rehabilitation of the Blind and Visually Impaired certifies graduates of university training programs.

A sizable number of mobility specialists work in larger school systems, where they provide training to blind students. In addition to direct training of children and youths, they also consult with teachers of younger children in the development of concepts that will later enhance travel independence.

REFERENCE

Bledsoe, C.W. (1980). Originators of orientation and mobility training. In R.L. Welsh & B.B. Blasch (Eds.), *Foundation of orientation and mobility*. New York: American Foundation for the Blind.

See also **Blind Learning Aptitude Test; Dog Guides for the Blind; Visual Training**

MODEL PROGRAMS FOR SEVERELY AND PROFOUNDLY DISABLED INDIVIDUALS

The purpose of model education programs for individuals with severe to profound disabilities is to look at the state of the art in the instruction of such individuals and to continue to innovate by investigating current practices in a variety of ways. Typically receiving funding from outside sources (e.g., Office of Special Education and Rehabilitative Services at the federal level), model programs may include demonstration projects in local school systems, work with nonschool personnel such as parents via parent training projects, or adult vocational and independent living skills training programs.

Three examples of model programs are the Community-Based Instruction Program (CBIP) in Albemarle County, Virginia (project director, Adelle Renzaglia), the Specialized Training Program (STP) in Eugene, Oregon (program director, G. Thomas Bellamy), and the Inclusive Education Project conducted by Syracuse University and Syracuse Public Schools (Rogan & Davern, 1992). The CBIP (Snell & Renzaglia, 1986) was a federally funded 3-year project that was established to serve school-age students with severe and profound handicaps. Prior to the start of the program, these students were being served inappropriately in preschool classes, in classes for students with mild to moderate handicaps, or in homebound instruction. Three classes were established in integrated settings: a high-school class serving individuals 16 to 21 years of age located in a high school that serves approximately 2000 nonhandicapped students; a middle-school class serving students ages 12 to 15 years that was located in a middle school housing approximately 375 nonhandicapped sixth through eighth grade students; and an elementary classroom serving students ages 6 to 11 years in an elementary school with approximately 225 nonhandicapped kindergarten through fifth-grade students.

The STP (Boles, Bellamy, Horner, & Mark, 1984) was implemented to develop, field test, and disseminate a structured employment model emphasizing benchwork assembly tasks for adults with severe handicaps. Initially developed within a university center as an on-campus vocational program for severely and profoundly mentally retarded individuals, the program moved into a field test phase in which community vocational training was offered in three states using the STP model. Currently, the program is in a model implementation phase in which a work support center is being developed to assist localities throughout the nation in developing STP sites.

The STP provides employment in the area of small parts assembly (e.g., electronic units). Work is procured from local industries and workers are trained on a one-to-one basis until they are able to enter a supported production setting. Applied behavior analysis procedures are used for training and areas of instruction include personal competence in the surrounding community as well as in the work place. Each model site operates as a small not-for-profit business and follows well-defined procedures for management, finance, and commercial operation.

Through careful planning of the site activities and training, as well as support for groups wishing to start replication sites, the STP model has provided multiple work sites for severely to profoundly handicapped individuals. Systematic instruction has enabled these individuals, heretofore unserved in competitive employment sites, to have a viable alternative to sheltered work or no-work options.

The Inclusive Education Project was designed to meet special problems of children with severe handicaps in regular education settings. Eight schools participated in building level process, leadership institutes, and community networking. A detailed report can be read in Rogan and Davern (1992).

The three models described indicate the types of programming that are being investigated and disseminated following demonstration of innovative practices. In general, model programs for individuals with severe or profound handicaps should include the following: data-based assessment of current and future needs; ongoing data-based evaluation of progress; integration of severely handicapped students/adults with their nonhandicapped peers; transdisciplinary programming; home-school interaction; chronological age-appropriate programs; objectives that are functional for students'/adults' current or future needs; and systematic instruction in specific domains such as the domestic (e.g., grooming, household chores), leisure/recreation, community (e.g., restaurant use, pedestrian skills, grocery shopping), and vocational (Snell & Renzaglia, 1986).

REFERENCES

Boles, S.M., Bellamy, G.T., Horner, R.H., & Mark, D.M. (1984). Specialized training program: The structured employment model. In S.C. Paine, G.T. Bellamy, & B. Wilcox (Eds.), *Human services that work* (pp. 181–205). Baltimore, MD: Brookes.

Rogan, P., & Davern, N. (1992). *Inclusive Education Project: Final report.* Syracuse, NY: New York Division of Special Education and Rehabilitation.

Snell, M.E., & Renzaglia, A. (1986). Moderate, severe, and profound handicaps. In N.G. Haring & L. McCormick (Eds.), *Exceptional children and youth* (4th ed.). Columbus, OH: Merrill.

See also **Applied Behavior Analysis; Functional Instruction; Transfer of Learning; Transfer of Training; Vocational Training of the Handicapped**

MONOGRAPHS OF THE SOCIETY FOR RESEARCH IN CHILD DEVELOPMENT

Monographs of the Society for Research in Child Development is one of three publications of the Society for Research in Child Development. Published irregularly by the University of Chicago Press, the *Monographs* series is perhaps the longest continuous publication in the field of child development.

In general, the series is intended for the publication of significant research articles that are longer than those normally published in journals. Of particular interest are longitudinal studies and research that appeals to a large number of developmentalists from a variety of fields.

MONTESSORI, MARIA (1870–1952)

Maria Montessori, who was Italy's first woman physician, originated the educational system known as the Montessori method. The major features of her method were a nongraded classroom, individualization of instruction, sequential ordering of learning tasks, sensory and motor training, use of concrete materials, abolition of punishment, discovery learning, and freedom of activity and choice. First used in 1899 for the instruction of mentally retarded children, Montessori soon found that her approach was equally effective with nonhandicapped children. Her influence is evident today in both special classes and preschool and lower elementary programs. Montessori taught and lectured in many countries and her schools sprang up throughout the world. A visit to the United States in 1914 led to the formation of the American Montessori Society, with Alexander Graham Bell as president.

REFERENCES

Goodman, L. (1974). Montessori education for the handicapped: The methods—the research. In L. Mann & D.A. Sabatino (Eds.), *The second review of special education* (pp. 153–191). Philadelphia: JSE.

Montessori, M. (1964). *The Montessori method.* New York: Schocken.

Orem, R.C. (Ed.). (1970). *Montessori and the special child.* New York: Capricorn.

Standing, E.M. (1962). *Maria Montessori: Her life and work.* New York: New American Library.

MONTESSORI METHOD

Maria Montessori was born in Chiavalle, Italy, in 1870; after receiving her doctorate she visited asylums, which spurred her interest in retarded children. Using some of the work of Itard and Seguin, she designed materials and an instructional method that was so successful that after one year of instruction, the retarded children had learned enough to pass the state examination given to normal children after one year of schooling. Montessori felt that if a retarded child could accomplish so much through her methods, a normal child should be able to accomplish even more. Gradually she devised materials and equipment to realize her goals and formulated an underlying philosophy based on the dignity and spiritual worth of the child. Between 1912 and 1917 she put her ideas into five key books: *The Montessori Method, Pedagogy and Anthropology, Dr. Montessori's Own Handbook,* and *The Advanced Montessori Method, Volumes I and II* (Gitter, 1970).

The Montessori classroom provides a prepared environment, organized by ground rules, in which the child is able to move and work constructively in relative freedom, without disruption from other children. The engineered classroom resembles this prepared environment, which is organized around activity centers designed to produce order. The centers include the mastery center, where academic tasks are offered; the exploratory center, which contains an array of manipulative materials for the pursuit of scientific exploration; and the order center, which is reserved for specialized supportive one-to-one instruction (Kottler, 1977). The child can work directly with the didactic material he or she has chosen, for as long as desired, creating an individual curriculum paced at an individual rate. This makes it more likely that the child will experience a pattern of success, rather than failure (Orem, 1969).

Many educators have turned toward Montessori as a possible solution to the educational problems of handicapped children. Individuation is central to special education and is attainable using the Montessori system. The nondemanding atmosphere is appropriate for children who cannot deal with pressure, and many children with sensory and perceptual deficits can benefit from the Montessori materials and methods. By applying several senses to a learning task, one sense can substitute for deficits in another sensory channel.

The early entrance age, as young as 3 years, is important in early intervention programs for children who need a head start. However the program's merits are not corroborated by results of objective evaluation, which offer little evidence to support the educational value of the Montessori method (Goodman, 1974). It is indicated that the Montessori environment may help handicapped children by its nongroup structure to feel more accepted by peers, a prime factor in the development of self-image (Krogh, 1982). However, Montessori does not emphasize transformational thinking, or acknowledge the importance of broad experiences. She does not make use of the unplanned as well as the planned environment and events. She does not place a high value on the early development of symbolic behavior, including language. These are important aspects in childhood development and present serious criticisms of Montessori's method (Bruce, 1984).

REFERENCES

Bruce, T. (1984). A Froebelian looks at Montessori's work. *Early Child Development and Care, 14*(1–2), 75–83.

Gitter, L.L. (1970). *The Montessori way.* Seattle, WA: Special Child.

Goodman, L. (1974). Montessori education for the handicapped: The methods—The research. In L. Mann & D.A. Sabatino (Eds.), *The second review of special education.* Philadelphia: O.S.E. Press.

Kottler, S.B. (1977, April). *The Montessori approach to the education of the exceptional child—Early childhood through high school.* Paper presented at the Annual International Convention, The Council for Exceptional Children, Atlanta, GA.

Krogh, S.L. (1982, April). Affective and social development. Some ideas from Montessori's prepared environment. *Topics in Early Childhood Special Education, 2*(1), 55–62.

Orem, R.C. (1969). *Montessori and the special child.* New York: Putman.

***See also* Ecological Education for the Handicapped**

MORAL REASONING

Moral reasoning refers to the manner in which a person cognitively processes information to arrive at a judgment as to whether an act is right or wrong. The research emphasis in this area is not on the factors that influence moral behavior, but rather how increasingly complex levels of moral reason evolve within the context of cognitive development. The prevailing theory of moral judgment is Lawrence Kohlberg's (1976); it has as its underpinnings the work of Jean Piaget (1965).

Kohlberg (1976) proposes three levels of moral reasoning, each with two stages. At the preconventional stage, the child cannot help but solve ethical dilemmas from an egocentric perspective. Thus what is wrong is anything that leads to punishment; the effects of one's actions on others is unappreciated. As egocentrism declines, the child is able to assume the viewpoint of another person, albeit in a concrete, individualistic way. Now an act may be considered right if it is based on an agreement, a deal, or some kind of fair exchange. During the conventional stage, the child begins to consider the perspective of society, yet still within a rather concrete framework. Moral reasoning has an authoritarian flavor in that the child is heavily influenced by adherence to interpersonal expectations and social standards. At the postconventional or principled level, the individual is able to engage in more abstract thinking about ethical matters, evidencing the emergence of formal operational thinking. A moral perspective is able to develop that recognizes universal ethical principles that are self-chosen. Laws or social agreements are usually viewed as valid because they are derived from universal principles. If a law is at variance with a principle, behavior should follow the principle. It must be emphasized that the level of moral reasoning displayed is not based on the final answer as to how one should behave or, for that matter, actual conduct. Rather, it is based on the rationale used to justify an action.

As a cognitive-developmental stage theorist, Kohlberg has assumed that his developmental stages were invariant (persons cannot skip a stage or change their order) and universal (stage sequencing and characteristics apply to all persons across all cultures, religions, and gender). These assumptions generated a great deal of controversy and research (Turiel, 1998). The invariance of stages has been generally confirmed in cross-sectional and longitudinal research that is also cross-cultural (Colby & Kohlberg, 1987; Colby, Kohlberg, Gibbs, & Lieberman, 1983). Those individuals who show moral development do progress systematically through the stages. However, it must be noted that in many cultures, including the United States, most individuals do not advance beyond the fourth stage into the level of postconventional or principled morality.

The universality of the stages has been controversial. Postconventional morality simply does not exist in some societies and may reflect a Western ideal. Many societies do not value individualism and individual rights, and therefore in those societies, the highest morality may be shown in sub-jugation of individual rights to societal or collective rights (Shweder, Mahapatra, & Miller, 1990).

Moral reasoning theory has been applied to many different disciplines including philosophy, anthropology, sociology, criminology, and education (Turiel, 1998). In general, there is a complex but only moderate relationship between moral reasoning and moral conduct. Persons in a higher moral reasoning level tend to act consistently, but situations involving high cost or high punishment may influence behavior consistent with a lower level of morality (Thoma, Rest, & Davison, 1991). Higher education tends to increase the level of moral reasoning, perhaps because of exposure to conflictual problems. Furthermore, nonretarded children and older retarded children with the same mental ages tend to have similar levels of moral reasoning (Weisz & Zigler, 1979). These results demonstrate that cognitive development may underlie moral reasoning but training can affect the level and upper limit of reasoning.

REFERENCES

Colby, A., & Kohlberg, L. (1987). *The measurement of moral judgment.* (Vol. 1). *Theoretical foundations and research validation.* Cambridge: Cambridge University Press.

Colby, A., Kohlberg, L., Gibbs, J., & Lieberman, M. (1983). A longitudinal study of moral judgment. *Monographs of the Society for Research in Child Development, 48,* Nos. 1–2, Serial No. 200.

Kohlberg, L. (1976). Moral stages and moralization: The cognitive-developmental approach. In T. Lickona (Ed.), *Moral development and behavior.* New York: Holt, Rinehart, & Winston.

Piaget, J. (1965). *The moral judgment of the child.* New York: The Free Press.

Shweder, R.A., Mahapatra, M., & Miller, J.G. (1990). Culture and moral development. In J.W. Stigler, R.A. Shweder, & G. Herdt (Eds.), *Cultural psychology: Essays on comparative human development.* Cambridge, England: Cambridge University Press.

Thoma, S.J., Rest, J.R., & Davison, M.L. (1991). Describing and testing a moderator of the moral judgment and action relationship. *Journal of Personality and Social Psychology, 61,* 659–669.

Turiel, E. (1998). The development of morality. In W. Damon & N. Eisenberg (Eds.), *Handbook of child psychology. Vol. 3, Social, emotional, and personality development* (5th ed.) (pp. 863–932). New York: Wiley.

Weisz, J.R., & Zigler, E. (1979). Cognitive development in retarded and nonretarded persons: Piagetian tests of the similar-sequence hypotheses. *Psychological Bulletin, 86,* 831–851.

See also **Conscience, Lack of; Piaget, Jean; Social Skills Training**

MOSAICISM

Mosaicism, the least common form of Down's syndrome, is found in about 1% of all cases. Mosaicism is not familial. Rather, it is thought to be due to an error in early cell division following conception. The first cell resulting from fertilization has the normal number of chromosomes. At some point after the egg is fertilized, the extra chromosome appears. At birth the child has some cells with 46 chromosomes and others with 47, thereby creating a mosaiclike pattern. Cells with 45 or fewer chromosomes usually do not survive.

The extra chromosome 21 is always associated with mental retardation and specific physical characteristics. Gibson and Frank (1961) list the most common features: large fissured tongue; short stubby hands; epicanthal fold at inner corner of the eye; single transverse crease across palm; inward curving little finger; flattened nose; fused ear lobules; cleft between big and second toe; small, flattened skull; short fifth finger; smooth simple outer earlobe; congenital heart problems; and a little finger with one lateral crease rather than two. All traits may not occur in any one individual with Down's syndrome. Mosaics may exhibit few if any visible signs. They may have normal intelligence (Koch & Koch, 1974). The number of symptoms present is thought to be dependent on the age of the embryo when the error of cell division occurs. The earlier the division, the more severe the effect.

The reasons that chromosomes do not divide properly are not clearly understood (Smith & Wilson, 1973). Suspect are radiation and X-ray exposure; viral infections; misuse of drugs; or problems of hormone or immunological balance. Mosaics can transmit Down's syndrome to the next generation. Some may not know they are mosaics until they produce a child with mosaicism or until cytogenetics reveals their condition. Amniocentesis can be performed during the first 12 to 16 weeks of pregnancy to determine if such chromosomal abnormalities exist (Dorfman, 1972).

REFERENCES

Dorfman, A. (Ed.). (1972). *Antenatal diagnosis.* Chicago: University of Chicago Press.

Gibson, D., & Frank, H.F. (1961). Dimensions of mongolism: I. Age limits for cardinal mongol stigmata. *American Journal of Mental Deficiency, 66,* 30–34.

Koch, R., & Koch, K. (1974). *Understanding the mentally retarded child: A new approach.* New York: Random House.

Smith, W.D., & Wilson, A.A. (1973). The child with Down's Syndrome: Causes, characteristics and acceptance. Philadelphia: Saunders.

See also **Chromosomal Anomalies; Congenital Disorders; Down's Syndrome; Heredity; Minor Physical Anomalies**

MOTIVATION

Motivation is generally believed to consist of two components, drive and incentive. Drive is something that invigorates activity without necessarily determining the type of activity. For example, a splinter in a finger may lead to a variety of energetic behaviors until the splinter is removed, even though it does not mandate any one specific behavior. Incentive is a stimulus that evokes approach or avoidance behaviors. For example, the availability of a tasty dessert may arouse approach behaviors even by people who are not hungry.

Many biologically determined motivations are described as homeostatic processes. A homeostatic process is one that tends to maintain constancy of some variable. For example, we use both physiological and behavioral means to maintain a nearly constant body temperature. Drinking enables us to maintain a nearly constant concentration of solutes in the cells and a nearly constant volume of blood. Eating enables us to maintain a steady supply of nutrients to the cells and a fairly steady body weight.

Many social motivations, however, are not homeostatic. Humans experience a need for affiliation and a need for achievement. Such motivations may remain at a high level over long periods of time. Fulfilling our affiliation or achievement needs does not weaken the motivation for further affiliation or achievement, however. In that way, such activities differ from drinking and eating.

Goals that people set for themselves can become highly effective motivations (Locke, Shaw, Saari, & Latham, 1981). Clear and specific goals lead to enhanced performance in many settings; vague goals such as "do your best" are ineffective. Generally, very high goals lead to the best performance, so long as the goals remain realistic. For a goal to influence behavior, the individual must make a commitment, preferably in public, to achieving the goal and must receive periodic feedback on progress toward the goal. It is also important to receive a reward for reaching the goal; otherwise, people become indifferent toward further goals.

Goals lead to enhanced performance in several ways. They focus attention and thereby reduce distraction. They increase persistence. They also motivate people to develop new strategies to achieve the goal, even at the expense of other worthwhile ends. For example, someone who sets a goal of increased quantity of output may decrease quality. Elements of motivation in students include: ownership of learning, confidence, positive self-esteem, and ability to transfer learning. Evidence of academic motivation is seen in the amount of goals set and achieved, positive classroom climate, and utilization of cooperative learning strategies (Phillips & Steinkomp, 1995).

REFERENCES

Locke, E.A., Shaw, K.N., Saari, L.M., & Latham, G.P. (1981). Goal setting and task performance: 1969–1980. *Psychological Bulletin, 90,* 125–152.

Phillips, L., & Steinkomp, M. (1995). *Improving academic performance.* Illinois: Saint Xavier University, Action Research Project.

See also **Achievement Need; Applied Behavior Analysis; Positive Reinforcement**

MOTOR-FREE VISUAL PERCEPTION TEST–REVISED (MVPT-R)

The Motor-Free Visual Perception Test–Revised (MVPT-R; Colarusso & Hammill, 1996) is a second edition of a popular test of visual perception first published in 1972. This test measures visual perception without motor involvement. It is designed for use by psychologists, educational diagnosticians, and others trained in individual assessment. The MVPT-R is easily administered in 15 to 20 minutes to children ages 4 through 11½ years. It is divided into five item types intended to measure the following components of visual perception: spatial relationships, visual discrimination, figure-ground, visual closure, and visual memory. The figure illustrates an item from the figure-ground grouping.

As the authors note, most of the tests used to assess visual perception (e.g., Bender Gestalt Test, Developmental Test of Visual-Motor Integration, and the drawing subtests of the McCarthy Scales of Children's Abilities) are actually measures of visual-motor integration skills, which require visual perceptual ability but make major demands on the child's fine motor skills. Children are frequently misdiagnosed as having visual-perceptual disorders on the basis of poor performance on tests requiring extensive motor performance. The MVPT-R avoids the confounding of visual perception with motor skills in its assessment.

Reliability of the scale is moderate (high .70s and low .80s for internal consistency estimates). Surprisingly, no reliability information is provided for children older than eight. Validity information is dated; only studies pertaining to the 1972 edition are provided. The MVPT-R is useful principally because of the lack of other instruments from which to choose. It is easy to administer and score and has considerable intuitive appeal.

REFERENCE

Colarusso, R.P., & Hammill, D.D. (1996). *Motor-Free Visual Perception Test–Revised.* Novato, CA: Academic Therapy Publications.

See also **Bender Gestalt; Visual-Motor and Visual-Perceptual Problems**

MOTOR LEARNING

Motor learning is necessary to acquire the skills required for effective movement of the body. Although some authors have distinguished between motor and movement activities, the terms are often interchangeable (Harrow, 1972). Oxendine (1984) has noted three types of motor (or perceptual motor) learning. First is the maturationally related behavior that typically is developed early in life. Walking, speaking, and general body coordination are in this category. The second group of skills is high in perceptual components and includes communicative behaviors such as handwriting. These activities are necessary for continued educational progress. A final set of motor behaviors is learned because the performance of these activities results in direct benefits to the actor. Much of vocational and recreational accomplishment is built on motor learning.

The sensorimotor deficits faced by many special education students make the issue of motor performance objectives particularly central in the design of education for those students. Motor learning is not only important for its own

sake, but as a component of cognitive and affective development. Activities learned in physical-education programs for the handicapped increase self-esteem and allow for social interaction in games (Moon & Renzaglia, 1982). Basic motor skills are necessary for the activities of daily living. Learning the motor behaviors required for communication is crucial for cognitive development.

Harrow (1972) has developed a taxonomy of tasks in the psychomotor domain. As with classification systems in the cognitive and affective domains, this taxonomy is designed to allow the teacher to specify educational objectives. Often the special education teacher must produce objectives aimed at needs of a given disability group. Motor learning behavioral objectives typically include motor skills of daily living and fine and gross motor performance (Fredericks et al., 1976; Hawkins et al., 1983).

Motor learning objectives for moderately and severely disabled students may involve behaviors that can be taught to most nondisabled individuals without any carefully constructed plan or method. The Hawkins et al. (1983) project is an example of the use of motor performance objectives to produce detailed activity programs for an enriched home and school environment. Such planning may be necessary to produce desired levels of simple motor learning. In general, motor learning has better outcomes the earlier it is initiated (Sanz & Melendez, 1992).

REFERENCES

Fredericks, H.D., Riggs, C., Furey, J., Grove, D., Moore, W., McDonnell, J., Jordan, E., Hanson, W., Baldwin, V., & Wadlow, M. (1976). *The teaching research curriculum for moderately and severely handicapped.* Springfield, IL: Thomas.

Harrow, A.J. (1972). *Taxonomy of the psychomotor domain.* New York: McKay.

Hawkins, R.P., McGinnis, L.D., Bieniek, B.J., Timmons, D.M., Eddy, D.B., & Cone, J.D. (1983). *The school and home enrichment program for severely handicapped children.* Champaign, IL: Research.

Moon, M.S., & Renzaglia, A. (1982). Physical fitness and the mentally retarded: A critical review of the literature. *Journal of Special Education, 16,* 269–287.

Oxendine, J.B. (1984). *Motor learning* (2nd ed.). Englewood Cliffs, NJ: Prentice-Hall.

Sanz, M.T., & Melendez, F.J. (1992). Early motor training in Down syndrome babies: Results of an intervention program. (ERIC Clearinghouse No. EC 301660)

See also **Movement Therapy; Perceptual Training; Visual-Motor and Visual-Perceptual Problems**

MOTOR SPEECH DISORDERS

Motor speech disorders are caused by a neuropathology that affects a person's ability to plan a program of motor activity (apraxia) or impairs their ability to carry out the movements that produce speech sounds (dysarthria). Motor speech disorders comprise more than 36% of all acquired communication disorders (Duffy, 1995). A motor speech disorder can be acquired or congenital, and may occur in both children and adults. Any type of language disorder is excluded from the category of motor speech disorder. Speech disorders caused by deficits or deviation in speech structures, such as laryngectomy, or delays in development, such as phonological processes, are also not classified as motor speech disorders.

Dysarthria describes a group of disorders in which speech movement errors are due to muscle weakness, incoordination, neural disinhibition, and sensory deficits. While problems can be focused on a single component of the speech system (i.e. respiration, phonation, articulation, or resonation), most dysarthrias impact all systems to some degree. The speech symptoms of different dysarthrias can be evaluated perceptually and these characteristics can be reliably related to distinct neuropathologic substrates. Therefore, dysarthric speech can be used to differentially diagnose certain types of neurological disorders. Treatment for dysarthria requires both behavioral and medical treatment.

In apraxia of speech, speech muscles and their neural supply are intact. However, the person demonstrates an impaired ability to map out a sensorimotor program—or plan of action—which determines the correct number and type of motor movements needed and the sequence in which they should occur. In speech apraxia, a person who produces involuntary movements of articulators effortlessly often cannot reproduce these same movements on command for speech production. Apraxia of speech can co-occur with apraxic dysfunction in other systems, such as nonspeech oral movements, oculomotor function, and limb movement. Treatment for speech apraxia is behaviorally-based. Very little evidence can be found for efficacy of medical treatments applied to speech apraxia.

Motor speech problems can be caused by vascular accidents, neoplasms, degenerative diseases, trauma, infection, allergic reaction, and metabolic abnormalities. Appearance of motor speech symptomology concomitant with the beginning of speech development is problematic for differential diagnosis unless a known neurologic etiology is present. Often, a motor speech disorder is found to coexist with other communication disorders which may result from neurologic (e.g. aphasia), developmental (e.g. delayed language), or musculoskeletal (e.g. cleft palate) disorders. Careful evaluation is needed to differentiate between multiple communication disorders in order to devise an effective treatment plan.

REFERENCE

Duffy, J.R. (1995). *Motor speech disorders.* St. Louis: Mosby.

MOVEMENT THERAPY

Movement therapy, creative movement therapy, body movement therapy, and dance therapy are all terms used interchangeably in the literature to describe a therapeutic approach that assists the disabled individual in the expression of his or her feelings and emotions in an acceptable manner through movement. Body movement therapy was described by Weisbrod (1972) as "the planned use of any aspect of dance, movement, and sensory experience to further the physical and psychic integration of the individual" (p. 66). It has been used successfully with the learning disabled, emotionally disturbed (e.g., schizophrenics and inhibited neurotics), deaf or hearing impaired, blind, aphasic, and retarded, as well as normal children and adults, to assist in language development and/or nonverbal communication skills (Chace, 1971; Weisbrod, 1972; Zumberg & Zumberg, 1979).

Movement therapy was greatly influenced by the psychoanalytic theories of Reich (1942), Jung (Hochheimer, 1969), and Sullivan (1953). Their contributions related to the expressiveness of body language, the therapeutic value of artistic experiences, and the interactive nature of personality. Influence was also exhibited by Laban's (1950) analysis of movement behaviors, Burton's (1974) improvision techniques, and Jacobson's (1958) and Schultz and Luthe's (1959) relaxation techniques.

The goal of movement therapy for childhood schizophrenics, who may be nonverbal or confused verbally, is to assist them to communicate and relate through movement. The goal for inhibited neurotics, who may be verbal but unable to express clearly certain ideas, notions, or convictions about themselves, the world, or others, is to confront blocked areas through the use of the body (Long, Morse, & Newman, 1971). The goal for all individuals is to present experiences that have underlying value to assist them in confronting their emotions (Weisbrod, 1972). This can be accomplished through activities that include imitation of nature or animals, expression of past, present, or future feelings of self or others, and use of music, voice, hand clapping, feet stamping, or environmental sounds in rhythm instruments (Shea, 1978). For example, having a child demonstrate the movement related to the loss of a toy may help him or her to express sadness or pain. Emotions such as anger, joy, and depression may be expressed by having the child perform the rhythm attached to rhythmic bases. Individuals with eating disorders may acknowledge body sensations and body image in creative movement (Williams, 1993).

REFERENCES

Burton, C. (1974). Movement as group therapy in the psychiatric hospital. In *Dance therapy–Focus on dance.* Washington, DC: American Association for Health, Physical Education and Recreation.

Chace, M. (1971). Dance in growth or treatment settings. In N.J. Long, W.C. Morse, & R.G. Newman (Eds.), *Conflict in the classroom: The education of children with problems* (2nd ed.). Belmont, CA: Wadsworth.

Hochheimer, W. (1969). *The psychotherapy of C.G. Jung.* New York: Putnam.

Jacobson, E. (1958). *Progressive relaxation.* Chicago, IL: University of Chicago Press.

Laban, R. (1950). *The mastery of movement.* London: MacDonald & Evans.

Long, N.J., Morse, W.C., & Newman, R.G. (Eds.). (1971). *Conflict in the classroom: The education of children with problems* (2nd ed.). Belmont, CA: Wadsworth.

Reich, W. (1942). *Character analysis.* New York: Farrar, Straus & Giroux.

Schultz, J.H., & Luthe, W. (1959). *Autogenic training: A psycho-physiological approach in psychotherapy.* New York: Grune & Stratton.

Shea, T.M. (1978). *Teaching children and youth with behavior disorders.* St. Louis: Mosby.

Sullivan, H.S. (1953). *The interpersonal theory of psychiatry.* New York: Norton.

Weisbrod, J.A. (1972). Shaping a body image through movement therapy. *Musical Education Journal, 58*(8), 66–69.

Williams, J. (1993). *Anorexia nervosa: Sociocultural factors and treatment.* (ERIC Clearinghouse No. CG 025009)

Zumberg, C., & Zumberg, M. (1979). Movement: A therapeutic technique for use with the learning disabled. *Academic Therapy, 14*(3), 347–352.

See also **Dance Therapy**

MOVIGENICS

Movigenics is a theory of learning disabilities developed by Raymond H. Barsch (1965, 1967), in which he postulated that learning difficulties are related to an individual's inability to interact effectively with space. The word movigenics was derived from two Latin words, *movere,* meaning to move, and *genesis,* meaning origin and development. "It is, therefore, the study of the origin and development of patterns of movement in man and the relationship of these movements to his learning efficiency" (Barsch, 1967, p. 33). The theory is based on Barsch's premise that human learning is related to movement efficiency. As a child adapts to his or her environment and learns to move effectively through it, he or she also develops language as a means of defining experience in connection with space (Lerner, 1971).

Barsch was highly influenced by Werner, Strauss, and Getman. He is one of the four main perceptual-motor theorists who are well known for their work with learning-disabled children. The other three theorists are Kephart, Getman, and Frostig (Hallahan & Cruickshank, 1973).

REFERENCES

Barsch, R.H. (1965). *A movigenic curriculum.* Madison, WI: Bureau for Handicapped Children.

Barsch, R.H. (1967). *Achieving perceptual-motor efficiency. A space-oriented approach to learning* (Vol. 1). Seattle, WA: Special Child Publications.

Hallahan, D.P., & Cruickshank, W.M. (1973). *Psycho-educational foundations of learning disabilities.* Englewood Cliffs, NJ: Prentice-Hall.

Lerner, J.W. (1971). *Children with learning disabilities* (2nd ed.). New York: Houghton Mifflin.

See also **Perceptual Motor Difficulties; Sensory Integrative Therapy**

MULTICULTURAL SPECIAL EDUCATION

The concept of multicultural special education abounds with controversies, one of which is the issue of overrepresentation of minority children in special education classes. However, there are other issues that demand even greater attention such as linguistic differences versus linguistic difficulties, minority-culture norms versus expected classroom behavior, and biases on assessment procedures as well in instrumentation.

Plata and Santos (1981) state that the purpose of bilingual special education "is to meet the academic, sociocultural, and psychological needs of non-English speaking handicapped pupils who cannot meet performance standards normally expected of a comparable group of English speaking handicapped pupils" (p. 98). Chan and Rueda (1979) refer to a "hidden curriculum" that interferes with learning and social adaptations by many children who come from a culturally different environment.

The concept of nondiscriminatory testing is a major concern regarding multicultural special education. Assessment of students referred for special education services, especially the mentally retarded and learning disabled, has been an intensely debated topic; a major issue is the fairness and usefulness of conventional practices (Reschly, 1982). However, this issue is far from simple. As Sattler (1984) points out, there are many different types of biases in assessment. Reschly (1982) indicates that there are many different ways to define the concept of test biases. Compounded by strong emotional feelings and the complexity of the assessment process, Reynolds (1982) suggests that the controversy over nondiscriminatory assessment will probably continue. Test developers, test authors, and test users (teachers, psychologists) must be sensitive to the many differences children from various cultures bring to assessment procedures. These factors, along with a commitment to interpreting test scores cautiously and objectively and in accordance with economic and cultural factors, may enhance efforts to meet the educational needs of multicultural students.

The issues concerning multicultural education have received serious consideration by those in special education because of the overrepresentation of minorities in classes for the mildly handicapped. The major challenge faced by educators is the ability to appreciate and understand the abilities of culturally and linguistically diverse children. Multicultural education and inclusion share a common goal: integrating the handicapped and the culturally different student and adult into the mainstream of school and society. We must insist on sound and effective instructional programs that are relevant to the students who come from different cultures (Garcia & Malkin, 1993).

REFERENCES

Chan, K.S., & Rueda, R. (1979). Poverty and children in education: Separate but equal. *Exceptional Children, 45*(6), 422–428.

Garcia, S.B., & Malkin, D.H. (1993). Toward defining programs and services for culturally and linguistically diverse learners in special education. *Teaching Exceptional Children, 26*(1), 52–58.

Plata, M., & Santos, S.L. (1981). Bilingual special education: A challenge for the future. *Teaching Exceptional Children, 14*(3), 97–100.

Reschly, D.J. (1982). Assessing mild mental retardation: The influence of adaptive behavior, sociocultural status, and prospects for nonbiased assessment. In C.R. Reynolds & T.B. Gutkin (Eds.), *The handbook of school psychology.* New York: Wiley.

Reynolds, C.R. (1982). The problem of bias in psychological assessment. In C.R. Reynolds & T.B. Gutkin (Eds.), *The handbook of school psychology.* New York: Wiley.

Sattler, J.M. (1984). *The assessment of children's intelligence and special abilities* (2nd ed.). Boston: Allyn & Bacon.

See also **Culturally/Linguistically Diverse Students; Culture Fair Tests; Mainstreaming; Nondiscriminatory Assessment**

MULTIDISCIPLINARY TEAM (MDT)

Multidisciplinary team (MDT) is defined by Golin and Ducanis (1981) as "a functioning unit composed of individuals with varied and specialized training who coordinate their activities to provide services to children" (p. 2). The MDT is often used interchangeably with the term interdisciplinary team. Teamwork in child guidance has been prominent since the early 1900s; it became even more evident in education in the 1950s. The use of the MDT with exceptional children increased because of the whole child concept and because of the legislative mandates passed by various states and then by the federal government. The whole child concept was developed by Whitehouse in 1951, when he described a human being as an "interacting, integrated, whole" (p. 45). Problems of exceptional children are interrelated and cannot be adequately treated in isolation. The various services needed by the exceptional child must be coordinated; therefore, the team approach was developed.

Possible team members include school administrators, school psychologists, special educators, physicians, parents, social workers, teachers, student teachers, diagnosticians, speech therapists, physical therapists, occupational therapists, audiologists, nurse counselors, curriculum specialists, optometrists, and vocational rehabilitation counselors (Jones, 1978). The role of the school psychologist can be augmented or supplemented by a psychiatrist, neuropsychologist, or an ophthalmologist. This will depend on the needs of the student and school experiences with local professionals. The physician, in many instances, will be either the family physician or the student's pediatrician. An occupational therapist can provide insight as to needed therapy concerning fine motor control. The student's regular classroom teacher will probably be the most reliable reference for components of the student's classroom performance beyond that indicated by formal tests.

The MDT is responsible for the individual evaluation and educational planning for public school handicapped children. The team decides if the student is eligible for special services. Through the individual education plan (IEP) conference, a written program is developed for the student. The intervention of the MDT must be evaluated periodically so the program can be adjusted if necessary for the child's best interests. The service can be only as good as the composition and functioning of the team.

The parents are important members of the team, yet many researchers report a breakdown of communication between parents and professionals. Professionals complain that parents are overprotective, interfering, and not understanding. Parents complain that professionals are intimidating and do not allow them to be active in the decision-making process (Golin & Ducanis, 1981). Many of the issues are culturally based and, with appropriate cultural competency training, can be avoided.

If MDTs are to serve the purpose for which they are intended, there must be a concerted effort by all members of the MDT to keep communication and participation at the highest possible level.

REFERENCES

Golin, A.D., & Ducanis, A.J. (1981). *The interdisciplinary team; A handbook for the education of exceptional children.* Rockville, MD: Aspen.

Jones, R.L. (1978). Protection in evaluation procedures criteria and recommendation. In *Developing criteria for evaluation of the protection in evaluation procedure provisions of Public Law 94-142.* Washington, DC: U.S. Office of Education, Bureau of Education for the Handicapped.

See also **Individual Education Plan; Individuals with Disabilities Education Act (IDEA)**

MULTI-ELEMENT DESIGN

The multi-element design is used to compare the effect of two or more conditions (treatments) on a dependent variable (Alberto & Troutman, 1999; Barlow & Hayes, 1979). This experimental design is also known as an alternating treatments design, multiple-schedule design, and simultaneous treatment design (Barlow & Hayes, 1979; Tawney & Gast, 1984; Wolery, Bailey, & Sugai, 1988). The multi-element research design allows the teacher to present two or more conditions in a rapid and interspersed pattern over a relatively short period of time in order to identify possible functional relationships between environmental variables and a targeted student's behavior. This design can be used by teachers to efficiently determine which treatment is most effective for an individual student (Cooper, Heron, & Heward, 1997) or which condition predicts when a targeted problem behavior may or may not occur in a particular setting or context. The latter is referred to as a functional analysis (O'Neill et al., 1997). Multi-element designs have been used to examine the effect of interspersal training on spelling word acquisition (Neef, Iwata, & Page, 1980); to generate and verify hypotheses of the function or purpose of problem behavior across a variety of settings and populations (Iwata et al., 1994; O'Neill et al., 1997; Taylor & Romanczyk, 1994); to investigate the effect of instructional strategies for increasing reading fluency (Daly, III, & Martens, 1994); and to examine the effect of low and high preference tasks on rates of problem behavior (Vaughn & Horner, 1997).

REFERENCES

Alberto, P.A., & Troutman, A.C. (1999). *Applied behavior analysis for teachers* (5th ed.). Upper Saddle River, NJ: Merrill.

Barlow, D., & Hayes, S. (1979). Alternating treatments design: One strategy for comparing the effects of two treatments in a single subject. *Journal of Applied Behavior Analysis, 12,* 199–210.

Cooper, J.O., Heron, T.E., & Heward, W.L. (1997). *Applied behavior analysis.* New York: Macmillan.

Daly, E.J., III., & Martens, B.K. (1994). A comparison of three interventions for increasing oral reading performance: Application of the instructional hierarchy. *Journal of Applied Behavior Analysis, 27,* 459–469.

Iwata, B.A., Pace, G.M., Dorsey, M.F., Zarcone, J.R., Vollmer, T.R., Smith, R.G., Rodgers, T.A., Lerman, D.C., Shore, B.A., Mazaleski, J.L., Goh, H., Cowdery, G.E., Kalsher, M.J., McCosh, K.C., & Willis, K.D. (1994). The functions of self-injurious behavior: An experimental-epidemiological analysis. *Journal of Applied Behavior Analysis, 27,* 215–240.

Neef, N.A., Iwata, B.A., & Page, T.J. (1980). The effects of interspersal training versus high density reinforcement on spelling acquisition and retention. *Journal of Applied Behavior Analysis, 13,* 153–158.

O'Neill, R.E., Horner, R.H., Albin, R.W., Sprague, J.R., Storey, K., & Newton, J.S. (1997). *Functional assessment and program development for problem behavior: A practical handbook* (2nd ed.). Pacific Grove, CA: Brooks/Cole.

Tawney, I.W., & Gast, D.L. (1984). *Single subject research in special education.* New York: Merrill.

Taylor, J.C., & Romanczyk, R.G. (1994). Generating hypotheses about the function of student problem behavior by observing teacher behavior. *Journal of Applied Behavior Analysis, 27,* 251–265.

Vaughn, B.J., & Horner, R.H. (1997). Identifying instructional tasks that occasion problem behaviors and assessing the effects of student versus teacher choice among these tasks. *Journal of Applied Behavior Analysis, 30,* 299–312.

Wolery, M. Bailey, D., Jr., & Sugai, G. (1988). *Effective teaching: Principles and procedures of applied behavior analysis with exceptional students.* Boston, MA: Allyn & Bacon.

See also **Functional Analysis**

MULTIPLE BASELINE DESIGN

The multiple baseline design is one of several single-subject applied behavior analysis research designs for evaluating the effects of interventions on the behaviors of handicapped children and youths. While intervention withdrawal or reversal designs are the most frequently used of the single-subject designs, there are instances in behavioral research where a return to baseline phase is not an appropriate alternative for evaluation purposes. Zucker, Rutherford, and Prieto (1978), Kazdin (1982), and Barlow and Hersen (1984) identify several situations where a return to baseline is not appropriate for either ethical or scientific reasons.

First, once some behaviors are acquired, they may no longer be dependent on the intervention and thus will be maintained by naturally occurring reinforcers in the environment. For example, if an intervention is initiated to increase an isolate child's cooperative behavior with peers on playground, the child may continue cooperative behavior through acquired peer social reinforcement despite the fact that the teacher intervention is reversed.

A second situation where the reversal design may be inappropriate occurs with behaviors that, once they are acquired, are essentially nonreversible. For example, if a behavioral intervention program is initiated to teach a child the letters of the alphabet, once the child has acquired this skill, it is unlikely that withdrawal or reversal of the intervention will result in a loss of ability to repeat the alphabet. Rate of response may decrease, but probably not the basic skill itself.

A third instance is when the teacher cannot accurately reverse the intervention procedures to return to baseline levels of functioning. For example, if the intervention involves systematic attention to student on-task behavior and ignoring of off-task behavior, the teacher may find it impossible to replicate baseline rates of attention and ignoring during the reversal phase.

The fourth situation involves children's behaviors that may be so dangerous or noxious that further instances of the behavior cannot be tolerated, even for a brief reversal period. If, for example, an intervention is effective in stopping a child's self-destructive behaviors, few teachers would want to withdraw the intervention and count the number of self-destructive behaviors.

The multiple baseline design is used in situations where the reversal design may not be appropriate for evaluating intervention effects. This design involves establishing baselines on several different behaviors concurrently, and then systematically applying the intervention to one of the targeted behaviors. If this behavior changes in the desired direction, then the same intervention is applied to the second behavior. If the second behavior also changes in the direction desired, the intervention is than applied to the third target behavior, and so on. If each behavior changes when, and only when, intervention is applied to it, experimental control is demonstrated.

The most important factors in research using multiple baseline designs are that baselines for all behaviors are begun at the same time and that ongoing measurement and recording of all behaviors is continuous throughout the procedure. Subsequent applications of the intervention are determined by their effects on the immediately preceding behavior. The most powerful conclusions regarding the effectiveness of the interventions can be drawn when there are closely related or functional behavior changes following repeated applications of the intervention across settings, behaviors, or subjects.

REFERENCES

Barlow, D.H., & Hersen, M. (1984). *Singlecase experimental designs: Strategies for studying behavior change.* New York: Pergamon.

Kazdin, A.E. (1982). *Single-case research design: Methods for clinical and applied settings.* New York: Oxford University Press.

Zucker, S.H., Rutherford, R.B., & Prieto, A.G. (1979). Teacher directed interventions with behaviorally disordered children. In R.B. Rutherford & A.G. Prieto (Eds.), *Monograph in behavior disorders: Severe behavior disorders of children and youth* (Vol. 2, pp. 49–61). Reston, VA: CCBD.

See also **Behavioral Objectives; Behavioral Observation; Behavior Modification**

MULTIPLE HANDICAPPING CONDITIONS

Students with multiple handicapping conditions are persons with two or more disabilities that result in handicaps within functional living experiences. Also called persons with severe handicapping conditions, dual diagnosis, and orthopedic disabilities, persons with multiple handicapping conditions include individuals who are deaf-blind, autistic, cerebral palsied, neurologically impaired, brain damaged, schizophrenic, or mentally retarded (Fewell & Cone, 1983). Labeling individuals as multiply handicapped should be done with caution and with particular focus on outcomes. Accordingly, the World Health Organization (1978) urges the adoption of a three-tier classification system including the terms impairment, disability, and handicap. Impairment refers to a physiological or anatomical loss or other abnormality or both. Disability is the limitation of an individual's capacity to perform some key life function because of an impairment. Handicap describes the limitation imposed by a disability on an individual's ability to carry on his or her usual activities. According to these definitions, a student with multiple handicapping conditions would have limitations in educational development as a result of two or more disabilities.

REFERENCES

Fewell, D., & Cone, J. (1983). Identification and placement of severely handicapped children. In M. Snell (Ed.), *Systematic instruction of the moderately and severely handicapped* (2nd ed.) (pp. 46–73). Columbus, OH: Merrill.

World Health Organization. (1978). *International classification of diseases* (9th rev.). Washington, DC: Author.

See also **Childhood Schizophrenia; Deaf-Blind; Labeling; Mental Retardation; Other Health Impaired**

MULTIPLE REGRESSION

Multiple regression is a statistical procedure in which a single continuous dependent variable is regressed on several continuous independent variables. Typical purposes are to predict dependent variable scores from the independent variables, model real world variable relationships, and explain dependent variable variation concisely.

There are two conditions in multiple regression that determine analysis and interpretation. In the first condition, all independent variables are statistically independent of each other. While this does not occur naturally very often, it can be occasionally obtained from theory or from judicious selection of independent variables. In this case, each independent variable is related to the dependent variable in magnitude equal to Pearson's correlation; the Pearson correlation squared equals the proportion of dependent variable variance accounted for. The sum of all the squared correlations for independent variables is equal to the squared multiple correlation, a measure of the total variance proportion accounted for by all independent variables. In a Venn diagram of these circles, the two independent variables intersect the dependent variable circle but do not intersect each other between independent variables.

The more usually observed condition is one in which one or more of the independent variables are not statistically independent of each other. This implies that the independent variables will be correlated with each other and with the dependent variable. In this case, there is overlap in the amount of variance accounted for in the dependent variable by two or more independent variables. In a Venn diagram, the circles representing independent variables intersect each other as well as the circle representing the dependent variable. The squared multiple correlation is still defined as the total proportion of variance in dependent variable accounted for. However, now the contributions of the individual independent variables are more difficult to discern because they overlap. The partial correlation between an independent variable $X1$ and dependent variable Y is defined as the Pearson correlation between two errors of regression. $X1$ is regressed on all the other independent variables and for each subject a predicted score is subtracted from the observed score to create one error score, $E1$. Similarly, the dependent variable is regressed on the other independent variables and an error score Ey is computed. The partial correlation is the correlation between $E1$ and Ey. Its square represents the unique or independent contribution of $X1$ to the variance in Y. The total squared multiple correlation is a function of the partial correlations but it cannot be simply stated (Darlington, 1978).

Uses of multiple regression in prediction are usually to make decisions based on past performance. For example, colleges make first-year selection decisions based on high-school percentile rank and Scholastic Aptitude Test (SAT) scores' prediction of the first year's college grade point average (GPA). High-school rank and SAT score are independent variables, termed predictors; college GPA is the dependent variable. Typical multiple correlation is about

.5, with about 25% of freshman GPAs predictable. The SAT score might add about 5% to the prediction based on high-school rank alone.

The use of multiple regression in modeling or theory building is based on specifying the order of including independent variables in the multiple regression. Thus contributions of the independent variables to dependent variable variance is dependent on the order of entry. This is sometimes called hierarchical regression or ordered regression. A special case is termed path analysis, in which the partial correlations are computed in specified order. They are interpreted as path coefficients, the direct influence of one variable on another (Pedhazur, 1982).

Often the purpose for multiple regression is parsimonious prediction when there are many possible predictors or independent variables. Not all are necessary or desirable owing to the expense of data collection, so a smaller subset of predictors that will perform nearly as well as all predictors available is sought. There are several strategies available to find this parsimonious subset: forward, backward, and stepwise regression. There are several variants available with each. Forward multiple regression begins with the best single predictor, the greatest magnitude Pearson correlation with the dependent variable. It adds new predictors according to some criteria for improving prediction or increasing squared multiple correlation with the dependent variable. When there is little change after adding a new variable, the procedure ends. Backward regression begins with all predictors and drops them out until there are large drops in the predictive criteria. For example, with both forward and backward regression, a criterion might be used that additional predictors must improve the squared multiple correlation by .05 (Draper & Smith, 1982). Stepwise multiple regression is a variant on either forward or backward regression in which variables previously entered are tested to see whether they are no longer needed after new variables have been included. This means that a new combination of predictors are now able to predict along with the previous set. Thus the first predictor entered might eventually be dropped. Multiple regression is widely used in the behavioral sciences. In its most general form, it encompasses most statistical techniques, including the analysis of variance, as the general linear model.

REFERENCES

Darlington, R.B. (1978). Reduced variance regression. *Psychological Bulletin, 85,* 1238–1255.

Draper, N.R., & Smith, H. (1982). *Applied regression analysis* (2nd ed.). New York: Wiley.

Pedhazur, E. (1982). *Multiple regression in behavioral research* (2nd ed.). New York: Holt, Rinehart, Winston.

See also **Discriminant Analysis; Research in Special Education**

MULTIPLE SCLEROSIS (MS)

Multiple sclerosis (MS) is a progressive neurologic disease affecting the brain and spinal cord. It generally is considered a disease of young adults, with symptoms rarely occurring before adolescence or after age 40 (Brown, 1971); mean age of onset is 30 years (Kaufman, 1981). Females are affected more than males (Kaufman, 1981; Magalini, 1971), and although no clear-cut hereditary component has been identified, the incidence is much higher in close relatives of afflicted persons (Kaufman, 1981; Thompson, 1979).

Multiple sclerosis is considered a demyelinating disease, in that the myelin (fatty sheaths surrounding nerve fibers) in the central nervous system is disseminated. Plaques or hardened patches of scarred nerve fibers are evident in the central nervous system of MS patients. The name multiple sclerosis derives from these scarred (sclerosed) masses, together with the multiple episodic nature of the disease (Kaufman, 1981; *Melloni's,* 1985). Multiple sclerosis is also known as *disseminated sclerosis* (Brown, 1971; Magalini, 1971).

Early symptoms of MS may be mild and vague, and hence may be dismissed by affected individuals or their families. Such symptoms include blurred vision, tingling or numbness in the trunk or extremities, vertigo, intention tremor, and clumsiness. Episodes of symptoms characteristically are followed by periods of remission, a pattern that may persist for several years. Despite the intermittent nature of the disease, MS is a progressive condition, and afflicted individuals demonstrate increasing neurologic impairment. Advanced symptoms of MS include ataxia (a gait disturbance characterized by a broad-based stance and lurching movements), scanning speech (evidenced by monotonous, staccato speech with slurring adjacent sounds), and nystagmus (tremor of eye movements). Other signs associated with the disease include bladder and bowel disturbances, partial or complete blindness (retrobulbar neuritis), and hyperreflexive movements (e.g., Babinski sign). While a number of experts report affective disturbances in MS patients, particularly emotional lability and euphoria (Kaufman, 1981; Magalini, 1971; *Mosby's,* 1983), Lechtenberg (1982) takes issue with such reports. He cites studies that indicate a high incidence of depression in MS patients, and suggests the symptom of euphoria may be better described as "a masked depression manifested by unrealistic or excessively optimistic attitudes" (p. 216).

The cause of MS is unknown, although commonalities have been identified among afflicted patients. Multiple sclerosis is considered a disease of temperate climates (Brown, 1971; Kaufman, 1981). While their role in transmission of the disease is unknown, many MS patients had small, indoor pets as children (Kaufman, 1981). Toxic viral and allergic metabolic etiologies have been hypothesized (Magalini, 1971). Diagnosis of MS relies largely on clinical symptoms and the multiple episodic nature of the disease.

Few beneficial therapeutic interventions have been identified in the treatment of MS. Physical or occupational therapy may facilitate optimal range of motion and may provide for environmental adaptations when necessary.

Corticosteroid treatments may shorten symptomatic episodes (Kaufman, 1981). Diets designed to reduce exposure to allergy-related foods reportedly have been associated with remissions of symptoms in some MS patients (*MS and diet*, 1984).

REFERENCES

Brown, J.A.C. (1971). *The Stein and Day international medical encyclopedia.* New York: Stein & Day.

Kaufman, D.M. (1981). *Clinical neurology for psychiatrists.* New York: Grune & Stratton.

Lechtenberg, R. (1982). *The psychiatrist's guide to diseases of the nervous system.* New York: Wiley.

Magalini, S. (1971). *Dictionary of medical syndromes.* Philadelphia: Lippincott.

Melloni's illustrated medical dictionary (2nd ed.). (1985). Baltimore, MD: Williams & Wilkins.

Mosby's medical and nursing dictionary. (1983). St. Louis: Mosby.

Thompson, W.A.R. (1979). *Black's medical dictionary* (32nd ed.). New York: Barnes & Noble.

See also Gait Disturbances; Physical Disabilities

MULTISENSORY INSTRUCTION

A multisensory approach to instruction involves presenting instructional content through several modalities such as the visual, auditory, kinesetic, and tactile modalities. The rationale underlying this instructional approach is that learning may be enhanced if the content to be learned is presented through several sensory modalities. The Fernald (1943) method and the Gillingham-Stillman (1960) method typify the multisensory approach to teaching reading. However, the two methods differ in emphasis. While the Fernald method emphasizes whole-word learning, the Gillingham-Stillman method emphasizes the teaching of phonics, specifically individual phonemes and sound blending.

Recently "multisensory" terms have evolved into "holistic" methods that infuse a wide range of activities into the teaching of academic subjects and the classroom (Fox & Thompson, 1994). The definition has evolved from a concrete delivery to a more interactive and integrated learner experience (Enz & Searfoss, 1993; McKeon, 1995).

REFERENCES

Enz, B.J., & Searfoss, L.W. (1993). Who evaluates teacher performance? Mismatched paradigms, the status quo, the missed opportunities. (ERIC Clearinghouse No. EA 025322)

Fernald, G.M. (1943). *Remedial techniques in school subject.* New York: McGraw-Hill.

Fox, L.H., & Thompson, D.L. (1994). *Bringing the lab school method to an inner city school.* Washington, DC: American University, School of Education.

Gillingham, A., & Stillman, B. (1960). *Remedial training for children with specific disability in reading, spelling, penmanship.* Cambridge MA: Educators Publishing Service.

McKeon, K.J. (1995). What is this thing called accelerated learning? *Training and Development, 49*(6), 64–66.

See also Reading; Reading Remediation; Teaching Strategies

MUNSON, GRACE E. (1883–1980)

Born in a sod house near Orleans, Nebraska, Grace Munson believed in self-growth and advancement through educational attainment. From one-room schools on the prairie, she moved through Peru (Nebraska) Normal School (1905) and the University of Nebraska (Phi Beta Kappa) for a BA (1911) and a PhD (1916) with time out for an MA from Wellesley College (1912), where she was an alumnae fellow.

Professionally, she was a rural Nebraska teacher near Geneva (1899–1903), teacher and principal in Harlan County (1905–1909), and instructor in education at the University of Nebraska (1912–1918) before moving to Chicago, where she was a school psychologist and teacher (1918–1935), director of the Bureau of Child Study (1935–1946), and assistant superintendent in charge of special education (1946–1949).

An innovative leader who welcomed suggestions, her criticism of others and of ideas was both trenchant and effective. Although her professional activity and leadership was usually limited to greater Chicago, she helped organize the Chicago Psychological Club in 1924 for psychologists in the bureau and the Institute for Juvenile Research, a group serving mental health needs. Through the club she was instrumental in bringing some of the great names from across the United States into dialogue with Chicago professionals.

MUSCULAR DYSTROPHY (MD)

Muscular dystrophy (MD) describes a group of inherited disorders characterized by severe, progressive weakness associated with atrophy of the skeletal muscles bilaterally. The most common forms of the disease typically have an early onset and produce increased wasting and eventual death. Because of the shortened life of afflicted persons, approximately two-thirds of muscular dystrophy patients are children ages 3 to 15 (Weiner, 1973).

Although classification systems for muscular dystrophy vary, there is general agreement that Duchenne's dystrophy (pseudohypertrophic type) is the most common variant. Other categories include faciocapulohumoral dystrophy (affects facial and shoulder muscles; onset in second decade) and limb-girdle muscular dystrophy (typically does not affect children) (Bleck, 1975; Buda, 1981; Rowland, 1979). Incidence figures vary widely by type, from 5 per million births for faciocapulohumoral type to 250 per million births for Duchenne's (Rowland, 1979). Duchenne's dystrophy is inherited via an x-linked mode of transmission, although spontaneous genetic mutation is reported to be fairly common, with perhaps two-thirds of afflicted children having no family history of the disorder (Rowland, 1979). It is by definition a condition that affects males exclusively, although female carriers have been reported to show mild clinical symptoms (Buda, 1981).

The onset of Duchenne's dystrophy generally occurs during the preschool period. Walking may be delayed, and early signs of the disorder may include difficulty in raising from a supine or sitting position or difficulty in climbing stairs. As the disease progresses and muscles in the pelvic girdle become affected, a characteristic waddling gait, with a sway back and protruding pelvis, may be observed (Bleck, 1975). Progressive weakness is characteristic of Duchenne's dystrophy, and children may be wheelchair bound by age 10 or 12 (Bleck, 1975; Kolata, 1985). Death typically occurs in the third decade, as a result of respiratory failure or involvement of the heart muscles. (Weiner, 1973).

Children with MD may require special education and related services. Adaptive equipment, attendant services, and appropriate therapies may be necessary for MD children. While a typical profile of neuropsychological strengths and weaknesses has not been established for boys with Duchenne's dystrophy, converging data suggest individual differences may be present that warrant a modified instructional program. Indeed, Kendall (1991) and Nielsen (1997) identify modified programs that call for trained educational personnel, flexible scheduling, continuum of services, parent support and training, and trained personnel in technological advances.

REFERENCES

Bleck, E.E. (1975). Muscular dystrophy-Duchenne type. In E.E. Bleck & D.A. Nagel (Eds.), *Physically handicapped children: A medical atlas for teachers* (pp. 173–179). New York: Grune & Stratton.

Buda, F.B. (1981). *The neurology of developmental disabilities.* Springfield, IL: Thomas.

Kendall, R.M. (1991). Unique educational needs of learners with physical and other health impairments. (ERIC Clearinghouse No. EC 300945)

Kolata, G. (1985). Closing in on the muscular dystrophy gene. *Science, 230,* 307–308.

Nielsen, L.B. (1997). *The exceptional child in the regular classroom: An educator's guide.* Thousand Oaks, CA: Sage.

Rowland, L.P. (1979). Diseases of muscle and neuromuscular junction. In P.B. Beeson, W. McDermott, & J.B. Wyngaarden (Eds.), *Cecil textbook of medicine* (15th ed.) (pp. 914–930). Philadelphia: Saunders.

Weiner, F. (1973). *Help for the handicapped child.* New York: McGraw-Hill.

See also Adapted Physical Education; Muscular Dystrophy Association; Physical Handicaps

MUSCULAR DYSTROPHY ASSOCIATION (MDA)

MDA is a national voluntary health agency—a dedicated partnership between scientists and concerned citizens aimed at conquering neuromuscular diseases. MDA is one of the world's leading voluntary health agencies, fostering research and patient care funded almost entirely by individual private contributors.

MDA combats 40 neuromuscular diseases through a worldwide research effort, a nationwide program of services to individuals, and far-reaching professional and public health education. Individual MDA research grants to scientific and clinical investigators in the United States and abroad number some 400. MDA's patient services program offers diagnostic services and rehabilitative follow-up care to children and adults with neuromuscular diseases through a nationwide network of some 240 MDA hospital-affiliated clinics. The association offers financial assistance toward the purchase and repair of selected orthopedic appliances, physical therapy, and transportation to and from clinics. MDA also offers a nationwide summer camping program for young people and sponsors ongoing self-help support groups and educational seminars. Educational literature and videos are available upon request. There are some 160 local chapters of the Muscular Dystrophy Association in the 50 states, Washington, DC, and Puerto Rico.

MUSCULAR IMBALANCE

Muscular imbalance occurs when there is difficulty or lack of integration in the interaction of opposing muscle groups. Normally there is a finely graded interaction of opposing muscle groups facilitated by reciprocal innervation of the muscles. Paralysis, weakness, or interruption in innervation may result in an imbalance. Depending on the location and severity of the muscle imbalance, the individual may not be able to remain upright, extend the arm, focus the eyes, or hop on one foot. Motor skills performance may be severely impaired or minimally affected. A muscle imbalance may lead to fatigue, difficulty in respiration, impaired oral-motor skills, pain, impaired visual focus, or numerous other conditions depending on the nature, location, and pervasiveness of the imbalance.

Signs of muscle imbalance may be observed in the classroom. Actions such as tilting the head to read, leaning to one side after being seated for a period of time, slumping, or significant deterioration of handwriting toward the end of a writing period may all be signs of a muscle imbalance or weakness.

See also Movement Therapy; Muscular Dystrophy; Physical Disabilities; Visual-Motor and Visual-Perceptual Problems

MUSEUMS AND INDIVIDUALS WITH DISABILITIES

Access of the handicapped not only to museums but to fuller appreciation of art itself was vastly extended with the passing of the Vocational Rehabilitation Act of 1973. Section 504 of that law prohibits discrimination against the disabled by government-funded organizations; this has had a significant impact on the way museums plan and implement their exhibits and educational programs. This is not to say that there were no programs for the handicapped prior to Section 504. The Mary Duke Biddle Gallery in Raleigh, North Carolina, pioneered the tactile approach for blind and visually impaired patrons as early as 1966, and the Lions Gallery of the Senses was established in Hartford, Connecticut, in 1972. These early efforts were exceptional, however, and they were not without their critics (Kenny, 1983). One important criticism stemmed from the fact that galleries and museums specifically for the handicapped, while admirable in their motivation, were unintentionally segregationist in their effect.

Museums responded in a variety of ways. To avoid segregation, the efforts generally revolved around an expansion of services and multisensory experiences for all visitors. But the museums had little experience with nonvisual efforts. Steiner (1983) points out some of the misapprehensions that surfaced as sighted curators began to plan for the visually impaired: that the legally blind have no sight at all; that most blind people read braille; and that the blind are automatically more sensitive to touch and sound than the sighted. Without conscious effort, it is also very easy to underestimate (or overlook altogether) the amount of background knowledge that the sighted pick up unconsciously from their environment and apply to the appreciation of art. In an effort to avoid mistakes that might easily result from such misunderstandings, museums across the country began organizing advisory boards made up of the handicapped to help guide and plan the new efforts.

Some museums across the country have been able to implement exemplary programs, maintaining continuous gallery experiences for the handicapped and interweaving them with other aspects of the art education program. The New York Metropolitan Museum in New York City, the De Young Memorial Museum in San Francisco, the Plimouth Plantation, a living history museum in Plymouth, Massachusetts, the Smithsonian Institute in Washington, DC, and the Wadsworth Antheneum in Hartford, Connecticut, are only a few examples. Horizons for the Blind of Chicago is a good source of further information on accessibility and special programs for the handicapped in museums, galleries, and art and science centers.

REFERENCES

Kenny, A.P. (1983). A range of vision: Museum accommodations for visually impaired people. *Journal of Visual Impairment & Blindness, 77*(7), 325–329.

Steiner, C. (1983). Art museums and the visually handicapped consumer: Some issues in approach and design. *Journal of Visual Impairment & Blindness, 77*(7), 330–333.

See also **Americans with Disabilities Act**

MUSIC THERAPY

Music therapy is the use of music in all of its forms to modify nonmusical behavior (Lathom & Eagle, 1982) and to promote mental health, social development and adjust-

ment, and motor coordination. At times it is used as a therapeutic tool in rehabilitation and for recreational or educational purposes. Perhaps the most important contribution of music to special education is that it can promote learning through activities that are enjoyable.

Music therapy in a variety of applications has been practiced in hospitals, schools, institutions, and private settings in a one-to-one or group approach. It includes moving to music, playing instruments, presenting musicals, attending concerts, dancing, creating music, singing, and listening.

The role of the music therapy should be distinguished from the role of music education in special education. Music therapy has remedial goals. Music education teaches the knowledge and skills of music as an aesthetic, enriching, and pleasurable experience for all children, including the handicapped (Alley, 1979). In special education, music therapy has been used to increase handicapped students' ability to follow directions and to attend to and respond to logical sequences of movement, voice, and music. Task analysis has assisted in these purposes (Alley, 1979). It is advised that in special education, the music therapist select musical activities that are within the students' skill levels; thus tasks may be as simple as listening to rock music or playing in the school orchestra.

After the passage of PL 94-142, music educators turned to music therapists, who had already established a tradition of success in teaching music to handicapped populations. As a result, many of the music materials and teaching procedures for the handicapped have their basis in music therapy. From 1975 to the present, music education and music therapy for individuals with disabilities have spread from private or residential programs to all aspects of special education under the aegis of IDEA. In fact, the CEC's Teacher of the Year in 1995 was Brenda Robbins, a music teacher and therapist.

REFERENCES

Alley, J. (1979). Music in the IEP: Therapy education. *Journal of Music Therapy, 16*(3), 111–127.

Lathom, W., & Eagle, C. (1982). Music for the severely disabled child. *Music Education Journal, 38*(49), 30–31.

See also **Dance Therapy; Recreational Therapy**

MUTISM

Mutism is defined as the lack of articulate speech (Kanner, 1975). According to Kolvin and Fundudis (1981), there are many forms of mutism. They may be divided into those with a presumed biological basis and those considered psychological in nature. Mutism with a biological basis is typically associated with profound deafness, serious mental handicap, infantile autism, or akinetic mutism. As a symptom of psychological disturbance, two further types are delineated. Traumatic mutism is identified as having a sudden onset immediately following a psychological or physical shock and is thus considered a hysterical reaction. Selective mutism is a condition in which speech is confined to a familiar situation or a small group of select others.

Differential diagnosis is important in distinguishing between elective mutism and mutism owed to other disorders. In severe and profound mental retardation there may be a general inability to speak reflective of a pervasive developmental disorder and developmental language disorder. Rutter (1977) notes that where elective mutism is typically a "pure" emotional disorder, mutism may develop as a reaction to an underlying speech or language handicap. Kolvin and Fundudis (1981) report that 50% of the elective mute children identified in the Newcastle Epidemiological Study displayed immaturities of speech or other speech difficulties.

Several considerations are important in distinguishing elective mutism from the mutism of the child with a language disorder. The chronicity of the symptom and premorbid verbal facility are important in the differential diagnosis. The child with a developmental or congenital language disorder is more likely to have a history of atypical speech and language development, whereas the elective mute child frequently has normal speech and language development during preschool years (Richman & Eliason, 1983).

According to the fourth edition of the *Diagnostic and Statistical Manual of Mental Disorders* (*DSM-IV;* 1994), only in selective mutism is lack of speaking the predominant disturbance. General refusal to speak, as seen in some cases of major depression, avoidant disorder of childhood or adolescence, overanxious disorder, oppositional disorder, and social phobia, should not be diagnosed as such.

Although there are few prevalence studies of this childhood disorder, some data currently available suggest that it is relatively rare. Morris (1963) reported an incidence of .4% of clinic cases and Salfield (1950) reported 1%. Existing incidence studies are not of the highest quality and these reported data cannot be trusted at this time. The number of treatment reports in the applied and clinical literature suggest that the disorder may be more prevalent than incidence data suggest. For example, Hayden (1980) and Sanok and Ascione (1979) suggest that many cases of elective mutism may go unreported because of the self-isolating nature of families of elective mute children, lack of acknowledgment of its severity, and general occurrence only in school situations. There is agreement that the disorder occurs most often in early childhood (5–7 years of age), is difficult to treat, and tends to be intractible over time (Kratochwill, 1981; Labbe & Williamson, 1984). The disorder is often accompanied by social withdrawal and even social skill deficits, but little research has focused on this aspect of the disorder.

There is a good deal of clinical literature in which there are reports of successful treatment; these studies have been reviewed in detail elsewhere (Friedman & Karagon, 1973; Kratochwill, 1981; Kratochwill, Brody, & Piersel, 1979; Labbe & Williamson, 1984; Sanok & Ascione, 1979). Both traditional dynamic therapy and behavior therapy treatment procedures have been employed with elective mute children.

Although it remains difficult to identify the specific psychodynamic strategies that appear most effective in the treatment of elective mutism, a consistently identified theme is difficulty in treatment. This is especially reflected in the overall length of treatment (several months to several years), lack of generalization from the treatment setting (e.g., clinic) to the problem areas in the natural environment where the mutism occurs (e.g., school), and lack of consistent follow-up and maintenance of results (Kratochwill, 1981; Kratochwill, Brody, & Piersel, 1979).

Labbe and Williamson (1984) developed a conceptual framework for linking assessment and treatment. Assessment involves direct measures of the child's speech in numerous settings (e.g., school, home, community) in the presence of various individuals (parents, teachers, peers). Treatment procedures are then linked to a possible assessment outcome. Five outcomes are possible: (1) the child speaks to most people in most situations, but with low frequency; (2) the child speaks to at least one person in all situations; (3) the child speaks to most persons, but only in one environment, (4) the child speaks to only one or a very few persons in only one environment: and (5) the child speaks to no one who is available for participation in a treatment program. As noted in the figure, various treatment procedures that have been developed in the operant literature are matched to the assessment outcomes that characterize the disorder.

REFERENCES

American Psychiatric Association. (1994). *Diagnostic and Statistical Manual of Mental Disorders* (4th ed.). Washington, DC: Author.

Friedman, R., & Karagon, N. (1973). Characteristics and management of elective mutism in children. *Psychology in the Schools, 10,* 249–252.

Hayden, T.L. (1980). Classification of elective mutism. *Journal of the American Academy of Child Psychiatry, 19,* 118–133.

Kanner, L. (1975). *Child psychiatry* (3rd ed.). Springfield, IL: Thomas.

Kolvin, I., & Fundudis, T. (1981). Elective mute children: Psychological development and background factors. *Journal of Child Psychology & Psychiatry, 22,* 219–232.

Kratochwill, T.R. (1981). *Selective mutism: Implications for research and treatment.* Hillsdale, NJ: Erlbaum.

Kratochwill, T.R., Brody, G.H., & Piersel, W.C. (1979). Elective mutism in children: A review of treatment and research. In B.B. Lahey & A.E. Kazdin (Eds.), *Advances in clinical child psychology* (Vol. 2, pp. 193–240). New York: Plenum.

Labbe, E.E., & Williamson, D.A. (1984). Behavioral treatment of elective mutism: A review of the literature. *Clinical Psychology Review, 4,* 273–292.

Morris, J.V. (1963). Cases of elective mutism. *American Journal of Mental Deficiency, 57,* 661–668.

Richman, L.C., & Eliason, M. (1983). Communication disorders of children. In C.E. Walker & M.C. Roberts (Eds.), *Handbook of clinical child psychology* (pp. 697–722). New York: Wiley.

Rutter, M. (1977). Delayed speech. In M. Rutter & L. Hersov (Eds.), *Child psychiatry: Modern approaches* (pp. 688–716). Oxford, England: Blackwell Scientific.

Sanok, R.L., & Ascione, F.R. (1979). Behavioral interventions for childhood elective mutism: An evaluative review. *Child Behavior Therapy, 1,* 49–68.

See also Elective Mutism; Language Deficiencies and Deficits; Speech, Absence of

MYOPIA

See VISUAL IMPAIRMENT

N

NARCOLEPSY

Narcolepsy is a disorder characterized by an abnormal need to sleep during the day along with pathological episodic attacks of REM sleep. Symptoms include sleep paralysis, cataplexy, and hypnogogic hallucinations. In the past, this disorder also has been referred to as Friedmann's disease and as Gelineau syndrome.

Narcoleptic attacks typically come at predictable times during the day; e.g., postprandial drowsiness is especially common among narcoleptics after they have ingested meals high in protein. The narcoleptic attacks are typically irresistible. The patient with narcolepsy is an individual who will usually be able to fall asleep easily at night but who may have trouble remaining asleep.

Age of onset for narcolepsy is typically in the late teens or early twenties. The symptoms may be controlled with medication, but the condition usually persists throughout adult life. The prevalence of the disorder is estimated to be 4/10,000, with males and females equally affected (Kaplan & Sadock, 1981).

Cataplexy occurs in the majority of cases of narcolepsy. Cataplexy refers to sudden transient loss of muscle tone in the trunk or extremities. It is often triggered by strong emotions, either positive or negative. During cataplexy, the afflicted individual is still conscious but is rendered totally immobile. Most narcoleptics can remember the events that occurred during the period of cataplexy.

Genetic studies have demonstrated a strong genetic loading for this disorder (Mignot, 1998). The etiology is still not fully understood. However, more than 85% of all narcoleptic patients with cataplexy share a human leukocyte antigen (HLA) allele, compared with 12–38% of the general population (Mignot, 1998). Treatment with tricyclic antidepressants may sometimes be useful. Imipramine is the tricyclic that has been most studied. In addition, amphetamines and methylphenidate have been used in the treatment of narcolepsy (Wise, 1998). In the treatment of youth with narcolepsy, management is educational and supportive with consistent follow-up (Wise, 1998).

REFERENCES

Kaplan, H.I., & Sadock, D.J. (1981). *Modern synopsis of comprehensive textbook of psychiatry.* Baltimore, MD: Williams & Wilkins.

Mignot, F. (1998). Genetic and familial aspects of narcolepsy. *Neurology, 50*(2), 16–22.

Wise, M.S. (1998). Childhood narcolepsy. *Neurology, 50*(2), 37–42.

NASH, CHARLES E. (1875–1953)

Charles Emerson (Ted) Nash served as a teacher at the Training School at Vineland, New Jersey, from 1898 to 1923, and as the institution's superintendent from 1923 until his death in 1953. A talented teacher and inspirational leader, Nash was a mainstay of the Training School during the years of growth to its preeminent position in the field of mental retardation.

REFERENCES

Commemorative issue: Charles Emerson Nash. (1948). *Training School Bulletin, 45,* 134–153.

Honoring Charles Emerson Nash. (1953). *Training School Bulletin, 50,* 31–37.

NATIONAL ADVISORY COMMITTEE ON HANDICAPPED CHILDREN AND YOUTH

The National Advisory Committee on Handicapped Children and Youth was authorized in Section 604 of Public Law 98–199.

Although funds were authorized to provide for the establishment of this committee, funds have never been appropriated. Consequently, this committee has never met and its membership has not been noted. It is possible that the administration has not used existing funds to create this committee out of concern that the committee would assume oversight responsibility for the programs operated by the department.

NATIONAL ASSOCIATION FOR GIFTED CHILDREN (NAGC)

The National Association for Gifted Children is an organization of parents, educators, and other professionals united to address the unique needs of children and youth with demonstrated gifts and talents as well as those children who may develop their talents with appropriate educational experiences. The association supports and develops policies and practices that encourage and respond to the diverse expressions of gifts and talents in children and youth from all cultures, racial and ethnic backgrounds, and socioeconomic groups. To this end, NAGC supports and engages in advocacy, communication, personnel preparation, collaboration with other organizations, and research and development.

Since its establishment in 1954, NAGC has become internationally recognized as an effective advocacy organization for gifted children, answering questions and providing expert information on gifted education. Affiliated groups are located in practically every state, and parents, educators, and policy makers are often referred to association contacts in Canada and Europe. Support generated by NAGC at the state and federal level is exemplified in the passage of the Jacob K. Javits Gifted and Talented Students Education Act which provides funding for research and demonstration projects and which targets high-potential young people who may not be readily identifiable as gifted by conventional means (e.g., the economically disadvantaged, those limited in English proficiency, the disabled).

NAGC welcomes participation through membership, attendance at conferences and regional meetings, and communication with elected leaders and professional staff. Headquarters are located at 1707 L Street, NW, Suite 550, Washington, DC, 20036.

NATIONAL ASSOCIATION FOR RETARDED CITIZENS

See ARC, THE.

NATIONAL ASSOCIATION FOR THE DEAF (NAD)

The National Association for the Deaf (NAD), founded in 1880, is a private, nonprofit federation of 51 state association affiliates, sponsoring and organizational affiliates, and direct members. Washington, D.C. and U.S. territories are considered state affiliates. Organizational affiliates may be nonprofit or for-profit. Direct members are classified as regular, senior, student, junior, or international. The NAD is a member of the World Federation of the Deaf.

The NAD promotes the accessibility and civil rights of deaf and hard of hearing Americans in education, employment, health care, social services, and telecommunications. It serves as a clearinghouse for information about the deaf community, culture, heritage, and language, as well as information about the programs and services that it provides. Those services include captioned media and certification of American Sign Language and Deaf Studies professionals and interpreters. In addition, it offers free legal representation to deaf and hard of hearing constituents in areas related to civil, employment, and education rights, and equal access as mandated by law. The NAD also provides programs to prepare deaf and hard of hearing youth for positions of leadership.

REFERENCE

National Association for the Deaf. About NAD. Retrieved October 29, 1998 from the World Wide Web: http://www.nad.org/about_nad.html.

NATIONAL ASSOCIATION OF SCHOOL PSYCHOLOGISTS (NASP)

Formed in 1969, the National Association of School Psychologists (NASP) is a 21,000-member professional association. The NASP was formed because many practicing school psychologists saw a need for uniform credentialing of school psychologists, a national identity for the profession of school psychology, a vehicle for communication among school psychologists, and a means for influencing legislation and regulations related to the delivery of school psychological services.

The NASP has been at the forefront of many issues affecting handicapped students. Its input has shaped numerous federal and state laws, including PL 94-142 (Rights of All Handicapped Children Act of 1975). It works in partnership with national education and special education groups to influence legislation and regulations affecting schoolchildren. The NASP has published position papers and adopted resolutions relating to nondiscriminatory assessment, parental rights in child evaluations, corporal punishment, and other issues relevant to the education of all students. The organization has a governmental and professional relations committee that provides information and technical assistance to a network of affiliated state school psychology associations. Its Social Issues Committee vigorously advocates for children's rights, cosponsoring a major international conference on the psychological abuse of children in 1983.

A primary objective of the NASP has been the promotion of high-quality professional practice. Toward this objective, the NASP, as a constituent member of the National Council for Accreditation of Teacher Education (NCATE), accredits school psychology training programs at the specialist and doctoral levels. Also, the NASP strives to meet its members' professional development needs. Members receive the *Communiqué* eight times a year and a highly regarded professional journal, *School Psychology Review,* containing theory, research, and opinions related to the profession.

***See also* American Psychological Association**

NATIONAL ASSOCIATION OF STATE BOARDS OF EDUCATION (NASBE)

The National Association of State Boards of Education is a nonprofit, private association that represents state and territorial boards of education. The principal objectives of the association include strengthening state leadership in educational policymaking; promoting excellence in the education of all students; advocating equality of access to educational opportunity; and assuring continued citizen support for public education.

The association serves over 600 individuals, including members of state boards, state board attorneys, and state board executives. These members are responsible for the educational interests of more than 40 million students in public schools and more than three million students in postsecondary institutions.

As the single organization representing state boards nationwide, NASBE seeks to further its goals by providing high quality training and technical assistance to members and the larger education community, sponsoring regional and national conferences on critical policy issues, and publishing resource materials tailored to policymakers' needs. Communicating with Congress, federal executive agencies, business and industry, national associations, and other state decisionmakers is another important service provided by the association.

Located in Alexandria, Virginia, NASBE has two affiliated bodies that provide the unique informational and training needs of related professionals who serve as state board members: the National Council of State Board of Education Executives and the National Council of State Education Attorneys.

NATIONAL ASSOCIATION OF STATE DIRECTORS OF SPECIAL EDUCATION (NASDSE)

The National Association of State Directors of Special Education (NASDSE) is an independent, nonprofit membership organization designed to serve the informational and professional needs of the chief administrators of special education at the state level.

Founded in 1938, NASDSE provides state directors of special education and related state education agency staff with information on national trends and activities; inservice training in program administration and policy development; and technical assistance in implementing programs at the state and local levels. Additionally, the association serves as the national representative for state directors of special education and their state agency colleagues, advocating on behalf of NASDSE membership before federal and state-level deliberative bodies and decision makers (including legislative and executive branch officials and commissions). NASDSE maintains a close affiliation with other national professional and advocacy organizations in order to effectively represent the positions and interests of the association members and to address the broader needs and interests of the special education community.

See also **Administration of Special Education; Supervision in Special Education**

NATIONAL CENTER, EDUCATIONAL MEDIA AND MATERIALS FOR THE HANDICAPPED

The National Center, Educational Media and Materials for the Handicapped facilitated the production and distribution of instructional media and materials designed for use in the special education of handicapped students. The center was founded in 1972 and had a staff of seven under the direction of Thomas M. Stephens. The center is now defunct.

NATIONAL CENTER ON EDUCATIONAL OUTCOMES (NCEO)

OVERVIEW

The National Center on Educational Outcomes (NCEO) was established in 1990 by the Office of Special Education Programs (OSEP) of the U.S. Department of Education. NCEO was the only national center at the time that focused its efforts on educational outcomes for all students, including students with disabilities (NCEO, 1999). In order to monitor educational results for students with disabilities, NCEO's mission was to provide leadership in identifying outcomes, indicators, and assessments that could be developed and used by state and federal agencies. NCEO's work is grounded in the belief that identifying indicators of educational outcomes and using them effectively and responsibly will allow students with disabilities to achieve better results from their educational experiences. Through the process of monitoring the educational results of students with disabilities, NCEO works to increase educational accountability for all students at both state and national levels.

Some of the major activities of NCEO include the development of a conceptual framework of educational outcomes to guide future efforts in collecting data, particularly data on students with disabilities. Surveys are conducted in order to gather information from states regarding their current methods of collecting data on students with disabilities. Other efforts include collecting and analyzing information from states related to educational outcome data on students with disabilities.

Since its establishment, the NCEO staff has collected and analyzed a vast array of information from state and federal agencies. By examining efforts regarding the implementation of standards, goals, and assessment systems, NCEO has been able to identify important outcomes for students with disabilities. Information has also been gathered by holding consensus-building working meetings with state directors, educators, parents, and others on the domains of educational outcomes for all students. Similarly, current state outcome policies and accountability practices have been studied thoroughly by NCEO (NCEO, 1999).

In order to provide technical assistance, the NCEO staff participate in three different types of activities. *Direct technical assistance* is provided through State Collaborative on Assessment and Student Standards (SCASS), which is sponsored by NCEO, the Council of Chief State School Officers (CCSSO), and the National Association of State Directors of Special Education (NASDSE). The staff at NCEO also review materials developed and drafted by states and provide feedback to them. Conference calls with state teams are used to provide assistance and support to states. At national conferences, clinics are often held by NCEO personnel on topics related to developing inclusive accountability systems (NCEO, 1999).

The National Center on Educational Outcomes also provides technical assistance by *working collaboratively with regional resource centers.* Staff at the center frequently provide states with resource materials, current research, and best practices related to improving state and national efforts of being more inclusive of students with disabilities within the educational accountability system. Regional resource centers also provide resource materials they have developed for states' use to NCEO for review. This review process enables regional resource centers to be assured that their materials consistently represent information about the full participation of students with disabilities (NCEO, 1999).

NCEO personnel also *work with other technical assistance providers* as a means of providing technical assistance to states. Working collaboratively, both NCEO and other technical assistance organizations have the opportunity to consult with one another about issues related to improving state and national practices, review resource materials developed by their organizations, and receive updates on current research (NCEO, 1999).

Since its establishment, NCEO's research has impacted and influenced policy development at both the state and national level. NCEO personnel have produced a large number of publications describing the data that have been collected from states; most can be downloaded from the NCEO website (http://www.coled.umn.edu/NCEO/). These include syntheses of state standards, policy briefs on important topics like alternate assessments, and technical reports. NCEO regularly publishes a summary of state assessment activities, and reports on state practices in providing testing accommodations. Self-study guides are also available for use by states in developing inclusive assessments and accountability systems.

REFERENCE

National Center on Educational Outcomes. (1999). http://www.coled.umn.edu/NCEO/.

NATIONAL COUNCIL FOR ACCREDITATION OF TEACHER EDUCATION (NCATE)

The National Council for Accreditation of Teacher Education (NCATE) was founded in 1954 to establish a national body for uniform application of standards in teacher preparation. The primary activities of the NCATE are at present the development and promulgation of standards for and review and accreditation of college and university programs for the preparation of all teachers and other professional school personnel at the elementary and secondary levels. The NCATE is the only appropriately credentialed organization to conduct such activities on a national level. It is authorized by the Council on Postsecondary Accreditation (COPA) to adopt standards and procedures for accreditation and to determine the accreditation status of institutional programs engaged in the basic and advanced preparation of professional school personnel. The NCATE is also recognized as the appropriate accrediting body in educational preparation by the U.S. Department of Education.

Thirty-three professional associations make up the NCATE coalition of teachers, teacher educators, content specialists, and local and state policy makers who represent over three million individuals. The professional associations appoint representatives to NCATE's boards, provide financial support, and aid in the development of standards, policies and procedures within four categories, including design of professional education, candidates in professional education, professional education faculty, and the unit for professional accreditation. The four categories "emphasize prospective teacher performance in the context of solid preparation in professional and liberal arts studies" (NCATE, 1998).

The NCATE offers accreditation in special education and in most of the related service categories as well, including school psychology, educational diagnosis, and school counseling. Any school that offers a 4-year or more degree in education or a related field is eligible for an evaluation for accreditation by the NCATE provided the school is approved by its appropriate state agency, has obtained the appropriate regional accreditation, is an equal opportunity, nondiscriminatory employer, and has graduated a sufficient number of students from its program to allow for an evaluation of the quality of the preparation. The specific standards for NCATE accreditations are revised frequently as are application procedures. Institutions, associations, societies, or individuals seeking to obtain more detailed information about the NCATE, its standards, or the accreditation process should contact the director at NCATE, 2010 Massachusetts Ave., N.W., Suite 500, Washington, DC, 20036–1023.

REFERENCE

National Council for Accreditation of Teacher Education (1998, August 16). *About NCATE.* http://www.ncate.org/.

NATIONAL EASTER SEAL SOCIETY

Founded in 1919 by a concerned Ohio businessman in co-operation with Rotary Clubs, the National Easter Seal Society, originally the Ohio Society for Crippled Children, became the first organization established for the purpose of helping children with physical disabilities.

Today in its 79th year of service, the national volunteer healthcare organization provides 1.5 million children and adults with disabilities and their families with services such as early intervention programs to help children with disabilities adapt and succeed in school, preschool and daycare programs for children with and without disabilities, adult vocational training and employment, and medical rehabilitation services. An advocacy role, ensuring equal rights for all disabled persons, is also assumed by the society and includes emphasis on elimination of environmental barriers, enhancement of positive attitudes, and increased recognition of individual abilities. Direct services are available to all persons with a disability resulting from any cause, including disease, illness, injury, or accident.

Easter Seals service sites are maintained in each of the 50 states, the District of Columbia, and Puerto Rico. The national headquarters of the organization are located at 230 West Monroe Street, Suite 1800, Chicago, Illinois, 60606 (National Easter Seal Society, 1998).

REFERENCE

National Easter Seal Society. (1998, August 3). *What's new?* http://www.seals.com/html/the_easter_seal.html.

NATIONAL EDUCATION ASSOCIATION (NEA)

As its mission, NEA advocates for the cause of public education, but also has a primary interest in the rights and welfare of teachers. Governmental relations, political action, and professional development are key components in the achievement of NEA goals. At the local level, the organization conducts workshops on topics relevant to school faculty and support staff, and is involved in negotiating contracts for school district employees; while at the state level, affiliates lobby government representatives for needed school resources and file legal actions protecting academic freedom. Work at the national level is wide-ranging and includes formulating inventive projects, restructuring how learning is achieved, and lobbying to prevent privatization of public education (NEA, 1998).

NEA policy is determined by its members, primarily through the annual Representative Assembly (RA) held each July and attended by more than 9,000 delegates who elect officers, debate issues, and set policy. In the interim, the Board of Directors and the Executive Committee make important decisions affecting education. NEA headquarters is located at 1201 16th Street, NW, Washington, DC, 20036 (NEA, 1998).

REFERENCE

National Education Association. (1998, February 12). *About NEA.* http://www.nea.org/.

NATIONAL ENDOWMENT FOR THE HUMANITIES (NEH)

The National Endowment for the Humanities (NEH) was created by the National Foundation on the Arts and Humanities Act (1965) for the advancement of scholarship and progress in the arts and humanities. NEH is a grant-making agency of the federal government supporting research in the humanities, educational opportunities for teachers, preservation of texts and materials, translations of various works, museum exhibitions, television and radio programs, and public discussion and studies. According to the 1965 act, the humanities broadly embraces such disciplines as archaeology; comparative religion; theory, history, and criticism of the arts; modern and classical languages; literature; the social sciences; and history, as well as other areas that study and apply the humanities to the present conditions of national life. Thus, NEH supports work promoting knowledge in all subject areas encompassing the humanities while complementing local and private efforts by increasing non-federal aid for high quality projects.

From its inception in 1965 through fiscal year 1996, NEH has awarded approximately $3 billion for more than 54,000 fellowships and grants, with some grants requiring one-to-one matching funds from private-sector donations generating more than $333 million in additional capital. The NEH Challenge Grants Program, begun in 1977, has resulted in some $1.15 billion in nonfederal support for America's libraries, colleges, museums, and other institutions (NEH, 1997).

Through its Public Information Office, the NEH publishes a variety of materials, including *Humanities,* a magazine reviewing current work and theory in the humanities, as well as an annual report, *NEH in the Digital Age,* The Media Log, Exhibitions Today, and Timeless Classics. Copies of these publications and application materials may be requested via email at info@neh.gov (NEH, 1997).

REFERENCE

National Endowment for the Humanities. (1997, February 4). *Welcome to the National Endowment for the Humanities.* http://www.neh.fed.us/.

NATIONAL FEDERATION OF THE BLIND (NFB)

Founded in 1940, the National Federation of the Blind (NFB) is a consumer organization that provides a vehicle for joint action and advocacy for blind people to improve their opportunities and increase public understanding of blindness. The largest organization of the blind in America, affiliates exist in all 50 states, the District of Columbia, and

Puerto Rico, and chapters are located in most major cities. NFB currently has over 50,000 members nationwide.

Services offered by the NFB include JOB, a highly successful program begun in 1979 and operated in conjunction with the United States Department of Labor to assist blind persons in finding competitive employment, and the International Braille and Technology Center for the Blind (IBTC), which provides evaluation and demonstration of adaptive technology used by the blind. Additional services include *Newsline®,* the first digital talking newspaper, and the Materials Center, offering over 1,200 publications dealing with issues about blindness.

NFB publications provide information to parents and educators of blind children, address the problems and concerns of blind diabetics, answer common questions about blindness, provide information about services and programs for the blind, and help to educate the blind and the sighted about a positive philosophy regarding blindness. *The Braille Monitor,* published monthly in braille, in print, and on cassette, is the voice of the National Federation of the Blind. With over 3,000 in attendance, the organization's annual convention is the largest gathering of the blind in the world. NFB national headquarters are located at 1800 Johnson Street, Baltimore, MD, 21230.

NATIONAL HEAD INJURY FOUNDATION (NHIF)

See BRAIN INJURY ASSOCIATION.

NATIONAL INFORMATION CENTER FOR CHILDREN AND YOUTH WITH DISABILITIES (NICHCY)

Founded in 1970 as the National Special Education Information Center and undergoing four name changes since its inception, the National Information Center for Children and Youth with Disabilities (NICHCY) is a project of the Academy for Educational Development within the Disabilities Studies and Services Center operated through a cooperative agreement with the Office of Special Education Programs of the U.S. Department of Education. NICHCY provides information and makes referrals on disabilities and disability-related issues for families, educators, and other professionals. A wide array of services is available through NICHCY, and among them are personal responses to specific questions; referrals to disability organizations, parent groups, and professional organizations; information from the center's databases and library; and disk and camera-ready originals in Spanish (NICHCY, 1998).

NICHCY also provides a variety of publications, including fact sheets on specific disabilities, state resource sheets, parent guides, bibliographies, and the NICHCY issue papers, *News Digest* and *Transition Summary.* Most publications are available in two formats, text-only and portable document format, on the organization's web site at http://nichcy.org/. NICHCY is currently developing the audiotape and booklet, "A Student's Guide to Jobs" and "Technical Assistance Guide: Helping Students Find and Keep a Job" (NICHCY, 1998).

REFERENCES

National Information Center for Children and Youth with Disabilities. (1998, June 11). *About NICHCY.* http://nichcy.org/.

National Information Center for Handicapped Children and Youth. (Undated brochure). *National Information Center for Handicapped Children and Youth.* Washington, DC: Author.

See also **SpecialNet**

NATIONAL INSTITUTE OF EDUCATION (NIE)

Founded in 1972, the National Institute of Education's mission was to promote educational equity and to improve the quality of educational practice. In carrying out this mission, the NIE supported research and dissemination activities that were designed to help individuals regardless of race, age, sex, economic status, ethnic origin, or handicapping condition, and to realize their full potential through education.

When the Department of Education was established in 1980, the NIE was placed within the DOE's Office of Educational Research and Improvement (OERI). A 1985 reorganization of OERI abolished the NIE as a separate agency, and its programs were spread throughout the rest of OERI.

NATIONAL INSTITUTES OF MENTAL HEALTH (NIMH)

The National Institutes of Mental Health, founded in 1946, is the federal agency responsible for supporting and conducting research into the causes, diagnosis, treatment, and prevention of mental disorders. To understand the causes and improve the treatment and prevention of mental illness, NIMH research utilizes a multidisciplinary approach to research on the human brain in health and in illness by integrating findings from the neurosciences, basic behavioral sciences, clinical research, epidemiology, prevention research, and mental health services research. With this overall approach, the Institute supports basic research and studies addressing the causes and treatments for specific mental disorders such as schizophrenia, mood disorders, anxiety disorders, eating disorders, Alzheimer's Disease, and childhood mental illness. NIMH research also focuses on the mental health needs of special populations including racial and ethnic minority populations, women, and residents of rural areas.

The Institute publishes *Schizophrenia Bulletin* and *Psychopharmacology Bulletin* as well as printed materials regarding basic behavioral research, neuroscience of mental health, and the diagnosis and treatment of mental disorders. Public and professional education campaigns include The Depression/Awareness, Recognition, and Treatment Program (1-800-421-4211); Anxiety Disorders Education Program (1-88-88-ANXIETY or 1-800-64-PANIC); and Eating Disorders. In addition, the Institute sponsors The Mental Health FAX4U (301-443-5158), a fax-back system containing a list of publications, order form, complete texts of PAs and RFAs, and other items of interest. The Resources and Inquiries Branch of NIMH may be contacted by calling (301) 443-4513, or by emailing nimhinfo@nih.gov. The Institute's offices are located at 5600 Fishers Lane, Rockville, MD, 20857.

NATIONAL INSTITUTE OF NEUROLOGICAL DISORDERS AND STROKE

The National Institute of Neurological Disorders and Stroke conducts and supports fundamental and applied research on human neurological disorders such as Parkinson's disease, epilepsy, multiple sclerosis, muscular dystrophy, head and spinal cord injuries, stroke, and neurogenetic disorders. The institute also conducts and supports research on the development and function of the normal brain and nervous system in order to better understand normal processes relating to disease states.

NATIONAL JOINT COMMITTEE ON LEARNING DISABILITIES (NJCLD)

The National Joint Committee on Learning Disabilities, founded in 1975, is a national committee of representatives of organizations concerned about the education and welfare of individuals with learning disabilities. Those organizations include the American Speech-Language-Hearing Association (ASHA), the Council for Learning Disabilities (CLD), the Division for Learning Disabilities (DLD) of the Council for Exceptional Children, the International Reading Association (IRA), the National Association of School Psychologists (NASP), the Association for Higher Education and Disability (AHEAD), the Division for Children's Communication Development (DCCD) of the Council for Exceptional Children, the International Dyslexia Association (IDA), the Learning Disabilities Association of America (LDA), and the National Center for Learning Disabilities (NCLD). Over 350,000 members of the various organizations are represented by the NJCLD, whose funding is provided by their contributions.

Numerous publications on issues relating to learning disabilities are available from NJCLD, 10801 Rockville Pike, Rockville, MD, 20852.

REFERENCE

National Joint Committee on Learning Disabilities (NJCLD). Fact sheet. http://www.ldonline.org/njcld/fact_sheet.html.

NATIONAL LEARNING DISABILITIES ASSISTANCE PROGRAM

Public Law 91-230, the Elementary and Secondary Education Act Amendments of 1970, repealed Title VI of the Elementary and Secondary Education Act as of July 1, 1971. The act consolidated a number of previously separate federal grant programs relating to handicapped children under a new authority, the Education of the Handicapped Act (EHA). The 1970 EHA also added Part G, a new authorization for funding programs for children with specific learning disabilities.

The purpose of the program under Part G of the EHA was to assist states in identifying, diagnosing, and serving children with specific learning disabilities. This discretionary grant program provided support for research efforts, training for teachers and supervisors of teachers of children with specific learning disabilities, and model demonstration service centers aimed at stimulating increased statewide services for the target population.

Public Law 94-142 amended the definition of handicapped children to include the category of specific learning disabilities. With that statutory change, funds under any of the other EHA programs could be used for children with specific learning disabilities. Part G was repealed in 1983 by PL 98-199.

NATIONAL MERIT SCHOLARSHIP CORPORATION

Founded in 1955, this independent organization is devoted to scholarship activities for intellectually talented young people. Organizations and businesses are solicited to support scholarships through the merit program. Annual testing by some 18,000 high schools for eligible juniors results in the naming of semifinalists. Semifinalists represent the top half of 1% tested in each state. Semifinalists compete for nonrenewable and renewable awards ranging from $1000 to $8000. Approximately 6500 awards are made annually.

Over 600 corporate foundations, professional associations, unions, trusts, and universities underwrite grants to support the program. Recipients must be U.S. citizens. The corporation has also administered since 1964 the Achievement Scholarship Program for Outstanding Negro Students. This separate program is devoted to increasing educational opportunities for promising black students. Over 650 black undergraduate scholarships are awarded annually. The corporation publishes booklets and other information for secondary students and interested individuals. Headquarters are located at One American Plaza, Evanston, IL 60201.

NATIONAL ORGANIZATION FOR RARE DISORDERS (NORD)

The National Organization for Rare Disorders (NORD) is a federation of voluntary health organizations dedicated to helping people with rare "orphan" diseases and assisting the organizations that serve them. NORD is committed to the identification, treatment, and cure of rare disorders through programs of education, advocacy, research, and service.

NORD has developed its own Rare Disease Database (RDB) Subscription Service. The RDB is a unique copyrighted consumer-based compendium of information on more than 1,100 rare orphan diseases. Selected portions (abstracts) of the RDB are currently available on the internet website and can be accessed for free. Subscribers can access the full text versions of the *Rare Disease Database* entries. Subscribers receive a user name and password that will provide them with unlimited access to the full text versions. In addition, two other databases are searched simultaneously. These include NORD's *Organizational Database* (containing information on over 1,400 organizations that serve people with rare disorders) and NORD's *Orphan Drug Designation Database* (containing information from the Food & Drug Administration [FDA] on newly designated orphan drugs). NORD can be contacted at The National Organization for Rare Disorders, Inc., P.O. Box 8923, New Fairfield, CT, 06812–8923. NORD's telephone number is 1–800–999–6673, and their internet site is located at http://www.rarediseases.org. Information for this entry was obtained from the NORD website.

NATIONAL REHABILITATION ASSOCIATION (NRA)

The National Rehabilitation Association (NRA) was founded in 1925. It consists of 15,000 members constituting 70 local groups. With its headquarters in Alexandria, Virginia, the NRA is a consolidation of counselors, therapists, physicians, disability examiners, vocational evaluators, and other individuals interested in the rehabilitation of disabled people.

Its newsletter is published six times annually; its *Journal of Rehabilitation* is published quarterly; and there is a Monograph of the Annual Mary E. Surtzer Memorial Seminar.

NATIONAL SOCIETY FOR AUTISTIC CHILDREN (NSAC)

The National Society for Autistic Children was incorporated into the Autism Society of America in 1981. It no longer exists as a separate organization.

NATIONAL SOCIETY FOR CHILDREN AND ADULTS WITH AUTISM

The National Society for Children and Adults with Autism was founded in 1965 and incorporated into the Autism Society of America in 1987. It no longer exists as a separate organization.

NATIONAL SOCIETY FOR CRIPPLED CHILDREN AND ADULTS

See NATIONAL EASTER SEAL SOCIETY.

NATIONAL SOCIETY FOR THE PREVENTION OF BLINDNESS (NSPB)

Founded in 1908, the National Society for the Prevention of Blindness (NSPB) has as its primary purpose preventing blindness and conserving sight. This purpose is addressed through nationwide programs of public and professional education, research, and industrial and community services. Services include promotion and support of local glaucoma screening, preschool vision testing, industrial eye safety, and collection of data on the nature and extent of the causes of blindness and defective vision.

Grants for medical research and research fellowships in ophthalmology are available through NSPB. The society publishes a quarterly journal and a newsletter. Pamphlets on eye diseases, children's eye care, and industrial, sports, and school eye safety are available. The NSPB distributes home eye tests for preschoolers and adults and issues testing charts, posters, films, and radio/TV material. A major thrust of the organization has been the promotion of safety eyewear for various occupations and athletics. Offices are located at 500 E. Remington Road, Schaumburg, Illinois, 60173.

NATIONAL TECHNICAL INSTITUTE FOR THE DEAF (NTID)

The National Technical Institute for the Deaf (NTID) was established in June 1965 by Congress and signed into law (PL 89-36) by President Lyndon B. Johnson. The law specifically included provisions relating to program size, program objectives, location, administration, curriculum, admission standards, duration of course study, and research.

Today NTID is the world's largest technical college for the deaf on a campus of primarily hearing students. NTID serves about 1,100 deaf students from across the United States and foreign countries. Students can enroll in diploma, associate, baccalaureate, and master's degree programs in a variety of career fields. NTID is one of the eight colleges of Rochester Institute of Technology (RIT). Approximately 94 percent of deaf RIT graduates have found jobs upon graduation. They are employed across the United States in business, industry, government and education.

Students at NTID must have good high school grades, at least an overall grade 8 achievement level on a standardized test, and a hearing loss of about 70 dBs or greater (without a hearing aid) in the better ear. Appropriate support services are available for students who need them. Further information may be obtained by writing NTID, P.O. Box 9887, Rochester, NY 14623, or by calling (716) 475–6219.

NATURE VERSUS NURTURE

The source of various traits has been debated throughout history. Some attribute honesty to genetic inheritance while others emphasize the modeling of family members, the influence of peers, or perhaps the mores held within a sector of society (Weinberg, 1983).

No area of human achievement has spurred greater controversy concerning the contributions of heredity and environment than the study of intelligence (Hallahan & Kauffman, 1986). Owing to the longstanding controversy and its social and political ramifications, it is vital that key issues be kept clear. Two issues are disputed: the validity of intelligence tests and the extent to which intelligence can be attributed to genetic inheritance. Intelligence tests, in particular the IQ test, contain items that probe an individual's ability to solve problems, comprehend words and passages, complete puzzles, and so forth. Such tests have been used in Europe and the United States for years, but have been under attack for being culturally biased. That is, the knowledge needed to do well on these tests is of value in some sections of society but not others.

The second major issue, the degree to which intelligence is inherited, is even more controversial. Some authorities (e.g., Jensen, 1969; Scarr & McCartney, 1983) have held that most of a person's intelligence is genetically determined. A majority of scholars in the field, however, have taken the position that intelligence is influenced mostly by environmental factors, or that the relative contributions of the two factors cannot be separated. (Block & Dworkin, 1976; Bouchard & McGue, 1981). Today, there is general agreement among geneticists that at least fifty percent of variance in IQ is genetic in origin (Carroll, 1992).

Nature does provide a promising method for evaluating the relative effects of heredity and environment. The crucial factor is to keep heredity constant. To study the offspring of the same parents is not sufficient, for each child has his or her own unique genetic makeup. It is only identical or monozygotic twins who share identical heredity; consequently, differences between these twins can be safely attributed to environmental factors.

Research on identical twins raised in different environments studies the extent of the contribution of the environment. A review of the literature on this topic by Farber (1981) reveals that identical twins who were separated but raised in similar environments had negligible differences in intelligence. However, identical twins' performances on intelligence tests could differ markedly if their environments were very different.

It is not possible to directly assess hereditary factors where there are no twins. Because some people have made unsubstantiated inferences about racial differences in intelligence, many psychologists are extremely cautious about speculating on the inheritability of intelligence (Block & Dworkin, 1976). Consequently, psychologists have favored the study of environmental factors, trying to determine how family factors, as well as the persons, institutions, and norms of the larger society, influence children's behavior, and how children themselves may affect their environments (McEwen & Schmeck, 1994).

The research clearly reveals that intelligence is influenced by both hereditary and environmental factors. Environmental influences come from birth weight, nutrition, and various familial sources. Consequently, hereditary and environmental factors continually interact to influence the child's development.

REFERENCES

Block, N., & Dworkin, G. (Eds.). (1976). *The IQ controversy.* New York: Pantheon.

Bouchard, T.J., Jr., & McGue, M. (1981). Familial studies of intelligence: A review. *Science, 212,* 1055–1059.

Carroll, J.B. (1992). Cognitive abilities: The state of the art. *Psychological Science, 3*(5), 266–270.

Farber, S.L. (1981). *Identical twins reared apart: A reanalysis.* New York: Basic Books.

Hallahan, D.P., & Kauffman, J.M. (1986). *Exceptional children.* Englewood Cliffs, NJ: Prentice-Hall.

Jensen, A.R. (1969). How much can we boost I.Q. and scholastic achievement? *Harvard Educational Review, 39,* 1–123.

McEwen, B.S., & Schmeck, H.M. (1994). *The hostage brain.* New York, NY: Rockefeller University Press.

Scarr, S., & McCartney, K. (1983). How people make their own environments: A theory of genotype-environmental effects. *Child Development, 54,* 424–435.

Weinberg, R.A. (1983). A case of a misplaced conjunction: Nature or nurture? *Journal of School Psychology, 21,* 9–12.

See also **Assessment; Intelligence; Intelligence Testing; Socioeconomic Status**

NAVANE

Navane (thiothixene hydrochloride) is a psychotropic drug used in the management of manifestations of psychotic disorders. It is not recommended for use in children under 12 years of age. Side effects can include drowsiness, especially on initiation of drug therapy, as well as agitation, restlessness, insomnia, and occasional instances of seizures and paradoxical exacerbation of psychotic symptoms. Overdosage symptoms can include muscular twitching, drowsiness, and dizziness, with gross overdose potentially resulting in gait disturbance and coma.

A brand name of Roerig Pharmaceuticals, Navane is available in capsules containing 1, 2, 5, and 10 mg, as a concentrate, and as an injection (intramuscular) vial. Dosages are individually adjusted, generally beginning with small doses of 2 mg three times a day, with increases up to 60 mg per day as needed.

REFERENCE

Physicians' desk reference. (1984). (pp. 1685–1688). Oradell, NJ: Medical Economics.

See also **Atarax; Benadryl; Compazine; Drug Therapy**

NCATE
See NATIONAL COUNCIL FOR ACCREDITATION OF TEACHER EDUCATION.

NEGATIVE PUNISHMENT
The removal of a stimulus to decrease inappropriate/interfering behaviors is referred to as negative punishment. Time-out from positive reinforcement and response cost procedures are commonly employed strategies for decreasing the future probability of targeted behaviors. When employing these strategies, the obtrusiveness with which the environment is altered deserves special attention. A recommendation for teachers is to provide the least amount of change in the environment that is most effective in reducing future occurrences of inappropriate behaviors. In a similar manner, the removal of previously earned points/tokens (response cost) can vary in intensity relative to the severity of the targeted activity to be decreased.

NEGATIVE REINFORCEMENT
Negative reinforcement is the removal or avoidance of an aversive stimulus from the environment that increases the future occurrence of the behavior immediately preceding the removal. Negative reinforcement includes both escape and avoidance components. In a classroom situation, escape from the loud sound of a fire alarm increases the future likelihood of vacating a room during a fire drill. Similarly, avoiding a verbal reprimand from a teacher by remaining on task during a math assignment is an example of negative reinforcement.

Negative reinforcement is often confused with and mislabeled as punishment. In negative reinforcement, the future probability of a behavior that is followed by the removal of an aversive stimulus increases. However, the future probability of the occurrence of a behavior followed by the removal of a positive stimulus (negative punishment) or the presentation of an aversive event (positive punishment) decreases.

See also **Behavior Analysis, Applied; Behavior Modification; Negative Punishment**

NEONATAL BEHAVIORAL ASSESSMENT SCALE (NBAS)
The Neonatal Behavioral Assessment Scale (NBAS; Brazelton, 1973, 1984) is designed to examine the behavior of neonates at not less than 37 weeks gestation or more than 30 days after birth. Characteristics of the normal, healthy, full-term newborn are measured, such as his or her adjustment to labor, delivery, and new environment. The sociability with caregivers and management of homeostasis are also assessed. How well a neonate adapts is primarily examined by looking at the newborn's states of consciousness.

The 1984 NBAS contains a test manual, an audiovisual tape, and a case of necessary equipment (shiny red ball, flashlight, rattle, bell, and tactile probe in a carrying case). There are 20 reflex items on the NBAS, and each are scored on a 4-point scale. The two global behavioral scales on the NBAS are (1) attractiveness (measuring the infant's organized response capacity, integration of behavior, and positive feedback to examiner), and (2) need for stimulation (infant's need for stimulation to organize responses). There are a total of 28 behavioral items that are scored on a 9-point scale. The exam itself takes approximately 20 to 30 minutes to complete. It is recommended that the exam be done on at least two different days to avoid making erroneous conclusions based on a single day.

Interpretation of scoring on the NBAS can be problematic (Silverman, Killian, & Burns, 1994) because some scales have varying "optimal" scores. For example, some items are considered optimal at a score of 9, while others are optimal at 5. An overall summary score cannot be obtained, but score clusters are available for the following: habituation, orientation, motor performance, range of states, regulation of state, autonomic regulation, and reflexes.

It is recommended that researchers and clinicians who plan to use the NBAS attend a training seminar to ensure interrater reliability. Because the score is based on clinical judgment, precise methods for administration are crucial, in addition to clinical experience with babies and a knowledge of infant development. The NBAS is quite time-consuming to learn to administer (Silverman et al., 1994). However, it is one of the most widely used scales in research. Silverman et al. (1994, pp. 474–475) state that the NBAS "appears to meet acceptable standards for basic research at this time, although it is not a clinically tested tool, as Brazelton will confirm." Caution must be used when administering the NBAS for clinical purposes, and generalizations to the general population cannot be made at this time.

REFERENCES
Brazelton, T.B. (Ed.). (1973). Neonatal Behavioral Assessment Scale [Special issue]. *Clinics in Developmental Medicine, 50.*

Brazelton, T.B. (Ed.). (1984). *Neonatal Behavioral Assessment Scale* (2nd ed.). London: Spastics International.

Silverman, C.R., Killian, G.A., & Burns, W.J. (1994). The Neonatal Behavioral Assessment Scale. In D. Keyser & R. Sweetland (Eds.), *Test critiques, Volume X.* Austin, TX: Pro-Ed.

See also **Infant Assessment**

NEPSY: A DEVELOPMENTAL NEUROPSYCHOLOGICAL ASSESSMENT
NEPSY, an acronym derived from the NE in neuro and PSY in psychological, is a reliable, valid, and comprehensive instrument that was designed to assess neuropsychological development in preschool and school-age children, ages 3 to 12 (Korkman, Kirk, & Kemp, 1998). NEPSY views learning

as a multifactorial process. The aim of NEPSY is therefore to take apart the components of learning and to view how the child functions in different areas.

NEPSY consists of a series of neuropsychological subtests that can be used to obtain a Core Assessment, providing an overview of a child's neuropsychological status, or an Expanded Assessment, providing a more thorough analysis of specific cognitive disorders. The NEPSY assesses the child's neuropsychological functioning in five domains: (a) Attention/Executive Functions; (b) Language; (c) Sensorimotor Functions; (d) Visuospatial Processing; and (e) Memory and Learning. When a deficit is apparent in a specific domain after the Core Assessment, all expanded subtests in that domain are administered in order to delineate the problem further. The results of an assessment are expressed by means of a scaled score for each individual subtest (mean=10, standard deviation=3), and a standard score for each domain, based on the domain's core subtests (mean=100, standard deviation=15). The core battery takes an hour to administer, and the expanded battery takes approximately 3.5 hours.

The NEPSY was normed on a standardization sample that was representative of the U.S. population of children (Korkman, Kirk, and Kemp, 1998). The standardization sample of 1,000 cases included 100 children in each of the 10 age groups ranging from 3 through 12 years. The sample included 50 males and 50 females in each age group. For each age group in the standardization sample, the proportion of Anglos, African Americans, Hispanics, and other race/ethnic groups was based on the race/ethnic-group proportions of children aged 3 to 12 in the U.S. population according to the 1995 census survey. Reliability coefficients for the core domains range from .72 to .87 for 5- to 12-year-olds. The NEPSY has been reviewed twice for content and bias by panels of experts that included pediatric neuropsychologists and school psychologists from all parts of the United States. The results of these evaluations indicated that the NEPSY has adequate content validity. The NEPSY also has adequate construct validity. The correlation coefficients between the NEPSY subtest scores and core domain scores indicate low to moderate positive relationships, between .34 to .85, for children aged 5 to 12. The pattern of correlations among the subtests within domains provides evidence that the structure of NEPSY is sound. Overall, subtests within domains are more highly correlated than subtests across domains. Various research studies also provide evidence for the convergent and discriminant validity of NEPSY domains and subtests (Korkman, Kirk, & Kemp, 1998).

REFERENCE

Korkman, M., Kirk, U., & Kemp, S. (1998). *NEPSY: A developmental neuropsychological assessment.* San Antonio, TX: The Psychological Corporation.

NETHERLANDS, SPECIAL EDUCATION IN THE

Special education services in the Netherlands are in a state of flux. Currently special education consists of ten types of special schools, including those for the deaf, the visually impaired, the physically impaired, the behaviorally disturbed or the severely mentally impaired pupils. Such schools are either located separately or attached in a department to another type of special education (e.g., a department for children with severe speech disorders in a school for hearing impaired children (see Table 1)). As a result of recent legislation, two former types of special schools, those for the learning disabled and the mildly mentally impaired, have been renamed special schools for primary education and are no longer part of special education legislation. Although most of these schools currently operate as segregated schools, it is expected that in the near future they will merge with regular schools (see "future trends").

Special school students re-entering regular education are entitled to certain facilities, as are students with sensory, physical, or multiple impairments, who although eligible for special education have not been referred to a special school. This so-called preventive peripatetic teaching is becoming increasingly widespread. In 1998, some .002 and .003% of all pupils received peripatetic teaching in primary and secondary schools, respectively.

Pupils eligible for special education may or may not have already been following regular education for some years. Although pupils are formally referred to special education by parents, the majority of referrals are initiated by

Table 1 Special Education in the Netherlands[1]

School Types/Departments	Schools	Pupils
Learning disabled (LOM schools)[2]	334	44,445
Mildly mentally impaired (MLK schools)[2]	328	40,426
Deaf	9	719
Hearing impaired	31	4,614
Children with severe speech disorders	2	410
Blind and partially sighted	4	743
Physically impaired	29	3,804
Chronically ill	36	3,928
Behavior disorders (ZMOK schools)	69	7,327
Multiply impaired	19	1,972
Children in schools attached to paedological institutes[3]	11	1,356
Severely mentally impaired children	103	9,229
Total	975	118,973

[1]Data are based on Central Bureau for Statistics, 1996; Min. OC & W, 1996.
[2]No longer part of special education legislation.
[3]These institutes are affiliated with a university.

regular school teachers in consultation with the school principal, the school support service, and parents. The placement decision is taken by the admission board of the proposed special school (comprised of psychologist, physician, social worker, and school principal).

Compared to many other European countries, Dutch special education is extensive, differentiated, and segregated, and since the sixties has evolved into a wide-ranging system for pupils who cannot keep up in regular schools. Almost 4% of all primary and secondary school-age pupils attend separate special schools, and over the past decades there has been a dramatic increase in their numbers. In October 1998, 4.3% of pupils between 4 and 11 (Dutch primary school age) attended a special school. In 1972, this was a mere 2.2%. The number of special education pupils depends on specific age groups. For example, almost 8% of eleven-year-olds are in separate schools. In general, boys and ethnic minority pupils are overrepresented. The growth has not been equal in each type of school.

Recent developments in the Netherlands have been influenced by two policy papers published in 1990 and 1996. The first, *Together to School Again,* aims to support the integration of pupils with learning difficulties (so-called LOM pupils) and mildly mentally disabled pupils (so-called MLK pupils). The implementation of this policy has resulted in all primary schools and special schools for these types of pupils being grouped into regional clusters; each cluster generally consists of one or more special schools working with 27 primary schools.

Plans to restructure parts of special secondary education into lower regular secondary education are fairly new. Special secondary education for pupils with learning difficulties (LOM) and mild mentally retarded (MLK) will no longer be part of separate special education legislation, but will become an integral part of new secondary education law. In keeping with integration policy for primary education, schools for secondary education and schools for secondary special education will also have to work together in clusters. In the near future, these clusters will also be funded equally according to the total enrollment in this sector. This reform was initially implemented on August 1, 1998 in the form of a number of pilot-projects nationwide in order to gain experience with several aspects of the new structure.

In 1996 the second policy paper, *The Back-Pack,* appeared, outlining separate plans for educating pupils with sensory, physical, and mental impairments and/or behavioral problems. The basic idea is that financing special school places for these pupils should be stopped in favor of linking the funding of special services to the pupil involved, regardless of the school type. The pupil does not follow the funding, but funding follows the pupil. An important characteristic of demand-oriented funding is that parents have an important voice in choosing a school for their child. If a pupil meets the criteria for a pupil-bound budget, parents and pupil can choose a school and decide together with the school on how to use the funding. Only in cases where a school could clearly demonstrate that it is incapable of providing suitable schooling for a special needs pupil would placement be denied. Directly linked to this new funding system is a reorganization of special (secondary) education. The number of different school types will be reduced to four: schools for the visually impaired, for pupils with communication disorders, for the physically and mentally impaired, and for pupils with behavior problems. In 1997, Parliament approved this new funding system and the changes are currently being implemented.

NEURAL EFFICIENCY ANALYZER (NEA)

During the past 20 years, a number of psychologists have argued that traditional intelligence tests are often inappropriate because they are culturally biased. In response to such criticism, many attempts have been made to develop measures of cognitive functioning that are both objective and culturally free.

A unique approach to culture-free assessment of cognitive functioning came in the late 1960s and early 1970s with Ertl's (1968) work with the Neural Efficiency Analyzer (NEA) (Tracy, 1972). Seen as providing an unbiased view of intelligence, the NEA was purported to measure the efficiency and speed of neuronal transmission.

While the NEA appeared to be an innovative attempt to minimize the cultural bias in intelligence testing, little empirical evidence exists to support the use of this measure on a clinical basis. Moreover, with the major goals of intellectual assessment being to portray an individual's functioning in a number of separate yet related cognitive areas as well as to predict potential for future development, any unitary measure of cognitive functioning would have questionable use.

REFERENCES

Ertl, J. (1968). Evoked potential and human intelligence. Final Report, VSOE, Project No. 6–1454.

Tracy, W. (1972). Goodbye IQ, hello EI (Ertl Index). *Phi Delta Kappan, 54,* 89–94.

See also Ertl Index; Intelligence

NEURODEVELOPMENTAL THERAPY (NDT)

Neurodevelopmental therapy (NDT) is an approach toward working with individuals who have cerebral palsy and other neuromuscular disorders. Originating in England with the work of Berta and Karl Bobath in the 1940s (Bobath, 1980), NDT was presented to professionals in the United States in 1959 (Campbell, 1982).

The main goals for NDT in the classroom are to analyze movement dysfunction accurately, to implement facilitation/inhibition procedures (to increase normal movement), to teach others necessary procedures for consistent management of the motor-impaired student across people and situations, to use adaptive equipment to the extent that equipment replaces unattainable functions, and to prevent the sequence of abnormal motor development from progressing to the point of formation of contractures and orthopedic deformities (Campbell, 1982). Studies on NDT have equivocal results (Degangi, 1994; Law et al., 1997).

REFERENCES

Bobath, K. (1980). *A neurophysiological basis for treatment of cerebral palsy.* London: Heinemann.

Campbell, P.H. (1982). *Introduction to neurodevelopmental treatment.* Akron, OH: Children's Hospital Medical Center.

Degangi, G.A. (1994). Examining the efficacy of short-term NDT intervention using a case study design. *Physical & Occupational Therapy, 14*(2), 21–61.

Law, M., Russell, D., Pollock, N., Rosenbaum, P., Walter, S., & King, G. (1997). A comparison of intensive neurodevelopmental therapy plus casting and a regular occupational therapy program for children with cerebral palsy. *Developmental Medicine & Child Neurology, 39*(10), 664–670.

See also **Cerebral Palsy; Physical Therapy**

NEUROFIBROMATOSIS

The neurofibromatoses are genetic disorders of the nervous system that affect growth and development of nerve cell tissues (National Institute of Neurological Disorders and Stroke, 1995). Researchers have classified the disorders as neurofibromatosis type I (NFI) and as neurofibromatosis type II (NFII). Both cause bone deformities, tumor growth on nerves, and multiple skin changes (Wong, 1995). They are autosomal-dominant diseases that occur in both sexes and are found in all ethnic groups (National Institute of Neurological Disorders and Stroke, 1995). They may be inherited or may arise through spontaneous mutation.

NFI is the most common type of neurofibromatosis, with symptoms, particularly of the skin, appearing at birth or during infancy (National Institute of Neurological Disorders and Stroke, 1995). Five or more brown spots (café au lait macules) are often visible, with the macules growing in size to over 15 millimeters in postpubertal children (Wong, 1995). Children 10 to 15 years of age afflicted with NFI develop neurofibromas or tumors on their nerves or on nerve tissue beneath the skin (National Institute of Neurological Disorders and Stroke, 1995). The diagnosis for NFI is based on two or more of the following physical findings: (a) five or more café au lait macules; (b) two or more neurofibromas; (c) freckling of the armpit or groin area; (d) benign growths on the iris of the eye; (e) tumors on the optic nerve; (f) severe scoliosis; (g) bone lesions; or (h) a parent or sibling with the disorder (National Institute of Neurological Disorders and Stroke, 1995; Wong, 1995).

Treatment of NFI is aimed at minimizing the symptoms. Surgical intervention is used to help bone malformations or scoliosis and to remove painful or disfiguring tumors (National Institute of Neurological Disorders and Stroke,

1995). In rare instances, tumors may be cancerous and require chemotherapy or radiation treatments (National Institute of Neurological Disorders and Stroke, 1995). Most individuals with NFI live normal and productive lives, but some forms of the disease are severely debilitating (Wong, 1995).

NFII is less common and primarily manifested in bilateral tumors on the eighth cranial nerve (National Institute of Neurological Disorders and Stroke, 1995). Progressive hearing loss is evident by age 10, and affected children often complain of ringing in the ears (tinnitus) and exhibit poor balance. Other symptoms include headaches, facial pain, and facial numbness. The diagnosis for NFII is determined through physical examination and a careful review of the child's medical history. Physicians assess for bilateral eighth nerve tumors when a family member has similar tumors or the family has a history of cataracts, gliomas, or neurofibromas (National Institute of Neurological Disorders and Stroke, 1995).

REFERENCES

National Institute of Neurological Disorders and Stroke. (1995, April). http://ninds.nih.gov/healinfo/disorder/neurofib/neurofib.htm.

Wong, D. (1995). *Whaley & Wong's nursing care of infants and children* (5th ed.). St. Louis: Mosby-Year Book.

See also **Café au Lait Spots; Physical Disabilities; Spina Bifida**

NEUROLINGUISTIC PROGRAMMING (NLP)

Neurolinguistic programming (NLP) is a model for effective interpersonal communication introduced by Bandler and Grinder (1975, 1976, 1979) for use in counseling and psychotherapy. The model is based on the belief that humans receive, store, and process information through their senses, or representational systems. Each individual has a preferred or primary representational system (PRS), either visual, auditory, or kinesthetic, through which information is most effectively processed. Interpersonal communication is enhanced, according to the theory of NLP, when dialogue reflects a match of preferred representational systems.

The NLP has recently been applied to the field of education. Torres and Katz (1983) suggest that if teachers are aware of their own PRS and the PRS of their students, and if the channels of communication are matched, learning is facilitated. Teachers who are aware of the multiplicity of receptive modes present within a group may develop greater flexibility and teach more effectively through a variety of communication channels.

Neurolinguistic programming and the implications derived from it remain controversial. Studies have shown that neither predicate analysis nor eye movement observations are reliable methods of determining PRS (Badderley & Predebon, 1991; Beyerstein 1990; Dorn, Atwater, Jereb, & Russell, 1983; Shaw, 1977). Further evaluation in classrooms and clinics will be necessary to determine the full value of these theories.

REFERENCES

Badderley, M., & Predebon, J. (1991). "Do the eyes have it?": A test of neurolinguistic programming's eye movement hypothesis. *Australian Journal of Clinical Hypnotherapy & Hypnosis, 12*(1), 1–23.

Bandler, R., & Grinder, J. (1975). *The structure of magic I.* Palo Alto, CA: Science and Behavior.

Bandler, R., & Grinder, J. (1976). *The structure of magic II.* Palo Alto, CA: Science and Behavior.

Bandler, R., & Grinder, J. (1979). *Frogs into princes: Neurolinguistic programming.* Moab, Utah: Real People Press.

Beyerstein, B.L. (1990). Brain scams: Neuromythologies of the new age. *International Journal of Mental Health, 19*(3), 27–36.

Dorn, F.J., Atwater, M., Jereb, R., & Russell, R. (1983). Determining the reliability of the NLP eye-movement procedure. *American Mental Health Counselors Association Journal, 5*(3), 105–110.

Shaw, D.L. (1977). *Recall as effected by the interaction of presentation representational system and primary representational system.* Unpublished doctoral dissertation, Ball State University.

Torres, C., & Katz, J. (1983). Neuro-linguistic programming: Developing effective communication in the classroom. *Teacher Educator, 19*(2), 25–32.

***See also* Ability Training; Cerebral Dominance; Hypnosis; Psychotherapy; Teaching Strategies**

NEUROLOGICAL IMPRESS METHOD

The neurological impress method was developed to facilitate reading among children with severe reading disabilities (Hecklman, 1969; Langford, Slade, & Barnett, 1974). It may be most effective with students beyond 10 years of age. In this approach, teacher and student read aloud at a rapid pace, with the teacher sitting slightly behind and directing his or her voice into the student's ear. At first, the teacher may read somewhat louder and faster, encouraging the student to maintain pace and not to worry about faltering or misreading. The teacher's finger slides along the print, underscoring the words as they are read. As the student becomes more comfortable, he or she may assume the vocal and pointing lead. Continuing through the passage, teacher and student alternate leading and following.

In a study using the neurological impress method, Lorenz and Vockell (1979) and Skinner, Logan, & Robinson (1997) found no significant gains in either word recognition or reading comprehension. On the other hand, improvement was noted in reading expressiveness, in fluency, and in students' confidence in their reading ability. Students' perceptions of gains using this method, however, have been subsequently refuted (Reetz & Hoover, 1992). Kann (1983) has suggested that the neurological impress method may be profitably combined with repeated readings, another approach that promotes fluency and syntactic competence (Samuels, 1979).

REFERENCES

Hecklman, R.G. (1969). The neurological impress method of remedial reading instruction. *Academic Therapy, 4,* 277–282.

Kann, R. (1983). The method of repeated readings: Expanding the neurological impress method for use with disabled readers. *Journal of Learning Disabilities, 16,* 90–92.

Langford, K., Slade, K., & Barnett, A. (1974). An explanation of impress techniques in remedial reading. *Academic Therapy, 9,* 309–319.

Lorenz, L., & Vockell, E. (1979). Using the neurological impress method with learning disabled readers. *Journal of Learning Disabilities, 12,* 420–422.

Reetz, L.J., & Hoover, J.H. (1992). The acceptability and utility of five reading approaches as judged by middle school LD students. *Learning Disabilities Research & Practice, 7*(1), 11–15.

Samuels, S.J. (1979). The method of repeated readings. *Reading Teacher, 32,* 403–408.

Skinner, C.H., Logan, P., & Robinson, S.L. (1997). Demonstration as a reading intervention for exceptional learners. *School Psychology Review, 26*(3), 437–447.

NEUROLOGICAL ORGANIZATION

Used generically, neurological organization refers to the functional organization of the brain, including the brain stem, the midbrain, and the neocortex. It is frequently encountered in neuropsychological research, a large portion of which is devoted to the investigation of individual differences in neurological organization and to the development of comprehensive theories of the functional organization of the brain. The term also has a more specific usage, as it is most often encountered in special education.

Special education and related services personnel are most likely to see the term used in the context of the Doman and Delacato approach to remediation of learning disorders (Delacato, 1959). The Doman and Delacato theory and the subsequently derived treatment methods rely on a systematic vertical and horizontal development and organization of function within the human brain. The neuropsychological theory that underlies the work of Doman and Delacato is based on the biogenetic principle that "ontogeny recapitulates phylogeny;" this principle contends that if an individual does not follow this sequential continuum of development, as prescribed by Doman and Delacato, problems of mobility and/or communication will develop. The therapeutic methods of Doman and Delacato are designed to overcome early deficiencies in development and to restore proper neurological organization.

Unfortunately, there has been virtually no research supportive of either the Doman and Delacato theory of neurological organization or its derived treatment programs. The developmental milestones appear to have been misplaced as well. Forty percent of normal five to nine year olds have mixed dominance (eye-hand preference), showing that complete dominance is not typically established by age six and one-half, as Doman and Delacato claim. The treatment programs of Doman and Delacato have been condemned by resolution by many major health organizations in the United States and Canada. It is unlikely that the Doman and Delacato concept of neurological organization will prove useful in working with the handicapped. A longer review of the approach is available in Reynolds (1981).

REFERENCES

Delacato, C.H. (1959). *The treatment and prevention of reading problems: The neuropsychological approach.* Springfield, IL: Thomas.

Reynolds, C.R. (1981). The neuropsychological basis of intelligence. In G. Hynd & J. Obrzut (Eds.), *Neuropsychological assessment and the school age child: Issues and procedures.* New York: Grune & Stratton.

See also **Patterning; Reading Disorders**

NEUROPSYCHOLOGY

Neuropsychology is the study of the relationships between behavior and the brain. Its emphasis is on understanding the mechanisms of the brain responsible for both simple and complex patterns of functioning (e.g., auditory discrimination, reading, memory). Since the mid-twentieth century, a good deal of professional attention has been directed to the understanding of specific loci of functioning in the brain. Indeed, Broca (1861) and Jackson (1874) observed a relationship between patients' behavior and specific areas of damage to the brain. In fact, some credit these observations of brain-behavior relationships as the birth of neuropsychology (Dean, 1986).

The clinical neuropsychologist's role has both diagnostic and therapeutic elements. Diagnosis concerns the identification of impaired neurological processes and the area of the brain implicated. Through therapeutic interventions, the neuropsychologist often works to structure experiences that maximize strengths and minimize weaknesses in an attempt to remediate processing disorders (Pfeiffer, Dean, & Shellenberger, 1986). In child neuropsychology, an increasing interest has been shown in the use of neuropsychological methods that use children's cognitive strengths to structure educational experiences for the remediation of learning and behavior problems.

The hemispheres of the brain can be viewed as processing information using different modes. The right hemisphere seems to use a more visual, spatial, simultaneous processing style whereas the left seems to use a more analytical, verbal, sequential style. The application of these processing differences recently has been attempted with some success in both educational assessment and remediation (Dean, 1981, 1984; Reynolds, 1984).

A number of neuropsychologists have begun to isolate the biological or organic factors involved in many of the emotional (behavioral) disorders (e.g., some forms of depression, hyperactivity, schizophrenia) that previously were thought to be functionally related to stress in the environment (Dean, 1985). These findings are important because they begin to tie brain functioning more clearly to human emotions and psychopathology. Additionally, these findings indicate that some disorders, or even subgroups of certain disorders, once considered environmentally caused actually may be biologically based. Therefore, in school remedial planning, an evaluation of the neuropsychological components of functioning may be as important as an evaluation of the child's current environment. In sum, neuropsychology has made significant contributions in the understanding of brain-behavior relationships and in providing distinct direction for the education and rehabilitation of children and adults with brain dysfunctions. Clearly, neuropsychology has the potential for becoming a major link between medicine, education, and the psychological sciences.

REFERENCES

Broca, P. (1861/1960). Remarks on the seat of the faculty of articulate language, followed by an observation of aphasia. In G. von Bonin (Trans.), *Some papers on the cerebral cortex.* Springfield, IL: Thomas.

Dean, R.S. (1981). Cerebral dominance and childhood learning disorders: Theoretical perspectives. *School Psychology Review, 10,* 373–388.

Dean, R.S. (1984). Functional lateralization of the brain. *Journal of Special Education, 18,* 239–256.

Dean, R.S. (1985). Neuropsychological assessment. In J.D. Cavenar, R. Michels, H.K.H. Brodie, A.M. Cooper, S.B. Guze, L.L. Judd, G.L. Klerman, & A.J. Solnit (Eds.), *Psychiatry* (pp. 1–16). Philadelphia, Lippincott.

Dean, R.S. (1986). Perspectives on the future of neuropsychological assessment. In B.S. Plake & J.C. Witt (Eds.), *Buros—Nebraska series on measurement and testing: Future of testing and measurement* (pp. 203–244). Hillsdale, NJ: Erlbaum.

Jackson, J.H. (1874/1932). On the duality of the brain. In J. Taylor (Ed.), *Selected writings of John Hughlings Jackson* (Vol. 2). London: Hodder & Stoughton.

Pfeiffer, S.I., Dean, R.S., & Shellenberger, S. (1986). The school psychologists in medical settings: Neurology section. In T. Kratochwill (Ed.), *Advances in school psychology* (Vol. 5). Hillsdale, NJ: Erlbaum (177–202).

Reynolds, C.R. (Ed.). (1984). The Kaufman Assessment Battery for Children. *Journal of Special Education, 18*(3).

See also **Cerebral Dominance; Hemispheric Functioning; Neurological Organization; Split-Brain Research**

NEW ZEALAND, SPECIAL EDUCATION IN

A variety of handicapping conditions are recognized for special education service provision in New Zealand; these include mental retardation, emotional/social maladjustment, speech/language impairment, hearing handicap, visual handicap, physical handicap/health impairment, and multiple handicap. However, recognition of learning disabilities is lacking and has been so for some time. It is hoped that new policies for "high incidence" special needs may change this as well as teacher preparation in the future (Chapman, 1992).

Recent epidemiological research in New Zealand has yielded prevalence estimates almost identical with estimates obtained in major studies in the United States, Europe, and Australia. While a sizable number of disabled children are currently receiving special educational services in New Zealand, little information is available on the extent or effectiveness of these services. Services for deaf-blind children are well developed, but there is concern that only a small proportion of children within other categories of handicapping conditions are receiving special education provisions (Wilton, 1984).

Perhaps because most of the special services for handicapped children are provided in segregated settings, the majority of students with disabilities attend regular schools without participating in special programs (Wilton, 1984). Off-site centers for disruptive secondary school pupils are an example of segregated service delivery. Initially formed on a voluntary basis by concerned community members, the off-site centers are now administered by the New Zealand Department of Education and are seen as a reflection on the failure of the schools to cater adequately to Maori and Polynesian students (Galloway & Barrett, 1984). There are presently seven off-site centers that are completely separated from mainstream facilities for disruptive secondary-level students. Recent administrative changes present schools as providers and parents as consumers; this stance is considered optimistic (Ballard, 1990).

REFERENCES

Ballard, K.D. (1990). Special education in New Zealand: Disability, politics, and empowerment. *International Journal of Disability, Development, & Education, 37*(2), 109–124.

Chapman, J.W. (1992). Learning disabilities in New Zealand: Where kiwis and kids with LD can't fly. *Journal of Learning Disabilities, 25*(6), 362–370.

Galloway, D., & Barrett, C. (1984). Off-site centers for disruptive secondary school pupils in New Zealand. *Educational Research, 26*(2), 106–110.

Wilton, K. (1984). Handicapped children of preschool- and school-age in New Zealand: Special educational needs and available services. *Exceptional Child, 31,* 173–184.

See also **Australia, Special Education in; Central America, Special Education in; China, Special Education in**

NIGERIA, SPECIAL EDUCATION IN

Nigeria's efforts to reform educational programs since independence are well-documented (Federal Ministry of Information and Culture, 1986). As indicated, any educational reform has a measurable impact on special education reform, and special education policies are integrated into overall educational policies set by the Federal Ministry of Education. The National Policy on Education contains Section 8, a directional policy that provides for educational services for persons with exceptionalities in Nigeria (Federal Ministry of Education, 1977). Section 8 has been a laudable effort by Nigeria. Its goals were to:

1. Give concrete meaning to the idea of equalizing educational opportunities for all children, their physical, emotional disabilities notwithstanding.
2. Provide adequate education for all "handicapped" children and adults in order that they may fully play their roles in the development of the nation.
3. Provide opportunities for exceptionally gifted children to develop at their own pace in the interest of the nation's economic and technological development. (Federal Ministry of Education, 1977, p. 1)

About a decade ago, a comprehensive case study sponsored by the Special Education Section (a unit created to facilitate special education programs/services) of the Federal Ministry of Education was undertaken by Oluigbo (1986) to evaluate the progress of special education in Nigeria. Oluigbo's study highlighted prospects and challenges facing special education in Nigeria. In more specific terms, Oluigbo found that (a) there was a remarkable increase in facilities; (b) there were large numbers of students with exceptionalities integrated into "normal" schools, and special school enrollments had more than doubled; (c) since some of the states were "new," it was difficult to compare the increased rate in enrollment in each state; (d) most of the purely vocational facilities lacked proper focus—they were only craft/skill training-oriented and were run by Ministries of Social Welfare, Youth, and Culture instead of the Ministry of Education; and (e) exceptional school-aged children were not receiving the benefits that could have been derived from Section 8 of the National Policy on Education.

In May 1990, Oluigbo prepared a monograph for the Federation Ministry of Education. This monograph, *National Curriculum for the Mentally Retarded,* became a landmark publication, because never in the history of Nigeria had there been any substantial attention on persons with cognitive disabilities. According to Oluigbo, "government determination to actualize its policy of equal educational opportunity for all her children irrespective of any disability has opened limitless opportunities for the educationally 'handicapped' in Nigeria, so much so, that disabled Nigerians now compete favorably with their non-disabled peers in every field of life" (p. 1). In referring to the revised National Policy on Education (Federal Ministry of Education, 1981), Oluigbo acknowledged that individuals with mental retardation have "not been equally opportuned to enjoy the same opportunities open to the blind, the deaf, the physically 'handicapped' and the learning disabled" (p. 1).

In Nigeria, there are problems of *who, when, why,* and *how* to admit exceptional individuals into school programs because of the lack of mandates. Educational programs are indiscriminately integrated without consideration for the specific needs of special students. Those students with serious integrative problems are admitted into residential programs or even institutions. In Nigeria, no systematic screening facility is available for exceptional children, and their admissions and placements do not follow organized sequences of special education (Algozzine, Wong, & Obiakor, 1996; Obiakor et al., 1991; Ogbue, 1981).

While special education placement is frequently geared toward programs that maximize the potential of exceptional individuals, this has not been the case with many special education placements in Nigeria. In some cases, students have been institutionalized—this kind of segregationary program hampers self-concept development and the ability to function in mainstream society (Obiakor, Bragg, & Maltby, 1993). In other cases, the procedure of indiscriminate integration or full inclusion into regular programs takes precedence over individual needs of exceptional learners. Bakere (1992), in his work, described problems of integration in Nigeria to include (a) large class size and inadequate placement procedures, (b) inadequate planning and teacher preparation, (c) lack of infrastructural facilities, (d) lack of materials and equipment, and (e) attitudinal problems. According to Bakere, integration is "an ideal shared by those who are well-versed in the problems involved. Idealism must, however, be combined with realism" (p. 260).

FUTURE CHALLENGES OF SPECIAL EDUCATION IN NIGERIA

Unlike many developing countries, Nigeria has a national policy on special education. The institution of Section 8 by the Federal Ministry of Education is an exemplary effort. The creation of a Special Education Unit is also a laudable idea—this unit disseminates information and creates policies for the State Ministries of Education. However, the future appears somewhat bleak because (a) Section 8 is not a national law promulgated by the legislators—there is no repercussion for not carrying out a policy; (b) the Federal Ministry of Education is operating under a transitional military government that disallows solid foundational policies and programs, and (c) there are socioeconomic, cultural, political, and educational problems inherent in developing nations—these problems directly or indirectly affect reform policies and programs in special education. In a 21st century Nigeria, educational policy establishment should positively correlate with policy implementation.

Nigeria appears to have made some efforts to combat problems confronting individuals with special needs. Section 8 of the National Policy on Education was created as a directional policy to address these needs. Despite this reform effort, special education has been theoretically approached. While Nigeria should be credited for recognizing and establishing a policy to help individuals with exceptionalities, this policy has not been legislated as a law by members of the Nigerian Parliament. Section 8 appears to be a pièce de résistance in content. However, there are current indications that it is a policy plagued by endemic problems of culture, socioeconomics, and politics in Nigeria. Special ed-

ucation reforms should be successful if and when the country focuses on (a) developing an appropriate philosophical foundation of education which would reflect the needs of the people, (b) evaluating educational policies and programs to reduce inconsistencies in program implementation, and (c) maintaining political stability which would have profound ramifications on overall special education policies.

REFERENCES

Algozzine, B., Wong, K., & Obiakor, F.E. (1996). Diagnosis and classification of children and youth with special needs. In E. De Corte & F.E. Weiner (Eds.), *International encyclopedia of developmental and instructional psychology*. Oxford, England: Elsevier Science.

Bakere, C.A. (1992). Integration in education: The case of education for the handicapped children in Nigeria. *International Journal of Special Education, 7,* 225–260.

Federal Ministry of Education. (1977). *Section 8 of the National Policy on Education.* Lagos, Nigeria: Author.

Federal Ministry of Education. (1981). *National Policy on Education.* Lagos, Nigeria: Author.

Federal Ministry of Information and Culture. (1986). *Education in Nigeria.* Lagos, Nigeria: Author.

Obiakor, F.E., Aramburo, D., Maltby, G.P., & Davis, E. (1991). Comparison of special education in Nigeria and the United States of America. *International Journal of Special Education, 6,* 341–352.

Obiakor, F.E., Bragg, W.A., & Maltby, G.P. (1993, July). *Placement of exceptional students in Nigeria and the United States of America.* Paper presented at the International Association of Special Education Third Biennual Conference, Vienna, Austria.

Ogbue, R.M. (1981, December). Experiments in integration: The Nigerian experience. *Educafrica,* pp. 136–152.

See also Africa, Special Education in

NIMH

See NATIONAL INSTITUTES OF MENTAL HEALTH.

NIND

See NATIONAL INSTITUTE OF NEUROLOGICAL AND COMMUNICATIVE DISORDERS AND STROKE.

NMR

See NUCLEAR MAGNETIC RESONANCE.

NONCOMPLIANT CHILDREN

Noncompliant children are those who fail to comply with the desires, rules, or policies established by others. They are norm-violating and frequently chronically disruptive. The term noncompliant is used in some states to describe youths who have come to the attention of the courts or the authorities. A noncompliant child is not necessarily emotionally disturbed or behaviorally disordered. Frequently, noncompliant children are socially different but not necessarily socially deviant.

Teacher-initiated interactions generally require compliance from the student. If the student complies, the teacher provides positive consequences. If the student does not comply, the teacher provides negative consequences first and then repeats the original direction. If the student then complies, the teacher provides positive consequences. If the student does not comply again, the teacher provides stronger negative consequences and the cycle continues until the student complies. The teacher then provides positive consequences.

Student-initiated interactions can be either appropriate or inappropriate behaviors. If behavior is appropriate, the teacher provides positive consequences. If behavior is inappropriate, the teacher provides negative consequences first and directs the student toward appropriate behavior. If the student then exhibits appropriate behavior, the teacher provides positive consequences. In all cases of teacher/student interactions, the end result should be the teacher's providing positive consequences. These consequences should also be communicated to the parents, who can then support the positive process (Alborz, 1993).

REFERENCE

Alborz, A. (1993). Parent input in education: An illustration. *Mental Handicap, 21*(4), 142–146.

See also **Applied Behavior Analysis; Classroom Management; Conduct Disorders; Engineered Classroom**

NONDISCRIMINATORY ASSESSMENT

Millions of tests are used yearly in schools for many purposes (e.g., grading, screening, placement, guidance, diagnosis, advancement, retention, formative and summative evaluation). While the public's attitudes toward testing are positive (Lerner, 1981), a number of authors (Black, 1963; Gross, 1963; Kamin, 1974; Mercer, 1972) have criticized testing generally; criticisms directed toward the uses of tests with minority students have identified additional abuses (Williams, 1974; Samuda, Kong, Cummins, Pascual-Leon, & Lewis, 1991). These abuses include assessing students in their nondominant language; using tests that reflect only white middle-class values and abilities; using inadequately prepared and culturally insensitive assessment personnel; overidentifying and placing minority students in mentally retarded classes and lower ability groups; allowing minority students to remain in inferior classes for years; restricting minorities' educational opportunities; not informing parents when important educational decisions are made; basing important educational decisions on meager and unvalidated information; and denigrating the dignity of racial groups in light of low test performance (Oakland, 1977; Oakland & Parmalee, 1985).

Once aware of these issues, educators, psychologists (Reynolds, 1982), politicians (Bersoff, 1981), judges (Sattler, 1981), and others sought different but often complementary ways of clarifying the issues and improving the assessment of minority children. For example, in their quest to obtain suitable measures, psychologists have tried to develop culture-fair and culture-specific measures, criterion-referenced measures, and behavioral assessment devices; translated tests from English to other languages; normed tests to include more minority children, developed ethnic and pluralistic norms; and developed statistical models to use tests fairly (Oakland & Parmalee, 1985; Jensen, 1980).

Traditional definitions of bias rely largely on the three conceptions of validity: content, criterion related (including concurrent and predictive), and construct (including internal and external). Statisticians seemingly favor those methods that combine judgment and statistics. For example, logical analysis may be employed to establish the relevance of items to the trait being assessed and to identify items that may offend members of particular groups. Statistical techniques then can be used to identify aberrant items—those operating inconsistently with other items presumably measuring the same trait. Judgment again may be used to examine possible patterns among the statistically biased items and to further refine one's understanding of the trait (Shepard, 1982). Methods using item bias (as opposed to criterion-related validity) may be preferred because they can be incorporated into the first stages of test construction, thus leading to the early elimination of biases that may eventually compromise the test's validity. Furthermore, regression methods to detect criterion-related bias and factor-analytic methods to detect construct bias may be employed later with greater ease and confidence following the use of item methods.

Psychometrists often define bias through definitions that emphasize the relation between test items and the total test (e.g., item-total correlations). However, others prefer definitions that emphasize the entire test and focus on possible bias in selection or placement decisions.

Three definitions of bias appear prominently. The regression approach holds that bias is present when a test predicts differently for one group than another. Thus, bias is defined in terms of differences in the regression of a criterion measure on an independent variable (Cleary, 1968).

A second model frequently used is the quota system. Using this model, persons are selected in the same proportion as they are found in the population. If a community's population is 80% white and 20% black, one black will be selected for every four whites. Two separate cutoff scores are set to allow this selection ratio when between-group differences in mean scores exist.

A third model, the corrected-criterion model (Darlington, 1971), allows social and political implications using various culture-fair models to be weighed. A choice of models depends on the relative importance attributed to selecting persons with the highest scores versus giving members of minority groups more opportunities to be selected. A practical effect of this model is to add bonus points to scores of members of certain groups to help ensure a larger selection ratio for them.

Tests are described as being culturally nondiscriminatory when they have been validated for the specific purposes for which they are being used, are administered by trained and competent examiners using standardized procedures, and assess multiple yet specific areas of education need. Information about the pupil's medical, social, psychological, and educational development should be collected and interpreted by trained professionals. When assessing pupils with sensory or other physical impairments, the tests must assess their capabilities unattenuated by their impairments. Submitting all information to a multidisciplinary team for evaluation and decisions constitutes a key feature of a nonbiased program. Specialists also are encouraged to propose helpful interventions (Heller, Holtzman, & Messick, 1982). School systems must fully reassess pupils every three years in order to note progress toward goals specified in the IEP and to determine continued eligibility for special education.

REFERENCES

Bersoff, D. (1981). Legal principles in the nondiscriminatory assessment of minority children. In T. Oakland (Ed.), *Nonbiased assessment.* Minneapolis: University of Minnesota.

Black, H. (1963). *They shall not pass.* New York: Morrow.

Cleary, T.A. (1968). Test bias: Prediction of grades of Negro and white students in integrated colleges. *Journal of Educational Measurement, 5,* 115–124.

Darlington, R.B. (1971). Another look at "culture fairness." *Journal of Educational Measurement, 8,* 71–72.

Gross, M. (1963). *The brain watchers.* New York: New American Library.

Heller, K.A., Holtzman, W.H., & Messick, S. (Eds.). (1982). *Placing children in special education: A strategy for equity.* Washington, DC: National Academy.

Jensen, A.R. (1980). *Bias in mental testing.* New York: Free Press.

Kamin, L. (1974). *The science and politics of IQ.* Hillsdale, NJ: Erlbaum.

Lerner, B. (1981). Representative democracy, "men of zeal," and testing legislation. *American Psychologist, 36,* 270–275.

Mercer, J.R. (1972). IQ: The lethal label. *Psychology Today, 6,* 44–47, 95–97.

Oakland, T.D. (Ed.). (1977). *Psychological and educational assessment of minority children.* New York: Brunner/Mazel.

Oakland, T., & Parmalee, R. (1985). Mental measurement of minority-group children. In B. Wolman (Ed.), *Handbook of intelligence.* New York: Wiley.

Reynolds, C.R. (1982). The problem of bias in psychological assessment. In C.R. Reynolds & T.B. Gutkin (Eds.), *The handbook of school psychology.* New York: Wiley.

Samuda, R.J., Kong, S.L., Cummins, J., Pascual-Leone, J., & Lewis, J. (1991). *Assessment and placement of minority students.* Toronto, Canada: Hogrefe & Huber.

Sattler, J.M. (1981). Intelligence tests on trial: An "interview" with judges Robert F. Peckham and John F. Grady. *Journal of School Psychology, 19*(4), 359–369.

Shepard, L.A. (1982). Definitions of bias. In R.A. Berk (Ed.), *Handbook of methods for detecting test bias.* Baltimore, MD: Johns Hopkins University Press.

Williams, R.L. (1974). Scientific racism and IQ: The silent mugging of the black community. *Psychology Today, 7*(12), 32–41.

See also **Cultural Bias in Testing; Individual Education Plan; Racial Discrimination in Special Education**

NONLITERAL LANGUAGE

Literal language is the ordinary, common construction or primary meaning of terms or expressions. *Nonliteral language* is the extraordinary construction or primary meaning of terms or expressions, i.e., going beneath the conventional code of language to interpret the intentions and attitudes of words, phrases, or sentences. The literal/nonliteral distinction is often a matter of degree; therefore, the notion of a continuum is used when discussing literal or nonliteral oral and written communication (Adamson & Romski, 1997; Kudor, 1997; Milosky, 1994; Nippold, 1998).

Nonliteral communication varies from culture to culture. Nonliteral language problems are common with speakers of English as a second language (ESL) and with individuals who have developmental or acquired communication-learning disorders. For the mainstream culture, the ability to understand and use nonliteral language forms begins to develop around age 5 and continues through life (Lane & Molyneaux, 1992). Being able to understand and use figurative language, humor, teasing, sarcasm, deceit, verbal aggression, and slang is necessary for social development. Comprehension and production of figurative language, deceit, advertising, headlines, multiple meanings, and ambiguity is important in academic settings. Knowing scripts and schemas, advertising language, and forms of deception are critical for employment and careers (Kudor, 1997; Lane & Molyneaux, 1992; Milosky, 1994; Nippold, 1998).

REFERENCES

Adamson, L.B., & Romski, M.A. (Eds.). (1997). *Communication and language acquisition: Discoveries from atypical development.* Baltimore: Brookes.

Kudor, S.J. (1997). *Teaching students with language and communication disabilities.* Needham Heights, MA: Allyn & Bacon.

Lane, V.W., & Molyneaux, D. (1992). *The dynamics of communicative development.* Englewood Cliffs, NJ: Prentice Hall.

Milosky, L.A. (1994). Nonliteral language abilities: Seeing the forest for the trees. In G.P. Wallach and K.G. Butler, (Eds.), *Language learning disabilities in school-age children and adolescents: Some principles and applications* (2nd ed.) (pp. 275–304). New York: Merrill/Macmillan College.

Nippold, M.A. (1998). *Later language development: The school-age and adolescent years.* Austin, TX: Pro-Ed.

NONSHELTERED EMPLOYMENT

Diverse employment options are available for graduates of special education programs. In the past, sheltered employment was a highly probable adult work setting for individuals with mental retardation. Today, several alternative employment options provide graduates with opportunities to experience work conditions in the mainstream of society (Rusch & Hughes, 1990). Nonsheltered employment comprises a range of work situations, including mobile work crews, enclaves within industry, competitive employment, and a supported work approach. These outcomes are enhanced through a commitment to a longitudinal progression of functional vocational curricular activities. The activities provide the mentally retarded with the requisite skills to function within integrated, community employment settings.

With systematic training strategies, trainers are paired with students/adults at an employment site and act as job coaches for the trainees. Acquisition strategies include varying the intensity of prompts prior to the occurrence of a behavior or providing varying intensities of feedback/reinforcement. Additionally, modification of the task itself may include altering the sequence of steps, modifying the physical nature of the materials, allowing the trainee to independently complete parts of the task, and rearranging duties of the trainee so that coworkers complete the more difficult steps of an activity.

Follow-along services are supplied in the final activity of the nonsheltered employment options. A critical dimension of nonsheltered employment is the fading of assistance from the trainer to allow the site supervisor of nondisabled workers to assume the same duties with the trainee. This fading process includes the analysis of supervisory feedback forms, the collection of data for rate and quality of work, the interviewing of parents to clarify incentives for long-term employment, and the willingness of a school/agency to be on call for crisis situations that, if not immediately handled, could result in termination of the trainee.

REFERENCE

Rusch, F.R., & Hughes, C. (1990). Historical overview of supported employment. In F.R. Rusch (Ed), *Supported employment: Models methods, and issues* (pp. 5–14). Sycamore, IL: Sycamore Publishing.

See also **Sheltered Workshops; Vocational Rehabilitation; Vocational Training of the Handicapped**

NONVERBAL LANGUAGE

Nonverbal language is commonly used to describe all human communication events which transcend spoken or written words (Wood, 1981; Knapp, 1980; Lane & Molyneaux, 1994). Nonverbal communication begins at birth and continues throughout life (Bretherton, 1991). The early development of nonverbal communication skills occurs in three phases (Mundy & Gomes, 1997): (1) the birth to 5-month dyadic phase where communication often involves face-to-face exchanges of affective signals between the infant and caregiver; (2) the 6- to 18-month phase where triadic exchanges occur more frequently (e.g., an infant points to a toy while making eye contact with a caregiver); and (3) the third phase, which overlaps with phase two (12–24 months) and involves the child's increasing utilization of verbal communication in conjunction with nonverbal signals. The third phase continues to be developed so that nonverbal communication serves at least four important functions:

- Taking the place of verbal communication (when verbal communication is unnecessary or impossible).
- Adding clarity to the meaning of verbal communication (by inflection, stress, tone of voice, intensity, gestures, and so forth).
- Revealing the general emotional state of the participants (e.g., comfort or anxiety; relaxed or fearful).
- Revealing specific feelings regarding topics under discussion (not only the nature of the emotion but its relative intensity).

Easily taken for granted, and often more difficult to observe and record systematically than verbal or linguistic behavior, nonverbal communication may convey as much as 80% of a message (Devito, 1997; Trenholm & Jensen, 1997). Although nonverbal communication is important in all social and academic communication-learning interactions, it is critical when negotiating meaning with prelinguistic infants and individuals with severe disabilities (Bretherton, 1991; Mundy & Gomes, 1997). Nonverbal communication varies from culture to culture and needs to be interpreted relative to the illocutionary (intent), locutionary (actual signals), and perlocutionary (interpretation by receiver) aspects of a situation.

REFERENCES

Bretherton, I. (1991). Intentional communication and the development of an understanding of mind. In D. Frye & C. Moore (Eds.), *Children's theories of mind: Mental states and social understanding* (pp. 271–289). Hillsdale, NJ: Erlbaum.

Devito, J.A. (1997). *Human communication.* New York: Addison Wesley Longman.

Knapp, M.L. (1980). *Essentials of nonverbal communication.* New York: Holt, Rinehart & Winston.

Lane, V.W., & Molyneaux, D. (1994). *The dynamics of communicative development.* Englewood Cliffs, NJ: Prentice Hall.

Mundy, P., & Gomes, A. (1997). A skills approach to early language development. In L.B. Adamson & M.A. Romski (Eds.), *Communication and language acquisition: Discoveries from atypical development* (pp. 107–133). Baltimore, MD: Brookes.

Trenholm, S., & Jensen, A. (1997). *Interpersonal communication* (3rd ed.). New York: Wadsworth.

Wood, B.S. (1981). *Children and communication: Verbal and nonver-*

bal language development (2nd ed.). Englewood Cliffs, NJ: Prentice Hall.

NOONAN'S SYNDROME (MALE TURNER'S SYNDROME)

Noonan's syndrome, which closely resembles Turner's syndrome phenotypically, primarily affects males; it may be a sex-linked chromosomal abnormality, but the specific cause is uncertain. Characteristics are similar to those of females with Turner's syndrome (Bergsma, 1979). Children with Noonan's syndrome usually are short in stature, have webbed necks or short broad necks with excessive skin folds, and swelling and puffiness of the extremities, especially the hands and feet. Swelling, present at birth, may disappear as the child develops. Testicular underdevelopment and missing secondary sexual development are often seen. Eyes are widely spaced, may slant, squint, or have epicanthal folds, and nearsightedness is often noted (Collins & Turner, 1973). Low-set ears are prominent and slanted. Hair is coarse and teeth may be misshapen. Fingers and toes may be shortened and nails will be short and poorly developed. Occasionally loss of muscle tone may be reported, as will visual and hearing deficits. Congenital heart disease is a common finding. Mild mental retardation is fairly common, although some children with Noonan's syndrome will have normal intelligence (Lemeshaw, 1982).

Educational placement should consider the degree of cognitive developmental disability that exists in the child although educable or trainable classes may often be necessary because of additional handicaps that may accompany this syndrome. Related services will be necessary if hearing and vision losses are documented. Secondary sexual characteristics may be lacking; therefore, psychological and guidance counseling may be necessary to remediate for self-image and adjustment conflicts that may arise as the male reaches puberty. This will be more necessary if the child is included in the general classroom. Medical care may often be necessary because of heart problems, as well as an adaptive physical education program. It is important to work with the student to make sure that academic and social goals are appropriate (Besag, Fowler, Watson & Bostock, 1993).

REFERENCES

Bergsma, D. (1979). *Birth defects compendium* (2nd ed.). New York: National Foundation, March of Dimes.

Besag, F.M., Fowler, M., Watson, J., & Bostock, R. (1993). The practical management of specific learning disabilities. *Educational and Child Psychology, 10*(1), 23–27.

Collins, E., & Turner, G. (1973). The Noonan syndrome: A review of the clinical and genetic features of 27 cases. *Journal of Pediatrics, 83*, 941–950.

Lemeshaw, S. (1982). The handbook of clinical types in mental retardation. Boston: Allyn & Bacon.

See also **Crouzon's Syndrome; Hunter's Syndrome; Mental Retardation; Physical Anomalies**

NORMAL CURVE EQUIVALENT (NCE)

Normal curve equivalents (NCEs) are an esoteric score system designed specifically for use in evaluating federal Chapter 1 programs (Tallmadge, Wood, & Gamel, 1981). The NCEs are standard scores that have been scaled to a mean of 50 and a standard deviation of 21.06 (Mehrens & Lehman, 1984). This unusual choice of metrics was made so that a score system would exist that has normalized standard scores, has equal intervals, and has the same mean and range as percentile scores (1 to 99). Many users apparently believe that NCEs are thus in direct correspondence with a percentile rank scale, however, this occurs only at three points on the NCE scale; scores of 1, 50, and 99 coincide with the percentile rank scale. This direct correspondence does not occur at other points on the scale because of the equal interval nature of NCEs (as with most other standard score systems) where the distance between scores of 20 and 30, 45 and 55, and 70 and 80 is the same. On a percentile scale, these distances are decidedly unequal. A gain in scores on a percentile rank score from the 90th to the 95th percentile is approximately twice as great as the gain in scores from the 80th to the 85th percentile.

Many achievement tests are now providing conversion tables for the derivation of NCEs expressly to make the tests eligible for use in Chapter 1 evaluations and reporting schemes. Outside of this use, NCEs have little purpose. More familiar systems, including percentile ranks and the familiar IQ-type scale, are more readily understood and accessible. The NCEs are easily confused with percentile scores.

REFERENCES

Mehrens, W.A., & Lehman, I.J. (1984). *Measurement and evaluation in guidance* (3rd ed.). New York: Holt, Rinehart, & Winston.

Tallmadge, G.K., Wood, C.T., & Gamel, N. (1981). *Users' guide: Title 1 evaluation and reporting system* (Vol. 1). Washington, DC: U.S. Department of Education.

See also **Percentile Scores; Z-Scores, Determination of Discrepancies in**

NORMALIZATION

The strong belief of parents and advocates that individuals with mental retardation have a right to live and function in what is considered a normal environment led to the concept of normalization. These advocates stressed the fact that the handicapped are citizens and should be provided with opportunities and programs similar to those provided to normal children and adults. The term normalization originated in Denmark and was first implemented successfully in Scandinavian countries (Wolfensberger, 1972). Nirje (1979) introduced the term to America and defined it as "making available to all mentally retarded people patterns of life and conditions of everyday living which are close as possible to the regular circumstances of society" (p. 173).

Recently, the term has been used to refer not only to the mentally retarded but to all handicapped individuals. Regardless of the type of disability, the individual should be included as much as possible in the community and society. This involves participation in what is considered normal daily living activities such as attending school (education), working at a job or sheltered workshop (employment), and attending movies and participating in activities at parks and YMCAs (recreation and leisure activities). The current trend is to place the handicapped closer to their families and communities. These environments include community residential facilities, group homes, and halfway houses.

REFERENCES

Nirje, B. (1979). Changing patterns in residential services for the mentally retarded. In E.L. Meyen (Ed.), *Exceptional children and youth: An introduction.* Denver: Love.

Wolfensberger, W. (1972). *The principle of normalization in human services.* Toronto, Canada: National Institute on Mental Retardation.

See also **Community Programs; Deinstitutionalization; Independent Living**

NORM-REFERENCED TESTING

Norm-referenced tests (NRT) refer to a broad array of standardized tests, the results of which are interpreted by comparing the performance of examinees with that of a specified population of individuals, or norm group. In a broader sense, NRT often refers to a type of test frequently defined by contrasting it with criterion-referenced tests (CRT), where test results are referenced to a particular content domain and provide information about the skills an examinee has acquired, not the rank of an examinee in a norm group (Anastasi, 1982).

Most standardized tests are norm referenced. They are designed to be administered under standard conditions, according to carefully specified directions, and scored in an objective manner so that the results may be referenced to norms based on a representative sample of the population who took the test under similar conditions during standardization. The normative frame of reference for most standardized tests used in schools is usually a national (U.S.) age or grade group such as eight-year-old children, sixth-grade pupils, or college-bound high-school seniors.

A variety of norm-referenced tests are used in psychology and education. Intelligence tests, aptitude tests, achievement tests, and interest and personality tests all rely mainly on norm group comparisons for their interpretation. The contrast between NRT and CRT refers specifically to achievement tests and, even more specifically, to those at the elementary school level that assess basic reading, arith-

metic, and language skills (Anastasi, 1982; Mehrens & Lehmann, 1984). Even though the items used in NRT and CRT may appear to be indistinguishable, norm-referenced tests are almost always broader in their content coverage than the narrowly focused criterion-referenced tests.

Benefits of both NRT and CRT come closest to realization when users exercise caution and sound judgment in the selection and interpretation of either type of measure. Since its introduction around 1920, NRT has undergone periodic episodes of both unrestrained use and enthusiasm followed by disenchantment and disillusionment. When introduced in mastery testing in the 1920s, CRT was subsequently abandoned because of its narrow focus and inability to capture the full extent of individual differences. Readers are urged to keep this historical perspective in mind when assessing the merits of NRT and CRT. A balanced view of both types of measurement procedures will undoubtedly yield the most benefits to test users and test takers.

REFERENCES

Anastasi, A. (1982). *Psychological testing.* New York: Macmillan.

Mehrens, W.A., & Lehmann, I.J. (1984). *Measurement and evaluation in education and psychology.* New York: CBS College.

See also **Assessment; Criterion-Referenced Testing; Measurement**

NORTHWESTERN SYNTAX SCREENING TEST

The Northwestern Syntax Screening Test, developed by Laura L. Lee, is purported to measure the syntactical language structure of students ages 3 to 8. This instrument was developed as a screening device and was not intended to be used as a measure of a student's overall language skills. It consists of 20 identical linguistic structures that compose the instrument's receptive and expressive portions (Lee, 1979).

This test has been criticized because of a lack of reliability data. Klein (1980) attempted to establish reliability data, but the time period between test-retest was 7 months. Based on this extended time period and the lack of reliability data, Pearson and Stick (1985) concluded that a need for these data still exists.

In addition, researchers have expressed concern over the lack of validity data. Most researchers reported that this screening instrument has been effective in identifying students with delayed syntactical language abilities, but there have also been reports of false positives (Pearson & Stick, 1985).

Normative data have been criticized based on the limitations of geographic area, economic class, and age intervals of 1 year. Norms were established on 344 students between the ages of 0–3 and 7–11. These students attended nursery or public school, were from middle- or upper-income families in which standard American dialect was spoken and were judged by their teachers as not having handicapping conditions that would inhibit normal language development (Pearson & Stick, 1985).

Lee acknowledges these criticisms and recommends that the clinician use the instrument for its intended purpose, as a screening device for students speaking standard English. Lee also recommends that clinicians establish their own norms dependent on their local population (Lee, 1979).

REFERENCES

Klein, A.E. (1980). Test-retest reliability and predictive validity of the Northwestern Syntax Screening Test. *Educational & Psychological Measurement, 40,* 1167–1172.

Lee, L.L. (1979). *Northwestern Syntax Screening Test.* Evanston, IL: Northwestern University Press.

Pearson, M.E., & Stick, S.L. (1985). Review of Northwestern Syntax Screening Test. In J.V. Mitchell, Jr. (Ed.), *The ninth mental measurements yearbook* (pp. 1059–1063). Lincoln: University of Nebraska Press.

NUCLEAR MAGNETIC RESONANCE (NMR) OR MAGNETIC RESONANCE IMAGING (MRI)

Nuclear magnetic resonance (NMR) or magnetic resonance imaging (MRI) is a technique for imaging the brain and body parts. This technique is based on the premise that atomic nuclei with odd numbers of either protons or neutrons possess a small magnetic field that is dependent on the spin of these nuclear particles. With the application of a strong external magnetic source, there is a weak torque that is exerted on the nuclei; the nuclear particles orient to the applied magnetic field. During this alignment process, the nuclei oscillate about the magnetic field like a compass needle aligning with Earth's magnetic field. The degree of oscillation is directly related to the strength of the magnetic field. The degree of magnetic field resonance emitted can be detected by measuring the magnetic field changes, which in turn relate to the density of the tissue or structure being examined. At this point, the process becomes similar to computerized axial tomography (CAT scanning) in that a density coding system is used to create the image. In CAT scanning this is based on the number of X-ray particles that pass through tissue. In NMR or MRI the density is dependent on the resonance of atomic nuclear particles to different magnetic fields. The physics of this procedure are outlined in the works by Bottomley (1984) and Pykett, Newhouse, and Buonanno (1982).

The NMR technique provides an image that approximates anatomical appearance of the structure being imaged (see Figure 1). In comparison with CAT scanning, there are some major advantages. Since no ionizing radiation is used, there is no hazard from X-ray irradiation. The NMR image better differentiates certain tissue differences so that in NMR brain sections there is a clearer image between brain and bone and white and gray matter (see Figure 1). The NMR also allows the detection of subtle tissue changes that

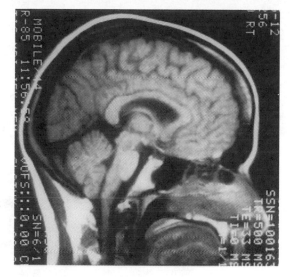

Figure 1. Sagittal section demonstrating NMR-MRI technique in visualizing cerebral structures. The detail obtained with NMR-MRI techniques approaches what would be observed with an actual anatomic specimen.

cannot be detected with CAT scanning and permits the topographic demonstration of the anatomic changes underlying neurobehavioral syndromes (DeMyer, Hendrie, Gilmor, & DeMyer, 1985; DeWitt, Grek, Buonanno, Levine, & Kistler, 1985). Current drawbacks to NMR include its cost, the fact that clinical studies are lacking, and the inability to scan patients with any type of metallic implants (i.e., pacemakers, artificial joints, aneurysm, clips, etc.) because of the strength of the magnetic field. Recent research has utilized this technology to visualize the development of perceptual and cognitive functioning (Thatcher, Lyon, Reid, Rumsey, & Krasnegor, 1996); to demonstrate the structural changes in psychiatric disorders such as schizophrenia (Potts, Davidson, & Krishnan, 1993); and to investigate higher cortical functions (Shaywitz, Shaywitz, Pugh & Skudlarski, 1996) and epilepsy (Cascino, 1998).

REFERENCES

Bottomley, P.A. (1984). NMR in medicine. *Computerized Radiology, 8,* 57–77.

Cascino, G.D. (1998). Neuroimaging in partial epilepsy: Structural magnetic resonance imaging. *Journal of Epilepsy, 11*(3), 121–129.

DeMyer, M.K., Hendrie, H.C., Gilmor, R.L., & DeMyer, W.E. (1985). Magnetic resonance imaging in psychiatry. *Psychiatric Annals, 15,* 262–267.

DeWitt, L.D., Grek, A.J., Buonanno, F.S., Levine, D.N., & Kistler, J.P. (1985). MRI and the study of aphasia. *Neurology, 35,* 861–865.

Potts, N.L.S., Davidson, J.R.T., & Krishnan, K.R.R. (1993). The role of nuclear magnetic resonance imaging in psychiatric research. *Journal of Clinical Psychiatry, 54*(12), 13–18.

Pykett, I.L., Newhouse, J.H., & Buonanno, F.S. (1982). Principles of nuclear magnetic resonance imaging. *Radiology, 143,* 157–163.

Shaywitz, B.A., Shaywitz, S.E., Pugh, K.R., & Skudlarski, P. (1996). Functional magnetic resonance imaging as a tool to understand reading and reading disability. In R.W. Thatcher, G.R. Lyon, J. Rumsey, & N. Krasnegor (Eds.), *Developmental neuroimaging: Mapping the development of brain and behavior* (pp. 157–167). San Diego, CA: Academic Press.

Thatcher, R.W., Lyon, G.R., Rumsey, J., & Krasnegor, N. (Eds.). (1996). *Developmental neuroimaging: Mapping the development of brain and behavior.* San Diego, CA: Academic Press.

See also Cat Scan; X-Rays and Handicapping Conditions; X-Ray Scanning Techniques

NUTRITIONAL DISORDERS

See MALNUTRITION, EATING DISORDERS, PICA.

O

OBESITY

Obesity is the most common nutrition-related problem in the United States today. Data from health and nutrition surveys indicate that the prevalence of obesity among adults ranges from 25 to 30% in various population groups. It is estimated that from 5 to 10% of school-age children and 10 to 15% of adolescents are obese (Pipes, 1985). The prevalence of obesity appears to be lower among low-income preschool children, but the trend is reversed for adolescents (Peck & Ullrich, 1985). There is a greater prevalence of obesity today than a decade ago (Meucke, 1992).

Obesity is defined most simply as excess body fat (Bray, 1979). It is characterized by an excessive deposition of adipose tissue. One criterion that is commonly used to indicate obesity is 20% above the recommended standard weight for height, age, and sex. Obesity is also classified by various authorities in relation to fat cell size and number, age when obesity first occurs, psychosocial factors, and degree of severity (Peck & Ullrich, 1985).

Peck and Ullrich (1985) cite psychological and social problems as the greatest health hazards for the obese child. Such problems include a poor self-image, sense of failure, and a passive approach to life. These authors point out that although health risks associated with childhood obesity are not so clear-cut, studies indicate that rigid weight control measures for children can interfere with normal growth and development, mental functioning, and reproductive capacity. The increase in disturbed eating behaviors such as anorexia nervosa and bulimia may be related to extreme and persistent weight reduction measures.

The fact that many obese children become obese adolescents and obese adults is cause for concern. Early onset obesity is usually more severe and resistant to treatment than adult onset obesity (Pipes, 1985) and is being linked to high-fat consumption/low physical activity lifestyles (Muecke, 1992). There is no evidence that psychopathology is the cause of obesity (Burgard, 1993).

Peck and Ullrich (1985) offer guidance for health professionals working with obese children. They suggest a progression of activities based on the magnitude and complexity of the problem. Any approach should be planned after assessment of the circumstances and needs of the person involved.

Regardless of other factors involved, excess weight results when more food energy is taken over time than is required for the growth, maintenance, and activity of the body. Preventive measures should be directed toward positive changes in attitude, lifestyle, and eating patterns in all segments of the population at risk of obesity. In addition, most school administrators and nurses believe that schools should be involved in weight management services (Stang, 1997).

REFERENCES

Bray, G.A. (Ed.). (1979). *Obesity in America.* Washington, DC: National Institutes of Health.

Burgard, D. (1993). Psychological theory seeks to define obesity. *Obesity & Health, 7*(2), 25–27.

Meucke, L. (1992). Is childhood obesity associated with high-fat foods and low physical activity? *Journal of School Health, 62*(1), 19–23.

Peck, E.B., & Ullrich, H.D. (1985). *Children and weight: A changing perspective.* Berkeley, CA: Nutrition Communications Associates.

Pipes, P.L. (1985). *Nutrition in infancy and childhood* (3rd ed.). St. Louis: Times/Mirror Mosby.

Stang, J. (1997). School-based weight management services: Perceptions and practices of school nurses and administrators. *American Journal of Health Promotion, 11*(3), 183–185.

See also Anorexia Nervosa; Eating Disorders

OBJECTIVE PERSONALITY TESTS

See PERSONALITY TESTS, OBJECTIVE.

OBSERVATIONAL LEARNING

Observational learning, the currently preferred term for imitation, is a basic process in the development of normal and abnormal behavior. As Bandura (1986) has said, "Through the years, modeling has always been acknowledged to be one of the most powerful means of transmitting values, attitudes, and patterns of thought and behavior" (p. 47). But that acknowledgment has not been explicit in many theories of learning, and only in recent decades has observational learning itself been extensively studied.

In Bandura's (1986) social cognitive analysis of observational learning, modeling is presumed to operate mainly by providing information. Bandura (1986) proposes a four-component model to account for observational learning. Because these processes become more sophisticated with age, observational learning shows important developmental trends. The processes may be briefly summarized:

Attentional Processes. In order to learn, one must attend to the modeled activities. Given the variety of models and other stimuli generally available, a child will selectively attend to relatively few. Observer factors that influence attention include perceptual capabilities and arousal level. Characteristics of the modeled activity such as conspicuousness and functional value also influence attention. Model characteristics and past experiences of the observer with the model are additional factors.

Retention. For delayed imitation to occur, the observer must be able to remember the modeled activity. Retention entails symbolic transformation into images and words. As with verbal material, transformation into meaningful terms and elaborated rehearsal facilitate retention of observed activities. Bandura (1986) stresses the importance of immediate and intermittent actual and cognitive rehearsal of observed activities.

Production Processes. Bandura (1986) suggests that "most modeled activities are abstractly represented as conceptions and rules of action which specify what to do" (p. 63). To produce the activity, responses must be organized in accordance with those conceptions and rules. A variety of evidence using verbal reports and recognition tests indicate that both children and adults can learn modeled activities without actually having performed them. Motor deficits may limit accurate imitation, and improvement may result from improvement in motor skills. Feedback is important in improving such skills. In complex motor skills such as those involved in playing a musical instrument, corrective modeling may be the most valuable. In corrective feedback, a skilled individual models the activity correctly; students then attempt to match it.

Motivational Processes. Behavior may be acquired through observational learning but not performed in the absence of appropriate incentive. Direct, vicarious, and self-produced rewards are all important in the actual production of learned responses, as is the observer's own motivation.

Modeled information can be acquired and retained without being immediately performed in the absence of appropriate incentives. For example, Bandura (1965) had groups of children watch a film in which a model displayed a high level of aggressive behavior toward another character. Different groups of children saw different endings to the film; the model was rewarded, punished, or suffered no consequences for aggressive behavior. In immediate testing, children who saw the model punished showed much less –aggressive behavior; girls were less aggressive than boys. However, when offered reinforcement for producing the modeled aggressive behavior, both boys and girls who saw all films reproduced a large number of the modeled behaviors. Thus, consequences to a model influence performance of modeled behaviors much more than learning of the behaviors.

Different models induce different degrees of imitation. Two factors that consistently appear as important in both experimental (Bandura, Ross, & Ross, 1963) and correlational (Hetherington & Frankie, 1967) research are power and warmth. Models are particularly likely to be imitated if they behave in an authoritative way, exerting control but showing care and concern.

An observer who is reinforced for imitating some modeled responses will also imitate other responses of the same model; this is important for the application of modeling techniques (Baer & Sherman, 1964). Thus a child who does not initially show high levels of imitation may be conditioned by appropriate reinforcement techniques to imitate in general.

Imitation begins to develop in infancy and becomes more exact during early childhood, with imitation of some responses developing earlier than others. For example, imitation of simple motor and social behaviors increases regularly from 12 to 24 months, whereas imitation of more complicated sequences may begin to occur only at 24 months or later (McCall, Parke, & Kavanaugh, 1977). Motor tasks not only use observation of the model, but self-observation as well (Ferrari, 1996).

Although most theories suggest that infants should not begin to imitate until several months of age, Meltzoff and Moore (1977) have reported that 12- to 20-day-old infants imitate simple facial expressions such as sticking out the tongue and gaping. Some subsequent studies failed to find any evidence for newborn imitation (McKenzie & Over, 1982), while others reported imitation in even younger infants (Field et al., 1982), leaving the phenomenon in considerable doubt.

A common recommendation to parents and teachers is to avoid using physical punishment with children because the punisher is providing a model of aggressive behavior that may be imitated by the child. Laboratory research (Gelfano et al., 1974) supports this recommendation. Young children imitate both punitive and reward control techniques, and the imitation persists over time.

Most children do imitate; others can be trained to imitate. Formal observational learning and reinforcement programs can be used to increase a variety of prosocial behaviors and to decrease antisocial or maladaptive ones. Additionally, children will imitate under informal circumstances. Teachers should remember that they generally have the characteristics that further imitation. If their behaviors are discrepant with their words, children are likely to follow the behaviors. "Do as I say and not as I do" is not likely to be successful. Finally, all who work with children would do well to remember that power and warmth, not power alone, are important characteristics of successful models.

REFERENCES

Baer, D.M., & Sherman, J.A. (1964). Reinforcement control of generalized imitation in young children. *Journal of Experimental Child Psychology, 1,* 37–49.

Bandura, A. (1965). Influence of models' reinforcement contingencies on the acquisition of imitative responses. *Journal of Personality & Social Psychology, 1,* 589–595.

Bandura, A. (1986). *Social foundations of thought and action: A social cognitive theory.* Englewood Cliffs, NJ: Prentice-Hall.

Bandura, A., Ross, D., & Ross, S.A. (1963). A comparative test of the status envy, social power, and secondary reinforcement theories of identificatory learning. *Journal of Abnormal & Social Psychology, 67,* 527–534.

Ferrari, M. (1996). Observing the observer: Self-regulation in the observational learning of motor skills. *Developmental Review, 16*(2), 203–240.

Field, T.M., Goodson, R., Greenberg, R., & Cohen, D. (1982). Discrimination and imitation of facial expressions by neonates. *Science, 28,* 179–181.

Gelfano, D.M., Hartmann, D.P., Lamb, A.K., Smith, C.L., Mahan, M.A., & Paul, S.C. (1974). The effects of adult models and described alternatives on children's choice of behavior management techniques. *Child Development, 45,* 585–593.

Hetherington, E.M., & Frankie, G. (1967). Effects of parental dominance, warmth, and conflict on imitation in children. *Journal of Personality & Social Psychology, 6,* 119–125.

McCall, R.B., Parke, R.D., & Kavanaugh, R.D. (1977). Imitation of live and televised models by children one to three years of age. *Monographs of the Society for Research in Child Development, 42*(5, Serial No. 173).

McKenzie, B., & Over, R. (1982). Young infants fail to imitate facial and manual gestures. *Infant Behavior & Development, 6,* 85–95.

Meltzoff, A., & Moore, M.K. (1977). Imitation of facile and manual gestures by human neonates. *Science, 198,* 75–78.

See also **Activity, Theory of; Behavior Modeling; Learning Styles; Phobias and Fears; Social Learning Theory**

OBSESSIVE COMPULSIVE DISORDERS

Obsession is defined by the American Psychiatric Association (1994) as, "A persistent, unwanted idea or impulse that cannot be eliminated by logic or reasoning" (p. 98). A compulsion is, "An insistent, repetitive, intrusive, and unwanted urge to perform an act that is contrary to one's ordinary wishes or standards. . . . Failure to perform the compulsive act leads to overt anxiety. Compulsions are obsessions that are still felt as impulses" (American Psychiatric Association, 1994, p. 20). In addition to the major attributes of obsession and compulsion, a number of additional responses are often present. Yaryura-Tobias and Nezirogly (1983) report that individuals who exhibit obsessive compulsive responses are also likely to be depressed (94%), anxious (90%), aggressive (65%), and dysperceptive (60%). Though occurring less frequently, individuals with obsessive compulsive disorders may also have sleep disorders (49%), family disturbances (45%), sexual dysfunctions (34%), or appetite disorders (33%); they may also be self-abusive (16%). Obsessive-compulsive disorder has been linked to pediatric autoimmune neuropsychiatric disorders related to rheumatic fever (Swedo, Leonard, Mittleman, & Allen, 1997).

The disorder has an extensive history in the psychological literature, with reports of obsessive compulsive behavior even appearing in ancient writings (Yaryura-Tobias & Nezirogly, 1983). It has also produced a substantial body of applied treatment research as illustrated in a review by Foa and Steketee (1980). Despite substantial professional interest, the incidence of obsessive-compulsive disorders is relatively low. Beech and Vaughan (1978) report that the incidence in psychiatric patient populations is between 0.1 and 4%. Among the general population, an incidence of approximately .05% has been reported (Black, 1974).

Common treatments have included psychotherapy, behavior therapy, pharmacological intervention, vitamin and diet therapy, and psychosurgery (Grados, Labuda, Riddle, & Walkup, 1997). Each approach has been demonstrated to be variably effective, and is more likely to be prescribed based on the orientation of the therapist rather than the clinical features of the individual.

REFERENCES

American Psychiatric Association. (1994). *A psychiatric glossary* (5th ed.). New York: Author.

Beech, H.R., & Vaughan, M. (1978). *Behavioral treatment of obsessional states.* New York: Wiley.

Black, A. (1974). The natural history of obsessional neurosis. In H.R. Beech (Ed.), *Obsessional states* (pp. 19–54). London: Methuen.

Foa, E.B., & Steketee, G.S. (1980). Obsessive compulsives: Conceptual issues and treatment interventions. In M. Hersen, R.M. Eisler, & P.M. Miller (Eds.), *Progress in behavior modification* (Vol. 8). New York: Academic.

Grados, M.A., Labuda, M.C., Riddle, M.A., & Walkup, J.T. (1997). Obsessive-compulsive disorder in children and adolescents. *International Review of Psychiatry, 9*(1), 83–98.

Swedo, S.E., Leonard, H.L., Mittleman, B.B., & Allen, A.J. (1997). Identification of children with pediatric autoimmune neuropsychiatric disorders associated with streptococcal infections by a marker associated with rheumatic fever. *American Journal of Psychiatry, 154*(1), 110–112.

Yaryura-Tobias, J.A., & Nezirogly, F.A. (1983). *Obsessive-compulsive disorders.* New York: Marcel Dekker.

See also **Emotional Disorders; Mental Illness**

OCCULOCEREBRAL-HYPOPIGMENTATION SYNDROME

See RARE DISEASES.

OCCUPATIONAL THERAPY

Occupational therapy is the art and science of directing man's participation in selected tasks to restore, reinforce, and enhance performance, facilitate learning those skills and functions essential for adaptation and productivity, diminish or correct pathology, and to promote and maintain health (p. 204–205, Council on Standards, 1972).

The primary concern of occupational therapy is response to activity. Special activities rather than exercise are used to increase function. These activities are purposeful and often medically prescribed. They may include manual, creative, or industrial arts. Occupational therapy activities are often part of the treatment plans for persons with physical, mental, and/or psychiatric disorders or disabilities. Although functional activity is the primary goal, the occupational therapist is equally concerned with the social, psychological, and communicative development of the patient.

Along with the implementation of PL 94-142 came the critical need for occupational therapists in public school settings. Here they became involved in direct services (e.g., screening, referral, evaluation, program planning and implementation, reevaluation, and formulation of individual education plans) and indirect services (e.g., administration and management and consultation) (American Occupational Therapy Association, 1980). This service continues today under IDEA (American Occupational Therapy Association, 1997). Many services that are critical to the development of severely handicapped children are provided by occupational therapists. The most important of these include the improvement of sensory integration, handling, and positioning. In many instances, it is necessary for the occupational therapist to adapt equipment for individuals. It is not uncommon for the occupational therapist to work with the physical therapist to provide services.

Increasing patients' daily living is another area for which occupational therapists assume responsibility. Patients may be physically disabled or developmentally delayed, young or old. Occupational therapists also may work with speech and language pathologists to develop strategies for improving oral motor functioning, thereby improving feeding and eating skills.

REFERENCES

American Occupational Therapy Association. (1980). Standards of practice for occupational therapists in schools. *American Journal of Occupational Therapy, 34,* 900–905.

American Occupational Therapy Association. (1997). *Occupational therapy services for children and youth under the Individuals with Disabilities Education Act (IDEA).* Bethesda, MD: Author.

Council on Standards, American Occupational Therapy Association. (1972). Occupational therapy: Its definition and functions. *American Journal of Occupational Therapy, 26,* 204–205.

See also **Career Education for the Handicapped; Physical Therapy; Rehabilitation**

OFFICE OF RARE DISEASES

The Office of Rare Diseases (ORD) is under the supervision of the National Institutes of Health. ORD offers information on more than 6,000 rare diseases, including research, publications, research resources, genetics information, patient support groups, reports on progress in research studies, and news and events. ORD has an extensive website on the internet that allows easy access to both the information that ORD disseminates and ORD itself. ORD can be reached at Office of Rare Diseases, National Institutes of Health, 31 Center Drive, MSC 2082, Room 1B03, Bethesda, MD, 20892–2082; telephone: 301–402–4336; fax: 301–402–0420; e-mail: sg18b@nih.gov; URL: http://rarediseases.info.nih.gov/ord.

OFFICE OF SPECIAL EDUCATION AND REHABILITATIVE SERVICES

The Office of Special Education and Rehabilitative Services (OSERS) supports programs that assist in educating children with special needs, provides for the rehabilitation of youth and adults with disabilities, and supports research to improve the lives of individuals with disabilities. To carry out these functions, OSERS consists of three program-related components:

The *Office of Special Education Programs* (OSEP) which has primary responsibility for administering programs and projects relating to the free, appropriate public education of all children, youth, and adults with disabilities, from birth through age 21.

The *Rehabilitation Services Administration* (RSA) which oversees programs that help individuals with physical or mental disabilities to obtain employment through the provision of such supports as counseling, medical and psychological services, job training, and other individualized services.

OSERS' third component, the *National Institute on Disability and Rehabilitation Research* (NIDRR) provides leadership and support for a comprehensive program of research related to the rehabilitation of individuals with disabilities.

All of the programmatic efforts are aimed at improving the lives of individuals with disabilities from birth through adulthood. The Office of Special Education and Rehabilitation Services maintains an extensive internet website at http://www.ed.gov/offices/OSERS/.

See also **Special Education Programs**

OLYMPICS, SPECIAL

The Special Olympics is the world's largest training and sports competition for individuals with mental retardation (Cipriano, 1980). Since its inception in 1968, over 2 million participants and volunteers have been involved in its local, regional, national, and international programs.

The goal of the Special Olympics is to train its participants to compete in individual and team sports. The Olympics emphasizes sportsmanship, skill development, cooperation through teamwork (Munson, 1997), working toward achieving athletic goals, competing for self-fulfillment. As is the case in the other Olympic Games, the importance of the Special Olympics lies in the training and preparation of individuals to compete, not in the games themselves. The games are intended to demonstrate the results of training progress (Henroid, 1979).

The first International Special Olympics was held in Chicago in 1968. There were 1000 competitors from 20 states and Canada on that occasion. By 1985 every state and 33 countries had organized Special Olympics training and competition programs. In the United States, over one million persons with mental retardation participate each year in local and state training and competition efforts in over 20,000 communities.

The International Special Olympic Games are held every 4 years. There are 16 different sports conducted during the summer and winter phases of the games. These include track and field, pentathlon, frisbee, swimming, diving, bowling, floor hockey, poly hockey, volleyball, team basketball, cheerleading, run-dribble and shoot, cross-country, soccer, equestrian, race walking, figure skating, alpine skiing, Nordic skiing, and snowshoeing.

A significant feature of the Special Olympics program is the large (now over 450,000 in number) volunteer force that organizes and administers the training and conditioning programs from local to international levels. The volunteers' tasks include fund-raising at the local and regional levels, transportation, and administrating local training clubs, as well as coaching and conducting competitions. Special Olympics volunteers come from schools, colleges, churches, social groups, and civil organizations such as the Rotary Club. They also come from the National Basketball and National Hockey professional sports leagues.

The International Special Olympic Games are fully sponsored by the Joseph P. Kennedy, Jr., Foundation. Local and regional programs and competitions preparing participants for the Special Olympics are funded through fund-raising efforts by the volunteer force. Contributions are secured from individual, group, and sources. The funds so raised are administered by a professional staff at regional and state Special Olympics offices.

REFERENCES

Cipriano, R. (1980). *Readings in Special Olympics.* Guilford, CT: Special Learning Corporation.

Henroid, L. (1979). *Special Olympics and Paraolympics.* New York: Watts.

Munson, D. (1997). The current research efforts of Special Olympics International. (ERIC Clearinghouse No. RCO20999)

See also **Equine Therapy; Recreation for the Handicapped; Therapeutic Recreation**

ON-LINE DATA BASES FOR SPECIAL EDUCATION

See APPENDIX.

OPERANT CONDITIONING

As conceived by Skinner (1938, 1948, 1953), operant conditioning is essentially learning in which behavior is affected by its consequences, as in the simple paradigm for positive reinforcement:

$$R \rightarrow SR$$

A contingency exists such that reinforcement (SR) occurs only if a particular response (R) has occurred. The contingent relationship between response and reinforcement is one of the factors that most differentiates operant from Pavlovian conditioning. The response becomes more frequent (increases in probability) when followed by a reinforcing stimulus. The paradigm is clearly related to Thorndike's (1911) Law of Effect, which says, in essence, that responses followed by satisfying consequences become more firmly connected to the situation. The classic example of operant conditioning is a rat in an operant chamber containing a lever. If the rat is deprived of food, presses the lever, and is reinforced with food, then lever presses increase. If the response is reinforced only in the presence of a specific stimulus, SD or discriminative stimulus, then the paradigm becomes:

$$S^D \rightarrow R \rightarrow S^R$$

For example, the rat may be reinforced (SR) for bar pressing (R) only when a light (SD) is on.

Skinner has proposed that the main task of psychology should be the functional analysis of behavior. That is, psychologists should determine of what antecedents and consequences behavior is a function. This approach has led to a model of behavior widely used by those who apply the operant approach to human behavior:

$$A \rightarrow B \rightarrow C$$

(Antecedents) (Behavior) (Consequences)

IMPORTANT ISSUES AND CONCEPTS

Nature of the Operant. Although we frequently talk about responses, Skinner's (1938) concept of the operant emphasizes a specified outcome rather than an actual response in terms of specific muscle movements. Thus if a child is reinforced for pushing a panel, panel-pushing is the operant. It does not matter whether the child presses with his or her left or right hand, left or right foot, or even the nose. The effects of behavior rather than the structure of the response itself are stressed.

Timing of Reinforcement and Punishment. Generally, reinforcing and punishing stimuli affect performance most if presented as soon as possible after the specified response. A reinforcing stimulus reinforces whatever response it immediately follows, such that a response that occurs between the target response and the reinforcement will be most reinforced. Punishment is actually most effective if delivered as the child just begins to make the undesirable response (Aronfreed, 1968).

In older children, time between response and reinforcement or punishment can be bridged by verbal mediators. At the time reinforcement or punishment is presented, words are used to reinstate the original situation where the child's behavior occurred. Aronfreed (1968) has demonstrated that such mediators increase the effectiveness of delayed punishment in inhibiting children's undesirable behavior.

Schedules of Reinforcement. Responses can be reinforced only intermittently rather then continuously (e.g., after every fourth response rather than after every response). One of Skinner's most important discoveries was that these partially reinforced responses are far more resistant to extinction than are 100% reinforced responses. Thus intermittent and unsystematic reinforcement increases the persistence of behavior. More detail on schedules and partial reinforcement can be found in most introductory or child psychology texts.

Primary vs. Conditioned (Secondary) Reinforcers. Primary reinforcers are stimuli that are intrinsically reinforcing such as food, water, and some kinds of tactile stimulation. Conditioned reinforcers are those stimuli that have acquired reinforcing power by being paired with another reinforcer. Thus money, grades, praise, and recognition are conditioned reinforcers. Conditioned reinforcers such as money can be very powerful because they are generalized reinforcers—they can be used to obtain a variety of other reinforcers.

Reinforcement History and Hierarchy. Different stimuli are reinforcing for different children and adults, making universal reinforcements hard to identify. Children will, partly as a result of their own histories, have different hierarchies of preferred reinforcers, although some items such as bubble gum are highly preferred by many young children. Further, reinforcement hierarchy generally changes with age: young children prefer tangible rewards, older children prefer social approval, and still older children prefer the intrinsic reinforcement from being correct (Witryol, 1971). However, tangible rewards may be more important for older low socioeconomic status children and for retarded children (Zigler, 1984), indicating that individual reinforcement hierarchies need to be considered in working with children.

Idiosyncrasies in reinforcer value led Premack (1965) to formulate a heuristic principle: preferred activities may be used to reinforce nonpreferred activities.

Positive and Negative Reinforcement. Reinforcement, by definition, increases behavior. Positive reinforcement occurs when a response is followed by presentation of a preferred event; negative reinforcement occurs when a response is followed by termination of an aversive event.

Shaping. Occasionally, a desired response may not be in the child's behavioral repertoire, in which case no response occurs that can be reinforced. In such cases, operant psychologists use shaping, or the method of successive approximations, to reinforce behaviors that increasingly resemble the target response.

IMPLICATIONS FOR EDUCATORS

Educators and others working with children should be sensitive to the effects of their behavior on children with whom they interact. Their behavior will frequently reinforce or punish children, sometimes inadvertently. Further, the child's perception determines whether a given event is rewarding or punishing. Using a common example, a teacher who yells at a misbehaving child views the yelling as a punisher, but to the child the attention may be reinforcing. On the other hand, to a very shy child, public recognition may be punishing. Of concern also is the possibility that adults will intermittently reinforce a child's undesirable response, therefore increasing its persistence and resistance to extinction.

In dealing with handicapped, particularly retarded, children, we need to consider that more tangible reinforcers and praise may be required to maintain performance than is the case with normal children.

REFERENCES

Aronfreed, J. (1968). Aversive control of socialization. In W.J. Arnold (Ed.), *Nebraska symposium on motivation* (pp. 271–320). Lincoln: University of Nebraska Press.

Premack, D. (1965). Reinforcement theory. In D. Levine (Ed.), *Nebraska symposium on motivation* (pp. 123–180). Lincoln: University of Nebraska Press.

Skinner, B.F. (1938). *The behavior of organisms: An experimental analysis.* New York: Appleton-Century-Crofts.

Skinner, B.F. (1948). *Walden two.* New York: Macmillan.

Skinner, B.F. (1953). *Science and human behavior.* New York: Macmillan.

Thorndike, A.E.L. (1911). *Animal intelligence.* New York: Macmillan.

Witryol, S.I. (1971). Incentives and learning in children. In H.W. Reese (Ed.), *Advances in child development and behavior* (Vol. 6). New York: Academic.

Zigler, E. (1984). A developmental theory on mental retardation. In B. Blatt & R.J. Morris (Eds.), *Perspectives in special education: Personal orientations* (pp. 173–209). Glenview, IL: Scott, Foresman.

See also **Behavior Modification; Conditioning; Generalization; Skinner, B.F.**

OPHTHALMOLOGIST

An ophthalmologist, sometimes called an oculist, is a medical doctor who specializes in the diagnosis and treatment of defects and diseases of the eye by prescribing lenses and, in some cases, drugs, performing eye surgery, and carrying out other types of medical treatment (Cartwright, Cartwright, & Ward, 1981, p. 71). Ocular disorders are of special significance because they often provide clues to the presence of systemic diseases and to other congenital malformations present in many handicapped children.

An important responsibility of the ophthalmologist related to serving visually impaired children and youths (which can also be performed by the optometrist) is a complete eye examination. This should include the following: developmental history, distance visual acuity, inspection of the eyes for evident physical problems, evaluation of ocular motility, determination of basic refractive status of the eyes, evaluation of accommodation of the eyes for near vision; visual field studies; testing of intraocular pressure; testing of color vision; and examination of the interior of the eye including the retina and vitreous (Goble, 1984; Nelson, 1984).

One of the subspecialists within the field of ophthalmology is a pediatric ophthalmologist, who focuses on the recognition, understanding, early treatment, and ultimately, prevention of ocular disease in childhood. This specialist is particularly skilled in areas such as visual development in the preverbal child, ocular genetics, amblyopia, and congenital cataracts (Nelson, 1984). He or she may be of particular value on multidisciplinary teams with special educators and parents to provide resources to meet the visually impaired child's developmental and educational needs.

REFERENCES

Cartwright, G.P., Cartwright, C.A., & Ward, M.E. (1981). *Educating special learners.* Belmont, CA: Wadsworth.

Goble, J.L. (1984). *Visual disorders in the handicapped child.* New York: Marcel Dekker.

Nelson, L.B. (1984). *Pediatric ophthalmology.* Philadelphia: Saunders.

See also **Developmental Optometry; Multidisciplinary Teams; Optometrist; Visual Acuity; Visually Impaired**

OPTACON

The optacon (optical-to-tactile converter) is a small electronic device that converts regular print into a readable vibrating form for blind people. When its tiny camera containing a transistorized retina lens module moves over print symbols, the image is converted to a tactual representation of the letter shape through vibrating pins. The blind person tracks the printed material using the camera with his or her right hand and reads the tactile image with the forefinger of the left hand, which is resting on the tactile array (Telesensory Systems, 1977).

Reading with the optacon is a slow process because the machine displays only one letter of a word at a time. It is not intended to replace braille. However, it provides the blind reader with instant access to printed matter such as personal mail, greeting cards, recipes, catalogs, applications for college or jobs, banking statements, bills, musical notation, and phone numbers. It also enables the blind student to read graphs and charts. In addition, there are special lens attachments that enable the blind user to read cathode-ray tubes and find employment using computers. Optacon use is not being taught in school programs as extensively as possible because of the time required and the wide variety of other skills needed by the visually handicapped student. In addition, braille translating programs in microcomputers are rapidly performing translation of data in multiple formats (Kapperman, 1997).

REFERENCES

Kapperman, G. (1997). *Project VISION: Visually impaired students and internet opportunities now.* Sycamore, IL: Research and Development Institute.

Telesensory Systems. (1977). *Optacon training: Teaching guidelines.* Palo Alto, CA: Author.

See also **Blind; Braille; Visually Impaired; Visual Training**

OPTOMETRIST (OD)

An optometrist (OD) is a licensed doctor of optometry who is trained to measure the refractive errors of the human eye and prescribe lenses to correct those refractive errors (Chalkley, 1982). Some optometrists specialize in prescribing lenses and other types of optical aids for low-vision students and spend a major portion of their professional time in low-vision clinics. These eye specialists work closely with special educators and base their decisions on information given and recommendations made by parents and other professionals on a multidisciplinary team. It is critical for the special educator and the optometrist to establish good communication to be sure that the student's corrective lenses are providing maximum vision for school activities. The aid of choice will vary, depending on the strength of the power needed, the visual fields and working distances required, and the low-vision student's motivation (Jose, 1983).

Some optometrists are involved in doing perceptual-motor training. The appropriateness of this role for the optometrist is questioned by many special educators.

REFERENCES

Chalkley, T. (1982). *Your eyes* (2nd ed.). Springfield, IL: Thomas.

Jose, R. (1983). *Understanding low vision.* New York: American Foundation for the Blind.

See also **Developmental Optometry; Multidisciplinary Teams; Ophthalmologist; Visually Impaired; Vision Training**

ORAL AND WRITTEN LANGUAGE SCALES

The Oral and Written Language Scales (OWLS; Carrow-Woolfolk, 1995) consists of measures of written expression, listening comprehension, and oral expression. The Written Expression Scale of the OWLS is normed for children through adults ages 5 to 21, and the Listening Comprehension and Oral Expression Scales are normed for children through adults ages 3 to 21.

The three scales of the OWLS were conormed on a sample of 1,795 children and young adults. The standardization sample was stratified to match basic demographic characteristics of the 1991 U.S. Census data, such as gender, race/ethnicity, religion, geographic region, and mother's education level. Mean internal consistency reliability values for each of the scales were 0.84 for Listening Comprehension, 0.87 for Oral Expression, and 0.87 for Written Expression. In examining the stability of the scales, the reliability coefficients were found to range from 0.73 to 0.80 for Listening Comprehension, from 0.77 to 0.86 for Oral Expression, and from 0.87 to 0.88 for Written Expression. Criterion-related validity was demonstrated with correlations to other measures of language and verbal ability. For example, the OWLS Language Composite correlated 0.88 with the CELF-R, 0.72 with the PPVT-R, and 0.77 with the WISC-III Verbal IQ.

There are several notable strengths of the OWLS. For example, its authors obtained clinical samples in addition to the standardization sample, so that statistical analyses could be performed to compare differences across the samples. Significant differences were, in fact, found between the control group and each of the following groups: language delayed, mentally handicapped, reading disabled, and hearing impaired. An additional strength of the test is that the content of the OWLS was carefully balanced for racial and gender representations and includes persons with physical differences. In addition, sensitivity to cultural and regional differences was built into the scoring methods, as the three OWLS scales do not penalize for regional and dialectic differences.

REFERENCE

Carrow-Woolfolk, E. (1995). *Oral and Written Language Scales: Listening Comprehension and Oral Expression.* Circle Pines, MN: American Guidance Service.

ORAL FACIAL DIGITAL SYNDROME (OFDS)

Oral facial digital syndrome (OFDS) appears to be a result of an X-linked chromosome that affects both males and females but that is said to be lethal in males. It is characterized by a midline cleft of the face with visibly abnormal structural defects of the mouth, teeth, tongue, and hands. Prominent clefting of the lips and palate and a marked lobulated tongue are highly visible; these may result in speech dysfunction. Teeth are abnormal. The nose tends to be broad and lacks demarcation from the skull. Growths may appear on the face and scalp hair may be sparse (Goodman & Gorlin, 1977). Fingers are broad, fused, and abnormal and extra fingers are often seen. Extremities may also have abnormal growth. No significant posture or neurological or motor problems are noted, although finger abnormalities may be apparent in fine motor development. In half of the cases, mild mental retardation is reported. No significant health problems are seen with this syndrome (Katzman, 1979; Lemeshaw, 1982).

Because deficits are so visible, counseling may be required and long-term emotional problems (particularly poor self-image) may be a result of this syndrome. For this reason, mainstreamed settings, while cognitively appropriate, may not be the optimal setting for a child with this syndrome. Team management of this child's educational plan will be necessary.

REFERENCES

Goodman, R., & Gorlin, R. (1977). *Medical aspects of mental retardation* (2nd ed.). Springfield, IL: Thomas.

Katzman, R. (Ed.). (1979). *Congenital and acquired cognitive disorders.* New York: Power.

Lemeshaw, S. (1982). *The handbook of clinical types in mental retardation.* Boston: Allyn & Bacon.

See also **Hurler's Syndrome; Mental Retardation; Physical Anomalies**

ORAL LANGUAGE OF THE HANDICAPPED

Language is defined as a coded set of rule-governed, arbitrary symbols, universally understood by a particular set of people and used to catalog or express ideas, objects, and events. There are five distinct but interlinked components of language: phonology, morphology, semantics, syntax, and pragmatics. Phonology refers to the rules associated with the ordering of phonemes. Phonemes are speech sounds that distinguish meaning in a language. For example, /m/ and /p/ are phonemes in English; if they are interchanged in words, there is a corresponding change in meaning. Morphology refers to the rules governing morphemes, the smallest meaningful units in language. There are free morphemes that can stand by themselves such as "happy" and "the," and bound morphemes that carry meaning but cannot stand by themselves. Prefixes such as un- and suffixes such as -ly are bound morphemes.

Semantics refers to the meaning of words in a language. Syntax describes the manner in which words are arranged in sentences. Pragmatics refers to the rules of communication in social interactions. The basic unit of pragmatics is a speech act; a behavior that communicates a single message. Speech acts include a locutionary act, an illocutionary act, and a perlocutionary act. A locutionary act is the actual surface form of the utterance and includes syntax, semantics, and phonology. The illocutionary act is the actual intent of the utterance. The perlocutionary act is the effect of the utterance on the listener.

Children with learning disabilities may display deficits in one or more of the following areas: oral expression, listening comprehension, written expression, basic reading skills, reading comprehension, mathematics calculation, or mathematics reasoning (Federal Register, 1977). Although language is one of many areas in which a child may evidence a learning disability, the ramifications are tremendous with language, as they may be associated with problems in reading, spelling, writing, and arithmetic. Preschool learning-disabled children are frequently not interested in verbal activities and may be delayed in their language development. Their syntax is primitive and may be accompanied by delays in the acquisition of morphological patterns. They may be unable to name pictures rapidly or identify colors, letters of the alphabet, days of the week, months of the year, and seasons (Bryen, 1981). School-aged learning-disabled children have an overall vocabulary that is within normal limits; however, they may have difficulty understanding that one object can be represented by several symbols. In addition, they may be unable to comprehend pronouns and the passive voice or to express comparative, spatial, and temporal relationships (Wiig & Semel, 1976).

Language impairment in an individual who is mentally retarded may reflect the degree of retardation. Investigators report that 45% of the mildly retarded, 90% of the severely retarded, and nearly 100% of the profoundly retarded have a language disability (Gomez & Podhajski, 1978; Schlanger, 1973; Spreen, 1965). Investigations of the language of the mentally retarded have yielded conflicting results. Lackner (1968) reported that retardation does not result in a different form of language; rather, language develops more slowly and terminates at a stage below that of a nonhandicapped child. Coggins (1979) and Miller and Yoder (1974) report similar findings. In contrast, Menyuk (1971) and Schiefelbusch (1972) report that retarded individuals use morphemes differently than their nonhandicapped peers. They do not generate rules of inflection; rather, they use only those inflections they have memorized through repeated use. Bliss, Allen, and Walker (1978) report limited use of the future tense, embedded sentences, and double-adjectival noun phrases.

Many researchers have demonstrated that hearing-impaired individuals are delayed in language acquisition (Goda, 1959; Myklebust, 1960; Pugh, 1946). However, it is still not clear whether hearing-impaired individuals develop language at a slower rate or whether their language is deviant. Investigators report that deaf children have smaller vocabularies than hearing peers and have difficulty with analogies, synonyms, and multiple meanings (Templin, 1963). Deaf children use more noun and verbs but fewer conjunctions and auxiliaries than hearing peers (Goda, 1964; Simmons, 1962). Results of studies of grammatical structure indicate difficulty with use of the passive voice (Power & Quigley, 1973), gerunds and infinitives (Quigley, Wilbur, & Montanelli, 1976), relative pronouns (Wilbur,

Montanelli, & Quigley, 1976), and verb constructions (Swisher, 1976). Pragmatic growth is also affected by hearing impairment. Deaf children have difficulty understanding how to communicate information to others, interact less frequently, and are less comfortable in social interchanges (Hoemann, 1972).

It is important to consider the interaction between the handicapping condition and delayed or deviant language development. For example, a child who evidences a language disorder may be unable to express feelings and concerns in a socially acceptable manner and may resort to disruptive and violent behaviors. Such a child may subsequently be labeled emotionally disturbed when, in fact, the language disability may be the primary handicapping condition. Conversely, a child evidencing Down's syndrome may be unable to respond appropriately to parental overtures of love and affection. Parents may find a lack of smiling and cooing discouraging and may inadvertently provide less verbal stimulation to their child. The child may subsequently be labeled mentally retarded but may also evidence a language disability. Educators are advised to consider the relationship between a handicap and a language disability when designing and implementing intervention strategies for handicapped children.

REFERENCES

Bliss, L., Allen, D., & Walker, G. (1978). Sentence structures of trainable and educable mentally retarded subjects. *Journal of Speech & Hearing Research, 20,* 722–731.

Bryen, D.N. (1981). Language and language problems. In A. Gerber & D.N. Bryen (Eds.), *Language and learning disabilities* (pp. 27–60). Baltimore, MD: University Park Press.

Coggins, T. (1979). Relationship meaning encoded in the two-word utterance of Stage I Down's syndrome children. *Journal of Speech & Hearing Research, 22,* 166–178.

Federal Register (1977, Dec. 29). (65082–65085.) Washington, DC.

Goda, S. (1959). Language skills of profoundly deaf adolescent children. *Journal of Speech & Hearing Research, 2,* 369–376.

Gomez, A., & Podhajski, B. (1978). Language and mental retardation. In C.H. Carter (Ed.), *Medical aspects of mental retardation* (pp. 51–65). Springfield, IL: Thomas.

Hoemann, H. (1972). The development of communication skills in deaf and hearing children. *Child Development, 43,* 990–1103.

Lackner, J.R. (1968). A developmental study of language behavior in retarded children. *Neuropsychologia, 6,* 301–320.

Menyuk, P. (1971). *The acquisition and development of language.* Englewood Cliffs, NJ: Prentice-Hall.

Menyuk, P. (1972). *The development of speech.* New York: Bobbs-Merrill.

Miller, J.F., & Yoder, D.E. (1974). An orthogenetic language teaching strategy for retarded children. In R.L. Schiefelbusch & L.L. Lloyd (Eds.), *Language perspectives-acquisition retardation, and intervention* (pp. 505–528). Baltimore, MD: University Park Press.

Myklebust, H. (1960). *The psychology of deafness.* New York: Grune & Stratton.

Power, D.J., & Quigley, S.P. (1973). Deaf children's acquisition of the passive voice. *Journal of Speech & Hearing Research, 16,* 5–11.

Pugh, G. (1946). Appraisal of the silent reading abilities of acoustically handicapped children. *American Annals of the Deaf, 91,* 331–335.

Quigley, S.P., Wilbur, R.B., & Montanelli, D.S. (1976). Complement structures in the language of deaf students. *Journal of Speech & Hearing Research, 19,* 448–466.

Schiefelbusch, R.L. (1972). Language disabilities of cognitively involved children. In J. Irwin & M. Marge (Eds.), *Principles of childhood language disabilities.* Englewood, NJ: Prentice-Hall.

Schlanger, B.S. (1973). *Mental retardation.* Indianapolis, IN: Bobbs-Merrill.

Simmons, A.A. (1962). A comparison of the type-token ratio of spoken and written language of deaf children. *Volta Review, 64,* 417–421.

Spreen, O. (1965). Language function in mental retardation. *Journal of Mental Deficiency, 69,* 482–489.

Swisher, L.P. (1976). The language performance of the oral deaf. In H. Whitaker & H.A. Whitaker (Eds.), *Studies in neurolinguistics* (pp. 53–93). New York: Academic

Templin, M.C. (1963). Vocabulary knowledge and usage among deaf and learning children. *Proceedings of the International Congress on Education of the Deaf.* Washington, DC: U.S. Government Printing Office.

Wiig, E., & Semel, E.M. (1976). *Language disabilities in children and adolescents.* Columbus, OH: Merrill.

Wilbur, R.B., Montanelli, D.S., & Quigley, S.P. (1976). Pronominalization in the language of deaf students. *Journal of Speech & Hearing Research, 19,* 120–140.

See also **Expressive Language Disorders; Language Deficiencies and Deficits; Language Delays; Language Disorders**

ORAL READING

Oral reading, or reading aloud, is a technique that is used frequently during reading instruction, especially in the early elementary school grades. Oral reading often occurs in small groups in which each child takes a turn reading aloud sections of text. Allington (1984) reports a general decline in the amount of oral reading across grade levels. The decline is more dramatic for good reader groups; poor readers spend proportionately more time reading orally than do good readers.

Oral reading has been used as a technique for reading practice, as an assessment technique, and as intervention for improving student reading motivation (Carr, 1995). Errors in reading aloud can be analyzed to determine what kind of instruction is needed. Much attention also has been given to the best procedures for handling oral reading errors.

Much debate has occurred over the relative merits and disadvantages of oral and silent reading. Some studies have suggested that the merits and disadvantages may vary as a function of the child's skill level. For example, Miller and Smith (1985) found that poor readers had higher comprehension scores when reading grade-level passages orally than when reading them silently, although performance levels were relatively low for both reading formats. Readers at a medium level of competence had higher comprehension scores when reading silently than orally; no differences were found for the best readers in the study. The researchers hypothesized that oral reading may improve the performance of poor readers by demanding attention to individual words.

Oral reading has been used frequently with handicapped children exhibiting difficulties. It provides practice for students who might otherwise not read; a method for teachers to determine the effects of their instruction; and a diagnostic function that indicates sources of difficulty for particular students (Jenkins, Larson, & Fleisher, 1983).

Several studies have been conducted on the effects of error correction procedures with handicapped students. In an investigation of the effects of two such procedures (word supply and phonic analysis) on elementary learning-disabled (LD) students' oral reading rates, Rose, McEntire, and Dowdy (1982) found both procedures generally more effective than no error corrections. The word supply procedure was found to be relatively more effective than the phonic analysis procedure. In contrast, delayed teacher attention to oral reading errors was more effective than immediate attention or no attention in reducing the number of uncorrected oral reading errors and increasing the number of self-corrections by moderately mentally retarded children (Singh, Winton, & Singh, 1985).

Allington (1984) notes that poor readers tend to receive instruction emphasizing accuracy over rate, fluency, or sensitivity to syntactic elements. Poor readers are corrected more quickly and more often than good readers, and are more often directed to surface level features of text. Poor readers have been found to make fewer self-corrections than good readers.

Another method to improve oral reading fluency is to have children read a passage silently before reading it aloud. However, classroom observations indicate that previewing is the exception, rather than the rule (Anderson, Hiebert, Scott, & Wilkinson, 1985).

Rose (1984; Rose & Sherry, 1984) and Sutton (1991) found previewing procedures (allowing the learner to read or listen to a passage prior to instruction and/or testing) to be effective in increasing oral reading rates of both elementary and secondary LD students.

REFERENCES

Allington, R.L. (1984). Oral reading. In P.D. Pearson (Ed.), *Handbook of reading research* (pp. 829–864). New York: Longman.

Anderson, R.C., Hiebert, E.H., Scott, J.A., & Wilkinson, I.A.G. (1985). *Becoming a nation of readers: The report of the Commission on Reading.* Champaign, IL: Center for the Study of Reading.

Carr, D. (1995). Improving student reading motivation through the use of oral reading strategies. (ERIC Clearinghouse No. CS012245)

Jenkins, J.R., Larson, K., & Fleisher, L. (1983). Effects of error correction on word recognition and reading comprehension. *Learning Disability Quarterly, 6*(2), 139–145.

Miller, S.D., & Smith, D.E.P. (1985). Differences in literal and inferential comprehension after reading orally and silently. *Journal of Educational Psychology, 77*(3), 341–348.

Rose, T.L. (1984). The effects of two prepractice procedures on oral reading. *Journal of Learning Disabilities, 17*(9), 544–548.

Rose, T.L., McEntire, E., & Dowdy, C. (1982). Effects of two error-correction procedures on oral reading. *Learning Disability Quarterly, 5*(2), 100–105.

Rose, T.L., & Sherry, L. (1984). Relative effects of two previewing procedures on LD adolescents' oral reading performance. *Learning Disability Quarterly, 7*(1), 39–44.

Singh, N.N., Winton, A.S.W., & Singh, J. (1985). Effects of delayed versus immediate attention to oral reading errors on the reading proficiency of mentally retarded children. *Applied Research in Mental Retardation, 6*(3), 283–293.

Sutton, P.A. (1991). Strategies to increase oral reading fluency of primary resource students. (ERIC Clearinghouse No. CS010683)

See also **Reading; Reading in the Content Areas; Reading Remediation**

ORAL VERSUS MANUAL COMMUNICATION

Oral versus manual communication refers to the debate surrounding the methodology used to educate individuals with hearing impairments. The oral method consists of speech reading, auditory training, speech, written expression, reading, and the use of common gestures (Chasen & Zuckerman, 1976). This method emphasizes maximum use of audition to develop the oral communication skills necessary for successful integration of hearing-impaired persons into society. The oral method has also been referred to as the auditory-oral, acoupedic, natural, and unisensory method (Bender, 1981). Strictly interpreted, the manual method includes the use of sign language, finger spelling, and common gestures. Rarely, however, do supporters of manual communication advocate exclusion of speech and speech reading; rather, they encourage simultaneous use of these methods (Pahz & Pahz, 1978).

Manual communication has been used interchangeably with total communication, a phrase coined in the late 1960s and formally adopted in 1976. Total communication actually refers to a philosophy of communication with and among hearing-impaired people. Deaf individuals select communication methods from a variety options including speech, speech reading, audition, finger spelling, sign language, reading, and written expression (Convention of Executives of American Schools for the Deaf, 1976).

Much of the debate surrounding oral and manual communication has focused on the merits of each. Advocates of oral communication express the following beliefs:

1. Maximum development of speech and speech-reading skills can be achieved only through maximum dependence on speech and speech reading. Using sign language interferes with the development of these skills.

2. Oral communication enhances integration into the mainstream of society. Use of sign language separates the child from family and friends (Berger, 1972).

3. A deaf child should be exclusively oral until it is established through repeated attempts that he or she cannot progress without some means of manual communication.

In contrast, advocates of manual communication express the following beliefs:

1. Oral communication gives the development of language a low priority after speech, speech reading, and auditory training.

2. Use of manual communication facilitates the development of language and other concepts and knowledge vital to normal mental development. Use of oral communication to learn language is a painfully slow process for most children and may waste many of the formative years necessary for language acquisition.

3. Reliance on speech reading to gain information is unreasonable as many speech sounds are not visible on the lips. Use of manual communication provides complete, accurate information that requires no educated guesses to fill in gaps.

Each of these methods has enjoyed a period of popularity only to be discarded in favor of the other in light of changes in public opinion or medical and technological advances. Participants in the oral/manual controversy have debated these methods for over 200 years.

Berger (1972) reported orally trained deaf students demonstrated speech-reading skills superior to those demonstrated by manually trained deaf students. Lavos (1944), in an early study, reported that orally trained students scored higher than their manually trained peers on language usage, arithmetic reasoning, and computation. Other studies have supported the use of manual communication. Manually trained deaf students have demonstrated superior performance on measures of word recognition (DiCarlo, 1964), reading (Delaney, Stuckless, & Walter, 1984; DiCarlo, 1964; Meadow; 1968; Orwid, 1970), speech reading (Delaney, Stuckless, & Walter, 1984; DiCarlo, 1964; Orwid, 1971), written language (Meadow, 1978; Orwid, 1971), and math (Chasen & Zuckerman, 1976; Delaney, Stuckless, & Walter, 1981; Meadow, 1968). It should be noted, however, that many of the manually trained students included in those investigations were educated in programs incorporating a philosophy of total communication. Therefore, they were encouraged to develop speech and speech-reading skills and to use any residual hearing.

It is apparent that no clear winner of the oral/manual debate has emerged as supporters on either side can easily document the superiority of their methods. This has led some school systems to offer a choice of communication options to hearing impaired students (Hawkins & Brawner, 1997). The trend appears to be toward manual methods as provided in programs embracing a philosophy of total communication. Whatever system the school system and educators propose, the future is colored by the growth and adherence to deaf culture (Gustason, 1997).

REFERENCES

Bender, R. (1981). *Conquest of deafness* (3rd ed.). Danville, IL: Interstate Printers.

Berger, K. (1972). *Speechreading: Principals and methods.* Baltimore, MD: National Educational Press.

Chasen, B., & Zuckerman, W. (1976). The effects of total communication and oralism in deaf third-grade "rubella" students. *American Annals of the Deaf, 121,* 394–402.

Convention of Executives of American Schools for the Deaf (1976). *Defining total communication.* Rochester, NY.

Delaney, M., Stuckless, E.R., & Walter, G.G. (1984). Total communication effects—A longitudinal study of a school for the deaf in transition. *American Annals of the Deaf, 129,* 481–486.

DiCarlo, L. (1964). *The deaf.* Englewood Cliffs, NJ: Prentice-Hall.

Gustason, G. (1997). Educating children who are deaf or hard of hearing: English-based sign systems. *ERIC Digest #E556.* Reston VA: ERIC Clearinghouse on Disabilities and Gifted Education.

Hawkins, L., & Brawner, J. (1997). Educating children who are deaf or hard of hearing: Total communication. *ERIC Digest #559.* Reston, VA: ERIC Clearinghouse on Disabilities and Gifted Education.

Lavos, G. (1944). The reliability of an educational achieved test administered to the deaf. *American Annals of the Deaf, 89,* 226–232.

Meadow, E. (1968). Early manual communication in relation to the deaf child's intellectual, social, and communication functioning. *American Annals of the Deaf, 113,* 29–41.

Orwid, H.L. (1971). Studies in manual communication with hearing impaired children. *Volta Review, 73,* 428–438.

Pahz, J.A., & Pahz, S.P. (1978). *Total communication.* Springfield, IL: Thomas.

***See also* Deaf Education; Sign Language Training; Total Communication**

ORDINAL SCALES OF PSYCHOLOGICAL DEVELOPMENT

The Ordinal Scales of Psychological Development (Uzgiris & Hunt, 1975) were designed to assess developmental abilities in infants up to 2 years of age. The scales were developed from a Piagetian principle that there is an invariant sequence of developmental landmarks, not linked to a specific age, that are characteristic of an infant's ability to manipulate and organize interactions with the environment (Gorrell, 1985). There are six basic abilities measured: (1) the development of visual pursuit; (2) the development of means for obtaining desired environmental events; (3) the development of vocal and gestural imitation; (4) the development of operational causality; (5) the construction of object relations in space, and (6) the development of schemes for relating to others.

Rosenthal (1985) has found the ordinal scales to have good reliabilities. Percentage of interrater agreement was found to be 96.1%, and agreement between sessions was

79.9%. The test was praised because it narrowed its focus for assessment, unlike its broad-ranged predecessors.

REFERENCES

Gorrell, J. (1985). *Test critiques* (Vol. 2). Kansas City: Test Corporation of America.

Rosenthal, A.C. (1985). Review of assessment in infancy: Ordinal Scales of Psychological Development. In J.H. Mitchell, Jr. (Ed.), *The ninth mental measurements yearbook* (Vol. 2). Lincoln: University of Nebraska Press.

Uzgirus, T.C., & Hunt, J. (1975). *Assessment in infancy: Ordinal Scales of Psychological Development.* Urbana: University of Illinois Press.

ORGANIZATIONAL CHANGE

During the remainder of this century, organizational change will be an important issue in special education. Organizational change refers to the process that any organizational unit (e.g., work group, department, school, school district) adapts to client needs, rules, regulations, and other factors. Organizational change acknowledges the fact that all organizational units are in flux and that they adapt to demands in either functional or dysfunctional ways. It is important for special education systems to be compatible and well-coordinated with regular education systems. Functional organizational change in special education, therefore, should take into account these important issues.

To accomplish functional organizational change, it is fundamental that a planned, systematic approach be employed by local level professionals. A planned, systematic approach is one that includes the following phases and constituent activities (Maher & Bennett, 1984):

Clarifying the Organizational Problem

1. Assessing the organizational problem
2. Assessing organization readiness for change
3. Defining the problem in measurable terms

Designing the Organizational Intervention

1. Describing purpose, goals, and objectives
2. Generating and selecting interventions to implement
3. Developing a written intervention design

Implementing the Organizational Intervention

1. Maximizing the degree to which the intervention is implemented in technically adequate, ethical, useful, and practical ways

Assessing the Organizational Intervention

1. Assessing the extent to which design elements were implemented
2. Assessing the extent to which goals of the interventions were attained

Process approaches to organizational intervention target relationships among organizational members for change (Beer, 1980). One approach to process intervention, survey feedback, encompasses both the collection of survey data and the communication of the survey's results to selected organizational members. Another process approach, team development, involves team members in a collaborative effort to improve their teams' effectiveness and efficiency. The system development process approach is intended to improve relationships between interdependent work teams. Though process consultation can overlap with the other process approaches, it is chiefly concerned with a consultant helping selected organizational members to understand and change problematic organizational processes.

Technostructural approaches to organizational change entail altering organizational structures as a means to improving worker satisfaction or productivity. One technostructural approach involves altering systems of reward, such as the manner in which wages or verbal praise are delivered to staff. The second technostructural approach is managing job performance. This approach may involve management by objectives (MBO), goal setting, performance appraisal, or performance review and development. Job design, also a technostructural approach, entails altering characteristics of work tasks or working conditions so that workers are more satisfied or productive. The fourth technostructural approach to intervention, organizational design, concerns making global structural changes such as decentralizing the decision-making process within an organization.

Organizational change focuses on the individual staff. An example of this approach, recruitment and selection, is concerned with matching the job role demands with abilities and skills of the individual. Another individual approach attempts to further organizational change by engaging individuals in continuing professional development activities. Finally, individual counseling can be used to reduce or alleviate interpersonal or personal problems that may be interfering with a staff's productivity (for a more extensive discussion of approaches to changing school organizations, see Maher, Illback, & Zins, 1984).

REFERENCES

Beer, M. (1980). *Organization change and development: A systems view.* Santa Monica, CA: Goodyear.

Maher, C.A., & Bennett, R.E. (1984). *Planning and evaluating special education services.* Englewood Cliffs, NJ: Prentice-Hall.

Maher, C.A., Illback, R.J., & Zins, J.E. (1984). *Organizational psychology in the schools: A handbook for professionals.* Springfield, IL: Thomas.

See also **Human Resource Development; Supervision in Special Education**

ORPHAN DISEASES

See LOW INCIDENCE HANDICAPS; NATIONAL ORGANIZATION OF RARE DISORDERS.

ORTHOGENIC SCHOOL

The Orthogenic School was established by Bettelheim (1950) to promote the application of Freudian principles of psychoanalysis to the treatment of behaviorally disordered children and youths. In the Orthogenic School of Bettelheim, teachers would create a permissive environment in which children could act on their impulses. Rather than correct behavior problems, teachers would work to help students achieve insight into their behavior through interpreting the symbolism of their actions. The Orthogenic School created a therapeutic milieu where the intrapsychic anxieties of troubled youths need not be contained. The Orthogenic School movement did not achieve widespread acceptance or implementation in special education circles although psychodynamic thought has influenced the development of various psychoeducational models of treatment in the schools.

REFERENCE
Bettelheim, B. (1950). *Love is not enough.* New York: Macmillan.

ORTHOPEDICALLY HANDICAPPED

With advances in legislation for individuals with disabilities (e.g., IDEA, Section 504 of the Rehabilitation Act), a greater number of orthopedically handicapped students are being included into regular or general education classes. In addition, students with multiple disabilities (e.g., severe mental retardation and cerebral palsy) are being served in public school settings with increasing frequency. The classroom teacher must take into account the specific needs of orthopedically handicapped students when planning instruction. An awareness of the types of orthopedic disabilities as well as intervention methods is useful for teachers of students with such disabilities.

Because the classroom teacher often has orthopedically handicapped students in class for most of the day, carry over of techniques used in special therapy sessions should occur in the classroom (Dykes & Venn, 1983). Classroom teachers should closely observe the general health and changes in health status of their students and make referrals as needed. Teachers should also be sensitive to and aware of negative attitudes of normal peers towards the child with orthopedic disabilities and adjust accordingly (Cohen, 1994). Knowledge of physical adaptations through consultations with specialists and attendance at in-service or preservice classes on management of the orthopedically handicapped will be necessary for the classroom teacher. Modification of instructional strategies and materials may be required to meet students' physical needs. Finally, awareness of the psychosocial aspects of physical disabilities (Carpignano, Sirvis, & Bigge, 1982) will be necessary in order to address the social and emotional needs of students with orthopedic handicaps. Indeed extracurricular activities should be encouraged to support social inclusion (Niva, 1994).

As technological advances in electronics and microcomputers continue, increased adaptation of seating, communication devices, and replacements for bracing equipment (e.g., the use of electronic stimulation) will be seen. Advances in medical care (e.g., computerized tomography [CT] scanners, position emission tomography [PET] scanners, computerized gait laboratories) will continue to allow doctors and physical therapists to make better use of their resources in managing neuromuscular problems in persons with handicaps. In addition, advances in surgical care will allow for more sophisticated analyses of pre- and postoperative conditions. In addition, prevention of deformities through surgery will continue to have successful results in coming years (Fraser & Hensinger, 1983). These advances will surely have an effect on students with orthopedic disabilities entering public school classrooms.

The teacher of students with orthopedic handicaps can provide appropriate instruction by working closely with specialists and providing carry over of techniques and adaptations suggested by specialists into the classroom. With a team approach in which all members of the staff, as well as the student where appropriate, have a share in program planning, education for students with orthopedic handicaps will allow such students to function as independently as possible.

REFERENCES

Carpignano, J., Sirvis, B., & Bigge, J. (1982). Psychosocial aspects of physical disability. In J.L. Bigge (Ed.), *Teaching individuals with physical and multiple disabilities* (2nd ed.) (pp. 110–137). Columbus, OH: Merrill.

Cohen, R. (1994). Preschoolers' evaluations of physical disabilities: A consideration of attitudes and behavior. *Journal of Pediatric Psychology, 19*(1), 103–111.

Dykes, M.K., & Venn, J. (1983). Using health, physical, and medical data in the classroom. In J. Umbreit (Ed.), *Physical disabilities and health impairments: An introduction* (pp. 259–280). Columbus, OH: Merrill.

Fraser, B.A., & Hensinger, R.N. (1983). *Managing physical handicaps: A practical guide for parents, care providers, and educators.* Baltimore, MD: Brookes.

Niva, W.L. (1994). The extent of participation in extracurricular activities at the secondary level of students with different exceptionalities in an urban school district. Paper presented at the International Conference of the Association for the Study of Cooperation in Education, Portland, OR, July 8–11, 1994.

See also **Cerebral Palsy; Multiply Handicapped; Spina Bifida**

ORTHOPSYCHIATRY

Orthopsychiatry is perhaps best described as a collaborative or interdisciplinary approach to the promotion of mental health and the study of human development. Psychiatrists, psychologists, educators, social workers, pediatricians, nurses, lawyers, and other professionals constitute the American Orthopsychiatric Association, founded in 1924. From its earliest years, orthopsychiatry as a field has served as a forum for uniting the contributions from many disciplines and attacking mental health problems with a unified approach (Levy, 1931).

Membership in the American Orthopsychiatric Association is open to all those working in the mental health fields who meet certain educational, or employment criteria. The association publishes the *American Journal of Orthopsychiatry,* a quarterly publication of selected theoretical, research, administrative and clinical articles; *Readings,* a journal of reviews and commentary; and the *Ortho Newsletter.* The American Orthopsychiatric Association is headquartered in New York City; it sponsors an annual meeting each spring.

REFERENCE

Levy, D.M. (1931). Psychiatry, and orthopsychiatry. *American Journal of Orthopsychiatry, 1,* 239–244.

See also **Ecological Assessment; Psychological Clinics, The; Psychology in the Schools**

ORTHOPSYCHIATRY MOVEMENT

Orthopsychiatry is a term that was adopted by a group of nine psychiatrists who first met in January 1924. The prefix ortho is a derivation of the Greek word for straight. Orthopsychiatry, therefore, literally means straight psychiatry. It was originally defined by the founding members as the "endeavor to obtain straightness of mind and spirt" (*American Orthopsychiatric Association,* 1985). By 1949 the American Orthopsychiatric Association (AOA) stated that "Orthopsychiatry connotes a philosophy . . . of interrelationships of various professions interested in learning about and shaping human behavior" (AOA, 1985). Since that time, it has "evolved to include the concepts of a preventive interdisciplinary approach and the interrelationship of social policy and mental health" (AOA, 1985).

The impetus to found the orthopsychiatry movement came from a group of psychiatrists, but it quickly moved to include psychologists and social workers (Lowrey, 1957). The initial meeting of the American Orthopsychiatric Association, held in Chicago in June 1924, had the topic of prevention as its major theme (Mohr, 1938). This interest in prevention became a primary focus of the movement, and was expanded on to include three types of prevention. "Primary prevention refers to preventing the disease before it begins. Secondary prevention involves diagnosing the disease and instituting immediate treatment. Tertiary prevention concerns itself with treatment efforts to prevent or minimize further progression of a chronic condition" (Wolman, 1977, p. 161). From the standpoint of prevention as well as of treatment, it soon became apparent that a need existed for services from more than one specialty or discipline. This need for teamwork among professionals was recognized and encouraged by the orthopsychiatry movement. Initially this teamwork was seen as being the strict domain of psychiatrists, psychologists, and social workers. The anticipated roles were for the psychiatrist to see the child, the social worker to counsel the parent, and the psychologist to perform needed testing. During the 1960s, as other disciplines became more involved in the counseling field, the movement expanded to include many other professionals.

The orthopsychiatric movement was a leader in the interdisciplinary approach to clinical practice, theory, research, and the study of social factors as they affect mental health.

Ortho has applied an interdisciplinary perspective to a wide range of issues affecting children, adolescents, adults, families, schools, and community mental health. Since the beginning, orthopsychiatry's philosophy has included an emphasis on prevention as well as treatment and has focused on the individual within the context of society. This broad-based interdisciplinary concept best characterizes orthopsychiatry and distinguishes it from the more specifically focused professional membership organization. (*Ortho: Interdisciplinary approaches to mental health,* 1985, p. 4)

REFERENCES

American Orthopsychiatric Association. (1985). Membership pamphlet. New York: Author.

Lowrey, L.G. (1957). Historical perspective. *American Journal of Orthopsychiatry, 27,* 223.

Mohr, G.J. (1938). Orthopsychiatry—fifteenth year. *American Journal of Orthopsychiatry, 8,* 185.

Ortho: Interdisciplinary approaches to mental health (1985, April). Paper presented at 62nd annual meeting of the American Orthopsychiatric Association, New York.

Wolman, B.B. (Eds.). (1977). *International encyclopedia of psychiatry, psychology, psychoanalysis, and neurology* (Vol. 8). New York: Aesculapius.

See also **Child Psychiatry; Clinical Psychology**

ORTON, SAMUEL T. (1879–1948)

Samuel T. Orton, a physician, is best known for his studies of children with severe reading disabilities. The children with whom he worked, although not otherwise handicapped, experienced extreme difficulty in acquiring the skills of reading, writing, spelling, or speech. Orton found that these language difficulties were constitutional and were often associated with confusion in direction, time, and sequence. Orton called this syndrome word blindness and set forth principles for its remediation. Teaching procedures developed by his associates, Anna Gillingham and Bessie W. Stillman, are widely used today in special education. The Orton Society, formed a year after Orton's death, carries forward the work that be began.

REFERENCES

Bulletin of the Orton Society. Pomfret, CT: Orton Society.

Orton, S.T. (1937). Reading, writing and speech problems in children. New York: Norton.

ORTON DYSLEXIA SOCIETY

See INTERNATIONAL DYSLEXIA ASSOCIATION.

ORTON-GILLINGHAM METHOD

The Orton-Gillingham method of teaching reading was developed by Anna Gillingham (Gillingham & Stillman, 1968) and is based on the theoretical work of the American neurologist Samuel Orton. Orton (1937) cultivated a special interest in dyslexic children (children of normal intelligence with a severe reading disability). He believed that weak associative power was central to these children's difficulties, stemming from incomplete suppression of the nondominant cerebral hemisphere. Gillingham translated these theories into a highly structured reading method that stresses the repeated association of individual phonemes with their sound, name, and cursive formation.

Often referred to as a multisensory approach (Oakland, Black, Stanford, Nussbaum, & Balise, 1998), the Orton-Gillingham method is one of several reading methods that emphasizes the phonetic regularities of English in its instructional sequence. It differs from other code-emphasis approaches by teaching letter sounds in isolation and requiring a considerable amount of individual letter blending (e.g., m-a-p = map). Its instructional format is highly repetitious. Within this method the teacher repeatedly combines reading with writing activities and relies heavily on drill techniques. The instructional materials include phoneme drill cards, phonetically regular word cards, syllable concept cards, little stories, and a detailed manual (Gillingham & Stillman, 1968).

Recent studies have found that students taught by this method for two years demonstrated significantly higher reading recognition and comprehension than control counterparts (Oakland et al., 1998). It has also been adapted for at-risk students learning a second language (Sparks, 1991).

REFERENCES

Gillingham, A., & Stillman, B. (1968). *Remedial teaching for children with disability in reading, spelling, and penmanship.* Cambridge, MA: Educator's Publishing Service.

Oakland, T., Black, J.L., Stanford, G., Nussbaum, N.L., & Balise, R. (1998). An evaluation of the dyslexia training program: A multisensory method for promoting reading in students with reading disabilities. *Journal of Learning Disabilities, 31,* (2), 140–147.

Orton, S.T. (1937). *Reading, writing, and speech problems in children.* New York: Norton.

Sparks, R.L. (1991). Use of the Orton-Gillingham approach to teach a foreign language to Dyslexic learning disabled students. *Annals of Dyslexia, 41,* 96–118.

OSBORN, ALEXANDER FAICKNEY (1888–1966)

Alexander Faickney Osborn, an advertising executive, financier, civic leader, author, and educator, was widely known for his emphasis on creativity as a teachable skill. He has been described as "a seminal thinker and gifted writer, whose clear and practical explanation of the basic concepts of creative thinking and problem solving would influence the thinking, teaching, and research of tens of thousands of others over at least a half-century" (Isaksen & Treffinger, 1985, p. 4). Among Osborn's accomplishments are his introduction and promotion of a technique of organized ideation called brainstorming and the development of a system for teaching creative problem solving.

His firm belief in the idea that people can be taught to become better creative thinkers led to the establishment of the Creative Education Foundation in Buffalo, New York (1954). The foundation was developed to disseminate information on the development of creative thinking skills and to sponsor the annual week-long Creative Problem Solving Institute. In 1967 the first issue of the *Journal of Creative Behavior,* a quarterly on creative development, was published by the foundation.

REFERENCES
Dodge, E.N. (Ed.). (1968). *Encyclopedia of American biography* (Vol. 38). New York: American Historical.

Isaksen, S.G., & Treffinger, D.J. (1985). *Creative problem solving: The basic course.* New York: Bearly.

Osborn, A.F. (1957). *Applied imagination. Principles and procedures of creative thinking.* New York: Scribner.

Staff. (1971). *The national cyclopedia of American biography.* (Vol. 53). New York: James T. White.

See also **Creative Problem Solving Institute**

OSGOOD, CHARLES E. (1916–1991)

Charles Osgood was born in Brookline, Massachusetts on November 20, 1916. He was a noted linguist, researcher, and Guggenheim fellow. He obtained his BA at Dartmouth College in 1939 and his PhD in psychology at Yale University in 1945. Osgood was an instructor at Yale from 1942 to 1945, conducted psychological research for the U.S. Air Force and Navy from 1946 to 1947, and was an assistant professor from 1946 to 1949. Beginning in 1950, Osgood was associated with the University of Illinois in Urbana as an associate professor (1950–1955), professor (1955–1981), and professor emeritus from 1981. Osgood also served as director of the Institute of Communication Research during his tenure there.

Osgood's model of verbal interaction provided the theoretical basis for the construction of ITPA (Illinois Test of Psycholinguistic Abilities), which was widely used in the late 1960s and 1970s for the assessment of children with learning disabilities. During his lifetime, Osgood authored or coauthored numerous publications, including *Measurement of Meaning* (1975), *Lectures on Language Performance* (1980), and *Language, Meaning, and Culture* (1990).

REFERENCES
Adams, F.M., & Osgood, C.E. (1973). A cross-cultural study of the affective meanings of color. *Journal of Cross-Cultural Psychology, 4*(2), 135–156.

Osgood, C.E. (1969). On the whys and wherefores of E, P, and A. *Journal of Personality and Social Psychology, 12*(3), 194–199.

Osgood, C.E. (1980). *Lectures on language performance.* New York: Springer-Verlag.

Osgood, C.E., Suci, G.J., & Tannenbaum, P. (1975). *Measurement of meaning.* Urbana, IL: University of Illinois.

Osgood, C.E., & Tzeng, O.C. (1990). *Language, meaning and culture: The selected papers of C.E. Osgood.* New York: Praeger.

OSTEOPOROSIS

Osteoporosis is the manifestation of the disorder known as osteopenia, meaning a reduction of bone mass (Behrman & Vaughan, 1983). Primary osteoporosis is most common in elderly postmenopausal women. Secondary osteoporosis is more common in inactive younger people such as hemiplegics, alcoholics, or those suffering from malnutrition. Adolescents possess several modifiable risk factors for osteoporosis (Lysen & Walker, 1997). Treatment with steroids and heparin may also cause the condition. It is generally asymptomatic until a fracture or cracking of a vertebrae has occurred while lifting a heavy object or from an unexpected jolt (Wandel, 1981).

Treatment of the condition may include dietary alteration, administration of sex hormones, and minerals to aid in calcification (Cooley, 1977; Rubin, 1985). Safeguards must be taught to both the individual and the family, including instruction on how to lift heavy objects safely. First-aid instruction for fractures is also essential (Wandel, 1981).

REFERENCES
Behrman, R., & Vaughan, V. (1983). *Nelson textbook of pediatrics* (12th ed.). Philadelphia: Saunders.

Cooley, D. (Ed.). (1977). *Family medical guide* New York: Better Homes and Gardens.

Lysen, V.C., & Walker, R. (1997). Osteoporosis risk factors in eighth grade students. *Journal of School Health, 67*(8), 317–321.

Rubin, K. (1985). *Osteoporosis in Prader-Willi syndrome.* Presentation at Prader-Willi Association National Conference, Windsor Locks, CT.

Wandel, C. (1981). *Diseases, the nurses' reference library series* Philadelphia: Informed Communications.

See also **Brittle Bone Disease; Prader-Willi Syndrome**

OTHER HEALTH IMPAIRED

Other health-impaired children include those pupils whose health problems severely affect learning. Federal law designates this group as including children with severe orthopedic impairments, illnesses of a chronic or acute nature that require a prolonged convalescence or that limit that child's vitality and strength (Acquired Immune Deficiency Syndrome), congenital anomalies (e.g., spina bifida or clubfoot), other physical causes (e.g., amputation or cerebral palsy), and other health problems including, but not limited to, hemophilia, asthma, severe anemia, and diabetes. This category constitutes about 4% of those children classified as handicapped (Ysseldyke & Algozzine, 1984). In addition, the overrepresentation of ethnic minorities in this category is much smaller than other categories, such as learning disabilities (Coulter, 1996).

Other health impairments may the be result of congenital defects or adventitious (acquired) disabilities. The tremendous heterogeneity associated with the term requires attention to the one obvious common factor of such children, a physical condition that interferes with normal functioning by limiting the child's opportunity to participate fully in learning activities by affecting the body's supply of strength and energy or the removal of wastes; by reducing mobility; and by creating severe problems in growth and development (Kneedler, Hallahan, & Kauffman, 1984).

REFERENCES

Coulter, A. (1996). Alarming or disarming: The status of ethnic differences within exceptionalities. Paper presented at the Annual Convention of the Council for Exceptional Children, Orlando, Florida, April 1–5, 1996.

Kneedler, R.D., Hallahan, D.P., & Kauffman, J.M. (1984). *Special education for today.* Englewood Cliffs, NJ: Prentice-Hall.

Ysseldyke, J.E., & Algozzine, B. (1984). *Introduction to special education.* Boston: Houghton Mifflin.

See also **Diabetes; Education for "Other Health Impaired" Children; Physical Disabilities; Spina Bifida**

OTIS-LENNON SCHOOL ABILITY TEST, SIXTH EDITION

The sixth edition of Otis-Lennon School Ability Test (OLSAT; Otis & Lennon, 1990) is the most recent in a series that began over a half-century ago with the publication of the Otis Group Intelligence Scale. The OLSAT is designed to assess individuals' abilities to cope with school learning tasks and to suggest their possible placement for school learning functions. The test may be administered to those in kindergarten through the twelfth grade.

All items in the OLSAT-Sixth Edition are new. The items are grouped into five clusters: Verbal Comprehension, Verbal Reasoning, Pictorial Reasoning, Figural Reasoning, and Quantitative Reasoning.

The OLSAT was standardized on a sample of approximately 175,000 students. Internal consistency estimates of reliability for the Total, Verbal, and Nonverbal scores range from the .70s to the low .90s across all grade levels. The reliability estimates for the clusters are lower with one as low as .24 and some in the .60s. Swerdlik (1992) noted that no data on the stability of scores are available. Anastasi (1992) noted that the treatment of the validity data uses an outdated approach, and that it would be beneficial to have an integrated, comprehensive discussion of validation procedures. Although there are limitations of this group-administered school ability test, the OLSAT represents a technically adequate test for screening purposes with a variety of strengths (Swerdlik, 1992).

REFERENCES

Anastasi, A. (1992). Review of the Otis-Lennon School Ability Test, Sixth Edition. In J.J. Kramer & J.C. Conoley (Eds.), *The eleventh mental measurements yearbook* (pp. 623–635). Lincoln, NE: Buros Institute of Mental Measurements.

Otis, A.S., & Lennon, R.T. (1990). *Otis-Lennon School Ability Test, Sixth Edition.* San Antonio, TX: The Psychological Corporation.

Swerdlik, M.E. (1992). Review of the Otis-Lennon School Ability Test, Sixth Edition. In J.J. Kramer & J.C. Conoley (Eds.), *The eleventh mental measurements yearbook* (pp. 635–639). Lincoln, NE: Buros Institute of Mental Measurements.

See also **Achievement Tests; Deviation IQ; Intelligence Testing**

OTITIS MEDIA

Otitis media is an inflammation or infection of the middle ear. Nasal secretions back up and infect the Eustachian tube so that the air pressure in the middle ear is no longer equalized and a partial vacuum is created, causing an impairment in hearing. The infection can also be caused by the puncturing of the eardrum. There are three types of otitis media—acute, serous, and chronic.

Acute otitis media and serous otitis media are the most prominent causes of conductive hearing loss in children. The symptoms of acute otitis media include ear pain, hearing loss, aural discharge, and a sensation of fullness in the ear. While commonly occurring in infants and children, it may occur at any age. The onset usually follows an upper respiratory tract infection. Fever is usually present. The common treatment is bed rest, analgesics, and antibiotics. Ear drops are usually of limited value but local heat is helpful. Oral decongestants may also hasten relief. Acute otitis media, if properly treated with antibiotics, usually is resolved. If treatment is terminated prematurely, resolution of the infection may be incomplete and a conductive hearing loss may persist. Studies suggest that chronic conditions, regardless of onset, can significantly interfere with language/speech acquisition (Cowley, 1996; Johnson, 1997).

Serous otitis media is characterized by the accumulation of fluid in the middle ear that results in a temporary hearing loss. The absence of fever and pain distinguish it from acute otitis media. The hearing loss is characterized by a plugged feeling in the ear and a reverberation of the patient's voice. Treatment consists of nasal decongestants. Antihistamines may be given if a nasal allergy is suspected as the cause. Tonsillectomy and adenoidectomy may be necessary to permanently correct the condition (Bluestone, 1982).

Chronic otitis media is nearly always associated with perforation of the eardrum. There are two types of chronic otitis media: benign and that which is associated with mastoid disease (Shaffer, 1978). The latter is more serious by far and is characterized by a foul smelling drainage from the ear as well as impaired hearing. If chronic mastoiditis occurs in infancy, the mastoid bone does not develop a good cellular structure. Antibiotic drugs are usually of limited use in combatting the infection, but they may be useful in treating complications. Local cleansing of the ear with antibiotic powders and solutions is one method of treatment. Surgery may be needed in other cases. The complications of chronic otitis media and mastoiditis may be meningitis and sinus thrombosis.

REFERENCES

Bluestone, C.D. (1982). Otitis media in children: To treat or not to treat? *New England Journal of Medicine, 306,* 1399.

Cowley, J. (1996). Longitudinal studies—Are they worth it? *Australian Research in Early Childhood Education, 1,* 225–226.

Johnson, D.L. (1997). The effects of early otitis media with effusion on child cognitive and language development at ages three and five. Paper presented at the Biennial Meeting of the Society for Research in Child Development, Washington, DC: April, 3–6

Shaffer, H.L. (1978). Acute mastoiditis and cholesteatoma. *Otolaryngology, 86,* 394.

See also **Deaf; Expressive Language Disorders; Language Delays**

OTOLARYNGOLOGIST

An otolaryngologist is a specialist who can treat diseases of and perform surgery on the ear, nose, and throat. An otolaryngologist may be consulted for disorders that might manifest themselves as speech or hearing disorders. An examination by an otolaryngologist will require an inspection of the nose, neck, throat, head, and ears. The otolaryngologist will locally anesthetize the area of the nose and use a series of probes to check for blockages and mucus. The Eustachian tubes are then checked for their functional efficiency. The physician checks for thick bands of adhesions or growths of adenoid tissue in the fossae of Rosenmueller behind the tubal openings. Using a tongue depressor and a mirror these can be seen by looking up the nasopharynx. The entire interior of the mouth is examined, including the teeth and tongue. Finally, the ears are examined using an otoscope (Sataloff, 1966).

The otolaryngologist may work in cooperation with other specialists. An audiologist may be consulted to do a hearing examination and consider nonsurgical remedies for a hearing problem or postsurgical services. A speech pathologist may work with an otolaryngologist for nonsurgical remedies for speech difficulties or for postsurgical services (Northern & Downs, 1974).

REFERENCES

Northern, J.L., & Downs, M.P. (1974). *Hearing in children.* Baltimore, MD: Williams & Wilkins.

Sataloff, J. (1966). *Hearing loss.* Philadelphia: Lippincott.

See also **Deaf; Otitis Media; Speech Pathologist**

OTOLOGY

Otology is the study of diseases of the ear. This includes deafness and other hearing defects as well as ear aches, discharges, and infections of the mastoid. An otologist is a medical doctor who specializes in the treatment of these diseases and problems. An otologist can diagnose causes of hearing problems and recommend medical and surgical treatments. An otologist may have an MD (doctor of medicine) or a DO (doctor of osteopathy) degree.

An otologic examination will involve far more than just an examination of the ear because the cause of some symptoms may lie in the nose, neck, or throat. An initial examination begins with a case history. Surgery for correction of otosclerosis and ossicular defects leaves no detectable scars; therefore questions regarding such surgery are necessary in taking a health history. Since otology deals with diseases of the ear, an otologist may call in an otolaryngologist to assist with a case when the source of the condition might originate in the nose or throat. An otolaryngologist deals with symptoms and diseases in which there is some relationship among the ear, nose, and throat.

See also **Deaf; Otitis Media; Otolaryngologist**

OTOSCLEROSIS

Otosclerosis is a common conductive hearing loss that occurs with the onset of middle age. The eardrum and middle ear appear to be normal through an otoscope. What develops, however, is the formation of spongy bone in the cochlear bone. The cause is unknown. Otosclerosis can occur without a resultant hearing loss. This occurs when otosclerotic changes affect areas of the bony labyrinth other than the oval window. When a hearing loss is associated with otosclerosis, it is referred to as clinical otosclerosis. The condition develops over a period of months or even years. The hearing gradually diminishes as the footplate becomes more fixed. In some cases, the hearing loss stops after reaching only a mild level. More frequently, the hearing loss stabilizes at 50 to 60 dB. The hearing deficit starts in the lower frequencies and progresses to the higher ones (Davis & Silverman, 1974).

Otosclerosis is a condition more common in females than in males and the symptoms may be aggravated by pregnancy. The condition is often found in several people in the same family. While there may be a genetic linkage to the condition in some cases, prediction based on genetic theory is not refined. Offspring of two people with otosclerosis have been found to have normal hearing. The condition could occur in just one ear. Surgery may help to restore some of the hearing loss (Sataloff, 1966).

REFERENCES

Davis, H., & Silverman, S.R. (1974). *Hearing and deafness.* New York: Holt, Rinehart, & Winston.

Sataloff, J. (1966). *Hearing loss.* Philadelphia: Lippincott.

See also **Deaf; Deaf Education; Otitis Media**

OVERACHIEVEMENT AND SPECIAL EDUCATION

Aside from those areas where children possess superior skills or abilities, overachievement would not usually be considered associated with special education. Achievement below normal performance, or underachievement, is more common, and most areas of special education focus on the inability to learn. For example, the mentally retarded, learning disabled, and emotionally disturbed manifest conditions that adversely affect educational performance; children with speech and language problems who are unable to comprehend language or express themselves adequately have difficulties in learning; and the physically impaired (e.g., those with hearing impairments, visual impairments, and health impairments) exhibit handicaps that affect achievement.

Special education has generally focused on these children's deficiencies, but in addition to weaknesses, these children also have strengths. It is these strengths that allow the special child to overachieve in some areas. For example, moderately retarded children generally do not learn to read beyond a first-grade level (Kirk & Gallagher, 1983). However, some of these children do read at higher levels. This ability to read at higher levels is probably owed to individual strengths in reading ability. In all likelihood, this reading ability would not demonstrate overachievement when compared with the normal population, but when compared with these children's other abilities, it may well demonstrate overachievement. Therefore, overachievement in special education must be considered in relation to each child's abilities and disabilities.

REFERENCE

Kirk, S.A., & Gallagher, J.J. (1983). *Educating exceptional children* (4th ed.). Boston: Houghton Mifflin.

See also Underachievement

OVERACHIEVEMENT AND THE GIFTED

While considerable attention has been given to the problems of the underachieving gifted student, overachievement in the gifted remains poorly defined. Generally, a discrepancy criterion is used to categorize students where a gap between expectation (as measured by aptitude and intelligence tests) and performance (as measured by achievement tests) indicates that a student is under or overachieving. Lack of uniformity in the measurement criteria makes it difficult to establish clear categories, and a child who may qualify as overachieving according to one system may be excluded when a different system is used (Tannenbaum, 1983).

Some reviewers identify psychosocial factors that may contribute to discrepancies between expectation and performance such as family dynamics (Gover, 1991). Whitmore (1980) suggests that the overachieving gifted student is more able to control feelings of academic anxiety, feels more adequate and confident, and has feelings of greater self-value than an underachieving counterpart. Furthermore, the overachieving gifted student tends to be more interested in academic pursuits than in social activities. Asbury (1974) found no consistent psychosocial factors underlying discrepant achievement. Interestingly, Tannenbaum (1983) proposes that any discrepancy between expectation and performance in the direction of overachievement points to an error in the measurements determining expectations. Overachievement is thus an "illusion resulting quite clearly from underprediction." Inasmuch as measures of expectation purport to indicate a child's capacity, it would seem that overachievement places a student in the absurd position of performing beyond his own capacity.

REFERENCES

Asbury, C.A. (1974). Selected factors influencing over- and underachievement in young school-age children. *Review of Educational Research, 44,* 409–428.

Gover, F.J. (1991). Children of alcoholics/addicts: Children at risk. Paper presented at the Annual Meeting of the California Peer Counseling Association, Anaheim, CA, March 4–5, 1991.

Tannenbaum, A.J. (1983). *Gifted children: Psychological and educational perspectives.* New York: Macmillan.

Whitmore, J.R. (1980). *Giftedness, conflict and underachievement.* Boston: Allyn & Bacon.

OVERCORRECTION

Overcorrection refers to a punishment procedure and includes the systematic application of prescribed strategies to decrease the future occurrence of targeted behaviors. An overcorrection package may include verbal reprimands, time-out from positive reinforcement, short verbal instructions, and graduated guidance. The two major procedures of overcorrection are restitution and positive practice. Restitution means restoring the environment or oneself to a state that is vastly improved relative to the prior condition. Positive practice involves the repeated practice of certain forms of behaviors relevant to the content in which the behavior occurred (Hobbs, 1985).

Foxx (1982) describes three characteristics of overcorrection acts, including the existence of a direct relationship to the student's misbehavior; implementation immediately following the misbehavior; and rapid administration of overcorrection acts. While administering overcorrection acts, the teacher employs a full or partial graduated guidance form of assistance followed by a shadowing procedure as the program develops. In a full graduated guidance technique, the teacher maintains full contact with the student's hands. In partial graduated guidance, the teacher uses a thumb and forefinger to gently guide the movements of the student. Eventually, the teacher shadows the student by placing a hand in close proximity to the student's hand and initiating contact only when the student fails to complete the movements of the overcorrection act.

In a review of behaviors that have been targeted for over-correction acts, Ferretti and Cavalier (1983) summarized the reported effectiveness with eating skills, toileting skills, aggressive-disruptive behaviors, stereotype behaviors, and self-injurious behaviors. In these research reports, the individual components of each overcorrection package of strategies were not evaluated. However, general observations of the effectiveness of overcorrection procedures were favorable. Overcorrection acts have been successfully implemented with individuals with mental retardation, autism, emotional handicaps, and behavioral disorders (Tyson & Spooner, 1991).

REFERENCES

Ferretti, R.P., & Cavalier, A.R. (1983). A critical assessment of over-correction procedures with mentally retarded persons. In J.L. Matson & F. Andrasik (Eds.), *Treatment issues and innovations in mental retardation* (pp. 241–301). New York: Plenum.

Foxx, R.M. (1982). *Decreasing behaviors of severely retarded and autistic persons* (pp. 91–111). Champaign, IL: Research Press.

Hobbs, S.A. (1985). Overcorrection. In A.S. Bellack & M. Hersen (Eds.), *Dictionary of behavior therapy techniques* (pp. 158–160). New York: Pergamon.

Tyson, M.E., & Spooner, F. (1991). A retrospective evaluation of behavioral programming in an institutional setting. *Education and Training in Mental Retardation, 26*(2), 179–189.

See also **Behavior Modeling; Behavior Modification; Destructive Behavior**

P

PALMAR CREASE

Human palms are covered by creases of different depths, lengths, and directions. The flexion creases are formed during early intrauterine life and are thought to be influenced by factors causing anomalies in the embryo. Variations in appearance of the palmar creases have been linked to certain medical disorders. Therefore, alterations have medical diagnostic value and usually are included in dermatoglyphic analysis. The three main creases have been the primary focus of most investigations. They are the radial longitudinal or thenar crease, the proximal transverse, and the distal transverse.

A single crease across the palm of the hand frequently is described as characteristic of Down's syndrome (Robinson & Robinson, 1965; Telford & Sawery, 1977). The proximal and distal transverse creases are replaced or joined into a single crease that transverses the entire palm. This has been referred to as a single palmar crease, single transverse fold, four finger line, or simian crease. The frequency of the single palmar crease ranges between 1 and 15% in controlled populations and possibly higher in groups with developmental defects (Schaumann & Alter, 1976). Researchers noted that the variability in appearance makes determination difficult and may partially account for the wide range in reported frequency.

REFERENCES

Robinson, H.B., & Robinson, N.M. (1965). *The mentally retarded child: A psychological approach.* New York: McGraw-Hill.

Schaumann, B., & Alter, M. (1976). *Dermatoglyphics in medical disorders.* Heidelberg, Germany: Springer-Verlag.

Telford, C.W., & Sawery, J.M. (1977). *The exceptional individual.* Englewood Cliffs, NJ: Prentice-Hall.

See also **Down's Syndrome; Physical Anomalies**

PARAPLEGIA

Paraplegia is a term used to describe a physical condition in which the individual is unable to functionally use the lower extremities of the body. The term describes the topography of the impairment and does not suggest the etiology of the physical limitations, which may be of varied origin (Best, 1978).

The environmental experience, is regarded as part of the educational process, will be impaired if provision for available alternatives to independent ambulation are not provided. The younger child with paraplegia who is deprived of free exploration of the environment may be impeded in concept development (Connor, Williamson, & Siepp, 1978). For the toddler, a device such as a scooter board or crawl-a-gator may assist in active environmental exploration. This device consists of a board on which casters are mounted. The child lies prone on the device and propels himself or herself around the floor by pushing the ground with the upper extremities. The older child may begin to use a wheelchair or a parapodium. The latter device allows the child and preadolescent with paraplegia to ambulate in an upright position to more freely explore and learn. Training in donning (putting on) and duffing (removing) the parapodium is essential to increasing the independent functioning of the individual. With developed upper extremities, the parapodium can also be used to climb stairs.

Within the classroom, a standing table may be used to support the child in an upright position, freeing the upper extremities for manual exploration of learning materials, and concomitantly avoiding static positioning. This table is ideal for use in the classroom where academics may require writing and other skills requiring hand use and lower body support. Thus for the special educator to accommodate the needs for education and management of the individual with paraplegia, a comprehensive understanding of methods and materials necessary to circumvent the functional impairedness becomes essential. This management includes positioning, locomotion, and the ability to attend in a learning situation, free from the distraction imposed by the disability. This also must occur on a case-by-case method to be successful (Mulcahey, 1992), and prevent further health complications (Herrick, Elliot, & Crow, 1994).

REFERENCES

Best, G.A. (1978). *Individuals with physical disabilities: An introduction for educators.* Saint Louis: Mosby.

Connor, F.P., Williamson, G.G., & Siepp, J.M. (1978). *Program guide for infants and toddlers with neuromotor and other developmental disabilities.* New York: Teacher's College Press.

Herrick, S.M., Elliott, T.R., & Crow, F. (1994). Social support and the prediction of health complications among persons with spinal cord injuries. *Rehabilitation Psychology, 39*(4), 231– 250.

Mulcahey, M.J. (1992). Returning to school after a spinal cord injury: Perspectives from four adolescents, *American Journal of Occupational Therapy, 46*(4), 305–312.

See also **Cerebral Palsy; Muscular Dystrophy; Spina Bifida**

PARAPROFESSIONALS

Various descriptors have been used to identify the paraprofessional in special education. MacMillan (1973) has identified as potential paraprofessionals, nonprofessional adults, older children in the role of tutor, and parents. Tucker and Horner (1977) identify a paraprofessional as any person other than the teacher who is engaged in providing educational opportunities for handicapped children. While not considered a fully trained professional, the paraprofessional is one who is expected to possess certain competencies that will promote a higher quality and more effective educational program for the handicapped.

The use of paraprofessionals in the special education classroom was first reported in the 1950s (Cruickshank & Haring, 1957). The conclusions drawn from this investigation were that the teachers who had paraprofessionals assigned to their classrooms felt that they were able to do a better job of teaching. The administrators of these programs concurred with this opinion, as did the parents of the children, who felt their children had profited from the presence of a paraprofessional in the classroom. In the 1960s, as a result of professional and legislative efforts, there emerged an increased interest in the establishment of a number and variety of educational services for the handicapped. As a result of this, there was an immediate critical shortage of professional personnel to meet the rapid expansion of special education programs (President's Panel on Mental Retardation, 1962). The paraprofessional was viewed as a potential solution to this problem (Blessing, 1967).

The position of the paraprofessional in special education programs has usually been one of a subordinate. The paraprofessional is expected to carry out his or her assigned duties in tandem with the fully trained professional. The assumption is that while paraprofessionals may be a valuable addition to the overall program, the teacher must be regarded as the one ultimately responsible for the teaching function. However, paraprofessionals have been used in a variety of ways in the educational setting. Their duties have usually encompassed activities such as clerical work, supervision of nonacademic activities, housekeeping, acting as parent surrogates, and sometimes even as active teachers engaged in the instructional process under the supervision of the trained teacher (Blessing, 1967; French & Pickett, 1997; Greer & Simpson, 1977; MacMillan, 1973).

Concerns for the extension of educational programs to a population of handicapped that has been unserved in an educational setting (e.g., the severely and profoundly handicapped) has created a potential new role for the less than baccalaureate trained (paraprofessional) teacher. Although Sontag, Burke, and York (1976) feel that teachers working with the severely handicapped should be rigorously trained and possess a number of specific and precise competencies, Burton and Hirshoren (1979) view the use of well-trained paraprofessionals as teachers as a resolution of problems that are indigenous to this level of programming (e.g., available manpower, individualization of instruction, and teacher burnout). Tucker and Horner (1977) have acknowledged the need for well-trained paraprofessionals in programs for the severely handicapped and agree that it is impractical to rely on fully trained teachers to provide the individualized instruction that is necessary in these programs.

While enjoying considerable discussion, the paraprofessional role in special education has not been clearly defined. However, the role continues to be evaluated, especially in light of inclusive practices (Doyle, 1997).

REFERENCES

Blessing, K.R. (1967). Use of teacher aides in special education: A review and possible application. *Exceptional Children, 34,* 107–113.

Burton, T.A., & Hirshoren, A. (1979). The education of the severely and profoundly retarded: Are we sacrificing the child to the concept? *Exceptional Children, 45,* 598–602.

Cruickshank, W., & Haring, N. (1957). *A demonstration: Assistants for teachers of exceptional children.* Syracuse, NY: Syracuse University Press.

Doyle, M.B. (1997). *The paraprofessional's guide to the inclusive classroom: Working as a team.* Baltimore, MD: Brookes.

French, N.K., & Pickett, A.L. (1997). Paraprofessionals in special education: Issues for teacher educators. *Teacher Education and Special Education, 20*(1), 61–73.

Greer, B.B., & Simpson, G.A. (1977). A demonstration model for training noncertified personnel in special education. *Education & Training of the Mentally Retarded, 12,* 266–271.

MacMillan, D.L. (1973). Issues and trends in special education. *Mental Retardation, 11,* 3–8.

President's Panel on Mental Retardation. (1962). *A proposed program for national action to combat mental retardation.* Washington, DC: U.S. Government Printing Office.

Sontag, E., Burke, P.J., & York, R. (1976). Considerations for serving the severely handicapped in the public schools. In R.M. Anderson & J.G. Greer (Eds.), *Educating the severely and profoundly retarded.* Baltimore, MD: University Park Press.

Tucker, P.J., & Horner, R.D. (1977). Competency based training of paraprofessionals training associates for education of the severely and profoundly handicapped. In E. Sontag, J. Smith, & N. Certo (Eds.), *Educational programming for the severely and profoundly handicapped.* Reston, VA: Council for Exceptional Children.

See also; **Teacher Effectiveness**

PARENTAL COUNSELING

Counseling parents of handicapped children has taken a number of different forms. Variations in counseling strategies reflect diverse professional orientations as well as differing family dynamics and needs. Because new challenges often arise as the child's disability interacts with increased demands at different developmental stages, counseling is frequently a recurrent need in families with handicapped children.

Increasingly, two theoretical notions, or frameworks, have informed many of the counseling approaches available to parents of handicapped children: stages of grief theory and family systems theory. Regardless of the particular approach (educational, psychotherapeutic, or parent training), many of those who counsel parents have been guided by, or at least sensitized by, one or both of these frameworks. The first reflects the prevalent view that many, if not all, parents of handicapped children undergo some version of a mourning process in reaction to their child's disability. To varying degrees, this represents a loss of the hoped for intact, healthy child. Variations on Kubler-Ross's (1969) stages of grief theory have been proposed to explain parents' emotional journey toward productive adjustment to their child's handicapping condition (Seligman, 1979). These mourning stages include denial of the existence, the degree, or the implications of the disability; bargaining, often evident in the pursuit of magical cures or highly questionable treatments; anger, often projected outward onto the spouse or the helping professional or projected inward, causing feelings of guilt and shame; depression, manifest in withdrawal and expressions of helplessness and inade-

quacy; and acceptance, the stage in which productive actions can be taken and positive family balances maintained. It is commonly believed that any of the earlier stages can be reactivated by crises or in response to the child's or the family's transitions from one developmental stage to another.

Family systems theory, particularly Minuchin's structural analysis (Minuchin, Rosman, & Baker, 1978) and Haley's (1973, 1976, 1980) strategic approach provides another highly valued conceptual framework for counseling. Within this framework, families are seen as interdependent systems whose problems are relational. This view offers concepts and techniques for considering the effects on all parts of the family of intervention with one member or with one subsystem. By focusing on the dynamics of a family's structure, hierarchy, and stage in the family life cycle, family systems theory offers a more complex, and therefore more accurate, understanding of the functioning, development, and needs of a particular family with a handicapped child (Foster, Berger, & McLean, 1981).

Both family systems theory and stages of grief theory are widely applicable conceptual influences within family counseling. Neither of these frameworks mitigates against using any of a wide variety of other educational, psychotherapeutic, or parent training methods to promote growth in families with handicapped children.

REFERENCES

Foster, M., Berger, M., & McLean, M. (1981). Rethinking a good idea: A reassessment of parent involvement *Topics in Early Childhood Special Education, 1*(3), 55–65.

Haley, J. (1973). *Uncommon therapy.* New York: Norton.

Haley, J. (1976). *Problem-solving therapy.* San Francisco: Jossey-Bass.

Haley, J. (1980). *Leaving home.* New York: McGraw-Hill.

Kubler-Ross, E. (1969). *On death and dying.* New York: Macmillan.

Minuchin, S., Rosman, B., & Baker, L. (1978). *Psychosomatic families.* Cambridge, MA: Harvard University Press.

Seligman, M. (1979). *Strategies for helping parents of exceptional children.* New York: Free Press.

See also **Family Counseling; Parent Effectiveness Training; Psychotherapy**

PARENT EDUCATION

Parents rarely receive direct instruction in how to parent. For many, such knowledge comes from their own personal experience of being parented, and from the advice of grandparents, friends, and neighbors. Parents of abused and neglected children are often reported to lack both effective parenting skills (Wolfe, 1985) and a social network of friends and neighbors who could be helpful with child rearing (Polansky, Gaudin, Ammons, & Davis, 1985).

The purposes of parent education programs are to help parents develop greater self-awareness, use effective discipline methods, assist in early intervention training programs

(Peterson & Cooper, 1989) improve parent-child communication, make family life more enjoyable, and provide general information on child development (Fine, 1980). Parent education is distinguished from parent therapy in that parent education is time-limited and has behavior change as a goal rather than personality change (Dembo, Sweitzer, & Lauritzen, 1985). Approaches have been developed from a wide variety of theoretical orientations, including behavioral (Becker, 1971; Patterson & Gullison, 1971), Adlerian (Dreikurs & Soltz, 1964), systematic training for effective parenting (Dinkmeyer & McKay, 1976), transactional analysis (James, 1974), humanistic (Ginott, 1965, 1968) and parent effectiveness training (Gordon, 1975). Each of these programs is delivered in a group format; all include reading materials for parents, demonstrations of techniques, and discussions of technique applications.

Given the variety of education programs available, program evaluation is essential. Dembo, Sweitzer, and Lauritzen (1985) published an extensive review of 48 evaluation studies. Only five studies comparing different educational approaches were identified in a Dembo et al. review, one comparing Adlerian and behavioral approaches, the other four comparing behavioral and PET approaches. These studies failed to find any significant differences between approaches. Each of these approaches focuses on changing parent behaviors and attitudes toward their children. They were developed prior to the current child-effects Zeitgeist in child development research (Bell, 1979); their effectiveness could possibly be improved by consideration of children's effects on their parents and by treating the family as a unit. Other concerns raised by Dembo et al. in their review involve the effectiveness of these programs with differing cultural groups including teenage mothers (Kissman, 1992), the lack of attention by researchers and program developers to differing needs of parents, the assessment of aptitude-treatment interactions, and the lack of methodological rigor in the majority of studies.

REFERENCES

Becker, W.C. (1971). *Parents are teachers.* Champaign, IL: Research Press.

Bell, R.Q. (1979). Parent, child, and reciprocal influences. *American Psychologist, 34,* 821–826.

Dembo, M.H., Sweitzer, M., & Lauritzen, P. (1985). An evaluation of group parent education: Behavioral, PET, and Adlerian programs. *Review of Educational Research, 55,* 155–200.

Dinkmeyer, D., & McKay, G. (1976). *Systematic training for effective parenting.* Circle Pines, MN: American Guidance Service.

Dreikurs, R., & Soltz, V. (1964). *Children: The challenge.* New York: Hawthorn.

Fine, M.J. (1980). The parent education movement: An introduction. In M.J. Fine (Ed.), *Handbook on parent education.* New York: Academic.

Freeman, C.W. (1975). Adlerian mother study groups: Effects on attitudes and behavior. *Journal of Individual Psychology, 31,* 37–50.

Ginott, H.G. (1965). *Between parent and child.* New York: Macmillan.

Ginott, H.G. (1968). *Between parent and teenagers.* New York: Macmillan.

Gordon, T. (1975). *P.E.T.: Parent effectiveness training.* New York: American Library.

James, M. (1974). *Transactional analysis for moms and dads.* Reading, MA: Addison-Wesley.

Kissman, K. (1992). Parenting skills training: Expanding school-based services for adolescent mothers. *Research on Social Work Practice, 2*(2), 161–171.

Patterson, G.R., & Gullison, M.E. (1971). *Living with children.* Champaign, IL: Research Press.

Peterson, N.L., & Cooper, C.S. (1989). Parent education and involvement in early intervention programs for handicapped children. *Educational Psychology, 17,* 197–234.

Polansky, N.A., Gaudin, J.M., Ammons, P.W., & Davis, K.B. (1985). The psychological ecology of the neglectful mother. *Child Abuse & Neglect, 9,* 265–275.

Wolfe, D.A. (1985). Child-abusive parents: An empirical review and analysis. *Psychological Bulletin, 97,* 462–482.

See also **Family Response to a Child with Disabilities; Family Therapy; Parent Counseling; Parent Effectiveness Training**

PARENTING SKILLS

Parents of students with disabilities are faced with needs not apparent to parents of students without identifiable disabilities. They are no longer passive recipients of services but assume a strong advocacy role on behalf of their children. Specifically, skills to be developed include learning to reduce stress, being involved in the individualized education plan (IEP), following through on home programming, helping the child to interact with friends and siblings, and managing behavior.

Active participation by parents is an encouraged and mandated aspect of the IEP. This participation occurs through systematic contact with school personnel regarding rights and responsibilities of home and school representatives. At the basic level, identification, evaluation, and placement decisions involve a due process component to ensure that decision outcomes are acceptable to all involved parties. Increasingly, teachers are assuming the role of consultant to parents and viewing the parents as the real experts in their child's life. With this perspective, teachers are initiating extensive questionnaires for parents to complete prior to the IEP conference. Included in these questionnaires are activities that are pinpointed as having the highest value to the parents for their child's development. Thus communication skills between home and school environments are essential for optimum development of the IEP.

A common characteristic of students with handicapping conditions is the lack of generalization from school to community-based settings without active planning. Accordingly, parents are increasingly solicited to continue teaching their child in the skills being addressed at school. Principles of applied behavior analysis common to many school-based programs can be acquired by parents to ensure continuity of instruction. These instructional strategies may include prompting hierarchies, reinforcement schedules, and task modifications. Increasingly, parents are provided training in these areas when the child is very young (Hanson, 1977).

Parents express concern about the impact of a child with handicaps on siblings and peers in the neighborhood (Powell & Ogle, 1985). Developing friendships, participating in community activities, and interacting with family members are activities that contribute to a quality of life for individuals with disabilities. Parents are obtaining information and support to foster these relationships through peer support groups, journals such as *Exceptional Parent,* peer tutors, community integration specialists, and parent training seminars.

REFERENCES

Hanson, M.J. (1977). *Teaching your Down's syndrome infant: A guide for parents.* Baltimore, MD: University Park Press.

Powell, T.H., & Ogle, P.A. (1985) *Brothers and sisters: A special part of exceptional families.* Baltimore, MD: Brookes.

See also Family Response to a Child with Disabilities; Individual Education Plan (IEP); Siblings of the Handicapped

PARENTS OF THE HANDICAPPED

Parents of handicapped children and youths have been one of the most influential factors in the education of and the delivery of services to handicapped youngsters throughout the history of special education. Over the past decade, groups organized by parents have been described as trailblazers in the crusade to win full acceptance of children with handicaps as human beings. These organizations have gained strength through painstaking and often self-sacrificing efforts. Parents have helped other parents, started schools, collected funds, collected facts and figures for unmet needs, lobbied for reforms, and initiated community services.

At the same time, parents persistently encouraged educators to recognize their rights as parents to seek relief for their children and to pass laws that would meet the needs of handicapped children (Webster, 1976). PL 94-142 and subsequent amendments and legislation such as IDEA mandate parental rights and involvement in the education of handicapped children and youths. Martin (1979) summarized these rights, as follows.

Children with disabilities are entitled to an independent educational evaluation that will be considered when placement and program decisions are made. Parents have the right to be told where an independent evaluation may be obtained at no expense or low expense, to have the agency pay for the independent evaluation if the agency's evaluation is not appropriate, and to be informed of the procedures for obtaining an independent evaluation at public expense and the conditions under which such an evaluation may be obtained.

Parents have the right to notice before the agency initiates, or changes (or refuses to initiate or change), the identification, evaluation, or placement of the child; to have that notice in writing, in their native language, or other principal mode of communication, at a level understandable to the general public; to have the notice describe the proposed action and explain why those other options were rejected; and to be notified of each evaluation procedure, test, record, or report the agency will use as a basis for any proposed action. Parents also have the right to give or withhold consent before an evaluation is conducted and before initial placement is made in special education; to revoke consent at any time; and to forfeit to the agency to proceed in the absence of consent to a hearing to determine if the child should be initially placed.

Parents are entitled to request an impartial due process hearing to question the agency's identification, evaluation, or placement of the child, or to question the agency's provision of a free appropriate public education; to be told of any free or low-cost legal or other relevant services available (e.g., experts on handicapping conditions who may be a witness at the hearing); to have the hearing chaired by a person not employed by a public agency involved in the education of the child or otherwise having any personal or professional interest in the hearing; to see a statement of the qualifications of the hearing officer; to be advised and accompanied at the hearing by counsel and to be accompanied by individuals with special knowledge or training in problems of the handicapped; to have the child present; to have the hearing open to the public; to present evidence and confront, cross-examine, and compel the attendance of witnesses; to prohibit the introduction of any evidence at the hearing that has not been disclosed at least five days before the hearing, to have a record of the hearing; to obtain written findings of fact and a written decision within 45 days after the initial request for the hearing; to appeal to the State Board of Education and receive a decision within 30 days of filing of an appeal; to have a hearing and an appeal set at a time reasonably convenient to the parent; to appeal a decision from the State Board of Education in court; and to have the child remain in his or her present educational placement during the pending of the administrative proceeding, unless parent and agency agree otherwise.

Parents also have the right to have a full and individual evaluation of the child's educational needs; have more than one criterion used in determining an appropriate educational program; have the evaluation performed by a multidisciplinary team; have child assessed in all areas related to the suspected disability; have a reevaluation every 3 years or more often if conditions warrant or if the parent or the child's teacher requests it.

Parents of handicapped children are entitled to have their child educated with nonhandicapped children to the maximum extent possible; have their child removed from the regular educational environment only after supplementary aids and services are tried and found unsatisfactory; have a continuum of alternate placements so that removal from the regular educational environment can be the least necessary deviation; have available supplementary services such as a resource room or itinerant instruction to make it possible for their child to remain in regular class placement; have their child placed within the school that he or she would attend if nonhandicapped unless the individual education plan requires some other arrangement; have their child participate with nonhandicapped children in nonacademic and extracurricular services and activities such as meals, recess, counseling, clubs, athletics, and special interest groups.

It is important that parents restrict access to their child's records by withholding consent to disclose records; be informed before information in their child's file is to be destroyed; and be told to whom information has been disclosed. In addition, the law stipulates that parents or guardians must be involved in developing the individualized education program (Turnbull & Schulz, 1979).

The roles of parents of handicapped children have been outlined as advocates, resources, teachers, and counselors by Knoblock (1983), Heyward and Orlansky (1984), Brown and Moersch (1982), Nowland (1971) and Volenski (1995). Parents may obtain information and listings of state and local agencies serving handicapped individuals from the U.S. Department of Education and the Office of Civil Rights.

REFERENCES

Brown, S., & Moersch, M. (1982). *Parents on the team.* Ann Arbor: University of Michigan Press.

Heyward, W., & Orlansky, M. (1984). *Exceptional children: An introductory survey of special education* (2nd ed.). Columbus, OH: Merrill.

Knoblock, P. (1983). *Teaching emotionally disturbed children.* Boston: Houghton Mifflin.

Martin, R. (1979). *Educating handicapped children: The legal mandate.* Champaign, IL: Research Press.

Nowland, R. (1971). *Counseling parents of the ill and handicapped.* Springfield, IL: Thomas.

Turnbull, A., & Schulz, J. (1979). *Mainstreaming handicapped students: A guide for the classroom teacher.* Boston: Allyn & Bacon.

Volenski, L.T. (1995). Building school support systems for parents of handicapped children. *Psychology in the Schools, 32*(2), 124–129.

Webster, E. (1976). Professional approaches with parents of handicapped children. Springfield, IL: Thomas.

See also Buckley Amendment; Family Counseling; Family Response to a Child with Disabilities; Individuals with Disabilities Education Act (IDEA); Special Education, Legal Regulation of

PARKHURST, HELEN (1887–1973)

Helen Parkhurst devised the Dalton Plan and founded the Dalton School in New York City. The essence of the Dalton Plan, based on Parkhurst's concept of the school as a laboratory where students are experimenters and not just participants, was individualization of instruction through student contracts, with each student working individually at his or her own pace to carry out contracted assignments.

Early in her career, Parkhurst studied with Maria Montessori in Italy; from 1915 to 1918 she supervised the development of Montessori programs in the United States. She left the Montessori movement to put her own educational plan into practice at schools in Pittsfield and Dalton, Massachusetts. She founded the Dalton School in 1920 and served as its director until her retirement in 1942. Parkhurst lectured throughout the world and established Dalton schools in England, Japan, and China. Her book, *Education on the Dalton Plan,* was published in 58 languages. After retiring from the Dalton School, Parkhurst produced radio and television programs for children and conducted a discussion program in which she gave advice on family life.

REFERENCE

Parkhurst, H. (1922). *Education on the Dalton Plan.* New York: Dutton.

PARTIALLY SIGHTED

The term partially sighted was used to classify and place students in special classes whose distance visual acuity was between 20/70 and 20/200 in the better eye after correction (Hatfield, 1975). In 1977 the classifications of levels of vision adopted by the World Health Organization omitted the use of partially sighted in its system (Colenbrander, 1977). As a result, this term has virtually disappeared from the recent literature (Barraga, 1983).

REFERENCES

Barraga, N.C. (1983). *Visual handicaps and learning.* Austin, TX: Exceptional Resources.

Colenbrander, A. (1977). Dimensions of visual performance. *Archives of Ophthalmology, 83,* 332–337.

Hatfield, E.M. (1975). Why are they blind? *Sight Saving Review, 45,* 3–22.

See also Blind; Visually Impaired; Visual Training

PARTIAL PARTICIPATION

The principle of partial participation entails the position that all students with severe handicaps (including the profoundly mentally retarded and the severely physically disabled) can acquire a number of skills that will enable them to function at least partially in a variety of least restrictive school and nonschool environments or activities (Baumgart et al., 1980). Because of the severity of their sensory or motor impairments as well as deficits in attentional and learning processes, some severely handicapped students have difficulty in learning skills needed to function independently in current and subsequent least restrictive environments. Rather than denying access to these environments, proponents of the principle of partial participation believe adaptations can be implemented that will allow students to participate in a wide range of activities (Demchak, 1994) as well as experience inclusive programming. The latter, however, may not always be the least restrictive environment for students with severe disabilities.

The classroom teacher will need to follow a number of steps to implement partial participation strategies successfully. These include: (1) taking a nonhandicapped person's inventory of steps/skills used in a particular task; (2) taking a severely handicapped student's inventory of steps used or skills exhibited for the same task; (3) determining the skills that the student with disabilities probably can acquire; (4) determining the skills the handicapped student probably cannot acquire; (5) generating an adaptation hypothesis; (6) conducting an inventory of adaptations currently available for use; (7) determining individualized adaptations to be used; and (8) determining skills that can probably be acquired using individualized adaptations (Baumgart, et al., 1982).

Several considerations are recommended when using individualized adaptations for severely handicapped students. These include: (1) empirically verifying the appropriateness and effectiveness of adaptations in the criterion or natural environment; (2) avoiding allowing students to become overly dependent on adaptations; and (3) carefully selecting adaptations to meet needs of individual students in critically functional environments (Baumgart et al., 1980). Appropriate applications of the principle of partial participation will enhance the access of severely handicapped individuals to integrated environments available to the nonhandicapped population at large (Brown et al., 1979; Ferguson & Baumgart, 1991).

REFERENCES

Baumgart, D., Brown, L., Pumpian, I., Nisbet, J., Ford, A., Sweet, M., Messina, R., & Schroeder, J. (1982). Principle of partial participation and individualized adaptations in education programs for severely handicapped students. *Journal of the Association for Persons with Severe Handicaps, 7*(2), 17–27.

Baumgart, D., Brown, L., Pumpian, I., Nisbet, J., Ford, A., Sweet, M., Ranieri, L., Hansen, L., & Schroeder, J. (1980). The principle of partial participation and individualized adaptations in education programs for severely handicapped students. In L. Brown, M. Falvey, I. Pumpian, D. Baumgart, J. Nisbet, A. Ford, J. Schroeder, & R. Loomis (Eds.), *Curricular strategies for teaching severely handicapped students functional skills in school and nonschool environments* (Vol. 10). Madison, WI: Madison Public Schools and the University of Wisconsin.

Brown, L., Branston-McClean, M.B., Baumgart, D., Vincent, L., Falvey, M., & Schroeder, J. (1979). Using the characteristics of current and subsequent least restrictive environments in the development of curricular content for severely handicapped students. *Journal of the Association for Persons with Severe Handicaps, 4*, 407–424.

Demchak, M.A. (1994). Helping individuals with severe disabilities find leisure activities. *Teaching Exceptional Children, 27*(1), 48–52.

Ferguson, D.L., & Baumgart, D. (1991). Partial participation revisited. *Journal of the Association for Persons with Severe Handicaps, 16*(4), 218–227.

See also Least Restrictive Environment

PASAMANICK, BENJAMIN (1914–1996)

Benjamin Pasamanick began his professional studies at Cornell University, where he received his BA in 1936. During this period, he began studying physiology and biochemistry, and was accepted as the sole undergraduate advisee of Nobel Laureate James Sumner. In 1937, he attended the University of Maryland School of Medicine, earning his MD in 1941. His internship psychiatry was completed at Brooklyn State Hospital and Harlem Hospital, both in New York City. Following his psychiatric residency at the New York State Psychiatric Institute in 1943, Pasamanick became an assistant at the Yale Clinic of Child Development, where he was accepted to study under Arnold Gesell. At the time of this death in 1996, he was research professor emeritus of pediatrics at Albany Medical College.

Throughout his illustrious career as a mentor, scholar, and clinician in child psychiatry, Pasamanick maintained an interest in exceptional children, particularly those with mental retardation. He challenged conventional practices, frequently promoting change and innovation, and sought a melding of basic research in child development with the practice and promotion of a clear conceptual framework for treatment.

Pasamanick is perhaps best known for his research on the multidimensional, multifactorial influences on children's development (Kawi & Pasamanick, 1979), particularly his longitudinal studies of the development of African American infants (Granich, 1970). He was the first to demonstrate that the behavioral development of African American infants, as an indicator of intellectual maturity, was indistinguishable from that of Anglo infants. He ultimately came to believe that, early in life, intelligence and related cognitive skills are primarily biologically determined but become increasingly chronologically and socially influenced with age, eventually being driven by socioeconomic factors.

Among his numerous contributions, he served as president of the American Orthopsychiatric Association (1970–1971), president of the American Psychopathological Association (1967), and president of the Theobald Smith Society (1984). Pasamanick was a familiar figure at professional gatherings where he presented scientific papers, and he authored or edited numerous books and articles in scholarly journals, with more than 300 publications to his credit. His service on editorial boards included *Child Development,* the *American Journal of Mental Deficiency,* the *Merrill-Palmer Quarterly,* and the *Journal of Biological Psychiatry.*

REFERENCES

Granich, B. (1970). Benjamin Pasamanick. *American Journal of Orthopsychiatry, 40,* 368–372.

Kawi, A., & Pasamanick, B. (1979). *Prenatal and paranatal factors in the development of childhood reading disorders.* Millwood, NY: Kraus.

See also American Orthopsychiatric Association

PASE v. HANNON

PASE (Parents in Action on Special Education) *v. Hannon* (Joseph P. Hannon, superintendent of the Chicago public schools at the time this case was filed) was a class-action suit on behalf of African American students who were or who might be classified as educable mentally retarded (EMR) and placed in self-contained special classes. PASE was established by a parent advocacy group assisted by the Northwestern School of Law Legal Assistance Clinic and the Legal Assistance Foundation in Chicago. The U.S. Department of Justice filed a friend of court brief on behalf of the plaintiffs. Defendants in the case were various officials employed by the Chicago Board of Education as well as the Board of Education of the State of Illinois. *PASE* resulted in a 3-week trial conducted by Judge Grady, who issued an opinion deciding the case on July 7, 1980.

Witnesses for the defendants contended overrepresentation reflected the genuine needs of black students, who were claimed to have a higher EMR incidence owing to the effects of poverty. This emphasis on socioeconomic status as an explanation for overrepresentation was also relied on by *Larry P.* defendants, though unsuccessfully. The association of EMR with poverty has been reported for many decades throughout the western world for diverse racial and ethnic groups. The defendants also contended that any biases that might exist in IQ tests were neutralized in the placement process through the use of procedural protections such as parental informed consent, the development of a multifactored assessment that focused on educational needs, and decision making by a multidisciplinary team.

Approximately two thirds of the space in Judge Grady's lengthy opinion was devoted to his analyses of the intelligence test items. Judge Grady provided the exact wording of the item, the correct answer, and the scoring criterion, where appropriate, for determining whether a response was awarded one or two points. This unprecedented breach of test security was initially shocking to many professionals, but no known harm or serious threat to normative standards has been reported.

Judge Grady concluded from his personal analysis of the IQ test items that eight of several hundred items were biased. He noted that four of those eight items were not on current versions of the tests, and that those that were generally appeared at the upper limits of the test. Items that appeared at the upper limits of the test typically would not be given to students who might be considered for classification as EMR. Grady concluded that any biases that existed on the test exerted a very small influence on classification and placement decisions, and agreed with the defendants that other safeguards, mentioned earlier, compensated for these negligible biases.

The plaintiffs appealed the *PASE* trial decision. However, before the appellate court ruled, the issues in the case were rendered moot by the decision of the Board of Education in Chicago to ban the use of traditional IQ tests with black students being considered for classification and placement as EMR. This ban was part of a negotiated settlement in still another court case concerning the desegregation of the Chicago public schools. The appeal was then withdrawn by the plaintiffs. The *PASE* decision is an interesting contrast to that in *Larry P.*, but it does not have the impact of *Larry P.* for a variety of reasons.

See also Diana v. State Board of Education; Larry P.; Marshall v. Georgia; Nondiscriminatory Assessment

PATH ANALYSIS

Path analysis is a technique developed in the 1930s by Sewell Wright (1934) for the purpose of studying causal relationships among variables. Path analysis provides mathematical models expressing the direct and indirect effects of variables assumed to have causal status on variables assumed to be affected by the causal variables. A direct effect occurs when one variable influences another in the absence of mediation by a third variable. An indirect effect exists when a causal variable affects a dependent variable by influencing a third variable, which in turn affects the dependent variable directly.

The mathematical models used to express causation in path analysis have their origins in regression analysis. The simplest path model is one involving the regression of a dependent variable on one or more variables assumed to explain variation in the dependent variable. For instance, student achievement might be regressed on an educational intervention assumed to affect achievement. Under this model, the intervention would have a direct effect on achievement. The residual term in the regression equation would also be included in the model. It is assumed to be uncorrelated with other variables in the equation. The residual would be treated as a causal variable indicating the effects of variables not explicitly included in the model on achievement. For instance, intelligence is a variable not explicitly identified in the model that might account for part of the variation in achievement. Many other variables that might affect achievement could be identified.

Models involving indirect effects require more than one regression equation. For instance, the example given involving the indirect effect of teacher training on achievement would require two regression equations. The first would include the regression of achievement on teacher training and teacher behavior; the second would include the regression of teacher behavior on teacher training. The general rule governing the number of equations is that one equation is needed for each dependent variable.

The two models discussed to this point assume unidirectional causation. For instance, in the indirect effects model, teacher behavior is assumed to affect achievement, but achievement is not assumed to affect teacher behavior. Models assuming unidirectional causation are called recursive. Ordinary least squares (OLS) regression can be used with recursive models. Nonrecursive models assuming bidirectional causation between one or more pairs of variables require procedures that go beyond OLS regression. Duncan (1975) provides an excellent discussion of nonrecursive models.

The Ps in the model represent path coefficients. In a recursive model, these are standardized regression weights. Each path coefficient is interpreted as that fraction of the standard deviation in the dependent variable for which the causal variable is directly responsible. For instance, P_{da} indicates that fraction of the standard deviation in variable D for which variable A is directly responsible. The standardized regression weights functioning as path coefficients in path models are no longer widely used in causal modeling. The assumption that all variables in a causal model should be placed on the same scale has been challenged. Unstandardized weights are now typically used. See Duncan (1975) for a discussion of the problems associated with standardized weights.

Path analysis may be regarded as a special case of a more general technique called structural equation modeling (Bentler, 1980; Joreskog & Sorbom, 1979). The major difference between path analysis as it was developed by Wright and structural equation models is that structural equation models may include latent as well as manifest variables. A latent variable is a variable that is not observed directly, but rather is inferred from two or more manifest indicators. For example, student achievement could be treated as a latent variable to be inferred from scores on two or more achievement tests. A structural equation model expresses the effects of one set of variables on another set of variables. The variables in the model may include both latent variables and manifest variables. For instance, a model might include the effects of sex on student achievement in mathematics. Sex would be a manifest variable in this model and mathematics achievement could be a latent variable inferred from two or more test scores. Structural equation modeling represents a powerful extension of Wright's pioneering work in path analysis. With structural equation techniques, it is possible not only to represent a broad range of causal relations among variables, but also to represent a wide variety of latent variables that may be of concern in educational and psychological research.

REFERENCES

Bentler, P.M. (1980). Multivariate analysis with latent variables. In M.R. Rozenweig & L.W. Porter (Eds.), *Annual review of psychology* (Vol. 31). Palo Alto, CA: Annual Review.

Duncan, O.D. (1975). *Introduction to structural equation models.* New York: Academic.

Joreskog, K.G., & Sorbom, D. (1979). *Advances in factor analysis and structural equation models.* Cambridge, MA: Abt.

Wright, S. (1934). The method of path coefficients. *Annals of Mathematical Statistics, 5,* 161–215.

See also **Multiple Regression; Regression (Statistical)**

PATH-REFERENCED ASSESSMENT

Path-referenced assessment (Bergan, 1981, 1986, Bergan, Stone, & Feld, 1985) is an approach that references ability to position in a developmental sequence. The path-referenced approach has been applied in the Head Start Measures Battery (Bergan & Smith, 1984; Stone & Lane, 1991), a set of six cognitive scales designed to assist in planning learning experiences to promote the development of Head Start children. Within the path-referenced framework, ability is defined as a latent (unobserved) variable estimated from overt performance on test items. The ordering of skills in a developmental sequence is indicated by variations in item difficulty. Items of low difficulty reflect tasks related to lower levels of development, whereas items of high difficulty are associated with higher levels of development. The examinee taking a path-referenced test obtains a latent ability score referred to position in a developmental sequence and used to indicate the probability of performing the various tasks in the sequence correctly. For example, a child taking the math scale of the Head Start Measure Battery might receive a latent ability score indicating high probabilities of performing simple counting tasks correctly and low probabilities of performing more complex addition tasks correctly.

The path-referenced approach applies latent trait models (Bock & Aitkin, 1981; Lord, 1980) to the problem of referencing ability to position in a developmental sequence. The general latent trait model asserts that the probability of performing a test item correctly is a function of latent ability and certain item parameters. Item parameters that may be reflected in a latent trait model include item difficulty, item discrimination (which gives the strength of the relationship of the item to the underlying latent ability), and a guessing parameter. Latent ability and item difficulty are placed on the same scale in the latent trait model. The path-referenced approach uses the latent ability parameter to estimate an individual's ability, described as his or her developmental level. Item difficulty parameters are used to quantify developmental sequences. The fact that latent ability and item difficulty are on the same scale is used to reference developmental level to position in a developmental sequence.

Path-referenced assessment differs in significant ways from both norm-referenced assessment and criterion-referenced assessment. Norm-referenced assessment references test performance to position in a norm group. An ability score is given indicating where the individual stands in the group. Ability is defined in terms of group position. In the path-referenced approach, ability is estimated from test performance using a latent trait model. Latent ability is then referenced to position in a developmental sequence. Path referencing indicates where the individual is in a sequence and in so doing specifies the competencies that have been mastered in the past and those that lie ahead as development progresses.

REFERENCES

Bergan, J.R. (1981). Path-referenced assessment in school psychology. In T.R. Kratochwill (Ed.), *Advances in school psychology* (Vol. 1). Hillsdale, NJ: Erlbaum.

Bergan, J.R. (1986). Path-referenced assessment: A guide for instructional management. In C.A. Maher (Ed.), *Special services in the schools.* New York: Haworth.

Bergan, J.R., & Smith, A.N. (Eds.). (1984). *Head Start Measures Battery.* Washington, D.C.: Department of Health and Human Services.

Bergan, J.R., Stone, C.A., & Feld, J.K. (1985). Path-referenced evaluation of individual differences. In C.R. Reynolds & V.L. Willson (Eds.), *Methodological and statistical advances in the study of individual differences.* New York: Plenum.

Bock, R.D., & Aitkin, M. (1981). Marginal maximum likelihood estimation of item parameters: Application of an algorithm. *Psychometrika, 46,* 443–459.

Lord, F.M. (1980). *Applications of item response theory to practical testing problems.* Hillsdale, NJ: Erlbaum.

Stone, C.A., & Lane, S. (1991). Use of restricted item response theory models for examining the stability of item parameter estimates over time. *Applied Measurements in Education, 4*(2), 125–141.

See also **Assessment; Developmental Delays; Head Start**

PATTERNING

Patterning is also known as the Doman-Delacato treatment method for children with neurological disabilities. The Doman-Delacato treatment was popular during the 1960s. Advocates of the treatment program have reported success with a wide range of disabilities, including mental retardation, brain damage, learning disabilities, physical handicaps, aphasia, language disorders, and dyslexia. Numerous reports from professionals, paraprofessionals, and parents have confirmed the success of the treatment program. The widespread acceptance of neurological exercises was enhanced through articles published in popular magazines such as *Good Housekeeping* and *Reader's Digest*.

Medical terms, educators, and persons serving in the human services field have studied, evaluated, and researched the claims of the advocates of neurological organization theories. The numerous studies and carefully controlled research reviews do not support the purported achievements of the patterning approach.

See also **Neurodevelopmental Therapy; Neurological Organization; Neuropsychology**

PDR

See PHYSICIANS' DESK REFERENCE.

PEABODY DEVELOPMENTAL MOTOR SCALES (PDMS)

The Peabody Developmental Scales (PDMS; 1983) is an early childhood motor development test for children birth through 7 years 11 months. The instrument includes a Gross-Motor Scale, which tests reflexes, balance, nonlocomotor, locomotor, and receipt and propulsion of objects; and a Fine-Motor Scale, which tests grasping, hand use, eye-hand coordination, and finger dexterity. The Gross-Motor Scale contains 170 items divided into 17 age levels, with 10 items at each level. The Fine-Motor Scale contains 112 items divided into 16 age levels, with 6 or 8 items at each level. Items are scored on a three-point system that distinguishes among mastered skills, emerging skills, and skills clearly beyond the child's reach.

The PDMS was normed on 617 children that were representative of the nation as a whole with regard to gender, race, ethnicity, geographic region, and urban/rural residence. Raw scores are converted into scaled scores (z-scores, T-scores, developmental motor quotients) and age scores.

Reviewers (Compton, 1996; Reed, 1985; Venn, 1986) have been generally complimentary of the PDMS, finding the instrument a comprehensive measure of a fundamental aspect of child development. Weaknesses noted include the cumbersome nature of test administration.

REFERENCES

Compton, C. (1996). *A guide to 100 tests for special education.* Upper Saddle River, NJ: Globe Fearon.

Reed, H.B.C. (1985). Review of the Peabody Developmental Motor Scales. In J.V. Mitchell, Jr. (Ed) *The ninth mental measurements yearbook* (p. 1119). Lincoln: Buros Institute of Mental Measurements, University of Nebraska Press.

Venn, J.J. (1986). Review of the Peabody Developmental Motor Scales. In D.J. Keyser & R.C. Sweetland (Eds.), *Test critiques: Volume V* (pp. 310–313). Austin, TX: Pro-Ed.

PEABODY INDIVIDUAL ACHIEVEMENT TEST–REVISED/ NORMATIVE UPDATE

The Peabody Individual Achievement Test–Revised (PIAT–R; Markwardt, 1989) is an individually-administered measure of academic achievement designed for children and adults, ages 5 to 22. The PIAT–R assesses six academic content areas with the following subtests: General Information, Reading Recognition, Reading Comprehension, Mathematics, Spelling, and Written Expression. The subtests are combined to yield a Total Reading score, Total Test score, and a Written Language Composite score. Administration time is approximately 60 minutes.

The PIAT–R was recently renormed, and is referred to as the PIAT–R Normative Update (PIAT–R/NU; Markwardt, 1997). A sample of 3,429 children stratified according to 1994 U.S. Census data comprised the standardization sample. Reliability of the PIAT–R/NU was demonstrated with split-half reliability coefficients of the subtests ranging from the low to mid 0.90s. The PIAT–R/NU was shown to be stable with test-retest values in the low to mid 0.90s. Validity was established by demonstrating strong correlations to other achievement measures such as the K-TEA (Kaufman & Kaufman, 1985), KeyMath–R (Connolly, 1988), and PPVT–R (Dunn & Dunn, 1981). Reviews of the PIAT–R are generally quite favorable.

REFERENCES

Connolly, A.J. (1988). *KeyMath Revised: A Diagnostic Inventory of Essential Mathematics.* Circle Pines, MN: American Guidance Service.

Dunn, L.M., & Dunn, L.M. (1981). *Examiner's manual for the Peabody Picture Vocabulary Test—Revised edition.* Circle Pines, MN: American Guidance Service.

Kaufman, A.S., & Kaufman, N.L. (1985). *Kaufman Test of Educational Achievement.* Circle Pines, MN: American Guidance Service.

Markwardt, F.C. (1989). *Peabody Individual Achievement Test—Revised.* Circle Pines, MN: American Guidance Service.

Markwardt, F.C. (1997). *Peabody Individual Achievement Test-Revised/Normative Update.* Circle Pines, MN: American Guidance Service.

See also **Achievement Tests; Assessment**

PEABODY LANGUAGE DEVELOPMENT KITS–REVISED

The Peabody Language Development Kits–Revised (PLDK–R; Dunn, Smith, Dunn, Horton, & Smith, 1981) are multilevel programs designed to facilitate development of oral language in young children. The areas targeted by the program are receptive, associative, and expressive language, and cognitive skills. The goals of the PLDK–R are to stimulate overall language skills in standard English and to advance children's cognitive skills about one year per level. Rather than training children in selected psycholinguistic processes, the PLDK–R focuses on overall language development.

The PLDK–R is a self-contained, comprehensive program designed to stimulate oral language and cognitive development for a diverse group of children. Speech-language pathologists, special education teachers, teachers of English as a second language, and regular-education teachers, will find the program beneficial.

REFERENCE

Dunn, L., Smith, J., Dunn, L., Horton, K., & Smith, D. (1981). *Peabody Language Development Kits–Revised Manuals Level P, 1, 2, and 3.* Circle Pines, MN: American Guidance Service.

See also **Oral Language of the Handicapped; Oral vs. Manual Communication**

PEABODY PICTURE VOCABULARY TEST–THIRD EDITION

The third edition of the Peabody Picture Vocabulary Test (PPVT–III; Dunn & Dunn, 1997) is similar to the original and revised editions published in 1959 and 1981. The PPVT–III is an individually-administered test of receptive vocabulary (of standard English) for children and adults ages 2.5 to 90. This untimed test requires examinees to examine four black and white pictures and choose which one best represents the meaning of a stimulus word that is presented orally by the examiner.

Although there are many similarities between the 1981 Peabody and the PPVT–III, there are also some notable differences. For example, the amount of test items for each form increased to 204, test items were grouped into 17 sets of 12 in each form (leading to a change in basal and ceiling rules), new illustrations were included to modernize the content, and the kit was packaged in a way that facilitates transporting test materials.

The PPVT–III is available in two parallel forms. The test was standardized on a stratified sample of 2,725 persons, including 2,000 children and adolescents and 725 adults over age 19. The alternate forms, reliabilities for the PPVT–III standard scores ranged from .88 to .96, with a median value of .94. The internal consistency values ranged from .86 to .97, with a median reliability of .94. Scores were also very stable, with all values in the .90s. The validity of the PPVT–III was examined by correlating its scores with other measures of intelligence and verbal ability. For example, the correlation between the PPVT–III and the Verbal Scale of the Wechsler Intelligence Scale for Children-Third Edition (WISC–III; Wechsler, 1991) was .91; between the PPVT–III and the Vocabulary Scale of the Kaufman Brief Intelligence Test (K-BIT; Kaufman & Kaufman, 1990), the correlation was .82; and between the PPVT–III and the Oral and Written Language Scales (OWLS: Carrow-Woolfolk, 1995), the correlation was .75.

The PPVT–III is a solid measure of receptive vocabulary. The revisions made from the last version have made scoring easier because of the new basal and ceiling rules. This test is an easy-to-administer task that is a good part of a comprehensive battery. However, it is not a measure of intelligence and should not be used alone as a criterion for placement or diagnosis of a language disorder.

REFERENCES

Carrow-Woolfolk, E. (1995). *Oral and Written Language Scales: Listening Comprehension and Oral Expression.* Circle Pines, MN: American Guidance Service.

Dunn, L.M., & Dunn, L.M. (1997). *Examiner's manual for the Peabody Picture Vocabulary Test-Third Edition.* Circle Pines, MN: American Guidance Service.

Kaufman, A.S., & Kaufman, N.L. (1990). *Kaufman Brief Intelligence Test.* Circle Pines, MN: American Guidance Service.

Wechsler, D. (1991). *Wechsler Intelligence Scale for Children-Third Edition.* San Antonio, TX: The Psychological Corporation.

PEABODY REBUS READING PROGRAM

The Peabody Rebus Reading Program is a representational symbol system designed to teach early reading skills to children. A basic vocabulary of pictographic symbols known as rebuses represent entire words or parts of words; they provide a foundation for developing reading and comprehension skills. Rebus symbols may be classified into four basic categories: combination symbols, which primarily depict objects or actions (e.g., ball = ⊘); relational symbols, which depict locations or directions (e.g., in = ▣, on = ▯); and abstract symbols, which are primarily arbitrary symbols representing ideas such as "at" = ⟍ and "too" = ⟂). The fourth category combines symbols with alphabet letters, affixes (e.g., doing = ⚶ ing), and other rebuses (e.g., into = ▣) (Woodcock, Clark, & Davies, 1969).

Initially, the spelled words are paired with their corresponding rebus symbols. The symbols are gradually faded to effect transition to standard orthography. On completion of the transition level, a student will be able to read 122 spelled words, sound out words, recognize punctuation, and read stories.

The Peabody Rebus Reading Program is designed to introduce children to reading by first having them learn a vocabulary of rebuses in the place of spelled words. The program has additional application for facilitating the development of language skills.

REFERENCE

Woodcock, R.W., Clark, C.R., & Davies, C.O. (1969). *The Peabody Rebus Reading Program.* Circle Pines, MN: American Guidance Service.

PEACE CORPS, SPECIAL EDUCATION IN

The Peace Corps is a volunteer program that was established in 1961 by President John Kennedy. Its goal is to help the people of interested countries and areas of the world in meeting their needs for trained manpower through the help of American volunteers. The promotion of a better understanding of Americans on the part of the people served, and a better understanding of other people on the part of Americans, are also basic goals of the program (Shute, 1986).

The Peace Corps offers a program for individuals interested in special education. Volunteers can be assigned specific placements working with children displaying mental retardation, learning disabilities, emotional disturbances, blindness or visual impairments, deafness or hearing impairments, multihandicaps, or speech problems. Assignments in special education cover teacher training and direct classroom teaching. Volunteers in the teacher-training program conduct needs assessments, organize and implement workshops and seminars, develop teaching aids using locally available materials, give demonstration lessons, establish criteria for evaluation, observe teachers, and monitor teachers' progress. Those participating in the direct-teaching program help to screen and assess the special child's abilities and progress; teach classes in academics, extracurricula areas, and self-help skills; and structure activities to facilitate interactions of the special child with the family and community.

To qualify as a special education volunteer, an individual must be a U.S. citizen and be at least 18 years of age. There are also medical and legal criteria. Finally, the special education volunteer should possess a four-year degree with some preservice teaching in special education (actual teaching experience is preferred but not obligatory). All volunteers receive a monthly allowance to cover housing, food, and spending money. On completion of the two-year service commitment required of all volunteers, an allotment for every month served is provided as a readjustment allowance on return to the United States (Shute, 1986).

REFERENCES

Shute, N. (1986). *After a turbulent youth, the Peace Corps comes of age.* Washington, DC: ACTION.

***See also* Community-Based Services; Voluntary Agencies**

PEDIATRICIAN

A wide variety of medical conditions may handicap a child's ability to learn. Some may be due to hereditary factors. Others may be prenatal and relate to the health of the mother or to direct dangers to the fetus such as infections or drugs. Some may be perinatal, occurring during or immediately following the birth process. This group includes complications resulting from the mechanics of labor and delivery. Some conditions may occur or be diagnosed only after the infant has gone home. Thus it is clear that the pediatrician has an important role in special education.

First, the pediatrician may be able to diagnose a condition that could have an adverse effect on the child's ability to learn and estimate the approximate extent of the handicap. Based on this and other relevant information, a plan for intervention and education can be developed. Second, school performance may be the first valid indication that a child is not developing normally. A comprehensive pediatric examination is a vital part of the overall assessment of such developmental problems so as to identify or rule out contributing medical factors, such as visual problems. If needed, detailed remedial measures may then be implemented (Berlin, 1975).

When necessary, the pediatrician can help by referral of the child to other specialists whose expertise may be needed to identify or treat the precise problems in question. Examples of medical specialists to whom such referral may be made include ophthalmologists for disorders of the eyes, neurologists for conditions related to the brain or other parts of the central nervous system, and ear, nose, and throat specialists for children with hearing impairments. Children's health problems may manifest themselves at school. If there is a medication or other treatment program in force, teachers can both monitor and encourage compliance with this program. Over 50% of all American parents have sought help from a pediatrician for school-related problems (American Academy of Pediatrics, 1978). For this reason, it is important that pediatricians and teachers maintain open lines of communication so that they may assist one another in helping children with both school-related and health problems.

REFERENCES

American Academy of Pediatrics. (1978). *The future of pediatric education.* Washington, DC: Author.

Berlin, C.M. (1975). Medical bases of exceptional conditions. In R.M. Smith & J.T. Neisworth (Eds.), *The exceptional child: A functional approach.* New York: McGraw-Hill.

PEDIATRIC ACQUIRED IMMUNE DEFICIENCY SYNDROME (AIDS)

Since the first cases of Acquired Immune Deficiency Syndrome (AIDS) were reported in 1981, the human immunodeficiency virus (HIV) that causes AIDS has presented an epidemic unknown in modern history. It has been estimated that there are 1,500,000 children with AIDS worldwide. Between 32,000 and 38,000 HIV-infected children will have been born in the US by the year 2000. In the United States, 6,309 cases of pediatric AIDS have been reported to the Centers for Disease Control to date. There were an estimated 12,000 children living with HIV in the US as of January, 1994 (Children's Hope Foundation, 1998).

It is predicted that by the year 2000 in the US, between 80,000 and 100,000 uninfected children will be born to mothers who will die from HIV. Approximately 25% of infants born to HIV-infected mothers each year in the US are born HIV-infected. Approximately 89% of all children with AIDS are perinatal cases—children who contracted the virus from their mother during pregnancy or birth. Other causes of pediatric AIDS include transmission through breast-feeding, tainted blood transfusions before 1985, and sexual abuse.

The average age for diagnosis of perinatal cases is 4.1. Only 54% of all perinatal cases are diagnosed by the age of 7.

Children with AIDS have special needs and concerns, as the variety of manifestations that occur with pediatric AIDS is larger than with adult AIDS. Children with HIV and AIDS often suffer from central nervous system complications, the inability to combat childhood diseases, and failure of growth and development (Children's Hope Foundation, 1998).

Newborns infected with HIV live an average of less than 18 months. Presently, hemophiliacs represent the largest HIV-positive school age group, but this number is declining due to an increasing safe blood supply (Adams, Marcontel, & Price, 1989). The school environment has one of the lowest exposure rates of HIV in terms of normal contact among children. This also applies for school personnel (Adams,

Marcontel, & Price, 1989). However, 25 states have mandated health education prior to graduation, and specifically education on HIV transmission and prevention (Kerr, 1989).

Curricula on HIV/AIDS education for special education populations have being focusing on defining health and prevention strategies (New Mexico State Department of Education, 1991). Unfortunately, it appears that very few school districts alter the HIV/AIDS curriculum to meet the needs of students with learning issues (Strosnider & Henke, 1992).

To date, nearly every court decision regarding the status of HIV-infected students and personnel attending school, has allowed the individual to stay in school in the absence of evidence that HIV can be spread by casual contact. Therefore, it is essential that school boards, administrators, and general personnel are thoroughly educated and repeatedly updated with information about AIDS. CDC guidelines recommend a team approach to decisions regarding type of educational setting for HIV-infected children. The team should be composed of the child's physician, public health personnel, parents, and personnel from the educational settings (Kirkland & Ginther, 1988). One other factor that should be addressed within the team approach is the involvement of the school's administration, counselor, psychologist, and social worker in providing emotional and social support to the HIV-infected child and children who make up his or her peer or support group, or classmates (Walker, 1991). It is crucial that at this stage of development of the AIDS disease, health policies and disease control concerns do not violate the individual's rights to privacy (Bruder, 1995) and an appropriate and humane education. Although to date, there have been no court decisions at the federal level on the application of the Education for All Handicapped Children Act or the Rehabilitation Act to children suffering from AIDS (Kirkland & Ginther, 1988), such decisions are most surely in the future of our educational institutions.

REFERENCES

Adams, R.M., Marcontel, M., & Price, A.L. (1989). The impact of AIDS on school health services. *Journal of School Health, 58,* (8), pp. 341–343.

Bruder, M.B. (1995). The challenge of pediatric AIDS: A framework for early childhood special education. *Topics in Early Childhood Special Education, 15*(1), 83–99.

Children's Hope Foundation. (1998). *Children and Aids.* http://www.childrenshope.org.

Kerr, D.L. (1989). Forum addresses HIV education for children and youth with special needs. *Journal of School Health, 59*(3), p. 139.

Kirkland, M., & Ginther, D. (1988). Acquired immune deficiency syndrome in children: Medical, legal and school related issues. *School Psychology Review, 17*(12), pp. 304–310.

New Mexico State Department of Education. (1991). *HIV/AIDS guidelines for special education populations.* Sante Fe, NM: Author.

Strosnider, R., & Henke, J. (1992). *Delivery of AIDS prevention education to students with disabilities: Implications for preservice education.* (ERIC Clearinghouse No. EC303726)

Walker, G.E. (1991). Pediatric AIDS: Toward an ecosystemic treatment model. *Family Systems Medicine, 9*(3), 211–227.

PEDIATRIC PSYCHOLOGIST

The past two decades have been a period of significant professional growth for pediatric psychology. In general, the number of psychologists in medical settings has increased rapidly and the scope of their activities has widened enormously.

There are three major types of pediatric settings in which pediatric psychologists work: (1) the pediatric hospital or multispecialty general hospital inpatient unit, (2) the ambulatory care facility (outpatient clinic or private pediatric office), and (3) the comprehensive care center (e.g., kidney dialysis center, burn hospital) for chronic illnesses or chronic medical conditions, which may provide outpatient and/or inpatient services. The primary clinical responsibilities of the pediatric psychologist in these settings are basically twofold: to provide direct psychological services to patients and to consult to a variety of pediatric medical subspecialties including nephrology, cardiology, hematology-oncology, endocrinology, neurology, genetics, and surgery.

Over the past 20 years, pediatricians have increasingly focused on the prevention of disease and the management of chronic childhood illnesses for which there are no known cures, such as cystic fibrosis, sickle cell disease, and juvenile diabetes. This shift in the practice of pediatrics has placed a new emphasis on patients' problems of daily living, issues of quality of life, and problems related to compliance with therapeutic regimens. It has further supported the active involvement of pediatric psychologists in the comprehensive delivery of health care to children.

Many children present in medical settings with physical symptoms of unclear origin or with symptoms having significant psychosocial components, including headaches, chronic abdominal pain, and failure to thrive. The psychosocial concomitants of physical illness in children represent a major source of referrals to pediatric psychologists.

Behavioral treatment procedures have shown considerable promise as an approach to alleviating or reducing the symptomatic behaviors associated with a number of somatic disorders in children (Siegel, 1983). Pediatric psychologists have used a variety of behavioral techniques such as biofeedback, relaxation training, and various operant conditioning procedures to successfully modify the symptoms associated with such disorders as asthma, ruminative vomiting, and enuresis.

Pediatric psychologists have also been concerned with the prevention of health-related problems. Among the problems that have received considerable attention in this area are the reduction of stress associated with hospitalization and painful medical procedures and the management of behaviors (e.g., overeating) that are associated with the development of physical disorders such as high blood pressure.

Finally, pediatric psychologists who work in hospital settings are often called upon to provide emotional support to health-care personnel who deal with children having life-threatening conditions. Professional burnout is a significant problem with staff who provide medical care to terminally ill children. The pediatric psychologist may consult with the staff to help them cope with the emotionally draining experiences that they encounter in these settings.

REFERENCE

Siegel, L.J. (1983). Psychosomatic and psychophysiological disorders. In R.J. Morris & T.R. Kratochwill (Eds.). *The practice of child therapy.* New York: Pergamon.

See also **Parent Education; Pediatrician; Psychosocial Adjustment; Psychosomatic Disorders**

PEDRO DE PONCE

See PONCE DE LEON, PEDRO DE.

PEER RELATIONSHIPS

The relationship between handicapped students and their peers is a complex phenomenon that is molded by many factors. Several of the more noteworthy factors are age of the child with disabilities, attitudes and behavior of the classroom teacher, type of handicapping condition affecting the student, self-concept and skill level of the handicapped student, and whether or not the regular class students have been prepared to understand the specific needs of some mainstreamed students. For example, it has been suggested that beginning in the early elementary grades (Rubin & Coplan, 1992), the influence of the peer group increases as the handicapped child gets older. In other words, during the early years of a handicapped child's school experience, parent and teacher acceptance are more important than peer approval or acceptance.

Methods to improve the peer relationships of the handicapped child can be found in the literature. As an example of one such approach, Schwartz (1984) provides a checklist for regular class teachers to follow when preparing for the arrival of a mainstreamed handicapped child. Among other activities, teachers are asked to give regular class peers information about handicapping conditions and allow for any questions students might have. Such procedures help increase the frequency of positive interaction between the handicapped child and his or her peers. This approach is particularly important with physically handicapped students. Some research suggests that the physically handicapped child is the least likely to be accepted by his or her nonhandicapped peers.

REFERENCES

Rubin, K.H., & Coplan, R.L. (1992). Peer relationships in childhood. In M.H. Bernstein & M. Lamb (Eds.). *Developmental psy-*

chology: An advance textbook (3rd ed., pp. 519–528). Hillsdale, NJ: Erlbaum.

Schwartz, L.L. (1984). *Exceptional students in the mainstream.* Belmont, CA: Wadsworth.

See also **Mainstreaming; Peer Tutoring**

PEER TUTORING

Peer and cross-age tutoring procedures have been identified in the literature as having success in the instruction of children with disabilities. Tutoring programs have been successful in improving a wide variety of academic skills. Peer tutors have been effective in teaching math (Bentz & Fuchs, 1996; Johnson & Bailey, 1974) and spelling (Harris, 1973), but have most often been applied for reading skills (Chaing, Thorpe, & Darch, 1980). Many authors identify the need to carefully prepare children before they perform as tutors (Martella, Marchand-Martella, Young, & Macfarlane, 1995; Schloss & Sedlak, 1986). Procedures for preparing children to function as tutors have not been extensively discussed in the literature. There are few sources readily available for a comprehensive description of tutor preparation techniques that have been successfully implemented.

Some studies in special education that have shown tutoring to be effective have older students tutoring younger students (Parson & Heward, 1979). Other reports indicate that large age differences are not critical to an effective peer tutoring program (Dineen, Clark, & Risley, 1977). In fact, one peer tutoring study demonstrated that learning-disabled (LD) elementary-age students were effective in teaching other elementary LD students placed in the same resource room (Chiang, Thorpe, & Darch, 1980). Therefore, based on information currently available, it is safe to conclude that tutor-tutee age difference is not in itself critical to the success of a peer tutorial program.

It appears that tutors can be selected from most special education programs. Research has demonstrated that effective peer tutors can come from either able or less able students. While studies within regular classrooms are common, low-achieving and special classroom students have also been effective tutors (Paine, Radicchi, Rosellini, Deutchman, & Darch, 1983). Several studies have shown higher functioning LD students to be effective tutors for lower functioning LD classmates. The success that tutees achieve in these carefully designed programs can contribute to important changes in previously unmotivated students.

REFERENCES

Bentz, J.L., & Fuchs, L.S. (1996). Improving peers' helping behavior to students with learning disabilities mathematics peer tutoring. *Learning Disability Quarterly, 19*(4), 202–215.

Chaing, B., Thorpe, H., & Darch, C. (1980). Effects of cross age tutoring on word recognition performance of learning disabled students. *Learning Disability Quarterly, 3*, 11–19.

Dineen, J.P., Clark, H.B., & Risley, T.R. (1977). Peer tutoring among elementary students: Educational benefits to the tutor. *Journal of Applied Behavior Analysis, 10*, 231–238.

Harris, V.W. (1973). Effects of peer tutoring, homework, and consequences upon the academic performance of elementary school children (Doctoral dissertation, University of Kansas, 1972). *Dissertation Abstracts International, 33,* 11-A, 6175.

Johnson, M., & Bailey, J.S. (1974). Cross-age tutoring: Fifth graders as arithmetic tutors for kindergarten children. *Journal of Applied Behavior Analysis, 7*, 223–232.

Maher, C.A. (1984). Handicapped adolescents as cross age tutors: Program description and evaluation. *Exceptional Children, 51,* 56–63.

Martella, R.C., Marchand-Martella, W.E., Young, K.R., & Macfarlane, C.A. (1995). Determining the collateral effects of peer tutoring training on a student with severe disabilities. *Behavior Modification, 19*(2), 170–191.

Paine, S., Radicchi, J., Rosellini, L., Deutchman, L., & Darch, C. (1983). *Structuring your classroom for academic success.* Champaign, IL: Research.

Parson, L.R., & Heward, W.L. (1979). Training peers to tutor. Evaluation of a tutor training package for primary learning disabled students. *Journal of Applied Behavior Analysis, 12*, 309–310.

Schloss, P., & Sedlak, R. (1986). *Instructional methods for students with learning and behavior problems.* Boston: Allyn & Bacon.

See also **Direct Instruction; Peer Relationships; Social Skills Training; Teacher Effectiveness**

PENNSYLVANIA ASSOCIATION FOR RETARDED CITIZENS v. PENNSYLVANIA (1972)

Commonly known as the *PARC* decision, the case of the *Pennsylvania Association for Retarded Citizens v. Pennsylvania* is one of two landmark court decisions granting educational rights to the handicapped (the other is *Mills v. Board of Education of Washington, DC.*) *PARC* and *Mills* were instrumental in the passage of state and federal laws guaranteeing equal access for the handicapped to all educational programs.

The *PARC* case was a class-action suit (the suit was certified by the court as representing all similarly situated individuals in Pennsylvania) brought by the Pennsylvania Association for Retarded Citizens and 13 mentally retarded students. The suit was brought because three students had been denied attendance in the public schools of Pennsylvania. The case was brought under the equal protection and due process clauses of the Fourteenth Amendment to the U.S. Constitution. In *PARC,* the plaintiffs argued that allowing the state to provide a free public education to some of its citizens while denying other of its citizens the right to attend the same schools or to receive an appropriate education at state expense was unfair and denied equal protection of the law. They also argued that handicapped children were excluded from public education without access to due process. (The Fourteenth Amendment does not deny the ability of a state to deprive a citizen of any fundamental right; however, before a right can be violated, the state must demonstrate a compelling interest and must grant the citizen a hearing and other such protection as may be deemed necessary under the due process clause.)

In deciding for the plaintiffs, the court clearly acknowledged that admitting seriously disturbing, profoundly retarded, physically handicapped children would be difficult and expensive at all levels; however, the court ruled that the interests of the handicapped were protected by the Fourteenth Amendment and that this protection outweighed the difficulties created by providing an education to the handicapped.

Following the *PARC* decision and the subsequent ruling in *Mills,* a flood of suits came forth arguing for the rights of the handicapped to equal educational opportunities. Few of these cases were even litigated, however, as most states during the period 1972 to 1974 passed and funded legislation requiring local school districts to provide special education programs for the handicapped.

The *PARC* decision and related cases had a profound effect on special education as currently practiced. *PARC* fostered a rapid change in American schools, bringing into local schools, for the first time in many cases, children with severe disabilities, including profound levels of mental retardation, deafness, blindness, multiple handicaps, and the severe orthopedic impairment.

See also Consent Decree; Equal Educational Opportunity; Equal Protection; Least Restrictive Environment; Mainstreaming; Mills v. Board of Education of District of Columbia

PEOPLE FIRST

People First is a self-advocacy organization run by and for people with mental retardation. It has the dual purpose of assuring the availability of the services, training, and support needed to maintain and increase the capabilities of people with developmental disabilities for leading independent and normal lives; and of demonstrating to society that the disabled are people first and handicapped second (People First, 1984). Groups of mentally retarded people are taught to organize their affairs, run meetings, and make decisions and carry them through. All of this is accomplished with minimal help from nonhandicapped advisers. To a large extent, these groups are not only concerned with the needs and problems of mentally retarded people, but also the needs and problems of all handicapped people. Statewide and national conventions of self-advocacy groups have been held and an international self-advocacy movement of People First groups is emerging.

Self-advocacy groups have sprung up in America and Britain. Such groups are challenging traditional views of mental handicaps, handicapped people, and mentally retarded persons who can speak for themselves. Self-advocacy groups stretch nonhandicapped people's expectations and attitudes, thereby helping to create a new independence for mentally handicapped persons. In California, People First was contracted by the State Council of Developmental Dis-

abilities to critique the current service system for the developmentally disabled. The unique aspect of this project is that it was entirely conducted by the consumers of the services and was not the work of professionals.

REFERENCE
People First of California. (1984). *Surviving the system: Mental retardation and the retarding environment.* Sacramento, CA: State Council on Developmental Disabilities.

See also Advocacy for Children with Disabilities

PERCENTILE SCORES

A percentile score is a score derived from the relative position of a raw score in the entire distribution of raw scores. The raw score must possess at least rank information; i.e., raw scores must be able to be ranked. Usually we assume at least intervals for the raw scores, so that a one-point difference has the same meaning for all possible scores. Percentile scores lose this interval quality.

The calculation of a percentile score is based on the number of scores lower than the raw score being changed or transformed. A percentile score of 50 means that half (50%) of the scores in the raw score distribution fall below the score under consideration. This percentile score is also called the median. A percentile score of 10 means 10% of the scores are lower, and a percentile score of 90 means 90% of the scores are lower.

Percentile scores are not equal intervals. That is, a 10 percentile point difference has a different meaning when examined for a score of 10 or 50. The difference between percentile scores of 10 and 20 may represent many raw score points, while the difference between 50 and 60 may represent only a few. This is because raw score distributions typically have most scores clustered around the average score, perhaps two thirds of the scores within one standard deviation, so that 10% of the scores will occur within a few points of each other. At the extremes of the score distribution there are few people, and 10% may represent a large raw score range. Percentile scores should not be treated as interval scores. They cannot be routinely added, subtracted, divided, or multiplied to obtain anything sensible. Their primary use is to inform the user of the relative position of a raw score with respect to all other raw scores. In standardized testing, in which a norm sample has been carefully sampled, the percentile score tells us how an observed raw score compares with the norm group distribution of raw scores.

See also Grade Equivalents; Measurement

PERCEPTUAL AND MOTOR SKILLS

Perceptual and Motor Skills (titled *Perceptual and Motor Skills Research Exchange* in 1949) is published bimonthly. Two volumes a year total between 2000 and 3000 pages. About 30% of the articles are submitted from outside the

United States. The purpose of this journal is to encourage scientific originality and creativity from an interdisciplinary perspective including such fields as anthropology, physical education, physical therapy, orthopedics, anesthesiology, and time and motion study. Articles are experimental, theoretical, and speculative. Special reviews and lists of new books received are carried. Controversial material of scientific merit is welcome. Submissions are examined by multiple referees, and critical editing is balanced by specific suggestions as to changes required to meet standards.

PERCEPTUAL CONSTANCY

Perceptual constancy refers to the ability to perceive objects possessing invariant properties such as size, shape, and position in spite of changes in the impression on the sensory surface. Essentially, this means that one recognizes a chair as not only a chair but as the same chair regardless of the viewing angle. Even though an object may have been seen only from a single point of view, we are often able to recognize that object from different distances and from nearly any angle of view (Martindale, 1981).

Perceptual constancy is an integral part of overall visual perception and is involved heavily in the early reading process. Disorders of perceptual constancy are relatively rare, but they do occur and can wreak havoc with early learning. Children learn to recognize letters and words even though they see them printed in a variety of orthographic representations. Much variability of printing by children and their teachers occurs during the early learning stages as well, yet children master these various representations with relative ease. The generalization necessary to performing such tasks of visual pattern recognition requires perceptual constancy. Children with mild disturbances of perceptual constancy or higher order visual pattern recognition will have great difficulty with many school tasks, but especially with reading. The disorder is low enough in incidence, however, that accurate estimates of its prevalence are unavailable.

REFERENCE

Martindale, C. (1981). *Cognition and consciousness.* Homewood, IL: Dorsey.

See also **Developmental Test of Visual Perception; Perceptual Development, Lag in; Perceptual Training**

PERCEPTUAL DEFICIT HYPOTHESIS

The perceptual deficit hypothesis, a once widely accepted view of learning disabilities, exerted a dominant influence on special education teaching and evaluation practices from the early 1960s to the mid-1970s. While the perceptual deficit hypothesis encompasses a number of variants, its central notion is that learning disabilities arise from perceptual-motor dysfunction of neurological origin (Cruick-

shank, 1972). Learning-disabled children are viewed as having deficient form perception and/or visual analysis, and these deficiencies are believed to be the central feature of their difficulties in learning to read.

This view of learning disabilities widely influenced special education practice through the writings and programs of Kephart (1960), Getman (1962), Barsch (1965), and Frostig (1961). Remedial programs reflected this orientation by emphasizing gross and fine-motor training, ocular exercises, spatial orientation, balance board training, visual discrimination, sequencing, closure exercises, etc., as necessary prerequisites to more direct teaching of academics. It was believed that such foundation training in sensory-motor functions would remediate underlying processing deficits and was a required prerequisite to higher order, conceptual, or symbolic learning.

Proponents of the perceptual deficit hypothesis were influenced by Piaget's theories concerning the role of maturation and motor functioning in perception, by gestalt psychology's emphasis on perceptual development, and by Strauss and Lehtinen's (1947) work with brain-injured children. In their programs for learning-disabled children, these pioneers of special education translated stage theories of learning literally into hierarchies of preacademic remediation activities that sought to develop motor, visual, and visual-motor skills prior to focusing on academic learning. In theory, the development of academic skills required mastery of these lower-level functions.

By the mid 1970s, the perceptual deficit hypothesis and its concomitant remedial programs began to receive severe and substantial criticism. Aspects of the underlying theory were questioned and fault was found with the early foundation research. The overly simplified and literal translation of theory into practice was decried as an essential misinterpretation of the concept of perception. New research indicated that learning disabilities, and reading disabilities in particular, were attributable more to problems in the verbal realm than to perceptual deficits (Vellutino, Steger, Moyer, Harding, & Niles, 1977).

The assumptions of a process orientation are that human performance can, in fact, be parsed into psychologically distinct categories, that any given parsing categories are valid compartments, that valid tests exist with which to parse, and that remediation based on underlying processing profiles will transfer to functional and academic learning. Currently, the state of the art in psychology and special education does not support any of these assumptions.

REFERENCES

Barsch, R.H. (1965). *A movigenic curriculum* (Publication No. 25). Madison: Wisconsin State Department of Instruction.

Cruickshank, W.M. (1972). Some issues facing the field of learning disability. *Journal of Learning Disabilities, 5,* 380–383.

Frostig, M. (1961). *The Marianne Frostig Developmental Test of Visual Perception.* Palo Alto, CA: Consulting Psychologists.

Getman, G. (1962). *How to develop your child's intelligence.* Luverne, MN: Announcer.

Kephart, N. (1960). *The slow learner in the classroom.* Columbus, OH: Merrill.

Strauss, A.A., & Lehtinen, L.E. (1947). *Psychopathology and education of the brain-injured child.* New York: Grune & Stratton.

Vellutino, F.R., Steger, B.M., Moyer, S.C., Harding, C.J., & Niles, J.A. (1977). Has the perceptual deficit hypothesis led us astray? *Journal of Learning Disabilities, 10,* 54–64.

PERCEPTUAL DEVELOPMENT, LAG IN

Lag in perceptual development has been hypothesized as a major cause of learning difficulties in children by Kephart, Delacato, and Getman, among others. In general, these theorists believe there is a sequential series of strategies children use to process information from the environment; if learned incompletely at any stage, these strategies will cause learning difficulties at higher levels. These theorists maintain that proficiency in perceptual functioning provides an essential foundation for academic learning. Furthermore, they presume children experience academic failure because of developmental lags in these perceptual systems, lags that can and must be ameliorated before academic learning can occur. Although varying somewhat in theoretical orientation, these researchers, as well as Frostig, Barsch, Ayres, Doman, S. Kirk, and W. Kirk, advocate perceptual training to both establish the necessary foundation for and enhance the acquisition of academic learning. Their research provides much of the foundation for current work in the field of learning disabilities (Smith, 1984).

Although numerous perceptual-motor theories and training programs exist, research findings to support the theories on which they are based or validate their efficacy have not been found. Hammill, Goodman, and Wiederholt (1974) reviewed studies investigating the effects of the perceptual training programs of Frostig, Kephart, and Getman on readiness skills, intelligence, and academic achievement. Of the studies reviewed, positive effects of training on intelligence and academic achievement were not demonstrated and readiness skills improved in only a few cases. In a study of the effects of Delacato's training method on reading ability and visual-motor integration, O'Donnell and Eisenson (1969) found no improvements in either visual-motor integration or reading ability. Further, a number of researchers, professional groups, and parent groups have severely criticized Delacato's theory and program (Aaron & Poostay, 1982).

Finally, in an evaluation of 38 studies employing Kirk and Kirk's psycholinguistic training model, Hammill and Larsen (1978) found only six demonstrating positive results and concluded that the efficacy of psycholinguistic training remains nonvalidated. Although perceptual and psycholinguistic training theorists maintain the efficacy of their treatment programs, others question the large amounts of time and money expended on these unsubstantiated perceptual-training programs (Hammill, Goodman, & Wiederholt, 1974). Research may validate their value in certain cases, but general use appears unwarranted.

REFERENCES

Aaron, I.E., & Poostay, E.J. (1982). Strategies for reading disorders. In C.R. Reynolds & T.B. Gutkin (Eds.). *The handbook of school psychology* (pp. 410–435). New York: Wiley.

Cratty, B.J. (1979). *Perceptual and motor development in infants and children.* New York: Macmillan.

Hammill, D., Goodman, L., & Wiederholt, J.L. (1974). Visual-motor processes: Can we train them? *Reading Teacher, 27,* 469–478.

Hammill, D., & Larsen, S. (1978). The effectiveness of psycholinguistic training: A reaffirmation of position. *Exceptional Children, 44,* 402–414.

O'Donnell, P.A., & Eisenson, J. (1969). Delacato training for reading achievement and visual-motor integration. *Journal of Learning Disabilities, 2,* 441–447.

Smith, C.R. (1984). *Learning disabilities: The interaction of learner, task, and setting.* Boston: Little, Brown.

See also **Neurological Organization; Remediation, Deficit-Centered Model of**

PERCEPTUAL DISTORTIONS

Perceptual distortion is a clinical term referring to aberrant reception and interpretation of stimuli by one or more of the five basic senses: vision, hearing, smell, taste, and touch. Perceptual distortion typically occurs in conjunction with schizophrenia, severe depression, and psychomotor and ideopathic epilepsies. Schizophrenics are particularly susceptible to perceptual distortion and often process incoming sensory information abnormally via attenuation or reduction. Schizophrenics traditionally have been thought to underestimate tactile, auditory, and visual stimuli in particular. Related to perceptual distortion is evidence that schizophrenics have a defective sensory-filtering mechanism that does not allow them to focus on the most relevant of stimuli at any given time (Pincus & Tucker, 1978). Perceptual distortions that mimic the schizophrenic's perceptual distortions also may be induced by various psychoactive drugs. Prolonged sensory deprivation can also produce perceptual distortions and full-blown hallucinations.

In contrast to schizophrenics, depressed and epileptic individuals exaggerate the intensity of incoming stimuli. Psychomotor seizures produce the most specific of the perceptual distortions but they tend to be ideopathic. Perceptual distortions may also be considered a soft sign of neurological impairment and may occur with learning disabilities, though the latter is far less frequent than commonly believed.

REFERENCE

Pincus, J.H., & Tucker, G.J. (1978). *Behavioral neurology* (2nd ed.). New York: Oxford University Press.

See also Childhood Schizophrenia; Perceptual Development, Lag in; Seizure Disorders

PERCEPTUAL-MOTOR DIFFICULTIES

Perceptual-motor development is recognized as a basic foundation for later learning. The perceptual deficit hypothesis holds that academic difficulties underlie perceptual deficits (Daves, 1980) and that improving the perceptual processes will bring about improvement in academic achievement. Frequently, children with serious learning disorders have difficulty with spatial orientation, eye-hand coordination, and body image. The early work of Strauss and Lehtinen (1947) described such disorders using the term brain-injured, but later such disorders were labeled the Strauss syndrome by Stevens and Birch (1957). They described the child with perceptual-motor difficulties as one who showed disturbances (separately or in combination) in perception, thinking, and emotional behavior.

There is little question regarding the importance of the development of perceptual-motor skills. Cratty (1975) notes that a child with perceptual-motor difficulties cannot translate thoughts into written and printed form with the same precision as a normally developing child. Such a child also may possess various perceptual deficits within one or more modalities (touch, kinesthesia, vision, audition) that may combine as evidence of a defective nervous system and lead to learning problems. Cruickshank (1979) also emphasized that perceptual processing deficits or neurological dysfunction underlie learning problems. Such problems are related to receiving, processing, and responding to information from outside the environment and from inside the child's own body. The ability to understand, remember, think, and perform perceptual-motor skills all precede the ability to read, write, or master arithmetic. Strategies to assist children in the overall learning process were developed (Kephart, 1963) based on the notion that perceptual-motor deficits are primarily organic in nature, and further, that they can be remediated by the development of specific skills such as form perception, eye-hand coordination, and temporal-spatial relationships.

Both Frostig (1975) and Kephart (1975) emphasized the need to develop skills in their natural order. They stressed the effect of motor processes on perception and the effects of perception on cognitive processes (i.e., the use of vision and motor skills or activities in the formation of a concept).

Controversy exists regarding the efficacy of such programs. Much of the research to replicate beneficial results linking perceptual motor training to academic achievement (Balow, 1971; Goodman & Hammill, 1973; Zigler & Seitz, 1975) suggests that the claims are unwarranted. Little evidence has been found to support the use of perceptual-motor activities in the treatment or prevention of disabilities in reading or other specific school subjects. However, other research tends to confirm earlier claims (Ayres, 1972; Gregory, 1978; Masland, 1976; Neman, 1974).

There is continued interest in and support for determining the benefits of specific sensory-motor training.

REFERENCES

Ayres, A. (1972). *Sensory integration and learning disorders.* Los Angeles, CA: Western Psychological Services.

Balow, B. (1971). Perceptual-motor activities in the treatment of severe reading disabilities. *Reading Teacher, 24,* 513–525.

Cratty, B.J. (1975). *Remedial motor activities for children.* Philadelphia: Febiger.

Cruickshank, W.M. (1979). Learning disabilities: Perceptual or other? *Association for Children with Learning Disabilities Newsbriefs, 125,* 7–10.

Daves, W.E. (1980). *Educator's resource guide to special education: Terms-laws-tests-organizations.* Boston: Allyn & Bacon.

Frostig, M. (1975). The role of perception in the integration of psychological functions. In W. Cruickshank & D. Hallahan (Eds.), *Perceptual and learning disabilities in children* (Vol. 1) (pp. 115–146). Syracuse: Syracuse University Press.

Goodman, L., & Hammill, D. (1973). The effectiveness of the Kephart-Getman activities in developing perceptual-motor and cognitive skills. *Focus on Exceptional Children, 4*(9), 19.

Gregory, R.L. (1978). Illusions and hallucinations. In E.C. Carterette & M.P. Friedman (Eds.), *Handbook of Perception: Vol. 9. Perceptual Processing* (pp. 337–358). New York: Academic.

Kephart, N.C. (1963). *The brain injured child in the classroom.* Chicago: National Society for Crippled Children and Adults.

Kephart, N.C. (1975). The perceptual-motor match. In W. Cruickshank & D. Hallahan (Eds.), *Perceptual and learning disabilities in children* (Vol. 1, pp. 63–70). Syracuse: Syracuse University Press.

Masland, R. (1976). The advantages of being dyslexic. *Bulletin of the Orton Society, 26,* 10–18.

Neman, R. (1974). A reply to Zigler & Seitz. *American Journal of Mental Deficiency, 79,* 493–505.

Stevens, G.D., & Birch, J.W. (1957). A proposal of clarification of the terminology and a description of brain-injured children. *Exceptional Children, 23,* 346–349.

Strauss, A.A., & Lehtinen, L.E. (1947). *Psychopathology and education of the brain-injured child* (Vol. I). New York: Grune & Stratton.

Zigler, E., & Seitz, V. (1975). On an experimental evaluation of sensory motor patterning: A critique. *American Journal of Mental Deficiency, 79,* 483–492.

See also Movigenics; Visual-Motor and Visual-Perceptual Problems; Visual Perception and Discrimination

PERCEPTUAL SPAN

Perceptual span is a term encountered in the study of reading. It refers principally to the amount of visual information useful to a reader during a single fixation. Readers are able to apprehend only a limited amount of information during the fixation of the eye's journey across a line of print; however, it has been long noted that skilled readers are also able to recognize words that are a short distance to the right and to the left of the fixation (Woodworth, 1938). This perceptual span (or span of apprehension) is useful to the skilled reader, increasing speed and comprehension of reading. Specifying the nature and extent of this span and its relationship to disorders of reading has been a controversial process (Pirrozzolo, 1979). Pirrozzolo (1979) has described the four major methods of measuring perceptual span, another controversial topic.

Over the last century, researchers and clinicians have hypothesized that disabled readers have a less efficient or possibly a dysfunctional application of their perceptual span. Frank and Levinson (1976) have recently suggested, as one example, that disabled readers have a lower blurring speed than nondisabled readers. This is believed to be due to a cerebellar-vestibular dysfunction that adversely affects the reading process by reducing clear vision and making correct orientation more difficult.

There is sizable evidence (overwhelming in Pirrozzolo's view) from studies of visual function in reading disabilities to indicate that visual-perceptual defects are unrelated to reading disabilities. Problems in occulomotor scanning, sensory and perceptual skills, and perceptual span are clearly not causative in the vast majority of cases of reading disorders, but these areas may appear abnormal as a result of the reading disability.

REFERENCES

Frank, J., & Levinson, F. (1976). C-V dysfunction in dysmetric dyslexia. *Academic Therapy, 12,* 251–283.

Pirrozzolo, F.J. (1979). *The neuropsychology of developmental reading disorders.* New York: Praeger.

Woodworth, R.S. (1938). *Experimental psychology.* New York: Holt.

See also Perceptual Development, Lag in; Perceptual Training; Reading Disorders; Sensory-Integrative Therapy; Visual Perception and Discrimination; Visual Training

PERCEPTUAL TRAINING

Many theorists believe that perception is a learned skill; therefore, it is assumed that teaching or training can have an effect on a child's perceptual skills (Lerner, 1971). Once perceptual abilities have been assessed, there are various teaching procedures and programs that can be used to improve perceptual skills.

Some of the most frequently used educational programs for children with learning disabilities have focused on perceptual training activities. While many of these perceptual training programs have emphasized visual or visual-motor training, there are also perceptual training activities in the areas of auditory perception, haptic and kinesthetic perception, and social perception. In spite of all the available material on these perceptual training programs, many researchers have questioned their effectiveness as a way to improve school learning (Hallahan & Cruickshank, 1973; Hammill & Larsen, 1974).

The book *The Slow Learner in the Classroom* (Kephart, 1971) presented Kephart's perceptual-motor training program, which included activities involving chalkboard training, sensory-motor training, ocular-motor training, and form-perception training. Because of Kephart's belief that motor activities influence visual development, the activities in the form-perception training include assembling puzzles, constructing designs from matchsticks, and putting pegs in pegboards (Hallahan & Kauffman, 1976).

Getman (1985) also proposed a model that attempts to illustrate the sequences of children's development of motor- and visual-perceptual skills. This model, called the visuomotor complex, is applied in a manual of training activities, *The Physiology of Readiness: An Action Program for the Development of Perception in Children* (Getman, Kane, Halgren, & McKee, 1964).

Frostig and Horne (1964) created a visual-perception training program designed for remediation or readiness training. The Frostig Program for the Development of Visual Perception has activities in the areas of eye-motor coordination, figure ground, perceptual constancy, position in space, and spatial relations.

Barsch's movigenic theory proposes that difficulties in learning are related to the learner's inefficient interaction with space. The training program that evolved from this theory has a series of activities that are a planned developmental motor program (Barsch, 1965). Chapters on each of these aspects of the program are included in the curriculum along with exercises to use with learning-disabled children.

Several books and training manuals that focused on training motor skills were written and developed by Cratty (1973). These materials present exercises similar to those found in physical education programs for the purpose of enhancing motor skills and improving a child's cognitive abilities.

REFERENCES

Barsch, R. (1965). *A movigenic curriculum* (Bulletin No. 25). Madison, WI: Department of Instruction, Bureau for the Handicapped.

Cratty, B. (1973). *Teaching motor skills.* Englewood Cliffs, NJ: Prentice-Hall.

Frostig, M., & Horne, D. (1964). *The Frostig program for the development of visual perception.* Chicago: Follett.

Getman, G., Kane, E., Halgren, M., & McKee, G. (1964). The physiology of readiness: An action program for the development of perception in children. Minneapolis: Programs to Accelerate School Success.

Hallahan, D., & Cruickshank, W. (1973). *Psychoeducational foundations of learning disabilities.* Englewood Cliffs, NJ: Prentice-Hall.

Hallahan, D., & Kauffman, J. (1976). *Introduction to learning disabilities.* Englewood Cliffs, NJ: Prentice-Hall.

Hammill, D., & Larsen, S. (1974). The relationship of selected auditory perceptual skills and reading ability. *Journal of Learning Disabilities, 7,* 429–436.

Kephart, N. (1971). *The slow learner in the classroom* (2nd ed.). Columbus, OH: Merrill.

Lerner, J. (1971). *Children with learning disabilities*. Boston: Houghton Mifflin.

See also Movigenics

PEREIRE, JACOB R. (1715–1780)

Jacob R. Pereire, an early educator of the deaf, was the originator of lip reading and the creator of the first manual alphabet for the deaf that required the use of only one hand. Pereire also demonstrated that speech can be understood by using the tactile sense to perceive the vibrations and muscular movements produced by the voice mechanism.

Pereire conducted schools for the deaf in Paris and Bordeaux, and his methods were further developed by de l'Epée and Sicard at the National Institution for Deaf-Mutes in Paris. In recognition of his work, Pereire received an official commendation of the Parisian Academy of Science, was made a member of the Royal Society of London, and was awarded a pension by King Louis XV.

PERFORMANCE INSTABILITY

Performance instability refers to inconsistent functioning on a given task across time. As a characteristic of handicapped children, performance instability often is confused with a second type of variability referred to by O'Donnell (1980) as intraindividual discrepancy. Whereas performance instability denotes changeability within a single domain across time, intraindividual discrepancy refers to variability across different performance areas within a similar time frame.

Nevertheless, the validity and usefulness of performance instability as a salient learning disabilities characteristic is weakened by at least two facts. First, work in two areas that are conceptually related to performance instability—attention disorders and impulsivity—demonstrates that learning-disabled children do not behave distinctively when compared with pupils with different labels of exceptionality. Second, research exploring performance instability among normal and mildly handicapped learning-disabled and behavior-disordered students indicates that the three groups are essentially comparable in the extent to which they manifest performance instability on academic tasks (Fuchs, Fuchs, & Deno, 1985; Fuchs, Fuchs, Tindal, & Deno, 1986).

REFERENCES

Fuchs, D., Fuchs, L.S., & Deno, S.L. (1985). Performance instability: An identifying characteristic of learning disabled children? *Learning Disability Quarterly, 8,* 19–26.

Fuchs, D., Fuchs, L.S., Tindal, G., & Deno, S.L. (1986). Performance instability of learning disabled, emotionally handicapped, and nonhandicapped children. *Learning Disability Quarterly, 9,* 84–88.

O'Donnell, L.G. (1980). Intra-individual discrepancy in diagnosing specific learning disabilities. *Learning Disability Quarterly, 3,* 10–18.

See also **Attention-Deficit Hyperactivity Disorder; Impulse Control**

PERINATAL FACTORS IN HANDICAPPING CONDITIONS

A number of perinatal factors increase the risk of handicapping conditions in the newborn. Social factors include lack of prenatal care; maternal age; inadequate maternal nutrition; use of alcohol, tobacco, or drugs (Alcohol, Drug Abuse, and Mental Health Administration, 1992); stress; work; handicapping condition (Lord, 1991); and fatigue. Maternal disease factors such as hypertension, diabetes, and heart disease may also affect fetal condition at birth. However, alterations in the birth process itself may contribute to the development of fetal handicapping conditions. Preterm labor, postterm labor, premature rupture of membranes, multiple births, antepartum hemorrhage, breech presentations, Caesarean sections, and forceps deliveries all add to the risk of unfavorable fetal outcomes and handicapping conditions (Avery & Taeusch, 1984).

Maternal age represents a nonspecific influence on fetal outcome at birth. Adolescent women 15 years and younger have increased incidences of newborns with neurologic disorders and low birth weights. Women 40 years and older are at increased risk for stillborns or infants with chromosomal abnormalities (Avery & Taeusch, 1984).

Inadequate maternal nutrition and insufficient maternal weight gain of less than 14 pounds have been associated with low infant birth weight. The heavy use of alcohol during pregnancy increases the newborn's risk for growth retardation, microencephaly, cardiac anomalies, and renal anomalies. Tobacco use during pregnancy increases the newborn's risk for low birth weight, prematurity, and even stillbirth. Prescribed, over-the-counter, or recreational drugs may have an adverse effect on the neonate. The probability of a drug causing harm is dependent on the drug itself, the dose, route of administration, stage of gestation, and the genetic makeup of the mother and fetus. Drugs increase the risk of low birth weight, chromosomal abnormalities, organ anomalies, and even fetal death. Further, drugs can create problems with resuscitation and potential withdrawal phenomenon in the newborn (Hobel, 1985).

Stress, work, and fatigue have been associated with an increased risk for poor fetal outcome. The association between stress, work, fatigue, and pregnancy complications is not clear, but it is related to growth retardation and/or low birth weight of the neonate (Creasy, 1984).

Maternal disease factors associated with poor fetal outcome and handicapping conditions include hypertension, diabetes, and heart disease. Hypertension is the most frequently identified maternal problem associated with growth retardation. Hypertension is also associated with preterm labor, low birth weight, cerebral palsy, mental retardation, and fetal death (Avery & Taeusch, 1984).

Poorly controlled maternal diabetes with associated high blood sugars is related to poor fetal outcome. The risk for growth retardation, congenital defects, and brain damage is increased by the complications of diabetes. Maternal heart disease with associated reduced cardiac output is also associated with the increased risk of prematurity and low birth weight. (Hobel, 1985).

Prematurity with its complications is associated with many handicapping conditions. Postterm pregnancy refers to pregnancy lasting longer than 42 weeks. Postterm pregnancy is associated with an increased risk for growth retardation, distress, and even death of the neonate (Hobel, 1985).

The premature rupture of membranes is associated with an increased risk of premature birth and an increased risk for neonatal infection (Oxorn, 1986). Multiple births, antepartum hemorrhage, breech presentation, Caesarean section, and forcep deliveries also increase the risk of handicapping conditions to the newborn. These alterations in the birth process increase the risk for neonatal mortality, central nervous system hemorrhage, asphyxia, and long-term neurologic disability (Avery & Taeusch, 1984).

REFERENCES

Alcohol, Drug Abuse, and Mental Health Administration. (1992). *Identifying the needs of drug-affected children: Public policy issues.* OSAP Prevention Monograph II. Rockville, MD: Office of Substance Abuse Prevention.

Avery, M.E., & Taeusch, H.W. (Eds.). (1984). *Schaffer's diseases of the newborn* (5th ed.). Philadelphia: Saunders.

Creasy, R.K. (1984). Preterm labor and delivery. In R.K. Creasy, & R. Resnik (Eds.), *Maternal-fetal medicine, principles and practice* (pp. 415–443). Philadelphia: Saunders.

Hobel, C.J. (1985). Factors during pregnancy that influence brain development. In J.M. Freeman (Ed.), *Prenatal and perinatal factors associated with brain disorders* (NIH Publication No. 85–1149, pp. 197–236). Bethesda, MD: U.S. Department of Health and Human Services.

Lord, C. (1991). Pre and perinatal factors in high-functioning females and males with autism. *Journal of Autism and Developmental Disorders, 21*(2), 197–209.

Oxorn, H. (1986). *Human labor and birth* (5th ed.). Norwalk, CT: Appleton-Century-Crofts.

See also **Etiology; Intervention; Low Birth Weight Infants; March of Dimes; Neonatal Behavior Assessment Scales; Prematurity**

PERKINS-BINET TESTS OF INTELLIGENCE FOR THE BLIND

The Perkins-Binet Tests of Intelligence for the Blind (Davis, 1980) were designed to assess the intellectual functioning (verbal and performance) of visually handicapped children. Shortly after their appearance it became evident that there were a number of significant flaws in the tests. Reviewers (e.g., Genshaft & Ward, 1982) found the test manual lacking in technical information. Instructions for administering were vague, and in some instances, incomplete. The tests were lengthy and difficult to administer, and scoring criteria

were unclear. There were also concerns about psychometric adequacy and the lack of reliability and validity data (Gutterman, Ward, & Genshaft, 1985). The tests have since been withdrawn from the market.

REFERENCES

Davis, C.J. (1980). *The Perkins-Binet Tests of Intelligence for the Blind.* Watertown, MA: Perkins School for the Blind.

Genshaft, J., & Ward, M. (1982). A review of the Perkins-Binet Tests for the Blind with suggestions for administration. *School Psychology Review, 11*(3), 338–341.

Gutterman, J.E., Ward, M., & Genshaft, J. (1985). Correlations of scores of low vision children on the Perkins-Binet Tests of Intelligence for the Blind, the WISCR-R and the WRAT. *Journal of Visual Impairment & Blindness, 79,* 55–58.

See also **Blind; Visually Impaired**

PERKINS SCHOOL FOR THE BLIND

The Perkins School for the Blind was the first private residential school for the blind chartered in the United States. It was founded by Samuel Gridley Howe in 1832 to serve two blind students and was originally called the New England Asylum for the Blind. At that time asylum was all that even the most fortunate blind person could expect out of life. However, Howe, a strong believer in education, changed the name to the New England Institution for the Education of the Blind. Today, it is known as the Perkins School for the Blind, after Thomas Perkins, a prominent Boston merchant and one of the school's early benefactors. Probably one of its most well-known students was Helen Keller, who attended Perkins from 1887–1892.

See also **Blind; Visually Impaired**

PERSEVERATION

Perseveration is used in special education to describe behavior that is continued by a child beyond the normal (Cuneo & Welsch, 1992) end point of the behavior and that is accompanied by difficulty in changing tasks. Perseveration is considered to be a soft neurological sign and is believed to be most common among learning-disabled and brain-injured children. Lerner (1971) discusses perseverative behavior as one of the four major behavioral characteristics of learning-disabled children.

Difficulties with adaptability may be a component of a general biological predisposition to inefficient attentional strategies. Children who cannot shift tasks, activities, or mental sets may be reflecting anxiety linked to issues of loss or fear of failure, or may be demonstrating neurological abnormalities associated with frontal lobe or possibly reticular function. Koppitz (1963, 1975) has reviewed a number of studies in which children with brain damage demonstrate higher levels of perseverative behavior than do normal children of the same age. Perseveration is one of the best indicators of neurological impairment on the Bender-Gestalt Test (Koppitz, 1963, 1975) and is one of the least subjective scoring categories.

The following clinical illustrations from Levine, Brooks, and Shonkoff (1979) are useful in understanding the different features of perseveration as well as its relationship to impersistence.

1. A child may find the daily progression of routines difficult to manage. Getting up in the morning, dressing, eating breakfast, and preparing for school may present problems. The youngster may linger over each activity. The same pattern may appear when the youngster returns from school; there may be problems initiating routines, coming in from play, disengaging from the television set, and preparing for sleep. Parental efforts to induce a shift of activities may result in severe temper tantrums and unbridled anger.

2. A child may persist at an activity, wishing to sustain it beyond a reasonable period. Such a youngster has difficulty in suspending a project for continuation. Sometimes the behavior reflects a child's wish to pursue some enterprise that is likely to yield success rather than to move on to a riskier endeavor that might culminate in failure; such tenacity may be an avoidance response. At other times perseveration may be a consequence of cognitive inertia with regard to shifting sets. For example, some children with memory deficits or difficulties in establishing object constancy may experience change as overwhelming.

3. A child may resist any changes in daily routine. His or her behavior may deteriorate at the prospect of an unexpected visit to a relative. Some children crave consistency, or a sameness that helps provide order in a world that seems chaotic. They do not appreciate surprises and instead insist on knowing exactly what is going to happen each day (pp. 240–241).

Painting (1979) has commented, appropriately, that perseveration may occur because a particular response is so gratifying to a child that it is repeated primarily for the pleasure involved. A child with learning problems who gets a test item correct or who has mastered a particular activity may perseverate in the behavior because it promotes feelings of success and aids the child's self-esteem.

Perseveration may occur for a variety of reasons. Good diagnosis must go beyond designation of the presence of perseveration to explaining why the child perseverates. Treatment choices are likely to be impacted significantly by etiology in the case of perseverative behavior.

REFERENCES

Cuneo, K., & Welsch, C. (1992). Perseveration in young children: Developmental and Neuropsychological perspectives. *Child Study Journal, 22*(2), 73–92.

Koppitz, E.M. (1963). *The Bender Gestalt Test for Young Children.* New York: Grune & Stratton.

Koppitz, E.M. (1975). *The Bender Gestalt Test for Young Children. Vol. II. Research and application, 1963–1973.* New York: Grune & Stratton.

Painting, D.H. (1979). Cognitive assessment of children with SLD. In W. Adamson & K. Adamson (Eds.), *A handbook for specific learning disabilities.* New York: Halsted.

See also **Bender Gestalt**

PERSONALITY ASSESSMENT

Personality assessment, defined as the description and measurement of individual characteristics, has traditionally been divided into four distinct types: interview, objective, projective, and behavioral. Clinicians frequently use one or more of these assessment methods as an integral component of psychological evaluations.

The interview, which has historical precedence over other methods, was formerly seen as unreliable and subjective. Interviewees are often unwilling to reveal negative things about themselves, and may present different information depending on the style and personal characteristics of the interviewer. On the positive side, an interview can be one of the most direct methods of obtaining information. Structured instruments such as the Schedule for Affective Disorders and Schizophrenia (SADS; Endicott & Spitzer, 1978) and the Diagnostic Interview Schedule (DIS; Robins, Helzer, Craughan, & Ratcliff, 1981) have demonstrated empirical validity and adequate reliability and thus reflect a resurgence of the interview method.

Objective personality assessment, which includes questionnaires such as self-report measures and inventories, is typically the most standardized and structured method of assessing personality. Questionnaires can be scored quickly and used for group administrations; however, they are prone to poor validity when people do not give truthful answers.

Projective techniques, which are less standardized, require good clinical judgment in interpretation. They include the Rorschach Test (Rorschach, 1942), the Thematic Apperception Test (TAT; McClelland, Atkinson, Clark, & Lowell, 1953), figure drawings, word association, and sentence completion tests. As there are no right or wrong answers, it is believed that projective techniques are better able to assess an individual's actual personality characteristics. Critics of these techniques argue that interpretation is subjective and highly dependent on the skills of the interpreter. Exner (1974) has developed a structured, comprehensive scoring system for the Rorschach in an attempt to increase the scientific validity of this measure.

Behavioral assessment examines present behavior, with the expectation that such observation aids in the prediction of future actions. Methods include naturalistic observation, analogue observation, self-monitoring, and participant observation.

Although personality assessment has been a widely used and valuable clinical tool, the validity has been problematic. Objective criteria for diagnosis has been provided by the

DSM-IV (the *Diagnostic and Statistical Manual of Mental Disorders*), but prediction of DSM-IV diagnosis via personality assessment is still a controversial issue. Ongoing research is therefore aimed at increasing predictive validity and reliability and the DSM-IV diagnostic compatibility with personality assessment (American Psychiatric Association, 1994).

REFERENCES

American Psychiatric Association. (1994). *Diagnostic and Statistical Manual of Mental Disorders*. Washington, DC: Author.

Endicott, J., & Spitzer, R.L. (1978). A diagnostic interview: The schedule for affective disorders and schizophrenia. *Archives of General Psychiatry, 35,* 837–844.

McClelland, D.C., Atkinson, J.W., Clark, R.A., & Lowell, E.I. (1953). *The achievement motive*. New York: Appleton-Century-Crofts.

Robins, L.N., Helzer, J.E., Croughan, J., & Ratcliff, K.S. (1981). The NIMH diagnostic interview schedule: Its history, characteristics, and validity. *Archives of General Psychiatry, 38,* 381–389.

Rorschach, H. (1942). *Psychodiagnostics*. Berne, Switzerland: Huber.

See also **Diagnostic and Statistical Manual of Mental Disorders (DSM-IV); Mental Illness; Mental Status**

PERSONALITY INVENTORY FOR CHILDREN (PIC)

The Personality Inventory for Children (PIC) was developed over approximately a 20-year period, primarily by Robert Wirt and William Broen. With its 600 items, 33 subscales (3 validity scales, 1 general screening scale, 12 primary clinical scales, and 17 supplemental scales), point of origin, and emphasis on profiling of scores for interpretation, it is similar in many ways to the Minnesota Multiphasic Personality Inventory (MMPI). At least one reviewer has characterized the PIC as a junior MMPI (Achenbach, 1981).

The PIC is a lengthy personality scale for children that is hard to understand. It has serious psychometric deficiencies with standardization, norming, and reliability and serious problems with the construct validity of the scale. As a research tool, however, it is ready for widespread but careful use in a variety of areas. As a clinical tool, it holds promise, but its widespread use in diagnosis and decision making is premature and must await, at a minimum, a complete renorming of the scale. Better interpretive scoring systems are also needed as an aid to clinicians. The present computerized scoring and interpretive system does little more than group statements checked by the respondent into coherent paragraphs, giving little new information. Though its use is growing in clinical settings, it has not been widely adopted in schools. An extensive critique of PIC can be found in Reynolds (1985).

REFERENCES

Achenbach, T.M. (1981). A junior MMPI? *Journal of Personality, 45,* 332–330.

Reynolds, C.R. (1985). Review of Personality Inventory for Children. In J.V. Mitchell (Eds.), *Ninth mental measurements yearbook*. Lincoln: Buros Institute.

See also **Personality Assessment**

PERSONALITY TESTS, OBJECTIVE

An objective test of personality is one in which the subject is required to make forced choices in response to questions or statements. The scale is objectively scored using templates to organize responses according to the factors measured by the scale. In objective tests of personality, the test items are likely to be interpreted as asking or stating the same thing by most respondents. In most instances, those items are constructed in a manner that avoids ambiguity. The possible alternatives are "yes" or "no" or "true" or "false." In other instances, they may be in a multiple choice format with up to five options.

The validity of the test is established by analyzing the responses and response patterns of persons who have been clinically identified as deviant and comparing the responses to those selected by nondeviant (control) groups. The Minnesota Multiphasic Personality Inventory (MMPI-2) is probably the best known and most widely regarded personality inventory of this kind. In contrast to a projective test of personality such as the Rorschach Test an objective personality test allows for psychometric manipulation and profile analysis.

Objective personality assessment procedures are used by clinicians and researchers interested in identifying psychological problems. The results are used to help them better understand the individual and to help them resolve problems. There is some concern that the use of the scales for excluding persons from employment or educational opportunities is inappropriate and may carry some legal liabilities. In the future, their use in clinical settings may be more applicable than for purposes of employment screening.

See also **Minnesota Multiphasic Personality Inventory–2; Personality Assessment; Revised Children's Manifest Anxiety Scale**

PERSONNEL PREPARATION FOR WORKING WITH DIVERSE INDIVIDUALS

In contrast to the increasing number of students from diverse cultural and linguistic backgrounds, the teaching force is predominantly white, monolingual, female and suburban (Zeichner, 1993). The culture clash resulting from this disparity between the characteristics of students and those of teachers is a contributing factor to the underachievement of culturally and linguistically diverse (CLD) students in both general and special education, with Hispanic/Latino, African American, and American Indian children and youth experiencing the most significant achievement difficulties. As a group, these students are disproportionately overrepresented in special education, underrepresented in gifted education, and have higher dropout rates when compared to their white counterparts (García & Dominguez, 1997).

ESSENTIAL KNOWLEDGE AND SKILLS RELATED TO DIVERSITY

Institutions of higher education must adopt training models that prepare special educators to be culturally and linguistically competent service providers. To effectively address the diverse backgrounds of the students in their classrooms, teachers must have both culture-general and culture-specific knowledge and skills. Culture-general knowledge emphasizes cultural phenomena that occur across cultures and that are widely applicable in a variety of settings (Brislin & Yoshida, 1994). This information provides the initial foundation for understanding cultural/linguistic factors in schooling and education. Culture-specific knowledge, on the other hand, provides an understanding of the customs, norms, traditions, and values of a specific racial/ethnic community and helps prepare teachers to better serve the communities in which they teach.

There are several efforts underway aimed at identifying essential knowledge and skills of novice and exemplary teachers. For example, the Council for Exceptional Children has developed professional standards for the preparation of special educators (Council for Exceptional Children, 1996) and is currently collaborating with its Division for Culturally and Linguistically Diverse Exceptional Learners to identify entry-level knowledge and skills associated with teaching CLD students. Similarly, the National Board for Professional Teaching Standards is preparing standards for what accomplished special education teachers should know and be able to do, and has designed a system for recognizing exemplary teachers of special needs students. All Board certificates include equity, fairness, and diversity standards which underscore the importance of respecting and responding to individual and group differences and of ensuring that all students have access to academically challenging curricula and opportunities to learn.

REFERENCES

Brislin, R., & Yoshida, T. (1994). *Intercultural communication training: An introduction.* Thousand Oaks, CA: Sage.

García, S.B., & Dominguez, L. (1997). Cultural contexts that influence learning and academic performance. *Child and Adolescent Psychiatric Clinics of North America, 6,* 621–655.

Zeichner, K.M. (1993). *Educating teachers for cultural diversity.* NCRTL Special Report. East Lansing, MI: Michigan State University, National Center for Research on Teacher Learning.

PERSONNEL TRAINING IN SPECIAL EDUCATION

See SPECIAL EDUCATION, TEACHER TRAINING IN.

PERÚ, SPECIAL EDUCATION IN

OVERVIEW AND DEMOGRAPHICS

Perú has an estimated population of 24,400,000. Using international estimation guidelines, there should be approximately 2,440,000 or 10% of the general population with disabilities. The last official census reported in 1993 indicated only a total of 289,526 disabled people, which must be assumed to be an incorrect count because it represents only 1% of the actual population. Assuming that 7% of the estimated number of people with disabilities are under 18, the number of children needing service would be 170,800. The Ministry of Education, however, remains responsible for students until they are 26, so that percentage would probably grow by another 5%, or 14,476 people, for a total of 185,276 people with disabilities eligible for special educational services (Census, 1993).

As of 1997, 20,373 people eligible for special education were enrolled in 356 state schools and 3,515 were enrolled in 88 private schools of special education. Regular schools integrated another 221 pupils. The total of 24,109 being educated represents only 13% of the eligible estimated population. The actual total population that is disabled is probably much larger than the world estimation of 10% because Perú has the second highest rate of malnutrition in South America. Thus, those served are likely less than 13% of the actual number of children and youths below 26 years of age (Demographic Statistics, 1997).

The quality of special education that is provided is generally considered inadequate because of poor teacher salaries, poor school conditions, difficult travel, lack of professional education for the majority of the teachers, and lack of government priority. The people who receive no education generally are those who have severe to profound disabilities or multiple handicaps, those in the severest levels of poverty, and those who live in the Andes and the Amazon jungle.

Most schools, state or private, do not accept students with severe to profound retardation, autism, behavior problems, or those with multiple handicaps. The one state psychiatric institution to which they can go is severely limited for funds and space. Thus, there are many adults and children with various types of disabilities living in the streets. The majority live at home with their families. There are two group homes, one in Lima and one in Trujillo, each serving about 20 students. There are many people with retardation who are abandoned and who live in the streets. Adults and children with disabilities have only one state psychiatric institution, located in Lima, to turn to if they have no family, and even then, they can only be admitted if there is space.

There are 30 state early intervention programs for children from birth to five years of age and their caregivers. This program is similar to the Portage Project operated by U.S. researchers in Perú in 1977, which did not flourish due to lack of government support. These programs are unable to serve large numbers of children, however, because they work with one family at a time, for two or three times a week. In 1995, the Ministry began a program of integration in four districts. Although a commendable program, most of the children are very mildly handicapped and many are placed into the program because of behavioral problems. Similar behavioral placements occur in special education classes (The Portage Project, 1995).

Perú does have one private internationally-known model center, Centro Ann Sullivan del Perú, founded in 1979, which is recognized for its excellent functional/natural curriculum, its required family participation program, its individualized life plans and integration into life for its student/workers, and its national and international professional and parent training. It serves 250 people with severe retardation, autism, and behavior problems who live with their families. The center has over 15 different programs ranging from early stimulation to supported employment. Students and professionals from Perú and many other countries come to study and the staff travels around the world to teach the procedures and programs of the center, which is recognized by the University of Kansas as a model center for international cooperation and multiplicative education. The dedicated staff, with help from consultants, has developed the various training programs around the theme of "Treat me like a person and educate me to succeed in life." Currently recognized best practices are used in this low-budget, small-staff, diversified program that serves large numbers of student/workers, ranging in age from birth through adulthood and their families.

The Peruvian government does not make special education a priority because of greater problems of street children, malnutrition, unemployment, and abject poverty which affect much larger numbers of the total population. Because of travel, communication, financial, and professional/parent education problems, creative approaches are needed if education of children with special needs is going to improve. The Ministry of Education continually seeks ways to upgrade the education of all of its teachers, but few resources go directly to special education. The Centro Ann Sullivan del Perú is currently developing a long-distance parent/professional education program, with donations and foundation projects aimed at alleviating problems of substandard professional education and communication in the next few years.

REFERENCES

Central Government of Perú. (1993). *Official census.* Perú: Author.

Ministry of Education of the Central Government of Perú. (1995). *The Portage project.* Perú: Author.

Ministry of Education of the Central Government of Perú. (1997). *Demographic statistics of education and services.* Perú: Author.

PESTALOZZI, JOHANN HEINRICH (1746–1827)

Johann Heinrich Pestalozzi, a Swiss educator, greatly influenced education in Europe and the United States. Believing that ideas have meaning only as related to concrete things and that learning must therefore proceed from the concrete to the abstract, he developed a system of education through object lessons that were designed to help the child develop abstract concepts from concrete experience.

Pestalozzi operated a number of orphanages and schools, the most notable being his boarding school at Yverdon, founded in 1805. His school demonstrated concepts such as readiness, individual differences, ability grouping, and group instruction, and contributed to the inclusion in the curriculum of the practical subjects of geography, nature, art, music, and manual training. Large numbers of educators visited Yverdon and hundreds of Pestalozzian schools were established in Europe. Pestalozzi's object method was first used in the United States in the schools of Oswego, New York; the Oswego Normal School trained teachers in Pestalozzi's methods. Of his numerous publications, Pestalozzi's *How Gertrude Teaches Her Children* best sets forth his educational principles.

REFERENCE

Pestalozzi, J.H. (1978). *How Gertrude teaches her children.* New York: Gordon.

PETS IN SPECIAL EDUCATION

Animals have long been used in classrooms throughout the world (Hulme, 1995). The classic goldfish and gerbils have been used to teach basic animal facts. Teachers have also used pets to foster responsibility in their students. Animals can provide valuable classroom or instructional assistance far beyond the traditional expectations. Sustenance instruction, responsible behavior training, and abstract concepts development can be enhanced by involving special education students with animals. These animals may be provided in the classroom or they may be pets from home.

Teaching responsibility is a multifaceted, often difficult task. Whenever special education students have the responsibility for pets in the classroom or at home, the teacher should be attempting to develop various components of responsible behavior. Students should learn to create feeding, watering, bathing, walking, etc., schedules. In creating schedules for their pets, students may learn to develop schedules for their own lives. Caring for pets also aids in developing task commitment, as well as relationship commitment. Another facet of responsibility, self-initiation, is readily taught when students must care, without reminders from the teacher, for classroom animals.

REFERENCE

Hulme, P. (1995). *Historical overview of nonstandard treatments.* (ERIC Clearinghouse No. EC303986)

See also **Equine Therapy; Recreation**

PEVZNER, MARIA SEMENOVNA (1901–1986)

As a physician-psychiatrist and doctor of pedagogical sciences, Maria Pevzner is known for her work on oligophrenia (mental deficiency). Her research was concentrated in the areas of child psychopathology and clinical assessment of atypical children. Well-known publications of Pevzner are *Children Psychopaths* (1941), *Developmental Assessment and Education of Oligophrenic Children* (1963), and *Children with Atypical Development* (1966).

PHENOBARBITAL

Of the many available anticonvulsant medications, phenobarbital is the least expensive, most effective, best known, and most widely used barbiturate. It is the drug of choice for tonic-clonic (grand mal) epilepsy, neonatal fits, and febrile convulsions (Maheshwari, 1981), and may be viewed as the drug of choice for childhood epilepsy except in cases of absence (petit mal) attacks (Swanson, 1979). It even may be used as an effective agent in pure petit mal epilepsy as a measure against the development of grand mal epilepsy (Livingston, Pruce, Pauli, & Livingston, 1979).

All anticonvulsant medications have side effects and the extent and severity of such side effects often influence medication choice. Unlike many anticonvulsant drugs, phenobarbital has few somatic side effects; however, it appears to have more pronounced effects on mental or cognitive functions in children (National Institutes of Health, 1980). Sedation or drowsiness is the chief side effect of phenobarbital in children. Common behavioral side effects include hyperactivity, extreme irritability, and aggression (Fishman, 1979; Livingston et al., 1979; Nelson, 1983; Wilensky, Ojemann, Temkin, Troupin, & Dodrill, 1981). Other side effects involving cognitive or higher cortical functions include impaired attention, short-term memory deficits, defects in general comprehension, dysarthria, ataxia, and, in some cases, poor language development (Shinnar & Kang, 1994). Fortunately, the side effects do not appear to be permanent, and withdrawal or replacement with other medications often produces significant amelioration of these deficits.

REFERENCES

Fishman, M.A. (1979). Febrile seizures: One treatment controversy. *Journal of Pediatrics, 94,* 177–184.

Livingston, S., Pruce, I., Pauli, L.L., & Livingston, H.L. (1979). The medical treatment of epilepsy: Managing side effects of antiepileptic drugs. *Pediatrics Annals, 8,* 261–266.

Maheshwari, M.C. (1981). Choice of anticonvulsants in epilepsy. *Indian Pediatrics, 18,* 331–346.

National Institutes of Health. (1980). Febrile seizures: Long-term management of children with fever-associated seizures. *British Medical Journal, 281,* 277–279.

Nelson, K.B. (1983). The natural history of febrile seizures. *Annual Review of Medicine, 34,* 453–471.

Shinnar, S., & Kang, H. (1994). Idiosyncratic phenobarbital toxicity mimicking a neurogenerative disorder. *Journal of Epilepsy, 7*(1), 34–37.

Swanson, P.D. (1979). Anticonvulsant therapy: Approaches to some common clinical problems. *Postgraduate Medicine, 65,* 147–154.

Wilensky, A.J., Ojemann, L.M., Temkin, N.R., Troupin, A.S., & Dodrill, C.B. (1981). Clorazepate and phenobarbital as anti-epileptic drugs: A double-blind study. *Neurology, 31,* 1271–1276.

See also **Absence Seizures; Anticonvulsants; Grand Mal Seizures; Medical Management; Seizure Disorders**

PHENOTHIAZINES

Phenothiazine is the class of drugs that historically has been most often prescribed in the treatment of psychotic disorders. This class of medications, which provides symptomatic relief from many of the disturbing symptoms of disorders like schizophrenia and borderline personality disorder in males (Andrulonis, 1991); has replaced the more radical methods of symptom control (e.g., psychosurgery). In addition, the significant behavioral changes that occur when medication regimens are optimally effective allow patients to be treated in outpatient clinics rather than be chronically hospitalized. There are three major classes of phenothiazines that are relatively similar in their overall actions but different in their dose/response ratios and the overall amount of sedation produced (Bassuk & Schoonover, 1977).

The major criticisms of phenothiazines revolve around the exclusive, long-term use of these drugs to control observable symptoms without an attempt to deal with etiology or overall adaptiveness (Marholin & Phillips, 1976).

Phenothiazines produce side effects that may be grouped into four classes: involuntary muscular contractions, especially in the area of the face; motor restlessness; parkinsonlike symptoms such as rigidity, motor slowing, excess salivation, slurred speech, flat facial expression, and gait disturbance; and tardive dyskinesia, a syndrome that consists of stereotyped, repetitive involuntary movements and persists even after medication is discontinued (Bassuk & Schoonover, 1977). Side effects in children are similar to those of adults; however, parents additionally should be aware of sun sensitivity, when children are outside for extended periods of time, and learning/concentration difficulties, especially during onset of treatment (Bassuk & Schoonover, 1977).

REFERENCES

Andrulonis, P.A. (1991). Disruptive behavior disorders in boys and borderline personality disorder in men. *Annals of Clinical Psychiatry, 3*(1), 23–26.

Bassuk, E.L., & Schoonover, S.C. (1977). *The practitioner's guide to psychoactive drugs.* New York: Plenum Medical.

Marholin, D., & Phillips, D. (1976). Methodological issues in psychopharmacological research: Chlorpromazine—a case in point. *American Journal of Orthopsychiatry, 46,* 477–495.

See also **Mellaril; Stelazine; Thorazine; Tranquilizers**

PHENYLKETONURIA (PKU)

Phenylketonuria (PKU) was one of the earliest biochemical irregularities associated with mental retardation. Folling noted in 1934 that a few institutionalized retardates had urine with a peculiar "mousy" odor, which was found to arise from the excretion of phenylacetic acid. Classic PKU results from the absence of the enzyme phenylalanine hydroxylase, which normally converts phenylalanine, an essential amino acid common to most proteins and many other foods, into tyrosine and its constituent components. The resulting high levels of phenylalanine damage developing brain tissue. Since brain damage is irreversible, permanent and severe retardation is a predictable outcome, as are seizures, tremors, and hypopigmentation of skin (Smith, 1985).

An autosomal recessive inborn error of amino-acid metabolism, PKU is expressed only in those homozygotic for the defective gene. Incidence is about 1 in 10,000 births in Anglos and Asians, but much lower in African Americans. Heterozygotes typically produce enough enzymes for normal metabolism. Affected homozygotes are usually normal at birth since prenatally they received already metabolized nutrients through the umbilical cord. If the disorder is undiagnosed and untreated, progressive brain damage begins. Until the 1950s, prognosis was poor; most affected individuals had IQs of about 30 and were institutionalized.

Neonatal screening is now universal. Although a urine test was originally used, diagnosis is now through the Guthrie test, which reveals excess phenylalanine through a blood test 24 to 48 hours after birth. If PKU is diagnosed, the infant is placed on a low phenylalanine diet, which is synthetic because of the ubiquitous presence of phenylalanine in protein. Dietary treatment must begin within a few days of birth for maximal effectiveness. Adult IQ of early treated PKU individuals is about 90; IQ becomes lower with delay of treatment so that by about 3 years of age, maximal damage has occurred. The diet is the sole nutrient fed in infancy. Some (e.g., Berkow, 1977) suggest that thereafter low-protein foods such as fruits and vegetables may be tolerated, whereas others (e.g., Smith, 1985) recommend strict adherence to the diet. The taste of the diet is aversive, and maintaining the child on it while the rest of the family eats regular food can be an increasingly serious problem as the child grows.

Since phenylalanine is toxic only to developing brain tissue, treatment can cease or be relaxed when brain development is complete. Authorities disagree on when the diet can be terminated, but common practice has been to return the child to normal food at about age eight. However, research suggests that longer dietary treatment may be advisable. Dietary treatment for PKU is a classic example of genetic-environmental interaction. On a normal diet, individuals with PKU genotype will develop phenotypic IQ of about 30; dietary intervention alters the predicted developmental pathway, resulting in nearly normal phenotypic IQ (Brown, 1986).

However, treated PKU children may show specific deficits in perceptual motor functioning and arithmetic achievements that are more serious than would be expected on the basis of their slightly below average IQs. They appear to have neuropsychological deficits similar to those of brain-damaged children (Batshaw, 1997; Brunner, Jordon, & Berry, 1983; Pennington, von Doorninck, McCabe, & McCabe, 1985), and have particular deficits in visuospatial and conceptual skills, which may partially account for their problems with mathematics. Pennington et al. (1985) suggest that the deficits may occur because the children are taken off of the diet before the completion of relevant brain development. Although the number of subjects in these studies was small and the findings need confirmation, those working with treated PKU children should be aware that such children may have some specific learning deficits.

The effectiveness of the diet has had one tragic and unexpected effect. In the late 1960s, it became clear that children born to PKU women who had eaten normal food during pregnancy suffered prenatal growth retardation, microcephaly, and brain damage, even though the children did not have the PKU genotype. Although the effects were variable, many of the children died early or became severely retarded. The problems may have been more serious than in untreated PKU itself (Lenke & Levy, 1980). The pregnant women had transmitted unmetabolized phenylalanine to their embryos and fetuses at the prenatal critical period for adverse influences on brain development. A common recommendation now is for PKU women to return to the diet throughout the time they may become pregnant. But regulation of optimal phenylalanine levels is difficult, and no dietary program is completely effective. The safest recommendation is for PKU women not to have children. Thus treated women have an additional responsibility during childbearing years, and some who are at a marginal level of functioning may need some social service assistance (Brown, 1986).

REFERENCES

Batshaw, M.L. (1997). PKU and other inborn errors of metabolism. In M.L. Batshaw (Ed.), *Children with disabilities* (4th ed.) (pp. 389–404). Baltimore: Brookes.

Berkow, R. (Ed.). (1977). *The Merck manual* (13th ed.). Rahway, NJ: Merck, Sharpe, & Dohme.

Brown, R.T. (1986). Etiology and development of exceptionality. In R.T. Brown & C.R. Reynolds (Eds.), *Psychological perspectives on childhood exceptionality* (pp. 181–229). New York: Wiley.

Brunner, R.L., Jordon, M.K., & Berry, H.K. (1983). Early treated PKU: Neuropsychologic consequences. *Journal of Pediatrics, 102,* 381–385.

Lenke, R.R., & Levy, H. (1980). Maternal phenylketonuria and hyperphenylalaninia: An international survey of untreated and treated pregnancies. *New England Journal of Medicine, 303,* 1202–1208.

Pennington, B.F., von Doorninck, W.J., McCabe, L.L., & McCabe, E.R.B. (1985). Neuropsychological deficits in early treated phenylketonuric children. *American Journal of Mental Deficiency, 89,* 467–474.

Smith, L.H., Jr. (1985). The hyperphenylalaninemias. In J.B. Wyngaarden & L.H. Smith, Jr. (Eds.), *Cecil textbook of medicine* (17th ed., pp. 1126–1128). Philadelphia: Saunders.

See also **Biochemical Irregularities; Inborn Errors of Metabolism**

PHILOSOPHY OF EDUCATION FOR THE HANDICAPPED

The philosophical beliefs and values that underlie special education are diverse, dynamic, and interrelated. They reflect broad social issues such as attitudes toward individuals with handicaps as well as specific educational concerns. Three key issues are access to education, placement, and instruction.

Issues of access to education involve questions relating to which children have a right to education and whether all children can benefit from instruction. Questions of access and educability were first raised with respect to individuals with severe and obvious handicaps—the blind, deaf, mentally retarded, and seriously emotionally disturbed. Concern for these individuals prompted the earliest intervention efforts, beginning in the United States as early as 1817.

The question of what organizational setting, or placement, is most appropriate for students with disabilities has been answered differently through the history of special education. Beginning with residential institutions, the range of placement options has gradually increased to include special schools, special classes within public schools, and, finally, integration into regular public school classes (mainstreaming) and inclusion. IDEA requires that handicapped students be placed, to the maximum extent appropriate, in regular educational environments with their nonhandicapped peers. This mandate is known as placement in the least restrictive environment. Inclusion and least restrictive placement are outgrowths of the broader philosophical concept of normalization—the belief that handicapped persons should, to the greatest extent possible, be integrated into society.

Without appropriate instructional strategies, any inclusive or least restrictive placement efforts are unlikely to succeed. Individualized instruction, first advocated by nineteenth-century educators such as Itard and Seguin, has been formalized through IDEA's requirement that an individualized education program be developed and its execution monitored for each child placed in special education.

The philosophical issues that have shaped special education have evolved and changed significantly over the past two centuries. A contemporary philosophy of education for the handicapped incorporates a diversity of complex issues that include those related to access to education, educability, placement, and instruction.

See also **Individuals with Disabilities Education Act (IDEA)**

PHOBIAS AND FEARS

Fear in children and youths is a very strong emotion and is associated with behavioral, cognitive, and physiological indicators of anxiety. When a handicapped child or youth experiences fear that is not age-related in a setting where there is no obvious external danger, the fear is irrational, and the person is said to have a phobia. When the person begins to avoid the nondangerous feared situation, even while maintaining that such action is foolish, the phobia is commonly referred to as a phobic reaction (Morris & Kratochwill, 1983). Fear, on the other hand, is an integral part of normal child development. Many children's fears are transitory, appear in children of similar age, and generally do not interfere with everyday functioning. In fact, some fears that occur during development provide children with a means of adapting to various life stressors.

Those fears observed in infancy typically occur as a reaction to something taking place in the child's environment (e.g., the presence of strangers or loud noises). As the child grows into the toddler and preschool years, the fears broaden and involve the dark, ghosts and other supernatural figures, parent separation, and fears of particular events, objects, or persons. With growth in to the early to middle school years, developmental fears continue to broaden and include such stimuli as animals, thunder and lightning, the dark, parent separation, bodily injury, and sleeping alone. As the child enters preadolescence and adolescence, the normative fears turn more toward school performance, physical appearance, bodily injury, peer acceptance, death, and imaginary figures (Morris & Kratochwill, 1983).

With respect to developmental or normative fears, studies have shown that young children, 24 to 71 months of age, experience on the average 4.6 fears (Jersild & Holmes, 1935). Forty-three percent of children who are 6 to 12 years of age experience at least seven or more fears (Lapouse & Monk, 1959). In preadolescent and adolescent youths, 66% of those sampled reported fears of violence (Orton, 1982). Although girls tend to be more fearful than boys in the early years, this difference does not seem to appear on a regular basis in pre- and early adolescence. No literature exists on the incidence or prevalence of phobias and fears in handicapped children and youths.

Numerous studies have been published over the past several years on intervention approaches for reducing fears and phobias. The assumptions underlying these approaches have generally followed a behavioral orientation. There are five major behavior therapy approaches for fear or phobia reduction in children and youths: systematic desensitization (including variations of this procedure); flooding-related therapies; contingency management procedures; modeling; and self-control procedures. Of these methods, the one that has been used primarily in research is systematic desensitization or variations of this method. Although there are many studies on fears and phobias available for study, with regard to handicapped children and youths, few research studies have been published on the treatment of fears and phobias; however, of those studies that have been published, the majority have used a procedure that is based on systematic desensitization.

REFERENCES

Jersild, A.T., & Holmes, F.B. (1935). Methods of overcoming children's fears. *Journal of Psychology, 1,* 75–104.

Lapouse, R., & Monk, M.A. (1959). Fears and worries in a representative sample of children. *American Journal of Orthopsychiatry, 29,* 803–818.

Morris, R.J., & Kratochwill, T.R. (1983). *Treating children's fears and phobias: A behavioral approach.* New York: Pergamon.

Orton, G.L. (1982). A comparative study of children's worries. *Journal of Psychology, 110,* 153–162.

See also **Anxiety Disorders; Emotional Disorders**

PHONOLOGY

Phonology is a study of the rule-based system underlying phoneme development and speech production. The focus is not on the emergence of specific phonemes but rather on sound classes such as stridency and nasality. The organizational schemata for the formation and use of the phoneme system is the focus of attention.

The need to convey meaning drives this system. At first, children may have only gross classifications like consonant versus vowel as tools to communicate. To get their needs met, they learn that words need beginnings and ends and that there are classes of sounds like stops and front sounds. They acquire the global classes and gradually refine within those classes to ultimately differentiate between a /t/ and a /k/. Children's productions, at any point in time, may be transcribed, analyzed and the rules written to describe the strategies they are using to articulate.

Children with phonological disorders have difficulty abstracting the rules for articulation from the input they hear from others. Their speech is generally unintelligible. The number of phonemes in error will be in excess of 10, and the errors will have a rule-based pattern. Children with phonological disorders generally use the same processes that younger, normal-developing children use, but they have more processes functioning and tend to maintain them longer (Ingram, 1976). In evaluating the severity of the disorder, two considerations are the age of the child and the number of processes being used. In addition, if there are vowel errors, a more complex disorder is signaled because vowels emerge very early in speech production. Similarly, if a child has truly been taught to self-evaluate and does not do so after a reasonable amount of time, it may be the first indicator of an accompanying auditory processing difficulty. Most children with phonological process disorders are normal developing children with intact systems who for no known reason are having trouble with the organizational structure of speech production. The prognosis for this latter group is very good. Children with auditory processing deficits and those with motor/neurological involvement also benefit from phonological process treatment but progress more slowly.

Prior to treatment, an extensive speech analysis is needed to determine the rules being applied and the extent of process usage. Treatment focuses on providing children with information that assists them in revising the rules they are using for speech production.

Phonological processes are most frequently discussed relative to developing rule systems, typically that of children. Older individuals with mental retardation or neurological involvement which presents as apraxia and/or dysarthria also benefit from process-based treatment. The person with retardation may not have mastered the rule-based system for speech. Focus on low level processes like ends-on-words, syllableness, front and back sounds, and others produces gains in intelligibility. Adults with dysarthria and apraxia have previously learned the rules for speech production but due to neurological insult, now have difficulty executing or planning movements. Broader-based treatment which organizes speech by category, assists these persons in improving their speech. For example, if a patient is substituting one sound for another, in-class substitutions will produce greater intelligibility than those which are out-of-class. Thus, the applicability of phonological process treatment is broad and not limited solely to young children.

REFERENCES

Ingram, D. (1976). *Phonological disability in children.* New York: Elsevier.

See also **Linguistic Readers; Reading Disorders; Reading Remediation**

PHOTO ARTICULATION TEST– THIRD EDITION (PAT–3)

The Photo Articulation Test–Third Edition (PAT–3; Lippke, Dickey, Selmar, & Soder, 1997) is a completely revised edition of the Photo Articulation Test. The PAT–3 enables the clinician to rapidly and accurately assess and interpret articulation errors. The test consists of 72 color photographs (9 photos on each of eight sheets). The first 69 photos test consonants and all but one vowel and one diphthong. The remaining 3 pictures measure connected speech and the remaining vowel and diphthong. Consonant sounds are differentiated into the initial, medial, and final positions within the stimulus words. A deck of the same 72 color photographs, each on a separate card, is provided for further diagnosis and may be used in speech-language remediation.

The PAT–3 was standardized in a 23-state sample of more than 800 public and private school students in prekindergarten through grade 4. The students have the same characteristics as those reported in the 1990 Statistical Abstract of the United States. Percentiles, standard scores (mean = 100, SD = 15), and age equivalents are provided. Internal consistency, test-retest, and interscorer reliability coefficients approximate .80 at most ages, and many are in the .90s. Information is provided for content, criterion-related, and construct validity.

REFERENCES

Lippke, B.A., Dickey, S.E., Selmar, J.W., & Soder, A.L. (1997). *Photo Articulation Test–Third Edition.* Austin, TX: Pro-Ed.

PHYSICAL ANOMALIES

A physical anomaly is any bodily attribute that deviates significantly from normal variation. Technically, physical anomalies need not be disabling or handicapping though, as will be noted, they often occur concomitant to a variety of handicapping conditions.

Physical anomalies can impose handicaps in one or many important domains (e.g., cognition, affect, and motor). Functionally, the individual may have difficulty in academic achievement (e.g., reading, mathematics), in social/emotional adjustment (e.g., making and sustaining friendships, attaining a positive self-concept), and in physical activities (e.g., locomotion, orientation).

Visual anomalies, depending on the age at onset, may be classified as congenital (present at birth) or adventitious (acquired sometime after birth). Generally, the impairment concerns visual acuity, field of vision, ocular motility, accommodation, color vision, or corneal opacity.

Like visual anomalies, hearing problems may be classified in different ways. For instance, classification may depend on age of onset (congenital vs. adventitious). Distinctions are also based on the degree of hearing loss (i.e., deaf or hard of hearing). Finally, hearing problems may be conductive or sensorineural in nature. A conductive hearing loss results from interference with the physical transmission of sound waves from the outer ear to the inner ear. On the other hand, a sensorineural hearing loss, as suggested by the name, is caused by neurological damage to nerve tissue in the inner ear. Sound may be grossly distorted to the listener or may not be transmitted at all. In general, sensorineural hearing losses have the more pessimistic prognosis.

Physical handicaps are varied but are commonly categorized as neurological or orthopedic in origin. The former results from injuries, congenital defects, or the progressive deterioration of portions of the central nervous system (CNS). Because most human functions are heavily dependent on an intact CNS, neurological disorders may present particular difficulty for the child and the educator. For instance, it is often difficult to determine a child's true intellectual ability because a motoric handicap may prevent the child from exhibiting it. Cerebral palsy, spina bifida, convulsive disorders, and poliomyelitis are common neurological disorders.

Orthopedic, or musculoskeletal, disorders may be congenital or adventitious. They affect the bones (including joints) and muscles. Accidents, diseases, and hereditary anomalies cause most of the orthopedic disorders. Some of the more common of these conditions are muscular dystrophy, amputations, osteogenesis imperfecta, scoliosis, arthritis, and Legg-Perthes disease.

Other children have conditions in which physical health is poor either permanently of intermittently. Although their conditions are frequently less visually apparent than neurological or orthopedic disorders, they may well face handicapping circumstances in many functional areas (e.g., academic performance, social acceptance). Among the most common of these conditions are epilepsy, cystic fibrosis, juvenile diabetes mellitus, sickle cell anemia, and hemophilia.

The physical anomalies that exist among the mentally retarded population are extensive. Over 250 have been classified so far. Even so, these represent no more than about 25% of the diagnosed cases of mental retardation in the United States. The American Association on Mental Deficiency (Grossman, 1973) has classified the known causal agents of mental retardation as follows: (1) infections and intoxication; (2) trauma and physical agents; (3) metabolism and nutrition, (4) gross brain disease; (5) prenatal influence; (6) chromosomal abnormality; (7) gestational disorders, (8) psychiatric disorders. As with other physical anomalies, individuals with mental retardation suffer from a wide array of affective and motor problems. However, it is their difficulty in cognition and adaptive behavior that best characterizes these children.

Physical anomaly is a term also used to describe a variety of physical aberrations that accompany a host of medical syndromes that typically require special education. Many of these syndromes are genetic disorders that are diagnosed by the specific constellation of physical anomalies apparent to the trained eye. In cases where only one or two minor physical anomalies are present (e.g., hair whorls and a palmar crease), they are often considered to be "soft signs" indicative of neurological problems. Observable minor physical anomalies are often related to neurological problems through coincidental development. The same initial tissue that develops during the embryonic stage into the central nervous system (the neural tube) also forms the epidermis, the outer covering of the body. Also, human chromosomes control more than one aspect of physical development and where one abnormality occurs, others are likely to be present.

Minor physical anomalies occur in many forms and in conjunction with a host of disorders. In Down's syndrome (trisomy 21) one finds a broad flat face, pronounced epicanthal folds, a small palate, and malformed ears. Trisomy 13 will result in microcephaly, physical cardiac defects, polydactyly, cleft lip and palate, and malformation of the eyes and ears. Both of these syndromes frequently result in mental retardation ranging from mild to profound. Marfan's syndrome, most often associated with learning disabilities, though occasionally resulting in mild retardation, occurs with elongated arms and legs, arachnodactyly (long, spider-like fingers), and malformations of the eyes and heart.

***See also* Down's Syndrome; Genetic Factors and Behavior; Mental Retardation; Minor Physical Anomalies**

PHYSICAL EDUCATION FOR STUDENTS WITH DISABILITIES

Physical education is a means of developing motor and sports skills and physical fitness with handicapped populations. Physical education programs for the handicapped have been ongoing throughout the United States in residential, private, and public educational institutions (American Association of Health, Physical Education and Recreation, 1981).

Many terms have been applied to programs of physical activity for the handicapped. Each of these terms represents a specific approach to improving motor and physical performance. Terms such as corrective, developmental, modified, therapeutic, or special physical education are representative of aspects of adapted physical education.

Corrective physical education is a means of remediating structural and functional dysfunctions through physical exercise or motor activities. The dysfunctions, although impairing, are generally correctable. Developmental physical education focuses on improving delayed motor and physical development through exercise and motor skill activities. Modified physical education has activities that are adapted to the learning levels of the handicapped regardless of individual differences. Therapeutic physical education denotes the use of physical education activities under the prescription of a medical doctor. Special physical education is a selected program of developmental activities designed to meet the limitations of those who cannot participate in unrestricted and regular physical education. This term has not gained nationwide acceptance owing to its controversial connotation.

Adapted physical education is a "diversified program of developmental activities, games, sports, and rhythms suited to the interests, capacities, and limitations of students with disabilities who may not safely and successfully engage in unrestricted participation in vigorous activities of the general physical education program".

By definition, adapted physical education includes activities:

Planned for persons with learning problems owed to motor, mental, or emotional impairment, disability, or dysfunction.

Planned for the purpose of rehabilitation, remediation, prevention, or physical development.

Modified so the impaired, disabled, or handicapped can participate.

Designed for modifying movement capabilities.

Planned to promote optimum motor development.

Occurring in a school setting or within a clinic, hospital, residence facility, daycare center or other locale where the primary intent is to influence learning and movement potential through motor activity.

Adapted physical education differs from regular physical education in that it has a federally mandated base and a multidisciplinary approach to individual program planning, covers an age spectrum from early childhood to adulthood, has educational accountability through the individualized education plan (IEP), and emphasizes cooperative service among the school, community, and home to enhance a handicapped person's capabilities (Sherrill, 1985).

The aim of physical education for the handicapped is to aid in achieving physical, social, and emotional growth commensurate with their potential. Objectives of adapted physical education programs vary from program to program depending on population characteristics, instructional expertise, facilities, and equipment.

Prior to participation in a physical education program conducted by a public school, the student with disabilities must have a thorough physical examination. Abnormalities are identified by the physician and suggestions for management are made to school personnel. The physician's suggestions usually include follow-through procedures to ensure proper class placement and appropriate educational placement based on the extent of physical activity needs and limitations. The adapted physical education teacher must be aware of the physician's guidelines and interpret them into an appropriate physical activity program.

Students with disabilities are required to take a battery of motor, physical fitness, and perceptual-motor tests for the making of the yearly IEP (AAHPER, 1981). Short- and long-term goals for the academic year are developed from the test results along with the specific activities recommended for each goal.

Once a pupil with disabilities is given an appropriate physical education class placement, it is the role of the physical education instructor to provide a program of physical activity throughout the school year. In addition to planning and implementing the IEP, the physical education instructor acts as a counselor to aid the student in:

Setting reasonable physical activity goals

Transferring class skills and habits to other environments

Promoting healthful practices

Coordinating program goals with the student's family and related services within the school and community

Providing a framework that fosters socialization skills in the least restrictive environment

Recording progress and continually evaluating needs and interests through physical activity

The aim of a physical education curriculum for the handicapped is to develop physical fitness and motor skills through exercise and sports. For effective learning to take place, it is necessary to know the different levels of functioning in motor learning that affect a student's performance in class. There are three levels of functioning in motor skill acquisition: (1) input functions, (2) abilities, and (3) motor skill.

For the handicapped student to meaningfully participate in a sport, it is often necessary to modify some aspect of the sport to suit the capabilities of the student. For instance, wheelchair basketball is an adaptation of regular basketball in which the participants wheel around and pass the ball as opposed to dribbling and running. General guidelines followed by most instructors who teach adapted physical education state that the activity must be adaptable for effective learning to occur. This means that equipment, rules, or the manner of play may need to be modified for the participants. For instance, to accommodate the limited motor capabilities of a developmentally delayed group, the soccer field could be smaller and the ball could be lighter for it to be kicked farther and more accurately. In addition, activities could be designed to suit the students' abilities and not their disabilities. For example, a student with spina bifida is capable of learning how to swim because of intact upper body coordination. Finally, the instructor should be able to sequence and time learning experiences according to the students' capabilities.

REFERENCES

American Association of Health, Physical Education and Recreation. (1981). Resource guide in adapted physical education. Reston, VA: Author.

Sherrill, C. (1985). *Adapted physical education and recreation* (3rd ed.). Dubuque, IA: Brown.

See also **Adapted Physical Education; Adaptive Behavior; Olympics, Special; Recreation for the Handicapped**

PHYSICALLY HANDICAPPED

The range of disability varies from mild to profound physical impairment. Nonetheless, it is current practice to categorize students with physical handicaps as having average to above average intelligence, and physically handicapped/multiply handicapped students as having additional impairments such as mental retardation, blindness, or deafness. Additionally, mild to moderate learning disabilities often are found with students whose only handicapping condition is physical.

It is estimated that the incidence of physical handicaps is 2% (Smith, 1984). In the school year 1984–1985, 73,292 multihandicapped, 58,924 orthopedically impaired, and 69,688 other health-impaired students received special education services (Office of Special Education and Rehabilitation, 1985). The most common physical impairments found in schools are cerebral palsy, myelomeningocele (spina bifida), and muscular dystrophy. Although children with communicable diseases such as cytomeglavirous, herpes, hepatitis, and acquired immune deficiency syndrome (AIDS) are being denied entry into some schools (Dykes, 1984–1985), the incidence of these diseases is on the rise and will have to be addressed within the public school system.

Most physically handicapped and health-impaired students are served in a combination of regular and special programs (Walker & Jacobs, 1984). Nevertheless, Dykes (1984–1985) suggests that 85% of health-impaired and 35% of orthopedically impaired children should be served solely in regular classrooms. Physically and multiply handicapped students are usually served in special education classrooms, separate facilities, or hospital/home-bound programs if their conditions do not permit inclusive programming.

The educational needs of physically handicapped students vary as widely as the definitions, etiologies, and educational placements. For most physically handicapped students, the regular academic curriculum is most appropriate. In addition, an emphasis is placed on helping the students to gain independent living skills such as grooming, dressing, and food preparation. Perhaps the greatest needs of these students are in the areas of adaptive equipment (Campbell, 1983) and technology (Vanderheiden & Walstead, 1982). Often physically handicapped students require wheelchairs, crutches, head pointers, arm and leg braces, etc. It is common for the physically handicapped child to use a nonverbal/augmentative communication system (e.g., Zygo 100, Tetra-Scan II, Omni) or use microcomputers for a variety of instructional purposes (Rushakoff & Lombardino, 1983). Technological advances have narrowed the gap in providing adequate educational instruction to students who cannot speak, move, or use their hands.

Another major area for intervention with physically handicapped students is in social and self-concept development. Often the physically impaired student is characterized as passive, less persistent, having a shorter attention span, engaging in less exploration, and displaying less motivation (Jennings, Connors, Stegman, Sankaranarayan, & Mendelson, 1985) and less self-esteem (Lawrence, 1991). Additionally, physically handicapped students are found to be more dependent on adults and to interact less with their peers. Programs serving these students must consider socialization and independence. Parents as well as teachers need to find ways to facilitate independence and build self-esteem.

REFERENCES

Campbell, P. (1983). Basic considerations in programming for students with movement difficulties. In M. Snell (Ed.), *Systematic instruction of the moderately and severely handicapped* (2nd ed.) (pp. 168–102). Columbus, OH: Merrill.

Dykes, M.K. (1984–1985). Assessment of students who are physically or health impaired. *Diagnostique, 10,* 128–143.

Jennings, K., Connors, R., Stegman, C., Sankaranarayan, P., & Mendelson, S. (1985). Mastery motivation in young preschoolers: Effect of a physical handicap and implications for educational programming. *Journal of the Division for Early Childhood, 9,* 162–169.

Lawrence, B. (1991). Self-concept formation and physical handicap: Some educational implications for integration. *Disability, Handicap & Society, 6*(2), 139–146.

Office of Special Education and Rehabilitation. (1985). *School year 1984–85 report of services by category.* Washington, DC: U.S. Department of Education.

Rushakoff, G., & Lombardino, L. (1983). Comprehensive microcomputer applications for severely physically handicapped children. *Teaching Exceptional Children, 16,* 18–22.

Smith, O.S. (1984). Severely and profoundly physically handicapped students. In P. Valletutti & B. Sims-Tucker (Eds.), *Severely and profoundly handicapped students: Their nature and needs* (pp. 85–152). Baltimore, MD: Brookes.

Vanderheiden, G., & Walstead, L. (1982). *Trace Center internationally software/hardware registry.* Madison: University of Wisconsin, Trace Center.

Walker, D.K., & Jacobs, F.H. (1984). Chronically ill children in school. *Peabody Journal of Education, 61*(2), 28–74.

See also Accessibility of Buildings; Augmentative Communication Devises; Other Health Impaired

PHYSICAL RESTRAINT

A structured procedure that involves the immobilization of limbs or the entire body is referred to as physical restraint. The intent of physical restraint is to decrease or eliminate the unacceptable behavior immediately preceding the onset of the physical restraint procedure. Physical restraint should be employed only after ample documentation is obtained that lesser intrusive interventions were ineffective.

Immobilization methods vary and may range from holding a student's hands by the side of the body to applying a mechanical arm restraint at the elbows to prevent self-injurious blows to the face. Several recommendations have been offered for implementing physical restraint procedures. Bitgood, Peters, Jones, and Hathorn (1982) recommend that the teacher be positioned behind the student and firmly grasp the student's shoulders to hold them against the back of the seat. A second method of physical restraint involves holding the shoulders while the student is in a bent-over position in a chair (Reid, Tombaugh, & Heuvel, 1981). A third method is holding both of the student's hands behind the back of a chair (Rapoff, Altman, & Christopherson, 1980). The exact method of restraint will vary along several lines, including the size of the student; the size of the teacher; the alternative activity to be taught to the student to replace previously observed unacceptable behaviors; and the position of the student relative to the activity being taught.

In addition to actively immobilizing parts of a student's body, mechanical restraints can be employed. These restraints can restrict the student's movements to strike parts of the body, or materials (e.g., elbow pads, helmets, face masks) can be worn over injured areas to prevent future injuries.

The duration of time during which each instance of physical restraint is employed has varied from 3 seconds to 15 minutes, with most reported studies containing recommendations of 10 seconds to 1 minute. That is, following the occurrence of an unacceptable behavior, the teacher would employ a restraint procedure for a pre-established time interval. If the student is calm, nonagressive and willing to verbally process the incident (Rich, 1997) at the end of the time interval, the restraint is removed. However, if the student continues to struggle as the time expires, an additional duration of time must elapse during which the student is calm prior to removing the physical restraint.

Applying physical restraint as a behavioral intervention should not automatically be associated with punishment. Researchers have observed that physical restraint may act as a reinforcer for continued maladaptive behaviors. Favell, McGimsey, and Jones (1978) evaluated situations in which physical restraint actually resulted in increased frequencies of aggressive behaviors. Similarly, Singh, Winton, and Ball (1984) documented an increase in out-of-seat behavior when followed by contingent physical restraint. Finally, Foxx and Dufrense (1984) evaluated the reinforcing effects of hinged metal splints on the self-injurious behavior of a mentally retarded resident within a large residential facility. Interestingly, the authors were able to fade a self-restraint of a preferred object (large plastic glass) to a socially accepted form of self-restraint in the form of a wristwatch and eyeglasses.

Reasons cited for the reinforcing properties of physical restraint include a relaxing feeling of being immobile and resultant drowsiness; physical contact from a reinforcing adult i.e. attachment (Bath, 1994); reduction in demands placed on the student who escapes from disliked activities by engaging in unacceptable behaviors resulting in physical restraint procedures.

Guidelines have been offered for the judicious application of physical restraint procedures, and teachers need to safeguard the rights of each student by adhering to at least the following:

1. Obtain informed consent from the student's guardian

2. Closely monitor the procedure to prevent intentional or unintentional abuse

3. Positively reinforce appropriate behaviors

4. Consider less restrictive alternatives prior to physical restraint

5. Use minimum physical force

6. Document length of time and frequency of instances of physical restraint

7. Administer physical restraint only in a contingent manner

8. Train all individuals in all environments frequented by the student

9. Maintain a resource file of successful documentations of the use of physical restraint to guide the development of the parameters for a targeted student

10. Fade the intensity of restraint materials to socially acceptable, nondebilitating materials (Foxx & Dufrense, 1984)

11. Identify functional, life skill activities to replace self-injurious or stereotypic behaviors when decreasing unacceptable behaviors via physical restraint

REFERENCES

Bath, H. (1994). The physical restraint of children: Is it therapeutic? *American Journal of Orthopsychiatry, 64*(1), 40–49.

Bitgood, S.C., Peters, R.D., Jones, M.L., & Hathorn, N. (1982). Reducing out-of-seat behaviors in developmentally disabled children through brief immobilization. *Education & Treatment of Children, 5,* 249–260.

Favell, J.E., McGimsey, J.F., & Jones, M.L. (1978). The use of physical restraint in the treatment of self-injury and as positive reinforcement. *Journal of Applied Behavior Analysis, 11,* 225–241.

Foxx, R.M., & Dufrense, D. (1984). "Harry": The use of physical restraint as a reinforcer, timeout from restraint, and fading restraint in treating a self-injurious man. *Analysis & Intervention in Developmental Disabilities, 4,* 1–13.

Rapoff, M.A., Altman, K., & Christophersen, R. (1980). Elimination of a retarded blind child's self-hitting by response-contingent brief restraint. *Education & Treatment of Children, 3,* 231–237.

Reid, J.G., Tombaugh, T.N., & Heuvel, K.V. (1981). Application of contingent physical restraint to suppress stereotyped body rocking of profoundly mentally retarded persons. *American Journal of Mental Deficiency, 86,* 78–85.

Rich, C.R. (1997). The use of physical restraint in residential treatment. *Residential Treatment for Children Youth, 14*(3), 1–12.

Singh, N.N., Winton, A.S.W., & Ball, P.M. (1984). Effects of physical restraint on the behavior of hyperactive mentally retarded persons. *American Journal of Mental Deficiency, 89,* 16–22.

PHYSICAL THERAPY

Physical therapists are responsible for physical restoration. Employing a variety of equipment, they use massage and regulated exercise to improve coordination and balance, reeducate muscles, restore joint motion, and increase the patient's tolerance for activity.

A physical therapist employs mechanical and muscle strengthening exercises to assist students who will benefit from these activities to improve their quality of life. Physical therapists are frequently members of interdisciplinary teams, where they contribute to the overall management of the patient. The goal of most client service is to obtain entry into independent living and competitive employment. An example of services might include deep heat, paraffin baths, hydrotherapy, mild stretching, or strengthening exercises for a person with a crippling arthritis; strengthening and coordinating exercises for a person with a cerebral palsy; development, frequently in concert with an occupational therapist, of exercises for mobility through walking, leg braces, a wheelchair, or some combination; and the appropriate use of any prosthetic devices. Braces, wheelchairs, and other appliances require instruction in their use and care. Physical therapists generally teach these skills. They also join with occupational, speech, hearing, or other therapists in assisting the patient in the use of the prosthetic device to accomplish independent living or vocational skills.

Physical therapy, then, is the act of teaching motor strengthening, motor control, balance, and other skills to handicapped persons. It combines these motoric trainings with prosthetic devices to help the patient to accomplish needed goals by reducing the effects of disability. Physical therapy is one aspect of the total training needed to reduce the effects of disability to enable the handicapped person to profit from residual (normal) bodily functions. Frequently, both the general public and the handicapped person, particularly the newly handicapped person, become overwhelmed at the presence of a handicapping condition. What frequently is not seen is the amount of usable function that remains. The principle involved is to provide the handicapped person with training of muscle groups, motor control, balance, etc., to promote the use of the residual, nonhandicapped functions.

See also Occupational Therapy; Physical Disability

PHYSICIANS' DESK REFERENCE (PDR)

The *Physicians' Desk Reference,* known popularly as the *PDR,* is an annual publication of Medical Economics Company. It reports information on more than 2500 drugs. The information is supplied entirely by the drug's manufacturer but is edited and approved by medical personnel employed by the publisher. The *PDR* contains descriptions of drugs (with pictures in many cases of the most common form), indications for use, recommendations regarding dosage levels, and antidotes for some drugs. Management information for overdosage developed by the Institute for Clinical Toxicology is also presented. The *PDR* is intended primarily for use by physicians and was developed to make readily available essential information on major pharmaceutical products. The *PDR* is useful to allied health professionals and to special educational personnel. It is particularly useful to the latter because of the high incidence of medication usage by handicapped children. The *PDR* is likely to be available in the reference library of any special education program.

PHYSIOTHERAPY

Physiotherapy or physiatry is the treatment of disease with the aid of physical agents such as light, heat, cold, water, and electricity, or with mechanical apparatus. The person responsible for physiotherapy is a physiatrist: a physician who specializes in physiotherapeutics or physiotherapy. Physical therapy, or the application of physiotherapy as practiced by physical therapists or occupational therapists, is supervised by the physiatrist responsible for the physical therapy unit.

The primary purpose of physiotherapy is to provide for the controlled movement of the extremities and for the other muscle and joint articulation necessary for the activities of daily living or competitive employment. Muscles are strengthened, coordination exercises are offered, and mechanical (nonchemical) applications to increase the range of motion and strength for each joint are provided.

The range of patients includes those suffering from damage to either the central or peripheral nervous systems;

those suffering from any disease or mechanical injury; and those afflicted with a birth defect affecting muscle and bone. Two primary systems treated are the skeletal and nervous systems. Some of the more common conditions treated are strokes (cerebral vascular accidents), cerebral palsy, head trauma, spinal cord injuries, arthritis, polio, and a number of inherited and acquired bone, joint, or muscle problems.

Diagnostically the two major groups of study are orthopedically handicapped and other health impaired. The orthopedically handicapped constitute the group that is neuromuscularly handicapped as a result of insult or trauma to the central nervous system or as a result of lower common neural-muscular-orthopedic (skeleton system) damage peripheral to the central nervous system. Other health-impaired conditions have numerous etiologies but have in common a condition that so weakens the individual that he or she must limit or modify the activities and therefore participate in physiotherapy to obtain relief.

See also **Orthopedically Impaired; Other Health Impaired**

PIAGETIAN APPROACH TO SPECIAL EDUCATION

Jean Piaget (1950, 1952, 1977), Switzerland's noted genetic epistemologist, proposed a developmental and constructivist model of human cognition from birth to adolescence based on biological processes. Although his theory has been applied to regular education for several decades, fewer efforts have been made to apply his work to exceptional populations (Gallagher & Reid, 1981; Reid, 1981; Wachs & Furth, 1980). One reason for this apparent lack of interest is Piaget's derivation of theoretical principles from observations of essentially normal children, with the consequent assumption of lack of applicability to handicapped individuals. A second obstacle has been an assumed lack of fit between more holistic and social/linguistic (Beilin, 1996) instructional goals and strategies compatible with Piagetian theory and the specific, step-by-step goals and methods typically prescribed for handicapped learners. Nevertheless, Piaget's cognitive-development theory provides a useful means of understanding and teaching children with exceptional needs.

Piaget himself made little reference to the application of his theory to educational practice. However, psychologists and educators have derived from Piaget's work several principles for instruction appropriate for both academic and social learning. Piaget's theory, applied to special populations, assumes that all children, handicapped and nonhandicapped, proceed through the same invariant sequence of stages using the same processes of assimilation, accommodation, and equilibration. Thus, while the rate of development may differ for exceptional learners, the instructional principles continue to be applicable. Experimental attempts to propel children (exceptional and nonexceptional) to a higher level of development through training generally have

been unsuccessful (Gallagher & Reid, 1981), theoretically because children's stage progression depends on maturation as well as environment. The instructional principles that follow are directed at the teaching of concepts, generalizations, and thinking processes rather than at increasing the level of cognitive development.

1. Because children's thinking is qualitatively different at the various stages of development, teaching objectives should be matched to children's level of development.

2. Learning is the acquisition of higher order structures transformed from and built on previous structures. Thus, learning involves the acquisition of broad, general rules or frameworks rather than particular, isolated facts. As such, learning proceeds through understanding rather than through incorporation of rote responses.

3. Children are internally motivated by a desire for achieving equilibrium. Thus, learning is facilitated by the presentation of optimally challenging tasks and discrepant events that predispose the child to disequilibrium.

4. Children learn best through interacting with and manipulating environmental stimuli.

5. Group interactions may present children with ideas that challenge their own, leading to disequilibrium, reorganization, and new structures.

Teaching methods consistent with these principles and guidelines include cooperative learning, hypothesis testing, discovery learning, inquiry, and other approaches that encourage inductive thinking. Cooperative learning is an instructional strategy whereby students work together in small groups to complete academic tasks. Potential benefits include gains in academic content, basic skill development, problem solving, and socialization. More research is needed on the efficacy of cooperative learning with exceptional students (Pullis & Smith, 1981). Gallagher and Reid (1981) describe hypothesis testing approaches for teaching exceptional students as another method consonant with Piagetian theory.

MENTAL RETARDATION

Although Piaget's writings reflect little interest in individual differences, his ideas have been used to interpret the cognitive behavior of exceptional individuals. For example, Inhelder (1968) noted that the level of cognitive development ultimately achieved by mentally retarded individuals depended on their degree of impairment, with the severe-profound fixated at the sensorimotor level, the moderately retarded at the preoperational stage, and the mildly retarded rarely advancing beyond the level of concrete operations.

During the 1960s and 1970s, Piaget's theory sparked a new view on the field of mental retardation. The developmental approach to mild, familial mental retardation provided a positive alternative to deficit approaches, which assume that mentally handicapped individuals by definition possess deficits (e.g., in processes such as attention, memory, organization, or in neurological structures) that require remediation. The developmental view, articulated by Zigler (1967; Zigler & Balla, 1982) and Iano (1971), suggests instead that the familial educable mentally retarded constitute the lower end of the normal curve and differ from the intellectually average only in terms of rate of development and final level achieved. Mental age serves as an indicator of current developmental level.

In general, proponents of developmental theory as applied to the mildly mentally retarded suggest that this approach enables teachers to view retarded children in terms of normal stages achieved at a slower rate. Klein and Safford (1977) concluded from their review of research literature that stages of development in the mentally retarded population parallel those described by Piaget for nonhandicapped children, but appear at later chronological periods. Hence, the mildly retarded can be expected to perform according to their mental ages. The implication for educators is that methods applied to normal children can be used effectively with mildly retarded students of similar mental age. Thus, these individuals can profit from many regular instructional techniques and a broader curriculum appropriate to normally achieving children. Iano (1971) noted that educators too often assume that the mentally retarded have deficiencies in learning rate, retention, and the ability to generalize and abstract. As a result, teachers emphasize great amounts of repetition, structure, concrete presentation, and slow, step-by-step introduction of new material. He asks whether the retarded child's failure to reason and problem solve is due to an inability to understand or to an emphasis in teaching on the rote and mechanical.

Although the developmental approach as applied to mental retardation has received serious criticism (e.g., Spitz, 1983), research has neither disproved the developmental approach nor proved the deficit position, and probably never will (Spitz, 1983). In the meantime, the application of Piagetian instructional methods with the mildly retarded merits serious investigation and offers an exciting alternative to teachers wishing to broaden their instructional repertoire. Most important, application of Piagetian approaches to instruction may provide variety and challenge to the children themselves.

Piaget's descriptions of the sensorimotor stage, normally covering birth to 18 months, have served as a basis for interpreting the behavior of the severely/profoundly handicapped, assessing their level of cognitive development, and developing appropriate curricula. The six sub-stages of the sensorimotor period can be summarized as follows (Stephens, 1977), together with sample instructional tasks appropriate to each.

Reflexive (birth–1 month). This phase is initially characterized by reflex actions (e.g., hand waving, kicking, crying, sucking, grasping) and visual tracking of objects. These actions become more coordinated and generalized. Sample task: To encourage visual tracking, hold a bright moving object 10 inches from the subject's eyes and move the object slowly across the subject's field of vision. If visual tracking fails to occur spontaneously, physically turn the subject's head to follow the object.

Primary Circular Reactions (1–4.5 months). Reflexive behavior becomes elaborated and coordinated. The infant becomes interested in movement itself, as in observing his or her own hand waving. Repeated as ends in themselves, these actions are "circular" responses. Sample task: Move a colorful, sound-producing object from side to side and up and down to encourage coordination of visual tracking and touching of the object with the hand. If visual tracking coordinated with touching the object does not occur spontaneously, physically guide the behavior.

Secondary Circular Reactions (4.5–9 months). The infant intentionally repeats chance movements that produce a desirable effect (e.g., shaking a rattle to produce a sound). Sample task: Demonstrate a squeeze toy and hand it to the subject. Guide the squeezing behavior to elicit the sound if the behavior does not occur spontaneously.

Coordination of Secondary Schema (9–12 months). The infant begins to discriminate between self and environment, to imitate speech sounds and movements of others, and to differentiate means and ends. Sample task: Demonstrate and guide a means-ends activity such as dropping an object into water to create a splash.

Tertiary Circular Reactions (12–18 months). The infant actively experiments and discovers new means to ends, such as pulling a blanket to reach a toy that is resting on it. Sample task: Provide opportunities for (and guidance as necessary) discovering a means-ends activity such as obtaining an unreachable object using a stick.

Invention of New Means Through Mental Combinations (18–24 months). The infant considers alternatives, solves problems, and completes development of object permanence. Sample task: Demonstrate and permit experimentation with fitting objects of different sizes and shapes into slots of various size and shape.

Based on her earlier work with severely retarded individuals, Woodward (1963) concluded that many of the seemingly inappropriate behaviors of this population are explainable within a Piagetian framework. Given that profoundly handicapped individuals operate at a sensorimotor level, mannerisms such as hand flapping in front of the eyes can be interpreted as sensorimotor patterns developed in the course of coordinating vision and grasping, as in the subphase of primary circular reactions.

Uzgiris and Hunt (1975) developed an assessment procedure for charting infant development founded on major areas of cognitive functioning during the sensorimotor period. Such an assessment procedure can be adapted for use with severely/profoundly handicapped individuals of various chronological ages. Areas of functioning assessed by Uzgiris and Hunt include visual pursuit and object permanence; means for achieving desired environmental events; gestural and vocal imitation; operational causality; object relations in space; and development of schemas in relation to objects.

Because severely/profoundly handicapped individuals generally do not proceed beyond the preoperational stage, curricula can be derived for this population based on the sensorimotor subphases and adapted according to chronological age. Development of appropriate curricula of a Piagetian nature for the severely/profoundly handicapped requires matching objectives to the individual's present level of development; active involvement of the individual; opportunity for the individual to proceed at his or her own pace; opportunities for exploration and manipulation; opportunities for repetition and practice; and adaptation for any associated sensory or motor impairments.

LEARNING DISABILITIES

By most definitions, learning-disabled students possess average to superior intellectual potential but manifest academic and social achievement at levels significantly lower than this potential would predict. Delays in cognitive and social-cognitive development have been explored through research as possible factors in explaining the discrepancy between potential and achievement in academic and social areas. Suggestions for teaching interventions based on Piagetian theory have also been offered in the literature.

Research. In general, the research suggests that learning-disabled (LD) children demonstrate performance inferior to that of nondisabled (NLD) children on tasks designed to measure cognitive development and social cognition. Speece, McKinney, and Appelbaum (1986) found a developmental delay in LD children's attainment of concrete operations compared with nondisabled (NLD) controls over a 3-year-period. However, their results also suggested that when the LD children attained the concrete operational stage, they acquired specific concepts in the same sequence and at the same rate as did NLD children. Moreover, for the LD but not the NLD group, Piagetian measures of cognitive development (conservation scores) and age better predicted academic achievement than did verbal intelligence. Most important was the finding that while the LD children as a group improved over the 3-year period, they failed to catch up with their NLD peers. Speece et al. (1986) concluded that delayed cognitive development may constitute an important explanatory factor for continued academic underachievement experienced by LD children despite intervention.

Dickstein and Warren (1980) reported similar delays in LD children's role-taking ability compared with NLD children in cognitive, affective, and perceptual tasks. Their analysis of the performance of children from 5 to 10 years of age suggested that larger differences in scores occurred in the younger age groups and that performance among LD children improved little between ages 8 and 10. Horowitz (1981) also found lower performance for LD children on an interpersonal role-taking task, but no significant differences between the two groups on a perceptual role-taking measure. However, as indicated by Horowitz, results were confounded by differences between the two groups in intelligence. Wong and Wong (1980) found significant differ-

ences between LD and NLD children in role taking, with LD girls demonstrating much poorer skills than LD boys.

Finally, investigations of LD children's referential communication skills corroborate the findings on role taking that LD children possess deficits in social cognition relative to their NLD peers. Noel (1980) found LD students less effective in providing descriptive information about objects than NLD controls because of the LD children's tendency to describe objects by shape rather than by label or name. Spekman (1981) further reported that LD speakers tended to give more unproductive, irrelevant, or repetitious messages than did NLD children on communication tasks. These findings suggest that LD children communicate less effectively than do NLD children.

As a whole, results of investigations on role taking and communication suggest that deficits in these skills may be one source of social problems evidenced by some LD children. Having difficulty in anticipating other people's views and accommodating their messages to others' needs reduces LD children's chances for successful social interactions.

Teaching. The literature has suggested Piagetian-derived instructional strategies for LD students both as tools for presenting academic content and for remediating deficits in social-cognitive skills. Gallagher and Quandt (1981) presented questioning strategies consistent with Piagetian theory for improving reading comprehension of LD students. They suggest, for example, the use of inference questions that require students go beyond the information given. Such questioning strategies present puzzling problems that stimulate equilibration. Moses (1981) offers examples of arithmetic instruction to illustrate the use of Piagetian guidelines for teaching LD students. Role-taking training through each child's sequential adoption of the various roles in a story also has been suggested (Chandler, 1973) as a vehicle for improving role-taking skills and social behavior.

OTHER CATEGORIES

A few investigators have examined the application of Piagetian principles to children with other types of exceptionalities: cerebral palsy, hearing handicaps, visual impairments, and emotional disturbance and giftedness. A review of these studies by Gallagher and Reid (1981) suggests that (1) intellectually normal children who have cerebral palsy progress at approximately the same rate as nonhandicapped children, although the former are slower to perform on tasks requiring manipulation, need more trials and encouragement, and have a lower frustration tolerance; (2) deaf children and blind children display minor or no delays in attainment of conservation compared with normal peers when accommodations are made for language and sensory differences and subjects are carefully matched; and (3) seriously emotionally disturbed children show deviations from normal developmental patterns.

In conclusion, the available research on cognitive development of exceptional learners suggests, for the most part, that exceptional individuals progress through the same sequence of stages described by Piaget for normal children, although they vary in rate of development and level ultimately attained. Application of Piagetian theory to practice suggests use of strategies that engage children in active problem solving appropriate to their current level of development. Additional research is required to demonstrate the efficacy of Piagetian-derived instructional strategies for handicapped and gifted learners. Such strategies have potential as additions to the instructional repertoire of special education teachers.

REFERENCES

Beilin, H. (1996). Mind and meaning: Piaget and Vygotsky on causal explanation. *Human Development, 39*(5), 277–286.

Chandler, M.J. (1973). Egocentrism and antisocial behavior: The assessment and training of social perspective-taking skills. *Developmental Psychology, 9*(3), 326–332.

Dickstein, E.B., & Warren, D.R. (1980). Role-taking deficits in learning disabled children. *Journal of Learning Disabilities, 13*(7), 378–382.

Gallagher, J.M., & Quandt, I.J. (1981). Piaget's theory of cognitive development and reading comprehension: A new look at questioning. *Topics in Learning & Learning Disabilities, 1*(1), 21–30.

Gallagher, J.M. & Reid, D.K. (1981). *The learning theory of Piaget and Inhelder.* Austin, TX: Pro-Ed.

Horowitz, E.C. (1981). Popularity, decentering ability, and role-taking skills in learning disabled and normal children. *Leaning Disability Quarterly, 4*(1), 23–30.

Iano, R.P. (1971). Learning deficiency versus developmental conceptions of mental retardation. *Exceptional Children, 58,* 301–311.

Inhelder, B. (1968). *The diagnosis of reasoning in the mentally retarded.* New York: John Day.

Klein, N.K., & Safford, P.L. (1977). Application of Piaget's theory to the study of thinking of the mentally retarded: A review of research. *Journal of Special Education, 11*(2), 201–216.

Moses, N. (1981). Using Piaget principles to guide instruction of the learning disabled. *Topics in Learning and Learning Disabilities, 1*(1), 11–19.

Noel, M.M. (1980). Referential communication abilities of learning disabled children. *Learning Disability Quarterly, 3*(3), 70–75.

Piaget, J. (1932). *The moral judgment of the child* (M. Gabain, Trans.). New York: Harcourt, Brace & World.

Piaget, J. (1950). *The psychology of intelligence* (M. Percy & D.E. Berlyne, Trans.). London: Routledge & Kegan Paul.

Piaget, J. (1952). *The origins of intelligence in children.* (M. Cook, Trans.). New York: International University.

Piaget, J. (1977). *The development of thoughts: Equilibration of cognitive structures.* New York: Viking.

Pullis, M., & Smith, D.C. (1981). Social cognitive development of learning disabled children: Implications of Piaget's theory for research and intervention. *Topics in Learning & Learning Disabilities, 1*(1), 43–55.

Reid, D.K. (Ed.). (1981). Piaget learning and learning disabilities. *Topics in Learning & Learning Disabilities, 1*(1).

Speece, D.L., McKinney, J.D., & Appelbaum, M.I. (1986). Longitudinal development of conservation skills in learning disabled children. *Journal of Learning Disabilities, 19*(5), 302–307.

Spekman, N.J. (1981). Dyadic verbal communication abilities of learning disabled and normally achieving fourth- and fifth-grade boys. *Learning Disability Quarterly, 4*(2), 139–151.

Spitz, H.H. (1983). Critique of the developmental position in mental-retardation research. *Journal of Special Education, 17*(3), 261–294.

Stephens, B. (1977). A Piagetian approach to curriculum development for the severely, profoundly, and multiply handicapped. In E. Sontag (Ed.), *Educational programming for the severely and profoundly handicapped* (pp. 237–249). Reston, VA: Council for Exceptional Children, Division on Mental Retardation.

Uzgiris, I.C., & Hunt, J.M. (1975). *Assessment in infancy ordinal scales of psychological development.* Urbana, IL: University of Illinois Press.

Wachs, H., & Furth, H. (1980). Piaget's theory and special education. In B.K. Keogh (Ed.), *Advances in special education* (Vol. 2, pp. 51–78). Greenwich, CT: JAI.

Woodward, M. (1963). The application of Piaget's theory to research in mental deficiency. In N. Ellis (Ed.), *Handbook of mental deficiency: Psychological theory and research.* New York: McGraw-Hill.

Zigler, E. (1967). Familial mental retardation: A continuing dilemma. *Science, 155,* 292–298.

Zigler, E., & Balla, D. (Eds.). (1982). *Mental retardation: The developmental-difference controversy.* Hillsdale, NJ: Erlbaum.

See also Cognitive Development; Direct Instruction; Individualization of Instruction; Intelligence; Piaget, Jean

PIAGET, JEAN (1896–1980)

Jean Piaget was a Swiss psychologist whose explorations of the cognitive development of children helped to revolutionize education in the twentieth century. He described the sequence of mental development in three phases: (1) the sensory-motor phase, from birth to about age 2, during which children obtain a basic knowledge of objects; (2) the phase of concrete operations, from about 2 to 11, characterized by concrete thinking and the development of simple concepts; and (3) the formal operations phase, from about age 11, emphasizing abstract thinking, reasoning, and logical thought. Piaget's theories and descriptions of developmental sequences have encouraged teaching methods that emphasize the child's discovery of knowledge through the presentation of developmentally appropriate problems to be solved.

Born in Neuchatel, Switzerland, Piaget was educated at the university there, was director of the Jean Jacques Rousseau Institute in Geneva, and professor at the University of Geneva. In 1955 he established in Geneva the International Center of Genetic Epistomology, where he and his associates published voluminously on child development.

PIC

See PERSONALITY INVENTORY FOR CHILDREN.

PICA

The word "pica" originates from the Latin word for magpie, a bird known for ingesting a wide variety of food and non-food items (Danford & Huber, 1982). Pica is seen in various species, including birds, fish, apes, and humans (Diamond & Stermer, 1998). Pica as a disorder is characterized by habitual ingestion of inedible substances (Kerwin & Berkowitz, 1996). It is frequently associated with mental retardation (Danford & Huber, 1982), but also occurs in normal young children (less than age 3) and pregnant women within certain cultural groups. As many as 90% of children with elevated levels of blood-lead may show pica behavior. Pica sometimes continues into adolescence and adulthood (Diamond & Stermer, 1998). In infancy and early childhood, children often chew on their cribs, wood, sand, and grass as a method of early exploration (Erickson, 1998).

Pica is a learned behavior, but its maintenance may owe to a number of factors. Since one of those factors may relate to a nutritional inadequacy, medical and nutritional analyses should precede any treatment program (Katsiyannis, Torrey, & Bond, 1998). If it is associated with some nutritional inadequacy, pica may be successfully treated with some dietary changes or mineral supplements targeted at the particular deficiency. In cases where no nutritional problem is found, a functional analysis of behavior should be conducted. Several types of behavioral interventions have been used successfully, ranging from less intrusive (e.g., differential reinforcement for non-pica behavior) to more aversive (e.g., overcorrection or brief physical restraint contingent upon pica). Obviously, any treatment program should begin with the least restrictive interventions unless the child's behavior presents an immediate risk. One interesting treatment uses a "pica box." A pica box is a small box containing edible items for a child. When a child attempts to eat a nonedible item, he or she is stopped, and after a brief time-out, is reinforced by being allowed to get a treat out of the pica box. This method has been especially useful in working with mildly retarded and autistic children (Hirsch & Myles, 1996). A particular source for those in special education is Katsiyannis et al. (1998), who not only describe several programs in detail but provide useful case studies.

REFERENCES

Danford, D., & Huber, A. (1982). Pica among mentally retarded adults. *American Journal of Mental Deficiency, 87,* 141–146.

Diamond, J., & Stermer, D. (1998). Eat dirt. *Discover, 19*(2), 70–76.

Erickson, M.T. (1998). *Behavior disorders of children and adolescents.* Upper Saddle River, NJ: Prentice Hall.

Hirsch, N., & Myles, B. (1996). The use of a pica box in reducing pica behavior in a student with autism. *Focus on Autism and Other Developmental Disabilities, 11,* 222.

Katsiyannis, A., Torrey, G., & Bond, V. (1998). Current considerations in treating pica. *Teaching Exceptional Children, 30*(4), 50–53.

Kerwin, M.E., & Berkowitz, R.I. (1996). Feeding and eating disorders: Ingestive problems of infancy, childhood, and adolescence. *School Psychology Review, 25,* 316–329.

See also Anorexia Nervosa; Eating Disorders; Lead Poisoning; Obesity

PIERRE-ROBIN SYNDROME

Hypoplasia of the mandible, prior to 9 weeks of intrauterine development, results in a posteriorly located tongue which, in turn, impairs closure of the posterior or soft palate. Children born with the syndrome of micrognathia (small lower jaw) are at risk for airway obstruction which may be present at birth or develop over the first month of life, requiring endotracheal tube or tracheostomy. Lack of oxygen can lead to damage to the heart and brain during this critical period. Most infants are otherwise normal and mandibular growth catches up, the long-term prognosis is good both for appearance and function. This anomaly is, however, also seen as part of other multiple malformation syndromes that may include mental retardation.

PIERS-HARRIS CHILDREN'S SELF-CONCEPT SCALE

The Piers-Harris Children's Self-Concept Scale (Piers, 1969) is a self-report inventory designed to measure self-concept in children ages 9 through 16. The 80-item scale consists of short statements reflecting concerns children have about themselves. There are 36 positive statements and 44 negative statements written at a third-grade reading level. Responses indicative of a favorable self-concept are worth one point and total scores can range from 0 through 80. Scores are also obtained on six subscales: behavior, intellectual and school status, physical appearance and attributes, anxiety, popularity, and happiness and satisfaction. Test-retest reliability has ranged from .62 to .75 (over a 2 to 7 month period) and from .80 to .96 (over a 3 to 9 week period; Hughes, 1984). Evidence of construct validity was reviewed by Piers (1977). Moderate relationships were reported with other measures of self-concept, and relationships with personality and behavioral measures were generally in the direction expected.

Although the norms for the Piers-Harris are several decades old, more recent research has provided general continuing support for the use of the instrument (Epstein, 1985). When integrated with other data on a child, the Piers-Harris may prove to be quite clinically useful. Therapists or counselors may find it to be a helpful screening tool or a useful introductory activity for therapy (Epstein, 1985).

REFERENCES

Epstein, J.H. (1985). Review of The Piers-Harris Children's Self-Concept Scale. In J.V. Mitchell (Ed.), *The ninth mental measurements yearbook.* Lincoln, NE: Buros Institute of Mental Measurements.

Hughes, H.M. (1984). Measures of self-concept and self-esteem of children ages 3–12 years: Review and recommendations. *Clinical Psychology Review, 4,* 657–692.

Piers, E.V. (1969). *The Piers-Harris Children's Self-Concept Scale.* Nashville, TN: Western Psychological Services.

Piers, E.V. (1977). *The Piers-Harris Children's Self-Concept Scale, research monograph No. 1.* Nashville, TN: Western Psychological Services.

See also **Children's Manifest Anxiety Scale; Self-Concept**

PINEL, PHILIPPE (1745–1826)

Phillipe Pinel, French physician and pioneer in the humane treatment of the mentally ill, served as chief physician at two famous mental hospitals in France, the Bicêtre and the Salpêtrière. Convinced that mental illness was not a result of demoniacal possession, as was commonly believed, but of brain dysfunction, Pinel released his patients from the chains that were used to restrain them and replaced deleterious remedies such as bleeding and purging with psychological treatment by physicians.

Through publications in which he set forth his methods for the care and treatment of the mentally ill, Pinel's ideas gained wide acceptance throughout the western world. France, through Pinel's efforts, became the first country to attempt the provision of adequate care for the mentally ill.

PITUITARY GLAND

The pituitary is a small gland located at the base of the brain immediately beneath the hypothalamus, above the roof of the mouth, and behind the optic chiasma. The pituitary lies in a bony depression called the sella turcia. The pituitary is also sometimes referred to as the hypophysis.

The pituitary regulates the secretions of a number of other endocrine glands and often is referred to as the master gland. However, its function is closely linked to the hypothalamus, and the pituitary and hypothalamus must be thought of as a system rather than independent entities. The hypothalamus and the pituitary are connected by a rich supply of nerves called the infundibulum.

Morphologically, the pituitary is a small gland. It weighs less than a gram and is only about a centimeter in diameter. It consists of two major lobes, the anterior pituitary (adenohypophysis) and the posterior pituitary (neurohypophysis). These two lobes are connected by a much smaller pars intermedia. The anterior pituitary manufactures a number of hormones that serve to trigger the release of still others. The hormones directly secreted by the anterior pituitary include growth hormone, thyroid-stimulating hormone (TSH), adrenocorticotrophic hormone (ACTH), and gonadotrophic hormones such as follicle-stimulating hormone (FSH), luteinizing hormone (LH), and lactogenic hormone (prolactin).

Adrenocorticotrophic hormone (ACTH) is intimately involved in stress reactions. Release of this hormone by the pituitary causes the adrenal cortex to produce cortisol and other steroid hormones that help prepare the body for fight or flight. Gonadotrophic hormones (e.g., follicle-stimulating hormone and luteinizing hormone) activate the ovaries and testes so that estrogen and testosterone, respectively, are produced.

Prolactin is a hormone that affects the mammary glands and that appears to be involved in the regulation of maternal behavior in vertebrates. Somatotropin (STH or growth hormone) is a hormone necessary for normal growth. Excesses of somatotropin result in the clinical condition of acromegaly.

The posterior pituitary (neurohypophysis) secretes antidiuretic hormone (ADH) and oxytocin. Release of these hormones is triggered by complex connections with other parts of the nervous system. The cells of the posterior pituitary do not produce hormones themselves but instead serve as storage sites for hormones produced by the anterior hypothalamus. When blood pressure falls, the secretion of ADH stimulates the kidneys to reduce their excretion of water into the urine. Lack of ADH can produce diabetes insipidus. Oxytocin plays an important role in inducing contractions during labor, and it is necessary for the contraction of the smooth muscles of the mammary glands, which are needed to produce milk in response to sucking.

It has been found that individuals with anorexia and bulimia have same pituitary atrophy due to nutritional and/or endocrine alterations (Doraiswamy, Krishnan, Figiel, & Husain, 1990).

REFERENCE

Doraiswamy, P., Krishnan, K., Figiel, G.S., & Husain, M. (1990). A brain magnetic resonance imaging study of pituitary gland morphology in anorexia nervosa and bulimia. *Biological Psychiatry, 28*(2), 110–116.

See also **Diabetes**

PKU

See PHENYLKETONURIA.

PLACEBOS

Placebos are substances or therapeutic interventions that produce their effects as a result of the expectations of the recipient and the therapist. As originally applied in medicine, placebo therapies improved patients' conditions despite the fact that the placebos had no direct physiological action. Placebos, therefore, became an aid to physicians who lacked a specific therapy and a nuisance variable to researchers studying therapeutic effectiveness.

The placebo effect is most powerful in social situations where an experimental approach produces high hopes for success (Orne, 1969). To differentiate between placebo and direct therapeutic physiological effects, it has become commonplace in drug research to use a double-blind procedure. In such a design, both the person administering the therapy and the subject are unaware (blind) as to whether a given dose contains the experimental substance or a physiologically inert placebo. If the placebo and treatment interventions result in similar effects, the value of the new therapy is called into question. Practical or ethical considerations often limit the applicability of double-blind studies, and the existence of potential placebo effects remains a problem in a variety of areas of research.

There has been great controversy concerning the use of the placebo concept in understanding behavioral change interventions. Simeon & Willins (1993) suggest that there has not been enough research done in the use of placebos with children. Critelli and Neumann (1984) have argued that the placebo effect is more than a nuisance variable and the display of empathy, nonpossessive warmth, etc., that may occur in a placebo intervention may be an important part of the therapy. In the classroom, the expectations of teachers and students about the probabilities of high student performance during an educational intervention may play a significant role in its effectiveness (Zanna, Sheras, Cooper & Shaw, 1975).

REFERENCES

Critelli, J., & Neumann, K.N. (1984). The placebo: Conceptual analysis of a construct in transition. *American Psychologist, 39,* 32–39.

Orne, M. (1969). Demand characteristics and the concept of quasi-controls. In R. Rosenthal & R. Rosnow (Eds.), *Artifact in behavioral research* (pp. 147–181). New York: Academic.

Simeon, J.G. & Wiggins, D.M. (1993). The placebo problem in children and adolescent psychiatry. *International Journal of Child and Adolescent Psychiatry, 56*(2), 119–122.

Zanna, M., Sheras, P., Cooper, J., & Shaw, C. (1975). Pygmalion and Galatea: The interactive effect of teacher and student expectancies. *Journal of Experimental Social Psychology, 11,* 279–287.

See also **Double-Blind Design; Teacher Expectancies**

PLACENTA

The placenta transfers life-sustaining supplies from the mother to the prenate, disposes of the prenate's wastes, and protects the prenate from some harmful substances. It begins to form during the germinal period and becomes differentiated as a separate disk-shaped organ during the embryonic phase (Annis, 1978). The umbilical cord extends from the center of the smooth fetal surface. The maternal surface is composed of many convoluted branches, creating a surface area of about 13 m2, which provides maximum exposure to blood vessels in the uterine lining. At term the placenta is about 18 cm in diameter and weighs about 570 g.

The placenta includes two completely separate sets of blood vessels—one fetal and one maternal. Only small, light molecules may pass through the placental barrier; maternal and fetal blood never mix. Although the exact mechanisms of transfer of nutrients and wastes between the two systems are not completely understood, transfer of gases and water is accomplished by simple diffusion (Hytten & Leitch, 1964).

The placenta protects the prenate from overexposure to elements in the mother's blood (e.g., hormones and cholesterol) by reducing their concentration in the fetal blood; it also prevents some teratogens from reaching the fetus.

In a small percentage of pregnancies, impairments involving the placenta create serious consequences. In about 10% of pregnancies the placenta fails to produce progesterone in the early weeks, resulting in spontaneous abortion. Infrequently, the placenta is small or malformed, causing retarded fetal growth or possibly stillbirth. When the placenta partially or entirely covers the cervical opening (placenta previa), the membranes usually rupture early in the third trimester, leading to a premature delivery.

Even during normal functioning, the placenta is an imperfect filter. As the fetus matures, placental blood vessels enlarge and stretch the placental barrier more thinly, thus decreasing its ability to filter larger molecules. Many harmful agents (e.g., bacteria) are kept out during the early prenatal stages, when teratogens are potentially most dangerous. For example, syphilis cannot cross until after the twentieth week. Viruses (including rubella), because they are so small, are able to pass through during this critical period. Many chemicals that the mother ingests that are potentially harmful (e.g., alcohol, caffeine, and carbon monoxide) pass through in ever-increasing dose levels as the placental barrier thins.

REFERENCES

Annis, L.F. (1978). *The child before birth.* Ithaca, NY: Cornell University Press.

Hytten, F.E., & Leitch, I. (1964). *The physiology of human pregnancy.* Oxford, England: Blackwell.

See also **Congenital Disorders; Prematurity**

PLANTAR REFLEX

The word plantar means "of, pertaining to, or occurring on the sole of the foot" (Rothenberg & Chapman, 1994). The plantar reflex is observed when the sole of the foot is scratched or stroked with a dull object and the toes bunch or curl downwards. The plantar response is a reflex that involves all the muscles that shorten the leg and the toes and is present in normal children (after the age of one year), adolescents, and adults.

Abnormal response to the plantar stimulation is usually in the form of the big toe extending upwards towards the head, the toes fanning out, and withdrawal of the leg. This response is known as the Babinski reflex or sign and is indicative of neurological damage.

REFERENCE

Rothenberg, M.A., & Chapman, C.F. (1994). *Dictionary of medical terms* (3rd ed.). Hauppauge, NY: Barron's.

See also **Apgar Rating Scale; Babinski Reflex; Developmental Milestones**

PLASTICITY

Plasticity in the human sciences is the absence in an individual of predetermined developmental characteristics and a concomitant modifiability by organismic or environmental influences. The concept is not limited to the capacity to change in accord with outside pressure. It includes the power to learn from experience and modify behavior while retaining predisposing genetic inheritance (Kolb & Whishaw, 1998). Educator John Dewey (1916) emphasized the characteristic plasticity of the immature child as a specific adaptability for growth. Basic to this concept is a person's power to modify actions on the basis of the results of prior experiences. In addition, plasticity implies the development of definite dispositions or habits. Habits, Dewey wrote, give control over the environment and power to use it for human purposes.

A study by Chess, Korn, and Fernandez (1971) of 235 victims of a 1964 worldwide rubella epidemic began when the youngsters were 2 years old. Development showed an overall delay during the first years of life, with characteristic impairment in language and motor sensorimotor functions. One-third of the children were diagnosed as showing varying degrees of mental retardation during the preschool period, while only one-fourth showed evidence of mental retardation at ages eight and nine. The IQs of the nonretarded children also showed progressive increases as they entered the school-age period. Detailed case studies of a number of the children who showed such improvement demonstrated that they came through a diverse and roundabout pattern to normal school functioning. Often they pioneered new territory in the acquisition of language, social development, and learning—thereby affirming the inherent plasticity of human brain function in the young child.

REFERENCES

Chess, S., Korn, S., & Fernandez, P. (1971). *Psychiatric disorders of children with congenital rubella.* New York: Brunner/Mazel.

Dewey, J. (1916). *Democracy and education.* New York: Macmillan.

Kolb, B., & Whishaw, I.Q. (1998). Brain plasticity and behavior. *Annual Review of Psychology, 49,* 43–64.

See also Intelligence; Zone of Proximal Development

PLATO AND THE GIFTED

Plato's three levels of public education included common elementary school, secondary school with selective admission, and a state university with admission still more selective. On the elementary level, the curriculum covered literature, music, and civics. On the secondary level, students were prepared for future military and civil service posts by studying in the curriculum areas of mathematics, arithmetic, plane and solid geometry, astronomy, and harmonics. In higher education there were 5 years of "dialectic" learning followed by 15 years of practical experience for those chosen to be the leaders of the ideal state (Brumbaugh, 1962).

The idea of gifted students within the educational system was especially evident in the republic during the open discussions on mathematics. Plato believed that all students should be introduced to mathematics and discussed how this subject had an effect on the mental powers of a student; he believed it sharpened a student's wits and helped to fix attention. The skills of higher mathematics were seen as needed by the chosen few future rulers. These gifted students would study with systematic thoroughness and exactness (Morrow, 1960). Students were chosen for this advanced curriculum if they demonstrated that they understood the general connection of the various curriculum areas. If a student successfully grasped both a practical and theoretical connection, at the age of 30 the student would be admitted to the highest and most complete of all possible studies—philosophy.

REFERENCES

Brumbaugh, R.S. (1962). *Plato for the modern age.* New York: Crowell-Collier.

Morrow, G.R. (1960). *Plato's Cretan city: A historical interpretation of the laws.* Princeton, NJ: Princeton University Press.

See also History of Special Education

PLAY

Regardless of its seemingly nonserious origins, play is a critical developmental activity. Many aspects of our social, motor, and cognitive lives have their origins in childhood play. The famous Russian psychologist Lev Vygotsky argued that play creates the conditions for the child's acquisition of new competence in imaginative, social, and intellectual skills. Recently, computers and the internet have provided a new form of play for many children and adolescents (Griffiths & Hunt, 1995).

One method of classifying children's play is based on interactions with other children. Five categories of play can be distinguished (Parten, 1932). The first type, solitary play, involves no interaction at all with other children. In onlooker play, the second type, the child simply observes other children at play. This is thought to be the first phase of a preschooler's interaction with other children.

When children begin to engage in the same activity side by side without taking much notice of each other, parallel play is said to occur. Associative play, the fourth type, occurs in older preschoolers; in this type, play becomes much more interactive. During this phase, two or more children partake in the same activity doing basically the same thing; however, there is no attempt to organize the activity or take turns.

Cooperative play, an organized activity in which individual children cooperate to achieve some sort of group goal, usually does not appear until age 3. At this stage children become more able and eager to participate in social forms of play. Solitary play does not ever disappear. Most children are capable of playing alone if a companion is not available. Onlooker behavior persists even into adulthood.

The symbolic nature of play is vital to the development of the child; it performs several functions in that development. First, children can use their symbolic skills, like language, in new and different ways, in a sense testing the limits of those skills. Second, children can, through play, do and say things that are normally difficult to express or taboo. Third, as children exit infancy they can use play in a cooperative, social fashion. "Make believe" allows children to explore social roles, work in cooperation with others, and experiment with social roles and rules (Damon, 1983).

Children who are handicapped may be less able to use play effectively and therefore may lose out on some of the important outcomes of play. For example, a physically handicapped child may not be able to engage in normal social play with other children. Hence, that child needs special arrangements or interventions to make sure that he or she has access to normal opportunities for play (Cattanach, 1995).

REFERENCES

Cattanach, A. (1995). Drama and play therapy with young children. *Arts in Psychotherapy, 22*(3), 223–228.

Damon, W. (1983). *Social and personality development: Infancy through adolescence.* New York: Norton.

Griffiths, M.D., & Hunt, N. (1995). Computer game playing in adolescence: Prevalence and demographic indicators. *Journal of Community & Applied Social Psychology, 5*(3), 189–193.

Parten, M.B. (1932). Social participation among preschool children. *Journal of Abnormal & Social Psychology, 27,* 243–269.

See also **Concept of Activity; Vygotsky, L.S.; Zone of Proximal Development**

PLAYTEST

The PLAYTEST procedure is recognized as one possible approach to screening and direct assessment of an infant's auditory functioning (Butterfield, 1982). The PLAYTEST system was originally developed by B.Z. Friedlander as a research tool for measuring infants' selective listening and receptive voice discrimination abilities within the home environment (Friedlander, 1968).

The system consists of a simple, portable, automated toy apparatus that attaches to the infant's crib or playpen. An audio or video-audio recorder and response recorder complete the equipment. The apparatii are attached at different locations on the crib or playpen. When the infant attends to either device, the responses activate the accompanying stereophonic tape recorder. The tape recorder is fitted with an endless loop audio tape. Certain systems are equipped to provide video-audio feedback instead of just audio feedback. Separate channels on the device carry different prerecorded sound samples.

The infant's frequency and duration of response to the various sources of auditory stimuli are used to infer the current level of auditory discrimination and selective listening abilities. Both the audio and the video-audio PLAYTEST systems use a response recorder to register the infant's differential response to the various auditory stimuli.

The PLAYTEST system has proven a valuable research tool in the investigation of auditory functioning in infants (Friedlander, 1968, 1970, 1971, 1975). One interesting finding is that very young infants show a clear preference for the mother's voice as opposed to a simple musical score.

It appears that the PLAYTEST system also provides an invaluable means of identifying infants at high risk for developing significant language disorders later in life (Butterfield, 1982; Friedlander, 1975). Butterfield (1982) envisions the PLAYTEST procedure as an instrumental screening and assessment procedure in the very early detection of auditory processing and/or discrimination problems in infants. He has described modifications of the existing system that would enable professionals to assess infants less than 6 months of age for possible auditory dysfunctions (Butterfield, 1982).

REFERENCES

Butterfield, E.C. (1982). Behavioral assessment of infants' hearing. In M. Lewis & L.T. Taft (Eds.), *Developmental disabilities: Theory, assessment, and intervention.* New York: SP Medical & Scientific.

Friedlander, B.Z. (1968). The effect of speaker identity, voice inflection, vocabulary, and message redundancy on infants' selection of vocal reinforcement. *Journal of Experimental Child Psychology, 6,* 443–459.

Freidlander, B.Z. (1970). Receptive language development in infancy: Issues and problems. *Merrill Quarterly of Behavior & Development, 16,* 7–51.

Friedlander, B.Z. (1971). Listening, language, and the auditory environment: Automated evaluation and intervention. In J. Hellmuth (Ed.), *The exceptional infant* (Vol. 2). New York: Brunner/Mazel.

Friedlander, B.Z. (1975). Automated evaluation of selective listening in language impaired and normal infants and young children. In B.Z. Friedlander, G.M. Sterritt, & G.E. Kirk (Eds.), *The exceptional infant* (Vol. 3). New York: Brunner/Mazel.

See also **Auditory Discrimination; Deaf; Language Disorders**

PLAY THERAPY

Play therapy is a therapeutic technique used with children that emphasizes the medium of play as a substitute for the traditional verbal interchange between therapists and adult clients. Direct work with a child was first initiated by Hug-Hellmuth (Gumaer, 1984), who applied Freudian analysis to children under age 7. It soon became apparent that children lacked the verbal ability, interest, and patience to talk with a therapist for an extended period of time. Thus in the late 1920s, both Melanie Klein and Anna Freud developed therapeutic methods that used play as the child's primary mode of expression. Anna Freud stressed the importance of play in building the therapeutic relationship, deemphasizing the need for interpretation. Klein, however, approached play therapy much like traditional adult psychoanalytic work, with free play becoming a direct substitution for free associations, and insights and interpretation retaining primary importance.

In the following decade, Otto Rank was an important contributor with his notion of relationship therapy. Rank stressed the importance of the emotional attachment between the child and the therapist, focusing mainly on present feelings and actions of the child. In the 1940s and 1950s, Carl Rogers client-centered therapy was modified by Virginia Axline (1947) into a nondirective play therapy. Axline's work, which has remained one of the cornerstones of current play therapy, is predicated on the belief that the child has within himself or herself the ability to solve emotional conflicts. According to Axline, it is the job of the play therapist to provide the optimal conditions under which the child's natural growth and development will occur. The basic rules of Axline's approach have become the standard for nondirective play therapy. They include the development of a warm relationship, acceptance, permissiveness with a minimum of limits, reflection of feelings, and giving the child responsibility for directing the sessions, making choices, and implementing change.

The effectiveness of play therapy has been attributed to its direct relevance to the child's developmental level and abilities. Woltmann (1964) stresses that play allows the child to act out situations that are disturbing, conflicting, and confusing and, in so doing, to clarify his or her own position in relation to the world around. Inherent to the success of play therapy is the make-believe element. Through fantasy and play, children are able to master tasks (drive a car, fly a spaceship), reverse roles (become parent or teacher), or express overt hostility without being punished. Woltmann believes that play therapy allows the child to "eliminate guilt and become victorious over forces otherwise above his reach and capabilities." Caplan and Caplan (1974) provide a further rationale for the effectiveness of play therapy. They contend that the voluntary nature of play makes it intrinsically interesting to the child and reduces the occurrence of resistance. The child is free to express himself or herself without fear of evaluation or retaliation. Through fantasy, the child can gain a sense of control over the environment without direct competition from others. Finally, play therapy is seen as developing both the child's physical and mental abilities.

The selection of the play media is an important part of the therapy. Gumaer (1984) notes that toys should be durable, inexpensive, and safe. They should be versatile (e.g., clay, paints) so that children may use them in a number of ways. Toys should encourage communication between the child and therapist (e.g., telephones, puppets). Some toys should be selected for their ability to elicit aggression such as a toy gun or a soldier doll. Finally, toys should be relatively unstructured; items such as board games or books leave little room for creativity. In addition to the toys already mentioned, Axline (1947) commonly employs a set of family dolls, a nursing bottle, trucks and cars, and, if possible, a sandbox and water.

In recent years, play therapy has expanded to include a number of settings, participants, and techniques (Phillips & Landreth, 1995). Ginott (1961) has developed a method that provides a specific rationale for toy selection and that emphasizes the importance of limit setting. Dreikurs and Soltz (1964) use play therapy that emphasizes the natural and logical consequences of a child's behavior. Myrick and Haldin (1971) describe a play process that is therapist directed and shorter in duration than Axlinian therapy, thus making it more practical for use in school settings. For further study, the reader is directed to *The Handbook of Play Therapy* (Schaefer & O'Conner, 1983), which describes specific techniques such as family play and art therapy, as well as play therapy directly tailored to such childhood disturbances as abuse and neglect, divorced parents, aggression, learning disability, and mental retardation.

REFERENCES

Axline, Virginia (1947). *Play therapy.* Boston: Houghton Mifflin.

Caplan, F., & Caplan, T. (1974). *The power of play.* New York: Anchor.

Dreikurs, R., & Soltz, V. (1964). *Children: The challenge.* New York: Hawthorne.

Ginott, H. (1961). *Group psychotherapy with children.* New York: McGraw-Hill.

Gumaer, J. (1984). *Counseling and therapy for children* New York: Free Press.

Myrick, R., & Haldin, W. (1971). A study of play process in counseling. *Elementary School Guidance and Counseling,* 5(4), 256–263.

Phillips, R.D., & Landreth, G.L. (1995). Play therapists on play therapy: A report of methods, demographics and professional practices. *International Journal of Play Therapy,* 4(1), 1–26.

Schaefer, C., & O'Conner, K. (1983). *The handbook of play therapy.* New York: Wiley.

Woltmann, A. (1964). Concepts of play therapy techniques. In M. Haworth (Ed.), *Child psychotherapy* (pp. 20–31). New York: Basic Books.

See also **Family Therapy; Play; Psychotherapy**

PLURALISM, CULTURAL

Cultural pluralism is a sociological concept that refers to the dual enterprise of acceptance and mobility within the mainstream, majority culture while preserving the minority cultural heritage. Cultural pluralism is seen by many as the most desirable cultural milieu and has been promoted in a variety of settings, including education and employment.

The term is recognized in special education in relation to the work of Mercer et al. (Mercer & Lewis, 1979) in the assessment of mental retardation. Mercer has argued that past efforts in assessment and placement in special education programs for mildly mentally retarded children have failed to recognize the pluralistic nature of American society.

The cultural competence movement in teacher education has grown considerably in recent years in terms of legislative support (IDEA, Part H in particular) and with the development of instruments such as the Pluralism and Diversity Attitude Assessment (PADAA) instrument, which assesses preservice attitudes of educators (Stanley, 1997). Cultural competence is becoming a consistent demand for special and regular education, and is promoting cultural pluralism.

REFERENCES

Mercer, J.R., & Lewis, J. (1979). *System of multicultural pluralistic assessment.* New York: Psychological Association.

Stanley, L.S. (1997). Preservice educator's attitudes toward cultural pluralism: A preliminary analysis. *Journal of Teaching in Physical Education, 16*(2), 241–249.

See also Cultural Bias in Testing; Cultural/ Linguistically Diverse Students; Disproportionality; System of Multicultural Pluralistic Assessment

POLAND, SPECIAL EDUCATION IN

Special education in Poland has a long history. In 1817, the Institute of Deaf-Mute and Blind was established in Warsaw. In 1922 Maria Grzegorzewska (1888–1967) established the Institute of Special Education, which conducted research and trained teachers. In 1924 a special education section of the Polish Teachers Association was established (Kirejczyk, 1975). In 1976 the National Institute of Special Education was reorganized into the Graduate School of Special Education.

In the 1950s programs for the mentally retarded were segregated into 120 self-contained schools. In the 1960s there were 331 special classes within elementary schools with an enrollment of over 5000 youngsters. By the 1970s the number of such classes increased to 698, with an enrollment of nearly 11,000. Currently, there are over 250 special schools in Poland, in addition to a considerable number of special classes within public schools.

Handicapped pupils in Poland are educated in special preschool facilities, special elementary schools, special vocational schools, residential boarding schools, and rehabilitation and therapeutic facilities; they also receive home instruction (Belcerek, 1977). Various levels of interaction of exceptional children within the mainstream of education are also provided (Hulek, 1979), e.g., regular programs with some supplemental instruction, special classes within regular schools (there are presently over 1100 such classes for the mildly handicapped within the Polish public schools and 57 within the vocational schools), selected activities within regular schools, and special schools in the vicinity of regular schools, with cooperative programs.

Special educators in Poland prefer the term therapeutic pedagogy, or special pedagogy, rather than defectology, a term widely used in the Soviet Union. The mildly retarded attend 8 years of basic special school, followed by 3 years of specialized vocational training. A new 10-year curriculum for the mentally retarded recommends the following areas of training and education: adaptation and social living, language stimulation, arithmetic, visual-motor tasks, music, physical exercise, technical-practical activities, and prevocational training. Training goals and objectives for the severely handicapped include physical development and acquisition of manual skills, development of self-help and everyday activity skills, development of basic information, appropriate interpersonal relationships, and prevocational training.

Special education teachers in Poland are prepared at 4-year teacher's training institutions which they enter after graduation from high school. Some experienced teachers of subjects enter universities that have a special education teachers' training program. Since 1973, in addition to the National Institute of Special Education, special education teachers are also prepared at 11 universities (Belcerek, 1977). In 1977 the Polish Ministry of Education opened postgraduate studies in special education at the Graduate School of Special Education in Warsaw. The areas of study at the school include diagnosis and assessment of exceptionalities and the study of deaf, hard-of-hearing, chronically ill, and socially maladaptive children. Special educators are also trained at the Graduate School of Education in Krakow.

Guidelines for the training of special educators have been developed by the special education team of the Pedagogical Science Committee of the Polish Academy of Sciences (Hulek, 1978). Guidelines recommend that a student in special education become familiar with teaching non-handicapped and subsequently handicapped children; teachers should cooperate with various agencies and institutions outside the school; and teachers should continuously be upgrading their education after graduation by attending in-service classes.

Special education studies in Poland are published in *Informator Szkolnictwa Specjalnego* (Bulletin of Special Education), *Nowa Szkola* (New School), *Szkola Specjalna* (Special School), and *Educacja* (Education; formerly *Badania Os'wiatowe,* Educational Research).

REFERENCES

Belcerek, M. (1977). Organization of special education in Poland. In A. Hulek (Ed.), *Therapeutic pedogogy.* Warsaw: State Scientific Publication.

Hulek, A. (1978, June). *Personnel preparation: International comparison.* Paper presented at the First World Congress on Future Special Education, Sterling, Scotland.

Hulek, A. (1979). Basic assumptions of mainstreaming exceptional children and youth. *Badania Oswiatowe* (Educational Research), 3(15), 99–112.

Kirejczyk, K. (1975). Half-century of activity of the Special Education Section of the Polish Teacher's Association. *Szkola Specjalna* (Special School), 1, 7–18.

POLITICS AND SPECIAL EDUCATION

Through the middle of the twentieth century, the politics surrounding special education can be characterized as the politics of exclusion. The primary decision makers were school officials who excluded from the public schools students with special needs requiring services not provided to the majority of students (Copeland, 1983). The grounds for exclusion tended to be observably inappropriate or disruptive behavior, rather than rigorous identification of the nature of students' needs or impediments to learning. Parents typically acquiesced in such decisions without questioning the denial of public school resources to their children.

Around the turn of the century, forces began to emerge that would contribute toward the inclusion rather than the exclusion of special needs students from public school systems (Sarason & Doris, 1979). Refinements in evaluation technology facilitated the identification of the special needs of handicapped students and suggested management and instructional methods appropriate to them. As a result, there was a widespread increase in the number of special classes within public schools (though outside the mainstream of regular students). State and federal legislative bodies enacted programs and provided funds for such classes. Parent advocacy groups and associations of special educators pressed for increased outlays to meet the needs of specific categories of handicapped children and youths.

Since services for different disabilities incurred different costs, there are indications that various funding formulas may have had a significant effect on local school policies and practices (Lynn, 1983). The proportion of students labeled as having particular disabilities varied from district to district and among states, often in relation to variations in the amounts of funds that could be obtained for specific handicaps. It also varied in relation to the type of diagnostic instruments used, the type of specialists in the school, and the type of specialized services already provided. The politics of inclusion were thus influenced by local practices and political configurations and maneuverings of special education interest groups, legislators, and bureaucracies.

Although emerging special education policies, funds, programs, and practices may not have always matched the needs of special education students, their legitimacy was increasingly accepted, and they provided the leverage for progressively including special needs students within the public schools. By 1975 mandatory legislation that provided for the education of special needs students had been passed in all but two states. By that time, the states' financial contribution had risen to more than half the total revenues allocated to special education. By 1979 approximately 140 different federal programs serving the handicapped had been enacted. By the early 1980s, localities and special districts were contributing a total of $5.8 billion; states $3.4 billion; and the federal government a total of $804 million (Lynn, 1983).

However, it became clear as support for special education advanced, that two separate systems had developed: one outside the public schools, the other inside. Parent advocates now moved to expand the one that had been established within the public schools by pressing for geographic, social, and educational inclusion of special needs students within the system. These efforts contributed to the exodus of the majority of special education students from state-run residential institutions into the public schools, and to considerable cost shifting from the former to the latter.

The legal basis for this shift came from landmark court decisions establishing the rights of special education students to free and appropriate public schooling (*Watt v. Stickney*, 1970; *Diana v. State Board of Education*, 1970 and 1973; *PARC v. Pennsylvania*, 1972.) The Fourteenth Amendment guarantees of due process and equal protection were invoked to affirm the rights of special needs children to the free public schooling offered to other children. The U.S. Constitution was applied to protect these students from discriminatory public school practices in the same manner in which it had been applied to protect minority group students in such decisions as *Brown v. Board of Education* in 1954.

While court action gave significant impetus to recognition of the rights of access of students with special needs to public schools, it did so by declaring prior school policies and practices unconstitutional. Yet such determinations tended not to specify what was or would be judged constitutional. Rather, the courts began to act as umpires, ordering plaintiffs and defendants to negotiate compromises that would be acceptable to both and not unconstitutional (Kirp, 1981). Their role was to set up a structured, adversarial process within state and local school systems in which the courts would act as mediators rather than lawgivers. The process would thus be open-ended in terms of its duration, given the lengthiness of legal proceedings, and unpredictable in terms of its possible outcomes.

The debates and conflicts as to placement of handicapped students, as well as services to be provided them, spread to the federal arena as well, where advocates sought to apply the inclusionary principles of court decisions to congressional enactments. These advocates rode on the coattails of the civil rights movement and the Civil Rights Act of 1964. They encountered countervailing forces similar to those that hampered civil rights activists in their efforts to obtain federal enactments and implement them through the federal system. The movement and the act and its numerous amendments sought to eliminate discriminatory practices by public schools that had denied students geographic, social, and educational inclusion because of their ethnicity, national origin, sex, or impoverishment (Bordier, 1983).

They provided the U.S. Congress with a model for a major legislative enactment designed to protect the rights of special needs students. Passed in 1975, the Education for All Handicapped Children Act, PL 94-142, affirmed their right to a free, appropriate public education in the least restrictive environment; required the identification, evaluation, and placement of students with special needs according to an individual educational plan (IEP); and guaranteed parental rights of participation in educational decisions concerning their children.

Under PL 94-142, the federal government was to pay a graduated percentage of average per pupil expenditures by public elementary and secondary schools, starting with 5% in 1979 and culminating in 40% by 1982. Implementation of the legislature was nominally nonmandatory. However, most school districts followed suit, presumably because they would have been hard pressed by the parents of special needs students if they did not seek to obtain available federal funds. Furthermore, an earlier law, Section 504 of the Vocational Rehabilitation Act of 1973; forbade discrimination against handicapped students in programs receiving federal financial assistance. Under 504, school districts were routinely required to sign compliance statements affirming that they did not discriminate against students on the basis of race, national origin, sex, or handicap. Since the law was initially interpreted to mean that failure to sign compliance statements could jeopardize receipt of federal financial assistance, compliance (at least on paper) via these statements became the norm.

By the middle 1980s, at the end of the first Reagan presidency and at the beginning of the second term, funding for implementation of PL 94-142 was curtailed. The law and its regulations were weakened by congressional interventions and Department of Education actions designed to lessen the federal role in education and to devolve social sector responsibilities (including education in general and special education in particular) to the states.

However, because PL 94-142 had assigned significant responsibilities and funds for implementation to state authorities, by the early 1980s, the latter had already adopted laws and regulations reflective of the principles and the delivery system the federal government had mandated earlier. Such legal frameworks, created at state levels, remained in force even after the federal law itself was weakened in the 1980s. Furthermore, state and local authorities had voted to increase expenditures in order to comply with PL 94-142.

When cutbacks in funding occurred at the federal level, and signs of backlash against rapidly increasing expenditures for previously underserved groups appeared at local and state levels, advocates seeking to protect the rights of special needs students used these policies and funding allocations as precedents to justify continuing aid to special education. The role and responsibilities of state and local authorities became established independent of federal laws and regulations. Local school systems followed suit, and the progressive inclusion of special education students proceeded, geographically, socially, and educationally, in more depth than ever anticipated (Brantlinger, 1997).

The enrollment of special needs students increased significantly. Schools formalized their identification, evaluation, and referral procedures, and included new participants in the process. These included committees on the handicapped, appointed by local school boards; parents and their counsels; new categories of special educators and clinicians; "regular" teachers, administrators, and ancillary personnel who had not previously had responsibility for special needs students; and multidisciplinary evaluation teams. The earlier politics of inclusion that affected the federal court system and the federal government had thus significantly increased the number of participants in the politics of inclusion at the local level. Their participation was focused on the legally specified, formalized procedures that court decisions and legislative enactments had established to improve educational services provided to students with special needs.

In the meantime, the signs of a new movement in the field of special education appeared; this would engender new policy approaches designed to integrate a whole spectrum of institutions providing services to handicapped students, including but not limited to school systems (Copeland, 1983). The needs of special education students for services beyond those provided by public schools had become increasingly apparent, and new service providers outside the schools had emerged. The institutions that provided these services, and the funding sources on which they drew, were separate from the public schools.

Interinstitutional cooperation and coordination was needed, but it would require the development of policies, regulations, and funding formulas that were complementary. For example, agencies dealing with public welfare (e.g., social services, aid for dependent children, foster care, Medicaid), health (e.g., maternal and child health), mental health/retardation/developmental disabilities, vocational rehabilitation, and corrections needed to work more closely. As the public schools incorporated the major portion of the children and youths who had previously been assigned to residential institutions, it became clear that the schools could not provide all the collateral services that these students would require.

Linking these services required interagency cooperation (as mandated by IDEA) and the development of coalitions of advocacy groups to formulate legislation and programs to link their budgets, staffs, and services into an integrated delivery system of which the public schools would be a part. It also required intricate planning that would continue to promote the inclusion of special needs students within the educational mainstream while at the same time requiring the differentiation of these students according to their needs for external services. This blueprint for the 1990s and beyond would require interagency policy making, programming, and budgeting. It would provide an ambitious and complex political agenda for the advocates of special and general education, as well as external social services for children and youths.

REFERENCES

Bordier, J. (1983). Governance and management of special education. *The Forum, 4*(3), 4–13.

Brantlinger, E. (1997). Using ideology: Cases of non recognition of the politics of research and practice in education. *Review of Educational Research, 67*(4), 425–459.

Copeland, W.C. (1983, January). Strategies for special education in the 1980s. *Policy Studies Review, 2* (Special Issue 1), 242–260.

Kirp, D. (1981). The bounded politics of school desegregation litigation. *Harvard Educational Review, 51*(3), 395–414.

Lynn, L., Jr. (1983). The emerging system for educating handicapped children [Special issue]. *Policy Studies Review, 2,* 21–58.

Sarason, S., & Doris, J. (1979). *Educational handicap, public policy, and social history.* New York: Free Press.

See also **History of Special Education; Inclusion; Individuals with Disabilities Education Act (IDEA); Mainstreaming**

POLYDIPSIA

Polydipsia is excessive drinking of water. It is often associated with water intoxication and polyuria (excessive urination). It is essential to distinguish polydipsia that is biologically based from psychogenic polydipsia (Singh, Padi, Bullard, & Freeman, 1985). Most cases of polydipsia are not due to psychogenic factors (Wright, Schaefer, & Solomons, 1979). Psychogenic polydipsia involves the consumption of excessive quantities of water over a brief time period that is often associated with water intoxication. Water intoxication symptoms include headache, excessive perspiration, and vomiting, as well as more severe symptoms such as convulsions and even death (Blum, Tempey, & Lynch, 1983). Psychogenic polydipsia in children is reported to be rare and there is a lack of epidemiological studies available reporting reliable incidence. Among psychiatric patients, the incident is reported to range from 6.6 to 17.5% (Singh et al., 1985).

Biological determinants of abnormal thirst and polydipsia include diabetes, hypercalcemia, congestive heart failure, intracranial disease, potassium deficiency associated with renal disease, and meningitis (Chevalier, 1984). Another physical form of polydipsia during infancy occurs when infants are fed on demand with an overly diluted formula (Horev & Cohen, 1994; Wright et al., 1979).

Psychogenic polydipsia is associated with a wide spectrum of psychopathology ranging from mild personality disorders to severe psychosis (Singh et al., 1985). Various explanations for psychogenic polydipsia have been provided including the psychodynamic concept of an oral personality (Singh et al., 1985) or an obsessive-compulsive personality (Wright et al., 1979).

There is presently no single treatment recommended in the literature for psychogenic polydipsia. The treatment would depend on the aspects of the aspects of the condition relative to a particular case. Polydipsic children with central nervous system (CNS) involvement would be at risk for learning disorders and possibly special education services. Those with more severe psychological disorders may be in need of special programs for behavioral handicaps.

REFERENCES

Blum, A., Tempey, F.W., & Lynch, W.J. (1983). Somatic findings in patients with psychogenic polydipsia. *Journal of Clinical Psychiatry, 44,* 55–56.

Chevalier, R.L. (1984). Polydipsia and enuresis in childhood renin-dependent hypertension. *Journal of Pediatrics, 104,* 591–593.

Horev, Z., & Cohen, H.H. (1994). Compulsive water drinking in infants and young children. *Clinical Pediatrics, 33*(4), 209–213.

Singh, S., Padi, M.H., Bullard, H., & Freeman, H. (1985). Water intoxication in psychiatric patients. *British Journal of Psychiatry, 146,* 127–131.

Wright, L., Schaefer, A.B., Solomons, G. (1979). *Encyclopedia of pediatric psychology.* Baltimore, MD: University Park Press.

See also **Medical History; Medical Management**

POMPE'S DISEASE

See RARE DISEASES.

PONCE DE LEON, PEDRO DE (1520–1584)

Pedro de Ponce de Leon, a Spanish Benedictine monk, is credited with creating the art of teaching the deaf. His method, as described by early historians, consisted of teaching the student to write the names of objects and then drilling the student in the production of the corresponding sounds. Whether lip reading was taught is not known, nor from the surviving accounts of his work can it be ascertained whether Ponce de Leon used any signs in teaching his students. It is known that his methods were successful with a number of children.

After Ponce de Leon's death in 1584, no one continued his work, but it is probable that his success, which received much publicity, influenced the development of methods to educate the deaf in Spain in the early seventeenth century.

POPLITEAL PTERYGIUM SYNDROME

See RARE DISEASES.

PORCH INDEX OF COMMUNICATIVE ABILITIES (PICA)

The Porch Index of Communicative Ability (PICA) is designed to assess and quantify gestural, verbal, and graphic abilities of aphasic patients. As a reliable standardized instrument, the PICA provides quantitative information about a patient's change in communicative function and enables the examiner to make predictive judgments relative to amount of recovery (Porch, 1971).

The PICA is a battery of 18 subtests; 4 verbal subtests ranging from object naming to sentence completion; 8 gestural ranging from demonstrating object function to matching identical objects; and 6 graphic on a continuum from writing complete sentences to copying geometric forms. For consistency, 10 common objects are used within each subtest (e.g., toothbrush, cigarette, fork, pencil). A multidimensional binary choice 16-point scoring system is used to determine the degrees of correctness of a patient's response. The scoring system judges responses according to their accuracy, responsiveness, completeness, promptness, and efficiency. Administration time is variable, usually averaging approximately 60 minutes.

Prior to administering the PICA, participation in a 40-hour workshop for test administration, scoring, and interpretation is required. Examiners must complete a rigid testing protocol to insure a high degree of reliability. The PICA is a valuable clinical tool for providing valid and accountable descriptions of an aphasic patient's current and future level of communicative performance.

REFERENCE

Porch, B. (1971). *Porch Index of Communicative Ability. Vol. 2. Administration, scoring, and interpretation* (Rev. ed.). Palo Alto, CA: Consulting Psychologists.

See also **Aphasia; Developmental Aphasia**

PORTAGE PROJECT

The Portage project was first funded in 1969 as a model home-based program by the Bureau of Education for the Handicapped under the Handicapped Children's Early Education Program (HCEEP). In rural Portage, Wisconsin, the project's staff traveled to the homes of children to help parents learn how to work with children in a home setting (Lerner, 1985). The experimental edition of the Portage project was developed during the first 3 years of the project and was published by McGraw-Hill in 1972. The revised edition (1976) was developed by Susan Bluma, Marsha Shearer, Alma Froham, and Jean Hillard (Bailey & Worley, 1984; Bluma et al., 1976; Thurman & Widerstrom, 1985). The project was a developmental, criterion-referenced, behavioral model that employs precision teaching to evaluate a child's developmental level and to plan an educational program for children from birth to 6 years of age. The complete guide came in three parts: a checklist of behaviors on which to record an individual child's developmental progress; a file card listing possible methods of teaching these behaviors; and a manual of directions for use of the checklists, card files, and various methods of remediation. The assessment procedure was administered in 20 to 40 minutes. The behavioral checklist consisted of a 25-page color coded booklet that contains 580 developmentally sequenced behaviors.

For a home-based program, children were assigned to a home teacher who spent about an hour and a half a week with each child assigned. Instruction during the remainder of the week was the responsibility of the parent. Prescriptions were modified according to each child's individual progress from week to week. Three new behavior targets were identified each week, and it became the parents' responsibility to provide instruction on these behaviors between the home teacher's visits. The home teacher collected data before and after instruction and helped parents with their teaching skills by modeling techniques and allowing parents to try the skills each week.

The success of the Portage model was seen in its wide dissemination and replication. Over 30 replications across the United States have been reported as well as international recognition (Mittler, 1990). The project staff provided training and technical assistance to the replicated sites while the sites provided input regarding changes and additions. (Thurman & Widerstrom, 1985; Southworth, Burr, & Cox, 1980; Bluma et al., 1976).

REFERENCES

Bailey, D., & Worley, M., (1984). *Teaching infants and preschoolers with handicaps.* Columbus, OH: Merrill.

Bluma, S., Shearer, M., Froham, A., & Hilliard, J. (1976). *The Portage project: Portage guide to early education manual* (Rev. ed.). Portage, WI: Cooperative Educational Services Agency.

Lerner, J. (1985). *Learning disabilities: Theories, diagnosis, and educational strategies* (4th ed.). Boston: Houghton Mifflin.

Mittler, P. (1990). Prospects for disabled children and their families: An international perspective. *Disability, Handicap, & Society, 5*(1), 53–64.

Southworth, L., Burr, R., & Cox, A. (1980). *Screening and evaluating the young child: A handbook of instruments to use from infancy to six years.* Springfield, IL: Thomas.

Thurman, K.S., & Widerstrom, H.A. (1985). *Young children with special needs: A developmental and ecological approach.* Boston: Allyn & Bacon.

See also **Homebound Instruction; Parent Effectiveness Training; Parents of the Handicapped**

POSITIVE PRACTICE

Positive practice is a behavior change technique whereby a misbehaving individual is required to practice correct or appropriate behaviors repeatedly. The term positive practice is frequently used as a synonym for overcorrection, a punishment technique (MacKenzie-Keating & McDonald, 1990). In fact, positive practice is actually a subcomponent of overcorrection. With overcorrection, a misbehaving individual is required to overcorrect the environmental effects of his or her inappropriate act and/or repeatedly practice correct forms of relevant behavior in situations where the misbehavior commonly occurs (Foxx & Bechtel, 1982). The first part of the overcorrection procedure outlined is commonly referred to as restitution and the latter portion of the procedure is often labeled positive practice. Foxx and Bechtel (1982) have recommended the terms restitution and positive practice be dropped and replaced by overcorrection for purposes of conceptual clarity and communication.

REFERENCES

Foxx, R.M., & Bechtel, D.R. (1982). Overcorrection. In M. Hersen, R.M. Eisler, & P.M. Miller (Eds.), *Progress in behavior modification* (pp. 227–288). New York: Academic.

MacKenzie-Keating, S.E., & McDonald, L. (1990). Overcorrection reviewed, revisited, and revised. *Behavior Analyst, 13*(1), 39–48.

See also **Applied Behavior Analysis; Behavior Modification; Negative Punishment; Overcorrection**

POSITIVE REINFORCEMENT

Behavioral psychology, in particular operant conditioning theory, is based on the supposition that behavior is maintained by its consequences. A consequence that leads to an increase in the frequency of a behavior is called a reinforcer.

The principle of positive reinforcement has two parts: (1) if in a given situation a person's behavior is followed close in time by a consequence, then (2) that person is more likely to exhibit the same behavior when he or she is in a similar situation at a later time. This consequence is referred to as a positive reinforcer and is roughly synonomous with the concept of reward.

The application of positive reinforcement is deceptively simple. Two important components in the successful application of positive reinforcement are the selection of a reinforcer and the schedule for delivering the reinforcer. Some stimuli are positive reinforcers for virtually everyone. For example, food is a reinforcer for almost anyone who has not eaten in several hours; money also is generally reinforcing. It is very important, however, to understand that one can actually determine if a stimulus is reinforcing only after it has been administered contingent on the appearance of a desired behavior. In other words, a stimulus is defined as a reinforcer only by its effect on behavior. Failure to select a stimulus that is reinforcing is one of the most common errors in implementing a behavior change program.

The relationship between a behavior and its consequence is called a contingency. Contingencies can operate continuously (i.e., the consequence follows every occurrence of the target behavior) or intermittently (i.e., the consequence follows only a portion of the occurrences of the target behavior). Most contingencies operate on intermittent schedules (e.g., variable ratio, variable interval, fixed ratio, fixed interval). Each reinforcement schedule has been demonstrated to have a different effect on behavior. In general, continuous schedules are used effectively to develop a new behavior, whereas intermittent schedules are used effectively to increase and maintain a behavior already in a person's repertoire. Ratio schedules generally produce high rates of response, and interval schedules produce lower rates of response. In summary, the selection of a stimulus that is reinforcing and the schedule by which it is administered will determine the strength of the positive reinforcement.

See also **Applied Behavior Analysis; Behavior Modification**

POST-INSTITUTIONALIZED CHILD PROJECT

One of the most devastating examples of early childhood neglect and deprivation can be seen in the experiences of children living in some foreign orphanages. It is known that maternal deprivation, neglect, and severe malnutrition in the early lives of children put them at greater risk for growth failure and developmental delays in the early years. Little is known, however, about long-term growth and development of these children. More and more of these children are being adopted by families within the United States. Individual reports suggest that these children may experience long-term growth failure, continued developmental delays and abnormalities related to the onset of puberty. Definitive data are not yet available.

Physicians from Emory University School of Medicine, The Marcus Institute for Development and Learning, and The Hughes Spalding International Adoption Evaluation Center are researching the potential problems that children adopted from international orphanages who are exposed to severe deprivation and/or neglect may struggle with as they grow. Currently, the research is focusing on children adopted from Romania. Efforts to expand this research may be taken.

Families who have experience with a child adopted from an orphanage or institution from any country and who are interested in assisting with the development of knowledge in the field are encouraged to contact the project.

Further information can be obtained on the Internet at http://www.emory.edu/PEDS/ENDO/orphan/ or http://www.adopt@oz.ped.emory.edu.

POST-INSTITUTIONALIZED CHILDREN

A wide variation of scenarios are envisioned when a child is described as neglected. Tangible resources that are considered primary needs of a child such as food, shelter, and clothing may not be provided by caretakers. Services such as appropriate medical care or education may be withheld. In addition, less tangible neglect may occur in the form of lack of emotional interaction with caregivers and/or lack of developmental or intellectual stimulation.

This emotional neglect, which is a product of social, developmental, and intellectual understimulation, may result from a variety of early environmental situations. The parent who is too busy or too overwhelmed by his or her own issues may not take the time to provide stimulation and attention that the child needs. Likewise, a child who has been moved from one overcrowded foster care home to another may also be exposed to such neglect. One of the most devastating examples of neglect and deprivation can be seen in the experiences of children living in some foreign orphanages.

After the fall of the Romanian communist regime in 1989, a disturbing system of state-run child care was discovered. The government was housing up to 300,000 children in an orphanage system. These orphanages became a dumping ground for either the country's most severely diseased and damaged children or for those that were without a home or family. Children were often placed into orphanages that provided minimal amounts of clothing and food, and little medical attention. The orphanages were also generally devoid of personal contact, with ratios of children to caregivers often as high as 60 to 1. Children were left unattended, with contact only for adding food to the bottle suspended above the crib and occasional diaper changes.

Studies suggest that approximately 80% of children adopted from foreign institutions show some developmental delay at the time of entry into the United States (Johnson et al., 1992). Long-term studies of these children are few due to the relatively short time that the majority of these children have been in the United States. One study demonstrated that after approximately 3 years in the United States, 30% of the children continued to demonstrate language delays, 28% demonstrated delayed fine motor skills, and 25% demonstrated delayed social skills (Groze & Ileana, 1996).

The exact mechanism in the brain for the cause or etiology of these developmental problems is usually unknown. Children in an orphanage system are at risk for factors before birth, at the time of birth, and after birth which may contribute to the injury of the brain causing developmental difficulties.

Whatever the cause may be, some of the diagnoses these children may have include symptoms of include post traumatic stress disorder (PTSD), attachment disorders, functional mental retardation, learning disabilities, sensory integration abnormalities, depression, anxiety, behavioral disturbances, personality disorders, fetal alcohol syndrome (FAS), partial fetal alcohol effects (PFAE), attention-deficit hyperactivity disorder (ADHD) and others. Children may also be diagnosed with pervasive developmental disorder (PDD) and/or autism. Dr. Ronald Federici, a developmental neuropsychologist who specializes in the care of post-institutionalized children, proposes a unique type of autism sometimes seen in these children. He terms this autism: an acquired syndrome.

Unique medical problems can also be seen in these children. These may include infectious diseases, gastrointestinal problems, and heart conditions. A common medical problem that may be related to the negative effects on the brain is growth retardation. Some research has also pointed to an increased risk of early puberty onset (Proos et al., 1991).

The adoptive parents and siblings may have difficulty integrating the child into the family. Unfortunately, some agencies organizing such adoptions may promise a perfect child who just needs a little TLC. Families may become very frustrated if the child continues to demonstrate delays or behavioral difficulties.

Likewise, the child may have great difficulty adapting to his or her new environment. Culture shock is common. A modestly decorated home in the United States may be as stimulating as a crowded, colorful amusement park to a post-institutionalized child. Some things that we take for granted may be threatening or scary to the child who has

been deprived. These things may include new foods; the introduction to warm and hot water at bath time; car rides; being outside; hugs, kisses, and other forms of physical affection. Professional assistance from individuals such as pediatric psychologists and/or pediatric and family counselors who are familiar with foreign adoption issues may be of great benefit to such families and children.

As for educational recommendations, Debra Schell-Frank, special education consultant for the Parent Network for the Post-Institutionalized Child, strongly recommends that initially these children be considered as special needs children. Parents, educators, and physicians must work together to evaluate the child's strengths and weaknesses and to offer appropriate intervention services early with close monitoring in order to help the child develop to his or her maximum potential.

RESOURCES

The Parent Network for the Post-Institutionalized Child (PNPIC)
Tel: (724) 222-1766
Fax: (770) 979-3140
E-mail: PNPIC@aol.com

The Hughes Spalding International Adoption Evaluation Center
Tel: (404) 616-0650
Fax: (404) 616-1982
E-mail: adopt@oz.ped.emory.edu

Help for the Hopeless Child: A Guide for Families by Dr. Ronald S. Federici.

Children with Backgrounds of Deprivation: Educational Issues for Children Adopted from Institutions by Dr. Debra Schell-Frank.

The above two books may be obtained through the PNPIC.

REFERENCES

Groze, V., & Ileana, D. (1996). A follow-up study of adopted children from Romania. *Child and Adolescent Social Work Journal, 13,* 541–565.

Johnson, D., Miller, L., Iverson, S., Thomas, W., Franchino, B., Dole, K., Kieman, M., Georgieff, M., & Hostetter, M. (1992). The health of children adopted from Romania. *JAMA, 268,* 3446–51.

Proos, L., Hofvander, Y., & Tuveno, T. (1991). Menarcheal age and growth pattern of Indian girls adopted in Sweden. *Acta Paediatrica Scandanavia, 80,* 852–8.

POSTLINGUAL DEAFNESS

Postlingual deafness is a general term for profound hearing loss that occurs after the normal acquisition of language and speech. It is also called acquired or adventitious deafness. Those who sustain this type of hearing loss are referred to as deafened rather than deaf.

Postlingual deafness is differentiated from prelingual

deafness. The latter interferes with the normal acquisition of language and speech, and frequently affects educational achievement to such an extent that deaf students leaving special schools at the age of 18 are often 7 or 8 years behind their hearing peers (Thomas, 1984). A postlingually deafened child has learned to speak before losing his or her hearing. The child has the memory of the sound and rhythm of speech and has acquired vocabulary and grammar normally. If the child had normal hearing, even for a short time, the outlook is improved (Webster & Ellwood, 1985) however not necessarily predictive of cerebral symmetry (Szelag, 1996).

The etiology of acquired or adventitious hearing loss may be familial, noise-induced, by accident or illness, or, in the case of adults, the result of old age (presbycusis). The onset of a hearing loss is sometimes so gradual that it may go unnoticed for a long time. However, any hearing loss, whether acquired gradually or suddenly, that is extensive enough to interfere with the normal communication process creates a myriad of problems so complex that coping with the hearing world becomes difficult (Giolas, 1982). Formal speech-reading lessons are required in most instances. Sometimes individual hearing aids and cochlear implants (Langereis, Bosman, van Olphen, & Smoorenburg, 1997) can supplement residual hearing to facilitate communication.

Children who lose their hearing between the ages of 3 and 12 sometimes complete their education in programs for the deaf and later become the leaders and spokespeople of the deaf community. Children who lose their hearing at ages older than 12 are more likely to remain with their former hearing friends and not join the community of deaf adults (Jacobs, 1980). Modern technological devices such as hearing aids, auditory trainers, TDDs (telecommunication devices), and television decoders that display captions, are of great assistance in the education of deaf and deafened children.

REFERENCES

Giolas, T. (1982). *Hearing-handicapped adults.* Englewood Cliffs, NJ: Prentice-Hall.

Jacobs, L. (1980). *A deaf adult speaks out.* Washington, DC: Gallaudet College Press.

Langereis, M.C., Bosman, A.J., van Olphen, A.F., & Smoorenburg, G.F. (1997). Changes in vowel quality in post-lingually deafened cochlear implant users. *Audiology, 36*(5), 279–297.

Szelag, E. (1996). The effect of auditory experience on hemispheric asymmetry in a post-lingually deaf child. *Cortex, 32*(4), 647–661.

Thomas, A. (1984). *Acquired hearing loss: Psychological and psychosocial implications.* Orlando, FL: Academic.

Webster, A., & Ellwood, J. (1985). *The hearing-impaired child in the ordinary school.* Dover, NH: Croom Helm.

See also **Deaf; Deaf Education**

POVERTY, RELATIONSHIP TO SPECIAL EDUCATION

Although the connection between poverty and special education is easy to establish, it is difficult to separate the many variables and determine which is the most critical to the child. This is because many of the variables are interwoven at points in the child's development. Malnutrition, poor maternal health, inadequate prenatal care, a child's poor health, homelessness (Masten, 1992) and general environmental deprivation demonstrate complex interrelationships that make it difficult to isolate a single and specific causal agent. Nevertheless, all of these factors associated with poverty have been shown to have an influence on an individual's cognitive and behavioral development.

Child rearing also takes a somewhat different form in many poor families than in middle-class families. Low-income families tend to have more children and fewer adults. Discipline in lower-income families tends to rely on punishment, especially physical punishment; middle-class families tend to rely more on reasoning, isolation, and appeals to guilt. Poor families also tend to delay training their children for independence until they are able to learn rapidly, which provides few opportunities for learning how to make mistakes without disgrace.

Another negative aspect of this environment is a restricted range of sensory stimulation. Low-income families are usually associated with restricted developmental stimulation because there are fewer objects for the child to react to (Smith, Neisworth, & Hunt, 1983). This restricted range of sensory stimulation will hinder a child's interaction with physical and social environments by providing fewer behavioral cues.

The environmental factors mentioned are not meant to be inclusive. There are many other factors associated with poverty that also influence learning and behavior. But these factors do point out that poverty is an underlying cause for many of the negative environmental variables associated with handicapping conditions. In some cases (e.g., poor maternal nutrition and health care), these factors can affect the child's development prenatally, resulting in an organic origin for the disability (e.g., damage to brain cells). In other cases, poor environmental circumstances cause children to be ill-prepared to start school. These children lack the experiences that are common to children of higher income families and can be overcome by preservice intervention programs (Barnett, 1998; Evans, Okifuji, Engler, & Bromley, 1993).

Even though these poverty factors underlie many of the negative variables associated with handicapping conditions, it must be remembered that these learning and behavior problems apply to only a small number of children. The large majority of children living in poor environments will show normal development. While these factors can cause cognitive and behavioral problems in some children, they produce no ill effects in others.

REFERENCES

Barnett, S.W. (1998). Long-term cognitive and academic effects of early childhood education of children in poverty. *Preventative Medicine, 27*(2), 204–207.

Evans, I.M., Okifuji, A., Engler, L., & Bromley, K. (1993). Home-school communication in the treatment of childhood behavior problems. *Child & Family Behavior Therapy, 15*(2), 37–60.

Masten, A.S. (1992). Homeless children in the United States: Math of a nation. *Current Directions in Psychological Science, 1*(12), 41–44.

Smith, R.M., Neisworth, J.T., & Hunt, F.M. (1983). *The exceptional child: A functional approach* (2nd ed.). New York: McGraw-Hill.

See also Cultural Deprivation; Cultural-Familial Deprivation; Socioeconomic Impact of Disabilities; Socioeconomic Status

POWER AND RESEARCH IN SPECIAL EDUCATION

The scientific method has evolved in such a way as to allow researchers to observe phenomena, question, formulate hypotheses, conduct experiments, and develop theories. In hypotheses testing, one compares scientific theories in the form of a statistical hypothesis (H^1) versus a null hypothesis (H^0). According to Kirk (1984), the "statistical hypothesis is a statement about one or more parameters of a population distribution that requires verification" (p. 236). An example is

$$H^1 : m > 80,$$

where the mean score of a population of children is hypothesized to be greater than 80 after participating in a remedial reading program. The statistical hypothesis is thus based on the researcher's deductions from the appropriate theory and on prior research. The null hypothesis involves formulating a hypothesis that is mutually exclusive of the statistical hypothesis. In other words, if the researcher believes that children's mean reading scores will be greater than 80 after participating in a reading program, a mutually exclusive hypothesis by which to test the researcher's premise is given by

$$H^0 : < 80.$$

If the null hypothesis is rejected, by default the statistical or alternative hypothesis is assumed to be true but not proven; it is retained as the most likely truth.

In hypothesis testing, rejection or nonrejection of the null hypothesis is based on probability. Incorrect decisions can occur in two ways. If the null hypothesis is rejected when it is in reality true, this is defined as a Type I error. Should the null hypothesis fail to be rejected when it is in fact false, a Type II error is said to have occurred.

Power is a basic statistical concept that should be taken into consideration in the design of any research study that samples data for inferential purposes. Rejecting the null hypothesis is dependent on whether the test statistic falls within a specified critical region at a particular level of significance, or alpha level (a). The probability of committing a Type I error depends on the alpha level specified. The alpha level also determines the probability of correctly accepting the true null hypothesis (1 − a). The probability of committing a Type II error is labeled b; the probability of a correct rejection is based on 1 − b, or the power level. One method of increasing the power of a statistical test is to increase the sample size.

Using power in an a priori fashion enables the researcher to compute the sample size necessary for testing the null hypothesis, given a level of power and alpha. Often, a researcher is faced with a restricted or small sample size on which he or she wishes to determine the power level. Furthermore, in many research situations, as in evaluating special education programs, assessing the impact of a new teaching technique, or exploring the effectiveness of new medication compared with existing therapies, power allows the experimenter to consider, while in the planning stages, what effect size is needed to detect a significant difference. Similarly, the use of two-tailed tests, greater alpha levels, and small population standard deviations contribute to studies with more powerful results. However, it is worthy to note that the cost of committing a Type I error can be as damaging as committing a Type II error. Adopting a new diet program for the treatment of attention deficit children by falsely deciding that the diet is more effective than behavior therapies and medications is as serious as denying the new diet plan any effectiveness as a springboard for future research. Although power is of central consideration in research design and planning, its contribution must be weighted with other important statistical, methodological, and practical facets of the study.

REFERENCE

Kirk, R.E. (1984). *Elementary statistics* (2nd ed.). Monterey, CA: Brooks/Cole.

See also Research

PRACTICAL INTELLIGENCE

The history of scientific research on practical intelligence is a short one (Sternberg, 1996; Torff & Sternberg, 1998). Neisser (1976) provided a theoretical distinction between academic and everyday intelligence, and Sternberg, Conway, Ketron, and Bernstein (1981) demonstrated that both laypeople and intelligence researchers had implicit beliefs that academic and practical intelligence were separate things. Ceci and Liker (1986) and Scribner (1984) did early research on how adult subjects performed much better on tasks of mathematical reasoning when these tasks were presented in the context of a more familiar domain (e.g., filling orders in a factory), showing subjects who may not do well on traditional intelligence tests may be able to solve similar problems if they are presented in the guise of their day-to-day work.

He defines practical intelligence as being similar to street smarts—the ability to apply one's knowledge in a hands-on, real-world manner. One key element required for practical intelligence is tacit knowledge (Wagner & Sternberg, 1985, 1986; Sternberg, Wagner, Williams, & Horvath, 1995), i.e., knowledge that is acquired without being explicitly taught. There are three features of tacit knowledge that are considered characteristic: (1) it is procedural; (2) it is related to the pursuit and achievement of valued outcomes; and (3) it is learned without assistance from other people. The third condition is one of the key distinctions between tacit and academic knowledge.

Empirical research by Sternberg, Wagner, and others (Sternberg, 1997; Sternberg, Okagaki, & Jackson, 1990; Sternberg, Wagner, & Okagaki, 1993; Wagner & Sternberg, 1986) has found several consistent results. Tacit knowledge increases with hands-on experience; measures of tacit knowledge have repeatedly correlated at significant levels with job performance, yet show only small correlations with traditional measures of intelligence; and early results show that if one wants to teach tacit knowledge, such training should improve results on tests of practical intelligence and tacit knowledge.

Practical intelligence has many important implications for education. Sternberg, Gardner, and other colleagues have combined to form a collaborative project called "Practical Intelligence for Schools" (PIFS; see Gardner, Krechevsky, Sternberg, & Okagaki, 1994). The authors defined the practically intelligent student as one who is aware of his or her individual learning styles; knows how to draw on individual strengths; understands the requirements for the variety of problems encountered across many different school subjects; and can function well interpersonally as well as academically. The authors propose a curriculum for enhancing PIFS that has three units: one that focuses on self-awareness and self-management, another that focuses on task management, and a final unit that shows students how to interact beneficially with others (Gardner et al., 1994; Sternberg et al., 1990). This curriculum resulted in improvement on a variety of measures of practical intelligence.

REFERENCES

Ceci, S., & Liker, J. (1986). Academic and nonacademic intelligence: An experimental separation. In R.J. Sternberg & R.K. Wagner (Eds.), *Practical intelligence: Nature and origins of competence in the everyday world* (pp. 119–142). New York: Cambridge University Press.

Gardner, H., Krechevsky, M., Sternberg, R.J., Okagaki, L. (1994). Intelligence in context: Enhancing students' practical intelligence for school. In K. McGilly (Ed.), *Classroom lessons: Integrating cognitive theory and classroom practice* (pp. 105–127). Cambridge, MA: Bradford Books.

Neisser, U. (1976). General, academic and artificial intelligence. In L. Resnick (Ed.), *Human Intelligence: Perspectives on its theory and measurement* (pp. 135–146). Norwood, NJ: Ablex.

Scribner, S. (1984). Studying working intelligence. In B. Rogoff & J. Lave (Eds.), *Everyday cognition* (pp. 9–40). Cambridge, MA: Harvard University Press.

Sternberg, R.J. (1997). Tacit knowledge and job success. In N. Anderson & P. Herriot (Eds.), *International handbook of selection and assessment* (pp. 201–213). New York: Wiley.

Sternberg, R.J. (1996). What should we ask about intelligence? *American Scholar, 65*(2), 205–217.

Sternberg, R.J., Okagaki, L., & Jackson, A. (1990). Practical intelligence for success in school. *Educational Leadership, 48,* 35–39.

Sternberg, R.J., Wagner, R.K., & Okagaki, L. (1993). Practical intelligence: The nature and role of tacit knowledge in work and at school. In H. Reese & J. Puckett (Eds.), *Advances in lifespan development* (pp. 205–227). Hillsdale, NJ: Erlbaum.

Sternberg, R.J., Wagner, R.K., Williams, W.M., & Horvath, J.A. (1995). Testing common sense. *American Psychologist, 50*(11), 912–927.

Torff, B., & Sternberg, R.J. (1998). Changing mind, changing world: Practical intelligence and tacit knowledge in adult learning. In R. Sternberg (Series Ed.), & C.M. Smith & T. Pourchot (Vol. Eds.), *Adult learning and development: Perspectives from educational psychology* (pp. 109–126). Mahweh, NJ: Lawrence Erlbaum Associates.

Wagner, R.K., & Sternberg, R.J. (1985). Practical intelligence in real-world pursuits: The role of tacit knowledge. *Journal of Personality and Social Psychology, 49,* 436–458.

PRADER-WILLI SYNDROME (PWS)

First described in 1956 by Swiss physicians A. Prader, A. Labhart, and H. Willi, Prader-Willi syndrome (PWS) is a complex disorder and a rare birth defect. Common characteristics include hypotonia in early infancy, hypogonadism, short stature, and, after age 2, excessive weight gain and obesity (Cassidy, 1984). Perhaps the most outstanding characteristic of PWS is the individual's constant preoccupation with food and the compulsion to be eating all the time (Otto, Sulzbacher, & Worthington-Roberts, 1982; Pipes, 1978). This voracious craving for food finds PWS victims often exhibiting unselective and bizarre food behaviors such as eating spoiled meat, rotten vegetables, and/or cat food as well as foraging, stealing, or gorging food (Bottel, 1977; Clarren & Smith, 1977; Dykens & Cassidy, 1996; Otto et al., 1982).

Characteristics of PWS individuals usually include erratic and unpredictable behavior such as stubbornness, outbursts of temper, depression (Watanabe & Ohmori, 1997), and even rage (Otto et al., 1982). Personality problems, behavioral disorders, and emotional problems are frequent though not consistent findings in people with PWS (Cassidy, 1984). Many of the more aggressive behaviors escalate out of anger or desire for food.

Current research indicates that an aberration in a portion of chromosome 15 may be the cause of PWS (Nardella et al., 1983). However, PWS is not a high-risk condition and is most likely a noninherited chromosome defect (Neason, 1978). Another prevailing theory is that PWS is due to a defect within the hypothalamus and thus PWS victims never reach a sense of satiety (Clarren & Smith, 1977).

Mental retardation, particularly in the borderline to moderate range, has been considered to be an integral part of the syndrome (Cassidy, 1984; Neason, 1978). However, recent reports by Holm (1981) indicate that for many of these people, cognitive functioning is more typical of learning disabilities. That is, the child has strengths in several areas and weaknesses in others, unlike a retarded child, who tends to be developmentally delayed across skill areas.

Educational intervention for individuals with Prader-Willi syndrome should begin in early childhood with a program that assists and supports parents and children in managing eating behaviors. Food and nutrition management must be the first and foremost objective of any school program. Deliberate and calculated attempts by the teacher must be made to rid the classroom of any and all food, including pet food. Alternate reward and reinforcement systems other than food reinforcers such as candy must also be instituted. All school personnel who come in contact with the child (particularly lunchroom aides) must be made aware of the child's condition and the consequences of additional caloric intake. The child should be encouraged to stay away from food at all cost.

Physical activity designed to enhance body awareness and activities that encourage social interaction should be stressed and deliberately planned in any class with a PWS child. Academic weaknesses should be addressed as well, and particular attention should be paid to eliminating or modifying temper tantrums or extreme stubbornness by using a behavior-modification approach (Cassidy, 1984). Secondary-level students should be prepared in independent living skills such as math in daily living and vocational/occupational skills, with an emphasis on increasing the child's responsibility for weight control. Competitive employment is rare and most adults are employed in noncompetitive structured workshops and centers. At all times, in any school or workshop program, students with PWS must be watched to prevent their consuming other people's leftovers and food items.

REFERENCES

Bottel, H. (1977, May). The eating disease. *Good Housekeeping,* 176–177.

Cassidy, S.B. (1984). Prader-Willi syndrome. *Current Problems in Pediatrics, 14*(1), 18.

Clarren, S.K., & Smith, D.W. (1977). Prader-Willi syndrome: Variable severity and recurrence risk. *American Journal of Diseases in Children, 131,* 798–800.

Dykens, E.M., & Cassidy, S.B. (1996). Prader-Willi syndrome: Genetic, behavioral, and treatment issues. *Child & Adolescent Psychiatric Clinics of North America, 5*(4), 913–927.

Holm, V.A. (1981). The diagnosis of Prader-Willi syndrome. In V.A. Holm, S. Sulzbacher, & P.L. Pipes (Eds.), *Prader-Willi syndrome.* Baltimore, MD: University Park Press.

Nardella, M.T., Sulzbacher, S.I., Worthington-Roberts, B.S. (1983). Activity levels of persons with Prader-Willi syndrome. *American Journal of Mental Deficiency, 89,* 498–505.

Neason, S. (1978). *Prader-Willi syndrome: A handbook for parents.* Longlake, MN: Prader-Willi Syndrome Association.

Otto, P.L., Sulzbacher, S.I., Worthington-Roberts, B.S. (1982). Sucrose-induced behavior changes of persons with Prader-Willi syndrome. *American Journal of Mental Deficiency, 86,* 335–341.

Pipes, P.L. (1978). Weight control. In S. Neason (Ed.), *Prader-Willi syndrome: A handbook for parents.* Longlake, MN: Prader-Willi Syndrome Association.

Watanabe, H., & Ohmori, A.K. (1997). Recurrent brief depression in Prader-Willi syndrome: A case report. *Psychiatric Genetics, 7*(1), 41–44.

See also **Chromosomal Abnormalities; Genetic Disorders**

PRAGMATICS AND PRAGMATIC COMMUNICATION DISORDERS

Pragmatics is the study of language use independent of language structure, rules, and principles that relate the structure of language to its use (Duchan, 1995; Duchan, Hewitt, & Sonnenmeier, 1994). The rules and principles of pragmatics define who can communicate (talking, writing, signing) what, to whom, how, when, where, and why. Pragmatics includes verbal and nonverbal dimensions of communication and the rules are often implicit and dynamic. Competence in pragmatics includes the development of scripts (the stereotypical knowledge structures that people have for common routines) and schemas (hierarchical cognitive categories of synthesized scripts) (Hedberg & Westby, 1993; Nelson, 1998).

Pragmatic theory suggests that every communication act has three aspects: (1) the illocutionary intent of the sender to accomplish some goal, such as to inform, request, persuade, or promise; (b) the locutionary dimension, i.e., the actual words and sentence structure of the communication act; (c) the perlocutionary effect that the act has on the receiver (e.g., did the receiver comply with the request, understand the information?; Haynes & Shulman, 1998; Hulit & Howard, 1997; Lane & Molyneaux, 1992; McLaughlin, 1998; Nelson, 1998; Owens, 1996; Paul, 1995; Wallach & Butler, 1994).

Communication style is a type of language variation that distinguishes individual speakers in different contexts. A formal, grammatically correct style, acrolect, would be appropriate for academic or some employment situations; a conversational, everyday style, mesolect, would be appropriate for conversations and some types of employment; and basolect (vulgarity) may be used by some individuals in certain situations (Muma, 1978).

Pragmatic communication disorders include violating the verbal, nonverbal, oral, and written rules of communication styles, codes, or scripts. They can interfere with social and academic aspects of the communication-learning process. Pragmatic communication disorders are seen frequently in persons with developmental or acquired disorders such as autism, blindness, deafness, language-learning disorders, mental retardation, and emotional-behavioral disorders (Duchan, 1995; Duchan et al., 1994). Individuals who are gifted and talented may also manifest pragmatic communication problems. Pragmatics of communication varies from culture to culture and should not be confused with a pragmatic language disorder.

REFERENCES

Duchan, J.F. (1995). *Supporting language learning in everyday life.* San Diego: Singular.

Duchan, J.F., Hewitt, L.E., & Sonnenmeier, R.M. (Eds.). (1994). *Pragmatics: From theory to practice.* Englewood Cliffs, NJ: Prentice Hall.

Haynes, W.O., & Shulman, B.B. (1998). *Communication development: Foundations, processes, and clinical applications.* Baltimore: Williams & Wilkins.

Hedberg, N.L., & Westby, C.E. (1993). *Analyzing storytelling skills: Theory to practice.* Tucson, AZ: Communication Skill Builders.

Hulit, L.M., & Howard, M.R. (1997). *Born to talk: An introduction to speech and language development.* Boston: Allyn & Bacon.

Lane, V.W., & Molyneaux, D. (1992). *The dynamics of communicative development.* Englewood Cliffs, NJ: Prentice Hall.

McLaughlin, S. (1998). *Introduction to language development.* San Diego: Singular Publishing Group.

Muma, J.R. (1978). *Language handbook: Concepts, assessment, intervention.* Englewood Cliffs, NJ: Prentice Hall.

Nelson, N.W. (1998). *Childhood language disorders in context: Infancy through adolescence* (2nd ed.). Boston: Allyn & Bacon.

Owens, R.E. (1996). *Language development: An introduction* (4th ed.). Boston: Allyn & Bacon.

Paul, R. (1995). *Language disorders from infancy through adolescence: Assessment and intervention.* St. Louis: Mosby.

Wallach, G.P., & Butler, K.G. (1994). *Language learning disabilities in school-age children and adolescents: Some principles and applications* (2nd ed.). New York: Merrill/Macmillan College Publishing.

PRECISION TEACHING

Precision teaching, a measurement system developed by Ogden R. Lindsley at the University of Kansas in the mid-1960s (McGreevy, 1984; Potts, Eshleman, & Cooper, 1993), involves daily measurement and graphing of student performance for the purpose of formative evaluation.

There are four steps in precision teaching. First, a precisely stated behavior or pinpoint is selected. An example of a pinpoint statement is "see word/say word." Next, frequencies of correct and incorrect responses are obtained and charted on the Standard Behavior Chart. Third, curricular events are modified to change performance in the desired direction. Finally, the graph is evaluated and instructional decisions are made according to trends in the data. Of course, these final two steps are repeated as necessary until progress allows for the attainment of aims.

The Standard Behavior Chart is a semilogarthmic or equal-ratio graph. Frequency is represented along its vertical axis as Movements/minute (M/m). Equal changes in the frequency of behavior are represented by equal distances along this Y-axis. Thus, the distance between 10 and 20 M/m is identical to the distance between 50 and 100 M/m since both represent a 2 × (times 2) change. In fact, any 2 × change, regardless of where along the Y-axis it occurs, will appear as the same distance on the Standard Behavior Chart. Behaviors ranging in frequency from 1 to 1000 minutes (.001 M/m) to 1000 in 1 minute (1000 M/m) can be represented on the Standard Behavior Chart. The unit along the X or horizontal axis is actual calendar days.

Data are obtained directly through observations of student behavior. For example, word recognition could be measured each day by counting the number of words said correctly and incorrectly per minute of reading. Also, in precision teaching, data are recorded continuously. Once recording starts, behavior is monitored without interruption until the recording period stops.

One of the principal measures used in precision teaching is celeration (Pennypacker, Koenig, & Lindsley, 1972). Celerations are standard straight line measures describing the trend of graphed data. For example, an upward trend or acceleration in correct responses and a downward trend or deceleration in incorrect responses, describe a desirable pattern. Precision teaching suggests that certain teaching decisions be based on a minimum acceptable celeration toward a performance aim. In practice, if the teacher sees the student's performance drop below acceptable minimums, then decisions are made to change some aspect of the curriculum (White & Haring, 1980).

Thus the process of precision teaching is an optimistic one. Once responses are precisely defined, observed, and recorded, the elements of a self-correcting instructional system are in place. Teachers may not interpret failure to maintain adequate progress toward an aim as a limitation of the student. Rather, such failure signals a limitation of the existing instructional program. Their ability to solve even the most difficult instructional problems of handicapped learners is limited only by their creativity in developing program adjustments.

The *Journal of Precision Teaching* is dedicated to dissemination of data-based information about human performance and is an excellent resource. The journal is available through Louisiana State University, Special Education, 201 Peabody Hall, Baton Rouge, Louisiana 70803.

REFERENCES

McGreevy, P. (1984). Frequency and the standard celeration chart: Necessary components of precision teaching. *Journal of Precision Teaching, 5*(2), 28–36.

Pennypacker, H.S., Koenig, C.H., & Lindsley, O.R. (1972). *Handbook of the standard behavior chart.* Kansas City, KS: Precision Media.

Potts, L., & Eshleman, J.W., & Cooper, J.O. (1993). Ogden R. Lindsley and the historical development of precision teaching. *Behavior Analyst, 16*(2), 177–189.

White, O.R., & Haring, N.G. (1980). *Exceptional children* (2nd ed.). Columbus, OH: Merrill.

See also Direct Instruction; Data-Based Instruction; Test-Teach-Test

PREHM, HERBERT J. (1937–1986)

A native of Aurora, Illinois, Herbert J. Prehm obtained his BS (1959) in elementary education and psychology from Concordia Teacher's College, River Forest, Illinois, later earning both his MS (1962) and PhD (1964) in education and psychology from the University of Wisconsin, Madison.

Trained as an elementary school teacher and experienced as a reading consultant for children with dyslexia, Prehm maintained an interest in the learning problems of children throughout his distinguished career. As a professor of education at various universities for some 20 years, his work primarily concerned the effective teaching of mentally retarded children (Hersh & Prehm, 1977; Prehm, 1967; Prehm & Stinnett, 1970). Prehm's publications regarding the elements necessary for preparation of students in the special education field at the doctoral level was a result of this experience as a teacher and advisor of those entering the profession (Prehm, 1980).

Among his numerous contributions, Prehm served as assistant executive director of the Department of Professional Development of the Council for Exceptional Children and president of the Teacher Education Division of the Council for Exceptional Children. Additionally, he was a fellow of the American Association on Mental Deficiency and recipient of the TED-Merril Award for Excellence in Teacher Education. The book he coauthored with Kathleen McCoy, *Teaching Mainstreamed Students* (1987), was published only a short time after his death in 1986.

REFERENCES

Hersh, R., & Prehm, H.J. (Eds.). (1977). Issues in teacher preparation. *Teacher Education & Special Education, 1*(1), 320–349.

McCoy, K.M., & Prehm, H.J. (1987). *Teaching mainstreamed students: Methods and techniques.* Denver, CO: Love.

Prehm, H.J. (1967). Rote learning and memory in the retarded: Some implications for the teacher-learning process. *Journal of Special Education, 1,* 397–399.

Prehm, H.J. (1980). Research training and experience in special education doctoral programs. *Teacher Education and Special Education, 3*(4), 3–9.

Prehm, H.J., & Stinnett, R.D. (1970). Effects of learning method on learning stage in retarded and normal adolescents. *American Journal of Mental Deficiency, 75,* 319–322.

PRELINGUAL DEAFNESS

Prelingual deafness refers to profound hearing loss sustained before language has been acquired. Age at onset of profound hearing loss is a major factor because of its implications for language development. The critical age at onset of profound hearing loss is about 2 years (Quigley & Kretschmer, 1982). Children born deaf, or deafened before the age of 2 years, are prelingually deaf. Deafness is a profound degree of hearing impairment, a bilateral loss of 90 dB or greater on the audiometric scale of –10 to 110 dB (Quigley & Paul, 1984).

Prelingually deaf children rely on vision as their primary channel of communication and language acquisition. Since language plays such a important role in thinking and in conceptual growth (Webster & Ellwood, 1985), prelingually deaf children require special educational programs with emphasis on all the skills related to language and communication.

Prelingual deafness is more than the inability to hear sound. It is a pervasive handicap that, because of its effects on language and communication, has an impact on almost all aspects of child development.

REFERENCES

Quigley, S., & Kretschmer, R. (1982). *The education of deaf children: Issues, theory and practice.* Baltimore, MD: University Park Press.

Quigley, S., & Paul, P. (1984). *Language and deafness,* San Diego, CA: College-Hill.

Webster, A., & Ellwood, J. (1985). *The hearing-impaired child in the ordinary school.* Dover, NH: Croom Helm.

See also **Deaf; Deaf Education; Speech, Absence of**

PREMACK PRINCIPLE

The original definition of reinforcement (Skinner, 1938; Spence, 1956) was circular. A stimulus could not be identified as a reinforcer until it had been tested and shown to increase the probability of a response. This left behavior modifiers with no a priori method of choosing effective reinforcers. However, Premack (1965) solved this problem of circularity by devising an independent means of determining the reinforcing power of different consequences. Premack found that under certain circumstances, an organism's own behavior can function as a reinforcer. More specifically, a less probable behavior within a person's repertoire can be strengthened by making the occurrence of a more probable behavior contingent on it.

Identifying reinforcers by the Premack principle requires assessing the relative probabilities of the reinforcing behavior and the behavior to be changed by counting their rate of occurrence in a free environment. This arduous task seriously limits the usefulness of the Premack principle in applied settings. Fortunately, behavior modifiers have found it adequate to identify high-probability behaviors by asking a person about preferred activities or by casually observing the person to determine the activities from which he or she derives overt pleasure (Danaher, 1974). Once the preferred behavior is identified, the behavior modifier will allow the person to engage in that behavior only after performing the targeted low-probability or less preferred behavior. Because of this formulation, the Premack principle is sometimes referred to as "Grandma's rule" (Becker, 1971; Homme, 1971) or "you do what I want you to do before you get to do what you want to do."

REFERENCES

Becker, W.C. (1971). *Parents are teachers.* Champaign, IL: Research.

Danaher, B.G. (1974). Theoretical foundations and clinical applications of the Premack principle: Review and critique. *Behavior Therapy, 5,* 307–324.

Homme, L. (1971). *How to use contingency contracting in the classroom.* Champaign, IL: Research.

Premack, D. (1965). Reinforcement theory. In D. Levine (Ed.), *Nebraska symposium on motivation.* Lincoln: University of Nebraska Press.

Skinner, B.F. (1938). *The Behavior of organisms.* New York: Appleton-Century-Crofts.

Spence, K. (1956). *Behavior theory and conditioning.* New Haven, CT: Yale University Press.

See also **Behavior Modification; Operant Conditioning; Positive Reinforcement**

PREMATURITY

Prematurity or preterm refers to infants born prior to completion of 37 weeks gestation. Although the overall survival rate of premature infants has steadily increased with advances in perinatal and neonatal care, the incidence of prematurity has not significantly changed in the past 20 years and remains at about 10% of all live births (Spitzer, 1996).

The exact cause of the majority of premature births remains unknown. The cause is hypothesized to be a combination of maternal, paternal, fetal, and environmental factors. Maternal risk factors for prematurity include pregnancy-induced hypertension, antepartum hemorrhage, infection, and premature rupture of membranes. Maternal social factors often contributing to prematurity are low socioeconomic status, age less than 16 or greater than 40 years, history of premature births, history of repeated abortions, maternal substance abuse (including cigarettes and alcohol), lack of prenatal care, and poor nutritional status (Spitzer, 1996). Paternal factors include genetic makeup and older age. Fetal factors related to prematurity include presence of congenital anomalies, fetal disease, and multiple gestation. Environmental factors include stress, injury, and exposure to teratogens (Johnson, 1986). The cause of prematurity continues to be elusive, making prediction of premature births difficult.

Gestational maturity is determined by both neurological and physical characteristics (Dubowitz & Dubowitz, 1977). The premature infant's head generally appears large for its small body and the skin is bright pink, wrinkled, and translucent. The eyes remain fused until about 22–25 weeks gestation and after opening appear large for the face. The abdomen looks distended, and genitalia are not fully developed (Merenstein & Gardner, 1998). The fingernails are thin and the body is covered with fine downy hair and a layer of sebaceous skin covering. The preterm infant's arms and legs are thin and muscle tone is poor, causing it to lie in an extended position unless supported against gravity. Reflex movements are only partially developed, and breathing and crying are often spasmodic and weak (Schuster & Ashburn, 1986).

Preterm infants have physiologically immature organ systems that cause many clinical problems. These problems include immature lungs, apnea, hemorrhaging into the brain, infections of the gastrointestinal tract, poor weight gain, inability to maintain body temperature, and infection (Merenstein & Gardner, 1998).

The clinical problems often require intensive management involving a team of healthcare professionals providing multisystem support. This support may include the use of incubators, ventilators, intravenous fluids, and physiologic monitoring. Survival rates are improving, with reports of 61% survival of infants born between 23–26 weeks gestation. Of those infants, 6% to 36% survived intact without long-term handicapping conditions. The more immature the infant, the greater the incidence and severity of long-term complications. Survival rates improve and incidence of complications diminish rapidly after 26 weeks gestation (Goldsen, 1996).

The long-range sequelae of prematurity are closely associated with both prenatal and postnatal complications and the disruption of the parent-infant attachment process. Long-term sequelae include breathing disorders, retinopathy of prematurity, increased incidence of SIDS, and neurologic impairment leading to sensorimotor and developmental delays (Merenstein & Gardner, 1998).

Other potential long-range effects of preterm birth include lack of parent-infant attachment and delays in growth and development. Lack of attachment can be caused by separation, guilt, fear, and poor parenting skills. Attachment can be strengthened by encouraging and supporting early parent-infant interaction and involving parents in the care of their hospitalized child. Teaching parents developmentally appropriate interactions, helping them to understand their infant's cues, and encouraging skin to skin contact all help in the attachment process (Merenstein & Gardner, 1998).

REFERENCES

Dubowitz, L.M.S., & Dubowitz, V. (1977). *Gestational age of the newborn.* Menlo Park, CA: Addison-Wesley.

Goldsen, E. (1996). The micropremie: Infants with birthweights less than 800 grams. *Infants and Young Children, 8*(3), 1–10.

Johnson, S.H. (1986). *Nursing assessment and strategies for the family at risk: High risk parenting* (2nd ed.). Philadelphia: Lippincott.

Merenstein, G.B., & Gardner, S.L. (1998). *Handbook of Neonatal Care* (4th ed.). St. Louis: Mosby.

Schuster, C.S., & Ashburn, S.S. (1986). *The process of human development. A holistic lifespan approach* (2nd ed.). Boston: Little, Brown.

Spitzer, A.R. (Ed.). (1996). *Intensive care of the fetus and neonate.* St. Louis: Mosby.

See also **Amniocentesis; Apgar Rating Scale; Baby Jane Doe; Birth Injuries; Low Birth Weight Infants**

PREREFERRAL INTERVENTION

Graden, Casey, and Christenson (1985) state that the goal of a prereferral intervention model "is to implement systematically intervention strategies in the regular classroom and to evaluate the effectiveness of these strategies before a student is formally referred for consideration for special education placement" (p. 378). The prereferral intervention model is intended to prevent unnecessary referrals for psychoeducational testing for purposes of determining eligibility for special education programs. The prereferral intervention model is an indirect, consultative service, and has several advantages as an alternative to the traditional process of teacher referral, psychoeducational testing, determination of eligibility, and special education placement. It has also paralleled the movement towards inclusion (Wilson, Gutkin, Hagen, & Oats, 1998).

First, while traditional psychoeducational testing assumes the child's problem resides in the child (e.g., a learning disability, low intelligence, or a personality disorder), the prereferral intervention model assumes that the child's problems are a result of the interaction of the child's characteristics with setting and task variables. When those setting and task variables that result in improved child performance are identified through careful observation and problem-solving efforts, modifications can be implemented in the classroom without removing the child from the regular class. Second, in the traditional testing approach, if the child is found ineligible for special education services, a great deal of resources are allocated to the child, but the child does not necessarily benefit from these resources. Third, because some testing does not use instructional data, the recommendations may not have instructional ramifications. Contributing to the problem of the relevance of recommendations is the fact that the problem for which the child is referred often does not show up in the testing situation. Fourth, when special education services are the only assistance available to children with problems, teachers will refer children whose needs could be met in the less restrictive environment of the regular classroom. If consultative help were available to the teacher, the child's needs could be served through an indirect model. Fifth, indirect services serve preventive goals. If teachers can request consultation from a school psychologist or special education teacher-consultant soon after a child's problem becomes evident, more severe problems can be avoided. In the traditional testing model, children who do not qualify tend to get referred again and again by teachers until the problems are severe enough to qualify these children for special education programs. Finally, the teacher develops new knowledge and skills in consultation that will assist in providing for the needs of other children.

Although there have been many studies evaluating the effectiveness of consultation, few of these have evaluated consultation as a systematic strategy for reducing inappropriate referrals for special education testing. An exception is the case study by Graden, Casey, and Bonstrom (1985), they found that four out of six schools that implemented the prereferral model experienced a decrease in referrals for testing and special education placements. The authors suggest that the model was not successful in the other two schools because there was a lack of system support and the model was not fully implemented.

REFERENCES

Graden, J., Casey, A., & Christenson, S. (1985). Implementing a prereferral intervention system: Part I. The Model. *Exceptional Children, 51,* 377–384.

Graden, J., Casey, A., & Bonstrom. (1985). Implementing a prereferral intervention system: Part II. The Data. *Exceptional Children, 51,* 487–496.

Wilson, C.P., Gutkin, T.B., Hagen, K.M., & Oats, R.G. (1998). General education teacher's knowledge and self-reported use of classroom interventions: Implications for consultation prereferral intervention and inclusive services. *School Psychology Quarterly, 13*(1), 45–62.

See also **Preschool Screening Consultation; Prevention, Primary**

PRESCHOOL-AGE GIFTED CHILDREN

Services for gifted children below kindergarten age have received increased attention as a means of encouraging development of the child's potential, stimulating interest in learning, and providing support for parents. Several authors (Fox, 1971; Isaacs, 1963; Whitmore, 1979, 1980) have pointed to lack of support and intellectual challenge in the early years as one source of later underachievement among the gifted. Programs for young gifted children facilitate early interaction between parents and educators that can promote supportive parenting practices and parent advocacy (Karnes, Shwedel, & Linnemeyer, 1982). Early identification and parent training are particularly critical for gifted children from economically disadvantaged backgrounds.

Despite the need, few programs exist that are specifically designed for preschool 3- to 4-year-old children (Roedell, Jackson, & Robinson, 1980). Several factors account for the sparsity of such programs. First, lacking state and federal incentives for providing appropriate education to preschool-age gifted and talented children, few systematic procedures have been implemented for early identification and service delivery. Second, critics have questioned the reliability and validity of currently available measures for identifying giftedness in 3- and 4-year-old children. Third, parents of young gifted children frequently have little access to information about referral characteristics, available services, and need for advocacy in initiating services.

A review of current literature on gifted education, however, reveals growing recognition of the special needs of gifted and talented children in the early years (Karnes, 1983; Whitmore, in press). Significant topics include identification procedures, characteristics, programs, and cultural issues (Sandel, McCallister, & Nash, 1993).

Characteristics of young gifted children are most readily observable in comparison with other children of the same age, sex, and cultural group. Cognitively, young gifted children often display advanced vocabulary and general information, early interest in books and numbers, long attention spans, persistence and creativity in solving problems, vivid imaginations, broad or intense interests, metacognition (Moss & Strayer, 1990) unusual memory for detail, and an intense desire to know "why."

Many young gifted children also possess social-emotional characteristics such as preference for associating with older children, capacity for intense emotions, and a high level of empathy, traits that render them vulnerable to stress. Additionally, young gifted children may become frustrated by their uneven development, e.g., when their advanced thinking but average fine-motor coordination results in products that fail to meet their goals. Kitano (1985) found characteristics of competitiveness and perfectionism in some children attending a preschool for the gifted. These socio-emotional vulnerabilities (Roedell, 1986) may become manifested in withdrawn, shy, aggressive, or attention-getting behaviors.

Many of the models employed in programs for elementary-age gifted children have been successfully applied to preschool-level programs. For example, programs at the University of Illinois, Champaign-Urbana (Karnes & Bertschi, 1978; Karnes et al., 1982) have incorporated Structure-of-Intellect and open classroom models. The Hunter College (Camp, 1963) and New Mexico State University (Kitano & Kirby, 1986a, 1986b) programs involve children in unit-based curricula and independent projects. The Astor program (Ehrlich, 1980) focuses on the higher level skills of Bloom's (1956) taxonomy as well as on academic skills and creative investigation. Taylor's (1968) multiple talent approach and Renzulli's (1977) enrichment triad model have also been applied to programs for preschool-level gifted children.

REFERENCES

Bloom, B.S. (1956). *Taxonomy of educational objectives, the classification of educational goals—Handbook I: Cognitive domain.* New York: McKay.

Camp, L.T. (1963). Purposeful preschool education. *Gifted Child Quarterly, 7,* 106–107.

Ehrlich, V.Z. (1980). The Astor program for gifted children. In *Educating the preschool/primary gifted and talented* (pp. 248–250). Ventura, CA: Office of the Ventura County Superintendent of Schools.

Fox, A.E. (1971). Kindergarten: Forgotten year for the gifted? *Gifted Child Quarterly, 15,* 42–48.

Isaacs, A.F. (1963). Should the gifted preschool child be taught to read? *Gifted Child Quarterly, 7,* 72–77.

Karnes, M.B. (Ed.). (1983). *The underserved: Our young gifted children.* Reston, VA: Council for Exceptional Children.

Karnes, M.B., & Bertschi, J.D. (1978). Teaching the young gifted handicapped child. *Teaching Exceptional Children, 10*(4), 114–119.

Karnes, M.B., Shwedel, A.M., & Lewis, G.F. (1983). Short-term effects of early programming for the young gifted handicapped child. *Exceptional Children, 50*(2), 103–109.

Karnes, M.B., Shwedel, A.M., & Linnemeyer, S.A. (1982). The young gifted/talented child: Programs at the University of Illinois. *Elementary School Journal, 82*(3), 195–213.

Kitano, M.K. (1985). Ethnography of a preschool for the gifted: What gifted young children actually do. *Gifted Child Quarterly, 29*(2), 67–71.

Kitano, M.K., & Kirby, D.F. (1986a). *Gifted education: A comprehensive view.* Boston: Little, Brown.

Kitano, M.K., & Kirby, D.F. (1986b). The unit approach to curriculum planning for the gifted. *G/C/T, 9*(2), 27–31.

Moss, E., & Strayer, F.F. (1990). Interactive problem-solving of gifted and non-gifted preschoolers with their mothers. *International Journal of Behavioral Development, 13*(2), 177–197.

Renzulli, J.S. (1977). *The enrichment triad model: A guide for developing defensible programs for the gifted and talented.* Wethersfield, CT: Creative Learning.

Roedell, W.C. (1986). Socioemotional vulnerabilities of young gifted children. In J.R. Whitmore (Ed.), *Intellectual giftedness in young children: Recognition and development.* New York: Haworth.

Roedell, W.C., Jackson, N.E., & Robinson, H.B. (1980). *Gifted young children.* New York: Teachers College Press.

Sandel, A., McCallister, C., & Nash, W.R. (1993). Child search and screening activities for preschool gifted children. *Roeper Review, 16*(2), 98–102.

Taylor, C.W. (1968). Multiple talent approach. *The Instructor, 77*(8), 27, 142, 144, 146.

Whitmore, J.R., (1979). The etiology of underachievement in highly gifted young children. *Journal for the Education of the Gifted, 3*(1), 38–51.

Whitmore, J.R. (1980). *Giftedness, conflict, and underachievement.* Boston: Allyn & Bacon.

Whitmore, J.R. (Ed.). (in press). *Intellectual giftedness in young children: Recognition and development.* New York: Haworth.

***See also* Gifted and Talented Children, Underachievement in the**

PRESCHOOL ASSESSMENT

Preschool assessment has been conceptualized as a "continuous, general-to-specific process of defining functional capabilities and establishing treatment goals" (Bagnato & Neisworth, 1981, p. 7) for children between the ages of 3 and 6 years. Broadly conceived, the process is carried out for the purpose of determining eligibility for services, obtaining information for individual program development, and evaluating program effectiveness (Neisworth et al., 1980). With these as broadly based goals, preschool assessment encompasses screening procedures, but it also involves in depth and comprehensive analyses of developmental strengths and weaknesses, the setting of instructional goals, and the evaluation of progress made by a child within a particular intervention plan.

To accomplish these purposes effectively, preschool assessment is comprised of multidimensional processes. It involves the synthesis of developmental information from multiple measures and sources and across multiple domains that include cognitive, social, language, motor, and adaptive behavior areas. The emphasis on multidimensionality is essential at the preschool level because of the lack of reliability of global scores and assessment devices for children undergoing rapid behavioral and developmental change.

Norm-referenced preschool measures typically yield developmental age and standard scores that represent the child's most stable level of skill development (Bagnato & Neisworth, 1981). A profile of strengths and weaknesses across developmental domain areas is also provided by these instruments. The standard scores are sometimes termed IQ scores (e.g., from the Wechsler Preschool and Primary Scale of Intelligence and the Stanford-Binet), but they have also been given alternative designations (e.g., the Mental Processing Index from the Kaufman Assessment Battery for Children and the General Cognitive Index from the McCarthy Scales of Children's Abilities). Regardless of the label used, the global standard scores are considered to represent a construct that is similar, yet different from, later IQ scores (McCarthy, 1972). Thus, the power of these instruments to predict later IQ and school achievement is an important practical and research issue that has encountered much debate (Bracken, 1994). Given this issue, all normative comparisons made at the preschool level must be made with an understanding of the influence of behavioral variation on the scores.

Balancing formal testing procedures with informal "testing the limits" procedures and "test-teach-test" approaches is also essential at the preschool level. Advocates of this approach, termed dynamic assessment (Lidz, 1983) or adaptive-process assessment (Bagnato & Neisworth, 1981), suggest a flexible yet systematic method of evaluating upper and lower limits of the child's ability to complete tasks. In particular, they stress the need to modify activities in a structured manner to compensate for a particular impairment and to allow for alternative response modes. Thus, this less formal approach combines testing and teaching as part of a single diagnostic process. Applying these procedures after the administration of tests in a standardized format provides a basis for comparing a preschool child's performance under standardized and adapted conditions.

Naturalistic observations and interview procedures comprise the cornerstone of nontest-based preschool assessment and provide information on the environmental influences that impact a preschool-age child. The Social Assessment Manual for Preschool Level (SAMPLE) (Greenwood, Todd, Walker, & Hops, 1979) is an example of a structured observation instrument that guides observation in a preschool classroom setting. The Home Observation for Measurement of the Environment (HOME) (Caldwell & Bradley, 1978) is an instrument for home observation. Additionally, there are numerous developmental checklists that structure analyses of developmental concerns from teachers and parents (Linder, 1983). Such procedures are essential in revealing adults' perceptions of a child's development, their teaching and coping strategies, belief systems, goals, and caregiving skills (Barnett, 1984).

Given the complexity of the preschool assessment process, it is clear that determining eligibility and establishing instructional objectives involve much more than the administration of a standard battery with one measure as the prime integral component. Similarly, the limitations of traditional test scores in evaluating program effectiveness have been enumerated (Bracken, 1994; Keogh & Sheehan, 1981) and should be noted.

REFERENCES

Bagnato, S.J., & Neisworth, J.T. (1981). *Linking developmental assessment and curricula.* Rockville, MD: Aspen Systems.

Barnett, D.W. (1984). An organizational approach to preschool services: Psychological screening, assessment, and intervention. In C. Maher, R. Illback, & J. Zins (Eds.), *Organizational psychology in the schools: A handbook for practitioners* (53–82). Springfield, IL: Thomas.

Bracken, B.A. (1994). Advocating for effective preschool assessment practices: A comment on Bagnato and Neisworth. *School Psychology Quarterly, 9*(2), 103–108.

Caldwell, B.W., & Bradley, R.H. (1978). *Home Observation for Measurement of the Environment.* Little Rock, AR: University of Arkansas.

Greenwood, C.R., Todd, N.M., Walker, H.M., & Hops, H. (1979). Selecting a cost-effective screening device for the assessment of preschool social withdrawal. *Journal of Applied Behavioral Analysis, 12,* 639–652.

Keogh, B., & Sheehan, R. (1981). The use of developmental test data for documenting handicapped children's progress: Problems and recommendations. *Journal of the Division for Early Childhood, 3,* 42–47.

Lidz, C.S. (1983). Dynamic assessment and the preschool child. *Journal of Psychoeducational Assessment, 1,* 59–72.

Linder, T.W. (1983). *Early childhood special education: Program developmental administration.* Baltimore, MD: Brookes.

McCarthy, D. (1972). *Manual for the McCarthy Scales of Children's Abilities.* New York: Psychological Corporation.

Neisworth, J.T., Willoughby-Herb, S., Bagnato, S.J., Cartwright, C.A., & Laub, K.W. (1980). *Individualized education for preschool exceptional children.* Germantown, MD: Aspen Systems.

See also **Preschool Screening; Preschool Special Education**

PRESCHOOL SCREENING

Preschool screening is the evaluation of large groups of children 3 to 5 years of age with brief, low-cost procedures to identify those who may be at risk for later problems. It is based on the assumptions that early intervention should produce a significant positive effect on development, that children with developmental problems must be identified accurately as their problems are developing, and that early identification and intervention programs should be implemented without prohibitively high costs (Holland & Merrell, 1998; Lichtenstein & Ireton, 1984). While also used frequently in the field of medicine, screening in special education and related fields refers to the early identification of risk factors associated with later school achievement and social adjustment. Because of the complexity of outcomes from many early childhood health problems such as otitis media (Mandell & Johnson, 1984), screening approaches that draw from several disciplines are considered the most comprehensive (Elder & Magrab, 1980).

Screening can be conceptualized as a process consisting of two components (Lichtenstein & Ireton, 1984). The first component, outreach, involves initial contact with parents, professionals, preschool centers, and community agencies to inform them about the services offered and to arrange for children to participate in the screening program. Other terms used to refer to this initial location of children are "child find" (Harbin, Danaher, & Derrick, 1994; Meisels, 1980), from the provisions of IDEA Part H, and "case finding" (Barnes, 1982; Harrington, 1984). The major goals are to locate a target population and to maximize attendance at the actual screenings.

The second component of the screening process consists of the assessment of those children found eligible, the synthesis of information, and the determination of need for further assessment. Generally, the structure of this component is based on: (1) the kinds of questions that need to be answered; (2) the types and severity of handicapping conditions to be assessed; (3) the ages of the children; and (4) the psychometric properties of available instruments (Harrington, 1984; Scott & Hogan, 1982). Specifically, screening activities should answer whether the child is delayed enough in one or more domains (cognitive, sensory, motor, social/ emotional, speech, language) to be considered at risk and in need of further diagnosis. If so, the screening should provide direction regarding what types of diagnostic assessments are needed to confirm or refute the screening impressions (Horowitz, 1982). The handicapping conditions should have a prevalence rate high enough to justify screening large numbers of children but not so high that every child must receive a diagnostic evaluation. Also, instruments should be chosen that have been normed on the ages of children represented in the target population and that have good reliability and validity. The precision of screening instruments is not as crucial as that of diagnostic instruments because of the general nature of the decisions made from them. A review of various screening systems and instruments, their psychometric properties, and their usefulness is provided by Buros (1985), Harrington (1984), and Lichtenstein and Ireton (1984). Although group and individually administered instruments are reviewed in these sources, it should be realized that individual administration maximizes the validity of test results with preschool-age children (Reynolds & Clark, 1983).

Generally, screening outcomes can be organized into screening positives (children regarded as high risk and referred for further assessment) and screening negatives (children regarded as low risk and not referred). For each child screened, four results are possible, based on the accuracy of the screening decision and the child's actual performance on criterion measures during a diagnostic evaluation. A child may be found to be in need of special services and referred by the screening procedures, or a child may be found to not need additional help. Given the possibility of error in screening decisions, however, a child may be referred by the screening procedure but not need special services (a false positive or overreferral error), or not referred but be in need of services (a false negative or underreferral error). To evaluate the consequences of using a given screening system, then, it must be determined whether children are referred at the rate intended, whether the right children are referred, and whether alternative procedures might accomplish the task more successfully. Other relevant issues are the appropriateness of the criterion measures used, the possibility of bias in the screening process (Reynolds & Clark, 1983), and strategies for maximizing parent involvement.

Given the long-held recognition that parents are vitally important in meeting the educational needs of their children, they should be involved in every phase of screening (Lichtenstein & Ireton, 1984). Not only is parent involvement mandated by IDEA, Part H but parents also constitute a rich source of information about specific aspects of their child's development that may be unavailable elsewhere. Parents can also make sure that the assessment of their child is culturally competent. The screening of environmental influences from home and classroom settings is a rapidly growing area of research and clinical attention (Adelman, 1982).

REFERENCES

Adelman, H.S. (1982). Identifying learning problems at an early age: A critical appraisal. *Journal of Clinical Child Psychology, 11,* 255–261.

Barnes, K.E. (1982). *Preschool screening: The measurement and prediction of children at risk.* Springfield, IL: Thomas.

Buros, O.K. (Ed.). (1985). *The ninth mental measurements yearbook.* Highland Park, NJ: Gryphon.

Elder, J.O., & Magrab, P.R. (1980). *Coordinating services to handicapped children.* Baltimore, MD: Brookes.

Harbin, G., Danaher, J., & Derrick, T. (1994). Comparison of eligibility policies for infant/toddler programs and preschool special education programs. *Topics in Early Childhood Special Education, 14*(4), 455–471.

Harrington, R. (1984). Preschool screening: The school psychologist's perspective. *School Psychology Review, 13,* 363–374.

Holland, M.L., & Merrell, K.W. (1998). Social emotional characteristics of preschool-aged children referred for child find screening and assessment: A comparative study. *Research in Developmental Disabilities, 19*(2), 167–179.

Horowitz, F.D. (1982). Methods of assessment for high risk and handicapped infants. In C.T. Ramey & P.L. Trohanis (Eds.), *Finding and educating high risk and handicapped infants.* Baltimore, MD: University Park Press.

Lichtenstein, R., & Ireton, H. (1984). *Preschool screening.* Orlando, FL: Grune & Stratton.

Mandell, C.J., & Johnson, R.A. (1984). Screening for otitis media: Issues and procedural recommendations. *Journal of the Division of Early Childhood, 8,* 86–93.

Meisels, S.J. (1980). *Developmental screening in early childhood: A guide.* Washington, DC: National Association for the Education of Young Children.

Reynolds, C.R., & Clark, J. (1983). Assessment of cognitive abilities. In K.D. Paget & B.A. Bracken (Eds.), *The psychoeducational assessment of preschool children* (163–189). New York: Grune & Stratton.

Scott, G., & Hogan, A.E. (1982). Methods for the identification of high-risk and handicapped infants. In C.T. Ramey & P.L. Trohanis (Eds.), *Finding and educating high-risk and handicapped infants.* Baltimore, MD: University Park Press.

See also Head Start; Preschool Assessment; Preschool Special Education

PRESCHOOL SPECIAL EDUCATION

Preschool special education is the delivery of therapeutic and educational services to handicapped infants and children from birth to age 6. These services are designed to provide optimum learning experiences during the crucial early childhood developmental period for children with a wide variety of handicapping conditions. The importance of the preschool years to future success has been documented by many child development authorities, who emphasize that the first 5 or 6 years of a child's life are the periods of highest potential growth in physical, perceptual, linguistic, cognitive, and affective areas (Lerner, Mardell-Czudnowski, & Goldenberg, 1981). These early periods of development are particularly important to the handicapped child, since the earlier that these children are identified and education begun, the greater the chances of lessening the impact of the handicapping condition on the child and society. A recent report by the House Select Committee on Children, Youth, and Families (1985) stated that for every dollar invested in preschool special education programs, there is a $3 reduction in special education cost later.

Identifying, screening, and assessing handicapped preschool children are meaningless tasks unless appropriate services are then provided to them (Hobbs, 1975). Once the child has been identified and diagnostic information is complete, then an appropriate program plan and curriculum must be developed. There are many different program delivery models that can be used, as well as a wide variety of philosophical bases for the programs.

Preschool special education programs have evolved from many varied theoretical positions, ranging from a child development model to precision teaching and systematic instruction. These approaches may be used with different populations, or in different environments, but they have all been shown to be beneficial. The child development model is mainly an enrichment model that provides multiple activity centers such as often found in many regular preschool programs. This is the model that many Head Start programs follow, and it is most successful with children with mild handicapping conditions. The sensory-cognitive model is based on the work of Maria Montessori. It emphasizes materials designed for the child's developmental level; these materials are presented in a carefully constructed environment. Other programs are based on the verbal-cognitive model, which draws heavily from the developmental theory of Piaget and stresses structured teacher-child interactions. Severely handicapped children often benefit from highly structured systematic instruction programs that rely on detailed task analysis and behavioral theory.

The age of the child often affects where the educational services are delivered; since it is difficult to transport infants for long distances, many of the programs for younger children are home-based, with the teacher traveling to the students. As the child becomes older, programs may be center-based, with the child attending a school program or a combination of home and school program. Another factor that affects where programs are delivered is the geographic region. Sparsely populated rural regions may not have sufficient numbers of children within a reasonable distance of a school; therefore, they may rely on more home-based services than might be found in large urban areas. Examples of home-based projects are the Portage project, the Marshalltown project, and Project SKI*HI; the Precise Early Education of Children with Handicaps (PEECH) project, the Chapel Hill project, and the Magnolia Preschool are all combined home- and center-based programs. Center-based programs include the Rutland Center, the Seattle Model Preschool Center, and the UNISTAPS project. These programs were all originally supported by HCEEP funding and are representative of many programs across the United States (Karnes & Zehrbach, 1977).

The actual curriculum content in preschool special education programs varies depending on the needs of the children; however, in most cases, the programs are based on one or more of the following approaches. Some preschool special education curricula are organized around an amelioration of deficits approach, which builds the curriculum based on an assessment of a child's problems; the content areas are directed toward correcting identified deficits. Other programs use a basic skills area approach. In this, curricula are organized around skills or processes such as attention, language, sensory motor processes, social skills, perception, auditory processes, gross and fine motor skills, self-help skills, and memory. The developmental tasks approach uses sequences of normal development to derive the curricula. The content areas in this approach are broad categories of child development that are task analyzed and sequenced. Finally, the educational content approach begins with areas of academic content; it defines areas of learning on the basis of preacademic or academic content. The most often included areas are prereading, numbers, music, art, dance, play, storytelling, social studies, and nature. In many cases these various approaches are combined to develop appropriate educational programs (Wood & Hurley, 1977).

A crucial component to any preschool special education program is parent involvement. As stated by Shearer and Shearer (1977), there are several reasons to involve parents in their child's education. The parents are the consumers and often want to participate in the education of their children. When parents are taught how to teach their children, they can help transfer what is being learned in school to the home environment. These teaching skills can also be used in new situations, and with the handicapped child's siblings, making the parents better teachers of all their children. Research has shown that significant gains made by children are often lost when the school programs end.

Recent research studies have demonstrated the effectiveness of preschool special education programs for handicapped young children. Karnes et al. (1981) presented a review of many studies that examined the efficacy of preschool special education. While there are some methodological questions about early studies by Skeels and Dye, the research, in general, has shown that early stimulation and preschool attendance make a significant difference in the rate of growth of children, and that these gains are maintained over time. It has been shown that diverse curriculum models can be equally effective in promoting school success if high standards of quality are maintained (Schweinhart & Weikart, 1981). In addition, inclusive programming for there children is being heavily supported (Cavallaro, Ballard-Rosa, & Lynch, 1998).

A longitudinal study of the Perry Preschool Program (Schweinhart & Weikart, 1981) has provided a strong argument for preschool special education programs. This study followed 123 children from age three through the school years. It found that those children who attended preschool had consistently higher school achievement, higher motivation, fewer placements in special education programs, and less delinquent behavior. An economic benefit-cost effectiveness analysis of the Perry Preschool Program was conducted; it found that there was a 248% return on the original investment when savings from lowered costs for education, benefits from increases in projected earnings, and value of mothers' time released when the child attended preschool were considered.

There are many reports of successful preschool special education programs. While many of these programs differ greatly in the populations they serve, their theoretical bases, and their curriculum content, their effectiveness has been demonstrated. It is essential that these benefits be recognized, and that programs for all handicapped pre-school children be supported.

REFERENCES

Cavallaro, C.C., Ballard-Rosa, & Lynch, E.W. (1998). A preliminary study of inclusive special education services for infants, toddlers, and pre-school children in California. *Topics in Early Childhood Special Education, 18*(3), 169–182.

Hobbs, N. (1975). *The futures of children.* San Francisco: Jossey-Bass.

Karnes, M., Schwedel, A., Lewis, G., & Esry, D. (1981). Impact of early programming for the handicapped: A follow-up study into the elementary school. *Journal of the Division for Early Childhood, 4,* 62–79.

Karnes, M., & Zehrbach, R. (1977). Alternative models for deliver-ing services to young handicapped children. In J. Jordan, A. Hayden, M. Karnes, & M. Wood (Eds.), *Early childhood education for exceptional children* (pp. 20–65). Reston, VA: Council for Exceptional Children.

Lerner, J., Mardell-Czudnowski, C., & Goldenberg, D. (1981). *Special education for the early childhood years.* Englewood Cliffs, NJ: Prentice-Hall.

Schweinhart, L., & Weikart, D. (1981). Effects of the Perry Preschool Program on youths through age 15. *Journal of the Division for Early Childhood, 4,* 29–39.

Select Committee on Children, Youth, and Families. (1985). *Opportunities for success: Cost effective programs for children.* Washington, DC: U.S. Government Printing Office.

Shearer, M., & Shearer, D. (1977). Parent involvement. In J. Jordan, A. Hayden, M. Karnes, & M. Wood (Eds.), *Early childhood education for exceptional children* (pp. 208–235). Reston, VA: Council for Exceptional Children.

Wood, M., & Hurley, O. (1977). Curriculum and instruction. In J. Jordan, A. Hayden, M. Karnes, & M. Wood (Eds.), *Early childhood education for exceptional children* (pp. 132–157). Reston: VA: Council for Exceptional Children.

See also Preschool Assessment; Preschool Screening

PRESIDENT'S COMMITTEE ON MENTAL RETARDATION (PCMR)

The President's Committee on Mental Retardation (PCMR) was formally established in 1966 to focus on mental retardation. The mission of the PCMR is to act in an advisory capacity to the President and the Secretary of Health and Human Services on matters relating to policy and programs affecting services and supports for people with mental retardation.

Since 1974, the committee has organized national planning; stimulated the development of plans, policies, and programs; and advanced the concept of community inclusion and participation for individuals with mental retardation. Several national goals have been adopted by the committee. These goals recognize and uphold the right of all people with mental retardation to create for themselves a life that reflects independence, self-determination, and participation as productive members of society. They include the assurance of full citizenship rights of people with mental retardation, the provision of all necessary supports to individuals and their families, the reduction of the occurrence and severity of mental retardation, and the promotion of the widest possible dissemination of information on policies, programs, and service models that foster independence, self-determination, and social and economic participation.

PCMR conducts forums and publishes numerous materials addressing the field of mental retardation and the needs, interests, concerns, and quality of life experienced by citizens with mental retardation. These publications include *Collaborating for Inclusion: 1995 Report to the President,* addressing the need for collaborative efforts among policymakers on all government levels, people with mental retardation, families, service providers, and advocacy organizations; and *Putting People First* (1994), presenting a new vision for people with mental retardation in the areas of healthcare, welfare, long-term care, housing, education, and employment. Additional information and single copies of publications may be obtained at no cost by contacting the U.S. Department of Health and Human Services at (202) 619–0634, (202) 205–9519 (fax), or *tlion@acf.dhhs.gov* (e-mail).

REFERENCE

President's Committee On Mental Retardation. (1997). *Voices and visions: Building leadership for the 21st century.* (DHHS Publication No. 520–562/90153). Washington, DC: U.S. Government Printing Office.

See also **Mental Retardation**

PREVENTION, PRIMARY

This term refers to efforts made to reduce the incidence or prevalence of handicapping conditions through the establishment of medical and social programs that attempt to change those conditions responsible for their development.

The President's Committee on Mental Retardation set a goal of preventing the occurrence of 50% of all cases of mental retardation by the year 2000 (President's Committee on Mental Retardation, 1976). As a result, research has been done on virtually all known causes of mental retardation. Patton, Payne, and Beirne-Smith (1986) indicate that for each cause, a specific preventive measure has been found. The most fruitful approaches to prevention include carrier detection, prenatal monitoring, and newborn screening. Combinations of these approaches appear to be more successful in preventing various handicapping conditions than the use of individual techniques (Sells & Bennett, 1977). Prevention is often approached within the framework of determining cause. The major causes appear to result from infections and intoxications, trauma or physical agents, disorders of metabolism and nutrition, gross brain disease, unknown prenatal influence, and chromosomal abnormalities (Grossman, 1983).

Preventive measures implemented during the preconception period can significantly reduce hereditary, innate, congenital, and other constitutional disorders. Adequate prenatal care and analysis for possible genetic disorders are two general approaches to prevention usually associated with the gestational period. Yet one out of every four women who gives birth in a hospital has never received prenatal care from a physician during her pregnancy (Koch & Koch, 1976). Anticipating potential problems that may occur at delivery can avert problems during the perinatal period.

Environmental intervention, adequate nutrition, and avoidance of hazards constitute the bulk of preventive measures during the childhood period. For example, a high correlation between ingestion of lead in drinking water and mental retardation has been reported (Gearheart, 1980; Needleman, 1994).

Blood-screening techniques can be used to identify some conditions (e.g., Tay-Sachs disease) transmitted through autosomal recessive genes or x-linked genes. Using several screening procedures, Thoene, Higgins, Krieger, Schmickel, and Weiss (1981) identified seven metabolic disorders caused by an enzyme deficiency. Because of the low incidence rate of most conditions, carriers are so rare that general screening procedures would have to involve massive numbers of people to be effective (Westling, 1986). Thus genetic screening is most often used by those who have already had one child with a disorder or who are aware that the condition exists in their family.

Monitoring the fetus prior to birth has resulted in the identification of over 100 inherited disorders (Sells & Bennett, 1977). Amniocentesis (drawing some of the amniotic fluid surrounding the fetus for cellular examination) is used to detect three types of problems: those identified through the chromosomal structure, those identified through enzyme deficiencies, and neural tube defects. Milunsky (1976) indicated that women who are over 35, couples in which one parent is a balanced carrier of translocation, and couples who have already had one Down's syndrome child are the three groups that most frequently seek chromosomal analysis through amniocentesis. The use of fetoscopy permits the physician to insert a small tube through the mother's abdominal wall to examine parts of the fetus. This permits the determination of physical characteristics that may be useful in determining whether a disorder exists. Senography consists of the use of ultrasound waves to outline the fetus and identify structures indicative of handicapping conditions (e.g., spina bifada, microcephaly) through different densities. Rh incompatibility may be prevented through Rh gamma globulin injections for the Rh-negative mother after the birth of her first Rh-positive child or after a miscarriage.

Newborn screening tests permit the identification of many infants with inborn errors of metabolism (e.g., galactosemia, phenylketonuria). In some cases, mental retardation may be prevented by altering the diet (Carpenter, 1975). Hypothyroidism can also be detected through birth screening using the same blood samples used with phenylketonuria (Dussault et al., 1975). Since some diagnostic indicators develop slowly during the first 6 months, the newborn screening should be followed with additional testing during later infant examinations.

Avoidance of certain substances (e.g., drugs, alcohol, X-rays) is the only current source of prevention for some disorders. Avoidance behavior can sometimes be the only method of prevention, as in the case of HIV/AIDS (Kelly, Murphy, Sikkema, & Kalichman, 1993). Preconceptual vaccinations can fight some bacterial infections (e.g., rubella, syphilis). Yet it has been estimated that 25% of children, older girls, and young women in the United States are not protected against rubella (Gearheart, 1980). A Caesarean-section birth may be used with women who have a herpes virus at the time of delivery. Postnatal causes that can often be prevented include direct trauma to the head, cerebral hemorrhage, lesions on the brain, infections that cause conditions such as encephalitis and meningitis, and electric shock. Although controversy still surrounds the role that chronic malnutrition plays in mental development, there is evidence that it can result in a greater risk of infection and increased likelihood of disease from other agents (Westling, 1986).

REFERENCES

Carpenter, D.G. (1975). Metabolic and transport anomalies. In C.H. Carter (Ed.), *Handbook of mental retardation syndromes* (3rd ed.). Springfield, IL: Thomas.

Dussault, H.H., Coulombe, P., Laberge, C., Letarte, J., Guyda, H., Khoury, K. (1975). Preliminary report on a mass screening program for neonatal hypothyroidism. *Journal of Pediatrics, 86,* 670–674.

Gearheart, B.R. (1980). *Special education for the 80s.* St. Louis: Mosby.

Grossman, H.J. (1983). *Classification in mental retardation.* Washington, DC: American Association on Mental Deficiency.

Kelly, J.A., Murphy, D.A., Sikkema, K.J., & Kalichman, S.C., (1993). Psychological interventions to prevent HIV infection: New priorities for behavioral research in the second decade of AIDS. *American Psychologist, 48*(10), 1023–1034.

Koch, R., & Koch, J.H. (1976). We can do more to prevent the tragedy of retarded children. *Psychology Today, 107,* 88–93.

Milunsky, A. (1976). A prenatal diagnosis of genetic disorders. *New England Journal of Medicine, 295,* 377–380.

Needleman, H.L. (1994). Preventing childhood lead poisoning. *Preventative Medicine, 23*(5), 634–637.

Patton, J.R., Payne, J.S., & Beirne-Smith, M. (1986). *Mental retardation* (2nd ed.). London: Merrill.

President's Committee on Mental Retardation. (1976). *Mental retardation: The known and the unknown.* Washington, DC: U.S. Government Printing Office.

Sells, C.J., & Bennett, F.C. (1977). Prevention of mental retardation: The role of medicine. *American Journal of Mental Deficiency, 82,* 117–129.

Thoene, J., Higgins, J., Krieger, I., Schmickel, R., & Weiss, L. (1981). Genetic screening for mental retardation in Michigan. *American Journal of Mental Deficiency, 85,* 335–340.

Westling, D.L. (1986). *Introduction to mental retardation.* Englewood Cliffs, NJ: Prentice-Hall.

See also Genetic Counseling; Inborn Errors of Metabolism; Phenylketonuria; Prematurity

PREVOCATIONAL SKILLS

Secondary handicapped students may have difficulty in learning vocational concepts because they have not mastered prerequisite basic skills that serve as the foundation for many vocational activities.

A student's success in a vocational program is influenced by his or her readiness to participate. Readiness skills are often identified as prevocational knowledge and attitudes. Brolin and Kokaska (1979) identified three curriculum areas with 22 major competencies. The areas and skills are (1) daily living (i.e., managing family finances, caring for personal needs, and engaging in civic activities); (2) personal-social abilities (i.e., interpersonal relationships, problem solving, independence); (3) occupational guidance and preparation (i.e., knowing and exploring occupational possibilities, work habits, and behaviors; being able to seek, secure, and maintain satisfactory employment).

Several factors can be considered predictors of vocational development for handicapped individuals. These include achievement of basic academic skills, adaptive behavior, verbal manners and communication skills, performance on vocational checklists, and actual samples of work behavior (Forness, 1982). A closer look at these predictors indicates that assessing a handicapped individual's vocational potential by evaluating his or her academic and social skills within the context of a work-related situation is valuable. Skills learned in a classroom setting may not generalize when applied to work settings. One step toward achieving generalization of academic skills is to develop a technique to assess applied academic and social skills. Neff (1966) suggested four approaches to the evaluation of the work potential of handicapped individuals. They are the mental testing approach, the job analysis approach, the work sample approach, and the situational assessment approach.

REFERENCES

Brolin, D.E., & Kokaska, C.J. (1979). *Career education for handicapped children and youth.* Columbus, OH: Merrill.

Forness, S.R. (1982). Prevocational academic assessment of children and youth with learning and behavior problems. In K.P. Lynch, W.E. Kiernan, & J.A. Stark (Eds.), *Prevocational and vocational education for special needs youth.* Baltimore, MD: Brooks.

Neff, W.S. (1966). Problems of work evaluation. *Personnel and Guidance Journal of Mental Deficiency, 44,* 682–688.

See also Vocational Evaluation; Vocational Rehabilitation; Vocational Training of the Handicapped

PRIMARY IMMUNODEFICIENCY DISORDERS

This classification of health-related disorders encompasses over fifty distinct, genetically determined illnesses and does not include HIV, AIDS, or secondary causes such as chemotherapy. The incidence of these disorders range from 1 in 500 to 1 in 1,000,000, with approximately 25,000 patients identified in the U.S. at the time of this submission. As the title suggests, these disorders affect the immune system, and though most are congenital (patients are born with them), symptoms may not become apparent until adulthood.

Perhaps the most famous case of primary immunodeficiency disorders involved David, "the bubble boy" in Houston, Texas. His particular type of disorder involved several different parts of his immune system, causing severe susceptibility to infections from all viruses and bacteria. David lived 12 courageous years inside a sterile environment. Though the immune system disorders were first recognized in the mid 1950s, David's ordeal advanced our understanding of immune deficiencies, autoimmune disorders, cancer, and infection process in general.

As with David, children and adults with primary immunodeficiency disorders are susceptible to infectious diseases. Some experience chronic, recurrent, unusual, invasive, or severe infections, and have multiple concurrent conditions before the immune system is evaluated. Some of these disorders are treatable by replacing the portions of the immune system that is missing. An example would be intravenous gamma globulin (IVIG; a product containing antibodies from pooled human plasma donations) for patients with X-linked aggamaglobulinanemia or Common Variable Immunodeficiency. Patients with one particular disorder were the first to undergo "gene therapy," in which affected cells were removed and DNA containing the normal genes was inserted. When these cells were reintroduced to the patient, the symptoms of their disorder were relieved, allowing a decrease in reliance on costly, complicated medical therapies. Similar to David's story, these patients have contributed to a very promising new field of study that may help most genetically determined illnesses (i.e. cystic fibrosis, sickle cell anemia, and so on).

Other special needs may be required on an individual basis, not as a direct result of the immune disorders but due to the sequelae of repeated infections. Some examples include special diets, frequent meals or special restroom privileges due to intestinal malabsorption, hall passes or scheduled nursing visits for medication administration, or assignment of classes to minimize absences.

Physicians, patients, and families should be flexible to work within the school system when possible, scheduling routine care around important times and dates; however, they must also rely on the patience, compassion, and understanding of others in their lives to reach the goals set by the patients themselves. Further information and support can be obtained from the Immune Deficiency Foundation at 25 West Chesapeake Avenue, Suite 206, Towson, MD, 21204.

REFERENCE

Immune Deficiency Foundation. (1998). *Informational brochure.* Towson, MD: Author.

See also **Chronic Illness; National Organization for Rare Disorders; Office of Rare Diseases; Other Health Impaired**

PRIMARY MENTAL ABILITIES TEST (PMA)

The Primary Mental Abilities Test (PMA; Thurstone & Thurstone, 1965) is a group-administered measure of both general intelligence and specific intellectual factors that the authors call primary mental abilities. In earlier versions of the PMA, six to eight primary mental abilities were identified. Subsequently, this number was reduced to the current five factors. There are six levels of the test (K–1, 2–4, 4–6, 6–9, 9–12, and adult). The adult test is identical to that for grades 9–12. No attempt was made to prepare adult norms, and no additional psychometric characteristics at the adult level are included in the documentation.

Historically, the PMA occupied a prominent position in the development of cognitive tests. The original series, published between 1938 and 1941, was based on extensive factor analytic work and represented a major contribution to test construction. The high aspirations held for the PMA battery reflected in early reviews were never realized (Schutz, 1972). While the Thurstones continued to contribute to both multifactor science and technology after the PMA was commercially available, very little of this new knowledge and technology found its way back into subsequent PMA revisions. Thus the PMA soon became outstripped by competing tests in terms of technical quality and functional utility. Because of the technical superiority of other instruments assessing similar abilities, reviewers have questioned the continued use of the PMA (Quereshi, 1972; Schutz, 1972).

REFERENCES

Quereshi, M.Y. (1972). SRA Primary Mental Abilities (1962 ed.). In O.K. Buros (Ed.), *The seventh mental measurements yearbook* (pp. 1064–1066). Highland Park, NJ: Gryphon.

Schutz, R.E. (1972). SRA Primary Mental Abilities (1962 ed.). In O.K. Buros (Ed.), *The seventh mental measurements yearbook* (pp. 1066–1068). Highland Park, NJ: Gryphon.

Thurstone, L., & Thurstone, T. (1965). *Primary Mental Abilities Test.* Chicago: Science Research.

PRIVATE SCHOOLS AND SPECIAL EDUCATION

Prior to the passage of the Education for All Handicapped Children Act of 1975 (PL 94-142), private schools that existed to provide services to handicapped children were mainly tuition-based, profit-making institutions that held the parents responsible for costs. With the passage of PL 94-142, it became the local education agency's responsibility to provide a free, appropriate, public education to all children regardless of severity of handicap.

Public Law 94–142 and subsequent amendments also mandated that it was the local education agency's (LEA) responsibility to provide the tuition for those students that the LEA placed in private schools (McQuain, 1982). Although it is clear that the LEA must be responsible for paying the tuition for students who are in private placement as a result of LEA placement, it is unclear as to the responsibility for payment for those students who are in church-related or other private schools at the request of the parent or a social agency (Wylie, 1981). For example, if a child's handicapping condition necessitates placement in a residential school to provide education, the placement, including nonmedical care and room and board, becomes the responsibility of the LEA. If placement is for noneducational concerns, home or community problems, then the LEA is responsible only for the educational costs. It sometimes becomes extremely difficult to separate education from other needs (McQuain, 1982).

Some decisions have been made by the courts related to placement issues. A program must be state approved to receive tuition payments from the LEA (Grumet & Inkpen, 1982). If an appropriate program exists within the LEA for a child, the LEA will not be responsible for private tuition (McQuain, 1982). Parents are not entitled to reimbursement for tuition as a result of voluntary placement in non-approved schools (Grumet & Inkpen, 1982), unless a clear case can be made that the program was appropriate and the LEA failed to take timely and appropriate action in evaluation or placement. The LEA must ensure that all children in private placement receive the same rights and procedures that they would receive if in public placement (Grumet & Inkpen, 1982). Therefore, the LEA, in conjunction with the state education agency, has the responsibility to monitor the programs in the private sector.

Within the continuum of services concept, a private placement is seen as most restrictive because of the inability to mainstream. Therefore, being placed in a residential setting, a child must first receive the full benefit of opportunities provided within the LEA (Grumet & Inkpen, 1982).

A recent Supreme Court decision has lifted restrictions on on-site instruction, and the 1997 IDEA amendments have helped to clarify an LEA's obligation to provide services to parochial school students (Osborne, DiMattia, & Russo, 1998).

Audette (1982) described additional areas of concern, including transportation, coordination of individual education plans, artificiality of environment of private placement, rising costs of placement, unanticipated placements, and due process issues. The questions about whether parochial school students with disabilities must have the same level of service as their peers, and on-site services remain and need to be satisfied (Osborne et al., 1998).

REFERENCES

Audette, D. (1982). Private school placement: A local director's perspective. *Exceptional Children, 49*(3), 214–219.

Grumet, L., & Inkpen, T. (1982). The education of children in private schools: A state agency's perspective. *Exceptional Children, 49*(3), 100–106.

McQuain, S. (1982). Special education private placements: Financial responsibility under the law. *Journal of Educational Finance, 7*(4), 425–435.

Osborne, A.G., DiMattia, P., & Russo, C.J. (1998). Legal considerations improving special education services in parochial schools. *Exceptional Children, 64*(3), 385–394.

Wylie, R.J. (1981). The handicapped child and private education. *Journal of Adventist Education, 8*(9), 35–36.

See also **Individuals with Disabilities Education Act (IDEA); Magnet Schools; Mainstreaming**

PRIVILEGED COMMUNICATION

Privileged communication is a legal concept which protects the communications within certain professional relationships from disclosure in a court of law without the client's consent. Privileged relationships have historically included the attorney-client and spousal privileges, which are based in common law traditions, and clergy-communicant and physician-patient relationships, which have been established by statute in all fifty states and U.S. territories. All fifty states have also enacted privileged communication laws covering licensed psychiatrists and psychologists and their patients. Only a few states, however, have included other counselors and psychotherapists, licensed or unlicensed, under their privilege statutes.

Legal privilege must be distinguished from confidentiality; though they are related in the sense that both address conditions in which professional communications may or may not be disclosed, they originate from different sources and provide different levels of protection from unwanted disclosure. Confidentiality is a professional duty to refrain from disclosing client information gained during the course of the professional interaction with a client, and is based upon the ethical standards and rules of the various professions. In addition, confidentiality requirements have been incorporated into legislation and the licensure laws of every state, prohibiting certain professionals from revealing client information without client consent, and specifying the conditions under which confidentiality may or must be broken (Knapp & Vandecreek, 1996). Confidentiality is not, however, protected when the professional is required to testify in court.

However, there are a number of statutory limitations to both confidential and privileged communications. The most common exceptions to privilege require the professional to disclose privileged information when (a) there is reason to believe the client may be a danger to him or herself or others (b) child abuse is suspected, (c) the client puts his or her own mental state at issue, and (d) various other conditions are present, as specified by individual state statutes, such as elder abuse, sexual abuse by a psychotherapist, in malpractice suits against one's therapist, among others.

A recent Supreme Court case has established new and important precedent regarding the psychotherapist-patient privilege. In the case of *Jaffe v. Redmond* (1996), the Court held "the confidential communications between a licensed psychotherapist and the psychotherapist's patient in the course of diagnosis or treatment are protected from compelled disclosure under Rule 501 of the Federal Rules of Evidence" (p. 338). This finding addressed two major problems in the privileged communication arena: it effectively established a federal psychotherapist-patient privilege for the first time, and it extended the privilege to licensed "psychotherapists," thus acknowledging the many professionals, other than physicians and psychologists, who provide mental health services that warrant privileged status. Although the Court's finding is binding only in federal courts, it delivers clear guidance to state courts and legislatures through its message about the importance the nation's highest Court gives to therapeutic relationships.

Privileged communication laws are not, however, applicable to most educational settings, including special education contexts. Educators have not been included in the groups whose communications with clients have been afforded privileged status, with the possible exception of doctoral-level, licensed school psychologists. The *Jaffe v. Redmond* case discussed above did extend privilege to a master's level therapist, but did not address whether privilege would apply to any educational setting. It is possible that school counselors, if they are licensed, could make a case for the need for privileged communication in certain circumstances, but this has not happened to date. Thus, communications with school counselors and other education professionals must be disclosed in court when required.

REFERENCES

Knapp, S. & Vandecreek, L. (1997). *Jaffe v. Redmond:* The Supreme Court recognizes a psychotherapist–patient priviledge in federal courts. *Professional Psychology: Research and Practice, 28,* 567–572.

Jaffe v. Redmond, 135 L.Ed.2d 337 (S. Ct. 1996).

See also **Confidentiality of Information; Parents of the Handicapped**

PROBLEM SOLVING, CREATIVE

See CREATIVE PROBLEM SOLVING.

PROCEDURAL SAFEGUARDS

See DUE PROCESS.

PROCESS TRAINING

See ABILITY TRAINING.

PRODUCTION DEFICIENCY

Production deficiency is closely tied to mediation theory (Flavell, 1970). Mediation refers to the intervention of some process between the initial stimulating event and the final response (Reese & Lipsitt, 1970). Special education students are often unable to "mediate" or use other task-appropriate strategies as intermediate steps in the learning process (Torgersen, 1977). Such inability may be due to special education students being inactive learners lacking goal-directed motivation (Torgerson, 1977). Or the learning environment not stimulating mediational interventions with the learner (Kozulin, & Falik, 1995).

Additional research in this area has resulted in an alternative explanation to those previously mentioned; special education students' poor academic performance may reflect a production deficiency (Naron, 1978; Wong, 1980). A production deficiency suggests that a student may have the ability to use the mediation strategy or another strategy but fails to spontaneously and appropriately produce it (Wong, 1980). For these children, prompting and training in metacognition and related processes might prove helpful.

REFERENCES

Flavell, J.H. (1970). Developmental studies in mediated memory. In H.W. Reese & L.P. Lipsitt (Eds.), *Advances in child development and behavior.* New York: Academic.

Kozulin, A., & Falik, L. (1995). Dynamic cognitive assessment of the child. *Current Directions in Psychological Science, 4*(6), 192–196.

Naron, N.K. (1978). Developmental changes in word attribute utilization for organization and retrieval in free recall. *Journal of Experimental Child Psychology, 25,* 279–297.

Reese, H.W., & Lipsitt, L.P. (1970). *Experimental child psychology.* New York: Academic.

Torgersen, J.K. (1977). The role of nonspecific factors in the task performance of learning disabled children: A theoretical assessment. *Journal of Learning Disabilities, 10,* 27–34.

Wong, B.Y.L. (1980). Activating the inactive learner: Use of questions/prompts to enhance comprehension and retention of implied information in learning disabled children. *Learning Disability Quarterly, 3,* 29–37.

See also **Mediational Deficiency**

PRO-ED, INCORPORATED

Pro-Ed is a publishing company that deals exclusively in the disability area (i.e., special education, counseling, rehabilitation, psychology, and speech/language pathology). The product line focuses on assessment measures, remedial and therapy materials, professional books, and periodicals. Among the latter are the following journals: *Journal of Learning Disabilities, Journal of Special Education, Remedial and Special Education, Intervention in School and Clinic, Reclaiming Children and Youth, Focus on Autism and other Developmental Disabilities, Topics in Early Childhood Special Education, Journal of Emotional and Behavioral Disorders.* Pro-Ed is a privately held corporation founded in 1977. Its current address is 8700 Shoal Creek Blvd, Austin, Texas, 78757-6897. In 1999, the company had approximately 1400 active titles.

See also **RASE; TECSE**

PROFESSIONAL SCHOOL PSYCHOLOGY

Professional School Psychology is the official journal of Division 16 of the American Psychological Association. *Professional School Psychology* is intended as a forum to promote and maintain high standards of preparation for professional school psychologists and effective delivery of school psychological services. The journal publishes empirically and theoretically based papers intended to reflect a cross-section of school psychology and suitable for a broad readership. Papers that analyze, synthesize, reformulate, or offer an empirical or conceptual perspective to issues involving the underpinnings of the profession, the delivery and evaluation of services, ethical and legal aspects, and approaches to education and training are encouraged. Of special interest are articles that outline innovative professional procedures with rigorous, theoretical, and empirical support. *Professional School Psychology* is published quarterly by Lawrence Erlbaum Associates.

PROFESSIONAL COMPETENCIES FOR WORKING WITH CULTURALLY AND LINGUISTICALLY DIVERSE STUDENTS

Students in public schools today look, sound, learn, and live in ways that differ from past populations. Of the 45 million students enrolled in public and private elementary and secondary schools, over 30% are from groups designated as racial/ethnic minorities (Gonzalez, Brusca-Vega, & Yawkey, 1997). In addition, many students are at risk for school failure because they live in poverty, live in a single-parent family, or have poorly educated parents (Pallas, Natriello, & McDill, 1989). Therefore, culture, as used in this article, refers to differences in race and ethnicity as well as socioeconomic status, beliefs, values, modes of expression, ways of thinking, and ways of resolving problems. The competencies listed below represent minimal competencies that teachers working with culturally and linguistically diverse students with exceptionalities (CLDE) should have.

The basic collaboration abilities needed by educators working with CLDE students have been identified by Harris (1991, 1996). The first is "to understand one's own perspective." Educators should be able to understand their own cultures and their relationship to other cultures. Educators also need to understand their own beliefs and expectations, especially regarding the abilities of students from various cultures.

The second collaborative ability is "the effective use of interpersonal, communication, and problem-solving skills." Educators must be caring, respectful, empathetic, congruent, and open in collaborative interactions. They must be able to communicate clearly and effectively in oral and written form. For effective cross-cultural communication, educators must be aware of cultural differences in communication and relationships and, when necessary, use interpreters appropriately. Educators should be familiar with the kinds of information that can be easily interpreted and conduct pre- and post-sessions with interpreters so that the language and intent of communications are clearly expressed. Educators must be able to grasp and validate overt as well as

covert meanings and affects in communication. They also must be able to interview effectively to elicit information, explore problems, and set goals and objectives for the collaboration (Harris, 1991, 1996).

The third ability is "to understand the roles of collaborators." In a multicultural society, educators should be able to facilitate problem-solving sessions with individuals with different values and problem-solving styles and collaborate with culturally diverse personnel (Harris, 1996). Therefore, educators working with CLDE students need to be familiar with familial and institutional objectives relevant to CLDE students, and understand the resources that can be provided by other personnel such as bilingual educators, ESL educators, parents, and paraprofessionals (Harris, 1991).

Alternative assessment models have been present over the last two decades in response to inconsistencies found with students from culturally and linguistically diverse backgrounds (Mercer & Rueda, 1991). Therefore, it is of critical importance for educators to be able to use a wide variety of alternative assessments with CLDE students. Because language assessment is key to documenting the difference between language difference and language disability, educators working with CLDE students should know existing assessment procedures and instruments in language proficiency, language dominance, and language development, as well as cognitive/intellectual development, social-emotional behavior, adaptive behavior, and achievement. They should also be able to adapt evaluation procedures to compensate for potential cultural and linguistic biases of the assessment process (Baca & Almanza, 1991).

Educators working with CLDE students should know sources for materials appropriate for students from various cultural and linguistic backgrounds and should be able to evaluate materials in terms of their quality, availability, and appropriateness. The materials educators use should stimulate active, meaningful, and purposeful involvement of students (Baca & Almanza, 1991).

REFERENCES

Baca, L.M., & Almanza, E. (1991). *Language minority students with disabilities.* Reston, VA: The Council for Exceptional Children.

Gonzalez, V., Brusca-Vega, R., & Yawkey, R. (1997). *Assessment and instruction of culturally and linguistically diverse students with or at-risk of learning problems: From research to practice.* Boston: Allyn & Bacon.

Harris, K.C. (1991). An expanded view on consultation competencies for educators serving culturally and linguistically diverse exceptional students. *Teacher Education and Special Education, 14*(1), 25–29.

Harris, K.C. (1996). Collaboration within a multicultural society: Issues for consideration. *Remedial and Special Education, 17*(6), 355–362, 376.

Mercer, J.R., & Rueda, R. (1991, November). *The impact of changing paradigms of disabilities on assessment for special education.* Paper presented at The Council for Exceptional Children Topical Conference on At-Risk Children and Youth, New Orleans, LA.

Pallas, A.M., Natriello, G., & McDill, E.L. (1989). The changing nature of the disadvantaged population: Current dimensions and future trends. *Educational Researcher, 18,* 16–22.

PROFESSIONAL STANDARDS FOR SPECIAL EDUCATORS

Professional standards for special educators are rules and guidelines governing the conduct of persons who work in special education. The development of competency standards is an attempt to increase the overall quality of service in the field and to strive for excellence in the profession. In 1966 the Council for Exceptional Children developed Professional Standards for Personnel in the Education of Exceptional Children. In 1979 the council approved Guidelines for Personnel in the Education of Exceptional Children. These standards did not include formal definable criteria for determining whether a teacher had acquired the necessary competencies. The most recent set of standards published by the council consists of three policy statements focusing on common requirements for the practice of special education: Code of Ethics, Professional Practice, and Standards for the Preparation of Special Education Personnel. These statements describe the philosophical position of special education professionals, the skills the specialists should exhibit in their jobs, and how training organizations should best prepare future special educators.

Once the development and implementation of the standards are completed, professionals in the field need to concentrate their efforts in three areas. First, the development of continuing or in-service education must address the competencies needed by professionals already in the field (Stedman, Smith, & Baucom, 1981). Second, as mentioned by Gersten (1985), efforts should focus on which teacher competencies actually make a difference to people with special needs (Englert, 1983). Interviewing experts to develop professional competencies (Zane, Sulzer-Azaroff, Handen, & Fox, 1982) is useful in developing a large number of skills and standards that seem logical, but such a strategy is insufficient in that it does not provide for a determination of whether such skills are functionally related to student improvement. Third, updating and changing of the standards must continue (Standards for the Preparation of Special Education Personnel, 1983). The validation process is one way that new skills and competencies will become known and incorporated into the standards as the nature of the field changes and the needs of the developmentally disabled shift over time. By validating them, updating as needed, and incorporating them into institutions that train special educators, the standards will become an integral part of the training of special educators and will achieve the original purpose for their development—producing qualified professionals and providing maximum improvement of persons with special needs.

REFERENCES

Englert, C.S. (1983). Measuring special education teacher effectiveness. *Exceptional Children, 50,* 247–254.

Standards for the preparation of special education personnel. (1983). *Exceptional Children, 50,* 210–218.

Stedman, D.J., Smith, R.R., & Baucom, L.D. (1981). Toward quality in special education programs. In D. Stedman & J. Paul (Eds.), *New directions for exceptional children: Professional preparation for teachers of exceptional children* (No. 8). San Francisco: Jossey-Bass.

Zane, T., Sulzer-Azaroff, B., Handen, B.L., & Fox, C.J. (1982). Validation of a competency-based training program in developmental disabilities. *Journal of the Severely Handicapped, 7,* 21–31.

See also **Ethics; Teacher Effectiveness**

PROFILE ANALYSIS

Profile analysis is the evaluation of scatter, or irregular performance, on the subtests and scales of a test. Whenever a profile of performance across specific areas is generated from a test, analysis of the profile is possible on a formal or informal basis. Thus, the patterns of scores from numerous intelligence, achievement, personality, aptitude, and vocational interest measures can be interpreted through the analysis of the relative positions of subtests and scales to each other (Goldstein & Hersen, 1984).

Of prime importance is that profile analysis is dependent on the presence of statistically significant differences among the subscales or among the subtests. Thus, before statements can be made about whether the examinee obtained higher or lower IQs, scaled scores, or subtest scores, significant differences among the subscales or the subtests must be present. Statistically significant differences among subtests or scales suggest that the differences are attributed to the abilities tapped by the respective subtests or scales rather than to measurement error.

Even with statistical differences, ideas generated must be viewed simply as hypotheses to be checked against other information about the examinee. Thus, a second caution is that profile analysis should be done with an understanding that uneven scores can be caused by many factors, including unreliability of the subtests, examiner/situational variability, background factors, physical disability, and minority group status (Sattler, 1982). In other words, experts agree that profile analysis is done only when the examinee's entire performance is evaluated to exclude the influence of other factors before specific strengths and weaknesses in cognitive ability are inferred.

REFERENCES

Goldstein, G., & Hersen, M. (1984). *Handbook of psychological assessment.* New York: Pergamon.

Sattler, J.M. (1982). *Assessment of children's intelligence and special abilities.* Boston: Allyn & Bacon.

See also **Intelligence Testing**

PROFILE VARIABILITY

Profile variability is an index of test scatter (individual variation in test scores between or within various psychological and educational tests) first defined by Plake, Reynolds, and Gutkin (1981). It is used as a diagnostic aid in determining the degree of intratest variability in an individual's performance on the subtests of any multiscale assessment device.

Test scatter has typically been determined by range (the highest minus the lowest score for an individual on a common family of tests), or by the number of test scores deviating at a statistically significant level from the individual's mean score on all tests administered (the latter sometimes is referred to as the number of deviant signs, or NDS). Profile variability is similar in some respects to range, but it is more accurate, more stable, and more powerful than older indexes of scatter. Profile variability encompasses data from all tests or subtests administered to an individual. It is not limited to the two most extreme scores as is the range.

Calculation of the index of profile variability is straightforward because it is the variance of a set of scores for one person on more than one measure, hence, the name profile variability. Profile variability for each member of a group or population can be estimated to be (Plake et al., 1981):

$$S^2 = \sum_{j=1}^{k} \frac{(x_{ij-\bar{x}_j})}{k-1}$$

where S^2 = the index of profile variability

x_{ij} = the score of person i on test or subtest j

$\bar{x}_j$ = the mean score for person i on all tests (k) administered

k = the number of tests administered

The resulting value can then be compared with data taken from the standardization sample of a test or some other group to determine whether the variance of the individual's profile is an unusual or a common occurrence. In a research setting, it may also be of interest to know if the mean S^2 for one group differs at a statistically significant level from the mean S^2 for another group. A statistical test of the significance of the difference has been developed and is detailed in Plake et al. (1981).

REFERENCE

Plake, B., Reynolds, C.R., & Gutkin, T.B. (1981). A technique for the comparison of profile variability between independent groups. *Journal of Clinical Psychology, 37,* 142–146.

See also Profile Analysis; Test Scatter

PROFOUNDLY HANDICAPPED, COMPETENCIES OF TEACHERS OF

Students considered to be profoundly handicapped (PH) may include individuals who have been diagnosed and labeled as either profoundly mentally retarded, autistic, deaf-blind, severely multiply handicapped, or severely emotionally disturbed. In recent years, increased emphasis has been placed on determining the competencies or skills needed by teachers of these students (Burke & Cohen, 1977; Horner, 1977; Southeastern Regional Coalition, 1982).

Among the specific competency areas considered to be most important in the area of behavioral programming and management are development of task analyses, understanding of behavior modification techniques, and the ability to arrange and manage reinforcement contingencies and principles. In addition, within this area, the ability to develop strategies for appropriate acquisition, maintenance, and generalization of behaviors, and the ability to measure behavior and competencies (Gresham, MacMillan, & Siperstein, 1995) precisely, are considered to be important competencies.

The ability to involve parents in educational planning and to function as an effective parent trainer are often suggested as important competencies for teachers of profoundly handicapped students.

The ability to maintain an ongoing assessment of learning is important. Knowledge of instrumentation and procedures appropriate for screening, diagnosis, and educational assessment, and the ability to comprehend and interpret diagnostic reports, are necessary skills.

Instructional delivery is an additional competency area that includes the ability to develop or select instructional materials, the use of a high percentage of minutes per day for instruction, and the ability to facilitate skill acquisition.

Knowledge of medical aspects has been determined to be an important area of needed competence. The skills of using modified equipment, administering medication, and providing assistance to a student having a seizure are often necessary competencies.

An understanding of the normative developmental sequence and early academic learning processes is paramount in the education of profoundly handicapped students.

A frequently stated competency is the ability to communicate and work effectively with other professionals. Other skills include the ability to supervise paraprofessional personnel and the understanding and use of support services in the school and community.

The final area includes the specific competencies of understanding cognitive, language, social, motor, and behavioral development and knowledge of clinical syndromes. Although an abundance of competencies have been suggested for teachers of PH students, the majority of these statements are based on the opinions of the author(s), groups of professionals, or citations from the professional literature.

According to Turner (1971), the highest criterion to judge effectiveness of teacher practices is to determine the effect to these practices on student learning over an extended period of time. Rather than basing the practices teachers use on opinion, it appears to be essential that the validity of the suggested teacher competencies be determined as a result of empirical research.

In reviewing the competency statements, it appears that many of those suggested may be applicable to all teachers and especially all special educators. However, teachers of profoundly handicapped students need to be much more proficient in their use. Sontag, Burke, and York (1973) noted an inverse relationship between the level of competence needed by the teacher and the functioning level of the student. Therefore, if profoundly handicapped students are to reach their optimal functioning levels, it is essential that their teachers demonstrate a higher level of competence than teachers of regular or other special students.

REFERENCES

Burke, P., & Cohen, M. (1977). The quest for competencies in serving the severely/profoundly handicapped: A critical analysis of personnel preparation programs. In E. Sontag, J. Smith, & N. Certo (Eds.), *Educational programming for the severely and profoundly handicapped* (pp. 445–465). Reston, VA: Council for Exceptional Children.

Gresham, F.M., MacMillan, D.L., & Siperstein, G.N. (1995). Critical analysis of the 1992 AAMR defintion: Implications for school psychology. *School Psychology Quarterly, 10*(1), 1–19.

Horner, R.D. (1977). A competency based approach to preparing teachers of the severely and profoundly handicapped: Perspective II. In E. Sontag, J. Smith, & N. Certo (Eds.), *Educational programming for the severely and profoundly handicapped* (pp. 430–444). Reston, VA: Council for Exceptional Children.

Sontag, E., Burke, P.J., & York, R. (1973). Considerations for serving the severely handicapped in public schools. *Education & Training of the Mentally Retarded, 8,* 20–26.

Southeastern Regional Coalition for Personnel Preparation to Work with Severely/Profoundly Handicapped. (1982). Developing personnel preparation programs to train personnel to teach severely handicapped individuals. *Teacher Education & Special Education, 5*(1), 46–51.

Turner, R.L. (1971). Levels of criteria. In B. Rosner (Eds.), *The power of competency-based teacher education.* Washington, DC: U.S. Office of Education, National Center for Educational Research and Development.

See also Competency Test; Mildly Handicapped, Teacher Competencies for Mental Retardation; Teacher Training

PROFOUNDLY RETARDED

See MENTAL RETARDATION.

PROGRAM EVALUATION

Program evaluation in elementary school and secondary school education has been an area of considerable activity during the past 20 years. Program evaluation has been such an active area largely because of public concern about program accountability as well as a desire by school professionals to provide quality programs, and outcomes services, (Cronbach, 1982). Although no universal definition exists, program evaluation can be characterized by two essential activities: systematic, purposeful data collection relative to one or more important evaluation questions; and the use of evaluation information to judge whether a program is worthwhile (Rossi, Freeman, & Wright, 1985).

In special education, program evaluation has become an area of avid interest and increasing activity at local school district levels nationwide, with collaborative efforts being undertaken among administrators, staff, and outside consultants. An important impetus to this avid interest and increasing activity at the local level was a two-day national conference on special education program evaluation held in St. Louis during December 1983 (Council of Administrators of Special Education, 1984). At that conference, which was jointly sponsored by the Council of Administrators of Special Education and the Office of Special Education and Rehabilitation Services, four proven models of local-level special education program evaluation were presented by their proponents. The invited audience of over 100 special education directors and supervisors from throughout the nation took part in workshops to learn about these practical approaches. Subsequent to the conference, local school district applicants were reviewed and the various models were field tested during 1984 at about 20 local sites (Associate Consultants, 1985).

Case study results of these field tests, along with empirical results from additional evaluations of local special education programs that occurred during 1985 and 1986 through state department initiatives, coupled with professional publications on special education program evaluation, have all coalesced to delineate and propose several important features and characteristics of this rapidly developing area. These features and characteristics are reflected in terms of the process of special education program evaluation, the foci of evaluation efforts, the methods, procedures, and instruments for conducting evaluations of special programs, and the enhancement of the use of evaluation information for program planning.

An emphasis on the use of special education program evaluation information seems to have been a positive outgrowth of practitioners' desires to act on the information for program planning purposes. In this regard, it has been found important that written evaluation reports be kept brief, that they be written in the nontechnical language of the school audience for which it is intended, and that the narrative be augmented with clearly developed tables, graphs, figures, and other illustrations to emphasize important points. Most important, recommendations for program planning should be specific as to how to take the next steps and clear as to how the steps were derived. To facilitate use of the information, it has been found useful to hold group meetings or forums between evaluation personnel and target audiences.

REFERENCES

Associate Consultants. (1985). *Results of the field tests of the special education program evaluation models.* Washington, DC: Author.

Council of Administrators of Special Education. (1984). *Proceedings of the national conference on special education program evaluation.* Indianapolis, IN: Author.

Cronbach, L.J. (1982). *Designing evaluations of educational and social programs.* San Francisco: Jossey-Bass.

Rossi, P., Freeman, H., & Wright, L. (1985). *Evaluation: A systematic approach.* Beverly Hills, CA: Sage.

See also **National Center for Educational Outcomes; School Effectiveness; Supervision in Special Education**

PROGRAMMED INSTRUCTION

Programmed instruction is a unique educational method based on principles emphasized by B.F. Skinner (1954, 1958). First, the use of positive reinforcement is preferable to punishment or lack of feedback. Second, positive reinforcement is more effective in producing behavioral changes if given frequently and immediately after each response. Last, there is value in presenting students with small chunks of information to learn that will eventually result in desired behaviors. Skinner sought to apply these principles through programmed learning and the use of teaching machines.

Programmed learning has been hailed as allowing truly individualized instruction permitting students to progress at their own pace. In many cases, it seems to be highly motivating to the student because of the immediacy of results, high density of reinforcement, and enjoyment from manipulating the machine (when a teaching machine is used). It has also been instrumental in showing how to teach complex tasks by breaking them down into small, teachable segments.

While the early application of programmed instruction used machines to present learning programs, programmed texts and workbooks soon followed. The increasing use of computers in special education has been revitalizing interest in variations of programmed instruction. An impressive characteristic of modern computers is the great degree of individualized instruction now possible for each student because of the development of branching programs (Rubin & Weisgerber, 1985; Schackenberg & Sullivan, 1997). Students diagnosed as learning disabled and mentally retarded (mild to profound) have learned a variety of skills on computers, such as addition, subtraction, word recognition, matching to sample (Richmond, 1983).

However, it is the application of learning principles and not the use of a computer that is the important issue. A computer does not automatically incorporate programmed instruction principles; in fact, much of the educational software in use today is to a large extent based on the traditional trial-and-error procedures that may result in academic failure in many children (LeBlanc, Hoko, Aangeenbrug, & Etzel, 1985). Integrating instructional principles of programmed learning into the development of educational methodologies, whether in software, textbooks, or other forms, is a way to maximize the chances for learning in special education students.

REFERENCES

LeBlanc, J.M., Hoko, J.A., Aangeenbrug, M.H., & Etzel, B.C. (1985). Microcomputers and stimulus control: From the laboratory to the classroom. *Journal of Special Education Technology, 7,* 23–30.

Richmond, G. (1983). Comparison of automated and human instruction for developmentally retarded preschool children. *Journal of the Association for the Severely Handicapped, 8,* 78–84.

Rubin, D.P., & Weisgerber, R.A. (1985). The center for research and evaluation in the application of technology to education. *Technological Horizons in Education, 12,* 83–87.

Schackenberg, H.L., & Sullivan, H.J. (1997). *Learner ability and learner control in computer assisted instructional programs.* Paper presented at the National Convention of the Association for Educational Communications and Technology, February 14–18, Albuquerque, New Mexico.

Skinner, B.F. (1954). The science of learning and the art of teaching. *Harvard Educational Review, 24,* 86–97.

Skinner, B.F. (1958). Teaching machines. *Science, 128,* 969–977.

See also **Computer-Managed Instruction; Computer Use with the Handicapped; Direct Instruction; Operant Conditioning**

PROJECTIVE TECHNIQUES
See PERSONALITY ASSESSMENT.

PROJECT ON CLASSIFICATION OF EXCEPTIONAL CHILDREN

In the early 1970s, Nicholas Hobbs was asked to direct a systematic review of the classification and labeling practices for exceptional children. Sponsored by 10 federal agencies and organized by Elliot Richardson, then secretary of health, education, and welfare, this review had several objectives.

The first objective was to increase public understanding of the issues associated with labeling and classifying handicapped individuals. The second objective was to formulate a statement of rationale for public policy, including suggestions for regulatory guidelines. The third objective was to educate professionals who were ultimately responsible for the provision of services to the population of exceptional children (Hobbs, 1975a).

The results of this review, known as the Project on Classification of Exceptional Children, were reported in the publication *The Futures of Children* (Hobbs, 1975b). Included in this report was a list of recommendations that detail actions to be taken as well as who should be responsible for the implementation, the cost of service, and the length of time required to accomplish the project objectives.

The specific recommendations of the project members included the formation of a national advisory committee for the purpose of establishing a comprehensive classification system. As a result of such a system, there would be increased understanding of the complexities of the characteristics and etiology of handicapping conditions. The changes proposed in the classification system were not regarded as an end product but rather as a vehicle for improving service and programming for handicapped individuals and their families.

Historically, there has been a great deal of controversy associated with the classification systems for handicapped populations. Since the introduction of the first special education textbook in the early 1920s, there has been a demand for more accurate classification systems (Kaufman & Hallahan, 1981).

Currently, there is little evidence in relevant literature that the recommendations resulting from the Project on Classification of Exceptional Children have been implemented on a national level. Individual agencies have made progress in several areas identified by the project report (e.g., improvement of diagnostic procedures, increases in services for the families of handicapped individuals, reclassification of mental retardation based on structural support needed [Gresham, MacMillan, & Siperstein, 1995] and protection of individual's right to due process). However, the major recommendation calling for a national advisory panel that would help to establish policy and direct relevant research has yet to be realized.

REFERENCES

Gresham, F.M., MacMillan, D.L., & Siperstein, G.N. (1995). Critical analysis of the 1992 AAMR definition: Implication for school psychology. *School Psychology Quarterly, 10*(1), 1–19.

Hobbs, N. (Ed.). (1975a). *Issues in the classification of children* (Vols. 1, 2). San Francisco: Jossey-Bass.

Hobbs, N. (1975b). *The futures of children.* San Francisco: Jossey Bass.

Kaufman, J.M., & Hallahan, D.P. (Eds.). (1981). *Handbook of special education.* Englewood Cliffs, NJ: Prentice-Hall.

See also **AAMD Classification System; Classification Systems; Labeling**

PROJECT RE-ED

The project on the Re-Education of Emotionally Disturbed Children (Project Re-ED) evolved after a 1953 study of mental health needs by the Southern Regional Education Board. The study indicated that there was great need for child mental health programs with demonstrated effectiveness, reasonable cost, access to a large talent pool of trained personnel, and potential for transfer of techniques to public schools.

In 1961 a NIMH grant of $2 million was awarded to George Peabody College for Teachers (now part of Vanderbilt University) and the states of Tennessee and North Carolina. Nicholas Hobbs was the primary developer of the 8-year pilot project for moderately to severely disturbed children (ages 6 to 12) in residential centers in Nashville, Tennessee, and Durham, North Carolina. Centers were in residential areas and provided services to groups of 24 and

40, subdivided into groups of eight. Program planning emphasis was on health rather than illness, teaching rather than therapy, the present rather than the past, and the operation of a total social system of which the child is a part rather than intrapsychic processes alone. Initial planning was pragmatic rather than theoretical; the theory developed with project research and experience. Hobbs (1978; 1983) later commented that one of the important ideas in the planning and development of Project Re-ED was that there should be no orthodoxy or dogma, but a "colleagueship" of discovery guiding the activities of professional individuals working together closely.

Follow-up studies of Project Re-ED children (Weinstein, 1974) indicated that although the reeducation program did not change the students into "normal" children, they were better adjusted than disturbed children who were not in the project. Since the average length of stay in centers was about 7 months (contrasted to several years in some other types of residential centers), it appears that the project met its goal, which was not to cure children, but to restore to effective operation the small social system of which the child is an integral part. Hobbs thought that Project Re-ED would be most likely to pay off when its concepts were applied in public schools. By 1983 about two dozen reeducation centers were established in nine states and several others were being planned. Professional consensus now is the Project Re-ED is a viable means of providing effective services to disturbed children.

REFERENCES

Hobbs, N. (1978). Perspectives on re-education. *Behavior Disorders, 3*(2), 65–66.

Hobbs, N. (1983). Project Re-Education: From demonstration project to nationwide program. *Peabody Journal of Education, 60*(3), 8–24.

Weinstein, L. (1974). *Evaluation of a program for re-educating disturbed children: A follow-up comparison with untreated children* (ERIC Document Reproduction Service No. ED-141–966). Washington, DC: U.S. Department of Health Education, and Welfare.

See also **Life Space Interviewing; Residential Facilities**

PROJECT SUCCESS (PS)

Project Success (PS) is an academic and social remediation program for the college-bound specific language-handicapped or dyslexic student. The intent of the program is for the language-handicapped student to become language-independent as well as socially and psychologically adjusted to the new environment.

Becoming language-independent means that the dyslexic individual learns how to read and spell any word by relying on his or her own integrated knowledge of the phonemic structure of the American-English language. Students in PS acquire this knowledge initially by memorizing how the 50 phonemes and 26 letters can be employed to identify 271 sound symbol assignments for reading and 245 sound symbols assignments for spelling.

This total number of assignments for both reading and spelling are taught using a multisensory approach. The instructional methodology used is Nash's (1984) adaptation of the original Orton Gillingham, Tri-Modal, Simultaneous Multi-Sensory Instructional Procedure (OG, TM, SMSIP). This procedure trains the learner to use the senses simultaneously to memorize and to integrate up to 84% of all American-English words. In addition to reading and spelling remediation, the program remediates math and writing deficits. There is also a social habilitation program.

REFERENCE

Nash, R. (1984). *Manual for remediating the reading and spelling deficits of elementary, secondary, and postsecondary students.* Oshkosh, WI: Robert I. Nash Language Training School.

See also **Reading Disorders**

PROJECT TALENT

Project Talent was conceived in the late 1950s as an ambitious survey of American youth. A two-day battery of specially designed tests and inventories was administered to a 5% sample of high-school students from across the United States. The intention was to follow-up those tested at regular intervals, and through this process develop an information base about the processes by which men and women develop and use their abilities. The goals of Project Talent were to develop a national inventory of human resources; to achieve a better understanding of how young people choose and develop their careers; and to identify the educational and life experiences that are most important in preparing individuals for their life work (Flanagan et al., 1962).

The results of Project Talent are far more extensive than can be covered in this report. The body of knowledge includes technical reports and published articles by the Project Talent staff between 1962 and the present, as well as articles by researchers accessing the information through the Project Talent Data Bank. Many of these reports are in university libraries; others can be obtained through Publications Service, American Institutes for Research, P.O. Box 1113, Palo Alto, California 94302.

The initial report of results from the Project Talent staff was in 1964; it described the inventory of talent in the United States (Flanagan et al., 1964). One highlight from the one-year, follow-up surveys was the tremendous amount of change in career plans. For example, those tested in 1960 were asked to indicate career plans. One year after high school graduation, more than half of those electing each of the career alternatives as high school seniors had changed their plans (Flanagan et al., 1966). Percentages were even lower for those graduating in 1961 to 1963. Of interest was the fact that changes were toward career choices more in line with abilities and interests.

Results of the fifth- (Flanagan, Shaycroft, Richards, & Claudy, 1971) and the eleventh-year (Wilson & Wise, 1975; Wise, McLaughlin, & Gilmartin, 1977) follow-up studies have also been reported. An important finding from the eleventh-year follow-up was that nearly 25% of the men and women at age 29 still planned to obtain further education toward various degrees (Wise et al., 1977).

The data collected in conjunction with Project Talent are available to scientists, stripped of identifying information and on a cost-recovery basis. The most comprehensive study done by an outside investigator using this data was that published by Christopher Jencks and his colleagues in the book *Inequality: A Reassessment of the Effect of Family and Schooling in America* (1972).

REFERENCES

Flanagan, J.C., Cooley, W.W., Lohnes, P.R., Schoenfeldt, L.F., Holdeman, R.W., Combs, J., & Becker, S. (1966). *Project Talent one-year follow-up studies.* Pittsburgh: Project Talent.

Flanagan, J.C., Dailey, J.T., Shaycoft, M.F., Gorham, W.A., Orr, D.B., & Goldberg, I. (1962). *Design for a study of American youth.* Boston: Houghton Mifflin.

Flanagan, J.C., Davis, F.B., Dailey, J.T., Shaycoft, M.F., Orr, D.B., Goldberg, I., & Neyman, C.A., Jr. (1964). *The American high school student.* Pittsburgh: American Institutes for Research.

Flanagan, J.C., Shaycoft, M.F., Richards, J.M., Jr., & Claudy, J.G. (1971). *Five years after high school.* Palo Alto, CA: American Institutes for Research.

Jencks, C., Smith, M., Acland, H., Bane, M.J., Cohen, D., Gintis, H., Heyns, B., & Michelson, S. (1972). *Inequality: A reassessment of the effect of family and schooling in America.* New York: Basic Books.

Wilson, S.R., & Wise, L.L. (1975). *The American citizen: 11 years after high school* (Vol. 1). Palo Alto, CA: American Institutes for Research.

Wise, L.L., McLaughlin, D.H., & Gilmartin, K.J. (1977). *The American citizen: 11 years after high school* (Vol. 2). Palo Alto, CA: American Institutes for Research.

PROSOPAGNOSIA

Prosopagnosia is a rare acquired defect in facial recognition that is a consequence of focal brain damage. Visual acuity remains intact. Individuals that develop prosopagnosia are unable to recognize faces as familiar and so do not know whose specific face they are seeing. This deficit in visual recognition of familiar faces occurs independently of any defect in language or cognition.

Prosopagnosia is often accompanied by other specific kinds of visual disturbances. Individuals with prosopagnosia usually have either a unilateral or bilateral visual field defect. That is, they are unable to see one portion of what ordinarily can be seen when the eyes are held fixed at mid position. This defect is secondary to brain damage or damage to the optic nerve radiations, not to eye damage. In addition, prosopagnosia frequently is accompanied by central achromatopsia, the acquired inability to perceive color as a consequence of central nervous system disease despite adequate retinal function. Visual agnosia also is often present. Visual agnosia is normal ability to see and perceive without the ability to give meaning to what one sees. Normal visual acuity, visual scanning, and visual perception must be demonstrable in an individual diagnosed with visual agnosia. Despite the adequacy of visual skills, the individual is unable to recognize what is seen. Difficulty in identification is not a consequence of deficits in language or cognition. Indeed, many of these patients can recognize objects once they touch them, or once their function is described to them.

See also **Visually Impaired; Visual Perception and Discrimination; Visual Training**

PROSTHETIC DEVICES

A prosthesis is any additional device, or artificial appliance, to support or replace a missing part of the body. Prosthetics are the dental and surgical specialties concerned with the artificial replacement of missing parts of the body. Examples of prosthetic devices are artificial legs, dental bridges, wheelchairs, and long leg braces. Devices supporting hand or arm control for eating or drinking such as specialized drinking cups, molded lower arm supports, or upper arm frames, are also examples of prosthetic devices.

Modern technology has not only added to the number of prosthetic devices, it has elevated their functional involvement to a considerable degree. The expanded use of microchips, lasers, and microcomputer technology has greatly expanded readers, laser canes, and opticons for the visually impaired. Technology capable of changing auditory signals into appropriate letters and reflecting them in eyeglasses, or capable of generally improving hearing aid quality, has been miraculous for the hearing impaired. Other important changes in signal systems that permit guided mobility for artificial limbs, stimulated by either movement or voice, now provide auto-regulating movement for the orthopedically handicapped and amputees.

Technology continues to push back the restrictions placed on the handicapped by disabilities. Rehabilitation engineering and rehabilitation technology are fields that, when connected to biomedical, electronic, and other areas of engineering, may well restore usable vision, hearing, ambulation, or upper arm control. The horizons of tomorrow are boundless in terms of the possibilities that technology offers in prosthetic development.

See also **Occupational Therapy; Physical Therapy**

PROTECTION AND ADVOCACY SYSTEM—DEVELOPMENTALLY DISABLED (P&A)

The protection and advocacy system (P&A) was established under federal legislation for the developmentally disabled (Section 113, PL 94-103). Each state or territory receiving funding from the Administration on Developmental Disabilities is required to have a P&A agency. The P&A agencies must be independent of any other state agency or governmental unit to ensure their ability to freely protect and advocate the rights of developmentally disabled (DD) individuals.

Activities of P&A staff may involve negotiation, administrative or legal remedies on behalf of clients seeking programs, services, or protection of clients' rights as DD citizens. The agency's staff is also responsible for information dissemination concerning the rights of DD clients. Activities include presentations and workshops for lay and professional groups on the rights of the disabled. Areas such as education, employment, transportation, housing, architectural barriers, and legal aid are concerns of a P&A agency. The P&A office for each state or territory may be located through the Office of the Governor or by contacting Commissioner, Administration on Developmental Disabilities, OHDS/HHS, Washington, DC 20201.

PRUNE BELLY SYNDROME

See RARE DISEASES.

PSYCHOANALYSIS AND SPECIAL EDUCATION

Newcomer (1980) discusses both the positive and negative contributions of psychoanalysis to special education. There is the notion in psychoanalytic theory that personality characteristics are determined by childhood events; thus, pathology would develop before a child arrives in school. The problems in school are caused by disorders that are within the child. Therefore the strategies for remediation focus on the child and the family rather than the school. This may result in the school having a passive role in resolution of the conflict.

Significant contributions to psychoanalysis and special education have been made by Bruno Bettleheim and Fritz Redl (Haring & Phillips, 1962). Their approaches have been primarily permissive in nature, and school work is often used as a vehicle to assist the child in bringing the unconscious conflict to a conscious level of awareness. In general, special education programs have moved from child-directed, psychoanalytic models to more teacher-directed behavioral models where emphasis is primarily on academics and behavior control. IDEA mandates teaching students in the least restrictive environment. Therefore, the emphasis in special education is on teaching children appropriate and acceptable behavior in school, which is in conflict with the free and open expression advocated by Freud and his followers.

REFERENCES

Haring, N.G., & Phillips, E.L. (1962). *Educating emotionally disturbed children.* New York: McGraw-Hill.

Newcomer, P.L. (1980). *Understanding and teaching emotionally disturbed children.* Boston: Allyn & Bacon.

See also **Child Psychiatry; Psychodrama; Psychotherapy**

PSYCHODRAMA

Psychodrama is a method of group psychotherapy devised and developed by Moreno (1946). Psychodrama requires a well-trained therapist, preferably one with special certification as a psychodramatist. Psychodrama consists of using dramatic techniques with clients who act out real-life situations, past, present, or projected, in an attempt to gain insight into their behavior and emotions. Psychodrama also provides the opportunity to practice specific behaviors in a supportive group atmosphere. The method of psychodrama integrates insight and cognitions with experiential, participatory involvement, taking advantage of the group therapy setting and using physical movement to bring nonverbal cues to the client's attention. This component of psychodrama can be crucial in therapy with individuals who have limited verbal skills, particularly children and delinquent adolescents (Blatner, 1973). Another significant advantage of psychodrama is its ability to convert the child or adolescent's urge to act out into a more constructive form of "acting in," with guided role playing.

Psychodrama can be a particularly useful form of psychotherapy with children and adolescents with a variety of behavior disorders. It offers an opportunity for understanding and gaining insight, but it also offers a setting for the development of alternative behaviors and an opportunity for rehearsal in a realistic and supportive setting.

REFERENCES

Blatner, H.A. (1973). *Acting-in: Practical application of psychodramatic methods.* New York: Springer.

Moreno, J.L. (1946). *Psychodrama* (Vol. 1). New York: Beacon House.

See also **Sociodrama**

PSYCHOEDUCATIONAL METHODS

Psychoeducational methods generally refer to the processes of psychological assessment and the subsequent design of remedial programs. Historically, special educators have attempted to develop a variety of psychoeducational methods, all with the goal of facilitating the learning of the exceptional child. This effort has been intensified in the years following the passage of federal and state special education laws mandating the link between psychoeducational assessment data and the development of instructional strategies in the form of the individualized educational plan (IEP).

Hundreds of different types of psychoeducational methods are currently in use. However, the choice of a particular psychoeducational method is often tied to the educator's assumptions or beliefs regarding the nature and etiology of a child's exceptionality (Quay, 1973; Ysseldyke & Mirkin, 1982).

Historically, psycholinguistic training programs (Kirk & Kirk, 1971; Minskoff, Wiseman, & Minskoff, 1972) tied to the Illinois Test of Psycholinguistic Abilities have represented some of the more popular psychoeducational methods. The level of empirical support of these psycholinguistic training programs suggests they should be implemented only for research purposes.

Another popular psychoeducational method based on the process dysfunction view of exceptionality is the perceptual-motor training program. This program includes training in visual discrimination, spatial relations, visual memory, auditory-visual integration, and auditory-perceptual skills (Ysseldyke & Mirkin, 1982). Little empirical support exists for any relationship between perceptual-motor processes and academic achievement (Larsen & Hammill, 1975) or for the effectiveness of these types of psychoeducational methods in improving academic performance (Ysseldyke & Mirkin, 1982).

Psychoeducational methods based on modality training (Johnson & Myklebust, 1967; Lerner, 1981; Wepman, 1967) have also received little empirical support (Arter & Jenkins, 1977). Modality training rests on the assumption that a child may learn better through one modality than through another.

Psychoeducational methods have also been developed based on process dysfunctions in intellectual skills (Cutrona, 1975; Jacobson & Kovalinsky, 1969). However, tasks on tests like the Wechsler represent only samples of behavior and inadequate performance on some of these samples should not automatically suggest the need to remediate those behaviors. Low scores should be viewed only as symptoms of problems that need to be corroborated to determine whether they represent global or pervasive deficits (Kaufman, 1979). Further, there is little empirical support that in isolation the psychoeducational methods designed to remediate deficits in cognitive skills are effective in facilitating academic learning (Ysseldyke & Mirkin, 1982).

Sensory integration (Ayres, 1972) and training in rhythm and balance (Rice, 1962) represent two additional psychoeducational methods designed to alleviate underlying dysfunctions. As is true for the other methods discussed, little evidence exists to support their use to improve academic achievement (Ysseldyke & Mirkin, 1982).

The opposite end of the continuum, in relation to views of the etiology of exceptionality, is represented by Quay's (1973) experience deficit notion. This viewpoint suggests that a student's learning problems are due not to deficits within the child but to the student's limited behavioral repertoire. The student's learning apparatus is intact and underlying process deficits are not assumed. The goal of the psychoeducational assessment guided by this notion of exceptionality is to identify experiential deficits and develop remedial or compensatory interventions or psychoeducational methods to eliminate them.

The task-analytic or skills-training approach represents a class of psychoeducational methods that is based on this experience deficit notion. Example methods include direct instruction (Carnine & Silbert, 1979) and precision teaching (Lindsley, 1971). Both of these methods focus on the academic and social skill requirements of the school program. They also share the characteristics of being sequential, systematic, and intensive, and are typically implemented in individualized or small group settings. Further, complex learning tasks are broken up into simpler component subskills so they can be taught more easily, using behavioral principles such as reinforcement and modeling. These various psychoeducational methods differ in the frequency and directness of their measurements. Precision teaching involves the continuous measurement of a student's performance in the mastery of academic or social skill objectives. The method also includes the direct assessment of skills that have been taught rather than the assessment of effectiveness through sampling from a larger domain. All of the task-analytic or skills-training psychoeducational methods are based on the assumption that the teacher cannot predict consistently the particular interventions that will be most effective with a particular child; therefore, the methods are used as tentative hypotheses that are always being tested and modified if necessary.

Compared with the other psychoeducational methods discussed, the task-analytic or skill-development approaches that use direct and continuous measurement tend to be the most effective in increasing academic achievement (Ysseldyke & Mirkin, 1982; Ysseldyke & Salvia, 1974). However, future research may indeed demonstrate that those who assess, develop, and implement psychoeducational methods for exceptional children should hold the belief that exceptionality is explained by an interaction view. Learning problems may well result from deficits resulting from process deficits and/or experiential deficits. However, most special educators exclusively use psychoeducational methods that are based on one or the other viewpoint (Ysseldyke & Mirkin, 1982). Special education needs more psychoeducational methods that rely on an interactive approach.

REFERENCES

Arter, J.A., & Jenkins, J.R. (1977). Explaining the benefits and prevalence of modality consideration in special education. *Journal of Special Education, 11,* 281–298.

Ayres, A.J. (1972). *Sensory integration and learning disorders.* Los Angeles: Western Psychological Services.

Carnine, D., & Silbert, J. (1979). *Direct instruction reading.* Columbus, OH: Merrill.

Cutrona, M.P. (1975). A psychoeducational interpretation of the Wechsler Intelligence Scale for Children-Revised (2nd ed.). Belleville, NJ: Cutronics.

Jacobson, S., & Kovalinsky, T. (1969). *Educational interpretation of the Wechsler Intelligence Scale for Children-Revised (WISC-R).* Linden, NJ: Remediation Associates.

Johnson, D., & Myklebust, H.R. (1967). *Learning disabilities: Educational principles and practices.* New York: Grune & Stratton.

Kaufman, A.S. (1979). *Intelligent testing with the WISC-R.* New York: Wiley.

Kirk, S.A., & Kirk, W.D. (1971). *Psycholinguistic learning disabilities: Diagnosis and remediation.* Urbana, IL: University of Illinois Press.

Larsen, S.C., & Hammill, D.D. (1975). The relationship between selected visual perceptual abilities to school learning. *Journal of Special Education, 9,* 281–291.

Lerner, J.S. (1981). *Children with learning disabilities* (3rd ed.). Boston: Houghton Mifflin.

Lindsley, O.R. (1971). Precision teaching in perspective: An interview with Ogden R. Lindsley. *Teaching Exceptional Children, 3,* 114–119.

Minskoff, E., Wiseman, D.E., & Minskoff, J.G. (1972). *The MWM program for developing language abilities.* Ridgewood, NJ: Educational Performance Associates.

Quay, H.C. (1973). Special education: Assumptions, techniques, and evaluative criteria. *Exceptional Children, 40,* 165–170.

Rice, A. (1962). Rhythmic training and board balancing prepares a child for learning. *Nation's Schools, 6,* 72.

Wepman, J. (1967). The perceptual bases for learning. In E.C. Friersen & W.B. Barbe (Eds.), *Educating children with learning disabilities: Selected readings.* New York: Appleton-Century-Crofts.

Ysseldyke, J., & Salvia, J. (1974). Diagnostic prescriptive teaching: Two models. *Exceptional Children, 4,* 181–186.

Ysseldyke, J.E., & Mirkin, P.K. (1982). The use of assessment information to plan instructional interventions: A review of the research. In C.R. Reynolds & T.B. Gutkin (Eds.), *The handbook of school psychology.* New York: Wiley.

See also **Assessment; Etiology; Measurement; Task Analysis; Teaching Strategies**

PSYCHOGENIC MODELS

Psychogenic models present causes of human behavior in terms of the psychological functioning of the individual. The cognitive and emotional aspects of personality are central to explaining behavior. The psychogenic approach emphasizes emotional distress as the root of deviant behavior (Bootzin, 1984). The model stands in contrast to the biogenic approach in placing little emphasis on the physiological factors underlying behavior.

Balow (1979) noted that psychological models are compatible with special education practice because most educational interventions are based on psychological principles. The models, techniques, and measurements of special education used to be expressed typically in terms of psychological function of individual students. The current focus in special education has moved away from the psychogenic model and is much more based in outcome assessments and are more focused on outcome.

REFERENCES

Balow, B. (1979). Biological defects and special education: An empiricist's view. *Journal of Special Education, 13,* 35–40.

Bootzin, R. (1984). *Abnormal psychology: Current perspectives* (4th ed.). New York: Random House.

See also **Biogenic Model of Behavior; Etiology**

PSYCHOLINGUISTICS

One of the factors responsible for the attraction of special education to psycholinguistics was recognition of the need to describe and explain normal language acquisition when attempting to assess the language problems of, for example, mentally retarded or autistic children (Rosenberg, 1982) or dyslexic children (Greene, 1996). At the same time, however, basic researchers in psycholinguistics began to recognize that their theories of normal language acquisition and functioning could be illuminated by observations of language disorders in children and adults. The fact, for example, that there are rarely any qualitative differences between normal and language-disordered children in the course of language acquisition or in the structure of the language acquired suggests "that there are strong specifically linguistic biological constraints on first-language acquisition that limit significantly the manner in which a wide variety of insults can affect language competence and its development" (Rosenberg, 1984, p. 228).

As indicated, psycholinguistics has been influential in the field of special education, with its longstanding commitment to children with language and communicative disorders associated with mental retardation, hearing impairment, visual impairment, learning disabilities, and other handicaps. This influence has been apparent in work with handicapped children on the assessment and remediation of disorders of linguistic competence (Bloom & Lahey, 1978), on linguistic coding and reading ability (Vellutino & Scanlon, 1982), and on the development of communicative competence (Donahue & Bryan, 1983). The work on communicative competence is the result of an increased emphasis in special education on preparing handicapped students for community living and mainstreaming.

Thus, progress has been made in the education of handicapped children in the areas of language and communication, although much remains to be done, particularly concerning the role of first-language competence in learning to read and mathematics (Osherson & Weinstein, 1995).

Recent applied psycholinguistic research that has particular implications for special education includes Abbeduto and Rosenberg (1980) who have shown that the conversational communicative competence of mildly retarded adults (and possibly moderately retarded adults as well) is mostly indistinguishable from that of normal adults. Therefore, although mentally retarded children tend to get off to a slow start in the area of conversational communicative competence, many of them may be able to catch up to their nonretarded peers. Such findings could inspire special educators to expand their efforts to facilitate communicative development in mentally retarded children.

REFERENCES

Abbeduto, L., & Rosenberg, S. (1980). The communicative competence of mildly retarded adults. *Applied Psycholinguistics, 1,* 405–426.

Bloom, L., & Lahey, M. (1978). *Language development and language disorders.* New York: Wiley.

Donahue, M., & Bryan, T. (1983). Conversational skills and modeling in learning disabled boys. *Applied Psycholinguistics, 4,* 251–278.

Greene, J.F. (1996). Psycholinguistic assessment: The clinical base for identification of dyslexia. *Topics in Language Disorders, 16*(2), 45–72.

Osherson, D., & Weinstein, S. (1995). On the study of first language acquisition. *Journal of Mathematical Psychology, 39*(2), 129–145.

Rosenberg, S. (Ed.). (1982). *Handbook of applied psycholinguistics: Major thrusts of research and theory.* Hillsdale, NJ: Erlbaum.

Rosenberg, S. (1984). Disorders of first-language development: Trends in research and theory. In E.S. Gollin (Ed.), *Malformations of development: Biological and psychological sources and consequences.* New York: Academic.

Vellutino, F.R., & Scanlon, D.M. (1982). Verbal processing in poor and normal readers. In C.J. Brainerd & M. Pressley (Eds.), *Verbal processes in children.* New York: Springer-Verlag.

See also **Language Disorders; Language Therapy**

PSYCHOLOGICAL ABSTRACTS (PA)

Psychological Abstracts (PA) provides nonevaluative summaries of the world's literature in psychology and related disciplines. Over 950 journals, technical reports, monographs, and other scientific documents provide material for coverage in *PA*. *Psychological Abstracts* includes bibliographic citations or annotations that are used to cover books, secondary sources, articles peripherally relevant to psychology, or articles that can be represented adequately in approximately 30 to 50 words. Since 1967 the abstracts have been entered into machine-readable tapes that now provide the basis for the automated search and retrieval service known as Psychological Abstracts Information Service (PsychINFO).

Further information about *PA* or the PsychINFO system can be obtained from the American Psychological Association, 750 First St., N.E., Washington, DC 20002-4242, or by telephone at (202) 336-5568.

PSYCHOLOGICAL CLINICS

University psychological clinics are generally student training facilities that have a cooperative relationship with the surrounding community. The clinics provide undergraduate and graduate students in disciplines such as education, counseling, and psychology with an opportunity to apply their theoretical and technical knowledge in working with a variety of clients in a closely supervised practicum. A number of types of services are usually offered in the psychological clinics, including: child assessment and treatment; parent training; family counseling; teacher consultation; program evaluation; and organizational consultation. Therefore, the clinic provides clients with a wide array of psychological services and the students in training with exposure to a number of different approaches to a particular problem.

See also **Child Guidance Clinic; College Programs for Disabled College Students**

PSYCHOLOGICAL CORPORATION

The Psychological Corporation is the world's oldest and largest commercial test publisher. It was founded in New York City in 1921 by three noted professors from Teachers College of Columbia University; James M. Cattell, Edward L. Thorndike, and Robert S. Woodworth. Over its 65-year history, the corporation's primary mission has been the application of principles of psychology and measurement to the solution of educational, clinical, industrial, and social problems.

The corporation is well known for high-quality educational and psychological tests. Names such as the Wechsler Intelligence Scales for Children-Revised, Children's Memory Scales, McCarthy Scales of Children's Abilities, Baley Scales of Infant Development, and Stanford Diagnostic Reading and Mathematics Tests are familiar to scholars throughout the world. The corporation now publishes over 200 tests and has a computer software development program.

PSYCHOLOGICAL REPORTS

Psychological Reports is published bimonthly, two volumes a year, the first with issues in February, April, and June and the second with issues in August, October, and December. Between 2000 and 3000 pages are published annually. Approximately one-third of the articles come from outside the United States. The purpose of this journal is to encourage scientific originality and creativity in the field of general psychology for the person who is first a psychologist and then a specialist. It carries experimental, theoretical, and speculative articles; comments; special reviews; and a listing of new books and other materials received. Controversial material of scientific merit is welcomed. Multiple referees examine submissions. Critical editing is balanced by specific suggestions as to changes required to meet standards (Ammons & Ammons, 1962a).

The journal has consistently maintained for 30 years a policy of being highly experimental, open to all defensible points of view, encouraging of new and often unpopular ways of looking at problems, and protective of authors by careful but open-minded refereeing and editing (Ammons & Ammons, 1962b).

REFERENCES
Ammons, R.B., & Ammons, C.H. (1962a). Permanent or temporary journals: Are PR and PMS stable? *Perceptual & Motor Skills, 14,* 281.

Ammons, C.H., & Ammons, R.B. (1962b). Permanent or temporary journals: PR and PMS become stable. *Psychological Reports, 10,* 537.

PSYCHOLOGY IN THE SCHOOLS

Psychology in the Schools began in 1964 with William Hunt serving as editor. He was followed briefly by B. Claude Mathis and then in 1970 by Gerald B. Fuller of Central Michigan University, who remains as editor. In an attempt to meet the practical needs of professionals in the field, this journal emphasizes an applied orientation. It addresses practicing school and clinical psychologists, guidance personnel, teachers, educators, and university faculty. Articles of preference clearly describe the relevancy of the research for these practitioners. However, occasionally important experimental and theoretical papers may be included.

PSYCHOMETRICS
See MEASUREMENT.

PSYCHOMOTOR SEIZURES

The term psychomotor was introduced in 1938 by Gibbs and Lennox (Lennox & Lennox, 1960) to describe epileptic manifestations composed of various multiple psychic or motor activities. These manifestations are associated with spikes, sharp or slow waves on the electroencephalogram over the anterior area of the temporal lobe; therefore, the manifestations are also called temporal lobe seizures. According to the classification of the International League Against Epilepsy (1981), the seizures are partial, as they begin locally, and also complex, as they are associated with "a clouding of consciousness and complete or partial amnesia for the event" (Livingston, 1972). They may be followed by generalized tonic-clonic seizures.

Psychomotor seizures are more frequent in older children, adolescents, and young adults (Currie, Heathfield, Henson, & Scott, 1971; Gastaut, 1953; Livingston, 1972). However, Holowach, Renda, and Wapner (1961) and Chao, Sexton, and Santos Pardo (1962) reported this kind of seizure in 11 and 15.7% of children with all types of epilepsy up to 15 years of age. The onset occurred before the age of 6 years in more than 50% and before the age of 3 years in almost 30%.

As in every partial seizure, the temporal lobe epilepsy may start with an aura that is the first subjective and remembered symptom of the seizure. This aura is indicative of the starting point of the fit, and sometimes of its spreading. Young children may, as an aura, run to their mother with fear or complain of gastric discomfort or unpleasant smell or taste before the loss of consciousness. The symptoms often start with an arrest of motion, with eye staring eventually followed by simple and/or complex automatisms such as repetitive oral movements (e.g., lip smacking, chewing, and swallowing) (Ebner, Noachter, Dinner, & Lueders, 1996; Serafetinides, 1996). The motor activities, like rubbing the face, fumbling with buttons of clothing, or wandering around the room, appear purposive but inappropriate at the time. Speech may become incoherent or mumbled. Autonomic disturbances such as urination, vomiting, salivation, or flushing of the face may be present. Awareness is impaired and amnesia of the attack is a fairly constant finding. The episodes are not very frequent (from one to five per day to one to five per month) and usually brief, 2 to 3 minutes, but the return to consciousness is often gradual. Mental or psychic seizures are variable, but visual or auditory hallucinations are frequent and owed to connections with the vicinity. Affective manifestations such as fear or aggressiveness are frequently present. The attack may terminate in a grand mal seizure. The symptomatology is often associated with mental retardation, cerebral palsy, and hyperkinetic syndrome (as with any organic brain disorder of childhood).

In children the etiology is most often the result of a chronic, nonprogressive neurologic disease. The seizures may be due to previous insult to the brain in the neonatal period as in hypoxia, infection, trauma, or congenital malformations, but also to severe or prolonged seizures in early life or to febrile convulsions. Tumors are rare. Often, no definite cause can be established (Gomez & Klass, 1983). The most common abnormality is mesial temporal sclerosis (incisural sclerosis). The prognosis is better than previously thought (Lindsay, Ounsted, & Richards, 1979; Staff, 1980), and treatment is mainly medical through drug therapy.

REFERENCES

Chao, D., Sexton, J.A., & Santos Pardo, L.S. (1962). Temporal lobe epilepsy in children. *Journal of Pediatrics, 60,* 686–693.

Currie, S., Heathfield, K.W.G., Henson, R.A., & Scott, D.F. (1971). Clinical course and prognosis of temporal lobe epilepsy: A survey of 666 patients. *Brain, 94,* 173–190.

Ebner, A., Noachter, S., Dinner, D., & Lueders, H. (1996). Automatisms with preserved responsiveness: A lateralizing sign in psychomotor seizures: Commentary Reply. *Neurology, 46*(4), 1189.

Gastaut, H. (1953). So called "psychomotor" and "temporal" epilepsy—A critical review. *Epilepsia, 2,* 59–99.

Gomez, M.R., & Klass, D.W. (1983). Epilepsies of infancy and childhood. *Annals of Neurology, 13,* 113–124.

Holowach, J., Renda, Y.A., & Wapner, J. (1961). Psychomotor seizures in childhood. A clinical study of 120 cases. *Journal of Pediatrics, 59,* 339–346.

International League Against Epilepsy. (1981). Proposal for revised clinical and electroencephalographic classification of epileptic seizures. *Epilepsia, 22,* 489–501.

Lennox, W.G., & Lennox, M.A. (1960). *Epilepsy and related disorders.* Boston: Little, Brown.

Lindsay, J., Ounsted, C., & Richards, P. (1979). Long-term outcome in children with temporal lobe, seizures. *Developmental Medicine and Child Neurology, 21,* 285–636.

Livingston, S. (1972). *Comprehensive management of epilepsy in infancy, childhood and adolescence.* Springfield, IL: Thomas.

Serafetinides, E.A. (1996). Automatisms with preserved responsiveness: A lateralizing sign in pscyhomotor seizures: Comment. *Neurology, 46*(4), 1189.

Staff. (1980). Prognosis of temporal lobe epilepsy in childhood. *British Medical Journal, 280,* 812–813.

See also **Absence Seizures; Drug Therapy; Epilepsy; Seizure Disorders**

PSYCHOMOTRICITY

An independent science firmly established in France, psychomotricity is based on the interdependence of physical, affective, and intellectual functions and thus covers a wide field that encompasses neurology, pedagogy, and psychoanalysis.

In France, psychomotricity was recognized as a discipline in the early 1960s. The first French Psychomotricity Charter (de Ajuriaguerra-Soubiran) was promulgated and a curriculum was created. A trade union and various publications came about.

As far as practice is concerned, a distinction is usually made between education, remedial work, and therapy. Education aims at stimulating the healthy child's psychomotor functions. This concept is slowly spreading in nursery schools. Remedial exercises aim at improving psychomotor symptomatology through a reprogramming of the neuromotor sphere. Model lessons by the well-known team of the Henri-Rousselle Hospital in Paris are available. Therapy aims at deblocking and developing the disturbed child's psychic structures through bodily and relational interaction with the therapist and mediatory objects. According to Aucouturier, technicity consists of working out sensorimotor pleasure and treatment of aggressive and fantasmatic productions. These various approaches are used primarily with children up to 7 years of age when symbolizing processes enable them to dissociate themselves from their bodily experiences. However, the concept of psychomotricity applies in theory to every stage of life.

PSYCHONEUROTIC DISORDERS

The term psychoneurotic as a description of childhood emotional disorders is associated with the psychoanalytic tradition of Sigmund Freud. It is a general term that has been applied to specific clinical syndromes, including phobias, anxiety reactions, obsessive-compulsive behavioral patterns, and hysterical or conversion disorders. Anxiety is postulated by all authorities as being the prime causal process in these clinical syndromes. Some authorities also include childhood and adolescent depressive reactions under the conceptual rubric of psychoneurotic disorders.

Most approaches to the study of psychoneurotic abnormalities follow either a psychoanalytic theory or a learning-behavioral approach. Each theoretical orientation has a substantial following and, at this point, there is no basis for rejecting or accepting the superiority of one approach over the other for the treatment of psychoneurotic dysfunction. Each of these two general theoretical frameworks also have application to the explanation and treatment of a wide range of abnormal behaviors.

Conversion reactions and obsessive-compulsive disorders have traditionally been treated with individual psychotherapy from a psychoanalytic approach. Behavioral approaches have been more frequently applied to the anxiety disorders such as phobias where their efficacy is well established. Noticeably fewer applications of behavioral therapy to obsessive-compulsive and conversion reactions have been reported. Psychodynamic individual therapy with children with these disorders is based on the intensity of the relationship between the child and the therapist. This approach attempts to examine the intrapsychic conflicts that produce the anxiety and then the psychoneurotic disorder. Play therapy is often used for younger children as part of the therapeutic process so that the child can express his or her conflicts through play. The Freudian approach emphasizes that the symptom must be removed by resolving the basic conflict. Otherwise, it is postulated that symptom substitution will occur where the intrapsychic conflict that is left unresolved will resurface in the form of a different pattern of abnormal behavior.

In contrast, behavior therapists reject the notion of symptom substitution and directly attack the symptom or problem behavior. Reinforcement contingencies may be set up by the therapist and implemented by the significant adults in the child's life. The problem behaviors would no longer be positively reinforced and may be negatively reinforced; more appropriate ways of responding would be positively reinforced with the goal that the child would learn new ways of coping with anxiety. For example, in the classroom setting, the teacher, after consultation with the therapist, would implement responses to compulsive behavior by the child that would encourage the child to be less perfectionistic and work at a greater rate of speed. The case of the 14-year-old with conversion reaction discussed at the beginning of the chapter illustrates a behavioral intervention following a psychodynamic formulation. The secondary gain from the conversion reaction behavior (i.e., failing to read) was eliminated. The child was not allowed to read and did not receive special tutoring at school. Emphasis was placed on normal social behavior involved with growing up and focus was shifted away from the symptom.

Family therapy is usually a valuable, if not necessary, adjunct to individual therapy for psychoneurotic children. Re-

cent trends are highlighting short-term dynamic psychotherapy, probably as a response to managed care as well as progression in theory (Davanloo, 1995). The traditional psychoanalytic point of view would assign a separate therapist to work with the parents while the individual psychotherapist worked with the child. More often today, the same therapist works individually with the child and consults with the parents. Family therapy sessions may also be held. The behavior therapist often consults with the parents on specific behavioral interventions that they could make at home. In this way, the parents become collateral therapists. School consultation is frequently a valuable adjunct to effective intervention. The therapist can educate the teacher on the nature of the problem and give suggestions for appropriate responses. These teacher behaviors might include being more patient, as in the case of a conversion reaction or excessive compulsivity; specific behavioral interventions by the teacher can play an important role in changing behavior. Drug therapy is generally inappropriate for these disorders, as there is little evidence of biological causes. An exception would be if a parallel disorder, such as depression in an older adolescent, called for antidepressant medication.

REFERENCE

Davanloo, H. (1995). Intensive short-term dynamic psychotherapy: Spectrum of psychoneurotic disorders. *International Journal of Short-Term Psychotherapy, 10*(3), 121–155.

See also **Anxiety Disorders; Childhood Psychosis; Depression; Emotional Disorders; Seriously Emotionally Disturbed**

PSYCHOPATHY

See SOCIOPATHY.

PSYCHOSIS, AMPHETAMINE

See AMPHETAMINE PSYCHOSIS.

PSYCHOSOCIAL ADJUSTMENT

Psychosocial adjustment refers to social and emotional functioning: the way a person relates to and interacts with other people in his or her environment. It is one noticeable area of difference between special needs students and those without disabilities. While problems in psychosocial development and intrafamily relations may contribute to later psychosocial difficulties (Erickson, 1963), a behavioral analysis position (Bryant & Budd, 1984) emphasizes the importance of environmental stimuli in reinforcing and maintaining appropriate social skills.

A number of remedial techniques have been used when an exceptional child exhibits psychosocial problems. Often parents can be taught to provide a more positive family environment and to more effectively communicate with their child. In school and during play, specific appropriate social behaviors, such as approaching other children, sharing, and playing social games, can be targeted for training and shaping using reinforcement techniques (Davies & Rogers, 1985). A high density of positive reinforcement for correct approximations of social contact may also be used to strengthen appropriate social relationships.

REFERENCES

Bryant, L.E., & Budd, K.S. (1984). Teaching behaviorally handicapped preschool children to share. *Journal of Applied Behavior Analysis, 17,* 45–56.

Davies, R.R., & Rogers, E.S. (1985). Social skills with persons who are mentally retarded. *Mental Retardation, 23,* 186–196.

Erickson, E.H. (1963). *Childhood and society* (2nd ed.). New York: Norton.

See also **Emotional Disorders; Family Counseling; Functional Assessment; Social Skills**

PSYCHOSOMATIC DISORDERS

The somatic expression of anguish is a frequent phenomenon in childhood and adolescence and is many times culturally dependent. More than 90% of children between the ages of 3 and 18 years have established a psychological relationship with the surrounding world and expressed a confusion in a psychosomatic form at some time during their development. Somatic expression in childhood is always bound with anxiety either in reaction to a situation objectively traumatic or in relation to the perceptive distortion of an objectively nontraumatic situation. Somatic expression in the child in regard to the adult is specific and evolutionary in relation to the maturational stage of the child (affective and neurological). It is associated with a quantitative or qualitative deficiency in the parent/child relationship, most often with the mother.

Psychosomatic diseases of children differ from those of adults and result from the conjunction of various factors. A calendar of psychosomatic diseases exists: colic at 3 months, vomiting at 6 months, eczema between 8 and 12 months, breath-holding spells at 2 years, abdominal pain at 3 years, asthma at 5 years, headaches at 6 years, and Crohn's disease at adolescence. The development of a psychosomatic syndrome is associated with (1) a genetically fragile somatic background (repetitive infections); (2) a precocious inappropriate parent–child relationship (rejection, overprotection, aggression, anxiety); (3) physical stress (allergene) or psychological reactivation of a previous problem of anguish until compensated; and (4) a familial functioning of the psychosomatic type. According to age, the prevalent etiology, and the therapeutic possibilities, the treatment will be made along an organistic or psychological point of view, individually or familial, and symptomatic or global.

The psychosomatic symptomatology of the child is the borderline of the physical and the psychical, of the inborn and the acquired, of the personal and the relational, and of the conscious and the unconscious. The approach to such a symptomatology needs a great deal of empathy, tact, and comprehension of the global context of the child, the family, and the society surrounding the child. Special educators are in an optimal situation to assist in the diagnosis of these disorders because of the consistent daily observations made by all teachers. School clinicians can refer to the Diagnostic and Statistical Manual of Mental Disorders (DSM-IV) for diagnostic criteria (APA, 1994). If physical complaints over a period of time alert the teacher to suspect a somatic disorder, the school psychologist and parents should be made aware of the situation. Referrals to support professionals in the community should be on hand to assist the family in diagnosis and treatment.

REFERENCE

American Psychiatric Association. (1994). *Diagnostic and statistical manual of mental disorders* (4th ed.). Washington, DC: Author.

See also **Emotional Disorders; Family Counseling; Physical Handicaps; School Phobia**

PSYCHOSURGERY

Psychosurgery is not an intervention that responds to a specific mental disorder. Instead, it is a neurosurgical procedure that was derived from observations made in animal aggression research (Fulton, 1949; Jacobsen, 1935) and applied to humans to control more violent psychiatric and neurological symptoms. Psychosurgical techniques were employed in the United States starting in the 1940s (Freeman & Watts, 1950). A variety of techniques that proceeded from gross frontal destruction by means of injections of alcohol into the frontal white matter (Kalinowsky, 1975) to sophisticated stereotaxic, electrically produced, ablative procedures (Kelly, Richardson, & Mitchell-Heggs, 1973) have been used. The location of lesions also has become more sophisticated. Initially, the goal of practitioners appeared to be to destroy enough anterior brain matter to create the desired effect, which was pacification of the patient. Contemporary techniques focus on greater localization of a lesion, hence avoiding large-scale brain destruction. Sites include parts of the limbic system, the anterior cingulum, and the posteromedial hypothalamus (Sano, Sekino, & Mayanagi, 1972).

Recent applications of neurosurgical procedures have noted success in dealing with pain (Culliton, 1976), obsessive-compulsive disorder (Rappaport, 1992) and uncontrolled seizures (Spiers, Schomer, Blume, & Mesulam, 1985). The latter approach is the best example of what psychosurgery was intended to do; that is, to remove a brain area that is intimately involved in producing a disorder. The goal of surgical intervention with an uncontrolled epileptic disorder is to remove the brain tissue that is producing a seizure focus. Thus, the techniques used to identify that focus are as important as the surgical procedure itself. This last point draws the most clear distinction between earlier psychosurgical procedures and current methods. When performed to alleviate behavioral dysfunction, psychosurgery was essentially an approach to limit reactivity without affecting the underlying disorder; in contrast, when surgery is performed to alleviate uncontrolled seizures, the underlying cause is removed with changes in behavior following.

REFERENCES

Culliton, B.J. (1976). In R.N. De Jong, & O. Sugar (Eds.), *The year book of neurology and neurosurgery: 1978*. Chicago: Year Book Medical.

Freeman, W., & Watts, J.W. (1950). *Psychosurgery*. Springfield, IL: Thomas.

Fulton, J.F. (1949). *Functional localization in the frontal lobes and cerebellum*. Oxford, England: Oxford University Press.

Jacobsen, C.F. (1935). Functions of frontal association areas in primates. *Archives of Neurology and Psychiatry, 33,* 558.

Kalinowsky, L. (1975). Psychosurgery. In A.M. Freedman, H.I. Kaplan, & B.J. Sadock (Eds.), *Comprehensive textbook of psychiatry-II* (pp. 1979–1982). Baltimore, MD: Williams & Wilkins.

Kelly, D., Richardson, A., & Mitchell-Heggs, N. (1973). Techniques and assessment of limbic leucotomy. In L.V. Laitinen & K.E. Livingston (Eds.), *Surgical approaches in psychiatry* (p. 201). Lancaster, England: Medical & Technical.

Rappaport, Z.H. (1992). Psychosurgery in the modern era: Therapeutic and ethical aspects. *Medicine & Law, 11*(5), 449–453.

Sano, K., Sekino, H., & Mayanagi, Y. (1972). Results of stimulation and destruction of the posterior hypothalmus in cases with violent, aggressive, or restless behavior. In E. Hitchcock, L. Laitinen, & K. Vaernet (Eds.), *Psychosurgery* (p. 203). Springfield, IL: Thomas.

Spiers, P.A., Schomer, D.L., Blume, H.W., & Mesulam, M. (1985). Temperolimbic epilepsy and behavior. In M. Mesulam (Ed.), *Principles of behavioral neurology* (pp. 289–326). Philadelphia: Davis.

See also **Electroconvulsive Therapy; Neuropsychology**

PSYCHOTHERAPY WITH INDIVIDUALS WITH DISABILITIES

Psychotherapy is defined as the application of psychological theories and principles to the treatment of problems of abnormal behavior, emotions, and thinking. The three major schools of psychotherapy are psychodynamic therapies, behavior therapies, and humanistic therapies.

The goal of psychodynamic, or insight, therapies is to help the client gain a sound understanding of his or her problems. Current behavioral and emotional problems are assumed to be the result of unconscious, intrapsychic conflicts and the unconscious mechanisms (i.e., defense mechanisms) employed to deal with them. It is a major goal of insight therapies to help bring this unconscious material into consciousness and thereby allow the client to exercise conscious, rationale control over his or her actions.

Contemporary psychodynamic therapists retain an ap-

preciation for unconscious influences on behavior but use more direct and focused techniques to help the client gain insight and exercise more rational control. The goal is to help clients find more realistic and effective ways to cope with their emotional needs. The client is helped to accept emotional needs and to find ways to meet them within the demands of external reality.

Behavior therapies differ from psychodynamic therapies in several ways. First, the presenting problem is viewed as the appropriate focus for the treatment rather than assumed underlying causes in the client's intrapsychic life. Second, principles of learning derived from experimental psychology studies are applied to modifying maladaptive behaviors and cognitions. Maladaptive behaviors and cognitions are assumed to be learned, and they can be modified through the application of learning principles. Behavior therapists focus on the here and now rather than on the historical causes of a problem. Behavior therapy is a broad term encompassing a wide variety of therapeutic techniques. A basic tenet of behavior therapy is that different problems require different treatments. Furthermore, the selection of treatment procedures are based on empirical studies of the effectiveness of different procedures with similar problems.

Humanistic therapies also incorporate a wide range of techniques. Therapies with a humanistic orientation share a belief that each client is a unique individual striving for personal growth, or self-actualization. Key therapy techniques include the therapist's positive regard for the client and empathic, or reflective, listening.

The rationale for providing psychotherapy to handicapped pupils is that handicapped persons have the same or greater need for improved psychological functioning as nonhandicapped persons. Some pupils may not be able to focus their mental energies on learning because they are experiencing psychological stress and emotional confusion. When a child's emotional and behavioral problems interfere with his or her learning and social behavior, educational interventions need to be supplemented by interventions that focus on the interfering emotional and behavioral problems.

See also **Adjustment of the Handicapped; Family Counseling; Family Therapy**

PSYCHOTROPIC DRUGS

The majority of drugs classified as psychotropic affect brain processes and thus indirectly produce behavioral changes. Their chemicals work by either increasing or decreasing the availability of specific neurotransmitters. The major classifications include hypnotics, major tranquilizers (antipsychotic agents), minor tranquilizers (antianxiety agents), stimulants, opiates, and psychedelics (hallucinogens). In most cases, these drugs increase or decrease activity level by producing effects on an individual's level of arousal. Potent psychedelic drugs add perceptual distortions to the more general effects.

Hypnotics are intended to produce drowsiness, enhance the onset of sleep, and maintain the sleep state (Katzung, 1982). These drugs produce a more profound depression on the central nervous system. They typically are referred to as barbiturates. Examples of this class of drugs are pentobarbital (Nembutal); secobarbital (Seconal); amobarbital (Amytal); and glutethimide (Doriden, Tuinal).

Barbiturates often are called "downers" because of their soporific action. Intoxication from barbiturates produces effects similar to those noted with alcohol. (For a complete review of barbiturate effects, see Blum, 1984, pp. 165–210). Of particular concern in the use of barbiturates is the tendency to produce physical dependence over time. Additionally, unless withdrawal is performed in graded steps under medical supervision, there is the possibility of mortality during sudden withdrawal.

Barbiturates are the drugs most involved in suicides, including accidental suicides (automatisms). The latter refers to a state of confusion during which an individual who habitually uses sedatives is unsure whether a pill has been ingested and proceeds to take additional pills (Ray, 1972).

Tranquilizers are intended to diminish the discomfort associated with anxiety states. Stimulants are intended to combat fatigue and have been used with children to limit hyperactivity. Moderate doses of stimulants (amphetamines) have been prescribed as adjuncts to weight reduction programs. Examples of these drugs are amphetamines (Benzedrine), caffeine (coffee, cola), cocaine, dextroamphetamine (Dexedrine), methamphetamine (Methedrine), methylphenidate (Ritalin), and nicotine (tobacco).

Negative side effects of chronic abuse include malnutrition, insomnia, impulsiveness, defective reasoning, delusional thinking, hallucinations, and paranoia (Blum, 1984). Owing to the affective lability of abusers, the associated hyperactivity, and the significant paranoia, abuse of amphetamines tends to set up conditions in which violence may occur.

Opiates are intended to provide relief from pain and appear to mimic natural analgesics (endorphins). Historically, morphine was used not only to provide relief from extreme pain, but also for diarrhea, cough, anxiety, and insomnia (Katzung, 1982). Examples of drugs in this class include opium, morphine, codeine, heroin, dihydromorphine (Dilaudid), and meperidine (Demerol).

Of particular concern with this class of drug is that, along with tolerance for a specific drug, physical dependence also occurs. Though central nervous system depressants, opiates produce feelings of euphoria in persons who are experiencing either physical or emotional pain (Leavitt, 1982). Persons appear to start abusing opiates secondary to situational stress, unenlightened treatment for severe pain, and comradeship (Blum, 1984). Chronic abuse produces periods of nausea, vomiting, constipation, respiratory inefficiency, and limited pain awareness. The latter produces

additional effects since abusers are unaware of physical distress (Leavitt, 1982). Mortality rates among heroine addicts under 30 are approximately 8 times that of nonaddicts (Leavitt, 1982).

REFERENCES

Blum, K.B. (1984). *Handbook of abusable drugs.* New York: Gardner.

Katzung, B.G. (1982). *Basic & clinical pharmacology.* Los Altos, CA: Lange Medical.

Leavitt, F. (1982). *Drugs and behavior.* New York: Wiley.

Ray, O.S. (1972). *Drugs, society and human behavior.* St. Louis: Mosby.

See also **Drug Abuse; Drug Therapy; Hallucinogens; Tranquilizers**

PSYC SCAN

During the past decade, a vast amount of information, traditionally available only in print, has been placed into computer-readable and retrievable form. Consequently, psychologists, special educators, and researchers have at their disposal a wealth of knowledge that has been classified, summarized, and stored for easy, quick, inexpensive retrieval by computer. Psyc SCAN is a service of Psyc INFO, which is part of the Psychological Abstract Information Services Department of the American Psychological Association.

Psyc SCAN provides computer-readable information and publications in various areas that are important to professionals involved in special education: applied, clinical, and developmental psychology, learning/communication disorders (LD) and mental retardation (MR). On a quarterly basis, Psyc SCAN offers subscribers an effective and efficient way of keeping up to date on practice and research in their fields by providing citations and abstracts from recently published journal articles.

Additional information about Psyc SCAN and related services can be obtained from Psych INFO Services, American Psychological Association, 750 First St., N.E., Washington, DC 20002–4242.

See also **Computer-Assisted Instruction; SpecialNet**

PUBLIC LAW 94-142

See INDIVIDUALS WITH DISABILITIES EDUCATION ACT (IDEA).

PUBLIC LAW 95-561

The Gifted and Talented Children's Education Act of 1978 was added, by PL 95-561, as Part A of Title IX of the Elementary and Secondary Education Act. The statute and its companion regulations describe gifted and talented children as individuals from birth through 18 years of age who require special educational services or activities because they possess demonstrated or potential abilities that give evidence of high performance capability in areas such as intellectual, creative, specific academic, or leadership ability, or in the performing and visual arts.

Financial assistance was provided under the Gifted and Talented Children's Education Program through two types of awards. Each state educational agency was eligible for a grant to plan, develop, operate, and improve programs for gifted and talented children. Eligible public or private organizations, agencies, or institutions also could compete for awards to conduct personnel training, model projects, information dissemination, or research.

On August 13, 1981, this funding program was consolidated into a block grant under Chapter 2 of the Education and Consolidation Improvement Act of 1981. States and localities may use the block grant funds, as appropriate, for continued services to gifted and talented children.

PUBLIC SCHOOLS AND SPECIAL EDUCATION

Interest in both special education and public schools in the mid 1990s is providing an unprecedented opportunity for educators to analyze and develop programs sharply contrasting from those of the past 50 years. Such evaluation and interest in developing effective schools has arisen from several major forces. First, concern is growing for the implementation of programs that truly enhance the academic and social skills of the nation's youth. Second, popular and accepted conceptions about handicapping conditions have changed, as have those toward the responsibilities of special and regular education. The result of this has been a drastic change in the procedures used in classifying students, in part as a function of the research providing an empirical critique of current practice, but also as a function of the consequences of such practice. Third, the relationship between special and regular education has been questioned both in terms of the content and the outcomes and reformed. These three forces have provided a major impetus behind the current efforts at designing our educational system.

The ideal that an appropriate education should be available to all children has profoundly influenced the direction of education in our country, especially the education of handicapped students. Special education services in public schools emerged in response to this ideal. However, the commitment to providing "education for all" is a recent development (Ysseldyke & Algozzine, 1983). In fact, the right of any citizen to a free and appropriate education began in the mid-1970s as a consequence of PL 94-142, the Education for All Handicapped Act. Up to the late nineteenth century, only a very small percentage of the population enjoyed the benefits of a formal education (Lilly, 1979).

In the late 1970s, Congress funded five research centers throughout the country to investigate the practices and procedures in use with learning disabled students. At one of these centers, the Institute for Research on Learning Disabilities at the University of Minnesota, a 6-year investigation was initiated to document the state of the art in assessment practices. In summarizing the results from the university's research program, Ysseldyke and Thurlow (1983) state that

1. Considerable variability exists in the assessment practices and classification criteria used by schools.
2. The instruments used in the assessment process are, for the most part, technically inadequate.
3. Generally, students are placed in special education programs because of a deficit between ability and achievement.
4. Current criteria for identifying learning disabled students are inadequate and inaccurate.
5. Classification decisions often are unrelated to the data generated during the assessment process.
6. Decision makers do not use assessment data reliably to identify students as learning disabled.
7. The focus of most teams is on reporting of data, with little time spent on integrating the data or attending to instructional interventions.
8. Professional opinions about the definition and prevalence of learning disabilities are discordant.
9. The most important determinant in placement in special education is the referral itself. Once a student is referred, the probability of assessment is 92%; once assessed, the probability of placement is 73%.
10. Placement in special education often does not result in substantive changes in educational programs that are different from those programs implemented in regular education.

Litigation pertaining to education began on a small scale during the 1960s, and evolved to a major area of concern among the special education community during the 1970s. In the 1960s, advocates for and parents of handicapped children first used the legal system to ensure the protection of the children's rights in the special education placement process. The area of special education litigation expanded greatly during the 1970s, and the courts became a primary arena for change in the field of special education.

An extremely significant legislative mandate emerged in response to the educational litigation of the 1960s and early 1970s. The adoption of PL 94-142, the Education for All Handicapped Children Act of 1975, which became fully effective October 1, 1977, had a profound effect on assessment procedures and the delivery of psychological and educational services for minority group children. Two of the most important changes mandated by the law were the establishment of due process procedures in each state to safeguard the rights of handicapped children and their parents or guardians in the provision of special education services, and the requirement of an individualized educational program (IEP). The IEP must include statements documenting the child's current level of performance, short term objectives, annual goals, educational services to be provided, the child's participation in regular education programs, anticipated length of the services, date of service initiation, and progress evaluation procedures (Lilly, 1979).

Legal action has been effective in drawing attention to a number of relevant issues such as nondiscriminatory testing and the use of multiple measures on the evaluation and placement of children. Furthermore, litigation can be recognized for encouraging our society to expect free appropriate public education for all children. This expectation has become well established and is widely pursued by the field of special education and our society as a whole.

The emphasis on litigation, and the still present inequities in the way students are identified and served in special education, has resulted in a renewed effort to more precisely determine the procedures for assessing and placing students in special education. The problem with current assessment and placement practices has had great impact on the provision of equal opportunity to all students. The most dramatic effect has been in the over-identification of minority children and males. The Office for Civil Rights (OCR) of the U.S. Department of Education has revealed that these two groups of students have been overrepresented in special education. This issue has continued for three decades and will most likely be monitored for three more.

Current practice in the delivery of special education programs is being reformulated. In part, this modification is based upon the lack of empirical support for the present procedures. As noted by Tindal (1985), the effectiveness of special education has been consistently questioned over the past 20 years by a number of reviewers. Most of these reviewers have found little evidence clearly indicating superior achievement gains as a result of special education. However, the methodology of the research in these efficacy studies has been sufficiently poor to question the validity of the findings.

In a related review by Epps and Tindal (1985), the analysis of special education programs was expanded to include not only the achievement outcomes, but also the definition of program components. In particular, this review investigated the differences between special and regular education programs in the content and context of instruction. Several studies were reviewed utilizing the process-product research paradigm, in which classrooms are observed in terms of organization and teacher behaviors and students' performance is monitored for gains in achievement. The major conclusion was that few, if any, differences exist between the two environments. Instruction has been defined in substantially the same manner in both special and regular education. Students receive approximately the same amounts of time and are required to engage in many of the same behav-

iors in receiving instruction. The only clear difference to emerge in the manner in which instruction is defined in special education is that students are instructed in one to one setting rather than the small or large group settings.

In response to both of these issues, the lack of markedly different or superior instruction in special education, evolved in to the reformulating of delivery of special education. The major model was the cascade of services originally proposed by Deno (1970) and revamped by Reynolds and Birch (1982). However, the regular education initiative and inclusion movements have changed the entire concept of the cascade of services, and research and outcome assessment will determine how delivery of services progresses.

Implementation of this system generally has acknowledged the importance of consultants and coteaches to regular classroom teachers. The consultation's content includes assessment procedures, development of individualized instructional procedures, direct instruction and evaluation of program outcomes.

In summary, current practice in the assessment and placement of students in special education generally has been judged inappropriate in the past. One new direction being proposed, in response to both empirical practices as well as legal mandates, is the implementation of inclusion. In this system, specialized staff serve as consultants and collaborators in the development of IEPs. By implementing such an approach, special education would indeed become a part of, rather than be apart from, the public schools.

REFERENCES

Deno, E. (1970). Special education as developmental capital. *Exceptional Children, 37*, 229–337.

Epps, S., & Tindal, D. (1985). The effectiveness of differentiated programming in severely mildly handicapped students: Placement options and instruction programming, In M. Wong, M. Reynolds, & H. Walberg (Eds.), Oxford England: Pergamon Press.

Lilly, M.S. (1979). *Children with exceptional needs.* Chicago: Holt, Rinehart, & Winston.

Reynolds, M., & Birch, J. (1982). *Teaching exceptional children in all America's schools* (Rev. ed.). Reston, VA: Council for Exceptional Children.

Tindal, G. (1985). Investigation the effectiveness of special education: Analysis of methodology. *Journal of Learning Disabilities, 18*, 101–112.

Ysseldyke, J., & Algozzine, B. (1983). *Critical issues in special and remedial education.* Boston: Houghton-Mifflin.

Ysseldyke, J., & Thurlow, M. (1983). *Identification/classification research: An integrative summary of findings.* (Research Report No. 142). Minneapolis: University of Minnesota Institute for Research on Learning Disabilities.

See also Assessment; Cascade Model of Special Education; Inclusion; Individual Education Plan; Individuals with Disabilities Education Plan (IDEA); Least Restrictive Environment

PUERTO RICO, SPECIAL EDUCATION IN

Special education services in Puerto Rico are administered under the legislative provisions of IDEA which are reflected in territorial law concerning the handicapped. Before IDEA and PL 94-142, there were few services. Since the legislation there has been greater consistency and continuity of services, improvement and expansion of personnel preparation, reduction of negative attitudes, and increasing movement of children toward the mainstream (Smith-Davis, Burke, & Noel, 1984).

Until a few years ago, the handicapped population in Puerto Rico was generally served in self-contained classes at the elementary level. Since 1979 programming has shifted to the mild and moderately handicapped, to mainstreaming, and to programs at intermediate and secondary levels. Prevocational and vocational centers for the handicapped have also been established (Smith-Davis et al., 1984).

Special education practices in Puerto Rico must be interpreted in light of the school system, which is highly centralized. It is organized into a central office responsible for all administrative and policy decisions, and six educational regions, each under a director appointed by the secretary of education (who is appointed by the governor at cabinet level). Each region is subdivided into districts run by superintendents. Within this structure, special education is largely centralized. It is directed by a special education director and is divided into four units: administrative, curricular, academic, and vocational. Regional special education supervisors are appointed to each region. Thus there are six plus two supervisors, one each for prevocational and vocational programs (Brown, 1977).

Unlike the United States, where Puerto Ricans are a linguistic minority, in Puerto Rico they are the majority. Consequently, all services and instructional aids and materials for special education are in Spanish. It is important that U.S. special educators be aware that Puerto Rico, through the governor's office and other agencies, is ready to offer technical assistance in these areas to anyone who requests it (Cruz, 1979).

REFERENCES

Brown, F.M. (1977, August). *Southeast Area Learning Resource Center: Final technical report, Sept. 1, 1974 through May 31, 1977.* Washington, DC: Bureau of Education for the Handicapped.

Cruz, D. (1979, June). Outreach problems in Puerto Rico. In G. Dixon & D. Bridges (Eds.), *On being Hispanic and disabled: The special challenge of an underserved population.* Chicago: Illinois State Board of Vocational Education and Rehabilitation.

Smith-Davis, J., Burke, P.J., & Noel, M.M. (1984). *Personnel to educate the handicapped in America: Supply and demand from a programmatic viewpoint.* College Park, MD: Maryland University College of Education.

See also Mexico, Special Education in

PUNISHMENT

Punishment, defined functionally, occurs when the presentation of an aversive consequence contingent on the emission of a behavior reduces the subsequent rate of that behavior. It is a commonly employed operant conditioning procedure. As Alberto and Troutman (1986) state, "Any stimulus can be labeled a punisher if its contingent application results in a reduction of the target behavior. A punisher, like a reinforcer, can be identified only by its effect on behavior—not on the nature of the consequent stimulus" (p. 245). Thus the mere application of an aversive stimulus (such as a spanking) or removal of a positive stimulus (such as a token or money) cannot be termed a punishment procedure unless a reductive effect on the target behavior occurs. Unfortunately, this reductive effect on behavior by a consequent stimulus is seldom evaluated in everyday use, thus resulting in inappropriate and ineffective use of the punishment procedure.

REFERENCES

Alberto, P.A., & Troutman, A.C. (1986). *Applied behavior analysis for teachers* (2nd. ed.). Columbus, OH: Merrill.

See also **Applied Behavior Analysis; Aversive Stimulus; Negative Punishment; Punishment, Positive**

PUNISHMENT, POSITIVE

The use of adjectives such as "positive" and "negative" are most frequently associated with reinforcement techniques, but occasionally have been employed to further define punishment techniques. Behaviorists use these adjectives to describe the contingent presentation of a stimulus (positive) or the contingent removal of a stimulus (negative). These terms should *not* be interpreted as value judgments synonymous with "good" and "bad." Therefore, *positive punishment* is the contingent presentation of an aversive stimuli for a misbehavior or rule violation. Spanking a child for fighting with a peer is a classic example of positive punishment. Socially more acceptable examples of positive punishment include undertaking a noxious task such as cleaning a restroom (i.e., the aversive stimulus) contingent on messing it up. *Negative punishment* is the contingent removal of a positive stimulus. Common examples of negative punishment techniques include response cost or timeout.

See also **Punishment**

PURDUE PERCEPTUAL-MOTOR SURVEY (PPMS)

The Purdue Perceptual-Motor Survey (PPMS) (Roach & Kephart, 1966) was developed to enable qualitative observations of problem areas of perceptual-motor development. Subtests include walking board, jumping, identification of body parts, imitation of movements (following the examiner's arm movements), obstacle course, Kraus Weber (requiring the child to raise first the upper and then the lower torso while prone), angels in the snow (differentiation of arms and legs in various patterns), chalkboard (e.g., drawing simple to complex patterns), ocular pursuits (visual tracking), and visual achievement forms (a paper and pencil copying task).

The theoretical and practical implications of the scale were described in Kephart (1971). The major assumptions that were controversial (Hammill, 1982) were that higher levels of learning are dependent on a motor base of achievement, and that perceptual-motor interventions are important for the remediation of academic deficits. The psychometric properties of the survey are now redundant and revisions were not done. Hence the survey is essentially obsolete.

REFERENCES

Hammill, D.D. (1982). Assessing and training perceptual motor skills. In D.D. Hammill & N.R. Bartel (Eds.), *Teaching children with learning and behavior problems* (3rd ed., pp. 379–408). Boston: Allyn & Bacon.

Kephart, N.C. (1971). *The slow learner in the classroom* (2nd ed.). Columbus, OH: Merrill.

Roach, E.G., & Kephart, N.C. (1966). *The Purdue Perceptual-Motor Survey.* Columbus, OH: Merrill.

See also **Perceptual and Motor Skills**

PUTAMEN

The putamen is the largest nucleus of the basal ganglia (caudate nucleus, putamen, globus pallidus, claustrum and amygdala) that function in background motor control via the extrapyramidal motor system (Carpenter & Sutin, 1983). The putamen also houses receptor sites for the dopamine containing neurons projecting from the substantia nigra. (The nigrastriatal system with the striatum is the putamen and candate nucleus.) The putamen is located lateral to the thalamus and internal capsule but medial to the external capsule and inner aspect of the Sylvian fissure. Since dopamine is an essential neurotransmitter for both normal motor and mental functioning, damage to the putamen may result in a wide spectrum of neurobehavioral changes. The prototype disorder of the basal ganglia that best exemplifies these motor and mental changes is Huntington's chorea. In Huntington's chorea there are specific motor deficits characterised by uncontrolled choreic movements as well as progressive dementia (Heilman & Valenstein, 1985). The disruption of any part of the nigrastriatal system will affect dopamine production and will have significant neurobehavioral effects. These are discussed in the section on the substantia nigra. Recent research has also implicated a greater role of the basal ganglia in language function than had been suspected (Segalowitz, 1983).

REFERENCES

Carpenter, M.B., & Sutin, J. (1983). *Human neuroanatomy* (8th ed.). Baltimore, MD: Williams & Wilkins.

Heilman, K.M., & Valenstein, E. (1985). *Clinical neuropsychology.* New York: Oxford University Press.

Segalowitz, S.J. (1983). *Language functions and brain organization.* New York: Academic.

See also **Huntington's Chorea; Substantia, Nigra**

PYGMALION EFFECT

According to Rosenthal and Jacobson (1966, 1968), one of the possible relationships between prophecies and events can be described as the pygmalion effect. The central concept behind the pygmalion effect is that of the self-fulfilling prophecy. That is, people behave in ways that increase the likelihood that their predictions and expectations will be realized. One person's expectation of another person's behavior becomes an accurate prediction as a result of its having been made.

Early researchers (Gottlieb & Budoff, 1972; Jones, 1972; Lilly, 1970) in the area of attitudes toward children labeled mildly retarded looked at what is expected of those who carry the label and how this expectation affects performance. Labels may engender specific behavioral expectations, particularly on the part of teachers. These expectations, in turn, may be reflected in the teacher's behavior toward the labeled child, and eventually in the child's level of performance.

Much concern about the pygmalion effect in special education was stimulated by minority groups who pointed out the disproportionate numbers of their children in special classes (*Larry P. v. Riles; Diana v. California Board of Education; Lora v. Board of Education of the City of New York*). The concern was focused on the consequences of special class placement as seen in the child's rejection by teachers, parents, and peers, poor self-image, and poor prospects for post school adjustment and employment.

REFERENCES

Gottlieb, J., & Budoff, M. (1972). Attitudes toward school by segregated and integrated retarded children. *Studies in Learning Potential, 2*, 1–10.

Jones, R.L. (1972). Labels and stigma in special education. *Exceptional Children, 38*, 553–564.

Lilly, M.S. (1970). Special education: A teapot in a tempest. *Exceptional Children, 36*, 43–48.

Rosenthal, R., & Jacobson, L. (1966). Teacher expectancies: Determinants of pupils IQ gains. *Psychological Reports, 19*, 115–118.

Rosenthal, R., & Jacobson, L. (1968). *Pygmalion in the classroom.* New York: Holt, Rinehart, & Winston.

See also **Labeling; Teacher Expectancies**

Q

Q-SORT

The Q-sort is a technique used to implement Q-methodology, a set of philosophical, psychological, statistical, and psychometric ideas propounded by William Stephenson (1953). The Q-sort was developed as a research tool, in particular a tool for exploring and testing theoretical formulations (e.g., about the existence of different educational philosophies). However, its use has been extended to both clinical assessment and to program evaluation.

The Q-sort is a way of rank-ordering objects. The objects ranked usually take the form of statements written on cards (though real objects, such as works of art, have been subjected to the Q-sort also). The sorter is given a set of cards—usually between 60 and 120—and instructed to distribute them into a fixed number of piles arranged along some continuum (e.g., approval to disapproval). The sorter is required to put a specified number of cards in each pile, resulting in a normal or quasi-normal distribution. This distribution permits the use of conventional statistical techniques, including correlation, analysis of variance, and factor analysis, in analyzing the results.

The results of the Q-sort typically are used to draw inferences about people (not the objects they are ranking) for theoretical, clinical, or program evaluation purposes. For example, a preliminary theory about the existence of two opposing educational philosophies can be tested by creating a set of statements reflecting each philosophy, having the combined set sorted on an "approval-disapproval" continuum, and analyzing the results to determine if there are groups of people who rank-order the statements in the same way. In the clinical setting, the patient's sort can be compared with those associated with known pathological syndromes. Finally, in program evaluation, sorts made before and after a program can be compared with one another or with a criterion sort meant to represent the desired outcome of the program.

REFERENCE

Stephenson, W. (1953). *The study of behavior.* Chicago: University of Chicago Press.

See also **Factor Analysis; Measurement; Philosophy of Education for the Handicapped; Research in Special Education**

QUADRIPLEGIA

Quadriplegia is often referred to as paralysis from the neck down. Although this definition may be accurate for certain conditions, it is also misleading. A more accurate description of quadriplegia is a nonspecific paralysis or loss of normal function in all four limbs of the body. The condition most often affects motor skills but also may affect sensory awareness. Quadriplegia may result from damage to or dysfunction of the brain (e.g., cerebral palsy, stroke, traumatic head injury), spinal cord (e.g., spinal cord injury, amyotrophic lateral sclerosis), or peripheral structures (e.g., muscular dystrophy, multiple sclerosis). The condition also may occur as a result of tumor, toxic chemicals, congenital abnormalities, or infection. The term sometimes includes quadriparesis, which is considered a weakness or incomplete paralysis of the four extremities. Quadriplegia is not generally associated with the head or neck, but it may involve these structures in some conditions (e.g., cerebral palsy).

The specific skills or functions that are lost or impaired for persons with quadriplegia may vary considerably and depend largely on the individual's primary impairment. For example, a person who experiences quadriplegia as a result of a spinal cord injury experiences a loss of sensation and movement below the level of the injury. When the injury occurs at the level of the third cervical vertebra (C3), the person has essentially no sensation or functional use of the body below the neck. On the other hand, a person with a C5 injury has some active movement available at the elbow (flexion and supination) and shoulder (abduction and external rotation), but most other movements are lost. In the latter stages of the Duchenne's form of muscular dystrophy, a person may be able to use the fingers to write, type, or manipulate other small objects. Because of progressive weakness in the large muscles of the body, people with this type of quadriplegia are unable to move their arms at the shoulder or wrist. Unlike quadriplegia from spinal cord injury, sensation in this type of impairment remains intact. Children with quadriplegia owed to cerebral palsy are almost always able to move the joints in their upper extremities. They usually experience normal tactile sensation, but they may have abnormal kinesthetic sensation. Because of abnormal changes in muscle tone in various groups of muscles, movements are either very rigid and stiff, uncoordinated, or limp and flaccid. Children with quadriplegic cerebral palsy also may experience abnormal muscle tone and movement patterns in their neck or facial muscles in addition to involvement in all four extremities.

The specific treatment, education, or other intervention for persons with quadriplegia also is dependent on the impairment that causes this condition. A team approach using multidisciplinary, transdisciplinary, or interdisciplinary models is essential in the care and management of an individual with quadriplegia. Team members may include physicians, nurses, teachers, physical therapists, occupational therapists, speech pathologists, rehabilitation engineers, family members, attendants, and, as often as possible, the affected individual. Sometimes individuals with quadriplegia need considerable assistance for even the most routine activities (e.g., eating a meal), while others are able to live independently, pursue a career, and raise a family.

Although quadriplegia usually results in extensive disability, a variety of electronic and nonelectronic devices may be used to facilitate more normal experiences or abilities. Electrically powered wheelchairs, specially designed passenger vans, adapted eating utensils, augmentative communication systems, and personal hygiene and grooming devices are only a few examples that may be used to compensate for impaired skills. These technologic advances have fostered a more independent lifestyle for many people with quadriplegia, but some advocates for people with disabilities would argue that social changes also are needed to permit the greatest level of independence. Elimination of environmental and attitudinal barriers and affirmative action for employment often are identified as essential components of a productive and satisfying life. References illuminating etiology, definition and management are cited below for further reading.

REFERENCES

Bobath, B. (1985). *Abnormal postural reflex activity caused by brain lesions* (3rd ed.). Rockville, MD: Aspen Systems.

Bobath, B., & Bobath, K. (1975). *Motor development in the different types of cerebral palsy.* London: Heinemann Medical Books.

Ford, J., & Duckworth, B. (1974). *Physical management for the quadriplegic patient.* Philadelphia: Davis.

Miller, B., & Keane, C. (1983). *Encyclopedia and dictionary of medical nursing and allied health* (3rd ed.). Philadelphia: Saunders.

Nagel, D.A. (1975). Traumatic paraplegia and quadriplegia. In E.E. Bleck & D.A. Nagel (Eds.), *Physically handicapped children—A medical atlas for teachers* (pp. 209–214). New York: Grune & Stratton.

Trombly, C.A. (1983). Spinal cord injury. In C.A. Trombly (Ed.), *Occupational therapy for physical dysfunction* (2nd ed., pp. 385–398). Baltimore, MD: Williams & Wilkins.

See also **Accessibility of Buildings**

QUESTIONNAIRES IN SPECIAL EDUCATION

Questionnaires are often used for gathering research data in special education. They are relatively inexpensive, can assure anonymity, and can be used with relative ease by novice researchers as well as seasoned professionals.

Pride (1979) has observed that the mail questionnaire in particular is useful in obtaining data from distant populations. It reaches subjects too busy to be interviewed, enables targeting subgroups of respondents, and is conducive in format to framing responses in a manner suitable for statistical analysis. The mail questionnaire can also "eliminate interviewer bias to questions that are sensitive or embarrassing when posed by an interviewer" (p. 59).

As popular survey research tools questionnaires (whether mailed, completed by telephone, or administered in person) require careful design. The design process includes separate decisions about (1) the kind of information sought (e.g., attitudinal, behavioral), (2) the question structure (e.g., open-ended, close-ended with ordered categories), and (3) the actual choice of words (Dillman, 1978, pp. 79–80). Every investigation presents special requirements and different problems. Oppenheim (1966), Dillman (1978), and Sudman and Bradburn (1982) provide thorough discussions about the many factors to be considered when designing questionnaires and detailed recommendations for writing and presenting questions.

Despite the fact that the mail survey is, in many cases, the most feasible approach for retrieving data from large, widely dispersed samples, many researchers have expressed concern about its methodological rigor and adequacy. This concern is based largely on the grounds of seriously deficient response rates. "The most common flaw is nonresponse of a size or nature which makes the answers nonrepresentative of the total sample and thus the total universe" (Erdos, 1970, p. 142). Returns of less than 40 or 50% are common. Additionally, there are limitations on the nature of data that may be obtained and the quality of responses to many mail questionnaires.

Kanuk and Berenson (1975) confirmed that, despite the proliferation of research studies (well over 200) reporting techniques to reduce nonresponse bias, "there is no strong empirical evidence favoring any techniques other than follow-up and the use of monetary incentives" (p. 451). Research on the topic generally has been narrowly focused, poorly integrated, and contradictory. Erdos (1970) and Dillman (1978) represent the few attempts to improve response rates to mail questionnaires from the perspective of addressing the entire mail survey process.

Dillman's recommendations offer a fully integrated, planned sequence of procedures and techniques that are designed to increase response rates and that are fully adaptable to research problems in special education. His total design method (TDM) attempts to present mail surveys in such a way that respondents develop proprietary attitudes toward the research project in which they are being asked to participate. Based on the tenets of motivational psychology, Dillman has postulated that the process of designing and sending a questionnaire, and getting respondents to complete it in an honest manner and return it, is a special kind of social exchange. His highly prescribed method and related strategies are designed to minimize the costs for responding, maximize the rewards for doing so, and establish trust that those rewards will be delivered. Readily adaptable in its present form, the TDM also provides a useful frame of reference against which the design aspects of each mail survey research problem may be considered.

REFERENCES

Dillman, D. (1978). *Mail and telephone surveys: The total design method.* New York: Wiley.

Erdos, P.L. (1970). *Professional mail surveys.* New York: McGraw-Hill.

Kanuk, L., & Berenson, C. (1975). Mail survey and response rates: A literature review. *Journal of Marketing Research, 12,* 440–453.

Oppenheim, A.N. (1966). *Questionnaire design and attitudes measurement.* New York: Basic Books.

Pride, C. (1979). Building response to a mail survey. *New Directions for Institutional Advancement, 6,* 59–69.

Sudman, S., & Bradburn, N.M. (1982). *Asking questions.* San Francisco: Jossey-Bass.

See also **Research in Special Education**

R

RACIAL BIAS IN TESTING

See CULTURAL BIAS IN TESTING.

RACIAL DISCRIMINATION IN SPECIAL EDUCATION

The right to education, nondiscriminatory treatment, equal protection, and due process protection for all handicapped children was first established by Congress with the Education Amendments of 1974 and the Education For All Handicapped Children Act of 1975 and continues in IDEA. Prior to this national policy, more than 36 court cases throughout the country brought convincing documentation that racially and culturally discriminatory practices existed in special education. Racially and culturally diverse school children continue to be disproportionately represented in special education programs while local and state education officials attempt to improve testing and classification procedures.

See also **Diana v. State Board of education; Education for All Handicapped Children Act of 1975; Hobson v. Hansen; Individuals with Disabilities Education Act (IDEA); Larry P.; Special Education, Legal Regulations of; Mattie T. v. Holladay; Mills v. Board of Education; PASE**

RARE DISEASES

POPLITEAL PTERYGIUM SYNDROME

Popliteal pterygium syndrome is also known as popliteal web syndrome and Febre-Languepin syndrome. It is a congenital syndrome consisting chiefly of popliteal webs, cleft palate, lower lip pits, and dysplasia of the toenails. A wide variety of other abnormalities may be associated with popliteal pterygium syndrome.

There is a web in the popliteal fossa that may present in several forms—from a dense, fibrous cord containing the tibial nerve to a large fold through the entire limb. There may be toenail dysplasia, the cleft palate can occur with or without a cleft lip, and the lower lip may display salivary pits. The syndrome is hereditary in acquisition and does not affect intelligence.

PRUNE BELLY SYNDROME

Prune belly syndrome, also known as Eagle-Barrett syndrome, presents with the congenital absence of the lower portion of the rectus abdominis muscle and the inferior and midportions of the oblique muscles. These patients also have marked dilation of the bladder and ureters, with small, dysplastic kidneys that are hydronephrotic. The testis are usually undescended. Because the anterior wall of the abdomen is muscularly unstructured, the wrinkled skin contains the intra-abdominal organs which bulge out, giving the appearance of a prune.

LEOPARD SYNDROME

Leopard syndrome is an acronym for Lentigines, ECG abnormalities, Ocular hypertelorism, Pulmonary stenosis, Abnormalities of genitalia, Retardation of growth, and Deafness. It is a hereditary syndrome, inherited as an autosomal dominant trait. The syndrome is manifested as multiple lentigines (tan, dark brown, or black pigmented lesions, measuring between one and two millimeters in diameter, oval, circular, or irregular in shape, located in any mucocutaneous surface). The heart defects do not usually produce any symptoms in spite of appearing on an ECG. Ocular hypertelorism refers to an increased distance between the eyes which may impair the patient's ability to focus on an object. Pulmonary valvular stenosis makes it difficult for these patients to engage in physical activities. Since the pulmonary valve connecting the heart to the lungs is narrowed, it does not allow for the adequate circulation of venous blood to be oxygenated in the lungs. With time, pulmonary stenosis produces many serious consequences. Also associated are retardation of growth and sensory-neural deafness. A profound impact on the patient's learning process occurs, especially when the input of information is verbal. It is necessary that diagnosis be made early.

MACROGLOSSIA

Macroglossia is defined by excessive tongue size. This can physically interfere with effective verbal communication and contribute to dysphagia. It should be considered when speech difficulties are encountered. It is readily diagnosed on physical examination by a medical health care provider.

LENZ MICROPHTHALMIA SYNDROME

Lenz's syndrome is an inherited syndrome, linked to the X chromosome. The patients have microphthalmia or anophthalmia (very small eyes or absence of eyes). It can affect one or both eyes. There may be many skeletal deformities, including finger anomalies, double thumbs, and narrow shoulders. Patients may have other defects affecting the cardiovascular, genital, or urinary systems. Dental defects are also found. It is present from birth and is detected due to the general physical appearance of the child. Special education programs directed at visual perception and dexterity enhancement are necessary in this group of patients.

MCCUNE-ALBRIGHT SYNDROME

The hallmark manifestation of this syndrome is found in children displaying hyperpigmented macules (very dark skin lesions), precocious sexual development, and thinning and hardening of bones with fractures. There are multiple endocrine alterations with increased glandular function. These can include goiter with thyroid disease, increased growth hormone secretion, Cushing's syndrome, increased prolactin production, hyperparathyroidism, rickets, and precocious puberty.

Precocious sexual development is the most common presentation and vaginal bleeding is the presenting feature in young girls. The ovaries are asymmetrically enlarged because of cysts and hormonal stimulation. Bone lesions may not be seen for years. The skin lesions are an inconsistent feature.

Each individual child will have some special needs to be addressed due to the varying presentations which directly depend on the endocrine organs involved.

MANNOSIDOSIS

Mannosidosis is a lysosomal storage disease due to a defective a–mannosidase with resultant oligosaccharide accumulation. Clinically there are coarse facies, upper respiratory congestion and infections, profound mental retardation, hepatosplenomegaly, cataracts, radiographic signs of dyostosis multiplex, and gibbus deformity.

Mannosidosis is divided into type I for infantile and type II for juvenile-onset, respectively. Mannosidosis type I will appear between three and 12 months of age; type II manifests itself between one and four years of age. The clinical presentation is very similar for both diseases. Patients have gargoyle-like facies, frequent and recurrent respiratory infections, mental retardation, hearing loss and impaired speech, cataract formation, corneal clouding, and abnormal bone structure (especially of the calvaria, long bones, and vertebral bodies). The liver and spleen are enlarged and there is a gibbus formation; the gingiva may be hyperplastic.

The diagnosis for this disease is based on finding a specific acid α-mannosidase deficiency in leucocytes, serum, or cultured cells.

MEDIUM CHAIN ACYL-COENZYME A DEHYDROGENASE DEFICIENCY (MCAD)

MCAD is a defect in mitochondrial beta oxidation due to deficiency of the acyl-Coenzyme A dehydrogenase acting on medium-chain-length fatty acids. It is characterized by recurring episodes of hypoglycemia, vomiting, and lethargy with urinary excretion of medium-chain decarboxylic acids, minimal ketogenesis, and low plasma and tissue levels of carnitine. MCAD occurs in 1 of every 10,000 births, and the patients may have severe hypoglycemia without hyperinsulinism, encephalopathies, floppiness, and an enlarged liver. The level of free fatty acids is elevated, as well as ammonia, creatine kinase (liver enzyme), and lactic dehydrogenase (muscle enzyme). Reye syndrome and SIDS are differential diagnoses considered with this condition. Fatty acid oxidation may be impaired at any of the steps.

The diagnosis is made when finding hypoglycemia in the absence of ketonuria. Treatment consists of increasing the frequency of oral feeding and oral carnitine replacement. Intravenous glucose may be essential during treatment periods of increased catabolism. The frequency of attacks diminishes with age, as the child grows into a larger body mass and develops fasting tolerance. In the absence of an attack, the illness may go undetected; about 50% of patients never have an attack and hence do not know they are medium chain acyl-coenzyme A dehydrogenase deficient. Such problems interfere with the education process of the individual, particularly due to episodes of hypoglycemia.

POMPE'S DISEASE

Pompe's disease, also known as acid maltase deficiency or α–1,4 glucosidase deficiency, is a type II glycogen storage disease due to a defective lysosomal enzyme. This disease stands in contrast with most other glycogenoses where the enzyme abnormality is cytoplasmic rather than lysosomal. The glycogenosis observed is due to the lack of hydroxylation of glycogen particles by the lysosomes. Symptomatology is then a result of accumulation of glycogen inside the lysosomes. Patients with this disease display marked hypotonia, cardiomegaly, cardiac failure, cyanosis, and death during the first twelve months of life. The pathological process is stored glycogen that is degraded, due to deficiency of the acid maltase enzyme, causing cellular swelling, dysfunction, and death.

There are other forms of the disease that present later in life, such as the skeletal muscle form. Demonstrating the deficiency of acid maltase in the patient's lymphocytes or tissue biopsy makes the diagnosis of this autosomal recessive genetic disease. There is no treatment available for this disease, and it ultimately results in the patient's death.

MIXED CONNECTIVE TISSUE DISEASE

This disease is a variant of systemic lupus erythematosus. It displays evident symptoms and signs of various connective tissue diseases. Mixed connective tissue disease commonly presents as a diffuse interstitial disease, and occurs more frequently in females than in males. The patient may present with features of three rheumatic diseases including juvenile arthritis, juvenile dermatomyosytis, and scleroderma. Because of the varied features that can be present, the management is geared to the specific problems of the individual patient.

This disease occurs only rarely in children. The prognosis is usually correlated to the degree of pulmonary involvement, with a five year survival rate similar to idiopathic pulmonary fibrosis. Young patients with minimal fibrosis and active alveolitis (inflammation of the alveoli) have a 90% survival rate, and those with minimum cellularity and severe pulmonary fibrosis have less than 25% survival rate. The educational approaches for these patients should be tailored to the specific needs and sequelae that require management.

OCCULOCEREBRAL-HYPOPIGMENTATION SYNDROME

This is an autosomal recessive syndrome that is also known as Cross syndrome and Cross-McKusic-Breen syndrome. Children with this problem present with microphthalmus (small eyes), small opaque corneas, and marked oculocutaneous (skin and eyes) albinism. These serious problems call for special educational efforts concentrating on the visual perception disadvantages manifested by these patients. Apart from the eyes, the skeletal structure is affected with scoliosis that may impact on the ability to participate in physical activities, gingival hyperplasia, and a high-arched palate.

ROBINOW'S SYNDROME

Robinow's syndrome is also known as Robinow's dwarfism and fetal face syndrome. Patients display dwarfism and ocular hypertelorism (an increased distance between the eyes), which may impair the patient's ability to focus on an object. The name "fetal face" is supported by the patient's bulging forehead, flattened nasal bridge, unaligned teeth, and short extremities.

ROTHMUND-THOMPSON SYNDROME

This syndrome is also known as poikiloderma congenitale because poikiloderma (a condition characterized by pigmentary and atrophic changes in the skin, giving a mottled appearance) is one of the predominant features. The skin is usually normal at birth, and begins to express the changes between the third and twenty-fourth month. The lesions begin as erythema (redness), followed by poikiloderma with atrophy, telangiectasia (dilation of blood vessels), and hy-

perpigmented and hypopigmented patchy areas. These lesions are seen in the face, extremities, and buttocks. During late childhood, some patients develop verrucous lesions (wart-like lesions) to the back and sides of the hands. These warts may also be found on palms and soles, as well as the other extremities. The verrucous lesions and the atrophic patches may predispose to squamous cell carcinoma.

Severe photosensitivity occurs in some 30% of the patients. Some patients will suffer alopecia of the scalp and secondary sexual hair (pubic and axillary), and the finger and toenails may be dystrophic. There is short stature and impaired sexual development. More than half the patients will develop juvenile cataracts (opacifications of the lens of the eye). There may be some skeletal deformities. Mental development and life expectancy are generally not affected. Special education targeting the visual disturbance of juvenile cataracts should be stressed.

RUBENSTEIN-TAYBI SYNDROME

This is a congenital disease. It is characterized by skeletal derangements that lead to motor development retardation. Mental retardation is also present. Special education needs should address both problems on patients with this syndrome.

The thumbs and toes are broad, and abnormalities of the vertebral bodies and the sternum (breast bone) are present. Patients display a characteristic facie due to a beaked or straight nose and a high, arched palate. Patients can develop pulmonary valvular stenosis and diverse eye abnormalities. Their skin undergoes keloid formation upon scarring, producing thick, white scars.

RUSSELL-SILVER SYNDROME

This syndrome is found in small babies who have grown slowly during most of the pregnancy. Babies experiencing slow growth before the 35th gestational week have increased potential for complications. They usually feed very poorly and will show asymmetry between the two sides of the body, clinodactyly, elfin faces and short stature. They will have an increased secretion of gonadotropins that will lead to precocious puberty.

SCHWARTZ-JAMPEL SYNDROME

Patients affected by this autosomal recessive disorder will display a variety of features including dwarfism blepharophimosis (abnormal narrowness of the eyelid fissures) and myotonic myopathy. Their joints also develop contractures, and they have flat faces. These patients have posture problems which need to be considered when developing a care strategy.

SMITH-LEMLI-OPITZ SYNDROME

This syndrome is characterized by a variety of congenital abnormalities. These may comprise incomplete development of the male genital organs, microcephaly, hypotonia, anterior inversion of nostrils on a short nose, syndactyly of toes, and mental retardation. This condition is hereditary and is transmitted as an autosomal recessive trait. Special education efforts should be geared toward the mental retardation status and the added complications caused by diverse physical impairments present.

TREACHER-COLLINS SYNDROME

This is also known as Franceschetti-Klein syndrome and mandibulofacial dystosis. Patients present with characteristic facies with the mandible and malar bones markedly hypoplastic, a cleft or high-arched palate, and dental malocclusion. The eyes show lids with an antimongoloid inclination and a coloboma (absence or defect of ocular tissue) is often found in the outer lower lid. The ears are affected with the absence of external auditory canal. All children with Treacher-Collins are assumed to be deaf until proven differently. There may be other malformations including congenital heart disease, mental retardation, and skeletal structural malformations. There may be milder variants of the syndrome. Patients with Treacher-Collins present a major challenge for special education.

RASE

See REMEDIAL AND SPECIAL EDUCATION.

RATIO IQ

A ratio intelligence quotient or ratio IQ is a type of score from a test of intelligence (or cognitive or mental ability). It is now obsolete as a statistical term and as a useful score. The ratio IQ has been replaced by most authors of mental ability tests with a standard score such as a deviation IQ.

The concept of a mental quotient to indicate the rate of cognitive development was introduced by William Stern in a paper to the German Congress of Psychology in Berlin in April 1912. With the Stanford Revision and Extension of the Binet-Simon Intelligence Scale in 1916, Lewis Terman introduced the term intelligence quotient and its abbreviation, IQ, as a prediction of the rate of future mental development (based on the rate of previous accomplishment). Early IQs were simply the ratio of the mental age to the chronological age, multiplied by 100 to eliminate the decimals (i.e., IQ = MA/CA x 100). However, mental ages represent ordinal not interval data and therefore the distance between two ages, e.g., 4 and 6, is not necessarily the same as between two other ages, e.g., 12 and 14. Also, test authors have not been able to construct tests with equal variability at each age level. As a result, the standard deviation of scores is not the same at each age and, therefore, the same ratio IQ obtained at different age levels may not be equal to the same percentile rank. (A ratio IQ that equals or exceeds 3% of the population might be 75 at one age, 68 at another, and 60 at another.) Whereas the statistical properties of a ratio IQ present too many difficulties for its use to be continued except as a concept for interpretation, the simplicity of the concept is still helpful in explaining performance to many consumers. With an IQ of 65, one can say that a 10-year-old child is functioning mentally much like most 6 to 7 year olds and is exhibiting about two-thirds of a year of mental growth each year. The concept of ratio IQ and mental age seem almost nonsensical when applied to adults. Since ratio IQs represent only ordinal scaling, they can neither be multiplied, divided, added, or subtracted across ages and are obsolete for most needs in diagnostic settings.

See also Deviation IQ; Intelligence Quotient

RAVEN'S MATRICES

The Standard Progressive Matrices and the Colored Progressive Matrices (Raven, 1938–1983) are a collection of figures that resemble swatches removed from a wallpaper pattern. The test requires the examinee to locate the swatch that best fits the removed pattern. The test is purportedly an excellent measure of *g* factor intelligence (general intellectual ability; Marshalek, Lohman, & Snow, 1983). The matrices have received wide use around the world because of their easy administration, nonverbal format, and high correlations with traditional measures of intelligence and achievement. The progressive matrices have been used in hundreds of psychological studies internationally.

The matrices are appropriate for individuals ages 5 through adult and are printed both in color (ages 5 to 11) and standard black and white versions (ages 6 and over). The test provides only percentile ranks as an individual's reported score, but even these are not complete; the manual reports performance level only at the 5, 10, 25, 50, 75, 90, and 95th percentiles. Thus, the test only approximates levels of performance. As such, the matrices are useful for the rough assessment of the nonverbal reasoning abilities of individuals 5 years and above. Because of the many deficiencies in the tests' manuals and standardized samples, it is best used as an assessment tool for research purposes and those occasional clinical instances in which an estimate of an individual's intellectual abilities are needed.

REFERENCES

Marshalek, B., Lohman, D.F., & Snow, R. (1983). The complexity continuum in the radex and hierarchical models of intelligence. *Intelligence, 7,* 107–127.

See also "*g*" Factor Theory; Intelligence; Intelligence Testing

RAY ADAPTATION OF THE WECHSLER INTELLIGENCE SCALE FOR CHILDREN-REVISED

Ray (1979) adapted the Wechsler Intelligence Scale for Children-Revised (WISC-R) performance scales for an intelligence tests designed especially for the hearing impaired. He introduced a set of simplified verbal instructions and added more practice items in an attempt to provide standardized test administration techniques to increase a deaf child's comprehension and performance. Therapists who are unskilled in American Sign Language are able to administer the test. In addition to Ray's version of instructions, several different techniques exist for nonverbal administration (Sullivan, 1982). Seven scores are yielded in the adaptation: Picture Completion, Picture Arrangement, Block Design, Object Assembly, Coding, Mazes, and Total. Administration time averages about 45 minutes.

The adaptation was normed on 127 hearing-impaired children from 6 to 16 years old. The sample used was not representative of the deaf school-age population, including no low-verbal deaf children and no multiply handicapped children (Sullivan, 1985). Norms provided in Ray's test should be regarded with caution, and thought should be given to other deaf norms developed. The WISC-R performance scales can be a suitable alternative to the Hiskey-Nebraska if the Anderson and Sisco norms are used with a total communication approach for administration (Phelps & Enson, 1986). Genshaft (1985) thinks that the most useful improvement in the adaptation would be separate, representative norms for deaf children.

REFERENCES

Genshaft, J.L. (1985). Review of the WISC-R: For the deaf. In J.V. Mitchell, Jr. (Ed.), *The ninth mental measurements yearbook* (Vol. 2). Lincoln, NE: University of Nebraska.

Phelps, L., & Enson, A. (1986). Concurrent validity of the WISC-R using deaf norms and the Hiskey-Nebraska. *Psychology in the schools, 23,* 138–141.

Ray, S. (1979). *An adaptation of the Wechsler Intelligence Scale for Children-Revised for the deaf.* Natchitoches: Northwestern State University of Louisiana.

Sullivan, R.M. (1982). Modified instructions for administering the WISC-R performance scale subtests to deaf children (Appendix B). In J.M. Sattler (Ed.), *Assessment of children's intelligence and special abilities* (2nd ed.). Boston: Allyn & Bacon.

Sullivan, P.M. (1985). Review of the WISC-R: For the deaf. In J.V. Mitchell, Jr. (Ed.), *The ninth mental measurements yearbook* (Vol. 2). Lincoln, NE: University of Nebraska.

See also Deaf; Wechsler Intelligence Scale for Children–Revised

REACTION TIME

The time required for a person to respond to a stimulus was one of the most frequent measures of human behavior by early psychologists. Indeed, E.G. Boring, a historian of psychology, characterized the late nineteenth century as the period of "mental chronometry." During this period Galton first used reaction time to an auditory stimulus as a measure of intelligence; similar reaction-time items were incorporated into several early intelligence tests. When reaction time was found to have negligible correlation with seemingly more valid measures of intelligence, however, interest in it waned. In retrospect, it appears that the failure of reaction time may have been due to unreliable measurement and other methodological difficulties. It is now recognized that a large number of trials are required to obtain a reliable average reaction time for an individual person.

As the computer analogy has come to dominate cognitive psychology in recent years, there has been a resurgence of interest in reaction time. The goal of current reaction time research is to measure the time required for the brain to perform a variety of elementary cognitive tasks. From such information it may be possible to infer how the mind is functioning.

Basically, the procedure is to measure reaction time in a task that requires a simple mental operation. The complexity of the mental operation is then increased, and the increase in reaction time is used as a measure of the time required for the brain to process the increased complexity. The following three basic paradigms have been frequently used.

Hick (1952) measured the increase in time required to choose among several visual or auditory stimuli as the number of stimuli increased. The time required is a log function of the number of stimuli, which can be interpreted as the amount of information involved in the choice. Thus the brain appears to be making a block-wise comparison among the various stimuli.

Sternberg (1966) presented subjects with a set of digits followed by a probe digit; the subjects then indicated whether the probe digit was included in the set. This task appears to measure speed of scanning short-term memory. Reaction time increases linearly with the number of items in the set, suggesting a sequential scanning mechanism.

Posner (1969) asked subjects to indicate whether two letters were same or different, with similarity being first defined as physical similarity, in which *A* and *a* are different, and then as semantic similarity, in which *A* and *a* are the same. The latter task requires considerably more time than the first, since the letters must be identified, evidently by a search of long-term memory.

Jensen (1980) has studied the relationship of individual differences in time required to perform these elementary cognitive tasks to scores on traditional psychometric tests of intelligence. The surprising finding is that, with careful measurement and allowing for certain sources of error, about half of the variance in psychometric intelligence test scores is predictable from the several measures of speed of mental processing.

REFERENCES

Hick, W. (1952). On the rate of gain of information. *Quarterly Journal of Experimental Psychology, 4,* 11–26.

Jensen, A.R. (1980). Chronometric analysis of intelligence. *Journal of Social & Biological Structures, 3,* 103–122.

Posner, M.I. (1969). Abstraction and the process of recognition. In G.H. Bower & J.T. Spense (Eds.), *The psychology of learning and motivation* (Vol. 3, pp. 43–100). New York: Academic.

Sternberg, S. (1966). High speed scanning in human memory. *Science, 153,* 652–654.

See also Culture Fair Tests; "g" Factor Theory; Intelligence Testing

READABILITY AND READABILITY FORMULAS

Readability refers to the difficulty level of a passage of text, and is often presented as a grade level number. Typically, reading curricula are designed to match the readability level of stories to the grade level in which the materials are to be used. Textbooks often are described in terms of their readability level. Various readability formulas are used to determine these readability levels.

Klare (1982) provides a general definition of a readability formula: "a predictive device that uses counts of word and sentence variables in a piece of writing to provide a quantitative, objective index of style difficulty" (p. 1522). More than 200 formulas have been published since the first one was developed in the 1920s.

To predict the readability level of a complete text, formulas typically are applied to 100-word samples drawn randomly from throughout the text. Formulas generally are based on regression equations, using weighted scores for word and sentence counts to predict a comprehension score that roughly corresponds to a tested reading grade level. Formulas either rely on word lists or counts of syllables that estimate semantic difficulty (Klare, 1982).

Many common readability measures are available in microcomputer format. A program may consist of a single procedure or as many as eight procedures. Kennedy (1985) provides information on nearly a dozen such programs. Duffelmeyer (1985) contends that although computer programs compute formulas quickly and easily, teacher judgment still is required to assess the conceptual difficulty of the material.

REFERENCES

Duffelmeyer, F.A. (1985). Estimating readability with a computer. Beware the aura of precision. *Reading Teacher, 38*(4), 392–394.

Kennedy, K. (1985). Determining readability with a microcomputer. *Curriculum Review, 25*(2), 40–43.

Klare, G.R. (1982). Readability. In H.E. Mitzel (Ed.), *Encyclopedia of educational research* (5th ed., pp. 1520–1531). New York: Free Press.

See also **Reading; Reading Disorders; Reading in the Content Areas**

READING

Reading is the process of deriving meaning from print. While people have been reading as long as language has been written down, at no other time in recorded history has interest in reading, both from a research and practical standpoint, been greater (Anderson, Hiebert, Scott, & Wilkerson, 1984). There has been a concerted effort to understand how the reading process occurs and to translate that knowledge into materials and strategies that more effectively teach reading. Reading educators, long concerned with reading research and its implementation, have recently been joined by cognitive, educational, and developmental psychologists, linguists, and sociolinguists in the attempt to unravel the mysteries of reading.

Although the word reading characterizes any meaningful interaction between an individual and print, we can subdivide reading into four basic types. Each of these types is differentiated by the purpose for which the reading act is undertaken. The four types of reading to be discussed are developmental reading, studying, functional reading, and recreational reading.

Developmental reading can be described as the activity undertaken for the purpose of learning how to read. As students progress through elementary school, developmental reading remains an integral part of their schooling, with the goal of increasing reading proficiency. Although developmental reading was confined to elementary grades in years past, it is now common to find developmental reading courses being offered at the college level. The rationale for this upward trend in developmental reading is the presence of larger numbers of college students who have not reached proficiency in reading, and who still require some instruction in learning how to read.

In the upper elementary grades, and throughout formal schooling, developmental reading is joined by another type of reading: studying. According to Anderson (1979), studying is a special form of reading that is concerned with the accomplishment of some instructional goal. The type of reading engaged in during studying is special for various reasons.

While the material used for developmental reading is mainly narrative text (i.e., storylike text), the kind of text students most often study is expository in nature. In terms of its demands on comprehension and recall, expository text appears to possess certain disadvantages over narrative text in that it has no identifiable elements such as plot, character, and setting. In addition, expository text is frequently less colorful, and filled with more technical language. Therefore, the task of studying may be more difficult than other forms of reading because expository text may be more difficult and less motivational to read. Not only is the text used in studying potentially more difficult to process, but when students study expository text it is often with the realization that they will be tested on the content; that fact is likely to make the studying experience less enjoyable.

Because of its nature, studying requires individuals to employ specialized learning and study skills. In addition to the well known SQ3R method (Robinson, 1970), there are such cognitive strategies as note-taking, outlining, paraphrasing, imaging, and rereading that might enhance student performance.

While developmental reading and studying are the forms of reading most directly associated with school, there is another form of reading that arises from real-world needs. This form of reading is called functional or survival reading. When we read road signs or find our way on a map, follow a recipe, or order from a menu, we are employing functional reading. Simply stated, functional reading is the reading that is required to accomplish some personal as opposed to instructional goal.

The final form of reading, recreational, is internally motivated. This form of reading is sometimes described as reading for enjoyment. Recreational reading serves no other goal than the reader's entertainment. When you read the comics, a novel, or poetry for pleasure, then you are engaging in recreational reading. There appears to be a strong relationship between the amount of recreational reading individuals engage in and their performance on other types of reading tasks such as studying. Because of this relationship, programs such as Sustained Silent Reading (SSR; McCracken, 1971) were developed to encourage schoolchildren to read more often. The hope of such programs is that students will begin to read more often and, ultimately, more effectively.

Whether developmental, for study, functional, or recreational, reading remains a complex and much investigated cognitive process. Although most reading researchers and educators would agree that reading is an extremely complex activity involving written language, there is much debate as to how the reading process takes place. Of course, how individuals view the reading process will directly affect the aspects of reading that they emphasize, as well as the instructional materials or strategies they select.

An individual's purpose for reading is directly linked to the type of reading (i.e., developmental, for study, functional, or recreational) engaged in. Likewise, an individual's purpose for reading impacts the nature of the process that occurs. Regardless of the type or view of reading, one fact remains clear: in an information-processing age, the ability to read well is an essential life skill. Further, reading and the investigation of the reading process will continue as long as there is written language.

REFERENCES

Anderson, T.H. (1979). Study skills and learning strategies. In H.F. O'Neil & C.D. Spielberger (Eds.), *Cognitive and affective learning strategies* (pp. 77–98). New York: Academic.

Anderson, R.C., Hiebert, E.H., Scott, J.A., & Wilkerson, I.A.G. (1984). *Becoming a nation of readers.* Champaign, IL: University of Illinois, Center for the Study of Reading.

McCracken, R.A. (1971). Initiating sustained silent reading. *Journal of Reading, 14,* 582–583.

Robinson, E.P. (1970). *Effective study* (2nd ed.). New York: Harper & Row.

See also **Reading Disorders; Reading Remediation**

READING AND EYE MOVEMENTS

Cognitive processes may be inferred from observation of a reader's eye movements (Pavlidis, 1985; Rayner, 1985). The reading process requires that readers focus their eyes on a relatively small region of the visual field. The eyes do not make a continuous sweep across the visual field. Instead, they make a series of jumps and pauses from left to right, across the line of print. Each pause is called a fixation. When the eye is fixated, the print is processed. A jump is called a visual saccade (interfixation movement). During the saccade, vision is blurred and detailed processing of the print is not possible. A backward movement and pause is made when a reader fails to process the print during the fixation. The good reader is assumed to have more regular, fewer, and shorter fixations than the poor reader, as well as fewer regressions.

It has been asserted that poor reading can be improved by training eye movement patterns (Getman, 1985). The nature of the relationship between eye movement behavior and reading has been fraught with controversy. Empirical evidence supporting the efficacy of this training with the reading disabled is sparse. Tinker (1958) reviewed studies in which the performance of poor readers was compared before and after such training. The studies that he reviewed suggest that poor readers could be taught to make more efficient eye movements, but that reading ability remained unchanged.

Evidence that eye movements cause reading disabilities is meager. Rayner (1985) reviewed the characteristics of eye movements during reading and concluded that eye movements are not a cause of reading problems. Rather, eye movement characteristics appear to reflect the difficulty that readers have in reading; they are caused by the reading disturbance and not vice versa.

REFERENCES

Getman, G.N. (1985). A commentary on vision training. *Journal of Learning Disabilities, 18,* 505–512.

Pavlidis, G.T. (1985). Eye movements in dyslexia: Their diagnostic significance. *Journal of Learning Disabilities, 18,* 42–50.

Rayner, K. (1985). The role of eye movements in learning to read and reading disability. *Remedial & Special Education, 6,* 53–59.

Tinker, M.A. (1958). Recent studies of eye movements in reading. *Psychological Bulletin, 55,* 215–231.

See also **Reading Disorders**

READING DISORDERS

Reading is a complex mental activity that involves the acquisition, manipulation, and retrieval of language symbols by the reader. When a failure to read exists, there is the tendency to examine that failure in terms of its etiology or cause. Familiar terms such as brain injury, damage, dysfunction, and neuropsychological disorder reflect a neurological etiology. Harris and Sipay (1980) summarize the symptoms of neurological problems as encompassing (1) a history of a difficult birth, perhaps involving prolonged labor, an instrumental delivery, or deformity of the head; (2) prenatal conditions or premature birth; (3) poor balance or general awkwardness; (4) marked language delay; (5) attention deficit, or (6) a history of seizures or brief lapses in consciousness.

According to Spache (1976), there has been a resurgence in emphasis on neurological factors over the past two decades. This resurgence may be accounted for, in part, by the increased awareness of the brain and brain functioning provided by expanding technology. However, Spache cautions that even though brain damage can result in such evident conditions as aphasias, cerebral palsy, or mental retardation, "it appears that almost any failure to learn to read is now being interpreted, by some medical and/or reading specialists, as proof of the presence of brain damage or dysfunction" (p. 177).

Among the most common neurologically related reading disorders are alexia, partial or total loss of reading ability, dyslexia, deficit language production, and learning disability, reading underachievement. Because of the widespread application of the labels of dyslexia and learning disability, we will consider these conditions in more depth.

Dyslexia is certainly one of the most widely applied and perhaps one of the most misused labels for reading problems. References to dyslexic conditions, which can be linked all the way back to Morgan's writings on congenital word blindness and Orton's research on strephosymbolia, have continued to appear with regularity in the literature. Although a multitude of definitions of dyslexia do exist, the root of the word relates to word distortion, and it is frequently associated with letter or word reversals. Critchley (1970) identified two types of dyslexia: developmental and symptomatic. Developmental dyslexia, in his opinion, has an organic source, while symptomatic dyslexia may be influenced by a variety of factors, both organic and psychiatric.

Despite the popularity of the term, many, principally in the educational community, prefer to believe that such a condition as dyslexia does not exist (Cartwright, Cartwright, & Ward, 1995). While it seems likely that the word dyslexia is too easy and invalidly applied by the general populace, it is equally difficult to discount the number of individuals who display an inability to encode, or to manipulate, written language, and problems in decoding language in written form is central to most current definitions of dyslexia (e.g., Reid, 1998).

Some of the same characteristics that apply to the condition of dyslexia apply as well to the condition of learning disability (LD). According to IDEA a specific learning disability is "a disorder in one or more of the basic psychological processes" required to understand language. "The term includes such conditions as perceptual handicaps, brain injury, minimal brain dysfunction, dyslexia, and developmental aphasia" (p. 65083, 1977).

Beyond this legal definition, however, there is ample disagreement about the nature, identification, and treatment procedures for learning disabilities. What is most interesting about LD is that in many ways the condition is primarily an educational problem. What frequently unites the vast numbers of students labeled LD is that there is a significant gap between perceived potential and demonstrated performance. In addition, there is no apparent cause for the significant gap between potential and performance. This gap may be related to a combination of affective and cognitive factors, and may be reflected both in learning and behav-

ioral problems within the learner. Often, teachers and specialists struggle to bring the LD student's performance up to potential through the application of medical and educational treatments.

Reading is a mental undertaking. Beyond its purely neurological aspects, however, the act of reading is very much a sensory activity, relying heavily on visual and auditory stimuli. There are several sensory deficits that can have an immediate and significant effect on an individual's acquisition and maintenance of reading proficiency.

While reading, particularly oral reading, depends on auditory skills, few severe reading problems can be directly linked to auditory factors. However, in our discussion of reading disorders, several auditory classifications should be considered. Those categories are auditory acuity, auditory discrimination, and auditory memory. Auditory acuity refers the state of having good hearing. Auditory discrimination involves the recognition of minute differences in speech sounds. Students' appropriate production of speech sounds is dependent on their ability to hear such differences. Many early reading programs stress phonic analysis, which relies on students' ability to recognize and reproduce the common sound-symbol patterns in language. Consequently, deficits in auditory acuity or discrimination would place the child at a disadvantage.

Also of importance in the reception of auditory stimuli is the individual's ability to mask or eliminate extraneous noises in the environment. As most of us know, the classroom, where so much information is transmitted auditorily, is anything but noise-proof. Focusing on important information in the classroom demands that the learner mask out sounds that would otherwise interfere with the acquisition of salient information. Overall, however, auditory deficits play a much less critical role in reading disorders than the visual or neurological conditions already discussed.

Beyond visual or auditory factors, there are other physical conditions that may contribute to reading problems. Among those conditions are illnesses, general awkwardness, glandular problems, poor nutrition, and allergics. It must be noted, however, that there is little direct evidence that such conditions significantly affect reading performance. For example, illnesses tend to come into play in reading problems when students suffer from prolonged or chronic ailments. Yet, in most instances, prolonged illnesses prevent the learner from attending school, and it is this lack of school attendance that contributes most to reading failures. General awkwardness is not, itself, a factor in reading problems, but it is of importance in that it is frequently a symptom of minimal brain dysfunction. Further, while glandular abnormalities can result in such physical abnormalities as dwarfism and obesity, there is limited understanding of the effects of endocrine treatment on reading disorders. The effect of malnutrition on reading disorders is also difficult to pinpoint since this condition is also closely tied to low socioeconomic status.

Psychosocial behaviors have been frequently related to poor reading performance. However, the significance of emotional and social factors in causing reading disorders is unclear. In part, we know little about the relationship of psychosocial conditions and reading disorders because the techniques for gathering data in these areas are somewhat unreliable. For example, teacher observation, which may be employed to gather information on a learner's emotional or social behavior, can be biased. Further, teachers generally conduct observations without the benefit of training. Interviews may also be used to collect data on these factors. Yet, even when these interviews are performed by training specialists, there is little assurance that what the learner says is an accurate reflection of the internal state. Personality measures are another tool for assessing an individual's emotional and social condition. While such measures may provide a better understanding of the condition of the learner than observations and interviews, the reliability of these measures is still a point of contention.

Two important points need to be made with regard to psychosocial behaviors and reading disorders. First, reading, as it occurs in the context of schooling, remains a social activity. The reader must not only process text to meet personal ends, but must interpret and verify understanding of text for teachers and peers in a way that is seen as appropriate. Therefore, whether or not social and emotional factors are significant in a causal way, they will continue to be related to reading performance. Second, schools tend to see themselves in the business of teaching reading skills, not of treating emotional and social problems. Consequently, in few classrooms or clinics are the emotional and social needs of the problem reader given serious attention. It would seem that those working with problem readers often feel that the emotional and social conditions of these individuals will be taken care of when the specific reading problems are dealt with. Others, however, would argue that to treat only the reading problem without treating the concomitant emotional and social concerns would result in only partial and temporary gains in learner performance. Continued research in the area of psychosocial factors is necessary if we are to understand how best to improve the performance of disabled readers.

REFERENCES

Cartwright, P., Cartwright, C., & Ward, M. (1995). *Educating special learners* (4th ed.). Boston: Wadsworth.

Critchley, M. (1970). *The dyslexic child.* Springfield, IL: Thomas.

Harris, A.J., & Sipay, E.R. (1980). *How to increase reading ability* (7th ed.). New York: Longman.

Reid, G. (1998). *Dyslexia: A practitioner: handbook. 2nd Ed.* New York: Wiley.

Spache, G.D. (1976). *Investigating the issues of reading disabilities.* Boston: Allyn & Bacon.

See also Ambloyopia; Developmental Delay; Dyslexia; Dyspedagogia; Learned Helplessness; Reading Remediation

READING IN THE CONTENT AREAS

For over at least half a century, reading and curriculum specialists have claimed that every teacher is a teacher of reading. Many books, articles, and research reports have been published during this period and courses in teaching reading in the content areas are offered in many colleges of education. Despite these efforts, content teachers have typically maintained that they are teachers of subject matter and not teachers of reading. In a comprehensive and critical review of the research in reading in the content areas, Dupois (1984) concludes that content teachers know too little about reading in general and reading in their subjects in particular. She further reports that teachers feel "helplessness and frustration in the face of students who cannot read classroom materials" (p. 1).

In 1981, 27 national organizations of teachers, supervisors, administrators, and lay groups endorsed a statement called "The Essentials Approach: Rethinking the Curriculum for the 80's", which proclaims the interdependence of skills and content as well as interdependence of knowledge in the several content areas. Interdependence of skills and content refers to the learner's use of reading, writing, talking, and thinking in learning literature, social studies, science, and math. The "Essentials" consortium argued that teachers will teach their subjects more effectively if they teach students the special reading, writing, and study strategies for acquiring and critically responding to knowledge in their disciplines. Ultimately, such a concerted effort will prepare students for a lifetime of learning but helping to make them independent learners. Clearly, the direction proposed is not limited to the relationship between reading and learning but rather extends to writing, studying, talking, and thinking.

The "Essentials" consortium warned against two related practices in many schools that stand in the way of fostering the interdependence principle. The first faulty practice defines basic skills by what can be measured at a time when tests are severely limited in what they can measure. Related to this is the practice of teaching the skills identified by such tests in isolation from significant content, i.e., from texts that look like the tests rather than real content texts. In short, reading skill has been fragmented away from the content areas and further fragmented into discrete subskills. Goodlad (1983) documented this state of the schools, which he characterized as being preoccupied with lower intellectual processes and boredom of epidemic proportions. The problem is exacerbated in special and mainstream classrooms for special educational populations, where it has been erroneously believed that there needs to be more emphasis on isolated subskills to remediate the poor reading skills of these students.

In 1985, the Commission on Reading of the National Academy of Education published *Becoming A Nation of Readers* (Anderson, Hiebert, Scott, & Wilkinson, 1985), which synthesized current sociopsycholinguistic theory and research on learning to read and reading to learn. This document provides a theoretical rationale for teachers who would implement the "Essentials" approach.

Reading is not defined as a product or as a set of sub-skills to be tested but rather as "a process for constructing meaning from written texts . . . a complex skill requiring the coordination of a number of interrelated sources of information" (p. 7). Those sources lie in the reader, in the text, in fellow students, and in the teacher. Readers bring to the reading task knowledge of the world, of language, of strategies for reading various texts, and of their teachers' purposes and expectations. They also bring their own interests and purposes. Texts present world knowledge in special ways; for example, literary texts have different conventions and structures from informational texts. They vary in purpose, content, and style. Fellow students constitute a community of comprehenders. Through interaction they can share relevant prior knowledge, text knowledge, and reading strategies.

The role of teachers is to orchestrate these interrelated sources, developing productive transactions among readers and texts that lead to more efficient strategies for information processing by students. Information processing involves such active mental searches as drawing on prior knowledge, predicting, questioning, elaborating, transforming, structuring, restating, summarizing, synthesizing, reflecting, and critically evaluating. In practical terms, content teachers can teach reading and study by modeling strategies that incorporate one or more of these searches by having students practice strategies in pairs and in small groups as well as on their own and by having students reflect on and share their experiences with each other in using the strategies.

Reading in the content areas today deals with how teachers can organize and plan for instruction so as to relate the basic academic competencies (language processes of not only reading, but also writing, listening, and speaking) to learning the basic academic subjects. That is true for all students, including special education students in mainstream classrooms as well as in learning centers.

From the point of view of special education, the proposed ways of teaching content reading would have the effect of providing for more learning and less isolation and fragmentation, less stigmatization and separation from peers, less isolation of teachers, and less fragmentation of language.

REFERENCES

Anderson, R.C., Hiebert, E.H., Scott, J.A., Wilkinson, I.A.G. (1985). *Becoming a nation of readers: The report of the Commission on Reading.* Washington, DC: National Institute of Education.

Dupois, M.M. (Ed.). (1984). *Reading in the content areas: Research for teachers.* Newark, DE: International Reading Association.

Goodlad, J.I. (1983). What some schools and classrooms teach. *Educational Leadership, 40*(7), 8–19.

See also **Reading Disorders; Reading Remediation**

READING MILESTONES (SECOND EDITION)

Reading Milestones, a basal reading series developed by Stephen P. Quigley, Cynthia M. King, Patricia L. McAnally, and Susan Rose, was designed specifically for individuals with hearing impairment and originally published in the early 1980s by Dormac, Inc. The series was then acquired by Pro-Ed, Inc. in 1995.

Reading Milestones is the most popular reading program of its kind. This successful alternative, language-controlled program is designed to take readers to approximately a fifth-grade reading level. It is especially effective for students with hearing impairments and language delays and is also widely used with others who have special language and reading needs, including individuals with learning disabilities and students learning English as a second language (ESL).

The *Reading Milestones* program includes student readers, teacher's guides, placement tests, and student workbooks at each of six levels. The *Reading Bridge* series includes extension materials for students reading at grade levels 4–5. Additional resources that adhere to the structured approach presented in *Reading Milestones* include the *Simple Language Fairy Tales, Simple English Classics,* and *Most Loved Classics* series.

Extensive revisions were made in the second edition of the program based on recent research, new practices in reading, and feedback from users of the series. Because most students with hearing impairments and/or other special needs lack a basic knowledge base in oral/aural aspects of language, there can be a resulting gap in their language experience and the assumptions inherent in the materials they are given to read. *Reading Milestones* was designed to minimize this gap by beginning with the simplest possible language to ensure initial success in reading and by increasing language acquisition. Students are guided to progress in small increments, accompanied by constant reinforcement and review of concepts, vocabulary, and language constructions, to ensure continuing success and motivation.

REFERENCE

Quigley, S., & King, C. (Eds.). (1991). *Reading milestones* (2nd ed.). Austin, TX: Pro-Ed.

READING REMEDIATION

Reading can be described as an essential and highly complex cognitive activity. As a cognitive task, the outcomes of the reading act require the successful completion of many simple and complex linguistic skills (Perfetti, 1983). To illustrate, consider the task of reading aloud the word *dog.* To accomplish this seemingly simple task, a reader must know the letters of the alphabet, must have internalized the sound/symbol patterns common to the English language, and must be able to decode or sound out the word accurately. Decoding alone can be a troublesome venture in the English language, where exceptions appear to out-number phonetic rules. Further, if an understanding of dog is also required, then the reader must relate the abstract symbols and sounds to the concept of dog stored in long-term memory.

If many skills are required to read and understand a single word, then the skills necessary to make sense of the previous paragraph are far more extensive. It is therefore not surprising that some individuals never acquire reading proficiency. Those individuals who consistently experience difficulties in processing print are part of a population of learners who require special instruction. This special instruction is referred to as reading remediation.

Reading remediation is a branch of language instruction that is concerned with the identification and treatment of reading problems.

Even before an individual is asked to read, there are factors that are likely to enhance or inhibit reading performance. Rupley and Blair (1983) identify two broad categories of variables that relate to reading performance: functional and facilitative factors. Functional factors are those variables that actually pertain to reading. Sight vocabulary, reading rate, and oral language development are examples of functional factors. In many ways, these functional variables are the outcome of other variables that are not directly part of the reading performance but contribute to it. These variables are called facilitative factors, and they are of particular importance in reading remediation. Facilitative factors fall under such broad headings as physical, cognitive, and emotional characteristics. Within each of these broad areas there are conditions that can significantly influence reading performance.

Cognitive factors also contribute significantly to the reading process. The cognitive ability an individual brings to the reading act is a major determinant of the level of proficiency expected. While there is no one-to-one correspondence between intelligence and reading ability, the relationship between the two is strong indeed. Cognitive factors may be assessed by means of achievement or intelligence test data, or school performance records.

Similarly, an individual's emotional well-being can positively or negatively affect the ability to read. The significant influence of affective factors on learning should not be ignored in the evaluation of reading problems (Cartwright, Cartwright, & Ward, 1995; Reid, 1998). Learners who have the cognitive potential may lack the desire or commitment that is required to do well in reading. Parent/student interviews and self-concept and personality tests may be used to gather information on the emotional condition of a reader.

When a reading problem is suspected, it is prudent first to determine whether existing physical, cognitive, and emotional as well as socioeconomic, cultural, or educational factors are potential sources of the problem. The systematic assessment of functional and facilitative factors is part of reading diagnosis, which, in turn, is a major component in the remediation cycle.

Much of the language of reading remediation is borrowed from medical science. The medical influence is particularly apparent in the cycle of reading remediation. This cycle is comprised of three phases: diagnosis, prescription, and treatment.

The diagnosis or data-collection phase of the remediation cycle refers to the systematic assessment of existing conditions: a search for evidence that might indicate the source of a reader's problems. It is in this phase that information about the reader and reading performance is gathered and analyzed. Knowledge about the reader may be collected in a spontaneous fashion within the classroom, or it may be amassed through a formal and extensive procedure.

On the basis of careful diagnosis, the second phase of the cycle, the prescription or program-specification phase, is put into place. Prescription is the delineation of the appropriate instructional treatment to be administered. It is expected that a carefully prescribed instructional program will ameliorate the reader's problems. As with the diagnostic procedure, the instructional plan may be informal or formal in nature. An informal prescription might entail little more than the teacher's specification of instructional objectives that seem appropriate for a reader. A formal prescription, by comparison, may be an elaborate instructional program to be administered by a specialist within a clinic or resource room.

Finally, there is the treatment or program-implementation phase of the cycle. In this phase, the prescribed instructional treatment is carried out and its effectiveness evaluated. From the knowledge gained during instruction and evaluation, additional information about the reader and reading performance is gathered. Based on these new data, a revised diagnosis may be rendered and the remediation cycle begins anew. This remediation cycle forms the basis of reading instruction, whether it occurs in the regular classroom or in the resource room (Cheek & Cheek, 1980).

Diagnosis can take place at several levels of complexity. Those levels, in order of increasing formality, are informal, classroom, and clinical diagnosis (Wilson & Cleland, 1985). In the previous section, the data gathering was apt to be part of the more extensive form of clinical reading diagnosis. Meeting the needs of most readers does not often require that diagnosis reach such a formal level, however. Rather, clinical diagnosis should be the last stage is the diagnostic procedure. For the most part, serving the needs of the reader entails only the first two levels in the sequence of diagnosis, informal, and classroom diagnosis.

Informal diagnosis is an ongoing process that takes place continuously in the regular reading classroom. This stage of diagnosis encompasses the teacher's monitoring of reading instruction to determine whether that instruction is appropriate for the learner. If found inappropriate or ineffective, the instruction should be adjusted in some fashion to suit more adequately the learner's needs and capabilities.

What if the minor adjustments in reading instruction were not successful in improving the situation? What would the teacher do next? In the second stage of diagnosis, the teacher would conduct some testing within the classroom in an attempt to identify the nature of the reading problem. Classroom diagnosis may involve the use of teacher-made or commercial tests that can be administered and interpreted by teachers who have no specialized knowledge of reading or assessment. Perhaps, as in the preceding case, the teacher constructs a cloze test (Tierney, Readence, & Dishner, 1980) from the basal text. From this cloze test, the teacher determines that the reading book that the child has been assigned is too difficult. The teacher then moves the child to a more appropriate reading group and the problem with oral reading seems to disappear.

Should the classroom teacher's attempts to identify or remediate the reading problem fail, then it is time to call in a specialist. It is at this point in the diagnostic sequence that a clinical assessment of the reading problem should be conducted. Following the assessment of facilitative factors, a battery of reading tests are given. Among the reading skills frequently tested in a clinical diagnosis are sight vocabulary, oral reading, silent reading, listening comprehension, and word analysis skills. The information amassed in diagnosis permits the clinical specialist to ascribe a remediation program for the learner that is likely to improve reading performance.

Because of the major role that diagnosis plays in the remediation cycle, it is imperative that the assessment provides valid and reliable information. Bond and Tinker (1973) have outlined some guiding principles for clinical diagnosis that should result in the more effective remediation of reading problems. Many of these principles can also be applied to informal and classroom diagnosis.

1. Diagnosis should be directed toward formulating methods of improvement.
2. Diagnosis should involve more than an appraisal of reading skills and abilities.
3. Diagnosis should be efficient and effective.
4. Diagnosis should be continuous.
5. Diagnosis should seek to identify patterns of behavior.

The determination to place a learner in a remedial reading program is often the result of a group decision-making process similar to that followed for other categories of special learners. While the primary responsibility for reading remediation falls to the reading specialist, the remediation program can and should involve parents, outside specialists, content-area teachers, and school administrators. Both long- and short-term goals are established for the reader, focusing on cognitive, metacognitive, and affective needs. Progress toward these goals are carefully documented, so that accurate evaluation of the program and the learner is possible.

The last reader profile is that of the slow learner. Like the remedial reader, the slow learner demonstrates reading skills that are far below grade level. However, unlike the remedial reader, the slow learner's reading performance is commensurate with cognitive ability. In other words, the slow learner is basically performing up to his or her potential.

As long as there is the complex process of reading there will be learners who encounter difficulties and who will require special reading instruction. It is the purpose of effective reading remediation programs to provide appropriate instruction to those learners for whom proficient reading is a goal yet to be achieved.

REFERENCES

Bond, G.L., & Tinker, M.A. (1973). *Reading difficulties: Their diagnosis and correction* (3rd ed.). Englewood Cliffs, NJ: Prentice-Hall.

Cartwright, P., Cartwright, C., & Ward, M. (1995) *Educating special learners* 4th ed. Boston: Wadsworth.

Cheek, M.C., & Cheek, E.H. (1980). *Diagnostic-prescriptive reading instruction.* Dubuque, IA: Brown.

Perfetti, C.A. (1983). Individual differences in verbal processes. In R.F. Dillon & R.R. Schmeck (Eds.), *Individual differences in cognition* (Vol. I, pp. 65–104). New York: Academic.

Reid, G. (1998). *Dyslexia: A practitioner: handbook* (2nd ed.). New York: Wiley.

Rupley, W.H., & Blair, T.R. (1983). *Reading diagnosis and remediation: Classroom and clinic* (2nd ed.). Boston: Houghton Mifflin.

Tierney, R.J., Readence, J.E., & Dishner, E.K. (1980). *Reading strategies and practices: A guide for improving instruction.* Boston: Allyn & Bacon.

Wilson, R.M., & Cleland, C.S. (1985). *Diagnostic and remedial reading for classroom and clinic* (5th ed.). Columbus, OH: Merrill.

See also Diagnostic-Prescriptive Teaching; Diagnostic Remedial Approach; Reading Disorders; Reading in the Content Areas; Remediation, Deficit-Centered Models of

REALITY THERAPY

Reality therapy is a method of psychotherapy that stresses the importance of clients learning more useful behaviors to deal with their current situations. Reality therapy stresses internal motivation, behavior change, and development of the "success identity." In terms of philosophical or theoretical stance, reality therapy can be described as strongly cognitive or rational in its approach, appealing to the client's reason and emphasizing the possibility of meaningful change, not just in feelings, but in behavior. The therapist takes an active, directive role as teacher, but remains supportive and non-punitive.

William Glasser, a physician, developed the theory of reality therapy over a period of years beginning with his psychiatric training. Both Glasser's reaction against traditional psychoanalytic psychotherapy and his experiences in working with delinquent youths at a California school for girls probably played major roles in the development of reality therapy (Belkin, 1975).

The therapist is viewed as a coach or instructor who provides clients with assistance and encouragement in evaluating the usefulness of their current behavior in satisfying their needs. Where the appropriateness of change is recognized, the therapist assists in the development and execution of plans for remediation. Development of the client's strengths and feelings of self-worth leading to a success identity is a key responsibility of the therapist.

Reality therapy has grown in popularity and influence. It is particularly well received in schools and the criminal justice system, and with counselors who work to rehabilitate handicapped individuals. This psychotherapeutic approach lends itself to short-term, direct, and active therapy.

REFERENCE

Belkin, G.S. (1975). *Practical counseling in the schools.* Dubuque, IA: Brown.

See also Psychosocial Adjustment; Psychotherapy

RECEPTIVE–EXPRESSIVE EMERGENT LANGUAGE TEST–SECOND EDITION (REEL-2)

The *Receptive–Expressive Emergent Language Test–Second Edition* (REEL-2; Bzoch & League, 1991) is a multidimensional analysis of emergent language. The REEL-2 is specifically designed for use with a broad range of infants and toddlers up to age 3 who are at risk. The instrument is a system of measurement and intervention planning based on neurolinguistic development to identify young children who have specific language problems based on specific language behaviors. Results are obtained from a parent interview and are given in terms of an Expressive Language Age, a Receptive Language Age, and a Combined Language Age.

Bachman (1995) reviewed the instrument and summarized that the REEL-2 covers a wide range of behaviors and could be used with direct observation to elicit information for developing a qualitative description of a child's early language development.

REFERENCES

Bachman, L.F. (1995). Review of the Receptive–Expressive Emergent Language Test, Second Edition. In J.C. Conoley & J.C. Impara (Eds.), *The twelfth mental measurements yearbook* (pp. 843–845). Lincoln: Buros Institute of Mental Measurements, University of Nebraska Press.

Bzoch, K.R., & League, R. (1991). *Receptive–Expressive Emergent Language Scale–Second Edition.* Austin, TX: Pro-Ed.

RECEPTIVE LANGUAGE DISORDERS

A language disorder in which there is a severe loss or impairment in the understanding or use of language owing to brain injury or dysfunction is known as aphasia. This disorder may be dichotomized into expressive or motor aphasia, in which the ability to form speech is impaired, and receptive or sensory aphasia, in which the ability to comprehend the spoken word is affected. In adults, aphasia is acquired through brain damage and results in cessation or regression from a prior ability to use language. In children, language disorders may be acquired as a result of brain injury, or they may be developmental in nature. That is, because of abnormal development or injury to the language centers of the central nervous system prenatally, perinatally, or postnatally during the first year, the child has difficulty in developing normal understanding and use of language (Gaddes, 1980). This condition is also known as a primary or congenital language disorder (Deuel, 1983). When the dysfunction in the language centers of the brain is mild, it may be referred to as a learning disability.

Receptive language disorders may be classified in several ways. Johnson and Myklebust (1967) discuss a generalized deficit in auditory learning in which a child hears but does not interpret. Other children, less affected, can interpret nonverbal, social sounds, but cannot relate the spoken word to an appropriate unit of experience. In cases of less severe receptive language deficits, the inability to comprehend may be limited to abstract language or to specific parts of speech. Benson (1983) cites four clinically distinguishable comprehension disturbances and suggests a neuroanatomical locus of pathology for each. These are (1) receptive disturbances, involving comprehension and repetition of spoken language; (2) perceptive disturbances (also known as Wernicke's aphasia), in which comprehension of written and spoken language is involved; (3) semantic disturbances, characterized by an inability to understand the meaning of spoken and written language despite relatively normal ability to repeat spoken language; and (4) syntactic disturbances, involving difficulties with syntactical structures and sequencing. Benson emphasizes that there is much overlap among these comprehension problems, and they are rarely found in isolation.

Receptive language disorders frequently are observed in conjunction with other disabilities. In the developmental hierarchy of language outlined by Myklebust (1954), expressive language follows and is dependent on inner and receptive language. In a similar way, reading and written language are dependent on the acquisition of earlier levels of language. Therefore, it is not surprising that reading, writing, and the problem-solving areas of arithmetic may be affected by receptive language disorders. Johnson and Myklebust (1967) suggest that auditory cognitive skills, including discrimination, rhyming, and blending, often are correlates of receptive language disorders. Such skills are prerequisite to the success of an auditory-phonetic reading program and indicate the need for a global language approach to instruction.

REFERENCES

Benson, D.F. (1983). The neural basis of spoken and written language. In H.R. Myklebust (Ed.), *Progress in learning disabilities* (Vol. 5, pp. 3–25). New York: Grune & Stratton.

Deuel, R.K. (1983). Aphasia in childhood. In H.R. Myklebust (Ed.), *Progress in learning disabilities* (Vol. 5, pp. 29–43). New York: Grune & Stratton.

Gaddes, W.H. (1980). *Learning disabilities and brain function: A neuropsychological approach* (2nd ed.). New York: Springer-Verlag.

Johnson, D.J., & Myklebust, H.R. (1967). *Learning disabilities: Educational principles and practices.* New York: Grune & Stratton.

Myklebust, H.R. (1954). *Auditory disorders in children: A manual for differential diagnosis.* New York: Grune & Stratton.

See also Aphasia; Auditory Discrimination;
Auditory Perception; Developmental Aphasia

RECIPROCAL DETERMINISM

Reciprocal determinism is a model of human behavior that effectively synthesizes the medical, behavioral, and ecological models into a single integrated perspective. Proposed by Bandura (1978) as a result of his extensive theoretical and empirical work on social learning theory, reciprocal determinism postulates that human activity is a function of the mutual and reciprocal interactions that occur between a person's behavior (B), cognitive and other internal events related to the person (P), and the external environment (E). The model hypothesizes that human behavior results from an ongoing interaction among the B, P, and E factors in each person's life. According to this point of view, meaningful insight into a person's behavior is best attained if one can discern (1) the salient B, P, and E factors operating on and within that individual and (2) how those factors interact and influence each other.

The reciprocal determinism model holds important theoretical and practical insights for special educators. Consider, for example, the hypothetical case of a fourth-grade boy who has developed reading difficulties. Approaching this child's problem from a medical model perspective would lead special educators to examine the IQ, neurological status, health, etc. Those who subscribe to a behavioral model would focus primarily on information such as the nature of classroom interactions with teachers, peers, and academic materials during reading lessons. If special educators were to use the ecological model, it would lead them to consider the nature of the school's reading program, the district's resources in the area of reading, the home environment, etc. From the perspective of reciprocal determinism, however, special educators can see that each of these pieces of information may be important and that none should be overlooked.

Even more significant, the reciprocal determinism model highlights that one cannot really understand the causal factors behind children's educational and psychological difficulties without understanding how the B, P, and E factors affect each other. For example, the behavior of this hypothetical child in reading class (B) is continuously affected by his intellectual abilities (P), which are in turn either heightened or diminished as a function of the school's academic programs and his home environment (E), which are themselves influenced by how the child behaves both in and out of school (B). By sensitizing special educators to this dynamic interaction among B, P, and E forces, reciprocal determinism provides a comprehensive framework within which children's problems can be conceptualized, assessed, diagnosed, and treated (Reynolds, Gutkin, Elliott, & Witt, 1984).

REFERENCES

Bandura, A. (1978). The self-system in reciprocal determinism. *American Psychologist, 33,* 344–358.

Reynolds, C.R., Gutkin, T.B., Elliott, S.N., & Witt, J.C. (1984). *School psychology: Essentials of theory and practice.* New York: Wiley.

See also Behavioral Modification; Ecological
Assessment; Ecological Education of the
Handicapped; Humanistic Special Education

RECLAIMING CHILDREN AND YOUTH: JOURNAL OF EMOTIONAL AND BEHAVIORAL PROBLEMS

Reclaiming Children and Youth: Journal of Emotional and Behavioral Problems is a quarterly journal publishing practical, research-validated strategies for professionals and policy leaders concerned with young people in conflict within school, family, or community. Each issue is topical. The journal was first published in 1992 under the title of *Journal of Emotional and Behavioral Problems.* In 1995, the title was changed to the present title to better reflect the journal's emphasis on a positive, reclaiming environment in which changes are made to meet the needs of both youth and society. The journal is owned by Journal of Emotional and Behavioral Problems, Inc. and is published by Pro-Ed, Inc.

RECORDING FOR THE BLIND (RFB)

Recording for the Blind (RFB) is an organization that was founded in 1951 for the purpose of recording textbooks at no charge for persons unable to use ordinary print, whether because of visual, perceptual, or physical conditions. Kirchner and Simon (1984), in a study conducted in 1982–1983, stated that RFB serves over 7300 students in higher education; 57% of the students served are visually impaired.

Recording programs such as RFB are invaluable to the education of visually impaired learners. Other service organizations provide audio-formatted materials for this population (Ferrell, 1985). The Talking Book Program, sponsored by the American Printing House for the Blind, is a source of materials for parents and teachers serving visually impaired students. American Printing House also distributes the variable speech control cassette recorder to be used with their audio cassettes. The National Library Service for the Blind and Physically Handicapped, of the Library of Congress, offers free library services to visually impaired persons. The Library of Congress also lends special talking book record and cassette players to applicants. Many of the materials available from these organizations are popular leisure books, magazines, religious materials, and newspapers.

Addresses for these organizations are:

American Printing House for the Blind
1839 Frankfort Avenue
Louisville, KY 40206

National Library Service for the Blind and Physically Handicapped
Library of Congress
Washington, DC 20542

Recording for the Blind, Inc.
215 E. 58th Street
New York, NY 10022

REFERENCES

Ferrell, K. (1985). *Reach out and teach: Meeting the training needs of parents of visually and multiply handicapped young children.* New York: American Foundation for the Blind.

Kirchner, C., & Simon, Z. (1984). Blind and visually handicapped college students—Part I: Estimated numbers. *Journal of Visual Impairment & Blindness, 78,* 78–81.

See also **Blind; Versabraille**

RECREATION, THERAPEUTIC

Therapeutic recreation is a form of play or physical activity that is used to improve a variety of behaviors that may occur in the cognitive, emotional, social, and physical domains. These activities include games, dancing, horseback riding, and a wide range of other individual and group games and sports.

The intellectual domain may be influenced through gross and fine motor movement activities. There are many theories of cognitive development occurring in sequential order in which motor abilities are the basis for higher thought processes (Kephart, 1960; Piaget, 1950). Theoretically, motor skills help to develop higher skill levels in handicapped persons by increasing memory, language, and problem solving (Major & Walsh, 1977). Forms of recreation may be used as an alternate to more traditional teaching methods. Humphrey (1976) used games and dancing to aid in reversal difficulties, sequencing difficulties, left and right directionality, and improvement in following direction skills. Physical movement helped to present concepts and skills in a more concrete form. Through imitation and role playing, children were able to use intellectual concepts they had already learned and developed (Yawkey, 1979).

Other forms of learning may be influenced by physical activities and games that have the objective of increasing motivation and attention span. Naville and Blom (1968) stressed educational achievements of concentration, willpower, and self-control through movement.

Emotions can be influenced through recreational activities, which may help individuals improve self-concepts and self-confidence. Being aware of one's body and feeling good about one's self can be associated with the pleasure of recreation. Socially, organized group activities may offer social skills learning through structured interpersonal play. Individuals have opportunities to work together, follow leaders, engage in appropriate behaviors, and develop various forms of self-expression. Recreation can be used not only as a medium for communication but also to help integrate the handicapped with the nonhandicapped and teach activities to decrease isolation.

Physically, recreational activities have endless limits. Movement may help individuals increase coordination and range of motion of body movement. For example, water sports, swimming, or water therapy can be extremely valuable to a variety of handicapped children and youths, as can free motion activities such as creative dance. These activities can increase physical strength and flexibility; having a strong, attractive body correlates with a positive self-image.

Specific programs such as bowling, folk dancing, and even competitive sports have incorporated recreational activities as therapy for different populations; a good example of one of these programs is the Special Olympics for various groups of handicapped students. Jacques-Dalcroze (1930) first developed eurhythmics for the blind to increase self-confidence and expression through music and rhythm. Gollnitz (1970) developed a rhythmic-psychomotor therapy that combined movement, music, and rhythm for individuals with psychic and developmental disorders. Lefco (1974) followed the idea of the integration of the body and mind when she used dance therapy to promote mental and physical well being. The Cove Schools in Racine, Wisconsin, and Evanston, Illinois, were designed for brain-injured students to provide play experiences that may have been missed because of slow rates of development. The Halliwick method deals with the swimming ability of the physically handicapped. Norway has a horseback riding school for the disabled. Mann, Berger, and Proger (1974) offer a comprehensive review of the research on the influence of physical education on the cognitive, physical, affective, and social domains in which movement was significant in helping the handicapped with different variables in these areas.

In summary, therapeutic recreation includes structured physical and social activities that are designed to have as objectives the enjoyment of leisure time, improved movement, and development of physical strength and social skills. Recreation, adaptive physical education, and physical activities increase or improve social, physical, and mental abilities.

REFERENCES

Gollnitz, G. (1970). Fundamentals of rhythmic-psychomotor music therapy: An objective-oriented therapy for children and adolescents with developmental disturbances. *Acta Paedopsychiatrica. The International Journal of Child Psychiatry, 37,* 130–134.

Humphrey, J.H. (1976). *Improving learning ability through compensatory physical education.* Springfield: IL: Thomas.

Jacques-Dalcroze, E. (1930). *Eurhythmics: Art and education.* London: Chatto & Windum.

Kephart, N. (1960). *The slower learner in the classroom.* Columbus, OH: Merrill.

Lefco, H. (1974). *Dance therapy.* Chicago, IL: Nelson-Hall.

Major, S., & Walsh, M. (1977). *Learning activities for the learning disabled.* Belmont, CA: Fearon-Pitman.

Mann, L., Berger, R., & Proger, B. (1974). Physical education intervention with the exceptional child. In L. Mann & D.A. Sabatino (Eds.), *The second review of special education.* NY: Grune & Stratton.

Naville, S., & Blom, G.E. (1968). *Psychomotor education: Theory and practice.* Denver, CO: University of Colorado Medical Center.

Piaget, J. (1950). *Psychology of intelligence.* New York: Harcourt & Brace.

Yawkey, T.D. (1979). More in play as intelligence in children. *Journal of Creative Behavior, 13,* 247–256.

See also **Equine Therapy; Recreational Therapy; Recreation for the Handicapped**

RECREATIONAL READING FOR THE HANDICAPPED

According to most dictionaries, recreation is an agreeable art, a pastime, or a diversion that affords relaxation and enjoyment. However, most handicapped students would not link recreation with reading because books symbolize failure and emotional distress (Schanzer, 1973). Therefore, the goal of education should be to encourage students to be independent readers who regularly choose to read. For this to occur, it is necessary for teachers, librarians, and parents to become involved.

Teachers are likely to be the only reading models for many students (Smith, Smith, & Mikulecky, 1978). Therefore, they should be active reading models, talking about what they have been reading and allowing students to see them carrying personal books or magazines. In the classroom, free reading time, when everyone reads without the threat of book reports or lengthy comprehension checks, should be scheduled (Smith et al., 1978). Teachers should be sure to have large classroom libraries of recreational reading materials. However, standard, off-the-shelf novels or biographies present frustrating hurdles such as reading level, subject matter, and length (Hallenbeck, 1983). Therefore, such books should be didactic, with important words repeated several times. The themes should relate closely to the lives of the students and the sentences should be short with simple verb tenses. In addition, pronouns should be placed near the nouns that they modify and characters should be human beings, not abstract things or ideas. Finally, the style of writing should be conversational (Slick, 1969). This will help to eliminate the selection of reading material that is too difficult.

Librarians can be helpful in encouraging recreational reading among handicapped students because they come in contact with all students in an average school week. The librarian should remove all stumbling blocks so that special education students feel free to use the library. For example,

the borrowing period may have to be adjusted because these students may need more time to complete a book. In addition, it is important to eliminate the frustration of book selection by establishing a one-to-one relationship with the student and having enough high-interest low-reading-level books available. As special education students begin to frequent the library, praise and commendation should be given. In addition, individual guidance and personal service are needed. It would also be helpful for the librarian to supply the special education class with a list of the new books in the library so that students can request a particular book when visiting the library. Finally, it is helpful to have students act as library aides to assure them that they are needed, are helpful, and are appreciated (Slick, 1969).

For many students, reading takes place at school or not at all. If reading is to become an enjoyable and lifelong experience, it is necessary for reading to occur at home. However, pressure from the parents to read is not the answer since pressure violates the spirit of free reading (Haimowitz, 1977). As early as the 1940s in Japan, there were two home reading programs. One was a 20-minute mother-child reading process in which parents and children sat for 20 minutes a day and the children read to the mothers. The second was scheduled reading hours once a week in which everyone in the family read (Smith et al., 1978). Programs such as these and others initiated by PTA groups and community groups can be helpful in encouraging recreational reading among handicapped students.

REFERENCES

Haimowitz, B. (1977, December). Motivating reluctant readers in inner-city classes. *Journal of Reading, 21,* 221–230.

Hallenbeck, M.J. (1983, March). A free reading journal for secondary LD students. *Academic Therapy, 18,* 479–485.

Schanzer, S.S. (1973, Fall). Independent reading for children with learning disabilities. *Academic Therapy, 9,* 109–114.

Slick, M.H. (1969, April 10). *Recreational reading materials for special education students.* Pittsburgh: University of Pittsburgh, School of Library Science. (ERIC Document Reproduction Service No. ED 046 173)

Smith, C.B., Smith, S.L., & Mikulecky, L. (1978). *Teaching reading in secondary school content subjects: A book-thinking process.* New York: Holt, Rinehart, & Winston.

See also **High Interest-Low Vocabulary Reading; Library Services for the Handicapped; Reading**

RECREATIONAL THERAPY

Recreational activities are necessary for the total wellbeing of any individual. They provide an important source of pleasure and relaxation. Most individuals learn how to use recreational activities from a lifetime of learning how to play. But as with other skill areas, the handicapped often experience difficulties in using free time appropriately. They may have been sheltered during much of their developmental period, or their disability may have prohibited them from acquiring the skills necessary for participation in recreational activities. Consequently, many handicapped individuals will require intentional and systematic instruction if they are to acquire those skills. In that regard, recreational therapy is a planned intervention process developed to promote the growth and development of recreational skills and leisure-time activities.

Recreational therapy attempts to eliminate or minimize an individual's disability. It uses recreation to assist the handicapped in changing certain physical, emotional, or social characteristics so they may pursue leisure activities and live as independently as possible (National Recreation and Park Association, 1978). Recreational therapy is also concerned with helping the handicapped participate in activities with the nonhandicapped as much as possible. This integration allows the handicapped to move into the recreational mainstream and become more involved in community recreational activities. Therefore, recreational therapy may be recommended to help the handicapped to maintain their physical skills, interact socially, and increase academic progress.

REFERENCE

National Recreation and Park Association. (1978). The therapeutic recreator. In W.L. Heward & M.D. Orlansky (1980). *Exceptional children.* Columbus: Charles E. Merrill.

See also Equine Therapy; Occupational Therapy

RECREATION FOR THE HANDICAPPED

Recreation for the handicapped includes individual and group programs of outdoor, social, sports, or educational activities conducted during leisure time. Such programs conducted in medically supervised institutions are identified as therapeutic recreation while those conducted in schools and the community are called community programs (Pomeroy, 1983). The overall goal of recreation programs is to enable each handicapped person the right to participate at the lowest effective care level as independently as abilities and disabilities permit (Stein, 1985).

Recreation services for the handicapped should be distinguished from therapeutic recreation. The latter is a means of intervention to bring about desired changes. In schools, therapeutic recreation is medically prescribed and programmed by recreational therapists. In contrast, the purpose of recreation programs for the handicapped is to provide these students with opportunities to realize their leisure and recreational needs whether on an individual or group basis. Recreation programs in schools or communities for handicapped students are voluntary in nature and programmed by recreational leaders.

Prior to 1960, most recreation programs for the handicapped were segregated or held in institutions (Robinson & Skinner, 1985). Since 1960 legislative forces and concerned professional organizations have sought to deinstitutionalize

and desegregate such programs. With the enactment of PL 94-142, recreation came to be considered as a related service in the schools. During the late 1970s the federal government provided grants to colleges and universities to set up training programs for recreation therapists and adapted physical education teachers and for the development of regional information and resource centers (Robinson & Skinner, 1985). Private organizations such as Wheelchair Sports and the Association for the Help of Retarded Children have also been active in promoting recreational programs in schools and communities.

Although only 5 to 10% of all handicapped persons are being reached by existing park and recreation service providers, the prognosis for the future appears to be positive. Statutes to promote barrier design, and the changing attitudes of service providers and participants, seem to indicate a trend toward more handicapped people availing themselves of school or community recreation programs.

Delineated on the basis of the degree of supervision required, there are four types of recreation programs for the handicapped. First, there are special programs limited to persons with specific disabilities, e.g. blind, deaf, or physically disabled persons. These programs often revolve around a single activity for the purposes of fun, socialization, and skill development. Second, there are semi-integrated services that allow the handicapped to mix with the nonhandicapped in activities that lend themselves to integration. Third, some communities have a buddy system where handicapped persons participate with nonhandicapped persons in the same activities and programs; scouting and Camp Fire Girls have used the buddy system extensively in their programs. The fourth type of program is one that provides opportunities for total integration in all activities, as is the case in many national parks and recreation areas.

The major categories of recreational activities for the handicapped listed by Russell (1983) are sports and games, hobbies, music, outdoor recreation, mental and literary recreation, arts and crafts, dance, and drama.

Handicapped programs at the national and international levels are usually of a competitive nature. Examples of these include the Para-olympics, which meets every 4 years in a different part of the world and has four disability groups: deaf, amputee, cerebral palsy, and paraplegic competition. Wheelchair Sports, sponsored by the National Wheelchair Athletic Association, provides competition in track, basketball, and weightlifting. The National Handicapped Sports and Recreation Association promotes sports and recreational activities through 29 regional offices across the United States.

Most state and regional programs are part of national structures such as the Special Olympics program. Some state programs are resident or day camps or outdoor activity centers. There are very few recreation centers that exclusively serve the handicapped. The majority are in large urban areas e.g., the Anchor Program in New York City and the Recreation Center for the Handicapped in San Francisco.

Many schools, colleges, and communities sponsor local recreational programs for the handicapped. Community swim programs seem to be the most popular and widespread. Hunter College in New York City conducts a recreation program for mentally retarded and physically disabled teenagers from the city, most of whom are minorities.

REFERENCES

Pomeroy, J. (1983). Community recreation for persons with disabilities. In E. Pan, T. Backer, & C. Vosh (Eds.), *Annual review of rehabilitation* (pp. 241–291). St. Louis: Mosby.

Robinson, F., & Skinner, S. (1985). *Community recreation for the handicapped.* Springfield, IL: Thomas.

Russell, R. (1983). *Planning programs in recreation.* St. Louis: Mosby.

Stein, J. (1985). Mainstreaming in recreational settings. *Journal of Physical Education, Recreation & Dance,* 5(56), 25–27.

See also **Equine Therapy; Music Therapy; Olympics, Special**

REDL, FRITZ (1902–1988)

Fritz Redl was born and educated in Austria, and obtained PhD in philosophy and psychology in 1925 from the University of Vienna. From 1925 to 1936, he trained as an analyst at the Wiener Psychoanalysis Institute, and was strongly influenced by the founders of child analytic work, particularly Anna Freud and August Aichhorn.

Redl maintained an interest in group psychology throughout his career. After coming to the United States in 1936, he accepted a teaching position at the University of Michigan and helped establish a guidance program at the Cranbook School, later moving to a position as professor of group work at Wayne State University, where he remained for 12 years. Redl's service to children and the field of mental health included his positions as clinical director of the University of Michigan Fresh Air Camp, chief of the Child Research Branch of the National Institute of Mental Health

Fritz Redl

(1953–1959), and president of the American Orthopsychiatric Association.

Redl's work focused on the exploration of children's behavioral controls, their defenses, and how to prevent or treat the disorganization that results when the behavioral control system is maladaptive (Redl, 1966, 1975). His development of the "life space interview," providing strategies and techniques for immediately dealing with crises in the lives of children, showed his keen awareness of the effects of temporal and spatial arrangements (e.g., the stress of transition) on children's behaviors. Redl also saw how studying the behavior of severely disturbed children helped to illuminate techniques used by the normal child. As an outgrowth of his studies, group work, camp experience, and involvement with social agencies, he established Pioneer House, a residential program for the study and treatment of delinquent children, and the Detroit Group Project, providing clinical group work with children and a summer camp for children from low-income families. Redl's Pioneer House work is summarized in his book, *The Aggressive Child* (Redl & Wineman, 1957).

A renowned lecturer and consultant worldwide, Redl was a Pinkerton guest professor in the School of Criminal Justice of New York State University, and a visiting professor in the Department of Child Psychiatry of University of Utrecht in Holland. He died in 1988 in North Adams, Massachusetts, where he had retired in 1973.

REFERENCES

Redl, F., & Wineman, D. (1957). *The aggressive child.* New York: Free Press.

Redl, F. (1966). *When we deal with children: Selected writings.* New York: Free Press.

Redl, F. (1975). Disruptive behavior in the classroom. *School Review,* 83(4), 569–594.

See also **Life Space Interviewing**

REFERRAL PROCESS

Referral is the process by which potentially handicapped or gifted students are identified for comprehensive individual evaluation by school officials. The identification of students for evaluation is a federally mandated activity for which all school districts and state education departments must have specific policies and procedures (U.S. Office of Education, 1977, sections 121a.128 and 121a.220). The law holds districts and state departments responsible for identifying all handicapped children within their jurisdictions who require special education or related services, including those in the care of other public and private agencies.

Students can be referred in one of two major ways (Heller, Holtzman, & Messick, 1982). The first is through the systematic efforts of school districts, community agencies, or government institutions. For example, districts may use very low or very high performance on annually administered achievement tests to refer students. Similarly, hospitals may screen newborns for referral to early intervention programs. Finally, state education departments may conduct print and electronic media campaigns and establish toll-free hotlines aimed at encouraging the referral of handicapped or gifted students currently not receiving services.

The second major referral mechanism involves the efforts of individuals who know the child. Such individuals include the child's teachers, parents, and physician. Of these individuals, the large majority of referrals appear to emanate from teachers (Heller et al., 1982). The advent of PL 94-142 increased the involvement of others both in and outside the school (Bickel, 1982).

Referrals made by teachers (and other individuals) are generally personal decisions based on subjective criteria. As such, these decisions are open to a variety of influences. The specific factors that influence teacher referrals are difficult to identify with any certainty (Bickel, 1982). However, research suggests that teachers are influenced by several considerations. One consideration is program availability; if no program exists to meet the student's needs, or if no room is available in an existing program, referral is unlikely. Second, teachers seem hesitant to refer if there is a large backlog in assessment. Such backlogs cause teachers to consider referral a meaningless action. Third, parents may influence the process. Teachers may hesitate to refer children whose parents would be likely to react in a hostile manner, or be quick to refer those whose parents exert positive pressure. Finally, eligibility criteria affect the decision. For example, some states and districts require that teachers refer students for placement in a specific program such as one for educable mentally retarded pupils. Hence, teachers may be encouraged to refer only children with particular characteristics.

The subjectivity inherent in the referral process has social and ethical implications. First, there is the possibility that substantial numbers of children are being referred inappropriately. Inappropriate referral is problematic because it wastes valuable resources; creates backlogs in assessment, thereby denying services to those truly in need; and subjects children to the potential stigma of special education placement and to education in an environment that may not meet their needs.

Second, inappropriate referral may disproportionately affect particular social groups. For many years, disproportionate placements of minority children and of males in programs for educable mentally retarded (EMR) students have been documented (Heller et al., 1982). The reasons for these disproportionate placements are many and complex. While these placements are not necessarily inappropriate, their existence raises the question of whether teacher referrals, too, are disproportionate.

Relatively little research has been conducted on the topic of disproportionate referral. Those studies that do exist have used two basic methodologies. Some investigators have analyzed existing referral data to determine whether disproportionate numbers of students from particular groups are referred. Other researchers have presented different groups of teachers with simulated data describing a

student and have asked them to make referral decisions. The data received by the groups differed only in the social group membership assigned to the student. While no definitive conclusions can be drawn, the studies have shown a tendency toward higher rates of referral for minorities even though these students presented problems that appeared little different from those of their majority peers (Bickel, 1982).

Concern regarding both the possibility that children are being inappropriately referred and disproportionate placement of minority students in special education has led many school districts to refine their referral processes. These refinements have primarily occurred with respect to teacher referrals. Such referrals were originally passed directly through to the pupil evaluation team. Most refinements have focused on inserting checks and balances into this teacher-to-evaluation team pathway.

REFERENCES

Bickel, W.E. (1982). Classifying mentally retarded students: A review of placement practices in special education. In K.A. Heller, W.H. Holtzman, & S. Messick (Eds.), *Placing children in special education: A strategy for equity.* Washington, DC: National Academy.

Heller, K.A., Holtzman, W.H., & Messick, S. (1982). *Placing children in special education: A strategy for equity.* Washington, DC: National Academy.

U.S. Office of Education. (1977). Education of handicapped children: Implementation of Part B of the Education of the Handicapped Act. *Federal Register, 42*(163), 42474–42518.

See also **Education for All Handicapped Children Act of 1975; Individuals with Disabilities Education Act (IDEA); Prereferral Interventions**

REFLEX

A reflex is an automatic connection between a stimulus and a response. One example is the knee-jerk reflex. Another is the reflexive constriction of the pupil in response to light.

Historically, the concept of the reflex has captured the imagination of many theorists who wished to emphasize the mechanical nature of behavior. René Descartes proposed a hydraulic model to account for the behavior of nonhuman animals. The Russian physiologist Ivan Sechenov (1863/1965) argued that all behavior, including that of humans, is reflexive (meaning that it is determined). Ivan Pavlov and other theorists of learning have used such terms as conditioned reflex to imply that even learned behaviors are mechanically determined and that they can be described as stimulus-response connections.

Certain human reflexes can be observed only in infancy (Peiper, 1963). For example, infants reflexively grasp any object placed firmly in the palm of the hand. Newborns grasp an elevated bar tightly enough to support their own weight, at least briefly. If someone strokes the sole of an infant's foot, the infant extends the big toe and fans the others (this is known as the Babinski reflex). If someone touches an infant's cheek, an infant who is awake will often, but not always, turn toward the stroked cheek and begin to suck.

Infant reflexes are suppressed in older children and adults, but the connections responsible for the reflexes are not destroyed. The infant reflexes may return as a result of brain damage, especially damage to the frontal lobes of the cerebral cortex.

REFERENCES

Peiper, A. (1963). *Cerebral function in infancy and childhood.* New York: Consultants Bureau.

Sechenov, I. (1863/1965). *Reflexes of the brain.* Cambridge, MA: MIT.

See also Behaviorism; Behavior Modification; Developmental Milestones

REGIONAL MEDIA CENTERS FOR THE DEAF

In 1959 the U.S. Office of Education implemented a program, under PL 85-905, to provide captioned films and related media to assist in bringing deaf persons into the mainstream of American life. The program featured the development and dissemination of highly specialized media services and products through four regional media centers. In the 1960s, 13 special education instructional media centers were established in addition to the four regional centers for the deaf. By the end of that decade, those 17 centers had been consolidated into four area learning resource centers (ALRCs). The ALRCs conducted activities related to educational media and technology for all handicapped persons, but specialized centers within the ALRC structure provided educational media and technology services for deaf persons. In 1972 the National Center on Education Media and Materials for the Handicapped replaced the ALRCs.

REGIONAL RESOURCE CENTERS (RRCS)

The Regional Resource Centers (RRCs) were created by the Elementary and Secondary Education Act, Title 6, of 1965. They were intended to assist state educational agencies (SEAs) in the implementation of special education services at a time when special education was just beginning to be recognized as a national concern. The RRCs were intended to help SEAs and local educational agencies (LEAs) in the development of special education services and resources by serving as agents in planning, programming, service delivery, training, and the creation of instructional materials. The actual operations of the RRCs proceeded through a variety of agencies, including state educational departments, universities, and LEAs.

See also Special education, Federal Impact on; Special Education Programs

REGRESSION (STATISTICAL)

Regression is a term widely used in behavioral research (multiple regression). It has come to mean both a statistical technique and a statistical phenomenon. The phenomenon or artifact of statistical regression is addressed here. Simply, regression is a way to say that two behaviors or variables are not perfectly related to each other. For example, high school performance and freshman year grade point average (GPA) typically correlate about .5. Regression refers to the fact that when a researcher uses one variable to predict the other (high school performance to predict freshman GPA), the predicted score will be less extreme than the predictor score. In the example just given, a predicted freshman GPA will be .5 times the high school rank in standard deviation units. A student one standard deviation above average on high school performance will be predicted to be one-half standard deviation above average for his or her class in GPA at the end of the freshman year.

The phenomenon was noted by Galton (and others before him) in his studies of human characteristics in the nineteenth century. He termed it regression to the mean, since the expected or predicted performance is always closer to the mean in standard deviations than is the predictor.

The significance of regression for special education is that the clients tend to be extreme in some way. Special education students by definition score differently, often extremely, on tests or observation scales with respect to the entire population of students. Thus when a second measure is made on the students, they will be observed, through regression, to be less extreme (see Figure 1, for example). Sometimes this artifact is confused with instructional or program improvement. Hopkins (1968), in a classic paper on the topic, detailed the problem for special educators. He pointed out that in attempting to test the effects of treatments for special education students, the students are sometimes matched with nonspecial education students. Matching is a keyword that should always force the researcher or reader to consider regression effect. In such studies, the special edu-

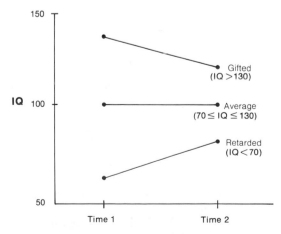

Figure 1. Examples of hypothetical regression effects between two testings for groups of children with IQs at three levels.

cation students, having been selected as extreme on one test, will exhibit regression on another test, perhaps the posttest in a research study. Their matched control group, also extreme owing to matching, will also show regression on the posttest. Unless the two groups have identical population means (a highly unlikely condition), they will show different amounts of regression, so that the difference between the groups found on the posttest may be due entirely to differential regression. Thus matching is a poor substitute for techniques such as randomization in comparative research. Similarly, single group designs, in which one treatment group is measured before and after treatment, is at risk to show regression effects. While the regression effect can be estimated in some situations, such designs are poor substitutes for carefully planned experimental designs.

REFERENCE

Hopkins, K.D. (1968). Regression and the matching fallacy in quasi-experimental research. *Journal of Special Education, 3,* 329–336.

REGULAR CLASS PLACEMENT

See MAINSTREAMING AND INCLUSION.

REHABILITATION

The term rehabilitation refers to any process, procedure, or program that enables a disabled individual to function at a more independent and personally satisfying level. This functioning should include all aspects—physical, mental, emotional, social, educational, and vocational—of the individual's life. A disabled person may be defined as one who has any chronic mental or physical incapacity caused by injury, disease, or congenital defect that interferes with his or her independence, productivity, or goal attainment. The range of disabilities is wide and varied, including such conditions as autism, mental retardation, muscular dystrophy, and a variety of neurological and orthopedic disorders. These disparate conditions may appear singly or in concert. Clearly, the process that is designed to assist persons in obtaining an optimal level of functioning is a complex one. The complexity of the rehabilitation process necessitates a team approach that involves a range of professionals almost as broad and varied as the types of conditions addressed.

See also Rehabilitation Counseling; Vocational Training of the Handicapped

REHABILITATION ACT OF 1973

The Rehabilitation Act of 1973 authorizes comprehensive vocational rehabilitation services designed to help physically and mentally handicapped persons become employable. The act also authorizes service projects for persons with special rehabilitation needs. For severely handicapped persons without apparent employment potential, the act authorizes services to promote independent living. Training programs are provided to help ensure a supply of skilled persons to rehabilitate handicapped persons. The act also authorizes a research program, a national council to review federal policy regarding handicapped persons, and a compliance board to help enforce accessibility standards for the handicapped.

The act authorizes state grants for comprehensive services designed to enable handicapped individuals to become employable. Each state receives an allotment of federal funding that must be matched on a 20% state to 80% federal ratio. Federal funds are allotted on the basis of population and per capita income, with the lower per capita income states receiving a relatively higher allotment on a per capita basis.

REHABILITATION ACT OF 1973, SECTION 504 OF

Section 504 of what is commonly called the Rehabilitation Act is frequently cited as an important precursor to the passage of PL 94-142 two years later (Bersoff, 1982). Section 504, among other things, protects the rights of handicapped children and precludes discrimination in employment and education. The stipulations of the Rehabilitation Act apply to the programs receiving federal financial assistance.

REFERENCE

Bersoff, D.N. (1982). The legal regulation of school psychology. In C.R. Reynolds & T.B. Gutkin (Eds.), *The handbook of school psychology.* New York: Wiley.

See also Larry P.

REHABILITATION LITERATURE

Rehabilitation Literature is a bimonthly journal published by the National Easter Seal Society. It is principally an educational service journal that abstracts articles published elsewhere and reviews books, journals, films, treatment programs, etc. dealing with the rehabilitation of all types of human disabilities. At least one original feature article appears in each issue. It is written at a level for professional personnel and students training to become professional service providers in all disciplines concerned with the rehabilitation of persons with handicapping conditions.

REITAN-INDIANA NEUROPSYCHOLOGICAL TEST BATTERY FOR CHILDREN (RINTBC)

The Reitan-Indiana Neuropsychological Test Battery for Children (RINTBC; ages 5 through 8), along with the Halstead Neuropsychological Test Battery for Children (ages 9 through 14) and the Halstead Neuropsychological Test Battery for Adults (ages 15 and older), constitute a global battery commonly referred to as the Halstead-Reitan Neuropsychological Test Battery. Each of these three batteries was devised as a tool for the assessment of brain-behavior relationships. The RINTBC was developed after it became apparent that many of the items on the battery for older children were too difficult for children below the age of 9 (Reitan, 1979).

The developmental research for the RINTBC, conducted at the Neuropsychology Laboratory of the Indiana University Medical Center, began in the mid-1950s. R.M. Reitan, a student of W.C. Halstead, modified several of the tests from Halstead's original adult battery (Halstead, 1947), and also created six new tests to complete this battery for young children. The modified tests include children's versions of the Category Test, Tactual Performance Test, Sensory-Perceptual Disturbances Tests, Finger Oscillation Test, and Aphasia Screening Test. New tests include the Color Form Test, Progressive Figures Test, and Matching Picture Tests; these were designed to measure cognitive flexibility and concept formation. The Target Test and the Individual Performance Test assess reception and expression of visuo-spatial relationships, while the Marching Test measures gross motor coordination (Reitan, 1979). The RINTBC customarily is supplemented by the Reitan-Klove Lateral Dominance Examination, the Reitan-Klove Sensory-Perceptual Examination, Strength of Grip, the Wechsler Preschool and Primary Scale of Intelligence, and the Wide Range Achievement Test (Reitan, 1974).

Reitan and Davison (1974) present a review of research that has demonstrated that the RINTBC effectively differentiates brain-damaged from normal functioning children, provided the test is administered and interpreted properly by trained professionals. An interpretive guide is available from Reitan (1987).

REFERENCES

Halstead, W.C. (1947). *Brain and intelligence.* Chicago: University of Chicago Press.

Reitan, R.M. (1974). Psychological effects of cerebral lesions in children of early school age. In R.M. Reitan & L.A. Davison (Eds.), *Clinical neuropsychology: Current status and applications* (pp. 53–89). New York: Hemisphere.

Reitan, R.M. (1979). *Manual for the administration of neuropsychological test batteries for adults and children.* Tucson, AZ: Reitan Neuropsychology Laboratories.

Reitan, R.M. (1987). *Neuropsychological evaluation of children.* Tucson, AZ: Reitan Neuropsychology Laboratories.

Reitan, R.M., & Davison, L.A. (1974). *Clinical neuropsychology.* New York: Hemisphere.

See also **Halstead-Reitan Neuropsychology Test Battery; Neuropsychology**

RELATED SERVICES

The Education for All Handicapped Children Act of 1975 (PL 94-142) was the first Federal law to hold education agencies responsible not only for the provision of special education services, but for the delivery of related services as well. Related services are defined as "transportation, and such developmental, corrective, and other supportive services...as may be required to assist a handicapped child to benefit from special education" (Section 4a). IDEA advances nearly identical language.

Among the services specifically included within the related services definition are speech pathology and audiology, psychological services, medical services (for diagnostic and evaluation purposes only), physical and occupational therapy, recreation, and counseling. However, because the phrase "other supportive services...as may be required" is included in the law, the precise definition of related services remains the subject of debate.

Disputes regarding the type and extent of related services required under PL 94-142 have been the focus of a series of court cases, including the first Supreme Court decision on federal special education law. Litigation has involved questions of eligibility, definition, and financial responsibility. All three issues were addressed in *Hendrick Hudson Board of Education v. Rowley.*

Dealing with the financial ramifications of providing related services is a continuing challenge. In its *Seventh Annual Report to Congress* (1984), the United States Department of Education described effective policies developed to provide related services in cost-efficient ways. One strategy has been to pool resources among local education agencies to make a range of related service specialists available to students. Another has been to seek third-party funding from public and private insurance providers. A third approach involves establishing joint funding and cooperative programming arrangements among education and human service agencies. For example, a school district and local mental health agency agree that the mental health agency will provide and assume the related services costs for the district's seriously emotionally disturbed children (Maher & Bennett, 1984). Each of these arrangements exemplifies efforts to share financial responsibility and work cooperatively to improve the quality of related services available to handicapped children.

REFERENCES

Maher, C.A., & Bennett, R.E. (1984). *Planning and evaluating special education services.* Englewood Cliffs, NJ: Prentice-Hall.

U.S. Department of Education. (1984). *Seventh annual report to Congress on the implementation of the Education of the Handicapped Act.* Washington, DC: U.S. Government Printing Office.

See also **Diagnosis in Special Education; Education for All Handicapped Children Act of 1975; Individuals with Disabilities Education Act (IDEA); Interpreters for the Deaf; Speech-Language Services**

RELIABILITY

Test score reliability refers to the precision of a test as a measuring device. If test results are to be meaningful and useful, precision of measurement is a highly desirable characteristic for the test or measurement procedure used. Test users must evaluate carefully information about test reliability provided in a test manual to determine the reliability of a test for its stated purpose.

Two types of statistical evidence of reliability are usually reported in test manuals: the reliability coefficient and the standard error of measurement. The reliability coefficient is a general indicator of test precision and is useful when making comparisons among tests. The standard error of measurement, on the other hand, is useful when interpreting the test score of an individual because it permits a statement of confidence to be placed in the particular.

Gulliksen (1950) notes that a basic definition underlying reliability states that an obtained test score (X_0) is composed of two parts: a true score (X_t) portion and error (X_e) (Formula 1):

$$X_0 = X_t + X_e. \qquad (1)$$

Formula 1 can be rewritten in terms of the variation among individuals, or variance (s^2), attributable to these sources (Formula 2):

$$s_0^2 = s_t^2 + s_e^2. \qquad (2)$$

Formula 2 states that the variance that occurs among observed, or obtained, scores (s_0^2) equals the true score variance (s_t^2) plus the error variance (s_e^2). Reliability (r_{xx}) is defined as the ratio of total variance attributable to true scores to the total variance of observed scores (Formula 3):

$$r_{xx} = \frac{s_t^2}{s_0^2}. \qquad (3)$$

The r_{xx} in Formula 3 indicates that the reliability coefficient is actually a type of correlation coefficient. In practice, the reliability coefficients for most published tests cluster in the .80s and .90s (Anastasi, 1982). If, for example, a standardized reading test for grade six reported a reliability coefficient of .90, this would mean that 90% of the variance among individuals was true variance, with 10% attributable to error. Obviously, the smaller the error, the greater the confidence in the accuracy of the test scores.

There are several procedures for estimating reliability. Readers of test manuals will encounter several types of reliability coefficients: test-retest, alternate forms, split-half, and internal consistency are the most common. Each of these permits different sources of error to be reflected in the test scores. Each type of reliability coefficient is estimated from either a single test administration or from two test administrations separated by a brief time interval (Thorndike & Hagen, 1977).

Test-retest reliability is determined by administering the same test twice, with an intervening time interval, and then correlating the scores. Differences in individual scores on the two testings would be attributed to the differential effects of factors specific to each test session. Alternate-forms reliability is estimated by administering two parallel test forms on separate occasions, with an intervening time interval, and then correlating the scores. Differences in individual scores on the two testings would be attributed both to differential factors affecting performance on each test occasion, and to different samples of content used in each test form. Alternate-forms reliability provides the most rigorous estimate of reliability (Thorndike & Hagen, 1977). Both test-retest and alternate-forms reliability require two separate test administrations; however, it is possible to estimate reliability from a single administration of a test. Split-half reliability estimates are obtained by dividing a test into two equivalent half-tests and correlating the results. Actually, the results are based on tests half as long as the total test and must be corrected to full-length estimates by use of the Spearman-Brown formula to adjust for test length. Individual score differences would be attributed to differences in the two content samples. Internal consistency reliability is estimated from item performance. Sources of error variance reflected include content and heterogeneity of the construct or trait measured by the test (Anastasi, 1982).

Reliability coefficients must be interpreted cautiously because a number of factors may affect their magnitude. Among these influences are the range of ability present in the group used to estimate reliability, the ability level of the group, and the extent to which test scores are dependent on speed or rate of work (Anastasi, 1982).

The size of a reliability coefficient is directly related to the range or extent of individual differences present in the group used to obtain reliability estimates. If, for example, an easy mathematics test were administered to a group of mathematicians, the reliability coefficient would be low owing to the fact that all the mathematicians would probably achieve perfect scores. There is little or no variability in a group such as this; hence, the reliability coefficient would be near zero. In a related sense, reliability coefficients may differ for groups different in overall ability or other demographic characteristics. The composition of a particular group must always be described clearly to sharpen the meaning of a particular reliability coefficient (Anastasi, 1982).

REFERENCES

Anastasi, A. (1982). *Psychological testing* (5th ed.). New York: Macmillan.

Thorndike, R.L., & Hagen, E.P. (1977). *Measurement and evaluation in psychology and education.* New York: Wiley.

See also Assessment; Measurement

RELIGIOUS EDUCATION FOR THE HANDICAPPED

Religious education for the handicapped refers to the moral and spiritual education of children with disabilities. It can be traced to l'Abbé de l' Epée and other ordained ministers who established schools for handicapped children with the specific purpose of bringing their students to the knowledge of God. Parents have also been instrumental in procuring religious education for their handicapped children by demanding that these children be given religious instruction and taught to participate in religious activities. Both priests and parents have insisted that handicapped children have the same need for spiritual development as other children and that they have the right to an equal place in the church or synagogue (Ellis, Ellis, & Warren, 1984).

Curriculum materials for the religious education of children with special needs are available (Hall, 1982), as well as suggestions for the adaptation of regular religious education curricula (Paul, 1983) and advice about religious education for parents and teachers of handicapped children (Hall, 1982; Paul, 1983).

Common difficulties concerning religious education for handicapped learners include complaints that religious development is a neglected area in the lives of handicapped children; that too few churches and synagogues provide programs on a national, regional, or local level for the religious involvement of handicapped individuals; and that many churches separate handicapped worshippers into special groups in special parts of the church or only provide opportunities for participation in part of the total worship experience (Denton, 1972).

REFERENCES

Denton, D. (1972). Religious services for deaf people. *Journal of Rehabilitation of the Deaf, 6*, 42–46.

Ellis, H., Ellis E., & Warren, G.T. (Feb. 1984). An open letter to pastors and parents. *The Exceptional Parent, 14*(1), 39.

Hall, S. (1982). *Into the Christian community: Religious education with disabled persons.* Washington, DC: National Catholic Educational Association.

Paul, J. (1983). *The exceptional child: A guidebook for churches and community agencies.* Syracuse, NY: Syracuse University Press.

See also **Private schools and Special Education; Privileged Communication**

REMEDIAL AND SPECIAL EDUCATION (RASE)

In 1982, Pro-Ed, Inc., purchased the journal *Exceptional Education Quarterly* from Aspen Systems Corporation. In 1984, the name of the journal was changed to *Remedial and Special Education* (RASE), and the journal became a bimonthly. That same year, Pro-Ed acquired two additional journals, *Topics in Learning and Learning Disabilities* (from Aspen Press) and *The Journal for Special Educators* (from the American Association of Special Educators); these were also merged into RASE. This journal is devoted to topics involving the education of persons for whom typical instruction is not effective. Emphasis is on the interpretation of research literature and recommendations for the practice of remedial and special education. RASE thus is alternative to practitioner-oriented teacher journals and pure research journals within the field. All published articles have been peer reviewed.

REMEDIAL READING

According to Smith (1965), the term remedial reading first appeared in the professional literature in a 1916 journal article by W.H. Uhl; however, like so many of the terms in the field of reading, the term remedial reading has no universally agreed on operational definition. The amount of confusion that exists with respect to the term was expressed well some years ago by Goldberg and Schiffman (1972), who noted:

Some educators refer to the problem category as remedial, strephosymbolia, associative learning disability, specific reading or language disability, congenital word blindness, primary reading retardation, or developmental dyslexia. One school district may refer to all retarded readers as remedial; another agency, in the same community, may use the term remedial for a small group of children with specific learning disabilities. (pp. 156–157)

A Dictionary of Reading and Related Terms (Harris & Hodges, 1981) provides a realistic, though somewhat vague, definition of the term remedial reading:

Any specialized reading instruction adjusted to the needs of a student who does not perform satisfactorily with regular reading instruction.

Intensive specialized reading instruction for students reading considerably below expectancy.

While there are apparently no clear-cut ways to diagnostically differentiate among remedial readers, the learning disabled, corrective readers, dyslexics, etc., one might wonder if there are any instructional methods or materials that are unique to remedial reading. Textbooks dealing with this topic imply that there are. For example, Bond, Tinker, Wasson, and Wasson, (1984) indicate that there are four important elements of remedial instruction: it is individualized; it encourages the reader; it uses effective teaching procedures; and it enlists cooperative efforts. While these elements are important to remedial reading, they are also important to all reading instruction. These authors go on to suggest that basal readers, the hallmark of developmental reading instruction, are a primary source of materials for remedial reading.

A careful reading of discussions of remedial reading suggests that the principles of teaching reading are the same regardless of whether we are concerned with remedial or developmental readers. The basic consideration is that remedial reading to based on a careful assessment of what the reader knows and needs to learn in terms of reading skills and that instruction then be at an appropriate level of challenge. Many of the techniques are similar to those used for teaching reading to achieving readers. For example, Rude and Oehlkers (1984) describe how a language experience approach to teaching reading, which centers around the use of reading materials that are dictated by the reader and written by the teacher, can be used for remedial reading; the language experience approach is also a major developmental technique for teaching reading.

REFERENCES

Bond, G.L., Tinker, M.A., Wasson, B.B., & Wasson, J.B. (1984). *Reading difficulties: Their diagnosis and correction* (5th ed.). Englewood Cliffs, NJ: Prentice-Hall.

Goldberg, H.K., & Schiffman, G.B. (1972). *Dyslexia: Problems of reading disabilities.* New York: Grune & Stratton.

Harris, T.L., & Hodges, R.E. (Eds.). (1981). *A dictionary of reading and related terms.* Newark, DE: International Reading Association.

Rude, R.T., & Oehlkers, W.J. (1984). *Helping students with reading problems.* Englewood Cliffs, NJ: Prentice-Hall.

Smith, N.B. (1965). *American reading instruction.* Newark, DE: International Reading Association.

See also **Basal Readers; Fernald Method; High Interest-Low Vocabulary Materials; Orton-Gillingham Method; Reading; Reading Disorders**

REMEDIATION, DEFICIT-CENTERED MODELS OF

Deficit-centered models for the remediation of children's learning problems have been the predominant model, though certainly not the only model, of special education worldwide throughout the twentieth century. Deficit-centered remediation focuses on the identification of underlying process deficiencies on the part of the child; it then directs any subsequent intervention at the remediation of these process deficiencies. The assumption of such programs is that once the underlying deficit has been remediated (fixed, removed, or cured), academic learning will occur at a more or less normal pace. Deficit-centered remediation has undergone numerous facelifts since the 1930s, although the strong influence of Samuel T. Orton is felt in most of these programs even today.

Many assessment techniques and programs exist to identify weaknesses or deficits in cognitive processes for subsequent intervention. Some of the approaches that emphasize treating the child's greatest area of weakness in cognitive processing include those of Ayres (1974), Bannatyne (1980), Ferinden and Jacobson (1969), Frostig and Horne (1964), Kephart (1963), and Vallett (1967). The efficacy of deficit-centered models has been the subject of considerable scrutiny by researchers in psychology and special education for some time. Unfortunately, support for the effectiveness of deficit-centered remediation programs for the remediation of academic deficits is nil, particularly when reading and math are the academic problem areas (Glass & Robbins, 1967; Kavale & Furness, 1999; Reynolds, 1981a, 1981b; and Ysseldyke & Mirkins, 1982). Perceptual and vi-

sual-motor functioning can be improved by deficit-centered remediation programs (Myers & Hammill, 1976), but there is, as yet, no documentable generalization for the remediation of the learning problems that trigger the referral.

Hartlage and Reynolds (1981) have criticized deficit-centered models of remediation as potentially harmful to children. The emotional trauma that may accompany the treatment approach of Doman and Delacato has been widely discussed and the method has been condemned (Levine, Brooks, & Shankoff, 1980). While it is unlikely that other deficit-centered models are as emotionally damaging, it is likely (though unproven) that making children work and practice for lengthy periods process skills in which they are deficient (in some cases, years) without noticeable academic gains is emotionally damaging, particularly to the child's self-esteem, motivation, and the likelihood of continuing in school. Glass (1981), in a meta-analysis of the effectiveness of what were deficit-centered models of remediation, reported that a significant number had net negative effects on academic skills—that is, many deficit-centered remediation programs resulted in less academic gains than no special education program at all. In some instances, then, doing nothing is superior to a deficit-centered approach to remediation, when only academic skills are considered.

Recently, cognitive psychologists have become interested in children's information-processing strategies and have made great strides in understanding how children organize, store, and manipulate stimuli. Concomitant with the revival of interest in cognitivism have been attempts to assess "new" cognitive deficits and provide remedial strategies. Haywood and Switzky (1986), among others, propose that through such techniques as Feuerstein's (1979) Learning Potential Assessment Device (known popularly as the LPAD), deficiencies in children's cognitive processes can be identified and targeted for remediation. Conceptually, this new "cognitive science" approach is no different from the approaches of the past—only the names of the processes thought to be deficient are new. The new deficit-centered models have been the subject of debate (Haywood & Switzky, 1986; Reynolds, 1986), and there is evidence that, through the use of a like set of materials, children's scores on tests such as Raven's Matrices (a nonverbal test of intelligence) improve.

There is no evidence that deficit-centered remediation programs aid in such real-world tasks as learning to read, write, or cipher. They remain popular largely on the basis of rational, intuitive appeal and personal testimony or anecdotal data. However, occasional children do improve without treatment and the same percentage or less improve under deficit-centered remediation. As Mann (1979) periodically reminds us, we are better off training or teaching for the task at hand, not for the latest process. In assessing the new cognitive science approach to remediation, we are forced to conclude, as has Mann in his review of process training, "The new scientific pedagogy was going to revitalize education, provide individual prescriptive correctives for learning problems, reclaim the cognitively impaired. Down with models of general intellectual incompetency! Down with medical models of noneducational etiology!" (pp. 529, 538). "The promised land was at hand. Alas, neither Moses nor we ever crossed to the other side" (p. 539). Process is not a useless variable, however. It is crucial to consider in the diagnosis of learning disabilities as well as certain other disorders; efforts to use process approaches to remediate academic problems seem better built on strength models of remediation than on deficit-centered models.

STRENGTH MODELS OF REMEDIATION

Strength models of remediation also invoke the concept of cognitive or intellectual processes and often measure them in the same way. The resulting approach and techniques differ greatly, however. Strength models argue that the best remedial approach for a child who cannot read is to teach the child reading, not metacognition, rehearsal strategies, auditory reception, or grouping and classification.

In strength models of remediation, direct instruction is encouraged in the area(s) of academic or behavioral difficulty. However, instruction is formatted around the child's best developed processes, taking advantage of the child's best intellectual abilities and avoiding those processes that are poorly developed, dysfunctional, or inept in this function. As Reynolds (1981b) describes this method, "The strength model is based on processes that are sufficiently intact so as to subserve the successful accomplishment of the steps in the educational program, so that the interface between cognitive strengths [determined from the assessment process]...and the intervention is the cornerstone of meaningfulness for the entire diagnostic-intervention process" (p. 344). In Lurian terminology, this would denote the need for locating a complex functional system within the brain that operates well enough to be capable of taking control and moderating the learning process necessary to acquire the academic skills in question. This view is hardly new, though it remains largely untested. Woodrow (1919) suggested teaching to cognitive strengths on the basis of scientific psychology.

Strength models do not tell us specifically what to teach children, as do deficit-centered models. The latter tells us to teach the specific process that has been found to be deficient. In strength models, the specifics of what to teach come from a detailed task analysis or a diagnostic achievement test that delineates precisely what academic skills are problematic for the child. The strength model of remediation tells us how to teach: how the material best can be organized and presented so that learning has the best opportunity to occur (Reynolds, 1985). The stress, anxiety, and self-denigration that may be fostered can be intolerable for many children. Using the child's strengths as building blocks for the acquisition of academic skills or even the remediation of behavioral disorders increases the probability of more positive and successful experiences, reducing stress and alleviating anxiety. Strength models of remediation may have other emotional benefits for children as well.

A strength model of remediation also can serve as a meeting ground for a variety of divergent theoretical models in use in the remediation of a child's problems. One can easily blend cognitive, behavioral, neuropsychological, and psychoeducational models in a strength approach. Behavioral and psychoeducational models that focus on academic skill delineation through task analysis or diagnostic achievement testing are needed to tell us specifically what to teach; cognitive and neuropsychological models that focus on how the child best thinks and processes information tell us how to organize, present, and teach the content and behaviors; behavioral models, particularly positive reinforcement programs using operant techniques, are best at giving the child reason, purpose, and motivation, the why of learning. Of the various processing theories from which to build the how, to implement strength models of remediation, the neuropsychological model seems the most promising (Reynolds, 1981b, 1985), and a blending of this model with others has been proposed on several occasions.

REFERENCES

Ayres, A.J. (1974). *Sensory integration and learning disorders.* Los Angeles: Western Psychological Services.

Bannatyne, A. (1980, September). *Neuropsychological remediation of learning disorders.* Paper presented at the NATO/ASI International Conference on Neuropsychology and Cognition, Augusta, GA.

Ferinden, W.E., & Jacobson, S. (1969). *Educational interpretation of the Wechsler Intelligence Scale for Children (WISC).* Linden, NJ: Remediation Associates.

Feuerstein, R. (1979). *The dynamic assessment of retarded performers. The learning potential assessment device, theory, instruments and techniques.* Baltimore, MD: University Park Press.

Frostig, M., & Horne, D. (1964). *The Frostig program for the development of visual perception.* Chicago: Follett.

Glass, G.V. (1981, September). *Effectiveness of special education.* Paper presented at the Working Conference of Social Policy and Educational Leaders to Develop Strategies for Special Education in the 1980s, Wingspread, Racine, WI.

Glass, G.V., & Robbins, M.P. (1967). A critique of experiments on the role of neurological organization in reading performance. *Reading Research Quarterly, 3,* 5–52.

Hartlage, L.C., & Reynolds, C.R. (1981). Neuropsychological assessment and the individualization of instruction. In G.W. Hynd & J.E. Obrzut (Eds.), *Neuropsychological assessment of the school-aged child: Issues and procedures.* New York: Grune & Stratton.

Haywood, H.C., & Switzky, H.N. (1986). The malleability of intelligence: Cognitive processes as a function of polygenic experiential interaction. *School Psychology Review, 15*(2), 245–255.

Kavale, K. & Forness, S. (1999). Effectiveness of special education. In C.R. Reynolds & T.B. Gutkin (Eds.), *The handbook of school psychology* (3rd ed., pp. 984–1024). New York: Wiley.

Kephart, N.C. (1963). *The brain injured child in the classroom.* Chicago: National Society for Crippled Children and Adults.

Levine, M.D., Brooks, R., & Shonkoff, J.P. (1980). *A pediatric approach to learning disorders.* New York: Wiley.

Mann, L. (1979). *On the trail of process.* New York: Grune & Stratton.

Reynolds, C.R. (1981a). The neuropsychological basis of intelligence. In G. Hynd & J. Obrzut (Eds.), *Neuropsychological assessment of the school aged child: Issues and procedure.* New York: Grune & Stratton.

Reynolds, C.R. (1981b). Neuropsychological assessment and the habilitation of learning: Considerations in the search for the aptitude x treatment interaction. *School Psychology Review, 10,* 343–349.

Reynolds, C.R. (1985, August). *Putting the individual into the ATI.* Paper presented at the annual meeting of the American Psychological Association, Los Angeles.

Reynolds, C.R. (1986). Transactional models of intellectual development, yes. Deficit models of process remediation, no. *School Psychology Review, 15,* 256–260.

Vallett, R.E. (1967). *The remediation of learning disabilities: A handbook of psychoeducational resource programs.* Palo Alto, CA: Fearon.

Woodrow, H. (1919). *Brightness and dullness in children.* Philadelphia: Lippincott.

Ysseldyke, J., & Mirkin, P.K. (1982). The use of assessment information to plan instructional intervention: A review of research. In C.R. Reynolds & T.B. Gutkin (Eds.), *The handbook of school psychology.* New York: Wiley.

See also **Frostig, M.; Illinois Test of Psycholinguistic Abilities; Information Processing; Kaufman Assessment Battery for Children; Learning Potential Assessment Device; Neurological Organization; Orton, S.T.; Perceptual Training; Sequential and Simultaneous Cognitive Processing**

REMEDIATION, STRENGTH MODELS OF

See REMEDIATION, DEFICIT-CENTERED MODELS.

REPEATED READING

Repeated reading is a remedial reading technique designed to improve fluency and indirectly increase comprehension. The method is based largely on the teaching implications of automatic information processing theory in reading (LaBerge & Samuels, 1974). In automaticity theory, fluent readers are assumed to decode text automatically; attention is therefore free for comprehension. Nonfluent, word-by-word readers, on the other hand, must focus excessive amounts of attention on decoding, making comprehension difficult. The purpose of repeated reading is to make decoding of connected discourse automatic, thus fluency is increased and the reader is able to concentrate on comprehension.

Moyer (1982) offers a theoretical rationale for the potential effectiveness of the method with disabled readers. She suggests that for some poor readers, the amount of repetition/redundancy offered by traditional reading programs is insufficient to permit the acquisition of reading. Repeated reading of entire passages, however, maximizes redundancy at all levels of written expression. Thus readers are given much practice in using syntactic and semantic cues, as well as in acquiring knowledge of graphophonemic word structure.

REFERENCES

LaBerge, D., & Samuels, S.J. (1974). Toward a theory of automatic information processing in reading. *Cognitive Psychology, 6,* 293–323.

Moyer, S.B. (1982). Repeated reading. *Journal of Learning Disabilities, 15,* 619–623.

See also **Reading; Reading Remediation**

RESEARCH IN SPECIAL EDUCATION

Research in special education is the means through which knowledge and methods of treatment are acquired and verified for application to persons exhibiting special needs. Such research encompasses a wide range of methodologies, data collection and analysis techniques, subjects, and issues. Although all special education research contributes to the ever increasing knowledge base of the field, all are different to some extent. Research ranges from case studies to single subject and group designs. Each method differs from the others in terms of ease of use, confidence and validity of results obtained, and generality of findings.

Through the process of research, advances are made in what is known about disabilities and how to prevent and treat them through education and training. The importance of research methodology in validating the findings of research must be emphasized. Many hypotheses related to developmental disabilities are advanced in the form of anecdotal reporting and logical analyses. But these hypotheses are speculative and before being applied to the special education field, they must be subjected to verification through research. Only by careful study through controlled research designs can research findings be considered useful and applied to persons other than those involved in the research study.

Special education research is usually applied research; in other words, it is conducted primarily in the places where handicapped persons live, work, and attend school. For example, research has been conducted in group homes, sheltered workshops, resource rooms, and the community. Although less rigorous than research in the experimental laboratory, special education research has the advantage of being relevant to and practical for the subjects involved; that is, the issues studied are usually of high priority for the well-being of the people involved because of their functional relevance. Through rigorously applied research programs, professionals in special education can confirm observations by testing hypotheses on persons with special needs and verifying known effects with different populations. In the long view, research provides a solid foundation of knowledge from which to progress and maintain the intellectual vitality of special education.

Observation of phenomena is inherent in all research and particularly in special education research. Naturalistic observation is one way to collect information about subjects. With this technique, the researcher observes a person (or group of people) and makes extensive records of the subject's behaviors. The purpose is to be as descriptive as possible to provide a post-hoc analysis of possible mediating factors.

Another important characteristic of research is that of systematically manipulating variables and observing the effects of such manipulations on other variables. Typically, a researcher wants to measure accurately how the dependent variable (e.g., subject behaviors targeted for change) is affected when the subject is exposed to the independent variable (one or more factors manipulated by the researcher). Some examples of dependent variables in special education research are number of words read, frequency of correct expressive signs made, number of problems solved, percentage of inappropriate social behaviors exhibited, and frequency of interruptions. Some examples of independent variables in research are teacher praise, repetition of task, removal of child from activity, use of a particular prompting strategy, and administration of drugs.

A third characteristic of most research is use of an experimental method to determine the extent to which independent variables are functionally related to changes in dependent variables. Researchers carefully design how and when their subjects are exposed to independent variables. Experimental designs minimize the possibility that uncontrolled, extraneous factors play a part in changing dependent variables. Research that is not adequately designed to decrease the impact of extraneous factors must be viewed with caution.

A final characteristic of research concerns analysis of findings. Typically, researchers have used statistical methods to determine whether their results demonstrate a strong (significant) change. Whether the research compares a pre- and postintervention difference, or whether the results obtained from one subject exposed to an independent variable is compared with those of another subject who is not exposed, the intent of the analysis is to assess the degree of difference and make a statement as to whether such a difference could be expected by chance. Statistical methods used in special education research include t-tests, analysis of variance, analysis of covariance, and regression analysis structural equation modeling, to name a few prominent examples. Researchers can determine whether their work has caused an observable practical change in their subjects. This determination is termed functional or clinical significance.

Meta-analysis is a research approach providing a quantitative analysis of multiple studies, allowing one to address specific research questions across many studies. Kavale and Forness (1999) provide multiple examples of how meta-analysis can be useful in special education, especially in the evaluation of intervention programs.

Research conducted in special education has increased knowledge in the field and at the same time raised new questions. One important concern is the ethical conduct of the special educator while doing research. Experimenters who use humans as subjects have the responsibility of providing stringent safeguards to protect the health and well-being of their subjects. Professionals in special education must be particularly sensitive to these concerns in that developmentally disabled subjects may not be capable of understanding the issues involved in the research and thus may not be able to give truly informed consent.

Research safeguards to protect subject rights do exist and professionals must abide by them. Kelty (1981) summarized several key guidelines for researchers to consider when planning studies using humans. Generally, these involve informed consent on the part of the subject so that the subject truly understands the purpose of the study, any risks benefits to the subject, and the option to volunteer or to withdraw so that there is maximum possibility for benefit with minimum possibility of harm.

A standard component of research studies is a description of reliability procedures to verify that the primary data collector is accurate in recording the responses of the subjects. Unfortunately, few researchers present a similar case verifying that an experimental treatment is actually applied as proposed. This issue has been termed integrity of treatment (Salend, 1984) and is crucial for confidence in research results. For example, if an experimenter inadvertently implements a different intervention than the one planned, relating the proposed experimental method to the results would be erroneous. Integrity of treatment may be verified with little extra effort on the part of the research designers. As reported in Zane, Handen, Mason, and Geffin (1984), the integrity check can be made part of the traditional reliability check. The reliability scorer notes whether the person implementing the experimental program uses the correct intervention and scores the subject response correctly. By presenting both sets of data, readers can judge to what extent the proposed intervention is actually implemented.

What are some recognized areas of special education in which more research could profitably be done? One area is diagnosis. Techniques that accurately assess the etiology of a person's deficits and discovery of the youngest age at which a true diagnosis can be achieved for various handicapping conditions would have a significant impact. Another area concerns the success of mainstreaming. Ideally, a solid research base should exist to support mainstreaming as well as to delineate ways of making it more successful. Several important questions can be addressed. What is the optimal class ratio of children labeled normal and developmentally disabled? How does mainstreaming affect the individual student in terms of academic and social success? What affect is there, if any, on the students labeled normal? Answers to these questions obtained from systematic research will shed light on the future direction of mainstreaming and lead to even further improvements for disabled people.

REFERENCES

Kavale, K., & Forness, S. (1999). Effectiveness of special education. In C.R. Reynolds & T.B. Gutkin (Eds.), *The Handbook of School Psychology* (3rd Ed.), pp. 984–1024. New York: Wiley.

Kelty, M.F. (1981). Protection of persons who participate in applied research. In G.T. Hannah, W.P. Christian, & H.B. Clark (Eds.), *Preservation of client rights: A handbook for practitioners providing therapeutic, educational, and rehabilitative services.* New York: Free Press.

Salend, S.J. (1984). Integrity of treatment in special education research. *Mental Retardation, 6,* 309–315.

Zane, T., Handen, B.L., Mason, S.A., & Geffin, C. (1984). Teaching symbol identification: A comparison between standard prompting and intervening response procedures. *Analysis & Intervention in Developmental Disabilities, 4,* 367–377.

See also **Measurement; Multiple Baseline Design; Multiple Regression; Regression (Statistical)**

RESIDENTIAL FACILITIES

Residential facilities in America have been provided a variety of labels, including school, hospital, colony, prison, and asylum. Both the role and the labels that institutions for the handicapped have taken on have been reflective of the social and cultural climate of the time (Wolfensberger, 1975). The periods that had major influence on residential institutions have been characterized as follows: early optimism, 1800–1860; disillusionment, 1860–1900; reconsideration, 1920–1920; ebb and flow, 1930–1950; new reconsideration, 1950–1960; and enthusiasm, 1960–1970 (Cegelka & Prehm, 1982).

The first residential institution designed for handicapped individuals was established in 1817. That year the American Asylum for the Education and Institution of the Deaf was established in Hartford, Connecticut. In 1819 a second school, for the blind, was established in Watertown, Massachusetts; it was named the New England Asylum for the Blind. During this period and continuing until the Civil War, a number of eastern states established residential schools for the deaf, blind, orphaned, and mentally retarded (National Advisory Committee for the Handicapped, 1976).

The development of residential institutions for the mentally retarded in the United States began in the 1840s. In 1848 Samuel Howe convinced the Massachusetts Legislature to allocate funds for the establishment of the first public setting for individuals with retardation. That same year Hervey Wilbur founded the first private institution for treating retarded persons. These institutions were designed to provide education and training to mildly, and occasionally to moderately, handicapped children and adolescents. After the Civil War, residential institutions fell into disfavor. However, the latter portion of the century was marked by continued growth, both in numbers of facilities and numbers of individuals within those facilities. As the nineteenth century came to a close, it became clear that institutions were not accomplishing training that would lead to the reintegration of handicapped individuals into the community. By 1900, 7000 handicapped individuals were housed in institutions. During this time, the role of residential institutions changed significantly. Their emphasis shifted from training to prevention of retardation through systematic segregation of the mentally retarded from society (Wolfensberger, 1975).

The view of institutions held by state legislatures and the general public fluctuated until after World War II. By this time institutions were overcrowded and understaffed. The effects of the baby boom in the late 1940s and the early 1950s placed further pressures on these settings. After World War II, a growing acknowledgment of the existence and needs of the exceptional person was experienced by the nation. This awareness was fostered by parental pressures, returning servicemen's needs, professional enthusiasm, and the availability of public and private funding. These factors led to a reevaluation of procedures, research, and a new understanding of the handicapped and the role of institutions in their treatment, care, and training. By 1969, 190,000 handicapped individuals were housed in institutions (Cegelka & Prehm, 1982).

By the 1970s a new view of the dangers and inadequacies of institutions was recognized. The courts played a major role in bringing this realization to the fore. *Watt v. Stickney* (1972) affirmed mentally retarded persons' right to treatment. *Lessard v. Schmidt* (1972) ensured due process for institutionalized individuals. *Souder v. Brennan* (1973) outlawed involuntary servitude of institutionalized persons. The federal government also caused major reforms with the passage of Title XIX (Medicaid) provisions in 1971. These provisions brought institutions under the same controls and review processes as other service providers for the handicapped. A nationwide push to return handicapped individuals to the community was experienced. Deinstitutionalization became a social, fiscal, and moral goal within each of the states. Between the late 1960s and the early 1980s, the number of handicapped persons being served by public residential institutions declined by over 50,000. At the same time, staff-to-client ratios improved along with the physical quality of many institutions. During the 1980s and 1990s, nearly half of state-operated residential facilities for persons with mental retardation were closed in favor of movement to group homes and other less restrictive environments.

To facilitate the deinstitutionalization process, community-based alternatives were developed and expanded during the 1970s and 1980s. During the same period, a number of small institutions (less than 100 residents) were built. Small group homes, foster placements, semiindependent residences, and nursing homes were heavily relied on to handle individuals leaving institutional placements and as alternatives to initial placement in large residential institutions. Although anticipated, few of the older large institutions were closed and many of the handicapped stayed within those larger institutions.

Large residential facilities continue to provide services for the handicapped. These institutions serve increasingly involved persons. This will be done at an increased actual dollar cost per resident. Community-based residential programs are growing as alternative residential settings for handicapped individuals. These community-based programs provide services to the majority of previously unserved handicapped individuals. Such settings provide financially and morally appropriate residential services to a large percent of all handicapped individuals, thus reducing, but not eliminating, the need for the large residential institutions.

REFERENCES

Cegelka, P.T., & Prehm, H.J. (1982). *Mental retardation.* Columbus, OH: Merrill.

Eplle, W.A., Jacobson, J.W., & Janicki, M.R. (1985). Staffing ratios in public institutions for persons with mental retardation. *Mental Retardation, 23,* 115–124.

National Advisory Committee for the Handicapped. (1976). *The unfinished revolution: Education for the handicapped, 1976 annual report.* Washington, DC: U.S. Government Printing Office.

Wolfensberger, W. (1975). *The origin and nature of our institutional models.* Syracuse, NY: Human Policy.

See also **History of Special Education; Philosophy of Education for the Handicapped**

RESOURCE ROOM

The resource room concept gained popularity following the *Hobsen v. Hansen* litigation, which declared tracking systems illegal and required reevaluation on a regular basis. This litigation was a forerunner for mainstreaming and the concept of least restrictive alternative (environment). This model of service delivery allows the handicapped child to remain in the educational mainstream as much as possible. With the passage of PL 94-142, and further emphasis on the least restrictive alternative seen in IDEA, the resource room gained even further popularity. There are over 100,000 resource room teachers in the United States today. Professional special educators have consistently cited the importance of the resource room concept and have noted its viability as a promising alternative to placement in self-contained classes or regular classes without support services (Cartwright, Cartwright, & Ward, 1995).

Usually, students attending resource rooms are identified as mildly handicapped (4 to 6% of the total school population). Resource rooms are a widespread means of service delivery for the mildly handicapped, and are gaining acceptance for use with gifted exceptional children.

Placement in the resource room is intended to be of short duration (Kasik, 1983). As students progress toward specified goals, they are returned to full-time placement in the regular classroom. Return to the regular classroom should

progress through a gradual phasing out of support services. The resource room is to be considered as one type of service delivery within the continuum of services available.

REFERENCES

Cartwright, P., Cartwright, C., & Ward, M. (1995). *Educating special learners* (4th ed.). Boston: Wadsworth.

Kasik, M.M. (1983). Analysis of the professional preparation of the resource room teacher. *Dissertation Abstracts International.* (University Microfilms International No. DAO 56766)

See also **Cascade Model of Special Education Services; Hobsen v. Hansen; Inclusion; Least Restrictive Environment; Resource Teacher; Self-Contained Classroom**

RESOURCE TEACHER

Much of the research literature calls for resource rooms to be staffed by highly trained special educators who are personable, demonstrate good human interactional skills, and are prepared professionally in the diagnosis and remediation of single or multiple groups of handicapped children. Wallace and McLoughlin (1979) identify the resource teacher's main role as including assessment, instructional planning, teacher evaluation, and liaison-consultant duties. Learner (1985) describes the resource teacher as a highly trained professional who is capable of diagnosing the child, planning and implementing the teaching program, assisting the classroom teacher, providing continuous evaluation of the student, and conducting in-service sessions with other educators and the community. Sabatino (1981) states that the role of the resource teacher includes direct service to individuals and small groups of children, consultant services to classroom teachers, and responsibility for assessment and delivery of individualized programs. Kasik (1983) states that the resource teacher needs to be well organized, flexible, self-directed, and effective in time management. Paroz, Siegenthaler, and Tatum (1977) suggest that the resource teacher be actively involved with the total school community, including students and staff members. They add that the "teacher's role is open ended and limited only by time, talent, and acceptance of the teacher by the school administration and staff" (p. 15). The resource teacher is a trained specialist who works with, and acts as a consultant to, other teachers, providing materials and methods to help children who are having difficulties within the regular classroom. Usually, the resource teacher works with the mildly handicapped population in a centralized resource room where appropriate materials are housed.

There are four different types of resource room teachers: (1) categorical, (2) noncategorical, (3) itinerant (or mobile), and (4) teacher-consultant. Categorical programs serve one specific population; noncategorical programs may serve one or more populations. The itinerant resource room teacher travels from one building to another and usually does not have an assigned room from which to work. The teacher-consultant resource room teacher provides consultation to regular class teachers, parents, and other service delivery personnel. Cartwright, Cartwright, and Ward (1995) provide a description of a typical day in the life of a resource teacher in today's schools.

REFERENCES

Cartwright, P., Cartwright, C., & Ward, M. (1995). *Educating special learners* (4th ed.). Boston: Wadsworth.

Kasik, M.M. (1983). Analysis of the professional preparation of the special education resource room teacher. *Dissertation Abstracts International.* (University Microfilms International No. DAO 56766)

Learner, J. (1985). *Learning disabilities: Theories, diagnosis, and teaching strategies* (4th ed.). Boston: Houghton Mifflin.

Paroz, J., Siegenthaler, L., & Tatum, V. (1977). A model for a middle school resource room. *Journal of Learning Disabilities, 8,* 7–15.

Sabatino, D.A. (1981). Overview for the practitioner in learning disabilities. In D.A. Sabatino, T.L. Miller, & C.R. Schmidt (Eds.), *Learning disabilities: Systemizing teaching and service delivery.* Rockville, MD: Aspen.

Wallace, G., & McLoughlin, J.A. (1979). *Learning disabilities: Concepts and characteristics* (2nd ed.). Columbus, OH: Merrill.

See also **Diagnostic Prescriptive Teaching; Resource Room**

RESPITE CARE

Respite care complements special education in providing support to families of handicapped children. Respite care may be defined as temporary care given to a disabled or otherwise dependent individual for the purpose of providing relief to the primary caregiver (Cohen & Warren, 1985). The concept of respite care is generally associated with intermittent services, although this term is also sometimes used to refer to regularly scheduled services occurring once or twice a week.

Respite care programs first appeared in the mid 1970s in response to the deinstitutionalization movement. Deinstitutionalization meant that many families who would probably have placed their disabled children in institutions, either out of choice or as a result of professional advice, no longer had the option to do so. In addition, some children who had been placed in institutions in earlier years were being returned to their families. Thus a substantial number of parents now had to cope with the care needs of their severely handicapped children each day. The natural breaks that parents of nonhandicapped children experience when their children sleep at a friend's home, or visit with relatives, or go to camp were usually not available. It was virtually impossible to obtain paid babysitters and even relatives were reluctant to assume this responsibility. The primary caregiver, usually the mother, found it impossible to engage in normal activities such as shopping, caring for medical and dental needs, or seeing friends. Parents rarely had time for each other or for their other children. Families experienced severe problems in coping.

Respite care is a family-support service, designed to improve family functioning and help normalize families of the disabled. This service is of particular importance to families with weak natural support systems, poor coping skills, or strenuous care demands. Difficulty in care provision may reflect the severity of the behavioral problems or the extensiveness of the physical and health care needs of the disabled person. Primary caregivers use the relief provided through respite care services to rest, meet their own medical needs, improve relationships with other family members, and engage in some of the common personal or social activities that other adults are able to enjoy (e.g., visiting with a friend, taking a vacation, going shopping).

Models of respite care may vary along several dimensions such as where the service is provided, what the content/nature of the care is, who provides the care, how the service is administered, and how much time is allotted. The most important variation in models is whether services are provided in the home or in some other setting. In-home services are preferred by a majority of families. In-home services are economical and minimize the adjustments that must be made by the disabled individual and the family. These services may be of short duration, as when the parents go to a movie, or for a period of a week or two when parents take a vacation. In-home services may be provided by a sitter with only a few hours of training or by a homemaker/home health aide with substantial training.

Babysitting and companionship are the major ingredients of respite care services that are of brief duration. Personal care and nursing care may be required when the client has severe physical or health problems. Social/recreational programming is usually a major component of longer respite care episodes.

Respite care services are often funded through state mental retardation/developmental disabilities agencies, with families obtaining services either directly through local offices of these agencies or through community programs supported by funds from these state sources.

REFERENCE

Cohen, S., & Warren, R.D. (1985). *Respite care: Principles, programs, and policies.* Austin, TX: Pro-Ed.

See also **Deinstitutionalization**

RESPONSE GENERALIZATION

Response generalization occurs when the effects of reinforcement or punishment of one response increase or decrease, respectively, functionally similar behaviors. Such generalization is an implicit goal of teaching because learning would be of little value if it affected only a specific response. Unfortunately, as Baer (1981) has emphasized, such generalization is not automatic and may be restricted in some handicapped children and adults, particularly persons with mental retardation (Robinson & Robinson, 1976).

REFERENCES

Baer, D.M. (1981). *How to plan for generalization.* Lawrence, KA: H & H Enterprises.

Robinson, N.M., & Robinson, H.B. (1976). *The mentally retarded child* (2nd ed.). New York: McGraw-Hill.

See also **Generalization; Transfer of Learning**

RESTRAINT

See PHYSICAL RESTRAINT.

RETARDATION

See CULTURAL-FAMILIAL RETARDATION; MENTAL RETAR-DATION.

RETENTION IN GRADE

Retention in grade or nonpromotion has been an issue of interest to educators since the turn of the century. The first comprehensive study of pupil progress was done by Ayres (1909) in his book *Laggards in Our Schools.* Literally hundreds of articles and studies have argued the pros and cons of nonpromotion. Since 1975 the number of students retained in grade has been on the increase. A great deal of this increase appears to be related to the establishment of performance standards in skill subjects. In 1979 and 1980 about half of the first, second, and third graders in Washington, DC, were retained in a grade because they failed to meet the new reading and math standards.

The results of studies conducted over the years on retention have generally borne mixed results. The quality of those studies has also been suspect (Jackson, 1975). Jackson concluded that studies that compared promoted students with nonpromoted students were biased in favor of promotion because promoted students did better than those retained. Using a technique called meta-analysis, Holmes and Matthews (1984) analyzed 44 studies that compared retained students with those promoted. In 18 of the studies they found matched subject designs that used control factors such as IQ, achievement, socioeconomic status, sex, and grades. The studies they analyzed used a variety of dependent means to evaluate the effects of nonpromotion. Included were academic achievement, personal adjustment, self-concept, and attitude toward school. On all variables, nonpromotion resulted in negative effects. The average size of effect for all variables was −.38. This means that students who were promoted performed about one-third of a standard deviation better than those who were retained.

The results from variable to variable were surprisingly consistent. For academic achievement, the size of effect was .44, for personal adjustment it was .27, for self-concept .19,

and for attitude toward school .16. All differences showed a more positive performance for students who were promoted than for those who were retained. The outcomes seem to demonstrate that the potential for negative effects far outweighs the benefits for nonpromotion.

REFERENCES

Ayres, L.P. (1909). *Laggards in our schools.* New York: Russell Sage Foundation.

Holmes, C.T., & Matthews, K.M. (1984). The effects of nonpromotion in elementary and junior high school pupils: A meta-analysis. *Review of Educational Research, 54*(2), 225–236.

Jackson, G.B. (1975). The research evidence in the effect of grade retention. *Review of Educational Research, 45,* 438–460.

See also **Developmental Delays; Prereferral Interventions; Research in Special Education**

RETICULAR ACTIVATING SYSTEM

The reticular activating system is the mass of cells in the brain stem associated with arousal, wakefulness, attention, and habituation. Its dysfunction may be associated with the hyperactivity and attention deficits often observed in brain-damaged children.

The major function of the reticular system is to provide for cortical activation via its connections through the diffuse thalamic projection system. If the reticular system is significantly impaired, as in severe head trauma, coma results. However, even with less severe impairment, wakefulness, perception (Livingston, 1967), or cognitive functions are attenuated. The second major function is through the posterior hypothalamus, an area that provides a similar activating influence on the limbic system (Feldman & Waller, 1962).

REFERENCES

Feldman, S., & Waller, H. (1962). Dissociation of electrocortical activation and behavioral arousal. *Nature, 196,* 1320.

Livingston, R. (1967). Brain in circuitry relating to complex behavior. In G. Quarton, T. Melnechuk, & Schmitt, F. (Eds.), *The neurosciences: A study program.* New York: Rockefeller University Press.

See also **Attention Deficit Disorder; Brain Damage; Hyperkinesis**

RETINITIS PIGMENTOSA (RP)

Retinitis pigmentosa (RP) was first described in the mid 1800s. The term pigmentary retinal dystrophy is more accurate, as retinitis suggests an inflammation of the retina although none is present. The condition is often hereditary and characterized by a progressive deterioration of retinal photoreceptor cells and associated layers of pigment epithelium and choroid (Krill, 1972). Clinical features include spiculated clumping of pigment in association with retinal vessels, pallor (atrophy) of the optic disk and thinning of the retinal vessels. The condition is always bilateral in familial cases, but sporadic unilateral cases have been reported. Pigmentary changes typically become noticeable during the first decade of life, and begin as fine dots that gradually assume the spidery bone corpuscle appearance. Unusual pigmentary distributions may be noted, including central and sector defect patterns. The pigment flecks may be sparse or absent (i.e., RP *sine pigmenti*) (Tasman, 1971).

Attempts at treatment have been disappointing. Current theory suggests the disease represents an abnormal sensitivity to light, with light being the agent leading to retinal photoreceptor degeneration. Occlusion of one eye, in an attempt to slow the progress of the disease, has been attempted with equivocal results. Injections of extracts from placental tissues have been tried in the past with no effect.

This disease tends not to affect school performance until late in its course. Clues for educators may include walking into objects (constricted or "gun-barrel" visual field defects), night blindness, and other defects such as hearing loss and degenerative central nervous system disease. Constriction of the visual field may make location of material on a chalkboard difficult. Braille instruction is typically ineffective unless no useful vision is present.

REFERENCES

Krill, A.E. (1972). *Hereditary retinal and choroidal diseases.* Hagerstown, MD: Harper & Row.

Tasman, W. (1971). *Retinal diseases in children.* New York: Harper & Row.

RETROLENTAL FIBROPLASIA (RLF)

Retrolental fibroplasia (RLF) was first recognized in the early 1940s, with the first literature description published in 1942. Over the ensuing decade, many unrelated and sometimes conflicting etiologies for the disease were considered. Among these were water miscible vitamins, iron, oxygen, cow's milk, and abnormal electrolytes, all of which have been shown in positive association to the incidence of RLF. Experimental evidence implicated vitamin E deficiency as a possible cause. Other factors that have been associated with RLF are viral infections, hormonal imbalances, premature exposure of infant eyes to light, and vitamin A deficiency in the mother. The observation that the incidence of the disease increases in direct relation to the duration and exposure of premature infants to oxygen was reported first in 1952. A controlled study was completed in 1954; it established oxygen as the most likely etiologic agent for the condition. The rise of this disease, called by some an epidemic, closely parallels the development of the ability to effectively concentrate oxygen administration to infants in incubators (Silverman, 1980).

The importance of oxygen concentration monitoring became apparent as experimental evidence of the early 1950s accumulated. Ambient oxygen levels were limited whenever possible to 40%, and measurements of oxygen concentration in the blood were made. This did not entirely resolve the issue for several reasons: the disease occurred in the absence of supplemental oxygen therapy; it occurred when 40% oxygen was administered "appropriately"; and this level of supplemental oxygen often was not sufficient to relieve the respiratory distress syndrome that often accompanies prematurity. The important relationship between arterial blood oxygen (PO2), the respiratory distress syndrome, and retrolental fibroplasia is now well established. However, numerous attempts to monitor and control arterial blood oxygen (PO2) have been fraught with great difficulties, both technical and physiologic.

Approximately 10% of infants under 2500 g birth weight are afflicted with the respiratory distress syndrome, accounting for approximately 40,000 infants per year in the United States; the incidence of RLF blindness following oxygen administration is a small percentage of the group, perhaps 2%. Recognizing this, many authors now designate this disease retinopathy of prematurity (ROP).

The full spectrum of consequences of RLF blindness to the child, family, social agencies, school, and community is beginning to be fully considered. Affected individuals tend not to see loss of sight as a major burden. Preconceptions, paternalism, and insensitivity of authorities in the visually oriented world often constrict the lives of those who wish to see this same world nonvisually. A number of factors—medical, legal, and societal—tend to perpetuate the stereotype that the blind wish to shed in their desire to move toward independence. Thus the complexity of this disease at several levels—visual, neurological, personal, and social—is only now being appreciated.

The visually disabling forms of RLF may impact on school performance by limiting sensory input, the degree of disability reflecting the severity of disease. Teachers may observe "blindness" where disability is severe. When bilateral retinal blindness is present, braille instruction is required. The educator should be aware of the complexity of problems for individuals with this condition.

REFERENCE

Silverman, W.A. (1980). *Retrolental fibroplasia: A modern parable.* New York: Grune & Stratton.

RETT SYNDROME

Rett Syndrome (RS) is a disorder that initially appears as a deterioration from apparently normal development in infancy or early childhood. It involves a slowdown in normal development, deceleration of head growth, disinterest in the environment, deterioration of motor functioning, loss of hand use and subsequently locomotion, hand stereotypies (typically hand wringing or clapping), loss of expressive language, autistic and self-abusive behavior, and eventual severe/profound mental retardation. Prevalence estimates vary. Hagberg (1995) recently has revised the estimate of prevalence of classic RS from 1:10,000 females to closer to 1:15,000. Cases have been reported in all parts of the world and in all ethnic groups (e.g., Naidu, 1997). First described by Andreas Rett (1966), it initially came to the world's attention largely through the work of Hagberg and his associates (Hagberg, Aicardi, Dias, & Ramos, 1983).

Unique to RS is apparently normal initial development followed by rapid mental and physical deterioration followed by stabilization or even reduction in some symptoms (e.g., Hagberg, 1995). Unusual in other ways, RS (a) apparently affects only women, whereas most gender-specific disorders affect only men; (b) is manifested in part through loss of acquired function, but is apparently neurodevelopmental and not neurogenerative (e.g., Glaze & Schultz, 1997); (c) presents in a fairly striking set of behavioral symptoms that have consistent developmental trends; and (d) is almost undoubtedly genetically-based, but no marker has been identified. Although the subject of hundreds of articles, it is still relatively unknown in comparison to many other developmental disorders of comparable prevalence. As would be expected, research on the genetic basis focuses on an X-chromosome abnormality. RS is associated with numerous neuroanatomical and neurochemical disturbances, summaries of which can be found in Brown and Hoadley (2000).

Owing to the lifelong impact of the disorder on parents and other family members, ranging from home care issues to decisions about educational and other placement, counseling for the family will be particularly important (Lieb-Lundell, 1988). Training of the parents in behavior modification may be helpful in managing some aspects of their RS daughter's behavior, including tantrums. Of importance, given the degree of care that RS adults may require and their relative longevity, parents will eventually need to face the issue of lifelong care and make financial arrangements for care of the woman after their death.

REFERENCES

Brown, R.T., & Hoadley, S.L. (in press). Rett syndrome. In S. Goldstein & C.R. Reynolds (Eds.). *Handbook of Neurodevelopmental and Genetic Disorders of Children,* (pp. 459–477). New York: Guilford Press.

Glaze, D.G., & Schultz, R.J. (1997). Rett syndrome: Meeting the challenge of this gender-specific neurodevelopmental disorder. *Medscape Women's Health, 2*(1), 1–9. http://www.medscape. com/ Medscape/WomensHealth/journal/1997/v2.n01/w223. glaze.html

Hagberg, B. (1995). Rett syndrome: Clinical peculiarities and biological mysteries. *Acta Paediatrica, 84,* 971–976.

Hagberg, B., Aicardi, J., Dias, K., & Ramos, O. (1983). A progressive syndrome of autism, dementia, ataxia, and loss of purposeful hand use in girls: Rett's syndrome: report of 35 cases. *Annals of Neurology, 14,* 471–479.

Lieb-Lundell, C. (1988). The therapist's role in the management of girls with Rett syndrome. *Journal of Child Neurology* (3 supplement), S31–S34.

Naidu, S. (1997). Rett syndrome: A disorder affecting early brain growth. *Annals of Neurology, 42,* 3–10.

Rett, A. (1966). Uber ein eigenartiges Hirnatrophisches Syndrom bei Hyperammonamie im Kindes alter. [On an unusual brain atropic syndrome with hyperammonia in childhood] *Wiener Medizinische Wochenschrift, 116,* 425–428. (As cited in Moser & Naidu, 1991, and Rett Syndrome Diagnostic Criteria Work Group, 1988.)

REVERSALS IN READING AND WRITING

The term reversals is usually associated with reading or writing disabilities. Reversals are difficulties characterized in either reading or writing by reversing letters, numbers, words, or phrases (e.g., *saw for was, p* for *q*), or what some have referred to as mirror reading or writing.

In Orton's first theoretical papers on reading disabilities (1925, 1928), he suggested that such reversal problems were due to poorly established hemispheric dominance. Orton (1928) cited the following examples of strephosymbolia (literally, twisted symbols): (1) difficulty discriminating *b* and *d;* (2) confusion with words like *ton* and *not;* (3) ability to read from mirror images; and (4) facility at writing mirror-like images. Orton further stipulated that these reversal problems were not caused by mental retardation. Other investigators have since promoted the concept of developmental lag in perceptual abilities as causally related to reading disorders (Bender, 1957).

Empirical support that reversals are due to perceptual deficits has been equivocal. It has been seen that many beginning readers reverse letters and words (Gibson & Levin, 1980). In fact, more than one half of all kindergarten students typically reverse letters (Gibson & Levin, 1980). This is considered a part of the normal component of discrimination learning when children first acquire reading skills. Gibson and Levin (1980) cite research that indicates that normal children continue to make reversal errors until the age of eight or nine. It was also found that single letter reversals account for only a small percent of total reading errors exhibited by poor readers. In addition, it has been questioned whether such reversals in learning-disabled students indicate underlying perceptual problems rather than, for example, linguistic problems (Gupta, Ceci, & Slater, 1978).

REFERENCES

Bender, L.A. (1957). Specific reading disability as a maturational lag. *Bulletin of the Orton Society, 7,* 9–18

Gibson, E.J., & Levin, H. (1980). *The psychology of reading.* Cambridge, MA: MIT Press.

Gupta, R., Ceci, S.J., & Slater, A.M. (1978). Visual discrimination in good and poor readers. *Journal of Special Education, 12,* 409–416.

Orton, S.T. (1925). Word-blindness in school children. *Archives of Neurology and Psychiatry, 14,* 581–615.

Orton, S.T. (1928). Specific reading disability-strephosymbolia. *Journal of the American Medical Association, 90,* 1095–1099.

See also **Agraphia; Dysgraphia; Handwriting; Remediation, Deficit-Centered Models of**

REVERSE MAINSTREAMING

Reverse mainstreaming is a procedure that involves introducing nonhandicapped students into special classrooms to work with severely handicapped students. The purpose is to maximize integration of severely handicapped and nonhandicapped students. Mainstreaming, a more familiar concept, refers to the integration of the handicapped into the nonhandicapped classroom to enable each individual to participate in patterns of everyday life that are close to the mainstream. Reverse mainstreaming is, as the name suggests, a procedure carried out in reverse of mainstreaming but striving for the same goals. Reverse mainstreaming can be used with all severe handicaps.

The primary use of reverse mainstreaming has been with the severely and profoundly mentally handicapped and the autistic. Until the early 1970s these severely handicapped students were educated in segregated environments that had only handicapped individuals. These environments included institutions and special education schools. Mildly mentally handicapped students, on the other hand, were more likely to be educated in closer proximity to nonhandicapped peers.

There has been widespread acceptance in the past 20 years of the philosophy of normalization. This philosophy implies that the handicapped should be able to live as similarly as possible to the nonhandicapped. Public Law 94-142, adopted in 1978, required that the handicapped be educated as similarly as possible to the nonhandicapped. For the mildly mentally handicapped, this has resulted in considerable integration into nonhandicapped classrooms. For the severely mentally handicapped, this has meant placement in buildings occupied by the nonhandicapped. It is frequently unrealistic to expect the severely mentally handicapped to participate in regular classrooms because of their low functioning levels and special needs. In these cases, in order to maximize interactions, special educators arrange for nonhandicapped students to participate in the classrooms of the handicapped as volunteers, or "peers"; hence, mainstreaming in reverse.

See also Inclusion; Least Restrictive Environment; Mainstreaming; Peer Relationships

REVISED CHILDREN'S MANIFEST ANXIETY SCALE (RCMAS)

See CHILDREN'S MANIFEST ANXIETY SCALE.

REVISUALIZATION

Revisualization has been defined as the active recall of the visual image of words, letters, and numbers (Johnson & Myklebust, 1967). Deficiencies in revisualization prevent students from picturing the visual form of printed material, and are related to difficulty in spelling and writing. By contrast, good spellers are able to compare their productions against an auditory or visual image when checking their spelling.

In terms of memory functioning, recall tends to be the area most substantially impaired for children with revisualization deficits, while recognition is somewhat less affected. Therefore, activities such as dictated spelling tests, number

sequencing, and drawing from memory are often extremely difficult for students with revisualization deficits. Such deficits will be less apparent when matching and multiple choice activities are employed.

REFERENCE

Johnson, D.J., & Myklebust, H.R. (1967). *Learning disabilities.* New York: Grune & Stratton.

See also Imagery; Visual Training

REYE'S SYNDROME

Reye's syndrome is an acute, frequently fatal disease of childhood. It is given the name of the Australian pathologist, R.D.K. Reye, who described the characteristics of this syndrome in the early 1960s. It is a rare condition with a reported risk of 1 to 2 per 100,000 children per year (Kolata, 1985). The onset of Reye's syndrome frequently follows an upper respiratory or gastrointestinal viral infection, such as may be associated with influenza B or chicken pox (*Mosby's,* 1983; Silberberg, 1979). Recovery from these relatively mild symptoms may appear to be under way when the life-threatening symptoms of Reye's syndrome ensue. These symptoms include persistent vomiting, fever, disturbances of consciousness progressing to coma, and convulsions. A characteristic posture (flexed elbows, clenched hands, extended legs) may be identified in some patients (Magalini, 1971). Deep, irregular respiration may occur, sometimes leading to respiratory arrest. The pathology associated with Reye's syndrome includes massive edema (swelling) of the brain and fatty infiltration of the liver and kidneys (Magalini, 1971; Silberberg, 1979).

The etiology of Reye's syndrome is unknown. A number of findings, including increased incidence following influenza B outbreaks and the localization of a virus in some Reye's patients, suggest a viral infection as the precipitating factor (Silberberg, 1979). Some studies have reported a link between aspirin given as a therapeutic agent during influenza or chicken pox and the subsequent development of Reye's syndrome. A study of 29 children with Reye's syndrome and 143 controls reported "children with chicken pox or flu who take aspirin may be 25 times more likely to get Reye's syndrome than those who do not" (Kolata, 1985, p. 391). In January 1985, Margaret Heckler, secretary of the Department of Health and Human Services, requested that manufacturers of aspirin include warning labels on aspirin products (Kolata, 1985). Further studies of the link between aspirin and Reye's syndrome are being conducted.

The course of Reye's syndrome is variable (Gillberg, 1995). A high percentage of afflicted children die. Estimates of mortality range from 25 to 50%, although more recent figures are consistent with the lower figure, probably as a result of enhanced medical management (Kolata, 1985; Silberberg, 1979). Survivors of Reye's syndrome frequently display significant neurologic sequelae, including mental retardation, seizures, hemiplegia, or behavior problems including hyperactivity and distractibility (Culbertson et al., 1985; Silberberg, 1979). There is evidence of an age effect on outcome for survivors of Reye's syndrome, with younger children exhibiting more severe impairment (Culbertson et al., 1985; Hartlage, Stovall, & Hartlage, 1980).

Although Reye's syndrome is an extremely rare condition, it is of relevance for educators since it afflicts children exclusively and is associated with sometimes devastating impairment. Because of the suspicion of an association between aspirin and Reye's syndrome, school officials should exercise caution in the use of aspirin with children. Survivors of Reye's syndrome may require special education or related services, which should be determined following a multifactored evaluation.

REFERENCES

Culbertson, J.L., Elbert, J.C., Gerrity, K., & Rennert, O.M. (1985, February). *Neuropsychologic and academic sequelae of Reye's syndrome.* Paper presented to the International Neuropsychological Society, San Diego.

Gillberg, C. (1995). *Clinical child neuropsychiatry.* Cambridge: Cambridge University Press.

Hartlage, L.C., Stovall, K.W., & Hartlage, P.L. (1980). Age related neuropsychological sequelae of Reye's syndrome. *Clinical Neuropsychology, 21,* 83–86.

Kolata, G. (1985). Study of Reye's-aspirin link raises concerns. *Science, 227,* 391–392.

Magalini, S. (1971). *Dictionary of medical syndromes.* Philadelphia: Lippincott.

Mosby's medical and nursing dictionary. (1983). St. Louis: Mosby.

Silberberg, D. (1979). Encephalitic complications of viral infections and vaccines. In P.B. Beeson, W. McDermott, & J.B. Wyngaarden (Eds.), *Cecil textbook of medicine* (pp. 836–839). Philadelphia: Saunders.

See also Encephalitis

REYNOLDS, CECIL R. (1952–)

Before receiving his BA in psychology in 1975 from the University of North Carolina at Wilmington, Cecil Reynolds was a professional baseball player with the New York Mets organization for five years. He received his MEd in psychometrics in 1976, his EdS in school psychology in 1977, and his PhD in educational psychology in 1978, all from the University of Georgia. There his mentors were Alan S. Kaufman and E. Paul Torrance, both of whom have continued to strongly influence Reynolds.

Reynolds became assistant professor at the University of Nebraska in 1978, and remained there until 1981. During that time, he was acting director and subsequently associate director of the Buros Institute of Mental Measurement, and was responsible for moving the Buros Institute to Nebraska. Reynolds was the first director to succeed the institute's founder, Oscar K. Buros, who served as director from 1928 until his death in 1978. In 1981, Reynolds went to Texas A & M University as an associate professor, and later became director of the Doctoral School Psychology Training Pro-

Cecil R. Reynolds

gram, which he led to American Psychological Association accreditation in 1985. He achieved the rank of professor in that year. He is currently a professor of educational psychology, professor of neuroscience, and a Distinguished Research Scholar at Texas A & M University.

Reynolds's primary interests are in the subject of measurement, particularly as related to the practical problems of individual assessment and diagnosis. He has also worked in the area of childhood emotional disturbance, and is the author of the Revised Children's Manifest Anxiety Scale (Reynolds & Richmond, 1985), the Behavior Assessment System for Children (Reynolds & Kamphaus, 1992), and the Test of Memory and Learning (Reynolds & Bigler, 1994), along with six other tests of affect and intelligence. He is best known in school psychology for his work in the area of the cultural test bias hypothesis (Reynolds, 1983) and as progenitor of *The Handbook of School Psychology.*

He is a member of the editorial board of more than 13 journals, including *Learning Disabilities Quarterly, Journal of School Psychology, Journal of Learning Disabilities,* and the *Journal of Forensic Neuropsychology.* With more than 300 scholarly and professional papers to his credit, he is the author or editor of 34 books. In addition, he is senior editor (with Terry Gutkin) of *The Handbook of School Psychology* (3rd ed.), and is editor of the Plenum book series *Perspectives on Individual Differences* and Plenum's *Critical Issues in Neuropsychology.* He is currently in his second term as editor-in-chief of the *Archives of Clinical Neuropsychology,* the official journal of the National Academy of Neuropsychology.

In 1983, Reynolds chaired the Special Education Programs Work Group on Critical Measurement Issues in Learning Disabilities of the U.S. Department of Education. The report of this task force and several related works (Reynolds, 1981, 1984) have been instrumental in developing practical, psychometrically sound models of severe discrepancy analysis in learning disabilities diagnosis.

He is the youngest recipient of the American Psychological Association (APA) Division of School Psychology's (16) Lightner Witmer Award, and has also received early career awards from the Division of Educational Psychology (15) and the Division of Evaluation, Measurement, and Statistics (5) of the APA. In 1995, he received the Robert Chin Award from the Society for the Psychological Study of Social Issues for his contributions to the scientific study of social issues. In 1997, he received the President's Medal for service to the National Academy of Neuropsychology and, in 1998, the Razor Walker Award for service to the youth of America from the University of North Carolina at Wilmington. In November of 1998, he received the American Board of Professional Neuropsychology's Distinguished Contributions Award in the areas of both science and service. He is the 1999 recipient of the American Psychological Association, Division of School Psychology Senior Scientist Award and the 2000 National Academy of Neuropsychology Distinguished Clinical Neuropsychologist Award.

Reynolds has also been politically active, serving a three-year term on the executive board of the National Association of School Psychologists and as vice-president of the Division of School Psychology of the APA. In 1986, he was elected to a two-year term as president of the National Academy of Neuropsychology, and served as president of the American Psychological Association Division (5) of Evaluation, Measurement, and Statistics (1997–1998) and the Division (40) of Clinical Neuropsychology (1998–1999). He is a diplomate and past-president of the American Board of Professional Neuropsychology, a diplomate in school psychology of the American Board of Professional Psychology, a Fellow of the American Psychological Association (Divisions 1,5,15,16, and 40), and a Fellow of the National Academy of Neuropsychology and the American Psychological Society.

REFERENCES

Reynolds, C.R. (1981). The fallacy of "two years below grade level for age" as a diagnostic criterion for reading disorders. *Journal of School Psychology, 19,* 250–258.

Reynolds, C.R. (1983). Test bias: In God we trust, all others must have data. *Journal of Special Education, 17,* 214–268.

Reynolds, C.R. (1984). Critical measurement issues in learning disabilities. *Journal of Special Education, 18,* 451–476.

Reynolds, C.R., & Bigler, E.D. (1994). *Test of memory and learning.* Austin, TX.: Pro-Ed.

Reynolds, C.R., & Kamphaus, R.W. (1992). *Behavior assessment system for children.* Circle Pines, MN: American Guidance Service.

Reynolds, C.R., & Richmond, B.O. (1985). *Revised-children's manifest anxiety scale.* Los Angeles: Western Psychological Services.

See also Buros Institute of Mental Measurement; Revised Children's Manifest Anxiety Scale; Severe Discrepancy Analysis; Test of Memory and Learning

RH FACTOR INCOMPATIBILITY

Rh factor incompatilibility (erythroblastosis fetalis) results from an antigen-antibody reaction with destruction of the fetal red blood cells (Sherwen, Scoloveno, & Weingarten, 1999). The most lethal form of Rh factor incompatibility is erythroblastosis fetalis. Generally defined, erythroblastosis fetalis is a type of hemolytic disorder found in newborns which results from maternal-fetal blood group incompatibility of the Rh factor and blood group (Anderson, 1998). When an Rh-positive fetus begins to grow inside an Rh-negative mother, it is as though the mother's body is being invaded by a foreign agent or antigen. The mother's body reacts to this invasion by forming antibodies that cross the placenta and cause hemolysis of fetal red blood cells. The fetus becomes deficient in red blood cells that transport oxygen and develops anemia; enlarged heart, spleen, and liver; and a cardiovascular system which easily decompensates. Without prompt treatment, hypoxia, cardiac failure, respiratory distress, and death may result (Anderson, 1998).

Prenatal diagnosis of erythroblastosis fetalis is confirmed through amniocentesis and analysis of bilirubin levels within the amniotic fluid (Anderson, 1998). The treatment regime may include intrauterine transfusions to combat red blood cell destruction or immediate transfusions after birth (Pillitteri, 1995). Preterm labor may also be induced to remove the fetus from the destructive maternal environment.

REFERENCES

Anderson, K.N. (1998). *Mosby's medical, nursing, & allied health dictionary* (5th ed.). St. Louis: Mosby-Year Book.

Pillitteri, A. (1995). *Maternal & child health nursing: Care of the childbearing and childrearing family* (2nd ed.). Philadelphia: J.B. Lippincott Company.

Sherwen, L., Scoloveno, M., & Weingarten, C. (1999). *Maternity nursing: Care of the childbearing family* (3rd ed.). Stamford, CT: Appleton & Lange.

RIGHT-HANDEDNESS

Right-handedness is a species-specific characteristic of humans (Hicks & Kinsbourne; 1978). Additionally, right-handedness, also called dextrality, can be considered universal in that 90% of the human population is right-handed (Corballis & Beale, 1983). Since the majority of individuals prefer using their right hands, and are also more skilled with their right hands, more positive properties and values have come to be associated with the right than with the left.

Although people classify themselves as right-handed or left-handed, handedness more accurately spans a continuous range from extreme right-handedness through mixed-handedness or ambidexterity to extreme left-handedness. Investigators always have been curious about the abundance of right-handedness and the rarity of the various degrees of nonright-handedness. However, studies of historical records and artifacts have revealed enough inconsistencies in incidence to preclude any simple choice between culture or biology to explain the origin of handedness. Consequently, combinations of these various nature and nurture explanations have been invoked. Harris (1980) provides an interesting and detailed account of these various theories.

Corballis and Beale (1983), in an extensive study of the neuropsychology of right and left, have argued that right-handedness is biologically rather than culturally determined. They cite the fact that right-handedness always has been universal across diverse and seemingly unrelated cultures; moreover, although right-handedness itself is not manifest until late in the first year of life, it is correlated with other asymmetries that are evident at or before birth. They acknowledge that there are environmental pressures to be right-handed and that some naturally left-handed individuals may be compelled to use their right hands for certain tasks, but suggest that these very pressures have their origins in the fundamental right-handedness of most human beings.

Today the relationship between right-handedness and the unilateral representation of language in the left cerebral hemisphere is well documented. Case studies linking the side of brain damage and the incidence of aphasia, or language impairment, have revealed that approximately 98% of right-handers use the left hemisphere of their brain for language. A similar conclusion has been drawn from studies in which linguistic functioning has been impaired in 95% of the right-handers whose left cerebral hemispheres were injected with sodium amobarbitol, a momentarily incapacitating drug.

The hemisphere of the brain used for language in left-handers is more variable. Two-thirds of left-handers have demonstrated the use of their left hemisphere. Almost half of the remaining left-handers use their right hemispheres for speech, while the remainder have some capacity for speech in both hemispheres (Rasmussen & Milner, 1975). In view of these data, many investigators suggest that both right-handedness and left cerebral dominance for language are genetically controlled expressions of some underlying biological gradient. This relationship further reveals the significance of right-handedness in the unique cognitive functioning of the human species.

REFERENCES

Corballis, M.C., & Beale, I.L. (1983). *The ambivalent mind.* Chicago: Nelson-Hall.

Harris, L.J. (1980). Left-handedness: Early theories, facts, and fancies. In J. Herron (Ed.), *Neuropsychology of left-handedness* (pp. 3–78). New York: Academic.

Hicks, R.E., & Kinsbourne, M. (1978). Human handedness. In M. Kinsbourne (Ed.), *Asymmetrical function of the brain* (pp. 267–273). New York: Cambridge University Press.

Rasmussen, T., & Milner, B. (1975). Clinical and surgical studies of the cerebral speech areas in man. In K.J. Zulch, O. Creutzfeldt, & G. Galbraith (Eds.), *Otfried Foerster symposium on cerebral localization.* Heidelberg: Springer-Verlag.

See also **Cerebral Dominance; Handedness**

RIGHT HEMISPHERE SYNDROME (LINGUISTIC, EXTRALINGUISTIC, AND NON-LINGUISTIC)

The role of the right hemisphere in communication was largely unknown 20 years ago (Meyers, 1997). Since then an extensive body of research has determined that the right hemisphere handles holistic, gestalt-like stimuli and visual-spatial information, and has identified a wide range of communication impairments that can occur subsequent to right hemisphere damage. Three types of right hemisphere syndrome (RHS) deficits are *extralinguistic* (discourse), *nonlinguistic* (perceptual and attentional), and, to a lesser degree, *linguistic* deficits (phonological, semantic, syntactical, and morphological; (Hegde, 1998; Myers, 1997; Payne, 1997).

EXTRALINGUISTIC DEFICITS

Discourse is the aspect of communication that transcends individual phonemes, words, or sentences. It links "the bits and pieces of language to create representations of events, objects, beliefs, personalities, and experiences" (Brownell & Joanette, 1993, p. vii). Discourse competence is context-driven, and context includes a variety of cues—not only words and sentences, but tone of voice, gestures, body positions, facial expressions of the speaker, and the overall purpose and relative formality of the communicative event. Discourse also involves organization, sequencing, and the generation of projections, predictions, and inferences so that sentences are not taken as independent units, but as part of a larger whole (macrostructure) in which central ideas are emphasized and supported. Four major areas make up extralinguistic deficits associated with RHS (Hegde, 1998; Myers, 1997; Payne, 1997).

Macrostructure—reduced number and accuracy of core concepts and inferences, reduced specificity or explicitness of information, and reduced efficiency of listening, speaking, reading, writing, and thinking.

Impaired non-literal language—reduced sensitivity and use of figurative language (similes, metaphors, idioms, proverbs), humor (cartoons, jokes, riddles, puns), teasing, advertisements, slang, verbal aggression, ambiguity, multiple meanings, deception (irony, sarcasm), and capacity to revise original interpretations.

Rhetorical sensitivity/affective components—reduced sensitivity to communicative purposes, shared knowledge, emotional tone, partner's communicative state, turn-taking, topic maintenance, gaze; increased impulsivity, excessive talking, shallow responses, and monotonal speech.

Impaired prosody—reduced sensitivity to affective prosody (comprehension of others' emotions as reflected in the voice) and use of prosodic features (production of personal emotional states).

NONLINGUISTIC DEFICITS

Nonlinguistic deficits associated with RHS include visual perceptual problems, left-side neglect, attentional deficits, and denial of deficits.

Visual perceptual deficits—reduced ability to recognize faces (prosopagnosia) and to construct or reproduce block designs, two-dimensional stick figures, or geometric designs.

Left-side neglect—reduced sensitivity to respond to information on the left, despite the motor and sensory capacity to do so. The definition of "left" may vary according to the type of neglect and the environment. In body-centered neglect, "left" may refer to the left of the body midline. In environment-centered neglect, "left" may refer to the left side of a group of stimuli, regardless of their spatial location, or to the left side of fixed environmental coordinates, such as the left side of a room or book. In other cases, neglect may occur on the left side of a given object, even if that object is located in the right visual field. Thus, neglect may occur in the left or right visual field, depending on the stimulus environment; left may, therefore, be considered relative. Left-side neglect can occur in all modalities (auditory, visual, tactile, smell, taste), but is most often noted and tested in the visual modality. In addition to ignoring the left, individuals with neglect also may demonstrate an orienting bias toward the right, i.e., right-sided stimuli "capture" the person's attention.

Attentional deficits—reduced arousal (alertness), vigilance (focusing on relevant pieces of information), and maintained attention to stimuli; selective attention.

LINGUISTIC DEFICITS

Unlike the communication deficits that occur with left-hemisphere impairment, linguistic deficits are less problematic in RHS. Word retrieval deficits (semantics) occur frequently. Defining categories (e.g., apple, peach, cherry are *fruit*) or identifying collective and single nouns through confrontation naming are characteristic linguistic impairments. Phonological, syntactic, and morphological errors do not characterize the communication patterns of RHS (Hegde, 1998).

Right hemisphere syndrome is associated with strokes, tumors, head trauma, and various neurological diseases in all ethnic groups (Payne, 1997). The syndrome can have significant effects on social and academic aspects of communication-learning.

REFERENCES

Brownell, H.H., & Joanette, Y. (Eds.). (1993). *Narrative discourse in neurologically impaired and normal aging adults.* San Diego: Singular.

Hegde, M.N. (1998). *A coursebook on aphasia and other neurogenic language disorders* (2nd ed.). San Diego: Singular.

Myers, P.E. (1997). Right hemisphere syndrome. In L.L. LaPointe (Ed.), *Aphasia and related neurogenic language disorders* (2nd ed.). New York: Thieme.

Payne, J.C. (1997). *Adult neurogenic language disorders: Assessment and treatment—A comprehensive ethnobiological approach.* San Diego: Singular.

See also **Nonverbal Language; Pragmatics**

RIGHT TO EDUCATION

The right to education refers to the legal concept that justifies a school-aged person's freedom to receive educational services. The conceptual and legal development of this right has occurred in conjunction with an increasing societal concern for individuals who exhibit exceptional educational needs. These changing social attitudes have been reflected in judicial decisions and legislative efforts that have substantiated the right of all school-aged children and youths to receive educational services.

The U.S. Constitution, although not explicit in its guarantee of the right to education, has been cited as the fundamental justification for the provision of educational services. Specifically, the right to education has been implied from the Fourteenth Amendment, which states in its equal protection clause, "a state may not pass laws, nor act in any official way, so as to establish for a group of citizens benefits or penalties which other citizens do not receive." Thus, this amendment requires that, where educational services are available, such services must be available to all on an equivalent basis.

Early court cases that addressed the right of the exceptional needs learner to receive educational services did not reflect this interpretation. Generally, litigation in this area prior to the 1950s resulted in exclusionary educational policies (e.g., *Watson v. Cambridge,* 1883; *Beattie v. Board of Education,* 1919). However, with the onset of the increasing civil rights awareness apparent in the early 1950s, right to education court cases evidenced a more positive trend. Some of the more influential court cases that have related to the development of the right to education concept for the exceptional needs learner include *Brown v. Board of Education of Topeka* (1954), *Pennsylvania Association for Retarded Citizens v. the Commonwealth of Pennsylvania* (1971), and *Mills v. Board of Education of the District of Columbia* (1972).

The *Brown* case dealt with the rights of a class of citizens (blacks in the South) to attend public schools in their community on a nonsegregated basis. The major issues in this case were suspect classification (i.e., classification by race) and equal protection. In a unanimous decision for the plaintiff, the Supreme Court emphasized the social importance of education and also ruled that education must be made available on equal terms to all.

The *Pennsylvania Association for Retarded Citizens (PARC)* case dealt more specifically with the educational rights of exceptional needs learners. Citing the Fourteenth Amendment right to due process and equal protection, the judge in this case ruled that Pennsylvania statutes permitting denial or postponement of entry to public schools by mentally retarded children were unconstitutional. The terms of the settlement reached in this case included provision of due process rights to the plaintiffs and identification and placement in public school programs of all previously excluded children.

More general in its plaintiff class, the *Mills* case challenged the exclusion of mentally retarded, epileptic, brain-damaged, hyperactive, and behavior-disordered children from public schools. Finding for the plaintiffs, the court required the defendants to provide full public education or "adequate alternatives." These alternatives could only be provided after notice and a reasonable opportunity to challenge the services that had been given. The progression from *Brown* (1954) to *PARC* (1971) to *Mills* (1972) reflects an increasing sophistication in the awareness of the educational needs of individuals with exceptional learning characteristics. This more complete view of the educational needs and rights of exceptional individuals is also apparent in recent legislation.

Two major legislative efforts that have addressed the educational rights of exceptional needs learners are the Rehabilitation Act of 1973, Section 504, and PL 94-142 (and its successor, IDEA). Section 504 of the Rehabilitation Act of 1973 is particularly important because it deals with all programs that receive federal funds. This legislation mandates nondiscrimination on the basis of handicapping conditions if these funds are to continue.

Public Law 94-142 and the IDEA embody the intent of all legislation that it follows in its highly specific delineation of the educational rights of exceptional needs learners. This law requires that all individuals, regardless of handicapping condition or its degree, be offered a free appropriate education at public expense. Public Law 94-142 further specifies that these services must be delivered in the least restrictive environment appropriate for the individual child.

The right to education for children and youths with exceptional learning characteristics has resulted from changing societal views of the needs and rights of these individuals. These attitudes have been reflected in increased litigation questioning the adequacy, availability, and appropriateness of the educational services offered this group. The outcome of these cases has established a legal basis for a right to education. This litigation has in turn led to legislation developed to ensure that right. For a comprehensive discussion of the right to education for the exceptional needs learner see Wortis (1978) and Sales, Krauss, Sacken, & Overcast (1999).

REFERENCES

Beattie v. State Board of Education of Wisconsin. (1978). In J. Wortis (Ed.), *Mental retardation and developmental disabilities.* New York: Brunner/Mazel.

Sales, B.D., Krauss, D., Sacken, D., & Overcast, B. (1999). The legal rights of students. In. C.R. Reynolds & T.B. Gutkin (Eds.), *The Handbook of School Psychology* (3rd ed.). New York: Wiley.

Watson v. Cambridge, Mass. (1978). In J. Wortis (Ed.), *Mental retardation and developmental disabilities.* New York: Brunner/Mazel.

Wortis, J. (Ed.). (1978). *Mental retardation and developmental disabilities.* New York: Brunner/Mazel.

***See also* Brown v. Board of Education; Education for All Handicapped Children Act of 1975; Individuals with Disabilities Education Act (IDEA); Mills v. Board of Education**

RIGHT TO TREATMENT

The term right to treatment refers to the legal concept that justifies an individual's freedom to receive therapeutic and/or curative services. Initially developed as an extension of litigation that targeted the availability of medically oriented services for institutionalized individuals, recent legal interpretations of this right have been broadened to include the right to habilitation and the right to education.

The development of the right to treatment reflects a trend of change in societal attitudes about providing services for individuals with exceptional learning or behavioral characteristics. As attitudes have changed, concerned individuals have organized systematic efforts to ensure the availability of these services. These changes have resulted in litigative and legislative efforts that have addressed both the availability and adequacy of treatment for institutionalized people.

The three major court cases that shaped the legal interpretation of the right to treatment are *Rouse v. Cameron* (1968), *Wyatt v. Stickney* (1970), a class-action suit, and *New York Association for Retarded Citizens v. Rockefeller* (1972). In these cases constitutional amendments and state laws were interpreted as requiring treatment services for institutionalized persons. The first court case that dealt with the right of an institutionalized person to receive treatment was *Rouse v. Cameron* (1968). In this case, a man was institutionalized for 4 years after having been found not guilty, by reason of insanity, of a misdemeanor. While institutionalized, Rouse did not receive treatment. Citing constitutional rights (due process, equal protection, freedom from cruel and unusual punishment) and basing the decision on state law, the court ruled that confinement for treatment purposes when treatment was not made available was equivalent to imprisonment. Rouse was subsequently freed.

***See also* Right to Education; Wyatt v. Stickney**

RILEY-DAY SYNDROME

Riley-Day syndrome, also referred to as Familial Dysautonomia (FD), is a rare, autosomal (non-sex-related chromosome) recessive, genetic disease primarily afflicting Jewish children of Ashkenazi or Eastern European heritage. First described in 1949 by Drs. Riley, Day, Greeley, and Langford, Riley-Day syndrome/FD is a malfunction of the autonomic nervous system and poses severe physical, emotional, and social problems for the afflicted patients.

Individuals affected with FD are incapable of producing overflow tears with emotional crying. Frequent manifestations of FD include inappropriate perception of heat, pain, and taste, as well as labile blood pressures and gastrointestinal difficulties. Other problems experienced by individuals with FD include dysphagia (difficulty in swallowing), vomiting, aspiration and frequent pneumonia, speech and motor incoordination, poor growth, and scoliosis. Other frequent signs are delayed developmental milestones; unsteady gait; corneal anesthesia; marked sweating with excitement, eating, or the first stage of sleep; breath-holding episodes; spinal curvature (in 90% by age 13); red puffy hands; and an absence of fungiform papillae (taste buds) on the tongue (NYU, 1999).

There is no cure for FD, but many of the symptoms can be treated through a variety of interventions and medication. Affected individuals usually are of normal intelligence, and FD patients can be expected to function independently if treatment is begun early and major disabilities avoided. Special education services may be provided under the category of Noncategorical Early Childhood or Other Health Impaired. Early identification and intervention is extremely important for FD children to address developmental delays, gross motor and walking delays, and failure to thrive due to feeding difficulties and excessive vomiting. Upon entering school, speech, physical, and occupational therapies may be beneficial. Specialized feeding techniques may need to be taught. Adapted physical education may be needed to prevent injuries due to insensitivity to pain, and to monitor difficulties with the inability to control body temperature. Individuals affected with FD are prone to depression, anxieties, and even phobias. Families of FD affected children may need psychological support to assist with the emotional demands of caring for a child with a debilitating disease. For additional information contact the Dysautonomia Foundation Inc., 20 East 46th Street, New York, N.Y., 10017 or call (212) 949-6644.

REFERENCE

New York University Health System. (1999). http://www.med.nyu.edu/fd/fdcenter. html.

RISK MANAGEMENT IN SPECIAL EDUCATION

Many times educational settings are unaware of the relationship between school practices and legal liability. Risk management is a proactive stance that attempts to identify potential areas of liability, evaluate current policy and standards, and provide workable strategies in an attempt to prevent injury and minimize liability (Phillips, 1990).

Common risk management strategies in educational settings include appropriate documentation when altering a child's instructional curriculum, specified protocol when a student has expressed suicidal feelings, adherence to state regulations and guidelines in diagnostic assessments, informed consent procedures for parents and children regarding school counseling, and maintaining adequate liability coverage (Woody, 1988). Risk management strategies for school personnel include knowing and following ethical guidelines, and keeping current with professional development and standards of practice (Phillips, 1990).

REFERENCES

Phillips, B.N. (1990). Law, psychology, and education. In T.R. Kratochwill (Ed.), *Advances in School Psychology* (Vol. 7, pp. 79–130). Hillsdale, NJ: Erlbaum.

Woody, R.H. (1988). *Fifty ways to avoid malpractice.* Sarasota, Florida: Professional Resource Exchange.

RITALIN

Ritalin, the trade name for methylphenidate, is a central nervous system stimulant commonly prescribed for children with an abnormally high level of activity or with attention-deficit/hyperactivity disorder (ADHD). Ritalin is also occasionally prescribed for individuals with narcolepsy, mild depression, or withdrawn senile behavior (Shannon, Wilson, & Stang, 1995).

Although all the intricacies of Ritalin are not fully understood, it increases the attention span in ADHD children (Deglin & Vallerand, 1999). Ritalin stimulates the central nervous system with effects similar to weak amphetamines or very strong coffee. Its effects include (a) increasing attention and reducing activity in hyperactive children, apparently by stimulating inhibitory centers (NIDAInfofax, 1998); (b) diminishing fatigue is in individuals with narcolepsy; and (c) increasing motor activity and mental alertness in individuals exhibiting withdrawn senile behavior (Shannon et al., 1995).

All individuals need to be advised to take sustained released Ritalin as a whole tablet and never to crush or chew the pill. Ritalin should be taken at regular intervals during the day and only by the individual for whom it is prescribed (Deglin & Vallerand, 1999). As a stimulant medication, Ritalin may cause sleep disorders if taken late in the day (Skidmore-Roth & McKenry, 1997). To minimize insomnia, the last dose of Ritalin should be taken before 6:00 PM. Weight loss is another potential side effect of this medication, and individuals should be advised to weigh themselves at least twice weekly (Deglin & Vallerand, 1999). Because of the combined effects of multiple stimulants, all individuals should be informed that they should refrain from drinking any caffeine-containing beverages such as cola or coffee (Skidmore-Roth & McKenry, 1997). As with any continuous medication regime, school personnel should be notified of the medication and any other health-related concerns (Wong, 1995).

Stimulant medications such as Ritalin have strong potential for abuse, and the United States Drug Enforcement Administration (DEA) has placed numerous stringent controls on Ritalin's manufacture, distribution, and prescription. Ritalin is documented to be a strong, effective, and safe medication, but the potential risks in long-term usage need further investigation (NIDAInfofax, 1998).

REFERENCES

Deglin, J., & Vallerand, A. (1999). *Davis's drug guide for nurses* (6th ed.). Philadelphia: F.A. Davis. NIDAInfofax. (1998, February 27). http://www.nida.nih.gov/Infofax/ritalin.html.

Shannon, M., Wilson, B., & Stang, C. (1995). *Govoni & Hayes drugs and nursing implications* (8th ed.). Norwalk, CT: Appleton & Lange.

Skidmore-Roth, L., & McKenry, L. (1997). *Mosby's drug guide for nurses* (2nd ed.). St. Louis: Mosby-Year Book.

Wong, D. (1995). *Whaley & Wong's nursing care of infants and children* (5th ed.). St. Louis: Mosby-Year Book, Inc.

See also **Attention-Deficit Hyperactivity Disorder; Medical Management**

ROBERTS APPERCEPTION TEST FOR CHILDREN (RATC)

The Roberts Apperception Test for Children (RATC) is a projective personality assessment technique designed for children ages 6 to 15. The RATC is an attempt to combine the flexibility of a projective technique with the objectivity of a standardized scoring system. Similar to the Thematic Apperception Test and the Children's Apperception Test, the RATC consists of a set of drawings designed to elicit thematic stories. The test consists of 27 cards, 11 of which are parallel forms for males and females. Thus 16 cards are administered during testing, which takes 20 to 30 minutes.

The RATC is said to have significant benefits over similar projective measures (McArthur & Roberts, 1982). The test manual is well designed and includes substantial information on psychometric properties of the test, administration, and scoring, as well as several case studies. The picture drawings were designed specifically for children and young adolescents, and depict scenes designed to elicit common concerns. For example, specific cards portray parent/child relationships, sibling relationships, aggression, mastery, parental disagreement and affection, observation of nudity, school, and peer relationships. The test has a standardized scoring system, with scores converted to normalized T scores based on data from a sample of 200 well-adjusted children.

Overall, the RATC appears to be a well-designed projective technique for children and young adolescents. The standardized scoring system, while lacking in evidence compared with purely objective measures of personality, appears to be relatively satisfactory compared with similar projective techniques.

REFERENCE

McArthur, D., & Roberts, G. (1982). *Roberts Apperception Test for Children: Test Manual.* Los Angeles: Western Psychological Services.

See also **Child Psychology; Personality Assessment**

ROBINOW'S SYNDROME

See RARE DISEASES.

ROBINSON, HALBERT B. (1925–1981) AND ROBINSON, NANCY M. (1930–)

Nancy and Hal Robinson have done extensive work in the areas of children with mental retardation, early child care, and gifted children. They coauthored *The Mentally Retarded Child: A Psychological Approach* (1976), an influential text defining the field of mental retardation and emphasizing its research base, and coedited the *International Monograph Series on Early Child Care* (1974), which offers descriptions of early child care options of nine nations, including the United States.

In 1966, with Ann Peters, Hal Robinson founded the Frank Porter Graham Child Development Center at the University of North Carolina (Robinson & Robinson, 1971), and in 1969 he accepted a position at the University of Washington, Seattle (UW) as a professor of psychology. While at UW, Hal also served as the principal investigator of the Child Development Research Group (CDRG, now the Halbert Robinson Center for the Study of Capable Youth). Child Development Preschool, formerly a CDRG program (later independent of UW), focused on the identification and development of curriculum for children with advanced intellectual and academic skills (Roedell, Jackson, & Robinson, 1980), while the UW Early Entrance Program admitted middle school-age students to the University, depending on their readiness, prior to entering high school (Robinson & Robinson).

Of their many honors, the Robinsons received the Education Award of the American Association on Mental Deficiency (1982). Additionally, Nancy has served as editor of the *American Journal of Mental Deficiency,* and after Hal's death in 1981, she assumed the directorship of the Hal Robinson Center for the Study of Capable Youth, a position she holds today. She is also a professor of psychiatry and behavioral science at UW, and has continued to publish on important topics including the counseling of highly gifted children and mathematically gifted children (Robinson, 1996; Robinson, Abbot, Berninger, Busse, & Mukhopadhyay, 1997).

REFERENCES

Robinson, H.B., & Robinson, N.M. (1971). Longitudinal development of very young children in a comprehensive day care program: The first two years. *Child Development, 42,* 1673–1683.

Robinson, H.B., Robinson, N.M., Wolins, M., Bronfenbrenner, U., & Richmond, J.B. (1974). Early child care in the United States. In H.B. Robinson & N.M. Robinson (Eds.), *International monograph series on early child care.* London: Gordon, Breach.

Robinson, N.M. (1996). Counseling agendas for gifted young people: A commentary. *Journal for the Education of the Gifted, 20*(2), 128–137.

Robinson, N.M., Abbot, R.D., Berninger, V.W., Busse, J., & Mukhopadhyay, S. (1997). Developmental changes in mathematically precocious young children: Longitudinal and gender effects. *Gifted Child Quarterly, 41*(4), 145–158.

Robinson, N.M., & Robinson, H.B. (1976). *The mentally retarded child: A psychological approach* (2nd ed.). New York: McGraw-Hill.

Robinson, N.M., & Robinson, H.B. (1982). The optimal match: Devising the best compromise for the highly gifted student. In D.H. Feldman (Ed.), *Developmental approaches to giftedness and creativity.* San Francisco: Jossey-Bass.

Roedell, W.C., Jackson, N.E., & Robinson, H.B. (1980). *Gifted young children.* New York: Columbia University.

ROBOTICS IN SPECIAL EDUCATION

Robotics in special education serves two potential functions. First, robotics can operate as an auxiliary to education by providing novel instruction to students, increasing motivation, and acting as an extension of the teacher in an instructional role. These auxiliary educational functions can be found in robots and robotic educational systems available today. They have been put to productive, albeit limited, use in special education. Little research has been conducted to test the efficacy of such uses.

A second, and perhaps potentially more dramatic, use of robotics for the handicapped concerns the robot as an extension of self. The robot is controlled by the individual to meet his or her personal needs and objectives and to control the environment. These functions demand a robot capable of a high level of sophistication in its logic and actions.

Speculation on the usefulness of robotics has focused on handicapped conditions that limit mobility, dexterity, and interaction with the environment (Kimbler, 1984). The robot has been conceptualized as providing missing or impaired human functions under the direction of the disabled individual. Remote control devices have been used in this manner to some extent, and individual robots have been employed in restricted environments to perform limited functions such as serving meals. However, these applications have required modification of the environment. Ideally, the capacity of the robot would be more generalized; it would perform its functions by interacting with existing environments. A second major type of disability for which robotics applications have been conceptualized is sensory impairments, including visual and auditory disabilities. In these cases, the robot would provide sensory interaction as a mobile, dextrous adaptive device, permitting individuals to perceive the environment and then to operate on the setting directly or to control the robot to interact for them.

To support these functions, certain performance characteristics are necessary. For example, mobility under internal control to accomplish external demands is required. This movement needs to be smooth, to vary in speed from very slow to quick, and to react to novel environments through sensory systems. Robotics for these purposes require both payload, or strength and manipulation for that which needs to be carried, and dexterity dimensions to support varied and precise functions. The intelligence of the robot must allow reception and transmission of information through sensory apparatus, coordination of basic motion with its command and sensory input, communication in a conversational mode, and adaptation to new settings and uses. Finally, the robot must combine these characteristics with reasonable size; for acceptable and practical use, the robot must approximate the size of an average adult but maintain adequate bulk, stability, and power.

REFERENCE

Kimbler, D.L. (1984). Robots and special education: The robot as extension of self. In T.S. Hasselbring (Ed.), Toward the advancement of microcomputer technology in special education, *Peabody Journal of Education, 62,* 67–76.

ROCHESTER METHOD

The Rochester method is an oral, multisensory procedure for instructing deaf children in which speech reading is simultaneously supplemented by finger spelling and auditory amplification. The language of signs is wholly excluded from this procedure of instruction. (Quigley & Young, 1965).

The Rochester method was established by Zenos Westervelt at the Rochester School for the Deaf, in Rochester, New York, in 1878. Westervelt was convinced that finger spelling was the best means of teaching deaf children grammatically correct language. He believed that the easy visibility of finger spelling could help in lip reading as well as in speech instruction (Levine, 1981). The Rochester method is directly related to the method used by Juan Pablo Bonet of Spain. He advocated the use of a combination of a one-handed alphabet and speech in his book *The simplification of sounds and the art of teaching mutes to speak,* published in 1620. This method had a resurgence in the Soviet Union in the 1950s under the name neo-oralism, and in the United States in the 1960s (Moores, 1982).

Various studies have assessed the effectiveness of the Rochester method as an educational tool. Reviewing these, Quigley and Paul (1984) reported that, in general, researchers concluded that deaf children exposed to the Rochester method performed better than comparison groups in finger spelling, speech reading, written language, and reading. They also found that, when good oral techniques are used in conjunction with finger spelling, there are no detrimental effects to the acquisition of oral skills.

REFERENCES

Levine, E. (1981). *The ecology of early deafness.* New York: Columbia University Press.

Moores, D. (1982). *Educating the deaf: Psychology, principles and practices.* Boston: Houghton Mifflin.

Quigley, S., & Paul, P. (1984). *Language and deafness.* San Diego, CA: College-Hill.

Quigley, S., & Young, J. (Eds.). (1965). *Interpreting for deaf people.* Washington, DC: U.S. Department of Health, Education, and Welfare.

See also **Deaf; Sign Language Training; Total Communication**

ROEPER REVIEW

The *Roeper Review*, published since 1977 by the Roeper City and Country School, is a journal on the education of gifted students. It originated as an information periodical for parents whose children attended the Roeper City and County School. The journal has three purposes: (1) presenting philosophical, moral, and academic issues that are related to the lives and experiences of gifted and talented persons; (2) presenting various views on those issues; and (3) translating theory into practice for use at school, at home, and in the general community (Staff, 1983, p. ii).

The audience and authors for *Roeper Review* include practicing teachers and administrators, teacher-educators, psychologists, and scientists. They are served by in-depth coverage of important topics in each issue. Some examples of issues discussed in past editions are teacher education for gifted education, social studies education for the gifted, special subpopulations among gifted students, and perceptions of gifted students and their education. The mailing address is *Roeper Review*, Box 329, Bloomfield Hills, MI 48013.

REFERENCE

Staff. (1983). Statement of purpose. *Roeper Review, 6*, ii.

ROGER, HARRIET B. (1834–1919)

Harriet B. Roger began the first oral school for the instruction of the deaf in the United States in 1863 when she accepted a deaf child as a private pupil in her home. With published accounts of the instruction of the deaf in Germany to guide her, she taught herself how to instruct the child. Her success in this undertaking led to the admission of other deaf children. One of these was Mabel Hubbard, who became Mrs. Alexander Graham Bell and whose father, a prominent lawyer, obtained legislation for the creation of an oral school for the deaf in Massachusetts. Hubbard formed this school by moving Rogers' school to Northampton, where, in 1867, they established the Clarke School for the Deaf, the second purely oral school for the deaf in the United States (the Lexington School for the Deaf having opened in New York City earlier that year). Rogers, the first teacher and the instructional leader of the Clarke School, remained there until her retirement in 1886.

REFERENCE

Lane, H. (1984). *When the mind hears.* New York: Random House.

RORSCHACH INKBLOT TEST

The Rorschach inkblot test is a widely-used projective personality assessment technique. The test is administered in a non-directive fashion (Exner, 1995). Respondents are asked to describe what he or she can see in a series of ten inkblots. Administration time with children is approximately 30 minutes, with interpretation taking 30 to 45 minutes. Examiners transcribe the respondent's words and identify the visual percepts, which are then coded and tabulated through an extensively researched, empirically-based system. Considerable examiner training is necessary to accomplish the administration, coding, and interpretation tasks.

The Comprehensive System (Exner, 1993) approach makes the Rorschach an objective multiscale performance and personality test. Its administration and coding standards, normative data, and accumulated research provide a sturdy empirical basis to the test. Test-retest reliability for children is as expected given developmental considerations: Some variables demonstrate relatively strong test-retest reliability for a year or two at a during the primary grade school years (Exner, Thomas, & Mason, 1985; Exner & Weiner, 1995). Test-retest reliability increases gradually, so that almost all measures of trait variables are relatively stable by age 18.

The test yields a large number of variables related to the domains of cognition, affect, interpersonal perception, self-perception, and coping styles, and also various characteristics related to diagnostic categories. Personality, coping, and problem-solving interpretations can be synthesized, along with observations about social, school, family, and problem behaviors, into a description of the psychological functioning of the child.

Criticism of the test has been a popular rallying cry, but empirical reports indicate adequate validity and utility, particularly for issues that are not readily accessible through self-report, brief interview, or observation (Exner, 1993; Viglione, in press). The fact that all responses are formulated by the subject without prefabrication from test developers allows the test to access personally meaningful information. For example, the Rorschach can shed light on issues that the respondent may be unwilling or unable to express. No other instrument yields such an efficient, yet comprehensive, empirically-based understanding of the individual. Criticism about the test may result from a misunderstanding of its so-called 'projective components'. This is not a test of imagination, and it goes far beyond projective processes, despite unfortunate and inaccurate characterizations (e.g., Dawes, 1994).

Rorschach variables have demonstrated concurrent and predictive validity for both academic achievement test scores and classroom performance by young children, even after the effects of intelligence were statistically removed (e.g., Russ, 1980, 1981; Wulach, 1977). These results support the belief that the Rorschach addresses cognitive motivational trends and real-life application of abilities.

As far as the special education evaluation goals of truly understanding a child, the Rorschach can help to identify the psychological factors associated with the expression of observed strengths and weaknesses. For example, the test can help to identify and to understand emotional and psychological disturbances that impede learning, difficulties with peer and authority relationships, inappropriate behaviors which interfere with school performance and socialization, and problem-solving styles which result in poor performance despite intellectual abilities. However, the use of the Rorschach remains controversial and an opposing view of its reliability and validity is available in Sechrest, Stickle, and Stewart (1998).

REFERENCES

Dawes, R.M. (1994). *House of cards: Psychology and psychotherapy built on myth.* New York: The Free Press.

Exner, J.E. (1993). *The Rorschach: A comprehensive system, Vol. 1: Basic foundations* (3rd ed.). New York: Wiley.

Exner, J.E. (1995). *A Rorschach workbook for the comprehensive system* (4th ed.). Asheville, North Carolina: Rorschach Workshops.

Exner, J.E., Thomas, E.A., & Mason, B.J. (1985). Children's Rorschachs: Description and prediction. *Journal of Personality Assessment, 49,* 13–20.

Exner, J.E., & Weiner, I.B. (1995). *The Rorschach: A comprehensive system, Vol. 3: Assessment of children and adolescent* (2nd ed.). New York: Wiley.

Russ, S.W. (1980). Primary process integration on the Rorschach and achievement in children. *Journal of Personality Assessment, 44,* 338–344.

Russ, S.W. (1981). Primary process integration on the Rorschach and achievement in children: A follow-up study. *Journal of Personality Assessment, 45,* 473–477.

Sechrest, L., Stickle, T., & Stewart, M. (1998). The role of assessment in clinical psychology. In C.R. Reynolds (Ed.), *Assessment,* Vol. 4 of A. Bellack & M. Hersen (Eds.), *Comprehensive Clinical Psychology* (pp. 1–32). Oxford: Elsevier Science.

Viglione, D.J. (in press). A review of recent research addressing the utility of the Rorschach. *Psychological Assessment.*

Wulach, J.S. (1977). Piagetian cognitive development and primary process thinking in children. *Journal of Personality Assessment, 41,* 230–237.

ROSS INFORMATION PROCESSING ASSESSMENTS

The *Ross Information Processing Assessment–Second Edition* (RIPA–2) provides quantifiable data for profiling 10 key areas basic to communicative and cognitive functioning: Immediate Memory, Recent Memory, Temporal Orientation (Recent and Remote Memory), Spatial Orientation, Orientation to Environment, Recall of General Information, Problem Solving and Abstract Reasoning, Organization, and Auditory Processing and Retention. The RIPA–2 enables the examiner to quantify cognitive–linguistic deficits, determine severity levels for specific skill areas, and develop rehabilitation goals and objectives.

The *Ross Information Processing Assessment–Primary* is designed for children ages 5 through 12 who have had a traumatic brain injury, experienced other neuropathologies such as seizure disorders or anoxia, or exhibit learning disabilities or weaknesses that interfere with learning acquisition. The eight subtests measure immediate and recent memory, spatial orientation, temporal orientation, organization, problem solving, abstract reasoning, and recall of general information.

The RIPA–P was standardized on 115 individuals ages 5 through 12. Reliability coefficients were found to be .81 or above, and more than a third of them were over .90. Valid- ity studies show that the test discriminates between "normal" and LD or neurological problems. Item discrimination coefficients for the RIPA–P range from .39 to .94. Norms include children who have learning disabilities.

REFERENCES

Ross-Swain, D. (1996). *Ross Information Processing Assessment– Second Edition.* Austin, TX: Pro-Ed.

Ross-Swain, D. (1999). Ross Information Processing Assessment– Primary. Austin, TX: Pro-Ed.

ROSWELL-CHALL DIAGNOSTIC READING TEST OF WORD ANALYSIS SKILLS, REVISED AND EXTENDED

The Roswell-Chall Diagnostic Reading Test was developed to evaluate the word analysis and word recognition skills of pupils reading at the first- through fourth-grade levels. It may also be used with pupils who are reading at higher levels where there is a suspicion of decoding and word recognition difficulties or for research and program evaluation.

Two comparable forms of the test are available. Each is individually administered. The test has 10 main subtests and 4 extended evaluation subtests. All of the subtests or only those deemed appropriate may be given. The following skills are measured: high-frequency words, single consonant sounds, consonant diagrams, consonant blends, short vowel words, short and long vowel sounds, rule of silent e's, vowel diagrams, common diphthongs and vowels controlled by *r*, and syllabication (and compound words). The extended evaluation subtests include naming capital letters, naming lower-case letters, encoding single consonants, and encoding phonetically regular words.

The test takes approximately 10 minutes to administer, score, and interpret. Score interpretations are provided in the manual. The test has good reliability and validity. Users should be concerned about the size and somewhat limited nature of the norm sample, therefore, the administrator should be knowledgeable in the kinds of skills needed in most individual testing situations and, in order to interpret the test accurately, be a relatively skilled reading clinician.

REFERENCE

Manual of instructions: Roswell-Chall Diagnostic Reading Test of Word Analysis Skills, Revised and Extended. (1978). LaJolla, CA: Essay.

ROTHMUND-THOMPSON SYNDROME

See RARE DISEASES.

ROUSSEAU, JEAN J. (1712–1778)

Jean Jacques Rousseau, French-Swiss philosopher and moralist, revolutionized child-rearing and educational practices with the publication, in 1762, of *Emile,* a treatise

Jean J. Rousseau

on education in the form of a novel. Rousseau contended that childhood is not merely a period of preparation for adulthood to be endured, but a developmental stage to be cherished and enjoyed. He enjoined parents and educators to be guided by the interests and capacities of the child, and was the first writer to propose that the study of the child should be the basis for the child's education. Probably every major educational reform since the eighteenth century can be traced in some way to Rousseau, and indebtedness to him is clear in the works of Pestalozzi, Froebel, Montessori, and Dewey. An eloquent writer, Rousseau's works on man's relationship with nature, as well as his writings on social, political, and educational matters, were major contributions to the literature of his day.

REFERENCES

Boyd, W. (1963). *The educational theory of Jean Jacques Rousseau.* New York: Russell & Russell.

Rousseau, J.J. (1969). *Emile.* New York: Dutton.

RUBELLA

Postnatal rubella (German measles) is a relatively mild viral infection that is generally inconsequential. It was first differentiated from measles and scarlet fever by German workers in the latter part of the eighteenth century. German scientists termed the disease *Roethelm.* According to *Black's Medical Dictionary,* the term German measles has no geographical reference but rather comes from the word germane, meaning akin to. Rubella comes from the Latin word *rubellus* meaning red (*Black's,* 1984).

The postnatal rubella virus is transmitted through contact with blood, bodily waste excretions, nasopharyngeal secretions of infected persons, and, possibly, contact with contaminated clothing (*Professional Guide to Diseases,* 1984). Because of the mild nature of rubella acquired postnatally, there is little concern for active treatment. The rash rarely requires topical ointments but aspirin may be taken to ease the discomfort associated with fever and body pains.

Children or adults with postnatal rubella should be isolated owing to the threat of infecting newly pregnant mothers.

Congenital rubella is a concern because of the 20 to 30% chance of damage to the fetus when a mother contracts the infection during the first trimester of pregnancy (Bonwick, 1972). Catastrophic damaging effects were first reported by Sir Norman Gregg, an Australian ophthalmologist, 1941. The classic congenital rubella syndrome as described by Gregg consists of fetal anomalies, ocular defects, and hearing impairment. Mental retardation was also shown to be a common result of early damage to the fetus.

Extensive investigations during the last 20 years have characterized congenital rubella as having pathologic potential much greater than was first assumed by Gregg. For instance, it is now hypothesized that congenital rubella, in addition to being responsible for the anomalies previously reported, may also be responsible for numerous abnormalities that appear later in life. These include dental problems, anemia, encephalitis, giant cell hepatitis, dermatitis, and diabetes.

Active prevention seems the key to reducing the impact of congenital rubella, as once the damage has been done in utero there appears to be little hope of reversing the effects. Of course, corrective surgery can be performed in cases where the fetus suffers cardiac damage or has cataracts, and hearing aids can be given to the hearing-impaired child, but the damage is not reversible.

Often the psychological impact of giving birth to a handicapped child can be as damaging as the virus itself. Parents of children with congenital rubella can obtain help and advice from the National Association for Deaf, Blind and Rubella Handicapped, 12 A Rosebery Avenue, London, England ECIR 4TD.

REFERENCES

Black's medical dictionary. (1984). Totowa, NJ: Barnes & Noble.

Bonwick, M. (1972). *Rubella and other intraocular viral diseases in infancy.* Boston: Little, Brown.

Professional guide to diseases. (1984). (pp. 384–386). Springhouse, PA: Springhouse.

See also **Cataracts; Congenital Disorders; Mental Retardation**

RUBENSTEIN-TAYBI SYNDROME

See RARE DISEASES.

RURAL SPECIAL EDUCATION

Approximately 67% of the 16,000 public school districts in the United States are classified as rural because of sparse population or geographic location (Sher, 1978). According to Helge (1984), educational characteristics of rural areas are distinctly different from those of urban areas. Rural areas have higher poverty levels and serve greater percentages of handicapped children. Populations in rural areas are increasing, however, their tax bases are not. Education costs more in rural areas than in nonrural areas because of transportation requirements and scarce professional resources.

Because of the remoteness of the areas, assessing the effectiveness of special education services to handicapped and gifted children has been difficult. One reason for this, according to the director of the National Rural Research Project (Helge, 1984) has been the absence of a consistently applied definition of the term rural among federal agencies, educators, and professional organizations. The definition that is most commonly used is the one developed for the 1978 to 1983 research projects funded by the U.S. Office of Special Education Programs and conducted by the National Rural Research and Personnel Preparation Project. This definition reads:

A district is considered rural when the number of inhabitants is fewer than 150 per square mile or when located in counties with 60% or more of the population living in communities not larger than 5000 inhabitants. Districts with more than 10,000 students and those within a Standard Metropolitan Statistical Area (SMSA), as determined by the U.S. Census Bureau, are not considered rural. (p. 296)

In an effort to focus on rural special education and the identified service delivery problems, the American Council on Rural Special Education was founded in 1981. This nonprofit national membership organization is an outgrowth of the National Rural Development Institute, headquartered at Western Washington University in Bellingham. The organization is composed of approximately 1000 rural special educators and administrators, parents of handicapped students, and university and state department personnel. The specific purposes of the organization are to enhance direct services to rural individuals and agencies serving exceptional students; to increase educational opportunities for rural handicapped and gifted students; and to develop a system for forecasting the future for rural special education and planning creative service delivery alternatives.

The American Council on Rural Special Education (ACRES) serves as an advocate for rural special education at the federal, state, regional, and local levels; provides professional development opportunities, and disseminates information on the current needs of rural special education. The ACRES has established a nationwide system to link educators and administrators needing jobs with agencies having vacancies. The ACRES Rural Bulletin Board communicates to interested agencies information regarding rural special education issues and promising practices through SpecialNet, the electronic communication system operated by the National Association of State Directors of Special Education. ACRES publishes a quarterly newsletter and a journal the *Rural Special Education Quarterly.* These publications include up-to-date information on issues facing handicapped students in rural America, problem-solving strategies, pertinent legislation and con-

ferences, and articles on rural preservice and in-service strategies. The ACRES also holds an annual conference each year in the spring, usually at the institute's headquarters. The conferences feature presentations to enhance services to rural handicapped and gifted children, media displays curriculum materials, and hardware and software exhibits.

REFERENCES

Helge, D.I. (1984). The state of the art of rural special education. *Exceptional Children, 50,* 294–305.

Sher, J.P. (1978). A proposal to end federal neglect of rural schools. *Phi Delta Kappan, 60,* 280–282.

RUSH, BENJAMIN (1745–1813)

Benjamin Rush, physician, teacher, reformer, and patriot, began medical practice in Philadelphia in 1769. He taught chemistry at the College of Philadelphia, and published the first American textbook on that subject. During the Revolutionary War, he served as surgeon-general of the Army and published a textbook on military medicine that was still in use at the time of the Civil War. Following his military service, Rush returned to the practice of medicine in Philadelphia, where he established the first free dispensary in the United States. He is believed to be the first physician to relate smoking to cancer and to advocate temperance and exercise to promote good health. An outspoken advocate of humane treatment for the mentally ill, in 1812 Rush published a work that would influence medical education for generations to come, *Medical Inquiries and Observations Upon the Diseases of the Mind.*

Despite his accomplishments as a physician, political and social issues were Rush's major interests. He was a member of the Continental Congress and a signer of the Declaration of Independence. He was active in the movement to abolish slavery, and was influential in the ratification of the federal Constitution in Pennsylvania. He involved himself in a number of educational causes, advocating improved education for girls and proposing a comprehensive system of public schools that would offer science and practical subjects as well as traditional academics.

REFERENCES

Hawke, D. (1971). *Benjamin Rush.* New York: Bobbs-Merrill.

Rush, B. (1962). *Medical inquiries and observations upon the diseases of the mind.* New York: Hafner.

RUSSELL-SILVER SYNDROME

See RARE DISEASES.

RUSSIA, SPECIAL EDUCATION IN

Special education in Russia first developed from the then-progressive ideas of Vygotsky, Luria, Boskis, Pevzner, Levina, Rau and other behavioral researchers. They approached the education of a child with special needs while considering his or her complex psychophysiological development, with the most complete possible social rehabilitation of a child as a goal. During the Communist regime these ideas were replaced by a pedagogy that was less child-centered, isolating a child with special needs from society, and establishing several boarding institutions (van Rijswijk et al., 1996).

Recently, Russia has entered a new phase in its thinking and attitudes about special education. A return to the individual child-focus has been augmented by the ideal for full participation or integration in society. Social rehabilitation continues to be valued, but social participation is also highly valued.

The modern phase into which special education has recently entered was necessary because of the absence of protective legislation for the civil rights of children with handicaps or with other special needs. This modern phase of special education in Russia places new emphases on preschool interventions and on staff training of teachers, psychologists, social workers, and others.

During the Soviet period in the republics of the former USSR, the rights of the child (as indicated in the UNO Convention, the UNO Declaration on the rights of the invalids and the rights of the mentally handicapped people) were not well-observed. Within the last decade, Russia's central government has taken firm steps toward ratification and realization of these international documents. Nevertheless, still there is inadequate legislation for special education, although there is some progress in this direction (Aksenova, 1997). The new phase for special education was signaled in part by a landmark Law on Education (1992), which was considered one of the most democratic in the history of Russia. This law was followed four years later by several further insertions and improvements to "About the Education;" these went into effect January 5th, 1996.

The Law on Education significantly improves the state guarantee of a free, appropriate public education to people with disabilities. Particularly, Article 50, Point 10 of the Law foresees the establishment of the special (correctional) educational institutions for children and adolescents with special needs, where they can have treatment, upbringing, education, social adaptation, and integration into society. Note that social rehabilitation is emphasized more than social participation.

A second law that marks the modern phase of special education in Russia is "On Social Care of Invalids," which went into effect on January 1st, 1996. Article 18 of this Law is dedicated to the upbringing and education of child invalids. According to the law, the educational institutions together with social and health care organizations must provide upbringing and education of children with disabilities, from preschool through secondary school, both within classrooms and outside, according to an individually defined program of rehabilitation. In both mainstream schools and special educational institutions, this education is free.

Another change in the modern phase is that the subjects of the Russian Federation (RF) have received the right to make legislation for solving their local problems, including the field of help and care of children and their families. This is appropriate because the financing of education, health, and other social services is carried out mainly at the expense of local budgets (which also brings about regional differences in type and quality of services). These legislative changes have encouraged public organizations to play a significant role in the improvement of children with special needs. In addition, public interest groups are beginning to attempt to influence regional decision-making in the field of special education. Newly active public organizations are representing the interests of children with disabilities and their families. However, the national networking and sharing of information is still minimal. For example, there is not a uniform data bank on children with disabilities and programs in operation, let alone data on program effectiveness.

Although the recent Russian legislation for the children with special needs is a major step forward, it touches only some aspects of special education. Now Russia must develop a new law specifically for special education; in fact, a draft has been worked out and is under consideration by the State Duma.

STRUCTURE OF SPECIAL EDUCATION

In Russia, several ministries are responsible for children with special needs, which causes a number of difficulties. The interdepartmental barriers interfere with creation of an integrated, harmonious, and effective system of social care and support. There is a whole complex of problems: social, scientific, practical. The largest obstacle to progress is the absence of high-grade statistical information about such children; in the Russian Federation there is no uniform state system to account for them.

The system of special education in Russia is based on five age designations and the specific type of disability.

Age structure. The vertical structure consists of 5 levels:

- Early childhood (from 0 to 3 years old);
- Preschool period (from 3 to 7);
- Compulsory education (from 7 to 16);
- Comprehensive education and vocational training (from 15 to 18 and up to 21 for the blind, deaf, and physically handicapped);
- Adults-invalid training.

Special (remedial) educational establishments for children with developmental problems offer programs of elementary regular education, general regular education, and general comprehensive regular education. These establishments must meet special state educational standards. They focus on special remedial work, education, treatment, social adaptation, and integration into the society.

Persons with developmental problems may receive both a regular education and vocational training in:

- Special average schools
- Special industrial workshops
- Centers of social-labor rehabilitation
- Special vocational schools.

DISABILITY-TYPE (HORIZONTAL) STRUCTURE

The horizontal structure of special education in Russia is by eight types of disability:

   I. For the deaf (classes for mentally retarded children)

  II. For the hard of hearing (classes for mentally retarded children)

 III. For the blind (classes for mentally retarded children)

 IV. For visually impaired (classes for mentally retarded children)

  V. With severe speech and language disorders

 VI. With emotional disabilities (classes for mentally retarded children)

VII. With learning disabilities

VIII. For mentally retarded (special classes for children with severe mental retardation, classes for children with multiple and complex disorders).

For children and teenagers with deviant behavior there exist three kinds of special educational establishments in Russia:

- Special educational school
- Special vocational technical school
- Special (remedial) comprehensive school and special (remedial) professional technical school for children and teenagers with problems

Russia is still marked by the existence of large numbers of separate special education boarding schools, where the majority of children get psychological, medical and pedagogical help. Such boarding schools became popular for two reasons. First, because of Russia's large territory, in rural areas the school is usually situated so far from home that daily attendance is impossible. Secondly, many of these children do not have parents, have been given up for adoption, or have been refused by their parents, becoming wards of the state.

INTEGRATED EDUCATION FOR CHILDREN WITH SPECIAL NEEDS

In the latter part of the 1990s, special education in Russia improved in two main ways: improvement in the existing network of special education programs and their expansion; and improvement in the integrated education of these children (Shipitsina, 1996).

Generally, in Russia, there are few statistics about the number of children with visual, hearing, and other impairments educated in mainstream schools. We do know that the majority of such children do not get any special help in ordinary schools. In recent years in Moscow, Saint Petersburg, and some other big cities of Russia, research began on the practical psychological and pedagogical guidance of children with sensory and moving problems in the mainstream school.

So far in Russia, the attitude to integrative education is restrained. Parents of children with impairments are commonly advised to place their child in a special boarding home from his or her very early life. The justification is usually that mainstream schools do not have the special staff and that the children cannot receive necessary support in mainstream classes in these schools. Unfortunately, this argument is partly true, as regular schools lack resources, expertise and philosophies of integration. Usually the nature of integration is not questioned; the majority agree that it is good in the abstract, but that the practical obstacles are too great. Where attitudes are the problem, they usually come from the teachers in the mainstream schools (Makhortova, 1996).

INCLUSIVE EDUCATION IN THE REGULAR CLASSROOM

Children with different disabilities are included differentially in general education classrooms in Russia. Children with hearing impairments have only recently been included. Today the process of integration of such children into mainstream establishments is steadily expanding (Shmatko, 1996). The integrated education of children with sight impairments in the mainstream school is a rare phenomenon, and most mainstream schools are not yet ready for it. Some of the hesitation is due to concern for the adjustment of the child with disabilities. Some contend that full integration may increase personal problems (Makhortova, 1996).

SPECIAL CLASSES IN THE MAINSTREAM SCHOOL

Today in Russia, one of the fastest growing models of integrative education is the organization of special classes in the mainstream school. They are organized:

—for the children with intellectual impairments (where there are not any special schools for this category of the children nearby), their number is rather small

—for the children with learning difficulties, the classes with special educational support or remedial classes

—for the children "of risk groups" (with learning difficulties, behavior problems, weak health), the classes of compensative education, special educational support, adaptation, and recreation.

In rare cases, due to the large distance from the special schools and unwillingness of the parents to refer their children to receive the education in the boarding schools, special classes or groups for children with sight, hearing, and speech impairments are organized in the mainstream kindergartens and schools.

Despite the positive results of the work of special classes in mainstream schools, serious problems are still not solved.

- First, students depend upon the existence of specialists (psychologists, speech therapists, special teachers), which are too few to service the children.
- Frequently, teachers refuse to work in special classes because of difficulties and lack of necessary knowledge about children with problems in development.
- Special classes often have a stigma attached, leading to aggressive social behavior and negative attitudes among peers.
- These classes promote the process of separating out children from the mainstream, permitting general educators to escape from their full responsibilities. Thus, the methods of selecting children for the special classed may be suspect.
- Mainstream education lacks the vocational training that many students with disabilities need in the secondary grades.

Despite all the problems and difficulties, it should be understood that in Russia the process of integration of the children with special needs into the mainstream schools is accelerating. Throughout the country, diverse models and forms of interaction between special and mainstream schools are developing; special schools are being de-emphasized; and conditions for both social adaptation and personal development are being more closely approached that ever before.

REFERENCES

Aksenova, L.I. (1997). Legal bases of special education and social care of children with problems in development. *Journal Defectology, 1,* 3.

State Report about the Situation of Children in Russian Federation-1996. (1997). Moscow.

Makhortova, G.H. (1996). Problems of psychological adaptation of children with visual impairments in the mainstream schools, *Journal of Defectology, 4,* 45–50.

Shipitsina, L.M. (1996). The topical aspects of integrative education of children with problems in development in Russia. *Integrative Education: Problems and Prospects.*

van Rijswijk, K., Foreman, N., & Shipitsina, L.M. (Eds.). (1996). Special education on the Move. Acco Leuven/Amersfoort.

See also **Luria, A.R.; Vygotsky, L.S.**

SAFETY ISSUES IN SPECIAL EDUCATION

Accountability, malpractice, due process, and liability insurance are all terms familiar to special educators. For teachers to gain protection from legal situations it is critical that children's safety become a high priority. In particular, physically impaired and severely handicapped children are more prone to accidents, medical emergencies, and injuries. Therefore, teachers must take certain precautions to protect students and staff from unnecessary risks. Specifically, educators must consider many facets of the classroom program in order to create safe environments for children. Four major areas related to safety must be considered: (1) basic first aid skills, (2) emergency weather and fire drill procedures, (3) safe classroom environments, and (4) parent consent and involvement in classroom activities.

Many states require teachers to obtain certification in first-aid procedures before they are eligible to obtain a teaching certificate. In particular, teachers should be trained in cardiopulmonary resuscitation (CPR) and anti-choking procedures such as the Heimlich maneuver. For teachers working with children who have seizures, a clear understanding of first-aid procedures for managing seizures is critical. Furthermore, basic instruction on poison management, eye injuries, and contusions must be included in first-aid programs. In the same context, children on medication such as Ritalin, Phenobarbital, and Dilantin, must be carefully monitored for signs of over or under dosage. Teachers should never be left solely responsible for dispensing any medications to children without the assistance of a physician or school nurse.

Much has been written on designing school facilities and classroom environments for handicapped students (Abend, Bednor, Froehlinger, & Stenzler, 1979; Birch & Johnstone, 1975; Forness, Gutherie, & MacMillan, 1982; Hutchins & Renzaglia, 1983; Zentall, 1983). Environmental designing of classrooms also involves a safety aspect for children in special education. For example, many classrooms for physically handicapped or blind students should have adequate storage space for bulky equipment (e.g., wheelchairs, walkers) and materials (e.g., braillers, books, canes). A classroom that is organized and neat ensures safety for children. Cabinets within the classroom holding harmful materials should be inaccessible to students in the classroom. Rossol (1982) discusses the possible hazards to students in special education using art materials.

In conclusion, safety in special education is a topic that is rarely found in the literature, yet it has enormous implications for teachers working with handicapped children. Although much of what has been discussed is commonsense, it is important to remind teachers of the many safety aspects in special education.

REFERENCES

Abend, A., Bednor, M., Froehlinger, V., & Stenzler, Y. (1979). *Facilities for special education services.* Reston, VA: Council for Exceptional Children.

Birch, J., & Johnstone, B. (1975). *Designing schools and schooling for the handicapped.* Springfield, IL: Thomas.

Forness, S., Guthrie, D., & MacMillan, D. (1982). Classroom environments as they relate to mentally retarded children's observable behavior. *American Journal of Mental Deficiency, 3,* 259–265.

Hutchins, M., & Renzaglia, A. (1983). Environmental considerations for severely handicapped individuals: The needs and the questions. *Exceptional Education Quarterly, 4,* 67–71.

Rossol, M. (1982). *Teaching art to high risk groups.* (ERIC Document Reproduction Service No. ED 224 182)

Zentall, S. (1983). Learning environments: A review of physical and temporal factors. *Exceptional Education Quarterly, 4,* 90–115.

See also Accessibility of Programs; Liability of Teachers in Special Education; Medically Fragile Students; Ritalin

SAVE THE CHILDREN FUND AND CHILDREN WITH DISABILITIES

Save the Children began when Eglantyne Jebb, the organization's founder, drew up the *Charter On the Rights of the Child* in 1919. Special mention was made of the disabled child, and this charter has now been enshrined in the UN Convention on the Rights of the Child. Disabled children are children first, and all articles in the convention that refer to children include disabled children.

Save the Children's current policy and practice on disabled children and education has developed from ongoing analytical reflection on a strong body of practical experience in a wide range of countries (in Asia, Africa, the Middle East, and Europe). Disabled children are defined as children with impairments (physical, mental, visual, hearing, speech, or multiple impairments) who are excluded or discriminated against in their local context and culture (Stubbs, 1997).

Many of the Western industrialized countries have a legacy of segregated special education provision and pro-

fessional special educators. In many economically poorer countries, there is more expertise on managing sparse resources, more community solidarity, and a strong tradition and experience of self-reliance. It is Save the Children's experience that pioneers in inclusive education are increasingly found in developing countries, and that there are many "lessons from the south" that can inform the international community (Holdsworth & Kay, 1996; Stubbs, 1997).

REFERENCES

Holdsworth, J., & Kay, J. (Eds.). (1996). *Toward inclusion: SCF UK's experience in integrated education.* Discussion paper, N.I. SEAPRO Documentation Series. Save the Children Fund.

Stubbs, S. (1997). *Education and geopolitical change.* Presented at the Oxford International Conference on Education and Development, Great Britain.

SCALES OF INDEPENDENT BEHAVIOR–REVISED

The *Scales of Independent Behavior–Revised* (SIB–R; Bruininks, Woodcock, Weatherman, & Hill, 1996) is used to assess adaptive behavior and problem behavior. It includes three forms—a Full Scale, Short Form, and Early Development Form. A Short Form for the Visually Impaired is also available. Administration time ranges from 15 to 20 minutes for either the Short Form or Early Development Form to 45 to 60 minutes for the Full Scale. The SIB–R is norm-referenced and nationally standardized on 2,182 individuals. It is appropriate for use with individuals from birth to 80+ years.

The SIB–R is easier to administer than its predecessor, the original SIB. In addition to the structured interview procedure, a checklist procedure is now available. It is also easier to score. Age-equivalent scoring tables are included in the response booklets for each subscale. A significant feature is the addition of a Support Score, which predicts the level of support a person will require based on the impact of maladaptive behaviors and adaptive functioning. Another unique feature of the SIB–R is the functional limitations index, which can be used to define the presence and severity of functional limitations in adaptive behaviors.

The test manual contains internal consistency reliabilities (mid to high .90s), test-retest reliabilities for the adaptive behavior scales (.83–.97) and the maladaptive behavior indexes (.69–.90), and interrater reliabilities (most correlations in the .80s). Extensive validity studies reported in the Comprehensive Manual support the developmental nature of the SIB–R adaptive behavior scales. The SIB–R is strongly related to other adaptive behavior measures and highly predictive of placements in different types of service settings. There is very little independent research on the SIB–R.

REFERENCE

Bruininks, R.K., Woodcock, R.W., Weatherman, R.F., & Hill, B. (1996). *Scales of Independent Behavior—Revised* (SIB–R). Itasca, IL: Riverside.

See also Adaptive Behavior

SCALES OF ORDINAL DOMINANCE

See ORDINAL SCALES OF PSYCHOLOGICAL DEVELOPMENT.

SCANDINAVIA, SPECIAL EDUCATION IN

In all Scandinavian countries, special education reform has been dependent on reforms in regular education systems and schools. As part of ongoing globalization patterns, higher priority has been given to values such as competition and education for excellence. These values have been embraced in general education. The guiding perspective of special education policy is an inclusive one, with special education support as much as possible integrated into regular education frameworks. Sweden and Denmark have traditionally been considered leaders in inclusion, and Norway and Finland were seen as following behind (Tuunainen, 1994). This is no longer the case, at least regarding Norway. Decisions on school laws and curricula during the 1990s by Norway's Parliament are more radically inclusive than in the other Scandinavian countries.

As in Sweden, a few general societal policy conditions greatly influence special education. There is ongoing decentralization of decision power and responsibilities from the national level to local municipalities (less evident in Finland). This process is happening concurrent with the effects of an economic recession during most of the 1990s (less evident in Norway). In combination, these two circumstances have meant that responsibilities and decision-making power have been moved from national and/or central bodies to local municipalities and schools. In Sweden, Denmark, and Norway, there are little or no resources earmarked specifically for special education any longer. School laws and other official guidelines stress that schools shall give high priority to the fulfillment of students' special needs. These resource allocation decisions, made on local levels of the system, have had to be made at the same time as severe budget cuts during most of the 1990s. These matters have raised sincere questions about what is possible to spend on students with special needs, especially compared to other school and student needs. This is most evident in Sweden and Denmark and, to a lesser extent, in Norway. Norway still has some stipulations for resource allocation for guaranteed support to students with certain severe disabilities. This is a small proportion (only around 2%) of all students, though, and is also a small fraction of all students given special education support in the schools. According to results from an evaluation study (Skårbrevik, 1995), the support given in this way to students with severe disabilities also covers only 20% to 30% of their weekly hours in school. In Sweden and Denmark, this support has to be financed within the frameworks of regular school budgets.

The process of closing down special schools and institutions has continued, and very few special schools are now in use. Most of those are for students who are deaf or hard of hearing, or who have intellectual or multiple disabilities. Again, this closing is going on at a slower rate in Finland than in the other three countries. Many of the former institutions and special schools are in the process of developing into resource centers. Their responsibilities are firsthand competence development and consultant support to schools attended by students with severe disabilities. They also often give shorter, intensive training courses for students, family members, and school teachers. They are still financed by government money, which is seen as necessary in order to guarantee qualified support to children with the greatest need, regardless of where they live or go to school. In most respects these resource centers and their consultant responsibilities are organized on a basis. At the national level, Sweden has a National Swedish Agency for Special Education, a separate administrative body parallel to the National Agency for Schools. In Norway, the same national administrative body monitors both regular and special education, as well as education for those with more severe disabilities.

Decreasing proportions of students attend special schools or special classes, usually less than 2% or 3% a year. It must be taken into account, though, that such proportion figures do not always give the full picture. This has to do with the decentralized and goal-based educational systems. Partly, this means that differences between local municipalities and schools are increasing, even affecting definitions for special education. There are some statistics from evaluation study reports on what could be a trend toward increasing proportions of students referred to special groups or schools again. For instance, clustering of special education resources sometimes means organization of special classes and schools turning up again on local or regional levels. This is the case in Sweden, according to special schools for students with intellectual disabilities, but corresponding trends are clearly seen in Denmark and, lately, Norway. One factor behind such trends is a lack of sufficient resources, which is related to elite and competitive values and priorities. Also, school officials hear parent worries and complaints that their disabled children are not being adequately supported in the integrated settings. Both circumstances lead to more segregated solutions.

From having been nearly culturally homogeneous until the 1960s, Scandinavia has become increasingly multicultural through immigration. During the first decades immigration was mostly a result of labor; more recently, immigrants have moved to Scandinavian countries as refugees for different reasons. This is so especially in Denmark, Sweden, and Norway, while Finland still has a comparatively small immigration rate. In many Danish and Swedish municipalities, the proportion of inhabitants with immigrant background reaches 30% or more, and there are schools in these places where the proportion of immigrant background students are up to 80% to 85%. This multicultural situation creates challenges for special education.

Scandinavian countries are still in the vanguard of special education development in inclusive education. However, there are many conflicting current trends and widening gaps between more privileged students and those who are less well off. The welfare state model, often thought of as guaranteed, has become at risk of being dismantled during the last decade. These trends also have great influence on education policies, and especially on special education policy and practice. Therefore, Scandinavia will continue to be a very interesting focus for studies of special education.

REFERENCES

Skårbrevik, K. (1995). Spesialpedagogiske tiltak pa dagsorden. Evaluering av prosjektet "Omstrukturering av spesialundervisning." Volda: Høgskulen og Møreforsking, Forskingsrapport no. 14.

Tuunainen, K. (1994). Finland, Norway, and Sweden. In K. Mazurek & M. Winzer (Eds.), *Comparative studies in special education.* Washington, DC: Gallaudet University Press.

See also France, Special Education in; Western Europe, Special Education in

SCAPEGOATING

A scapegoat is generally defined as a person or group that bears the blame for the mistakes of others. Typically, this is manifested as a group singling out an individual for unfair attack. In schools such systematic victimization of one child by a group of others can isolate the child from the social life of the class and cause the child to feel unworthy of inclusion in the peer group. At times handicapped children may be scapegoats, particularly those with low self-esteem, which is usual with handicapped children owing to academic, emotional, or physical problems (Gearheart, 1985).

Nonhandicapped children require help with social skills as they interact with handicapped peers in mainstreamed classrooms. One problem that may arise is the calling of names, which can be dealt with in a variety of ways. Salend and Schobel (1981) described one strategy that they implemented with a fourth-grade class. Discussion included the meaning of names, how names differ, and the positive and negative consequences of names. The last topic included a discussion of the negative effects of nicknames and the importance of considering another person's reaction to the nickname. It is obvious that educators must seriously consider the effects of scapegoating and must continue to develop strategies to counteract the negative effects of scapegoating on handicapped children.

REFERENCES

Gearheart, B.R. (1985). *Learning disabilities.* St. Louis: Times Mirror/Mosby College Pub.

Salend, S.J., & Schobel, J. (1981). Coping with namecalling in the mainstream setting. *Education Unlimited, 3*(2), 36–38.

See also Self-Concept; Social Skills

SCHIZENCEPHALY

Schizencephaly is a disorder of grossly abnormal neuronal migration patterns with onset during fetal development. It is characterized by clefts in the parasylvian region of the brain along with additional openings in the regions of the pre- and postcentral gyri. These anomalies may or may not be symmetrical (Baron, Fennell, & Voeller, 1995). Other regions of the brain may also be involved in ways that are not predictable solely on the basis of the diagnosis of schizencephaly. The disorder is diagnosable via fetal ultrasound but CT and MRI studies after birth are necessary to view the extent of the abnormalities in brain structure.

Outcomes vary widely and may range from microcephaly and severe or profound levels of mental retardation to normal intelligence, although at least some neuropsychological impairment will always be present. Children with schizencephaly may have a variety of neurological problems including hydrocephalus, seizure disorders of various types, mental retardation, and coordination disorders of varying degrees of severity (Baron, Fennell, & Voeller, 1995). Special education programming will be necessary in virtually all cases, but only after careful assessment due to the highly variable expressivity of symptoms. As the child develops, the behavioral and mental symptom complex may change significantly and frequent, comprehensive neuropsychological examinations are recommended.

REFERENCE

Baron, I., Fennell, E., & Voeller, K. (1995). *Pediatric neuropsychology in the medical setting.* Oxford: Oxford University Press.

SCHIZOPHRENIA

See CHILDHOOD SCHIZOPHRENIA.

SCHOOL ATTENDANCE OF HANDICAPPED

School attendance of students with disabilities, and of all children, is affected by the following factors: motivational level, home and community problems, levels of stress, academic underachievement, rate of failure, negative self-concept, social difficulties, external directedness, improper school placement, inconsistent expectations by parents and teachers, employment outside of school, aversive elements in the school environment, and skill deficiencies (Grala & McCauley, 1976; Schloss, Kane, & Miller, 1981; Sing, 1998; Unger, Douds, & Pierce, 1978). Absenteeism is learned; as it becomes habitual, it increases and continues to reinforce itself (Stringer, 1973).

Schloss et al. (1981) evaluated factors related to adverse aspects of attending school and pleasant aspects of staying at home. An intervention program was individually developed to assist the student in increasing the amount of satisfaction received from going to school, decreasing the amount of satisfaction gained from staying home, and actively teaching skills that enhance the student's ability to benefit from going to school. Not only did school attendance improve, but test scores also increased. Unger et al. (1978) described a program that taught students the skills necessary to succeed in school. Each student's attendance pattern was examined, reasons for truancy evaluated, and individual lessons devised. Students' attendance and attitudes toward school both improved.

School attendance for handicapped children is mandated by the Individuals with Disabilities Education Act (IDEA). It is extremely important that absenteeism be evaluated constantly by the local educational agency and that steps be undertaken to remediate the situation on an individual basis whenever possible.

REFERENCES

Grala, R., & McCauley, C. (1976). Counseling truants back to school: Motivation combined with a program for action. *Journal of Counseling Psychology, 23,* 166–169.

Schloss, P.J., Kane, M.S., & Miller, S. (1981). Truancy intervention with behavior disordered adolescents. *Behavior Disorders, 6*(3), 175–179.

Sing, K. (1998). Part-time employment in high school and its effect on academic achievement. *Journal of Educational Research, 91*(3), 131–139.

Stringer, L.A. (1973). Children at risk 2. The teacher as change agent. *Elementary School Journal, 73*(8), 424–434.

Unger, K.V., Douds, A., & Pierce, R.M. (1978). A truancy prevention project. *Phi Delta Kappan, 60*(4), 317.

See also **Individuals with Disabilities Education Act (IDEA); Parents of the Handicapped**

SCHOOL EFFECTIVENESS

School effectiveness is a term adopted in the late 1970s to refer to a body of research on identifying effective schools and the means for creating more of them. The movement to research effective schools has been driven largely by three principal assumptions. According to Bickel (1983), these are that: (1) it is possible to identify schools that are particularly effective in teaching basic skills to poor and minority children; (2) effective schools exhibit identifiable characteristics that are correlated with the success of their students and these characteristics can be manipulated by educators; and (3) the salient characteristics of effective schools form a basis for the improvement of noneffective schools.

Bickel (1983) has traced the origins of the school effectiveness movement to three factors. The first is the backlash that developed in response to the Coleman studies (and like research) of the 1960s. These studies left the unfortunate impression that differences among schools were irrelevant in the education of poor and minority children. The second basis, according to Bickel, was the general psychological climate of the 1970s. Principals, teachers, parents, and others seemed ready for a more positive, hopeful message, one that said schools could make a difference and that effective schools did exist in the real world. The final factor described by Bickel is the readiness of the educational research community to accept the findings that to date include such intuitively appealing variables as strong instructional leadership, an orderly school climate, high expectations, an emphasis on basic skills, and frequent testing and monitoring of student progress.

Rich, facilitative environments enhance the results of ability differences, allowing the maximum possible levels of growth; deprived, restrictive environments slow and constrain growth. This does not mean that group differences will necessarily increase. If schools and instruction are particularly effective for all groups, as should be the case, then the overall level of achievement should increase for all groups along with the within group dispersion. This, at least in theory, is currently being attempted in terms of school accountability movement, in which expectations for schools now include test results of special education students (CISP, 1998).

As promising as the school effectiveness literature appears to be, and even with the consensus on the core elements of school effectiveness, a variety of valid criticisms have been offered. These have been summarized and reviewed by Rowan, Bossert, and Dwyer (1983). The technical properties of the research have been criticized as (1) using narrow, limited measures of effectiveness that focus only on instructional outcomes; (2) using design that allows an analysis of relational variables from which cause and effect cannot be inferred; and (3) making global comparisons on the basis of aggregate data, without assessing intraschool variations in organizational climate or outcomes across classes within schools. Rowan et al. (1983) also caution that the effect sizes present in this line of research are questionable. They have argued that the traditional methods of research in school effectiveness resemble "fishing expeditions" that spuriously inflate the probability of finding significant results. Despite these and other problems, the school effectiveness movement has rekindled optimism that schools can be organized and restructured to enhance student performance. As yet, the application of the methods and concepts of the school effectiveness literature have not been applied to special education programs. Special education programs are typically excluded from the data in such studies and desperately need to be assessed. It remains to be seen whether special education programs that can be identified as particularly effective in educating the handicapped are affected by the same variables and with the same form of interaction as are regular education programs. The time to apply the concepts and research methods of school effectiveness to special education is past due. It holds much promise for understanding what makes special education effective and how to effect such changes.

REFERENCES

Bickel, W.E. (1983). Effective schools: Knowledge, dissemination, inquiry. *Educational Researcher, 12,* 3–5.

Rowan, B., Bossert, S.T., & Dwyer, D.C. (1983). Research on effective schools: A cautionary note. *Educational Researcher, 12,* 24–32.

See also **Special Education Programs; Teacher Effectiveness**

SCHOOL FAILURE

Failure in school often occurs when children come from environments characterized by economic hardship, deprivation, neglect, trauma, divorce, death, foster parenting, drug abuse, poor school attendance, or lack of adequate instruction. Indeed, dyspedagogia carries more of a role in school failure simply because of the theoretical paradigm in Western schools of individualism as opposed to social/ interactive paradigms such as those favored in Russian schools for so many years. Some change may be noted in the teacher preparation and involvement in inner-city schools (Yeo, 1997).

Children who exhibit behavior problems in the classroom also experience school failure. Some children have conduct disorders in which they disrupt the class, constantly irritate the teacher, do not follow directions, are easily distracted, are impulsive, or fail to attend. Other students who are fearful, anxious, withdrawn, or immature have difficulty in responding freely in the classroom and fail to learn to the limits of their abilities. Children whose self-esteem is so low that they believe they are of little worth often learn to be helpless. These children stop trying in school because they think they cannot learn. When children with behavior problems do not conform to the standards of the school environment, they may become socially aggressive, reject the values of the school and society, and come into conflict with authorities. A student may openly confront teachers and administrators, begin using drugs or alcohol, join gangs, break laws, steal, and eventually be expelled from or drop out of school (Knoblock, 1983; Long, Morse, & Newman, 1980; Quay & Werry, 1979).

Specific learning disabilities can result in failure in school. A learning disability is a dysfunction in one or more of the psychological processes that are involved in learning to read, write, spell, compute arithmetic, etc. In some cases, a child may have an attention disability and may not be able to direct attention purposefully, failing to selectively focus attention on the relevant stimuli or responding to too many stimuli at once. A memory disability is the inability to remember what has been seen or heard. Perceptual disabilities cover a wide range of disorders in which a child who has normal vision, hearing, and feeling may experience difficulty in grasping the meaning of what is seen, heard, or touched. An example is a child who has difficulty in seeing the directional differences between a "d" and a "b," or who requires an excessive amount of time to look at a printed word, analyze the word, and say the word. Thinking disabilities involve problems in judgment, making comparisons, forming new concepts, critical thinking, problem solving, and decision making. A disability in oral language refers to difficulties in understanding and using oral language. All of these specific learning disabilities might cause difficulty in learning to read, write, spell, compute arithmetic, or adopt appropriate social-emotional behaviors (Kirk & Chalfant, 1984). Recent research cites the need for school-family partnerships (Poole, 1997) and intensive case management (Reid, Bailey-Dempsey, Cain, & Cook, 1994).

REFERENCES

Kirk, S.A., & Chalfant, J.C. (1984). *Academic and developmental learning disabilities*. Denver, CO: Love.

Knoblock, P. (1983). *Teaching emotionally disturbed children*. Boston: Houghton Mifflin.

Long, N., Morse, W., & Newman, R. (Eds.). (1980). *Conflict in the classroom: The education of emotionally disturbed children* (4th ed.). Belmont, CA: Wadsworth.

Poole, D.L. (1997). The SAFE Project. *Health & Social Work, 22*(4), 282–289.

Quay, H., & Werry, J. (Eds.). (1979). *Psychopathological disorders of childhood* (2nd ed.). New York: Wiley.

Reid, W.J., Bailey-Dempsey, C.A., Cain, E., & Cook, T.V. (1994). Case incentives versus case management: Preventing School Failure? *Social Work Research, 18*(4), 227–236.

Yeo, F. (1997). Teacher preparation and inner-city schools: Sustaining educational failure. *Urban Review, 29*(2), 127–143.

***See also* Emotional Disorders; Learned Helplessness; Learning Disabilities; Mental Retardation**

SCHOOL PHOBIA (SCHOOL REFUSAL)

School phobia has been the subject of hundreds of research studies and dozens of literature reviews over the past several decades. The phenomenon was first described in 1932 when Broadwin distinguished a type of school refusal from truancy by an anxiety component. The term school phobia was coined in 1941 (Johnson, Falstein, Szurek, & Svendson, 1941). A common definition of school phobia cited in the more recent literature includes the following characteristics:

Severe difficulty in attending school often amounting to prolonged absence.

Severe emotional upset shown by such symptoms as excessive fearfulness, undue temper, misery or complaints of feeling ill without obvious organic cause on being faced with the prospect of going to school.

Staying at home during school hours with the knowledge of the parents at some stage in the course of the disorder.

Absence of significant antisocial disorder, such as stealing, lying, wandering, destructiveness, or sexual misbehavior. (Berg, Nichols, & Pritchard, 1969, p. 123)

In contrast to school phobia, truancy is characterized by behaviors that are the opposite of the last two behaviors.

Contemporary writers who use the term school refusal generally describe it with the same set of characteristics that defines school phobia that lack intensity (Kearney, Eisen, & Silverman, 1995). An exception is the American Psychiatric Association's (1994) classification system (DSM-IV), which describes school refusal as one possible concomitant of separation anxiety disorder, while reserving the term school phobia for a fear of the school situation even when parents accompany the child.

The occurrence of school phobia is relatively rare when one considers the abundance of literature devoted to it. Estimates of the incidence of school phobia range from 3.2 to 17 per 1000 schoolchildren (Kennedy, 1965; Yule, 1979). The wide discrepancy may be due in part to the age at which children are sampled. Prevalence is thought to peak at three different ages: 5 to 7, on entry or shortly after entry to school; 11, around the time children change schools; and 14, often concomitant with depression (Hersov, 1977). Many writers consider school phobia to occur in three girls for every two boys (Wright, Schaefer, & Solomons, 1979). However, this ratio has not appeared in several studies of school phobics reported in the literature (Baker, & Wills, 1978; Berg et al., 1969; Hersov, 1960; Kennedy, 1965).

As Atkinson et al. (1985) noted in their review, the construct of school phobia is too heterogeneous to be described by a simple dichotomy. They examined five variables related to school phobia, some of which overlap more than others—extensiveness of disturbance, source of fear, mode of onset, age, and gender of the child. The extensiveness of fear can be conceptualized along a continuum with the dichotomies of neurotic/characterological or type 1/type 2 at the end points. Generally, acute or sudden onset is characteristic of type 1 and chronic or gradual onset is characteristic of type 2. When researchers have operationalized acute mode of onset as the occurrence of school phobia after 3 or more years of trouble-free attendance, other correlates emerge. For instance, chronic onset tended to be associated more than acute onset with poor premorbid adjustment, dependency on parents, low self-esteem, and a poor prognosis.

During the past 20 years a proliferation of behavioral treatments of school phobia have occurred. Yule (1979) and Trueman (1984) provide critical reviews of the behavioral treatment of school phobia. Trueman (1984) reviewed 19 case studies between 1960 and 1981 that used behavioral treatments based on classical, operant, or a combination of those techniques. Of the eight studies reviewed that used techniques based on classical conditioning, six used reciprocal, one used implosion, and one used emotive imagery. Six of the studies involved boys aged 10 to 17; two studies involved girls aged 8 and 9. Trueman noted considerable variation among the reciprocal inhibition treatments, making conclusions difficult concerning the most efficacious component. Additionally, he noted the difficulty in distinguishing between systematic densensitization and shaping.

Among the 10 case studies reviewed by Trueman that used operant procedures, five involved boys aged 7 to 12 and five involved girls aged 6 to 14. The change agents varied among studies as well as the specific techniques and the criteria for success. Thus comparisons between procedures are hard to make. The procedures included training parents in positive reinforcement methods, contingency contracting, prompting and shaping, and school-based contingencies. It is important that resolution is long-term for these cases, because longitudinal studies indicate lifelong outcomes (Flakierska, Lindstroem, & Gillberg, 1997). Home-school collaboration essential (Jenni, 1997).

REFERENCES

American Psychiatric Association. (1994). *Diagnostic and statistical manual of mental disorders (3rd ed.)*. Washington, DC: Author.

Atkinson, L., Quarrington, B., & Cyr, J.J. (1985). School refusal: The heterogeneity of a concept. *American Journal of Orthopsychiatry,, 55,* 83–101.

Baker, H., & Wills, U. (1978). School phobia: Classification and treatment. *British Journal of Psychiatry, 132,* 492–499.

Berg, I., Nichols, K., & Pritchard, C. (1969). School phobia–Its classification and relationship to dependency. *Journal of Child Psychology & Psychiatry, 10,* 123–141.

Flakierska, P.N., Lindstroem, M., & Gillberg, C. (1997). School phobia with separation-anxiety disorder: A comparative 20 to 29-year follow-up study of 35 school refusers. *Comprehensive Psychiatry,, 38,* 17–22.

Hersov, L.A. (1960). Refusal to go to school. *Child Psychology & Psychiatry,, 1,* 137–145.

Hersov, L.A. (1977). School refusal. In M. Rutter & L. Hersov (Eds.), *Child psychiatry: Modern approaches* (pp. 455–486). Oxford England: Blackwell.

Jenni, C.B. (1997). School phobia: How home school collaboration can tame this dragon. *School Counselor,, 44*(3), 206–217.

Johnson, A.M., Falstein, E.J., Szurek, S.A., & Svendsen, M. (1941). School phobia. *American Journal of Orthopsychiatry, 11,* 702–711.

Kearney, C.A., Eisen, A.R., & Silverman, W.K. (1995). The legend and myth of school phobia. *School Psychology Quarterly, 10*(1), 65–85.

Kennedy, W.A. (1965). School phobia: Rapid treatment of fifty cases. *Journal of Abnormal Psychology, 70,* 285–289.

Trueman, D. (1984). The behavioral treatment of school phobia: A critical review. *Psychology in the Schools, 21,* 215–223.

Wright, L., Schaefer, A., & Solomons, G. (1979). *Encyclopedia of pediatric psychology*. Baltimore, MD: University Park Press.

Yule, W. (1979). Behavioral approaches to the treatment and prevention of school refusal. *Behavioral Analysis & Modification, 3,* 55–68.

See also **Childhood Neurosis; Phobias and Fears; Separation Anxiety and the Handicapped**

SCHOOL PSYCHOLOGY

Some (Brown, 1982) view school psychology as a profession separate and independent from the professions of psychology and education; others (Bardon, 1982) view school psychology as a specialty within the profession of psychology. In fact, most school psychologists straddle the professions of psychology and education. They provide many services that are unique and drawn from psychology as well as education. A comprehensive study of the expertise of school psychologists (Rosenfeld, Shimberg, & Thornton, 1983) found the practice of school psychology to be similar to the practice of clinical and counseling psychology. In fact, school psychologists devote considerable attention to assessment and organizational issues.

A comprehensive review of the school psychology literature (Ysseldyke, Reynolds, & Weinberg, 1984) identified the following 16 domains as ones in which school psychology has expertise: classroom management, classroom organization and social structure, interpersonal communication and consultation, basic academic skills, basic life skills, affective/social skills, parent involvement, systems development and planning, personnel development, individual differences in development and learning, school-community relations, instruction, legal, ethical, and professional issues, assessment, multicultural concerns (Rogers & Ponterotto, 1997), and research and evaluation.

While school psychology is a dynamic specialty and one not easily categorized or described, its work in five broad areas is described briefly. School psychologists frequently conduct psychoeducational evaluations of pupils needing special attention. The evaluations typically consider a student's cognitive (i.e., intelligence and achievement), affective, social, emotional, and linguistic characteristics, and use behavioral, educational, and psychological including psychoneurological (D'Amato, Hammons, Terminie, & Dean; 1992 and psychoanalytic) techniques.

School psychologists also participate in planning and evaluating services designed to promote cognitive, social, and affective development. Their services can include teaching, training, counseling, and therapy. While their principal focus frequently is on individual pupils, they also work individually with parents, teachers, principals, and other educators.

School psychologists also offer indirect services to pupils through educators, parents, and other adults. Their indirect services typically involve in-service programs for teachers, parent education programs, counseling, consultation, and collaboration. Their consultative and collaborative activities involve them with groups composed of students, teachers, parents, and others. Their work as members of the education staff enables them to effect important changes in organizations by working on broad and important issues that impact classrooms, school buildings, districts, communities, corporations, or a consortium of districts and agencies.

Most school psychologists work in the schools or within other organizational structures (e.g., mental health clinics, juvenile courts, guidance centers, private and public residential care facilities). State certification is important for these school psychologists. Forty-nine states presently certify school psychologists—an increase of 42 since 1946. Many school psychologists also want the option to practice privately. Although those who have doctoral degrees typically can be licensed by their states as psychologists, those holding subdoctoral degrees typically have been denied a license to practice psychology independently and increasingly are seeking the right to be licensed and to practice privately.

Five professional journals are devoted to advancing the knowledge and practice of school psychology: *Journal of School Psychology, Professional School Psychology, Psychology in the Schools, School Psychology International, and School Psychology Review*. An additional 16 secondary and 26 tertiary journals add to the literature (Reynolds & Gutkin, 1999). Persons interested in further information about school psychology are encouraged to consult the professional journals, *The Handbook of School Psychology* (Reynolds & Gutkin, 1999), textbooks discussing school psychology (Whelan & Carlson, 1980), and the National Association of School Psychologists (Dwyer, & Gorin, 1996).

REFERENCES

Bardon, J. (1982). The psychology of school psychology. In C.R. Reynolds & T.B. Gutkin (Eds.), *The handbook of school psychology* (pp. 1–14). New York: Wiley.

Brown, D. (1982). Issues in the development of professional school psychology. In C.R. Reynolds & T.B. Gutkin (Eds.), *The handbook of school psychology* (pp. 14–23). New York: Wiley.

D'Amato, R.C., Hammons, P.F., Terminie, T.J., & Dean, R.S. (1992). Neuropsychological training in American Psychological Association-accredited and non-accredited school psychology programs. *Journal of School Psychology, 30*(2), 175–183.

Dwyer, K.P., & Gorin, S. (1996). A national perspective of school psychology in the context of school reform. *School Psychology Review, 25*(4), 507–511.

Reynolds, C.R., & Gutkin, T.B. (1999). *The handbook of school psychology* (3rd ed.) New York: Wiley.

Rogers, M.R., & Ponterotto, J.G. (1997). Development of the multicultural school psychology counseling competency scale. *Psychology in the Schools, 34*, 211–217.

Rosenfeld, M., Shimberg, B., & Thornton, R. (1983). *Job analysis of licensed psychologists in the United States and Canada.* Princeton, NJ: Educational Test Service.

Whelan, T., & Carlson, C. (1980). Books in school psychology: 1970 to present. *Professional School Psychology, 1*, 283–293.

See also **Educational Diagnostician; Psychology in the Schools**

SCHOOL PSYCHOLOGY DIGEST

See SCHOOL PSYCHOLOGY REVIEW.

SCHOOL PSYCHOLOGY REVIEW

School Psychology Review, first published in 1972 as *The School Psychology Digest,* is the official journal of the National Association of School Psychologists (NASP). The primary purpose of the *Review* is to impact the delivery of school psychological services by publishing scholarly advances in research, training, and practices. *School Psychology Review* is a quarterly publication with an editor and appointed editorial advisory board.

A content analysis of the *Review* indicates that approximately 10 to 20% of the articles concern professional issues in school psychology, 30 to 40% relate to interventions for academic and behavior problems of children, and 30 to 35% involve testing and measurement issues. The remaining articles cover a wide array of topics, including program evaluation, psychological theories, and special education practices.

The *School Psychology Review* enjoys the largest circulation (over 20,000 subscribers) of any of the journals representing the field of school psychology, and is the second most widely distributed journal in the entire discipline of psychology. *School Psychology Review* is published by the National Association of School Psychologists and is a benefit of membership; it may also be purchased separately.

SCHOOL RECORDS

See FERPA (FAMILY EDUCATION & PRIVACY RIGHTS ACT).

SCHOOL REFUSAL

See SCHOOL PHOBIA.

SCHOOL STRESS

Stress is the nonspecific response of the human body to a demand. It is not simply nervous tension but a physiological response of the body. Stress occurs in all living organisms and is with us all the time (Selye, 1976). Stress comes from mental, emotional, and physical activity.

School stress results from the impact of the school environment on children. Physical stress is accompanied by feelings of pain and discomfort, but physical stress is seldom a major factor in school stress. In schools the stressors are most often psychological and result in emotional reactions with accompanying physiological changes in the body. Exceptional children experience more stress, less peer support, and poorer adjustment than peers without disabilities (Wenz-Gross & Siperstein, 1998).

In school stress, the demands usually result from significant others in the school, i.e., teachers and peers, or those who are expectant about school activities (e.g., parents). School stress is dependent on cognitive processes that lead to emotional reactions and a form or style of coping behavior. The coping behavior may or may not be effective, or the coping behavior may only appear to be effective. When this is the case, the body has changed from a state of alarm and is in the resistance stage. When in the resistance stage, one's ability to deal effectively with other stressors is reduced. Resistance can be maintained only so long before physical or psychological problems occur (Selye, 1976).

School stress can be prevented by intervening in the environment to eliminate or modify stress-producing situations before they have a chance to affect children; by intervening with children to protect them from the impact of stressors by building up their resistance and personal strength (i.e., self-concept); by intervening with children to increase their tolerance for stress; and by putting children who are adversely affected by stress in an environment that minimizes stress (Phillips, 1978). There are many techniques and strategies that can be used with children suffering from school stress. Most involve a focus on learning and motivational processes.

REFERENCES

Phillips, B. (1978). *School stress and anxiety.* New York: Human Sciences.

Selye, H. (1976). *The stress of life.* New York: McGraw-Hill.

Wenz-Gross, M., & Siperstein, G.N. (1998). Students with learning problems at risk in middle school: Stress social support, and adjustment. *Exceptional Children, 65*(1), 91–100.

See also **School Phobia; Stress and the Handicapped Student**

SCHWARTZ-JAMPEL SYNDROME

See RARE DISEASES.

SCOLIOSIS

Scoliosis, a lateral curvature of the spine, is the most common type of spinal deformity. Functional scoliosis results from poor posture or a difference in length of the legs. It is not progressive and usually disappears with exercise. Structural scoliosis, however, is a more severe form, involving rotation of the spine and structural changes in the vertebrae (Ziai, 1984).

Most cases of structural scoliosis are idiopathic—of unknown cause (Benson, 1983). Idiopathic scoliosis occurs most frequently in adolescent females during the growth spurt, ages 12 to 16. If untreated, the condition progresses rapidly throughout the spinal growth period (ages 15 to 16 for girls and ages 18 to 19 for boys). Scoliosis can also accompany neuromuscular disorders such as cerebral palsy and muscular dystrophy, or can develop as a result of infection, trauma, or surgery.

Early diagnosis of scoliosis is essential to prevent progression of the curvature. Treatment varies with the type of scoliosis, the age of the child, and severity of deformity. Mild curvatures require only observation, while more pronounced curvatures require bracing and exercise. In severe cases, surgery is required. Recent treatment approaches have also included electrostimulation (Benson, 1983) and use of biofeedback techniques (Birbaumer, Flor, Cevey & Dworkin, 1994; Ziai, 1984).

REFERENCES

Birbaumer, N., Flor, H., Cevey, B., & Dworkin, B. (1994). Behavioral treatment of scoliosis and kyphosis. *Journal of Psychosomatic Research, 38*(6), 623–628.

Benson, D.R. (1983). The spine and neck. In M.E. Gershwin & D.L. Robbins (Eds.), *Musculoskeletal diseases of children* (pp. 469–538). New York: Grune & Stratton.

Ziai, M. (Ed.). (1984). *Pediatrics* (3rd ed.). Boston: Little, Brown.

See also **Cerebral Palsy; Muscular Dystrophy**

SCOPE AND SEQUENCE

Scope and sequence information play an important role in the special education of exceptional individuals. In academic areas where curriculum is not readily available, the use of scope and sequence information and task analysis provides the special educator with ways of determining a set of skills (Hargrave & Poteet, 1984).

To provide appropriate programs, special educators need a clear understanding, in the form of a sequence of skills, of what each of the academic domains include. This array of skills is referred to as scope and sequence information. Scope and sequence charts provide schemata of an instructional domain. Scope refers to those skills that are taught; sequence refers to the order in which they are taught. Sequences may be determined from the work of others or may be synthesized by the special educator from experience (Wehman & McLaughlin, 1981).

Scope and sequence charts vary in structure and format among special educators and programs. Scope and sequence information provide a link between assessment and the specification of instructional goals and objectives (Wehman & McLaughlin, 1981). It is essential in developing individual educational programs. Knowledge of the scope and sequence of skills provides the teacher with a clearer profile of those skills that the student has acquired and those that he or she still needs to acquire (Mercer & Mercer, 1985).

REFERENCES

Hargrave, L.J., & Poteet, J.A. (1984). *Assessment in special education.* Englewood Cliffs, NJ: Prentice-Hall.

Mercer, C.D., & Mercer, A.R. (1985). *Teaching students with learning problems.* Columbus, OH: Merrill.

Wehman, P., & McLaughlin, P.J. (1981). *Program development in special education.* New York: McGraw-Hill.

SCOTT CRANIODIGITAL SYNDROME WITH MENTAL RETARDATION

Scott craniodigital syndrome with mental retardation is a rare, X-linked recessive genetic disorder. Children with this syndrome have mental retardation and various craniofacial and extremity abnormalities. Craniofacial features include a small, wide head; small, narrow nose; excessively small jaw; and eyes set far apart. Other head and facial characteristics include an extended hairline, thick eyebrows, and long eyelashes. A startled expression on their face is found among some children (National Organization for Rare Disorders [NORD], 1997).

Extremity abnormalities have also been found among these children, including webbing of their hands and feet. The heels of these children's feet are turned inward as well. Excessive hair growth on different parts of their body have also been reported (NORD, 1997).

Mental retardation is present; therefore, it will be important for the child to enter an early childhood intervention program at age 3, with continued special education services as the child progresses through school.

REFERENCE

National Organization for Rare Disorders (NORD). (1997). *Singleton-Merton syndrome.* New Fairfield, CT: National Organization for Rare Disorders, Inc.

SCOUTING AND THE HANDICAPPED

The scouting movement for boys and girls has made a significant effort to involve youths with handicaps. This was not always the case (Stevens, 1995) but currently in America, all levels of scouting have provisions to mainstream scouts in community units and to develop specialized troops for youngsters with severe disabilities or unusual needs. Scouting organizations catering to members with given disabilities are capable of designing adapted activities. For example, Stuckey and Barkus (1986) reported that the Boy Scout Troop of the Perkins School for the Blind went on a special camping trip at the Philmont Scout Ranch in New Mexico.

Scouting offers youths many opportunities for developing motor, cognitive, and social skills, increasing self-esteem and a sense of achievement, and obtaining a feeling of enjoyment. Boy Scout and Girl Scout programs have worked toward making these benefits available to all youths. Many publications and other materials are available to interested persons from the national offices of Girl Scouts and Boy Scouts and from various local scout executives.

REFERENCES

Stevens, A. (1995). Changing attitudes to disabled people in the Scout Association in Britain (1908–62): A contribution to a history of disability. *Disability & Society, 10*(3), 281–293.

Stuckey, K., & Barkus, C. (1986). Visually impaired scouts meet the Philmont challenge. *Journal of Visual Impairment & Blindness, 80,* 750–151.

See also **Recreation, Therapeutic**

SECKEL SYNDROME

Seckel syndrome, also known as nanocephaly, is a genetic disorder. The incidence of Seckel syndrome is higher in females than males and is due to an autosomal recessive gene (Thoene, 1992). The primary characteristics of the disorder include a very small head (microcephaly); intrauterine and postnatal growth failure, resulting in dwarfism; and sharp facial features with an underdeveloped chin (Rudolph, 1991). Prominence of the midface is typical in children with Seckel syndrome. Children with this disorder have a beak-like nose, large, malformed eyes, and low-set ears without lobes. They are short in stature, ranging in height from 3 to 3½ feet as an adult (Jones, 1988). Other physical abnormalities may include permanent fixation of the fifth finger in a bent position, malformation of the hips, and dislocation of the radial bone in the forearm (NORD, 1998).

Children with Seckel syndrome have moderate to severe mental retardation (Jones, 1988). These children often exhibit hyperactive behavior and have attention and concentration difficulties (Jones, 1988). These children would benefit from a small group educational setting that provides one-on-one instruction and allows them to progress at their own speed. A structured, educational setting with expected rewards and consequences would be optimal. The standard treatment of Seckel syndrome is symptomatic and supportive. Parent training with a pediatric psychologist including behavioral management techniques may be beneficial. Genetic counseling may be helpful as well (Thoene, 1992).

REFERENCES

Jones, K.L. (Ed.). (1988). *Smith's recognizable patterns of human malformation* (4th ed.). Philadelphia, PA: W.B. Saunders.

Rudolph, A.M. (1991). *Rudolph's pediatrics-19th Edition.* Norwalk, CT: Appleton & Lange.

National Organization For Rare Disorders (NORD). (1998). *Seckel syndrome.* New Fairfield, CT: Author.

Thoene, J.G. (Ed.). (1992). *Physician's guide to rare diseases.* Montvale, NJ: Dowden Publishing.

SECOND LANGUAGE LEARNERS IN SPECIAL EDUCATION

Special education is a field addressing many challenges, one of them being working with second language learners. Today, many children across the United States come from countries and homes where English is not spoken or used as a language in which concepts are discussed. If, as projections suggest, 10% to 20% of any given population has some or several disabilities, then special education serves a number of these children. For many such students, English is their second language. This condition currently presents challenges to educators and service providers, impacting the outcomes of evaluations and interventions (Ortiz, 1997). Unlike a child brought up in an English-only environment, the learner of English as a second language shows developmental lags in articulation, vocabulary, insights on syntax, and comprehension of complex oral and printed texts. These conditions, coupled with limited understanding of the stages of second language acquisition, tends to promote overreferral to and placement in special education. For example, Ochoa, Robles-Pina, Garcia, and Breunig's (2000) study across eight states with large populations of second language learners revealed that oral language-related factors (acquisition and/or delays) were the third most common reason for referral of second language learners. Further, Ochoa, Robles-Pina, Garcia, and Breunig (2000) state that eight of the top 13 most commonly cited reasons for referral of these learners could be linked to language; in their study, language reasons accounted for 54% of all responses provided. Equally, limited awareness of conditions that suggest a disability promote patterns of under-

referral of this population among general educators who consider the students' problems as typical patterns of second language learners (De León & Cole, 1994).

Until recently, special education in general invested modest efforts attending to the specific communication needs of second language learners and their families, and most support focused on attending to their conditions or disabilities. However, literature within the last ten years reveals a change in this trend, the effects of which will be reviewed perhaps five years from now. Consequently, increasing research, training, and publication efforts raise awareness and educate professionals. For example, guidelines and recommendations based on best practices for children without disabilities are advocated for second language learners with disabilities (California Department of Education, 1997; Fernández, 1992; Gersten, Brengelman, & Jimenez, 1994). Currently, the literature reflects continuous appeals to special educators and speech clinicians to incorporate modified approaches like English as a second language (ESL) and/or Sheltered English into their practice (De León & Cole, 1994; Garcia & Malkin, 1993; Gersten et al., 1994). However, the appropriateness and effectiveness of such practices are yet to be validated.

REFERENCES

California Department of Education. (1997). *Guidelines for language, academic, and special education services required for limited-English-proficient students in California public schools, K–12.* Sacramento: Special Education Division.

De León, J., & Cole, J. (1994). Service delivery to culturally and linguistically diverse exceptional learners in rural school districts. *Rural Special Education Quarterly, 13,* 37–45.

Fernández, A.T. (1992). Legal support for bilingual education and language appropriate related services for limited English proficient students with disabilities. *Bilingual Research Journal, 16,* 117–140.

Garcia, S.B., & Malkin, D.H. (1993). Toward defining programs and services for culturally and linguistically diverse learners in special education. *Teaching Exceptional Children, 26,* 52–58.

Gersten, R., Brengelman, S., & Jiménez, R. (1994). Effective instruction for culturally and linguistically diverse students: A reconceptualization. *Focus on Exceptional Children, 27,* 1–16.

Ochoa, S.H., Robles-Pina, R., Garcia, S.B., & Breunig, N. (2000). School psychologists' perspectives on referrals of language minority students. *Journal of Multiple Voices for Ethnically Diverse Exceptional Learners.*

Ortiz, A.A. (1997). Learning disabilities occurring concomitantly with linguistic differences. *Journal of Learning Disabilities, 30,* 321–332.

SECONDARY SPECIAL EDUCATION

Few models for service delivery of secondary special education services exist, therefore university training programs have traditionally prepared teachers with an elementary emphasis, many secondary systems have relied on the elementary resource room as a model for service delivery. If the school adopts the philosophy of providing assistance only in the acquisition of basic skills in language and mathematics, then the traditional elementary model might be useful. If the school recognizes, however, the special demands and circumstances of the exceptional student as well as the unique problems associated with the onset of adolescence, then different programming is needed (Marsh, Gearheart, & Gearheart; 1978).

Lerner (1976) holds that resource room teachers in high school must be familiar with the entire curriculum of the school to be successful in remediating and programming for exceptional students. This familiarity would enable the teacher to assist the students in a variety of courses rather than in the remediation of specific academic skills. Remediation must be tied closely to what happens in the mainstream classroom.

Goodman and Mann proposed a different model in 1976. They theorized a basic education program at the secondary level that restricts the activities of the teacher to instruction of mathematics and language arts. Enrollment of students would be limited to those who lacked sixth-grade achievement. The goal for the secondary teacher in special education would be to remediate students to a sixth-grade level to allow for mainstreaming into regular education classes.

Program options, in fact, lie somewhere between the two extremes, with decisions regarding the thrust of programming often dictated by local custom and philosophy. The main objective should be to provide a system of instruction that reduces the complexity without sacrificing quality. A carefully balanced program should include the provision for specific remediation as well as assistance in addressing course work through the accommodation of individual needs. Equal opportunity should allow each student to benefit from academic training and career education to the fullest extent possible. Insufficiency in reading should not deny a student the opportunity to participate and learn in an academic class; nor should it limit the student to training that leads to entry-level skills in low-status jobs. The verbal bias evidenced in the instruction of many schools should not limit the pursuits of intelligent but inefficient learners.

REFERENCES

Goodman, L., & Mann, L. (1976). *Learning disabilities in the secondary school.* New York: Grune & Stratton.

Lerner, J.W. (1976). *Children with learning disabilities* (2nd ed.). Boston: Houghton Mifflin.

Marsh, G.E., Gearheart, C., & Gearheart, B. (1978). *The learning disabled adolescent.* St. Louis: Mosby.

See also Resource Room; Resource Teacher; Vocational Training

SECTION 504 OF THE 1973 REHABILITATION ACT

See REHABILITATION ACT OF 1973.

SEEING EYE DOGS

See ANIMALS FOR THE HANDICAPPED; DOG GUIDES FOR THE BLIND.

SEGUIN, EDOUARD (1812–1880)

Edouard Seguin, who demonstrated to the world that mentally retarded individuals can be educated, studied medicine under Jean Marc Gaspard Itard in Paris, and applied the training methods of that famous physician and teacher to the education of the mentally retarded. In 1837 Seguin established the first school in France for the mentally retarded, with remarkable success. In 1848 he moved to the United States, where he practiced medicine, served as director of the Pennsylvania Training School, and acted as adviser to numerous state institutions. He was a founder and first president of the Association of Medical Officers of American Institutions for Idiotic and Feeble-Minded Persons, now the American Association on Mental Deficiency.

Seguin's methods, which provided the foundation for the movement for the education of the mentally retarded in the United States, were based on a number of principles: that observation of the child is the foundation of the child's education; that education deals with the whole child; that the child learns best from real things; that perceptual training should precede training for concept development; and that even the most defective child has some capacity for learning. Seguin incorporated art, music, and gymnastics into the educational program, and emphasized the use of concrete materials in the classroom.

Seguin's influence on the early development of special education services can hardly be overstated. Samuel Gridley Howe, who was responsible for the formation of the first state school for mentally retarded children in the United States, obtained much of his methodology directly from Seguin. Maria Montessori gave credit to Seguin for the principles on which she based her system of education. Today, more than a century after his death. Seguin's influence is evident in the methods being used to instruct children with learning handicaps.

REFERENCES

Kanner, L. (1960). Itard, Seguin, Howe—Three pioneers in the education of retarded children. *American Journal of Mental Deficiency, 65,* 2–10.

Seguin, E. (1907). *Idiocy and its treatment by the physiological method.* New York: Teachers College, Columbia University.

Talbot, E. *Edouard Seguin: A study of an educational approach to the treatment of mentally defective children.* New York: Teachers College, Columbia University.

SEIZURE DISORDERS

Seizures are relatively common in children and are the most common basis for a referral to a pediatric neurologist (Haslam, 1996). A seizure is a "paroxysmal involuntary disturbance of brain function that may manifest in an impairment or loss of consciousness, abnormal motor activity, behavioral abnormalities, sensory disturbances, or autonomic dysfunction" (Haslam, 1996, p. 1686). In many cases, seizures can be directly related to head trauma resulting from brain injury or high fever. Approximately 8% of children can be expected to have at least one seizure before adolescence (Brown, 1997). Epilepsy may be diagnosed only in an individual who has a series of seizures. Although descriptions of childhood seizures by parents and others may be very helpful in diagnosis, some different seizures (for example, absence and complex partial) may present almost identically in different individuals. Thus, EEG records are an important aspect of diagnosis (Haslam, 1996). Seizure disorders frequently occur in association with more severe degrees of mental retardation and cerebral palsy.

CLASSIFICATION OF SEIZURES

The International Classification of Seizures divides seizures into two major categories: partial and generalized. Partial seizures begin in unilateral (focal or local) areas and may or may not spread bilaterally. Generalized seizures begin with immediate involvement of bilateral brain structures and are associated with either bilateral motor movements, changes in consciousness, or both.

Partial Seizures

Partial seizures are divided into: (1) simple partial attacks that arise from a local area and do not impair consciousness and (2) complex partial attacks that begin in a local area but spread bilaterally and therefore impair consciousness. They are the most common type of seizure disorder, accounting for 40%–60% of all childhood seizures (Brown, 1997; Haslam, 1996). In simple partial types, consciousness is unimpaired; in complex partial types, degree of altered awareness or unresponsiveness is involved.

Simple partial seizures often exhibit primary neurologic symptoms that indicate the site of origin. Partial seizures involve motor activity from any portion of the body. They usually involve the limbs, face, or head, and sometimes cause speech arrest. Hallucinations and visual illusions may occur, depending on the site of the seizure. Partial seizures that progress with sequential involvement of parts of the body that are represented in contiguous cortical areas are termed Jacksonian. Benign rolandic epilepsy is common and may result in the child awakening from sleep and showing motor symptoms. Localized paralysis or weakness that may last for minutes or days sometimes occurs and indicates an underlying structural lesion. Partial motor seizures also can be continuous for extended periods of time.

Complex partial seizures, previously called psychomotor or temporal lobe seizures, are the most common shown in older children and adolescents and occur in over 50% of adults with seizure disorders. The seizures characteristically begin with emotional, psychic, illusory, hallucinatory, or special sensory symptoms. Sometimes, consciousness becomes impaired at the onset of the attack. After the aura, the individual becomes completely or partially unrespon-

sive and may perform apparently purposeful activity. The seizure consists of involuntary motor movements such as eye blinking, lip smacking, facial grimaces, groaning, chewing and other automatisms, but more elaborate behavior can occur. In the state of depressed awareness, patients may actively resist efforts to restrain them. A complete attack usually lasts between 1 and 3 minutes; on recovery, there is complete amnesia for the attack except for the aura or partial motor onset. Complex partial seizures usually begin in the temporal lobe but may originate from the frontal, parietal, or occipital regions.

Generalized Seizures

Generalized seizures involve bilateral brain regions and begin with immediate involvement of both hemispheres. Five types are recognized; (1) absence seizures with associated 3-Hz (cycles per second) generalized spike-and-wave discharges in the electroencephalogram (EEG); (2) atypical absence seizures; (3) myoclonic seizures; (4) tonic-clonic seizures; and (5) atonic seizures.

Absence seizures are not as common as other types of seizures, and account for only 5% of all seizure disorders. These seizures are short interruptions of consciousness that last from 3 to 15 seconds each. They are not associated with auras or other evidence of focal onset. Absence seizures begin and end abruptly and recur from a few to several hundred times per day. Ongoing behavior stops. While otherwise immobile, the individual may show inconspicuous flickering of the eyelids or eyebrows about three times per second; there may be simple automatic movements, such as rubbing the nose, putting a hand to the face, or chewing and swallowing. Falling does not occur because of the ability to retain muscle tone. Immediately following the short interruption of awareness, the individual is again mentally clear and fully capable of continuing previous activity. Patients with absence seizures of this type show bilaterally synchronous 3 Hz spike-and-wave discharges, usually occurring against an otherwise normal background activity. The age of onset of these short absence seizures is almost always after age 2; they almost never occur for the first time after age 20. Individuals with short absence seizures rarely have other neurological problems, but 40% to 50% of the patients have infrequent, easily controlled, generalized tonic-clonic seizures. Photic sensitivity is present in some cases.

Generalized tonic-clonic seizures occur at some time in most patients with seizure disorder regardless of the individual's usual pattern. This type of seizure can be triggered by many various events (e.g., fever, CNS infection, brain abnormality, and hereditary tendency) and also is commonly seen in childhood seizure disorders. A tonic-clonic seizure is classified under generalized seizures if the attack itself, the neurological examination, and the EEG all indicate that bilateral cerebral structures are simultaneously involved at the onset. A tonic-clonic seizure is classified as a partial seizure evolving to a secondarily generalized one if the same criteria indicate that the attack began in one hemisphere and then spread to produce a major generalized attack. Tonic-clonic convulsions usually last 3 to 5 minutes, and are characterized by a complex loss of consciousness and falling. As the patient falls, the body stiffens because of generalized tonic contraction of the limb and axial muscles. The legs usually extend and the arms flex partially. After the tonic stage, which usually lasts less than 1 minute, jerking or clonic movements occur in all four limbs for about 1 minute. Next, a period of unconsciousness follows (about 1 minute) during which the patient appears more relaxed. Consciousness then is regained and the patient usually is confused, sleepy, and uncooperative for several minutes prior to full recovery.

Atypical absence seizures generally result in blank stares that can last longer than the typical absence seizure. Atypical absence seizures are often associated with various types of seizure patterns including tonic-clonic, myoclonic, and atonic seizures. Atonic seizures usually begin in childhood and are characterized by sudden loss of postural tone which can cause slumping, a head drop, and even sometimes resulting in abrupt drops to the floor. These episodes occur without warning, are extremely short, and frequently cause injury. Myoclonic seizures are involuntary contractions of the limb and truncal muscles that are sudden, brief, and recurrent. Slight bilateral symmetric myoclonic movements often occur in persons who have absence seizures, but rarely are severe bilaterally symmetric myoclonic jerks the predominant symptoms of individuals with absence seizures.

TREATMENT

Seizure disorders can typically be treated with anti-epileptic drugs (AEDs). In treating seizures, it is initially important to identify and eliminate factors that potentially cause or precipitate the attacks. Different medications are used for various types of seizures. Medications are used until seizure control is achieved or until toxic side effects limit further increments. In more severe cases, when pharmacological treatments prove completely ineffective, surgery is often the only alternative. Removing lesions or tumors from the brain is often risky and later impairs cognitive functioning. The anterior portion of the temporal lobe is the most frequent site of surgical excision in individuals with medically intractable seizures.

GENERAL CONCERNS

People, particularly children, with seizure disorders frequently and understandably are often fearful and feel that they have relatively little control. In addition to medical management, parents and children may need counseling. Rarely are any special restrictions on activity needed except during swimming and bathing, and parents should be encouraged to allow their children to behave as normally as possible.

An excellent source for further information is the Epilepsy Foundation of American, 4351 Garden City Drive, Landover, MD 20785; phone: (800) EFA-1000; email: webmaster@efa.org; and website: http://www.efa.org/index.html.

REFERENCES

Brown, L.W. (1997). Seizure disorders. In M.L. Batshaw (Ed.), *Children with disabilities* (4th ed., pp. 553–593). Baltimore: Brookes.

Haslam, R.H.A. (1996). Seizures in childhood. In R.E. Behrman, R.M. Kliegman, & A.M. Arvin (Eds.), *Nelson textbook of pediatrics* (15th ed., pp. 1686–1699).

SELF-CARE SKILLS

See SELF HELP SKILLS.

SELF-CONCEPT

Self-concept is an individual's evaluation of his or her own abilities and attributes. It includes all aspects of an individual's personality of which he or she is aware. Although some authors have drawn distinctions between self-concept and self-esteem (Damon & Hart, 1982), the terms are frequently used interchangeably. Several theoretical models of self-concept exist in the literature. For example, Coopersmith (1967) has suggested that four factors contribute to an individual's self-concept: significance (feeling of being loved and approved of by important others), competence (ability to perform tasks considered important), virtue (adherence to moral and ethical principles), and power (the degree to which an individual is able to exert control over self and others). Recently, Harter (1982) found that self-concept can be broken down into three specific components, cognitive, social, and physical competence, and a general self-worth factor.

Self-concept begins to develop early in life, with children as young as 18 to 24 months able to discriminate between self and others (Lewis & Brooks-Gunn, 1979). As children's thought processes become less concrete and more abstract, there are corresponding changes in self-concept. Younger children (e.g., 9 year olds) tend to describe themselves in categorical terms (name, age, gender, physical attributes, etc.), while older children take an increasingly abstract view, describing their personal and interpersonal traits, attitudes, and beliefs (Montemayor & Eisen, 1977). There is not, however, any consistent evidence of age-related changes in the level of self-esteem (how positively or negatively one views oneself). The one exception to this is a temporary decline in self-esteem around the time children enter their teens (Simmons, Blyth, Van Cleave, & Bush, 1979).

A number of factors influence an individual's self-concept. Parents appear to play a particularly important role (Coopersmith, 1967). Children with high self-esteem tend to have parents who themselves have high self-esteem and who are warm, nurturing, and accepting of their children while setting high academic and behavioral standards. They set and enforce strict limits on their children and are fair, reasonable, and consistent in their use of discipline. Parents of low self-esteem children alternate unpredictably between excessive permissiveness and harsh punishment. A close relationship with the same-sex parent is typical among high self-esteem children. Findings of higher self-esteem in only children and first-born children suggest that parental attention is important. Other factors associated with high self-esteem include academic success, the presence of a close friendship, and the perceived opinions of others. Physical attractiveness and height are unrelated to self-esteem (Coopersmith, 1967). It is very important for educators to remember that different ethnic groups perceive self-concept and its measurement in different ways (Obiakor, 1992).

REFERENCES

Coopersmith, S. (1967). *Antecedents of self-esteem.* San Francisco: Freeman.

Damon, W., & Hart, D. (1982). The development of self-understanding from infancy through adolescence. *Child Development, 53,* 841–864.

Harter, S. (1982). The perceived competence scale for children. *Child Development, 53,* 87–97.

Lewis, M., & Brooks-Gunn, J. (1979). *Social cognition and the acquisition of self.* New York: Plenum.

Montemayor, R., & Eisen, M. (1977). The development of self-conceptions from childhood to adolescence. *Developmental Psychology, 13,* 314–319.

Obiakor, F.E. (1992). Self-concept of African-American students: An operational model for special education. *Exceptional Children, 59*(2), 160–167.

Piers, E.V. (1969). *The Piers Harris Children's Self-Concept Scale.* Nashville, TN: Counselor Recordings and Tests.

Simmons, R.G., Blyth, D.A., Van Cleave, E.F., & Bush, D.M. (1979). Entry into early adolescence: The impact of school structure, puberty, and early dating on self-esteem. *American Sociological Review, 44,* 948–967.

See also **Depression; Emotional Lability; Self-Management; Social Skills**

SELF-CONTAINED CLASS

The first self-contained special classes were established in the late 1800s and early 1900s as public school classes for the moderately retarded, deaf, hard of hearing, blind, emotionally disturbed, and physically handicapped. Esten (1900) states that special classes for the mentally retarded were established to provide slow learners with more appropriate class placement. A self-contained classroom for the handicapped can be defined as one that homogeneously segregates different children from normal children. Children are usually segregated along categorical groupings. As a result of Dunn's (1968) article on the detrimental aspects of self-contained placements for the mildly handicapped, students receiving special education in self-contained classes today are usually "low-incidence," exhibiting more severe problems Dunn was later refuted by Walker and McLaughlin, (1992). However, Kirk and Gallagher (1983) report gifted students are also grouped into special classes according to interests and abilities.

A self-contained class is a place where special education students spend more than 60% of their school day and receive most of their academic instruction. Typically, caseloads are small, ranging from 5 to 10 students in a class. A wide variety of instructional materials are available to the students. The self-contained class provides the opportunity for highly individualized, closely supervised, specialized instruction.

It is possible that a student may be assigned to a self-contained classroom and receive additional resource room assistance or partake in inclusive programming. Placement depends on what is best for the students in terms of least restriction. Usually, students are mainstreamed into regular education for nonacademic subjects such as music, physical education, and art, or academic areas of proficiency.

REFERENCES

Dunn, L.M. (1968). Special education for the mildly handicapped: Is much of it justifiable? *Exceptional Children, 35,* 5–22.

Esten, R.A. (1900). Backward children in the public schools. *Journal of Psychoaesthenics, 5,* 10–16.

Kirk, S.A., & Gallagher, J.J. (1983). *Educating exceptional children* (4th ed.). Boston: Houghton Mifflin.

Walker, J.G., & McLaughlin, T.F. (1992). Self-contained versus resource room classroom placement: A review. *Journal of Instructional Psychology, 19*(3), 214–225.

See also **Least Restrictive Environment; Resource Room; Special Class**

SELF-CONTROL CURRICULUM

The self-control curriculum was a product of the work of Fagen, Long, and Stevens (1975). They contended that emotional and cognitive development are closely related and therefore both need to be addressed simultaneously in the instructional process. They held that learning is impaired when learners have negative feelings about themselves. Fagen et al. believed that in many cases of behavior disorders there was an inability on the part of the individual to exert self-control. The self-control curriculum had as its goals the development of self-control and positive feelings.

There were eight enabling skills in the self-control model. Four of these were in the cognitive area and four in the affective area. The eight skills are:

1. *Selecting.* Paying attention to directions/instruction.

2. *Storing.* Remembering directions/instructions.

3. *Sequencing and ordering.* Organizing materials/work areas to perform work.

4. *Anticipating Consequences.* Realizing that behavior has consequences and predicting those consequences.

5. *Appreciating Feelings.* Expressing feelings by words and actions.

6. *Managing Frustrations.* Behaviorally maintaining control in stressful situations.

7. *Inhibiting and Delaying.* Delaying actions and reflecting on consequences of possible actions even when excited.

8. *Relaxing.* Consciously relieving bodily tension.

The curriculum has pupil activities and guidelines for teachers for developing more lessons in each unit. The activities involve games, discussions, and role-playing activities. The position taken in the curriculum was that self-control must be taught just as any other subject. Little research has been conducted over the past years to validate the curriculum.

REFERENCE

Fagen, S.A., Long, N.J., & Stevens, D. (1975). *Teaching children self-control.* Columbus, OH: Merrill.

See also **Self-Monitoring; Social Behavior of the Handicapped; Social Skills Training**

SELF-FULFILLING PROPHECY

See PYGMALION EFFECT.

SELF-HELP TRAINING

The skill areas typically included under the domain of self-help are toileting, eating, dressing, and personal hygiene. An obvious reason for training the developmentally disabled in these skills is that there are widespread self-help skill deficits among this population. Another reason is that the acquisition of these skills represents a critical step in the developmental process and can increase self-esteem, promote positive social interaction, and maintain physical health and well-being (Kimm, Falvey, Bishop, & Rosenberg, 1995). Once the skills are acquired, the caregiver's time devoted to the routine maintenance of the developmentally disabled person is reduced. The acquisition of self-help skills can have meaningful social consequences. It can increase the possibility of gaining access to valued places and activities.

Each self-help skill area has some unique characteristics that have affected the direction of research and training in that particular area (Reid, Wilson, & Faw, 1980). Training in independent toileting has become more complex and focuses on a more naturally occurring sequence of toilet behaviors. Automatic devices are being used to signal trainers when a trainee is about to have a toileting accident or has eliminated into the toilet. Nighttime toileting skills have also been trained to reduce the frequency of enuresis (bed wetting).

It is believed that training independent eating through behavior modification procedures has been relatively successful because food is an inherent reinforcer. In addition to focusing on the acquisition of independent eating skills, researchers and practitioners have attempted to eliminate or reduce inappropriate mealtime behaviors (e.g., eating too quickly and stealing food).

As in training eating skills, dressing has focused on acquisition of appropriate skills and the reduction of inappropriate behaviors (e.g., public disrobing). The generalization of dressing skills to other contexts has been an issue when developing training programs because training typically occurs when dressing is not naturally required. Maintenance over time has also been an important training issue because dressing is less inherently reinforcing than toileting and eating.

There are several areas of concern for research and practice (Whitman et al., 1983). Often there is a discrepancy between the development of an effective training technology and its day-to-day application by caregivers. Consequently, it is important to understand what factors contribute to caregivers' willingness to carry out training. A component analysis of the multifaceted training strategies, like the intensive training package, could assist practitioners in selecting the most effective and efficient training. As increasing numbers of developmentally disabled people live and work in the community, it will be necessary to train more advanced and complex skills in community contexts. It will also be necessary to determine the social validity of certain self-help skills, particularly in the areas of dressing and personal hygiene. By assessing social validity, practitioners will know what to teach in order to bring a skill into a socially acceptable range. Finally, effective and practical self-help training procedures need to be developed for the physically disabled.

REFERENCES

Kimm, C.H., Falvey, M.A., Bishop, K.D., & Rosenberg, R.L. (1995). Motor and personal care skills. In M.A. Falvey (Ed.), *Inclusive and heterogeneous schooling: Assessment, curriculum, and instruction* (pp. 187–227).

Reid, D.H., Wilson, P.G., & Faw, G.D. (1980). Teaching self-help skills. In J.L. Matson & J.A. Mulick (Eds.), *Handbook of mental retardation* (pp. 429–442). New York: Pergamon.

Whitman, T.L., Sciback, J.W., & Reid, D.H. (1983). *Behavior modification with the severely and profoundly retarded: Research and application.* New York: Academic.

See also **Daily Living Skills; Functional Skills; Habilitation; Rehabilitation**

SELF-INJURIOUS BEHAVIOR

Self-injury is one of the most unusual and probably least understood form of aberrant behavior. It may take a variety of forms, including biting, head banging, face slapping, pinching, or slapping. Such behavior has been reported to affect approximately 4 to 5% of psychiatric populations. Approximately 9 to 17% of normal young children (9 to 36 months of age) also exhibit self-injurious behavior (Carr, 1977).

Through a series of unrelated, yet complementary, studies, researchers were able to demonstrate that self-injurious behavior is regulated by the same laws that affect other human behaviors. The data from these early studies clearly point to the validity of applying the learning theory model to the treatment of self-injurious behavior (Lovaas, 1982).

The etiology of self-injurious behavior has been in debate for some time. There appears to be an organic basis for some self-injurious behavior. There are data to support the contention that self-injurious behaviors are seen in the Lesch-Nyhan and de Lange syndromes, which are both genetically caused. In Lesch-Nyhan syndrome, a rare form of X-linked cerebral palsy found in only males, there is repetitive biting of the tongue, lips, and fingers. It is thought that this behavior is biochemically related. Considerable research has gone into finding a chemical cure for these characteristics. In de Lange syndrome, which is also genetic in origin, a broad variety of self-injurious behaviors have been reported. A biochemical association has not been presented. The data on organic causes of self-injurious behavior are contradictory, and limited chemical and medical mediations have been found. Those who deal directly with handicapped individuals should recognize that medical screening is necessary at the onset of any treatment program, and in some cases medical intervention may be appropriate (Carr, 1977; Evans & Meyer, 1985).

Iwata et al. (1982) have provided the practitioner with a method for functionally analyzing self-injurious behavior. Using this method it is possible to identify the specific motivational factors causing self-injury in many handicapped persons. Employing this approach requires observing the individual in four situations: under negative reinforcement, social attention, play, and alone. Mean levels of self-injurious behavior across each situation are determined. Specific patterns of behavior are manifested in a specific setting that often clearly reflects a specific motivational cause for the behavior.

As previously noted, medical interventions are occasionally appropriate and successful in reducing or eliminating self-injurious behavior. Psychotherapy and other psychological methods have also been used to treat self-injurious behavior. Clearly, the most successful and effective interventions have been behaviorally based. Such interventions should be selected on a least-restrictive model and monitored by systematic data collection procedures. Behaviorally based intervention strategies include the use of punishment. Punishment has been shown to be highly successful, at least on a short-term basis, for the treatment of self-injurious behavior. In cases of chronic self-injurious behavior, where life or irreversible damage is threatened, steps as drastic as electrical shock have been used (Lovaas, 1982). These procedures are generally used to suppress serious self-injurious behavior until other approaches can replace them.

Self-injurious behavior poses many problems to the practitioner in its treatment. Although often misunderstood, recent work has provided both a theoretical explanation and a new direction for finding practical, effective, treatment methods for self-injurious behavior (Symons, 1995).

REFERENCES

Carr, E. (1977). The motivation of self-injurious behavior: A review of some hypothesis. *Psychological Bulletin, 84,* 800–816.

Evans, I.M., & Meyer, L.H. (1985). *An educative approach to behavior problems.* Baltimore, MD: Brooks.

Iwata, B.A., Dorsey, M.F., Slifer, K.J., Bauman, K.E., & Richman, G.S. (1982). Toward a functional analysis of self-injury. *Analysis and Intervention in Developmental Disabilities, 2,* 3–20.

Lovaas, O.I. (1982). Comments on self-destructive behaviors. *Analysis and Intervention in Developmental Disabilities, 2,* 115–124.

Symons, F.J. (1995). Self-injurious behavior. *Developmental Disabilities Bulletin, 23*(1), 90–104.

See also **Applied Behavior Analysis; Self-Stimulation; Stereotypic Movement Disorders**

SELF-MANAGEMENT

Self-monitoring refers to the observation, discrimination, and recording of one's own behavior. A child in the classroom, for example, may record on an index card each math problem completed. Self-monitoring has been demonstrated to have both assessment and therapeutic use with exceptional students who present a wide range of social and academic behaviors. Common problems associated with using self-monitoring as an assessment procedure include the inaccuracy and reactivity (spontaneous behavior change) of self-monitoring, both of which may result in a distorted picture of the initial levels of behavior. When self-monitoring is used as a treatment strategy, however, reactive effects are desired and inaccuracy may not interfere with obtaining this desired reactivity.

Self-evaluation, or self-assessment, is the comparison of one's own behavior against a preset standard to determine whether performance meets this criterion. Standards may be self-imposed or externally determined. In one study, special education students were asked to rate their behavior as "good," "okay," or "not good" when a timer rang at the end of 10-minute intervals. As is typical, self-evaluation was used as one component of a more comprehensive package; this resulted in reductions in disruptive behavior and increases in academic performance in these students (Robertson, Simon, Pachman, & Drabman, 1979).

Self-consequation refers to the self-delivery of positive consequences (self-reinforcement) or aversive consequences (self-punishment) following behavior. Self-reinforcement is preferred over self-punishment when possible and frequently is used in combination with other procedures. As an example, continued low levels of disruptive behavior or increased on-task behavior have been observed in special education students when self-reinforcement procedures were added to multicomponent programs (Shapiro & Klein, 1980).

Self-instruction is a process of talking to oneself to initiate, direct, or maintain one's own behavior. Children with attention deficit disorder, for example, may be taught specific coping self-statements that compete with such classroom problems as distractibility, overactivity, and off-task behavior. Typical training components include cognitive modeling, overt and covert rehearsal, graded practice on training tasks, and performance feedback (Meichenbaum, 1977).

Self-management training frequently combines these and other procedures in multicomponent self-management packages. In one example, disruptive developmentally disabled individuals were taught skills of self-monitoring, self-evaluation, self-consequation, and self-instruction that successfully reduced their chronic and severe conduct difficulties in a vocational training setting (Cole, Gardner, & Karan, 1985; Cole, Pflugrad, Gardner, & Karan, 1985).

Although total self-management is not possible for many special education students, most can be taught to be more self-reliant. Further, evidence suggests that self-management procedures are at least as effective as similar externally managed procedures in facilitating positive behavior change and in ensuring maintenance of this behavior change. Thus, in addition to its therapeutic effects, self-management offers economic, philosophic, legal, and professional benefits for use in special education.

REFERENCES

Cole, C.L., Gardner, W.I., & Karan, O.C. (1985). Self-management training of mentally retarded adults presenting severe conduct difficulties. *Applied Research in Mental Retardation, 6,* 337–347.

Cole, C.L., Pflugrad, D., Gardner, W.I., & Karan, O.C. (1985). *The self-management training program: Teaching developmentally disabled individuals to manage their disruptive behavior.* Champaign, IL: Research.

Meichenbaum, D. (1977). *Cognitive-behavior modification: An integrative approach.* New York: Plenum.

Robertson, S.J., Simon, S.J., Pachman, J.S., & Drabman, R.S. (1979). Self-control and generalization procedures in a classroom of disruptive retarded children. *Child Behavior Therapy, 1,* 347–362.

Shapiro, E.S., & Klein, R.D. (1980). Self-management of classroom behavior with retarded/disturbed children. *Behavior Modification, 4,* 83–97.

See also **Attention Deficit Disorder; Cognitive Behavior Modification; Self-Control Curriculum; Self-Monitoring**

SELF-MONITORING

Self-monitoring is one component of a more general process variously known as self-management, self-regulation, or self-control. The process of self-monitoring first involves a person's recognizing that a need exists to regulate his or her behavior. To recognize this need, the person must be observing his or her behavior and comparing it with some preset standard. This self-observation and assessment then combines with recording the behavior to create the self-monitoring component (Shapiro, 1981). Other components in the self-management process can include self-reinforcement, standard setting, self-evaluation, and self-instruction. These components have been used in various combinations with self-monitoring to modify many different types of behaviors (e.g., overeating, temper outbursts, negative statements, attending to task) in the developmentally disabled (Cole, Gardner, & Karan, 1983; Marion, 1994).

The variable results obtained with self-monitoring are probably due to several intervening factors that can impact on the reactivity or therapeutic value of self-monitoring (Nelson, 1977). The following comments are only suggestive, because the empirical evidence is limited and most of the supporting research has been done with nondevelopmentally disabled people. First, a behavior's valence or a person's desire to change the behavior can affect reactivity. Positively valenced behaviors tend to increase and negatively valenced behaviors to decrease. Generally, reactivity is enhanced by the frequency of self-monitoring; however, there are situations where the act of monitoring can interfere with reactivity, particularly with positively valenced behaviors. Reactivity also tends to be augmented when the recording device is visible and apparent to the person doing the self-monitoring. In addition, if several behaviors are monitored concurrently, the likelihood of change in any of them is suppressed. Finally, training in self-monitoring seems to enhance reactivity, particularly if the behavior is negatively valenced.

REFERENCES

Cole, C.L., Gardner, W.I., & Karan, O.C. (1983). *Self-management training of mentally retarded adults with chronic conduct difficulties.* Madison WI: University of Wisconsin, Rehabilitation Research and Training Center, Waisman Center on Mental Retardation and Human Development.

Marion, M. (1994). Encouraging the development of responsible anger management in young children. *Early Child Development & Care, 97,* 155–163.

Nelson, R.O. (1977). Methodological issues in assessment via self-monitoring. In J.D. Cone & R.P. Hawkins (Eds.), *Behavioral assessment: New directions in clinical psychology.* New York: Brunner/Mazel.

Shapiro, E.S. (1981). Self-control procedures with the mentally retarded. In M. Hersen, R.M. Eisler, & P.M. Miller (Eds.), *Progress in behavior modification.* New York: Academic.

See also **Impulse Control; Self-Care Skills; Self-Control Curriculum; Self-Management**

SELF-SELECTION OF REINFORCEMENT

When the student involved in a contingency management program is permitted to choose a reinforcer or determine the cost of a reinforcer relative to a target behavior, the technique of self-selection of reinforcement is being used. It is one of several self-management methods. It may be used in isolation or in combination with self-recording or self-evaluation (Hughes & Ruhl, 1985). However, a recording and evaluation system (controlled by either the teacher or the student) must be in operation prior to implementing self-selection of reinforcement.

As with other self-management techniques, self-selection of reinforcement appears to be more effective with students previously exposed to a systematic, externally controlled reinforcement system. Consequently, it may function as a helpful transition step for students being weaned from externally controlled systems. Studies (Cosden, Gannon, & Haring, 1995; Dickerson & Creedon, 1981; Rosenbaum & Drabman, 1979) have indicated that student-selected reinforcers are more effective than those selected by the teacher. This may be true because students are more capable of identifying what is of value to them and what they are willing to work for.

REFERENCES

Cosden, M., Gannon, G., & Haring, T.G. (1995). Teacher-control versus student-control over chance of task and reinforcement for students with severe behavior problems. *Journal of Behavioral Education, 5*(1), 11–27.

Dickerson, A.E., & Creedon, C.F. (1981). Self-selection of standards by children: The relative effectiveness of pupil-selected and teacher-selected standards of performance. *Journal of Applied Behavior Analysis, 141*, 425–433.

Hughes, C.A., & Ruhl, K.L. (1985). Learning activities for improving self-management skills. In B. Algozzine (Ed.), *Educators' resource manual for management of problem behaviors in students.* Rockville, MD: Aspen.

Rosenbaum, M.S., & Drabman, R.S. (1979). Self-control training in the classroom. *Journal of Behavior Analysis, 12*, 467–485.

See also **Applied Behavior Analysis; Behavior Modification; Contingency Contracting; Positive Reinforcement**

SELF-STIMULATION

Self-stimulation, also called stereotypic behavior, includes "highly consistent and repetitive motor posturing behaviors which are not outer directed in the sense of being explicitly disruptive and harmful to others" (Forehand & Baumeister, 1976, p. 226). Examples of self-stimulatory behavior include flapping the hands at the wrists, light gazing, excessive laughing, repetitive humming, head weaving, twirling in circles, hand staring, spinning or banging objects, finger posturing, and masturbation. Approximately two-thirds of the individuals living in institutions exhibit self-stimulatory behaviors (Snell, 1983).

Another class of self-stimulation is self-injurious behavior. This occurs when a person repeats a behavior that causes injury to himself or herself. Examples of self-injurious behaviors are eye gouging, head banging, self-biting, scratching or pinching, and face slapping. It has been estimated that between 4 and 10% of the institutionalized population engages in some form of self-injurious behavior (Snell, 1983).

Although not always disruptive to others in the environment, self-stimulatory behavior disrupts the individual's learning environment, precludes participation in normalized educational, vocational, and leisure activities, and, in the case of self-injurious behavior, poses a threat to physical well-being. Self-stimulatory behaviors, especially self-injurious behaviors, are high priorities for intervention.

Intervention techniques need to be carefully evaluated to determine their potential for alleviating a particular individual's self-stimulatory behavior. Before any behavioral or environmental intervention is begun, the medical status of the individual must be evaluated. Physical discomfort may be responsible for the self-stimulatory behavior. If no medical factors are revealed, other approaches should be explored.

According to Alberto and Troutman (1982), the techniques of first choice are those that apply a positive approach to behavior reduction; i.e., strategies of differential reinforcement. The technique of second choice would be the use of extinction procedures or the withdrawing of reinforcers that maintain the behavior. Third choice employs a punishing consequence, in that a desirable stimulus is contingently removed in order to decrease behavior. Fourth choice is the application of unconditional or conditional aversive stimuli.

Interventions that have aversive consequences (e.g., physical punishment, noxious odors and liquids, electric shock) are interventions of last resort. These interventions may be justifiable when self-injurious behaviors are life-threatening and all other less intrusive techniques have failed. In cases where aversive techniques are used, continuous program monitoring is critical both for programming and for ethical and legal justification.

REFERENCES

Alberto, P.A., & Troutman, A.C. (1982). *Applied behavior analysis for teachers.* Columbus, OH: Merrill.

Forehand, R., & Baumeister, A. (1976). Deceleration of aberrant behavior among retarded individuals. In M. Hersen, R.M. Eisler, & P.M. Miller (Eds.), *Progress in behavior modification, 2.* New York: Academic.

Snell, M.E. (1983). *Systematic instruction of the moderately and severely handicapped.* Columbus, OH: Merrill.

See also **Autistic Behavior; Self-Injurious Behavior**

SENSORINEURAL HEARING LOSS

A sensorineural hearing loss is a hearing impairment resulting from a pathological condition in the inner ear or along the auditory nerve (VIII cranial nerve) pathway from the inner ear to the brain stem. If the pathological condition or site of lesion is confined to the inner ear or cochlea, it is known as an inner ear or cochlea hearing loss. If the site of lesion is along the auditory nerve (as is the case with an acoustic nerve tumor), it is known as a retrocochlear hearing loss. Several audiological, medical, and radiological special tests have been developed to assist in the diagnosis of whether a sensorineural hearing loss is due to a cochlear or retrocochlear site of lesion.

An individual with a sensorineural hearing loss has reduced hearing sensitivity and lacks the ability to discriminate speech sounds, especially when listening in a noisy environment. Tinnitus is a common symptom of a sensorineural hearing loss. Tinnitus is any sensation of sound in the head heard in one or both ears. It may be described as a hissing, whistling, buzzing, roaring, or a high-pitched tone or noise. Dizziness is also a symptom of sensorineural hearing loss; it can range from light-headedness to a severe whirling sensation known as vertigo, that leads to nausea.

A sensorineural hearing loss can occur in varying degrees ranging from mild-moderate to severe-profound. The degree of sensorineural hearing loss is determined by averaging the decibel amount of hearing loss across the frequencies needed to hear and understand speech or the speech frequencies (500, 1000, and 2000 Hz). Individuals with a mild to severe hearing loss are usually classified as being hard of hearing, while individuals with a profound hearing impairment are classified as deaf. A sensorineural hearing loss can occur in just one ear (unilateral) or in each ear (bilateral). If the hearing loss occurs in each ear, one ear may be more affected than the other.

A sensorineural hearing loss can be caused by many factors, including genetic diseases (dominant, recessive, or sex-linked), diseases acquired during pre-, peri-, and post-natal periods, and childhood diseases. Adults can obtain sensorineural hearing loss from noise exposure, diseases, medication, and the aging process. Many sensorineural hearing losses are due to unknown etiology. A sensorineural hearing loss also may be part of a syndrome that affects the individual in other ways. A congenital sensorineural hearing loss is one that has existed or has an etiology from birth; an adventitious hearing loss is one that occurred after birth and in most cases is due to injury or disease. If the sensorineural hearing loss occurred prior to the development of speech and language skills, it is known as prelingual; if it occurred after the development of speech and language skills, it is known as postlingual. Standardized batteries of cognitive abilities and memory are currently being used to assess concurrent learning disabilities and skill strengths and weaknesses (Plapinger & Sikora, 1995; Sikora & Plapinger, 1994).

In children having sensorineural hearing losses, about half the cases are due to genetic causes and half to acquired causes. Meningitis and prematurity are the leading acquired causes of sensorineural hearing loss in children. For adults, the leading cause of sensorineural hearing loss is the aging process, known as presbyacusis, and excessive exposure to noise. Typically, the sensorineural hearing loss from presbyacusis or noise exposure is a progressive reduction of high frequency (1000 to 8000 Hz) hearing sensitivity that causes problems in understanding speech.

It is important that individuals with a sensorineural hearing loss have audiological and otological diagnosis and management. In almost all cases, there is no medical treatment for sensorineural hearing loss from a cochlear site of lesion. However, a retrocochlear lesion from a tumor, or some other growth along the auditory nerve may benefit from an operation. Cochlear implants are now available, but their use is controversial (Carver, 1997).

Children and adults with cochlear sensorineural hearing loss can benefit through the use of hearing aids. Most children are fitted with a hearing aid for each ear (binaural amplification) and require auditory and speech reading training, speech and language therapy, and academic tutoring. Adults are usually fitted with either a hearing aid on one ear (monaural) or with binaural amplification. Generally, adults do not need specialized training; however, many adults benefit from speech-reading therapy. References for in depth discussion of sensorineural hearing loss are cited below.

REFERENCES

Carver, R. (1997). *Questions parents should ask about cochlear implants.* British Columbia, Canada: DCSD.

Plapinger, D.S., & Sikora, D.M. (1995). The use of standardized test batteries in assessing skill development of children with mild to moderate sensorineural hearing loss. *Language, Speech & Hearing in Schools, 26*(1), 39–44.

Sikora, D.M., & Plapinger, D.S. (1994). Using standardized psychometric tests to identify learning disabilities in students with learning disabilities. *Journal of Learning Disabilities, 27*(6), 352–359.

See also **Deaf; Deaf Education**

SENSORY EXTINCTION

Sensory extinction is a procedure developed by Rincover (1978) for reducing various pathological behaviors in developmentally disabled children. It has been used to suppress self-stimulation (Maag, Wolchik, Rutherford, & Parks, 1986; Rincover, 1978), compulsive behaviors (Rincover, Newsom, & Carr, 1979), and self-injury (Rincover & Devaney, 1981). In a sensory extinction paradigm, stereotypy is considered operant behavior maintained by its sensory consequences. For example, repetitive finger flapping might be conceptualized as being maintained by the specific proprioceptive feedback it produces, while persistent delayed echolalia may be maintained by auditory feedback.

Sensory extinction involves masking, changing, or removing certain sensory consequences of behavior. If the sensory reinforcement received is removed, the behavior will be extinguished. For example, if a child continuously spins a plate on a table, a piece of carpet could be placed on the table to remove the auditory feedback resulting from this behavior. Similarly, the stereotypic behavior of a child who ritualistically switches a light on and off could be extinguished by either removing the visual feedback (if seeing the light were reinforcing) or removing the auditory feedback (if hearing the light switch click were reinforcing).

When sensory extinction is used to suppress stereotypy, the preferred sensory consequences of the behavior can be used to teach appropriate behaviors. For example, the child who spins plates could be taught to spin a top instead, since this would provide the same sensory consequences as the maladaptive behavior. Rincover, Cook, Peoples, and Packard (1979) found that children preferred to play with toys that provided sensory reinforcement similar to the sensory reinforcement previously found in the stereotypy.

REFERENCES

Maag, J.W., Wolchik, S.A., Rutherford, R.B., & Parks, B.T. (1986). Response covariation of self-stimulatory behaviors during sensory extinction procedures. *Journal of Autism & Developmental Disorders, 16*, 119–132.

Rincover, A. (1978). Sensory extinction: A procedure for eliminating self-stimulatory behavior in developmentally disabled children. *Journal of Abnormal Child Psychology, 6*, 299–310.

Rincover, A., Cook, R., Peoples, A., & Packard, D. (1979). Sensory extinction and sensory reinforcement principles for programming multiple adaptive behavior change. *Journal of Applied Behavior Analysis, 12*, 221–233.

Rincover, A., & Devaney, J. (1981). The application of sensory extinction principles to self-injury in developmentally disabled children. *Analysis & Intervention in Developmental Disabilities, 4*, 67–69.

Rincover, A., Newsom, C.D., & Carr, E.G. (1979). Using sensory extinction procedures in the treatment of compulsive-like behavior of developmentally disabled children. *Journal of Consulting and Clinical Psychology, 47*, 695–701.

See also Behavior Modification; Self-Stimulation

SENSORY INTEGRATIVE THERAPY

Sensory integrative therapy is a technique for the remediation of sensory integrative dysfunction developed by A. Jean Ayres (1972). Sensory integrative dysfunction is believed by Ayres and others (Quiros, 1976; Silberzahn, 1982) to be at the root of many learning disorders. Ayres uses the term sensory integrative dysfunction to describe children whose learning problems are due to the failure of the lower levels of the brain (particularly the midbrain, brain stem, and vestibular system) to use and organize information effectively. The principal objective of sensory integrative therapy is to promote the development and the organization of subcortical brain mechanisms as a foundation for perception and learning. Treatment procedures consist of the use of gross motor activities and physical exercise to achieve this goal. Sensory integrative therapy has gained its greatest popularity among occupational therapists.

Carefully controlled studies of the outcome of sensory integrative therapy are lacking, particularly in regard to improvements in academic skills. The therapy is a deficit-centered approach to remediation, though not strictly a process approach. However, it seems unlikely that learning disabilities can be corrected through the use of gross motor activities and physical exercise.

REFERENCES

Ayres, A.J. (1972). *Sensory integration and learning disorders.* Los Angeles: Western Psychological Services.

Quiros, J.B. de. (1976). Diagnosis of vestibular disorders in the learning disabled. *Journal of Learning Disabilities, 9*, 39–47.

Silberzahn, M. (1982). Sensory integrative therapy. In C.R. Reynolds & T.B. Gutkin (Eds.), *The handbook of school psychology.* New York: Wiley.

See also Ayres, A.J.; Remediation, Deficit-Centered Models of

SENSORY MOTOR INTEGRATION

See SENSORY INTEGRATIVE THERAPY.

SEPARATION ANXIETY AND CHILDREN WITH DISABILITIES

Separation anxiety is defined by Bowlby as anxiety about losing, or becoming separated from, someone loved. It is the usual response to a threat or some other risk of loss. This fear of abandonment can not only create intense anxiety, it can arouse anger of an intense degree, especially in older children and adolescents, and cause dysfunction (Bowlby, 1982). Adverse separation experiences have at least two kinds of effects: They make the individual more vulnerable to later adverse experiences and they make it more likely that the individual will have such experiences (Bowlby, 1982; Klein, 1995).

In infants and young children, separation anxiety is a normal part of the developmental process; it is related to the formation of positive attachment behavior. Sears (1972) says that attachment is completed during the second half of the first year of life, while separation anxiety appears after the child reaches 6 months of age. Ainsworth (1972) also states that an attachment if formed when definitive separation causes anxiety, although Yarrow (1972) believes that environmental conditions that influence the strength of positive attachment behaviors determine the strength and character of response to separation anxiety.

The presence of a handicap can put significant stress on the attachment process, increasing the vulnerability of both the infant and the caregivers (Ulrey, 1981). By viewing the attachment-separation process as a system, it follows that any change will produce disequilibrium, with different implications for various handicaps. A child with motor deficits may be at increased risk because the infant may not be able to adjust to the physical comforting offered by the parents, possibly minimizing parental contact. Abnormal muscle tone may influence the child's activity level and facial movements, affecting the child's emotional expressiveness, while other motor deficits may make it impossible for the child to physically move away from the caregivers, delaying the separation process. A visually handicapped child will develop attachments more slowly than a sighted child, but, once formed, attachments persist longer, delaying separation. Children with impaired hearing may also be at increased risk for disruption of the attachment process (Ulrey, 1981). A caregiver's anxiety about a child who is handicapped may make it difficult for appropriate interaction with the child to provide the stimulation necessary to form a quality attachment.

Separation anxiety has been linked to obsessive-compulsive disorder, panic attacks and life-long issues with separation. (Brynska & Wolanczyk, 1998; Klein, 1995).

REFERENCES

Ainsworth, M.D.S. (1972). Attachment and dependency: A comparison. In. J.L. Gerwitz (Ed.), *Attachment and dependency* (pp. 97–139). New York: Winston/Wiley.

Bowlby, J. (1969). *Attachment and loss: Vol. 1. Attachment.* New York: Basic Books.

Bowlby, J. (1982). Attachment and loss: retrospect and prospect. *American Journal of Orthropsychiatrics, 52,* 664–678.

Brynska, A., & Wolanczyk, T. (1998). Obsessive-compulsive disorder and separation anxiety. *Journal of the American Academy of Child & Adolescent Psychiatry, 37*(4), 350–351.

Klein, R.G. (1995). Is panic disorder with childhood separation anxiety disorder? *Child Neuropharmacology, 18*(2), 7–14.

Sears, R.R. (1972). Attachment, dependency and frustration. In J.L. Gerwitz (Ed.), *Attachment and dependency* (pp. 1–28). New York: Winston/Wiley.

Ulrey, G. (1981). Emotional development of the young handicapped child. In N.J. Anastasiow (Ed.), *Socioemotional development: New directions for exceptional children* (No. 5, pp. 33–52). San Francisco: Jossey-Bass.

Yarrow, L.J. (1972). Attachment and dependency: A developmental perspective. In J.L. Gerwitz (Ed.), *Attachment and dependency* (pp. 81–96). New York: Winston/Wiley.

See also **Borderline Personality Disorder; School Phobia**

SEPTO-OPTIC DYSPLASIA

Septo-optic dysplasia, also known as De Morsier syndrome, is a rare disorder characterized by visual impairments and pituitary deficiencies. The etiology of Septo-optic dysplasia is not known; however, this birth defect is found in a higher percentage of infants who are the firstborn children of young mothers. Both genders are affected equally by this rare disorder.

Visual impairments include dimness in sight, especially in one eye (often referred to as lazy eye), and dizziness. These symptoms result from small, not-fully-developed optic disks associated with the visual system. In this disorder, the pupil (the opening in the eyeball through which light enters) does not respond appropriately. Instead of a consistent response, the pupil's response to light of the same intensity varies from one occasion to another. Occasional field dependence has also been noted. Besides visual impairments, an underactive pituitary gland is present either at birth or later in development. If left untreated, a child's growth is stunted. Jaundice may also be present at birth.

Standard treatment for Septo-optic dysplasia is symptomatic and supportive. Hormone replacement therapy is used to treat the pituitary hormone deficiencies. Children with Septo-optic dysplasia are usually of normal intelligence; however, mental retardation or learning disabilities may occur (Thoene, 1992). Occasional sexual precocity has been reported (Jones, 1988).

If a child experiences learning problems or developmental delays, a comprehensive neuropsychological evaluation is recommended to determine cognitive strengths and weaknesses. Based on those results, recommendations can be made, and an individualized educational plan can be developed and implemented in the schools.

REFERENCES

Jones, K.L. (Ed.). (1988). *Smith's recognizable patterns of human malformation* (4th ed.). Philadelphia, PA: W.B. Saunders.

Thoene, J.G. (Ed.). (1992). *Physician's guide to rare diseases.* Montvale, NJ: Dowden.

SEQUENCED INVENTORY OF COMMUNICATION DEVELOPMENT, REVISED

The Sequenced Inventory of Communication Development, Revised Edition (SICD-R; Hendrick, Prather, & Tobin, 1984) is a diagnostic assessment tool to evaluate the communication abilities of normal and retarded children, ages 4 months to 4 years. The SICD-R utilizes both parental report and observation of communication behaviors. The inventory includes 100 items which are broken into Receptive and Expressive Scales. Responses may also be recorded on the Behavioral Profile that examines awareness, discrimination, understanding, imitation, initiation, response, motor, vocal, and verbal areas. There is also a Process Profile that examines semantics, syntax, pragmatics, perceptual, and phonological areas.

The normative data are from a sample of 252 children, all Caucasian from monolingual homes, who were believed to have normal hearing, language, physical, and mental development. The reliability data must be viewed with caution because of the small number of subjects in the reliability studies (Mardell-Czudnowski, 1989; Pearson, 1989). Validity data are not complete enough to warrant the SICD-R's use for determining delays (Pearson, 1989).

REFERENCES

Hendrick, D.L., Prather, E.M., & Tobin, A.R. (1984). *Sequenced Inventory of Communication Development.* Seattle, WA: University of Washington Press.

Mardell-Czudnowski, C. (1989). Review of the Sequenced Inventory of Communication Development. In J.J. Kramer & J.C. Conoley (Eds.), *The eleventh mental measurements yearbook* (pp. 740–742). Lincoln, NE: Buros Institute of Mental Measurements.

Pearson, M.E. (1989). Review of the Sequenced Inventory of Communication Development. In J.J. Kramer & J.C. Conoley (Eds.), *The eleventh mental measurements yearbook* (pp. 742–744). Lincoln, NE: Buros Institute of Mental Measurements.

See also **Verbal Deficiency; Verbal Scale IQ**

SEQUENTIAL AND SIMULTANEOUS COGNITIVE PROCESSING

Sequential and simultaneous are two of many labels used to denote two primary forms of information coding processes in the brain. These coding processes are the primary functions of Luria's (1973) Block II of the brain (the parietal, occipital, and temporal lobes, also known as the association areas of the brain). They have been proposed as fundamental integration processes in Das, Kirby, and Jarman's (1979) model of Luria's fundamental approach to human information processing. Other labels commonly used to distinguish these forms of processing include successive versus simultaneous (Das et al., 1979), propositional versus appositional (Bogen, 1969), serial versus multiple or parallel (Neisser, 1967), and analytic versus gestalt/holistic (Levy, 1972).

No matter what label is applied, the descriptions of the processes corresponding to each label appear to be defining similar processes though some minor distinctions may exist. Thus sequential processing is defined as the processing of information in a temporal or serial order. Using this coding process, analysis of information proceeds in successive steps in which each step provides cues for the processing of later steps. This type of processing is generally employed, e.g., when an individual repeats a series of numbers that have been orally presented. Each stage of processing is dependent on the completion of the immediately preceding stage.

Simultaneous coding processes are used when all the pieces of information or all the stimuli are surveyable at one time and are thus available for processing at one time; i.e., at the analysis of parts of information can take place without dependence on the parts' relationship to the whole. When an individual discerns the whole object with only parts of the picture available, this is usually accomplished using simultaneous processing.

Determining whether to process information sequentially or simultaneously is not solely dependent on the presentation mode of the stimuli to be processed (e.g., visual or auditory). Rather, the form of processing used appears to be more dependent on the cognitive demands of the task and the unique sociocultural history and genetic predisposition of the individual performing the task (Das et al., 1979; Kaufman & Kaufman, 1983). This may become habitual and individuals do develop preferred styles of information processing.

Sequential and simultaneous processing have been indirectly linked to various areas of the brain, but psychologists do not agree on the exact location of each of these functions. Some contend that processing abilities are best associated with the two hemispheres of the brain (Gazzaniga, 1975; Reynolds, 1981), with sequential processing being a left hemisphere function and simultaneous processing being a right hemisphere function. Luria (1973), on the other hand, located successive or sequential processing as a function of the frontal regions of the brain, with simultaneous processing carried out in the occipital-parietal or rear sections of the brain.

The Kaufman Assessment Battery for Children (K-ABC; Kaufman & Kaufman, 1983) was introduced into psychological and educational circles in the 1980s. This instrument was designed as an individually administered intelligence test for children ages 2½ and 12½; it is composed of several subtests that according to factor analytic data, measure sequential and simultaneous processing abilities. Focused on process rather than content as the major distinction of how children solve unfamiliar problems, this instrument has resulted in more controversy and discussion than any intelligence test in recent history (Reynolds, 1985).

Controversy has arisen over the Kaufmans' assertion that knowledge about a child's information-processing abilities, as measured on the K-ABC, in conjunction with other sources of data, can more easily translate into educational programming for children with learning or behavioral problems than traditionally had been possible from data gathered on other, content-based intelligence tests. Primarily employing an aptitude × treatment interaction (ATI) paradigm (Cronbach, 1975) and the habilitation philosophy of neuropsychology (Reynolds, 1981), the Kaufmans propose using knowledge regarding a child's individual strengths in information processing (e.g., simultaneous processing) as the foundation for any remedial plans thus developed. The notion of a strength model of remediation is in direct contrast to the deficit-centered training models that have dominated special education remedial plans for years, but that have proven largely ineffective in improving academic abilities (Ysseldyke & Mirkin, 1982).

Although preliminary data seem encouraging regarding the efficacy of using knowledge of a child's individual processing style to remediate learning or behavioral difficulties (Gunnison, Kaufman, & Kaufman, 1983), the data are not sufficient to support this assumption unequivocally. Much research remains to be done in this area.

REFERENCES

Bogen, J.E. (1969). The other side of the brain: Parts I, II, & III. *Bulletin of the Los Angeles Neurological Society, 34,* 73–203.

Cronbach, L.J. (1975). Beyond the two disciplines of scientific psychology. *American Psychologist, 30,* 116–125.

Das, J.P., Kirby, J.R., & Jarman, R.F. (1979). *Simultaneous and successive cognitive processes.* New York: Academic.

Gazzaniga, M.S. (1975). Recent research on hemispheric lateralization of the human brain: Review of the split brain. *UCLA Educator, 17,* 9–12.

Gunnison, J., Kaufman, N.L., & Kaufman, A.S. (1983). Reading remediation based on sequential and simultaneous processing. *Academic Therapy, 17,* 297–307.

Kaufman, A.S., & Kaufman, N. (1983). *The Kaufman Assessment Battery for Children.* Circle Pines, MN: American Guidance Service.

Levy, J. (1972). Lateral specification of the human brain: Behavioral manifestations and possible evolutionary basis. In J.A. Kiger (Ed.), *Biology of behavior.* Cornallis: Oregon State University Press.

Luria, A.R. (1973). *The working brain: An introduction to neuropsychology.* London: Penguin.

Neisser, W. (1967). *Cognitive psychology.* New York: Appleton-Century-Crofts.

Reynolds, C.R. (1981). Neuropsychological assessment and the habilitation of learning: Considerations in the search for the aptitude ¥ treatment interaction. *School Psychology Review, 10,* 343–349.

Reynolds, C.R. (Ed.). (1985). K-ABC and controversy [Special issue]. *Journal of Special Education, 18*(3).

Ysseldyke, J., & Mirkin, P. (1982). The use of assessment information to plan instructional interventions: A review of the research. In C.R. Reynolds & T.B. Gutkin (Eds.), *The handbook of school psychology.* New York: Wiley.

See also **Information Processing; Kaufman Assessment Battery for Children; Perceptual Training; Remediation, Deficit-Centered Models of**

SEQUENTIAL ASSESSMENT OF MATHEMATICS INVENTORIES: STANDARDIZED INVENTORY

The Sequential Assessment of Mathematics Inventories: Standardized Inventory (SAMI; Reisman & Hutchinson, 1985) is designed to measure the achievement of specific mathematics content objectives and to compare students' performance to national norms. It may be used to assess children in kindergarten through the eighth grade.

The SAMI is presented to students in an easel format, with the questions read aloud by the examiner. Students respond by pointing, writing, or verbally responding. Nine scores are obtained on the SAMI: Mathematical Language (grades K–3 only), Ordinality (grades K–3 only), Number/Notation, Computation, Measurement, Geometric Concepts, Mathematical Applications (grades 4–8 only), Word Problems, and Total. Subtest standard scores have a mean of 10 and a standard deviation of 3.

The SAMI was normed on a sample of about 1,400 students in kindergarten through eighth grade. Test-retest reliability values over a 6-week interval ranged from .43 to .89 with a median of .66. However, five of the subtests have reliability values below .50. Internal consistency values range from .72 to .97 with a median of .93. Validity evidence is limited to one study comparing the SAMI and two standardized achievement tests, as well as the reported intercorrelation of subtests. Fleenor (1993) states that the SAMI has promise as a measure of mathematics performance, but needs more data supporting its reliability and validity.

REFERENCES

Fleenor, J.W. (1992). Review of the Sequential Assessment of Mathematics Inventories: Standardized Inventory. In J.J. Kramer & J.C. Conoley (Eds.), *The eleventh mental measurements yearbook* (pp. 817–819). Lincoln, NE: Buros Institute of Mental Measurements.

Reisman, F.K., & Hutchinson, T.A. (1985). *Sequential Assessment of Mathematics Inventories: Standardized Inventory.* San Antonio, TX: The Psychological Corporation.

See also **Assessment; Mathematics, Learning Disabilities in**

SERIOUSLY EMOTIONALLY DISTURBED

The term seriously emotionally disturbed (SED) has been defined by federal legislation (IDEA) as a condition with one or more of the following characteristics occurring to a marked degree and over a long period of time: (1) inability to learn not explainable by health, intellectual, or sensory factors; (2) inability to develop or maintain appropriate interpersonal relationships with students and teachers; (3) inappropriate behaviors or feelings in normal circumstances; (4) a pervasive mood of depression; (5) a tendency to develop physical symptoms or fears in response to personal or school difficulties [Code of Federal Regulations, Title 34, Section 300. 7(b) (9)]. According to the legislative definition, the term specifically includes childhood schizophrenia but specifically excludes children who are socially maladjusted except when the maladjustment is accompanied by serious emotional disturbance.

The U.S. Department of Education (1997) reports that the incidence of emotional disturbance in children and youth served in the public schools for the 1995–96 school year was 438,217. The causes of emotional disturbance are varied and include factors such as genetics, trauma, diet, stress, social skills deficits, and family dysfunction. Children and youth exhibit psychiatric disorders in different ways than adults. Therefore, emotional disturbance may be seen in behaviors such as immaturity, hyperactivity, self-monitoring deficits, social skill deficits, learning difficulties and aggression or self-injurious behavior. Children with the most serious emotional disturbances may exhibit distorted thinking, extreme anxiety, abnormal mood swings, and other symptoms indicative of psychoses (NICHCY, 1998).

The entrance to special education for SED students has changed over the years to reflect the least restrictive environment (LRE) principle of IDEA and similar legislation. Placement of these students in psychiatric residential facilities has declined in recent years due to LRE and to financial constraints; however, the need for comprehensive treatment is still present. The inclusion movement has advocates that suggest that SED students are best served in the regular classroom with special education support. However, again, the least restrictive environment for SED students should be determined on a case-by-case method. What is least restrictive for one SED student may be a dangerous or nonadvantageous placement for another.

The difficulty of placement, treatment, and education for SED students has probably steered the field to look towards the identification of at-risk students and culturally competent intervention (Lago-Delello, 1996).

Ongoing teacher training for regular and special educators has been identified on many levels; and much of it has targeted multicultural competencies (Singh, 1997). The more that SED students are included in regular education, the more competencies are essential for all personnel involved in the regular education process.

Outcomes for SED students are not as good as they are for students with some other disabilities. Greenbaum (1996) has found that serious problems in these students tend to be present even seven years after the initial identification. These problems many times become lifelong adjustment issues and are highly correlated with adult high-risk behaviors in crime and substance abuse. The magnitude of the problem with the SED population is supported by data on these students concerning academic outcomes, graduation rates, school placement, school absenteeism, dropout rates, encounters with the juvenile justice system, and identification rates of students of varying socioeconomic backgrounds. Seven interdependent strategic targets have been identified by the Chesapeake Institution (1994) to address the future of policy, funding, and treatment of SED by federal, state, and local agencies: (1) expand positive learning opportunities and results; (2) strengthen school and community capacity; (3) value and address diversity; (4) collaborate with families; (5) promote appropriate assessment; (6) provide ongoing skill development and support; and (7) create comprehensive collaborative systems. Three universal themes are also stressed: first, collaborative efforts must extend to initiatives that prevent emotional and behavioral problems from developing or escalating; second, services must be provided in a culturally sensitive and respectful manner; and third, services must empower all stakeholders and maintain a climate of possibility and accountability.

The federal government is currently revising the definition of SED (NICHCY, 1998). Hopefully, more emphasis will be placed on prevention. The identification of at-risk children is the key to preventing serious adjustment problems for many children and youth. The field is moving towards being able to identify, in an objective and a culturally competent manner, young students who are having problems meeting the demands of everyday living. Once identified, this population can receive sensitive programming that includes family participation. Together, the school and family can help those young children who have not yet developed serious emotional difficulties to adjust and to meet the demands of their age group. The alternative is the present situation, where hundreds of thousands of children and youth are already suffering and in serious jeopardy of losing their ability to receive the benefits of an appropriate education.

REFERENCES

Chesapeake Institute. (1994). *National agenda for achieving better results for children and youth with serious emotional disturbance.* Washington, DC: Author.

Greenbaum, P.E. (1996). *National adolescent and child treatment study: Outcomes for children with serious emotional and behavioral disturbance.* (ERIC Clearinghouse No. EJ53063)

Lago-Delello, E. (1996). *Classroom dynamics and young children identified as at-risk for the development of serious emotional disturbance.* Paper presented at the Annual International Convention of the Council for Exceptional Children, Orlando, Florida, April 1–5.

National Information Center for Children and Youth with Disabilities (NICHCY). (1998). *General information about emotional disturbance.* Fact Sheet Number 5 (FS5), Washington, DC: Author.

Singh, N.N. (1997). Value and address diversity. *Journal of Emotional & Behavioral Disorders, 5*(1), 24–35.

U.S. Department of Education. (1997). *Nineteenth annual report to Congress on the implementation of the Individuals with Disabilities Education Act.* Washington, DC: Author.

See also Childhood Psychosis; Childhood Schizophrenia; Emotional Disorders

SERVICE DELIVERY MODELS

Service delivery models are programs, processes, and safeguards established to ensure a free, appropriate public education for handicapped children and youths. The models that have been developed for the delivery of services to handicapped school-aged children generally reflect in their form and operation the influence of at least three factors: (1) the statutory requirements and congressional intent of Individuals with Disabilities Education Act (IDEA); (2) the nature of the particular state or local education agency providing the services in terms of physical size, population distribution, and, to some extent, the available fiscal and human resources; and (3) the specific needs of the children being served. IDEA requires that children with disabilities to the degree possible be educated with nonhandicapped children and that removal from the regular education environment occur "only when the nature or severity of the handicap is such that education in regular classes with the use of supplementary aids and services cannot be achieved satisfactorily" (U.S.C. 1412(5)(B)). The regulations for the Act elaborate on this condition and refer to a continuum of alternate placements that must include instruction in regular classes with access to resource room services or itinerant instruction if necessary, special classes, special schools, home instruction, and instruction in hospitals and institutions. The regulations also require assurance that the various alternative placements are available to the extent necessary to implement the individualized education program for each handicapped child. The congressional intent clearly was to ensure the design of models for the delivery of services to meet the instructional needs of each child with disabilities rather than to allow assignment of a child with disabilities to whatever special education services happen to be available at the time, unless those services also happen to meet the needs of the particular child as detailed in that child's individual education plan (IEP).

The continuum of alternative placements as listed in the U.S. Department of Education regulations together with the language of IDEA suggest the basic models for the delivery of special education and related services. The number of children placed in different educational settings are reported every year. Reynolds (1962) originally laid out a chart showing various organizational patterns for instruction. His work was later modified by Deno and illustrates a cascade of services for handicapped children (Reynolds & Birch, 1992). The placements can be classified according to the amount of direct intervention provided by someone other than the regular classroom teacher; the more direct services necessary, the more a child moves away from the first level placement, the regular classroom. As the triangular shape of the illustration might suggest more children with special needs should be found in regular classrooms with access to consultant or itinerant support or resource room assistance and fewer in the special classes, special schools, residential schools, or placements outside the school setting. The figure has been adapted to include collaborative/consultative teaching arrangements that allow the special education student to remain in the regular education classroom with direct instruction from the regular and special education teachers.

IDEA and its regulations intend for regular class placement to be the goal for handicapped students. There will always be some students whose educational needs cannot be met in the regular class, however, without some adaptations, special equipment and/or materials, or extra help (Cartwright, Cartwright, & Ward, 1985). Because the regular class teacher may not be adequately trained to make those adaptations, secure the special equipment or materials, or provide the specialized instruction, full-time regular class placement for some children may be enhanced by the provision of consulting teachers who collaborate with regular class teachers and provide up to and including direct instruction.

Educators, parents, advocates, and others who promote appropriate inclusion of students with disabilities in general education classes believe that doing so will provide those students with greater access to the general education curriculum, appropriate education with their nondisabled peers, raise expectations for student performance, and improve coordination between regular and special educators. They also believe that greater inclusion will result in increased school-level accountability for educational results (U.S. Department of Education, 1998).

In 1994–95, 2.2 million of the total 4.9 million students with disabilities ages 6 through 21 spent at least 80% of their school day in general education classes, and more than 95% of all students with disabilities attended regular schools. The environments in which students receive services vary according to the individual needs of the child. Although 87% of students with speech and language impairments were served in regular classes for 80% or more of the school day, only 9.7% of those with mental retardation were served in regular class placements. Students ages 6–11 were more likely to receive services in regular class placements than students ages 12–17 or 18–21 (U.S. Department of Education, 1998).

A resource room program can enable some children who need more intensive instruction in some or all of the basic skills, or whose behavior at times goes beyond what is appropriate or tolerable in the regular class, to remain in the regular class except for limited periods of time each day or week. The resource room model has been particularly popular for learning-disabled students, although students with other handicapping conditions also profit from additional help provided by resource room teachers. Some resource room programs are organized by disability area while others, particularly in more recent years, accommodate children with a variety of handicapping conditions but whose instructional needs are similar.

Placement in a special class for all or part of the school day is considered necessary for some children. Frequently, the deciding factors for inclusive programming, resource room, part-time special class, or full-time special class placement are the amount of time the handicapped child can benefit from time in the regular class and the severity of the needs of that child. Interestingly, there seems to be considerable overlap in the types of students, the amount of time spent in the regular class, and the ways teachers actually use their time in resource room classes, self-contained special classes, and even residential classes, at least for emotionally disabled students (Peterson, Zabel, Smith, & White, 1983). This suggests some inconsistencies in determining appropriate placement for children and in defining responsibilities for special and regular education personnel.

Some children with disabilities are placed in special schools for their daily instructional programs. Such children, by the nature of their placement, have limited access to participation in social, academic, extracurricular, or spontaneous activities with nonhandicapped children. These children are, therefore to be placed in special schools and residential settings only when the severity of their conditions warrants such placement and only for so long as that placement is necessary. The same holds true for those students in settings such as hospitals, treatment centers, and detention facilities that are outside the educational system.

The overriding principle in selecting appropriate placement for a handicapped child who needs special education and related services is that of the least restrictive environment. No one placement or service delivery system described here can be cited as the best for all handicapped children, and that includes the regular classroom, although some proponents of full inclusion would argue this point. Rather, selection must be made on the basis of what setting permits the implementation of the IEP designed for a given child and allows for meaningful involvement with nonhandicapped children, if possible in the same community where the handicapped child would attend school if there were no handicapping condition necessitating a special education program.

In summary, the cascade of service delivery models emphasizes the place where children with special needs might be assigned for instruction. These models have collected criticism because of their focus on placement more than program content. Inherent in the instructional cascade is the goal of equipping the regular classroom to be a learning environment where the diverse needs of many children, including handicapped, gifted, and handicapped gifted learners, can be accommodated (Reynolds & Birch, 1992).

Service delivery models in the context of special education have changed over the years as laws, the inclusion movement, court decisions, local needs, parental pressures, fiscal and human resources, and community concerns have made their influence felt. Ysseldyke and Algozzine (1982) have suggested that change will continue but primarily in response to economic needs. More recently, Crowner (1985) has presented a taxonomy of special education finance and an analysis of funding bases, formulas and types and sources of funds for special education. The balance between congressional intent and legal necessity, local control, fiscal reality, and administrative expediency is delicate at best. For the benefit of all children currently in school and those to come, efforts must continue to be directed at designing and operating service delivery systems that meet the needs of all children, those who have conditions requiring special education and those who do not.

REFERENCES

Cartwright, G.P., Cartwright, C.A., & Ward, M.E. (1985). *Educating special learners* (2nd ed.). Belmont, CA: Wadsworth.

Crowner, T.T. (1985). A taxonomy of special education finance. *Exceptional Children, 51*(6), 503–508.

Peterson, R.L., Zabel, R.H., Smith, C.R., & White, M.A. (1983). Cascade of services model and emotionally disabled students. *Exceptional Children, 49*(5), 404–408.

Reynolds, M.C., & Birch, J.W. (1992). *Teaching exceptional children in all America's schools.* Reston, VA: Council for Exceptional Children.

U.S. Department of Education. (1998). *Nineteenth Annual Report to Congress.* Washington, DC: Author.

Ysseldyke, J., & Algozzine, B. (1982). *Critical issues in special and remedial education.* Boston: Houghton Mifflin.

See also **Cascade Model of Special Education; Individuals with Disabilities Education Act (IDEA); Least Restrictive Environment; Resource Room; Self-Contained Classroom**

SEVERE DISCREPANCY ANALYSIS (SDA)

Severe Discrepancy Analysis (SDA) is a computer program developed by Reynolds and Stowe (1985) to assist in the diagnosis of learning disabilities. The program provides an analysis of the severe discrepancy component of the federal definition of learning disabilities, which is also one of the most prevalent of the five major components of definitions of learning disabilities nationwide. The program also strongly recommends that all remaining aspects of the definition be assessed prior to arriving at a diagnosis of learning disabilities.

The program performs the two fundamental analyses recommended in the Federal Work Group Report on Critical Measurement Issues in Learning Disabilities (Reynolds, 1984): it assesses (1) the statistical significance of the difference between the child's score on an aptitude measure and an achievement measure and (2) the relative frequency of occurrence of the difference between the child's current achievement level and the average achievement level of all other children at the same IQ level. These two analyses and the principles underlying them are explained in detail in Reynolds (1984, 1985).

REFERENCES

Reynolds, C.R. (1984). Critical measurement issues in learning disabilities. *Journal of Special Education, 18,* 451–476.

Reynolds, C.R. (1985). Measuring the aptitude-achievement discrepancy in learning disability diagnosis. *Remedial & Special Education, 6,* 37–55.

Reynolds, C.R., & Stowe, M. (1985). *Severe discrepancy analysis.* Philadelphia: TRAIN.

See also **Grade Equivalents; Learning Disabilities, Problems in Definition of; Learning Disabilities, Severe Discrepancy Analysis in**

SEX DIFFERENCES IN LEARNING ABILITIES

Popular stereotypes and epidemiological research both suggest that boys have more learning and adjustment problems than girls. Boys are more readily referred for psychological services than girls with similar problems (Caplan, 1977). In addition, boys of all ages are more likely than girls to be evaluated or treated for learning problems (Eme, 1979). The reasons for apparent gender differences are widely debated. Some suggest that (1) boys are at some biological or developmental disadvantage that affects learning and adjustment (Ullian, 1981); (2) classrooms, teachers, or professionals are less tolerant of boys than girls (Pleck, 1981); and (3) the problems manifested by girls are perceived differently or considered to be less important. This debate leads one to question whether recognizable gender differences exist in children's learning abilities.

Many persons believe the cognitive abilities of boys and girls differ. The common notion is that boys have better developed quantitative abilities while girls are better in verbal areas. After reviewing literature on psychological gender differences, Maccoby and Jacklin (1974) conclude that three cognitive gender differences are well established: girls have greater verbal ability than boys, while boys have better visual-spatial and mathematical ability than girls. The authors further conclude that gender differences in verbal ability emerge after age 11, gender differences in quantitative (i.e., mathematical) abilities emerge at around 12, and gender differences in spatial ability emerge in adolescence.

Do sex differences exist in school achievement? The evidence is contradictory. Few gender differences in learning were found in a five-year longitudinal study of students ages 5 through 9 (Anastas & Reinherz, 1984). However, a review of the cross-national data on gender differences in achievement found that boys' mathematics achievement is higher than that of girls at both the elementary and secondary levels, that boys score higher in all areas of science, and that girls have higher achievement in verbal areas involving reading comprehension and literature (Fennema, 1982; McGuinness, 1993).

Assuming achievement is affected by opportunities to learn (e.g., participation in courses, amount of instruction), and that boys generally have more opportunities to learn mathematics and science than girls (Finn, Dulberg, & Reis, 1979), we may conclude that girls perform lower in math and science because of fewer opportunities in these areas rather than intrinsic factors. While research infrequently has considered the extent to which differences in socialization and educational experiences may account for differential performance and attainment, many social scientists believe most or even all sex differences in ability and achievement are due to differing cultural and social opportunities and expectations for boys and girls (Levine & Ornstein, 1983). Still, we know little about the origins of sex differences. When gender differences appear, we should be cautious in speculating about their etiologies.

REFERENCES

Anastas, J.W., & Reinherz, H. (1984). Gender differences in learning and adjustment problems in school: Results of a longitudinal study. *American Journal of Orthopsychiatry, 54,* 110–122.

Caplan, P. (1977). Sex, age, behavior and school subject as determinants of report of learning problems. *Journal of Learning Disabilities, 10,* 314–316.

Fennema, E. (1982, March). *Overview of sex-related differences in mathematics.* Paper presented at the annual meeting of the American Educational Research Association. New York.

Finn, J.D., Dulberg, L., & Reis, J. (1979). Sex differences in educational attainment: A cross-national perspective. *Harvard Educational Review, 49,* 477–503.

Levine, D.U., & Ornstein, A.C. (1983). Sex differences in ability and achievement. *Journal of Research & Development in Education, 16,* 66–72.

Maccoby, E.E., & Jacklin, C.N. (1974). *Psychology of sex differences.* Stanford, CA: Stanford University Press.

McGuinness, D. (1993). Gender differences in cognitive style: Implications for mathematics performance and achievement. In L.A. Penner and G.M. Batsche (Eds.), *The Challenge in Mathematics and Science Education:* Psychology's Response (pp. 251–274). Washington, DC: APA.

Pleck, J. (1981). *The myth of masculinity.* Cambridge, MA: MIT Press.

Ullian, D. (1981). Why boys will be boys: A structural perspective. *American Journal of Orthopsychiatry, 51,* 493–501.

See also **Hemispheric Asyymmetry, Sex Differences in**

SEX EDUCATION OF THE HANDICAPPED

Many professionals and parents believe the sexual needs of the handicapped should be met (Craft & Craft, 1981; Fitz-Gerald & Fitz-Gerald, 1979; Love, 1983). The principle of normalization promoted in the United Nations Declaration of Rights of the Mentally Handicapped (United Nations, 1971) underscores this belief. The declaration states that handicapped people have the same basic rights as other citizens of the same country and the same age. In the United States, normalization is espoused in the Rehabilitation Act of 1973 (PL 93-380) and the Individuals with Disabilities Act (IDEA), which provide for the individualized education of the handicapped in accordance with the requirement of the least restrictive environment.

The advocacy of inclusion in school and the movement away from custodial institutional care and toward community living supply the impetus for focusing on the sexual rights of the handicapped (Bass, 1974; Jacobs, 1978). In conjunction with the philosophy of protecting basic human rights, sex education is advocated to achieve the same ends for the handicapped as for the nonhandicapped: to develop sexually fulfilled persons who understand themselves, their values, and resulting behaviors (Harris, 1974). Moreover, many persons agree that sex education is bound to the practical tasks of improving the social and sexual functions of the handicapped. The need to moderate educational goals on the bases of age, gender, type of handicap and severity of handicap is inherent in the nature of sex education of the handicapped.

Great strides have been made in the individualization of sex education (Johnson & Kempton, 1981). A wealth of curriculum guides exists that identifies programs to meet the varied needs of the handicapped. Adapted sex education enables even the severely retarded to improve their sexual knowledge (Edmonson, 1980).

Normalization frequently entails the sexual development of the handicapped to enable them to assume more normal lives. While there has been progress in designing and offering sex education program for the handicapped, several areas of concern have hampered their acceptance. These include (1) constraints imposed on the design and implementation of curricula owing to legal and social restraints that pertain to sexual taboos; (2) neglect by teacher training institutes in the preparation of professionals in special education who are trained in sex education; (3) problems in assessing the effects of teaching because of the nature of affective instructional goals interacting with a diversity of abilities in this population; and (4) conservatism on the part of parents that tends to place limitations on expectations of instruction. These problems hinder but do not preclude change. Models for the successful institutionalization of sex education for the handicapped exist elsewhere, as in Sweden (Grunewald & Linner, 1979). Public policy regarding sex education for the handicapped is desirable given the obvious needs in this area (Craft, 1983). The handicapped should understand their sexuality, should be safe from sexual exploitation, and should become responsible in their sexual behavior (Cole, 1993; Craft, 1983).

REFERENCES

Bass, M.S. (1974). Sex education for the handicapped. *Family Coordinator, 23,* 27–33.

Cole, S.S., & Cole, T.M. (1993). Sexuality, disability, and reproductive issues through the lifespan. *Sexuality & Disability, 11*(3), 189–205.

Craft, A. (1983). Sexuality and mental retardation: A review of the literature. In A. Craft & M. Craft (Eds.), *Sex education and counseling for mentally handicapped people.* Baltimore, MD: University Park Press.

Craft, A., & Craft, M. (1981). Sexuality and mental handicap: A review. *British Journal of Psychiatry, 139,* 494–505.

Edmonson, B. (1980). Sociosexual education for the handicapped. *Exceptional Education Quarterly, 1,* 67–76.

Fitz-Gerald, D., & Fitz-Gerald, M. (1979). Sexual implications deaf-blindness *Sexuality & Disability, 2,* 212 215.

Grunewald, K., & Linner, B. (1979). Mentally-retarded. Sexuality and normalization. *Current Sweden,* 237–239.

Harris, A. (1974). What does "sex education" mean? In R. Rogers (Ed.), *Sex education: Rationale and reaction.* Cambridge, England: Cambridge University Press.

Jacobs, J.H. (1978). The mentally retarded and their need for sexuality education. *Psychiatric Opinion, 15,* 32–34.

Johnson, W.R., & Kempton, W. (1981). *Sex education and counseling of special groups.* Springfield, IL: Thomas.

Love, E. (1983). Parental and staff attitudes toward instruction in human sexuality for sensorially impaired students at the Alabama Institute for Deaf and Blind. *American Annals of the Deaf, 128,* 45–47.

United Nations. (1971). *Declaration of general and special rights of the mentally handicapped.* New York: UN Department of Social Affairs.

See also **Pediatric AIDS; Sexual Disturbances in Handicapped Children; Social Behavior of the Handicapped; Social Development; Social Isolation; Social Skills Training**

SEX INFORMATION AND EDUCATION COUNCIL OF THE UNITED STATES (SIECUS)

The Sex Information and Education Council of the United States (SIECUS) is a nonprofit, voluntary health organization dedicated to the establishment and exchange of information about human sexual behavior. The SIECUS provides information and responds to requests for consultation from churches, communities, school boards, and any other national or international health or educational organizations interested in establishing or improving their sex education programs.

The SIECUS guide provides instructional, curricular, and counseling information that will be useful in helping the mentally retarded individual to achieve this understanding. Finally, information is provided regarding printed materials, films and filmstrips, tapes, and other teaching aids that may be useful in sex education for the mentally retarded individual.

SIECUS also presents a listing of sexuality and disability materials published between 1982 and 1992 (Shortridge, Steele-Clapp, & Lamin, 1993).

REFERENCES

SIECUS. (1971). *A resource guide in sex education for the mentally retarded.* New York: Author.

Shortridge, J., Steele-Clapp, L., & Lamin, J. (1993). Sexuality and disability: A SIECUS annotated bibliography of available print materials. *Sexuality & Disability, 11*(2), 159–179.

SEX RATIOS IN SPECIAL EDUCATION

As concern grows about sexual bias in society and its effect on children, attention is focusing on the classroom. Sex bias in education is of particular concern to the field of special education. Research indicates that more males than females are served in special education programs, and that the gender label has been recognized as having a profound impact on the education of handicapped children.

Rubin and Balow (1971), in a longitudinal study of 967 kindergarten through third grade students, discovered that educationally defined behavior problems were exhibited by 41% of the children participating in their study. When results were reported by gender, the number of boys far exceeded the number of girls; boys were reported to have more attitude and behavior problems, to be receiving more special services, and to be repeating more grades. The authors suggested that teachers accept only a narrow range of behaviors, and that deviations outside this range are viewed as cause for intervention. This is supported by later research (Callahan, 1994).

Further evidence for the disproportionate number of males in special education comes from a study reported in Young, Algozzine, and Schmid (1979). McCarthy and Paraskevopoulos (1969) examined behavior patterns of average, emotionally disturbed, and learning-disabled children, and found that boys outnumbered girls 8:1 in the emotionally disturbed sample and 9:1 in the learning-disabled sample.

A variety of theories have been proposed to account for the sex ratio discrepancy in special education. Caplan (1977) suggested that the boy/girl learning problem report ratio is aggravated by behavioral differences. Caplan and Kinsbourne (1974) discovered that girls who fail in school tend to behave in socially acceptable ways, but their male counterparts tend to react punitively and aggressively. On the basis of this discovery, the authors suggested that because teachers view aggression as the most disturbing type of behavior, they would be more likely to notice boys who are failing in school than their well-behaved, silent female counterparts. Consequently, boys would be more likely to be recognized as needing special attention, if only to get them out of the classroom.

Physiological explanations for the higher incidence of males in special education also have been offered; several categories of exceptionality such as that of learning disabilities have been explained on the basis of sex-linked genetic traits (Rossi, 1972). However, according to Singer and Osborn (1970), there are no known physiological causes to explain the higher number of males treated for mental retardation. Singer and Osborn explain the high ratio of males to females receiving treatment as stemming from sociocultural expectations such as behavior differences and less societal tolerance for boys with academic problems.

REFERENCES

Callahan, K. (1994). Causes and implications of the male dominated sex ratio in programs for students with emotional and behavioral disorders. *Education and Treatment of Children, 17*(3), 228–243.

Caplan, P.J. (1977). Sex, age, behavior and school subject as determinants of report of learning problems. *Journal of Learning Disabilities, 5,* 314–316.

Caplan, P.J., & Kinsbourne, M. (1974). Sex differences in response to school failure. *Journal of Learning Disabilities, 4,* 232–235.

Rossi, A.O. (1972). Genetics of learning disabilities. *Journal of Learning Disabilities, 5,* 489–496.

Rubin, R., & Balow, B. (1971). Learning and behavior disorders: A longitudinal study. *Exceptional Children, 38,* 293–299.

Singer, B.D., & Osborn, R.W. (1970). Special class and sex differences in admission patterns of the mentally retarded. *American Journal of Mental Deficiency, 75,* 162–190.

Young, S., Algozzine, B., & Schmid, R. (1979). The effects of assigned attributes and labels on children's peer accepted ratings. *Education & Training of the Mentally Retarded, 12,* 257–261.

See also **Prereferral Intervention; Sex Differences in Learning Abilities**

SEXUAL DISTURBANCES IN HANDICAPPED CHILDREN

Attitudes have always played a large part in viewing the sexuality of the handicapped. Sexual disturbances or problems of physically handicapped individuals, especially those with essentially normal intelligence whose physical disability resulted from postnatal accident, injury, or trauma, have been something of an exception among the general handicapped population. Professionals, and probably society in general, seem more willing to recognize the sexual rights of this group and to provide the understanding, support, and even the aids or prostheses to help them regain normal sexuality (Thorn-Gray & Kern, 1983). This view is markedly different than that found when dealing with mentally retarded persons.

Where education has been unsuccessful in preventing sexual disturbances or counseling has been ineffective in eliminating inappropriate sexual behaviors, a variety of behavioral approaches have been found to be successful in individual cases. Hurley and Sovner (1983) describe case reports on the effective use of response cost procedures, aversive conditioning, overcorrection, in vivo desensitization, and positive reinforcement in dealing with problems such as exhibitionism, public masturbation, public disrobing, and fetishism. Assaultive and inappropriate interpersonal sexual behaviors were successfully eliminated in an adolescent male with Down's syndrome through a combination of differential reinforcement of other behaviors and naturalistic social restitution. The control of this behavior was able to be generalized to the student's teachers (Polvinale & Lutzker, 1980).

Sexual problems noted in learning-disabled populations have often been attributed to conceptual difficulties, disinhibition, or inadequate impulse control. Insights into sex-related difficulties in blind and visually impaired persons can be found in Mangold and Mangold (1983) and in Welbourne et al. (1983). Information on sex deafness can be found in *Sexuality and Deafness* (Gallaudet College, 1979).

REFERENCES

Gallaudet College. (1979). *Sexuality and deafness.* Washington, DC: Outreach Services.

Hurley, A.D., & Sovner, R. (1983). Treatment of sexual deviation in mentally retarded persons. *Psychiatric Aspects of Mental Retardation Newsletter, 2*(4), 13–16.

Mangold, S.S., & Mangold, P.N. (1983). The adolescent visually impaired female. *Journal of Blindness & Visual Impairment, 77*(6), 250–255.

Polvinale, R.A., & Lutzker, J.R. (1980). Elimination of and inappropriate sexual behavior by reinforcement and social restitution. *Mental Retardation, 18*(1), 27–30.

Thorn-Gray, B.E., & Kern, L.H. (1983). Sexual dysfunction associated with physical disability: A treatment guide for the rehabilitation practitioner. *Rehabilitation Literature, 44*(5–6), 138–144.

Wellbourne, A., Lifschitz, S., Selvin, H., & Green, R. (1983). A comparison of the sexual learning experiences of visually impaired and sighted women. *Journal of Blindness & Visual Impairment, 77*(6), 256–261.

See also **Masturbation, Compulsive; Mental Retardation; Self-Stimulation**

SHELTERED WORKSHOPS

Special education programs help prepare young adults with disabilities to work in sheltered workshops. According to Bigge (1982), the special education curriculum should include transition skills, work evaluation, work adjustment, work experience, vocational skills, and on-the-job training programs.

The sheltered workshop is the most widely used type of vocational training facility for adults with handicaps. Sheltered workshops can be classified into three general types: regular program workshops; work activities centers; and adult day programs. Regular program workshops (or transitional workshops) provide therapies and work intended to foster readiness for competitive employment. The Department of Labor requires that workers earn no less than 50% of minimum wages. Work activities centers (WACs) provide training, support, and extended employment in a sheltered environment to more severely handicapped adults. A wage ceiling of 50% of minimum wage has been set for WACs clients. The Fair Labor Standards Act, as amended in 1966, defines regular program workshops and work activities centers. Both are monitored by the Department of Labor. Adult day programs, managed by state developmental disabilities agencies, provide nonvocational services such as socialization, communication skills, and basic work orientation. The primary goal of adult day programs is the acquisition of basic living skills, leading to a decrease in maladaptive behavior and movement toward more vocationally oriented programs.

A sheltered workshop operates as a business. It generally engages in one of three types of business activities: contracting, prime manufacturing, or reclamation. In contracting, there is an agreement that a sheltered workshop will complete a specified job within a specified time for a given price. Workshops bid competitively for each job. Prime manufacturing is the designing, producing, marketing, and shipping of a complete product. A reclamation operation is one in which a workshop purchases or collects salvageable material, performs a reclamation operation, and then sells the reclaimed product. Recently, sheltered workshops have been closing and competitive employment (supported employment, for example) has been substituted. The closure of some workshops has created a division of scholars as to what is the best interests of persons with disabilities' employment (Block, 1997).

REFERENCES

Bigge, J.L. (1982). *Teaching individuals with physical and multiple disabilities* (2nd ed.). Columbus, OH: Merrill.

Block, S.R. (1997). Closing the sheltered workshop. Toward competitive employment opportunities for persons with developmental disabilities. *Journal of Vocational Rehabilitation, 9*(3), 267–275.

See also **Vocational Rehabilitation; Vocational Training of the Handicapped**

SIBLINGS OF THE HANDICAPPED

Siblings of the handicapped have received little research attention compared with the literature available on the effects of a handicapped child on parents (Crnic, Friedrich, & Greenberg, 1983; Drew, Logan, & Hardman, 1984; Trevino, 1979). The available research, however, suggests that nonhandicapped siblings are a population at risk for behavioral problems, the degree to which is influenced by a number of variables and factors (Crnic et al., 1983; Gargiulo, 1984; Trevino, 1979). Specific factors that appear to interact and contribute to sibling adjustment include the number of normal siblings in the family (Powell & Ogle, 1985), the age and gender of siblings (Crnic et al., 1983; Grossman, 1972), and parental response and attitude toward the handicapped child (Trevino, 1979). Trevino (1979) reports that prospects for normal siblings having difficulty in adjusting increase

when (1) there are only two siblings in the family, one who is handicapped and one who is not; (2) the nonhandicapped sibling is close in age to or younger than the handicapped sibling or is the oldest female child; (3) the nonhandicapped child and the handicapped child are the same sex; and (4) the parents are unable to accept the handicap.

The psychological and behavioral problems that may result from having a handicapped sibling is a reality that must be dealt with by parents and professionals. Siblings can benefit from the experience of having a handicapped sibling if they are introduced to the situation in an understanding and compassionate way. Siblings and parents should seek support from family counselors, religious organizations, nonprofit agencies, and sibling support groups that focus on the individual needs, attitudes, concerns, and feelings of the nonhandicapped sibling. Teachers should be alerted to the child's family situation to provide additional support and information.

REFERENCES

Crnic, K.A., Friedrich, W.N., & Greenberg, M.T. (1983). Adaptation of families with mentally retarded children: A model of stress, coping and family ecology. *American Journal of Mental Deficiency, 88*, 125–139.

Drew, C.J., Logan, D.R., & Hardman, M.L. (Eds.). (1984). *Mental retardation: A life cycle approach* (3rd ed.). St. Louis: Times/Mirror Mosby.

Gargiulo, R.M. (1984). Understanding family dynamics. In R.M. Gargiulo (Ed.), *Working with parents of exceptional children* (pp. 41–64). Boston: Houghton Mifflin.

Grossman, F.K. (1972). *Brothers and sisters of retarded children: An exploratory study.* Syracuse, NY: Syracuse University Press.

Powell, T.H., & Ogle, P.A. (1985). *Brothers and sisters in the family system.* Baltimore, MD: Brookes.

Trevino, F. (1979). Siblings of handicapped children: Identifying those at risk. *Social Casework: Journal of Contemporary Social Work, 62,* 488–493.

See also **Family Response to a Child with Disabilities; Respite Care**

SICARD, ABBÉ ROCHE AMBROISE CUCURRON (1742–1822)

Abbé Roche Ambroise Cucurron Sicard, educator of the deaf, studied with Abbé Epée at the National Institution for Deaf-Mutes in Paris and, in 1782, opened a school for the deaf at Bordeaux. Sicard succeeded Epée at the National Institution and, except for a few years during the French Revolution, served as its director until his death in 1822. Sicard made many improvements in Epée's educational methods. His most important publication was a dictionary of signs, a work begun by Epée.

The beginning of education for the deaf in the United States was greatly influenced by Sicard. He invited Thomas Gallaudet, who was planning the first school for the deaf in the United States, to observe the methods employed at the National Institute in Paris, with the result that Gallaudet became proficient in Sicard's methods. In addition, Sicard provided Gallaudet with his first teacher, Laurent Clerc.

REEFERENCES

Bender, R.E. (1970). *The conquest of deafness.* Cleveland, OH: Case Western Reserve University Press.

Lane, H. (1984). *When the mind hears.* New York: Random House.

SICKLE-CELL DISEASE

Sickle-cell disease is an inherited blood disorder that occurs as two conditions, sickle-cell anemia (SCA) and sickle-cell trait (SCT). Sickle-cell anemia is the more serious of the two conditions; it can be defined as an abnormality of the hemoglobin molecule, the oxygen-carrying protein in the red blood cells. Oxygen-carrying red blood cells are usually round and flexible. Under certain conditions, the red blood cells of a person with sickle-cell anemia may change into a crescent or sickle cell. This unusual shape causes the cells to adhere in the spleen and other areas, leading to their destruction. This results in a shortage of red blood cells, which has serious consequences for the individual with SCA (Haslam & Valletutti, 1975; March of Dimes, 1985). These consequences include fever, abdominal discomfort, bone pain, damage to the brain, lungs, and kidneys, and, for some, death in childhood or early adulthood (Haslam & Valletutti, 1975; March of Dimes, 1985; National Association for Sickle Cell Disease [NASCD], (1978). Individuals with SCA will experience episodes of pain known as sickle-cell crisis. During these periods, the sickled cells become trapped in tiny blood vessels. This blocks other red blood cells behind them, which lose oxygen and become sickle-shaped, totally blocking the vessels. When the bone marrow inadequately produces red blood cells, the child experiences an aplastic crisis and requires blood transfusion (Weiner, 1973). These crises and their effects vary greatly from person to person. Most people with SCA enjoy reasonably good health much of the time (Conner-Warren, 1996; March of Dimes, 1985; NASCD, 1978).

Sickle-cell anemia occurs when a sickle-cell gene is inherited from each parent. A person with sickle-cell anemia has sickle cells in the bloodstream and has sickle-cell disease. The second condition, sickle-cell trait (SCT), occurs when a sickle-cell gene is inherited from one parent and a normal gene from the other. A person with sickle-cell trait does not have sickle cells in the bloodstream and does not have sickle-cell disease. Persons with SCT may pass the sickle-cell gene on to their offspring (March of Dimes, 1985; NASCD, 1978; Whitten, 1974). As an autosomal recessive disorder, children of parents who both carry the sickle-cell gene have a 50% chance of inheriting SCT, a 25% chance of being a carrier, and a 25% chance of having SCA (Whitten, 1974).

In the United States, sickle-cell disease occurs most frequently among blacks and Hispanics of Caribbean ancestry. About 1 in every 400 to 600 blacks and 1 in every 1000 to 1500 Hispanics inherit sickle-cell disease (March of Dimes, 1985). Approximately 1 in 12 black Americans carry

a gene for sickle-cell trait (NASCD, 1978). Less commonly affected peoples include those whose ancestors lived in countries bordering on the Mediterranean Sea (Greeks, Maltese, Portuguese, Arabians; NASCD, 1978).

There is no known cure for sickle-cell anemia. However, a number of new therapies for reducing the severity and frequency of crises are being tried (March of Dimes, 1985; Weiner, 1973). A blood test for sickle-cell anemia and its trait is readily available; it is called hemoglobin electrophoresis. There is also a prenatal test to determine whether the fetus will develop sickle anemia or be a carrier.

REFERENCES

Conner-Warren, R.L. (1996). Pain intensity and home pain management of children with sickle-cell disease. *Issues in Comprehensive Pediatric Nursing, 19*(3), 183–195.

Haslam, R.M.A. and Valletutti, P.J. (1975). *Medical problems in the classroom.* Baltimore, MD: University Park Press.

March of Dimes. (1985). *Genetics series: Sickle cell anemia.* White Plains, NY: Author.

National Association for Sickle Cell Disease. (1978). *Sickle cell disease: Tell the facts, quell the fables.* Los Angeles: Author.

Weiner, F. (1973). *Help for the handicapped child.* New York: McGraw-Hill.

Whitten, C.F. (1974). *Fact sheet on sickle cell trait and anemia.* Los Angeles: National Association for Sickle-Cell Disease.

See also **Genetic Disorders**

SIDIS, WILLIAM JAMES (1898–1944)

William James Sidis was a famous child prodigy of the early twentieth century who came to a tragic end after leading a short, largely unfulfilled life. Sidis's history and early demise are often cited in early literature opposing acceleration and other aspects of special education for the intellectually gifted. Much of Sidis's life has been distorted in various informal accounts. Montour (1977) has characterized the use of Sidis's story deny acceleration to intellectually advanced children as the Sidis fallacy. Simply stated, the Sidis fallacy denotes "early ripe, early rot."

In 1909, at the age of 11, Sidis entered Harvard College. A year later he lectured on higher mathematics at the Harvard Mathematical Club. Sidis had performed remarkably in intellectual endeavors throughout his life. By Montour's (1977) account, by the age of 3 he read fluently with good comprehension; he was writing with a pencil 6 months later. By age 4, Sidis was a fluent typist. When he was 6, Sidis could read English, Russian, French, German, and Hebrew; he learned Latin and Greek shortly thereafter. At the age of 8, Sidis passed the entrance exam at the Massachusetts Institute of Technology, developed a new table of logarithms employing base 12 instead of base 10, and passed the Harvard Medical School exam in anatomy. He was well qualified to enter Harvard at that time but was denied entrance based on his age. Sidis earned his BA in 1914, although it has been reported that he completed his work for the degree 2 years earlier. Sidis pursued some graduate study in several fields, including a year in law school, but never earned an advanced degree. He spurned academia after an unsuccessful year as a professor at Rice University at age 20. He became sullen, cynical, and withdrawn from society (Montour, 1977). Sidis chose to live as a loner, working at low-level clerical jobs until his death in 1944, at the age of 46, from a stroke.

"It was not extreme educational acceleration that destroyed William James Sidis emotionally and mentally, but instead an interaction of paternal exploitation and emotional starvation" (Montour, 1977, p. 276). The events of Sidis's life are often exaggerated and misstated. The Sidis fallacy has restricted the education of the gifted and persists in some educational programs even today; it is yet another myth that afflicts programs for the gifted.

REFERENCE

Montour, K. (1977). William James Sidis, the broken twig. *American Psychologist, 32,* 265–279.

See also **Accelerated Placement of Gifted Children; Study of Mathematically Precocious Youth**

SIDIS FALLACY

See SIDIS, WILLIAM JAMES.

SIECUS

See SEX INFORMATION AND EDUCATION COUNCIL OF THE UNITED STATES.

SIGHT-SAVING CLASSES

For much of the present century it was common to educate children with low vision in "sight-saving classes". This was done in public schools as well as in residential facilities. Such classes for partially sighted children were begun in public schools as far back as 1913 (Livingston, 1986).

The notion behind these sight-saving classes was that a low-vision child's residual vision would be damaged by overuse. The emphasis, thus, was on conserving the child's vision as far as possible. This meant that children whose vision was impaired but still usable were removed from presumably visually stressful situations by reducing visual demands made on them. Some were even educated in dark rooms or blindfolded. The situation today is dramatically altered. It is now believed that all children, including visually handicapped ones, benefit from using their visual abilities as much as possible.

REFERENCE

Livingston, R. (1986). Visual impairments. In N.G. Haring & L. McCormick (Eds.), *Exceptional children and youth* (4th ed., pp. 398–429). Columbus, OH: Merrill.

See also **Low Vision; Partially Sighted**

SIGN LANGUAGE

Sign language is a general term that refers to any gestural/visual language that makes use of specific shapes and movements of the fingers, hands, and arms, as well as movements of the eyes, face, head, and body. There is no international system that is comprehensible to all deaf people. There exists a British Sign Language, a Spanish Sign Language, an Israeli Sign Language, and probably a sign language in every country where deaf people have needed to communicate among themselves rapidly, efficiently, and visually without the use of pad and pencil.

American Sign Language, sometimes called Ameslan or ASL, was created over the years by the deaf community in the United States. In American Sign Language, one hand shape frequently denotes a concept. American Sign Language must be differentiated from finger spelling or dactylology, which is the use of hand configurations to denote the letters of the alphabet. In finger spelling, one hand shape stands for one letter. Sometimes finger spelling is used to spell out the English equivalent for a sign (especially proper nouns) when ASL is used. In ASL, interpreters frequently finger spell the word for a technical or uncommon sign the first time it is used during a conference. Finger spelling with speech and speech reading for additional acoustic and visual cues is called the Rochester method (Quigley & Paul, 1984).

Research into the linguistic nature of American Sign Language has shown that the grammar of ASL, like the grammar of all languages, consists of a finite set of rules with which an infinite number of sentences can be created or generated. Deaf children and hearing children of deaf parents who use ASL acquire these rules in much the same way that hearing children abstract linguistic rules from the spoken language to which they are exposed (Bellugi & Klima, 1985). Courses in sign language are offered in many colleges, schools for deaf students, centers for continuing education, and some public libraries. Courses in sign language for hearing learners may also enhance language acquisition because of the multimodal advantage (Daniels, 1994).

REFERENCES

Bellugi, U., & Klima, E. (1985). The acquisition of three morphological systems in American Sign Language. In F. Powell (Ed.), *Education of the hearing-impaired child.* San Diego, CA: College Hill.

Daniels, M. (1994). The effect of sign language on hearing children's language development. *Communication Education, 43*(4), 291–298.

Quigley, S., & Paul, P. (1984). *Language and deafness.* San Diego, CA: College Hill.

See also **Lipreading/Speechreading; Rochester Method; Total Communication**

SIMULTANEOUS PROCESSING

See SEQUENTIAL AND SIMULTANEOUS COGNITIVE PROCESSING.

SINGLE-SUBJECT RESEARCH DESIGN

Increasingly, researchers are recognizing the importance of single-case investigations for the development of a knowledge base in psychology and education. Single-case time series designs involve observations before, during, and after interventions in order to describe changes in selected dependent variables. The development of time-series methodology, especially single-subject design, has been advantageous for researchers for several reasons. First, single-case research designs provide an important knowledge base that is unobtainable through traditional large-N between-group designs in clinical research. Single-subject designs are uniquely suited to evaluation of treatments involving a single client, a characteristic that is important given that it often is impossible to conduct group comparative outcome studies because of the limited number of subjects for a particular type of disorder or problem.

Another major advantage of single-case designs is that they provide an alternative to traditional large-N group designs about which various ethical and legal considerations are often raised (Hersen & Barlow, 1976). These concerns include the ethical objections of withholding treatment from clients in a no-treatment control group or randomly assigning clients to a particular treatment type.

Single-subject designs have been important in promoting the development of a measurement technology that can be used repeatedly throughout the intervention process. For example, various outcome measures such as direct observation, rating scales and checklists, self-monitoring, standardized tests, and psychophysiological recordings, can be used as ongoing measures of client functioning over the course of a research program. Such repeated measures taken over time allow for an analysis of individual variability as well as monitoring of potential response covariation within a single client. Perhaps the most important aspect of repeated measurement technology is its flexibility in the modification of treatment if the data indicate that this modification is necessary.

Single-case research strategies have also provided options for practitioners to be involved in research and evaluation of practice. There are differences of opinion, however, as to how feasible it is to implement well-controlled designs while providing clinical services. Carefully constructed single-case designs are usually difficult to implement (Kratochwill & Piersel, 1983). The use of a particular design may compromise the on-line clinical intuition of the therapist, yielding either a threat to internal validity of the evaluation or less appropriate treatment of the client. Finally, while clinicians may be concerned with the potential threats to being most responsive to patient needs, others may take the position that formal evaluation increases efficacy of the intervention itself (Barlow, Hayes, & Nelson, 1984). By implementing careful observation and measurement of behavior change, the therapist can measure type and degree of improvement and also know whether the treatment is responsible for change. The issues are readily subject to debate.

REFERENCES

Barlow, D.H., Hayes, S.C., & Nelson, R.O. (1984). *The scientist practitioner: Research and accountability in clinical and educational settings.* New York: Pergamon.

Hersen, N., & Barlow, D.H. (1976). Single case experimental designs: Strategies for studying behavior change. New York: Pergamon.

Kratochwill, T.R., & Piersel, W.C. (1983). Time-series research: Contributions to empirical clinical practice. *Behavioral Assessment, 5,* 165–176.

See also **Applied Behavior Analysis; Research in Special Education**

SINGLETON-MERTON SYNDROME

Singleton-Merton syndrome is a rare disorder of unknown etiology. The primary features of this syndrome include aortic calcification, dental abnormalities, and osteoporosis. Children with Singleton-Merton syndrome have abnormal accumulations of calcium deposits in their aorta, the major artery in the human body, and valves of their heart. Progressive calcification of the aorta and heart valves is life-threatening, as heart block or heart failure may result. In contrast, progressive loss of protein of the bones, resulting in osteoporosis, occurs in individuals with this disorder. Dental abnormalities in the form of poorly developed teeth and/or premature loss of primary teeth are seen in children with this syndrome as well (National Organization for Rare Disorders [NORD], 1997).

Other features of the disorder include generalized muscular weakness and hip and foot abnormalities. Motor delays are not uncommon. These children tend to be relatively short in stature due to growth retardation. Skin lesions, especially on their fingers, are also common among these children (Gay & Kuhn, 1976; NORD, 1997).

Physical therapy and occupational therapy may help motor development and increase muscle strength. Children may receive these support services through the school based on an Other Health Impaired diagnosis.

REFERENCES

Gay, B.B., Jr., & Kuhn, J.P. (1976). A syndrome of widened medullary cavities of bone, aortic calcification, abnormal dentition, and muscular weakness (the Singleton-Merton syndrome). *Radiology, 118*(2), 389–395.

National Organization for Rare Disorders (NORD). (1997). *Singleton-Merton syndrome.* New Fairfield, CT: National Organization for Rare Disorders, Inc.

SIX-HOUR RETARDED CHILD

The term 6-hour retardate first appeared in the report of the Conference on Problems of Education of Children in the Inner City (President's Committee on Mental Retardation, 1969). The conference was charged with developing a new set of recommendations regarding the problems of mentally retarded children living within the ghettos of U.S. cities. After reviewing the papers of the 92 participants, 7 major recommendations were developed: (1) provide early childhood stimulation education as part of the public education program; (2) conduct a study of histories of successful inner-city families who have learned to cope effectively; (3) restructure education of teachers, administrators, and counselors; (4) reexamine present systems of intelligence testing and classification; (5) commit substantial additional funding for research and development in educational improvement for the disadvantaged; (6) delineate what constitutes accountability and hold the school accountable for providing quality education for all children; and (7) involve parents, citizens, citizen groups, students, and general and special educators in a total educational effort. However, one outcome overshadowed all of these recommendations. It was the conclusion that "we now have what may be called a 6-hour retarded child—retarded from 9 to 3, 5 days a week, solely on the basis of an IQ, without regard to his adaptive behavior, which may be exceptionally adaptive to the situation and community in which he lives."

The concept of the 6-hour retarded child survived into the mid 1980s. Today many psychologists and educators have accepted as a given that children identified as mildly retarded during the school-age years manifest retarded functioning only in the school setting, and that outside of school, during childhood and in their work lives as adults, they function successfully. Often their retardation is invisible to their employers, families, neighbors, and friends.

REFERENCE

President's Committee on Mental Retardation. (1969). *The six hour retarded child.* Washington, DC: Bureau of Education for the Handicapped, Office of Education, U.S. Department of Health, Education, and Welfare.

See also **Educable Mentally Retarded; Mental Retardation**

SKEELS, HAROLD M. (1901–1970)

Harold M. Skeels, pioneer researcher in the field of mental retardation, was responsible for a large number of studies of institutional populations during the 1930s and early 1940s. These studies showed that children placed in unstimulating institutional environments failed to develop normally, and that the longer they remained, the greater their deficits became. Skeels reached the conclusion that it is possible to improve intellectual functioning through early stimulation, and he advocated early adoption as an alternative to institutionalization. His findings set off a nature-nurture controversy, and Skeels and his associates were the targets of vehement attacks.

Following service in the armed forces during World War II, and subsequent employment with the U.S. Public Health Service and the National Institute of Mental Health, Skeels made a follow-up study of some of the subjects of his earlier research. The results showed dramatically the long-term ef-

fects of differences in childhood environments. By the time his report was published, many of Skeels's concepts from the 1930s had become commonplace: adoption at an early age had become routine, institutional placements were decreasing, and a variety of early childhood services had been developed, including some programs, like Head Start, aimed specifically at early stimulation of disadvantaged and handicapped children.

REFERENCES

Crissey, M.S. (1970). Harold Manville Skeels. *American Journal of Mental Deficiency, 75,* 1–3.

Skeels, H.M. (1966). Adult status of children with contrasting early life experiences. *Monograph of the Society for Research in Child Development, 33,* 1–65.

Skeels, H.M., & Dye, H.B. (1939). A study of the effects of differential stimulation. *Proceedings of the American Association on Mental Deficiency, 44,* 114–136.

See also **Head Start; Nature versus Nurture**

SKILL TRAINING

The skill training model rests on the premise that assessment of a student's performance should focus on classroom tasks. Such assessment is usually tied to some hierarchy of skills. Instruction, then, follows directly from the results of the hierarchical assessment, and often uses direct instruction skills (Mercer, 1983).

Skill training is a commonly used approach in special education. It provides the teacher with an opportunity to evaluate specific skills, skills that are of immediate and direct concern to classroom instruction. The skill training process usually begins with the administration of a criterion-referenced or teacher-made assessment device. The analysis of the results of the assessment provides the teacher with additional information that is specifically related to classroom interventions. That is, the analysis, focusing on a hierarchy of skills, helps to pinpoint the specific error the student is making, allowing a more precise instructional decision to be made. This instructional decision will usually result in the teacher using some direct instructional technique, concentrating the teaching efforts on a specific academic skill (Gable & Warren, 1993). Pupil progress is continuously measured to ensure that instruction continues to focus on appropriate skills. On mastery of one skill, the teacher and student progress to the next hierarchical skill.

REFERENCES

Gable, R.A., & Warren, S.F. (Eds.). (1993). *Strategies for teaching students with mild to severe mental retardation.* Baltimore, MD: Brookes.

Mercer, C.D. (1983). *Students with learning disabilities* (2nd ed.). Columbus, OH: Merrill.

See also **Mastery Learning**

SKINNER, BURRHUS FREDERICK (1904–1990)

B.F. Skinner was born in northeastern Pennsylvania in 1904. He continued to write and work until his death on August 18, 1990. Skinner studied English and classics at Hamilton College where he received his AB (1926) in literature. After his aspirations of becoming a writer were discouraged, he entered the graduate program in psychology at Harvard, earning his MA in 1930 and his PhD under E. G. Boring in 1931. Regarded as a classic, his dissertation reflected his theory that a reflex arc, a then widely-debated concept, was nothing more than the relationship between a stimulus and a response. He argued that all behavior, in fact, could be explained by looking at the stimuli that result in its occurrence. These themes were the root of his theoretical orientation throughout his distinguished and remarkable career.

Skinner is considered by many to be the most important figure in 20th century psychology. In the field of education, he is perhaps best known for the development of programmed instruction and teaching machines as well as his behavior modification techniques. These areas allow the special educator to analyze and develop a systematic and situation-specific plan of instruction for learning or behavior. He denounced theoretical explanations of psychology, viewing the discipline as scientific and empirically driven, concerned with the observation of behaviors and the stimuli that bring them about. This Radical Behaviorism, as it has been termed, involves strict adherence to behavioral principles.

Skinner's concept of behaviorism, known as operant conditioning, as well as the results of numerous experiments, were outlined in his first major publication, *The Behavior of Organisms* (1938). The term *operant* refers to the identification of behavior which is traceable to reinforcing contingencies rather then to eliciting stimuli. Skinner believed speculation about what intervenes between stimulus and response or between response and reward to be superfluous.

The idea of creating a utopian community using his principles of conditioning, controlling all aspects of life using positive reinforcement, continued to interest him throughout his life. The notion of this ideal community was delineated in his 1948 novel, *Walden Two*. Another of his major books, *Science and Human Behavior* (1953), dealt with the application of behavioral principles to real-life situations including social issues, law, education, and psychotherapy. In this work, he postulated that the human organism is a machine like any other, thus behaving in lawful, predictable ways in response to external stimuli.

Skinner advanced behaviorism by distinguishing between two types of behavior, respondent and operant, and showing how varying contingencies of reinforcement can be employed to modify or control any type of behavior. Controversy was raised once again by his publication of *Beyond Freedom and Dignity,* a 1971 book in which he dealt with the application of these principles. In this book, he interprets concepts of freedom, value, and dignity in objective terms, suggesting a society designed by shaping and controlling the behavior of citizens with a planned system of rewards (reinforcements). Among his numerous publications, *The Technology of Teaching* (1968) and his autobiographical trilogy (the last part, *A Matter of Consequences,* published in 1984) are of particular interest.

In later years, Skinner extended his studies to psychotic behavior, instructional devices, and the analysis of cultures. Despite the criticisms and his unwavering position on a broad range of issues, his significant influence and impact on contemporary psychology assures him a place in its history.

REFERENCES

Skinner, B.F. (1938). *The behavior of organisms: An experimental analysis.* New York: Appleton-Century.

Skinner, B.F. (1948). *Walden two.* New York: Macmillan.

Skinner, B.F. (1953). *Science and human behavior.* New York: Macmillan.

Skinner, B.F. (1968). *The technology of teaching.* New York: Appleton-Century-Crofts.

Skinner, B.F. (1971). *Beyond freedom and dignity.* New York: Bantam.

Skinner, B.F. (1984). *A matter of consequences.* Washington Square, NY: New York University.

See also **Behavior Modification; Operant Conditioning**

SKINNER'S FUNCTIONAL LEARNING MODEL

B.F. Skinner's functional learning model, known as operant conditioning, describes the relationship between behavior and the environmental events that influence it. The basic principles of operant conditioning include reinforcement, punishment, extinction, and stimulus control. These principles describe the functionality of events that precede or follow behavior. Reinforcement, for example, serves the function of increasing the strength of behavior. Skinner (1953) described two types of reinforcement. Positive reinforcement refers to the presentation of an event, commonly called a reward, following behavior. For example, a teacher smiles and says, "Good work" following completion of a child's assignment. Negative reinforcement refers to the removal of an event presumed to be unpleasant following behavior. For example, a child's aggressive behavior may cause a teacher to remove an unpleasant request. In both cases, the effect of reinforcement is the same—the child is more likely to engage in that behavior (assignment completion or aggressive behavior) under similar conditions in the future.

The application of operant conditioning to special education involves the arrangement of contingencies of reinforcement to ensure effective learning. Skinner (1968) noted that although students obviously learn outside the classroom without such systematic procedures, "teachers arrange special contingencies which expedite learning, hastening the appearance of behavior which would otherwise be acquired slowly or making sure of the appearance of behavior which might otherwise never occur" (p. 65). Operant techniques have been applied in classrooms more than in any other setting and have been extremely successful in improving a variety of academic and social behaviors in diverse student populations (Kazdin, 1978).

REFERENCES

Kazdin, A.E. (1978). *History of behavior modification: Experimental foundations of contemporary research.* Baltimore, MD: University Park Press.

Skinner, B.F. (1953). *Science and human behavior.* New York: Free Press.

Skinner, B.F. (1968). *The technology of teaching.* Englewood Cliffs, NJ: Prentice-Hall.

See also **Behavior Modification; Conditioning; Operant Conditioning; Skinner, B.F.**

SLINGERLAND SCREENING TESTS

The Slingerland screening tests are comprised of four forms with designated grade levels (Form A, grades 1 and 2; Form B, grades 2 and 3; Form C, grades 3 and 4; Form D, grades 5 and 6) (Slingerland & Ansara, 1974; Slingerland, 1974). There are eight subtests for Forms A, B, and C that may be either group or individually administered. These subtests require the students to copy letters and words from a board, copy from a page, perform visual matching exercises by selecting a stimulus word from an array of distractor words with various letter reversals, copy words presented in flashcard fashion, write dictated words, and detect initial and final sounds. For children that exhibit difficulties with portions of the eight subtests, there are individually administered auditory tests designed to assess auditory perception and memory. The student is asked to repeat individual words and phrases, to complete sentences with a missing word, and to retell a story. As noted by Fujiki (1985) and Sean and Keough (1993), the purpose of the Slingerland is not to identify linguistically handicapped children, but to assess auditory, visual, and motor skills associated with learning to read and write.

Local norms are advocated to interpret the results of students' test performance. This recommendation is necessary because of the notable omission of adequate normative data. Also absent in the manuals is an adequate discussion of reliability, stability, or validity.

REFERENCES

Fujiki, M. (1985). Review of Slingerland Screening Tests for identifying children with specific language disabilities. In J.V. Mitchell (Ed.), *The ninth mental measurements yearbook* (Vol. 2, pp. 1398–1399). Lincoln, NE: University of Nebraska Press.

Sean, S., & Keough, B. (1993). Predicting reading performance using the Slingerland procedures. *Annals of Dyslexia, 43,* 78–79.

Slingerland, B.H. (1974). *Teacher's manual to accompany Slingerland Screening Tests for Identifying Children with Specific Language Disability-Revised Edition* (Form D). Cambridge, MA: Educators.

Slingerland, B.H., & Ansara, A.S. (1974). *Teacher's manual to accompany Slingerland Screening Tests for Identifying Children with Specific Language Disability-Revised Edition* (Forms A, B and C). Cambridge, MA: Educators.

See also **Assessment; Basic Achievement Skills; Language Disorders**

SLOSSON INTELLIGENCE TEST (SIT)

First published in 1961 by Slosson Educational Publications, the Slosson Intelligence Test (SIT) is a highly verbal, brief screening measure of intelligence intended to approximate the lengthier Stanford-Binet Intelligence Scale. A second edition was published in 1981. The SIT is a popular screening measure used by many special educators. Unfortunately, its use for any purpose is largely unsupportable on psychometric grounds and its status as a brief screening test precludes use in placement decisions.

See also **Deviation IQ; Kaufman Assessment Battery for Children; Stanford-Binet Intelligence Test; Wechsler Intelligence Scale for Children—Revised**

SLOW LEARNER

Historically, the slow learning child has been described in numerous ways. Ingram's (1960) book, the *Education of the Slow-Learning Child,* discussed the education of the educable mentally retarded child. Johnson (1963) noted that "slow learners compose the largest group of mentally retarded persons" (p. 9). Today, however, the term slow learner most accurately describes children and adolescents who learn or underachieve, in one or more academic areas, at a rate that is below average yet not at the level considered comparable to that of an educable mentally retarded student. Intellectually, slow learners score most often between a 75 and a 90 IQ—between the borderline and low-average classifications of intelligence.

It is unusual to find the slow learner discussed in the standard special education textbook. Indeed, slow learners are not special education students. There is no individuals with disabilities education act (IDEA) label or definition of slow learner, and these students are not eligible for any monies or services associated with that law. When slow learners receive additional supportive services, it is typically in the regular classroom or in remedial classes that may be supported by federal title funds or programs. These remedial classes are not conceptualized as alternative educational programs; they are used to reinforce regular classroom curricula and learning. Some slow learners are inappropriately labeled learning disabled to maintain the enrollment (and funding) of some special education classrooms, or because they would otherwise fail in the regular classroom, despite not having special education needs.

There is no consensus on a diagnostic or descriptive profile that characterizes the slow learner. Indeed, there is very little contemporary research with samples specifically labeled as slow learners. Many slow learners are now described by their specific academic weaknesses; research and/or remedial programs are applied to these academic areas—not to the slow learner labels. Because of this shift in emphasis, earlier research describing slow learners as being from low socioeconomic and minority family backgrounds, academically and socially frustrated, and devalued by teachers and peers, and as having low self-concepts, do not apply (Cawley, Goodstein, & Burrow, 1972).

REFERENCES

Cawley, J.F., Goodstein, H.A., & Burrow, W.H. (1972). *The slow learner and the reading problem.* Springfield, IL: Thomas.

Ingram, C.P. (1960). *Education of the slow-learning child* (3rd ed.). New York: Ronald.

Johnson, G.O. (1963). *Education for slow learners.* Englewood Cliffs, NJ: Prentice-Hall.

See also **Classification, Systems of; Educable Mentally Retarded**

SMITH-LEMLI-OPITZ SYNDROME

Smith-Lemli-Opitz syndrome is a genetic disorder due to an autosomal recessive gene. A larger number of males are affected by the syndrome than females (Jones, 1988). Smith-Lemli-Opitz syndrome is characterized by facial, limb, and genital abnormalities. Children with Smith-Lemli-Opitz syndrome have small heads; long, narrow faces; slanted or low-set ears; heavy or thick upper eyelids; anteverted nostrils; and small jaws. Squinting of the eyes is also a common characteristic found among these children. These children tend to be short in stature as well. On the palms of their hands and soles of their feet, simian creases are present and webbing often appears between their toes (Jones, 1988; Thoene, 1992). Some children with Smith-Lemli-Opitz syndrome experience seizures, and have cardiac anomalies, abnormal EEGs, kidney defects, and cataracts (Jones, 1988).

There are two forms of Smith-Lemli-Opitz syndrome: types I and II. Type II, also known as Lowry-Miller-Maclean syndrome, is a more severe form of the disorder. Stillbirth is a common characteristic of the type II form. Those who do survive have a low birth weight and failure to thrive. A shrill cry, vomiting, and feeding problems are typical in early infancy.

Moderate to severe mental retardation is evident among these children (Thoene, 1992). Special education programs focusing on life-skill training would be beneficial.

REFERENCES

Jones, K.L. (Ed.). (1988). *Smith's recognizable patterns of human malformation* (4th ed.). Philadelphia, PA: W.B. Saunders.

Thoene, J.G. (Ed.). (1992). *Physician's guide to rare diseases.* Montvale, NJ: Dowden.

See also **Rare Diseases**

SNELLEN CHART

The Snellen chart is a measuring device used to determine an individual's central distance visual acuity. The chart contains eight rows of letters of the alphabet in graduated sizes. There is a version for young children and for people who cannot read that replaces the alphabet with the letter E in different orientations and sizes. The letter sizes on the chart correspond to the estimate of the ability of a typical person to read the material. It is constructed so that at a distance of 20 ft, a person reading the figures on the chart corresponding to what a normal eye sees at 20 ft is said to have 20/20 vision (Bryan & Bryan, 1979). A person with 20/20 vision and both eyes working in a coordinated fashion is considered to be normally sighted. When a person sees at 20 ft what a normal person sees at 70 ft or 200 ft, that person has 20/70 or 20/200 vision. Individuals who have low vision or who are visually limited may be legally blind (visual acuity of 20/200 or less), or partially sighted (visual acuity between 20/70 and 20/200; DeMott, 1982).

The Snellen chart is widely used as a screening device for detecting eye problems because of the ease and speed with which it can be administered, its low cost, and its wide range of applicability.

Bryan and Bryan (1979) list three shortcomings of the Snellen chart:

1. It is not a good predictor of competence in visual processing of objects and tasks.

2. It does not tell how a child uses vision in terms of discriminating light or darkness, estimating size, or determining spatial location.

3. The results are not translatable into educational programs. Children with the same visual acuity may respond differently to school tasks, and, therefore, require different programming.

However, DeMott (1982) holds that the most important initial screening device for detecting eye problems is one that measures central visual acuity. Combining results from the Snellen chart with other screening measures is important for early diagnosis and remediation of eye problems.

REFERENCES

Bryan, J.H., & Bryan, L.H. (1979). *Exceptional children.* Sherman Oaks, CA: Alfred.

DeMott, R.M. (1982). Visual impairments. In N.G. Haring (Ed.), *Exceptional children and youth.* Columbus, OH: Merrill.

See also **Visual Acuity; Visually Impaired**

SOCIAL BEHAVIOR OF THE HANDICAPPED

Evidence from Lerner (1985) and Stephens, Hartman, and Lucas, (1983) has clearly documented that many exceptional children experience difficulty in the area of social skills. This difficulty could range from mild problems to severe disorders. Minskoff (1980) considers social perceptual difficulties as among the more serious problems of learning-disabled children.

In most instances, children who are receiving special education services have more than one problem and disabilities produce different behaviors in different children (Cartwright, Cartwright, & Ward, 1984). Bloom (1956) proposes a system whereby all education-related activities would fall into three major domains—affective, psychomotor, and cognitive. Cartwright et al. (1984) define the affective domain as the social domain; this deals with an individual's social abilities, such as establishing and maintaining satisfactory interpersonal skills, displaying behavior within reasonable social expectations, and making personal adjustments. Social skills and the ability to get along with others are just as important to the handicapped student as they are to the nonhandicapped student. In fact, these social skills are even more critical to the person who is handicapped because the handicapped are often compared with the norm and must compete for grades, social status, and employment.

Social skills have been hard to define and even more difficult to measure according to Wallace and Kauffman (1986), and Strain, Odom, and McConnell (1984). Direct observation is perhaps one of the most reliable methods used in assessment of social skills problems. Other procedures used to assess competence in social behavior are self-reporting and screening instruments, clinical judgment, analysis of antecedent events, interviews, sociometric procedures, behavior and rating scales. However, when assessing an individual's social skills, one must be aware of the situations, circumstances, and culture in which the behavior occurs.

Eleas and Maher (1983) suggest that well-adjusted children have certain social and academic skills that many mildly handicapped students do not possess. Such skills as sensitivity to others' feelings, goal-setting persistence, and an adequate behavior repertoire are just a few mentioned. Many more social skills deficits that often plague students with disabilities such as poor self-concept, withdrawal, rejection, attention problems, compound the academic problems. School personnel need to address these social skill problems of the handicapped student. Mercer and Mercer (1985) indicate that teachers can "help foster the student's emotional development as well as the acquisition of social skills" (p. 132).

Perhaps social competence might be a better term to describe the skills necessary to get along with others. Schulman (1980) defines social competence as "getting along with people, communicating with them and coping with the frustrations of social living" (p. 285). Girls tend to achieve social competence more frequently than boys (Merrell, Merz, Johnson, & Ring, 1992). Nearly all of us need to feel accepted and socially competent. However, many handicapped students and adults have difficulty, to some degree, in developing those skills necessary for adequate social acceptance.

REFERENCES

Bloom, B. (1956). *Taxonomy of educational objectives: The classification of educational goals.* New York: Longman.

Cartwright, C.P., Cartwright, C.A., & Ward, M.E. (1984). *Educating special learners.* Belmont, CA: Wadsworth.

Eleas, M.J., & Maher, C.A. (1983). Social and effective development of children: A programmatic perspective. *Exceptional Children, 4,* 339–346.

Lerner, J. (1985). *Learning disabilities: Theories, diagnosis, and teaching strategies* (4th ed.). Boston: Houghton Mifflin.

Mercer, D.D., & Mercer, A.R. (1985). *Teaching students with learning problems* (2nd ed.). Columbus, OH: Merrill.

Merrell, K.W., Merz, J.M., Johnson, E.R., & Ring, E.N. (1992). Social competence of students with mild handicaps and low achievement: A comparative study. *School Psychology Review, 21*(1), 125–137.

Minskoff, E.H. (1980). Teaching approach for developing nonverbal communication skills in students with social perception deficits. *Journal of Learning Disabilities, 13,* 118–126.

Schulman, E.D. (1980). *Focus on retarded adults: Programs and services.* St. Louis: Mosby.

Stephens, T.M., Hartman, A.C., & Lucas, V.H. (1983). *Teaching children basic skills: A curriculum handbook* (2nd ed.). Columbus, OH: Merrill.

Strain, P.S., Odom, S.L., & McConnell, S. (1984). Promoting social reciprocity of exceptional children: Identification, target behaviors selection, and intervention. *Remedial & Special Education, 1,* 21–28.

Wallace, G., & Kauffman, J.M. (1986). *Teaching students with learning and behavior problems* (3rd ed.). Columbus, OH: Merrill.

See also Adaptive Behavior; Social Skills; Social Skills Training; Sociogram

SOCIAL COMPETENCE

See ADAPTIVE BEHAVIOR.

SOCIAL DARWINISM

Social Darwinism, a social philosophy that was developed in the latter half of the nineteenth century, was based on the application of Darwin's principles of natural selection and survival of the fittest to the problems of society. Mental retardation, insanity, epilepsy, alcoholism, and other disorders were explained in terms of heredity, genetics, and Darwinian principles. Adams (1971) describes social Darwinism as follows: "the people of above average intelligence by previous standards become the norm in the next evolutionary phase, and the slow ones drop back to become the social casualties of the new order." Social Darwinism was also associated with attempts to interpret mental retardation as deviance rather than incompetence (Farber, 1968).

Social Darwinism and related social movements have had a profound impact on the treatment of the mentally retarded and other disabled individuals. However, not all of the effects of the social Darwinism movement were negative. Its popularity, along with the development of special educational services, has been credited with providing an impetus for the systematic study of the prevalence of mental retardation (Farber, 1968).

REFERENCES

Adams, M. (1971). *Mental retardation and its social dimensions.* New York: Columbia University Press.

Farber, B. (1968). *Mental retardation: Its social context and social consequences.* Boston: Houghton Mifflin.

See also **Eugenics; Heredity; Jukes and the Kallikaks**

SOCIAL INTEGRATION OF HANDICAPPED IN SCHOOL

See INCLUSION.

SOCIAL ISOLATION

There is a lack of agreement among investigators regarding the specific behaviors that need to be performed to indicate social skillfulness or competence, and the appropriate behaviors that are not performed, or the inappropriate behaviors that are performed, that indicate a lack of social skillfulness or competence. The contribution of several variables such as age, sex, social status, and situationally specific factors, in determining the presence or absence of social competence is poorly understood. Also, the criterion measures used to assess social isolation (behavioral observations, peer sociometric ratings, teacher ratings) may affect what is labeled as social isolate behavior (Conger & Keane, 1981). These criterion measures may not tap the same dimensions of behavior and may identify different subtypes of children (Gottman, 1977; Gourgey, 1998). The behaviors that have been selected as indicators of social isolate behavior have not been empirically determined. They have been chosen on the basis of the face validity of their relationship to the behavior pattern of social isolation, and single measures of social isolation typically have been employed (Conger & Keane, 1981). Additionally, little or no relationship has been found between the two main types of criterion measures used to assess social isolate behavior when they have been compared (i.e., global peer sociometric ratings of acceptance or rejection and behavioral observations of rate of discrete social interactions; Gottman, 1977).

The principal approaches in the conceptualization of social isolation in childhood have been in terms of withdrawal indicated by low rates of social interaction relative to other children and rejection or lack of acceptance by peers (Gottman, 1977). These two groups of social isolates may represent different populations; however, the infrequent use of both methods of assessment with the same groups of children does not allow for a determination of how well these measures agree on or discriminate among different subtypes of children. Also, given the lack of agreement on what behaviors or lack of behaviors are related to social isolation, it is unclear whether low rates of social interaction imply a lack of social skills or a lack of exhibiting social skills that the child possesses. In terms of peer acceptance or rejection, it is not clear whether this is based on a lack of social skills or on behaviors perceived as negative by peers such as aggressiveness. The grouping together of various behaviors within the category of social isolate behavior obscures assessment and intervention efforts and reduces the likelihood of heterogeneous grouping.

Intervention approaches used with socially withdrawn children increasingly emphasize the training of social skills. Social learning procedures (Coombs & Slaby, 1977) have constituted major treatment methods for teaching social skills to socially isolated children (Conger & Keane, 1981; Hops, 1983). The use of instructional packages with multiple components appears to be the best method for teaching social skills. The packages may include a combination of shaping, modeling, coaching, and reinforcement. Cognitively oriented interpersonal problem-solving interventions have also been employed; they emphasize the training of cognitive processes to mediate performance across a range of situations rather than discrete behavioral responses to various situations (Urbain & Kendall, 1980). The cognitive-behavioral approach uses many of the same instructional methods as the social learning approach, but it focuses on teaching problem-solving strategies and verbally mediated self-control (e.g., self-instruction). Music therapy has also been used successfully (Gourgey, 1998).

REFERENCES

Conger, J.C., & Keane, P. (1981). Social skills intervention in the treatment of isolated or withdrawn children. *Psychological Bulletin, 90*(3), 478–495.

Coombs, M.L., & Slaby, D. (1977). Social skills training with children. In B.B. Lahey & A.E. Kazdin (Eds.), *Advances in clinical child psychology* (Vol. 1). New York: Academic.

Gottman, J.M. (1977). Toward a definition of social isolation in children. *Child Development, 48,* 513–517.

Gourgey, C. (1998). Music therapy in the treatment of social isolation in visually impaired children. *REView, 29*(4), 157–162.

Hops, H. (1983). Social skills training for socially withdrawn/isolate children. In P. Karoly & J.J. Steffen (Eds.), *Improving children's competence.* Lexington, MA: Lexington.

Urbain, E.S., & Kendall, P.C. (1980). Review of social-cognitive problem-solving interventions with children. *Psychological Bulletin, 88*(1), 109–143.

See also **Social Behavior; Social Behavior of the Handicapped; Sociogram**

SOCIAL LEARNING THEORY

Social learning theory is a term that has been applied to the views of a relatively wide range of theorists and researchers. Without question, the theorist who has done the most to conceptualize and advance the ideas of social learning theory is Albert Bandura of Stanford University. His more recent work has moved away from the early environmental determinism that characterized behavioristic social learning theory. His most comprehensive presentation is in his 1986 book in which he extensively details his social cognitive theory. No socialization theory has as much careful empirical support as social cognitive theory. Bandura has added significant arguments for why internal evaluative processes must be included in any behavioral theory. At the core of Bandura's theory is the concept of reciprocal determinism. Similar to but more limited than Bronfenbrenner's ecological model, reciprocal determinism conceptualizes behavior as a continuous reciprocal interaction between an individual's thoughts, behaviors, and environmental factors.

This triadic model views human functioning as a three-way interaction among behavior (B), cognitions and other internal events that affect perceptions and actions (P), and a person's external environment (E). An interesting aspect of this view is that each element of the triad affects the other two elements. Thus, not only do internal and environmental events affect behavior, but behavior also affects internal events and the environment in reciprocal fashion.

Bandura's (1986) emphasis on internal mediators can be seen in work on observational learning, enactive learning, predictive knowledge and forethought, interpretations of incentives, vicarious motivators, self-regulatory mechanisms, self-efficacy, and cognitive regulators. Bandura demonstrates how cognitive factors determine what we observe, how we evaluate our observations, and how we use this information in the future. For example when students take tests, they read the questions, answer according to their interpretations of what the teacher wants, receive feedback in the form of grades, and then adjust depending on how successfully they believe they answered the questions graded by the teacher. No behavior occurs in a vacuum without prior internal processes and external effects.

A key component in most social learning theories is observational learning, which is based on the process of modeling. Through modeling, children learn a wide array of complicated skills, such as language and social interaction. Moreover, these skills are learned without reinforcement. This is in stark contrast to radical behavioral theory, which posits that complex behaviors are learned through the reinforcement of gradual changes in molecular response patterns. Teachers make use of observational learning many times a day. For example, some teachers will verbally reinforce a child who is behaving appropriately just so other children will be encouraged to imitate the modeled behavior. Most socialization is the result of observational learning, because it is much more efficient and realistic than the step-by-step shaping advocated by radical behaviorists.

Another key component that has received considerable research attention is the concept of self-efficacy. Self-efficacy is a complex process in which persons assess the likelihood of successfully performing a task based upon their previous mastery (e.g., training), vicarious experience (e.g., modeling of others), verbal persuasion (e.g., encouragement), physiological condition (e.g., health), and affective state (e.g., happy). Persons high in self-efficacy will make realistic judgments of their abilities to perform tasks, will tend to seek appropriately difficult tasks, and will persist in them until completed (Bandura, 1997). Teachers with high teacher self-efficacy will be more likely to believe they can teach a classroom of difficult children. In special education classes, high teacher self-efficacy will result in greater progress and competence in the students.

Social learning theory has also emphasized the concept of internal dialogues. These dialogues, or internal speeches, are used by people to learn information (e.g., to rehearse a phone number), for self-instruction (e.g., "Now what do I do next?"), and for self-reinforcement (e.g., "Way to go!"). These internal dialogues fit in nicely with Vygotsky's developmental theory postulating a cognitive self-guidance system in which these dialogues eventually become silent or inner speech. Teaching internal dialogues to children with learning disabilities may help them become better problem solvers (Berk, 1992). Social learning theory is seen by many as being very comprehensive in its ability to handle a diverse range of human experiences and problems.

REFERENCES

Bandura, A. (1986). *Social foundations of thought and action: A social cognitive theory.* Englewood Cliffs, NJ: Prentice-Hall.

Bandura, A. (1997). *Self-efficacy: The exercise of control.* New York, NY: Freeman.

Berk, L. E. (1992). Children's private speech: An overview of theory and the status of research. In R.M. Diaz & L.E. Berk (Eds.), *Private speech: From social interaction to self-regulation.* Hillsdale, NJ: Erlbaum.

See also **Impulse Control; Mediational Deficiencies; Mediators; Observational Learning; Reciprocal Determinism**

SOCIAL MATURITY

See ADAPTIVE BEHAVIOR.

SOCIAL SECURITY

Social Security is based on the concept of providing income and health maintenance programs for families in such instances as retirement, disability, poor health, or death. In general, to be eligible for Social Security a person must first pay into Social Security by working and allowing a certain amount of income to be deducted from earnings. Sixteen percent (over 3 million people) of the population in the United States receive Social Security checks. Individuals over 65 (about 25 million) are covered under health insurance called Medicare. In the category of disability, the number receiving benefits are about 3 million.

To be considered disabled under Social Security law a person must have a physical or mental condition that prevents that person from doing any substantial gainful work. The condition must be expected to last for at least 12 months, or expected to result in death. Examples of such conditions include diseases of the heart, lungs, or blood vessels that have resulted in serious loss of heart or lung reserves or serious loss of function of the kidneys; diseases of the digestive system that result in severe malnutrition, weakness, and anemia; and damage to the brain that has resulted in severe loss of judgment, intellect, orientation, or memory. The World Health Organization revised the mental health aspects of the International Classification of Impairments, Disabilities, and Handicaps (ICIDH) in 1995 to assist in the planning of care. Children of individuals who are eligible disabled persons can receive benefits if they are under 18 or 19, still in high school full time, or disabled before age 22, unmarried, and living at home. If an individual is blind, there are special considerations such as a disability freeze on income averaging for retirement purposes. Work situations for all individuals must require skills and abilities that are comparable to those of the individual's previous work history. If, however, the person is disabled before 22 and the parents are paying into Social Security, they can receive disability benefits. In order to qualify, the person must be unable to work in gainful employment and the person under whose credits they are applying must be retired, disabled, deceased, or fully insured under Social Security.

Another federal program administered by the Social Security Administration for low-income individuals is Supplemental Security Income (SSI). Supplemental security income is not based on work credits. Eligibility is based on age (over 65), income guidelines, and disability at any age for persons who earn below a specific income. In general, individuals living in institutions are not eligible for SSI unless they are classified under the four exceptions listed by the Social Security Administration (1986):

1. A person who lives in a publicly operated community residence that serves no more than 16 people may be eligible for SSI payments.

2. A person who lives in a public institution primarily to attend approved educational or vocational training provided in the institution may be eligible if the training is designed to prepare the person for gainful employment.

3. If a person is in a public or private medical treatment facility and Medicaid is paying more than half the cost of his or her care, the person may be eligible, but the SSI payments limited to no more than $25 per month.

4. A person who is a resident of a public emergency shelter throughout a month can receive SSI payments for up to 3 months during any 12-month period (pp. 9–10).

In the early 1990s the eligibility for SSI based on childhood disability was expanded because of a Supreme Court decision in Zebley v. Sullivan (Ford & Schwann, 1992).

To receive SSI under a disability option, the individual must have a physical or mental disability that prevents him or her from gainful employment. The disability must be one that will last at least 12 months or be expected to end in death. For individuals under age 18, the decision is based on whether the disability would not allow the person to work if he or she were an adult.

REFERENCE

Ford, M.E., & Schwann, J.B. (1992). Expanding eligibility for SSI based on childhood disability: The Zebley decision. *Child Welfare, 71*(4), 307–318.

See also **Disability; Rehabilitation; Socioeconomic Status**

SOCIAL SKILLS/COMPETENCE TRAINING

Social skills training is a method of teaching children effective social coping strategies. It is used as an intervention to manage disruptive behavior, a method to prevent future disruptions, and a tool to foster emotional growth in children (Gresham & Elliott, 1984). The adjustment problems of many children with disabilities have been related to social skills deficits; social skills training attempts to address these dysfunctional areas. Drawing from behavioral, cognitive, and humanistic theories of psychology, social skills training employs an educational approach to remediating behavior problems.

An individual's social skills determine important social outcomes such as peer acceptance and ascribed personality characteristics. Those children with poor self-control may learn inappropriate social strategies because their behavior leads to peer rejection (Gresham & Elliott, 1984). Socially incompetent children are reported to continue having socialization difficulties through adulthood (Rathjen, 1984).

Handicapped students with inadequate social perception need training in basic interpersonal skills (Speer & Douglas, 1981; Swanson & Malone, 1992). They may need to learn appropriate social gestures such as smiling and making eye contact. Learning-disabled children may also need instruction in interpreting and labeling facial expressions, and in moderating their verbal behavior. Language-deficient children must be taught appropriate verbal responses in social conversation. Communication training for language-impaired youngsters should teach them to be aware of four critical factors: personalities and roles of the participants, setting, topic, and objectives (Minskoff, 1982). Reality therapy, an approach to social skills training that stresses the relationship between behavior and natural consequences, has been used to encourage emotionally disturbed children to use more effective interpersonal strategies (Fuller & Fuller, 1982).

Social skills training has also been used with retarded children. Meisgeier (1981) has outlined a program stressing problem solving, personal responsibility, and communication skills. Students are taught to replace aggressive behaviors with assertive ones. The program consists of a series of structured success experiences stressing positive self-statements and relaxation.

Social skills training has been employed to increase the probability of mainstreaming and inclusion (Iannaccone & Hwang, 1998) effectiveness, and to help nonhandicapped children to accept their handicapped peers (Gresham, 1982). Gresham suggests that social skills assessments be included in all mainstreaming decisions.

As critics (Gerber, 1983) have argued that social skills training takes up valuable academic learning time, Shure and Spivack (1981) suggest that evaluation components be integrated into all social skills training programs to judge student growth and program effectiveness. One commonly used instrument is the Means-Ends Problem Solving measure (Platt, Spivack, and Bloom, 1971). This consists of a set of hypothetical social problems in which children are required to formulate a variety of possible solutions. Ratings can be made on the quantity and quality of these proposed solutions. Another popular evaluation approach uses sociometric procedures. Sociometric data are gathered by asking peers to rate each other in terms of popularity and desirability. Behavior rating scales also offer a means of assessing social skills. These scales attempt to define skills in terms of observable behavior, and are usually completed by the classroom teacher.

REFERENCES

Fuller, G.B., & Fuller, D.L. (1982). Reality therapy: Helping LD children make better choices. *Academic Therapy, 17*(3), 269–277.

Gerber, M.M. (1983). Learning disabilities and cognitive strategies: A case for training or constraining problem solving. *Journal of Learning Disabilities, 16*(5), 255–260.

Gresham, F.M. (1982). Misguided mainstreaming: The case for social skills training with handicapped children. *Exceptional Children, 48*(5), 422–433.

Gresham, F.M., & Elliott, S.M. (1984). Assessment and classification of children's social skills: A review of methods and issues. *School Psychology Review, 13*(3), 292–301.

Iannaccone, C.J., & Hwang, Y.G. (1998). Transcending social skills oriented instruction within integrated classrooms. *Emotional and Behavioral Difficulties, 3*(1), 25–29.

Meisgeier, C. (1981). A social/behavioral program for the adolescent student with serious learning problems. *Focus on Exceptional Children, 13*(9), 1–13.

Minskoff, E.H. (1982). Training LD students to cope with the everyday world. *Academic Therapy, 17*(3), 311–316.

Platt, J.J., Spivack, G., & Bloom, M.R. (1971). *Means-ends problem solving procedure (MEPS): Manual and tentative norms.* Philadelphia: Hahnemann Medical College and Hospital.

Rathjen, D.P. (1984). Social skills training for children. Innovations and consumer guidelines. *School Psychology Review, 13*(3), 302–310.

Shure, M.B., & Spivack, G. (1981). The problem solving approach to

adjustment: A competency-building model of primary prevention. *Prevention in Human Services, 1*(1–2), 87–103.

Speer, S.K., & Douglas, D.R. (1981). Helping LD students improve social skills. *Academic Therapy, 17*(2), 221–224.

Swanson, H.L., & Malone, S. (1992). Social skills and learning disabilities: A meta-analysis of the literature. *School Psychology Review, 21*(3), 427–443.

See also Behavior Modeling; Developing Understanding of Self and Others

SOCIAL VALIDATION

In an educational context, social validation is the philosophy of providing psychological services that emphasize the importance of the student's or teacher's subjective opinions about intervention methods. Social validity differs from the statistical notion of validity in several aspects. Statistical validity refers to how well treatment results correlate with an objective set of criteria or other treatment methods. Social validity is concerned with the subjective opinions of teachers, parents, and/or students and how these subjective opinions affect the overall treatment outcomes. In social validity it is assumed "that if the participants don't like the treatment then they may avoid it, or run away, or complain loudly. And thus, society will be less likely to use our technology, no matter how potentially effective and efficient it might be" (Wolf, 1978, p. 206).

Consumer satisfaction differs from treatment acceptability mainly in the timing of the measurements. Treatment acceptability requires teachers and students to judge treatments before they begin. Consumer satisfaction requires teachers and students to judge treatments during the treatment or after the treatment is over. In applied behavior analysis, it is believed that the outcomes of treatments are easily judged based on behavioral changes from baseline measurements. However, according to the social validity paradigm, the usefulness of school interventions can only be judged by the subjective evaluations of the teachers and students participating in the treatment program.

REFERENCE

Wolf, M.M. (1978). Social validity: The case for subjective measurement or how applied behavior analysis is finding its heart. *Journal of Applied Behavior Analysis, 11,* 203–214.

See also Applied Behavior Analysis; Teacher Expectancies

SOCIAL WORK

Social work in special education traditionally falls within the realm of the school social worker. The functions performed by social workers within the school include individual and family casework, individual and group work with students, and community liaison services. School social workers have stated their goals as helping students to maximize their potential, developing relationships between the school and other agencies, and offering a perspective of social improvement in the education of students (Costin, 1981).

The school social worker often participates in the evaluation of students who are being considered for special education. In this regard, the case history is an extremely important tool that the social worker uses to gain environmental, developmental, social, and economic information about the student.

Often, family members of the children with disabilities need support from the social worker in their efforts to program for their impaired youngsters. The primary goal of the social worker in providing services to family members of the handicapped is to help them face and accept the limiting condition (Dickerson, 1981). The family is encouraged to follow through on recommendations designed to enhance their child's functioning. The social worker helps the family to recognize that the problem is real and that it can be helped by the development of an accepting, positive attitude about the child.

Pupil services such as counseling, sex education, prevocational development, and child advocacy are often performed by the school social worker. As an advocate, the social worker attempts to create systemic changes that improve the quality of the impaired child's school life. The social worker may assume responsibility for shaping a school system's attitudes to reflect more adaptive, relevant, and socially responsible positions (Lee, 1983).

School social workers may be responsible for developing communication links within the school so that teachers, administrators, and other staff can exchange information necessary for student programming. They may also plan in-service workshops in areas related to student welfare. Future trends in special education social work will continue to expand the systems approach to service delivery. To this end, an increase in coordinator and liaison roles for special education social workers is predicted (Randolph, 1982), and mandated in inclusive programming (Pryor, Kent, McGunn, & LeRoy, 1996).

REFERENCES

Costin, L.B. (1981). School social work as specialized practice. *Social Work, 26,* 36–44.

Dickerson, M.O. (1981). *Social work practice and the mentally retarded.* New York: Free Press.

Lee, L.J. (1983). The social worker in the political environment of a school system. *Social Work, 28*(4), 302–307.

Pryor, C.B., Kent, C., McGunn, C., & LeRoy, B. (1996). Redesigning social work in inclusive schools. *Social Work, 41*(6), 668–676.

Randolph, J.L. (1982). School social work can foster educational growth for students. *Education, 102,* 260–265.

See also **Multidisciplinary Teams; Personnel Training in Special Education**

SOCIODRAMA

Sociodrama was developed by J.L. Moreno (1946) as an extension of a group-therapy technique, also devised by Moreno, known as psychodrama. (Moreno is often credited with having initiated group therapy in Vienna just after the beginning of the twentieth century.) Though he developed the technique, Moreno did little with sociodrama, preferring to continue his efforts in the development and application of psychodrama. E. Paul Torrance, a psychodramatist who studied with Moreno, later reconceptualized and refined sociodrama as a group problem-solving technique based on Moreno's early work but also incorporating the creative problem-solving principles of Torrance (1970) and Osborn (1963). Sociodrama can be used with all ages from preschool through adulthood.

The primary uses of sociodrama, largely reflecting Torrance's interests and influence, have been in primary prevention of behavior problems with the disadvantaged and other high-risk populations. Sociodrama has also been used in specific treatment programs with adolescents who engage in socially deviant behaviors and with status offenders. Sociodrama seems particularly helpful in introducing and teaching new social behaviors as well as in improving the problem-solving skills of the youngsters involved, giving them more behavioral options.

During sociodrama, a problem or conflict situation that is likely to be common to the group is derived from group discussion. Members of the group are cast into roles, which they play as the situation is acted out. Many production techniques are brought into play to facilitate solution of the conflict; these include the double, the soliloquy, direct presentation, mirror, and role reversal.

The director's role is to keep the action moving in the direction of a resolution, or, preferably, multiple resolutions of the conflict. Each session should end with a series of potential resolutions that can be discussed by the group. Appropriate behaviors can also be practiced. By teaching participants to brainstorm alternative behaviors and to rehearse for real-life problem situations, sociodrama has proved a useful method for treatment and prevention of behavior problems in children and adolescents.

REFERENCES

Moreno, J.L. (1946). *Psychodrama.* Beacon, NY: Beacon House.

Osborn, A.F. (1963). *Applied imagination* (3rd ed.). New York: Scribner's.

Torrance, E.P. (1970). *Creative learning and teaching.* New York: Dodd, Mead.

See also **Group Therapy; Psychodrama**

SOCIOECONOMIC IMPACT OF DISABILITIES

There is a well-established relationship between parents' socioeconomic status and children's school performance, (Barona, 1992). Caldwell (1970) reports that many of the children from lower socioeconomic classes live in restricted and nonstimulating environments. As a result, low socioeconomic profile is one factor that is significantly related to poor cognitive functioning. There are many more children from lower socioeconomic classes with poor cognitive functioning than from higher socioeconomic classes.

There are many factors associated with socioeconomic status that are considered contributing factors to some disabilities. These include poor health care, inadequate pre and postnatal care, improper diet, and lack of early stimulation. Zachau-Christiansen and Ross (1979) state that infants from lower socioeconomic families are at greater risk for experiencing or being exposed to conditions that may hinder development. These conditions include low birth weight, lead poisoning, malnutrition, and maternal infections during pregnancy. Kagan (1970) discusses other psychological differences between lower class and more privileged children. The differences are evident during the first 3 years of life and tend to remain stable over time. Variables include language, mental set, attachment, inhibition, sense of effectiveness, motivation, and expectancy of failure. All of the factors play a crucial role in influencing school performance. Deficits in any of these areas limits the child's ability in various cognitive skills. Young children raised in an environment lacking in stimulation and healthy interaction with adults will often be retarded in motor, language, cognitive, and social skills.

Many other correlates of low socioeconomic status are associated with poor school learning. Some of these correlates are delayed development of language; greater impulsivity; lower intelligence on standard intelligence tests that predict success in standard curricula; lower parental educational levels; families with children over five; poor home climate; lack of variety in sensory stimuli; minimal encouragement of scholastic success within the home; and less time spent on tasks in the classroom and on homework.

MacMillian (1982) and Podell and Scodlak (1993) have emphasized the dangers of class stereotyping. Determining socioeconomic status and the relationship between the ratings and developmental outcomes can be misleading; there are some exceptions to every rule. It is very important that special education personnel are trained in cultural awareness programming that includes socioeconomic variables. The major concern should be placed on the overall impact of socioeconomic factors in preventing or enhancing the possibility of physical, social, emotional, and intellectual disabilities.

REFERENCES

Barona, A., & Faykus, S.P. (1992). Differential effects of sociocultural variables on special education eligibility categories. *Psychology in the Schools, 29*(4), 313–320.

Kagan, J. (1970). On class differences and early development. In V. Denenberg (Ed.), *Education of the infant and young child.* New York: Academic.

MacMillian D.L. (1982). *Mental retardation in school and society.* (2nd ed.). Boston: Little, Brown.

Podell, D.M., & Soodlak, L.C. (1993). Teacher efficacy and bias in special education referrals. *Journal of Educational Research, 86*(4), 247–253.

Zachau-Christiansen, B., & Ross, E.M. (1979). *Babies: Human development during the first year.* Chichester, England: Wiley.

***See also* Culturally/Linguistically Diverse Students; Gifted and Talented Children; Socioeconomic Status**

SOCIOECONOMIC STATUS (SES)

Davis (1986) defines socioeconomic status (SES) as a person's position in the community. There are many factors involved in determining SES. These factors include income, employment, location and cost of home, and social status of the family. Socioeconomic status influences various behavior patterns. For example, the number of children, the year and model of the family car, and the number of vacations per year will vary according to SES.

Society places a high value on wealth and material possessions. There is a tendency to rank individuals based on their wealth and power within the community. Wealth is highly correlated with education, income, and occupation.

Kohn (1969) states that middle-class mothers value self-control, dependability, and consideration, while lower class mothers value obedience and the ability to defend oneself. The middle-class family raises the child in an environment where achievement and getting ahead are encouraged. The lower class family raises the child in an environment that emphasizes the immediate and the concrete. The child is taught to shy away from the new or unfamiliar. According to Boocock (1972), the family characteristic that is the most powerful predictor of school performance is socioeconomic status. More specifically, the higher the socioeconomic status of the family, the higher the child's academic achievement. Socioeconomic status also predicts the number and type of extracurricular activities the child will be involved in and social and emotional adjustment to school. Other areas highly correlated with socioeconomic status include grades, achievement test scores, retentions at grade level, course failures, truancy, suspensions from school, dropout rates, college plans, and total amount of schooling.

REFERENCES

Boocock, S.S. (1972). *An introduction to the sociology of learning.* Dallas: Houghton Mifflin.

Davis, W.E. (1986). *Resource guide to special education* (2nd ed.). Boston: Allyn & Bacon.

Kohn, M. (1969). *Class and conformity.* Homewood, IL: Dorsey.

***See also* Socioeconomic Impact of Disabilities**

SOCIOGRAM

A sociogram (Moreno, 1953) is a graphic display of interpersonal relationships within a group. It is considered one of the most common sociometric techniques used by teachers. In most instances, a sociometric test is administered to a group of children by asking each child who he or she would like to work with on a particular activity. The sociogram displays a diagram of students with whom other students prefer to study, play, or work. It also displays a diagram of students who are rejected and tend to be isolates. Each child is asked such questions as, With which three students would you prefer to study? Which three students do you like best? Which two students do you prefer to play with at recess? Which three students are your best friends? The students' responses to these types of questions are used to construct the sociogram.

The information obtained from a sociogram can be used for assessing students who may be isolated, socially immature, unhappy, and who have disabilities (Conderman, 1995). Once this information has been obtained from the sociogram, the teacher may begin to ask questions to determine why some students are considered isolates and often rejected. This information can assist the teacher with assigning students to groups for class projects and making changes in classroom relationships. It may also alert the teacher to the possibility of an existing or potential handicapping condition. Almost 40% of all teachers use sociometric techniques (Vasa, Maag, Torrey, & Kramer, 1994).

REFERENCES

Conderman, G. (1995). Social status of sixth and seventh-grade students with learning disabilities. *Learning Disability Quarterly, 18*(1), 13–24.

Moreno, J.L. (1953). *Who shall survive? Foundations of sociometry, group psychotherapy, and sociodrama* (2nd ed.). New York: Beacon House.

Vasa, S.F., Maag, J.W., Torrey, G.K., & Kramer, J.J. (1994). Teachers' use of and perceptions of sociometric techniques. *Journal of Psychoeducational Assessment, 12*(2), 135–141.

See also Social Skills; Social Skills and the Handicapped

SOCIOMETRIC TECHNIQUES WITH THE HANDICAPPED

Sociometric techniques originated by Moreno (1953) are a set of questions used to determine the social organization of a group. There are various types of sociometric techniques that are used with the handicapped. The two most common forms are peer nomination and roster and rating methods. Most peer nomination techniques ask questions such as, With whom would you most like to study? Who would you most like to sit with at lunch? Who would you most enjoy working with on an art project? Who would you most enjoy being with during break? (Mercer & Mercer, 1981 p. 109).

With handicapped children social acceptance is considered a very important aspect of school adjustment and educational achievement. Sociometric techniques may help the teacher determine whether the handicapped child is ac-

cepted by his or her nonhandicapped peers (Conderman, 1995). If the child is not accepted, the next step is to decide which interventions will help to improve the child's social status.

REFERENCES

Conderman, G. (1995). Social status of sixth and seventh-grade students with learning disabilities. *Learning Disability Quarterly, 18*(1), 13–24.

Mercer, C.D., & Mercer A.R. (1981). *Teaching students with learning problems.* Columbus, OH: Merrill.

Moreno, J.L. (1953). *Who shall survive? Foundations of sociometry, group psychotherapy and sociodrama* (2nd ed.). New York: Beacon House.

See also Social Skills; Sociogram

SOCIOPATHY/ANTISOCIAL PERSONALITY DISORDER

Sociopathy is a diagnostic label applied to adults of 18 years or older who exhibit a lifelong pattern of conduct problems or antisocial behavior. The most valid predictor of sociopathy is antisocial behavior in childhood. Fighting, stealing, persistent lying, delinquency, and chronic violations of rules at home serve as markers for the disorder. Conduct problems at school are chronic. It is not uncommon for these children to have a sociopathic father. In fact, irrespective of socioeconomic status, the more family relatives that display antisocial behavior, the greater the likelihood that the child will engage in antisocial acts (Robins, 1972).

As is true for most psychological disorders, specific patterns of parenting or family dynamics have not been clearly identified as leading to sociopathy. Nonetheless, several authors have noted two styles of child rearing that may contribute to the development of the syndrome (Meyer, 1980). One consists of cold, aloof parents that fail to demonstrate, and thus inculcate, a sense of empathy and a capacity for intimacy. The other parental style is characterized by a lack of consistency in administering reinforcement and punishment. The child then fails to learn abstract rules of right and wrong and instead responds to short-term consequences, fails to trust, and does not react to interpersonal consequences such as disapproval. In addition, exposure to an antisocial adult, usually a male, provides a model for nonnormative behavior.

Several studies have found electroencephalogram (EEG) abnormality in 31 to 58% of sociopaths. The most common abnormality is nonlocalized slow-wave activity, typical of infants and young children (Ellington, 1954). Among extremely impulsive and aggressive sociopaths, temporal lobe EEG abnormalities have been found and positive spikes of 6 to 8 cycles per second (cps) and 14 to 16 cps have been observed (Hill, 1952; Syndulko, 1978). These data are difficult to interpret as causal factors in sociopathy because not all sociopaths show such brain wave activity. Perhaps there are subtypes of this personality disorder that when identified will allow for a different etiological theory of each type. Nevertheless, Hare (1970) has speculated that slow wave brain activity is indicative of a dysfunction in behavioral inhibitory mechanisms. This is consistent with the belief that sociopaths have difficulty in learning from experience, and despite social or physical punishment continue their maladaptive behavior.

Despite the protestations of some that sociopathy is a wastebasket category, the concept is considered meaningful by most clinicians (Gray & Hutchinson, 1964) and is reliably diagnosed. Indeed, interrater agreement for this disorder exceeds that commonly found for most other categories in the *Diagnostic and Statistical Manual* (Spitzer, Cohen, Fliess, & Endicott, 1967). No doubt the definitional criteria for antisocial personality will continue to shift, most likely in the direction of subtypes, as researchers continue to bring this complex syndrome into focus. It is hoped that these efforts will also lead to effective measures for prevention and treatment. With the exception of isolated reports (Meyer, 1980), the most optimistic prognostic statement is that the sociopathic behavior pattern seems to lessen as the person reaches middle age. However, special education personnel must deal with the conduct-disordered youth and hopefully prevent the antisocial adult from developing.

REFERENCES

Ellington, R. (1954). Incidence of EEG abnormality among patients with mental disorders of apparently nonorganic origin: A criminal review. *American Journal of Psychiatry, 111* 263–275.

Gray, H., & Hutchinson, H.C. (1964). The psychopathic personality: A survey of Canadian psychiatrists' opinion. *Canadian Psychiatric Association Journal, 9,* 450–461.

Hare, R.D. (1970). *Psychopathy: Theory and research.* New York: Wiley.

Hill, D. (1952). EEG in episodic psychotic and psychopathic behavior: A classification of data. *EEG & Clinical Neurophysiology, 4,* 419–442.

Meyer, R.G. (1980). The antisocial personality. In R.H. Woody (Ed.), *Encyclopedia of clinical assessment.* San Francisco: Jossey-Bass.

Robins, L.N. (1972). Follow-up studies of behavior disorders in children. In H.C. Quay & J.S. Werry (Eds.), *Psychopathological disorders in childhood.* New York: Wiley.

Spitzer, R., Cohen, J., Fliess, J., & Endicott, J. (1967). Quantification of agreement in psychiatric diagnosis: A new approach. *Archives of General Psychiatry, 17,* 83–87.

Syndulko, K. (1978). Electrocortical investigations of sociopathy. In R.D. Hare & D. Schalling (Eds.), *Psychopathic behavior: Approaches to research.* New York: Wiley.

See also **Conduct Disorder; Drug Abuse**

SOFT (NEUROLOGICAL) SIGNS

Neurological soft signs are defined by Shaffer, O'Connor, Shafer, and Prupis (1983) as "non-normative performance on a motor or sensory test identical or akin to a test of the traditional neurological examination, but a performance that is elicited from an individual who shows none of the features of a fixed or transient localizable neurological disorder" (p. 145). Some sources (e.g., Buda, 1981; Gaddes, 1985) suggest soft signs have a strong age-related component, in that many of the behaviors judged to represent soft signs in children of a certain age would be considered within the range of normal behavior for chronologically younger children (Ardilla & Rosselli, 1996). The term is contrasted with hard neurological signs, which are medically documented symptoms of neurologic disease.

To be considered a soft sign, Shaffer et al. (1983) state there should be no association between the observed behavior and a positive history of neurologic disease or trauma. Furthermore, clusters of neurological soft signs should not be pathognomonic of neurologic disease or encephalopathy. Soft signs, by definition, are not indicative of specific central nervous system pathology. Soft signs are not additive in the traditional sense: "the presence of more than one soft sign does not make a hard sign" (Spreen et al., 1984, p. 246).

Nearly 100 different neurological soft signs have been identified (Spreen et al., 1984). Such signs encompass a wide variety of behaviors, including impulsivity (Vitello, Stoff, Atkins, & Mahoney, 1990) attention, concentration, fine motor speed, activity level, and affect. Gaddes (1985) lists the following as among the most common neurologic soft signs: motor clumsiness, speech and language delays, left-right confusion, perceptual and perceptual-motor deficits, and deficient eye-hand coordination. Soft signs may occur in conjunction with hyperactivity and specific learning disabilities, but the presence should not be considered pathognomonic of these conditions (Gaddes, 1985).

The relationship between neurologic soft signs and learning and behavior disorders in children has been investigated widely. In a comprehensive review of studies of children conducted prior to 1983, Shaffer et al. (1983) reported these investigations demonstrated consistent relationships between neurological soft signs and IQ scores, as well as diagnosed psychiatric disturbances and behavior problems. The authors described a study of 456 children participating in the Collaborative Perinatal Project of the National Institute of Neurological and Communicative Disorders and Stroke (NINCDS). The subjects were examined for the presence or absence of 18 neurological soft signs at age 7. Specific signs included movement disorders (e.g., tics, tremors, mirror movements) and coordination difficulties (e.g., dysmetria, dysdiadochokinesia). Subjects were rated blind on 15 behaviors (e.g., fearfulness, verbal fluency, cooperativeness, attention span). As in previous studies, the authors reported increased incidence of cognitive dysfunction, learning problems, and behavior disorders in children who exhibited neurologic soft signs.

The etiology of neurological soft signs has not been delineated clearly, and it is likely there are multiple causes. Soft signs may constitute one end of a continuum of neurologic signs, and thus may be a result of mild central nervous system impairment. For other individuals, soft signs may represent a genetic variation (Shaffer et al., 1983). The high incidence of neurologic soft signs in the general population suggests that caution should be exercised when interpreting their significance.

REFERENCES

Ardilla, A., & Rosselli, M. (1996). Soft neurological signs in children: A normative study. *Developmental Neuropsychology, 12*(2), 181–200.

Buda, F.B. (1981). *The neurology of developmental disabilities.* Springfield, IL: Thomas.

Gaddes, W.H. (1985). *Learning disabilities and brain function: A neuropsychological approach* (2nd ed.). New York: Springer-Verlag.

Shaffer, D., O'Connor, P.A., Shafer, S.Q., & Prupis, S. (1983). Neurological "soft signs": Their origins and significance for behavior. In M. Rutter (Ed.), *Developmental neuropsychiatry* (pp. 144–163). New York: Guilford.

Spreen, O., Tupper, D., Risser, A., Tuokko, H., & Edgell, D. (1984). *Human developmental neuropsychology.* New York: Oxford University Press.

Vitello, B., Stoff, D., Atkins, M., & Mahoney, A. (1990). Soft neurological signs and impulsivity in children. *Journal of Developmental & Behavioral Pediatrics, 11*(3), 112–115.

See also Laterilization; Neuropsychology; Visual-Motor and Visual-Perceptual Problems

SOMPA
See SYSTEM OF MULTICULTURAL PLURALISTIC ASSESSMENT.

SONICGUIDE
The Sonicguide is a mobility aid and environmental sensor for the visually handicapped. It operates on the principle of reflected high-frequency sound, which, when converted into audible stereophonic signals, provides the user with information about the distance, position, and surface characteristics of objects within the travel path and immediate environment. Users of all ages (Hill, Dodson-Burk, Hill, & Fox, 1995) learn to locate and identify objects up to a distance of approximately 5 meters.

A transmitter in the center of a spectacle frame radiates ultrasound (high-frequency sound inaudible to the human ear) in front of the wearer. When the ultrasound hits an obstruction such as a wall, a person, or a tree, it is reflected to the aid and received by two microphones below the transmitter. The microphones transform the reflected signals into electrical signals, which are shifted to a much lower range of frequency and converted into audible sounds by two small earphones in the arms of the spectacle frame. The sounds are then directed to each ear by small tubes. These tubes do not interfere with normal hearing and the user learns to integrate the sounds of the Sonicguide with natural sounds to enhance a concept of the environment. The microphones are deflected slightly outward so that sounds produced by objects to either side of the user will be louder in the ear nearer to the object. This process of sound localization occurs in normal hearing and therefore is a natural indication of direction. The pitch of the signal indicates the approximate distance of a reflecting object; it is highest at the maximum range of the aid and gradually reduces as the object comes closer. By interpreting the comparative loudness at each ear of the signal and its pitch and tonal characteristics, the user is able to judge the direction, distance, and surface qualities of reflecting objects. The aid's sensors are built into a spectacle frame to encourage the user to develop the same head movements and posture as a sighted person. When the skills of the aid are mastered, safer and more confident travel and a heightened awareness of the environment is assured. In outdoor situations, the device is to be used in conjunction with a long cane or guide dog, unless the area of travel is both familiar and free from hazards at ground level, which the Sonicguide may not detect.

REFERENCE
Hill, M.M., Dodson-Burk, B., Hill, E.W., & Fox, J. (1995). An infant sonicguide intervention program for a child with a visual disability. *Journal of Visual Impairments, 89*(4), 329–336.

See also Blind; Electronic Travel Aids; Visual Training

SOUTH AFRICA, SPECIAL EDUCATION IN
Special education provision during the period prior to 1994 (commonly referred to as the apartheid era) is characterized by disparate provision of services in terms of race. As a result of apartheid policy the state classified four groups Africans, Coloreds, Whites, and Indians, who were exposed to different education systems that were controlled by the Apartheid State. During this period there were 17 different education departments in South Africa.

Between December 1990 and August 1992, the National Education Policy Investigation into Education Support Services was conducted. This was a component of a wider investigation that included all areas of education with the aim of building a unitary and efficient education system for all South Africans.

Besides providing policy options that suggested equality in special education provision for all South Africans, this policy investigation challenged the conceptualization of special education need (SEN). The challenge centered around the lack of consideration of extrinsic factors as a possible cause of SEN. The report indicated that by locating the problem within the learner and ignoring societal factors, the system "perpetuates categorization, labeling, and separation of the child from mainstream education and community life" (National Policy Investigation into Education Support Services, 1992:78). This statement was particularly significant because the majority of Black children in South Africa face adverse social conditions that could result in a breakdown in learning (Naicker, 1995). As a result, many universities and colleges of education injected a sociological dimension in SEN preservice and inservice teacher training courses to provide a more comprehensive understanding, thus ensuring more appropriate intervention strategies. In 1992, the National Party Government, after an investigation into all areas of education, presented the Education Renewal Strategy (ERS). With regard to special education, the report called mainly for an equitable dispensation for all South Africans (ERS, 1992). There were no significant shifts in conceptualization.

After the advent of the new democratic order in 1994, the National Ministry of Education transformed the 17 education departments into a single system of education for all South Africans. As part of the transformation initiative, the National Ministry of Education appointed a National Commission for Special Education Needs and Training (NCSNET) and the National Committee for Education Support Services (NCESS) in 1996. Both NCSNET and NCESS were charged with the task of making recommendations on all aspects of special needs and support services in education and training in South Africa. As part of its terms of reference, the NCSNET and NCESS were to appropriate the principles of the Constitution of South Africa, the White Paper on Education and Training, and major international declarations, such as the Salamanca Statement, that were underpinned by a rights culture. With regards to a rights culture, the new Constitution in South Africa states very clearly that nobody should be discriminated against on the basis of race, disability, or gender (Constitution of South Africa, 1996).

The investigation was completed in the latter part of 1997 and the report was submitted to the National Minister of Education in November of the same year. The recommendations of the NCSNET and NCESS were radically different from previous policy initiatives. While other policy investigations focused on equity and minor conceptual shifts, the central thrust of the recommendations was a move away from a dual system of education to a single one. "Key strategies to achieve the vision include: transforming all aspects of the education system, developing an integrated system of education, and infusing 'special needs and support services' throughout the system. It also has the strategy of the holistic development centers of learning to ensure a barrier-free physical environment and a supportive and inclusive psychosocial learning environment, and developing a flexible curriculum to ensure access to all learners. By promoting the rights and responsibilities of parents, teachers and learners, it provides effective development programs for educators, support personnel, and other relevant human resources. While fostering holistic and integrated support provision (intersectoral collaboration), it develops a community-based support system which includes a preventative and developmental approach to support, and developing funding strategies that ensure redress, sustainability, and ultimately access to education for all learners" (NCSNET & NCESS report, 1997, p. xi).

Therefore, the recommendations of both NCSNET and NCESS suggest that education centers (schools) should

have the capacity to respond to diversity. Further, those barriers to learning should be identified and broken down. More emphasis should be placed on the limitations of the system instead of the deficits in individuals. For example, a learner who is physically disabled and uses a wheelchair would gain access to mainstream schools by removing the barrier of lack of access (since no ramps are provided). It also suggests a range of learning contexts offering diversity in terms of the curriculum, and that 'high need' support (severe difficulties) to a small percentage of learners should be made available, taking into account the need to promote their full participation and inclusion in the education process and in society at large (NCSNET & NCESS, 1997). In order to bring about these radical changes, the NCSNET and NCESS recommended that the implementation plan will be put into place over a 10-year period.

REFERENCES

Department of National Education. (1992). *Education renewal strategy.* Pretoria: Government Printer.

Department of Education. (1997). *Report of the National Commission on Special Needs in Education and Training and National Committee for Education Support Services.* Pretoria: Government Printer.

Naicker, S.M. (1995). The need for a radical restructuring of special education need in South Africa. *British Journal of Special Education, 22*(4), 152–154.

National Education Policy Investigation. (1992). *Support services.* Cape Town: Oxford University Press.

Parliament of South Africa. (1996). *The Constitution of South Africa.* Pretoria: Government Printers.

SOUTH AMERICA

See ARGENTINA, SPECIAL EDUCATION IN; MEXICO, SPECIAL EDUCATION IN; PERU, SPECIAL EDUCATION IN.

SOUTHERN AND EASTERN AFRICA, SPECIAL EDUCATION IN

A brief history, statements on current status, and the future prospects of special education in twelve East and Southern African countries are presented here. The countries discussed include Botswana, Ethiopia, Eriteria, Kenya, Lesotho, Malawi, Namibia, Swaziland, Tanzania, Uganda, Zambia, and Zimbabwe. The availability of information on the aforementioned topics and between these countries differs widely. Thus, some countries are discussed in greater detail (Tanzania, Uganda, and Zimbabwe) than others (Eriteria, Malawi, and Swaziland).

INCIDENCE OF HANDICAPPING CONDITIONS WITHIN THIS REGION

Reliable data on the incidence of childhood disorders within this region are unavailable. Various problems associated with incidence surveys preclude obtaining accurate data. Parents may need to register their disabled children in special centers, and they often are reluctant to admit their children display handicapping conditions (Kisanji, 1997; Whyte & Ingstad, 1995). Also, community attitudes toward the handicapped often are negative (Devlieger, 1995; Jackson & Mupedziswa, 1989). These and other qualities are believed to contribute to grossly underestimated incidence figures for handicapping conditions.

This large region in East and Southern Africa is home to an estimated 59,800,000 children. Population details for children ages 5 to 16 years for the year 1996 are provided below (UNICEF, 1996):

Botswana	700,000
Ethiopia	15,600,000
Eritrea	1,600,000
Kenya	12,100,000
Lesotho	600,000
Malawi	3,200,000
Namibia	700,000
Tanzania	8,700,000
Uganda	10,500,000
Zambia	2,900,000
Zimbabwe	3,200,000

If we accept the World Health Organization's general incidence estimate that 10% of a country's population is likely to be handicapped, almost six million children in this region can be expected to have one or more handicapping conditions. We believe this estimate substantially underestimates the number of handicapped children, given the region's substandard medical, health, and early childhood education facilities. Among children with handicaps, less than 1% attend formal school (Tungaraza, 1994; Kann, Mapolelo, & Nleya, 1989).

GENERAL HISTORY OF EDUCATIONAL SERVICES FOR HANDICAPPED CHILDREN

The availability of special education services and other resources for children with physical, sensory, and cognitive disabilities occurred recently. Historically, native African societies integrated learning and other developmental activities within their everyday home and community activities (Kisanji, 1997). Home and community-based activities provide various advantages: a favorable ratio between the young and elders, accommodations to match the child's developmental levels, and utilization of the child's natural milieu within which to promote development and transfer of training. The extent to which homes and communities provide appropriate adaptations to accommodate children with disabilities is unknown. The beneficial effects that professional services can have on children with disabilities are well-established.

The introduction and evolution of professional services for these children in East and Southern Africa closely follows a pattern found in other developing areas: first, national or regional institutions, often residential in nature and initiated by religious, humanitarian, and philanthropic

agencies, are established. Professional services for middle-class children then develop in metropolitan centers. The widespread provision of services to children with disabilities in public schools occurs only after general education services, at least through the elementary level, are well-developed and nationally available. Children with handicapping conditions who reside in rural areas are least likely to receive professional services. Stronger special education services generally are found in countries with stronger and well-established regular education programs (Saigh & Oakland, 1989).

The majority of countries in this region have inadequate basic education programs (UNICEF, 1991, 1994), lack formal special education policies, and experience school dropout rates in the range of 15% to 60% involving disadvantaged children, which includes those with disabilities (Kann, Mapolelo, & Nleya, 1989; Stubbs, 1997; UNICEF, 1994).

CURRENT STATUS OF SPECIAL EDUCATION IN EAST AND SOUTHERN AFRICA

Special education services in East and Southern Africa generally follow a functional integration (resource room) model in which children with disabilities attend class part-time to full-time with their non-disabled peers and receive support of a full-time specialist teacher (Charema & Peresuh, 1997). Specialist teachers maintain the resource room, provide intensive individualized instruction to children with disabilities, and work closely with mainstream teachers in planning and effecting integration strategies for children with disabilities. A functional integration model generally is preferred for children with mild to moderate sensory, physical, and cognitive handicaps. Children with more severe handicaps generally attend special schools and rehabilitation centers, typically those residential in nature, which provide more specialized resources. With few exceptions, most integration units for the visually handicapped and hearing impaired are residential, whereas those for children with moderate to mild physical and cognitive handicaps are nonresidential.

Compared to current needs and potential demand, special education facilities in the twelve East and Southern countries of this survey are severely limited. Botswana has approximately 20 special schools and resource units for children with visual, auditory, mental, and physical handicaps. Current enrollment figures by handicapping condition were unavailable. However, previous enrollment was vision (35 students), hearing (88), mental (176), and physical (18) (Kann et al., 1989). There are no facilities in the country for children with severe disabilities.

Lesotho has twelve special schools (Stubbs, 1997). Enrollment figures by handicapping condition were unavailable. Lesotho's Ministry of Education, with support from international nongovernmental organizations and United Nations agencies, recently opened integration units for children with a variety of handicaps in eight of the country's ten districts.

Namibia's school for children with visual impairments has 71 students and its school for the hearing impaired has 185 students (Bruhns et al., 1995). Twenty-four specialist teachers work in these schools. Two schools and 15 specialist teachers serve 125 children with severe learning disabilities. Two additional schools staffed by 67 teachers provide instruction to 733 children with mild learning difficulties. Twelve schools and 16 teachers offer remedial education to 385 children with specific learning disabilities. Namibia also has 28 integration units attended by 507 children with moderate to mild disabilities and taught by 40 teachers.

In Tanzania, services for students with visual impairments are provided in twelve special schools and 23 integrated (18 primary, 5 secondary) schools that offer education to 979 children with visual disabilities (Possi & Mkaali, 1995; Tungaraza, 1994). Sixty-four specialist teachers and 157 regular education teachers provide education to children with visual handicaps. Services for children with auditory impairments are provided through 14 special schools and three integrated primary (one residential and two nonresidential) schools to approximately 980 pupils and staffed by 100 specialist and 26 regular class teachers. In addition, 6 schools serve 305 deaf-blind students. About 930 children with physical disabilities attend 61 specialist and integration units staffed by 185 specialist and regular class teachers. The vast majority of children with physical disabilities either attend schools in their communities or do not attend school at all. Tanzania also has four residential special schools for children with moderate mental handicaps and 15 nonresidential integrated units that serve 980 children with moderate to mild mental handicaps. Sixty-seven specialist and 128 regular class teachers teach these children. Twelve children with autism and 14 with cerebral palsy attend four units taught by 6 specialist teachers. Thousands of children with severe mental handicaps do not receive any schooling. In contrast, more than 90% of Tanzanian children with epileptic conditions attend ordinary schools (Whyte, 1995).

Uganda has at least 6 special schools and one integration unit which serve about 500 children with visual impairments, two special schools for 150 children with hearing impairments, and one special school for 124 students with physical handicaps (Ross, 1988). An estimated 32,134 children with mild to moderate disabilities are attending ordinary schools (Onen & Njuki, 1998). The Ugandan government's goal was to have the country's estimated 325,000 children with disabilities attend school in 1997 (Kristensen, 1997; Uganda Ministry of Education, 1992). However, the country lacked the resources for meeting this highly ambitious target then, and it still does today (Mpofu et al., 1997).

Zimbabwe's twenty special schools provide educational and rehabilitation services to 5,000 children with visual, hearing, physical, and mental disabilities. The country also has 162 integrated resource units: 69 for those with hearing disabilities, 46 with mental disabilities, and 47 with visual disabilities. A total of 1,315 children with disabilities are served by the integrated resource units: 552 with hearing impairments, 409 with mental impairments, and 354 with visual impairments. Additionally, about 4,300 children with moderate to mild generalized learning difficulties attend 270 part-time special classes in regular education settings. At least 50,000 children with learning difficulties receive part-time remedial education in classes or clinics in general education schools.

The current status of special education programs in Swaziland, Eriteria, Kenya, and Zambia is unknown. However, information from respondents to a survey on school psychology practices in these countries (Mpofu et al., 1997) suggests special education programs may be better established in Kenya than in other East and Southern African countries. Such programs generally are limited to urban areas in Zambia, and may not exist to any significant degree in Swaziland and Eriteria.

Although the need for more special education facilities in all of the East and Southern African countries is quite apparent, a paradox exists in that attendance is below capacity in many existing special education schools and units in some countries, including Tanzania and Lesotho (Kisanji, 1995; Stubbs, 1997). This under-utilization exists because the facilities are not well-known to parents of children with disabilities and parents in some rural communities are suspicious of their intended purposes. In addition, government departments and international aid agencies often established special education schools and units in certain communities in response to requests by local politicians or parochial interest groups, but without adequate consultation with traditional and other community leaders. Thus, resistance to utilizing these facilities often occurs regardless of their need.

Some countries in this region have mounted comprehensive community outreach programs aimed at educating citizens on the nature of disabilities, their prevention, and appropriate educational interventions. In addition, teachers have walked from village to village to locate children with disabilities to attend school (Kisanji, 1995). The teachers' door-to-door, village-to-village approach can effectively reach families and significant community leaders, and it often yielded larger enrollments of children with disabilities in areas that seem to have few if any such children.

FUTURE PROSPECTS OF SPECIAL EDUCATION IN EAST AND SOUTHERN AFRICA

Nearly all countries in East and Southern Africa provide some forms of special education programs. The work of Christian missionaries and nongovernmental agencies often resulted in the establishment of special education programs. The continued involvement of missionaries, although desired, is unlikely to match prior levels of involvement. Nongovernmental agencies increasingly are recognized by international agencies (like the United Nations and the World Bank) as effective implementers of needed social programs. Although their involvement is likely to continue for some years, their resources also are limited in time. Thus, special education programs in this large and important region must depend more heavily, if not exclusively, on local and regional resolve and resources.

A government's involvement in special education programs and teacher preparation programs (through policies enacted and funded by its legislature and implemented by its ministries of education) provides demonstrable evidence that they support special education as an essential component of its national education program. Although the degree to which federal governments are involved in special education programs differs among the twelve countries within this region, all are involved to some degree. However, beneficial policies often are enacted and either not funded or not implemented by ministries of education. For example, the governments of Uganda and Botswana both established policy underscoring the importance of school attendance among children with disabilities as a national priority. However, this policy remains to be implemented.

The adoption of the principle of universal primary education by these governments implicitly recognizes children with disabilities as having the right to education. This, and other positive trends in educational thinking, eventually can be expected to translate into more favorable policies and practices governing special education programs. Moreover, most governments continue to support the further development of their elementary and secondary regular education programs—conditions prerequisite to the strong support of special education programs. Thus, prospects for the continued growth and availability of special education programs in these countries are somewhat encouraging.

However, one should not underestimate impediments to the further development of sustainable special education programs in East and Southern Africa. These impediments include inadequate personnel and financial resources for the provision of basic and regular education and inadequate leadership from advocacy groups.

Given other pressing responsibilities, federal governments in this region are unlikely to prioritize special education programs without some form of external support. Uncertainty exists as to the willingness and commitment of some governments to fund special education programs at current or higher levels than that currently provided by international development agencies (like DANIDA and SIDA).

The sustainability of donor-supported special education programs in East and Southern Africa will depend on the extent to which donor agencies build into their aid packages policies and practices that cultivate a cadre of local personnel willing to lobby for future programs, to implement genuine partnerships with federal and regional government to establish and maintain special education programs, to employ phased donor-funding withdrawal, and to help developing vibrant self-advocacy organizations at the local and national levels. For example, the Swedish Federation for the Blind has financed an advisory project in Eastern Africa aimed at improving the organization and self-advocacy of persons with disabilities (Ross, 1988).

Greater involvement of parents and community members in founding special education schools and integration units would strengthen a sense of ownership for special education facilities in communities, leading to greater attendance and school retention. In addition, the importance of community education programs on disabilities to the future of special education programs in East and Southern Africa cannot be over-emphasized. Most parents of children with disabilities are not involved with any special interest groups or agencies providing special education services (Kisanji, 1995; Ross, 1988).

The significantly limited material and manpower resources within most of these countries constrain the establishment and growth of special education programs (Tungaraza, 1994; Ross, 1988). Most countries are grappling with the provision of basic education and health facilities. The countries have very few personnel specifically prepared to work with children with disabilities in either special or mainstream school settings. The future of special education programs in the region could be considerably enhanced if countries pooled resources to promote professional preparation and research on effective methods to promote basic education of students in special education.

REFERENCES

Bruhns, B., Murray, A., Kanguchi, T., & Nuukuawo, A. (1995). *Disability and rehabilitation in Namibia: A national survey.* Windhoek: The Namibian Economic Policy Research Unit.

Charema, J., & Peresuh, M. (1997). Support services for special needs educational needs: Proposed models for countries south of the Sahara. *African Journal of Special Needs Education, 1,* 76–83.

Devlieger, P. (1995). Why disabled? The cultural understanding of physical disability in an African society. In B. Ingstad & S.R. Whyte (Eds.), *Disability and culture* (pp. 94–106). Berkeley: University of California Press.

Jackson, H., & Mupedziswa, R. (1989). Disability and rehabilitation: Beliefs and attitudes among rural disabled people in a community based rehabilitation scheme in Zimbabwe. *Journal of Social Development in Africa, 1,* 21–30.

Kann, U., Mapolelo, D., & Nleya, P. (1989). *The missing children: Achieving basic education in Botswana.* Gaborone: NIR, University of Botswana.

Kisanji, J. (1997). The relevance of indigenous customary education principles in the education of special needs education policy. *African Journal of Special Needs Education, 1,* 59–74.

Kisanji, J. (1995). Interface between culture and disability in the Tanzania context: Part 1. *International Journal of Disability, Development and Education, 42,* 93–108.

Kristensen, K. (1997). School for all: A challenge to special needs education in Uganda–A brief country report. *African Journal of Special Needs Education, 2,* 25–28.

Mpofu, E., Zindi, F., Oakland, T., & Peresuh, M. (1997). School psychological practices in East and Southern Africa. *Journal of Special Education, 31,* 387–402.

Onen, N., & Njuki, E.P. (1998). *Special education in Uganda.* Unpublished manuscript.

Possi, M.K., & Mkaali, C.B. (1995). *A brief report on special education services in Tanzania.* Paper presented at the South-South-North Workshop. Kampala, Uganda.

Ross, D.H. (1988). *Educating handicapped young people in Eastern and Southern Africa.* Paris: UNESCO.

Saigh, P.A., & Oakland, T. (Eds.). (1989). *International perspectives on school psychology.* Hillsdale, NJ: Erlbaum.

Stubbs, S. (1997). Lesotho integrated education programme. *African Journal of Special Needs Education, 1,* 84–87.

Tungaraza, F.D. (1994). The development and history of special education in Tanzania. *International Journal of Disability, Development, and Education, 41,* 213–222.

Uganda Ministry of Education. (1992). *Government white paper on the education policy review commission report.* Kampala, Uganda: Author.

UNICEF. (1991). *Children and women in Zimbabwe: A situation analysis update, July 1985–July 1990.* Republic of Zimbabwe: Author.

UNICEF. (1996). *The state of the world's children: 1996.* Oxford: Oxford University Press.

Whyte, S.R. (1995). Constructing epilepsy: Images and contexts in East Africa. In B. Ingstad & S.R. Whyte (Eds.), *Disability and culture* (pp. 226–245). Berkeley: University of California Press.

SOVIET EDUCATION

Soviet Education is a journal of English-language translations that started publication in 1959. It made Soviet education literature available through English-language translations for the first time. The founding editors of *Soviet Education* were Myron Sharpe, Murray Yanowitch, and Fred Ablin. From 1967 through 1969, Seymour Rosen served as editor, followed by Harold Noah in 1970. The editorial load was shared with Beatrice Szekely, who assumed the full role of editor in the late 1970s.

A topical journal, *Soviet Education* draws material from Russian-language books and works in teacher training texts, educational psychology, sociology, comparative education, and educational administration. The journal tends to focus on educational policy issues. It is published monthly.

SOVIET UNION AND EASTERN EUROPE, SPECIAL EDUCATION IN THE

See RUSSIA SPECIAL EDUCATION IN.

SPACHE DIAGNOSTIC READING SCALE

See DIAGNOSTIC READING SCALE.

SPAN OF APPREHENSION

See PERCEPTUAL SPAN.

SPASTICITY

Spasticity is a type of cerebral palsy involving a lack of muscle control. Spastic children make up the largest group of the cerebral palsied, constituting 40 to 60% of the total.

Another term that has been used to refer to spastic cerebral palsy is pyramidal. This term was coined because the nerves involved are shaped like pyramids. Spastic cerebral palsy is produced by damage sustained to the nerve cell that is found in the motor cortex. The motor cortex is the gray matter of the brain containing nerve cells that initiate motor impulses to the muscles. The nerve cells have tracts that extend from the neuron in the cortex to the spinal cord. These cells eventually connect with nerve tracts that innervate the limb so that muscle movement can be carried out. If these nerve cells or tracts are injured, spasticity results.

Because spasticity can affect one or all four extremities, it is subdivided into several types. Monoplegia involves one extremity only, either an arm or leg. This type is extremely rare. Triplegia involves the impairment of three extremities; it is an unusual occurrence. Hemiplegia means that the abnormality is confined to half of the body, either the right or left side with the arm more involved than the leg. This is the most common locus of involvement. Bilateral hemiplegia or double hemiplegia involves weakness or paralysis of both sides of the body with the arms compromised more than the legs. Another type, quadriplegia, occurs in all four extremities with more disability of the legs than the arms. Diplegia means that all four limbs are affected, with minimal involvement of the arms. Paraplegia is neurologic dysfunction of the legs only. Spastic hemiplegias are the most common group, representing approximately 40% of the total cerebral palsied population, while spastic quadriplegias represent 19% of the total (Capute, 1978).

In mild cases, the spastic child has an awkward gait and may extend his or her arms for balance (Kerrigan & Annaswamy, 1997). In moderate cases, the child may bend the arms at the elbow and hold both arms close to the body with the hands bent toward the body. The legs may be rotated inwardly and flexed at the knees; this causes a "scissoring gait." In severe cases, the child may have poor body control and be unable to sit, stand, and walk without the support of braces, crutches, a walking frame, or other support (Kirk & Gallagher, 1979).

REFERENCES

Capute, A. (1978). Cerebral palsy and associated dysfunctions. In R. Haslam & P. Valletutti (Eds.), *Problems in the classroom* (pp. 149–163). Baltimore, MD: University Park Press.

Kerrigan, D.C. & Annaswammy, T.M. (1997). The functional significance of spasticity as assessed by gait analysis. *Journal of Head Trauma Rehabilitation, 12*(6), 29–39.

Kirk, S., & Gallagher, J. (1979). *Educating exceptional children* (3rd ed.). Boston: Houghton Mifflin.

See also Cerebral Palsy; Physical Disabilities

SPEARMAN, C.E. (1863–1945)

C.E. Spearman grew up in an English family of established status and some eminence; he became an officer in the regular army. He remained in the army until the age of 40, attaining the rank of major. He then obtained his PhD in Wundt's laboratory at Leipzig in 1908 at the age of 45. He was appointed to an academic position at University College, London, where he remained for the rest of his career.

Spearman is known for his theory of general intelligence and for a number of contributions to statistical methodology, including factor analysis, the Spearman rank correlation, and the Spearman-Brown prophecy formula. Spearman's primary interest was in the study of general intelligence, which he preferred to call g. His methodological innovations were directed toward the better definition and measurement of g.

Spearman's original two-factor theory (Spearman, 1904) included only g and a factor specific to each task. Subsequently, he expanded the theory to include group factors, which are factors common to a group of tasks independent of g. However, his major emphasis was always on g (Spearman, 1927). Subsequent development and mathematical refinement of factor analysis by Thurstone and others emphasized the group factors; g became obscured in the correlation among the primary factors. Today g is recognized as a second order factor accounting for the correlations among the primaries. There is still disagreement concerning its importance.

REFERENCES

Spearman, C.E. (1904). "General intelligence" objectively determined and measured. *American Journal of Psychology, 15,* 201–293.

Spearman, C.E. (1927). *The abilities of man: Their nature and measurement.* London: Macmillan.

See also **"g" Factor Theory; Intelligence; Reaction Time**

SPECIAL CLASS

The first special classes were established in the late 1800s and early 1900s as public school classes for the moderately retarded, deaf, hard of hearing, blind, emotionally disturbed, and physically handicapped. Esten (1900) stated that special classes for mentally retarded were established to provide slow-learning children with more appropriate class placement.

A special classroom or self-contained classroom for the exceptional can be defined as one that homogeneously segregates different children from normal children. Children are usually segregated along categorical groupings. As a result of Dunn's (1968) article on the detrimental aspects of special class placements for the mildly handicapped, students receiving special education in self-contained special classes today are usually those with more severe problems. However, Kirk and Gallagher (1983) report gifted exceptional students are also grouped into special classes according to interests and abilities. As low-incidence students demonstrate proficiency in specific skill areas, they are mainstreamed into regular classes.

REFERENCES

Dunn, L.M. (1968). Special education for the mildly handicapped: Is much of it justifiable? *Exceptional Children, 35,* 5–22.

Esten, R.A. (1900). Backward children in the public schools. *Journal of Psychoaesthenics, 5,* 10–16.

See also **Cascade Model of Special Education Services; Inclusion; Resource Room; Self-Contained Class; Service Delivery Models**

SPECIAL EDUCATION, EFFECTIVENESS OF

See EFFECTIVENESS OF SPECIAL EDUCATION.

SPECIAL EDUCATION, FEDERAL IMPACT ON

The impact of the federal government on special education occurs through two independent, but overlapping, functions: (1) the administration and development of programs, and (2) the compliance monitoring of state education agencies. The administration and development of programs involves the disbursement of discretionary grants and contracts as well as the disbursement of formula grant funds under Part B of the Individuals with Disabilities Education Act (IDEA) and under Part H and the Preschool Grant Program. Discretionary grants are awarded to individuals and organizations in states and territories on a competitive basis. Depending on the specific program for which awards are made, these funds are to be used for research, program/materials development, technical assistance, demonstration, or training. For the most part, these projects do not directly serve handicapped children and youths, but rather, are intended to support existing programs, demonstrate new or more effective ways of delivering services, train special education and related services personnel, or increase our knowledge of current or promising components of special education (i.e., research efforts).

In addition to discretionary grant awards and contracts, states also receive annual funds based on the total number of handicapped children and youths receiving special education and related services. The history of funding for the PART B entitlement program under IDEA, state grant program from 1977 to 1996, is shown in Table 1 below.

Each state education agency (SEA) must distribute at least 75% of the total funds to local education agencies to be used directly for the education of handicapped students. The remaining funds may be used by the SEA, with some portion going toward administrative costs. Thus federal funds are used to offset some of the additional costs associated with educating handicapped students.

Until 1994, children and youth with disabilities were also served under the Chapter 1 Handicapped Program. In October 1994, the Improving America's School Act (IASA) was enacted, which reauthorized the Elementary and Secondary Education Act of 1965 (ESEA). However, the Chap-

Table 1 IDEA, Part B State Grant Program: Funds Appropriated, 1977–96

Appropriation Year	IDEA, Part B State Grants[a]	Per Child Allocation[b]
1977	$ 251,770,000	$ 71
1978	566,030,000	156
1979	804,000,000	215
1980	874,190,000	227
1981	874,500,000	219
1982	931,008,000	230
1983	1,017,900,000	248
1984	1,068,875,000	258
1985	1,135,145,000	272
1986	1,163,282,000	279
1987	1,338,000,000	316
1988	1,431,737,000	332
1989	1,475,449,000	336
1990	1,542,610,000	343
1991	1,854,186,000	400
1992	1,976,095,000	410
1993	2,052,730,000	411
1994	2,149,686,000	413
1995	2,322,915,000[c]	418
1996	2,323,837,000	413[d]

[a]The figures from 1977 through 1994 include amounts appropriated to the Federated States of Micronesia and the Republic of the Marshall Islands. In 1995, those entities received no appropriations.
[b]The per child allocation excludes children and funds for the Outlying Areas and Bureau of Indian Affairs (BIA) and is based on the child count information available as of July 1 of the fiscal year.
[c]This amount includes $82,878,000 added to the Grants to States appropriation because of the elimination of the Chapter 1 Handicapped Program.
[d]This allocation was derived by dividing the total appropriations for the 50 States, District of Columbia, Outlying Areas, and BIA by the total number of children served in all of those areas.
Source: U.S. Department of Education, Office of Special Education Programs, Data Analysis System (DANS).

ter 1 Handicapped Program was not reauthorized. Beginning with the FY 1995 appropriation, all children with disabilities were served under programs authorized by IDEA. The IASA included a number of amendments to IDEA to provide for a smooth transition to serving all children. (U.S. Department of Education, 1997).

Part H of the Individuals with Disabilities Education Act (IDEA) was adopted by Congress in 1986. Part H was designed to address the needs of infants and toddlers with disabilities and their families through a "statewide system of coordinated, comprehensive, multidisciplinary, interagency programs providing appropriate early intervention services to all infants and toddlers with disabilities and their families" (20 U.S.C. §1476 (a)).

The increase in the number of infants and toddlers served under PART H (22.4 percent) since 1992 has been greater than the growth in the number of children served under Part B. The growth rate is, however, comparable to the number of 3–5 year olds served under Part B (U.S. Dept. of Education, 1997).

Thus one of the primary ways special education is impacted by the federal government is through a direct infusion of funds that assist state and local educational agencies in offering special education and related services, or through efforts that further state and local programs (discretionary grants and contracts).

The second major area in which the federal government impacts special education is through compliance monitoring. To accomplish this objective, special education programs engage in program administrative reviews that involve on-site and off-site reviews of information. Where deficiencies are found, corrective actions are requested from the SEA. The corrective actions report includes a description of the steps to be taken by the SEA, timelines for completion, and the documentation to be submitted verifying that deficiencies have been corrected. Should substantial noncompliance be noted, the U.S. Department of Education is authorized to withhold federal funds. Considerable leeway exists within the department's administration of its compliance monitoring efforts to ensure that each state receives funding. Nevertheless, the possibility that a state may not receive federal funds can be persuasive in altering special education programs in that state. Thus this is one further way in which special education is impacted.

Audette and Algozzine have suggested that the dearth of legislation monitoring, and regulations from the federal level have increased bureaucratic paperwork and procedures to the point of being a major hindrance: That special education is "costly rather than free." (Audette & Algozzine, 1997).

REFERENCES

Audette, B., & Algozzine, B. (1997). Re-inventing government? Let's re-invent special education. *Journal of Learning Disabilities, 30*(4), 378–383.

U.S. Department of Education. (1997). *Nineteenth Annual Report to Congress on the Implementation of the Individuals with Disabilities Education Act.* Washington DC: Author.

See also Demography of Special Education; Politics and Special Education; Special Education Programs

SPECIAL EDUCATION, GENERIC

See GENERIC SPECIAL EDUCATION.

SPECIAL EDUCATION, HISTORY OF

See HISTORY OF SPECIAL EDUCATION.

SPECIAL EDUCATION, PHILOSOPHERS' OPINIONS ABOUT

See PHILOSOPHY OF EDUCATION FOR THE HANDICAPPED.

SPECIAL EDUCATION, PROFESSIONAL STANDARDS FOR

See PROFESSIONAL STANDARDS FOR SPECIAL EDUCATORS.

SPECIAL EDUCATION, RACIAL DISCRIMINATION IN

See RACIAL DISCRIMINATION IN SPECIAL EDUCATION.

SPECIAL EDUCATION, SUPERVISION IN

See SUPERVISION IN SPECIAL EDUCATION.

SPECIAL EDUCATION, TEACHER TRAINING IN

The training and practice of special educators have undergone rapid development and change over the past three decades.

The reality of the 1990s is essentially economic in character. Given the increase in the number of children being served and the fact that federal, state, and local budgets do not have unlimited resources, the 1990s have become a period of retrenchment and uncertainty in special education. There is a clear and pressing need to increase the number of teachers qualified to work with handicapped children, but at the same time newly trained teachers are being asked to do more with less. Teachers in special education are being called on to be more resourceful, more organized, and more precise in creating, planning, and executing instructional interventions and more directly involved in general or regular education.

In addition to these broad political and economic factors, the quantity and quality of research in human learning and development and pedagogy has had an impact on the preparation of teachers for handicapped pupils. Out of the massive research and development efforts with handicapped and nonhandicapped children that began in the 1960s, special educators have acquired a substantial base of knowledge concerning effective instructional practices. With this large and growing body of information and the complex roles that special education teachers are currently being asked to assume, effective training of special educators in the 1990s and beyond will require greater breadth and depth of preparation than ever before.

While there is a lack of agreement concerning specific knowledge and skills that teachers of the handicapped should possess, the general parameters include the following: First, teachers need a firm foundation in general literacy and in the basic disciplines of the humanities, liberal arts, and sciences as prerequisite to entering the teaching profession (Denemark & Nutter, 1980). Second, special education teachers must be well versed in general education requirements as well as those specific to special education; i.e., they must be education generalists as well as education of the handicapped specialists (Reynolds, 1979). Their training should include acquiring knowledge of school development, basic academic skill curricula, instructional methods, including the effective use of computer-assisted instruction, and instructional and behavioral management strategies. In return, the inclusion movement has mandated that general educators have same training in special education. General education teacher license requirements in 22 states include a requirement that teachers have some coursework related to students with disabilities. Eleven states require some practical work with students as well as coursework (U.S. Dept. of Education, 1997).

Third, as a key to participation in inclusion efforts, special education teachers must function as team members and as consultants, providing interaction with the general education faculty on questions concerning handicapped pupils. Fourth, regardless of the nature and severity of a pupil's disability, all special education teachers must possess effective communication skills to work with parents of handicapped children.

Lastly, teacher training programs should provide extensive practical experience for their students. This practical experience should be initiated early in the students' training, with greater amounts of professional practice provided as students progress through the program (Scannell & Guenther, 1981).

The American Association of Colleges of Teacher Education Commission of Education for the Profession argues that the presently constituted teaching profession is, at best, a semiprofession (Howsam, Corrigan, Denemark, & Nash, 1976). The commission recommends a 5-year initial teacher preparation program combining the bachelor's and master's degrees, plus a sixth year of supervised internship to improve the quality of teacher education. Such an effort would enhance the profession of teaching and lead to outstanding pupil achievement. In view of these collective recommendations, it appears that preparation of special education teachers will require the extension of teacher education into graduate training.

Unfortunately, due to declining enrollments in teacher preparation programs and reductions in university budgets, few university faculties have decided to make their programs more rigorous by incorporating the recommendations of leaders in the area of teacher education and special education.

Attrition of special education teachers has been a major concern nationally. Moreover, lack of quality in preservice training has been related to teacher attrition rates. With the extensive and culturally competent (Miller, Miller, & Schroth, 1997) course work, practica, and internship training required in new programs, graduates will be better prepared to meet the challenges and demands of special education instruction. As a consequence, they may continue to teach handicapped youngsters for a longer period of time and in a more effective manner.

REFERENCES

Denemark, G., & Nutter, N. (1980). *The case for extended programs of initial teacher preparation.* Washington, DC: ERIC Clearinghouse on Teacher Education.

Howsam, R.B., Corrigan, D.C., Denemark, G.W., & Nash, R.J. (1976). *Education as a profession.* Report of the Bicentennial Commission on Education for the Profession of Teaching of the American Association of Colleges for Teacher Education. Washington, DC: American Association of Colleges for Teacher Education.

Miller, S. Miller, K.L., & Schroth, G. (1997). Teacher perceptions of multicultural training in preservice programs. *Journal of Instructional Psychology, 24*(4), 222–232.

Reynolds, M. (1979). *A common body of practices for teachers: The challenge of Public Law 94–142 to teacher education.* Minneapolis, MN: The National Support System Project.

Scannell, D., & Guenther, J.E. (1981). The development of an extended program. *Journal of Teacher Education, 32,* 7–12.

U.S. Department of Education. (1997). *Nineteenth Annual Report to Congress on the Implementation of the Individuals with Disabilities Act* (IDEA). Washington DC: Author.

See also **Human Resource Development; Teacher Effectiveness**

SPECIAL EDUCATION, TELECOMMUNICATION SYSTEMS IN

See TELECOMMUNICATION SYSTEMS IN SPECIAL EDUCATION.

SPECIAL EDUCATION AND POLITICS

See POLITICS AND SPECIAL EDUCATION.

SPECIAL EDUCATION INSTRUCTIONAL MATERIALS CENTERS (SEIMCS)

More than a decade before the passage of the Education for All Handicapped Children Act, the United States Office of Education recognized that one of the main obstacles to education of quality for handicapped students was the dearth of appropriate instructional materials and services both for the students and for those responsible for their education (Alonso, 1974). The federal government hoped to have established a network of service centers to address this problem by 1980.

The initiation of this effort began in 1963, when two projects were funded—one at the University of Southern California and the other at the University of Wisconsin—to serve as demonstration models for the development and dissemination of effective instructional materials and methods. From this modest beginning was to come 13 regional special education instructional materials centers (SEIMCs); four regional media centers for the deaf and hearing impaired (RMCs); a Clearinghouse on Handicapped and Gifted Children in the Educational Resources Information Center (ERIC) Network; an Instructional Ma-

terials Reference Center at the American Printing House for the Blind; and a National Center on Education Media and Materials for the Handicapped (NCEMMH).

The official scope of the centers was not strictly defined by the government. It was acknowledged that needs varied widely from one service area to another, and each program was encouraged to respond to its local situation appropriately and to take full advantage of the special strengths of its staff. In general, however, the activities tended to break down into three categories. The first involved identifying, collecting, evaluating, circulating, and, when necessary, developing or stimulating the development of instructional materials. The second category consisted of field services of various sorts: the training of teachers in the choice, evaluation, and use of instructional media and materials; coordination activities that established or improved the delivery of services to special educators and their students; and technical assistance to state departments of education to ensure the institutionalization of ongoing support services within each state. Finally, the centers were all involved to some extent in the systematic dissemination of information regarding current research, methods, and materials for special education.

REFERENCE
Alonso, L. (1974). *Final technical report of the Great Lakes region special education instructional materials center.* Washington, DC: Bureau of Education for the Handicapped. (ERIC Document Reproduction Service No. ED 094 507)

See also **On-Line Databases for Special Education; SpecialNet**

SPECIAL EDUCATION IN THE UNITED KINGDOM

See UNITED KINGDOM, SPECIAL EDUCATION IN THE.

SPECIAL EDUCATION PROGRAMS (SEP)

In 1982 Special Education Programs (SEP) succeeded the Office of Special Education as the primary federal agency responsible for overseeing federal initiatives in the education of the handicapped. Although SEP's mission has basically remained the same since the creation of the Bureau of Education for the Handicapped in 1966, its organizational structure has changed. Special Education Programs is divided into five divisions.

The Division of Assistance to States (DAS) has four areas of responsibility. Its primary function is to monitor the extent to which states are implementing the requirements of PL 94-142 and PL 89-313 state-operated programs. The DAS is also SEP's liaison with the Office for Civil Rights when parent complaints are received. The DAS provides technical assistance to states either directly through its program officers or through a national network of regional resource centers. Finally, DAS oversees the awarding of grants to centers that serve the deaf-blind.

The Division of Innovation and Development (DID) carries out SEP's mission for generating new information to help the handicapped. The DID administers several grant competitions.

The Division of Personnel Preparation administers grant programs to prepare special educators and related services personnel, parents of handicapped children, and doctoral-level professionals, among others, to serve the needs of handicapped students.

The Division of Educational Services is responsible for grant projects that develop model programs in the areas of early childhood education, youth employment, services for the severely handicapped, transitional services for students changing their least restrictive environment placement, and captioning of films for the hearing impaired.

The Division of Program Analysis and Planning has responsibility for managing the planning and budgetary processes within SEP.

The current address of SEP is U.S. Department of Education, Special Education Programs, 400 Maryland Avenue, SW, Washington, DC 20202.

See also **Office of Special Education**

SPECIALNET

SpecialNet, is an education-oriented computer-based communication network in the United States, and is operated by the National Association of State Directors of Special Education. SpecialNet makes it possible for its more than 2000 subscriber agencies to use the system to send electronic mail (messages, forms, reports, questions, and answers) instantaneously to one or many participants. The system also contains electronic bulletin boards, which are topical displays of various information bases, administered by content experts around the country

SpecialNet can be accessed on any computer. Access through a local or toll-free 800 number is available nationwide via the GTE Telenet public data network, through which SpecialNet information is transmitted and stored. Access to SpecialNet is obtained through an annual subscription fee. Further charges accrue for on-line time spent accessing the system. SpecialNet may be contacted at LRP Publications, 747 Dresher Road, Suite 500, Horsham, PA, 19044; 1-800-341-7874, or http://www.lrp.com.

See also **On-Line Databases for Special Education; Special Education Instructional Materials Centers**

SPECIAL OLYMPICS

See OLYMPICS, SPECIAL.

SPECIAL SERVICES IN THE SCHOOLS (SSS)

Published by Haworth Press (New York City), *Special Services in the Schools* (*SSS*) is a quarterly, refereed journal with an applied focus. It is now in its seventh volume. The *SSS* is intended to be read by multidisciplinary professional audiences who provide special services in schools and related educational settings, including school psychologists, guidance counselors, consulting teachers, social workers, and speech and language clinicians. It is the journal's policy to disseminate available information of direct relevance to these professionals. As such, information published in *SSS* includes reviews of relevant research and literature, descriptions and evaluations of programs, viewpoints on latest trends in policy development, and guidelines for designing, implementing, and evaluating special service programs.

Articles are aimed at being informative and instructive to special educators, psychologists, counselors, nurses, social workers, speech and language clinicians, physical and occupational therapists, and school supervisors and administrators. The material is intended to assist these professionals in performing a wide range of service delivery tasks.

Manuscripts that focus on the topical areas and service delivery tasks noted are routinely considered for publication. All manuscripts undergo blind review by editorial consultants.

SPECIFIC LEARNING DISABILITIES

See LEARNING DISABILITIES.

SPEECH

In the context of special education, the word speech may have two different meanings. Sometimes, it is used to refer to the whole of linguistic skills. Such is the case in compounds such as speech pathologist and speech therapy. In other cases, the meaning is narrower, with the word referring to spoken language. The use of the word speech to denote the whole of verbal abilities is indicative of the cardinal importance of spoken language. Oral language is by far the most frequently used form of verbal communication. It is also the first linguistic ability to be acquired by the child.

Speech (i.e., spoken language) is produced by means of the speech organs. These organs make up parts of the respiratory system and the digestive tract. Usually, expiratory air is used to generate audible speech sounds. If air from the lungs activates the larynx, voiced sounds such as vowels or voiced consonants are produced. If the vocal cords are kept apart and consequently do not vibrate during exhalation, egressive air is turned into voiceless consonants (such as /s/ or /f/). Speech movements are rapid, complex, and finely timed sequences of gestures. Therefore, it takes the child several years to learn to perform them.

See also **Language Disorders; Speech Disorders**

SPEECH, ABSENCE OF

Many children use their first recognizable word at age one and by two are using some type of sentence. When a child has not started speaking by age two, parents often become concerned about the child's development. However, it is not unusual for the normally developing child not to use his or her first word until some time after the second birthday. However, if a child has no speech by age five, it is likely that a serious difficulty exists (Bloodstein, 1984).

The most common cause of a lack of speech is a cognitive disability. While many children exhibiting severe cognitive disabilities have the potential to develop some language, those with a profound disability are likely to have no speech throughout their lives (Robinson & Robinson, 1976). Cognitive disabilities may sometimes be due to genetic factors. In other instances, traumatic brain injuries are the known cause of intellectual difficulty. Children with intellectual disabilities who do develop language typically do so in much the same manner as normally developing children but slower (Naremore & Dever, 1975; Van Riper & Erickson, 1996). They do, however, tend to exhibit limitations in their vocabulary and syntax usage.

Congenital deafness is another possible cause of a child exhibiting no speech. When a child is born with a profound hearing loss, he or she does not generally develop speech without special intervention. A number of children are born with some degree of hearing loss, but the impairment is not so severe that they cannot use hearing for the development of speech and language. However, a child with profound deafness typically experiences severe problems in developing speech because they have no way of monitoring their own speech production. Surprisingly, a profoundly deaf child's difficulty with hearing is often not noticed until the child is about age two and has not spoken his or her first word. This is due in part to the fact that many children with hearing impairments appear to go through the babbling stage in much the same way that children with hearing do.

Once a hearing loss is identified, most children with hearing impairments are fitted with a hearing aid. If the child has more than a 90 dB loss, he or she will probably not learn speech and language through hearing alone. The speech and language training of some children begins with the oral method, where language instruction is carried out primarily by requiring the child to lip read and speak. During the last 20 to 25 years, however, language instruction for children who are deaf has changed. Now most children are exposed to a sign language system once they are identified. It is important to make a distinction between speech and language when referring to children with hearing impairments because many children with profound deafness acquire language without having usable speech.

An additional problem that can cause an absence of speech is the presence of social/emotional disturbances, specifically childhood schizophrenia and early infantile autism (Van Riper & Erickson, 1996). Typically, a child with schizophrenia appears to develop normally for the first few years of life, and then begins to regress, possibly losing all language and speech. Schizophrenia, characterized by periods of remission, has been found to be resistant to treatment. Unlike schizophrenia, autism seems to be present in a child from birth. Many children with autism fail to develop language. Language usage that does develop can be quite deviant. Some children with autism have been known to speak fully formed sentences, but only once or twice in their lifetimes. Others develop what is known as echolalic speech, where they parrot back what is spoken to them. Other children do use some sentences meaningfully, but these seem to be memorized strings of words and are often simple demands. A smaller percentage of children with autism eventually attain a fair degree of speech and language.

In the past, many children who did not acquire speech were institutionalized, receiving little or no educational services. With the advent of PL 94-142, many of these children were able to live at home and were provided schooling on a regular basis. Continued refinement of public educational laws (e.g., Individual with Disabilities Education Act Revisions of 1997) and a broader base of services have resulted in marked improvement in the communication skills of a number of who have difficulty in this area.

REFERENCES

Bloodstein, O. (1984). *Speech pathology: An introduction.* Boston: Houghton Mifflin.

Fuller, C.W. (1975). Maternal deprivation and developmental language disorders. *Speech & Hearing Review: A Journal of New York State Speech & Hearing Association, 7,* 9–23.

Naremore, R.C., & Dever, R.B. (1975). Language performance of educable mentally retarded and normal children at five age levels. *Journal of Speech & Hearing Research, 18,* 92.

Robinson, N.M., & Robinson, H.B. (1976). *The mentally retarded child* (2nd ed.). New York: McGraw-Hill.

Van Riper, C., & Erickson, R.L. (1996). *Speech correction: An introduction to speech pathology and audiology* (9th ed.). Boston: Allyn & Bacon.

See also Autism; Elective Mutism; Mutism; Speech Therapy

SPEECH AND LANGUAGE HANDICAPS

See COMMUNICATION DISORDER; LANGUAGE DISORDERS.

SPEECH-LANGUAGE PATHOLOGIST

Speech-language pathologist is the recognized title of a professional who evaluates and treats persons with speech and/or language disorders. There is some confusion about this title because there are other equivalent titles for speech-language pathologist including speech (-language) therapist, speech pathologist, and speech (-language) clinician. In addition, speech-language pathologists sometimes use the informal abbreviated title of SLP. Different titles are used depending on the preferences of speech-language pathologists as well as the particular work settings (schools vs. hospitals, etc.). Different titles do *not* necessarily reflect any differences in educational or skill levels.

See also Communication Disorders; Speech Therapy

SPEECH-LANGUAGE SERVICES

The provision of services to children and adults who have speech and/or language disorders is a complex process. According to Cleland and Swartz (1982), delivery of services includes such factors as funding, transportation, and consumer resistance, in addition to problems of keeping service providers up to date in the latest techniques and tools. Speech and language services are provided in a variety of settings (Van Riper and Erickson, 1996), but always by professionals trained as speech pathologists having appropriate certification or a state license. The greatest number of speech pathologists are employed in school settings, ranging from preschool through high school. Services provided include screening for speech and hearing disorders, diagnosis, treatment, and referral for more complex disorders. Since children make up the caseload in public schools, the majority of disorders treated are those concerning speech, language, voice, and stuttering. Many hospitals provide speech and language services. Speech clinics are usually established in rehabilitation departments. Speech-language pathologists work with occupational and physical therapists to treat people with physical disorders. Sometimes hospitals also provide services for children, thus offering an alternative to the free services of public schools.

REFERENCES

Cleland, C.C., & Swartz, J.E. (1982). *Exceptionalities through the lifespan.* New York: Macmillan.

Van Riper, C., & Erickson, R.L. (1996). *Speech correction: An introduction to speech pathology and audiology* (9th ed.). Boston: Allyn & Bacon.

See also Speech Therapists; Speech Therapy

SPEECH SYNTHESIZER

A speech synthesizer is an electronic device that attempts to duplicate the human voice. Essentially, it allows a machine to talk to a human being. Of course, a human being must program the synthesizer and tell it what to say.

There are two different techniques for producing speech output that account for almost all the current synthesizer designs. The first is called linear predictive coding (LPC), which attempts to make an electronic model of the human voice. It creates tones much like those of the human vocal folds. These tones are passed through a set of filters that shape the tones into sounds the way that the articulators (tongue, lips, teeth, etc.) shape tones into sounds. This is a popular technique because it requires only enough computer memory to store the filter configurations and therefore is relatively inexpensive to make. Sound quality is acceptable but not realistic because the modeling of the voice is not exact enough to duplicate all the subtle vocal characteristics of human speech. The result is a machinelike speech quality.

The second method of producing speech is referred to as digitized speech. Actually, digitized speech is not synthesized speech. In digitized speech, the sound waves of the speech signal rather than the throat positions are recorded. These waves are then digitized—converted to digital codes and played back when needed. The advantage to this method is that the speech quality is good, sounding like a high-quality tape recorder. Nonetheless, it still takes time for the average listener to adjust and understand synthesized speech (Venkatagiri, 1994). The disadvantage is that great amounts of memory are required to store the speech waves.

Aside from the industrial application of speech synthesizers, the synthesizers are being used as communication devices for nonspeaking handicapped individuals and to prompt handicapped individuals using remediation software (Lundberg, 1995).

REFERENCES

Lundberg, I. (1995). The computer as a tool of remediation in the education of students with reading disabilities. *Learning Disability Quarterly, 18*(2), 89–99.

Venkatagiri, H.S. (1994). Effect of sentence length and exposure on the intelligibility of synthesized speech. *American Journal of Speech-Language Pathology, 4,* 36–45.

See also Augmentative Communication Systems; Computer Use with the Handicapped

SPEECH THERAPY

Speech therapy includes all efforts to ameliorate disordered speech. Treatment activities include attempts to improve the speech of persons who have never spoken normally (habilitation) as week as to improve the speech of persons who formerly had normal speech (rehabilitation). A variety of treatment approaches are used, depending on the speaker's age, speech disorder, and the professional training and experience of the speech pathologist. Speech therapy usually includes teaching a person with a speech disorder to speak differently. Concerning adults and older children, however, therapy may consist of play activities during which treatment is indirect.

Although many research investigations have been conducted into the nature and treatment of speech (and language) disorders, much remains unknown. Therapy remains, therefore, often more of an "art" than a science. The speech pathologist must often rely more on intuition and experience than on research results. Often, no attempt is made to determine the cause of the speech disorder because, in most cases, the cause(s) cannot be found (e.g., Van Riper and Erickson, 1996). Although some speech disorders can be completely "cured" so that no traces of the original behavior remain, some speech disorders cannot be completely eradicated. For instance, some children and adults who stutter will continue to have vestiges of stuttering despite successful speech therapy.

Clients receive therapy in group and/or individual sessions, and therapy may be short-term (a few sessions) or long-term (several years), depending on the nature and severity of the disorder. The length and frequency of therapy sessions also depend on a variety of factors.

Speech-language pathologists typically assess clients before therapy actually begins, although a period of "diagnostic therapy" may also be used to help determine the nature of the disorder. Sometimes, clients are referred to other professionals by the speech-language pathologist (e.g., audiologists, dentists, physicians.).

REFERENCE

Van Riper, C., & Erickson, R.L. (1996). *Speech correction: An introduction to speech pathology and audiology.* Boston: Allyn and Bacon.

See also **Augmentative Communication Systems; Communication Disorders; Speech-Language Pathologist**

SPELLING DISABILITIES

Spelling is a traditional element of the elementary school curriculum and an integral part of the writing process. The primary goal of spelling instruction for both handicapped and nonhandicapped students is to make the act of correctly spelling words so automatic that it requires only a minimal amount of conscious attention. If students master the ability to spell words with maximum efficiency and minimum effort, it is assumed that they will be able to devote more of their attention, and consequently more of their effort, to higher order writing processes such as purpose, content, and organization (Graham, 1982).

It is commonly believed that the majority of students who are labeled handicapped exhibit spelling problems. This is particularly the case for handicapped students with reading difficulties (Lennox & Siegal, 1993).

Spelling instruction for the handicapped has, in large part, been based on the use or modification of traditional spelling procedures and techniques. Although handicapped students may not progress as rapidly through the spelling curriculum or master all of the skills taught to normally achieving students, their spelling programs commonly emphasize the traditional skills of (1) mastering a basic spelling vocabulary; (2) determining the spelling of unknown words through the use of phonics and spelling rules; (3) developing a desire to spell words correctly; (4) identifying and correcting spelling errors; and (5) using the dictionary to locate the spelling of words. There is considerable

controversy, however, surrounding the issue of which skills should receive primary emphasis. Some experts, for example, recommend that a basic spelling vocabulary should form the core of the spelling program, while others have argued that spelling instruction should take advantage of the systematic properties of English orthography and stress the application of phonics and spelling rules (Graham, 1983).

A final point concerns the use of behavioral and cognitive procedures. Although the evidence is not yet conclusive, spelling procedures based on behavioral and/or cognitive principles appear to be particularly effective with handicapped students. McLaughlin (1982) found, for example, that the spelling accuracy of students in a special class improved as a result of group contingencies. In terms of cognitive procedures, Harris, Graham, and Freeman (1986) found that strategy training improved learning disabled students' spelling performance and, in one study condition, improved their ability to predict how many words would be spelled correctly on a subsequent test. Others have found that computers assist in spelling skill acquisition in a meaningful way (Gordon, Vaughn, Schumon & Shay, 1993; Van Daal & Van der Leij, 1992).

REFERENCES

Gordon, J., Vaughn, S., & Schumon, J.S., & Shay (1993). Spelling in instruction: A review of literature and implications for instruction for student with learning disabilities. *Learning Disabilities Research and Practice, 8*(3), 175–181.

Graham, S. (1982). Composition research and practice: A unified approach. *Focus on Exceptional Children, 14,* 1–16.

Graham, S. (1983). Effective spelling instruction. *Elementary School Journal, 83,* 560–568.

Harris, K., Graham, S., & Freeman, S. (1986). *The effects of strategy training and study conditions on metamemory and achievement.* Paper presented at the American Educational Research Association, San Francisco.

Lennox, C., & Siegal, L.S. (1993). Visual and phonological spelling errors in subtypes of children with learning disabilities. *Applied Psycholinguistics, 14*(4), 473–488.

McLaughlin, T. (1982). A comparison of individual and group contingencies on spelling performance with special education students. *Child and Family Behavior Therapy, 4,* 1–10.

Van Daal, V.H., & Van der Leij, A. (1992). Computer-based reading and spelling practice for children with learning disabilities. *Journal of Learning Disabilities, 25*(3), 186–195.

See also **Writing Remediation; Written Language of the Handicapped**

SPERRY, ROGER W. (1913–1994)

Born to a middle class family in Hartford, Connecticut on August 20, 1913, Sperry dedicated his professional life to understanding two basic questions in psychology: 1) what is consciousness? and 2) what roles do nature and nurture play in the regulation of behavior? Educated at Oberlin College in Ohio (BS in English and MS in psychology), Chicago (PhD in Zoology), and Harvard (post-doctoral fellowship in psychology), Sperry always went against the conventional wisdom of his day, tending to question established fact through simple but brilliant studies. Most of his important studies were completed as Hixson Professor of Psychobiology at the California Institute of Technology.

Together with surgeons Joseph Bogen and Phillip Voegl, Sperry designed a series of studies aimed at discovering the functions of the two sides of the brain and if the brain was as hard-wired as the peripheral nervous system. About a dozen patients with intractable epilepsy had their corpus callosum severed in what is now called "split-brain" preparation. Over numerous studies, some of which are still are still being carried out, it was discovered that the brain was indeed hard-wired, much like the peripheral nervous system. Further, it was found that the left hemisphere was primarily responsible for verbal information while the right hemisphere controlled visual information.

Additional studies revealed that the patients had two separate minds. Hence, their behavior was not integrated. After further study, Sperry concluded that consciousness was a function of the integration of both sides of the brain simultaneously. Also, he believed that the consciousness emerged from brain function and, in turn, had a downward control on the brain function from which it had been produced.

For his scientific work, Sperry shared the 1981 Nobel Prize in Medicine and received the highest awards in the disciplines he worked in, including psychology, neuroscience, and philosophy with over 300 publications, close to 100 students doing research in 9 different continents, Sperry's contributions extend way beyond his half century of research and modern-day psychology. He died at the age of 80 in Pasadena, California from complications of ALS. He is survived by his wife and two children.

REFERENCES

Puente, A.E. (1995). Roger Sperry (1913–1994). *American Psychologist.*

Sperry, R.W. (1952) Neurology and the mind-brain problem. *American Scientist, 40,* 2910312.

Sperry, R.W. (1982). Some effects of disconnecting the cerebral hemispheres. *Science, 217,* 1223–1226.

SPINA BIFIDA

Spina bifida (myelomeningocele) is a congenital abnormality present at birth. The defect begins early in embryogenesis (the first 30 days of gestation), as the central nervous system is developing with a failure of the spinal cord to close over the lower end (Haslam & Valletutti, 1975). Without such closure, normal development of the spinal column cannot occur; the spinal cord and covering membranes bulge out and block further development.

It is a fairly common developmental anomaly present in .2 to .4 per 1000 live births (Haslam & Valletutti, 1975). The risks increase dramatically to 1/20 to 1/40 following the birth of one affected infant. It is possible to test for spina bi-

fida through amniocentesis. The amniotic fluid is analyzed by testing for abnormally high alpha fetal protein and acetyl cholinesterase levels. Both are normally present in the fetal cerebrospinal fluid, which, in myelomeningocele, leaks into the amniotic fluid (Behrman & Vaugh, 1983).

Detection at birth is due to the presence of a large bulging lesion or swelling, with or without a skin covering, at the lower part of the back (lumbosacral region). It is the damage to or the defect of the spinal cord that results in a variety of handicapping conditions. Eighty percent of children with spina bifida have hydrocephalus, a condition caused by the accumulation of fluid in the ventricles of the brain (Haslam & Valletutti, 1975). If left untreated, hydrocephalus can result in severe mental retardation. Treatment consists of diverting the cerebrospinal fluid to some other area of the body, usually the atria of the heart or the abdominal cavity (Wolraich, 1983).

Children with spina bifida will require extensive medical, orthopedic, and educational services. This is often expensive and time consuming, creating frustration and financial hardship for the family. Educational programming for these children must consider the need for personnel trained in toileting techniques and physical therapy. While some children with spina bifida may require a self-contained special education class setting, others who are less severely impaired cognitively may be able to perform successfully in a mainstream classroom with support services.

Incidence of spina bifida can be significantly reduced owing to the discovery of a strong link between neural tube defects in general and folic acid deficiency. Folic acid is now known to protect against such defects, although the mode of action is not clear. Women who have had one child with spina bifida who take folic acid supplements during subsequent pregnancies have a 70% reduction in recurrence. Further, folic acid supplements can reduce incidence of new cases of spina bifida by 50%. Thus, all women who may become pregnant are advised to take daily folic acid supplements both before and during the first 12 weeks of pregnancy. Such supplements are now planned for common foods such as bread, flour, and rice (Liptak, 1997).

REFERENCES

Behrman, R.E., & Vaughn, V.C. (1983). Defects of closure tube. In W.B. Nelson (Ed.), *Nelson's textbook of pediatrics* (pp. 1560–1561). Philadelphia: Saunders.

Haslam, R.A., & Valletutti, P.J. (1975). *Medical problems in the classroom: The teacher's role in diagnosis and management.* Baltimore, MD: University Park Press.

Liptak, G.S. (1997). Neural tube defects. In M.L. Batshaw (Ed.) *Children with disabilities* (4th ed.) (pp. 529–552). Baltimore Brookes.

Wolraich, M. (1983). Myelomeningocele. In J.A. Blackman (Ed.), *Medical aspects of developmental disabilities in children birth to three: A resource for special service providers in the educational setting.* Iowa City: University of Iowa.

See also **Hydrocephalus**

SPINAL CORD INJURY

Damage to the spinal cord frequently, but not always, result in paralysis or paresis to the extremities. The specific impairment or dysfunction that occurs in the extremities depends on the corresponding spinal level and the severity of the injury. In some situations, the injury may be only temporary and the individual may not experience any permanent effects. More often, the injury results in permanent damage and loss of function in the involved extremities.

The most common causes of spinal cord injury are accidents in or about the home, falls, bullet wounds, sports injuries, or motor vehicle accidents. The injury is often associated with fractured bones of the spinal column but also may occur from dislocation of one or more of these bones on the other. When the spinal cord is damaged, the nervous pathways between the body and the brain are interrupted. All forms of sensation (e.g., proprioception, touch, temperature, pain) and muscular control are typically lost below the level of the damage. Although nerves outside the spinal cord may be repaired or heal spontaneously, damaged nerves within the spinal cord will not regenerate. If the injury is low on the spinal cord (usually below the first thoracic vertebra), only the lower extremities are involved. This type of injury is called paraplegia. If the injury is higher on the spinal cord (cervical level), all four extremities and the trunk may be involved; this condition is referred to as quadriplegia. Injury to the highest levels of the cervical spine may cause death because of the loss of innervation to the diaphragm. Occasionally, only one side of the cord is damaged. This type of condition is called Brown-Sequard syndrome. Loss of proprioception and motor paralysis occur on the same side as the injury, while loss of pain, temperature, and touch sensations occur on the opposite side.

During the initial stage of spinal cord trauma, autonomic and motor reflexes below the level of the injury are suppressed. This flaccid paralysis is called spinal shock and may last from several hours to 3 months. As the spinal shock recedes, spinal reflexes return in a hyperactive state. This spasticity or muscular hypertonicity may vary initially at different times of the day or in response to different stimuli, but it becomes more consistent within one year of the injury. The most common form of acute treatment is traction to the spinal column to bring about a realignment and healing of the fractured or displaced vertebrae. Special beds may be used to permit people in traction to be turned from their back to their abdomen, thereby reducing the chance of pressure sores (decubitus).

Artificial ventilation usually is necessary for persons with injuries at or above the level of the third cervical vertebra (C3). Decreased respiratory capacity is present in injuries from C4 through T7 (the seventh thoracic vertebra), making coughing difficult and often necessitating suctioning when the patient gets a respiratory infection. Dizziness or blackout may occur from pooling of blood in the abdomen and lower extremities when a person is first brought to an upright position following a period of immobilization. This is a normal reaction and is avoided through the aid of a reclining wheelchair or a tilt table that allows gradual adjustment to a full upright position.

Rehabilitation procedures begin within a few days of the injury and usually continue for several weeks or months after the healing process is complete. The general goal of rehabilitation is to improve the physical capacities and develop adapted techniques to promote as independent a lifestyle as possible. Unfortunately, rehabilitation's goals all too often focus on participation rather than performance (Dudgeon, Massagli, & Ross, 1997). Educational performance for a person with a spinal cord injury is hampered only by the individual's physical limitations. However, the individual may have problems with self-image, coping strategies, accessibility support, and unresolved feelings, all of which may affect educational performance (Mulcahey, 1992). Persons with high-level injuries may require numerous assistive devices such as an electronic typewriter with mouthstick or mechanical page turner. Persons with low-level injuries may not require any specialized assistance to benefit from education. Counseling to help a person adjust to new physical impairments and to develop future vocational pursuits may also be in order.

REFERENCES

Dudgeon, B.J., Massagli, T.L., & Ross, B.W. (1997) Educational participation of children with spinal cord injury. *American Journal of Occupational Therapy, 51*(7), 553–561.

Mulcahey, M.J. (1992). Returning to school after spinal cord injury: Perspectives from four adolescents. *American Journal of Occupational Therapy, 46*(4), 305–312.

See also Paraplegia; Quadriplegia

SPINOCEREBELLAR DEGENERATION

See FRIEDREICH'S ATAXIA.

SPITZ, RENE ARPAD (1887–1974)

Rene Arpad Spitz, educated in his native Hungary and in the United States, was a leading representative of psychoanalysis in the United States. He served on the faculty of the New York Psychoanalytic Institute, was professor of psychiatry at City College, City University of New York and the University of Colorado, and was clinical professor of psychiatry at Lenox Hill Hospital in New York City. The author of some 60 monographs and papers, Spitz is best known for his extensive studies of infant development.

REFERENCES

Spitz, R.A. (1962). *A genetic field theory of ego formation.* New York: International Universities Press.

Spitz, R.A., & Cobliner, W.G. (1966). *The first year of life.* New York: International Universities Press.

SPLINTER SKILL

See IDIOT SAVANT.

SPLIT-BRAIN RESEARCH

The technique of cerebral commissurotomy (split-brain surgery) was first introduced by Van Wagenen in 1940 as a surgical solution for severe and intractible forms of epilepsy. Van Wagenen performed the operation on approximately 2 dozen cases, hoping to be able to restrict the abnormal electrical activation characteristic of epilepsy to a single hemisphere. Unfortunately, the early operations were not successful and the procedure was largely abandoned until the early 1960s, when it was taken up by Roger Sperry working in collaboration with Joseph Bogen and Philip Vogel (Beaumont, 1983). The refined operation proved to be effective in many cases and, more important from scientific perspective, the procedure allowed a unique opportunity to study cerebral organization. Sperry's work with split-brain patients was deemed so important that he shared the Nobel Prize in Medicine in 1984. This award appropriately reflects the tremendous advances that were made in the neurosciences following this seminal work.

The technique of cerebral commissurotomy involves the complete section of the corpus callosum, including the anterior and hippocampal commissures in the massa intermedia. This technique effectively isolates each half of the cortex and prevents transfer of information from one side of the brain to the other. Despite the operation's dramatic nature, postsurgical patients appear to function quite well. Fairly sophisticated testing procedures are necessary to isolate and identify the effects of surgery.

Detailed study of postsurgical split-brain patients reveals that, in fact, a number of problems do exist for these patients (Springer & Deutsch, 1981). The patients frequently report trouble with associating names and faces. This may be due to the differential loci for naming and facial recognition, with the assignment of names occurring in the left hemisphere and the recognition of faces more intimately linked to the right hemisphere. Patients also report difficulty with geometry, and many complain of memory loss. Finally, many postsurgical patients report cessation of dreaming; however, this has not been supported empirically and these patients continue to show REM sleep postsurgically.

Levy and her colleagues have completed a number of studies with split-brain patients employing chimeric stimulae (Levy, Trevarthen, & Sperry, 1972). These are stimulus items that are composed by joining two half-stimuli. The stimuli are presented in such a way that each half goes to the isolated contralateral hemisphere. On the basis of these studies, Levy has argued that the left hemisphere is best described as analytic while the right is best described as holistic.

Split-brain patients make ideal subjects for dichotic listening experiments in which different stimuli are presented simultaneously in each ear. In addition, for those patients who receive a commissurotomy, divided visual field studies can be employed with less concern for saccadic eye movements. However, considerable experimental skill is necessary to avoid the phenomenon of cross-cuing. This occurs when a patient deliberately or inadvertently develops strategies for delivering information to both hemispheres simultaneously. For example, a subject who is palpating a comb may rub the teeth of the comb with the left hand. Although the tactile information will reach only the right hemisphere in the split-brain patient, the associated sound goes to both ears and may reach the left hemisphere and allow for linguistic identification.

Increasingly, neurosurgeons are performing partial commissurotomies with good success. These procedures allow still more detailed information about the localization of transference fibers in the corpus callosum. For example, it has become clear that somatosensory information is transmitted via the anterior corpus callosum while the rear portion, the splenium, transfers visual information. In addition, there is an indication that some perceptual judgements may be made sub-cortically (Corballis, 1994).

The work done to date on split-brain patients may offer important clues to help the teacher better understand and educate the child with special needs. Levy (1982) has used split-brain data to develop a model of handwriting posture; Obrzut and Hynd (1981) have applied these findings on cerebral lateralization to children with learning disabilities; and Hartlage (1975) has developed a plan for predicting the outcome of remedial educational strategies based on a model of cerebral lateralization. Perhaps it is only through understanding how each half of the brain works that we will ever approach an understanding how it works as a whole: a concept supported fully by Sperry (Corballis, 1998).

REFERENCES

Beaumont, J.G. (1983). *Introduction to neuropsychology.* New York: Guilford.

Corballis, M.C. (1994). Split decisions: Problems in the interpretation of results from commissurotomized subjects. *Behavioral Brain Research, 64*(1), 163–172.

Hartlage, L.C. (1975). Neuropsychological approaches to predicting outcome of remedial educational strategies for learning disabled children. *Pediatric Psychology, 3,* 23–28.

Levy, J. (1982). Handwriting posture and cerebral organization: How are they related? *Psychological Bulletin, 91,* 589–608.

Levy, J., Trevarthen, C., & Sperry, R.W. (1972). Perception of bilateral chimeric figures following hemispheric disconnection. *Brain, 95,* 61–78.

Obrzut, J.E., & Hynd, G.W. (1981). Cognitive development and cerebral lateralization in children with learning disabilities. *International Journal of Neuroscience, 14,* 139–145.

Springer, S.P., & Deutsch, G. (1981). *Left brain, right brain.* San Francisco: Freeman.

See also Cerebral Dominance

SPORTS FOR THE HANDICAPPED

Currently, federal mandates regulate physical education services and sports opportunities for individuals with disabilities. IDEA requires a free appropriate public school education, which includes instruction in physical education, in the least restrictive environment. Section 504 of the Rehabilitation Act, specifies nondiscrimination on the basis of handicap, and states that equal opportunity and equal access must be provided for handicapped persons, specifically including physical education services, intramurals, and athletics. The most direct mandate for sports opportunities is the Amateur Sports Act of 1978 (PL 95-606) (DePauw, 1984).

As a result of this law, the U.S. Olympic Committee initiated a Handicapped in Sports Committee, which changed its name to the Committee on Sports for the Disabled (COSD) in 1983 (DePauw, 1984). Committee membership consists of two representatives from each major national organization in the United States offering sports opportunities for disabled individuals. At least 20% of COSD members must be, or have been, actively participating disabled athletes.

Sports activities for the handicapped are sponsored by many nonschool groups, however, guarantees of equal opportunities for disabled students require that educators and psychologists give more attention to school-sponsored sports programs (Ashen, 1991). Unique and innovative approaches are needed so that these individuals can participate in sports within the schools. One possibility is to have special sections for the disabled as part of regular track, swimming, and gymnastic meets. It also may be possible to mix people with different handicapping conditions with able-bodied individuals in some sports programs. One promising program is the Paralympic movement. The paralympic games as one of the largest sporting events in the world (Steadward, 1996.)

REFERENCES

Ashen, M.J. (1991). The challenge of the physically challenged: Delivering sport psychology services to physically disabled athletes. *Sport Psychologist, 5*(4), 370–381.

DePauw, K.P. (1984). Commitment and challenges, sport opportunities for athletes with disabilities. *Journal of Physical Education, Recreation & Dance, 55*, 34–35.

Steadward, R.D. (1996). Integration and sport in the paralympic movement. *Sport Science Review, 5*(1), 26–41.

See also **Olympics, Special; Recreational Therapy**

STAFF DEVELOPMENT

Staff development is necessary to improve the product of an organization by raising the skill level and awareness of the human resources of that organization. In the public schools, the product is education. Teachers design and deliver the product; students consume; and the public evaluates the product based on their observations of its effects on the consumers (children). Education must be accepted as meaningful and pertinent to the children before they learn. The motivating and technical skills of teachers, as salespersons, are vital to the success of the enterprise. The delivery of the product—instruction—requires teacher performance, materials, physical plant, technology, and student motivation. These variables determine the amount of the product the consumers buy or, in some cases, refuse. The teacher's skills, as those of the producer and delivering agent, are the key input in the process. Because of the importance of those skills, development of the staff as a key resource should be continuous and planned, as with any of the other resources of an organization. Development must be perceived as required, meaningful, and attainable by the staff.

The administration should develop a plan for the enhancement of the school's staff resource. The plan may encompass several areas: curriculum; instruction; personal skills; licensure; advanced education; stress management; work environment; administrative support; school, home, community relations; student management; and school organization. Once the needs of the organization have been identified, each staffer's part in the scheme is drawn up and agreed to. The individual's role is contracted for and evaluated in the routine teacher evaluation process. Methods for enhancing the skill level of the organization may include professional in-service training, team teaching, internships, remedial plans of development, individual guided education units, school visitations, outside instruction, and role modeling.

Once needs are identified, a positive environment established, and a plan designed and implemented, monitoring of the professional staff is recommended. Positive feedback to personnel regarding their teaching performance is essential for it identifies the organizational expectations. Monitoring/supervising can be the same activity. Being visible, asking curriculum-directed questions, acknowledging instructional changes, encouraging staff reviews and faculty support groups, organizing creative instructional changes, providing evaluative feedback, and holding teacher conferences are all supervisory techniques under the heading of monitoring. Classroom visitations are important to monitoring. These activities deliver a clear message of administrative interest. When these components are addressed, an environment of trust develops. The teaching staff becomes more accepting of staff development programs once positive staff development has occurred in the school among the staff.

The administrator is the key person in preparing the staff for a resourceful plan, but only after the staff has been provided the opportunity for in-house planning and leadership. The assets of an organization, human and physical, must be known. A development system can allow for a committee of teachers to help decide in-service and other needs. As the human resources are assessed, staff should be placed in positions where personal/professional talents are best used. An extension of the effort can complete the plan for achievement of the overall objective of the organization.

See also **Personnel Training in Special Education; Supervision in Special Education**

STANDARD DEVIATION

The standard deviation is a measure of the dispersion of sample or population scores around the mean score. It is the most important and most widely used measure of dispersion for quantitative variables when the distribution is symmetric. We compute the standard deviation for a population of n scores by first averaging squared deviations of scores (X) from the mean population (m) using Equation 1:

$$\sigma^2 = \frac{\sum_{i=1}^{n}(X_i - \mu)^2}{n} \qquad (1)$$

This yields the variance of the scores, s2. The square root of this value, s, is the population standard deviation. For a sample of n scores, the variance is computed using Equation 2:

$$s^2 = \frac{\sum_{i=1}^{n}(X_1 - \overline{X})^2}{n - 1} \qquad (2)$$

where

$\overline{X}$ is the mean sample score. Here we use $(n - 1)$ as the divisor instead of n because this produces an unbiased sample estimate of $\sigma 2$. Dividing by n produces a biased estimate. The square root of this value, s, is the standard deviation of the scores in the sample; i.e., the average dispersion of the scores around the mean score.

This measure of dispersion is widely used in the behavioral sciences to describe the spread of scores around the mean score when the distribution of scores is normal. Then we can state the proportion of scores that fall above or below any given value or between any two values by first converting the value(s) to z score units using

$$z_1 = \frac{X_i - \overline{X}}{s} \qquad \text{or} \qquad z_i = \frac{X_i - \mu}{\sigma} \qquad (3)$$

for a sample or population. For example, for a sample of scores with computed statistics $\overline{X} = 40$ and $s = 5$, the value $X_i = 50$ is two standard deviations above the mean. Thus from a normal table, we find that 97.72% of the scores fall below 50 while 0.28% are larger than 50.

The size of the standard deviation also indicates the relative spread of two comparable distributions. For example, given that $s = 3$ for males and $s = 5$ for females on a given test, where the mean score, 15, is the same for either group, we can tell that the female scores span a wider range than the male scores, with 16% of the females scoring at least 20 while only 5% of the males obtain this score or higher.

In addition to describing a distribution of scores, the standard deviation is used widely in inferential statistics for describing the spread of the sampling distribution. For example, the standard deviation of the sampling distribution of the sample mean, $\overline{X}$, is given by $(\sigma/\sqrt{n}$, where s is defined in Equation 2. We may also obtain the standard deviation of the sample proportion, variance, correlation coefficient, or

any other statistic. When so used, the standard deviation is called the standard error of estimate of the statistic. Further, in regression estimation procedures, the standard deviation of the errors of prediction is used to judge the precision of the predicted values. This measure is called the standard error of estimate of prediction. In measurement, we define the standard deviation of the errors of measurement, the standard error of measurement, and use it to infer the value of true scores (Hopkins & Stanley, 1981). Further information on the standard deviation is found in the following references.

REFERENCE

Hopkins, K.D., & Stanley, J.C. (1981). *Educational and psychological measurement and evaluation* (6th ed.). Englewood Cliffs, NJ: Prentice-Hall.

See also **Central Tendency; Normal Curve Equivalent**

STANDARDS FOR EDUCATIONAL AND PSYCHOLOGICAL TESTING (SEPT)

The Standards for Educational and Psychological Testing (SEPT) is a joint effort of the American Psychological Association, the American Educational Research Association, and the National Council on Measurement in Education.

The SEPT is divided into four major sections: technical standards for test construction and evaluation; professional standards for test use; standards for particular applications (including testing language minorities and testing individuals with handicapping conditions); and standards for administrative procedures. The principal purposes for the SEPT are to provide criteria for the evaluation of tests, testing practices, and the effects of test use. While these evaluations depend an the judgment of professionals with appropriate training and certification/ licensure for the use and construction of test, the SEPT provides the key frame of reference and ensures that all relevant areas are addressed in making such judgments. Tests and testing are rapidly changing and the SEPT does not provide precise numbers or cutoffs for meeting the various standards. Rather, the SEPT requires that specific types of information be reported so that appropriate evaluations can be made on the basis of evidence and not various fallacies such as the "expert opinion" or appeal to authority. The SEPT is a document that all test users and consumers of test results should have intimate knowledge of and should apply in practice. Tests not reporting the required information or conforming to the standards should not be used because their appropriateness cannot be evaluated adequately.

See also **Buros Mental Measurement Yearbook; Test in Print**

STANFORD-BINET INTELLIGENCE SCALE–FOURTH EDITION

The Stanford-Binet Intelligence Scale–Fourth Edition (Thorndike, Hagen, & Sattler, 1986) is an individually-administered intelligence test appropriate for ages 2 to young adult. It consists of fifteen tests designed to appraise four major areas of cognitive ability: Verbal Reasoning, Abstract/Visual Reasoning, Quantitative Reasoning, and Short-Term Memory. Each individual test has a Standard Age Score (SAS) mean of 50 and a standard deviation of 8. The Area Scores and the total test Composite SAS have a mean of 100 and a standard deviation of 16. The total test Composite SAS provides the best measure of general reasoning ability, or *g*.

The Stanford-Binet traces its origins to Lewis M. Terman's 1916 Stanford Revision and Extension of the Binet-Simon Scale. Major revisions of the Stanford-Binet were completed in 1937, 1960, and 1986. Historically, the Stanford-Binet has had its leading applications in the assessment of preschool cognitive-intellectual functioning, mental retardation, learning problems, and intellectual giftedness.

Extensive validity, reliability, and fairness studies have been published in the Technical Manual (Thorndike et al., 1986) and professional journals. Validity studies reported in the technical manual document factor analytic investigations, correlations with other measures of intelligence (e.g., Stanford-Binet Form L-M, Wechsler intelligence scales, K-ABC), and mean test performance among several exceptional samples (e.g., individuals who are designated by their schools as intellectually gifted, learning disabled, or mentally retarded). Studies of test score reliability in the Technical Manual show internal consistency reliabilities typically in the .80s and .90s, with the total test Composite SAS having a median KR-20 reliability of .98 across ages. Test-retest scoring stability over an average of four months yields median total test Composite SAS reliabilities at or above .90, with the stability of the four Area Scores ranging from .51 to .88. Fairness studies reported in the Technical Manual include expert bias and sensitivity reviews of items and procedures, as well as quantitative studies of item properties using both traditional and Rasch procedures. A more extensive report of statistical analyses of the test's fairness in terms of sex, race, and ethnic membership is available from Riverside Publishing.

Critiques of the Stanford-Binet have generally noted its "high level of technical quality" (Anastasi, 1989) while suggesting that its clinical utility and advantages over other intelligence tests remain to be established (e.g., Anastasi, 1989; Cronbach, 1989). The discontinuation of the traditional age-scale format, in which all items of any type for a given age are administered before proceeding to the next set of items for adjacent ages, has led some reviewers to note that the Stanford-Binet may be "less game-like" (e.g., Cronbach, 1989) than previous editions and other tests. Even with these limitations, contemporary test usage surveys show that the Stanford-Binet ranks as the second most commonly used intelligence test among school psychologists after the Wechsler scales (Reschly, 1998).

REFERENCES

Anastasi, A. (1989). Review of the Stanford-Binet Intelligence Scale, Fourth Edition. In J.C. Conoley & J.J. Kramer (Eds.), *The tenth mental measurements yearbook* (pp. 771–773). Lincoln, NE: Buros Institute of Mental Measurements.

Cronbach, L.J. (1989) Review of the Stanford-Binet Intelligence Scale, Fourth Edition. In J.C. Conoley & J.J. Kramer (Eds.), *The tenth mental measurements yearbook* (pp. 773–775). Lincoln, NE: Buros Institute of Mental Measurements.

Reschly, D.J. (1998). *School psychology practice—Is there change?* Paper presented at the Annual Convention of the American Psychological Association, San Francisco.

Thorndike, R.L., Hagen, E.P., & Sattler, J.M. (1986). *Stanford-Binet Intelligence Scale: Fourth edition technical manual.* Itasca, IL: Riverside Publishing.

***See also* Assessment; Binet, A.; Intelligence Testing; Mental Retardation**

STANFORD DIAGNOSTIC MATHEMATICS TEST–FOURTH EDITION (SDMT4)

The Stanford Diagnostic Mathematics Test–Fourth Edition (SDMT4, 1996) is designed to measure which areas of mathematics are of specific difficulty to a student. The test is intended to be used for diagnostic purposes as well as to help create appropriate intervention. The test may be administered from grade one through community college. Two response formats are provided: multiple choice and free response. A group or individual format may be used in administration.

The standardization sample of the SDMT4 involved over 40,000 students that were representative of the US school population. Internal reliability coefficients were generally above .80, and interrater reliability for the free-response items is very good (above .95). Evidence for validity was provided by correlations with the Otis-Lennon School Ability test, with correlations among the two instruments in the .60s and .70s.

Generally, the SDMT4 has been favorably reviewed (e.g., Lehmann, 1998; Poteat, 1998). It provides much detail in terms of diagnostic information. The psychometric qualities are strong, and lead to obtained scores that are reliable and valid. The SDMT4 is not useful for simply obtaining achievement test norms. It also does not provide information about algebraic operations. It is best used for assessing students that are below average, rather than those that are at or above average functioning.

REFERENCES

Lehmann, I.J. (1998). Review of the Stanford Diagnostic Mathematics Test, Fourth Edition. In J.C. Impara & B.S. Plake (Eds.), *The thirteenth mental measurements yearbook* (pp. 932–936). Lincoln, NE: Buros Institute of Mental Measurements.

Poteat, G.M. (1998). Review of the Stanford Diagnostic Mathematics Test, Fourth Edition. In J.C. Impara & B.S. Plake (Eds.), *The thirteenth mental measurements yearbook* (pp. 937–938). Lincoln, NE: Buros Institute of Mental Measurements.

Stanford Diagnostic Mathematics Test–Fourth Edition. (1996). Cleveland, OH: Harcourt Brace Jovanovich.

See also **Assessment; Mathematics, Learning Disabilities and**

STANFORD DIAGNOSTIC READING TEST–FOURTH EDITION (STRT4)

The Standford Diagnostic Reading Test–Fourth Edition (SDRT4; Karlsen & Gardner, 1996) is intended to diagnose students' strengths and weaknesses in the major components of the reading process. There are several components that are specifically assessed: Phonetic Analysis, Vocabulary, Comprehension, and Scanning. The SDRT4 may be administered in a group or individual format. Students may be assessed with the SDRT4 from the end of grade one through the first semester of college. In addition to assessment of reading, the SDRT may be used to develop strategies for teaching reading or may be used to challenge students who are doing well.

The SDRT4 is a diagnostic test, not an achievement test, and as such it provides more detailed coverage of reading skills and places a greater emphasis on measuring the skills of low achieving students. Both norm-referenced and criterion-referenced information is available on reading skills. The normative sample was based on data collected from approximately 53,000 examinees from 1994 to 1995. The sample was found to closely match the total US school enrollment statistics. Engelhard (1998) evaluated the reliability statistics in the SDRT4 manual and found that the use of the shorter subtests for the diagnosis of an individual's strengths and weaknesses is not recommended. No evidence for stability of scores over time is provided.

Overall, the SDRT4 is found to be a sound measure of reading. It provides adequate traditional psychometric information, clear administration directions, and scoring strategies. Teaching suggestions are also described, but the base of the interventions is not clear. Interpretation and intervention based on the SDRT4 should be done by those with specialized knowledge in clinical practices in reading.

REFERENCE

Engelhard, G. (1998). Review of the Stanford Diagnostic Reading Test, Fourth Edition. In J.C. Impara & B.S. Plake (Eds.), *The thirteenth mental measurements yearbook* (pp. 939–941). Lincoln, NE: Buros Institute of Mental Measurements.

See also **Reading**

STEINART'S DISEASE (MYOTONIC DYSTROPHY)

Steinart's disease (myotonic dystrophy) appears to be caused by an autosomal dominant characteristic that results in varying degrees of mental retardation, poor muscle development, bilateral facial paralysis, and general muscular wasting. Overt myotonic does not usually occur in early infancy. Most often, it manifests itself in late childhood or adolescence. Many children display behavioral characteristics of suspiciousness and moroseness and are asocial and submissive in treatment needs. Mental retardation is often present; although it may vary from mild to severe, it tends to be severe, particularly with early onset of the disease (Carter, 1978).

The older toddler or young child with myotonic dystrophy may have muscular weakness and wasting with psychomotor delay, drooping eyelids, and an open, drooling mouth. Cataracts are present in most individuals. High-arched palates and weak tongues are seen, as is an open, drooling mouth, even in older children. Children often have difficulty in feeding and swallowing. Abnormal curvature of the neck and back is seen. Atrophy of the extremities is often seen and clubfoot may be present. Premature baldness is also seen. Hypogonadism causes premature loss of libido or impotence in affected males. Nasal speech and articulation problems are common, as are vision problems associated with cataracts. Diabetes, heart arrhythmias, and cardiac abnormalities may be present, as well as increased incidence of diabetes mellitus (Lemeshaw, 1982).

Educational planning will often include categorical placement in classes for students with mild mental retardation; however, this disorder may not manifest itself until much later in life but then will remain constant (Tuikka, Laaksonen, & Somer, 1993).

REFERENCES

Carter, C. (Ed.). (1978). *Medical aspects of mental retardation.* (2nd. ed.). Springfield, IL: Thomas.

Lemeshaw, S. (1982). *The handbook of clinical types in mental retardation.* Boston: Houghton Mifflin.

Tuikka, R.A., Laaksonen, R.K., & Somer, H.V.K. (1993). *Cognitive function in myotonic dystrophy: A follow-up study.* European Neurology, *33*(6), 436–441.

See also **Diabetes; Mental Retardation; Muscular Dystrophy**

STELAZINE

Stelazine is the trade name for the generic antipsychotic agent Trifluoperazine. It is of the class of drugs known as phenothiazines and demonstrates many of the expected side effects. The piperazine subgroup of phenothiazines is very potent in its actions. In relation to Thorazine (Chlorpromazine), the dose/response ratio is approximately 20 to 1. Stelazine also appears to be more long-acting than Thorazine; thus fewer administrations are necessary to maintain therapeutic blood level.

In addition to the general side effects produced by phenothiazines, the piperazine subgroup has been related to a consistent pattern of extrapyramidal symptoms called the Rabbit syndrome, owing to distinctive facial movements (Bassuk & Schoonover, 1977). These side effects are reported most commonly in women over age 45. Characteristic symptoms include tremor of the lips and masticatory muscles that resembles a rabbit chewing. In contrast to tardive dyskinesia, tongue movements do not appear to be involved.

REFERENCE

Bassuk, E.L., & Schoonover, S.C. (1977). *The practitioner's guide to psychoactive drugs.* New York: Plenum Medical.

See also **Thorazine**

STEREOTYPIC BEHAVIORS

Stereotyped behaviors are highly persistent and repetitious motor or posturing behaviors that seem to have little or no functional significance (Baumeister & Forehand, 1973). They are rhythmic movements that are coordinated and apparently intentional. They are repeated in the same fashion for long periods, often an hour or more at a time (Mitchell & Etches, 1977). Stereotyped movements are voluntary, brief, or prolonged habits or mannerisms that often are experienced as pleasurable (American Psychiatric Association, 1994). Stereotypic behaviors result from conditioning (in some form) and appear to be related to the achievement of homeostasis (Nijhof, Joha, & Pekelharing, 1998). Sometimes present in children of normal intelligence, they are most common among individuals with mental retardation or autism. The stereotyped behaviors, mainly seen in infancy and early childhood, may persist into adolescent and adult life, especially in institutionalized retarded persons.

The most typical movements are head rolling, head banging, and body rocking. Other rhythmic repetitive movements have been described as foot kicking, hand shaking, hand rotation, finger and toe sucking, lip biting, and tooth grinding. According to Sallustro and Atwell (1978) and Mitchell and Etches (1977), head rolling from side to side on the pillow occurs mainly before the infant falls asleep, but it also may be seen during sleep and while awake; it is usually encountered in early infancy up to the first 2 to 3 years of life. Head banging, seen more often in the sitting position but sometimes on hands and knees or even standing, typically starts toward the end of the first year. It sometimes follows head rolling and ceases before the age of 4 years. The child repeatedly and monotonously bangs the head against the pillow or the bars of the cot, and sometimes against a wall or the floor. This generally occurs before sleep, but it may be seen at any time of the day or night, may continue for an hour or longer, and may alternate with other rhythmic movements. Body rocking, the most frequent stereotyped behavior, is a slow, rhythmic backward and forward swaying of the trunk, usually while in the sitting position, beginning in the first year of life (Sallustro & Atwell, 1978).

The true significance of these movements is still unknown as to their anatomical and functional levels. Their high frequency among severely mentally handicapped children suggests the failed development of cortical control and that most of these movements are probably infracortical in origin. The element of volition appears to indicate participation of the cerebral cortex in their initiation and maintenance. La Grow and Repp (1984) have reviewed various treatments and strategies used to suppress the stereotyped patterns from the behavior repertoire.

REFERENCES

American Psychiatric Association. (1994). *Diagnostic and statistical manual of mental disorders* (4th ed.). Washington, DC: Author.

Baumeister, A.A., & Forehand R. (1973). Stereotyped acts. In N.R. Ellis (Ed.), *International review of research in mental retardation* (Vol. 6). New York: Academic. p. 55–96.

La Grow, S.J., & Repp, A.C. (1984). Stereotypic responding: A review of intervention research. *American Journal of Mental Deficiency, 88,* 595–609.

Mitchell, R.G., & Etches, P. (1977). Rhythmic habit patterns (stereotypies). *Developmental Medicine and Child Neurology, 19,* 545–550.

Nijhof, G., Joha, D., & Pekelharing, H. (1998). Aspects of stereotypic behavior among autistic persons: A study of the literature. *British Journal of Developmental Disabilities, 44*(86) 3–13.

Sallustro, F., & Atwell, C.W. (1978). Body rocking, head banging, and head rolling in normal children. *Journal of Pediatrics, 93,* 704–708.

See also **Autism; Mental Retardation; Self-Injurious Behavior; Self-Stimulation**

STEREOTYPISM

People generally are classified and fit into molds or groups that have certain attributable characteristics. With handicapped individuals, the characteristics especially focused on are disabilities rather than abilities. Labeling an individual or fitting a person into a specific handicapped group or category according to certain characteristics has a few advantages and many disadvantages. The traditional handicapping labels are basically used to explain a medical problem or to aid in educational intervention, but the result generally is stereotyping of individuals, which may lead to misleading and inhumane side effects.

Today, misconceptions arise from stereotyping the handicapped. Although many visually handicapped individuals have no mental retardation, the term visually handicapped often carries the connotation that these individuals are physically disabled and severely mentally deficient (Hollinger & Jones, 1970). Goffman (1963) writes extensively of the negative stereotypes and stigmata associated with the mentally retarded. People with cerebral palsy may have an IQ of average or above average, but their physical rigidness and slurred speech often make people talk to them as if they were unable to understand. The hearing impaired have fought against the stereotype of being deaf and dumb. People interacting with blind individuals believe they have to talk loudly in order to be heard. Learning-disabled students and students with attentional problems (Cornett-Ruiz

& Hendricks, 1993) are frequently associated with the retarded even though their mental capacities are generally average or above.

The misconceptions have caused many sociological, economic, and other types of barricades for the handicapped. These individuals have been denied access to a life that is as normal as possible, not only in the physical environment but also in the social environment. Many of the handicapped are still isolated, laughed at, and criticized. Their problems may be increased because of added emotional stress.

Mainstreaming has helped regular classroom students to better understand special education students; mainstreaming has also helped special education students to develop feelings of belonging and self-worth. Exposure to the regular classroom student has given the special education student a model from which to learn.

REFERENCES

Cornett-Ruiz, S., & Hendricks, B. (1993). Effects of labeling and ADHD behaviors on peer and teacher judgments. *Journal of Educational Research, 86*(6), 349–355.

Goffman, E. (1963). *Notes on the measurement of spoiled identity.* Englewood Cliffs; NJ: Prentice-Hall.

Hollinger, C.S., & Jones, R.L. (1970). Community attitudes toward slow learners and mental retardates: What's in a name? *Mental Retardation, 8,* 19–13.

See also **Attitudes Toward the Handicapped; Family Response to a Child with Disabilities; History of Special Education**

STERN, WILLIAM (1871–1938)

William Stern, German psychologist and pioneer in the psychology of individual differences, introduced the concept of the intelligence quotient, in 1912. This quotient, used to express performance on intelligence tests, is found by dividing the subject's mental age as determined by the test performance by the chronological age and multiplying by 100. In the United States, the intelligence quotient, or IQ, was used by Lewis M. Terman in his 1916 Stanford Revision of the Binet Scales.

REFERENCES

Murchison, C. (Ed.). (1961). *A history of psychology in autobiography.* New York: Russell & Russell.

Stern, W. (1914). *The psychological methods of intelligence testing.* Baltimore, MD: Warwick & York.

STIGMATIZATION

See LABELING.

STIMULANT DRUGS

Stimulant drugs are a commonly used class of medications for the treatment of inattention, impulsivity, and restlessness in school-age children and adolescents, and, less often, for the treatment of narcolepsy and drowsiness or disorders of arousal in the elderly. Children and adolescents having an attention deficit disorder (American Psychiatric Association, 1994) are the ones most often given these medications because of the significant effects of the drugs on sustained attention. In fact, stimulants are the most commonly prescribed psychotropic medications in child psychiatry (Wilens, & Biederman, 1992). The drugs are so named because of their stimulation of increased central nervous system activity, presumably by way of their effects on dopamine and norepinephrine production, and reuptake at the synaptic level of neuronal functioning (Cantwell & Carlson, 1978). The drugs may also have effects on other central neurotransmitters as well as on peripheral nervous system activity. The changes in central neurotransmitter activity result in increased alertness, arousal, concentration, and vigilance or sustained attention, as well as reductions in impulsive behavior and activity or restlessness that is irrelevant to particular tasks (Barkley, 1977, 1981). While a number of substances such as caffeine fall into this class of medications, those most typically used with children and adolescents are methylphenidate (Ritalin), d-amphetamine (Dexedrine), a mixture of dextroamphetamine and racemic amphetamine salts (Popper, 1994). Despite similar behavioral effects and side effects, the mechanism of action of each of these stimulants is somewhat different.

The stimulants are relatively rapid in their initiation of behavioral changes and in the time course over which such changes are maintained. Most stimulant drugs, taken orally, are quickly absorbed into the bloodstream through the stomach and small intestine and pass readily across the blood-brain barrier to affect neuronal activity. Behavioral changes can be detected within 30 to 60 minutes after ingestion and may last between 3 and 8 hours, depending on the type of stimulant and preparation (regular or sustained release) employed. Traces of medication and their metabolites in blood and urine can be detected up to 24 hours after ingestion, perhaps corresponding to the clinical observation of persisting side effects after the desired behavioral effects are no longer noticeable.

The most commonly experienced side effects are diminished appetite, particularly for the noon meal, and insomnia, although these are often mild, diminish within several weeks of treatment onset, and are easily managed by reductions in dose where problematic. Increases in blood pressure, heart rate, and respiration may occur, but they are typically of little consequence (Hastings & Barkley, 1978). Other side effects of lesser frequency are sleeplessness (Day & Abmayr, 1998), irritability, sadness or dysphoria, and proneness to crying, especially during late afternoons, when the medication is "washing out" of the body (Cantwell & Carlson, 1978). Some children experience heightened activity levels during this washout phase. Headaches and stomach aches are infrequently noted and, like all side effects, appear to be dose related. Temporary suppression of growth in height and weight may be noted in some children during the first 1 to 2 years of treatment with stimulants, but there appear to be few lasting effects on eventual adult stature. Between 1 and 2% of children and adolescents may experience nervous tics while on stimulant medication, but these diminish in the majority of cases with reduction in dose or discontinuation of medication. A few cases of Gilles de la Tourette's syndrome (multiple motor tics, vocal tics, and, in some cases, increased utterance of profanities) have been reported after initiation of stimulant medication (Barkley, 1987). Children with a personal or family history of motor/vocal tics should use these drugs only with caution because of the possible emergence or exacerbation of their tic conditions, observed in more than 50% of such children.

Despite generally positive behavioral improvements in most children with attention-deficit/hyperactivity disorder taking stimulants, these drugs have shown little, if any, significant, lasting effect on the long-term outcome of such children in late adolescence or young adulthood once medication has been discontinued.

REFERENCES

American Psychiatric Association. (1994). *Diagnostic and statistical manual of mental disorders* (4th ed.). Washington, DC: Author.

Barkley, R. (1977). A review of stimulant drug research with hyperactive children. *Journal of Child Psychology & Psychiatry, 18,* 137–165.

Barkley, R.A. (1981). *Hyperactive children: A handbook for diagnosis and treatment.* New York: Guilford.

Barkley, R.A. (1987). Tic disorders and Tourette's syndrome. In E. Mash & L. Terdal (Eds.), *Behavioral assessment of childhood disorders* (2nd ed.). New York: Guilford.

Cantwell, D., & Carlson, G. (1978). Stimulants. In J. Werry (Ed.), *Pediatric psychopharmacology.* New York: Brunner/Mazel.

Day, H.D., & Abmayr, S.B. (1998). Parent reports of sleep disturbances in stimulant-medicated children with attention-deficit/hyperactivity disorder. *Journal of Clinical Psychology, 54*(5), 701–716.

Hastings, J., & Barkley, R. (1978). A review of psychophysiological research with hyperactive children. *Journal of Abnormal Child Psychology, 7,* 413–447.

Popper, C.W. (1994). The story of four salts. *Journal of Child & Adolescent Psychopharmacology, 4*(4), 217–223.

Wilens, T.E., & Biederman, J. (1992). The stimulants. *Psychiatric Clinics of North America, 15*(1), 191–222.

See also **Attention-Deficit Hyperactivity Disorder; Dopamine; Hyperactivity; Ritalin; Tourette's Syndrome**

STIMULUS DEPRIVATION

Stimulus deprivation refers to an increase in reinforcer effectiveness that occurs following a reduction in the availability of or access to that reinforcing event. The effectiveness of reinforcers, especially of primary reinforcers such as food, depends greatly on the deprivation state of the individual. Using edible reinforcers with a student who has just returned from lunch probably will not be as effective as using the same reinforcers immediately prior to lunch, when the student is more likely to be in a state of deprivation for food. Most stimulus events serve as effective reinforcers only if the individual has been deprived of them for a period of time prior to their use. In general, the longer the deprivation period, the more effective the reinforcer (Martin & Pear, 1983).

Ethical and legal issues should be considered prior to use of a deprivation procedure. Major objections typically focus on deprivation of essential primary reinforcers (e.g., food, water, shelter, human contact) on the basis that it constitutes a violation of basic human rights. A decision to use deprivation, or any other aversive technique, requires careful consideration of the kind of deprivation, the duration of the program, the availability of alternative treatment strategies, and the demonstrable benefits resulting from its use (Kazdin, 1980). As a precautionary measure when using a deprivation procedure, an individual should never be completely deprived of the reinforcing event for a lengthy period of time.

Fortunately, intentional deprivation of reinforcers usually is not necessary, as the natural deprivation that occurs in the course of an individual's daily activities often is sufficient to increase reinforcer effectiveness. Since children in the classroom, for example, do not have unlimited access to free time, they normally experience a mild form of deprivation during the course of a school day. As another example, when using small amounts of edible reinforcers to increase appropriate responding, the only deprivation required may be the natural deprivation that occurs between meals. Thus a variety of events may serve as effective reinforcers simply as a result of natural deprivation without the introduction of more formal deprivation procedures.

REFERENCES

Kazdin, A.E. (1980). *Behavior modification in applied settings* (revised ed.). Homewood, IL: Dorsey.

Martin, G., & Pear, J. (1983). *Behavior modification: What it is and how to do it* (2nd ed.). Englewood Cliffs, NJ: Prentice-Hall.

See also **Behavior Modification; Operant Conditioning; Stimulus Satiation**

STIMULUS SATIATION

Stimulus satiation refers to the reduction in reinforcer effectiveness that occurs after a large amount of that reinforcer has been obtained (usually within a short period of time). Thus an event that initially shows reinforcing qualities may become ineffective or even aversive for a period of time if experienced too frequently or excessively. Teacher praise may be effective the first few times if it is provided in the morning, but may gradually diminish in value with additional use during the day. Treats and certain activities may be highly reinforcing if used sparingly but may lose their effectiveness if used frequently. The special educator should be sensitive to the principle of satiation and provide alternative reinforcing events when loss of effectiveness is noted (Gardner, 1978).

Satiation is especially common with primary reinforcers such as food. These reinforcers, when provided in excessive amounts within a short period, may lose their reinforcing properties relatively quickly. To prevent or delay satiation, only a small amount of the reinforcer should be provided at any one time. Satiation of primary reinforcers is usually temporary, as these events regain their reinforcing value as deprivation increases.

Secondary reinforcers such as praise, attention, and recognition are less likely than primary reinforcers to be influenced by satiation effects. The category of secondary reinforcers called generalized reinforcers is least-susceptible to satiation. This is due to the fact that the reinforcers themselves (e.g., tokens, grades, money) can be exchanged for a variety of other reinforcing events called back-up reinforcers. Thus satiation of generalized reinforcers is not likely to occur unless the individual becomes satiated with the items or events offered as back-up reinforcers. The greater the number and range of back-up reinforcers available, the less likelihood that satiation will occur (Kazdin, 1980). This would suggest that teachers consider the use of tokens, exchangeable for a wide variety of back-up reinforcers, when tangible events are required to ensure effective learning and behavior (Gardner, 1978).

Educators can enhance the effects of a satiation procedure by ensuring that, during the interim period in which the maladaptive behavior is absent or of low strength, other more appropriate replacement behaviors are taught and strengthened (Gardner, 1978).

REFERENCES

Gardner, W.I. (1978). *Children with learning and behavior problems: A behavior management approach* (2nd ed.). Boston: Allyn & Bacon.

Kazdin, A.E. (1980). *Behavior modification in applied settings* (Rev. ed.). Homewood, IL: Dorsey

See also **Applied Behavior Analysis; Behavior Modification; Stimulus Deprivation**

STRABISMUS, EFFECT ON LEARNING OF

Strabismus, also called heteropia, is a visual condition in which the two eyes are not parallel when viewing an object. While one eye is fixed on an object, the other eye will be directed elsewhere. Strabismus can be classified in two ways. The first concerns the angle of separation. In concomitant strabismus, the angle of separation is fixed; in noncomitant strabismus the angle between the eye that is fixed and the deviant eye varies. Strabismus also can be classified as to whether the visual paths of the two eyes converge or diverge (Harley & Lawrence, 1977).

Some form of strabismus occurs in approximately 5% of all children. The percentage increases to 40 to 50% for children with cerebral palsy; it is noted in as many as 60% of the children who are visually impaired at birth as a result of their mother's having contracted rubella during pregnancy.

Strabismus can be corrected through lenses if it is detected early in a child's life (Flax, 1993). Freeman, Nguyen, & Jolly (1996) suggest that amblyopia and strabismus deviation are the major components of visual acuity, loss and should be reduced by whatever means are available. Additionally, some doctors recommend eye exercises as a way to correct the condition. This recommendation is controversial. Eden (1978) notes that strabismus often starts early in life, before the child is capable of following any rigorous exercise schedule. Once the child is capable of following such a schedule, permanent visual damage may already have occurred. In school, close work should be limited for students with strabismus, and these students should be given frequent rest periods.

REFERENCES

Eden, J. (1978). *The eye book.* New York: Viking.

Flax, N. (1993). The treatment of strabismus in the four to ten year old child. *Child and Adolescent Social Work Journal, 10*(5), 411–416.

Freeman, A.W., Nguyen, V.A., & Jolly, N. (1996). Components of visual acuity loss in strabismus. *Vision Research, 36*(5), 765–774.

Harley, R.K., & Lawrence, G.A. (1977). *Visual impairment in the schools.* Springfield, IL: Thomas.

See also **Ambliopia; Blind; Cataracts; Libraries from the Blind and Physically Handicapped**

STRAUSS, ALFRED A. (1897–1957)

Alfred A. Strauss was born in Germany and received his medical degree and subsequent training in psychiatry and neurology there. He left Germany in 1933, became visiting professor at the University of Barcelona, and helped to establish Barcelona's first child guidance clinics. In 1937 Strauss joined the staff of the Wayne County (Michigan) School, where he served as research psychiatrist and director of child care. In 1947 Strauss founded the Cove School in Racine, Wisconsin, a residential institution that gained an international reputation for its pioneering work with brain-injured children. Strauss served as president of the school until his death.

Strauss made major contributions in the areas of diagnosis and education of brain-injured children. He developed tests for diagnosing brain injury. His studies of children without intellectual deficit who showed characteristics of brain injury in learning and behavior resulted in the first systematic description of a new clinical entity, minimal brain dysfunction. His 1947 book, *Psychopathology and Education of the Brain-Injured Child,* written with Laura Lehtinen, was the major guide for many of the numerous school programs for minimally brain-injured children that came into existence during the 1950s and 1960s.

REFERENCES

Gardiner, R.A. (1958). Alfred A. Strauss, 1897–1957. *Exceptional Children, 24,* 373.

Lewis, R.S., Strauss, A.A., & Lehtinen, L.E. (1960). *The other child.* New York: Grune & Stratton.

Strauss, A.A., & Kephart, N.C. (1955). *Psychopathology and education of the brain-injured child* (Vol. 2). New York: Grune & Stratton.

Strauss, A.A., & Lehtinen, L.E. (1947). *Psychopathology and education of the brain-injured child* (Vol. 1). New York: Grune & Stratton.

See also **Birth Injuries**

STRAUSS SYNDROME

The term Strauss syndrome was coined by Stevens and Birch (1957) to focus on an expanded set of behavioral characteristics of children who could not learn and did not easily fit into other classification systems. It also extended the work of a leading pioneer in the field, Alfred Strauss. Strauss's ideas regarding the education of brain-injured, perceptually handicapped children were presented in works coauthored first with Laura Lehtinen (1947) and later with Newell Kephart (1955).

REFERENCES

Stevens, G., & Birch, J. (1957). A proposal for clarification of the terminology used to describe brain-injured children. *Exceptional Children, 23,* 346–349.

Strauss, A., & Kephart, N. (1955). *Psychopathology and education of the brain-injured child* (Vol. 2). New York: Grune & Stratton.

Strauss, A., & Lehtinen, L. (1947). *Psychopathology and education of the brain-injured child* (Vol. 1). New York: Grune & Stratton.

See also **Brain Damage; Etiology; Learning Disabilities; Lesions; Minimal Brain Dysfunction**

STRENGTH MODELS OF REMEDIATION

See REMEDIATION, DEFICIT-CENTERED MODELS OF.

STREPHOSYMBOLIA

Strephosymbolia is a Greek term that literally means twisted symbol. Originally used by Samuel T. Orton, strephosymbolia is most commonly used in discussions regarding dyslexia. Orton and others noticed that when certain children read, they often reverse letters, syllables, or words. These children see all parts of a word, but not in the accepted order. So, instead of "pebbles," a strephosymbolic child might see "pelbbse" (Johnson, 1981). This twisting of reading material is viewed as a primary symptom of dyslexia (Clarke, 1973).

Currently, Orton's theory has little credibility as there has been no substantiation that mirror images are projected onto the brain (Kessler, 1980). Mercer (1983) notes that these difficulties are referred to as severe reading disabilities and are treated according to the specific difficulty.

REFERENCES

Clarke, L. (1973). *Can't read, can't write, can't talk too good either.* New York: Walker.

Johnson, C. (1981). *The diagnosis of learning disabilities.* Boulder, CO: Pruett.

Kessler, J.W. (1980). History of minimal brain dysfunction. In H.E. Rice & E.D. Rice (Eds.), *Handbook of minimal brain dysfunction: A critical review.* New York: Wiley.

Mercer, C.D. (1983). *Students with learning disabilities* (2nd ed.). Columbus, OH: Merrill.

See also **Dyslexia; Reading Disorders**

STRESS AND THE HANDICAPPED STUDENT

Stress results when physical and psychological demands on an individual exceed personal coping skills. Stress is activated when a threat to security, self-esteem, or safety is perceived. Schultz (1980) suggests that stress is often triggered by environmental interactions, which may be more problematic for handicapped children than for nonhandicapped ones. Handicapped children may also develop stress reactions to personal thoughts.

Mainstreaming and inclusive practices may produce increased social stress in the handicapped student. Tymitz-Wolf (1984) analyzed mildly mentally handicapped students' worries about mainstreaming as related to academic performance, social interactions, and the transitions inherent in split placement. A range of worries were reported in all three areas, with worries concerning transitions being the most prevalent.

Schultz (1980) contends that stress-management programs for handicapped students should emphasize instruction in adaptive coping skills, including relaxation training. Relaxation training has been used to decrease stress in learning-disabled students (Hegarty & Last, 1997; Omizo, 1981).

In addition, it has been found that parental support is very important and can be enhanced by the school providing parent support and parent support training for students (Volenski, 1995).

REFERENCES

Hegarty, J.R., & Last, A. (1997). Relaxation training for people who have severe/profound and multiple learning disabilities. *British Journal of Developmental Disabilities, 43*(85), 122–139.

Omizo, M.M. (1981). Relaxation training and biofeedback with hyperactive elementary school children. *Elementary School Guidance & Counseling, 15*(4), 329–332.

Schultz, E. (1980). Teaching coping skills for stress and anxiety. *Teaching Exceptional Children, 13*(3), 12–15.

Tymitz-Wolf, B. (1984). An analysis of EMR children's worries about mainstreaming. *Education & Training of the Mentally Retarded, 19,* 157–168.

Volenski, L.T. (1995). Building support systems for parents of handicapped children: The parent education and guidance program. *Psychology in the Schools, 32*(2), 124–129.

See also Self-Concept; Social Skills

STRONG INTEREST INVENTORY

The Strong Interest Inventory (SVIB-SCII, Fourth Edition; Hansen & Campbell, 1985) assesses an individual's interests in occupations, hobbies, leisure activities, and school subjects. The test has a long history, with its first edition, the Strong Vocational Interest Blank, being published over 70 years ago. There have been major changes since the SVIB, most notably a gender equity process that began in 1971.

The SVIB-SCII is a paper-and-pencil measure in which the respondent is asked to indicate "Like," "Dislike," or "Indifferent" to the items. The test takes an average of 30 minutes to complete and was designed for use with adults and 16–18 year olds with a 6th grade reading ability. The SVIB-SCII is machine-scored and responses are compared to the interests of people in a wide variety of jobs. The test yields five types of information: scores on 6 General Occupational Themes, 23 Basic Interest Scales, and 207 Occupational Scales. Additionally there are 2 Special Scales (Academic Comfort and Introversion-Extroversion), and Administrative Indexes (validity scales). Interpretive information includes a profile with an optional interpretive report.

The psychometric properties of the SVIB-SCII are excellent. Over 48,000 people taken from 202 occupational samples were used to construct the Occupational Scales. The fourth edition of the *Manual for the SVIB-SCII* describes the reliability, validity and sampling procedures for all the scales in detail.

The SVIB-SCII is easy to administer and provides easily understood interpretive results. Critiques of the inventory praise its outstanding interpretive information and excellent psychometric properties (Busch, 1995). One issue with the test is the authors' failure to report response rates for the occupational samples; response rates can affect the representativeness of the sample, and thus the predictive validity of the scales (Busch, 1995; Worthen & Sailor, 1995). However, despite the concern, the SVIB-SCII has been described as "by far the best available interest inventory" (Worthen & Sailor, 1995).

REFERENCES

Busch, J.C. (1995). In J.C. Conoley & J.C. Impara (Eds.), *The twelfth mental measurements yearbook.* Lincoln, NE: Buros Institute of Mental Measurements.

Hansen, J.C. & Campbell, D.P. (1985). *Manual for the Strong Interest Inventory* (4th ed.). Stanford, CA: Stanford University Press.

Worthen, B.R. & Sailor, P. (1995). In J.C. Conoley & J.C. Impara (Eds.), *The twelfth mental measurements yearbook.* Lincoln, NE: Buros Institute of Mental Measurements.

See also Habilitation; Vocational Rehabilitation

STRUCTURE OF INTELLECT

J.P. Guilford (1967), in his work *The Nature of Human Intelligence,* developed a model of intelligence based on his factor analysis of human intellect. The structure of intellect theory (SI) grew out of experimental applications of the multivariate method of multiple-factor analysis.

Although Guilford's model has not been widely used, it has pointed to a theory that has been lacking from the beginning of the era of mental testing—i.e., to give the concept of intelligence a firm, comprehensive, and systematic theoretical foundation. Guilford maintains that a firm foundation must be based on detailed observation; that the theory itself should include all aspects of intelligence; and that the result must be systematic, embracing numerous phenomena within a logically ordered structure. The outcome is his structure of intellect.

REFERENCE

Guilford, J.P. (1967). *The nature of human intelligence.* New York: McGraw-Hill.

See also Intelligence; Intelligence Testing

STUDY OF MATHEMATICALLY PRECOCIOUS YOUTH (SMPY)

The Study of Mathematically Precocious Youth (SMPY) was officially begun on September 1, 1971, by Julian Stanley. Stanley had become intrigued by a 13 1/2-year-old boy who scored extremely well on several standardized mathematics tests. A fear that students such as this one might fail to be identified and appropriately served led Stanley to devise the SMPY at Johns Hopkins University.

The SMPY is essentially a summer program. Students are identified, evaluated, and selected for the program throughout the year. Once selected, students participate in an eight-week program, meeting one day a week for slightly less than 5 hours per day. Throughout the instruction, the student-teacher ratio never exceeds 1:5 (Stanley, 1980). All instructors are former SMPY graduates and usually range in age from 13 to 20. During this approximately 35-hour program, students will typically demonstrate mastery of material 2 school years beyond where they began (Stanley, 1980).

To achieve such dramatic results, SMPY uses a "diagnostic testing followed by prescriptive instruction" method of instruction (Stanley, 1980; Stanley & Benbow, 1983). An evaluation determines what the student does not know. The instructors then help the student learn the information without taking an entire course (Stanley & Benbow, 1982; Stanley, 1997).

REFERENCES

Stanley, J.C. (1980). On educating the gifted. *Educational Researcher, 9,* 8–12.

Stanley, J.C. (1997). Varieties of intellectual talent. *Journal of Creative Behavior, 31*(2), 93–119.

Stanley, J.C., & Benbow, C.P. (1982). Educating mathematically precocious youth: Twelve policy recommendations. *Educational Researcher, 11,* 4–9.

Stanley, J.C., & Benbow, C.P. (1983). SMPY's first decade: Ten years of posing problems and solving them. *Journal of Special Education, 17,* 11–25.

See also Acceleration of Gifted Children; Advanced Placement Program; Gifted and Talented Children

STUTTERING

Stuttering is the most common of several disorders of fluency (Manning, 1996), all of which affect the rhythm or "flow" of speech. All speakers are sometimes disfluent, though not all speakers stutter. The causes of stuttering remain unknown despite decades of research. Recent speculations (e.g., Guitar, 1998) are that stuttering probably has several causative factors, including genetic predisposition, as well as neurophysiological and psychological influences. Research has consistently shown that more boys stutter than girls, a fact which has sometimes been used as evidence of a biological explanation.

Stuttering has both overt and covert aspects. The overt dimensions of the disorder include part-word repetitions, sound prolongations, and a variety of so-called "secondary" (learned struggle and avoidance) behaviors. The covert or hidden aspects of stuttering include word and situation avoidances, and feelings of anxiety, embarrassment, fear, and frustrations.

Treatment for stuttering varies depending on the age of the person and the severity of the disorder, as well as the training and orientation of the speech-language pathologist. Therapies designed for young children who stutter include working with the child's parents to help reduce stressors, reducing the parents' speaking rate, discovering and eliminating fluency disruptors, and teaching the child a slower and "easier" way to speak.

Treatments for older children and adults tend to fall into one of two large categories. The first group of therapies is the "stuttering modification" or "stutter-more-fluently" therapies. Stutterers are encouraged to confront their fears and to stop avoiding their stuttering. They learn how to stutter in a more fluent and controlled manner. The emphasis is on reducing the struggling and the abnormality of the disorder rather than on trying to eliminate the stuttering.

The second family of therapies is the "fluency shaping" or "speak-more-fluently" therapies. Using slow speech and other methods, stutterers are taught to speak fluently (i.e., without stuttering), first in the therapy room and later in other speaking situations. Maintaining fluent speech has been the greatest challenge to therapists who use fluency shaping therapies.

Both types of treatments are effective with at least some stutterers, and, recently, speech-language pathologists have begun combining aspects of stuttering modification and flu-

ency shaping therapies (e.g., Guitar, 1998). As yet, however, there is no single, accepted treatment for stuttering. As with the cause of stuttering, its treatment remains controversial.

REFERENCES

Guitar, B. (1998). *Stuttering: An integrated approach to its nature and treatment* (2nd ed). Baltimore: Williams and Wilkins.

Manning, W. (1996). *Clinical decision making in the diagnosis and treatment of fluency disorders.* Albany, NY: Delmar.

See also Speech Instruction; Speech Therapy

SUBSTANCE ABUSE

Substance abuse is often said to be one of the major public health concerns in this country. The term "substance abuse" describes abusive or harmful use of any substance. A drug is any substance that crosses from the bloodstream into the brain and that somehow changes the way the brain is functioning. By this definition, some common substances such as alcohol, nicotine, and even caffeine are considered "drugs." Although caffeine, nicotine, and alcohol are by far the most common drugs in the United States, some other drugs of abuse include marijuana, cocaine, amphetamines ("speed"), heroin and other opiates, hallucinogens (LSD, psilocybin mushrooms, peyote), depressants (barbiturates, benzodiazepines, or "downers"), and prescription drugs. In recent years, the development of "designer" drugs and newer chemical compounds has gotten a good deal of media attention. Such substances as the "date rape drugs," including Rohypnol and GHB, have been gaining in popularity in recent years. Although the use and abuse of these drugs are not nearly as prevalent as some other substances, they are causing some alarm within the community of substance-abuse treatment professionals.

A number of variations of substance abuse are included in the Diagnostic and Statistical Manual of Mental Disorders-Fourth Edition (DSM-IV; American Psychiatric Association, 1994). Criteria are specified in DSM-IV for substance intoxication, withdrawal, abuse, and dependence. The major criterion for diagnosis of substance abuse according to the DSM-IV is identified as "a maladaptive pattern of substance use manifested by recurrent and significant adverse consequences related to the repeated use of substances." A child or adolescent who is abusing a substance may show a number of behavior changes, including failure to complete school work, marked decreases in academic performance, behavior problems at school and home, problems with the legal system, fighting, arguing, and problems with peers. Substance dependence, by contrast, is more severe than substance abuse. According to the DSM-IV, substance dependence is indicated by at least three of the following symptoms: marked tolerance, withdrawal symptoms, using more of the substance than was intended, inability to control or stop using, a desire to stop using, disruption in normal everyday functioning and activities, and continuing to use the substance even after knowing that the use is causing physical or psychological problems. Note that while tolerance and withdrawal are typical "hallmarks" of addiction, these criteria are neither necessary nor sufficient to indicate substance dependence. One of the reasons that these criteria are not necessary for a diagnosis of substance dependence is the fact that some substances, such as marijuana and most hallucinogens, cause few marked physiological withdrawal symptoms. Thus, substance dependence may be indicated by a disruption in functioning in a number of areas of an individual's life (American Psychiatric Association, 1994).

Although many people assume that the highest rates of substance abuse are in adults, the highest rates of heavy alcohol use and of marijuana use are in those of ages 18–25 years (U.S. Department of Health and Human Services, 1993; American Psychiatric Association, 1994). The initial substance use that may eventually lead to abuse or dependence generally begins in adolescence. Adolescents who show symptoms of abuse or dependence are less likely to complete school than those who do not (American Psychiatric Association, 1994). Therefore, and obviously, educators and health professionals need to pay particular attention to the problem of substance abuse in adolescence and young adulthood.

Apparently, little research is available on substance abuse in children enrolled in special education programs. One study on the possible association between special education status and substance abuse yielded alarming results. Gress and Boss (1996) surveyed students from grades 4–12 and found differences in substance use between students in special education and noncategorical classes, especially for students in intermediate (4–6) and junior high (7–8) grades. Some of the most striking differences were found between students in the intermediate grades. For instance, 20% of severely behaviorally-handicapped but only 2.3% of noncategorical students used marijuana. Interestingly, whereas a high percentage of students with severe behavioral handicaps and specific learning disabilities used alcohol, amphetamine, and inhalants, a lower, percentage of students with developmental disabilities used these substances than did noncategorical students. The authors suggest that substance abuse among students in special-education programs is related to several factors, including unmet needs for attachment and close relationships, difficulty establishing a "self-identity," a need to have a certain image within the eyes of their peers, and a need for immediate gratification. Common to all children, these factors may be especially important to students in special education who want to "fit in." Gress and Boss (1996) suggest that students with serious handicaps may lack some of the necessary internal skills to deal with unmet needs. Risk of substance abuse may increase as a result of psychological, emotional, and social problems related to their specific disabilities (Gress & Boss, 1996).

Many different treatment methods exist to help people with substance abuse problems. Formal counseling or psychological treatment is available for individuals with substance abuse problems in inpatient, outpatient, and day treatment facilities, depending on the needs of the individual. Many people choose to attend self-help groups, such as Alcoholics Anonymous, Narcotics Anonymous, Women for Sobriety, or Rational Recovery.

REFERENCES

American Psychiatric Association. (1994). *Diagnostic and statistical manual of mental disorders–4th ed. (DSM-IV)*. Washington, DC: Author.

Gress, J., & Boss, M. (1996). Substance abuse differences among students receiving special education services. *Child Psychiatry and Human Development, 26*, 235–236.

U.S. Department of Health and Human Services (USDHHS). (1993). *Alcohol and Health*. Rockville, MD: Author.

See also Chemically Dependent Youth; Drug Abuse

SUBSTANTIA NIGRA

The substantia nigra houses the cell bodies of dopamine containing neurons that project to the striatum (putamen and caudate nucleus). This the so-called nigrostriatal pathway is the major dopamine pathway in the brain. The substantia nigra is a midbrain structure and is darkly pigmented, hence its name (i.e., black substance or black body). The nigrostriatal pathway is an important pathway in the extrapyramidal motor system, which controls background movement. Because of the importance of dopamine in the regulatory control of motor as well as emotional functioning, the nigrostriatal system has been implicated in a variety of neurobehavioral disorders (Andreasen, 1984). In particular, a breakdown of normal functioning of the dopaminergic system has been strongly implicated in schizophrenia (Andreasen, 1984). Also, other lines of investigation have suggested that dopamine plays a role in hyperactivity and attention deficit disorder (Shaywitz, Shaywitz, Cohen, & Young, 1983) and Rett syndrome (Segawa, 1997). The motor maladroitness frequently seen in learning-disabled children may be related in some fashion to basal ganglia/nigrostriatal irregularities (Duane, 1985; Rudel, 1985). The prototype neurologic disorder with primary substantia nigra involvement, and hence dopamine loss, is Parkinson's disease (Kolb & Whishaw, 1985).

REFERENCES

Andreasen, N.C. (1984). *The broken brain*. Cambridge, England. Harper & Row.

Duane, D. (1985). Written language underachievement: An overview of the theoretical and practical issues. In F.H. Duffy & N. Geschwind (Eds.), *Dyslexia: A neuroscientific approach to clinical evaluation*. Boston: Little, Brown.

Kolb, B., & Whishaw, I.Q. (1985). *Fundamentals of human neuropsychology*. New York: Freeman.

Rudel, R.G. (1985). The definition of dyslexia: Language and motor deficits. In F.H. Duffy & N. Geschwind (Eds.), *Dyslexia: A neuroscientific approach to clinical evaluation*. Boston: Little, Brown.

Segawa, M. (1997). Pathophysiology of Rett syndrome from the standpoint of early catecholamine disturbance. *European Child & Adolescent Psychiatry, 6*(1), 56–60.

Shaywitz, S.E., Shaywitz, B.A., Cohen, D.J., & Young, J.G. (1983). Monoaminergic mechanisms in hyperactivity. In M. Rutter (Ed.), *Developmental neuropsychiatry.* New York: Guilford.

See also **Dopamine; Putamen**

SUBTEST SCATTER

Kaufman (1994) points out that scatter, such as significant differences in abilities measured by the Wechsler Intelligence Scale for Children (WISC-III), occurs frequently in the normal population. On the basis of this finding, he emphasizes the importance of being certain that the intersubtest variability is indeed rare in comparison with that of normal children before associating the scatter with abnormality. However, certain characteristic scatter has been consistently found for specific groups. Low scores on arithmetic, coding, information, and digit span subtests of the WISC-III have been shown to characterize the performance of many groups of learning-disabled children. This recently has been refuted (Dumont & Willis, 1995). It has been concluded however, that learning disabilities are more likely to be indicated by intraindividual differences than by set profiles.

Scatter has been applied to problems other than learning disabilities. Different types of mental deficiencies have been described in terms of scatter (Roszkowski & Spreat, 1982). Organically caused mental deficiency exhibited more scatter in Wechsler Adult Intelligence Scale (WAIS) scores than environmentally caused deficiency, but not to a significant degree. Greater scatter may be linked to lower functioning individuals. Large amounts of scatter on intelligence tests can also be associated with high degrees of maladaptive behaviors (Roszkowski & Spreat, 1983) and social-emotional problems (Greenwald, Harder, & Fisher, 1982). Thus scatter can be associated with behavioral, emotional, and organic disorders, as well as with the more commonly thought of learning disabilities.

There may be evidence linking scatter to various disorders, but it is questionable whether it is strong enough to warrant its use as a diagnostic tool. The greatest portion of the evidence says no (Kavale & Forness, 1984). Subtest scatter may be useful in specifying particular strengths and weaknesses of an individual's performance, and in educational intervention planning. Caution is needed with interpretation of scatter and profile analysis, and flexibility is recommended when selecting tests for a particular population (Kamphaus, 1985).

REFERENCES

Dumont, R., & Willis, J.O. (1995). Intrasubtest scatter on the WISC-III for various clinical samples vs. the standardization sample: An examination of the WISC folklore. *Journal of Psychoeducational assessment, 13*(3), 271–285.

Greenwald, D.F., Harder, D.W., & Fisher, L. (1982). WISC scatter

and behavioral competence in high-risk children. *Journal of Clinical Psychology, 38,* 397–401.

Kamphaus, R.W. (1985). Perils of profile analysis. *Information/ Edge: Cognitive Assessment & Remediation, 1,* 1–4.

Kaufman, A.S. (1994). *Intelligence testing with the WISC-III.* New York: Wiley.

Kavale, K.A., & Forness, S. (1984). A meta-analysis of the validity of Wechsler scale profiles and recategorizations: Patterns or parodies? *Learning Disability Quarterly, 7,* 136–156.

Roszkowski, M., & Spreat, S. (1982). Scatter as an index of organicity: A comparison of mentally retarded individuals experiencing and not experiencing concomitant convulsive disorders. *Journal of Behavioral Assessment, 4,* 311–315.

Roszkowski, M., & Spreat, S. (1983). Assessment of effective intelligence: Does scatter matter? *Journal of Special Education, 17,* 453–459.

See also **Factor Analysis; Intelligence; Intelligent Testing; Profile Analysis; Test Scatter; WISC-III**

SUICIDE

There has been much concern about the adolescent suicide rate that dramatically increased from 1950 to 1990. Seven percent of high school students attempt suicide in a one-year period, and 60% of them use handguns (O'Donnell, 1995).

The origins of suicide in children and adolescents have been cited as (1) lack of stable support in a home or family situation; (2) family problems that lead the young person to feel powerless and without control of his or her own life; (3) lack of supportive social relationships; and (4) inability to successfully solve problems (Wagner, 1997; Weiner, 1982). Clearly, these factors, singly or in concert, are likely to affect many exceptional children and youths, particularly those who experience institutionalization or social stigmatization. In addition, there are clear parallels between these factors and theories of learned helplessness and depression (Steer, Kumar, & Beck, 1993). Seligman (1975) has defined learned helplessness as the belief that one's actions do not affect or shape one's destiny. It has been further hypothesized that children who grow up with the sense of having little control over their own lives typically feel unable to cope with problem situations and become depressed (Dweck, 1977; Miller & Seligman, 1975).

Recent research dealing with affective disorders among the mentally retarded suggests low levels of social support do lead to depression and learned helplessness within this group (Reiss & Benson, 1985). Reynolds and Miller (1985), in an initial investigation, found educable mentally retarded (EMR) adolescents to be more depressed than their nonretarded peers. In addition, higher than normal rates of suicide have been reported among other exceptional groups, including persons with alcohol and drug abuse problems, for which children and adolescents are at increasingly high risk (Farmer, 1978; McIntire & Angle (1980), and mental illness (Dunham, 1978; Wagner, 1997) a disorder for which the retarded are at high risk (Lewis & MacLean, 1982; Szymanski, 1980).

To reduce the risk of suicide among exceptional children and adolescents, intervention must occur on a basic level, addressing those needs that have been identified as preceding learned helplessness, depression, and suicide. The construction of stable family or familylike support groups, the involvement of the exceptional individual in planning and control of his or her own life, assistance in forming supportive peer and social relationships, training in problem solving and coping skills, and appropriate treatment for related disorders such as alcohol, drug abuse, or mental illness should substantially reduce the risk of suicide in this population.

REFERENCES

Dunham, C.S. (1978). Mental illness. In R.M. Goldenson, J.R. Dunham, & C.S. Dunham (Eds.), *Disability and rehabilitation handbook*. New York: McGraw-Hill.

Dweck, C.S. (1977). Learned helplessness: A developmental approach. In J.G. Schulterbrandt & A. Raskin (Eds.), *Depression in childhood*. New York: Raven.

Farmer, R.H. (1978). Drug-abuse problems. In R.M. Goldenson, J.R. Dunham, & C.S. Dunham (Eds.), *Disability and rehabilitation handbook*. New York: McGraw-Hill.

Lewis, M.H., & MacLean, W.E., Jr. (1982). Issues in treating emotional disorders. In J.L. Matson & R.P. Barrett (Eds.), *Psychopathology in the mentally retarded* (pp. 1–36). New York: Grune & Stratton.

O'Donnell, C.R. (1995). Firearm deaths among children and youth. *American Psychologist, 50*(9), 771–776.

McIntire, M.S., & Angle, C.R. (1980). *Suicide attempts in children and youth.* New York: Harper & Row.

Miller, W., & Seligman, M.E.P. (1975). Depression and learned helplessness in man. *Journal of Abnormal Psychology, 84,* 228–238.

Reiss, S., & Benson, B.A. (1985). Psychosocial correlates of depression in mentally retarded adults: I. Minimal social support and stigmatization. *American Journal of Mental Deficiency, 89,* 331–337.

Reynolds, W.M., & Miller, K.L. (1985). Depression and learned helplessness in mentally retarded and nonmentally retarded adolescents: An initial investigation. *Applied Research in Mental Retardation, 6,* 295–306.

Seligman, M.E.P. (1975). *Helplessness: On depression, development, and death.* San Francisco: Freeman.

Steer, R.A. Kumar, G., & Beck, A.T. (1993). Self-reported suicidal ideation in adolescent psychiatric inpatients. *American Psychologist, 61*(6), 1096–1099.

Szymanski, L.S. (1980). Individual psychotherapy with retarded persons. In L.S. Szymanski & R.E. Tanguay (Eds.), *Emotional disorders of mentally retarded persons.* Baltimore, MD: University Park Press.

Wagner, B.M. (1997). Family risk factors for child and adolescent suicidal behavior. *Psychological Bulletin, 121*(2), 246–298.

Weiner, I.B. (1982). *Child and adolescent psychopathology.* New York: Wiley.

See also **Depression; Emotional Disorders; Learned Helplessness**

SULLIVAN, ANNE

See MACY, ANNE SULLIVAN.

SULLIVAN PROGRAMMED READING

The Sullivan Programmed Reading system comprises an individualized programmed workbook approach to teaching reading to students in grades one through three. The sequence of the three-year system extends from Reading Readiness through Series III, with diagnostic prescriptive teaching aids and student activities that are designed to optimize individual pacing. Pupils systematically progress from letter discrimination to word recognition or to reading sentences and stories. The first ten weeks of the program are spent in the development of a basic vocabulary and the acquisition of skills that are necessary for the use of programmed material. This part of the series is teacher directed or oriented and must be done as a class or group. Afterward, the program allows each pupil to progress according to his or her own rate of learning. The pupil is provided with a minimal amount of information, a problem is posed, a response is solicited, and the response is corrected or reinforced. The child makes the response, then checks his or her answer against the correct response that is revealed as a slider moves down the page to reveal the next frame (Hafner & Jolly, 1972; Moyle & Moyle, 1971; Scheiner, 1969; Sullivan Associates, 1968).

The Reading Readiness and Programmed Readers Series I, II, and III provide sequential instruction in consonants, vowels, sight words, punctuation, suffixes, contractions, possessives, capitals, and comprehension. Placement tests indicate at which point in the series to enter a pupil who begins in the system after first grade. The Programmed Reading Program is comprised of 23 levels, with one book per level. Pupils progress through each book and are expected to pass an end-of-book test before proceeding to the next book. A total of 3266 words are introduced in the complete program (Hafner & Jolly, 1972; Sullivan Associates, 1968). For use with exceptional children see Lerner (1985).

REFERENCES

Hafner, L., & Jolly, H. (1972). *Patterns of teaching reading in the elementary school.* New York: Macmillan.

Lerner, J. (1985). *Learning disabilities: Theories, diagnosis and teaching strategies* (4th ed.). Dallas: Houghton Mifflin.

Moyle, D., & Moyle, L. (1971). *Modern innovations in the teaching of reading.* London: University of London Press.

Scheiner, L. (1969). *An evaluation of the Sullivan Reading Program (1967–1969) Rhoads Elementary School.* Washington D.C.: U.S. Department of Health, Education and Welfare. (ERIC Document Reproduction Service ED 002 362).

Sullivan Associates. (1968). Sullivan Associates programmed reading Sullivan Press. New York: McGraw-Hill.

See also **Reading Disorders; Reading Remediation**

SUMMER SCHOOL FOR THE HANDICAPPED

Extended-year programs for individuals with handicapping conditions have been a highly debated issue for many years. The position of many individuals is that extended school year programs are needed for students with handicapping conditions to prevent the loss of existing skills, accelerate the acquisition of new skills, and provide recreational programming and respite care for the parents.

Empirical support for the current policy on extended-year programs for individuals with handicaps is difficult to find in the literature. Browder, Lentz, Knoster, and Wilansky (1984) found that the primary methodology for determining both eligibility for and effectiveness of extended-year programs was the subjective judgments of teachers and parents (Bahling, 1980; McMahon, 1983). This information, while not surprising, does not provide empirical support for extended school year programming. Ellis (1975a) studied the effects of a summer program on possible regression of 16 multihandicapped blind children, and found that none of the students had regressed in eight target skill areas (e.g., communication skills). In a second study, Ellis (1975b) examined the skill levels of 145 physically and neurologically handicapped students and found a significant improvement in skill areas for the summer program participants. In contrast, Edgar, Spence, and Kenowitz (1977), in a study that examined the findings of 18 summer programs, found that the data (e.g., teacher observations, rating scales) did not strongly support the premise that such programs facilitated the maintenance of skills. However, these results are possible when there is not a coherence between the school year objectives and those of the summer program. Therefore, there are conflicting data concerning the effectiveness of extended-year programming in either maintaining or extending the learning repertoire of handicapped students.

REFERENCES

Bahling, E. (1980). *Extended school year program, Intermediate Unit #5, June–August, 1980.* Paper presented at the annual international convention of Council for Exceptional Children, Philadelphia. (ERIC Document Reproduction Service No. 208 609)

Browder, D.M., Lentz, F.E., Knoster, T., & Wilansky, C. (1984). *A record based evaluation of extended school year eligibility practice.* Unpublished manuscript.

Edgar, E., Spence, W., & Kenowitz, L. (1977). Extended school year for the handicapped: Is it working? *Journal of Special Education, 11,* 441–447.

Ellis, R.S. (1975a). Summer pre-placement program for severely multihandicapped blind children. *Summer 1975, Evaluation Report.* New York City Board of Education. (ERIC Document Reproduction Service No. ED136489)

Ellis, R.S. (1975b). Summer education program for neurologically and physically handicapped children. *Summer 1975, Evaluation Report.* New York City Board of Education. (ERIC Document Reproduction Service No. ED136489)

McMahon, J. (1983). Extended school year programs. *Exceptional Children, 49,* 457–460.

See also Tutoring

SUPERVISION IN SPECIAL EDUCATION

Current emphasis in special education is on the employment of a program administrator specifically for exceptional children. Other titles used are special education director and supervisor of exceptional children's programs. For most states, the administrator or director of special education must have an academic degree at the master's level in the education of exceptional children or a related field. The educational program for the preparation of exceptional children's program administrators is basically the same as for preparing general school administrators. The major difference in their preparation is in the specific exceptional children's program content requirement.

Program administrators should have competencies in the administration of exceptional children's programs, including assessment; planning and implementing programs; budgeting; communicating with parents, central office staff, principals, other service providers, and state and local agencies; staff development; and program evaluation. Another area of expertise necessary for program administrators is the application of school law administration of exceptional children's programs. This includes knowledge of legislation about the handicapped as it relates to IDEA other state and federal statutes; confidentiality guidelines; due process procedures; procedures for auditing and evaluating compliance; authority of the hearing officer; and schools' responsibility for various placements, transportation, suspension and expulsion, related services, competency tests, and evaluations.

Program administrators should be well versed in supervision of instruction centered around personnel management. He or she should be able to interview and select qualified exceptional children's teachers, observe and evaluate teachers to identify teaching strengths and weaknesses, and develop professional growth plans for teachers and support staff. The administrator should be able to design instructional units that specify performance objectives, instructional sequences, learning activities, and materials and evaluation processes, and prepare an educational plan that includes curriculum content and level, activities, alternative teaching strategies, and evaluation of learning outcomes (Sage & Burrello, 1994). The program administrator should also be able to evaluate the quality, utility, and availability of learning resource materials.

REFERENCE

Sage, D.D., & Burrello, L.C. (1994). *Leadership in educational reform: An administrator's guide to changes in special education.* Baltimore, MD: Brookes.

See also **Administration of Special Education; Politics, Special Education and**

SUPPORT, BEHAVIORAL

Behavioral support is the outcome of a collaborative process of systematically creating comprehensive and effective behavior support plans for individuals with severe behavioral challenges. Behavior support plans typically focus on data from functional assessments that result in environmental modifications and specific instructional procedures that teachers, family, and support personnel can implement which decrease the problem behavior, increase alternative behaviors, and result in attributions of self-determination, inclusion, and independence for the person of concern (Field, Martin, Miller, Ward, & Wehmeyer, 1998; O'Neill et al., 1997; Sugai & Horner, 1994; Turnbull & Turnbull III, 1990). Behavioral support planning is a nonaversive approach for reducing challenging behaviors that incorporates systems-level change and skill development based on an understanding of the purpose or function of the problem behavior within the context of targeted environments (Horner et al., 1990; Sugai & Horner, 1994; Turnbull, Turnbull, Shank, & Leal, 1999). O'Neill et al. (1997) write that the outcome of behavioral support is "not just to define and eliminate undesirable behavior but to understand the structure and function of those behaviors in order to teach and promote effective alternatives" (p. 8). An additional outcome of behavioral support is the promotion of durable and generalizable change that positively affects each individual's access to the general education curriculum, community settings, and preferred activities and persons across environments (Horner et al., 1990).

O'Neill et al. (1997) offers four considerations for building effective behavioral support plans. Behavioral support plans should describe our behavior; that is, behavioral support planning is a process of examining the changes that teachers, family, and support personnel will make across environments with the intent of teaching the student more effective alternatives to the problem behavior. Behavior support plans also should always build upon the results of comprehensive functional assessments; that is, the behavior support team should incorporate both indirect and direct functional assessment methodologies as a means to understand the purpose or function that the problem behavior serves for the individual. Behavior support plans should be technically sound; that is, effective behavioral support plans should include strategies that make the problem behavior irrelevant, inefficient, and ineffective by implementing empirically-validated behavioral principles across settings, persons, and time. Behavior support plans should also fit the setting where they will be implemented; that is, the behavior support plan should provide a good fit for the behavior support team and the person of concern by taking into account the values, time, and resources of those that will implement the procedures. In summary, effective behavioral support is a process of creating responsive environments that take into account the preferences, strengths, and needs of the person with severe challenging behaviors in their current environments by incorporating data from functional assessments, by promoting systems-level change across environments and persons, and through skill development activities that teach the individual effective alternatives to the targeted problem behaviors (Sugai & Horner, 1994; Turnbull et al., 1999).

REFERENCES

Field, S., Martin, J., Miller, R., Ward, M., & Wehmeyer, M. (1998). *A practical guide for teaching self-determination.* Reston, VA: The Council for Exceptional Children.

Horner, R.H., Dunlap, G., Koegel, R.L., Carr, E.G., Sailor, W., Anderson, J., Albin, R.W. & O'Neill, R.E. (1990). Toward a technology of "nonaversive" behavioral support. *The Journal of the Association for Persons with Severe Handicaps, 15,* 125–132.

O'Neill, R.E., Horner, R.H., Albin, R.W., Sprague, J.R., Storey, K., & Newton, J.S. (1997). *Functional assessment and program development for problem behavior: A practical handbook* (2nd ed.). Pacific Grove, CA: Brooks/Cole.

Sugai, G., & Horner, R. (1994). Including students with severe behavior problems in general education settings: Assumptions, challenges, and solutions. In J. Marr, G. Sugai, & G. Tindal (Eds.), *The Oregon Conference Monograph* (pp. 102–120). Eugene, OR: University of Oregon.

Turnbull, A.P. & Turnbull, H.R., III. (1990). A tale about lifestyle changes: Comments on "toward a technology of 'nonaversive' behavioral support." *The Journal of the Association for Persons with Severe Handicaps, 15,* 142–144.

Turnbull, A., Turnbull, R., Shank, M., & Leal, D. (1999). *Exceptional lives: Special education in today's schools* (2nd ed.). Upper Saddle River, NJ: Merrill.

See also Functional Assessment

SUPPORTED EMPLOYMENT

Supported employment is a vocational alternative that has been described in rules published by the U.S. Department of Education in the *Federal Register* (June 18, 1985) as "paid work in a variety of integrated settings, particularly regular work sites, especially designed for severely handicapped individuals irrespective of age or vocational potential." Traditionally, individuals with severe disabilities have been served in day activity centers in which the intended goal is to prepare these clients for vocational rehabilitation services and, ultimately, employment. However, this readiness model of service delivery has not prepared these individuals successfully for vocational rehabilitation services or employment. Supported employment provides employment opportunities to those individuals with mental and physical disabilities so severe that they are not eligible for vocational rehabilitation services.

Supported employment (Will, 1985) includes four characteristics that differentiate it from vocational rehabilitation services and traditional methods of providing day activity services. First, the service recipients are those typically served in day activity centers who do not have the potential for unassisted competitive employment and thus are ineligible for vocational rehabilitative services. Second, ongoing support, which is unavailable in a traditional day activity program, as well as supervision and ongoing training is involved. Supported employment is not designed to lead to unassisted competitive work as are vocational rehabilitation programs. Third, the employment focus of supported employment provides the same benefits typically obtained by people from work (e.g. income, security, mobility, advancement opportunities, etc.). It does not seek to identify and teach prerequisite skills and behaviors needed for employment as is usually done in day activity centers. Last, there is flexibility in support strategies to assist individuals with severe disabilities in obtaining and maintaining employment. This may include the provision of a "job coach" by a community agency. The coach provides training and supervision at an individual's work site, direct support to employers to offset training and special equipment costs, or salary supplements to coworkers who provide regular assistance in the performance of personal care activities while at work.

Examples of four supported employment options are enclaves, mobile work crews, specialized industrial programs, and supported competitive employment.

Supported work options have been initiated at state and local levels to meet the vocational needs of individuals with severe disabilities. The purpose of these work options is to provide these individuals with real work opportunities and the support necessary for them to keep their jobs. Supported work has been found to be cost-effective (Mc-Coughvin, Ellis, Rusch, & Heal 1993). The assumption is that all persons, regardless of the severity of their disabilities, have the ability to work as long as appropriate, ongoing services are provided.

REFERENCES

McCoughvin, W.B., Ellis, W.K., Rusch, F.R., & Heal, L.W. (1993). Cost-effectiveness of supported employment. *Mental Retardation, 31*(1), 41–48.

Will, M. (1985, Autumn). Supported employment programs: Moving from welfare to work. *Office of Special Education and Rehabilitative Services (OSERS) News in Print, 1*(1), 8–9.

See also **Transition; Vocational Rehabilitation**

SURROGATE PARENTS

The Individuals with Disabilities Education Act (IDEA) included parental participation as a major component in the educational planning for children with disabilities. The purpose of including parents was to ensure that the rights of the child and the parents are protected. This component of IDEA officially recognized the parents as a crucial and viable force in the life of their child and required their input in the educational planning and decision-making process. However, there are instances when a handicapped child's parents, for various reasons, are unable to represent him or her in the educational decision-making process. This is when the public agency responsible for educating the child appoints a surrogate parent. According to federal regula-

tions, a surrogate parent is appointed when (1) no parent can be identified; (2) the public agency, after reasonable efforts, cannot discover the whereabouts of a parent; or (3) the child is a ward of the state under the laws of that state (*Federal Register,* 1977 p. 42496).

Surrogate parents are individuals who are responsible for ensuring that the handicapped child receives a free appropriate education in the least restrictive environment. The surrogate parents' role is limited to the educational needs of the child. However, more and more grandparents are taking on this role (Rothenberg, 1996).

Shrybman (1982) listed the following rights of surrogate parents:

1. Review all written records regarding the child's education
2. Take part in the evaluation and development of the individual education plan (IEP)
3. Reject, accept, or recommend changes in the IEP
4. Request and/or initiate a second evaluation
5. Initiate mediation, hearing, or appeals procedures
6. Receive legal help at no cost if such assistance is necessary in the furtherance of the surrogate's responsibilities
7. Monitor the child's program
8. Recommend changes in the pupil's placement
9. Take advantage of all the rights afforded to natural parents in the special education decision-making process (pp. 267–268)

Each state is required to develop specific requirements for the selection of the surrogate parents. Once the need has been proven by the local agency, the criteria and responsibilities are specifically defined. A surrogate parent does not have to be a professional person; however, it is important that the surrogate have a general knowledge of state and federal laws relating to the handicapped. In addition, knowledge of the rules and regulations of the public school system and specific information about the child's handicap and educational needs are crucial areas. The state is responsible for education and training of the surrogate parent to ensure adequate representation of the child.

REFERENCES

Federal Register. (1977). Washington, DC: U.S. Government Printing Office.

Rothenberg, D. (1996). *Grandparents as parents: A primer for schools.* (ERIC Digest No. ED401044).

See also **Individuals with Disabilities Education Act (IDEA); Parent Education; Parents of the Handicapped**

SURVIVAL SKILLS

Survival skills are essential components of functional teaching. Many educators use the terms survival skills and functional teaching synonymously. Heward and Orlansky (1984) define functional skills as skills that are "frequently demanded in a student's natural environment" (p. 340). Cassidy and Shanahan (1979) suggest the term survival emphasizes the need to develop skills that will help individuals to attain personal goals and social responsibilities. A few examples of survival skills include balancing a checkbook, riding a bus, completing a job application, reading a menu, and shopping for groceries (Alcantara, 1994). Survival skills have also been extended to self-management skills in the classroom (Synder & Bambara, 1997).

An essential component of survival skills in the area of reading is selection of materials. Cassidy and Shanahan (1979) identified the three basic criteria for selection as relevance, necessity, and frequency. Relevance implies considering the student's age, current level of functioning, and geographical area when selecting materials. In terms of geographical area, using materials such as a phone book or a bus schedule from a student's hometown is more appropriate than using commercial materials. Necessity suggests selecting materials that are representative of tasks required in the real world. Frequency deals with the number of times the student will deal with the materials selected. Activities such as reading menus and container labels occur often in the real world.

Potential strengths of the functional curriculum model identified by Alley and Deshler (1979) include the following: (1) students are equipped to function independently, at least over the short term in society; (2) students may be better prepared to compete for specific jobs on graduation from high school; and (3) instruction in the functional curriculum may have particular relevance for the high school junior or senior who is severely disabled (p. 50).

REFERENCES

Alcantara, P.R. (1994). Effects of videotape instructional package on purchasing skills of children with autism. *Exceptional Children, 61*(1), 40–55.

Alley, G., & Deshler, D. (1979). *Teaching the learning disabled adolescent: Strategies and methods.* Denver: Love.

Cassidy, J., & Shanahan, T. (1979). Survival skills: Some considerations. *Journal of Reading, 23,* 136–40.

Heward, H.L., & Orlansky, M.D. (1984). *Exceptional children.* Columbus OH: Merrill.

Synder, M.C., & Bambara, L.M. (1997). Teaching secondary students with learning disabilities to self-manage classroom survival skills. *Journal of Learning Disabilities, 30*(5), 534–543.

See also **Daily Living Skills; Functional Instruction; Functional Skills**

SWEDEN, SPECIAL EDUCATION IN

See SCANDINAVIA, SPECIAL EDUCATION IN.

SWITZERLAND, SPECIAL EDUCATION IN

Switzerland is a confederation of 26 cantons which include 2,929 political municipalities. The cantons are autonomous states. Their population varies from 14,100 to 1,178,800 citizens.

Switzerland does not have national school/educational legislation. The cantons remain the highest authority in this area, except for certain fields of vocational education. Article 69 of the Swiss Federal Constitution specifies the responsibilities of the 26 cantons for an adequate, sufficient, and free compulsory education. Compulsory education (pre-school, primary school, lower secondary school) is subordinate to the Cantonal Departments of Public Education. Each canton is highly independent with regard to school administration and organization, which leads to an extreme decentralization of the school authority in Switzerland. Only few institutions on the tertiary level (e.g. universities, advanced vocational training, higher vocational schools) are administered and supported by the Federal Government. The Federal Government also promotes and supports the cooperation and coordination between the cantons.

Small children with disabilities and/or developmental problems are taken care of by early childhood special education services. Early education of children with special needs can be extended from birth to kindergarten, special kindergarten, or the start of school. The most common kind of early childhood interventions are the mobile education programs: They take place at the child's home where the specialist works with the child and the family in their usual environment once or twice a week. Most services are staffed with professionals with a degree in special education; some services also employ other specialists such as speech therapists, physiotherapists, or specialists for the education of children with sensory impairments.

If a child needs special help, he or she usually attends a special class (tied to the regular school) or a special school (managed partly by private organizations and partly by the canton, subsidized by Federal Disability Insurance). Thus, children with special educational needs are mostly segregated from the regular school. Actually, 5.6% of all school-age children are schooled in classes with a special curriculum (Bundesamt für Statistik, 1997). A good number of children in regular classes, special classes, and special schools get additional support and assistance from itinerant support services (between 10% to 20%, depending on the area they live). These services mostly provide psychological counseling, speech/language and psychomotor therapy. School services also includes school medical service, school dental service, vocational counseling, and support teaching for immigrant children with a foreign mother tongue. Over the past 15 years, an increasing trend towards the integration of children with special educational needs into the regular school system can be observed; in some cantons, a restricted kind of integration is already practiced. As mentioned above, special schooling embraces all the school and education-oriented endeavours for children and youths with special needs. On the compulsory education level, this function is assumed by special classes and special schools.

After their compulsory education, a good part of those exiting special classes take up vocational training (apprenticeship) or they enter an individualized vocational program which takes into account the trainee's difficulties and problems. The vocational training runs on a dual basis: The young people are trained in practical work in a particular enterprise 3 to 4 days a week; and 1 to 2 days a week they go to a vocational training school, where they attend general education classes as well as specific classes referring to their professional field. The training ends with a Federal diploma. Some of the young persons with minor disabilities do not go through a vocational training, but they might work on their parents' farms or carry out some unskilled work.

Young people who have difficulties training for a job in the free market because they suffer from physical handicaps (visual or—rarely—hearing impairments) get their training in specialized institutions. Many of the youths with mental retardation are occupied in sheltered workshops. On their way towards professional life, young persons with disabilities are supported by professionals of the vocational guidance services, run by the Federal Disability Insurance. For further information on special education in Switzerland refer to Bürli (1993).

REFERENCE

Bürli, A. (1993). *Special Education in Switzerland.* Aspects 50. Lucerne: Edition SZH. Swiss Institute for Special Education.

See also Western Europe, Special Education

SYDENHAM'S CHOREA

Sydenham's chorea is more commonly known as St. Vitus' Dance, but it also may be called minor chorea, rheumatic chorea, or acute chorea. It is generally regarded as an inflammatory complication of rheumatic fever, tonsillitis, or other infection; it also can be associated with pregnancy (chorea gravidarum). The condition is most prevalent in young girls between the ages of 5 and 15 and more common in temperate climates during summer and early fall. The condition has declined substantially in recent years owing to a similar decline in rheumatic fever. It is characterized by involuntary choreic movements throughout the body and occurs in about 10% of rheumatic attacks.

Choreic movements are rapid, purposeless, short lasting, and nonrepetitive. The movements usually begin in one limb and flow to many different parts of the body; they may resemble athetoid cerebral palsy. Fidgety behavior, clumsiness, dropping of objects, facial grimacing, awkward gait, and changes in voice or slurred speech are common symptoms that may occur at onset. A month or more may pass before medical attention is sought because these symptoms initially may be mild. Anxiety, irritability, and emotional in-

stability also may occur because of the uncontrolled movements. The involuntary motions disappear during sleep and occasionally are suppressed by rest, sedation, or attempts at voluntary control. Sydenham's chorea is nonfatal and recovery usually occurs within 2 to 6 months. Recurrence may happen two or three times over a period of years in almost one-third of the people affected.

Differential diagnosis depends on ruling out other causes through history and laboratory studies. There are no characteristic laboratory abnormalities, and pathologic studies suggest scattered lesions in the basal ganglia, cerebellum, and brain stem. No deficits in muscle strength or sensory perception are found during neurologic examination. The course of the impairment is variable and difficult to measure because of its gradual diminution.

There is no specific treatment, but some medications (phenobarbital, diazepam, perphenazine, or haloperidol) can be effective in reducing chorea. In most situations, the person with Sydenham's is encouraged to return to school or work, even if residual symptoms continue. In severe cases, protection from self-injury by using restraints may be necessary. The prognosis for recovery is variable but the condition inevitably subsides. Reassurance that the condition is self-limiting and eventually will decline without residual impairment is in order for people with Sydenham's, their families, teachers, and classmates. Behavioral problems, mild motor abnormalities, and poor performance in psychometric testing have been reported after the chorea dissipates. It is important that affected individuals receive Therapeutic Support (Moore, 1996).

REFERENCE

Moore, D. (1996). Neuropsychiatric aspects of Sydenham's chorea: A comprehensive review. *Journal of Clinical Psychiatry, 57*(9), 407–414.

See also Chorea; Huntington's Chorea

SYNAPSES

The synapse is the structure that mediates the effects of a nerve impulse on a target cell, permitting communication among nerve cells, muscles, and glands. It is a synapse that joins the terminal end of an axon of one neuron with the dendrites or cell body of another. The synapse was first described by Sir Charles Sherrington in 1897. The word itself means connection.

Synaptic transmission can be electrical or chemical, although the former is uncommon in the mammalian brain (Gazzaniga, Steen, & Volpe, 1979). With chemical transmission, one cell, the presynaptic, secretes molecules that cross a synaptic cleft and join with a postsynaptic cell. The presynaptic cell endings contain mitochondria and synaptic vesicles that hold various neurotransmitters. The neurotransmitter substances are released in tiny packettes called quanta. These substances can serve excitatory or inhibitory purposes, and not all are currently identified. However, major excitatory neurotransmitters include acetylcholine, noradrenalin, seratonin, and dopamine. Important inhibitory transmitters include gamma-amino-butric acid (GABA) and glutamate. Specific receptor molecules that receive these neurotransmitters have been identified on the postsynaptic cell.

Synapses generally are classified as axiodendritic or axiosomatic. The typical pattern is axiodendritic; this pattern occurs when an axon meets a dendrite. Somewhat less common is the axiosomatic pattern, in which an axon meets a cell body.

REFERENCE

Gazzaniga, M., Steen, D., & Volpe, B.T. (1979). *Functional neuroscience.* New York: Harper & Row.

See also Dendrites; Dopamine

SYNTACTIC DEFICIENCIES

See CHILDHOOD APHASIA, LANGUAGE DISORDERS EXPRESSIVE; LANGUAGE DISORDERS.

SYSTEMS OF CLASSIFICATION

A system of classification can be developed in an effort to identify individuals as members of one of the major handicapping conditions (e.g., learning disabilities), or it may be used to provide a subclassification within a major area of exceptionality (e.g., Down's syndrome as a subcategory of mental retardation). Contemporary special education services rely heavily on the classification of general handicapping conditions and, to lesser extent, on subclassifications.

The historical origins of the use of classification systems are dominated by two events. First, special education represents a unique educational development derived from the discipline of psychology. As such, it emerged in light of that discipline's intense interest in the measurement and study of individual differences. Subsequent refinements in measurement, including the development of classification systems based on reliable individual differences, were transferred to special education practice in the first part of the twentieth century. A second related influence arose from the attempts of early special educators to provide a science of treatment. That is, the study of individual differences led to the acceptance of a nosological orientation in treatment. Long practiced in medicine, the nosological orientation presumes that disorders can be isolated with reference to etiology, that etiology can ultimately be treated, and that subsequent cases can be similarly addressed (i.e., treatment proceeds from symptom to diagnosis of etiology to specification of treatment). In this approach, the development of a precise system of classification and subclassification is essential.

Possibly the most influential classification system now in effect is that provided within Individuals with Disabilities Education Act. Ysseldyke and Algozzine (1984) indicate that through this legislation, the U.S. Department of Education recognizes 11 categories of exceptionality, although some states recognize more or less categories. In most states, the categories represent an effective determinant of service: If an individual is not a member of the specified handicapping condition, services are not mandated. Thus, systems of classification, and related entry procedures, are essential in the selection process that ultimately determines entrance to special education.

Despite these criticisms, classification systems remain an important consideration for special education. Kauffman (1977) provided a rationale for the continuation of attempts to classify behavior: classification is a fundamental aspect of any developing science of behavior; classification is of importance in organizing and communicating information; and classification systems, if scientifically investigated, may ultimately assist in the prediction of behavior and offer insights into the preferred method of treatment. As noted by Kauffman (1977), the alternative to continued development of classification systems is "an educational methodology that relies on attempts to fit interventions to disorders by random choice, intuition, or trial and error" (p. 27).

REFERENCES

Kauffman, J.M. (1977). *Characteristics of children's behavior disorders.* Columbus, OH: Merrill.

Ysseldyke, J.E., & Algozzine, B. (1984). *Introduction to special education.* Boston: Houghton Mifflin.

See also Diagnostic and Statistical Manual of Mental Disorders (DSM-IV); Learner Taxonomies

SYSTEM OF MULTICULTURAL PLURALISTIC ASSESSMENT (SOMPA)

The System of Multicultural Pluralistic Assessment (SOMPA) (Mercer & Lewis, 1979) was designed to provide a comprehensive measure of the cognitive abilities, perceptual-motor abilities, sociocultural background, and adaptive behavior of children ages 5 through 11 years. It employs three models of assessment and attempts to integrate them into a comprehensive assessment: (1) the medical model, defined as any abnormal organic condition interfering with physiological functioning; (2) the social system model, determined principally from labeling theory and social deviance perspectives taken from the field of sociology, which attempts to correct the "Anglo conformity" biases of the test developers who have designed IQ tests for the last 80 years; and (3) the pluralistic model, which compares the scores of a child with the performance levels of children of a similar ethclass (that is, the same demographic, socioeconomic, and cultural background) correcting for any score discrepancies with the white middle class. English and Spanish language versions of the scale are available.

The SOMPA is a complex and somewhat innovative system of assessment designed to ameliorate much of the conflict over assessment in the schools. The senior author,

Mercer, a sociologist, conceptualized SOMPA in the late 1960s and early 1970s from her work in sociology's labeling theory and her sociological surveys and studies of mental retardation, particularly mild mental retardation, as a sociocultural phenomenon. The SOMPA has been extensively reviewed and debated (Humphreys, 1985; Nuttall, 1979; Reynolds, 1985; Reynolds & Brown, 1984; Sandoval, 1985). Unfortunately, presentation of the SOMPA for clinical application as opposed to pure research appears to have been premature. Major conceptual and technical issues pertaining to the scale have not been resolved adequately, even considering that a complete resolution of most of these issues is not possible. As a result, the SOMPA has contributed to the controversy over assessment practices in the schools rather than moved the field closer to a resolution. Even though controversy frequently can be stimulating to a discipline, in many ways, SOMPA has polarized the assessment community.

REFERENCES

Humphreys, L.G. (1985). Review of System of Multicultural Pluralistic Assessment. In J.V. Mitchell (Ed.), *Ninth mental measurements yearbook.* Lincoln, NE: Buros Institute.

Mercer, J., & Lewis, J. (1979). *System of Multicultural Pluralistic Assessment.* New York: The Psychological Corporation.

Nuttall, E.V. (1979). Review of System of Multicultural Pluralistic Assessment. *Journal of Educational Measurement, 16,* 285–290.

Reynolds, C.R. (1985). Review of System of Multicultural Pluralistic Assessment. In J.V. Mitchell (Ed.), *Ninth mental measurements yearbook.* Lincoln, NE: Buros Institute.

Reynolds, C.R., & Brown, R.T. (Eds.). (1984). *Perspectives on bias in mental testings.* New York: Plenum.

Sandoval, J. (1985). Review of System of Multicultural Pluralistic Assessment. In J.V. Mitchell (Ed.), *Ninth mental measurements yearbook.* Lincoln, NE: Buros Institute.

See also **Adaptive Behavior; Cultural Bias in Testing; Mercer, J.R.; Vineland Adaptive Behavior Scales**

T

TACHISTOSCOPE

The tachistoscope, or t-scope, is an instrument for presenting visual stimuli for very brief times at a controlled level of illumination (Stang & Wrightsman, 1981). The t-scope may be a self-contained unit or mounted on a slide projector.

Often the goal of tachistoscopic presentation is to determine the threshold at which subjects verbally report recognition of a stimulus. Research using the tachistoscope also has been carried out concerning the existence of subliminal perception where stimuli are said to affect behavior below the conscious threshold of perception.

REFERENCE

Stang, D., & Wrightsman, L. (1981). *Dictionary of social behavior and social research methods.* Monterey, CA: Brooks–Cole.

See also **Perceptual Span**

TAIWAN, SPECIAL EDUCATION IN

HISTORICAL OVERVIEW

The early development of special education in Taiwan has its root in the tenets of Confucianism: "education for all" and "instruction by potential." In this context, efforts are made both by government agencies and private sectors to ensure that all exceptional individuals are entitled to a right to appropriate education. The protocol of educational alternatives for students with disabilities in Taiwan can be traced back to the late years of the nineteenth century. Interestingly, early attempts to educate the individuals with disabilities were inaugurated by the clergy. To illustrate, the first special day school (built in 1886 for children who are deaf and mute) was funded by English churches and staffed by ministers. This day school served as a catalyst for establishment of similar facilities throughout the island. Public schools did not provide special education programs until 1961, when the Dong-Men elementary school of Taipei developed the first self-contained class of its kind for children with emotional disturbances.

Educational programs for children with mental retardation (MR) have played a major role in the development of special education within the public schools. Actually, special education and classes for students with MR were considered one and the same. The confusion was attributed to overemphasis on developing programs for MR children and the lack of programs for other exceptional children and youth, which in turn was associated with the overrepresentation of students with mental retardation.

Few efforts had been organized before the 1980s to fight

for the rights of populations with disabilities. The stimulus for increased public interest in and governmental attention to the welfare of people with disabilities is attributed in part to political parties and academic scholars who had their advanced studies abroad. In the late 1970s as the major opposition political party emerged, the rights movement for people with handicaps became overwhelming. The outcome has been passage of the Special Education Act of 1984 and similar legislation, plus significant changes in schools and communities.

The Special Education Act of 1984 provides the framework for special education policies and its regulations delineate a broad guideline for criteria for the identification, placement, and delivery of educational services for children with special needs. Specifications of the regulations include classroom organization, instructional objectives, and teaching methods and materials. Much of the impetus for the laws passed in the 1980s stems from issues surrounding education of children with MR, including (a) the assumed negative impact of labels, (b) expansion of special class placement, and (c) excessive reliance on single assessment measures—primarily the intelligence test.

In each locality, the Ministry of Education develops a Special Education Coordination Committee in charge of programming and monitoring of enforcement of laws and regulations associated with special education. The local government designates the Identification, Placement and Consultation Committee (IPC) to deal with special education practices in schools. The revised Special Education Act of 1997 is characterized by an addition of zero rejects to the array of special services and an extension of children from school-aged to preschool. Specifically, public schools are now open by law to all children and youths with disabilities aged 3 to 18.

Many educational problems of exceptional children and youth can be prevented or minimized through the provision of comprehensive services. The revised Special Education Act of 1997 applies to handicapped individuals ages 3–18. Many more special needs children are eligible for special education services. The role of the public school has been extended both in the nature of services and the ages of students served. Identification of exceptional children and high-risk children as infants or preschoolers has become a widespread practice, and early childhood programs designed to enhance development of the handicapped and prepare them for school have been demonstrated to be effective. Several metropolitan cities have already mandated the provision of preschool programs for children with disabilities. Career programs designed specifically for post-junior-high adolescents are under assessment across the island and the programs are gaining in popularity. Community resources are being applied to help young adults with handicaps establish themselves as active members of the community. While full inclusion is in practice in the West, it appears that Taiwan has a long way to go yet. Quite against the worldwide trend of normalization, special day schools are recently flourishing in Taiwan.

REFERENCES

Ministry of Education. (1984). *Special Education Act.* Taiwan: Author.

Ministry of Education. (1997). *Revised Special Education Act.* Taiwan: Author.

TALENTED CHILDREN

See SPECIFIC TALENT, E.G., ACADEMICALLY TALENTED CHILDREN.

TALKING BOOKS

Talking books are books recorded on cassette tapes or, more often the case in recent years, on compact disks that are used principally by the blind. These modified records are played on special talking book machines and recorded on modified machines as well. Talking books and the modified recorders are available to all visually impaired students registered through the American Printing House for the Blind. Severely reading impaired students with a diagnosis of dyslexia may also qualify for the use of talking books.

See also **American Printing House for the Blind**

TASH

Formerly the Association for Persons with Severe Handicaps, TASH is an international advocacy association of people with disabilities, their family members, other advocates, and professionals working toward a society in which inclusion of all people in all aspects of community is the norm. The organization is comprised of members concerned with human dignity, civil rights, education, and independence for all individuals with disabilities. Creating, disseminating, and implementing programs useful for the education and independent lifestyles of persons who are severely handicapped is a primary objective of TASH. Formed in 1975, TASH is a membership-supported, not-for-profit association with chapters in 34 states and members in 35 countries.

TASH seeks to promote the full participation of people with disabilities in integrated community settings that support the same quality of life available to people with disabilities. This task is accomplished through its facilitation of training in best practices, systems change, Americans with Disabilities Act (ADA), and Individuals with Disabilities Education Act (IDEA). TASH also strives to provide information, linkage with resources, legal expertise, and targeted advocacy. The organization accomplishes its work by disseminating information via a monthly newsletter covering current disability-related issues and a quarterly academic journal containing cutting-edge research. TASH also sponsors an annual conference and topical workshops, and advocates on behalf of people with disabilities and their families through building grassroots coalitions.

TASH'S central office is located at 29 W. Susquehanna

Avenue, Suite 210, Baltimore, Maryland, 21204. The association can be reached via telephone (410-828-8274), fax (410-828-6706), TDD (410-828-1306), e-mail (info@tash.org), or by visiting TASH's web site at www.tash.org.

TASK ANALYSIS

Task analysis is a teaching strategy that encompasses the breaking down and sequencing of goals into teachable subtasks. Moyer and Dardig (1978) noted it is a critical component of the behavioral approach and it serves a dual role in the instruction of learners with handicaps. First, it serves an effective diagnostic function by helping teachers pinpoint a student's individual functioning levels on a specific skill or task. Second, it provides the basis for sequential instruction, which may be tailored to each child's pace of learning. A thorough task analysis results in a set of subtasks that form the basic steps in an effective program. In essence, task analysis is both an assessment and a teaching tool (Ysseldyke & Elliott, 1999).

According to Mithaug (1979), the procedures that define task analysis have evolved from Frederick Taylor's work measurement studies and Frank and Lillian Gilbreth's motion studies conducted in the late 1800s. Motion analysis was the precursor of today's task analysis, although many elements critical to motion analysis have not been included in the educational applications of task analysis. The term task analysis came into increasing use during the 1950s, whenever tasks were identified and examined for their essential components within the workplace. This foreshadowed subsequent applications of task analysis to teach individuals with disabilities in the late 1960s.

Guidelines for designing and implementing task analysis programs have been suggested (Moyer & Dardig, 1978; Siegel, 1972):

Limit the scope of the main task

Write subtasks in observable terms

Use terminology at a level understandable to potential users

Write the task in terms of what the learner will do

Focus attention on the task rather than the learner

The ability to analyze tasks, a skill that can be acquired by any teacher, enables the detection of trends in a student's performance and the modification of task components during an instructional session (Junkala, 1973). Thus it is an extremely effective instructional method and diagnostic tool in special education.

REFERENCES

Junkala, J. (1973). Task analysis: The processing dimension. *Academic Therapy, 8*(4), 401–409.

Mithaug, D.E. (1979). The relation between programmed instruction and task analysis in the pre-vocational training of severely and profoundly handicapped persons. *AAESPH Review, 4*(2), 162–178.

Moyer, J.R., & Dardig, J.C. (1978). Practical task analysis for special educators. *Teaching Exceptional Children, 11*(1), 16–18.

Siegel, E. (1972). Task analysis and effective teaching: *Journal of Learning Disabilities, 5,* 519–532.

Ysseldyke, J., & Elliott, J. (1999). Effective instructional practices: Implications for assessing educational environments. In C.R. Reynolds & T.B. Gutkin (Eds.), *The Handbook of School Psychology* (3rd ed.). New York: Wiley.

***See also* Behavior Assessment; Behavior Modification; Behavioral Objectives**

TAT

See THEMATIC APPERCEPTION TEST.

TAXONOMIES

Taxonomy is the science of systematics. It incorporates the theory and practice of classification, or sorting and ordering significant similarities and differences among members of a system to facilitate precise communication about members, enhance understanding of the interrelationships among members, and suggest areas where additional relationships might be discovered. Early attempts to design taxonomies date back to the third century BC and Aristotle's efforts to classify animals as warm- or cold-blooded. Theophrastus, Aristotle's pupil, concentrated on a system for sorting plants. In the eighteenth century in Sweden, Linnaeus designed a classification system for botany that has served as a basis for almost all subsequent systems.

Among the more commonly used taxonomies today are the Library of Congress and Dewey Decimal systems for the classification of books and the taxonomies developed for the classification of plants and animals. The latter contains categories that permit the identification of individual organisms according to species, genus, family, order, class, phylum, and kingdom.

Stevens (1962) developed a taxonomy for special education that focuses on physical disorders. He observed that classification systems then in use were typically based on a medical model with an emphasis on disease, etiology, and symptomatology. His intent was to improve communication regarding educationally relevant attributes or somatopsychological or body disorders and the special education procedures students with such disorders might require. Stevens stressed the differences among the terms impairment, disability, and handicap and provided for attributes that carried significance for planning special education programs.

More recently the World Health Organization (WHO) has published its *International Classification of Impairments, Disabilities, and Handicaps* (1980). This publication relates consequences of disease to circumstances in which disabled persons are apt to find themselves as they interact with others and adapt to their physical surroundings. The purpose of WHO's efforts was to prepare a taxonomy that would ease the production of statistics regarding the consequences of disease, facilitate the collection of statistics useful in planning services, and permit storage and retrieval of information about impairments, disabilities, and handicaps (WHO, 1980). Diagnosis, a useful precursor to treatment, is a form of taxonomic classification (e.g., see Kamphaus, Reynolds, & McCammon, 1999).

Ultimately, taxonomies should be comprehensive, improve communication, stimulate thought, and be accepted by professionals in the field for which they were designed (Bloom, 1956). Whether the taxonomies available for special educators lead to the achievement of these goals remains to be seen, but without taxonomies as a guide, communication would be surely impaired (Kamphaus, Reynolds, & McCammon, 1999).

REFERENCES

Bloom, B.S. (Ed.). (1956). *Taxonomy of educational objectives: The classification of educational goals: Handbook I. Cognitive domain.* New York: McKay.

Kamphaus, R.W., Reynolds, C.R., & McCammon, C. (1999). Roles of diagnosis and classification in school psychology. In C.R. Reynolds & T.B. Gutkin (Eds.), *The Handbook of School Psychology* (3rd ed.) New York: Wiley.

Stevens, G.D. (1962). *Taxonomy in special education for children with body disorders.* Pittsburgh, PA: Department of Special Education and Rehabilitation, University of Pittsburgh.

World Health Organization. (1980). *International classification of impairments, disabilities, and handicaps.* Geneva, Switzerland: Author.

See also **Classification, Systems of**

TAY-SACHS SYNDROME

Tay-Sachs disease is a disorder of fat metabolism that results in loss of visual function and progressive mental deterioration. It is one of a variety of demyelinating diseases of the nervous system characterized by cerebral macular degeneration. The disorder is named after Warren Tay, an English physician (1843–1927), and Bernard Sachs, an American neurologist (1858–1944). The disorder is transmitted by an autosomal recessive gene and is found with dramatically increased frequency among Jewish infants of eastern European origin. Approximately 90% of cases of Tay-Sachs syndrome can be traced to Lithuanian or Jewish ancestry.

The disorder typically first manifests itself in infants between the ages of 4 and 8 months. Early signs include an abnormal startle response to acoustic stimulation, delay in psychomotor development or regression with loss of learned skills (e.g., loss of the ability to roll over), spasticity, and cherry red spots in the retinas, the result of degeneration of retinal ganglion cells. Head size typically increases in the second year while the cerebral ventricles remain relatively normal. There are frequently tonic-clonic seizures and blindness may occur. Infants typically become weak and apathetic. Death usually occurs at 3 to 5 years. At autopsy, the appearance of the brain is one of widespread atrophy. Treatment is aimed at the symptoms of the disease with anticonvulsant medications used to suppress seizures.

See also **Congenital Disorders**

TEACCH

Treatment and Education of Autistic and related Communication handicapped Children (TEACCH) is a unique program offering comprehensive services, research, and professional training for autistic children of all ages, and their families, in the state of North Carolina. TEACCH is a division of the psychiatry department of the University of North Carolina School of Medicine, Chapel Hill.

The program was founded in 1966 by Eric Schopler and Robert J. Reichler as a research project supported in part by the National Institute of Mental Health. Its purpose was to investigate the following misconceptions about autism: (1) that the syndrome is primarily an emotional disorder that causes children to withdraw from their hostile and pathological parents; (2) that these parents are educationally privileged and from an upper social class; and (3) that autistic children had potential for normal or better intellectual functioning. The research results clarified these misconceptions by demonstrating that autism is a developmental disability rather than an emotional illness; that parents come from all social strata and, like their children, are the victims rather than the cause of this disability; and that in spite of peak skills, mental retardation and autism can and do coexist.

These empirical research findings led to the development of the TEACCH program based on the following principles:

1. Parents should be collaborators and cotherapists in the treatment of their own children.

2. Treatment should involve individualized teaching programs using behavior theory and special education.

3. Teaching programs should be based on individualized diagnosis and assessment.

4. Implementation should be by psychoeducational therapists or teachers who function as generalists rather than specialists in a technical field such as physical therapy or speech therapy. Treatment outcome is evaluated according to the interaction between improved skills and environmental adjustments to deficits.

The TEACCH program provides comprehensive services, including professional training and research efforts that are integrated with clinical services. Training is provided for various specialists, including teachers, psychologists, psychiatrists, pediatricians, speech pathologists, and social workers. The main emphasis is on the involvement of parents in all facets of the program directed toward adjustment in all areas of the child's life—home, school, and the community.

School adjustment is fostered through special education classrooms in the public schools that include four to eight children with a teacher and an assistant teacher. These classrooms (about 54 currently) are under TEACCH direction according to individual school contracts. TEACCH functions often include hiring teachers, intensive in-service training of teachers, diagnosis and placement of children, and ongoing classroom consultation for behavior problems and special curriculum issues.

Community adaptation is facilitated through parent groups. Each center and class has a parent group affiliated with the North Carolina Society for Autistic Adults and Children, and a chapter of the National Society. The main goal of this collaboration is to improve community understanding of the client's special needs and to develop new and cost-effective services. In recent years, this involved services for the older age group, including group homes, respite care, summer camps, vocational training, social skills training, and the development of a learning-living community program.

The outcome studies of various TEACCH services have shown that autistic children learn better in a structured setting, and that with appropriate training, parents become effective in teaching and managing their own children. Such gains carry over into the home situation.

See also **Autism; Filial Therapy; Journal of Autism and Developmental Disorders**

TEACHER CENTERS (TC)

A teacher center represents a centralized setting that facilitates teacher development, in-service programs, and the exchange of ideas (Hering, 1983). Initially, TCs were funded directly with federal dollars. The basis for this funding was the passage of PL 94-482. Approximately 110 TCs were directly supported by the federal government. However, as noted by Edelfelt in 1982, "The categorical assignment of funds for teacher centers . . . [was] terminated in the fiscal year 1982 federal budget" (p. 393). The majority of TCs have continued as a result of their funding from other local and state sources. Their continuation supports the contention that the original concepts that premised their initiation are still valid.

REFERENCES

Edelfelt, R.A. (1982, September). Critical issues in developing teacher centers. *Education Digest, 48,* 28–31.

Hering, W.M. (1983). *Research on teachers' centers: A summary of fourteen research efforts.* Washington, DC: National Institute of Education.

See also **In-Service Training of Special Education Teachers; Instructional Media Center**

TEACHER EDUCATION AND SPECIAL EDUCATION

Teacher Education and Special Education is the official journal of the Teacher Education Division (TED) of the Council for Exceptional Children (CEC). The purposes of *Teacher Education and Special Education* are to support goals of the TED, and to stimulate thoughtful consideration of the critical issues that are shaping the future of teacher education.

The journal is published four times a year and the first issue of each volume is a potpourri issue that includes articles dealing with a wide range of topics. The second issue focuses on either preservice, in-service, or doctoral preparation. The third issue focuses on a topic of timely interest in personnel preparation. The last issue focuses on research and/or evaluation activities related to personnel preparation.

See also **Council for Exceptional Children**

TEACHER EFFECTIVENESS

Over the last three decades, field-based studies have been conducted on the teaching process that related specific teaching behaviors to student achievement outcomes. The results of the early studies (Crawford et al., 1978; Anderson, Evertson, & Brophy, 1979) were that there is a common set of process variables that can be observed or documented in effective teachers across grade and subject areas. It is further indicated that less effective teachers do not demonstrate these same behaviors to the appropriate degree. Continued research demonstrated clearly that teachers do make a difference in children's lives, especially with regard to classroom learning (see review by Gettinger & Stoiba, 1999).

The body of this research clearly speaks to a technology of teaching, making it increasingly clear that teachers and what they do are important determinants of student achievement. We know that effective teachers (1) optimize academic learning time; (2) reward achievement in appropriate ways; (3) use interactive teaching practices; (4) hold and communicate high expectations for student performance; and (5) select appropriate units of instruction. There are, of course, exceptions to these and other principles, and as such, teachers need to be adaptable. The research does not say that there is one best system of teaching but rather that the teacher must constantly be analyzing the feedback from students and performance data and making decisions to modify the instruction. Therefore, the findings from the teacher effectiveness studies and related research should be viewed as road maps with the teacher constantly making decisions regarding the best route to pursue and sometimes alter the selected route based on new information. In general, the literature strongly addresses the need to train teachers as accurate decision makers. It is not level of effort or the aspiration to teach well that differentiates effective instruction; it is rather knowledge, skill, and confidence (Elmore et al., 1996).

Various authors have separated the major components of effective teaching practices into different configurations. One possible organization places these practices under the domains of management, decision making, time utilization, and instruction, all of which interact with each other and result in the development of a supportive classroom climate. These domains and their subdomains are based on the experimental and correlational research reported regularly in journals on studies involving instructional strategies.

Effective teachers use effective classroom management. Effective classroom management means (1) organizing the physical classroom to minimize disruptions; (2) establishing teaching rules and procedures and adhering to those rules and procedures; and (3) anticipating problem situations and having action plans to prevent problems or deal with them when they occur. Effective teachers have a strong command of their subject matter and a keen awareness of how children think and learn (Elmore et al., 1996).

Effective teachers practice effective instruction a large percentage of the day. Instruction requires explanation, demonstration, and clarification. Effective instruction requires that material be explained and reviewed so that new material can be linked to old. Using demonstration and practice while focusing attention on the relevant dimension of a concept is a teaching art. The science of instruction followed by effective teachers is comprised of modeling, questioning, providing prompts and cues, providing feedback, and providing opportunities to practice newly learned skills. Students in classes taught by effective teachers know the goals and the expectations of the teachers for meeting those goals. Finally, research substantiates that effective teachers are people who believe they can make a difference in student achievement.

REFERENCES

Anderson, L.M., Evertson, C.M., & Brophy, J.E. (1979). An experimental study of effective teaching in first-grade reading groups. *Elementary School Journal, 79,* 193–222.

Elmore, R., Peterson, P., & McCarthey, S. (1996). *Restructuring in the classroom: Teaching, learning, and school organization.* San Francisco: Jossey-Bass.

Gettinger, M., & Stoiba, K. (1999). Excellence in teaching: Review of instructional and environmental variables. In C.R. Reynolds & T.B. Gutkin (Eds.), *The Handbook of School Psychology* (3rd ed.). New York: Wiley.

See also Teacher Expectancies; Teaching Strategies

TEACHER EXPECTANCIES

The general area of teacher expectancies involves investigating the effects of teachers' perceptions, beliefs, or attitudes about their students. Rosenthal and Jacobson (1968) tested kindergarten through fifth-grade children and then randomly identified some of them by telling their teachers that they had the greatest potential to show significant academic achievement over the school year. Results demonstrating that these children made significantly greater IQ gains than the control groups were interpreted to suggest that the teachers' expectations for the higher potential children influenced their teaching interactions with them, positively affecting the children's learning, as manifested in the higher scores. These results and interpretations were rejected by some owing to methodological flaws; e.g., the failure to measure the teachers' changed expectations and their teaching interactions. Later studies (Hall & Merkel, 1985) failed to replicate these results and indicated that teachers base their expectations for the most part on criteria relevant to academic performance and that they do not bias children's education.

With respect to the handicapped, teacher expectations have been discussed mostly in conjunction with the effects of labeling. Within this field, there is a fear that children's special education labels will cause teachers, parents, and others to lower their expectations for these children's academic and social development. The term self-fulfilling prophecy has been used to describe teachers' expectations and resulting instructional interactions that reinforce handicapped children to act in a manner consistent with the stereotypical characteristics of their handicap. There is the possibility that these children will have difficulty in learning because "they are handicapped," and may master skills only up to a level popularly ascribed to their handicap. This self-fulfilling prophecy, then, might lower teachers' and others' expectations for handicapped children, lower the children's expectations for themselves, and significantly limit the educational opportunities for them because they are not exposed to more advanced work or complex learning situations.

The research investigating teacher expectancies with handicapped individuals has been inconclusive. While some studies have demonstrated that labels do affect teacher perceptions and expectations of handicapped children, others have shown no significant negative effects. MacMillan (1977) appropriately concludes:

Although it [the evidence] does not demonstrate convincingly that calling attention to people with [for example] intellectual deficiencies by giving them special attention is always a bad thing, the controversy over labeling should make us all more sensitive to its potential hazards (p. 245).

Hobbs (1975), who coordinated a national study on the effect of labels and their resulting expectancy effects, similarly noted no simple solution to the issues as long as labels are required for entrance into special education programs and for the reimbursement of federal and state funds to finance these programs. What appears necessary are ways to minimize the potential expectancy effect of labels while permitting their continued use in the field.

REFERENCES

Hall, V.C., & Merkel, S.P. (1985). Teacher expectancy effects and educational psychology. In J.B. Dusek (Ed.), *Teacher expectancies* (pp. 67–92). Hillsdale, NJ: Erlbaum.

Hobbs, N. (1975). *The future of children.* San Francisco: Jossey-Bass.

MacMillan, D.L. (1977). *Mental retardation in school and society.* Boston: Little, Brown.

Rosenthal, R., & Jacobson, L. (1968). *Pygmalion in the classroom.* New York: Holt, Rinehart, & Winston.

See also Pygmalian Effect

TEACHING EXCEPTIONAL CHILDREN (TEC)

Teaching Exceptional Children (*TEC*) is a professional journal that is a joint production of the Council for Exceptional Children Information Center and the Instructional Materials Centers Network for Handicapped Children and Youth. It was first published in 1968 and now has a circulation of 55,000.

Edited by Dave L. Edyburn, *TEC*'s objective is "to disseminate practical and timely information to classroom teachers working with exceptional children and youth." Published quarterly the journal deals with various topic areas such as practical classroom procedures for use with the gifted and handicapped, educational-diagnostic techniques, evaluation of instructional material, new research findings, and reports of educational projects in progress.

Information concerning subscriptions or manuscripts should be referred to Publication for Council for Exceptional Children, 1920 Association Drive, Reston, VA 22091.

See also Council for Exceptional Children

TEACHING: INCLUSION AND CO-TEACHING

Co-teaching is a form of instruction in which a general education teacher and special education teacher work together in an inclusive classroom consisting of students with and without disabilities. Typically, the types of students with disabilities found in a co-teaching environment are students considered to have mild disabilities (i.e., learning, behavioral, and speech/language disabilities). Because students with mild disabilities bring a number of general and specific weaknesses to classrooms that may be structurally rigid and where information may be poorly organized, too abstract, uninteresting, and assumes a great deal of prior knowledge, a teacher who specializes in learning processes is a critical support.

TEACHING STRATEGIES

Teaching strategies are those activities that are conducted by a teacher to enhance the academic achievement of students. A teaching strategy is based on a philosophical approach that is used in conjunction with a learning strategy. Teachers generally choose a particular approach based on their educational background and training, their personal beliefs, the subject being taught, the characteristics of the learner, and the degree of learning required.

Training backgrounds of special educators can range from the behavioral to the process-oriented. Teachers with behavioral backgrounds will use approaches that are task specific and focus on observable behaviors. Those coming from a process background are more inclined to follow approaches that focus on underlying processes. They try to treat the hypothesized cause of the problem or deficit rather than the observable behavior. Approaches such as perceptual-motor training or cognitive training may be followed by teachers with process orientations. Perceptual-motor training approaches are controversial and have questionable effectiveness in regard to academic achievement (Kavale & Forness, 1999). Cognitive training approaches focus on thinking skills and learning how to learn rather than specific content skills. The research on this approach is promising. Examples of behavioral approaches are direct instruction and applied behavior analysis. These approaches focus on identifying the specific content to be taught and teaching that content in a systematic fashion using a prescribed system of learning strategies. There are also subject specific approaches. For example, in reading, some of the different approaches available are the linguistics approach, phonics, sight word, Fernald, multisensory, language experience, and the neurological impress method. These approaches focus on the organization of the materials needed for instruction and also prescribe, in some cases, specific strategies to be used.

In addition to an approach, the application of a learning strategy to a situation is needed to create a teaching strategy. A learning strategy becomes a teaching strategy when the teacher systematically plans, organizes, and uses a learning strategy with a student to achieve a specific outcome. In many texts, these learning strategies are referred to as generic strategies or principles of instruction. These strategies generally are used in conjunction with a particular phase of learning (e.g., acquisition, retention, or transfer), or for a particular type of learning (e.g., discrimination, concept, rule, problem solving). Generic strategies used for the acquisition phase include giving instruction (verbal, picture, modeling or demonstration, reading), revealing objectives to the learner, providing appropriate practice on a skill, providing feedback to the learner, organizing material into small steps and in sequential order, checking on student comprehension through questions, and offering positive and negative examples of concepts. However, it is also important for students to learn to teach others through the development of their own strategic and skillful processing of information (Alexander & Murphy, 1999).

REFERENCES

Alexander, P., & Murphy, P. (1999). What cognitive psychology has to say to school psychology. In C.R. Reynolds & T.B. Gutkin (Eds.), *The handbook of school psychology* (3rd ed.). New York: Wiley.

Kavale, K., & Forness, S. (1999). The effectiveness of special education. In C.R. Reynolds & T.B. Gutkin (Eds.), *Handbook of School Psychology* (3rd ed.). New York: Wiley.

See also Ability Training; Applied Behavior Analysis; Direct Instruction; Mnemonics; Teacher Effectiveness

TECHNIQUES: A JOURNAL FOR REMEDIAL EDUCATION AND COUNSELING

Techniques originated in July 1984 with Gerald B. Fuller and Hubert Vance as coeditors. The journal provides multidisciplinary articles that serve as an avenue for communication and interaction among the various disciplines concerned with the treatment and education of the exceptional individual and others encountering special problems in living. The orientation is primarily clinical and educational, and reflects the various types of counseling, therapy, remediation, and interventions currently employed. The journal does not mirror the opinion of any one school or authority but serves as a forum for open discussion and exchange of ideas and experiences.

TECHNOLOGY FOR THE DISABLED

If there is one word that summarizes the impact of technology in the last 25 years, it is zeitgeist, the spirit of the time. The inculcation of silicon chips and microprocessors into our everyday lives irrevocably changed us from an industrial society to an informational society (Toffler, 1982). If disabled persons are to function fully in this society, they must have access to the myriad technologies that can improve communication, information processing, and learning. While technological advances are making in-roads in the reduction of the impact of motoric, sensory, and cognitive disabilities, the real potential is yet to be met. The following section is an introduction to some of the technologies that are currently affecting the lives of disabled persons. It also offers an overview of some of the technologies that have yet to fulfill their promise.

The computer is second only to the printing press in its impact on the way in which humans acquire and distribute information. As computers are reduced in size and cost, their impact is multiplied geometrically. The computer has two characteristics that are particularly significant for disabled individuals: (1) as hardware decreases in size, it generally increases in capacity; and (2) the more sophisticated computers become, the easier they are to use. These characteristics are very important for handicapped individuals in several respects. First, as computers become smaller, they also become more portable. For example, hand-held microcomputers can be attached to wheelchairs to improve mobility. Second, as computers become easier to use, they are more accessible to the handicapped. For example, reducing the number of keystrokes required to perform certain computer functions has greatly facilitated their use.

Microprocessor-based technology facilitates communication in two ways: as a compensatory device for sensory disabilities and as an assistive device for individuals whose physical impairments make communication difficult. Examples of compensatory devices include talking computer terminals that can translate text into speech (Stoffel, 1982); special adaptive devices for microcomputers that can provide visual displays of auditory information by translating sound into text (Vanderheiden, 1982); and Cognivox, an adaptive device for Apple personal computers that combines the capabilities of voice recognition and voice output (Murray, 1982).

For individuals with motoric disabilities, communication aids have been developed that allow them to operate computers with single-switch input devices. These devices may be as simple as game paddles and joysticks or as sophisticated as screen-based optical headpointing systems. Keyboard enhancers and emulators help individuals with restricted movement by reducing the number of actuations necessary for communication. For example, Minispeak is a semantic compaction system that can produce thousands of clear, spoken sentences with as few as seven keystrokes (Baker, 1982). Adaptive communication devices can also be linked with microcomputers to help the disabled control their living environments (e.g., by running appliances, answering the telephone, or adjusting the thermostat).

The term telecommunication means communication across distance. It is a means of storing text and pictures as electronic impulses and transmitting them via telephone line, satellite, coaxial and fiber optic cables, or broadcast transmission. Telecommunication offers several advantages over traditional means of communication. First, telecommunication is relatively inexpensive when spread across time and users. Also, telecommunicating helps alleviate the problems associated with geographic remoteness or the isolation imposed by limited mobility. Information-gathering and dissemination need not be limited to schools. It can occur in the home or office; a local area network (LAN) can link several microcomputers or terminals to a computer with expanded memory. Such a system permits several operators to use the same software and data simultaneously. A wide-area network links computers from distant geographic regions. Examples of this networking capability can be found in several states where all of the local agencies are linked to the state agency. Statewide systems greatly reduce the time and paperwork necessary for compliance with special education legislation.

SpecialNet is another example of a wide-area network. Subscribers use it primarily to access electronic bulletin boards and to send messages through electronic mail. Electronic bulletin boards function much the same as traditional corkboards found in most schools. Users can post messages to obtain information, or they can read messages to find out the latest information about a given topic. For example, the employment bulletin board on SpecialNet posts vacancies in special education and related services. The Request for Proposals (RFP) bulletin board has information on the availability of upcoming grants and contracts. The exchange bulletin board is for users to post requests for information. Electronic mail, as the name implies, is a system whereby computer users can send and receive messages through their computers. On the SpecialNet system, each subscriber is given a special name that identifies his or her mailbox; with the aid of word processing and telecommunication software, users can send short or long documents in a matter of seconds.

In addition to capabilities offered by electronic bulletin boards and electronic mail, individuals with telecommunication hookups have access to information from large electronic libraries that store, sort, and retrieve bibliographic information. For example, the Educational Resources Information Center (ERIC), operated by the Council for Exceptional Children, is the largest source of information on handicapped and gifted children. Other important sources of information are the Handicapped Exchange (HEX), which contains information on handicapped individuals, and ABLEDATA, which is a catalog of computer hardware, software, and assistive devices for the handicapped.

Another important form of telecommunication is teletext, a one-way transmission to television viewers. Teletext uses the vertical blanking interval (VBI), the unused portion of a television signal, to print information on television screens. Applications of teletext include news headlines, weather forecasts, and information on school closings. Closed captioning is a form of teletext that allows hearing-impaired individuals to see dialogue (JWK International, 1983). Experiments are now under way to use teletext to transmit instructional material. Broadcasters can transmit public domain software into homes and schools that have microcomputers and special transmission decoding devices.

A videodisk is a tabletop device that is interfaced with a monitor to play video programs stored on 12-inch disks. When interfaced with a microcomputer, the videodisk becomes interactive, and thus becomes a powerful instructional tool. Part of the videodisk's power comes from its storage capacity; it can hold 54,000 frames of information, including movies, filmstrips, slides, and sound. When combined with the microcomputer's branching capacity, videodisks allow students to move ahead or go back according to the learner's needs. Information can also be shown in slow motion or freeze frame. One of the earliest educational videodisks was the First National Kidisc, a collection of games and activities for children. The California School for the Deaf in Riverside also developed a system to use the videodisk to teach language development and reading. With this system, students use light pens to write their responses on the screen (Wollman, 1981). In the past, videodisk technology has been very expensive because of the cost in developing the disks. Now, however, educators and other service providers can have customized disks made at relatively low cost.

Artificial intelligence refers to the use of the computer to solve the same types of problems and to make the same kinds of decisions faced by humans (Yin & Moore, 1984). Because scientists do not fully understand how humans solve problems and make decisions, they have debated whether true artificial intelligence is possible. So far, the closest they have come is the development of expert systems, natural systems, and machine vision. Expert systems are computer programs that use knowledge and inference strategies to solve problems. The systems rely on three kinds of information: facts, relations between the facts, and methods for using the facts to solve problems (D'Ambrosio, 1985). An example of an expert system is Internist, which makes medical diagnoses. Natural language processing is the use of natural speech to communicate with computers and to translate foreign language texts. Machine vision takes advantage of sensory devices to reproduce objects on the computer screen. These technological applications, like many others, offer potential benefits to disabled individuals, but their use for physical or cognitive prostheses hinges on the commitment of vast resources for their development.

A robot is a device that can be programmed to move in specified directions and to manipulate objects. What distinguishes a robot from other technologies and prosthetic devices is its capacity for locomotion. Robotic arms can pick up and move objects, assemble parts, and even spray paint. Robots of the future will not only be able to move, they will also be able to sense the environment by touch, sight, or sound. More important, the robot will be able to acquire information, understand it, and plan and implement appropriate actions (Yin & Moore, 1984). While robots offer great potential as prosthetic devices for the disabled, their current use is limited primarily to research and manufacturing. To some extent, robots are being used in classrooms to teach computer logic.

Specific technologies are in use today in special education classrooms for nearly all categories of disabling conditions, including communication disorders, health impairments, hearing impairments, visual impairments, and students with learning disabilities in particular (e.g., see Cartwright, Cartwright, & Ward, 1995). Technology is growing most rapidly in areas where it was first used and seems to have the greatest impact on quality of life issues in the sensory impairments and communication disorders. Computer-aided instruction is on the rise as well, especially with children with learning disabilities, but is a late-comer. As recently as 1990, the major textbook in learning disabilities (Myers & Hammill, 1990) makes no mention of technology for learning disability interventions.

REFERENCES

Baker, B. (1982). Minispeak: A semantic compaction system that makes self-expression easier for communicatively disabled individuals. *Byte, 7,* 186–202.

Cartwright, P., Cartwright, C., & Ward, M. (1995). *Educating special learners* (4th ed.). Boston: Wadsworth.

D'Ambrosio, B. (1985). Expert systems—Myth or reality? *Byte, 10,* 275–282.

JWK International. (1983). *Teletext and videotex* (Contract No. 300-81-0424). Washington, DC: Special Education Programs Office.

Murray, W. (1982). The Cognivox V10–1003: Voice recognition and output for the Apple II. *Byte, 7,* 231–235.

Myers, P., & Hammill, D. (1990). *Methods for learning disorders* (4th ed.). Austin, TX: Pro-Ed.

Pfaehler, B. (1985). Electronic text: The University of Wisconsin experience. *T.H.E. Journal, 13,* 67–70.

Stoffel, D. (1982). Talking terminals. *Byte, 7,* 218–227.

Toffler, A. (1982). *The third wave.* New York: Bantham.

Vanderheiden, G. (1982). Computers can play a dual role for disabled individuals. *Byte, 7,* 136–162.

Wollman, J. (1981). The videodisc: A new educational technology takes off. *Electronic Learning, 1,* 39–40.

Yin, R.K., & Moore, G.B. (1984). *Robotics, artificial intelligence, computer simulation: Future applications in special education.* Washington, DC: U.S. Department of Education.

See also **Computer Use with the Handicapped; Robotics; SpecialNet**

TECSE

See EARLY CHILDHOOD SPECIAL EDUCATION, TOPICS IN.

TEGRETOL

Tegretol (carbamazepine) is an anticonvulsant medication indicated for the treatment of various types of seizure disorders. In addition, Tegretol may also be prescribed for the treatment of manic-depressive disorders, resistant schizophrenia, rage outburst, or alcohol withdrawal management (Shannon, Wilson, & Stang, 1995). With any continuous medication regime, school personnel should be notified of this medication and any other health related concerns (Wong, 1995).

REFERENCE

Shannon, M., Wilson, B., & Stang, C. (1995). *Govoni & Hayes drugs and nursing implications* (8th ed.). Norwalk, CT: Appleton & Lange.

Wong, D. (1995). *Whaley & Wong's nursing care of infants and children* (5th ed.). St. Louis: Mosby-Year Book.

See also **Absence Seizures; Anticonvulsants; Grand Mal Seizures**

TELECOMMUNICATION DEVICES FOR THE DEAF (TDDS; TTYS)

Telecommunication devices for the deaf (TDDs or TTYs) make communication by telephone available to the hearing-impaired population by providing video or printed modes of communication across regular phone lines. Using a modem, or acoustic coupler, a TDD user types out a message to another user. This message either moves across a video display screen or is typed on a roll of paper. In this fashion, conversations can be held and information exchanged as far as telephone wires extend.

A TDD uses a regular or slightly modified keyboard. Some special terminology is used to facilitate ease of transmission. GA, for go ahead, indicates to one user that the other is waiting for a reply. SK, for stop keying, denotes the completion of a conversation. Often a Q is typed to imply a question.

The number of TDDs in public and private use is increasing rapidly. Public service agencies such as libraries, schools, and airlines are using TDDs to enable the hearing-impaired population to use their services. Police and fire departments use TDDs to ensure the safety of hearing-impaired individuals. The TDD has been hailed as a great contributor to the independence of hearing-impaired persons.

See also **Deaf; Electronic Communication Aids**

TELECOMMUNICATIONS SYSTEMS IN SPECIAL EDUCATION

The use of telecommunication technology for special education mirrors the explosion of technology in society. In the same way that commercial electronic network services such as Compu-Serve and The Source have become widely known to the general public, SpecialNet is an electronic mail service and information source specifically for special educators. Similarly, transformation of the telephone system from copper to fiber optic wire will facilitate rapid data transmission for any use, including perhaps transfer of data on special education students as they move from district to district.

Certain types of telecommunication technologies (e.g., computer-assisted instruction) delivered over telephone lines from a central location, as in the University of Illinois' PLATO system, are being made obsolete as modifications are made for personal computers, thus reducing the costs of instruction delivery. Other technologies involving electronic memory and telephone transmission are expanding, notably ABLEDATA, a bibliographic source of information on assistive devices for the disabled.

Telecommunications technology, currently in a period of rapid change, may transform special education practice in much the same way that it is transforming communication worldwide. However, in contrast to other technologies developed specifically for the disabled, special education will benefit from technological advances for all citizens. Thus the average modern family may use a personal computer, modem, and telephone line as a link to specialized news sources, stock quotes and discount brokers, specialized electronic news services, and targeted mailboards or electronic mailboxes. Disabled persons, using the same systems, may communicate with other persons with similar interests, scan specialized information sources, work in competitive employment from their homes, and avail themselves of services provided for all citizens. Special educators in public schools and higher education may use telecommunications for much the same purposes, targeting their efforts toward the acquisition of information from rapidly expanding specialized information networks.

See also **Computer-Assisted Instruction; Electronic Communication Aids**

TEMPERAMENT

Individual differences in temperament have been recognized for centuries. The Greeks talked of four basic dispositions. Yet, the notion of constitutional contributions to behavior received only limited formal attention from American psychologists and educators until relatively recently. Major impetus to the study of temperament has come from the work of psychiatrists Alexander Thomas and Stella Chess and their colleagues (Thomas & Chess, 1977), but independent support for the notion of temperament may be found in pediatric and psychiatric research, in longitudinal studies of development, in research on infants and on child-family interactions, in twin studies, and in work in behavioral genetics. Temperament is an important area of concern from both research and applied perspectives. Its relevance to special education and the development and adjustment of handicapped children is increasingly recognized.

Definitions. Although intuitively appealing, temperament has somewhat different definitions, depending on the investigator. Thomas and Chess (1977) view temperament as a stylistic variable. They consider that temperament describes how an individual behaves, not what an individual does or how well he or she does it. Thomas and Chess identified nine dimensions of temperament or behavioral style: activity level, adaptability, approach/withdrawal, attention span and persistence, distractibility, intensity of reaction, quality of mood, rhythmicity (regularity), and threshold of responsiveness. The dimensions were derived in part from Thomas and Chess's clinical observations, and were formalized in major longitudinal research, the New York Longitudinal Study (NYLS). In Thomas and Chess's view, these temperamental variations are, in part, constitutional in base.

The constitutional or biological anchoring of temperament is apparent in other definitions. Buss and Plomin (1975, 1984) propose that to be considered a temperament, a behavioral predisposition must meet criteria of developmental stability, presence in adulthood, adaptiveness, and presence in animals, and must have a genetic component. They define four dimensions that, in their view, meet these criteria: emotionality, activity, sociability, and impulsivity. Rothbart and Derryberry (1981), based primarily on their studies of human infants, suggest that temperament is best conceptualized as individual differences in reactivity and regulation that are presumed to be constitutionally based. Their formulation emphasizes arousal (or excitability) and the neural and behavioral processes that regulate or modu-

late it, a formulation consistent with that of Strelau (1983). Goldsmith and Campos (1986) adopt a somewhat different perspective, defining temperament as individual variation in emotionality, including differences in the primary emotions of fear, anger, sadness, pleasure, etc., as well as in a more general arousal; they consider both temperament and intensive parameters. It should be noted that a major definitional issue relates to distinctions between temperament and personality (Goldsmith & Campos, 1982; Rutter, 1982). Many investigators consider temperament a constitutional and genetic component of personality. This view is well reflected in the definition that emerged from the 1980 New Haven Temperament Symposium: "Temperament involves those dimensions of personality that are largely genetic or constitutional in origin, exist in most ages and in most societies, show some consistency across situations, and are relatively stable, at least within major developmental areas" (Plomin, 1983, p. 49). Thus, despite differences in specific components and in emphases, there is some consensus that temperament is an individual difference that has its basis in biological or constitutional makeup, has some stability across setting and time, and is linked to differences in behavioral or expressive styles (Bouchard, 1995).

The formal application of temperament constructs to educational practice is relatively recent but is growing. Overall, the evidence suggests that temperament and cognitive ability are partially independent contributors to educational achievement. In addition to achievement in academic content, there is considerable evidence to suggest that temperamental variations are related to children's personal and social adjustment in school. The impact of temperament may be particularly powerful where children have other handicapping or problem conditions (Keogh, 1982), although there are temperamental differences within groups of handicapped children (Hanson, 1979). Field and Greenfield (1982) suggest that temperament patterns may be associated with particular handicapping conditions. There also is some tentative evidence linking temperament to adjustment and achievement problems of learning-disabled pupils (Keogh, 1983).

Temperament may contribute to school achievement and adjustment in several ways (Keogh, 1986) and is related to intellectual performance (Brebner & Stough, 1995). It may be a factor in a generalized response set; i.e., some temperaments may fit well with the complex and changing demands of school whereas others do not. Temperament may affect a child's specific preparation for learning by allowing activity and attention to be modulated and directed easily and quickly. Temperament may interact with particular subject matter to facilitate or impede learning. Individual differences in temperament are also significant contributors to children's personal-social adjustment in school. Intuitively, at least, interpersonal problems have a strong foundation in child-peer and child-teacher interactions. Thus, personal style, or temperament, may be a major factor in problem behavior. If the relationship between children's temperament and their achievement and behavioral adjustment in school is considered within Thomas and Chess's "goodness of fit" notion, then both child characteristics and setting or task demands and conditions must be taken into account. Goodness of fit has important implications for identification, diagnosis, intervention, and treatment.

REFERENCES

Bouchard, T. (1995). Longitudinal studies of personality and intelligence. In D. Saklofske & M. Zeidner (Eds.), *International handbook of personality and intelligence,* NY: Plenum.

Brebner, J., & Stough, C. (1995). Theoretical and empirical relationships between personality and intelligence. In D. Saklofske & M. Zeidner (eds.), *International handbook of personality and intelligence.* New York: Plenum.

Buss, A.H., & Plomin, R. (1975). *A temperament theory of personality development.* New York: Wiley.

Buss, A.H., & Plomin, R. (1984). *Temperament: Early developing personality traits.* Hillsdale, NJ: Erlbaum.

Field, T., & Greenberg, R. (1982). Temperament ratings by parents and teachers of infants, toddlers, and preschool children. *Child Development, 53,* 160–163.

Goldsmith, H.H., & Campos, J.J. (1986). Fundamental issues in the study of early temperament: The Denver twin temperament study. In M.E. Lamb & A.L. Brown (Eds.), *Advances in developmental psychology* (pp. 231–283). Hillsdale, NJ: Erlbaum.

Hanson, M.J. (1979). A longitudinal description study of the behaviors of Down's syndrome infants in an early intervention program. *Monographs of the Center on Human Development.* Eugene, University of Oregon.

Keogh, B.K. (1982). Temperament: An individual difference of importance in intervention programs. *Topics in Early Childhood Special Education, 2*(2), 25–31.

Keogh, B.K. (1983). Individual differences in temperament: A contribution to the personal-social and educational competence of learning disabled children. In J.D. McKinney & L. Feagens (Eds.), *Current topics in learning disabilities* (pp. 33–55). Norwood, NJ: Ablex.

Keogh, B.K. (1986). Temperament and schooling: What is the meaning of goodness of fit? In J.V. Lerner & R.M. Lerner (Eds.), *New directions for child development: Temperament and social interaction in infants and children.* San Francisco: Jossey-Bass.

Plomin, R. (1983). Childhood temperament. In B.B. Lahey & A.E. Kazdin (Eds.), *Advances in clinical child psychology* (Vol. 6, pp. 45–92). New York: Plenum.

Rothbart, M.K., & Derryberry, D. (1981). Development of individual differences in temperament. In M.E. Lamb & A.L. Brown (Eds.), *Advances in developmental psychology* (Vol. 1, pp. 37–86). Hillsdale, NJ: Lawrence Erlbaum.

Rutter, M. (1982). Temperament: Concepts, issues and problems. In R. Porter & G.C. Collins (Eds.), *Temperamental differences in infants and young children* (pp. 1–19). London: Pitman.

Strelau, J. (1983). *Temperament-personality-activity.* New York: Academic Press.

Thomas, A., & Chess, S. (1977). *Temperament and development.* New York: Brunner/Mazel.

See also **Body Image; Hyperactivity; Learned Helplessness; Personality Assessment; Teacher Expectancies**

TEMPER OUTBURST

The temper outburst or temper tantrum, as it may be referred to more frequently, is familiar to any professional who works with children. The temper tantrum occurs more frequently among younger children who exhibit a variety of learning, physical, or emotional problems. In almost every instance where a temper tantrum occurs, it is obvious to the attending adults that the child is attempting to gain some personal objective(s) through this staged outburst.

The temper tantrum is usually easily recognizable because it is characterized by explosive kinds of behavior. Such behaviors as cursing, kicking, hitting, biting, destruction of property, and related behaviors that may be dangerous to those around as well as to furnishings. The wild rage and anger, the intense yelling and crying signify a child that is out of control emotionally. It often appears that the usual defenses of the child have fallen apart and that he or she can only vent intense, uncontrollable rage.

In general, the temper outburst seems to occur only when the child is in the presence of an adult in charge. Typically, this behavior may occur in the presence of the parent, but it may also occur with teachers or in an institutional setting with child-care workers. Trieschmann, Whittaker, and Bendro (1969) present a comprehensive treatment of the nature, causes, and possible treatments for temper tantrums. In general, the authors view the temper tantrum as an effort by the child to gain control and deal with developmental problems.

In many instances, the parent or child-care worker reports that there seems to be no reason for or warning that the child is going to erupt into wild, uncontrollable anger. However, most educators and psychologists who have made a thorough investigation of children's temper tantrums discover that there are precipitating or contingent factors. For example, the child usually exhibits tantrum behavior only around adults and always around other people. Usually, the child receives an intense amount of attention, albeit negative. In fact, adults present will often need to exhibit a great deal of attention (e.g., restraint) to prevent the child from hurting others or from destroying property. Mullen (1983) provides an extensive description of the occurrences of temper tantrums among children institutionalized in a youth development center. Some of these children are strong teenagers who can, and do, inflict injury on professional child-care workers. A temper outburst in this setting is characterized by fear on the part of other children and the staff. In all cases, the person having a temper tantrum captures the attention of others.

REFERENCES

Mullen, J.K. (1983). Understanding and managing the temper tantrum. *Child Care Quarterly, 12,* 59–70.

Trieschmann, A.E., Whittaker, J.K., & Bendro, L.K. (1969). *The other 23 hours: Child care work in a therapeutic milieu.* Chicago: Aldine.

See also **Behavior Modification; Behavior Observation; Restraint**

TERATOGEN

A teratogen is an agent that causes developmental malformations or monstrosities. The causes can be environmental, genetic, multifactorial, maternal-fetal, or unknown. Environmental agents include drugs and similar agents (e.g., alcohol, anticonvulsants, LSD), hormones, infections (e.g., cytomegalic inclusion disease, influenza, mumps, rubella, syphilis, toxoplasmosis), radiation, mechanical trauma, hypotension (low blood pressure), vitamin deficiency or excess (hypervitaminosis A), and mineral deficiency (zinc). Genetic causes include chromosomal abnormality (e.g., Down's syndrome, trisomy 13) and various hereditary patterns—sporadic, dominant, recessive, and polygenetic. Maternal-fetal interactions are exemplified by advanced maternal age and maternal hypothyroidism. Finally, a variety of dysmorphic syndromes are undetermined as to etiology. Many congenital abnormalities may be detected prior to birth. The primary means for such diagnosis has been through amniocentesis. Additionally, imaging systems such as ultrasonography demonstrate relatively gross abnormalities late in development (Spaeth, Nelson, & Beaudoin, 1983).

The timing of development helps to clarify the spectrum of associated malformations. Injuries prior to the fifteenth day of gestation affect development of primary germ layers; such abnormalities are usually so global that survival of the fetus is unusual. Between weeks two and seven, insults cause major abnormalities that affect whole organ systems. Following the first trimester (the period of differentiation of organ detail and organ interrelationship), abnormalities tend to be more limited and specific. While timing of embryonic or fetal insult relates closely to manifest anomaly, certain substances may cause varying malformations, though the time of insult is constant.

REFERENCE

Spaeth, G.L., Nelson, L.B., & Beaudoin, A.R. (1983). Ocular teratology. In T.D. Duane & E.A. Jaeger (Eds.), *Biomedical foundations of ophthalmology* (Vol. 1, pp. 6–7). Hagerstown, MD: Harper & Row.

See also **Central Nervous System; Genetic Variations**

TERMAN, LEWIS M. (1877–1956)

Lewis M. Terman received his PhD in education and psychology from Clark University, where he studied under G. Stanley Hall. Experienced as a schoolteacher, principal, and college instructor, in 1910 he joined the faculty of Stanford University, where he served as head of the psychology department from 1922 until his retirement in 1942.

With an interest in mental tests dating from his graduate studies at Clark University, Terman became a leading figure in the newly born testing movement, developing dozens of tests during his career. The best known and most widely used of his tests were the Stanford-Binet tests of intelligence, which he adapted from the Binet-Simon Scale of Intelligence in 1916 and revised in 1937. He also developed the Army Alpha and Beta tests (the first group intelligence tests) for use in classifying servicemen during World War I. With the publication of the Stanford-Binet tests in 1916, Terman introduced the term intelligence quotient (IQ), a term that quickly became a part of the general vocabulary.

Lewis M. Terman

In 1921 Terman initiated the first comprehensive study of gifted children. His staff tested more than 250,000 schoolchildren to identify 1,500 with IQs above 140. This sample of boys and girls was studied intensively and followed up periodically in a study that continues today. Terman found that, contrary to the popular belief at the time, children with high IQs tend to be healthier, happier, and more stable than children of average ability. In addition, they are more successful in their personal and professional lives. Terman, who can be credited with founding the gifted child movement, used his findings to promote the provision of special educational programs for able students.

REFERENCES

Fancher, R.E. (1985). *The intelligence men.* New York: Norton.

Hilgard, E. (1957). Lewis Madison Terman: 1877–1956. *American Journal of Psychology, 70,* 472–479.

Murchison, C. (Ed.). (1961). *A history of psychology in autobiography.* New York: Russell & Russell.

See also **Stanford-Binet Intelligence Scale**

TERMAN'S STUDIES OF THE GIFTED

In 1911, while at Stanford University, Lewis M. Terman began a systematic collection of data on children who achieved exceptionally high scores on the Stanford-Binet Intelligence Test. In the early 1920s, working with Melita Oden, he administered the Stanford-Binet test to students referred to by teachers as being "highly intelligent." Studies of their traits and the extent to which they differed from unselected normal children were begun in 1925.

Terman's subjects were in a 1500-child sample (800 boys and 700 girls) that was in the top 1% of the school population in measured intelligence; i.e., they possessed tested IQs of 140 or higher (Terman & Oden, 1925).

Terman and Oden (1951) summarized the characteristics of the students in their gifted sample as (1) slightly larger, healthier, and more physically attractive; (2) superior in reading, language usage, arithmetical reasoning, science, literature, and the arts; (3) superior in arithmetical computation, spelling, and factual information about history and civics (though not as markedly as in the areas covered in (2); (4) spontaneous, with a variety of interests; (5) able to learn to read easily, and able to read more and better books than average children; (6) less inclined to boast or overstate their knowledge; (7) more emotionally stable; (8) different in the upward direction for nearly all traits.

Follow-up studies in 1947, 1951, and 1959 were completed to obtain a comparison between promise and performance. Follow-up studies by other authors have obtained less "perfect" findings, in that not all of the subjects were found to be geniuses in the sense of transcendent achievement in some field (Feldman, 1984). Recent studies have supported Terman's findings on emotional stability (Schlowinski & Reynolds, 1985), spontaneity and creativity in play (Barnett & Fiscella, 1985), and reading aptitude (Anderson, Tollefson, & Gilbert, 1985).

The entire set of data sources for Terman's original group is maintained in closed files at Stanford University. It is estimated that less than half of the coded responses of this source of data have been transferred to tabulation sheets.

REFERENCES

Anderson, M.A., Tollefson, N.A., & Gilbert, E.C. (1985). Giftedness and reading: A cross sectional view of differences in reading attitudes and behavior. *Gifted Child Quarterly, 29*(4), 86–189.

Barnett, L.A., & Fiscella, J. (1985). A child by any other name.... A comparison of the playfulness of gifted and non-gifted children. *Gifted Child Quarterly, 29*(2), 61–66.

Feldman, D.H. (1984). A follow-up of subjects scoring about 180 IQ in Terman's "Genetic Studies of Genius." *Exceptional Children, 50*(6), 518–523.

Schlowinski, E., & Reynolds, C.R. (1985). Dimensions of anxiety among high IQ children. *Gifted Child Quarterly, 29*(3), 125–130.

Terman, L.M., & Oden, M.H. (1925). *Genetic studies of genius: Mental and physical traits of a thousand gifted children.* Stanford, CA: Stanford University Press.

Terman, L.M., & Oden, M.H. (1951). The Stanford studies of the gifted. In P.A. Witty (Ed.), *The gifted child.* Boston: D. C. Heath.

See also **Gifted Children and Reading**

TEST ANXIETY

Test anxiety is such a universal phenomenon that it hardly requires general definition. In school, on the job, or for various application procedures, tests are required. Performance on a test can impact negatively on the test-taker. Thus an essential component for an anxiety arousal state exists when the individual is placed in a test-taking situation. Test situations are specific and thus present an opportunity to investigate the nature of anxiety.

Test anxiety is usually regarded as a particular kind of general anxiety. Ordinarily, it refers to the variety of responses—physiological, behavioral, and phenomenal (Sieber, 1980)—that accompany an individual's perceptions of failure. The person experiencing test anxiety often has a fear of failure as well as a high need to succeed. Both the fear of failure and the drive for success may be internalized. In some instances, either may seem more of a desire on the part of the test-taker to please a parent or other significant individual. Regardless of the originating causes of test anxiety, it can be a debilitating state of arousal.

One of the major challenges for theorists and researchers on test anxiety is to ascertain why anxiety appears to motivate some persons yet limits seriously the performance of others. Findings from several researchers suggest that the individual's expectations of success or failure on a test are strongly correlated to the development of test anxiety (Heckhausen, 1975; Weiner, 1966). For example, it may be argued that those who are low in motivation to succeed attribute failure to a lack of ability whereas those who are high in motivation to succeed see failure as emanating more from a lack of effort. Heckhausen (1975) cites data showing that those persons with a high fear of failure tend to attribute success more to good luck than those persons with a high expectation of success. Thus, for those who expect to succeed, anxiety may be more of a motivating force than for those who fear failure. For the latter group, initial anxiety may become a debilitating form of test anxiety.

Much of the available research and numerous self-reports suggest that test anxiety is a recurring problem for children and adults. Moreover, test anxiety often appears to inhibit the usual maximal level of performance of the individual. Thus if a test situation is to be used as an effective means of assessing human potential, it is important that we understand more fully the origin of test anxiety as well as its impact on individual performance.

REFERENCES

Heckhausen, H. (1975). Fear of failure as a self-reinforcing motive. In I.G. Sarason & C.D. Spielberger (Eds.), *Stress and anxiety* (Vol. 2). Washington, DC: Hemisphere.

Sieber, J.E. (1980). Defining test anxiety: Problems and approaches. In I.G. Sarason (Ed.), *Test anxiety: Theory, research, and applications.* Hillsdale, NJ: Erlbaum.

Weiner, B. (1966). The role of success and failure in the learning of easy and complex tasks. *Journal of Personality & Social Psychology, 3,* 339–344.

See also **Anxiety; Stress and the Handicapped Student**

TEST EQUATING

Test equating is a technique for making the characteristics of two tests similar or identical, if possible, so that an individual's scores on the two tests mean the same thing. This process is accomplished currently through statistical means. There are two different problems associated with test equating. One is the problem of equating scores on two tests that were designed to be of the same difficulty, for the same kind of student, with the same content. This is called horizontal equating. The other problem is how to equate tests that were designed for different populations, often younger and older students, in which the content overlaps. In this case, one test will be hard for the younger students and the other will be quite easy for the older. This is called vertical equating.

See also **Assessment; Measurement**

TEST FOR AUDITORY COMPREHENSION OF LANGUAGE–THIRD EDITION (TACL-3)

The *Test for Auditory Comprehension of Language–Third Edition* (TACL-3) is an individually-administered measure of receptive spoken language that assesses a subject's ability to understand the following categories of English language forms: Vocabulary, Grammatical Morphemes, and Elaborated Phrases and Sentences. The TACL-3 consists of 142 items, divided into three subtests, each of which corresponds to a category of language form. Each item is composed of a word or sentence and a corresponding picture plate that has three full-color drawings.

Percentile ranks, standard scores, and age equivalents are available for children ages 3-0 through 9-11. The TACL-3 provides a variety of norm comparisons based on a standardization sample of 1,102 children, relative to socioeconomic factors, ethnicity, gender, and disability that are the same as those estimated for the year 2000 by the U.S. Bureau of the Census. Studies have shown the absence of gender, racial, disability, and ethnic bias. Reliability coefficients are computed for subgroups of the normative sample (e.g., individuals with speech disabilities, African Americans, European Americans, Hispanic Americans, females) as well as for the entire normative group.

See also **Auditory Processing**

TEST OF ADOLESCENT AND ADULT LANGUAGE–THIRD EDITION (TOAL-3)

The *Test of Adolescent and Adult Language–Third Edition* (TOAL-3; Hammill, Brown, Larsen, & Wiederholt, 1994) is a revision of the Test of Adolescent Language originally published in 1981 and revised in 1987. A major improvement in the test is the extension of the norms to include 18- through 24-year-old persons enrolled in postsecondary education programs. This improvement required that the name of the test be changed to indicate the presence of the older population in the normative sample. TOAL-3 yields 10 composite scores: Listening—the ability to understand the spoken language of other people; Speaking—the ability to express one's ideas orally; Reading—the ability to comprehend written messages; Writing—the ability to express thoughts in graphic form; Spoken Language—the ability to listen and speak; Written Language—the ability to read and write; Vocabulary—the ability to understand and use words in communication; Grammar—the ability to understand and generate syntactic and morphological structures; Receptive Language—the ability to comprehend both written and spoken language; and Expressive Language—the ability to produce written and spoken language. The Overall Language Ability quotient and the other 10 composite quotients have a mean of 100 and a standard deviation of 15.

The normative sample exceeded 3,000 persons in 22 states and 3 Canadian provinces. It was representative of the U.S. population according to 1990 U.S. Census percentages for region, gender, race, and residence; the sample is stratified by age. Internal consistency, test-retest, and score reliability were investigated. All reliability coefficients exceed .80. Content, criterion-related, and construct validity have been thoroughly studied. In addition, the TOAL-3 scores distinguished between groups known to have language problems and those known to have normal language. Evidence is also provided to show that TOAL-3 items are not biased with regard to race or gender.

TEST OF EARLY MATHEMATICAL ABILITY–SECOND EDITION (TEMA-2)

The *Test of Early Mathematical Ability–Second Edition* (TEMA-2; Ginsburg & Baroody, 1990) measures the mathematics performance of children between the ages of 3-0 and 8-11 years. Items are specifically designed to measure the following domains: concepts of relative magnitude, reading and writing numerals, counting skills, number facts, calculation, calculational algorithms, and base-ten concepts.

The TEMA-2 standardization sample was composed of 896 children representing 27 states. The characteristics of the sample approximate those in the 1980 U.S. Census. The results of the test, which takes approximately 5 to 15 minutes to administer, may be reported as standard scores, percentiles, or age equivalents. Reliabilities are in the .90s; validity has been experimentally established. Test results are reported in terms of a standard score (M = 100, SD = 15) and a percentile rank. The TEMA-2 now includes a book of remedial techniques for improving skills in the areas assessed on the test.

REFERENCE

Ginsburg, H.P., & Baroody, A.J. (1990). *Test of Early Mathematical Ability–Second Edition.* Austin, TX: Pro-Ed.

TEST OF EARLY READING ABILITY–SECOND EDITION (TERA-2)

The *Test of Early Reading Ability–Second Edition* (TERA-2; Reid, Hresko, & Hammill, 1991) measures the actual reading ability of young children from ages 3–0 to 9–11. Items measure knowledge of contextual meaning, alphabet knowledge, and book and print conventions. Performance is reported as a standard score (M = 100; SD = 15), percentile, or normal curve equivalent. The TERA-2 has two alternate, equivalent forms. Although subtests are not provided, items can be profiled to reflect abilities in the areas of contextual meaning, alphabet knowledge, and book and print conventions. The TERA-2 was standardized on a national sample of 1,454 children. Normative data are given for every 6-month interval. Both internal consistency and test-retest reliability are reported in the test manual. In all instances, coefficients approach or exceed .80. Validity coefficients are available based on correlations of the TERA-2 with other tests of reading, language, intelligence, and achievement. The TERA-2 Picture Book is in an easel format. A computer scoring system is available.

REFERENCE

Reid, D.K., Hresko, W.P., & Hammill, D.D. (1991). *Test of Early Reading Ability–Second Edition.* Austin, TX: Pro-Ed.

TEST OF EARLY WRITTEN LANGUAGE–SECOND EDITION (TEWL-2)

The *Test of Early Written Language–Second Edition* (TEWL-2; Hresko, Herron, & Peak, 1996) measures early writing ability in children from ages 3–0 to 10–11. It includes two forms, each with a Basic Writing and Contextual Writing subtest. The Basic Writing subtest requires responses to specific items (spelling, capitalization, punctuation, sentence construction, and metacognitive knowledge) while the Contextual Writing subtest depends on the authentic assessment (story format, cohesion, thematic maturity, ideation, and story construction) of a writing sample. Detailed scoring instructions are provided. Each subtest measures conventional, linguistic and conceptual components of writing. Further, each subtest may be given independently.

Three quotients (Basic Writing, Contextual Writing, and Global Writing) are provided each based on a mean of 100 and a standard deviation of 15. The TEWL-2 norms represent more than 1400 children from 33 states. Normative information is reflective of the nation as a whole with respect to gender, race, ethnicity, geographic region, and urban/rural residence. Internal consistency and reliability coefficients all exceed .90. Substantial content-description procedures, criterion-prediction procedures, and construct-identification procedures are presented.

REFERENCE

Hresko, W.P., Herron, S.R., & Peak, P.K. (1996). *Test of Early Written Language–Second Edition.* Austin, TX: Pro-Ed.

TEST OF LANGUAGE DEVELOPMENT–PRIMARY: THIRD EDITION

Originally published in 1997, the *Test of Language Development–Primary* (TOLD; Newcomer & Hammill, 1997) is now in its third edition. It is a nine subtest, individually administered test designed to measure a child's language ability relative to three types of linguistic systems (listening, organizing, speaking) and three types of linguistic features (semantics, syntax, phonology). The results of the subtests are combined to form six clinically useful composite scores, one for each of the systems and features listed above. The test is for children ages 4–0 through 8–11 and takes about an hour to give.

The test is widely used by speech and language pathologists and educational diagnosticians who need to obtain a normative comparison of a child's language skills. Because the third edition of the TOLD has just been published, no reviews of the test are available. However, reviewers of earlier editions have generally found the norms and reliability of the test to be adequate. References to these reviews are listed below.

REFERENCE

Newcomer, P., & Hammill, D.D. (1997). *Test of Language Development–Primary* (3rd ed.). Austin, TX: Pro-Ed.

***See also* Language Disorders**

TEST OF MEMORY AND LEARNING (TOMAL)

The TOMAL (Reynolds & Bigler, 1994a) is a comprehensive battery of 14 memory and learning tasks (10 core subtests and 4 supplementary subtests) normed for use from ages 5 years 0 months 0 days through 19 years 11 months 30 days. The 10 core subtests are divided into the content domains of verbal memory and nonverbal memory that can be combined to derive a Composite Memory Index. A Delayed Recall Index is also available that requires a repeat recall of the first four subtests' stimuli 30 minutes after their first administration.

Memory may behave in unusual ways in an impaired brain and traditional content approaches to memory may not be useful. The TOMAL thus provides alternative groupings of the subtests into the Supplementary Indexes of Sequential Recall, Free Recall, Associative Recall, Learning, and Attention and Concentration. These Supplementary Indexes were derived by having a group of "expert" neuropsychologists sort the 14 TOMAL subtests into logical categories (Reynolds & Bigler, 1994b). To provide greater flexibility to the clinician, a set of four purely empirically derived factor indexes representing Complex Memory, Sequential Recall, Backward Recall, and Spatial Memory have been made available as well (Reynolds & Bigler, 1996).

Table 1 summarizes the names of the subtests and summary scores, along with their metric. The TOMAL subtests

Table 1 Core and Supplementary Subtests and Indexes Available for the TOMAL

	M	SD
Core subtests		
Verbal		
Memory for Stories	10	3
Word Selective Reminding	10	3
Object Recall	10	3
Digits Forward	10	3
Paired Recall	10	3
Nonverbal		
Facial Memory	10	3
Visual Selective Reminding	10	3
Abstract Visual Memory	10	3
Visual Sequential Memory	10	3
Memory for Location	10	3
Supplementary subtests		
Verbal		
Letters Forward	10	3
Digits Backward	10	3
Letters Backward	10	3
Nonverbal		
Manual Imitation	10	3
Summary scores		
Core indexes		
Verbal Memory Index (VMI)	100	15
Nonverbal Memory Index (NMI)	100	15
Composite Memory Index (CMI)	100	15
Delayed Recall Index (DRI)	100	15
Supplementary indexes (expert derived)		
Sequential Recall Index (SRI)	100	15
Free Recall Index (FRI)	100	15
Associative Recall Index (ARI)	100	15
Learning Index (LI)	100	15
Attention Concentration Index (ACI)	100	15
Factor scores (empirically derived)		
Complex Memory Index (CMFI)	100	15
Sequential Recall Index (SRFI)	100	15
Backwards Recall Index (BRFI)	100	15
Spatial Recall Index (SMFI)	100	15

are scaled to the familiar metric of mean equaling 10 and a standard deviation of 3 (range 1 to 20). Composite or summary scores are scaled to a mean of 100 and standard deviation of 15. All scaling was done using the method of rolling weighted averages and is described in detail in Reynolds and Bigler (1994b).

TOMAL SUBTESTS

The ten core and four supplementary TOMAL subtests require about 60 minutes for a skilled examiner if the delayed recall subtests are also administered. The subtests were chosen to provide a comprehensive view of memory functions and, when used together, provide the most thorough assess-

ment of memory available (Ferris & Kamphaus, 1995). The subtests are named and briefly described in Table 2.

The TOMAL subtests systematically vary the mode of presentation and response so as to sample verbal, visual, motoric, and combinations of these modalities in presentation and in response formats (Reynolds & Bigler, 1997). Multiple trials to a criterion are provided on several subtests, including selective reminding, so that learning or acquisition curves may be derived. In the selective reminding format (wherein examinees are reminded only of stimuli "forgotten" or unrecalled), when items once recalled are unrecalled by the examinee on later trials, problems are revealed in the transference of stimuli from working memory and immediate memory to more long-term storage. Cueing is also provided at the end of certain subtests to add to the examiner's ability to probe depth of processing.

STANDARDIZATION

The TOMAL was standardized on a population-proportionate stratified (by age, gender, ethnicity, socioeconomic status, region of residence, and community size) random sample of children throughout the United States. Standardization and norming was conducted for ages 5 up to 20. Details of the standardization and specific statistics on the sample are provided in Reynolds and Bigler (1994b).

The TOMAL subtests and composite indexes show excellent evidence of internal consistency reliability. Reynolds and Bigler (1994b) report coefficient alpha reliability estimates that routinely exceed 0.90 for individual subtests and 0.95 for composite scores. Stability coefficients are typically in the 0.80s.

Reynolds and Bigler (1994b) review a series of prepublication studies that demonstrate evidence for the validity of the TOMAL as a measure of memory functioning. The TOMAL scores correlate around 0.50 with measures of intelligence and achievement, indicating the TOMAL is related to but not the same as these measures. Measures of intelligence typically correlate with one another (around 0.75 to 0.85) and with measures of achievement (around 0.55 to 0.65).

Since publication of the TOMAL, several studies have provided evidence of convergent and divergent validity of the TOMAL subtests as measures of various aspects of memory by examining patterns of correlations among TOMAL subtests and the Rey Auditory Verbal Learning Test and the Wechsler Memory Scale-Revised. The verbal components of the TOMAL correlate well with these measures but the nonverbal sections are relatively independent. The TOMAL nonverbal subtests, unlike a number of other purportedly visual and nonverbal memory tests, are difficult to encode verbally, making the TOMAL nonverbal subtests more specific and less contaminated by examinees' attempts at verbal mediation. On the nonverbal or visual memory portions of existing memory batteries, examiners should expect larger differences across tests than on verbal memory measures.

Validity is a complex concept related to the interpreta-

Table 2   Description of TOMAL Subtests

Core

Memory for Stories. A verbal subtest requiring recall of a short story read to the examinee. Provides a measure of meaningful and semantic recall and is also related to sequential recall in some instances.

Facial Memory. A nonverbal subtest requiring recognition and identification from a set of distractors: black-and-white photos of various ages, males and females, and various ethnic backgrounds. Assesses nonverbal meaningful memory in a practical fashion and has been extensively researched. Sequencing of responses is unimportant.

Word Selective Reminding. A verbal free-recall task in which the examinee learns a word list and repeats it only to be reminded of words left out in each case: tests learning and immediate recall functions in verbal memory. Trials continue until mastery is achieved or until eight trials have been attempted: sequence of recall unimportant.

Visual Selective Reminding. A nonverbal analogue to WSR where examinees point to specified dots on a card, following a demonstration of the examiner, and are reminded only of items recalled incorrectly. As with WSR, trials continue until mastery is achieved or until eight trials have been attempted.

Object Recall. The examiner presents a series of pictures, names them, has the examinee recall them, and repeats this process across four trials. Verbal and nonverbal stimuli are thus paired and recall is entirely verbal, creating a situation found to interfere with recall for many children with learning disabilities but to be neutral or facilitative for children without disabilities.

Abstract Visual Memory. A nonverbal task. AVM assesses immediate recall for meaningless figures when order is unimportant. The examinee is presented with a standard stimulus and required to recognize the standard from any of six distractors.

Digits Forward. A standard verbal number recall task. DSF measures low-level rote recall of a sequence of numbers.

Visual Sequential Memory. A nonverbal task requiring recall of the sequence of a series of meaningless geometric designs. The ordered designs are shown followed by a presentation of a standard order of the stimuli and the examinee indicates the order in which they originally appeared.

Pair recall. A verbal paired-associative learning task is provided by the examiner. Easy and hard pairs and measures of immediate associative recall and learning are provided.

Memory for Location. A nonverbal task that assesses spatial memory. The examinee is presented with a set of large dots distributed on a page and asked to recall the locations of the dots in any order.

Supplementary

Manual Imitation. A psychomotor, visually based assessment of sequential memory where the examinee is required to reproduce a set of ordered hand movements in the same sequence as presented by the examiner.

Letters Forward. A language-related analogue to common digit span tasks using letters as the stimuli in place of numbers.

Digits Backward. This is the same basic task as Digits Forward except the examinee recalls the numbers in reverse order.

Letters Backward. A language-related analogue to the Digits Backward task using letters as the stimuli instead of numbers.

---

tion of scores on tests and many approaches to the question of meaning of performance on tests such as the TOMAL are appropriate. Case studies, group comparisons, and views of the internal structure of tests all add to this knowledge. These are provided in Reynolds and Bigler (1997).

REFERENCES

Ferris, L.M., & Kamphaus, R.W. (1995). Review of the Test of Memory and Learning. *Archives of Clinical Neuropsychology, 10*(6).

Reynolds, C.R., & Bigler, E.D. (1994a). *Test of Memory and Learning.* Austin, TX: Pro-Ed.

Reynolds, C.R., & Bigler, E.D. (1994b). *Manual for the Test of Memory and Learning.* Austin, TX: Pro-Ed.

Reynolds, C.R., & Bigler, E.D. (1996). Factor structure, factor indexes, and other useful statistics for interpretation of the Test of Memory and Learning. *Archives of Clinical Neuropsychology, 11*(1), 29–43.

Reynolds, C.R., & Bigler, E.D. (1997). Clinical assessment of child

and adolescent memory with the Test of Memory and Learning. In C. Reynolds & E. Fletcher-Janzen (Eds.), *The Handbook of Clinical Child Neuropsychology* (pp. 296–319). New York: Plenum.

TEST OF NONVERBAL INTELLIGENCE–THIRD EDITION (TONI-3)

The *Test of Nonverbal Intelligence–Third Edition* (TONI-3; Brown, Sherbenou, & Johnsen, 1998), a major revision of the popular TONI-2, was designed to be a language-free measure of abstract-figural problem solving for children and adults ages 6–0 to 89–11. The TONI-3 measures a specific component of intelligent behavior by testing an individual's ability to solve problems without overtly using language. The directions, content, and responses of the test are all language-free, which makes the TONI-3 an ideal test for those who are deaf, language disordered, non-English speaking, or culturally different.

The abstract-figural content of the test ensures that each item presents a novel problem. The TONI-3 items contain no words, numbers, familiar pictures, or symbols. The drawings in the TONI-3 Picture Book have been substantially improved in this revision. Because the TONI-3 has 2 equivalent forms, it is ideal for situations where both pre- and post-measures are desirable. Each 45 item form contains problem-solving tasks that progressively increase in complexity and difficulty. Raw scores are converted to percentile ranks and to deviation quotients that have a mean of 100 and a standard deviation of 15 points.

The TONI-3 was normed over 3,000 subjects tested in 1995 and 1996. Their demographic characteristics matched those of the United States population according to the 1996 Census data. The normative group was stratified on the basis of age, gender, race, ethnic group membership, geographic location, community size, principal language spoken in the home, and socioeconomic status as indicated by educational attainment and family income.

Almost 20 years of research has established the test's reliability and validity. Extensive research is reported in the manual, including the authors' own research and all published research conducted by independent investigators since the test was first published in 1980. Considerable validity data are reported as well. These data document the test's relationship to other measures of intelligence, its relationship to measures of achievement and personality, its efficiency in discriminating groups appropriately, and its factor structure. The potential bias of test items was studied and found to be insignificant.

REFERENCE

Brown, L., Sherbenou, R.J., & Johnsen, S.J. (1997). *Test of Nonverbal Intelligence–Third Edition.* Austin, TX: Pro-Ed.

TEST OF PHONOLOGICAL AWARENESS (TOPA)

The *Test of Phonological Awareness* (TOPA; Torgesen & Bryant, 1994) measures young children's awareness of the individual sounds in words. The TOPA can be used to identify children in kindergarten who may profit from instructional activities to enhance their phonological awareness in preparation for reading instruction. The Early Elementary version of the TOPA can be used to determine if first- and second-grade students' difficulties in early reading are associated with delays in development of phonological awareness.

The TOPA is provided in a Kindergarten version (measuring same and different beginning sounds) suitable for administration any time during the kindergarten year and in an Early Elementary version (measuring same and different ending sounds) suitable for first- and second-grade children. Both versions can be administered either individually or to groups of children, with group administration taking about

20 minutes. The test has been standardized on a large sample of children representative of the population characteristics reported in the U.S. census. The manual provides information to generate percentiles and a variety of standard scores. Internal consistency reliabilities range from .89 to .91 at different ages. Evidence of content, predictive, and construct validity also is provided in the manual.

REFERENCE

Torgesen, J.K., & Bryant, B.R. (1994). *Test of Phonological Awareness.* Austin, TX: Pro-Ed.

TEST OF WORD FINDING (TWF)

The *Test of Word Finding* (TWF; German, 1989) assesses an important expressive vocabulary skill. An examiner can diagnose word-finding disorders by presenting five naming sections: Picture Naming: Nouns; Picture Naming: Verbs; Sentence Completion Naming, Description Naming; and Category Naming. The TWF includes a special sixth comprehension section that allows the examiner to determine if errors are a result of word-finding problems or are due to poor comprehension. The instrument provides formal and informal analyses of two dimensions of word finding: speed and accuracy. The formal analysis yields standard scores, percentile ranks, and grade standards for item response time. The informal analysis yields secondary characteristics (gestures and extra verbalization) and substitution types. Speed can be measured in actual or estimated item response time.

The TWF is an individually administered test consisting of a primary form (80 items) for grades 1 and 2, and an intermediate form (90 items) for grades 3 through 6. Administration time is between 20 and 30 minutes. Age norms for ages 6–6 to 12–11 and grade norms for Grades 1 through 6 are available.

The instrument was nationally standardized on 1,200 individuals residing in 18 states. The sample was stratified based on the 1980 census. Reliability and validity are reported in the technical manual.

REFERENCE

German, D.J. (1989). *Test of Word Finding.* Austin, TX: Pro-Ed.

See also **Aphasia; Learning Disabilities**

TEST OF VARIABLES OF ATTENTION

The Test of Variables of Attention (TOVA; Greenberg, 1988/1996) is an individually-administered visual continuous performance test. It is designed primarily for diagnosing children with attentional disorders and for monitoring the effectiveness of medication in treating attentional disorders. The TOVA is a 23-minute computerized test that requires neither language skills nor recognition of letters or numbers. The task is relatively simple: one of two easily discriminated visual stimuli is presented for 100 milliseconds at

2-second intervals, and the subject is required to click a button whenever the target appears, but must inhibit responding whenever the non-target appears. The target stimulus is a small square adjacent to the top of a larger square and the non-target stimulus is a small square adjacent to the bottom of a larger square. There are two conditions during the test: 1) infrequent presentation of targets that is designed to measure attention; and 2) frequent presentation of targets that is designed to measure impulsivity.

Seven scores are obtained on the TOVA: errors of omission, errors of commission, mean correct response time, variability, anticipatory responses, multiple responses, and post-commission response time. The TOVA kit provides a manual for interpretation of test results and the test itself provides computerized test interpretations. The TOVA kit also provides two videotapes that demonstrate how the TOVA may be used to screen for ADHD, to predict response to medication, and to monitor the psychopharmacological treatment.

REFERENCE

Greenberg, L.M. (1996). Test of Variables of Attention. Los Alamitos, CA: Universal Attention Disorders, Inc. (Original work published 1988).

TEST OF WRITTEN LANGUAGE–THIRD EDITION (TOWL-3)

The *Test of Written Language–Third Edition* (TOWL-3) measures language in spontaneous and contrived formats. Using a pictorial prompt, the student writes a passage that is scored on Contextual Conventions (capitalization, punctuation, and spelling), Contextual Language (vocabulary, syntax, and grammar), and Story Construction (plot, character development, and general composition). The contrived subtests (Vocabulary, Spelling, Style, Logical Sentences, and Sentence Combining) measure word usage, ability to form letters into words, punctuation, capitalization, ability to write conceptually sound sentences, and syntax. Composite quotients are available for overall writing, contrived writing, and spontaneous writing.

The TOWL-3 was standardized on a 26-state sample of more than 2,000 public and private school students in grades 2 through 12. These students have the same characteristics as those reported in the 1990 Statistical Abstract of the United States. Percentiles, standard scores, and age equivalents are provided. Internal consistency, test-retest with equivalent forms, and interscorer reliability coefficients approximate .80 at most ages, and many are in the .90s. The validity of the TOWL-3 was investigated and relevant studies are described in the manual, which has a section that provides suggestions for assessing written language informally and that gives numerous ideas for teachers to use when remediating writing deficits. In addition, the TOWL-3 is shown to be unbiased relative to gender and race and can be administered to individuals or small groups. Because two equivalent forms (A and B) are available, examiners can evaluate student growth in writing using pretesting and posttesting that is not contaminated by memory.

TEST SCATTER

Individuals who take intelligence, achievement, and other educational and psychological tests seldom, if ever, earn precisely the same score on all tests or even on the subparts of one test. This variation in performance across tests by individuals is known as test scatter. There are three principal measures of test scatter present in the testing literature: the range, the number of deviant signs, and profile variability.

The range is simply the highest minus the lowest score for an individual on a battery of tests once the scores have been placed on a common scale such that the means and standard deviations are equal. The Wechsler Intelligence Scale for Children-Revised (WISC-R) has 10 regularly administered subtests and two supplementary subtests. As one index of test scatter, one might locate the highest subtest score and the lowest subtest score for a particular child and then subtract the two. The resulting number is the range. The range for a particular child can be compared with the average range of scores for individuals in the standardization sample of the tests or some other relevant reference group to determine the degree of "usualness" of the observed range of scores. Sometimes, as with the WISC-R verbal and performance scales, a range will be calculated with only two scores.

The number of deviant signs (NDS) refers to the number of subtests or other component parts or a battery of tests that deviate at a statistically significant level (typically, p # .05) from the mean score of the individual across all tests taken or at least all of those used in the comparisons. Six subtests constitute the WISC-R verbal scale. It may be of interest of know whether the number of subtests that differ significantly from a child's own mean subtest score is unusual or whether it is a common occurrence to show so many strengths and weaknesses in an ability profile. Normative comparisons would again be made.

Profile variability is another prominent index of test scatter and one that appears to be the most stable. Profile variability is simply the variance of a set of scores for one individual, i.e., the average squared deviation from the mean score of all the scores.

Since perhaps the inception of the field of learning disabilities, learning-disabled (LD) children have been characterized as having a large or unusual amount of intra- and intertest scatter (Chalfant & Scheffelin, 1969). Until the mid-1970s, this assumption was made largely in ignorance of the degree of test scatters that characterizes the test performance of normal children. Although normative data on test scatter for the WISC had been presented as early as 1960, these data went largely ignored until Kaufman's studies of the WISC-R were published in 1976 (Kaufman, 1976a, 1976b). Prior to his examination of test scatter for the 2200 normal children in the WISC-R standardization sample, myths regarding such indexes abounded.

In an informal survey, Kaufman (1976a) reported that

Table 3 Percentage of Normal Children Obtaining WISC-R V–P Discrepancies of a Given Magnitude or Greater, by Parental Occupation

Size of V–P Discrepancy (Regardless of Direction)	Parental Occupation					
	Professional and Technical	Managerial, Clerical, Sales	Skilled Workers	Semiskilled Workers	Unskilled Workers	Total Sample
9	52	48	48	46	43	48
10	48	44	43	41	37	43
11	43	40	39	36	34	39
12	40	35	34	31	29	34
13	36	33	31	28	26	31
14	32	29	29	25	24	28
15	29	25	26	21	22	24
16	26	22	22	19	19	22
17	24	19	18	15	16	18
18	20	16	16	14	15	16
19	16	15	13	12	14	14
20	13	13	12	10	13	12
21	11	11	8	9	10	10
22	10	9	7	7	9	8
23	8	8	6	6	8	7
24	7	7	5	5	6	6
25	6	6	4	4	5	5
26	5	5	3	3	4	4
27	4	4	2	2	3	3
28–30	3	3	1	1	2	2
31–33	2	2	<1	<1	1	1
34+	1	1	<1	<1	<1	<1

Source: Kaufman, Alan S. Intelligent testing with the WISC-R. © 1979, New York: Wiley.

when asked to estimate the range of subtest scores on the WISC-R for normal children, most practicing psychologists and other diagnosticians suggested a range of only two to four points. The mean range for normal children in the WISC-R standardization sample turned out to be more than seven points, more than twice the typical estimate. A similar phenomenon occurred with regard to verbal-performance IQ differences on the WISC-R.

Conventional diagnostic beliefs, prior to the publication of Kaufman's work, held that a verbal-performance IQ difference of 15 points or more was a primary indication of learning disability. Even Wechsler (1974) indicated that this degree of scatter was of clinical significance and deserving of follow-up study. At it turns out, approximately 35% of the population of normal children have a verbal-performance IQ difference of 12 or more points, representing a statistically significant difference between the two scores, and 24%, or nearly one out of four, of normal children demonstrate a difference of 15 or more points. These data are extremely similar to those reported in 1960 for the WISC.

A complete tabulation of Kaufman's (1979) findings regarding verbal-performance IQ differences is presented in Table 3.

Since these seminal studies, a number of authors have investigated test scatter for normal children on such widely used tests as the Wechsler Preschool and Primary Scale of Intelligence (Reynolds & Gutkin, 1981) and the Kaufman Assessment Battery for Children (Chatman, Reynolds, & Willson, 1983). It is now clear that normal children exhibit much variation in their abilities, exploding the myth of the normal child's "flat" ability profile and that only exceptional children show large amounts of test scatter. Recent revisions of the Wechsler scales including the WISC-III and WAIS-III continue to show distributions of test scatter similar to what was seen in Kaufman's (1979) early work.

Large amounts of scatter in the profiles of normal children do not negate the importance of variation in children's test scatter. If the differences among a child's test scores are large enough to be considered real (reliable), then chances are that real differences exist among the child's cognitive skills and abilities, differences that mandate attention and that have relevance to the development of instructional strategies. Unusual differences among test scores will continue to have diagnostic use as well, but only when determined with regard to normative standards.

REFERENCES

Chalfant, J.C., & Scheffelin, M.A. (1969). *Central processing dysfunctions in children* [NINDS Monograph No. 9]. Bethesda, MD: U.S. Department of Health, Education, and Welfare.

Kaufman, A.S. (1976a). A new approach to the interpretation of test scatter on the WISC-R. *Journal of Learning Disabilities, 9,* 160–168.

Kaufman, A.S. (1976b). Verbal-performance IQ discrepancies on the WISC-R. *Journal of Consulting & Clinical Psychology, 44,* 739–744.

Kaufman, A.S. (1979). *Intelligent testing with the WISC-R.* New York: Wiley-Interscience.

Reynolds, C.R., & Gutkin, T.B. (1981). Test scatter on the WPPSI: Normative analyses of the standardization sample. *Journal of Learning Disabilities, 14,* 460–464.

Wechsler, D. (1974). *Wechsler intelligence scale for Children-revised.* New York: The Psychological Corporation.

See also **Profile Variability; Verbal-Performance IQ Discrepancies**

TESTS IN PRINT

Tests in Print (Buros, 1961, 1974; Mitchell, 1983; Murphy, Conoley, & Impara, 1994) are volumes that provide a comprehensive index of commercially available educational and psychological tests in English-speaking countries. The volumes contain descriptive information about each test (e.g., the age or grade levels for which the test is designed, author, publishing company, scale scores); literature related to the specific test; an index to all reviews of the test in previous Buros *Mental Measurement Yearbooks;* and references to test descriptions and related literature cited in previous *Test in Print* volumes.

The most current, *Tests in Print IV* (Murphy, Conoley, & Impara, 1994), contains thousands of descriptions of commercially available tests; references for specific tests; an alphabetical listing of test names, a directory of publishers with addresses and an index to their tests; a title index showing both in print and out-of-print tests since previous listings a name index for test authors, reviewers, and authors of references; and a classified subject index for quickly locating tests in particular areas.

REFERENCES

Buros, O.K. (1961). *Tests in print.* Highland Park, NJ: Gryphon.

Buros, O.K. (1974). *Tests in print II.* Highland Park, NJ: Gryphon.

Mitchell, J.V., Jr. (1983). *Test in print III.* Lincoln, NE: Buros Institute of Mental Measurements.

Murphy, L.L., Conoley, J.C., Impara, J.C. (1994). *Test in print IV.* Lincoln, NE: Buros Institute of Mental Measurements.

See also **Buros Mental Measurements Yearbook**

TESTS

See SPECIFIC TEST; MEASUREMENT.

TEST-TEACH-TEST PARADIGM

The Test-Teach-Test Paradigm (TTT-P) is representative of an instructional concept that is similar to the concept of teaching students how to read by using the phonics approach. Fundamentally, the TTT-P represents an instructional sequence. The instructional concept and postures of both Bateman and Engelmann are regarded by many as representing a kind of pioneering methodology of the 1970s that distinguished special educational instruction from regular education.

See also **Diagnostic-Prescriptive Teaching**

THALIDOMIDE

Thalidomide was among the first drugs for which teratogenicity was established. A teratogen is a chemical agent that can cross the placenta and cause congenital malformations. Effective as a sedative and a tranquilizer, thalidomide is an example of a teratogen that had positive effects on the mother but devastating consequences for the embryo. Even after decades of study, the mechanism by which thalidomide causes deformities is not understood (T.J., 1999).

Teratogenicity became suspected with the birth of a relatively large number of babies with phocomelia (seal-flipper limbs) and a variety of other deformities in Europe in the late 1950s and early 1960s. Phocomelia is a condition in which arms and/or legs are drastically shortened or absent and fingers/toes extend from the foreshortened limbs or the trunk. Thalidomide was widely distributed in Europe, where it is estimated to have affected over 7,000 individuals. It was withdrawn from the market in late 1961 before it passed Food and Drug Administration approval in the United States (Moore, 1982). Teratogenicity was unusually high; over 90% of women who took thalidomide during a particular period in pregnancy had infants with some type of defect (Holmes, 1983).

Despite the horrific consequences of prenatal exposure to thalidomide, research on its potential benefits began again shortly after it was withdrawn from the market. In 1964, thalidomide was given to a patient with leprosy because of evidence of the drug's anti-inflammatory benefits; within days the patient's symptoms subsided and stayed reduced with continued use of thalidomide (Blakeslee, 1998). It has received FDA approval for use in treatment of leprosy, and may be of benefit in treatment of a number of other diseases, including brain and other forms of cancer, inflammatory disease, and autoimmune disorders. Thalidomide is now being used experimentally with AIDS, and appears to relieve symptoms such as oral ulcers and severe weight loss. Some research suggests that thalidomide may inhibit HIV replication (Blaney, 1995). Thalidomide has been said to be non-toxic among those taking the drug; researchers have yet to find a lethal dose (Blakeslee, 1998).

REFERENCES

Blakeslee, D. (1998). Thalidomide. *Journal of the American Medical*

Association [HIV/AIDS Information Center]. http://www.ama-assn.org/special.hiv.newsline.briefing.thalido.htm [11/15/98].

Blaney, C. (1995). Second thoughts about thalidomide. *Medical Sciences Bulletin.* http://pharminfo.com/pubs.msb/thalidomide.html

Moore, K.L. (1982). *The developing human* (3rd ed.) Philadelphia: Saunders.

T.J. (Feb 20, 1999). Theorizing about the dark side of thalidomide. *Science News, 155*(8), 124–125.

See also **Early Experience and Critical Periods; Etiology; Teratogens**

THEIR WORLD

Their World is the annual publication of the Foundation for Children with Learning Disabilities (FCLD). The FCLD was founded in 1977 and began publication of *Their World* in 1979. The publication is presented each year at FCLD's annual benefit in New York City. *Their World* is a public awareness vehicle, intended to educate the public about learning disabilities generally while emphasizing the accomplishments of the learning disabled. *Their World* publishes real-life stories about the way families cope with learning-disabled children. *Their World* supports after school, summer, athletic, and creativity programs as a support network for the learning disabled and their families. The publication is distributed to over 75,000 parents, educators, legislators, and professionals each year.

See also **Foundations for Children with Learning Disabilities**

THEMATIC APPERCEPTION TEST (TAT)

The Thematic Apperception Test (TAT) is a projective assessment instrument developed by Henry Murray (1938) as a means of investigating his theory of personality. Designed for use with subjects ages 7 and older, TAT has become one of the most widely used assessment techniques. The test materials consist of 31 black and white pictures depicting characters in various settings. Each picture is designed to elicit particular themes or conflicts. Subsets of pictures (typically 8 to 10) are selected for administration depending on the individual's age and sex and the nature of the presenting problem. Subjects are asked to tell a story about each picture as it is presented. Typical instructions stress that subjects use their imagination and include in their response a description of what the characters in the scene are doing, thinking, and feeling, the preceding events, and the outcome. Responses are recorded verbatim by the examiner. An inquiry is usually conducted after all pictures have been presented.

REFERENCE

Murray, H.A. (1938). *Explorations in personality.* New York: Oxford University Press.

See also **Emotional Disorders; Personality Assessment**

THEORY OF ACTIVITY

The theory of activity is a general theoretical paradigm for psychological and developmental research that has its historical roots in work carried out in the Soviet Union between 1925 and 1945 by L.S. Vygotsky, A.R. Luria, A.N. Leont'ev, and their colleagues (Leont'ev 1978, 1981; Minick, 1985; Wertsch, 1981, 1985). Activity theory is among the most important intellectual forces in contemporary Soviet psychology, providing a unifying conceptual framework for a wide range of psychological theory, research, and practice. As a consequence of linguistic, political, and conceptual barriers, however, it was only in the late 1970s that psychologists and social scientists in Western Europe and the United States began to become aware of activity theory.

The theory of activity is the product of an effort by Vygotsky's students and colleagues to extend the theoretical framework Vygotsky had developed between 1925 and his death in 1934. Vygotsky had been concerned with two fundamental limitations in the psychological theories of his time. First, he felt that many psychologists had underestimated or misrepresented the influence of social and cultural factors on human psychological development. He was particularly concerned with the failure to clarify the mechanisms of this influence. Second, Vygotsky felt that the disputes between the traditional psychology of mind and the behaviorist theories that were emerging in the 1920s reflected a widespread tendency in psychology and philosophy to represent mind and behavior in conceptual isolation from one another rather than as connected aspects of an integral whole (Davydov & Radzikhovskii, 1985; Minick, 1987). Vygotsky's work and the subsequent emergence of activity theory were attempts to develop a theoretical paradigm that would overcome these limitations in existing theory.

A central premise of the theory of activity is that human psychological development is dependent on a process in which the individual is drawn into the historically developed systems of social action that constitute both society and the life of the mature adult. Within this framework, psychological development or change is dependent on the individual's progressively more complete participation in social life. Modes of organizing and mediating cognitive activity are mastered and the relationship to the external world of objects and people is defined in this process.

As a general perspective on psychology and psychological development, the theory of activity has had an important impact on theory and practice in the broad domain of special education in the Soviet Union. While a detailed discussion of the nature of this impact is impossible in this context, a useful illustration is available in the English translation of a volume by Alexander Meshcheryakov in which he reviews his work with deaf and blind children (Meshcheryakov, 1979).

REFERENCES

Davydov, V.V., & Radzikhovskii, L.A. (1985). Vygotsky's theory and the activity-oriented approach in psychology. In J.V. Wertsch (Ed.), *Culture, communication, and cognition: Vygotskian perspectives* (pp. 35–65). New York: Cambridge University Press.

Leont'ev, A.N. (1978). *Activity, consciousness, and personality.* Englewood Cliffs, NJ: Prentice-Hall.

Leont'ev, A.N. (1981). *Problems of the development of mind.* Moscow: Progress Publishers.

Meshcheryakov, A.N. (1979). *Awakening to life: Forming behavior and the mind in deaf-blind children.* Moscow: Progress Publishers.

Minick, N. (1985). *L. S. Vygotsky and Soviety activity theory: New perspectives on the relationship between mind and society.* Unpublished doctoral dissertation, Northwestern University, Evanston, IL.

Minick, N. (1987). *The development of Vygotsky's thought. Introduction to L. S. Vygotsky, Collected works: Problems of general psychology* (Vol. 1). New York: Plenum.

Wertsch, J.V. (Ed.). (1981). *The concept of activity in Soviet psychology.* New York: Sharpe.

Wertsch, J.V. (1985). *Vygotsky and the social formation of mind.* Cambridge, MA: Harvard University Press.

See also Vygotsky, L.S.; Zone of Proximal Development

THERAPEUTIC COMMUNITY

The therapeutic community as a model for psychosocial rehabilitation was developed following World War II by Maxwell Jones, a psychiatrist, in Great Britain. This approach developed out of Jones's experience in working with soldiers on a psychiatric unit who had suffered emotional trauma and with persons with personality problems. Jones's approach was a reaction to the traditional psychiatric hospital practice that produced dependent patients who needed resocialization in addition to treatment of their illness if they were to be discharged. He believed the hospital could be purposefully employed as a significant therapeutic milieu by facilitating full social participation by the patients (Main, 1946). Providing appropriately organized social environments, rather than just psychotherapeutic or medical approaches, was the method of effecting change in patients. Jones's work was significant for the development of social psychiatry, in which emphasis is placed on the environmental sources of stress that cause persons to learn maladaptive ways of coping rather than on illness or deviancy, the traditional psychiatric emphases.

Jones initially presented the principles and practices of the therapeutic community in *Social Psychiatry: A Study of Therapeutic Communities* (1952), but the book was limited in detail. A clearer explication of the underlying themes that guided and shaped the social interactions in the therapeutic community was provided by R. N. Rapoport, an anthropologist, in *Community as Doctor* (1960). Themes identified by Rapoport were those of (1) democratization—an equal sharing among community members of the power in decision making about community affairs; (2) permissiveness—the toleration of a wide degree of behavior from members of the community; (3) communalism—the free exchange of information and observations among all members of the community, including patients and staff; and (4) reality confrontation—the continuous presentation to the patients of interpretations of their behavior from the perspective of other members of the therapeutic community.

The principal social methods used in the therapeutic community were the discussion of events that occurred within the context of frequent community group meetings by all community members; the facilitation of exchange of information among members of the community; the development of relationships between staff and clients that emphasized their status as peers in learning through interacting with each other; the provision of frequent situations in which patients could learn more adaptive ways to cope with problematic situations by interacting with community members; and the continued examination by community members, especially staff members, of their roles to find more effective ways of functioning.

REFERENCES

Jones, M. (1952). *Social psychiatry: A study of therapeutic communities.* London: Tavistock.

Main, T.F. (1946). The hospital as a therapeutic institution. *Bulletin of the Menniger Clinic, 10,* 66–70.

Rapoport, R.N. (1960). *Community as doctor.* London: Tavistock.

See also Community Residential Programs; Psychoneurotic Disorders; Social Behavior of the Handicapped

THERAPEUTIC RECREATION

See RECREATION, THERAPEUTIC.

THINK ALOUD

Think Aloud is a cognitive behavior modification program designed to improve social and cognitive problem-solving skills in young children. Based on the pioneering work of Meichenbaum, Goodman, Shure, and Spevak, and tied to theory regarding development of self-control. Think Aloud was conceived as a training program to decrease impulsivity, encourage consideration of alternatives, and plan courses of action. It emphasizes the use of cognitive modeling as a teaching tool in which teachers model their own strategies for thinking through problems. Students are then encouraged to "think out loud" while systematically approaching each problem through asking and answering four basic questions: What is my problem? How can I solve it? Am I following my plan? How did I do?

Development and study of Think Aloud classroom programs was supported in part by ESEA Title IV grants to the Denver public schools. Few of the classroom program studies could be conducted with random assignment to experimental or traditional teaching programs. However, within limitations imposed by a nonequivalent control group design, children in the Think Aloud classrooms improved on measures of both social and cognitive problem-solving skills more than children in nonprogram classrooms at all grade levels. Cognitive differences between children in the Think Aloud classroom programs and comparison children were most reliable for the program for grades 1 and 2 and the program for grades 5 and 6. Differences in social problem-solving skills were reliable at all grade levels. The classroom programs can easily be adapted for use in an individual or tutorial program to intensify and individualize the experience. The materials now provide challenge to children over a broad range of developmental levels, making them suitable for special education classrooms as well as regular classrooms, for some middle school children, and for children with special needs for social skills training or assistance in curbing impulsivity.

See also **Impulse Control**

THINKING CENTERS

See CREATIVE STUDIES PROGRAM.

THORAZINE

Thorazine is the trade name for the generic antipsychotic agent chlorpromazine. Though Thorazine was among the first synthesized drugs that were found effective in the control of behavioral symptoms associated with psychotic disorders, it is no longer as widely prescribed as it was 30 years ago. However, Thorazine is still used as a benchmark against which new antipsychotic agents are compared in terms of frequency of side effects and efficacy. Thorazine is of the drug class phenothiazine and tends to produce the classic panorama of side effects associated with the phenothiazine group.

In addition to use as a major tranquilizer with psychotic individuals, Thorazine also is used in emergency situations to limit the effects of LSD and to control prolonged behavioral reactions after intoxication with other hallucinogens. One of the major criticisms of Thorazine as a therapeutic agent has been its reported abuse as a chemical restraint (Leavitt, 1982).

In use with children, several cautions must be considered: children are more likely to show side effects; dose-related attentional problems can develop and thus create interference in learning (Seiden & Dykstra, 1977); and seizures may be potentiated in children with a preexisting seizure disorder (Bassuk & Schoonover, 1977).

REFERENCES

Bassuk, E.L., & Schoonover, S.C. (1977). *The practitioner's guide to psychoactive drugs.* New York: Plenum Medical.

Leavitt, F. (1982). *Drugs and behavior.* New York: Wiley.

Seiden, L.S., & Dykstra, L.A. (1977). *Psychopharmacology: A bio-* *chemical and behavioral approach.* New York: Van Nostrand Reinhold.

See also **Stelazine**

THORNDIKE, EDWARD L. (1847–1949)

E. L. Thorndike was an early theorist and writer who applied psychology to education. He was educated at Wesleyan, Harvard, and Columbia universities, with most of his professional career spent at Teachers' College, Columbia University. He is best known for his contributions to learning theory (Thorndike, 1905, 1931, 1932, 1935, 1949) and intellectual assessment (Thorndike, 1901, 1926, 1941).

Thorndike's major contribution to learning theory, termed the Law of Effect, is well known as a basic behavioral principle. The Law of Effect states; "any act which in a given situation produces satisfaction becomes associated with that situation, so that when the situation occurs, the act is more likely to recur also" (Thorndike, 1905, p. 203). His theory of connectionism was cognitively oriented, and viewed both physical and mental acts as involving the establishment of neural pathways. Learning was viewed as taking place when pathways were established through repetition.

Thorndike's measurement interests were diverse, as reflected by his famous dictum, "If anything exists, it exists in some amount. If it exists in some amount, it can be measured" (Thorndike, 1926, p. 38). His multifactored approach to measurement viewed intelligence as comprising abstract, mechanical, and social abilities. Intellectual assessment to Thorndike also involved the dimensions of attitude, breadth, and speed (i.e., level of difficulty, number of tasks, and rate of completion, respectively). This multifactored approach was in contrast to the approach of others of his time, who viewed intelligence as a general or unitary factor. Thorndike developed many tests, especially college entrance and achievement tests.

REFERENCES

Thorndike, E.L. (1901). *Notes on child study.* New York: Macmillan.

Thorndike, E.L. (1905). *The elements of psychology.* New York: Seiler.

Thorndike, E.L. (1926). *The measurement of intelligence.* New York: Teacher's College, Columbia University.

Thorndike, E.L. (1931). *Human learning.* New York: Century.

Thorndike, E.L. (1932). *Fundamentals of learning.* New York: Columbia University.

Thorndike, E.L. (1935). *The psychology of wants, interests and attitudes.* New York: Appleton-Century.

Thorndike, E.L. (1941). Mental abilities. *American Philosophical Society, 84,* 503–513.

Thorndike, E.L. (1949). *Selected writings from a connectionist's psychology.* New York: Appleton-Century-Crofts.

See also **Measurement**

THOUGHT DISORDERS

Disorders in thinking, although most commonly associated with schizophrenia, may also occur in paranoid disorders, affective disorders, organic mental disorders, or organic delusional syndromes such as those owed to amphetamine or phencyclide abuse (*Diagnostic and Statistical Manual of Mental Disorders* [DSM IV], 1994). Schizophrenic patients, however, tend to show more severe and specific forms of thought disorders, and may continue to show some degree of idiosyncratic thinking when not in the acute phase of the disease (Ginsberg, 1985). According to DSM IV (1994), at some point, schizophrenia always involves delusions, hallucinations, or certain disturbances in the form of thought most often expressed by the patient in disorganized speech. A thought disorder is but one of the criteria needed for a diagnosis of schizophrenia; the illness is also characterized by disorganization in perceptions, communication, emotions, and motor activity. The term thought disorder encompasses a large array of dysfunctions, including disturbances in the form of thought, structure of associations, progression of thought, and content of thought.

Several theories have been advanced to account for the existence of thought disorders. The more psychogenic of these theories point to inadequate ego functioning, such that the patient creates his or her own reality to cope with overwhelming stress and anxiety. Biological theories view thought disorders as being genetically transmitted. Research in this area has focused on chemical neurotransmitters such as dopamine; it found differing levels of such chemicals in disturbed and healthy individuals. The effectiveness of drug therapy in treating thought disorders lends credence to biological theories. Other theories such as learning, cognitive, and family approaches are more environmentally based, and hold that persons with thought disorders may learn maladaptive ways of thinking or acting in response to live circumstances or unhealthy family situations (Worchel & Shebilske, 1983).

REFERENCES

American Psychiatric Association. (1994). *Diagnostic and statistical manual of mental disorders* (4th ed.). Washington, DC: Author.

Ginsberg, G. (1985). The psychiatric interview. In H. Kaplan & B. Sadock (Eds.), *Comprehensive textbook of psychiatry/IV* (Vol. 1, pp. 500–501). Baltimore, MD: Williams & Wilkins.

Worchel, S., & Shebilske, W. (1983). *Psychology: Principles and applications.* Englewood Cliffs, NJ: Prentice-Hall.

See also **Diagnostic and Statistical Manual of Mental Disorders (DSM-IV); Emotional Disorders**

TICS

Tics are recurrent, rapid, abrupt movements and vocalizations that represent the contraction of small muscle groups in one or more parts of the body. Motor tics may include eye blinking, shoulder shrugging, neck twisting, head shaking, or arm jerking. Vocal tics frequently take the form of grunting, throat clearing, sniffing, snorting, or squealing. These abnormal movements and sounds occur from once very few seconds to several times a day, with varying degrees of intensity. Although tics are involuntary, they often can be controlled briefly. However, temporary suppression results in a feeling of tension that can be relieved only when the tics are allowed to appear. Tics increase with anxiety and stress and diminish with intense concentration (Shapiro & Shapiro, 1981).

The *Diagnostic and Statistical Manual of Mental Disorders,* fourth edition, delineates three major tic disorders that are based on age of onset, types of symptoms, and duration of the condition: transient tic disorder, chronic motor tic disorder, and Tourette syndrome (American Psychiatric Association, 1994).

Tourette syndrome, the most severe condition, is differentiated from the other tic disorders by the presence of both motor and vocal tics and a pattern of symptoms that waxes and wanes as the tics slowly move from one part of the body to another. Complex movements such as jumping and dancing are often exhibited. Not always present, but confirmatory of Tourette syndrome, are echolalia (repetition of words or phrases spoken by others), palilalia (repetition of one's own words), coprolalia (involuntary swearing), echopraxia (imitation of the movement of others), and copropraxia (obscene gesturing). Although the nature and severity of these symptoms vary over time, the disorder rarely remits spontaneously and usually remains throughout life (Shapiro, Shapiro, Bruun, & Sweet, 1978).

REFERENCES

American Psychiatric Association. (1994). *Diagnostic and statistical manual of mental disorders* (4th ed.). Washington, DC: Author.

Shapiro, A.K., & Shapiro, E.S. (1981). The treatment and etiology of tics and Tourette syndrome. *Comprehensive Psychiatry, 22,* 193–205.

Shapiro, A.K., Shapiro, E.S., Bruun, R.D., & Sweet, R.D. (1978). *Gilles de la Tourette's syndrome.* New York: Raven.

See also **Echolalia; Echopraxia; Tourette Syndrome**

TIME ON TASK

The amount of time that students spend on task has been an issue that concerns teachers in all fields, not just those involved with special education. Squires, Huitt, and Segars (1981) have identified three measures of student involvement that may be used to determine time on task. The first, allocated time, is simply the amount of time that is planned for instruction. Obviously, students will probably not be on task for the entire time that has been allocated. The second measure, which addresses this observation, is known as engagement rate. It is defined as the percent of allocated time that students actually attend to the tasks they are assigned. The third measure, engaged time, is the number of minutes per day students spend working on specific academic or related tasks; it is an integration of allocated time and engagement rate. Stallings and Kaskowitz (1974) found that, given certain maximum time limits based on a child's age and the subject matter at hand, engaged time is the most important variable that is related to student achievement. Given this finding, many researchers have focused on increasing time on task.

As an example, Bryant and Budd (1982) used self-instruction training with three young children who had difficulties in attending to task in kindergarten or preschool. The researchers trained the children to verbalize five separate types of self-instruction: (1) stop and look; (2) ask questions about the task; (3) find the answers to the questions posed in (2); (4) give instructions that provide guidance; and (5) give self-reinforcement for accomplished tasks. The results indicated an increase in on-task behavior for two of the children and, when used in combination with an unintrusive classroom intervention of reminders and stickers, all three of the children exhibited marked increases in their engaged time.

A somewhat different approach to the study of on-task behaviors was undertaken by Whalen et al. (1979), who examined the effects of medication (Ritalin) on the on- and off-task behaviors of children identified as hyperactive. They found clear differences in a maladaptive direction in the behaviors of their subjects who had been diagnosed as hyperactive under placebo conditions when compared with peers who had no diagnoses of hyperactivity. However, while the authors acknowledged that the medication did result in more on-task and prosocial behaviors in many of their subjects, they cautioned against a wholesale reliance on medications since many long-term effects had not yet been studied. Rather, the researchers felt that careful study of all variables in individual situations (e.g., teacher tolerance, cost effectiveness, environmental adaptations) must be undertaken when making treatment decisions.

REFERENCES

Bryant, L.E., & Budd, K.S. (1982). Self-instruction training to increase independent work performance in preschoolers. *Journal of Applied Behavior Analysis, 15,* 259–271.

Squires, D., Huitt, W., & Segars, J. (1981). Improving classrooms and schools: What's important. *Educational Leadership, 39,* 174–179.

Stallings, J.A., & Kaskowitz, D. (1974). *Follow through classroom observation evaluation, 1972–1973.* Menlo Park, CA: Stanford Research Institute.

Whalen, C.K., Henker, B., Collins, B., Finck, D., & Dotemoto, S. (1979). A social ecology of hyperactive boys: Medication effects in structured classroom environments. *Journal of Applied Behavior Analysis, 12,* 65–81.

See also **Attention Deficit Disorder; Attention Span; Hyperactivity**

TIME-OUT

Time-out is an individual behavior management technique typically used to reduce or eliminate inappropriate atten-tion-getting behaviors of children and sometimes adults (institutionalized disturbed). Time-out occurs when access to reinforcement is removed contingent on the emission of a response (Sulzer-Azaroff & Mayer, 1986).

The reductive effect is best demonstrated when time-out is implemented as follows:

Total removal of opportunities for reinforcement (e.g., removal from the reinforcing environment and placement in a nonstimulating environment).

Time-out durations of short to medium length (e.g., 3 to 10 minutes following the cessation of the inappropriate behavior).

Clear communication of conditions to the subject prior to use of time-out (e.g., the inappropriate behavior that will occasion time-out).

Consistent use of time-out after each occurrence of the inappropriate behavior until reduction has been maintained.

Reinforcement of desirable alternative behaviors to the inappropriate behavior to occur in conjunction with the use of time-out once the subject has returned to the natural environment.

In addition to its reductive effect on inappropriate behaviors, time-out allows for management of behaviors without the application of aversive stimuli.

REFERENCE

Sulzer-Azaroff, B., & Mayer, G.R. (1986). *Achieving educational excellence using behavioral strategies.* New York: Holt, Rinehart, & Winston.

See also **Aversive Stimulus; Behavior Modification; Punishment**

TIME SAMPLING

Time sampling is an intermittent means of recording behavior by observing the subject at certain prespecified times and recording his or her behavior in a manner prescribed by the time sampling method in use. According to Arrington (1943), the major impetus to developing various time sampling procedures was provided by the National Research Council between 1920 and 1935. The council, which controlled many research fund allocations, had become concerned because the diary records typically used in research on the behavior of children were neither comparable nor exact. This group began to encourage research that used quantifiable and replicable methods of data collection.

In more recent times, a common terminology has developed that defines the various types of time sampling methods. In a landmark study, Powell et al. (1977) discussed three different types of time sampling procedures: (1) whole interval recording, (2) partial interval recording, and (3) momentary time sampling. In all of these procedures, the observation session is divided into a series of intervals. When the intervals are equal, the procedure is known as fixed interval (e.g., every 30 seconds). When the interval lengths are assigned at random but still average to the desired length (e.g., on the average, every 30 seconds), the procedure is known as variable interval.

The Student Observation Scale (SOS) of the Behavior Assessment System for Children is an example of a standardized time-sampling procedure that uses a fourth approach successfully. The SOS employs brief intervals, and at the end of each, the examiner/observer records all behaviors occurring at any time during the 3-second observation (Reynolds & Kamphaus, 1992). After recording, behavior is again observed, and the process is repeated for a 15 minute total time sample.

REFERENCES

Arrington, R.E. (1943). Time sampling in studies of social behavior: A critical review of techniques and results with research suggestions. *Psychological Bulletin, 40,* 81–124.

Powell, J., Martindale, B., Kulp, S., Martindale, A., & Bauman, R. (1977). Taking a closer look: Time sampling and measurement error. *Journal of Applied Behavior Analysis, 10,* 325–332.

Reynolds, C.R., & Kamphaus, R.W. (1992). *Behavior assessment system for children.* Circle Pines, MN: American Guidance Service.

See also **Behavioral Charting; Behavior Assessment; Behavior Assessment Scale for Children; Behavior Modification**

TOFRANIL

Tofranil is the proprietary name for the drug Imipramine, which primarily is used in the treatment of major depression and nocturnal enuresis. It has been suggested that Tofranil may be useful in the treatment of school phobia (Hersov, 1985).

Though Tofranil has proved to be an effective treatment for major depression in adults (AMA Drug Evaluations, 1983), its use with children is questionable. Shaffer (1985) reports that there have been few well-designed studies of the effectiveness of Tofranil and childhood depression. In one reported study in which Tofranil was compared double blind with a placebo, a 60% response rate was reported in both groups. In adults, Tofranil has a mild sedative effect that serves to lessen anxiety, though it is not intended to be used for this symptom. It has been suggested that it is this anxiety effect that may be helpful in a multidisciplinary approach toward school refusal (Hersov, 1985). In the 1990s, use of Tofranil has declined in favor of selective serotonin reuptake inhibitor, such as Prozac and Zoloft.

In children, Tofranil is most frequently used to ameliorate nocturnal enuresis. Numerous studies have demonstrated Tofranil's effectiveness in decreasing nighttime enuresis in most children (Shaffer, Costello, & Hill, 1968).

The effect is seen rapidly, and almost always within the first week of treatment (Williams & Johnston, 1982). Unfortunately, research also has suggested that once the medication is withdrawn, many of these children begin wetting again.

REFERENCES

AMA Drug Evaluations (5th ed.). (1983). Philadelphia: Saunders.

Hersov, L. (1985). School refusal. In M. Rutter & L. Hersov (Eds.). *Child and adolescent psychiatry: Modern approaches* (2nd ed., pp. 382–399). St. Louis: Blackwell Scientific.

Shaffer, D. (1985). Enuresis. In M. Rutter & L. Hersov (Eds.), *Child and adolescent psychiatry: Modern approaches* (2nd ed., pp. 465–481). St. Louis: Blackwell Scientific.

Shaffer, D., Costello, A.J., & Hill, I.D. (1968). Control of Enuresis with Imipramine *Archives of diseases in childhood, 43,* 665–671.

Williams, D.I., & Johnston, J.H. (1982). *Pediatric urology* (2nd ed.). London: Butterworth Scientific.

See also **Depression; Enuresis**

TOKEN ECONOMICS

A token economy is basically a miniature monetary system in which clients work for generalized, secondary reinforcers that are exchangeable for a variety of backup reinforcers. The token economy was first described in detail in the late 1960s (Ayllon & Azrin, 1965, 1968); it has since become one of the most popular means of providing reinforcers in special education settings. Successful token economies have been documented with such diverse populations as psychiatric patients (Ayllon & Azrin, 1965), sheltered workshop clients (Welch & Gist, 1974), and students in special education classes (Heward & Eachus, 1979).

When developing a token economy, the service provider needs to consider a number of different points. First, the token itself must be established. Just about anything can be used, however, some of the most popular items are plastic chips, check marks, and points. What is important in deciding what to use for tokens is that the tokens be easily administered and not easily counterfeited. A second consideration is the choice of backup reinforcers and their token prices. These reinforcers must be desirable for the clients and reasonably priced. A wide choice and constant variation of backup reinforcers will make the system appealing. A third consideration is access to the purchase of backup reinforcers. Regular times that provide access to the reinforcers on at least a weekly schedule are desirable. A fourth consideration is the record-keeping system devised by the service provider. Both clients and teachers should be aware of storage options or means of recording tokens earned. Finally, as with any behavioral procedure, the service provider must ensure that tokens are administered consistently. The clients and teachers must be clearly aware of what behaviors can earn tokens and what behaviors can result in fines, and these rules must be strictly enforced.

Kazdin (1982) and Kazdin and Bootzin (1972) have provided reviews of token economy systems. Most recently, Kazdin (1982) has commented on the progress within the profession on four critical issues (enhancing effects of token economies, staff training, client resistance to the program, and long-term effects) and has identified three emergent areas of concern (integrity of treatment, administrative and organizational issues, and dissemination of the token economy). In the first area of progress, enhancing effects, Kazdin (1982) notes that varying the strength of the reinforcers, emphasizing the economic aspects of the token system, and involving peers have all been helpful in improving the efficiency of token systems. Second, Kazdin (1982) points out that a number of studies have focused on effective means of training staff to administer token programs. Generally, training that includes several facets (e.g., modeling and informative feedback) has been most effective. When clients resist the program, Kazdin (1982) feels that providing opportunities that are not usually available (e.g., negotiating reinforcers) might help to reduce negative behaviors.

The issues discussed by Kazdin (1982) are generally administrative in nature and focus on (a) whether or not the program was conducted as intended, (b) how various organizational variables (e.g., authority to make decisions) affect the token program, and (c) how well program methodologies and results are shared with others. Kazdin (1982) feels that currently, methodology for token economies has been well established, and that "the next step for research is to explore and evaluate procedures to integrate token economies routinely into settings where programs are likely to be of use" (p. 441–442).

REFERENCES

Ayllon, T., & Azrin, N.H. (1965). The measurement and reinforcement of behavior of psychotics. *Journal of the Experimental Analysis of Behavior, 8,* 356–383.

Ayllon, T., & Azrin, N.H. (1968). *The token economy: A motivational system for therapy and rehabilitation.* New York: Appleton-Century-Crofts.

Heward, W.L., & Eachus, H.T. (1979). Acquisition of adjectives and adverbs in sentences written by hearing impaired and aphasic children. *Journal of Applied Behavior Analysis, 12,* 391–400.

Kazdin, A.E. (1982). The token economy: A decade later. *Journal of Applied Behavior Analysis, 15,* 431–445.

Kazdin, A.E., & Bootzin, R.R. (1972). The token economy: An evaluative review. *Journal of Applied Behavior Analysis, 5,* 343–372.

Welch, M.W., & Gist, J.W. (1974). *The open token economy system: A handbook for a behavioral approach to rehabilitation.* Springfield, IL: Thomas.

See also **Applied Behavior Analysis; Behavioral Charting; Behavior Modification**

TONI

See TEST OF NON-VERBAL INTELLIGENCE.

TONIC NECK REFLEX, ASYMMETRICAL

See ASYMMETRICAL TONIC NECK REFLEX.

TOPICS IN EARLY CHILDHOOD SPECIAL EDUCATION

Topics in Early Childhood Special Education (*TECSE*) is a refereed, quarterly journal publishing articles on timely issues in early childhood special education. Three issues per year are topical; one is nontopical. The topical issues address an identified problem, trend, or subject of concern and importance to early intervention. Persons interested in services provided to infants, toddlers, and preschoolers who display developmental delays and disabilities and the families of such youngsters will find *TECSE* informative. *TECSE* has been published continuously since 1981. Pro-Ed, Inc. purchased the journal from Aspen Press in 1983.

TOPICS IN LANGUAGE DISORDERS

Topics in Language Disorders, an interdisciplinary journal that is published quarterly, addresses topics within the general fields of language acquisition, language development, and language disorders. Contributors include speech and language pathologists, psycholinguists, pediatricians, neurologists, and special educators, especially remedial reading and learning disabilities teachers. This journal originated in 1980 to meet the need for published interactions across professional boundaries on specific topics.

As the title implies, each journal presents a variety of issues surrounding one topic. A guest editor is responsible for soliciting manuscripts; in doing so, he or she seeks equality among disciplines as well as several views. Both clinical and educational application are sought with balance between theory and practice.

Members of the American Speech and Hearing Association may earn continuing education credits by reading each volume and responding to the questions at the end of the volume. Responses are then submitted to the address included in the journal.

TORCH COMPLEX

TORCH complex is a phrase used by some authors (e.g., Thompson & O'Quinn, 1979) to group a set of maternal infections whose clinical manifestations in children are so similar that differentiation among them on the basis of those symptoms alone may not be possible. TORCH stands for *TO*xoplasmosis, *R*ubella, *C*ytomegalovirus, and *Her*pes. Generally speaking, with the exception of herpes, the infections have only mild and transitory effects on the mother, but through pre- or perinatal transmission, they may produce severe and irreversible damage to offspring. The major manifestations are visual and auditory defects and brain damage, which may result in mental retardation.

The infections generally destroy already formed tissue rather than interfering with development; infants are frequently born asymptomatic, but gradually develop symptoms in the early years of life.

Although the major symptoms of the members of the TORCH complex are similar, the detailed symptoms, mechanisms of action, and times of major action differ.

REFERENCE

Thompson, R.J., & O'Quinn, A.N. (1979). *Developmental disabilities.* New York: Oxford University Press.

See also Cytomegalovirus; Herpes Simplex I and II; Rubella; Toxoplasmosis

TORRANCE CENTER FOR CREATIVE STUDIES

The Torrance Center for Creative Studies is a research center dedicated to investigations of the development of creative potential. Its research and development program honors and builds on the legacy of Ellis Paul Torrance, a native Georgian and a University of Georgia Alumni Foundation distinguished professor emeritus. This legacy is best reflected in the following statement:

In almost every field of human achievement, creativity is usually the distinguishing characteristic of the truly eminent. The possession of high intelligence, special talent, and high technical skills is not enough to produce outstanding achievement.... It is tremendously important to society that our creative talent be identified, developed, and utilized. The future of our civilization—our very survival—depends upon the quality of the creative imagination of our next generation (Torrance, 1959, p. 1).

Torrance, a pioneer in research on the identification and development of creative potential, is best known for his work in the development and refinement of the Torrance Tests of Creative Thinking (TTCT), the most widely used tests of creativity in the world.

The goals of the research and instructional program of the Torrance Center are to investigate and evaluate techniques and procedures for assessing creative potential and growth; to develop, apply, and evaluate strategies that enhance creative thinking; and to facilitate national and international systems that support creative development.

Four components—assessment, development, education, and evaluation—provide the organizational structure for the research and instructional programs of the center. Each component has been designed to contribute research that verifies and expands our understanding of creativity as a major ingredient in the development of human ability and that carries out the further development of instructional and evaluation technology to enhance the development of that ability.

A major program initiative of the Torrance Center is the Torrance Creative Scholars Program. This program provides educational services to those individuals who score in the top $1\frac{1}{2}\%$ of the national population on the TTCT, verbal and/or figural. The program is consistent with Torrance's assertions (1984) that

a common characteristic of people who have made outstanding social, scientific, and artistic contributions has been their creativity. Since we are living in an age of increasing rates of change, depleted natural resources, interdependence, and destandardization, there are stronger reasons than ever for creatively gifted children and adults to have a fair chance to grow. We must find these "world treasures" and give them support so that they can give society those things it so desperately needs.

A unique aspect of the Torrance Creative Scholars Program is its use of a mentoring component. This component provides a year-round mentoring network for the creative scholars. Individuals selected by Torrance are designated Torrance creative scholar-mentors; they provide mentoring services to the scholars in a variety of ways. These mentors are also eligible to become Torrance creative scholars and to receive the services of the program.

The third component, education, provides training for educators interested in creativity. This component operates in conjunction with the degree programs (master's, sixth year, and doctoral) offered through the department of educational psychology at the University of Georgia. Training programs offered through the center include the Torrance Center Summer Creativity Institute, the Challenge Program for preschool through fifth graders, and the Visiting Scholars Program for national and international scholars. In addition, there is the annual E. Paul Torrance Lecture and the library and archives donated to the university by Torrance. A future goal of the Torrance Center is to endow an E. Paul Torrance Research Professor Chair. The final component, evaluation, focuses on quantitative and qualitative evaluations of assessment techniques, educational strategies, and support systems for the various programs of the center.

The Torrance Center for Creative Studies was formally established at the University of Georgia in the spring of 1984. It is located in the department of educational psychology, College of Education, 422 Aderhold Hall, University of Georgia, Athens, GA 30602.

REFERENCES

Torrance, E.P. (1959). *Understanding creativity in talented students.* Paper prepared at the Summer Guidance Institute Lecture Series on Understanding the Talented Student, University of Minnesota.

Torrance, E.P. (1980). Creativity and futurism in education: *Retooling Education, 100,* 298–311.

Torrance, E.P. (1984). *The search for a nation's treasure* (Keynote address). St. Louis: National Association for Gifted Children.

See also Creativity; Creativity Test

TORRANCE TESTS OF CREATIVE THINKING

The Torrance Tests of Creative Thinking (figural form) can be used from kindergarten to graduate school (Torrance, 1974). Thinking Creatively with Words is useful from fourth grade to graduate school. Thinking Creatively in Action and Movement is designed for 3- to 8-year-olds. The test's author defines creativity as a process of becoming sensitive to problems, deficiencies, gaps in knowledge, or missing elements.

The Torrance Tests of Creative Thinking (figural forms A and B) use tasks that require drawing. They report scores in terms of fluency—the ability to think of many ideas for a given topic; originality—the ability to think of new and unusual ideas; abstractness of titles—the ability to sense the essence of a problem and know what is essential; elaboration—the ability to add details to a basic idea; and resistance to premature closure—the ability to "keep open" in processing information and to consider a wide variety of information. The Torrance Test of Creative Thinking (verbal forms A and B) require written responses and report scores in terms of fluency, originality, and flexibility (the ability to shift thinking and produce ideas in different categories). Thinking Creatively in Action and Movement uses action, movement, and verbal responses to test creative thinking ability. It measures this in terms of fluency, originality, and imagination.

Test results indicate an individual's creative thinking as compared with other adults or children in the same grade. In addition, the test results may be used to give additional insight into a student's style of thinking, learning, and creating. Several studies indicated that the Torrance Tests of Creative Thinking (figural and verbal) and Thinking Creatively in Action and Movement show no sexual, racial, or socioeconomic bias (Torrance, 1962, 1971, 1973, 1974). The Torrance Tests of Creative Thinking are not used prevalently today despite being the best available measures of creative thought processes.

REFERENCES

Torrance, E.P. (1962). Guiding creative talent. Engelwood Cliffs, NJ: Prentice Hall.

Torrance, E.P. (1971). Are the Torrance tests of creative thinking biases against or in favor of disadvantaged groups? *Gifted Child Quarterly, 15,* 75–80.

Torrance, E.P. (1973). Assessment of disadvantaged minority group children. *School Psychology Digest, 4,* 3–10.

Torrance, E.P. (1974). *Norms-technical manual: The Torrance Test of Creative Thinking.* Lexington, MA: Personnel Press/ Ginn.

See also **Gifted and Talented Children; Insight**

TORSIONAL DYSTONIA

The term "dystonia" was first used by H. Oppenheim in 1911 to denote the coexistence of muscular hypotonia and hypertonia. Since that time, the term has been used to describe a symptom of abnormal muscle contraction, a syndrome of abnormal involuntary movements, and a disease that has either a genetic or ideopathic origin. Torsional dystonia is commonly referred to as a progressive disorder characterized by slow, twisting movements that ultimately may result in bizarre, twisting postures of the extremities or trunk. Some causes of torsional dystonia are identifiable while other causes remain unknown, making classification of the condition difficult.

The disorder has a gradual onset, beginning between the ages of 5 and 15, and commonly involves the foot or leg. Torsional dystonia may spread to several parts or all of the body, but the condition is not present during sleep. Contractures or permanent muscle shortening and joint deformity ultimately occur. Treatment of torsional dystonia generally has been disappointing.

See also **Physical Anomalies; Physical Handicaps**

TOTAL COMMUNICATION

The expression total communication can be used in the general sense of communication through all possible channels, not only vocal (including verbal) communication, but also communication provided by such other means as mimicry, gestures, etc. Recently, total communication has been used mainly in a more restricted field, namely the education of deaf children. It presents itself not as a method, but as "a philosophy incorporating the appropriate aural, manual, and oral methods of communication in order to ensure effective communication with and among hearing impaired persons" (Garretson, 1976, p. 300). It advocates the use of various modes of communication, such as speech (which should not be neglected, as the deaf live among a majority of hearing people), written language (reading and writing), sign language, finger spelling, pantomime, etc.

In recent years, methods of teaching deaf children applying this philosophy have been used in a steadily increasing number of schools in the United States and in Europe. These schools gave up the oral method that had prevailed since the end of the nineteenth century, mainly in Europe, where the resolutions of the International Congress held in Milan in 1880 were accepted and recommended almost unanimously (Lane, 1980).

According to the defenders of total communication, the oral approach, including lip reading, gives unsatisfactory results as far as linguistic and cognitive development are concerned (Conrad, 1979). It is argued that even if the hearing loss is discovered early, poor parent-infant communication delays the acquisition of language considerably and irretrievably, except with children whose residual hearing is sufficient to make communication possible. Ensuing education in specialized institutions is slower and less differentiated than with hearing children and, instead of reducing the gap, increases the retardation of the deaf children.

Total communication advocates the use of signing as the most appropriate mode of early communication between parents and hearing-impaired children. The double exposure to sign and speech (about 9 out of 10 deaf children have hearing parents) should allow partially hearing children equipped with appropriate audiological aids to be educated together with their hearing peers; children whose residual hearing is insufficient should be educated through a wide network of activities, of which "spoken language, finger spelling, signing, and written language constitute the linguistic core. Being capable of consistent transmission and internal symbolization of linguistic signals, these are the media of special relevance to linguistic and cognitive growth" (Evans, 1982, p. 91).

Opponents of total communication think that signing may prove harmful and impede the acquisition of a spoken language and that too much time spent on teaching signs (finger spelling, etc.) could be used more appropriately to teach the spoken language. They stress the fact that some deaf children, albeit a minority, educated through the oral method succeed in obtaining a satisfactory level in spoken language perception and production.

REFERENCES

Conrad, R. (1979). *The deaf schoolchild: Language and cognitive functioning.* London: Harper & Row.

Evans, L. (1982). *Total communication: Structure and strategy.* Washington, DC: Gallaudet College Press.

Garretson, M.D. (1976). Total communication. In R. Frisina (Ed.), A bicentennial monograph on hearing impairment: Trends in the U.S.A. *Volta Review, 78.*

Lane, H. (1980). A chronology of the oppression of sign language in France and the United States. In H. Lane & F. Grosjean (Eds.), *Recent perspectives on american sign language.* Hillsdale, NJ: Erlbaum.

See also **American Sign Language; Deaf Education**

TOURETTE SYNDROME

Tourette syndrome is a tic disorder characterized by the appearance between the ages of 2 and 15 of involuntary muscular movements. A single, simple tic is generally the initial symptom and takes the form of an eye blink, head shake, or nose twitch. However, the symptoms gradually change over time, becoming more complex and involving other body parts. Complicated movements of the entire body are often observed, including kicking, jumping, and turning in circles. Vocalizations such as throat clearing, coughing, grunting, or barking are present. Later these noises may change into words and phrases. Echolalia (repetition of phrases made by others), palilalia (repetition of one's own words), coprolalia (utterance of obscene words), echopraxia (imitation of the movement of others), and copropraxia (obscene gesturing) frequently accompany the disorder.

While the frequency and severity of the symptoms fluctuate over time, the disorder is chronic and rarely remits spontaneously (Shapiro, Shapiro, Bruun, & Sweet, 1978). Associated features often include obsessive-compulsive be-

haviors, an attention deficit disorder with hyperactivity, school-related problems, and an increased incidence of learning disabilities (Jagger et al., 1982). The etiology of Tourette syndrome remains unknown. However, the discovery of the efficacy of haloperidol in the treatment of the disorder has led researchers to postulate that Tourette syndrome may result from a biochemical imbalance in the nervous system (Snyder, Taylor, Coyle, & Meyerhoff, 1970). This hypothesis is further substantiated by the tendency of families of individuals with the disorder to have a positive history of Tourette syndrome or simple motor and vocal tics (Shapiro & Shapiro, 1982).

REFERENCES

Jagger, J., Prusoff, B.A., Cohen, D.J., Kidd, K.K., Carbonari, C.M., & John, K. (1982). The epidemiology of Tourette syndrome: A pilot study. *Schizophrenia Bulletin, 8,* 267–278.

Shapiro, A.K., & Shapiro, E.S. (1982). Tourette syndrome: Clinical aspects, treatment, and etiology. *Seminars in Neurology, 2,* 373–385.

Shapiro, A.K., Shapiro, E.S., Bruun, R.D., & Sweet, R.D. (1978). *Gilles de la Tourette's syndrome.* New York: Raven.

Snyder, S.H., Taylor, K.H., Coyle, J.T., & Meyerhoff, J.L. (1970). The role of brain dopamine in behavioral regulation and the action of psychotropic drugs. *American Journal of Psychiatry, 127,* 199–207.

See also **Echolalia; Echopraxia; Tics; Tourette Syndrome Association**

TOURETTE SYNDROME ASSOCIATION

The Tourette Syndrome Association, a voluntary nonprofit organization, was founded for the purpose of assisting individuals with Tourette syndrome, their families, friends, and concerned professionals. The primary objectives of the association include disseminating information regarding symptomatology and treatment of Tourette syndrome and raising funds to encourage and support scientific research into the nature and causes of the disorder.

In an effort to promote understanding of Tourette syndrome, the organization publishes quarterly newsletters, pamphlets, medical reprints, and films, and publicizes the disorder in newspapers, magazines, radio, and television. It provides support groups at a regional level for sharing current information about research, treatment, and management of Tourette syndrome. Information may be obtained from the Tourette Syndrome Association, Bell Plaza Building, 42–40 Bell Boulevard, Bayside, NY, 11361.

See also **Tics; Tourette Syndrome**

TOXOPLASMOSIS

Toxoplasmosis is caused by an intracellular protozoan, Toxoplasma gondii, which is transmitted via the blood to the prenatal fetus. This congenital infection causes mild to severe mental and motor retardation. The largest number of newborns will be asymptomatic in the neonatal period so they must be observed for ocular and central nervous system disability. The newborn with symptomatic toxoplasmosis will present at birth with one or more of the following: head abnormalities (large or small), cerebral calcifications, brain damage, muscle spasticity, convulsions and seizures, visual and hearing impairments, and eye infections. An enlarged liver and spleen, which cause an extended abdomen, are often present. Rashes and jaundiced skin may be seen in infants. Motor impairment as a result of brain damage may be seen. Prognosis is poor; death occurs in 10 to 15% but a high percentage of children have neuromotor defects, seizure disorders, mental retardation, and damaged vision (Behrman, 1977; Carter, 1978).

Many children with toxoplasmosis may need to be placed in a fairly restrictive setting because of mental retardation and visual, hearing, and motor impairments. Children often need self-help skills training (including feeding and toileting) from an early age. Related services may be required for speech, vision, and hearing deficits. Physical and occupational therapy may also be needed. Since a variety of health problems may be present, a medical consultation will probably be needed. Team placement and management will be necessary for adequate educational programming.

REFERENCES

Behrman, R. (Ed.). (1977). *Neo-natal-perinatal diseases of the fetus and infant* (2nd ed.). St. Louis: Mosby.

Carter, C. (Ed.). (1978). *Medical aspects of mental retardation.* (2nd ed.). Springfield, IL: Thomas

See also Functional Skills; Mental Retardation

TOY LENDING LIBRARIES

Toy libraries, occasionally named a Toybrary, are lending libraries with a broad range of toys, learning materials, and equipment appropriate for young children. Many traditional public libraries offer a toy section that includes puzzles, games, stuffed animals, blocks, etc., that can be checked out and taken home by children and adults. However, the real growth in toy lending libraries is as a part of the increasing need for child care outside the traditional home setting. Toy lending libraries and resource centers are becoming more common across the country as child-care needs and services grow and as people become more interested and involved in meeting the needs of children and those who care for them. Such libraries allow the various child-care programs in a specific geographic area to pool their resources and share equipment, as well as to exchange ideas and information. These libraries are particularly useful to people in isolated areas or those who work alone. When these libraries limit their use to certified day-care providers, they may also serve as a motivating force that results in a greater pool of licensed and certified day-care providers.

Types of equipment typically found in such libraries include recreational equipment, sand and water play sets, transportation equipment, farm and animal sets, blocks and other manipulatives, housekeeping materials, make believe materials, infant toys, puzzles, perception, alphabet, and math materials, and large and small motor toys. Funding for toy lending libraries comes from a number of sources. The most common would be government (national, state, or local) grants, foundation awards, local United Ways, and dues from members. Special groups such as state (Councils for Exceptional Children) have also been known to provide start-up funds for such libraries.

See also Day-Care Centers; Play

TRACE MINERALS

Trace minerals are minerals found in very small quantities in the human body but having significant relationships to certain metabolic events necessary for normal function. Severe deficiencies of trace minerals can result in a variety of handicaps, including orthopedic and learning disabilities. Some minerals and their relative levels in the body affect memory and attention as well. An overabundance or improper metabolism of some minerals also may produce problems. Depending on the particular mineral and the chronicity of the deficiency (or oversupply), mineral-related handicaps may or may not be reversible, though all are treatable to a large extent.

See also Etiology; Nutritional Disorders

TRAINABLE MENTALLY RETARDED

Trainable mentally retarded (TMR) was a diagnostic category in the 1960s and 1970s, referring to those people whose IQ scores ranged between 25 and 50 (based on the IQ tests of those days; Smith, 1998), and who were believed unable to benefit from the standard educational curriculum. This group represents roughly 10% of the mentally retarded population.

The term "trainable" is outdated and misleading, since it implies that the person is unable to profit from educational efforts. Most people with this level of mental retardation learn communication skills during early childhood, can benefit from vocational and occupational skills training, and usually adjust well to community life, generally in supervised settings.

The most appropriate diagnostic category currently is "moderate mental retardation," which requires an IQ within the 35–55 range, as well as impairments in adaptive behavior that adversely affect the person's ability to perform ordinary, everyday activities of living (American Psychiatric Association, 1994).

REFERENCES

American Psychiatric Association. (1994). *Diagnostic and statistical manual of mental disorders* (4th ed.). Washington, DC: Author.

Smith, D.D. (1998). *Introduction to special education: Teaching in an age of challenge.* Boston, MA: Allyn and Bacon.

See also Arc, The; Mental Retardation

TRAINING SCHOOLS

Training schools were an intricate part of the larger multipurpose residential facilities known as the "colony plan" that were established in the late 1800s. These schools served children and adolescents who were not considered eligible for public school education because of their unique educational needs.

The evolvement of the training school concept was based on earlier work by Samuel Gridley Howe (1801–1876). Howe's Perkin School for the Deaf (1848) led to the development of other self-contained schools (e.g., Massachusetts School for Idiots and Feeble-Minded Youth, 1855). Although Howe's 10-bed unit was the first residential facility established, it was not until 1848 that the first large facility, the Syracuse Institution of the Feeble-Minded was developed. Harvey B. Wilbur (1820–1883), a physician, became the first superintendent of this facility. Like Howe, Wilbur was very much influenced by the philosophy and principles of Edward Seguin; he placed a great deal of emphasis on education.

Although institutions for exceptional individuals were initially viewed as beneficial by many throughout history, their purpose, programs, and administration changed drastically. The small homelike educational establishment was replaced by the larger, overcrowded, and underfinanced multipurpose facility that would typify institutions for generations to come.

Initially, training schools in institutions were intended to serve school-aged exceptional needs children and adolescents. As years passed, it became increasingly clear that individuals who reached the age limit for school programming had few choices for continued educational services. Typically, these adults were sent to almshouses or other similar institutions.

As early as the 1860s, however, advocacy of education in public schools was being heard. Although it is difficult to determine precisely when the first public school special education program was initiated, credit is usually given to the public school system of Providence, Rhode Island. An auxiliary school for 15 mentally retarded students opened in December 1896 (Woodhill, 1920). By 1898 the city of Providence established three more auxiliary schools and one special education classroom in a public school.

Other cities soon followed Providence's example. By the turn of the century, special education provisions for the mentally retarded shifted from total residential training schools to generally accepted, though not always implemented, education in public school systems.

REFERENCE

Woodhill, E. (1920). Public school clinics in connection with a state school for the feeble-minded. *Journal of Psycho Asthenics, 25,* 14–103.

See also History of Special Education

TRANQUILIZERS

The term tranquilizer is a superordinate that may be applied to two general classes of psychoactive drugs: antipsychotic agents (major tranquilizers) and antianxiety agents (minor tranquilizers). Both major and minor tranquilizers produce sedative effects, though to different degrees. Minor tranquilizers tend to produce fewer neurotoxic side effects, but appear to be more likely candidates for abuse (Blum, 1984).

The major tranquilizers were developed in an attempt to humanize the treatment of psychotic individuals, who were being given long-term treatment in psychiatric hospitals. The drugs were developed based on observations of related agents that produced calming effects on wild animals. Like the minor tranquilizers, the major tranquilizers have not been found to be physically addictive. Abrupt withdrawal, however, has been reported to induce insomnia, anxiety, and gastrointestinal symptoms (Brooks, 1959).

In terms of the general public, the minor tranquilizers are more familiar and also show more pervasive, popular use. The benzodiazapines are often used to reduce the effects of chronic stress, tension, and emotional discomfort. Valium has been described as the most prescribed drug in the United States, with 75% of the prescriptions being issued by nonpsychiatrists (Blum, 1984). Blum also reports that annual revenue of the antianxiety drug market in the United States is approximately $500 million. When added together, the prescriptions for Librium and Valium would account for approximately one out of five American adults (Blum, 1984).

REFERENCES

Blum, K.B. (1984). *Handbook of abusable drugs.* New York: Gardner.

Brooks, G.W. (1959). Withdrawal from neuroleptic drugs. *American Journal of Psychiatry, 115,* 931.

See also Mellaril; Stelazine; Thorazine

TRANSDISCIPLINARY MODEL

Originally conceived by Hutchison (1974), the transdisciplinary model is one of several team approaches for the delivery of educational and related services to handicapped students. The other team models are the multidisciplinary model and the interdisciplinary model. In a multidisciplinary model, team members maintain their respective discipline boundaries with only minimal, if any, coordination, collaboration, or communication (McCormick, 1984). The interdisciplinary model differs from the multidisciplinary model in that there is some discussion among the involved professionals after their individual assessments have been completed and at least an attempt to develop a coordinated service delivery plan. However, the programming recommendations are often not realistic. The teacher may not have the skills to implement the recommendations or the authority to arrange for their provision (Hart, 1977). Another problem is the lack of provision for follow-up and feedback in the interdisciplinary model.

The transdisciplinary model assumes the following: (1) joint functioning (team members performing assessment, planning, and service delivery functions together; (2) continuous staff development (commitment to expansion of each team member's competencies); and (3) role release (sharing functions across discipline boundaries; (Lyon & Lyon, 1980). The professional makeup of a transdisciplinary team varies depending on the needs of the student. It may include few or many professionals, but whenever possible they coordinate their assessment procedures and plan as a group for the student's daily programming.

REFERENCES

Hart, V. (1977). The use of many disciplines with the severely and profoundly handicapped. In E. Sontag, J. Smith, & N. Certo (Eds.), *Educational programming for the severely and profoundly handicapped.* Reston, VA: Council for Exceptional Children, Division of Mental Retardation.

Hutchison, D. (1974). *A model for transdisciplinary staff development* (United Cerebral Palsy. Technical Report No. 8).

Lyon, S., & Lyon, G. (1980). Team functioning and staff development: A role release approach to providing integrated educational services for severely handicapped students. *Journal of the Association for Severely Handicapped, 5*(3), 250–263.

McCormick, L. (1984). Extracurricular roles and relationships. In L. McCormick & R. Schiefelbusch (Eds.), *Early language intervention.* Columbus, OH: Merrill.

See also **Itinerant Services; Multidisciplinary Team**

TRANSFER OF TRAINING

Transfer of training, also referred to as stimulus generalization or generalization, takes place when a behavior that has been reinforced in the presence of one stimulus event occurs in the presence of different but similar stimuli. Using the behavior analytic $S > R > C$ paradigm, the emphasis of this learning construct is on (1) the characteristics of the events that precede a behavior, and (2) the relationship of these characteristics to the occurrence of the behavior under similar stimulus conditions.

From this viewpoint, increasing similarities in events that precede a behavior result in an increased likelihood of stimulus generalization. Conversely, there is a decreased likelihood of the trained behavior occurring as these preceding events become more dissimilar. Applied to educational programming, the influence of these similarities might be beneficial or problematic. Thus a student may be trained to respond to questions asked by an adult male teacher by raising his or her hand. If this student responds likewise in other classroom settings to questions asked by female adults, a beneficial transfer of training has occurred. However, if the student responds to his father's inquiry, "Why are you late?" by raising his or her hand, the transfer

of training that has taken place might be viewed as potentially problematic.

This example highlights some of the problems that relate to transfer of training and also touches on the fundamental role of this learning explanation in the educational process. Almost without exception, students are exposed to information and material with specific stimulus characteristics or in specific stimulus settings. Traditionally, this stimulus-specific training is assumed to automatically transfer to similar stimulus events. The accuracy of this assumption is highly questionable when teaching the learner with exceptional needs. As the severity of an individual's learning problems increase, so does the need for implementation of more specific interventions that are geared toward systematically promoting transfer of training.

The effectiveness of education to a large extent relates to the amount of training that is transferred from one stimulus event to another similar events or settings. With the exceptional learner, this transfer must often be directly encouraged. For a comprehensive explanation of transfer of training and related teaching considerations, the reader is referred to texts by Sulzer-Azaroff and Mayer (1977) and Alberto and Troutman (1977).

REFERENCES

Alberto, P.A., & Troutman, A.C. (1977). *Applied behavior analysis for teachers: Influencing student performance.* Columbus, OH: Merrill.

Sulzer-Azaroff, B., & Mayer, G.R. (1977). *Applying behavior-analysis procedures with children and youth.* New York: Holt, Rinehart, & Winston.

See also **Generalization; Transfer of Learning**

TRANSFORMATIONAL GENERATIVE GRAMMAR

In 1957 Noam Chomsky revolutionized the field of English grammar and research with the publication of the book *Syntactic Structures.* Chomsky, considered the father of the theory of transformational grammar, proposed a finite set of operations (called transformations) that produce (or generate) sentences of infinite number and variety without producing nonsentences. These operations are acquired during the first few years of life through exposure to conversation rather than through formal study. They are internalized by the speaker without his or her being aware of or able to state them.

REFERENCE

Chomsky, N. (1957). *Syntactic Standards.* The Hague: Mouton.

See also **Language Deficiencies and Deficits; Linguistic Deviance**

TRANSITION

Transition is the process of changing from one condition or place to another; it is common to individuals at various times throughout their lives. Transition from preschool to school environments as well as transition from school to postschool environments present problems for the young child and the adolescent. For individuals with special needs who are graduating or leaving school, this process is frequently more difficult than for others. The entitlement to a free appropriate public education may not necessarily culminate in opportunities for employment, integration into the community, or adult services. In recognition of the concerns of parents, educators, and service providers regarding the futures of handicapped students leaving publicly supported education programs, a national priority on transition from school to work for all individuals with disabilities was announced by the Office of Special Education and Rehabilitation Services (OSERS) in 1983. The need for transitional services and the provision of some degree of financial support for these activities are addressed in PL 98-199, the Education for All Handicapped Children Amendments, and in IDEA.

The transition from school to work and adult life requires careful, systematic preparation and planning in the secondary school; cooperative support of interagency teams on graduation; and awareness and support of multiple employment options and services as needed by the community and professionals.

Transition services may be grouped into three classes that reflect the nature of the public services used to provide support as the passage is completed: (1) transition with no special services—vocational technical schools and work experience; (2) transition with time-limited services—vocational rehabilitation, Job Training Partnership Act; and (3) transition with ongoing services—supported work environments for individuals with severe disabilities (Will, 1984).

Finally, one of the major issues surrounding transition is the lack of information about the status of special education graduates. Hasazi et al. (1985) cited the need to develop a body of data regarding the employment status of these individuals for use as a basis for future planning regarding transition activities.

REFERENCES

Hasazi, S.B., Gordon, L.R., & Roe, C.A. (1985). Factors associated with the employment status of handicapped youth exiting high school from 1979 to 1983. *Exceptional Children, 51,* 455–469.

Will, M. (1984). *OSERS programming for the transition of youth with disabilities: Bridges from school to working life.* Washington, DC: Office of Special Education and Rehabilitative Services.

See also **Vocational Rehabilitation; Vocational Training of the Handicapped**

TRANSPORTATION OF HANDICAPPED STUDENTS

Transportation of handicapped students is usually viewed as an administrative requirement to ensure access to public education. It is seldom viewed as an opportunity to teach students community mobility skills. However, community mobility is the dynamic concept within the issue of transportation of handicapped students. The ability of an individual to participate independently or semiindependently in all aspects of community life (e.g., domestic, recreational, and vocational) is dependent on community mobility (Wehman, Renzaglia, & Bates, 1985). Community mobility refers to movement from one place to another within a particular setting and travel between two community locations. The concept of community mobility was originally developed in program practice and literature related to working with visually handicapped individuals. In this literature, community mobility is referred to as orientation and mobility training.

For visually impaired individuals, orientation and mobility training has long been a well-respected component of the curriculum. As the rights of all citizens to participate in the least restrictive environment have been acknowledged, the concept of community mobility has been broadened to include the physically handicapped, mentally retarded, emotionally disturbed, and other special education consumers. Assurances for meeting the basic transportation needs to and from school have been established within PL 94-142 for all special education students and continued in IDEA. However, the transportation needs of handicapped students are complex.

The ability of a person to be independently mobile is dependent on several factors. One of the primary factors that influences the degree of mobility attained by handicapped individuals is the opportunity for travel from one place to another. Opportunity for mobility can be restricted by both physical and attitudinal barriers. In many communities, extensive physical modifications have been made, including construction of ramps, widening of doorways, installment of elevators, cutting out of curbs, and purchase of lift buses. Although these modifications have removed many barriers to independent mobility, obstacles still exist in all communities. Realistically, many of these obstacles are not going to be eliminated. Some of these obstacles are outside of the control of engineers and educators (e.g., weather conditions, natural terrain). Since mobility obstacles are likely to remain in every community, efforts must be directed toward teaching individuals to overcome these problems. By combining environmental changes with specific instruction programs, handicapped citizens are provided easier access as well as more skills for traveling independently within their communities. Community mobility training programs should reflect this dual concern for improving physical accessibility and training skills that compensate for various environmental barriers.

Overprotectiveness and lowered expectations can combine to present attitudinal barriers that severely limit a person's opportunity to acquire independent living skills. However, the development of responsible and effective community mobility training programs can alleviate fears and concerns regarding safety and consequently raise the expectations of parents and professionals for independent living by handicapped individuals. The development of such programs will significantly increase the opportunity an individual will have to acquire independent living skills.

Recently, more community mobility training programs have began to emphasize the functional relationship between public transportation and access to community services. For example, Sowers, Rusch, and Hudson (1979) used systematic training procedures to teach a severely retarded adult to complete the following 10-behavior sequence to ride the city bus to and from work: (1) cross controlled intersections, (2) cross unmarked intersections, (3) use bus tickets, (4) walk to bus, (5) identify the correct bus, (6) board, (7) ride, (8) depart, (9) transfer, and (10) walk to work. Further, Marholin, O'Toole, Touchette, Berger, and Doyle (1979) taught four moderately and severely retarded adults to use public bus transportation to travel between a public institution and various community locations for shopping and eating in a restaurant.

The responsibility of public schools for transporting handicapped students to and from school programs must be expanded to include greater sensitivity to the unique community mobility needs of individual students. In meeting these responsibilities, educators should promote the development of a normalized repertoire of transportation skills. At a basic level, this could involve assistance that enables handicapped students to use the same transportation system in association with their nonhandicapped peers. At a more complex level, this would require a commitment to teaching a variety of mobility skills that would enhance a person's ability to access community activities throughout his or her lifetime.

REFERENCES

Marholin, D., Touchette, P., Berger, P., & Doyle, D. (1979). I'll have a Big Mac, Large Fries, Large Coke, and Apple Pie—of teaching adaptive community skills. *Behavior Therapy, 10*, 236–248.

Sowers, J., Rusch, F.R., & Hudson, C. (1979). Training a severely retarded young adult to ride the city bus to and from work. *AAESPH Review, 4*, 15–22.

Wehman, P., Renzaglia, A., & Bates, P. (1985). *Functional living skills for the moderately and severely handicapped.* Austin, TX: Pro-Ed.

See also **Electronic Travel Aids; Mobility Training; Travel Aids for the Handicapped**

TRAUMATIC BRAIN INJURY AND SCHOOL REENTRY

Traumatic brain injury (TBI) involves a physical injury to the brain caused by an external force, resulting in diminished consciousness or coma (Stratton & Greogory, 1994). There are two types of traumatic brain injuries: open and closed-head injuries. Open head injuries occur when an object (e.g., a bullet or shell fragment) penetrates the skull and produces damage to the brain. The damage tends to be localized about the path of the penetrating object (Lezak, 1995). In contrast, closed head injuries are more common

than open head injuries and are more likely to produce diffuse damage (Begali, 1992). A blow to the head without penetrating the skull is an example of a closed head injury. In closed head injuries, the direct impact causes the brain, which is floating in cerebrospinal fluid within the skull, to strike the inside of the skull in one or more places. The movement of the brain within the skull causes shearing and tearing of nerve fibers and contusions (i.e., bruising; Lezak, 1995). In addition to the primary effects (e.g., the bruising, shearing, and tearing), secondary effects are often present in the form of brain swelling and hemorrhaging. The secondary effects compound the damage, resulting in a wide variety of neural structures being affected (Stratton & Gregory, 1994). As a result, diversity in behavioral sequelae (i.e., consequences) in TBI patients is the norm rather than the exception. Impairments in cognition, language, memory, attention/concentration, conceptual functions, abstract reasoning, judgment, academic achievement or new learning, and perception have been reported in traumatic brain injured children and adolescents. Motor and sensory deficits have also been noted along with behavioral and socioemotional problems (Begali, 1992). For additional information on the sequelae associated with TBI, see the entry on traumatic brain injury in children.

Children with TBI are not new to the schools; however, the number of severely injured children surviving and returning to schools has grown. Sophisticated medical technology has resulted in an increased survival rate among children following a traumatic brain injury (Rapp, 1999). Federal law mandates that these children are to be served by the schools; however, educators and parents often lack the knowledge on how to best serve these students (Blosser & DePompei, 1991).

In 1990, traumatic brain injury was added to the list of eligibility categories under the Individuals with Disabilities Education Act (IDEA). IDEA, or Public Law 101-476, is the major special education law in the United States. P.L. 101-476, now P.L. 105-17, defines a traumatic brain injury as:

An acquired injury to the brain caused by an external force, resulting in total or partial functional disability or psychosocial impairment, or both, that adversely affects a child's educational performance. The term applies to open or closed head injuries resulting in impairments in one or more areas, such as cognition; language; memory; attention; reasoning; abstract thinking; judgment; problem-solving; sensory, perceptual and motor abilities; psychosocial behavior; physical functions; information processing; and speech. The term does not apply to brain injuries that are congenital or degenerative, or injuries induced by birth trauma (Federal Register, 1992, p. 44802).

According to the federal law, children and adolescents who experience a brain injury resulting from internal as opposed to external trauma are excluded from this definition and services. In other words, children whose injuries are caused by internal events, such as brain tumors, cerebral vascular accidents, exposure to environmental toxins, or central nervous system infections cannot be served under the TBI category, but may be eligible for services under another special education category (e.g., Other Health Impaired). Some states, however, have opted to identify, classify, and serve a broader range of children whose injuries are the result of either external or internal trauma (Rapp, 1999). State rules and regulations should be consulted to determine whether children whose brain injury is the result of internal trauma are eligible for services under the TBI category.

To be eligible for services under the TBI category of IDEA, children's educational performances must be adversely affected by their injury. For those individuals with TBI who are not eligible for special education and related services under IDEA, Section 504 of the Vocational Rehabilitation Act of 1973, a civil rights law, may provide sufficient services and protections in the general education classroom. Section 504 outlines the school district's responsibility to provide educational accommodations and related services to allow disabled students to have equal access to all publicly funded programs available to their nondisabled peers. In either case, the federal law is quite clear. Children with TBI who are eligible under IDEA or Section 504 must be served. Thus, plans must be developed and services implemented in order to successfully reintegrate these children into the classroom following their injury.

A number of resources must be mobilized and activities planned and implemented prior to a child's return to school to ensure successful school reentry, including assignment of a case manager, formation of a school or interdisciplinary team, inservice training for school personnel, family education, peer education, notification to the State's Vocational Rehabilitation Office, and collaboration among the systems (home, school, hospital/rehabilitation unit). Successful school reintegration is dependent upon collaboration and open communication among the family, school, and hospital/rehabilitation systems. Open communication is imperative in all stages of recovery. Information exchanged should begin immediately following the injury, when the child is first admitted to the hospital (Clark, 1997); however, controversy exists as to which system is responsible for making the initial contact. Haak and Livingston (1997) suggest the school should take the initiative and contact the parents to obtain permission to contact the medical facility. Opening communication channels helps ensure that the child will be appropriately served.

The school should appoint a representative (i.e., a case manager), who is knowledgeable about TBI, to serve as a liaison among the different systems. The case manager's role should be to establish and maintain communication and coordinate services among the systems on behalf of the child. The case manager should relay information to the school from the hospital regarding the severity of child's injury, current behavior, medication management (Clark, 1997), progress, and expected discharge and school reentry dates (Haak & Livingston, 1997). Through the case manager, assessment results and the hospital/rehabilitation unit's recommendations can be forwarded to the school. The case manager provides the medical facility, on the other hand, with information from the school regarding the child's educational history, any preinjury assessment results, classroom assignments, and the school's progress in preparing for the child's reentry (Clark, 1997); for example, removal of architectural barriers, if needed. The case manager also communicates with the parents to obtain information about the child's current status and any problems the child may be experiencing.

Family education is also critical to a child's successful school reentry. The child's family needs to receive general information on TBI and TBI sequelae. They also need to be informed about the child's specific needs (e.g., educational needs) and abilities. Medical professionals and the case manager can help educate the family in these areas. Medical professionals can also provide the family with information on TBI and TBI sequelae, whereas the case manager can provide the family with information on IDEA and Section 504. The child's family needs to know what services are available in a school district, eligibility criteria to receive these services, process to obtain these services, and child and family's rights in relation to these services under the federal law (Ylvisaker, Hartwick, & Stevens, 1991).

Inservice training is another essential activity needed to facilitate a child's successful reentry back into the school setting. The professional with expertise on TBI should provide information on the specific needs and abilities of the child as well (Ylvisaker et al., 1991). Information about intervention strategies that may be beneficial to the child in and outside the classroom should also be included (Clark, 1997).

Besides inservice training, in-class meetings should be held between the case manager and the child's peers to educate classmates about TBI and discuss the child's condition and possible changes in his/her behavior (e.g., changes in personality). A discussion with the student's classmates about the child with his/her permission (Ylvisaker et al., 1991) may help peers to develop a better understanding of the situation and support for the student.

The state's Office of Vocational Rehabilitation should also be contacted in the likelihood that a child with TBI will need their services in order to obtain employment upon graduation from high school. Many vocational rehabilitation offices have tracking systems. Notification results in the youth's name being entered into the vocational rehabilitation system for future services. In addition, the school counselor and vocational liaison specialist for the school district should be made aware of the need to develop community-based work experiences for the child. On-site training will help the individual with TBI develop work skills needed to succeed in a competitive employment market (Ylvisaker et al., 1991).

Before the child with TBI is discharged from the medical facility, the formation of a school or interdisciplinary team is needed to develop a plan for school reentry. The team is composed of a variety of professionals, the child's parents, and the child. The team usually consists of a general education teacher, special education teacher, case manager, school psychologist, parent, and student. Other team members may include a neuropsychologist, counselor, rehabilitation specialist, speech pathologist, physical therapist, and occupational therapist. The team's composition is dependent upon the child's needs (Clark, 1997). The team develops a tentative plan consisting of accommodations and intervention strategies and addresses the possibility that special education and related services will be needed.

Transitions from the medical facility to home and from home to school, along with the injury and its aftermath, are stressful periods for most children with TBI and their families. Guidelines exist to assist families with these transitions (e.g., Cohen, Joyce, Rhoades, & Welks, 1985). For example, Cohen et al. provide guidelines to help families and school personnel determine when a child is ready to return to school and will benefit from the school experience. According to Cohen and colleagues, a child is ready to return to school when he/she is able to attend for 10–15 minutes at a time, tolerate 20–30 minutes of classroom stimulation, function in a group setting, follow simple directions, engage in meaningful communication, and demonstrate some degree of learning. These guidelines are means of helping families reduce the stress associated with the transitions.

For the child with TBI, the transition and return to school can be very stressful and upsetting. The return to school highlights the losses in cognitive abilities, academic skills, physical functioning, and changes in behavior. These losses and changes can be demoralizing to the child and make the child a target of misperceptions. An increase in risk-taking behavior (Begali, 1992), social isolation, and withdrawal may result. Classmates' understanding and support are essential during these critical periods.

The transition from home to school can result in parental frustration and stress as well. In her review, Begali (1992) reported that common parental frustrations have been found, including lack of teacher understanding about TBI, reduced parental contact with support networks, inappropriate class placements, and social isolation of the child. For the family of a child with TBI, the injury and recovery process never occur in an interpersonal vacuum. Brain injury affects both the child and his or her family (Haak & Livingston, 1997). The family may have difficulty accepting their child's limitations and possible changes in personality. Moreover, financial difficulties, injury to other family members, and weariness may exist as the result of the accident. Schools can assist the family in the aftermath of TBI by empowering the family to play an active role in their child's education, teaching the family about TBI, and offering support and counsel. Family stress and frustration highlights the importance of developing a school reintegration plan and the value of having a knowledgeable and well-prepared school staff (Begali, 1992).

When a child with TBI returns to school, questions arise concerning the most appropriate placement for the child to receive his or her education. Not all children with TBI will require special education. Some students will need only monitoring in the classroom with slight adjustments made in the curriculum based on teacher observations. Others, on the other hand, will require special education and related services. To receive these services, a student must be "educationally diagnosed" (Begali, 1992). In other words, an evaluation needs to be conducted to determine a child's eligibility for special education.

Assessment plays a prominent role in determining eligibility and treatment of traumatic brain injured children and adolescents (Begali, 1992). Assessment results provide invaluable information and help determine educational placement, related services, and instructional goals. Psychoeducational, ecological, neuropsychological, and neurological evaluations should be conducted and results should be integrated in order to determine appropriate accommodations and modifications needed in the school environment to provide optimal learning experiences for children and adolescents with TBI. Standardized testing supplemented with testing of the limits and process procedures will provide invaluable information for designing appropriate accommodations and interventions (Kaplan, 1988).

A standard psychoeducational evaluation consists of an intelligence test, achievement test, and behavioral rating scales (Rapp, 1999). A psychoeducational evaluation can predict future learning potential and learning disabilities; however, children and adolescents with TBI are more likely to have problems with attention or concentration, memory, new learning, problem solving, and socioemotional behavior, which will not be appropriately assessed using only a standard psychoeducational battery (Rapp, 1999; Reitan & Wolfson, 1992). Therefore, other evaluation procedures are needed.

In contrast, a neuropsychological evaluation assesses a broad range of brain-behavior relationships, current cognitive strengths and weaknesses, and new learning. Educational and vocational program goals can be developed based on these assessment results. Neuropsychological evaluations and neurological evaluations, consisting of physical assessments conducted by medical specialists, should be used to augment standard psychological assessments (Goldstein, 1984). A neuropsychological evaluation should be conducted before the child reenters school and reevaluations should be conducted frequently during the first year (Rapp, 1999). Begali (1992) recommends conducting a reevaluation every three to six months for the first two years postinjury. Following the first or second year postinjury, reevaluations should be conducted before major school transitions, when new problems arise, or when lack of educational progress is reported (Rapp, 1999).

Ecological evaluations consist of observations of children or adolescents in a variety of settings. Students with TBI usually have difficulty monitoring and regulating their own behavior in the real world, generalizing skills and abilities, and cognitive organization. Formal testing cannot assess these skills with any degree of accuracy, nor does formal testing have any resemblance to the real world or classroom environment. Thus, observations complement formal testing. Observations of children and adolescents with TBI provide a means of monitoring these students' progress and evaluating educational programs and interventions (Rapp, 1999). Observations should be conducted on a frequent basis.

Informal testing such as curriculum-based and criterion-based assessment is also recommended. Curriculum-based and criterion-based assessment may be used to guide instructional efforts and provide feedback. Program deficiencies can be identified and revisions of instructional objectives can be made. The main point to remember in the assessment of children with TBI is that frequent formal and informal testing will be needed to monitor these children's progress, as these children can recover substantial cognitive, physical, and behavioral functioning in short periods of time (Clark, 1997).

If a child is found to be eligible for special education based on assessment results and other relevant information, the Individualized Education Program (IEP) team, the members of the school, or interdisciplinary team will develop an IEP. The IEP is a document stating the educational goals and objectives and specific educational and related services that will be provided. The IEP is required to address the child's current level of educational performance in the areas affected by the disability (Clark, 1997). This requirement can be a challenge to the IEP team, as dramatic changes are seen in individuals with TBI during the first three months of recovery (Lezak, 1995). Thus, constant review and updating of educational goals and objectives is needed to keep pace with the child's recovery. A review of the IEP within three months of its implementation is recommended. After the initial review, the IEP should be reviewed periodically thereafter (Clark, 1997). For those who do not qualify for special education and related services under IDEA, but do qualify for services under Section 504, the school's 504 team will need to develop a plan to ensure that children with TBI are adequately served as well.

Because of the dramatic changes seen in children with TBI during the recovery process and the fact that no two traumatic brain injuries are alike, educational programs for children with TBI must be individualized, flexible, and delivered in a timely manner. Educational programs for children with TBI should ensure that professional training, instructional methods, and program practices parallel the state-of-the-art in head trauma rehabilitation. Quality educational programs should include the following options: environmental control, low student-to-teacher ratio, individualized and intensive instructional techniques (Begali, 1992), flexible class scheduling, and community-based experiences.

Some children with TBI need a more controlled environment in the schools, such as a self-contained placement. Common characteristics found among children with TBI are their limited ability in interpreting environmental cues and responding to these cues in socially appropriate ways

(Wood, 1990), hypersensitivity and hyposensitivity to sensory stimuli (Savage & Wolcott, 1994), and difficulty remembering class schedules and organizing their materials. Temporary placement in a self-contained classroom may provide these individuals with the time needed to develop coping strategies to interact appropriately and to handle the less predictable and more demanding general educational environment (Begali, 1992).

Flexible class scheduling is another mark of a quality educational program for children and adolescents with TBI. Children with TBI often lack the stamina needed to attend school on a full-time basis when they first return. Shortened school days and reduction in class load and number of classes may be needed to combat fatigue. Appointments with specialists, such as an occupational or physical therapist, may need to be scheduled into the school day as well. Thus, the actual time spent in the classroom may be very limited upon initial reentry (Begali, 1992).

Small classes where the student-to-teacher ratio is low may be beneficial to some children with TBI, especially those with severe head injuries. In these smaller classes, children with TBI can receive more intensive training, closer supervision, and more frequent feedback. In addition, distractions in these classes are more likely to be held to a minimum in comparison to the larger regular education classes (Begali, 1992).

Individual and intensive instructional opportunities are other key features of quality education programs for children with TBI. Children with TBI may need individual instruction or additional instructional assistance due to cognitive impairments, problems with new learning, loss of specific skills, or behavioral problems. Remediation, compensation, and accommodation strategies may be helpful in addressing these children's difficulties. For learned maladaptive behaviors, changes in the environment and setting clear limits may be beneficial. Accommodation strategies are often the initial intervention methods used when children with TBI return to the classroom. Remediation of specific lost skills is also an appropriate strategy to use with children with TBI. Practice, repetition, and more time to relearn specific lost skills are examples of remediation strategies. Teaching compensatory strategies is another set of intervention methods that may be used to circumvent cognitive impairments. With compensatory strategies, such as the use of mnemonics, new ways of performing and learning tasks are acquired (Rapp, 1999). To maximize instructional time, limits on transitional time and extracurricular classes may be set. Attendance in an extended school program during the summer months, if eligible, may be helpful in preventing regression in learning. Due to the rapid changes in cognitive, physical, and behavioral skills and abilities, dynamic and responsive instructional approaches tailored to the individual will be required (Begali, 1992). For additional information on more specific intervention strategies to use with students with TBI, see the entry on traumatic brain injury in children.

Community-based work experience is another indicator of a quality educational program for children with TBI. In 1990, IDEA required school districts to provide students in special education with transitional services. Children with TBI who are in special education and are 14 years of age or older qualify for these services. Participation in community-based work experiences occurs during the school day. These students go to work sites located in their community to receive on-the-job training. These work experiences are arranged to help students develop good work skills, work habits, and social skills needed in today's competitive employment market. The goal of the school-to-work experience is for students to develop the skills needed to obtain meaningful employment and to have independent living opportunities upon graduation (Haak & Livingston, 1997).

School reentry is a challenging experience for the student, family, and school. At present, limited information exists on school reentry programs for children with TBI. In addition, empirical research demonstrating the effectiveness of school reentry programs for children with TBI is lacking. Collaboration among the systems (home, school, medical, and community) and drawing upon the technical expertise of these resources are needed in order to assist these children on their road to recovery.

REFERENCES

Begali, V. (1992). *Head injury in children and adolescents.* Brandon, VT: Clinical Psychology Publishing Company.

Blosser, J.L., & DePompei, R. (1991). Preparing education professionals for meeting the needs of students with traumatic brain injury. *Journal of Head Trauma Rehabilitation, 6*(1), 73–82.

Clark, E. (1997). Children and adolescents with traumatic brain injury: Reintegration challenges in educational settings. In E.D. Bigler, E. Clark, & J.E. Farmer (Eds.), *Childhood traumatic brain injury: Diagnosis, assessment, and intervention.* Austin, TX: Pro-Ed.

Cohen, S., Joyce, C., Rhoades, K., & Welks, D. (1985). Educational programming for head injured students. In M. Ylvisaker (Ed.), *Head injury rehabilitation: Children and adolescents* (pp. 383–411). San Diego: College-Hill Press.

Diamond, R. (1987). Children and head injury. In A. Thomas & J. Grimes (Eds.), *Children's needs: Psychological perspectives.* Washington D.C.: The National Association of School Psychologists.

Federal Register. (1992, September 9). Individual with Disabilities Education Act. (IDEA), U.S. Department of Education Regulations. Washington, DC: U.S. Government Printing Office.

Goldstein, G. (1984). Neuropsychological assessment. In G. Goldstein & M. Hersen (Eds.), *Handbook of psychological assessment* (pp. 181–211). New York: Pergamon.

Haak, R.A., & Livingston, R.B. (1997). Treating traumatic brain injury in the school: Mandates and methods. In C.R. Reynolds & E. Fletcher-Janzen (Eds.), *Handbook of clinical child neuropsychology* (2nd ed., pp. 482–505). New York: Plenum.

Kaplan, E. (1988). A process approach to neuropsychological assessment. In T. Boll & B.K. Bryant (Eds.), *Clinical neuropsychology and brain function: Research, measurement, and practice* (pp. 129–167). Washington D.C.: American Psychological Association.

Lezak, M.D. (1995). *Neuropsychological assessment* (3rd ed.). New York: Oxford.

Rapp, D.L. (1999). Interventions for integrating children with traumatic brain injuries into their schools. In C.R. Reynolds & T.B. Gutkin (Eds.), *The handbook of school psychology* (3rd ed., pp. 863–884). New York: Wiley.

Reitan, R.M., & Wolfson, D. (1992). *Neuropsychological evaluation of older children.* South Tucson, AZ: Neuropsychology Press.

Savage, R.C. & Wolcott, G.F. (Eds.). (1994). *Educational dimensions of acquired brain injury.* Austin, TX: Pro-Ed.

Stratton, M.C. & Gregory, R.J. (1994). After traumatic brain injury: A discussion of consequences. *Brain Injury, 8*(7), 631–645.

Wood, R.L. (1990). Neurobehavioral paradigm for brain injury rehabilitation. In R. Wood (Ed.), *Neurobehavioral sequelae of traumatic brain injury* (pp. 3–17). New York: Taylor & Frances.

Ylvisaker, M., Hartwick, P., & Stevens, M. (1991). School reentry following head injury: Managing the transition from hospital to school. *Journal of Head Trauma Rehabilitation, 6,* 10–22.

TRAUMATIC BRAIN INJURY IN CHILDREN

INCIDENCE & PROBLEMS

Traumatic brain injury (TBI) in children remains as a major health problem and has been reported to be the leading cause of death between the ages of 2 to 44 (Hay, 1967). Actual incidence records are only available for those with more severe injuries who sought medical treatment but it is estimated that approximately 15,000 suffer severe traumatic brain injury in the US each year (Di Scala et al., 1991). Severe TBI produces many observable changes, and even more changes in a child's cognitive functions. In less severe TBI, or later in the recovery, the child may appear to be functioning normally but subtle cognitive deficits may remain which influence behavior in diffuse ways or which remain unnoticed until later stages of development are reached.

Assessment of the nature and extent of the consequences of TBI in children is more difficult and challenging than with adults, yet effective treatment and remediation requires an objective appraisal of cognitive strengths and weaknesses. Underestimating the capacity of recovery may lead to delayed rehabilitation with efforts aimed at the consequences of the injury rather than at preventative therapy (Stover & Zeiger, 1976). On the other hand, underestimating the extent of the impairment may lead to excessive stress or difficulty in emotional adjustment (Taylor et al., 1995). Clearly, even mild head injury can become a significant disruptive event to a child and his or her family unless the consequences are properly evaluated and effective rehabilitation is instituted.

DEVELOPMENT AND TIME TO RECOVERY

For a time it was generally believed that TBI sustained early in life was associated with less deleterious effects (Kennard principle). Children were thought to have a more resilient nervous system since they appear to recover more rapidly than adults, experience less persistent symptoms (Black et al., 1969), and seldom report post-concussion symptoms (Rutter et al., 1983). However, this notion is at best only partially accurate (Bolter & Long, 1985). Recent research has suggested that the likelihood of residual cognitive deficits is greater with early injury (Max et al. 1997; Taylor & Alden, 1997).

Children can "grow out" of some early deficits, but not others. In some cases, dysfunction may only appear later in the course of development (Teuber & Rudel, 1962; Goldman, 1971, 1972, 1974; Wrightson et al., 1995). For example, damage to the immature frontal lobes of a young child may not produce behavioral manifestations until much later in development when those cortical areas would normally assume functional prominence (Russell, 1959). It is likely that the effects of head injury in children combine with other functions in their development and may have widespread effects (Korkman, 1980). Age is only one variable of importance in determining the extent of recovery. In addition to age, one must consider location, nature, and the extent of the injury in order to determine the effects of the injury upon subsequent behavior.

SEVERITY OF INJURY

The pathophysiology of brain injury is similar in children and adults. Severity of injury is usually measured by duration of coma and/or post-traumatic amnesia (PTA), although both are difficult to assess in younger children (Leigh, 1979). As a general guide, children experiencing coma of over 7 days seldom recover to their pre-injury level. Even coma of less than 7 days or PTA of less than 3 weeks is usually associated with permanent cognitive impairment (Stover & Zeiger, 1976).

COGNITIVE CONSEQUENCES

After severe head injury, obviously impaired physical functions tend to improve rapidly, whereas cognitive dysfunction may resolve less quickly. Head injury frequently affects intelligence, memory, speech, language, and other functions. The effects upon cognitive functions are pervasive during the first 6 months following injury. Later in recovery, the effects are often characterized by slowed information processing, poor problem solving ability, impulsivity, distractibility, and poor stress tolerance with irritability and emotional lability. In addition, researchers have documented memory impairment, decreased visuospatial processing (Lord-Maes & Obrzut, 1996) and decreased attentional shift (Ewing-Cobbs et al. 1998). Common behavioral symptoms also include hyperkinesis (32%), discipline problems (10%), and lethargy (87%; Black et al., 1969), as well as ADHD (Max et al., 1998). These effects are observed in school performance and in neuropsychological testing. More important is the finding that children suffering even mild head trauma, with little or no coma and/or PTA, demonstrate attenuated cognitive abilities.

Children are undergoing significant developmental changes and even mild TBI can cause developmental setbacks leading to immature behaviors. Such damage may cause a loss of previously mastered skills and compromise future ability for the acquisition of new skills.

EMOTIONAL AND SOCIAL FACTORS

In addition to physical impairment and cognitive dysfunction, the brain injured child is at risk for the development of emotional problems (Max et al., 1998). The risks are greater in those with low premorbid I.Q., from low socioeconomic class, or from broken homes (Rutter et al., 1983). Pre-injury family environment has also been shown to affect recovery (Yeates et al., 1997). Survivors of TBI are at a greater risk of developing psychiatric disorders as well, which is positively correlated with injury severity (Max et al., 1997, 1998).

ASSESSMENT STRATEGIES

Proper assessment strategies leading into the development and enactment of an individually-tailored intervention plan are critical in facilitating the successful reentry of the brain injured child into his premorbid environment. These assessment strategies focus on cognitive, emotional, and environmental factors which interact and shape subsequent behavior. Initial assessment should focus on the neuropsychological consequences of the injury. This assessment examines the relationship between the functioning of the brain and the cognitive processing abilities exhibited by the child. This assessment of cognitive abilities, coupled with a consideration of the type and severity of injury, developmental factors, and emotional functioning of the child, affords a view of basic strengths and weaknesses in cognitive functioning which can serve to identify initial intervention strategies.

Repeated neuropsychological assessments are not necessary in most cases. Rather, a psychoeducational assessment should be of greater value later in recovery. Aptitude and achievement tests are not sensitive to the impact of a brain injury on functioning immediately following a TBI. However, they become critical components later in the assessment process for evaluating the impact of the child's processing strengths and weakness on school performance. The comparison of performance on aptitude and achievement tests given before and after the injury is valuable in evaluating changes in the child's ability to acquire and retain new information.

The child's emotional functioning and reaction to the environment in daily life is another key component of the assessment process. Observation of the child at home, within class, while interacting with peers, and so on is most likely to add to an understanding of the child's problems within these environments. Other assessment strategies include interviewing and utilizing scales of adaptive and emotional functioning. Evaluation of the appropriateness of the child's environment to his level of cognitive ability, emotional functioning, and behavioral control is needed.

INTERVENTION STRATEGIES

Examination of interacting cognitive, emotional, and environmental factors should be considered in the development of treatment plans. Traditional behavior management strategies may be helpful, but not completely adequate, for aiding the recovery of function in children with TBI. Because individuals with TBI often exhibit impaired concentration and memory and also have a low tolerance for frustration, environmental considerations must be made. Children with TBI should be afforded less distracting and more structured environments for study. Allowing children more time to complete their tasks can combat slowed processing. The lowered stamina of a child with TBI can be accommodated by providing frequent breaks and shortening the school day. The child's reentry into the normal school situation should be a gradual process. Care should be taken to insure that they are working at a level that will produce some successes. Resources such as special education and speech/language specialists should be utilized as needed. Additionally, consideration of emotional functioning should determine the need for psychological intervention. The reader is referred to a more extensive discussion of an ecological model of assessment and intervention (Farmer & Peterson, 1995, Long & Ross, 1992, Sbordone & Long, 1996).

REFERENCES

Black, P., Jeffries, J.J., Blumer, D., Wellner, A., & Walker, A.E. (1969). The posttraumatic syndrome in children. In A.E. Walker, W.F. Caveness, & M. Critchley, (Eds.), *Late effects of head injury* (pp. 142–149). Springfield, Illinois: Thomas.

Bolter, J.F., & Long, C.J. (1985). Methodological issues in research in developmental neuropsychology. In L.C. Hartlage & C.F. Telzrow (Eds.), *The neuropsychology of individual differences* (pp. 41–59). New York: Plenum.

Di Scala, C., Osberg, J.S., Gans, B.M., Chin, L.J., and Grant, C.C. (1991). Children with traumatic head injury: morbidity and postacute treatment. *Archives of Physical Medicine and Rehabilitation, 72,* 662–666.

Ewing Cobbs, L., Prasad, M., Fletcher, J.M., Levin, H.S., Miner, M.E., & Eisenberg, H.M. (1998). Attention after pediatric traumatic brain injury: a multidimensional assessment. *Child Neuropsychology, 4*(1), 35–48.

Farmer, J.E., & Peterson, L. (1995). Pediatric traumatic brain injury: promoting successful school reentry. *School Psychology Review, 24*(2), 230–243.

Goldman, P. (1971). Functional development of the prefrontal cortex in early life and the problem of neuronal plasticity. *Experimental Neurology, 3,* 366–387.

Goldman, P.S. (1972). Developmental determinants of cortical plasticity. *Acta Neurobiologica Experimentalis, 32,* 495–511.

Goldman, P. (1974). An alternative to developmental plasticity: Heterology of CNS structures in infants and adults. In D. Stein, J.

Rosen, & N. Butters (Eds.), *Plasticity and recovery of function in the central nervous system* (p. 109). New York: Academic.

Hay, R. (1967). Head injuries. *Canadian Medical Association Journal, 97,* 1364–1368.

Korkman, M. An attempt to adapt methods of Luria for diagnosis of cognitive deficits in children. Convention paper INS, 1980.

Leigh, D. (1979). Psychiatric aspects of head injury. *Psychiatric Digest,* 21–34. Levin, H.S. & Eisenberg, H.M. (1979). Neuropsychological impairment after closed head injury in children and adolescents. *Journal of Pediatric Psychology, 4,* 389–402.

Long, C.J., & Ross, L.K., (1992). *Handbook of head trauma: Acute care to recovery.* New York: Plenum.

Lord-Maes, J., & Obrzut, J.E. (1996). Neuropsychological consequences of traumatic brain injury in children and adolescents. *Journal of Learning Disabilities, 29*(6), 609–617.

Max, J.E., Lindgren, S.D., Knutson, C., Pearson, C.S., Ihrig, D., & Welborn, A. (1997). Child and adolescent traumatic brain injury: Psychiatric findings from a pediatric outpatient specialty clinic. *Brain Injury, 11*(10), 699–711.

Max, J.E. Koele, S.L., Smith, W.L., Sato, Y., Lindgren, S.D., Robin, D.A., & Arndt, S. (1998). Psychiatric disorders in children and adolescents after severe traumatic brain injury: A controlled study. *Journal of the American Academy of Child and Adolescent Psychiatry, 37*(8), 832–840.

Max, J.E., Arndt, S., Castillo, C.S., Bokura, H., Robin, D., Lindgren, S.A., Smith, W.L., Sato, Y., & Mattheis, P.J. (1998). Attention-deficit hyperactivity symptomatology after traumatic brain injury: a prospective study. *Journal of the American Academy of Child and Adolescent Psychiatry, 37*(8), 841–847.

Russell, W.R. (1959). *Brain, memory, learning: A neurologist's view.* Oxford: Clarendon.

Rutter, M., Chadwick, O., & Shaffer, D. (1983). Head injury. In M. Rutter (Ed), *Developmental neuropsychiatry* (pp. 83–111). New York: Guilford.

Sbordone, R.J., & Long, C.J. (1996). *Ecological validity of neuropsychological testing.* Delray Beach, Florida: St. Lucie.

Stover, S.L., & Zeiger, H.E. (1976). Head injury in children and teenagers: Function/recovery correlated with the duration of coma. *Archives of Physical Medicine and Rehabilitation, 57,* 201–205.

Taylor, H.G., & Alden, J. (1997). Age-related differences in outcome following childhood brain insults: An introduction and overview. *Journal of the International Neuropsychological Society, 3,* 555–567.

Taylor, H.G., Drotar, D., Wade, S., Yeates, K., Stancin, T., & Klein, S. (1995). Recovery from traumatic brain injury in children: The importance of the family. In S.H. Broman & M.E. Michel (Eds.), *Traumatic head injury in children* (pp. 188–216). New York: Oxford University Press.

Teuber, H.L., & Rudel, R.G. (1967). Behavior after cerebral lesions in children and adults. *Developmental Medicine and Child Neurology, 4,* 3–20.

Wrightson, P., McGinn, V., & Gronwall, D. (1995). Mild head injury in preschool children: evidence that it can be associated with a persistent cognitive defect. *Journal of Neurology, Neurosurgery, and Psychiatry, 59*(4), 375–380.

Yeates, K.O., Taylor, H.G., Drotar, D., Wade, S.L., Klein, S., Stancin, T. & Schatschneider, C. (1997). Preinjury family environment as a determinant of recovery from traumatic brain injuries in school-age children. *Journal of the International Neuropsychological Society, 3*(6), 617–630.

TRAVEL AIDS, ELECTRONIC

See ELECTRONIC TRAVEL AIDS.

TRAVEL AIDS FOR INDIVIDUALS WITH DISABILITIES

The United States Department of Justice provides a guide to disability rights and laws to ensure equal opportunities for people with disabilities. Encompassed within this document are guidelines for access to public transportation, public accommodation, and air carriers (Disability Rights Section, 1996). America adheres to these guidelines and provides disabled travelers with various options for traveling. Numerous opportunities for accessible travel by car, boat, train, or airplane are available to those with handicaps. Airlines have made themselves more accessible by arranging for an aisle seat (many of which have removable arms for easier access), notifying the crew that a special needs traveler will be on board, and meeting special requests such as dietary needs or supplemental oxygen. Wheelchairs may be gate-checked for easier accessibility as they will be the first items offloaded at the traveler's destination or at any change of planes. Travelers with disabilities should ask the airlines or their travel agent to make reservations for the most direct route and to allow ample time to change planes if necessary.

Train travel is another option for the handicapped traveler. Amtrak provides information and details about station accessibility along its routes. Train aisles are narrow, so wheelchair access may be limited. However, often meals are served at the handicapped person's seat. Conductors give hearing-impaired travelers necessary announcements in writing. Guide dogs travel free, and most trains are equipped with signs in braille.

Avis Rent-a-Car and Hertz Car Rental companies offer hand-control cars if reserved well in advance. Other car companies also have vehicles to offer special needs clients, including wheelchair-accessible vans.

If traveling by ship, the handicapped traveler should check accessibility before making a reservation. Most major cruise lines have handicapped accessible cabins and public areas, but some small ships have limited access. The special needs traveler should check with each ship to find out what provisions have been made for the disabled and if specific needs can be met.

Quick handicapped travel answers can be found from sources such as Fodor's Great American Vacations for Travelers with Disabilities (1994). The internet also provides multiple sites providing travel information and answering specific questions. Project Action (1999) has a comprehensive database with city and state listings of accessible travel options. National 800 numbers are listed on the Project Action website with public transportation, airport transportation, hotel shuttles, private bus, and even tour companies' information links. Information can be located online.

Access Amtrak
400 N. Capital Street, NW
Washington, DC 20001

American Foundation for the Blind
Travel Concessions for Blind Persons
15 W. 16th Street
New York, NY 10011

Centers for the Handicapped, Inc.
10501 New Hampshire Avenue
Silver Springs, MD 20903 (301-445-3350)

Diabetes Travel Service
349 E. 52nd Street
New York, NY 10022

INTERMEDIC
777 Third Avenue
New York, NY 10007

International Association for Medical Assistance for Travelers
350 5th Avenue, Suite 5620
New York, NY 10001

National Easter Seals Society
Information Center
2023 W. Ogden, Avenue
Chicago, IL 60612

Society for the Advancement of Travel for the Handicapped (SATH)
"The United States Welcomes Handicapped Visitors"
(cassette or braille available)
5014 42nd Street, NW
Washington, DC 20016 (202-966-3900)

Travel Tips for the Handicapped
U.S. Travel Service
Department of Commerce
Washington, DC 20230

Wheelchair Wagon Tours
P.O. Box 1270
Kissimmee, FL 32741 (305-846-7175)

Whole Person Tours
137 W. 32nd Street
Bayonne, New Jersey 07002 (201-858-3400)

REFERENCES

Fodor's great American vacations for travelers with disabilities. (1994). New York: Fodor's Travel Publications.

Project Action. (1999). http://projectaction.org/paweb/index.htm.

US Department of Justice. (1996). *Disability rights section.* Http://www.pueblo.gsa.gov/cic_prog/disability-law/disrits.html.

TREACHER-COLLINS SYNDROME

See RARE DISEASES.

TREATMENT ACCEPTABILITY

Treatment acceptability is a form of social validation that asks consumers how they feel about treatment methods prior to treatment. "Judgments of acceptability are likely to embrace evaluation of whether treatment is appropriate for the problem, whether treatment is fair, reasonable, and intrusive, and whether treatment meets with conventional notions about what treatment should be" (Kazdin, 1980, p. 259). The most basic assumption of the acceptability hypothesis is that the acceptability of a treatment method will influence the overall efficacy of the treatment. Methods that consumers feel are the most acceptable will be more effective than methods that are judged to be unacceptable. As Wolf (1978) stated, "If the participants don't like the treatment then they may avoid it, or run away, or complain loudly. And thus, society will be less likely to use our technology, no matter how potentially effective and efficient it might be" (p. 206).

REFERENCES

Kazdin, A.E. (1980). Acceptability of alternative treatments for deviant child behavior. *Journal of Applied Behavior Analysis, 13,* 259–273.

Wolf, M.M. (1978). Social validity: The case for subjective measurement or how applied behavior analysis is finding its heart. *Journal of Applied Behavior Analysis, 11,* 203–214.

See also Teacher Effectiveness; Teacher Expectations

TRIARCHIC THEORY OF INTELLIGENCE

The triarchic theory of intelligence is founded in the notion that intelligence has three primary aspects: analytical intelligence, practical intelligence, and creative intelligence. Analytical intelligence involves the ability to analyze, to make judgments and comparisons, and to evaluate. Practical intelligence is similar to "street smarts"—the ability to apply one's knowledge in a hands-on, real-world manner. Creative intelligence, finally, is the ability to create, to be imaginative, and to discover. However, all three of these intelligences work together (Sternberg, 1999).

Sternberg (1993) developed the Sternberg Triarchic Abilities Test, which measures these three intelligences; examining the different types of items used in the test can help define the three intelligences. The practical intelligence subtests include such tasks as route planning (reading maps and finding the shortest route from one place to another) and everyday verbal reasoning. Questions of the latter type require solving problems such as: How can a would-be college student who needs $1000 per year to supplement her scholarship obtain money yet remain financially independent? How can a teen-age boy who just moved from Arizona to Iowa, who has had a hard time making friends, and who enjoys writing stories, best solve his problem? Analytical intelligence questions include some interesting variations on traditional intelligence test items. An analogies subtest, for example, includes a "pretend" statement, such as "Money falls off trees." The subject must "pretend" the sentence is true, and then complete the statement: "snow is to shovel as dollar is to." The correct answer, hidden among words like "bank" and "bill," is "rake." Another analytical subtest invents algebraic operations such as "graf" and "flix," which take on specific meanings. The creative intelligence part includes such subtests as sentences that include nonsense words, such as "yip" or "tems," that have specific meanings that can be figured out from the context of the sentence. All three components are also measured via essay questions (Sternberg, 1993).

Neither creative nor practical intelligence have been shown to be highly correlated with IQ (Sternberg & Kaufman, 1996, 1998), which leads to a central implication of the triarchic theory: Two-thirds of a child's capacities are not being adequately measured by schools. In addition, because nearly all standardized tests focus on analytical intelligence, schools often over-reward students who are high on analytical intelligence while penalizing low-analytical students who may be quite intelligent in practical or creative abilities. Teachers may end up presenting their lectures and materials in an analytical manner, hoping (consciously or subconsciously) that students will be helped on the analytic-oriented standardized tests. But through this process, students who excel in other areas are unfairly penalized.

One final aspect of Sternberg's triarchic theory is his theory of mental self-management. In this conceptual framework, considered part of his theory of a triarchic mind, there are three mental processes used in thinking: metacomponents, performance components, and knowledge-acquisition components. Metacomponents, or "white collar" intelligence, are higher-order processes that are similar to analytical intelligence, while performance components, or "blue collar" intelligence, are lower-order processes that are similar to practical intelligence. Knowledge-acquisition components, finally, involve the process of learning and acquiring knowledge (Sternberg, 1988, 1999).

REFERENCES

Sternberg, R.J. (1999). *Cognitive Psychology* (2nd ed.). New York: Harcourt Brace.

Sternberg, R.J., & Kaufman, J.C. (1996). Innovation and intelligence testing: The curious case of the dog that didn't bark. *European Journal of Psychological Assessment, 12,* 175–182.

Sternberg, R.J., & Kaufman, J.C. (1998). Human abilities. *Annual Review of Psychology, 49,* 479–502.

TRICHOTILLOMANIA

Trichotillomania is a low-incidence disorder (occurring in less than 1% of pediatric referrals) of self-injurious behavior that consists of pulling out one's hair; it is often accompanied by trichophagia, subsequent eating of the hair. The etiology of trichotillomania is unknown, but it has long been held to be of a psychoanalytic or Freudian nature. It occurs most often in conjunction with a major psychological or psychiatric disorder, particularly schizophrenia and lower levels of mental retardation, though it also occurs with narcissistic personality disorders. In special education programs, it is most often encountered among mentally retarded populations. Incidences of trichotillomania have also been reported in conjunction with episodes of child abuse. Incidence is generally greater in females than males.

A variety of treatment approaches have been attempted with this unusual disorder, including psychoanalysis, traditional psychotherapies, hypnotherapy, and a variety of operant and other behavior modification techniques. Generally, the earlier the age of onset, the greater the likelihood of successful treatment (Sorosky & Sticker, 1980). Behavioral techniques appear to be the most successful methods of treating trichotillomania and trichophagia, particularly when competing responses can be developed, although success has been reported with a variety of techniques and the role of spontaneous remission is not known.

Some recent animal research suggests that a variety of self-injurious behaviors, including trichotillomania and trichophagia, may, in some cases, be of neurological origin. Relationships to damage of cells around the substantia nigra have been suggested.

REFERENCE

Sorosky, A.D., & Sticker, M.B., (1980). Trichotillomania in adolescence. *Adolescent Psychiatry, 8,* 437–454.

See also **Self-Injurious Behavior**

TRICHORHINOPHALANGEAL SYNDROME

Trichorhinophalangeal syndrome is a relatively rare hereditary condition which is traced to a defect on chromosome 8. Children born with this disorder have thin, sparse hair; thick, heavy eyebrows along the bridge of the nose, thinning out toward the distal portions of their faces; a pear-shaped or bulbous nose; large eyes; thin upper lip; small and /or extra teeth; small jaw; and a horizontal groove under their chin. These children are short in stature and have thin fingernails. Abnormalities of the skeletal system, including short, stubby fingers and toes, are common. Problems in bone growth appear around age 3 or 4 years and persist and worsen until adolescent growth is completed. Degenerative hip disease may develop in the young adult and senior years (Rudolph, 1991; Jones, 1988).

Trichorhinophalangeal syndrome comes in two forms: Types I and II, with Type II more severe than Type I. Besides the degree of severity, other distinguishing characteristics of Type II include a smaller head circumference and susceptibility to upper respiratory infections. Moreover, these children have mild to moderate mental retardation and delayed onset of speech. Children with Type I are usually of normal intelligence. Some children with Type II may have a hearing loss. Standard treatment for the syndrome is symptomatic and supportive. Surgery may be performed to correct limb and extremity abnormalities. Genetic counseling may also be helpful (Thoene, 1992).

For children who are mentally retarded or speech delayed, it will be important to begin services through an Early Childhood Intervention (ECI) program. Based on the child's progress and development, he/she may continue to require additional support through special education or speech therapy.

REFERENCES

Jones, K.L. (Ed.). (1988). *Smith's recognizable patterns of human malformation* (4th ed.). Philadelphia, PA: W.B. Saunders.

Rudolph, A.M. (1991). *Rudolph's pediatrics-19th edition.* Norwalk, CT: Appleton & Lange.

Thoene, J.G. (Ed.). (1992). *Physician's guide to rare diseases.* Montvale, NJ: Dowden.

TRISOMY 18

As indicated by its name, trisomy 18 is a congenital disease owed to the presence of three chromosomes 18 instead of two. Trisomy 18 symptomatology was first described by Edwards et al. (1960); therefore, the term Edwards syndrome is sometimes used instead of trisomy 18. As in many autosomal trisomies, severe polymalformations are observed. Moreover, affected patients show many common features, so that trained physicians are able to diagnose the syndrome on clinical inspection. Generally, trisomy 18 newborns are postmature (42 weeks of pregnancy), but nevertheless show a birth weight below 2500 g (Hamerton, 1971); hydramnios (too much amniotic fluid) is the rule. An elongated skull with prominent occiput is noted, together with microcephaly. Micrognatia (small mandible), low-set ears, short neck, short sternum, prominent abdomen with umbilical hernia, and narrow hips are usual findings. The extremities are also characteristic: fingers are in forced flexion, very difficult to unfold, and deviated so that the third one is recovered by the second and the fourth. Arches are present in most, if not all, fingers. These dermatoglyphic configurations are rare in normal people or in those with other chromosome diseases. Clubfoot is frequent, and the big toe is in dorsiflexion. Internal malformations include severe congenital heart anomalies in more than 95% of all cases, either intraventricular, septal defects or patent ductus arteriosus. Indeed, premature death can be related to these heart defects. Failure to thrive is the rule and, despite palliative treatment, death occurs in a mean time of 70 days (Hamerton, 1971). Developmental retardation is always observed, but accurate testing is difficult.

REFERENCES

Edwards, J.H., Harnden, D.G., Cameron, A.H., Crosse, V.M., & Wolff, O.H. (1960). A new trisomic syndrome. *Lancet, 1,* 787–790.

Hamerton, J.L. (1971). *Human cytogenetics* (Vol. 2). New York: Academic.

See also **Chromosomal Abnormalities; Genetic Counseling**

TRISOMY 21

Trisomy 21 or Down's syndrome is a combination of birth defects characterized by mental retardation, abnormal facial features, heart defects, and other congenital disorders. Approximately one in 800 to one in 1,000 infants is born with this disorder (March of Dimes, 1997). Trisomy 21 occurs in all races and economic levels; however, incidence is highest among Caucasians. Over 250,000 individuals with Trisomy 21 (March of Dimes, 1997) live in the United States. Life expectancy and quality of life has greatly increased over the past twenty years due to improved treatment of related complications and better developmental educational programs (Ball & Bindler, 1999). Mortality rates for infants with Trisomy 21 and congenital heart defects remain high at 44%. However, overall life expectancy among adults has improved to over 55 years (March of Dimes, 1997).

The cause of Trisomy 21 is unknown. A number of theories including genetic predisposition, radiation exposure, environmental factors, viruses, and even infections have been proposed (Wong, 1995). Trisomy 21 does result from an aberration in chromosome 21 in which three copies instead of the normal two occur due to faulty meiosis (nondisjunction) of the ovum or, sometimes, the sperm. This results in a karyotype of 47 chromosomes instead of the normal 46. The incidence of nondisjunction increases with maternal age and the extra chromosome originates from the mother about 80% of the time (Wong, 1995). Mothers over the age of 35 years are at the greatest risk for rearrangement of their chromosomes and their risk of having a child with Trisomy 21 increases greatly with age. At age 35, the risk is calculated to be 1 in 385 births, at age 40, the risk increases to 1 in 106 births, and at age 49, the risk of having a baby with Trisomy 21 is 1 in 11 (Wong, 1995). Prenatal testing through amniocentesis or chorionic villus identifies Trisomy 21 (March of Dimes, 1997). Both procedures carry a risk of infection and miscarriage. Genetic counseling is available for couples with

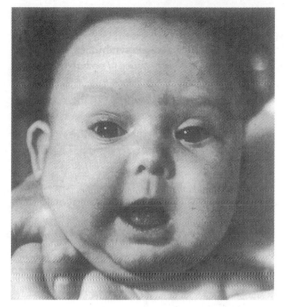

Characteristic facies of a trisomic 21 child.

a known family history of genetic birth defects and is also indicated for mothers over the age of 35 (March of Dimes, 1997).

The physical signs of Trisomy 21 are apparent at birth. The newborn is lethargic and has difficulty eating. Trisomy 21 newborns have almond-shaped eyes with epicanthal folds, a protruding tongue, a small mouth, a single palmar crease (simian crease), small white spots on the iris of the eye (Brushfield spots), a small skull, a flattened bridge across the nose, a flattened profile, small and low-set ears, and a short neck with excess skin (Wong, 1995). Slowed growth and development are characteristic of this syndrome, especially in speech formation. Other physical abnormalities include dry, sensitive skin with decreased elasticity, short stature, broad hands and feet, abnormal fingerprints, and hypotonic limbs (Ball & Bindler, 1999). Premature dementia similar to Alzheimer's disease usually occurs during the fourth decade of life, and an increase in leukemia, diabetes mellitus, thyroid disorders, and chronic infections are all common in individuals with Trisomy 21 (Wong, 1995).

The degree of mental retardation with Trisomy 21 varies greatly and ranges from mild to profound. Although children with Trisomy 21 can usually do most things that any child can learn to do (walking, talking, dressing, self-feeding, and toileting), they develop at a slower rate and at a later age (March of Dimes, 1997). The exact age of achievement of developmental milestones and skills cannot be predicted. However, early intervention programs beginning in infancy encourage these special children to reach their greatest potential.

Special education programs are available around the country with many children fully integrated into regular classroom situations (March of Dimes, 1997). The future for special children with Trisomy 21 is brighter than twenty years ago. Many will learn to read, write, take care of themselves, and hold partially supported employment while living semi-independently in group homes (March of Dimes, 1997).

REFERENCES

Ball, J., & Bindler, R. (1999). *Pediatric nursing: Caring for children* (2nd ed.). Stamford, CT: Appleton & Lange.

March of Dimes. (1997). *Down syndrome: Public education information sheet.* http://www.noah.cuny.edu/prenancy/march_of_dimes/birth_defects/downsynd.html

Wong, D. (1995). *Whaley & Wong's nursing care of infants and children* (5th ed.). St. Louis: Mosby-Year Book.

See also **Chromosomal Abnormalities; Down's Syndrome; Genetic Counseling**

TUBERCULOSIS

See CHRONIC ILLNESS IN CHILDREN.

TUBEROUS SCLEROSIS

Tuberous sclerosis is an inherited disorder transmitted as an autosomal dominant trait with variable penetrance affecting the skin, brain, retina, heart, kidneys, and lungs. It belongs to the group of diseases called phakomatoses, characterized by malformations, the presence of birthmarks, and the tendency to tumor formation in the central nervous system, skin, and viscera. The estimated frequency of occurrence is 1 per 30,000 live births (Berg, 1982). About 25% of the patients are sporadic owing to new mutations.

Tuberous sclerosis is a protean disorder chiefly manifested by epilepsy, mental deficiency, and cutaneous lesions. Convulsions are the most frequent initial symptom (up to 88%), presenting often in early life as infantile spasms (about 70%), usually between the fourth and sixth months of life. The convulsions later become generalized grand mal epilepsy and focal or akinetic seizures (Gomez, 1979; Hunt, 1983; Jeavons & Bower, 1964; Pampiglione & Moynahan, 1976). Mental retardation, when present, is usually severe; one-third of the patients may have normal intelligence (Gomez, 1979). Only 12 to 15% of affected subjects are free of epilepsy and mental retardation. The cutaneous lesions are multiple. Adenoma sebaceum is the characteristic sign of the disease. It appears in the face between 1 and 5 years of age (usually after 4 years), starting as a macular rash over the cheeks in a butterfly appearance, then increasing in size and covering the nose, lips, and chin with a granular aspect. Those adenoma named Pringle's are seldom absent but they may grow very slowly. Hypopigmented leaf-shaped spots called white or achromatic spots or depigmented nevi are the most frequent sign in up to 95% of cases (Hunt, 1983); they are disseminated over the trunk and the limbs and are present at birth (Gold & Freeman, 1965), but they increase in number during the first 2 years of life. They appear more numerous under Wood's light and may be demonstrable in clinically asymptomatic parents. Shagreen patches are thickenings of skin best seen in the lumbos-acral region. Periungueal fibroma (Koenen tumors) are more often present on the toes than on the fingers and appear after the first decade and in adults; they may be the only sign in parents of an affected child.

The pathology in the nervous system shows the presence of cortical malformations, variable in size (called tubers), that contain neurons, astrocytic nuclei, and giant cells. The tubers also can be located in the subependymal area and contain calcium deposits that can be identified on X-rays or CAT scans. They may grow into the ventricles, interfering with cerebral spinal fluid circulation, blocking the foramen of Monro or the aqueduct of Sylvius, and producing hydrocephalus and signs of raised intracranial pressure. Tumors can also be present in the heart, the lungs, and the kidneys, but they can be discovered easily by ultrasound examination showing angiomyolipoma or even cystic tumors (Avni et al., 1984). The examination of the ocular fundus may reveal tumoral lesions at the nerve head or about the disk, even in the absence of vision complaints.

Diagnosis of the disease is based on the association of epilepsy, mental retardation, and skin lesions. It can be made very early in life on the presence of infantile spasms and achromatic spots in correlation with the cerebral calcifications seen on CAT scans of the brain (Lee & Gawler, 1978).

REFERENCES

Avni, E.F., Szliwowski, H., Spehl, M., Lelong, B., Baudain, P., & Struyven, J. (1984). Renal involvement in tuberous sclerosis. *Annales de Radiologie, 27,* 2–3, 207–214.

Berg, B.O. (1982). Neurocutaneous syndromes. In K.F. Swaiman, & F.S. Wright (Eds.), *The practice of pediatric neurology.* New York: Mosby.

Gold, A.P., & Freeman, J.M. (1965). Depigmented nevi: The earliest sign of tuberose sclerosis. *Pediatrics, 35,* 1003–1005.

Gomez, M.R. (1979). Clinical experience at the Mayo Clinic. In M.R. Gomez (Ed.), *Tuberous sclerosis pp.* 16–20. New York: Raven.

Hunt, A. (1983). Tuberous sclerosis: A survey of 97 cases. *Developmental Medicine and Child Neurology, 25,* 346–357.

Jeavons, P.M., & Bower, B.D. (1969). Infantile spasms. *Clinics Developmental Medicine, 15,* London: Sime/Heinemann.

Lee, B.C., & Gawler, J. (1978). Tuberous sclerosis. Comparison of computed tomography and conventional neuroradiology. *Radiology, 127*(2), 403–407.

Pampiglione, G., & Moynahan, E.I. (1976). The tuberous sclerosis: Clinical and EEG studies in 100 children. *Journal Neurology Neurosurgery & Psychiatry, 39,* 666–673.

TURKEY, SPECIAL EDUCATION IN

Turkey has a centralized education system. The Ministry of Education has an Office of Special Education which monitors all special education services in Turkey. These special education services are regulated by the new Special Education Law (KHK/573), which replaced the old law in 1997. Basic principles of special education, as cited in the new Special Education Law, are as follows:

1. All special needs individuals should be provided special education services according to their interests, desires, sufficiencies, and abilities.

2. Special education should be started as early in one's life as possible.

3. Special education services should be planned and administered without segregating the special needs individuals from their social and physical environments to the greatest extent possible.

4. Priority should be given to educating special needs individuals with other individuals (i.e., in regular education environments) by considering their educational performances and modifying the instructional goals, contents, and processes.

5. Collaboration should be made with other organizations and institutions providing rehabilitation services in order to prevent the interruption of services.

6. Individualized education plans should be developed and education programs should be individualized for special needs individuals.

7. Families should be encouraged to take part in every process of special education actively.

8. Opinions of nongovernment organizations of special needs individuals should be considered in developing special education policies.

9. When planning special education services, elements should be included to facilitate special needs individuals' interactions with and adaptation to society.

There are guidance and research centers affiliated with the Office of Special Education in every major town to monitor the local special education services in Turkey. Main responsibilities of the guidance and research centers are as follows:

• To accept referrals from schools and conduct assessments
• To identify special needs individuals
• To place identified individuals in regular or special education environments
• To follow-up the special needs individuals
• To conduct inservice training to education personnel.

There are various placement alternatives for special needs students in Turkey. Until 1997, most special needs students were placed in special schools or special classes where available; they were integrated in regular classes when

special education placement was not available. In a sense, special students used to be integrated whenever they did not have a chance to be segregated. However, the new Special Education Law has a principle mandating integration to be considered as the preferred option for special needs students. Hence, this principle is expected to facilitate special education placements according to the "least restrictive environment" concept.

The number of special needs students from various disability categories enrolled in special schools, special classes and regular classes in 1997–98 in Turkey is 31,215. When all special needs students are considered, it is observed that 41% of them are educated in special schools, 26% of them are educated in special classes, and 33% of them are educated in regular classes.

The total number of students enrolled in elementary and secondary education programs is 11,355,736 (according to the records of the Ministry of Education). These data show that 0.3% of all students are special needs students. This means that the percentage of special needs children receiving special education services is rather low in Turkey.

The new Special Education Law mentions the need for special education support services for the integrated special needs students. Integration was started in Turkey without providing any support services to the integrated students and /or to their teachers. Therefore, integration did not prove to be a successful placement for many special needs students in the past. Now that special education support services are considered in the Special Education Law, regular schools are expected to have support personnel for providing services such as teacher consultations, in-class support, or resource room services when necessary.

Special education is a rather new and rare professional discipline in Turkey. Special education teacher training programs exist in only three universities, Abant Izzet Baysal University, Anadolu University, and Gazi University. The oldest of these programs, Anadolu University Special Education Teacher Training Program, started to graduate special education teachers in 1987. Thus, many teachers working with special needs students were originally trained as regular teachers and completed special education certificate programs, which are no longer offered.

Special education teacher training programs offer BA degrees in three special needs categories: developmental disabilities, hearing impairments, and visual impairments. Teacher training programs for the developmentally delayed have a behavioral orientation and emphasize direct instruction for teaching concepts and skills. Teacher training programs for the visually impaired aim to equip their students with knowledge necessary for teaching partially sighted and blind students. In teacher training programs for the hearing impaired, the auditory-oral approach is followed. Most of the graduates of special education teacher training programs apply to the Ministry of Education to be appointed as a special education teacher in a school or a guidance and research center, and some graduates choose to work in private schools. The total number of teachers working in special schools and special classes is 2653 at present, 435 of which are special education teachers.

Regarding special education research in Turkey, in addition to the quantitative methodologies, single-subject and qualitative research methodologies are two popular trends of the past few years. Although these research methodologies differ remarkably in terms of philosophical orientations as well as data collection/data analysis procedures, both are perceived to be very appropriate for improving special education knowledge and practices. Accordingly, the number of research projects, theses, and dissertations conducted qualitatively or by single-subject designs is increasing considerably in Turkey.

TURNER'S SYNDROME

Turner's syndrome is a sex chromosome abnormality characterized by the absence of all or part of one X chromosome in females (Reed, 1975). That is, rather than having the two sex chromosomes of the normal female (XX), about 80% of females with Turner's syndrome have only one X chromosome, symbolized as XO. The remainder have a variety of mosaic patterns involving variability in cells with chromosome deletions or translocations (Bender, Puck, Salbenblatt, & Robinson, 1984). Physical and developmental stigmata are less pronounced for some of the mosaic types (Bender et al., 1984). Only a small percentage of fetuses with abnormal sex chromosomes result in live births and the estimated incidence of all types of Turner's syndrome is 1 out of 2500 female live births (Reed, 1975). Physical sequelae often associated with this syndrome are short stature, webbing of the neck, deformity of the elbow (i.e., cubitus valgus), sexual immaturity, and congenital heart defects (Park, Bailey, & Cowell, 1983). Medical treatment primarily involves estrogen replacement during adolescence.

Learning disorders have been consistently associated with Turner's syndrome. While earlier studies reported a greater risk for mental retardation (Haddad & Wilkins, 1959), several recent studies have replicated a finding that only visual-motor abilities rather than verbal and global cognitive skills are decreased (Bender et al., 1984). Children and adolescent girls have been found to have lower performance than verbal IQs on the Wechsler Intelligence Scale for Children Revised. Neuropsychological studies have reported reduced capabilities in the right cerebral hemisphere and particularly the right parietal lobe (Money, 1973). Hence girls with Turner's syndrome appear to have a particular risk for the neuropsychological learning disorder type of visual-spatial dyslexia. There has been no particular vulnerability to general behavioral problems or psychopathology other than attention deficit disorder with hyperactivity (Hier, Atkins, & Perlo, 1980).

The primary implication for special education practitioners is that girls with Turner's syndrome should receive a comprehensive psychoeducational and perhaps neuropsychological evaluation to detect possible learning disorders. Behavioral practitioners also could provide anticipatory guidance to the child and family regarding such issues as sterility.

REFERENCES

Bender, B., Puck, M., Salbenblatt, J., & Roninson, A. (1984). Cognitive development of unselected girls with complete or partial X monosomy. *Pediatrics, 73,* 175–182.

Haddad, H.M., & Wilkins, L. (1959). Congenital anomalies associated with gonadal aplasia: Review of 55 cases. *Pediatrics, 23,* 885–902.

Hier, D., Atkins, L., & Perlo, V. (1980). Learning disorders and sex chromosome aberrations. *Journal of Mental Deficiency Research, 24,* 17–26.

Money, J. (1973). Turner's syndrome and parietal lobe functions. *Cortex, 9,* 385–393.

Park, E., Bailey, J.D., & Cowell, C.A. (1983). Growth maturation of patients with Turner's syndrome. *Pediatric Research, 17,* 1–7.

Reed, E.W. (1975). Genetic abnormalities in development. In F.D. Horowitz (Ed.), *Review of child development research* (Vol. 4, pp. 283–318). Chicago: University of Chicago Press.

See also **Genetic Variations; Kleinfelter's Syndrome; Mosaicism**

TUTORING

Tutoring is a method of instruction in which one or a small group of students (tutees) receive personalized and individualized education from a tutor. Tutoring is widely used with students of all ages and all levels of ability. However, in elementary and secondary schools, it is most often used as an adjunct to traditional classroom instruction: (1) to provide remedial or supplementary instruction to students who have difficulty learning by conventional methods, including mainstreamed, handicapped children; (2) to provide students with increased opportunities to actively participate in the learning process and receive immediate feedback; and (3) to help relieve the classroom teacher of instructional and noninstructional duties.

In most cases, tutoring is provided to students by someone other than the regular teacher. This may be an adult who volunteers or is paid, a college student, a programmed machine or computer, or, in many cases, another student. The term peer tutoring is used when children serve as tutors to others close to their age who are functioning at a lower level. The term cross-age tutoring is used when older children or adolescents work with tutees who are several years younger than themselves.

The practices of peer and cross-age tutoring were recorded as early as the first century AD by Quintilian in the *Institutio Oratoria.* However, the practice was not formalized and instituted on a widespread basis until the late eighteenth century by Andrew Bell in India and later by

William Lancaster in England. Tutoring was standard practice in the one-room schoolhouses of America until graded classes helped reduce the heterogeneity of student ability. Renewed interest in children teaching children began in the early 1960s because of shortages in professional teachers. Educators argued that disadvantaged children might learn more from a peer than from an adult. Several large-scale tutoring programs in New York City, Washington, DC, Chicago, Michigan, and California were successful (Allen, 1976).

Since 1970, numerous research studies and anecdotal reports have documented the benefits of tutoring for both the tutee and the tutor. Both have been found to benefit in terms of increases in achievement, school attitudes, peer acceptance, and self-image (Devin-Sheehan, Feldman, & Allen, 1976). Successful outcomes of tutoring have been reported for nonhandicapped tutees, tutees in special education including the moderately retarded, and those with aggressive behavior disorders (Maher, 1982).

Research further indicates that the effectiveness of tutoring depends greatly on how it is organized and structured and the nature of the relationship between the tutor and tutee. Some guidelines for developing a successful tutoring program follow.

Tutors must be carefully selected, trained, and supervised. Prospective tutor recruits must be dependable, responsible, and knowledgeable in the skill to be taught. They must be trained in tutoring skills (e.g., praising, task analysis, direct instruction, communication) and be provided with specific materials. A designated tutor supervisor must be available. Tutors and tutees should be matched carefully so that they have good rapport and work together conscientiously. Contracts are helpful in spelling out the responsibilities of each. If possible, tutoring should be held twice weekly for at least 30 minutes each session over a minimum of 10 weeks. The program should be continually monitored to determine its effectiveness. Meetings should be scheduled separately with the tutors and tutees to discuss any problems.

Extensive descriptions of tutorial procedures can be found in Allen (1976) and Ehly and Larsen (1980). The use of handicapped students as tutors for the nonhandicapped has been discussed by Osguthorpe (1984).

REFERENCES

Allen, V.L. (1976). *Children as teachers: Theory and research on tutoring.* New York: Academic.

Devin-Sheehan, L., Feldman, R.S., & Allen, V.L. (1976). Research on children tutoring children: A critical review. *Review of Educational Research, 46,* 355–385.

Ehly, S.W., & Larsen, S.C. (1980). *Peer tutoring for individualized instruction.* Boston: Allyn & Bacon.

Maher, C.A. (1982). Behavioral effects of using conduct problem adolescents as cross-age tutors. *Psychology in the Schools, 10,* 360–364.

Osguthorpe, R.T. (1984). Handicapped students as tutors for nonhandicapped peers. *Academic Therapy, 19,* 473–483.

See also Teaching Strategies

TWINS

Twins may pose a number of educational problems because of their close relationship and their strong attachment to one another. For instance, they often show language delay. Because they are content with each other's company and consequently socialize less with other children and adults than singletons, they tend to be less influenced by the linguistic environment (Luchsinger, 1961). Indeed, they may develop a jargon that enables them to communicate with one another but that is incomprehensible to others. This private idiom is called cryptophasia. Cryptophasia is not a language sui generis (as some have thought it was), but a sort of pidgin based on the language of the adults (Lebrun, 1982). Despite reduced vocabulary and absence of grammar, it makes communication possible between the twins; they have so many affinities that they can understand one another with just a few words. To improve the twins' language command, speech therapy may be necessary. Moreover, it may be desirable to separate them part of the day so that they can learn to socialize.

REFERENCES

Lebrun, Y. (1982). Cryptophasie et retard de langage chez les jumeaux. *Enfance* (3), 101–108.

Luchsinger, R. (1961). Die Sprachentwicklung von ein- und zweiengen Zwillingen und die Vererbung von Sprachstörungen in den ersten drie Lebensjahren. *Folia Phoniatrica* (13), 66–76.

U

ULCERS AND HANDICAPPED CHILDREN

While little empirical evidence exists to substantiate the relationship between ulcers and handicapped conditions, it appears that handicapped children may be more predisposed to ulceration than their nonhandicapped peers. Kim, Learman, Nada, and Thompson (1981) found that 5.4% of the residents in a large institution for mentally retarded children had peptic ulcers.

Other factors often associated with handicapping conditions also appear to lead to ulceration. For example, ulcers are more likely to occur in children with lower IQs. Additionally, ulcers occur more often in children who are withdrawn and less likely to express their feelings or frustrations, similar to some emotionally handicapped children. Finally, children who come from extended family situations (e.g., divorced or separated parents) are more likely to have ulcers, a factor that has been shown to be more likely to occur in handicapped children than in their non-handicapped peers (Beattie & Maniscalco, 1985).

Particular types of ulcers, particularly ulcerative colitis, may result in growth retardation and cosmetic problems that may lead to eligibility for services under the IDEA (Gillman, 1994; McClung, 1994).

REFERENCES

Beattie, J., & Maniscalco, G. (1985). Special education and divorce: Is there a link. *Techniques, 1,* 342–345.

Gillman, J. (1994). Inflammatory bowel diseases: Psychological issues. In R. Olsen, L. Mollins, J. Gillman, & J. Chaney (Eds.), *Pediatric psychology.* Boston: Longwood.

Kim, M., Learman, L., Nada, N., & Thompson, K. (1981). The prevalence of peptic ulcer in an institution for the mentally retarded. *Journal of Mental Deficiency Research, 25,* 105–111.

McClung, H. (1994). Inflammatory bowel diseases: Medical issues. In R. Olsen, L. Mullins, J. Gillman, & J. Chaney (Eds.), *Pediatric psychology.* Boston: Longwood.

***See also* Antisocial Behavior; Divorce and Special Education; Emotional Disorders**

ULTIMATE INSTRUCTION FOR THE SEVERE AND PROFOUNDLY RETARDED

The criterion of ultimate functioning (Brown, Nietupski, & Hamre-Nietupski, 1976) refers to a method of prioritization that may be used in developing programs for the severely or profoundly handicapped learner. Although the type of handicapping condition may vary, this program development philosophy has most often been applied to individuals who have been classified as mentally retarded.

Use of this type of rationale to develop curricula for such persons extends from three major assumptions (Brown et al., 1976). First, the exceptional needs learner should be taught skills that increase the student's independence in and access to less restrictive environments. Second, transfer of training, response generalization, and response maintenance cannot be assumed to occur with such learners. Third, programming efforts with the severely or profoundly handicapped learner should address the wide variety of individual learning characteristics of this group. Thus application of the criterion of ultimate functioning in developing curricula for these students requires that the skills and behaviors taught to such individuals should relate directly to the behaviors that will be expected of them in nonschool environments.

Brown et al. (1976) developed the concept of the criterion of ultimate functioning in response to inadequacies of educational programs that had been generated based on alternative curriculum philosophies. With the severely or profoundly handicapped learner, these philosophies have often been either developmental or nontheoretical in nature (Haring & Bricker, 1976).

In response to the limitations of most curriculum development approaches with the disabled, the criterion of ultimate functioning (Brown, et al., 1976) suggests teaching skills that are (1) relevant to student needs in light of individual learning characteristics; (2) immediately useful in terms of the environment(s) in which the student functions; and (3) able to increase the independence and ability of the student to attain access to more normative social environments. The teaching methods that are used from this perspective are based on specific analysis of the skills of the student and the requirements of the environment. Differences between these two assessment areas become the teaching objectives.

The criterion of ultimate functioning, used as a rationale for curriculum development with the severely or profoundly handicapped learner, breaks with the traditional developmental curriculum orientation. The skills that are taught are directly relevant in terms of the environments in which the student does, or is expected to, function. Building on techniques that emphasize specific analysis of student behaviors and environmental requirements, this approach systematically teaches the exceptional needs student skills that increase independence in and access to less restrictive settings. Theoretically, the degree to which the student might access social environments is a direct function of teaching the skills necessary for effective adaptation to those environments. Accordingly, the skills that are taught address not only the immediate relevance of learning experiences but also the long-term relevance of such skills.

REFERENCES

Brown, L., Nietupski, J., & Hamre-Nietupski, S. (1976). The criterion of ultimate functioning. In M.A. Thomas (Ed.), *Hey! Don't forget about me.* Reston, VA: Council for Exceptional Children.

Haring, H., & Bricker, D. (1976). *Overview of comprehensive services for the severely/profoundly handicapped.* New York: Grune & Stratton.

See also **Curriculum for the Handicapped; Profoundly Retarded**

UNITED CEREBRAL PALSY (UCP)

United Cerebral Palsy (UCP) is a national voluntary association comprised of state and local affiliates and the national organization, United Cerebral Palsy Associations (UCPA), which is headquartered in New York City. A governmental affairs office is located in Washington, DC. Local affiliates provide direct services to individuals with cerebral palsy and their families, including special education, transitional services, and community living facilities. State affiliates coordinate the programs of local affiliates, provide services to areas not covered by locals, and work with agencies at the state level to further UCP goals. United Cerebral Palsy Associations assists state and local affiliates by formulating national policies on which affiliates are organized, managed, and supported. It also represents the UCP on a national level.

There are five district offices: UCP of Northeast in New York City; UCP of Midwest in Des Plaines, Illinois; UCP of southwest in Dallas, Texas; UCP of Western in Burlingame, California; and UCP of Southeast in East Point, Georgia. United Cerebral Palsy Associations' district offices were established to bring national services closer to affiliates and to transmit affiliate needs quickly to the national organization.

UCPA works in many ways to generate new programs and services. In representing UCP in national affairs, UCPA cooperates with federal government agencies that administer programs that affect individuals with cerebral palsy. In addition, UCPA articulates UCP's positions on national issues such as national health services and transportation for people with disabilities. The UCPA develops model services for people with disabilities that are designed to be replicated in local communities (Cohen & Warren, 1985). The UCPA also supports national standards for the conduct of community programs. Through the UCP Research and Educational Foundation, UCPA promotes research into the causes of cerebral palsy, means of prevention, training of medical and allied personnel, and biomedical technology to improve mobility and communication. In addition, UCPA supports professional education by granting clinical fellowships and student traineeships

and by running conferences and institutes. The UCPA uses national communications media to educate the public about cerebral palsy and to raise funds (e.g., public service messages are contributed to UCPA by television networks, radio and press syndicates, and national magazines). Public education and information materials are available from UCPA.

REFERENCES

Cohen, S., & Warren, R. (1985). *Respite care: Principles, programs, and policies.* Austin, TX: Pro-Ed.

Nielsen, C. (1978). *The cerebral palsy movement and the founding of UCPA, Inc.* Unpublished manuscript.

United Cerebral Palsy Associations. (1983). *Annual report 1983.* New York: Author.

United Cerebral Palsy Association. (undated). *Meet your national organization.* New York: Author.

See also **Advocacy for the Handicapped; Cerebral Palsy**

UNITED KINGDOM, SPECIAL EDUCATION IN THE

To suggest that special education is undergoing change in the United Kingdom is an understatement. The rethinking of policies and practices in dealing with children with problems since the publication of the Warnock report in 1978 has produced massive changes, both tangible and attitudinal. Policy has altered from one of removal from normal schooling to one that attempts to integrate. A new set of procedures designed to keep children within the mainstream of society has been developed.

The United Kingdom has had special schools for over 200 years and legislation for special education since 1893. The principles of this education provision have been sound in their concern for children and their potential. Educational provision has been based on an extension of a medical model in which assessment allows diagnosis, which in turn leads to treatment. Following the medical model, it is the individual who is treated. For children in the United Kingdom, this has meant screening, diagnosis, and classification into groups such as deaf, blind, educationally subnormal, maladjusted, delicate, physically handicapped, autistic, and so on. In turn, the classification has led to segregation, partly to regularize ordinary schools and partly to provide special treatment in institutions. It is only since 1971 that all children have been included within the education system. Prior to that date, there was a further classification of ineducable. Severely mentally handicapped children were kept at home, in hospitals, or in junior training centers.

By the mid-1970s, the climate of opinion had changed sufficiently for there to be a major rethinking of this approach (Brennan, 1981; Fish, 1985). Pressures from parents, the mainstreaming lobby, sociological theorists, and the report of the Warnock Committee (1978) produced a new Education Act in 1981 that rejected the previous classifications in favor of "children with special educational needs":

A child has 'special educational needs' if he has a learning difficulty which calls for special education provision to be made for him. . . . A child has a 'learning difficulty' if: (a) he has a significantly greater difficulty in learning than the majority of children of his age; or (b) he has a disability which either prevents or hinders him from making use of educational facilities of a kind generally provided in schools within the area of the local authority concerned, for children of his age. (1981 Education Act)

By the time this Education Act came into force, provision was being made for 156,384 children in the United Kingdom (Fish, 1985). Of these, 45% were children with moderate learning difficulties, 20% had severe learning difficulties, 14% were maladjusted, 9% were physically handicapped, 5% were partially hearing or deaf, and 2% were partially sighted or blind. Following 1981 legislation, these categories were no longer used except where they would aid in the specification of need.

The Education Act requires local education authorities to be responsible for educational provision from birth if the parents request it and for the discovery of special educational needs from the age of 2. In addition, the procedures require parents to be active participants in every aspect of their child's assessment and placement. Within the school, procedures may be implemented differently from area to area but they must largely observe the following pattern:

1. The teacher concerned with pupil progress or behavior implements a program to assess and then develop those areas where problems arise.

2. Where change does not occur, alternative possibilities for the child are discussed at school meetings.

3. The parents are involved in these discussions.

4. Continuing difficulty leads, with the parents' permission, to outside professional involvement.

5. No progress leads to a full statement prepared on the child.

6. The local education authority acts on the basis of the statement in conjunction with the parents to place the child in a setting where special educational needs, as specified, can be met.

7. Reviews occur at least annually.

The central feature is the statement. This is the official document containing the local education authority's proposed placement of the child. In theory, the statement enforces multidisciplinary assessment of the child and allows the parents to offer evidence as well as their own opinions. In an ideal setting, the parents have considerable power in this process, as they must be consulted at every stage. The proposals for placement of the child and the statement of special education needs will be couched in positive terms to allow parents and education authorities to monitor progress and determine whether the child's needs are being met. Often, however, parents' involvement is small despite receiving written details on their rights. The proportion of parents offering evidence on their child is still very low. In effect, parents may not feel any more involved than before.

The whole process whereby professionals assess and deliver special education has been questioned. In effect, it has been proposed that those involved have had a vested interest in maintaining levels of provision that highlight their own roles. As a result, what is determined as need is what can be catered to by that group of professionals. This criticism strikes a chord with the increasingly heard views of people who have come through the system. Campling (1981), using self-assessment by disabled people, shows the strength of group identity. Thomas (1982), in examining how the experience of disability affects a person's ability to contribute to society, indicates how a special education system maintains the lower social status of disabled people. There is no simple response to criticism in this area since it is an attack on the most fundamental aspects of special education itself. It does require a response, however, and as yet there has been none that would lead to more positive integration and a more sensitive education system.

There was radical reorganization of services throughout the United Kingdom in the wake of the 1981 Education Act. It is not surprising that the discussion of special educational provision has meant a clarification of the respective roles of different agencies. In the preschool years, which for children with severe problems means only up to age 3, there has been greater cooperation between educational and medical professions. Legally, education can begin at birth if the parents or health services request it. This requires increased contact between health personnel and education services and should provide a much higher level of response to children and their families. In the school years, the peripatetic teams support not only the child, but also the teacher. In fact, the job of educating the classroom teacher about disability has largely fallen on the support teaching service.

In the postschool period, there has been greater attention to the child's transition to membership in adult society and continuing education for special needs. The former has meant the development of new curricula for young adults that are more relevant to society's demands. The latter has simply extended all special education issues into the areas of further education and adult education. The questions of integration and minority provision are no more easily answered in a college of further education than in an ordinary school.

While the 1981 act did not discuss teacher training in special education, at the center of all these issues are the teachers themselves. The structure of special education training is now undergoing marked change, with an increase in control from government (Galloway, 1998). All initial teacher training programs throughout the United Kingdom now include a special education component. To teach as a specialist in special education now requires additional second-tier training in special education. Training for work with special handicaps such as teaching the deaf or blind may ultimately become a third tier rather than the second tier it is at present. The picture is one of more extensive and more thorough training for all teachers at both the initial and in-service stages, but these changes will take many years to affect the system.

The current bureaucracy of professional practice in Britain prevents educational psychologists from paying any more than lip service to cultural diversity, parent involvement, and child-centered services (Galloway, 1998). Many are being used as consultants rather than in assessment (Marsh, Jacobsen, & Kanen, 1997). The latter may well be a reflection of tasks suggested by the Warnock Committee and realized in integration and inclusive practices taking place and succeeding (McNeill, 1996).

REFERENCES

Brennan, W. (1981). *Changing special education.* Milton-Keynes, England: Open University Press.

Campling, J. (1981). *Images of ourselves.* London: Routledge & Kegan Paul.

Fish, J. (1985). *Special education: The way ahead.* Milton Keynes, England: Open University Press.

Galloway, D. (1998). Special education in the United Kingdom: Educational psychologists and the effectiveness of special education. *Educational & Child Psychology, 15*(1), 100–108.

Marsh, A.J., Jacobsen, E., & Kanen, L. (1997). The impact of new legislation on school psychology in the United Kingdom. *School Psychology International, 18*(4), 299–324.

McNeill, B. (1996). Behavior support in a mainstream school. *Support for Learning, 11*(4), 181–184.

Thomas, D. (1982). *The experience of handicap.* London: Methuen.

See also **France, Special Education in; Western Europe, Special Education in**

UNITED STATES OFFICE OF EDUCATION

The United States Office of Education, a precursor to the current federal Department of Education, was created by an act of Congress in 1867. Its original mission was to collect and disseminate information on the condition of education in the states and U.S. territories. According to Campbell et al. (1975), the Office of Education was responsible for establishing a system to identify and advance promising educational practices in school districts throughout the country.

Public Law 96-88, passed by Congress and signed by President Carter in 1979, created the U.S. Department of Education. The new department assumed all of the functions previously assigned to the Office of Education, and also included education-related programs and functions previously administered by other entities within HEW such as rehabilitation.

REFERENCE

Campbell, R.F., Cunningham, L.L., Nystrand, R.O., & Usdan, M.D. (1975). *The organization and control of American schools.* Columbus, OH: Merrill.

See also **Politics and Special Education**

UNIVERSAL NONVERBAL INTELLIGENCE TEST (UNIT)

The Universal Nonverbal Intelligence Test (UNIT; Bracken & McCallum, 1998) is an individually administered instrument for children and adolescents ages 5 through 17 years. Although the UNIT can be administered whenever an intellectual assessment is warranted, the test was designed to be useful particularly when a traditional language-loaded intelligence test would create an unfair disadvantage for examinees. That is, the UNIT is especially useful when assessing students who are limited English proficient, speak English as a second language, deaf, hearing impaired, linguistically learning disabled, selective mute, or autistic.

The UNIT assesses intelligence through six culture-reduced subtests that combine to form two Primary Scales (Reasoning and Memory), two Secondary Scales (Symbolic and Nonsymbolic), and a Full Scale. Each of the UNIT subtests (i.e., Symbolic Memory, Cube Design, Spatial Memory, Analogic Reasoning, Object Memory, and Mazes) are administered in a totally nonverbal format (i.e., no receptive or expressive language is required of either the examiner or examinee) through the use of eight standardized gestures, task demonstration, and sample items.

REFERENCE

Bracken, B.A., & McCallum, R.S. (1998). *Universal Nonverbal Intelligence Test.* Itasca, IL: Riverside Publishing.

UNIVERSITY AFFILIATED FACILITIES (UAF)

Today's network of university affiliated facilities (UAFs) grew out of the recommendations of the 1962 President's Panel on Mental Retardation, which stressed the need for a "continuum of care" for mentally retarded persons, parents, and volunteers. In the following year, federal funds for construction of facilities to house services affiliated with universities or hospitals were authorized in PL 88-164. Maternal and Child Health, now the Division of Maternal and Child Health (DMCH), was the first agency to provide program support. In keeping with the mandate of this agency, funding was limited to support for faculty positions and trainees within the traditional maternal and child health disciplines that focused on children's services. The UAFs were the first major federally backed initiative to provide interdisciplinary training and diverse health care for persons with mental retardation.

The developmental disabilities legislation in 1979 expanded the scope of concern to include other disabilities, and the Developmental Disabilities Act (administered by what is now the ADD [the Administration on Developmental Disabilities]) provided core support for administrative costs of UAFs. Today, 19 programs receive DMCH funding for training and ADD core support goes to 36 UAFs and 7 satellite programs. Additional support is generated in each UAF from a variety of federal, state, and local sources. In addition to the DMCH and ADD-funded UAFs, 5 programs have elected to become members of the national association of UAFs, so that the present network of UAFs includes 55 programs in 38 states and the District of Columbia.

The mission of the UAFs includes four major elements: interdisciplinary training, exemplary services, applied research, and technical consultation/dissemination. The UAFs reduce both the incidence and the impact of mental retardation and developmental disabilities through a range of activities designed to prevent these disabilities or to enable persons who have these conditions to achieve their fullest potential. The latter is accomplished through early diagnosis, treatment, training in self-help and employment-related skills, and education tailored to specific needs and capabilities. These goals are pursued through four distinct programmatic activities that are the components of the mission: (1) interdisciplinary training for professional, administrative, technical, direct-care, and other specialized personnel to work with children and adults who are mentally retarded or developmentally disabled or at risk for developing such conditions; (2) a continuum of a full range of services; (3) technical assistance and dissemination of information to state, regional, and community-service programs through in-service training, continuing education, publications, development and dissemination of training materials, and conferences; and (4) applied research into related disorders and the efficiency of prevention, treatment, and remedial strategies.

See also **Metal Retardation**

VAKT

VAKT is a multisensory method of instruction that uses visual, auditory, kinesthetic, and tactile senses to reinforce learning (Richek, List, & Lerner, 1983). Unlike most other teaching strategies, the VAKT method emphasizes the kinesthetic sensory input provided by tracing and the tactile sensory input provided through varying textures of stimuli. The VAKT method is based on the principle that some children learn best when redundant cues are provided through many sensory channels (Mercer & Mercer, 1985). During instruction, the student sees the stimulus, listens to the teacher pronounce the stimulus, and then traces the stimulus over some textured material (e.g., sandpaper, corduroy, Jello). Thorpe and Sommer-Border (1985) contend that the kinesthetic-tactile component increases students' attention to the task. Under VAKT instruction conditions, students are more likely to attend selectively to distinctive features of the target letters and words. In addition, they tend to persevere or stay on task for longer periods of time at higher rates of engagement.

Many variations in the types of sensory activities have been devised. Depending on the style of learning of individual students, emphasis may be on one sensory channel over another. Some students may need more involved sensory experiences. More potent stimulation may be provided by such activities as tracing stimuli in sand trays, cornmeal, or Jello. Other activities include tracing in air, tracing in air while blindfolded, and tracing over raised stimuli of varying textures. Since the activities used with the VAKT method are time-consuming, it has been recommended they be used particularly in cases of severe learning deficits (Richek et al., 1983). However, VAKT activities can be used with milder deficits or even everyday learning.

REFERENCES

Mercer, C.D., & Mercer, A.R. (1985). *Teaching students with learning problems* (2nd ed.). Columbus, OH: Merrill.

Richek, M.A., List, L.K., & Lerner, J.W. (1983). *Reading problems: Diagnosis and remediation.* Englewood Cliffs, NJ: Prentice-Hall.

Thorpe, H.W., & Sommer-Border, K. (1985). The effect of multisensory instruction upon the on task behavior and word reading accuracy of learning disabled children. *Journal of Learning Disabilities, 18,* 279–286.

See also **Fernald Method; Gillingham-Stillman Approach; Multisensory Instruction**

VALETT DEVELOPMENTAL SURVEY OF BASIC LEARNING ABILITIES

The Valett Developmental Survey of Basic Learning Abilities was developed in 1966 by Robert E. Valett. The survey is designed to emphasize the use of psychoeducational diagnosis and evaluation to ascertain specific learning and behavioral problems in children ages 2 to 7 (Valett, 1967). A total of 53 learning behaviors that may appear in a deficit form have been grouped under seven major areas of learning as follows: motor integration and physical development; tactile discrimination; auditory discrimination; visual motor coordination; visual discrimination; language development and verbal fluency; and conceptual development. A graded range of one to four items for a particular age level constitutes a 233-task survey. Each of the seven major areas is operationally defined and arranged developmentally in ascending order of difficulty. The instrument, educational rationale for remedial programming, and remedial materials are presented in a loose-leaf workbook format that are number-keyed to the major areas and subtasks. Scoring is based on correct, incorrect, or partial development.

REFERENCES

Valett, R.E. (1966). The Valett Developmental Survey of Basic Learning Abilities. Palo Alto, CA. Consulting Psychologist Press.

Valett, R.E. (1967). A developmental task approach to early childhood education. *Journal of School Psychology, 2,* 136–147.

See also **Psychoeducational Methods; Remedial Instruction**

VALIUM

Valium (diazepam) may be used for the management of anxiety disorders or for the short-term relief of the symptoms of anxiety. It also is used for the relief of skeletal muscle spasms or for spasticity caused by upper motor neuron disorders such as cerebral palsy; thus, it may be used for some children in special education classes. In some cases, it also may be used as an adjunct in status epilepticus and severe recurrent epileptic seizures. It has a central nervous system depressant effect, and is thought to act on parts of the limbic system, the thalamus, and hypothalamus. Side effects may include drowsiness and fatigue, with less frequent reactions of confusion, depression, headache, hypoactivity, and slurred speech. Overdosage may produce somnolence, confusion, or coma, and withdrawal symptoms such as convulsions, cramps, and tremor may occur following abrupt discontinuance.

See also **Anticonvulsants; Drug Therapy**

VALPROIC ACID

Valproic acid is the recommended nonproprietary name for dipropylacetic acid. The common (proprietary) name for this drug is Depakene. In the United States and Europe, the sodium salt of dipropylacetic acid is used. In South America, the magnesium salt of dipropylacetic acid also is marketed.

Valproic acid is effective in the treatment of absence seizures. It is considered of some use in the treatment of myoclonic seizures, and in tonic-clonic seizures (Dreiffus,

1983). It is also used to treat certain forms of bipolar disorder, cyclothymia, and may be used with ADHD children who are unresponsive to or have problems with stimulant medication. The major side effects that are reported are drowsiness, gastrointestinal discomfort, and changes in appetite. The Committee on Drugs of the American Academy of Pediatrics lists valproic acid as having minimal adverse effects on cognitive functioning (Pruitt et al., 1985). The most significant and rare side effect of valproic acid is hepatic failure.

REFERENCE

Dreifuss, F.E. (1983). How to use valproate. In P.L. Morselli, C.E. Pippenger, & J.K. Penry (Eds.), *Antiepileptic drug therapy in pediatrics* (pp. 219–227). New York: Raven.

Pruitt, A.W., Kauffman, R.E., Mofenson, H.C., Roberts, R.J., Rumack, B.H., Singer, H.S., & Speilberg, S.S. (1985). Behavioral and cognitive effects of anticonvulsant therapy. *Pediatrics, 76,* 644–646.

See also **Depakene**

VALUES CLARIFICATION

Values clarification, an approach to moral instruction used with both handicapped and nonhandicapped pupils, stems from the humanistic education movement of the 1960s. Students trained in values clarification are taught to investigate the facts pertinent to a moral issue and to examine their feelings in a systematic manner. Values clarification teaches students the process of obtaining values and encourages them to explore personally held values and examine how they affect their decision-making processes (Casteel & Stahl, 1975). Rather than defining values in terms of good or bad, students learn to see values as guiding principles that affect choices. Critics of this approach have argued that values cannot be taught from a relativist position, and have questioned the appropriateness of using schools as settings for the teaching of values. As a result, values clarification started to lose its popularity as an educational force by the late 1970s (Brummer, 1984).

Special education students are often faced with value decisions relating to their handicaps. For example, vocational programs for special education students may rule out certain academic options. The handicapped adolescent, limited in career opportunity, needs to explore the implications of vocational choices. Values clarification can help these youngsters to pick appropriate career directions and to learn decision-making principles necessary for adequate socialization at the work place (Miller & Schloss, 1982).

Some emotionally disturbed and learning-disabled children have been found to act without carefully considering the implications of their behaviors (Miller & Schloss, 1982). Values clarification provides a structure within which behaviorally disturbed children may find consistency. Thompson and Hudson (1982) found values clarification effective in reducing the maladaptive behavior of emotionally disturbed children. These children were also reported to be happier and less anxious.

Values clarification has also been used to help regular education students accept mainstreamed handicapped pupils. Simpson (1980) trained students to examine the effects of social influence and group affinity, and found that it eased the mainstreaming transition for both regular and handicapped students. Future research might focus on the long-range effects of values education on the attitudes of the general population toward handicapped individuals.

REFERENCES

Brummer, J.J. (1984). Moralizing and value education. *Educational Forum, 48*(3), 263–276.

Casteel, J.D., & Stahl, R.J. (1975). *Value clarification in the classroom: A primer.* Santa Monica, CA: Goodyear.

Miller, S.R., & Schloss, P.J. (1982). *Career-vocational education for handicapped youths.* Rockville, MD: Aspen Systems.

Simpson, R.L. (1980). Modifying the attitudes of regular class students toward the handicapped. *Focus on Exceptional Children, 13*(3), 1–11.

Thompson, D.G., & Hudson, G.R. (1982). Value clarification and behavioral group counseling with ninth grade boys in a residential school. *Journal of Counseling Psychology, 29,* 394–399.

See also **Conscience, Lack of in the Handicapped; Moral Reasoning**

VAN RIPER, CHARLES (1905–1991)

A native of Champion, Michigan, Charles Van Riper received both his BA (1926) and MA (1930) from the University of Michigan, and his PhD (1934) from the University of Iowa. His degrees are in speech pathology and psychology. He is a professor in the department of speech pathology and audiology of Western Michigan University. He also has been the director of the Speech and Hearing Clinic at that University since 1936.

One of the premier authorities in the field of speech correction, Van Riper contributed to the theory and correction of stuttering and has developed methods for understanding, evaluating, and altering speech behavior. In 1978 the sixth edition of his textbook, *Speech Correction: Principles and Methods,* was published.

Van Riper was concerned with involving the family in the therapy of any child with a speech problem. He believes that parents who know what they are doing are frequently better speech therapists than formally trained therapists. He began his book *Your Child's Speech Problems* (1961) with the statement that "once parents understand what the speech problem (of their child) is and what should be done, they can do great deeds" (p. xi).

A member of Phi Beta Kappa, Van Riper received the honors of the Association of the American Speech and Hearing Association. He has been included in *Leaders in Education, Who's Who in the South and Southwest,* and *American Men and Women of Science.*

REFERENCES

Van Riper, C. (1961). *Your child's speech problems.* New York: Harper & Row.

Van Riper, C. (1978). *Speech correction: Principles and methods* (6th ed.). Englewood Cliffs, NJ: Prentice-Hall.

See also **Speech and Language Handicaps; Speech Disorders**

VELO-CARDIO-FACIAL SYNDROME (SHPRINTZEN SYNDROME)

This is the syndrome most commonly associated with cleft palate. The symptoms of this autosomal dominant syndrome may include: small stature, slender and long hands and digits, cleft palate, pharyngeal hypotonia, velopharyngeal incompetence, structural facial anomalies, microcephaly, cardiac anomalies, pulmonary atresia, seizure disorder, personality disorder, intelligence ranging from normal to below normal (McWilliams, Morris, & Shelton, 1990). These symptoms result in speech problems which reduce intelligibility such as nasal resonance disorders due to a velopharyngeal valving deficit and articulation problems due to motor speech disorder. Hearing function is often impaired by conductive hearing loss associated with the occurrence of cleft palate, deficits in the muscles which dilate the Eustachian tube and structural narrowing of the Eustachian tube itself. Feeding difficulties can be present during infancy. Language development is frequently delayed and subsequent language deviations appear. Learning disability is a common outcome for this population.

The variety and range of severity of symptoms in Velo-Cardio-Facial syndrome complicates diagnosis and often delays effective treatment. Due to the wide range of medical and behavioral deviations, transdisciplinary team management is recommended for intervention with an individual who is diagnosed with this syndrome (Shprintzen & Bardach, 1995).

REFERENCES

McWilliams, B.J., Morris, H.L., & Shelton, R.L. (1990). *Cleft palate speech* (2nd ed.). Philadelphia: B.C. Decker Inc.

Shprintzen, R.J., & Bardach, J. (1995). *Cleft palate speech management: A multidisciplinary approach.* St. Louis: Mosby.

VELOPHARYNGEAL INADEQUACY (VPI)

Velopharyngeal inadequacy (VPI) is an inclusive term which refers to deficiencies in structure or function of the velopharyngeal mechanism. Such deficiencies result in loss of control of nasal resonance in speech. This can significantly affect intelligibility and may also cause swallowing dysfunction. The velopharyngeal mechanism includes the velum (soft palate) and posterior and lateral walls of the uppermost portion of the pharynx.

One problem area subsumed under VPI is anatomical structure anomalies, termed velopharyngeal insufficiency.

In this case, there may be a lack of tissue in the velum which means it is too small to make contact with the posterior pharyngeal wall, thus compromising the seal necessary for disconnecting the nasal area. Another structural problem may involve interference from or loss of tonsilar tissue. Large palatine tonsils can obstruct the movements of the velum or lateral pharyngeal walls. In addition, pharyngeal tonsils (adenoids) can temporarily reduce the distance to be covered by velar elevation and their disappearance, due to surgery or maturation, may reveal a latent velar insufficiency. Finally, oral surgery techniques used to correct craniofacial deficiencies (e.g., maxillary advancement) may increase the diameter of the velopharyngeal portal beyond the capability of the existing velopharyngeal mechanism.

VPI also encompasses the term velopharyngeal incompetence. This term describes physiological dysfunction affecting movement of the velum or pharyngeal walls. The muscle fibers in these structures can be misdirected so that appropriate movement, such as medial motion in the lateral pharyngeal walls or elevation of the velum, is impossible. Muscle pairs may be asymmetric or asynchronous in their contraction response. Nervous supply to the muscles may be deficit, resulting in paralysis or paresis (weakness).

Velopharyngeal inadequacy can also describe the mislearning of the nasal/oral balance of specific speech sounds that occurs in the presence of hearing impairment and deafness. In addition, idiosyncratic phonological development or dialectical differences can also produce nonstandard nasal resonance patterns during speech.

Differential diagnosis of this condition involves perceptual and acoustic analysis of speech, examination of oral motor structures and functions and visualization of the velopharyngeal mechanism using videofluoroscopy and/or endoscopy. VPI can be reduced or corrected with surgical or behavioral intervention. Determination of the best treatment options for an individual can best be made by consulting a Cleft Palate Team which includes surgical and speech-language pathology professionals.

VERBAL DEFICIENCY

Verbal deficiency is a term with multifaceted meaning in the field of special education. It refers to the use and understanding of language and indicates abilities that are either deficient in terms of an individual's overall level of functioning or clearly below the norm for individuals of a certain age. Frequently, verbal deficiency is diagnosed when a child's verbal IQ on an individually administered intelligence measure such as the Wechsler Intelligence Scale for Children-III, is significantly lower than performance IQ (Kaufman, 1994). Verbal deficiency is also inferred from a child's relative difficulty on those portions of group-administered standardized achievement tests that rely heavily on verbal skills. Parents and educators often note that a child's verbal skills are not age appropriate. A child may exhibit difficulty in following directions given orally or comprehending information presented orally. The child also may have difficulty with verbal expression. Language arts skills such as reading, composition, and spelling may be impaired. Speech pathologists working with children may use the term verbal deficiency when referring to subnormal development of language structures, verbal fluency, and knowledge of vocabulary.

A verbal deficiency may have roots and causes that are primarily medical. Hearing impairment, especially if mild, can be an undetected cause of verbal deficiency. A history of chronic otitis media (middle ear inflammation) and resulting intermittent hearing loss can be a factor as well. Neurological impairment can result in deficiencies in verbal skills while leaving other areas of functioning relatively intact. Although mentally retarded children often show depressed functioning in all areas, this possible cause must be considered when a child presents with verbal deficiency.

It is sometimes possible to infer through evaluation and testing specific developmental difficulties that lead to verbal deficiency. These include expressive or receptive language deficiencies or a central auditory processing disorder. A learning disability (as defined by failure to learn at a normal rate despite average intellectual ability) in the language arts area also can be associated with a verbal deficiency.

Sattler (1982) and Kaufman (1994) provide a more detailed discussion of the nature and causes of verbal deficiency. A single or combination of causes may be present with a child presents with verbal deficiency. Causes not described here may exist as well in individual cases.

REFERENCES

Kaufman, A.S. (1994). *Intelligent testing with the WISC-III.* New York: Wiley.

Sattler, J.M. (1982). *Assessment of children's intelligence and special abilities* (2nd ed.). Boston: Allyn & Bacon.

See also **Expressive Language Disorders; Receptive Language Disorders**

VERBALISMS

Verbalisms is a term coined by Cutsforth (1932) to describe the use of words by the blind that represent terms or concepts with which the blind could not have had first-hand experience. Color words are one example. Blind children learn quickly that sighted individuals refer to green grass, blue sky, and a bright orange sun and use such terms freely in their own language although they never experience these colors. The development of verbalisms is important to the mastery of language and communication by the blind; however, the blind should also be encouraged not to rely exclusively on verbal learning.

REFERENCE

Cutsforth, T.D. (1932). The unreality of words to the blind. *Teachers Forum, 4,* 86–89.

See also **Blind**

VERBAL-PERFORMANCE IQ DISCREPANCIES

When interpreting the results of any of the three Wechsler scales, WAIS-III, WISC-III, or WPPSI-R, particular attention is focused on whether or not a discrepancy exists between the verbal (V) and performance (P) composite IQs. Other intelligence tests (e.g., McCarthy Scales of Children's Abilities) yield similar verbal and performance IQs. Tests assessing only verbal or nonverbal (performance) intelligence are also available. Although this discussion will focus on interpreting V and P discrepancies of the commonly used Wechsler scales, much of content is also applicable to these other intelligence tests.

The interpretation of IQ test data often focuses initially on the V-P discrepancy because it possesses particular diagnostic and/or prognostic value. The value lies in indicating particular strengths and weaknesses of the examinee as they apply to present or future educational or vocational pursuits (Kaufman, 1994; Sattler, 1982).

When considering a V-P IQ discrepancy, the test user must determine whether the observed discrepancy reflects a real difference rather than one that could be attributed to chance error. Sattler (1982) and the individual test manuals of many of the intelligence tests provide useful tables to allow the examiner to associate critical magnitudes of V-P IQ discrepancies with their levels of statistical significance. For the purpose of interpretation and planning appropriate remediation programs, the 95% (.05) level of confidence is recommended to determine whether a V-P IQ difference is real or should be attributed to chance (e.g., error measurement; Kaufman, 1994).

In addition to the determination of the statistical significance of an observed V-P IQ discrepancy, the clinical or practical importance of such information must also be assessed. A method to evaluate the value of a particular V-P IQ discrepancy involves determining how common or rare the discrepancy is for normal individuals. This is accomplished by calculating how often V-P IQ discrepancies of a given magnitude occurred in the test's standardization sample comprised of normal individuals. By inference, this information provides data or base rates as to how often particular discrepancies occur in the general population. For example, Kaufman (1976) reported that as many as 50% of normal children in the WISC-R standardization sample had V-P IQ discrepancies of 9 points or greater and 34% of the sample obtained V-P IQ discrepancies of 12 points or greater. One out of every four children in the standardization sample earned V-P discrepancies of one standard deviation (15 points) or greater. Matarazzo and Herman (1984) presented similar base rates for the WAIS-R standardization sample. These statistics suggest that although statistically significant, discrepancies of these magnitudes are relatively common. Kaufman (1994) argues that when a verbal-performance difference is significant, examiners have a basis for making remedial suggestions; when it is both significant and abnormal (i.e., occurring infrequently in the normal population), they also may have a basis for interpreting the test information in the context of other test scores and clinical evidence to reach a diagnostic hypothesis.

Based on analyses of the various standardization samples for the different Wechsler scales, equal percentages of subjects earn V greater (>) than P IQ discrepancies and P > V differences. Further, no pattern of V-P discrepancies were observed based on age, race, or sex. However, V-P IQ differences were related to overall IQ level (full-scale IQ) and background characteristics including parental occupation and socioeconomic status (SES). More V > P discrepancies were found at the higher IQ levels (average and above average) and for those from advantaged backgrounds, including individuals from professional families. Based also on standardization sample data, P > V discrepancies were more frequent in the lower IQ ranges (below average) and for those from lower SES backgrounds, including children of unskilled workers. These findings suggest that an examinee's background experiences help to influence the development of verbal and performance (nonverbal) cognitive skills. Also related to interpretation, the statistics suggest that a P > V discrepancy is particularly noteworthy for an individual from a professional, high SES background and a V > P difference is unusual for an examinee from a low-SES environment.

REFERENCES

Kaufman, A.S. (1976). Verbal-Performance IQ discrepancies on the WISC-R. *Journal of Consulting & Clinical Psychology, 44,* 739–744.

Kaufman, A.S. (1994). *Intelligent testing with the WISC-III.* New York: Wiley.

Matarazzo, S.D., & Herman, D.O. (1984). Clinical uses of the WAIS-R: Base rates of differences between VIQ and PIQ in the WAIS-R standardization sample. In B.B. Wolman (Ed.), *Handbook of intelligence: Theories, measurements, and applications.* New York: Wiley.

Sattler, J.M. (1982). *Assessment of children's intelligence and special abilities* (2nd ed.). Boston: Allyn & Bacon.

***See also* Information Processing; Intelligence Testing; Wechsler Scales**

VERBAL SCALE IQ

The verbal scale IQ is a standard score (with mean of 100 and a standard deviation of 15) derived from a combination of five of the six subtests that comprise the verbal scale of the Wechsler Intelligence Scales. Every subtest on the verbal scale requires that the examinee listen to an auditorily presented verbal stimulus and respond verbally. The abilities measured include vocabulary, general information, verbal reasoning, and auditory-verbal memory. The verbal scale IQ is interpreted as a good indicator of verbal comprehension and expressive language skills. It is also considered to be an indicator of "crystallized" ability or intellectual functioning on tasks calling on previous training, education, and acculturation. Auditory attention is also reflected in the score.

Because of the verbal orientation of most American schools, the verbal scale IQ is by far the best predictor of academic achievement for students. Persons for whom English is a second language, or those from a low socioeconomic background or minority culture often earn a verbal scale IQ that is lower than their actual intellectual ability. Significant differences between verbal scale IQs and performance scale IQs are often used to document the presence of a learning or language disability.

See also **Verbal-Performance IQ Discrepancies; Wechsler Scales**

VERBO-TONAL METHOD (VTM)

The verbo-tonal method (VTM) is primarily an auditory method for the education of deaf children. It was developed by Petar Guberina in Zagreb, Yugoslavia (Guberina, Skaric, & Zaga, 1972) and reformulated by Asp and Guberina (1981). The term verbo-tonal was first coined to characterize an original audiometric technique that measured the perception of speech segments called logatomes (hence the term *verbo*) of variable main frequency spectrum (hence the word *tonal*) from the low, such as *bru-bru,* to the high such as *si-si.*

REFERENCES

Asp, C., & Guberina, P. (1981) *The verbo-tonal method.* New York: World Rehabilitation Fund Monographs.

Guberina, P., Skaric, I., & Zaga, B. (1972). *Case studies in the use of restricted bands of frequencies in auditory rehabilitation of the deaf.* Zagreb, Yugoslavia: Institute of Phonetics, Faculty of Arts.

See also **Deaf; Deaf Education**

VERSABRAILLE

Versabraille, a device for the blind, is a microcomputer with a braille keyboard. In lieu of a screen, there are 20 electronic braille cells, each containing the usual six dots that can be selectively raised to form braille characters. After a period of machine familiarization, reading speed on the 20-cell display is comparable to paper braille reading rates.

One of the main advantages of this system is that it can store much braille information on small floppy disks. Furthermore, it does not necessitate any printing on paper, and makes word processing and the production of tables and charts possible.

See also **Blind; Braille**

VIDEOFLUOROSCOPY

Videofluoroscopy is a method of obtaining fluorographic/radiographic and images of anatomical structure and phys-

iological function. This procedure offers the benefits of low radiation levels, synchrony of visual and sound data for speech, and multiple viewing planes. The procedure requires an interface between common medical fluoroscopy equipment and a video recorder. The patient is observed in multiple positions to produce different views of the area of interest. A barium solution is administered to highlight soft tissue structures. The procedure is usually conducted by a team composed of a speech-language pathologist, radiologist, and an imaging technician. Two common applications of this procedure are to observe the functioning of the velopharyngeal mechanism during speech production and to track the movement of food and liquid during swallowing (Skolnick & Cohn, 1989).

Velopharyngeal inadequacy (VPI) may be suspected because an individual's speech contains inappropriate nasal resonance (i.e. hypernasality, hyponasality, assimilative nasality, cul de sac resonance). Videofluoroscopy is then used to evaluate the structure and function of the velopharyngeal mechanism while the individual produces selected speech samples which stress the valving capability of the mechanism. The information gained during this procedure aids in differential diagnosis, supports decisions regarding the efficacy of surgical or prosthetic and/or behavioral management of VPI, and can indicate the course of therapy.

Another form of the videofluoroscopy procedure, a modified barium swallow (MBS) study, can be used where neuromuscular problems have resulted in problems with swallowing. The MBS study is utilized to identify specific points of dysfunction in the upper gastrointestinal tract during eating and swallowing. The occurrence of foreign material entering the airway (aspiration) is of particular interest during the MBS study since this condition can lead to aspiration pneumonia. During this procedure, the patient is fed different consistencies and amounts of food/liquid containing a barium trace. The information gained includes how the individual is able to organize material in his or her mouth, prepare to swallow it, and how that material moves through the pharynx towards the esophagus and stomach. A treatment regimen, which can include dietary management, postural changes, and muscle stimulation, will result from an MBS study. The procedure is usually conducted by a speech-language pathologist, a radiologist, and an imaging technician, and the results are presented to a team of professionals for recommendations and followup.

REFERENCE

Skolnick, M.L., & Cohn, E.R. (1989). *Studies of speech in patients with cleft palate.* New York: Springer-Verlag.

VINELAND ADAPTIVE BEHAVIOR SCALES (VABS)

The Vineland Adaptive Behavior Scales (VABS; Sparrow, Balla, & Cicchetti, 1984), a revision of Doll's Vineland Social Maturity Scale, is an individually-administered questionnaire given to a person familiar with the individual being tested. The purpose of this scale is to assess personal and social sufficiency of people from birth to adulthood in a variety of settings, including clinical, research, and treatment planning. The Vineland is available in three forms including Survey, Expanded, and Classroom editions. Administration time of the VABS depends on the form used; however, it ranges from 20 to 90 minutes.

Four domains exist within this Scale: Communication, involving the skills needed for receptive, expressive, and written language; Daily Living Skills, including the practical skills that are needed to take care of oneself; Socialization, pertaining to those skills a person needs to get along with others; and Motor Skills, including how the individual uses his/her arms and legs for movement, coordination, and manipulation of objects. The Adaptive Behavior Composite is derived from these domains. The VABS also contains a Maladaptive Behavior domain, which assesses the presence of problematic behaviors interfering with an individual's ability to function effectively. Percentile ranks and age equivalent scores can also be obtained.

The examiner's manual offers information regarding technical aspects such as norming, reliability, and validity. Stratified using sex, race, size of community, region of the country, and level of parental education, a nationwide sample of 3,000 people was used for the Survey and Expanded forms. The Classroom edition was standardized using 2,984 children ranging from 3 years to 12 years, 11 months and was stratified using the same variables (sex, race, size of community, and so on). In terms of reliability, split-half, test-retest, and interrater were reported for the Survey form. Median split-half reliability coefficients range from .70 to .98. Median test-retest reliability coefficients range from .80 to .90. Finally, interrater reliability coefficients range from .62 to .75. With regard to validity, concurrent validity was established using such assessment tools as the Kaufman Assessment Battery for Children (K-ABC), the Peabody Picture Vocabulary Test—Revised (PPVT-R), Hayes-Binet, and Wechsler Intelligence Scale for Children (WISC and WISC-R). These coefficients range from .28 (PPVT-R) to .82 (Hayes-Binet).

REFERENCE

Sparrow, S.S., Balla, D.A., & Cicchetti, D.V. (1984). *Vineland Adaptive Behavior Scales.* Circle Pines, MN: American Guidance Service.

See also **Adaptive Behavior; Mental Retardation; Vineland Social-Emotional Early Childhood Scales**

VINELAND SOCIAL-EMOTIONAL EARLY CHILDHOOD SCALES

The Vineland Social-Emotional Early Childhood Scales (SEEC; Sparrow, Balla, Cicchetti, 1998) is designed to measure the emotional functioning of children from birth to 5 years, 11 months. The SEEC scales were derived from the Socialization domain of the Vineland Adaptive Behavior Scales. There are three scales on the SEEC: Interpersonal Relationships, Play and Leisure Time, and Coping Skills. A Social-Emotional Composite score is also available. The types of behaviors assessed include those such as paying attention, entering social situations, understanding emotional expression, developing relationships, and developing self-regulatory behaviors. The scales are designed to help develop early intervention plans and to chart developmental progress in preschool and kindergarten programs.

Administration of the SEEC Scales is done via a semi-structured interview with a child's caregiver. Items are scored based on how often a child is reported to perform a certain behavior: a score of 2 indicates that the child "usually performs," a score of 1 indicates that a child "sometimes or partially performs," and a score of 0 indicates that a child "never performs." Age-based standard scores (M=100, SD=15), percentile ranks, and descriptive categories are obtained from the scales. The entire SEEC Scales administration time is usually 15 to 25 minutes.

The norms of the SEEC scales were computed from the normative data of the Vineland Adaptive Behavior Scales (Sparrow et al., 1998). The standardization sample was comprised of 1,200 children from birth to age 5 years, 11 months.

REFERENCE

Sparrow, S.S., Bala, D.A., & Cicchetti, D.V. (1998). *Vineland Social-Emotional Early Childhood Scales.* Circle Pines, MN: American Guidance Service.

See also **Adaptive Behavior; Vineland Adaptive Behavior Scales**

VINELAND TRAINING SCHOOL

The Training School at Vineland, New Jersey, has had a long and influential role in the history of mental retardation in the United States. Originally founded in 1888 by Olin S. Garrison as a private school and institution for the "feebleminded," the Training School maintained a reputation for high standards of care and for pioneering experimental and research work. Rather than being a medical setting, it was designed to provide care and research within a psychological-educational context.

In 1901 Edward R. Johnstone became director of the Training School, a position he held until 1943. The genesis of many of the institution's later activities was the establishment in 1902 of the Feebleminded Club by a group of interested professionals and financial backers (Doll, 1972). In 1904 Johnstone started the summer school, one of the first programs designed to provide training for teachers of the mentally retarded. This program subsequently established university affiliations, and many leaders in the field were graduates of the program. In 1913 the Department of Extension was founded to publicize findings in the field. This led in 1914 to the Committee on Provisions for the Feebleminded, which undertook the first organized efforts of national scope to promote better state laws and increased institutional care for the retarded.

In 1906 the first psychological laboratory for the study of mental retardation was established at the Training School and Henry H. Goddard was appointed director of research. It was here that Goddard did his most famous work, translating and adapting the Binet intelligence scales, helping develop World War I army tests, and conducting extensive research on mental retardation. Goddard's (1912) study of the family history of Deborah Kallikak, a resident of the institution, became one of the most widely read research projects of the day; it gave impetus to the eugenics movement.

The laboratory Goddard directed continued to be considered a center for research on mental retardation for decades after his resignation in 1918. As director of research from 1925 to 1949, Edgar A. Doll made several important contributions, the most well known of his efforts being the establishment of criteria of social functioning. In the early 1960s the Training School changed its name to the American Institute for Mental Studies and in 1981 the Elwyn Institute assumed management responsibility for the facility.

REFERENCES

Doll, E.A. (1972). A historical survey of research and management of mental retardation in the United States. In E.P. Trapp & P. Himelstein (Eds.), *Readings on the exceptional child: Research and theory* (2nd ed., pp. 47–97). New York: Appleton-Century-Crofts.

Goddard, H.H. (1912). *The Kallikak family*. New York: Macmillan.

See also **History of Special Education; Mental Retardation**

VISION TRAINING

Optometric visual training (vision therapy) is the art and science of developing visual abilities to achieve optimal vision performance and comfort. Training techniques are used in the prevention of the development of vision problems, the enhancement of visual efficiency, and the remediation and correction of existing visual problems.

Visual training encompasses orthoptics, which is a nonsurgical method of treating disorders of binocular vision. Orthoptic techniques were used as early as the seventh century by a Greek physician, Paulus Aeginaeta, who used a mask with small perforations to correct strabismus. The mask was still in use in 1583 by George Bartisch, the founder of German ophthalmology.

Many of the current visual training techniques developed by Brock, Nichols, Getman, MacDonald, Schrock, Kraskin, and Greenstein emphasize development of smooth eye movement skills (fixation ability). These include pursuit, the ability of the eyes to smoothly and accurately track a moving object or read a line of print, and saccadic movement, the ability to move the eyes from one object or word accurately.

Additional skills emphasized in visual training are eye-focusing skills, eye-aiming skills, eye-teaming skills (binocular fusion), eye-hand coordination, visualization, visual memory, visual imagery, and visual form perception. These techniques have been found to be effective in eliminating or reducing visual symptoms even when the visual acuity is 20/20 at distance and near on the Snellen acuity charts.

Techniques employing lenses, prisms, the steroscope, and rotator are used to align the eyes and maximize optimal visual efficiency. Visual training procedures also are used when there are overt eye turns such as those encountered in constant, intermittent, or alternating strabismus (esotropia or exotropia). Prism therapy is often used in conjunction with lens therapy in the correction of horizontal and vertical deviations of the eye.

Visual training techniques also have been used in the treatment of amblyopia, learning-related problems, and juvenile delinquency; in sports training programs; and with older adults and workers having visual difficulties on the job.

The optometrist often works on a multidisciplinary team that includes the educator, psychologist, social worker, rehabilitation specialist, orientation and mobility instructor, and child development specialist who specializes in the remediation of the child, teen, or adult with a learning or visual disability. These methods are effective only if learning problems are related to vision system problems as opposed to a central processing dysfunction.

See also **Developmental Optometry; Optometrists; Visual Acuity; Visually Impaired**

VISUAL ACUITY

Visual acuity refers to the degree to which the human eye can distinguish fine detail at varying distances. It is dependent on the eye's ability to bend light rays and focus them on the retina (Cartwright, Cartwright, & Ward, 1994). Tests of visual acuity provide measures of the smallest retinal formed images distinguishable by someone's eyes. The results of such tests are influenced by such factors as the area of retina stimulated, the intensity and distribution of illumination, the amount of time of exposure, the effects of movement, and whether the visual acuity test is conducted with each of the eyes separately or both together (Duke-Elder, 1968).

When assessing children's visual acuity, particularly those with low vision, it is important to use visual displays with high-contrast letters and to avoid glare and visual distractions. In instances where a child has difficulty in localizing the symbols to be discriminated, e.g., when testing a child with cognitive difficulties, it may be necessary to occlude parts of the chart (Jose, 1983).

When assessing young children, those who are learning disabled, or those who have multiple handicaps that limit their ability to identify the letters on the Snellen chart, it may be necessary to use alternate methods to assess visual acuity. One of these methods, the Snellen E, requires the student to indicate the position of the *E* symbol (whether left, right, up, or down). Caution must be used in administering this test since a grasp of directionality and some eye-hand coordination is required to succeed; some training of the child may facilitate the application.

Other methods of approximating visual acuity include the use of an optokinetic drum, Sheridan's Stycar miniature toys, the Rosenbaum Dot Test, and the New York Lighthouse Symbol Flashcards. The last test employs three symbols, a house, an umbrella, and an apple, that conform to the sizes of the Snellen letters. The child can identify the symbols on the chart by naming them in any understandable way or by pointing to a symbol placed in front of the table where the child is seated (Faye, Padula, Gurland, Greenberg, & Hood, 1984).

In addition to testing for distance visual acuity, it is important to assess a child's near distance acuity because so many school and work-related tasks are performed at close distances. Near tasks, required in much of school learning, are usually performed from a distance of 14 to 16 inches. A major problem confronting the assessment of near vision is the lack of standardization in the types of chart systems that are currently used for this purpose. The Snellen near-point card uses the metric system to indicate close distance visual acuity. The Jaeger consists of 20 different type sizes in increasing graduations; it indicates the type sizes that the student is able to identify. The Point system uses type sizes in which one point equals 1/72 of an inch. Thus a student who can read newspaper print has a near point Snellen equivalent of 20/40, a Jaeger recording of J4–5, and a Point recording of 8; a student who can only read newspaper headlines has a Snellen rating of 20/100, a Jaeger recording of J17, and a Point recording of 18 (Jose, 1983). A lay person may find it difficult to reconcile such diverse findings. For them to be understood by teachers and parents, the visual examiner should explain their nature and implications. Information respecting the visual acuity, both far and near, of all children, but particularly the handicapped, is an essential guide for children's instruction.

REFERENCES

Cartwright, G.P., Cartwright, C.A., & Ward, M.J. (1994). *Educating exceptional learners 4th ed.* Boston: Wadsworth.

Duke-Elder, S.A. (1968). *Systems of opthalmology.* St. Louis: Mosby.

Faye, E.E., Padula, W.V., Padula, J.B., Gurland, J.E., Greenberg, M.L., & Hood, C.M. (1984). The low vision child. In E.E. Faye (Ed.), *Clinical low vision* (pp. 437–475). Boston: Little, Brown.

Jose, R.T. (1983). *Understanding low vision.* New York: American Foundation for the Blind.

See also **Visually Impaired; Visual-Motor and Visual-Perceptual Problems; Visual Training**

VISUAL EFFICIENCY

Visual efficiency, as defined by Barraga (1970, 1976, 1980, 1983), relates to a variety of visual skills including eye movements, adapting to the physical environment, attending to visual stimuli, and processing information with speed and effectiveness.

In keeping with this definition is Barraga's (1983) definition of the visually handicapped child as a child whose visual impairments limit his or her learning and achievement unless there are adaptations made in the way that learning experiences are presented to the child and effective learning materials are provided in appropriate learning environments.

The basic idea behind the notion of visual efficiency is that children learn to see best by actively using their visual abilities. As applied to the visually handicapped (i.e., low-vision children), this means that they should be provided with such opportunities for learning and should be taught in such ways that they learn effectively to use their residual vision. Low-vision children, without proper opportunities and training, may not be able to extract much useful information from their visual environments simply by being provided with appropriate visual environments, but they can learn to use their visual information with proper opportunities and training so that they eventually can make sense out of what were previously indistinct, uncertain visual impressions. Barraga's program to develop efficiency in visual functioning, intended for the training of low-vision children (1983), is one that emphasizes structured training for visual efficiency.

Associated with the idea of visual efficiency is the concept of functional vision. This concept is concerned with the ways that children use their vision rather than with their physical visual limitations, although the latter improves with specific training as well (Cartwright, Cartwright, & Ward, 1994).

REFERENCES

Barraga, N.C. (1970). *Teacher's guide for development of visual learning abilities and utilization of low vision.* Louisville, KY: American Printing House for the Blind.

Barraga, N.C. (1976). *Visual handicaps and learning: A developmental approach.* Belmont, CA: Wadsworth.

Barraga, N.C. (1980). *Source book on low vision.* Louisville, KY: American Printing House for the Blind.

Barraga, N.C. (1983). *Visual handicaps and learning.* Austin, TX: Exceptional Resources.

Cartwright, G.P., Cartwright, C.A., & Ward, M.J. (1994). *Educating exceptional learners 4th ed.* Boston: Wadsworth.

See also **Functional Vision**

VISUAL IMPAIRMENT

Godfrey Stevens, in his study on *Taxonomy in Special Education for Children with Body Disorders* (1963), used the term impairment to mean any deviation from the normal. Thus impairment was interpreted by many to mean a disorder at the tissue level. Visual impairment, therefore, would mean the medical cause of the handicap. For example, cataract would be the impairment; diminished eyesight would be the disability or handicap. It would, therefore, be correct to refer to individuals with visual impairments.

In recent years, however, the term visual impairment has taken on a broader meaning. In many cases it denotes visual loss other than total blindness, such as the "blind" *and* the visually impaired, thereby separating the functionally blind from those who have some remaining vision. It is common also for experts in the field to refer to an individual with a visual impairment as anyone with a measured loss of any of the visual functions such as acuity, fields, color vision, or binocular vision (Barraga, 1983). Used in this context, visual impairment almost becomes synonymous with visual disability or visual handicap.

REFERENCES

Barraga, N.C. (1983). *Visual handicaps and learning* (rev. ed.). Austin, TX: Exceptional Resources.

Stevens, G.D. (1963). *Taxonomy in special education for children with body disorders.* Pittsburgh: Department of Special Education & Rehabilitation.

See also **Visual Perception and Discrimination; Visual Training**

VISUAL-MOTOR AND VISUAL-PERCEPTUAL PROBLEMS

Many researchers have emphasized the importance of perceptual-motor skills to the development of children. Piaget and Inhelder (1956) stated that early sensory-motor experiences are basic to more advanced mental development, and Sherrington (1948) proposed that the motor system is the first neurological system to develop and the foundation for later perceptual growth. The concern for perceptual-motor development is a recurring theme in many areas of the history of special education. While this perceptual-motor framework can be used to discuss all areas of perception that relate to motor responses—auditory, visual, haptic, olfactory, etc.—the relationships between visual-motor perception and discrimination and learning problems have received the greatest attention.

Although early researchers reported that visual-perceptual and visual-motor problems were evident in individuals with brain damage, a distinction between these two types of disturbances was not always made. While Goldstein and Scheerer (1959) considered visual-motor and visual-perceptual deficits as separate entities, Bartley (1958) viewed perception as being either experiental or motor. Some of the assessment instruments used to measure visual perception are actually visual-motor copying tasks; for example, the Bender Gestalt Test, the coding subtest of the Wechsler scales of intelligence, and the developmental test of visual motor integration, all require motor responses.

The failure to differentiate between visual-perceptual and visual-motor tasks may have far-reaching consequences. Perception is most directly tested when objects or pictures of various shapes, positions, or sizes are matched, or in some other way differentiated; it is then a task of interpreting what is seen. When the difficulty is demonstrated in a task that requires reproducing designs or spatial relationships, it is described as a visual-motor difficulty; i.e., the acts of perceiving and reproducing an object are combined. It may be possible that the child who displays a visual-

motor difficulty also has a perceptual problem, although that inference cannot be made on the basis of a reproduction task. In normal development, visual perception of form precedes the visual motor reproduction of the form (Piaget & Inhelder, 1956), and copying requires skills of an order different from perceiving (Abercrombie, 1964).

Children who have visual-motor problems have difficulty coordinating their movements with what they see. Kirk and Chalfant (1984) reported that breakdowns in three areas may occur when a child displays problems in visual-motor perception and discrimination. First, a child may have problems with laterality, or lateral dominance. This type of problem becomes apparent when both sides of the body perform the same act at the same time when that is not part of the task, or when a child uses only one side of his or her body when two sides are called for. Second, a child may have a directional disability. Directional disabilities manifest themselves when the child fails to develop an awareness of basic directions such as right from left, up from down, and front from back. Very young children will have problems in directionality; this is normal during the early stages of development, but as the child matures, this problem usually corrects itself. If these difficulties continue, the child may have problems in learning. Finally, a child is said to have a breakdown in visual-motor perception when the child's development is limited to the stage where the hand leads the eye. As visual-motor perception is refined, the eye should lead the hand.

Problems in visual-motor perception and discrimination can be seen in both academic and nonacademic tasks. In particular, visual-motor difficulties are most evident when children are involved in pencil and paper activities, play with or manipulate toys and objects, or catch or throw a ball, or when they are involved in any tasks that require good eye-hand coordination. Subsequently, numerous training programs have been devised to improve visual-motor skills with the stated objective of improving academic skills. Critics and advocates of these programs abound.

However, unfortunately, both the critics and advocates of these training programs have based their arguments on highly questionable research reports (Hallahan & Kauffman, 1976). Detailed, recent meta-analyses demonstrate no real benefit to academic learning with perceptual-motor training programs (Kavale & Forness, 1999).

REFERENCES

Abercrombie, M. (1964). *Perceptual and visuo-motor disorders in cerebral palsy.* London: Heinemann.

Bartley, S. (1958). *Principles of perception.* New York: American Orthopsychiatric Association.

Goldstein, K., & Scheerer, M. (1959). Abstract and concrete behavior: An experimental study with special tests. *Psychological Monographs, 83.*

Hallahan, D., & Kauffman, J. (1976). *Introduction to learning disabilities.* Englewood Cliffs, NJ: Prentice-Hall.

Kavale, K., & Forness, S. (1999). The effectiveness of special education. In R. Reynolds & T.B. Gutkin (Eds.), *The Handbook of School Psychology* (3rd ed.). New York: Wiley.

Kirk, S., & Chalfant, J. (1984). *Academic and developmental learning disabilities.* Denver: Love.

Piaget, J., & Inhelder, B. (1956). *The child's concept of space.* London: Routledge & Kegan Paul.

Sherrington, C. (1948). *The integrative action of the nervous system.* New Haven, CT: Yale University Press.

See also **Perception; Perceptual Motor Difficulties; Perceptual Remediation**

VISUAL PERCEPTION AND DISCRIMINATION

Visual perception is a difficult concept to define and measure because it involves complex interactions between the individual and the environment. Basically, visual perception and discrimination is the ability to interpret what is seen. Frostig and Horne (1973) describe it as the ability to recognize stimuli and to differentiate among them.

Visual-perceptual problems are concerned with disabilities that occur despite the fact that a child has physiologically healthy eyes. A child may have 20/20 visual acuity and adequate eye muscle control, and still have visual perceptual problems. These disabilities may include problems in form perception: discriminating the shapes of letters, numbers, pictures, or objects; position in space: discriminating the spatial orientation—left/right, top/bottom, etc.—of letters or words; visual closure: discriminating pictures or words with parts missing; and figure-ground discrimination: the ability to perceive a figure as distinct from the background (Hallahan, Kauffman, & Lloyd, 1985). A child who has problems with visual perception and discrimination may have difficulty in school because most academic activities require good visual-perceptual skills. In particular, the areas of math and reading will be difficult for the child who cannot distinguish between a multiplication and an addition sign, or who has difficulty discriminating pictures, letters, numbers, or words. During the early stages of a child's development, these problems are normal, but as a child matures, parents and teachers should become concerned if these difficulties persist.

REFERENCES

Frostig, M., & Horne, D. (1973). *Frostig program for the development of visual perception.* Chicago: Follett.

Hallahan, D., Kauffman, J., & Lloyd, J. (1985). *Introduction to learning disabilities* (2nd ed.). Englewood Cliffs, NJ: Prentice-Hall.

See also **Bender Gestalt; Developmental Test of Visual Perception-2; Illinois Test of Psycholinguistic Abilities; Visual-Motor Perception and Discrimination**

VISUAL TRAINING

See VISION TRAINING.

VISUOMOTOR COMPLEX

Visuomotor complex is a term used by Getman (1965) to describe his model of the development of the visuomotor system and its relationship to the acquisition of learning skills. This model reflects Getman's training as an optometrist by emphasizing the visual aspects of perception. It illustrates the developmental sequences that a child progresses through while acquiring visual-perceptual and motor skills, and emphasizes that each successive stage is dependent on earlier stages of development.

The six systems of learning levels in this model are (from the lowest to the highest) the innate response system, the general motor system, the special motor system, the ocular motor system, the speech-motor system, and the visualization system. These systems all contribute to vision or the perceptual event that results in cognition when many perceptions are integrated (Lerner, 1971).

REFERENCES

Getman, G. (1965). The visuomotor complex in the acquisition of learning skills. In J. Hellmuth (Ed.), *Learning disorders* (Vol. 1, pp. 49–76). Seattle, WA: Special Child.

Lerner, J. (1971). *Children with learning disabilities.* Boston: Houghton Mifflin.

See also **Visual Perception and Discrimination; Visual Training**

VOCABULARY DEVELOPMENT

The knowledge of vocabulary, that is, the ability to recognize words and understand their meanings, is recognized as possibly the most important factor in being able to use and understand spoken and written language. Vocabulary knowledge is very closely associated with the ability to comprehend what is heard or read, and may be related to general intelligence and reasoning ability.

The essence of reading and writing is communication, and the crucial variable in communication seems to be vocabulary knowledge. What distinguishes the fluent, successful reader from the poor reader seems to be a knowledge of words and what they mean. A successful and appropriate program of vocabulary development in the school, coupled with the child's preschool experiential background, may provide that key ingredient to becoming a successful language user. Johnson and Pearson (1984) give a complete and detailed account of how to provide an appropriate program of vocabulary development in school.

REFERENCE

Johnson, D.D., & Pearson, P.D. (1984). *Teaching reading vocabulary* (2nd ed.). New York: Holt, Rinehart, & Winston.

See also **Intelligence; Reading; Reading Remediation**

VOCATIONAL EDUCATION

The goal of vocational education programs is to prepare students to enter the world of work. Astuto (1982) described vocational programs as focusing on the development of basic academic skills, good work habits, personally meaningful work values, self-understanding and identification of preferences, skills and aptitudes, occupational opportunities, the ability to plan and make career decisions, and the locating and securing of employment.

The basic program components for vocational education are recognized as remedial basic skills, specific job training, personal and social adjustment skills, career information, modified content in subject areas, and on-the-job training. Further, Ondell and Hardin (1981) delineated four types of occupational activities that would be part of a vocational program: paid work experience during the day, paid work experience after school hours, unpaid work observation, and in-school vocational laboratory.

The Vocational Education Act, as amended in 1976 (PL 94-482, Title II), designated vocational education for handicapped persons as a national priority. This mandated that 10% of federal monies be used, in part, to pay up to 50% of the cost of additional services handicapped students need to succeed in vocational education.

Public Law 94-142 unequivocally established that every handicapped youth be given the opportunity to participate in free and appropriate vocational education programs. According to Greenan (1982), the law states that

Vocational education means organized education programs which are directly related to the preparation of individuals for paid or unpaid employment, or for additional preparation for a career requiring other than a baccalaureate or advanced degree. (121a.14(b)(3))

And in addition

vocational education is "included as special education" if it consists of specially designed instruction, at no cost to the parents, to meet the unique needs of a handicapped child. [121.14(a)(3)]

The Carl D. Perkins Vocational Education Act, PL 98-524, replaced the Vocational Education Act of 1963. The new act ordered federal involvement in vocational education around two broad themes. First, equal access to vocational education must be provided to handicapped persons. Second, the quality of vocational education must be improved. The act specifies that 10% of its funds must be allocated for vocational education services and activities designed to meet the special needs of, and enhance the participation of, handicapped individuals. This is accomplished through allotments to local school districts on a formula basis. Each local school district has to comply with five prescriptive requirements. The first of these is to provide information to handicapped students and parents concerning opportunities available in vocational education at least 1 year before the student enters the grade in which vocational education programs are first generally available, but in no event later than the beginning of ninth grade. Each handicapped student who enrolls in a vocational education program shall receive an assessment of his or her interests, abilities, and special needs; special services, including adaptation of curriculum; guidance, counseling, and career development activities conducted by professionally trained counselors; and counseling services designed to facilitate the transition from school to postsecondary environments.

Vocational education for students with disabilities generally entails at least two different approaches, depending on the severity of the disability. A major thrust at the state level has been to provide the necessary supportive services to handicapped persons enrolled in regular vocational education programs.

REFERENCE

Astuto, T.A. (1982). *Vocational education programs and services for high school handicapped students.* Bloomington: Council of Administrators of Special Education, Indiana University.

Greenan, J.P. (1982). State planning for vocational/special education personnel development. *Teacher Education & Special Education,* 5(4), 69–76.

See also **Rehabilitation; Vocational Evaluation; Vocational Training of the Handicapped**

VOCATIONAL EDUCATION ACT OF 1963

Public Law 88-210, the Vocational Education Act of 1963, provided priority allotments of state funds for vocational education programs for the handicapped. Under 20 USCS, Section 2310, for each fiscal year, at least 10% of each state's allotments under Section 103 (20 USCS Section 2303) from appropriations made under Section 102(a) (20 USCS, Section 2303(a)) shall be used to pay up to 50% of the cost of programs, services, and activities under Subpart 2 (20 USCS, Section 2330 et seq.) and of program improvement and support services under Subpart 3 (20 USCS, Section 2350 et seq.) for handicapped persons.

See also **Rehabilitation; Vocational Training of the Handicapped**

VOCATIONAL EVALUATION

Vocational evaluation is a term that encompasses the processes undertaken in determining eligibility and appropriate program plans for students entering vocational education. Specific components and processes used in vocational evaluation include assessment of skills, aptitude, interests, work behaviors, social skills, and physical capabilities (Leconte, 1985). The area of vocational assessment is affected by the Carl Perkins Vocational Education Act of 1984, which mandates that schools provide each handicapped or disadvantaged student who enrolls in a vocational education program an assessment of the individual's interests, abilities, and special needs with respect to the successful completion of the vocational education program (Cobb & Larkin, 1985).

Levinson and Capps (1985) discussed vocational assessment as a process that yields critical information with which vocational programming decisions may be made. They include the identification of appropriate goals and instructional methods in the process.

Peterson (1985) suggested six guidelines for effective vocational assessment: (1) use trained personnel; (2) develop and use locally developed work samples; (3) obtain access to a vocational evaluation center; (4) plan to develop and expand vocational assessment in phases with a team; (5) ascertain that vocational assessment is instructionally relevant and useful; and (6) ensure that the vocational assessment is used for vocational guidance and the identification of appropriate career and vocational service.

Peterson (1985) stated that vocational assessment can be "a powerful tool in the education of special students" since it can provide a link between special education or Chapter 1 services and vocational education. The challenge to fully operationalize these services with respect to students with disabilities remains.

REFERENCES

Cobb, R.B., & Larkin, D. (1985). Assessment and placement of handicapped pupils into secondary vocational education programs. *Focus on Exceptional Children, 17*(7), 1–14.

Leconte, P. (1985, December). *Vocational assessment of the special needs learner: A vocational education perspective.* Paper presented at the meeting of the American Vocational Association Convention, Atlanta, GA.

Levinson, E.M., & Capps, C.F. (1985). Vocational assessment and special education triennial reevaluations at the secondary school level. *Psychology in the Schools, 22,* 283–292.

Peterson, M. (1985, December). *Vocational assessment of special students: A comprehensive developmental approach.* Paper presented at the meeting of the American Vocational Association Convention, Atlanta, GA.

See also **Vocational Rehabilitation; Vocational Rehabilitation Counseling; Vocational Training of the Handicapped**

VOCATIONAL REHABILITATION ACT OF 1973

Section 504 of what is commonly called the Rehabilitation Act is frequently cited as an important precursor to the passage of PL 94-142 two years later (Reschly & Bersoff, 1999). Section 504, among other things, protects the rights of handicapped children and precludes discrimination in employment and education. The stipulations of the Rehabilitation Act apply to the programs receiving federal financial assistance.

REFERENCE
Reschly, D., & Bersoff, D.N. (1999). Law and school psychology. In C.R. Reynolds & T.B. Gutkin (Eds.), *The handbook of school psychology* (3rd ed.). New York: Wiley.

See also **Education for All Handicapped Students Act of 1975; Individuals with Disabilities Education Act (IDEA); Larry P.**

VOCATIONAL REHABILITATION COUNSELING

According to the 1984–1985 edition of the *Occupational Outlook Handbook,* "Rehabilitation counselors assist physically, mentally, emotionally, or socially handicapped individuals to become self-sufficient and productive citizens." While this general definition is correct, the actual activities engaged in by rehabilitation counselors and the resources available to them vary considerably depending on their work setting.

The profession of rehabilitation counseling emerged with the passage of PL 236 (Smith-Fess Act) in 1920, which established the civilian vocational rehabilitation program in the United States. However, it was not until the passage of PL 565 in 1954 that federal funds were available to encourage formal academic training for rehabilitation personnel.

The most prominent professional organizations for rehabilitation counselors are the National Rehabilitation Association, the National Rehabilitation Counseling Association, and the American Rehabilitation Counseling Association. Within the past decade, certification procedures for rehabilitation counselors have been established through the efforts of various professional organizations. Certification is based on a combination of education, experience, and the successful completion of a national examination. While certification procedures do guarantee minimum standards of competency, they may be criticized for restricting entrance into the profession by those who are otherwise qualified but lack formal credentials. Many rehabilitation employers expect applicants to be certified, but this is by no means universal and the eventual status of certification is unclear at present.

The high social validity of rehabilitation counseling is indicated by the continuing bipartisan congressional support that rehabilitation legislation has enjoyed for over 65 years. Studies estimate that once disabled persons return to work they earn, and pay taxes on, between 8 and 33 times the amount of money that was spent on their rehabilitation (Bitter, 1979). Additional economic benefits accrue to society from the reductions in welfare, disability, and medical assistance payments after the disabled person enters the work force. In human terms, state DVR agencies rehabilitate between 300,000 and 400,000 handicapped persons per year. The dignity and self-esteem these individuals feel when they become contributing members of society cannot be measured in dollars.

REFERENCE

Bitter, J.A. (1979). *Introduction to rehabilitation.* St. Louis: Mosby.

See also Vocational Evaluation; Vocational Training of the Handicapped

VOCATIONAL TRAINING OF HANDICAPPED

See VOCATIONAL EDUCATION.

VOCATIONAL VILLAGE

A vocational village is a cloistered community in which handicapped and nonhandicapped persons live and work. It is often referred to as a sheltered village. There is a strong work ethic in the community. The setting is not usually designed for transition but rather as a permanent living/working arrangement for the handicapped. There is usually a deep religious undertone in such villages and a majority of the time they are church sponsored. The nonhandicapped residents of the village are often volunteer workers who have made a long-term commitment to the village. There are also some nonhandicapped workers who are students working in practium arrangements or in work-study activities. Baker, Seltzer, and Seltzer (1977) explain that

common to all sheltered villages is the segregation of the retarded person from the outside community and the implicit view that the retarded adult is better off in an environment that shelters him/her from many of the potential failures and frustrations of life in the outside community (p. 109).

It is a delivery model that espouses the principle of separate but equal.

REFERENCE

Baker, B.L., Seltzer, G.B., & Seltzer, M.M. (1977). *As close as possible: Community residences for retarded adults.* Boston: Little, Brown.

See also Community Placement; Community Residential Programs; Sheltered Workshops

VOICE DISORDERS (DYSPHONIA)

Aronson (1985) says that, "A voice disorder exists when quality, pitch, loudness, or flexibility differs from the voices of others of similar age, sex and cultural group." What constitutes an abnormal voice is a relative judgment which is made by the speaker, the listener, and professionals who may be consulted. Causes of voice disorders are usually classified as either organic (physical) or functional (behavioral). The parameters by which a voice can be judged as abnormal are considered in context. For example, a voice that is so hoarse that it distracts the listener or interferes with intelligibility can be identified as disordered and in need of treatment. The pitch of a female voice considered to be appropriate during her school-aged years may be too high for effective function as she enters the business world. The person who cannot produce a voice loud enough to be heard in a typically noisy classroom or one whose voice is so inflexible that the speaker seems emotionless may also be identified as abnormal. In some cases, such abnormal voice symptoms indicate the presence of an underlying illness which is in need of medical diagnosis and treatment. If a hoarse voice quality exists for an extended period of time (i.e. longer than two weeks), it could indicate the presence of a mass lesion in the larynx (voice box) which could be benign or malignant. An inability to alter pitch or loudness to convey meaning could signal a neuromuscular problem associated with incipient neurological disease. An inappropriately high pitch, used habitually, might point to endocrine dysfunction or to psychosocial issues which require attention (Colton & Casper, 1990). Evaluation and treatment of voice disorders requires the combined efforts of the speech-language pathologist and an otolaryngologist (ENT).

REFERENCES

Aronson, A. (1985). *Clinical voice disorders.* New York: Thieme.

Colton, R.H., & Casper, J.K. (1990). *Understanding voice problems.* Baltimore: Williams & Wilkins.

See also Speech

VOLTA REVIEW, THE

The Volta Review was founded in 1898. It is published four times a year, with a monograph issue in September. The publication is a product of the Alexander Graham Bell Association for the Deaf, a nonprofit organization founded by Alexander Graham Bell in 1890 that serves as an information center for people with hearing impairment. Bell believed that people with hearing losses could be taught to speak and, through lip reading, could learn to understand others.

Only articles devoted to the education, rehabilitation, and communicative development of individuals with hearing impairment are published by *The Volta Review.* The target audience includes teachers of the hearing impaired; professionals in the fields of education, speech, audiology, language, otology, and psychology; parents of children with hearing impairments; and adults with hearing impairments. The articles are peer-reviewed for possible publication and vary in length, and the journal includes advertisements as well as illustrations. Topics include issues related to hearing impairment such as language development, parental concerns, medical/technical and psychosocial issues, teaching, and computers.

See also Deaf; Deaf Education

VOLUNTARY AGENCIES

Voluntary agencies are those agencies that use volunteers to deliver services or to serve on decision-making boards. Volunteers are those members of the community who give their time on a nonpay basis to agencies that serve particular groups in an area. Approximately 84 million Americans serve as volunteers in such agencies each year (Shtulman, 1985). Women have provided a large portion of volunteer service but the entry of large numbers of women into the work force has limited their availability for volunteer service. However, an increasingly active senior citizen population is providing a pool of dependable, dedicated volunteers. Another developing source is through the work place. Some firms make it possible for their employees to have released time for community service; these firms say that this "loaned executive" program contributes to a better work force through the opportunity for workers to apply or develop skills, a lower rate of absenteeism, and increased productivity (United Way, 1985).

Volunteers on agency governing boards make decisions on the purchase of property and capital equipment, organizational policy, specific human services that will be available in the community, allocation of funds to other agencies (United Way, foundations, etc.) or within their own agency, and fund-raising.

REFERENCES

Shtulman, J. (1985). *A question-and-answer session on voluntarism.* Holyoke, MA: Transcript-Telegram.

United Way. (1985). *Volunteer notes.* Alexandria, VA: United Way of America.

See also **Advocacy for Handicapped Children; Library Services for the Handicapped**

VON RECKLINGHAUSEN, FRIEDRICH (1833–1910)

Friedrich von Recklinghausen, a German pathologist, was a major contributor to the development of pathological anatomy as a branch of medicine. He is best known for his description, in 1863, of neurofibromatosis, or von Recklinghausen's disease, characterized by multiple small tumors affecting the subcutaneous nerves. The disease is hereditary and is associated with mental retardation.

REFERENCE

von Recklinghausen, F. (1962). Multiple fibromas of the skin and multiple neuromas. In E.R. Long (Trans.), *Selected readings in pathology* (2nd ed.). Springfield, IL: Thomas.

See also **Neurofibramatosis; Mental Retardation**

VYGOTSKY, LEV S. (1896–1934)

Lev S. Vygotsky was a Soviet psychologist and semiotician. His work had a tremendous impact on the development of psychology in the Soviet Union and is currently attracting a great deal of interest outside the Soviet Union as well (Wertsch, 1985a, 1985b).

In the West, Vygotsky is known primarily for his work on the relationship between the development of thinking and speech in ontogenesis (Vygotsky, 1962, 1978, in press a). In Vygotsky's view, the more complex forms of human thinking, memory, and attention depend on the individual's mastery of historically and culturally developed means of organizing and mediating mental activity. Vygotsky argued that words and speech are first used in social interaction to organize and mediate the mental activity of several individuals working cooperatively on a task, and that these same linguistic means are later appropriated by the individual and internalized to be used in organizing and mediating his or her mental activity when working alone on similar tasks. In this sense, Vygotsky felt that certain kinds of social interaction between children and adults (or more competent peers) can create a "zone of proximal development" that raises the level of the child's cognitive functioning in the context of social interaction and helps move the child toward the next or proximal stage of independent functioning.

For Vygotsky, however, this work was only part of a much broader program of theory and research that was concerned with the relationships between historically developed modes of social behavior and the psychological development of the individual in all its aspects (Minick, 1987). In the decade following his death, the efforts of his colleagues and students to develop this broader theoretical framework led to the emergence of what is known as the theory of activity, a theoretical and research paradigm that illuminates the work of many contemporary Soviet psychologists.

Vygotsky had a lifelong interest in developing theory, research, and practical intervention techniques relevant to abnormal psychological functioning and development in both children and adults. He wrote extensively on these topics (Vygotsky, 1987) and founded several institutes that continue to play an important role in Soviet work in this area. Through this work and that of colleagues and students such as A.R. Luria (Luria, 1979), Vygotsky played a central role in the development of Soviet work in this domain.

REFERENCES

Luria, A.R. (1979). *The making of mind: A personal account of Soviet psychology.* Cambridge, MA: Harvard University Press.

Minick, N. (in press). The development of Vygotsky's thought. *Introduction to L.S. Vygotsky, Collected works: Problems of general psychology* (Vol. 2) (N. Minick, Trans.). New York: Plenum.

Vygotsky, L.S. (1962). *Thought and language* (E. Hanfmann & G. Vakar, Eds. and Trans.). Cambridge, MA: MIT Press. (Original work published 1934).

Vygotsky, L.S. (1978). *Mind in society* (M. Cole, V. John-Steiner, S. Scribner, & E. Souberman, Eds.). Cambridge, MA: Harvard University Press.

Vygotsky, L.S. (1987). Thinking and speech. In V.V. Davydov (Ed.), *L.S. Vygotsky, Collected works: General Psychology* (Vol. 2) (N. Minick, Trans.). New York: Plenum. (Original work published 1934).

Vygotsky, L.S. (1978). In A.V. Zaporozhets (Ed.), *L.S. Vygotsky, Collected works: The foundations of defectology* (Vol. 5) (J. Knox, Trans.). New York: Plenum.

Wertsch, J.V. (1985a). *Vygotsky and the social formation of mind.* Cambridge, MA: Harvard University Press.

Wertsch, J.V. (Ed.). (1985b). *Culture, communication, and cognition: Vygotskian perspectives.* New York: Cambridge University Press.

***See also* Theory of Activity; Zone of Proximal Development**

W

WAIS-III

See WECHSLER ADULT INTELLIGENCE SCALE–THIRD EDITION.

WALKER PROBLEM BEHAVIOR IDENTIFICATION CHECKLIST (WBPIC)

The Walker Problem Behavior Identification Checklist (WBPIC) was published in 1983 (Walker, 1983). This edition consists of a teacher problem behavior rating scale for preschool through grade 6. The 50-item checklist contains six scales: acting-out, withdrawal, distractibility, disturbed peer relations, immaturity, and total. Separate forms are provided for boys and girls. The checklist is to be completed by a teacher who has known the child for at least a 2-month period. Raw scores on each scale are converted to T-scores for interpretation. The latest version was standardized on a sample of 1855 children from sites in Oregon and Washington. Norms are presented separately for males and females. The demographic characteristics of the norm group (e.g., socioeconomic status) are not specified in the manual.

REFERENCE

Walker, H.M. (1983). *Walker Problem Behavior Identification Checklist.* Los Angeles: Western Psychological Services.

***See also* Assessment; Behavioral Assessment**

WALLIN, JOHN EDWARD (J.E.) WALLACE (1876–1969)

J.E. Wallace Wallin, a pioneer in the fields of special education and clinical psychology, was born in Page County, Iowa on January 21, 1876 to Henry and Emma M. (Johnson) Wallin, originally from Sweden. Wallace was the third of nine children. He attended the public schools of Stanton, Iowa. On June 21, 1913, at the age of 37, he married his wife, Frances Geraldine Tinsley. The couple had two daughters, Geraldine Tinsley Wallin Sickler (1919), and Virginia Stan-

ton Wallin Obrinski (1915), who also became a psychologist.

Wallin obtained his BA degree in 1897 from Augustana College in Rock Island, Illinois. He attended Yale and studied under Dr. Edward W. Scripture and George Trumbull Ladd. Scripture had done his own thesis under "the great German psychologist," Wilhelm Wundt. While at Yale, Wallin completed an MA degree in 1899, and a PhD in 1901. Wallin also worked as an assistant to Dr. G. Stanley Hall at Clark University in Worcester, Massachusetts. Wallin served as head of the psychology department and vice-president of the East Stroudsburg State Teachers College in Pennsylvania. While at Stroudsburg, he taught courses in physiological, child, genetic, educational, and abnormal psychology and mental retardation. Wallin held numerous positions in the following years. He was the head of the department of psychology and education at the Normal Training School at Cleveland, Ohio, from 1909 to 1910, where he developed the field of special education, psychoclinical examinations, and one of the first group intelligence tests. By 1912, he established a psychoeducational clinic at the University of Pittsburgh, which was one of the first such clinics in the country. Wallin went on to become the director of numerous other clinics and special schools and affiliated with more than 25 colleges and universities (Wallin, 1958).

Outspoken, argumentative, critical, and at times cantankerous, Wallin was a crusader and a pioneer for disabled children. He was a leading advocate for the use of clinical psychology in education, especially as it relates to identification, diagnosis, and prescription for handicapped children (P.I., 1979), and was a strong advocate for the proper training of clinicians. He worked to establish the principle that all children would benefit from an education, regardless of degree of handicap, and helped to establish special classes in Western Pennsylvania, Ohio, Missouri, and Delaware. Wallin also made extensive contributions to the area of special education and the field of psychology by publishing over 30 books and 350 articles throughout his career, including psychological textbooks. He was a political activist for policies, regulations, and change to ensure appropriate education for children with special needs. He was a member of numerous professional organizations and served on many committees such as the secretary of the committee on special education for the White House Conference on Child Health and Protection from 1929–1930. He continued to write into his 90s. Wallin died on August 5, 1969.

REFERENCES

P.I. (1979). John Edward Wallace Wallin (1876–1969). A biographical sketch. *Journal of Special Education, 13,* 4–5.

Wallin, J.E.W. (1955). *The odyssey of a psychologist: Pioneering experiences in special education, clinical psychology, and mental hygiene with a comprehensive bibliography of the author's publications.* Wilmington, DE: Author.

WATSON, JOHN B. (1878–1958)

John B. Watson developed and publicized the basic concepts of behaviorism, which in the 1920s became one of the major schools of psychological thought. Watson obtained his PhD at the University of Chicago and continued there as an instructor until 1908, when he accepted a professorship at Johns Hopkins University. Watson's behaviorism explained human behavior in terms of physiological responses to environmental stimuli and psychology as the study of the relationship between the two. Watson sought to make psychology "a purely objective experimental branch of natural science," with conditioning as one of its chief methods.

Watson's zealous environmentalism led him into some extreme positions, such as his assertion that he could train any healthy infant, regardless of its heredity, to become any type of person he might designate: "doctor, lawyer, artist, merchant-chief, and . . . even beggar-man and thief." Hyperbole aside, Watson's behaviorism was a dominant force in American psychology for decades and underlies many of today's behaviorally oriented instructional approaches. Watson eventually left the academic world, completing his career as an executive in the field of advertising.

John B. Watson

REFERENCES

Skinner, B.F. (1959). John Broadus Watson, behaviorist. *Science, 129,* 197–198.

Watson, J.B. (1919). *Psychology from the standpoint of a behaviorist.* Philadelphia: Lippincott.

See also Behavior Modification; Conditioning

WECHSLER, DAVID (1896–1981)

Known primarily as the author of intelligence scales that played, and continue to play, a critical role in the lives of millions of individuals throughout the world, David Wechsler had a humanistic philosophy about testing as a part of assessment. His professional writing includes more than 60 articles and books that emphasize the importance of motivation, personality, drive, cultural opportunity, and other variables in determining an individual's functional level.

Born in Rumania, Wechsler moved with his family of nine to New York City at age 6. At 20 he completed a BA degree at City College (1916) and an MA the following year at Columbia University under Robert S. Woodworth. The next few years were spent with the armed forces, where Wechsler helped evaluate thousands of recruits, many of whom could not read English and who had little formal schooling. Near the end of his Army tour he studied with Charles Spearman and Karl Pearson in London and then, on a fellowship, with Henri Pieron and Louis Lapique in Paris. These studies provided the foundation for his continuous enthusiasm for the "nonintellective" components of intelligence.

While completing his PhD at Columbia (1925), Wechsler worked as a psychologist in New York City's newly created Bureau of Child Study. After serving as secretary for the Psychological Corporation (1925–1927) and in private clinical practice (1927–1932), Wechsler became chief psychologist at New York's Bellevue Hospital, a post he held for 35 years. In that position he developed the tests that carried both his and the hospital's name in the early editions: the Wechsler-Bellevue Intelligence Scale I (1939) and Scale II (1942), the Wechsler Intelligence Scale for Children (1949), the Wechsler Adult Intelligence Scale (1955), and the Wechsler Preschool and Primary Scale of Intelligence (1967). He continued to help with the revision of his scales in retirement. The utility of the scales has warranted periodic updating by the publisher.

Wechsler believed his most important work to be his article "The Range of Human Capacities" (1930), the seminal work for his book by the same name that was published in 1935 and revised in 1971. A more popular contribution is the concept of a deviation quotient used for reporting adult intelligence test scores in place of mental age and ratio IQ used with the Binet tests for children and youths. Today nearly all cognitive ability tests use standard scores patterned after the deviation IQ.

The many honors Wechsler received from professional groups and universities around the world include the Distinguished Professional Contribution Award from the

American Psychological Association (APA) (1973), similar awards from APA's Division of Clinical Psychology (1960) and Division of School Psychology (1973), and an honorary doctorate from the Hebrew University in Jerusalem.

See also Assessment; Intelligence Testing

WECHSLER ADULT INTELLIGENCE SCALE–THIRD EDITION

The Wechsler Adult Intelligence Scale–Third Edition (WAIS-III) is the newest member of the Wechsler family of tests. It is an instrument for assessing the cognitive abilities of individuals ages 16 to 89. The WAIS-III has fourteen subtests that yield three IQ scores (Verbal, Performance, and Full Scale) and four factor indexes (Verbal Comprehension, Perceptual Organization, Working Memory and Processing Speed). Each of the IQs and factor indexes are standard scores with a mean of 100 and a standard deviation of 15. The subtests on the WAIS-III provide scaled scores with a mean of 10 and a standard deviation of 3.

The Verbal IQ is comprised of six verbal subtests (Vocabulary, Similarities, Arithmetic, Digit Span, Information, and Comprehension). In addition to these Verbal subtests, a new supplementary subtest (Letter-Number Sequencing) has been added which may substitute for Digit Span if necessary. The Performance IQ is comprised of five non-verbal subtests (Picture Completion, Picture Arrangement, Block Design, Matrix Reasoning, and Digit Symbol-Coding). In addition, there are two supplementary subtests on the Performance scale: Symbol Search (may be used to replace Digit Symbol-Coding) and Object Assembly (which is an optional subtest that may be used to replace any Performance subtest for individuals younger than 75) (Kaufman & Lichtenberger, 1999; 1998). The Digit Symbol-Coding subtest also has new optional procedures, called Digit Symbol-Incidental Learning and Digit Symbol-Copy, that may be used to help the examiner rule out the cause of poor performance.

The WAIS-III was standardized on 2,450 subjects stratified according to age, gender, race/ethnicity, geographic region, and educational level. This sample was selected to match basic demographic characteristics provided in the 1995 US Census data. An additional 200 African American and Hispanic individuals were administered the WAIS-III without discontinue rules during the process of normative data collection, in order to perform item bias analyses (The Psychological Corporation, 1997).

The reliability data for the WAIS-III are strong. The average split-half reliability coefficients, across the different age groups, were 0.97 for the Verbal IQ, 0.94 for the Performance IQ, and 0.98 for the Full Scale IQ. Numerous factor analytic studies were reported in the WAIS-III manual (The Psychological Corporation, 1997). The underlying four-factor structure of the WAIS-III was validated. However, one important exception to this finding should be noted: in the 75 to 89 age range, more subtests loaded on the Processing Speed factor the Perceptual Organization factor

(Kaufman & Lichtenberger, 1999). Only one Performance subtest, Matrix Reasoning, had a factor loading above 0.40 on the Perceptual Organization factor for the oldest age group.

The relationship between the WAIS-R (Wechsler, 1981) and the WAIS-III was examined to see how well the old and new versions of the test related. Subjects tended to perform about 2.9 points lower on the WAIS-III Full Scale IQ than on the WAIS-R Full Scale IQ. This would be predicted based on work done by Flynn (1984) that has shown similar patterns from the WAIS to WAIS-R. The overall correlations between the WAIS-III and WAIS-R were high: 0.94 for the Verbal IQ, 0.86 for the Performance IQ, and 0.93 for the Full Scale IQ (Kaufman & Lichtenberger, 1998).

Many improvements were made in this latest edition of the WAIS. Administration is not difficult with the clear and easy to read WAIS-III manual, in addition to the record form with ample space and visual icons (Kaufman & Lichtenberger, 1999). The floor and ceiling of the WAIS-III were extended from its earlier version, providing better assessment of high and low functioning individuals. The WAIS-R's method of using a reference group (ages 20–34) to determine everyone's scaled scores was not retained in the development of the WAIS-III, which is also an improvement. The four-factor structure of the WAIS-III is a strength of the instrument that may aid in interpretation. The addition of Matrix Reasoning and Letter-Number Sequencing to the overall battery have made assessment of abilities such as fluid reasoning and working memory possible (Kaufman & Lichtenberger, 1999). Although there are still a few areas that could be improved, Kaufman and Lichtenberger (1999) note that the WAIS-III's strengths seem to outweigh its weaknesses. The WAIS-R has proven itself as a leader in the field of assessment, and the WAIS-III is likely to follow suit.

REFERENCES

Flynn, J.R. (1984). The mean IQ of Americans: Massive gains 1932 to 1978. *Psychological Bulletin, 95,* 29–51.

Kaufman, A.S., & Lichtenberger, E.O. (1999). *Essentials of WAIS-III Assessment.* New York: Wiley.

Kaufman, A.S., & Lichtenberger, E.O. (1998). Intellectual Assessment. In A.S. Bellack & M. Hersen (Series Eds.), & C.R. Reynolds (Vol. Ed.), *Comprehensive clinical psychology: Volume 4. Assessment* (pp. 203–238). Oxford, England: Elsevier Science Ltd.

The Psychological Corporation. (1997). *Technical manual for the Wechsler Adult Intelligence Scale–Third Edition.* San Antonio, TX: The Psychological Corporation.

Wechsler, D. (1997). *Administration and scoring manual for the Wechsler Adult Intelligence Scale–Third Edition.* San Antonio, TX: The Psychological Corporation.

Wechsler, D. (1981). *Administration and scoring manual for the Wechsler Adult Intelligence Scale–Revised.* San Antonio, TX: The Psychological Corporation.

See also Intelligence Tests; Stanford-Binet Intelligence Scale; WISC/WISC-III; WPPSI-R

WECHSLER INTELLIGENCE SCALE FOR CHILDREN–THIRD EDITION

The Wechsler Intelligence Scale for Children–Third Edition (WISC-III) is an instrument for assessing the cognitive abilities of children and adolescents ages 6 to 16. The WISC-III, like the WISC-R, is easily the most popular and widely researched test of children's intelligence. The WISC-III has thirteen subtests that yield three IQ scores (Verbal, Performance, and Full Scale) and four factor indexes (Verbal Comprehension, Perceptual Organization, Freedom from Distractibility and Processing Speed). Each of the IQs and factor indexes are standard scores with a mean of 100 and a standard deviation of 15. The subtests on the WISC-III provide scaled scores with a mean of 10 and a standard deviation of 3.

The five subtests that comprise the Verbal IQ include Vocabulary, Similarities, Arithmetic, Information, and Comprehension. In addition to these Verbal subtests, a supplementary Verbal subtest (Digit Span) is also administered and may substitute for other Verbal subtests if necessary. The five non-verbal subtests that comprise the Performance IQ include Picture Completion, Picture Arrangement, Block Design, Object Assembly, and Coding. In addition, there are two supplementary subtests on the Performance scale: Symbol Search (may be used to replace Coding) and Mazes (which is an optional subtest that may be used to replace any Performance subtest; Kaufman & Lichtenberger, 1998). Because of the significantly stronger psychometric properties of Symbol Search in comparison to Coding, Kaufman (1994) strongly recommends that Symbol Search be routinely substituted for Coding as part of the regular battery and in calculation of the Performance IQ.

The following provides a brief description of each of the scales and subtests on the WISC-III.

The WISC-III was standardized on 2,200 subjects stratified according to age, gender, race/ethnicity, geographic region, and educational level. This sample was selected to match basic demographic characteristics provided in the 1988 U.S. Census data. The excellence of the WISC-III's norms have been noted by several reviewers (e.g., Braden, 1995; Kaufman, 1993; Sandoval, 1995).

The reliability data for the WISC-III are strong. The average split-half reliability coefficients for individual subtests, across the different age groups, ranged from 0.69 to 0.87. The average reliability values for the IQs and indexes were 0.95 for the Verbal IQ, 0.91 for the Performance IQ, 0.96 for the Full Scale IQ, 0.94 for the Verbal Comprehension Index, 0.90 for the Perceptual Organization Index, 0.87 for the Freedom from Distractibility Index, and 0.85 for the Processing Speed Index (Wechsler, 1991). Factor analytic studies were performed for four age groups: ages 6 to 7, ages 8 to 10, ages 11 to 13, and ages 14 to 16. The underlying four-factor structure of the WISC-III was validated, and provides evidence of the WISC-III's construct validity. Descriptions of what each of the four factors measure are listed along with descriptions of the subtests above. Substantial loadings on the large unrotated first factor also provide support for the construct of general intelligence (g) underlying the Full Scale IQ.

Verbal Scale

This scale measures verbal comprehension and expression, verbal reasoning, and memory.

Verbal Comprehension Index. This factor index measures verbal knowledge, expression, and conceptualization.

- *Vocabulary.* Child orally defines a series of orally and visually presented words.

- *Similarities.* Child explains how two common words are conceptually alike.

- *Information.* Child answers a series of questions tapping knowledge of common events, objects, places, and people.

- *Comprehension.* Child answers questions that require an understanding of social rules and concepts or solutions to everyday problems.

Freedom from Distractibility Index. This factor index measures number ability, sequential processing, and verbal short-term memory.

- *Arithmetic.* Child mentally solves a series of arithmetic problems.

- *Digit Span.* Child repeats a list of orally presented numbers forward and backward.

Performance Scale

This scale measures nonverbal reasoning, visual motor cooordination, and processing speed.

Perceptual Organization Index. This factor index measures nonverbal thinking, reasoning, and visual motor coordination.

- *Picture Completion.* Child determines which part of an incomplete picture is missing.

- *Block Design.* Child replicates geometric patterns with red and white colored cubes.

- *Picture Arrangement.* Child rearranges a set of pictures into a logical story sequence.

- *Object Assembly.* Child assembles puzzle pieces into a meaningful whole.

Processing Speed Index. This factor index measures response speed.

- *Digit Symbol-Coding.* Child uses a key to write symbols underneath corresponding numbers.

- *Symbol Search.* Child indicates, by marking a box, whether a target symbol appears in a series of symbols.

How to interpret or clinically use WISC-III results is not clearly delineated in the WISC-III manual, but there are many sources for obtaining such information (e.g., Kaufman, 1994; Prifitera & Sakolfske, 1998). The process of WISC-III profile interpretation is a complex one. It is recommended that individual subtests not be evaluated in isolation; rather, subtests should be grouped and combined with other supportive information in order to make hypotheses (Kaufman, 1994). Differences between the Verbal IQ and Performance IQ are regularly evaluated by examiners, but with the WISC-III, it may at times be more beneficial to compare differences between the factor indexes (i.e., Verbal Comprehension and Perceptual Organization; see Kaufman, 1994 for a detailed explanation). To best interpret a child's scores, the context of the referral question, background information, behavioral observations during the testing, and situational factors must all be considered together.

The WISC-III has obtained very favorable reviews (Braden, 1995; Sandoval, 1995). The improvements from the WISC-R include updating the testing materials and artwork, reducing item biases, and others. The norms for the WISC-III are excellent and its psychometric properties overall are very strong (Braden, 1995; Sandoval, 1995). However, Mazes is considered a weak subtest on the WISC-III, with an average stability coefficient of 0.57. This subtest is so poor psychometrically that Kaufman (1994) has stated that it should have been dropped. The addition of the Symbol Search subtest to the WISC-III was a good addition as it has allowed the four-factor structure. Some reviews of the WISC-III have been mixed, but it continues to be one of the most frequently used tests in the field of children's intelligence testing (Kaufman & Lichtenberger, 1998).

REFERENCES

Braden, J.P. (1995). Review of the Wechsler Intelligence Scale for Children–Third Edition. In J.C. Conoley & J.C. Impara (Eds.), *The twelfth mental measurements yearbook* (pp. 1098–1103). Lincoln, NE: Buros Institute of Mental Measurement.

Kaufman, A.S. (1993). King WISC the third assumes the throne. *Journal of School Psychology, 31,* 345–354.

Kaufman, A.S. (1994). *Intelligent testing with the WISC-III.* New York: Wiley.

Kaufman, A.S., & Lichtenberger, E.O. (1998). Intellectual Assessment. In A.S. Bellack & M. Hersen (Series Eds.), & C.R. Reynolds (Vol. Ed.), *Comprehensive clinical psychology: Volume 4. Assessment* (pp. 203–238). Oxford, England: Elsevier Science Ltd.

Prifitera, A., & Saklofske, D. (Eds.). (1998). *WISC-III clinical use and interpretation.* San Diego: Academic.

Sandoval, J. (1995). Review of the Wechsler Intelligence Scale for Children–Third Edition. In J.C. Conoley & J.C. Impara (Eds.), *The twelfth mental measurements yearbook* (pp. 1103–1104). Lincoln, NE: Buros Institute of Mental Measurement.

Wechsler, D. (1991). *Wechsler Intelligence Scale for Children–Third Edition.* San Antonio, TX: The Psychological Corporation.

See also **Assessment; Intelligence Testing; WAIS-III**

WECHSLER PRESCHOOL AND PRIMARY SCALE OF INTELLIGENCE–REVISED

The Wechsler Preschool and Primary Scale of Intelligence–Revised (WPPSI-R; Wechsler, 1989) is a measure of cognitive functioning of children from ages 2 years, 11 months to 7 years, 3 months. The WPPSI-R overlaps with the Wechsler Intelligence Scale for Children–Third Edition (WISC-III) in the age 6 to 7 range. Examiners are likely to find the WPPSI-R a better measure for low functioning children in this age range, but the WISC-III a better instrument for normal or high functioning children in this age range.

The WPPSI-R is comprised of two scales: Performance and Verbal. Each provides standard scores with a mean of 100 and a standard deviation of 15. Mainly motor responses are required on the Performance Scale (pointing, placing, or drawing) and spoken responses are required on the Verbal scale. The two scales are each comprised of five subtests,

Performance Subtests	*Verbal Subtests*
Object Assembly. Child is required to fit puzzle pieces together to form a meaningful whole.	*Information.* Child must either point to a picture or verbally answer brief oral questions about commonplace objects and events.
Geometric Design. In the first part of the task, the child must look at a design and point to a matching design from an array of four. In the second part, child copies a drawing of geometric figure.	*Comprehension.* Child verbally responds to questions about consequences of events.
Block Design. Child reproduces patterns made from flat, red and white colored blocks.	*Arithmetic.* Child demonstrates ability to count and solve more complex quantitative problems.
Mazes. Child solves paper-and-pencil mazes of increasing difficulty.	*Vocabulary.* Child names pictured items and provides verbal definitions of words.
Picture Completion. Child identifies what is missing from pictures of common objects.	*Similarities.* Child chooses which pictured objects share a common feature or child completes a sentence that contains a verbal analogy.
Animal Pegs (Optional subtest). Child places pegs of the correct colors in the holes below a series of pictured animals.	*Sentences (Optional subtest).* Child repeats verbatim a sentence that is read aloud.

plus one optional subtest. Each of the subtests provides scaled scores with a mean of 10 and a standard deviation of 3. The section below lists and describes each of the WPPSI-R subtests.

The WPPSI-R was standardized on a sample of 1,700 children who were chosen to closely match the 1986 US Census data. The reliability and validity information are presented in the WPPSI-R Manual (Wechsler, 1989). The average internal consistency coefficients are 0.95 for the Verbal IQ, 0.91 for the Performance IQ, and 0.96 for the Full Scale IQ. Internal consistency values for individual subtests ranged from 0.54 to 0.93 (median = 0.81). The WPPSI-R is a fairly stable instrument with test-retest reliabilities of 0.90, 0.88, and 0.91 for the Verbal, Performance, and Full Scale IQs, respectively. Construct validity of the WPPSI-R is supported by the factor analytic studies described in the manual. Validity is further supported by strong correlations with other instruments such as the Stanford Binet-Fourth edition.

The original version of the WPPSI was criticized because of its drab color and lack of appropriate preschool activities. However, the WPPSI-R is more suitable for young children, and includes simplified directions (Bracken, 1992). Although the floor of the WPPSI-R for young, low-functioning children is weak, Bracken (1992) notes that it is generally stronger than many similar instruments. Another weakness of the WPPSI-R is the lack of information provided in the manual on interpretation. Kaufman (1992) notes that there is age-inappropriate stress on solving problems with great speed on the WPPSI-R. Overall, the WPPSI-R is a useful assessment tool, but it possesses certain strengths and weaknesses that should be considered upon deciding to use it.

REFERENCES

Bracken, B. (1992). Review of the Wechsler Preschool and Primary Scale of Intelligence–Revised. In J.J. Kramer & J.C. Conoley (Eds.), *The eleventh mental measurements yearbook* (pp. 1027–1029). Lincoln, NE: Buros Institute of Mental Measurements.

Kaufman, A.S. (1992). Evaluation of the WISC-III and WPPSI-R for gifted children. *Roeper Review, 14,* 154–158.

Wechsler, D. (1989). *Wechsler Preschool and Primary Scale of Intelligence–Revised.* San Antonio, TX: The Psychological Corporation.

See also Assessment; Intelligence; Intelligence Tests; Kaufman Assessment Battery for Children; Stanford-Binet Intelligence Scale; WISC-III

WELSH FIGURE PREFERENCE TEST

The Welsh Figure Preference Test (FPT) was developed by George Welsh in 1949, for his doctoral thesis, as a projective assessment of psychopathology. More recently, it has been used as a measure of creativity more than as a diagnostic tool for the evaluation of psychopathology.

The Welsh FPT (Welsh, 1959) consists of a booklet containing 400 black and white line drawings. The scale was re-vised by Welsh in 1980. It is designed for use with individuals aged 6 years and up. It requires nearly an hour to complete and, despite being intended as a projective, provides objective scoring. Instructions to the test taker are simple. Individuals are asked to view each drawing and indicate on an answer sheet whether they like or dislike the drawing. The intent was to provide nonlanguage stimulus materials suitable for a wide range of individuals who could not be assessed with language-laden measures such as the MMPI, or projective measures such as the TAT, requiring extensive verbal expression.

The Welsh FPT can separate artists from nonartists, as can many other tests; it can also separate clinical from nonclinical populations. However, it has not been extensively researched considering its publication date. Welsh (1986) contends that the Welsh FPT is useful as a measure of creativity; it has been used in creativity research since at least 1965. Its uses in creativity research seem well established at this time, but its validity as a measure of psychopathology is questionable.

REFERENCES

Welsh, G.S. (1949). *A projective figure-preference test for diagnosis of psychopathology: I, A preliminary investigation.* Doctoral thesis, University of Minnesota, Minneapolis.

Welsh, G.S. (1959). *Welsh figure preference test.* Palo Alto, CA: Consulting Psychologists.

Welsh, G.S. (1980). *Welsh Figure Preference Test, revised edition.* Palo Alto, CA: Consulting Psychologists.

Welsh, G.S. (1986). Positive exceptionality: The academically gifted and the creative. In R.T. Brown & C.R. Reynolds (Eds.), *Psychological perspectives on childhood exceptionality: A handbook.* New York: Wiley-Interscience.

See also Creativity

WEPMAN'S AUDITORY DISCRIMINATION TEST–SECOND EDITION

The second edition of Wepman's Auditory Discrimination Test (ADT; Reynolds, 1986; Wepman, 1975) is a revised version of the Auditory Discrimination Test, first published in 1958. The ADT is a measure of a child's auditory discrimination that can be used as a reliable screening measure to identify children with problems in the areas of auditory, cognition, speech, and language abilities. The test is designed to be administered to children ages 4 to 8 years, 11 months who are suspected of having auditory discrimination problems.

The ADT contains 40 pairs of words: 30 pairs that differ in a single phoneme and 10 same-word pairs. The word pairs are read aloud to the child with the child's back to the examiner, so that visual cues cannot be used in responding. The demands of the ADT are minimal; the child may respond yes or no either verbally or nonverbally. The number of correct responses on 30 different-word pair items yields the total raw score. The same-word pairs serve as control items for checking the validity of the test. The test is considered invalid if a child scores 9 or less in the different-word pairs category or a score of 6 or less in the same-word pairs category. Raw scores may range from 10 to 30 and these are converted into a qualitative score, a standard score (T-score), and percentile ranks.

REFERENCES

Reynolds, W.M. (1986). *Manual for Wepman's Auditory Discrimination Test* (2nd ed.). Los Angeles: Western Psychological Services.

Wepman, J.M. (1975). *Auditory Discrimination Test manual.* Los Angeles: Western Psychological Services.

See also Auditory Discrimination

WERNER, HEINZ (1890–1964)

Heinz Werner received his PhD from Vienna University in 1914 with highest honors. Perhaps the beginning of his scholarly career began when he read about the evolution of animals, man, and the cosmos. He became increasingly interested in philosophy and psychology while at the University of Vienna. His work in the field of psychological phenomena is relevant to psychologists, educators, anthropologists, students of animal behavior, and scholars investigating aesthetic phenomena.

His contributions to the field have been many. He has published over 15 books and monographs and more than 150 articles within a 50-year period. His principal publications include *Comparative Psychology of Mental Development* and *Developmental Processes: Heinz Werner's Selected Writings.* His selected writings include his general theory and perceptual experiences in Volume I; Volume II focuses on cognition, language, and symbolization.

Werner was a great teacher and researcher, and he inspired others to follow his example in the search for understanding of psychological phenomena. His theory was interdisciplinary because all of his developmental principles apply to all the life sciences. He founded an Institute for Human Development at Clark University in 1958. This institute made Clark an "international center directed toward the developmental analysis of phenomena in all the life sciences" (Werner, 1978). Werner's contributions to the field of developmental psychology are steadily gaining recognition.

REFERENCES

Werner, H. (1940). *Comparative psychology of mental development.* New York: Harper & Brothers.

Werner, H. (1978). *Developmental processes: Heinz Werner's selected writings.* New York: International Universities Press.

WERNICKE'S APHASIA

Wernicke's aphasia is one of several subdivisions of fluent aphasia. This is the first type of aphasia described, and it is one in which the localization description still holds true in terms of the symptoms correlating with damage to particu-

lar location in the brain. Those possessing communicative deficits consistent with Wernicke's aphasia have pathology in the dominant superior temporal gyrus (typically the left, but not always). A lesion in the superior posterior temporal is obligatory for Wernicke's aphasia.

Major language characteristics of Wernicke's aphasia are defective auditory comprehension; disturbed reading and writing; defective repetition of words and sentences with speech which is incessant at normal prosody with a rapid rate; good articulation but paraphasic speech, containing semantic and literal paraphasias and possible extra syllables added to words (Graham-Keegan & Caspari, 1997; Hegde, 1994).

REFERENCES

Graham-Keegan, L., & Caspari, I. (1997). Wernicke's aphasia. In L.L. LaPointe (Ed.), *Aphasia and related neurogenic language disorders* (pp. 42–62). New York: Thieme.

Hegde, M. (1994). *A coursebook on aphasia and other neurogenic language disorders.* San Diego: Singular.

See also Aphasia; Dysphasia; Language Disorders

WHOLE WORD TEACHING

The term whole word teaching has been used as the label for two different approaches to beginning reading instruction. Mathews (1966) in *Teaching to Read: Historically Considered* describes the first approach as a "words-to-letters" method that was introduced into reading instruction in Germany in the eighteenth century and later brought to the United States.

The development of the words-to-letters method was motivated by dissatisfaction with the ABC method, the prevailing method of reading instruction since the invention of the Greek alphabet. Critics of the ABC method did not disagree with its underlying philosophy that mastery of the alphabet and syllables (combinations of vowels and consonants such as *ba, bē, bu*) were prerequisite skills for learning to read. However, they took issue with the procedures used to teach those skills, namely, years of drill, which they described as senseless, tortuous, desperately dull work. The method that eventually evolved presented beginning readers with whole words in their total form followed by an analysis of the sounds and letters. This was an analytic approach to teaching the alphabet, whereas the ABC method was a synthetic approach under which students were taught to combine syllables into words only after having mastered their pronunciation as isolated units.

Mathews (1966) refers to the second approach that has been called whole word teaching as a "words-to-reading" method. This method, commonly called the "look-and-say" method, also had its roots in Germany and may have been used by some teachers in the United States as early as the 1830s. Horace Mann, a strong advocate of the method is often credited with having brought about its widespread use (Betts, 1946).

During the first two decades of the twentieth century, it

became firmly entrenched in elementary reading programs and remained so until the mid-1950s, when Rudolf Flesch (1955) captured the growing public alarm over what was happening in the nation's elementary schools in his book *Why Johnny Can't Read.* Flesch challenged the prevailing practice in beginning reading instruction that emphasized a look-and-say approach. He advocated a return to a phonic approach using existing research as support for his position.

Flesch's book led to a great deal of public debate, which in turn spawned numerous research efforts to identify the best method(s) for beginning reading instruction. Among these were 27 U.S. Office of Education grade 1 studies and a study funded by the Carnegie Corporation of New York (Chall, 1967).

REFERENCES

Chall, J. (1967). *Learning to read: The great debate.* New York: Mc-Graw-Hill.

Flesch, R. (1955). *Why Johnny can't read and what you can do about it.* New York: Harper & Brothers.

Mathews, M.M. (1966). *Teaching to read: Historically considered.* Chicago: University of Chicago Press.

See also **Phonology; Reading Disorders; Reading Remediation**

WIDE RANGE ACHIEVEMENT TEST–THIRD EDITION (WRAT-3)

The Wide Range Achievement Test–Third Edition (WRAT-3; Wilkinson, 1993) and the Wide Range Achievement Test–Revised (WRAT-R) are both instruments used to measure skills in the area of spelling, arithmetic and reading. The revised 1993 WRAT-3 has returned to its original format with two alternate test forms (Blue and Tan). Both forms provide information in three areas: 1) Reading—recognizing and naming letters and pronouncing words; 2) Spelling—writing name, writing letters and words to dictation; and 3) Arithmetic—counting, reading number symbols, solving oral problems, and performing written computations. The three subtests may be administered in any order. Each form can be given to individuals between the ages of 5 to 75 and can take between 15 to 30 minutes to administer depending on the skill level. The Blue or the Tan form can be used separately or both forms may be administered together (Combined Form) to measure the respective academic skills and convert the resulting raw scores to absolute scores, standard scores, grade scores and percentiles. The WRAT-3 was designed to take out the comprehension factor. This enables the examiner to use the results obtained from this measure and compare it to a measure of intelligence such as the Wechsler scales in order to determine the areas of difficulty for an individual.

REFERENCE

Wilkinson, G.S. (1993). *Wide Range Achievement Test–Third edition administration manual.* Wilmington, DE: Wide Range, Inc.

See also **Achievement Tests**

WIDE RANGE ASSESSMENT OF MEMORY AND LEARNING (WRAML)

The Wide Range Assessment of Memory and Learning (WRAML; Sheslow & Adams, 1990) is a test to assess one's ability to learn and to memorize different types of information for children between 5 and 17 years of age. The WRAML is an individually-administered test used to clarify memory deficits in children with a learning disability and/or who have suffered some type of head trauma. The WRAML is comprised of three index scales yielding a Verbal Memory Index, a Visual Memory Index, and a Learning Index, each consisting of three subtests. The nine total subtests yield a General Memory Index. It can be administered by a trained clinician with experience in administration of testing under the direct supervision of a psychologist.

The Verbal Memory Index Scale measures the learner's ability to utilize language as it relates to enhance or detract in remembering. The Visual Memory Index serves to compare rote memory demands as it relates to memory, and the Learning Scale is used by the evaluator to assess the performance over trials. The WRAML also utilizes several delayed subtests in the area of Verbal Learning, Visual Learning, Sound Symbol, and Story Memory procedures. This group of tasks requires only 1 to 2 minutes each and can provide the examiner with important information regarding the learner's capacity to remember. The total administration time of the WRAML ranges from 45 minutes to one hour if all the Delayed Recall tasks are given.

The WRAML is not an intelligence test, nor is it designed to measure all aspects of memory. Specifically, this instrument lacks the ability to assess the function of long-term memory. Instead, the test provides useful information with the Delayed Recall subtests by assessing immediate recall and then measuring the learner's ability to recall that information after approximately 20 to 40 minutes have elapsed.

Because the WRAML does not utilize one theory, but instead uses various theories, the test does not seem to be a consideration of the developmental aspects of memory, such as the idea that children do not systematically use active encoding strategies until about the age of 8 or 9 years and that children older than 10 gradually refine their use of strategies, making them both more effective and more flexible (Kail & Hagen, 1982). In addition, the concept that children will vary in the degree to which they benefit from multiple trials as a function of developmental status are not addressed by the authors (Boyd, 1988).

REFERENCES

Boyd, T.A. (1988). Clinical assessment of memory in children: A developmental framework for practice. In M.G. Tramontana & S.R. Hooper (Eds), *Assessment issues in child neuropsychology* (pp. 177–204). New York: Plenum.

Kail, R., & Hagen, J.W. (1982). Memory in childhood. In B. Wolman, G. Stricker, S. Ellman, P. Keith-Siegel, & D. Palermo (Eds.), *Handbook of developmental psychology* (pp. 350–366). Englewood Cliffs, NJ: Prentice Hall.

Sheslow, D., & Adams, W. (1990). *Wide Range Assessment of Memory and administration manual.* Wilmington, DE: Jastak Assessment Systems.

WIEACKER SYNDROME

Wieacker syndrome, also known as apraxia, involves the inability to execute familiar voluntary movements. A child with Wieacker syndrome is physically able to perform motor acts and has a desire to perform the acts, but is unable to perform the movements upon request (Merck, 1987). When motor movement does occur in a child with this syndrome, the movement is often uncontrolled, unintentional, inappropriate, and clumsy.

Selective apraxias do exist. For example, a child with constructional apraxia is unable to draw, whereas a child with oculomotor apraxia is unable to move his or her eyes (Thoene, 1992).

Apraxia results from a lesion in the neural pathways of the brain associated with the memory of learned patterns (Merck, 1987). The lesion may be due to a stroke, head injury, dementia, congenital malformation of the central nervous system, or metabolic or structural disease (Merck, 1987; Thoene, 1992).

Physical and occupational therapy is recommended to help a child with apraxia to relearn voluntary movements. If apraxia is a symptom of another disorder, treatment of the primary disorder is required (Thoene, 1992).

REFERENCES

Merck manual of diagnosis and therapy. (1987). (15th ed.). Rahway, N.J: Merck & Co.

Thoene, J.G. (Ed.). (1992). *Physician's guide to rare diseases.* Montvale, NJ: Dowden.

WILBUR, HERVEY BACKUS (1820–1883)

Hervey Backus Wilbur, physician and educator, established the first school for mentally retarded children in the United States when he took a group of retarded children into his home in Barre, Massachusetts, in 1848. With the published accounts of the educational work of Edouard Seguin to guide him, Wilbur fashioned out of his own experience a system of teaching that was successful to a degree not previously thought possible.

In 1851, the New York State legislature established an experimental residential school for mentally retarded children, the second state school for the mentally retarded in the United States, with Wilbur as superintendent. Residential schools were opened in a number of other states during the next few years, many of them patterned after the New York School. This school, over which Wilbur presided until his death, is today the Syracuse Developmental Center.

Wilbur was a founder and the first vice president (with Edouard Seguin as president) of the Association of Medical Officers of American Institutions for Idiotic and Feeble-Minded Persons, now the American Association on Mental Deficiency. He produced numerous pamphlets and articles dealing with the care and treatment of mentally retarded persons.

REFERENCES

Godding, W.W. (1883). In memoriam: Hervey Backus Wilbur. *Journal of Nervous & Mental Diseases, 10,* 658–662.

Scheerenberger, R.D. (1983). *A history of mental retardation.* Baltimore, MD: Brookes

See also **AAMD Adaptive Behavior Scales**

WILD BOY OF AVEYRON

The Wild Boy of Aveyron—or Victor, as he later came to be known—first was noticed by a group of peasants who witnessed him fleeing through the woods of south central France. He was spotted on subsequent occasions digging up turnips and potatoes or seeking acorns. He was captured in the forest of Aveyron, France, by three hunters in July 1799. It was determined that the boy was about 11 or 12 years of age, was unable to speak, and had been living a wild existence. He was taken to the Institution of Deaf Mutes in Paris and was assigned to the care of Jean Itard.

Itard, a young French physician, believed that this wild creature was physiologically normal and that his intellectual deficiencies were due to a lack of "appropriate sensory experiences in a socialized environment" (Scheerenberger, 1983). Itard was convinced that with an adequate training program, Victor would show great intellectual development and could be transformed from a savage to a civilized being. Because Victor's intellectual deficiencies were not seen as physiologically based, but were attributed to isolation and social and educational neglect, this was viewed as an opportunity to substantiate the effectiveness of educational methods being developed at the time (Maloney & Ward, 1979).

Over the next 5 years, Itard worked intensively with Victor and established a sequence of educational activities designed to teach him speech, self-care, and manners, and to develop his intellectual functions and emotional faculties. Itard employed socialization techniques and sensory training methods much like those he had used with deaf children (Robinson & Robinson, 1965).

Victor's progress was sometimes frustratingly slow, despite Itard's affection, effort, and ingenuity. Still, the doctor made tremendous gains in his 5 years of work with the boy, later documenting this in great detail (Kirk & Gallagher, 1979). Victor accomplished a great deal: he was able to recognize objects, identify letters of the alphabet, and comprehend the meaning of many words (Maloney & Ward, 1979). However, he never learned to speak, and Itard felt his program of instruction had failed. The physician decided to terminate the program after 5 years of intensive work with Victor.

Itard's experiences with the Wild Boy of Aveyron are particularly notable since his work was the first documented, systematic attempt to teach a handicapped person. Although his attempts to make the boy "normal" failed, Itard did make significant gains, and showed that even a severely handicapped individual could make great improvements with training.

REFERENCES

Kirk, S.A., & Gallagher, J.J. (1979). *Educating exceptional children* (3rd ed.). Boston: Houghton Mifflin.

Maloney, M.P., & Ward, M.P. (1979). *Mental retardation and modern society.* New York: Oxford University Press.

Robinson, H.B., & Robinson, N.M. (1965). *The mentally retarded child.* New York: McGraw-Hill.

Scheerenberger, R.C. (1983). *A history of mental retardation.* Baltimore, MD: Brookes.

See also History of Special Education; Itard, J.M.

WILLIAM'S SYNDROME

See INFANTILE HYPERCALCEMIA.

WILLOWBROOK CASE

The Willowbrook case, or *New York State Association for Retarded Children v. Carey,* was litigation tried by Judge Orrin Judd in which the conditions in the Willowbrook State School in New York State were challenged. Specific charges included widespread physical abuse, overcrowded conditions and understaffing, inhumane and destructive conditions, extended solitary confinement, and lack of therapeutic care. Brought on behalf of more than 5000 residents of the Willowbrook State School, this class-action suit is recognized as a landmark in protection from harm litigation.

During a series of Willowbrook trials, witnesses appeared and provided court testimony documenting the inhumane conditions and the physical, mental, and emotional deterioration of residents. On April 21, 1975, the New York Civil Liberties Union, the Legal Aid Society, the Mental Health Law Project, and the U.S. Department of Justice announced that the parties to the Willowbrook litigation had agreed on a consent judgment that would resolve the suit. This consent decree, which was approved on May 5, 1975, established standards in 23 areas to secure the constitutional rights of the Willowbrook residents to protection from harm.

See also Deinstitutionalization; Mental Retardation

WILSON'S DISEASE

See KAYSER-FLEISCHER RING

WISC-III

See WECHSLER INTELLIGENCE SCALE FOR CHILDREN–III.

Lightner Witmer

WITMER, LIGHTNER (1867–1956)

Lightner Witmer established the world's first psychological clinic, at the University of Pennsylvania in 1896, an event that marked the beginning not only of clinical psychology but also of the diagnostic approach to teaching. Previously director of the psychological laboratory at the University of Pennsylvania, where he succeeded James McKeen Cattell, Witmer moved psychology from the theoretical concerns of the laboratory to the study of learning and behavior problems of children in the classroom. Proposing a merging of the clinical method in psychology and the diagnostic method in teaching, Witmer developed an interdisciplinary approach to education; his clinic provided training for psychologists, teachers, social workers, and physicians. He formed special classes that served as training grounds for teachers from across the nation and as models for many of the special classes that were established in the early part of the twentieth century. Anticipating special education's strong influence on mainstream education, Witmer suggested that learning-disabled children would show the way for the education of all children.

REFERENCES

Watson, R.I. (1956). Lightner Witmer: 1867–1956. *American Journal of Psychology, 69,* 680.

Witmer, L. (1911). *The special class for backward children.* Philadelphia: Psychological Clinic.

WOLF-HIRSCHHORNE SYNDROME

Wolf-Hirschhorne syndrome, also known as Wolf Syndrome or 4p-Syndrome, is a genetic disorder resulting from a defect in chromosome 4. The incidence rate of Wolf-Hirschhorne syndrome is 1 out of 50,000 births (Thoene, 1992). The syndrome occurs more often in females than males by a ratio of 2:1. Approximately one-third of the children who are born with the syndrome die in the first two years of life as a result of either cardiac failure and bronchopneumonia (O'Brien & Yule, 1995).

Primary features of the disorder include low birth weight, deficit or low muscle tone, physical and mental retardation, and a very small head. Prominent facial characteristics are also found in this syndrome, such as cleft lip, cleft palate, downturned mouth, small jaw, low-set ears, high forehead, and beak-like nose. Squinting of the eyes is another common feature. Heart and kidney problems and seizures occur in approximately 50% of the children with this disorder. In some cases, reconstructive surgery is needed to address facial abnormalities.

In schools, special education may be needed to address learning disabilities. Due to delayed psychomotor development and speech/communication abilities, physical therapy, occupational therapy, and speech services will be needed (O'Brien & Yule, 1995). Vocational services may be helpful. Genetic counseling may also be beneficial (Thoene, 1992).

REFERENCES

O'Brien, G., & Yule, W. (Eds.). (1995). *Behavioural phenotypes*. London: Mac Keith Press.

Thoene, J.G. (Ed.). (1992). *Physician's guide to rare diseases*. Montvale, NJ: Dowden.

WOODCOCK DIAGNOSTIC READING BATTERY

The *Woodcock Diagnostic Reading Battery* (WDRB; Woodcock, 1997) is a set of carefully engineered (Woodcock, 1992) tests for clinical measurement of reading achievement and important abilities related to reading. Continuous-year norming, based on a nationally representative sample of 6,026 individuals ranging in age from 4 to 95 years, produced highly accurate normative data—10 points at each grade level and 12 points at each age level for school-aged individuals.

The WDRB is comprised of six tests from the WJ-R Tests of Cognitive Ability (Woodcock & Johnson, 1989b) and four tests from the WJ-R Tests of Achievement (Woodcock & Johnson, 1989a). The tests were combined into one format to be "more useful to those who are reading specialists and researchers" (Rudman, in press). That is, one short battery of tests includes (1) tests of basic reading and reading comprehension skills, (2) important reading-related tests (phonological awareness and oral comprehension), and (3) reading aptitude tests.

The reading tests include Letter-Word Identification, Passage Comprehension, Word Attack, and Reading Vocabulary. The phonological awareness tests include Incomplete Words and Sound Blending. The oral comprehension tests are Oral Vocabulary and Listening Comprehension.

Four tests comprise the Reading Aptitude cluster: Memory for Sentences, Visual Matching, Sound Blending, and Oral Vocabulary. These tests are based on tasks that are statistically and logically associated with proficiency in reading, but are uncontaminated with reading content. The median correlation between the WDRB Reading Aptitude cluster and Broad Reading achievement clusters is .78.

REFERENCES

Rudman, H.C. (in press). Review of the Woodcock Diagnostic Reading Battery. The fourteenth mental measurements yearbook. Lincoln, NB: University of Nebraska Press.

Woodcock, R.W. (1992, April). *Rasch technology and test engineering*. Invited presentation to the American Educational Research Association annual conference, San Francisco.

Woodcock, R.W. (1997). *Woodcock Diagnostic Reading Battery*. Itasca, IL: Riverside.

Woodcock, R.W., & Johnson, M.B. (1989a). *Woodcock-Johnson—Revised Tests of Achievement*. Itasca, IL: Riverside.

Woodcock, R.W., & Johnson, M.B. (1989b). *Woodcock-Johnson—Revised Tests of Cognitive Ability*. Itasca, IL: Riverside.

WOODCOCK-JOHNSON PSYCHOEDUCATIONAL BATTERY– REVISED

The Woodcock-Johnson Psychoeducational Battery–Revised (WJ-R) contains a variety of tests that measure cognitive and academic achievement abilities and is, therefore, applicable in educational, clinical, and research settings. The WJ-R has two major components: The Tests of Cognitive Abilities (WJ-R COG; Woodcock & Johnson, 1989b) and the Tests of Achievement (WJ-R ACH; Woodcock & Johnson, 1989a). Each component is further divided into a Standard and Supplementary Battery. These batteries yield several Cluster Standard Scores as well as age and grade equivalents and percentiles. The components are designed so that the clinician may select only the tests required to provide additional information regarding particular abilities or skills in question. The test may be administered to children and adults between the ages of 2 and 90. In general, administration of the WJ-R can range from 40 to 180 minutes.

Derived from the Horn-Cattell intelligence model, the WJ-R COG is comprised of 21 subtests that yield seven factors including Long-Term Retrieval, Short-Term Memory, Processing Speed, Auditory Processing, Visual Processing, Comprehension-Knowledge, and Fluid Reasoning. In addition, the WJ-R COG generates predictions about an individual's achievement abilities based on reading, mathematics, written language, knowledge, and oral language. The WJ-R ACH includes nine standard subtests and five supplemental subtests. The following ten cluster scores are derived from this component: Broad Reading, Basic Reading Skills, Reading Comprehension, Broad Mathematics, Basic Mathematics Skills, Mathematics Reasoning, Basic Written Language, Basic Writing Skills, Written Expression, and Skills. Further detail regarding each cluster is provided in the WJ-R manuals.

The examiner's manual offers information regarding technical aspects such as norming, reliability, and validity. The tests were normed using a national sample of 6,359 subjects between the ages of 2 and 95. In a separate norming sample, college and university students were used. With regard to reliability, coefficients were not reported for timed tests, such as Visual Matching, Cross Out, and Writing Fluency. The Spearman-Brown split-half statistical procedure indicated that, on the cognitive subtests, median reliability coefficients range from .72 (Visual Closure) to .94 (Concept Formation). On the achievement subtests, median reliability coefficients range from .75 (Writing Fluency) to .94 (Letter-Word Identification). Content, criterion-related, and concurrent validity were established. For the WJ-R COG, content validity was established with the aid of the Horn-Cattell model of intelligence, while being established by outside experts and experienced teachers for the WJ-R ACH. Concurrent validity was reported with such tests as the Kaufman Assessment Battery for Children (.74), the Stanford-Binet Composite (.77), and the Wechsler Intelligence Scale for Children–Revised (.75).

REFERENCES

Woodcock, R.W., & Johnson, M.B. (1989a). *The Woodcock-Johnson Tests of Achievement–Revised.* Chicago: Riverside.

Woodcock, R.W., & Johnson, M.B. (1989b). *The Woodcock-Johnson Tests of Cognitive Abilities–Revised.* Chicago: Riverside.

See also **Achievement Tests; Criterion-Referenced Tests**

WOODCOCK LANGUAGE PROFICIENCY BATTERY–REVISED

The *Woodcock Language Proficiency Battery–Revised* (Woodcock, 1991; Woodcock & Muñoz-Sandoval, 1995; WLPB-R) is designed to provide an overview of a subject's language skills in English (or Spanish), to diagnose language abilities, to identify students for English as a second language instruction, and to plan broad instructional goals for developing language competencies. The instrument is appropriate for individuals aged 2 to over 90 years of age. For interpretive purposes, each WLPB-R provides cluster scores for Broad Language Ability (English or Spanish), Oral Language Ability, Reading Ability, and Written Language Ability. When the entire battery is used, the WLPB-R provides a procedure for evaluating the strengths and weaknesses among an individual's oral language, reading, and written language abilities. When both the English and Spanish forms are administered, examiners can obtain information about language dominance and relative proficiency in each language.

The WLPB-R oral language tests measure linguistic competency, semantic expression, expressive vocabulary, and verbal comprehension/reasoning. The WLPB-R reading tests measure the ability to identify sight vocabulary, to apply structural analysis skills, and comprehend single-word stimuli and short passages. The written language tests assess a broad range of writing tasks. These include tasks measuring the ability to produce simple sentences with ease, writing increasingly complex sentences to meet varied demands, and other tasks measuring punctuation, capitalization, spelling, word usage, and the ability to detect and correct errors in spelling, punctuation, capitalization, and word usage in written passages.

Administration time varies depending on the purposes of the assessment and the number of tests administered (20 minutes to over one hour). A wide variety of interpretive scores are available, including age and grade equivalents, instructional ranges, standard scores, and percentile ranks.

The English form was standardized on more than 6,300 individuals ranging in age from 2 to over 90. Lehmann (1995), who reviewed the WLPB-R primarily from a psychometric perspective, commented favorably on the development of continuous (gathered throughout the school year), rather than interpolated, norms. The Spanish form was standardized on more than 2,000 native Spanish-speaking subjects. The Spanish form uses equated US norms for interpretive purposes.

REFERENCES

Woodcock, R.W. (1991). *Woodcock Language Proficiency Battery–Revised, English Form.* Itasca, IL: Riverside.

Woodcock, R.W., & Muñoz-Sandoval, A. (1995). *Woodcock Language Proficiency Battery–Revised, Spanish Form.* Itasca, IL: Riverside.

See also **Nondiscriminatory Assessment; Woodcock-Johnson Psychoeducational Test Battery**

WOODCOCK READING MASTERY TESTS–REVISED

Available in two forms, the Woodcock Reading Mastery Tests–Revised (WRMT-R; Woodcock, 1987) is an individually-administered test designed to assess a variety of reading abilities of individuals between the ages of 4 and 75. The WRMT-R is useful in various settings, such as instructional placement, individual program planning, and progress evaluation (Cohen & Cohen, 1994). The test consists of six subtests, including Visual-Auditory Learning, Letter Identification, Word Identification, Word Attack, Word Comprehension, and Passage Comprehension. Visual-Auditory Learning involves learning several unfamiliar visual symbols representing words. Letter Identification assesses an individual's ability to identify by name or sound the letters of the alphabet. Word Identification requires the test taker to read words ranging in difficulty. Word Attack evaluates the ability to pronounce nonsense words using phonic skills. Word Comprehension is comprised of antonyms, synonyms, and analogies. Finally, Passage Comprehension is designed to evaluate reading comprehension skills. From these subtests, five cluster scores are obtained: Readiness, Basic Skills, Reading Comprehension, Total Reading-Full

Scale, and Total Reading-Short Scale. Percentile ranks, grade and age equivalent scores, instructional ranges, and strengths and weaknesses can also be obtained. Depending on the form used, administration time ranges from 30 to 60 minutes.

The WRMT-R was recently renormed, and is now referred to as the Woodcock Reading Mastery Test–Revised/Normative Update (WRMT-R/NU; Woodcock, 1997) The examiner's manual for the WRMT-R/NU offers information regarding technical aspects such as norming, reliability, and validity. The WRMT-R/NU was normed using approximately 3,700 subjects; however, new norms were not collected for subjects in grades 13–16 or ages 23 and older. Subjects were randomly selected using a stratified sampling method based on variables such as geographic region, community size, sex, and so on from 1994 US Census data.

REFERENCES

Cohen, S.H., & Cohen, J. (1994). Review of the Woodcock Reading Mastery Tests–Revised. In D.J. Keyser & R.C. Sweetland (Eds.), *Test critiques: Volume X.* Austin: Pro-Ed.

Woodcock, R.W. (1987). *Woodcock Reading Mastery Tests–Revised.* Circle Pines, MN: American Guidance Service.

Woodcock, R.W. (1997). *Woodcock Reading Mastery Tests–Revised/Normative Update.* Circle Pines, MN: American Guidance Service.

WOODS SCHOOLS

The Woods Schools, located in Langhorne, Pennsylvania, was established in 1913 to provide educational and training programs for students with development delays, retardation, brain damage, and learning disabilities. The school is primarily a residential facility that features group home life in small cottages with an intensive staff ratio that provides for direct care and services to meet the individual needs of students. The school provides for day and residential students on a coed basis.

The school programs offer a wide range of educational experiences to students who are severely handicapped and who require therapeutic services. Vocational training is provided. Students are trained in a wide range of vocational exploration experiences that establish appropriate work habits, basic working skills, and prevocational experiences that lead to job training. Remedial services, tutorial instruction, and therapeutic services are designed to meet the individual needs of students as they progress through the programs.

See also Vocational Training

WORD BLINDNESS

Congenital word blindness, word blindness, dyslexia, developmental dyslexia, specific dyslexia, developmental alexia, visual aphasia, and strephosymbolia are all terms that have on some occasions been used interchangeably in the special education literature (Evans, 1982; Orton, 1937; Wallin, 1968) to indicate a child's inability to learn to read. Developmental dyslexia was defined by Critchley (1964) as a specific difficulty in learning to read, often of genetic origin, which existed in spite of good general intelligence, and without emotional problems, brain damage, or impairments of vision or hearing. Ford (1973) defined congenital word blindness or dyslexia as the inability of a child to learn the meaning of graphic symbols.

REFERENCES

Critchley, M. (1964). *Developmental dyslexia,* London: Heinemann Medical.

Evans, M.M. (1982). *Dyslexia: An annotated bibliography. Contemporary problems of childhood #5.* Westport, CT: Greenwood.

Ford, F.R. (1973). Developmental word blindness and mirror writing. In *Diseases of the nervous system in infancy, childhood, and adolescence* (6th ed.) Springfield, IL: Thomas.

Orton, S.T. (1937). *Reading, writing, and speech problems in children.* New York: Norton.

Wallin, J.E.W. (1968) Congenital word blindness (dyslexia) in children. *Journal of Education, 151*(1), 36–51.

See also **Dyslexia; Reading Disorders; Reading Remediation**

WORDS IN COLOR

Words in Color is a one-to-one sound-symbol approach to teaching reading that was devised in 1957 by Caleb Gattegno. Gattegno, a scientist, approached the problems of reading as he did the problems of mathematics and physics. He introduced the concept of temporal sequence into reading methodology (Gattegno, 1970) and proposed that our language is coded into a series of sounds that, when uttered in sequence, produce wholes that we call words. The timing of the sounds in sequence is essential learning for correct pronunciation (Aukerman, 1971). Words in Color is based on the premise that reading is a process of decoding printed symbols and translating them into sounds and words. Color is used in the initial stage of reading to help the learner make an association between the symbol and the sound.

REFERENCES

Aukerman, R.C. (1971). *Approaches to beginning reading.* New York: Wiley.

Gattegno, C. (1970). The problem of reading is solved. *Harvard Educational Review, 40*(2), 283–286.

See also **Reading Disorders; Reading Remediation**

WORKFARE

Workfare is a term that was coined in the 1980s to describe welfare reform efforts that require able-bodied AFDC parents to work in public service projects in exchange for monthly benefits. These unpaid jobs were typically at the city or county level and involved entry-level positions in clerical, human services, or park maintenance work. The majority of the participants were single females with children over the age of 6.

See also **Rehabilitation; Socioeconomic Status**

WORLD FEDERATION OF THE DEAF (WFD)

The World Federation of the Deaf (WFD) was founded in 1951. It consists of 83 members representing the languages of English, French, and Italian. Its central office is in Rome, Italy. The WFD is a collection of associations of the deaf from various countries. These national or international organizations encompass societies and bodies acting for the deaf, health, social, and educational groups related to the aims of the federation, professionals involved with deafness or performing special assignments for the federation, and parents and friends of the deaf. Through social rehabilitation of deaf individuals, the WFD is a leader in the fight against deafness.

Among its services, the federation makes available social legislation concerning the deaf as well as statistical data. It also serves as consultant to the World Health Organization and UNESCO. The WFD sustains a library and bestows awards for merit and special achievement in education and social rehabilitation of the deaf. The federation holds commissions in the areas of communication, arts and culture, pedagogy, psychology, medicine, audiology, social and vocational rehabilitation, and spiritual care. The federation publishes a journal triannually entitled *Voices of Silence,* in addition to the *Proceedings of International Congresses and Meetings* and a dictionary.

See also **World Health Organization**

WORLD HEALTH ORGANIZATION (WHO)

The World Health Organization (WHO) is a specialized agency of the United Nations with primary responsibility for international health matters and public health. Created in 1948, it comprises of delegates representing member states and is attended by representatives of intergovernmental organizations and nongovernmental organizations in official relationships with WHO. Assemblies are held annually, usually in Geneva.

The official functions of WHO are varied; they include (1) directing and coordinating authority on international health work; (2) assisting governments in strengthening health services; (3) furnishing technical assistance and emergency aid; (4) stimulating and advancing work to eradicate or control epidemic, endemic, and other diseases; (5) promoting improved nutrition, housing, sanitation, recreation, economic and working conditions, and other aspects of environmental hygiene; (6) encouraging cooperation among scientific and professional groups that contribute to the advancement of health; (7) promoting material and child health and welfare, and fostering the ability to live harmoniously in a changing total environment; (8) fostering activities in the field of mental health; (9) working for improved standards of teaching and training in health, medical, and related professions; (10) studying and reporting on administrative and social techniques affecting public health and medical care from preventive and curative perspectives; and (11) assisting in developing informed public opinion on health matters.

Several WHO activities relate directly to diagnostic and classificatory issues in special education. First, WHO produces key writings concerning the use of health statistics and undertakes psychiatric epidemiology devoted to comparative research on mental disorders. Second, WHO compiles the International Classification of Diseases (ICD), a statistical classification of diseases; complications of pregnancy, childbirth, and the puerperium; congenital abnormalities; accidents, poisonings, and violence; and symptoms and ill-defined conditions. The ICD has been adapted for use as a nomenclature of diseases, with mental disorders constituting one major category. Subsumed in this category are classifications along with operational definitions of handicapping conditions.

Several other systems are tied to the ICD, including the *Diagnostic and Statistical Manual* (*DSM*) as well as the *Grossman Manuals on Terminology and Classification* of the American Association on Mental Deficiency. Third, the Mental Health Unit of WHO has implemented an intensive program to acquire systematic data on variables in diagnostic practice and use of diagnostic mental disorder terms. This has resulted in a multiaxial scheme for the classification of childhood mental disorders, with three main axes: clinical psychiatric syndromes, individual intellectual levels of functioning regardless of etiology, and associated physical, organic, and psychosocial factors in etiology.

See also **World Federation of the Deaf**

WORLD REHABILITATION FUND

The World Rehabilitation Fund, also known as the International Exchange of Experts and Information in Rehabilitation (IEEIR), seeks to identify, "import," disseminate, and promote the use of innovative rehabilitation and special education knowledge from other countries. Information about unique programs, practices, and research, as well as the policies of other nations, is sought for dissemination to professionals in the United States.

The IEEIR program is substantially supported by the Office of Special Education and Rehabilitation Services (OSERS) of the U.S. Department of Education. It is an outgrowth of the National Institute of Handicapped Research (NIHR, an OSERS division) mandate to facilitate the use of selected ideas and practices generated in other countries. Selection of knowledge or problem areas to guide the program staff are set jointly by OSERS, NIHR, and IEEIR staffs.

The IEEIR engages in the awarding of fellowships, the publication of monographs, and the dissemination of information. The fellowship program enables qualified U.S. experts to study and report on either special education or rehabilitation developments in other lands. This group includes rehabilitation and special education faculty, researchers, and administrators. Other specialists such as rehabilitation engineers, physicians, psychologists, independent living leaders, and consumer advocates also participate.

See also World Health Organization

WPPSI–REVISED

See WECHSLER PRESCHOOL AND PRIMARY SCALE OF INTELLIGENCE–REVISED.

WRAT-III

See WIDE-RANGE ACHIEVEMENT TEST–THIRD EDITION.

WRITING ASSESSMENT

Competence in writing requires the mastery and automation of a vast array of skills. To ensure that these skills develop in an efficient and efficacious manner, it is generally believed that assessment should be included as an integral part of handicapped students' writing programs. This belief is primarily based on the assumption that information from the assessment process should make it possible for teachers to more readily determine a student's writing strengths and weaknesses, individualize instruction, monitor writing performance, and evaluate the effectiveness of the composition program.

The assessment of handicapped students' writing should focus on both the written product and the process of writing (Graham, 1982). There are a host of procedures for evaluating the various attributes embodied in the written product; the most popular of these will be reviewed at length. Relatively few techniques, however, are available for examining the process by which students compose. The most common procedures include: (1) observing and, in some instances, timing the various activities and behaviors that the student engages in during the act of writing; (2) interviewing students about their approach to writing and questioning them about their reasons for particular composing behaviors; and (3) asking students to verbally report what they are thinking while they write. Regrettably, the reliability and validity of these procedures have not been adequately established and the results from such assessments may, as many critics have suggested, yield a distorted picture of the writing process (Humes, 1983).

Both formal and informal assessment procedures have been used to examine the relative merits and/or shortcomings of handicapped students' writing. The most frequently used standardized test is the Test of Written Language (TOWL). According to the authors (Hammill & Larsen, 1983), this instrument "can be used to ascertain the general adequacy of a product written by a student and to determine specific proficiency in word usage, punctuation and capitalization (style), spelling, handwriting, vocabulary, and sentence production" (p. 5). The TOWL consists of six subtests. Scores for three of these subtests (vocabulary, thematic maturity, and handwriting) are derived from a spontaneous sample of writing. The remaining word usage, spelling, and style subtests employ a contrived format; e.g., a student's proficiency in word usage is determined by a sentence completion activity. Although the TOWL appears to have a sound theoretical basis and to be reasonably valid and reliable, there is some question as to the value of the vocabulary and thematic maturity scores (Williams, 1985).

Informal assessment procedures have been used to assess a variety of factors ranging from story quality to writing mechanics. Not surprisingly, the quality of students' writing has proven to be the most difficult factor to define and measure. Probably the oldest measure of writing quality is the holistic method. With this method, an examiner makes a single overall judgment on the quality of a student's writing (Mishler & Hogan, 1982). Each paper is read at a fairly rapid pace and the examiner attempts to weigh the various factors (e.g., content, organization, grammar, etc.) in roughly equal proportions. The examiner's overall impression is quantified on a Likert-type scale, ranging from poor to high quality. To increase accuracy and reliability, most holistic scoring systems include representative examples of specific scores.

A more complex procedure for determining the quality of a student's writing is the analytic method. With this method, the student's paper is analyzed and scored on the basis of several different factors such as ideation, grammar, and spelling (Moran, 1982). The scores for each of these factors are then averaged to produce a single grand score. Although the analytic method may provide more useful information for instructional purposes, it is much more time-consuming than the holistic method.

A more recent development in the measurement of writing quality is the primary trait scoring method. With this procedure, different scoring systems are developed for different writing tasks. For a task such as writing a short story, the examiner would decide ahead of time what traits should be evaluated and what type of responses will be considered appropriate and inappropriate for each trait. For example, for a short story one of the primary traits might be the introduction and development of the protagonist (Graham & Harris, 1986). Consequently, stories that adequately present and develop the leading character would receive credit for this trait.

A number of procedures have been used to evaluate the various elements embodied in the written products. Writing fluency has typically been assessed by examining total number of words written, average sentence length, and number of words written per minute. Vocabulary diversity has been measured by counting the occurrence of particular vocabulary items such as adjectives or adverbs and by computing the corrected type/token ratio (number of different words divided by the square root of twice the number of words in the sample) or the index of diversification (average number of words that appear between each occurrence of the most frequently used word in a composition). Proficiency with the mechanics of writing is generally determined by tabulating the occurrence of a particular behavior (e.g., spelling errors), while syntactic maturity is often defined in terms of the average length of T-units (main clause plus any attached or embedded subordinate clauses).

It is important to note that students' knowledge of their writing performance can be a powerful motivator and have a potent effect on learning. Nevertheless, the value of circling every misspelled word, writing "AWK" above every clumsy wording, or red-marking each deviation from standard English is questionable. Intensive evaluation may have little or no effect on writing improvement and may, in fact, make students more aware of their limitations and less willing to write (Burton & Arnold, 1963). Feedback on the positive aspects of a student's composition, in contrast, can have a facilitative effect on writing performance (Beaven, 1977). It also is desirable to dramatize a student's success through the use of charts, graphs, verbal praise, and so on.

REFERENCES

Beaven, M. (1977). Individualized goal setting, self-evaluation, and peer evaluation. In C. Cooper & L. Odell (Eds.), *Evaluating writing: Describing, measuring, judging.* Urbana, IL: National Council of Teachers of English.

Burton, D., & Arnold, L. (1963). *The effects of frequency of writing and intensity of teacher evaluation upon high school students' performance in written composition.* (Research Report No. 1523). Tallahassee, FL: USOE Cooperative.

Graham, S. (1982). Composition research and practice: A unified approach. *Focus on Exceptional Children, 14,* 1–16.

Graham, S., & Harris, K. (1986). *Improving learning disabled students' compositions via story grammars: A component analysis of self-control strategy training.* Paper presented at the American Educational Research Association, San Francisco.

Hammill, D., & Larsen, S. (1983). *Test of written language.* Austin, TX: Pro-Ed.

Humes, A. (1983). Research on the composing process. *Review of Educational Research, 53,* 201–216.

Mishler, C., & Hogan, T. (1982). Holistic scoring of essays: Remedy for evaluating the third R. *Diagnostique, 8,* 4–16.

Moran, M. (1982). Analytic evaluation of formal written language skills as a diagnostic procedure. *Diagnostique, 8,* 17–31.

Williams, R. (1985). Review of test of written language. In J.V. Mitchell (Ed.), *Ninth mental measurement yearbook.* Lincoln: University of Nebraska Press.

See also Written Language of the Handicapped; Writing Remediation

WRITING DISORDERS

While research on writing disorders in context is limited, the sources of difficulty emerge when they are considered within a framework or model of writing. Writing is a complex cognitive activity (Hayes & Flower, 1980) that requires writers to coordinate and regulate the use of task-specific strategies during three overlapping and recursive writing stages (i.e., prewriting, drafting, and revising). During prewriting, task-specific strategies focus on planning and organizing. Writers generate and select writing topics, decide on a purpose for writing, identify the audience, generate and gather ideas about the topic, and organize the ideas into a network or structural plan (e.g., text structure such as story narrative, compare/contrast, sequence). During drafting, task-specific strategies involve the activation of the structural plan, translation of ideas into printed sentences, fleshing out of placeholders in the plan with details, and signaling of relationships among the elements of the plan. During monitoring and revising, task-specific strategies pertain to evaluation and analysis. The writer reads the draft to see whether the objectives concerning audience, topic, purpose, and structure have been achieved, and applies correction strategies to portions of the text that fail to meet expectations.

Though these task-specific strategies are necessary, they are not sufficient for skilled writing. A second domain involves the execution of these strategies. Metacognitive knowledge is the executive or self-control mechanism that helps writers activate and orchestrate activities in each of the writing stages. Metacognitive knowledge includes the ability to self-instruct or direct oneself in the writing stages, to monitor strategy use, and to modify or correct strategy use on the basis of outcomes. Without metacognitive knowledge, writers fail to access writing strategies and monitor their use even when the strategies are in their behavioral repertoire.

A third domain includes the mechanical skills that make writing a fluent process. This domain involves writers' knowledge of rules related to spelling (orthographic knowledge), writing conventions (punctuation, capitalization), and language (syntactic knowledge). These skills are of primary importance to writers in the stage of final revision in light of the importance of legibility to the audience. In addition, for the successful strategic employment of these skills, writers must not only acquire mechanical skills, they must acquire the task-specific strategies and metacognitive knowledge governing their use. For example, writers who lack task-specific strategies may not know how to rehearse or study spelling words to improve recall, whereas writers who lack metacognitive knowledge may learn to accurately spell words for the weekly spelling test, but fail to accurately spell or monitor their spelling of the same words in written compositions. Skillful writers not only acquire the mechanical means to produce text, they acquire the cognitive tools that help them know when and how to use those means, how to monitor their use, and how to correct errors when they occur.

The literature suggests that several deficiencies may impede students' writing performance. Deficiencies in spelling, grammar, and writing conventions have been reported—though these may not be the barriers to writing success as much as students' lack of task-specific strategies and metacognitive knowledge. Research is still needed to determine the impact of other elements of the writing process (e.g., audience, prior knowledge) on performance in each of the writing stages. However, it is certain that writing competence will be associated not only with the acquisition of efficient strategies pertaining to the use of each element, but with the metacognitive knowledge that helps the writer know when and how to use the element in planning, drafting, monitoring, and revising compositions.

REFERENCE

Hayes, J.R., & Flower, L.S. (1980). Writing as problem solving. *Visible Language, 11,* 388–399.

See also **Writing Assessment; Writing Remediation; Written Language of the Handicapped**

WRITING REMEDIATION

The writing difficulties exhibited by many handicapped students necessitate the development and use of instructional procedures aimed at improving writing competence, particularly in terms of handicapped students' functional writing skills. The remediation of handicapped students' writing difficulties, however, has not received much attention in either the research literature or in school settings. Leinhardt, Zigmond, and Cooley (1980) found, for example, that handicapped students may spend less than 10 minutes a day generating written language. Although there are many possible reasons why writing remediation appears to receive a limited amount of time and emphasis in handicapped students' instructional programs, teacher attitudes and backgrounds may be the key factors in determining the quantity and quality of writing instruction for these students. According to Graham (1982), many teachers do not enjoy writing and are not prepared to teach composition. Furthermore, many special education teachers may feel that writing is not a critical skill for their students and may choose to spend their instructional time teaching what they consider to be more important skills (e.g., reading and arithmetic).

For the most part, writing instruction for handicapped students has drawn heavily on techniques used with normally achieving youngsters. One commonly recommended instructional procedure has been to use a phase approach. This approach emphasizes the various stages of the composition process (prewriting, writing, and revising) and is designed to develop security in the use of these stages. In a phase approach described by Silverman et al. (1981), the teacher first structures the writing process with prewriting activities that involve thinking, experiencing, discussing, and interacting. The student and the teacher then develop a series of questions that are used to guide the writing process. During the revising stage, the teacher critiques the student's writing and they jointly revise the student's paper. Although empirical support for this particular model or other phase approaches is limited, this writing procedure does stress the development of two important skills: thinking as a preliminary facet of composing and revision of the initial draft of the written product. In addition, a phase approach to writing may be especially suitable for handicapped students since it helps reduce cognitive strain by taking a large complex problem such as writing and breaking it down into smaller sub-problems.

Another traditional approach that has been used to teach specific writing skills to handicapped students is modeling. With this approach, students may be asked to imitate a specific type of sentence pattern, a well-known style of writing, a certain type of paragraph, and so on. There are two basic approaches to modeling. One approach stresses strategy explanation and model illustration; the other emphasizes problem solving. With the former, a student may be asked to mimic a specific type of paragraph (e.g., topic sentence located at the start of the paragraph) following an examination and analysis of several examples that are representative of the style to be emulated. The latter can be illustrated by examining a procedure developed by Schiff (1978). With this procedure, examples of a particular type of paragraph are selected. Sentences for each paragraph are then written on a separate strip of paper and their order randomized. Students rearrange the sentences in each paragraph and compare their arrangements with the original model. At present, it is impossible to draw any definitive conclusions on the relative effectiveness of these procedures, as there is virtually no research that examines them.

A great deal of attention has been directed at teaching handicapped students information about language and writing with the aim of promoting the correct use of structure, form, and language. One of the most consistently held beliefs in the history of writing instruction is that the teaching of grammar and usage is critical to the development of writing competence. Formal grammar, however, is difficult to master and knowledge of grammatical concepts does not appear to be necessary for the skillful use of written language (Blount, 1973). This is not meant to imply that teachers should not attend to handicapped students' use of structure or form in their writing or that these skills cannot be improved. Rather, improvement of usage and form "may be more effectively achieved through direct practice of desirable forms when the need arises" (Graham, 1982, p. 6).

An interesting alternative to traditional writing approaches is the use of procedures that seek to minimize or circumvent handicapped students' poor writing skills. The most commonly used alternative is dictation. Traditionally, dictation has involved having a student furnish the content or ideas orally while the teacher or a peer structures the form the material takes on paper. The conventional dictation process can be adapted by using a tape recorder as an aid to organizing content; i.e., ideas are taped and later written and edited by the student. In some instances, dictation is employed as a temporary aid and its use diminishes as the student becomes more adept at the mechanics of writing. Dictation may represent a viable alternative for students with adequate oral language skills who have been unable, after years of intensive instruction, to automate and integrate basic writing skills.

A recent alternative to traditional writing instruction approaches is the cognitive-behavior modification (CBM) procedure. Typically CBM training involves teaching students to regulate task-specific and metacognitive strategies through processes such as self-instruction, self-assessment, and self-reinforcement (Harris, 1982). For example, Harris and Graham (1985) reported a CBM composition training procedure that significantly increased learning-disabled students' use of verbs, adverbs, and adjectives and resulted in higher story quality ratings. Further, generalization and maintenance probes taken up to 14 weeks after training yielded positive results. The CBM training regimen in this study included skills training (instruction on specific task-appropriate strategies), metacognitive training (instruction in the self-regulation of those strategies), and instruction concerning the significance of such activities. In a second study, Graham and Harris (1986) found that CBM procedures also could be used to improve the overall structure of learning-disabled students' compositions through the use of a story grammar strategy. Training procedures were similar to those in the first study; however, strategy training consisted of instruction in story grammar elements: setting, goal(s), action(s), emotional responses, and ending.

Educators also have attempted to improve handicapped students' writing skills by further refining or developing their reading, oral language, and thinking skills. Since reading, writing, thinking, and language skills are interrelated, it is assumed that intensive and generalized instruction in an area such as oral language, for example, will have an indirect and positive effect on a student's writing ability (Groff, 1978). Although these skills may be interrelated, they do not necessarily function in an interactive and supportive way. Generalized instruction in an area such as reading or oral language appears to be of limited value in the immediate improvement of a student's writing (Graham, 1982).

A recent development in the teaching of writing to the handicapped has been the advent of the computer, particularly the word processor. The word processor, with its various capabilities for storing and editing texts, has the potential to both strengthen and significantly change the nature of writing instruction. The word processor and other technological advances should not, however, be viewed as a cure-all for handicapped students' writing problems. MacArthur and Graham (1986), for instance, found no major differences between handwritten stories and those composed on a word processor, even though the learning-disabled students in their study had considerable experience using the computer.

Additional instructional recommendations for teaching writing to the handicapped have been summarized by Gra-

ham (1982). These include (1) providing students with plenty of opportunities to write and exposing them to a variety of practical and imaginative assignments; (2) having writing assignments, whenever possible, serve a real purpose and be directed at an authentic audience; (3) having a pleasant and encouraging composition program; and (4) de-emphasizing writing errors.

REFERENCES

Graham, S. (1982). Composition research and practice: A unified approach. *Focus on Exceptional Children, 14,* 1–16.

Graham, S., & Harris, K. (1986). *Improving learning disabled students' compositions via story grammars: A component analysis of self-control strategy training.* Paper presented at the American Educational Research Association, San Francisco.

Groff, P. (1978). Children's oral language and their written composition. *Elementary School Journal, 78,* 181–191.

Harris, K. (1982). Cognitive behavior modification: Application with exceptional students. *Focus on Exceptional Children, 15,* 1–16.

Harris, K., & Graham, S. (1985). Improving learning disabled students' composition skills: Self-control strategy training. *Learning Disability Quarterly, 8,* 27–36.

Leinhardt, G., Zigmond, N., & Cooley, W. (1980). *Reading instruction and its effects.* Paper presented at the American Educational Research Association, Boston.

MacArthur, C., & Graham, S. (1986). *LD students' writing under three conditions: Word processing, dictation, and handwriting.* Paper presented at the American Educational Research Association, San Francisco.

Schiff, P. (1978). Problem solving and the composition model: Reorganization, manipulation, analysis. *Research in the Teaching of English, 12,* 203–210.

Silverman, R., Zigmond, N., Zimmerman, J., & Vallecorsa, A. (1981). Improving written expression in learning disabled students. *Topics in Language Disorders, 1,* 91–99.

See also **Writing Assessment; Writing Disorders; Written Language of the Handicapped**

WRITTEN LANGUAGE OF THE HANDICAPPED

In addition to other academic problems, it is generally agreed that handicapped students have difficulty using the medium of written language to express their ideas and thoughts (Graham, 1982). It would be difficult at present, however, to substantiate this belief since the written language problems of the handicapped have received little attention from either researchers or the educational community in general. While there are many possible reasons why there has been a notable lack of interest in this important language skill, two factors merit special attention. First, it is likely that handicapped students' writing problems have not received much emphasis because most special educators lack specific training in this particular area and feel that writing is not a critical skill for their students. Second, the difficulties inherent in measuring written language have proven to be formidable obstacles to researchers interested in describing the writing characteristics of the handicapped. Adequate procedures for measuring a complex phenomena such as composition quality, for instance, do not exist.

The information that is available on the written language of the handicapped has primarily centered on two disabilities: learning disabilities and hearing impairments. Even though some students with visual impairments and/or physical disabilities may require special writing programs and technological adaptations (Napier, 1973), no information is available on the writing characteristics of these students. Furthermore, the definitive source on the writing problems of students with emotional/behavioral difficulties, mental retardation, and speech and language disorders is a single large-scale study conducted by Myklebust (1973).

Even in areas where a more solid research base exists, knowledge of students' writing characteristics is extremely limited. For example, considerable information has been gathered on the length, syntactic complexity, vocabulary diversity, etc., of learning-disabled students' compositions. Most of our knowledge concerning these factors, however, is restricted to elementary-age students and a fairly narrow range of writing tasks (primarily creative writing assignments). Our understanding of how handicapped students' writing skills develop is, at best, spotty. Virtually no attention has been directed at determining how they plan and revise their compositions, and the effects of different audiences on their writing performance is unknown.

Although it is generally agreed that written language development may be influenced by a variety of factors (Bereiter, 1980), surprisingly little research has been conducted with handicapped students to determine the relationship between their writing performance and various genetic and environmental variables. If research conducted with normal students can be used as a benchmark, then handicapped students' writing performance may be related to and, in some instances, influenced by the following: general language development, intelligence, maturity, reading achievement, sex, socioeconomic status, personality characteristics, school locale, and specific cognitive abilities such as short- and long-term memory (Graham, 1982).

An examination of the available literature reveals that students who are labeled mentally retarded have severe writing difficulties that tend to persist over time. From elementary to high school, they score significantly lower than normal students on a variety of written language tasks. Retarded students make consistently more grammatical and spelling errors and their written compositions evidence less vocabulary diversity (Sedlack & Cartwright, 1972).

Studies examining the writing performance of students with hearing impairments have primarily been restricted to examining sentence structure, vocabulary diversity, spelling and grammatical errors, and productivity. In comparison with normal students, sentences composed by the hearing impaired tend to be less complex, with more errors and less diversity in vocabulary usage (Powers & Wilgus, 1983;

Yoshinaga-Itano & Snyder, 1985). Wilbur and Nolen (in press) have indicated that stories written by the deaf often lack creativity, cohesiveness, and complexity in terms of temporal sequence. They further point out that the material written by these students is generally stilted and vocabulary choice is restricted to a small number of words. Although hearing-impaired students' poor performance on measures of written language is, in part, due to their hearing loss and resulting language deficits, instructional variables also appear to be a contributing factor.

Learning-disabled students typically have a great deal of difficulty expressing themselves in writing. In terms of overall quality and content, their writing has consistently been found to be inferior to that of average students. Graham and Harris (1986), for example, compared the stories of sixth-grade learning-disabled and average students using holistic ratings of quality. With the holistic method, raters make a single overall judgment about the quality of the writing sample based on a variety of factors, including content, imagination, structure, word choice, and writing conventions. Mean scores for the learning-disabled and average groups, on a scale ranging from 1 to 8, were 2.2 and 4.5, respectively.

In addition, Poplin and colleagues (1980) compared learning-disabled and normal students in grades three through eight on the thematic maturity subtest of the Test of Written Language. This subtest reportedly measures whether the student's story has been written in a logical manner that efficiently conveys meaning. The differences between the learning-disabled and normal students on the thematic maturity subtest increased with age. There were no significant differences between third to fourth graders, but at fifth through eighth grades, average students outperformed the learning disabled.

Other investigators have studied the structure and completeness of stories written by the learning disabled. MacArthur and Graham (1986) used an analytical scale based on the common elements contained in most short stories. Most of the stories written by learning-disabled students included main and supporting characters, action, and an ending, but few included explicit goals, starter events, or emotional reactions. Nodine, Barenbaum, and Newcomer (1985), on the other hand, had 11-year-old learning-disabled, reading-disabled, and normal students write narratives in response to a sequence of pictures. The students' compositions were classified as stories, storylike, descriptive, or expressive. To be judged as a story, a composition had to include a setting, conflict, and resolution. Complete stories were written by 71% of the normal students, 47% of the reading disabled, and only 30% of the learning disabled. Nearly half of the learning-disabled students (48%) wrote compositions with no story line.

Research has also shown that learning-disabled students write stories and essays that are shorter than those of their normally achieving peers. For instance, Nodine et al. (1985) reported that learning-disabled students' stories were on the average 54 words in length, while normal children wrote stories with approximately 104 words. Limited fluency may be related to lower overall quality and content. MacArthur and Graham (1986) found significant correlations between length and story structure and a measure of overall quality.

An additional difficulty exhibited by most learning-disabled students involves the mechanics of writing. On both standardized tests and informal measures of contextual writing, these students demonstrate considerable difficulty in spelling words correctly or using proper punctuation and capitalization (Moran, 1981). Spelling problems appear to be particularly pronounced among learning-disabled students.

Although it is generally assumed that learning-disabled students have difficulty with written grammar and vocabulary, research has yielded conflicting results concerning this issue. Morris and Crump (1982), for example, reported that learning-disabled students' written vocabulary is less varied than that of normal students. In contrast, Deno, Marston, & Mirkin (1982) found no differences between normal students and the learning disabled on several vocabulary measures. In terms of grammatical or syntactical difficulties, several studies have found no differences in the syntactical maturity of learning-disabled and normal students' compositions (Nodine et al., 1985). Learning-disabled students, however, tend to make more grammatical errors than their normal peers (Moran, 1981).

Finally, only one study was located that examined both the product and process of writing. MacArthur and Graham (1986) videotaped learning-disabled students as they composed stories using three different methods: handwriting, dictation, and word processing. Results from the study revealed that dictated stories were over three times as long as stories produced under the other conditions and that they were rated significantly higher on overall quality. Regardless of the mode of writing, students engaged in almost no planning prior to writing their stories. Furthermore, students made a few revisions (on average, about 24 per 100 words), but most revisions (57%) involved surface changes such as changing the spelling of a word. Only 10% of all revisions affected the meaning of what the student wrote. Further research on the writing process of learning-disabled and other handicapped students is needed to understand how these students write so that teachers can help them learn to write more effectively.

REFERENCES

Bereiter, C. (1980). Development in writing. In L. Gregg & E. Steinberg (Eds.), *Cognitive processes in writing.* Hillsdale, NJ: Erlbaum.

Deno, S., Marston, D., & Mirkin, P. (1982). Valid measurement procedures for continuous evaluation of written expression. *Exceptional Children, 48,* 368–371.

Graham, S. (1982). Composition research and practice: A unified approach. *Focus on Exceptional Children, 14,* 1–16.

Graham, S., & Harris, K. (1986). *Improving learning disabled students' compositions via story grammars: A component analysis of self-control strategy training.* Paper presented at the American Educational Research Association, San Francisco.

MacArthur, C., & Graham, S. (1986). *LD students' writing under three conditions: Word processing, dictation, and handwriting.* Paper presented at the American Educational Research Association, San Francisco.

Moran, M. (1981). Performance of learning disabled and low achieving secondary students on formal features of a paragraph-writing task. *Learning Disability Quarterly, 4,* 271–280.

Morris, N., & Crump, D. (1982). Syntactic and vocabulary development in the written language of learning disabled and non-learning disabled students at four age levels. *Learning Disability Quarterly, 5,* 163–172.

Myklebust, H. (1973). *Development and disorders of written language: Studies of normal and exceptional children.* New York: Grune & Stratton.

Napier, G. (1973). A writing study relative to braille contractions to be mastered by primary level children. *Education of the Visually Handicapped, 5,* 74–78.

Nodine, B., Barenbaum, E., & Newcomer, P. (1985). Story composition by learning disabled, reading disabled, and normal children. *Learning Disability Quarterly, 8,* 167–179.

Poplin, M., Gray, R., Larsen, S., Banikowski, A., & Mehring, T. (1980). A comparison of components of written expression abilities in learning disabled and non-learning disabled students at three grade levels. *Learning Disability Quarterly, 3,* 46–53.

Powers, A., & Wilgus, S. (1983). Linguistic complexity of the written language of hearing-impaired children. *Volta Review, 85,* 201–210.

Sedlack, R., & Cartwright, G. (1972). Written language abilities of EMR and nonretarded children with the same mental age. *American Journal of Mental Deficiency, 77,* 95–99.

Wilbur, S., & Nolen, S. (in press). Reading and writing. In *Gallaudet encyclopedia of deaf people and deafness.* New York: McGraw-Hill.

Yoshinaga-Itano, C., & Snyder, L. (1985). Form and meaning in the written language of hearing-impaired children. *Volta Review, 87,* 75–90.

See also Dysgraphia; Handwriting; Writing Disorders

WYATT v. STICKNEY

The case of *Wyatt v. Stickney* established constitutionally minimum standards of care; in the last two decades, *Wyatt* has been credited with establishing the legal precedent for a constitutional right to treatment for involuntarily committed mentally ill patients. Directly addressing Alabama's state institutions for the mentally ill and mentally retarded, this case represented a landmark federal judicial intervention in the mental institutions of a sovereign state, and signaled dozens of *Wyatt*-type "right to treatment" lawsuits in nearly every part of the country.

As a result of the unrefuted "atrocities" documented in *Wyatt* (1972), the "shocking" and "inhumane" conditions in New York's Willowbrook State School for the Mentally Retarded (1973), and 25 other suits involving the U.S. Justice Department (1979), congressional legislation for financial assistance and a "Bill of Rights" for institutionalized persons were enacted.

Only six decisions based on the Wyatt case have ever been published in the law reports (1971–1981), although it is cited in over 200 judicial decisions and is the subject of numerous law reviews and other professional journal articles.

Ricky Wyatt was one of about 5000 mental patients at Bryce State Hospital, Tuscaloosa, the same hospital established in 1861 through the urging of the advocate Dorothea Dix. Stonewall B. Stickney was a psychiatrist and the chief administrative officer of Alabama's Mental Health Board. The case was filed initially by 99 of 100 dismissed staff members plus Ricky Wyatt's aunt and other guardians on October 23, 1970. The plaintiff employees alleged that this reduction in staff would deprive patients at Bryce of necessary treatment and sued for reinstatement. Stickney had released over 100 of the 1600 employees at Bryce owing to reduced state cigarette tax revenues allocated to the department, while redirecting the limited funds to community mental health services. Stickney believed in preventing institutionalization.

The employee plaintiffs withdrew their reinstatement claim prior to Judge Frank M. Johnson's initial reported decision on March 12, 1971. The court found that more than 1500 geriatric patients and about 1000 mentally retarded patients were involuntarily committed at Bryce for reasons other than being mentally ill, and were receiving custodial care but not treatment.

Judge Johnson ordered the development and implementation of adequate treatment standards and a report within 6 months; he requested the U.S. departments of Justice and Health, Education, and Welfare, as "friends of the court," to assist in evaluating the treatment programs and standards. On August 12, 1971, the court allowed the request. All involuntary patients from Partlow State School and Hospital in Tuscaloosa, housing nearly 2500 mental retardates with segregated facilities for blacks, and Searcy Hospital in Mount Vernon, a formerly all-black hospital for the mentally ill, were to be included in the class suit. Defendants filed the court-directed report on September 23, 1971, and Judge Johnson ruled on December 10, 1971, allowing the state 6 months to correct three basic deficiencies. He called for "a humane psychological and physical environment, . . . qualified staff in numbers sufficient to administer adequate treatment, and . . . individualized treatment plans." Following additional testimony, briefs, and standards proposed by "the foremost authorities on mental health in the United States," the parties agreed to standards that mandated a "constitutionally acceptable minimum treatment program"

for the mentally ill at Bryce and Searcy as ordered by the court on April 13, 1972.

Judge Johnson also ruled, in a supplemental order issued the same day, that unrebutted evidence of the "hazardous and deplorable inadequacies in the institution's operations at Partlow was more shocking than at Bryce or Searcy." He said that "The result of almost 50 years of legislative neglect has been catastrophic; atrocities occur daily"; Judge Johnson published these findings (1972):

A few of the atrocious incidents cited at the hearing in this case include the following: (a) a resident was scalded to death by hydrant water; (b) a resident was restrained in a strait jacket for 9 years in order to prevent hand and finger sucking; (c) a resident was inappropriately confined in seclusion for a period of years, and (d) a resident died from the insertion by another resident of a running water hose into his rectum. Each of these incidents could have been avoided had adequate staff and facilities been available.

Judge Johnson ordered the defendants to (1) implement the standards for adequate habilitation for the retarded at Partlow; (2) establish a human rights committee; (3) employ a new administrator; (4) submit a progress report to the court within 6 months; and (5) pay attorneys' fees and costs to the plaintiffs.

The defendants appealed both decisions to the Fifth Circuit Court of Appeals in May 1972. The review court, on November 8, 1974, upheld the constitutional right to treatment concept and ruled that the federal judicially determined standards did not violate the state's legislative rights.

Although subsequent implementation and compliance with the court's orders continue to produce controversies, numerous motions, briefs, hearings, and additional opinions have been issued. However, no legal changes have occurred in *Wyatt* as of the last published order of the court on March 25, 1981.

REFERENCE

Civil rights of the institutionalized. Report of the Committee on Judiciary United States Senate on S.10 together with minority and additional views. (1979). Washington, DC: U.S. Government Printing Office.

See also **History of Special Education; Legal Regulations of Special Education; Philosophy of Education for the Handicapped**

X-LINKED DOMINANT INHERITANCE

The consequences of the presence of a recessive gene on one X chromosome are well known. X-linked dominant inheritance, however, follows a different pattern. First, males and females can show the trait equally, and, if a pathologic gene is concerned, patients of both sexes are affected. Second, if a male carrier of the dominant trait "A" marries an homozygous recessive female "aa," all his daughters will exhibit the trait "A" (they are heterozygous "Aa," having received one X from the "aa" mother and the paternal X with "A"), and all his sons will show the trait "a" (they have received the X chromosome from their mothers and the recessive "a" behaves like a dominant). This mode of transmission, from father to daughter, is in fact so characteristic that, when it is observed, the presence of an X-dominant gene is almost demonstrated. Only a few rare diseases are known to be X-linked dominants. X-linked dominant inherited diseases, though rare, result in a variety of handicapping conditions. Not all genetic disorders need result in handicaps, however. Proper care during pregnancy and throughout life can avoid many natural consequences of genetic disorders.

See also Etiology

.

X-LINKED RECESSIVE INHERITANCE

It is well known that the same gene may present different forms, called alleles. All alleles are located at a fixed place of a chromosome, the locus. In any person, only two alleles are present, one at each locus of the same chromosome pair. One of the two alleles originates from the father, the other from the mother. Alleles can be either dominant (usually represented by a capital letter: "A"), or recessive (represented by a small letter: "a"). As indicated by its name, the dominant form prevails over the recessive one. This means that the carrier of "Aa" (heterozygote) will show the character "A," the recessive "a" being masked. To express itself, "a" must be in the homozygote state "aa." This happens when two "Aa" heterozygotes marry: 25% of all their children will be "aa."

This general rule does not apply to the sex chromosomes. In the XX female, only one X is active in any cell, the other one being inactivated (Lyon, 1961). In a heterozygote female "Aa," the gene "A" will express itself in half of the cells, and "a" in the other half. Most often, the fact that the normal allele is active in half of the cells is enough to determine normal characteristics. For instance, if a woman is a carrier of the recessive mutation responsible for blindness for the red color (daltonism), half of the cells of her retina will be blind for red, but the others not and this will be sufficient to give almost normal color vision. The male has an XY sex chromosome set: only one X, transmitted by the mother, is present. The Y chromosome is very small and has only a few genes.

Any boy has a 50% chance to inherit one of the two maternal Xs. If he receives the X with a normal dominant allele, there will be no problem. If he receives an X with a recessive abnormal allele from an heterozygous mother, all his cells (not half of them, as in his mother) will be affected. The gene "a" alone, although recessive, behaves like a dominant (e.g., in the case of daltonism, he will be blind to the red). In short, an X-linked recessive gene is transmitted by the mother to half of her sons. If the gene determines a disease, half of the male progeny will be affected, the mother herself being apparently normal. Moreover, half of her daughters will be "normal carriers" and thus will be at risk of having half of their sons affected. When an affected male marries, all his children will be normal. The boys receive their X chromosome from the normal mother and the girls are heterozygous (the problem concerns their future children). Only the exceptional and seldom reported marriage of a heterozygous woman "Aa" with an affected man "a" can produce affected "aa" homozygous females.

The striking fact in this sort of X-linked recessive pedigree is that only males are affected (black squares). Inversely, when a family is found with only males presenting a disease, the transmission of an X-linked recessive gene is likely.

From a preventive point of view, it is important first to diagnose correctly any X-linked disease with mental retardation, and to detect the normal heterozygote mothers at risk. This is not always possible, but it is a new area of research and it is hoped, with the help of biochemistry and molecular DNA analysis, to prevent in the near future the birth of affected males.

REFERENCE

Lyon, M.F. (1961). Gene action in the X-chromosome of the mouse. (Mus musculus). *Nature, 190,* 372–373.

See also **Congenital Disorders; Genetic Counseling**

X-RAYS AND HANDICAPPING CONDITIONS

Irradiation of the developing fetus during the early stages of development as a consequence of maternal X-rays is now clearly recognized as a potential cause of later physical and cognitive abnormalities. There may be dramatic effects associated with irradiation that are clearly recognized at birth.

There may be other, more subtle effects appearing at later ages such as reduced head size. Pioneer studies on the subject were done by Zappert (1926), Murphy (1929), and Goldstein (1930); (Berg, 1968).

Though the potential dangers to the fetus from X-ray radiation were recognized before World War II, the dangers of radiation were most dramatically brought into focus by the events of that war. It was found that there was a direct relationship between the distance of a pregnant woman from the point of impact of the atomic bombs at Hiroshima and Nagasaki and the degree of damage suffered by her unborn child. Women who survived the bomb explosion but were within a half-mile of it were found to have miscarriages, while there was an extremely high incidence of microcephalic children born to those who were 11/4 miles away (Wood, Johnson, & Omiri, 1967). Still farther away, there was no clear evidence of cognitive or physical damage to the children that were later born, but some 20 years later, as adults, they had a high incidence of leukemia (Miller, 1968).

One major study of pregnant women who were receiving cobalt treatments for cancer discovered that 20 out of 75 of the infants born to them had definitive central nervous system abnormalities. Sixteen of these were microcephalic (Cooper & Cooper, 1966). The corroboration of these findings in later studies has resulted in caution and forbearance on the part of physicians with respect to the use of X-rays with pregnant women. Normally, women should not have abdominal X-rays more than 2 weeks after the last period. X-rays during the first trimester are discouraged on any but the most necessary grounds. X-rays as diagnostic tests, such as those once carried out to establish fetal size, have been replaced with less invasive procedures like ultrasound. Indeed, there has been recent evidence suggesting that some of the more subtle kinds of handicaps, e.g., those associated with learning disabilities, may be the consequence of X-ray use.

On the positive side it should be observed that X-rays have played a role in assisting in the assessment of handicapped individuals. Thus X-rays of the bone structures of hands and wrists have provided estimates of carpal ossification in cases where delayed maturation has been suspected. X-rays also are essential for the diagnosis of various physical problems and deformities, e.g., dislocations, fractures, internal injuries, and congenital defects.

REFERENCES

Berg, J.M. (1968). Aetiological aspects of mental subnormality: Pathological factors. In A.M. Clarke & A.D.B. Clarke (Eds.), *Mental deficiency.* New York: Free Press.

Cooper, G., & Cooper, J.B. (1966). Radiation hazards to mother and fetus. *Clinical Obstetrics & Gynecology, 9,* 11.

Miller, R.W. (1968). Effects of ionizing radiation from the atomic bomb on Japanese children. *Pediatrics, 72,* 1483.

Wood, J.W., Johnson, K.G., & Omiri, Y. (1973). In utero exposure to the Hiroshima atomic bomb. An evaluation of head size and mental retardation: Twenty years after. *Pediatrics, 39,* 385.

See also Cat Scan; Neural Efficiency Analyzer

X-RAY SCANNING TECHNIQUES

The history of X-ray scanning techniques of the brain is eloquently outlined in the text by Oldendorf (1980). Up until the advent of CAT (computed axial tomography) scanning in 1973, the image of the brain could only be grossly inferred by either bony abnormalities of the skull as seen on routine skull X-rays or by a technique (pneumoencephalography) in which air was introduced into the brain ventricles (either directly or via spinal puncture). The resultant shadowy contrast between ventricle, brain, and bone would permit some visualization of major cerebral landmarks sufficient to detect some types of gross structural pathology (e.g., hydrocephalus, tumor). However, the technique of pneumoencephalography had significant morbidity risks and was invasive. The pneumoencephalogram has been replaced by CAT scanning.

An historical predecessor of CAT scanning was the radioactive isotope scan (based on differences in rate of absorption of radioactive particles in normal and abnormal brain tissue), which began clinical use in 1947 and continued until the advent and clinical implementation of CAT scanning. The CAT and other neuroimaging techniques have essentially replaced the radioactive isotope scan. This is also the case with routine cerebral arteriography, which used to be the only way to visualize blood vessels of the neck and head; it has been replaced in large part by digital subtraction angiography (DSA). The DSA is an X-ray scanning technique that uses a computer program to "subtract" background tissue in the X-ray image that is not of the same density as blood vessels. Comparisons of these techniques, sample figures, and a more complete discussion of their diagnostic usefulness are presented in Bigler (1988).

Positron emission tomography (PET) is a new technique that permits the mapping of brain metabolism by using radioactive-labeled glucose or oxygen. Based on different metabolic rates, an image of the major cerebral structures can be obtained with specific indication of which brain areas were using the most glucose or oxygen (e.g., the brain area most involved in a particular task while PET scanning was being done).

REFERENCES

Bigler, E.D. (1988). *Diagnostic clinical neuropsychology* (2nd ed.). Austin: University of Texas Press.

Oldendorf, W.H. (1980). *The quest for an image of brain.* New York: Raven.

See also **Cat Scan; Nuclear Magnetic Resonance; X-Ray, Associated with Learning Disorders**

XYY SYNDROME

Polysomy Y or XYY syndrome is a sex chromosome variation characterized by an extra Y chromosome in males. That is, rather than having two sex chromosomes of the normal male (46, XY), those with the XYY genotype have an extra male sex chromosome (47, XYY). There are no dysmorphic factors associated with this syndrome other than most males with it are tall (i.e., height is typically above the ninetieth percentile by age six and older). There are also no chronic health disorders associated with the syndrome, but XYY males were found to have a higher rate of broken bones and infections than normal peers (Stewart, 1982). Fertility appears to be normal (Cohen & Durnham, 1985). The incidence of XYY syndrome is 1 in 700 to 1 in 1000 live male births (Cohen & Durnham, 1985). Many XYY males are never identified because they are generally indistinguishable from the general male population.

There have been misconceptions in the past regarding the behavioral and developmental sequelae of XYY syndrome. Research with biased samples indicated that XYY males were typically violent criminals and mentally retarded (e.g., Jacobs et al., 1965). More recent and well-controlled studies have indicated that only 1 of every 950 is institutionalized. While this is higher than the general population, it is much less than suggested earlier (Jarvik, Klodin, & Matsuyama, 1973).

Research has identified the following developmental and behavioral problems when comparing school-age XYY males with normal peers and siblings: (1) IQ scores are slightly lower than normal but there is no increased risk for mental retardation; (2) fine-motor coordination and language development tend to be mildly decreased; (3) reading difficulties and a wide spectrum of learning disorders are more often present; (4) aggressive behavior does not have a higher frequency of occurrence rate; (5) behavioral problems related to general immaturity, impulsivity, and low frustration tolerance are more often present (Robinson, Lubs, & Bergsma, 1985; Stewart, 1982).

Cohen and Durnham (1985) have provided a comprehensive review of school management of children with XYY syndrome as well as other sex chromosome variations. It is suggested that children with suspected XYY syndrome be referred to school health personnel. Once identified, psychoeducational assessment is typically needed to identify possible learning and behavioral disorders. Anticipatory guidance concerning the risks of XYY syndrome is especially needed in view of the typical misconceptions cited earlier. Cohen and Durnham have listed the following resources for school personnel and parents for gaining further information about sex chromosome variations:

March of Dimes Birth Defects Foundation
1275 Mamaroneck Avenue
White Plains, NY 10605

Metropolitan Turner's Syndrome Association
P.O. Box 407C
Convent Station, NH 07961

National Center for Education in Maternal and Child
    Health
3520 Prospect Street NW
Washington, DC 20027

National Health Information Clearing House
Box 1133
Washington, DC 20013

National Information Center for Handicapped Children
1201 16th Street, NW
Washington, DC 20036

REFERENCES

Cohen, F.L., & Durnham, J.D. (1985). Sex chromosome variations in school-aged children. *Journal of School Health, 55,* 99–102.

Jacobs, P.A., Brunton, M., Mellville, M.M., Brittain, R.P., & McClemont, W.F. (1965). Aggressive behavior, mental subnormality, and the XYY male. *Nature, 208,* 1351–1352.

Jarvik, L.F., Klodin, V., & Matsuyama, S.S. (1973). Human aggression and the extra Y chromosome. *American Psychologist, 28,* 674–682.

Robinson, A., Lubs, H.A., & Bergsma, D. (1985). *Sex chromosome aneuploidy: Prospective studies on children.* New York: Liss.

Stewart, D.A. (1982). *Children with sex chromosome aneuploidy: Follow-up studies.* New York: Liss.

See also **Chromosomal Abnormalities; Genetic Counseling**

Y

YALE, CAROLINE A. (1848–1933)

Caroline A. Yale, teacher and principal at Clarke School for the Deaf in Northampton, Massachusetts, from 1870 to 1922, was a leading figure in the development of educational services for the deaf in the United States. She developed a system for teaching speech to the deaf and was a founder, with Alexander Graham Bell and others, of the American Association to Promote the Teaching of Speech to the Deaf. At Clarke School, she organized a teacher-education department that was responsible for the training of large numbers of student teachers. Through her teacher-training activities and numerous publications, Yale was a major contributor to the acceptance of instruction in speech as an essential element in the education of deaf children.

REFERENCES

Taylor, H. (1933). Caroline Ardelia Yale. *The Volta Review, 35,* 415–417.

Yale, C.A. (1931). *Years of building.* New York: Longmans, Green.

See also Deaf Education

YEAR-ROUND SCHOOLS

The concept and use of year-round schools for special and general education has developed, in part, as a result of changing expectations and roles of public education in the community (Hanna, 1972). The traditional answer to the question of school responsibility was simple: transmit the heritage, or at least that part of it considered to be important to the educated person. The traditional school said, in effect, fit children and youths into the fixed curriculum of academic subjects. If they do not care, or in the case of many exceptional students, cannot cope with it, that is unfortunate. In the cases of many exceptional students, traditional education models forced them out or openly expelled them if attendance laws permitted. In other cases, students were tracked into vocational education or home economics. More progressive educators organized schools around a child-centered orientation in order to more effectively stimulate student interest, provide for the exploration and expression of those interests, and, therefore, assist in desirable personality growth (Olsen & Clark, 1977).

A system embracing year-round schooling is able to affirm the central values of the earlier concepts while providing programming in light of the school's basic responsibility to help improve the quality of living in the local community or region. The traditional school curriculum is still almost standard practice (Ysseldyke & Algozzine, 1983). The approach involved in year-round schools, however, provides

curriculum flexibly structured about the enduring life concerns of humans everywhere. These concerns, with their attendant problems, are those of earning a living, communicating ideas and feelings, enjoying recreation, and finding some measure of self-identity.

REFERENCES

Hanna, P. (1972, May). What thwarts the community education curriculum? *Community Education Journal* (pp. 27–30).

Olsen, E.G., & Clark, P.A. (1977). *Life-centering education.* Midland, MI: Pendell.

Ysseldyke, J., & Algozzine, B. (1983). *Introduction to special education.* Boston: Houghton Mifflin.

See also Licensing and Certification of Schools; Summer School for the Handicapped

YPSILANTI PERRY PRESCHOOL PROJECT

The Perry Preschool Project, which operated from 1962 to 1967, was a program to help poor black children in Ypsilanti, Michigan, overcome the apparent effects of their disadvantaged environment. The project evolved from the recognition that a disproportionate number of low-income or minority children with no specific organic etiology were labeled mentally retarded. David Weikart and his associates who initiated the project sought to provide an equal educational opportunity at the preschool level for underprivileged children. Schweinhart and Weikart (1986) believe that effective programs for preschool children can compensate for socioeconomic factors that correlate with school performance. By providing preschool programs, Weikart's goal was to increase the probability of children succeeding in elementary and secondary school as well as the probability of their gaining employment.

Enrolled in the project for 2 years were 3- and 4- year old children (except for four-year-olds enrolled during the project's first year). The school year lasted for seven and a half months; classes ran for two and a half hours each morning, 5 days a week. Teachers also made home visits once a week for one and a half hours to work with each parent and child. The preschool was staffed with four classroom teachers with graduate degrees and extensive in-service training at a ratio of five students for every teacher (Schweinhart & Weikart, 1986; Thurman & Widerstrom, 1985).

The Perry Preschool Project used a Piagetian-based curriculum consisting of a set of cognitive/developmental objectives (Thurman & Widerstrom, 1985; Weikart, 1974). Emphasis in the curriculum was on children developing the ability to reason and to understand their relation to the environment. Activities were designed so that learning to think and to solve problems took place through direct experiences. Development of cognitive abilities was viewed as more important and useful at the preschool level than direct instruction of academic skills. Consequently, preacademic and academic skills (i.e., reading and math concepts) were not emphasized in the curriculum. Rote memory and drill activities typically used in academic skills instruction were not part of the instructional format. Instead, an open format of instruction was used to allow teachers to devise activities that they believed would help individual children through the stages of cognitive development. Ispa and Matz (1978) contend that "because each child works at activities that are developmentally appropriate, he or she has the opportunity to grow and experience success without infringing on the needs of other children for a faster (or slower) pace or for an activity that is more personally interesting" (p. 171).

Extensive longitudinal research on the effects of early intervention has been generated from the Perry Preschool Project. Researchers from the project monitored five sets or "waves" of children from the time of enrollment until age 19. In the south side of Ypsilanti, where the preschool was located, project staff surveyed neighborhoods to identify preschool-aged children. A variety of socioeconomic and ability measures were taken on the children and their families, including parents' education, level of employment of the head of household, ratio of rooms in the home to persons in the household, and IQ levels of the preschool-aged children (Schweinhart, Berrueta-Clement, Barnett, Epstein, & Weikart, 1985). Neighborhood 3 and 4 year olds were then randomly assigned to the preschool group and the nonpreschool group.

The outcome variables measured in the longitudinal study were divided into three domains: scholastic success, socioeconomic success, and social responsibility (Schweinhart et al., 1985). In terms of scholastic success, at age 19 individuals enrolled in the preschool were more likely to have graduated from high school, receive college or vocational training, and perform better on measures of functional competence. In addition, fewer of them were subsequently labeled mentally retarded and they spent a lower percentage of their school years in special education programs. On measures of social responsibility, fewer of the preschool group were ever arrested or detained by police and fewer of the females had teenage pregnancies. In terms of economic success, nearly twice as many individuals from the preschool group were employed and half as many were receiving welfare (Schweinhart et al., 1985).

A benefit-cost analysis of the project indicated that the Perry Preschool Project paid dividends in the long run. The return on investment was estimated to be three and a half times greater than the cost of the 2 years of preschool. The results of the analysis showed that the benefit of the project was in the areas of increased earnings and reduced educational costs for those who had been enrolled in the program (Schweinhart et al., 1985).

REFERENCES

Ipsa, J., & Matz, R.D. (1978). Integrating handicapped preschool children within a cognitively oriented program. In M.J. Guralnick (Ed.), *Early intervention and the integration of handicapped and nonhandicapped children.* Baltimore, MD: University Park Press.

Schweinhart, L.J., Berrueta-Clement, J.R., Barnett, W.S., Epstein, A.S., & Weikart, D.P. (1985). The promise of early childhood education. *Phi Delta Kappan, 67,* 548–553.

Schweinhart, L.J., & Weikart, D.P. (1986). What do we know so far? A review of the Head Start Synthesis Project. *Young Children, 41,* 50–55.

Thurman, K.S., & Widerstrom, A.E. (1985). *Young children with special needs: A developmental and ecological approach.* Boston: Allyn & Bacon.

Weikart, D.P. (1974). Curriculum for early childhood special education. *Focus on Exceptional Children, 6,* 1–8.

See also **Early Identification of Handicapped Students; Socioeconomic Impact of Disabilities; Socioeconomic Status**

YUNIS-VARON SYNDROME

Yunis-Varon Syndrome is a rare genetic disorder caused by an autosomal recessive gene. Children with Yunis-Varon Syndrome have skeletal ectodermal tissue (e.g., nails and teeth), and cardiorespiratory defects. Skeletal defects include complete or partial absence of the shoulder blades, digital abnormalities (i.e., absence or underdeveloped thumbs, big toes, and fingertips), and abnormal growth of the bones of the cranium (i.e., the skull). These children have abnormally large hearts and respiratory difficulties, along with feeding problems, which can be life-threatening, especially in infancy (National Organization for Rare Disorders [NORD], 1997). In fact, neonatal death is a significant feature of Yunis-Varon Syndrome (Lapeer & Fransman, 1992).

Other physical features of this disorder include abnormal or unusual facial characteristics. Children with this syndrome have sparse or no eyebrows and eyelashes, thin lips, and excessively small jaws. These children are also short in stature due to pre- and postnatal growth retardation (NORD, 1997).

Twelve cases of the syndrome have been reported in the literature, which suggests a rare disorder and/or a high mortality rate associated with the disorder. Children who have survived the infancy period have been reported to have additional problems, including bilateral hearing loss, spinal defects, and impacted teeth (Lapeer & Fransman, 1992). Special education support services, such as speech services, may be helpful, especially if a hearing loss is evident.

REFERENCES

Lapeer, G.L., & Fransman, S.L. (1992). Hypodontia, impacted teeth, spinal defects, and cardiomegaly in previously diagnosed case of the Yunis-Varon syndrome. *Oral Surgery, Oral Medicine, and Oral Pathology, 73*(4), 456–60.

National Organization for Rare Disorders (NORD). (1997). Yunis-Varon syndrome. New Fairfield, CT: Author.

Z

ZEAMAN, DAVID (1921–1984)

After receiving his PhD from Columbia University in experimental psychology in 1948, David Zeaman embarked on a lifelong career developing and elaborating on an attention theory of retardate discriminative learning. In the early 1950s, he conducted pilot studies specializing in animal learning with his wife, Betty House, at the Mansfield State Training School in Connecticut. They thought that the techniques developed for studying animal behavior could be adapted for retarded children with low ability to speak or understand language. That early work proved promising, leading to funding by the National Institute of Mental Health for a project that lasted 20 years. The Mansfield State School administrative provided space for a permanent laboratory that is still in existence.

The initial target behavior for Zeaman and House's research was a discriminative learning task disguised as a candy-finding game. Early results convinced them that the deficiency they observed in retarded subjects was due to attentional deficits rather than slow learning. They developed a mathematical attention model with the basic assumption that discriminative learning requires a learning chain of two responses: attending to the relevant dimension and approaching the correct cue of that dimension.

Their approach to retardation was to look for changes in parameter values of the model related to intelligence. The parameter that was most affected by level of intelligence turned out to be the initial probability of attending to the colors and forms that were the relevant dimensions of the tasks. Later work related this finding to three factors: (1) breadth and adjustability of breadth of attention—subjects of higher intelligence can attend to more dimensions at once and can narrow attention when necessary; (2) dimensionality of the stimulus—subjects of low intelligence are likely to attend to stimuli holistically rather than analytically; and (3) fixed as well as variable components of attention such that strong dimensional preferences interfere with learning—salience of position cues in retardates slows learning about colors, forms, sizes, and other aspects of stimuli. A history of research and theory development from the first publication of the model in 1963 to 1979 can be found in Ellis's *Handbook of Mental Deficiency* (1963).

Zeaman served as editor of the *Psychological Bulletin* and as associate editor of *Intelligence*. He received many awards and honors from organizations such as the American Psychological Association and the National Institute of Mental Health.

REFERENCE

Zeaman, D., & House, B.J. (1963). The role of attention in retardate discrimination learning. In N.R. Ellis (Ed.), *Handbook of mental deficiency: Psychological theory and research.* New York: McGraw-Hill.

See also **Zeaman-House Research**

ZEAMAN-HOUSE RESEARCH

David Zeaman and Betty House, along with other researchers located primarily at the University of Connecticut and the Mansfield Training School, have contributed substantial research on attention theory to the literature on mental retardation. Though more than 100 years of psychological and educational research on attention has concluded that the process is multifactorial (Alabiso, 1972), the Zeaman-House, and later Fisher-Zeaman, focus on selective attention has provided several learning theories useful in understanding and teaching mentally retarded persons.

Using a series of simple visual discrimination tasks, Zeaman and House found that plotting of individual, rather than averaged, group responses produced learning curves that differed significantly from traditional learning curves. The former curves stayed around the chance (50%) correct level, then jumped quickly to 100% accuracy. Prior to plotting individual data with backward learning curves, the expectation would have been for a gradual, incremental curve from chance to the 100% correct level. This discontinuity caused these researchers to postulate two processes, one controlling the length of the first part of the curve, and one determining the rapid jump to correct problem solution. Mentally retarded learners in the 2- to 4-year mental age range performed more poorly on these tasks than children of normal intelligence at comparable mental ages. Also, Zeaman and House determined that, among mentally retarded subjects, IQ was a more accurate predictor of better discrimination, independent of mental age (Robinson & Robinson, 1976).

REFERENCES

Alabiso, F. (1972). Inhibitory functions of attention in reducing hyperactive behavior. *American Journal of Mental Deficiency, 77,* 259–282.

Robinson, N.M., & Robinson, H.B. (1976). *The mentally retarded child: A psychological approach.* New York: McGraw-Hill.

Zeaman, D., & House, B.J. (1963). The role of attention in retardate discrimination learning. In N.R. Ellis (Ed.), *Handbook of mental deficiency.* New York: McGraw-Hill.

See also **Zeaman, David**

ZERO INFERENCE

Zero inference is a term that refers to the instructional needs of individuals with severe handicaps (Brown, Nietupski, & Hamre-Nietupski, 1976). Typically, teachers of nonhandicapped students teach a series of core skills using a variety of materials (e.g., counting using wooden cubes). It is assumed that these students will then learn strategies, roles, and concepts necessary to the use of such core skills in other natural settings. It cannot be inferred that severely handicapped students can be taught critical skills in an artificial (i.e., nonnatural) setting using artificial materials and be expected to perform the same skills in more natural settings.

Characteristics of the zero-degree inference strategy of instruction include the belief that no inferences can be made about training a student to perform at a skill level that he or she will be able to use in postschool settings. In order for severely handicapped students to generalize skills taught in more natural (i.e., nonschool) settings, strategies must be used to ensure that generalization will occur (Stokes & Baer, 1977). Training across multiple settings, materials, and trainers may be included in instruction of students with severe handicaps. General case programming (Horner, Sprague, & Wilcox, 1982), in which common characteristics of several materials or settings are assessed in an effort to teach students a strategy that can be used in a variety of postschool settings, may be used. Additionally, techniques of systematic instruction, including data-based instruction and assessment of student progress, are necessary to ensure the acquisition of usable skills on the part of severely handicapped learners (Lynch, McGuigan, & Shoemaker, 1977).

Employing training techniques including generalization or general case strategies and systematic instruction will ensure the acquisition of skills that can be used by severely handicapped students in all necessary environments. Teachers who make zero inferences regarding student performance will be more likely to see success in student performance across situations requiring similar skills.

REFERENCES

Brown, L., Nietupski, J., & Hamre-Nietupski, S. (1976). Criterion of ultimate functioning. In M.A. Thomas (Ed.), *Hey, don't forget about me!* Reston, VA: Council for Exceptional Children.

Horner, R.H., Sprague, J., & Wilcox, B. (1982). General case programming for community activities. In B. Wilcox & G.T. Bellamy (Eds.), *Design for high school programs for severely handicapped students* (pp. 61–68). Baltimore, MD: Brookes.

Lynch, V., McGuigan, C., & Shoemaker, S. (1977). Systematic instruction: Defining the good teacher. In N. Haring (Ed.), *An inservice program for personnel serving the severely handicapped.* Seattle: Experimental Education Unit, University of Washington.

Stokes, T.F., & Baer, D.M. (1977). An implicit technology of generalization. *Journal of Applied Behavior Analysis, 10,* 349–367.

***See also* Self-Contained Class; Self-Help Training; Transfer of Learning; Transfer of Training**

ZERO-REJECT

The term *zero-reject* identifies a policy of providing to all children with handicapping conditions a free, appropriate, and publicly supported education. The constitutional foundation of zero-reject is the Fourteenth Amendment, which guarantees that no state may deny any person within its "jurisdiction the equal protection of the laws." The courts have interpreted this to mean that no government may deny public services to a person because of his or her unalterable characteristics (e.g., sex, race, age, or handicap). Advocates of children with handicaps claimed that these children have the same rights to education as children who are not handicapped. If a state treats children with handicaps differently (e.g., by denying them the opportunity to attend school or by inappropriately assigning them to a special education program), then it is denying them "equal protection of the laws" on the basis of their unalterable characteristics.

***See also* Education for All Handicapped Children of 1975; Public School's and Special Education**

ZONE OF PROXIMAL DEVELOPMENT

The concept of the zone of proximal development was outlined by the Soviet psychologist L.S. Vygotsky in several papers published in the years immediately preceding his death in 1934. This concept was a critical component of Vygotsky's more developed perspectives on the role of social interaction in cognitive development and offered the theoretical foundations for alternative approaches to the assessment of cognitive development. As part of Vygotsky's general theoretical framework, the concept has influenced the development of important traditions of theory, research, and practice within the Soviet Union, in particular, the theory of "activity" as it has been developed by Vygotsky's students and colleagues. In the past decade, as the work of Vygotsky et al. has become more widely known and more fully understood in the West, the concept of the zone of proximal development has stimulated theory and research on cognitive development (Rogoff & Wertsch, 1984; Wertsch, 1985a, 1985b) and its assessment (Brown & French, 1979; Lidz, 1988, Minick, 1988).

Four postulates were central to Vygotsky's theory and research:

1. The agent of complex cognitive processes such as thinking or remembering is not always an individual. It is often a dyad or larger group whose common activity is organized and mediated by speech. According to Vygotsky, cognitive functions are often intermental rather than intramental.

2. The development of certain cognitive processes in the individual is the product of his or her mastery and internalization of means of organizing and mediating cognitive activities that are first encountered in social interaction or intermental functioning.

3. These means of organizing and mediating complex cognitive activities represent one aspect of the historical development of human social and cultural systems.

4. These socially and historically developed means of mediating cognitive activity are transferred from one generation to the next through the child's interaction with adults and more capable peers in cooperative activity.

The concept of the zone of proximal development is a natural extension of these postulates. Vygotsky argued that two different measures of the individual's cognitive development are possible at any point in ontogenesis. First, focusing on the individual's activity when he or she is working alone, one can assess what Vygotsky called mature cognitive processes. In his view, these processes reflect the individual's mastery of modes of organizing and mediating cognitive activity that are first encountered in social interaction. It is this aspect of the individual's cognitive development that is tapped by traditional methodologies of experimentation and assessment. Second, Vygotsky argued that by analyzing the activity of the individual when assistance is provided by someone more skilled in a particular task or by someone at a more advanced level of cognitive development, it is possible to assess cognitive processes that are maturing. By focusing on the level at which the individual performs when acting in collaboration, one can gain insight into the individual's current development state and the next or proximal stage that will emerge in his or her development given adequate experience with appropriate social interaction or collaboration.

Vygotsky defined the zone of proximal development as the difference between the child's actual level of development as defined by his or her independent activity and the level of performance that he or she achieves in collaboration with an adult or more competent peer (Vygotsky, 1978, pp. 85–86). Strictly speaking, the upper range of the zone of proximal development is not a characteristic of the child. It is created in the interaction between the child and those who provide the child with assistance. The level at which the child is able to participate in cooperative cognitive activity is determined simultaneously by the adult's interest and skills in facilitating the child's participation and by the knowledge, skills, and interests that allow the child to participate in intermental activity and benefit from this experience.

Reflecting his lifelong interest in developmental disabilities and delays, Vygotsky felt that one important application of the concept of the zone of proximal development would be in assessing cognitive development in abnormal populations and designing techniques to facilitate that development. In his view, the application of the concept in assessment practice would permit a qualitative assessment of the child's strengths and weaknesses and help identify the kinds of assistance needed to move the child to more advanced levels of cognitive functioning (Minick, 1988). These ideas are currently being developed and applied in the West by Brown and Campione (Brown & French, 1979; Campi-

one, Brown, Ferrara, & Bryant, 1984) and are compatible with work being done by Feuerstein and others in developing dynamic assessment techniques (Feuerstein, 1979; Lidz, 1988).

REFERENCES

Brown, A.L., & French, L.A. (1979). The zone of potential development: Implications for intelligence testing in the year 2000. *Intelligence, 3*, 255–273.

Campione, J.C., Brown, A.L., Ferrara, R.A., & Bryant, N.R. (1984). The zone of proximal development: implications for individual differences and learning. In B. Rogoff & J.V. Wertsch (Eds.), *Children's learning in the "zone of proximal development"* (pp. 77–92). San Francisco: Jossey-Bass.

Feuerstein, R. (1979). *The dynamic assessment of retarded performers: The learning potential assessment device, theory, instruments, and techniques.* Baltimore, MD: University Park Press.

Lidz, C.S. (Ed.). (1988). *Foundations of dynamic assessment.* New York: Guilford.

Minick, N. (1988). The zone of proximal development and dynamic assessment. In C.S. Lidz (Ed.), *Foundations of dynamic assessment.* New York: Guilford.

Rogoff, B., & Wertsch, J.V. (Eds.). (1984). *Children's learning in the "zone of proximal development."* San Francisco: Jossey-Bass.

Vygotsky, L.S. (1978). *Mind in society.* Cambridge, MA: Harvard University Press.

Wertsch, J.V. (1985a). *Vygotsky and the social formation of mind.* Cambridge, MA: Harvard University Press.

Wertsch, J.V. (Ed.). (1985b). *Culture, communication, and cognition: Vygotskian perspectives.* New York: Cambridge University Press.

See also **Activity, Theory of; Vygotsky, L.S.**

Z SCORES, IN DETERMINATION OF DISCREPANCIES

Since the passage of PL 94-142 (Education for all Handicapped Children Act of 1975) several measurement discrepancy models have been recommended in the measurement and special education literature for defining a child as learning disabled (Berk, 1984; Boodoo, 1985; Reynolds et al., 1984; Willson & Reynolds, 1985). These models are all used to estimate the difference between a child's aptitude and achievement, and to determine whether such a difference constitutes a severe discrepancy. The models recommended for use involve the use of standard scores. Under each model, a true discrepancy between a subject's aptitude and achievement is estimated using the subject's standard score on the respective aptitude and achievement test. Many of the standardized aptitude and achievement measures used for individualized testing are normed using the standard score scale with a mean (X^-) of 100 and a standard deviation (S) of 15.

An alternative scale that simplifies the statistical formulas used in the discrepancy models for assessing a severe discrepancy is the Z score scale (Hopkins & Stanley, 1981). This scale has a mean of 0 and a standard deviation of 1 and has the advantage of representing the scores directly in standard deviation units. The following illustrates its use with the Simple Difference Model. Under this model, a difference is defined as [Aptitude (X)–Achievement (Y)] with the standard deviation of this difference, S_D, given by

$$S_D = (S_X^2 + S_Y^2 - 2r_{XY}S_XS_Y)^{1/2}$$

where r_{XY} is the correlation between X and Y. The standard error of estimate of a difference, SE, is given by

$$SE = [S_X^2(1 - r_{XX'}) + S_Y^2(1 - r_{YY'})]^{1/2}$$

where $r_{XX'}$, $r_{YY'}$, are the reliabilities of X and Y respectively.

Using the Z score scale, each of the aptitude and achievement scores is converted to the corresponding Z score using

$$Z_X = \frac{X - \overline{X}}{S_X}$$

and

$$Z_Y = \frac{Y - \overline{Y}}{S_Y}$$

Then, a simple difference is ($Z_X - Z_Y$). The standard deviation of this difference is

$$S_D = (2 - 2r_{XY})^{1/2}$$

where r_{XY} is the correlation between X and Y, and the standard error of estimate is given by

$$SE = (2 - r_{XX'} - r_{YY'})^{1/2}$$

REFERENCES

Berk, R.A. (1984). *Screening and diagnosis of children with learning disabilities.* Springfield, IL: Thomas.

Boodoo, G.M. (1985). A multivariate perspective for aptitude-achievement discrepancy in learning disability assessment. *Journal of Special Education, 18,* 489–449.

Hopkins, K.D., & Stanley, J.C. (1981). *Educational and psychological measurement and evaluation* (6th ed.). Englewood Cliffs, NJ: Prentice-Hall.

Reynolds, C.R., Berk, R.A., Boodoo, G.M., Cox, J., Gutkin, T.B., Mann, L., Page, E.B., & Willson, V.L. (1984). *Critical measurement issues in learning disabilities.* Report of the USDE, SEP Work Group on Measurement Issues in the Assessment of Learning Disabilities.

Willson, V.L., & Reynolds, C.R. (1985). Another look at evaluating aptitude-achievement discrepancies in the diagnosis of learning disabilities. *Journal of Special Education, 18,* 477–488.

See also Discrepancy from Grade; Learning Disabilities, Severe Discrepancy Analysis in; Severe Discrepancy Analysis

ZYGOSITY

Zygosity is twinning that may result in monozygotic (MZ) or identical twins and dizygotic (DZ) or fraternal twins. The cause of MZ twinning remains unknown while the cause of DZ twinning is largely the result of multiple ovulation (Groothuis, 1985). Placentation helps to explain zygosity of twins, where dichorionic placentas take place in all DZ pairs and in about 30% of MZ twins. Monochorionic placentas occur only with MZ twins (Siegel & Siegel, 1982). A twin birth occurs in approximately 1 in 80 pregnancies. For women who already have given birth to twins, the incidence of having a second set rises to 1 in 20. The incidence of MZ twins is 3.5 per 1000 live births independent of race and maternal age. With maternal age DZ twinning increases. It is slightly more frequent in blacks and most unusual in Orientals (Groothuis, 1985; Siegel & Siegel, 1982).

Twinning is of relevance to special education personnel because there are increased risks for medical, psychological, developmental, and educational problems. Twin pregnancies have been associated with higher rates of such symptoms as nausea and vomiting. The greatly increased mortality of twins at birth (i.e., 15%) has been attributed to the high prematurity rate (i.e., 60%) in terms of both gestation time and birth weight. Twins also experience a higher rate of such perinatal problems as entangling of cords, prolapsed cords, hypoxia anemia, respiratory distress syndrome, and jaundice. These risks are generally higher for MZ twins and the second born of both MZ and DZ twins (Young et al., 1985). Twins also experience congenital anomalies such as heart disease, cleft lip, and cleft palate about twice as frequently as children of single births.

There is a general consensus that twins experience higher rates of developmental and behavioral problems than the general population. Like the medical difficulties, these risks are generally more severe for MZ and second-born twins. During the preschool years, problems are focused in such areas as verbal and motor development, discipline, sharing, toilet training, separation, and individual needs. Many of the problems continue for school-aged twins with classroom assignments, school avoidance, peer relations, and academic performance as special concerns. During adolescence, the identity crisis could be exacerbated for twins who have not resolved separation and individuation issues earlier. Regarding school-related abilities, the degree of impairment has been found to be dependent on birth problems and illness as antecedents (Matheny, Dolan, & Wilson, 1976). Moreover, Matheny et al. reported that twins in comparison with the general population have higher rates of learning disabilities and social immaturity. Siegel and Siegel (1982) point out that IQ deficits are questionable, especially when antecedent and environmental factors are controlled.

Typical recommendations for management and guidance follow: (1) encourage parents to avoid emphasizing similarities; (2) separate twins at school as soon as possible but delay if problems are encountered; (3) establish individual expectations for school performance; (4) give psychoeducation assessment to twins with early medical problems. Parents are referred to the National Mother of Twins Club for information and resources.

REFERENCES

Groothuis, J.R. (1985). Twins and twin families. A practical guide to outpatient management. *Clinics in Perinatology, 12,* 459– 474.

Matheny, A.P., Dolan, A.B., & Wilson, R.S. (1976). Twins with academic learning problems: Antecedent characteristics. *American Journal of Orthopsychiatry, 46,* 464–469.

Siegel, S.J., & Siegel, M.M. (1982). Practical aspects of pediatric management of families with twins. *Pediatrics in Review, 4,* 8–12.

Young, B.K., Suidan, J., Antoine, C., Silverman, F., Lustig, I., & Wasserman, J. (1985). Differences in twins: The importance of birth order. *American Journal of Obstetrics and Gynecology, 151,* 915–921.

See also Siblings; Twins

AUTHOR INDEX

SUBJECT INDEX